A Muse To Follow

A MUSE TO FOLLOW

The National Library of Poetry

Richard Schaub, Editor

A Muse to Follow

Copyright © 1996 by The National Library of Poetry
as a compilation.

Rights to individual poems reside with the artists themselves.
This collection of poetry contains works submitted to the Publisher by individual authors who confirm that the work is their original creation. Based upon the authors' confirmations and to the Publisher's actual knowledge, these poems were written by the listed poets. The National Library of Poetry does not guarantee or assume responsibility for verifying the authorship of each work.

All rights reserved under International and Pan-American copyright conventions. No part of this book may be reproduced, stored in a retrieval system or transmitted in any form, electronic, mechanical, or by other means, without written permission of the publisher. Address all inquiries to Jeffrey Franz, Publisher, P.O. Box 704, Owings Mills, MD 21117.

Library of Congress
Cataloging in Publication Data

ISBN 1-57553-062-7

Proudly manufactured in The United States of America by
Watermark Press
One Poetry Plaza
11419 Cronridge Dr., Suite 10
Owings Mills, MD 21117

Editor's Note

Inspiration comes in waves and often floods our emotions with the urgency to communicate. A poem born from a "spontaneous overflow of powerful feelings," as Wordsworth said in the preface to his <u>Lyrical Ballads</u>, originates from a source of energy poets commonly refer to as the Muse. The Muse is the personification of inspiration sparking ideas in the shadowy vale of our minds. Wandering lonely through the folds and mists of memory, the Muse of legends stirs the sleeping mind of an artist from the slumber of reality. Questions burn inside the minds of poets who wish to understand the source of their creativity. Why does the muse call upon a poet to create, and what is significant about that moment of poetic conception?

Wordsworth had his opinion on the Muse, though he did impose a condition on his idea. Poetry according to Wordsworth was indeed the "spontaneous overflow of powerful feelings," but it is important to note that he also believed "poems to which any value can be attached" were produced by someone who possessed a "more than usual organic sensibility," and who "had also thought long and deeply." Too often, the Muse's presence is felt only as the emotional reverie that inspires a poet to put pen to paper. What really makes poetry meaningful, however, is that the poet thoroughly works and reworks his or her poem until it is *alive*. Poets have the ability to endow words with meaning and sculpt feeling into experience. Thus, when we read poetry we are entrusting our minds and emotions to the hands of an artist.

To follow a muse, in poetry, is not merely to search blindly for inspiration but to trust our experiences and our intellect and fashion meaning into words. Perhaps Alexander Pope put it more eloquently when he said:

> *True ease in writing comes from art, not chance,*
> *As those move easiest who have learned to dance.*

Among the many talented poets in **A Muse to Follow**, Gary Lafleur demonstrates a "true ease" of poetic skill in his work, "The Rhetoric of Poetry." LaFleur presents an intriguing image that demands examination and fully displays the poet's virtuosity in dealing with a multi-dimensional poem.

> *Framed*
> *six crows sit on a line*
> *between two utility poles*
> *characters unsupported, sponsoring*
> *themselves, inventing themselves*

On a literal level, the image is visually true to life while still being poetic. The poet asks you to imagine "six crows on a line between two utility poles." From a distance these crows give the appearance of being "unsupported," because the line between the two poles is barely perceptible. LaFleur's insight into the nature of perception is also seen in the crows' ability to invent themselves. Considering the seemingly mundane existence of a crow, one might assume that it could invent and re-invent itself on a daily basis, like a child's imagination, for mere amusement. LaFleur, however, reveals that there is a deeper significance to the crows' invention since they "invent themselves with necessity" and "urgency." This invention shows the function and "necessity" of the imagination in the lives of these creatures.

In a similar way, human beings are continually inventing themselves with the aid of the imagination. As humans, we imagine before acting or making a decision. The imagination helps us to see the possible outcome of any action. It is through the imagination that we understand patterns of behavior and change or alter the aspects of behavior that cause negative results. The imagination also helps us to create the kind of life we wish to live, and understand the life choices others have made. In short, it is the resulting understanding from the imagination that brings meaning into our lives. Humans then, as well as crows, "invent themselves with necessity" and "urgency."

LaFleur takes the paradigm of the crows one step further by building on the image a model for the creative process. The poem continues to expound upon the scene with the crows but it soon becomes apparent that the poet is working on a new level of meaning.

> *...inventing themselves*
> *with necessity, urgency, in a voice and*
>
> *Tone*
> *(let me kiss your neck and)*
> *what do I mean the crows*
> *squabble inadequately, changing*
> *places, balancing themselves*

LaFleur triggers a response by mentioning the literary term "tone" in the opening of the second stanza, and we are aware that he is also speaking about writing, particularly poetry. It is apparent that the crows mentioned in the previous stanza are the first six words of a poem the persona is currently writing. Line two of the second stanza represents this poem as it sits between two utility poles, or parantheses, and consists of six words. In this second stanza we see the poet struggling to make sense of his expression through the metaphoric image of the crows who "squabble inadequately" and change places while trying to "balance themselves," like a poet who often rearranges words in a poem. LaFleur enhances the meaning of his work by showing an aspect of truth that is completely self-contained within the work. Just as the crows *need* to invent themselves in order to find meaning -- (as both animals and as a metaphor for words) -- so too does the poet. The poet is inventing himself by trying to express a meaning through poetry.

The third stanza continues to unfold the persona's work in progress, alighting on an important aspect of poetry: rhythm. In many ways poetry is very much like music: the poetic equivalent to a single measure of music is a "foot." LaFleur also refers to another commonality poetry shares with music when he speaks of "melody and syncopation."

> *Feet*
> *(how many syllables to a sigh)*
> *six black crows now look*
> *like a melody, syncopating*

The final stanza represents a kind of poetic confession that helps us understand why the poem is titled "The Rhetoric Of Poetry." LaFleur asserts that these "crows," or the words within a paranthetical line of verse, have a "secret life" as they "whisper to each other." On one level, a parenthetical break in a line of prose or verse can be seen as a whisper because it is extraneous information revealed to the reader. From a strictly poetic view, however, where words are used to allude to larger meanings, these whispering crows reveal the inherent nature of what LaFleur would term "the rhetoric of poetry."

A good title can open a poem to new and deeper levels of interpretation. The American Heritage Dictionary defines rhetoric as "1. The art or study of using language effectively and persuasively. 2. Language that is pretentious or insincere." Both definitions show the poem's insight into the poetic process. A poem is a persuasive piece of writing since its intention is to make you feel and believe what you read. It is the second definition, however, that LaFleur is speaking of in the final stanza

> *I, too, dislike it (its secret life)*
> *Without it: silence or banality inadequacy and embarrassment*

The persona here confesses that he does not like the exclusiveness of poetic language, which is often misread as pretentious or insincere language. But "without it," the poet cannot fully express him or herself. Gary LaFleur's careful rendering of this intriguing and revealing poem earned for him the Grand Prize for **A Muse to Follow**.

Of the many prolific poems entered for the contest connected with **A Muse to Follow**, Jessica Tilley's poem, "November," shone brilliantly among the second place winners. "November" displays a high level of excellence in composition and imagery. The poem offers a graphic description of a drug addict's confrontation with herself through the disturbing metaphor of a "freak circus." With macabre imagery, Tilley forces the reader to experience the horror of an addict's self-awareness.

> *Remove the shroud, let the show begin!*
> *Skin taught to stretch tight over the bones*
> *Creating a circus tent.*

The persona's addiction competes with her reason in order that she remain an addict, and the price she pays is to live as a "caged beast" in a bleak existence.

> *An infection is here among the poppies,*
> *among caged beasts, a competitor of reason.*

Perhaps the most revealing and insightful information about the persona's mental state is disclosed in the last three lines:

> *plead desperately for the ring master*
> *to once again, for pity,*
> *cover the mirror, replace the shroud.*

These lines reveal the addict's inability to confront the horror that is herself. She relinquishes control of her situation and desires only to "cover the mirror," a tradition associated with death. Tilley commands an amazing ability to forge frightening images into a blunt and candid vision of the darker side of human nature.

Philein Wang's "Asia" displays exceptionally well crafted verse within a tight and carefully framed narrative. The poet depicts the ambiguous thoughts of a person visiting the homeland of his or her parents.

> *I can only as a distant outsider surmise*
> *about the country of my genetic dissension*
> *...about the wondrous and dichotomous place*
> *from which a geographical presence of me by my parents was once erased*

The poetic structure of Wang's verse shows more than competent proficiency in line structure. Wang's delicate and mellifluous language provides an excellent counterbalance to the dynamics of the verse. With fresh and inventive imagery, the poet creates a subtle bond with the reader that draws one into the unfolding narrative. Wang makes use of a difficult poetic technique known as "concrete poetry," which attempts to form a picture through the shape of a poem by using very specefic line placement. It is only after experiencing the poem that we come to recognize Wang's line structure as a graphic representation of the clouds the poem describes; like the poem itself, the clouds "traverse to the left from right." Wang's ability to shape words, in both a literal and figurative fashion, is executed with such a high degree of finesse and subtlety that it is barely noticeable on an initial reading.

The clouds
here never stop
merging
no individual puffs in the sky
just a blanketed full array of white
traversing to the left from right.

Philein Wang's poem, as well as all the prize winners of **A Muse to Follow**, exemplifies a thorough knowledge of the many facets of poetic invention. Other poets of exceptional ability are Candice Rawls's "Vaddie" (pg.43), Sarah Hildebrandt's "Garden Of My Inner Child" (pg. 183), Areti Georgopoulous's "preface to migration" (pg. 93), Robert Cameron's "Values" (pg. 182), Heather Hanford's "Stale?" (pg. 53) and Kathy Peterson's "Helpless" (pg. 201).

It is fair to say that these poets demanded of themselves more than what at first their respective muses had to offer. Their abundant creativity allowed them to follow their muses with a vigor and persistence that yieded brilliant results. There also lies within the pages of this anthology hundreds of highly creative poets whose work is a tribute to their art form. As you peruse this volume, keep in mind that the many innovative and artistic works within **A Muse To Follow** are the results of long and arduous dialogues with creativity. The pursuit of artistry is rewarded with gifts of truth when on the path of self you choose to follow the Muse.

Richard Schaub, Editor

Acknowledgements

The publication of **A Muse to Follow** is a culmination of the efforts of many individuals. Judges, editors, assistant editors, customer service representatives, graphic artists, layout artists, office administrators, data entry, and the mail-room staff have all brought their respective talents to bear on this project. The editors are **grateful** for the contributions of these fine people.

Howard Ely, Managing Editor

Cover Art: Tracy Hetzel

Winners of the North American Open Poetry Contest

(Held in connection with the anthology *A MUSE TO FOLLOW* -- ISBN - 1 - 5755 - 3 - 062 - 7)

Grand Prize Winner

Gary LaFleur / Richmond, KY

Second Prize Winners

Robert Cameron / Spokane, WA
Areti Georgopoulos / Providence, RI
Heather Hanford / Montoursville, PA
Sarah Hildebrandt / Duluth, MN
Henry Mucha / Macomb, MI

Kathy Peterson / Rosemount, MN
Candice Rawls / Jackson, MS
Anna Soter / Columbus, OH
Jessica Tilley / Hartford, CT
Philein Wang / Sherman Oaks, CA

Third Prize Winners

Damien Aherne / Chicago, IL
Elisabeth Allen-Smith / Spartanburg, SC
Ephraim Alexander / Ames, IA
Rae Arrington / Idaho Falls, ID
D. V. Arthur / Los Angeles, CA
Judith Bean / Oakland, CA
Mumtaz Bengali / Corvallis, OR
Joe Bradley Jr / Knoxville, TN
Sandor Boulter / Bolinas, CA
David Brooks / Santa Monica, CA
Ted Carson / Sublette, KS
Ian Cheverton / Key West, FL
Jan Clements / Aurora, IL
Sherry Colombaro / Vernon, CT
Glenn Cooley / Philadelphia, PA
Douglas Croyle / Kodiak, AK
Margie Donohoo / Evansville, IN
Linda Durnbaugh / Kirtland, OH
Lawrence Etue / Bakersfield, CA
Juliane Gallina / Waipahu, HI
Buddy Gray / Cincinnati, OH
Chris Gulino / Las Vegas, NV
Chris Fillie / Gainesville, FL
J. Maurice Hourihane / Portland, OR
Kristen Kappel / Salt Lake City, UT
Esther Keller / San Francisco, CA
Olga Kokino / Long Beach, CA
Kathleen Kolar / Lakeside-Marblehead, OH
Esaku Kondo / Bloomfield Hills, MI
Cynthia Kovar / College Station, TX

Kelly Krenning / Overland, MO
Rosalind Levine / Los Angeles, CA
Brynn Lopez / Chandler, AZ
Joan T. MacKenzie / Menlo Park, CA
David Massey / Decatur, GA
Matt McClure / Cumming, GA
Bobbi Meislohn / Lewisville, NC
Richard Metzner / Los Angeles, CA
David Minjares / South San Gabriel, CA
Munir Nassar / Brockport, NY
Bertrand R. Norman / Seattle, WA
Teri Pavone / Hilton Head Island, SC
Dan Q. Posin / Millbrae, CA
Dee Pye / Austin, TX
Wendy Riesterer / Sandusky, OH
Norma Shelby / Louisville, KY
Sharon Sitton / Townsend, MT
Marlene Smith / Stone Mountain, GA
Brian Sommers / Stevensville, MD
Charles Stromeyer / Concord, MA
Bradley Tice / Cupertino, CA
Jerry Trimmell / Wichita, KS
Bartholomew Villa-McDowell / Los Angeles, CA
Valerie Virgona / Tangerine, FL
Mike Weltz / Washington DC
Teresa Wilcox / Aurora, IL
Kathleen Wood / Houston, TX
Odessa Zeromus / Chicago Heights, IL
Myrtle Zimmerman / Sarasota, FL

Congratulations also to all semi-finalists.

The National Library of Poetry · 11419-10 Cronridge Drive · PO Box 704 · Owings Mills, MD 21117

Grand Prize Winner

The Rhetoric Of Poetry

Framed
six crows sit on a line
between two utility poles
characters unsupported, sponsoring
themselves, inventing themselves
with necessity, urgency, in a voice and

Tone
(let me kiss your neck and)
what do I mean the crows
squabble inadequately, changing
places, balancing themselves
with fluttering, annoyance, in a panic.

Feet
(how many syllables to a sigh)
six black crows now look
like a melody, syncopating
itself, whispering to each other
in pairs, secretly, they know

I, too, dislike it (its secret life)
Without it: silence or banality inadequacy and embarrassment

Gary B. LaFleur

Violet Window

The man that she married gives her few gifts
just wraps her in misery and pain
he kicks her and slaps her but won't let her cry out
she knows only smolders, she wants to know flame

The only relief from a day full of shadows
is a violet window in this room where they stay
frayed drapes are a mouth, smeared glass is a smile
dull panes capture pain but have nothing to say

This time she won't cower, recoil from his slap
he hits her but she pushes him back to the wall
he slips on the rug, through soiled drapes he does crash
the window shatters like leaves frozen in fall

Diamonds of glass echo long broken dreams
falling panes release misery to spill through the night
the screaming blackbirds are loosed from her cage
they leave her body on their enraged flight

The violet window, its glass broken and gone
in front of this window a widow now stands
drapes torn and bloody tell what has gone on here
Freedom she sees in the blood on her hands

VIOLENT WIDOW
Jim Hay

The War

A long long time ago
in a far away land
there was a thing called the war.
And the people who are old now or dead now.
Are the people who were in the war.
I Arielle I felt I fell sorry for the people who died in the war.
You know my great grandfather died in the war.

Arielle Feit

Summer

A summers day gone all too soon,
Leaves us with darkening gloom,
For winter is around yon corner,
Think I need a blood donor.

For the winters wind thickens the blood,
And makes us feel like a dud,
And staying warm is a chore,
Don't think I like winters anymore!

So now I dream of summers warmth and light,
Could I but sleep and wake to summers bright
And shining glory, with green everywhere again,
And enjoy the sparkling summer rain.

Franklin J. Warren

Daddy You Lose

You left me when I was two years old
a drunk, a bum I was told
It doesn't matter now, my heart closed

I wonder if you think of me on Father's Day
Have any regrets or does the bottle make it ok

Don't ever come back it's much to late
Leaving this child was your biggest mistake

You'll go to your grave not knowing me
I'll go to mine
Having a father I never did see!

Cindy Nicolelli

Bubbles

A tiny crystal world,
Seemingly almost perfect in shape.
Glistening with the reflection of the sun.
Translucent,
Filled with the colors of the rainbow.
It contains within it,
A super-natural life.
A life so innocent,
Not even a blemish.
Nothing able to harm it.
Nothing but,.... Time that is.

It is free from the world
Lighter than the air.
It floats without power, without a conscience.
More fragile than glass, softer than silk.
It is the definition of freedom.
For once one attempts to capture it.
It sheds its outer skin,
And disappears into eternity.

Evan Harris

The One I Love

You are truly a friend to me
Better than I ever thought could possible be.
You are not only my best friend
You are the one I'll love till the end.

You are the only one I love
You are truly an answer from above.
I never thought my dreams would come true
Until the day that I met you.

When I look in my future, what do I see
Nobody else but you and me.
I will always want to be with you
And love you today, tomorrow and forever.

Erma Whetstone

The Golden Years

"The golden years" as some would say
are often dimmed with shades of gray.
A special lady who has given to all
accepts today another call.

A life that's been so full of giving
must now depend upon receiving
her body weakening from years of pain
disease laying claim to her once strong frame.

This day, unwanted, has finally come
when this pillar of strength must leave her home.
A home she cherished, her haven of rest.
Now others say that they know best.

She recognizes that this is true
but to never return is hard to do.
Thoughts of all who have had a part
years of memories flood her heart.

Her faith that always has kept her strong
will not diminish in this new home.
Though limited she will think of others.
This special lady is my dear Mother.

Dee Elson

Amber Sunshine

We have a little bundle of joy that we call Amber Sunshine,
and although she's only four year old she looks forward to our funtime.

She's Grandpa's little angel and Grandma's little brat,
and mom and dad both agree she can be either of that.

She started preschool last week and already has a beau,
and Grandpa knows the time will come when she will have to go.

But let's not rush that time too fast when Amber graduates,
because in the meantime we have memories to create.

Memories of the amusement park, stuffed animals that we won,
and trips to the Discovery Zone where we always had lots of fun.

I know we'll never forget the fun times that we shared,
little Amber Sunshine and a Grandpa who cared.
    George L. Clark

"Big Blue Marble"

A big blue marble as we see it.
A big blue marble called planet.
A big blue marble we except as home sweet home.
A big blue marble we live, and die for.
A big blue marble with beauty, and destruction.
A big blue marble with living creatures.
A big blue marble of water, and land.
A big blue marble precious as a diamond.
A big blue marble seek for refuge.
A big blue marble with the purest breathing substance.
A big blue marble sister of planet moon.
A big blue marble suspending in space.
A big blue marble that shines like a star in sky.
A big blue marble with hemisphere of good, and bad.
A big blue marble that holes our faith.
A big blue marble admired by millions.
A big blue marble with endless promises.
A big blue marble with wondrous colors.
A big blue marble with liberty, and justice.
A big marble the brother of Mr. Sun. Mr. Earth!
    Johnny V. Silvas

"The Amazing Baby Jessica Show"

All of a sudden one wonderful day
A call came that Jessie was comin'
And all of a sudden that wonderful day
The trees and the wind started hummin'

Soon the sun and the stars added their sound
As they sang of a beautiful child
Whose arrival was met by a thunderous applause
While the world went collectively wild

There's a time and a place for a miracle
I know cause I watched one come true
I saw the whole world made decidedly brighter
And the reason sweet baby is you

Of all of the children in all of the world
You're among the most fortunate few
You're surrounded by people who love you a lot
Whose love you'll find lasting and true

Well I'm a recipient of this magical aura
Of this "Amazing Baby Jessica Show"
So I'll love you forever and ever and ever
You can count on your ol' grandpa Joe
    James J. Brown

What Can I Do

As I pass you
A cry from your spirit I can't ignore
Artistically displayed on the curve
The sun highlights the beauty of dark skin
Bold features signify a queen
A portrait of you has touched me
Steps of fear lead me to come closer
Unpleasant arms to greet me
Food from my heart to serve you
Only for you to drape the street
With
Love I tried to show you
What Can I do
    Annette Flowers

The Personal Ads

A dating column for today's successful singles
A different approach than the bar scene
Gone are the days of a school mingle
No more church socials like when I was a teen

Now I read "country boy or officer and a gentlemen"
Sounds more like I am reading TV guide
Will these individuals really be a ten?
I would settle for a four or five who does not hide

I want a man who is honest, sincere, and fun
Yet, all these ads say everything but the above
Tall, educated and a communicator would be a bonus by a ton
As I read I circle very few who want love

One man, one relationship, one day
As my pen makes it way through the ads
I wonder, yes, no, maybe or no way Jose!
Talking, meeting, dating, I rule out the cads

Maybe one day I will meet my dream guy
Until then I will continue reading as I try.
    Cheryl Hollister

Delayed Tears

There's a river to cross,
A dragon to slay;
But I first must remember to welcome the day.
And a mountain to climb to its snowiest height.
And a bluebird to watch as it drifts on its flight.
So, I'll cry later.

With a baby to hug,
And a gift to unwrap,
And a kitty to stroke as he purrs in my lap,
I'm a busy old girl with a smile on my face.
But when I am alone in my own special place,
Then I cry later.

I can never express the emotions I own.
I just write them all down when I am alone.
It is then I tell God of my heart's heavy ache.
It is then I'm forgiven my every mistake.
That's why I cry later.
    Jo Piper

Snowflakes

They come tumbling down in their dresses so white
And the sun makes them glisten and glitter so bright
They look like little fairies as they dance and they play
Then they lie close together and sleep for the day.
    Jeanette Middleton

Life Beyond Flesh And Time

A crack
   A fissure in the human spirit.

A cosmic string
   A whip to chastise planets.

Futility lies in keeping the flesh and soul married.

The shedding
   The relieving of corporeal stagnation.

Life's singularity is alleviated with death.

Pure beings
   arrow through the lightless cold

The knowledge of all
   The pain of none.

   Donald W. Caves

There Is A Story To Be Told

Once when I was 5 years old
A funny story was told
By my grandpa just getting bald
Lapping my body he was so proud

Once there was a balding grandfather
And a 5 year old boy
Grandpa, I am tired of all my toys
Please tell me a story with for ever joy

Once there was a grandfather, and a little boy ...

One day I will also get old
Facing my grandchildren, I also have a story to be told
An endless story with true meaning of the world
Only the future of our tradition,
Can price the value of gold

On that day might not be too far away
Our mother earth may too get old
Her hair falls off, the forest land become bald
Her milk runs dry, the river bed turns cold
On that day, there will not be any story
To be told

   Ellis C. K. Hsing

Life And Nature

A blackbird crows in a tree
A Gopher peeks out of the ground
Two butterflies entangled in a love dance
A humming bird drinking sweet nectar

Nature and Life move on

Cool water moves down the creek bed
Hugh Oak and Pine swing to the breeze
A single leaf drifts down to mother earth
A rock sits going this time daily

Nature and life move on

You sit and wonder why people die
Why can't we just go on forever
Your blessed with a beautiful granddaughter

Nature and life move on

You realize your part of nature
Moving thru life as life moves thru nature
For they are both one in the same
Life is nature and nature is life

Nature and life move on

"There is no time for death."

   Abel J. Flores

Traces

A small white sock with a bit of lace,
A green Pterodactyl with a chewed-up face.
A peanut butter smear on the arm of a chair,
A little bow barrette that belongs in red hair.
A dirty ring going 'round the tub,
A white cake of soap melted down to a nub.
A couple of plastic cups with teeth-marked rims,
A couple of stepped-on M & M's.
A small hand print on a French door pane,
A rocking horse with a straggly mane.
A hole in my heart as big as the sea,
Oh, please, bring my grandchildren back to me.

   Elisabeth Allen-Smith

Melancholy Hysteria

These walls cage me like a jail
A jail — that can't be escaped
So desperately I want to be free, free
Free as the bird that flies the wind
Free as the naughty ocean that crashes about
Free as the lily that sits by the pond
Free as the fieldmouse that leaps and creeps
Oh, how I yearn—Eagerly I wait
My sanity is but a delicate vase.
Easily it can crack, tremble, and break.
Causing my whole being to become a mistake.
I wish not to be crazy!
I wish to be free.
I wish to know of the joys that lurk behind my evil walls.
I desire richly to stand in a chilling rain
Barefoot and benign.
But I can't, I shan't, so I won't think of the glories
that linger around me.

   Ben Weiss

Where Robins Go

A Robin came in the Early Spring
A little girl with a broken wing
Alone and afraid in the tempest blast
Of a broken home - of a marriage past
Of a father gone to another life
Of a new strange family, more bitter strife.
A little girl - no place to run.

Did you ride the blast of your daddy's gun
To another land in the setting sun?
To that secret place where the Robins go
To escape the cold of a winter's snow?

Do you know that your eyes, ne'r filled with glee
Now help another child to see?
Your wounded heart that longed for joy
Now beats in the breast of a little boy

Do you know dear Robin, after all these years
Of a mother's anguish, of a Grandpa's tears?
The springs return, but they're not the same
As that early spring when a Robin came.

   Charles M. Pickett

Untitled

I take it's only memento
A little piece of my soul.
Wonder if it would mind; ponder if it would care.
I eject this memory.
I say they can't cry; just a reaction to pain.
This comical warble is not in jest.
I blush our sky light; I paint our blood with crayon color.
But it stakes back and the facts remain.
We lose our virgin mind.
I face the horror of needless death.
What power could bring back innocence?
As I experience it's necessity;
Bleeds back into our world
I realize my strongest emotions are
Blind are apathetic,
As we face this together.

Jared Kusmit

"The Gate"

I dream of a gate, at night when I sleep
a lonely old house, and a forest so deep.
We sit on the gate, and wonder why.
Mamas not here, why she had to die,
We set here in silence, afraid to complain,
that we might let each other, know each others pain
My little brother, is sleepy and scared.
I look down the road to see if daddy was there.
We will set on the gate, and feel so alone.
I wish mama was here, or daddy would come home.
I hold my brother, tight in my arms
and try to tell him we would come to no harm
We can sit on this gate, but what would we eat
Would we die of hunger, and where would we sleep,
This gate cannot hurt us, or die or go away.
So we will sit here together, and silently prey.
For someone to come, and take us away.
from all of this sadness, where we used to play.

Betty Rinehart Pevehouse

Justice Served?

In the night of summer heat,
a man lay dead, out in the street
police arrive, and he does not run
the suspects charged with murder one!
For his reason, he will not tell
he thinks, he will probably burn in hell
his pride won't let him say why,
he's sentenced to life... Condemned to die
to tell the people, he sees no point
he'll go like man, and rot in the joint
the dead man could have kept his life,
but the bastard, raped his wife.
That's why he fell victim to the knife
decades go by...
He is old, and ready to die
I search the corners of my mind,
there is a question that I find,
when he goes, to meet his maker,
will he again be judged...
As a life taker?

Adam John Tate

Mystery Of Life

I am that which is not what was;
a mere being, here without much cause,
why the mystery of life knowing what could've been;
And knowing not what might've been.
Is it possible why it isn't known;
What we are seeking for and that alone,
Makes mystery of life seem twisted,
Could never in an index find listed.
Castle in the air day dream;
More fantastic then reality would seem,
For all this would rather be an optimist
Then just an unreal pessimist,

Alyce Marie Dellien

Little Genes

On that day which seems so far away,
a miracle occurred, that I cannot convey.

Happiness, joy, it brought to my eyes
Such a feeling, that money cannot buy.

Each one looked up to me as if to say,
I am me in my own little way.

Appearance like one other, hopefully
I look like my mother.

But, inside I am like no other,
I am me, and happy to be.

As light crept upon them for the very
First time, tears formed upon my eyes.

I know they will stay, special, in their
Own little way.

I shall never forget the feeling when six kittens
Were born on that summer day in May.

Brittany Garratt

"A Moment To Live"

A moment to live
a moment to cry
a moment to realize how suddenly we die

A moment of laughter
a moment to capture
this moment that is fading ever so faster

A moment to unwind
a moment this is so kind
a moment that many of us try to find

A moment of peace
a moment to unleash all the pain and experiences
that have kept us out of reach

A moment of grace
a moment that keeps us out of the race
a moment to thank God for
his love that keeps us in his place

But the moment of all...
Is the biggest moment that is important
To us all...

Gabriella Maria Pilato

My Friend

My friend, my friend, you've come to be
A most special gift God gave to me.
You make me laugh when you're around
You pick me up when I am down.
We share our thoughts, our trials and dreams
We find in each other, respect it seems.
Each day that passes I thank God anew
For I know I have a true friend in you.

Donna E. Lent

A Mother's Love

A mother's love is true
A mother's love is real
A mother's love is good
A mother's love is sincere
A mother's love is harsh
A mother's love is sympathetic
A mother's love is suspicious
A mother's love is aggressive
A mother's love is determined
A mother's love is forever

No matter how mad at her you may get
A mother's love is always there when you need it.

Jennifer M. Ryan

Waterfalls

Water cascading down a mountain Abyss,
A multitude of color caught up in the mist.

Turbulent pools at the base of its fall,
Encompassed by boulders in the valleys hall.
Reaching across in a natural bridge

Fallen trees make a path to the other ridge
An abundance of creatures are called by its song,
Lured by its promised for that which they long.
Leading quietly away, its fingers reach out,
Soothing the land on its rivery route.

Annette D. DeClue

What Then My Son?

In this great time of peace or war, where shall we go my Son?
A Nation so strong and yet so weak, if only our Hearts could be as one
Would we this day rewrite the Laws, to enslave our Hearts to fun?
Or would we just burn and riot or loot? Is this Great Nation done?

To school you go to learn to read, the history of the past
To set the pace of future men, to see that peace will last.
As we grow older and go to war, to keep our Country strong
We know that war is not our thing, we do our neighbor wrong.

To see the world as it really is, without it's Hallowed Crown
With people yelling in the streets, let's burn this college down.
Where then my Son shall we go, or what things shall we do?

We are only small compared to those, who in violence shout and boo
The crowd is right most of the time, suppose we go along
To see the law and schools destroyed, to sing their happy song.

Once more we are victorious in our fight for love and peace.
To learn what we might choose, slaves we will release.
Our guilt, our burdens, our fight is finally won.
Only our conscience can say, where then shall we go my Son?

Harry T. Albright

Arranged Marriage

The myriad of colors overwhelmed me
A New England autumn had come to our household
The rhythmic beat of the drums echoed through my ears
Announcing my fate to the world
The aroma of Eastern spices toyed with my nose
I sat on the cold ground quiet and motionless
Sequins on my dress sparkled in the intense light
The gold necklaces felt like chains on my neck
I was deep in thought
They told me it was a perfect match
I didn't know him
I hadn't even seen him
A single tear escaped down my cheek
I could hear voices praising and laughing
I dare not look up
My reluctance would shine in my moist eyes
I swallowed my pain and smiled for my parents
It was a celebration to remember
A celebration of my rape.

Farah Rasheed

I Love You Because...

I love you because you are you,
a person inside of yourself
and I a part of your person.

I love you because you are warm,
a fire happiness lies within you
and I am a log in your place.

I love you because you are gentle,
a softness in your touch
and I the cotton which you are made of.

I love you because I am all these things to you
and you are all these things to me
I love you because, you love me back.

Dianna Malone

Friend From Afar

He came to me in my thoughts,
A pleasant face with questioning eyes.
But when I would speak to him,
There was never any response.

His appearances were regular, never frightening,
But his attempts at communicating
Were always on the edge of my comprehension.
Then he would hurriedly be gone.

Who was this man who invaded my thoughts?
His unclear face seemed somewhat familiar.
Perhaps he was a troubled spirit,
Simply wandering, trying to touch someone.

Time passed and we did not "speak" for awhile.
Suddenly he was before me with a request.
He asked me to care for his dearest treasure.
I then recognized my visitor.

"Be good to my lady for I must leave."
"Where are you going," I sadly inquired.
But before the sun set again, I had my answer.
My vision was gone — to be with his Eternal Friend.

Filomena D'Elia

Sport

I married a sport
A real down-to-earth sport, that is.
During our courtship we went
To see many a race-car event.
When my hand he won,
I found I wasn't the only one,
   love, that is.
Because I married a sport, you see.
Oh what a sad tale - my rivalry!
First there were the various games of ball
Which I could help him watch, if I desired,
But I'm a party girl - not a sport - I soon grew tired.
Then there was and is, the game of pool - not water.
But my ability didn't give him the competition it orter.
My worst rival (I thought) was bowling.
The only time he was happy was when the ball was rolling.
But alas, in my old age when unable to cope,
I have a new rival and there is no hope.
I am doomed to widowhood!
I have lost to irons and a wood.
   Clara West

Grieving Wind

In my deep solitude, during the tranquil silence of a winter night,
a restless wind, brushes against my room-window, with a wailing sound,
and I, being free of slumber with my ears and heart, listen intensely,
wondering why the grief and why the lamentations are so profound.

The wind's lonely cry, is soul-breaking and seems to be full of sorrow
and I with active imagination, sympathetically try to guess the reason.
Is it because of the daily damage done to the environment,
or is it because of the gloominess of the long winter season?

Why all the melancholic anguished and sad lamenting, dearest wind?
Do you wail, because of the many troubles and misfortunes of mankind?
Or is your crying, because of the loneliness and cruelty of the world?
Please tell me... and the solutions you seek I shall try to find.

Please tell me. I humbly ask you to completely trust and confide in me.
My heart aches a little, and my eyes become misty with tears,
thinking that you grieve for all the injustices that you daily see
and because you find no one to tell your sadness, no one to
   soothe your fears.

Why are you grieving, dearest wind?
   Amelia Rios

An Old Trunk

Open an old trunk and look inside,
   a sentimental feeling will sit by your side.

A lace dress worn by mom,
   from her wedding or maybe a prom.

An old photograph faded with time,
   just signed "Love Warren", on one single line.

A top, a ball and some jacks,
   isn't it nice to be able to go back.

A pair of baby shoes worn at the toes,
   whose they were we may never know.

A wind-up clock not making a sound,
   it used to keep time all year round.

A war torn letter states, "I wish to come home.
   I am scared and so alone."

A tear just fell from my eye,
   I knew the soldier who chose to die.

Close the lid on this old trunk
   and know that the memories are not just junk.
   Barbara Rayfield

The Search

Last night
A shapeless phantom whirled into my bedroom
And instantly the room became icicle cold.
It rose high, it dropped low, its misty fingers
Reaching everywhere as it searching for something.
I pulled the covers up to my head watching,
Fearfully watching its every move.
Hesitatingly I asked, "What are you looking for?"
The phantom answered, "My peace of mind.
I lost it and I want it back".
Sarcastically I said, "I don't have it."
The phantom replied, "I know you don't.
I'm merely helping you to find it."
Unassured I asked, "Why do you want to help me?"
The phantom answered, "Because I am your inner-self.
I am you."
   Doris K. Shockley

A Pastoral Hymn

She sits in quiet contemplation,
   a shattered wineglass by her side.
A tear, poised on her cheek,
   reflects the sadness in her eyes.
Her thoughts, they mingle with the breeze,
   scattering o'er the land barren seeds.

In the fields of her distant gaze,
   the grasses seem to bend and sway to melodies so sweet,
     as that gentle breeze caresses her cheek.
The petals which she holds so dear in hand,
   fall like raindrops on the barren land.

As she rises, her skirt billows up as if a cloud
   on its journey through the azure sky.
The tear breaks free,
   unleashed by a mournful sigh.

The glass catches her reflections as she makes her retreat.
   The tear stained petals swirl about her feet.
The grass gives up the evidence of her descent.
   The breeze carries off the memory of her scent.
All that's left is sadness, sadness, and emptiness.
   Benjamin Page

A Transient Love

Crossing the Mackinac Bridge over a decade ago,
A sign greeted my eyes that set my heart aglow.

The U.P. Loves You! Were the words up head,
And little did I know the truth that they said.

Our mutual attraction was love at first sight,
In fresh air and sunshine from morning 'till night.

Like a child I've wandered past the rivers and falls,
And tramped through jack-pine forests that know no walls.

My mind has meandered from shore to shore,
And my heart was lost by some backwoods door.

I've left once before, and returned once again;
Each time attached more to my northern friend.

The ice-castle winters are breath-taking 'tho long,
And summers seem to arrive sudden - like the robbins song.

Now I find once again that it is farewell for me,
But please, just remember: I love you U.P.!
   Carol Lee Heller-Church

Love Betrayed

The maelstrom seethes in a vortex of passion
A silent scream permeates the being
Anger wells into a torrent of rage
Why, why does the aching heart reach for hatred
Because there can be no peace?

The loathing and shame that makes the
Quietude erupt into hot spasms only begets
The sameness of sorrowful pain

Silent longings of the soul never to be known
Slowly writhing in agony, bound by chains of doubt.

Deceit - the unholy name of Evil, spawns the
Cataclysm of destruction

Mockery with empty sounds and scorn with
Movements abounds, unborn yearnings reaching out,
Searching.

The darkness of lonely despair withers by neglect
Soon to be smothered.
   Elmo M. Schilling

"Slow And Tranquil Voice"

Someone calls your name outside the door.
   A slow and tranquil voice you've heard before.
Words and revelations you can't ignore,
   Burning in your mind forevermore.

Lucifer sits on the steeple high.
   The church will burn, and the people die.
There he sits, while the hypocrites,
   Conceal their lust, and make it fit.

The church of invisible fire turns its ear.
   The slow and tranquil voice it will not hear.
Invisible fire they cannot see,
   Their eyes are hid in apostasy.

Crows and vultures gather in the night,
   Prepared for judging sins against the light.
In the churchyard the bodies lie,
   Look away to the eastern sky.

That tranquil voice, you would not hear,
   Now they've come, the days of fear.
A crimson sky, aglow with wrath,
   The world is purged in denial's blood bath.
   Jeremy Doss

Surcease

A burst of light flashed through the vibrant air
A streak short-lived and yet so very bright
That naught but this could make us feel so near
To tragic death and all its agony.

A roar of thunder and a trembling crash
That pealed to warn us of the pending storm.
Oh Lord, we pray, please let the deluge fall
To ease the torture of unending fear.
   Helen T. Patterson

Shadow On The Wall

Look there, who do you see? Only to discover it's only me
a shadow on the wall for all to see...

Did you say what's my name? All of our faces look the same
shadows on the wall playing the same old game

Time is up to leave that wall, you might stumble and you
might fall; But you want be just another Shadow on the wall
   Gwendolyn Jones

"Devotions"

I admit I have trouble preparing "Devotions".
A task that leaves me with mixed emotions.
I shouldn't, I know, wear my heart on my sleeve.
Yet with prayers and bible verses, I tend to grieve.

Words are the harp-strings of the soul.
They lilt and twang, thunder and roll.
They call up tears, prayers and blessings,
Contrite hearts and rude confessions.

A touch of compassion is more than enough,
To salt and pepper all of this stuff.
But thinking and praying, I go overboard.
I'm a sucker, I guess, in the name of the Lord.

I'm only one man, yet He did it for me.
And His death on the cross, at last set me free.
When I think what He did for the whole human race,
The blessings, the love, the power of His grace,

Then I, prostrate before Him, come up a winner.
Forgiven forever, though I'm always a sinner.
With poems, and songs, and prayers without ceasing,
I'll cherish my Jesus, my faith still increasing!
   Cletus E. Melick

To My Son, The Fisherman

Cloudy grey skies on Honey Lake,
A ten-foot boat of leaky-drab make,
Creaky oar- locks, Zebco poles,
Floating-white lilies and fishing holes,
A rugged son in patched up pants,
Huckleberry Finn in a Red-Skins cap.

His rod and real, gripped white knuckled,
Whipped in that air a lure to rustle
The hushed lagoon to a wild splash
Stirring the flurry of boy and bass
Where fearful eyes with chills down the spine
Dreaded the loss yet brimmed with pride.,

In the war of nerves on that troubled bay
The boy and the fish made a pact that day
To stop the battle of untamed instinct
And go with the flow of currents linked
To the pulse and bend of a throbbing rod
Giving neither the bass nor the boy the nod.
   Gus Wilhelmy

The Performers

The sound whistles by as the dawn breaks the mist.
A thrumming as soft as the hummingbirds beat,
Swarms across the streets like the ants moving gist,
The quartet rambles away at the bright larks way,
And growing sun's heat.
By noon the throng dances away,
At the lively groups play.
As the luncheon is served
The currency box rings,
While the soprano sings,
To lull the afternoon away.
The early dusk sets the announcer to the fore of the affray,
For it was the end of the show,
And they really must go,
They left the town at the end of day.
   Christopher Bogardus

Vanishing Sun

It is time of war not peace
A time dreams die in their infancy and go cruelly unburied and left
to remain on top soil as a recurring reminder of what never was or
could never be I swear, I swear, I swear

In doubt reach out only to grope the darkness for the sunshine is
fleeing from hope leaving a path of darkness and nothing here in
the universe to care, to care, to care

Life must be to the end and each day is a end in itself with no
will power to journey on although one must wake up to a sadness we
must bear, must bear, must bear

What I see is complete despair everywhere, everywhere, everywhere

Where is the sunshine of life to blind out that evil demon known
as doom nowhere, nowhere, nowhere

Hope said it too was taking a vacation in pursuit of the vanishing
sun who dares to remain hidden somewhere, somewhere, somewhere

If a change for the better is to come and has yet to arrive trust
not your feelings of well being and be on guard with the strength
of your soul, beware, beware, beware

Betty Alford

Rain

"Come with me, Do not be afraid."
A voice begs me to come out.

The wind, my mother's hand, held on tight.
The cold wetness enveloped me like a warm blanket.
I felt safe for that brief, fluttering moment.
Sadness melted,
I was left alone in a new world.
A world where no sadness could ever reach me.
My fears left. My tears were dry.
I never had to face the pain of death ever again.

The rain fell. Grief found the door, and left.
Understanding filled my soul.
Laughter was my breath.
I invited sweet thoughts to fill my heart.

A memory whispers goodbye.
God smiles sunshine.
The voice, for now, is quiet.

Ascenza Montalbano

Carry Yourself

Your talent can only carry you so far,
after that you carry yourself
Whatever you do it's been done before
that's why you have to give just a little more;
Doors will open as they will close...
take your opening and fly away
People will put you up, just as they
will bring you down, rise to the occasion
and smile over the frowns
You can if you believe, no one can
steal that or make you mean
If you choose to be a success then the world
is at your mercy,
If you choose to fail then the world
is a thousand enemies
You can if you will and you will if you can,
Your talent can only carry you so far
after that you carry yourself.

Jami L. Bauer

A Deeper Peace

Country against country, brother against brother.
  A war is the same, if one hates the other.

Must the end result always be war?
  Why can't we learn from battles before?

Do we really care who our enemies are?
  Or will our battle lines continue to scar?

We all look like enemies from a distant glance,
  If guns are drawn and hate given a chance.

For the attacks of hatred inside each man's heart,
  Continue to tear our countries apart.

What will make our nations whole?
  To learn the name of another man's soul.

The name of the greatest in a war gone by?
  Was the hero who listened to the other man's cry.

A cry to put down the gun in your hand,
  "Please bandage my wounds and by you I'll stand."

Who knows the difference between right and wrong?
  Lay our guns on the ground, that's where they belong.

This is the answer that will turn the tide.
  It must always begin with a deeper peace inside.

Jon H. Wentzel

Untitled

As I gaze into the night sky
All that I know and feel becomes no more
Reality is meaningless
Often I dream of times when the problems of everyday life were
insignificant
Nothing lasts forever
Sadly I awaken from my sleep
Wondering if the world will ever be as I dreamed
Or as...
Others may have dreamed

Aaron Woo

Choices

Our lives are filled with choices,
About families, jobs and friends.
From the time we get up 'till we go to bed
To them, there is no end.

Do we want to laugh or cry?
Sometimes smile or frown
Do we solve problems easily,
or find we often compound?

Sometimes with problems we're too involved
And can't see the trees for the forest.
If we don't look at them objectively
Our emotions can destroy us.

There is no one else we control,
Yet others are part of our lives.
How much they influence what we do
Is up to us to decide.

We'll forever be faced with decisions,
And there's only us to blame
If life is not going the way it should,
Then it's our choices we'll have to change.

Bette Berger

"Lord, Help Me"

Lord, don't let me grow tired and discouraged,
About the things You have for me to do...
Help me to keep my mind focussed,
Knowing that whatever I do is for You.

Help me to know what to say to the one
Facing surgery and who is afraid,
Help us to know that it's all in Your hands
And You have heard all we asked as we prayed.

Send me the wisdom to know how to comfort
The one for whom doctors say there's no hope!
They say that there's no more options,
And what's left for them is just to cope.

I know when I feel frail and helpless,
I'm thinking I'm just here alone...
I've lost sight of the fact that You're with me,
The strength comes from You; it's not my own!

I wonder why You picked such a weak vessel?
Yet, You know me better than I do!
Let me continue to do what I can for others...
Praising God and giving glory to You! AMEN
   Daphne Phillips

You Were Born Only Yesterday

You were born only yesterday, and already, there's change,
absolutely for better, and not a bit strange.
I counted your fingers, and then, all your toes.
Your skin was so soft, you had a little pink nose.

We read lots of stories and played peek-a-boo,
then for a moment I blinked, you were suddenly two.
We laughed and we played with cars, trucks and dolls.
I bandaged your boo-boos and comforted your falls.

You brought home a dog, a lizard, a cat,
a hamster, a rabbit, I said "NO" to the rat.
The day you turned six, you climbed your first tree.
You were born only yesterday, how could this be?

For dessert we had cake, the candles were ten.
I looked at you closely, then counted again.
You went on to college to earn your degree.
You were born only yesterday, how could this be?

The years have passed quickly, then before I knew,
you were up on the altar, saying "I do".
You're all grown up now, your kids, there are three,
YOU were born only yesterday, how could this be?
   Danielle M. McCoy

With You

In the darkness I can see it all.
Across the room you stand so tall.
Do you know I am here with you?
I watch the tears roll down your cheek.
Your fists close tight, you are feeling weak.
Can you see I am here with you?
I hate it that you feel this way
I know it hurt when he went away.
Do you know I am here with you?
Soon the pain will disappear.
The memories you will hold dear.
I will be there with you.
Through this you will regain strength
Life goes on, Love you may thank.
Because I am here with you.
   Jayne Eastman

Calm The Sea

Calm the sea and walk with me,
across the sea of life that's shaken me.
Calm the sea and walk with me,
upon the shores of this wretched world
that's taunting me.
Calm the sea and walk with me,
show me peace and tranquility.
Calm the sea and walk with me,
are you truly what you seem to be?
Can you calm the sea and raging rivers
that's whelming up inside of me?
Lord calm the sea and walk with me,
I can not with stand the storm that's taunting me.
Lord calm the sea and walk with me,
It's beating at my soul and ripping at my sails,
as I crash against the rocks of life
and ever lasting hell.
Calm the sea and walk with me,
Lord please calm me.
   Jackie Rice

Expression Of A Mother's Love

My dear American beauties
Adorned with grace, charm and brilliance,
Growing on a stem covered by thorns
Protecting the delicate petals which unfold
To embrace the life you so richly enhance,
The hearts you so warmly touch.
The storms ahead will tear your lovely petals apart
Leaving their gentle perfume scattered about
Only to have your loveliness extend beyond
The confines of your nurturing place.
The clinging thorns will dry and die,
Preparing you to blossom in the years ahead.
You need not feel trapped by the thorns
For you are American beauties
In the realm of your being.
Soon you will both grow into
A beautiful rose.
   Christine French

Gifts From Aunt Will

Occasions like these

Simple times around the table after Mother prepared the meal;
After Daddy's special blessing gave a warm delightful appeal.

There's always plenty served. Prepared by Mother's faithful hands.
I remember her biscuits. I smell bacon in the pan. The fresh milk, eggs, potatoes, cabbage, peas and the rest came from our farm and garden. We always ate the best. Fried chicken from our yard made a favorite dish. Lemon pie and chocolate sometimes answered our fondest wish. The home made 'safe' stood by filled with goodies good and fine. Seemed like mother's tea cakes were the top of the line!

Daddy would tell a tale about his childhood ways. We laugh and ask questions concerning by gone days.

I wish I could go back in time to enjoy occasions like these. To hear Daddy ask the blessing and to see Mother pass the peas.
   Frankie Hultz

Ocean

The waves handed the shore their water.
As they came near they began to yell.
As it crashed on the shore it began to crawl
up the shore.
At the end it looked like it died and was beheaded!
   David Robert Quintana

The Danish Dresser

"I want this," she said, touching it tenderly...meaning
after I'm gone and won't need earthbound treasures.
What she wants is my sturdy, Danish, dresser.
Ah, yes, in her solitary childhood, this was not
just a dresser. It was her Fantasy Land:
brand-new then, with a four-foot mirror on the right;
slender but functional with nine drawers, spaced
three in a row; colored like papershell pecans
and a three-inch ledge near the bottom
where she stood, moving "Windsong," "Chantilly,"
and miniature perfume bottles all around.
She called them *people*.
What do Bottle People do?
Eat lunch on a roundtable, dusting powder box,
recline beneath a pink shade, treelamp,
or ice skate on white, dresser-scarf lake?
She shall have this dresser.
Her scuff marks on the ledge prove squatter's rights.
Some special day, she'll look at it and remember
the little girl, who stood on the edge of Fantasy Land.

Adeline C. Erwin

A Rose By Many Other Names

I plucked it that afternoon from her bouquet,
  after saying my last goodbye.
Though it was set in honor of me,
  only with her light did it shine.
Placed on my windowsill illuminating the shadows,
  It glowed with a halo of purest beauty:
  A blood red divinity, shaming the darkness.
Yet as it intrigued me, its frailty also repressed me.
  Longing to touch its delicate form,
Daring not lest my impurity soil its sacred grace.
No matter how mystical the rose, it could not compete with time,
  And soon my vigils were replaced with works still
yet to be done.
  Taken for granted and ignored,
  It had no reason to remain.
  It seemed I only turned away for a moment,
  But the rose was gone.
  And all that remained was a single petal,
  And a memory of its grace.

Heather Greenwell

The Wall

The wall
all around me,
tempting me, mocking me,
stands but four feet high,
a small wall compared to most,
yet no one ever climbs it,
simply this.. no one in, no one out,
as I approach this wall, that perfect, handsome wall,
it grows in size,
but in reality it is I who shrinks, smaller and smaller,
so I retreat before I fade,
back to my origin,
and so starts the cycle again.

Anthony Colon

Untitled

"Should have" and "could have" are phrases we use every day,
Because of things we did not do, or words we did not say.
We must be more positive and not procrastinate.
Let's learn to say and do the things our hearts seem to dictate.
But if by chance this can't be done, we "should have" no regret.
What "could have" been is in the past and that we must forget.

Ann Guida

Untitled

I didn't like my little brother, he was such a pest
All he did was run and screech, he never stopped to rest
Slopped his food, he ate with his hands
Made loud useless noises, like an old rock band
He crawled on me with pokes and kicks from elbows and toes
Mom says "He's only a baby, just wait this stage he'll outgrow"
He followed me everywhere, just being a bigger pest
Sharing a room with him, really put me to the test
We had our fights and arguments, how I loved to tattle and tell
There were times when, shared as friends,
  on the beach gathering shells
He flirted with all my girlfriends, which made me really mad
He took my favorite girlfriend, she dumped him, that made me glad
We kinda grew apart through the college years
Going on our separate ways, at times we shared a beer
Baby brother got married, and lived not too far away
Visiting became the same old problem, its the price I pay
Crawling and kicking all over me, sloppy food, messy hands
Running and bouncing, screeching as a loud rock band
I watch and wait see him grow
Somehow it reminds me of the someone else I knew

Carlene Wyrich

Untitled

The silence of the room was almost to scary to bear.
All I could hear were the sounds of the walls cracking
As the earth settled in it's place.
As I listen to the silence I thought, is life dead as we know it?
Suddenly my heart started pounding and I realized I was
scared by the silence in the air.
Then I realized I was scared of death!
The silence made me want to scream, to be able to say "I
will never die, I am Immortal!"
By saying I was Immortal was even more scary than Death.
Then I realized, I was scared of Life!

Angela Born

Thoughts Are Things

Our thoughts have wings, they flit and fly
All over the earth and all through the sky
Sometimes we think no one will know
But then the actions start to show
For our thoughts come back in the form of things
To bless or hurt us, to make us sad or sing

They hold the power over us in the end
They can be our worst enemy or be our best friend
For our thoughts are things measured and weighed
That's why it's so vital our mind is stayed
On the thoughts of mercy, goodness and love
So we can reap from the bounties above

For regardless of where our thoughts go
That's where they take root and start to grow
And as they grow they become stronger and stronger
Molding and changing us until we no longer
Are the person who thought that very first thought
But we are the end result of what it brought.

Frances C. McArthur

Deceptive Illusions

Upending misery, shattered dreams,
are life's constant companions, it seems.
The dream always out weighs the truth
in excitement and vigor, as in our youth.
The dream is perfect, the truth is not,
It never measures up to what you thought.
Wouldn't life be perfect if the truth was the dream
and all life's hardships we could redeem?

Bonnie Soderquist

Christmas In America

T'was the night before Christmas and all through the town,
all the homeless were searching for a place to lie down.
Their clothes were few, all tattered and torn,
the looks on their faces were sad and forlorn.
They were all cold and hungry, no hopes of food in sight,
as they wandered around aimlessly, alone through the night.
To visit with family or a very close friend,
had been long forgotten as their days come to end.
The food that they eat is not turkey or hams,
but scraps from the street or half-empty cans.
As they wander the streets and search for hope,
they silently remember Mary's struggle to cope.
For just like her they are in a way,
alone, cold and hungry with no place to stay.
So as we sit down to our food and good cheer,
let us not forget that we too could be there.
For in a blink of an eye our whole life could change,
if we become greedy, forgetting the pain
of the homeless and hungry alone in the streets,
searching for shelter and a small bite to eat.

Jennifer Hooks

The Keymaster To My Safehouse

Pent up anger, love, stories, creativity.
All these things building up inside of me, growing swarming,
festering, screaming to escape.
She gave me a key to the problem, a safehouse for my expression.
A journal or diary, a notebook or single pieces of paper.
Many thoughts jumbled up and running together spewed out on paper.
It is all the same, a way to have freedom for what needs to be expressed.
She told me to let the thoughts flow, that whatever was created
would be pure and beautiful because it had been set free to run
and scream as it pleased.
She was not only a teacher, but also a mentor, a friend and a
person with many feelings and insights into life.
Susan taught me to love myself, my feelings, and my ideas.
She gave me a ticket to freedom, a ticket to a new way of life.

Cherish Booth

Cats Are People, Too

Some people say that cats are not people because they cannot talk
All they do is play, but that is not true, not true at all
Cats talk in their own special language, in their own special way.
Some people say that cats are not people because cats have paws,
Not hands, but that shouldn't matter because they use their paws the
same way we use our hands, but in their own special way.
Some people say that cats are not people because cats have fur not
Hair, but that should not matter because they take care of their fur
the same way we take care of our hair, but in their own special way.
So now you see that cats are people, but in their own special way.

Carolyn M. Beaudet

Missing You

There are people you forget, after they move on.
And some you never forget, no matter how long they've been gone.
Some will always stay in the corner of your mind.
That thought is so comforting knowing it's there to find.
It can bring sorrow to your heart, and tears to your face.
When someone is gone, whom you can never replace.
But they're looking down on you from some place in the sky.
And always comforting your pain, when you stare and wonder why.

Jordan Hugh Lee

"The Dead Friend Whom I Never Met"

Oh Lord, I've gone and done it again
All those stupid, idiotic geniuses finally got to me
They won't understand and be peaceful to my pleas
And my grave is getting colder
Lord, you and I get along so well together
I will never have one to be this way
I sit and watch from my early days of childhood
They hear the silence and blame me
They harp on me until I turn into my elder self
I now care no more for what has ever happened
I'm better, but no one is here to welcome me
There is never anyone, and I fear, there never will be
As the real ones approach me, the bricks within me flux
Like the rapid compensations of a bio-mechanical man
I always did like Lost in Space
There will never be a revolution of my kind
Probably a fault within our secretly engineered plague of deliverance
Yes, the vials were beautiful, with their labels made of negatively
charged happy face stickers
Oh love of loves, show me the way, come to me, and never leave me
alone and dead again

Dillon Smith

I'd Rather Be Dead

On you it is my heart that is set
Allowing things to come between us, I wouldn't let
For you, I'll do all I possibly can
So by my side, I hope you'll always stand
I'm opening my heart to show you that I love you so
And no matter what happens, it would be hard for me to let you go
If you ever told me you didn't want my love anymore.
Then I'd have nothing left to live for
Just the thought of you not lying next to me in bed
I'd rather be dead
Not having you close to my heart
Will tear it all apart
Tell me you'll always stay
Leaving your love with me each and everyday
Let me know that your love will always be true
Because I'd rather be dead than be without you

Edwina Bryant

Untitled

I use to walk all day for miles,
along abandoned tracks.
One step after another,
breaking up the ground to back when
our lives were open and lived
with thunderous direction.
A locust jumps. Quick like thought.
A dusty place stirred where I stop,
and bury myself feet first,
down, down to the headspring
of our once shared memory.
Here the line is broken:
Under the bed and milepost,
further still beneath the rose.
Countless currents enfolded the world around us.
Our sheet flew away with the sky.
And so breaths held we reveled,
in the billowing reach of love's cry.

Bethany Woodward

Special Friend

A special friend is a treasured golden thread,
Always there to share moments of joy, laughter, and delight.
When a day turns to grief and sorrow a true
  friend can help make it bright.
Sharing thoughts and caring helps heal life's problem days.
This human touch will help us through the darkest maze.
Years fly by — pleasant memories grow
  the size of the tallest mountain.
Often we stop to recall memories from this special treasure fountain.
Sometimes I stop and say, "This friend means so much to me."
Many years ago God helped our paths to cross we both agree.
Joy and sorrow we have shared together making our friendship stronger.
May both of us continue to live and share this friendship longer.
    Ethel M. Shannon

So Thankful

Looking into their sweet innocent eyes,
Am completely overcome...love...
Responsibility.....the kind of wife...
The kind of mother I must be.

Parents mirrored in the eyes of their children.
Eyes of love...reflecting eyes of love.
Looking into their eyes...so trusting...pure love...
Complete fulfillment...so glad they are mine.

Looking into his eyes...so sincere...
Am lost in two pools filled with love.
Eternal love....eternal devotion.
Love him so much....so glad he is mine.

Sacred calling....wife and mother...
Guiding them in their tender years.
Praying for wisdom....guidance...strength...
So thankful...so thankful.
    Eva Murphy Phelps

"South Africa's Yesterday"

There's a South Africa,
America knows all too well,
A South Africa...hopefully...of yesterday,
That resembles America's segregated hell;

With little black children in this nation,
Being sent to one set of schools,
As little white children...at another (set),
Were taught to hate—by big white fools;

Racially "separate, but equal" accommodations,
Of all varieties and kinds,
Supported by ignorant and bigoted folks;
With equally small, narrow minds;

And though now, both countries...no longer have apartheid laws,
People can still be judged by skin color—by those with biased views,
And so, equal justice and opportunities...can still be dreams deferred
Of the type once described by poet, Langston Hughes;

Sadly...the promise of true racial equality for all,
Still lacks fruition—in either nation,
And Dr. King's "dream"...has yet to match the reality,
Since, the content of mankind's character still needs reformation.
    Jerrold Kleiman

Unity Of Islands

We are each an island, unique
  Amid a sea of individuals
We direct our course in life
  Stumble, but continue on

And we are not alone

Along this rugged path
  We gather our values and beliefs
Surrendering some,
  While strengthening others

We meet someone special and we know we are not alone

When we join hands with another it reveals our inner self
We share what was our own, join together and begin anew

Encourage one another and harvest the good of your lives
Battle together and overpower the trials and obstacles.

Remember that you are individuals and
  Your differences cannot harm your unity
You are together for the good of both
  And together you become one island

May the best years of your lives begin every day.
    Dale Dehoff

Definition Of Self

Among glances, I am the second one,
Among footsteps, I am the thunder,
Among scissors, I am the cutting edge,
Among keys, the one which opens the door.

Among weapons, I am the peace,
Between sighs, I am the heartbeat.
Among nights, I am the brightest star,
Among letters, the true friendship.

Among questions, I am the answer,
Among windows, the one which is unbreakable.
Among the dreams you find in the heart,
The one that came true was mine.
    Christina R. Lynch

To My English Teacher

Today an era has passed.
  an African country is calling my teacher of English prose
To join with a drum beat
  and fall-in with a roll call.
"Come, wake me up to the other side of the sun
  taste water from crystal streams
  never imagined in dreams.
  Hear tales of brotherhood
And unite us in your dignified way.
Teach us to laugh with grace
  and school us as you have our white brothers."

Miles and Miles away from me here,
  schooled by her words of aged repute
  travels my teacher.
And whether or not
  we meet again,
  I revere her
  by reading English.
    Clare Ventura Butchart

A Tear For A Child

A tear for a child is shed by millions, the river cried has become
   an endless ocean.
A tear for the touch that can only linger, a tear for the laugh that haunts.
A tear for the tears that were kissed away, and replaced with a
   sunshine smile.
A tear for the light that's been lost.
A tear for the little Prince who's pockets were full of string, and
gum on his shoes, the frogs that he liked to chase.
A tear for the little Angel who stands in shoes too big, and wears
a dress too long with pearls and lipstick.
A tear for a child is shed for all who have been senselessly lost.
The hugs that can't be felt, the "I love you's" that will never be
heard, the empty playgrounds that scream their silence.
A tear for a child is shed, and their loss has been felt.
   Judith Russell-Mannick

An Artist

Bottles and bowls sitting alone on the horizon are his past
An unformed innocence, his awakening dream
But it is the present that fires his soul
"Now" is when he wedges moments into stone
Painting life into clay with bright colors of liquid glass

His strong hands caress life into sleeping limbs
As unformed eyes wait with anticipation for his mind
   to create a world unknown and alive
Softly and patiently the reclining figure becomes reality
Through a glaze of pink she melts into soft clay under his touch
The firing of her soul bringing her farther and farther from
   the frozen past
She lies drenched in life within the tropical heat
   and naked before his eyes
   Amy Eagan

Christmas

A glass of whiskey
and a shot of rum
gives my heart a tickle
and warms my belly
readying me for the winter
of icy cold months
of indoor fires
blazing with the glow
of marshmallow madness.
With greedy children running and roaming
seeking the rustle of wrapping paper presents.
He can Ho Ho Ho, but they don't care
All they want are the presents
in the sack over there.
The sack over there!
   Chris Edwards

"The Dreamer"

If dreams were given to lonely men,
And lonely men's dreams come true,
I'd force myself to sleep so I could dream of you.
If wishes were given to lonely men and I was granted two,
I'd wish for you to always love me,
And the other wish I would save for you.
If tears could write a love song and love songs were made for two,
You'd know just how I feel inside and how much I do love you.
But dreams are just for dreamers and wishes seldom come true,
My tears won't write a love song, but when they fell,
They fell for you!
   Brett P. Short

You, So Lovely...

Alone in the rain, heart bruised
And a tear in your smile tonight, in my arms
You said: It's cold at home please love me, hug me
A rose crushed
with her petals exposed to the whims to the wind.
Blood red, pain eternal and reflective like a love poem.
The eyes says it all; It's midnight at the threshold of life
When the heart is waiting for a beat to sing to
Night is a time good for hanging the sorrow
Of the soul away from the mind, I say.
The shine of the moon always reminds me of silky skins
Moon a glowing, sweat glittering hope glimmering
Love simmering, happiness lingering on the steps to forever.
Reality shimmers with the dreams of yesterday
The image that is reflected on the wings of time
Paper moon for paper dreams. Therefore I,
When it's my time to dream I'll dream platinum
I'll dream of you, so lovely,
Waiting, with the sun a shining in your heart
For me to make you mine.
   Frantz Guichard Israel

How Did I Let It All Pass Me By?

As I say good-bye to all those years of piggy-tails
and adolescent fears
of making fun of playing dolls
of velcro shoes and horrible falls

I sit here this morning and realize that
all those years have passed me by

I try so hard to remember when
I lost my first tooth or made my first friend

I sit here and think
then begin to cry
Why can't I remember,
was it all just a lie?

How will it be when I'm eighty-eight
Will I remember the time I was on my first date?
The time I got braces or learned to drive
Or the time I turned the big 1-5.

As I sit here this morning
tears in my eyes
I ask myself this-
How did I let it all pass me by?
   Cheryl Birkey

If Only

If only things were different
and although they're not,
I can't help but long for
your gentleness, your passion, your touch!

If only for a moment and not only in my thoughts,
you make me quiver when our bodies lock!
You kiss me, you caress me and
then you fill me up.

If only I could stop myself
for when I think of you, my heart starts to pound
and I feel certain sensations
upon which I could expound.

If only I could stop thinking of you
and the moments that we've shared.
Can we survive with just reminiscing?
Only time will tell!
   Cheryl Delander

Choices

Choices - decisions of desperation - determined at last by exhaustion and despair
I know what I want and need to fulfill myself, I always have, I always will
In the knowing there are no unknowns for me - no personal risks
The mirror's reflection is clear, penetrating through the mass to my soul
Yet, like a giant magnet, the needs and the wants of the many tug viciously at my poles
Until once again I am drained of my own identity
The decision has been made
And now, as if drugged and unconscious, I am adrift
Floating powerlessly in a sea of surrender
Afraid to risk the happiness and security of others for my own gratification
I choose what is best for the many
A bittersweet trade off for the agony and disappointment of my own self denial
Where lies the honesty and virtue in the final decision?
When will I find the strength to be true to myself?
And after I pass from this life how will the many remember the one?
What glory, honor and dignity is there in the remembrance of a martyr?
Should I count myself fortunate to know the gift of CHOICE
Or would my life be rich with joy and peace if I were but a pawn of destiny?

BonnieAnn Callahan

"I Wonder"

Is a heart really whole?...
And does it have one single destiny?
Or is a persons heart only half
Of it's opposite self existing in another?
Could be, Love is: Two hearts,
with one destiny,..in two parts.
Opposites everywhere, just look around, from sky to ground.
It's so plain to see, so I had to wonder of my heart inside of me.
Am I lacking? Or is my heart already whole?
Is ones heart Love? Or...is love, heart spirit and soul?
Have I only half a heart, waiting to become whole?
Or do I exist to know my other part?
Then to what do I explain, In solitaire I am the same?
Yes I wonder, could it possibly be, my heart waits for unity?

Cynthia L. Belanger

My Dream Boy

I meet him when I close my eyes
And drift off to sleep...dreaming.
He is there often, popping up anywhere.
Then we are together
Laughing and talking like any normal twosome.
Will it ever be in the real world?
I feel I have known him all my life.
I know everything about him.
If someone asks for his description,
I would not be able until I actually meet him.
Everything is closed up in secrets,
Under lock and key in my dreams.
When I do spot him in the real world,
His face will come into focus.
The future holds our encounter.
I am constantly watching and waiting;
But I am not unhappy.
I will always have him in my dreams-
My mysterious dream boy forever!

Debra J. Schuld

Ethos Of Her

She seeks the truths of life through crystal teardrops
And eyes of deepest darkest brown
How often must her gentle heart be broken
Before she reaches for her golden crown

She knows the joy of everlasting friendship
Has felt the sweetness of her child's touch
Accepts the finer things in life as tokens
And trusts the wisdom of the Lord above

Yet there is an emptiness within her
Unfounded by her lust for love and life
She has yet to fulfill the dreams she has spoken
To allow herself to be free from strife

Although she says "one day I'm going to do it"
She needs a hand to hold along the way
To love and gently guide her through it
When all around her look the other way

Diane M. Hubiak

A Greater Ride

I always dreamed that I would ride.
  And follow the Rodeo circuit.
Going from town to town there seemed to be
  Great Romance in it.
But as it goes, we all should know, it's God's will
  and not our own
We live our lives by his Great plan
  to let his lite be shown.
So I am not famous, no bareback Trophies
  sitting on the mantle
But blessed I am, you see I am called mommy
  and I am thankful
The ride you get from motherhood
  There's nothing to compare
So I tell you now look up be proud
  It's this I want to share
Rodeo and Cowboy days are written in the past
Content I'll be "I am Mommy"
  It's more than I can ask.

Betty Klassen

Two Hearts

They say that a man has only one heart
And for some that may be true
But I am not the average man,
For in truth, I have two.
One beats inside my mighty chest
Pumping blood throughout my being,
The other is inside the breast of a woman
Without whom I cannot long survive without seeing.
My first heart beats ever faster and faster
Whenever she enters my mind,
For I know a finer woman was never made
Nor a better wife could I ever find.
"Therefore shall a man leave his father and his mother
And shall cleave unto his wife"
These were the words spoken so long ago
By the Giver of all life.
They say a man has only one heart
Tell me, my love, is this saying true?
Alas, my darling, I think not,
FOR MY SECOND HEART IS YOU.

Ian L. Ketterer

There Is One

There is One who knows the ocean's depths
And has walked IN those depths as well;
There is One who knows where heaven is
And also the location of hell.
There is One who knows the foundation of earth,
And just where the cornerstone lays;
There is One who knows the exact end of time,
And how many more will be our days.

There is One who commanded the morn to appear
And caused the dawn to rise in the east;
There is One who fashioned the woman and man,
And formed from the clay each beast.
There is One who knows the extent of the earth
And the location of the gates of death,
There is One whose Son died on a cross,
And will conquer His foe with a breath.

Cynthia Cochran Kinard

Affair With A Sailor

My love is a sailor, the sea has his heart,
And he's never happy when they're far apart.
A lifetime he spent, in courting her there,
Unafraid and courageous, with a smile and prayer.
For many have perished at her fickle desire,
She's cruel, unforgiving, like brimstone and fire.
With fury and rage, no mercy has she,
For a brave fearless sailor, who dares go to sea.
Deep like a woman, she's calm for a while,
Then she'll take him down, without even a smile.
Unsuspecting and trusting, he may soon find that he,
Is on a bottomless journey to eternity.
Flirting, yes daring a man to be brave,
She entices him down to a watery grave.
Yet this man has rode her, and conquered her moods,
Forgiving her dearly, as a true sailor could.
Like a mountain to climb, a challenge remains,
And he'll rush to meet her, to woo her, to tame.
On ships large and small, he has traveled afar,
A steady set course, he has followed his star.

Duana Schaefer

Out Of Reach

Will you have me put into words the love that I have for you;
   And hold the torch out while the winds are howling.
I drop at your feet.
I cannot teach my hand to hold my spirit so far off from myself -
   me, that I should bring you proof in words of love hid in me,
   and out of reach.
Am I cold, ungrateful for all you have done for me?
   You think I have rendered nothing back at all.
Not so, not cold, but very poor instead. Ask God who knows.
   For frequent tears have run the colors from my life and left me dull.
And the words turn within myself, forming thoughts but no sounds;
   Only I can hear when I say to you, "I love you with the breath,
   smiles, tears, of all my life;
and, I shall but love you better in another time and place,
   and, out of reach.

Anne Polise

The Basketball Jersey

A basketball jersey is filled with hundreds of wins and the joy of being the best possible. The smell of success fills the jersey. It is cold like a championship game that was lost, and warm like a game winning shot that was made at the buzzer. It is smooth like the texture of a basketball running through your fingers and being gently pushed downward again. It sounds like the cheering of the crowd after a game that has just been won.

Andrew Taegel

Ben

He knows how it feels to be the "responsible one"
and how great it can be to let loose and have fun.
He's always here for me—just a phone call away,
to give me advice or help me through the day.
He's understanding, supportive, and helpful too,
and he's always here for me when I'm feeling blue.
He's trusting and caring and fun to be around,
and he always lifts me up when I'm feeling down.
I look up to him as I do my big brother,
and I wouldn't trade our friendship for any other.
Wherever I go, I'll take my stuffed cow
to remind me and be a symbol of just how
a good solid friendship will win in the end.
That's why I cherish my good friend, Ben.

Jennifer S. Coleman

Love In The Eyes Of A Child

Love in the eyes of a child, is for believing.
And I possess no value of greater worth.
It's warm in innocence and undeceiving.
And I have found no greater feeling on this earth.
If I have known true love, it is from my children.
God bless them, will remain my constant prayer.
Other forms of love may prove bewildering.
But in their eyes I see that love is there.
It's warm and sweet, and never too demanding.
When giving me my children, God has smiled.
Their love is always filled with understanding.
And the purest love I've known, is from a child.
Well, I've never had much wealth, or worldly treasure.
But in their presence, I became a king.
Their love gives me a joy I can not measure.
But without them, I become a wretched thing.
God give me grace, that I may watch them growing.
Til the fury of my life is reconciled.
And when I go, I'll leave this old world knowing,
That the purest love I've known, is from a child.

Don Underwood

"Sometimes"

Sometimes the sky is painted in blue,
And I remember the day I first met you

Sometimes a flower will bloom and live forever,
While I think of times we shared together

Sometimes the clouds hide away the sun,
And two hearts mend together to become one

Sometimes the winter grows long and cold,
While you are the only one I want to hold

Sometimes the rain washes away the day,
And I can only wish you were here to stay

Sometimes the summer breeze blows through a tree,
While I dream of a day when you'll be with me

Sometimes the sky is painted in blue,
And all I want to say is I love you

Bobby Barringer

Car Horns

Car horns passing by my city dwelling -
Blaring, insistent, irritating
Sparring with other horns
Revealing their owner's state of mind -
Frustration, anger, rage
At their sudden and unwanted helplessness

Christa R. Fordham

'Round The Bend

In a distant land flows a river,
And in this river is a bend.
With steadied hand and studied eye,
Schooled by daily tide and sudden storm,
The ferryman ferries his passengers
Back and forth from shore to shore
But never 'round the bend.

But once his hire
Be destined 'round the bend,
The ferryman, though sailing the same river
And returning now and then to familiar shore,
May not want to sail again
The charted course
He sailed so many times before.

Edward Zerin

"The Gazebo Retreat:"

Come sit inside my gazebo retreat,
And inhale the breath of the Lilacs, sweet;
Feed the squirrels, — see them scurry around,
Picking up treasures from the ground:

I sprinkled birdseed just after dawn,
For my feathered friends banquet out on the lawn
Their food and their drinks are provided free;
They drink from the fountain and sing with glee:

They have a free community bath,
Just outside the garden path;
See the flowers in shades of the rainbow's hue;
And Roses, kissed by the morning dew:

The Butterfly bush draws the butterflies;
Hummingbirds on wing seem to hypnotize, —
Not much bigger than a bumble bee,
With an ariel show for all to see:

Before the curtain of night-time falls,
Listen, with me, to the Whippoorwill's calls;
You'll be intoxicated by the floral perfume,
In my garden gazebo, where Roses bloom.

M. Jane Turano

In Loving Memory Of Nannie J. Worthy Fleming

The angels are singing
And Jesus is here

We are all now together
With no worries or fears

With hope in our hearts
For those left behind

That they too will join us
When Jesus calls time

Don't cry but rejoice
For we are happy not sad

We no longer hurt
Nor ever feel bad

There are no tears up here
And we never get bored

Every day is filled with gladness
And praising our Lord

Joyce H. McDaniel

The Pilot Within

To Parents and Teachers
Teach them to find the Pilot within,
And let them fly, fly with the wind.
Tell them the Highest should be their aim;
Then let the Pilot show them the way.

Teach them of faith in the Pilot within.
Faithfulness means to have wings as eagles.
Show then your faith in the Pilot within you,
And let them fly, fly with the wind.

The how to fly, and the when to fly,
The way to fly and the where to fly,
Is for the Pilot Himself to decide,
And each of His eagles He expertly guides.

Show them a glimpse of the limitless universe.
And tell them to heed the Pilot within.
Then, heed yourself the Pilot within you,
And just fly, fly, fly with the wind.

Clementina Ceide Leist

Flying

Let me soar through the orange crescent skies,
And look at God's creation from on high.
As a pilot may I feel the power of escalate through
The silvery blue clouds.
Guide my plane through the storms or the soft
Blue sunny skies.
Let me gasp in awe at the majesties of the mountains
And rippling rivers below.
May I always be reminded of the power source from on high.
Let me take control of my journey
And be reminded that power and control needs an energized source
And a manager of performance to maintain balance beyond the
Starry skies.
For in the twinkling of an eye,
We will meet the Pilot bye and bye.

Jane Thompson

Care For Free Or Less

My self-esteem ran away from home.
And my confidence went on vacation last week.
Why not?
It's summer.
It's time to bask at the beach among strangers
While our blood boils
And our skin hatches cancerous growths.
It's time to sip lemonade
And flaunt our sexuality.
Yet here I am - alone;
Picking paint off the walls
And dreaming myself complete.
Where did February go?

Jennifer M. Sanders

Raw Suit

Let us go out among the trees, my love,
Among the confidential trunks and leaves,
Discreetly rustling in the warm night breeze.
Let us go out beneath the stars, my love,
Beneath the slyly winking summer stars,
That witness everything and keep their secrets.
Let us go out into the field, my love,
Where wildflowers run riot in the day
And shut their pretty eyes up in the night.
Let us go out into the night, my love,
And f***

James de Weese

Forever

If my Kingdoms turn to sand
And North winds carry them through
How will I then be able to think you?

When mountains crumble to oceans blue
Crest of waves come shining through
My every thought will be of you

When the stars lose there place in the sky
There I'll be - holding one for you

For when rivers run dry
And my eyes begin to cry
There I'll be - waiting for you

When the walls of ruins tumble
Drifting into seas of silence
Under the dark skies I'll sail
In hopes to find you
And tell you I love you
Ella Mieszkowski

Hi, God, Are You There?

  Are you listening to me?

I'm really confused, as to whom I'm to be.

  I wish you could help, I really feel lost.

  Acting out of control,
and not considering the cost.

  I sometimes talk to myself,
and then make myself cry.

  Feeling alone, and not knowing why.

I think its my dad, I miss him you see.

  He was my bestfriend, but he died and
left me.

  Since he's been gone, its myself I don't know

  I forgot how to trust, and how
to let go.

  He was always my strength and my honesty too.

Knowing just when to say,
"Its ok, I love you."

  So God don't you see,
I have to go on

But how do I start, when my father is gone.
Ginger Martin

Love Is

  Love is for the strong,
    and not for the weak
Love can be as simple as a kiss on the cheek
  Love is always right,
    and very seldom wrong
Love can be shared by two who get along
  Love is simply magical,
    but sometimes it takes time
Love is why you are always present in my mind
  Love is sugar sweet
  Love is always true,
and I know love is what I feel when I'm around you.
John Czerwinski

Our Love

As our love blooms, and goals and desires become one.
And our children have grown.
Now you see it's our time, for our love.
The young love, the powerful love, has come and gone.
A sensitive love remains.
One of understanding, one of pride.
As we become one !
Our dreams, and life's realities have come and gone.
Now, we know one another as we have ever known before.
No more secrets, no more lies, because we have become one.
Once young, and foolish, so carefree.
But, now secure and slow to anger.
But, now wise and careful with responsibilities,
with grandchildren to spoil and send home.
A peace and harmony rain in our home, we have become one!
Now, we have our tender years.
The gray hair, and wrinkles, and lost memories.
Our eyes, and speech have astray,
but we have become one! Till death do us part.
As our love has become one!
Irene J. C. Morris

To A Friend

I looked into your eyes,
   and saw the past ablaze,
Beautiful the memories
   showed and unfolded
As if on a moving screen.
Life in all it's greatness
   projected for me to share.
A place in time I knew not where
But somehow our minds reached out and touched
The communication was so dear.
As if we had meant and been the closest
   of friends in yester years.
The minutes were but a precious few
That I will treasure
in a secret niche within my soul..forever more.
As times years fly by
Often I will unlock the door
That stores within the meeting of two human souls
And will again relive the feeling of friendship
That was so instant but in our troubled times
Anita L Hahn

Friendships Found In Secret Places

I awoke this morning with a tear in my eye
   and a burden on my mind.
I could not remember what would make me cry,
when nothing had upset me or given me cause to sigh.
I have so much, what more, Lord, am to do?
It must be this message that I need to send to you.

Today I said a prayer for you.
I asked the Lord to see you through
the stress and heartache that you might feel
and the burdens that you fight to conceal.

May you be blessed by His loving touch
   and be granted, Oh, so much.
So be thankful to the Lord for all He's done for you,
He's taken what is troubling and making it all work through.

Go now and find a secret place,
to share a moment face to face.
And send a message to a friend,
that they might too find a place
to thank the Lord for all His grace.
Janet Cockriel

Untitled

Take a ride on a moonbeam
   And shake hands with the man in the moon
Or ride on the wings of a butterfly
   During the month of June
Some things are quite complex
   And quite difficult to do
Such as telling you the things
   My heart has hidden for you
You see, my heart longs for you
   Yet it feels obligated to me
Afraid that you may not care
   And someday set it free
But then you give me that certain look
   The one I feel down to my toes
And before I can keep my heart any longer
   Straight to your arms it goes.
   Gaila Bagsby

"Have A Good Day, Anyway"

THERE ARE PEOPLE, PLACES
   and situations,
NO MATTER WHAT YOU SAY,
always out there, they seem to be waiting
JUST TO DESTROY YOUR DAY!
So, I've GOT A MOTTO I WANTED TO SHARE
ESPECIALLY WITH YOU BECAUSE I CARE:
"BAD DAYS ARE FOR LOSERS"
and I'm not in that crowd
so, each day when I start out - I say real loud
"I REFUSE TO HAVE A BAD DAY!"
then I just go on my way
after I take time to pray
YOU TOO CAN BEAT THE ENEMY AT HIS OWN GAME
AND YOUR LIFE WILL NEVER BE QUITE THE SAME
REMEMBER TO PRAY, THEN JUST SAY:
"I ABSOLUTELY REFUSE TO HAVE A BAD DAY!"
   Hadiya S. Barnes

I Soared

I went to bed late one night,
And soared with great wings of flight.
I went so high above the ground,
There wasn't a whisper or a sound.

The people looked small and unimportant to me,
But the earth looked beautiful and
   wonderful to see.
The animals and trees were so full of life,
The humans were so full of hatred and strife.

The sky was so blue, gray and white,
And off in a distance I saw a great light.
It was pointed at the earth as if to see
If there was any hope for you and me.

The animals and the trees seemed natural to be.
But man was wanting to abuse it you see.
As I flew by that light that I saw,
I heard a voice say, "I'll give one more chance to all."

I ended my soar and went back to bed,
knowing that the people could have been dead.
   David Hufstetler

"The Greatest Mom"

   She raised six children of her own,
and some of her Grandchildren to.
   Then along the way she offered her hand
and her home to most of us in need.
   It's good to recall old memories, all the good
times spent with this great Lady called Mom!
   Her home was where I could find a smile,
Welcome hand and love, so true where memories
dwell from the pass, with it's joy and pain often
replaced, by tears at the end of the day,
   So today as she sleeps, I stop and pause
awhile, to thanks thee Lord for happiness she gave,
   I will not doubt thou eyes be damp with
tears, as I go through life to remembrance,
   This great lady called mom is walking
down the sun shinning path, and vision of God
As she walks in peace, and through the Golden gates
   Evelyn L. Messel

All Things Need Love

Have you ever had a puppy run and jump into your lap
And start licking your face, right down onto your neck
It's telling you it loves you, with all it's little heart
Showing everything needs love, and has right from the start
Have you ever seen an old person, looking lonely and sad
Just say hello and smile at them, and see how they react
Perhaps they aren't outgoing, so afraid to speak first
But will beam all over, just to be noticed by you
Even when we take the flower and plant it in our yard
And give it the care it needs, right from the start
It will reward you abundantly, for the love and care you've shown
By giving in return to you, many beautiful blooms
Even when we pray to our God, so high up above
To tell him we love him and his word he gave to us
He won't answer with words you can hear with your ears
But your heart will confirm he loves you, and always will
Love is something the world certainly does lack
So let's put forth the strength we have and try to put it back
We all need to have love, but need to give it to
To exist thru each day, and each night to.
   Evelyn J. Hiryovati

How Could I Not Be Among You?

Think of me in Spring when violets push through dampened sod,
And tender shoots show forth new evidence of God.
On summer nights when fields are softly trod,
Recall the feel of dew-wet grass on feet unshod.
Think of me when rain pelts upturned faces in the morn
When all the world seems pink and newly born.

But mostly think of me in Fall
When Autumn lets her beauty out in all
Her gold from vaults unseen
And glory leaps the void between;
Who says we die when all this comes anew
Whether I am gone or sitting close to you.

Then think of me again when snow falls softly down
To give you rest and peace and surcease from your frown.
Let sorrow cease, wipe all lines clear —
Remember me with joy — not with a tear.
   Helen M. Sheldon

Blue Time

Somewhere between the last scarlet rays, of the winter sunset,
And the arrival of total darkness, over a snow covered landscape,
   Lies.... Blue Time........
Old folks, given to country ways and simple pleasures,
Felt it was a time for terminating a winter day's activities....
   A time for gathering livestock.........
A time for securing one's family, before darkness envelopes,
   The rolling countryside....
The warming glow of a solitary oil lamp, now braces against....
   Yet another January evening,
As Blue Time...descends over the shadowed hill sides....once again.
   Gerald Yokely

To Dorothy, On Our Fiftieth Wedding Anniversary

You're the beat of my heart
And the breath of my life
My wonderful jewel of perfection.
Since you entered my life
In becoming of my wife
You've had all of my love and affection.
You have filled all my days
In such wonderful ways
That time has raced by without rest.
You have guided our years
Through their joys and their tears
In a way that has made them the best.
Our first fifty years was a measure
Of time to look back to with pride,
But now I look forward in pleasure
To sharing still more at your side.
I know that whatever the future
You'll be there with me still to the end
And I'll ever be calling you sweetheart,
My lover, my darling, my friend.
   Cyril W. Johnson

There Is God

When the mask is pulled away,
And the excuses are used up,
and the games have been played.

When all the lies have been exhausted,
And the excitement and thrill of the "greener grass"
In secret places has died.
And the outward chaos and confusion has ceased;
There is God.

In the hurt and the pain
Of broken pieces
That can never be repaired
With human hands;
There is God.

In the self-righteous justifications
And rationalizations
Of acts committed at the expense of hurting
Loved ones; to gain the whole world
(For a moment of pleasure)
and to risk losing your soul
(For all eternity); There is God.
   Cheryl K. Nash

Untitled

If we would take the time to pause, once or twice a day
And think of some kind deed to do, or a thoughtful word to say.
It could brighten someone's spirits who is feeling rather blue
It would only take a minute, but the nicest thing to do.
"Love they neighbor as thyself" is taught by Him above,
But how many of us take the time to think of brother love.
To be considerate of others is the thing we lack the most.
We're busy thinking of ourselves and much to quick to boast.
A thoughtful word, a kindly deed, has great reward for you
You'll find much more contentment in everything you do.
   Jean Muller

Journey

One a virgin to love,
and the other quite experienced
unite tonight, once again,
on a journey of the mind

On this journey,
this far away destination,
the lights are low
and the emotions high

Bodies pressed tightly together
shadows as one;
the two lovers embark on their journey once again

Softly, slowly, nature takes it's course,
the puzzle falls into place..... and once again
the two bare bodies awaken in the morning
holding one another
as they did the night before
yet.... not physically connected

The lovers, you and I, we lie so close,
and yet so far away...
connected by our innerselves..... only in our minds
   Destiny D. Calzadias

The Homeless

They say this is the land of the free and plenty.
Where birds sing and the sky is always blue.
But as we look closer between me and you,
has this society become a plastic jungle that's cold and without justice?

Please lets put a little love in our
hearts and do something about the homeless.

They have no place to go and have been cheated by fate.
Please let's help these people for it's not too late.

If it was your mother or brother, how would you feel;
get concerned because this sad situation is very, very real.

The homeless are suffering, the children are even ridiculed in school.
It's no fault of theirs that in today's times, the dollar bill rules.

All of these poor people are without, and live from day to day.
Something is terribly wrong with the system.
We must pray to God to show us the way.

The homeless will bear scars that time can't erase. Hey, this is
America, let's recapture the dream and clean up this place.
   Adrienne V. Lewis-Ross

In The Spring

In the spring when the snow has melted
And the sky is clear;
The world is right.

In the spring the leaves on the trees, hide the blackened wounds.
The grass grows up through the soil,
And those deep bitter wounds of long ago, seem to mend.

In the spring, the sod is no longer torn by the hooves of horses.
In the spring the air is filled with the scent of flowers,
And alive with the songs of birds.
No more does the crack of the rifle and gun smoke befoul the air.

In the spring all of man's transgressions are forgiven.
All black stains are wiped clean by the hand of God.

Here all ideas forged of hate and conceived in iniquity
Are purged by the soft rains;
Washed clean.

In the spring
The bleached bones of man and beast,
Find solace beneath the watchful eye
Of the gentle poppy.
    Joel Sheridan

A Letter To My Husband On Our 50th Anniversary

I awakened in the night — one night
and thought I had a dream.
I saw a child — and then a crone
and I was in between.
I've shared that time with you, my love
and something special we have had,
The "ups" were pretty wonderful
the "downs" were not that bad.
For 50 years we've traveled
that ribbon of a road
And shared each other's burdens
so they wouldn't be a load.
I wouldn't change a thing, my love,
a perfect match we are;
Or marriage has God's blessings
an ever filling reservoir.
The dream was one of happiness
for both of us, God knows,
As our lives are full of it
and thank you, Lord, it shows.
    Helen V. Campbell

The Fine Attorney

If they stumble over words and stammer in their speech -
And though they choke upon the phrase which tumbles out of reach -
The truth is hard in coming and can be so hard to find -
Until the fine attorney helps to bring it back to mind.

He knows the law and wields it well - he's mastered his profession.
To squeeze the truth from out of those who've yielded no confession -
Is such an art in use of words and rare as precious gold.
But when one does have chance to hear - it's awesome to behold.

How language purrs or cuts straight through those lies they dare to tell -
Attorneys fine can linger there with phrases that will dwell -
Beside the heart that's dark inside until the light is shown -
Upon the truth which shows its face and is at last condoned.
    Betty J. McLeod

Passion's Enlightenment

    The light hits the angle of the rounded sky,
and though time is continuum it stands still — why?
    The touch is soft - the heart is deep, as the strong face
awakens my girlish cheek.
    A strong, firm grip — I am held secure. His lips caress,
no intent, so pure.
    The world whirls 'round, as the boxed in hues of the rainbow
sky clearly diffuse.
    Brilliant eyes have the power, lips gently unite. Energy
climaxes — life is so bright.
    Prism colors explode! My mind is released, to a world of
contentment, a world of peace.
    I am taken away by the angled light; the moment is graceful -
the sense of delight.
    Radiant shapes soon connect; illumination begins. Vivid
patterns ignite — the spectrum opens.
    Pure light is now focused, the beams reach the soul, the
mind's thoughts so trust in the heart's firm control.
    Embracing through time in the mind's dim eye, is the scene
that replays again with a sigh.
    Aimee Bubb

Fishin' Dreams

I think I'll go down to the old fishin' hole,
And try my luck today.
Dad says there really are fish in there,
They just always get away.
I don't have a fancy rod and reel,
And things like they use on TV.
But I got determination, and a lot of faith in me.
So I'll just cast my line out, as far as the eye can see.
And me and my dog, my bestest friend ever,
We'll sit here and wait patiently.
And I'll catch that big trout, and run home to my mom.
And yell "Get out your big frying pan."
For I've just caught a fish, the biggest old fish,
Ever was seen by man.
By gosh Prince, we've been here a while,
It's beginning to be a bore.
So I think if we're gonna eat fish tonight,
We better fish down at the grocery store.
    Jessie H. Good

Untitled

Maybe now the bad times are over
And we will again be back in the clover.
It has been a very long fight,
But, no more will we have lonely nights,
Wondering what will come in the early morning light.

We can finally see the rainbow
And the end of the tunnel.
There are hopes and good times coming,
Now we can slow down the running.

We are now at peace with the Lord on our side,
To cover and protect us while we must abide,
Till we meet our Lord and Saviour
In the great Revelation in the sky.
    Jan Williams

My Loyal Friend

You're my second self; I'm your comforter
And when I myself have problems, you become my listener

I never leave empty-handed whenever we have to part
For your sweet sayings and kind gesture stays in my heart

No matter what I say or do, you never scold me cold
But when I need a shot in the arm, that's when you need to be bold

Friends see things we ourselves cannot perceive alone
I remember many times, our conversations on the phone

We have gone through our struggles with emotions and other dealings
Never were we left in despair, for God knows our feelings

Going through life is not all bruises and bumps
We learn by examples, from our mistakes and triumphs

Take courage, my friend, someday we'll make it through
When paradise is on the horizon, I'll be there to meet you
   Adee DeJoya

Anticipation

'TIS AUTUMN
  and, where did the summer go?
  we played, shared, loved and made merry
  and, now we must think

WINTER
  with furry wraps, hot chocolate
  and fireplaces to keep us toasty warm
  and smiling
  and, next comes the breath of

SPRING
  with its new life and beginnings;
  the buds on the trees and green grass
  and flowers for those we love
  and, before we know it, it's

SUMMER
  with warmth of the sun for picnicking,
  bathing and sports

HOW LUCKY WE ARE TO HAVE THIS WONDERFUL HOME
ON EARTH TO CALL OURS. OH, TO BE THANKFUL FOR
THE SIMPLE, EVERY DAY BLESSINGS!
   Cynthia J. Gifford

Lazy Summer

The fresh wash swaying in the breeze,
and whirring hum of honey bees,
a picnic lunch, a fishing pole,
a dug-out boat by the fishing hole.
Small puffy clouds go sailing by
white ships across a sea-blue sky
a long, cool dip in the swimming pool,
reflection of the days at school,
bright flowers, green grass, and trees that blend
together at the rainbows end.
Long, hot days and crystal rain,
The distant whistle of a train.
A game of ball, and children's laughter,
and strawberry ice cream that comes after.
Revelations of Mother earth
and growing things that give life "worth".
The chores we do, the church bell's tone
this dream belongs to me - alone.
   Audrey D. Hitchen

Selfishness

As I sit here
And wonder, what to do
I should think how, selfish, I am, too
What is selfishness?
Selfishness is something that holds you back
So there must be something that I lack
Lacking in caring about someone else
And only thinking, of myself
Why is it, that I feel all alone?
Because selfishness is something that really, I own
Wondering, why I have such a sad face
Not! Giving a damn, but the whole human race
And thinking that, the ones I love always owe me
Just thinking of selfishness all the years through
When no one will be there only, just you.
   Carol L. Allen

You Can't Spill Peanut Butter

Today are the smears on ivory keys
And yesterday the crackers were gone.
Oh little one - I forgive your dirty knees
But, peanut butter on the telephone?

Is Kale and Spinach such cause to complain?
Are cakes so sweet, pizza so dear.
That you forgot the price of pain
Ain't worth the dentist chair each year?

Unbeknowest I watch the wonder of your years
Don't run to the playground with your mouth so full!
And watching you I'm moved to tears —
This child - this gift - this miracle.
   Harry Hirschman

A Once And Future Regina: Sonnet

To enter you was now, I know, repose.
And yet the touch so dark, so deep did foil
the reachings of my mind that would compose
an understanding searching not for toil.
O yes the fires of the night did burn,
A fever shook us with its mighty storm.
An energy unlocked no one could urn.
A Palace found; a mesmerizing form.
Shakespeare, in all his wit, in all his guile
could not do justice to your flame, I burn.
Your distance a punishment for my smile-
I ache, I dream, I love. Banished, I adjourn.
Our dreams of the past, of the future, laid bare
My nightmare transforming to love, the Queen is near.
   Bertrand R. Norman

Abiding

As dual winds leaves us asunder,
enthralling autumn to swoon;
nature hints other seasons aspire
with frost and fiery dyes shone;
still a cycle will fashion earthly attire;
so on some sunny day, when nothing apposes,
I will beckon your heart, to set on fire,
desiring you at my side, with poetry and roses.
   Anthony D. Brooks

Be Not Afraid

The passage into darkness and fear has been long and cruel
   and you have gone deep into it this night.
I feel your torment of rage against the fading of the light.

I offer you gentleness and hope but take back humble despair.
I offer you my hand and my heart but bring back hollow air.
I offer you strength and courage but you seem not to care.

I search your eyes through to the deepest core of your soul
Be not afraid young man, so near to death's door, soon your
   pain will disappear and you will find peace in place of war.

Release your hostilities and seek the bright shining light,
I too, shed tears along with your fierce tears of the night.

Your fight is over and the light is waiting there for you
Be not afraid, young man, for it is beginning anew.

Your heart and soul are in His almighty hands, therefore abide.
For He will never forsake you, but bring you safely home to
   the other side.

Be not afraid, young man, so near to death's door
Give up to Him your illusions and your dreams foretold
For He will gently lift you with His angels at your side to
a perfect world that awaits you with Him forever as your guide.
   Joanne Michelle Buck

"Be Encouraged"

If your life seems worthless and you are without hope;
And you have tried everything possible, but still cannot cope;
No amount of worry could possibly remove your despair;
There are no friends around, no one who seems to care;
To you, your plight is despicable, deplorable at best;
The world is a jungle, lacking joy, peace, and rest;
Destitution has set in, and being alone is even lonely;
Comfort and security has escaped, so you crave anything homely;
Now you know you are poor, and bankrupt of worldly possessions;
Your epitaph could read "Inventor of personal recessions;"
It is time to wake up and realize your true calling;
That is to make a difference in the world, to keep others from falling;
Who understands character and perseverance better than you?;
Press on with the message that others can make it too;
Submit yourself to God, He will use your precious life;
In a way that encourages others to deal with their strife;
Call on Him who has the answer and can satisfy your every need;
He will water the plant, make it grow, but you must plant the seed;
Seek ye first His kingdom so He can fully show you His love;
Only then can you share with others His blessings from above.
   Donnell Hilliard

Weigh The Gravity

As dusk awakens the cyclopes of wonder,
And Zeus of Libra beckons S.L. Nine.
Countless searching souls will look to ponder,
This awesome display of cosmic design.

In rare audience to plumes of such scale,
One must retreat to weigh the gravity.
For in truth life's revelations seem pale,
Near the text of natures obscurity.

Reflecting this infinite orchestra,
Directed by the hand of creation.
Man may find himself eternal's quanta,
A simple flavor of God's sensation.

Then deterministic complacency,
May be lost to divine contingency.
   Brian Aguilar

Creations

Birds and blooms, leaves and breeze
are all related to the trees.

Would we consider some form of trade
for any of the above when on parade?

Of course we wouldn't, we couldn't even entertain
a thought so embellished with disdain.

We dare not think in terms to discard
items we hold in such high regard.

All nature's creations are here to stay
Ours to enjoy in their magnificent array.
   Frank Cortello

Words Within

These words in my mind
   Are flowing all the time

These words within are like a rush,
   They are a part of me

Where have they come from?
   Where have they been?

These words within are like a certain spint
   Appearing and disappearing,

Coming from the depths of my soul
   They cannot wait,

For they are strong-willed, you see,
   Trying to escape, the master of my fate.

These words within, my words
   I'm glad they are here.
   Catherine Frazier-Allison

A Journey

The rhythms of love
Are of the mind and spirit,
Our bodies add flavor and smells.
Our spirits are joined.
We levitate together,
The music of our voices blend,
Establishing shared pleasures,
Directing us towards each others fulfillment.
Then the memories in silent contemplation,
Bond us even closer.
Comfortable with the knowledge,
That we will share this again.
Then to doze as one,
Awakened to the dream of agape.
   Edward J. Wermann

Old One

Old one, no one really knows
Are you truly old or do you simply tease
Old us out of ancient pasts
Through time and lives into the present?
Haunting sounds so familiar recalling
Ancient friends stirring within
Memories on the edge of darkness
Expanding into the light of our conscience
Pulled outward on strings of harmony
Dancing still lightly out of reach
Illuminated briefly by flickering fires
Retreating apprehensively into primitive caves
Always there with no escape.
Knowing is possible,
Not knowing, too comfortable.
   Bob Jones

Opportunity

I dreamt I was a hunter
Armed with bow
Standing atop a snow-crested hill
The winter wind singing shrill in my frozen ear.
In the valley my quarry
Waits for the arrow
Patient the deer
Whose gaze in the white stillness
Chills my marrow

The string I draw taut
In silent prayer
My frantic thought rushes
Like the ice-laden streams
Lord, let this one
Escape my blow
Let me not hear the screams
Or see the crisp scarlet bright
On ruined snow
Elaine Daley

Making Love

To feel your arms so strong and gentle with care
Around my shoulders soft and bare.
Tender kisses from your lips divine
Make me feel drunk as if from wine.

Our bodies together in a warm embrace
Your tender hands softly caress my face.
I feel your every heartbeat quick and fast
This moment for us forever will last.

We'll love 'til early light
Locked in each others arms oh so tight.
We'll make love whenever we feel
All through the hours these moments to steal.

Our hearts were once torn and tattered
Now have mended with all troubles scattered.
A beautiful love like a rose has bloomed
Sweet words to each we shall croon.

You whisper softly in my ear
"You are mine and I love you dear."
These words so strong and true
I whisper, "Babe, I love you too."
Deanna McCarkindale

Art

Art is the sparrow flying in the blue sky
Art is the bear walking on the black soil
Art is the rose growing in the fertile ground
Art is the tree grasping the ground with its muscular roots
Art is a diamond shining in the sunlight
Art is the eye of a person
Art is the people who created long ago
Art is the ticking of the clock
Art is the time that ticks by
Art is the decoration of the world
Art is nature
Elizabeth Kim

Cherish

Cherish love, hope, joy, and all your dreams.
But above all cherish your good memories.
Memories of love.
Memories of happiness.
Memories of comfort, laughter, and joy
of togetherness.
Cherish them because of what they mean—
everything to you and me.
Erica Nicole Herron

October

My mug of cider, I will sip soon;
As baking apples perfume each room.
And my favorite bowl sets by me;
Filled with walnuts from a nearby tree.

October and its Indian summer haze;
Has about twenty gorgeous days.
The wild geese know what it's all about;
Their v-formations fly down south.

Grab your suitcase, camera, and flee;
Up to crisp New England, God's country.
Where a miracle of nature will unfold;
Watching forests transform to brown and gold.

Holidays are few and far between;
Only Columbus day and halloween.
If autumn is wine, let us drink our fill;
While a harvest moon floods each windowsill.

Like the blink of an eye, this month will go;
Just remember that I told you so.
Thank the good Lord we're here and alive;
To enjoy October in nineteen ninety five.
Austin F. Stebor

Barriers

Majestic stance upon inking board
as fleeing hopeless from human hoard.
Shoot keen slicing through gloomy dark wave
where souls contain a futile brave
who once never in struggling fight
twill asunder among wretched might.
Flee the depth and lingering pasts
of glowering beings with fallen masts.
Too late to rise, too wise too swim,
drowns lonely clown on forgotten whim.
Silver Surfer you've been told
better to die than be bold.
Gregory D. McKay

Looking Within

The joy in my heart seems oh so clear
As I day by day release my fear
Holding in thought those things that are dear
While refusing to believe all that I hear

Arising each day I make the choice
To choose to acknowledge that internal voice
That will guide and direct if attention I'll pay
Letting chaos and noise fall by the way

For just as joy is found in my heart
So too is all that I sought from the start
And though I spent years looking without
Within was where I found the fount

The answer of course, the American dream
Or perhaps being crowned the beauty queen
Or maybe a star of stage and screen
Busyness and greed allay the internal scream

To come to that place of serenity and peace
And behold all that is, if and when I will cease
To believe that forms will calm the beast
When it is within where lies the feast
Carolyn Blumberg

Green

Green is the grass
As I merrily pass
Through the bushes and the green trees too.

As I look at the sky,
Oh me, oh my,
There's a grasshopper stuck on my shoe.

I took off my shoe and said, "How do you do,
What does it feel like to be green?"
"Like spinach, like peas, like green slimy goo,
But most of all like a green bean".

As he said this he flew
Right off of my shoe
And left me thinking of green.
David Toney

You Mean So Much

The warm winds blow through my soul
As I remember the days of long ago
When sadness filled my every day
And nothing seemed to go my way
But then I found you like a match in the dark
Came upon me and lit a spark
My life has been turned around by you
And I want you to know that my love will be true
Till all your aches are cured inside
And all your shame has been replaced with pride
Then all will be happy and full of love
Like a bird in flight; like a pure, white dove
Soaring through the sky so free.
This is all you have meant to me.
Amy Beth Combs

Interment

I had been hungry so many days,
As I saw the fields of gazing grain.
I saw the apple orchard so grand;
From beyond barbed wire so full of pain.

When my mother put me down with a pain
That had no name, I carried myself with fatigue.
To the barrack we walked,
Where I would sleep till early morn.

Be awakened again, and again be with
Other children, with no mother there.
Nor days nor mornings nor evenings with family.

I missed my mother, I missed her so.
She so worn from work and war.
When finally with her;
Our eye lids were heavy with sleep.

Many days have passed and my mother is at rest.
She who had faith and always prayed,
Believed in the joy of salvation.
Rest now peacefully my mother,
In God's loving embrace.
Barbara Stefania Sveitis

Awaken

Rays of light, artificially shining through my bedroom window
As if into the tunnel of my weary restless mind
They are all reflections of the sun
Illuminating the earths moon, just before dawn
Faintly blinking, I have experienced sleepless slumber

My mind fumbling for conscientiousness
The wooing creativeness of Gods holy spirit reminding me
There is no darkness in him, he is the light
Our Christ, the bright morning star, a sinless savior
Light the path, to my hearts door, my Lord

Awaken my soul, my sleeping spirit, well up within me gladness
Surely my joy can overcome all sadness
When I recount your many thoughtful blessings
And meditate on your word, the holy scriptures of righteousness
Peace, love, joy and forgiveness return to my continence

From the dark place, day dawns, day star appears, day springs forth
from on high I have been visited, brought out of the shadow of death,
the agony of my anguish the sun of righteousness arise, with healing
in his wings my Lord God, my sun and shield, illuminates, invigorates
warms and sustains, faith heals my broken body and my injured soul
Frank W. Friedlander

Virtue

How gentle her touch in the crowd that day
As Jesus, the Physician passed her way.
How quickly He turned, aware of her presence,
Knowing her faith was her balm of essence.
"Who touched Me?" He asked, in His gentle way.
The crowd pressing 'round Him, laughed in dismay.
Who touched Thee? They asked, "Why all of us hath!"
Yet, one was different by virtue and faith.
As He turned to look on each face around,
She crumpled in trembling fear, to the ground.
He tenderly touched her, knowing her plight.
Her faith in Him brought a song to her night
Of suffering and pain, which now was released.
Christ's gentle response, "Daughter, go in peace."
I, too, felt the touch of Your robe today,
Aware of Your presence passing my way.
Feeling accepted, understood, and loved,
A gift of the Spirit sent by a dove.
'Twas healing for me, faith's balm of essence,
Transformed by love alone in Your presence.
Jeanette Kay Labaj West

Hope Saves Planet Earth

As long as planet Earth continues to turn on it's axis
As long as life giving oxygen is in the air
As long as human-kind work together for love and peace
Hope shall prevail on earth everywhere
As long as the sun rise every morning
As long as the moon sheds it light in the night
As long as the stars spangle the dark sky
As long as they twinkle with all their might
Hope shall spring forth with glory and continue its marvelous flight
As long as the beautiful flowers blossom in early spring
As long as the rain drops keep falling on land, rivers and streams
Hope shall inspire us as we lift our voices and sing
God save, God bless Planet Earth
Grant to us your saving Grace
Jomarian L. O'Neal

Cryptography By Poe And Miss Emily

By 1845 Poe's THE GOLD BUG was very well read
As many as 300,000 copies circulated — and then
It was printed in Poe's TALES — soared his fame
Poe offered to solve any cryptograph — anytime

Poe wrote — "In English — the letter most frequent
Is E—Afterwards the succession runs A O I D H N
R S T U Y C F G L M W B P Q X Z" — thus in BUG
His hero solves — EASILY — an "encoded" message

Note that Ms and Bs are near the bottom of usage
So one must know — by late 1850 — that higher usage
Of Ms and Bs — especially in poetry — say POEMS by
Miss Emily — they would beg crypto-analysis some day

In Letter 622 Miss Emily — " Of Poe — I know too
Little to think" — but at least She knew his NAME
Her brother Austin told how his sister would put
On a special "pose" for Her famed Boston Editor

Either way — there YOU have it — between 1858-1864
Miss Emily wrote a "heated" thousand "Secret Love"
POEMS with SAM B LETTERS in a vast cryptograph
Any computer — any analysis — unravels Her Intent!
Bill Arnold

The Child In Me

As I look back in time, painfully I watch
As seasons come and seasons go, if we could only be young again
And know what we know now, I'd let time roll on forever

I remember when we met all the magic and the glitter
The first time we touched I soared and left the ground
I've got to hold on to this dream for just another hour
Before we wake up to tomorrow

All the laughter and the merriment as we go round and round
The winds of your mind that silly child I love
You'll leave me broken hearted and saying goodbye to yesterday
And life is moving on again and again

It's the child in me, playfully I watch as seasons go
A cheerful heart and a melody, how did it slip away
Where is that child in me???
Jan Short

Untitled

I have a song within my heart
As soft and low as a lullaby
But there are times its seems to start
To swell and grow and reach the sky

I have a light within my heart
As a small and thin as a candle's flame
Until it's glow becomes a part
Of a roaring searing flame

I have a hope within my heart
And its seems somehow to grow
Until it becomes a living part
Of all I see and know

That song that seems to reach the sky
That light that turns to roaring flame
That hope that makes me long to fly
Are a part of something I can't name

A groping within the human mind
A search that's endless for the soul
A longing for something we may find
When we reach our final goal.
Grace Arioli

Sounds Of Divine Silence

The pain just doesn't go away,
as tears continue flowing downwards - making their way.
Numbness bloats the reddened cheeks,
while in anguish - the human heart reeks.

Tens of thousands - ghastly vaporized
   in the early morning suns.
Countless lives shattered - violence echoes
   in the sounds of loud guns.

Silent screams of millions - in a macabre way herded to their
   steel chambers of gaseous death.
Muted cries of billions - hopelessly anguished while of
   food, shelter and health bereft.

Is the Divine silent because - so futile are our prayers, our
rituals, our ceremonies, and our votive supplications?
Are Hiroshima, Nagasaki, Bataan, Okinawa, Aushwitz, Bangladesh
and Bosnia - the fruitless results of our unanswered petitions?

The sounds of Divine silence like - deafening atomic bombs
   burst in my brain!
While clutching to ancestral faith, hope and deeply in pain,
I ask why, - Why continue to call upon the Divine Name?
Frank J. Bober

The Last Rose Of Summer

The last rose of summer lingers of a soft fragrance
   as the days of summer fade into days only remembered
   over the fires embers that stir yesterdays moment.

The last rose of summer whose beauty brought love and caring
   in the cool evening breeze to a heart
   touched briefly by its petals of soft color.

The last rose of summer that but briefly spoke of tenderness
   to a heart in the stillness of the night
   to be remembered in the quiet fragrance of a rose.

The last rose of summer whose petals are pressed to a book
   hiding its treasure of yesterdays love
   remembering days held in time
   not to be forgotten.
Elaine E. Brebner

Astonishing Tree

There is an astonishingly beautiful tree.
As the green leaves wave through the sky,
I see baby birds crying for mama bird to give them some worms.
There is a sparkling stream by the tree
There is bridge by the tree.
The bridge takes me to a bright clean trail,
The trail goes in a circle back to the tree.
There are flowers to adorn the brown branches.
There are joyful squirrels up in the tree.
As I stood there amazed
Watching that big beautiful tree.
Chuck Cohen

The Family

The rain falls softly to the earth
As the family sits inside,
Each in a separate room,
Not acknowledging one another's presence.
They are related, but non inter-related.
Alone in their own time and space,
Consumed by thoughts they sit emotionless.
Then suddenly the phone rings,
And realizing someone else is there —
No one stirs to answer it.
Heather McKaig

Condescending Lies

Dreams of naked ladies in their Ivory Towers
As they stare at the walls and don't see the flowers
And what of the smashed pumpkins on the floor
And all the muck that was there before
In the night will they let down their long velvet hair
So we can ascend on a hope and a prayer
Has someone pulled out their eyes
Or are they so blind of my disguise
And what of the flying monkey's that circled the spires
Why were they cast out into the fires
Their blood stained swords that caused so much pain
Didn't they know I could see them through the rain
Now the sun shines down as Ice forms on the lake
The color of the woods like a hand painted snake
I hear the wails into the night
My heart pounds with lust until it's light
And what about the unborn babies that cry
Who will live for them and who will die
What about your promises, were they all lies
And why have you forsaken us without any goodbye's

Andrew Balasa

Bliss

You and you alone, follow my mind for a ride through eternity.
As we enter the world of the subconscious your mind becomes
    foggy, but that will all pass soon.
Your sight becomes dim, now you have arrived in the beginnings of time
Your senses are dull, nothing is what it seems in this world where
    fantasy and reality blend to one.

Anything is possible in this deranged state of total bliss.
As your spirit is freed from your body, you look down to what
you might have been.
Soon you forget about that as you go on a thrill ride to a higher
    place of being.
You lye down to rest, you had a long hard journey and you still
    have a long way to go.

Derick Dean Ditzler

To A Wild Duck

I marked your flight through smoke gray air,
    As you came alone out of nowhere.
Over slate gray water in your lone flight,
    I held you poised in my bright gun sight.
Carefully on you I drew that bead,
    And just as carefully judged the lead.
The moment to fire came and passed,
    And I watched you over the horizon till the last
I could not end your solitary flight in air.
    I too, may spend eternity going from gray nowhere to
Gray nowhere.

John F. Beeson

"Judi One Of A Kind"

Judi is a jewel has came into my life,
As you see she is my grandson's wife.
She's honest, true and faithful too,
And you would love her if you knew her as I do.
She among other things, brought me joy,
When she produced a girl then a boy,
Because of this mother and the care she gives,
Make my great grand children the greatest that lives.
To have my grandson to love me so,
That he brought his wife for me to know.
Makes life ever so wonderful and great,
That he was so lucky to find such a mate.
Takes the worry from my mind,
To know your great-grands will grow up just fine.

Betty Duffey

Dreaming

Your head is laid to rest upon the softness of her breast;
As your body is crying out in hopes of little peaceful rest.
Your mind wonders over the sweet serenity of the night,
And your dreams enter without a key, proceeding without the light.
Your dreams carefully select the time and place to appear;
Whether it's day or night, as long as it erases all your fears.
You may be alone in your thoughts as you so peacefully lay down;
But you're not alone in your dreams for there is always,
Someone around.
You can be in a crowd and leave your body for them to admire;
But your in a world with enough desire to create "fire".
Upon awakening with caresses so soft and real,
You ask, "Am I dreaming, or is this how I really feel".

Evelyn Williamson

I Don't Have To Go Alone

Hello Lord! It's one of your children again.
Asking your help and how to begin!
To feel the power of strength from above,
Because, Dear Lord! I need your tender love!
My heart feels so heavy with fear.
For what I may or may not see or hear!
I am frightened of the unknown,
And allow myself to feel so alone!
WHY? Is it so easy to forget you are
    right at my side,
And that from YOU my fears I don't
    have to hide!
Lord, SHAKE me and make me see,
YOU! Are the shadow that always
    walks with me!

Janet L. Engleman

Window Of The World

Looking out the window....
at green prairies so full of life,
at happy families, picnicking by the calm and peaceful river,
at joyous children, running through the rolling hills,
at tree branches reaching for the sky.
Looking out the window at a perfect world.

Looking in the window.....
at the hustle and bustle of the big city,
at down-hearted children walking home from school,
at weary parents arriving home from work,
at criminals awaiting a victim,
at trees wilting from deadly pollution.
Looking in the window at today.

Can't we look out instead of in?

Alison M. Walls

America, We Yearn

Take us back, Oh; time in your flight.
Back to the days gone by, when all through the night
came sounds of nature, now so rare,
were denizens of woods and fields
to rest and sleep, rest secure.
From day's toil, people did seal off
toil and sweat of the field.

The trees, forests, stones beauty that gave
So generously from Heaven above
By a Creator who so clearly loved
The people and world He created alone
By His divine hand for His own,
Not mutilated, not wasted.

Juanita F. Jones

If It Doesn't Fit...You Must Acquit!!!

O.J. Simpson killed Ron and Nicole
At least that's the way the story is told
He was arrested after a high speed chase and carted off to jail
Where over 365 days, he was held without bail

He hired the dream team
His eyes held no gleam
Until the closing arguments began
And attorney, Johnny Cochran took his stand

Said Johnny, "If it doesn't fit
My client, O.J., you must acquit
The jury did just that
Once Johnny tried on that hat

Saying, "I'm still me
O.J. Simpson was set free
The evidence, tampered with, just didn't fit
So O.J., the jury, did acquit

Grace Weaver Fletcher

"Touch Me"

Touch me...in the morning when night still clings,
at midday when confusion falls upon me,
at twilight as I begin to know who I am,
In the evening when I can see you and hear
you - best of all.

Touch me...like a child who will never have
enough love
for I am a man who wants to be lost in your arms.
A man who has known enough pain to love,
A man who sometimes is strong enough to give.

Touch me...In crowds when a single look
says everything,
In solitude when its too dark to even look,
In absence when I reach for you through
time and miles.

Touch Me...with your lips, your hands, your
words, your presence in a room.

Touch me...Gently for I am fragile, firmly for I
am strong, often, for I am...alone.

Bob Roberge

Statue Of Liberty

As we sit and ghastly gaze
   At Miss Liberty with her arm upraised;
She reminds us of our heritage
   As her pleasant smile does spread.

She stands 151 feet tall
   And weights 250 tons in all;
Her crown has seven points
   To remind us of our seven continents.

In her right hand is a torch
   A light to welcome others from their porch;
When their ships arrive from other soil
   She welcomes them to rest from their toil.

Emma Lazarus says, "Give Me Your Tired, Your Poor"
   So America has boldly become an open door;
To welcome those who are weary
   As they turn from a life so dreary.

The Statue was given to us by France
   She wanted friendship with us per chance;
We, too, are sharing the lasting bond
   As many have to the Statue thronged.

Gladys M. Donovan

Higher Power

During the day I grieve in the sun
At night alone, I cry to the stars
I have meditated at the ocean at sunrise
Stood on the top of mountain in prayer

Constantly looking, forever seeking
Asking myself and questioning others
My God, where do I find your wisdom
How do I capture your continued love

I have grown tired in this world I live
My heart is heavy without your love
The light of my mind dims, my soul dies
All my life I have searched and not found you

I have to find the peace and calm
That the elders have spoken to the young
Your wisdom and love is a dependable force
God, find me and rock me in your arms

Jessie A. Honeywood

Oklahoma City

Innocent children laid to rest,
At the hands of men; and their quest

Years of anguish for the rest,
Their loved ones gone none the less

Is this America; land of the free,
Where people hurt each other needlessly

Where people set off bombs for all to see,
They hurt innocent people like you and me

Oh, these people; I wish they could see,
This is not the answer, it is not the key

For with this action, we will cease to be,
America the beautiful, the land of the free

Jeanne Harris

De Profundis (L. out of the depths)

Again on the chiseled cliff with a late
August moon slowly ascending over the water.
Damp grass cushions the minutia of collective
thoughts; ineffable. Hunger has taught us
many things, we inhale salt air suspended
in a twilight canopy between full moon and
swelling sea - where are the whales arching
among shadow and light, searching the silence,
their soft spray reaches even here.
Baptized, I enter your profile at the wicket -
no further. The fine lines at the corner of
your eye; a feeling
that it is close to pain, your departure
into arcana. I say macte animo!
Do not look for me riding the high waves. I'll
be cutting through the darkest depths in a
rapid, fluid motion where only giants leave
their scent. If you never see me you will know
I have found my own way home.

Julia Y. Manuel

Back In The Day

Back in the day when things were so simple,
Back in the day when we gathered in God's holy temple,
Back in the day when everyone worked for a living,
Back in the day when it was more than receiving it was giving,
Back in the day when people were more thoughtful,
Back in the day when we trusted one another and weren't so doubtful,
That's the way it used to be, but to some people it's all a mystery,
They just don't know and they don't understand,
They don't ask for anything they just demand,
But if we'd all slow down and look around,
We'd realize what we were doing and notice it was ourselves
we were fooling,
Maybe we thought we were doing right but times have changed,
And all we want to do is fight,
Negative thoughts is on everyone's mind,
And back in the day that would be hard to find,
Hatred, anger and tears is something you never saw,
Back in the day you'd be happy and never selfish at all,
Back in the day when things were so simple,
Back in the day when we gathered in God's holy temple,

Jackie Bridges

The Knight And The Dragon

From the canyon deep in shadow, rode a knight of old
Banner flying, armor shining, fearless and so bold
Into a land he had not seen the dragon he pursued
But the dragon did avoid him, until he paid his due

For many years he wandered far, and suffered many pains
He learned the meaning of despair, and felt it's freezing rain
He knew the ache of loneliness, and somewhere lost his pride
On bended knees he felt the steel of swords thrust in his side

Through all his years of struggle, the knight had paid his due
And when he grew old and weary, somehow the dragon knew
Only then did he appear, with sword and coat of mail
A valiant battle, one last fight, but the dragon did prevail

Dale C. Looney

All Grown Up

She's all grown up or so she thinks,
Barbies' the rage, Barney stinks,
Barely wears a new outfit before it seems to shrink,
She's growing up too fast!

She's all grown up or so she says,
And she's showing it with each passing phase,
Just when you think you know her she changes her ways,
How long can these phases last?

She's all grown up or so it seems,
With grown up wishes, hopes, and dreams,
Her future to do with as she well deems,
The amount of choices are vast.

She's all grown up with a little girls mind,
Not really quite ready to leave childhood behind,
There's plenty of time, her horizons to find,
Maybe her age, her maturity has surpassed.

Goldie Howard

Unity

Fantasizing our accomplishments that appear beyond our control,
Copulating our thoughts while searching for a solution,
Materializing our discovery to fight for what
We feel impossible,
Uniting our hearts forever to become as one.

Carolyn E. W. Henderson

Paradise

Being with you where ever you are
Bearing your children
Sharing your life
The good and the bad times
The happy and sad times
Teaching our children the importance of the
individual and not the immorality of colour and race
teaching and learning from each other
growing old together
loving you

Isabelle McConnell

Wants, Wishes, Dreams And Tears

I want, I want to fly away,
Be a bird, come back some other day.

I wish, I wish I had wings of blue and gold.
That could take me places I could never behold.

I dream, I dream of a song full of harmony.
A song that could help me be who I wish to be.

I cry, I cry for you and me.
And the people we wish to be.

And maybe one day,
all my wants, wishes, dreams and tears will wash away.
And take me to a place,
a place I look for each and every day.

Carissa Nason

Let Me...

Let me
Be where the grass is green
And the soil fertile.
Let me linger awhile where the river waters
Sing a song of it's own
As they rush over rock and stone.
Let me take a bath in a crystal clear pool
And as a towel use the rays of the morning sun.
Let me run for miles, naked and unashamed
And shout of my happiness to the mountains,
And laugh as it echoes back at me.
Let me sit with a loved one and stare at the moon
With eyes that twinkle like the stars above
Let me listen for the concerto of nature
Crickets and frogs in harmony
With the rustle of leaves in the breeze
Let me with my lover's love to heaven rise
Let me
And I'll be in paradise.

Andy Oosthuizen

The Truth

As I walk along the road of life, sometimes I may fall,
But Jesus leads me back again, he's the greatest Lord of all,
Though I sometimes get in valleys my Lord knows the way,
He's like a shepard, I'm the lamb,
God loves me each and every day,
When I don't read the Bible or think about him,
I have so sense of peace within,
When we all go to heaven, what a glorious time it'll be,
I just hope that you'll be there to see him and me.

Brandy Rogers

Our Grandmother's Love

Our Grandmother's love is a precious thing,
   beautiful and bright like a butterfly's wing.

It's cherished and nourished and stored in our hearts,
   and always remembered even when we're apart.

With heart warming smiles and kind words to say,
   you always knew how to brighten a day.

You mended our clothes and our hearts with love,
   such a wonderful grandmother sent from above.

You never condemned us or turned us away,
   and loved us regardless of what we might say.

We're attached by our hearts in our own special way,
   never to be forgotten or stolen away.

You'll live in our hearts and be remembered each day,
   with a rainbow of memories no one can ever take away.

Candace Welch

Grandma's House

A pretty white house at the edge of town,
Beautiful shade trees all around.
Green grass and gardens of wonderful foods
And flowers all over the grounds.

The white coop of chickens, a little brown cow
That Grandpa milked every day.
The old water pump outside the back door
Where kittens would meet to play.

A grape-vined pagoda house made of white laths
Was a resting place from the sun.
A rock garden built by Grandpa's own hands,
And a stone bath where birds had fun.

This was my home for many long years,
With grandparents I loved so dear.
These are the things I'll never forget,
Though I'm aging year after year.

Arleen J. Wadzinski

Swift Things Are Beautiful

Swift things are
Beautiful; swallows and
Deer, and lightning that
Fall bright-veined and
Clear, rivers and
Meteors, wind in the
Wheat, the strong -
Withered horse, the
Runner's sure feet.

And slow things are
Beautiful; the closing of
Day, the pause of the
Wave that curves downward
To spray, the opening
Flower, and the ox that
Moves on in the quiet of
Power.

Derrick Gladney

When My Soul Was Sad

My soul was sad when I said good-bye,
because I didn't realize that my hands weren't tied,
My soul was sad when your tears touched my hand,
It was because I didn't understand
My soul was sad from the burden of shame,
which was only eased by the sound of your name
My soul was sad when I didn't know how to say,
That I was sincerely sorry and begin a new day
But now my soul is no longer sad,
'cause you said to me "Please take my hand
and together we can make our stand
for we have found the Love that we've always had."

Isabella Kelly

Untitled

It's a mistake to doubt me,
because it shows you don't trust me,...
It's a mistake to leave me,
because it shows you don't love me,...
It's a mistake to give up on me,
because it shows that I really didn't matter,...
But it's okay to share your feelings
because then I know what you're feeling
And it's okay to smile
because then it'll make me feel good inside
And when you feel good
you know I feel good
But it's a mistake to blame yourself
because if it's your fault, it's as much, mine too

Joy Toda

"The Purpose"

Was proud of the fact I have no strings attached.
   Been building this wall for so long now.
Lost in a maze I alone have created.
   To get out — I don't really know how.

There's nothing to hold me, and yet I am trapped.
   Feel I'm choking, no air left to breathe.
Just spinning in circles for so many years now.
   Want to go — 'fraid to go — just can't leave.

This life must have a purpose — but I just can't find it.
   And Lord knows — there is no one who'll tell.
Ever searching, always crashing up against all the barriers.
   It's as though I've been sentenced to Hell.

There are no bounds to hold me, and yet I'm imprisoned.
   Losing ground now — no space left to breathe.
Spinning in circles for so many years now.
   Want to go — 'fraid to go — just can't leave.

My life must have a purpose — when will I ever learn it?
   Will I find someone, someday, who'll tell?
Who'll give me a reason, a purpose, some meaning....
   Or is this 'final sentence' to Hell?

Janet Wyse

Family Affair

The family started long ago, before the cadillac
before the radio, now that I have your attention
I got the fact's I feel I must mention, I say the
family unit is in trouble help them out on the double
don't walk away or turn your back, the family can't
survive like that and when you out there on your own
you know the family needs unity, and love to keep it
strong, but some times people don't take the time they
look for excuses, they close they're minds, with delusions,
with reality believe nothing what you hear, and half
what you see concerning your family, check it out thoroughly.

Del Stewart and Gary Stewart

How Many More Summers Must The Leaves Fall

How many more summers must the leaves fall
Before we come to humanities beck and call

There's unrest and hatred these days
But I know there's a light beyond the haze

How many more summers must the leaves fall
I wish I could tell you,
But I have no crystal ball

As I peer out of my window the leaves are falling fast
I wonder how it will be next year, I hope we last

For there is no love, no shelter, no kindness of old
It seems those feelings are left in the cold
How many more summers must the leaves fall...

Jesse E. Dixon

Your Mark

Momma always used to say,
before you die, leave your Mark along the way...
As a child I used to think...
Gee, if I plant a tree,
will they remember me?
As I reached puberty, I thought about
all the things I could be...
But what I didn't see, was the real me...
I become bolder, but not older,
I was not wise and saw with clouded eyes...
It took a death to help me see,
the real life left in me...
The secret to your Mark,
is leave open your heart...
With each day give part of you away,
until you are no more...
But your Mark will be your Love,
for evermore.

Janice Bowers

Untitled

God gave us parents to help him take care of his children
Best of all; God gave me
The best parents in the world...

Together in life; as man and wife you walked that road together,
Each day you rise you hope and pray things got a little better.
Over the years the love that grew for one another,
One now my father; the other my beautiful mother.
The love and care to be divided; keeping a family all united.
Love and respect for my father; who taught me wrong n' right,
Love for my mother; who was my bestfriend in life.
Our hair grows white as we grow old,
I've learned to pass on what I've been told.
To clean my room; eat all my food,
To stay out of trouble; always be good.
To study in school; come straight home,
To take care while I'm out on my own.
As I lay my head down at night, I say my prayers
before each morning light.
I thank the Lord for the love we share,
and for giving me my parents; I know who care.

Arlene Ryan

Change Of Mind

After awhile you learn the subtle difference...
Between holding a hand and imprisoning a soul.

And you learn that love doesn't mean security,
While you begin to understand that kisses aren't binding contracts.

Words or gifts aren't promises of forever
You accept defeats in reality.

With your head held high and your eyes open wide,
Take it as the grace of a woman, not the grief of a child.

Then you learn to build all your roads on today,
Because tomorrow's ground is too uncertain

future have a way of failing in full flight,
After awhile you learn that sunshine burns when you get too much.

So you plant your own garden and decorate your soul,
Instead of waiting for someone else to bring you flowers that will
whither in the wind.

It's then that you learn to endure... and endure...
Endure even more

You discover that you really are strong, a survivor.
And you learn that you really are worthwhile...
You learn and learn... that's life!

Jay Warren Downs

Voice In The Cemetery

Here I am, under the maple tree
Come closer child and talk to me
Look down here, yes, look down and see
That tombstone, child, that tombstone's me
Look, child, look at the cold gray stones
Look down, child, down to where I've gone
Stare, child, stare at the green green grass
Growing, child, growing on the dirty mass
The upturned dirt, child, the dirt you see
Is all that separates you from me.

Jenny Bell

In Depth Insanity In Yellow And Black

Sunlit straw, as I draw, back my arrow;
Between trees so narrow.
The flight of the sparrow.
The fields we harrow.
The days of our youth, searching for the truth...

Memories of yesterday, they seem okay.
But we must see today, and take time to pray; for tomorrow.
Because today doesn't stay.

We can't go back, or ahead.
The cards we stack are stacked instead...
The lies we tell, tell us so; on us too.
Yet nothings true. So what do we do?

Giving up... is worth than death...
What is death... you should ask yourself.
It's a one way ride; suicide!
A place inside, where we hide.
A sea with a never ending tide, no one to lay beside.
You won't here the ones that cried...

Gone into nothing...blackness...silent and cold
NOTHING! NOTHING AT ALL

Bill Fleming

When The Heron Died

At morning's first light, a startle of wings shatters the stillness
   beyond my window:
The shock of a heron, soundlessly thrashing on the shadowed grass.
All angles and sharpness, sweet tenderness gone, wingtips and beak
   aimed high, toward the black hurtle that dives from the clouds,
And dives, and dives again, tearing the morning air.

And in the treetops—precise against the lifting dawn
A black and silent flock, perfect sculptures of simple line
   and essential mass, bear witness to the clash below,
And watch through round and brilliant eyes
the solitary stranger's dying,
At dawn, in heavy dew.

He must have lost his way—strayed from the tangled edge of his world.
But—lose his way?
At any rate, he trespassed,
A stranger in a strange land, besieged.
No sound comes through the barrier between us,
No silent plea, no heron-cry for rescue,
No mercy for the fear, and pain, reflected in the glass
The mirror of our separate wars.
Dorothy Causey

Something

There is a place beyond,
beyond the perils of life —
a place where goodness reigns —
where darkness does not abound.

But ask you, "Where can this place be found?"
   In the peace of the soul,
   in the stillness of the eye —
In this, do I testify.

This "somewhere" waits beyond,
beyond the trials of day —
this "somewhere" is a "something"—
the center core of all.
Only there, shall harm not us befall.

Now ask you, "What is `something'?"
   'Tis what we receive,
   'tis what we give —
What "something" is, we live.
Jenna Miller

Perils Of Night

Shadows do stretch over saw grass and clover,
bidding farewell to the sun as it flees.
It has come time for the rogue and the rover,
to stop on their trek and make camp for the eve.

The moon it does rise in the herald of night,
it's silver face, does shine like a pearl.
Standing amidst the lover's own light,
makes one lonely for the warmth of a girl.

Stars do glitter and fill the night sky,
feeling so small as you gaze into ink.
You hear in the darkness the sound of death cries,
the stillness and shadows do make the mind think.

Pray to your Gods that the night may pass swiftly,
carrying with it the peril of night.
You lay down your head as thoughts start to drift,
bringing you into the dawn and new light.
James E. Mosser

In Memory Of My Friend Bruce Morgan

Big Bruce, a gentle man. Best friend I ever had.
Big smile, always glad to see you. Big hands, but gentle hands.

Right by your side through thick and thin. Reach out to Jesus
Christ. Right choices, he always tried to do his best.

U need him as a true friend. U all can learn many things from him.
U can do all thing with Jesus Christ's help.

Came to meet me 'most every Saturday morning for breakfast.
Company, just to have him by your side. Courage, he gives to all men.
Consider other's needs and heartaches.

Eyes that light up like a star. Ears that listen and understand.
Eternal things he spoke of often.

Mind that is open to other's needs. Many log truck and fishing trips
together. Many talents - mechanic, needlework, painting, etc.

One person you enjoy being with. Oars a boat to battle the wind at
Horsetheif Lake. One to turn to, Jesus Christ.
One day at a time, precious Lord. Reaches out to reach others.
Right friend to stand by your side when needed.

Great friend in many ways. God was his personal savior.
GENTLE-GREAT

A great friend I will never forget. Always right there to help and assist.
Now, man of all men. My friend, Bruce Morgan.
Carl Leo Bliss

A Prayer For My Mom

Bless my mom, when she's cooking.
Bless my mom, when no one's looking.
Bless my mom, on a rainy day,
   and help her keep the bad away.
Bless my mom, when its cold outside, and
   when I run to her for a place to hide.
Bless my mom, when she's driving her car.
Bless my mom, she is like a movie star.
Bless my mom, through thick and thin.
Bless my mom, till the end.
Bless my mom, for all the good done for me.
Bless my mom, for helping live, learn and see.
Bless my mom, for she's done her best.
Bless my mom's soul when its put to rest.
Bless my mom, for she's done what she should.
Bless my mom, and please bless her good.
Cherise M. Jones

The Gray Steel Day

The whispering, whistling, howling wind
blew to and fro over the rolling hills.

While the sky grew threatening
in darker shades of gray
on an emerging canvas
with whisps of white dancing
and whirling wildly around.

Trees stretched out on the horizon
bending and bowing as the wind
whipped through them
leaving an awesome feeling in chilling bones.
Debbie Doherty

The Garden Of Life

We are all flowers in the garden of life,
blooming amidst this world's trouble and strife.

Each emitting its own fragrance so sweet and so rare,
Contributing assets that no other could share.

The colors of each flower are beautiful to see,
as they bloom in varied colors and varieties.

Some blooms reach boldly into the heavens on high,
while others hover near the ground ever so shy.

From the moment each life begins as a very small seed,
it matures ever changing into a beautiful blossom indeed.

Each day offers new beauty and mysteries to behold,
as the bud blossoms into a beauty so bold.

Each flower lifts its face to the sun every day,
basking in its warmth as it grows and sways.

But alas, its life must end all too soon,
and its time to say goodbye to the lovely bloom.

Don't despair for life will continue on as before,
as new buds appear daily for others to adore.

As day after day, God's plan for life begins once again,
as a new seed takes root and a new journey begins.
Faith Davis Yost

Untitled

We all do some things for the last time... smile,
Blow the last trumpet, run the last mile.
Turning our heads we see the blowing sand cover our footsteps.
Then if we would stand quietly still and listen, we might hear
Remembered moments whisper in our ear.
Quietly still, looking at what we have;
Older we are, but maybe just as brave.
There always were so many trysts to keep,
And when the work is done, tired we sleep.

We all do all things sometime for the last.
The footsteps end...that which has passed is past.
Diana I. Harvie

Windowpane

I see the world through my windowpane.
Blue Skies tease Cotton-Candy clouds
into Silver Streaks of rain.
The golden Sun fills my room with
dazzling light, showing off his
    "Holy" might.
A majestic Eagle, screeching, circling,
darts out of my sight.
Irish velvet fields are adorned with Jewel
colored Flowers. A Pansey and a Perriwinkle
welcome a Petunia into their bouquet of Life.
I look out my windowpane and see the world.
I see beauty; I see God; I see harmony.
Above all, my world plays a Symphony.
What lies beyond your windowpane? It can be
Bliss, Comfort, Peace of Mind and the
discovery of your TRUE SELF.
Elaine M. Adams

Oklahoma

Death and despair
Bodies strung out between levels of rubble.
Screaming for help.
Hoping the pain will stop.
Hoping to live
Hoping to die
Hoping to be saved.
Mothers waiting for their babies to be saved.
Waiting for the phone, hoping.
Hoping for the news
Praying for their babies
Hoping they catch the bombers.
The bomb was like a storm of
fury - demolishing, killing,
everything and everyone in it's path.
Joshua Abbott

Blame!?

"Baby Boomers" offspring not by choice,
born into a failing and often corrupt society,
but blame we must take for the evils we don't make!

Still wet behind the ears they say,
yet some are ready to embrace politics,
but no ills have we created being only recently procreated!

Look! The young are drugs, sex and rap n' roll,
they kill and rob each other without moral and guilt,
Yeah, we were born in your sins to the hilt!

Protect them from abuse and hate,
for they are still young and don't understand,
Yeah, blame the "Generation X", even if they were born
in a sinful hex!
Daniel Malone

Looking For Love

Look for love at any cost looking for love not with your,
boss. Looking for love when friends are not around, looking,
for love, can't be found. Looking for love when you want to,
change your name.
After looking for love things won't be the same.
Looking for love, when your name is on the line.
When you looking for love it won't take to much time.
Looking for love for someone to hole you tight.
Looking for love all for one night.
Bertha Mae Johnson

Lombardy Poplars

Lombardy poplars stand tall and straight
Branches folded as if hands praying, pointed skyward
Golden harps in the wind, strummed by the high winds
of an approaching storm,
Small golden leaves tinkle like golden bells
Swiftly the winds send a rush of leaves to
decorate the green lawns
Like a thousand amber gems, they strew the area
around the foot of the statuesque giants.
Soon the mighty trees will be skeletons, plucked
of all their glory,
Left only to sing the songs of the winter winds
Until again summer returns to pin on green gems
to rustle and tinkle until once again the
Winds of autumn completes the age old cycle of seasons.
Inez M. Mezyk

The Birth

On one late September's eve, as Autumn's
Breeze touched the leaves. A tiny cry was heard.

It did not sound around the world,
Nor by all was it heard.

The soft wail was greeted by just two ears,
Touched a heart, marking it for all the years.

Two tiny hands frailed in the air,
Reaching out, clutching, nothing was there.

Then softly a pale hand touched the one.
Fingers groped and curled around,
An anchor there was found.

Something magical then appeared,
A bond that would not break, midst all lifes fears.

A smile, a tear, a mothers face,
The birth of a child into this race.

Betty Chester Gravitt

The Way Life Goes Around

Skies so bright
Broad day light

Hopes and dreams
More they seem

Hearts filled with fears and eyes filled with tears
Prayer not near to overcome the fears

Is pain shown
Pain not known

Anger, fear, pain, fright
All happen in broad day light

Skies grow dark
Stars make their mark

Times get tougher
And roads get rougher

So stick to your path, Follow your heart
Be patient and play your part

What happens has happened, no matter what you do
But if you don't give up chances of failure are few

So learn to live and live to learn
Wait and see you'll get your turn

Angela K. Hassan

Lost Love

What I thought to be true love turned out to be unreal;
Broken hearts and mixed emotions of how she made me feel.
She took me by the hand, and said she'll lead the way;
She would be with me forever, until my dying day.
But as you see she's gone, a love I felt so deep;
Who left me for another, and so I sit and weep.
It came to me as a shock, as she said I wasn't the one;
For I'd thought we'd be together, cause our love had just begun.
I loved her with all my heart, treated her like a Queen;
I guess she had it planned, for she had me by the string.
I guess that's what love does, when you try to rush things through;
As for the games and when they'll end, I haven't got a clue.
So once again I'm all alone not knowing what to do;
Sitting here beside myself waiting for my dream come true.

John Thomas Williams III

Woman Of The Moon

In the shadows of an October moon a stillness rises
Broken only by the sound of footsteps
On a carpet of twigs and leaves.
Through the fog the figure makes her way
Down the hillside to the swamp, to
The boat made of reeds.
She is a frail shadow of a woman
The 'black widow' to some
Across the countryside they whisper
And talk, a father warns his child,
'watch out for the witch, my son'.
Her last voyage in the mist to the Avalon shore
The last night on her boat, to be seen no more
The days have gone, tambourines still,
She'll not dance again
She's the curse of a queen, child like princess
Gwynever's bane.

Cyd McMillian

Journey Through Motherhood

Dedicated to my English Teacher from 1978, Charla Wear

A newborn was she,
Brought into this world by me.
We were all strangers.

From diapers to school,
She faced the good and cruel.
Love surrounded her.

Graduation Day!
Time has taken her away.
A life of her own.

She married in June,
Had children, but all too soon,
The miles kept us apart.

They've grown up and gone,
Her only love passes on.
She was all alone.

In her rocking chair,
Thinking back to her mother's care.
Her life was fullfilled.

Julie Shockey Henderson

Coral Reefs In Jamaica

The coral reefs are dying in Jamaica.
Brown algae strangles out their polyp life.
The fish that cleaned the coral in Jamaica
Are harvested by trap and net and knife.

The coral reefs are broken in Jamaica
By hurricanes whose surging waves crashed down,
By pleasure boats and snorkelers in Jamaica
Whose fatal touch soon turned the coral brown.

The coral reefs are smothered in Jamaica
By sediment and sewage from the land,
By lack of ways to give them some protection,
By people who just will not understand.

The coral reefs are crying in Jamaica,
Their diadena urchins have died out
No longer cleaning coral in Jamaica..
No longer is there really any doubt

The coral reefs are ending in Jamaica.
The time to save them now lies in the past.
Will other places perish like Jamaica,
Or can we choose ecology at last?

Helen Tripp Davidson

Spring Is Coming

The gentle beams from the sun
Brushed upon my face
And sweetened my body gently
And then sailed along the textured forest floor
And across wide open fields.

I gazed upon the blue sky
With fluffy clouds hovering silently
Above my squinting eyes.
And I looked swiftly towards the dangling trees
That move quietly above.

The wind whispers through my ears
Sending quick shivers up my spine
Letting me know
That spring is coming
From a distant outlook.

Eric Jackson

The King And The Guard

She came a knocking at the gate
but all was locked up tight,
walls and bars and secret alarms
guarded it day and night.

She tried to climb and tried to dig,
she tried all the other sides,
she tried to use keys of old
but still she was locked outside.

Then one night she approached the guard,
she came with open arms,
she tried to prove she was unarmed
and showed him all her charms.

The guard was nervous and raised his shield,
his sword ready at the quick,
he would fight to protect his King
and save him from this trick.

Some say she never opened that gate
even though she found the key,
at the entrance was the shield and sword
and a sign, "ADMITTANCE FREE."

Derek Barton

Books

Reading a book is not only good for your education,
But also makes you use your imagination:
   Spaceships and stars,
   Saturn and Mars.
   Adventures and dangers,
   Family and strangers.
   Mountains and hills,
   And lots of great thrills.
   Swimming and hiking,
   Shopping and biking.
   Summer, spring, winter, and fall,
   Do you really think that is all?
No, there's lots of adventures just waiting for you,
So pick up a book and see what's new!

Ashlee Pruett

Untitled

I watch,
but always from a distance. I speak,
only silently to my self. I feel,
the loneliness grow as you walk further away. I touch,
only things you have accidentally brushed against. I wish,
that you knew of the love I have for you. I breathe,
in the same rhythm as you. I hear,
the sound of your voice talking always to someone else. I want,
to do everything with you. I wonder,
if I could ever have you. I hope,
one day my dreams will come true.
I need,
You now.

Elizabeth Lisa Gregory

Strength Through Adversity

I have my troubles, as does everyone,
But I also have hope with each rising sun.
Discouragement enters and tries to take hold,
But my thoughts are of blessings as hours unfold.
Pain signals the presence of something that's wrong.
Could it be that the suffering will make me grow strong?

I remember a tree atop Sentinel Dome,
All gnarled and crooked its trunk had grown.
Mid Yosemite's beauty that tree had withstood
Years of weathering storms, the bad with the good.
Now my body is twisted and bent like that tree.
I, too, have found strength through adversity.

Emma Lou Boatwright

Kitchen Aid

"I am more important than you," said the cup to the saucer.
"But I am the one that holds you up," He replied.
The tea bag sitting near, and smiling with a sneer:
"You should be nothing without me— your Majesty likes ME in her tea!"
"Who's more important than I?" asked the Creamer sitting by.
"A little bit of sugar," was the sweet reply.
"Well, I really hate to meddle," said the kettle steaming up.
"although it isn't my manner to be so abrupt
but without me — there would be no tea!"
The Table haughtily remarked,
"Just where do you think you would park"
Feeling defeated, the tea cup made her apologies -
"Dear friends, I seem to recall - Success depends on All for One
and One for all — and now that that's agreed,
"Ring for the Butler!!!!!! He's all we need!"

Jane Hanson Harris

A Moment In The Sun

I glow, as if I've had a moment in the sun.
But I have had a moment in the sun
For that brief moment when she turned my way
And called my name.
She merely said "Hi", as she does to everyone each day.
But when she followed that greeting with my name
I glowed, as if I've had a moment in the sun.
The brightness of her smile was the cause, I know.
Or was it the warmth of my cheeks as I turned away?
I thought about her throughout the day
And I waited for the 'morrow,
For my next moment in the sun.

Jeff Balaban

Happy Anniversary, Little Church

This Church House is getting old,
But it keeps out the rain, snow and cold.
Some neighbors made available, a nice piece of land,
125 years ago. This Church was built to stand.

For a place to worship GOD, in peace and love,
We raise our voices in prayer, to GOD above.
HE hears and blesses us, in every way,
We take good care of HIS Church each day.

It's good to have a Church, to worship GOD in,
We sing HIS praises, HE forgives every sin.
If this Church could only talk, what a story it could tell,
How many sick have been brought in? How many left here well!

Since 1870, this old world has changed a lot,
People were born, people died. Some were saved, some were not.
Wedding were held here, Funerals too, and lots of preaching against sin,
But the little Church keeps standing, welcoming people in.

We wonder how much longer, will it still be here?
125 More years we hope, with faithful up-keep, never fear.
So, HAPPY ANNIVERSARY LITTLE CHURCH, you have done real well,
You provide us a place to worship GOD, so For You,
WE RING THE BELL.

Alma F. Dye

"A Tree Is A Tree"

What a hiker sees after a mountain hard-won is a tree,
   but it's a shelter from the burning sun.
What a bird sees from high in the thunder-clap is a tree,
   but it's only a dot on a map.
What a scientist sees from deep in the laboratory is a tree,
   but in one of its many categories.
What a dreamer sees behind a small flower he plucked is a tree,
   but it's a support for one side of his hammock.
What a giraffe sees high above the ground is a tree,
   but it's free food that's been flower-crowned.
What a painter sees imposed on a white canvas is a tree,
   but it's Beauty sprung from the grass.
But when asked, the tree politely replied,
I am nothing as complex as what you have implied.
My purpose is singular, one that I embrace,
With my roots I hold this unsteady Earth in it's place.

Erik Benson

Standing In The Doorway

Once through the door, all happiness is obtained
But what is happiness, a frame of mind?
An instant held within emotion
Suspended throughout time?

Without thought
We react

Acting in ways we don't feel true
Trying to find happiness
With bruised emotion
Re-thought to be new

Search for the difference
To find the key
Or look on from the outside
Questioning all that may be

The choice is up to you
But the key is easy to find
Simply open your heart,
Soul, spirit, and mind

Aaron Wing

We'll Always Be Together

Knowing your suffering is over is some relief
But leaving us now has left us so much grief

And though there is nothing to ease our sorrow
Just more time for you we wish we could borrow

So many things we still needed to do
Picnics, family, grand kids were just a few

Through the years many things you taught
Your guidance and wisdom many sought

You gave an extended hand to those in need
Always wanting and willing to do a good deed

Always the friend to someone who was new
Always the great man to those close to you

So many lives you've touched through the years
And now the time has come to shed some tears

The broken hearts and tears will someday end
For the memory of you will help us all mend

Please remember dear husband, grandpa and dad
You'll be with us forever, great memories we've had

And as you begin your journey home
We'll always be together, never alone

Cindy Gibbons

What Christmas Is All About

Yes, Christmas is on it's way
But let us not forget to help,
some unfortunate person along the way

Making sure that their day is a bright, happy, and joyous reason
Before we jump up to toast the season

If you know of a fellowman in need
You are to help him, that's if you are a Christian indeed
Don't stand back looking and knowing that
Some little child did not receive a single toy
And be first to say "Christmas brought us Oh, Oh, Oh, great joy"

And while we are out cheering the season to be jolly
Let's try and make sure everyone has a hall
to deck the ribbons and the holly.

In essence let's help where we can and how we can
And God will shower down on us a blessing,
Because that man everything he understands
So, if you keep these lines somewhere in a corner or in a bottle
Or just in the back of your mind
You'll find out that everything about Christmas, will be just fine

So to my girls and boys and to my young at heart
Merry Christmas to you in all that you do
This is from me and St. Nicholas too!

Frederick V. McBryde

Alone

I can try to pretend I'm not cold
but my will doesn't stay quite as bold
when I lay alone at night
when covers aren't warm enough, pulled around me tight
I think of you and try to be tough
and sometimes your memory is enough
to keep me warm
but, sometimes, I feel torn
and I'd rather be with you
but what can I do?

Ami Shipley

Un-Named

I wanted to try my hand at writing,
  But no title have I in store,
    So where to start and when to stop,
      Is truly mounting chore.

Should I talk about the rainbow
  With its majestic, beautiful hues,
    Or about the towering, needled pines
      Bedecked with sparkling morning dew?

Could I expound on the ocean's swirling tides,
  Or the aroma of new-mown hay?
    Would I reflect on the morning sunrise
      That ushers in a brand-new day?

Will my thoughts bring in the soaring birds
  With their chirping songs of joy?
    Could the care-free days and laughter.
      Tell of little girls and boys?

Seems all subject matter is over-crowded,
  So just what am I to do?
    I'll lay my thoughts and pen aside,
      And bid my poetry attempt adieu!
    Ersel M. Kidwell

The Old Homestead

I walk again where as a youth I roamed
But now so many things have changed—
Where then I dared to bound in careless glee,
I walk sedately as befits a grown-up me.

The pasture that the cows kept velvet-shorn
Is now a ragged urchin-patch of weeds,
The brook, remembered as a green enchanted space
Has only dry rock-bed to mark its place.

The barn once filled with fragrant summer hay
Crumbles and sags upon its ancient base
My childhood home, unoccupied and bare
With vacant windows' cold and gloomy stare.

A tangled mass of weeds engulfs the yard
Where childhood games and chatter then held sway,
The fir trees we planted by the garden wall
Lift scraggly giant arms—aloof and tall.

The curving bower of the lilacs' scented arch,
Which was our playhouse in those bygone days,
Has disappeared, as do all childish things
When Time comes stealing on its silent wings.
    Elva I. Sullivan

Treasures Of The Heart

I seek not a share of your beautiful silver and gold,
But rather in my arms your body I'd love to hold,
I ask of you no wealth and riches to lend,
But the treasures you have that I long to possess,
Are those of your happy heart my friend.

For every real true heart holds so precious a store,
That it bubbles with happiness as time goes on more,
Oh, the gifts that this wonderful weary world needs,
Is understanding and forgiveness in someone who leads.

So I'm wishing for pearls and ivory your kindness and trust,
Your loyal friendship and smile is always a must,
I love the bright diamonds of your very generous deeds,
May you have lifelong blissfulness without any needs,
Each moment of life should be lived to the brim,
For it's a gamble to know how soon it will dim.
    Chester Reeve

The Letting Go

She told me we'd go walking together
but she couldn't walk...anymore
after that day in the hospital
when she held my arm so tight...I bit my lip.
Sorry I didn't know then
the difference between living and alive.

She told me we'd go out to eat
but she couldn't eat by herself....anymore
I fed her babyfood
and held her hand when she threw it up.
I learned then to look at her
...with my eyes closed.

She would have told me that she loved me
but she couldn't talk...anymore
she would stare at me
and I would hug her with my fingertips.

The last day that I saw her
she didn't know who I was.
...It was then that I let go
...And it was that night that...she died.
    Dana Fraser

Black And White

Black is all colors
But the absence of light
Black is your eye
After losing a fight
Black is the horrible
Bleak winds of December
Black is the dread
Of each dying ember
Black is the creature
We all know as death
Black's what you'll see
When you breathe your last breath

White is a daisy a pretty primrose
White is the water when you turn on the hose
White is a diamond, a crystal, a pearl
White is the dress of a very young girl
White is the body of a very pale ghost
White is the foam on the smooth sandy coast
White is a flower on a beautiful tree
White is my color, white's the color for me
    Ashley Lucas

Yesterday

The world is a lonely place, when away from ones so dear
But the one fact of life we all must face, on this you can rely
No matter where we are and no matter how long we stay
We must leave those close to us and it's hard to say goodbye

Time is so short when with loved ones from far away
Soon the happy times we have had are just a fond yesterday
But yesterdays become great memories to cherish and to hold
So gather those great yesterdays and cling to them as fine gold

Just as time goes on my dear, life for us must do so too
We may want to change our destiny, but there is nothing we can do
So cling to those yesterdays and let them warm your heart
Let them draw us close together though we are far apart

No matter where you go, No matter how long you stay
Soon it's time to leave and always so hard to go away
But soon the hurt grows dim and we wipe the tears away
Then we begin to look forward to another happy yesterday
    Don Meyers

A Hopeful Dawn

Commending another's similarities is an all-too-familiar game.
But, to appreciate his differences, first erase all fear and shame.
There awaits a cultural cornucopia of riches not yet seen.
To perceive them requires a vision both willing and surely keen.
Judging an individual's worth by his pigmentation alone
Can lead to quick misunderstanding, a friendship forever blown.
Pause just long enough to travel beyond the epidermal layer
Where along every highway a hopeful soul kneels in silent prayer.
To achieve mutual understanding takes an outstretched hand,
Plus open-minded determination and a cleverly crafted plan.
Just how many are willing to cast aside such bias and hate,
Making room for affection and understanding on their plate?
Quenching this appetite should be its own best prize,
Revealing a heightened awareness equally loving and wise.

Julie Shearer

White Car

We could have been physically together
but you got in her white car with a smile
on your face and she drove you away
You hung around for a couple of years and we
even said a few nice words on different
occasion to each other. Including the
first time you told me you'd take the guy
outside the door who bothered me on that second
meeting about four years ago I'd say.
So we could have been physically
together but you got in her white car with
a smile on your face and she drove you away.

Carolyn Irene Schaugaard

Left Behind

They say it gets easier as time passes by;
  but you still find yourself asking why.
You put on your best face for everyone to see;
  but inside you're afraid and somewhat empty.
It's been sometime since they passed away;
  but they're still thought of, each and every day.
You still live in the house you used to call home;
  but now most of the time you're all alone.
You try your best not to dwell on the past;
  but sometimes it's necessary, for memories don't always last.
Your days past quickly with many things to do;
  but nights seem to go on forever, when sleep eludes you.
You get up every morning to face the day;
  for those of us left behind, there is no other way.

Geraldine Manfredi

Father Stranger

I am of your blood.
But your blood to me
Is like blood at the scene to a crime.
Victim unknown?
I was the victim!
But you were a victim too,
(Of something only you knew.)

What made you turn your back,
close the door, and throw away
the key to my heart?

The fire has long been burned out.
Unable to be rekindled.
It's a shame.
I probably would have made you proud of me,
And been proud of you.

Jason Thomas Gnau

Long Trip

I've been flying high all day
But you're always on my mind
I've been singing with the birds
You don't even know I'm gone
I want you to come fly with me
Come join me on this cloud
Let's go touch the stars
Take a walk across the moon
I want to know your feelings
I want to know your thoughts
I want to know you
I just want to be with you
Just us and our own perfect world
Without worrying about the reality that is beyond it
But you don't care
So why should I care
Why should anybody care
You don't need anybody
So I'll just stay in my world
And you can stay in yours.

Jennifer Harper

Gifts From Mother Nature

In summer, Mother Nature gives the bright and shining sun;
Butterflies, the singing birds and little things that creep and run.
There are lovely flowers, speckled frogs and park visits can be fun.
A sudden cooling rain might fall and refresh everyone.
Nature paints a twilight sky and starlit night when the day is done.

She provides falls chilling frost and many brilliant leaves,
Apples, vegetables to store, while the farmer cuts the sheaves.
The days are growing shorter, the nights are growing long.
The birds are packed and leaving as they sing their "good-bye" song.
Fall is the brightest time of year but a squall may come along.

Nature's wonderland in winter should be fun in snow and ice.
Quiet times and family fun can make this cozy season nice.
Cold winter walks and quiet talks in the crisp and snowy air
Might create a love of nature which could make each one aware
Of little creatures who need a shelter and some care.

Nature gives spring "wake up" sounds to most everyone around.
Baby birds and baby plants and baby animals abound.
The howling wind, the gentle rain and the warming sun,
The budding trees and meadows green should cheer up everyone.
Mother Nature gives it all, winter, summer, spring, and fall.

Donna K. Brant

Pretense Without Art

That once held mystic, of the American Life
By neglect, has now withered and shrunk
From the Biblical concept of 'Love One Another'
To that of greed and delinquency of self.

We now pretend, stutter and shout
Claiming to be, what we are not
While wanting more than we've got
We insist on upsetting, the American cart.

Education, being the curriculum of wisdom
Requiring the energy of youth to pursue
STAND UP AMERICA! In recitation and give,
Education's definition, of truth, honesty,
And how to live.

Harvey E. Clendenen

Welcome To The Little Church

Welcome to the little church
by the busy highway of life.
Enter into the small sanctuary
and sit on the old wooden pews,
as the sun shines through the stained windows.

Welcome to the little church
where children learn about Jesus
as a choir sing songs of praises.
Welcome, as the preacher speaks the word
of God from Thy Holy Bible.

Welcome to the little church
where families are formed and nurtured
and loved ones are honored and remembered
where the life-cycle is unbroken.

Welcome to the little church
by the busy highway of life
to a place of serene quietness,
that God has truly blessed.

David Paul Duncan

Fantasy Of Love

Do you know my fantasy deep within my heart?
Can you feel the fantasy my soul wishes to impart?

Do you know the longing for your sweet caress?
Can you feel the love there, and the tenderness?

Do you know the magic I feel by loving you?
Do you know my fantasy of dreams I wish were true?

If you too had my fantasy-such music you would hear
Playing from each other's hearts and in the atmosphere.

If you too, had my fantasy-how happy we would be-
For as much as I am loving you, you would be loving me!

Judy Danridge

The Homeless Man

Candle in the sill
can't know what it feels
The homeless old man
don't know if he can,
hold on to another day

He sleeps his nights out in
desolation
doesn't know if it's real or illusion
Don't know if he can handle the match
that must light the candle

The homeless man is about to die
just like Catcher in the rye
The homeless man's life is just like a candle
in the wind
out in a flash without any
sound...

Edward M. Balas

In The Stillness Of The Night

If, in the stillness of the night you can't sleep,
Count your blessings instead of sheep.
As you name them you will find
Your reward is peace of mind.
Just remember when fears assail
That the love of God can Prevail.
If you trust Him Day by Day
He will guide you along your way.

Edna Zimmerman Prentis

Elysian Fields

Hope will decease as pressure comes down
Care becomes worry as concern surrounds
You long for elysium as Pandemonium reigns
Dream of a heaven beyond the grave
The curtains seem closed as fate takes it bows
The fields are now dying and you wonder how
Spirits expire from wrists which are bound
You long for devotion that can never be found
Though in distress some light will remain
Even in heaven some things can not change
Friendships will show what it means to be loved
Life's energy comes from not places above
Vigor will come from attachment to friends
Whether they will or not be there in the end
Familiars will shelter your soul from the storm
Bliss can still thrive when you being is torn
In the abyss rebirth may expound
Stress disappears as comrades are soon found
Look still for affection, from problems don't run
Rest not yet now for your kingdom has come

Christopher R. Horting

The Will

Behold the sweeping movements of her majestic heart, carefully kept untethered by the darkness that surrounds her. Bring forth the corruption!
It affects her naught. She cries for previous privies on life's lonesome journey.
She remembers the fun has only just begun. You think you know everything, you know nothing at all. She holds the knowledge of a BILLION stars. She carries it with her in a little pouch hung around the back of her left hand. Carefully balanced so to not disturb the precious cargo. I wish to see it! I demand it! Why should you want to see...this, she teases. It will most certainly consume your giant head like a weed at harvest. Give me a peek PLEASE! I beg of you. Ah, but the bag has already been open. You've glimpsed inside before.
Don't you remember?

Ephraim Alexander

High Hopes

My hopes were floating high in the sky.
Cares were there, but never seen.
Ignoring sounds as the wind cried,
Suddenly, they came crashing through my dreams.
My hopes came crashing down.
Grasping my cares in my fist,
I ran from the moon and let it drown,
Choking on the summer mist.
Now the sounds haunt my dreams.
There are no more moon beams.
The wind howls and it burns my ears,
Drowns out the sound of lonely tears.
Now I'm left in darkness,
Begging for forgiveness.

Jeanine Olszewski

The Definition Of Saderia

Do you remember your first sunset, the beauty of it? Do you remember your first falling star, the excitement of it? Do you remember your first car, the joy of it? Do you remember your first ride on a roller coaster, the thrill of it? Do you remember your first real love, the awe of it? Do you remember the first time you held your newborn child, the miracle of it?
The words used to describe these feelings are the same words to define Saderia.

Angela S. Kinyon-Wilson

The Breeze

The summer breeze blowing warmly through my mind,
caressing me with arms I cannot see. I close my
eyes to feel the strength surrounding me. I spread
my arms in search of flight, to soar the open spaces,
free within the breeze. I feel the need to give of
myself; to make love to the strength that surrounds
me. I lay down in the meadow, awaiting the touch of
the warmth in my mind, on my body. Soft touches, deep
sighs, as the warmth moves within me. I shudder as
the moment draws near. So tender, so loving; I cry
out in ecstasy. Then, as I lay in the meadow, my body
wrapped in flowers of wild, the breeze that warmed my
body, my mind, moves slowly, ever so slowly, to the
next meadow

   behind the hill,
     beyond my mind.
   Chris Stanton

A Backward Journey

As a small boy, I fished this river, never
caring about the changes that were sure to come.

Then, Daddy and I could put our boat
in the river most anywhere.
Now, fences mark boundaries and hold in possessions.
"Keep out" signs are everywhere.

From our wooden bateau, we cast our fishing lines,
used chicken liver for bait.
Fished deep, on bottom with a heavy weight.
Wait! Wait! Set the hook hard
in the mouth of a long whiskered cat
with a forked tail fin.

As I sit on the river bank,
and listen to the tires click
across the cement bridge,
watch water rings ripple from rock splashes
the sunlight dance on the river,
like disco lights on a skating rink floor.
in my mind I fish the swift Sabine again
a small boy forever.
   Anna M. Grayson

Love Is A Flower

What's this, my love, you bring to me? A Rose for love so rare
  Carnations for, the road ahead, shows rest beyond compare.
Orchids are, the symbol of wealth, the love that we both share,
  Gardenia's for, narcotic nights, we're high on love so fair.
Magnolia's for, soft southern winds, love blossoms in the air,
  Daisies for, stability dear, they show we'll always care.
Sunflowers for, our stately love, so quaint and debonair,
  Azaleas and, Camellias dear, love's resting in their lair.
The honeysuckles, from the vine, shows love without despair,
  Two Lilies of, the Valley dear, we make a loving pair.
Orange blossoms smell, so sweet my love,
  As winds blow through your hair.
What's this, my love, you bring to me? A flower I can wear.
   David R. Clukie

The Flag Bearer

Into the morning mist he strides
Carrying Old Glory at his side.
The flag-bearer approaches the hallowed pole
And pauses as he reaches his goal.
One glance toward the top of the lofty spire
Then clasps the flag with heartfelt desire.
Just a moment to lower the ropes
That are the resemblance of many a hope.
Then putting the clasps and rings together
While loosening the folds and unwinding the tether.
A gentle tug moves it away from the ground,
And for a moment there isn't a sound.
The first breath of wind nudges the stripes
The stars ripple as if in slight.
Then pulling aloft the colors,
While the morn watches from the parlors.
Hand-over-hand the flag is raised
While the group below is appraised.
Then reaching the top of the stately shaft
It makes its decision at long last.
   Bill Clark

Going Down

Life's leading down the drain,
  cause there is nothing left to gain.
Elephants in pink tutus,
  dancing around saying I won't forget you.
People turn all look and stare,
  but you can't tell for you must glare.
warm damp cloths enclose your mind
  would you ever even leave me mile behind.
Bloodshed milk stands in a trance,
  with only a time warped mind that is enhanced.
Stand beside me for a while,
  then drops pore down in denial.
A swirl of flowers overwhelms my destination.
  takes over my body and leaves no explanation.
A senseless interruption invades my thoughts,
  twist and ties my tissue into knots.
Left with no direction or any last words,
  just unforgiven hearts and eternal lures.
   Jamie Morris

The Garden

In a time of my life where fear with little
Cheer had became and unwelcome sight,
I see a garden where I can walk without
A trail of lingering misery and sheer despair

Times of fear with no end insight
I walk in a garden of joy and delight

When a loved one passed into the other
Light I cried for my joy had became the
Darkness that I feared all my life

I wept for my only love had said the words
I avoid to hear goodbye with no tear
In his eyes

The garden appeared before me once more
With rainbows and sun, flowers and more

The pain in my life turned to ashes
Like people without chances

For my garden then had a name I
Call it God a garden without pain
   Jodie Carter

A Tribute

Many people, veteran or not,
Come to the wall for the men who have fought.

Memories here still can be found,
As strong as they were on the battle ground.

Questions lead into empty space,
Of why we went to Nam, that was the place.

Experiences of pain, fear, and death,
Were an everyday occurrence, like taking a breath.

Although the war has ceased and we're gone,
In the minds of servicemen, it still goes on.

The wall, a small tribute, was long overdue.
Still the same, Vietnam vets, it stands for you.
   James Bottger

Fraudulent Quest

He endured scars difficult to heal
Confused fantasy from what is real
Was rejected and abused
And in search for answers grew up confused

The dilemma of origin and birth
His weary soul bewitched by presage
Reflected a mirror image of outrage
Absent the family resemblance from his face.

Memories of chastised youth
A turmoil of painful tears
Nightmares of darkness and fears
Sources of a quest for identity and truth.

With no legacy claim but a will to forgive
He began the journey toward destiny
Defeated by death his kin outlived
But later found by whom he was conceived

Angel of heavenly visions, womb that beard him
Your love could efface fears and dissipate grief
But his presence, reminder of shame, betrayal, and sin helped you
build a wall of conditions that destroyed his hopes and dreams.
   Aurora Munoz

"Uncle Wayne"

Pain and anger rage inside me.
Confusion fills my thoughts.
My mind an endless maze
Searching for a better explanation,
Interrupted by disbelief.

I can't help but picture the scene,
What it must have looked like
The thick rope, the blue face,
And his arms dangling loosely by his sides.

Pleasant memories appear vaguely
Like an old slideshow.
Quickly am I to comprehend
His bright blue eyes, his smile, his voice, but now...
Where are you now, Uncle Wayne?
   Andrea Renae

No Big Deal

Bullets. Tanks. Bombs.
constant rattling of guns.
The mighty blasts of cannons.
   Bloodshed.
Explosions of bombs form
out of the ground like sprouting mushrooms.
radiation. Diseases. The Unexpected.
Air crafts. Helicopters. Sirens.
Figures with red-crosses. Nuns.
Help. Too late for many.
One by one. Falling on to
the mist of the unknown.
Falling into a black Abyss.
More soldiers charge
with rage and determination
at their enemies. While others
lifelessly bathe in a pool of Blood.
Wounded. Infected. Sick.
Dying. Dead. Left behind. Forgotten.
The price of War.
   Harrison Luong-Tran

Fall Reverie

The changing of the seasons, though God forbid,
Could bring that one most often feared.
With hoary head and flowing beard,
his scythe in hand and hourglass aloft.

"It isn't time," one thinks; "Life's span's too short!"
But yesterday a youth he stood, with shining eyes and face upturned;
Aware and eager his race to run.

But now with footsteps slowed and back bent low
He pushes forward lest he fall,
His body crying, "Quit," his spirit urging, "On!"

"What's wrong?" he says; "What's happening?
I used to do these chores in half the time!"
So philosophically he reasons yet.

But sands keep running still, while daylight flies.
The hours, weeks, and months have turned to years;
The clock will not go back, but soon 'twill stop!

The season's changed, life's cycle's spent;
A baby's born, a sire has died;
The yellow leaf has fallen, the spirit gone to God!
   Frances Kinlaw Moore

Hallelujah Story

   A lot of people are always talking about the
Doomsday Story. I say let's live life to it's fullest and give
God the Glory!

   Let's not be full of gloom and depression. Let's be full
of happiness and think of successes.

   The Lord wants us to be happy and filled with joy and
think of God's glory and say Oh Boy!

   Let's not think of the worlds news and all it's sad
stories. Let's think of God's Good News and say
"Hallelujah!" and give God the Glory!
   John J. Jordan

Acquainted With The Nite

I am one acquainted with the nite, from my growing up years in the country, to my adult life in the inner-city I began with the very dark, unless moonlit-nites, with people all asleep and crickets, 1000's it seemed, chirping their screeky, leggy noises; and occasionally in the wee hours of the nite, long-distance soulful whistle of the train, blowing for a crossing, long and deep. Then to the city, at first hard to sleep, since it seemed, there were always people and machines that never sleep, all beneath my 14th floor window, echo-ing between the concrete streets and rows of tall brick buildings. Voices in stress, or high in terror, fighting intoxicated, or children playing late on concrete, or hot muggy polluted summer, poverty stress, many nitely screams of our city's women being battered, on lonely, unsafe, nite streets or echoes imprisoned in an apartment with the abuser. Cops often siren-maniacs, racing dangerously down dark, skinny, populated sheets going the wrong way down one-way streets chasing one individual. The flood of voices and cars of the well-to-do in evening gowns oblivious to the stress, ending their social event, in the wee AM hours from music hall across the street. Just before dawn, the whirring, brushing sound, of the city's street sweeper. Through many all nites work projects at the shelter, or sleepless, tossing nites, I've heard and seen it all.
  Buddy Gray

Vaddie

Wide-backed wicker, like a southern throne
Crackles like a shaking maraca.

The blades of a rusty fan sing from the window sill
Sweet tunes of dry country.

Vaddie smooths her tabby child.

Crooked hands draped in loose silken skin groom with Mother strokes,
with lonely old lady love.

Hunching shoulders shaded in white and green garden polka dots.
Wheaty hat brim shading gray lash eyes.

My hair was in great black curls, fore
You came to me, sweet kitty.

Now it is fuzzy white like the cat's every whisker.

Douglass used to work those fields out there
Come in for a Coca-Cola now and then.

He brought me this ring from St. Louis...
Now you're my boyfriend, aren't you kitty?
Want a Coca-Cola?

Purr words, echo true love.
  Candice Rawls

Red Waves

Red waves dancing in the wind.
Creamy white, dotted satin.
Pools of deep green sadness.
I saw into her soul, though she never knew.
I knew her sadness, knew her pain.
Knew her emptiness, for I was the same.
Held my hands out, grasping with fear,
Please help me stop it, the running hand of time!
The waves now straw, white now yellow,
The pools are now empty, everything lost.
I hold the dust in my hands, drifting softly,
To dance on the waves, deep and blue,
One last time, I beg God, LET HER STAY!
And ask why has AIDS washed my mother away?
No answer, just silence, I pray and she stays,
She lives locked in my heart, for the rest of my days.
  Heather Hutchins

Untitled

Inventors are thinkers, and strange at best
Creating wonderful things, their only quest

With heads in the clouds, their thoughts abound
Never distracted, with daily mundane sounds

Peering aloft, with a condition of intention
Necessity of course, is the mother of invention

Trial and error, plodding without fear
Regardless of the criticism, that they hear

Research and development, known as R and D
Are results and facts, for all to see

Patent potential, is "State of the Art"
This is goal, from the very start

The odds of obtaining, this pinnacle state
Are astronomical figures, as of this late date

Nevertheless they continue, with undaunted vision
Why they do it? It's their very own decision

a slogan they use, expresses without slants
"SUCCESS COMES IN CANS! NOT IN CANT'S!"
  Clyde Wilson

Unwanted Creatures

There are unwanted creatures in all of us.
Creatures we don't want others to see.
They are the creatures of hate, violence, and death.
They lurk in the shadows of our minds,
waiting for an escape.
We try to ignore them,
but sometimes they come out from the darkness
and into the light.
They hurt those who love us
and push our friends away.
When this happens there is nothing we can do.
I try to hide my unwanted creature,
but sometimes it gets the best of me.
  Allma Bockelman

Sweet-Associations

I offer you...

Almond roca and sweet tapioca
Crisp apple struddle and fresh danish noodles
Grilled shishkebabs with spiced baklava
Striped candy-canes and tart tangerines
Frozen snowflakes and frosted rum-cakes
A fresh summer's rain with moist sugar cane
The 'Sunset Grill' and late evening thrills
An ice and 'Snickers' with a hot rum jigger
Spiced caviar and fresh crab dujour
A full moon's mid-night as two lovers delight
Fresh calabash with peppered corn-beef-hash
Tangy filet-mignon with roasted beef boullion
Grapes souffle and a lobster pate, a gourmet stew with cajun shrimp too
Waterchestnuts with shredded coconut
Chicken-ala-king in an oven baked cuisine
An evening with a gent and after-supper mints
First snow outside and a warm fireside
A crisp and chilly breeze and a walk down by the sea
Such sweet associations delighteth me....
  Herquelies Bond

"Components Of Time"

How long will I love you? That question never
crosses my mind, for the hours and minutes of each day
spent with you are too cherished to define.

A clock's time may be measured by seconds, a year
by the sands in a glass, but my love can't be contained by
the hands of time, nor limited to season's past.

My heart does not know what times is, or recognize
the ending of a day, for my love for you is evergoing only
guided by the grace of his spirit that lights my path
every step of the way.

Darryl L. Williams

The Clearest Day

When the snows fall, the animals
cry. Of hunger their stomachs groan
with the cold, wanting something to
eat. Their furs twinkle in the distance.
The birds flutter to shelter as the sun
sets before them. As all the animals
nestle by their Mom and Dad, they fall asleep.
As the wind blows and the snow falls.

Jessica Michels

Reflecting Pool

What stories churn behind those magazine eyes
Crystal blue with the illusion of transparency
No hint of truth or lies
Without the fire of pain
Or the hooded shadows of sorrow ...

Did they ever drown
In the watery grave of disappointments
No shimmer of the warming rays of youthful innocence
To beckon the suitor of your charms ...

What dark and brooding waters
Lay stagnant beneath your crystals of blue
Feelings and emotions dammed up within your timid soul ...

Who were thy to hurt you so
Making you a master of disguise ...

Open your soul   there is no reason to hide   magazine eyes.

Glenn Cooley

Target Practice

Mama...
Daddy...
What do you think of me?
Am I all that you had dreamed
A little girl should be?

 I tried so hard
 To make you see
 The best me inside of me.

 With band-aid knees
 And curly locks,
  Saggy pants and droopy socks
 I performed my best on each occasion
 Sending a message 'bout the kid you were raising.

Fell short of the target, I know I did.
Please
Want me forever, 'cause I'm your kid.

Donna Renee Frye

A New Day

As the sun begins to rise, the
darkness fades away,

The first ray of sun peeks over the
mountain, it is the beginning of a new day,

The crisp, cool morning air is warmed
by the sun,

Now it can be said that the new
day has just begun,

The sun grows higher in the clouds
up above

The sight of the morning sun, I love,

A new exciting day has now begun,

Full of new surprises that are yet to come.

Alisa Renee Schleper

Discovery

In Steel City's early morning
Daylight dawning bleak and gray
He came to her
warm hands, warm lips, warm breath
Engulfing and smothering her.

Ecstasy etched on his shadowed face
He took her with such passion
She could not speak
Nor see, nor breath, nor think
Drowning and possessing her.

In that moment life stopped
Spun on a cobweb, balanced in space, suspended
Having neither beginning nor ending
Tracing a circle complete unto itself.

In another city
Not yet known
It is predestined they shall meet again
To drink in each other, to taste each other, to plummet each other's
  deepest depths
Letting the moment lengthen to forever.

Chloe Pollock Molnar

My Truest Friend

Days have come and as quickly have gone
Days which many have sung a sorrowful song
Be near! Be dear! Is what they proclaim
Yet near nor far they never came
Only one has earned a special right
One whose been closest through all that I fight
You may not be able to see with your own eyes
It has never been hidden behind any disguise
Calming the seas of troubled storms
Calming the eves corrupt by emotions torn
Finding my heart is many ways
The same heart so many throw away
Unconditional love is what I receive
From the only one who will never deceive me
There shall never be an end
For I have found my truest friend

Bonnie Lee Hunsberger

Neptune's Funeral

In those ancient underwater gardens,
Deep below human minds' fantasies,
My body is floating down that sparkle fog,
My eye touches the beauty of a thousand princesses,
Hazardous reflections dipped in everlasting harmony,
The gentle flood brings me further down,
Until I touch that undulating surface.
Driftwood is flying across the blue colored sky,
It is further but more visible than before,
The sea is a fierce power — careless,
Now they become silent, those gossipers,
Now that I am here, far away and deep below,
Sitting on my bed of pain with that cureless body,
I see myself sick, pale and empty,
"Deliver me," I cry, "let me sleep forever slow and deep."
Daniel Pantano

Its Beautiful At Night

Its beautiful at night, when you can't see the writings on the walls.
Deep in the dark where graffiti appears as a work of art,
　rather than a sign of corruption.
At night when the homeless are travelers; tourists.
At night when trash can be leaves on the sidewalk.
At night when freeway lights are fireflies.
Now its morning, Los Angeles awakens.
The tourists are gone, smog over our castles, congested traffic on the freeway, and we face the fact Picasso wasn't here.

Its beautiful at night.
John Melcombe

Remembrance

Firelight brightens my darkened room
Dispelling slowly my deep-etched gloom.
Drowsily I sit as its glow and flicker seem
To warm my inner self, and I fondly dream
Of things long past - of a young boy
Fretting over some favorite broken toy,
Of snowy skies and gleaming icy ponds
Where skaters slip and glide midst fronds
Of frozen pond lilies, and bright fires
Warm cold toes and nose, and desires
Swell within us big enough to send
One whirling to find his ultimate bend
In the curve of time; by dying embers,
When wind is calmer, a heart remembers
But can't fully recall those days gone by,
But it can try - yes, it can try.
Ernest G. Scholz

Almost Perfect

She was alone with her children four;
He was alone with his three;
When they met in the spring and wed in the fall
Their future looked bright as could be!

The kids got along, each one had a bed;
Most problems were solved without wrath;
But it's not easy it seems keeping everyone clean
As their old house has only one bath!
Charlene Johnson

Tender Years Of Youth (An Ode For June Mary)

Tender years of this child's youth
devoid of maternal love and acceptance.
Starved for attention, eager for praise,
yearning for mother's embrace in attendance.

Tender years of this child's youth,
prayers answered by a touch of another.
Angelic voice, warm laugh, freckled arms
appeared in a form of a mother.

Tender years of this child's youth
graced by her brief tender embrace.
She modeled courage, love abundant,
harboring a sense of safety in her face.

Tender years of this child's youth,
legend of a woman I once called mother.
Living among illuminating memories,
her legacy in the hearts of my father and brothers.

Tender years of youth, days of yore,
memories of childhood forever tarry.
A father's wisdom, a youngster's fate.
this child's Mother known as June Mary.
Judith Simone Skotnica

What Did You Give Today

What did you give as you passed along my way?
Did you give a smile to help me make my day?

Did you give gladness or did you give woe?
Did you plant a seed that you'd want to grow?

Did you give a hug to your family or to a friend?
Did you try to help a broken heart mend?

Did you try to help a co-worker cope?
Did you give your neighbor a word of hope?

Did you give some deserving child a word of praise?
Did you purposely rain upon his parade?

Did you give the Beggar a financial lift?
Did you hold tight to your precious gift?

Now, just tell me what did you give today?
As you passed along some poor soul today.
Barbara Redding

The Ancient Ruins

Boldly sitting, staring at history, and daydreaming.
Dismissing knowledge of things more important than me.
Could it possibly be?....yes
One has withstood time. One has experienced so little.
A tangible breathing being - a distant memory.
So obvious which more worthy of attention...the here, the now, no!
What once was carries more weight.
The ruins possessing more substance than petty, everyday,
"all-important" life. Time, so obvious in everything.
Aging both but only distorting one. Changing both slightly but only killing one. Which will survive longer?...
Not a question but sarcastic mockery.
Others, daring to ignore the greater of the two,
The victor continuously laughing at the weak, the lowly,
the fleeting moment in history.
Choose to learn or be com placement....no matter.
Choose to be enlightenment or remain in darkness....who cares.
A personal choice with no one to hurt but yourself.
Accept the sad truth....
One will remain. One will not even be remembered.
Jennifer Pukach

"Divorce Is Not An Easy Thing"

When you have children, and things don't work out.
Divorce maybe the only way out.

Divorce is not an easy thing.
For children, it can be devastating.

Sometimes they get caught between the fights.
Only to lay awake at night's.

It's always hard for them you know.
To see there Mother, and Father's love go.

When the family bricks up you see.
There the one's that lose, not you and me.

For love is no longer there for you and me.
But for them, they love us both you and me.
David L. Beliveau

Stars

Where do stars go when they lose their sparkle?
Do they keep on shining just for you and me?
Do they stay bright for everyone to see?

Or do they just fade out and eventually die?
Retreat into nothingness without asking why,
And the only one's who'll know that they are not there
Are the ones who knew the stars, and the others will not care.

Way up in the sky, shining star I see tonight
Do you glimmer with happiness, or shake with fright?
Do you hide your troubles in all your shining light?
No one thinks a thing when they see you so bright.

Do you quiver at the thought of burning out one day?
Or couldn't you care less to have it either way?
Do you take like as it comes, and try to have some fun?
Do you shine your shiniest so they'll think you're number one?

Shine for me, O little star
Way up there, so far,
I wish I may, I wish I might
Have the wish I wish tonight.
Jessica Pizzuli

The Turtle

The creature moves slow.
Does it think show?
It eats slow. Maybe it just moves slow.
Maybe it's just thinking.
It's possible it just reacts and doesn't
  think at all.
Maybe it just moves.
Maybe it just flows with the course of the earth.
Like a tree, it just grows, feeds off what
  the earth gives it.
It basically hugs the earth with its' vines.
The earth created everything.
It created the thoughts of everything.
It lets only some close to its' secrets and
  some totally just beyond the thought.

The ones that don't think about it are
  the ones that destroy the earth.
They don't even care.
As for the slow ones, they can just think
  about it and cry.
James M. Boldosser

Stop The War Of People

Because of what's on the outside
Doesn't mean we're not the same inside
Who gives us the right, to pick out the best
When we all have hearts within our chest.

The world is full of race segregation
Why not stop to think of our equal creation
Why can't we be united as brothers
And make the world a pretty rainbow of colors.

Yes, there's good and bad in everyone
Why blame the bad on certain ones
Can't we join together, hand in hand
And make America, a peaceful land.

Lets stop the war, the war of people
And bring America to its highest steeple
Oh yes we can do it, if we try
We can make hatred, walk on by.
Cathy Abston Zwack

"The Proof Was In His Hand"

I had a dream - I thought... I was dead
Don't be afraid - a man's voice said
Then a hand reached down - to take hold of mind
A presence so sweet - so gentle and kind
I caught a glimpse of scar in His hand
As He helped me up - so I could stand
I'm weak - I cannot walk; I began to cry
Do not worry, He smiled - as he wiped my eye
I am here to help you now... And I will never leave
I am not real to all - you know... Only to those who believe
As we stepped into the light - His face I now could see
His eyes were like blue water - as he stood and smiled at me
I watched Him in amazement - not knowing what to say
Do not be afraid, He said - I am coming again someday!
Suddenly I was awake again - and I was in my bed
I realized - that NOT knowing Him - was why that I felt dead
He had always been there - I just didn't understand
He had loved me all along - "THE PROOF WAS IN HIS HAND"
Denise McVay Penny

Untitled

Descending on this man-made invention - the escalator - it breaks
down from time to time...
descending into a man-made hell, into a hell of life of work and
slavery to a God called money and its son named society
finding one's way through the dark twisting subterranean tunnels
down more escalators, plunging deeper and deeper into the flames
ignited by man's desires
waiting impatiently, the masses fidgeting and incessantly glancing
at their watches..
as if they could speed up time
the lights on the platform begin to blink and flicker
the beams of light emerge from a large hole blasted out of the
inside of victim earth
the train cars approach, the brakes squeaking, squealing and
moaning as it laments its oppression
the doors open and crowds emerge from its belly
like a cocoon cracking open
and the dormant life escaping from within, reawakening and I,
too, step into that train
adopting the state of unconsciousness I must to survive
Emilie F. Young

Who Are We?

Have you heard that we're sinking?
They say we're obsolete and believe too much in firm foundations.
Pressure is placed on us to conform.
We are as vessels upon stormy seas.
The winds and waves press for change, change, change...
 We hold fast to the hope of a better tomorrow where neighbors help
each other with a love for GOD and country,
where evil is called "a sin" not an illness.
 One day we'll come to shore and reclaim our rights. As of now we
are overtaxed, overregulated, and overworked. We are up before dawn
and labor past midnight to do our daily tasks.
 Who are "we"? You ask.
We are the old fashion working American Family.
With the father as captain, mother and children as crew working
together to guide the ship to peaceful shores.
 As the storm rages on, I can see other similar type ships headed
to the same shores to unite there voices as one saying we are still
here strong as always.

Joanne Gillespie

Lament Of The Monkey

Softly shrieks the monkey, loudly thumps his heart,
as hopes and dreams, weak thoughts of slumber plumb his mind and numb
his arts, still unencumbered wishes lumber, limber as unholy dark.

Loudly shrieks the monkey, softly thumps his heart,
his hopes and dreams cryptic numbers
purge his mind and plumb his senses,
of what becomes his soul in slumber,
through the yeasts of baker's art—and still the creature lacks
defenses; too soon, his mind, forever dark.

Lost, vain vagaries, vague, soiled beliefs have and steamed the nubile mind.
A quest for meaning, learning, ends, spawns countless moors of endless kinds.
Religion and its counterpart twine and twist and coil, then bend;
a golden peach without a core, our world splits, seems to read,
When, as if by occult design,
The monkey shrieks no more;
just an empty, fruitless rind,
the wound, unkindest kind,
His heart's beat is no more...

Frank Lesser

The War Is Over

There's no turning back, life had begun, you were chosen by God to
 be the son
Of a marriage. Never meant to be, of a sister, who needed thee
Your sister, she loved you so, but being so small, you couldn't know
You gave her support, you gave her love, to her, you were sent from above
So little but yet so wise, it was seen, in your eyes
You didn't have to speak a word, everything unsaid was heard

As you were leaving, you said your good-byes, they all saw it in your eyes
"I love you all, I have to go, I'm not leaving now, I'm going slow,
I'll watch over you and be your guard, don't cry please I know it's hard"
Hospitalized for a year of pain and sorrow, hoping you'd recover by 'morrow
It didn't happen, nothing could be done, the war was over and nobody won.

As you were going, you had said, "My life is over, no need to dread
No more suffering, no more pain, for I'll see you once again
I have to go, I'll miss you all, I have to go, I hear my call
Don't be sad, everything's alright, no more need for me to fight
I have to go, my time has come, the war is over, and I have won"

You died at such a young age, no chance to write a page
But you did, you wrote a chapter, now you're "happily ever after"
Brother, I miss you so, I didn't want to let you go
At 3, you died with a heart of gold, so I saw it necessary,
 your story be told.

Flora Markaj

"Superman Forever"

The flowing red cape lays still
draped over the quiet window sill.
The phone booth door is frozen in time
while fictitious villains
perpetuate frightful crime.
The powerful body lays limp
there is no walk
It is even a struggle
to breath and talk.
Gaze into his x-ray eyes
Absorb the radiant smile
Let the bright glow over take you for awhile.
Honor, loyalty, truth and justice you will feel
Oh superman you will always be forever
Lucky and real.
Your mind shrouds a cape
Your heart beats super love
Your warm soul will fly
So none of us will ever cry.

Perspective

I wonder what happens to a bird when it falls
Does his brothers and sisters continually call
Does his mother and father look every day
Maybe our son has just gone astray
Or do they think deep in their head
I know he's not missing he is certainly dead
Maybe they don't know what has happened at all
They probably don't care when one of them fall
They don't even realize something's not right
Lost in themselves so free in their flight
Do they sing a short sacred song
To let the world know one is now gone
Everyone see but don't be afraid
We'll always be free never in chains

David S. Mason

Fantasy

Deep hypnotic eyes
draw the dreams to my chin, I sleep
Drowsy thoughts into my mind of you
the image, the moment I keep

Meditation strays
from the pores of your skin and crawls into mine
Oh phantom of fantasia whisper into me,
your tranquil thoughts, so sublime

So near to my heart,
from classical years two hundred before
Sing with your feathered fingers of age,
your hands, I so adore

Play the fantasy
on ivory keys across my dreamy mind
Oh phantom of fantasia whisper into me,
your tranquil thoughts, so sublime

Hillari Zimpelman

"The Angels Are Crying"

The angels crying will flood the
Earth's valleys with endless pain and grief;
The demons we've allowed to enter our lives
Have cracked our shield of peace.

Death is on its rampage, stealing souls one by one;
The angels are crying for all to hear
Stop the killing far and near.

The angels are crying, and want you to know;
We are all God's children and must be allowed to grow.

Gregg William

The Forever Ones

There She is.
Dreaming.
She loves to watch the rain fall.
She sleeps all day not knowing why.
She loves them and their white ivory skin.
She wants to be one with him, but she cannot.
She tries to understand him and feel what he's feeling.
She drags her soft, gentle hand along the long wondering scar upon his face.
There she is standing looking in his deep blue eyes of sea, thinking.
What does everybody see wrong with him.
He is so gentle he just looks a rough and frightening
Will she ever lean on his head again crossing bridges.
She only sees him in her dreams watching her from a distance.
He is so far, but he has been right there all along.
    Jessica Murphy

He Cares

Oh, wonderful story of deathless love;
Each child is dear to that heart above.
He fights for me when I cannot fight,
He comforts me in the gloom of night,
He lifts the burden, for he is strong,
He stills the sigh and awakes the song;
The sorrow that bows me down he bears,
And loves and pardons, because he cares.

Let all who are sad take heart again;
We are not alone in our hours of pain;
Our father stoops from his throne above
To soothe and quiet us with his love.
He leaves us not when the storm is high,
And we have safety, for he is nigh.
Can it be trouble that he doth share?
Oh, rest in peace, for the Lord doth care!
    Alex B. Profitt

Tears

Tears of love, tears of hate,
Each flowing through a singular gate.

Entwined the many, spared the few,
Each beginning anew.

Each tear drowning him in sorrow,
Now hopes he must borrow.

And with a silent cough there comes,
A downward glance there is from.

And with a cough more violent,
Her eyes open, the color violet.

And in her soaked skin there does appear,
A rosy color, crystal clear.

There eyes meet, paralyzed as one,
A new life has begun.

And as he helps her to her feet,
One thought they do meet.

And with soft lips he does say "Heather",
They now know they will always be together.
    Jane P. Tergis

The La In Love

I hear a whisper in the night, for I will sing to you tonight.
Each la in love that I will sing comes from deep with in me.
For when I cry, don't be afraid. For every tear, don't turn away.
Each tear I cry withholds the love you have shared with me in life.
For I have not dared to express these feelings that I have not sang for you before.
You comfort me with open arms, each word I say,
each song I sang was never turned away.
In the icy air of night all the heavens say a prayer for you tonight.
The la in love that I will sing, listen carefully and hear it ring.
Remember me with every laughter that comes from every child,
and with every rainbow in the morning sky,
remember the la in love that I will
provide for you in my song tonight.
    Christina Corrales

I Have A Mission

Each of us has a mission in life
Each of us has a task to perform
Some tasks may seem to be
More glamorous than others
Working in a foreign land
Making a movie - writing a book
Each task requires great discipline, dedication, and patience
Every task great or small is important
As we all know, this is the "Space Age"
All space personnel are entirely
Dependent on "Mission Control"
Astronauts must have enough trust
To place their lives completely
In the hands of "Mission Control"
Our "Mission Control" is God
Sometimes we tune Him out
But if we listen to Him
He will guide, sustain, and strengthen us
Listen to God!
He will help you fulfill your mission in life
    Dorothy J. Melton

Another Chance

Christine my love for you goes unnoticed.
Each passing moment I am tortured for being forever isolated from your warm sweet caring love.

How I remember my foolish mistakes of letting you go from my unsteady grasp.

I throw myself in despair each day remembering how you left me.
My fear has conquered my love for you dear Christine.
My cowardly attempts to bring you back to my side have failed.
Everyday my heart agonizes and yearns for you my sweet Christine.
Oh how my heart aches for the past,
A past in which I had my true love.
Yes my heart wishes it could feel
   the soft smooth skin of my dear Christine.
If I could only have one more chance with my only love.
Oh to feel my heart sing in harmony once again.
I cannot live in despair much longer, If I only had another chance.
Only if I could swim back into the past
   and leave my fear behind in the future.
Then I could be with my love again.
Please, I need another chance...another chance.
    Gavin Lindsey

Elephant! Elephant!

Earth Mother you are! True composition of
earth, wind, fire, and water! Forbearing!!
Unique in class. A style all your own!
Elephant! Elephant! Monarch of power!
Leader of life, love, good and sad...
Delicate, and dedicated... in your way!
   "Jumbo", in Africa! Beauty to me!
A gift from the Lord! Understanding, strength!
Reminder of life, and hazard! Memory, and care!
Composed of magnetic, energy from the sun!
Magnificence in stance... ivory... trunk of sound!
   Eyes so small they see to understand,
and understand all they see!! Wisdom!... Love!
   Ears so large they flap in the wind... yet...
so gentle they give a butterfly, and bird a lift!
Poised in stance!... Wisdom of understanding!
Bubbles of delight in the river... happiness!!
"Jumbo," in Africa, kiss the sun... and God!
Thank you Lord for the garden, and, beauty
in Africa... and the elephant in my eyes!!!

Anita M. Diaz

Flight From Omaha To Minneapolis

She was a well dressed lady who sat calmly as the daring box
elder bug walked in trembling steps from hair to hair and tuft
to tuft across the vast pompadours from a middle part on top of
her head. I gasped a bit myself as he came to the ravine of
hairdo and almost slipped and fell to the roots below. It was
a treacherous gangplank that the pirate tread, but oh so carefully,
he made his way around the blonde tundra. I thought for
sure he had been detected, but it was only her shift from the
left cheek to the right. How could you be so brave as to risk
your very life with the clasp of her hand on feeling a moving
thing that may have been more than the breeze from the air vent.

You must feel safe that even with an error in judgment that you
could spread your wings and fly away. I can not dare to walk so
boldly on willowy hairs because if I should bend too deeply, my
wings would hold no air. Even if they would, I could only try
to break the fall. So many others depend on my safe passage
that wings could not take me away from it all.

Donald Comer Brown

Beauty In Motion

She moves with grace and song, yet a quiet dignity envelops her
Elegance is her gait, yet she possesses a quiet pride
Her movements flow delicately and still show her strength
She is beauty in motion

I have seen much beauty, however none compares to hers
Her enchanting eyes, her seducing smiles
Are more than able to eclipse an average beauty
It is clear to see that
She is beauty in motion

When she walks into a room, all actions are halted
Glances drift toward the door and her smile puts all at ease
Time resumes
She is beauty in motion

She is the prize; the trophy
To strive for; to try for
To me she is more
She is living contentment, the embodiment of love
She is beauty in motion
She is you

Anthony Rodriguez

The World Does Not Remember Those Who Never Forget

It wasn't crazy - a mirage - or an impossibility,
Elephants seen deep inside the desert or swimming far out at sea —
Evidence, by witnesses and taken on film,
has proven it a fact to be.
These astounding stories,
have now appeared recently,
in newspapers and on T.V.
Years ago, one man knew,
(He was named Hannibal)
the elephants great potential.
They easily crossed that Alps,
blowing their trumpets over loud cheers and shouts.
For years, elephants faithfully served in many armies,
obeying orders in their ears.
Malaya, Burma, Vietnam, Laos, Thailand, and in India.
But, the world does not care, or know,
any one of these big, and brave, fighting soldier veterans,
it just adores and remembers the performing circus troops and,
Jumbo and Dumbo.

Hendryk Zenon Kenna

Awakening of a Soul

The autumn wind surrounds me,
embracing me as if I am a child.
Waves of colored leaves whisk the thoughts away.
As the lazy sun slowly retires,
my eyes become heavy,
I drift into a sweet slumber.
Time ceases to exist.
In what seems like what has been forever
I am happy.
I am loved.
I know the shadows are floating past through
   the nothingness.
I am not scared, and this scares them.
My light of armor protects me.
Is it all in my head?
Does it come from within?
Or is it a greater force, of which I can not imagine?
I choose to live not to question.

Amanda Engelman

The Moving Waters Of Life

Upon the placid lake
emerges a reflection of you,
A spirited image of vitality stands before your being,
Casting a transparent body upon the moving waters of life.
Living amongst such a diverse forest of visages,
You challenge yourself to raise your sights to the majestic view above.

You make the first few steps into the waters,
And among those river depths
You find the compass for success
You learn to work against the current
and create a path of your own.
Storms may loom on the horizon,
But your sight is direct upon mountainous achievement ahead of you.

As the undertow of life's challenges grasps your chances,
You cling to the banks you have solidified
through knowledge and understanding.
Casting off the damp shadows of defeat,
and lifting you toward the shores
holding courage for tomorrow.

Courtney M. Chamberlain

Absent Picture Tube

Angels cry
emotions
scream.
Dreams fall
life
shatters. And the television plays on and on.

Abstract reality
insomniac
bed.
Thoughts dancing
fugitive
sunshine. And the news is always on.

Lifejacket drowning
hungry
fruit.
Roadless map
mountains
growing. And the images go on and on.
   Cynthia Kay Marek-McConkey Kovar

Landmark

The one-room Woodside School squats there.
Empty.
Bare flagpole, books stacked neatly; homes for silverfish.
Eaves lined with mud nests of long-dead swallows.
Cold, cold ashes in the jacketed old stove;
Long dead wood sticks piled beside it.
The school turns blind vacant eyes to the roadway;
Dreaming shadows coil and recoil,
Crouching, ready to spring
From the door locked long ago.
Shadows waiting, waiting
For the door to spring open once again.
So that once again they may drink up the young lives.
   Julia E. Lind

Leaving

Will I leave you with words
Empty as coffee cups filling the night,
And hide you away as a somber memory,
When your arms welcomed me?

Will I offer an ending to the echoes I hear
Through melody ranges now sharp, now soft,
In shadows following the sun?

What is North when you took the clouds from my eyes
And freed the laughter
Dancing before you?

   When sunsets drip nightfall
   In heated colors against the sky,

   When the scent of honeysuckle urges us
   To linger by the soft breathing of a stream,

   When waves step over beach stones
   And break endlessly against the shore—

Remember that once, we filled this room
As the moon now fills the night.
   Claire W. Traveler

A Day's Journey

Awaken to a pillow
   Empty as the night sea
Reach for the answer
   Darkness questions another day

Search to inspire
   As hope feeds the soul
Eyes struggle, but faith sees the light
   Encouraged, a spirit provides the strength

Educate with your tools
   Motivate through his voice
Reflect, relax, and smile
   Admiring the seagull brushing along the waves

Appreciate the undeserving peace
   Cry, in the amazement of greatness
Rest now, enjoy the fruit
   Capture the warmth, preparing for another day.
   Bill Dincognito

Within A System Malfunction...

Enveloped in folds of cosmic dust,
Encased in failing ship of steel,
Engrossed in future death we must,
Engrave our destined pattern field.
Our mothership, the Tesn'lar,
Damaged by the waves of a dying star,
Must carry our message, far to home,
To explain our deaths, within this tomb.
Without stones we cannot build cairns to bury our dead with pride.
This vacuum perishment of we and our bairns lets loose ship's
   oxygen, leaves us inside.
Within a capsule, three days in flight,
Lay farewells to kin, and our recorded plight.
Ten years from completing its harbinger ride.
A decade within, grievous tiding reside.
When relations learn and begin to mourn, our bodies linger,
   maintained in airless freeze.
A drifting hulk, shall our corpses adorn, afloat in the endless
   astro-seas.
With shared fading dream of colony founding,
We reach our journey's end, deficient grounding.
Now joined in fate, and lamenting verse,
Five hundred souls wed the universe...
   Brian Thomas Maher

Ellipsis

Hark ellipsis, to the way of the wind, hidden treasure, of
endless knowledge. Wisdom do cry in a child's eyes, fear
within the changed mind.
Hark ellipsis, seek to find.

Sage to a cage within much rage, 'tis truth I say 'tis truth!
Seek her seek her if thou may this day, 'tis thy way to life,
with much strife.

Hark ellipsis, Hark ellipsis, to where have they gone,
golden crown of glory, gifts upon gifts to the giver, 'tis
blinding, 'tis binding.
   'Tis Ellipsis!
   Frank J. Florio

My Mother-My Friend

Sitting alone I can feel her presence, as the combined
energy of life surges through my veins.
She is able to sense when I'm hurt or feeling lonely,
and wills me a map to re-route the pain.
By herself, she has taught me survival in a world
so unjust and unkind.
I've learned to forgive those who judge and degrade
for they were raised to be prejudiced blind.
Our bond is so strong that communication may be silent,
understanding without having to talk.
She is the light which surrounds me each day of my life,
revealing the footsteps that I will soon walk.
Since being the only hero I revere in my heart, on top
of the pedestal she will always stay.
I ask God to protect and bless her with a much deserved
long happy life for she is My Mother, My Friend, who has
paved my way.
Biley Riddlesperger

Slim Death

In between his forefinger and middle,
engaged a long, thin cigarette,
Its graceful rising smoke listlessly floating
in an abstract, ghostly ritual.
Hand candidly fluttering up to his mouth,
He lifts the slim death, drawing in its lethal toxins.
Oh but how this process is presented,
So sensually enticing!
Then, exhaling in languid fashion, from full accentuated lips.
Within a cadaverous bloom rests upon his brittle respiration.
Although aware of this prolonged internal torture,
He resumes with his fetish of abuse.
He falls prey to this addiction of seemingly innocent smoke,
escaping from the poisonous demon, clutched fervently between
his fingers.
Chryssa Brazil

The Splendor Of Autumn

Wonderful is the splendor of autumn
Golden leaves a beautiful sight,
Soon they will fall all over the ground
Where they will be blown afar by the wind.
Others will lie on the ground to decay
One can hear their sound as they rustle about,
Then a quiet settles over the land
As winters snows cover the earth everywhere.
Clarence S. Pittard

Friends

Friends are my life, just like a husband is to a wife.
I don't understand why we fight.
Maybe the timing is just right. I'll stay their friend no matter what.
I'll always keep their spirits up.
And when their lonely or feeling down I'll be their till the end.
After all what is a friend?
And I've know from the first time,
They'll always be a special part, deep down inside my precious heart.
Deanna Riggle

Tho'ts

A poets tho'ts, a net of gossamer hue
  entraps words drifting out of the blue.

Words glowing like fireflies gliding by
  softly selected by his critical eye,

To be smoothly crafted, a picture to tell,
  as his idea coalesces and begins to jell.

Then the poet strings words like glittering beads,
  marshalling his tho'ts to serve his needs

With word-colors blending, harmonious, whole,
  a message from his immortal soul.

He hopes some pleasure will be brought
  to those who will read what he has wrought.

So he casts his tho'ts down time's placid stream
  that others may read, and mayhap dream,

Entrusting their tho'ts to the same placid flow
That the cycle, unbroken, may onward go.
Harry J. Cooke

'Forks Of Steel'

No need to pour panic into the blender,
Escape, the chaos will only tend to hinder
No need to risk any future personal harm,
Because, there'll be no help from added alarm

To stalk nightly, with Forks of steel,
The hunger, so causes the mind to reel
Such apparatus, becomes the sword we feel,
As we go, in search of another meal

Before we go, on our knees we kneel,
Praying for fruit, not meat to peel
Carrying not any bow, arrow or quill,
No bandages, for there'd be no time to heal

Praying for a shower, upon our parched lands,
Remaining quick and faithful, with cupped hands
Never expecting the indulgence, of precious sips,
Feeling blessed, should we be allowed, to wet our lips

Hunger seems so rampant amongst our lot,
Forgetting wine, we no longer recall Noble Rot
Perhaps a few morsels, to cover the thin bone,
Once again, we venture into the 'No Eating Zone.'
Dane S. Jester

Morning, You Are Gone...

You are gone and none of you remains.
Even the bed is half as warm,
my pillow the only pillow.

First light and the dull glissando
of a distant train draw away
the echo of your voice.

A hint of grace is lost
in the soar and dive of dry leaves.
Martins thrown by silence.

Now the air quickens through the open door.
The hanging plant begins to twist...

Like a mime pounding for release.
Charles Stromeyer

Innocence Revisited (It's About Childhood)

Silence enveloped the skies
even the wind's soft whisper ceased
yet the silent turmoil grew inside
a deafening rumble rolled over unmoving fields
this I knew to be love cascading my soul
the ones who grew up to forget tremble
yet the childlike giggle tickled with joy
familiarity breeds indifference, adult proverb
remember how the child's world is filled
with an endless variety of new and wonderful experiences?
Taste for a moment if you will the timeless
perpetually churning kaleidoscopic embrace of love
    Chad Gall

Departing Friend

A friend of mine is going away
Even though I would like him to stay.
Neither her nor I have control over the situation,
But a higher arch who has declared his restitution.
Although he hasn't gone away yet,
Mourning undoubtedly has already set.
Such emotional ties grip the heart,
As not to experience an emotional gain,
But only to experience the emotional pain.
I have to question our very existence
As the loss of my friend grips the heart
With powerful persistence; I'm the one left
To sort out the reasons, his soul
Will move on no matter the season.
As with every season there is a new beginning
I hope my friend is delivered what he is deserving.
Let his peace be shared with those left behind
To comfort our soles as well as our minds.
    Deborah L. Ellis

Until We Meet Again

I can see her, far off in the distance against the amber glow of an evening setting sun. She's statuesque.
Her smile and laughter lingers in my thoughts.
It was always there; the richness of acceptance she gave unselfishly.

Look toward a creek which ebbs waters of peace and tranquility.
You know its quiet strength by its unending courage to never bend.
So as her courage.

She understood love, a love so strong and trusting that she put
    others before herself.
Out of this love her courage came.

The love shared between a mother and daughter never bends.
They travel through life together;
The mother the provider and protector, sharing her knowledge and
life's treasures with grace and dignity, and the joy of giving to
    the one of lesser year.

I questioned the bond we shared at times, because she is no longer
    here to reinforce my fears, but when I recall her beauty,
I regain my strength and the trust returns to me.

My mother walks with God now. I miss her. Until we meet again...
    Barbara A. McCoy Giera

"Unborn Love"

Just for one minute if you could feel
Every bit of heartache I'm trying to heal
No one you meet could help you forget
Nothing you do stops the regret
If only I had been stronger inside
Far less tears would have been cried
Even if I could have seen that things would work out
Reality is there was too much doubt
Believe me I wish I could
Leave the past I know I should
Unborn love that wasn't meant to be
The absence of what was special burning inside me
Tender first love I had to let go
You meant so much more than I can let you know
    Jennifer B. Lutty

"The Soul"

Way down deep where it doesn't show
Everyone has soul of this, we all know.
It doesn't matter if your black or white,
you need to be kind and do what's right.
Stop all this hate and, hurting each other,
look past, the surface and help one another.
We all have a soul and, right from the start,
we should look with our eye's, and see with our Hearts.
We might be surprised if, this would catch on,
soon all the hate, and distrust would be gone.
This world would be a much better place,
for all of us, the Human Race.
Then God could smile, from up above,
were all his children, we have his Love.
We must be careful you and me,
as we walk through this world toward eternity.
To stand before God all alone,
and hope that, He welcomes all of us home.
    Janice Naslund

Kissing

Bring two lovers together by touching lips;
evoke the inner feelings through a gyrating kiss.

Every turn of the neck/every movement of the mouth
Grows we as a rain forest, no question of doubt.

As the soft we lips caress the ear lobe;
the warmth of breath like a Santa Ana flow.

Your mind is elated/your eyes are close
Body heat rises you lose control.

This is a kiss of exceptional beauty;
perpetuating lips a raving ruby.

A kaleidoscope of colors travel in your mind;
tingling sensations run up your spine.

It's the stimulating kiss that tells us all;
that love conquers summer, spring, winter and fall.
    James Berkowitz

Untitled

Sitting in a room of my past, cold memories fall by my eyes in silent reflection, stories read and books stacked high, words flowing by the fire, these things I hold dear, longing for the chance to experience, embrace once more the feelings, spirit of the moment that tamed my soul, and warmed my heart, and of those times, some forgotten too long to regain, and of those remembered and relished, like those of my love now, something's flourish and something's die, but in my years I will know only but a constant, my memories and my love.
    James Moriarty

Sweet Gentle Poet Of Scarred Language

God is not here for him. Nor will be.
Except when running through woods in words
only, silently screaming for heartwood.

He wants to be in love, but cannot.
Knows commitment, once committed, is
loss. His lover, poetry, weans herself on his darkness.

Slender hands and a scalloped ear lobe
invite caresses, remind he has
never been tough enough for himself. He

sharpens words on razor straps and whittle
thoughts till they sting, but quietly,
then no one will notice until afterwards.

Consumed in sadness, he dies now,
slowly rather than waiting for an end. This
keeps him from being afraid of death, temporarily.

When he really dies he will be wrapped in words
before the burning. Afterwards, she will
scatter whatever is left.

Elaine Woodruff

My Life!

My life is eternal; my life is external; my life is eternal and external of itself. My life, as known by me in my fullest conscious-awareness, is complete;

My life surges forward to new horizons, awaiting the newness of the rising sun; my life revolves as the earth repositions itself in perfect harmony with all the elements of life;

My life is committed to the highest order of perpetual motion, constantly in tune to the harmony of all things. My life has full meaning and understanding, abounds with omnipotent spirit;

My life is Spirit, enclosed in this fantastic kingdom called the human body, with knowledge and wisdom abound for the asking;

My life, with knowledge and wisdom, has come into a peaceful coexistence with my indwelling Spirit; My life breathes, moves and has its being from only one source, GOD!

My life IS GOD; it's omnipresent, omnipotent and omniscience; my life is your life, for the same omnipresence within me is within you. Your life has become my life, for I'll accept nothing less, for there is only love; peace and happiness; for without YOU... there is nothing!!!

Edward Ellis Jackson Sr.

Thread

Thread is an essential and versatile item. It can hold two pieces of fabric together, binding them into one unit. The thread allows the two pieces to be joined and be larger, warmer or stronger than they could be individually.

While it is strong when used to mend or join, an individual strand is not and it can be easily broken. Even with delicate handling, seams let go, tears develop and the threads can quickly unravel, fraying the fabric or separating the halves. If the two do begin to separate from one another, or a tear develops, new thread can be used to mend the material so it can be whole again. Neglecting the situation could lead to a larger tear or a complete separation of the two pieces.

Prompt attention and repair is always the best course of action. Only mindful, close sewing, strong thread and care will allow the union to last. Our thread is love.

Edward H. Ryan

Stale?

Can you shuffle through these thoughts I breed?
Face these wounded impossibilities...
This distance brings an ache for tomorrow...
Your yesterday. Step through their worlds, into mine.
They've been choking on rotting words...
I promise something more substantial.
Just close your eyes to this drought and
Dream of rain, wet with kisses.
A balm for your submission?
As I plaster unassuming stars with your name...
Rip them right out of their velvet beds...
I am aware of your ebbing...your digging
From shallow graves. Don't let me drown in
These rivers...this spill of ocean.
This splinter is the only thing holding
Me together. Am I something sweet
For your sore? Everything sour for your affection...
I've swallowed half the moon. Just give me
Something for the pain...or you could always suffocate
On this breath between us, stale as the distance that falls upon us.

Heather Hanford

Quaking And Shaking

Quaking and shaking all around.
Falling, crashing, I hate the sound.
Running I am doorway bound.
Jolt out of bed, leap to the floor,
Run and go stand under the door!
Quaking and shaking all things are
  breaking.
I'm so scared, stop the time it is taking.
Yelling, screaming above the sound.
Quaking, shaking all around.

Courtney Mooney-Arrington

Untitled

Since childhood he's sheltered me.
Fathering my every step
Holding my hand to see me off.
To tucking me in at night.

So young gazing through old eyes.
Always with an eye on me and
an eye on himself.
Never had a chance to play.

Now in our best years
Were at our worst times
endless arguments echo in my head
So close in age, yet so far in personality.

We no longer hold hands
He no longer watches me
Am I at fault for your deep anger.
I'm sorry! You couldn't play.

Anthony DeStefano

Gray

Gray is a lonely heart; Waiting,
  for someone to come along.

Gray is like a cold rainy day, in the fall,
  bringing sadness and broken hearts, together
Gray is a lazy, when you can't move in the morning
Gray is when it's black outside, and
  not a big 'Yellow sun'
Gray is when your big 'Red balloon flies away.
Gray is when your best friend moves away

Donna Lee (Bromm) Algren

Sea Of Peace

Turmoil was around me and pain cut my heart
Fear caused my hands to shake and tears filled my eyes
I am running daily, not for physical strength
Running to win the race of my life

Water cleanse me, slow my fast feet
Sea of serenity let me float calmly
When the waves knock me down, cushion me
Water give me peace

Wounds of the heart burn like fire
My mind is tied up with confusion
Thoughts are fogged with clouded emotions
I know I must find rest

I dive deep to sink the pain
I slowly rise to the top
Emotions are freed, washed clean and made new

Cynthia L. Jones, M.D.

Untitled

    Against my thoughts since being conceived. In the cold and fear I tremble, while the lights so bright I wish it would blind me. Voices a jumble with disconcerting intonations to calm. The sterile indifference confuses my emotions hovering from up above to beneath the floor, moving quickly and slowly. To my anguish tears so deep they can only be ripped out of my most inner center. The drinking of red thick and lumpy then spitting it away, coming sharper and sharper till I turn away only to turn right back. Unbearable, with a small world closing tighter around my morals. How will I live with me after the crash. To ashamed for any one to know and no peace with one too many memories being hidden. Nothing to fill the empty grave in my soul. Simple, justify to no one earthly creature and go on day after day after day.

Elizabeth Barrett

Life's Knowledge

Life's days are strange. The nights are long.
We really don't feel like we belong.

But do not fear for you will persevere,
and end with knowledge you can adhere.
For every time and every season
there is always a perfectly good reason.
and end with knowledge you can adhere.

For we shall learn from our mistake,
along the paths we seem to take.

But if shallow minds can not reach,
then wiser ones can not teach.

If we do not accomplish these things,
then wasted is all knowledge that time brings.

John J. Dolan

Silent Night

Silent night and it's christmas.
Holy night and I feel I am dieing
Crying your name, it's just not the same.
You've gone away on Santa's sleigh.
Silent night and it's christmas
Wishing you back, praying you were near.
Dreams and wishes, I'll never forget our kisses
Holy night and I feel I'm dieing.
Silent night and it's christmas.

Alice M. Mills

The Agony Of Truth

Clouds above, blocking the light
Feel my mind losing its sight
Deep inside, not much to see
Just dreams of what I think I should be

Standing alone, seeming so tall
Everyone wanting to see me fall
No one feels the pain, in me
Just keep pounding, and you will see

They try destroying all my dreams
Fighting hard, or so it would seem
Reaching, so deep inside!
Still trying to hide?

They never expected me, to live!, for "Me"

Jonathon Rupp

The Star

The wee angel sat on a fleecy white cloud
Feeling so lonely and blue,
And complained to the angel in charge of all things
That she wished she had something to do.

Then the angel in charge said: "This tarnished old star
Won't shine it's so battered and old,
Now take it and see if the polish you use
Can bring back it's glitter of gold."

The wee angel polished so hard and so long,
And worked while the other ones played,
That the oldest star there, on the junk pile once thrown,
It's brilliancy once more displayed.

So the angel in charge hung the star out once more
In a space over Bethlehem Town
And the night when the infant Jesus was born
'Twas the brightest of stars to shine down.

Howard A. Woodard

They Saw The Dream

Remembrance in the little white sailing boat...
Feminine seaway, singing to the prey of a bird...
Like a woman's dream, dancing on rippling screens...
Strong tides pick up the pages of a wave...

They wanna leave their homeland...
They pull the anchor, out of the sand...
Likewise to choose a different land...
Rushed out, run off the fatherland...

Once they take a breath away...
Once they bring you back to the wake...
All are dying, all are crying...
All are living off a mother's diamonds...
Once their destination comes, their faith sails to the,
crossroads of decisions...

Remembrance in the little white falling star..
You wished upon, in your golden heart...
It seems like yesterday, when you fell apart...it seems like
today, when you walked the new land...

Christopher J. Williams

I Love The Flowers

Dandelions, Roses, so many kinds
I can't think of one more because they
Smell very fine!
Red, Pink, Yellow, Blue any color will due.
Vases, Water, Cups too it will keep
them fresh for you!

Gina Ann Zippo

A Lost Love

In shallow moonlight and splendid silver;
fields of untarnished gray, filled in flood.
In the grasp of an untold bloom
Filled the bosom to make one swoon.

A quick dash down the shadowed path,
let me see, at last,
a million geese in flight
sounds apart from their light!

To join them, I thought
would be so easy, so I fought.
But alas, gravity saw my quick descent
as I pierced the body of cool torment.

All the feathers afloat remind me of my loss,
pinning me onto a red and hot cross.
Mere seconds later, calm was the lake,
haunting and oh, so fake.

For I was sure that the lake had been distraught
my love had been destroyed much.
But my deep pool seemed to me, nature's sin
For what can I do now? I cannot swim!

Alexander W. Lee

Mindchild

Child of my mind,
Fleeting, illusive, undefined.
Like an orphan, left to find it's way,
Taking first steps on legs unsteady.
Groping, searching, the time nearly ready
To burst forth alive, strong and sure,
Just born new, still virginal pure.
Somewhere deep inside received,
From the deepest depths of my soul conceived,
Your birth came not on easy pain,
At times rejected, only to surface again.
Child of my mind,
It is you I sought.
Child of my mind,
I named you, Thought.

Bonnie Jean Lance

Flying With One Wing

It's hard to fly with just one wing when you've
  flown with two for so long.
And you look around and the wind is so cold
  and storm clouds are very strong.
It's hard to find your balance and you feel
  so all alone.
You sometimes wonder where your dreams
  and hopes have gone.
And here you're left, with just one wing to
  weather the storms of life.
But praise the Lord He sends His spirit to
  help us through our strife.
And so on the wings of the spirit of God,
  He gives us strength for the hour
So we learn to fly with just one wing
  with the presence of God and His power.

Elmeta Fine

The Day God Closed The Shutters On The Sky

It was the day - brilliant sunshine
Fluffy white clouds floating in an azure blue sky
And on the earth we saw it, as we did on other days
And accepted it as our due, and went our merry ways

But there came a bolt of thunder with roaring belching sounds
And lightning so sharp it would cut you like a knife
You can't believe it, nor can I
But it happened, it really happened

Most people tho't 'twas the end of the world
Got down on their knees and prayed
But all Hell broke loose that fateful day
All black, no sun nor moon - the people screamed

They cried "Oh God, Why, Oh Why, we're not ready to die"
Just speak to us, Please God and tell us
The earth and the sky were as one
And if the earth is round, we will fall into space

Give us one more chance or put us
In a very special place where we can atone
Just tell us Dear God! What do we do?
"Are we to be damned as we have damned you?"

Dorothy Nicklin

A Jaunty Prelude For The Birds

Little birdies soft and sweet
Fly too and fro for food to eat.

Their coming and going in constant flight
Causes us to wonder...What will be their plight.

It's not for us to know
Why at will they come and go.

They're just a creation for our delight
Not made by man but by God's might.

So we look forward day by day
For them to come play, bathe, eat and sing
Bringing cheerfulness to our day
As they wing beautifully on their way.

They hop about on little web feet
Building nests, hatching eggs, just procreating
While we enjoy their coming and going
Just watching...and waiting....

Always singing-in weather good or bad
Is their song for their delight or make us glad?
It doesn't matter, what the case maybe
I can truly say it works for me.

Isedora Wilson

Getting Back

Returning like a sailor on a voyage of discovery,
Full of memories,
Full of hope for the changes he wished,
Full of desire to know what has become of what he left behind,
Full of love to share with family unseen for years,
Full of dreams inexplicable but to one like he,
He is home,
Dreams are shattered,
Desire is flustered with futility what has become,
Hope is crushed with what he sees
Memories and love remain,
But they are dying.

Gordon Gilbert

"An Afternoon Goes By"

An afternoon goes by as time,
folds the room into origami shadows.
I lie staring at undecipherable cracks,
on a water-stained stucco ceiling.
Absent-mindedly I listen,
to an anonymous sidewalk radio.

In the noontime heat she peels an orange,
her sweat blends bittersweet with citrus.
Carelessly she tosses the orange peel,
onto an overflowing littered ashtray,
embedded onto the sticky varnish,
of spilled cheap whiskey like an offering,
made to the Gideon nightstand shrine.

Time unfolds the room's tense shadows,
into the cool blue-black of evening dusk.
We make small talk and agreeably laugh,
desperately avoiding the certainty of desire.

It's night when we leave that guiltless room,
parting into opposite streetsign geometry,
our faces masked by our departing backs.
   Cesar M. Abrajano Jr.

True Love

As we touch I feel our souls connect
   for a brief moment in time.
That precious moment leaves a scar of love,
   which even I can not hide.
As the gentleness of your lips touch mine,
   soft as rose petals falling on still water.
Never knowing when the sun shall set for the final time
   and we shall not awaken.
My love stronger than if you shall not awaken.
I shall claim that day to be the last that I see
   the blindness of life,
The black tears I shed for my life,
   for now I am with you!
   Cyndi Zwank

Just For You

You are my friend and I know you care,
For all of the times that you were there.

I took advantage of you and, sometimes, I still do,
But you never seemed to care; just said, "I love you."

When I hurt, you would hurt; I can now realize,
It was pain and anguish I saw in your eyes.

I'm getting older and now I can see,
Just how much you have sacrificed for me.

I can never repay you for all that you've done,
Truly, I've been blessed by being your son.

I wish I could tell you how much I really care,
These words on paper are only a few to share.

I know how much I have taken and feel the love you've shown,
Where does your strength come from and when will it be gone?

Mother, you're the greatest and can never be replaced,
I don't understand how you do it, but don't let your smile be erased.

Thank you! Thank you, a million times twice,
And always remember — I love you thrice.
   Craig Wilton Tucker

To A Special Friend

My friendship is kind, great and true,
   For an image brought and thought through.
Many times we have caused great pain,
   Up's and down's so we have gained.

Peace to us now and ever more,
   Together forever rich or poor.
Meaningless treasures brought in the past,
   Things that meant nothing and did not last.

Your touchable face, your delivered kiss,
   Something through time that I will miss
Your captured eyes, your heart of gold,
   Something great in value and never to be sold.

But future lies and troubles me,
   I shut my heart, my eyes - I can't see.
For pain is wicked, evermore!
   Bloodless pain, I will not sore.

So in this poem I truly tell,
   Not a story, not a spell.
But what I feel, in my heart,
   Every word in every part.
   Amy Olson

Journey

Sometimes I think of life and wonder my purpose...
For, do we not, all, enter alone down one tunnel, the birth canal?
And, do we not all leave along that other one with two branches,

One toward the bright, almost-blinding light and the other,
into total absolute darkness?

So, that being said, our being, our life has often been described
as the "roadway of life"

Along this roadway, there are many paths, some clearly marked
and some less distinct, a mere trail, heavily shrouded with
branches and obstacles.

One thing, that has become clear in hindsight, is that, sometimes
the clear, easily discernible path often leads to a rocky trek and
even a dead end, causing one to arrive miles from the original destination.

While the treebranch - overhung, briar-filled path can sometimes
yield a shortcut and move us physically and spiritually toward our
chosen mecca.

So, on one moves, frequently skipping merrily along, stopping to
sniff wild flowers and pick bouquets while enjoying the sun
warming the body and encouraging the continuance of the journey.

Ah, but other times, the sun is nowhere to be seen and the clouds
overhead are so dark that the path is almost obscured and one wonders
"Should I continue on or should I pause or even stop..."
   Alice Green

Spellvasion

Unclear shapeless shadows linger in my soul
I feel an urge to grasp the vagueness
A want to understand, a need to control
Not spellbinding - I'd say mysterious
To wipe smudged window clear
Or wave a wand to conjure up
To stare at face with inner fear
   Craig Rule

Cigarette

Why am I smoking this damn cigarette?

It must be what you do to me,
for I am opposed to the thought of
 my own blackened lungs.

I am not, however, opposed to you.

I thought it blissful to ride aside you today,
 your hair laying across my shoulder,
 your laugh trickling out,
The sun biting your face like an apple.
(If I could govern weather, you'd never have burned)

Man, I am so damned lucky to have someone like you.

I just don't understand, though,
Why I'm smoking this bloody stogie,
 my head reclined,
 the horse before me, whinnying.

It must be what you do to me.

I can enjoy myself in the worst of circumstances.
Daniel Hickey

Me As A Tree

 I am like a tree, a young sapling,
for I have not the wisdom of the old.

 I am quiet,
unless my leaves are shaken by the wind.

 My roots are firm in the soil from which I grow,
but yearn to explore the unknown darkness below.

 I stretch my branches grasping for the sky,
hoping to reach the blue dome above.

 Knowledge is rain which I soak in thirstily,
taking in as much as possible.

 I do not grow alone,
the elder trees stand tall protecting me from the cruel onslaught of
the weather,
Other saplings are near, each growing in their own way
but all trying to stay the same.

 I am a tree,
a young sapling, gaining wisdom from the old,
knowledge from the world,
and growing with each day.
Edward G. Hiser Jr.

Songs Unsung

Oh sing to me of songs unsung, of lovers passion deep,
For if tomorrow I shall not awaken from bitter sleep.
I need to find myself within the fabric of my mind,
To love and hold the things I need and not want left behind.
Oh sudden joys of victories past are sweet but not the same,
I search for words to elaborate but words escapes my brain.
I feel the passion in my heart, a fire controls my soul,
For the need to be the best I can and a reason to be whole.
So raise your voice in sweet content to ease a troubled mind,
And turn the pages on my life to leave the pain behind.
I need a song that turns my head so I can search within,
And rearrange the things I find and move on out again.
The voices of the demons there all echo in my head,
And seem to come out at night to haunt me in my bed.
I need to hear the song unsung so I may befriend myself,
So sing to me of treasures found and of my inner wealth.
Oh sing a song of time, and ages creeping by,
For I feel my life's in ashes, but from the ashes the Phoenix flies.
David R. Hutton

A Forsaken Generation

Aging or sickness is like a mirror that we prefer not to look in
For it brings out the fear and uncertainty that we feel within
We remember a loved one that once stood strong and tall
Now we see a frail person who can barely move at all

We make little excuses for not coming around
We're just so busy and can't slow down
Fooling ourselves into believing, if we ignore it, it'll go away
Not realizing that we all must cross that bridge someday

It's a known fact that wisdom often accompanies age
Like someone who has lived a book page by page
Not taking advantage of the knowledge that they've acquired
We toss aside our elders with a label that says "retired"

The backbone of this country for so many years
Building up his nation with their blood, sweat, and tears
They taught us to believe in ourselves, to strive to be the best
Now we cop out on them, when life puts us to the test

So Lord, forgive us, for we know not what we do
We have again forsaken someone, who's very close to you
People, open up your hearts as well as your mind
Discover all the treasures that you're trying to leave behind
Jimmy Copeland

Team Player

The fans were jeering with delight
for the time had come to end this fight.
He helped bring them here to see this show
knowing soon he'd be going home.
He knew there would be no shame
for He played well at this game.
But He seemed weary, worn and fray
and thought his Mother would see him this way.
So He stood upright fast and tall
knowing that He better not fall.
So proudly He carried the wood aloft
winching and gasping with pain so soft.
A sting in his hands the wood would claim
So He drew in a huge breath to prepare for fame.
And He called to his Father
so proud, so long,
and darkness fell and the fans were gone.
He rose to the occasion once again
that Great team player, towards the sky He ascends.
John R. Foreman

Remnants Renewed

I was a house resplendent, a hearty haven
 For those weathered and worn weary.
Tea and sympathy in my kitchen quaint, cozy and content.
Children squealed in my nursery
 Uproarious and gay.

Where once I towered tall and rooted,
 Only ashes and cinders in smoldering silence;
 Blackened bleak obliteration.
The flicker of candle-lit love flared full
 Engulfing me in the inferno of infidelity.
It seared me and scorched me, then slowly
 It burned me down.

Like Phoenix from the ashes - a quickening.
 Brick and mortar, travail and tears,
 Course by course, column and beam
The Master Carpenter recreated and raised
 Grandeur, strength and wisdom.
A house most resplendent, a hearty haven
 For those weathered and worn weary.
Cecile Jeannette Durand

Thanks To God

We thank thee our Father, for the love that you gave.
For thy son that you sent us, our souls for to save.
We thank thee our Father, for being so true.
Though often we hurt thee, by the deeds that we do.
We thank thee our Father, for all of our joys.
For we are thy children, as small girls and boys.

We thank thee our Father, for thy spirit divine,
Who leads us in mercy, to our Father sublime.
We thank thee our Father, for thy holy word.
It helps us to know thee, makes our sins seem absurd.
We thank thee our Father, for our pastor and friend.
He helps in all trials, our God to defend.

We thank thee our Father, for our guiding light,
In the person of Jesus, who makes our days bright.
We thank thee our Father, for trials of this world.
They help us to know, of thy goodness unfurled.
We thank thee our Father, for all of these things.
We pray we'll remember, the blessings you bring.

Charles F. Dunton

The Mask

The rigid, tight mask embedded upon my face.
For with it, there is barely room to breathe.
Brown coloring pasted upon my skin.
What a sad, confusing sight I see when I look in the mirror.

This mask I wear defines my social and economic standards.
As I go throughout the day, I am looked upon with hatred.
Injustice constantly slaps me upon my cheekbones.
Inequality stomps on me repeatedly, hoping I will eventually
   give up on life.

This mask I wear is filled with unfair treatment, stares, glares, and fears.
This world we live in will never change.
Like the sun, it shines down upon my face,
   illuminating the color of my skin.

No matter where I go, no matter what I do, no matter what I say,
I am not the person being viewed...It is the Mask.

Jennifer Pressley

Our Love

Our love is true, I know it is Dear,
For you have shown that you are sincere.
A ring you have placed upon my left hand.
And soon in the chapel together we'll stand.

The joy I feel when we walk hand in hand
Makes me feel more important than all in the land.
As a leader you are wise, and soon you will rise
To be master of a household in which we two abide.
You use common sense and are always thinking ahead
Of the joys we will have and the sorrows we dread.

Let's always communicate the thoughts we are thinking
As that makes a family so strong and enriching.
May we not take for granted the love that we have
For some couple's love has turned into sand.
But keep it forever as strong as can be
Until we both shall reach eternity.

Beth E. Loesch

A Poem Of Love And Praise To Jesus My Lord

Jesus I want to say "Thank You" so much
for your saving healing touch.
You left your throne on high and came down
to earth to die.
You gave your life so free on the cruel
cross of calvary.
We can never repay the debt of love we owe
that I truly know.
We can try to work until that glorious day
that you will break through the sky in that
great by and by.
I know that you are coming back again to catch
your bride away; for in heaven we will stay.
with loud Hosannas we will shout forever
more on that beautiful heavenly shore.
So long until then, I will say
Amen and Amen.

Helen Dickson

"Lady In Red"

Send me some forget-me-nots; anybody, that would make my day
Forget-me-nots from the lady in red with the blinding blue eyes
For her and the governor to deliver my pardon, now that would
   truly make my day!
But who could this lady be?
I have touched love with many;
Chris, the dashing red bone with the black and grey eyes,
Rose, the shy, gentle dove who carries a piece of my heart
   around her neck
Diane, the adventurous chick who can turn around on a dime
   and give you eleven cents change
Cindy, the snow girl, who looks at me everyday within a set of twins
Holly, the only pecan tan to ever propose to me
Evil, a gentle teddy bear with a lust for life and second to none
Rhonda, a tenderoni, on a quest for a no-static-love
Laverne, the lith tigeress who can devour a heart at the
   blinking of an eye
But Red, the most understandable woman in the world
Pound for pound, she's untouchable
Oh how I wish for a future or even a past with the Lady in Red
Let the victor come forth and claim their prize.

Grant Rogers Jr.

She's Back And Safe — Again

She came home today, after an absent spree
From a disease her family tries faithful to see
Our daughter, our sister, our lovely Lea.

One day at a time, never two the same
Her troubled spirit she tries hard to tame

When very young, headstrong and so gullible
Her life before her leading only to trouble

Conduct that persisted through out the teen years
Drugs and alcohol continued our fears
Watching and waiting with worry and tears

No future, no peace, only constant running
An altered mind, unstable and cunning

While the devils persisted to rape her mind
And steal the peace she only knows a short time

Ever searching, but finding no place to go
Until a higher power intervenes with the foe

With constant vigilance and a family's love
Reaching and praying to the power above

That peace and serenity and love unfurl
Around our loved one, until we leave this world.

Freda Hurley

"How Time Slips By"

Known only to me...In silentness you stood...
From a far I watched as you grew to manhood...
Many memories I have carried to heart...
How time slips by...
Our paths have crossed over the years...
As we faced the battle on life's crowded street...
Never forgotten...Nearest to me...
Waiting to be called on...when in need...
You were not a stranger...unloved and unknown...
You were a brother with a heart that is much like my own...
How time slips by...
Our Heavenly Father knows what is best for us...
For we always want sunshine..but we know there must be rain...
He gently placed his hand upon thy heart...
Quietly he said...Close your eyes my child...
I have come to take you home...
Known only to me...In silentness you stood...
How time slips by...
Until we meet again...

Esther Frances Gilland

Mother Earth

Our planets dying, you know I'm not lying,
From deep down inside her she spews out
The chemicals we've put in her now flooding,
Our planets frying,
With her forests on fire burning, our planets choking,
With her air polluted and smoking, our planets trembling,
With her earthquakes and volcanos a coming
Up from the bottom rumbling, our planets dying,
you know I'm not lying
We've probed her drilled her stripped her and
Raped her its no wonder she's dying,
And we oughta be ashamed and crying,
With our plutonium in her oceans leaking,
With our power plants radiation in the air leaking,
With our nuclear warheads pointed up at her skies
Ready to start flying, blowing,
Her and us too bits and pieces its no wonder she's screaming,
And with God fed up and steaming,
I'm sure that's why were stuck down here with her
Doomed until it's all ending,
Our planets dying, you know I'm not lying.

David Martin Johnson

Admirabilis (A Butterfly)

A butterfly has chased the goose way
from my November chill and touched my frame
with such a tinder spark that I can stay
no more cocooned in cold than she in flame.

Is it a face that fires me, or a hope,
a curl, a smile that flutters in her lips
and gambols through my shivers like a rope
teasing the anchors of a thousand ships?

I've courted butterflies before and learned
the warm breath flapping in an admiral's beat,
but chasing, I've been chastened too, and burned
my face with wind rather than face retreat.

Oh, I have lost my chill alright, and yet,
what is this species that I can't forget?

David Aikman

Colorado

There are a million reasons why I love this state.
From the eminent mountains to the graceful landscape.
When the Aspens dance in the gentle breeze,
beholding the mountains in blissful-harmony.
It soothes my soul, my worry escapes,
I feel so proud to live in this state.
The opulent beauty of a mountain silhouette,
that warms of heart, least I forgot.
The Colorado river flows like blood in my veins,
a life time to all as it fiercely reigns.
Cutting through rock in a deep canyon floor,
Kindly nurturing forever more.
When beautiful was our creations intent,
Colorado was truly what he meant.

Deborah M. Vanderwood

Lava Lamp

Hot wax ascends the glass tower,
  Full of power.
Forming balls,
The light calls,
  "Come to the top, make a spectacle."
We want to know,
About the show.
Soundless, rounding
Toting circles,
  Floating wax.

Waning buoyancy,
  Bring the spheres, set them free.
falling they become part of the heart.
Spitting offspring to the top, where they stop.
Cool wax descends the tower,
  Void of power.

Guy Olivieri

The Brown Teddy

The little girl in the faded raincoat
Gazed longingly at the brown teddy
On the back window of Kelly's Hillman.

She shivered as she remembered her Dad
In the pub across the road since mornin'
As she waited for him to drive her home
To the top of the hill above the town.

She knew he'd be cross with her Ma,
Shouting and striking her maybe hard
And they'd all run out in the fields to hide.
When he'd finally collapse on the ground,
They'd creep inside as he slept noisily.

It was cold in the car across the road from the pub
But it was coldest of all in her heart.

Joanne Norris

God And The Doctor

God and the doctor, as one person be;
God through the doctor lets blind people see;
No matter where they travel, throughout this land;
The doctor says "Oh God, be kind to me thy humble slave,
Let me a way of cure find, and this person let me save."
If it's God's will that the person die,
it's not really by the doctor's hand,
For God is always right you know,
He gives and takes of man.

Jean Giambra

Spouse Abuse

Women of all ages have this happening to them
Getting beat up- who am I talking about - him
They wear shades to cover their black eyes
Living a life full of lies
Wearing their hair hanging across their faces
So no one else can see their swollen places
Having on long sleeves in the summer time
So they won't hare to hear that same line
He hit you again, he ain't going to stop, you need to leave
Having the long pants to hide the abused legs
Keep it up and they will need pegs
Those men, are not their dads
They should be willing to get out and glad
The women should tell the men to get the hell out
Because they already know what he's about
I don't like the fact that men abuse their girlfriends or wives
The rest of all those women's lives will be called lies
   Danielle Vereen

"Aids" "Wanted Dead Or Alive"

Aids is a disease most commonly known
given little understanding it comes
into your home. Its doesn't care if you
like it or not, it's there to ruin your life.

Aids is not bashful, nor is it shy it comes
in all colors, shapes and size. It doesn't worry
of whom the next victim will be, not caring
that it is a deadly disease.

Aids is something that does not discriminate,
if given the opportunity it diminishes your health
this can be very gruesome you see. Let's pull
together in peace and harmony.

The muggers, the robbers, prostitutes and pimps, the crackheads,
and gangs or no exempt. Aids has no respect for you
or me so now we must look up towards heaven
for God is our only key.
   Delisa Phillips

One of Those Days

Ever had one of those days when things don't go just right?
Well I had one and it gave me a fright!

Last week after my first patient
I thought I was going to get blown up!
The gas fumes in the truck cab were so strong -
I thought I was going to throw up!
So— I held my nose - put the window down,
drove to my second patient's house with a frown -
I thought to myself - this just isn't right!!!
I called my son and traded rigs
He said, "Gee Mom, your sure lucky that this didn't blow!"
the gas was certainly not leaking slow!,
but a steady stream, just under the hood —
we both know, that that wasn't good!
Well, I guess you'd call it my lucky day,
the problems all fixed and I'm on my way!!!!
   Janet Frey

Life

The answers are hidden
I go searching thru time...
The bumps and the bruises collectively shine
The magical moments, laughter, and friends
I gather like chestnuts to help and to mend
My aura is dimming... weep not for me;
My pains were lessons-be happy for me.
   Donna V. Stokes

You Made Our Lives Worth Living

You didn't ask to be born.
God sent you to us for our pleasure, and treasure.
We didn't do as much for you as we could,
or as much as we should.

We accepted and enjoyed the privilege of raising you.
Just thought this was what we were supposed to do.
If either of you were complimented or praised,
we took pride because we had raised you.

As you all grew older we were having so much fun,
we forgot to consider anything we had done.
You were making your mark's at school, church, and work.
Home responsibilities you didn't shirk.

We are careful to give the Lord thanks
for letting us be,
the couple given the privilege
of raising you three.
   Clara B. Bailey

Autumn Teases

Autumn teases,
Golden blankets cover the lush green earth,
Red bushes set the hillsides on fire,
The sun and the moon compete for brightness,
These days will never end.

Autumn teases,
Balmy winds play hide and seek with the leaves,
Warm gentle rain falls lightly.
These days will never end.

Autumn teases,
Winter lurks quietly in a shadowy corner
not yet announcing it's coming.
   Dorothy Bernd

Daydream

I'm here today.
Gone tomorrow.
I travel to my day dreams and out I come.
I wonder in the misty land were no man has been.
I'm loud one day quiet the next.
I follow my dreams to see were they go.
When I awake from them I'm in the twilight zone.
I'm here today.
Gone tomorrow.
I travel everywhere.
I wonder what my future holds for me.
I'm short one day and tall the next.
I follow the wind to see were it blows me.
But someone bring me back.
Day in.
Night out.
I here today.
Gone tomorrow.
   Alicia Denise Brown

To Maureen, With Keats' Poems

I cannot give you what some men can give
Gowns made of silk, glittering rings of gold,
And though I could, I wouldn't. Primitive
Is that which greedy men love to behold.
I cannot make to you the vows which warm
The coldest hearts. I cannot say "My Love,
You are so sweet that bees around you swarm
And angels fear they've lost you from above."
But what I give shines infinitely bright
When Sleep or thought have cast their silent spell;
When snow is falling on a Winter's night
But Summer's joy within you starts to swell;
Or when in Spring, you see a flower bloom
And think of Autumn dreaming up its doom.

Jamison Ashley Oughton

There Went A Demon

Photo albums fall, open in wounded memories,
Grainy concrete images of sliced life
Stand aching. My heated pulse oozes,
Joining hollow beats and hallucinogenic screams.
Twisted worlds of anger reverberate black doors of
Dark nightclubs. Bullets throbbing, bleeding,
Choking life. He lies.
Victory passes and sighing pompoms lead
Undauntingly to captain popularity,
Scholarships, smiles so straight and white,
They hurt.
Vegas memorial service. Slight tears evaporate for a
Gunman leaving pools of pain in Denver streets.

Alison Ewert

Age Spots, Liver Spots, Good Deeds Or Bad?

I remember the first time I saw them on my
Grandma Anna's hands, and then her face
I wondered what they meant,
I was young, newly married but
I saw them again on my Mom's hand, and arms,
and watched
Till I saw them on my husband's mothers hands,
and arms
And as the years passed I saw them come to my
husband's arms, and then he left to live with God
and now I see them on my hands, and arms, and face
and wonder, what do they really mean?
Age spots, liver spots, good deeds or bad?

Bettie Norman Noble

My Grandmother in Her Rocking Chair (A Picture)

On her veranda space
Grandma looks like time
Rocking backward and forward
Knitting complicated patterns
 for her children,
And with a tonal tinge to match:
"Just listen to that owl,
"Every night about this time;
"And, oh! the wind blew the garland
"From the crucifix in the garden,
"Poor John! may his soul rest in peace."
She puts down her needle
And her cotton unrolls itself
 along the floor
Stopping at the wall like a future;
And her hair grew grey
As she looks at the moon
Remembering when John ploughed the garden
Where flowers bloom.

Euton I. Beckford

Rain

Heat without movement, still and bright
Grass burnt brown and curled up tight

The air smells of dust and things dry
Everything lingers under the clear sky

The hush is patient and long has been the wait
Without moisture soon, for much it will be too late

Something is different, it has a smell
Moisture is a tease and only time will tell

The air makes a move, ever so slight
The sun still bakes everything in sight

The scent is real and ever so sweet
The move is now a breeze shifting the heat

So small and so precious, it is the first drop
Hope consumes all, will it continue or stop

The brightness dims and then a streak of light
A splitting crack then rumbles from great heights

Rain is here in torrents and with a great rush
Replenishing those who had waited with patience and trust

Howard M. McCain

His Skillful Care

The future waits, and holds
great rewards for those who not only dream
but rather tend their fields, and pray
drawing vigor from the Living Stream.

Many times a dream must wait
through seasons long and often dry;
during such times one's faith can grow -
That cherished vision not die!

So take heart! O trust in Him -
though your load be much to bear;
Understand your dream does rest
on the wings of His skillful care.

Jennifer Anne Messing

Colors

Red, orange, yellow,
Green,
Blue, indigo, violet
These are the colors of the rainbows.
These colors look good together;
they agree with each other to give us beauty.
Why can't we be the same?
Humans are different colors,
but humans don't agree with each other all the time.
Why?
If we'd only agree with each other all the time,
life would be beautiful.
Yet, our differences add to the beauty of life.
Maybe, we don't have to agree with each other.
Maybe, our differences are like the colors of the rainbows
We agree that we have differences.
Maybe, we need our differences to live a beautiful life.
Our differences are colors themselves
Each a shade of our being.
Each making us uniquely beautiful.

Jason Aloysious Wong

"Merry Christmas"

Season of GOOD WISHES, Season of MERRIMENT
Greet good morning and make this eve silent;
Select us Peace and Joy for the coming new year;
And leave us with laughter, fun, and family cheer.

Season of WONDROUS LOVE, Season of GOODWILL
Send us red stockings, some we'd like to fill;
Bestow us splendor bright, like stars radiant beauty;
And leave gratitude and thanks to serve as our duty.

Season of GREAT HARMONY, Season of FRIEND
Gather us together and make skin-colors blend;
Let this special way be blessed with lasting love;
And leave us resounding, like music from up above.

Season of ST. NICK, Season of GIFT
Offer us the best time to give someone a lift;
Wrap precious presents that will not pull apart;
And leave us everlasting with Jesus in our heart.

Season of THANKS, Season of WORLD PRAYER
Seek out the weak and the poor people out there;
Offer richness and newness that they cannot afford;
And leave us today, a holiday to celebrate the Lord.

Carol A. Masterson

Windswept

The white heads move swiftly overhead,
Grey, angry, touched with fire and crimson red.
The dead reminders of the past rustle,
And the spring tipped shoots stand erect against the Force.

The wind sweeps from the crest of the hill,
Bending the trees to and fro.
My skirt molds to my frame like a second skin.
Part of me and yet pulling me away from all that I am.

The Dandelions bob up and down, up and down.
My hair whips around my face.
I am lost in the world around me.

The pump shoots waves of emotion around me.
I am ecstatic and open my arms wide to embrace the cresting sea.
I am lifted to where the eagle soars and spirit becomes one
    with the never ending music.
The buds reach for me, trying to return me to where I have been.
I struggle with returning.

My cheeks flame with undeniable ecstasy.
I cry out like the panther that roams the wind raped mountains.
My body tingles where the hands have moved over me,
And then returned to the crest of the forest.

Georgia Huff

Messy

Juice from a lemon, juice from a lime
Ground carrots, onions, sage, and thyme,
Moldy cheese spread, covered with dirt,
I guess it's time to change my shirt.

Stepped on berries and their leaves,
Sap that dropped down from the trees,
Old honey that is crawling with ants,
It may be time to change my pants.

Tomato juice that was spilled on the floor,
Purple gum that was stuck to the door,
All kinds of mold, gray-green and blue,
It's probably time to change my shoes.

I'm in this state, it's really true!
Gray-green and purple, red and blue.
I think you'll agree its probably best
To tell me that I am a mess!

Ingrid Sakrison

Bonnie Rae

Bonnie Rae was a young girl,
Hair of auburn and eyes of brown.
She was just a tomboy, who made life full of joy.
Bonnie Rae was a young girl, when God took her that day,
Awards she hadn't seen, and the years of being a teen.
She showed me one day, how to jitterbug the time away.
Her love of Elvis and Johnny Ray, I laugh to this day.
My sister, I remember our times of yesteryear,
But now, your an angle in the clouds.
The year 1958, and the summer had just begun,
Why did God take you before our fun was done?
Bonnie Rae, my sister, I miss you everyday!

Jane Grodi

Loneliness

Loneliness is my life's intention,
Happiness, a feeling I have in its suspension.
I am left alone and afraid,
I want to be left in my darkest shade.
Ignorance is the twist to loneliness,
So unpure with its unholiness.
Emptiness is the loneliness mate,
With that feeling I want to end my fate.
Why isn't my life meant for the better or great?
I got the inheritance of the loneliness trait.

I want to be alone hidden away,
The loneliness has got me and I'm feeling afraid.
Everybody wants to spend their time with someone else,
The happiness I have left away it welts.
Why couldn't I have quite a different fate?
Instead I got the inheritance of the loneliness trait.

Amy Pierzchalski

The Ant Hill Of Life

When first we met, eyes looked into eyes,
    Happy music played.
We had met our fate, everything was great,
Forgotten was problems and strife.
    Never did I dream, he was a piss
Ant in the Ant Hill of Life.

Great ideas were relayed, thoughtful music played.
Hands entwined meeting of the minds,
Long, long talks, gentle walks
    Never did I think, he was a p**s
Ant in the Ant Hill of life.

More than hands entwined, exciting music played.
What did anything matter, body heart and soul on a silver platter.
Never did I feel, he was a p**s ant in the ant hill of life.
This is my reward, heart broken as by a sword,
Funeral music played.
He liked a clean kitchen floor.
So he took his cleaning lady for his wife
    Now I know for sure.
He was a p**s ant in the Ant Hill of Life.

June Ball

Untitled

Memories of long ago come rushing to my mind,
Happy thoughts of carefree days seem to ease the passing time,
The long nights of winter we'd have oyster stew,
When finding a pearl we'd add to our treasures anew.
The meadows were covered with blossoms galore,
A wonderland we had discovered before
For sheep showers we'd look and the blossoms we'd eat,
With the dew of the morning covering our feet.
The vines that were dormant all winter long,
An entanglement of green round the windmill grew.
Never knowing the cares of the passers by,
The toils, labors and their sighs.
In the midst of the grove
Each year we'd find,
Luscious red and white mulberries
In the open air we would dine.
The walnut tree stood close by the road,
Withstanding the rain, wind, and snow.
As faithful as those who passed by through the years
Time passes on with happy memories that brings cheer.

Dorothy Kuxhausen

"A Mother And Wife"

The biggest dream of my life
Has always been to be a great mother and wife.
Material things don't mean much to me
Just as long as my family is happy you see.
My husband and my children always come first.
May they never be hungry or have an unquenched thirst.
If one of them hurts, I hurt too
As a wife and a mother that's what you do.
When one of them needs me I try to be there
Because nothings more important than their well being and care.
Sometimes things can kind of get rough
But, I stick it out and try to be tough.
When things begin to fall apart.
I take a deep breath and make a fresh start.
I try very hard to be perfect you see
But no one is perfect, not even me.
When it's all said and done.
How am I as a mother and wife?
No one can deny the fact that they
Are my life!

Debra Brabham

Continuation

An old-fashioned town of some content
Has folks who modern changes resent.
Mother Earth with abundance and glory
Has reason to show quite another story;
By the turn of our planet, the settling of shelves,
Rocks, water and soil adjusted themselves.
What was newly borne became old,
Minerals materialized, like oil and gold.
Alterations in living had to be made
To continue progress of life's charades.
Games of chance are meant to be
To homes and business as necessity.
To fritter away on thoughts alone
Is like moss gathering on a stone.
Deeds are accomplished by trial and error
And renews a course that duties incur.
What is ancient can be treasured
While latest developments are measured
By good souls who participate
And live uncertainly in the hands of Fate.

Helen Sheehan

The Pinnacle

Like a flower whose petals have fallen from the wind,
Has my life changed in youthfulness, year upon end.
Strength and beauty and fragrance that must descend,
Within the grace of fulfillment of what it has been.
As the thorn is meant only to protect the flower,
So is mortality to bring meaning in its hour.
The cloud with shadows of darkness also brings the rain of growth,
As do trials of hurt and pain invoke new strength and hope.
Within the fullness of the rose in timely bloom,
Is its peak of performance, as it passes all too soon.
The greater value is not that one moment of glory,
But of all the time in coming and going.
As each flower thrives on both sunshine and rain,
Must each life reside in both happiness and pain.

Bill J. Buzzo Jr.

A Lament Of A Child

I am so young still a child, not sinned not viled, did not yet
have friends or mates, and I am told I have Aids,
O heavens blue, what wrong did I do, what wrong could I have
done to thee, to be born with H.I.V.
I am only five, already designated to a miserable short life,
I want to live, play, jump, run, bath in the shining sun, like
other children having fun, why did you me choose, to put on
that miserable noose, to depress my youthful days,
darken the rays, filled with fear, for every coming year,
please do not leave weep give me a chance, will earn my keep,
and in knowledge advance, I want to study and learn,
give back to society come my turn, and please society young
and old, take me in your fold, I am your mold, do not leave me
out in the cold, I am not contagious there are written pages,
that make clear the stages, of my misfortune as it ages.
and when time comes, I will not stay in your homes,
I will not be a mourner, I will retire to my lonely corner,
without friend of mate, will patiently wait, to accept my fate.

Jacob Haruvi

Ginger

How many times
Have you looked at the pain
In the eyes of the dog
Tied on a chain?

I am tied there for life
With no-one to care
I cry and howl
So lonely, in despair

If I could just hear my masters voice
Or feel his soft touch
I need very little
And don't ask for much.

Keep my water bowl clean and feed me once a day
And when you do these chores please take time to play.
I don't understand
When you just walk away.

But if you do, I'll still love you
When the time comes to part
Because there is no-one
So dear to my puppy heart.

Frank Horn

The Baby Of Love

Have you looked in the eyes of a baby
  have you touched his hands
Did you feel the warmth of his body.
  The body of love warming this land.
Have you felt his soul, go through you.
  His touches, kisses, and joy, rolling in the sand
Think like a baby, feel like one
  Live like one, than you will understand
That love is something to share
  Not a product, or a new brand.
Like the excitement of a baby, taking the first step
  or thinking to escape the sun, by blocking it with one hand
Love is the freedom to the slave
  Freedom is the slave of love and its golden band
Lets go back and become babies
  Give the soul a chance to fly to wonderland.
Like the sent of flowers enchants us
  so is the fire of desire, elusive yet so grand.
Love is the hope and renewal,
  Let me be in your dreams, and next to you stand.

Dr. Antoine Nacouzi O.M.D, PH.D.

World Wide Web Woes

My husband said it couldn't be done.
He didn't know I'd be having such fun.
I surfed the net, and oh! What a breeze!
The game and it's virus brought our Mac...
To it's knees.
Try as we may, our disk was fried.
The jumbo freeware took us down a slide.
My great little system is now broken.
Infected by virus... the dead disk our token.
My advice to those who surf
Is don't download till you cover your turf.
Virus protection is there for a reason...
'Cuz an infected system ain't very pleasin!

Cheryl Poole

"God Gave Me A Reason"

God gave me reason for everything;
He gave a reason to walk..... so that someday,
I could walk along side of you.

He gave me reason to talk.... so that someday,
I could share my goals and dreams with you.

He gave a reason to hear.... so that someday,
I could hear your most intimate thoughts and learn from you.

He gave me a reason to see.... so that someday,
I could see all of the beauty that exist within you.

He gave me a reason to feel.... so that someday,
I could embrace the warmth and softness of you.

He gave me a reason to think.... so that someday,
I could combine all of my thoughts with you.

He gave me a reason to laugh.... so that someday,
I could share my joy and laughter with you.

He gave me a reason to cry.... so that someday,
I could immerse myself into a pool of tears with you.

But most of all. He gave me a reason to love..... so that someday,
We could share a life of love, meant for me and you.

And that is why.... God gave me a reason for everything!

Espie Sandoval

The Beautiful World

I've always known that God was good,
He had a plan and I conclude,
That every human in this world,
Black, brown, yellow, or white
Tall or short,
Is part of God's tapestry
And braided in with symmetry
He hold us all in his loving hands
He works his spools
Our lives in the strands
And as our lives connect and meet,
He accomplishes no mean feat
As through our difference of lives he gave,
His choice perfect, our friendship gift.
And so, it is no coincidence
So far it makes such perfect sense
That through no accident, it's true
That out of all, he gave me this world.

Dina Nagamine

The Gardener

My Dad isn't a man of many words,
he just likes to garden and feed the birds.
Watching things grow is his main cup of tea,
one look at his yard and you would agree.

Every spring my Dad prepares his soil,
Long into the day he happily toils.
Loose, fertile, and not a rock in sight,
everything has to be just right.

Soon it is ready to plant many seeds,
and do battle with bugs, rabbits and weeds.
up and down the perfect rows he does trod,
now for rain and a little help from GOD.

Green beans, corn, turnips and potatoes,
onions, squash, red beets and tomatoes,
cabbage, eggplant, pickles and lima beans,
peppers, hall peas, lettuce and other greens.

Just as the garden needs a lot of care,
the heart needs to have JESUS planted there.
Dad has gone to the heavenly garden,
thanks to JESUS who gave him his pardon.

Joanne Quinn

How Much Longer??

Soft brown eyes hide the pain well.
He looks so healthy. It's too hard to tell.

His head's in his bucket: He's pretending to eat,
Meanwhile in his mind, he's admitting defeat.

I have to turn away. I can't bear to see
this beautiful creature in such misery.

He never showed off, he didn't have to;
he had medals of gold and ribbons of blue.

There's a ride in August, that I'm sure we can win.
I sent an application; looks like we got in.

I'll wait till next Tuesday, that's when they'll call;
but I already know we're not going this fall.

Early tomorrow, I'll hear from the vet,
but I don't want to know, at least not yet.

Caroline Renfro

The Gifts Of God

He created the clouds that float high and gently overhead,
He made all the flowers that bloom prettily in their beds.
He made the sunbeams that forever dance and play,
God in all his wisdom made every thing today.
He made the humming birds sipping nectar from the flowers,
Seeing the flowers needed rain, he made the soft rain showers.
He created those beautiful lofty things, he called them trees,
And to make the music through their leaves, he made the breeze.
He made day so things would grow, for rest he made the night,
His sign, the rainbow, showed that everything would be alright.
He made the lightning that lights up the sky so bright,
His thunder shakes the ground, showing all his might.
He made us and made all the things that we need and use,
He gave his son to die, to pay for all his laws that we abused.
He made it all, the hills, valleys, the lakes, the streams,
He made the moon, the stars and gave us our beautiful dreams.
He gave us his promise that there will always be a heaven above,
He did all this but best of all, he gave us his eternal love.

James Hoogland

The Baseball Game

I hit the ball and so did Flynn,
He ran to third and then came in.

Fat was up next, he made an OUT
And then we all began to shout.

"Hurrah, hurrah" for us we cried,
Taking our caps and tossing them high.

The Pitcher got mad, then so did we,
Now you shall see, what you shall see.

We hit the ball as hard as we could,
It went over the fence in a farmer's wood,

The farmer came out and ran about,
He came 'round the fence and chased us out.

We fell over each other and he caught me,
And then he turned me over his knee.

One by one he spanked us all,
And then he gave us back our ball.

Eleanor Panck Van Hoy

Untitled

He spoke of the past like it was tomorrow,
He spoke of decisions and reasons-

He spoke of respect, admiration, and devotion,
He spoke of an endless need never forgotten,
He spoke of feelings that have no description-

He spoke from his heart,
speaking with a conviction as only he could.

He wrote of blood, fate, and second chances,
He wrote of time with fearful knowledge-

He wrote of passion, hope, lust, and death,
He wrote of relentless dreams,
He wrote of memories only we could share-

He wrote from his heart,
writing with a conviction as only he could.

The love we shared was true and unequalled,
our love will last forever.

Garry Leiker

The Little Songbird

The little songbird could not sing.
He tried but nothing would come out.
He simply made a tiny sound
That sounded just like tweet, tweet, tweet.

I sadness he was filled with grief.
And tried so hard to forget his need.
But one day he travelled high into the sky
When a strong wind hit his throat.

The vibrations of that mighty wind
Made connection with his vocal cords.

He landed high upon a tree top
Not thinking of making a sound.
He opened up his tiny bill
And music came flowing out.

Albert A. Cox

Ole Tree

The "Ole Tree" stood bare and brown
He was lonesome without his leaves around.

He watched his foliage that windy day,
The yellow, brown and red - flit around so gay.

They rolled along the road - then flew into the air
And swirled and danced without a care.

They flew against the window and through the door.
As if to say, "Hello - we're free - not prisoners anymore".

But "Ole Tree" was wise and strong.
He knew their dancing wouldn't last long.

He had seen it happen time after time.
The birth of his beauty so green and fine.

At first, his leaves would be happy and content
To sway on his branches without lament.

But as fall neared, he knew they would leave
To roam around until the winter freeze.

Then shrivel and rot and turn back to the earth.
And "Ole Tree" just stands and waits for new birth.

Helen Rose Bohman

He Was One Of Many

He was one of many who answered the call,
he was one of many who landed abroad.
Days, weeks, months went by,
without word from my soldier guy.
An enemy shell had found its mark,
on that young soldier so close to my heart.
While he lay wounded on that far away land,
he wrote these few words before God took his hand.
For my country and family I have given my life,
for no greater cause can any man die.
He gave his young life no yet twenty three,
so that we may live in a country that's free.
I will never forget that young soldier of mine,
his bravery and courage will live in my mind.
May God be with him in his other life,
my soldier, my son, who laid down his life.
He was one of many who answered the call,
he was one of many who had to fall.

Fernand Frechette

As I Knew Him - Grandpa

An old mountaineer - "Grandpa" to me;
He was short and fat,
Wore a sweat-stained felt hat,
Chawed tobacco and spat
From the porch where he sat
Reading, reading, reading with his one eye.

He wore longjohns, cold or hot;
He bathed once a year, need it or not;
White turned yellow in his curly hair -
He was as grouchy as a grizzly bear,
Had no false teeth to wear
And his nose almost touched his chin.

He would lean back in his straight chair
Against the porch wall and he sat there
For hours, with his hat pulled down
Over his red face; wearing a frown.
Splat! A tobacco stream hit the ground
(The grass never grew in that spot again!)
And he wiped his mouth with a faded red bandanna.

Reading, reading, reading with his one eye!

Jeannette Huckaby

The Fractured Jewel

Oh cast down blue, at once death darkened
hear the angels harken near,
once it was green dreams now is brown and drear.
The fear, the fear has he once spoken
old weariness, his courage only token,
steals upon the grave.
What was once fresh and new is
grey with decay, the retching
sky is now defiled.
Hey harken, harken, the befouler
man give heed to what thou
hast done for naught but greed.

Ann E. Meritt

Legacy

Walking through the roads of life,
hearing what only can be sung,
doing what only can be done,
wondering why you can't put down the knife.

Visions, dreams, yet experience yields,
knowing that you have to deal
knowing that it's all so real,
wondering why you hide behind these shields.

Voices, pressure, it's hard to resist,
living the only moments left,
leaving the ones you have already left,
but it's those who, have to realize that
you no longer exist ...

Jen Wozniak

"Wants And Tries"

I want to be what my mother tries to instill in me,
  I fail
I try to be what my friends seem to be,
  I fail
I want to be what my teachers try to train me to be,
  I fail
I try to be what my spouse desires of me,
  I fail
I gave my want to be's and my try to be's to the Lord,
  I discovered me.

Carolyn Henderson-Shepard

The Reason

I saw you and you saw me,
Heaven knows we were meant to be,
We laughed and we talked all day and all night,
Then I knew I found Mr. Right,
Days went by and a few weeks had been,
I could hardly wait until I see you again,
We fell in love, it was love at first sight,
My little heart melted and you became my guiding light,
My life has changed and we've only just begun,
Our feelings will grow like the rays of the sun,
Sometimes I cry when I'm thinking of us,
It means that I'm happy and your the one I can trust,
Whenever your gone and far far away,
I sit and think of you every minute of every day,
Every problem we have we always seem to work it out,
We've never had to fight, scream, holler, or shout,
I know we will be together for the rest of our lives,
I pray to God that our love will never die,
The reason I say these things and feel the way I do,
The reason why I wrote this poem is because "I love you"!

Deniese Mathis

An Old Man's Prayer For Growing Old Graciously

Almighty God of all that is fair and good.
Help us in the twilight of our days
To remember and to honor Thee.
We would humbly raise our voice in praise
Of thy great works, and thank Thee for the years
Thou hast bequeathed to us. Grant we my find

Time to serve Thee well. Awake our hearts
To preserve both with the heart and mind
In all humility, and always let us live
In Thy precepts. Let Thy unspoken voice
Guide us in the paths of dignity.
Give us assurance that we may rejoice
To walk with Thee. We pray Thee for new strength
In the obligation of our duty
Cleanse our hearts of all unfaithfulness
Keep us aware of hope and love and beauty.
Let our lives stand a monument to Thee,
Safe in the knowledge that we are Thy own.
Forgive us our transgressions that we may
Some day join Thee at Thy celestial throne.

Julia Hanan

Computer Files

I can hear only our shadows rustle
Helplessly crawling between spots of light,
Rehearsing lists of "things to do" next day...
I call it home...or just a place to stay
Ready to battle one more fearful night,
And disappear by sunrise from castle...

  Cool logic, challenge - no room for emotion
  In the name of future and the life-time chance...
  Closed-loop controlled, high frequency brain
  Trips over simple, forgotten refrain
  And opens files of "life at a glance"
  Scrolling chaotic fragments in slow motion...

Wordless lullaby!...This tune casts the spell...
Shadowy figures transmute into faces,
Memories rattle in restricted shell...
And take me back to long-forgotten places...

  Cradle, soft tune, and smiling face above...
  Why did I try to forget what I saw?
  First kiss...first love...green eyes sparkle, glow...
  I must save these files - Smiles beaming with love...

John Gallar

And Love Grows

Marriage, Family, and Commitment
-helps love grow

You start out with just two
-and love grows

You spend time together
-and love grows

You receive a special gift-a little girl from God
-and love grows

You work, play, have dogs, a cat and go to PTA
-and love grows

You struggle together through the good times and bad
-and love grows

You grow older and sickness comes
-and still love grows

You find it hard not being able to be together as much
-and still love grows

When God comes to take one of us home and we will think we can't go on
-but our love still grows

Carmen S. Bridick

I Remember...My Wife's Tragedies

My wife has been saddened by much despair
Her experiences are almost too much to bear
Death and illness can be a terrible thing
Without end
It can seem more like an enemy
And never a friend.
My illness
The loss of her sister
And now her first cousin's son
The stories make you sick and numb
How much can a person bear?
But there's a brighter side
If you don't stop there
Your experiences help to make you strong
You draw closer to others if you bear long
And if you stay close to God
that is a sweet song.

Joseph Armstrong

"Immigrant Woman"

"God Bless America" my Godmother would say
Her eyes see Liberty
an orphan from Greece seeking hope.
With a dollar in her pocket and a house of her own
She purses her happiness.

A decade of life, seeing it all
J.F.K., Martin Luther King
She wept for them all
Surviving everyday reality with her faith
Understanding none of it.

Seasons come and go.
Forgetting her birthdays gone by
But remembering her snowfalls

Lying in her hospital bed
giving me hope
and blessing America for it all.

George Zaverdas

Change Of Address

My mother had an address change, she's no longer at the old,
   Her new address is Heaven's Gate, where streets are made of gold.
No more waiting for the mailman to bring mail up to her door.
   She has become a messenger to those who went before.

My mother no longer feels the pains, no doctors now to see,
   For at her new address, her body is set free.
Those shaking hands, those eyes so dim, are things that now are past,
For at her new address, her health will always last.

Her clothing there is different too, a robe so clean and white,
   An address with an open door, where no one fears the night.
So even though she left us, should we be in distress?
   She really didn't die you see, she simply changed address.

John C. Banker Jr.

"If My Nation..."

God Almighty created this greatest nation on Earth.
Here in the Land of Liberty, I celebrated my birth.
Daily by prayer and His Holy Word, I discover my worth.

As a citizen of this most special and hallowed land,
I bow on my face in gratitude, as I'll take a stand.
To pray for my nation and brethren as a dedicated and committed man.

"If my people who are called by My Name will humble
themselves and pray - repent, seek my face and
walk in My way...My Word obey - I will hear from
Heaven, forgive their sin and I will repair the break and heal this place."

Great and mighty things will be accomplished by this
nation as they return and obey my Word.
Not of strange new thoughts of their own,
But by My Written commands, which for hundreds of years
have been spoken and heard.

Hear me my children, turn again to Me, be exalted,
be liberated, help one another and be blessed
I desire to heal the wounded nation, I created from
being racially distressed and sorely oppressed.

James S. Russell Sr.

High On The Mountain Have I Come

High on the mountain have I come,
Here where the air is thin and free.
High on the mountain have I come,
But thoughts of the valley have followed me.

Days in the valley were warm and sweet,
Soft were the mists from the sea.
My cottage was sheltered and safe from the thrust
Of the cold wind which now lashes me.

Here on the mountain, this bitter-won crest,
This summit of rocks grey and bare
Sends a chill to my heart, for one who stands here
Stands alone in the rarefied air.

So I must return to the valley,
The warm-time, the spring-time, the rain,
Turn back to my home in the valley,
Never to leave again.

Agnes G. Hohmann

"Restless Nights"

I long to feel him in the night, his arms around me, oh, so tight,
His breath in my ear, his body so near.
I want to wake up in his arms so strong,
I've dreamt of the moment for so long.
The thought of it sends chills down my spine
I wonder if he'll ever really be mine.
To hold and to love and to cherish,
Without him I feel that I will perish.
My love for him is just so great, I want him so much I cannot wait.
My heart is aching - I can feel it breaking.
I hope that soon he'll understand
That only he is the one man
Whom I will always want to be with,
So near, so close, I long for his kiss.
His hugs so strong and warm and tight
I will never give up without a fight!
He is the one man that I do need
He sends my heart racing at top speed!
I long to feel him in the night, his arms around me, oh, so tight!

Janet Lynn Eklund

Prophets Of Peace

Bobby said, "Don't worry; be happy."
His philosophy is nice, but his mind is not cognizant to reality.
The time is now for humanity to take a stand.
Instead of white for white, black for black; its time for man for man.
Will we ever know the true meaning of justice?
Will we ever live to see a world free of prejudice?
The answer is unknown; the search for the answer will take long.
I have faith that we as elements of the human race will someday sit at
   the table of unity and that our capability to love one another will
   be strong.
It seems like an eternity ago that God sent two advocates of peace
   born with the name Kennedy.
They both died by assassin's bullets, but neither could find a remedy.
Gone are Gandhi and Martin Luther King.
These men-these prophets of peace died trying and we still have not
   heard the bells of freedom ring.
Our objective should be continue to fight; continue to strive.
Continue to live Jessie's philosophy and keep hope alive!

Charles Edrick Neal

The Partner

If the shadows and valleys of a man's inner mind
Hold misery and secrets you'll not ever find,
He may be neurotic
Or at worst a psychotic,
And you'll find in the end that he isn't your kind.

For you'll note with surprise that his reasoning's wrong.
By the standards you live with they just don't belong.
And he's got this sad quirk,
And his mind doesn't work
In the manner in which you've been taught all along.

And now you regret that long-ago day
When you took him as partner and first heard him say,
"I'll be like a brother,
you'll not need another.
By working together, we'll sure make it pay."

But the business is ended and everything's right.
You're no longer faced with a long, endless fight.
For he's deep in the ground
And he'll never be found,
And nobody knows that you shot him last night.

John L. Burrows

Dearest Mom

May 8th, another Mother's Day
Hope it's great in every way
You're so special to us and others
You're a "Mother" amongst mothers.

When we needed help you were always there
It seemed you could be just everywhere
With a smiling "Yes" or a firm "Nay"
You guided us every step of the way.

With love and kindness you gave your best
With God's love and help we did the rest
May God love and keep you every day
And bless you especially this Mother's Day.

Betty Murphy

Hope

Hope is one of the greatest words we can keep in our heart.
Hope that we put away our selfish pride and all do our part.
Hope for our nation is not fighting wars all the time.
Hope is faith in God that all will change their mind.
Hope is treating everyone equal regardless of their race.
Hope is looking at their heart and not the color of their face.
Hope for our children is not taking God out of school.
Hope for our children is teaching them to live by the golden rule.
Hope for tomorrow even when today things are so dim.
Hope because we know we can put our trust in Him.
Hope for our family is raising them to know God in our homes.
Hope is not abusing our children and sending them out alone.
Hope for the little babies who never get a chance to be born.
Hope for the young mothers, unwed, all alone and torn.
Hope for the gangs who only know to fight and kill.
Hope they will hear about God and there is a better way to live.
Hope that they will learn that Jesus died for them too.
Hope they will find God's love can save them like me and you.
Hope is something to hold onto no matter what the cost.
Hope, if we ever give it up, our world will surely be lost.

Grace Wilson

"A Wife's Thoughts"

I sit here thinking and I can't forget
Hour God was with me the night we met
You are a good man and they are hard to find
All the good things you do is what comes to mind
I know I am not what you want me to be
But if I left you I'm sure you would miss me
If I die before you I won't you to know
I will still love you no matter where I go
We are growing old and don't have much longer to live
So we should change our ways and learn to give
Each day you come home safe and sound
Then I know that God is still around
So you go do your work and return to me
I have loved you more as you will someday see

Freida Marsh

The Dreaming Heart

I never knew how lonely it is until I was without you.
I had a walk through the pines and all I could do was,
pray of loving you, only you. But that's alright honey
everybody gets a little loving. Now and then, once or twice,
bye and bye, through and through. This lonely heart is seeking
you. Only you, but if miles are permitting us to be apart
then what's wrong with me dreaming in my lonely heart...

Billy Amiotte

Why, O Lord?

Why O Lord? Why the suffering?
How can I bear this suffering?
It is in our brokenness, that we are
   ministered to; and out of our brokenness,
   that we minister to others.
It is in our wounds, that we are
   healed; and out of our wounds,
   that we heal others.
It is in our powerlessness, that great
Joy and growth in loving ourselves
   and others is born.
The gift, from God of laughter in our
   suffering.
The gift, from God, of weeping in our
   joyousness.
It's Gods paradox:
In the midst of our human suffering;
   comes healing laughter.
Out of our joy-filled humanness;
   comes a joyous, weeping heart.
   George E. Hansen III

Beginnings

How can it be so wonderful just sitting and watching you,
How can it be so special to see everything the way you do?
I count myself so lucky, far beyond human words can say,
How can you be so real, to love me as you do today.

You show amazing strength, and kindness beyond measure,
I respect, admire, adore you - you are far beyond a treasure.

I've never known this kind of love, given from the depths of your heart,
I only hope you'll see it - I know this is just the start!
I'm falling for you father, deep within my heart,
And want to please you always, just like I did at the very start.

I pray that you will see in me, a reflection of yourself,
That we can be a team together, beyond anything this earth has felt.

I regret the time I've wasted, by not searching high and low for you,
But now I'll make the most of it, by spending time with you!
I love the way you look at me, and hold me in your smile,
I hope I'll always please you, just like I did as a little child.

Remember this if nothing else, I'll put your needs above myself,
You gave me life not once but twice, for me that is truly very nice!
   Debra Ellingson

I Weep

For those who have no love of country within their breast,
   How can they know the crest of great emotion felt
When "Old Glory" is displayed or when the national anthem is played?
   For those who know this not, I weep.

For those whom hate has shriveled the heart and soul
   And causes of nobleness have no hold,
For those to whom honor, truth and beauty are lost
   And eyes are unseeing and cold, I weep, I weep.

To behold the world when once more dawn makes it new
   To touch a flower diamonded with dew
To be a part of God's great plan, no matter how small
   That's given free to all, I will stand tall
And for him who cannot see this beauty given to him and me, I weep.
   Audrey Wright Miller

The Funeral

"How sad!" "How terrible." A dear friend has died
"How did it happen?"... We all asked at once.
"It was all very sudden", the family replied.

The widow was crying, she looked so distraught,
The people kept asking, "You need help?...just ask."
She replied very softly, "I do need the help,
"One thousand dollars to pay off my debts."
At this, the sad wishers, just quickly dispersed.

"How peaceful," "How natural," "He looks so good,"
Were words quietly said as he laid there in state
In his blue coveralls, blue T-shirt,
and red wide suspenders to boot!

Lots of nice things were said of the man in the casket
When all of the sudden this jazz music erupted
Surprise hit the mourners who looked one another,
Should they cry, sing, or dance with each other??

The dead man had wished, no one should bereave,
So the procession was happy and all seemed to have
A good time as they wished him a peaceful voyage.
   Betty L. Williams

Trapped Within

Oh, imprisoned heart of crying pain
How did this come to be
That my tears are the only comfort to come and visit me.

I'm locked away for none to see
Just what I have inside
And I dare not tell for they will know
Just that I'm trying to hide.

Emotions swell, my nerves are tense
Pease of mind cannot be found
As I locked it all inside of me and utter not a sound.

I dare not let my feelings show
For fear I cannot contain
Then the sadness that has locked me in
Will pour forth too much pain

I cannot change what has happened
Nor return what I have lost
So I'm left to bear the burden
And with pain I pay the cost.

So I continue on and maybe time will shut the pain outside
And replace it with love and I won't ever have to hide.
   Brenda Gilbert

"My Valentine Heart"

Though February is a cold month,
I am still always warm inside,
Because my heart is big, loving and caring,
For the woman, whose love I don't hide.

There's a day set aside, for love in all hearts,
It's the 14th of February, as everyone knows,
It's a time for people to put their troubles aside,
A time to make up, and show how your love grows.

Within the past couple months, I've been told,
My heart has expanded and touched someone near,
Not the love that people claim is real,
No, my love is for only one woman, and that's you dear.
   James A. Pionke

"Oh Sweet Baby Of The Vine"

Oh, sweet baby of the vine; you are mine, you are mine...
How I look at you in awe and wonder and see; the magic in your eye.
Oh, tiny newborn that you are; you are such a delight to me!
Even though you are weak and small; I'll make sure I hear your plea;
I'll make sure I hear your call.

Oh, sweet baby of the vine; you are mine, you are mine...
Elephants could come from deep and afar;
But they wouldn't touch my little star.
Tigers could gnash their teeth and snarl;
But they wouldn't touch my little pearl.

I shall protect you like no other could;
I can hide you like my deer, deep within my wood.
Not rain, nor snow, nor blizzard storm; could come against my
  mighty form.

Not crocodiles in the deep; nor snow covered feet;
Nor wolves at the fountain can go beyond my mountain,
Nor my joy, nor my peace; not even the enemy in fur-lined fleece.

None of these things shall ever threaten thee.
Because, you are mine...
Nor shall anything ever come between us,
Not even that thing they call time.

Cynthia Austin-Thorn

Beneath The Oak Tree

I often wonder
How it would be now,
If I'd taken the chance they kept giving.
I feel a great loss,
But don't know how
Since I never met him in the living.

As I sat there
And watched strong people, cry,
I realized the hurt could be greater.
I wanted to meet him,
but don't know why,
Since it would only cause more pain later.

If I'd known him before the last grain fell,
Would my eyes be free of tears that grieve?
I wonder if my heart will ever tell
My mind what it should believe.

No matter how little
Or great the pain,
His place in my heart
Will always remain.

Jennifer Clarkson

Wake-Up, Wake-Up

Wake-up, wake-up, let me whisper in your ear,
How much I love you, how I'll always be near.
Your rugged faced, so peaceful in slumber,
Every muscle relaxed, I hear your murmur.
You groan as if you wish the day was slow coming,
But it's here, waiting for your smile, a sight most becoming.

Wake-up, wake-up, the day is nearly dawning,
This is our time, to satisfy a wanting.
The arms once relaxed, are now taut and strong,
This is where I want to be, this is where I belong.
Hair dripping, a towel around the waist,
Now the day has begun, hurry don't be late.

Escorita Lewis

"What A World Without You"

We met in springtime our hearts were carefree,
How we enjoyed each day.
But when it ended a cloud descended,
The things I loved so faded away.

Summer nights with no stars, city parks with no flowers,
Not a trace of morning dew.
No setting sun when day is over, no fragrant fields of clover.
What a world without you.

August nights with no breeze, country lanes with no trees,
Not a rainbow trail in view.
No fairy tales with happy endings, no children's voices blending.
What a world without you.

Holidays with no fun, new years eve with no one,
Not a crocus peeking thru.
No spring for me around the corner, your love is growing warmer,
But for somebody new, what a world without you

James J. Stalter

"Days Gone Bye"

Don't you remember in days gone by
How we played in under the old plumb tree
And how we swung in the wing on high.
You my sisters and me.
Some times we would play house and store
or sometimes we would make a mud pie.
Gosh I would give a million or more,
for those days that's gone by.
You were then a little boy,
and we were three little girls.
We were all so filled with joy,
in those days that were precious as pearls.
Grandma and grandpa would look on,
with eyes so full of delight.
To see us flop about on the lawn,
or to see us wrestle or fight.
And little dog Prince would bite at our heels
as we would chose around the tree.
Gosh, it all seems like a picture show real
the times of you my sisters and me.

Evelyn Elmore

Lasting Memories

The years are passing by without you.
How's your new home, your new friends,
your new life? You've started your eternal
journey, and all I have are memories.
Memories that started long ago but feel
as if they've just begun. Memories that
I confuse with dreams. Was it real
when you held me in your arms
to comfort me? Was it real when
I was the pitcher and you were
my catcher? Was it real when you
knelt down so I could jump into
your open arms? I will never know
until I arrive at my new home,
with my new life, to begin my
eternal journey. Only then will you no
longer be a memory - but a father
again to your seven year old son.

Greg Gottberg

The Rat King

The Rat King had riches and rooms of gold
hundreds of maids and thousands to scold
His feast were enough for a town
and made of jewels he wore his crown
He sat in a chair two stories high
The King he told not a lie
Yet the King he told one single tale
that his Queen Ruth was born with a golden tail
And whenever they went out he hid her tail of hair
for the town would tell him he lied without a care
But it was this day when young Cat Purr
found this rat was nothing but fur
And without hesitation he ate Queen Ruth and Rat King
took all their riches and their rings
Now it just might be better to tell the truth
or you could be eaten like Rat King and Queen Ruth

Cortni Creamer

"In Between"

Tangible sanity escapes me.

My awakening consciousness torments me,
Hurling issue after issue at logic
only to succumb to the lack of reason;
My heart refusing to deal with the pain,
Leaving my brain to sift through the rubble,
Searching for reason that flashes and is gone,
As quickly as the camera of life can snap still photos.

My sleeping subconsciousness terrifies me,
Staging dreamy scenarios of helplessness,
Only to fight to the bitter meaningless ends;
My eyes refusing to open and cry "Uncle",
Forcing my emotions to run the gauntlet,
Exchanging fear for sorrow
Faster than my eyes would blink if only open,
As furiously as if I were awake in hell.

Peace lies somewhere in between.

Joyce Kilkenny

Mother, The Unbroken Circle

I am your mother! I am your grandmother! I am your great grandmother!
I am all the mothers that have come before, and
all the mothers that are yet to be.

I have brought you laughter and tears.
I have brought you sorrow and joy.

I have not left you - I have only crossed over!

I will visit you on the wings of the butterfly
and speak to you thru the whistling of the wind.

I shall be with you in times of joy and happiness,
and in times of heartache and pain.
I shall be with you when the heavens are filled with sunshine,
and when the clouds bring you teardrops and rain.

I shall be with you as you walk on a rainbow path
and when the journey up the mountain never seems to end.
I shall be with you as you travel through the valley
and when you think you have no friends.

For...
I am your mother! I am your grandmother! I am your great grandmother!
  I am your past!
    I am your future!
      I am forever!

Irma Sun Woman Epps

Why, Grandpa?

My dearest, loving, Grandpa,
I ask myself so much...
Why was it that cigarette you just had to touch?
It was death between your fingers,
Didn't you understand?
I miss you so much, Grandpa!
But you're in a distant land.
It was the gurgle of your last breath,
The struggle for some air...
That made me sadly realize
You had left from here.
I still remember, Grandpa,
When you were here with me,
The times we spent together
When you held me on your knee...
But all of that is gone now and I must admit
That it was that dumb cigarette you unfortunately lit!

Annette N. Joyner

Untitled

Feeling so alone and full of fear
  I ask the dear Lord to lend me a ear,
  I said Lord I just lost a good
friend you see
  And now I wonder what's to
become of me
Feeling so sad and depressed
  I didn't have the heart to try and guess
Just sitting so sad and alone,
  all of a sudden I heard the phone
The call come from many miles away,
  And the words that were said
made my day,
A family I worked for and dearly Loved
Sent a message to me from the good
Lord above,
It gave me the strength to get up and go and
  I thank you Lord from whom all blessings flow.
  I thank you Lord for hearing my prayer
Thank you dear mannings you all know I care.

Jessie Dennis

My Silver Wedding Anniversary

Twenty five years ago my love
I ask you to married me sweet heart
It seems like it was yesterday my love
But now on our silver wedding anniversary
The flame still burning in my heart for you

Thank you for caring and been so devoted
Thank you for the beautiful moments wee shared together
Thank you for being there when I needed you to

Sorry if I hurt you when I did not mean to
Sorry for the tears when I make you cry
Sorry for my wicked ways when my heart would listen to me

You was like a chunk of coal
But father time turn you into a beautiful diamond
And you reward my love
With three wonderful jewels

Words cannot express how much I love you
I will always love you today more than yesterday
But less than tomorrow
And my love for you will never die, your husband

Joe Romero

Nightmares

Last night I saw you in my sleep.
I asked myself was it a dream.
You were standing at the door engulfing in a beam.
Your face hidden by the shadow of hate.
I tried to run to no avail, as you were already on my trail.
I felt a blow across the face.
I knew right then I was not safe.
I tried to scream as loud as I could,
but next thing I knew I was on the floor.
I felt your heavy body against mine,
and the brutal separation of my thighs.
I tasted my tears streaming down my face,
as this penetration was too much to bear.
I woke up by the sound of my screams,
and was distracted by the knock at the door.
I jumped quickly to my feet, and was
dumbfounded to see you standing there.
I then grabbed the next thing I could find, for
this nightmare shall never be.

Enette Charles Jean Pierre

Cancer

I come in a form dark as night invisible as can be
I can conform in this life by using your own pity
I hate all races for I am none I can take your life———DONE
Then on the next like a leech
Sucking nectar breathless with out speech
I take the rich, I take the poor
I'll slap you around like some cheep ass whore
for I fear no evil no pain
'Cuz I am that plague that will drive you insane
And then I leave you wishing and wishing to someone to blame
for this heinous act that is unexplained
I settle deep inside your bones
Deep to the point that can make one moan
You pray that I go away
Pray so much there's nothing more to say
I show back up with in months to come
Now it's time for to have fun slipping deep into my trace
Now I'm the man that's in command
Don't think for a second that you may have the answer
'cuz silly fool there is no cure for my CANCER

Antonio Caggiano

I Can Hear My Momma Cry

Through the thin walls of our run down shack
I can hear my Momma cry.
I lay on my cot and whisper my prayers
"Why, dear God, why?"
Suddenly I can hear my Momma being slapped
and I think, oh God, help us please 'cause he's back.
My Daddy used to be so happy,
before the liquor came.
Now we consider it good
when he remembers his own name.
Coming back into reality, I sneak into the hall.
I'm present when he slaps her, and when my Momma falls.
I run back to my room because I do not want to pry,
and lying on my cot again I can hear my Momma cry.

Amber L. Woods

The Prize Of A Puzzle

My life is like a puzzle, Lord, each piece is scattered apart.
I can not see the outcome tho' I try with all my heart.
From time to time I'm amazed to find a piece has found a place.
It's then I'm encouraged by a smile as I look into Your face.

Isn't it customary to arrange outside pieces and protect with a border
while trying to connect this puzzle resulting from traditional order?
I can see Your way is not mine, what You see as whole, I see in part.
Thus, trusting my inside to You, placement truly needs to start.

My life is like a puzzle, Lord, someday every piece will create
a likeness so lovely by hands of a Master place without a mistake.
Each piece of puzzle a story to tell, a Banner of Victory as upholder.
Beauty has been arranged with care by eyes of the Heavenly Beholder.

Gail Merrill

The Sea And The Sand

Standing in the tears of God, the rain
I can release all of my guilt-filled pain.
So let the rain soak me and drown my fears;
It's only to hide my own mournful tears.
I realize now that it was all in my head
And that I must have dreamt it all in my bed.
So run to her arms, I can't hold you again
You're like the sea and I am the sand.
Each time we meet you wash a bit of me away
And leave me standing there with nothing to say.
I can no longer pretend that every thing is fine
When all I do is pray for you to be mine.
You made your choice and now I must face reality
So I'm leaving town to end my personal brutality
Because I can no longer watch you kiss her
And pretend I don't love you, sir.
May your love be wonderful and grand
And never become the sea and the sand.

Faith E. Bruner

Endlessly

In my dreams and fantasies,
I can see you loving me.
But it's not real, when I awake...
it's all gone, then I ache...
to feel the touch, that love can give,
I need that touch to really live,
to find the one - is the hardest part,
the one that reaches deep inside...
The one from which my heart can't hide.
The one that's different from all the rest,
He who will love me the best...
Who will never hurt or let me down, without
his love, I'll surely drown, in this
world full of pain.
Are you the one? Am I insane?
I don't know, my hearts not sure.
Unlock the door - inside your heart,
So I will know if you are he...
The one who will love me Endlessly!

Cora L. Wilhelm

Wistfully Wandering

I had a dream, wistfully wandering in a meadow
I changed upon a girl, a beautiful girl
laughing, singing, enjoying
Enjoying all the good things, the flowers in the meadow
The wind in the grass, bright sun on high
So I called to her, for my heart felt sad
I longed to sing and dance with her on meadow grass in spring
She answered me, crossed the meads to talk with me
I asked her name she called herself Lasari
That means meadow child
We spoke of many things, the sun on tree leaves,
The birds and the bees, the breeze of bygone days.
Of children and their silly ways,
We spoke of old dreams, cold rain on starless nights.
I woke from my dream, wished not to, and cried out
Please do not leave me but I knew she was gone
Only the cold hearth stone, the fires dying embers.
Only the cold north wind, only sleepless resentful remembering.
All night when I wish for my meadow child
To dance on the grass in spring.
Douglas C. Robins

Wail Of A Lonely Man

Soft, my heart is like mush.
I cry out, but no tears come.

My eyes remain dry,
unlike the bottle in my hand.
I pour it down the drain - my life -
and I wonder if that's where
my tears have gone, as well.

I gather the possessions we used to share.
You would dust them with your soft, over worked hands.

Now everything we own
is covered in dust.
I blow and memories fly everywhere.
I must catch them;
they are full of you.

I put what is left of my life
in a box—I begin to shake.
I see you and you're so close;
covered in dust, nestled in a box.

I open my mouth to a noise
that sounds like your name.
Heather Thompson

Fifty

Fifty; what a drag; when I was young,
I knew it all.
GOD, what gall! I thought I had it all in the bag.
Now, at fifty what I thought, really is not.
I've stumbled and fallen and gotten up again.
I keep trying to find the right path once again.
I have tried to make the road easier for those after me;
to teach them to know their GOD,
themselves and maybe me,
however, they take some wrong turns just like me.
Dennis Mantas

Disappearance

I sit alone; common place.
I dagger my innermost self,
  making sure each thrash I inflict is fully felt.
My innermost self must be eliminated,
  it is from there that my hurt is felt.
My life has ended...I have died.
Why does God insist on pumping breath into my lonely heart?
  my shattered soul?

Do I have the strength to stop this breath?
The pain would end; your happiness planted.
...alone...numb...lifeless...my only choice clear...

DISAPPEARANCE

Remains of none is my gift to you;
...that is how strong I love
  ...that is how strong I hurt.

I am so in love, and for that I will spend my eternity
...never forgiving my innermost for causing you pain...
  -stopping your breath; instead of mine.

Outcome clear, problem solved...
  hurt no more, breathe no more...DISAPPEARED.
Brent Kelly Szabo

"Ode To Knowledge"

I was born pure and innocent.
I danced on the water, I laughed at the wind.
I had no limits or expectations,
I did not want, I did not need.
I was a light in your black world.

You Came Along.

As I got older you taught me words like, better, evil and right,
I conformed, I loved my new found knowledge,
And you laughed at my fading innocence.

I KNOW HATE, I know evil,
I feel it running through my veins like a venom squeezing my heart.

I WAS DIFFERENT, I FOUGHT A LONG WAR.
You told me to grow up... I laughed with pity.
You ask me if I know your GOD... How can I?
I don't even know myself.

I KNOW I CAN'T GO BACK, I TRY TO ACCEPT THAT,
I'VE BATTLED THE LOST WAR
YOU TOOK MY LIGHT AND SHATTERED IT.
YOU'VE MADE ME COLD AND INDIFFERENT,
I'LL DIE SAD AND ALONE...
Jason Pietropaulo

Running

Running, running, when there is no race
I have to keep going to keep my place
How can I carry on — how can I win?
Over this thing that is called sin
I have to keep running to find my niche
And I don't even have a pitch
Will you help me when I start to fall
Will you listen to me whenever I call
I would like to be somebody grand
To stand up straight and take my stand!
Come over here and take my hand
And lead me to that promised land.
Helen A. Harris

Awe of the Moon

Did you see the moon last night?
I did
it was beautiful, it held me in awe and wonder
at who or what could create
it's perfect circle of autumn yellow
against the backdrop of early night
low in the sky
almost as if I could walk right to it
and I looked around and realized
no one,
no one else seemed to notice
and I then felt special
but a little alone
that this moon was shining just for me
reminding me
that there is beauty, awe and wonder
everywhere, everyday, always
all you have to do is take a moment
and look and see
did you see the moon last night?

Caryn F. Hatalla

God Led Me Home

I walked a path home today
I didn't bother to seek the Lord
So I didn't ask, I didn't pray
I presumed I'd find my way.
The path became dark and colder
The world remained on my shoulders
I tripped and stumbled
And everything before me tumbled.
The tears I couldn't hold back any longer
And wondered why I wasn't stronger
I asked God why he let me
Fall to my knees in agony
He told me "sometimes I have to let you fall
for you to see alone you can not overcome it all."

I came to another cross-road
I prayed to God for my hand to hold
I asked so I would not be alone
And today, God led me home.

Debbie Roman

My Echo Of The Past

In memory of Leslie W. Johnson
When I left that day, Your mother said we're through
I didn't know that I was also losing You

When I left that day so many years ago,
My thoughts were always with You
But I know I had to go

When I returned to see You, a few months had gone by
And when I could not find You, I hung my head to cry

The search has never ended, that has left me in despair
But ECHO my little darling, I want you to know that I care

Many years have gone by, my hair a touch of gray
Still waiting and wondering, will I see my ECHO again some day

You looked just like your Mother
When you were born that special day
That's why we named you ECHO, Your Mother's name was Faye

"I hope someday to find you" My ECHO of the past
Your Daddy really loves you, that love will always last.

Beverly Jones-Johnson

The First Rose Of Spring

The calendar said spring, the weather said winter,
I didn't know which to believe.
The north wind was blowing, the rain was pouring
And I thought I was going to freeze.
But as I stood watching by my window that day,
And much to my surprise,
Was a beautiful white rose, out in all that cold,
As bright as a morning sunrise.
And as I beheld this beautiful sight,
The answer suddenly came to me,
That spring was exploding and winter was going,
And a warmth filled up inside of me,
This white virgin flower, out in that cold shower,
Was a promise of what was to come.
Of birds and bees and flowers and leaves, and
The warm rays of a summer sun.
So I thank you dear Lord for this beautiful rose, and
The answer that was given to me.
That this delicate spring flower, the rose of the hour,
Was a sign of the spring to be.

Gene Adamek

The Letter

I got a letter the other day.
I didn't know who it was from.
Now I get them every week.
Another soon should come.
They keep me entertained when there's nothing else to do.
I say a special prayer at night that they will get through.
I don't mind helping those in need.
Or helping them through times that are hard indeed.
Also I've found a new friend to help and listen to me.
When everyone is busy and I need someone to see
The happiness or sadness that's exciting me!
In the letters it is clear she has a lot to say.
And she always tells her news in her own way.
It's enjoyable to read and enjoyable to write.
During the Morning, afternoon or in the bright moonlight.
There is one reason why this fact is so.
It's that I never know what's coming next.
I have to wait and see.
And every week a new surprise always waits for me.

Casey Becker

Sun Times

I looked out of my window at the chilling day.
I long for the California sun.
Where is the California sun?
The wind rattles the doors and windows.
Dare I go out?
There is no California sun,
Thee is a chilling in my heart and soul.
I long for the California sun.
I long for peace of mind.
Days when there were better times,
The California Sun Times.
The warm heart and soul times
I look out at the chilling day.
I have dreams of the California day
Not so very far away.

Jean Dixon

A Broken Friendship

So much has happened that has changed our lives forever.
I don't even know if we will ever recover.

That is why I must tell you how I feel,
My love for our friendship is real.

At the end of this school year,
Neither of us will be here.

We will both go our separate ways
And hope that someday we will meet by the waves.

That was once a dream for you and me,
But now it seems like only a memory.

How could I believe that this could still be,
When my "roomie" has made other plans that don't involve me.

We were once the best of friends we could be,
Now you can barely stand talking to me.

I want to tell you how much I care
But when I try, I get knocked down by your cold glare.

I never thought that I would give up
But now it seems as though I've ran out of luck.

The time has come for me to say Good-Bye,
Maybe someday I'll understand why.
Amy Garcia

What I Did Not Learn In Kindergarten

Hurry! Hurry! I am late for work - not for class;
I don't ride the bus - I stop for gas.
In my seat it's eight o'clock not nine
Whew! I barely made it this time!
Papers shuffled I take a break;
Not milk and cookies - coffee and smoke.
I don't play with toys; I stand outside and joke.
A staff meeting? I goofed, OK?
I'll do better if that coworker stays out of my way!
After lunch I don't sleep on the floor;
If I pretend I am reading I can grab 10 seconds or more!
I go home to cook and clean;
Homework is now with many machines.
Clothes are laid out for the next day;
I wash and iron them then spend my pay.
I must have had chicken pox the last day of school,
Because if I would have learned THIS I would have said
"I AM NOT LEAVING! Do you think I'm a fool?"
Cheryl Grothjan

Untitled

Deep in thought and lost in mind,
I enter a whole new world of wishes.
A place where every person seems to be,
To drift away from pain and evil.
A chance to be the birds in flight,
That fly away from the unending outpour of rain.
A moment of silence and security enters my thoughts,
And all is gone except for the gentle breeze that slowly
    transforms into a deep vision of my life.
A feeling of never waking up surges through me,
But a sudden jolt wakes me from my quiet reverie.
I see darkness, nothing is in sight except for the trees
    swaying in the night beyond my room.
Back deep into my head I again dream my past,
Both good and bad occurrences are brought back to life.
I see a bright light making me shield my eyes,
I look again and see the sun reflecting its light on a window.
I realized that the window was calling me,
Calling me back to the real world.
Cristina Poscablo

Halfway Up

Leaning against the bones of an ironwood tree,
I feel all nature's warmth wash over me.
I'm halfway up on this broomed mountain side
Watching the sun catch his last evening glide,
Hurling his tipped lance of orangy glow,
Spilling off still waters that lie below,
Casting velvet painting of purple and red
To this mountain I've climbed before the day has fled.
I sense as I rest on the musty pungent grass
That this day's radiance like life itself must pass.
I stand in awe of the magic of the scene,
Of the beauty more brilliant than eyes have ever seen.
These amber rays that flood the mountain's girth
Are the embers of day, consumed by the fire of its birth.
Don Johnson

Ghost Dance

As I stand upon this great plain and look to the sun for answers
I feel great disaster coming our way
The presence of something immoral and vile coming from the east
A genocide with an utmost intention to plaque us with extinction
This will be our primitive defeat
Join me in this chant people and spirits of the dead
Take back and feel the knowledge you have given me
Dance with me, for you cannot fight no more
Our mother shall drink our blood for the last time
And all we can do is hope that this will strengthen her
For the time to come
As I look below, thousands of bodies lie scattered about
With their balance shattered
Raped and slain like helpless sheep
And there will be thousands more before the next equinox
But I will not let them kill me; I still have my pride and honor
So the sound of my soul tells me
I will take my own life before I let them clutch and contaminate my
    kind
I will not take orders from the illusion of greed.
There is nothing I can do. As I lay down on this cold barren soil
    suspended in space, I will get in touch for the last time.
Chris Gulino

The Storm

I smell the scent of a single rose,
I feel the rain upon my face.
I dance naked beneath a field of thunder,
And curl my toes between the earth.
I live with the lightning,
And die with the darkness,
I run upon the eerie light.
And I laugh at the heavens,
And tremble in fear,
As the booming sky lights up the night.
Overgrown grass tickles my feet,
And the howling wind whips at my hair.
The taste of fresh rain gathers on my out-thrust tongues,
And the smell of ozone fills my nose.
Then, deep, and in the center of my being,
A rose unfolds,
And I awaken.
Adam Lapayover

Change The Wind

Step by painful, struggling step
  I finally reached the mountain top.
The wind was biting, swirling,
  Wailing like a vigorous wave.
I thought the force would
  Never stop.

It flung my hair and stung my eyes
  It pierced my ears with a mighty howl.
It tried to push me off the top
  With a stinging, mournful, penetrating growl.

I pushed against it with trembling hands-
  Could I change its course, I wondered aloud?
If I took but one more powerful step
  I could reach up and catch a cloud.

  Bertha Susman

"The Memories Of You"

In the long, soft shadows that fill the fields and lawns;
I find the memories of you.

As summers long sultry days slip into the days past,
and Autumn wraps me in golden leaves and crisp evenings;
I find the memories of you.

All to soon the days will hold a cast of grey, and the night sky
will steel away even afternoon hours.
Winters quiet sullen days will be an ever present emphases on the moods of the world;
and I will find the memories of you.

The crisp, clean breezes and fluttering of newly arriving Robins
on the wing will soon
be a part of a fresh clear spring morning;
and I will find the memories of you.

  Dorrie Humphries

Ode To A Legacy

I found comfort in your lyrics, on those dark, lonely nights
I found a kindred spirit—someone who really understood
I was a freak, a nerd, a geek, and a dork
But in your music I found some relief

No matter how much you denied
Because of our generation—you died
A heartless man tripped over your body
Called the media for his fifteen minutes of fame

I love you, I love you—but what could you do?
The pain was too much to bare
Your sorrow too horrible to share
The agony has finally hindered

It was like you looked deep within my soul
Like we shared something no one else would know
You left this world too soon
Wings that flew too close to the flame

I'm sorry, I'm sorry you died alone
I'm sorry you had to chose the easy way out
Your story will live on in history
And in the heart and eyes of your precious daughter

  Lisa Lippert

Dreams And Nightmares

Walking through the woods one day,
I found a path, with signs that say,
"This is the road for none to take."
"It leads to a place where all is fake."
"It's similar to heaven, it feels like hell."
"It's a place of evil, for none to dwell."
I read the signs and took their heed,
I proceeded to walk I felt no need.
I walked with quickness, I walked with fear,
I walk toward a light, that drew me near.
It was so wonderful, is was so great,
I found such wonder, and knew no hate.
A material possession, any at all,
Could be mine, upon my call.
Then I remembered, my family's true love,
The calmness and caring, like that from above.
And then I realized, the signs were so right,
It was an illusion, a twist of my sight.
Because if you are living for possessions alone,
Your soul has no love, your heart is a stone.

  Dustin L. Bender

The Journey Wasn't Easy

Walking in faith through my cultural background,
I found multitudes of emotions, deeply bound.
Represented by strength and determination,
From my African ancestor's immense dedication.

The journey wasn't easy, as my history I retraced,
Through trials and tribulations courageously faced.
Growing as a family supporting the cause,
Coping with the pressures and all the downfalls.

The journey wasn't easy, though tattered and torn,
They upheld the pride so deeply worn.

A culture symbolizing strength and unity;
A purpose in life to fulfill their destiny.
They became strong leaders, progressing day by day;
Incorporating dreams, of those who've paved the way.

The journey wasn't easy, but we're firm to believe,
Through the grace of God, we will succeed.
Visions of the future, our foundation allayed,
Trusting in each other... Sacrifices being made.

No, the journey wasn't easy; Dreams linger on,
Captivating the moments of which we've overcome.

  Anne Anderson Copeland

Wonder

As I walk I wonder, as I wonder I walk.
I look, I see, I try to live my love for thee.
I shed a tear as I think, I step on the
Tattered sand and watch the world turn before me.

I look over in the horizon and see a blank,
As I watch, the wind blows and I wonder.

As I wonder I look to see the purpose in
Life and take a step backward into the sea,
The water cold and murky, but nothing stands between you and me.

  Cori L. Huenink

"A Message From John Sent From Heaven"

Happy birthday Mom you've reached "52"
I had a special wish and I wished it for you

Although I'm not with you, I an actually here
But not with my presence as my spirit is near

I know there were times when we had a fight or two
But all in all Mom, I'm glad that God gave me you

You were everything a mother could ever be
And I knew in my heart that you did love me

You never left my side during that one night
You held my hand and helped me "see the light"

You told me it was okay if I was "ready to go"
I finally made peace with myself and drifted away slow

I have been watching closely from high up above
How wonderful it is to see a family filled with love

It's been two years now since I said my goodbyes
I smile looking down as tears of joy fill my eyes

You brought me into this world and you helped me exit out
You are truly a wonderful mother, there is no doubt

You have made me proud Mom, more that I thought I would be
Have a wonderful birthday, cheers to you from me

Amy D. Hinson

Crossroads

Fate has dealt me what seems like a destined hand
I have become one of the grains in the sand
My life now lacks all enchantment, it has become many things
Two of which are solitude and confinement

How unequivelent it seems to me
One who has bathed and basked in life's beauty
For when I perceived that life would be grand
That's when fate dealt me that arduous hand

Of this world I belong like the tree
Yet there is no ground beneath me
I look up and see the endless brilliant sky
But I am rooted and cannot fly

I am of this world but hope to be of the Earth's soul
There I will be able to guide my loved ones giving them control
Shielding them from the pain that I have had to endure
Making their lives beautiful and pure

Often alone I feel great pain
The flesh is weak but the spirit will sustain
Just like the Eagle soars in his domain
One day I will do the same.

Chaxy Hurst

"Old Windmill"

I went outside to play one day, I noticed the sky was very gray,
I looked to the left and I looked to the right... still no one
    to play with in sight!
Then I noticed something way out yonder,
"could that be someone to play with I wonder?"
I noticed this object was on a huge hill.
I climbed and climbed till I reached the top of the hill,
out of breath and against my will....
to find nothing up there, but an "Old Windmill!"

Jessica Wilson

The Tree That I Am

As once I was a tree, I am now a stump, cut down many years ago.
I have seen many a fisherman catch a trophy fish
from the pond a my right,
I have had many a lover carve his love's name into my trunk,
I have witnessed children growing into adulthood,
and I have witnessed them passing into death.
It is not a dreary thing, death that is, for in death there is life.
The trees I grew with, most of them, are dead,
but from their death new life springs.
From their decayed remains springs new trees,
eager saplings ready to take on life.
In the hollow trunk seeds lay,
someday to sprout roots I feed off of all that is the befallen tree.
So you see, there is no death, only new life.
Though my bigness of trunk and limb is gone I am still alive,
bounding through the children of all living things.
My trunk and limb will never grow again,
but I will thrive from all that I learn every day.
In my youth I was blind and dumb,
but now I can see and have wisdom.

Cory L. Fisher

True Love

To my princess Di on this special day,
I have so many wonderful things that I want to say.

Who would have thought fourteen years ago,
That we would have so much love and so little dough.

We have been through tough times and fun times too,
But we were never bored with nothing to do.

You have worked with me through my difficult times
And you never charged me a single dime.

I wouldn't change this precious marriage
For a husband and wife who are just average.

You have cared for loved ones in their times of need
Not worrying about your gardens with all those weeds.

You're beautiful, thoughtful, caring and full of love.
You soar through life like a carefree dove.

I couldn't imagine life not being with you
I'd have this empty feeling and I'd feel real blue.

So, because of you, I'm content to stay.
Let's both cherish our anniversary day.

Now this is the end of all those rhymes,
But I will always love you till the end of time.

Jay C. Albright

God's Work In The Fall

While out walking one brisk fall day
I noticed a leaf floating my way.
The color had changed from green to brown
Letting me know God still is around.

I noticed the sun had changed from hot to warm
Letting me know God would help in the storm.
I noticed the birds had all disappeared
They had all flown south they never fear.

I noticed the frost so shiny and white
Glistening on the still green grass.
I knew at last as I walk on a way
That God up in heaven is with me to stay.

Johnnie Lockhart

How Great This Love

How great this love?

So much so that when the birds sing,
I hear them herald our love,
Yet their song cannot match
The lilt and texture of your sweet voice.

So much so that when the stars shine,
They signal the glow in your beautiful eyes,
Yet pale in the presence of
Such a shining soul as yours.

So much so that when soft, warm breezes blow,
They toss gently your flowing hair,
Yet cannot match the
Softness of your touch and caresses.

How great this love?
So much so that
Words provide the way to express
My deepest thoughts,
Yet fail to fully express
How truly great and sincere
Is this a love.

David Borden

Battle Of The Flocks

As I look into the dark night skies,
I hear two bird flocks let out there deafening war cries.
They collide into a battle so evil and vital,
That even the Devil himself not dare interfere.
For the pain he would feel would be so great,
That death would be his most pleasant of fate.
Their powerful bodies swoop down in the night,
Causing all natures creatures to flee in a fright.
In ten more years this battle will end,
But the bodies of the warriors will be impossible to mend.
And to the leader of the last standing tribe,
Goes all known power and the world to ride.

Jarrett Csupo

"Waiting For That Special Girl"

   I've been looking for that special girl all my life.
I keep getting rejected, my heart becomes more
infected. I can't wonder why I feel so lonely. It's so
hard getting your heart broken so many times.
Everybody laughs at my pain. When I have all that love
to gain. If I get that special someone, I will hold her
in my arms. I just don't know how I can get a girl
like you. When I look deep into your eyes, it's like
looking at the sunset and looking at your smile, it's
like watching a rose rise from the ground. I'm
patiently waiting for the time when I can say "I
love you". I'll never let you go. I'll be beside you
during the good and tough times even when loves not
worth a million dimes. Here I am sitting in the rain
crying, cause I can't find that special someone. Don't
keep me waiting any longer even when my love for
you will become even stronger.

   As you can see, I am so very sweet. I dream about
you, think about you and can't get you off my mind.
There's pain in my heart that only you can release.

Bryan Reynolds

A Prayer For You

Every night before I sleep.
I kneel by my bed side with praying hands.
I ask of God to hear my prayers.
A prayer for you I pray each night.
To keep you safe, and always away from evils harm.
To bless you with his presence in so many ways.
To let you have no fear's to share.
He knows I care so very dear.
To keep the one's that I do love.
So if you should say that no one cares.
That's so untrue, because there's God and me,
Yes me! Who cares as a friend, and as a loved one too.

So when your far, near, or no matter where.
Just remember, God and this prayer are with you.
So when you sleep just think of what I say.
Because this prayer is from me to you.
So God Bless, and may He always be with you.
As each night I pray.....A prayer for you.

Joseph P. Galindo Jr.

Feelings

From the moment we had spoken,
   I knew that there were feelings.
      Feelings that for me would never fade.

Feelings
   I would never have the courage
      To express

Living in fear, wondering if I'd lose you.
   Lose you to feelings,
      Said to be so wrong.

Quivering in your presence,
Shattered by your touch.

I slowly opened my heart,
   Leaving you
      To fill in my every emotion.

Now you are gone,
My fear becomes greater.

Yet my fear has changed.
   I fear
      I will never love again,

Love anyone again, the way I love you.

Janine Tancredi

This Feeling For You Cannot Be Spoken

I knew you through days and nights and years
I knew you through lonely and want and tears
I knew not your face or shape nor size
But I knew your smile would be a gentle surprise

And then one day you came to me
The power of you filled the air I breathe

And now I'm like a tree in bloom
though spring is gone and winter calls

And now I'm like a branch that bends
to grasp the sighs of whispering winds

Ever gently now it fills my being
Ever softly now it opens the door
drawing me closer, restoring my soul
arousing a passion I have yet to know

Christine Burroughs

Untitled

It was in a little box
I know it's important
So I smiled when she pulled out a pair of round, shiny, tiny shoes
"They'll protect your feet when you walk, Son."

Then I watched every step
so as not to ruin a family nest
or to crush a baby ant

Years gone by
shoes start howling many moons
and shoelaces drumming

The more I grow, the less I know
and later, shoes are long forgotten

Just one more thing, she didn't tell me,
"Shoes will always be between the earth and who I am."
David Adiv

A Beautiful Day In Paradise

The sun comes streaming in my bedroom window.
I lazily stretch, slowly open my eyes.
The flowers are brilliant, the birds singing.
It is a beautiful day in paradise.

Heavy dew sparkles like jewels on the verdant grass,
Soft, fluffy clouds float across the skies,
Humming birds dart in and out of crimson blossoms,
What a beautiful day in paradise.

Later, storm clouds begin to gather,
Lightning paints designs in the darkened skies,
But soon the sun peeks out, a rainbow appears.
It is still a beautiful day in paradise.

Slowly daylight begins to fade,
Brilliant colors fill the Western skies,
The sun seems enormous as it sinks into the sea.
It was a beautiful day in paradise.
Alice B. Remus

At Long Last Peace! Perhaps?

Since I was young and battered in whole
I lived my life in anger and doing wrongs;
Now I want to feel safe, warm and consoled,
All I really wanted was to feel I belonged.
As I grow older and wiser, the anger still exists.
It busts my guts, making me scream in unphysical pain.
Tell me when this madness no longer will persist?
Tell me that it's easier to let go than have my energy drained.
As I step out of my apartment, I hear a child's cry.
Will he be who he doesn't want to be?
This horrible screech makes me want to die.
Will he be like me and never have the thoughts to see?
Ironically my anger makes me want to crush the kid's head!
In the glorious momentum of it all I have been stung,
I don't wish for the child to be dead!
Is this a passing sentiment or has my life's work just begun?
I dream I can hold this boy and touch him with care,
Whispering in his ear of a place called serendipity.
For most of my life I would have never dared.
At last for me and this child, for the moment, a place called serenity.
Andres J. Wrath

"Weighting"

Lying in wait for the Golden Kiss,
I long to feel your love.
Sleepless tosses and turns fill my bed.
The night is so long.

I close my eyes and you are with me.
All of your beauty and splendor I see.

When in your arms, my soul sings of love never before known.
Oh, how quickly my passions has grown.
All men with all the words of all tongues could not join together
The feelings burning deep within me for you.

Trite babbling and lofty logic
Often pry hard against we two.
What strong chords have we that we shall claim?
Commitment, Romance, Caring, or Friendship to be our bond?
Oh no! 'Tis true love that beckons us forth.
'Tis true love that grows strong when we want to fail.

Lying in weight for the Golden kiss,
I long to feel your love.
Sleepless tosses and turns fill my head,
The night is so long, the night is so long.
Geoffrey B. Bruschi

Brian (1976-1994)

Where are you? Love divine
  I look and look, I can not find
you were, you are, one of a kind
  Eyes of blue, teeth of pearl - a straight line.

There you are! I have you
  So near; yet out of reach
So young, so strong, so true
  A propelled force; waves on the beach.
Wonderful! The gaze on sky blue.

I search; far and near
  Room to room; he can't be far
Come to me my love, never fear
  Make you stay; never so close to the bar.

Come to me, my love, hold my hand
  Take me to your never, never land
On the clouds. Oh! I ran
  To get a glimpse, as fast as I can.
'Tis Heaven, this land everything; beautiful and grand
One day to see such wonderful wealth
  Up the ladder of life; down the slope of death.
Alma Ann Williams

Heavenly Reassurance

On a midwinters night, retiring to the porch
I look to the heavens above.

Thinking of Vikkie, my second daughter the Lord has taken;
My heart fills with sadness and love.

The stars and the moon shine down on me, as I search
The heavens above;

The tears begin to fall, and I have to wonder, "Why Lord?"
"Why do you take the ones we love?"

The stars and the moon continue to shine, but my sadness
Was lifted by the wind.

In the silence of the night, I knew I'd be alright

My daughters were happy... they were together again.
Fannie Hicks

"A Big City"

Overlooking the city and contemplating the view
I look upon life's busy portal.
People with plastic faces — rushing about with meaningless causes
anticipating the last reward.

Plastic people with plastic lives — look up and see the true beauty
the truth of life's eternity.
Behold the sweeping grandeur of God's day —
He sends an ever changing picture —
Glorious prisms of light —
Wondrous to the eye.

Why then do we rush through life's door —
anticipating the last reward
Only to miss this life's Heavenly view.
    Carol Coles

Perfect Love

I looked far and near for my perfect love.
I looked in book's and T.V.'s. I looked in
magazines. I went from state to state, town to
town, from girl to girl, from up to down, and
still my perfect love could not be found. I
opened the cabinets, the fridge, the stove, I
went to the basement, I looked through the
clothes, and still my perfect love could not be
found. I went outside and looked at each
tree, in both directions, as far as I could see.
Then I went inside again, and still I could not
find my perfect love. Then it came to me (still
have eyes and cannot see) that my perfect love
was inside of me. My perfect love sent from
heaven above. My perfect love is God, true love.
    Brian M. Bryant

Nature's Gift

I love to see a snowflake — watch it fall;
  I love to see a beam of sunshine steal down the hall.
I love to see a baby — tiny, sweet;
  I love to see an aged person trudging down the street.
I love to see a flower — beautiful, rare;
  I love to see a thorny, ugly prickly pear.
I love to see the Springtime — its freshness know;
  I love the cold, brisk Winter with its glittering snow.
I love to see a cottage — cheery, bright;
  I love to see a castle and to hear about its knight.
I love to see a river — swift or still;
  I love to see a little stream trickle down a hill.
I love to see a common thing — or dear;
  I love to be made happy by the things which God put here.
    Charles E. Hunter

Love is a Many Splendored Thing

I love you more with every breath I take
I love you more with every step and I make
In wind or rain in sunshine or in shade
I love you wildly as the waves in storm
And gently as the willow in the breeze
From dawn til dusk and through the still of night,
  I love you more
But most of all when I behold the wonders of "His Hand"
The sky the stars the sea the sand,
Above all you, the more in thee is "He"
  I love you more
    John S. Clemence

River Of Dreams

I loved you so much for twenty three years
I loved you so much through laughter and tears
But one day you ripped my heart from my chest
So mean so cruel not even in jest
The words that you spoke left me in shock
To see this new side of you come out from the dark
Because of our son who got caught with pot
I wanted him gone from our house and lot
You defended his actions his honor his deeds
By putting me down with shame and bad creeds
I kept my head stone faced my emotions inside
I had no great come back I wanted to hide
For I could not hurt you as you have hurt me
For I could not hurt you I just let it be
It bothers me now four years have gone by
The flame that burnt bright is starting to die
I feel we're so close yet so far apart
I don't want to lose you but this is the start
My feelings have changed with no self esteem
I've gone with the flow down the river of dreams.
    Hartwell L. Gauthier Jr.

Walk Slowly

Come walk with me, but don't go too fast;
I may want to sit
In a rocker on my front porch,
A hot cup of coffee at my lips,
Gazing out over the flowering fields
As the frail morning light plays games
Among the trees that bend and wave;

I may linger beside a giggling brook
To let it tickle my dangling, bare feet
As a sweet breeze cools the hot, noon-time heat;

I may want to stop
And pat my child's head
Or kiss the tip of their nose,
Or listen to their most inner thoughts
Or teach them a song to sing;

I may want to hold your hand
And lean against your shoulder
As we stand beside a shimmering, shadowy pond
Watching the sun hide behind dark hills;

Walk slowly, so each moment will last.
    Evelyn J. Lewis

A Baby's Point Of View

Life as a baby "sucks".
I mean burping up isn't fun.
Every little thing you do is so cute.
You sit and watch older kids running and jumping around.
You are held hours upon hours having people admire your clothes.
I am not saying being admired is bad; but you try being admired
twenty four hours a day.
Night is a whole worse story.
There is air pockets, dirty diapers, toilets flushing.
Then that loud beepy thing goes off everyone starts rushing around
The whole things starts over again.
    Amanda Rachael Roberts

"My Prayerful Plea"

Lord I am just a stranger here in this old barren land,
I need your help to make it Lord-please take me by the hand.
Sin runs a very rapid course, and evil keeps a watchful eye
But Lord I'm trying to walk upright, please help me as I try.

I can't go this journey alone-too many traps I cannot see,
So I invite you in dear Lord, to come and dwell in me.
Lord I will do my very best to keep this vessel clean
For nothing good I know Dear Lord, is in a fleshly thing.

Sometimes the storms of life they beat-upon my bodily tent,
And sometimes Lord I do wrong things -for which I must repent.
Sometimes dear God I do not love in a way that pleases you
But teach this evil heart of mine to love the way you do.

I can't even imagine Lord, how you felt on that dreadful day,
When Jesus died on Calvry's cross-to wash all my sins away.
Now I can never repay you Lord for all you have done for me.
But Lord as dirty as I may be, I give my life to Thee.

Please use me Lord as you see fit to lift Jesus up on high,
In words, in poems, in songs dear Lord, in praise and in reply.
Help me to maintain the course that you have planned for me,
And as I end, My Prayerful Plea, I pray that it pleases Thee.
Diann F. Moulden

Untitled

As I stare gazing at a hole in the floor,
I notice you standing beside me smiling.
Nothing in this world matters except us,
There is nothing that can cure me of such inner peace.

As we sit close to one another on the porch swing.
I can't help but to think that this is all I want.
I want this forever, never let it end.
As I see this as selfish, I think of it no more.

As we exchange vows on the night of our marriage.
I turn to you to repeat the minister and you smile.
I don't believe there was ever a time when your frowned
You made me so happy the day we become one.

As we await the birth of our first,
we hold hands and you make everything perfect,
the baby is born, a little boy, he's beautiful,
he has your eyes, we name him after you.

Sadly the day arrives, over the grave we stand.
The air is so cold it stings our weeping eyes
As we turn to leave, junior drops a single rose
and I drop my heart with you to show our undying love.
Christy Hutzel

Positive Negation

Sweet love, I wrote no Valentine;
I suppressed the need to tell
I'd loved unwisely once, too well,
And call nobody mine.
I spared myself a needless tear;
I've lately found it rarely pays
To roam forbidden yesterdays,
Imagining you here.
I saved myself a useless pain
By passing up that lover's time;
I read no verse, recalled no rhyme
To light the past again.
Forget you? Till I cease to be, it's foolish, just to say;
But sometime, do the same for me: Turn down an empty day...
Annabel Alderman

I Stand Alone

I stand here all alone to watch my brother grow.
I once was a newly planted seed and
I grew under the watchful eyes of those before me.
Today they are gone
and you and I are here to take their place and
I have been left to show you the way
to follow in their footsteps.

You ask me why I did not follow those before me?
I am of the rare breed,
the one that would not develop as those before me.
I am the one that would not take the path
to seek fulfillment.
I am the one that stands alone
with no direction, no purpose to my life.
I have always had the love and support
but lacked the courage to trust the words:
"Go forth and be all you can be."

I know I still have a chance
to go forth and follow those before me.
Will I, can I? I don't know!?!
Connie Coleman-Lacadie

I Remember

I remember, you're gentle touch,
I remember, that I loved you so much.

I remember, your warm embrace,
I remember, your sweet gentle face.

I remember, that first special kiss,
I remember, the way you held me that, I will miss.

I remember, when we watched the sun set,
I remember, that beautiful day that we met.

I remember, when you played our song,
I remember, I cried all night long.

I remember, when I use to call,
I remember, when you helped me through it all.

I remember, when we laid outside,
I remember, when you tried to hide...
And now these wonderful times are gone,
I loved you so much but, for now so long.
Heather R. Chafin

Escape

To forget sorrow, and painful memories
I retreat into the recess of the mind,
Sink into the pages of a good book,
And down in insignificant busy work.

To stop the torturous thoughts
I drug myself with sweet and healing music,
Becoming the light and floating melody
Drifting out of the window and everywhere.

To laugh, joke, and join in free laughter,
I hide my true emotions from the world,
Masking eyes clouded with tears
And a badly scarred heart.

To cease endless hours of thinking,
I travel to the peace of Dreamland
Until fear invades and transports me
To a world of nightmarish terror.

To end all thought,
I banish all feeling,
Kill all emotion,
And escape.
Jen Viloria

Peace Of Mind

While sitting and looking out of my window,
I see a great quietness and peace;
but where is my peace of mind?

Trouble arises far and near;
but where is my peace of mind?

My home and family is so dear;
but where is my peace of mind?

I've helped and loved others as I should,
and this is good;
but I still have not found my peace of mind.

The world is a beautiful place;
so where is my peace of mind?

The world is big enough for all of us;
but I'm still looking for that peace of mind.

I've been told that life is gold,
it's a blessing to get old and
that through God he watches over all souls.

If we believe and do all good deeds;
then we will find that great and wonderful
Peace of Mind.
   Hattie Foster

A Wanders Reminiscence

I wander back in memory, my Paddy's in my hand:
I see again the hills of Kerry and Sligo's golden strand.

In the heart of Country Kerry, Castleisland's bustling scene;
each friendly pub alive with hope for an "All Ireland" team.

The barman sips his Murphy's, as the conversation flows;
From forwards, backs and frees, to center fielders and to goals.

I down my Paddy's gently and bid a fond adieu,
for I'm off to County Sligo, to visit kin anew.

I cross the mighty Shannon. I hear the "wave of song!"
The voice of Connacht calling; whispers to guide me along.

I arrive at a cottage in Rathlee; where greeted by kin at the door,
I can smell the sweet scent of turf fire, as another Paddy's I pour.

I have lived again through memory; a holiday so grand.
I have seen again the "Golden Vale" and Sligo's golden strand.
   John F. P. Finnerty

Heartsong

On thee, soft winter morning, frosty white
I see the river flowing ever on.
The mighty sun reflects its brilliant light,
The touch of snow is gentle as the dawn.
No sound can pierce the silent, cold-white air,
My cares are heavy, pushing on me so.
I move alone, as slowly as a bear,
My heart must let its sadness freely go.
For even as the seasons always bend
And yield to Nature's ever-circling flow,
I wish this frosty day would never end
And that this treasured moment need not go.
But in this life, both good and bad depart.
And what is left, a measure of the heart.
   Eric Eide

Magenta

I do not see the world through eyes of obvious cliche
I see the world through eyes of words, each its own colour

When I step, they are footprints of silver not yet gold saved for my
   yonder years
When I smile, it is the bluest of oceans mysterious the truth
   beneath if
When I sigh, there but the purple of royalty lost not forgotten
When I miss you, I miss you colour magenta

Rainy day, magenta
Legs entwined, solitude embraced magenta
Whispers, tingling, shutter magenta
Nay red nor black or common blue no, not blue
Hot, sweet, slow, passion I miss you
Words hardest to speak, I love you magenta
   Donna M. Richardson

Live

Many will get on; few will get off
   I shall be one to get off
Many will die; few shall live
   I shall live
The flames enfold many a person who comes my way
We have stopped.
Led to the crematories where the air smells of burning skin.
   I must wait in line for my turn...
My turn is now...
The flame enfolds me...
   I scream, "My spirit shall live!"...
   and it has...
   Alexi Burns

Moonstone Beach

On just a bone cold day as this,
I sometimes walk the beach, not
Remembering summers past, nor lazily imagining
Impending springs,
   for the beach is at its best in winter.
The barren edge of two worlds stretching endlessly,
Erupting wherever land and sea collide, unable
To bring peace to their everlasting struggle,
A demilitarized zone of coexistence.
Scattered along this no man's land are remains
Of abandoned assaults, quahog shells, fish bones,
Fragments of rolled glass...
   All's calm today...silent, except for
   squawking gulls, as they police the front lines.
   John-Robert Curtin

If I Were Black

If I were black
I think my heart might cry each day
To see the obstacles an unkind fate
Placed in my way.

If I were black
I'd still no less a person be
Than others dreaming whiter skins create
Humanity.

And yet the paths I love might be forever barred
The cobweb of my life forever torn
The beauty I have seen forever marred
In payment for the crime of being born.

If I were black
And saw the white me turn my back
I'd hate my whiteness with a special hate
If I were black.
   Eleanor M. Schetlin

Never Again

While he lie there dying
I stand there crying
Wondering why
At a time like this
that he opened my eyes to the world
that he could not close them
As I walked out of the room
I knew never again would I see him
at the parlor he lie there motionless
I thinking he'll wake up at anytime
But he never did
when the preacher said
ashes to ashes and dust to dust
I knew when they lowered him into the ground
Never again would I see him
But I knew that his guardian angels
would take him to his final resting place
and the roots of his flowers
would grow to touch our hearts.
Carey Morris

Mother

As I look down the corridor and see nothing ahead,
I start to get cold and tremble wondering am I alive or dead.

A life without purpose is full of darkness indeed;
Despair, destruction and a life full of greed.

I gaze down the corridor once again and I see a spark.
I gain a little courage and feel a flutter in my heart.

The brighter the spark gets the more courage I gain.
And as it gets brighter and brighter, it eases the pain.

Because just when I thought no more happiness I will see,
It is always brought back by the woman who gave birth to me.

Finally, the darkness dispels and I can see a bit further.
The spark of light I saw coming to my rescue was my mother.
Carlus Delonte Koonce

Begger In The Park

I met a man the other day as I strolled through the park.
I stopped and talked to him till' well after dark.
I said I must be going now, I have to get some rest.
The man only looked at me and buttoned up his vest.
He said, kind sir, will you loan me a dime?
I may be able to catch my friends if I call them in time.
They are going on a train ride, I know not where, but, if I catch
them in time, I too will be there.
It's cold and lonely here all alone at night.
You have to find a place to stay well out of sight.
I said come home with me we'll find a place for you, some food and
warm bed too. He said, sir that is so kind of you, but I'm on my way
to find a job I can do.
I want to straighten out my life and be respectable too.
A few years passed, I took another stroll.
I went down to the park just above the knoll.
A well dressed man sitting have his noon lunch, said to me, please
join me in some brunch. I look at him, could it be, he said, sir it
is he. You helped me to see myself and what I had to do.
I now hope you receive my many thanks to you.
Allen Randy Coy

Lost In A Dream

I fly through the night on my little pet star
I tell my grandkids how a certain sword gave me an ugly scar
I get tired and take a nap on the moon
I battle a monster in a big black lagoon
On my unicorn we ride through the hills
I'm an evil villain longing to kill
I rescue a fair maiden trapped in a tower
I watch the pink sun set with my prince as he
  hands me a flower
I'm an celebrity on my Hawaiian Yacht
I am a slave and try to keep warm on my cot
I sit all alone up in my room for my dreaming is over
But I'll dream again soon.
Emma Tomingas

Once Then Twice

They like you once and hate you twice,
I think another fight is going to happen again tonight.
Beans and rice Spanish sacrifice,
Ham and peas African needs, noodles and sauce Caucasian cost,
A merry-go-round made from ups and downs,
They hate when you lie, cheat or spy,
The day is here when we should all fear,
Just like a kite we'll all take flight,
Leaving the ground wiping away all of our discontented frowns,
Quickly and swiftly he'll come to the place,
He's up in the trees, and even the sky,
Tears fall from his many eyes and we still pretend why,
Hope is still there ready to share, buried with snow,
Drenched with rain, and even camouflaged as pain,
African spice, Spanish rice, Caucasian dice,
This is just a small part of life, and don't forget,
The African bees, Spanish flees, and Caucasian weeds,
All spelling freedom please, wrapped around,
Greed, needs, and pleads, because they like you once,
Then hate you twice.
Jacqueline Sorrells

Untitled

In February 1981, I heard about you,
I thought it sounded so wonderful and exciting too.
The first thing I knew we had fallen in love.
Oh! What joy just like the stars above.

In March 1981, our vows were said,
So much love, happiness and joy was spread.
We pledged to be true till death do us part,
And the thoughts of each other will always remain in my heart.

We had so much pleasure in showing our love.
Getting up in the morning and receiving a great big hug.
My God! My God! How can this be?
That you left this life so unexpectedly.

Now my darling you are gone.
No never again on this earth to roam.
But to walk by the River of The Crimson Tide.
Where you'll never again will need a guide.

My heart is lonely and so sad,
That the reality of your death seems like only a fad.
The children and I can hardly stand thought of loosing you,
Because you are such a wonderful grand dad and dad.
Eunice F. Erdei

Injury

I used to jump I used to play
I used to play basketball but now it's not the same way

I got hurt playing football I played it every day
But when I got to the hospital they said "no way"

They told me I was paralyzed from my neck down to my toes
I had to stay in a wheelchair the nurse and doctor chose

My mom and dad helped me from morning until night
They told me I'd get better just if I fight

My friends told me to get better I told them I would try
They bought me gifts and I started to cry

The doctor came to my house one day in the summer
He said he had bad news I said "That's a bummer"

Doctor said I was dying the year of '97
I couldn't believe I was going to heaven.
    Andrea Lee Watts

The Father's Snowy Mountain

Once as I sat and thought of you
I viewed myself as a rugged mountain,
And you as a majestic ice peak.
As our Creator melted and pulled you away
Down the stream beds that
Took you distances I hate to say,
My stomach turned and my heart ached
When I imagined your crushing fate.
I was forced to watch Jesus twist and roll you
Around the cliff's far, far below my base
Destined for the sea's salty bay,

Finally, I saw you at a distance having grown
Into a beautiful, crystal clear lake.
Then I remembered when you blanketed me
All around in a wonderful coat of snow,
And my heart started to yearn
For you and your return.
When the Father will you back
In a floating sea, to pour you upon
His lonely peak, me.
    Jason Vick

Vacuum

As I gaze inwardly into the depths of my soul,
  I visualize a vacuum;
    empty and longing to be filled.
Unless this bottomless pit is filled and sealed,
  my body dies and withers
    like the leaves after the fall rains.
I begin to frantically search for fulfillment, but
  soon realize that it comes not from wealth
    or possessions but from love, mercy, and grace.
During my search for the pieces to complete my inner puzzle,
  I sense a Being far greater than I
    who fills both Heaven and Earth.
I sense His emptiness, too, even though
  He is Creator and Giver of Life to all;
    myself included.
He also is incomplete: a far, far greater Vacuum.
I then understand that in His heart, He
  is missing a piece, as am I.
    But together...together
we fill one another's void perfectly and become One.
    Chris Dickens

Cat's Eyes

Cat's eyes
I want those beautiful eyes
I look at such beauty that shines through
A beautiful creature with such beautiful eyes

Cat's eyes
I look at them and I can see so much

Imagine with your eyes what I saw
Cat's eyes

Can he evil but good
and also full of weird mysterious
ideas of the unknown but the cat

I can hear the beauty calling out
The beauty of Cat's eyes
They come alive with me and also you

I want them
I want the beauty of everything
through the Cat's Eyes.
    Jennica Goulet

Teen Wishes

I have to live with myself and so
I want to be fit for myself to know
I want my looks to do me proud
I want to feel adequate in any crowd
I want to strike verbal abuse off my list
I want to keep my cool when the heat resists
I want to take time to respect truth in all
I want to be myself but listen to my Master's call
I want my soul all clean so that God is proud
I want to represent God well in every crowd
I want to be able to sort out the good from the bad
I want to accept the happiness, but handle the sad
I want to hear whispers, "There goes a good teen"
I want the experience: not all teens are mean
I want to shun funky deeds that are never real
I want to grow graceful in right way GOD! Please reveal
I have to live with myself and so
I want to be fit for myself to know.
    Bess Shannon

The Tennis Match

It was the day of the tennis match and all through my veins,
I was feeling tension, stress, and all sorts of pains.
We started to volley and practiced our serves,
Butterflies went up my spine and through my nerves.

The first serve was served and flew past my face,
I couldn't believe it, it was an ace.
The first couple games were all really fast,
And I was wondering about how long I would last.

The next couple games were not all that good,
I was down 4-2 but playing as I should.
The first set was completed, the first set was done.
The score was 6-4 and first set he won.

The second set started and the match was in his hand,
I told myself to get my head out of the sand.
It was at match point, and he was to serve,
The ball came to me with some spin and some curve.

He followed his serve and came to the net,
He put it away and completed the set.
The match was all over, and I wasn't at all mad,
Cause I put up a fight that I didn't know I had.
    Chanda Kumar

The Day Is Coming

I was truly looking forward, your birth was drawing near,
I was in no way ready for the news I had to hear.
The word when it came, seemed so hard to bear,
my comfort was knowing that God would take care.

I don't understand, and it is hard to cope,
but His word assures me in God is my hope.
You're parents are brave, though pain's in their eyes,
they wait for the day there'll be no goodbyes.

Eternal life will be ours, we read in First John,
if we remain true to God and His Son.
Grandma loves you dearly and will eternally,
I'm looking for our Lord's return, when you're sweet face I'll see.

I let you in His keeping, I know His word is true,
He says the day is coming, we'll meet again Matthew.
Doris Musselman

My Kids

It started many years ago, probably thirty,
I was just eighteen with the world in hands.
I wanted a happy marriage...that would last forever,
I wanted a large family, boys and girls,
I got my wish, In found Johnny, love brought us together.
We had our family of four girls and two boys...
We proceeded to have fifteen wonderful years,
Until a mess up in the plan...God took him away...
I don't question God's plan, I know he had reason...
I went on with my life...I did a good job...
I raised my children, they were great kids,
I did what I had to make things work,
I missed him terribly but never let it show
I prayed daily for strength to help my kids grow.
A brief remarriage brought a seventh child...
Today I'm a grandparent and can not believe
That I made it this far by myself, but I did...
You might say, like a famous singer once said...
I did it my way...
Carmel Castlevetro

Untitled

My mind was all set, the depression was strong;
I was losing my grandpa, and something seemed wrong.

Compassion was there, my love was so great;
Was the man, himself, ready to go through the gate?

He reached for a hand, and I held it in mine;
The warmth that went through us, I still can't define.

For just a brief moment, we both were as one;
My life still beginning, and his was all done.

Now all those long years, as we hid what we felt;
Came up just like gang busters, God, what a belt!

I held him in close, for my strength he could use;
I remembered the times, when he filled those shoes.

I'm glad that I saw him, to just let him know;
That I cared, and I loved him, and let the tears flow.

We both found some peace, in that moment of grace;
When grandpa and grandson, could touch face to face.
James G. Hoffman

The Empty Plate

As you prepared our dinner, you held your empty plate...
I watched as your gaze focused on each of us,
and I wondered why you would wait...

You filled us up on staples, some beans and rice and such,
making sure we were never hungry,
that was your "Special" touch...

But still, your plate was empty, and we had not left you much.
You cleaned our plates and ate our scrapes...
You could not have gotten enough...

Many years have passed and still I think upon your empty plate.
You have shared so much, you gave your all,
and to me that says you are Great!

The lessons you have taught me have lingered throughout my life...
Your strength and faith has helped me as I became a mother and a wife.

For what I saw as empty was filled with warmth and love,
you gave to all so freely, a true example of God above...

Of all the things you could give me, I have but one request to make.
"As you discard your old things,
please give to me your empty plate..."
Carol Westbrooks Williams

To My Son

As I anxiously await your arrival I often think of the moment that
I will be able to hold you in my arms for the first time. It will
be one of the most important moments of my life.

Important not only because your father and I have been wanting a child,
but also because I will be sharing a very special bond with you.

For my little Brendan,
you will be the first part of me I've ever known.

I often wonder if you will have my eyes,
smile or maybe even my stubborn disposition.

Because of you I will no longer feel alone.
Alone in the sense that I have wondered for many years if there is
someone else out there like me
for now I will know because you are
MY SON.
Elizabeth Anne Seeger

Song Of Love To A Trumpet Player

How can I compete with that silver beauty?
I wish to be with you but you have eyes only for your music.
True, you play with such feeling that passion
stirs within the being of a sensitive ear.
Yet, how I wish I could be held in your arms,
Your lips caressing mine,
Your eyes embracing my soul;
if only for a brief moment.
Your voice, were that it speaking words only for my ears,
opening me up to you, that I might feel your trust and gentle love.
Here is my song of desire and longing —
place it upon your stand and play.
Soft and muted...forever.
Ellen Rose Dillon

Waiting

He left in early Spring when the world awakened bright and new.
I wondered why he would leave and miss the magic of it all.
Then Summer came with colors bursting brilliant on flowers and
　birds and trees
And I questioned why he would go and miss the glory of it all.
In Fall as Summer green turned Autumn gold and children played
　in falling leaves
I sighed to think he would miss the beauty of it all.
Then Winter's crystal snowflakes danced in icy winds
And I cried knowing he would miss the wonder of it all.
Alone I've watched the seasons pass and though
I know he won't be back, I keep waiting.
　　Joyce M. Clark

Past

If I were to walk in someone else's shoes,
I would be an Indian of two hundred years ago,
I would walk in the forest without a sound,
I would plant corn in a field for my village,
I would play like a child in the river or in the woods pretending I
was older with a hunting party ready to face a angry bear.
If I were to walk in someone else's shoes
It would be an indian of two hundred years ago,
I would walk to the mountains in the winter,
I would follow the deer were they roam
If I were to walk in that Indian's shoes,
I would die of illness and hunger,
I would be called a savage by the white man who stole my land,
I would be called a killer by the white man,
If I were to walk in someone else's shoes,
It would be an indian of two hundred years ago,
I would look out on the land one last time as they take me away forever.
　　Caryn Charlton

To Be Reborn

If I could relive my life over, what would I be?
I would be the wind-
As free as the open sea.
Because no one could ever own me, possess me, test me or
depress me.
I would be free to go here or there or anywhere.
If I were the wind-
I would not be closed or confined.
I would have a peace of mind.
I would live forever.
I would not die.
I would not have to hurt.
I would not longer have to cry.
I would not have to worry about pain nor sorrow.
I would not have to face the trials and tribulations of tomorrow.
　　Cheyney Richardson Whitaker

Untitled

Baseball is a game I'd get out
I'd prefer to play soccer
I'd rather wander about
Or talk next to a locker
Even though the hot dogs are good
And catching fly balls is fun
I'd rather stand in the rain without a hood
Or be eating a sticky bun-bun
If I had a choice between baseball and soccer
I'd definitely pick the second
I'd rather sit in a rocker
Than by this game be beckoned
　　Jared Ritter

Letting Go

If I had been a bird
I would have pushed him from the nest,
but being the human that I am
I held him to my chest.
A lifetime of bonding seem to be of another day,
when I watched him leave to fly
so far away.

Does he feel what I feel?
Does his heart feel torn in two?
Does he feel the need to reach out
for that warm embrace the way I do?

Letting go is not easy,
I've lived it so I know
I can only hope he's happy in his life
wherever he may go.

A mother's love is forever and
for her children she wishes the best,
and she'll carry the joys and heartaches
of motherhood with pride
until she's laid to rest.
　　Anna Marie Crews

Cast To The Curb

Why each time I visit thee, you treat me
　ice cold and insipid deliberately?
Why do you cast me off like worthless
　debris, while I unfold my creativity?
There is no competition between you and me,
　you are my sister and I love thee!
　　Eleanor Lynar-Cohen

In Nature There Is No Silence

You cannot make a person believe in light and beauty
If all of their life has been dark and ugly,

You cannot make a person see something
That is, to him, an illusion,

You cannot make a person hear the sound of music
If they prefer silence or hear only noise,

You cannot make a person savor a taste
If their taste buds are deadened or numb,

You cannot connect with and touch a soul
If it closed to awareness long ago,

You cannot hold hands with a tightened fist
If the clenched hand has no sensation,

You cannot reach out to another
If you've shut down all movement within yourself...
　　Cynthia L. Ferguson

Glad, I Am Me

Sometimes I wonder how my life would be
If I were someone else instead of me.
If the eyes that I see through were not my own
If I were a child instead of grown.

But then I see the faces of those I love
And dream of things yet to be
My heart is full of memories of the past
And I thank the Lord, that I am me.
　　Evelyn C. Brown

Why I Cry

"If I die will you cry? Or will you just say goodbye?
If I'm hurt will you be hurt? Or will you just say too bad?
If I cry will you cry? Or will you just say bye?"

"Time flies as I cry. Cry for the pain I hide inside.
No one knows not even my sole why I cry for the pain I hide.
Do you know why I cry?
Or is it some thing that happens time after time.
If you cared you'll say those three words. The words that may
change mine pain I hide in side."

"Do you love me? Or feel sorry?
Sorry because you don't want to hurt me?
No one may share no one may care.
Care for the feeling deeply down me."

Amy Koh

A Centimental Mother's Thoughts

Mother's Day - how nice - what more can I say?
If it wasn't fer the three of yuz, I'd have no new shoes.
I wouldn'a got know billfold or a new poice.
Of coarse they was empty - but things coulda been woice.
There'd be know purfume, powder and a poiple puff.
Jest think, I got awl that stuff!

Suppose sumtimes ya wonder what really makes me tick.
But then, ya shrug it off and say "Oh, she's just sick!"
I hope I can learn ya to dew good each day,
Bee good and kind too others in every sorta weigh.
Have lottsa smiles — bee happy — don't think nuthin mean.
Cuz what's in the inside, on the outside is scene.

Yuz awl aint poifect, I will admit,
But I wouldn'a wanna change ya, not a little bit.
I luv yuz awl — I want yuz to no
And I hope yuz lov me two.
Cuz if'n yuz didn't, don't no what I'd dew!
No refund - no exchange - trade-in aint so hot.
Sew will ya settle fer the mom that ya got?

Alberta June Hugunin

Goodbye, From A Soldier's Wife

To hear a breaking heart is so profound
If only it were a more silent sound

Emptiness rings loudly within my ears
Chorused only by my falling tears

A steady cadence my heart now cries
Forever echoing those sorrowed goodbyes

It is sad and cold my blackened stare
Dreams that danced like fire, no longer there

Never, will I forget this fateful day
My true love has gone so far away

Deena L. Germani

Untitled

As I lay awake dreaming of you
I'm here alone just thinking of us too.
When you say I love you, I know it's true
So I won't have to watch or worry about you
I know how much you love me
And I know how much you care
But I just couldn't imagine you not being there.
I love you so much and I want you to see
Just what your love does to me.

Jennifer Smith

Where Do I Belong

I'll get by myself,
If they'll only let me try myself.
Oh, I know I won't deny myself,
   Where do I belong?

I'll just find my place,
If they'll only let me set my pace.
Oh, I know I'm gonna win the race-
   Where do I belong?

Oh, I know sometimes the going gets rough,
And I may start to fall.
But, if I don't dare to go far enough,
I know I won't find out at all.

Let me free myself.
If they'll only let me be myself.
Oh, I know I wanna see myself,
   Where do I belong.

Let me prove myself.
If they'll only let me do myself.
Oh, I'm gonna make it through myself,
   For that's where I belong.

Catherine Baker

A Distant Cry

An infant child is crying near, it cries from loneliness and fear.
If you can't hear it must not be, but it is real for few like me.
What this means is most don't care, nor does its mother standing there.
The love for life she does not know, for a child she did not grow.
She to was treated much the same, a loveless life of endless pain.

The distant cry is far away, it grows more louder every day.
Abort its life before it's free, or live on Earth in Hell like me.
Suffer child, you'll suffer long, the right you do is also wrong.
No one care for who you are, so ruin your life and run afar.

The crying child it has no name, fatherless and feels shame.
It guides itself most on its own, the streets you see is place call home.
Full of rage and no control, inflicted pain has taken toll.
Failed at home and in the school, to seek the church it feels a fool.
Fights, drugs, sex, the gun, appears the streets already won.
A child whose life was born in violence, now begins its final silence.

Why? For what? Can they not see, another child in misery.
Worship, pray with no intent, is this why the Lord was sent?
Save the children, save them all, if we do not then we should fall.
It's very sad a child should die, because we can't hear a distant cry!

Eric Charles Green

Brother

In December
I'm open like a walnut.
Once the seed has fallen from the tree,
Who will treasure it?

On the frigid January nights
I lie on the floor
Too cold and too tired to take my shoes off.
Bald heart, a night removed from my brother.

In February I am
singing like an Angel.
Warm and shoeless, I swoon over you.
Brother, ageless and unknown, I am with you.

David Cho

What Age Would You Be

Have you ever been asked what age you would be
If you could be any age you wanted to be?

If you find the present easy or hard
Would you want to be young and have a guard?

Someone to watch over you while you played
And when you were ill, to come to your aid.

Or would you be older and just starting life
On your own, filled with joy and strife?

Would you go back to a time less hurried
When living was easier and you weren't worried

About where the money came from or where it went
And you didn't care how fast it was spent?

Back to a time when radio reigned supreme
And a dime-store novel helped you to dream

Of places to go and things to see
And people to meet for afternoon tea.

Or would you stay the age that you are?
I would, now that I've gotten this far.

If I could be any age that I wanted to be,
I'd be the age that belongs to me.
Doris Upchurch

Going On, Because

Because, bird sing and trees dance
  I'll Go On.
Because, children laugh and elders sigh
  I'll Go On.
Because, of whippoorwills and cold frost chills
  I'll Go On.
Wind of strength blow cares away
the Lord does walk beside
I am meek, but still his child
with nothing I can hide.
No more hurt, pain or sorrow
praying for a new tomorrow,
  I'll Go On.
  STOP!
    What is this?
"My" child's sweet and tender kiss
because, of all that I would miss...
  I'll Go On!
Bambi Joy Shine

Mothers Touch

Night falls and she whispers go to sleep, Mama's here your grace I'll keep. Through the cuts and bruises, and skinned knees. Countless hours of walking in the cool breeze.
My son, my son she cries and scurries, seems like a thousand times of frantic worries. Oh what if he dies, I won't forgive myself. She looks at the second hand of the clock hits twelve. The years have gone by but you learn to trust. A mothers will you know you must. A dreaded heart disease often fatal, yet treated with respect it needed not be cradled. He has had that handicapped since the early years and she's watched him grow to overcome his fears. The Lord had given him a gentle hand to clutch, to love and guide, a mothers touch.
Derrick Arincorayan

If You Are Not There

If you are not there on Judgement Day
I'll know you went the other way
For all the pain and suffering
As well as many other things
I could never bare the painful sting
That being away from you would bring
And just so you know what I would do
I would go to Hell for you
Because I couldn't live without you
This can not mean that we are forever through
I realize that from now on we can never be
But can't you see just what this is doing to me?
Casey Coble

When I Have Time

When I have time I heard her say, I'll watch the children as they play
I'll look around not straight ahead, at corporate challenges I dread
I'll break the glass and scale the wall, then finally I'll have it all
Giving my heart to tender care, lighting fires that linger bare
I'll laugh and dance and not forget to fulfill the needs I've left unmet.
Believing that she knew it all I watched her rise in silent awe

So bittersweet the news today, the sand ran out and washed away
As she descends into the ground, the die is cast I'll wear her crown
But remembering the words she said about how years and minutes fled
A simple smile, a gentle touch, the little things that mean so much
The sunrise setting on a distant shore, a falling star, a lover's snore
I won't forget my inner dreams, balancing out the frantic scheme
So just relax and ease your mind, I'll do it all when I have time
Betsy Ramsey

Last Words To A Friend

I'll miss your hearty laughter and the sparkle in your eyes.
I'll miss your loving advise so insightful and so wise.
I'll miss our conversations and all the time we've shared.
I'll miss your open, giving heart and the ways you showed you cared.
Thank you for your time, it meant the world to me.
Thank you for all you taught me and your candid honesty.
Thank you for your laughter when I was feeling down,
you always put a smile on my face where once I had a frown.
When you reach the pearly white gate and come face to face with
  the Maker,
let Him know you lived your life as a giver and not a taker.
If He happens to give you a test, when it comes to friends, tell Him
  you were the best.
Oh, my loving caring friend they say all good things must come to an end.
I'll hold the memories close to my heart as you pass the final test.
Good-bye my closet, dearest friend it is time for you to rest.
Once the gates are open and you enter life ever after, save a place
  for me,
I'll follow the echo of your laughter.
Dymphna O'Connor

My Valentine

The moment that we met
In a dream so far away
I found my sun within your eyes
And skies of blues and greys
I watched as all my hopes an dreams
Went dancing on your smile
That's when I got down on my knees
And asked to stay awhile
And though we've grown throughout the years
Our hearts now live entwined
It was at that first moment
You became my Valentine....
Daniel Ford

To Become

I'll never know where until I'm there
I'll never know why until I die.

All I want is to become
But in my mind it can't be done.
We fly, we try and try
And then we die.

The wind blows hard against my face,
I beg to be taken to a different place...
Sometimes I feel love in my heart
Not knowing what to say or where to start.

I'm up against the dark, I'm losing it all.
I sit here waiting as my dreams are fading.
I see no light, I must take flight.
I keep on trying cause I know I'm dying.

I want so much that I can't touch
As happiness and love, but that's asking too much...
When I die, where will I go?
I'll be dead, that much I know.
There will be a dawn when I'm gone
Remember me.

Ario Cibas

Memories Of Yesterday

I'd like to sit and write a poem" I'll write about yesterday.
I'll write about many simple things" like playing in the hay.
I'll write about poppa's chicken coup painted all white inside.
I'll write about many happy things like when I
Played a tool sharpener" was my ride.
I remember when I played back then" there were many games to play.
Poppa had the hay stack piled so high "I loved playing in the hay.
Poppa didn't mind at all" to see me having fun.
I'd climb all the way up to the top "I'd roll back
Down and away I would run.
Poppa had a rooster he had named "Bandie you see"
Whenever he saw that I was there" around the yard he would chase me."
I remember going to sleep at night" I couldn't wait
Till morning came" to run back out into our yard"
And play my happy games...

Angelina Paone Hurd

Somewhere In The Silence

Somewhere in the silence I've been longing for you.
I'm not going to be asking-those days are through,
Because somewhere in the silence I'm not thought about by you.
I've learned I'm not so hard to love and my
Intentions are only good
But somewhere in the silence I've been
Misunderstood.
Your time is so precious, of this you've made so clear.
"Everyone" wants your presence and loves to have you near.
Somewhere in the silence I hold on to the fear
That "Everyone" will always
Be more dear.
While all the others needs are met you've forgotten the one
who loves you best.
But my love goes the distance and this I know is true
That somewhere in the silence I'll always be waiting for you.

Joni Derwingson

Forgive And Forget

To forgive and to forget is said to be divine.
I'm not sure it is.
I know you wish that I would forgive you.
To forget what you did.
But I can't.

Forgiveness is for sweet, innocents.
Not me.
I lost my innocence a long time ago.
But that is already known.

To forget is impossible.
The memories are burned into my brain.

To forgive and to forget is a wish that never comes true.
To forgive and to forget is a dream never reached for.
To forgive and to forget what you did is a miracle that God
    can't do.

Audrey M. True

Patiently Waiting

Lights out again another day is done,
I'm patiently waiting for that long-away one.

When I finally leave this God-awful place,
when the sweet smell of freedom
flows to my face.

I look up at the fence,
at the razor wire,
I feel the burning inside,
my heart is on fire.

The flame is running through mind, body, and soul,
I curse myself often for losing control.

I've broken the law, for that I now pay,
still I'm patiently waiting
for that long-away day...

Jeffrey Dare

Endlessly

Blue seas comfort me, whispering in my ear the joys of life.
I'm surrounded by this endless blue. Crystal clear, mysterious
and powerful.
Sometimes enraged, sending mountains of liquid glass to crash.
Men and women rush to the challenge to ride your immense
walls of water.
With their flimsy guns, they're paddling and racing for that
Never ending ride of exhilaration that is unexplainable to those
who fear you.
Yet sometimes you're calm, inviting, very tame.
The treasures you hold are gifts only God could bless us with.
The predator, the prey, the coral reefs, the giant mammal, the
humble turtle glides by.
I realize the ocean is Gods greatest creation and here I am in
the middle of it, endlessly.

Jamesy U. Gonsalves

The Kitten

In the fall the kitten plays in the leaves.
In the winter, he plays in the snow.
In the summer, he plays with the butterflies.
In the spring, he plays with the flowers.
But when the sun sets,
The kitten shuts his eyes and rests,
Dreaming about the leaves, the snow,
The butterflies, the flowers,
But most of all,
The time when he's no longer a kitten,
But a cat.

Emily Meyer

A Measure Of It

His pains hang inside him
in a bag on a string on a hook in his brain.
Every time he thinks too hard
about his dream thrown life, he gets a pain.
No....he gets a rush of pains. Inside his head he squeals softly
until the bag settles and he can glide again.
He walks that way, glides to appease the bag. It works, mostly.

Once he tried to float the damn thing
in the clean burn of ten thousand Smirnoff labels.
it wouldn't float, just go wet.
Wet pain hurts more than any dying thing.
And dying he wasn't, dreaming to, but not.

He makes his good dreams pay out, tho.'
A very high percentage, anyway.
The ones that don't, they go in the bag.
The overflow from that thing
would kill a couple of bankers on the wing,
a stock clerk and a ballplayer or so.

When they shut his music off
Nobody'll be able to dance with that bag. Nobody.

Jon VanNess

I Have Not Left

I have not left I am in the beauty all around,
in brilliant colors of fall,
in clouds that roll by,
a wild flower, in any field,
in a snow flake, that softly fell,
in mountains that are high,
The feeling of a breeze,
in rain drops to fall a cheek,
rustling leaves from a tree,
most of all, I'm in the heart,
even if I must depart.

Ethel Beuhler

The Moth

As a moth is drawn by a fire,
in fascination to its bright light.
It is consumed by the burning intensity
that has enticed it from it flight

It occurs to me on loves occasion
to a moth I can compare.
For I am drawn by the alluring persuasion
to love if only I dare

Loves eye glow a soft invitation
they beckon warmly, come and see
all the mysteries contained and reflected there in
she soon would reveal to me

My desire to share in her secrets
compels me to brave the bright heat
of the flames of love that cause two hearts.
To ignite and burn with one beat.

Glenn D. Johnson

"Silent Regard"

Last night, for just a moment, I stood in from the barn,
in the capitol moonlight, gazing out towards the pond.
Nothing could have seemed more passionately frozen,
more a moment in the Creator's perfect plan.
All else about me, too, seemed still,
deft field and distant stand of pine,
lying frozen in the rich, unshaken air,
to the selfsame, moonlit absence of sound.
Everything there reminded me of a tiger's grace
that my son and I had read of, one summer's night.

David J. Marcou

Citizen Of Tomorrow

Citizen of tomorrow,
In my class this year
Beckoning to learning's call
In a voice so clear.

You depend on me to be your guide,
Your instructor, counselor, and friend;
To awaken your talents and inspire your thoughts
As a means unto an end.

I'll give to you the very best
Of all I have and know;
Then guide you carefully along
As you seek to learn and grow.

The things you'll learn
Will help you build a foundation firm and strong,
To help you solve life's challenges
On the paths you walk along.

So, citizen of tomorrow,
In my class this year,
Make every moment count
For tomorrow is very near!

Arlene Hobaugh

Winter Time

I just can hardly wait for spring
In my heart all the loveliness it brings
The out of doors I shall walk and talk
To strangers all along.

Feel the grass so green upon my feet and
Between my toes to clean the mud
That has warped my soul.
All these winter days.

The snow comes from East and South
and then back again,
In another direction the North wind blows.
It tears my soul.

Grace Wohlenhaus

The United States Of America

Fifty magnificent states!
In my heart how high it rates!
One country with beauty all around
And where you find freedom does abound,
Freedom to worship and to express
All our feelings, more than you can guess,
Seas, mountains, lakes, and rivers galore,
Wheatfields, corn, fruit trees growing and more.
Beautiful scenery everywhere
God gave us this land and made it fair.
How I appreciate this great land,
Created by God's powerful hand!
Red, white, and blue — our colors so true!
They mean liberty for me and you!

Ernestine Green

"You'll Never Know"

You were not always there for me
In my heart its just the same
No matter what people say
You were never to blame

I wish I could've seen you more than I did
But I guess it was for the best
You worked all day and worried all night
But you didn't love me any less

I looked up to you
You're everything I wanted to be
Believe it or not Dad,
I loved you more than you could see

I just hope that when the day comes
Whoever first leaves
I want you to know....

Dad, I know you love me
I just knew it was true
You never have to say it
Because I could see it shinning through
Dad, I have always loved you too!

Brian L. Wyatt

My World

In the world I see, beyond and below me
In the air I breathe, polluted and impure
In the grounds I hear, whispers and shouts,
grieves and more.
The flames of fire in your eyes makes me wanted to cry
All sadness of blues, all blames are not to you but me
Seeing the world fall down right under my nose
Dosing off to the grave and being the Devil's slave
Hidden in a dark cave, knowing no one will be save
No thing will be alive;
Like a spell or a curse, a shell which cannot be burst
My world in flames of fire - drifting off and far away
Watching it like a movie or game.

Farmmary C. Saephan

Windows In Heaven

Have you ever wondered about the stars?
In the sky at night, as they glow?
From up above
Could it just maybe, be windows in Heaven?
For which the Angels, to watch us, with heartache.
And love.
You know some stars, are brighter then others
And I have often wondered, could it be so?
The star is a window in Heaven and what we see is,
the Angels glow,
Sometimes at night when something wet hits,
And we just pass it off as the on coming dew.
I wonder, could it be an Angel?
Crying, from the window, in Heaven, over?
Me and you?
So the next time you watch, the stars, in the sky at night,
Are they stars, or windows in Heaven who's? To know?
But maybe if you look hard enough,
you just might see, a face looking
back at you from out of the glow.

Jimmy M. Franco

Spring Is Here!

The abnormal red diamond danced
  in the sky cutting the wind.
The kid below hung on tight to the umbilical
  cord-like attachment.
His feet were sunk into the yellowing field
  making squishy sounds.
In the woods to the left were white trilliums
  popping up.
From the shack to the right came the smell of maple
  syrup cooking that filled the air.
The sun caressed the boy with love, until
  suddenly it faded away and incessant rain fell.
The kid reeled in the kite and ran home
  causing worm tunnels to their homes to collapse.

Becky Oertel

Plaint Against Civilization

We force ourselves into a set mold,
Inch by inch against nature.
We follow the path civilization has worn.
Cutting off some part that doesn't fit.
Stretching here to fill some corner
Until we find ourselves as others want us.

Warped and missing things cut from our lives,
Dissatisfied and disappointed Beings,
We look back over the way we have come.
Wishing we had grown as nature intended,
Had had a little more courage to fight for our course,
And the fortitude to stand for what we truly believe.

Some few mortals escape this mark of civilization,
Have the courage to stand for their convictions
Regardless of the opinions of others,
Live up to the mark of human perfection
Of which most of us are capable
Could we but throw off the tyranny of our friends.

Icil Anne Parks

"Letter To An Angel"

Dear Mother,
  I'm writing to an Angel in Heaven where its always fair,
today down here is Mother's Day and I wish I were with you
up there.

  I'll get down your sweet faded picture and your Bible all
ragged and old, but today in my Heart my Darling Mother,
you are as bright to me as new gold.

Dear Mother,
  I long once more to see your gentle bright smiling face,
and I long to hold you once more in my arms, and to feel your
tender embrace.

My Dear Mother,
  I'll follow your teaching, and each day to Jesus I'll
pray and who knows, I may be with you Dear Mother next year
on Mother's Day.

Bessie L. Howard

He Is A Good Man (My Grand Father)

If a good man lives a good life and gives praises and thanks to his creator.
From the beginning; Since he remembered, the good man has been offended
First from his color, by his age and then numbers.
But, having lived a good life, this good man chooses a wife.
The good man along with his wife has watched his seed multiply.
And as the years have past, multiplying is just what his seed has done.
The good man seemed to be happy and content,
   by the way his life had went.
But then the day came when the good man was left in a lot of pain.
The wife he'd chosen had passed on leaving him the seeds which they
   had produced and a good name.
As these seeds continued to multiply and multiply into great numbers,
   in which you had add and even divide.
Being lead in the right direction, giving praises and thanks to his GOD.
   And this good man and his good life was called to join his wife.
He must enter through the pearly white gates, with nothing but his
   soul, his love and his faith.
Having live to be one hundred and five, with no doubt he live
   a good life.
Just look around and you will see the multiplication of the good man's seed.
This is truly a good man, a great man indeed.

Donnie R. Andrews

"My Prayer"

"Yesterday brought discouragement, I felt cornered and in despair".
"I wanted to pray and repent, but it didn't seem God heard my prayer."
"I tried to tell him my feelings, that things weren't alright inside"
"As if the didn't already know, there were things I'm still trying to hide!

"I thought on my plight for a while, how to handle the hurt I didn't know,"
"I wanted him to forgive me, things I done to worry him so!"
"I'd lived my life just thinking, that God really was every where,"
"And the things I'd often done wrong, He'd cover for me up there,"

"Then it dawned on me how unfair I'd been, my life I had tossed away!"
"And when I really need him, not thinking its going to come its going to come a day!"
"All my friends had left without notice, to parts all over the Earth,"
"I know of no one to turn to, and my life of despair grew worse!"

"My heart cries out within me, I try to live each day at a time",
"If only I could get right with God, and break this spell on my mind!"
"For some day I know I must meet him", and confess I threw that rock,"
"And I'll lay down my cross and go with him, for I want him my heart to unlock!

"I want to Sing Praises and shout Hallaya!
"I want Angels to lift me above!
"I want to tell all my friends when I see them"!
"How Jesus died and saved me with love"!

Helen Turner

Time

I'm not afraid of Judgment Day, even when the mist lies cold in the
fields; I will come running on that Last Day and when the sun is up,
the path of justice will run as broad and golden as the Pilgrim's Way.

I shall always lift up mine eyes to the hills, where dwells that
everlasting City, however far I roam, travelling the paths of all the
world until the daffodils and the first brave crocus,
are bidding me come home.

What is over that hill? Has the jay or lark sung there?
Have primroses the next spring's golden gossip spread?
Or is it all so new that no blossom glistens there?
Are the seasons yet to be established?

Right here when the green leaf crumbles, when the birds have ceased
to sing and the robin's gone, it is no valiant dream, but life itself
that tramples down the dark avenues, and passes on.

A swallow cannot hold back time, even for an hour, nor anything but
naked fact prevail, for you cannot fight the future with a flower,
nor halt redemption with a nightingale.

Andy Marshall

"Tattoo"

A rose tattoo adorned her breast
A bold co-worker "let us see",
And in queasy fascination
I looked and thought," not me".

Well all the girls were talking
Each had her point of view.
Then things got kinda heavy,
Somewhat depressing too...

So to lighten up the moment
I asked them all in jest
If they thought maybe I could get
Some t**s'tood on my chest?!

Deborah Morgan

Reflections

The snow is gently falling
a chill is in the air
you're in my thoughts again
and I wish that you were here

I remember all the good times
the laughter and the fun
But memories are all I have
and I wonder where you've gone

If I could find my way to you,
would you feel the same?
Would you take me in your arms,
and gently speak my name?

Or would you turn away
and leave me as before
with the memories I cherish
and the closing of the door

Another night is ending
The darkness turns to dawn
You're in my thoughts again
And you will be from now on

Carolyn McCullough

Poem

Its a Westmont home located on
   a corner lot which is fine
and its priced at a whopping $299,900
Three bedrooms - two baths
   and a huge family room too
Its an older home that looks fairly new
A lock box is located on
   the front door
As you enter a screeching
   Parrot gives you "what - for"
Its been freshly painted and
   has great curb appeal
So lets get together and
   make a deal
As you can see poetry
   is not my forte
So show it and sell it
   and make my day!

Evelyn C. Hoppy

A Voice Not Wanting

Here I will lay, and here will they find me without words for my
escape. My staring nearing blue and my eyes nearing. A clenched hand
and another refusing as I pass an unsettling glare. Too real to be
fashionable, and cloth that cries a dirty tear. Too week to stand
and too awake to speak. Here I rest and work and play, left to mingle
with a reprimanding cage that raises a finger to its detest. Fear for
nothing, pity for everything. Focused on a dot ending in a sphere.
The curvature of a triangle leads me astray. And a voice with sting
in an open field trying to reach a language I cannot speak. To my
dear, fair thee spear, a net or a fish two times returned from its end
And in these lines of endless pursuit I find no end. To a
conversation turned comfortable and a shade of red turned familiar.
The flickering of the day runs like disappointments brought together
over families distances away. And here I lie too close to the ground
to be noticed but too high to want. And still the sun burns my image
onto the ground with each passing mark. And thus if follows that an
empty hat brings no joy to a gentleman that flaunts it from his head
to passing pedestrians each to each alike but to himself familiar. In
my verticality I close my eyes and stare and here I can see myself
lying, and an empty hat on a blue and white day scaring its owner away
waiting to be found.

Andres Hecker

Remembering Mama

Now I lay me down to sleep/I learned those words at Mama's feet.
I said them daily as I did grow/Mama made sure my head I'd bow.
And as I grew she still would say,/"Now make sure to talk to God today."
I sometimes seemed it was a chore/sometimes I thought, "Oh what a bore
God won't miss my prayer tonight/So I'd just crawl in bed and curl up tight.
I knew it was myself I fooled/And I was listening to the way of the world
Then I turned myself around/and got back on safer ground.
As time went by we had a child/And, in just a little while
It was time to teach those words again/So with words so careful and greatest pain
The words came freely and from the heart/For Mama's words never did depart.
And as they grew I'd always say,/"Make sure you talk to God today."
Then when Mama laid so ill/It seemed I could hear those words, still
I thought of the worlds Mama used to say,/"Now, make sure you talk to God today."
Oh, how my heart ached as she searched my eyes/She knew I didn't want to cry.
I held her hand so very tight/That always seemed to make things right,
She whispered, "Please don't wish for me to say./Just be sure you talk to God each day
Now Mama's gone, the children grown/I still pray the prayer I've always known.
And when I ask the Lord to bless us all/And never from His grace to fall,
Bless us as we work and play-and/Help us remember to talk to God each day.

Donna M. Poyet

The Peach Rose

The first time I laid my eyes on it, 'twas growing in my neighbors
garden, fresh and beautiful, with such a wonderful scent, reaching out
to possess me. I was filled with envy and desire, wanting to
transplant, but my ground was starting to harden. Could I attempt to
revive the one I had growing or wasn't it meant to be.

The other gardener let mine and his be together from time to time,
they became close, I didn't mind, only hoping to enjoy and be near.
By now your wondering if flowers are really the subject of my rhyme.
Sensing my desire, he took his rose and moved far away, would I see
  again was my fear

The closeness of mine and his, allowed me the joy of nearness once again.
When in his garden, his was wilting, no water or fertilizer, or very much care.
Could I revive if mine, with love and tenderness, and would it be such a sin.
I would give up mine to watch his bloom, anytime or anywhere.

Finally his started blooming in my garden, all that I had I did give.
Such a wonderful sight to see, the petals opening to receive the sun everyday.
Before this Peach Rose came into my life, I had very little desire to
live, would it really be mine forever or simply wilt again and die away.

Time will only tell, the rest of the story, still yet to unfold,
Would the Peach Rose continue to bloom and grow in my garden,
or will it want to grow somewhere else, where the ground is filled with gold,
or someone else's desire cause them to steal, not caring about it or even my pardon.

John Nichols

Mother's Day Prayer

Dear Lord, we thank you for sending someone so dear;
for without her contribution we would not be here.

The character that you have instilled in a mother's heart;
makes us feel alone when we are far apart.

Mothers nurture, care and share their love;
just as you do from the heavens above.

Mothers intercede lending a helping hand;
Why that's their nature; don't yoo understand?

She always wants the best for her children in life;
so fervently she prays they will choose what is right.

Without a mother to tend and care for her babe;
we would find ourselves wrapped in an early grave.

So, Lord, we thank thee for this very special day;
to give tribute to our mothers in a mighty, mighty way.

Amen.

Judith A. Drummond

preface to migration

shells have gathered
in your ears,
bringing the sea
and i wait, patiently,
for you to fly.
apprehension
clings to your voice:
the lilacs haven't
thought of blooming,
yet.
we continue
the ritual: every day,
we eat tangerines together,
growing older in the sun.
soon, you will discern the evocation
of migration
and in twilight, body tilted
towards luring landscapes,
you will breathe the possibility
of new lives.

Areti Georgopoulos

Heaven Sent

I,
Wrote a letter to heaven,
Addressed to God up above,
asking him to please send me
A special lady to love;

But an angel opened the letter first,
and she began to cry,
It wasn't the words that I had written,
It was the love, I had sealed inside.

"Lord I promise to love her,
Like no one else,
and cherish her love,
the love you send from heaven above."

After she finished the letter,
The angel showed the Lord above,
He than granted me my wish,
and now! I'm so deeply in love.

Byron Brown

Enter The Light

Quantum caverns
caked and choked

Desolate spaces
undifferentiated and dry

Eyes blank
bemused and blind

Hearts desires
halting and heavy

Enter the Light
lavish and loving

Caverns
coalesce and create

Spaces
differentiate and delight

Eyes
blink and behold

Hearts desires
happen

Eileen McGowan

Tears For Tomorrow

Thirsting for knowledge
The hands of time
Fill my hourglass
And
Slipping thru the empty void
The crystal grains become
Salty tears of pain.

Darcianne M. Ernce

Prayer for the Quickening

Dear God,
Help my eyes to be open
Aid my ears to hear
Assist me in recognizing
The things I should hold dear

Let my hands fly open
Show my arms to swing away
Allow my breath to spit outward
The garbage I might hold on to today

For my life is a journey of assessment
What would you approve or reject
Please grace me with the insight
To live and love as you expect.

David J. Boswell

The Photo

It's just a photo that I hold
a memory I can touch
with my hands, my heart
I reach for you every night
and every morning whisper your name
of course you cannot hear me
at least not with your ears
but somehow just in saying your name
and staring at out smiling eyes together
my heart feels warm and comforted
with just this photo to hold.

Julie Speight

Kittens

A kitten
A ball
Together they play.
Brown, black,
White and grey.
Colors here
Colors there
Kittens kittens everywhere.
Playful ones
Shy ones
Sleepy ones
Sly ones
All kinds of different ones.
Big, fat, skinny ones
Short, hairy, lazy ones.
Kittens here
Kittens there
Kittens kittens everywhere.

Brianna Mendoza

Winter's Dance

The snowflakes performed
 a ballet in the air.
Their white toes pivoted in time
 with the tune of
  the winter's breeze.
They swirled with the
 rhythm of the wind.
They leaped,
 they looped,
  they spun,
   they tip-toed in space.
They danced until they became
 outstretched upon the earth
  and gracefully melted
   after their performance
    while the audience
     visioned with awe.

Beverly A. Hopkins

Indomitable Man

What hath God wrought?
A basket full of stars flung
by a mighty hand;
against a flannel graph
of black and blue.

Agreed, but what of man
and his new star that knows,
the earth by a slender span?
Man's satellite may stub its toe,
as others things of man can do.

But man will dust his star,
spin it back heavenward,
to search eternity's hue.

Gladys L. Britt

Untitled

A single tear, a broken praise.
A heart that cannot mend.
A half-felt smile, and hollow laughter.
A life-time without a friend.
A ray from the sunshine;
hair tossing in the wind.
A lost and lonely soul -
wishing for the end.

Connie Meadows

The Darkness Within

Stuck between collapsing walls
A darkness from within me calls
Thorny, spiny weeds have grown
In place of all I've loved and known.
Those things are distant memories
Hell is now a part of me
Living under darkened skies
I watch the world through cloudy eyes
Surviving in a world of doom
This body has become my tomb
Like all good things that once were mine,
The sun's bright rays now make me blind
Stripped of all I've cared about
I now have learned to live without
I understand the word "alone"
The dreary side of life is shown
Living in nightmarish dreams
I hear the echo of my screams
Bouncing off these canyon walls
As the darkness from within me calls.

Amanda Davis

Ye Flower

Beneath a shadow of pain
a Flower lays in a grave yard
cry's in a painful way such
as the one of Love,
No one to look for, no one to hug,
only the one in the grave yard.

Crying thy most beautiful love,
tide up in the chains of pain,
Drown in the tears of love,
although there's no one to look for
no one to hug
only the one in the grave yard

She's ye Flower that lays beneath a shadow
She's ye Flower that sleeps in a grave yard.

I cry but I won't forget
ye Flowers love.

juan gonzales

Forever My Love And I

Sweet love who came from nowhere
A gift from paradise
You brought a timeless wonder
No words could yet describe

But oh how short the visit
And oh how long the pain
And how the memory lingers
Like sunshine in the rain

And though the days have flown away
On wings of solitude
The sweetness of the memories shared
Are like a warm prelude

But never a moment lost
And never a day goes by
For we walk in the shadow of time and space
Forever my love and I

Doreen Naser

Nearly Autumn

In the backyard
 A gate opens
To the winter garden

Claudia Van Dyke

Grace

Grace is fine lace
A gift to lift
One's face to pace
The race now won
To God's Son...

Grace is freely givin'
For the livin' not for sinin'
Grace's to be drivin'
By Spirit-Breath not by demon-death!
Grace can be merited!
Even inherited!
Grace can not not be learned,
Easily spurned, readily discerned!
It can only be earned
  By a sweet
    "Yes"
      To God
        Nothing "Less!"
    Albert P. Boettcher

Four Days

A needed friend or buddy
A hand to hold, a smile to give,
Someone to warm wounds of heart
and body.
Attention to get, acceptance to
give,
Had been too long to walk alone.
Though Four Days can not lie to the
want,
In boat or field...
  Betty Rogers

Sweet Wine

Gushing from the vine
a healing, sweet wine.
"Healing the one way,"
we who are healed say.

"It's finished!" was cried.
It slumped and then died.
"Forsaken but why?"
"Your will God, but why?"

The vine lives today
and again we say,
"Healing the one way,
yes, for you this day."

God's son is the vine.
His blood is sweet wine.
So, today believe
and healing receive.

"Though you die today
you'll live," he did say,
"with Me forever
Die again? Never."
  Dewey E. Williamson

The Smoking Lip

A poorly rolled cigarette.
A random flicker from a lit pipe.
Has consumed the hairy forest.
Down to the last follicle.
Exposing a naked and weak mouth.
  Bradley S. Tice

Performance

Little tyke, jumping
  A hop, skip and twirl.

With impish smile
  And eyes dancing.

Small one, flinging
  Arms up, down, around,

With legs pumping
  And skirt in a swirl.

Little tyke showing
  That talent abounds,

Reaches for hand clinging
  And ends in crumpled pile.
  Georganne G. Tiemann

Roses Are Lovers

A rose among others.
A king among brothers.
Scarlet red roses.
That tickle the noses.

Endless achievement.
Imagination's conceivement.
A rose of achievement.
Makes a king of a peasant.

These roses are rare.
Like a Unicorn Mare.
But still can be there.
By imaginations' flare.

A king among brothers.
When he finds his lover.
Above all the others.
He soars and he flutters.

A king among brothers.
He forgets all his bothers.
Sees all the worlds lovers.
And becomes a rose among others.
  Jorge L. Rivera

"Mother"

The many heartaches
a mother holds
within her heart
will one day experience
the sacrifice
to be paid,
Her many prayers
have kept her working
at her daily tasks
as God has held
her true to Him
free of doubt
free of sin;
Yes, a mother
knows within her heart
there is a place to hide her fears,
a place to store
her quantity of tears.
She's a Mother!
  Dorothy E. Cedarleaf

To A Mother

To a person, I will always love and dear
A person that times I fear,
But a person that will always be there
A person that knows my life
A person will be there in strife Mom
I remember, the Chinese
Laundry you went every week
So that I could be clean and neat.
Things sometimes wasn't peaceful
But you made it glow and meaningful.
If I marry and she carry my name
Nothing will ever change
you will always be my main-squeeze
  Barney Wayne Vardell

Untitled

Lost in a world of make belief,
a place where my heart can get relief.
From which the pain that I bare,
I can not hide it any where.
It seems to hold on and follow me,
causing misery for every one to see.
For when I try to fight this pain,
there seems to be a massive rain.
running down my aching face,
and off I go to this make believe place.

Thinking of you and all I have done,
wishing I laid here with a gun.
To pierce a bullet threw my head,
left in life to be known as dead.
All the misery and agonizing pain,
stored in my heart to finally drain.
Easing my mind from lost control,
and saving the remains of my puzzled soul.
  James Thomas Williams

Rejection

Rejection is an under view
A reality oversight
People and their strong
Minds and thick wallets
Break under pressure
Known as rejection.

Except for the bums, tramps
And the losers who
Know the meaning of
Rejection
It's not to put away
Just to put down.

Rejection is the evil twin of love.
It lurks in everyone's heart.
It lives in stuck up noses
And under four hundred
Dollar suits.
It lies in a race that deals
With matter not thought
money, not life.
  Josh Holmes

Nymphette

She says she has a ghost in her body
A saturn of horses
Feathering in the forest
Standing long on her white bones
Lightening gassing across the trees
Waiting for the charge of weather
Horses and horns enough to panic the heart
Blind the eye
The nymphette trembles
To blood foreign ghosts
Through her loins
Into the hammock lap of fear
Set for her
To lie in
To expose herself up to
To spread herself for
For she is the hosting
She is the home.
David Brooks

Known Of Wild

Brazen knight, the moon of dark,
A shadowy, form with liquid fire
That of the ball of gleaming spark
With night ere high, the graceful crier
Who deems the wolf is worthy of play
Beckons through golden moonlight
Over plains molded by carried wind of clay
The fronds of the earth obscure the light
Bemoaning whispers sworn from end to end
A prevalence of surmised great
To shorn upon the known wild's bend
A softer fly of wooden straight
Make upon the stones great form
A moss of greener tone to lay
Upon its moonshined gleam it now worn
And wield its weapon may
To the sigh that lack not of night
Nor the handsome facade of moon
Given a tail sky glorious flight
Entrance to nature's womb.
Julie DeMorier

My Sister's Shadow

Looking back in time
A sister of mine I envied.

When we were together,
people always noticed,
how beautiful and lovely she was
while I lingered in her shadow,
forgotten...

It has been difficult for me,
to love this sister of mine.

But she was not to blame,
if people can be so mean.

As we grew up, I had to accept,
hearing it so many times...
that she was better than me.

Because I was never good enough,
for anyone to notice me.

And so I stay, lingering...
in my sister's shadow.
Giovannie Monica Eugenio

Cold Dark Night

On a cold dark October right,
A small child was full of fright.
Taken from her soft warm bed,
she never knew what lay ahead.

Hair of gold, eyes of blue.
Taken by someone she knew.
We can only guess what she went through.

She went to heaven that cold dark right.
While we all searched by the days new light.

She was a child of only four,
when death came walking through her door.
She's an angel now, no one can hurt
  her anymore.
Betty Jane Sabol

Coping

I did not know until too late
A son was of a different fate.

His loving, caring ways would be
For too long the same, same mate.

This dreaded and feared way of life
May take this precious, precious life.

In years to come I will try
To be a loving caring hope to he.

If God prevails and takes his hand
And helps nurse him back to health.

To live on earth far quite a spell
And live his life as he will.

Ever thankful will I be
To know that he is finally free.
Justine Walker

Love Letters

And he played to his lover,
a song for her to enjoy.
A pen his flute,
Words his band.

Across the page they danced.

With shouts and laughter,
they curl and twist.
Spinning a song of love,
singing the song of his soul.
John Caldwell

"I Stopped To Think"

I stopped to think yesterday
about the people that are working today,
women bearing but working too,
men drilling, singing, sculpting too,
but when you think about this, women too!
When I stopped to think yesterday
about the people that are working today
it gave me a clue that maybe
God is a woman too!
Jennifer S. Blair

Hats

The caveman was the first to wear
a square of fur upon his hair.
Next the Greeks with rings of flowers,
others chose hats that looked like towers.
Cone shaped hats and some of lace,
stove-pipe hats were a fellows grace.

Berets of wool, by both were worn,
to top the head and keep it warm.
A fine cloth print was Grandma's bonnet,
stiffly starched with ruffles on it.
Hats of velvet, silk and leathers
adorned with flowers, fruit and feathers.

Special hats were for Easter Day
as ladies paraded to church to pray.
Many refused an old hat to part,
but a new one helped a troubled heart.
Again the hats are being worn,
the perfect shape to the head adorn.
Hats are really here to stay,
used for church, work and play.
Charlene Patterson

Untitled

When I look into the heavens at night,
  a star shines
  a moon glows
  a sky deepens

White to
  yellow to
    orange to
     red to
      dusk to
       dark

My heart slows
the day slips away

Cares float
  disappear

I search the sky
  and I am there:
   I am that star, moon, sky
   the colors of the twilight

I am in the heavens
David Doty

Space Love

You set my heart on fire
A super nova explosion
The birth of a new love
Still after all these crazy years.

Burnin' up in my atmosphere
you've got my stars fall in like rain
My brains are cloudy and unclear
must be love or there's
been a nuclear blast inside there.

Oh can't have this feelin' alone to long
N- listening to your so pretty love song.

Groping in loves deepest space
Longing for a and friend
Sun shining billions of degrees
But quickly dies without
your smiling face.
Jack Lane

Awakening River

I am thirsty - parched and lifeless
A Tearless Rut

Dark Cloud rising - murky dusk
A drop falls

Roaring through my soul
Overflowing my banks
Refusing to ebb the tide

Yielding to His current
Submitted to the stream
Swept by His Spirit

In this fluid flux
Obstacles pervade
Rigid Rocks of Reason persuade

Stones of Suggestion slung
Pelting Preponderant flung
Spirits pressing - trying

Discovering the Peaceful Ford
Beneath Foolish Falls
Pools of Compassion form

Brad Francis

God's Little Flower Garden

I looked upon my tiny child.
   A thought reminded me of a flower bud.
To think that she would blossom forth.
   To brighten my heart,
And bring joy for years to come.
   But alas this was for naught.
God sent his angel gathering.
   For the garden up above,
And there she will remain.
   For God and all to see,
And when that day comes my way.
   I will see her there,
And she will never fade away.
   For in God's care.
Her beauty will remain for eternity.

David W. Gary

For Jennifer

Sitting in a lonely room
A thousand miles away
Wondering what I'm gonna do.
My soul is weary
And I think I've lost my way
But at least I know I still have you.

The LORD has called me
To a work I can't explain
Sometimes I doubt I know myself.
But which you beside me
Through the sunshine and the rain
We can do all things with His help.

Once in a lifetime that someone comes along
To help you through your struggles
And help to keep you strong.
I thank the LORD each day
That he brought you my way.
It's you and Jesus
That help me make it through the day.

Bryan Ready

The Thought In My Mind

A picture is worth
A thousand words
A dream leaves
A thousand thoughts
One can dream
And not think
And he can think
And not dream
A blind man may see better
Than a person
With perfect vision
Knowledge is the key
But power rules the world.

Billy Lewis

Anna Belle Beneath The Magnolia

Fish still jump in the stream,
A tire swings over the old hole,
It's rope and it periodically replaced,
And time never grows old.

In the pantry coffee is hot,
Pie cools on the window sill,
Peering out, mist appears,
As time silently stands still.

Straw flowered hat ragged not torn,
Clothed in homemade flour-sack frock,
You lie beneath the Magnolia tree,
The hands on the clock, stopped.

How on earth I wonder,
Could Time so deceive...
It was only yesterday, or today?
You laid beneath the Magnolia tree.

Years it seems, or only moments passed,
The pie lays mist before my eyes,
The youth, the love, so real, so fresh,
Beneath the magnolia still lies.

Johnny W. Piver Jr.

I'd Like To Be

I'd like to be
A unicorn
With a golden horn
That lived in an enchanted forest
I'd like to be
A little bee
Smelling beautiful flowers
With flying powers
And tasting sweet honey
I'd like to be
A mermaid under the sea
With Orcas to be my friends
And of course I'd never get the bends
I'd live among the coral
And toil with the fish
So to be what I'd like to be
I just set in a shady spot
And dream, just dream away.

Amanda Miller

Awakening Flame

Approaching with a mesmerizing step
a warming smile, a longing gaze
speaking boldly, passionately
arousing emotions
with a trembling, aching need

Bewitching, beautiful eyes
igniting passions that
carelessly brush my face
with tantalizing, energizing
craving, unbridled desire

Our spirits entwined
dancing, leaping fires
rising and falling
magnetizing
one last caress

Our rendezvous ending
on a satisfying smile
a sweet remembrance
simmering and waiting
as passion embers fade

George Edward Kimball

Light Phoenix

In dreams, I am Light Phoenix,
  A Warrior,
  A Hero,
  A Fighter,
  A Wizard,
  A Master of Animals;

In dreams, I live on a planet with no evil,
  No Pollution,
  No Wars,
  No Drugs,
  No Killing,
  No Hatred;

In dreams, I live with other creatures,
  Foxes,
  Dogs,
  Doves,
  A Phoenix,
  A Dragon,
  And Friends.

Brian Stanley

Refuge

On an island of its own
A weather-beaten house stands alone.
Nearby, a giant gnarled tree
Swoops nearer the house for company.
Mist swirls and hangs heavy there;
Gray moss and vines are everywhere.
The wind is well-known by this isle;
It lies calm but once in a while.
It slams the house and bends the tree
And whips the water angrily.
But inside the house is home
To the bent old man who lives alone.
The home is cheerful, warm and bright
With a leaping fire and twinkling light.
The tree leans closer on this lonely isle
While the mist is heavy and the wind is wild.

Ione M. Hargis

Vanity

How brief is beauty
a withered flower in a hand
Fleeting elegance
    cast down
Slipping silently and unknown
from finger's failing grasp to hold
And caught by earth's ensuing brown
it withers
    and fails
        and weeps upon the ground
For time record its final day
in a mirror
full of emptiness

Douglas B. Hirst

To Be A Human Being

A Mensch
A Womensch,
Capable of the Supreme Bench,
and the workplace,
whatever place,
she may desire,
to set afire,
to amaze,
how the blaze,
takes hold,
with the bold,
tickles their senses,
these mensches.

Harriet F. Rutchick

Am I Dreaming

I lie here awake, wondering
about what?
I do not know.

I can not understand death,
it happen's so fast, but why?

It comes and that's it.
Its like a gunshot to the head
bang bang and your dead

Will you ever wake up, maybe
in another life time
or just somewhere in between

I stare at the shadow on my wall,
making funny pictures out of it all
trying to understand its purpose
why is it there?
does it mean to be?

I look over my tape has ended
has my life? No I'm still here,
wondering like always,
I wonder am I dreaming?

Debra Webb

Untitled

Mellow moon, falling stars,
A touch of warmth held in your arms.
Reaching up, to share the light
Never knew the dawn that night.
Moving thimbles, wasted thread
And all the miles our lives have tread,
And all the miles our lives have tread.

Amelie Cooper Yonge

Justice

"Burden the Garden of
    Adam and Eve,"
        demanded the devil of God.
"It's their path to maturity."

It took a moment and,
    God said,
"Let me put magic in
    Mom's pie filling
And leave the tops of mountains
    to argumental ribs."

"And let it be forever by the process
    of killing,"
        suggested the devil, delighted.

"Wow," proclaimed God,
    in all his wisdom,
    Willing.

Junia Lorain Dubbs

The Monument

I stand,
Admonishing,
Amidst garden grasses
Vibrating with Summer rains.
Rekindled light reflects upon
One solitary bush,
Gracing my presence.
Forest-green leaves
Cup rose clusters of reposeful radiance.
Bluish blooms blossom into
Pale pink profusions of perfume,
Emitting fragrance,
Pulsating through my senses.
The power of thousands!
Yet, only one.
Alone in a forgotten garden
Neglecting not, its purpose
For being.

Jane L. Wiseman

True Love

He came to me in the late afternoon
After a whole lot of pain.
I found that he was well worth it
Especially as I saw he was perfect.
    My life began again.

I was so scared to become a mother,
A single one at that,
But after all was said and done,
I was where I was meant to be at.

I watch him sleep at night
And thank the Lord above.
He gave me the greatest blessing of a life...
    My one true love.

Callie A. Hartley

My Sister

You're my sister,
And all through the years,
You will always care,
No matter sad or mad,
You will always give and share.
And now I'm not young anymore,
And soon I'll be driving up to your door,
But I'll always be your sister.

Danielle Edgar

Choices Of Freedom

I can be free, you can be free.
All by God's divine decree.
Free to succeed, free to frail.
Free to be ignorant, free to be wise.
Free to love, free to hate.
Free to be good, free to be bad.
Free to be happy, free to be sad.
Free to be or not to be.
It's our own responsibility.
All by God's divine decree.

Edith L. Weigner

Eden

The memory is a field,
all planted under snow;
sun and earth are sharing
and love begins to grow.

The heart is a vast garden,
planted in every seed;
love is the fruit and flower
and rain is all it needs.

The soul is the sprout that reaches,
that breaks through all the dark;
the hope of a rich harvest
and a spring that never stops.

The time in the garden is autumn,
the earth and the sun grow apart;
the faith of winter tomorrow
and the promise of a new start.

Donald Foster

Untitled

Death, I fear not thee
All that peace and tranquility
I know someday you must visit me
Death, I fear not thee

Death, I fear not thee
For you must come to set me free
Then on celestial shores I'll be
Death, I fear not thee

Death, I fear not thee
For I shall live for eternity
With my father in heaven, whom I shall see
Death, I fear not thee

Carolyn Creamer

Heaven

Death I fear, pain and anger-
although Heaven seems somewhat stranger,
to run from death and danger.
My heart is turning into stone
is this what He condones?
That I feel lost completely alone?
These cruel harsh devils all surround me
I scream at them I plea,
it's as if God does not see.
Yet my dear and Holy Father
I know you care, I know you bother,
so I love my Lord no other.
My eyes are blurred, not very clear
a war-song death is what I hear,
and yet I feel His presence near.
This bitterness of my life dead-
everlasting life in heaven, I wed,
and sleep eternally in an entities bed.

Heather Brantley

A Memory Of Faith

Familiar voices laded with tears
All the while your captivating,
Heart becomes as stone

The pounding of your inner walls
Becomes shattering to the
Silence found from within my
Soul, now avoid of love

Happiness now just a thought,
For your silence has taken
Apart even the walls I have
Instilled as I though as I
Think, as your thoughts were of
Lasting faith

For now I remain conquered, by
The dreams.(I have lost you...)

I have banished all that was
Clear, only to dream of lasting
Faith now gone

Issac Romero

We Are As "One" "To My Darling Husband"

We are as "one" we "two",
alone, in crowds, apart; adieu!
no time; forever, the clock beats cry;
"a like, my soul; until we die
how strange was fate to bring you near;
now evermore your voice I hear;
in prayer, in poem, in song at night,
your tender arms that hold me tight,
thy lips that kiss away my tears.
Thine eyes whom understand my fears.
its "you", "my love", my life, my "all",
that makes life sweet instead of gall;
we are as "one we "two" you know,
as years may pass; as years may go;
and "after time we shall not part,
For how can "one" just leave her "heart";
So "eternity keeper" of life's "old fate.
Keep room for "two" at "Heavens Gate,
For we are as "one," we "two" you know.

Dorothea Kotsakor

"Heaven's Valentine"

Everyone's valentine is what you still are
Although you are in heaven, in our
hearts you are not far.

Love and laughter fills your soul,
while we keep you in mind
And that is the reason, you are
Heaven's and our valentine.

So as we commemorate February 14th
and think of Elizabeth in Heaven above.
Your love is thought of, as a white dove.

Diane Doyle

What I See

 I used to see the sun...
But now I see gray clouds all through the sky
 I used to see a rainbow...
But now I see a plain sky
 I used to see flowers...
But now I see brown leaves
 I used to see you...
But now I see nothing.

Amanda Olbrys

A Kiss

It was only a kiss I asked for,
And you finally gave your consent.
Then I asked if ever before
Your kisses you had lent.
You said "no" in tones so meek,
My heart swelled with pride.
But, when you showed me your technique,
I knew darn well you lied.

Joseph Longo, Ed. D.

Firefly

May love and beauty,
always be your guide,
radiant sweetness, and personality,
your innermost pride,
blossoming Womanhood understood.

Today an unlimited horizon,
the beckoning warmth of a glowing Sun
Tomorrow flying high,
navigating your dreams
by a starlit sky.

Soon the runaway will clear,
flashing takeoff beams, will appear
But I'll never say goodbye,
you've touched my heart,
Firefly.

Eugene S. Hewett

The Whisper

When I was lost and lonely,
An angel came to me.
I heard its gentle whisper
Above the roaring sea.

It spread its golden wings
Above my drowning soul
And calmed the raging storm
Before the bell would toll.

And by an angel's grace,
A call within my dream
Lead me to the brightest light
That I had ever seen.

It was an angel's voice
That filled my life with love.
O that I was worthy
Of the whisper from above.

Carol Caponiti

My Poem

To write a poem,
 an experience,
 my feelings.
To laugh
 to cry
  to sing
on paper.
To shape the words
 into sounds, feelings, colors.
To write a poem.

To show the poem to
 someone respected.
To feel rejected
 and misunderstood.

Christine E. Rideout

My Life What It Was To Me

Looking to the mountain I see
an ole' gnarled cedar tree
Next to it a sapling,
standing straight and tall,
trying not to look so small

Once, I was as the young sapling,
able to stand straight and tall,
trying not to look so small

Looking to the mountain, I see
I am like that ole' gnarled cedar tree

Darlene Mae Tucker

Pearl

I thought of a special friend today
and a smile came across my face
Remembering her gentle touch,
Her busy loving hands
and especially her warm embrace.

She has touched my heart in many ways,
My life is not the same.
Her thoughts and Prayers are with me,
I have no need of shame,
She knows me inside out
and loves me just the same.

She is truly a special friend
although across the miles,
My heart knows not the distance,
but cherishes the smiles.

The loving touch of her friendship
Is like none I've ever known,
This precious friend of mine,
I'm proud to call my own.

I love you Pearl.

Celia Bowen

The Game

Through all the years you've played,
and all the things you've done.
Like you I love the game,
But you'll always be number one.

Better than Cy, Nolan, and Sandy,
You are the greatest of all.
But when they step to the mound to pitch,
all the batters seem to fall.

Strike one, two, and three,
That is all I hear,
As you throw your fast ball harder,
The scouts all watch from near.

That is all I dream of
to be like you in a game.
Your desire overpowered everything,
That's why you belong in the Hall of Fame.

I wish to follow your footsteps,
in the great American game.
That is why someday I hope,
I could be the same.

Bobby Welch

Surrounded By The Light

They say the light surrounds you
And Angels softly sing
The memories of loved ones
Are all that you may bring
And in our hearts we'll see you
The special times we've shared
The good things that you taught us
The special way you cared
And in those quiet moments
When we wish that you were here
We'll unfold all those memories
And we will feel you near
We'll miss you, oh so deeply
With each passing day and night
But in our hearts we'll know
That you're surrounded by the light

Jodi Woloszyn

Benji

We have a cute little dog
And Benji is his name.
But everyday is different,
It's never quite the same.
Susan is his master though
But she has moved away
She comes to visit often so
He has a fun-filled day.
Benji likes to run and walk
And play with friend, Maxine
Except they fight, go
round the block
They're really quite a team.
We've had hamsters, birds,
and bunnies
Fish, turtles and gerbils too,
But I think it's worth the money
To keep a dog and not a zoo.

Dorothy M. Gillis

With You

To hold your hand
And dance all night,
To watch you smile
Till mornings light.

To walk with you
On a sunset beach,
To a point in time
Together we reach.

Tender the touches
We will share,
Always together
Showing we care.

When we are yet
A memory in time,
I will remain
Forever, with you!

Donald J. Nelson

Untitled

It comes quietly
And lingers calmly
Not realizing its presence
But knowing something is different
And the ache starts
The hushed breath begins
The sight of her excites
The thought of her elates
Yes, love has come
With its pain and joy

Clyde L. Borg

Like Daddy

I took my little laddie one,
And drew her to my knee
And whispered to my little Lad,
"Do you want to be like me?"
"Like daddy", said my little lad."
"I'm gonna be like you."

I bowed my head in humbleness,
And suddenly I knew
If my small girl would be like me
There's one thing I must do,
The step's I take, the things I say
Had better all ring true.

As in the night I lay awake
While my wee lad slept on
Her word's re-echoed thought we need.

To help to keep us straight
Upon the way we fathers walk
Depends on out children's fate.

Cathy Mitchell

The Wonder In Your Eyes

Even though you are very young
and everything is so new to see
the wonder in your eyes
is always amazing to me.

The world is so big
and you strive to be a part of it
you have no worries or fears
I envy you, I must admit

The world is your play thing
more than mere toys
you have lots to discover
and you'll have lots of joys

Your blue eyes light up
like firecrackers in the sky
everything is thrilling to you
just like a roller coaster ride

Your smile and your laughter
will always brighten my day
and so, as your Aunt, I'll love
you every day and in every way.
In honor of my niece,
Mary Catherine Scott

Debra A. Scott

"Colorama"

As the Summer slowly disappears
and Fall arrives upon the scene,
Mother Nature waves her wand,
the trees re-do their leaves of green.
The woods becomes a fairyland,
the trees take on the sunset's glow,
brilliant orange, scarlet red and
bright sunshiny gold.
As an accent to her masterpiece,
she leaves the deep green pine,
so elegant her work of art,
we know her guidance is Divine.
One more of God's great miracles,
surrounding us each day.
His gift another pleasure
to enjoy along the way.

Betty Poyer von Lutzow

This Winter: A Love Poem

My spirit rises, this time soundless
and gently, like its very dissension:
  is the way a day began
  is the way evening later led
to belief and movement.

Ev Vroyevu: Waiting-in-patience
this same self-spirit
eases through itself
to meet its own meek fitting darkness;

And
while the light burden of touch
changes this timeless moment
a simpler fire turns within,
lost in silence, and found,
in a modest, tender mercy

Moving and curious
I am borne
inside this gossamer, grace-filling
Opening-
not enlightened, thank God, but stilled

Deborah D. Jackimek

Time Is A Crook

Even though I'm always busy
And have things to do
There's not a day that goes by
When I don't think of you

I could be working very late
Or trying to get some sleep
I could be out on a date
With my Country Dancing feet

I could be cleaning house
Or studying a book
All of this takes time, you know
Time is a crook

I just want to let you know
How much I love you both
Forgive me for not being there
Just remember, I do still care.

Donna Costello

"Follow Me"

Will you follow in my footsteps,
And help me on my way?
For your caring, love, and guidance
will help me through my days.
I'm not quite sure you understand
The impact of your love.
It's the force that keeps me going,
Combined with God above.
If you follow these small footprints
The challenge becomes yours,
To become the raft that saves me,
And brings me to your shore.
So give careful thought to this path,
Follow - if it's your will.
I hope my loving in return,
Can someday pay the bill.

Cara D. Main

Voice of Experience

And so you have suffered me
and I have marked your flesh,
I am with you now eternally
to know each day in tenderness.
You'll soon forget my closeness:
let me fade into a trace.
Still, when you give yourself
in birthing or in radiance,
like sunlight on a wall,
look back, and you will see my face.
So cherish me, for I am yours
and won't forsake you anymore.

Anesa Miller

To Whom It May Concern

I am a new born baby
and I see many colors;
what do they mean?
I see black, white, red, yellow
what color am I?

I wonder.
What does color stand for?
Can I go into the world
and not be laughed at?
Am I safe or is there danger?
All I want is peace and harmony.

I want to explore new things, seek
the unknown, and look for adventure.
Will this happen?
I have so many question to ask
To whom it may concern

Ebony Coleman

"Sweet Surrender"

Smile at me
  and my eyes
  begin to twinkle

Touch me
  and my heart
  jumps for joy

Love me
  and a million flowers bloom
  all over the world

Day H. Oshiro

If I

If I could be anything,
I would be the wind
And I would fly endlessly
In a direction all my own.

If I could be anything,
I would be a flower
And I would lay in the sun
Hour after hour.

If I could be anything,
I would be a star,
I would watch the earth from afar.

If I could be anything,
I would be an ocean
And I would let my salty tears caress the sand.

If I could be anything,
I would be a drop of rain,
And I would cry for my lost love,
Although my sorrow is in vain.

Daniela Machuca

Happy Thanksgiving

Thanksgiving was coming,
  and I'd prepare.
All of the family,
  would soon be there.
The turkey was done,
  the aroma, was great.
The candles were lit,
  I could hardly wait.
We shared our love,
  at times like this.
A favorite story,
  you wouldn't miss.
I cherish the memories,
  time goes so fast.
I often relive them,
  to make them last.

Ann Jones-Markwood

Commitment For The Future

I'm living for lovin'
and I'm lovin' my living
without doing some giving
so give me the love
that I gave from my heart
let's hold on to each other
now that we've got a new start
let the past be the past
the future lays bright ahead
now we got something
which before we never had

Irina Creaser

Love

I love you, love you.
Can this be true?
I love you, love you.
Your love is so blue.

The faith in your eye,
I can not deny
How much I love you;
For the pain in my eye.

Jenna Neely

Fantasy

If I could rub Aladdin's Lamp
And it would grant one wish of mine,
I'd ask for an Island all my own
And just one year away from time
Where I could rest and sleep and dream.

I'd build me a cabin, crude and small,
By a willow tree on that lonely isle,
Where the warm sea waves would wander in
To pause with me and rest a while
And time itself perchance would sleep.

Yet, if one morn in the dreamy mist
The shape of a shadowy barque appeared,
In a beat of my heart I'd fly to the shore
To breathlessly wait as my lover neared
And wish for Aladdin's lamp no more.

Edna M. Campbell

My Darling

I never knew of love before
And knew not what I missed
But life with you is wonderful
When we hold hands and kiss.

I always felt strong alone
But strength has lost its meaning
For nothing will come between us
And dull the love that's gleaming.

God has blessed the both of us
By giving us each other
I will never feel the need
To be with any other.

Cecilia Forbis

Mom

To see the years that have passed,
and knowing I'm not the me of
yesterday.
To wonder at a life so different
and to know it will forever
change.
To have reached for help knowing
you'd be there when I needed you
most.
To be afraid like a child
yet knowing it's time to
grow up.
To leave the port and sail away
knowing the shore will be there
always.

Dawn M. Sterr

To Larry — Too Late

I knew it could not last,
And that it shouldn't begin,
But your intriguing eyes
And your flippant grin
Held me fascinated;
Would not let me go.
Why didn't you come around
A year or so ago?

Harriet Kimball Ross

Reasons

There's a world beyond reasons
and like a life with no soul
A season that has no end
or a wheel that doesn't roll

A person that's better than the rest
or one that shatters your dreams
Like a relationship that grows stronger
or one that falls apart at the seams

There's an answer to every question
like there's a woman for every man
A world sometimes with no meaning
or one that just doesn't understand

A love that's stronger and growing
or a love that sad and ugly at heart
Times to be shared with love
too rich and pure to be torn apart

A flower without a sun
like a love throughout every season
There's power and magic in everyday
like a love that's stronger without any reasons

Diane McEachen

Beauty

Where does beauty end,
And loveliness begin?
Is it a passing trend
That no-one can attend?

Beauty is mightier than the rock,
And swifter than lightening.
It tends to be a shock,
And even sometimes frightening.

Beauty is the essence of life,
In every creature that lives.
And shows itself through strife,
With the soul and spirit it gives.

John Briedis

A Friend; A Friend

I wandered off into a cave
And now I fear my life to save,
I looked around to find a light
I struggled with all the rock to fight.

Alas, a ray of light I see
My name - my name, it's all so clear
Could this be truth or mere despair?
A prayer - a prayer, please rescue me!

A voice, a call, a friend - a friend
Ha, ha, I laughed with all my might.
I followed the sound to hallowed ground,
And found myself upon a mound.

The sun was bright, the grass was green
To me this was a lovely scene
I looked around, a friend stood near,
Thank God, I had no more to fear!

A friend, a friend, I cherish this dream!

Estelle Thompson

Sister

You used to call me "Sister"
And now it can be true.
Those days we spent together
I could always talk to you.
And those letters that we wrote,
When you moved so far away,
Brought us very close
With each and every day.
You have become a part of me
That no one else could take.
And you have taught me many things
That no one could replace.
My brother is very special.
He means a lot to me.
He too has taught me many things
That no one else could see.
I could picture him with no one
Unless it could be you
So now I call you "Sister"
And know it will always be true.

Heather L. Fago

To My Lover, Gone Away

Love has come, and Love has gone
  And now life must go too
I Loved you and I lost you
  Oh God, what can I do.

I can't replace you with another
  No one else could do
There's only one who was meant for me
  And Heaven only knows it's you.

You meant a lot to me, so very much
  Even though you've gone away
I loved you then, I love you still
  I'll get you back someday.

And if that day should never come
  I don't know what I'd do
You know as long as I'm without you
  Darling, I'll be blue.

Carl Broniman

True Love

I look into your eyes
And see your happiness
Clear as a bolt of lightning
True as a sweet caress.
I wish the best for you
That's all that I can say
I hope he brings you joy
As I know he will today.
I hope it's true love
That's what it seems
I hope he's sweet and caring,
The man of your dreams
So I wish only this
On this great day
The truest of true
Love forever stay.

Jay Ann Farkas

Untitled

Angels in the heavens are beautiful
Clouds in the sky are white
at night as we gaze at the sky
and see a fallen star
we hold each other tight and smile
as we know we belong.

Candice Parsons

Magic

Sometimes people come,
and sing a joyful song,
And other times they don't,
but when they do magic appears.
The magic of a magician,
or the magic of a person,
they pull a rabbit out of a hat,
or a corner of a bat.
They pull money out of peoples ears,
or flowers out of someone's hair.
But when the show is over,
the people long to go,
because it is a place,
that they are safe,
from all the violence,
of the crazy world,
today.

Andrea Roy

Endings

And so the day has come to end,
And so the time has come.
At last, the soul, not you or I,
But us, has dripped
From the ends of our fingers,
From the tips of our tongues,
As we now glimpse of what will be,
And accept.
There are no shadows in our smiles,
Nor in our words or deeds,
But now, at last, we find the truth:
There are no good goodbyes,
As we pass each other
As no more than friendly strangers.

James Maher

The Song

You hear a certain song
And tears will flow.
It once made you happy,
Made you give off a glow.

Made you feel warm
And bring out a smile.
Now it makes you sad
For quite a while.

Brings back memories
Of a happier time,
Of hugs and kisses,
When you were mine.

Now all I have left
Is memories and this song.
The holding and loving fade
But the song lingers on.

Try to focus on the future,
Put the memories behind,
But the song is forever
Always there on my mind.

Fanny Lee Baker Shaw

A Letter To Mom

It's a little cold and damp, Mom
And the food isn't so good.
The ground is cold and wet, Mom
And soaked with human blood.
I have a bullet in my leg, Mom
But, it doesn't hurt me much;
When an orphan boy goes by, Mom
Without a leg, or a crutch.
Their coming down the hill, Mom
One thousand men strong;
I'd better write you now, Mom
We can't hold them very long!
Tell sister not to cry, Mom
I'll see her again, someday;
And please, please tell my girl, Mom
I had to go away.
Now don't you cry for me, Mom
After all, I am just one man;
United States soldiers are everywhere, Mom
Fighting for our land.
(I LOVE YOU, MOM!)

Adren L. Ogden

Waiting My Turn

as the fires burn
And the gasses flow,
I lay here starving and weak
wondering when I'll have to go.

As I watch many people die,
I lay here scared and trying to hide.
At night people sleep but don't wake
all because of a thing called hate.

I lay here, naked shivering and cold,
as soldiers rip out teeth and steal our gold.
I can hear all of our screams of pain.
I can feel all of the horrors untamed.

We have no money,
but they make us pay.
Not with cash,
but with pain.

I wish this all would quickly end.
They've killed my family and my friends.
I hear them coming to scar and burn,
they're coming for me; it's now my turn.

Benjamin Shafer

I've A Key To Heaven

I've a Key to Heaven
And the keeper is dear to me.
That keeper is my Mother
Who long preceded me.

I see her in the morning sun
And the rainbow in the sky.
I know she'll never leave me.
Her constancy is nearby.

When the day comes to meet her
She'll be waiting there for me
With arms outstretched and a smile so big
The angels will envy me.

My stay on Earth is happy.
My deeds are for the best.
By Faith I am contented
As Mother gave me Happiness.

Glenn Ferris Bennett

Reverie

In the evening as the sun goes down
And the night is falling fast -
Memories that come to mind
Are of days that are long past -

I close my eyes and remember well
The times of joy and sorrow -
Then bow my head and with my prayer
Comes the hope of a new tomorrow.

Imogene Ragan

Dirge Singer

Within the desecrated dreams
and the raging hatred
of self-immolation,
lies the graveyard
of the almost-Gods.

The agony of their
daily suicide
imprinted in their eyes,
their words,
in the hollowness
where laughter once danced.

I, dirge singer,
walk gently inside their graves,
probe their pain softly,
   weaving mourning melodies,
     their deaths my legacy.

Gale Sutton

Haunted Heart

I remember soft summer nights
and the restlessness of our youth.
Fearless and wild, searching in vain
for what we thought was truth.

You were there, so true a friend
and we became as one.
Our laughter filled the moonlit sky.
Then suddenly you were gone.

You left without a warning.
For years I've cried alone.
You left your memory to burn my soul
when you left your name in stone.

The years have flown so quickly by
and I'm a woman now.
Often I've wondered what may have been
if you were here somehow.

You must know I love you
though death keeps us apart.
I know you'll forever live
deep inside my haunted heart.

Cindy M. Williams

Untitled

The black ribbon reaches forth
  as a palm upward asking;
Thousands of raids so nobly made
  from the past begging;
The requests extending from
  another time remembered;
The voices held in the hearts
  of the remaining remembering
Do you hear the plea

David James Cooper

As The river Ran Wild

As the water seemed to climb
and the trees and rocks went,
we felt an inner fear
as if it weren't meant;

As all we knew was changed,
before our very eyes,
As we all said a prayer
Mother Nature changed our lives;

She took some of our land
and even a life too:
She showed us what she could be
and made us feel blue;

But as the river ran wild
we grew a lot inside,
And opened up our hearts
some of us even cried:

We helped our next door neighbor
and gave a friend a hand,
We showed we could be civilized
and life could still be grand!

Joanne Borello

We Must See The Need

When values are misplaced with greed
And the young view life as short
Each of us must see the need
To help them in our heart.

However gloom the future seems
Filled with war, and destruction, too;
Our vision must be on the dreams
That make life better for our youth.

There's so much untapped talent around
This we all know for sure.
And it will be evident when found
In new art, and medicine, and cure.

A creative mind needs a place
To carry out its deeds.
Our challenge is to make it safe
For those who have that need.

Let's join together in peace and love
To lend our helping hand.
Our strength comes from the One above;
We must do all we can.

Doris L. Huntley

Life's Legacy

I opened my eyes on a winter's day
  And there in Mother's arms I lay;
She rocked me with the rhythmned rain
  And lulled me with an old refrain
Of fairy tales and lullabies
  And angels watching from the skies.

I blinked my eyes on a winter's day
  And in my arms my girl-child lay;
I closed my eyes on a winter's day
  And in HER arms HER baby lay.

I shut my eyes this winter's day
  And as I rock alone I pray
That fairy tales and lullabies
  And angels watching from the skies
Will still be heard when I am gone.
  And part of me will thus live on.

Barbara S. Weppener

The Healing Touch

My hands are anointed
And through them healing flows.
I lay hands on the sick
Just as Jesus did so long ago.

There's healing in my hands
Everywhere I go.
I must seek out who to touch.
I must be bold.

There are people everywhere
To minister to and reach.
After healing their bodies,
They're ready for me to teach.

Hearts are changed
And bodies are healed.
I've done my part-
That which the Lord revealed.

Barbara S. Barrow

The Ring

A spontaneous gesture of love
and trust...
A circle unbroken.
Becoming whole...
Sealed by God.
An angel awaits Your Presence.
A heart healed, a new life begins
Hold The Ring...it's part of me
Diamonds... Angel glitter
Radiant sparkle... God's love, my love
You are loved...

Cheryl Detwiller

A Day In The Country

I look upon a meadow
  And what do I see?
Little rabbits scampering
  And a horse sleeping by a tree.
Tiny bees and lots of little flowers.
Sit under the warm sun
  And watch for hours.

Stops and look at the glittering trees,
  That make our homes,
  And suit our needs.
Look at the big, lumberous branches,
  And the small, delicate leaves.
The tree is a beautiful creation
  That God has given to you and me!

Little flowers dotting a dull field.
  White ones soft and mellow,
  Pink, purple, orange, red and yellow.
Blooming up in the spring,
  Bringing joy to everything!

Jessica Urban

Legacy Of Marie

Floral bouquets painted in pastel hues,
  Children's rhymes in animation,
Old world treasures of gold and crystal,
Soft, romantic gowns of white and pink,
Piano chords drifting across the hills,
  Sunlit days, sunshine spirit,
Gray days endured with humor and grace.
A legacy of memories and inspiration.

Donna Dreier

A Time Of Sorrow

Your loved one has been taken away....
And with the sweet sting of death
His pain is gone.
He is asleep and at peace
And has left you alone
To bear the pain of his leaving.
The emptiness and loneliness
Are more than you can endure.
And dear friend.....
I feel your pain
as you weep.

Ann P. Russo

Sympathy

Have you ever seen the sunset
And wondered where it went?
Or seen a ship sail out of sight
With noise and merriment?
You know they didn't really get
Away forevermore,
The scene is very different
Than what it was before
The sun still bright
The ship still plies
Although its under different skies.
Your loved one too is going on
To newer scenes and other songs.
May this message comfort you
And help you understand
Your loved one's on a journey
There's no reason to be sad!

Elaine E. Feig

A Summer Garden

In summer sun, the bright green leaves
Are dancing in the jolly breeze
On waving branches of the trees.
The border flowers are many hued
There's red and purple, pink and blue
All smiling on this happy day
When light and life are holding sway.
The yellow jackets swoop and swoon
And pause to light on chosen blooms
The short green grass, a carpet laid,
To cushion and for comfort made.
A butterfly goes sailing by
Its beauty to delight the eye.
And in this tranquil state I lie
While quiet dreams doth cloud my eyes.
For peaceful thoughts bring soothing sleep
To those who close to nature keep.

Joyce M. Kirkpatrick

Memories

Memories become precious
  as the years pass by,
What you did in the past
  is seen only in the eye.

Memories are pictures that
  are formed in the mind.
Visions of happiness, sadness
  and treasures of all kind.

Cling to those memories
  for they are all we have left,
As the years rush by us
  and we're left in the past.

Joy R. Formica

Heaven

Is there a stream that never ends,
Are there snow covered mountains,
Is there peace and everlasting life,

We are told it exists,
And have read that it does,

But, to try
And convince our minds,
Is the biggest chore of all,

I choose to believe,
Believe that the peace is there,
That love is all around,
And that our family and friends,
Will always be present,

If not only to watch over us,
And protect us,

To watch as we grow,
Mature,
And never stop,
Believing in ourselves!!!

Edith A. Dunn

Crossing Over To The White House

Who are those devils in the white-house?
Are they hearing from God Almighty?
No, I don't think so!
Taking from the poor to feed
the rich, Mr. Louis Farrakhan
let's march to the white-house
one million strong can't be
wrong, crossing over to the white house.
Mr. President!
Look out! We are coming!
We are crossing
over to the
white house!

Evon R. Clarke

Dreamer

I am a Dreamer,
as are you,
I dream, dream
that come true,
and some that will never be reality.

When I dream
I am like all of you,
when I sleep
I am as you are
running as you run,
playing as you play.

In the waking hours
of the morning sun,
when my dream
is no longer reality,
I lie there wondering
Why I dream
then I realize,
better in my dreams than not at all.

Jennifer Henkel

Reincarnation

I long to see you
As each idea
Of you
Creeps into my restless thoughts
Day after day

O Mother

The mother I haven't seen
In a lifetime

A soothing touch
A warm smile
The welcoming you so incautiously give
Makes me certain
We have a bond
Much more than meets the eye

Please, Mother
Gather me in your arms
Comfort me
As you did long ago
When we knew each other

Amy Irons

See Thy Beauty

Thy pigeons, thy trees
as far as my eye can see
there is beauty.
Thy flowers, thy clovers
are everywhere I look and
they are beautiful.
Thy sky, thy flys
are always there, they
are beautiful too if
you know what I mean.
Thy grass, thy cats
go good together, they
are beautiful.
Thy vines, thy fence
thy fence is not beautiful
but thy vines make it
lovelier than you or I.

Jackie Piascik

Immortal Kiss

On the brink of things eternal,
 As He writes my final journal
And I face His hell infernal
 Or His everlasting bliss,

In the dusk of suns descending,
 'Neath the peace of shadows blending,
As my mortal life is ending,
 I shall ask my God but this:

May His angel, now before me,
 Softly weaving her life o'er me,
Come to seal the love she bore me
 With one last, immortal, kiss.

Daniel Canfield Payne

The World

The World around is madness,
As I look around in wonder,
I feel a certain sadness.

A pang within my heart,
If only more could see,
If only we were smart.

We blow apart the World we love,
We poison seas below,
We ionize our skies above.
Now how far will we go?

If we could see the future,
I wonder what we'd give?
Would we try to clean our World?
Could our World forgive?

Would you?

Brandon C. Alt

Untitled

I see her;
 As if yesterday.
I see a baby;
 Blond and blue eyes
I see a child;
 Walking and talking
I see the shyness;
 Hiding in side
I see a teenager;
 Maturing before my eyes
I see her;
 My daughter
I see her;
 I see myself

Denise Skriapas

Will Tomorrow Come?

There are those who look at life
As nothing but a bed of strife,
Whose lives are just one long lament,
Filled with worry and discontent.

Why can't we take a brighter view,
Appreciating each day anew,
Instead of wasting it away
Lamenting our fate along the way?

Why can't we see how blessed we are,
And hitch our dreams upon a star,
Instead of wasting today in sorrow,
When God never promised us tomorrow?

Clarence N. Wesson

The Strength Of My Father

The strength of my father
as strong as an oak
Although stubborn at times
few negative words has he spoke

If the strength of my father
would rub off on me
I could be as strong
as the crushing sea

All that he's been through
the hurt and the pain
The strength in his heart
let sun shine through rain

I admire the courage
and the strength that he shows
I love him so much and
I hope that he knows

Heidi Kaliher

Ecstasy

Your touch is icy but comforting.
As the oil seeps into my skin, I'm
lost in a world unknown to man.
Now slippery hands are on
my thighs and I can taste the
wine on your breath. I can
smell the savory steam of passion.
All I hear are your whispers in my ear,
sending warm chills down my back.
Satiny sheets slide beneath me as
I fall into a trance of your
lustful powers. Not wanting to
give into your manly charms,
I protest. But I am lost in
the sweet tenderness of ecstasy.

June Julander

Heavens Great Gate

I will never be with you again,
At least not on this earthly plain.
And although your gone my darling,
So much of you remains.
Your children, your grandchildren.
Your great grand children too.
None of them would be here, if it
were not for you.
And as for me my darling, there are
not enough words to say.
All the love, and the joy, you brought
into my life, each and every day.
you were my husband, my lover, and
my best friend. Ill miss you more
than I can say.
But darling I know, that at some later
date, I will see you again,
at heavens great gate.
Goodbye my love

Betty Britton

"In Search"

I stand, I look
at the chance I had
I wish I took.

To seek, to know,
to finds, to grow;
an experience now
to show.

A gift we give
is that of trust;
with simple thought
in which we must:

Let live, let dream,
let find new hope,
in seeing past with
ways of cope.

The future holds a
definite truth.
A self to find...
   in search of youth.
Craig J. Crawford

Jessi Cries

When daddy comes to visit,
at the end of every week;
Jessi gets excited,
and she can hardly speak.
She runs into his open arms,
to kiss him on the face;
then puts her arms around his neck,
with a child strong embrace.
Then Jessi tells her mommy;
that she will soon be home;
because Jessi knows that Mommy,
doesn't like to be alone.
But Jessi doesn't understand,
and often she will cry;
when daddy brings her home again,
and has to say goodbye.
Janet Nardini

The Simple Life

The simple life is what I like
At the lake, both day and night
Where troubles fade away, and so
The "city place" where others go
Appeals not to me, nor to my kind
No "big time" lights are on my mind.

The quiet and calm of life and bliss
As sun and moon the lake doth kiss
Chipmunks and the birds that fly
Traffic noises, go straight by
Grass grows green, there's flowers, too
And ripples small on lake of blue
Mother Nature shows her face
Thanks be to God! I LOVE THIS PLACE!
Ina A. Firth

Dinosaurs

Dinosaurs are told.
Dinosaurs are mold.
Dinosaurs maybe sold.
But they are gold.
Chrissy Thompson

What If...

The bird is tapping again,
  at the window,
coming to annoy me
  and turn me into Poe.
Breaking my calmness
  like a dropped mirror.
Shattering my facade of
  security into
    thousands of
  doubts.
Once steadfast in my decisions,
  now unsure of what
I've become
  because
  two words echo in my head.
Danielle Pennock

Air

Two balloons
Attached themselves
In harmony one day.
They were with
One another with
Their contrasting colors.
They embarked
Upon a fantasy
For a lifetime;
Only to have
An abrupt ending
That shriveled
Them into infinity.
Elizabeth Schroeder

"For The Love Of Life"

  As life weaves it's sharp
barbed-wire threads around
me, despair oozes from each
caress that it inflicts.
  The sorrow that it's touch
provokes, kisses my flesh
like a knife.
  Exposing my deepest
desires for the world to
dance upon.
  Misery rages within the
confines of my heart, crying
out for it's seductions.
  Darkness encloses me
as I weep.
  There is no escape from
this hell for I am my own captor.
Christin Nile-Heald

Encouragement

Believe in yourself
Be all that you can be
Turn your dreams
into reality!

Hold your head up high
Stay right on track
CONFIDENCE goes forward
FEAR holds back.

Believe in yourself
DO all that you can do
DOUBT may slow you down
DETERMINATION will befriend you.
Cathy M. Brandt

Live Every Moment

Live every moment.
Be the best that you can be.
Take time to smell the roses
And share a cup of tea.

Live every moment.
Enjoy life while you can.
Love one another.
It's all part of God's plan.

Live every moment.
Build memories that last.
For when this day is over
It becomes part of the past.

Live every moment.
Laugh and cry and sing.
Make each day a Masterpiece
No matter what it brings..

Live every moment
Too soon this life is done.
Live every moment.
Live them one by one.
Grace Mitchell

In The Heart

Just remember that the physical
beauty of that rose which you have
gazed upon day after day, will soon
vanish. You will miss that rose
and maybe even shed a tear or two
for it. But you soon will realize
that it wasn't it's shade of color
or sweet scent that enticed you -
it was how it made you feel and the
memories it has given you that you
will miss. But it will never be
missed or truly gone if you keep
it within your heart forever.
The rose in the Heart will Bloom
Forever.
Jaclyn De Jacquant

When All Is Gone

The children are crying
because of their place,
where all is dying
because of our waste.
Why do we do this?
Nobody knows.
Why do we do this and
cause all these woes?
The children are fighting,
and continue to fight,
to defend their home
with all of their might.
The children are pleading.
Please, won't you stop?
They need all they have
to stay close to the top.
When all is gone
it won't be best,
for nevermore, their
souls be blessed.
Jammie Carufel

"Matthew Andrew Ezekiel Ritchie"

In the beginning
Before he was named,
The devil sent doctors
To put him to shame

He wanted to end him
And Oh! How he tried
I'll never forget how
Often we cried.

Then the Lord sent a message
And he let us know
We should leave it to him
who comes and who goes.

Then he sent Matthew
He filled him with love,
Matthew is an angel
Sent from above.

Carol Lee Ritchie

The Con

Chuckles, snickers and chortles
  Behind the pelting tears
Pranks, jokes, games and tricks
  been going on for years

Trust and hope are on the way
  Beginning more seriously than before
Working toward a new beginning
  The cheating ways - nevermore

Seeking out that special one
  Believing it to be for me
Hanging on to every fragment:
  Is this how it is to be?

You're with me now, I know
  You promised me you'd stay
It's hard to trust those few words
  For others have gone away

I believe it though,
  I know I must
You said it truly
  And you I trust!

Bonnie K. Cady

Wallflower

Sitting in a field of worrying,
being not sure of who I am.
I feel alone, so isolated
being not sure of when it will end.

Falling backwards in my dreams,
knowing that will not come true.
Things are clearly not what they seem,
Lord help me out, I need a clue.

I'm a man who needs respect,
but how can you earn what you can not get.
Don't know what the future holds,
I only know that I'm stuck in a hole.

Highway man walks the line,
never sure of when comes his time.
With my back against the wall,
I listen and hear the voices call.

But I do not go....

Jason Andrew Barkus

Beneath The Raven's Wings

It is cold,
Beneath the solid ground.
I lie straight and still,
With death and decay around.

Outside,
The future I can hear.
It beckons and calls,
My forth coming is near.

All my thoughts,
Of hatred and loneliness.
Turn towards escape of ground,
For my sins I have confess.

Finally the day comes,
The ground above me parts.
Eagerly I push ahead,
My resurrection starts.

My hand touches the cool air,
My heart of freedom sings.
As I reach the living world,
I find I am the raven's wings.

Cheryl Clayton

Painted Letters

Looking out the window
Between the painted letters
Homemade, Hometown Goodness.
A street lamp painted green
Waits for the first signs of night
To illuminate the matching green shutters
Of the brick building behind it.
The number is 159.
The name is probably Main Street.
The town is disappearing.

Diana Ellworth

The Splendorous Creation

Although the Sun is setting fast
  Beyond the mountains yon,
The rising of that Wondrous Light
  In me, is just begun.

The bluish sky of radiant hue
  With amber streaks, behold,
And cumulus clouds heaped oh so high
  Speak of the Artist bold.

No man dare ever duplicate
  What God himself has done,
To stand in awe (with mouth aghast)
  Portrays the race man's won.

Such great magnificence Creation bares
  Of splendor, and so grand,
Reveals the handiwork so plain
  From God's artistic hand.

Though some might think the Sun has set,
  And darkness reigns and falls,
Created truth belies such thought
  Sunlight illumines all.

Boyd D. Pendleton

Untitled

Homo sapiens
Bipedal dweller of Earth,
Heir of the flame,
Conqueror of the beasts,
Breaker of soil,
Molder of all around,
Lord to all creatures,
Less equipped than all,
Maker of war,
The ultimate weapon,
Shell of the finest computer,
Doubter of own existence,
MAN.

Joshua Defoor

Autumn Smoke

Blue, red, green
  Black, yellow
    Smoke.

Rising, twisting, climbing
  Floating, drifting
    Stretching out.
    Smoke.

Grass, leaves, straw
  Twigs, branches
    Sticks, bark
      Turning to ash.
    Smoke.

Wispy, soft, wild
  Fragile, fragrant
    Sharp, sooty
    Smoke.

Rising, curling, drifting
  Stretching out.
  Smoke.

James G. Francis

Wind Of Fear

The wind blows,
blows out the light,
the light of my small candle,
quick,
quick as a whip.
The whip snaps,
snaps and brings the cold,
the fears,
the dark fears of the night.
Far faster than I can re-light.

Anne Haberkorn

"The `X'"

"Her eyes were"
  Blue!
"Her hair was"
  Blond!
"As she sits"
  in the sun.
"She thinks."
"How it once was"
  "A flame."

Charles A. Saige

"Ocean In A Bottle"

My emotions are trapped in a
bottle with carrying tides that drift
away, then drifting ashore. I feel
drained away. The lost feeling of
forever and then being carried back
into the ocean of thoughts. This
never ending feeling of regret, powerless
uncontrol of my wandering
mind. Knowing that this process
moves some of the most important
things in life. One day the
cork will turn loose of my bottle
and the tides will have an endless
ocean of forgiveness.

Jamie Deserto

The Perfect Rose

His sweetest fragrance fills the air,
  breathes grace and mercy everywhere.
What Wondrous Rose so fair, so pure
  blooms in my heart-salvation sure.
Such splendor, beauty glory rare
  excites my soul His love to share.

Such worship, praise and joy of heart
  His faithful promise n'er depart.
Touched by His grace — God only knows
  my deepest love for this His Rose.
This song of love and honor goes
  to this Majestic, Perfect Rose.

Amazing Graze, Redeeming Love
  yearns for your heart in Heaven above.
The Way, the Truth, the Life is He;
  Repent, believe, His child you'll be.
Lord, Saviour, Priest and King 'tis true-
  This Perfect Rose died just for you.
    He died for you.

Bessie Evers Gooch

Fuchsia On My Mind

Fuchsia is the color of my dreams
Bright and bold
Storng and forceful
Fuchsia is the color of my thoughts
Screaming loud
Drawing attention
Fuchsia is my soul
Too violent to calm
But calm against another color
Black
Black is the background
On which my fuchsia falls
As eye-catching as black and white
But with more character
Black is the color of choice
On which to lay my fuchsia self.

Elizabeth Pride

One Life

One life to live, one life to give.
Christ gave it all for me
That I might have abundant life
Through all eternity.

Help me to live my life on earth
In service, Lord, for thee.
That I might have something to give
The one who died for me.

Audrey C. Harlow

Schindler's List

The once colored, full face.
Bright-eyed smile that went from
cheek to cheek is replaced with
dark sunken eyes that
reveal the pain that's been
afflicted upon him, tattered clothes which
show the riches he once owned.
The pale, slim figure
displays the body that no longer exist.
He can't speak nor think
in fear of what may happen
His dream, hopes, and peace of mind
have all been striped from him.
Heartache and frustration
is all he shows millions of them,
who look the same, feel the same.
Men, women and children lost
Lost among the list of names,
The names of the spirits,
The spirits of the Schindler's list.

DeChà S. Reid

Lightning

Lightning is coming,
Brightly flashing,
Streaking through the sky,
What is it? What does it want?
Will it punish the guilty?
Or will it reward the innocent?

Lightening is coming,
Barely touching the mountains,
Lighting up the trees,
Oh why has it come?

Lightning is coming,
Glowing in the night,
Like a firefly,
Dancing around.

John En Hsieh

Reasons

Eyes of comfort full of caring
Bring feelings that grow ever strong
Soft smiling lips full of loving
Make time apart seem not so long

A touch that soothes when pressure grows
Brings calming peace and sets me free
Unselfishness that always shows
Your love and trust you've given me

Your smell your essence fills the room
Overcoming me with desire
Apart for now I'll be home soon
My passion like a raging fire

A face so bright with beauty filled
Upon it I stare in wonder
Feelings so deep in me instilled
My defenses torn asunder

Standing so tall and so erect
Confident yet soft and tender
Our life together seems perfect
To you my heart I surrender

Barry Amrich

"Abyss"

Blackened by our darkest skies
Broken by our deepest lies
Stricken by our piercing cries
These are the challenges which
We must endure in our quest to
Secure our Edenistic setting.
Words are shot
Dreams are caught
We are taught
All to find
The elusive mind
That is the holder
Of all that is bolder
In this dream-state.

Justin Potter Christman

Winter Commute

No balmy breeze is this
But could be called instead
A horribly wicked storm
Of terrible dimension.

Blast!

So piercing thru thin coat
Those brittle shards of ice
That leave my nostrils thus
So pinched and tightly shut.

Br-r-r!

And slithery feet I do so fear
Are cold and simply do not feel
Yet wearily as head bends down
It gratefully reveals - the door.

Bliss!
Arouse be quick undo the latch
As stiff and frosted fingers tremble
Just give a shove and push to inward
A smile of relief to be home at last.

Janice Sjurseth

Animals Of The World

Daylight comes to us each day
But for some animals, they must pay
For what we don't know,
Some people don't care,
but some dare to dare
Through our times we have shared
and also cared.
Animals are as old as the sun,
as old as the moon
I think we should thank our
dear friends
and not let it come to an end.
So I leave you with this;
Reach forward, and
help a life reach its fullest.
Not it's dullest!

Adrian Osland

Silence Is Galling

"My wife", I say, you see, "she says."
But in fact, to tell the truth,
She really doesn't speak.

No! Now!? Not to say she doesn't speak
But she really doesn't say,
Not with a tongue, or teeth,
Not even puff of cheek.

But I'll say, "You'll see,"
She can more than speak!
By hand, that is!
With squint of eye and nose a'tweek.

"Not as you'd say," I'll say
"But more," I'd say, "like you'd see,"
She speaks her silent say.

With love, and scorn,
And not without
A little pique.

John J. Parnow

The Quiet Man

Some will stand and watch me,
but most will back away.
They fine solitude a fearful place,
cause I don't have much to say.
I've learned the painful facts of life,
completely trust only yourself.
Most will show face value,
And time will show what is felt.
I know my limitations,
how and where I stand.
I have no need to brag or boast.
I'm just a quiet man.

James F. Nesselroad

Gone

You're here in my heart
But not by my side
We are forever apart
Cause you went and died

Never more will I see you
Or hear you call my name
Never more will I hold you
Things will never be the same

I think of you and cry
Memories go thru my mind
Remembering times of years gone by
And loving you all the time

A tear for you, a tear for me
For life is not a song.
The future can never be
For you are now gone.

There is nothing left, or so it seems
Yet life goes on despite my dreams.

Elaine Moore

Peace

P eace
E verybody wants it
A society is destroyed without it
C orruption and greed confine it.. the
E ntire world needs it.

Edward Enriquez

Brotherhood

God made us different colors,
But our blood is all the same,
And in His sight were all alike,
Each one of us He claims.

No one race is the better,
No color best of all,
And each one is our brother,
We should care for if he falls.

The sun shines down on all alike,
With no discrimination,
And we should love them one and all,
And share all God's creations.

Put forth a friendly hand each one,
For to all this earth belongs,
And in this whole vast universe,
There's room for all God's sons.

Arlene Windom

Puddles And Brooks

May life not find me in a puddle
But rather in a brook.
Would murky and stale suit my being?
No! A brook with laughing clear ripples
Is more appealing.
A clean bubbling brook shows life's fullness.
A muddy puddle never shows life's goodness.
Forego sadness for a plunge into happiness.
Bathe in the brook of constant laughter.
Dwell not in the unending puddles of disaster.

Crystal Davenport Jones

"Peace"

Peace - what a wonderful word;
but who really knows,
what it means?
War - what a frightening word,
and we all do know,
what it means.

Everybody looks at life
in a different way.
One likes the sunshine,
the other the rain,
and it doesn't help
just to complain.

Too many misunderstandings,
too many foreign words,
a lack of communication,
some laughter and some tears.
Why don't we try harder,
to figure out the word: PEACE!

Ilse Roffler

Untitled

Life is my darkness
Death my freedom and light

Amber Tappan

At This Time...

You said your love for me was true,
but you knew I could see through.
We've been through so much,
and God knows I'll miss your touch.
But I need someone to care,
someone to always be there.
You're not the one for me,
and you may never, ever be.
So for now we must part,
and hope to find a new start.
You mean more to me than you'll ever know,
but at this time, I must go.

Alice Hooser

Perceive

When your mind is veiled
by merciless pain.

Do not slumber in dreams
of shimmering wealth and
physical bliss. They
cannot perceive.

But make radiant of your
thoughts to guide your path.
A circle you make if you astray.

The tormented and suffering
shell you leave when the
passing is made. No more
agony as the road you
ascend.

Arise your spiritual energy
with a messenger awaits, to
leave forever the world of
Cain.

George Shields

Future Vows

Being visited
By my dream
I'm not really in control
Though it seems

I order nothing
I'm not selfish
Though I smell like
Yesterdays shellfish

Keep your pennies
Way back in the back
Save them for
The people who lack

When will they produce
A produce liquid pill
Everyone on Earth
Will always be filled

A little plug in
Somewhere it is said
The lacking 90% percent
Will come to the head

But You Know Best

Rusty

He will answer by that name
call him and see
Such a fine animal
Full of heart and compassion
His eyes shine and sparkle
  with love and devotion
A pat on the head and a pal he will be
Such a bond between man and animal.
This is love between two friends
That will exist until one ends.
   With life.
   Charles Linde

The Heart Of An Angel

Already touch by God.
Came to us with much love,
So sweet and innocent as can be,
She brought to us what we could not see.

How one little angel,
With bright shining eyes,
Took all our love up to the skies,
With a sprinkle and a shake,
She shook us free,
Opened our hearts for us to see,

God needed AMY ROSE more than we.
   Cindy Kane

Undefined Love

The love shared between our hearts,
Can ever be grasped by the human hand.
It will never be explained by
the smartest man.
It is free; a living spirit
full of life and joy.
The art of language cannot make it clear.
A measure of music can never flow
like the music of our souls.
To define it would destroy
its identity,
would mask it and make it unfree.
So I leave it like it is—
nothing added, nothing gained.
So love spread your wings,
Fly free and take us to eternity.
   Brandi Key

Life's Song

A song whose beginning is never ended
can have no middle.
A song whose middle has had no beginning
can have no end.
A song unended is always in a state
of expectation....

Waiting
for
something
to
happen.

Somewhere between
Alpha
and
Omega.
   Janet A. Lee

Baby's First Words

Upon my birth, I cannot speak.
Can I express that which I seek?
For I need them.. will they need me?
I fear that they may never see.
But wait...I feel a warm embrace,
A gentle kiss upon my face.
What joy! I need not say a word
To have my inner feelings heard.
What is this silent bond which flows
From my heart to heart I've come to know?

Why do they smile? T'was I who reaped.
Yet, those are tears of joy they weep.
Did I touch every heart that's here
By simply wanting someone near?
It's really true! They do need me!
It seems we knew instinctively
That all must share, from deep inside,
The nourishment our souls provide.
I guess that's why as life begins,
We first must learn to speak within.
   Debbie Jackson

Cancer Patient Man

My brother the
Cancer patient man
Trouble seeing, mistaken
for a drunken clown
A bulge, in the forehead
unable to stand
Emergency, emergency
the Doctor, looked and said
Operation, immediately
blanked out, to understand
My brother the
Cancer patient man

Dreams shattered
broken hearts
Cries, tears, and fear
unpleasant sight
Thirty years old,
will not see the light
My Brother the
Cancer patient man
   Fayez Salaita

You Don't Understand

You don't really understand how much I do
care, I wish I could be with you instead
of being here, your always on my mind and
I miss you all of the time the only
happiness that I can find is when I'm
with you, right by your side, but lately
it seems you keep letting me down, you
seem to make promise and that's all
they are. I feel so lonely I just want
to cry what have I got into, this just
doesn't seem right.
   Carole L. Johnson

Homestead

Old as a family Bible,
Fields hold in dust blown spears a heritage.
Bladeless, a sentinel stands waiting
To voice the past with its cry of water,
As warped boards of house and barn
Shelter emptiness embraced by webs
and echoes reminisce.
   Jackie Roby

Of Celebrity's Passing

These pristine palliates
Cheered and revered;
These brightly burnished briolettes
To us endeared;
These guttering candles
With hallowed glow,
Now flickering,
Now burning low...
These joyless curtains
Of deeper blackness
And ever deepening sadness
Drawing down
O'er these lauded lamps,
'Till doused and darkened
'Till in inkyness lost
Never to be revisited
Nor reclaimed
Nor for us
To twinkle again...
   George Hlinka

Untitled

Wind sounds with elegant poise
Children laughing
Noise
Balloons sight
Drifting moods
Summer nights
Loving you
Woman's craze
Month of days
Remembering conversations
Waiting
Lost dreams stir desires
Experience
Need
   Catherine Frinier

Time Wise

A child is born
Choice through will
Less lineage a blank chalice
In wait for the filling

With knowledge as nectar
Then served
And if sweet
Matches past to a future
Puzzling as the witness

My closet door is now glass
My bones are there for all to see
Both cracked
From stones thrown few
Reluctantly
I age
   Jeff Baumann

Fresh Start

Clean your house of garbage
Clean your life up too
And soon you'll find that someone
Who is meant for you.
Don't dwell in self pity,
For it's a waste of time
Instead, think of all you do have
And you will be just fine.
For God will guide where you should go
And, if you listen, you will know.
   Elizabeth Weidemann

Clocks

Clocks
Clocks
Clocks
Wood clocks
Metal clocks
Large, medium, small clocks
VCR, microwave, TV clocks
Cuckoo clocks too!
Alarm clocks
Weird clocks
Old, new, school clocks
Brown, gray, black clocks
White clocks too!
Those are just a few clocks.
Don't forget the blue clocks.
Last of all, best of all
Grandfather clocks.
Joshua Gillespie

Shadows

Looking at shadows,
clouds of darkness.
Wondering if they know
my heart.

Will they take away
all my tears.
Will they take away every wrong
and make it right.

Then the sun appears,
it was only a shadow.
France V. Caffey

Spirit Coming To Life

I feel like I'm on another roller
coaster ride that is taking me up,
down, over, under, and around.
But this ride won't take me up so high
I can't come down, down so low I can't
get up, over a mountain I can't
possibly climb, or under an ocean so
filled with despair I sink and drown,
or around a world filled with people
so unloving and uncaring, I want to die.
No, this ride will take me up to the
Heavens to talk to God, a forgiving God.
Down to the depths of my soul
to talk to me, a forgiving me.
It will take me over mountains,
for I am learning to climb under oceans
for I am learning to swim.
I will travel all around the world
and I will love all people for I am
learning to love myself.
Janice Blankenship

Looking Inside

Love dances in an
endless twirl and
shines throughout her like colors
within rainbows
aura so strong
down deep she
is complete and
she is wrapped
into the color
of love...
Debbie Kehaulani Graham

An Ode To Luke

Cuddly and yet
Cold and tough as leather
In the darkness of the night
He worships the climax of winter....
She longs for the hotness of summer;

Yet, they had a lot in common.

What was it?

If Luke wants to find out
He can ask the
Goddess of Crete...
Angella A. Focas

The Midnight Prayer

Holy Spirit descending dove
Come to us with all thy love
Sent from our Father up above
Holy Spirit descending dove.

Holy Spirit with all thy light
Rain down on us, with power and might
Oh come Holy Spirit, come this night
Holy Spirit with all thy light.

Holy Spirit with all thy power
Let us know that this is the hour
Ring from the rooftop and the tower
Holy Spirit with all thy power.

So Holy Spirit from this night
Fill us with your guiding light
Let us share your love and power
And be more like you hour by hour.
Darlene M. Armstrong

"We Are Growing Up"

Our fun years are
   coming closer to an end
We will never have fun
   like we usually did then

Now we will be going
   our separate ways
We will never forget
   those good old days

We are growing up
   everyday
to tell the world
What we have to say

We will meet new people
   Now and then
And make new friends
   till the end

No matter what we've
   been through, good or bad times
there is nothing but friendship
   will bring all of us closer together again.
Elsielyn A. Abad

Barking All The Time

 Barking, barking, barking
Everytime I hear my dog bark, I want
to scream.
Today, I would love to hear my dog bark.
Wouldn't you love to hear your dog bark.
Or would you want him to be quiet.
Jennifer Beaty

Sumiko

Silent,
Confused,
Life she may lose.

Emptiness,
Loneliness,
Unable to move.

Dependent,
Helpless,
Is there any justice?

Silent,
Confused,
Life she may lose.
Brandi Mitchell

School

School is so cool.
Cool is school. I
think school is totally
cool. The boys are hot,
the girls are cool.
Some people think school
is not, so cool. Stay cool,
stay in school.
I got to go be cool so
see you later.
Amy Moffet

Most Especially You

To say, "I love you Mother dear"
Could never quite convey,
The very special thoughts of you
Recalled this special day.

In looking back to long ago
To time when life was new,
Containing all its precious joys
There's most especially you.

This special day brings memories
To linger in my heart,
A place to sort them wistfully
And set each one apart.

Nostalgic recollections now return
To flood my soul,
And there in secret sanctum dear,
Your love collects its toll.

And once again, dear Mother mine,
I long for just a few,
Of simple joys, when life was young
But, most especially you.
Bertha Torbert

Little Wonders

A good night kiss,
Embracing love.
A sparkled eye,
A pure white dove.
Innocence lost,
Experience gained.
Living love,
A Spring's fresh rain.
James S. ClearyLittle Wonders

A good night kiss,
Embracing love.
A sparkled eye,
A pure white dove.
Innocence lost,
Experience gained.
Living love,
A Spring's fresh rain.
James S. Cleary

Love Whisper

The earth is still
Crickets sing their nightly song.
Something is in the air.
I feel calm.

What stories must be told
I think to myself,
I have so much to say,
Where to begin.

Love is always in the air it seems.
It is us who must catch it.
Touch it.
Feel it.
Be with it.
Yes that's it, this night
LOVE is the story being told.
Joseph M. Cresta

"Please Tell Me Why"

I look at his face and start to
cry, but the only thing he could
do is look back and sigh.
I look in the mirror and ask myself
what has he done wrong? Then I look
back at myself and say I have
to be strong. I tell him that I
love him alot, and hope that I
can keep the memories that I have got.
I tell him that he's got to be strong,
and to stay in my life with out
anything going wrong. Every night
when I kneel on my bed to
pray, I am hoping he will be
with me each and every day.
Ashley Geiger

Guilt

Sensations of birth
crystal icons of life
fleeing from the hellhound
through the urban bedrooms
and country mudrooms
of an atrophied spirit
flesh tears and loss
celebrate failure's pain
which restrains the soul
and destroys the body
now the silence of soil
the scentless neurons
and the recreant thoughts
of the life lived
are all memories
and the invisible leash
of morality
is leather with definite spikes
capable of piercing pain
and true suffering
Jae Emerling

"Garden Of Life"

Harvest the love in your heart
Culturing lives
In happiness;
Bury weeds of hatred
That lingers in a soul of malice;
Display a manifesto
Of goodwill
To facilitate an
Achievement of success;
Honor the genteelness
Of the artistic progress
In the fertile garden.
Hazel Smithson

Our Love

Out of darkness came Light
   Daring to shine.
Out of loneliness you gave Love
   Daring to live.
Love feeding your light,
   You read my secret pages
In the closed book of my life
   And released my spirit
With your touch.
   Filled by love our dream grows.
Come! Let us join lives!
   Let the tidal swell of passion
Sweep our fears asunder.
   Come! Let us be one!
A lasting embrace of intimate truth.
   Sharing our lives, our unity in
One eternal moment of time.
   United endlessly, forever.
Joann A. Payne

I, Antigone

Yes, I am called Antigone
Daughter of Oedipus,
Granddaughter of my mother.

When my brothers died
And Creon decreed that one
Should be left unburied,
I defied him.

Yes, I buried my brother.
Though my sister, older
And wiser, tried to stop me.
But I honored him,

And I paid the price.
I died by my own hand,
Leaving Creon without a niece
And his son without a bride.

Yes, I am called Antigone
I died, but my act
Of conscience lives on.
Isabel Martin

Untitled

Flowers grow almost everywhere.
flowers grow in many different places.
flowers grow in many different kinds.
flowers grow like people.
but there is one difference,
flowers grow in peace.
Jennifer K. Morrissette

Just One Day In My Life

Up all night and this is just one
day in my long enduring life.
Lied to my mom let sin take over a
once precious, pure soul. Let my
addiction have complete and total control
Loud music playing that I don't really
even like. Smile on my young face, body
fallen over welcoming the ground.
Partying till we all lose control
3:00 in the morning retching in pain,
a small heaving heap looked down
upon with faces of pity. That's
just another day in a less then perfect
life. Regretting my stupidity, my
mistakes. Now I feel the pain, unseen
damage. I hate and love the person
I've become. So young with an
old and ancient mind. So much
wonder and pain can happen in
just one day of my life, my reality.
Becky Reed

Searing Soul

Fires burn
Deep in the sky
Searing bolts
Singe the soul
Shrill shrieks
Pierce the ears
The light goes out
The sounds are silent
Isn't it divine.
Anthony N. O'Grady

It's Just Something The Demons Should Know

It's just something the
Demons should know: I
Don't owe you anything.

When they haunt me
And taunt me

When through the night
I hear their laughter
Ring

When they engulf my
Soul in torment and
Pain

When to God they
Complain

I am your demon

It's just something the
Demons should know: I
Don't owe you anything.
Jeremy Willis

Ode To A Dewdrop

Little dewdrop
Happy little dewdrop
Why do you dewdrop around?
Don't you know you dewdrop
that when you do drop
your dewdrop make no sound.
Bernice M. Ostendorf

Dreams

Dreams in our lives
Don't always come true
Hopes that we rely on
Don't always come through
But without dreams, what would we do?
Life would be hopeless
During our toughest time
With nothing to pull us through
So don't give up on your dreams
They lead to true success
Keep believing in yourself
And never settle for less.

Ashley Houser

Earthwalkers

Two guiltless forms
descend the marble stair.
They clasp hands lightly
and walk
with urgent steadiness
toward a common goal

It seems a shady descent,
yet a faint glowing
emanates, somnolent
from the end of their intent.
They stare with limitless eyes.
Searching
into the deep.

As of yet,
they cannot see
the light.

Autumn McClintock

Colors

Black and white
Determined the fate
Then fade to form
A present grey
To fill the void
It occurred just now
A miracle
To see
Throws splashes
Of color at
You and me
Then we look
Out of ourselves
And through
Our fantasies
At happy faces
That in a
Cruel reality
Fade once again to
Black and white

Julie Ann Curtiss

Fantasy, Lover

It's always you from night to night
From time to time I fantasize
It's never a face I know or see
Just someone there on top of me
Rising and falling like the tide
The faceless one plodding on inside
There's no guilt attached to it.
Even if you find out about it.
I wonder do you fantasize?

Diana Simmons-Martin

The Cherry Tree

The cherry tree
Did not bloom this spring.
It's proud expressions,
Once constant and fruitful
Had vanished in the winter skeleton.

And though it pained me
I cut the branches
It did not need,
Leaving a stump
And stubs in recovery
A bare heart pumping
For itself alone.

For the tree had to choose
To remain a splinter or to push,
Against wooden walls
Against twisted enclosures
Enter the air and bloom.

Ian Williamson

The Wonder Of Nature

Take a soft brush
Dip it in azure blue
Paint heavenly skies
An ever brilliant hue

Dip your brush in white
To touch soft clouds above
Perhaps to form a pattern
Of the angels we love

Dip your brush again
In a soft but cheery yellow
Let the sun come smiling thru
He's such a happy fellow

Then as evening falls
Let silver be your guide
Touch each tiny star
That twinkles side by side

Brush a bit of lustrous gold-
Bring the moon into sight
Watch the wonder of nature
As day blends into night

Bess M. Robertson

Sing A Little Lover's Song

Do re do re sing a little lover's song
Do re do re everyone sing along
Sing it swing it either high or low
Do re mi fa so la ti

Do re do re sing a little lover's song
Do re do re everyone sing along
Day time night time any time you go
Do re mi fa so la ti do

Love is always in the air
Love is always everywhere
In the fall and in the spring
In the lover's heart that sings

Do re do re sing a little lover's song
Do re do re everyone sing along
Sing it swing in the rain or shine
Sing it swing it for your love and mine

For your love and mine

Fred F. Heitzig

"Thorns Of Love"

My friend do you know Jesus?
Do you feel the power in his name?
Now's the time to follow him
To understand why he has came.

Jesus has brought salvation
To a world that's not his own,
He endured more than any other human
Mankind has ever known.

He walked among many people
Who betrayed him along the way,
But still in all he preached the gospel
Even on the sabbath day.

Thorns were placed upon his head
As punishment for his love,
Nails scarred his outstretched arms
As he ascended up above.

Faith is not seen by vision
It comes from deep within,
Trust in he who's spoke to you
The beginning and the end.

Janice Reed

Twice Upon A Time

Through your silence
Do you hear
My song?
The song I sing
For you alone.

Not wanting to
Do you want me to
Fly away from you,
You, already alone.
You, already lonely,
Among three million.

I am one in three million...
Open your eyes.
See me.
Open your heart.
Love me.

Arlene B. Rice

Does He?

Does he listen when you talk?
Does he hear what you say?
To keep you happy.
Does he go out of his way?

Does he give you his time?
Does he give you his heart?
If he writes you a poem
Does he know where to start?

Does he open the doors?
Does he pull out your chair?
If you're not around
Does he wish you were there?

Does he buy you roses?
Does he treat you right?
Whenever you're cold
Does he hold you tight?

Does he love you completely?
Does he cherish you?
Because if he doesn't
I certainly do.

Eric Thorpe

Ducks

I stopped my car,
   Down by the river
Then I got out to look around,
   About that time.

About forty mallard ducks appeared,
   Gliding across the water,
The sun was going down,
   Oh! what a beautiful sight.

Inch by inch I moved slowly,
   To get my camera from my car.
I turned around,
   The ducks were gone
There down by the dam,
   Quacking away,

Gladys E. Walker

Her Essence

She slips beneath her cloudy veil
Dressing maybe, naked moon.
Perfect whiteness bathed in stardust,
Omnipresent is she still.
Basking in her only light,
She is the moon in ageless night.
More radiant than an angel's glow,
Her secrets we may never know.
Her pale, marble, timeless face
A cold yet harmless fall from grace.
Where is she on those moonless nights?
Her presence lingers; starless flight.
She plays her part in fairytales.
Werewolves call her; doth she smile.
She's only whole twelve nights a year
And doth she worry, doth she fear?
Forever worshipped and adored,
Her luminescent silence pours.

Dena Loree Sweigart

Stand Alone

I stand alone watching the storm clouds
drift away with my childhood dreams.

I stand alone watching the angry river
carry away my memories.

I stand alone watching the serpent
within me surround my soul.

I stand alone watching the demons
devouring my friends and family.

In my hour of need
I stand alone.

Deana Rae Nethers

"Child Of The Universe"

You are a bit of stardust
Endowed with dreams.
The world, it seems,
Clamors for "reality"
Draining your vitality
To live the dream.
Recall — "We are such stuff
As dreams are made on"
Come, walk, with eyes
Fixed on the heavens
Whence you came
Not progeny of Mars,
But, offspring of the stars.

Dan Q. Posin

The Raindrops

Drip drop, drippedy,
Drop go the raindrops,
Oh when oh when
will it leave,
Drip drop drippedy
Drop there goes a
song
When will the raindrops
stop when will
they be gone.

Raindrops raindrops
lets go in and let
the fishes swim
drip drop drippedy
drop go the raindrops

Ashley Smith

How Precious The Time

How precious the time that passes
Each day seems so small
What really is our purpose here...
To struggle through life, then fall?

Oh, how often I stop and wonder
And often I stop and cry
For all those we do not know
Our lives will pass them by

Mother, can you hear me?
You have such a pleasant smile
Will you comfort me tomorrow?
Will you see my unborn child?

Have I told you how much I love you?
What can I do to comfort you?
How can the day be so warm and bright?
And I so cold and blue

There's a fate from which we cannot hide
It's only one that we all must see
That those we hold so dear today
Tomorrow, they may not be

John Hooks

The World In Touch With Nature

We are all in touch with nature,
   Each in our own little way;
     We admire the beauty,
     We cherish the sight,
Of a graceful animal on display.

We are all in touch with nature,
   Protecting it everyday;
     We study it's course,
     We follow it's path,
Yet we don't know how much it pays.

Though we are all in touch with nature,
   We do not realize all it's pain;
     We cut down forests,
     We hunt for fur,
And deride in it's rain.

To be in touch with nature,
   We need not know it's ways;
     Just accept it's here,
     And respect it's future,
And know that it's here to stay!

Erika Dahlstrom-Roadruck

Kittens And Cats

Kittens and cats don't both
eat rats. Kittens are too
small so cats eat them all.
When the rest of the mice
move out the cat catches trout.
When the trout are all gone
the cat finds a new home.
There he catches many mice
and thinks he is in paradise.

Amber Leigh Whitehurst

One Remains

I am
empty
and
a helpless, sexless
tumor
floats
in a silver bag

I am
empty
and
a man in green
drops
a crimson
bundle
in a can

One ceases movement
one moves on
and one
remains
empty

Charlie Harlan

The Unloved

In the motion he pulled her inside
Engulfing emotion as a silent notion
There is no light to find
Under her black eyes
Shines the surprise
To be shaker from heaven
To blind our damned eyes
To release this prison of passion
That keeps we as alive
In hell we rejoice
In a room pitted with cries
While I eat your soul ripe
In a sexual high
You need to unwind
The deep secrets I hide
I release it all inside your mind
In a naked gesture
In hateful nature
I enjoy hear you
Scream my name.

Edward Moussouris

"One"

Was their ever a reason
for me to call us one
one meaning two hearts
together joined in love
I guess I got my wish
for I'm stuck now with two hearts
but both belong to me
for mine was torn apart!

Dorian R. Bullock

Entelechy

Rolling thunder
   Enigmatic light
Untrampled footsteps
   Cool air nights

Unfought battles
   Biased swings
Moving cloths
   Outspread wings

Dismal days
   Hearts striving
Methods cursed
   Innocence dying

Racist thoughts
   Locked inside
Ancient skulls
   Freedom hides

Christopher Rice

Madoc

Yesterday I walked alone.
Enjoying life
friends family
working playing
companions
solitude.

Today I walk with you.
Enjoying life
friends family
working playing
companions
solitude
and something more.
Peace.

Helen Marie Iles

Two Becoming One

We are two becoming one
Entering into this holy place of God
When the day is finally done
Our lives together will have begun
And His presence will forever abide

As my bride walk the aisle
I see what I've been searchin' for
She have been here all the while
God's destiny for me since a child
The woman who I love and adore

Standing in front of the altar
Is the man for whom I've waited
We will share many laughter
As our love becomes richer and stronger
This I sincerely anticipate

We want to let all of you know
As you witness this special occasion
We want our love to flow
Our trust and understanding to grow
We were two now we are one.

Gregory Darty

Fate's Broken Thread

Illusive of choice in the womb,
   even as aging and death beset you,
Brought forth already gasping
   in air of defiance,
   as if you already knew.

Conflict secretly grinding the soul,
   burdened low with heaping ashes,
Settling a course for steady pace
   to walk as a sluggard,
   among the bleached white bones.

Imagined fate crushed underfoot,
   aroused from a veil of darkness,
Into light sketched with a hope
   to preserve the days ahead,
   as the eyes grow dim.

Wisdom, a golden frond to grasp,
   forever guarding it from silence,
The vine drinking in nourishment,
   from the root of good pleasure,
   Who foreordains the cupholder.

Betty Gallas

NaNa

You are no forgotten
Even though you are not here.
You are remembered
Year after year.

The tears I shed
Upon my face,
When I saw you buried
In that big white case.

Nobody knows why.
Nobody to be blamed.
A memory remembered.
A picture framed.

I will be with you soon.
I don't know when.
So, wait patiently
And I'll see you again.

Amy Pananen

Faith

Faith is knowing
Even when the strong winds are blowing
faith is the key to all you will see
faith is believing God,
when everything else seems like a phased
faith is keeping your dreams alive
when there is thousands of enemies
moving in on every side -
faith is knowing you have a place to hide
the father has a place for us,
all write bye his loving side,
faith knows when the battle is tough,
it can see the other side of your dreams
and visions and gives you wisdom
to endure all the hard stuff.
Faith is knowing that you can put it
in Gods hands and He alone will bring it
to pass and remember, never fear, doubt or
be dismayed,
keep praying and believing, you will see
your dreams and vision come to pass
because God is Faith

George A. Farrugia

God's Gifts

Every tree and all its branches
Every bird that sings
Each sunrise bright and shining
God made each and everything

Each little petal on a flower
Each cloud up in the sky
Every sunset warm and glowing
God made each and everything

Every mountain tall and glorious
Every hill small and green
Each wave out in the ocean
God made each and everything

For our God is good and giving
He made each and everything

Angel M. Stephens

Untitled

I used to go and visit him
Every now and then
I was never quite sure why I was there
It seemed I was somewhere I did not belong
Yet I yearned to belong to him

We never ate real dinners
And I stayed up way too late
Singing songs together
He sang songs about freedom
And I sang songs about refuge

What an odd couple we were
Thrown together by blood
They say I have his eyes
I wish I had his genius
Without the obsession

Now sometimes while I lie in bed
Wrapped in the arms of my husband
I sing a sweet song of refuge
And I think that somewhere in heaven
He is singing a song of freedom

Allyson Atwell

My Love's Love

Love....what is love?
Everyone describes it differently.

My portrayal of love is the love you devote to me. You give me passion yet firmness. You give me joy with happiness. You grant me security but allow freedom. You protect and guide. You listen but share. You cherish me and show it ever so much. The love you offer me goes without comparison to anyone in this earthly world. You, Jeff are the rarest example to all mankind of that word. That word which has many different meanings, yet is known throughout the whole world, is love.

Jennifer Coulter

Sweat Of God

The sweat of God flood's the earth
Everything below is destroyed
Pain of man
Pain of woman
Feel the rain of God

He washes down the dirt
Dirt from the sins of man
Collecting all the evil thoughts
The sweat of God is your land

God's tears of Holy water
Cleanses the land
But, Us, man can lend a hand
I can hear the Angel's band

No more impure thoughts
That's why he fought
Because he taught, His people to live
And to give

The sweat of God is your land
You need to lend a hand
Remember the Angel's band

Donna Bonacum

Child's Awakening

The absence of light prevails,
except for the tall pillars,
man made light
bugs flock to it.

The heaviness of the air; a weight.
I clasp the cold hard aluminum,
and approach my fate.

Then it comes, slowly at first.
I can count the red stitches
One-Two-Three-Four.
My muscles tighten,
My hands feel the vibration,
I watch it fly away.

I run, faster, harder.

The crowd up on their feet,
Their voices echo my pounding heart.
I smell the grass,
taste the victory,
immortalized forever,
then I blink.

Jayne Polizzi

Life And A River

Life and a river
flowing through time,
growing to the climax,
slowing down, dying.

Life and a river,
start as a baby and a creek,
grow to a stream and toddler,
advance to a child, a tributary.

Life and a river,
continue to grow, a teen, a river,
a raging river, an adult,
a senior, a lake.

Life and a river,
an ocean, death.

Christopher Appleton

Gghist

Fire outlines six circular faces
exchange smiles tongues roam
A hand. Gloating laughter
Howls,
Begins to question satisfaction
Soot - covered guardians dust
outlines the insides
Flavor of nothing in between
tongues circling exchange and
fire laughter begins satisfaction
Howls in between tongues
Guardians exchange faces
Hand outlines soot - covered flavor
Faces begin circling laughter
in between howls exchange
begins a fire of six
Dust tongues the insides
Circular flavor of circling
laughter howls roam

Jerry Trimmell

Viking

Mountainous cheekbones of his land
   Eyes reflecting icy fiords of blue

Mouth carved of granite till it
   softens at my touch

Capable hands engulf my eager face
   Lifted to receive his kiss of grace

Voice deep and gentle
   reassuring and kind

Set my heart afire, rekindle this
   past love of mine

Rumbling laughter deep within
   Captures my soul

As we begin again...

Jeannette Spencer

Shattered Dreams

"She enters the door
face down to the floor
In hand two little boys
so quiet no noise."

"Her long lived dreams
shattered for sure
Her pride she did swallow
she'd learn to endure."

I watched her daily
through pain and through strife
As she picked up the pieces
to mold their new life.

"I'll be her friend
to the very end
Like a sister indeed
I'll come to her need."

"Living and learning
loving and sharing

Our hearts will soon mend
from all of the caring."

Cindy Sue Fullen

No Way To Escape
dedicated to my father (Al Paser)

I walk lamely
failures cover my heart
tightly like a web of spider
tear it into pieces
without pity for my future.

I struggle with all my might
to get away from it
but I fall headlong onto its lap
with no way to escape!

Darkness surrounds me
catching my hands
dragging me to the edge
of a rocky ravine
surrounding me with misery.

I shout loudly
but no one answers.
I'm simply
alone
in the darkness.

Francis de Sales

Reminders Of You

The tears that
Fall down my cheek
Wash away the anger
And I am filled
With melancholy memories,
Memories of long ago.
Those reminders of
Harvest moons and
Sun-drenched days
In each other's arms.
Memories of times spent together
And short times apart,
Of idle chatter
And late night talks.
But most of all— memories of you.
Fond memories they are.
The mind is sweet
To the past and omits failures.
The past is delightful,
At least the past I recall.

Johanna Curry

Tears

  A single tear
falls from a lonely eye
  She'll love him forever
never knowing why

  The love is strong.
  The devotion high
but he could never see it
with his naked eye.

The pain is forever.
The heartache is shroud
His name in her mind echoes so loud.

His very words,
His very touch,
His very looks, means so much to her.

A single tear
falls from her eye
As she turns around
And tells him good-bye!

Amanda Johnson

A Place Of My Own

A place of my own
far, far away;
no people no places
no sorrow no play.
I'm all by myself
no one else in sight;
it seems to get darker
with only a faint yellow light;
in the morning I'll awake
going back in the night.

Crystal Zett

Lost Muse

My summer Muse is hidden
far from intrusive chords
of power tools and clattered pipe
high decibeled next door

My fury falls on brawny shrugs
my toothless wrath is spent
curdled rage is what I drink
my thirst for peace unquenched

Wrinkles etch my once smooth brow
my voice is split to gravel
no longer sweet on tender peace
my Muse's skills unravel

Frustration bores a deeper hole
in this fabric of my life
months of hard-hat society
have made my patience rife

With bedeviled tasks and angry stance
rich fodder for a place
far from my present domicile
deep within a quiet space

Elisabeth S. Kassan

Watchman

The watchman stood with
fearsome strength, so little ones
in fearless sleep, would wake
to shining songs.

He worked the fields by
full moon skies, with lighted
windows in home of homes,
to fill his heart with pride.

His splendid spirit eyes
would roam and gaze and gather in.
At end of watch he slowly walked,
All remembered and nothing lost.

Watchman who with gentle words
Saying what he saw,
Taught little ones to see,
And sing a shining song.

Jeff Anderson

Survival

The tree that never had to fight
   for sun and sky, air and light,
But stood out in the open plain
   and always had its share of rain,
Never became a forest king
But lived and died
A scrubby thing.

Elene G. Thomas

The Snow Bird

Feed little snow bird
   Feed while you may.
The storm is coming
   'Twill be here today.

Hide little snow bird
   Hide in the hay.
When the storm is over
   You can come out and play

Busy, lively snow bird
   In your coat so warm;
It is scant protection
   In this kind of storm.

Berniece Doudna Shults

Contemplation

I wake up in the morning
Feeling just fine
I look up into the Heavens
And speak what's on my mind.
I talk about my love for Him
My deep desire to please;
My humbled heart grows heavy
And brings me to my knees.
The tears that flow remind me of
The sinful state I'm in.
But if I am obedient
I know that I can win.
The prize that's set before me
Is everlasting love
Coming from the Father
And from His son above.

Julia King

Winter

Gentle, soft, snowflakes
fell to the ground.

In the winter sunlight,
the snow glistened.

Christmas cheer was
all over the place.

People hurried to stores
to get their special gifts,

Carolers went door to door,
singing their spiritual songs.

Families gathered around
their fireplaces with cocoa.

Even though it's cold,
everyone feels warm.

It should be like this
all the time.

Jen Jeffers

Hummingbird

You sit on a thistle, sipping
from the bowl of a purple cup.
Could that I but join you,
together we would sup.

Dancing to and fro,
zipping like a bee.
In a world both up and down,
What better way to be?

Glenn Lee LaRocque

As You Walk Along

As you walk along the lane of life
Filled with loneliness and strife,
The choice is yours as how you go,
Traveling along fast or slow,
With holes in your shoes
Or floating in air.
The choice is yours,
The choice is there.
If you go along with smoke and booze
Or if you ride in a Cadillac
With no pack of worries on your back,
The choice is yours,
The choice is there.
With Cadillac and wafting air
You educate yourself, my boy.
Cram in for all you can
So you can ride in comfort
And follow life and be, in life, a man.

Fred I. Patterson

Inspiration

The sunset
Flames in me,
The sunrise stirs.
Life's zest and beauty
I sense and see,
As though reflected
By inner pools
Of soulful symmetry
I cannot forget.
In awesome wonder.
I write as led
To share of
Something lovely
That flows through me,
A dimension immortal
I must tell.

Jane Huelster Hanson

Mother Teresa

You bring light to the darkest corner,
   Food, where there is no bread.
Love, for the ones forgotten,
   Hope, to replace despair.

Poverty knows no boundaries,
   And charity no frontiers.
You are where the help is needed,
   And bring joy instead of tears.

Reward, you don't ask for any,
   Just follow the world of God.
That guides you to do some good,
   For people the world forgot.

Example, that few will follow,
   All we do is sit back and cheer
For the job you do so well,
   On the ones you hold so dear.

A coin in the extended basket,
   A smile for the person there.
With that we have done our duty.
   Two steps, and we "cease to care".

Diego Parra

Untitled

Together again
For a few hours
A moment, a smile

Our eyes meet, and
Mentally take a picture
To last the lonely
Nights ahead

We touch, we feel
Without saying, we
Know our love is
For real

Together again
For a few hours
We had everything
Charlotte Hartman

Beauty

Beauty is in the mountains —
for all the world to see.
With all its springs and fountains,
flowing so wild and free.

Beauty is in the rivers of green —
that race to oceans so blue.
Making one feel peaceful and serene,
knowing each day will be new.

Beauty is in the trees —
standing so tall and proud
As the wind rustles the leaves,
making their voices sound out loud.

Beauty can be in everything —
If we only choose it to see.
The beauty that life can bring
Will someday set us free.
Darlene Phillips

Grandma-Ing

We walk in the Park
Hand in hand
Grandma and Grandson.

See ducks, geese,
Squirrels and fish,
Kids and nannies, too.

You grow, we go
No longer hand in hand, for
You run, play, swing and slide.
Grandma sits quietly by.

A few years later
You are a teen.
Go to the Park
Walk hand in hand with
A lass, a sweet sixteen.

Grandma strolls by.
You meet, greet, chat a bit.
She smiles, waves
Walks on alone.
Esther M. Nelson

Indian Wanderer

Indian Drums
beating steadily
Imagine:
Copper skinned natives
by a fire
chanting rhythmic chants,
listening to their leader.
Talking
about ancestors,
the spirits,
wind, rain and fire.
Asking
for blessings
a good harvest,
plentiful hunting.
Joy.
Some, dancing native dances
Some, donned in colorful feathers.
Peace.
The fire glows softly, some watch for
signs, all wait for answers.
Jenni L. Poole

Praise To Him

Praise to HIM this morning,
For hope has come to me.
No more have I a restless soul
Without my Lord it could not be.

Praise to HIM today,
For faith has come to me.
No more do I walk in darkness,
For instead HIS light I see.

Praise to HIM today,
For I am able to live, with HIM
No more will I be tossed about
giving in to every whim.

Praise to HIM today,
For keeping me strong
Through thick or thin,
No matter how long.

Praise to HIM tonight,
Rich am I, for God has revealed
Himself to me, cleansing my soul,
my life to HIM I yield.
Jason Jaenicke

One Simple Miracle

You and I a miracle
Gave every wish ethereal
Moment of happening I knew
You and I were true.

There you are away afar
Present in spirit spoke that star
Time or space shall not erase
Vision of loveliness beheld in your face.

If GOD is all and all is one
May eternity link our hearts
Until kingdom come united above
In love that never departs.
Gary Abraham

The Creator

To you, I give life,
For I am your death.
I live in your nightmares,
I consume your dreams.
I am all that is beautiful,
Yet evil lives within.
I am not what you see,
For you can never be.
I was, in the beginning,
And shall be in the end.
To you, I give my tears,
For your blood, I have shed.
Your life, which is mine,
Can you only borrow.
I give you today,
But I take your tomorrow.
You can run from my light,
But I will seek you in the darkness.
For I am the light, that shows the way,
Yet I am the darkness,
which will always stay.
Brenda K. Jackson

Mount Fuji Sunrise

Appreciate this sky,
for it lasts only once in this eternity.
A new moment
changes its shade completely,
and looking at it in the evening
casts a shadow
in every pocket of light.
So live in the morning
where it becomes luminous
with each passing cloud.
Courtney Chiba

Willow

A willow weeps
For love has pass'd

The one I longed to last

Drifting leaves
Of memories
Sleep upon the grass

The wind awakes
To breathe a sigh
Light about the sky

And tender dream
Is whisk'd away
As cloud upon the air

Tho' lingers long
The wish of you
With love we once did share.
Amber Howe

In Loving Memory

There comes a day for everyone
 for when they must go away.
Why you had to leave us
 no one can ever say.
Our memories are all you left us with
 when our hearts were pierced with pain.
For you were taken from our lives
 is what we must face each day.
There comes a day for everyone
 for when they must go away.
James Thomas Williams

Some Say...

Love is blind,
For that
I am thankful.
For if Love
Wasn't blind,
Then..
Who would have it?
You must have Love
Or you have nothing.
For Love
Overlooks the wrong,
Sees only the right.
Oh! If only everybody
Was blinded by Love!

Joshua Hernandez

Only Through Love

Do not take only the colors,
  for the ocean underneath
  is yours.

It is only a prism,
  holding the promise,
  that the resurrection is
  in your eyes.

It is only through Love
  the ascension happens.

It is, as it always will be.

It is only in Love
  the gift is made complete.

I see your face, even
  when you are not before me.

And I fall to my knees.
  The taste of your sweetness,
  resting always in my soul.

Janine C. Murray

The Soul

The heart and mind do not make up the soul
For the soul belongs to a higher authority
Which can give it life
Or take it away.
A soul can be saved
But only through one way.
The Way is seen to those who believe
But the blind fools must pay a price
The price of the death of their soul.
The soul.
Not the mind
Not the heart.
For the mind can be deceived
And the heart tampered with.
But the soul is protected.
It is safe
In the arms
Of our Creator.

Joan Marie Sladky

Call Me Friend

Colour of skin doesn't mean a thing
For we were centuries apart
Yet heart to heart
A Friend said to me
"Girl, you need to get smart"
Look at her skin ___ milky white
Look at yours ___ black as night
Touch her hair - smooth as silk
Then touch yours - kinky, fibre, filth

But I was determined to start anew
To change history I knew what I had to do
I looked beyond the surface
I saw beyond the lies
Then I looked into her eyes
And saw a heart with no disguise
We shared a past - developed a bond
And now it was time for us to move on
'Call me friend', I said to the lady

For she was "white"
She was humanity.

June Marcelle

Ode To The Turkeys

What a sad sight
For your life you have to fight.

No one else to blame
You have no shame.
Sand traps tracks are proof,
No blame to Nene goose nor
prints of human hoofs.

I have given you names,
Three Toe, Bill, Blue, Ken, and Joe.
We spent a lot of time together
Playing toss and catch the corn games.
How I wish you didn't have to go.
I saw an arrow...
Oh, my special blue.
None more friendly than you.
What have they done....
Goodbye, my friend, my special one.

Alfred Lauro

"Our Veterans"

V - Stands for our veterans who
    fought for the red, white and blue
E - Is everything they have done not
    only for me left for you
T - Is all the tears we shed when
    they were far away
E - Everything we praise them for
    day after day
R - Is right they are and right
    they will always be
A - Is all the fighting done in air
    and land and sea
N - Stands for never forget them
    whether here so far away
S - Means to salute them on
    this great Veteran's day.

Eugenia W. Spaldo

Lingering Love

Like a sigh in the warm wind of a
    fragrant summer eve,
My desire, to store away and save
    for day-dreaming on an idle day
    with time to spare.
It's like spring water rising
    on a wooded hillside
To recall my lingering love.
I can feel it — I can't say it
    isn't there — and even if I
    cover it with rocks and leaves
And things to stem the flow,
I still can hear a happy murmuring
    below.....
That effervescent memory of love
    long ago.

Cyra G. Renwick

Best Friends

  We will always be best
friends, everyday until life
ends. We will be each other's
guiding light even if we
sometimes fight. When we
are very far apart we'll
always be in each other's
heart. We'll never forget
the good times we've had,
even when life's treatin'
us bad. We will always be
there for one another,
especially when we need
each other, so whatever
happens at the end we'll
never have to worry because
we'll always be best friends!

Elaine Mealy

Come Play The Game

Mummied in sheets
From our heads
To our feets
Time was no matter
Just up and down game
Of shoots and ladder
Chances seeming precarious
Venturing to unveil
Exactly what's sleeping
Beneath the skin
Surrounding monotones of silence
And prestigious glances
Hinting to come play the game
Of seductive forbidness

Janelle Phillips

My Own

Some day I'll sing my freedom
From the chains that bind me still.
I'll walk along the path I choose
And bend the world to my own will.
On that day the sun will rise,
In utter glory I will stand
Exactly where I want to be,
So far from where I first began.
But now I'm just a frightened child,
Cold and naked, afraid and alone,
Sitting, sobbing, in the shadows,
With nothing but myself to call my own.

Adrienne Kiser

Forcing Death To Pass Me By

Let me go, I cried
From the depths of my soul.
But she wouldn't listen,
Replacing water with air,
Breathing life into me.

Let me go, I cry
From the depths of my soul.
But they can't hear me.
My silent scream only a
Behavior dealt with.

Let me go, I cry
Softly from my soul.
But no one's listening
As I drool in my wheelchair
Shackled by life-worship.

Let me go
I cry silently
With my soul

Candon Aelfdan Clannach

Light

Twilight or evening star,
   Forever noble and marvelous;
A true companion
   For the solitary travelers.

Or, standing aloft
   In a cold stormy night;
You lead the way
   For a stray ship to fight.

Search endlessly for
   The end of darkness.
You are - an enemy
   To failure; a friend to success.

Helen Li

Funny

Funny how love can be...
Funny how you wanted me.
Funny that I should choose you,
Hoping I would never lose you.
I dreamed of holding you,
Funny how my dreams came true.
Funny how dreams can leap,
When someone tells you,
"I'm yours to keep."
Funny how love can turn cold,
After only a few months old.
Funny how easy hearts can break,
When the love was only a fake.
Funny how love can die.
So funny, that I want to cry.

Cindy Smith

"Life"

Life is hard, did you say?
Have you walked in
Someone else's shoes today?
Once you've opened your eyes
Your problems might
Seem like a prize!

Dottie J. Johnston

Please Let Me Go

You are a thing,
from the past.
That I don't have any feelings for,
and never will again.

I haven't had feelings for you,
since our relationship ended.
Now that I have changed,
and still am changing.
I know that I,
will never love you again.

What you need to know,
and understand is that.
I don't want anything,
from you or to be,
a part of your life.
You also need to know,
that I am in love with someone else.
So if you would,
would you please let me go?

Christine B. Trenary

An Afternoon Drive With Vida

We emerge
from the trees

And suddenly

The landscape
is so piercing

So wide open

So much the way
I wish my heart to be

With rows and rows
of emerald green corn

Gleaming
in the distance

My eyes
fill with tears.

And I hear you say
there is nothing
quite like the beauty
of a corn field.

And silently I agree.

Christine Rodgers

Revenge

Head throbs, eyes strain
have to focus on the pain
hands shake, eyes twitch
have to get back at the witch
set the bait, have to wait
set a date, don't be late
broken back, stomach aches
a hypochondriac is one that fakes
veins pound, as does my head
wait much longer and I'll be dead
blackness calling, fastly falling
life's appalling, life's appalling.

Angie Iler

An Ode To Julie

How I have loved you
from the very depths of me
I wonder how I can go on
when you, I can never see.

Never to touch nor hold you again
not even to feel your warmth
not ever to see that crooked grin
nor you looks of triumph.

The rolling laughter from your lips
shall never again touch my ear
and your wonderful silly wit
again I'll never hear.

I never thought a heart could break
Oh! I was so wrong
when the wind your soul did take
I found I was not so strong.

You will always be the breeze
the wind in my hair
and when I ask, will you please
brush my cheek - I'll know you're there.

Loving you forever, Mom

Frankie R. Smith

Ashes

I belong in the air, everywhere
From there you can see
Where there is no fear
There's no need to hide
Up and away far and wide
Up in the air
Where everything's clear
At times you can hear
A voice that is dark
Darkness can hide
All that is you
All that is me
Far and away, where
There is no need
No need to be seen
No need to be heard
Now it's all clear
For now I can see
Because you see
It's all of me.

Anna Diaz

The Foot Of The Mountain

Why stand at the foot of the mountain
Gazing at the top?
Hurry and put your sneakers on,
Start climbing, and do not stop.

For there's room and there's knowledge,
Opportunity, and there's peace of mind.
There's also your unfortunate brother
Whom you have left behind.

There's so many helpless children
That's running in the street,
And begging on every corner
For just a bite to eat.

So don't stop climbing, just hurry,
Where there's love and grace,
Then look up to Heaven,
And pray for the human race.

Dotsie Jefferson

Thank You My Friend

Sweet words
From your lips they fell
Their meaning to me
Deeper than a bottomless well
From your heart
Taking it so sincere
Though the moment is long past
I'm still standing here

Listening to you
Again and again
Listening to you say
Thank you my friend

Simply spoken
In your inimitable way
It's your love that says more
Than those words can ever say
Shining clearly through
And I understand
Why it is I'm here
In that evening I still stand

Charlene Ralph

Children

Children! Children, everywhere.
Full of fun, frolic and play.
Scampering here, there and yon,
Hardly knowing what to say.

Eyes, bright and filled with wonder,
Minds questing for enlightenment,
With imaginations going full sway,
In their heads, dreams of enchantment.

Let's not take away their hope,
Nor their dreams of tomorrow.
We don't want them lost forever,
To our shame and sorrow.

Let us protect these fragile beings,
Let us lead them by the hands,
Not by what we say alone,
But what we do throughout the lands.

Our resources for tomorrow.
Our endeavors quite rewarding.
When we do what God requires,
Our precious children we are guarding.

Bonell Fields

Our Sweet Mom

She's a beautiful lady
Full of grace
A pretty smile
Adorns her face
Whenever we were lonely or
Whenever we were blue
Our Sweet Mom
Knew just what to do
We know we will miss her
We know we will cry
But we know we will have to
Say good bye
And when tomorrow comes
And she is not here
We'll have her sweet memory
To hold close and dear
So don't worry Mom
We'll be ok
We'll have God's guidance to show us the way!
We love you Mom, please go in peace.

Barbara Forstrom

"Gift From Above"

Gifts of clothes
Gifts of toys
Pretty little girls
Rowdy little boys

Precious tears
Treasured hugs
Golden smiles
A child's love

Mom knows best
Daddy's love
A newborn baby
Sweet gift from above

Imaginary friends
A game of peek-a-boo
A child whispers
I love you

Being a parent
A double edged sword
Really a gift
That has it's own reward

Jim Bass Jr.

Embrace God's Love

A promise of a rainbow.
God's love so great and bold.
A promise of a savior
With joy His words are told.

God's love so divine.
A gift of His Son He gave,
To cover your sins and mine.
Through faith we are saved.

God's loving Spirit to guide
A heart full of bubbling praise.
His love in us will abide.
The name of Jesus Christ we raise.

God's mercy He shows
With love and grace.
Open your heart, in love flows
To all the human race.

Faith in God's Holy Love,
Faith in God's Holy Son,
Faith in God's Holy Spirit,
Eternal life we have won.

Eva Bell

Help Me!

Lord, I ask not only,
For an honest living,
But to have a heart forgiving.
And let me confess all the wrongs,
From this old heart,
That you have known.
The one you turned,
In me that day,
That very time I went astray.
You showed me what,
A good life could be,
If from sin I would flee,
Into the arms of one who waits,
Standing there at Heaven's gate.
To love and duty I am bound,
For the joy of the Lord,
Which I have found.

Emile A. Cantrelle

It's Not What Everyone Think

Everyone that laughs is not
happy, everyone that cries is not sad.

Everyone that Pray is not righteous.
Everyone that sin is not bad.

Everyone that hear you, is not
a good listener and everyone that
listens does not hear you.

Life is so confusing in so many ways.
I can be up for a while and
down for many days.
The key thing to that is stand up
for self and know when to say NO
always keep the faith and ever lose hope.

One day you are here the next day gone.
One day you have
friends next day you are alone.
Just stay on your knees and continue
to pray the Lord will hear you each and
every day.

Barbara Jean Carpenter

Collecting Point

A park bench resting in the rain
Has nothing but our butts to fear
Brooding softly in a pool of disdain

For those who do nothing but complain,
Drip-dried wood, hears us all too clear
Omniscient bench resting in the rain

Faded green slats creek under the strain
Of the bald fat man, sitting in tears,
Brooding softly in a pool of disdain

Listening to humanity go insane
A cacophony produces a sneer,
At a park bench resting in the rain

Old and tired with nothing to gain
Its immanent destruction is near,
Brooding softly in a pool of disdain

Only the frame is left to stain,
A faded green, skeleton so queer,
As a park bench resting in the rain
Brooding softly in a pool of disdain

Chip Olson

Polonius

Waiting behind the curtain
for the prince to draw his sword;
he will ask: "A rat?"
And will stab me through the arras.
I hear his voice talking to his mother:
Is getting closer and closer,
as I have to stand here
to fulfill my destiny.
Don't condemn him yet,
ladies and gentlemen of the jury:
I depend on him to die,
just as he can't seal off his own fate
without killing me;
we need each other
to complete this tragedy.

Arnold M. Krockmalnic

Apaches

Great warriors
Have stopped fighting.
White tepees stick out.
The desert is still.
Boom!
Deer skins hang.
Rain drops from the sky.
Deadly warriors sleep.
Spanish widows morn their husbands.
In the village
There are scalps hanging.
Day breaks.
Brett Goodman

For Daniel On His Seventh Birthday

Once there was a mighty train
He had a song
He sang, "Choo-ooo Choo-oooo".

And to the woods
And to the hills
And to the valleys wide and deep
He gave his song
While he rolled along
For a secret he did keep.
He loved his valleys, woods and hills
When he passed them every day
And in his song
So loud and long
They learned his secret too,
In locomotive language
"Choo-oooo choo-oooo" means,
"I Love You".

I hope you will remember this
Each time you hear his song
And know we both are singing
And both will love you long.
Becky McCarley

"My Friend"

What a friend of mine
He is so divine
What a friend of mine
He made my world shine
For my God above
Took my friend of love
His legacy is gone
But, mine lives on
His fullness of life
Never gave him a wife
What a friend of mine
Who even helps me at this time
What a Great Friend
I'm glad you were mine
Delena Cheryl Frye

The Parrot That Got Stung

There was a parrot that talked a lot,
He lived in Africa where it was hot.
He flew around a coconut tree,
Then he got stung by a bee!
He got stung on his wing,
He could no longer sing.
Gia Elie

Master, 7th Don

Man of knowledge, man of care
He who came from the Shoalin Temple
Best of students become best
Of teachers, as in the high priest
The wisdom of the old masters
Is fading away from tomorrow
Purity in mind and spirit
In protection of righteousness
Of the ying yang
Sea and waves
Chung Do Kwan
Korean, Chinese, Japanese
Masters of the art
Complementary to North American
Symbols of life
Heaven, sun, moon and stars
Katas into a jump sign side
Giving thus the terminology
Bloodshed only if necessary
From the Master, 7th Don
Jeffery Grant Amsden

Peace

And so the wind rolls on.
Hear the thunder crashing.
Reach deep within,
follow that thread
which leads you blindly
through the dark,
Your eyes will accustom.
Weave with your mind,
the story of your healing.
A tapestry of great colors
bright visions, was created
within your smile.
And so the storm blows on.
Peace.
Jenny Mead

Music

Listening to my music
hearing the words
As the beat fades away
    now all is silent
    there is nothing to hear
    no one to care
    the music has died
But the words stand tall
teaching of its own
so many stories
    not enough time
    no time at all
there is nothing
without music
nothing exists
without a beat
There are no lyrics
and no one can listen
or watch the faded shine again
Jess Mpelezos

A Journey Into Life

All began blessedly a miracle from
heaven, an adventure beyond
distance far in earth, life, space,
world; planted, rooted, soiled,
life in a prairie tree.
Charmaine Glover

Ecstasy

Her lips loomed large - all I could see,
Her tongue stood still - yet beckoned me,
And finding myself mesmerized
I looked once more - then shut my eyes
And leaned toward her - under her spell,
Then locking souls we gently fell
Into the place I longed to be-
Into her arms of ecstasy.
John Hartz

At The End

How did we come to this?
Hearts no longer in tune
Souls no longer mate
Thoughts that once we shared
No longer communicate.
Did we try hard enough
Did we quit to soon.
Was it too little effort
Or too little play
Or just that life's routines
Got in loves way.
How did we forget to remember
What did we forget to say
When did we sacrifice tomorrow
For today.
Forever promises and dreams
So easily set aside
Not enough love left
To give it a try.
Judy Dankers

"Bobo" A Black Labrador

Like morning mist,
Her spirit drifts
O'er wooded hills,
And races swift
Through flowered Alpine fields
To play amongst the giant trees
And swim each mountain stream,
The droplets shaken from
Her black and shining coat,
Appear as morning dew on grassy banks,
Each bloom refreshed to sweetened scent;
Long since, her joyous bounding form
Returned its sustenance to earth,
But on these shadowed forest trails
She's with me still,
By death, her spirit given birth.
Harry J. November

Life's Sand

Life is very much like sand.
Hold it tightly in your hand.
Gently, some will say they can.
All find some will fall to land.

Gritty, rough when held too tight
Keeping more, but why the fight?
Grasping hides your spirit bright.
Held up and out your sand is light.

Open wide your hands then see
What freely falling sand can be...
Not piled up but spreading free
More fun when it's not just for me.
John E. Reaves

The Wonder Of Christmas

December 25th - a glorious day -
Heralded by the melody of bells,
A day for many that begins when they pray,
And with joy and hope does slowly swell.

A time when men remember one
Who showed us a better way of life.
Such peace and serenity we had never known,
With days and nights devoid of strife.

Upon us the hush of heaven descends
As we reflect upon His birth;
A day when the fullness of time had come,
Bringing Good will and peace on earth.

Our hearts and homes are warmer then,
As we pause to sing and praise His name.
Families grow closer and dearer are friends,
And our lives will never be the same.

And when the day ends as surely it must,
All the world's troubles will not have gone;
But with spirits refreshed and faith rekindled
Our hopes anew will be reborn!

Eddiemae Livingston

View

View from my large window,
High grass like a flaxen hair
Waiving on the windy day
Wide open spaces over there.

Black dead tree stands in front,
Makes a picture card view well,
Wish to have a camera handy
To put the art in the frame.

Group of like halloween houses,
Bright lights shining warning you
Trick or threat voices you expect to hear
The witches are having a fun with you.

Then there is that beautiful sky,
Changing colors every day,
Light blue like the girl's skirt,
Dark clouds on the rainy day.

Hedy W. Formanek

Untitled

There I was in the middle of the land
Holding onto someone else's hand
Thinking maybe I maybe make it
Thinking maybe I give it a try
There I was in the middle of the night
Holding onto someone maybe too tight
Thinking I could do no wrong
Playing the same old song
There she was in the middle of a field
Holding onto all the love in her heart
Thinking maybe she'd send a flower
A gift across the rift

John Ruffing

Untitled

The sun is my light
It brings me hope for a new day
Flowers and trees come alive
It warms my smiling face
Life is back in the land and me

Chris McWilliams

"Home Makers Lament"

When I was so busy with "children and
home" time flew by so fast - I had
no time "alone to leisurely bathe"
do my nails even floss!!
But, the time was well
spent" - now, the "children" are
"grown"!
But the teeth in my mouth
are "no longer" my own!!

Ginny Dawson

The Hidden Pain

How heavy is my heart
   How empty is my soul
My tears ceased to flow

Many thoughts are of you
   Deep are my sighs
Oh, how my heart cries

Cheerful I appear
   There's laughter and play
Life goes on they say

I gaze at the ocean
   I stare at the sky
I know you are nearby

You come to life
   In familiar places I see
Where many times we chose to be

It's the magic of love
   I feel your warm touch
Our spirits bind
   From your world to mine.

Daisy M. Lem

My Cocoon

I'm doing fine, but for how long?
How long will it last?
I still feel sheltered, enclosed, and safe.
Yet, slowly escaping my past.

I sense some changes, subtle still;
but I'm changing nonetheless.
But, do I like what I'm becoming?
Am I at my best?

I really am scared inside.
there exists this frightened child.
I'm a butterfly inside my cocoon,
waiting for someone to let me go wild.

What I wonder is...do I have my wings?
Am I ready to fly?
If I make an attempt at this point in my life,
will I fall to the ground and die?

Jennifer Liguori

Depression

Depression, what is it?
I don't know myself
It lurches on to you like a leech,
Not letting go
But how do you get rid of it?
I don't know that either
Because my depression is still
Lurching on

Anna M. Gill

Ode To My Brother

Today I stood beside your grave,
How peacefully you slept;
As I recalled the years gone by
Silently I wept.

Those beautiful precious memories
That time cannot erase;
Kept flowing back in my mind
As tears streamed down my face.

The joys we knew, the happiness shared
Although there were moments of pain
Were I rich, my wealth I'd gladly give
To relive those years again.

I placed a rose upon your grave,
Hoping somehow to impart
The deep sorrow and grief
Your death leaves in my heart.

As I stood there in my reverie
Knowing that my life had been blest
I thank God that you were my brother
So sleep, you have earned your rest.

Edna F. Holsey

Night Sea

I see the sea waves at night;
how they sparkle all in fright
   running from the moon so bright.

I hear them beat upon the sand;
  playing conch shells in a band
   drumming up a march so grand.

I feel the waves upon my feet;
cold ice cubes that rob my heat
   stealing for Poseidon's eat.

I taste them with their salty kiss;
slapping my lips with a laughing hiss
  whispering to me, "Drink of this."

Night waves call and beg to me
"Come and join us in the sea.
Forever we will always be."

Hilary Helding

Observe

Isn't it funny
how we see things -
wee things,
things that move
in the corners of eyes
that lie.

A tree becomes moving leaves
on a branch, a single leaf
with the beetle on it,
and bird-s**t.

A crowd becomes people,
become a woman
with one blue eye,
one green,
with dark-thick eyebrows.

The night sky
filled with stars twinkling,
one flashing brightly.
Who stares back?

Benjamin N. Adler

Heart's Desire

The subject of my desire
How you rekindled that new love fire
Now it burns so out of control
Within my heart and thru my soul

Now in time by chance or fate
So desirable, I can not wait
What I thought was lost
And tremendous emotions were tossed

He claimed me to fantasy
A reality I could not see
For a touch, a kiss so strong
How could this be wrong

Quenching unrealized needs
Now I only feel pleads
To maintain a promise "no pain"
Reality sets me insane

Now all this is probably to deep
It's because he taste so sweet
And these memories forever I'll keep
For our relationship, the emotions are deep.

Evie L. Karlovec

Untitled

A young man rushes off to work,
   Hurried and heedless,
His mind attacked from all sides,
   By worries that are needless.

A sparrow is on the housetop,
   Singing at the sun;
He never wonders where he is,
   Or from where his food will come.

Are not two sparrows
   Sold for a single penny?
How much more are we worth
   To the wondrous Almighty?

The man will return home,
   Discouraged and depressed;
The sparrow joyfully will sing,
   Once he's reached his nest.

Yet both the man and the lowly sparrow,
   Knowing not by whom or when,
As they scan the vast world around them,
   Are cared for and guided by the great unseen hand.

Christina M. Rankins

Unforgiven Pain

Unforgiven pain
I carry deep inside,
unaware of the work
it takes to hide.
Laughing, loving, talking,
but still the pains remain.
What is the pain I hide
that little wounded child inside?
How quiet how sweet
never to let me know
the anger that lies so deep.
Unforgiven pain so hard
to let it go, because
I know it's me
who has hurt me so—

Gail Yandell

"Love Remains"

You are from one side of the tracks
I am from the other.
Not only my best friend,
But also my lover.

You grew up hard,
Much difficulty and woe.
I was given everything,
But true love I did not know.

You were in love with the needle,
My best friend was the drink.
We somehow found each other,
An undeniable link.

Fate brought us together,
Jealousy tore us apart.
Left alone with our habits,
And pain in our hearts.

You returned to your needle,
I went back to my drink.
Even with these renewed practices,
Each other we could not replace.

Debra J. Ayers

Power How Sweet It Is

I am in charge...I have power,
   I am gifted....I am free.
At my command, I have five senses
   Just to serve, thou me.

My two eyes, have both sight and vision,
   My two ears, bring the sounds to me.
One nose, one mission
   Sniff the air, that's free.

My two hands, can touch with feeling.
   All power, have the above:
Looking, listening, sniffing, feeling
   Serving me, with love.

Such talent have my senses,
   Each separate...each apart,
With the awesome mystery of science,
   The grace and beauty of art.

My two lips can seal, with kisses,
   Can sip my tea,
Can taste my honey,
   And can tell me...How Sweet It Is!

Frances G. Knight

Ode To An Ex-Boyfriend

I saw you on the road
I did not stop you to say hello
Memories arose of long days passed
Remember when we were young?
Starry nights out in the desert,
Half naked under the moon
Illusions of grandeur.
Disappointments.
Then goodbye.

Debbie G. Varelas

A Note From Grandpa

Do not stand at my grave and weep
I am not there, I do not sleep

I'm way beyond the tree tops far
I'm way beyond the highest star

I'm way beyond the deepest sea
So when you dream, you'll dream of me

So please forget the emptiness
That's being filled with sorrowness

Way down deep, within your soul
It soon will leave it soon will go

And think of all the fun times we've shared
Laughing, running and being scared

One day we will meet again
Perhaps this time in heaven

Do not stand at my grave and cry
I am not there, I did not die.

Erin McKinstry

"Unique And Genuine"

I am unique, and genuine
   I am, one of a kind.

No one, can take my place,
   In this, "Christian Race"

For, I, have a place in God
   Created, just for me.

There is a calling, that is uniquely mine,
   Just between God and me.

"For You see,"
   He made You...You,
And He made me...me.
I am one of a kind,
   "I Am Me!"

Dorothy R. Booker

Visions of Twilight

You fear what I am.
I am what you will become.
You and I are one.

Mirrors without sight
Reflect life's dissolving child
Image without depth

The children depart
A window reveals a ghost
Silent days alone

I am not old yet!
Gray whiskered grandpa would say
Chasing faded dreams

Shadows overhead
Angels patiently waiting
Gentle departure

Ellen R. Kirkpatrick

Burning Candle

Nights when I lay awake at night
I burn a candle and stare into the flame
I look into the flame as I think of you
Your soft touch; your tender kisses;
the sweet words you whispered to me
I stare into the flame as I feel the
warmth overcoming the room
all I can remember is feeling your
warm soft skin as you held me tightly
all through the night
As I glance at the candle
I see the flame dying
I think of all the lonely nights
I've sat here crying
I wish you would come back to me
So my eyes can start drying

Christie Bruno

Candle - Life

St - ri - ke !
I can feel a hot flame hovering over me.

Slowly...., my radiance springs abruptly
into a once-gloomy atmosphere.

My yellow-white flame flickers, wavers,
and reaches higher upward.

Shadows darken..., dance..., quiver,
and shake.

Suddenly, a door is opened!
A gust of wind engulfs me -

I....., expire!

Edward F. Willett

Autumn

It's autumn once again,
  I can feel it in the air,
There's a sign upon the billboard,
  Advertising the county fair.

The leaves on the trees are turning,
  Mother Nature has her brush,
Mid-October we'll all be going,
  To the mountains in a rush.

Clothing stores are full of people,
  Buying clothes right off the rack,
Dressing up the little children,
  Autumn means that school is back.

Autumn leaves the Autumn colors,
  Oh, how beautiful to see,
And of all the changing seasons,
  Autumn is the best for me.

Dixie C. Bickley

The Void

I reach out into the blackness,
I touch no one.

I cry out into the void,
I hear no one.

I have no direction,
I am lost.

The darkness surrounds me,
and I am alone.

James M. Szczublewski Jr.

Desire

Come to me in the darkness of the night
I cannot see you but I hear your footsteps
and your breath
Circle me with your arms
Cradle my head
Take my mind
Make me reach for you
  but be near
Let me push you away
  but don't go
No - I do know what I want
I just can't always tell you
Take the time to know me well
enough so words aren't necessary
Between us two
in the darkness of the night

Heidi J. Lemberger

My Thought

I'm lost in thought.
I can't find my way back.
I need to find peace,
but of it I lack.
The world's full of hate;
it needs love and cheer.
I'm calling for help,
but no one will hear
the sorrow of mind;
the grief I face
everyday of my life;
everyday in disgrace
from all the unkindness
the children face today;
they need lots of help;
We must hope and pray
for a better life
because it's not just a myth
that the world's in trouble,
and that's what I close with.

Brianne Fuss

Untitled

I laughed
I cried
I had fun
I died

He was my sun
He was my earth
He brought me pain
He brought me mirth

I thought we were as one
I thought we were but two
I hoped to be eternal
But I also knew

He was the one I wanted
He was my friend
He was what I hoped to be my life
And now this is the end.

Donna Falter

My Adoption Story

I cross the ocean,
I cross the sea,
waiting for someone to discover me.
I wait and wait until,
the midnight hour,
waiting for the hoot owl to howl.
Mother crossed the ocean,
she crossed the sea,
trying to discover me.
I found her,
she found me,
now we are a family!

Heather Keegan

A Struggler

I am a struggler from dusk to dawn
I don't know why but I carry on
Nothing comes easy
Nothing seems fair
I'm over here, when I should be there

Should have been done an hour ago
But because of my struggling
I have hours to go
Slip slide and fall is my normal day
And I wonder who else will get in my way

So if you see a struggler
Look up in the sky
And thank the good Lord
That he passed you by

Edward Wesolowski

Senseless Killings

Senseless killings.
I drive.
The street lights zoom by.
Arching palm trees wave as I pass.
Hollow buildings surround me.
Where am I going?

Senseless killings.
I work.
Clanging silver echoes.
Laughter fills the room - my head.
Stick-figure people surround me.
What am I doing?

Senseless killings.
I sleep.
Oatmeal occupies my senses.
Colors deafen me - I scream!
Fear and despair is all I see.
What can be done?
How can I stop
Senseless killings?

Anadel Baughn

Minimum Wage

Minimum wage
I earn minimum wage
Big business is my overseer
My life's incomplete, I'll never see her

Minimum wage,
I earn minimum wage
I'm working with people twice my wage
Who make less than minimum wage.

Adam Fuller

Untitled

Poetry is the way
I express myself
I love the rhythm of my poems
Beating like the rhythm of my heart.

How bright you are
Sliver of moon,
On this October night
Blinding me with your light.

There is no one but you
Trying with you is better
Than trying with anyone else
Partner, friend, beloved.

Emily Loube

"My Heart"

Every time our eyes meet
I feel my heart skip a beat
Your touch, so soft and tender
A feeling, I will always remember
Feelings for you, I've never felt
Ice on my heart, your love will melt
Love so strong, it can't be wrong
You've filled a need, I've forever longed
My love for you flows through my veins
Like a river flows after it rains
I would climb the highest mountain
Swim the deepest sea
Fly on a cloud across the sky
To make this love last for you and I

Jai Underwood

Reflection

Sometimes when we are alone,
I feel sadness in the air.
It becomes difficult to breathe,
I close my fingers around my neck
And so do you.
Then I can see the sadness,
All of it in your eyes.
And it hurts me to look at you.
I wonder why you stay with me.
You can be free,
But only if I free you.
That's when I walk away from the mirror.

Julia Petitfrere

Sign

Loneliness
I feel the rain come down,
Kissing me with every drop,
Touching me,
Securing me with its warmth
It surrounds me,
Comforts me,
It's there for me when no one else is,
It heals my wounds,
cleanses me,
Hugs me tight and cries to me,
And I remember my love,
Falling for an eternity,
I miss the rain.

Jill Carlin

"Dawn"

I am the moon's lover
I flow with the seas
I dance around the stars and
  sing with the sun
I sleep with the wildflowers and
  cry through the rain
I run beside storms and
  shout with the thunder

I am warmth and woe;
I am forever and I am whole

I am a dream and I am a memory
I am infinity;
I am the beauty that grows in you
I am the joy that speaks to your soul

I am a cloud angel. I am the grace
  that breathes within.

Elizabeth Aiken

Transcendence

As soon as I came upon the rose;
I fluttered.
I blossomed up against this specimen
  as if it were a spectacle of God.
And in my own mighty power...
  I became beautiful.
Not in the sense you may think,
  but in the sense of humanity.
I listened from deaf ears through the
silence. And in my own way, I saw
through darkness with blinded eyes.
  I touched each element of air.
And space became nonexistent.
As the wind blows upon the surface
  I reach down even deeper.
  I pick the elemented rose
and lift it to a higher element...
  much higher than man.
  and there...
  it takes it's place forever...

Brenna Dickerson-Czarnecki

Me

I come alone,
I go alone.

I am me,
By myself.

If no one else was left in this world,
I would still be me.

People influence me,
But I make me.

They change me a little,
I change me a lot.

You can't make me into someone else,
Neither can I.

I am me, by myself,
And don't ever try
And change that.

Athena Kazantzis

The Little Oak Tree

When I was just a little girl
I had only one little curl
It was on my forehead
And on my face
Everyone said "oh what a disgrace."

I think I'm like someone
Someone just me
I compare myself to the little oak tree

The oak tree is different
The oak tree is proud
In a forest of trees
It stands out
from the crowd

It reminds me of someone
That someone is me!
I think of myself
As the Little Oak Tree

Emily Wiesemann

A Loving Mother's Prayer

God I know
I have an appointment
with you, but please
let me help my
children out before
I do. Thank you Lord

Delores Holdren

The Daily Grind

Everyday it's up before dawn;
I jump into my car, and drive
to the city,
I'm choking on other car's
fumes all the way-it's really
quite a pity.
I spend all day behind a desk
and then back into traffic I go,
Why is it when I'm in a hurry
everyone else goes so slow?
Don't they know I'm rushing home
to get some rest-
so in the morning I can be fresh
and at my best?
Woe is me... and the daily grind.

Dorothy Peters

True Story

Telling you this, no disgrace
I put the gun to my face
couldn't stand life's ugly pace
Believe me it was loaded.
Couldn't stand as you winners goaded.
Pulled down on the trigger
Grandness in after life so much bigger
The gun only jammed
All my anger slammed
I just can't win
Living now worthlessly
Living in sin.

Caleb Clark

Silent Stores

Beside you
I lie,
gravity weighting
my truth.

In my body's darkness
I ensile my hate,
nurture the wonder
when will it burst forth,
knock you down, bury you?

A kernel of rage
brands my throat
with silence.
And, beside you,
I curl into myself
like a fist.

Holly Brooks

"My Mother-In-Law"
To Brother Tom

My mother-in-law is a dear.
I just married her daughter
and she was there in my hair.
I can't get through a sermon
without a mention of her name.
Bless her heart, I use her
as examples to explain.

Sometimes I poke playful fun
at things she says and does.
In return she shows what
good mother-in-laws are made of.
She takes it all on the chin
with love and kindness, she just grin.

I must have a talk with this ole dear
and let her know how much I care.
After all if it wasn't for her.
I would not have my bride, so dear.
I kneel in prayer and as I pause
I just thank you God,
for mother-in-laws.

Gladys Walls

Somewhere

Thou, I cannot meet them all,
I know that God has reserved a hall,
A hall which in majestic splendor stands,
Beside the Nile in heavens land.

A hall for those, as grand as she,
Who, were never meant, for boy's like me.
A hall where she shall reign supreme,
O're a land of those, as meek as me.

A land where girl's like she shall dwell,
As if under, Gods own great spell.
Where God will grant to those like she,
Eternal life so earned by thee.

Maybe he shall grant to me,
Just one chance to be with thee,
But if my fate shall be forever dim,
I shall never loose my faith in him.

Arthur L Harberg

Not Too Perfect

People are strange
I know this is true.
But have you ever thought,
the strange one might be you?
We look in the mirror,
and think we're alright.
Yet we're so quick to judge others
just by their sight.
It's so unfair to judge one's looks
you know the old saying
About "The cover of a book".
We need to look deeper,
And into one's soul.
We all need to stop being
So very cold.
The next time you see someone
Take time to say, "Hi",
For beauty can be seen
by anyone's eye.

Chris Torgersen

Knowledge Of The Heart

Knowing only what's to be learned
I learn over a summer's time,
the rules of life, a key to a smile
All the days pass, leaving only memories.
I spend these days of my life
only worrying about others
never about myself,
Should the days of our lives
only be meaningful if we smile,
Wherever I see a frown
I always ask what is wrong,
I try to help in any way I can,
Telling myself to smile and be happy
I learn more about the world,
Being able to see visions and understandings
through others eyes is sometimes good
The world is a scattered place
of a lot of dreams, wishes and pain
I know only what was supposed to be learned

Georgia Rangel

Sky

In the twinkle of an eye
I listen to the sky
Crushing my space
In a quiet place
A place of peace,

In the rapture of the heavens
I kneel to the sky
Clinching my space
In a quiet place
A place of peace.

In the illumination of the moon
I dance to the sky
Choosing my space
In a quiet place
A place of peace.

In the aura of my soul
I transcend to the sky
Collecting my space
In a quiet place
A place of peace.

Gale Ragan

Why I Travel

Oh world you're just so beautiful
I must see more of you.
There are so many places
that I must travel through.

To stand atop a mountain
and nearly touch a star
Is to realize that Heaven
really isn't very far.

To gaze out the ocean
in the silence of the night
I've never seen a diamond
whose sparkle is as bright.

Elaine Fornero

An Agnostic Prayer

If there should be a God on high
I pray you save land sea and sky
Spare the people set them free
In a seamless unity.
Give me hopeless in their pain
Strength to rise and start again
guard the children at their play
Bless the start of each new day
Keep sun and moon forever bright
Light up every star each night
Save the flowers birds and trees
Little dogs and bumble bees
Lead the lonely and the old
Through summers heat and winters cold
Guide each country race and creed
Far from war and lust and greed
And save mankind from souls so ill
Who dream to save but wake to kill
Should you be there be this thy will

Geraldine Allen Shields

I Love You, Will You Love Me Too?

I love you
I really do
Oh, will you
love me too?

I am hoping and waiting
for a clue
all the time praying
my dreams will come
true.

Oh, my friend told me
is it so?
That instead of
loving me you love
Rose?

Bethany Webb

Untitled

"Today" is just another day
I wake up and wish you were
beside me. And I tell my
self soon it should be very soon
that we meet cause we were
in love and that's something I thought
not even marriage can defeat.
Love the beginning of life has
me watching everybody else's
Waiting for you so you can take
me higher

John T. Yazinsky

Untitled

That night on the phone,
I sat all alone
Wondering if you'd ever come home.
That night when we talked,
I felt so lost
Wondering if it was worth the cost.
You're like a dream,
That flows like a stream
Into my penetrating heart
I'm back at the start.
It has been really tough
Without you here,
But when it gets rough
I know you're near.
Whenever you're away
I can only pray,
But if it's meant to be
Eventually, we'll see!

Angel Myers

Fairy Frolics

One golden, summer dawn,
  I saw a fairy on the lawn;
When I came close to look my fill,
  It turned into a daffodil.

There was a brownie in a tree;
  He was laughing down at me;
When I drew near to speak to him,
  It was a robin on a limb.

An elf was perched upon a blade
  Of grass, in the noonday shade;
I sat upon the ground close by,
  And it turned into a butterfly.

I heard a leprechaun call to me,
  From the heart of an old oak tree;
When I bent my head closer to hear,
  The wind's soft sighing filled my ear.

If I don't try to go too near,
  Their games to see and songs to hear,
The brownies, elves and leprechauns
  Will play each morn upon my lawn.

Dorothy Summers

Fleeting Dreams Of Youth

To things undone and dreams untold,
I scoff at thee and sigh.
T'was thrust upon this world so cold
To grow, yet surely die.

No melodious tunes of life,
to close to sorrow's friend.
My spirit broken down by strife,
my hopes gone with the wind.

I saw myself amongst the stars,
upon life's silver screen.
Traversing, through great lands afar
dining with royal queens.

But alas, our fondest desires,
concealed within our youth,
will burn out like smothering fires
during our quest for truth!

Jarrett Hallcox

Too Late

"Don't do it! Don't do it!"
I screamed
But he didn't listen to me
He never had.

"Kiss me! Kiss me!"
I pleaded.
But his lips clamped shut
And his eyes rolled right
He had already died that night.
"Too late! Too late!"
I cried.

Edith Devine

A Friend

When last he is no more,
I search my distressed heart,
For times I chose to spend,
Away from his warm hearth,
In search of what I had so near,
A Friend.

As breath no longer comes,
My thoughts will serve me well,
To find regret for bitter end,
As pride let ego swell,
And tore the bond that made him,
A Friend.

Please take from me this chore,
Of counting ways I turned aside,
A shoulder that would help in mend,
A hurt he felt inside.
How rich my life to have him as,
A Friend.

George Hartigan

"The Search"

Throughout this castle
I search the white room
I left so long ago to meet
With your needs and my expectations
To love and hold you
Who stole the key to
The room where I alone
Can find my peace and
Quiet, now I sit
As I search the light
Which met me with darkness
As I met you, that day
The sky was grey as is
The room I find myself in now
With coldness at my feet
Unwilling to lead me into
Brighter shades because my punishment
I now deserve what fate suggests
That I might never find
My white room again...

Carmen Albu

My Pencil

My pencil's very friendly
It writes words easily
and when I do not know it
It speaks out loud for me

Jill Kollar

The Silence Of Emptiness

As I look into her eyes
I see a mirrored reflection
Of my own sadness and despair
And so I say all that words can say
And so I do all that can be done
But it is all to no avail
So now I turn painfully around
And walk away from it all
But my heart is still there
Taking its bow at the end of a show
The lights dim away to darkness
The curtain slowly comes down
But there is no applause resounding
No roses awaiting it offstage
Just the silence of emptiness
A failed performance at the height of its career
Nothing left to do now but become a memory
So it is released but it does not know to where
Only that it cannot seem to walk off that stage

Eric D. Maack

White Mare

In her eyes
I see integrity and innocence
There is no regret
And there is no fear

Her white mane is flowing
Like wisps of satin lace
Her coat is smooth as silk
And it shines in health

In a gentle, rhythmic manner
She walks gracefully
Through the meadow
Expressing herself
Without saying a single word.

Danielle Steele

Our Flag

I see my home, I see my state
I see my country;
When I look at the red, white and blue
I see our ships, I see our schools,
I see our freedom.
I see our boys, who fought for her too

I see our plains, I see our fields,
I see our mountains;
Old Glory, when I look at you....
I see our towns, I see our farms,
I see our churches
Where we thank God....
Who made it all come true.

Iva Cieslewski

Life's Garden

Quiescent is the rosebud,
In chrysallid silence waiting
The pinpoint penetration
Of early morning dewdrop.

Lethargic the gardenia,
Releasing velvet fragrance
From blossoms heavy-petaled,
In the sunlight of fulfillment.

Majestic is the lily,
As a swan upon the shadow
Of the twilight's cool approaches,
Gliding gracefully into evening.

Diane L. Engstrom

To A Cloud

Upon a hill
I see my dreams go by
Misty and unearthly
they fill the sky
Thinking I'll succeed
to my heart I often lie
Thinking I can reach
something so high
Yet looking from the grass
is all I try
I hope and dream
but here I'll die
Seeing my dreams
as clouds go by.

Jessica Martineau

The Bird

As I look upon the window sill,
I see this little bird.
As he chirps away at the others,
In the fate air.
He thinks of nothing.
He turns around his little head
And stares at me with the sweetest grin.

He looks at me like he's saying
"Don't worry there's always a new day."
He turns again and says a chirp
That sounded like goodbye.
He takes off again and flies away
With no worry in the wind.

I wish thy little bird was I,
So I'd have no worries
And fly far beneath the big blue sky.
As he the bird of no worries
And no thoughts.

Julie Stamp

Lord Inspite Of Myself

Lord inspite of myself in behavior and ways,
I seek for myself a more promising place,
a place in my life with someone
who is authentic like you,
Who is worthy of all the
wooing I do, who give to me
a joy of life, a lasting love
which is twice as nice,
that shalt not be taken for the
breaking of hearts, but a
bearer of secure ending as
well as it's start, that why
my love for the heavenly
Father shall never do part.

Albert Jasmine

Let The Morning Rise

Night owl hoots cease for awhile.
Let the morning rise.
Rooster perched on a fence post
near by, gives a wake-up call.
Let the morning rise.
Flowers open-up from their nightly sleep.
Let the morning rise.
The Morning are in their Glory!

Joan A. Hartman

Dawn Light

The Morning Dew brought something too
I sent a thought to someone new
   A thought of Love to I know not who
They did receive it that I know
Because their answer upped the flow
of Light it flashed not, just a glow
   Light years away a mind did reach
and perhaps upon a sandy Beach
   Someday that someone us shall Teach
of Paradise in our own hands
and on the Shores of distant lands
because last night at thought Traversed
of Love throughout the Universe

Brian J. Racin

"Sunbeams"

While walking down a wooded path
I stopped and I did see,
Sunbeams shining through the trees
They danced in front of me,
And as they touched the cool green earth
With golden lights aglow,
Brought sunshine to this world of ours
For all our hearts to know,
That God had placed them there for us
His beauties to bestow,
Upon this lovely world of ours
The golden sunbeams glow.

Eleanore M. Rudewicz

The White Wolf

I see a white wolf in a field.
I turn for a second.
Then I look back.
He's gone.
I look everywhere,
But he's nowhere.
I run to where he was standing.
His tracks are in the snow.
I follow the tracks.
They lead over to a mountain.
I look at the mountain.
There's the wolf.
He howls.
I wake up.
It was only a dream.

Jessica Ann Rodriquez

"Seasons"

I once held Springtime in my arms
I was enticed by all her charms
Raindrops, filling ponds and streams
Wind blown kites, soar high tethered
   by a string
My heart was given in springtime song
I gave all I am, my dreams now are gone
Summer-time came bright and warm
The birth of a son to sooth and charm
A child's joy ..... youth soon lost
What do you want? At what cost?
Fall came swiftly, and brought sudden death
Sweet smell of decay with each labored breath
Winter closed in with its bone numbing chill
A still small voice cries out...
I'm still living and live I will!

Earl Snyder Jr.

Modesty

I watched a Lady undress today
I wasn't ashamed- I'll have to say
It filled my heart with very much pain
My sorrow matched that of the falling rain.

The colors of her garments were gay
They reminded me of the rainbows ray
I thought- oh my- what a lovely sight
She seemed unaware of her terrible plight.

It took a while these clothes to shed
She stood as one wrapped in death
I felt an urgent need to weep
For not one garment did she keep.

Then all of a sudden she took new height
The place I sat was illumed with light
She shook her limbs with pure delight
I knew just then that all was alright.

Our tree in the garden is now undressed.
She's stripped to the bark for needed rest,
But I'll never forget her gracious ways,
As she shed her garments for winter days.

Helene Treadway

To My Father's Memory

After he's gone, I feel alone,
I wish he'd never leave.
I find myself asking me why,
and thinking of eternity.

I wonder why in the world,
he left me wondering why.
One day he's being happy at home,
the next day he's forever gone.

As I look for words in vain,
to try to describe my pain,
I still tremble with the fear,
somebody could see me crying.

It is then, that I realize,
through the struggles
and the tears,
that he is not gone,
that he is right here,
in my heart and in my soul.

Abimeleth Roman

Starvation Of The Innocents

I wish I could be a part of someone's life,
I wish someone would be a part of mine.
I wish I could see what would happen,
I wish I could know the depth of time.

I wish I could hear the distant sounds,
I wish to feel each life, each pain.
I want to touch each of my dreams,
I'd like to know if I am sane.

If I could only stop the music,
If I could just have an over-view.
I want to see the sounds of moonlight,
I want to feel the endless blue.

I want to know when it is over,
I'd like to see how it could end.
I want to know who she is,
I hope that we will meet again.

I need to have a constant rhythm,
I wish to belong to one more dream.
I'd like to know just one more thing,
Are things really the way they seem?

Eric Farber

Love

Once I had a real love,
I won't forget her soon,
And every night the stars do shine,
Her love shines like the moon.

The morning dew is like her lips,
And the weeping willow is her hair,
The gentle wind is her hand,
As it drifts through my ruffled hair.

Although the raging fire is gone,
The embers of my love burn on,
And now your love for me is ash,
So its time to give my heart a gash!
Anthony R. Nathe

Untitled

On my tombstone
I would like
a single word
It's shape I want
the image of
a flying bird
It's texture smooth
the color white
and with no date
A single rose
deep velvet red
to decorate
a final place
infinite peace
in no-man's land
my life irrevocable
a last symbol
of my journey's end.
Conchita Altuner

Why

Times in life to be nice or wild
If anyone why take it out on a child
The feelings of not to hear a sound
The thought that the child is underground

Abuse is common but doesn't have to be
The thought of the child you don't see
In your home where it's nice and warm
The feelings of the calm before the storm

Just remember as parents if you try
Be thoughtful to your children and then
No one will say WHY
Danny Minton

Entheoxicity

How does the tiger run
In the glow of the good Titan's gift.
Hammered Earth in muscle tone
And claws of Time's absinthe.

Saturn as the father
Soon the tiger slows.
Hourglass and Life are flowing
All the Threads are wove.

As Earth the mighty beast
Will fall with its last breath.
What tremendous Power it must feel
OF life before its death.
Chris Fillie

The Pain Of A Broken Heart

The pain is strong, and just won't go;
If I should tell you, then you will know.

My heart beats fast, and will not stop;
I feel so weak, my legs could drop.

You cannot fight it when it is here;
it's more painful than your biggest fear.

I never knew it would be this strong;
but now I know that I was wrong.

I let you go, and you won't come back;
the cause of this pain is love I lack.

Please, come mend my broken heart;
When it is gone, my peace will start.

The war inside is destroying me;
my life is going, why can't you see?

If I can help heal a broken heart;
it would be to say don't let it start.

If you're in love, make it work well;
ask a question, and I will tell.

A peace of pain is a pinch from a dart;
but the real pain comes...from a broken heart.
Jerry Vandiver

The Sun Was Shining

The sun was shining bright today
If only it would stay that way
My heart is heavy, inspite of that,
My love is slowly giving way.
I felt my life was passing by,
I had little time to say goodbye
To loved ones far and near
Some that showed me love, and
Others shied away - afraid they
Might show their love in some
Mysterious way
Love is the essence that I bequest
You - no song, no psalm is sweeter
Than "God Bless You!"
Alice A. Stiles

Would We?

I often wonder, sitting here,
If we could see the road ahead,
If we would have the courage fine,
To join our hearts and choose to wed.

If we could know the trials and grief,
The disappointments and the pain,
Would we throw caution to the winds,
And do the same thing o're again?

Would all the heartaches and the tears.
Or'e balance all the joys we've known,
Or would the happiness we've had,
For all the cloudy days atone?

I know not what reply you'd give,
To all these questions that I write.
But were it mine the choice to make.
I know I'd marry you this night.

Grief comes to all who tread this earth,
We pass through bright and stormy weather,
But how much easier is the load,
If we can share the weight together.
Earlene Willette

Drifting In The Abyss

Don't worry me, don't envy me:
I'm already in pain.
Don't speak to me, don't laugh at me:
I'm falling like the rain.
Don't hate of me, don't lie to me:
I've been to hell and back.
Don't harp on me, don't pick on me:
I've been stabbed in the back.
Reach out before me, take my soul:
It's all been washed away.
Reach out before me, rip my heart:
It's all that knows the way.
I'm not alone in misery:
All those before me, were.
I'm not alone in agony:
All those before me, sure.
Before I die I know the end:
Defeat is what will sting.
Before I die I know the truth:
Defeat like glue will cling.
Brian Rice

Don't Cry For Me

Don't cry for me, Mommie
I'm contented as can be
Setting here in heaven
Bounching on Jesus knee

Don't cry for me, Mommie
I'm well as can be
No pain, no tears here
It's peaceful, don't you see

Don't cry for me, Mommie
I'm safe as can be
Playing with the Angels
The heavenly star lights, I see

Don't cry for me, Mommie
I'm dressed in satin white
Living here with Jesus
So precious in His sight

Don't cry for me, Mommie
Up here we don't grow old
When you get here, Mommie
We'll play in streets of pure gold.
Carolyn Jane Donohoo

Untitled

She lives on
Inside of me.
From her soul
I will never be free.
I can see her beauty
Flowing within,
The child she bore
Through original sin.
The mystical touch
Of her hand,
Lives on in the babe
Of earthly land.
For God has taken
The one I adore,
In place of another
To love even more.
Arthur Batista

A Grandmother's Prayer

I'm so thankful Dearest Savior
I'm so blessed throughout my soul
My heart is full to bursting
   And I'll praise you 'till I'm old.

I am so very grateful
I'm humbled through and through
For it is so very awesome
To see what God can do

It is so very healing
To know that you can take
All our sorrows and our heartaches
And makes them into cake.
And we thank you, Blessed Jesus,
For the little life you give
And pray that all goes well with him
And a healthy baby lives.

With hearts overflowing
And our eyes full of tears
We thank you for this baby
Who'll being pleasure to our years.
Barbara Ann Humphreys

Silence Of Sound

On the corner of two streets
in a city of no particular name
I look down into the silence
which the night has tamed

The night holds an unconscious silence
for which I cannot explain
There is silence among the many cars
in the street's painted lanes

The sleeping drunk in a phone booth
mumbles many words
but from the steel balcony above
his mumbles are not heard

A bird soars past
towards the music from far away
And as the young dance and sing
I hear not what they say

It's then that I realize
Despite the noise from all around
the only true silence is
the silence of sound
Alex Ross

The Power Of Love...

Love is strong,
It binds two hearts,
To hold them tight.
To never part,
Through ups and downs,
And highs and lows,
Through both our hearts
Love always flows,
I love you dear,
And this is true,
For in my heart
There's always you.....
Billy Joe Rea

To The American Soldier

Alone, and yet not alone
In a world of turmoil and hate;
Alone, and yet not alone
Waiting, waiting for fate.

Forget not thy mother's prayers,
As onward to battle you go;
Forget not thy mother's prayers
When the lights of the world are low.

Fight the foes with hands of steel
Bearing the "Gospel of God" as shield
Peace be to you where'ere you be
On foreign land or rolling sea.

Some will live while others die
Marching boldly with battle cry;
Each man has but one life to give
So others may in freedom live.

Oh that freedom flags would soon unfurl
O'er a battle-scarred and weary world;
And the winds of war again would cease,
To usher in a "time of peace."
Elizabeth M. Carter

Simply You

To lay with you,
in bed and bliss
Naked, yet comfortable;

To look at you,
and feel the world is right
Beyond the trivial and meaningless;

To be with you,
and know love
Undeniable and unconditional;

To ache for you,
and feel halved when you are gone
Incomplete and anxious;

To simply have you,
To have you,
  Simply.
    You.
Alexander R. Messerli

Astray Unprepared

The storm approaches
In eerie calm
As if life before it
Goes on an on

It's scary
In these last days
Observing the feeble
mind of man

No time for Truth
Love
Or Preparation

Carrying on
Believing what's best
For their new generation

I worry not
For the trap will fail
With heavenly winds
and horrific hail.
David W. Domansky

A Room Full Of Writers

A room full of writers
In fourth grade you say?
Yes, yes talented, creative writers
And you know this already today?

Yes, all of these children write
With feeling, emotion and love.
About many different topics
So beautiful they're way above.

Those boring little lines
Never do exist in here.
Only words they treasure
And hold to their hearts so dear.

For as time passes
Writing ideas will only grow.
And the memories will last.
For their words will always be here
And loved by their teacher
For the words are written so sincere.
Denise Mancini

Trumpet Player

He stood separate
In his own pool of
Light and shadow
The silver trumpet
Poised in readiness
Concentration flickered
On his face as
He counted the notes
In time
Then through the
Sudden silence
Rose the haunting
Refrain of the trumpet
Transforming player and
Instrument
From Mortality
to
Life
Angela L. Bennett

Loose Change

He fingers the coins
in his pocket,
nickels scrape dimes,
quarters scratch pennies,
scarring the faces
of liberty.
Sounds scarcely hiding the
shattering of his heart.
Sadness seeping
through tired shoulders,
suffering etched
about a silent mouth,
signal of fear
sighted in knowing eyes.
Sorrowful change
of plans.
The freedom of
his beloved's health
invaded
by the enemy.
Joyce Carr Stedelbauer

Your Eyes

As I look at you across the way-
in my heart I want you to stay.
As I look into your eyes-
I hear all the ways that my heart cries.

All of these years I have waited-
waiting to be with someone like you.
Now I am glad your love is true-
for years I have waited without a clue,
now I wonder what I would do without you.

There's something about your eyes
there's no way I can disguise.
Looking at you across the way
I hope you say you will stay.

Angela Eilene Hewitt

Gone A Little While

I seize the moment
in my mind
I seize the moment
here in time
I make the moment freeze

My mind tends to believe
the pictures that it paints
fantasy the state
in which I walk into

Dreams of passion
dreams of fun
doing things I've never done
being in places I've never been
then it all so quickly ends

A tug on my sleeve
I'm forced to leave
and look into
small eyes of blue
of the child at my side
"daddy, when is suppertime?"

Gary Thomas

In Memory Of Mary Ann Lambert

There's been too much sadness
In our hearts today,
We never thought we would
Lose one of our own
She touched the hearts of
Both young and old.

Oh - oh - oh that Mary Ann Lambert
Had a heart of gold,
She saved many lives
And healed many souls.

Always a kind word
She would say
Please do not mourn or
Be sad today.

For twenty long years
She did her best,
Mary Ann Lambert is not gone,
For within our hearts;
She just took a little rest.

Geraldine Green

The Seasons

The sun will rise, the moon will fall
In Summer, Winter, Spring or Fall.
The days will shorten, then get long
As the fiddler plays his morning song.
The song is lively, full and sweet,
Till Winter comes with snow and sleet.
When Winter goes, it leaves with us
The Springtime, then the Summer months.
Summer temperatures elevate
And you seek coolness by the lake.
Then you think that after all,
A few more weeks, and there'll be fall.
Fall will hurt some enormous trees
By making these to lose their leaves.
Then you will get your broom and rake,
And wipe away the crackling flakes.
And when you think you've done your share
You look at all the trees so bare,
And you will say that it is true,
Another year is finally through.

Jared Azzone

The Absence Of

In the absence of war,
In the absence of gore;
In the absence of kills,
In the absence of bills.
In the absence of pain,
In the absence of gain;
In the absence of fears,
In the absence of tears.
In the absence of the hungry,
In the absence of the sundry;
In the absence of drugs,
In the absence of bugs.
In the absence of sex,
In the absence of checks;
In the absence of race,
In the absence of Face.
In the absence of hate,
But with the greatest of faith
You Will have Peace!

Dennis A. Burke

Harmony

If you were to see me
in the country I love best,
  You'd see me sing.

I learn from jobs I take tasks
I need for country living,
building of my homestead of wood.

Here I lay with the moon
  light across the skies.

I walk the shore line
glancin' at the shadows.

I was not born in century today,
  but only to rejoin the friend
    of long ago.

River goes down, seeking places to go,
critters to water - plants to feed,
for life generates in each cycle of time.

There is an open road - I must go
  on to meet the one, and life of
    solitude.

Heidi Lee Johnson

The Pearl

You are like a reflection of a pearl
in the Deep Blue Ocean.
Difficult and rare to find, but full
of splendor and beauty.
Brave men risk their very own lives
diving for such precious gems.
As the same when I gaze into your beautiful
wonderous eyes, I plunge deep into
the beauty I see losing my breath
and getting lost in the sea.
Only one thing can save me!
That's your love and friendship
only I can find in One of a kind, in
a person such as you no other jewel
can compare, nor diamond, anywhere.
No! Not even the most lustrous gem.
But, no matter what, no matter when,
I'll always be a lover, companion and friend.
Whatever I encounter or find, you'll
always BE ONE OF A KIND.

Alvin E. Hernandez

A Rose Is...

As beautiful as the warm shining sun
In the east that's slowly rising,
As fragrant as a fresh spring breeze
Why, no... that's not surprising!

As lovely as this rose my be
It's looks can be deceiving,
That when uprooted from the ground
It's thorns can leave you bleeding.

As white as a day, or black as night
This rose is not complete,
Without sunshine, rain, or love
It willows with defeat.

A rose is like a human being
Or a candle in a tree,
If perceived in it's own true light,
A rose is just like me!

Amanda Bond

The Llama

There little drama
in the life of the llama
A crittur that is quite hirsute
and led by a peasant playing a flute
Toting necessities in heavy packs
a long way over narrow mountain tracks
The llama yields as well a milk
both nutritious, and smooth as silk
Upon his back he'll willingly carry
a young child whose begun to tarry
The llama's wanton wooly coats
are shorn and shipped afar in boats
to be into sweaters woven and thatched
with a prestigious label attached
Now at dusk appears the evening star
The llama reclines, and smokes a cigar
Of the llama sure there's much to be said
yet this never seems to go to his head.

Jim Hunter

Omnipresence

There was spectacular beauty
In the magnificent twilight
The creator paints his sunset
The ball of fire drops out of sight.

The entire western horizon
Revealed colors not made by man
Deep purple, pale pink and some gray
Covering God's canvass like a fan.

An orange color appeared on the
Kaleidoscope from a light peach
As the pattern changed in the dusk
It felt as if God were in reach!

As we travel the road of life
There are changes along the way,
The master artist knows the plan
As He sketches the scenes each day.

Jesus Christ communicates love,
Working through his loyal children's lives
Entering the gates of heaven
It's beauty will be a surprise.

Carolyn F. Marquis

The "Fir" Coat

The call came
In the middle of the day.
And the lady's husband
Had this to say.

"Tonight my darling
I'll bring home a lovely fir".
She became ecstatic!
When he said this to her.

She called all of her friends
"My husband is bringing me a fur.
I hope it's a mink or fox,
Hmmn! I'll even settle for a cur."

Well folks,
Night couldn't come quick enough!
And she was disappointed
As one could ever be.
For instead of a lovely fur coat,
He brought home a lovely fir tree.

Eleanor I. M. Coombs

A Scribble

What is a scribble?
Is it-
  A testing of a pen?
  An indication of boredom?
  A vent of anger?
  A sign of blooming artistry?
  A stimulant for the imagination?
Or-
  Just another human behavior
  Studied beyond need,
  Causing something so simple
  To be turned into a thing
  Of great complexity.

Amy Tag

The File

There's a file marked "confidential"
In the recesses of my mind
Behind the darkened shadows
Amidst the cobwebs built in time.

In this file one would find
All the past I put behind.
The pain, the hurt, the misery
All the dreams of what could be.

Anger's carefully tucked inside
An emotion that's been much denied.
Shattered fragments of trust and hope
Lie inside stamped "what a dope!"

All the love a heart can hold
Split in half and not so bold.
A child's laughter, hopes, and dreams
Torn apart right at the seams.

Present and Future are lost in the Past
Given up and fading fast.
Who can see the potential
In this file marked "confidential"?

Cheryl DeVore

Emotions

We dance with the clowns
in the tent of emotions.
We go from happy to sad
in one look it goes away.
We laugh, we cry,
we have to say good-bye.
We can't so we stay.
Our path has been laid
on the ladder of emotions.
They lie, cheat and steal,
come in go out,
we can't pout,
we can't leave,
We can be deceived,
by the dance of clowns
in the tent of emotions.

Heaven Wilson

Thunderstorm

On dark nights
In tranquil places,
Lightning traces
Fiery fingers
Through stormy clouds.
Pulse quickens,
The heart races,
As booming thunder loud
Rolls through the land
The sky embraces.
With furious claps
The earth it shakes,
Bringing fear
To men's faces.
Until the glorious sun
Breaking through,
The clouds erases.
Restoring calm once again;
Returning all
To normal paces.

John M. Ochiltree

Whispers In The Night

Dark skies out the window
inside blackness encloses the room
hearing only stillness and silence
all others sleep, deep into their dreams
and you call

low voices
soft sighs
whispering secrets and feelings
laughing quietly
crying silently
wishing to reach you and touch you

sharing stories....
and becoming closer
holding on to words that are so important

it's only me and you
no one to hear us, no one's listening
the only noise to be heard is my heart
pounding
from the truths that are being spoken
from the intimacy that's partaken
from the whispers in the night

Diana S. Gliem

The Seed

Seed lies dormant
inside our minds
waiting
plant it and feed it
start it to grow
into something that's good
you didn't even know
the roots are growing
a stem I do see
coming from within
for all to see
cover it not
or stump it's growth
strong are the branches
the season is here
ripe is the fruit
for others to feed
nourishing their seed
that lies dormant
waiting

Jackie Hines

The Chamber Of Whispers

Awaken out of asleep
into a white beam
around my body
a faint whispering

Turning my head
focussing where it came from
Tilting my head toward the beam
the indication of my left ear

The surrounding is black
total darkness but the present of light
whispering are increasing tone
in a high pitch

A screech sound
dropping me to my knee's
covering my aching ears
woke up to a hospital bed

Dripping with blood from head to toe
Accusing me of a crime
that I myself have not acted upon!

Donna Cole

"Alternatives At Daybreak"

You walk in softly, tiptoeing
   into my dreams
To haunt me, stealing
   my thoughts at dawn
When buds are waking
   to dewdrops melting
From dreamless sleeps.

Hasn't it been what seems
   two scores or so ago
When you and I were weaving
   campus memories?

Let us review and compromise,
   baring apostasy
And cling to tender moments,
   kiss yesterday's echoes,
Adorn our past with wreaths
   of redemption,
Or better yet -
   Compose a song

Elma Diel Photikarmbumrung

Sarah

The little girl in the picture
is a precious child.
A gift from heaven,
God given with love mild.

Looking ahead to her future
bright and bold.
A tiny child,
innocent and fair,
with a story yet to be told.

SARAH, the little girl in the picture
is a precious child.
Full of wonder and
life abundant.

Generous with her sharing
of a life flourishing.

With the innocence of a flower,
awaking to the early morning dawn,
she holds the world in her palm.

SARAH, the little girl
in the picture is a precious child.

Dolores Harvell

Individual

  I am a single person who
is strong and whole.
  I radiate my beliefs deep
within my soul.
  No matter what it is I see
or hear.
  There is nothing I should
ever fear.
  No matter what others
say or think I should be.
  I will decide what is best
for me.
  I am an individual who
stands among all.
  And I am one who will
never fall.

Chris Chester

"A Beautiful Canada, In A Dream"

"A beautiful Canada, in a dream"
is about a land of vast opportunities.
It is a land of Mass Cultures, that
bond together nicely, that add the
colors of just what is healthy, full
of life, with a purpose to build,
create, enjoy and learn, from others.

A land, where people help people,
a place to enjoy, Marvel at Nature,
and her wonders, and a place where
faith, hope, and charity rule the
consciences of the Masses of Minds
that bond and create a beautiful
nation. A beautiful county, that is open,
to all peoples, from around the world.

When I vision Canada, I see the Cultures,
the bonding together, of all people in
building a stronger Nation, for all the
World to enjoy, and love.
"A Beautiful Canada in a dream," is what all
hearts, and souls dream of.

Blayne McKay

Midnight Ride

The horse I ride in my dreams
is black as night. Big and
powerful. Full of speed.

I ride my horse in the day
when the sun is high. Ride until
the sun goes down. Riding
through the star filled night
listening to the wind whistle by.

On and on forever I ride until
the sun shines—it's light! As the
day comes and the sun is high in
the sky again, my dream begins
to fade and my ride comes to an end.
I wake to the light of a new day.

Colleen MacDonald

The Last Day

Finally, it
is here.
The day of days was
never so near.
Slowly, Sweetly,
Gently and neatly,
it has come so
dear.
Days and nights,
I've waited so long.
For this day to finally
be sung.
And so it is
finally here,
But pardon me
while I wipe my
tear.

Rebecca Muroski

Anyone Can Write A Poem

The art of writing poetry
is simple - just like A - B - C.
At work, at play, or going home
   anyone can write a pome.

Just try to think of words that rhyme.
You can do it any time!
And wherever you may roam
   you can come up with a poam.

Try some pairs, like fork and spoon;
dawn 'til dark, or morn 'til noon;
soap and water, brush and comb.
   Now you've got 'er; it's a pomb.

This has gone from bad to worse
but, nonetheless, it's still a verse.
And now the final touch: The chrome!
   Once again, we've got a phome.

That's the lesson for today
but, before I go away,
I'll leave you with this little gnome:
   Anyone can write a gpome!

Dianne Shultz

My Guardian Angel

The evening dew upon the grass
is sparkling like a jewel
and the fragrance of the roses
fill the air, that now is cool.

I shiver in the moonlight
as I rest beneath the sky
and allow my thoughts to surface
as the clouds drift slowly by.

This day has been a joyful one
and tonight my spirit's free
I thank my Guardian Angel
for watching over me.

Della Coffee

Reflections

That face in the mirror.
Is that really me?
Can this be the same face?
The one others see.

All those wrinkles and lines,
that I didn't know were there.
Someone just asked me.
"Do you color your hair?"

That's why I have no mirrors
in the house where I live,
I don't need those reminders.
The kind mirrors give.

I use windows or pictures
when combing my hair.
The reflection's much kinder.
Mirrors aren't fair.

John Edward Laurel

On The Outhouse Door

When fate or age have bid thee "run"
Lest bowels or bladder have their "fun"
Pass through these portals on the "run"
And we'll not ask ye - which one "won"?

Carol M. Althaus

Growing Up

A fact of life in Nature's plan,
Is walk one's happy way.
A boy must grow into a man,
But not in just one day.

For change is quietly taking place,
The best is yet to be.
So say farewell to youthful face,
Move on with spirit free.

Our youth is only half the song,
As tenor turns to bass.
Be steadfast as you grow along,
With others in the race.

Know too, more phase of Life's travail,
Adds more to living's zest.
One's bound to learn that without fail,
Each age will seem the best.

And when you've finished Nature's plan,
With sorrow and with joy.
Remember friend in every man
You'll always find a boy.

Alfred G. Bussey

Just A Thought

Just a thought as a leaf leaves a tree.
It floats to earth so effortlessly.
Finally free and on it's own.
Has it lost or found a home,
Family high and family low.
Only the wind seems to know.
Where it's travels will finally end.
To be alone, or with a friend.
Surely it's fate it close at hand.
As the wind dies and it starts to land.
The Seasons have struggled and fought.
What of the leaf now...just a thought.

James N. Moore

Invite

It's fine to invite
It gives us a chance
To unite
Keep this in mind
Before things get
Out of site
Once we have begun
There could be
Much fun
To look forward
Is very nice
To acquire
Some of the spice
Our lives tend to
Give us a lift
Perhaps to
A new shift
A good grip
Tends to give
Us a better trip.

Edward T. Philpitt

"Expression"

In art there is no abuse
  it is for all to use
Take this poem for instance
  it is meant as reference
Just a simple guide
  used to describe
The essence of poetry
  the expression without enemy
As the pen's ink flows
  the paper starts to glow
It becomes a great release
  for the anxiety ridden beast
It can also amaze
  as cheeks become glazed
No need for commotion
  poetry is meant to spring emotion
Just like all art which is true
  poetry's presence is for you

Daniel B. Norton

A New Generation

  Our world is so quickly changing,
It is no longer the same.
It's filled with hatred and war,
But most of all it's shame.

  It seems we can't get along,
No matter how hard we try
When I think of all the hate,
It makes me want to cry.

  But we are a new generation,
And hate is an old word.
We are all joining together,
And making sure we're heard.

  So we are saying lookout,
For world here we come
We are all joining together,
And we've only just begun.

Barbara Nevins

Untitled

It's my nightmare
it keeps me awake
no one in the room
no light of day
something there is watching me
I know it to be true
just around the corner
its eyes are crystal blue
I'm hiding here
I'm trying to
It sees me move
and it comes too
something there is watching me

Diane Brennis

On Parting

When we part, my beloved
My heart cries a little
And turns
Seeking comfort
To memories
Still warm

Dorothy W. Lytle

Joy

The word, itself, is unique,
  It makes a lovely feeling in the mouth;
Try it and see; you have to smile.
  Since the mere word is so pleasant,
Learn to find joy in everything around you -
  the birds
  the trees
  the flowers
  the animals
  the people.

As poet William Blake exclaimed
  "Catch joy on the wing!"
And send a paean of praise
  to the universe!"

Enjoy!!!!

Dorothy A. Newsom

2 - U - 2

When you two had married,
  it seemed war was everywhere.
But identities were clear
  and decency was always there.

When you two had children,
  it seemed conflict was everywhere.
But provision was made sure
  and guidance was never impure.

When you two had careers,
  it seemed discontent was everywhere.
But generosity was effervescent
  and aid to the needy ever present.

When you two travelled the world,
  it seemed fear was everywhere.
But resolve and faith prevailed
  and thousands of postcards were mailed.

To you two on your fiftieth anniversary,
  it seems Grace is everywhere.
As God pours forth upon us His Spirit,
  I praise Him for you as my parents!

Janette Louise Foley

But, Thank You

I didn't ask for your help,
It seemed you were there.
Overlooking a pathetic form.
Me, Standing near a rail.
The bridge was high,
The water deep.

My sorrows, encased the space.
Between, the bridge and the river below.
All, I wanted was freedom from pain.
Yet! You were there,
Holding a imaginary lasso,
To keep me from harm.

I wonder and I ponder,
Over your moments here.
My heart gave way and I walked away.
Once looking back to see,
If you where still there,
You where not, and I went my way.....

Anna Evanosich Geary

Lean On Lord

I heard a voice from deep within,
It was my Lord, "please don't sin",
He's always there to take my hand,
But if I'm wrong he takes a stand.

When I'm troubled and very sad,
I pray and then it's not so bad,
For Jesus shows the path to take,
It's up to me the choice to make.

A friend can let you down indeed,
But Jesus knows your every need,
So call upon him loud and clear,
He's always there to lend an ear.

Look up to the sky and see,
What he has done for you and me,
The sun, the clouds, the beauty there,
He's unselfish and let's us share.

Why do we sin and give him pain,
When we have love and peace to gain,
You have no reason to stumble and fall,
Remember that he loves us all.

Barbara L. Baldwin

One Life

Your life is valued highly
It was ordained by God above
Yes! You are important
Your destiny is love!

Come out of the darkness
Look up to the Light
Trust in His direction
You know it will be right

One life...what's it worth?
Your destiny put in place at birth
One life...created above
You'll find your hope and strength
...In love

Glenda Taylor

Arlene

Long ago on a hot July day,
it was then that my best
friend was taken away.
She lived just 16 short years,
leaving behind many eyes filled
with tears.
It is the living that are filled
with sadness, so it is up to
us to stop the madness.
So while you are about to
take that drink, please pause
a moment to think.
out with the gang running a tab,
do us a favor and call yourselves a cab
don't be too proud to hand a sober friend
the keys to your car,
For the ones who pay for the drinks
never even sat at the bar...
   Thank you for cooperating,
   for the results of your
   ignorance can be devastating...

Alphonsina Sochuck

Untitled

It's not supposed to be this way
It wasn't supposed to happen
Yet here I am in love with you
Isn't this strange
Though I tell you every thing
Else without a qualm, I somehow
Have troubles with this.

I know I've said it once,
But I have to say it again
It's not supposed to be this way
It wasn't supposed to happen
How do you suppose it did?

I am not supposed to feel this way
Yet I do somehow

I love you, yes I said it I love you
How did this happen

Ashli Brooke Turner

The Uncharted Path

Where have you gone to Father dear?
It's a place I do not know.
Although I see you sitting here -
Just where - oh where did you go?

At times you seem to know me
When I come to visit you
As though I've found a magic key
When you smile with a word or two.

Where have you gone to Father dear?
As you stare blankly in space?
It's a land I do not know, I fear,
But I hope it's a happy place.

Diane Reese Petitpas

"Sea Of Love"

Men and dating, constipating,
it's all the same to me,
nonproductive...
There's not enough of
a catch left in the sea.

My bait is old, the water's cold
everything is soon going wrong.
I get a bite, bring it in.
It's a throwback once again!
I've been in this boat too long.

Winds berating, hopes deflating,
up to my knees in brine...
back to land I go
worn out net in tow
one more big waste of time.

The very next day, up, up and away
my good sense all but goes,
to my boat, out to sea...
Singing songs, gleefully,
I ignore what I already know.

Cheryl D. Wagner

Untitled

Dear Mom,
Music to my ears
On top of things
My mom
Superb
Dream come true
Always there
You make me feel good

Eric Siegel

Untitled

I have a little telephone I use at anytime,
It's lines are always open
and it doesn't cost a dime.
The way I always use it in,
I fall down on my knees and ask the
Lord in heaven, Lord help me,
help me please.
Each time I use it I always get reply
dear children your call I answered
and your needs I will supply.

Charlotte C. Wilson

Untitled

When Hanukkah falls on Christmas Eve
Its more than I can handle,
For its up to me to trim the tree
Then light my Hanukkah candle.

I place the toys around the tree
Put sisters doll in her cradle,
And then I run to the other room
And spin my Hanukkah dreydel.

If God in Heaven were looking down
He'd smile if he could see us,
Santa and I and the other guy
Judas Maccabeus.

Irvin Pollak

The End Of The Road

The end of the road, I cannot see.
Its path gives me no clue.
At each new fork, I pause a while
to determine what to do.

A time of peace to clear my thoughts —
explore some new insight.
Each dendrite path implores me
to choose its path outright.

Each path stems from common seed
planted deep inside of me.
The end can only yield the fruit
of my thoughts' pedigree.

Greeting me at the end of the road,
whether good or catastrophe,
is consequence of one root cause
—desires' heredity

Go here. Go there or go no where,
are choices I can make.
What meets me at the end of the road
is never a mistake.

Hazel J. Goodwin

Time....What Is Time?

Naked trees, white covered grass,
It's wintertime....
Our love is growing quietly
Under the cold, clear nights.
When spring arrives,
It will shower our hearts
With its morning mist.
Our love will grow even more...
Let it be indelible in our souls.
Together, we perpetuate the feeling,
So it could never be forgotten...
Even on the days
When the sun is not shining.
Soon, time will lose importance.
Summertime will embrace us with
Its warmth and bright days,
Keeping our love intertwined and happy.
Then, we'll experience
The greatest love of all...
You and I, together, until the end of time.

Edna Elliott

Mask

I've got my day mask
I've got my night mask
Neither one can be removed!
The day mind
The night mind
Not of the same kind!
With one I'm in tune with myself.
The other with everyone else.
In the day I am blind
The night is where I'm able to find!
"Find what?," you might ask.
I'll never tell.
This is my night mask.
And it's not for sell!

Anthony E. Barr

For A Reason Of Life

For hours one day
I've searched through my soul
For a reason of life
That was not there no more,
I looked through every corner
of my mind
And up into the heavens
 into space
But I could not find
Purpose for my role
In the human race,
I ask myself questions
For things I need to find
But I can't get this pounding feeling
of life off my mind,
What do I got that I can give
What can you give me
 to make me want to live.

John Adam

Life

A post-modern
neo-retro
docu-dramady

Doug Dewing

Concept by Jeff Smith

The Fishing Day

Come on fish,
jump on my dish.
Don't delay,
jump today.
I don't want a snail,
give me a whale!
Don't give me a hard time
or I won't make this poem rhyme.
Come on fish,
jump on my dish,
jump on my dish
you ugly little fish,
or I will throw my fishing pole,
right into your water hole.
Come on, come on, come here to stay,
join the fun on our fishing day.
Cast the line, that will be fine,
just come to our fishing day.
Don't be a crook, bite on my hook
and come to our fishing day!!!

Jesse Wright

To Lety, With Love

Flowers are blooming in may
Just like you dear on your birthday
Everybody is really happy.
To see you very pretty.

Everyone says I'm lucky
To have you as a friend, Lety
For they all know your generosity
As well as your honesty.

Keep on your philosophy
That simplicity is beauty
Because you'll never regret when I say
Your prince charming is on his way.

So now my dearie, you've got to cheer
For God's blessing is beyond compare
He'll make you more clever
As long as you'll love him forever.

Always and ever, don't fail to remember
That true friends are friends forever
Start counting your birthdays by friends not years
And you will feel life and love better.

Elena A. Ching

Separated

Space can not stop
My heart from loving you.
Distance can not tumble
The bridge between us,
Love will keep us together
No matter how much time
Passes by us.
Imagine if life were timeless
And space was not relative;
The sun would shine,
The moon would glow,
And I would follow you
Wherever you go.

Charna M. Horne

The Old House

Alone I stand in the cold, open field
Just waiting for someone to see
How awfully tired and lonely
Year after year, it gets to be.

No one understands the pain
I try so hard to convey,
All that keeps me standing
Are memories of forgotten days.

I was once painted and proud,
I rang with laughter and tears,
I was the envy of the hillside —
Now I cry and no one hears.

Gone is the winding, wooded road
That graced my front so beautifully,
There are fields now up to my doorsteps
Leaving so little room for me.

I am so weary standing alone,
You look, but you don't see,
Please put me out of my misery —
Love me, or let me cease to be.

Judy Rogerson Cox

Sleep

You did not know
Just why I cried
You loved me true
Until you died
Your support was strong
You held me up
With a heart made of gold
You're my undying pup
But then one day
That heart it stopped
In the bitterest pain
My barriers dropped
I am forced to continue
Without your sweet face
But your memory lives on
As you sleep in God's grace

Debbi J. Lugo

To All Of God's Men

 You are a man of God's! this I
know for sure, because after all the
hardship your love still endures. Take
God's advice you'll have a good life
and a very loving wife.

 Being a man of God's, means,
you're very good for me, Help raise your
family, lead us to God the way it suppose
to be. Its all about God you see!
Since you are son of man, you'll always
make a very true friend. So keep God
first in your life and he'll stay with
you till the very end.

Donna Hall

Outdoors

Biking, hiking having fun.
Mountain climbing is so fun.
Swimming diving is exciting.
Now is night Jupiter in sight.
The moon is bright like alight.
Crickets chirping, frogs aburping.
Sleep, sleep, sleep.

Aaron Anthony Bynum

Forever Wishing

Seeing the light
Knowing it's there
Wishing to hold it and have it hold you
Dreaming of having a reason to smile
Yet what holds you back
There is no wall
There are no restraints
One step maybe two
But you stay in the dark
Crying and screaming
Begging the light to come
But it does not care
Those painful steps
Is it worth it
The dark is so much easier
So you sit
And the darkness takes you to its deepest deeps
But you'll never forget the light
And you'll always wish you had taken those steps

Genevieve Krause

Sands Of Time

Time rolls on like waves
landing on shores golden with sand
Time pulls us further
away from a moment as we reach
trying to grasp it to
hold to it
Our minds filled with faded
memories, courtesy of time
Time the remedy for hurt
and pain
Time lends us our goals and
dreams, changes our feelings
and points of view
Sands of time flowing eternally
and untouched by the human hand
The sands of time from which
all creation evolves.

Adrienne Hill

I Saw You

At a distance
Last year
Between the last of spring
And the first of summer
I say you standing
In the company
of tranquility
The shifting afternoon wind
Caressed your hair
While the golden sunlight
Peacocked your face
Your handsomeness ventured
The four chambers in my heart
And dazzled my curious vision

By the witness of time
The petals of your beauty
Shroud my soul with love
And fragrance my senseless
Lifeless feelings with
Sweet atonements of life

Bernice Price

Autumn

Red and yellow
Leaves so bright
Forest on fire
A special sight

A gift for eyes
So tired and bored
As autumns flies
Her colors stored

This time so short
With winter near
Behold the fire
Of autumns tears

John Brimsek

O Heart, O Heart

Whilst yet you beat so strong,
  lest silence come to soon
  and still the inner eye

My conscious soul does sing and cry
  to beat a hearty heart.

Yet nor can I bestill the soul
  when last you go to rest O heart.

So be I conscious self or deepest,
  blindest soul when you depart

May all my inner senses be beyond you
  please my beating heart.

I pray, if possibility of thought beyond
  my realm may be bestowed,
  to understand, midst bodiless
  life anew,
  those cares and woes of yesterday
  that hastened your adieu.

Claudette S. Mautor

To Cia

From your distant peak
let fly your thoughts to soar...
to float...as dreams to me.

Take all wind from the air
and make it your voice to whisper...
to call...to me.

Make the sun and moon your eyes,
with all the sky your face,
and look into the depths of me.

And when you ride down into your valley,
across the field from pain,
take the trail that makes you free...
the way that leads to me.

Glenn L. Adamson

Passing Thru

Life is a dream
Life is a short.
Life is peaks and valleys,
Bits and drabs.

Commitments need not
Be a prerequisite,
Reach out.
Grab the moment!
Do not deny yourself!

George Shapiro

Eternity

Away beyond this earthly home
  lies the bounty of the feast;
Someday I shall no more roam
  after the coming of the beast.

The mansions there will unfold
  the various treasures of the mind.
We will walk upon streets of gold,
  no one there will be unkind.

The Lamb will be the shining sun
  that brightens up the night.
The humble souls will have won
  everlasting light.

The ones I loved so long ago
  and now are out of sight,
are waiting on that distant shore
  where there is no night.

I'm on my way to going there,
  I know within my soul,
because my sins Christ did bear;
  that balances the scroll.

Darlene Brown

"Resurrection"

As soon as the seed is planted
Life begins to sprout
And from this infinite beginning
We question and we doubt

As soon as the seed is planted
Death is on the way
But that which subsists
We refuse to throw away

With ageless stretches of anguish
And 21 gallons of guilt
We assail with indignation
And destruct what we have built

A fresh divergent seed is planted
And life begins to form
And from this infinite beginning
We have been reborn

With the icon independence
We astound with potency
The blessedness of manumission
We are liberty

Joe Sutter

The Candle

Daybreak and the candle ends,
Life ebbs, as the long trail bends...
Will it go to horizon's edge
Or mesh with the clouds sailing by?

What is in store for the soul?
A passing over, and out?
A sailing and a rout?
What does it mean - the candle's end?
What portends the dreams that rend?

I treasure most, I think,
The gift I was given . . .
I did deliver
Hope for the driven.

Goldie R. Scherberg

Spring

The winter chill is gone.
Life is blooming everywhere.
   It is but a resurrection.
Come, and share it's warmth!

Birds are returning from their journey.
   To awaken the peaceful hibernators.
The sun shines down on earth
   to many joyful smiles.

Trees open their arms,
   and welcome the long-lost birds.
Flowers emerge and sing,
   welcoming the busy hummers.

It is Spring! It is Spring!
   Can you hear the joyful sounds?
Awaken yourself to this day,
   It is but a resurrection!

Emily Collins

Epistemology

Each of us is born in innocence whose
life is entrusted to
guardians whom we do not choose.
They, who will determine what
we come to know
as truth, in our
destiny to grow.

Nurtured form birth, with deeds,
to satisfy our basic needs.
Bodies cleansed and clothed and given food.
All five senses cared for,
to pacify each mood.

Strange sounds entrap our tiny ears,
as we watch the World, wide-eyed, unfold.
Our keepers - wise - move fervently,
to school our minds,
in prudent things to know.

And as our sense are fulfilled from birth,
Our minds, as well, will tell -
how we know, what we know.

Anita Kingsley

Blue Toil

The simple essence of life,
Life which weighs eternity,
Looks for balance on the
Scales of time.
3 Boards slide along
The parabellum holding life.
Waves bombarding,
Etching, Chiseling, Life.
Renewed in it's Destruction
Bares a new face.
Cavernous chasms yield
Tunnels of labyrinthic life.
Ports and passages in which to travel.
March to the pounding,
Pounding, pounding of the drum.
Like a heart pulsating
Shoot through the chasm and open the door.
Is anyone there? Only if you want.
And so on the waves toil -
Chiseled face, Changed life.

Christopher L. Van Loan

Friendship Is...

Friendship is life's up and downs,
life's ins and outs, life's losses
and gains, life's thick and thin.

Friendship is lost loves
and reborn lovers,
lust and anguish.

Friendship is anger and joy
sorrow and grief, similarities
and differences.

Friendship is kind-hearted
and soothing, thoughtful
and endless.
Friendship is funny or full,
solid or hollow, complete or
not yet completed.

Friendship is trust and respect,
honesty and truthfulness.

Friendship is us, forever!

Heather L. Walker

Swinging High

Up in the air, the air so high
Like a diamond in the sky
There goes my grandson swinging by.

Up in the air, the air so high
Like cream puffs in the sky
There go the clouds passing by.

Up in the air, the air so high
Like a rainbow in the sky
There go the birds flying by.

Up in the air, the air so high
Like a buttercup in the sky
There goes the sun shinning by.

Up in the air, the air so high
Like a shinning star in the sky
There goes an airplane flying by.

Up in the air, the air so high
Like an angel in the sky
There goes my grandson swinging high.

Carolyn Ulmer

Untitled

You came unbidden
like a dream...
softly...
disturbing
the oh
so carefully drawn
patterns

I had forgotten...
left no space for you
My Friend

Yet
how quickly
you made your way
there...
entering
(to be held
gently now
and cherished)
in my heart

Dear Heart

Bonnie Mangold

To Say I Do

Our hearts are filled with love
Like a flock of flying doves
Precious moments with you
Has never turned me blue
Your sweet kisses are just great
Ever since our first date
Your soft touch hurdles through me
Emotionally I am free
Event less times with you
Has lead me to say I do

Dana R. Huffman

A Pearl Of Hope

When I hear you sob
like a little boy,
frail hands fold
like a clamshell
not to expose the pain.
When I hear you spirit scream
to be set free
as crashing waves
beat upon your shell
wearing you down to nothing,
Your pearl of hope slipping
quietly into the sea
leaving nothing of your
body but tired empty
sadness and, goodbye.
And when I hear seagulls cry
For You
I add to a string of Pearls and,
I stand up
through your descent I stand up.

Bridget Humphries

Untitled For Sarah

Her voice flowed:
like ice melting
in a tall glass
with two drops of tea
and a slice of lemon left
in a august heat.
Like a soothing bath of
warm soapy water
when you've worked hard all day.
Like the touch of his hands
when the time is right.
Like the safeness of a warm embrace
on a cold, cloudy day
when you've forgotten your coat.
Like rhymes and jonin'
when good friends get together.
Like a good wine with bird and dizzy.

I cried when she died but now I smile
When she sings she lives and so will we.

Alyce D. Emory

Cold As Ice

My blood is cold and black.
It freezes in my veins.
I cannot touch,
I cannot love,
My soul is as cold as ice.
I can kill, and I can hate,
But it does not keep me warm.
Roll it up, and lay it out,
It numbs me from all pain.

Jody Ratti

Winged Friends

Earthy amber shadows
Linger on an ancient plain
Bathed in the glow
Of shimmering stars
Encircling a gentle moon

An angel of light
Embraces her winged friend
A dove
Earth's symbol of peace
Wings of heaven and earth unite
And we give thanks
For the gift of peace
And a heart to hold it in

Emelda Darlene Shirinian

Sheep Dog

Walking through a field of sheep
Little sheep, white little sheep
Sleeping in a bed of fleece
With a little dog.
Little dog herds little sheep
Little sheep that never weep
Never weep, just always sleep
With a little dog.
Little dog with little teeth
Little teeth herd little sheep
Little sheep that never weep
Sleeping in a field.

Jim Glenn

The Sentry

Mr. Cohen likes me
loans me money
calls me the school-teach

Tells me about
summer nights in Warsaw

And how the guard at Duchau
wore a black-handled Luger
strapped to his thigh.

He shows me a blue-steel pistol
tells me he'll keep us safe
from mad dogs, vandals, thieves.

When the weather's warm
he patrols, up Oak
and down forty-third.

Today he sits outside
in overcoat, earmuffs
and red snow boots

Watching the icicles drip
loading and unloading the gun.

Allene Calderone

"Love, Is"

Love is reality,
Love is hell,
Love is sweet,
Love can kill,
Love is a pain,
Love is insane,
Who needs love?
I don't know.
Do I need love?
I think so!

Cynthia Caudill

New Beginnings

As the grayness of the
   long winter's days
   transforms from bleak
   to sunshine,
With the kiss of Spring time rains
   and the rising Summer sun,
The skeletons of the forest's trees
   and the dead matted carpets
   of the meadows,
Give birth to new beginnings
   from that which never died
   but lived in dormant stillness,
   shed of its worn out cloaks.
The seeds of yesterday's blossoms
   blown by the winds of Nature
   find home in new beginnings,
Nurtured not from where they came,
   but by the life within them and the soil
that feeds their growth.
We, too, can form new beginnings with
what is born within us
   and new soil to nourish our rebirth.

Arlena Rodriguez

A Venturing Forth

All faced the passage—
longer, crueler—but with
end in mind and eventually sight.
Rough seas, rocky shore.
Coolness of a winter setting in.

Legends they began,
strangers in the land.
Fortress-builder Guardian
Standish to the fore.
Craftsmen not of the persuasion
needed now. Fearsome red men
at the edge. The ship is gone
alone we tread.

Winter cruel, winter harsh.
Each day sorrowful mourning.
Slings, arrows not a threat.
Disease, hunger, cold and dread
Which of us may see not a
Spring dawn's early light?

Curtis E. Grassman

Look Away

Look at me

My life is shattered
Look at him
His life is lost
A mirror can be fixed
A soul can be found
You run I hide
It's a game we all play
Love It's coming
Hurry
Look away
When it comes for you

It will come for me
The clocks are ticking
It will have to be
No running no hiding
Game over
Love It's coming
Hurry
Look away

Christina Tuzzolino

Green, Green, Green

It's a green world.
Look at the map.
See someone's cap.
Check somebody's bookbag.
Check somebody's jacket.
Walk through the jungle.
Walk on the grass.
Leaves on the trees.
Seeds from the trees.
Even soda cars.
Or sour cream chips.
Even a chair,
Or a bucket.
A notebook or a poster,
A T-shirt or a car.
They are all green.

Billy S. Au

"I'm Not A Bitch But A Lady"

A bitch is a female who likes to be
looked at as low.
A lady is one who is highly respected
and does not answer to the term ho.
A bitch is a female who likes to look
for trouble.
A lady is the type who likes to get
things done on the double.
A bitch is a female who likes to fight
people as if it was a job.
A lady is the type of person who ignorant
people considers a snob.
A bitch is a female who likes to play
around with ten to twenty guys.
A lady is the type of woman who is
faithful to her boyfriend till they
say it's over and goodbye.
A bitch is a female who gives up things
and winds up having a baby.
That's why I'm not a bitch but a lady.

Donneisha Williams

Sitting On A Cloud

Sitting on a cloud
Looking down at God's creation
What wonderful sights we would see
No details would be denied us
He might be sitting there beside us
Explaining with great modesty

Why there are so many races
With different names and faces
Why they live in different places
And are gifted with various graces
Because the world is round
We can sit here looking down.

God would lend His wisdom to us
If He could, to make us see
He meant all man to be brothers
With no conflicts between you and me
But His wisdom He cannot lend us
Only His eternal love can He send us
Between us He sees only equality.

Edna M. Lowell

"Gazing Toward Heaven"

As I gaze toward the heavens
looking for God's face,
I'm searching for an answer
that has put me in this place.

With struggles before me
and triumphs behind,
I know that with God's help
the answer I will find.

God is always faithful
and is looking after me,
even when His plan
is something I don't see.

I know that it is written
that all things work for good,
so I'm trusting in the Lord
the way I know I should.

When this battle's over
and another was begins,
I'm know that God is with me,
and I will surely win!

Annette Pitts

Over The Horizon

Sitting at the top
Looking out
With memories
Past and present
I've cried a lot
Since you went away.
But I have no regrets
Knowing you'll be back
To start a new day.
And if by chance
You are close by now
Remember our first dance
Will be here.
Among the sand, the sea,
The birds, the deer.
And by our poplar,
Maples and evergreen tree.

Joanne Marie Rumford

The Face

The face upon the wall
looks out at me
through searching eyes,
darkening with thought.
The face of a dream,
once held so tightly.
Made bright by imagination
and kissed repeatedly
by deep emotion.
So desired, and polished,
like the finest of silver.
Untouched by time,
that smile lights up still
in memory's warm reflection.
Then, like a bubble,
opening into the air,
it vanishes,
bursting into eternity.

Carole Perrin Fishkind

The White Candle

One night I was
lying in bed
thinking of you, as I
looked out my door
and saw this
white glowing candle
As I watch this candle glow
I remembered the day
I saw you,
you made my heart burst into flames
The more I think about you
and watch the white candle glow
I think about the love I
feel for you, that will never
stop glowing inside of my heart.

Crystal Shibles

Status Quo

The elite on the mountain
maintain status quo
Like marble and granite
their movements are slow

Only heat and great pressure
exerted from the deep below
Can cause magma to rise
and lava to flow

John F. Zaengle

Pleasant Memories

Funny how a roosters crowing
Makes me think of spring.
Soft warm winds upon my face
Kite upon a string.

Shiny bits of broken glass
I called them, my dishes
In a house all tumbled down
Where I made my wishes.

A wooden box I had for table
Another for a chair
And still another for my guest
Although he wasn't there.

For years in that small house I played
With pleasure never ending.
A game I never quite forgot
Of silly, sweet, pretending.

And though all wishes don't come true.
Still it's worth the knowing
That pleasant memories will return
When a rooster's crowing.

Gertrude Hartigan

I Will Always Love You

  Great grandma, you saw
me when I came home
as a baby. You have seen
me grow up for 12 1/2 years.
I am sorry you will not
see me as a grown up.
But you will someday
see me again. And I will
always love you and I know
you will always be apart of me.

Antionette Williams

"My Precious Friend"

There are...
   Many things in life
      That I hold precious.

But...
   Not one...
      That is more precious
         Than the likes of you!

It couldn't be...
   The promise...
      Of that wonderful gift
Friendship
   That makes you so
      Precious.

Because...
   I knew you were
      Precious before we were
         Friends!

Earle Edward Vine

Masterpieces

In life's great gallery, I have seen
Masterpieces of flawless sheen,
Whose beauty has never met
Brushes wet and artists' skill,
Has never realized a painter's dream.

I stood in a trance and behold
Three leaves of rusty gold,
Burning with midsummer's fire
Crumbled, curled, spent, and tired,
Blew in and lingered on the threshold.

A simple butterfly in flight,
Wings of yellow moon and black night,
Soaring, dropping, in graceful motion,
Touching earth and upon a notion
Dwindling and moving out of sight.

The old clock on the mantle-piece
Ticking the hours in dreamy peace.
Worn, glorious with age and when
The hour strikes, musically then,
It chants and sings again.

Betty Paul

A Poem?

So you're having a poetry contest,
maybe I should write a poem.
But oh, I'm just so busy,
i've got chores to do at home.

You see, I'm just a simple housewife,
And my duties never end.
There's the dishes, the laundry
and some pants that need a mend.

As I run the vacuum sweeper,
I start to fantasize,
that the National Library of Poetry
Would choose mine for Grand Prize.

Then I come back to reality,
and start making up the bed,
as I wrack my brains and try
to find a poem inside my head!

Julie Ann Bapst

Seniors

Sure we're older
   Maybe stronger,
We're just young folks
   Who lived longer.

We greet each day
   With a prayer of hope,
Whatever happens
   We try and cope.

We have our shares
   Of aches and pains,
Take all them pills
   And don't complain.

When things get bad,
   And they sometimes do
We just look up,
   And talk to, "You know who."

So when we think of where
   We've been, and the things we've done,
If you work it right,
   Being a senior, can and should be fun.

Edward J. Ferruzza

Poems

Poems can be about anything,
Maybe troubles with your sibling
A mystical egg made of gold,
Heirlooms inadvertently sold,
A story of a love gone bad,
An epic of man gone mad,
Dark birds spread evil through the night,
The courageous hero is in a plight,
Lost at sea, a lone ship wanders,
In a village, a thief plunders,
So to discuss some great caper,
Please pull out a pen and paper.

Brian Foster

The Petal On The Ground

The petal on the ground reminds
me of the love that was never found,
The love between you and me that
was never meant to be
we had love in our eyes beyond all
skies, but it really wasn't there, we
didn't seem to care
then it became a mix that we could
never seem to fix.
The love we thought we had ended, and
everything became bended,
but the petal on the ground still moves
around although it's purpose was never found.
It moves into another broken heart
where it makes it's new start.

April Benton

"Untitled"

So, what do you think
of this novel subject,
filled with distorted consequence
and innuendos abundant
as a spellbound gaze
upon delicate leaves
twittering - dancing
frivolously free
yet taunted and swayed
by the changing song
of Spring's promising winds.

Diana Randall

Memories

As life goes on and time passes
   Mental pictures are taken,
Whether the pictures are good or bad
   They shall remain forever.

As more time passes, we often reflect
   And recollect on days far gone,
Those mental pictures taken long ago
   Come to visit us once again.

Pictures of lovers, friends, and foes
   Whose images we once knew,
Clear, vivid, crystalline pictures
   Reenacting life from yesterdays.

Tears, fears, hugs, and kisses
   Feeling we have had during times past,
Some painful, others are charming
   Yet these, our memories, keep us alive.

Heather Rhoton

The Style Show

Fancy fabrics;
Models all aflutter.
Swirling skirts;
Narrow runaways.
Soft music
Chicken salad.
Sticky buns.
Cups of tea!
Fancy hats;
Dressy clothes.
High heels!
Fun for all to see!

Jeanne M. Cavender

Untitled

If our dreams are more than dreams —
More than midnight picture shows —
Could it be that what now seems
To be the world that we all know
Is nothing more than fine illusion
Compelling us to wake each day,
And spend our lives within delusion
That what we own and do and say
Makes up the one and only world
A waking conscious that we keep
While never knowing of the true world
Alive within us as we sleep?

John Richter

Star Wars II

The people came from miles around
More than you could count.
For spicy off-camera bedroom scenes
And to learn the amount.

After weeks and weeks of argument
At last they heard the score:
Mary kept the unpainted wagon
But Michelle got a hundred and four.

It set a legal precedent
For any girl that lucky,
Who can find a willing lawyer.
We all should be that lucky.

But most girls must settle for less—
A mortgaged house and car.
Not a scent for rehabilitation.
Let's go and catch a falling star.

Betty A. Baker

Untitled

I see the sun sink
Morsel by morsel
Into the ravenous earth

Blue mountains
Extensive sea horizons
Swallow its energy

And leave me dark and wondering
Before the black pebbles
And the surf

The sand is cold now
No birds fly
Across the subdued sky

I accept nightfall
It is the price
Of a new day.

Eileen J. Wall

Muguet Des Bois

May day...
Muguet day in Paris....
May day, Muguet Day
Spring-time in Paris, Au Printemps...
   Smell it, feel it
     Live it, love it
     - And, buy it
Vendors at every coin Dans Les Bois
Selling a single spray
"Muguet, Muguet, Muguet Des Bois
Achetez, Achetez, Madame"
   Selling such happiness!
   Buy a spray.... and
   Fly, fly, fly-away with
     Muguet, Muguet Des Bois

Jeanne Tyson Hoover

Empty Days

The nights are cold,
my dawns are empty,
the pillow next to me
has not one fold.

I stare into space
for hours at a time.
A picture in my hand,
I long to see your face.

Will you come back
Or will you stay?
Am I enough for you?
What do I lack?

Every day I miss you more.
Every night I lie awake,
and impatiently wait for the day
you return through that door.

Helen B. Rossiter

Fairy Footprints

Fairies danced
on my window
last night.
Their feathery footprints
are still etched there.

Must have been
some party...
The confetti still
falls.

Joanna Amren

It Never Rains In Ireland

It never rains in Ireland.
My father did insist.
For what we think is pouring rain
Is merely morning mist!

The morning mists can last all day,
Dad said they're magical.
They come and go across the bogs
And end near Donegal.

It never rains in Ireland.
That's what the Irish say.
It's just that water from the sea
Blows in from Galway Bay!

It never rains in Ireland,
'Tis plainly to be seen,
But morning mists are everywhere
To keep the land so green.

So take rain gear and walking boots
To see these morning mists.
It never rains in Ireland.
My father told me this!

Howard Mackin

Untitled

I sit on the bank with
my feet in the water.
Memories nibbling
on my toes.
The water sparkles
like diamonds
in the sunlight.
The winds caresses
the land so gently.
Frogs bellow with joy,
as the butterflies
dance on the breeze.
So, this is life.

Jan D. Toomer

Mixed Feelings

I sat down today feeling insane.
My heart and mind with so much pain.
Looking for place to hide.
Alone in the corner I cried.

This crazy madness
fills my eyes with sadness.
Just too much thinking on my mind.
Makes the world seem so unkind.
I've got to make it through this day.
By tomorrow it will have gone away.

I'll be at peace again.
Thanks to God my friend.

Denise Vargas

Untitled

The tears are gone now.
Only silent resignation remains.
Someone said to accept the things
I cannot change but no one told me how.
The path we walked is overgrown with
weeds of anger and distrust.
I searched for it the other day but
hedges of fear blocked the way.
Oh if I could but turn back time to
when we walked among the poppies and
you loved me.

Amanda N. Shales

Released From Despair

I sat alone in darkened room
My heart and soul amidst with gloom
Day after day night after night
The end of sorrow not in sight
I stood at the edge of sanity
And wondered what was left for me
Then it came one desperate night
The music that would set things right
The soul stirring sounds that filled my air
Sparked memories of love we shared
I knew right then what I had to do
I had to make things right with you
And now your mine I've been set free
From the darkened gloom that imprisoned me

James A. Wiskochil

Waiting

When I think of you
my heart makes a fast thumping sound,
Then I feel sad
and start to frown, I feel as if
you are so far, may be that's
because you are, I think
of you and sometimes cry, later,
I must tell a lie,
I think there's dust in my eye,
I said to my friend the little guy,
I wait for you to come home,
I am here all alone, you have been gone
only two weeks but it seems
more like two century's, when you come
home I will be here, weather it
a week, as month, or even a year,
I will be awaiting here,
I will be waiting!

Chris Barnes

When I Must Go...

There'll come a time when I must go,
my journey will be done.
I'll gather all my memories,
to watch the setting sun.
And in my thoughts, my life goes by,
and shows me all I've learned.
I see how proud I have become,
from all the smiles earned.
With comfort then, I'll realize,
it's time to move along.
I'll kneel down and bow my head,
and sing my Fathers song.
My heart will stop, my mind will fade,
my body disappear.
And everyone I ever knew,
will then become a tear.
And even though I'll miss them much,
I'll never, ever cry.
With all their love I keep inside,
my soul will never die...

Christopher Geeting

Defining My Love

When I try to define
my love for you,
Words come to my mind
that others use.

But, they don't describe the
core of my love
Which is sweet and tender
soft as a dove.

Then I allow myself
to face my fear...
The loneliness I feel
when you're not near.

An ache develops deep
within my soul,
Opens my heart - my love
for you exposed.

The blood pumping through my
heart and body,
Much better depicts what
you mean to me!

Cheri R. Baugh

My Father My Friend

You're my father and also a friend;
My love for you will never end.
You'll always have that golden touch;
That's one reason why your loved so much.
Your inner beauty shines so bright;
Like a shiny star on a cloudy night.
Throughout the years you held my hand;
And always tried to make me understand.
Your heart is filled with a ton of gold;
Not hard to reach or hard to hold.
A part of you is a part of me;
You gave me life and dignity.
You always understood my fears;
And wiped away those dreadful tears.
You give me courage, you give me love;
Your a saint from up above.
Always willing to lend an ear;
Spreading nothing but good luck cheer.
And now it is time to say;
I love you more every day.

Carol O'Donnell

Dry Eyes

Apathy, neutrality.
My mind is numb.
Thoughts unclogged of thought.
I gaze stupidly at the void,
a gape drops my jaw, and
I am unfeeling of feeling.
Thoughtless thoughts through the
day make my mind cluttered.
My body yearns for rest,
my brain is a sputter.
Unconscious of reality,
if it is really there.
Unconscious to emotion
with only a blank stare.
 Nothing going in,
 nothing going out.
Am I awake? Is this a dream?
Indeed, even these thoughts
are too much thought
to put into one poem.

Chris Powell

Native Blue Morning

Deep in my soul, never lost in my mind,
My native blue morning trapped under ice.
The pine trees are touching, adding color
   to the snow.
Green ivy covers the path below.
A boy, with a stick, hitting the trunk of
   a pomegranate tree.

A girl, with a smile, waits at the fence
   so patiently.
The sky is a grey cloud, just hovering the ground.
Still, my native blue morning, makes no sound.

Beverly Royse

Used

A single tear rolls down my cheek,
   my soul is lost,
     and cold,
Trying to get over the heartbreak again,
everything you use me,
   over and over again.
The would cuts deeper and tears me apart.
   I try, try my hardest
     to stay away
but no matter
how much, you hurt me
   over and over again,
I will be here,
the love I feel, deep in my heart
I know will never leave.
So I sit here, without you,
lonely and abandoned
waiting to be used again.

Christie Rich

Untitled

If I am strong,
   my strength comes from tragedy;
If I am calm,
   my calmness comes from storms;
If I am hopeful,
   my hope comes from despair;
If I am serene,
   my serenity comes from acceptance.

If I am joyful,
   my joy comes from sorrow;
If I am tranquil,
   my tranquility comes from peace;
If I am peaceful,
   my peace comes from the Lord —
Who gives me all good things.

Estelle Lowe Kaczenas

For My Pal

Life has never meant much before.
My time was spent often alone.
Going nowhere and doing nothing.
Speaking with no one,
nor did anyone talk.
Till you came seeking.
With something to say.
To rid me of my lonely days,
and fill them with bright, sunny rays.
To lend a hand when one is needed.
Now I'm going places and doing something.
Making with you funny faces.
Laugh I shall for you are my pal.

Bridget Welscher

Sweet Little Child

sweet, little baby child
   never know the wrong down here
sweet, little love child
   God has to Him drawn you near
never play in metal play grounds
   you have clouds to sleep on
never see this world again
   free from earth's wrong
sweet, little angel child
   never learn to hurt
sweet, little free child
   dead, marked at birth

Casanya Herndon

My World

I as a child was always afraid
Never to be loved
As a girl, I found that love in you

Now a woman, I know the hurt
And joy of love
As a mother, I adored the lives we made
Our love was growing everyday

When the children, grew and moved away
You showed me loving sometimes
Means letting go

Now once again I am afraid
I ask, I pray
Show me how to let
My world go!!!
As you walk away

Dar McFarlane

"The Road Of Life"

Life is a struggle for all of us,
no matter what we do
You can't accomplish anything,
unless you just be you

We have our ups, we have our downs,
we even have the blues
Our minds may tell us one thing,
but it's the heart that has to choose

We go through life, day by day,
wondering what's in store,
Have we made the right decision?
Or regret it forever more

We travel down the road of life,
thinking of the past
Should we do this? Should we do that?
And how long will it last?

So if you wonder, which way to turn,
just listen to your heart
Your mind may tell you one thing,
but the truth, is in your heart

Barbara J. Grant

Reach Out To Him

When things look down and hard to bear,
Reach out to Him and He'll be there.
He'll comfort you and all you do.
His tender guidance will see you through.

Time heals all things, how well I know,
With age comes wisdom as you grow.
Remember dear when things look dim,
He'll help you through, Reach out to Him.

Alice Carol Lazzeri

Silent Cries

Silent cries - always
No one must hear
No one must know
Must make no sound

Wrenching sobs - gulp
Tears well up in eyes
Can't stop the hurt
But make no sound

Stare straight ahead
Blink back the pain
Bite down hard
Gasp quickly, make no sound

Concentrate now
Don't think about that
No one knows
Don't forget, no sounds

Breathing slower again
That feeling is gone
Just remember next time
Make no sound

Jessica M. Crosby

Lost

No clue,
No trace,
Just a weird look on the teacher's face.
I don't know.
I can't see.
Is there something wrong with me?
I need help.
I need correction.
Could you show me the right direction?
Lost my place,
Lost my feel,
Now I've even lost my will.

Aria Campbell

"Peace"

Sometimes I feel so all alone
No where special to call home,
I sometimes drift off,
Where there is peace, every where
from Chicago to Rome
There no crimes committed
No police needed
It's a place where our
children can be free,
to play and do whatever passes thee,
My world is a place
of freedom and love
Where nothing can go wrong
and people sing and play
our favorite song of unity and peace.
Maybe someday it will come to be.

Carolyn Wilson

A Small Surprise

Small drops of happiness
Rare magic moments
Waiting for one who appreciates
A bit of color
In the darkened wood.
Violets in a clump
Uplifting the spirit;
Take only a small bouquet —
Leave some to delight another passerby.

Ada Weygandt

A Shade Of Gray

Neither black
nor white.
Blending into the woodwork
is a shade of gray
like a mist
barely visible
it envelops my being
I stand on the outside
looking in
I am nothing but a shade of gray
except for the crimson
on my sleeve
dripping down my arm
pooling around my feet
and yet everyone passes me by
for I am no one

Jody Hamilton

Death

Death has come,
Not an end to life,
But a new beginning.
Without death,
We would have no understanding of life.
Death is all around.
Whether a tree, or even you or me.
Death we live with,
Death we take with us,
For we do not know where,
Nor do we know when,
Or how soon, or how far off,
All we know for sure is
Death will come.

Claudette Drake

The Flow

My feelings do not flow
Not like water
Not like the wind
Not like energy
They are not visual
They are not verbal
They are, however
Internal
And there they flow
Like a great river
Like an ocean wave
Like a long, lonely stretch of highway
Flowing, till it disappears from sight
But not from my memory

Cabrina A. Gilbert

Under The Roof

No one to look up to
nothing to look forward to
in criss-crossed lands
painted in a color I can't see
pictures made to fit the frame
with a lock that looks like me
in a foreign way of blurred decisions
and boredom has blocked the visions
of escape into the jaws
of what I hate in red-stained claws
lies what no treasure can erase
no gift is greater
or more constantly raped
my optimism is in the basement
filling with self-depravation
and hanging on a rope of my own creation.

Jody Eastman

Sweetest Lady

Sweetest lady, I knew the day would come.
Now it's time to say goodbye.
It has been a long, such a long labored day.
Now it's time to rest your eyes.
But it's gonna be alright,
Because when you go to sleep tonight
The world will be by your side.
The sun is going to shine again,
The heavens will find another friend.
Our farewell is so justified.
Sleeping eyes will turn themselves to dreams
And find a home in the night.
Sweetest Star, I knew the night would come.
Now you shine beautiful and bright.
And it's going to be alright.
Because when I go to sleep at night
The stars will be in the sky.
The night is going to shine again.
The heavens have found another friend.
Your warm star light will never die.

John M. Fanning Jr.

Tomorrow Comes

Tomorrow comes with the grace
Of a frightened doe
Chased by wild dogs
Along a rock spotted
Mountain hillside.

The dew in the shade
Looks black like tar.
I watch it drip
On her back.

She growls,
Chasing a wild cat in her sleep.
She bears her teeth,
I wake to the day.

David Jones

November 22, 1963

The burning shame
of a nation wronged
Has seared men's hearts
Which lonely throb
amid motionless stupor.
A shaken world
Unknowingly pleads for Time,
The sole constant,
capable of soothing,
Like rolling waves smoothing
jagged edges of suddenness,
Washing away
the sting from our wounds
So that only a sorrowful ache
remains to remind us.
With voices regained,
We bellow our outrage
to the winds, which briefly dispel
Our helpless humiliation
And then blow it back again.

Josephine Bell

My Tribute To Desert Storm

Stormy Norman lead the band
Of America soldiers.
In desert land
Modern weapons were at the test.
In desert storm they proved the best.
Back at home America prayed.
American flags.
We watched them wave.
Yellow ribbons.
Were every ware.
In Jesus love.
We showed we care
For those who died.
In desert storm.
America will pray.
America will Morn.
For hero's brave.
And soldiers true.
From desert storm.
We'll remember you.

David Lee Knepp

Memories

   We have an old lighthouse at the end
of my street.
   When I was little, my friends and I
would go there to meet.
   We would play all the day, games like
hide and seek.
   Until it was dark and the
sky turned bleak.
   But over all the darkness the
lighthouse would shine.
   So my friends and I would feel
safe all of the time.
   I went back one day when I got
older to see.
   The lighthouse was dusty and
didn't shine on the sea.
   It had cracks in the bricks and no
glass for the windows.
   But it still give me warmth
like no body knows.

Dyan Spain

My Angel On Earth

I have seen life through the eyes
Of one of God's greatest gifts
This gift is my special child
And my spirits she always lifts
I watch her as she grows
And she continues to amaze me
She is an angel sent from above
Just look at her and you can see
Her smile lights up a room
Her laugh is as sweet as can be
Her hugs make you warm all over
And her kisses are always free
She has had many battles to fight
To stay here on earth
And each battle that she wins
Is like a new birth
She gives me a reason to live
To be the best that I can be
God sent this angel to earth
And I'm glad He sent her to me

Alice J. Massey

Upswing

Riding a crest
  of positive emotion
Hangin' ten on
  happiness
Even as I enjoy
  the ride,
I look ahead apprehensively
  for the break point.
So as not to end up
  wasted
On the rocks
  of utter despair.

Jim Lamoreaux

Just A Thought

In the realm
Of relative logical collective
Thinking
I
Too
Am merely a bug
Easily squashed
And
Swept under a rug

A moment
Of clarity
Is better than none
Clarity
Is a blessing
Flavor it
Savor it
Some lives live
A
Long life
Never having one

Aubria R. Becker

Forgiveness

I saw the ugly beauty
  of the crucifixion scene.
I had not always realized
  how people can be mean.
Quietly I went to Christ,
  trembling all the way.
Dear Lord, I said, how do you feel
  about that dreadful day?
If I were you, I said to him,
  my grudge would last forever.
To actually forgive those guards,
  never, ever, ever!!
Listening to his reply,
  I sensed a caring love.
My dearest child, he said to me,
  That was so long ago.
We'd best not hold too tightly to things,
  nor pull them from the past.
definitely we can survive,
  provided we forgive.

Carol Stromswold

"God's Awesome Way"

I've seen the beauty
of the midnight sky
I've shared with the morning
it's glorious sunrise,

I've walked on the shore
of a peaceful bay
I've gathered tranquility
in God's Awesome Way,

In search of my sanity
I listen to the gulls
As they fly so graceful
in the heavens above,

I will, find my rest
at the end of this fight
I'll no longer be troubled,
by long sleepless nights,

Yes, my time will come
If soon, that's okay
Because, I've found my peace
in God's Awesome way.

Alton A. Akin

The Picture

There's a picture in the corner
Of the table by my bed,
To comfort and relax me
When I lay down my head.

The smiling dimpled face
Encourages me each day,
Knowing the fight she fought
Before she was called away.

Her spirit touched our hearts
In, oh, so many ways,
Happiness surrounded her
Through each and every day.

Even to the very last
When pain engulfed her so,
She had a smile upon her face
So nobody else would know.

Now she's gone and out of pain.
God called her home, you see.
But still she loves within my heart
Through all the lovely memories.

Dorrice S. Rayburn

My Guardian Angel

Oh my guardian Angel
Please whisper in my ear
I need your thoughtful inspiration
To guide me through my fear

Oh my guardian angel
Brush your wings against my cheek
And keep me safe from harm
Your weight upon my shoulder
Gives me the reassurance
That I can make each day
Better than the one before

Gina DiPietro

A Union

If you must carry the weight
of this cold, cold world
upon your shoulders,

Let me be your blanket
of warmth.

I will engulf you
with my love.

I will tantalize your senses
with pleasure.

I will caress the pains
of your soul.

I will smooth away the creases
of worry
that furrow your brow.

I will stand beside you
as the global pressures
begin to take flight.

And thus, I will remain,
until in this world,

All is right.

Anna Roberson

Song To Susan

Remind me not, remind me not
  of those beloved those vanished hours,
when all my soul was given to thee,
  hours that may never be forgot,
till time unnerves our vital powers,
  and thou and I shall cease to be.

Can I forget, can'st thou forget
  when playing with thy chestnut hair,
how quick thy fluttering heart did move,
  O by my soul I see thee yet
with eyes so languid breast so fair,
  and lips though silent breathing love,
when thus reclining on my breast.
  Those eyes gave back a glance so sweet
as half reproached yet raised desire,
  and still we near and nearer pressed,
and still our glowing lips would meet
  as if in kisses to express.

Denson D. Croxson

Can't We All Just Be Winners

  They say the determination
of what place you take is based
on how many games you've
won and lost but, what about
the team that played the
hardest, that showed up willing
to play during rain and
played with hurt players.
What about the team who was
put down because of the color
of there shirts, who tried to
beat all adds in winning just one
game. It seems we could do it if
we had a little more time. Can't
we all just be winners? Not always
is the first place team the best
or the last place team the worst.
Our team played with
glory and determination to win.
Can't we all just be winners.

Jennifer Johnson

Wondering Vision

Their sweet song is a reminder
of your gentle voice
when you lovely speak to me.
I hear you call from a land afar;
I turn to look for you,
to search your eyes, for some truth
of where to go from here.
Your vision touches my eyes
and you are here with me.
We walk together by the shores.
Your hand touches mine,
the water gently encircles our feet.
Looking back, our prints,
which were once in the sand,
are now washed out to sea.
Still here we are together
looking each in the other's eyes
wondering where this has brought us,
and in what direction it will take us.

Andrea Nafziger

"Arizona, I Salute You"

As I stand above you
  oh, great battleship,
I salute you and
  your gallant men
who lie eternally
  in your underwater tomb.

Your hallowed decks lie
   submerged below the surface
gentle waves splash
   against your vents and stacks
berthed here forever
   the flag waves in your honor.

A thousand men still
   serve your rusty hidden
hulls, await the day
   to rise and march
with throngs of comrades
   who also died
for their country.

Glenn A. Souders

Ten Little Indians

Ten little Indians,
oh what a mess,
Running Wolf will not sit down
and Falling Star has ripped her dress.

Little Bear lost his lance
while trying to spear White Rose,
Spotted Fawn pushed Two Feathers down
which bloodied up his nose.

Three Rivers began to create
a river of her own,
Angry Eyes stubbed his toe
and he wants to cry alone.

All the while Hopping Black Crow
from under the table gazed,
as mischievous Fox fell of his chair
looking totally amazed.

Ten little Indians
caused me to loose my wit,
my patience and my temper
I'll never baby-sit for....
TEN LITTLE INDIANS.

Gypsy Lundberg

For Life

In the gray morning fog
on a busy commuter highway,
a Canada goose
paces back and forth,
perilously close to traffic
on the edge of the road,
while waiting for his mate
lying dead
in the wet, morning grass,
to mount up with him once again
to the safety of the skies.
A Canada goose mates for life.
Fine line,
fine line.

Bruce K. Friesen

When I was ten, a poor kid from queens,

A rich aunt sent me to camp in Maine;

I heard chamber music for the first time

The violinist studied sheet music
On a silver filigree stand
As the pianist rapped for silence.
The cellist, thighs outspread
As a woman receives her lover,
Bowed her head,
Then drew back on a bow
Sounding the first note
Of Haydn's Allegro.
From the dark
Moon-lillied lake
Came an answering loon.

Hallie Wells

She

She sits in the sun,
on a stone, in a field.
She sits in the snow,
by a fire deep in thought.
She is in the moss,
is the tree, is the pond.
She is in the fish,
in the sea far away.
She is everything,
everyone, everywhere.
She knows many things,
about life and the world.
she is old mother earth,
she is life, death and rebirth.

Annie Green

Love Is Beauty

I can't say her name
Or love at her being
All I know is love.

I live eternity
Studying before beginning
With my need growing.

Mirror mind meditating
With her mirror mind
Silence is our conversation.

Carl R. Miller

My Brother, My Sister

A forlorn figure
  on the bus ascending
Head bowed in shame
  the piercing stares to fend.

Starkly before me stands
   life's pained Ambivalence incarnate
A captive battleground
   for sport
Between the Gods
   Hermes and Aphrodite
Oozing chagrin
   tormented without cause.

Blaspheme the Satan-Gods
  so ruthless and sadistic
God-Child of tortured days
  and mournful nights.

Aris F. Yanibas

"Destiny Tolled The Bell"

It was an ominous night
On the ebony sea,
Brave men on the Clipper Ship prayed;
But Heaven was deaf, Hell's fury reigned
And doomed were the ship and crew.

The lightning flashed
And the thunder rolled,
Howling winds blew torrential rain.
Lost was the sound of splintering wood,
Tattered sails and masts blown away.

One water— soaked page from the ship's log
Riding the crests at dawn of day
Was a legacy left for man's eye to see;
Fate wrote the script, destiny won,
Relentless waves had claimed their prey.

Anne J. Pierre

Untitled

The Land is Reality, -
On the other side of the
Forest, -
Listen, - for a Pine Needle
Dropping, -
On the White Cushion
Far, - Far, -
Below.

Listen for the Lone Cry
Of a Bird, - so far above -
It can hardly be heard -
On the other side of the
Forest.

The Fields Swing down to
The Sea, — Where Waves so
Distanced, — are Motion - Slow, -

Suddenly, Caught, - in an
Unreal Glow,—
On the Other Side of the
FOREST.

Joan Julien Grant

Lingering Love

Dare not let me linger
  on thoughts of yesterday,
Regarding our past friendship
  that appears so far away.

The richness of a friend
  always willing to give,
Everything that is needed
  for a fuller life to live.

Dare not let me linger
  on what you meant to me,
Lest the days be full of sadness
  and that should never be.

So, let me ask a little prayer
  to Him in heaven above,
Let me meet someone like you
  to whom I can give my love.

Douglas A. Slingerland

Another Night

All night I sit and wait
Once again there's no call.
My tears flow like raging rivers,
But they do no good.
My heart breaks once again.
I lay in bed dreaming,
Dreaming of white horses and Prince
  charming
Even though my heart breaks
My mind and body are ready to move on.
My heart puts the memory on the shelf
  with the rest.

Jennifer Anderson

Untitled

It nearly always ends this way,
One must go and one must stay;
One is rescued out of pain,
And one must learn to live again.

Grace H. Chinault

Anxious Pressures In My Chest

Anxious pressures in my chest
One so young is laid to rest.
Bullets fly to our distress.
Law enforcement tries their best.

Parents morning for their young
Minor shooters never to be hung.
Countless shots to be rung
How many deaths must be sung?

NRA is much too strong
Don't you see where's the wrong?
Stopping guns shouldn't take so long
How much more of the mourners song?

Three years old and shot in his bed
Seven-in the crossfire to her dread.
Thirteen with a gun and eyes that see red
Seventeen with a revolver to his head.

Anxious pressure in my chest
Can't we stop this tremendous mess
Peace on earth from my heart and soul.
Please dear God we pray for gun control.

Denise De Terlizzi

Tomorrow

Tomorrow is another day,
Only time can help us now.
Maybe some day you will see,
Memories of our precious vows.
Yes it's true I loved you,
Kept deep inside.
Ending only in bitterness,
Telling me to run and hide.
Touches we've once had,
Is enough for us to see
Reality is around the corner,
It's here that you should be.
Never give up I say at night,
Guiding my every dream.
But in that dream you're with her.
Please tell me what does it mean?

Julie Diane Eckard

Today

  Oh Day you do bore me
only your gloom do I see
your rain is today's fee
taken from some mighty sea

The sun cannot see through your cloud
your thunder is much too loud
your wind does blow proud and wild
tomorrow will be your child
the moon is your tombstone
in heaven it roams

Allan H. Lambert

What A Dump!

When John Jason Smocker
Opens up his locker,
We all evacuate,
We never hesitate.
John grumbles,
As junk tumbles
Onto the floor.
Paper wads galore.
Report cards, failing slips,
Bags of broken potato chips,
Sandwich bags, grey rocks,
Dirty, smelly gym socks,
Math papers, beat up books,
All around he gets dirty looks.
Lost papers, glass jars,
Half-eaten candy bars,
Broken pencils, apple cores,
All around the students roar
With laughter as John Smocker
Stuffs his junk back in his locker.

Cortney Pickering

People

People are noisy
People are choosy
People can talk
Baby's 1, 2, 3 can not
People are all different kinds
Some are deaf some are blind
People go through many phases
Kids go through many mazes
People are cool
I think we rule!

Gerrish Craig

Surrender

Simply I surrender
Raise the flag I've held so high
This has gone on long enough
It's time to say goodbye

For I just cannot stand it
As we grossly go to war
As if we had no mind in store
And tell me what's it for

Revenge, or test of guns perhaps
Who has the biggest force
Well, now we're minus one and strong
I'm walking our the door

Chris Armstrong

Strength

Must I be strong
or can I cry
and If not why?

Can I be weak
and let you know
I need your love
Allowing my emotions to show

The strength is acknowledging
the urgency does exist
to be held and comforted
holding out my hands
held open,
not balled into a fist

You are my might
although I tried to hide
I must confess that the real strength occurs
when you are at my side

I now know there is no weakness
for it is the strong
that can cry

Bob Macke

Through The Window

Bursts of orange and yellow
or even shades of grey,
her eyes gaze out into the brilliance
or the dullness of the day.
She sits and stares and thinks
while time strolls idly on —
through the dusky evening
and then again at dawn.
Her time is spent entranced,
enthralled in how and why.
What of this, what of that.
Suddenly she begins to cry.
For her there is no present.
For her there is but past.
Where has all her time went?
She ponders as she stares
through the window, through the glass.

Jennifer Marie Goff

Witch's Brew

Coffee is a bean,
Tea is a leaf,
Both caffeine-mean
Make potions brief!

Bella Wein

Insomnia, Insomniac

Sleep is upon me, yet
plays to deprive me.
Surreal images of
dreamland lost.
As stars fall, night continues
its journey toward dawn.
INSOMNIA ever present.
Eclipsing pink and white
combinations as they dissolve.
Franchon Lane

Listening To God

In the quiet of the evening,
Or the early morning hours,
Is the time my God gives whispers,
Of His wonders and His powers.

To listen is a choice,
I have to try to hear His voice,
And when He finally comes,
It is then that I rejoice.

His message, always clear,
His presence, always near,
When we harden not our hearts,
His voice we can hear.

So, take some time today,
And listen to what God has to say,
Through His Word
It is near we will stay.
Jeanette A. Wilson

"A Woman's Lamentations"

Will God create a man again
Or will a woman, He Begin
To form again a human race
For planets in our Outer Space.

What will God, this time devise
To make a woman twice as wise
No aches, no pains, for her to chafe
No troubles, dangers, she'll feel safe

Now God, we're thinking of a perfect place
Where does Man enter in this race
Your World, Dear God, cannot increase
That's the human point, to say the least.

So we'd best, I guess, let God alone
To rule us humans from His Throne
We'll keep Gods rules for a perfect wife
And go to Him for Eternal Life.
Helen Scott - A.P.

Storms Of Life

Extraordinary thunder crashing through
   our heavens above
Vivid white lightning jagging to earth
Rain swiftly tapping at the windows
While the wind sweeps away the stifle air
To a fresh, soothing, sweet aroma of
   new beginnings.
Nature is grateful for the showers of
   life today.
Even I feel content and at ease within
   the storm
Right now I feel cleansed in the
   moment and free.
Cathy McConnachie

Dreaming

Oh, how the waves are trying to
   out do themselves
As if say, "Come see me act."

The grey clouds meeting the sea;

The sprays' as tall as a mountain,
   As noisy as a freight train -
      Going through a tunnel.

The winter storm is howling,
   The sea gulls
Are sailing like kites in the wind.

The seals are slumbering on the beach,
   As if to say,
   I'm having a rest—
before the tides take me away.

I sit in my warm yellow cottage,
   sipping my morning coffee,
   As I dream the time away.
Dollie Buehner

Friend To Friend

There is a rainbow
Over our lives and state
In which I live, Joan.
Do enjoy, cause every day is great.

So much to see and do
As changes in our lives mature.
And being a widow, Joan
I still have a wonderment of nature.

Your living in one era, Joan.
I miss my children and friend!
Changes cannot compensate us
We now take what life offers, again.

To live one day at a time
And see the world, Joan, as is
To say a prayer for everyone.
And never forget, or cry, what we missed.
Jean Mathis

What A Gift

A dull cloudy day life's mysteries
overwhelmed me today,
A sudden shock, a gasp of air,
Not knowing what to expect
Not knowing what to do
something so precious
should be a gift I was told.
Yet I stood there stunned
frozen, lost without words.
How could I tell my parents?
of something from God
only to them it would be a disgrace.
Something that happened
with no band upon this finger.
Disgrace.... how awful a word.
To them this maybe an ungodly sin,
But in the long run everything will be changed.
Something so special look them right in the face.
Something so innocent surely this is a gift
from Gods Heavenly embrace.
Angie Sutton

dawn

i walk the placid hills
   past verdant fields
in amber hues of sunlight —

i gaze upon the jewelled sky
   face upturned
to catch the gentle breeze —

arms upraised
   I lift my voice
in song —

tears of joy I shed
   at this wondrous miracle
dawn of a new day —
Bobbi Meislohn

The Reluctant Lady

The reluctant lady
Peaks out of her shell
She's finally completed
Her stay in Hell.

Understand her awkwardness
For so long she did grieve
It might take her a while
To trust enough to believe.

The reluctant lady
Is careful for fear
That her love her in vain
And she shed a tear.

Be patient, her uncertainty
Walk ever so gently the path
As the warm rays of love touch her
She relaxes to bath.
Angelia Flores

"God Will Make You Stop And Think"

God will make you stop and think
Pray and you'll stay in the pink
He can bring you to hells brink
God will make you stop and think

God will make you stop and think
Hates filthy words so low you sink
You could end up in the clink
God will make you stop and think

God will make you stop and think
Think of God when you wear mink
Animals to God we link
God will make you stop and think

God will make you stop and think
Pray and you'll stay in the pink
He can bring you to hell's brink
God will make you stop and think
Daniel Andrade

Untitled

The weeping of the willows
signified the end,
Where the lost journeys of
youth are resting,
Bringing peace to the
fields of laughter,
And restoring solemn quiet
through the years of maturity.
Jason Hodge

Colorblended

When this white hand
pressed his of black
his pride of him
yet clasp of me
the twain did pierce
our minds once set
to feel so strange
this black and white
palms each on each
this then we knew
so plain as black and white
so true as blood is red
that all Earth's creatures
framed for kindred love
are human-kind
who joy can share
in this our common lot
since pressed as one
within God's circling arm.
Donald R. Daniels

Notre Dame

Football tradition for the country
Pride and fame
Home of college football
Golden is thy name

They tell me you are famous
  I have seen the Golden Dome
They tell me you are strong, and I say, "Yes"
  I've seen the defense crush the "O"
They tell me you are dedicated
  I've seen the great comebacks
They tell me you are spirited
  You have some awesome crowds
You still carry tradition, like:
    "Moose" and Dan
    The Four Horsemen
      and Lehey
Fierceness, power, domination and tradition
Show me another place that has the same
Touchdown Jesus! This is Notre Dame.
Joseph Leik

Blood Ties

A red-haired, blue-eyed baby girl
Proud of her first word, "Daddy"
My childlike heart closed against you,
Couldn't see life through your lies.

The teenager, strong-willed and brave
Detached with mastered skill
I grew away, my spirit soared
Hate's energy sustains short flights.

The once natural bond harshly severed
Legacy of hate, anger, fear
I still don't know you, nor you me
Exactly what is my duty here?

We've both tried and failed to mend before
Pain is the prize for such fools
But I kid myself, whatever my choice
Your ties, our ties, are blood ties.

The damage we've done, part of both of us
Like the steel-blue eyes we share
Our futures enmeshed, these blood ties so strong
Together we must choose the path to new life.
Jennifer Bailey

Grand Mesa

On soft brown beds of needles fallen
  Quietly plays your dappled fawn
A deadfall breaks the peaceful silence
  The sound there echoes on and on

There you rise between two rivers
  To these you send your thaw in spring
To folks who dwell within your valleys
  Your cool and sparkling waters bring

Grand Mesa! You're my kind of mountain
  A gift of God you are to man
Giving freely season's colors
  Rising proud upon this land

It's summer now and once again
  I'll look upon your vast domain
Of shadows cool and Columbine
  Such treasures these I claim for mine

Away and out toward the sky
  You cast a mighty shadow
Thank you Lord for giving us all
  Grand Mesa, Colorado!
C. Guy Wallace

Why Me

As I sit here feeling the
rain pound against my face,
hearing the tiny droplets - the
water's soundless pace,
I close my eyes and ask myself.
why am I me and why am I here,

Why not a racing horse or a
running deer.

Why not on a far away land,
by the sea on heated sand.

Why not somewhere soaring
through the breeze, being a
little bird and hoping
through the trees.

Why not somewhere old and
gay, I ask myself, but
here I lay.

As I decided all these
thoughts I'd write down and keep.....
my mind went blank and I fell asleep.
Janice Kelley

Silent Rain

I sit and speak in silence:
Rain falls
around a beautiful, silent, butterfly
floating somewhere in my mind.
Kind,
sensitive flutters
following the spoken silence.
A butterfly,
in a world that sits to cry,
blinded by the uncertain-
the unwanted.
A butterfly floating in the rain,
soft,
and beautifully silent.
Jeff Hawkins

Endless Sea

The swell of the sea
Reached up and kissed the
Moisture of mist
From the early haze of morning.
Merging together, as one
each swell of the sea had a
slow, rhythmical motion and
with each rising mound,
The sea kissed, so lightly
The mist, until the mist seemed
To disappear into the sea,
Embracing it forever
Together, like passionate souls.
The mist.
The endless sea.
Carole Jean Saleh

Dreaming

Darkness all around
Reality at rest
Ethereal mood surrounds
Animation at its best
Momentary peace is found
Images with zest
Nervousness is unwound
Gigantic fears undressed
Christine Finnegan

"Sometimes I Forget"

Sometimes I forget what life
really means to me, and
I drown in tears my pain
and I just want to disappear
cause - sometimes I forget.

Sometimes I forget how happy
life can be, and because of
my scarred heart, I want
to simply die! Cause - sometimes
I forget.

Sometimes I forget... but
then you - you make me
  remember.
Eliza Bozek

Perpetual

Willows oblique toward the river
Reflections mirrored in the stream
Magnificent their beauty captures
As a painting so supreme.
Sweeping low along the river
Sodden leaves which makes them weep
Changes amber in the autumn
A beauteous memory that we keep.
Willows stark along the river
Icy droplets every where
Frozen water slows the flowing
Willows standing slim and bare.
Green tipped willows skims the river
Springtime thaws and river flows
Breathes again the ancient beauties
Sunlight cast its golden glows.
Willows drape as lacy curtains
Casting hanging branches o'er
The summers lazy lukewarm water
Perpetually forever more.
Clytie N. Pickard

Welfare

Dramatic democrats
Responsible republicans
Wanting to help people
Generation after generation

The poor and rich
The poor and rich

Parts of the world
Keep getting
Hungrier and sicker
Hungrier and sicker

Danielle Bennett

Romantically Inclined

Wear away our vitality
Reveal the nakedness
The shame that cloaked the truth
Has drained away to a vast ocean
To mingle with pollution.
Purity lives but a short time
is fleeting
for the young.
All the saints are dead
All the dead are saints
And effluvium becomes our legacy
We cry at man's tendency
And wonder at women's parity
to ask, what is liberty?

David Palmer

Above And Below

Through the eyes of above and below
Riding on the waves,
My spirit sails
Through the haze of life.
With passion free to discover
The beauty in my soul,
The ocean heals;
It's where I feel so whole.
My spirit's in the ocean
Its always been my home.
My strength is the mountains
When I'm feeling so alone.
I've always felt that I belonged
Beneath the crashing of the sea.
With the spirit of a dolphin
And in his eye I see...
Freedom from my body
And freedom from my world
Free to live and free to play
The freedom of my soul.

Amy Welch

Contemplation

So quick; So brief;
  So infinitesimal is Life -
That one has barely just
  begun its journey
When, suddenly - it is no more!

What lies beyond the arms of death?
A dream? Heaven? Hell?
Who can tell -
Until he answers the eternal beckon!

Jean S. Trott

The Essence Of An African-American Man

I don't want to Physically touch you right now;

I want to embrace the aura of your spiritual being;

I want to intensify your desire by mentally bonding with you;

I want to caress your mind with the sincerity in my eyes and the fire in my heart;

I want to feel your passion by penetrating the flames of your soul.

At the peak of your emotional longing and lusting - then, I'll pierce you with my thrusting manhood and introduce you to eternal ecstasy.

Dane C. Lutcher

Lost Hope

Torn
Ripped between dreams and reality
Pulled apart, so that
neither side wins
neither side tries
Hope's lost
Disappearing in the wind
Blowing away like
scattered fragments of life
Death or Silence
One and the same
For no one hears
the whispering echoes of dreams

Elizabeth A. Harney

Pebble

Losing my support
Rocks crumbling, falling
I grab a ledge
A small niche
Hanging on
Only to realize
In time
It, too will
Give way
And down I'll go
Into oblivion
Pebble
  in
    my
      hand.

Danyel Hermes

The Circle Of Life

The circle of life, goes round and round, the first one lost is the first one found, you can't get by if you can't get through, but the circle of life will wait for you, so go through the middle to reach the end and the circle will open up again half stays their to point the way and the other half goes to a brand new day.

Brent Porter

Bed Time Story

Children play games in the park
  Running around in the dark.
  A frisbee sails up to the sky
For someone to catch or to try
Mothers swing babes in the air
  Wondering, wondering where
Like a cylinder whirling around
Careful to not touch the ground
Lights in the inn cross the way
Proclaiming the end of the day
  Aeroplanes fly overhead
Nine o'clock, "Time you're in bed!"

Helen F. Atkins

Ski Boats in the Sun

I'll listen to what you my friend,
Say is number one.
But the finest things I'll ever see,
Are ski boats in the sun.

Rays glisten off clear-coat glass,
Ride low 'til they gun.
Single, double, triple, ten,
Boy! They make it fun.

Deck girls in their two piece suits,
A group that thinks as one,
Radios all on a hit,
Ready for your run?

And when it seems as though
A red ball is the sun,
They bob and wait in waves,
For crystal yet to come.

The green-red flash of that last turn,
When the day is done,
Ends a day of paradise,
For ski boats in the sun.

Joellen Petrey

A Ray Of Hope

Send a ray of hope to me,
Say word of praise
Show me a little kindness
Don't let me go astray.
This weary heart of mine
Is lonesome as can be,
Without hearing a word of hope
What good is this life too me.
For a Day without Love
Is a cold, cold day
A day without hope has no dreams
A day without Faith is a dreary day
Please bring life back to me.

Jennie Scurti

Bird

Like a bird
Soaring above the clouds
The eagle
Proud and Free
And
Alone
Likeme.

Bonita Whitmire

Loss Of Seed

The expression was without words.
Screaming birth of silence,
The child I did not set free.
Under the sarcastic rule
I can not speak equality.
It is eaten like that
Delicate man,
I will never know.

Empty shells remind of dependency,
A lighter wanting fuel.
Things unsoft waiting,
To plant themselves somewhere
other than anger, only wanting.

The ripening still to come,
Pride drowns hope.
Then none of it matters,
Sand is not soil,
Love can not convert it,
And desolation was
Never meant to be gardened.

Dina Gerhauser

The Ladder Of Life

The builder building a building
Seeks support from his ladder.
The ladder doesn't dangle in mid-air.
It needs a system of support.
The support is as important to the
Ladder as the ladder is to the builder.
The climber in life seeks support.
That support is as the ladder is to
The builder building a building.
Yes the climber in life
Frantically seeks support.
Finding it, he succeeds.
With no support, the discouraged
Climber falls or recedes.
His story could have had a happy ending
If he had found a supporter to
Help him climb the ladder of life.
So, I'll gladly help someone..
Somewhere climb the ladder of life.
May a climber or two depend on you?

Florence M. Jones

A Love Weakened

Baby when we started
seemed like we were the same
Each thinking that the other
was the end of all the pain
Your past was safe and solid
a life so trouble free
Me - I came from somewhere
of the opposite degree
And the somebody it made me
changed your reality.

Nothing good comes easy
so we try to work things out
just lovin' through the good times
is not what love's about.
The work load's gettin' heavy now
how long can we hang on
to a love that's slowly turning weak
intending to be strong?

Debi Callaizakis

Backyard Baseball Of My Youth

The backyard of my youth
Seems now a far and distant place.
Where players of great skill once played
Combining speed and style and grace.

Rendered mute by the stroke of time
Lying vacant yet still exposed
Through the window of its grandstand home,
I gaze in memory on its repose.

The ghosts of all the greats were there.
We were they and we were great.
Cobb stole a base, Mickey slid home,
Lou Gehrig's at the plate.

In truth, just one hitter took his stance.
Calm, and with a smile upon his lips,
The rest were fielders on this team,
This team of a father and his kids.

Its venue was in our neighborhood
Behind the driveway, out from the stoop.
It was here baseball and life were taught,
In this backyard of my youth.

Charles L. Roberts, Jr

The Angels Are Within You

The angels are within you
   Set them free
Allow their wings to carry you
   to your destiny

Some will say you're crazy
   to believe
For all you know they're missing out
   on what they can receive

So close your eyes and go inside
   to meet your angels there
For they will be with you today
   each and everywhere
Don't look into the future
   it will come to you
Let the angels guide the way
   they will see you through

Alice F. Zimak

The Rush Hour

Hurry and bustle! Through the street
   Sets the pattern for the day
Until the darkness draws once more
   And lonely streets can have their play.

Hurry and bustle! Rings our ears
   Down the Stately Avenue
Until the thoroughfare runs out
   Unto the fields beneath the blue.

Car after car - hat after hat
   Numerous colors are seen
Blended together upon the street
   Bright as the valley is green.

Let us enter in this doorway.
Stand here in the farthest corner.
Watch the people crowding by
   Never pausing once for rest.
You friend, take a warning!
   But me? I hurry with the best.

John K. Crawford

First But Last

Keeping pace with what the world
Sets to be my goals
Never minding whose behind
All those wounded souls.

Running fast
Can't lose a beat
Crushing all the promises
I swore to keep.

Lord, I want to serve you,
Be your good and faithful one,
But how can I leave this task
'til all my chores are done?

I seek you in the morning,
Love you all through the day,
But when it comes to quiet time,
I faithfully slide away.

First but last, you're always there for me.
First but last, your love has made me free.
First but last, that's not how it's supposed to be.
Lord, let me put you first not last.

Brenda Thomas Davidson

The Prospector

Scratching in the river bed
Shakin' in the pan
Lookin' for some color is
A prospecting man

Friends and family all are gone
No one left to care
Back all bent from diggin'
And just tryin' to get his share

Saw a trace the other day
Got his hopes up high
Got so hot by noon that day
He thought his brains would fry

Still he digs and claims for sure
Today will be the day
He'll have a strike so rich he'll have
To give a bunch away

His motions always hurried
His back forever bowed
Hurry or some stranger's
Gonna hit the mother load

Barbara Nielsen

My Dream Girl

My girl is dream, possessing charms untold
Let me tell you about her,
   if I may be so bold
Chocolate brown hair, with traces of red
A bundle of charisma, sex and wit,
   from her toes to her head
I love her, I do love her, from
the bottom of my heart
We shall be as one forever,
   and never, ever part
When she casts her eyes upon
   me, I blush, yes I do
Believe me, if you were the
   recipient, you would blush too
Her every wish is my command,
   which is as it should be
She is my source of happiness,
   health and longevity

James Maull

"Donna And Her Animal Friends"

She collects frogs,
She collects worms,
She collects fishes
On her own terms.

She collects puppies
She collects guppies
She has a rat
A pair of cats
A turtle or two
A cocka too, a bunny
That's oh, so funny.
She has a caterpillar
Soon to metamorphisize
Oh, what a surprise
A beautiful butterfly!
I could go on and on
About her love for all life.
Best of all
She is my wife.

Joseph R. Johnson

The Awful Truth

Sue said, "You sure look fat!"
She has a nasty tongue.
Decked in my pretty new dress,
I wanted praises sung.

"Yellow and so snug, it looks
Like a banana skin!"
She looked more like one,
So long and much too thin!

Should I retort smart words,
And stop her saucy tune?
Now, how could that help me?
Couldn't make me less balloon!

I suppose I am a chunk.
Those word I'll make her eat,
By losing twenty pounds,
So she cannot repeat.

Critical, hurtful words
Blossomed fine in the end.
They brought me compliments.
I now call Sue my friend.

Grace Pierce

The Love of A Child

The love of a Child
  So Precious to hold,
    The Gleem in their eyes
      As you watch them grow.

The love of a child
  As they play outside
    You watch from the window
      And feel a warmness inside.

You ask the Lord to guide you
  With wisdom, strength, and faith,
    With the trouble that they find
      Pray you handle without mistake.

I hope you always know
  The love you bring to me,
    And know I did my best
      To raise you lovingly.
        I love you, Mom

Jamie Boothe

Rainbows

Rainbows gold, yellow, bright
Shining in my night
Wishing upon a star
Hoping daylight won't be far
Seeking peace in my light

Rainbows green, blue, new
Binding me with hope
Hanging on to truth
Building bridges strong
Giving me my throne

Rainbows purple, orange, red
Thank God, I'm not dead
Feeling sunshine on my head
Seeing love in a stranger's eyes
Hear my mama sing a sweet lullaby

Rainbows, Falling in that pot of gold
Sweet substance eating at my soul
Healing my every desire
Giving me my quest for life's fire
Rainbows seeking peace in my light -
this night!

Angela Cain Wilkins

Seasons

Spring, Summer, Winter, Fall.
Should I like one or two?
Should I like them at all?

Spring is cool, calm, and wet.
My birthday's in spring,
How can I forget?

Summer is hot, sticky, and humid.
School starts after Summer,
Oh man what a bummer.

Winter is cold, ice, and snow.
I don't like the cold and ice,
But the snow's pretty nice.

Fall is bright with the leaves that fall.
Oh how I love the game football!

Jessica Patterson

"Sister Day"

Once a month was sister day when we 5
sisters got together, we talked of kids, old
times and friends, and yes, about the
weather. We laughed and joked, and ate,
and sang, we shared our worries and
our pain. And as the year went speeding
by we watched one sister slowly die,
we watched the cancer make her weak as
through her body it did eat. We helped her
bear her pain and fear as we watched the
final day draw near. We prayed to God
to help her through and knew that she
was praying too.
  She read her Bible everyday, asking God
to show the way to understand
the reason why, the time had come
for her to die. A part of us has
died with her, there will be an empty chair.
But we 4 that's left will carry on
until sister day in our heavenly home,
for not our will but thine be done.

Faye Gowan

Life Is All One Way

A melancholy girl
Sits all alone
No one to talk to
Afraid of the phone

Her cynical friends
Never really care
They just walk around
With a superlative air

Who can she talk to?
No one will ever know
About all the confusion
That is too tangled to show

So she writes it all down
All the problems and fears
Releasing all the pressures
And also a few tears

She knows she'll be fine
She knows she'll be okay
She has to move on
Life is all one way

Holly Reindl

Sweet Silent Dove

A sweet silent dove
Sits way up there.
As a short gust of wind
Sweeps right by.
He's so silent
I don't know why.
Now there's a coo
And off you fly.

Jessica Johnson

Show Me!

Who are you
sitting behind that face I love?
I have slept with you all my life,
and have no idea
if you are fog or myth or dream.
Come out!
Show me you!
Let me have you in fullness.
Better the truth than fancy,
than the floating to never catch.
Please come to me,
hard to lean against,
and know
whoever you may me.

Donna T. Griffiths

"Rules Of Reality"

In this world today
So many obstacles are in my way
I forget the important things
The new day each sunrise brings
I forget the moon and stars
And think of the way people are
Sometimes I can't see
The unwritten rules of reality
The limits that are put on us
On the surface look fine and just
Race, religion and color
Don't cross the border to each other
I realize these are not uniting tools
But some group's prejudice rules.

Jessica Reilly

The Rhetoric Of Poetry

Framed
six crows sit on a line
between two utility poles
characters unsupported, sponsoring
themselves, inventing themselves
with necessity, urgency, in a voice and

Tone
(let me kiss your neck and)
what do I mean the crows
squabble inadequately, changing
places, balancing themselves
with fluttering, annoyance, in a panic.

Feet
(how many syllables to a sigh)
six black crows now look
like a melody, syncopating
itself, whispering to each other
in pairs, secretly, they know

I, too, dislike it (its secret life)
Without it: silence or banality inadequacy
and embarrassment

Gary B. LaFleur

Sisters

To a great couple that wed
Six daughters were born
It was said
There was Velma, Wilma and Gladys
You see
Then before long here comes Bea
Then there was Johnnie
That was not enough it seems
In six years here comes Darlene
Then there were Others
In all of this mixing
There were two brothers
Henry and Louis to our surprise
They made a great difference
In all our lives
So thanks Mom and Dad
For having six sisters
I am so glad
The oldest was the Cats Whiskers

Bea Wallace

Simple Gifts

Outside the air is crisp and clear
  slightly cool yet refreshing.
Bodies warm the hallowed hall
  eyes and hearts focusing
  on the center of the room.
Flames flicker,
  light permeates
    all dark recesses.
Slowly, faintly the fresh baked
  aroma wafts throughout
and mingles with the
  fragrance of crushed fruit.
Portions given
  gratefully grace received,
  empowered from above,
    called out
      to be.
Joyous songs of praise resound
and enlivened love abounds.

Denise A. Ryder

Ever So Restful....

You meander
Slowly
Shimmeringly
Peacefully
Over flat stones
Sand washed to silkiness
Flowing under over hangs
Of windfall trees
Rocks
Banks
Only to re-appear
Calmly unaffected as
Leaf and twig join
Circular swirl slow of motion
On to seemingly
Endless journey of
Existence
Only for those fortunate enough
To come upon
A tiny woodland stream

Dottie Campbell

Spring

Colors of green dominate the land,
Smells of spring freshens each breathe
And the sun reaches out to demand
That you pay tribute to winter's death.

Birds chirp the song of the new season.
Like town criers call the time,
And many find the birds song pleasin'
Just as much as one of Lowell's rhymes.

Bouquets of flowers blanket the land
In never-ending array of hues,
They were put there by God's loving hand
As one of His many gifts to you.

Christy Chandler

Dear Little One

Dear little one, so newly born
Smiling mother, though birthing worn.
Daddy, in awe, looks at his son
A miracle, that love has done.
Happy parents with dreams to fill
As days evolve by God's good will.
Oh to be young and full of dreams.
My dreams are gone, or so it seems.
I look at you, Dear little one
How far must your little feet run?
How many hurts must you endure?
How can you keep your heart still pure?
My thoughts go back to days of youth
My heart cries out with voice of truth.
Days of frolic, they bring a smile
Hard work and tears, but all worth while.
The gift of life, clouds, sun, and birth
I've loved them all, my days on earth.
By your birth, life's circle is done
Run - and Godspeed, Dear little one.

Elsie Aune

Music

Music is warm,
The silence gets torn.
Music is fast,
Like a hunting dog.
Or music is slow,
Like the morning fog.

Garrett Thor

God's Gift

A permanent fuxture shining
So bright
Illuminating all
That's right
Uniting and advising a family of
Twelve
To stay in touch and treat each other
Well
Thank you Lord for what
You've done
Cause we still have our moms
At age "81".

Helen J. Zackery

Hope Is In Our Hands

Like two, rays of light meet,
so do triumph and defeat.
We are so far ahead,
other nations we have led,
but there is something missing deep within
and the search for it must begin.
So short our lives,
to be overcome with violence and crime.
Prejudice and hate separate us all
and only we can break this racial wall.
What can we do? What can we say?
It is up to our youth to pave a new way.

Jill Meyer

Moma's Purple Coat

My mother wore a purple coat.
  So many years ago
She never really liked it.
  Though she never told me so.

The lining was torn and ragged
  the buttons .. there were few.
This year she'll get a new one
  but the old one would always do.

The purple coat was the reason,
  I had nice clothes to wear.
The reason for my love for her
  and memories of her care.

The purple coat is a symbol
  of what I'd like to be.
Of love and understanding
  and what she meant to me.

In time of ease and plenty
  the purple coat is rare today.
But the love within it's meaning
  will never pass away.

Ina Hazel Tarver

Cascade Mountains

High in the cascade mountains
South of the cascade trail

We climb to Red top mountain
to dig for G-O's of old

On the way through the land of
the lost, we find the wild and free.

They roam through the meadow
And valleys (living their life as
it was meant to be.)

Gerald L. Kirschenmann

The Creek (Beside My House)

She moved along in Rhythm style
So peaceful in her bed
A gentle sound moved with her
As on her way she sped

I sat in silence gazing at
Her locks of snowy white
I thought perhaps she's getting old
Like people do with time

Then I was but a simple child
Who did not understand
That folks get old and pass away
While creeks go on and on

No tranquilizer ever was
Or ever yet will be
As soothing as that gentle sound
That meant so much to me.

Helen Thompson

A Sip Of You

I long to win your heart my love
So this I'll promise you
I'll treat you right and cherish you
And make you feel brand new

If you were wine drank from a cup
I would not drink for long
For I fear I would drink too quick
And soon you would be gone

So I will sip and savor you
So you can last my life
For should you spill and drift away
From thirst I'd surely die

So wine of love please quench my thirst
My love it's now or never
Then I can show and you will know
That love can last forever

Jack B. Walton Jr.

To My Daughter

The day you were born
So tiny and sweet
You were given a name
for you to keep.

It was passed on to you
With love and a smile
To honor and cherish
And use for a while.

It carries the family
From whence you came
Proud and honorable
Is your name.

Carry your head high
And don't be ashamed
For the name that you bear
Is all that I claim.

One day you will change it
When you marry, my daughter
Remember the honor
When given another.

Cathy Guerin-McDowell

The Baby No One Wanted But God

In careless love it was conceived,
So tiny its hard to believe.
Blue eyes from her or
Brown eyes from him?
Dark skin or light
Which will it be?
Still unwanted by them
Who will care if not them?
Oh yes there is one
Who cares what it will be.
And He takes it and
Makes it after Him eternally.

Elizabeth Pledger

Lasting Moments

All of life is made up of moments:
Some are born, then dwindle and fade.
But some are stored indelibly
Where secret dreams are made

They touch the heart, they stir the soul
Like the thundering tide of the sea,
And when they're gone, they still remain
Forever a part of me.

So I keep my faith, and wend my way
Along the shores of life
And 'though I'm bruised and battered.
I am calm amid the strife

Fannie Freedman

It's A No. 1 Nation

In looking back at these our states
   Some things do come to mind,
We hear complaints from our people
   Good words are hard to find.

They talk of floods and forest fires
   of rape and murders, too.
The Earthquakes often take some lives
   Tornados often do.

Now stop and think about our flag
   Let's keep it flying high
The freedoms it has brought to us
   We surely can't deny,

In spite of all our trouble spots
   There's just one thing to say,
You cannot find a better place
   Than this, our U.S.A.

Buryle W. Marvin

Two Pine Trees

Two stately pine trees
   swinging in the breeze
one holding the other
   because its got weak knees,
hold on tight the tall
   one seems to say
and maybe just maybe
   you'll last another day
but there comes the wind
   blowing oh so high
down goes the pine tree
   with a great big sigh.

Alice C. Van Cour

I've Got To Be Me

Some think that I'm cute,
Some think that I'm fine,
Some think that I'm ugly,
Now somebody's lying;

But see I don't care,
Cause who I am is myself,
I will always be me, and nobody else;

Some think that I'm smart,
Some know that I am,
Some think that I'm stupid,
But I know who I am;

So to me who they see,
Really doesn't matter,
Cause, who I am is myself,
I will be no one else;

So if you're the type, who always
Talks down someone else,
Stop! Go look at yourself,
I'm sure that you'll find,
A person who is not, ONE OF A KIND.

Helen L. Brown

Untitled

We have something more you see
something that will always be
True as blue here to stay
Here tomorrow as yesterday
Never does it leave me sad
hurt confused are extremely mad
it yields a hand and helps me through
and reminds me there is always you
yet things may not always go well
of that I'm sure I've lived to tell
but what we have it means so much
and so lets always keep in touch
lets make it work and see it through
Depend on me as I count on you
What do we have some may ask
a friendship that will always last

Brandy Sparrow

"Troubled Heart"

Why, dear friend, do I worry so,
spirits at times very low,
when often you don't seem to care
how other's feelings you lay bare.

Searching always for life's pleasure,
spending too much time at leisure.

Our body which is very frail
The Lord did give us as a grail,
our spirit and our soul to hold,
life and character to mold.

Drifting onward without aim
eventually can but maim
the things most precious in our life,
values for which all should strive.

Of such serious thoughts I cannot speak,
only in writing can I seek
your understanding for my true concern.

Irene Osburn

Balloons

A clown
standing alone
holding his balloons

Red, yellow, blue, white
bright, bouncing
tugging upward at their strings

A boy
innocent, harmless
asks for a balloon
What's just one of so many?

Children of all ages
wanting balloons
just like the boy
What's a few more?

A crowd
loud, menacing
demanding balloons
There aren't enough

A clown standing alone
holding nothing.

Jeffrey May

Untitled

A mountain of frozen custard
Standing always there.
A mountain of frozen custard
Sweet but bare.
I told you everything I could
All that I could share.

Upon a frozen mountain top
A tree stands tall and sere.
Upon a mountain top it stands
Strong but bare.
I told you everything I could
All that was right and fair.

I told you everything I could
All that I should
All that was good
The rest I did not dare.
The rest I did not dare.

Florence Campi

Serenity

The old oyster-bed guard-house
Stands vacant
Silently guarding our creek.
Trees on the bank
Sway slightly in the gentle breeze.
Cat-tails and marsh reeds
Beckon.
Gliding silently along the creek
We paddle.
The hoot-owl hoos in the distance.
In the deepening dusk
Frogs croak.
Crickets chirp.
Geese fly noisily by
Honking.
Peace and serenity
Shroud us
Quietly.
My soul is at rest.

Edith Killmon

Winter

Frosty, frigid midnight blue
Stars to earth that look askew
Fleeing hermits seen on high
Do well your footsteps cover nigh.

Pole and stance there to see
They cycle all to each his lea.
Bolder turned to side the vent.
Canvas pulled behind a tent.

Nagging shays are at the gate
Downcast, trodden vandals wait
Morning dews freeze at the sight
Brought to all from heaven's light.

Joane Harmon

The Child Inside

The child inside cries out in vain
still haunted and tortured
still full of pain.
No one can soothe her tormented heart
her world so cold
lonely and dark.
For she'll never grow old
and she'll never die
she'll always remain
a child inside.
There's no more laughter, only tears
as she tries to hide
from all she fears.
For we are one, she and I
an outer shell
in which we hide.
Restless we'll forever be
for the child inside
is inside of me.

Dawn Cavanaugh

Shovelling The Driveway

The narrowness of winter,
street-light dark by five p.m.,
snow falling since noon,
a few inches now on the driveway
the perfect catharsis before
going inside to face them.
Again the shovel serves its purpose.
Scooping, lifting and tossing
loosens the shell built-up
in layers through the day.
Shovelling hard, shoulders and back
broad and exposed in the trench coat,
the shell slides
to the driveway
where it freezes so quickly,
the next downstroke creates thousands
of shards tossed aside
with dirty snow.

Jeff Levi

The Setting

Goodbye sun, your fading away...
The moon is shining, the stars
are crying, all for the hope
of a new day. Hello darkness
with your beautiful array...
Your hiding the creatures of
a day away. Goodbye sun until
another day, your gleam is
only a dream away.

Joe Morrow

The Tide

The tide is before me
strong and alluring
ever glistening
consuming
unable to move
I feel its tug at my feet
sand washing away
the wave crashes
again I feel its gentle caress
tighten its hold
then release and pull
the force becomes stronger
will I be able to stand
or be caught in the wave
and carried away

Julianne Blommer

After Pachabel's Canon In D

Unwavering is your love,
Strong, secure, enfolding,
Never ceasing, always growing.

It whispers exaltations of joy,
Which leap into golden harmonies
Of constancy and warmth.

New themes play upon the old.
Our constant transformations
Surpass all ancient dreams.

The might and glory of eternal love
Sing out interwoven melodies
Of enduring ecstasy.

Denise Auch Olson

Autumn

Forest of color touches the sky
Sunlight sparkles overhead high
A cool chill settles over all
On this beautiful enchanting day of fall.

Trees sway in the breeze
Sunlight dances on the leaves
A peacefulness settles within
Renewed energy as the new day begins.

Red, yellow, green, and brown
Dot the roadside from town to town
Warmth of the sun penetrates the inner soul
Falling leaves form a yellow pool.

Forest of color touches the sky
Bids farewell to the summer gone by
Seasons changing across the land
Touched by God's very own hand.

Georgianna M. Weese

"Thank You God"

Thank you God for the food I eat.
Thank you God for my hands and feet.
Thank you God for the clothes I wear.
Thank you God for my ears to hear.
Thank you God for my eyes to see.
Thank you God for making me.
Thank you God for the birds and the bees
Thank you God for the flowers and trees
Thank you God for the buildings so tall.
And all of the animals big and small.
For all these nice things to you I pray.
Thank you God for each new day.

Deloris Fenske

Misty Waters

Misty waters on the lake
Surround me as I wander.
I take my time to stop and think,
To look around and ponder.

For life withholds so many truths,
Yet tells so many lies.
How can we create a world
If no one really tries?

So I just sit here by my lake
And think all to myself,
"How can we create the truth,
If it's hidden upon some shelf?"

"Locked away up tight somewhere
Is the key to unlock that door."
This is something I once said,
But listen to no more.

For truth lies there waiting,
Floating in the breeze.
One day if you look close enough,
You'll find that you believe.

Cassandra D. Earles

The Vessel

Tranquil waves upon the shore
Surround me day by day,
Until the lulling is a roar
Beckoning along the way...

To a better time, a greater joy
As those I've yet to know;
A sense of peace, a calm resides
From whence it came, it goes.

Now weathering the silence
The wind so high and strong,
I tenuously return to the enigmatic path
I once was on.

Listless as I wander
A part of me escapes,
To travel to that sacred place
Where pleasure does await.

The reality at once I find...
Imagination at it's prime.
This deafening dream bestows to me
The grace of change in history.

Denise Aileen Humphrey

Unconditional

So in love you were
That you decided
To walk the path of life
Together side by side
With the watchful eye
Of the Lord as your guide.

Those vows you did take
Through the good times and bad
This union thou shall not forsake
For only in death shall you part.
So in love you are—-
Embedded deep in your heart.

Take this time to reflect
Upon the friendship and respect
That has grown through the years
So stay on this path and you
Will always be so in love

Eric Proctor

Standing Still In Time

I am standing still in time;
Suspended as I wait patiently for you.
My focus on you takes away all pain, all
 doubt, all misery.
Wishing you were with me now as I'm filled
 with infinite anticipation.
Afraid to even blink, because in that
 small piece of eternity,
That tiny block of being,
I might miss you.
You know I'm waiting for you...
I can feel it;
But we must come together when we are
 both ready,
There is no rush.
Love does not know Time;
Nor does love expire.
Love is with me-
Standing still in time;
Suspended as I wait patiently for you.

James W. LeGrand

Untitled

The tempestuous sea
Swaying moorings
Thunderous in its' approach.
Waves glistening in moonlight.
The tides hunger
Drawing, taking me.
I feel the wind.
A roughness against my skin.
The mist upon my face.
A taste of salt.
Water crashing against me.
The icy warmth caressing.
Bellowing waves calling me further
Into the gray, the darkness,
The murk of things.
The illusion and confusion.
The ever changing flow.
The ebbing and withdrawal.
I feel the sea.
A turbulent sea in me.

Geri Swift

Special Day

Special days, part of life's encounter
Some recur, others need a reminder
When being on the job was number one
Days off with pay were fun
Now, New Year's Day's not all that
Tool old for celebrant's hat
Washington and Lincoln's dates of birth
No longer stand-alone worth
Come days of prayer and sparkle
Like liberty, thanks and ecclesiastical
None can ever be as special as May one
First son born that May in 1941
Loved from the start
This master of cello and kind heart.

Joseph J. Rutkowski

The Robbery

It comes like a thief in the night,
taking item by item, piece by piece
anything of value. Some items
small, some large. Take all while
it can-memory by memory.
Childhood experiences, high-school
dances, college graduation, wartime
buddies, golf games, wedding glimpses,
piano skills, parenting trials,
and the joy of being a grandparent.

What is left is a house with no
memory of bygone days-asking the
question - who am I? And who are you?

Jeanita Tidwell

Old House

Old House, talk to me.
Tell me of the footsteps
 coming to my bed softly
 like a gentle rain of new life.

Old House, tell me of the ghosts
 who lived and loved here
In the night
While I wait for her caress.

Old House, bless the shadows
And the echoes, the creakings
 and the darkness
When she doesn't come tonight.

Old House, give me patience
 while I wait with you forever,
For the dawn
And for her light.

Alan Nichols

Untitled

Lilly was a lady
Tender in her years;
Her tries at growing flowers
Only brought her tears.
 She tried - they died. She cried.

Grandma said to Lilly
I have a plan.
Let's plant water bulbs
In the meadow land.
 Too damp to camp. Re-vamp.

Later at the meadow edge
They did a double-take.
Now, the flowering meadow
Is called 'Lillys' Lovely Lake!
 The lake does take the cake!

Geraldine Villa

By Example

O' mother how tender your heart,
The gifts of love and laughter.
Pure beauty and joy,
Through your womb I enter this world.
Through your eyes I see peace
and acceptance.
Through your example I find
passion for wisdom.
It is our existence here,
now - together.

Cindy M. Dietz

The Wind

Slowly the breeze goes through the trees.
Tenderly touching all the leaves.
Sometimes bending them to the ground.
Swirling the tree tops round and round.
Ever so slowly, then sometimes fast,
But very seldom does it last.
We stand and watch it as it grows,
At first its gentle, then it blows.
It lifts and throws sand in the air,
Tosses and curls and blows our hair,
It touched us like a special friend,
Engulfs us like the night descends.
A sadness comes at this poems end,
Because we will never touch the "wind"

James C. Jouget

Forgiveness At Wounded Knee

I felt the fear of my shadow moon
That ancient stalker of the night.
The rushing blood, the hot breath
The angry sword, arcing and flashing
With might of right.

Trembling children, running women
Devoured by a raging father.
Gentle flowers of the earth.
Discarded as worthless.
Beauty scattered from my sight.

Precious child, flowering in the dawn.
Your heart I will not see.
I've cut you down, and snuffed you out,
That gentle part in me.

Alexander Neervoort

A Feeling Inside

There's a feeling inside
That can make you feel ill
It needs no invitation
It arrives upon will

If you choose not to call it
And keep it inside
It may mean you stay silent
And swallow your pride

My mind tells me often
This should not be allowed
It can almost consume you
And won't make you proud

It's anger I speak of
And it makes me feel sad
That more often than not
This feeling I've had

So I do all that I can
To forget this exists
I speak now with my heart
Instead of my fists.

Gregg Neff

Last Words

I need not epitaph
  There'll be no headstone
    I'll be free forever
      Riding the surf in the bay

Henry A. Sarkissian

No Tears

I like things
  That go bump in the night

A roller coaster ride
  Now that's out of sight

That big balloon
  Way up in the air

Would never give me
  An awful scare

Whenever I'm free falling
  It's almost like crawling

As you see
  I have no fear

Except when it comes
  To a baby's tear.

Bertha Pentleton

"A Endless Times Forever"

Life is an endless times
that go on over and over
Without knowing its good or bad
cause only time will tell
The reasons, that we learn is
not clear until then
knowing not the reason
until it to late
life can be of beauty
that's heavenly host
Or life can be of darkness
and despair
Without no place to turn or hide
If we do not learn, life experience
Then we as a peoples have
been in an endless times forever.

Christina C. Sanders

My Old Rocking Chair

The old rocking chair
  that I love so
Where my grandfather sat
  so long ago
I remember him still
  in his quiet way
Looking thru the window
  on a sunny day
Looking out, at the garden below
  a smile on his face
    so many years ago.
Today, as I sit
  in that Old Rocking Chair
I remember my grandfather
  who often sat there
I remember his smile
  and his quiet way
And the love we knew then
  Is with us today!

Hilda Beltz

Ice Cream Cone

There's an ice cream cone in the sky.
Too much of a sight to pass by.

I wonder what it could be from,
It sure would be filling in my tum!

Boy, it sure is getting low.
WHAT?! You say it's a tornado!

Carrie Kuecker

Untitled

You tell me that you love me
that is something I can't say
you tell me that you need me
and I slowly turn away
you tell me that you care for me
and I know the words are true
you tell me that you want me
now all my hopes are new

So
if I say I love you
will you turn around and stay
if I say I need you
will you never go away
if I say I care for you
will you make my dreams come true
and if I say I want you
will you take away my blues

Audra J. Leland

Gate Of Promise

There is a gate of promise,
That is there for you and I,
In the morning we'll meet at sunrise
Then there we'll be on high.
Open wide the promise gate.
It stands beyond compare,
Get ready before it is too late.
I'm hoping to meet you there.
Come and dine the master calls.
He waits in blessed hope,
There is no time to falter.
The gate just might be closed.

Flora Lovelace

Untitled

There is a deer
That plays around here
Right at our back door;

We chase him away,
He thinks it's play,
And always comes back for more.

T.W.'s his name,
Time wasting's his game,
This dear little buck of ours;

We love him a lot,
But hope that he's not,
Here just to eat our flowers.

Some day he will go,
At the first sign of snow,
Never to visit again;

But until then
We will play with him,
This little time waster of ours.

Helen B. Wysocki

Survival

So many times I have felt
  that you have beaten me.

Still I have - to my own surprise -
  risen again.

But
  now you have beaten me.

Someone rises though it is no longer
  anyone any of us recognizes.

Carol Duefrene

Frozen Flowers

Silver gray the color,
that shades this Winters day.
Frost etches on my window,
flowers, but not of May.

Silently no sound,
from the softly falling snow.
But underneath this blanket,
the flowers wait to grow.

Will the snow cover,
all the scars of pain?
From sorrow filled hearts,
will thawing come with rain?

Not gentle has been the Winter,
cold upon the land.
I long for the Summer,
to hold flowers in my hand.

Claire Brogren

"Reasons For Loving You"

I love you for your eyes
That sparkle in the sun;
I love you for the memories
Of all the things we've done.

I love you for your sweet embrace
That always holds me tight;
I love you for your caring ways
That make me feel just right.

I love you for your protectiveness
That lets me know you care;
I love you for your forgiveness
That is so very rare.

I love you for your honesty
For when I'm wrong you set me straight;
I love you for your determination
To withstand the hands of fate.

I love you for the things you say
And for everything you do;
But I love you most of all....
For just being you.

Cindy Fulks

A Mother Is

A mother is like the wind
that surrounds you,
like your body is surrounded by skin.
A mother is always there
through thick and thin;
and always there to pick up the
broken pieces no matter where or when.
A mother is someone who cares
when all of your bad times begin.
She is someone who falls to her knees
to pray for you and your sin
A mother is one who is loyal and kind
and always, from day to day,
has you on her mind.
A mother is an ocean
that runs deeper and deeper with love,
mother is like the sky
and all the heavens above.

Charles E. Stevenson

Dreamy Thoughts

We yearn for the bond
That will make us one
And hold us together
To outlast the sun.

With a ring on the finger
And love in the heart
It will bind us together
Till death do us part.

To wake up with you
Each day by my side
Oh how I dream
Of being your bride.

To walk down the aisle
And say "I do"
While looking at eyes
Of beautiful blue.

Marry me today
Love me tomorrow
And promise me Brett
You'll take away this sorrow.

Christi Dugas

Death Of A Friend

I know the Lord is happy now
That you are there with him.
But how I miss your happy face
And ever present grin.
There is so much we left undone
That we had planned to do.
You'll have to wait for me "Up There"
And hope I make it too.
The tears I shed are not for you
But for myself, I fear.
Because I lost a friend so true,
So loyal, kind and dear.
I know that I will have to strive
To be both good and true.
But that's my goal while I'm alive
I want to be like you.

Harriett Scott

Someday

Someday the world will be right again
(that's if it ever was.)
It'll go back to the days when people,
helped out "just because."
Back when people were honest
and there wasn't a lot of crime.
When there was respect for the elderly
and you wouldn't steal a dime.
Back to a time when parents taught values
and children really learned in school.
Not like now, where parents abuse
and teenagers are just "too cool."
Someday the world will be right again.
I wonder if it was always this wrong.
The dream of peace and brotherhood
is a journey much too long.
A smile should be automatic
a handshake black and white.
That can be the beginning
of making this world right.

Joelle M. Schultz

I'm Thankful

Voting on election day,
That's our privilege and choice.
We all have this great freedom
To lend action to our voice.

Veterans and Remembrance Day,
They just seem to go hand in hand.
  People we never forget
  Keeping America grand.

Let's give thanks for what we have
And share it with everyone.
We have so much to be thankful for,
Like the sunrise of a day begun,
The food that we can grow and eat
The knowledge that we can obtain.
Sharing ideas for a good life,
The more we learn means the more we gain.

I'm thankful for many reasons
  For good friends and times to share.
  There's something to do in each day,
  To let others know you care.

Diane Adler

Stillness Be My Guide

As I sit here and ponder
The absolute wonder
My mind loses position
To gain my recognition
My heart opens wide
Because stillness is my guide
Finally I am free
To forget the one who's me
Her name now is holy
She finally left her story
Peace on earth
Good will towards men
Makes living on this planet
  comparable to Zen
Buddha was my teacher
Christ was my redeemer
God - All - Mighty
When will LOVE be our
  only demeanor?

Candace Netzel

Celebrate The Hues

Celebrate the Hues!
The African American Hues!
We the African American,
our hues range from Blue Black
to light bright and damn near White.

Celebrate the Hues!
Like a rainbow in the sky,
we look up and smile, smile,
for we do not have the blues.

Celebrate the hues!
The hues that make us one,
the hues that divide us,
and the hues that compliment us!

Celebrate the hues!
Do not fault the light one.
Do not fault the black one.
Celebrate, Celebrate the Hues!!

Gloria Graham

Moving On

You can tell she is tired,
the bags under her eyes sag.
Her wrinkles seem to deepen,
as she frowns.
She straightens her long gray hair,
that is matted, pulled back in a braid.

She sits near the window,
and stares into a world she's never seen.
Again and again she opens her mouth,
but all that comes out is a sigh.

Her hand moves across the table,
as if trying to wash away old memories.
and then and again,
she reaches up to shield her eyes,
from the mist that is overcoming them.

She is afraid to move on, to a different life.
The only one she's ever known, is right there.

But she knows she must, so she stands up,
and taking one last look,
steps out of her world.

Anna Malinoski

The Prisoner's Lament

The steel gates clanged behind;
The bank heist wasn't mine:
And without reason, I did time.

I was old, alone and crushed
During sly looks so obvious
And whispers declared
With distance, oh distance,
Which means to beware.
When you could not take a stand, my son,
Although truth was half-noted;
A chance was too risky to take
With your professional status at stake
And your silence condemned me.

But I am free again
And the years beyond—-
It will not matter then
When a spirit, midst the clouds, wings by
Looking down on a stone,
  Dust to dust.

Isabella R. Stirpe

On Being A Grandparent

Each grandchild is
  the best
    the smartest
      the quickest
        the most beautiful/handsome
          the most adorable
            the most responsive
When they're small
  and then

Each adolescent grandchild is
  just like the "other" family
    and then

Each grandchild is
  the best
    the smartest
      the quickest
        the most beautiful/handsome
          the most adorable
            the most responsive
  when they're young adults

Joy Goldstein

Nature's Symphony

Nature is a symphony
The birds sing in harmony,
The calmness of a summer mist
Is like the concertmaster's fist
Like violins in nature's song
Butterflies dance along.
In the grass a duck is born
With a distant sound of a French horn.
And all the busy bees...
Move like fingers on piano keys.
And the owl lets out a hoot...
I hear woodwinds and a single flute.
An eagle flies on guilded wings...
Like the sound of harp strings.
The bullfrog is a lonesome fellow...
He moves slowly like a single cello.
The humming bird makes a hum...
Like the pounding of a drum.
Nature is a symphony
An orchestra of harmony.

Dennis Vernon Poe

Northern Autumns

Up North when autumn settles in
The changing wildlife roles begin.
Calls blend with wonderment
Of woodland scenes and scent.

Within the pageantry of trees
Nests fragment in the reckless breeze.
The feathered, in fall chill,
Note time for farewell trill.

When geese honk in their V flight forms,
Ground creatures stock their winter dorms.
Their senses indicate.
The time to hibernate.

The wondrous northern fall that frays
Both blooms and leaves to fragrant sprays,
Relinquishes its glow
To sparkling ice and snow.

Helen L. Youngstrand

A Baby's World

A baby's bewitching face conveys
The chapters of candor to me.
Its silent, shifting gaze surveys
Both innocence and duplicity.

What wonder is it to watch this world
In that delightful, unaffected vein.
To sight no evil; to have the ego furled
With no emotions of pretext or feign.

In that privileged kingdom of fame
Misery has no reason to thrive;
It renders all incongruous instincts lame,
And secures a mirth-filled hive.

Bala Raghunath

Courage

It takes a lot of courage,
To get through life.
To handle all the hardships,
To handle all the strife.

It takes a lot of courage,
To handle your fears.
But you overcome them,
Through the years.

Jason Bowman

Seasons

The flowers bloom
The children sing
The winters gloom
Has turned to spring

All the things that were asleep
Have come awake once more
The baby birds begin to peep
Their mothers in the blue skies soar

Then summer comes and with the heat
We wipe the dampness from our brow
The beaches sand against bare feet
It's time for fun, it's summer now

Then once again the earth grows still
The season now is fall
And soon will come the winter chill
The seasons to recall

Colleen Sineway

Childhood Memories Of The White Carnation

On Mothers' Day in school each year,
The children went to church to pray.
They wore carnations to celebrate,
The love and joy of this great day.

Children whose mothers were alive,
Were given carnations red and bright.
Those whose mothers were deceased,
A white carnation told their grief.

Eleven boys and girls would tell,
With white carnations in their lapel,
That their mothers had departed,
And left them sad and brokenhearted.

They longed to be with the majority,
Wearing red carnations happily,
Giving thanks to God Almighty,
For mothers who were hale and hearty.

Alas! They must be brave and strong,
To carry this burden, oh! so long.
Mothers' Day will always be sad,
They cannot remember and be glad.

Ethel P. McKenzie

Music Of The Wild

As the winds churn
The clear river water,
The cattails wilting in the
Wind.
Frogs croaking,
Birds and crickets
Both chirping,
Water rushing down the
Waterfall.
Leaves getting caught in
The uproaring wind,
Crackling as they fly up in
All directions!
If you listen
Close enough you
Might just be able to
Make out the
Music of the wild!!!

Carrie Pelland

He Maketh No Mistakes

When the Lord put the world in place,
   the creation was no disgrace
Every thing happens in succession
   this is our daily confession.

Nothing happens out of turn
   this is our daily concern
as we see that the world is in place
   we see this happen with our face.

When God let's things happen
   regardless of where it will be
We know that God still rules
   this is some thing we'll all agree

Nothing happens before its time
   that is very sublime
Everything happens as it should
   this is very good.

Dolores Mahan

A New Day

Each morning as I rise to greet
The dawning of a brand new day,
I'm thankful I have another chance,
To fulfill my life in another way.

So many opportunities for sharing
Are out there awaiting me.
Just to make a sad face smile
What a joy for others to see!

But only I live in my world -
Everyone else has their own place.
I only know what I can do
To put a smile on someone's face.

And maybe help to make their life
Perhaps a little bit different -
With just a wink, or a little smile,
My day for me will be better spent.

Betsy Gibson Porter

The Day

As the sun rises,
the day holds many surprises,
for what does the day hold,
live it and watch it unfold.

On this day you should not fret,
your mistakes do not regret,
for there is tomorrow,
so do not wallow in your own sorrow.

But yet never overlook today,
the chance will never be again,
and remember the day,
for what it could have been.

"That will be the day."
This could be that day.

Brent Alexander

"Ancient Rule"

An ancient rule
When practiced through
Would peace and harmony bring,
An ancient rule
Elementary pure and true
Simply,
Respect others
As you would have them
Respect you.

Joan Reego Gully

Confusion

The yearning to be needed.
The desire to be wanted.
The feelings of love,
But in reality, her loneliness.

Always striving to be number one.
The constant efforts to succeed.
The competition that still awaits,
But in reality, the emptiness of people.

Needing to tell all fears,
But having no one to tell.
Searching for some answers,
But finding none anywhere.

Reality isn't here loneliness,
But the vacancy in her life.

Drena Forthuber

Untitled

I often sit and ponder
the enormity of this wonder;
This wonder we call love.
Do we learn it at
our Mother's knee,
or is there a grander key?
Could it be possible
we're missing the point,
the obvious point;
that we all have it in us
but some are more
willing to share it,
While others fear they'll never
get it back?

Angela C. Sanabia

Bits And Pieces

The drifting snow,
the falling snow.
Where it comes from,
I do not know.
Like bits
and pieces
of falling cloud,
it drifts
to the ground,
falling, proud.
Maybe angels
are shearing their sheep,
shearing, shearing,
while we sleep,
and when we wake,
we have our keep,
of silky wool,
from angel sheep.

April Graves

Untitled

At night, while I lie in bed
   waiting to fall asleep,
I think of the person I would like
   close to my heart.
I see this person all the time,
   but She never sees me. Why?
I just don't know how to tell Her
   what I feel and why.
I am scared because, what if
   She feels the same???

Donovan Randolph

Unbridled, You

With you, I cannot shake the fact
the feeling that
the fairytales come true.
Sword in hand
you conquer me.

For you, I could not make
vast empires create
the world strong enough to hold you.
Take me there
I beg of thee.

To you, I could not give the joy
my heart, your fragile toy
you have, thus, to me.
The tops that spin
you shatter me.

Corbett Lynch

The One Who Stood

The battle was long,
the fight it was hard
but victory went
to the one who stood.

While others ran
and cried with fear
he stayed there,
the one who stood.

Thousands dead,
millions hurt,
they all ran, except
the one who stood.

Now alone
in his victory
the land of waste
to the one who stood.

He wonders now
as he lays to rest
the ones he loved,
should he have stood?

Caroline Rea

Temporary Gift

He came gift little warning,
the first of three,
a curled up bundle of wrinkles
and down that reeked of talcum
powder and sour milk and
wailed like a siren.
He invaded my life and soon
there were diapers among dolls and
bottles among bows.
We competed for attention and a
fan-toed, stiff-legged,
air-gasping scream was always
the winner.
Who was this thief that stole my
parent's affection and many
precious hours of my sleep?
He was an annoyance and a treasure,
a gift from God that for years
grew in value—
And then the angels came. . .

Diana Lockwood

Second Life

I'm starting on my second life,
The first one ended a year ago.
The first life with marriage and children,
A job, money worries and so.

My first life was very fulfilling,
As I rushed through it day after day,
With little time to enjoy or thank
The Lord, who had blessed my way.

My first life came to an end,
The children grew up, my husband died,
So I started on my second life,
A different person, alone, untried.

My second life comes with time
To think and try avenues never trod,
To give of myself in a different way,
And to soar where I used to plod.

Who knows the overall plan,
The blessings a second life may bring,
The mission yet to be fulfilled,
The songs that are yet to sing.

Carol K. Dunnagan

"Drinking Too Much"

Sometimes people drink around
the ghetto.
Too much beer to do right.
Now don't all of you,
go to holler slang baloney.
You don't think right
So you don't do right,
I think the whole table,
needs discipline.
And to scare some of you,
Out of here,
I said, I don't play the mess.
But now, I see I have to,
throw you out of here.
Now, get out of here

"Grandma, when we drink
you know, we ain't fitting
to cook after it." "Can I get a witness."

Constance Davis

God's Blessing

To the son and daughter I never had
The good Lord has supplied
The two most perfect people
That are always by my side

Through trials and tribulations
Joys and sorrows as well
The good Lord has smiled on me
I can surely tell

Without the two of you
I don't know what I would do
Always with a helping hand
No matter what the demand

Never can I repay
For the joy and help
You've given to me

May the good Lord
Smile on both of you
Through all eternity

Harry L. Vern Speth

Shamanistic Sensations

Today is the first of October
  the greatest day of my life
A day that will spin in fury
  simultaneously appearing passive
delivering me from pain and strife

  I call upon the blue sky
the cool wind, gentle breeze
  Autumn sunshine and all that
appeals to the senses
  transient trust and elegant ease

When night befalls
  decisively devouring the day
Tomorrow I will call
  petitioning fate in yet
A more consuming way

Jon Paul

"Matilda"

If I could stop
  The hands of time
I'd keep you here with me

Or catch my thoughts
  In a simple rhyme
For all the world to see

If only I could
  I'd make you smile
And laugh so joyfully
For in my eyes
  I'm but a child
When you are here with me

Bernard Scott Guenthner

Untitled

The bird jumped over the hawk
The hawk swoops under the tree
The birds lays an egg on the mouse
The mouse really has to go pee
He goes pee on the ant
The ant screamed raining
And then it makes a flood in the mud.
The plants start to sprout
And then is a little doubt
Cuz the mouse had to go to a meeting.
His little house
Had a little couch
And a big fat tree house
He puts on his belts
And then he melts
And then he feels like a piece of felt
And then he lets out a big fat belch.

Brandon Csupo

Under The Night Sky...

The land below bathed in
the glider of the moon,
a pair of eagles glided
through the fresh crisp
air with smooth grace.

All living in harmony with
the land only taking what
was needed.

In one last grand gesture,
the elder gave back all
that he had taken.

JoAnn Latzke

Applaud

Applaud!
the horse, so graceful
in step.
Praise! his mane
flowing with no pain!
Cheer for his
rear, as he jerks his front
upward!
Congratulate his rate,
a ten in the pen.
Rejoice in his splendid
towering might.
A creature of feature
so wonderfully in tone.

Take a glimpse!
Tell a prince!
Of his outrageous gracefulness.
He's Nature's Pride

Jennifer VanderVeer

"The Island"

Do you ever think of
The islands in the sea
One of them is ours
You and of course me

This place is full of romance
And lots of other things
But most of all its love
Between you and me

The place I have in mind
Is so beautiful as you
Its called Island of Beauty
And you are the Island Queen.

Dustin Hardin

To Virginia

T'was in the fair state of Oklahoma
the land of summer and sunshine;
on a warm September day
a baby girl was born.

She was the pride in her parents eyes,
for she was fair of face
and filled with grace.

As the baby grew and blossomed
She dearly loved this land;
the birds that sang,
the wild flowers that bloomed,
the creeks that flowed,
the hills She roamed.

The years have slipped by
  one by one;
Her youthful years
  have faded and gone;
But her heart is young
  and her memories strong...
For this fair state where Virginia was born.

Emma Cummins

Attitude Adjustment

This is
the last time
my sun
is going down.
Sunsets
are so final,
like a
disapproving frown.
Tomorrow,
in the evening
when the chickens
go to bed,
I'll watch
a golden sunrise —
standing
on my head.

Betty Edmondson

Untitled

The burbling creek,
The laughing wallow,
The whispering woods,
And rustling leaves.

The creaking swing,
The chirping birds,
The moaning of the wind,
The clapping of thunder.

Crash! Bang! Pop!
A banshee screaming
In the night.
The ripping teeth,

The tearing claws
Shredding the clouds apart.
Pounding water
And cascading mud.

Calm, quiet
The storm is over.
The sky is clear.
No more shall I fear.

April Brazee

An Ineffable Smile

The date I don't remember,
the moment I know well,
what you did to enchant me,
to hold me in your spell.

We looked at something,
of what is of no import,
for you were close, at peace
with yourself and the world.

I made some comment,
inane or humorous,
that made you smile,
a smile so wondrous.

That ineffable smile
is the one that burned
itself into my memory,
and captured my heart.

Hal Marsh

Calling

Ice glides over the water reflecting
The murky depths below.
The shadows crawl over
Her face;
pale, white, dark, red - sliding, creeping
As the silent orbs watch, trapped inside.

Green crunches as the foot falls closer toward
The sinking edge. Frozen wind reaches her
Skin as breath escapes in cloudy exhaust.
Lap
After lap kisses soil, dewy and calm.

Moonlight drifts over the ice and stops on
Her. Cold ecstasy envelopes in a sheet
The soundless. Ice, slivered and separated
From the ripples that form. All is restored.

Courtney Piver

My Life

I wonder when
The pain will end
I wonder why
I always cry
The sky is blue
And so am I
As days rush past
I stay still
Nothing has changed
I wonder if it ever will
To put the pain to rest
Will be the ultimate test
To find the way to peace
Is to conquer the beast
Why do we give up
Are hearts to the past
To make the pain go away
We must face it at last

Heather Robinson

Sunflowers In The Snow

There's a part of me so empty,
The part I try to ignore.
That to me it seems as though,
My whole life gets wa shed ashore.
The nights only grow colder,
I still search for this I know.
And I'm so close to finding it,
As near as finding sunflowers in the snow.
My future draws a blank to me,
As far as two glass eyes can see.
Where's my intuition?
Haven't I any ambition?
I lost my self security somewhere
along the way.
My younger years sucked up my purity,
that I now long for today.
I feel the best of my years are over,
It may be too late to grow.
Like an icicle in the summertime,
Like a sunflower in the snow.

Jenny Mancini

Joyous Me

I can now be the guitarist at
   the party:
desired since the age of fourteen.
My instrument is my voice,
   my songs are my poems.
I can now offer beauty through
   the words inspired by
   unseen hands.
I can act and perform, and
   wherever there is an
audience, I can now create a
   stage.
I can now sing, and never be
   off key,
   for, I created the tune.

Judi Rittel

Other Faiths

I walked through your church today
The place where you meet your God.
I was impressed by its grandeur
And paeans to your faith.
The skill with which you constructed your world
To worship as you see fit.
You follow a mortal, with beginning and end
Placing those teachings above all others.
You spend your lives in search of truth.
It's so simple.
It's been here all the time.
Look inside and see your God,
For He sees you.

Bobbie Burks

God Is Not Dead

The sun still rises day by day.
The planets move their ordered way.
All nature shows His mighty power.
He rules it surely, hour by hour.
   God is not dead!

Our Saviour died upon a tree
That life might come to you and me,
But He is risen and He lives!
Light and hope to all He gives.
   God is not dead!

He is our ever present friend,
Our judge whose mercy knows no end,
Our Lord and Master, yet our slave
Whose sacrifice destroyed the grave.
   God is not dead!

He lives! He reigns! Blest be His name,
Who bore upon the cross our shame!
He lives to reign eternally
And cares for us most tenderly.
   God is not dead!

Ione B. Orr

Autumn Leaves

Come little leaves said
the wind one day,
Come over the Meadows
With me and play.
Put on your dresses of
reds and yellow an Gold.
Summer is gone and
the days grow cold.

Audra W. Runner

The Bride

Beautiful
the powdered cheek
likened to frost
turned a slight blue.
Her silken curls lie
silent across a
pale, cool forehead.
Calmly she lies in wait
listening
as beetles call
with frost-bitten tongues,
Drawing her to sleep
upon her satin sheets
where dreams are
wrapped in lacey
worm-worked earth,
And the roots
of the pine lie branching,
patient for their porcelain
princess.

Angela Ramseyer

Just Try It

It really seems amazing,
　the power of a prayer.

But just try it and you'll see,
　there's an answer there.

You may not understand it,
　it's a mystery indeed.

But if you put it in God's hands,
　you'll get exactly what you need.

The answer may not come as
　quickly as you think.

Then again, it may come as
　quickly as a blink.

For he hears every prayer,
　no matter how small.

If your faith is unfaltering.
He will answer them all.

Alicia M. Shannon

A Place In Time

The ticking of the clock,
the quietness of solitude
rings ever true to remind
us of our mortality.
Because of the wonderment
the ever sense of awe,
being, brings us closer to
one another. A place in time
brings us nearer our destination,
which may be scattered by
life's ironies and lessons.
We humans so small but so
giving in our humanities,
realizing our dreams but
understanding our sorrows reach
out for that place in time.

Bradford J. Sage

My Love Is Raining

I can't stop thinking about you
The rain's still falling down
I don't know why I want you so bad
But my heart is calling out
Whispering the love I have for you

Like rain sinking into the ground
Love is sinking into my soul
My mind and body too

But there's another feeling there
It's falling down with the rain
What is this emotion?
I've felt it once before
It's the feeling of not having him
That special person you need
Of seeing him love someone else

Someone that would be me
If only I had been there
Been there when he needed me
But I wasn't
And my love is nothing but rain.

Carrie L. Joyce

Dunes—The Sand Blades On Block Island

Long green and straw blades housed in
dunes above
　the shore
Dance to the song of the seductive wind
which they
　submissively endure.
While particles of sand play tag among the blades
shadows cast their tones of grey, climatic shades
　Alas, the wind does cease.
The blades now still - the shadows demure
The only sound, is the song of the waves
　which frames the placid shore.

Iris Kitagawa

He's The Son Of God, You Know?

Mary had a little LAMB,
The SON of GOD, you know?

He came to be the SAVIOR of the world,
And wash us white as snow.

His blood of red, that's sweet as love,
Will bring us all back home.

And we will live with JESUS CHRIST,
In a mansion all our own.

And in this land of milk and honey,
There will be no tears or woe,

For JESUS CHRIST is full of love,
He's the SON of GOD, you know?

David Glen Callahan

My Heritage Tree

I remember
when I first saw my father cry
With that tragic,
yet tranquil look in his eye
He was leaving his mother
to go back home
He felt so cold,
looked so alone
This memory will always be with me:
This
is part of my Heritage Tree

Charlene Kannankeril

The Sea

Star twinkling in an indigo sky
the sounds of the ocean, echoing softly
in my ears, ever so gently.
Beckoning me closer, closer.
　Ships out on the horizon, looking
back as if to say, come, come
where you belong, with me.
　Together we will the air is
filled with a salty mist and
the heavens seem to touch
the briney depths.
　Here is where I feel the
closest to the one true meaning,
the beauty of the universe.
I am home, I am free to be me.

Barbara H. Troia

Mood Manhattan

Not for us
　the stridence of Village guitarist
　　singing songs, contrived,
　of love and despair.

Not for us
　the young eccentrics
　　sprawled on Macdougall Street,
　flaunting false wisdom
　　and sadness unearned.

For us
　the pregnant sound of silence,
　the erratic rhythm of stumbling words,
　remnants of doubt and anguish
　　and yearning
　torn out
　　and offered
　with childlike trust.

Felix Laumann

A Day Goes By

Night falls...
The sun goes away
I plead...
Will you please stay?

You go...
I cry all night
I sleep...
It will be alright

Day comes...
The sun awakes too
I think...
All day about you

Wind blows...
I look up above
There you are...
Like a peaceful dove

Sun setting...
I look at you
You smile...
I love you too.

Deborah Stitt

Failing Body

Skies are gray
the sun gone today.
Heart heavy, tears
fall upon my bed.
Lonely, lonely. Fears
fill my soul of dread.
Where's the flowers,
the smell of fall?
Where's the body, sours
the weight of it all?
Oh! Youth devoured
body, now soul!
Come spring beauty
unfold the dying desire.

Annie Tweton

Beginning

It's Spring.
The sun warms the earth,
flowers wake from their sleep
   and come into bloom.

Leaves on the trees swell
and wait to unfold,
the grass does not wait
   turning green as we watch.

Spring is the essence of awakening,
the promise of things to come,
our reward for surviving the winter.
   It is the season of life.

Joni Evans Barnett

Laughter And Love

I remember when I left.
The sun was shining bright
as it fell out of the sky that day.
Tears fell hard with no sign of light.
Then I awoke.
The moon grew dim.
The sky grew bright.
That was the day the wind
carried you into my life.
Like a world pool you drew me in.
You carried me with you through
the sky on your cloud of bliss.
We looked down upon the world
of reality as we danced our dreams.
Day after day.
Night after night.
We floated on laughter and love.

Destiny Joiner

Each Day

Each day I'm thinking of you
The times that we both shared
What were these words
We used to part?

Each day grows with my sadness
No utter sweetness twined
The sweetness that I knew as wine,
The times that we both shared.

Each day my heart goes searching
In this small world of mine,
For the love I knew one season,
For the time when you shared thine.

David D. Bruner

Skeletons In Stone

In a population explosion
The universe is born
Life evolves in uncertain ways
Microscopic creatures abound
Echoes
As the dinosaurs die away
Bleached bones, tarpits and time
Skeletons in stone
Remnants of an age long gone bye

Ride the Gobi Desert train
Through the rice paddies of China
Hear the echoes?
Ancient fossils in mountainsides
Excavated skeletons in stone
Species or specimens?
All pieced together
To link an immense spectrum of space with time
Expanding the knowledge of great minds

Adelia M. Belveal

Untitled

The world is falling apart
The walls are crashing down
Anyone trapped inside is gone
Forever they slowly disappear
Falling into Fate's bloody hands
No one able to stop them
Nothing to slow their fall
Soon everyone will be gone
No one to hear the cries
Infant's teary eyes staring at the sky
A world cleansing itself of filth.

George D. Markle

"You've Captured My Heart"

Words could never express to you
The way I feel inside
For all the little special things
You've added to my life.
You make my life so special
In each and every way
With the special things you do
And the special things you say
When it comes to my life
I know you'll always be a part
Because I truly love you
and you've truly captured my heart!

Douglas M. Cox

Alone

Alone I walk, with silent steps,
The wind is with me as I go.
And gentle boughs sway to and fro,
And whispers softly, just as though
They're watching over me.

Alone I walk, while silver stars,
From heaven smile and seem so near.
And dew-kissed flowers scent the air,
And softly, softly, I can hear
the gentle voice of night.

Alone I walk, with certain steps,
The moonlight guides me as I go.
And I find peace within my soul,
And I smile softly, for I know
That I am not alone.

Janis Kiper

Alton Bay At Evening

'Tis evening!
The western sky and clouds
Are mirrored in the bay
Not a ripple is seen.

   The trees stand tall
    Against the evening sky
   Lifting tall branches upward
   To their creator.

Dusk falls!
Here and there lights dot the
Boats and homes along the shore.
The evening stars appear
As little lights
In God's vast window on the world.

Not a sound is heard
Save the crickets
Which sing their even song.

Night has fallen!

Janet M. Niklaus

"Our Lord"

The sunset so mild,
The wind so mellow,
A scene full of grace;
A beautiful angel stands upon a hill,
Smiling softly as tears run down
His face;
Triumphant is He,
So powerful,
With love he rules this land,
And to his people;
Gives life,
A promise so grand —

AnneMarie K. Bazan

So You Say You Love Me

You say the words
The words are there
The words mean nothing
Unless you show you care

Show me the words
Show me you care
But I know you don't dare
Because it's just words that are there

I know to speak them is rare
But, please, if you would
Just show me you care

So you say you love me
My heart and mind want it believed
But when you don't show it
Am I being deceived?

Janeen Robichaud

The Feelings Of A Lonely Husband

Hot summer days, sleepless nights,
what a horrible plight.
   Loneliness, terrible loneliness.

Boredom at work, misery, thinking of
you, a short reprieve from reality.
   Loneliness, terrible loneliness.

I caress your face, my soul gives chase,
my heart will race.
   Loneliness, terrible loneliness,
   Most horrible loneliness.

Chris L. Dittman

Profile

What the days counted dear
The years took away.
Time formed a veneer
That would overlay
Memories too sweet to erase,
And the cameo of your loving face

That perished like a falling star
Lost and out of sight.
Leaving a vestige lingering afar
Like fragments of shattered light,
Then the void of an empty space
And the dim design of your fading face.

Episodes, events, chosen sections
Come to my mind's view,
Dismal decades have made selections
Trading old for new,
Longing to barter back, and trace,
The outline of your vanished face.

Billie Houston

Thanks

The blue hues of morning,
The yellows and golds.
And whites of a clouds bank,
Each dawn does behold.
The greenery now flourishes,
As spring touched the land.
As birds and bees harmonize.
Oh isn't life grand.
To enjoy every morning,
Created with love.
By God who is watching us,
All from above.
So little we thank Him,
For wonders of life.
So thanks for each morning,
And the rest of my life.

Danny Ray Anderson

Winter Sonnet

Outside the trees seem drooped and sad,
Their limbs so cold and dark and bare,
All frozen o'er in silence clad
With not a songbird anywhere.
No songs to cheer, no warmth of flowers
To brighten up the day in part.
How sad to bear these gray-tinged hours
That press so coldly on the heart.
My body shivers with despair,
A lawn so lifeless before me
All crinkled in the chill out there.
I snuggle in my shawl, then see
God's gift - a crocus in the snow,
Gives all the joy one needs to know.

Elna Rogers Worts

Loneliness

I guess you'd call it loneliness,—
 This hunger that's inside me,
For a hand to hold, a smile to share,
 Someone to walk beside me.
But I'll smile in my mirror,
 and go walking alone.
And the hand I hold — will be my own.

Dorotha W. Dye

Oh My Love, My Love....

Oh my love my love
There are atoms
And worlds
Surging around us
And between us
And through us
And so, what are we
But spirits reaching
Across the world of oceans
And the world of space
To find one another
To love and briefly hold
Each other in our arms and hearts
But no matter where or when
You are there

Joy Fearnhead

Spirit Is All

SPIRIT, spirit and spirit,
There really is but one.
Not a jewel, not a dragon,
Not a whit was spun,
'Till such greatness unfurled...
Ahh!...here comes the sun.

How splendid this SPIRIT,
That is all, and still one.
Immersed in bright lights,
With chaos undone,
We've a home in a world,
To be born and become.

Such mystery this SPIRIT,
All power is to Thee.
Oh, so troubled I was,
When I could not see,
How the world is spirit,
And Spirit!!!.......is me!

Gloria Rose Choquette

Makes Sense

I am just a penny
They call me one cent.
How much I am worth
Is how I am spent.

Alone I buy little
My currency is low.
But save me up
And watch how I grow.

Save me in jars
Or just use a pot.
When it becomes full
I'll be worth quite a lot.

Spend me wisely
Or just have a ball.
When I am all spent
It's then I become small.

Roll me in wrappers
I'll be safe in a bank.
Save me for years
And it's me you will thank.

Anthony F. Zanghi

Hidden Heroes

This land is full of heroes,
they live from coast to coast.
I'm speaking of the silent ones
they never brag or boast.

Heroes go that extra mile
but not for personal gain.
They do it 'cause it breaks their heart
to see someone in pain.

A person who will risk their life
to help someone in danger.
Not just friends and family,
but even a total stranger.

To those who help our fellow man
or animals in need.
And those who love an orphan child
and homeless folks, they feed.

Thank God for hidden heroes.
They deserve a warm embrace.
And thanks to people such as them,
the world's a better place.

Darla Ferriell

Broken Glass

On one side the world turns,
Things are full of life.
On the other death awaits,
Standing with his scythe.
He looks at us and smiles,
Shadows us with fear.
Life is just a game to him,
a simple two way mirror

Jeramiah Martin

My Husband, Your Wife

I lay here holding you close, wondering if
 this is all a dream?
Your body still wet from the shower, my
 lips still wet from your kisses.
The room heavy with the scent of lilacs,
 and just made love.
Your bodies warm next to mine,
I see your chest rise and fall as you
 drift off to sleep.
I smile softly and lean over to kiss you
 good night.
The touch of my lips wakes you, your arms
 fold round me holding me tight.
As I close my eyes and snuggle up to you.
I thank the two people who made this
 all possible
My husband and your wife.

Jo Ann Wood

The Question

Why did you do that?
Throw away my poems,
Heart-born pieces
Slashed across the page,
Letter perfect processor lines,
Thoughlessly tossed away
Like a used tissue in your pocket,
The deepest pictures of my soul.

Angela Conrad Staub

People Born Of Yester-Year

History is etched in the hearts of babes,
This is what I'm told.
By the people born of yester-year;
Born of the days of old.

   They tell stories of the slavery days,
   Of that boat ride over here.
   The tears and blood that was shed,
   Of people chained and filled with fear.

Sun up to Sun down they worked in fields,
Men and women all the same.
Babies strapped upon their backs;
With death the only victory claimed.

   They lifted their hearts unto God,
   Cried for mercy upon their poor souls.
   These are the stories I've heard tell,
   By people born of the days of old.

This history is etched in my heart,
It paints a vision of blood and tears.
I cry out in pain for my people;
The people born of yester-year!

Charles Selwyn McGary

Check Me Out

Here I stand in the checkout line
This old cowpoke right behind
Said "excuse me mom wonder if you knew
I only have one item but you have two
could I step in front of you?"

I said "how about women in front of me?
I only have two items, she has three
I wonder if she'd step behind me?"
he scratched his head and looked around
then gave me a big old frown.
"Ask her if she will do, the thing that
I just asked of you"

"You gotta be crazy, gotta be sick,
ask me to pull that kind of trick."
he hung his head and looked real sad
"I know this must sound awful bad
pardon me lady but you see
I really have to take a pee.

Donna Hall

Summer Thoughts

Lovely, lazy summer brings,
Thoughts of many pleasant things,
Children playing in the streets,
Lemonade and ice cold treats.

Golden blossoms, leafy trees,
Clear blue skies, and busy bees.
Snow white clouds, and golden dawns,
Sunny days, and shady lawns.

The fire flies, and the sudden showers,
The starry skies and the lovely flowers,
The dewy morns, and the new mown lawn,
The rosy sky at the break of lawn.

All these things do fill my mind,
When I am trying hard to find,
A thought or two keep me going,
When winter comes, and the wind is blowing.

Julia Grace Pavlic

"Where Did It Go?"

I saw the first snow
through my sleepy eyes.
It was a happy and
exciting surprise.
I rushed in to dress warm
and to see
If I made a snow man,
Would he play with me?
I went outside and there I found
No snow but just plain
Dry, hard ground
Where did it go?
Where did it go!
I'm sure I saw some new
White snow but where did
it go? I just don't know
I don't think I will ever know.

Ivon Sutak

Wonders

Can you see me through the clouds,
through the sun or the rain?
Can you hear me as I pray,
as I mention your name?
Do you know that I still cry,
and I still feel the pain?
Even though the years have gone by,
I still miss you just the same.
Do you know that I hold strong
to the title that you gave?
Yes, I am still your daughter,
and that will always remain.
Do you know that I still love you?
Do you know that I still care?
Do you know I think about you?
And I wish you were here.

Christine Ann Barnes

Resonance

Your song plays on this life
thrumming counterpoint sometimes,
sometime synchronizing,
always stepping up the dance
vamping sad garden to new bud-
which in one two three cadenzas
open as waltzing blossom.
  Dance me.
   Swirl me.
    Swing me 'round.

Trill my time for two
four six turns more till,
your presence missed,
the petals fall.
The silence of loss
re-asserting
leaves life on hold...

  Dance me, Love.
  Swirl me, Love.
  Swing me alive.

Joe Scully

A Poem For Mike

Once I had a big balloon
Tied to a ribboned strand,
And nothing in the world could pry
That ribbon from my hand.

But days passed and I lessened
The firm grip of my fist.
My hand grew tired, so I just
Tied the long string to my wrist.

I didn't even notice
That my knot had broken free
'Til my balloon was floating in the sky
Up and away from me.

I jumped frantically to grab it,
But, alas, it was too late.
The ribbon was just out of reach,
The gap was just too great.

And as it faded from my sight,
I wished I'd seen before,
Though I might hold a million others,
Not one could I love more.

Cheryl L. Myrick

Broken Promises

They promise to love you
  'Til death do you part
To honor and cherish you
  Right from the start

Promises, sometimes
  Seem meant to be broken
Your future seemed certain
  With the vows you'd once spoken

Your fairy tale life
  Holds your hopes and your dreams
But the breaking of promises
  Tears your heart at the seams

I'll never give up
  In my search for true love
'Cause God watches over me
  From the heavens above

I know I'll soon find him
  My "happily - ever - after"
And we'll grow old together
  Through our love and our laughter

Julie A. Stevenson

Untitled

Our lives are nearly over
Time I hope well spent
We've lost two houses
Should we pitch a tent?

We worked so hard to save them
But to no avail
Should we carve out a tree trunk
  And let her sail?

We could climb a mountain
Over rock and boulder!

Time is racing past us
Can I cry on your shoulder?

We could find an Eagle
And ask her for a ride.

We'd be close to heaven
And you would be by my side!

Joan C. DePietro

Time

Time is!
Time is not!
And time will never start before it stops
Time moves on
Or simply freezes still!
Time moves by program
Time moves at will
Time changes everything
Leaving nothing the same
Time, makes us much wiser,
To life's webb-infested game
Time is the real medicine
We need to get well
You can never cheat, on time
For time will surely tell
Time is the essence,
Of our very existence here
But what time is, before it's up,
Is simply grace
From year to year

James H. Donald

Where Are We Now?

When I look around I see pain
Time is not on your side
The earth rotates, the sky moves
   You and I breathe
People live, fight and sleep
   Love, hate and die
When do we learn?
   Where are we now?

Do you sit and wonder
   Where you are now?
Remind yourself -
Where you wanted to be many years ago
   Always different
   Never the center of the fork
Remove the left and right side
Hard to walk straight
   Easy to be a robot
Where are we now?
   Live.

Belinda M. Ellerbe

Mass

Mass is such a sweet delight
time spent in presence
Causing one to reflect,
consider things often left undone
Thoughts mostly put under the rug.
It bring a deep descent into
the unknown part of your soul,
Pickings of your heart
lie dormant no more.
But, rush to the surface
With a jolt of surprise.
Sprinkles from life drip
into constant rhythm time.
Reminders of moment past
words spoken or a touch.
Love so precious comes to the top
one does not feel alone now.
It is a moment to connect.

Janet Lee Frazier

A Child's Prayer

Have you ever listened closely
   to a child as he prays
Have you ever really wondered
   what lies beyond his small eyes
If you will listen closely
   to a child as he prays
Then you will learn of kindness,
   of sadness, and of truth.

For a child doesn't pray
   with big fancy words
Nor with ever thinking,
   "Does God hear my prayer"
But a child prays with kindness
   for those that he loves
A child prays with sadness
   for those that mistreat him
And a child prays with truth
   for it comes from the pureness
   of his heart.

Jean McKelvey Carson

I Awake

I awake and hurry away
to a temple toward the sky.
Until I a support gives way
and suddenly there is a cry.

I awake and I leave
with my shield and mighty sword.
When I engage and head is cleaved
and my family never got word.

I awake and I see
an evil man held on high.
He cries aloud kill for me
and I believe his lie.

I awake and now I'm here
in this present time and event.
And I sincerely do fear
that I will awake in a moment.

David Sellors

Broken In Two

  I lost the one I love
to another person's heart.
But I will never forget him
even though we part.
For he was the one I kissed,
I kissed for the very first time.
Our lips touched so gentle,
it was as if it were a crime.
But now he doesn't love me,
he will never love me again.
That thought tears me in two,
but in my heart our love was like a gem.

Hillary Rose Davis

Untitled

The Ending
which began at the beginning
Bespeaks
of the all to familiar facade.
Family, friends
and faces on the photo,
Forceful Reminders
of rainy days.
and Raggedy Ann dolls

David Gaddie

New Horizons

If from every corner turned we strive
To cling to places past,
From whence we came;
If spirits crave a haven once alive
For sanctuary, in times of agony.
Embrace the comfort memories
Can give;
Dwell in her arms
And feed upon her breast.
Rest awhile; yet linger not
Too long,
She can't replace what's now
With what was then.
Allow the loom of destiny her way,
To guide our souls with courage
To move on;
To weave in her design
A new resolve
To leave the past, with love
Where it belongs.

Jo Shrader

Stoned Again

Stoned again can't wait
to come down.
So I can roll another
with a frown.
Cause I know when
I'm done I'll have to smoke
and endure the fun.
Smoke filled rooms and
still the sparks fly.
Christ if I keep on
smokin' I'm gonna die.
Well I made up my
mind I'm going to
quit,
damn that's a big joint,
smells good, s**t.
Okay so I lied.
But look at it this way
at least I tried.

Gordon S. Senz

Let Me....

Ah me, oh me. Let me, oh Lord,
To come from far to west,
A hymn of love, a nourishment,
A life to test the crest.

A chance to see, to feel, to be,
All merged in sound and revelry,
To taste the thought, a world reprieved.
A knock awakes, oh no,...not me?

A molecule awaits your will,
To ponder what, would be in you?
To some a value high and good,
And moral more in ethic...too?

And then its back, a distant shout,
A lass, alone, a spirit free!
To sail the shores of nothingness,
To flea and sea, a universe at ease.

Jonathan Tallfoot

You Could Count On Her

You could count on her,
  to do more then her share.
You could count on her,
  to always be there,
You could count on her,
  to be a loyal friend.
You could count on her,
  right up to the end.

But this is not the end,
  it's a brand new beginning.
So join her now, Lord,
  with Husband, Sister and Brother.
You're getting a most devoted wife,
  and a wonderful Mother.

Charles F. Miller

Man's Folly

A star flickers in the moonlight and falls
to earth unknowing.
It's journey down through sky and clouds
to rivers overflowing.
The beauty abounds.
A wonderland of light and dark.
A paradise all here.
And yet
And yet
What man has done
to render hate and fear.
The greed, the lust, the lawlessness
Oh, what has man done?
A world so freely given,
Its rich and fruitful earth,
Is man so harshly driven?
Is that all man is worth?

Joy Deflavio

Hug

It would be wonderful
To embrace and to give a hug
To every single living being
On this earth
With love, compassion, kindness and caring
That would not result in
Any more problems
Like hate, jealousy, angry and attachment
And wars as well...
Thus, I visualize myself
Giving all my hugs and embraces
To everyone with no preferences
That permeates warmth and joy
With golden light radiating
Onto them...
With much happiness
And dispel all kinds of misery!

Joan Germany

Warm

Why does the clock tick?
Why do people get sick?
Why do jackets keep you warm?
Why do bees swarm?
The thing that makes me feel warm
is knowing that I have a family.

Benjamin Todd Hencye

Ode To Gelayne

For this guy,
To feel high,
It isn't heroin or cocaine,
Just a girl named Gelayne,
How to describe her?
Well one word for sure,
Stunning, is it,
And there are others that fit,
She sets me on fire,
With passion and desire,
I want her for mine,
So I tell her in rhyme.

Anonymous

The Willing Wonka

To be my willing Wonka bar:
To have your foil unfurled,
To break

  A part.

To slide between my fingertips,
To rest atop my tongue,
To lie

  Square.

To melt.

Juliane Gallina

Her Tender Kiss

Her loving look and tender touch,
to me that meant so very much.
Oh how I miss her tender kiss.

Her smile of approval and anticipation
was the greatest kind of inspiration.
Oh how I miss her tender kiss.

She enjoyed traveling from place to place,
with a look of excitement on her face.
Oh how I miss her tender kiss.

To have loved and lived with my wife
was the greatest pleasure of my life.
Oh how I miss her tender kiss.

Joseph D. Rudloff

My Mother's Day

    Mother's day was not very important
to me, when I was young and free. Now
I am a mother to be, there are so
many wonders to see.
    A tiny life which grows inside
me, makes me very happy too. Seeing
and feeling this miracle gives me more
joy than I ever knew.
    Yes, there are many things to
learn, and I have so much love to give.
More than ever I want nothing to go
wrong, I want this little life to live.
    There is a miracle in this body
and I can't wait to see. When my baby
comes into the world, his bright eyes
staring back at me.
    Yes, Mother's Day is more important
to me. I can't wait to see, just
how great a mother I can be.

Jonelle Gibson

The Flight Of The Leaves

When the leaves fall, they want us
to recall their beginnings.

They start out as a bud in the
spring, wondering their meaning.

Then slowly peek through to a
delicate, green hue, each of great stature.

Each leaf so well defined and
greatness from above, rain makes
its way to show it's love.

Then summer finds the leaf well
formed and secure in its surroundings.

Through the dryness of summer and
the heat of time, the leaves endure.

Then fall comes and the leaves
say goodbye to their homes.

They show their appreciation by
the sigh of their colors

Yellows, oranges, reds, and browns make
a great sight, all in the name of the leaves in flight

Cinda L. Smith

"Fly High"

Fly high and above the sky
To soar the rising word "why?"

It keeps motivation and enquiring
About the things required.

Needed for the growing of the seed
That develops during the way it's weed.

Keep flying, and fly to reach the sky
Because it's the way one is intrigued.

Go far up high and take a dive and
Plunge into a drive (go position).

Go fast and fast and one will last
In the sky on high air with good
Loving care.

Jennifer Anderson

On The Threshold Of A Dream

On the Threshold of a dream
to the clash of the Gods
In the days of future passed
meet our city and the stars
to our fortress of solitude

Near the threshold of a dream
as we reach our nights dream
to the meeting of the Gods
in the days of future past
all is quiet on the western front

Close to the threshold of a dream
how green is my valley
a quiet man
the devil is a woman
the scarlet empress

At the threshold of a dream
in the days of past
meet the temple of doom
and in our last, crusade
on the threshold of a dream

Alden W. Sibley III

Hark! My Tree Has Fallen

Hark! My tree has fallen
To the ground in hollow thud.
The roots the sky they witness,
Leaves do drown in shallow mud.

Once it stood to tower;
With the clouds it danced and played.
But now it lies conquered
By the earth to be unmade.

Hark! My tree has fallen
By result of withered pride,
And now no more traveled,
It's lain down; of spirit died.

No child may captain play
Of ship sailed on open sea,
Nor king of castle reign
To war with those against thee.

Hark! My tree has fallen
And now sleeps quiet and sound.
Its life of one fulfilled;
Of battles won and new worlds found.

April Lynn Manteris

Mom

Today's the day we set aside
to treat our mothers well.
If there's a better mom in this world
well, I certainly can't tell!
You've given me all I'd ever need,
and even so much more.
When you seek my help, I know,
I often act like it's a chore.
But I hope you know in spite
of all I say or do,
Without a second thought,
I'd give my life for you!
So please enjoy this special day
and know that you're loved tons
Especially by me mom
the youngest of your sons!

Cary Jimenez

Silent Moon

To gaze upon a silent moon,
To try to touch its hue.
The shadowed silk its rays emit
Make me think of you.

Its deepest pools of sheltered light
Create a velvet sky.
I look for things I cannot see
In your darkened eyes.

I think of other nights of mine
Where thoughts I've had won't stay.
To gaze upon a silent moon,
So very far away.

Jason Tyler Rhodes

Incubus

The long descent of night begins
With darkness spreading its poisonous wings.
It touches all avoiding none,
A creeping silence and the fear it brings.
Slaying each ray that day had known;
Replacing each hope with anguish and pain,
This specter cold moves swiftly on
Advancing and conquering days domain.

Gene N. Sutherland

Forever

Forever does my heart belong
to you my beloved...

Forever may our love grow strong
together my beloved...

Forever will I stay with you
a wish to my beloved...

Forever may our words hold true
content in life beloved...

Forever do I have a prayer
pledged to thee beloved...

Forever trust, I will be there
to help you my beloved...

Forever as an endless sea
reflects my sweet beloved...

Forever means eternity
in heaven dear beloved...

David Rogers

Sundancer

Sundancer, sundancer
    today you make the sacrifice,
    today you pay the price.

Sundancer
    see the blood offering on the
    buckskin string.
    Hear the drummers song in
    Sacred sing.

Sundancer
    blow the eagle bone and make
    it cry.
    Make it heard where eagles fly

Sundancer
    with the pain, you dance all day,
    the spirits talk of you and pray.

Sundancer, sundancer
    today you make the sacrifice,
    today you pay the price.

George Shields

Happy Birthday Dad

Today is your birthday.
Today, you're 54,
and we all hope you live
to see many, many more.

You worked and cared for us
your children, all ten
and we all love you;
you're The Man among men.

We know that you love us.
We know that you care.
For if we ever need you,
you're always right there.

We know we disappoint you
in some of the things we do;
but just always remember
that we all do love you.

You stand by us all
when things are so bad
and we thank the Good Lord
that YOU are our DAD.

Jo Ann Rhodus

Mortal Perception

Incessant thermonuclear sensations
Transcendental neurotic mutations
A metaphysical pilgrimage
Elusive external images

Come with me to serenity
Make eternity our reality
Caress the confusion, put to rest
This other kingdom seems by for the best

Rainbow haze
Midnights dream
Tranquil, serene, a mountain stream
Pure, deep, and cold
You're the reflection
On the pupil of my soul
Sunset of crimson Gold
Illuminants my outer body
Against celestial murals of immorality

Beauty is not a thought, nor seen
Beauty gets perceived
when your spirit is freed

Jason Ploskonka

The Crimson Tear

The crimson tear
    trickled down your cheek,
Yet you gaily donned a smile.
—Pain was wailing through your eyes.
Your eyes are your enemy.

Feelings chained deep within your
    Perpetual Prison of Pride,
You never looked back — the Crimson
Pain trickled throughout your memories.
You hesitate towards your future —
    but you must proceed.
You clenched onto the present —
    and you knew you wouldn't go far!
This tear is your trademark
    the one you try to hide so well.
Your claim to fame is to bury a living hell.

Must I watch your Crimson tear
    and consciously walk away?
Knowing your eyes are begging me
    to wipe your pain away.

Corde Marie Bednar

Untitled

A chance meeting,
Turned my world around.
I'd look at you,
From a distance
Thinking how I wish you were mine.
Never did I feel
In the depths of my heart
The way I feel for you.
Everytime we're together,
I melt like ice on a fire.
You make me feel special,
Then quickly, you leave again.
And I hold the memories strong
Never letting go of you
For I love you.

Darcy Holmes

Valley Of Life

Walking in peace of the valley
T'ward war of the land

Hearing the songs of love
before the cries of hate

Seeing the beauty of life
Then the echoes of death

Smelling the essence of perfume
For then the puddles of blood

Feeling the sense of eternity
For those in hell

Touching happiness of earth
How sadness touches the planet

Talking the truth of our Lord God
Cut down by the evil devil

Deborah Darland

Good-Bye

It's hard to say these
two words,
when you're leaving this in
a simple letter.
When that person hasn't
even gotten better.

It's hard to say these
two words,
when a friend has to say
it so soon.
But you'll never have to
say good-bye forever
if you're going to
see your
Heavenly Father.

Allison Randolph

"A Dream Of Light"

In a distant land
Under the silence of the night
I am wrapped in a dream
That makes me tremble inside.
In my mind I see
The low Swaying palms
And the tears of the waves
The bathe in their grief
A slumbering alligator
Stained with red,
Who dreams of a light
Shining over the ocean.

Argelio Del Valle

Time Goes By

As we get older by the day
Time just flies by the way
Sunrise comes, sundown goes
Many happy times, many woes
Then we look at all the beauty
To find it, is our duty
God made many natural scenes
Made us up of many genes
As the population grows
Crime and disaster has it's cons and pros
As the great years go by
Many times we ask why, why, why?

Enid M. Bork

Death Erases A Time Haven,
unique to each living thing;
disbursing the molecules of life,
to mix for what else may bring.

Eventually as it must be,
life in every form will end;
leaving in part the abstract soul;
needing elsewhere to transcend.

All that is here with today,
in one form cannot always be;
but legacies are made to transpire,
for all those left to see.

Timeless solitude is unimaginable,
a dark mystery of the unknown;
theories of what it is really like,
envisions our creator upon a throne.

Heaven or hell whichever it is,
is not the real fear we deny;
it's having to live with the idea
of just how it is we will die.

Bruce Crandall

Taking A Rest

I walk through the woods.
Up ahead I see a clearing.
I stop to watch the snow fall gently down.
What a beautiful sight.

I sit on a rock to rest.
I close my eyes.
The only sound I hear
is the wind blowing
through the trees,
and the trot of a deer
walking on dead leaves.

I stand to walk back,
and I think;
What a beautiful sight that is.

Angela Young

Heat

Beings being cast
upon a passion verge
eyes behold blissful mold
heat magic feat a soul.

Awake night plight
right chill fright
knife bleeding deed
waste away bearing seed.

Melancholy jaundice breasts
metamorphose rue distress
passions frigid nights
mourning privilege rights.

Tear fall eyes cry
waver silence nature's bye
heat set free
may have been will never be.

Charles G. Harding

Time

It lurks in the shadows
Waiting for its victims
With gleaming fangs
And razor sharp claws
Its beady red eyes stare me down
As I feel now paralyzed
I stand there helpless
As anxiety fills my body
Just as I begin to feel again
It tears away at me
I can feel its cold, icy claws
I am unable to regain my loss
This horror takes its toll
On each one of us
We may fight and try
But to no avail
In the end it is it
That triumphs over us
This beast that we call time
Keeping us from our dreams...

Bryan Schmidlapp

Remembering My Father

How unhappy life can be
Waiting in the rain
For the joyous return
Which never came

Time full of sorrow
Eternal agony is
Hope deep despair and sadness brings
It is too late my son
My eyes closed forever
No more can cry
Hoping to see you up there in the sky

Dominic Scolaro

Untitled

I remember walking.
Walking down that old,
old path. The one that had
had so many things.
Things so hard to see-
see at night. I wished;
wished upon the black sky.
"Sky," I begged, "please,
please let me out!"
Out of this old,
old path, the one that had
had so many untold things.
Things untold in the night.

Erica Jump

I Can

There are fifty nifty states
Where freedom is the place
From San Diego to Key Largo
The flag is red and white
With blue for all our might
From the mountain tops
To the sea shores
We fight for human rights
I am proud to be an American
Because the last four letters spell I can

Brent Carinder

All Alone

All alone.
Walking in the rain.
Looking for something to do.
Searching for someone to love.

All alone. All alone.

All alone.
Sitting at a desk.
Looking for something to do.
Searching for someone to love.

All alone. All alone.

All alone.
Lying in bed.
Looking for something to do.
Searching for someone to love.

All alone. All alone.

All alone.
Moving through life.
Looking for something to do.
Searching for someone to love.

All alone. All alone.
Brad Dresbach

Temple Of Doom

Belief in you tonight
Warning of my fright
Desirous rage of beauty
Oh what a night

Words so smooth
Hands so strong
Can I really believe
Lips so calming

Eyes filled with freedom
Voice strong with confidence
I trust you tonight
Face of knowing

Blues a singing and playing
Our feet a dancing
Your stronghold in my belief
Bodies entangled for strength

I gave you trust
How I had faith
All I did was believe
All you did was leave...
DiDama Star Tucker

A Kiss

A kiss,
Was just a kiss,
Until it was your lips.

For at,
The first touch,
Love replaced my lust.

A kiss,
Is just a kiss,
Unless it is your lips.

For they,
Are my wine,
So sweet and so divine.

That a kiss,
Has no bliss,
Unless it is your lips.
Dan Everett

Hot Springs Pool

Bubbles
Washing away troubles
In cramped legs
And tired muscles.
Bubbling water
Hot, refreshing.
Very hot, relaxing.
Very, very hot
Getting out...going out.
Cool air, aaah!
Back in again,
Basking
Until I'm like a prune.
Soon
Time to get out
Dash for home room.
Fun
For everyone!
Hilda Kellis

Grandma's Garden

Children love to play and sing
Watch the songbirds flap their wings
There's a peace one can't explain
Here in Grandma's Garden

Seeds are sprouting from the ground
Crickets hopping all around
Butterflies are always found
Here in Grandma's Garden

Flowers blooming everywhere
Sweetly scenting up the air
Sun and rain provide their share
Here in Grandma's Garden

Frost will come to end the season
Plants may die but they're not leavin'
Come next spring they'll all be gleamin'
Here in Grandma's Garden
Arlene Mason

Only In My Mind

In my minds eye, I see us.
We are connected.
We are one.

We share this moment,
this place, and this time.
Yet I feel alone.

In my minds eye, I see us.
We are lovers.
We are one.

We share everything.
We have passion and desire.
Yet I feel distant; cold.

In my minds eye, I see us.
We are connected.
We are one.
But it's only in my mind.
Faye E. Macey

Untitled

Just as I believe
we are each here for a
reason, I believe
that as each day
unfolds we see more
of the gold and less of
the tarnish. Our lives are
only a spark from the whirl
of time. We may write a
story, pen a rhyme, and then life is
gone - or is it? For Jay, a very
special person I believe it has
just begun - He left this earth
just as he lived - quietly
and with great dignity
Leaving behind a
golden thread in
the tapestry of
life - binding
us to him forever,
Elizabeth McKethan

In The Age Of Innocence

In the age of innocence
 we are very pure.
In hope and love
 we are very secure.
In the age of innocence
 everything is possible.
With the world at our feet
 we are ever so gullible.
In the age of innocence
 we accept all things;
We trust in everyone
 and in everything.
In the age of innocence
 our hearts know not labels.
We are the personification
 of living angels.
Cesarina Maria Rossetti

With God's Grace

With God's Grace
we cannot fail
on wings of an eagle
we can sail

With God's Grace
we can and we will
live the life of dreams
to its fill

With God's Grace
He'll answer our prayers
we will not worry
for He is always there

With God's Grace
We are loved and blessed
He'll carry us through
so that we might rest

With God's Grace
Victory is won
He shed His blood
and said "it is done"
Brenda J. Baptist

My Love

In times like these with money tight
We have to try with all our might
To make our future life secure
Not overnight but safe and sure

Look back on many silly times
We couldn't even find a dime
But we each have the love we share
So in other words were millionaires

Our home has been exactly that
Not just a place to hang our hat
Not fancy big or even fine
But cozy cause it's yours and mine

So what came up will work it out
But our love we'll never doubt
It's nice to love and have love to share
And know some one is always there

With all that happening all around
It's great to have what we have found
And know there never be another
Thank God my love we have each other...
Donna L. Britt

Horses

We spend our lives running
We see only what's ahead of us
We don't care what happens behind us.
We are nameless;
"Horses" is what everybody calls us.
We don't weep.
We don't laugh.
We keep quiet.
We listen.
Eat what is set before us,
Go where we are told.
None of us is keen of mind.
The steed mounted by a king
Had a lofty post.
The steed mounted by a princess
Had a saddle of gold.
The peasant's horse
Had a saddle of straw.
The wild horse slept outdoors all his life.
But vis-a-vis man, we have been and
remain just horses!
Gjeke Marinaj

Gone But Not Forgotten

To you who are unknown,
We sing your praises long.
And honor you for the freedoms you won,
For those of us who stayed at home.

The tomb in which you lay is cold,
But all our hearts are warm,
With thoughts of all the things you did
To keep us free from harm.

Not one can know the heartaches
You suffered day by day,
Nor all the loving comrades
You laid to rest along the way.

In our sight, you are heroes all,
Though medals you have none.
But you answered the call of duty
Without a place in the sun.
Beverly M. Jacob

Flight

Upon our wings
  we take flight,
    as the cool evening breeze
      lifts us above the earth.

A dozen pairs of wings
  join in the graceful dance,
    tilted and gliding
      we trace the rising shadows.

A silent rhythm is followed,
  like a song from heaven
    that only we can hear.

We beat our wings
  to the melody of angels,
    and sail on
      towards the setting sun.
Jill L. Johnson

Our Anniversary

Although it seems like yesterday
  We went walking down the aisle
We were young and so in love
  With our future stretched before us
It seemed we fought so many battles
  In the very early years
But our love like a raging river
  To never dry and disappear
When times were hard and there were many
  We held each other close
No children we will ever have
  It never stopped our love
You said its me you always wanted
  And will always be enough
We have worked very hard together
  To get to here today
For its our sixteenth anniversary
  With love, hope, and happy years ahead.
Bonnie Lou

Shame

Slavery
What a shame
Forcing people to work
For nary a dime
Nor freedom
People like you and me
Except color of skin
Never having a taste
Of freedom
Unless they
Ran away
Boy, am I glad
That I didn't have to
Witness
This
Shameful
Deceit.
Ashley Brooke Summerhill

As I Gaze In The Mirror

As I gaze in the mirror
what do I see?
An unbelievable image of me

Hair of silver, wrinkled face
A figure that moves a slow
steady pace

My husband of fifty years
has died
And since that time I feel
empty inside

All my loved ones has gone astray
To lead their own lives
from day to day
Deep in my heart the loneliness lies,
And my tear stained eyes begin to cry

As I gaze in the mirror what do I say
Take me away Lord, take me away
Joan Cleland

Your Best

People say you're too good
what do they mean
can't accept kindness
rather be treated mean
taking advantage of kindness
leads to disrespect
for kindness is not a weakness
It's a strength that comes from within
show not your ignorance
by excepting anything less
for their is only one that is good
and he's expecting your best.
Jacqueline Smoot

Time

Time passes by, so that
What was new, becomes old.
Feelings out in the open
are long forgotten.
Words once spoken are lost
Everything you gave, all
that was felt, now
has been dealt with.
What was yours, is now his.
And you wonder, "How did I get to this?"
Dreams as the rainbow,
Once alive with colors,
Have all but faded away.
Where once skin was without blemish,
There are now wrinkles.
The hair you tinted, has now
Tinted itself gray.
Once upon a time, you
would have stayed.
But now, no way!
Bonnie Seefeldt Kaminski

The Sun

The sun
will it set
in the east or the west
over what?
A lake or a city
a farm or a mountain
what will happen next?
Who will know
it is a magical thing
Denise Bonvouloir

A Friend Is Someone

A friend is someone to be there
Whatever the time of day.
A friend is someone who listens
To whatever you have to say.
A friend is someone to confide in
With your most secret thoughts
A friend is someone who will be there
When things are good,
Or when they're not.
A friend is someone you can count on
And reminds me a lot of you,
So I write this poem
To thank you
For a special friend like you

Joie Jones

What Can I Do?

What can I do, to save our world
When all people seem to hate
Jealousy, greed, and envy
Might just have sealed our fate.

What can I do, when our children
Carry guns to school
Our teachers are afraid to teach
And that alone is cruel.

What can I do, my hands are tied
When parents show no concern
And what are children going to do
When adults refuse to learn.

What can I do, when media news
Speak only of O.J.
"Why can't we all just get along"
One king was heard to say.

What can I do, I can pray to God
And teach children right from wrong
If I'm successful, I've done a small part
To keep this nation strong.

Andre Patterson

Remember The Days

Remember the time, not long ago
When all the earth seemed new?
When the birds did sing,
And it was spring,
And the sky was a beautiful blue?

Walk in the woods amid the trees
Not alone was I.
The wind was blowing a playful breeze,
And the sun above was high.

I spent those days in rapture true,
Never a moment blue.
Though often for those times I mourn,
I know a new day will be born.

Aesha Al-Saeed

Teach Me To Be Silent

Lord, teach me to be silent
When fellow-men spurn me
When I feel, tired, weary, discouraged
And adversity spawns its will
When things become so chaotic
That I realize, I am not as strong and
  mighty as you

Teach me to be silent
Lead me to a quiet place
Where I can find serenity, solace
Comfort, consolation, understanding
For I too at times am a weakling
With a babbling tongue
Please, Lord, I know you are the way
I chose your path
So look down on me, show me
Teach me to be silent

Anna Gilmore

The Halloween Night

On Halloween night
When goblins are out,
I will scare people,
And ghost's will shout

You can see cats,
As the scary costumes go by,
Witches on brooms
In the Sky.

The kids go trick or treat,
People in costumes can be seen,
When scary people dress up,
On Halloween.

Chastity Olemaun

I'm In Love With You

It was just about three years ago,
When I asked you into my heart.
I didn't realize then,
My life was about to start.

You promised me salvation,
And washed away my past.
People called me a fanatic,
They said it wouldn't last.

I know I have a place,
When you came to take me home.
I hope my friends will see,
And want to go along.

I don't miss my old life,
I never will look back.
Because you died for me,
There's nothing that I lack.

I want to say Thanks,
For everything you do.
I pray you always know Jesus,
How much I'm in love with you.

Diana Hollenback

I Dare To Dream

There was a time
When I have become divorced from myself
I made mistakes
Just when I thought I was in control
I lost control, I went out of control
Time has been a very good teacher
It has taught me the error of my ways
I've learned not to let what I cannot do
Interfere with what I can do
It's hard sometimes to face reality
So I have proposed to myself
To be bold in what in stand for
And careful what I fall for
No matter how far I go
It's what I achieve along the way
That truly counts
I dare to dream

Jerome Hill

A Poet's Thoughts

I always let my thoughts run free
When I start to write some poetry.

As I think of a line, I jot it down
Then read aloud to check the sound.

When an inspiration comes to mind
Those proper words I need to find.

As soon as the ink starts to flow
It seems my pen knows where to go.

Sometimes my thoughts go on ahead
To find the words that I have read.

Now the great challenge has begun
To compose this poem just for fun.

Expressing some feelings is a goal
If it gets exciting, I'm on a roll.

By using my heart for ammunition
It drives away all the competition.

I want each poem to be just right
So to please the reader's appetite.

Howard Golley Jr.

From This Life To The Next

Heaven is the place I want to go
When my time on earth is done.
I will spend my ever-after
Praising God's only Son.

The toils that life can bring
Are sometimes more than we can bear.
And I know there will be no heartache
No sorrows to endure there.

When I meet my Lord and Savior
I will fall upon my knees
And thank Him for all He has done
And answering my needed pleas'

When it is the next ones turn
And I see my home built, as the Bible told.
I will see my loving family.
On the street, made of gold.

Jamie M. Clegg

Laughter

God filled my mouth with laughter
When tears there should have flowed
And filled my heart with faith
On such a rocky road

And in the midst of praising
I felt the victory
As I remembered promises
In His word for me

His promises remembered
Caused my heart to rejoice
And as I read His word
I seemed to hear His voice

His word hid in my heart
Kept my heart with Him in tune
Filled me with joy and hope
For it says He's coming soon

Earth's trials will soon be over
We'll leave them all behind
Our mouths be filled in Heaven
With laughter that's Divine

Helen Gleason

I Think Of You

I think of you
When the sun shines bright
When the breeze softly whispers
The stars a goodnight.

I think of you
When the skies turn grey,
And it seems the clouds
Won't go away.

I think of you
Each day I rise,
And you fill my dreams
When I close my eyes.

I think of you
When the leaves turn gold,
And the flowers bloom
And spring unfolds.

I think of you
Every heartbeat true,
Every breath I take
I think of you.

Erica Reed

Trumpet's Song

Do you know what it sounds like
When two angels meet?
Sometimes in the air
Sometimes in the street
It can sound like stars
Colliding in space
Or the sound of a kiss
On a new baby's face
It's a sound when bird's wings
Glide in the air
It's the sound of a greeting
From someone who cares
It's the sound of the wind
As it stirs up the leaves
It's the sound of the rain
As it drips from the eaves
It can be as noisy
As a brass trumpets blare
Or as quiet as the sound
Of your own whispered prayer

Connie J. Cornwell

"An Evening To Remember"

It was a wonderful evening in September
  when you and I
Chose to be together, admiring a
  full moon in the sky.
We toasted, laughed, danced, and shared
Because it was enjoyment of the now
  for which we cared.

Even strangers befriend us and
  wanted us to know
That we radiated with a personable
  warmth and a glow.
But not until our joy, peace, and tenderness
  combined into a special blend,
That this Delightful, Wondrous, evening
  came to an end.

Anthony J. Composto

Courtney Ann

Our hearts were filled with so much glee
When you came to us in October '93.
Our life was now so complete
A boy and girl - each one so sweet.
Our prayers were answered - one by one
With two grandkids to bring us fun.
Your little face always wore a smile
We'd sit and rock for a little while.
Beautiful eyelashes, so curly and long
you liked all music and enjoyed a song.
With your cute head of golden curls
We longed to watch your life unfurl.
God needed an angel - a very special one
We've had to accept his will was done.
You're our guardian angel above
You watch over us and send your love.
We're thankful for your time on earth
Just 20 short months from your birth.
In our heart your memory will always be alive
Since you left our world in June '95.

Charlotte Cushing

Untitled

The door will open
When you stop crashing against it
With your orphaned self

When you see
The armed guard, the barbed wire,
The land mines

When you feel
The infinite sorrow, the endless rage,
The ancient pain

When you begin to understand
The exquisite fragility
Of the newborn soul

When you know
That you have the right
To exist

Dianne Crismond

"Our Most Magnificent Gift"

Glory to our heavenly king
Where around the throne the angels sing.
As their trumpets fill the skies
Our messages of love and hope arise.

"Peace On Earth!" the angel said.
Where wise men found his stable bed
They knelt in reverence to behold
With gifts of incense, myrrh and gold.

God's gift to all - there lies the key
His love - hope for our eternity.
By sending his only son to earth
So, we might live and have rebirth.

What a gift! Oh, how we treasure
God's love for us that has no measure
For in the lowly manger where Christ was born
Was our most Magnificent Gift
That Christmas morn!

Darlene M. Reynoldson

Times

What can you do?
Where can you go?
When you're feeling blue,
And you no longer know.

The forces is beyond
Your control,
So then you're left
Standing alone
Out in the cold.

For those you didn't care for,
You leave them behind.
And for those you love,
They stay in your mind.

You could never forget
The memories from the past,
For those are the ones
That forever last!

Emily T. Hall

I Wish I Were In The Country

There is a place in the country
Where I would like to be
There is a place in the country
Not far from the sea
A place to run
A place to play
A place where I could have fun all day
I wish I were in the country
I wish I were far away.

There is a place in the country
Where I would like to be
There is a place in the country
With a stream that flows to the sea
With a waterfall
And a rocky edge
And a tree that's just above my head
I wish I were in the country
I wish I were far away.

Ian P. McDole

A Beautiful Dream

I dream of a place
Where mankind meets face to face
With a smile upon every brow-
I ask you - "do you know how?"
An experience like this can
take place
Among every kingdom, tribe,
And race.
No more hate
No more war
For love and beauty abound
No thought of uncertain sound
All is peace
Tis heaven at last.
Carol Jane Hargett

"Fear"

Trapped in a world of hatred.
Where no one bothers to care.
Looking around and seeing this
I wonder why were here.
People love the things that scare
them, and hate the things
that are right.
No one cares to help each other,
all they want to do is fight.
Hatred is everywhere.
I wonder why we are all
trapped down in this awful
place.
Look around, you can see
the fear in people's faces.
They know what's going to be.
Bang!
They can't take being trapped,
so they take their lives from
you and I.
Andrea Ross

Remembering

God's house now stands
  where once grew trees,
    tall pines and oak
      as far as the eye could see.

I saw the broken ground,
  the sweat and tears
    it took to raise
      this house.

I watched the bowed
  down heads in earnest
    prayer, with children of
      Each man and spouse.

Now, quite complete with
  memories still, this house
    of God among the trees
      itself-stands tall in
        summer breeze.
Ella Ray Weese Bates

Under My Willow Tree

Under my willow tree
Where the clouds roll by,
Nobody finds me
Nobody's nigh.

Under my willow tree
Is joy and gloom,
Go there for fun, joy and play.
Under there to suffer and die away.

That's where it is,
My fun and my play.
That's where it is,
Where my fears blow away.

That's where it is,
Under my willow tree.
Cheri Phillips

Wake - Up - Walk

Come walk in the woods with me
Where there is so much to see.
Windflowers nodding in the breeze
Welcomes the shade of budding trees.
Jack-in-the-pulpit standing so tall
Wears a striped robe to make his calls.

The umbrella leaves of May apples there
Shelters toads from the hot sun's glare.
It's bloom looks like a china cup
Inviting all bees to come and sup.
A round green apple soon appears
With ants marching like legionnaires.

Chipmunks scampering to and fro
Appear not to know which way to go.
A flash of color in the tree's canopy
With joyful sounds for you and me.
The sweetest music ever heard
Comes from the throat of a little bird.
Dorothy M. Goerke

The Race To Heaven

This race that we run in is life
which causes troubles and strife

I dream of the day I will see His face
the day that I will finish the race

The day when all my dreams come true
and I can finally say I am through

This will be when I can ask Him why
why He sent His son to die

Then maybe, just maybe they will see,
what they're missing and come to believe

And we'll apologize for it all
all we didn't do when we heard His call

I may be only 27 or even 111
but I will be with HIM, up in heaven.
Christy Owen

"Love's Refrain"

Your eyes
which I shall
never see again,
for our paths
have come to an end.
Love cannot exist
working only one way,
so from your life
I must stray.
For in your heart
I am dead.
While within my chest
you remain.
Hoping you will
find love to this I pray,
but not knowing that
I will know that day.
For constantly I ponder
the reason
to love's refrain.
Douglas Sousa

Fire And Ice

One side's ice, and one is fire
which one do you desire.

One side's sin, and one is hate
there ain't no pearly gate.

Just remember, it was you
who was turning all the screws.

You said they've paid you well
to build the path you built to hell.

Now walk, in your footsteps
Walk, cause your children will to.

Just walk, in your footsteps
Because I've decided this is for you.
John Ferris

"They Didn't Fit, So We Must Acquit"

Everyone saw the demo
  which the prosecution put on;
Everyone howled a cry
  cause the gloves were difficult
    to put on.

Many efforts were made
  to bring home the point.
New gloves were presented;
  New explanations given
    cause the gloves simply
      did not fit.

"Since they did not fit", said Cochran
the jury, must acquit.
And indeed they certainly did.
Herbert Collins Jr.

A Distant Stranger

One day you met a stranger,
   while sitting in a great hall.
He just kept staring at you,
   from the mirror upon the wall.

Now his hair is turning gray,
   but his eyes are bright and clear.
As he looks upon you with desire,
   remembering and knowing a yesteryear.

Time has a way of passing by,
   the lonely hearts that stand still.
But his love for you is forever,
   as his faithfulness always will.

Perseverance and patience are virtues,
   keeping his memories safely within.
Hoping someday with time permitting,
   you and he will share life again.

Elmer Rasmussen II

"Slumber"

Yes it is I upon, a great
   white stallion,
Mates hoisting, bellowing sails,
   Me captain of the gallion.
Lord of a kingdom, most faithful
   by my side, wielding a
broad ax, into battle we'd ride.
Lived a pleasant's life, I held
out, the cleanest hand,
   Adrift on a raft, I sighted
land.
   Embraced with my love,
so deep in passion, tied to a
post, across my back a whip lashes.
Tasting vintage wine, the grapes
were sour, cutting trees ten
cords an hour.
The sun brazed my lids.
From the incoming light.
With a jolt oh my God.
What a restless night.

Dennis J. Ross

Hear These Cries

Hear these cries...
who are they you say?

They're the new born babies.

Why are they crying. Because
they want a certain someone
to teach them to talk shh.

Their cries are crying because
they want someone to teach
them to walk.
   Shh

Their cries are crying because
they want someone to teach
them how to dress properly

Their cries are crying because
they want someone to teach
them how to eat properly.

They want someone to teach
them their skills about life
shh, they're still crying.

Domeka Harrison

A Brother's Love

A brother's love is shared by someone
who cares,
A brother's love is given to everyone
who needs it
A brother's love will never be broken.

A brother's love is always seen,
no matter how old you are,
A brother's love is the inspiration to
all success.
A brother's love will never die.

A brother's love is stronger than the
strongest man,
A brother's love is better than the
best friend's love.
A brother's love is all within, and
it will always remain the best thing
in the world.

Andrea Turner

A Little Diddy For My Daddy

I once knew a man;
who couldn't cook.
So, I bought him a book.
With recipes in hand;
he decided to take a look
He put the water on the stove,
and turned the fire on.
Later; as the pot spouted
He just sat, and pouted!
His gravy wasted, and meat not tasted;
He made a dish, that would be fine.
It was tomatoes; right off the vine!
He added then; some white bread,
And a little mayo too!
He ended up with a simple meal.
Oh! My Gosh! He forget the veal!

Donna Long Moritz
Dedicated to the Memory of My Late Father
Mr. Conrad Lee Long

A Yearn For Love

Who do I yearn for,
Who do I love,
Who's touch do I lust for,
Who's body do I crave,
Who's soft lips do I wish to touch,
Who's muscular biceps do I yearn for,
Who's sweet words do I wish to hear,
Your's, your's, your's,
You are the only man I want to be with,
Tonight, tomorrow, forever,
I want, I need, I yearn,
For you, for me, forever.

Jessica Minnick

My Big Black Hole

If love is a big black hole,
Why am I always falling in it?

When you like someone
It seems to be the same,
Why do they play
Their selfish little game?

Life isn't always fair
I know
But sometimes love is like a
BIG BLACK HOLE!

Ellie Syvrud

Me?

Who are you; who am I,
Who do I want you to be,
Why do I ask; why do you talk,
What am I suppose to say,
You don't know; where I am,
Who am I suppose to be,
Are you loving; loving I,
Who am I suppose to be,
It's kind of hard; to understand,
You and I... infinity,
Am I rich; poor you are not,
Am I smart; dumb you are not,
Am I skinny; fat you are not,
Who are you suppose to be,
Am I loving; loving you,
Who are you suppose to be,
I don't know; where you are,
What are you suppose to say,
Why do I talk; why do you ask,
Who do you want I to be,
Who am I; who are you, you and I are Me?

Brent D. Sheehan

Soldier Lament

For all the soldiers
who fought in wars
Fell on boulders
Died on sandy shores
In all the wars

Blood that was spilled
Fathers who died
Brothers who were killed
In all the wars

Anger which held
Letters of peace that were mailed
Stop the blood that was spilled
Causing soldiers to be killed.

Jessica Coyle

Who Is The Winner

There was a coach named Steve Yoder
Who helped put B.S.U. in order,
Then moved on to higher ground
Which doesn't seem very profound.
The man had a way
And definitely could convey
The basketball is "round."
And if you don't win
The citizens send you to the "pound"
To master a sport where
Everyone is puzzled,
Has led the best player/coaches
To the depths of getting guzzled.
   Mikan had the hook,
    Cousy the eyes,
   Dr. J. the brains
   Hubie the cries.
   But the curtain call
   Is overdue, for the man who tries.
Jesus is the answer for these who thirst!

James Francis Ziegler

The Perfect Friend

Today I found a friend
Who knew everything I felt
She knew my every weakness
and the problems I've been dealt.

She understood my wonders
And listened to my dreams
She listened to how I felt
About love and what it means.

Not once did she interrupt
Or tell me I was wrong
She understood what I was going through
And promised to stay long.

I reached out to this friend
To show her that I care
To pull her close and let her know
How much I need her there.

I reached to hold her hand
To pull her a bit nearer
And realized this perfect friend I found
Was nothing but a mirror.

Courtney A. Reimer

Life Part II

As this young child
  who lay a forth,
Who's body is limp and cold
Never really experienced love,
  or had a chance to grow old.

Yet this young one
  wanted it this way.
This was yet her final decision.
She chose to give it all up,
and that's exactly what she did...
  She gave up on living

Now as she is put into her grave,
  I can't help but wonder
If she a second chance...
  would she choose to live,
  or would she still be asleep
    six foot under?

Davina Lynn Garber

Here Lies A Union Soldier

Here lies a Union Soldier
Who stood so brave and true.
His face turned up to Heaven,
His body wearing Union blue.

Here lies a Union Soldier
His body resting on the sod.
An unknown face without a name,
Known only but to God.

Here lies a Union Soldier
His shoes and rifle gone.
His eyes forever closed,
Never to see the morning dawn.

Here lies a Union Soldier
With other Soldiers in a row.
And music playing over head,
The notes held long and low.

Here lies a Union Soldier
Now buried beneath the sod.
His Mother knows not where,
Known only but to God.

James D. Miller

Memories Not Forgotten

I have memories of a loved one
who was so dear to my heart.
Someday we will meet again,
and never again will we part
we spent so little, time with each other
it was my dear sweet little brother
God gave him to us for only a short
While. He loved me so very much
and he trusted in me too,
and he told me everything I told him
was true, but now he is gone
God called him home and he had to go,
and we will miss him so, we don't
understand. But God knows best,
and now he has gone to rest.

Annie Mitchell

With Open Arms

I've always wondered
Why I bother to care
When I needed someone near
You pretended you didn't hear
When out of my eyes came a tear
All I needed was for you to be near
For you I always had open arms
to you I was willing to give my heart
Instead you decided to move apart
I just don't understand the way I feel
I wish I had a heart of steal
Instead its made of pencil lead
I feel sharpened till the end
And still I wait with so much faith.
With open arms
hoping for no more harm
With open arms I wait for your return
Yet inside I know I have too much of a burn.

Andrea Christine

Why

Why is the moon, she thought
Why is the moon, why love
And she watched the golden ball
Tossed on the puff of a cloud,
And the tree, cold, stiff,
Black 'gainst the gloom of the sky.
I'm alone, she thought,
Lost in this silence, this emptiness,
But no peace
No peace in the night
No peace in this cool quiet light
And she knew.

Dagmar Hegland

This Bond

This is what dreams are made of.
Wishes that come true,
Two hearts that become one life,
An understanding of one another,
Putting each other first.

Whatever we have
We have together.
Nothing is mine.
Nothing is yours.
The truth is what holds us together.
The honesty of love,
This bond of ours.

Janet Worrell Burton

Why Grow Old

Why being born
Why me
Why walk
Why live
Why white hair
Why drink water
Why make love
Why wake up
Why drown
Why fishing
Why drink
Why on the floor
Why happy
Why question
Why ridiculous
Why fools grow old
Why white skin
Why peach
Why voices
Why not at all.

Charles W. Budetto

Silence

Unasked questions
Will I ever know
The location of the keys
That guard your soul
Deep in your eyes
That penetrate
Nothing but time
I choose to wait
Longing for answers
Hidden within
Unrequited feelings
Omission is sin
Silence is loud
But you do not speak
Love is for the strong
I am but meek
I get no response
So I look ahead
Full of regret
For things left unsaid

Jennifer Mariner

At The Crossroads

I'm right here beside you
will you hold my hand?
My mind wants to travel
it takes me to another land.

My eyes are wide open
yet I can scarcely see.
I'm coming to a crossroads
which way shall it be?

You nourish my body
you feed my soul,
but I'm still very weak
time has taken its toll.

The road is long and lonely
another day is here
I smile as you greet me
you've just erased the fear.

So I close my eyes and dream
of that other place and land
because you're right here beside me
and you will hold my hand!

Barbara A. Kearsing

Missing You

When I say that... I love you
will you turn and walk away
will your eyes grow cloudy on a sunny day
Can I go beneath your skin
to touch you deep within
let me in...Please let me in.

When I've hurt you deep inside
and your soul runs and hides
I am lost in your pain
without you again.

I'm sorry I am a man
imperfect as I am
You are the world to me
so you have to believe...
I love you.
James R. Lieurance

The Road To Albuquerque

The road to Albuquerque
Winds thru sun baked fields
Doted here and there
With stubby green shrubs
And seared brown trees
Wind bent like little old ladies
Carrying a heavy load.
The fields stretched to a distant rim
Of gray and lavender hills
And whipped cream clouds
Melting into a pale blue sky.
This is the road to Albuquerque.
Dorothy J. Forrester

On Christmas Day

On Christmas day you
wish for something neat, but
when you open a package
you get, stockings for
your feet! You say, "Oh Ma,
oh Pa didn't you read my
Christmas list I put this and
that and got not even a cat!
I put stuff from A-Z
couldn't you see I didn't
put stockings for me?!"
You open another package
and you get something neat
you say, "Oh Ma, oh Pa I
guess in a mist just maybe
you did read some of my Christmas list."
Ashley Duffin

A Loving Hand

Learn we must from the birds,
Who speak so well with not a word,
They tell of how a loving hand
Provides for them in every land
And gives them hope and courage too,
As this same hand looks after you,
To care for you in every way
And carry you through another day.
Andrew Villarreal

How

How can I find you
  with a propeller in my arm
with a propeller in my arm
  with a love of the air
with my face in the sky
  with my eyes in the sky
with the love in my face
  in the brilliance of flying
  the of the air
the love in the air
a dove in the air
and my face falls gently
with my body in air
  my love in the sky
lonely dove in the sky
broken wing in my arm
falling dove through the heavens
  blinking eyes in the sky
can I love you gently
Aaron R. Martz

Untitled

I, stand here all alone
With an emptiness deep inside...
Feeling as though this life,
Has somehow passed me by...

I, share my life with others,
Its their leftovers I endure...
They toss their discarded dreams at me,
Why I'm not so sure....

I'd like to shout with all my might,
That hey this isn't fair...
I, have feelings too my friends,
I, know they don't really care....

So, I'll stand here as a monument,
With all hopes and dreams inside...
Crying with a empty heart... trying to abide

My life will be emptied soon,
They'll come to take me away...
Be gentle with me, dear sir, for it's here that
I must stay...

I, stand here all alone, as if I got a plan...
I, guess it doesn't matter though, after all
I'm just a ... can.
Gilbert Zendejas Sr.

Jaguars Tonight

Jaguars tonight
With black and gold spotted bodies
Are jumping fiercely
From damp, leafy ground
To thick bamboo branches
Is sweet smelling trees above.
Seeking their prey
Roaming quietly around the misty jungle.
Rippled waters are a mirror.
Ka-lu-lu birds coo their lullaby songs.
Tonight this mysterious jungle
With all its majesty and might
Paints a picture
Captured in my mind forever.
Allison Christy Hoover

December Fountain

Silent winter fountain
where once we laughed, we three.
In our youth and happiness,
like children, we swam, in innocent gaiety.
Gestures brought forth smiles,
sitting we on this grass now wet,
beneath the sun, and shared our lunch,
waves of greetings,
the tears of jokes,
throwing acorns into the fountain.

Now my gaze catches on every tree.
Restlessly I search for,
what, what could it be?
A ray of love's hope,
a ray of light in the winter rain,
a way of walking
which speaks to me, a love again.
So I return to you
still December fountain,
quiet, dry, empty, lifeless fountain.
David Marks

Silent Storm

My stomach knots as storm clouds gather.
A lightning flash and the wind starts to blow.
My chest feels constrained—unlike the weather,
and a feeling of danger will not let go.

My heart pounds hard and my face feels flush
as the sky darkens and wind blows the thistles.
Except for thunder there's a tangible hush
as the dog's ears perk and the cat's hair bristles.

The clouds roll on and the sun peeks through.
The wind slows to a gentle breeze.
My stomach relaxes and chest takes the cue
which gives me a feeling of ease.

The dog stretches lazily, the cat starts to purr.
They sense that it was only a game.
The dog goes to sleep as the cat grooms her fur,
and I am left with a feeling of shame.
Ruby B. Britt

God's Child To Love

Who has given to us this child to love?
A fragile child to keep from harm.
Our heart aches to see our child so weak.
Where is the strength to run and play?
A beautiful child full of love and trust.
Our love is strong for this child we have.
We pray for God's healing hand from above.
Can this child be made well?
Only God can tell.
We teach our child to pray, and to look above
For strength each day.
Can I do the same, I say?
I pray that my faith can stay strong, for I know
God can touch all.
Day by day I thank God for this child I have.
For you see - it is they who teach us, that with
Love and trust in God; all are made well.
Sharron Baker

Silent Angel

Were all here today to show our love,
To an energetic little boy, who now shines from above.

He sees us cry, he feels our pain,
Now he's in heaven, home once again.

Sometimes things happen, we just don't know why,
But his name is Jesse, now a twinkle in the sky.

We'll always remember the smile on his face,
His cute little dimples, and state of grace.

No longer the same, the home where he lived,
Keep shining son, you still have a lot to give.

He feels no more pain, he sees no more fear,
Life will be sweat for him up there.

We'll see you again soon, this you can be sure...

You were our little man, now your our light,
When we look up, we'll see you at night.

Our love is with you Jesse, our hearts our souls,
We give our lives so your star will always glow.

Lori Bedwell

On Angel's Wings

One hour set aside in another hectic week
Mothers huddle together in a room to speak
Boldly aloud so the rest can hear
Engaging us all in a melody so dear.
Thoughts lifted on angels wings become a song
A sweet-smelling aroma fills the throne-room of God.
Hearts full of love for our children that hour
Their names leave our lips-oh! The Spirit's power!
He continually intercedes for those anxious cares
The mothers believing the answers to prayers.
Assured He has listened to our earnest words
We gratefully acknowledge the plans of the Lord.
For in the heart of Jesus lies his children's best
The mothers go separate ways and confidently rest.

Linda Pfeifle

Volunteering

I volunteer my time.
I don't get, or ask for a time.
I do this because I think it is kind.
I do it all the time, I really don't mind.

This makes me feel good from the inside out
Sometimes I really want to shout!
To see all the children come out
This is something to talk about.

Giving up my time is very fine
When I do this I make my light shine
This makes me feel glad
If you do this you won't feel bad

When I see the glow on the children's faces
I can say I have reached some bases
I want to do this even more.
This shows I care, I am sure

Volunteering my time is the best thing to do!
I try very hard to make dreams come true
Maybe someday I'll be able to help you too,
This makes a big difference when I serve you!

Susan Braxton

A Lonely Dirt Road

Wondering barefoot
down a lonely dirt road,
the burning sand beneath my feet.
When in the distance
someone appeared,
just a stranger I chanced to meet.
As he came closer, it seemed so strange.
Do I know you I ask, when he spoke my name.
There were tears in his eyes,
he could sense my fear.
Don't be afraid he said, as he walked near.
I just wanted to know,
I wanted to see.
What you'd be like today,
and if you'd recognize me.
Then he walked away, the same as he came.
On a lonely dirt road never saying his name.

Virginia Wynne Tucker

CHRONIC PAIN

Living with pain each day,
This young and old body rebels against pain,
To an unfortunate and incurable chronic disease.

This body is in misery,
Wanting to be free,
And wanting a life that will never be.

Every second, minute, and hour of each day,
Pain takes it's toll on my body, mind, and spirit.
A life of despair, fighting pain, isolation, and loneliness.
Pain is my lesson in life,
To find courage in a world that forgets I'm alive.

Loneliness, isolation, and rejection are my world.
Something in me in lost forever.
Alone I'll be to a world of pain,
Fighting for a life that has been taken away.

Hoping to find peace, in body, soul, and spirit.
Something in me in lost forever.
My life has been taken away, torture I must feel.
I continue to struggle and carry this burden,
And fighting chronic pain, will always be forever!

Karen Meanea

"Kisses To The Wind"

The last time you saw him, you'll never forget,
You blew each other kisses, and in the wind they met.
A life's great love it was, one too close to close...
In your heart will remain, special feelings which arose.

The passion you've felt through shared times, good and bad...
Have enriched each other's life with experiences felt and had.
The true love that you gave, will come back to you two fold...
You'll make great life choices, memories more there to hold.

You've learned oh, so much, as the bridge of youth you do cross...
Let pain flow right through you, cry out from the loss.
The black and white life issues are transcended with time by true colors of love...
So send heaven your prayers, on the wings of a small white dove,

All your heart, mind, and soul you gave, blossomed as a fresh fragrant lilac...
He knew in life what it meant, to have a precious sweet"Love, love him back"...
And to desire his child; I ask, "what else can compare to that?"
We all make our choices which inspire, heartfelt passionate deep fires where at.

A life's great love it was, one too close to close...
In your heart there will remain, special feelings which arose.
You blew each other kisses, and in the wind they met...
Your soul's time is eternity, Heaven's Angels guide memories never both to forget!

Michael J. Chassion

Okinawa

Ah lovely Okinawa! Keystone of the Pacific
One would think living on this enchanted isle would really be terrific,
A lovely two hour flight from Japan - 800 miles from China's coast,
You would never believe you were in the middle of no where,
The way the propaganda boasts.
The exciting tourist attractions - you really all should come,
The fantastic beaches and suicide cliff,
Not to mention the tropical sun
Of course there are the taxi-cab drivers,
Who in a moment will turn your hair gray,
Not to mention the occasional typhoon
Which always heads this way.
A couple of jolts from an earthquake,
Just to keep you on your toes,
And when will water rationing be called off,
Only the officials and heaven knows.
So lets hear it for Okinawa - a bronx cheer will do,
And until the summer of '75
Just call me Mister Blue.
  Pan Taylor

Illusions

The dinosaurs (an illusion) are not visual to the eye;
This picture may cause confusion because they're almost
invisible. WHY?
Because it's an optical illusion, of course you can see it by now;
It causes a lot of delusions. It can make you scream and shout,
WOW!

You see purple and orange and green and blue
And all of the colors you know,
But you might see some weird looking objects, too.
Did that baby dino just grow?

The dinosaurs are for you to see.
If you can't see them, don't worry.
It's the same way for you as it is for me.
It may look a little bit blurry.

Are they hiding or walking or fighting or chewing?
They can't be — pictures don't move.
Just what in the world are those dinosaurs doing,
Just what are they trying to prove?

It seems like we've come to a simple conclusion
That might seem to people quite strange.
Delusions, confusions are caused by illusions;
That's a fact that we just cannot change.
  Nicole Ronae Merkledove

Respect

Respect is the bluish color of a naval officer's uniform after
  winning a battle.
It sounds like people cheering in a grandstand.
It tastes like a sweet victory.
It smells like a crisp, fall morning.
It looks like the face of a person who has just achieved an A+ on a test.
It makes me feel proud.

Respect is the color of the raging waves at the beach.
It sounds like a judge saying you've won.
It tastes like a box of chocolates.
It smells like a freshly baked loaf of bread.
It looks like a parade held in your honor.
It makes me feel important.

Respect is getting a sweet slice off the onion of life.
  Katie Polatsek

Archives

Lessen your trial, lesson your trial.
A bursted arm lies on the floor
Your lies on the floor.
The clean sweep finished at last
A forged leader coming in fast.

Homes of charcoal and pointed blame
Minds of programs and useless games
A spray of bolts in their heads
With bottled tongues, little said.

The few alive in a restless recluse, for now.
After They exhumed their shortened fuse, allowed.
  Wendy Whitehead

His Song

Their music pulsates the campus,
a celebration of the invincibility of youth,
its heartbeat enhancing the daily task of living.
Not content with mere accompaniment,
they play melodies uniquely their own.
And they dance their own dances.
And they sing their own songs.
But as they travel life's rugged terrain,
the music stops when they encounter the rain.
They have met disappointment,
or experienced great pain.
Then all from amateurs to
accomplished musicians surmise:
If we all tune together,
a symphony will arise.
And they dance His dance.
And they sing His song.
  Shirley M. Johnson

Computer Class

In a small school, there is a cute classroom.
A charming computer class.
The teacher elegant looking,
Has blond hair, green eyes, wears glasses.
How good looking he is!
Eastern and Western languages are two different ones.
The students have grey hair,
Are not intelligent as they were before,
But they are very assertive, patient, and determined.
I understand that my teacher tried hard,
How difficult to teach slow learners!
Word by word, he teaches with joy,
Without anger but love.
He has a good heart and is intelligent,
He is happy when I understand.
Oh! My teacher, don't you know?
That I have determined to be your student,
How happy I am, I could type my poem!
I am grateful to my teacher's.
Love which is large as a river, an ocean.
  Thua Thi Nguyen

Today

Today it has been 15 weeks.
Today it has been 105 days.
Today is has been 2,520 of the longest, hardest hours of your life.
Today you have been given 151,200 more minutes.
Today makes 9,072,000 seconds that we are grateful for.
AND
I LOVE YOU!
  Sharon L. Taylor

Deliverance

Moving ever so slow but moving still,
A cold war grips and binds my soul.
When will Truth return and set Despair to flee?

Like tunnel-work, jeering and blasting,
Darkness invades and burrows deep.
Moving ever so slow but moving still.

Tenderness evades my withered grasp;
Mirth succumbs to grief and droops to frown.
When will Truth return and set Despair to flee?

Cynical dullness shadows mine eyes
As pandemonium denies the warming Sun.
Moving ever so slow but moving still.

Scalding humiliation tempers my tears
And long my cross, no more can I bare.
Pray! Truth will return and set me free.

Exhaustion overcomes and drowns me in slumber
Whilst Hope soothes my ragged-born blunder.
Moving ever so slow but moving still,
Patient Truth will ever be and send Despair to hell!

Tamatha Anne Pooler

Till We Shall Meet Again

I have long been haunted by a face from a distant memory,
A dark romantic fantasy, and I never understood how and why
It moved something so deep in me. This is a scene I have often seen
In the depths of an epic dream; a sunset by a distant sea

Two warriors stand poised for a fight, swords drawn, ready for attack,
One crouched low and dressed in black, the other noble and upright
My eyes are fixed on that tall young man, the long brown hair and shining eyes
Call to me across the skies, across the seas to another land.

Yesterday I saw the face from my vision, same sad eyes and chiseled features,
Tall Japanese boy with the regal stature of an old and proud tradition
But he walked by me unseeing, unknowing. How could he know?
Of that battle on a wild and rocky shore, and the memories that he set stirring.

My only love, I've lost this chance, but our story will never end
You promised me forever, someday we shall meet again
In the future, in Japan, our paths will cross once more
And we'll begin our love anew on that wild and rocky shore.

Thasneem Manzur

Values

A crown around a cloudy brow makes sleep to seep away
A deeply sleeping king may bring a crowd too proud to pray
The mass will pass a classy lass in deeply cheap array
To will their fill of chilly thrill against their brazed display

Who knew these two unruly fools whose wit seems not to fit
For where they go and what they know matters not a whit
One's job's to rob the unruly mob and take away their pay
One alibis and slyly tries to trade their pay for play

Once duressed or duly blessed by either of these two
Your pockets torn or truly worn from fingers passing through
We lose our truths in booths with sleuths; the life we spent is bent
They bind our mind and then we find we don't know where it went

When all is said, it's those in bed who slice our life so thin
We share and care, though unaware of regal vicely din
The king has wed the wench in bed and fleeces us with ease
Why do we work when a mere dirk would rid us of disease

Robert W. Cameron

"Lover's Cove"

I know a place beyond the water's edge
A distant cove where only lovers dwell
Here exists the sweetest temptation of the heart and mind
Along with the heavens, the body and soul of two lovers will combine

Underneath a spring-lit shower where rain droplets taste of red wine
Two people will make love forever, for the very first time
At night the sky would forever be clear, full of stars and their
   constellations
And during the day, the sunbeams will project a gallant optic
   presentation

Amidst golden pyramids that seem to reach the heavenly skies
Will run streams of succulence filled with beauty seen through each
   lover's eyes
The wind will gently flow with the aroma of poppies and pines
While the sounds of chirping doves echo through the tunnels of love

This place is a special one, where only a chosen few will come
It's found deep within the heart and soul of two people eternally
   bound as one
Seeing its beauty and sharing the depths of it's wonders is truly
   a blessing from above
To find this place, let down your guard, step off the edge, and fall
   in love

Vann G. C. Jones

The Winds

The winds of words that sweep you into
a dream are what can create the nightmare
that the dream never began.....

Resist the winds for the rain will accompany it.
The sun will soon appear with its own winds,
But you will know these winds are true,
And the difference is love....

Michelle Landis

Untitled

Maybe I'm a dreamer but what's a dreamer for?
A dreamer dreams the dreams that opens up all doors.
Sensations and images thoughts and ideals,
Vision of another world far away from here,
I can dream myself to the stars are deep beneath the sea.
I can dream myself young again are old as I can be.
I can dream myself into the
Past a million years ago.
Or I can be a dreamer of things still yet to be.
I know I'm a dreamer, because that's what dreamers are for.

Wanda Lynn Washington

Fire

Saw a house today gutted by
a fire — still steaming. Wondered
who got hurt, who lost. I remember fire

compressed in a stick, made blood red
by the touch of a trigger. Scary never knowing
if he'd pull it. Poured fire too from a bottle, every night

and day — its burning scent. Damn, he lived on that golden
fire. Worst fires I remember rose up from within
his belly, flared out his mouth, darting

into the bellies of others. Never
missed. Gutted them — just
like that house.

Pat Long

Garden Of My Inner Child

mangled rusting iron fence
a gate flinging itself at the haze,
sanguine raven-scream
the orange sky strangles a seething sun
one swing, tire and heavy chain
asphalt everywhere, heaved and crumbled
in the barren tree the crooked fort is black where fires played

the ghostly babe that lives in me sings a twisted rhyme
goes about her play, head shorn, shaking the dead tree limbs
gathering brown weeds into desiccated bouquets
she laughs and pelts the fence with stones,
shrieking into darkening air
   Sarah Hildebrandt

Gifts

A gift once was given to me;
A gift - truly given, bought with only love.

So long that gift warmed my soul,
Illuminating corners and depths of an
   inner being I'd longed for,
   but never known.

Gradually, the light of the gift grew dim,
   and the vastness of my soul shrunk into
   darkness.

Was the gift, as all worldly things, only
   a victim of mortality?

Or, does its beams lay buried among the
   ashes of pain and hurt?

My soul quivers in the coldness of the dark;
   and warm beams of light seem only a distant
   dream of yesterday.

Gifts are to be treasured for before realized,
   the gift may only be a memory.
   Karen S. Ward

By Moon I Sat

By moon I sat alone upon a pier of stone,
A guest who'd walked along the river's edge with quiet tread.
It was as if a tent around me had been spread —
The grand expanse of placed waters and a dappled sky.
There was no sound that broke the calm but, by and by,
A spectral crest of swishing seaweed, reed, and sedge,
And lazy, lapping waves upon the rocky ledge.

I knew I there was drawn by some unearthly song
To raise my voice in prayer within that airy temple's nave.
And when I had at last discharged my heart-felt praise,
Then quickly came across His silver stool a whispered sigh:
The Spirit's breath of peacefulness, 'twas His reply,
That brushed aside the scudding billows in the air
And turned the night's uncertain sky so bright and fair!
   D. Silas Peterson

Morning's Sun

When the mountains uncover the morning's sun,
A new day for me and you has begun
As the fresh, new flowers, begin to unfold
I dream of us growing together, growing old
As I gaze through the window, at the sparkling dew,
I feel so happy, so lucky, to be lying here next to you
Your warm lovely cheek rests gently upon my chest,
Your eyes twitching in your sleep, as you dream of happiness
I could lye here forever, holding you tight in my arms,
Just as long as I know when this day is done,
I'll awake again to see the mountains uncover the mornings sun
   Mark M. Schell

The Shackles Of Faith

A vast kingdom-constructed upon a consecrated infern O
A hellfire kindled by your self-serving hand illuminates all darknes S
Except for that which dwells within your sou L
The hearts of the righteous lain in universal blacknes S
Only the blind are san E
But the blind are the blin D
And it is those of us who think who are crucifie D
Pseudo shepherds lead their flocks into the pasture of their si N
Bound by the shackles of faith the sheep will follow and serv E
Behold and all was vanit Y
Lurid demons lurk behind many masks and manifestations of the sou L
In one final act the monster is unveile D
The naive see no T
The blessed see al L
And I remain in the shadows of your hat E
   Micah J. Larripa

"Mary"

The beginning, a new life
A joyous day, a baby girl
Blessed we are, Mary was born
For each year, we celebrate.
The joys you have brought
To each and everyone you hold dear
The wisdom and beauty you give
Each and everyday through out the year
Like a rose each pedal so beautiful and delicate
You've touched our lives, so we celebrate
The glorious day of the year
Happy birthday dear
   Kathy D. Eaton

Teardrops Are Glistening On The Christmas Tree Tonight

Shades of night had fallen the ground was white with snow!
A little boy was writing a letter amid the candle glow!
With tear stained cheeks he finished it and sealed it with a kiss;
"God bless him Lord" he whispered and the letter went like this!
Now daddy dear they say you've gone across the sea to fight!
And mommy says you wont be home to share our "Christmas Night!"
So I helped mommy trim the tree and when we lit the lights!
Teardrops were glistening on the Christmas Tree Tonight!
Now the tears that fell there came from mommy's face;
When asked why she was crying she held me in embrace!
She prayed to God above for you while she held me tight;
And the teardrops were glistening on the Christmas Tree Tonight!
Now daddy dear please tell all those bad men;
The story of the "Jesus Child" tan all the wars will end.
"For Peace On Earth" good will towards men, its so wrong to fight;
Then no tears will glisten on the Christmas Tree Tonight!!!
   Leah P. Mapes

Romance At Sea

San Juan at midnight when we met.
A time I won't soon forget.

The Celebration our ship at sea.
How very special when you looked at me.
Emotions unfold, locked up for so long.
How can these feelings be so wrong?

Tender moments we shared together,
Wanting to last forever and ever.
You said you were the best thing that happened to me,
Yet, I knew, just a romance at sea.
   Lawrence James Gladstone

Reflections

I look in the mirror and what do I see
A little old lady — I daresay that's me
Though I'm now in the eighth decade of my life
And it's been years since I was a dutiful, loving wife
A Mother and a Grandmother I shall always be.
That's the joyous part of being "Little Old Me"
In reflecting upon the years that have been spent
There were times when I sorrowfully had to repent
But I shall remember those who touched my heart
Alas, from this Earth they long did depart
No matter the hows, whys or when
Yesterday can't ever come back again.
So, as I gaze about me and ponder anew
Life's really been a blast, lots of dreams came true
So, if I ever sinned, I've gotten my reprieve
As I rejoice in the legacy that I leave
My family and friends will remember me with love
When I am called to meet my Maker from above
I fervently pray with all my heart and soul
That I'll be sent to heaven — for that is my goal

Ruth Stalerman

Untitled

A thousand times I've said "I love you";
A million more, "You set my soul on fire".
Many times "I'll put no other above you";
And always called my pain a liar.
A hundred times I've promised forever;
Twice as many, it was promised to me.
"If you're true, I'll leave you never",
Was always followed by, "I must be free".
I have searched my soul for expressions of desire;
I have wrung my heart for feeling true;
Of loving diction I have never tired -
Each inspiration reaching something new.
With every syllable uttered, I exposed the depth of my fears
Now, I finally see that all the expressions of my soul were
just words wasted on empty ears.

Kristina Clay

Sailing: The Realm Of Relaxation!

Once aboard my sailboat,
A new attitude captures me,
Allowing me to escape my cares
By leaving reality;
Through the glass-like water
My sailboat glides away;
Occasionally upon my tanning skin
I feel the salty spray;
As we sail away from shore,
Passing boats and noisy birds,
What I feel inside of me is too wonderful to express in words!
Out in open water, I allow the sails release,
Relaxing while my boat sets forth to a realm of joy and peace;
I dread when my adventurous journey must all-too-quickly end,
For once sailing has settled in my bones I seek a way to extend
The time I have with my lovely boat, abandoning comforts of home,
Never as happy as I am when away from the shore I roam;
I'm happy to be known by all as a "Man of the Sea";
It doesn't take much to achieve this goal,
Just the sea, my sailboat, and me!

Leda McElhiney

Morning Delight

A handsome woman sat alone, eating a light breakfast and reading
a novel; such a woman could inspire.
He sat across the way, trying hard not to stare, with his newspaper,
toast and coffee. Oh, for a Roman chin.

No wedding ring. Her friend was late. Tardiness, a saving trait
against those doting suitors; sly dog.
(Conclusions drawn during one self-conscious gaze).

When no one came to join her, encouragement set in;
Much better not to overstay; just use the clock
as if to say — this man has an agenda!

Of course, he passed her table on the way. She raised her head
and blushed a smile. Was that excitement in her eyes?
Hold the moment. Plan the next. He nodded simply and politely.

Too near the bud to realize, he spied the fruit of her surprise,
and what he saw can be inferred and should be gently told.
"He looks so much like Dad," she thought, "It's been so long and I must call."
How kind, to never know.

In days to come, same time and place, he'll smile at the waitress
and joke with the cook; over newspaper, toast and coffee.

William C. Martin

Decide

Sometimes I sit alone, and comes to me a poem
A poem to say how I feel, to let me know that life is real
For sometimes I feel as if I am dreaming
In a world which I don't belong
Then I will catch myself seeing, myself in a song

For without poems and songs
To express how someone feels
Life would be wrong, like a rod without a reel
I can take my pen in hand, and a poem then begins
I really don't understand

I feel as if I am a writer trapped inside
Within this body, I try and hide
I take my pen in hand, and on the paper place it
It seems to write its own words, I must face it
To be a writer or not, I must decide

Olivia Michaels

Remembering You

It was great anticipation and joy to welcome a baby boy.
A prayer of thanksgiving was said.
The weeks then months slipped away as we watched you
Roll over and sway, then sit erect with nurturing enchantment.
The day, place, and time is vividly clear,
When your first faltering steps you took.
Loving eyes watched you, caring hands were there to steer.
Time did not stand still, the baby boy became a man.
Handsome, loving, and charming, but obviously in search of something.
Perhaps you heard that voice calling you.
Unlike your entry, there was no anticipation of your exit.
Only shock and dismay, as we recaptured the good
And not so good moments we shared.
Then suddenly we wondered why should we be drowned in despair,
When we know you are happy there.
And can see your smiling face, adding more brilliance to that place.
You are not alone for sure, we see smiling faces more and more,
All seemingly saying, don't you worry we all are happy.
Now we can smile remembering you,
Realizing you did have the last laugh after-all.
Dedicated to the memory of Aubrey Leon Springer.

Norma Springer

Promise Land

I'm looking for the promise land,
A promise of peace, contentment and harmony.
I'm looking for my dream,
my soul, and things I cannot seem to find.
I've searched the world over and looked many places,
Looking to find where my heart belongs.
I've looked and lived with many people
only to find, I was unhappy with these things,
these people and these towns.
I ask myself why I am so sad?
I am sad because I forget to look inside of myself,
This is where my dreams, my love and peace lives.
It was just buried so deep, I lost sight of it all.
Inside myself I know now,
Where the promise land lies,
IN THE HEART ITSELF.
  Katie Sorrels

As A River

Sometimes I feel I'm like the river,
  A river that run's free
Confines between two boarder lines,
  for all of life to see.

The water's run rough-the water's run soft
Under society's pressures
  time has come to say enough

As I look within, I compare
  I see myself in the river
It runs on forever
  searching somewhere

Eye's above try so hard to recognize
  piecing together shattered scar's
Beyond the surfaced.
  Their I can see
Their; is were the truth speaks loud to me
Mysterious as a river
  those who ponder are curious

As I feel I'm like the river
  I am as a river
  Shannin Vatalaro

I Saw Her Sadly Standing

She was standing on a street corner
A sad portrait of a lady
Whose days go by so slowly oh so lonely
She and others like her they all are wishing only
To relive the moments passed
have a chance at youth again
and make those moments last

Age has not refined her
Nor has time fulfilled her dreams
The wishes and wants of yesterday
They've disappeared it seems
Replaced with said reflections
Now the loneliness the need

That lady on the corner waiting for the bus
knows time has not been kind to her
It's dragged her through the dust
The freedom of her youth exists for her no more
Life is now a prison and the child is inside
Age has locked her up and she's waiting now to die
  Kymberly van Konijnenburg

Stormy Seas

Darkest night on stormy seas -- ravaged, raped, and left to bleed
A sea of tears, fathoms deep, forever fed by eyes that weep
Grabbing, clutching, dragging down, confusion, madness, fear abound

A trace of light, the faintest beam, beckoning softly as if a dream
Cutting through the dark of night, offering hope and strength to fight
Calming, soothing, urging on, promising days of peace beyond

Battles rage, long and fierce -- nature wounds, the heart is pierced
Agony gnaws, like a dog on a bone
There is no comfort on the sea all alone
But through it all the light remains
Burning brighter until it flames
Blazing its way straight into the heart
Healing and warming and mending the parts
Together anew in the warmth of the glow
Lifted and carried, the sea far below
Never again to drown in the tears
The flame burns inside year after years
  Kenneth M. Blahut

Out Of Control

Controlled completely yet completely out of control
A short lived chemical high
For just one moment you are content
Those utopian moments seem heaven sent
So as you fly high, high in the sky
Everything important to you as died
The earth is no longer a place you want to be
For you don't even see the honesty in me
Everything to you is a paranoid illusion
So there you stay in your depressed confusion
Yes, I must say I understand
One day I hope that you will land
And are able to find love within
So maybe the ice you walk on won't seem so thin
Instead of wishing upon a false star
Close your eyes and find out who you are
  Renee Antaya

Silence

BANG!
A shot echoes through the air.
The sounds of sirens in the distance are beginning to overcome
  the intense screams of pain.

HELP!
Someone points to the victim of the drive-by shooting.
The EMT's climb out of the ambulance. One of them starts
  repeating the all-too-familiar questions to the wounded woman.

OH!
The woman moans while clutching her belly.
The EMT's scurry around preparing for an on-the-spot birth.

HURRY!
She's going, going...damn.
Pulse: Nothing. Breathing: Stopped.
Her body has become limp and impassive.

STILLNESS.
All motion has stopped; the beeping of a pager breaks the silence.
A few words are mumbled. The EMT's fidget with their supplies
  before cleaning up to respond to the next call.
  Naomi Heimeyer

Sighs From Atop The Widow's Shelf
I am a shadow made of glass,
a silent scream inside a jar,
left to sit atop a widow's shelf,
listening for the tide.
The spider builds its home around me,
the months die before my eyes,
a swinging bulb without a shade,
lights my vacant room.
I can hear the steps on the floor above me,
feel warmth thru the crack of the door,
imagination is the world around me,
sealed tight inside my jar.
   D. Judson Cooper

A Cowboy's Prayer
Lord, I'm a just cowboy, out here on the range;
a simple man, workin' hard every day.
I'm tryin' my best to do just and right,
but sometimes I feel like I'm slippin' a mite.

I look at the beauty you've surrounded me with
and pray every day to be worthy of this.
You gave me a life that I'd never trade
for all of the gold that the world's ever made.

I got me good friends, enough money to live,
respect for all that this land's got to give.
I sleep with your stars keepin' watch in the dark,
and waken to sunrises that quicken my heart.

Help me make the most of this time that I borrow.
Though it's mine for today, it might not be tomorrow.
And if I should stray from ways that are right,
watch over me still; I'll look for your light.

Lord, help me remember with each step I take,
that these steps put together form the path that I make.
Lead me and guide me as I chose the way
of the trail I will travel on each brand new day.
   Kathy Malinski

The Choice
There is something alluring in the void
A siren's yearning, beckoning whisper
Rising to a call, a wail from the depths of my darkest self;
A drawing, tugging desire, a perverse curiosity
A moment spent at the crossroads of feeling;
   a time of assessment -
To the right, an ascension on an arduous slope
   reaching for gentle promise;
To the wrong, a decline
   cutting out of sight at the switchback down,
Posing the seductive question,
   If I inch around that first dim corner, will I, can I climb out?
If I investigate temptation
   Will I control the descent,
   or stumble and tumble helplessly into my own chasm?
How deep and steep are my canyons of fear?
How starkly dark are the tunnels of my loneliness?
How near, how dear will I find the specter of death?

I choose — and step tentatively onto my path.
   Maureen Bucek

My Face In The Mirror
Eyes looking around, as new happenings go by,
Always thinking, I'm one of a kind.
Always smiling, but hiding bad feelings inside.
As time goes, I think I'm going to die.
But not knowing, how long I will survive
   Tony Ho

Kimiko's Grandpa
On Grandpa's lap, I share
a spot, its always soft and warm and when I come to
visit, its him that I adore.
He gives me lots of hugs
and loves, he always shares his bites.
I am his only granddaughter
and precious in his sight.
   Pamela Bennion

Rekindling The Flame
In the summer heat
a small fire begins to burn
In no time the flames have doubled
but, just as fast as they grew
the flames are doused with water.
All that is left is mud and used wood
Time goes on and dries the wood
The sun shines down and begins
the tiniest of flames.
Over the span of a year the fire intensifies
growing and spreading, but somehow its contained
It wants to get out
It wants to breath and grow stronger
But it stays where it is
Scared that it might be put out again
not knowing what the future will bring
So for now the fire remains
until it builds up enough courage
to love again.
   Matthew Gold

This Way
Felt your words today
A speckled victory
Our first raw transference;
first pure path to understanding-one made lucid by pain

Can't help wonder if your disillusionment
stems from insecurity, from deliverance;
not humility, not banishment

You only needed to hold instead of grasp, to both
listen and hear, to love rather than possess

A grain of trust, a hint of hope, a
willingness of the heart
Such an endowment surely joins

Feel my words today
Reflect upon thy and my - in no way discrediting
Let love be the founding recurrence

Connect with me again
The trail's not engulfed
Let more than your words refrain

Leave me with more than memories
as one too desperately loved
   Tempo Bierley

Voices
From within the mind the side unused
Alter egos lie varied and mused.
They would all be named if left turn right
escape through the ear be seen in the light,
Then more would there be to fill the earth
Many personalities sharing one hearth.
Quiet now these thoughts in my head
Right back to left now they all are dead.
   Terry S. Waltz

Grandma

A tall woman
A strong mind
Not the typical grandma you would usually find
A gentle man
A hug, a kiss
Now gone and sadly missed
Now all alone
Stuck in a room
Hoping someone will be there soon
But when we are there,
Does she really know?
Does she feel that we love her so?
It is really doubtful
The memory is tossed
A tall woman,
A mind lost...
Robin Boyle

What Is Love?

What is pure and clean
A thought that is sure and real
What a person perhaps may feel?
Love is what that means.
Kindness and respect
Time with a certain person takes on a big affect
No lies, the truth are in the eyes
That is proof enough with what one does say
Love is what that means.
A touch, a tender kiss
to see how one truly feels cannot be missed
A precious gift from God
When one is sad, a word of care bring up an enormous lift
Love is what that means
A pleasant smile, a warm laugh
A desirable heart, causes no harm to a child
To understand and have patients
Are honest qualities that make a man
You are what loves means.
Tammy Lane

The Willow's Secret

Somewhere in this ornate world, a young girl sits alone under a towering weeping willow tree. When the quiet wind blows, it mysterious removes the suspended ginger branches of the willow from her few. Soon, she can witness the sun's farewell to the day and its welcome to the night. For in instant, the girl sees the dilatory marshmallow clouds that drift though the countless pigments of the exquisite sun set. Soon, the wind's sojourn comes to an end and the willow's branches return to lock away the magical beauty of the ocean sky. The young girl knows that the sun has completed its grand finale and has retreated for the night, leaving the sky a shade of ebony for the stars to dance in. The girl leaves her place beneath the weeping willow, but will return again to witness its magic.
Megan O'Neill

Prayers, Isaiah's In Heaven

Isaiah's dead. The thought keeps running through my mind.
A wake up call. A reminder for safe driving and seat belts.
A goal to be done. A determination for myself to accomplish for both of us.
A respect for life and death. Teenagers are not immortal.
A way to stick together. A unity of mourners, both school and community.
Released feelings. The feelings bottled up from other problems.
Hung up jerseys, memorial services. Knowledge that we will be remembered after death.
Prayers. Isaiah is now in heaven.
Stephanie Tezak

Wind On The World

I feel the wind hard and cold,
A trouble world in a death hold.

People die without cause.
Others rush by and never pause.

To consider the life that might have been.
A president. A poet or some next of kin.

To seek a reason, for what is lost.
The price we pay what hatred cost.

Day by day hate takes its toll.
A little heart a lot of soul.

How long before we learn to care.
About the hearts of others, the lives we share.
Steve Pflum

My Sweet William

My sweet William you'll always be
  a very special part of me
Tho we no longer can show our love
  it was as pure as the soft white
    clouds above
Someone watches over us you see
He'll guide us through the way it should be
  My Sweet William you'll hear him say
Follow your heart and I'll show you the way
  My Sweet William you'll hear me say
I'm very sorry it couldn't be that may
Never let go for the love we have shared
  And always remember that I'll still care
My Sweet William when my life must end
Always remember if nothing else you had a friend
With so much love that wouldn't end
My Sweet William don't feel any blame
I know now that my life can never be the same...
Tammy Marie Stark

Embered Tunes Gasping

They hauled sixteen tons, and what did they get
a walk - in grave though they weren't dead yet.
Their wages paid Charron the price he required,
but they couldn't dig out so their bodies were pyred.

Two raps were levied by the company store.
Their voices shouldered their way to the floor.
The company store declared, "Your souls are mine!"
So the Faustian minors just bided their time.

Saint Peter can't call, hell's store prevails
for the lifeless souls sound widow's wails.
Then to stay their keep, the young boys they give,
Mama's babies are buried before they live.

Oh the throat of darkness swallows their boys.
Bituminous teeth break their carbon toys.
But they soon learn to call the grave their home
as props talk a eulogy that never is known.
Sean Flannery

Glimmer Of Light

She has stood in many a doorways to watch us go,
and wave goodbye till she could see no more.
The glimmer of light stays in our heart,
no darkness nor storm could break us apart.
Margaret A. Brogdon

Nature's Teachers

I walk on this path deep into the shaded Forest
A wall of heavy stones all sitting like the rest
The trees stand erect with the multi-colors of Summer's defeat
And all that I hear is that of my own two feet

Ahead I see an opening of soft green moss
A bed for the deer on their journey across
The down graded slope brings me to a cold crystal stream
Where fish must thrive it does so seem

An old rotted log lies as nature's own bridge
Maybe felled by the fat beaver I see on the ridge
I look above and see the many well constructed nests
Way up high to keep out their pests

But what surrounds me is an animal society
Like us yet simple and left so carefree
And now I wonder how much we take after all creatures
As we superior-minded learn so much from these teachers.
   Robert J. Smith

My Only Angel

Once upon a time, an angel saved my soul,
A woman of untamed beauty, and a heart of solid gold,
She came in like a lightning bolt, and took my heart away,
My everlasting love for her, grows stronger everyday,
I hold a torch so bright and hot, a flame of burning love,
I thank the Lord everyday, for sending her from above.
Sometimes I have to pinch myself to make sure she is real,
Words can not explain, how strongly I feel.
It's a passion like no other, that I can not explain,
A mystical vision of beauty, that sets my heart a flame.
Without this angel in my arms, my heart will no longer beat,
For only when I am with her, is my heart complete.
   Robert Cohen

A Woman's Heart

Sunlight or moonlight sparkling in her eyes, a woman's heart grieves.
A woman's heart knows loss.
It is not the travail and pain of pushing life into this world that
   hurts her so.
It is the inability to contain, to hold, to protect that life that
   wounds her heart.

Insistent and so brave, life bursts forth and draws it's own daring
   breath.

Earth born, woman born, she can but hold out her woman's hands;
To steady, to comfort, to guide, to touch...to pray?

Life sparkles in her eyes. She knows joy.
Yet the knowledge of the loss remains, within her woman's heart.

Does she grieve the ocean, the stars, the sun, the moon, the sky?
She cannot...they belong to her.
Constant and brilliant in her eyes they mirror her hope.
She goes to them, when she chooses - when she must.
They lighten, but have not the power to replace the grief that lies within.

It is then that her wailing will be heard.

She's learned by now...that they live there together...joy and grief.
Within her woman's heart.

Creating at the last, simply, a heart beat strong here within this
   circle of life.
   Sharon Skywater

Volunteer

Volunteer, volunteer
A word we very rarely hear.
They give up hours of their day,
To spread joy and kindness along the way.
How can we ever repay?

They are beautiful people with hearts of gold.
What they do for others is seldom told.
Hats off to volunteers young and old!!
What more can I say,
How can we ever repay?
   Nancy J. Huratiak

The Unspoken

Out of the mouths of babes came the wind.
A Zephyrling that bore the name of the who spoke it.
They unearthed the shadow of its soul,
Only to be uttered in silence.

So tell the stars, the sun, the moon, the sea.
Then, and then and they are freed.

The rage of dreams reeks passionless among them.
Their honorless patrons sought solace in it.
Speak once, twice, thrice and hush now.
The dormant ones are the martyrs of time.

So tell the stars, the sun, the moon, the sea.
Then, and then and they are freed.

Their timid whispers, food for her.
They fueled the fortress of her ancient being.
Empowerment is in its name, she said.
They spoke the traitorous Unspoken.

So tell the stars, the sun, the moon, the sea.
Then, and then and you are freed.
   Tracy P. Rud

The Bet

I made a bet with John today
About a game that's on Sunday.

The bet was a million dollars times ten.
It's alright, I know I'll win.

I jump and shout but never fret.
I just know I'll win this bet.

That pitiful guy is gonna lose.
I might as well take a snooze,

'Cause the game I don't need to see.
I already know who the winner will be.

Now the day of the game is here.
Poor John, he'll owe me till next year.

The game's almost over, the score is close.
But I dream of money, I'll be so grandiose.

Then I stop to look at the score.
I'm not dreaming anymore.

And now my face is wet with sweat
His team throws a touch down and.....
   A A A A A H H! I lost the bet!!!!
   Matt Schmidt

Addictions

Wasted time is tugging on your shoulder
Acceptance of expectations wrongly unfulfilled
Waiting, wanting, wishing

Normal states seem unappreciative
Harmony exists on unrealistic levels
Selfishness, self-pity, self-indulgence

Repetitions of events known only too well
Disappointment is a major reoccurrence
Guilt, greed, gloom

Escapism? Maybe
Relief? Maybe
Sorrow? Maybe
Reality? Always
Doubt, disturbance, destruction

Finding never
Searching ever for what is desperately needed
An addiction worthy of my addiction
Lesa Sirmon

Easy She Walked

Easy she walked,
across the barrenness of her own being.
Her left was strewn with the untold multitudes
of a race forgotten and abandoned by its very maker,
drowning eternally in an abyss of their own construction.
Her right was the grave, lonely, dark, chilled with memories
of things which never were nor ever would be.
She left behind a husband, a son, and a life she never loved.
Her future was a boundless dessert
quenched by the rays of a dying moon.
Her tears lay unshed.
Her heart unmoved.
Through the smell of brimstone,
Easy she walked.
Mark McQueen

If Flowers Could Be Sisters

If flowers could be sisters I would pick you.

I would sprinkle you with sunshine and
add a splash of dew.

If flowers could be sisters I would make just enough rain,
to shower you lightly so you would grow every Spring.

If flowers could be sister I would color you bright!
I would hold you ever so gently, but never too tight.

If flowers could be sisters, I would pick you,
and you would pick me too.
Muriel Pitts

Life's Lesson

Life holds many things, some that can change
and some that stay the same.

If you see life thru eyes of a learner, and
not a spectator, you'll be able to see and
feel very thing to its greatest extent.

With each lesson learned, remember to smile
because your that much closer to peace and
happiness within.
Sherrie Hugunin

Rain Dance

A gusty wind came down the street,
Adding dirt and leaves to the oppressive heat..
The sky grew dark and thunder cracked,
And rolled from cloud to cloud and back.

The rain, at first in whispers blurred
My window, then it washed, and stirred
A boiling caldron in the street,
And beat upon my roof with thunderous beat.

Through the rain swept glass was born,
A vision of heathen dancers leaping in the storm.
My blood began to rise, my heart to race.
I was being drawn to a wild imaginary place.

Run out, run out, into the street,
And lose all thought but the pounding feet.
Leap and turn to the maddened drum,
Splash through gutters, brimming...run...

Then suddenly... just as it had begun,
The rain stopped...and the peeping sun
Set emeralds sparkling in the grass.
The glistening trees sighed happily at last.
Robert Peterson

A Leaf's End

One leaf hangs on a tree's stem,
Afraid of the merciless wind
Autumn brings: He knows his life
Will soon be over.

He has seen his brothers drift
From the tree — their dear mother
Who bore them as small buds
That distant spring day.

Old and wrinkled, he clings, scared,
Wishing for the past, when he was young,
Green, and strong enough to withstand
Nature's horrendous wind.

With a sigh to the wind, he releases his hold
And gusts take him in his final dance.
His sacrifice allows another to be born...

And so the dynasty continues.....
Lisa Boggs

My Friend

I don't ask much, only that you accept what I extend.
After all, isn't that an important part of being a friend?

I can't honestly say I want nothing in return from you,
for I'd be lying if I denied I need to be needed too.

I laugh with you; cry with you,
and share so much of what you do.

We are connected, yet separate;
  living individually,
but bonded by more than what we view.

Yet, I wonder if you trust anyone
enough to open your heart—-
or have all the battles made you feel alone—-
so retreating is safer than another start?

Please, dear friend, don't keep your fears from my eyes.
Don't tell me what I want to hear—I don't want lies.

I'm never going to be perfect, but I will allow you inside
to all the facets that make me who I am—-
as long as you don't hide, and to the same principles abide.

I love you!
Libbie Richman

When She Cries

Do you see her heart aching,
After you were breaking her heart.
Don't you know she cries at night,
Hoping that everything be all right.
She has so much love in her eyes,
She promised that she wouldn't tell any lies.
She has always been scared,
Until you helped her to be prepared.
She has so much love for you,
And you will always know its true.
Please love her with all your might,
For that she will never leave your sight.
Right now she is in pain,
And she will never be the same.
Are you going to leave or stay,
She doesn't want you to go away.
If you do decide to leave let her know,
Then she will let you go.

Kylee Templin

Starless Nights I

These streets are paved with silver and gold
Ah, yes the golden streets.
But we tend to laugh and then ignore
The sound when midnight weeps.

Belittled by the mockery,
Supplied by bright lights and cars.
True beauty seems to elude us all,
For the night's too bright for stars.

To stare into the moonlit night,
With unsuspecting eyes.
And listen with ears that cannot comprehend
The sobs as midnight cries.

So we walk the streets of silver and gold,
Surrounded by the lights.
And frown to face another day
And cry to face the night.

Melvin C. Perrow II

A Fish Story

They say that fish is food for the brain
And who am I to deny that it's true
Because its been proving by scientist of fame.
That there are suck things as fish schools.
And in these schools they must teach these fish
To bite and dart quickly away.
and the ones that we catch.
Are the bad little fish.
That played hokey from school that day.

Mickey Aubuckon

It Was Needed

The house is old, and empty here.
All alone it stands from year to year.
Snow drifts up against the door.
Pushing the cold air across the floor.
Everyday the old house creeks.
All alone on an empty street.
It was once filled with warmth and beds.
Now it's nothing but boards and webs.
It use to be an Orphan home.
For Children who were left alone.
It's walls, are still full of laughter and love.
As its served it's purpose from the man above.

Merla Lingle

"My History"

African History is mine and I want to know it all
All about the rising of the Songhay Nation and the fall
I want to hear about Askia the Great, and how he took Songhay
The way he made it rise and multiply.

I want to know about Antar, the poet and slave
To hear about all the things he did, how he was so brave.
I want to hear all the beautiful poems he wrote,
About all the love for his wife he was willing to promote.

A lot of my history is orally passed,
From generation to generation is how they made it last.
Although this is true, there's a lot written down
So that people like me can finally wear their crown.

Lakeshia Williams

One Minute In Oklahoma City

One minute and they were gone.
All because one person decided to be mean.
Floors caving in, children crying.
One minute and they were gone.

I came home from school and heard the news.
Innocent children crushed to death.
Average, working Americans killed at their desks.
One minute- and they were gone.

Broken bones, bloody bodies.
Gore that was not needed.
There are other ways to express oneself.
One minute- and they were gone.

Teddy bears, blue sheets of paper, roses.
Nothing can replace the lives lost.
One man, a truck full of death.
One minute- and they were gone.

I can only say I'm sorry.
I can only keep you in my prayers.
For I am only one person, but one can make a difference.
One minute- and they were gone.

Kelly K. Faulstich

I Saw God Wash The World

I saw God wash the world today,
All dirt and slime were washed away.
Every blade of grass was clean,
Making the lawns cleaner than I had ever seen

The birds and beasts all got a bath,
But to count them all would be a lot of math.
God has the power to do all things,
including cleansing ponds, rivers, streams and birds' wings.

When I see how clean all outside things are,
I feel as if I am seeing them from afar.
Oh! how I wish God had also washed me,
As clean as He did that old magnolia tree.

Modine G. Schramm

Photo Album

As I open the book to my past
And see how different things were then
I sit there turning page after the page
Wishing I was there again
Where people had more time for one another,
And we see each as sister and brother
But now a-days, everyone is each to their own,
Always in a hurry, but never knowing where to go.
So far to enjoy things as they were
I open my book to my past
And wish, I could bring those days back.

Sheila Bax

Last In My Memory

Just in an instant my thoughts of you take over without warning.
All else fades around me then my dreams carry me until morning.

In the midst of the confusion-through the laughter-
Your memory hits me.
And the lights seem to grow dimmer, the music turns to silence,
And you are with me.

In the middle of the night, I awake abruptly, reaching for your arm.
And in the eyes of a stranger, I see YOU in his charm.

In the middle of a conversation, I lose track of thought.
And I can hear your voice whisper memories- and in them I get caught.

My eyes see the pictures I had taken in my mind. All else disappears.
If only you could measure my love by the amount of fallen tears.
All my lost feelings seem to show up in a musical display,
When a song reads my mind of all I long to say.

You fill my eyes with memories and with dreams-You leave me no choice.
You steal my quiet time of Silence when I can only hear your voice.

Just in an instant, your love takes me back to a moment far passed.
And even if not in the future, there will always be a place
where our love could last... In my memory.
   Melinda Wells

I Want A Cat

I really want a cat,
all fluffy, and fuzzy and fat,
to meow and purr sweet melodies all day,
and jump around, and pounce and play.

I really need a kitten,
one that's nice so I'll never get bitten.
He'll run, and play and sleep with me,
Please, can't I have a KITT-Y?

They love to play ball,
they balance and don't fall!
They eat fish, and that's cheap,
They sneak around and don't make a peep!

They don't bark, or make messes on the floor,
They don't whine and scratch at the door,
They will rub so sweetly on your leg,
and when you eat they will not beg!

Now you see why I need a cat,
all fluffy, and fuzzy, and fat!
To keep me happy when I'm blue.
Now you see why I need a cat, don't you?
   Susana Churion

Frances And The Mud Pies

I used to make mud pies, when I was just a child.
And feed them to my sister, it drove my Mother wild.
My hands were always muddy, my apron never clean.
To feed them to my sister, my Mother said "was mean"
Now I make sculptures with a different kind of clay.
Some that can be fired, some that harden right away.
With plastic that is soft, and colors that are bright.
Directed by the hand of God, I sometimes get it right.
I used to make mud pies, when I was just a child.
I'd feed them to my sister.
How could I know she'd die so young, and
how much I would miss her.
   Laura T. Krieger

Untitled

As the day goes by, I think of you.
   All I get are feelings of blue.

I think of all the good times; and the bad.
   Wondering why we are always so mad.

When we try, our Love is Great.
   But when we don't, there is only hate.

I thought Love was supposed to come out ahead.
   Where is our Love? Is it dead?

No, no. Our Love is too strong, it can not die.
   Then why is it leaving, tell me why?

Let us put down our sword and our shield.
   Our Love is one we have yet to build.

It's not too late, I know it's not.
   We know we love each other, for this we taught.

So let's really try to forgive and forget.
   And try to remember when we first met.
   Terri Rollins

Soldier Boy

A lonely boy so far from home in a desert he is sent to roam;
A tent set up for dorm, in a war known as Desert Storm.
Because of a man named Hussein who seized a country in his name,
to hold in his possession, we were sent to fight aggression.
Nations form an allied force, war is set to run its course;
But in the end, when all is done, we'll see the fall of an Iraqian son.
And when the soldier has time alone, his mind wanders to a distant home,
He thinks about his family and his wife, and how the war changed his life.
Alone with his thoughts and his fears, a single tear on his cheek
   did appear
But amidst his heartache and his sighs, he knows where his duty lies.
And as the soldier sits and waits, so much support back in the states;
Yellow ribbons, flags held high "'Til they all come home" will be
   our cry.
   JoAnn Koppenhaver

"World's Greatest Dad..."

I can still remember your laugh and smile,
Along with the joy, you brought to our hearts
You were always willing to walk that extra mile,
To see that your family would never split a part.

You gave us all of your tender loving care,
never once asking, "What can you'll give me?"
At times we thought you were mean and unfair
But the love for us, in your heart, we couldn't see.

You worked extra hard to give us all we had,
while all we done was keep asking for more
our memories of you are sometimes happy and sad,
But your life here with us, was never a dull or bore.

It's been 8 years ago since you left us that day,
with us never knowing whether you were happy or sad,
The good Lord sent his angels to carry you away
Saying, "Bring forth Billy Martin", the World's Greatest Dad!
   Tina Lester

Pondering

Personal destiny our edge of reality,
Alter or advance perspectives understanding.
Thoughts programmed in memories,
Between self and spiritual world sifting.

Small part of brains imagination,
Pondering what struggle was about.
Thee trail stretches on timelessly,
Flowing onward humanities river route.

Ponders feeling of deep spirituality,
Mystery of past present overwhelms.
Eternities vistas awesome search,
For us a vibrant question realm.

Dusk falls upon rescinding era,
Earth brushes heavens yard.
Tomorrow are today's yesterday,
Weep not the changing guard.
   Margaret Scholl

Trick And Treat

The weather went tricking and treating before Halloween.
Although October was still in her teens
Snow had fallen all through the night
Shrouding everything in a ghostly white.

The treat arrived with the break of day
With the feeling that Christmas was on it's way.
The trees presented a beautiful sight
As they stretched their boughs to reflect the light.

Since winter had decorated the place
The windows now sported a new pattern of lace.
Except for the steepest the roofs were snow covered
As if to keep warm together they hovered.
   Rachel Farmer Raska

Always And Forever

Always and forever, you know that I am there.
Always and forever, you know that I do care.
A friend is not just anyone, together a team.
Always and forever, a friend will share your dreams.
A friend is someone special, a friend is always near.
Always and forever, you know that I am here.
Always and forever, through happiness and tears,
Always and forever, a friend will share your fears.
At times a friend may hurt you and wonder what they've done.
Always and forever, we forgive them every one.
Through happiness and laughter, sorrow, heartbreak, and tears,
Always and forever, friendship last through years.
Unconditional, loving, strong friendship will endure.
Always and forever, in pain friendship's a cure.
Always an forever, is more than what you see.
Always and forever is what friendship means to me.
   Laura Van Wye

Abortion

An outrageous number of
Babies, seeds that have not yet sprouted, are being brutally
   murdered everyday
Out of
Reckless acts without
Thinking of what precious life may be lost
In the future
Only to
Never know existence
   Victoria Helmer

Ownership, <u>My</u> Freedom

I did it. I took me
amongst the red woods and pine trees,
on a cliff,
on a bed of pine needles on the warm earth.

The waves were crashing,
the icy breeze caressing,
and the sun was warm and tender
all through my body.

I came to the understanding with myself.
That *my dad does no longer own my body.*

I have taken charge and won.
Standing in the breeze and letting the wind cleanse
   my ahead, shoulders,
      breast and belly,
   my femaleness, and all through me.

I took delight in me, I took myself where I've never been before.

Feeling freer and more whole and more solid.
And really claiming me
to be for me *and me alone*,

Unless, and when I *choose* to share.
   Pnina T. Loeb

Life...

I taste the sweetness each time I savor
an apple from a tree,
a berry from a bush.

I hear the music every moment I linger to listen
to the wind in the air,
to the crickets at night.

I smell the purity always as I breath in
the aroma of flowers,
the scent of every season.

I feel the love indefinitely as I embrace
the touch of a kiss to my lips,
the touch of a helping hand to my soul.

I see the miracles everywhere as I open up
my heart,
my mind.

I cherish the precious moments
of life.
   Tara Kaffenberger

Sundays In The Paradise Garden

There hovers in the Paradise Garden
An atmosphere of expectation.
But perhaps it is the ruby-throated humming birds,
Flitting through the dewy mist of morning that I hear,
And not the muffled cries of unborn cactus blossoms,
Struggling, to burst their budded bonds of nature,
That they might effloresce in brilliant colored triumphs
To greet the grand magnificence of morning
In this, my private Eden.
But no matter.
I still thank God for nature and my life,
And as for all the joy and quiet serenity
Of my Sundays in the Paradise Garden,
I thank the gardener by whose love and care
I am embraced by beauty everywhere.
   Larry Gaskill

Salvation Army

She hides behind her hair flowing like a muddy river,
an attempt to disguise her shame,
victim of the cards that have been dealt to her.
She scratches up a few meager
coins from the cushions of the sofa she doesn't have
to buy enough clothe her child's frail body
and feed their hungry mouths.
The cold December winds blow her hair back,
away from her dirty face aged beyond its years.
She pulls her shawl close around her bony shoulders
and throws a furtive glance to the sides,
though checking if they had been seen,
scurrying 'cross the street
filled with busy Christmas shoppers.
her timid child huddles close,
clutching a tattered stuffed animal
nervously tugging on her momma's
sleeve, as if to question their very existence.
The spenders push by them,
not even acknowledging their presence.

Kristin Mumper

Something Other Than The Night

Picture a place, the face of a ghost
an engraved image conjured by sleep
an accumulation of loneliness and longing
heaving upward and inward
a rising vibrato imbuing all senses
as the presence draws nearer
dark and smooth atop my pale stillness
a razor sharp silhouette of a lover long passed
eyes cut of crystal cobalt fall upon mine
raw mirrors of human desire
aligned in the needle point of time
for a moment
a distant vibration interrupts
the dream is broken
image fragments, rising in flight
swept heavenward
leaving the residue of yearning on my lips
and the lingering memory of
something other than the night.

Robert Reese

One Precious Spring

As tender drops float softly to the ground,
an exuberant ecstasy is my dream.
O, wish I to awake and find it so,
that fields of dust could be wet by God's love.
Then might my bounty, once vibrant and lush
from springs gentle sun and delicate rain,
come alive again as if in rebirth
to a vivid green and a fresh new life.

Harsh fiery waves burst forth from heaven
to awaken men from glorious dreams,
and to whither the fields which once were green.
So shall my soul whither in yonder dust.
Should I expect any less? Is it not
true that man has but one precious spring?

William Urban

What Do You See?

What do you see when you are looking at me?
An old woman who should have died years ago?
A bag of twisted bones, with dried up,
wrinkled skin?
Unable to care for herself,
Lonely and miserable,
I am the last one.

Do you know what I see?
I am young and beautiful, in my mind's eye,
My mother was so kind,
And taught me all I needed to know,
To help me grow into the warm,
and compassionate woman I am.

I am young, in my mind,
And I don't have much time,
So please be kind and gentle with me,
What do you see as you look at me?
What do I see when I look at you?
All that I was and wanted to be.

Shirley Tsosie

The Heat

The southern sun
And a blue sky
Causes an explosion of heat
Where cactuses can hardly survive

   And you
   You and you
   Want to be in love
   And even want hotter sky at night
   With stars around
   And the sun every day in your life.

Because; as you know
The desert on the hottest days of summertime
Under the southern sky
Can be green and shadowy
When the essence of life
   Does exist

And you feel it
And you know it
Just love
Is the essence of our life.

Wojtek Mozdyniewics

Recollection

With deep affection
   and a constant recollection;
I often find myself thinking of you.
   On this I ponder,
   as my mind begins to wonder;
   What ever happened
   between us two?

The pleasant waters that flow
   from my mind;
   slowly trickles down to my hearts oasis.
For there is where all the
   memories are dwelling;
As I recall all our happy meetings places.
Back then the torrents of your love were
   as flood waters;
   that just keeps running in deep
   to water my ever waiting soul.
I miss you; I really do!

Theodore L. Mungin

Springtime

In spring all nature comes awake
And a new lease on life we seem to take.
The streams are full and rush along,
The birds are singing a beautiful song,
Woods are dressing in many greens
And flowers are blooming as new blown queens
Farm animals - the poultry too
Are taking on a life a new.
So are the animals in the wild.
And look! There goes a barefoot child
Though he is young and I am old
A new lease on life we seem to hold.

Myrtle Price Massey

Lost In A Dream

I know a big deep canyon where a lone pine grows
And a small creek wanders cool and slow.
All mother's children come and go
A coyote, a rabbit, then a gentle doe.

Then in dreams I see it all.
The ground shakes, dust clouds rise and fall
While thunder echoes from the canyon wall.
Echoes that proclaim, "I'm king of it all."

No, not a hungry lion with kill in his eyes
But a firey stallion and his band he drives.
Wild as the wind and with a challenge in his eyes
This land was his; they called it Wild Horse Paradise.

He roamed his kingdom wild and free
Now, dim trails and dry bones are what you see.
They're gone now, his kind just not meant to be,
I weep with the little creek and the old pine tree.

Leland E. Peters

His Call

As the final day of life closes, and the disease meets God's request,
and answers the call of his sweet gentle voice, to lay his soul to rest.

Love ones come from near and far, to pay their last respect, with
their eyes filled with tears, and a heart so sincere, they weep but hold no regrets.

Although you cannot see them, they still live in your heart and as
long as your love is forever strong from you they will never depart.

No man can define the reason for death, or knows when the hour will
fall, but trust in God, have faith in his word, for we all must answer

His Call

Rodney Lawson

What Would It Take To Win Your Love?

If I could capture the light of a million stars
  and brighten your days forever,
  I would do it.

If I could sail you away on a soft gentle breeze
  and float across oceans into endless tomorrows,
  I would do it.

If I could give you the peace of a walk in the woods
  and help you feel oneness with His divine plan,
  I would do it.

And if I could stretch out my arms and hold your soul
  and show you how truly beautiful you are,
  I would do it.

Yes, I would do all these things and even more,
  because to me that's what loving you is for.

Marsha M. Mauro

Origin

What ancient man of my blood has given my eyes,
and brought shape to my limbs?

Where lies the begin of me?

I have been in the past
and will go on forever in my limbs.

They will change some to little to die,
or to lose what I was before I am,
and what I am before I'd been,
and what had been still lives to have.

So when my turn of limbs have felt the last
my son; they are yours to grab
hold to what feast your eyes
and relish the day of realize

Ancient blood is not a was but is; today
a never ending change unchanged.

I will always touch, feel, and live for me,
for vein I know.
Their was no me to form just form to me.

I am no origin for it will always be
unknown; and so will me.

R. Michael Gallegos

Daughter

It came like a blackness covering her youth
  and changed her life forever.
It stays like the shadows on a snow covered night
  that the moon will always uncover.

Though she's gifted and bright and happy with a joy
  that only angels could know.
It rears its ugly head just when
  we'd hoped it finally did go.

It's a dark and lurking monster
  who has no mercy or fears
Of drugs, of doctors, of growing up,
  of prayers, of wishes, of tears.

If wishing could make dreams come true,
  I'd wish my life for hers
So she might once again feel free
  of this terrible demon she serves.

But even through this Darkness Veil
  it's rainbows that she sees.
She lives her life like a butterfly
  for the day she again will be free.

Kathy Brumbaugh

Life's Wonders

When autumn leaves begin to fall,
And clutter slowly upon the ground,
They represent a change for one and all;
It's a beautiful change to be found.

Lovers walk among the swaying trees,
And the cool winds blow to make their stand.
There is beauty there for those who see,
And Love for the opened heart and hand.

Life is so dear to us
With its many wonders and changes;
It holds a lot for those who find
Some beauty and goodness in all mankind.

Renee Mickle Smith

Escape From The Slum

I slam my fist against my chest
And declare loudly that I protest
To this life that I am living, which is not meant for me,
Because I cannot smile, I only sulk in misery.
I watch the roaches as they crawl,
In and out of the holes on my wall.
Somewhere in the streets, I hear a woman yelling,
Shouting out how good the stuff is that she's selling.
I can't wait until my boy get back,
Cause he's gone to buy us a few rocks of crack.
We'll get high and move to Beverly Hills,
Driving those big Coup De Villes.
We'll spend money and mingle with only the rich,
And get away from here, ain't life a bitch.
Damn the high will be over soon,
And I'll be stuck back in this world of gloom.
I know that one day I'll be found dead,
From an overdose or a bullet in the head.
Someone will find me and say t hat Odis has past,
But my tombstone will read Odis has escaped the "SLUMS" at last.

Odio Harris Jr.

My Family And Me

I have a father and mother,
And double one brother.

I'm their sister, the only one,
And they don't think I'm any fun.

I'm short compared to both of them,
I'm like a tiny flower stem.

They're in college unlike me,
I'm still in elementary.

We have three horses that I ride every day,
And sometimes I go to their stable just to play.

I like to recycle cans and all,
And my brothers, they like to play basketball.

First it's Jason, my brother,
Then it's Nathan, my other.

I really love my family,
I'm as happy as a kid could be.

Stephanie L. Vaughn

This Thing Called Love

It encircles the universe
   and every inch of space,
It even covers the earth
   and embraces the human race,

You can't really see it
   even though it is there,
It's really nice to keep it
   but, feels much better to share.

God, gave it to us freely
   the supply will never run out,
When you share it with others
   the wonderful feeling makes you want to shout.

From the top of Mount Everest
   to the bottom of the Mariana Trench,
Covering the entire globe
   it's thirst you cannot quench.

God, gave it to mankind
   like the wings of a dove,
There is plenty to go around
   this thing called love.

Steve Faulkner

Discovery Beach

I temporaled on the beach one balmy day
and gazed to the sun shooting out deep rays.
The winds from the east beckoned to the sand,
the water splashed and splithered in my wrinkled hand.

I wrestled in the air as I jumped to the sky,
and all at once it seemed my mellifluous heart could fly.
My mind was overflowing with dreams and thought galore,
and discovery was idle with an open door.

My feet were truly gliding against the rapid sea,
I locked myself in imagination and threw away the key.
I whisked across the blazing sand where rainbows shot out stars,
and looked up through capacious skies, where grief was kept in jars.
I quickly found the mind was blithe in this little kid,
so GO, DISCOVER! I DARE YOU!
You'll be glad that you did!

Molly Reed

One Fine Day

One fine day

I am going to get down on one knee
And gently kiss your outstretched hand

I am going to hold you tight
And tell you about my future plan

One fine day

We are going to promise each other
Eternal joyous love and seal it with a kiss

We will then go on a honeymoon
To the enchanted land of mystical bliss

One fine day

We are going to climb lovers mountain
And stroll up among those stars

We will float like two beautiful
Butterflies aboard magic carpet cars

One fine day

We are going to dance the light fantastic
Until the final story is told

We will then go visit the glorious rainbow
And slide down to the pot of gold

Terry Lee Kerr

Marriage

Sincerity is solid ground with love as its foundation,
And honesty erects the walls of truth,
Commitment is the roof above that shelters out dissension,
The fireplace inside keeps warm the loving of our youth.

Enthusiasm is the bread of happiness forever,
Devotion is the meat that keeps us strong,
We satisfy our daily thirst with wine of thoughtful sharing,
And eat the fruit of true humility when we are wrong.

The darts of animosity can find no place to anchor,
The soothing sword of laughter quells the pain,
Affection stabs an angry heart, its loving blade, a comfort,
The spear of our forgiveness is the love that will remain.

We warm our souls with photographs, nostalgic thoughts to guide us,
Before our eyes our younger years burn bright,
But growing old together is the lightning of our loving,
And our embrace as man and wife sets fire to each night.

Kamal A. Saadoon

My Mother

I often think of my mother
And how hard she worked for us all,
But never did she complain
Luxuries of life she had none
But never did she complain
She would wash and iron our clothes each day
for we had little to wear, but never did she complain
She would read her Bible each day
and pray for us all to live right
Now she's resting up there I know
For rest she had none her below.
I will always remember the
Wonderful mother I had, and how hard she worked for us all
and never did she complain.
   Tommie F. Hume

When The Rose Is Truly Blue

I see brilliant colors everywhere I look,
and I feel as if I'm dreaming.
But the air I breathe smells clean and pure,
and sweet like dew drops gleaming
on the early morning blades of grass,
and the flowers as they 'waken.
I see glitter dancing all around me
and I realize as I'm shaken,
that it's just the sunbeams bouncing off the drops
of moisture in the air.
I hear laughter and I feel the thoughts
of others off somewhere.
I remember how the world was when
I knew the day was near.
I pass a bush off to my right,
and I know it's finally here.
It's not a dream, this world I see.
It has been born anew.
And right beside me, living proof,
The rose that's truly blue.
   Rosemarie E. Bishop

Outside My Window

It is spring,
and I look out my window to see,
beautiful birds chirping, people bike riding, everything blooming,
and the wind in a peaceful breeze.

It is now summer,
and I look out my window to see,
flowers, trees, birds, and bees, and fruit,
and children laughing, playing, and having fun.

Now it is fall,
and I look out my window to see,
leaves falling from trees, birds flying south for the winter,
and dogs barking at trees.

Now cold winter is here,
and I look out my window to see,
smoke rising from chimneys, trees with no leaves,
and cold winds blowing.
   Nazia M. Siddiqi

I Walk Alone

I walk the streets and people make a crowd,
And in that crowd I feel no one is around.
The steps I take don't lead me nowhere,
The pain I feel no one else knows it's there.

The tears I shed are lonely ones,
The smile I wait for feels like it will never come.
My heart beat is slowing down each day,
Sometimes I feel that from this world I should walk away.

I cry out to the presence that I feel,
I know it's the Lord and to him I kneel.
I pray for guidance of my lonely heart,
I ask for safety of this world that by me falls apart.

The place I visit is the house of God,
When the door is opened I say Lord I've come
Visit because I felt of me you had forgot.

Lord I humbly fall to you on my knees,
I pray that my heart and soul for you you'll keep.
Lord I ask of you to give me light to the darkness I'm in,
Lord forgive my mistakes and all of my sins.
   Maria Gonzalez

Time

The pain I have no one can see
And it doesn't hurt anybody but me.
Would I do it over to cause me such pain?
Oh yes, oh yes, again and again.
I listened to the lies, the excuses.
the compliments, the funny things,
bad things and the good things.
Boy I'll say I listened, and I believe it all.
   I enjoyed, I laughed, I cried, I kidded,
I gave, I took, it was never dull.
   The pain is sharp, the pain.
is deep, the pain is real, the pain
is mine...
   But the love will always be there...
just like time...
   Patty Goston

Terror

I am trapped inside a maze
And it frustrates me to a point
Where I slam my fist into the cement wall before me
Blood is dripping from my knuckles
But the pain is not as agonizing
As the maze itself
Every way I turn
A tall brick barrier
Keeps me farther from my destination
I scream out in terror
As I run, the tears sting my blood-shot eyes
Slowly my body weakens
My legs will carry me no further
I fall, letting my hand scrape along the wall beside me
Blood staining the cement - my eyes close
Never to open
Never to see the door before me.
   Shannon Charles

The Gift

Have you ever paused from your daily chores
And looked at the world around you
Have you ever wondered how this came to be
As the beauty of nature surrounds you.

The grass so green, the sky so blue
The geese on the wing up above.
You look at the trees just getting their leaves,
And you hear the song of the dove.

The breeze is blowing so gentle and warm
And the birds are singing so sweetly.
The world is alive with spring in the air
Everything is changing completely.

The sun is shinning so warm and bright
The children are busy at play.
Thank the Lord above for these beautiful things,
Thank you God for these wonderful days.

Ralph H. Lampe

Cowboys Ruled

In a time where hands were calloused
And most the money was round.
A man could see forever
With both feet on the ground.

A fence weren't to keep your neighbors out,
But to hold your cattle in.
And a jail was called a jail
Not a pokey or a pen.

Where you could tell a stranger
By the way he wore his hat.
And every porch in miles around
Laid out a welcome mat.

Only thing you had to worry 'bout
Were your cattle gettin' thin.
And they didn't work on Sundays.
Back then it was a sin.

I wish I lived back then.
I believe that it was best.
Where men were men and really were.
And cowboys ruled the west.

Stacey Dawn Knowlton

My World Of Friends

In this world I live in my own little space,
And my thoughts are not biased by creed or by race.
I accept any friendship that is offered to me,
And if you're in need, a friend I will be.

I feel sorry for those who live in a clique.
They only have time for friends that they pick.
And those who aren't picked and are left in the dust;
Acceptance in a cliques is all that they lust.

All of those people with greed as their friend,
Who want everything but don't want to spend;
Power and money is all they live for.
I wish they'd realize that a friend would give more.

Everyone is different in this world of mine,
But my friends are as numerous as stars that shine.
So next time you're feeling lost and alone,
Just come to me and you'll feel right at home.

Melissa Olson

Oppression

Long beneath the mist of time there lies a silver grass,
and never growing seasons find their winter slipping past.
The only sound is careful feet stepping over crystal paths
to shuffle gently till they meet with latent shards of glass.

There clear air suffers silently, and flowers cannot grow,
for evil cackles blatantly to make the death wind blow.
The sunshine cannot warm, nor does the evening chill.
The neutral, sunless, moonless sky changes not with will.
Ill wishes cause the motions here; effects of actions harm;
the cloud of overhanging fear aids constant alarm.

In frozen soil young seed dies, this all before life knows.
Drowning nature's strangled cries, the coldest liquid flows.

Speaking sordid melody, ashen lips say a prayer;
asks that pain use sparingly its need to hold them there:
a blissful torture chamber catered to the mind,
made to thrash and tamper, delude and help to blind.
This parallel dimension draws one deep inside,
preys on their confusion, begs them to confide.

The ghosts here now imprisoned will travel soon through time,
act on their present vision, and boost their quick decline.

Michelle Dexter

Autumn Cleaning

I missed my spring cleaning, it didn't get done,
And now it is fall and I want to run.
Nowhere to run, nowhere to go,
So I get out the rake, the shovel and hoe.
I won't clean my closets, not this season,
Fall is for planting, can't question the reason.
Dig in the dirt, the rich Earths soil
Planting a tree, it take lots of toil.
Turn over the dirt, my spirit and soul,
Help make me feel new, I want to be whole.
Dig way down deep, get to the bottom,
I look for the answers, but only He's got'em.
He's been with me, through rain and snow
And now is the time to finally let go!
They say that spring is the time for growth
I say Autumn, my solemn oath...
To grow in His love, His mercy and care,
No need to run, I'm already there.

Linda Gauck

Oneiric Octave

In a lecture hall, filled with erased blackboards
and numerous blank stares, our eyes have met many times.

Once, in a crowded hallway, our eyes even met openly
as you went down and I came up, the staircase.

I should have pinched my leg to suppress the fear
which gnawed within me not to say hello.

Still...I have tumbled euphorically with you,
on avocado green, and powder blue sheets.

My lips have glided over yours —
like a kitten glides its tongue over silky fur.

I have stared blankly out windows at elbow-shaped trees,
to suddenly find your arms about my waist, as you nestled
your smooth chin in the nook between my neck and shoulder.

I have shivered while driving down highways, watching
streetlights flickering reflections upon payments glazed with ice,
as instantaneously you drove the chill from my body...
placing your head on my chest; resting your hands in my lap.

I have shared all of this with you, and so much more...but,
I dare not flitter my eyelids when the alarm rings
for you may not be there.

Tony Smeaton

A Voice Through Time

I was here for all of it,
And on that ship I had to sit.

In that ship with people sick and dying,
Families and friends left for crying.

Mean and nasty are what they are,
Taking us to a different land so far.

The crack of the nasty whip is all we heard.
When we stopped to take a breath or look at a bird.

Since we can't turn back the time,
A paper of freedom we will sign.

Giving us equal rights and such,
It's hard to believe we've conquered so much.

But even now in the world today,
People can't walk around and be ok.

People must understand that we are all the same,
No one should down their race or be ashamed.

Someday I hope for people to be treated equally,
Only then can I sleep peacefully.
Stacey Ann Lewis

Dayz

Days pass slow, like big rivers flow
and once there gone, you wonder where they go

Turbulent waters
to trinkling streams
many symbols to life
or so it seems
flooded banks
then prolonged drought
abounding happiness
or impending doubt

Reluctantly proceeding
with a tangled mind
knowing it'll get better
its just a matter of time
years and years latter
its better at last
open your eyes from dreaming
your days have passed
Randall Lee Smith

Dead Poets

Poe stabbed the hearts of the poets
And slit their jugular vein
Starless nights and crimson tides
Drank their blood, and went insane
Jim sang the most to me,
He made me laugh, and he made me weep
Dante's "Inferno", brought me down
Where there's demons, monsters, and creeps

Dead poets
I love them all
Though some are big, and some are small
Dead poets
I love them all
They speak to the heart of us all
Robert D. Duggan

Aged Wisdom

"Wisdom comes with age" says she,
And so "Grow old along with me, the best is yet to be?"

But, wisdom, age and me? I burst with laughter tears
At my snow-mountain top and wobbly knees.

How odd? We strut across life's stage
With our smug lips and fretful scowls.
Character act each scene with intensity-pomposity.

But, wisdom, age and me? Another belly laugh
At what I do perceive in youth so tight; adult so cool.

A sniff, a taste again of fools food fed
Me long ago.

Oh, I recall so well tick-tock-time
And gulped that Siren's call: succeed! succeed!

But now, chuckle ripples tickles
Touch the ivory black and white of hoary age
To relish sound sense newness symphony.

But, wisdom, age and me?
Roar out, old lion, roar.
Mark-seal on time no fretful sigh
But laughter tears to tease at what you spy.
William A. Beaver

Unfair

God, why is life so unfair?
And so hard to bare.
Why did you have to take my baby cousin away?
He never got the chance to wake up to see the very next day.
His blond and precious big blue eyes;
Only left his family and parents filled with cries.
A smile that cannot be forgotten because it always ran
   a thousand miles.
Mickey was his favorite toy;
and he always brought his parents joy.
His soft, baby white skin that always smelled so fresh
   and clean;
A child that loved to laugh and to never act mean.
Oh baby Justin how it's so unfair how God took you away
   before the break of day.
I miss you a lot;
And I will never forget you;
Even though life's so unfair;
Baby Justin you'll have a part in the middle of my heart.
Katherine Byal

Magic

I saw a sun setting a while ago.
And the colors reflected on the water below.
I heard the waves gurgle as they met the shore.
I never saw anything so beautiful before.

I'd seen my share of sunsets in my time.
So, what made this moment stick in my mind?
I've seen the water turn fire as it dipped and waved.
So, why is this memory so deeply engraved?

Because, when my mind forms this picture, I see,
You're there, too, standing right next to me.
Everything is beautiful if you're there, too.
You add a touch of magic to everything we do.
Kristi Maitilasso

All At The Back Of My Mind

There are so many feelings of things I've seen,
and so many hopes no one can find.
So many places I have been,
all at the back of my mind.

All at the back of my mind there'll be,
a place only for me.
Feelings of caged and those of free,
all at the back of my mind.

Seasons come and seasons go,
Songs at rhythm and those of rhyme,
Stars shine and Milky Way flow,
all at the back of my mind

Love may come once or many times
dreadful horror and scenes of crime.
Church bells ringing...the sound of chimes,
all at the back of my mind.

People trickle in and out
colors from white to golden lime.
Imagination of how the world will turn out,
all at the back of my mind.

Kimberly Belika Osmond

My Dad

The years have flown since he was young
And some would say his song has been sung.
They would be satisfied and content
But not this octogenarian gent.

His body's now frail and weary and worn
But he refuses to fret and mourn
There's cleaning and laundry and cookies to bake
Pay no mind to an occasional ache.

He cares for his wife, who once nurtured him
Bathing her gently and wiping her chin
His work worn hands now gently hold hers
Blinking through tears as a memory stirs.

He lives his life for me to see
What God meant commitment to be
Through simple and tough, through thick and thin
He sets his mind, then digs right in.

How do you measure a man of worth?
Not by height or weight or girth
For though he's only five feet tall
My dad stands highest of them all.

Laverne Jorgensen

A Squirrel Named Nick

Nick is the name.
And Squirrel is the game.

I love to run and play all day.

In the summer it's climbing through the trees.
In the fall, it's rustling through the leaves.

In the winter, it's running across the snow and making tracks.
In the spring, it's time to chase the other squirrels around.

I really like to eat bird seed.
Sunflower seeds are the best.

I'll eat just about anything left out for me.
Leave me some crackers and you will see.

I live to eat, run and play around.
You can see Squirrels like me all over town.

Think of me when you see them.
A squirrel named Nick, that's me.

Roseanne Lesko

If

If I could just crawl out of bed
And start another day,
If I could just stop the tears, then I'd be okay.

If I could just forget about you and think about me,
Then I could get out of life
All that was meant to be.

If I could just sleep without dreaming of you,
I could get rid of those visions
That are in my head, too.

If I could forget what you did
Instead of just forgive
Then maybe this life would be less painful to live.

If the tears would stop falling
Down my cheeks,
If I could stop being
So naive and weak,
If true love could find me,
And tell me no lies,
Then I wouldn't have to
Say good-bye.

Melinda A. Matthews

Untitled

Take from the ocean the sedentary sand which rests calmly at the deep
And stir it up to remind the grains that in them our security we keep.
Rustle the leaves of the mighty tree which commands, in the forest,
    the winds
And whisper to them acknowledgment of the protection which they have
    devotedly afforded our kin.
Tickle the tail of the softest rabbit with the most delicate hand
And perhaps the warmth which she radiates to us, she will understand.
Dance with the monkey who dupes you out of a finely-crafted meal
And let him hear the rhythm of your laughter in response to his
    cunning steal.
Give me the vision to journey to the peripheries of her joy
Whereby I may stumble upon knowledge which fantastically I shall employ,
And with it, to all the world I will sign, about her harmony, about her worth.
As loud as I can, I will sing of the glories of our beloved Mother Earth.

Priti Joshi

To My Loving Sister: Regina

My rebel years I remember well,
And stories of them I seldom tell.
Yours were walked in kindness and grace,
Why couldn't I find that loving place?

You are a true disciple, in every word and deed,
Who am I then, to not take heed.

You are consecrated with reverence and love,
Surely we know, this comes from above.

You walk without fear, in to the hearts of adversity,
While we stand here, with such diversity.

You embrace the world with love and gentleness,
It is we who walk, in daily nothingness.

And so! In fading years I pine.
That I too may someday find.
The treasures and knowledge; your daily traits.
If only I could duplicate.
I Love You

Margaret Watts

A Lovely And Precious Flower

I found a lovely flower one bright and sunny day
And thanked the Son above me for bringing her my way.
I loved my precious flower - her beauty, oh so rare -
Her petals were as soft, soft silk - I wanted her to care

Me and my lovely flower together warmed the sun
As if we did not need him - love and lives had just begun.
I'd shield my precious flower from life's often too bright glare
And hope she'd one day lean on me - I could not help but care.

Oh, life is an uncertain thing - sometimes the sun can't shine.
I see the storm! Its here! Its come! I pray it's not that time!
Please mister sun, this storms too big, our warmth is not enough!
Please won't you help us fight it? Three warmth can be so tough!

But flowers sometimes fade away when storms will block the sun.
Oh how I pray my flower stays, this storm might make her run.
For the beauty of my flower is rare and oh so hard to find -
If someday she would leave me I would surely lose my mind!

So I show my precious flower my ways
How much I care - what she means to me
And promise her if she dares to stay
The sun will again shine and set us both free

Robert Adee

When August Comes

When August comes
and the air is free and spirited with the gentle breeze of summer
The Lion emerges from the den, as youth springs forth from the womb
and mangoes fall ripened from the tree.

But He knew how to lie - 'cause He grew on the streets
And He's hungry for money; for food; for love; for touch...
And He feels the pain of all of the lies, For the truth lies
somewhere off in the distance, flickering at the end of a tunnel.

But August has come and gone
And Your youth lies warm in someone else's arms
While you lie in rest and the herb grows about your head; or is it your feet?
Let down your locks, Jah-Man, and the Truth will awaken -
As the lightening flashes across the horizon;
Our beach is deserted and white.

Remembering images of You and the future that has long ago passed
The love we once had, the dreams we shared
All fade into the Caribbean mist on the dusty mountainous path
And on Lynch's Road you lie in the earth
And the lies you one told echo down caves and cane fields
blowing gently in the wind; when August comes.

Michelle Martin Gonzalez

Life Force

Alive on the crest of the wave,
Alive like the wind in the cave,
Alive like the blue, white and green
Of the waters astonishing sheen

Alive, every atom unseen
Alive, like the seals as they gleam
Alive and still in the sun as they sleep
And dream of the fish alive in the deep

The power, the force, the life of the world
Of the gravitational fields that are curled
In the spinning, whirling, whipping and swirling
Life, in the life, in the life forever unfurling.

Sheila Brooks

"Where's My Daddy Going?"

Where's my Daddy going, a small boy was heard to say,
   And the answer he was given, was, your Daddy must fly away.
He's going with your Mommy, to a state not far from here,
   But they'll be back before you know it, so dry those big, big tears

Little did the President know he'd said his last goodbye,
   Or gazed upon his son's fair face for the last time in this life.
For on that fateful journey, in the year of sixty-three,
   The President was shot and murdered as he rode down a Dallas Street
His death came without warning, his life no more to be,
   And so a small son waiting, his Father he'd never see.

As the shadows cast by men, over wheels of his Dad's last ride,
   One small boy stood straight and tall to salute as the Casson rolled by.
He watched as the big bronze casket was drawn far out of sight,
   And wondered where his Dad was, and how long would be his flight.

On a grassy hillside, they laid his Dad to rest;
   An eternal light was lit, forever to be blessed.
And as the sounds of taps were played, the President's last farewell,
   And all American's knelt to pray, you could hear a small voice well
   "Where's my Daddy going, a Small boy was heard to say:"

And who of us could answer, "Your Daddy died this Day."

Modena Abney

Untitled

Many the times I wanted to pray
And the words so desperately wanted to say
Just seemed to vanish and fade away
I was lost in doubt with much dismay

My burdens grew with no one to share
I asked Lord Jesus don't you care?
Many sleepless nights till break of dawn
Asking Jesus to listen I was so alone

I tried again for words to say,
For I knew our Savior lives to day,
Trying again my problems to solve,
More trials and discouragements seemed involved

If we let Jesus take over and have His way
Our burdens grow lighter each passing day
Don't wait again for words to say,
When you claim His promises before you pray

Jesus will listen when you ask,
He'll give you courage and strength to last
Our days will be brighter and happier too
His love is so deep and His promises true

Nona C. Moore

Teardrop

A single teardrop falls from my eyes,
As I realize how deep my soul is in lies.
I feel so alone, worried, afraid,
Nervous, exposed, even a little bit nave.
As I look into my true love's eyes,
I realize he doesn't know this demise
For he loves one of my best friends
And as I sit an watch them
I wonder, will the pain ever end?
Oh, what can I do? I start to think,
as this solitary teardrop rolls down my cheek.

Laura DePierre

The Man In The Glass

When you get what you want in your struggle for self
And the world makes you king for a day,
Just go to the mirror and look at yourself
And see what the man has to say.

For it isn't your father or mother or your wife
Whose judgment upon you must pass.
The fellow whose verdict counts most in your life
Is the one staring back from the glass.

Some people might think you're a straight shooting chum
And call you a wonderful guy.
But the man in the glass says you're only a bum
If you can't look him straight in the eye.

He's the fellow to please, never mind all the rest,
For he's with you clear to the end.
And you've passed your most dangerous test
If the guy in the glass in your friend.

You may fool the whole world down the pathway of years
And get pats on the back as you pass.
But your final reward will be heartache and tears
If you cheated the man in the glass.

Roy G. Hawley

Money $$$$$

While walking down a road one day, I stopped, looked,
and then said "HEY".
Any soon to come to my surprise, a penny, before my very eyes!
I thought I'd buy a pickle, just before I found a nickel!
Then I said I'd buy a lime, but then soon, I found a dime!
After a while, I "crossed the boarder," until I found a shiny quarter!
And then I just had to holler, because I found a new, flat dollar!
I wanted to go home, but then I just found a ten!
I gave myself a little snitch and said out loud,
"I'M RICH, I'M RICH."
I went home to show my mom, but no one was home, except for Tom.
Tom is my big brother, you see and greedy, greedy, greedy is he!
He took my money away from me!
You'll be in trouble with Mom and me!
I'll show you, you'll see, you'll see!
I got my money back and then...
I found even more again and again!

Kelly Marie Butler

The Dream Of The Perfect Day

Sometimes late at night I close my eyes;
And think of a world that never lies;
I dream I am walking hand in hand;
With a variety of people of this land;
I dream that all fighting and hate would cease;
And we would all get along in perfect peace;
That all racism would be erased from this country;
And all people would sing in sweet harmony;
There would be no poverty or people poor;
There would be no bloody, hateful wars;
A man would be paid for the work he does;
And our tax money would go for a real good cause;
All people would work like they should;
And people were sincere and gave what they could;
Our justice system would be equal for all;
All people would have to obey all laws;
This world would be happy-never blue;
And love would be so precious and true;
I fear my perfect day will never exist;
But only in my dreams in the mist;

Tracy Ann Kidder

I Walked

I walked by a tall tree
And thought of its age, and the strength of its life.
I walked by a stream
And thought of its consistency and ever flowing.
I walked by a nest of birds
And thought of the warmth of a family.
I walked by a group of wild flowers
And thought of the pureness of nature.
I walked by a flock of geese
And thought of togetherness and how one is loyal.
I walked by a mother and daughter playing
in the park
And thought of love and the bond one shares.
I walked by age, strength, consistency, loyalty,
warmeth, pureness, togetherness, and love
Today I walked by you.

Katherine C. Elliott

Revelation

As souls were born into the world, God handed each a box,
and told them what they'd treasure most, were sealed behind their locks.

"But don't despair!" He comforted, "just place your faith in me..."
"I would not hand your dream to you, and not provide the key."

But off each went upon a quest to find their key instead,
and spent their lives in constant search, ignoring all He said.

When time expired at last—they died, and went from where they came,
and begged the Lord to please reveal the answer to His game.

"Where was it?" asked one puzzled soul, "I looked most everywhere,"
"I made my life a living hell—t'was more than I could bear!"

"T'was lack of faith in me," God roared, "and angst about those locks..."
"YOU made your key your TREASURE, so...I locked it in your box."

Oren Dodge

Among Revolutions Mine

T'was in the aperture November condemnation became find
and t'was only by divine sensation I hath changed my mind
alone a hollow sentinel so far from further sheep
and from astray thus I can say what memories I keep
vintage withered fell apart so decadent and compound
the shadow stayed my hell bound heart disastrously profound
disease drew quickly at my thoughts befell my self control
and this obsession is that wrought a cancer in my soul
in my conditions aptitude I silenced innovations
for in such state I desecrate all once loving relations
but as the weapons of the Lord endow us with their chore
so was I felled by spirits sword to make new seed once more
and in times passing slowly though I came to realize
that thus angelic knowledge know a blessing in disguise
and so through intervals of time my blessed soul fulfilled
that stays temptation so sublime less apt and yet more skilled
be steady heart and do not falter nor follow carnal wrath
that when approached the heavens altar 'tis said I stood my path.

Victor Frank Tarros

Helpless

I live between the rock of perfect timing
and the hard place of Chance
watching the shred
I tore from the innuendos in your words
flutter in the breeze of your laughter.
This longing
pressed with your image,
nose on a windowpane,
believes like a child
that all good things come to those who wait.

Kathy A. Peterson

The Bargain

She showed up late for dinner
and was breathless, a bit
sloppy, the cake she had for him
had flipped on its lid
and her guitar was out
of tune
still, she was ready to pick his brain,
play a song or two, and eat his food

He seemed prepared for indifference
still he showed her some chords, threw out a line
just to see if he could reel her in

After a meal, a few beers and
a guitar lesson—their fantasia
they struck a bargain, though unspoken
that it would be a wait and see
game, nothing decided too soon
He'll fish, perhaps for others, and she'll hide
for now
and something started that night will either
fade or bloom

Lauren Bielski

Don't Dance With The Devil

Dazed and confused as we look into the hour glass.
And watch the time diminish as we live within our past
We hold on to our loved ones thinking that there's a chance.
Hoping to catch a firey stare but settling for a glance.

The room is full of faces none of them which you know.
I feel there hearts beating from somewhere down below.
But over in the corner there is a face that's recognized
A little girl in the distance with bright and shining eyes

You hear her calling come over here
I am the light and you have nothing to fear
I am your strength and wisdom I will guide you on your path
The road that lead to righteousness is well within your grasp

To avoid a dance with the devil let the angels in
It won't be an ending it will be a new begin

Lorri Ann Bruner

"Miss Ethel"

Ethel Benson was her name. She stood not five feet
And weighed ninety-eight pounds. Yes, she was petite.
This little lady left the city behind
To live in Edesville and mold the little one's mind.

Tiny but powerful how she won her fight
Against hostile parents lacking in foresight!
For school was folly; there were seeds to be sown,
Fields to be plowed, corn and wheat, yet, to be grown.

She founded the first school of grades one through eight
With kids of all ages; she didn't discriminate.
Her aim was to teach; so, she took no sass.
Thus, one smart boy learned as she tossed him from class.

Lo! seven years this lady taught in one room.
How respect and love for "Miss Ethel" did bloom!
She married Will Johnson, gave birth to her own,
And raised five girls from experience she'd known.

Their names—Louise, the eldest, Carolyn, Elois,
Dorothy, and Bernice. There were no boys.
"Get knowledge with understanding" was her theme.
Our Mom, "Miss Ethel", we hold in high esteem!

Louise J. Bankins

Therapy

You are all the magic that makes the world so dear,
And when you touch me gently, ecstasy is near.
And where we walked together and looked across the sea,
I've marked the spot forever in fondest memory.

I can hear the wanton waves crashing land's devotion,
But none of it compares to passion's grand emotion.
I love the feel of wind in my face,
The joy of living when we embrace.

And in the darkness of the night,
Bodies blurred in pure delight,
You hold my trembling breath so tight,
And give me sun and moon and light!

The happiness we always shared,
The love that showed you really cared,
The taste of your lips whene'er we met,
These are the things I won't forget.

And now that you are gone, your face I'll never see,
I'll know that part of Heaven came down just for me.
For I can go on living as you watch me from above,
For I know a better world since I've felt your love.

Patricia Coulter

Grandparents

They're older than us,
And wiser most will say, and nothing is so special,
As when they hug you, that certain way.
When as a child, you looked at them in awe.
Ever so special, perfect without a flaw.
Spoiling you with attention, as if you could never commit a crime.
Laying you to sleep at night, with a poetic nursery rhyme.
But as you grow older, and spend more time apart.
There's nothing that compares, to their loving feeling in your heart.
It's that extra warm feeling, that makes you feel good inside.
Makes you feel good, with lots of family pride.
They gave you their best, they gave you your parents.
But above all they stand, they're my Grandparents.

Kevin Smith

The Suicide King Is The King Of Hearts

My heart is broke,
(And you have the glue)
You picked up my sword, and then ran me through
My life's bloody hell,
How is it for you?

Your game is done
(I hope you've had fun)
Tell me, where did you sleep last night?
(Who's secret did you keep last night?)

You say I don't need you
(You don't need me)
But tell me Queenie,
(Don't you know?)
You thought you knew me
(Who did you know?)

You tore it out of my chest
And stuck it with darts
Don't you know Queenie?
(The suicide king is the king of hearts.)

Katy Davidson

America's Precious Colors

Our flag's red, white, and blue
  Are precious to me; are they to you?

To some, colors may seem so insignificant,
  But as an American these three should be magnificent.

For red symbolizes the hardiness
  Of our young soldiers who fought regardless.

White symbolizes the purity
  of freedom from England, our mother country.

And blue symbolizes that which is just
  And as a nation in God we trust.

So the next time you see that "Star-Spangled Banner"
  Please don't respond in an apathetic manner.

Remember the reason why it's there to see,
  A high price was paid for our liberty.

Our flag's red, white, and blue
  Are precious to me; are they to you?
    Patricia Spaulding

Farewell My Friend

Why have you gone away, my friend,
Are you watching over me?
Are you finally home, my friend,
are you now finally free?

In the season of white you departed, my friend,
A season of despair.
Nine years ago you left us, My friend,
While still young, and strong, and fair.

You walk with me in my dreams, my friend,
We laugh, we run, we play.
Often I've wished to follow my friend,
To seek our yesterdays.

It seems you're with me now, my friend,
Your memory fresh in my mind.
And 'though I'll join you in time, my friend
For now I shall remain behind.
    Thomas N. Hines

Untitled

Memories of days past tug at my thoughts
As a child I bounced, jumped and tossed
I remember sunshine, green grass, trees galore,
fishing, swimming, camping trips and more

I remember you having a stern hand
when we were bad, correction would land
You were quick to love when hurt we felt
And fast to protect when danger was dealt

You were my idol, a man I'd seen
the kind of man I'd like mine to be
Oh how I cherished my younger years
because that was before all of the tears

The children married, suddenly gone
leaving you with too much time alone
False deception day in, day out
from the bottle your life laid out

Now you're divorced, children you don't see
You're even lonelier than you use to be
    Ruth E. Smith

Untitled

As a youth I only knew of today
As an adult I've found myself scouring the news
High rates of crime keep me searching for better todays
Better to search than to be writing the blues
I once read about World War II
The beginning of a time when parents were taken
You see, World War II were trying times too
I'm so sure I'm not mistaken
Centers developed for the children were taught skills
Yet past ideas are considered over the hill
The idea that government take charge is not new
But cutting of monies means never avenues
Every community is integrated
Yet we survive on our own so often segregated
Too many wandering youths with all of their little
I've noticed how it gives you and I the jitters
Consider the idea of a Community Arts Fund
And a place to gather the old and the young
The value and skills of World War II are not so old
Yet centers in small towns never happen I'm often told
    Linda A. Mull

Quagmire

Your sight dyes my view like a carbuncled fall,
As an image of you that haunts past this hall
Of bricks with light hue, crosses two windows, small,
Where the other resides on the opposite side.

The sun silvers through from the side where you stand,
Between birches that newly are bleached until bland,
By Autumn's adieu and Hades' dark hand,
And bleakness resides on the opposite side.

Tattered but true, I resign and retain
This different view that is always the same;
And still I stare through from pane to pane,
But silence resides on the opposite side.

I don't like the view, what the consequence costs,
But I must get through or my destiny's lost;
So I search for you through the trees and the frost,
But sad I reside on the opposite side.
    Kilian St. Michael

The Poet's Pen

The poet has his life in his hand
As he puts his passion on the line.
Immortality may or may not be his plan
As his tangled thoughts unwind.

Deriving pleasure from a consistent flow
Of rhyming words and rhythmic phrases,
The intensity of his stroke continues to grow
While his stream of consciousness races.

Swimming through the spontaneous stream of life,
Rising to feed on the spawn of my own kind,
Finding offense in society's sentiments and strife,
I drown in the flood of resistance in your mind.

From crude charcoal, then the quill,
The pen has evolved over time.
The ink flows freely from my printer, still,
And the thoughts flow freely from my mind.

It is not the poet's pen that is crude,
This fact must be clearly understood.
For in the mind of a true poet who's nude,
The pen is not ugly or bad. The pen is good.
    Mel Bon

Walk And Think

I took a walk,
As I didn't want to talk.
But to dream, and think and,
Once more from the spring, drink.

My mind stays busy going back over
each day of our lives.
Where we used to live, love...and play.
I went over each second, minute, and hour
of each memorable day.

I wanted to take each step we had
taken together.
To take them again, hand in hand, would
be much better.
Touch each thing we had touched along
the way...and pretend we were together again,
and it was yesterday.
   Pauline Young

The Tide

I walked alone to the sea that day to watch the water flow
As if I had a purpose and knew which way to go.
Arriving a few breaths before the dawn's appointed rise
I stopped to rest beside a Rock and raised my face to the skies.

The glorious moment awoke my soul and my spirit began to climb
The ladder of hope left for me there when I was taught to shine.
Soaring above God's earth below I thought that I could see
The reason why my Spirit has such a hunger to be free.

I sat there wondering, waiting and watching as the day passed slowly by
Should all this beauty be the cause I should still want to try.
To live my life for the One who came and put my Spirit here
The son's rays shot into the sea, in its reflection my mind did clear.

As I sat on the shore, I picked up the Rock and wrote my heartaches
  in the sand
Looked up above in time to see the outline of my Master's hand.
As it pushed the sea a little and then once again
I smiled inside when I realized the tide was rushing in.

I walked alone to the sea that day to watch the water flow
As I turned to leave He tugged my sleeve not wanting me to go.
Until I looked down upon His feet that stood on that awesome shore
And saw that all my heartaches were not there anymore.
   Linda L. Smith

Oakey Ridge Farewell

While on a journey through the South, I suddenly lost my way
At Oak Ridge, Alabama, a sweet, time-forgotten place.
Two old houses, stood weathered and gray, high upon a hill;
Death had made a stop that week, and everything was still.

On a beautiful sunny November day in the early afternoon,
Neighbors gathered, black and white, to sing a mournful tune.
In respect, all heads were bowed, as someone said a prayer.
Red clay dust was everywhere, even hanging in the air.

South Alabama back roads, beautiful hill country, high!
Red and gold autumn leaves under a clear blue sky
All witness the silence of those who grieve,
Sitting on an old porch, folded hands on knees.

An old house, shotgun straight, facing the empty road
Was filled with loving "company," as callers come and go.
Country folks, proud and true, come to call this day
To pay their kindly last respects in their humble, personal away.

Washed and ironed overalls, a forty-year old suit,
Cotton-fields behind the house, standing in salute,
As silent soldiers in a row, standing very high,
Like "White flags," dear friend today, sadly wave "goodbye."
   Lorraine A. Golden

Life As I See It Today

Life has its many pleasures,
As it did in days gone by,
We have to take more safety measures,
For the crime rate is quite high,
People move at a faster pace,
Than they did when I was young,
So many are in the rat race,
You'd think some traps were sprung!
They need to make money galore,
Which slips through their fingers like sand,
"Never enough", always need more,
As everything new they demand,
Many friends they gather fast,
Bought with the money they spent,
Friendships like those never last,
Only those do, that are God sent,
So turn your eyes to God, and you will see,
His best friends will love you for free.
   Kathryn Shaak

Grandma

Your smile fills my memories,
as it did in the past.
Remembering your loving ways,
Your patience, a beacon, it's light cast,
Guiding our troubling days

How many nights did you kneel by our beds?
Helping us say our prayers,
How many times did you just hold our heads?
Showing us how much you cared.

Now Grandma, I know you're listening
And I sure bet you're mighty proud,
Cause just look on down here tonight,
Just look at the size of our crowd.

And, even though you're not with us
Well, you know you're in our hearts,
For if ever there lived a special lady
For each of us Grandma, you filled the part.
   Randy Brower

The Family Reunion

My heart in joyous rapture rings,
As overhead the robins sing,
The old folks sit around and talk,
While others choose to take a walk.

From miles around they came to see
Their parents names on the family tree.
Whose name in high regard we hold
Began with John and Rachael long ago.

The greatest miles traveled, I understand,
Were Gertrude's kids from Alabam'
The oldest one there was none-other
Than our dear Clara, a devoted grandmother.

The youngest of course, was sweet little Paige.
May God bless her at this tender age.
Let her grow up to be strong and tall.
And tell of God's love to one and all.

Smiles and laughter and plenty to eat
Were there for all you happened to greet.
Make your plans now, please don't delay.
The next reunion is just two years away.
   Myra Fercy

My Guardian Angel

My Guardian Angel is drawing near
as she brushes her wings against my hair
Softly she whispers oh so low
I can hear her voice, I'm all aglow.

She's forever watching and leading the way
as I go about my busy day.
She gently takes me by the hand,
and as I follow without a care
I know there isn't danger there.

But should I be frightened or maybe confused
she'll sing to me until I am soothed.
At the end of the day she'll lead me home,
and even though no ones there
I'm never alone...
In moments of silence when all is hushed
I feel her presence at the coming of dusk.
Marilyn S. McCollum

It Must Be

Confuse me with your everyday clothes
  as some faceless thing that I am not.
That is the fastest way to get sap from the rose.
  A sticky, poor substitute for a caress, a blot.
Let me hold you close and clasp you to my heart.
  With all the strength in this carrier of emotion.
I want to make a happy life to love from the start.
  And spend days through time with perfect devotion.
Do I love? I hope, I dare to feel all.
It makes me shiver. I want it to be.
Maura Leigh Keese

Everything I Need

His eyes may not be sapphire
As the proverbial shimmering sea
His hair not the golden perfection
Everyone thinks it should be.

Yet he tempers my "strengths" with his "weakness"
And speaks gently of family ties
He reminds me that we are mere humans.
In a voice like a soft lullaby.

He grounds me with calm words of wisdom
And shelters with true loving care.
With him I will always be safe and complete
In a love that's as warm as it's rare.

So, he may not be a "knight-in-shining-armor"
Riding in on the fabled white steed.
He's not what I thought that I wanted
But, he's everything I really need.
Shari Lu Ahner

From A City Dweller

I must be out on the trail again.
Away from the cities of pale-faced men.
Out where legions of tall pines raise
their twisted arms to the sun's bright gaze.
Again I must walk dim, silent trails
where softly, coolly a thin wind wails
and sun warmed shadows kiss my face.
I search for a sweetly scented place
Pungent needles of pine piled deep.
A quiet place where I may sleep.
Kaye Jamison

The Rose, My Friend

A rose is like a friend, fragile and beautiful
As the rose gains strength and the petals open
so does the heart
When the rose reaches full bloom
The friendship is complete
Surely, the rose is the most beautiful of flowers
As a friend is the most beautiful of treasures
Your friendship has forever endeared my heart
As the rose will forever bloom, the friendship will grow

But, even as roses are transplanted
The memories of their beauty are not forgotten
As you will always be remembered
In my mind, a special rose blooming
A rose defining her path
As the rose climbs the trellises
You will climb to greater heights
As I look on in admiration of the rose
I cherish the rose, my friend
Phyllis Brookover

Wedding Poem

Just as the day will give way to the night,
As the sun will spread warmth to the earth,
So may the two who sit before us,
Cherish what lies in this birth.

The birth of a life shared by two new beings,
  a promise of love and devotion.
May their promise stay strong as trees' roots in the earth,
And stay deep as the glorious oceans.

For yesterday it was Two of One and One and today it is Two as One.
Great Destiny that guides our way had no hesitation in crossing
these paths...in bringing these two together.

She knew it would bring gifts
  of trust, of laughter, of dedication,
    of love, of faith and of simplistic bliss.

It was the joining of two who could not remain apart.
Two, whose souls would draw them North or South,
East or West to at last find the soul of the other,
To at last become a unique endless One.

Take care of your love and of each other...
  You have purity in the palms of your joined hands.
Kris Adams

Mylo

Envelop the infant in my trembling arms,
as the tide rushes in,
of images too bold and fierce to deny;
A boy, A teen, A man, A corpse.
The foam recedes into the crystal blue brine,
and I go with it,
seeking the strength in this fragile being's eyes,
to go forth with him into darkness
of future waning moons
where dolphins careen
in early morning mist of his dreams.
Potential met, his gurgling revelry
awakens me to the present
and I am soothed of the panic,
which is new life.
Keith F. Malinsky

Goodbye

Cold wind blows
as waves break over the wall
mist hides my tears
but it doesn't catch them all
peaceful were those nights
walking hand in hand
melted to your touch
as we became one in the sand

Still all alone as your so far away
wasting what time we had
going our separate ways
didn't know what I wanted
didn't think it was so bad
took you for granted, never knew what I had

Candles burn bright
find little comfort in their glow
the heat they provide
does little for my sole
watch you lie before me, tears fall like rain
resting there so peacefully, I never felt such pain
Robert Stewart

Once Again

I remember when we met, her smile was warm and new
As we walked by we both said hi-our words were short and few.
Her voice was sweet, her eyes were soft, and her smile could melt a heart.
If that was the scene from a romance movie I'm glad I got the part.
But time went on and life did too
And I sometimes wondered of my beautiful friend.
As I was yearning to hear her sweet voice
She suddenly said, "Hello. It's nice to see you once again."

My lungs collapsed, my body ached, and my heart had skipped a beat.
As I turned around to see her smile
I suddenly felt my life complete.
She shook my hand, her skin so soft, and gently whispered her name.
I replied with mine, though it took some time, and the sparks
   transformed to flames.
We struck up some silly conversation, but it sadly came to an end.
And as she winked a goodbye she said with a smile,
"I hope I see you once again."

Since that time, we fell in love
And there's no one else that I could ever dream of.
And I often dream of how we first met; I know she does too every now and then.
When I hear her voice and I see her smile as she gently holds my hand
It's that moment in time when we look in our eyes that we dream of
   that moment once again.
Richard A. Bernal

Anniversary 50

As you see us - as we were then
aspiring to live a life worth living
bursting upon the scene
Janie, Judy and Juste in a God's world
values were simple - love abounded
there was the cabinet maker of high repute
the fisherman, gleeful in his catch
the little lady watching over her brood
and he was all loving and giving
the lady and her other family.
Children of the future, teaching them right from wrong
aside from the basics
oh! those days spent away from home
traveling - here and there,
days at Cape May, bicycling all over the place
abruptly facing the now in our lives
wondering, reminiscing - a smile on our face
it is a great life
Phillip J. Paulle

Song Of Deseree

Wide eyed, innocent, lovely and brave. She is a wonder at fours years of age.
She is but one of many we see. Could I an adult, be so brave as she.
In her I see the lessons most of us will fail to learn
all the years of our lives, as we continue to hurt our children,
our husbands and wives.
Each day we should live as though it were our last.
Close the door on a hurtful past.
Forgive the wrongs of feet made of clay, live and forgive, let Christ show the way.
Grandma says she, "The doctors gave me a hat cause I'll lose
my hair and a magic button cause my medicine goes there
Sometimes I'll get mad at the sickness I have, so they gave
me a ball to squeeze, or bite and smash when I'm maddest of all.
"I hope I can get better 'cause I'd sure like to grow.
I have leukemia, it's a cancer you know".
Rebecca S. Snyder

The Guardian

Though time has passed, tonight I stand
at your grave, my grief an open wound
that begs for the healing touch of your hand
and absorbs the soothing light of the moon.
My toes sink into soft black earth,
give birth to roots that twist and turn
in graceful arcs as they venture forth
to embrace you. My veins burn
as water replaces blood. I close my eyes,
feel my fingers form leaves, my arms breed branches
that reach toward the heavens. I realize
my prayers have finally been granted.
Above you I stand guard: Your lover, your shelter,
at peace. Once more, we are together.
Leslie D. Duvall

The Poor Mouse

This morning I watched the cat
Attack the poor mouse.

She pulled him from the
Roadside foliage.
What seemed to her prey and me an eternity,
She tossed him around and around.
She cuffed him vigorously;
She gently pushed him along the road.
Again—she tossed him around and around
Again—she cuffed him vigorously;
Again—she gently pushed him along the road.

When the poor mouse played dead,
She crept away.
She didn't go far.
Suddenly! She sprang back,
Grasped the motionless figure,
And hurried to serve
Breakfast to her anticipating family.

The poor mouse.
The poor mouse.
Ruby L. Gabbard

No Title

To lose is an instant death that you're a witness to. I swim just below the surface of this exquisite pain, yet how many times can I broach the surface with sleep?
The pain is not everlasting if the heart beats strong, love will come again. Unlike fear the pain won't travel through, it will try to stay for the long hall.
Winning is relative.
Dew Neh Loh Moh on your MR. pain.
Michael A. Richardson

To Aunt Lucille On The Occasion Of Her 87th Birthday

Through life's troubles great and small,
Aunt Lucille endures them all
With patience, kindness and gracious style,
And whenever you see her,
There's always that smile.

Though the years may come and go
And the body weakens and movement is slow,
Still the inner strength is always there,
Because she knows she is in God's care.

On this, her birthday, we contemplate
What gifts we can give her to celebrate.
But as we look into her smiling eyes,
We know she already has the greatest prize.

Peace and love and a cheerful heart,
A life well-lived right from the start.
Compared to these, our gifts to her are small,
And she keeps on giving to us all.
Wilma Peebles

History Of "The Last Mile"

The "Last Mile" was composed by the
author while serving a term at the California
correctional facility, San Quentin. He was
assigned to a clerical position for the
then Protestant chaplain Byron E. Eshelman in
1955, his duties as a clerk to the
Protestant chaplain was to accompany the chaplain
to Death Row and distribute religious
literature to the residents of Death Row.
The poem was inspired by the feelings
and attitudes, and perhaps the regrets,
of the animates whom had received a
execution date.
Royal T. Groomes

A New Life

Your eyes, so soft and warm
Awakened me this morning.
A new life awaits you.
Seize it now; it may never be offered you again.

Look into yourself with humility,
Trust yourself in your honesty;
Most of all, be true to yourself.

Examine each thought before acting
Then move swiftly and deceptively toward your goal,
Lest old patterns spring forth
Like barriers before you.

Life's changes can seem painful.
Do not fret should you err at first.
We all do. Only then can come
Balance and self-esteem.

A new life beckons you; hasten toward it.
You know not of it's pleasures.
Trust that each step you take
Is a leap toward freedom.

A freedom you know not exists
Saundra Coon Gardenias

Step By Step

Each day is a game that I play with zest,
Awakening from placid night, I project the best.
Imagining adventures to fulfill and time to taste,
One move after the other, no hours to waste.
Yet, a greater overall plan always takes effect,
Altering and refining, guiding me quite correct.
This Divine sport has subtle meanings galore -
Jousting about performing chores and things I adore.
Yes, the best drama around is the one in which I heartily engage
Deciding which mores and leaps to incorporate that are all the rage.
Not always a winner or a loser to be,
All manifold experiences that are sent help me to see
That each step is purposeful and is leading the way
To a personal pattern woven intricately each day.
Sheilah Strauss

Reflections

"You don't experience life, you just stand
back and watch," I told that girl.
  She wasn't moderately pretty; just a little
brown mouse. She was shy, and didn't say much,
and for some reason I felt sorry for her.
  Then, trying to give her advice, I said,
"You know, if you'd try things, and not care
what other people thought, you would enjoy life more."
  But the girl never replied. And sadly
I turned away from the mirror, and wondered
why I had even tried to help that poor
defenseless girl.
Paula Hodges

Bang (The Pain)

  Bang, that's what the gun said
  Bang, a bullet to the head
  Bang, a three year old dead
  Bang, I hope you're proud now
Why does the sun shine on this day I'm filled with pain?
Misery has now beset me, there are no morals, there is no shame
Life is being taken for granted by an army of uncaring fools
My God if you can hear me, why do the innocent always lose?
My daughter just a baby, a lovely woman who shall never be
All hope and desire gone, taken away by a coward in the street
Boys will remain boys, because violence is their only tool to talk
My daughter would be alive today if men would teach little boys to walk
  Bang, my little girl is gone
  Bang, she did nothing wrong
  Bang, laid to rest this morn'
  Bang, I hope you're proud now
Oliver W. Hill Jr.

There Is Nobody As Beautiful As You

There is nobody as beautiful as you,
Because when I look into your eyes
They shine like a star in the night sky.

To me your the Goddess of Love, Aphrodite.

I think Cupid has struck me with his arrow of love,
And your beauty is like a rose in the morning of Spring.

Your smile is as brilliant as diamonds.
My love for you is above all the riches in the world.
Matt Nguyen

Tragic Meeting Never Come

Wind blew soft through skeletal trees.
Bare branches vines
like fingers, arms,
crept up the red-brown bricks
of the manor wall.

In an open window drapery fluttered, flapped.
Beneath an arched entry,
alone, concealed in dark, vague cloak,
she waited, long,
silent.

Dark, night winds moaning.
Invisible clouds blocking moon, star,
the hour chimed twice — a distant clock.
The night grew older, the figure paced
with growing agitation.

Pale tendrils of light,
fingers pulling back cloaking night,
shedding newborn morn into the dark alcove.
The huddled figure revealed
slumped, still, stone — He never came.

Kristy J. Halseth

Life

Life in cycles
Bares no resemblance to dreams
Vignettes pretending to be real
When truth comes, shock waves
rip through our conscious minds
reminding us...
Goodness and beauty come in small portions.

LaLoie Johnson

Purge

As I move in silence to the holy waters,
bathing in the burning sun, I just fall over.
Intuition speaks to me while my head grows narrow,

A place that is nearly empty, staring far from tomorrow
"Lie down and die!" A thousand voices try to tell.
Here I ponder to find my own way out.
I'm afraid I'm here again, somewhere in-between

Let it all go, an adoring pleasure,
send everything away to rest in darkness,
sleep to be free and lose only emptiness,
spill upon the end, relax just fall under.

I hear my eyes peel apart, to see I've left my sorrow,
and forth upon the sand a blind man begs me for more.
I'm to turn away and find compassion,
leaving broken pity for the holy waters.

My pace unbinding, I leave all of it behind...

To rinse myself clean.

Skylar R. Rathbun

Black Me

Look in the mirror, what do you see?
Black eyes looking back at me
Look at your hair, what do you see?
Black, strong, kinky and pretty
Look at your lips, what do you see?
Soft, luscious and lovely
Look at your nose, what do you see?
I see beautiful wide flat nose that what I see
Look at your skin, what do you see?
I see flawless beauty, black beauty, that's what I see

Karen A. Hall

One Thousand Thoughts...

One thousand thoughts in my head, will the baby be fed, will the dogs be dead? Will the bills be paid, will the cable be on, I tremble with anxiety from noon until dawn. From thinking so much sometimes I go numb, I won't tell anybody they may think I'm dumb. Sometimes I feel like I might explode. Am I carrying too heavy a load? I'm embarrassed to admit, but I'm scared as s**t. The longer I sit the more I think, by the end of the day I need a stiff drink. Even at night when I lay to sleep, my thoughts to me are still really deep. I worry about things all over again, Oh Dear God when will it end? The thoughts, I mean not my life. There's no need to hide that knife! I need to sleep, I need to rest, maybe I should talk to someone to get these worries off my chest. I feel like a nut, but that's how I am, oh well it's almost morning, time to start over again.

Natosha Randall

Keys To The Family Fold

Acceptance is forever saving face
Bear with the stagnant pace
Cooperation it has it's place
Deal with it the family race
Ere there has not been a role yet writ
That will ever master in script
Or sorted means and ways with majestic airs
Nor scroll endowed with might ever compare
To mother the first teacher
Brother and sister listen to the preacher
First to use our own good eyes and ears
Few to know how wise
Free to be our unity
Four to surely be our ecstasy
Five to thrive harmoniously
Familiar to enhance our flight
Father who keeps our peace and light
Favors to reach and branch our highest heights
Fields to yield or fight
Farewell to our burdens removed the heavy weight

Melvin P. Hunter

My Body The Shape Of The World

My long black hair is like a seed growing from a
beautiful brown strong root of shiny brown skin,
as it ages with the world passing by like day
and night, as the sun goes down the moon appears.
My mouth catches the rain as it falls down
deep inside my body.
My breast and hips round with life so lovely as a
flower growing in full bloom, my heart is hot
with red hot blood ready to burst out with so much love.
My eyes full of light, like the burning hot sun,
but at night you see beautiful tear drops falling down
as I make love.
My ears hear the wonderful sounds of beautiful
song birds singing a love song, my nose smells the fresh
crisp air as I sit and stare at the world around me.
My legs, arms, fingers and toes remind me of beautiful
tree limbs, ready to stretch out and say world I love you.

Nancy Ann Ligon

The Line Dancers

Figures gracefully moving, gliding
Bodies on a merry-go-round, up, down
Robots skipping to the beat
Clapping like puppets when strings are pulled
Turning to the rhythm, right, left
Shadows in the grey haze
Emotionless faces staring nowhere
Engulfed by a web
A force without thought
Following the circle

Robert Alan

Test Of The Believers

A tale recorded 3000 B.C.
Became a legend, through Holy you'll read
The time was that of Sadam and Gomorrah
Yet the man to mention, His glory adored
The man was told to prepare for the worst
A storm, a deluge. Numbered days were cursed
For years, of gofer, a vessel was built
To deliver his family, shown fear of guilt
Along with his family, on this great voyage
He was requested, take both genders, all species of the age
Always following his master, led them two by two
From a to z all accounted for an the cruise
Then the day came for the water to rise
Many cling and grasp, only hearing cries
The water then carried the vessel away
For forty days and nights continuous rain
Awakened by the sun, wings were sent
With olive branch return the storms relent
So in the end brought to a beginning
On the mount of Ararat he prayed for no more sinning

Matt Mutschler

"Angels Wings"

I heard a whisper from afar and knew that he was
beckoning. Oh Lord! How you have tested me.
The pain is sometimes excruciating. You sent for
my love and took him from me. I could not give
him up readily.

I heard the whisper of the Angel's wings, when his
illness laid him low. First disbelief then despair,
then know I must let him go.

Oh! The suffering, but my love accepted, because
he had also heard the angel beckoning him to go.

Oh my God, my God, not again I pray; I have heard
your call before. The soft gentle angels wings whispering
near the door.

You took my first love, sweet and gentle was he.
In my innocence and trust, I accepted your Holy Will.
Never to be free of the pain of losing him.
Now again I hear the whisper of the "Angel's Wings"

Laura M. Doyle

Hymn

Mid-hum I stop to listen - the melody - it haunts unconscious mind
Begins again the search for memory in halls my soul can never find

Frantic thoughts unfurl, unknown emotions awake;
Heart-beats skip in hurry, reign over conscience it takes.

Melody that charms my soul to sway through hypothesized cue.
Refreshes while unravelling, sweet music in enhanced hue.

And it plays as before un-interrupted, so evasive as appears,
this melody stranger to my tongue, familiar to my ears.

Triggered by HOLY SPIRIT its essence never captured,
Fleeting silence exorcised, I listen again enraptured.

Susan Lorrine Varghese

The Mist

A mist came upon me early one morn,
   bringing thoughts that had long been scattered and torn.
Circling, engulfing the depths of my mind,
   seemingly probing and hoping to find,
The me that was lost so far back in time,
   to the days of roses, wine and rhyme.

Katheen J. Robinson

Walls

Looks can be deceiving for many of us hide,
Behind the many walls we have created over time.
People sometimes look at us saying we have it all together,
But inside we are falling apart, the sadness seems to go on forever.
They say we are strong and can win any fight,
But they don't see us when we are alone and cry through the night.
Sometimes people think, "If I could only have it as easy as her,"
But they don't see behind the mask to the trials she also must endure
So be careful as you look at the faces of others,
Not to judge them by the picture on the cover.
Be willing to take the time to look deep inside,
Chances are you'll find much of the cover is just a mask behind
which to hide.

Lori Yancey

Space Fantasy

Past the steel gate our slick, silver shuttle soared,
Below us we left a crowd which roared.
For all they could see
In the darkness of night
Across the sky, the fiery flame; their only light.
With a click, clack, click, the engines shut off.
About ten seconds later I was weightless as a gray moth.
Through my side window, I saw a diamond filled sky.
Beside me I saw the moon which looked like a sweet lemon pie.
Until we drew closer, I did not see, the man in the moon,
   winking at me.
Between the stars and planets, I was glad to see
Beneath the darkness, Earth; home to me.
During the trip back home
By my window I cried goodbye
To the big black mass which held my diamond sky.

Nicole Heino

Untitled

The women was old and blind and grey,
Bent with the chill of the winters day.
the many people that passed her by,
Nary a one would turn their eye
as she sat on her porch, they could
hear her cry, "Please somebody help me."

I remember the day as I rode through town
Seeing her there in her nightgown.
Her little old hand as she waved it on
crying, "Please somebody help me.'

What's wrong with people today,
they turn their heads and walk away
when they see a women blind and grey
Who is lost on her porch and can't find her way.

She wont get lost on her porch no more,
For the angels will her thru the door.
She won't have to cry, I'm sure no more,
"Please somebody help me."

Wanda Andrewlavage

Brown Eyes

Your big brown eyes, so sweet and true,
But when I looked into those sweet eyes,
I saw the pain and I felt it too.
But this pain I've never found in you before,
But, just now I saw it in those big Brown eyes.

Sabrina Xavier

Attraction

I feel like a hostage, under your control.
Betrayed by these feelings, deep in my soul.

I have ruined my image, shattered my name.
Filled all my desires, for lustful shame.

I've felt affection, that I cherish so near.
Lost in a search for fate, forbidden to clear.

I was aroused by the charm, swept in a daze.
Alone in your world, like a forgotten page.

I explored your world, like imagination was true.
Got a glimpse of your heart, felt affection come through.

The fantasy is real, the emotions are true.
Lost in an endless search for love, attracted to you.

Tonya Ashe

A Patch Of Blue

A patch of blue graces the sky,
Birds of beauty flying by;
While pollution and poison fill the air.
Who sees any of it?
Who will care?

Flowers blooming in the spring,
Happy children angelically sing;
While machine noises are harder to bear.
Who hears any of it?
Who will care?

Lakes and rivers shimmer brightly,
Sailboats skip across water lightly;
While wastes and oil enter our waters fair...
Who sees the problems?
Who will care?

Oh, give us strength to make amends,
For all the problems, before the End;
Before we cannot see a "patch of blue".

Phillis Denmark

What's Wrong With Being Black?

What's wrong with being Black?
Black hair, brown eyes, brown skin down my back.
Tell me, I ask, what's wrong with being brown?
I'm happy with my color, so don't put me down!
What's wrong with being Black and having green eyes?
Yes, I'm Black, does it come as a surprise?
Look at my skin, brown as the bark of a tree.
Nature is the creator, of this mahogany.
Look at foundation, "King" and queens at the root.
I am beautified by Nature's pure suit.
My hair may have kinks and broad may be my nose,
but beauty coats this body, from my head down to my toes.
Wisdom fills my mind, and experience coats my face.
When I walk down the streets I project nothing but grace.
All is what I have, there is nothing that I lack.
So answer it for yourself, there's nothing wrong with
   being Black!

Tunisia L. Riley

The Old Place

Sand once washed upon this ancient shore,
Bleached white by yesterdays sun,
While high above the hawks still soar,
And down below the deer still run
Here on this old place, sacred placed that I hold in my heart.

A breeze brushes my skin and cools the sand,
Like a spirit of old only seen by touch,
Stirring around me, calling me from where I stand,
To a time and place of old things and such,
To an old place, sacred place that I hold in my heart.

I listen closely to the whispers that drift on the wind,
From the voices of my grandfather's father who called this place
   "My Land",
Telling me of my past and what was then,
The blood, the sweat and the callused hand,
That made this place an old place,
a sacred place to hold in my heart!

Sheila M. Bender

Mother Nature

I know a mother. Her name is Nature. She has a baby and that's her blessing - her present from life. I love the daughter. The precious daughter and lovely mother, are a real blessing to watch. The baby and mother "Nature" bring beauty to life. The beautiful life of the young daughter, and pretty mother - is a great blessing indeed! The baby is tiny and "Nature" is full grown. "Nature" teaches the good life, and with her daughter, the lovely mother - also is blessing the future. The baby is pure. The baby is joyful. "Nature", the pretty mother, loves her sweet daughter ... and I love there life, it's a great blessing to see. The blessing for the sweet baby and "Mother Nature"...is happiness. Life loves a sweet daughter ...and pretty mother...

   The baby is life, daughter, and blessing, to "MOTHER NATURE".....

Willard R. Fox

Brand New Day

When I open my eyes to a brand day I thank God for blessing me
Given the opportunity to start a new day, I envision all I can be
There are great dreams and lofty goals I still have yet to achieve
And I know in my mind's eye, they will all someday come true
That's why all praises go to my Savior, for each day He
   brings me through
The Lord provides day after day His forgiveness, strength and love
All He asks in return is for our love and to walk in His light
A small price to pay when you consider His huge sacrifice
So when you open your eyes to a brand new day
Thank God that you've awaken
This may be the day you accomplish your goals
And realize life is not to be forsaken

Rhonda R. Gary

Respect Is

Recognizing that you must first respect yourself before you
can gain the respect of any fellow human.
Earnestly seeking to reach your fullest potentials and goals in life
Striving to make a good reputation for yourself.
Protecting yourself from all the drugs and violence in the world.
Enhancing your education to the highest degree.
Continuously construct a life built around respect.
Trusting in yourself.

Tyronica Scott

The Blossom

Wrung out hearts beat slowly.
Blood impacts overburdened feet.
Overburdened by gravity suffocating wandering.
Hopelessly lost in a world of illusion and control.
Yearning for peace of mind and uplifting promises.
Sighs of shortened breath seep life.
Reminiscing illusions flash during sleepless nights.

Tear drops impact the Earth with heartfelt pain
Mixing the body's natural fluids with the dust.
Hardened experience builds walls of granite emotions.
Listlessly breaking down mountains of remorseful sorrow.
Blackened by the sting of a lost love- a true love,
Crows fly never to return home- only a predator now.

Trudging onward is a task of uncertainty.
Viewing the silhouette of the setting sun- a darkness come early.
Chilling winds- a sign of fall to come, dries teary eyes.
Glancing down as the colors of Earth fade to gray.
Flowers breathing their last moments of life
On the verge of withering only to vibrantly rejuvenate next season.

Yes, some things must perish before they blossom again.
Todd Nelson

The Train

Life is riding a horse; on your face
   blows the winds of breath.
Alongside rides a train; the dreary
   train of death.
Those on the train long to be
On the passing horses riding happily.
Though, some on horseback do long
For their Time to come along.

The Riders dodge obstacles and
   seek treasures
While the Passengers suffer with
   no pleasures.
Onward and forward the Riders do quest,
As the Passengers look on, finding no rest.
When a horse grows tired, the ride comes to an end.
And fellow riders must say good - bye to a dead friend.

When the whistle blows, the Riders fear
And all their eyes fill up with tears.
Because they know one Rider will feel the pain,
As they pass from Horse to Train.
Karen Ruth Brumbaugh

Late Bloomer

Late into spring through the world's winter crust,
Break tender young leaves impeded by dust.
Cautiously seeking a place in the sun,
Nourished by rain with battle half won,
The young plant endures.
The young plant survives.

Struggling for space, seeking the sun,
Growing slowly but green, now budding for fun,
Urged on by life but hindered by time,
Proclaiming at last a purpose divine,
The young plant matures.
The young plant survives.

With glorious message to all that surround,
With budding gone flowering but roots grasping ground,
Exalting Creator, establishing worth,
Its beauty in air but welling from earth,
The plant now produces.
The plant still survives.
Kate Stevens

Jetstreams

Jetstreams brace extended the twilight
Blue clear crystal evening sky
Echoing vibrantly the vanishing rays
Of a sunshine summer love
In the August heat of a dusty world.

Blue skies...green leaves...warm yellow winds,
Enigmatic women...shady ladies...crimson sundowners.

The sky falls thundering
With harsh early evening realities
Into mauve night moods reflecting hues
Of passionate human coloration
Within the timely depths eternal.

And of the evening sun of our true everlasting life love;
Only the crazily angelic dreams persist passionately
Throughout the doggedly recurring memories
Of having once danced quixotic
Across the face of earth time.

Glorianna, my love!
We have dwelt passionately fixed and transfixed
Within our enchanted visions of the world's existence.
Thomas R. Knowlson

Behind The Eyes Of A Stranger

Eyes of a priest
Body of a beast
Beauty that cuts time like a razor blade
A walk that reaches out and licks you with a wet inviting tongue
Symbolism that transcends thought

A stare that arrests
and leaves you stupefied
wondering about the connection to the dynamic night sky;
hallucinating cosmic connections
and looking for a new way to the same home.

Childhood innocence lost -and gained back,
trapped in a flashcube second.
One glance that releases the flood of
all night hide 'n go seek or red masher marbles,
thoughts of Norman Rockwell and your first sweetheart conspire.

Cold as marble in a cemetery
quick as a ravens heart beat
disconnected...
left wondering...
beating your heart against your insecurity.
Michael T. Hale

Puzzled By My Thoughts

I don't know what to expect from these words,
but all I hear is just a few little birds,
trying to tell me to listen and think.
But I close my eyes and begin to wink.
The pieces are so hard to fit
when you seem like you just want to quit.
It's so hard to say good-bye to the past
when it flew by so very fast. I hope
the puzzle will one day link. And it
won't be so complicated to think.
Robbin C. Akin

Schools Blues

Schools bells and classes and ten cent lead pencils
Book bags and bus stops and paying the lunch bills
List'ning to teachers until the bell rings
These are the things the schools blues brings

Getting up early and gobbling my breakfast
Hours of cramming for that really hard math test
Mom is so happy she literally sings
Heralding in the school blues things

Blackboards, erasers, ink pens and spitballs.
Sitting in time-out midst snickers and catcalls!
The odor of chalkdust what memories it brings
These are a few of the school blues things

Caf'teria lunch lines and checking the menu
Called on the carpet for the book that is past due.
Bags full of gym clothes and smelly old shoes
These are the things that create schools blues.

Volleyball practice and football games too.
Secretly pass notes and hide gum to chew
Childhood crushes or getting his ring
These are the things that school blues bring

Marlene Kruse

Before And After The Showers

Walking on a hot humid day in August. Not a
breeze is stirring and the air is full of hot
dry dust. In God and through prayers we
trust, waiting for the showers to fall that
covers the earth with a wet shinny crust.
The smell after the showers leave a precious
smell more valuable than gold dust. The air
is so fresh that the flowers stand up with a
brilliant lust and the streets shine with such
a gust. The wind blows gentle rain drops off
the leaves on the trees. Sometimes the drops
of rain fall on my head or fingertips
allowing me to know that it is time to give
God thanks for the blessings of the showers.
I continue walking and the children are
playing, while dogs and cats are doing their
tricks. I reach down to pick a rose and it
leaves a thorn prick in my palm. Then I
remember to ask God one more thing and that
is to forgive us for our lust.

Susanne A. Jimenez

Friendship For Ever

Friendship- the master that unlocks the key to the heart,
bringing closer two souls separated by silence;
breaching the barriers that hatred erected,
destroying the boundaries that kept love in chains.

Friendship- the captain of ships that sail unhindered forever,
the reaper of the fruit that was planted for the sharing;
gathering bits and pieces of love and caring,
to fulfill the quota given by Him in the beginning.

Friendship- the one who sits quietly holding your trembling hand,
whispering in your ear words that ease the ache within you;
embracing your weak and frail body with strong arms,
soothing your fears with words that heal the festering wound.

Friendship- it understands your tears and your laughter,
reuniting the feelings and longings that were once lost;
rekindling the dying flame that almost perished,
preserving the true love that lives in friendship- forever.

Ruben Matos

An Evening Dance

Red rock towers merge with yellow feathery clouds.

Their dark mysterious bases enhance the chill of the brisk cold winds.

Light from the last of the firey sun edges the canyon rims.

Life radiates amid the hearts of One.

A flashing Yellow Hammer dips from tree to tree.

The evening light intensifies the winter color of the
   feeding bluebirds.

Nature's song fills the air being carried everywhere.

Light filled eyes meet knowing Who is there.

Splashes of fading sunlight cast dark rhythmic shadows
   Creating life like figures.

The clear crisp air deepens rosy checks atop loving smiles.

Darkness nears the edge of light with pressing winds
   whistling for the night.

Laughter signals the two to dance, back and forth, hand held
   whirling, round and round.

Life's One heart sparkles in the Light.

Louis F. Baum Sr.

Silicon Chip — Blessing or Blight

It's sure till now, in human's dealings, hand of bone and blood has
built sweet commerce.
So why this subtle, this gradual supplanting of so effective a communion?
Can carved silicon as bravely chart tomorrow's unknown destinies?
Do we casually forget their cyber ways, though keen, are still
Not more than bias exchanging down a thin, cold wire?
Dare we afford to risk earth's kind on systems so untried?
Who can say, if failing, could we return to yesterday's utility?

I see a present anomaly. It's us of bone and blood increasingly to them
Deferring what, till now, we've built with bloody intellect.
I will allow they've proved fair helper to our fleshly hand,
I will allow tasteless chores they always execute, but flawlessly.
But why no voice, no push to somehow slow this chip's ubiquity?
For I see a subtle inverse — a cost not seen in human record.
That while we, unthinking, yield to a Cyberchip
what flesh till now has wrought us,
Diminishing,
Within us is our lively, human center.

Thomas D. Stirling

A Displaced Person: A Poem

Nothing is left for you
but agony for country lost
home, friends, work and you

Not even a grave,
desecrated, your soul alone

Once happy memories
of an old country,
a birth place, of schools and churches
and worn out benches
of loved ones and marriages
of laughter and tears
of passing dreams
fading into darkness

City noise all around you, and inwardly silently despair
yearning for friendly voices mixed with laughter
to love and be loved, to work and rest
there by the tall grass under the cedar tree
a humble refuge by the sea
wizened face, silent
I, unhappy and free.

Munir E. Nassar, MD

Life

Beauty is found not only on the outside,
But deep within ones soul.
The love found in ones heart,
Is what makes that person whole.
You must look inside yourself and others.
Look for the person hidden within.
Life wasn't meant to be easy.
It's an experience,
both painfully and pleasurably.
Take time out, sit back, and watch this
world of ours.
It's full of wonderful and beautiful people.
Some will crush your heart, and others...
will melt it with every spoken word.
And all; all was created by our glorious Lord.
Our father of guidance, Jesus Christ.
He has given us victories and defeat,
But never left our side.
We must all thank him,
For the gift of life.
Shannon Lee Giordano

The Hurt

I watch the puddles collect rain,
But, I can not feel your pain.
I can not begin to understand,
What has been planned.

Sometimes you tend to forget,
What you have already gotten.
And, you do not appreciate them,
Until you no longer have them.

You sit back and realize what is going on,
Even though the feeling stays strong.
You are being deprived of what you took for granted.
And, all of your prized possessions, that you no longer have.

Yet, all of the problems,
Seem to stay with you.
Those problems that seem to have snuck up on you.
Will not now or ever leave. They are permanent.

So, now what is left,
Do you have anything that you really want?
That question you ask.
But, you are the only one who can answer that.
Stephanie Perry

Untitled

I want to write sadness-melancholy is nice -
but I can't seem to do it-it just doesn't fell right.
It used to-it did-that's all that I know.
But now I know more-and I know better, too!

It's great-it's wonderful-this thing we call life.
What a great party-there's really no strife.
You know it and I know it, but what of the rest?
I guess will just show them, will teach them the best!

Please take my hand and share with me the way.
I've got to say there's tons more inside-
I'll just let it keep flowing till the huge waves subside.

What an experience this is. To put ourselves in this game.
We came here with love and we still gave the same.

Nothing can take it-it can't leave if it wants.
It's ours forever-we can hold it real tight.
Doesn't that feel good? Isn't it great? Even if we
don't try we're still love innate.
Tremaine

"Illusions/Delusions And Juxtapositions"

Volcanic emotions burned and liquefied,
But I didn't cry when my father died,
For our family had long been torn asunder.

His imagined enemies and voices cursed,
Imploding his brain until it burst,
And death became his ultimate surrender.

Hated him for leaving before his time,
As if mental illness was a crime,
Changing a beloved civic leader into leper outcast.

Prescription drugs didn't keep him sane,
However alcohol eased his pain,
Thus reality became a monster unmasked.

Children laughed and people whispered condemnation,
Shunning our family for fear of "crazy" contamination,
Adding explosive fuel to a troubled schizophrenic's mind.

Time exorcises disturbing memories and people forget.
Yet, "Your just like him!" is a silver bullet,
Ripping my soul, erupting molten tears that blind.
Peter R. Hardell

Lessons Learned

As a child, I treasured my carefree days,
but I looked with dread to school.
Would that lonely prison end it all, crush my childish ways?

As a schoolboy, I thrilled to the playground's games,
The happy friendships made, secrets shared, curiosity sated,
And worldly knowledge gained.

But, oh, how I feared the end of youth, duties of manhood loomed,
  not far.
The grind of college, the distant place, would they sever my
  boyhood's cord?

As a young man, I rejoiced in the strength of my arm,
The fire of life, the pursuit of love's reward.

But, oh, how I grieved at what the future would hold,
Middle age—my God!
How can I face the specter of myself, fat, bald, and slow?

As a man mature, I tasted the fruits of the Earth,
My labor rewarded, my family a joy, my home a comfortable berth.

But oh, how I gasp at the rushing days,
At the pounding hooves of death on its way.

As a man on the brink, I look to my past:
If every dread is unfounded, if the future reflects the past,
If lessons learned can be counted, then I have no fears, at last.
Ken Wilson

My Life

I don't have a wonderful life,
But it is good enough for me,
Full of happiness and sadness,
Exactly how a life should be.
I have some friends and some enemies too,
But they don't stand in my way and if they do,
I push and I shove and come up on the top,
And if I come up on bottom,
I don't give up I'll never stop,
Trying and prying to be the best I can,
Because that is how my life is,
That is my goal, my major plan.
Stephanie Gran

General Lies

I know all there is to know in life, every card in the deck
But I'm a constant strife, like a vampire to a neck
My point of views are black or white, don't waste my time with grey
Don't cloud the issues when I'm right, it's easier that way

Opinions are my stock and trade, my drug, my alcohol
My motto needs to be conveyed - you've seen one you've seen 'em all
Rich and Poor, Left and Right, Gays and Welfare Mothers
Man and Woman, Black and White, Jews and all the Others

How do you do, I'm General Lies, my fingers are in all your pies
Targeting humanity, I'm good at making tensions rise
Peace on Earth, goodwill towards men? You must be putting me on
As long as I appear again, the battle lines are drawn

All the talk shows know my name and politicians play my game
I anger, hurt, divide, inflame, and pinpoint scapegoats I can blame
I infiltrate the hearts and minds, and cause the eyesight to go blind
I separate all humankind and cut communication lines

For those of you who dislike me, reality is cruel
My influence is everywhere - at home, at work, at school
I come, I see, I conquer - everybody's in this duel
I look, I lump, I label - no exceptions to the rule
   Keith Steinbaum

The Tea Party Mess

I invited my friends to a tea party
But my friends said they didn't like tea
No apple juice!
What shall we have?
How about cookies and milk?
But my friends didn't like cookies with nuts
And we didn't have the jelly filled kind
So we baked our own cookies
With chocolate chips
Oh! What a mess!
A very tasty mess!
And my friends said they'll be back
Again for tea
Tomorrow at 5:00
   Lisa Karpinski

Soul Mates

You have touched not only my heart,
   but my very soul.
Is there not a word more beautiful
   than love to describe it?

As our eyes met I was captured in an
   abyss of knowing
To break away with a sob as my
   soul soared to touch a star.

Let us be together now for this
   moment in eternity that our souls may touch
To expand our very consciousness
   To teach and to learn
Travelling upon a star of wonder and might
   Bid us adieu.
   Lynn Marlowe

Almost Over You

Once in awhile I still see your face,
but not as clearly.
Once in awhile I still feel the pain,
but not as deeply.
Every now and then I find myself laughing out loud,
freely and without one thought of you.
It gives me hope.
   Lynn F. Kollar

Untitled

Dashing girl, long lost in plodding woman-
But now and then when warm breezes stir, and clouds whirl by-
I feel her stretch with joy—inside,
and long to run toward distant hills, with arms out-stretched
to catch the coming spring.
   Leanna Mae Collins

Puddle Hopping

I used to be a small rambunctious child,
But now I am more graceful, soft and mild,

The shadows used to come pouring out of the night,
But now they have gone, as well as the fright.

I used to have small worries, like "Where did my dog go now?"
But now I think of questions, like "When, where, why and how?"

I used to hop and skip in puddles,
but now I realize that brings more troubles.

As I've grown up through the years,
I've grown, matured and conquered my fears.
   Kelly Fick

Wallflower

Because you attached that stigma to it, it sounds so bad
But now, it's "okay", it's part of my melody
You see, at first, I was angry every time you called me that
I mean, how DARE you?!
   How dare you try to define my character or try to label me
WHO ARE YOU?
   You—with your deficient bodies
    They're pathetic; gaps above and gaps below

See, you became the artist trying to paint my picture
   Completely unaware that all along you had the WRONG canvas
But be that as it may
   I'm still here hurting
Some friend you are, calling yourself building me up
   when all you're really doing is tearing me down
I wish I could show all of you
   who I really am
Then you'd know...and be ashamed
Flowers are beautiful
   even on the wall
Thanks for the compliment.
   Myrshia L. Woods

He Was Sent By His Father

He was sent by his father to meet our needs,
But some of us are too blind to see.
He came to save, not to condemn,
That was very gracious of him
He shared his knowledge that we might learn.
And taught us how to live as one.

He was sent by his father to help us all.
Not to harm us but to save a lost cause.
He gave his life for you and me it is hard sometime for us to see.
His occupations were many, a carpenter by trade,
A physician for many and never used a blade.

He is Alpha and Omega, the beginning and the end.
That is why our salvation is in his hands.
It's free to all, but you must obey this is one debt that
we will never repay.
   Minnie L. Nettles

Yet.....Again......Forever

I failed you and hurt you,
But that was never my intention
Because all I have are precious dreams of you.
Yet you still come to me with your radiant smile,
Soft brown eyes, and tender touch
In spite of the pain I've caused.
You instill in me the desire
To please you and make you happy.
Warming my heart with your smile
And touch, you make me feel loved
Despite my gross inadequacies.
In spite of my failures you give me hope
Telling me to keep my chin up.
My only prayer is that you will come
To me yet......again and forever.
Rebecca K. Wetzel

A Lost Love

You said that you'd be with me forever.
But that wasn't true.
To feel this bad I thought I'd never.
Because now that you're gone, I have nothing to hold onto.
But you left and I feel a part of me is lost.
I'd give anything to have you back with me.
I wouldn't care what it cost.
How much I loved you I guess you'll never see.
You were the most beautiful person I'd ever met.
I'll remember all the times we had together.
For your departure, I wasn't set.
All your memories I have to collect and gather.
For one last time I'm going to say goodbye.
As I kneel down by you and pray.
I asked God why you had to die.
His answer came to me, he said,
"I guess, just like everyone's comes, it was her day."
Epilogue:
Your parents are still trying to find out how much you had to drink.
And when you left the party and arrived.
Whenever they ask questions, my eyes fill with tears and my heart sinks
Because I ask myself why that fateful night you had to be the one to drive.
Luke Hubbard

Changing Of The Seasons

Summer is not gone.
But, the dried, burnt grass is a reminder
of what may come.
Breakdown. Destruction. Crumbling.

Approaching Autumn.
Beautiful life all around.
One by one, falling. Just a memory
of what used to be.

Snow-white Winter.
Precipitation exciting through the wonders
of the sky. Slowly and surely, fading...
to a warmer and wetter presence.

Finally, Spring bouquets.
Gardens of wild, frilly colors
extending for miles... miles of
black tar covering over.

What has happened to the
existence of the place we were once proud of?

Replacement... Disintegration of our world... Our Earth...
Our HOME.
Kellee S. Kissinger

Retarded Girl

Thoughts invade with bells and whips
But the girl can't heed them
Through the more stuporous roar

That yells upon her in drips and drops
And splashes uncalled for
Against the top of her proud, straight spine.

Thoughts of mom and boys and God and learning
Surge curious to reach the banks
Of awareness that laugh, falling forever away.

"Plant and live and grow and die"
The pleading wail sounds from a shore
Parched desperate for the young girl's thoughts

But the seduction finds no listener.

The roar whips her along
Without real delight
Smothering its bottled and stuffed-up cargo.
Todd West

Created In His Own Image

I may not develop as all children do,
But the Lord says all things work together for me and you.

I may appear different than most kids do,
But God created me in his own image too.

I may be able to walk or maybe just stand,
But nonetheless that is in the Lords hand.

I may open my mouth to say one word or two,
But I pray dear God I can say Mom and Dad I love you,

I may appear silent as far as you know,
But the Lord knows on the inside there's joy that over flow.

I may show sorrow sometimes on my face,
But please Mom remember I'm kept by Gods grace.

I may feel lonely sometimes down here,
But God has said he will always be near.

I may be used that the works of God can be manifest,
But please have no regrets for he promised me joy, peace and rest.

I may be a little burdensome on this life's run,
But remember our latter end will be joy, laughter, worship and fun.

I love you Mom and Dad!
Marie A. Hudson

Blue Eyes

On July 2, my mother told us that our daddy went away.
But then my mother told us his memory would always stay.
Now, a year later, my memory is not as good.
And I cannot remember all the things I should.
But I do remember his smile. And his heart was oh so true.
But what I remember most, are his eyes of brilliant blue.
When I was just a little girl, I'd see his loving stare.
And I knew my dad would always love me. I knew he'd always care.
And as I grew older, the same thing still held true.
Whenever I looked into my daddy's eyes of brilliant blue.
Then one day he closed his eyes, never to be seen again.
Until we meet in heaven, but I can't bear to wait 'til then.
So whenever I look up into the clear blue summer skies.
I will always be reminded of my daddy's brilliant eyes.
Kathleen Johnston

No Longer Ask Why

They say I'm just quiet perpetually shy
But there's something more and I often ask why
These feelings I harbor they are my hearts voice.
In need of no change they were not by choice.
With bodies alike man pleasing man
How can we be happy they don't understand
I've but one regret and it is quite mild.
I'll never see my eyes
In the face of his child
I'm still just as quiet though not quite as shy
Having found my true soulmate
I no longer ask Why!
   Tony Spencer

Just Browsing

I seek solitude amid Science Fiction,
But they only blast me with their laser diction,
I get verbally beaten and mugged among crime novels,
Searching for cryptic analysis where Psychology dwells.

Why do these people continue to pester?
An answer lies through Medieval History, they are like the court jester,
I resolve to be patient, not to be fussed,
When they consider my browsing capabilities unjust.

I threaten to wear a 'Do not disturb' sign,
Before I get to that checkout line,
Jesus, can't they see it's only half past four,
I've got to flick through rows and rows more.

I only want to spend relative time, like Einstein,
I really pose no threat, I am benign,
It all seemed so easy once before,
To spend idle time by the score.

Is someone looking after you?
Can I redirect you to aisle two?
Have you found what you're looking for?
Please, please, no more questions, I implore.
   Paul Griffin

Nothing Left

I tried to reach for a star,
But they told me my grasp was too short;
and the distance too far.
I tried to walk upright and tall,
But they belittled my stride to a crawl.
I tried to live doing others a good deed,
But they hastily took and left me in need.

Now with nothing left, no dignity or pride,
I tread an internal sea of uncertainty in
search of steadfast freedom the other side.
But nothing is found except the skeleton's remains,
Of a heart that once bled kindness but now bleeds pain.
Where do I go from here? Where do I look?
To restore that which this world so selfishly took?
   Nahshon Collie

Shining Bright Love

It stands alone with no strings attached.
Burning bright, that shining light stating that love is near.
The symbol of hope and faith so high.
Sharing the warmth from inside.
Seeing it everyday is such a joy.
So God decided to share it with all of his children.
The sun is so bright, so big and so warm.
That it brings great happiness to my days alone.
   Priscilla A. Owens

I'm Not An "I" - I Am A "We"

*I have been crucified with
Christ, and I no longer live
But Christ lives in me
Gal. 2:20*

There are things ahead which I truly fear,
  But WE don't.

There are obstacles that I cannot face,
  But WE can.

There are loads that are too heavy for me,
  But not for US.

There are sorrows that I can't bear,
  But WE can.

There are times I simply grow tired of the fight,
  But WE don't.

There are barriers that I have no strength to climb over,
  But WE do.

I seek happiness, WE seek holiness.
  I seek to be loved, WE seek to love.

I can't walk the Christian life,
  But WE can.

I'm so grateful that I'm no longer an I,
  I am a WE!
   N. Elizabeth Holland

Caregiving

Caregiving is a calling which we may never need pursue
But we must always remember what a caregiver goes through.

We, as caregiver's need lots of love, appreciation and most of all, relief
For we are living constantly with monotony, sadness and grief.

Most people ask about your loved one but hardly ever
  ask about you
Who may be so hurting on the inside and tired through
  and through.

To see our loved ones weak of body, mind and soul,
deeply saddens us but makes us ever mindful of our role
Which is to make them comfortable as the days stretch out
  in front
And try to deal with reality which daily we must confront.

And so we, as caregiver's willingly carry on day after day
And for God's strength and patience, we do constantly pray!
   Margaret Johnston

My Little Home

My little home is very small
But the love in it is felt by all
No fancy furniture, no ritzy stuff
Just plain and clean and that's enough
I make all welcome with a smile
And hope they enjoy my visit once in awhile
So if you get lonely and want to chat
Just knock on my door and we can do that
Now that we had our visit
And you go home
Then it's me again
  All alone.
   Theresa Glogowski

Hearts

I gave you my love
but what wasn't enough.
You had to have my heart, too

You took my heart,
claiming it as yours
taking it under your possession.

The blood in my heart
pumped for you.
Leaping with joy
every time it saw you.

But you took my heart crushed it
broke it and ripped it up
until it lay in a broken mass
where my love for you had once grown strong.

Now I lay
letting my heart drip its last drop
Now I realize that
what I didn't realized before
was that when I gave you my heart,
my soul went with it too...

Kelly Schneider

Tribute To "Gram" Grandma

For my dearest friend the end has come
but yet a new beginning has begun.

For permanent peace and forever content -
The Lord sent His angels and away she went.

Away disappeared her pain and her grief -
Upon her arrival she felt only relief.

The angels above gathered to sing -
When Grandma appeared to meet the Great King

He held out His arms when Grandma came near -
Away went her sadness and all of the fear.

"Everlasting life" as he always vowed -
Was His very first words as she stood there so proud.

Under His arms He held her away
Where days from now on will never be grey.

She left us her wisdom, courage and pride
And now lives with Jesus right by His side.

How great thou art to have such a place
To take Grandma where there's continuing grace.

Nancy E. Mann

Oklahoma

The children are gone
but yet they are here,
the darkest of nights,
and the blackness of fear

Their souls were lost and now they've been found,
the silence of death, not even a sound

Their souls were taken to the heavens up high,
just look at the moon, and the stars in the sky.

Trevor Albertson

The Mind Game

As I lay down and try so hard to breathe
but you are a heart into my body I receive.
Cannot sleep at night, I toss and turn
'cause when I close my eyes I feel my body's being burned.
As I think to myself of what to do
then for some reason I set my mind on you.
If you wouldn't trip so much maybe you could see
all the pain you're causing you, all the pain causing me.
Going down a dead end road
where you will end, no one knows.
Lost in the dark 'cause you can't stand the light
going to leave you wrong 'cause you don't want to be right.
Coming to reality you say this is no mind game.
Whatever you want to call it, you have no one to blame.
Can't think with your mind cause it's not straight.
Not a normal body 'cause you've speeded up your heart rate.
Can't talk too much, we all sound the same.
You are the one who is a joke
you are the mind game.

Tiffany Beatrice Peters

Sleeping Beauty

Dragonfly
Butterfly
Pheasant in my favorite colors
Soft blossoms
Moon on silver and gold
I think of you every moment of the night and day.
A huge part of me is with you. I know I am not completely here.
I dreamt that you woke up.
Thank God.
We all prayed for you from the cellars of our heart and soul.
Thank God you survived.
I need you.
We all need you.
Greg called you Brenda Babe.
I cried.
I want to be with you.
Talk with you.
And mostly listen.
Know my heart is full of love for you.
My sister, my friend.

Patricia L. Arnold

Line Four

Early Morning- Thin fog and heavy smog
By my side, there are people standing like sticks
From ages seven to seventy
I am cold and quiet
They are warm and noisy
Red, white, black, and blue with whizzing by
Just to form more goose bumps on me.

Early Morning- Sleepy eyes stare into
The end of the boulevard
Patiently waiting for a face
To pop out of the horizon
A face so vivid
It takes you where you wish.

Early Morning- I rise
To pursue my daily routine
The waiting
The loneliness of having myself for company
Is it?
Can it be what I've been waiting for?
Ah yes... line four is finally here.

Thangsy Yort

The Price Of Silence

I was told along time ago that silence is golden
  by someone who was very old.
But sometimes the price of silence,
  can trouble our very souls.

Today I witnessed a human being take another human's life.
However, everyone was afraid to talk about the crime
  that took place that night.
Once again silence claimed another life.

When I lay my head down to sleep,
  my heart (mind) keeps telling me I should speak.
But this silence has a serious hold on me.

But what can I do?
I don't have the courage to set myself free,
  from the things that this silence has done to me.

How long will this silence have a hold on me?
  the price is more than I can pay,
  the price is too much for me.

I can't live a life of silence.
I can't suffer this pain all alone,
  knowing what I did was wrong.
    Walter V. Clark Jr.

"Beautiful Autumn Day"

The trees have been painted in the night.
By the masters hand that touched the leaves,
They are so colorful and bright.
The wind is softly blowing them down.
Upon the lawns and all around.
A whirlwind catches the brilliant
colors, and blows them up in heaps.
Another whirl, they disappear,
In the field across the way.
It is a beautiful autumn day.
    Virginia W. Holbrook

The Concrete Forest

Buildings tall and small of concrete all
Cables, pipes, roots to nourish the artificial forest
Vehicles scurry about as do forest insect life
Paint to give the concrete forest many colors of
A living forest
Human life inhabits the concrete forest
They emerge out of subway tunnels as animals do
From their burrows
Among the humans, predators lurk, as they do
Among the animals in a living forest
Alas on this forest land an artificial monument
To the destruction of natures bounty by man.
    Pen Rose

Childhood

Childhood is a time to have tons of fun.
Childhood is a time to swim in the sun.
Childhood is a time to skip rocks with a friend.
Childhood is a time that should never end.
    Tyler Keyser

Midnight Widow

  Your voice softly whispers, chiming in the night:
Calling out to me, from a mystical light.
  Stepping toward me, but paralyzed in place;
I can faintly see, a kind, innocent face.
  Reaching for you, my arms in mid-air,
But Oh! my darling angel, you are not there.
  Awakened by the realization it seems,
Gone in a blink of an eye, 'twas only a dream.
  My arms to be around you, will just have to wait,
till I am free to walk, through heaven's gate.
  Only in body, absent from soul, I lie here in the dark,
Painful aches soar, from my breaking heart.
  With all strength, or so it appears,
I close my eyes, to console my tears.
  Blinded by God-driven hope, my hand then strays,
to where you slept, many a night and days.
  As my hand rests, where you did lay,
Lord! take me too, my last breath I pray.
    Loretta Petry

Too Late?

Do you hear the past
calling to OUR uncertain future,
or will YOU ignore and ignore and ignore it
until convenience approaches
or nothing better arrives.

I must not be alone.
Others must feel the urgency
pounding away from within and without.
Such audacity we must have to think
that WE can dictate THIS future.

No matter, the balance is gone.
We have tipped it too far to right this mess.
WE will pay and THEY will pay,
if they are they and not the
should haves, could haves, the why didn't I or we
see this in time, in time, in time...
    Tanya Albert Swindell

Untitled

I have a beautiful picture in my mind, that time
  can never erase
A picture of a little girl that gives me the courage the
  future to face
I miss so much the times I spent with her on a friday night
There was so much love between us, I made everything seem all-right
We spent so many happy hours racing along the sea shore
I can hear her voice like an echo calling "NaNa lets run some more"
Her little face would glow and her eyes were like dancing lights
She's wrap her arms around me and hug me oh so tight!
"I love you NaNa" she would so often say
She looked like an angel captured in the suns golden rays
Those days have gone forever, but the are implanted in my mind
No where else except God garden a more beautiful picture could I find.
    Terrie Mavis Fischer

Snow In The Night

So quietly, so softly, the snow drifting down,
Covering each fence post, the trees, and the ground,
Blanketing the earth with a veil of white,
So quietly, so softly, the snow in the night.
    Kathie Brush

What Exactly Is Love?

What exactly is love someone asks the answer I
cannot explain
It's that special feeling for someone that causes you
to smile even when in pain.

It's wanting to be near someone all the time and willing
to give your life that they can live
It's having tender feelings for someone and always
expecting less from them than you give.

It's working with them sometimes and it's worrying
when they are sick or away
It's thinking of a dreary life if they were gone
it's pulling together every single day.

It's being content with very little earthly goods as
long as this loved one is with you
and it's sharing your deepest feelings but mostly
it's a feeling between God and you.
Laverne Puckett

All Hallows' Eve

Autumn is gone from the Crystal Hills.
Carved pumpkins sit by old doorsills.
Trees, bare in sunlight, stand silver gray
Still lovely in a different way.
Chalk white birch bark brightly shines
Beside the green eternal pines.
Against the earth, curled brown and dry,
The leaves have settled down to die.
The air is crisp like brand new wine.
The harvest moon looms large and fine.
Gourds are gathered in a pile.
October takes her leave in style.
Memory C. Lane

Do They Know?

   All around me the chitter chatter of conversations. I
catch bits and pieces here and there; what she did last weekend, how
lucky he got last night, how much she gets on her nerves,
the grade he made on his biology test, how cute her outfit is.
All around me the chitter chatter of conversation.

   But do they know? Don't they realize how fast it all goes?
How unimportant their conversations sound? That we're
just tiny specks on a huge, round, globe?
So caught up in acceptance, image, looks;

   Do they know? Tomorrow may not be theirs? That when they're
gone the world will carry on as if they never existed; their
conversations long gone, and forgotten, but their harsh words
an immortal imprint in someone's mind?

   Don't they want to be remembered for the things that matter?
Don't they want to leave that protective corner they call home, and
explore, experience, fly? Make a difference, make a change?

   All around me the chitter chatter of conversations, how
unimportant their content seems. Do they know? Do they know?
It goes so fast, it will not last... We're just tiny specks on
a huge round globe.
Kwaseera Dixie

Star-Kissed Snowmist

Moonlit dunes ever shifting on the sighing wind...
Crying winds sheds a tear,
Crystal clear frozen rain
Like silent pain
The Star-kissed snowmist
Margaret Domeny

From Afar

Kissing bitter wind as my journey proceeds
Caught between time and the span of my needs.
I lash out at injustice and the hate that it brings
Wishing for loving and the song that it sings.

I've searched to the end of this fading light
With every last bit of my now dying might.
Pain and tears have erased the good I once had
And my feelings have become these new shades of sad.

Why can't he see by this weak look on my face
Why can't he see for him I have fallen from grace?
My days without him are always empty and long
I know I need to survive but I fail to be strong.

From afar I admire and wish only he'd hear
The things that I know that make him so dear.
His picture is engraved in my love-starved mind
And my fate is too clear to let it be kind.

The reasoning of this need has long since faded
And my outlook on life is nothing but jaded.
It's deadly vice, knowing that he's never known
He'll stay eternally ignorant to feelings not shown.
Rachelle S. Miller

The World As I See It

As I walked down the city street, the wind blew my hair.
Caught by the wind was the long flowing skirt that hung from my waist.
As I walked on a great feeling of joy came across;
A smile suddenly broke through my frowning face.
For some unknown reason I felt as it I were an angel.
An angel cast down upon this great earth not knowing my purpose,
   but knowing I had one.
Then I thought of you and my smile grew; it was no longer a smile.
Now my face glowed with eyes sparkling and teeth gleaming.
What was I feeling; I was feeling love.
Not just love for you, but love for everything.
I saw the world.
I saw the good the bad and I loved it all.
The country the city, it didn't matter what it was all I knew was
   that I loved it all. Then I saw you.
My smile broke and a tear shed. This was a tear like no other;
A tear that will never be forgotten. I cried when I saw you.
I cried because you showed me the love I felt.
You showed me how to love the world;
And for that you will always be loved.
Stacey Heisler

Candor Of Another Lesion

He's back on creation with a webbed cryptic sword.
Caught standing in his life without a braided billfold.
Flipped in concept and begging bulk rate madness.
Yells are consistent canes of hampered acknowledgment.
Snap shots cease to instill strangled muscle tones.
In the middle of an absolute decent spring board.
Bleak recommendation on top of beaten sophistication.
Study introspection while chewing red meat and nicotine.
He vanishes in the jacket of long ago behavioral childhood.
While maturity hovers in the face of elongated eyelashes,
glasses pick the dust off of eager repetitious levels.
A penguin sits in the booth farthest from his sight.
Passers by cling to the ground while I sway away.
Just look before your eyes and stop that whiny rant.
He is not a genius worthy of biochemical capitalization.
Laurie Christenson

"Season Holiday"

When I see the leaves,
Change from green to gold...
I often realize I feel the first of winter's cold!

I start dreaming of the turkey,
on Thanksgiving Day!
And sleigh rides down Hill,
when we were youth at play!!!

But the biggest thrill I get, when I often think back,
is trying to locate where Santa
hides his sack:

I love to see the sparkles, up and down the street,
everyone knows Christmas is better then
trick or treat!!

And at night when it gets peaceful,
and all has settled down
I like to watch the lights on the tree
and hear the choirs sound!

So everyone please remember, don't forget to pray,
that everyone you meet and know,
have a wonderful holiday...
   Marquintala Cuffee

A Child Within

Children are God given.
Children need looked over.
Children need love and understanding.
For if we desert a child,
we desert our inner self.
For in each of us there lies a child,
of yesterday year that will not grow up.

For if we force a child to grow up before it is time,
we deprive them of sliding boards,
swings, sand boxes, and water battles,
bumps and scraps.
We deprive them of learning and loving.

For if we desert our selves, it is
like deserting a child. We need to learn and love.
Not just some, but every one has
a child within.
   Sandra K. Pease

Lost Little Girl

It's hard to imagine here I am a woman grown with
   children of her own;
For buried deep inside me is a little girl lost;
I strive to keep her well buried and in the place where she belongs;
But, now and then when I'm down and feeling all alone;
I can feel her begging to come forth;
And then she silently takes over and deep inside I still feel her pain;
Tears run like a river over torrents of frustrations and
broken dreams;
No one to hold and comfort her, no one to say "it will be all right;
Just the silent whimpering of a little girl lost;
No one to understand or care whether she finds her way back home;
Why I'm being silly, I'm a woman full grown with children of her own;
I look at them and pray;
To never feel the sadness of the little girl lost;
And maybe one day, I will look back and finally see a smile;
To finally become the little girl lost found.
   Sharon Parker

Memories Of Christi

Happy Seventeenth Birthday to our daughter
Christi
We think of you and our eyes grow misty,
Thinking of other birthdays of yesteryear
When the circle was unbroken and you were here.

We remember you as a baby, little things that mean so much...
Your first tooth, your first step, things you said, things you touched.
We think of you in your growing years
We shared happy times and also the tears.

You loved your Church, your school, your family and friends,
Your car, your horse, the trail rides on weekends.
Many things come to mind - - - like your love for flowers,
The phone calls you would get your talking for hours.

We miss you so much! No tongue could ever tell.
We just were not ready to say, "Farewell."
To a very special teenager who loved life and fun,
Whose memories are ever with us, we cherish every one.
   Louise Hester

Love Eternally

Morning dawns like every other. Summer sun shines brightly.
Cloudless sky. Work is waiting. I tiptoe through the house as not to
wake them. Never even say good-bye. Thank you, thank you.
Schedule change. Home early. Thank you.

In haste I collect them at the sitter. Sun still shines brightly.
Few clouds are in the sky. "Mommy!" Up they jump. My two blond
darlings quickly rushing to my side. "I love you so much!"
They're singing. They're laughing. They're bouncing, in the back seat,
full of joy.

Wonderment! That my heart can hold such love. Endless
Summer. Clouded skies. Daddy's home! Out they jump excitedly.
My little girl and my little boy. "Daddy, Daddy. Where are you
going?" "Can we come, Daddy?"
They're singing. They're laughing. They're bouncing, in the back seat,
full of joy.

They turn and wave. Bright smiles. Two little faces.
I raise my hand and wave. Then stand forlorn.
We didn't give kisses! What was all the rush?
No "au revoir!" I watch them drive off. Push the button.
Mechanically. The garage door screeches as it slowly closes.
The day ends unlike any other.

Catapulted through searing sharpness of grief. Unrelenting waves of
grief's pain. Their absence has a presence all its own.
It's everywhere I go. It's in everything I do.
No longer "Mommy" or someone's wife. "Now, who am I?"
"Where do I belong?" Hope flashes when suddenly I see -
   that I am also journeying through eternity.
   Karin L. Ford

Remember?

Remember when the eyes were clear and you
could face the world without fear; when all
body parts moved without forewarning and
there was no problem in performing?

And remember when to vigorously exercise
was a way of life, that did not bring on body
aches nor mental strife?

And what about those days when a spontaneous
decision to go on an adventure, did not mean
you had to first find your...DENTURE!
   Lillian L. Braxton

Lonely

I know the way a lonely person feels,
Cold, dark, and empty, a vacuum in his heart,
Days that are cloudy, nights that are dark,
Waiting for sunrise while wandering thru a park.

I know the way a lonely persons acts,
Alone with his thoughts, the shadows of his mind,
Fear, fright, remorse, when he dares to think back,
To the years of regret, he chose to be alone.

I know the way a lonely person dreams,
Big, bold, beautiful, the conquest is in sight,
For tomorrow, tomorrow may even be tonight,
But back to being lonely, someone turned out the light.

And now I'm alone and I know me,
Wishing, waiting, wanting; someone, something set me free,
Show me the place where I have to be,
And please God take all the loneliness from inside of me.
    Richard Sheehan

Mirroring

I met a man who said to me
Come take my hand that you might see
God's secret place inside of thee
Let go of fears and feelings past
That you might breath fresh air at last

So I took a chance that I would find
God's hidden nature in this heart of mine.

And so we travelled, my friend and I,
To virgin isles within my mind.

Afraid and uncertain I'd hold back my hand
I cannot go further, I know not his plan.

Take trust in the Lord and hear what I say,
Should you ever feel lost, he'll point out the way.

As the wind comes up from I know not where
I found my soul given into his care.

As a reflection seen in a pool of glass,
I saw myself in another at last.

I knew at once why I'd come to be
The image I saw in front of me.
    Viki Lopatka

Walk With Me

Take my hand.
Come walk with me, I've much to say,
But you must lead, show me the way.

We must go back these long past years,
Too long I've waited to dry your tears.

Hold my hand.
The stones, the weeds, the thundering skies
Are mine alone, my faults, my lies.

Children, flowers and ever always birds,
Your gifts alone, by acts, by loving words.

Take hold my hand
You were love, all songs, the cloudless blue,
Could you believe and know I needed you.

Your gentle smile, but why your touch so cold?
Did I wait too long, your hands to hold?
    Walt G. Nimtz

Untitled

It began as a single drop
Coming from the sky,
And then was hidden deep within as time went on.

Then suddenly, like a spring,
It bubbled up - called upon by God
To grow and flow; to stand the tests of time.

A creek, fragile in the beginning,
It struggled around curves of destruction,
Though at times it seemed to disappear
Hidden from sight.

It reappeared around the bend,
Stronger than before,
Somehow that brook became a stream.
A stream, overflowing with peace and happiness
Full of the gentle assurance few know.

Larger with each drop,
Stronger with each moment,
Like a river, crashing over rocks
Yet going on..to a pool of calm.
    Robyn Scott

Umbilicus

I live in the recesses of mind
Confined to the body
Waiting to explode into eternity.

I see, I hear, I touch through corporal senses;
Give birth to weary questions
Blinded by the foggy labyrinth of my brain;
Dead, synaptic end. Refrain!

I am more than the sum of my genetic pool;
DNA harp strings playing wise man or fool.
More than a moral or ethical seal
Stamped to a culture demanding appeal.

I am more than the pattern of my design
Schooled by clocks that tick and chime
And tell me when to go and where
As if the rules we share/create
Will lead us to that pristine state we seem to long for.

Alas! No!
I say what we can fathom isn't day,
And truth is more than you or I can imagine.
    Pamela A. Barletta

To Fall In And Out Of Love

Is it possible for one to fall in and out of love?
Confused about his life, he thought "Never"
Then one morning, sprouting wings, he left like a dove
Leaving the woman to cry and hating him forever
Hair of fine black thread
Skin of white satin
Wishing that she was dead
Wanting him to speak in Latin
Their love was not planned
Nor was its demise
He built his dreams on sand
Only to be destroyed by the tides
True love is something that happens and happens strong
When you look the next day, it can never go wrong
    Lyle L. Schmerz

"Enrapture"

Delve into my world and let me experience the energies of you.
Connect me to the heavens that allow our clouds to mingle.
Soothe my mind with sweetness.... Awaken me !!!!!
As our bodies respond to the rhythm of heartbeats
Mine, yours, ours, raise me to heights unknown.
Soaring above the clouds let me drift up into eternity
  And then ....maybe I'll smile.

Perforate my sous with rapture, discover me!
Glide through my aperture with inquisition.
Stimulate my intellect as only you can.
Entice the anatomy I never knew I had.
As I reach out to your warm embrace
You appease me with harmonious ecstasy.
On ascent as high as I want to, you want to, we want to.
  Then linger there...as we explore unchartered abreaction.

As you forge through my prohibition I enwrap you
With tentacles of mind, body and soul while the heavens shriek
With glorified unity the clouds burst and sun shines through.
As we fill the air with unbridled paroxysm and resounding cries of
  Yes Yes Yes....by golly this is living!!!!!!!
Sharon A. Miller

Soul Spring

Maintaining thought's creative flow
Conscious awareness of the voice
Of gracious Sophia, my spirit muse
Is easier some days than others.

Sometimes, like a well stripped dry
Pumping sand and muddy gurgles
The life-spring of intuitive insight
Slows to a soul-sludge trickle.

Things must then rest for awhile in silence
As pure water refills my depths
Fed by clean unknown mountain snows
Raising and renewing the water table.

Then creation's private garden
Can be irrigated and refreshed
By the life-giving moisture of the muse
The crystal fountain of the soul.
Ronald T. Diephuis

"Children Shamed"

The knot in my stomach and screams in my mind.
Could this be the 100th or 200th time.

The rage in his voice and hate in his eyes
Blaming and cursing and tainted with lies.

Maybe the booze will deaden his brain
So tears will cease like summer rain

Oh God, how can I continue on
The sky is grey; it's almost dawn.

Send me hope or a sign to see
Do you hear my universal plea.

I am the children of tomorrow
Existing in a world deadened by sorrow.

No hope, no love, no future to see
Blame flowing, from us, you and me.
Linell C. Hallman

Cold Silence

Cold silence filled the air,
Crept down to the dank basement,
Shaded people lay against the wall,
Unpure emotions cries in her face,
Weak and weary she falls upon the ground,
In a black world,
The beating of her heart as tears roll,
Alone, all alone,
She fancies a sparrow,
She quaff of blood in the night,
Her pain punctured her like a scorpion bite,
Her look was as scythings cut.
Kari Longanecker

Shadows

The sky was dark, t'was black as coal, and evil filled the air.
Creatures of the night made sounds and shadows everywhere.

Silently, the sad face child slipped through the darkened streets
Eyes huge and wide with rampant fear, heart racing, skipping beats.
No one knew that she was leaving, no one would ever care
All alone she faced the evil world and the pain that she would bear.

The shadow moved on silent steps and followed her in flight
Till near the woods, way down the road, he stopped her in her plight.
His eyes were glazed and evil red, his hands were icy cold.
The knife he held against her breast said all that must be told.

He did the deed, t'was Satan's task; he left her where she lie.
As her life's blood poured on the ground she wished that she would die.
She didn't die, t'was not to be, t'was simply not her fate.
Now she lives with memories and never ending hate.

A rage that eats up her control, a rage that she can't touch,
A heart felt pain that she denies, a pain that's just too much.
Daily now she wills it dead, those memories and pain.
She tried to kill it once but failed. Should she try again?
A. Elaine Powers

Changes

Yesterday we had...
  Cried at the first feeling of hunger or pain;
  Spoken for the first time trying so hard to be heard;
  Problems over rights and wrongs; struggling to determine which is which,

Yesterday I...
  Talked too much in class and got into what I thought was trouble
  but would soon find out what trouble was;
  Listened to the constant fighting of my parents not knowing what
  disaster was soon to be; fell asleep with not a care in the world.

Today we...
  Awake to drugs, violence, and crime in our perfect little world;
  Strive so hard to be the perfect person with the perfect grades and
  life, but not realize we are far from perfect; leave our loving
  homes and witness the harsh reality of the real world.

Today I am...
  Remembering the old friends I used to have while gaining new ones;
  Comparing my memories to my friend's memories and finding a lot are
  the same; changing in so many ways as the days go by.

Tomorrow will be...
  New memories; beginnings; changes
Renee Devere Hudspeth

Westampton

Farmers in their fields, policemen in their cars,
Crossing guards in the street; green, grassy, busy, kind.

It was whispered that you were small and now I know the truth.
I have reached your boundaries.

The rumor is that the nights are well noisy. I myself have heard
the truck's racket and the endless sound of car horns.

There is a myth your weather is your own and skeptical eyes
presently see the construction of your weather station.

It is reported your library is the biggest in the country and all
doubters watched it expand.

Calmness. Hypnotic,
Tranquil Location. Traffic.

Between the houses and playgrounds are children's voices full of joy.
In the malls and supermarkets are workers' voices full of joy.

Neighbors and friends seeing each other morning, noon, and night have
voices full of joy! Sounds of joy are everywhere in this town's air.

Farmers singing in their fields, policemen waving as they go by.
Crossing guards protecting as children walk, and crickets in the grass
singing hypnotic songs

Make up Westampton.
Terica Lynn Swangin

"Liberty"

Liberty, the love of our fathers long ago,
Crossing the Potomac through thick sheets of snow,
Fighting the Redcoats with powder and shot,
Their hope for freedom burned fiery and hot.

Shackled and beaten the slaves could not see,
The numerous attributes of true liberty.
Segregation and hatred tore them apart,
The sadness they felt surely broke many hearts.

Oppression and strife now block the way,
On the road to freedom for many these days.
Liberty so desired by millions on earth
We often have taken for granted since birth.
Ryan Scoville

Brick Black Red

There is an ugly red chair
crouching in the corner of my grandmother's parlor.
I remember it being in my house
when I was small.

I would fall asleep lying crossways in it;
my head resting on the right arm, my legs hanging over the left,
my bare feet dangling over the side
-white cotton pajamas thin at the knees.

They say that I was a pretty child
-blonde hair hanging straight or in pigtails.
They say that I was a happy child
-before I started hiding under desks at school.

I remember closing my eyes lying in the red chair,
and waking up in my father's arms;
my head resting on his right arm,
my legs hanging over his left.
-feeling his strong arms as he carried me up the stairs
to place me in my small bed.
He must have loved me then.
—Didn't he? Even for that small time?
Karen Dwyer

"The Light"

For the world is darkened with so much
cruelty, from the threats of life's endangerments,
there stands only one man in my heart.
He longs for the warmth of love to enter his
soul, seeking survival from the cold. Then the
passion begins.
With the storm rolling into his veins, the rush
of lightning darting at his heart, and the sound of
thunder in his mind.
He becomes to frightened and scared to see that
I am beside him, the love that we share being
the only real truth in this world.
There will come a time when that will be his
guiding light through an endless tunnel called love.
Only when that time comes will he know the value
is more than what is waiting at the end of the
rainbow, where the darkness is over come by
such a beautiful light.
Nathalie L. Herring

Treasures Of Raindrops

Treasures of raindrops
    dance from the sky,
    tantalizing doves soaring high.

The sun is bursting with colorful rays,
    comes out of nowhere
    precisely at that time of day.

Gazing up at the sky, I'm inclined to stare,
    treasures of raindrops dance in my eyes.

As the long days go by and by,
    the earth takes on a vastness of mysterious shape
    in a richness of textures and tones;
    silently waiting until the next time of day.
Lori Guinn

Relentless

The weary soldier of love
    dances with fate and the Gods above.
Playing their game he bides his time
    on the path of chance, but he's the last in line.
Never flinching, in the bright sunlight
    he waits and waits for her alone at night.
Marching on and on each day
    watching others laugh, make love, and play.
Relentlessly he looks beyond
    and hums his sorrow song.
Pining for the love he knew
    hoping against hope that she's longing for him too.
Maybe seen his shattered heart will mend,
    but if not he'll march until the very end.
Neil Arends

If One Door Closes, Another Two Doors Open

Why is it that when my dreams seem so bright
darkness approaches and I stand without light?
I thought that my vision would unfold and extend
but instead it just vanished all because of a friend.
Time after time it just happens once more
my visions collapse as my heart has been torn.
It seems so unreal how the pain lies within,
how a few words can bruise me again and again.
I'm hoping to see that the tables will turn
so I won't reminisce and again feel this burn.
Vanessa Santana

Transcending Vacancy

"So", she said to me. "You can't love what you do not know.
Dare you know me?" She's been mad, and told me so.
Terrified, I see her ravaged visage. Blue-green eyes,
impaling me, taunting plead, "You stay or you flee: Decide!"

Childhood's wilds, abusedhood's refuge, "schizophreniforms."
Dossiers expose. Touching, loving, plunge embracing storms.
Sane saddens awareness. Impairments we rearranged.
Her madness, treasure, pleasure. Unmeasured laughs exchange.

Lunacy's the sublimity. Hers, fuzzy logic.
Honed humanity, spirit shaved-naked, not tragic
like unsullied mentality always unborn
unto peaks amaranthine, stark, erudite, sun-warmed.

Fractals' portals, madness for mortals. Infinity
fascinates,enervates. How she enucleates me!
Basking, abiding. Delighting requiting, I sing
apprehension's suspension. So, I mention a ring.

"So" she told me. "Logic is the irrelevancy.
You are brave, you see. Few dare transcending vacancy."
I stand the cost. Dreadful, illusive normality burned,
out of being. Lost to rational. Freedom returned.

Mathew K. Kiel

Resurrection

Gnashing her rotten teeth; writhing her gnarled, crippled hands
Dark shadows slinking behind her
Small black eyes, glazed with terror,
Glowing from the swarthy complexion.
Her twisted fingers grasped for mine
Puckered gray lips parted
Her dry, raspy voice whispering unknown secrets
Her eyes darted to the left
A shrill scream escaped her twisted mouth
Echoing throughout the dark street
Her mangled body shrunk back into the bleak darkness
Trembling fingers clutched the gold cross around her neck
Glassy eyes transfixed on the illusion lurking behind me
Her body shook, went limp, and crumbled to the pavement
A halo of light radiated around her sullen face
Still pressed to the cold ground she looked up
Shedding all evidence of desolation and despair
Rose without a word, a passionate resurrection
Her fragile body moved toward the immaculate light Crooning softly

Lisa Ann Wilcox

The South Has Risen

In this country, but not this century,
conflict lived, and exploded in fury.
Brothers in blue battled brothers in gray.
Freedom and more were issues of the fray.

Beaten and down, the South bided her time
as her forced facade complied like a mime.
But, in her heart to herself she stayed true.
Slowly with patience her influence grew.

Congressmen and Senators from the South
often voted with a regional mouth.
Change by loyal Southern voters is rare.
Return the same men. What is to compare?

The mood of the nation shifts a bit right.
The South looks, sees, and expresses delight.
Strom, Armey, Helms, Gramm, Lott, and even Newt;
And the nation asks, "How deep is the root?"

Clinton is president...who else will run?
The South seems assured to have some more fun.
So citizens, have you learned the lesson?
True to her promise, the South has risen.

Marie B. Huntsman

Happy As Can Be (1945-1995)

Bertha Ann "Bert" Quinn and Wilton Sanfort "Cat" Nichols
In "Cat's" 40 Ford, he went through the iron bridge of Otter Creek to
find his lover 50 years ago. "Bert's" eyes so bright to see "Cat"
that night. After they courted many nights, they were— Happy As Ca

Later "Cat" said, "Bert," 'Come now, be my bride. I'll always be by
your side." On May 11, 1945, with Reverend George F. Dyer,
We said, yes I do- - - You were a happy bride by my side.
This made me—- Happy As Can Be!

We'll have children, one, two or three. Gail will build us homes one,
two or three. Our farm home we'll share with Karen and Kevin with
delight— A sight to see! They will be happy to add to our genealogy
tree. This will make us— Happy As Can Be!

Rook will be played until one, two or three— With family, friends,
you and me. This made many people— Happy As Can Be!

The Old Iron Bridge on Otter Creek is out of sight, what a delight.
There will be the Great Golden Bridges. We'll go with delight— To
cross to the golden shores— To eternity— Just you and me. Will go
hand in hand with thee— We'll be— Happy As Can Be!

Edith McGhee Sigmon

Tying Ribbons Into Bows

Slow planning and patience, with gentle persistence;
Giving individual attention not only to contour and texture,
But to a new color emerging
And feeling yourself bloom.

Michael Korhnak

The Christmas Patch Quilt

Trimming the tree with ornaments and lights, Hanging balls, bells, berries and bows,
Placing a wreath on every door, Lighting candles in all the windows

Smelling pine, holly and spice after spice, Sipping cider and nibbling fruit cake,
Crunching candy canes and chocolate Santas, Cutting batches of Christmas cookies to bake

Celebrating together with family and friends, Remembering Christmases past,
Enjoying the season's festivities, Making memories that will surely last

Spreading cheer with fruit-filled baskets, Taking sleigh rides in the frosty snow,
Caroling around the neighborhood, Sneaking kisses under the mistletoe

Licking stamps for Christmas cards, Rushing around 'til the 25th gets here
Standing in endless lines at the mall, Rushing about as Christmas draws near

Joining the kids in the final countdown, Leaving milk and cookies for St. Nick,
Crossing your fingers for time to pass quickly, Watching time pass slowly, tick...tick

Checking at dawn for white Christmas morn, Gathering everyone around the tree,
Keeping in mind those less fortunate, Thanking God for all that you see

Waiting for a cue for the opening to begin, Pondering what's in the biggest box,
Scattering it's paper all over the floor, Oh Santa fooled you! It's only a pair of socks!

The Christmas quilt with all its patches can warm heart with memories dear.
Christmas by Christmas, memory by memory, your patch quilt grows larger each year.

Ah, the joys of the holiday seasons, but don't limit them to only December.
Just pull out your Christmas Patch Quilt anytime you want to remember.

Sandra Lee Heim

The Night Comes Early In December

The night comes early in December,
Darkness descends before the day in through.
There is no dusk, just daylight and night.
Afternoons are short and nights are long.

Some days even daytime seems not to be day
But a somber gray absence of night.
The sun is lost in the cold murky air,
And one can but dream of brightness of summer.

The bare trees reach toward the darkening sky
As if asking for the daylight to stay,
But too soon it has vanished, darkness returns,
And the long night has arrived once more.
   Marguerite Comiskey

Prince Of Forbidden Dreams

Once upon a time, in a land of forbidden dreams, the earth dawned a new day. As the water rushed through the land and the flowers blossomed with the wondrous colors of the rainbow, the dew of the morning frost left a fresh, undisturbed sensation as far as the eye and could see.

As life began to awaken from a peaceful dream, a love was also awoken. A love that is exiled by many and understood by few. But yet a love that could last FOREVER.

For many, FOREVER is a forbidden word, but to me, FOREVER has a deep and unforgettable meaning. FOREVER is the eternal commitment of love, honor, cherishment, loyalty, and forgiveness.

Although love may perish for some, I have found love's true form. The purest form of love that has ever touched or will ever touch my heart and soul. To love with all my heart is an everlasting and true commitment. I have never loved so deeply as I love YOU! May we never lose sight of the land of forbidden dreams and eternal peace.
   Helen Reneé-Hair

My Truest Friend

Days have come and as quickly have gone
Days which many have sung a sorrowful song
Be near! Be dear! Is what they proclaim
Yet near nor far they never came
Only one has earned a special right
One whose been closest through all that I fight
You may not be able to see with your own eyes
It has never been hidden behind any disguise
Calming the seas of troubled storms
Calming the eves corrupt by emotions torn
Finding my heart in many ways
The same heart so many throw away
Unconditional love is what I receive
From the only one who will never deceive me
There shall never be an end
For I have found my truest friend
   Bonnie Lee Hunsberger

Success

Who is to say what is success and what is not.
For each person, success may be measured with mind or heart.
Then again, how can you measure love, hope and joy in a pot.
Perhaps, life measured is not...
   Mariko R. Pope

Untitled

I have stood on the hill of opportunity.
I have seen the result of defeat.
I'm not afraid of failing, I just don't like to be beat.

I could not try at all; I could sit and cry;
I could look and lie and know that I'm hiding myself from me.
But to shame myself with guilt would be something I could not do.
For what and who would I coincide with?

I am not dull or beaten down. I just like to be calm and peaceful.
I don't have a problem with my walk or pace, it's just a slow gait.
My back is straight and my head is held high. I have a heart.

Being in a single place can drive one to insanity.
But being strong is the way to go.
Don't let others who lack talent for life, bring your dreams down.

Being you is the best thing in the world.
Don't let others label you.
Be untitled
   Kristin M. Gosline

Game Over

I step forward to try my luck,
Defending her title,
My grandmother, unrelenting
Eyes, silver steel balls, loaded for a game
CHAMPION CHAMPION CHAMPION

Intimidation I deposit my quarter in the pinball machine of her mind.
THE COIL IS COCKED IN SPRING IS SPRUNG
I take my shot
I'm fine (20 pts.)
WHO IS THE PRESIDENT (5 pts.)
WHAT DAY IS THIS? (0 pts.)
WHERE ARE YOU? (10 pts.)
I'm not leaving (20 pts.)
SHH THEY'RE LISTENING! (0 pts.)
I can take care of myself (20 pts)
WHAT DAY IS THIS (0 pts).

Machines do not know they are machines,
Loss is not understood
Though the game may have just begun,
For Alzheimer patients, it is already over.
   Susan D. Wilson

Exodus

Isn't it time to wash away the mud,
Discard that ancient, paining rib,
Arise from the soiled and stony past,
Remove the rusting nails and cleanse the wounds.
Forget that broken body of Thought!
Let it be consigned to that "Shadowed Cave",
And raise your spinal shaft, parting the light
Like a shimmering, crimson sea, running...
To meet her; that patient informed touch.
Yes, now-time to give her a reasoned kiss
That lingers with the taste of ripened fruit.
   Robert E. Tager

Who Am I?

Here I sit in total darkness,
even though the sun's as bright as can be,
   wondering why I did the things I did,
and what will become of me.
   I shall look deep inside for the answer
I am searching for and I will open many doors,
   but while I wait that long lonely wait,
I'd like to know... who am I?
   Shawn Michael Toombs

"Sisterhood"

There are those who tried to crucify; mortify; justify; with a lie.
Defile; degrade; deface; deject. Strip me of my self respect.
All hail the women of Sisterhood.
Those who stood by me and made me feel good.
Those who sheltered me from harm. Made my heart full and warm.
Every day you've shown me the light at the end of the tunnel.
Even when I felt my strength being drained through a funnel.
You've made me proud to call you friend and Sister.
You've healed my heart of the internal blister.
So strong is the bond we share. Like the smile I force my face to wear.
The love that's shared may not always be spoken.
But, as sure as there's a GOD our bond will never be broken.
When I'm feeling lost and all alone.
All I have to do is pick up the phone.
We've had our ups and downs it's true.
But, I've never felt stranded when I was blue.
You truly understand my inner beauty.
Advocating freely, you've made it your duty.
The vibes that flow are Heaven sent.
Like a caterpillar to a butterfly a friendship that was meant.
So in closing I'd like to say, on this your very special Mother's Day.
All hail you Sister with our voices loud. To be a part of your entity
I'm truly proud.
  Michelle G. Birt

Beginning To Grow

Running through patches of greenery
Delighting from the smallest touch.
I take hold of a most beautiful creature
  Quite dear to me.
I vision a look of happiness.
Brightening to me at present
Suddenly beginning to sit
I take hold of this living being embracing his soul to mine!
For a while I begin to smile.

Words adventuring forth from my mouth
  Travel to the listener.
If this living being understand these words
  He will understand me!
But this living creature is quite like a baby:
Besides adventuring words.
  My expressions are to be physically shown.

I hold his body near mine as I relax here on this earth
He brings forth a sound and utter a sound I've heard before.
This living creature being so small in size
Actually as we know is just "Beginning to grow".
  Mary A. Daniels

Love Song

One early spring when I awoke feeling sad and blue,
Depression is what some call it; have you had it too?

I heard the sparrows singing a cheerful joyous song.
And suddenly I realized my feelings were so wrong.

If God gives the birds a song, then I should have
one too. Because for me Jesus died; He also died for you.

You too can hear this love song, just open up your
heart. Let Jesus in to make a change, he will not depart.

Now when I awake, feeling sad or blue, I listen for
the sparrows song and I start singing too.

Because I know God loves me and that his love is real.
He will always be beside me no matter how I feel.
  Wanda Lussier

The Stars Are Mine

As I reached for the stars, I would stumble and fall
determined, I'd struggle back up, to answer perfectionist' call

Why do I reach for the stars, you may ask of me
that my burdens may be lifted, and I be set free

My beloved, since you died and have gone away, sadness and fear
filled every day, until I realized I am loved in a very special way

My Lord and my Master gives me all the joy and peace I need
as I travel on this journey, my own life now to seek

He tells me I am His. He paid the price for all. "Go forth
proclaim my good news. Fear not. Go!! And Stand Tall"

I follow His loving advice. Now my heart reaches heights sublime
I touch the stars each evening. I know they are mine.

Replacing sadness and fear with indescribable peace and serenity
I now live my life fruitfully, as I go towards my own eternity
  Milli Marks

Daughter's Love
Excepts from my free writing

It's been thirteen months since my mother's death.
Died on January 19, 1989.
I'm left with an empty void never to be filled again.
There are so many things that I want to say, but now it is too late.
Letting go is the hardest part, and letting the healing process begin.
Trapped between the two worlds of insecurities and bitterness.
Feeling cheated that one day when I marry, and have children, she
  will never to be there to see it.
But these last thirteen months, God has tested my new founded faith.
And Mom, I just want to said - I Love You.
  Wendy Levinson Maiello

This Is The Garden Of Life

All kinds of flowers growing together.
Different colors and creeds of flowers.
When the rains come, each flower shares the water.
No one flower chokes out another.
Each has its own place in the garden.

When the sun shines, the tall flowers bend
for the small flowers to get their light.
The roots of these flowers grow together
to keep out the weeds that choke them.

When one flower dies, all flowers die.
When one flower smiles to the sun,
All flowers smile.
No one flower is more gallant than another.
All flowers are equal in beauty.

This is the Garden of life
These flowers will grow forever,
for these flowers are never at
War with each other
For every man, woman that dies, a flower grows.
This garden can be seen where it is not.
  Timothy Lawrence White

Beauteous Unjaunt

Kingly beauty shining gently at the world,
Disguised by shades of pastel and textured curls.

Oft times surveyed with jaded glasses,
Potential finite, progress molasses.

Unabridged by the world around,
Bravely forging, pioneering new ground.

Restructuring within to fortify the outward view,
Brow bloodied, vision askew.

Head abound, Focus restored,
Beauty shines boldly with discernment and lore.
Lubertha McClairen

Hurricane Luis

I beg of you please stay away
Do not come St. Thomas' way

We suffered through that Hugo Hurricane
First the watch, then the warning, then the rain

Thunder roared and lightening struck
And filled our hearts with fear

Five years, eleven months and eighteen days ago my dear
Not nearly time enough to wipe away the fear.

Veer away, although we wait and trees
Are madly swaying

The gusts of wind are reminiscent that
now all should be praying

Why do hurricanes love to strike
In the darkness and at night?

Though when I really think of it
There is no time, that is really right

The demons prowl, the godly pray
Don't let the devil, have his way

Dear God make Luis veer away.
Olga Rasmussen Lopez

About The Color Of One's Skin

Is the color of another skin an issue with you?
Do you judge someone by their color, before you hear the
words from their month, that pass through?
Do you ever stop to think that, that person may be
loving and compassionate, and unto God may be true?
If you ever thought those thoughts, would that change
your point of view?
If you ever see this poets arms, chest
and back, you will see many, many tattoos. And
I have seen on many different faces their judgement
of me, by what their eyes did view.

And oh what a wrong judgement they made of me, for
you see within my heart and soul unto almighty God,
I am totally committed loving and true.
Please wait until you are around a person for a while,
and have listened unto their words, before you pass your
judgement upon that one. And never, never pass judgement
for ones color, for if you do
it is a gross wrong that you have done.
Michael D. Jones

Destiny...

What is destiny?
Does anyone know?
Can you make it with a recipe?
Can you shape it out of snow?

Can you find it in the trees?
Can you find it under rocks?
Can you get it out of text books?
Can you get it from your socks?

Can you taste it with your tongue?
Can you see it with your eyes?
And if you're looking upward;
Will it be there in the skies?

Well, you can't see destiny, and it can't see you.
Destiny is that special thing; you were always meant to do.

In your heart you can feel one,
And in your soul you can shape it.
But one thing is for sure; you decide, to make or break it.

What will it bring in the future?
What has it brought in the past?
I'll make it what it will be; a special destiny, at last!
Kristen Delgrego

Late Bloomer

Am I too fat?
Does my hair look right?
Which dress should I wear?
Will I get a date to the prom?
Can I pass the test?
Has my essay enough research?
Why am I shaking about my report card?
Should I try out for the cheer leading team?
I am slim.
My hair has just been weaved.
The dress is the latest style.
I have a date to my favorite place tonight.
I just completed multiple budgets on time.
I'm confident about my Board presentation on Tuesday.
I got promoted last week.
I'm part of the corporate team.
Molly F. Seamons

Death is Forever

Death is forever, so live life today.
  Don't ever let anything, get in your way!
    Enjoy the large things, as well as the small,
      All of your desires, are at your beck and call!

What are some big things, that happened to me?
  That all depends on, now, let me see!
    There was the day, I met the love of my life,
      And the children I shared, with my former wife.

What are the small things, that I can recall?
  There's never been one - not one time at all.
    'Cause each tiny moment, of each fleeting day,
      Grew bigger and bigger, like a wave in the bay!

Wouldn't it be great - to relive the time?
  To be young folks, at the peak of our prime.
    We wouldn't waste a second, of each precious day,
      Just enjoy all our work, and relish our play!

So this is the reason, that I think you should try,
  To live, and 'get with it' - don't let life pass you by.
    Not once again, will you hear someone say:
      "Death is forever", but, "Have a nice day!"
Richard E. Nickel

Violence

Violence is something I may never understand.
"Don't kill me over my new shoes
just take them man."
The horror lynching's by the klan,
Yeah! Violence truly dominates the land,
And you wonder why that kid got shot
by the over anxious cop?
The kid had a toy gun
he thought it was fun!
Now the kid's life, which has just begun
is confined to a wheelchair
"He will never Run"
It's hard to explain the pain I feel
when an innocent is killed
over a senseless act.
Bombing buildings full of kids
"what kind of sense is that?"
Violence is something that we all must face
Violence doesn't limit itself to just one race
Not one person not one place
Violence must be erased!

Kendrick N. Cross

Follow Your Dreams

Follow your dreams, where ever they lead you
Don't let your pride, or fear impede you

Follow your dreams, where ever they go
They may come true, you never know

Follow your dreams, you may be surprised
They may bring back, the gleam in your eyes

Follow your dreams, they may slip away
Life is too short, we're not here to stay

Follow your dreams, believe in yourself
Follow your heart, not anyone else

Follow your dreams, they may make you smile
Don't get discouraged, if it takes you a while

Follow your dreams, don't sell yourself short
Don't take put downs, of any sort

Follow your dreams, not for anyone else
Follow your dreams, and live for yourself

Susan D'Angelo

Problem Solver

When all of life's problems are rushing in upon your door
don't try to fight in your own strength just turn toward the Lord
He takes us through the toughest times when all seems so lost
He even suffered all our pains when He died upon the cross.

He knows the troubles we have at times seem to drag us down
But He wants to put a smile in place of all the many frowns
He has never left us nor shall He ever let us fall
Unless it's to pick us up with greater love involved.

Never let troubles leave your heart feeling empty and afraid
Remember there's a Savior standing in for us each day
Don't ever think that you have lost, cause this is the way
Victory was won for us when He arose from the grave.

Venus D. Painter

Another Chance?

Dazing out through the driver side window, my eyes were
drawn to yours. You, standing hunched, dirty, with too
big boots that had eaten gray frayed woolen socks, cuffed
unrolled work pants, half-out plaid flannel shirt, yesterdays
five o'clock shave, muffled hair and broad hands clutched
to worn carboard sign which read, "Will Work For Food."
Our eyes meet. Do I see a warm spirit?
Did you loose love?
Did you love? Can you love?
Was life too hard on you?
Are you a remind of humbleness?
Are you humble? Will you really work?
Do you want to work?
Passers-by ignore you. Stone faces keep straight forward.
You have eyes that shine. Do they mirror your soul? Do you
need someone to believe in you?
Love is patient. Love is kind. Love never gives up.
I believe in you.
I smile- You smile-
Do I take a chance?

Twinkle Williams

"Midnight Dreaming"

Midnight dreaming, in the midst of natures mighty throne
Dreaming not only of you, but of your world alone
The sky so clear, and the stars so bright
I pray to the heavens on this cold December night
I ask the queen of angels to shield thee from dread
But I read in the eyes of others, that their hope is dead.

Finally as a cold, brisk wind hits my face,
I awake from my dream, and move from my place.
As I walk through the towering forests of sycamore
I fear the reality that I will see you never more
As the snow gently falls, and down my cheek run the tears
I feel your presence near, and remember back through the years

Midnight dreaming, while admiring natures universal throne
I walk through the deepening snow, all alone
I remember you on this cold December night,
As the stars above shine so purely bright.
From the tears, my cheeks have been tendered,
And with a midnight dream, I keep you in my heart, remembered.

C. Moffitt

"Dreams"

Dreams are the stars twinkling in the sky
Dreams are the rainbows arched so high
Dreams are the raindrops that pitter, patter and fall
Dreams are the trees that grow so tall
Dreams are the flowers that brighten up the day
Dreams are the clouds that float along and play

Dreams are the pictures I see inside my head
Dreams are the journeys I take when I lie in bed
Dreams are the things I want to grow up and be
Dreams are the places I'm yearning to see
Dreams are the sunrays in a child's smile
Dreams are the wings that carry us mile after mile

Dreams are the love lights inside you and me
Dreams are anything you want them to be
Dreams are wishes and hopes you have within
Dreams are the steps that you take to win
Follow the dreams in your heart wherever they lead
Start with a book and begin to read!

Patrice A. Arnold

Myself

Kristen, Humorous, Active, Responsible
Wishes to succeed in life.
Dreams of going some place in the world.
Wants to travel to a Tropical Rainforest.
Who wonders if her dreams will come true.
Who fears of going in allies by herself.
Who is afraid of big spiders.
Who loves animals and running cross country.
Who believes in everything she wrote down here.
Who likes horseback riding.
Who likes shopping at the mall.
Who likes babysitting.
Who likes winter when it snows.
Who plans to go to college and get a degree.
Who plans to make her dreams come true.
Who plans to save the Rainforests.
Who hopes (or choices) she will have a good school year.

Kristen M. Catalano

Sunrise Beach

The sand feels smooth and warm like new woven silk freshly
    dried in the sunshine.
The ocean reverberates like a lover's intimation
Satisfying one with an intimate valentine.
The beach is the essentiality of a natural sensation
Freshly created for the enjoyment of the imagination.
A light taste of salt touches the taste buds and leaves a craving
    for more.
The morning sun's fingers of light stroke the ocean with friendly
    persuassion.
The seagulls make a melody with a harmony of sea life along
    the shore.
The gentleness of the ocean encases the world like a warm
    blanket's clutch.
The sky is kaleidoscope of many blues, reds, oranges and pink.
The fragrance of life awaking is almost tangible enough to touch.
The simplistic elegance of the early morning ocean's wink
Is as breathtaking as a new rose opening to the sun.
The peace of early morning by the beach brings a sense of
    life just begun.

Mandy Satterfield

Why I Love My Biological Father

Thinking
Drinking
Sinking
Thinking

Alcoholics and drug addicts swim around tainting,
diluting the murky fluid that fills my gene pool.

Father, viewed through child's eyes, a monster,
on our pain and suffering he thrives.

I guess I'll really never understand,
Why he spoke of love, but struck her closed hand.

Noise
Silence
Confusion
Delusion

Why were the moments of happiness quickly
drowned out by the pain and fears?

Maybe it wasn't the pain and fears,
probably just the blood and tears.

Ryan Weathers

N.A.

Cackling monkeys wave their paws to
drown the tides of life.
With gourded pickles served as holders for
their jagged knifes.
Trooped as Gods with silver shawls the lions
place there crowns.
Along the stream where fishes dream and
sinners all fall down.
The putrid seas collide and mingle along the
ocean floor.
All happy days now fade away replaced
by blood and gore.
The tales told that rise so bold will only
soon see.
The world apart, a severed heard all as
dead as me.

Victoria L. Simonsen

Suffocation

Forever strangled by peoples acts of racism
due to their insecurity.
My pain increases as my patience wears thin.
When will it stop when does this foolishness end?
To what joy do we gain from suffocating each
other from the joys and happiness that life itself brings?
To what extent do we end this madness and
resolve it with a profound love which we
ourselves can give.
As the inanimate praise God for their very
creation, to what sweet blessings do we give
as animate creatures of God's creation?
Love is nothing but a dream in a world full of hate.
But the love inside each of us causes our
goodness grace. To receive love, we must
first give love in order to untangle ourselves
from this suffocating hate.

Marlene Mais

The Lily And The Cross

The lily and the cross stood side by side —
Each a master of its own,
The lily was the pureness of an unselfish friend —
The cross — a sympathetic end, alone.
'Twas honesty and forgiveness that were tried
By hearts of stone that wouldn't melt away,
As Jesus heard them shout the he be crucified
(The thorn in their ignorance thus to slay.)
The lily before the cross stood silent and still —
No words would it offer — its life to save;
The cross stood firm on Calvary Hill —
A somber, lonely grave.
The cross was taken down upon the dawn;
The sky lay a brilliant blue,
And where once both had stood upon the lawn,
Now alone the radiant lily grew.

Margaret L. Schroeder

Aikido

He glides forward as if on wheels.
He encounters opposition with which he deals,
without pitting force against force.
Their energies meld, and become as one,
the movement executed, aggression undone.
Another comes with hurt in mind,
but hurt reflected he will not find.
It's practiced with reverence nice and slow,
this is the heart of aikido.

Michael Sosa

The Enemy

He creeps inside of us
each chance he gets,
And uses subtle tactics
to strengthen egos
and increase ruthlessness.
We never suspect him to be the
demon that grows inside of us,
but he always gets the last cruel remark
in an argument.
We often mistake him
for the winner
or the other team.
He becomes fatal when
taken to an
extreme degree.
The relentless force that pressures us
not only to content,
but to win.
We desire more than to succeed,
we desire to sin.
Treena Zimbelman

"Friends"

Throughout our lives, it seems as though,
each day that passes, new friends come
and go, living each day by day; having
good ones, along with some bad.
At times, when feeling as though we've
met up with the worst, our friends are there
to lend a helping hand, and sometimes even
that shoulder needed to cry on. Supporting
each other, on those days needing support.
along with sharing some of the best days too.
Relieved, when realizing, that those times shared,
will last a lifetime, later becoming memories
we can cherish forever. Regardless, of how
far apart we become, real friends, those who
really count, never let go.
        I'll never let go!
Sandee Bishop

Memories Of War 1939-1945

The war was a game to six year old twin sisters, at first.
Each day we walked off to school carrying gas masks in cardboard boxes.
At night we listened to the siren howling its melancholy warning.
From the safety of the air raid shelter we heard the thud of
bombs, the silence, then the tinkling of broken glass falling like
icicles on frozen seas.
Our parents held us, but we were more afraid of the spider on the ceiling.
Then off to the country, London evacuees settling on another planet.
Walking through country lanes to school, watching the war on the movies.
The war ended when I was twelve years old.
The nightmares began later.
Chased by German soldiers in boots.
Running, hiding, running again.
Now in my sixties, those nightmares have gone like mist in the morning.
But memories still return to haunt me in sad and unexpected ways.
One day I come across an antique Prussian plate stamped with a swastika.
I quickly find some paint and carefully cover the sign with liquid gold.
And at a park one summer Sunday afternoon, I see a small Japanese
man, about my age, dancing with his wife to the music of a band.
He wears a camouflaged cloth cap, the kind worn by Japanese soldiers.
As he smiles and executes some fancy steps, I suddenly see
A prisoner of war camp with Japanese guards beating women to death.
Ashamed of my thoughts, I turn away. A shadow crosses the sun.
Olive Evans

Velvet Chains

You bind me to you with velvet chains
Each link forged by words of love.
So strong upon me these chains have lain
Yet soft and gentle as wings of a dove.

I've tried so hard to break these chains
To free myself from your strangling hold.
Just when I think my freedom's gained,
You whisper again those words of old.

So once again the chains hold fast
As your words strengthen the weakest link,
And again I know, as in the past
My hopes for freedom begin to sink.

I loved you so in days long past,
And you killed my love with a lie,
But your velvet chains still held me fast
And they will - until I die.
Wilda Lee Rogers

Dedicated To Dad

All the things we've said and done I hold close to my heart
each moment that I spent with you until we had to part.

Moments will now come no more, it's memories I must cherish
soldier down the road of life because you had to perish.

For some unknown it must have been that God was in your need,
he must have had some other plan than to have you here with me.

I may not know what the reason is or fully understand,
but I have faith that how he works is within his perfect plan.

So I'll believe that your above, an angel in the wings,
guiding me through the good and bad that life will surely bring.

You may not be within my touch or nor within my sight,
but rest assured you're by my side within the guiding light.

And all I've become and all I am I owe to you today,
Thank you Dad so very much for showing me the way.
Susan Schrom

Masquerades

Blind guides, not knowing the way,
Each putting on their showy display;
Pretending they are right when they have not a clue
Of what is proper to say or proper to do.

Pretty lies make us feel good
When we are not doing all that we should.
We build ourselves up by tearing others down;
And paint on a smile to cover a frown.

Masquerades. Life is a game.
What we act like and are never the same.
Why we choose to live these lies is not very clear.
Maybe it serves to easy the pain or quiet a hidden fear.
Lita C. Miller

"Two Candles"

Two candles represent the bodies,
Each with their own characteristics and personalities.
Candle-holders are the solid base for the bodies symbolizing stability
Which is found in a nurturing, growing friendship.
A match allows the chance to ignite...
A spark which steadily grows into...
A flame...
The flame has a chance of dying because it may go unnoticed.
But, how can the flame ever grow if the match has never been lit
Allowing the spark to start the flame?
Melanie Celeste Stephenson

Lost And Found

Cozy and secure, snuggled under his blanket,
Ears twitching, a hero in his dreams? or just scared,
Remembering the time he was lost, wishing
Someone would find him, or feed him.
Remembering!

Remember him, running anxiously through the woods,
And me, running desperately through life.
Fear would keep him alone, who would rescue him?
Alone. Who would comfort me?
Searching!

Two rescues, safe from danger, and together!
A chance meeting, perfect timing, is that what it was?
But no. He who sees the sparrow fall saw us both.
Safe!
We remember...

Mary Jo Rothenberg

A College Friday Night

My to do list:

Write my biology report, write half of it, do the outline;
Eat a banana split, eat two, awe eat three banana splits;
Have your stomach pumped;
Call your friends and ask for money, just demand money,
awe black mail them for money;
Take a break, have an Alka-Seltzer on the rocks, take your temperature
Quilt bedspreads for the Kickapoo Indians;
Mend my shirt, sew doll clothes, just clean the lint in the sewing machine;
Sell fingernail clippings, string beads for money, just empty your piggy bank;
Grow rice in your water glass;
Hang it in your ear, hang in your closet, hang it in your car;
Leave it where it was!
Write my biology report, do the outline; settle for a reasonably good topic!
Call it a night!

Virginia Mohler

"Through The Eyes Of A Child"

I awakened to the smell of crisp bacon an
eggs frying on Saturday morning;

While getting out of bed to wash my face,
thinking of what cartoons to watch, as I stare
in the mirror wondering.

Suddenly I hear a knock on the bathroom door from
my Big Brother - trying to rush me out; because he has
a basketball game to play with is friends.
I yell to him Okay, okay as I began to pout.

Mother calls to all of us, to come and eat breakfast,
before it gets cold;
Of course I am the first one downstairs.
As mother asked me, did you wash you hands?
Of course yes, I tell her - my face and my toes!

Mother turns, then gives me a look that could melt steel;
Although I know she loves me,
I am always making jokes - and oh what a thrill

We all sat down at the table to say our blessings;
While we begin to eat, I look around the table and
say to myself - God! Thank you for such a great family.

Thomas White Jr.

"Just One More Day"

As the Autumn leaves rustle quietly, in shades of amber,
  emerald and crimson...
A brisk northern wind threatens their very existence...

Yet, they cling to their lifeline, desperately...in hope...
A glimmer of radiant sun, blankets them in warmth,
and gives promise, for yet another day...

Suddenly, the alarm sounds...

Deepening gray layers, frigid swirling wind,
and the gentle tapping rain, colour the ominous pathway,
to yet another brief encounter with mortality...

A life, a soul, delicately clings to me, with hope, as its lifeline...
With relentless fervor, and all human interventions exhausted,
a hand to hold, a soft blanket for warmth, we give promise...

Quietly, a presence with unparalleled power, consumes the life,
and with a shroud of cold and darkness, it is finished...
Winter Begins...

Life has come full circle. Yet as all within the universe...
We cling...disparately...

For Just One More Day...

Patricia Melle-Yohe

Conclusion

Summer's sun is dying
ending its season of primacy.

An unwelcome chill has displaced
its once vibrant warmth.
The rays now a pale imitation of past glory.

Later and later it rises
weakened, lifting itself reluctantly above the horizon.
Owing more to habit than vigor.

There are good days yet
of sparkling light and glowing heat.
But they are few.

So begins an orderly withdrawal
an eagerness to cut short the day.
A removal from the center to the periphery.

Impressions of the golden days remain
when robust strength and energy poured forth, spilled over
when days were long, and then longer still.

They will see us through the dark times ahead.

Martha Zvonik

Untitled

Love is a truth and a trap. Possessive as a father, yet
evasive like the autumn wind. Known, but never understood;
Believed, but never quite grasped. It is a weapon, a knife
cutting through the heart with swift ease. The wounds may
heal, but the scars will always remain, present ever in the
depths of thought, actions, words spoken, and decisions made.
Never be fooled by love, or what love is believed to be. No
eyes can see the truth that lie within, nor the lies that
hide inside. Look beneath the word, behind it, inside of
it. It is there that you will find the true meaning of the
word 'love'. Always sought and so very hard to find, it is
eternally found, forever in the heart.

Shawn P. McKern

False Vision

Is there a religion for which we can trust
Even a superpower God who created us
Do we belong in a world of logic and science
Or in politics in a world of war and defiance
It is hard to believe what I can not recognize
The philosophy of life and death through believable lies
By ignoring the strength of a political move
Searching for a reason science can not prove
Here I cry without a religion
Living my life through a false vision

Kevin R. Gines

To Karen From Her Grandmother

A spring baby! The month of May
Even then she stole our hearts away.

And now, six springs later

This girl of ours, has changed - and stretched and grown
So tall and so sophisticated, we hardly know her for our own.

Ready for school, ready for play,
Ready for the fun each day

Of change and challenge
Of love and tears

This little girl of six short years.

Marion Elmer

The Happiest Age

I will not grow old,
Even tho, I look old.
Because I have joys to share,
With all the young who pass my way.

I love to hear their laughter,
All about the cares of their day.
Why should I burden them with something,
That would make them worry on their way?

I won't bring up thoughts to trouble them,
Or sing them songs of woe.
Goodness knows there's enough of that,
No matter where they go.

Let my life bring something into their world,
Instead of taking it away.
And make their lives all worthwhile,
And never from happiness stray.

Marjorie E. Shaner

My Garden

Far beyond this vicious earth lies my garden that gave me birth.
Every rose upon this garden greets me with the aromas of a sweet
  sensation.
I swear I touch the doors of heaven every time a plant
  bears a new creation.
Every flower petal so perfectly formed, every leaf ever so green.
My feet have been were no feet have been, my eyes have seen
  what no eyes have seen.
Embraced by the spirits of my garden comfort is all I feel,
  I gently rub my sore eyes to see if such perfection is real.
And then all the love and innocence slowly disappears.
I return to this world overcome with fears and harms but
  for some reason sad I am not.
And then I remember that the word tomorrow is something my
  garden has not yet forgot.

Laura Cruz

Ballgame Dream

All my life I've been hitting the single,
Every time it's been just what I need
To get to first where I can recover,
And they wonder why I can't ever lead
When I take my swing at the at the line of life.
At times I connect my bat with the ball,
To soar the path that fortune's found,
But with the wrong stick, I often miss
And must look for the luck around
Again the next when I am up.
All my life I've been running the one-by-one,
Just once I'd like to starry the stands,
And jump up two in the upward climb,
To run the four without a pause,
To break the never happen laws.

Susan J. Shaw

Sapphire Summer

Your sparkling eyes like sapphires catching the sun's precisely extracting precious stones from ordinary pebbles, mining the rivers of our senses, stripping extraneous terrain yielding gems of possibility, protection, promise

Sister Moose lolling in meadow grasses, sunlit rays dancing on your silken back we pray in flowered fields roaming with abandon drinking from forest's splashing stream at dawn sharing life's communal pool with Black Bear Brother

Creaking echoes ascending narrow, leaning stairs, parade of miners' expiring ghosts removing coats, hats, boots, socks, burly hands warming by fiery furnace awaiting a bed, a meal, a bath, counting futures in the sack

Moonlight sweetly painting the room in dusky starlight your familiar gently treading upon my afghan cover at the first sign of my stirring as if to reassure himself I'm not a ghost

Piercing wail announces burnt breakfast toast sending Rosebud into panicked flight, fearing to lap her kibbles, awaking your tired robe, fanning the dissipating smoke while I prop the kitchen window, escaping hope

My cards admonish me to cease the frantic, whirling dervish to recognize the exhaustive, spinning of the grouse; look into sapphire, stream, furnace and familiar to ground my nascent energy and find my compass upon the earth

Olga Kokino

Untitled

Rugged
Faceless figures
Walk alone inside the bottle
Depressed,
Blacken' faced brothers
Die without honor on the battlefield forgotten
While a God overhead laughs
And pours burning hot oil upon naked babes
The mothers of the forsaken weep
Their tears slowly drowning each other
Death brings the God a smile
For everything is tainted by hope
A baby's births
Brotherhood
Motherhood
Even life.

Matthew Whitmire

Untitled

Dignity, what a beautiful word to hear,
falling softly from thoughts,
sinking deep in my inner ear.

Success? Now I've had little of that,
Wealth? Only the sunsets flame.
Honesty? Yes, and dignity and my name.
Money? Only lovely flower growing on the earth.
Stocks and Bonds? Only the birds singing of joy and mirth.

Acclaim? Only a humble cottage, needing paint and renovation,
but doubtless I will leave this earth and never have a vacation.
But after studying all this complicated situation,
where I am going, what I wanted to be in this conglomeration,
No, I never achieved them no not one,
My dreams and goals were lost on life's sea,
But when my craft sails off from this old world,
I will have with me my Dignity.
La Hom Ham

Change

Softly the winds of change call,
falling upon deaf ears, that hear nothing at all.
It seems in darkness it all begins,
and then, again, it ends.
Yet, when the end might come,
there shines a bright new beginning.
Sometimes the candle flames are hard to see,
as they flicker in the strong winds of indifference and
injustice.
Rise up! Listen, to the sound of change
See the flickering light of reason.
Be whole again!
Susanne C. Toro

Midnight Run

Time for fun, Midnight Run
Fantasies and nightmares come alive

Midnight Run, there is no Sun
I hope this will open up your eyes

Discoveries abound, look at what I found
Roaming on my Midnight Run

Quiet streets, trees and stars galore
Gave me much more than I was looking for

Aliens, vampires, terrorists and queens
Situations, from my wildest dreams

They follow me every step of the way
All with incredible things to say

The quiet and stillness makes my mind wander
The fog, rain, and bats make my heart thunder

Midnight Run, almost done
Running is a natural high

Nightly fun, Midnight Run
People ask me why

Midnight Run, now I'm done
Look at all the stars in the sky
C. Brian Law

Snow

Crystalline flakes caress my skin
Fantasy and reality - threads worn thin
Crisp are the words in the frozen stratosphere
Calling to me - bringing me near
Sharp are the images painted in the clouds
Free from the blur of shadowy doubts
The tundra's rainbow opens a vision in my head
Reminding me that I am not dead
The arctic breeze blows wide the aperture of my mind
Revealing to me what I hope to find
A warm open hearth with love surrounding
Blessed appreciation and contentment abounding
Games being played by the roaring firelight
Affection and joviality shine through night
Outside the window snowflakes fall like fleece-
But I am inside - one at peace.
Matthew G. Barber

God On My Side

Darkness is the river that carries thee across the land of lies
fear is the bear that tears thy flesh and whips thy golden eyes
hate is the hand that pushes thee to the shores of regret
death is the crumbled earth that lets thee fall without a net

I am the bear of darkness, I am the hand of fear
I am the cyclone of hate that draws ever near
I am the magus of death in my nightmare paradise
I am the malevolence that bears me away to ritual sacrifice

I am my God, I decide what is
I destroy life even as live
R. Carroll Monroe

'God Knows'

When things around you are going bad, and you can't be happy for
feeling sad, God knows. He knows exactly what to do,
he'll be the one to carry you. God knows.

When you've prayed for things to change, but another day brings
the same old pain, God knows. He'll be your guide to a brighter
day, give him your hand, he'll lead the way. God knows.

You've struggled, sacrificed and given your best, still you worry
and some nights you can't rest, God knows. He'll be the shelter in
your storm, his mighty arms will keep you warm. God knows.

God sees your heart and knows what you feel. Just keep the
faith cause this God is real. Like Job be patient, learn to wait.
God may not be there when you want him, but he's never late.
And when you need strength to face a new day, just
call on him, he's not far away. Remember your strength comes
from above, wrapped in his mercy and unconditional love.
Kirk D. Harris

I Have Been Watching A Butterfly Die

I have been watching a butterfly die, not quite understanding why,
God has chosen such a beautiful creature, the butterfly shudders
with a painful sigh — the butterfly is dying.

I reach over and touch it, it draws its wings up tight, it has no
strength to fly away, though it tries to hold it in, life keeps
slipping out — the butterfly is dying.

A puff of wind, it blows the butterfly on its side, it cannot upright
itself, and I sit here watching the butterfly die — I feel a cool
rush of air nearby, and I know the butterfly is dead.

I wonder if a single death is all the deaths of butterflies still to come.
Laura Kenkel

The Day I Thought You'd Never Stop

Pound, pound, scream, scream; crash as the skillet of ground meat
  fell to the floor.
Shrieks came from around the house as we headed for the door.
Anger boiled through my bones as I watched you hit her face.
Pound, pound, scream, scream, "Stop David stop!"
I walked out quietly, everyone staring and I was stark raging mad;
my heart was crushed from that day forward.
I went for help and on my way back in my mind I was thinking,
"I can take him by myself I don't need anyone's help."
I felt I had the strength of a raging bull.
I came back to the house and all I could hear was her scream;
it was a cry for help. I stormed back into the house still angry and mad.
All I could do was pace the floor.
You looked at me with your crystal clear mind and said,
"What's wrong baby?"
I could see my self fighting you with my bare hands,
but I was too mad to do anything but cry.
From that day on when ever we told the story they laughed.
I never though it was a laughing matter,
because in my heart that was the day I thought you'd never stop.

  Tomeka Smith

A Little Boy That Wanted To Turn His Life Around

Once there was this little boy who wanted to change his life, but he
felt like if he got out of the gang he would be killed. So he went
to his mother in tears one day. She took him in her arms and said!
My son what's wrong. He said mother! I'm in this gang and I want to
get out of it, but it's so hard...His mother replied to him and said,
no son it's not hard talk to God ask him to help you.

God can do anything that you want him to do just trust in Him, and
  turn your life around in his direction.
God will fulfill any dreams are problems that's in your life...

But my child you have to trust Him and believe in your heart and soul,
  that God is real.
My son I have seen God change and turn many lives
around, you have to go down on your knees in prayer, and just say
father give me that strength to let go of this life of sin.
For I know there's no one but you God that can step in and just
turn me around from this unjust world.
Lord Jesus take my hand and walk with me each day to come...Amen

  LaFaye Price

Untitled

The river runs imperfectly
  Fighting rocks and banks that are
Hostile to serenity
  The river rushes on

And then a dew migrates
  To the river
From the lonesome tranquility of the grass
  until the dawn it played hide and seek with the sun

Now, the river runs more strongly
  Yet it will not last
Once the sun is back
  The river will weaken fast

  Niloufar Haghighi

Pennies And Peanuts

On a Sunday morning drive, she and daddy could be seen,
Going to the place with a penny peanut machine.
In daddy's pocket pennies would easily be found,
She'd hold them tightly, so they were safe and sound!
Into her little hands those red-skinned pearls would fall,
And the smile that blossomed was caught, by daddy and all.
That memory with daddy stays very much alive,
Especially, when pennies make those red-skinned peanuts arrive!

  Linda Lee Jacobsen

Rainbow's End

I walk among the awesome beauty of life.
Filled with love, sorrow, and anticipation of the morrow.
There are no regrets for what might have been.
I have had it all when I have my kin.

The world is not ours it's only on loan.
No amount of money can claim it as your own.
There are straight, narrow, and winding roads to God knows where.
There are mountains to climb and valleys to go through to get there.

You ask to where?
My friend—the yellow brick road at the Rainbow's end.

  Pauline Henry

"Pyramids"

A beautiful secret design
Filled with the ages of time
Awed by the artistic craft
Scents of ancient kings and queens of the past.

Undaunted by nature's blend
In hopes of listing courageous grins
Beset by beautiful unknown signs
To be deciphered by scientist of our time.

To be in such a cascade of mathematical spheres and shades
God's design of infinite keepsake
To be adored by all man's watch-bake.

  Linda Mitchell

Crystal Memories

Crystal memories and images of the past
filter through our lives each day.
They beckon us, "Return once more!
Come journey with me down the paths of yesterday."
But, today stands silent
while we reach into yesterday,
filled with joys and sorrows,
played out like scenes in a play.
Today cries out a mournful plea,
"Please come back soon! Return to me!
For I need you here with me today,
Before I become your yesterday!
For in the twinkling of an eye
I too will be a memory,
and I'll entreat thee, return once more.
Come journey with me for a while."

  Karen R. Martin

A Dream

Future Astronauts, Princesses, and Presidents
follow your dreams, create or invent
a road that will lead you and guide you inland
For it's as much the dream, as it is the man.

Believe in the unknown - it's uncovered space.
But forfeit your dream, and you'll forfeit your place.
You'll distort every vision your mind has instilled
and deny your heart all it so deeply has willed.

PROCLAIM TO THE WORLD:
WHAT YOU SEEK YOU WILL GET!
Believe in your self, then prepare for it.
Reach out for the brightest, the highest thus far-
Display to the doubtful, you're half-way where you are.
SO AIM. INSPIRE. INTRIGUE. FULFILL.
ZOOM! RACE! SOAR! BEG! APPEAL!
But never let go of the DREAM at hand
For it's as much the dream as it is the man.

  Rhenetta Witherspoon

Going To Church

On Sunday morning we go to church
   Five or six children ready to go.
Stay in the house and don't get dirty.
   Eat your breakfast and don't be so slow.

Brush your hair and wash your hands and face.
   Come on, let's go; don't run out to play.
Just once a week is a time of praise
   Of meeting together to sing, to pray.

Get in the car so we won't be late
   Hurry! Blow the horn, where are the boys?
Now, fasten your seat belts, buckle up.
   We're all here, but you can't take your toys.

Let's sing a song. Which one will we sing?
   "Jesus Loves Me" is the one we like
We'll all sing and make a joyful noise;
   Get started now and listen to Mike.

Here's the church, go to the restroom first.
   Take a front seat so we all can hear.
Be still. Don't talk. Stand up. Don't look back.
   Hear our Pastor who is very dear.

Leona M. Auer

Archie

He is just a guy named Archie with whom I've spent my life
For 52 years, I have been blessed to be his wife

We were 17 and 19 when we signed-on for our life's trip
Confident we could overcome any problem without a slip

A kaleidoscope of memories fill me with such joy
Of this 71-year old man with the heart of a boy

He is wonderful with children, and each little one
Is convinced, through love and warmth, he is special and fun

In this world of ambition, he is quick to confess
No, he has never really been much of a success

I protest - disagree loud and clear
As husband, father and grandfather, he has no peer

Now old age has descended and shadows begin to fall
Ah, what a trip it has been - we have had it all

He is just a guy named Archie filled with contentment and peace of mind
He is a treasure, a keeper, a real find!

Marguerite Page

An Untamed Treasure

To everyone out there with care and concern
For a majestic wilderness that may never return
you see there's a river, we call the payette
And its free flowing waters are under great threat
Fellow Idahoan's please make no excuse
Don't let this wild river suffer endless abuse
Just think of the many who will miss this rare wonder
Never hearing the roar of its white water thunder
This river holds bounties far greater than gold
Leave its waters free flowing for all to behold
The payette is a legend, our grand monument
Untamed, undeveloped was NATURE'S intent!!

Pamela E. Price

Lavish Blossom Cup

Am most certainly warm besides gay
For a reason particular lustrous sunbeams
Reached Sarasota the present day.
Sunlit blossoms produce highly agreeable,
Enjoyed dainty feathered companions
Come forth fully gay,
In addition in similar manner
The Supreme Being is the way
About sun coming up,
Likewise about what time planets come, from earth, up.

"Oh! California Poppy allow us imbibe of your lavish blossom cup,
Take in sun gladness you portray
In Supreme Being's chosen day."

Rosa Leonora Galfano

When Angels Cry

   The angels rain tears of red,
for all the pain and sorrow shed.

   Somewhere in the world a child dies,
from the pain of hunger that grows inside.

   Night falls and a mother weeps,
for her little babe forever sleeps.

   The angels rain tears of red,
but love for the children turn them clear instead.

   Is there but one who knows our woes,
and has forever claimed our souls?

   Are there many who meet in between,
that share our pain of griefs unseen?

   The angels tears fall as rain,
as we all fight in honor and die in vain.

   I search to solve the mystery,
of why there is such misery.

   Could the new star that twinkles in the sky,
be a life beginning as you and I?

   The angels live in heaven high,
and spill their teardrops from the sky.

Teresa Joy Moreland

Guess Who?

If there was a medal that I could give
For all the years for all the tears
I'd give it to....guess who?

She held me when I was very small
I couldn't even talk or walk at all
Her love was the greatest love I knew...guess who?

Now I'm older and able to do all the things she taught me to
I visit her as much as I can, she has alzeheimers you understand.

That far away look with a familiar glance
She looks at me just by chance
She refers to me as if I'm small
Not realizing I've grown at all
For her everything I try to do...guess who?

The answer is so plain to see, there's only one person this could be
Who'll always love me truthfully
No other than
"My Mother".

Linda Marie Benitez

Untitled

I just want to hold you close,
For as long as I live and more,
But as I enter the house you call your heart,
I seems you've closed the door

If I could hold you in my arms,
and be yours and yours alone,
Would you run to me and come to me,
as the girl you call your own?

To spread my love and touch your soul,
would please me oh, so much.
But years would pass before your soul
could ever feel that touch.

I never expected for you to give
me gold or jewels or fur.
But I also never expected
for you to be with her.

Rachel Howard

Hallmark

O, human beings, how can you rejoice!
For every thing there is "multiple choice."
It starts already with greeting cards,
splendidly written in various arts.
From birth to death your life unfolds,
squeezed into funny and serious molds.
The Thesaurus (you have one?)
can dust on your shelf.
Don't torture your brain
with a rhyme word on "elf."
One reads the texts,
and one nods in consent:
  This one will do,
it's the one, I shall send.

Maidi Leibhardt

Reality

I am nothing,
  for I did not fight in the
  Civil War that killed so many;

  for I did not drop the bomb
  on Hiroshima that paralyzed so many;

  for I did not walk through
  the Jungles of Vietnam that
  scared so many;

Instead I have listened to my mother
talk about killings, killings that never cease;

I watched my fathers grief and sorrow,
sorrow that we did not expect, but
which became reality;

Reality is something I fear,
for in reality my brother was shot,
shot in the back to take a fall of mine;

I pray to God everyday,
but everyday reality comes into effect;

For I am nothing without my brother,
and my brother is dead.

Richard Shermer Jr.

No More Sinking Sand

On sinking sand I no longer stand
for I've taken a hold to the masters hand
and safely he leads me across the troubled seas
and his face I'll some day see
and there I'll thank him for his grace
that can be found in no other place
for he is there in my time of need
and any hour when on my knees
I call upon his precious name
nothing of this world is the same
for he leads me on a different journey
and fills my soul of all it's yearning
I would not trade what his touch means
for at all times on him I lean
great it is to be his child
his blessing he bestows all the while

Laura L. Johnson

His Love

Look to God in everything,
For only He knows what the future holds.
Place all of your trust in Him,
He will see you through.
When you are unable to walk he will carry you.
When you are weary he will lift your spirits.

God renews our hope with each new day,
He places smiles on our faces and joy in our heart.
Only He can satisfy a hungry soul.
He provides us with words of comfort when we are sad,
And places a new song in our hearts everyday.
God is so good.
He is faithful even when we let Him down,
He will never forsake us nor leave us.
His love will see us through.

Pek Hu Liu

Contemplation Nation

We the people need a socialution
For our amended constitution

Liberty has lost, with the medias decision
To misspell personal tragedy
And private lives grief-stricken

Mistakes of innocence can be subjected
By unnamed sources that remain protected

The influenced believe
Such guise of reality
To contempt the naive
May foretell our society

A notion tales the truth just to beat a deadline
Read with a cynics eyes all the foreboding headlines

We must quash the medias subpoena on our very lives
By the people - democracy
It is ours to protect - our survive

Troy A. Karash

Everyone Has A Story

Everyone has a story to tell
for some everyday life is a living hell
Bullets shooting out of guns
Claiming life's of mother's sons
People with homes on wheels
Praying if tomorrow will be their next meal
Baby's being brought up in the wrong.
But anything has a sad song.
Innocent baby's dying so young.
Never knowing all their life work was done
It makes my heart bleed my soul weep.
When I see 2 and 3 years olds already in their eternal sleep.
Everyone did not come out of their mothers womb.
With in their mouth a golden spoon
Tears that they shed are real from inside.
People have been stripped of their dignity and pride
But who's to say it's wrong or right.
When everyday is a struggle, a fight.
Everyone has a story to tell.
Too bad everyone doesn't want to listen.

Lakisha Waters

"The Harvest"

The mountain spirit is singing for the dream of his heart,
For songs of love touch the maiden living in its shadows.
As the white moon roams through the twinkling skies,
His dancing feet wanders to the hidden places of the forest.

Through the cedars mystic flutes call to the willows,
As the autumn leaves fall down the roaring rapids.
Mother Earth is coming to him walking past the rainbow,
Over the paths of the forest, into the hidden fields.

Her breasts bring gifts of a plentiful harvest,
She will lie with him in the cool leaves of joy.
Descending she will bring him gentle peace,
Waiting under the clear sky with gifts of plenty.

As the spirit of the mountain draws near to her,
The sunshine of the gods gazes over the land.
Bending and swaying in the river's breeze,
They reached their vision of the holy dream.

Now the eagle can spread his giant wings,
For he has been given the strength to defy foes.
Trust the Mighty One to hear us pray,
Then good will come from the powers of the sky.

Marcia Schwartz

Believe In Dreams

Believe in dreams that may come your way
For soon they'll be gone just like yesterday
Hold on to the ones that make your heart sing
for they may fly by as if they had wings
Remember the warmth you feel in the night
Store it inside before it takes flight
Keep in your mind the ones that ring true
believe in those dreams they're meant just for you
So when you awake try to think back
Don't ever forget for you may lose track
And during the day some dreams may still last
Hold on to the moment for it may just pass
Again at night your dreams will come by
Before you let go try to think why
These dreams I dream will they really be
Believe in those dream they're just yours to see

Vincent Cea

"The Artist"

Who could be the painter, of this unforgettable sky,
For the colors on His canvas are imitated,
but not nearly as beautiful
I only know of One.

Who could be the poet, that wrote the songs of the animals,
For we try to make the same ones on instruments,
but aren't quite the same tune.
I only know of One.

Who could be the sculptor,
that molded those unclimbable mountains,
For we try to see the top, but there is always one higher.
I only know of One.

I would like to meet this Painter, this Poet, this Sculptor,
For I know the time will come,
But it is for Him to decide when.

Megan Suarez

Blackness

Crazy hot Cars waxed down ready
for the cruise through Black Forest
park And you know why they call it that
even though ain't no trees there.

'Cause in the summertime the air
is so thick with Black people it's as
deep as a forest. Can't hardly see clear
to the other side; with heat as thick as butter,

Giving everybody in view a wet gleam
of perspiration. Brothas screamin' on the
court to pass the ball while you feel the
bass thumpin' from one of the many cars

Passing by comin' straight from the car wash;
with the tops down, sunroofs open, a woman's
freshly done head peekin' out her man's ride
to wave at her jealous friends, poppin' gum and

Noddin' to that fly new song by the brother from
around the way as they drink lemonade
and bribe their little sisters to go get them some
more pop from the corner store....

Kristi Jordan

My Garden

As I kneel in my garden, I am at peace,
for there is no other place I would rather be.

My toil is for naught, as I labor diligently,
for my garden will be a wondrous sight to see.

I think back to the Fall, and the bulbs I spent laying,
and how they will soon begin their Spring awakening.

My Primrose, my daisies, all the varieties,
will begin to arise from their long Winters sleep.

And as their buds open, their sleepy eyes,
they will each display the beauty kept hidden inside.

I treasure there many colors, that tease and delight,
for how dull the world would be in just black and white.

I feel a sadness when a bloom, is near its end,
but I smile knowing there is another to begin.

And I think how empty, our lives would become,
if there were no flowers for us to gaze upon.

I see my garden as a lesson, from the Lord above,
how beautiful life is when it is nurtured with love.

Theresa Dischinger

The Dreamer

Pity on them, the ones without dreams,
For they will not experience the things your eyes have seen.
You are the dreamer; you will suffer much pain,
But the dreams are your life, and Dreamer is your name.
Because of your gift, you will be scorned by the rest.
But the nondreamers aren't you, oh, what things they will miss.
To live without dreams is to live without soul.
They will not live in sorrow, for what they miss they will not know.
Though you will know great despair and great sadness,
With each tear of pain there will be one of gladness.
For you the dreamer, a full life you will live,
And for the world, precious gifts you will give.
To achieve your goal you will endure much pain,
But the dreams are your life, and Dreamer is your name.
Rebecca Long

Time

We are all trapped, in this neverending trance,
For time never seems to want to cease.
Every single second, of our very important lives,
Goes by like the wind, is lost forever-
Far away, into our pasts, never to be returned to us, ever again.
Trying to get the best out of every little minute,
Because a minute gone is a minute lost forever.
However we musn't have regrets, of a wasted minute,
Instead we must cope with looking towards the future-
Thinking of ways to put our pasts, far behind us,
Then perhaps we can correct the mistakes we made-
before, long ago in the past.
We don't know much about the future,
But we always have the chance to make it a better one...
Sharon Im

"Life Is An Everyday Thing"

Do not let the poverty of living bring desolation to your heart.
For we can help another by the loving we impart.
For life is built on love that we can freely give,
To bring hope and joy to another and renewed desire to live.
We often judge another by an indiscreet moment,
not considering their repentance or atonement.
A painful Barb is often thrust by a word we speak in jest.
How often we inflict an injury to the one we love the best.
Do not live in loneliness as you live each passing day.
Just reach out to a fellow traveler on your way.
I will keep a faithful spirit that there's goodness in the land,
and we can all live together with Jesus guiding hand.
Linda King

Vintage Auto

Love is akin to vintage auto
Forever warming with the anticipation
or reaching a destination.

Value may increase with time
　a chance you take with emotion
And you can never neglect maintenance
　least you run into expensive repair
Which you almost always have to borrow for.

And on a beautiful day the paint will shine.
A faraway glance will notice, but not appreciate
The hours of dedication preparing for one moment
No matter,
Beauty is intrinsically reflected.
Mark Williamson

A Mundane Reality

Brothers and sisters we are all
For we come from a sole creator
Living on a planet far from small

Color and race, still separate us

We fight one another in pursuit of a bountiful tomorrow
Destroying and raping our mother-Earth
We show our primitive sorrows, calling it natures's side

Proclaiming that we are civilized

Centuries have passed
Transformation has taken place
Forsaking evolution

Living in havoc, for we still haven't learned to share

Politicians, they embrace our hand
A gesture a greedy lie
Dictating freedom

Ironically enough dictating nothing but our lives

For the best of all concerned
And all who want to know
SOCIETY, is what it's called.
Sandra L. Valdivia

The Other Song Of History

How many years of my life on earth should I apologize
For what my great grandfather did to yours?
Just how deep, really, are your sores?

How many more demands for your rights will you insist be due
Because your ancestors suffered from mine?
Tell me, when will it all be fine?

How many willful injustices were suffered years ago
From bigots, racists, despots and bullies
Who jerked lives like grips and pulleys?

How many years before you demand responsibility
In your own way to behave,
And not ride someone else's wave?

How many pints of blood do you want so that you can watch me squirm?
Let go of your safari
And accept my, "I'm sorry."
Kay Lohner

Jenny

I don't think it's fair that you have no voice
For when you were born they gave you no choice.
Or maybe they did and we just couldn't see...
That you were sent here to influence me.

With your eyes of beauty you give me such hope,
And when you smile at me the tears I must choke.
That's when I know that God sent you here
To bring to our grey world happy colorful cheer.

You are a symbol of perfectness even though you may not be...
Just like all of the other kids every day that we may see.
You reach out with your heart instead of with your hands,
And you walk with eyes of brightness even though you do not stand.

For all this I must thank you for everything I see
For without your influence who knows what I might be.
So when I go away to school, we may be far apart
Please know that even though I'm away I love you with all my heart.
Wendy Kelley

Untitled

The most obscure door is the one that will hold the key
for you, so do not pass it by.

And do not be afraid of the thorns and ivy that seem to
knot themselves so tightly that the threshold seems
impossible to cross - these things are only the creations
of some other mind.

And once the door is in full view, do not chance to peek
through the hole first, for the key will fall into the
abyss and you will be lost.

Nay, turn the key forcefully and step right in, for your
Paradise has been well-earned.
    Marjorie Schmidt

Different

Condemned, alone.
Forsaken for differences of mind and soul.
Disgraced in today's world.
Society is cruel.

Someone so loving, kind, and tender,
crushed by his love for the same;
forbidden to be true—to himself, to others.
Difference is frowned upon,
harsh judging awaits those who dare.

So locked in a cell of make-believe,
he awaits freedom—total acceptance—
with or without Differences.
He knows he is not alone in his world of thought,
others long also to be Different.

Unforgiving is the society
which frowns upon loving souls, yearning to belong.
Thus, yearning sustained in this cold world,
longing to be true to mind, body, soul—
Themselves—are the Different.
    Robbin J. Brown

The Quest

In my youth I sought recognition in all things.

   I sought recognition for my robust health and energy and
found I was only ordinary.

   I sought recognition for wit and cleverness and found the
folly and poverty of my mind.

   I sought recognition in illuminating the frailty and weakness
of others and found only the infirmity of my own character.

   I sought recognition in knowledge and conversation that
I might be wiser and more learned than most in all matters.
I found this boring to myself and others.

   I sought recognition for my possession and importance and
and found only vanity, deception, and loneliness in my pursuit.

   I sought recognition for light verse and prose only to find
the domain reserved for the gifted. I agonized over shattered
dreams and disappointments.

   In my quest for recognition I found a quiet desperation
and knew the malady was within.

   Therein I searched for recognition and found a truth — a truth
that rang through every crevice and recess of my mind and heart;
Know Thyself, Be Thyself. I searched no more.
    Neal Roberson

I.S.P. - The Wonderful People

I - INTERNATIONAL wealthy and elite group of poets building
     universal friendship
S - mall world the magnificent intellectual people achievers whose
     accomplishments in their chosen field of endeavor are
     worth emulating
O - pen, accessible, admirable warm hearted human beings
C - aring, loving men and women to your family and country
I - mpressive personalities inspiration and pride of your countrymen
E - nergetic self motivated highly creative thinkers who often
     develop new and exciting ways of doing things
T - he world's finest poets togetherness like brothers and sisters
     in one big family
Y - our talents and accomplishments a treasure forever

O - f all the good things you have done you'll always be remembered
F - oundation of I.S.P. 1990 to the whole world you are great

P - romote peace, ecucation, accomplishments, charity and equality
O - nly you can make your dreams come true
E - verlasting love and harmonious relationship to everyone
T - riumphs and full of possibilities, to be humble, toward God
     and toward one another
S - uccessful poets, writers articulate and very supportive
    Leonides S. Sales

"Two Best Friends"

Ever since I turned thirteen years old
Friendships I had were worth more than gold.
But when I was a little child
I was too serious to be wild.
My best young friend asked me to play
and all I did was drive her away.
I just couldn't laugh or smile
and it's been like this for a while.
Now I'm different, I love to play
I wish I could laugh every day.
But life is so different now
I don't know why, but I do know how.
More than ever I want that friend to laugh with me
Because I am better than I used to be.
She is very different, too
Her eyes are no longer a happy blue.
She takes drugs and fools around
I hate to see her with the wrong crowd.
I think our friendship is at its end
Oh, how I wish she was the same friend.
    Maribeth Hegadorn

Our Children

   Our children are so special so sweet,
from the tops of their heads, to the tips of their feet.
   Our children are a breath of fresh air
when we need to breathe.
   Our children are the lights in our eyes,
the glow in our hearts.
   Our children are us you see,
when we were young and growing up free.
   Our children are examples of love
what it can do and what they can be.
   The children you see are special to me,
they warm my heart and give me joy.
   Our children are the foundation
of a new beginning and brighter tomorrows.
   Thank God for the children
so special so sweet.
    Kami Fryberger

The Girl In The Picture

Where is the little girl who looks out at me,
From a picture that is an old memory?
Her face is filled with an innocent delight,
Before her she sees a life that is so bright.

But life was not meant to be for the taking,
So she went to a world of her own making.
Surrounded by her own dreams and fantasies,
She refused to face life's own realities.

Her days were all filled with magical musings,
Where there was none of the usual rueings.
Nights continued with these mystical wendings,
With perfect dreams that all had perfect endings.

When suddenly forced to face the world outside,
The pain of it forced the child to run and hide,
Back to where promises are never broken,
And only cheerful words were ever spoken.

The poor babe is lost with her imaginings,
Not a chance for any new awakenings.
I must learn to let go of the little dear,
There is nothing to keep a daydreamer here.

Sally Rose

"The Lover's Destiny"

Reaching up I found Him laid upon an outer limb
From garden well below, I danced on tiptoe to and fro.
He dared to leap - Lovers reap! 'Tis not a fleeting whim —
Now the violet vine of mine drops the around so low!

Freedom's flight abandoned night, Dawn first glance Lovers wed
And flung upon silken bed around which rosy wreathes doth glow.
Captured free, dwellers Be within a tripping aura red —
Destined for Eternity ne'er to know a dead foe!

Rays of promise in promenade fan like fingers long
Touch my dewy eyelids, the Iris mirrors only You.
A fiery plumed alights then quivers with His Morning Song,
Lo the dance becomes so light, He scarcely knows I wear a shoe!

On the Songbird's last note the Fortunate float and rise above the din
Melodious is He invariably, the Dance begun is ne'er to end
And so is Lover's Destiny unfailingly to win —
For like the bending of Yore, Dancers Lovers' Fate defend!

Leslie N. Todd

Blessed Storm

Our Earth has endured a great many changes;
from Hurricanes, twisters, to flooding rampages.
Here at our home we've experienced Drought,
with sun-drenched skies, all about.

There was anxious hope when I awoke
to rapid moving clouds.
The breezes strong brought me to song
and thanks; I sang aloud...

A flash of lightening, thunder sounds,
the rains begin to fall;
Proceeding weeks of intense heat
come relief for our Earth after all.

Through the night the sky lit bright
with lightening from above.
Rain, rain, blessed storm
just fills my heart with love...

Today a gentle, precious rain
continues soft and warm...
So Graciously, I thank you Lord,
for Nourishing this storm.

Michelle C. Clymer

Euphoria

Not long ago I was awakened
from my placid state of sleeping and waking.
My eternal waters, which for so long lay dormant and muted,
now ebbed and flowed with pleasures unknown.
The reverberations from my muddied waters
resonated from my toes to the skies.
My impassioned soul, in transient flight,
caressed the clouds and drank the sun's fires.
I had tasted heaven.

Like Icarus, I had flown too high.
My feet were off the ground, my head in the sky.
My fall was brief but hard-
my wings singed and charred.
I had re-learned one of life's hardest lessons:
Mere mortals are not meant to fly.
I had tasted heaven...
and it was you.

Zachary Zakour

Mom And Dad

As future years have come
from one September day
thirty years ago,
in Heavens own will I continue to believe
you two were made for each other.
To be blessed with such a gift from God,
for it is certain, I have, a father and mother
who have given so much of themselves.
Memories of love remain,
even from that which fades from the world,
because your compassion and strength
are never ending.
In my prayers I thank God
I was chosen to belong to you.
As I, counting myself so fortunate,
have been shown that love and
friendship are enough.
Yet knowing the truest part of my heart
comes from the influence of
my mom and dad.

Shelly Lynn Smith

A Portrait Of My Husband

A man who has more waves than the ocean, sometimes
gentle and still, sometimes attacking, raging, turbulent and glistening.

A man full of emotions, erupting like a volcano spewing
out joy, humor, sadness, happiness, disappointment and
most importantly, is deeply concerned about love.

A man as independent as a thin penny - he chooses his
location and audience with forethought and strategy.

A private man whom only the few with keen observation
skills can catch a glimpse of his special character.

Finally a man whose attraction to me were his dancing
eyes and genuine voice that paved the way for the
giving and receiving of love.

A spiritual being whom I want to be with.
A genuine, true watercolor!

Therese M. Wheaton-Harkins

Winter's Eve

It falls with silence, no sound to be heard.
Gently it covers the ground, and all that surround.
It falls once the cold Autumn sun has hidden itself from the eyes of all.
Everything is hushed, no sound is heard.
Just the unbounding sound of snow.

The fire inside pops and crackles with life.
Red and orange flames dance around, with piercing warmth.
Sparks frolic up the chimney, to meet their frozen sisters.
The ash, black as night itself, tells that the warmth will end.

Again the sun rise, releasing its rays of warmth.
The snow melts as graceful as it came.
And the fire has died, only the cool ash remains.
Trey Crane

Walking With The Lord

I'm walking sinking my feet in the sand
gently you came and walked with me
The movement of the ocean waves
so violent and brave
Walking on my bare feet
hearing the waves make a beat
As I listen to the shore make a roar
The ocean glistened and looked like white diamonds
Walking me through this deserted island
You're not visible nor are you able to be see
But, LORD, I believe you are always walking with me.
Victoria Ortiz

The Master Plan

God tells us to be patience, so we wait before him and
get very still. Revelation knowledge come then, of His divine will.

He loves us, oh so very much: He does not want us
to flounder around, but to know the depth of his riches
in glory and on earth, how to abound.

He never will leave us nor forsake us down here.
He gave us the holy ghost and we do not need to fear.
Just trust him wholly and walk in the faith
delivered unto us, by all of the saints.

Jesus went before us, to show us the way, and we
follow Him unto a brighter new day.

Nothing will overtake us, but such as is common unto
all men: So we follow in His footsteps because.....
   He has the Master Plan!

He walked this way before and he knows every trap and
snare: He will keep us from stumbling, if we hold to
His hand with care.

He picks us up and carries us along because.....
He is the burden bearer, and he will take us up with Him,
   A home in glory to share!
Shirley M. Hathaway

The Lurking Monster Under My Bed

I'm afraid of the monster under my bed.
He has a pointy chin and green hairs on his head.
I'm afraid to go to sleep
Because under my bed the monster will creep.
He has bumps and warts and pimples and boils.
And when he gets made his green hairs coils.
I know that at midnight he'll be a nightmare.
That's why I hug my teddy bear.
I know that at midnight he'll lurk under my bed,
The monster with bumps and green hairs on his head.
Travis Faulhaber

Give Thanks Everyday

Give thanks to God for His abounding grace,
Give thanks to the Lord for letting me live in this place.
Give thanks to the Creator for my birth,
Yes, give thanks because He created us, heaven, and earth.

Give thanks to our Lord for the food that we eat,
Especially thank God for the friends that we meet.
Give thanks to God for the clothes that we wear,
But most of all - thank God for our faith in Him we share.

Give thanks to the Lord for a helping hand, and our creative mind.
Thank God for our sense of humor or we'd all be left far behind
Give thanks for our dreams, family joys, and sorrows,
For these are what bring us the memories for our tomorrows.

Give thanks to the Heavenly Lord above,
Who has touched us and the ones we love.
So, give thanks for your blessings one by one,
In the morning, at noon, and during the setting of the sun.
Theodore Friedman

I'll Be Here, My Child

Let me wipe the teardrops from your eyes,
give you courage in a world of compromise.
Let me shield your innocence from pain,
and instill in you a love that will sustain.
Let me walk the uphill roads for you,
climb the mountains, swim the seas, and oceans, too.
Take the burden from your days that lie ahead,
and place them gently in my willing hands instead.
Soon you alone will grow and learn your way,
and look back on my guidance every day.
You will need me less and less, you'll see,
as you become whom I've prayed for you to be.
So hold your childhood moments ever dear,
knowing that forever I'll be here.
Lisa B. Newman

Victory Is Theirs

Row by row they proudly stand - brightly in the sun.
Giving mute testimony to brave, proud men who lie beneath the
   soft green carpet.

Name, rank and duty carved deeply in the pure white marble.
As they stood at attention in life - they lie at attention in their
   final sleep.

They have answered their country and God's final call - good men - all.
Sons, brothers, husbands and fathers, grandfathers - loved by someone - everyone.
But the grave holds only that which was - notthat which is -
Shining souls, having fought valiantly side by side with their comrades -
they are now reunited in an unbreakable bond - to which only they belong.
These were their glory days - when they felt all man invincible -
united in their unquenchable thirst of freedom for all.

We, mere mortals, civilians, if you will, cannot enter this select
   group of real men.
We grieve for those we have lost - but some solace comes from
the sparkling white headstones, deeply carved with name,
rank and duty - which is our country's final commitment and vow
   to never forget -
These brave men who gave their all - their future, to the country
   and people they loved so well.
Their final sacrifice was for us all -
left behind, grieving, for that which was,
and can never, ever be again.
Tacey M. Hoban

We Gather Now The Harvest

We gather now the harvest — the bounty of the Lord;
God's blessed us with abundance; give thanks in one accord.
We've scattered o'er the good land the seeds of Life and Love;
Through faith they have been nurtured by God who reigns above.

Our task is never easy; we're called to persevere;
Reality confronts us; we pray for vision clear
To deal with disappointment, to bend, but never break.
We would with deep thanksgiving forge on for Jesus' sake.

Our pilgrimage continues, each day — a challenge new;
Sustained by God's far purpose — great glory to pursue.
We're modern-day disciples; Christ beckons to us all;
We find our full fruition responding to Christ's call.

H. V. Lloyd Jr.

My Recipe For Life

Looking up at the ceiling, there isn't any healing
Going through the battles of life, just isn't easy anymore
Friendships, relations, heartbreaks; just plain life
One has to go through a great deal of pain
And for what you may ask, when we all going to die someday
Well, let me tell you why
Cause that's what life's all about
There are good and bad times, for everyone and anyone
No one said life was easy
It's an experience - a useful one
Imagine if no one had any problems
We wouldn't be able to look for better days to come
There would be no problems and no solutions
No one would use their heads
So just take life as it comes; don't be impatient
And run ahead, don't be lazy and stay behind
Take charge of your life and the opportunities
It has to offer and everything will fall into place
Remember that you get to live life only once
It's too precious to waste.

Lydia Monteiro

"Lights Of Love"

Lights of love;
Gone from our lives;
Torn from our hearts,
Seared from our souls!
Lights of love:
Each one unique,
Loving and kind,
Brave and strong!
Lights of love:
Unite us in grief,
Urge us to heal,
Bond us in hope!
Light of love, DAVID,
Young, handsome, soldier of Christ!
A "GIVER," not a "TAKER," BROTHER, SON, AND FRIEND,
Now whispers with the wind, "PEACE AND LOVE TO ALL!"
Lights of love unite to guide us.
"THROUGH" the "VALLEY."
"TOWARD" the "ALTAR OF LIGHT."
"TO" the "SOURCE OF ETERNAL LIFE!"

Sondra S. Mathews

"Christmas Time"

Suddenly it's Christmas time again,
Greeting, have been sent to our dearest of kin.

And to our friends with love so true.
Gifts neatly wrapped in ribbons of red, white, and blue.

A symbol of our nation, and God in
whom we trust.

But let us not forget the reason
why we celebrate this joyous season.

But let us have hope, and spread
good cheer.

For God is watching, and standing
near.

Nolan Gillispie

A Place In Time

Little round aspens all in a line
Guarding the forest's spruce and pine
The north country.. a place in time...
Each dark yellow leaf dancing free, like
Golden Buddhas they watch silently.
The maples bristling in costumes of red
Like Chinese lanterns...   hung overhead
Lining the roadways as if someone... an
Ancient emperor had ordered this done
That passing motorists might be impressed
By his kingdom... in confetti dress.
Golden light shining through falling leaves
Within the silence of oak and elm
Resembles the temple's golden eaves...
Mighty God... don't take fall away please,
Put the leaves back up in the trees...
With your power and your reason
Can't you just..... reverse the season?

Tobi Kumar

Life

Life of treasures stored up in our minds,
guided by God are gifts to hand down.

Life is a pleasure if dealt as should be,
with peace everlasting as life travels on.

Life is precious as precious can be,
if only kept sacred as life should always be.

Life is a present in which to behold,
never knowing how your day will unfold.

Life is eternal if only kept right.
Live with God's book which is holy and right.

Madeline Schaeffer

God's Special Breed

God made the moon, the stars, day and night
He made the trees, the ponds, dark and light
But none of these things can barely succeed
In over doing humans, God's special breed.

He made us from sand, his own special touch
He made us to eat break fast, dinner and lunch.
We're his own special creation, he made us by hand
He is as nice as he possibly can.

We have arms and legs, fingers and toes
He knew what he needed, all things he knows.
Well this was my survey on God's special breed.
I hope you go to heaven. I know you can succeed.

Keisha Sandusky

Lindsey's Pantoum

Lindsey's from a magical land - an angel flying near.
Hair like golden aspen - sweet petite sugar-pie.
Eyes that sparkle with mischief - a welcoming smile.
A round little bottom - feet that race to meet you.

Cute as button and bows - a tiny turned-up nose.
Full of poise and grace - a very special charisma.
A wiry bundle of love - a monkey with a funny face.
Fresh as a daisy - smells like powder and candy.

Lights a room with joy - a little wiggle worm.
A quick little mind - curious about everything.
Tiny hands so soft and warm - little arms to hug you.
Precious gift of life - with a juicy kiss or two.

A girl blooming softly - a clown that laughs.
The sparkle of stars - warmer than sunlight.
An atom with a soul - beautiful innocent eyes.
Lindsey's from a magical land - a tiny footprint in life.

Stella L. Brooks

Hate

We act like puppets, our life in your
hands, hate pulls the strings, but we're in command.

We go to war but for what?
As if there where no families, no lives to destroy.

Some fight for revenge, others fight
for their lives. It's not just a game
to play with your guns and your knives

See whose better that you can do, but
there's another way than violence, it destroys you too.

Open your eyes, can't you see that hate
solves nothing but causes pain and death.
Love hurts no-one and its the only hope we've got left.

Mary F. Copley

The Faded Rose

Today, I caressed the hand of a beautiful faded rose.
Hands once so hard working and strong,
Now soft and withered.
Her crown of lovely hair,
Turned so thin and gray.
Sparkling blue eyes, once full of life,
Now tired and lost.

Many tiring journeys she has endured.
Nurturing and giving with all her love.
As special and unforgettable as the eucalyptus,
She once bundled to sale.
Warm like the quilts so lovingly made.
Our lives she touched,
In gentle caring ways.
She has loved us for so long.
As she is on her final journey,
We send her with all our love...
While holding in our hearts all the wonderful memories.

Katrina W. Ellis

Believe In Me

Drunken drop outs. Pregnant teens,
Homicide, suicide, murder in the first degree.
Shout out at gun point and gang bang of three.
Misdirection and misery.
This is what the world's coming to.
    Can't you see?
    I believe in you.
    Will you believe in me?

Rosa Vasquez

Why?

She stands alone on the jagged dark cliff, as she
has many times before.
The torn white gown flows behind her in the
chilling breeze.
Slowly she raises her arms to the heavens
and falls to her knees on the cliff's cold dark heart.
A single sunbeam peeks out and shines down on her beaten face,
as a bittersweet tear falls to the ground.
She seems to whisper softly into the breeze, "Why?"
And, then in the blink of an eye, she jumps.

Susan Phillips

The Magic Of Love

At one time our love was true
Happiness was being with you
Love is something money can't buy
Love is just a feeling inside
Love is a friendship that should never die
Love is always being there right by your side
Love is much, love goes on and on
But if your in love and forever you want to be
The magic of love is best friends both of you got to be
I was in love but what happen to me
We didn't stay together because his best friend wasn't me

Katrina Martinez

Death Of Innocence

An affection for pure passion
has altered my perception for wanting Love
with replacement of an eagerness
for erotic enticing pleasure

An inclination from her
meaningful will have meaning
and ever so precious will be our Love

To have been reborn
my heart's wish is yours

My glowing soul is vigorous
to join with yours

Everything I have learned
is not carved in stone
all I have felt
is numb till I feel
your tenderness of delight

Slowly I create your trust
from my truth of being
showing all I am, to become one
innerheart...innersoul: United before all

Michael K. Cushing

Untitled

The one and only man I love,
Has gone to heaven in the sky above:

We went to sleep, and there he stayed,
A part of me has gone away;

It is real my pain inside,
Because my Gilbert just instantly died:

Wish it was a dream, and I would all go away,
My heart is broken, so I cry everyday:

Life's not fair is what I say,
But together forever, we will stay!!

Margie Romero Sosa

The Hourglass

Never before, since I can remember
  has summer passed so quickly.
The humid days - the torrid heat
  was more than we could bear.
What was it like so long ago
  without AC or ice?
Ah, there's a question we can ponder
  as pollution fills our air.
No wonder our fun filled days have flown
  and the hurricane winds have frightfully blown.
Nature's not happy with what we've done
  with all this leisure time we've won.
The sand thru the hourglass has
  quickened its pace.
Could it be something that we've done?
  Are the days getting shorter - the time running out?
The problem is ours, may it not be too late.
  Retribution will come, of that I've no doubt.

Nan Spivak

A Walk On Water

Only a quivering illusion
Haunts the wavering grayness of perception
Taut with tension
We dangle
Precariously balanced
Like the delicate legs of a skittering spider
Lacing a pattern on a seemingly calm summer pond
Juxtaposed between the lightness of air
And the enveloping darkness of a drowning mass
Longingly following the parade of rainbowed droplets
Floating to a higher plane
Battered by the whimsical rains of fortune
Reprieved by the warmth of a gentle sun
Forestalling the gravity of transience
Just beneath the sliver of shimmering water

Kristen Kappel

Self Control

Hold your self back don't throw that punch.
HAVE A LITTLE SELF CONTROL.

Take a DEEP BREATH
Don't YELL AT THE LITTLE CHILD
HAVE A LITTLE SELF CONTROL.

Put down the bottle of whiskey
Don't get drunk
HAVE A LITTLE SELF CONTROL.

Calm yourself
Don't YELL OUT THAT SECRET
HAVE A LITTLE SELF CONTROL

Don't blame the enemy for that punch you threw
YOU SHOULD'VE HAD SELF CONTROL.

Don't blame that child for an early GRAVE.
YOU SHOULD'VE HAD SELF CONTROL

Don't blame the car for running into that tree.
YOU SHOULD'VE HAD SELF CONTROL.

Don't blame your ex-friend for your ex-relationship.
YOU SHOULD'VE HAD SELF CONTROL.
SELF CONTROL IS THE WAY OF LIFE DON'T BLOW IT!

Marini Brown

Past Somethings

Have you ever felt like no one cared?
Have you ever felt alone or scared?
Have you ever felt like life should end?
Have you ever felt lost a really good friend?
If you have then you're like me,
Betrayed and sad, never giddy with glee.
But if you ever want, to get on with life,
Then listen to me, take my advice.
The past is just that and nothing more,
You cannot change what was in store.
What happened was fate, nothing more, nothing less,
And even though you think that life's a mess,
You can go on, you should and you will,
You must cross that stream,
You must climb that hill.
For if you don't you are throwing away,
A life, that could have been something, someday.

Tiffany Rhodes

Untitled

The seed that is within you is my own.
Having once bathed in streams gushing, like snakes
Slithering mindless to blood-filled lakes,
I now have a place that is home.
Did you ever think you'd be alone
In space, hoping that somehow you'd wake
To find the pure flowing of a flake
Falling gently, gently, to softness like foam?
The currents have ceased and the floods have become
Forgotten wounds with scars to forsake,
And give me that which is mine to take.
The union's complete and what's done is done.
Lonely and wandering, once we were two;
The planted seed will blossom anew.

Ken Menke

"The Great White Hunter"

The great white hunter wounds but doesn't kill,
he allows his prey to die a slow, lingering death
as he sits and waits for all of life to flow away,
but death does not come and a healing begins.

The prey has life but no spirit to live,
the wound is so deep that it leaves what was once whole,
almost empty now.

So who really won
the great white hunter
or the prey who supposedly survived,
or did no one win
at this game called love?

Susan Margaret Clark

"Ideal Sir"

I once met the ideal sir.
He wasn't rich, he didn't own a business.
He wasn't the first man on the moon.
Infact, he wasn't an intellect.
He was normal.
He had respect from everyone he saw.
He was a man of truth.
Thus, never denying his faults.
He was full of humor and wisdom.
Never did his anger overtake his love of life.
But all I saw him in was a dream.
If I ever saw the Ideal sir
he was just a blur beneath my tears.
He'll always remain a dream,
But he'll never change.
My ideal Sir.

Miriam Limon

God Bless My Dad With Alzheimer's

"Hello Dad, how are you feeling today?"
He answers in a soft frail voice, "Oh, not bad I guess."
Although, with a confused look on his face, tries to remember his
  daughter, the faithful guest.

Dad tries to speak again, but forgets what he wanted to say.
So with a smile, points to a chair to sit with him awhile.

You see, my Dad is in a nursing home because he has gone astray.
A non-existent father and husband we visit on Sunday an hour's
  drive away.

They say it's the "Disease of the Century", the Alzheimer's Disease.
A brain deteriorating condition which affects the thinking and
  behavior of elderly.

I read about the dementia and just can't understand,
Why did it have to attack this poor innocent old man?

Such an active and hard working his entire life.
Today he is helpless, and a stranger to his wife.

Visions I have of those summer days in the past,
Dad's tireless hands planting our garden and mowing the grass.

Mom still recalls the sacred marriage vows on their wedding day. . .
"Together in sickness and in health, till death do we part."
But God understands the sacrifice mom made for dad,
She made unselfishly from the love for him in her heart.

I'll cherish our visits together, and this forever holds true,
You'll always be my Dad no matter what, and I will always love you.
Sheila I. Potts

Soldier

The solider of loneliness is a poor man
he fights the world, armed only with his hands
seeming everyone against him
for no one to love him.
He can't control his feelings, or what he does
he only destroys, what he loves
he looks at the blood
on his hands and face
full of shame and disgrace
if he uncovers
he is hit by a blow
so he never opens up or shows
hit him and kick him while he's down
he'll never crack a smile, for all he knows is frowns
fighter of good luck
solider of eternal peace
tougher then leather, so not to decease
but to age and harden
as a soldier of loneliness
and unforgiven peace
Mike Bryant

Hollowed Heart

Unable to truly love, because of lack of that in his youth.
He has no friends or an intimate lover to be with.
He truly has nothing to live for.
When he tries to love, and he gives his heart away it still remains
the same, it had been hollowed out too long ago to ever be filled.
Even if there was a chance to fill it, who could care enough to do so.
He was a virgin to true love, and would never know what it would ever
feel like to give his heart to someone without it crumbling when it
  touched them.
He then decided a life with no love wasn't a life worth holding onto.
So he ended it, and died wondering if anyone would give a damn.
R. David Bush

Uncharted Love

A captain of old, on a sailing ship upon a stormy sea.
He held the wheel when the gale hit,
Oh! How the strong wind blew.
Mighty waves pounded the ship and the storm raged on
It split the mask, ripped the sails, and washed the deck of Captain and crew.

Afloat in the sea, among the ships debris, he found a plank and
  rested his weary head.

In a dream like daze he drifted and dreamed, of such wondrous things.

An angel of rare beauty and grace, held him in her wings and kissed
  His windburn face.

"Don't fear," she said. "Rest and sleep for you are in God's keep."

He woke and found he'd been washed ashore onto a beautiful
  uncharted land.

His heart filled with ecstasy, he sang joyous phrases of:
  "Hallelujah! Great is God's love."
Norma Overmeyer

Mother

God made many wonders in this world,
He made man, woman, boy and girl.
He made everything, in its awesome beauty,
The mountains, the seas, the flowers, the trees.
But I know the greatest wonder from the start,
Was the sweet, sweet love of a mother's heart.
Words can't express or ever reveal,
How much I love you or how I feel.
I cherish each day together or apart,
Because I know, I'm always in your heart.
So don't be troubled or worried, you see,
Because our God watches over me.
One day we may part for a short time,
But we'll meet again, in God's kingdom so fine.
But as we remain here on earth, til the end,
I'll always know that you're my best friend.
Louise H. Barbour

Unspoken Feelings

There once was a man who was thought to be made of stone.
He seemed so strong, and never to fail,
especially to his Son, who sought to follow,
his father's trail.

As time went by, the two, Father and Son grew apart.
The Son felt he was a failure in his Fathers' eyes,
and in his Fathers' heart.

Now, they work side by side, day after day,
and I see the Pride, fondness, and love each has
for the other in his heart.
But from their lips, these words never part.

I wish the two, Father and Son, could tell each other,
just how they feel.
For one day, Fate will come; and neither will know when,
and where there were two, there will be only one.
Wishing he'd spoken his unspoken feeling,
whether it be the Father or the Son.
Kathy L. Gresham

Peace Within My Heart

I heard the voice of God today through the ruffling in the trees,
He spoke to me so softly I fell right to my knees.

Please don't be angry Lord for I know that I have sinned,
I want you to forgive me for I know where I have been.

He wrapped his arms around me to comfort all my fears,
And told me to be patient that his son is very near.

He will come as a thief in the night, everything will be all right,
He'll take you up to heaven where the light is shining bright.

So be patient dear child my son Jesus will come to rule,
You will be with your loved ones and no one's cruel.

So stay just the way you are and follow only me,
And my son will bring you to me for a life of eternity.

Just remember I will always love you and I will never depart,
As long as you keep me deep within your heart.

I must leave you now to spread the word to others,
Just remember what I said and that is to always love one another.

I heard the voice of God today as it departed from the trees,
He left me with so much peace within my heart I got up off my knees.

Kimberly Joan White

The Greatest Man I Ever Knew

The greatest man I ever knew was a man you might know too.
He was a friend to me and a friend to many
If you look for enemies, there weren't any
He was a man that loved to work and work
all night was not uncommon
for days are too short when your a farmin'.
He was a good farmer for many years
and earned every dollar with blood, sweat and tears.
He was the kind to always help.
And took very little in spite of himself.
He was the kind to always listen and even care,
not just listen, but he would be there.
He's the kind you could trust with your most valuable possession,
And time spent with him you could learn many a lesson.
He's the kind to work only at his pace
he's not here to win any race.
Not only was he the kind I just told
but he's the kind whose memories will never grow old.
Not only did I lose my grandpa
but my best friend who was loved by all.

Teresa Copas

Promenade For Paradise

A wonderful promenade for paradise on high
Hear the voice of angels singing, come abide
The door is always open for welcome wide
All your needs for eternity are received inside
Open your heart to be filled with care
Requiring abundant relief for to share
Chiefly love for our neighbors to sow
Patience for ourself and give everywhere we go
A request of wisdom for all to have faith
Strength as courage, essential for today's heavy pace
As burdens are heavy, yet our reward be grace
Plentiful salvation, when ask is free
Sufficiently there, to share with all you see
Seek prayer for Holy Ghost you will receive
Peace and joy will flow within ourself
As songs of praise we share, yet many left
An angel's reply for our debt, Jesus gave His self
A plea for love and peace to do our Master's will
For reward of such mortal deeds, eternity seal
And our promenade in paradise will be forever real

Willie M. Jordan

The Children

Where are the children? Do you hear their laughter?
Do youhear them singing and playing?

Where are the children? I can't even see their smile.
Their faces are pressed against the window panes, locked behind
barred doors, longing, but not daring to come out and play.
With bullets flying, friends dying, mothers crying, how can
we expect our children to survive!!! I pray for the children
because many won't see tomorrow.

Where are the children? Do you see them in the schools?
With strife and destruction all around them, how can we expect
the children to study hard and learn well.
How can we expect them to survive.
I pray for the children in hopes of a better tomorrow.

God bless the children, they are our future, our leaders,
our decision makers.
Our lives are in their hands. There will be no tomorrow, unless
Jesus is accepted today by you, and you, and you...

Give our children a chance for tomorrow...
love one another right now!!!

Patsy McAfee

Living Hell

A tortured soul, death in the flesh,
Heart of compassion in the mind of madness;
The battle of thoughts and emotions rage on,
But finds no one with whom they can confess.

Loved by none they know, despised by all they see,
They pray for death to come and set their soul free.

Silent whispers for help, from the abysmal night,
The end of mother's twisted memories nowhere in sight.

The loss of two innocent lives,
The weight none should have to bear;
The outpouring of worldly neighbors,
We begin to see how America cares.

What could bring a person to such a crime?
How did their morals go so sublime?

Becoming like so many others,
We're losing our sisters and brothers!

No one showing concern to help, until after the crime,
Then comes help they don't need, as they do their time;
We must start early, to lend our neighbors the helping hand,
We must not wait for them to ask, we need to take a stand.

Rhyet

Dusk

There is a time each evening, between the night and day,
Heaven holds a special kind of quiet, one hear when one begins to pray.
A stillness and peacefulness as my memories seem to return,
Nearer to a place somewhere between the earth and the home for which I yearn.
Kind and gentle in it's solace, like the beauty of a sunset, or a newly risen moon.
You can hear this magic music just as the stars come out to play their tune.
One can hear natures wondrous symphony filling up the silent air.
Uttering no sound at all, but the soul delights in its melodic flares.
Loving and caressing, with entwining threads of light,
Opalescent colors, of orange, red and violet twilight
Resounding echoes of a place with timeless dimensions,
Dusk should only be described in such poetic mention.
Thank You Lord, say I.

K. R. McElroy

Rapture

You released my inhibitions and caused me to soar heights unexpected,
Removed from the gallery of insignificant etchings,
I arose a magnificent masterpiece.
The mixtures of aromas still rise to engulf my own nostrils,
Never before nor since, Have pleasures felt then been rebirthed.

Rarely; will one find the intense and provocativeness alluringly present,
If there be the slightest chance to recapture a minute flicker, I would not hesitate once to seek it out.
Time has not erased from the pages of my memory, that which would cause molten substances to flow.

Mere imagery fosters the reincarnation of something so delicate, yet profound,
Held within the boundaries of my keepsake; I bend for a moment, Not in sadness, But to raise to the grandeur embroidered upon my clothe.

J. McKnight

Sun Child

She looked like an orphan-waif. Probably was.
Her dingy hair cascaded over her shoulders like sun-drenched water, falling.
Her head bent low between her knees, pulled up to her chest, held there by strap-like arms.

She sat on a throne of garbage, this girl, so close to my own suede saddle-shoes, on the street.

My curious nudge sent her head up,
her hair flying through the air and
coming back down like Apollo's chariot.
Her eyes looked up; ours met in a quick glance
then looked away.

This girl, my age, in the brown-stained Keds,
with the fire-ball eyes and a crown of ashes.
Go back to sleep, sun child,
and return to your castle of dreams.

Morgan Currie

To The Maestro

Maestro, you were so adept at your instrument, you knew how to stroke her exactly.
When to pressure her chords when to woo her with words
through her strings you did soar breaking speed, taking wing
while her vibrating ring made spirits song sing as she trembled beneath you chin.

Maestro, how you fondled her bow with your hands she did flow
while your fingertips flew on her carved curving skin.
You touched her, caressed her, so gently , so fine.
You held her like satin, like fine splendid wine.
Her arched sides ached out for the notes you incited
as she searched for the end that she sought.
The frenzy of light you instilled and inspired choked her breath,
pulled her tight and in final crescendo she peaked.

You rocked her, oh Maestro, so soothingly slow as she clung to your trunk with her life.
She kissed you with notes from a distant day dream, that blessed you with days filled with reverent ways
through the joys that were known from the notes that you played on her vibrant, voluptuous scale.

Oh Maestro, sweet Maestro her ecstasy swelled to her final and full refrain.
Oh Maestro, dear Maestro come play her again, and again, and again, and again.

Saundra J. Aguilar

Lover's Awakened

Silken lips caress her body
Her mane cascades softly to the ground
A delicate sea breeze kissed her nudity
Callused hands journey timidly over her breasts.

Daylight has dawned
A lover's whisper
Eyes meet in romance
Their bodies basked in the summer sand
Hands meet at midpoint.

Kim Field

The Young Bride And Groom

The music, a hush, the young bride appears,
Her mother stands, and wipes at her tears.
Her father, so solemn, is holding her steady,
Silently wondering, "Dear God, is she ready?"

She's a sight to behold, this vision in white
As she stares straight ahead, not left or right.
For there, right before her, is her reason for being
And despite all the people, he's all that she's seeing.

The young man turns, and his eyes fill with tears,
This beautiful woman dispels all his fears
For there, in that aisle, is all that he's longed for,
A wife, a friend, a lover, and more.

As softly the solemn vows are spoken,
And promises made, ne'er to be broken
A union is made between man and wife,
A bond to sustain them throughout their life.

Together, they'll face what the world has to give,
And together they'll stay for as long as they live.
For their love, like a flower, will bloom.
And they'll always glow like that young bride and groom.

Melanie I. Hilbert

Storm

She looks at me with golden eyes, deep in her tiny face.

Her tiny velvet ears listening, listening to
  everything even that, that cannot be heard or seen.

She looks at all, not the outside but the soul.

Her colors of black and silver grey show her
  wisdom, her power, and her furriery.

She is as fast as the wind of hurricane, but
is as steady as the oldest, tallest, and strongest tree in the world.

She plays like a child, but is as old as the earth is young.

The storm I see will be with me until the day
I die, may it be tonight or never.

Michael W. Nedrow

A Glorious Day

Coming soon is a glorious
Holiday for celebrating the birth of our
Redeemer who was born of a virgin-lady
In a manger while a brilliant
Star shone brightly in the sky, guiding
Three wise men, bearing gifts for the child,
Many heavenly hosts cried out, singing,
Alleluia! Praise ye the Lord-the new born king!
Shepherds, watching their flocks, were awed.

Katy Lynn Hudson

What Life's All About

If you're uncertain, of where you are going
Here are some tips, that are worth knowing.
Make sure you enjoy, all that you do
Or else you'll grow old, feeling down and blue.

Take time out to smell a fresh flower,
Stay outside during a warm summer shower.
Keep awake to watch the gorgeous sun rise,
Or watch the sun set in the red western skies.

Run barefoot through the tall grass,
Call up old friends and have some good laughs.
Dip your toes, in the water of a fountain,
Take your lover away, for a week in the mountains.

Find that special someone, go fall in love.
Stare at the stars in the sky way above.
Build a snowman in the fresh snow,
Go to that place, you've always wanted to go.

Reflect on your past but never dwell,
Because all that has happened is good and well.
Don't think sadly on days long ago,
Because life is too short, and it won't go by slow.

Ryan Silverman

Here I Stand

Here I stand 20 years old and do not have any plans.
Here I stand.
Here I stand lost and depressed and made fun of by man.
Here I stand.
Here I stand and a home of drug and violence and no one to take my hand.
Here I stand.

Here I stand wanting to be somebody but the way of the world
I do not understand.
Here I stand.

Here I stand with hope and prayer because I have let Jesus in the plan.
Here I stand.

Krystal Truss

Asia

The clouds
 here never stop
  merging
  no individual puffs in the sky
just a blanketed full array of white
  traversing to the left from right.

   Yet, the tranquil splendor of this sight defies
   the corruption milling amongst the millions below.
   For centuries, a selected ring floated in royalty
    while the remaining band was admonished and inert:
    on a level equitable to slavery.
     Countless who never served the sights
     removed such as I:
      bathing in the translucent beauty
      of harbor waters dark as ebony
     reflecting silvery shimmery spots on the surface;
     like a circle, a ball of jelly
       rotating over and over - directly before our eyes.
      And all this, all that, and all how they live now
      I can only as a distant outsider surmise
      about the country of my genetic dissension
      ...about the wondrous and dichotomous place
from which a geographical presence of me by my parents was once erased

Philein Wang

Reminded Of Your Spirit

I can't help to wonder, how minuscule my time is,
 here on this planet.

As I gaze outward and above, I see this universe,
 realizing infinity overwhelms my soul.

For we are each merely a particle, comprising
 this vast world.

It makes me aware of our duty to ourselves and,
 you, even more prevalent notwithstanding.

For we all have a small amount of time,
 to make an imprint worthwhile.

Interestingly enough, I'm profoundly enchanted with
 your challenge you've presented us.

Graciously, I embrace it and accept all that
 you have given. Every act, word, deed, thought,
 and creativity has me captured as well as renewed.

Emphasizing your importance with certainty, reinforces
 our own inner strength, courage, mortality and beauty,
 which stimulates us back into the universe.

Sophia C. Mack

The Eagle

As he flies through the sky so gracefully,
He's the master of the sky.
Soaring towards the sun like an arrow just shot,
He's the master of the sky.
Shining, Glimmering, Flying high
He's the master of the sky.
Wounded crying out aloud
He's the master of the sky.
Dying, gasping, tears in his eyes
He's the master of the sky.
Dead, limp, cold, lifeless
He was the master of the sky.

Rachel Roberts

The Dream

There in the darkness lies a dream once lost, never to be found.
Hidden beneath shrubbery that grew faster than it was cut. The
thought of something better had slipped from the mind in too big
a hurry, one that was overcome by the trials. There it lay,
buried below the surface-beyond eyes view, where no one would
notice. Like the winter snow falling softly, silently, covering
the essence of what could have been. The sun melting the ice that had
frozen around its very being, footsteps trampling, one by one
pushing the dream further into the earth. As time passed - the
dream began to corrode, flaking off gradually until the wind
blew...sweeping the ashes away...becoming dust particles,
landing on clothing; brushed aside. In hair to be washed out,
tickling the nose of yet another, only to be sneezed beyond the
recipient. As the light shone brighter, darkness was dispelled.
Another sits in wonder and behold...a particle of a buried dream
impregnated into the mind of an African-European American
 boy who became inspired with possibilities.
A dream that was once cherished, yet invisible.
Beneath the surface and treated by the "elementals."
The boy held the dream securely, protected it, hiding it until the dream
 gained strength, finally to be born anew.

Patricia Shelton

Sailorman's Dream

An old sailorman hunched over a crowded dock rail.
His thoughts returned to the time of his first sail.
"To love the Sea!" the sailors oath, he swore.
That first time his spirit left the main shore.

At night in his bed, feeling the sea surge in his mind.
The sea and his life will be forever entwined.
Rising and falling with each cresting wave;
His heart was purged; his soul she did save.

As a young man, he wished to concur with the sea.
Out on the sea; his spirit was set free.
Carried away from loneliness, calmed by her roar;
With the wind in his sails, his heart would soar.

But now, weathered are his hands, wrinkled is his face.
No longer can he move at a young man's pace.
The sailorman awoke to a seagulls scream;
Realizing with pity that it was just an old dream.

Theresa King

"Dancing Leaves"

There was a man his hair was white,
his twisted hand held onto a cane.
He sat on a bench, alone, head held high.
As I walked toward him he gave a beaming smile.
His free hand waved toward the trees.
"Look, "he said," the dancing leaves.
I just sit here by myself remembering
days gone by.
I use to play a fiddle when my hands
were young and strong."
I saw a tear trickle down his wrinkled skin.
"Do you have family, Sir?"
"No family," he sighed," Just some good memories
of happy dancing folks. Look, can't you see them
in the leaves? God sure has been good to me."
As I walked away — he smiled again —
looking at the dancing leaves.

Sophia Simmons Borger

Second Coming Of Christ

Everyone had just celebrated New Years eve bringing in the most historical year ever, the year is now two thousand. 1999 had brought a massive heat and dry spell causing Wells, streams, lakes to go dry and food crops to dry up. People came out of nightclubs, neighbors homes, etc. complaining about the heat, turning on water faucets and getting nothing but hot air, and worse people, animals dropping like flies survivors seeing angels flocking to earth, mysterious smoke on the mountain, Saint Peter blowing his horn,
The ending of the world was near, everyone knew Christ was here.

Paul Andrew Pease

Love Can Be...

Summer nights, stars so bright.
Holding each other, walking hand in hand.
Love is in the air, only if you dare.
Falling down, doesn't mean you fail.
Learning is the key to life.
Put it to use, let it help you from day to day.
Put down your walls, learn to be happy.
Being content and in love,
    doesn't have to hurt anymore.

Feelings can be shared, and not ridiculed.
Thoughts can be expressed, and not criticized.
Dreams can be revealed, and not laughed at.
    Love can be...

Sharon Lill Angel McCulloch

To The Reconciliation Of Opposites

"Let me not to the marriage of true minds admit impediments".

I thought it time to tell you,
Hopefully, you will agree that Freud and Jung
are one.

Their mythical journey ending, threads left undone.
We weave anew

But, alas, we too must journey carrying our
collective consciousness to the very mountain peak
a White Hotel of Love
Shall the two become one? The Animus and Anima
of each heart and soul
Behold the beauty of the other
and you will be made whole

To the reconciliation of Opposites
I say, Let East meet West and find the
answer within - toward common ground

Let each man reconcile the world to
himself and let the Mystics of the mind
Join hands and Love prevail.

Linda Gelshenen

Flowers For Vallecitos

For Sheri
In the morning light the unswept floor is white and dusty.

A woman gathers clothing into a wicker basket.
Hours before the children awake she walks to a river
Swimming naked as the rising sun clears the cedar water,
She feels the push and pull of the current
Like an argument-a strong and steady seduction.

She washes the clothes.

At the market on the corner there are flowers today.
She buys a new straw broom pausing to count the change.
There is enough left over for two yellow roses,
One tightly fisted but, the other in bloom
The lost promise of the first.

As she sweeps the floor clean, she wears a distant look
Of a dreamer recalling perhaps, an old lover
Laughing coming around a corner
The sound of milk bottles in the morning.

The clothes are drying in the sun
When she kisses the children, waking them gently
One by one...

Shawne Rose Mimna

"Love Is Waiting"

What am I going to do?
How can I forget about you?
I still feel the love inside of me,
I hope your eyes of blue will again see.

I hoped our love would last for eternity,
One thing that still remains is sensitivity.
I know you still love me somewhere down deep,
To say you care for me makes me just weep.

Is the love lost, or is it hiding in your eyes?
I have a feeling it's just hidden under disguise.
I really don't understand what happened to us,
From the very first moment there was love, there was trust.

This is what I want you to know,
I just hope I have the strength to let it show.
We should be like we used to be,
Please, just for awhile, please come back to me.

Mishalle Roza

"Tell Me How"

Tell me how, what do I do?
How do I stop loving you?
Tell me how to let you go.
How do I stop all these tears that flow?
How do I erase these memories we had?
We had some rough times, but they weren't all that bad.
How do I fill this emptiness inside?
How do I revive this part of me that's died?
Tell me how to mend this old broken heart.
I'd fix it if I could; but, where do I start?
Tell me how did you stop your love for me?
It didn't seem to hard. You made it look so easy.
Woman, only you can help me. I'm counting on you.
So, tell me how. What do I do?
   Steven R. Jones

Yumpin Yiminy

My name is Yumpin Yiminy and I went to school to see
How many people could a person really be
Could I be a doctor or a teacher or maybe trim a tree
I went into my schoolroom and yumped into my seat
The teacher said to me, "I've never seen such fidgety feet"
Then I found you have to start with A, B and C
And begin to count with 1, 2 and 3
I remember my Mom said you have to use your sense
So when you go to the store you can count your cents
When at the end of the day I could count to 1, 2 and 3
And recite real easy about A, B and C
I then decided that I'll have to wait and see
If to learn to be a doctor or a teacher or trim a tree
Would that be the person I really wanted to be
So I came home to Mom to tell her about my day
She listened and said, "Son, you're really on you way
When you decide what you want to do
Buckle down and study and really follow through
So that as a doctor or a teacher or trimmer of a tree
You'll be best that anyone can be."
   Norman T. Leavitt

Sweet Cakes

My little Sweet Cake,
how sad that you do not recognize
the LOVE which is all around.

It must be hard being alone during this, your early years.
A teenager of just fourteen, my little niece take comfort.
I LOVE YOU with all my heart, now close your eyes, feel my embrace.

Although miles separate us, you're never out of my mind, my heart,
   or my prayers.
Since the day of birth we've been one, Please, my Sweets, be calm.
For this time of hormonal combat will soon be gone.

When you ache and feel all alone, close your eyes, feel my loving arms
   and let me enter your heart, now you know your not alone.
Never have been, never will be, and when you feel you are,
   just read this poem.
   Richard Eldred

Untitled

My heart,
hungry for love,
grows angrily at me.
It has been emptied and forgotten long ago.
"Feed Me" it cries.
"Don't doom me to this fate"!
Frustrated, it rumbles in a slow deep voice.
   Kellie Dawn Arrowood

Reason

I realized I was broken when I was swimming on my feet.
How terribly broken, I was too wet to cry.
But tears are for the afraid, and I have seen truth.
What is there to fear in death?
Pain is bad, but gone when you die,
That is, of course, if you're Heaven bound.
If Christianity is so dangerous as they say,
Then why are they afraid of death?
If there is no God, it still makes people happy
To believe.
Be happy, they say, with psychics and dianetics.
Why can't you let us be happy with Christ?
Am I really harming you?
God must really be real if you hate Him
For no reason.
No reason at all.
A reasoning age of geniuses.
You're all so stupid.
Dim!
Dim!
   Stephen Thomas

Mother

Mom in your celestial world do you remember me?
How we talked and you corrected me?
On ordinary days we could get along;
But those hectic one's you'd wish me gone.
Now that I'm older and reminisce,
You were, oh, so clever and ominous,
Six children you had, I but one.
But you, Mom, are compared with none.
How I loved your artistic style,
So creative and festive when all was done.
You protected me because I was dumb,
But now, Mom, I have overcome the
   disabilities that shadowed our fun.
When we meet again we both shall be whole,
And enjoy our friendship clear to the soul.
   Lisa Lewis

Flashback Of 50 Years Ago

Not dwelling on the past, I have not clearly remembered
   How we were thrown into buses, like cattle for the slaughter.
'Take only what you can carry' is what my folks were told
   Not knowing where we were going, or how long we would be away.
Don't know how mom managed, with eleven little ones to care
   While poppa crated up household goods to leave behind with friends.

First to the race track, horse stalls were our home,
   They called it an Assembly Center, while the camps were being built
Over ten Relocation Centers, erected on desolated land,
   For humans of Japanese heredity, whether U.S. born or not

Barb wired fences with watch towers, surrounded the camps.
   MPs with rifles were always aimed at us,
We were at war
   Why were they not fighting our enemies? Not us.
   Youko Yamasaki

"I Believe"

I believe that a fire must start with a spark
I believe that with out light, it would be dark
I believe in true love, it's getting hurt that I fear
I believe time is precious, every minute is dear
I believe that the moon reflects light from the sun
I believe it is how you play the game, not who won
I believe good things come to all those who wait
I believe life is destiny, and when we met it was fate
   Nikki R. Howard

"Summer"

The cold flat dust lies in solitude, where lovers once promised in hushed voices,
while children strove to create.
A whisper in the breeze echoes of laughter and balm,
but abruptly whips away in a gust down the stretch.
The large, gray scavengers comb the dust, searching for some remnants of life...
but none remain.
On half-hearted wings, they once again take flight, their shrill cries momentarily
drowning out the thrash and crash of the tumultuous body.
Storm clouds brew and loom overhead, threatening to join in the lonely reminisce
...how long has it been?...Days, nights, nights, days
Oh endless time!

    OminousSilencetoomuchtobear,thedankgreen
    depthsCRYOUTforattentionasthedustdisappears
    inchbyinchswallowedupfornowbutyet.......

It will know the solitude again. There is no escape, no reprieve
But look! A lone figure strides purposefully forward with great intention.
A shiver envelops me and I feel welcomed into the gloom
Take heart desolate strip! I am here as promise of warmth and spirit!
I know your despair so take comfort in me.
Let me sit with you in all your loneliness and we will dream of summer.

    Kimerri Noel Leonardo

"The World Within"

I am a spiritual being.
I am an Eternal Spirit.
I am a soul on a journey.
Let God's truth pass through me.

I have a spiritual partnership.
I have a divine purpose.
I have aligned myself with His perfect order.
Let God's truth pass through me.

I am at peace.
I am in harmony.
I am in quiet acceptance.
Let God's truth pass through me.

I will go to the secret place within.
I will discard my self-imposed limitations.
I will create the magic that I need.
Let God's truth pass through me.

I am in awe.
I am a miracle.
I am willing.
Let God's truth pass through me.

    Sally A. Meyers

Becoming Beige

Somewhere between the pink tattered taffeta and the tainted white,
I am becoming beige.

The liquid swan's song replaced by the quack of a domestic duck,
More real than inspirational.

It would take too much thread to weave my life, not gold cord,
But unraveled yellow yarn.

Rebroadcast my life in technicolor,
Televised sunsets and sappy endings.

I dreamed of a butterfly catcher, superfluous and beautiful
To dance across the sphere
Giving cosmic deliverance.

Shrouded in broken buttons and stained drapes
I inhale deeply, sip my diet soda and
Watch my thighs spread.

    Lisa Michelle Remmert

Depression

Sometimes there is nothing inside me,
I am hollow,
but only the inside hurts.

Sometimes you die and leave me,
and my tears flow for someone who is too far to feel.
(Or were you alive only in my mind?)

Sometimes I am sick and sink deeper,
but no one knows
and no one cares to pull me out.

Sometimes you are right in front of me,
but I cannot find you,
because I am blind,
but they are the ones who do not see,
for we hide.

We are isolated,
separated by the pain
that has frozen my once-human heart.

Sometimes when I smile I weep,
my eyes full of emptiness,
because I am depressed.

    Margalo Astrid Connolly

Heaven

Roses are red, Violets are blue
I am on my way to Heaven, how about you?
Some apples are red some are green
Heaven is the most beautiful place ever seen
Some clothes are grey some are black
When I get to Heaven I am never
coming back, but while I am going
along, help me dear Lord, make me strong.
Fill my soul with your marvelous love
Make me fit for Heaven above.

    Violet P. Hadden

"The First Shall Be Last"

"Who's next?" The clerk asked, it was spring break vacation,"
"I am" she announced, stepping forward with no hesitation.

An accident ahead chokes traffic down to one lane,
Let that car cut in front of me, "Do you think I'm insane?"

My garden's so plentiful this year, to eat all
  its produce, we're just not able,
So share it, give it away - why I couldn't
  do that, who will provide for my table?!

As a nation that fears cancer and dreads that word AIDS,
  how can we be so blind and not see,
A plague more destructive to our body and
  soul is the silent killer that centers around ME!

You ask, "what's the answer, is it too late, has the lot been cast?"
America let's turn it around and instead of me
  always being first, I'll choose to be last.

    Pat Bryant

Shadows

All around me I see shadows of what I want to be.
I am wife, mother, friend, but nowhere
Do I see the shadows of whom I want to be.
I see shadows of dreams that have not yet come true,
All around are shadows of years that just slipped by,
I see shadows of us together and of mistakes
that should not have been made;
All around me are shadows of whom I want to be.
I see shadows of us, walking hand in hand to
a better tomorrow,
All around me are shadows that proclaim our
Love for each other;
And I realize the shadows are whom I want to be.

Loisita Rodriguez

I Am A Nurse

I was caring for you before I knew what I was
I am your Mother, your sister, your brother
Throughout time I made my mark and became what I am
I was the first, though many came before me
I know not what to call myself, for I have always been there
I am a nurse

I have cared for those who have made this country free
I have served in wars, on battlefields, in foreign lands
I ease their pain, cleanse their wounds and hold them through the last
hours of life their pain touches me but I endure I am a nurse

I have touched your life when it first began
I care for your children, your parents, your spouse, your loved ones
I am there when others may not be, I am the guardian of wellness, I am
your friend I am a nurse

I work not for rewards, for money or fame
Your smile, your touch, your thanks is my gain
I will give my life, to help those that I serve
I am dedicated to life, dedicated to healing
dedicated to caring, dedicated to you
I am a nurse

Patrick Ahearne

Autumn

As I wander along the winding dirt path,
I breathe the clean smell of nature,
breaking the congestion that was causing all those headaches.
My mind begins to open,
taking in the scents of fallen crisp leaves browning in the fall,
and the breeze beginning to chill.
My eyes begin to search over the hazy blue sky in hopes to catch a
glimpse of the ones who's goodbye calls echo towards the south.
But all I see is the last of the green trees.
The pines who's peak pokes the edge of the sky.
All is still.
Realizing the goose bumps set upon my bare arms,
I watch as smoke from each home slowly releases itself from
   crackling fireplaces.
The outdoors is a world of death.
But the spirits of life rejoice in my heart.
For in just a few months, the sun will again shine.

Kelly Ann Lavin

The Cry Of The Coyote

I hear the cry of the coyote again and again
I look but I can't find it, 'till I look within
For the cry of the coyote comes from my heart
Calling for the pain to stop, for the joy to start

I run through my days and even play
But when the moon rises in the sky
I sit on my mountain and howl and cry

Keith H. Kline

Shadows Move

I am not alone or so I fear
I can feel something very near
my skin crawls and I'm terrified
nowhere to run-nowhere to hide
and in midnight's unholy gloom
the shadows move-in my bedroom

I feel the urge to just flee
but if I move then it gets me
it's all the things that I dread
haunting me from the dead
out of the darkness spirits loom
and the shadows move-in my bedroom

Ghosts from a child's tormented past
creeping in but coming fast
whispers of doubt cross my mind
will you love me for all time
or will my past spell our doom
as the shadows move in our bedroom

Olen Segers

"The Story's Untold"

   Come to me, let me hear your mighty sound,
I can feel the moisture coming from your sweet breath,
As I stand on your soft floor, I feel satin on my feet,
How I wish I could know for certain what you have found.
   Your salt I taste, It's as tears on my face,
Bright stars all around you, they twinkle in the night,
The moon up above you, a glowing halo I can see,
Through God you were created, He touched you with His grace.
   Come and share with me the secrets that you hold,
Tell me of the laughter and happiness you have seen,
A whisper of the sadness, and hearts so full of fear,
I know when I look at you, there's stories waiting to be told.
   You travel so very far, your journey has no end,
As you come and go with a spirit that is easy and free,
With peaceful tranquility, you lure me to your side,
The wisdom that's within you, my mind can't comprehend.
   "The Ocean"

Louise Weddington

Baseball

I'd love to join in that game of baseball across the street,
I can hear the umpire making his calls so discrete.
He calls out loud safe, foul, strike, and your out,
Maybe he'll let me play or maybe he'll shout.
Get off the field boy you've been there all day,
Oh please, Oh please let me play.
I promise there won't be any mistakes on my part,
"Are you sure", he said? Oh yes baseball is an art.
Okay, okay one game you may play,
Thank you sir, oh sure that'll be okay.
I played and played until it was dark,
I was so happy he let me be a part.
Be a part of a game I love a lot,
It's time for me to go its almost eight o'clock.
I thanked my mom for letting me stay out after the sun
I'm very tired now that the day is done
I'm going to go and get in the bed
I have no choice that's what my mom said.
Good night!!

Tonyell F. McDay

"Memories"

My darling Grandma to whom I hold real dear
I cannot believe; it was my biggest fear.
   For it is reality one month to the day;
that my heart broke in two and you went away.
   I'll always remember the times that we shared;
when you and I Grandma were always a pair.
   I'll always remember you until the day I die;
and I will look forward when I reach the sky.
   For you and me Grandma together again,
at last I can say my sorrow will end...
Kimberly Cecilia Jaramillo

What Is The Wind?

   What is the wind, I'd like to know?
I can't see it, as it blows.
It has such power,
It can destroy everything, in an hour.
   I was in the yard, it was in may,
The wind got stronger, nearly blew me away!
I ran in the house, looked through the window-pane,
It rooted up trees, I was amazed in vane.
   Next the roof, was blown-off the house,
I was scared as a "Little-Mouse".
Why can't I see the (WIND), I'd like to know?
I can only see the things it "BLOWS!
Winifred Bullard

"Runaway Brain"

When I'm alone
I can't stop thinking about the past
It flashes
Assaults in angry bursts
The memories penetrate
The guilt is residual
A deposit from the past I have trouble shaking
Please
Give me something to do with myself
I'm too tired to solve the problems anymore
Please
Keep me busy
Keep me tame
Please
Keep me from thinking
Put the brakes on my runaway brain
Tom Brazelton

Promises

Broken like glass, fragile to the touch
He who keeps them, is encased in gold
Those promises can seal a love
They can break a heart of goodness
   and tarnish a man of potential
They can make a man of nothing into a man
   of power
So why do we make them, break them, seep them
   and keep them?
Just look into a child's eyes and you will see
   them.
I promise
Santo

Graves

When I call'd upon my love whose soul from life has fled,
I chanc'd to see a new grave as if the earth had bled,
The small proportions of the mound sadly testifies,
That taken from this life too young a tiny child lies.

A grieving widow down the path weeps in dress of black,
Her husband gone she must face he's never coming back,
For she is young and so was he how we all have tried,
To comprehend why from life so many young have died.

And further on soldiers stand in honor they do pray,
For a fallen comrade whom to rest they sadly lay,
A man so young and live was so full of power,
A life the war did deny it toll'd his final hour.

When the tatter'd spectral visage at last comes to stand,
Beside my bed to call my name and reach to take my hand,
I will know the time has come when all my days are past,
I'll bid farewell to those I love and smiling breath my last.

In the lonely graveyard winter's silence is the sound,
Symbolic of the end of life while snow does dust the ground,
As if children dancing the breeze leaves that trees bequeath,
Stop to tickle the new mound I see from underneath.
J. Gregory Crapo

"Us"

I think of you every night and day
I close my eyes and hope our love will always stay,
I want you to know that your the one for me
I am telling you right now that my love for you
   will always be,
I close my eyes right now and see
   us together forever happily,
I'm praying that we will never part
   but if it happens it will brake my heart,
I want to tell you something that is very true
I want to tell you that ... I love you.
Laura Yousif

Puppet On A String

One day as you were shopping, something caught your eye,
I didn't understand it, and still do not know why.
But you took it home and polished it and really made it shine,
Then you sat and just admired it and fed it a few lines.
You thought the cracks gave character; they made it so unique,
You thought it might be fun to maybe keep around a week.
You attached some little strings to it, and painted on a smile,
Then you went to shop for something new, something else you could defile.
You made my heart a puppet, a brand new toy for you,
And when the novelty wore off, you broke my heart into.
Sandra Lee

Brief Time

All that we shared was a brief time
I feel so all alone, never having the chance to
Say goodbye, or to hold you tenderly once more.
Oh why, oh why, was your life such a brief time.
Still remembering the vows we took. Gazing into your
Eyes feeling that special love inside. Oh why, was your life
Such a brief time. Scattered and torn, where do I go from
Here, yesterday forever in my mind. Your touch and the way
You smile. I sit and stare of how it use to be, it's so
Strange how I miss you even more when the seasons change. Oh
Love you may be gone, but not to me...I still sense your
Presence here, and when I use to touch you it's your memory
I'm holding dear.
Sherilynn Pacheco

Dreams Become A Reality

Many many years before I traveled
I dreamed of traveling to far-away places
From state to state
From coast to coast
From country to country

Many years before I traveled
I wished that I could fly
From state to state
From coast to coast
And to foreign lands

Many years later
My dreams became a reality
Travelling by car, plane and train
Visiting every taste in the USA
In winter, spring, summer and fall

Many years late
I traveled to foreign lands
By plane, cruise ship and freighters too
In winter, spring, summer and fall

Nettie Y. Schwartz

Dissolutions Within

As I sit inside my domain of silence,
I fear the impossible happening to me,
I lower my eyes till I see full blackness,
I'm falling down upon my dream.

The sun progresses it's daily routine,
But through my eyes, a different scene,
Rotting bodies of dust and bones,
cries for help, screams and moans.

Grappling hands, pulsating strides,
the shadows are lurking, hiding inside,
street lights now flicker, one thousand stares,
I start to hallucinate, corpses appear.

Dragging limbs, fists of soil,
vivid graphics, ground has spoiled,
let me live, demons shackled,
all around, fires crackled.

Surrounding walls of ancient history,
the dying are dead, let me be,
I awake alone, drenched in sweat,
tomorrow repeats, they will kill me yet!

Michelle Jeffries

God's Star-Studded Night

On God's Star-studded night, with the heavens so bright,
I feel I can reach out and touch Him.
He gives me new strength, when the way seems so faint,
Lets me know He's the one I can trust in.

It works like a balm, to help keep me calm,
When the stresses of life over-take me.
I feel Him so near, when the night is so clear,
The stars seem to twinkle to cheer me.

When I star-gaze at night, when the heaven's so bright,
It seems like a peek into heaven.
I can't help but say may God's name be praised,
For all of the beauty He's given.

Lillie D. Wilder

To Feel This Way

I lay awake
  I feel my body tremble deep inside
And though it's late
  I see your image everytime I close my eyes
    There's a brand new feeling growing strong
    Without your love I can't go on

Deep in your eyes
  I see the things I've searched for all these years
I don't know why
  but when you touch me you comfort all my fears
    This time I'm going to listen to my heart
    And nothing is going to tear this love apart

Hold me tight
  So when our bodies meet the two of us are one
All through the night
  Keep me close until the rising sun
    I want to be in your arms to start each day
    I want the rest of my life to feel this way

Margaret Kleintop Heine

My Daughter

Now that you have grown and left the fold
I feel that I am growing old,
My dearest daughter child of mine
Now that you have left those teens behind
Set your goal and mark it well
The paths through life, can be hell
But, I have brought you up to trust in God
And you can walk where wise men trod
The end of the rainbow, the pot of gold
Work hard my love, they are there to unfold
Life is not an easy path to tread
But, then again, it's nothing you should dread
You have brought me joy and caused me pain
If I had it all to do again
I would want you just the way you are
Now and forever, my bright and shining star
Good luck my darling, may your joys increase
May you always find
  Love, happiness and peace.

Marjorie M. Peacock

Together And Apart

In the night
I feel your touch.

And that feel I keep,
it seems so much.

When you leave me, I shed a tear.
And when I'm with you, I have no fear.

That love you gave to me
could never be what it is today.

But the love you give to me
is not what it seems night and day.

Now that we're apart
the pain of an arrow is going through my heart.

And the pain that is there,
it just seems to me, like you just don't care.

And the more and more it hurts with pain,
it seems to me like you're going insane.

With the names that you call me, I really don't care.
And the love that you gave to me, was not really there.

The love and affection that could never
be, I am sorry to say, but you're not the person for me!

Nicole Wilson

In Fantasy Free

When you were here near to my heart,
  I felt that you cared, —well, maybe you cared,
So I dared to fair you with me,
  For I cared so much,
In fantasy free.

I joyed at your looks;
  The touch of your smiles,
Daringly, —I held on to your hand,
  While still hoping you'd fall,
In fantasy free.

Suddenly we danced to the strains of our song,
  the miracle refrains brought love to our life,
My darlin', —say you'll be mine,
  We'll live up this joy,—-
In fantasy free!
ASCAP, Na Hoku, Hanohano Academy
    Marcelliano Villaverde

Road Of Life

Everywhere I turn on my road through life
I find many people living in strife
Wandering aimlessly as they walk the earth
Never knowing how much they truly are worth

Why me!?! They would often shout and cry
Wishing for the struggles of life to die
Never realizing the true answers are here
How happiness can rule their life instead of fear

The instructions from God in heaven above
Teaches us how not to hate, but to love
Obeying his oracles is how life should be
For discipline in his word sets us free

Works done faithfully to glorify God shows
For He forever blesses those whom He knows
Lord Jesus Christ, God's only begotten Son
Will help to guide us until this life is done

Everywhere I turn on my road through life
I find many people living in strife
Wandering aimlessly as they walk the earth
Never knowing how much they truly are worth
    Melissa Beth Nelson

The Journey

The ocean waves move back and forth on the sand
I go and travel with my merry band
In search of this mysterious land

It's said that things are better there
Everyone gets a really fair share
Nobody's hands are seen to be bare

We travel high, we travel low
How long it has been, we all don't know
But we have seen each other grow

Soon enough we see something
Far, far away, a big structure shining
It was so bright, it was so blinding

What a frightening thing, we all thought
We're in a trap, we have been caught
This isn't the mysterious land we sought

A voice spoke up and we quieted down
We looked around and each face had a frown
We were happy, though, for we didn't drown

The voice came from this colorful object on a mound
We knew in our hearts that the land we sought, we had found.
    Meliza B. Fuentes

"My Opponent"

I had a dream late last night,
I had been in a dreadful fight.

My opponent wasn't a man, woman or child,
It wasn't an animal, fierce and wild.

This frightful creature took hold of my being,
I found myself running, hiding, fleeing.

I couldn't break loose from its powerful clutch,
The pain was unbearable - it hurt so much.

When the fight was over I realized I'd lost,
I bought the farm at an outrageous cost.

My opponent comes without warning, no sign,
My opponent...cancer of the spine.
    Suzanne K. High

Seasons Of My Life

In Spring I came to life
I had no burdens to bear
God planned it that way
When He placed me in another's care

Then Summer arrived
I felt such carefree bliss
It seemed like I was in heaven
Constantly soothed by an angel's kiss

Fall settled in without warning
My time was no longer full of glee
I was faced with many responsibilities
When I'd rather still have been running free

But Winter brought it's recompense
And I've learned to go to the Source
Neither snow, sleet, rain, or hail
Can lure me from my final course
    Marie H. Dawson

Far From Home

As I write this my dear,
I have in my eye a tear.
For it has been almost a year
Since I have seen you, my dear.

The threads of love that bind me to your heart
Will forever keep you near.
And even though we are miles apart,
You will always be so dear.

This is the first time that I have been gone
And I pray to God that I will soon be home.
For to me it is no joy to roam,
Away from you and our dear home.

I have always held you in my mind
And this has helped to pass the time.

I look forward to that day
That I can see and hear our children play.

Take care of yourself and the children my dear
And never worry or fear.
For if the Good Lord is willing,
I will be home by next year. And I will always be, your dear Bill.
    William H. Conley Jr.

Dreams

There is a show in my head,
I have it every night when I go to bed.
  Sometimes I dream in color and sometimes
in black and white,
  it all happens when I turn out the light.
I see people walk by and I say Hi,
  and they don't see me and I wonder why?
Am I here? Am I alive? Am I a dream in a dream?
  Life is not what it all shims.
When I awake in the day,
  I wonder did I dream it all my way.
The illusion of the walking in a dream
  and no one around, no people no birds no sounds.
Then the clock wakes me up for a new day,
  I wonder did I dream it any way.
    Nancy Jordan

Learning To Live

It was something that happened only to someone else.
I have never thought it would happen to me.
I am no different inside or out.
My surroundings begin to slowly isolate... I cry helplessly.
Thinking back on that moment pushed my emotions over the edge.
I wanted so bad to end everything I have.
It was just a waste.
All that exists is pain.
Wondering what will be next I cannot say.
I am alone and lacking something desirable.
But that cannot be received.
I sit quietly watching the time go by... alone.
    Kelly Matsuda

Back Of My Mind

I hear the thunder
I hear the rain
You could never understand the depths of my pain
All is gone that, matters to me
I'm left to try to understand all the things I can't see
The way of the world I've tried not to question
The many things of joy are not in my possession
At night, my mind throbs with screams
With memories of truth that I can't redeem
What could I do to console my mind, body and soul
Just anticipation of what maybe to come
Makes me shake and my world quake in a way that would not worry some
Give me love or fortune, for both I have none
I wonder which would make me happy
I'd love to have both, but that maybe too much to ask
Give me which either one, which would stop the storms of my every task
For tranquility and serenity is what I long for maybe this security of life,
I'll know one day for sure
But from this point in life, I could never guess the score
    Wanda Blackwell

"Where Am I"

I know where I'm going
I even know what I want to be
I can see my future just around the corner
but my heart is beating to two different drummers in the same band,
Can you play double dutch with one rope? I can
I can live in two different time zones without leaving the room
Why can't I live my life in the same body that I live out my other life
Why can't I live and not look into my mind to find myself.
    Teri Marie Shepard

Time

They grew up so fast. Wasn't it just yesterday
I kissed their boo-boos and chased their fears away?
It was like playing house with my little girls,
their china doll faces and hair brushed in curls.

How could I think there was plenty of time
to guide them and love them? They'd always be mine.
But time slipped away too quickly it seems,
and now all I have are memories and dreams.

Somehow life has its way of giving us more,
a new generation, a new open door.
Now there is someone who calls me grandma,
with great big brown eyes and hair like her mama.

I hope there is time in my life to see
more little grandkids being bounced on my knee.
This time I won't let the time slip away;
I'll play with them more and treasure each day.

I'll hold them and love them and make sure they know
how special they are, feeling pride as they grow.
We are all blessed with gifts from the heavens above
and the most precious of all are the children we love.
    Linda S. DeJohn

My True Love

The first time I met you,
I knew it would be our destiny.
To be together, to love each other,
For eternity.

I used to shudder at the thought of losing you,
The fact that you would never be there.
There would be no one to share my love with,
No one else's beautiful eyes in which I may stare.

You left me for a little while,
And how I made it through, I don't know.
But now you are back in my life,
And my love I will ever greater show.

In my heart, there will be no one higher.
For my love, no one will ever be above.
'Cause in the deepest part of my heart,
It tells me that you are my only true love.
    William Walker

My Grandparent's House

I'd go walkin' to your house in the afternoon,
I knew that I would see your faces soon;
Those were such happy times for me,
'Cause my grandparents house, was where I wanted to be.

Chasin' rabbits till they were mine,
Whittlin' sticks on the old stone grind;
Hidin' from the cows behind the big oak tree,
Takin' rides in the ol' model T.

Edgehill sippin' from a coffee cup,
Sittin' 'round watchin' dippy duck;
Drinkin' water from an old tin cup,
Those were some of things that I loved.

Takin' naps in your big feather bed,
Lovin' pats on the top of my head;
Grandma whistlin' a religious tune,
Grandpa restin' in the afternoon.

Just thinkin' about you, yet today,
Makes me feel in a special way.
Those were such happy times for me,
'Cause my grandparents house, was where I wanted to be.
    Suzanne Shaner

What Is Good?

"What is good?" a boy asked his father and his mother.
"I know it isn't bad," he said, "Must it include another?"
"Another what?" his mother asked. "Another you or me?"
"I'm sure it does," his father said, "What other do you see?"
"Some other, one or more, maybe even God
  or power that's more than we!"
"There might be better kinds of good," his mother said to him.
"If there are greater kinds of good, where would the greatest lie?"
Almost as a voice within came forth this reply:
  The greatest good you can ever do
  Should be what is best for every other
  Just as well as you.

This is something you may never know nor totally believe,
But you should try at least to show what you are trying to achieve.
   William Winfield Armentrout

Corner Of My Mind

When I'm standing all alone in the corner of my mind
I know just where I am
And I'm sure of what I'll find
Sometimes when its dark outside, and I can't quite find the light
It's a place where I can stay awhile
And the mood there feels just right
Looking out from the inside, a place no one else can go
Where I can stay and hide to lock inside
feelings I just can't let show
I can hold the thoughts that comfort me
when emotions fall down like rain
I can shed the tears and hide the fears
Or I can throw away the pain
A place where a calmness comforts me
And there's a strength down every hall
Where faith doesn't tumble and my spirit won't crumble
And my hands don't shake at all
So when life becomes overwhelming and I want to be by myself
I'll go back in the corner of my mind
And put my thoughts back on the shelf
   Lisa Greenwood Bushey

You Are My Song

I know there is a sun that always rises
I know that life will often bring surprises
And so I always knew
that someday you
would come along
You are the song
I've always wanted to hear
You are the one
I'll always want to be near
You are my song, the song of life

I know tomorrow's face wears nine disguises
I know the mind believes what it devises
So yes, I knew someday
you'd come my way
and I'd belong
You are the song
I've always wanted to hear
You are the one
I'll always want to be near
You are my song, the song of life
   Michael C. Berker

"Crying Heart"

My heart is dead and filled with sorrow.
I know you are here today, but will you be gone tomorrow?
I know my love is true and real as can be.
I feel things when I'm with you that you might not ever see.
I think you love me, I know I love you.
In the past you were done wrong, but now the love is true.
I love you more than ever, more than any one before.
And every time I think of you I always love you more.
I love you more and more each and every day.
And I'll keep on loving you in every which way.
I'll always want your love, I'll always love you.
I'll treat you nice and sweet, just show you love me too.
Our love has great purpose and head a great start
I once was hurt bad, but you fixed my "crying heart."
   Buck Wright

I Still Love You

I talk to you each night, each day.
I know you don't hear the words I say.
I can't give up the closeness we once knew.
You see honey, I still love you.

Some times at night I feel you near me.
For that brief moment I live in ecstasy.
Your love helps me make it through.
I hope you know honey, I still love you.

I see you in my dreams each night.
Just as you were when all was right.
As morning comes, so do the blues.
For you see honey, I still love you...
   Russell C. Cornwell

Bagg'n Under The Stars

In the back of my Chevy truck
I lay on foam pad resting in my sleeping bag.
The midnight blue sky of March dances twinkles from the stars.
Vibrant full moon echoes of Halloween Eve.

Scarce clouds wisp by in hurried scuttle.
The Boulder pines crystallize the frosty dew
And winds nudge the mountain ridge.

Below, the stream wears upon it icy cover
Tunnelling sounds as from a cavernous fort.

A blast of images.
   Scott J. Behan

The Value Of My Life

The value of my life was always stressed
I learned and learned well, but when I forgot
I was reminded, I was taught
The intelligence of my teachers was so great, so wide
That there was always something new
Something hiding behind that wall, waiting to be learned
Through many books was this value expressed to me
So many, I can't remember
After Mr. and Mrs. Young were through with their teachings
Mom and Dad would tuck me in
Goodnight Mom, Goodnight Dad
I would lay there and think about that value book
They had just read, or that story they had just told
Then I would smile and go to sleep
  Thank you Mom
  Thank you Dad
   Zachary Young

Shadows

Can't see what I'm doing, I just want myself back
I let go of my hope, my dreams to become someone else's shadow
I was me, I am me
To see my footsteps, to hear the sound of thunder rumbling
through a dark hallway
All is quiet to them, not to me.
It comes when least expected, isolating yourself from others
To wake up, all is around me, you see nothing but a haze.
Not understanding where you've been all this time.
Fearing what will overcome you next
You descend into a eternal sleep
  Tatiana Rasa

A Life Without

My life has no joy without you in it.
I long to see your smiling face brightening up my life for that time.
When you're with me I feel content, even peaceful.
But all I feel now is the pain of loss.
Thrown into a maelstrom of emotions.
Rage! Denial! Pain! Sorrow! Fear! Regret! And ultimately loss.
Sitting in my miasma of dismal thoughts of life and suicide.
I try to take my life, but fail!
Whatever Gods, beings, or entities there are, they want me to stay and
live without you.
I don't want my life to be one without you.
You were my emotional anchor.
With you gone my stability collapsed.
My days are filled with remorse of the things we didn't do, things I
  didn't tell you.
My nights are filled with the tears of what could've been.
Someday soon I will see you again.
  Ryan Bush

That Old Bench

I sit alone on that old bench, pondering over all my woes.
I look about and see the people; yet I see none.

A blind fool I seem to be, one that sees all I want
And nothing more. I see not the homeless man
Looking for food in a trash can, the child running,
Gasping and panting while a crowd chases
Screaming obscenities.

I sit there wrapped in my ego, oblivious to others.
I sit and wonder on that old bench, down by the Green,
Looking but not seeing what goes about.

A woman screams as a teen wrestles her down to the ground;
He stands beside her and pulls the firmly held bag
Holding the savings of a lifetime. He kicks her,
And she lets go. And off he runs with her worldly goods.

Cops come! I saw it all; yet I don't know
What the man wore, if he was white, black or gold.
For all I know he had no color, he was a ghost.

I ponder some more on that old bench,
Wondering why we spin ourselves into a cocoon,
And look about yet see not what is all around.
  Maria A. Ortiz

My True Love

I thought I saw my true love walking past the gate.
I looked, then looked again;
But, alas, searched too late.
Could it have been really he... my king among men?

My eyes must have played a prank for he was not there.
How I yearn that he be,
Thus, seek him everywhere
And hope time might reveal my true love's identity.

Yet, will I recognize him if somewhere we meet?
Shall I even know him
If we pass on the street?
Does "my true love" exist or is he "my heart's whim"?

Oft I have wondered if my true love looks for me
And if he ponders, too,
Where it is I could be.
Might we know each other, not be aware we do?

I pray the day will come when he may glance my way,
And, having once seen me,
Perchance decide to stay.
Then this dream of my true love could become reality!
  Millicent E. Lutz

One Of Grandma's Days

I woke up in the morning, and I rubbed my eyes;
I looked to see what time it was; it was past sunrise,
I jumped out of bed and took my shower,
I slipped on the rug going ninety miles an hour.
I got myself together, I was bruised here and there;
I guess it doesn't matter, I am still breathing air.
I can walk and I can talk so I'm doing all right.
I suppose people think that I am not that bright.
No one seems to give a care, and they do not keep in touch;
But now I'm old and all alone it doesn't matter much;
I keep on smiling and laughing and doing whatever I like,
I'm happy and contented so things may turn out all right.
  Leah M. Bodily

This Little House

This little blue house had a white picket fence
I looked upon it and knew that it was right for me
It had charm and warmth and possibility

It offered me a little home of my own
And, it became my retreat in my time of pain
It sheltered me and helped me to start anew
I began to heal, at last - at last

Though I was not young, it was the place in which
I finally could learn to grow - to stand tall and alone
I would become proud of who and what I was

It was the place, where at long last
I found the peace that had always eluded me
I discovered acceptance within myself, and
Learned how to walk forward, ever forward

It was just a place you say, but not to me - not to me
It was a haven where I learned to let down the walls of my soul
Where I learned to love, and to be loved
I learned to be, just to be

It can never be "just a place" to me
For there I became whole
  Sandra M. W. Gursky

Love

Love is more then just three words,
  I love you.
Love is an intimate vulnerability,
  full of passion and desire.
Love is a yearning waiting to be redeemed,
  touched in the most intimate way.
It goes beyond the body and hands,
  that touch. Pass the heart,
  Penetrating the soul.
Love is colliding lovers into an eclipse,
  intertwining the depths and heights,
  reaching the Spirit and consuming
  it with fire.
Love is more then just three words
  I love you.
It is an intimate relationship seen
  in the eyes of those who dare to,
  love in its most intimate form of passion and desire.
Love is vulnerability.
  Sarah Gonzalez

To The One I Love The Most

To the one I love the most,
I love you from coast to coast
Your so great, I can hardly wait,
till you come home where you belong.
I love you so, I never want you to go.
I want you to stay close, so with you I can be.
You'll always be mine, in my heart, soul and mind.
For only you can satisfy me, the way it ought to be.
I'll love you forever, as long as you will leave me never.
All through your strife, don't forget I'm your wife.
I'll always be your best friend, even until the end.
I'll love you until you die, you are my sugar pie.
I know this sounds silly, but I thought it was a dilly.
  Marie Terrell

My Special Love

While I was visiting a friend one time,
I met a man I wanted to be mine.
He was tall, handsome and good,
Made me feel special as only he could.
The days were long when we were apart,
But I held him close to me in my heart.
One day he came to me, I'll never forget,
He promised me a ring next time we met,
My heart was so thrilled, it pounded inside,
One day soon I'd become his bride.
A few days later a letter arrived,
Just a few lines, he'd changed his mind.
My heart was broken, I thought I'd die.
The man I loved was saying, "Good-bye."
Many years passed after that letter came,
But my love for this man never changed.
There must be a reason we kept in touch,
God surely knew I loved him so much.
I believe it was meant I was to be his wife,
We are married now for the rest of our life.
  Mary K. Bennington

The Summer Crawled

The summer crawled throughout these many days;
I neither felt noon heat nor evening breeze,
It might as well have been the winter snows
Through which I trudged these endless, empty hours.

It was in autumn when we formed our plans;
Each vibrant moment lent the perfect touch,
Retreats where-in we thrilled were picturesque
And wrapped us close in nature's warm embrace;
The rustling, burnished leaves all flashed their smile
And as they whirled, our spirits joined their dance.

The dance is over...plans we made are gone;
Our dreams, like autumn leaves, could not endure,
For when chill winter screamed in fierce attack,
You shivered with the leaves and slipped away.

The summer crawled throughout these many days...
It might as well have been the winter snows.
  Martha Fowler Reichle

First Kiss

"Meet me at the playground," he whispers
I nod, my brown eyes round with wonder
The moment finally comes
We are there...alone
Our eyes meet
Those blue eyes highlighted with excitement
They move closer
The drum in my chest is pounding
Closer
Time has stopped
Closer
Darkness surrounds me
Closer
Our lips meet
Every cell, every atom is suddenly warm
My body is tingling
It ends
I grow numb
Brown eyes meet blue eyes
He whirls around and runs while I stand in dismay...and smile
  Larissa Salas

Eternal Flame

Looking across this desolate wasteland of ash
  I often reflect.
On what?

A children's song in minor played by rag dolls in the rain,
The cheerful fat dolts in the taverns
  who threw bits at the skeleton performers.
  How they laughed at our misery
  stuffing their mouths to the rhythm
  of Waltzes;
As we marched on toward the light,
Our smoke filled the sky, we rained upon you
  yet no one stopped to ask...

The itsy-bitsy spider mocked me
  from atop the barbed wire;
Twinkle twinkle little star
  how I wonder where you are!
  Nicole C. Bayer

Silence

I watch your breathing, you seem to stop, is this the end?
I reach across the rail and brush my hand across your brow
I feel the sweat and clammy coolness of your skin
I watch closely as your chest rises again
I breath a sigh of relief, brush, you brow,
and wait for your final breath and silence

Now you're breathing so hard and your heart beats so fast!
I know you are tired and want only to rest
But your my mom, and I'm frightened by this final quest
As I wait for the silence

I lay my head on your tired breast
I remember the years of friendship and battle
I weep and I wait for the final heart beat and silence

You slowly open your eyes, murmur, and glance my way
Your eyes fill with tears as your glance meets mine
We speak no words but connect in thought
I allow my tears and I wait for the silence

I remember the fun and allow a glimpse of the pain
I speak no words, but stare into your eyes,
that suggest through your tears that you've done the same-
I squeeze your hand, I feel the pain and I wait for the silence

Suzanne Goen

October

As I turn up my collar on this cool, crisp evening
I remember last winter.....
the month of our break up, seems like so long ago
now it's the end of summer
I can't face it, the beginning of October
I hate it
I recall wearing your oversized sweater, tucked away in your house,
our corner of the world
felt like I belonged
nothing or no one could move me - so I thought
last October...
when I found lipstick traces and her possessions
where we shared our love
foolish me, love has no guarantees
and baby, you are not worth my sanity
I must hold on and not fall to pieces
remember..
last October
wish I could forget!

Linda McBee

Memories Of Stephen

I dreamt about you again last night.
I saw you in the distance, at the place
  where we once met—
Your eyes were lit with the glow of excitement, as were mine.
We ran to one another, but stopped suddenly as a sadness
  pervaded our souls.
I begged for you to kiss me, but you were afraid of the
  intimacy, knowing that it could not last...
Finally, your quivering lips touched mine before you faded
  away into the darkness.
I awoke then, reaching for you...
But you were gone.

Mindy Tunis

"For Elizabeth"

Somewhere in my mind, in a chasm of a dream
I saw you sitting atop a grassy hill, in a T-shirt and Cut off jeans.
Under an ancient willow tree, beneath a purple sky
You were puffing on a hooka pipe, getting really high.
As I climbed through the fragrant clouds to reach your resting place.
I was inspired by your radiant smile, the beauty of your face.
You appeared to be a goddess, the very daughter of Mother Earth
The very essence of my soul, the very reason for my birth.
When I finally reached your lofty perch your shrouded realm of mystery
You took me by the hand and introduced me to my destiny.
What happened next I cannot recall, it is lost within my mind
Lost within the morning light and the sinking sands of time.
But I felt no disappointment from my dreamless memory
Because I realized you are more than a dream and exist in reality.

Oscar Barroso

Peace

Sometimes I sit and wonder why can't people get along?
I say to myself what could possibly be wrong?
Some people pick their friends by looks,
That is a disgrace
Others prejudge by color, nationality or race
I'm no respecter of a person, that puts God to shame.
No matter how you look, I treat everyone the same
If we took different races of kids
that were not taught to hate.
They would play together and get along so great.
If you judge a person by outward
appearance, you are truly blind
their beauty on the inside is
what you should try to find.
Every day I hear about violence
raging on our streets
the day we learn to love
all mankind is the day
that we find peace!

Vincent E. Green

Search And Find

Where Columbus sailed off the edge of the earth,
I search the watery depths for my dreams and my soul.
In less exalted company I search for my wavering thoughts,
Even though I don't know what I am looking for.
All my life I have strived to gain independence;
Now that I have achieved that goal, I don't know what I was
  liberating myself from.
I would do anything to blend in;
To find my dreams and escape to where only my imagination can take me.

I dare you to look me in the eye and say that you've truly found
  yourself.
You disappear into the crowd,
All the while the ground beneath you drops,
I am turning into something you are not.
I just sit here while my insides fall to pieces.
I seek to escape the pain and the injustice of the real world.

I search the darkened sky for a distant light called hope; there all
  is calm and all is safe.
I sit across the table from you asking why should we hope if we
  can not even dream.
The person with the dreams will always beat the person with the truth,
Yet we can not get past the physical and factual parts of ones being.
And as I look to the horizon, I hope that everyone can find their own dreams;
'Second star to the right and straight on till morning; Neverland.'

Matthew Stinnett

"I Am Me"

I am me! I wonder why I am here?
I see the hate all around us, I hear crying in the distance.
I want to help, I am me.
I pretend not to notice,
I feel sad!
I touch your hand, I worry when you leaves,
I cry when you don't come back.
I am me!
I understand when you go, I say good-bye.
I dream of when you come back.
I try to understand when you don't come back to me?
I hope you don't hate me because— I am Me.
David Maddocks

Fish

I see them swim
I see them caught on a hook
I see them eat
I see them in oceans
I see them in ponds
I see them in tanks
I see them rest
I see them blow bubbles in the water
I like fish
I like the way they swim
I like the way they eat
I like the way they rest
I like the way they blow bubbles in the water
I love the way they taste
I just love fish
Rychael Lewis

Stages

I see you there hiding in the fear I find familiar
I see you there struggling to save yourself from defeat
I see you there in my shoes, running for your sanity
I remember myself as you are now
Memories taunt me with the wicked anticipation
Innocence in the discovery
Horror and shame of the knowledge
I see you there powerless to help you
I see you there wailing quietly to myself
Despair, a hot acid eating at me from the inside
Viral emotions lyse my souls I see you there
Blind faith tells me you will be fine
The author of your life
Will grant you the ending we all search for after a while
You'll stop fighting when the stars seem to fade
Their brilliant intensities no longer a worthwhile goal
Fear of the unknown subsides
Yet nothing is scarier, that surrender.
Matthew A. Walker

Gift Of Giving

As I reflect on my life today,
I shared with another the gift of praise.
To be thankful for the gifts from above,
And all that was given, was given in love.

The talents we have, to share what can be,
To make this world a better place to see.
And in giving of ourselves with all our heart,
We are given back much more than our part.

More love to share and talents to see,
More life to live, friends to meet,
More sunshines and smiles to lighten our load,
That brighten our paths wherever we go.
Leslie Anne Bower

Like A Canary

Like a canary locked within a cage,
I sing a blessed song of wanting to be free.
Free from the inflicting pain of my owner's rage,
Something that is hurting me.

Like a canary who waits behind its cage bars,
I sit and await for my freedom to return.
Though I am patient, I carry many scars
But I bear it quietly, for in my heart, freedom still brightly burns.

Like a canary who waits for its opportunity to fly,
I wait and dream about my triumph over the suppressor of my freedom.
For now I must be strong, I shall not cry
For someday my freedom will surely come.
Olotania Alalamua

Gang Members Secrets

I sit and wait as seconds tick by
I sit and wait too tired to cry
I watch the headlights of the cars that go by
Only more disappointed when I don't see your car

I only wait for you to come by
You said you were leaving but didn't say why
Your clothes are still here, your magnum is gone
Where did you go, what have you done?!

Why not a note, or even a call?
I'm said you were leaving a right to know
How do I know you'll be back alive
How do I know we didn't say goodbye

The traffic slowed down, my tears start to flow
You have three kids, you're supposed to be home
I hear a ring, I dash for the phone
It was hospital...They said you were gone.
October A. Pawlik

Crazy Moose

I sit and wait for the wooden gate, to open wide and turn us loose.
I sit on a thousand pounds of hate, a horse by the name of Crazy Moose.
Between my legs, snorts the devil's brother.
Complete with red eyes and a tail.
He plans to toss me one way or the other.
I have no serious doubt that he'll fail.

I'm sittin' and thinking of why I'm here, can't come up with one single thing.
Yesterday I had a promising career...night manager at Burger King.
I sense by my fear, the moment is near. We rocket away with the tide.
Old Moose turns it loose, like corn through a goose...
I just go along for the ride.

Like old John Brown at the ferry renowned,
this horse is determined to soon set me free.
The crowd does a wave, as I dance on my grave.
My insides discover the outside of me.
He bounces me right, up, down and left,
my teeth play a tune when they rattle.
My very own screams are making me deaf,
I land upside down in the saddle.

But it's a cowboys life to toe the line and suffer the bruises and pain.
So, as soon as I get down from this Budweiser sign, I'll probably do it again.
H. Ernie Hardie

"Perfidia"

Because it seemed the only thing to do,
I smiled to keep the pain from showing through.
A cigarette grasped firmly 'tween my lips
Kept them from trembling. Nervous finger tips
Beat out in quick staccato to some tune
That I alone could hear within the room.

But it was you who placed me on a throne,
Defined my words with meanings all your own,
Designed the godly raiment that I wore,
And then doubt dashed your dream against life's shore!
Your pretty picture blurred, the colors ran,
And there I stood, not God, but merely man...
Then it was you devised the perfect frame,
Selecting me on whom to place the blame.

Who'd guess our love, so wondrous at the start,
Would end up murdered by a jealous heart.

Wayne Hamilton

Train

Then there was train.
I spied red lights and could see the fog light cutting a path through the night.
I watched this scene from my stairway window: the train up the hill from my house, as I looked at it through sticks and tree branches.
Toot, toot
Whir, whir
Chug-a-lug-a
Chug-a-lug-a
Bridge.
Clickity, clickity clack
Clickity, clickity clack
Down the railroad track.
Silence.
For a moment time was frozen, nothing else moved.
Finally, I made a motion to my bed-to dream of green apple jellied
Sandwiches.
The snow would be light with crystals in the early morning sun.

Richard S. O'Connor

Winters In Afghanistan

It is snowing in Wardaq
I stand naked by a tree
the field of snow separates us
I imagine my friend Raouf reading the letter to you
I imagine you cursing my name
Banishing your son
to the trunk of a frozen walnut tree
Are you closing your mind for the winter, Father?
I push my cap down on my eyes
as it starts to snow again
I shove my hands deep, deep into my pockets
No tears come
It is too cold for tears
And it has been winter in all my memories.

Zuhal Osman

"How Long Must I Wait..."

How long must I wait
I only have a limited time on this earth, my love
I can only wait so long...
But with every waking hour
My heart grows weak with need
Of your love yet you see not
Beckon me with your lips and see the desire within my eyes
But as time passes and so shall I one day...
Do remember, this heart can only wait for an eternity and a day...

Rafia Lodhi

"Brain Dead"

Wind blows through the window like the wrath of judgements call,
I suddenly feel my mind blow as my will begins to fall.
At times I feel like falling from this painful amusement hall
But still I keep on trying in a world that's just too small.
I've seen once in, now in my sin hell glistens of amber might,
Now back again I think twice then, this world is not quite right.
I sit and ponder, then gather and wonder of these claims which lay on me
I walk, then sit, as I pace this trip of life and how it should be.
These times of life are trying and the loneliest of all
Through all these times I'm crying but still I have yet to fall.
Through times of change the clock must wane
My feelings in painful strife,
But remember when these feelings thinned
Yet long lasting and still as the night.
The dew from rain drops falling
They're glistening on my brow
I feel as if I'm calling, yet still I'm not sure how.
My mind in cranial illusion from hallucinogens in my head
Constant state of confusion: That's it, it's through, Brain dead.

Thomas G. Highfield

Every Night

As I lie alone, surrounded by darkness,
I think about you.
I peer through the window at the moon and stars,
and I'm hoping you are looking too.
On a clear night,
there sits our star, alone in the dark sky,
shining so bright.
The moon is full and so round,
I feel like I can reach it,
but my feet are still touching the ground.
As I look out the window,
I can see the bright city lights,
they aren't formed in rows,
but scattered throughout the night.
When I look out the window,
I will close my eyes too,
and for the rest of the night,
I will dream about you.

Wendy Wray

Echoes

Echoes in the morning of people waking up in the past.
I think I'll wake up where I have before.
I think I'll wake up in my house.
I think I'll wake up in my own room
I think I'll wake up in my own bed

I wake up.

Stare into the darkness, smile.
But something's wrong,
Something feels wrong.
I shiver. A shiver of frozen fear.

Then,
Then it all comes back.
In a flood of feelings,
False hopes,
And too many broken dreams.

I think I'll wake up where I have before
But I don't.

Michelle Angell

Be By My Side

I only feel this way when
  I think of you.
You're my inspiration
  and my spirit too.

I'll be by your side dear Lord. You keep my head up
as I bow it down, but as I go walking you are right here

By my side
Lord just lean on me. Be by my side
cause I need you as the days go bye

Be on my side
Lord, Lord, Lord
You lift me up when I'm feeling down
You give me the strength as you guide me around.

Dear Lord be on my side
I give you the praises, without you
I would not be alive
You are my savior and
I thank you Lord
Cause I'm walking
With you and I'm on your side

Yolanda Curry

My Cardinal

Pretty, pretty red bird so high up in the tree,
I think you are singing your melodious song for me.
Pretty, pretty bird I've loved you for so long,
And when I whistle, you answer me with your song.

Pretty, pretty red bird, glistening in the sun,
I hear you in the morning and when the day is done.
Sometimes you fly away and I really miss you so,
Do you have a family; where do you go?

Pretty, pretty red bird I hear your song once more,
I stop what I'm doing and rush right out of my door.
Pretty, pretty bird I'm happy as can be,
There you are once again high up in my tree.

Pretty, pretty red bird winter's drawing near,
If you fly away from me I will shed a tear.
Pretty, pretty red bird come live high up in my tree,
As long as I can hear your song, forever happy I will be.

Pretty, pretty red bird now you're gleaming in the snow,
You've made me so happy, I'm glad you didn't go.
Pretty, pretty red bird, I hear the song you give,
We will be the best of friends as long as I live.

Velma Carstensen

"Danielle"

  Overwhelmed with feelings that I can not yet explain,
I thought I felt your presence before I knew your name.
  A sense, of growing nearer, I felt your need inside
To be all that you can be with dignity and pride,
  I fight all that is in me, to do as I must do,
To make a choice, a sacrifice, a pain I must go through...

  Her name is Lynne, as I give in, to call her on the phone.
A silent prayer, someone to care; we bond, we live as one.
  She can't conceive, I can't believe how much I fill her void.
it's clear, I see, my reason here to be part of her joy.

  So many cannot understand the minds of the inquiring,
I find more peace, a grand release, of ever more inspiration.

  As days go by, she doesn't cry, I always see a smile.
In my heart, though we're apart,
  my legacy,
      her life.

Patricia A. Fleming

The Garden Of Truth And Reality

All most! All most like you Michelle,
I to found a little seed of kindness and held it close to me as well.
But my wisdom was filled with blindness.

But of cause my wisdom never read between a line,
or read minds know matter how define.

But I — I remember searching the world over and found,
beautiful flowers all around. But I pass them all by,
for a little seed laying on the ground, but then I wondered why?

The Rose: I thought was rather too bold!
even if it had a heart of gold.

The Violet: Was all very well and sometimes it would do,
but much - much to lonely and blue

Then there was the Forget-me-not who's passion was too hot.
Not one you'll what to tie with a love - knot.

But in the garden of earthly pleasure,
I too! Thought I found my earthly treasure.
For I pass by them all.
For that little seed and her love - call.

Until!! Until I awoke in the garden of truth and reality,
for her love was created artificiality.
For there, were once laid my lovely seed
was now nothing but a hateful weed.

Ronald D. Rose

Looking Between The Did Not

I did not go swimming this morning.
I told my friend I ought to have gone.
He asked, "Did the family of Should's visit this morning?"
I replied, "Yes, and the Expected-Of's and the Ought-To's came
   along as well."
In quiet understanding he commented, "Uh, Huh."
I asked, "Could we make sure they all have homes?"
He concluded, "You do not want to look after them all?"
In relief I replied, "No."

Laurel Gauld

Awakening

This time joy dawned slowly in my soul.
I usually became aware right away,
Of the towering green trees and billowy blue sky,
Which failed to arouse my woeful senses that day.
But slowly, oh so slowly, as days passed I became aware,
Of the beauty and majesty of God's eternal nature.
As I rested my body, my soul came alive,
To appreciate and admire its creatures and features.
The crystal blue water, the scent of fern and fauna;
The trail of the sea gull, the duck and the loon,
Fully lulled my spirit into a peaceful calm,
As my eyes beheld the full red Sturgeon moon.
Time flies too quickly in this land I love,
I long forever to view the shimmering still lake,
As the sun flings showers of glittering diamonds,
Onto a mirror image of the sky, its picture taken.

My heart grows sad at thoughts of leaving,
Twill be too long 'till I return, for my awakening I will yearn,
Seasons will pass featuring beauty unseen by my eyes,
Alas, next time I promise I'll be ready your lessons to learn!

Susan K. Arnold

Free

Full of life and exuberance,
I walk on the deserted beach.
I see the angels of mystified beauty,
And the Lords of eternal life.

Alone, I dance to the song of the heavens.
I think with a mind that knows no limits of exploration.
It is in this state of solitude, that I am free.
I have finally put my heart and soul out of a misery that
it felt for so long.

I lay upon the sand and let the waves wash ashore on my body.
I feel my soul journey into the sea.
It is now that I am forever cured.
For my soul, which is undeniably full of life, will reach it's
life long destiny.
It is this state of solitude that will become my companion
for an eternity.

Kimberly Trimblett

Halloween Scare

The clock struck 12, one Halloween night,
I was all alone; it gave me a fright!
As I listened there, it was as silent as death,
I could manage to hear my very own breath.

I looked out the window; the moon was full,
I had nothing to do; it was awfully dull,
When all of a sudden the light flickered low,
As I turned my head, something started to glow.

Along the wall, I began to creep,
I fell a couple of times 'cause I was half asleep.
The hair stood up on the back of my neck.
I heard something behind me; I decided to check.

As I turned around with horror and surprise,
I saw myself staring into two glaring eyes.
I shut my eyes, and shuddered with fear.
When they opened again, I saw it was only a mirror!

Katie Hamlin

First Love

This was a very long time ago.
I was as pure as anyone can be,
   Until you got a hold on me.
You made love to me in your special way,
   I'll never forget, 'til this day.
You stole my soul, and my heart,
   Then with my love, you did part.
Goodbye my love, for it was true,
   You didn't love me, but I loved you.
The saddest part, is that you'll never know.

Margaret Lisa

The Day The Sun Dies

The day the sun dies
I will not be here to bid it farewell
Every trace of my existence has long since vanished
yet I will still mourn

All my struggles were for naught
As the cold and darkness have forgotten my being
Yet I will still mourn
the day the sun dies

Matt L. Harris

My Love Creature

In a library is where our eyes first met,
I was majoring in engineering and you pre-vet.
From that day forward I knew you would be my pet,
our days were limited as members of the single set.
Later in the games room we began to mingle,
it was then I realized I no longer valued being single.
Less than a year later when we tied the knot,
I felt like I had won a million dollar jackpot.
By day you are my sweet love creature,
and after dark in bed you become my teacher.
Out of our union came the sweetest kitty creature,
in a Disney movie he's sure to be the feature.
Then came the cutest pooch you've ever seen,
no doubt about it Disney would star her as queen.
Is it any wonder my love is so great,
for in this whole wide world I could find no better mate.

Neal C. De Witt

Fading Away

I remember the days when we were as one,
I was the earth and you were my sun.
You kept me warm, with the love we shared,
and I truly felt then that you really cared, but
with the passing of time, you're love grew cold,
Constantly my love, you were always told, of
my love for you and how much you meant, to
a man like me, "you seemed heaven sent,"
but no matter how tight I tried to hold on.
you're warmth grew less with every dawn, and
little by little with each passing day, I started
to realized that you're fading away, "I need you with
me, and in my heart." So stop fading away, it's
tearing me apart, cause I don't know, If I
Can face one more day, knowing inside,
"you're fading away."

Raymond Eads

I Just Don't Understand!

When I was young and growing up-
I was told to be nice to others.
One day when I was out playing-
a boy came walking by and said hi-
He then started to hit and kick me.
I started to cry! I just don't understand!

A new boy moved in next door-
We then became good friends.
One day I went over to get him-
his mother told me he had died.
She tried to explain. I just don't understand!

I was also told to earn and save money.
This way I could buy things I wanted.
I bought a new bike.
One day I went out to ride my bike-it was gone!
I just don't understand!

I had a new neighbor move in across the street.
I would see him with his girlfriend and wave.
One day I saw her alone and crying.
I asked her why? I just don't understand!

Roy Moreno

A World Away

Flesh of my flesh, flower of my seed,
I watch with a mother's pride and pleasure
as you tumble and play carelessly
amid the lush greenery.
Caring not yet from where you come
unaware of your golden-skinned legacy
of an ancient sun-baked land steeped in time
that time itself may have forgot.
Dressed in your prerequisite blue denim chic
and speaking classic childish gibberish
in an accent foreign to your grandmother's ears,
you know nothing yet of temples, dust, and shimmering saris;
of incense, bullock carts and fiery curries;
of hunger, resignation and misery; or
of the multitude of humanity striving for and seeking this...
This place of endless opportunities;
of pine-studded hills and blue mountain lakes,
a mere twenty-four hours and a world away
from the land of your mother's birth.

Mumtaz Bengali

The Place Where My Heart Should Be

I feel the wind blowing through the place where my heart should be.
I will stand the pain to it's full intensity of this terrible
    emptiness within my heart.
For the lack of love that create this feeling that embody's me.
I'll give myself permission to be more easy and be free.
But not from the heart again, so it can not be torn apart from me.
This way I can not blame anyone for what happens to my life,
    but only me.
I feel the wind blowing through the place where my heart should be.
This terrible feeling that distorted my perception of how life
    should really be.
This emptiness occurring and unforgivable acceptance that keeps
    haunting me.
Although rejected and lonely perhaps of betrayal of your insincere
    love that has made this change within me.
I feel the wind blowing through the place where my heart should be.
Until I feel the warmth of love, again in my heart.
Which you selfishly destroyed of me, I'll take the hurt and pain to
    its full intensity
But remember this clearly that this terrible emptiness within my heart
    will not always be.
So no matter what you tried to do to me.
It will only make me a stronger person you can count on that,
    you'll see.
I feel the wind blowing through the place where my heart should be.

Lillian Lydia Garcia

Jealousy

I am cruel, I am cold, and I am unkind
I will talk in your ear, and I will make you mine
I will show you things. That I want you to see
And you will carry them out, the way I want them to be.

I am strong in power, all you need is me
And you can have what you want, if you listen, and learn from me
I have a way of doing things, I will lie, I'm cunning,
two-faced I will be
You won't have a friend, but all you need is me
Just us two, to walk and agree
Jealousy is rage, in the hearts of men you see
And he will not spare thee, in the day of vengeance.

It's best not to listen to a smiling face you know
For all smiles are not a friend, some like people, you know
So be like the ant, be wise in what you do
Seek God in all things, and let nothing persuade you.

Sandra Bankston

Wishes For A Granddaughter

I wish you a rainbow, I wish you a song.
I wish you blue birds all your life long.
I wish you sunshine, I wish you soft rain.
I wish you blue skies again and again.
If you're ever lonely, sad as can be,
Remember these wishes, these wishes from me.

I wish you music, your favorite tunes.
I wish you flowers, the prettiest blooms.
I wish you an angel, the guardian kind,
To sit on your shoulder for your peace of mind.
If you will listen, just take her hand,
She'll guide and protect you in all you have planned.

I wish you a true friend to stand by your side,
A friend you can talk to with nothing to hide.
I wish you courage to meet each new day,
To laugh at the mishaps that may come your way.
If you're ever lonely, sad as can be,
Remember these wishes, these wishes from me.

Leslie Carlisle

If We Try

As I sit and wonder where you are, and what goes thru your mind,
I wonder if your memories, are anything like mine.
It's really such a scary thing, to wonder and not know,
And now you stay so bottled up, that it may never show.

I do believe we got off track, yes waylaid but not lost.
And yes we almost lost our way, at what a precious cost.
And now if we are patient, and loving, true and kind...
I do believe the path will lead, to what we want to find.

I'm trying, Oh so very hard, to be the patient one...
To give the space, support and love, until your battle's done.
But oh, it's not so easy, I'm not sure just what to do.
For I only want to hold you close, and for you to hold me too.

I miss you oh so very much, your smiling playful eyes...
Your laugh, your little cocky grin, the way we both would sigh.
I'm so afraid that I may never know those things in life again...
I'm trying to hold on because I know, together we can win.

I think you could be happy Babe, with life, and love, and me,
Inside we are so much in tune, if you could only see!!
So, take the chance and just reach out, be patient and be kind.
Yes, time and love will heal the wounds, just put your hand in mine.

Pam Bickford

"I Am"

I am a kind and fun loving person.
I wonder what life would be like in the year 2000.
I hear the cries for help from young women and children.
I see a Leprechaun hiding his pot of gold.
I want to stop all the violence and drug abuse.
I am a kind and fun loving person.

I pretend to be older than I really am.
I feel the desperation of starving and homeless children.
I touch the sky wishing for world peace.
I worry about the future of the world.
I cry for the homeless, starving, and battered children.
I am a kind and fun loving person.

I understand that no one is perfect.
I say all races are equal.
I dream all of the wars would end.
I try to get along better with my siblings.
I hope all of the fighting would stop.
I am a kind and fun loving person.

Nicki Jo Agro

The Pages Of My Life

As I watch the pages of my life fly by...
I wonder where the time has gone.
I think back to see if time has been good to me.
Eluded me, or maybe even stopped for me.

As I watch the pages of my life fly by...
I look to see if anything has slipped by me.
Maybe something important, like the meaning
of life. But, I see nothing. And still, I wait with
time, to finally have the chance to say:
"Hey! Look at me. Look what has become of me."

I know one day this will happen. I'll see it,
flying by, in the last few pages of my life; in due
time.
Michelle A. Spano

If I Could

If I could go anywhere on Earth
I would go to a place where the sun shines long
and the moon guides me at night
Where soft rains gently wash my back
and the shade of a blossoming tree is always a stone's throw away.
Beautiful mountains could be seen
from a sparkling crystal beach
with only swaying meadows
and enchanting forests between them.
The birds in the air have the freedom to soar to great heights
and the mighty lion can roam without being feared.
Where humans can live together with nature,
yet more importantly,
where humans can live together as one.
Ryan Coffey

My Friend Forever...

If you weren't my friend
I wouldn't have a care in the world.
But we have started a trend,
that our friendship would never end.

The special ways you've helped me through,
I really know your someone true.
You always give what's in your heart,
But now it's time to make a new start.

You can't change yourself to please everyone,
your a unique person for you are one.
Life has its ways of getting you down,
But the sun doesn't shine on any frowns.

I will never forget the fun we had,
just the good times not the bad.
But someday as we go our separate ways,
I'll always remember the good old days.
Temple Turner

Paracite
(In A,B,C)

Hey, english books give me fleas
I try to scratch but get only bees
between da lines I looks and sees
while da teacher asks me what are dese?
If I knows what's best I'd better freeze
that ain't too hard I can do it with ease!
Mark Vineyard

Cold As Death

Immobilized - Frozen - Stiff
Icy grief, my sculptor,
Death, the glacier-cover over me.

And in this empty Arctic world,
    abstract heights and concrete depths collide,
    chasms rend my being's wall.
My soul so panes my eyes
    that every day is jagged, torn and so unwhole.
Ice-age survivors speak,
    showering words of warmth:
"Time heals, time mends,
    time will see you be the same again."
But time, my friend,
    has not the chasms closed;
Has rather smoothed some edges
    and let me learn self-sculpture once again.
New light and warmth now passes through this shaft
    and glacier-death, in waterfall
    baptizes a recreated whole.
S. Jeannine Norton

A Lovely Secret

There's much the very young don't know.
I'd rather keep them in the dark for now.
Let them believe, as I once did,
That they alone taste passion and desire,
That only young, strong bodies are afire
With hunger and the need to touch and hold,
With yearnings, tender, aching, fierce, and bold.
Let them suppose, in their young pride,
That for those elders over forty, love has died.
Let them imagine that a starry night
Holds magic just for their delight.
And when they've lived and loved and lost and won,
Then let them know the joy of the sun!
B. J. Sherman

Worth It

Sometimes I sit here and I wonder,
If all the hard work is worth it.
I wonder if all the sprints, pushups,
Situps, stretches, and drills are worth it.
I wonder if all the techniques, blocks,
Patterns, and plays I must learn are worth it.
I wonder if all the days, weeks, and months
Of lifting and training are worth it.
I wonder if that quick second or moment
Of victory over one man or team is worth it.
I do realize that when I'm there
With the blood dripping off of my fingers,
The snot running out of my nose,
The wind in my face, and the smell of sweat
And hard work is all around me.
It is then that I realize all of my hard
Work is worth it!!
Matthew P. Palladino

The I Unknown

If I danced, naked, among damp ferns...
If I swayed to an unheard beat, moist from gentle mist..
If I caressed the rough back of ancient oaks
    and wore cherry blossoms petals in my hair...
If I climbed moss covered rocks...
If I cleansed my soul in emerald waters...
If I exposed my heart for all to see...
    Would I stand alone?
Theresa La Whon

All Alone

It would be a hard, hard life to live,
If I lived on the streets, and not a soul would give.
I'd have to stand in line forever, to get my daily meals,
I'd have to live in a shelter, where everybody steals.

Drug dealers would always stand on the corners of the streets,
Trying to persuade little kids to buy their "grownup treats."
Ragged clothing would be the only thing I own,
Sometimes sleeping in a cardboard box would be my only home.

All those people who are well-off, give me pitied looks,
Maybe even a little money, to buy food, and possibly books.
Then again some people would make fun of me and stare,
As if I was a piece of dirt, and shouldn't breathe the same air.

But the good news is that I'm living happily at home,
The bad news is that still some people don't own a single comb.
Every person deserves a chance in life to be all they can be,
So spare some extra love and care, for those less fortunate than we.

If I lived on the streets, and not a soul would give,
Yes, it would be a hard, hard life to live.
Kerry Christensen

At The End Of The World

At the end of the World, at the last of the Earth
If I'd flee, If I'd see
Where a song sings, a bird
I would be.

At the blue of the sky, at the mountains of high
If I'd try, if I'd fly
Where of green shines, the eye
I would be.

At the wind of the fall, at the sun cool and warm
If I'd bow, If I'd low
Where of green smells, the grass
I would be.

At the bless of a kind, at the wonders of heart
If I'd find, if I'd land
Where of always fells, Time
I would be.

A bird I would be, the eye I would be
The grass I would be, a Time I would be
At the end, of the World
I would be.
Liviu Nedelescu

Desperation Calling

Feeling lost, feeling confused,
I'm drowning in a sea of emotions,
Don't know which way to go,
Don't know which way to turn.

Time slips through my hands,
like water evaporates in the sun,
Dreams that I'm trying to hold on to
are slowly fading away.

Yet here I am, still standing and hoping,
Waiting for that light to shine,
A light that will lead me to the promised land,
A land full of hope, and a land full of glory.

Tell me, is it real or just an illusion,
Am I blind or just a fool,
I need to know for the sake of my heart,
and the sake of my soul...
Peter M. Bietenholz

Two Ships In The Night

At the helm of my ship, in the dark, on the sea.
If it storms, what will happen to my men and to me?
What if winds whip the water into a mountainous wave
That beats us and sinks us. Will there be anyone to save?

Deeper and deeper we plow into the brine
Decisions...Decisions...can only be mine,
For I am ship's Captain, a most thankless rank
No glory, no medals, no money to bank.

What's that to starboard, can it be a light?
Could it be a friendly ship to help us this night?
What a pounding we're taking, can we keep her afloat?
Have we the strength of a great ship and not a toy boat?

Up again, down again, twirling around
We're like a giant corkscrew, but a friend we have found.
Is the sea getting calmer at the horizon beyond?
Will this raging ocean soon be but a pond?

Where's our good friend? We so depended on her.
She's disappeared completely...she's no longer there.
We'll be all right now, but we sure needed her light
To comfort each other's souls...two ships in the night.
Marvin P. Roth

If Only...

Rowing on a river, or dive into sea
If it were a perfect world, it would just be me

Drinking by the case, or sipping of a can
If it were a perfect world, people would lend a hand

Rising of the nation, or vision that's far
If it were a perfect world, there would be no war

The shot of a gun, no drugs is what they say
If it were a perfect world, children would play

Held in captivity, or set free as a dove
If it were a perfect world, we would all know how to love...
Krystal Gonzalves

A Fairy Tale Love Story

Do you realize who and what you are in my eyes?
If not pray let me tell you a tale
of a lover so precious he reigns my world

In a majestic kingdom of glitter and gold
  Resting upon clouds of the softest fold,
    Lived a maiden who knew the story of old
      Of the wonders and splendor of love untold.

A life rather lonely though she chose to live
Shutting off people she knew she couldn't believe;
Withdrawn into herself, silent is the air she breathes.
Designing for herself only patterns she could weave.

In a resplendent palace, scintillating not too far away,
  Was a prince whose eyes were set on her that magical day;
    Wanting to win her heart, yet not daring to look her way,
      Her iciness froze his passion, turning all hope misty grey.

Until the day Goddess Venus decides to manifest her power,
Delivering the maiden to her prince, waiting for that magical hour;
At a Crystal Ball, they danced to the mystical rhythm of the night's desire,
As history unfolds a youthful and romantic love, both united in ardor.
Kim Jin Chew

Family Tree

Ellie May, baby, I'll see you tonight.
If with my mother, I don't have to fight.
Mother don't like you, 'sez, son can't you see
She just won't fit on our family tree.

Jerry, my darling, you'll see me tonight.
If with your baby, you don't want to fight.
Your mother don't like me, it's so plain to see.
So let's both cut loose, from the old family

We'll start a tree together,
in a comfy, cottage small.
'Twill grow to be a big one,
so broad, so strong and tall.
Soon, there'll appear a little sprout,
happiness to us 'twill bring.
Then lots of branches all about,
like a tree in early spring.
As we grow old together,
our life will fruitful be.
For there'll be lots of branches
to cut loose from our tree.
Nellie M. Alders

Peace

Do you want peace enough to fight for it?
If you study these words you will see,
That they are as ambiguous as ever they will be.

In the name of peace we fight a war
And hope all things will be better than before.

But bodies lie broken all over the land
And peace is no more permanent than words written on shifting sand.

When Jesus walked the earth so very long ago
He told all who would listen the truths we should know.

"Love Ye One Another" your neighbor - yourself,
Be not mindful of gain and glory of self.

Lift not your voice in anger for like a pebble once thrown,
It's ripples spread ever wider and peace no longer is known.

Instead, remember that Jesus died on the cross that we
Might someday be in His Kingdom and know peace eternally.
Sylvia B. Scocozzo

From Omnivore To Herbivore

The holidays are coming and with a little luck,
I'll get a Christmas goose, or maybe just a duck.

A roast of beef would be quite nice, a turkey, or some fish,
Pork chops fried up golden brown, and piled upon my dish.

And to you Veg-e-tar-i-ans, who look at me with dread,
How about your little lettuce, who had to loose his head?

And out in the garden, trembling with the cold,
Some radishes and onions know they're never growing old.

A tomato turns to a cucumber, and is heard to sadly say,
"My God, they said a salad, I guess we'll die today!"

Then I hear a little soybean cry, "Stay away with all that goo,
I want to stay a soybean, and not become tofu!"

I'll not try to change your mind, nor tell you what to eat.
But why are you sitting there with leather shoes upon your feet?
Winifred Williamson-Ater

Mother

In the month of May of every year
　A day is set aside
To honor her and cherish her
　And do it with great pride.

Her untiring ways of doing things
　To make the day complete
Made the tasks more tolerable
　Her method was unique.

Through good and bad events in life
　Her support was always there.
She left you know within your heart
　How much she really cared.

Within your children, you can see
　Her success in every way:
Their love, concern and thoughtfulness
　They use day by day.

The day that I'm referring to
　The one above all others
The day in May that's set aside
　Is the gracious one for Mother.
Robert Adams

I Hear A Shot

I hear a shot, I feel the pain.
A deer has died. So what's the gain?
Once, caught your eye, a beauty, rare,
has been reduced to meat and hair.
The only creature with a gun
puts other creatures on the run.
The elephants and tigers, too,
will soon be only in our zoo.
A clarion call goes out to MAN!
Please stop this slaughter, if you can!
Phyllis Brackett Bradley

Drifting

Drifting from my life
A distant fight to shore
I fight for my life.
Drifting free and far
I no longer control my life.
The life I live
Is no longer
A life
But a distant dream
Of a life.
Drifting to a dimension
Far and wide.
I lay upon a string
The last string of hope.
Drifting from my life.
Krissy Doughty

Faithful

I've never wanted lots of friends
A few faithful ones that's all
For the most will stay
While skies are fair
But leave when the shadows fall.
So I wish not for a host of friends
But to this I will confess
If all my friends were just like you
I'd never want one less.
Lorraine M. Samano

"Terrible Two"

Now that I am finally two, there's lots of things that I can do.
I go to the potty when I have to pee, mommy don't have to buy pampers for me.
I drink my milk now from a glass, mommy got rid of my bottles at last.
I don't have to wait to be fed anymore, sitting in that high chair was always a bore.
I now feed myself, I have my own booster seat, I get to throw peas, oh boy how neat.
I no longer wonder whats up on a shelf, I climb in a chair and see for myself.
Mommy and daddy says I'm a terrible two, they say it's because of some things that I do.
Sometimes I do things that even scare me, like the time I played with buttons on the TV.
Oh boy, it got loud, it scared me so bad, I screamed and cried, then ran to my dad.
Mommy says sometimes I do things kind of cute, like the time I tried to walk in daddy's big boot.
Daddy says I must learn things I'm not allowed to do, mommy says it's
gonna be tough, cause I'm a terrible little two.
Yvonne S. Lucado

Whispers

They whisper so loud, I hear what they say - No matter what...she'll find her way
Well, whisper again, I'm lost this time see - He took all my strength and I lost most of me
They all whisper loud, and always say - She just needs time and she'll be okay
Time's a dumb cure, he's not here no more - I know that time can not settle this score
So just whisper again but say something true - Maybe say something like what will she do?
And stop saying you know, when I know you can't - You don't have a clue of the pain I enchant!
Please learn how to whisper, what you do is yell - What's wrong with people it's clear as a bell!
You whisper dumb things like - well it was his time - or he's in a good place with the divine
Well I want to know just who are these two - What kind of time and divine are you?
I'll tell you right now - I know them both well - They are rotten and cruel and sent straight from hell!
They took him from me without even a sign - They did this to me and you call this divine?
They took him from me without even a sign - They did this to me and you call this divine?
Well its my turn to whisper and I do it right - I whisper real low and keep my voice light
SHSHSHSHSH! Now listen to me you cruel evil force - You took most of me when you took him of course
You remember the night you visited right? - You took all the insides, all that gave me might!
You took all that's dear my strength and my cheer - Now there's nothing inside but horror and fear!
The insides you left are a big empty stack - So listen real close and give me - "me" back
I'll listen real close, for a whisper - of course - and I'll hope from you or your force
So please hurry and bring these whispers of mine and maybe some day
I'll think you're divine!
Sally Notaro

Because I Have To....

Dreaming
   I was Flying through the water with a pack of Dolphins, not knowing where they were taking me. When I came upon a Mermaid of exquisite beauty. She then spoke in a kind, angelic voice and inquired, "Why do you hold on?" All that my Heart could reply was "Because I have to..." She gave me a sweet, sympathetic look, and winked at me. I was then swept off towards a tunnel in an underwater mountain, as I went through, images that were my memories flashed all around me. I came out of the tunnel in a whirlwind of brilliant Light. The Dolphins lead me to the surface at a lightning quick speed. I broke through to the Air in a roar of water, visions, and feelings. I was flying through the Sky at an amazing speed. Memories still passing through my mind, the Dolphins pushed me high into the Sky towards the Sun. Closer and closer I came to the fiery ball, accelerating in speed as I approached. Until my heart could not take any more, it burst from the searing heat and painful Memories. I awoke in a hot, passionate sweat, holding on to what little breath I had left. My mind was numb with exhaustion, but that still could not block out the continual phrase I heard. "Because I Have To...."
The Dreamer.

Monsters

Grrr roar!! I know that sound, the sound of monsters all around.
I'm getting a little scared right now.
My pulse is racing-afraid of what I might be facing,
My goosebumps are large-my brain is running on super charge!
I hear one right behind me now—I'll have to take my final bow!!
He'll rip me up and feed me to his nasty, scary, gruesome crew-
Wait a second, what's that I hear? My mom's voice and it's very near.
Now that I'm awake, the monsters were fake.
As a rule, I'll keep my cool. When my mom wakes me up for school!!
Laura A. Baldine

My Love

I looked into your eyes

and saw your soul

and then I fell in love.
Nancy L. Haney

Feelings

Feelings come in different ways.
Some are sad and some are hurt,
Some are glad and childish ways,
Some are clean, some hold some dirt.

The feelings of love are very strong
It's so good to feel this way,
Mostly when generously given,
But not when taken away.

So pay attention to your feelings,
and handle them as you should.
for if handled in a correct way,
It will make you feel real good.
E. Willadson

jill

he looks out at the world
through the shape of her eyes
her words pass by from between his lips
a well fitted thing of beauty
made by his builders' hands
she is the child of her father

but

watch her walk
svelte and grace
see the tilt of her head
and the turn of a wrist
inborn elegance passed on from
hands to hands
she is her mother's daughter
d. l. dunaway

If I Could Give the World a Gift

Sometimes I worry and wonder what to do
About the worldly battles that are
affecting me and you.
it ought to be;
I'd like to care for all and
have all care for me.

So if I could give the world a gift,
I'd give the gift of love,
For love mellows, grows and heals,
And helps us rise above
The struggles and differences that mount,
With a "treasure-trove" of values that
One could never count.

We have to love our fellow man
Whatever or whoever he may be,
For only this can bring world trust,
peace and security.
We have to give our caring best
In the chain we weave in life,
Only adding links of love and peace
Instead of wrath and strife.
Kerri O'Brien

Shame, Shame

Many times we hear the thunder
Long before the storm arrives
But choosing not to see the clouds
We simply close our eyes.

Though some may choose to look aside
Pretending its not there.
I trust they'll be reminded
When they're called to lead in prayer.

They'll meet you at the entrance
With an extended hand.
They'll pray for God to lift them up,
And then refuse to stand.

Now search your heart, and know God's Will
That you too, may be inspired
For to him whom much is given,
Much will be required.

The moral of this story is
That all the world should see,
It's recorded in God's Holy Word,
Jeremiah, Chapter Twenty Three.
Lewis H. Rooks

Burial At Sea

On the day we buried Bernie
a thousand dolphins swam around
his watery grave
They leapt in gray profusion
Their happy dolphin dance
tore us
away from our pain...
so clouds parted
so ceased the rain
The experienced sailors were awestruck
by this sight
To mother and his children
it seemed glorious right
No tombstone with epitaph
to mark a spot
No urn of ashes
dust to dust
The vast sea is his resting place
to satisfy his wanderlust
Stephanie Cole

"The Final Time"

A silence fills the night, like
a blanket around a child, you see the
bitterness of life reflect and you go
insanely wild. The cold falls upon
your body like a cascade of light;
you try to take a deep breath but
before you do you loose the sight.
You feel the pounding of your heart
as you think back to memories, can
you move the land, can you still the
seas. There's a hand that's there
waiting for your grasp, if you decide
to take it will your life forever last?
As an aching of torture pursues
throughout your soul, you take the hand
of an angel and away to paradise you go.
You see light and you see gold, this new
world before you is so little and yet
so bold. You close your eyes and say a
prayer, knowing you're finally there.
Misty Starleen Wykle

My Mother

A happy smile
a cheerful face;
one who's love
could fill this place.

Bad times and good times
my mother has them all.
No matter where I am
she will be there when I fall.

Minutes pass;
days go by,
I will love her always
and that's no lie.

She has a beautiful voice
and a wonderful heart.
Oh, did I mention
She's also very smart.

I guess what I am trying to say
is she's my best friend,
and the way I see it:
our friendship will never end.
Lea Rene DeLay

"What's A Child's Life Worth?"

How do you balance out,
a child's life, in worth?
from the time, of conception,
'til the time, of birth?

And from the time, of birth,
thru' the remaining years?
With all the joy and laughter,
and thru' the many tears?

For there are no words to express,
the inflating, feelings, of joy.
When one's to pick and hold,
a baby girl, or boy.

And there are no precious elements,
to compare to a child's life.
That can measure up to the happiness,
even in time of strife.
Mel Ruckman

No Ordinary Man

One day I saw a man walking along
a dark road. As he walked, I asked,
"Can I go with...Only me?"
It looked kind of funny; I a bit
lonely, he a bit pigeon-toed.
His pockets were empty, his heart full
of gold. We talked of rockets and
lockets. Time never got old.
He has silvery hair and blue blue eyes.
He often laughs like a bear and even
Sometimes cries, Together we would
talk, sifting out all the bad of the good
times, Softly he touched my hand; I
Saw a twinkle in his bright blue eyes
and I knew that this was no
Ordinary man....
This was my Grandfather!
I love you grandpa!
Tina Louise Sokolowski

A Mother's Alarm

I wake this morning and I hear,
A funny noise come to my ear.
I run right down the stairs to see,
Two silly children drenched in tea.

I see you found something to play,
What is this mess you made today?
It's goo and slop and looks like clay.
"It's just pancakes and tea", you say.

"You made a bowl of flour goo,
With eggs and milk and shortening too.
The mixing part had just begun,
When I came in and spoiled your fun."

Except, I see you spilled the tea.
How did you do this, please tell me.
"You took the tea down off the shelf,
And poured it down upon yourself."

The party's over as you know,
Please change your clothes, and don't be slow.
I then want you to go and play,
I'll clean this mess you made today.
Mary Matthews

If I Could Give The World A Gift

If I could give the world a gift,
A gift of freedom, A gift of peace,
The world would be a better place.

If I could give the world a gift,
No wars, No fights,
Mostly freedom rights.

If I could give the world a gift,
No quarrels among race,
No lives to replace.

If I could give the world a gift,
A gift of loving and no hurt,
Would bring us together to love one another.

If I could give the world a gift,
That is what I would give,
So all among the human race can live.
Larkin Wilde

Disillusioned Rogue

Seeking to find what was always there.
A guiding voice, or light to shine thru.
The impending darkness smothering...
The little desire of truth.

It became the ruthless fight of the two.
Each face fought with great strength.
Only to find...
The little desire of truth.

In every move and every thought,
A new one had emerged.
What was, had gone,
only to see....
The little desire of truth.
Mary Cabrini Costanzo

Abortion

You loved him,
and he loved you.
Oh why,
why,
couldn't you love me too?
Kathy Bacon

The Epitome Of Love

A soft and gentle whisper,
A heart so big and kind,
A touch to reassure me,
And a kiss to ease my mind.

How lovingly she taught us
What was right and what was wrong.
She filled our lives with constant
Chatter, laughter, joy, and song.

Indeed, the Lord has blessed us,
With an angel from above,
When He gave us our sweet mother,
The Epitome of love.

Karen J. Dyer

U.S.A.

Now, let us sing a song of U.S.A.,
　A home for great and small;
A place of winding rivers,
　Of mountains, grand and tall!

Oh, let us tell of hidden caves,
　Beneath a wide valley floor;
Or lakes so full of fishes,
　To be found, if we explore!

There are many fine old places,
　Where we hunt, or fish, or rest;
Great heritage of wonders,
　Our dear U.S.A. is blest!

Let us sing a song of praises
　For many homes along the sea;
Let us watch the billowing whitecap,
　Where we frolic rich and free.

Let us never change dear U.S.A.;
　May we strive with all our might
To protect these things of beauty;
　Let's keep U.S.A. clean and bright!

Orda Hood

Mother And Wife

Mother and wife
a job well done during life.
Lots of love you did share
for at all times we knew you cared.
Your smiles was brighter than the sun,
for a new life you have begun.
We send you love,
to the heavens above.
Rest in peace mother and wife
at ease in a whole new life.

Theresa Guy

Day Into Night

A sunrise melts into the horizon
A night dies amidst a fiery diamond

A sun ascends from within the trees
A sky of blues brighter than the seas

A sunset fades away to black
A day is lost amongst a star attack

A moon rises from behind the earth
A sky of lights begin a night birth

Michelle Speros

"Despair"

DEPRESSION, the depth of despair
A long, lonely road will lead you there.

It won't cost you nothin'
Yes, the ticket is free!

The Company is 'solitary'
It'll be "you" and "me".

The Train will be leavin'
'bout a quarter-to-four.

Just bring what you're wearin'
You won't need much more.

The Reaper, he'll join us
On the Night Train "goin' down".

You'll see his teeth shinin'
And shudder at his frown.

It means life is over,
You didn't do it right.

DEPRESSION is comin'
By the Night Train's gray light.

Tawny Wolf

What Time love

Time we shared together
A long time; moved like the wind
Time is sunrise and sunset
Our love deep, never ending
Time passed, children away from home
Another sunrise another sunset
Happy, sad, age, illness, alone
What is time-time is love
Many sunrise, many sunset
Our love on earth, somewhere out there
Times ends, times goes on
So precious, yet so unfair
One life gone, one life to stay
Time now to find my way
Life ends - life begins

Mary A. Banning

Songbird

The song bird sings,
A lovely tune.
From suns first light,
Until the moon.
All day it sings
The joyful song
So happy when,
You sing along.
A tweet tweet here,
A tweet tweet there.
Just tweets away
Without a care.
You just can't help
But tweet it's tune.
From suns first light,
Until the moon

Ramon R. Castillo Jr.

I Am

I am a man
A man I am
A man of passion
And compassion
With hurt and pain
Joy and shame
Wants and needs
Hope and dreams
A life to share
With loving care
Put to the test
Have done my best
Stand out from the rest
Paid my dues unused
Drifted apart; perhaps
Doomed from the start
Shared failures blame
Time for a change
Feel no shame

Val Munroe

A Look At Life

To look at life, one set of eyes
A narrow-minded view.
Don't just walk a well known path
In your worn out shoes.

Experience the most you can
In everything you do.
Compare the homeless to the rich,
A fine line between the two.

The middle ground feels safer,
But it doesn't take much thought.
How would you know what's missing
If you're not sure what you've got?

Cross the stream, upon the rocks,
Get a little wet.
Don't be afraid of challenges
You haven't taken yet.

Peace of mind and honesty
It comes to in the end.
Build up strengths and character
And live life while you can.

Tami Naylor

Misled Rebel

I don't want to go to
a parochial school
where everyone looks the same,
a uniform is the rule.

I want the freedom to choose,
no matter what our means,
what I want to wear each day,
like a tee shirt and jeans.

LaVerne M. Emanuel

A Loving Touch

A loving touch can bring
a special moment where
heart meets heart and
mind flows into mind.
It knowing a tenderness and
and understanding that can't be
shared in any other way but in
the remembering of that
loving touch.

Sue Byard

Mother's Memory

Lord, why have you taken,
A part of me away?
You took her simple beating heart,
And left me here to stay.
Why did she leave my family,
Here alone to cry?
A feeling of such emptiness,
Is all that's left inside.
How can I go on,
When her memory lingers here?
And every waking moment,
Is only left with fear?
How can I forgive you,
When my heart may never mend?
You've not only taken my mother,
But you've taken my best friend.
Maybe one day I'll understand,
Maybe one day I'll see.
That all the love my mother had,
Is the love that lives in me.

Michele McLaren

Who Am I?

Who am I?
A pretty girl face
Who am I?
The sunshine of your day
Who am I?
A friend to all who come my way

Who am I?
Your worst enemy
Who am I?
The one who can destroy without feeling
Who am I?
The sanity of insanity

To all who wonder
To all who stare
Here is your answer
Who am I?
I am me.
Just like you.

Laurie Grubb

The Red Bicycle

One whole week of riding the red bicycle.
A pro for sure,
Well almost,
for a six year old.

Who are your little boy of many dreams?
Where do you go when you ride?
To Toledo?
The nearest Dairy Queen?
Are there things to outrun?
You can outrun anything,
your bicycle is the fastest of all.

So ride with the clouds.
Let your wind carry you
wherever you care to go,
and may you stop
on top
of a rainbow.

Peter Hessman

Trace Of A Heart

Double dragon to swords on
a rack to not be for attack
just the pure mind of art in
fantasy land of the twin dragon
hands to twin by the heart's win
for two in mighty tiger as double
dragon sworn the love in art
form by history all of a thorn
to your dojo room in a Gene Autry
trail by cowboys and indians drinking
with a tap of lusty gals riding
on your men's rails, that's
a short story tail, do I fail
or do I sworn another round
of art form double dragon on
my wall of rack, no one
ever for attack.

Sheila Y. Bohler Conner

The Last Ride

In the twilight the sound comes clear,
A raven's caw as the pale horse nears.
Friends and family so long adored,
Their bedside whispers I hear no more.
When my heartbeat starts to fade,
My mind grows strong with yesterdays,
And when I sense the end is near,
I close my eyes and face my fears.
Mount the pale horse for one last ride,
Into the darkness, into the light.
Secrets hidden within my mind,
Are brought to light one last time.
In boundless vistas before my eyes,
The truth comes home as do the lies,
Now I judge the wrongs and rights,
To free my spirit from its earthly life.
Will my spirit fall or rise,
Down into darkness or up to the light?
Look closely there upon my face,
A final smile reveals my fate.

Patrick A. Younger

Lovely Rose

Here comes sweet Eve,
a rose she is, full of life,
how kind she says "Hi".
She's holding the promised
fruit for me to eat, I have
not sinned. If I could just
taste, kiss her tender lips,
someday I would know that
by the kiss from a rose, I
have not done wrong.

Sweet lovely rose loves my eyes
more then my words. If she could
just sit still and hear my song,
maybe I would play a beautiful tune,
so that she can dance everytime I
speak to her about dreams. If I could
find the perfect time in place, I will
let her know why I call her my lovely rose.

Kerwin Romero

To Ryan White

Your young life was dealt
A rotten card,
But you rose to the occasion
With your big heart

You fought with courage,
As well as faith,
You never gave up
As you fought AIDS

To those who hurt you
By words and deeds,
You could have hated them
But you never did

We bid farewell
With a broken heart,
To us, you are a young hero
Named Ryan White

Paul Cepero

Duplicity

Duplicity wore
A silver mask,
That passed as affectation.
Shimmering, exciting
False expectation.

Duplicity clad
In gleaming black,
Cloth of her own creation.
Woven with glints of light
Conjured of ulterior motivation.

Duplicity astride
A fiery steed,
Races through your imagination.
You fall beneath her hooves,
Sharp iron of truth scarcely
Scratches your adulation.

Rose Marie Smith

A Single Tear

A single tear is all that falls.
A single tear is all he'll see.
A single tear is all I have to,
spare on this pain I feel.
A single tear is all I see,
that fall upon my tender breast
A single tear is all I shed because
for him I gave my best.
A single teat is all he gets
A single tear is what I have to spare
Because a single tear is all
I got to share

Tatiana Leahwood

Davenport

Davenport Home -
All for girls was built;
Viewed by all to be a place,
Ever useful, and full of grace.
Now in these days is kept alive;
Propagated before one's eyes.
On, yet in, a cottage home,
Rooms of treasures for one to behold -
Today, tomorrow, future untold.

Marlene B. Moir

Our Gal, Lil

Our Gal, Lil
  A soft spoken Gal,
    With a sweet smile,
      And a big heart!

Our Gal, Lil
  Caring and loving,
    But retirement gave
      Our Gal, Lil a call,
        And she'll soon be missed.

Our Gal, Lil
  "Thanks for the memories",
    We have "high hopes" for you.
      "When you wish upon a star",
        It makes no difference
          Where you are,
            You know we will be there,
              "Wishing, wishing" for you!

        "My best to you",
        May your dreams,
        Come true!

Marlene Jeziorski

A Song To Revere

I write you a song to revere
A song that will keep you near
My goodness of thought shall prevail
Because you are a special tale
An angel of God that brings joy
You are that special person not coy
That's why I love you so much
And you cannot consider that as Dutch
It's Greek as it comes on the vine
And it is the finest of the wine
Do not be ashamed of your fate
And we did not meet too late
I am coming back for you sooner or later
As it is your destiny not a tater
I mean it with heart, body and soul
And beautiful lady that is my ultimate goal
And so I end my song
That is not far from wrong
From America I tell you this
I am sending you a Big Kiss

Michael A. Martin

Mom Is God On The Lips Of Babies

So it begins, light, sound, and fury
A strange new world, cold and hurried
Only one touch is calm and warm
Only it silence the storm

When all's a mass of confusion
An unknown frightening illusion
When thoughts don't form to console
And you have no knowledge nor control

A gentle powerful love is there
A single spirit who truly cares
A blessed caress to dissolve your fright
A guardian angel through the night

Primitive memory bright like the sun
For you and her till life is done
When reality is foreboding and odd
She's there, like the hand of God

William A. Morey

The Village Rose

A Spring Day, a Village Rose,
A sweet perfume, a captive nose;
A garden gate, a peaceful state,
My inner voice says hesitate.

Slow it down and drink it in;
You'll never pass this way again...

A vision coalesces there,
Perceived perfection everywhere;
An overwhelming tapestry
of sights and sounds surrounding me.

With watering eyes my heart takes wing.
I briefly taste eternal spring.
And now I know my God does care,
Even when I'm not aware.

A spring day, a village rose,
A sweet perfume, a captive nose;
A summer breeze, the swaying trees:
God created all of these.

Michael F. Conway

Untitled

I want to tell you about
a very special place that everyone has.
A place that makes your dream come true.
Where you can make yourself a pirate or
even a kings knight.
You and your friends can be stranded
on an island.
Even you in an animals point of view.
If you would like to eat dog food
you are welcomed to.
Would you like to know why?
Well, because silly you can eat anything
you please.
You could dress in fish scales or even
amphibian skin.
It's all up to you, because it's your
imagination.
Won't you come and imagine?

Nicole Ball

Rambling Thoughts Of Joy

Bright blue skies in the heavens above.
A wedding date with the one you love.

Sharing a swing on an evening mild.
Awaiting the birth of your very first child.

A crackling fire on a winter night.
The nativity scene, a wondrous sight.

Eternal hope that springs anew.
Precious moments with a love so true.

On a hillside, cattle lowing.
Safe in the womb, a baby growing.

The thoughtful gift of a single rose.
Counting a newborn's fingers and toes.

A rainbow arcing the sky above.
A whispered promise of undying love.

Birds and deer, all creatures wild.
Bringing a smile to the face of a child.

Rain on the roof in early fall.
Treasured photographs lining a wall.

Snow on a mountain, ice on a tree.
Remembered thoughts bring joy to me.

Mildred Oram

Our First Year

We recently got married
A year ago in August
It's a new life for us
And we're still trying to adjust

Our's wasn't a big wedding
None of the fancy frills and fuss
Not even a wedding dress
Just the judge, himself, and us

Newly weds we still are
Until we learn the rules
Which forever keep changing
With never any clues

It's amazing what can happen
In just a month or two
By signing that legal paper
Now who's in charge of who

Though it's been rough now then
We've both done our share
Our love is stronger than ever
And for each other, we really care.

Kim Sieler-Randolph

Life

Life to me is beautiful. To be able to see the grass grow green, the flowers in bloom. To be able to hear the laughter of children at play. It would be wonderful if life were never sad, but with the changing of time and so many problems facing us today I know this can never be. And in this great life of mine I pray that God will always be with me, to give me the strength to be the wife I should, to be a good Mother to my children and the knowledge and patience to be a good person. God has given me this chance and I pray I make the most of all the wonderful things in this wonderful life of mine. I know all these things are possible because you see, I have God on my side.

Williadine Eblin

Time And Time Again

Thinking about your life,
  About Jesus, the rain;
Reoccurs to your mind,
  Time and time again.

To want to live forever,
  Never waiting for an end;
Do you think about that,
  Time and time again?

The peace, the harmony,
  everyone a friend;
This thought occurs to me,
  Time and time again.

One day this will happen,
  No one knows when,
You really need to think about it,
  Time and time again.

Teresa I. Lara

Alone

I am reason that you might think
about not leaving,
But I am not reason enough
for you to stay.
In a world where cruelty has become
a value, it does not frighten me.
Where hopes and dreams are shattered
by the shots of a gun,
I will live.
But you I can not replace.
Please understand -
It is not alone in life,
but alone in love.
That is the most frightening
place to be.
Melissa L. Plowden

Our Present Future

We love the moon and Stairs
Above
They shower us with
their heavenly love
We love the people here
below
They all guide us where
ever we go
we often go to bed at night
wondering about tomorrow
will their be peace and
will their be joy
or will it be filled with
sorrow?
Patricia A. DeRocher

Across The Water

Slave ship lights shine out,
across the evening waters.
Ride their anchors silently,
to fill the coffers.
But the cup in never full enough,
the weak are dead, what's left are tough.
To build the farms, and work the fields,
Across the water
Across the border
It's been two long years
since I've seen my home.
I must give my master
what I have grown.
But I keep for me a freedom seed,
and dream of the day I will be freed.
Free my brothers of the storm,
Across the water
Across the border.
Rachael Lynn Smith

Love

Love is unpredictable.
Actually very rare.
Sometimes you don't know what it is.
When love is in the air,
Love is love, it can be cruel.
Sometimes your heart gets broken.
If it does you must remember,
There might be words unspoken.
So in conclusion.
To this rhyme.
Don't give up on love.
This time.
Michelle Windle

"Ashes"

The fire so brightly burning,
Aglow with love and warmth
Drenched with the wind and the rain,
flickers and slowly turns to embers.
Little fire, why must you go,
Your flames no longer touch and glow.

Nothing left but smoldering embers
That a gentle breeze will stir
and kindle a spark, a flame
begins to glow...the breeze has
gone...the fire sadly burns away.

At your feet lay the ashes
That were once a glowing fire
Grey dry ashes, so cold and dead
Only the curling smoke remains,
The flame is gone,
Don't stir the ashes.
Leona S. Ayars

Loneliness

Loneliness sits
  all alone on the stairs
   noticing everything,
   the comments and glares.

Loneliness walks
  like a fool in the dark
   as an extinguished flame,
   searches for a spark.

Loneliness cries
  as it sits unaware
   that someone somewhere,
   really does care.

Loneliness dies
  as all things must end
   all alone, with no one,
   not even a friend.
Richard T. Morgan III

My Magic Horse

From a distance you can see,
All the branches of the tree.
Then up close there is one part,
That is closest to my heart.
It is the branch on which I played
On my royal steed I made.
My magic horse so still, so calm.
While I put his bridle on.
His bridle and his reins, so grand
Were a jump rope in my hand.
We rode all day to a far away place,
And when the sun began to lose its face.
I fed him water from a pail,
Took off his bridle and brushed him well.
I said, "good night", to my dear friend
Until the morning comes again.
Megan Sublett

Untitled - Haiku

Wildflowers in bloom
A world of beauty to see
Don't pick, let them be
Yoshiyuki Otoshi

Untitled

I have no time for you
All you do is hold me down
I have nothing for you
My life is mine to own

I have no consciousness
Of what you're trying to do
I have no consciousness
Lived my whole life for you

You tried to break me up
But I've taken back control
You tried to make me up
As something you could rule

Give me some time to be
What I have missed in life
Give me some time to be
What I couldn't find in death
Nathan Kutemeier

"Poetry"

Allegories alter abstraction,
Allusions allure audiences,
Ballads bestow bravado,
Elegies elicit eloquence,
Epics extend endlessly,
Metonyms master meaning.
Monologues mark my selves,
Narratives note news,
Odes orate overtures,
Oxymora outdo opposites,
Personifications people-ize,
Puns present purposely,
Rhymes richly repeat,
Riddles remonstrate reasoning,
Serenades sweetly soothe,
Soliloquies solicit self-revelation
Sonnets soar sunsets.
Kathleen Wood

Untitled

  Holding back my feelings for
almost all my living years.
  Trying to stay strong by
not crying any tears.
  Disliking certain things
and all I could do is sigh.
  Still living but not afraid
to die.
  We can not throw a fit if
something isn't our way.
  We can ignore people who
have something negative to say.
  Thinking only of my family
to others I'm greedy.
  For nobody helped us out
when we were the ones, needy,
Thank you to God I'm on
the wright track, and I'll never
  give up because the Lords got
my back.
Misty McFarlane

"Her In My Life"

She's kind and considerate
Also very lovely and bright
Such a beautiful lady
Always trying to do what's right

She's a classic homemaker
With such style and grace
Her things always so neat
I feel sometimes out of place

She's always so happy
A living joy to be around
I thank my God up above
It's her that I found

I'll tell you I'll love her always
For the rest of my life
I know I have been really blessed
To have "Her In My Life"
  Victor Wilkins

Reflections In The Shadow Of Shasta

Today, a snowy Sphinx
Always, silent and serene
Except for inner rumblings
Like a woman's disquiet
For no discernible reason

Lovely lady, up thrusting
Empurpled in majesty
Capricious as a real-life woman
Changing colors like dresses
From dawn gold to sunset pink
From unadorned starkness
To snowy peak
Capturing us

Forever there
Unless... volatile
Like a bad-tempered woman
Spewing pent up fires
Explosive release
Softening angles, creating subtle contours
Wondrous woman of fire and ice...
  Megann Purdy

Song Of Praise

I praise God in the morningtime
Among the birds and flowers.
I thank Him in the eveningtime
Mid sunsets and the showers;
But His presence is the sweetest
When I lie upon my bed.
He fills my heart with happiness.
'Tis then my soul is fed!

In those wee, small hours of morning
When I wake and feel Him near
And my heart sings out with gladness.
I never, never fear.

When the mocking bird is singing,
When I hear the thunder roll
Or the soft and quiet darkness
Lifts the burdens from my soul,
His presence fills my heart with joy
As I lie upon my bed.
He fills my heart with happiness
'Tis then my soul is fed!!!
  Nell S. Reeves

Moms Like You

Moms like you are
Among the chosen few
With your arms open wide
You can feel the love from inside
You share your smiles
And give us your strength
Our arms will forever hold you tight
For you are our beginning
And our light
We are here to protect you
And keep you near
Inside our hearts you will always be
The warmth, the love and security
If there are times
When you feel alone
Look up
And feel the love
Coming from the rainbow
Up above
  Tracy Kinney

The Pocket Filled With Rage

Tonight I feel the hole in my heart,
an opening of pain that only comes from
the pocket filled with rage
tonight I feel all the hate,
the mistake of needing someone
who won't remove the pain
tonight I wish I could confine
all my rage and find the days
that weren't shattered by mistakes
but when I close my eyes
all I see is the pocket of pain.
  Lynn M. Korn

A Moment In Time

The stars glittered like silver points
and
the white-faced moon
stared
as the wet, cool sand
enveloped
my bare feet.
The waves tumbled and splashed
as the sea
called to me
to place my feet in its foamy white edge.
As I watched my feet disappear and reappear
beneath the bubbly foam
I tried to taste
the misty, salty sea breeze
or
catch a bit of moonlight
on
the tip of my tongue.
  Patricia Fischetti

Flight

Winds wailing ceased,
and became gentle in me,
like a lover in ocean time.
Tin can churches light
false candles. The real fire
grows in my belly.
Dirty feet dance on the earth stage.
All the faces blend
with the ivy, oak, and sky white
  Michelle Marks

Eternal Love

There was love in their hearts,
And a gleam in their eyes.
As they walked hand in hand
Under moonlit skies.

They talked of the future,
They talked of the past,
They talked of the things
That made their love last.

They had been side by side
Throughout all the years,
The good times, the bad times,
The laughter, the tears.

They knew as they walked
That their end was near,
But they weren't about
To shed a tear.

For together they have been,
Together they will be,
Forever in love
Through eternity.
  Suzy D. Sullivan

Terrorist

You took away the child
And all the life it had to live
before the kid could read
he had no more love to give

You took away the smiles
You took away the toys
You took away the tears
You took away the boys

You made glass shatter
you made children die
you made the people hurt
you made the nation cry
  T. Marie Taylor

Peace

If you never venture forward
And always look behind
Time will steal your life away
And that's no peace of mind.
Our time is short and our desire strong
Are we doing right
Or are we doing wrong.
Whether in your body
Or whether in your mind
Your actions will judge
The person you are inside.
Its really very simple
And here's a friendly cue
"Do unto others
As you would have them do unto you."
So make your life a good one
And don't throw it away
Do what you know is right
And do it every day.
  Mark T. Miller

War

War in its name
and back ground so red
Pon many foreign countries
Our proud bloods been shed
Year after year
It has always been the same
Some lowly man would cheat and kill
Just for sake of fame
It's not only now
That makes our blood just boil
It happened years ago
When our forefathers tilled the soil
They pounced upon us then
Little did they realize
The strength, courage and power
Of a country of this size
We will win this war
No matter what they say
Whoever had an idea
They could beat our USA

Roger Abrahamson
Jamestown NY

"Change"

The golds, yellows, reds, oranges,
and browns.
Is it possible for such beauty
to occur at a time
of passing?

Can such life-filled colors
exist in a season
of change?

One cannot say they have
been a witness to beauty
until they have seen such
a change.

If it only would stay
longer.
But it leaves.

And let us face the winter
alone.
With only the memory of its
beauty to keep us warm.

Michael John Penko

One Tear

He sing's a song, so sweet
 and clear.
He sing's his love, and hold's
 me near.
With every word, my heart is
 full, I shed one tear.
Upon my lips, he placed a kiss,
So hot and sweet, our tongue's
 did meet,
His touch is hot upon my breast.
I shed one tear.

Susan Gardner Ryan

Life's Gentle Fray

Each day I fly
 But brake before delight
And in my wake, a dream unreached
 A fancy yet to ply

Maxine Ilah Rude

Sempiternity

Intense passion ebbed
and flowed through tangled limbs,
As day danced into night and in a moment,
dawned again.

Pasts surfaced and lingered
until absorption,
While eyes spoke words
not yet formed.

Musical laughter filled a void
left by broken dreams,
As destiny smiled upon two stars
falling into one.

Desire glistened and warmed
these kindred souls,
Lovingly touched by moon's silver
and sun's gold.

So when reality came and wildly
reared its wedge,
Two hearts entwined yet whole and free
softly kissed its edge.

Marty Waltman Bond

Matthew

 To you all I can say is hello
And goodbye; I wish I could stay
But I can't and you cry.

 You were the spice of my life for
the last two years; but we dismembered
to problems and do to fears.

 I want to do for the better and
teach you right; I can not accomplish
this until we reunite.

 When we are together we will live
happily; I promise this will last for eternity.

 Everyone makes mistakes and you'll
make them too; never let them take you
under you can always make it through.

 I'm gonna end this with the words
I love you; remember them forever
alright "Matthew".

Tony D'Ambrosio

"Bless Me"

Bless Me, oh Lord, with knowledge,
 and grant me the wisdom to use it.
Bless Me, oh Lord, with compassion,
 and grant me the love to give it often.
Bless me, oh Lord, with health,
 and teach me to appreciate it.
Bless Me, oh Lord, with understanding,
 and help me to give it freely.
Bless Me, oh Lord, with patience,
 and help me to practice it always.
Bless Me, oh Lord with faith,
 and teach me to trust like a child.
Bless Me, oh Lord, with love for others,
 and grant me ability to express it.
Bless Me, oh Lord, with honesty and truth
 and let me never fail to uphold them.
Bless Me, oh Lord, with strength,
 that I might uphold my fellowmen
And Bless Me, oh Lord, with your presence,
 that your love might be expressed
through me.

Linda Ferguson

There Is No Place Like Home

I have crossed this earth's great oceans
And have flown it's endless skies.
I have seen the tombs and temples
Of the famous, rich, and wise.
I have walked among the people
Observing customs in each land.
I have even met their leader
And shook his outstretched hand.
I have delved into their history
Many centuries back in time.
Then I walked among the ruins
With a thousand steps to climb.
I have looked upon these treasures
With astonishment and wonder
In these far away exotic lands
Where monsoons unleash their thunder.
I have crossed the highest mountains
As around the world I roam
And I have reached the grand conclusion
"THERE IS NO PLACE LIKE HOME."

Leslie A. Cole

Revelation

I dreamed death came the other night
And heaven's gate swung wide.
With kindly grace an angel came
And ushered me inside
And there to my astonishment
Stood folks I'd known on earth,
Some I'd judged and called "unfit"
And some of little worth.
Indignant words roes to my lips
But never were set free,
For every face showed stunned surprise
Not one expected me!

Mildred V. DesLaurier

Our Mother

Mother took each little child
And held it to her breast
With Gods grace from above
She gave us all love
Then each one grew and left the nest.

But always there were more to love
And she never seemed to tire
When each grandchild came
Her love was the same
And it spread like a burning fire.

It wove around the nine of us
And twenty two grandchildren too
Then one by one
Twenty seven great grandchildren came along
And each time her love rekindled anew.

Children and grandchildren, other family
and friends
Each one felt her loving touch
Now she's in Gods embrace
In that heavenly place
Dear Mother we'll miss you so much.

Rudeen Estacio

Forlorned

I leapt alive, astride the silken fray.
But only to notice, too late as
if to say. There was but one,
'cept another found today. The other
finding no one, but alone and swept away.

Max Hair

In My Dreams

I dream about you all the time
And hope some day that you'll be mine.

I dream of us out on the beach
It keeps happiness within my reach.

Reality will always be
So save your dreams just for me.

A dream is yours, yours to see
It will take you where you want to be.

Allow yourself some time to dream
And you will see just what I mean.

So close your eyes and take a chance
Dream of love and sweet romance.

Remember Grace that dreams come true
Cause in my dreams you love me too.

You're in my dreams, your sweet embrace
You're in my heart, I love you Grace.

Mike Martagon

Coming Out Of Darkness

A light shines through my window,
and I see a shadow against the wall;
It belongs to me.
I am in control of it.
I can move my shadow from side to side,
up and down;
wherever I go,
it must follow.
My shadow is no longer in control of me.
For now,
I make my own movements.
I am no longer in the darkness,
or afraid of the light.
I now welcome the light,
and fight back at or change
what I don't like to see.
In fact,
I think sometimes now,
my own shadow is afraid to me!

Paige Owens

Colorful Moment

The laughing brook caught my attention...
and in contrast to the sky
are the leaves of many colors
and the twinkle in your eye.

   The rocks are wet and shiny
   in streams of purest blue
   the stream bed closely bounded
   by grass bedecked in dew.

   The blue expanse above our heads
   with fragile puffs of white
   is home to sun and moon and stars
   which live to share their light.

   The swaying trees adorned with leaves
   their colors bright and smart
   unnumbered shades of red and green
   can't help but cheer the heart.

I share this awesome moment
God's gift of land and sky
with you my special lady
with the twinkle in your eye.

Roger G. Riedel

"Harmony"

Hark! I see an angel
And it is telling me
Be black or white
We shall not fight
But live in harmony
He said there shall be love
To the bitter end
To make this world a happy place
We shall all be friend
Be you yellow, be you white
Be you red, black or brown
We shall live in harmony
And make the world go round
I'm a poet and I know it
My creativity is fine
It's the finest dinner
With an expensive glass of wine
We thank each other, we all agree
Long live the world, in harmony

Steven H. Arviso

Did You Ever?

Did you ever love someone
And know he didn't care?
Did you ever feel like crying
And know it wouldn't get you anywhere?
Did you ever see him dancing,
When the lights were really low?
Did you ever whisper, "I love you,"
but didn't let him know?
Don't ever fall in love, my friend
The price to pay is high
Don't ever fall in love, my friend
I think I'd rather die
So don't ever fall in love, my friend
You'll be hurt before it's through
See my friend, you ought to know
I fell in love with you...

Sandra Neese

Insight

I'd rather see one lose the race,
   And let another win,
Than see him quit and give up hope,
   And never run again.

I'd rather see a baby's tears,
Whose hunger pangs have brought.
Than hear his mother weep aloud,
   Because she has him not.

I'd rather see a broken heart,
That makes ones teardrops fall.
Having lost the one they loved,
   Than never loved at all.

I'd rather not see prejudice,
Toward those whose minds are slow.
   And turn our backs in apathy,
     Pretending not to know.

I'd rather not my eyes be dimmed,
To hunger pain and strife.
Than blinded to the needs of those.
Who share this road of life.

Mike R. Vandine

Children

Create their moods enjoy their thoughts
and listen ever clear
Before too long their growing fast
So soon to not be near.

They feel your distance, watch you close
their self-esteem on line
Your every move they memorize
developing their mind.

So give them all you have to give
Rewards are all but few
The love you showed will be in them
and will come back to you.

Suzy Eastwood

First Snow

I woke up in the middle of the night
And looked out the window
By the front porch light
And I saw the greatest wonder of all
The first snow of winter
Had started to fall
Thoughts of fun danced through my head
I went to the closet
And got out my sled
Finally I saw the bright light of day
I dressed really warmly
And went on my way
My sled in my hands and snow on the ground
I was so happy
The first kid around
Others would come and that would be fine
But the first snow of winter
At that time was mine.

Michael W. Kinney

Keep On Trying

Hello to you across the miles
And may your days be filled with smiles.
Look up to God as days go by
And He'll be with you if you try.
When things get rough and you are down
Remember to smile and never frown.
For when you smile your joy will show
To all around you and you will know
How good it feels to help someone
To reach the top, but not alone.
For when you help a friend who's down
You help yourself to wear a crown.
So love yourself and love a friend
Just keep climbing to the end.

Margaret Good

Untitled

My mind is the sieve of reality
And my heart is the bowl which
Catches the incongruous hope.
I hope to catch the train
To Bethlehem where I can
Witness the birth of Jesus.

Steve Ross

Life's Crossroads

Where dreams,
   and nightmares
     flow from the
       same fountain;
Schweitzers,
   and Ecihmanns,
     Building hospitals,
     and crematoriums,
       For the ecstasy of love;
       For the voracity of hate.

Hunger,
   Piercing, the soul,
     Flowing outward
       Toward others.

Ralph J. Caro-Capolungo

Warm Blue

No bony jam
And no slave away
You could cruise with me too
You could snooze with me too
Look at my picture
Make it a fixture
Or throw it away

I could wash my car
I could clean my house
The map said I was here
Though I was still at home
Look at my money
Make me your honey
Or throw me away

Look at my picture
Make it a fixture
Look at my money
Make me your honey
Freedom can cost love
But dreams are free

J. Michael Stewart

"Friendship Turned To Love"

I look into your blue eyes
And now I truly know
The feeling for you as my friend
Has started to grow.

You come to mean so much to me
In so very many ways,
I'd like to stand beside you
For all of my days.

The timing in our lives
For friendship that's so strong,
Is right in many ways,
But in many ways it's wrong.

I need to be patient
For both of us indeed
But if the reward is what I want
It will be worth it indeed.

Lynn Zakrajshek

Love

Love looks like pink hearts
and taste like ice cream
and smells like red roses
love makes you feel good
and lets you know that
someone loves you.

Shaunda Carter

Fall

Sweet smell of fall
and of you
Gradual learning
is what we need
What ever happens
is meant to be
Wind
Kisses my eye's closed
and makes me dream
Last night
Seeing you
Standing there
Drawn towards you
No hesitation
Dance with me
Sweetly
we are one
If only for a moment
You have added to me
For a lifetime

Katherine E. Hills

"Her Eyes"

She's such a jewel
and oh what a flirt!
I guess that's what-
really hurts.
the idea that she
cannot see me.

does it really bother me?
or...
am I worried I would hear
them say...

"Oh, what a shame, what's wrong
with her eyes - any ways?"

The one question remains...
do we really see "love"

with our eyes - or in many
different ways.

Karin R. Brandt

A Toast To The Disillusionment

Here's to lost loves, forgotten dreams, and old times. Here's to days gone by, days now living, and days yet to come. Here's to the lonely man in the rain, the single mother in the streets, and the rich woman drinking to her death with brandy. Here's to those who've lost the game on a fluke, lost their lives for governments, and lost causes always fought for. Yes, here's to them, and hope, and fear, and to love, and hate. Here's to laughter, and tears. And, of course, here's to life. Even at its most unfair and worst, here's to life. And dreams, and love, and laughter, and hope. Yes, friends, here's to us.

Tracy L. Allen

Friend

Come, sit with me, my friend,
And rest here now as we
Explore the twisting, endless maze
Of life's inconstancy.

My thoughts I give to you,
While you with subtle skill
Reveal your secret inner self
To meld with mine, at will.

The shuttered past we open wide
and see us, young and free,
Restricted not by duty's bonds
Both as we wish to be.

Our maiden's dreams we dream again,
While passion still untried
And feelings yet to bud and bloom
Lie dormant, deep inside.

And when the time has quickly gone
Then you must leave; But know —
Friendship is the heart of life,
For you have made it so.

Sharon Hansen Jensen

Return To Innocence

One heart breaks open
and ruby shards
kaleidoscope
into multitudes of desires,
unfulfilled, fueled and radiating
a cascade of promise;
a milky way of fruitful crossings
into unchartered turf
where blindness grazes
in the alfalfa field,
where lovers weave clover,
warp and woof
the longitude and latitude of luck
compassing hot dreams,
while warm wine
spills over cheeks
poised, puckered, petulant
against a sinless salvation
that might return us to innocence.

Natalija Nogulich

God's Creations

As the children play
   and scream,
the sun is leaving
   for the day,
the birds are tucking
   in their young,
and the wind dances
   in the sky,
we hear the noises
   that God created.

Tiffany Luke

Sunset

When the day is almost over
And the sun begins to sink,
God seems to tell you how He feels
Through the colors that He paints
Like ribbons reaching toward the earth,
Promising tomorrow another birth.

Lori Sue Grieb

Giver And Receiver

God gives me love and happiness.
And sometimes sorrow. The
door to happiness is wide and
narrow and sometimes painful,
we don't know why we all
can't be receivers. But in
this world some of us must
be givers as well as receivers.
That's what the Lord made
us to be in this world.

Margaret Calderon

The dove at witherspoon

at dawn
the morning dove
sings her song
a
sad
sad
sad
dove
crying
But soft,
what bird
sings for peace
in these troubled times?
Do you know?

Beatrice Cackle

To Still A Broken Heart

Alas, the sorrow
and the bleakness of the morrow
with no respite
always darkness, never light
he sobs in his solitude
with no one to blame but himself
ah, how he loved so
and as his tears flow
he raises his chalice
and toasts the malice
bequeathed him.
And as his soul dies
the poet cries
and closes his eyes
for the last time

Phillip D. Mitchell

Erotica

With a thunderous pounding in my chest
    and the gasping of my breath
my inner desires are heated to a boil.

    Can you
      kiss me
        hotter
          than the
            flame
      singeing
        my body?

My deeper soul screams
    whispers of want
  steaming from smoldering lips
Quench my lust
  Ignite my body unrestrained
Storm my being
If you dare
    create an inferno to devour my hell
You too shall I consume in my craze.

Susan K. Donohoe

Friends

When we've been through so much together
And the time of separation grows near
May we remember the good times and bad
As it was and will always be dear
As we hug and begin to part
We will always and forever remember in our hearts
The friendship between us that was pure and good
As we part, and shed a tear, we smile

Shelley Irene Zacherl

Foreign Lands

Look at the men who fight and die
And think of the people who will cry
Some are young and some are old
Some are cowards some are bold

There all like brother on foreign lands
Where each of them must lend a hand.
Some are black, red, yellow and white
But each of them must stay and fight

So mother, fathers and the rest
I'm sure that he is doing his best
To bring the peace back to our lands
And make the worlds all join in hands

So let us all kneel down and pray
And hope the men don't have to stay
In foreign lands across the sea
'Cuz that's a dirty place to be.

Paul Soyring

A Sequal

I came to the road not taken
And thought I'd never be back
But there I stood one day
Looking far down the track

The leaves were falling gently.
My mind turned to yester-year
It didn't seem so long ago.
Way led onto way and I was here.

My footsteps are not now so sure
And faltering
I took a step.
I straightened up my shoulders
And down the road not taken, I went.

Ruth E. McMillen

End Prejudism

We've gotta stick together
And try to get along.
Don't listen to what people say,
Don't let them tell you wrong.

Don't judge us by our color,
Cause we are all the same.
We've gotta realize that
this is not a game.

We know there is no difference,
if you're black or if you're white.
Together as a team, we're
sure to stop the fight.

So listen very carefully,
and you are sure to see.
How the best of friends,
black and white, can truly be.

Veronica Aguilar-Medina

My Ocean

Cometh morn, awaken I to the ocean's roar
And walk across the sands to the ocean's door
To sit and meditate by her side
Gaze I upon the waves as they collide.

Warm friends are we, deep down she's cold
For in the ocean's bed lie sad tales of old -
Warmed am I from sun in high noon
Soon, the dark of night, a glowing moon.

Vanish my time, cometh the tide
Sorrowful my being, to leave ocean's side
This moment in thought with grave emotion
The morrow come, returneth my ocean.

Samuel J. Tarantino

Precious Friend

I never came to you, my friend
And went away not knowing.
You have turned my world upside down,
Giving me faith and less doubt.
Encouraging me in days ahead.

How can I find the right words,
The right phrase, that tells you
how much you mean to me?
There is no word, no phrase,
for you on whom I rely.
All I can say to you is this.
I love you, precious friend!

Scot Wisniewski

"My Thanks To You"

I look to the Heavens
And what do I see
My father's face smiling at me.

He watches me by night
He watches me by day
He's with me every step of the way.

When I am anxious and forlorn
And feel like giving up
My Father's voice speaks to me
About my overflowing cup.

I remember to give Him daily
My thanks and my praise
And look to Him as my source
All the rest of my days.

Verdell Cray

Awareness Asleep

We talk to people of all disguises
and when the question arises
the answer most often spouted
"He is everywhere - all about us"
if we think this be so true
why do we do the things we do
if we are so aware of his essence
why do we not practice his presence
while our minds and bodies sleep
may our hearts a vigil keep

Robert F. Hughes

Missing You

Tonight God came down
and whispered your name,
as the angels encircled your bed.
"My child you are needed in Heaven,"
they said.
With a touch of your heart,
and a lift of your soul,
they moved you to that place in the sky.
But they forgot to stop and tell me why.
So now I'm left to think
of the reason you could have went,
when you ascended with the angels
God sent.
And I just can't imagine what He
possibly needs you for,
Knowing I will always need you more.
So now as you rest
way up above,
Know that you are missed.
Know that you are loved.
  Michele Ann Ryan

Second Chance

Thru sleepless nights I toss and turn
And, wide awake, I often yearn
For little hands I used to hold,
One pair of which has long been cold,

If I could live my lifetime o'er
I'd hurry less, and give much more
Of all the things that children need,
And this, I vow would be my creed:

"Take time to love and laugh and play"
For all too soon there comes the day
When little hands no longer cling,
And little feet have left the swing
That hung beneath the old oak tree.

And when my children say to me,
"Grandma, you spoil my children rotten,"
I hope perhaps that they've forgotten
The busy Mother who never knew how
To live, and laugh, and love - 'til now.
  Verna J. Walker

Forget - Me - Nots

Do you remember us from spring?
And will you come again for us to sing?
We wait for you in a quiet spot.
To bloom and to wait that is our lot.

Forget-me-not that is our name.
We love you, songful child of fame.
So come to us, yes do.
Our beauty and love is all for you.
  K. G. Schmidt

The Rose

The petals on a rose
Are so carefully placed,
I wonder how God knew
The pattern to be made.

The colors... many hued,
The fragrance — sweet and mild
Intoxicates one's senses
Its beauty to behold.
  Sally H. Garner

Sunset

Oh to turn back the pages
And write a new book!
To stand at the mirror
And like how I look.
To sit on the porch in
The cool of the day.
Watching the children,
Busy at play.
To run through the meadow,
With the wind in my hair;
To wake up each morning
And not have a care.
To sit in my rocker
And make up a song,
And sing to my babies
All the day long.
And when the sun sinks
For the very last time,
Remember the wonderful things
That were mine!
  Nora Jones

"It's Only Time"

You've heard it said a hundred times,
And yet it's really true.
It seems like only yesterday,
I pledged my love to you:

I've wondered where the years have gone,
Where can they really be?
I pray they've been as good for you,
As they have been for me.

Yes, there have been the heartaches,
And there have been the tears.
We both have had our problems,
But all of yesteryears.

I can not see the future
The past just fades away.
I can not tell what tomorrow brings,
I can only count today.

So that is why I need you,
Always by my side.
I couldn't make it on my own,
Even if I tried.
  Keith Bridges

My Love

Out of no where you came to me
And you changed my life history.
Like the moon rising out of the sea
Perhaps, an angel directed you to me.
You are making my life so complete,
You give my life meaning and a chance
To dream again.
Dreams of many tomorrows.
You make my life beautiful, because you
Are beautiful.
If this is love this must be heaven.
If this is only a dream,
Let me dream forever.
  Kathleen N. Clark

"The Punished Bully"

You pushed me against the wall
and you thought that I was weak.
But I read in the Bible
to turn the other cheek.

One day you whipped me good
and this I shall admit.
I put you behind bars
because you wouldn't quit.

Maybe I should feel sorry
think I should even frown?
Well, I don't think so
but look who's laughin' now.
  Nicole Lester

My New Day

Being able to touch you
And you touch me
Carries with it a message
Of what life can be.

Full of the sensations
That are good and so right
And don't disappear
When we lay down at night.

They linger forever
In the mind of the free
And can never be stolen
From deep within me.

You've written on the pages
Of a brand new book
Making a brilliant beginning
That I can't over look.

You gave them to me
Don't take them away
I'll keep them forever
To begin my new day.
  Olivia L. Isenberg

A Love That Will Never Die

When the sky starts to fall
and your stars fade away,
My love is with you all
like a bright shining ray

When your world starts to crumble
and you can take no more,
Try and be humble
for my love is at your door

For when I leave this place
I will never truly disappear,
Just picture my face
and you will know my love is near

I will be up in the sky
looking down at you,
Hoping you will try
to remember a love that was true

And know that I am with you
and I will always be,
for a mothers love is true
a love that will never leave
  Toni Gurley

Prayer To The Angels

angels in the sky
angels up on high
i have but one single prayer
i have but one final care
please take care of my baby
keep him warm and keep him safe
take care of my sweet special love
it 'tis for when i keep my faith
angels you must listen closely
he gets so scared so easily
help him to live more peacefully
angels you must hear me now
please grant me this, my last request
he needs your guidance and your care
angels i'm sure you will try your best
please ease his pain and dry his tears
give him love with a tender touch
please take care of my sweet special love
angels i thank you so very much

Michele Parvis

The Fickle Sea

The fickle sea is once again changing:
Angry torrents of water break,
Against the rock;
That vast blue stuff, ranging;
As if into infinity, pounds at the earth,
As if life
Were a mere mock.

Once again quiet,
As if in a beautiful sleep,
The sea...caressing it's shore,
I try not to weep.
So like a person,
In his fit of rages;
Then gentle and serene,
As precious time ages...

Marian Kelley Walls

Diamonds In The Snow

This winter day our Lord has made
Another day and I have prayed.
I look outdoors. What do I see?
Beautiful snow on every tree,
Like heaven on a starry night,
When all the stars are twinkling bright.
Shining diamonds in the snow
Lord are you trying us to show?
From earth a place where we are going,
To another world of our now knowing,
Up to a place of Eternal light,
Like this new snow so pure and white.
Our lovely birds have gone away.
I hope they all come back someday.
In Spring she will come back again,
To build her nest out little wren.
Hope Eternal is in our breast
Also hers as she builds her nest
I hope in God whose message I know,
Sparkling diamonds in the snow.

Ruth Ardys

Regretful Past

Another day has set,
another light gone dim,
and I will stand there in the dark,
face to face with sin.

Fear is my companion,
love stands at my side,
I give away my purity,
security and pride.

I looked upon the rest that day,
their faces full of hate,
I could have been there earlier,
I should have shown up late.

Shaun Muis

Another Night

Another night without knowing,
another night of tears,
another night of wondering,
of all my deepest fears.

As I lie here crying,
into the silent night,
knowing no one hears me,
no one can make it right.

I feel like I am drowning,
sinking ever more deep,
I think I might go crazy,
and I am losing sleep.

My situation is drastic,
and it gets worse every day,
I wish someone could help me,
I wish there was a way.

Another night without knowing,
another night of tears,
another night of wondering,
of all my deepest fears.

Norma Aponte

Anxiously

For his little heart beats for me
anxiously he awaits;
I wonder what he thinks of me.

So small, tender and unaware
how that heart can break and tear
Long days, short nights
all I do is think of him.

For my heart beats for him
anxiously I await.

Kathy Myers

The 90's Woman

See me as a woman
  and I will be a woman.

Care for me as a woman
  and I will respond like a woman.

Treat me like a woman
  and I will behave like a woman.

Touch me like a woman
  and I will melt in your arms.

Above all else
  respect me for the woman who I am.

Marlo Ramnarine

Lil' Piggy

Oh your lil' piggy eyes,
Are in your lil' piggy face,
And your lil' piggy knees,
Make your legs look out of place.

And your lil' piggy hair,
On your lil' piggy head,
Makes me wish, each time I see you,
You were some place else instead.

And your lil' piggy ways,
When I see you eating food,
Makes me know in just an instant,
That you manners are so crude.

And your lil' piggy feet,
Have piggy toes I'll bet,
You should be in a circus,
Or a barnyard, better yet.

So remember Lil' piggy,
No matter what you do,
You could have a brother, or a sister,
That looks exactly, just like you!

Paul E. Borusky

From The Hayloft

From the hayloft I can see for miles
Around the countryside—
A more pleasant view I could not find
No matter how I tried.
The valleys wide, the mountains tall,
And snuggled in between,
The rooftops of the country town
Can now and then be seen
Among the graceful treetops
Swaying softly in the breeze—
I drank my fill of beauty
And put my heart at ease.
The hawk and eagle soaring high
Above the fruited plain
Scanning all the earth below
Surveying their domain.
A little puff of cotton cloud,
The wide blue sky above,
And all around and in between
Our Heavenly Father's love.

Lorna M. Stewart

What Was It Really Like

The barefoot boy had shoes on
As he play in the silt of the sand,
For the beach was covered with litter
As far as the eye could scan.

He started to ask questions
As only a small boy can do:
"Were sunsets really pretty
And was the sky really blue?

Before all the pollution
What was it really like?
Were there really trees on hillsides
When you went there for a hike?

Could you really see the ocean
Before all the smog
And were there really birds and animals
And boys who played with frogs?"

The old man sat in silence
And hung his head in shame,
For he realized far too late
It was he who was to blame.

Murray Kofoid

Bed Of Green

Fingers touch my bare stomach
As I lay alone.
The blue surrounds me.
The white.
The green tickles my skin.
A buzzing and silence.
It flies away.
I fly away, into the blue.
  Mackensie Wolf

Rendezvous

So far, and yet so near!
As I musingly shed a tear
Your voice comes back again
Making sweeter "Lover's Lane."

Hearing you say, "Don't fret,
I shall be with you yet."
You sound so true and real
That only certain joy I feel.

Too, I see your smile
As it thrills me yet the while
It comes as balm to pain
As sunshine comes in place of rain.

You walk and talk with me
No, not for the passing eye to see
Stealing away thus with you
We keep our secret rendezvous
  Virginia Ashby

Untitled

Raindrops hitting upon my bare knee
as I sit in my car
At the local Arby's

Bolts of lightning carve into the
sky and asphalt rumbles beneath me
while torrents of water rush by

They call it fast food
but I'm in no rush
sitting here watching the show

The earth will keep spinning and
Stars always glowing are signs that
I must start to slow

For I now understand that this is
all grand and there is more to life
than a baked stuffed potato
  Keith A. Brown

Silence

I sit in silence,
As I sit in silence
I observe the natural
World in all its beauty
Around me. Just sitting
And watching the birds
Fly to and fro, the ants out
On a hard days work. So
Many small yet wonderful acts
Of nature that people just
Pass by without a thought or glance
Or even a care. I watch them, I
Take notice of them, I give them
Respect. And peacefully and
Contentedly observe them, as
I sit in silence.
  Mike Thiel

My Savior

Hot tears stream down my face
As I think of you who took my place
And, gave your life on Calvary
To save a sinner such as me.

You took the stripes I so deserved
And did not say a single word.

A crown of thorns placed on your head,
And oh the blood so pure and red.

A sword did pierce your blessed side,
And all my sins were covered wide.

Your precious blood was shed on Calvary
So all mankind may be set free.
  Wanda P. Grace

Untitled

The Dancer moved like the butterfly
as the lightning sang her song,
the moon had left the party,
but the rain stayed and played on;
feel the heat in her movements,
as the steam rolled from her eyes;
as the deer all fled for cover
I longed to be at her side;
rain dancer in the storm forest
dance Dancer, dance
rain dancer in the storm forest
dance Dancer, dance . . .
  Steve Sniezak

"The Princess And The Poet"

Foreboding the sky
As the rain does fall,
Look there men approach
And they do give call.
The princess lies still
Is what they declare,
Messengers of doom
My sorrow lay bare.
So onward I ride
My heart cold from pain,
Through deepest forest
In bone chilling rain.
I enter the shroud
And my tears do start,
My true love lies still
As still as my heart.
Is there any hope
I can not surmise,
I kiss her cold lips
And look she does rise.
  Mark Samuel Smith

The Traveler

If I were the traveler,
back in time I'd go,
to a more simple era,
were love and life would flow.
I'd sit by peaceful waters,
and mountains towering high,
but I am just the dreamer,
the traveler denied.
  Tina Borders

Drowning The Fears

There's something about the darkness
As the shadows dance around
The fear creeps in and engulfs you
As though you donned your gown

Then your imagination intensifies
Watching the shadows move up and down
And the thoughts of strange possibilities
Play tricks on the mind, profound

Then the beasts and demons within you
As though they had come from the ground
They overwhelm your imagination
Then play with the mind they've found

As the rays of light crest the horizon
When the morning finely comes around
Then the beasts and demons disappear
They've withdrawn, as though they were drowned
  R. C. Stamper

The Eternal Day

I lay and watch the people
as they weep or cry for me.

I'd like to comfort them,
And tell them it's okay.

But somehow I can't do it,
For I must remain so still.

My body is no longer mine;
My wish will move it not.

My mind is still quite clear
Though now it is my soul's.

I never thought I'd see the day,
When I'd know that I am dead!
  Kaye Leazier

Hiroshima

On August sixth in forty-five
At eight fifteen
The bomb was dropped
in far Japan.
A glaring blast
Inferno - at 2,000 C
Heard you the flutter
of soaring souls?
78,000 we believe
13,000 never found
37,000 left to bleed
From this carnage
The earth took strength.
Rampant foliage - lustrous green
Pretties the rippling waters
Where near perfect children swim!
  Rose Marie Scheel

Shadows

The sun hid
behind a cloud today

Secreting my sorrow
in its shadow.

Beauty all around me
and yet
I can not see

Nor share, even in
the tranquility of
a midsummers eve.
  Michael James Brown

Dad

I can still see you:
  bald head,
    broad shoulders,
      strong muscles and
hairy arms.
I can still see you:
  photographing family events,
  planning army reunions,
  remodeling neighbor's houses and
walking crying babies.
I can still see you:
  kneeling on the job pounding
    nails,
  sitting at your desk paying
    bills,
  standing at the grill turning
    bratwurst and
lying in bed-dead.

Mary T. Gellings

Two Fish

Two fish
Beautiful and innocent
As they
Can be
Taking on
The life dangers
That lies
Within the
Sea.

Holding on
To that
Precious gift
That God
Has given
To thee
And That
Is to be
Forever free.

Tracey Christopher Rice

My Best Friend (A Tribute To Teri)

Her smiling face was like the
  beautiful sun setting in the
  west breeze.

Her laugh and talk was like
  the beautiful singing of a
  thousand birds.

But most of all she was a
  best friend to me, like a
  mother to her daughter.

She always knew what to
  say when I was down,
  she was by my side helping
  me through sad times and
  helping me through bad times.

But now she is gone forever,
  but not forgotten,
  she is my best friend
  she was so near to me.

She shall always live in my
  heart and soul.

Tracy Linette Yon

The Half Full Glass

The half full glass I say,
Because after I had reckoned
It was half empty.
In a flash, I saw a rain drop
Fall into it;
Just as I started to walk away.
It came from somewhere up above.
A leak in the ceiling,
condensed moisture or
what? I can't say.
All I know is; that I
measured twice,
before I conclude this truth.
The glass was half full.
And from the weavers nest
I reason; there has to be
a loving God.

Ray O'Neal

After The Dawn

Since the dawn of life, this world has
been home. Sometimes filled with
pains and thorns, yet I love and enjoyed
it so well. Now the twilight is here,
to signal the end is near. Maybe tomorrow,
anytime I know not when.

I thank God for this dear life. Thou
I had enough I wanted more. I must confess
I have sinned. I did it my way
without intent. I am aware I cannot be
an Angel. The numerous faults I've done
will tell. Because I am too human to be a Saint.

I know I can't stay here forever.
After the dawn, twilight must come.
Not even God has the power to alter the
route he gave us. Just like the sun and
I each morning. We arise together for the
day's journey that ends only in the
simple peace of night.

Mike A. Caguin

Paper Weigh's

I know
Behind that
Nimbus cumulus sky
Are you pounding your voice

But down in here
Where you want me to
My feet down
Deep in snow
And my eyes towards
The celestial vault
To the silence
I attest
your aubade
Will be heard
For I once
Have seen days
This very night
Will grow bright
O my God
Glory to Thee

RDTRS

To Be

I want to be, and I am
Being as desired to be —
Healthy with zest, upright with smile —
Keeping relations so fine tuned
As I am.

I want to be much, and I am
Striving for wisdom and wealth.
I go to school learning the books,
Then go to work earning the bucks,
I join a club to have some fun
With no booze or drug to get me high.
I go to church to search my soul
For inner peace — that's my goal
While I am.

I want to be many, so I am
A warden of a family I have raised
In a community I help build
In a country that I love.
I give them all I learned and earned
After I am.

Lorenzo S. Camacho

Spring Cleaning

Pictures far back in a drawer
Beneath the bills and the letters,
Remind me of what I have no more.
But perhaps it's for the better.

Our favorite books hide under the stack,
All those words now lost.
Still I carry the weight on my back
Of the pages I long ago tossed.

The golden locket now covered in dust.
I pry it open to look inside.
I n your face I always found trust,
But as the years past,
That idea died.

So now I wipe all of this clean,
Though it takes me many hours.
For the empty drawer and all it means
Still holds all of its old powers.

Nicole J. Miranth

Night Flights

Two hearts danced again tonight
Beside a silver stream
Entwined in perfect harmony
Without a line or seam

Two hearts danced again tonight
With silent passion known
Bathing in the stream of life
In love's symphonic song

Two hearts danced again tonight
Upon a radiant beam
And with reluctance, took to flight
Back into a dream

Peggy Spencer

"On The First Years Of Marriage"

Bitter though the berry be,
  but sweetness there,
and leaves of gold.

Rod Pike

Untitled

From God a gracious gift
beyond human thoughtfulness.
Autumn seeds are deep
growing so silently.
Spring gently showers us,
summer delivers innocence,
bringing a newborn scent.
A petal soft touch
   of tenderness.
We can conceive,
   what nature brings.

Tese Hardy

A Woman Broken

A woman broken
beyond repair

To tired to despair
a woman without means
tears stream

Barely able to face another day
wishing quietly she could slip away

The sun rises and with it another day
in her heart she prays

But only in her mind
does she see

Linda B. Rosenfield

The Last Sigh

Rose petals are falling.
Bleeding hearts are aching.
Forget-me-not-s are sighing.
Tear-drops are running.

   Need no more tender touch,
   Caressing kisses, songs of love,
   Just tell me, you forget me not!

Silver, gold, cold shining rocks
I do not need. I'm not!
Just bring me one forget-me-not.

   Send me no more roses,
   Carnations, carrousels.
   I'm no more. I'm not!
   Just tell me, you forget me not!

Kathleen Pentek

Untitled

   Lord, you knowest tho my heart.
and you have from the very start.
Knowing, understanding, growing in your spirit.
Walking in your light.
Trusting in your everlasting grace.
I've finally come to a restful place.
   I hide myself in you. I lovest you
oh my soul. My God how much you've
loved me more, your arms have held me or and or.
   I've just begun to understand the depth
of love you demand. Even tho love is
a choice, we must know your heavenly voice,
of the one who speaks the truth.
   Seek and you shall find.
All I have is time.
My time and God's
time are not the same.

Sissy Temple Ratliff

"Delusions Purified"

   The beast is banging on his cage
Blinded by my effigy's rage.
   His teardrops cascade onto the ground
The angels threw this passion down

   Your newborn ambience is purified
By an unfamiliar will to try
   You can't forget your illustrious dream
Sleep to realize your everything

   The gate has opened by request
Now your conscious never rests
   Demons dance inside your head
To steal your fears, the beast is fed

   I'm not the beast, don't run away
You hold my only reason to stay
   I see your essence through your eyes
My perfect life is realized

   I can't pretend I'm someone else
I'll only love you for myself
   Someday I hope you'll finally see
I give you the purest part of me

Richard Carpenter

Dawn

The sun blazes across the ashen sky,
Blood crystallizes in the golden heat,
From the morbid wounds of soldiers,
Lying there, lifeless.
Sands of time,
Echo,
In the valley of death.
Troops march on,
Unmoved by the terror and tragedy,
That encompasses them,
Forced to move on,
For survival,
And more importantly,
To feed their insatiable appetite,
For belligerence.

Pat Chiu

A Portrait Of An Old Friend

Eyes like the ocean,
Body like bamboo,
He casts the shadow of
An eagle, a skunk, and sometimes
The Lochness Monster.
Colors are: black, gray, and blue
Also pink, yellow, and green
But, mostly white

Susan Y. Chen

Weather

Today again the sun is shining
   But soon it will be blinding.
For high heat is here
   Let's look at the magic mirror.
Why high heat magic mirror?
   No answer which brings on fear.
Drought may soon be here
   If rain does not appear.
Why high heat Dear God I ask
   Have faith for the heat will soon pass.

Pamela Schenkelberg

Going To Town

Drive slowly along the country lane,
Boiling dust coats the window pane.
Rolling farmland quietly passes by
Wildwood edges flaunt secrets and defy.

Stagnant, noonday air stifles fields
Cool forest's dark shadow ne'er yields.
Fairies, ghosts and goblins live there
'Neath leaves, bark and toadstools rare.

Seen laughing with the moon and stars
Whilst peeking through the fence row bars.
Breezes are their breath sent to find
Wayward children, with a willing mind.

Play away sweet summer days with abandon
And pluck the wildflower weed at random.
Measured and treasured, by the aged sleuth
Time eludes the grasp of ardent youth.

Captured spirits still hear the call
Whimsy lights within; mirth does crawl.
Memory finds that old country lane
When dust bowls formed the bane.

Kathryn J. Davis

Mind Magic

Night creatures raise above the darkness
Breaking stillness - hear their cries!
Are there really - tiny people
Does one ever trust his eyes?

Hush - a twig has snapped
Be still, my heart, breathe
Stop - o roaring in my ears
Sometimes senses do deceive!

Will I ever see a fairy?
Scattering magic glitter dust.
Spying on a leprechaun
Now, is very much must!

Follow me - walk stealthily
I know a glade where we can't stay
Where will o wisps and fireflies
And all night creatures works and play

Such a try no mortals dare
Available to one of a kind
Wait for me, within my reach
It's in the castles of my mind.

Lucille J. Boudreaux

Without Perfections

Without a clue,
breath and death renew
where joy meets tears
of laughter and fears
as something to pursue —
perfections neither come nor go
of great illusion things to know
and oh to see from such a show
the smallest little thought will glow.

In nameless insight of an age,
wisdom is sublime,
a chariot of heaven
sounding as a chime —
the thought of man
in action speaks
the movement of ideas
and all the worlds have so appeared
cast images revered.

Marvin Blevins

Gay

Good, kind, honest,
bright ruler of
your mind.
Mend your ways
Gaye, who for, what
for, the beauty
of the earth; sand
upon the beach.
Be gay, happy, kind
and good, have
a mind of your
own. Wake up, take
time to be gay, happy
and kind to your
friend. Who is my
friend, I do not know.
Some day away, I will say,
"Hello, how are you?"

Martha G. Essi

The Ultimate Price

That sapphire blue machine
Brought back the memory of that day.
That event—which in a single moment,
Left such a price to pay.

A day which began with gaiety,
Laughter, and future thoughts.
Routine and ordinary; Without a clue
Of devastation to be wrought.

After work, gathering with friends,
Sipping that sour grape nectar.
Hearing the words "last call;"
Hoping it didn't affect her.

Only a short drive home—
A cautious, steady, pace.
OH NO! Forgot that curve!
The windshield embraces her face.

The cop wrote reports, the wrecker came;
Neighborhood locals stared—dismayed.
The black station wagon door opened
In front of her parents, praying where she laid.

Wilma A. Rice

Lonely Is The Night

Luminary rays drop beyond the hill,
Burning embers turn to ashes;
The house grows strangely still.
As I slip beneath a quilt of patches,

Heavy is my heart.
Shadows fade into the night;
I lie alone here in the dark.
Hands lifted toward the moonlight,

I go to Him in prayer.
Knowing He'll be with me,
I find my solace there.
Awakened from a peaceful sleep

By the rising of the sun,
Once again, a new day has begun.

Margery Lusk Mitchell

Cherish

Cherish love, hope, joy and all your dreams.
But above all cherish your good memories.
Memories of love.
Memories of happiness.
Memories of comfort, laughter and joy
  of togetherness.
Cherish them because of what they mean—
  everything to you and me.

Erica Nicole Herron

"In This Place I Don't Belong"

You may wonder why I'm here,
but, believe me I'm sincere,
when I say, I won't stay too long...
in this place I don't belong.
I was born, but shall I live?
It wasn't my choice to be here,
but now that I'm here, it's not clear...
Whether I should go or stay,
in this place I don't belong.
No I, say - I don't belong,
in this place that's not for me.
I'm just a limb from the family tree,
cut a limb from the family tree.

Scott C. Shafer

Home Alone

How still and quiet is the morning
  but for the sound of my own breath
Shallow as it seems to be
  as if in a state of quietude and rest.

I peer 'round this empty room
  devoid of another living soul
Realizing that I am now alone
  and have gotten frightfully old.

Oh! to go back to the days
  when the children were around
And fun and games were played
  with love and happiness abound.

How sad and lonely is our home
  with but memories of yesteryear
Looking through old picture albums
  to recall cherished times held most dear.

But tomorrow will be different
  gone to see my loving kids
To relive, once again, the days
  now but memories of things we did.

William Henry Jones

Wake Up

Why must we judge one another,
By appearance, religion, race or color?
Do we not know, we were sent here to live;
Each with a special talent to give;
With a purpose to live in peace and love;
To fervently strive for the "Home above?"

Stacy L. Francis

Victory

It's easy to hide from life
But how long,
and how much will have gone by,
before you are found?

The ultimate hideaway
is probably death.
Also the easy way out
where nothing is felt,
and no victories are won.

But if you have the courage,
the faith,
the love in your heart,
then you will not hide.

You will be found,
and then you can feel,
life's little victories.

Steven D. Himmelsbaugh

Evolution?

They say it's evolution
But I just don't understand,
What part of evolution
Taught my cat to hold my hand?...

No scientist can ever prove
Enough so I'd believe,
That creatures that we love so well
Don't "Miss us" when we leave

They know some things about us
That they never have been told,
Like when we're feeling blue inside
Or "think" we're getting old

They see inside our eyes so deep
They reach into our soul,
Passing up the "ugliness".
See diamonds where there's coal

If someone grunts in disbelief
"It's only just a pet!"
Just realize with empathy
They haven't been "adopted" yet!

Rita A. Martin

Mom

I feel you're here beside me
But I still get very sad
I always took for granted
What I'm wishing now I had
I want to feel your touch
To hear your voice to see your face
I long for how I felt
So safe and warm in your embrace
I do some crazy things
Like start to call you on the phone
Forgetting that you're gone
And then I feel so all alone
I know you're in a better place
But still I'm sad for me
I wonder if you miss me too
Now that your soul is free
I know you're there to meet me
When my days on earth are through
Till then I'll do my best
Till then I'll still be missing you

Sonya Barnes

Recovery

Swift and sudden it came
But I survived, depending
On others for my very life!
Now I have learned some patience,
And am content to wait
To see what comes each day.
It seems like living again
To watch the glories of a sunset
and the autumn landscape!
"Sweet are the uses of adversity"
And I have tried them all!
With cane, I venture out
to new adventures,
And watch my empty reservoir
of life fill up again!
Kathleen J. Henderson

Daddy

I'm just so tiny now,
But I'm sure I'm going to grow.
This is for both of us,
I guess you probably know.

I look so forward to learning,
To run, to skip and play.
With a Dad like you to teach me,
I'll do it all someday.

There are other things you'll teach me,
Things all "men" should know.
Respect, humility, love and praise,
At life you're such a pro.

We'll grow together and learn a lot,
The future has no end.
I'll try to learn your every way,
I'm so glad I've got you as a friend.

I love you, Daddy.
Shari Murray

Silence Is Galling

"My wife", I say, you see, "she says."
But in fact, to tell the truth,
She really doesn't speak.

No! Now!? Not to say she doesn't speak
But she really doesn't say,
Not with a tongue, or teeth,
Not even puff of cheek.

But I'll say, "You'll see,
She can more than speak!"
By hand, that is!
With squint of eye and nose a'tweek.

"Not as you'd say," I'll say
"But more," I'd say, "like you'd see,
She speaks her silent say."

With love, and scorn,
And not without
A little pique.
John J. Parnow

Do They Really Listen

You tell them how you feel,
but is your message clear
Have they paid attention
Do they even hear

They never tell you how they feel,
so how will you know
what the future will be like,
where the relationship will go

And if they put it off
to another day
Will things be the same
Or will it all fade away

Then comes the moment
You've been waiting for
Everything starts going great,
but then your back to where you well before

He's not listening at all
To a word you say
The relationship is ending
And both you hearts will pay
Mendi McClure

Special Friend!

I tried to be a friend
But it was at an end
  When you blamed it on me
I was ashamed to have a friend
  that didn't trust me

  I couldn't understand
when you went and grabbed his hand
  You knew, you knew
he was special didn't you

  Is that why,
did you try
  To hurt me, make me cry

And did you believe
  all those people
who told you that lie

  I couldn't understand
when you went and grabbed his hand
  you knew, I knew
he was special to me too
Melissa Templeton

Fear

Fear to do what is right,
Can into our life bring blight.

As we study and grow,
Let's put to work what we know.

God has given to each of us,
Talents to use for Him without fuss.

So if a tomorrow we are granted,
Let's use our gifts to get seeds planted.

Forget the fear, hope for the best
Go and do, the Lord will surely bless.
Peggy Bogle

Emotion

I never knew I knew her,
but know her yes I do.
She caught me by surprise to say,
"Nathan I know you."

She always knew she knew me,
and played her game she did.
She wrapped herself inside my heart,
and there is where she hid.

She filled me with despair and grief,
with happiness and joy.
In her hands she held my heart,
as if it were a toy.

Then after she had shaped my heart,
her work with me was fair.
But as she stepped out of my life,
I noticed she was there.

More beautiful than anything,
I ask her who she was.
And as she turned away from me,
she whispered, "I am Love."
Nathan Galvin

Untitled

They think they keep me prisoner
but little do they know,
that these four walls that I'm inside
just make me love you more.
My body may be locked away
but my heart belongs to you,
and while they keep us separate
my heart stays there with you.
No matter how long they keep me,
no matter how far away,
my heart will always stay behind
waiting for reunion day.
So let them try to break me,
as long as your around,
I'll always know my heart is safe
and home is where I'm bound.
Martha R. Clark

Autumn

Summer is over, days are still sunny.
  But now shadows are much longer.
Often the air is crisp
  And tree tops sway in a cool breeze.
It's autumn and time for colored leaves.

Green leaves slowly change to
  Red, brown, orange and gold.
The landscape is so colorful
  That I wish time would stand still,
And leaves would not fall from the trees.

But time does not stand still.
  Already leaves are falling:
Some spinning, some swirling,
  Some gliding gracefully in the breeze.
It's autumn and time for falling leaves.
Philip Wicke

Dead End

Slavery has ended now
but racism has not.
I cannot go to bed
without the thought
of terror in my mind.

The future looks like it ought
to be that I find
even more racism
and the though of terror comes
back to mind.

I go to look for work and food
but a dead end I find.
To me no one is kind.
I have heard news about many
beatings.
I feel that in this world
all I can find
is a
dead end.

Tyrus B. Cooper Jr.

Tomorrow

Can't yet it isn't,
   but soon will be.
Sooner than was,
   but later than is.
Was after now,
   but before then.
Hasn't yet happened,
   and soon will have past.

Later than before,
   sooner than later.
Closer than that,
   yet father than this.
A little bit of now,
   and yet more of later.
And is yet, and
   never to be now!

Marshall W. Lile

Alma

She said she was allergic to dust
But we were pretty sure it was
   cleaning she was allergic to.
She sat in her beveled house
Fancy, grand, on the hills of course,
And dictated the morés
   of the people in our town.
She was an awesome sight.
Folks said that once a month
She went to the city
For the Treatment
And came back twenty years younger.

She lived by herself, for herself,
And of herself
Just as our Constitution says.

But Alma was her most spectacular
That day, made up by specialists,
Dressed in sequins and silver
Against the coffin lining.

Myra L. DeChaine

Butterflies: New Life

I look out at you each morning
Butterflies symbolize new life
I think of each day's dawning
Sometimes filled with strife
As I watch you at the flowers
You have a purpose there
And so do I, I can find hope,
new meaning and people who really care
Oh, beautiful Butterflies
made by our Creator's hand
How special at the window
As I go thru sifting sand
For tomorrow is Forever
But today brings new life and change
And like your metamorphis
I too, can break my cocoon
And find answers within my range.

Shirley Campbell Horton

Untitled

A sunny six pack sitting
by an open window

A cool breeze flowing
Through the hot music
Hits me
Hard enough to knock me to my feet
To shake my hips to the beat
I look up and give thanks
That I can dance dance dance

And that the window was
open

Gustavo Acosta

So Long

   The years have flown
by its almost time to
move on, it hurts deep
inside to see you go,
Our time has been short
but I won't cry even though
its hard to say good-bye.
I want you to know
I'll miss you, as we part
I'll tell you once more I love
you more than ever before
all I want to ask you is
please don't say good-bye.

Malena Given

The Choice

Deuteronomy says it all:
   Choose life! - Or, death's appall.
She heard The Voice
They made The Choice
To spare a life
To face the strife
To care and nurse
For better or worse

Rita A. Merritts

I've

I've Been Seduced
By Sin

I've Been Abused
By The Madness
Of The man
Within

I've Been Reduced
By A Mindless
Whim

Led Upon A Tour
By A Blindman
Who Swore
He Could See
And What He Saw
Swore He'd Win

I've Been Obliged
To Choose
A New Road
To Begin

Robert Andrew Montefusco

"The Bay"

I walked along to-day,
By, the beautiful shimmering bay
I gazed out to the sea,
It reminded me of things to be.

The rocks that lay upon the shore,
Brought memories of the past that I adore,
The waves dashing so free,
Reawakened, wonderful years to me.

The azure blue of the sky,
Sea gulls gliding by,
Soft white clouds, like billowing cotton,
Awakened memories, long forgotten.

I bowed my head, in silent prayer,
Thank God that they're still there,
For others to share with me,
The awesome delight of the sea.

Nola G. Ramsey

My Little Dream

My little dream
   came many years ago.
She became reality
   ever so slow.

My little dream
   such a small package indeed.
So sweet and innocent,
   stay that way I plead.

My little dream
   so treasured and rare.
What a beautiful life,
   we will share.

My little dream
   fills my heart with love.
I thank the good Lord
   in the skies above.

My little dream
   threw me for such a whirl.
My little dream,
   is my new baby girl.

Rhonda K. Hogan

Can You See Jesus?

Can you see Jesus in you?
Can you see Jesus in me?
Does His life come shining through
So that all the world may see?

Do we behave as He did
When He walked upon this earth?
Or do we blink an eyelid
And continue with our mirth?

Do our actions give a clue
To what He wants us to be?
Can our lives pass in review,
And will they be found sin-free?

Would Jesus do as we do
In order to have some fun?
Shouldn't we His life pursue
And listen for His "Well done"?

As we seek to walk with Him
We should leave the world behind,
Let the love of it grow dim,
And in Christ our joy to find.

Mary L. Shelton

Grandchildren

Carrots on his fingers
Carrots on his toes
Some actually made it to his little mouth
More was smeared upon his nose.

Carrots on his forehead
Carrots on his knees
Here comes another mouthful
Please! Oh please! Don't sneeze. Yum!

May I have a cookie? Please?
Eyebrows raised in question sweet
I know he'd think a cookie
Quite a treat for him to eat.

But, with his busy little hands
He crumbles it upon his tray
And with an impish little grin
He swishes it away.

Tsk! Tsk! Tsk! No more today!

Sandra Greiwe

Unusual Animal Life

Dogs are hogs.
Cats were hats.
Birds come in herds.
Fishes have wishes.
Mice are nice.
Worms always swarm,
Bunnies are honeys.
Beavers are weavers.
Monkies are honkies.
Bees pay fees.
Hens live in dens,
Cubs eat subs.
Otters have daughters.
Animals are weird aren't they?

Michelle Calhoun

"The Magic"

An Illusionist sat wiping his tears,
Cause his "magic" no longer brought cheers.
But, unwilling to quit,
He smiled as he sit
And said, "It's not as bad
as it appears."

Teresa Heilman

Summer

Summer memories like
chocolate linger:
Inboard motors rumbly, rumbling
on Marine stadium waters.
The smell of mown grass fresh
Children murmur playing
mumblety-peg.
Kittens mewing mom's milk pleading.
Full moon orange hung low
over the marsh
Minus mooing cow to jump over.
Steeple bells muffled by
municipal order
Memories echo louder
And Laura La Bar humming.

Susan E. Crockett

Ghosts

A vague hint of whispered scent,
Christmases long past,
A Halloween mask.
A card made of hugs and kisses,
Love and good wishes.
A smiling face on the mantle.
A birthday candle.
Teddy bears with tattered faces.
A shoe without laces.
A voice that calls from the wind
Searching for a friend.
Silent tears only I can hear,
In my heart she is near.
These are the ghosts that haunt me
Even in my sleep.

Teresa Dezern McKinney

Funny Things

Birds got funny legs,
Clams got funny lips,
Scallops have the bluest eyes,
And Snakes got skinny hips.

Bears waddle when they walk,
And Rats have draggy tails,
Bumble Bees got funny wings,
And Fish have silver scales.

Horses all have funny feet,
And Porkies funny spines,
Elephants the longest nose,
And Zebras funny lines.

Hyenas have a funny laugh,
Raccoons a silly grin,
Bats they all sleep upside down,
And Owls have head's that spin.

Frogs, they all have funny tongues,
Chimpanzees a funny hand,
But the one who takes the cake, I say,
Is the species known as Man.

F. L. Darling

Untitled

You shadow me with dead rain.
Cliff edges are in your eyes,
the coming of clouds in your dreams.
Locks of spoken words
entangled in broken wind,
yet your eyes look low upon me.

Mika Handelman

At Command

Quiet.

Be very still.

Can you hear it?
    Close your eyes -
    Listen very closely.

    - (it's hissing) -

WHY ARE YOU BEING SO QUIET!

RAISE your voice,
    SHOUT your prejudices OUTLOUD!

WHO told you to be so quiet
    and WHY do you always LISTEN!

Why do you play dead
    when you are told.
- Why are you yelling at me -
Apologize and say -
    thank you.

Breathe, you damn fools.

Be still.

Wendy C. Riesterer

Days Alone

Darkness, blackness, velvet night
Clouds hide starlight from our sight.
Thunder, lightning, terror, flight
Emptiness.

Husband, lover, sweetheart, friend,
When will darkness ever end?
All to thee, my love I send
Forever.

From the past, we've come somehow.
And in that past I made my vow.
When will our future days be now?
Silence.

Though for a time, apart we stay.
Constantly for you I pray
Hoping soon for light of day
Together.

Mellie E. Miller

'Magic Man'

When first he took me
By the hand,
I thought he was
A magic man.
But, the hand is quicker
Than the eye —
He never even said
Goodbye.

Phee Richards

Whispering Sands

the beaches horizon
confuses and eludes
it paints a solid picture
that comforts and soothes

whispering sands
delight and entice
each grain mystifies
with wondrous spice

it rolls and it curls
to the beat of the wind
the softness possessed
could never be dimmed

the world could learn
from the whispering sands
that we're all tiny specks
in God's mighty hands
Robert Lesco

The Quest For Divinity

The essence of our existence
Consideration should be imperative

Establish a precise foundation
Its beneficial in your search

Acknowledge the absolute source
Demonic energy is discrete

Seek all that is pure
Acquire its caring sense

Pursue all the testimony
It will render you the truth

Confess always in prayer
Recognize the substance of reality

Our assurance is the message
The nature of our concern

Faith is what we hope
Certain of what we do not see

Perseverance produces character
Character displays belief
William H. Krueger Jr.

Old Grandma Thompson

Old Grandma Thompson baked
cookies all day.
 She took a short walk while
the children were at play.

 When she got back to her house
all that she found
was the displeasing pleasure
of a mouse on the ground.

 She searched through the house
and all she could find
were the crumbs from the cookies
that they left behind.
Kyle Thompson

Said She

What a world this would be, if I
 could break free
I'd do things so different, I'd be the
 real me.
Oh yes, I could paint or sail the
 high seas
I'd write the great novel or walk
 among trees
What a world this could be, if
 I broke away
I'd never count hours, I'd breathe
 in the day
I'd fill up my soul with wonderful
 things
I'd be so contented - my heart would
 grow wings
What world this would be,
 said she, at sixty three.
Mary J. Tippett

Will To Shine

Tragedies in our life
could destroy ones will to live,
our happiness no longer shines
our emotions are not free to give.
You awaken every morning
wanting it to end,
you just exist, lost somewhere
hoping soon your heart will mend.
Then one day, given time
you awaken and can see,
your strength has truly shone for you
you've gotten through this tragedy.
What triggered my emotions?
I feel alive again,
Did I forget or just accept?
Have I moved on - but when?
It's not that you forget
you simply let it fade,
accept what you can't change
this too is what God has made.
Lisa Roy

"Simply Love"

How simple!
Count to One
For you to find
Your own True Love.

One thought,
One mind,
One being,
One Love,
This is the stuff
We're all made of.

When One finds it,
It helps all,
For the Love of One
Is the love of all.

Let's begin now
And count to One
For all to find
Their One True Love!
Mary Louise Palumbo

Yes I Am Woman

Yes I am woman
created from flesh of a man
but I need not a man
to make me whole
for my strength
comes from within my soul

I want to be all that I can
on my own two feet
I will stand
shall I fall, I will rise again
why do you ask
because woman I am

Here I am, proclaiming myself
independence is what I'm made of
I need not a man for his money
nor his pity
all I need is his love
and if that he can not give
then I need not a man at all.
Monique Z. Mbarga

Untitled

A thousand leaves
danced on the limb of
a single tree. Harmony
whispered in the wind and
the sun was a symphony
 Rows of dancers
line the walk, the sound
of foot steps, the faint
echo of idle talk.
 An applause of
traffic glides by this
lonely street, while the
angels began to sigh and weep.
 Few had taken
notice the orchestra
of natures way. They've
missed the gift of
solitude in this moment
of the day.
Wayne A. Check

Native American

Tall
Dark
Proud Men
Died for their country not of sin
To keep the land their ancestors hold
Till the first white man came for gold
Many were shot
Many were killed
Many are buried on the hill
So proud to live
So proud to die
To keep their kin alive
Their culture lost
Their land dying
But many keep on trying
They want to see before their gone
The land their ancestors loved so long
Raechel Wempen

Untitled

Two o'clock in the morning
Dark as jet,
Thoughts running wild,
Voices of old friends
Ringing in my ears
Touch of old loves,
Running cold.
Ruby lips,
Taste of salt in my tears.
Throaty laughter
Deep and clear,
Big band music,
Beautiful girls,
Handsome boys gliding by,
Floor so slippery
Can't stand up -
Music stops
Everyone's gone
Black as jet.

C. W. Genszler

Adoration Gone Sour

Always
dealing with
overly sensitive emotions.
Rare occurrences in private
and
timely glances.
Instead of being
overjoyed at your presence, I am
nauseated.

Sheri L. Wesson

Voices

Cold wet smoke of repression
defending the remote unconscious
against colonization
by an ego
abstracted to unreality
where pain was hardened
to succulent jewels
dissolved in the stale mouths
of gossips.

Wilbur J. Childs

Isn't Life Strange

Life is what you make of it
Depends upon your style,
Because you have the power
To make it worth your while.

Sometimes you may not have control
Of things that come your way,
So try to make the best of it
And live each day, by day.

And when some people make mistakes
The others criticize,
But when you do the right thing
They turn and close their eyes.

I know, because I've been there
And from my experience,
You feel as though you're put on trial
And no one comes to your defense.

I hope that in the future
These people, look and see,
That when it comes down to it
They are no better than me.

Sharlene Frazier

Happy Birthday

There is sorrow in the air
Despair is everywhere
Where did the last year go?
Where so many have gone before

Aches and pains you start to feel
All of life seems uphill
When you strain to be someone
The pain you feel will not heal

Yet there is a spark of light
Barely able to be seen at night
and when you wish upon a star
You think the spark can be seen from afar

But from afar there is nothing
and from close there is less
Has the whole world passed you by
What have you missed?

At this frantic time
You look for some hope
But there is none
And tomorrow you strive no more

Robert J. Stilwell

Did You Mean It?

When you said you loved me...
Did you mean it?
I did
When you said you cared...
Were you telling the truth?
I was
When you said we'd be forever...
Did you want it?
I did.
When you broke my heart...
Did you mean to?
When you say your sorry...
Do you mean it?
How can I tell?
I said I love you, and I do.
I said I care, and I always will.
I thought we'd be forever,
but I was wrong,
and for that I'm sorry.
Can we at least be friends?

Todd Michael Vittoria

Paradise

Happy
enjoying life
in a place
where time stops
her eyes
filled
with excitement
her thoughts
in lost times
her small smile
spreading
slowly
across her face
as she stares
into space
in a black and
white world

Lisa Murphy

Borderlines

As the world turns,
as days pass,
they say things change,
not borderlines.

We see the world over the top of walls
of steel, through iron bars.

Why do we hide?
Why do we divide?

Ever since the human race came to
earth to stay, we've lived this way.

Some say this way, helps
peace and order stay.

But how many friends have been
made across a fence of chain?

A fence is to defend,
not make amends.

Yet peace begins with friends,
with enemies it ends.

Why are we so blind? Is it because
we lives our lives by borderlines?

Lisa Newman

Untitled

Broken sand dollars on Sandy Shores
Discarded dreams forgotten.

Soft whispers on the wind
Voices of those gone.

Raindrops of tears
A crooked smile to hide the pain.

Shattered pieces of glass
A heart broken.

Petals fall from a wilted rose
Hopes crushed and delusioned.

Soft brown eyes of a wounded doe
Loneliness surrounds you.

A clock with no hands, no time to tell
Future plans misplaced, discarded.

hazy reflections in smoky windowpanes
Tumultuous thoughts unspoken

A gentle touch of a baby's hand
Things best not remembered

A bright light at tunnels end
Fading fast...just beyond a grasp.

Nyta Dooley

Careless Heart

Careless Heart,
Do you not listen?
Told you to be careful,
Did you not hear?
Told you not to fall;
You did not heed my warning.
Now you are broken
And I must feel the pain.

Keli Adell Killingsworth

Under The Sun

When you look at me what do you see?
Do you think I even care,
Or does it seem like every word.
Or every thought from everyone
Means everything Under The Sun

A touch for comfort, just a word,
Do you think inside me burns
To feel belonging to the world,
A longing deep for promised sleep,
A shoulder from everyone Under The Sun?

A passing glance into a trance
Does it seem to make me dread
Or furious at looking dead
To everyone who passes me,
From everywhere Under The Sun?

With every broken piece of me
Do you know I am being sold
In little chips for chunks of gold
But everyone that I hold dear
Is every person, in my dream,
That pertains to anyone and everyone
Under The Sun?

Melinda Martin

Don't Forget

Don't forget the sound of his voice
Don't forget his baby eyes
He left so suddenly and painfully
Sheltered by dreadful lies

Don't forget the tears you shared
Don't forget the laughter and shouts
He always said he would be here to care
Instead he found the quickest way out

Don't forget the touch of his hand
Don't forget the plans that were made
His last words of his love
On his bed, which we laid

Don't forget him, no matter what
While standing at his graveside crying
He died instantly, feeling no pain
After being hit by a man, drinking and driving.

Linda Barela

Gift Of Friendship

In all your many travels,
Down life's bumpy road.
You may fill the weakening,
From such a heavy load.

One thing you must remember,
You're never there alone.
But it may seem at times,
As you turn, look, they're gone.

They're not always in site,
At all times, you should know.
With each happiness and sorrow,
In each heart, you both shall go.

Traveling through life together,
Helps brighten each others day.
Once you have the gift of friendship,
Know one can take it away.

Mike Nowlin

Okinawa Night

The crew chief was waiting
Down on the line
E models were rumbling
As turbo props whine

I was on the night shift
The duty was fine
Cause the days were long and lonesome
But the Okinawa night was mine

The barracks were quiet
Except for the roar
As engines turned over
When I opened the door

I Stopped for a moment
In the tropic moonlight
And felt the wonder
Of an Okinawa night

The trade winds kept blowing
The sea grass on the hill
As I headed for the flight line
The Okinawa night grew still

Richard G. Micka

The Burning Candle

Alone one walks,
Down the vast, cold
Streets of life,

Eager to satisfy
The incessant yearnings within.
But feelings of

Discouragement, despair and bewilderment
Assail the mind.
Let not these emotions

Alter one's predisposition.
Remember, life is like
A lighted candle

In the breeze;
One lacks the knowledge
Of knowing when

An abrupt wind
Will subside
This vital flame.

Sounthaly Neena Thattanakham

My Light

Every day we
Dream our dreams,
Shine our lights
Fight our fights
The struggle each day is nothing new
Some how we just make it through
Grab my hand, don't let go
Squeeze it tight, here we go
Be brave stand firm
Or we will fall
There's someone there
To stop us all
Don't look back
To see who's there
He's in our shadow's everywhere
My wings will guide us safely to
The man in white who sees us through
All our troubles will be sent away
When faith brings hope in every way

Sonya Andrus

Autumn

The autumn winds
Drift slowly through the trees,
Bringing down around them
Red and orange leaves.

As I look in wonder
And pure delight,
My heart swells
As I behold this beautiful sight.

The colors so true
Unusual and yet the same,
Every year I feel it
A beauty beholding, without any pain.

It lightens your heart
When your feeling unsure,
Because God's creation
Is wondrous and pure.

Treica Winkler

Untitled

Dreams
   drifting in and out of lonely nights,
   changing shape and color
   elude the light of day.
But you, my love, are here
   strong and warm—
A dream in my arms.

Karen Nordmann

Hummingbird

Abundant nectar and blossoms full,
Drink until sweet intoxication.

Little bird over my shoulder,
Darting, flying, here and there,
Perched upon a wire high.

Warrior colors and feathers wide;
Ready, swift, acrobat.
Guard your fountain, pool of sugar,
Chatter, chatter, don't talk back.

Medy Dronet

Dungarvan Water Dance

Night comes quickly
dropping her star-studded velvet drape
across the green hills,
tucking in the distant villages
till Morning's arrival.

Brightly colored row boats
tired from the day
nestle-bob peacefully
along the harbor's wall.

The Moon's light
spills her still song
along the silent waters.

And the waters gracefully dance,
dance toward the twinkling shore.

The waters keep on Dancing
dancing, dancing

Yes, the waters
keep on dancing,
dancing toward the twinkling shore.

Kathleen Galvin Grimaldi

Sunlight Through Evergreens

bathes my
drowsy unclothed body
warm silent water
covers my eyes
runs over my neck
breasts
legs
and lingers at my feet.
A tinkling creek
breezes
awakens me
as shivers
race
down my arms.
Sunlight through evergreens
dries my skin
as warmth
embraces
my soul.

Lauree Sayler

Anniversary

Twin projectors flicker
dust and light
across a space too cluttered, tight
with time and need,
to clear a path the way most do
with simple shovel, sweat, bared teeth.

But elevated each,
at proper height,
beams forth beside the other, bright
in word and deed,
to glance a medium unseen
then bend, refracted, so to meet.

Nancy Middleton

A Dream Of Love

I walk through the day in pain,
Dwelling on every little thing,
I throw down ideas,
Like the drops of rain,
Some collect in puddles,
While others go down the drain.

Love is a conflict,
Which we all must endure,
The broken hearts and flowing tears,
The cashed out bowls,
And the empty beers.

The classic virgin,
Innocent and pure,
Love is a disease,
It has no cure.

Kenneth Hammer

Oceans

The water seems cold, dark, deep
Dying off in numbers while we sleep
Feed each other from scraps of flesh
Caught in oil, trapped in mesh
Gasoline smell on which they feed
So corrupted they cannot breed
A whole new ocean is what they need
Millions of miles away from you and me
Save the earth last
Need a rebirth fast
Kingdom come thy will be done
Save them all before their gone!

Ronald R. Neslein

Untitled

Stars in the sky
Each blink out with a day gone by.

Slowly falling.
Years go by.
Youth is over.

Growing up too fast,
Or at least seems so.

Kindergarten,
Nothing mattered
Except an untied shoe.
You might trip!

Tripping
Down you go,
You can't get back up.

No one is there
To help you up!

There goes another star.
Another day just blinked out.

Katherine L.W. Krazmien

That Part Of Me

There's a part of me I lose,
each time I go away.
When I have to say goodbye,
knowing I want to stay.

That part of me I lose,
I watch it drift away.
When I have to say goodbye,
knowing I want to stay.

Stephanie Rushton

Twilight Magic

Darkness descends upon the
earth like a veil covers a
grieving widow's face.
The silence is deafening as day,
is by night replaced.

The shadows move on silent
winds as they dance on unseen wings.
This is just the beginning of the
lovely sights that twilight always brings.

The petals soft flowers bend
and bow to the night,
As stillness comes across the
land behind fast fading light.

Shelia Petrey

Early Morning

Early morning, seen through my
eyes is dark, and cold and lonely;
yet I'm not afraid.
For there are many, who know
my fears, and know my pain.
We are the people called the weak,
the helpless, and the blind,
But in reality; we are the strong;
the fearless and the brave.
Go forward to learn;
not backwards to remember.

Thomas E. Farris

Carrie

I was six; she was seven.

School paste whispers
Edible plastic scent.
White cells swell
Her blood.

Orange chill leaves
Cracker slap feet.
Red Rover Red Rover
Send Carrie right over!
Leukemia blasts fast
Her blood.

Raining music drops
Angelic cedar sound.
Hopscotch heaven wins
Her life.

I was six; she was dead.

Kelly Krenning

Watch

Watch me
  emerge from the ashes
Become something no one smashes

Watch me
  as my thoughts take form
  as I walk away from the norm

Watch me
  as my soul ascends into the sky
  as I become cosmically alive

Watch me
  as I become whole
As I venture inward for more

Watch me
  as I destroy the teeth
Of shallow thought and belief

Watch
  for when you recognize what I am
  I will no longer be there for you to
understand

Marcotulio Camacho-Martinez

Be Yourself

Be yourself -
False fronts fool no one.

Be conscientious -
Dryrot can destroy a mansion.

Set goals and climb the ladder
One rung at a time.

Recognize your faults -
A leaky roof can be repaired.

Be assertive -
So the life you live is your own
not the shadow of another.

Victoria Strash

Precious Time

Time is a precious thing
Equal portions for commoners and kings
Precious time from God is given.
Pack it full of joyful living.

Each day presents opportunities
The dressing room for eternity
Fill each day with faithful duty
To the best of your ability.

The present moment is supreme
Strive to fulfill your dearest dreams.
Service to mankind denote.
For tomorrow is a promissory note.

Time is the passing of life
Spread joy not a strife
Time will spent today
Makes tomorrow a better day.

Live life without regret
As the hours you regiment
Your days are numbered by the Lord
Trust and obey his holy word.

Shirley Brigham

Steppin'

Steppin' through the alley of my life
Ever steppin' — a constant fight.
Steppin' to the corner blues
Got no time for hearsay views.
Steppin' off the syndrome high
   To the people's cry.
Steppin' to the rhythm of my heart
   A definite start.
Steppin' from a tear to a smile
In tune to a new born child.
Steppin' right beside my mate
Life's pleasures limited by fate.
Steppin' from dawn to midnight
Into the sunlight.
Steppin' to the music of my mind;
Steppin', steppin', steppin' all the time...

BitterHoney Scott-Joynes

Careless Heart

Why do you run and hide from life,
Every chance that you get,
Has a love from your bitter past,
Made your heart sad and lonely,
I know you need and want love,
You're just afraid to start,
I know that I'm not your first love,
I can wait and be your last,
I will steal you away,
From a careless heart.

Melvin Thayer

Rain

Sitting Alone
Feeling Sad
Not a Body Around
Undecided
Actions
Passive Reactions
Popular Opinion
Losing Opposition
Nothing worse than a Rainy Day alone.

Matt Garadis

Untitled

Fragile connections to
everything
from a distance,
with no commitment, no responsibility
like icy-hot Teflon coated bullets
training, weaving
gossamer tendrils
voiceless thoughts
through space
in air
of whispers
of faint
echoes
on
webs of
fragile connections.

Maria Markovic Cathcart

The Preacher's Kid

As a preacher's kid I heard say,
"Evil tempts us day to day-so-
To the Lord we must pray."
When my eighteenth year came 'round
I was bound for Tinseltown —
Mama did scold and preacherman told
The wages of sin;
I left the fold.
Still not heeding what I knew
The place I craved I ventured to
There I sang my heartbreak songs
Aware that I did not belong.
Many years and tears - did take -
To learn I made the big mistake,
I should have reached for stars at night
Instead - I reached for neon lights.
From the pulpit I now pray,
(For all sinners gone astray)
"Save us Lord from evil ways."

Laura Witkin-Kaufman

The Rose Bush

They sat beside me
Exchanging words of love,
Holding hands, the girl and he,
Beneath the moon above.

I was so young
And so were they
As their faces hung
Together, so dear, that day.

I saw their kiss
And sweet caress
In joy and bliss
That had no stress.

As the sun came down
I unfolded my flower;
It was like a crown
To approve their hour.

Parting, the lovers went;
Heartsick, I bloom alone,
Old, and all glory spent
As my last rose feels like stone.

Phyllis Breves

Shadows in the Night

Remove your mask
experience the joys of life
leave out the pain.
The sun does not shine for one reason,
so you can feel my heart tonight
in the October rain.

We will soon come together
through the mischief of the night
where we will lose our shame.
We will then live forever
unmoved by the loss of light
since we will feel the same.

Steve Liarakos

Wayward Soldier

He wore a hospital bracelet
Face brownish-red like leather
A cough growled from his depths
From living each day by the weather.

Eyes locked in endless surveillance
Gray stubble speckled his face
Hair as white as if from fright
Mouthing disgust at the human race.

He spoke of the wars he'd known
And the dangers of the street
He looked around and whispered
Of being rolled while fast asleep.

He huddled eyes down and shaking
Spent last night in the rain
Waiting for government money
A soldier's reward that never came.

(Writer's Note: This man was no bum,
he was homeless
Never asked me for a dime
I shared with him my coffee
And I wrote for him this rhyme.)

Sandee W. Daniels

The Magic Wheel

So soft upon the summer's air
Faint strains have lured her to the fair.
He's waiting there, so tall and white,
So handsome in the dazzling light.

Bejeweled, the charger stands at bay
Inviting her to ride away.
Enchanted scenes call from afar.
Perhaps they'll even touch a star.

With hot blood racing in her veins,
She leaps astride and grabs the reins.
The shivers down her spine are cold.
Flashing by is a ring of gold.

Around they fly, but in dismay
Feel time race by as fast as they.
Dismounting then, and teary-eyed,
She gathers up the dreams that died.

Willie Ann Gurlacz

Etiolation (Lilies for Medusa)

Filigree of serpents
entwined within
this corporeal coil

Matthew L. Anderson

On The Grave Of My Baby Grandson Eric

Sweet rain above,
  Fall softly here

Swift winds about,
  Blow gently here

Bright moonlight glow,
  Shine sweetly here.

Do not disturb my sleep.
Silvia Cirne Parker

Autumn Of Life

I saw the autumn leaves
falling; and arrayed in color so fair.
I knew the Lord had painted
them and placed them so beautifully there.
Like the leave's I too
was; in the Autumn of
life with His paint brush
He silvered my hair, and
on my face he painted a
story of a life that's been
placed in His care. Ever so
gently a line of love, a
line of grace, He painted
in wonderful hue's for
other's to observe the
beauty of life, with a
celestial land in view.
Over there time is endless
no season's life Autumn,
or spring. Yet t'will be a
place of glory
for there we'll dwell with our king!
Peggy L. Herron

A Child's Love

To sacrifice one's
  family ties
When a yearning for love
  is unfulfilled.
To open one's arms and
  reveal a warming heart,
Heed not to seek
  this parental advice.
So deny that name
  which is so unworthy
  of someone so loving,
  honest and caring.
Revel in this new life
Overabundant with love.
Marvelling at a child's antics
Treasuring such precious moments
Like the wondrous colors
  of the rainbow,
This is the true
  pot of gold.
Mary Lou Tillinger

Dreams

Dreams are fragile
For if dreams die
life, like a shattered mirror,
we cannot deny.
Lucie Ciciarelli

Seasons

Listen to the Spring,
  Feel it bring to the lips
    A song of happiness on wings.

Listen to the summer,
  Hear the cheers at games people play,
    Growing to a roar at end of day.

Listen to the Autumn,
  See the leaves turn many colors,
    Then dance away, one, then another.

Listen, look and see, the Winter
  With it's cover of white, white snow,
    And the silence of the cold.

We, like the seasons,
  Sing out songs, play our games,
    And dance our time away,
    Then, like winter, become silent.

Count the days my friends,
  Make the most of what they give;
    And in each fleeting moment,
    Enjoy...Enjoy...Enjoy.
Virginia Holzkamp

September

September days, soft and golden
Filled with promises for keeping
September makes one beholden
For God's gentleness - no weeping.

September days all gold and green
Seem etch'd 'gainst skies of purple blue
This oddity goes all unseen
Lest we peer closely, me and you.

September days tho they linger
Soft and sweet and a paler hue
They follow God's tracing finger
As He show His way to me and you.
Ruby Nifong Tesh

Broken Freedom

Mystic Music
Fills my soul
Careless hearts
Are yours to hold
Cold feeling on a pain of glass
Feel the mist
A journey through the sun and rain
In a clench fist
Something fills my soul
With happiness but then pulls it back
It seems like mold
Mystic sounds
Are yours to hold
Fills my soul
Cold chill of the past
Now you may regret
One friend that's destined to die
Now...you let him go —
  Corner clouds of the east
  I do not express.
Sam Jade
Alias David Michael Conway

My Unknown Certainty

My soul will be forever changing
First life then death next the unknown
Desiring only the perfect final resting
I simply want to return home

But home for me will always be
The life I've surely lived on earth
Complexities of my life and purgatory
Between heaven and hell I have no worth

My path was prepared long ago
There's nothing to do except be me
Entering into the unknown is my fortune
I've accepted whenever my resting will be

Where, I wished I could truly say
With certainly no doubts or wavering
About the unknown of my after life
That has given birth to my obsession

Being good or bad is worthless now
My diary will painfully be closing
Still, I wish I could speak honestly
About my unknown certainty.
Robert L. Miller Jr.

First Things First

First the larva, then the bee;
First the seed, then the tree.
  FIRST THINGS FIRST
First the bricks, then the school;
First the school, then the pool.
  FIRST THINGS FIRST
First the bee, then the honey;
First the work, then the money.
  FIRST THINGS FIRST
First the tooth, then the fairy;
First the ring, then the merry.
  FIRST THINGS FIRST
First my mom, then comes me;
That's the way God planned it to be.
Nathan Arnold

Lady Luck

Lady Luck is a fickle one
Flirts at will as she pleases
She's a coquette surpassed by none
And cares not whom she teases.

She's a one-sided little wench
Who will lead you on and on
If not careful your hopes she'll wrench
And leave you sad when they're gone.

Lady Luck is a game of chance
One you seldom win but lose
No matter what the circumstance
There is no way you can choose.

Her playful personality
Belies her kindly spirit
For Lady Luck in reality
Will come to those who earn it.
Lucienne Corriveau Walker

Termination

In my mind are darkened shadows
floating and swirling and taking form
into creatures without shape or substance
grabbing, reaching...to carry me away

No one hears my continuous screams
there's no one here to listen
The cries of terror are in my mind
hidden away from all possible salvation

I cannot see the battered hands
that's pushing me from reality
As an inescapable force keeps dragging me
to my own destruction
  Tenna F. Stafford

Floating

A sailing ship
floating upon currents in the sea

Silently
it moves in its direction

Existence
floats upon the currents of life

Silently
it moves in its direction

Each appear guided
A hand firmly at the tiller

Yet
Each are subject
to the winds of change

Each
subject to the currents of life

Each
afraid yet aware, choosing to move
Sailing
willingly
into the unknown
  Richard Mednick

"Pen"

Thoughts like a river
Flow from my pen
Feelings spill out
Through the ink
My own life's blood
Emotions soak the page
Bring to life
This dead piece of paper
A piece of the soul
Covers a piece of the tree
It sets aflame
The forest of my mind
The fire within
Drives me so
Nothing can keep me from my pen
My paper
The veins of my soul are cut
It bleeds forth
Onto the tree.
  Todd Thatcher

Free As A Butterfly

Butterfly, butterfly
  flying free.
Would that I
  could join with thee.

Flitting here
  and lighting there.
Existence filled
  without a care.

No bills to pay,
  no job you hate.
I could live
  with such a fate.

Butterfly, butterfly
  flying free.
Where e'er you're going,
  please take me.
  Linda DiCristina

The Anchor

Jesus is the Anchor
For all my life on earth;
Be is the one I must adore.
The source of my new birth!

Jesus keeps me safely
Fastened to Him, the Rock;
Keeps me from what's deadly
Guides me in His flock!

Jesus prevents my heart
From drifting far from God
He's the unshakable — ne'er to part;
Only security on the sod!
  Susan M. Aderman

Be Happy For Me

Be happy for me
For even though I am gone,
I still exist.
BE HAPPY FOR ME
For now I see, and breath,
only that of beauty.
BE HAPPY FOR ME
For now I will protect, and
watch over you.
BE HAPPY FOR ME
for my undying love will mend
your broken heart.
BE HAPPY FOR ME
For now I am truly free.
BE HAPPY FOR ME
For again we shall meet.
BE HAPPY FOR ME
and I for you.
BE HAPPY FOR ME
  Kymberly Henderson Graham

My Prayer

I knelt in humble thanks to pray
For God's prodigious gift of day.
I closed my eyes His face to see
That I might feel Him nearer me.
With grateful heart my blessings viewed -
For they are many, brightly-hued -
I let them sing a melody
To God in their infinity.
I thanked my God for this day's peace,
For all its beauty He released,
For every trial that I surpassed.
His infinite love that held me fast,
His mercy for a slave so weak
Who all too often knows defeat.
And, yet, with faith I can reach Him
And touch His golden diadem...
With faith I climbed His throne's steep stair
And left my soul to linger there.
  Wray Christine Stewart Jones

Ignorance

  I do not see you
For I cannot hear
  I do not hear you
For I cannot see
  I do not speak
For you will not listen
  I am not weak
I am a strong person

  You are a stubborn bastard
Society reflects your fate
  Your time is coming
So you just wait

  No sweeter time will be
When your presence leaves me
  Paul A. Pelon IV

The Mountain

I come to the mountain
For it knows my name
It calls out to me
Calling, calling, calling

I come to the foothills
To stand
And I feel grounded in
It's awesome serenity and peace

I stand atop the mountain
Looking out into the vastness below
Amongst the clouds I feel
The endless ebbs of time

I am safe on the mountain
For it knows my people
It was here before they came
It survives when they are gone

I come to the mountain
Seeking answers
And it replies
I am, I am, I am
  Trish A. Holmes

Memories

Memories were made
For moms to cherish
When daughters grow up
Move away and marry

It seems you only just arrived
When it's time to say good-bye
Time has stolen you away
Memories, I need you now

Don't give me diamonds
Don't give me gold
Give me my little one
Once again to hold

Build for today
As there's no tomorrows
Or special memories
You will seek from someone to borrow.

Linda Wilkinson

My Aunt

The Clock ticks very fast
for my Aunt is gone away
I can't imagine how you feel
with you so high and me so low
I will never know how you feel
For you have left in sorrow

Then today, I write to you
to tell you how I feel
for only if I could of said
Goodbye just once
But I couldn't
so I'll say it now

Goodbye

Maria Moraga

Untitled

He smoked his pot an awful lot.
For ten years I had gagged and sneezed.
I'd often say "Your mind will rot,"
And "My God, listen to you wheeze."
He enjoyed the roach at breakfast.
A joint for lunch and dinner too.
Blood shot eyes and hacking would last
As Mary Jane is nearly through.
No more could I take the beatings
When he would get drunk and/or stoned.
From the dope head I was fleeing
Once again, safely on my own.
"God help me," I had prayed each night.
Yes, leaving to live. That was right.

Susan M. H. Erskine

Entreaty

Be gentle with her, God,
For she's my mother
And I love her.
She softly rests on angels' wings
Awaiting what each new day brings...
So fragile now, transparent, frail,
Let dignity alone prevail.
And someday through eternity
She'll live with thee and not with me;
Attend her as she once watched me
When I was small and knew not thee...
Be gentle with her, Lord,
This treasure is my mother.

Virginia P. Oren

"Unseen Love"

No one can give you,
for they have not received.
Nor can anyone show you,
for they have not seen.
Neither can anyone tell you;
for they have not heard.
I'm the one who told you,
for I know all your needs.
Am I not the one who showed you,
fore I've done the greatest deeds.
Who was the one giving you all
the love you'll ever need?
But it was all unseen,
due to your selfish greed.
Now that you know this my love;
come to me with great speed.
Fore if you linger long my dear,
I fear our love won't be...

Ursula A. Flynn

Life

Life is full of dreams
   for those who cherish it.
Life is full of wonders
   for those who want it.
Life is full of love
   for those who accept it.
Life is full of hope
   for those who need it.
Life is full of terror
   for those who are afraid.
And life is full of happiness
   for everyone.

Sara Weisfelner

Untitled

Seagulls gracefully soaring
Forest fires a roaring
Animals feeding on grassy plains
From grass grown by acid rains
Seals playing in the snow
Silenced by a club's heavy blow
Fish swimming in the ocean
Dying from pollution potion
Man continues to destroy this earth
Never considering his lowly self worth
We live on
For how long?

Millie Leuz

Drifting Away

I saw you in the clouds today
   Floating freely
     Drifting away.

I heard you in the breeze today
   Whispering sweetly
     What did you say?

I felt your hand on my cheek today
   Caressing softly
     Like a sunray

I kept you in my heart today
   Constantly dreaming
     Drifting away.

Margaret Gilbert

Dear

You cursed the expense.
For what? You said
terrine and cheese.

No, it was the wine,
I said in silence,
the passion thirst
that costs.

Instead I tried to
spread the taste
into your mouth.

A farewell kiss
to bid my price, as you
climbed in a cab
to go six blocks.

I walked ten or twelve,
I didn't count,

Yes, along the Limmat
part gone with you.

Sonjia Weinstein

The Bar Mitzvah

Today was quite a day,
For you and yours alike,
As you attained a milestone
In the journey of your life.

You've studied the traditions
And the rituals of your faith;
You read the Torah and perform Mitzvot
As your heritage does dictate.

Health and happiness is wished for you
On this very special day.
May wisdom and prosperity
Always lead your way.

Wear your Tallit with pride,
Go with values in hand;
And, hold your head high.
Mazel Tov to a fine, young man.

N. Loy Higgins

The Great Cacapon

The river goes north to Cacapon
Forking its way, at certain intervals
Through the mountains of Appalachia

Early this spring I came to see
How far the snow had gone
I noticed, some trees cut down
I thought maybe someone
Will build a dam or bridge
I suspect, the beavers had a hand in it.

I would like a dam or a bridge
There is no landing for a boat.
The river bank is too steep
Its bottom covered with stones
And branches knocked down
By the winter storms
I fear, on foot is not the way to go,
To cross to the other side.
Where the mountain top promises a great
Overlook.

I lingered on my side, till the sun's
Gold and crimson light, vanished into the night.

Roela Weber

I Am A Child

I live in a little shanty
Found deserted after the war
The journey I have travelled
Can take me no more.

I am a child who knows pain
I walk this earth alone
There are times when I lie in the street
And hear my echoing groan.

The clothing on my back is all I have
There are no shoes to be torn
Each day I walk by strangers
Each day I feel their scorn.

My family now gone
No hope dwells within
My life has been destroyed
By poverty, not by men.

Sandy Robinson

Who Shall I Be?

Six o'clock
   Friday night
Out to impress
   everyone in sight.

Every flaw
   covered so neat.
My mask is on
   I'm almost complete.

I'm now ready
   to begin the game.
To avoid reality
   I'll need a new name.

They don't need to know
   the real me.
For if they did
   alone I would be.

Linda Engler

Nature's Creed

I believe in the brook as it wonders,
From hillside into glade
I believe in the breeze as it whispers,
When evenings shadows fade.

I believe in the roar of the river,
As it dashes from high cascade
I believe in the cry of the tempest,
'Mid the thunders cannonade.

I believe in the light of shining stars,
I believe in the sun and the moon
I believe in the flash of, lightning,
I believe in the nightbird's croon.

I believe in the faith of the flowers,
I believe in the rock and sod
For in all of these appeareth clear,
The handiwork of God.

Mary Townsend Cook

The Eagle's On Course (Almost)

The Eagle lifted off in its flight,
From Independence Hall.
And it has soared through the centuries,
Tugging us along, not letting us fall.

The Eagle is awesome in its flight,
As it searches for prey.
With its spirits high, it generously
Helps weaker ones along the way.

Some say the Eagle, in its flight,
Has lost its sense of direction.
That it has no useful purpose now,
And is not a symbol of perfection.

The Eagle maybe lost, in its flight.
And the critics may be partially right.
For it has led only three-fourths
Of the world to freedom, by its might.

Lester W. Boyd Jr.

Isle Royale

I hear a wolf howling
From Isle Royale in Superior,
A wolf howling on that cold lake island,
To which moose who walked winter's ice
And winter wolves followed, howling.
To which mainland Indians canoed
In search of copper with which
To stone-beat amulets,
To make good medicine.
Indians hear the wolves' cry
But between, the greatness of silence
That sings this needle-green isle.
As wolves howl against the great silence
Indians invoke the great spirits
That reside within the silence.
Both howls and invocations fade to silence
And even that silence
Has been silenced.

Matthew W. McGregor

Autumn

"Autumn beauty brings mixed memories
From my child-hood long ago
Some solemn and some happy ones,
Some somber in the twilights glow
The pretty "Black eyed Susans"
And the beautiful "Golden-rod"
For me was such a joy to gather,
Created by the Hand of God.
With the flower's yellow beauty,
I'd fill vase's here and there
"Cheering" all the lonely places,
With their fresh beauty rare.
I imagine I'm a child again,
With no cares and fancy free
Listening to the "Whippoorwill",
Bringing "Echo's" back to me."

Ruby Savell

Inevitability

There's no turning away
from the pain that precedes me
It lures me on into the night
and bears me up on its heated wings

There's no turning away
from the sin that precedes me
My eyes go blind from its temptations
with an open pit of regret before me

There's no turning away
from the death that precedes me
It takes my hand in its steely grip
and leads me into the depth

There's no turning around
to see the angel that succeeds me
She whispers out softly my name
but her beckons dies within my heart

There's no sweet dreaming
of the Heaven that made me
There's no peaceful sleeping
in the grave that claims me

Travis J. Lohrer

The Colors Of A Rainbow

Red is for the blood which drips
   from wounds that we create.
Black is for the darkness seen through
   eyes filled with pain.
Green is for envy, the sin which has
   destroyed many lives.
White is innocence, which so many
   people are lacking.
Blue is the color of bruises made
   without thinking of the consequences.
Yellow is the light, that we wish to
   reach without attempting to gain entrance.
Orange is for the fire which fills up
   the depths of darkness.
Why are rainbows described as
   beautiful when the colors which
apparently put together this entity
   are filled with evil?

Maria Palmieri

Seasons Turn

Winter sunrise, crystal dawn
Frozen landscape, shadows long
Stark white snowfall, coats the scene
Melts as Springtime, sprouts with green

Gentle rainfall, bathes the land
Brings the flowers, on command
Sunshine strengthens, warms the soil
Soon gives rise to, Summer's boil

Sweetest season, Summertime
Livin's easy, days sublime
Farmers working, in their fields
Brings the harvest, with its yield

Leaves are turning, red and gold
Days are shorter, nights turn cold
Autumn showers, soon give way
To the Winter's icy haze

Just like clockwork, seasons turn
Such is Nature, and we learn
To accept this, simple plan
Given freely, from God's hand

Tom Cummiskey

Untitled

A crispness fell
Frozen tear drops
as I walked the icy shore
A dance of crimson
broke a sky of violet black
Dreams inverted taking me back
The sun rose pinked caps
we lay in our bed of snow
You laughed I smiled
We new the day would last
A sparkle of Gold
Reflected to my soul
Embracing Utopia
How was I to know
Shocking reality
tore me away
Ice flowing above me
Cried my last breath I have to stay

Regan Leflar

Untitled

The tide swallows me deeper and deeper
Gasping for breath
Bruised and limp
Limbs mangled with seaweed

Gasping for breath
My lungs fill with salt water
Limbs mangled with seaweed
Sand plasters my pallid body

My lungs fill with salt water
Haze of blood
Sand plasters my pallid body
Helplessly floating

Haze of blood
The tide swallows me deeper and deeper
Helplessly floating
Bruised and limp

Valerie Palmer

"Let Go My Love"

Pull the dagger out of my heart
Give me back the love I had
You're killing my trust in faith
that I can love and be glad

Glad to feel happy, joyous, and free
With another who loves me too
The way I've loved him for so long
Just hoping his love was true

My eyes. Did they see what was real?
They couldn't have, they were blind
My love for you was so strong
That my head overlooked every sign

Was I in love with love
Or was I in love with you?
Did the romance of our affair
Excite me more than you?

You've left me so we'll never know
But I'm sure you'd be curious to see
Regardless, you're a thing of the past
Except for your love inside me

Terry Johnson

"Mother Of The Teenage Driver"

Oh Lord, how'd I get myself in this situation?
I'm at my wits end and no longer have patience,
I must have been crazy to hand this kid keys,
Just let me live through this "I'm BEGGING YOU PLEASE",

We started this driving lesson, with a dozen or so bunny hops,
Next came the intersection, he was shifting and couldn't stop,
We went the wrong direction on a busy one way street,
Our lesson in left-turn yielding was really quite the treat,

I think my son is colorblind, we've gone thru four yellow lights,
I swear there are holes in this dashboard, I'm hanging on so tight,
He tailgates, speeds, and switches lanes as if this were a race,
I hope the judge has a sense of humor, when it's time to hear his case

Mary Jo Baker

A Fine Line

Where, oh where, has my sanity gone?
I'll just hope against hope it's gone upstream to spawn
Some new reinforcements to brighten my dawn.
But the line is so fine between insane and out,
My well-trodden path has worn crooked, no doubt.
I'll continue my search, hoping someday to find
Mere bits and pieces of what once was my mind!

Sally Vilim Gunsteen

June 14, 1995

When he received the James L. Quinn award
   For teaching excellence.
As I did once stare in wondrous awe,
   at the image there...nothing I awe
as he had once looked and with time
   did see.
with much care, what he soon did impart to me
How awesome a change it is to behold,
Amorphous then, but a sculpture to mold.
With fear and uneasiness I once cumbersome strode,
Eager mind, keeping hand, learning to bear the load.
Once feeble, uncertain, yet now I walk strong,
For in times of defeat when he did keep me along.
For the time and the knowledge I could never repay.
I will pass to another what he did freely give away.

Lisa H. Lowe

"Soaring Love"

It wasn't very long ago that my mind was free
Like a magnificent hawk soaring thru the sky.
Then you so beautiful arrived, overwhelming me
With your smile, my love was not to be denied.

I am sorry I appear to be selfish for wanting
To be with you to share your laughter and sorrow.
But my heart is unrelenting and continues taunting
My love for you as if there is no tomorrow.

Oh how I want to feel your breath on my face,
As I watch your ruby red lips in conversations:
But I know I am compelled to remain in my place
For only in my dreams will I feel such sensations.

Milton Thomas Staples II

Untitled

As I lay and stare at the clear blue sky
I think of heaven and begin to cry.
A place where I will someday be
all of a sudden comes so clear to me.
Somewhere there are no worries at mind
Memories of earth will be hard to find.

NaKesha Welch

Like The Wind

Like the wind you passed my way
Gently you moved like the sea breeze
All I could smell was the scent of
Fresh roses in early spring
Which you left behind.
My heart enjoys still
But you are miles and miles away
I can't seem to reach you.
Between love and hate I hate I lay.
Judge me with warmth not apathy
Sugar is sweet but not as sweet as sweet as you
Judge me by my heart not by my looks
Like a gentle breeze
You whisper freely into my ears.

Premil Chery

Hidden

Cold stones
get buried
deepest
when they F
       A
        L
         L

Onto
warm
soft
dirt

Teri K. McMenamin

Untitled

The lion roars
gladly we follow,
for love knows no walls
My spirit takes flight to be noticed by
the king
To feel his breath at my neck
All who see high with longing,
for to be touched by him gives
new birth to the soul
I am chosen, I am reborn.

Susan Monson

Lost Seasons

Shattered sunlight
glistening on broken souls
exposing dreams to the day
that are still wet from their birthing.

Sharp edges
leaving tattered ridges
a line of redness seeps
showing the world that I am hurting.

Who among you understands
the summer illusions left behind
the chances unattempted
lost to time's passing.

Autumn winds blow cold
I always thought it a cliche
but not anymore
as I feel, not see, the snowflakes forming.

My friends around me
we huddle close to curb the chill
enshrouded in silence
as we hear the angels singing.

Theresa Anne Carvey

To Slawa

Such a friendly little lady
God has taken home today,
And we'll miss her, though we're happy
She will not in illness lay.

A smile lit up her little face
Each time someone stopped by,
And she lived her life at her own pace
With Dottie by her side.

In her chair that sat behind the door
She worked on her crocheting,
She turned out so many pretty things
But today a harp she's playing.

Her boys did what they could to help
Their lovely little mother,
Now her children will stand side by side
To try to help each other.

Goodbyes are hard, but now they're done
And Slawa's life is through,
So today we're gathered here to say
We'll miss you, we love you.

Lill Clark

God

God is holy,
God is true,
God is precious,
He loves you.

God makes the breeze
And leaves that fall.
He makes the world
That seems so small.

For God is holy,
God is true,
God is precious
And He loves you.

Melanie Rieger

God Knows

God knows that I was lost
God knows that I've been found
God knows that lately
I've been losing ground

God knows that sooner or later
I'll give all of my life to Him
God knows that if I persist
I'll regret what I've been
Somewhere down the line...
I am running out of time
God knows

Leonard H. Brisbon

War

Love
Gone.
Life.
Gone.
Living
eliminated.

Kim Headley

"Angel"

To our very sweet Angel...

You don't remember when
God sent you as a special gift
and you made our life begin.

I know that it was not easy,
because we were strict with you.
It was only because we cared about,
the things that you might do.

When you became a teenager,
we couldn't communicate.
We knew someday that you would grow up,
and all we could do was wait.

Now you're grown up and married,
and have your very own kids.
Perhaps by now you will realize,
why we did the things that we did.

Lenora Sullivan Stark

Seasons Change

Seasons change, life goes by, time goes on they say.
Life is what we make of it, each and everyday
Season begins the trees have leaves
as green as they can be.
the children play everyday and love flows so free.
The leaves fall on to the ground,
we rake them everyday, school begins,
but yet-we still want to play.
Chilly nights; the snow falls
we sing Christmas songs, a new year
begins, our hearts filled with love
the nights seen so long.
The birds start singing, the trees
bloom, the animals come out to play,
the days get longer, homework ends,
as school goes away
Once again its hot!

Sandra Ebel

Moment

Ticktack-Ticktack
Goes the grandfather's clock
All throughout the day
Both through night and day.

Two ticktacks make two moments.
There's two ticktacks per second.
There's sixty seconds in a hour.
Don't waste a precious moment.

It may make a big difference
Between life or death.
Jesus made His consummation;
The Good Thief's last moment!

Don't think this is funny.
It's serious as ever.
One moment may save your life.
It's just like the blink of an eye.

In everyone's life
There is an idea or intuition
That lasts just but one moment.

Thaddeus Capek

Untitled

The Northern Star has
guided decades of people
guide us forever

Regina Scannell

Jade

The great American beauty
Hair the color of dark chestnut
Eyes breathtakingly emerald
Tall and slim a girl firm with youth

Like a doe, she represents simplicity,
Beauty and strength
Appearing weak but always ready
to defend what she loves

Wise beyond her years from
A year her glass world was shattered
Strong enough to mend it

Always there to offer a smile
Ready to heal someone else's wounds
Even when hers are still healing.

Nichole Miller

The Sunrise of You

The last rays of the sunset
have gone. Even tho the darkness
is here, the warmth of you
linger's on, the moon reflects a lot
of your bright light. Darkness
surround us again, for the lost
of someone, we hold very dear.
But we do not fear for you
have taught us, there will
always be another dawn, another
day of warmth and beauty.
A day of sunshine and happiness
it may not be as bright as
the one's we hold so dear, but
it will be, for we all have our
own special memories of the love
we shared and the sunrise of
Tomorrow

Theresa Whitt

The Angel Spoke (Aids Victims)

The Angel spoke and I leaned near
He gave me hope - He shared my fear
The trumpet sounded far away
If I have Aids how can I stay
But Angels now will help delay
The scene I fear. I hope I pray
How brave the fight - I have nearly won
And friends have gathered - one by one
The Angel spoke - I heard a hymn
Oh winged one - Oh seraphim.

Marty Martin

Me

I can dream so far away and so close too
I am a snake slivering in the morning dew

I can fly like an eagle and
Walk like a weasel
But I will always be just plain me
For there is only one true me to be

Teresa Cervantes

Out Of Sight

He knows your face but not those eyes
He knows of darkness but not of lights

The colors of flowers - birds in the sky
Not able to see that certain smile

When summer turns into autumn leaves
And falling snow in a winters breeze

A running horse - a boxing fight
And also miss a guiding light

Not to notice the grasses grow
To miss a sunset an evening's glow

That autumn forest - a rivers stream
He heard of these but has not seen

Rainer W. Raumer

Rose Petals

As she plucked rose petals she counted,
He loves me, he loves me not
All night she plucked trying to get
   the answer she sought
She plucked till she was pallid
   with sorrow
Till she knew for love she'd
   die by tomorrow
When the sun rose in an
   elegant light
There she lay a sorrowful
   heartbroken sight
A single rose stem elegantly
   wrapped around her wrist
While crimson rose petals were
   clenched within her fist
To show her love she threw
   her life away
Now he'll love her till his dying day

Rena Myers

Grandmother's Love

When the Lord was making Grandmothers
He picked you from the rest.
He knew that for a grandma
He had to make the best.
So he molded all the grandma's
With your love and patience to
And hoped that in the future
They would all turn out like you.
Well we can't speak for the others
But there's one thing we all know
The love that you have given us
Is the kind that grows and grows,
You always seemed to worry
Was there food enough to eat
Was there hats and gloves for winter
Were there shoes upon our feet.
Well now the time has come grandma
For you to get some rest.
The Lord is taking care of you
You sure did pass his test.

Norma J. Henry

He Lead Me To Sin

I've loved once, but never again;
He said he loved me, and lead me to sin.
He told me he loved me;
And this fool was taken in.

His arms were so warm;
And so inviting.
This gal was young;
And love seemed so exciting.

The things that he told me;
Now I know weren't true.
The things that he told me;
Now he's saying them to you.

Now he's told you that he loves you;
So be careful my friend.
Be sure he really loves you;
Before he leads you to sin.

Sandra K. Moore

Taking Up Your Cross

"Take up your cross and follow me",
He said to me so tenderly
"Not now Lord, my hands are full."

"I don't have room a cross to bear,
it's not cool, why should I care?
Maybe tomorrow——we'll see."

So on my merry way I went
without a worry or a hint
——of what it all meant.

And then one dreadful day
a sorrow came my way
and to the cross I ran.

As I was to recall,
how He gave His all,
this JESUS who emptied His arms,
laid down His life and died for me.
How could I NOT give Him my all?

Marva M. Watson

Weaknesses

He weakens everytime
he sees me
his eyes want to
lead him to me
but his mind
pushes him away
he walks pass me
several times
as if to speaks to forgive
but everytime he does not
he glimpses at me
waiting for me to apologize
But I am to stubborn
to do so
why is it my heart cries to him
yet he just waits and waits
for him to win this battle
but I cannot let him win
for the words he wants to
hear me say I cannot say.

Lilia Urias

My Cat Max

My cat Max
He sleeps all day,
And he never ever wants to play.

My cat Max,
I love him so,
And I'll never let him go.

My cat Max,
Is really fat.
He really is a lazy cat.

My cat Max,
He ran away,
And I miss him every day.

J. Lynne Boule

The Rose

In the stillness of the night
he stole into the beauty's room
to glance upon in pale moonlight
the one for whom his heart did swoon

She lay in silence beauty slept
her auburn hair spread all around
Her perfect form the Gods did bless
visible through her lace-made gown

He watched the beauty through the night
till dawn's faint light began to grow
then out the window silence crept
left behind a single rose

Beauty woke to find the gift
the giver she may never know
but she too harbored love's intent
for the stranger who had left the rose

Michael S. Sprabary

TAMELESS

Powerful Princeley bEAST
 He was bathing in a
 moonlit pond.
A pair of amber eYes
SPARKLED against the bLaCkk
 A gentle murmur
expressed a Contentedness
then
glorius
with a grace,

The tiger slowly strolled
        away.

Katarzyna Kochany

Scotland

Scotland, Scotland
Home of my ancestors.
Home of the beautiful dancers,
Who are always wearing plaid.
Home of the bagpipers,
Who are so loud.
Scotland so close
Yet so far
How beloved you are!

Thayer Low

To Soar Again With You

I woke one day to find
he was no longer at my side.
The shifting sands of time had
spirited him away.
The only true love
I had ever known was
now beyond my reach.
My majestic eagle
all strength and grace
no longer soared with me,
over our field of dreams.
You who so loved
flowers and trees,
I pray to see one day
in a special place
cultivated with such love
it will take our breath away.
A place more beautiful than before,
just waiting for us to forever soar
over our field of dreams.

Wava J. Nelson

I Love Him

He was always there for me
He was their at sad times and
happy times. He helped me when I cried.

But at times
he made me mad.
But I still love him
He's in my heart, I know he's
Watching me like a guardian angel,
When I have no one to talk to
he is there, I wish he was
here but his gone,
I still have my mom,
and I love her, but it's
not the same.
Dad, I miss you.

Laura Hutson

Innocence Guided

She whom I fear,
He whom I hate,
They who confine me
To a cold world.
Let me see light,
Let me see love.
Help me clear a
Path.
Guide me to my
Freedom.
and,
I shall help you to
see
My world,
My light,
My love.

Leah Recor

Changes

Times may change
Hours may fly but
our love stays
the same all our lives.

Sandi Gigantino

Magical Match

I love the exotic appeal,
Heart murmurs beating breast;
For the magical junction
Where east meets west

She said she was a poetess
Explorer of metered measure
I said I was a diver
Searcher of lost treasure

In the waters of south sea dives
I discovered emerald jade eyes

She recounted the legendary city
Where Emperor's palaces lay
Buried below briny depths
Amidst coral, squid N stingray

Slowly, I descended to the
Treacherous ocean's floor
She fed my life by line
From the clipper's bobbing moor

Betwixt whale N shale; arose royal spires
Lightning heart fires for beauty,
Love...desires

Thomas Bonner

Our Baby Girl

When I heard you cry, I thought my
  heart would burst.
But I kept thinking, let me see her
  first.
I couldn't believe how tiny you were.
I kept thinking, she'll break for sure.

As they gave you to me to hold
I felt my heart swell triple-fold.
As I held you in my arms
I felt the urge to protect you from
  all harm.

We named you after a sweet flower
Now over our hearts you have complete
  power.
When you smile, we leap for joy.
As will one day all the boys.
So for now sweet little baby girl; sleep.
For you'll always be ours to keep.
For now have no worries or cares in the world.
Sleep for now our baby girl.

T. Fularz

In The Crowd

People Together
"Hello, How Are You?"
Pain Hidden Beneath
The Smiling Faces
A Secret Sorrow
Strangling the Soul
While the Grinning Mask
Lies
"I'm fine, and You?"

Rebecca J. Kubiak

"Pain"

Unexpected turns,
Heartaches that burn.
Your life's true fate,
Apologies too late.

Choices not chosen,
Years that are frozen.
Chances not given,
Fears so hard driven.

Staking the pain,
Hard as the rain.
Placing the blame,
Living with shame.

Hurting inside of you,
Lies that are spoken, too.
Nightmares are made,
Friends start to fade.

Harden my heart,
End before start,
I reached in, with outstretched arms,
I came back, with forever harm.

Lisa Simmons

Grandma's House

I think
Heaven is a lot like Grandma's house,
Where joy and peace abound.
Heaven is a lot like Grandma's house,
Where family and friends are found.
There are little angels everywhere
making hearts feel warm.
A place to go whenever
another child is born.
I see Grandma and Grandpa waiting there
at the old front door.
Their love is overflowing with
fond memories evermore.
With smiles on their faces
and arms out open wide,
looking down upon us,
with their hearts full of pride.
Grandma's house is special.
It's where everyone wants to be.
That's why Heaven is a lot like Grandma's house,
At least it is to me.

Peggy (Anthony) Cook

Love's Night

Oh! Night of flowing embers
High above thee reign
In glowing rapture thy splendor
Only if one could tame

Heavenly this world beyond me
A peaceful space entwine
Joy filled night of glory
My own true love and vine

Oh! Hear the call this day
Of love and joy filled heart
For in this sky so bountiful
God's love doth shine about

This land of light in shadow
Cast all one need to see
And moonlight on ebb-tide
For thee and me born - free

Val Kohlman

Dreams

Stars are like dreams,
Held in the mind of the sky.
If you truly believe,
Your dreams will never die.

Dreams are like angels,
Sent from above.
But if you're not careful,
They'll fly away like a dove.

Hold on to what you believe,
And try your very best,
If you try hard enough,
You'll soon end your quest.

Dreams are only special,
In the mind of the beholder.
Keep them in your heart,
And remember them as you grow older.

Everything may not always be,
As bad as it may seem,
But if you only believe,
You can achieve your dreams.

Malisa Lovette

Prayer For Assistance

Oh God, my Creator
Help me to play the role of peace,
In life's theatre —
O Lord of the earth
And of the firmament,
Let me represent,
The spirits of love and harmony,
Teach me honesty and decency,
Instruct me in the art of modesty-
Assist me to create my psalms,
Glorifying Your Name,
Anoint me with Thy healing balms,
And sooth the wounds of painful emotions,
With Your miraculous potions,
Comfort my aching heart,
And let me start a new episode
On life's station,
Perform on me, the great miracle
Of Regeneration-

Magda Herzberger

My Friend "Dog"

Soft and furry,
Helpless;

Nurturing love,
Loyalty;

Chasing through the fields,
Happiness;

Frolicking in the snow,
Delight;

Long evenings by the fire,
Companionship;

Years of friendship,
Love;

Slowing down and vision dim,
Dependent;

Lay down to nap and never to awake,
I miss you.

Marilyn E. Williams

The Girl

Baby barrettes gently pull back
  her thin, dark hair.
Her almond eyes shine through
  the darkness
Roses worship her perfect, blood-red
  lips.
She is cloaked in the dark cape
  of perfection.
Drowning in the bottomless pool
  of brilliance.
Her aura is a shield
Trained
To reflect love.

Sasha Pasulka

The Deceptive Sound

We heard the fear in
her trembling voice at
the mighty lion's roar!
The voice of conceit and
racial defeat stained
the bloodied jungle floor.
Who else did this feat?
We all repeat, we heard
the lion roar!

Lula M. Haines

Not Right

The world is not right
Hiding behind what is real
Confusion is all the world can feel
And we curl up in the night
And hope things will be all right
When were still alone amongst a crowd
What right is ours to feel proud
We challenge the gods to a fight
Then pray to them to show us the light
No understanding-just skimming the text
Millions of teenagers longing for sex
Something to make us feel all right
'Cause lately this world is never right
I think everyone wants to hear the voice
Open your eyes and make a choice
I'll just continue to rub and write
Brace yourselves! And hold on tight...

Matthew L. Brophy

Longing To Feel Alive

I stood amidst a pile of rocks
High above the Ocean's Rage
Longing to feel alive
And as I sensed the Danger
Of the crashing waves
Climbing up the Rock I stood on
I heard your words echo
Clearly through my mind...
"Be Fearless" you once said...
And instantly that Rock became a vessel
Carrying me far away from here
To the other side of that Horizon
And I felt Alive
As ecstasy surged through my Body
Like a long awaited lover
Setting myself free!

And for all of this
I have You to thank
Over and over and over again

Liliana Amador

Near Somewhere We Were

Walking from the hips,
hiking the Nameless Trail,
getting hotter in down vests.

Glancing at the view
  over left shoulder,
climbing higher
  now right shoulder,
snaking our way to the top
no end in sight.

Did we touch did we kiss did we
on nameless mountain?

Breathing pulsing pounding-out
that unclaimed destination:
how would it feel now to
reach some scenic overlook
and come back down with you?
Forget specifics.
They say it's safer
walking from the knees.

Nancy Nicol

Wisdom Ordained

To the bride of Christ
his chosen.

Let me leave this thought
behind, modern thoughts
are facts established,

They don't always seek and find.

But new ways and revelations
come thru faucets in the mind.

I will call this, (God's conception)
Meditation — Revelation

It's use leads you when
your blind.
  A servant of God
Proclaim his covenant of Acts 2:38

Sam C. Romo

Gone

His eyes were made of the sea
His hair was beams of sun
I loved him like a brother
We came together as one

I wish that he was clean
Clean of what he'd done
I wish that he had stopped
But he wanted to have fun

He never was home
He never was there
He came home dazed
Why he didn't share

About one year later
One day I awoke
To find that he had died
Of drugs, alcohol, and smoke

His funeral was on Saturday
I went where I sat on,
The bench where I saw his body
Now he's surely gone

Lauren Chrissos

Camp Fire Song

The all trees,
hitch hiker leaves-
an unstable fire
waving with the breeze

Story book friends that come
dandelion songs that always go;
there's a trail that leads
to the house of tomorrow,

There's the traveler
who remembers it from the day before.

The fire ballet
before audience stars-
an applause of silence to be broken by
a curtain of cars

Richard Possel

The Enigma

Hold to everything
Hold to nothing
Nothing makes sense
Time continues on
Turning like windmills in my mind
Revolution
Governments rise and fall
Wars rage
Peace reigns
Everything is a paradox
Unobserved circles
Continue through space
Not knowing where to go
So it returns to end at the beginning
And continues starting over

Timothy J. Franks

Will I Find?

Look at you wish I could
hold you close know you will
if you would smile at me.
In the sky the pretty eyes
you wear always
think nothing more
then to adore more and more.
I see you and you me
dream to be your every destiny.
My heart beats out your name.
L for Love like a dove,
O in hope all about you,
V in forgiving worth our living,
E for eternity
faithfully until then.
What I say day after day.
This I know how to be
friend to you and to me.
When we meet dreams come true
every time I think of you.

Patrick Michael McKinstry

Voices

The vespers
  in the Aspens
Would say more
  if they were heard.

Vera L. Logan

"I Never Realized"

I guess I never realized,
  How hard it was for you
I never understood
  The things you went through
I never realized
  That I was only thinking of me
There were other people there
  But I just couldn't see!
It really showed me
  How much you cared
That you have your love for daddy
  And you want it to be shared
Now I finally realized
  That you went through a lot of pain
I never knew before
  That it was such a strain
Mommy, I love you!
  I really do - and this love that I feel
Will always be true

Terry Kouw

"Mother's Day"

I may not show enough
  How much I love you,
Trust me I do.
  You mean the world to me.
Even the blind man can see,
  The love that lives
Between you and me,
  You are so special
No matter where you may be
  You'll always be near
I'll have you here,
  In my heart,
And if you call my name, I'll dart
  To your side.
Because your voice will always
  Be deep inside.

Kyle Oels

Alone

How much we hide behind these walls,
How much of we are not us at all;
Beneath a fabric, oh so frail,
We feign our way along life's trail.

Throughout the hollows of the night,
Parched from the long lost day,
The searching soul mounts itself
And rides into the chasm

Deep within our meager minds,
Or far beyond its realm,
The wonders of the firmament
Swallow up identity.

Lost, we grope in the wilderness,
The awesomeness created by you and me;
Lonely, we cry unheard,
Afraid of those who see

Hoping through the darkest hour
To find the hand of sharing;
Sadly, wandering on —
Nobody, nobody caring.

Mike Lally

True Colors

You've made me realize
how the world can be
how something so foolish
can make me see

We may be different
but were still the same
the colors of our skin
have the world to blame

We cannot control
what's in the past
but only look forward
to a friendship to last

This world is so sheltered
if it only knew
that skin is so deep
and the heart is true

If there is one thing
this world needs to know
is it should step back
and let the true colors show.
Mercedes Smythe

Autumn Song

Winds of autumn, winds of autumn,
How they touch me when they sigh!
Winds of autumn, winds of autumn,
As the leaves go hurrying by.

Sometimes my heart
Is like the winds of autumn,
Sometimes my heart
Is like the winds of autumn,
Sometimes my heart
Is like a lonely sigh,
When autumn leaves
Go drifting by.

Winds of autumn, winds of autumn,
How they touch me when they sigh!
Winds of autumn, winds of autumn,
As the leaves go hurrying by.
Rilla Black

Thoughts Of An Unborn Child

I often sit and wonder
how you would have grown
what kind of man you would be,
if you would make it on your own.
Would you be a blonde,
and would you have blue eyes,
or would you be a genius,
who could never tell lies.
Would you grow to be the president,
and have the whole world in your hands,
or would you be a poor man,
trying to keep up with the worlds demands.
Tomorrow would be your birthday,
I can't believe it's been four years,
tomorrow I would like to be alone,
alone with your memories and my tears.
Even though I abandoned you,
and even though you're not real,
I still hold you close inside,
and my love for you no one can steal.
Michele Forcade

"Winter"

On a hillside a coyote
Howls with the cold winter breeze.
A full moon glows behind the clouds,
Icicles shine in the moonlight.
A flock of birds fly through
The sky, as snowflakes float
to the ground.
Rabbit tracks are found
In the woods,
And a doe stands by her young.
The trees are beautiful with
Frost on each branch,
One star twinkles alone
In the lonely sky.
Soon the sun will rise,
Leaving a memory of last night.
Lindsay Huth

"Analyzation Realization"

Why am I afraid of you?
I always have feelings of
"Dejavue" around you
I am in fear...
Yet, I am attracted to you!

Are you the one...?
I've been searching...
Looking and longing for
Wanting, waiting for
Needing but forever missing...
I thought I'd never find...

My heart aches for you
My being yearns for yours
I want you...but...
Are you the one?

Then why am I afraid?
Marlene N. Johnson

Bored

Bored, boring, bored
I am looking toward

A teacher in front of the room
I wish he'd get done soon.

My mind is wandering
Help me! Quick!

The seconds seem to go by
Tic by tic

The room isn't colorful anymore
Just broken old desks and a dusty chalkboard

Remember how elementary was so fun
'Cause we had a recess to play and run

Time did fly
But and since junior high

In junior high, time doesn't fly anymore
And I'm sitting here bored, bored, bored.
Miranda Breding

Little Girl

Little girl sit as you please
in that wonderland of trees.
Little girl sing as you may
on this pretty autumn day.
Little girl please don't cry;
Let no rain drip from your
sparkling eye.
Teresa Bearden

Forever

When I think of you,
I am no the same,
You are much better,
Than fortune or fame.
I can be happy,
I know I will be,
As long as your love,
Is promised to me.
Forever in Love with thee.

You are always,
the thought on my mind.
I've never met anyone,
As generous and kind.
You don't have to own,
A Limo or a Caprice.
Just act like yourself,
That's all I ask you to be.
Forever in Love with thee.
K. J. Thompson

The Past: The Jailer It Be

First says I then he to me,
I am not the coward ye came to be.

Then comes I, I says to he,
A Sunday soldier ye came to be.

I do not march about for all to see,
All I did to earn myself free.

Then he says to I you see,
I march about 'cause I'm not yet free.
S. L. Mowry

"Dear Lord Jesus"

I thank you when
I arise from sleep
I thank you for watching
over all of your sheep

I thank you for
the birds that sing
yes I thank you dear
Jesus for everything

I thank you for
us big and small
I thank you dear
Jesus for us all

I thank you when
the day is done
I thank you dear
Jesus for the sinking sun

I thank you when
I lie down to sleep
It's then time too
count the sheep
Ralph Winfield Toll

To You And Yours

To you and yours
I bid you happiness,
the secret of life.
I wish you glowing orange sunsets
and bright, cheery sunrises
to bring you to your tomorrows.
I wish you fields of wildflowers
that you can run through.
I wish you beautiful oceans
and blue skies above
that you can see.
I wish you the sweet scent of
fresh spring grass
that you can smell.
But, most importantly,
I wish you the will to
treasure all of these,
and the knowledge to
notice real beauty.

Susan Wiechelman

Inside My Mother

Inside my mother,
I breathe the air she breathes
and no one bothers me.
   My home is built by her Love
I don't even need a key.
   I eat whenever I please
each meal is on time and is free.
   I am a man or woman you will see.
   There's no need for light for me.
   Inside My Mother,
I can be care free just with her and
me, and we don't mind waiting for the
world that's waiting for me.

Wynona Ray

Memories

Alone on the cliff,
I call to my lost love
only seagulls answer.

Alone at the fireside,
I sip sherry in silence
hugging memories of memories.

Alone, lying in the clover field
I watched rolling clouds,
memories sinking into oblivion.

Naomi Y. Brown

How Do I Feel?

How do I feel?
I can not say
I go through these things
Every single day
How do I feel?
I do not know
It's very hard for me to show.
I can't explain it but,
A part of me is torn away
Every time I hear a laugh or snicker.
You wouldn't know or understand
Because you are not me
Or what I am.
When you feel the hurt and pain
Everyday like me
Then you can ask,
"How do you feel?"

Tracey Tuttle

Stream Of Consciousness

In a timeless glimpse of mortality
I can see the lines receding
An epic of youth unfolds
As the last tomb of innocence
Is put into the ground
Leveling off into waves
Of unconscious brooding
The mind frays and sways
Knowledge evades me
The curtains are drawn
And all I thought I believed
Vanished when the lights came on
I would open myself unto you
If I thought you would be accepting
But your eyes betray
What your words fail to tell
So with this last diminishing
Ray of introspection
Call on your minions
And see if they can break me

Lori Varjabedian

Mother

Why is that when looking back
I cannot remember your admiration in me?
You never showed me how to do
But always how to overcome
You sent me off into a world
much bigger than I could ever dream of
You watched me as I taught myself
about love, labor, pain, success
And I learned
I learned well
To be like you in certain ways
but mostly to be myself
You caught me when I stumbled
A step
A fall
Another try
Yet you were always there
watching me from behind

Kitty Elshot

Ti Ameny Net, Princess Of The Nile

A thousand, thousand years it seemed
I danced above the sands.
Saffron I wore and golden crown
Beside the dripping well,
My face of dew, my hand held high,
Beneath the pear and the palm.

A thousand, thousand years it was
I lay beneath the sands
In crown of gold and saffron gown
Beyond the cold choked well.
Footsteps so dim, and silent song
Below the palm and the pear.

Immensely time rehearses me
In light of your watching eyes,
As lips unsung sing life to yours-
Oh, dance yes dance for me now!
Pear of gold and glancing palm,
My high-held hand and face of dew
around the glistening well.

Patricia Marshall

The Day I'll Die

-The day I'll die
I don't know
-Should a holiday
It doesn't matter
-By a car accident
Or an airplane crash,
it is possible
-By hold up or murdering,
I believe
-Attack by a lion, or any force animal,
Why not?
-Falling down the steps, my neck broke
I don't know
-In an hospital, lying in the bed
Will be my last trip,
-Still a mystery—-
The day I'll die, I don't know
How, when or where!

Kozowali Nzinga

Wrong Feelings

I don't like the pain.
I don't like the tears.
To not have you near,
Is one of my fears.
You said you loved me,
This was just a week ago.
But when I said the same to you,
The only thing you said was "So?"
A few days have gone by,
But I still feel the same,
I love you forever,
And that will remain.

Tasha England

Untitled

*When I dream
I dream of that endless feeling
as I fall
but never reach the bottom.
I dream fear
as crimsoned blood rushes to escape
my lifeless body.
I dream of being alone
so often that I die
from the loneliness...
Then I never wake up.*

T. Popielski

The Chance

I see you in the sky tonight
I dream; that's where you are
A moment in a guiding light
A wish; a shooting star

If ever once an angel flew
Or butterflies spoke in dance
If roses flourished in winter's bloom
If ever there was a chance

If under moonlight's wax and wane
A heaven glowed beneath your touch
If rainbows sang in summer's rain
If laughter wept in songs as such

So what is it you dream at night?
What visions have I brought?
If only there's a chance I might
In you, inspire thought

William WL Shy

"Your Touch"

Your touch is like warm wine
I feel the warmth inside.

My flesh is all aglow
Wanting to love you so.

When we kiss, and you hold me close
You are the one I want the most.

I miss you so when we're apart
I feel lost and in the dark.

Then your touch and warm embrace
Brings me back from another place.

I know you are real and warm
I get lost in all your charm.
Sue Johnson

The Angels Took My Daddy Away

One day when I was feeling low,
I felt the nearness, Lord, of Thee.
As I dried my tears of sorrow,
These words suddenly came to me.

I heard the fluttering of their wings,
On that freezing winter night.
I knew they had come for him,
And he would soar to new heights.

It seemed like just yesterday,
When he held me safely on his knee.
I truly wanted him to stay,
But his name on the list I did see.

The music was sweetly playing,
And they said, "this is the day."
I was softly crying, and praying,
When the angels took my Daddy away.

He was a good and faithful one,
His work on earth fulfilled.
The pain and heartache are all gone,
Now he's resting in his mansion on the hill.
Virginia A. Jones

Love, Mommy And Daddy

The day you entered my life
I felt whole, a mother, a wife.
I waited for you for so long,
Our mother and daughter bond, strong.
Mommy and daddy love you dearly,
We hear your tiny cries clearly.
It's a race to get home to my little love
To my little girl, my little dove.
Your blue eyes, your blond hair,
Skin so soft, so fair.
Don't ever worry about us,
Everything for you, and a lot of fuss.
Some day you'll have a sister or brother,
Then after that, another.
Remember, we are your mom and dad,
Come to us, no matter how happy, how sad.
For there is no one who cares more about you,
As much as we do.
Karen T. Cabak

Unloved

I knew this day was coming
I guess I should've known
That you were in love with someone else
And now I'm on my own

What we had isn't worth saving
Now that I can see clearly
You brought me so much pain and
suffering
Even though you knew I loved you dearly

I sit here all alone
Wondering how it could've been
If you didn't betray me
And done that awful sin

I picture a pretty dress
And everything in white
But I know it'll never happen to us
Because it's just not right

And now I'm very lonely
With no one here to love
I guess deep down inside
It's always you I'm thinking of.
Sandra Arnal

Isabella

Everytime Isabella smiles
I hear a little voice say....

Hey loser you just won!!
...Look at that precious face!

I've never succeeded in anything
I've never had that luck or faith

My childhood was sad and lonely
My teenage days were much the same

But now I have my daughter
Isabella is her name

I love to feel her happiness
To feel her warm embrace

To wipe her tears that come down
When she gets a bump or scrape

I've succeeded as her mother
In her eyes, I am great!

And so that's what makes me
feel like a winner...
Day after day after day....
Linda E. Burgos

Hatched

On life support
I imagined you a swimmer
engaged
in a complicated
back stroke
breast stroke...

The Butterfly.

I wanted to touch
your foot,
brown and near,
but when I looked
I saw you only has wings now

And means
to take
your leave.
Stephanie Carson

Beloved Man And Parent To Be

With my small hand in your larger one
I heard you speak my name
and whisper softly into my ear
but my head was in a state of fog

You breathed heavily into the air
your hand perspired whilst holding mine
and the room seemed to spin around
and the walls of white became a swirl

My stomach heaved and tugged again
and my feet in silver stirrups were held
sweat lay upon my brow
our labor was going well

you my husband standing there
a new life emerging from within
we sharing a common dream
of love, unity, and family.
Natasha Jarvis

The Grass Blade

Although I am just a blade of grass,
I hold my own. I am full of strength
always stretching for the sky. I am
cut down by aliens, but I fool them,
I regain my strength and grow anew
trying to gain my point. What I am
trying to tell the aliens is there
is a force within, that can not be
destroyed, by you or anything. I am
ready to hold my ground.
Patsy A. Murdoch

Poetry

I could be a poet
I just can't show it
Hard to explain
Paper covered with pain
That falls like tears
Which no one hears
Hiding all the true
Not from me but from you
These are my lines
Attached by rhymes.
Rachel Flournoy

They Say It Comes In 3's

When I see people begging,
I kick them,
because it's easier to forgive,
when their on the ground.

She has 3 teeth,
no hope,
a day old bagel,
and their all in her pocket.

My head is throbbing,
her T-Shirt reads "NO SPARE CHANGE".

Does she give more than she has,
but has nothing to give?
Does she love without measure or regret?
Is that why Justice wears a blindfold?

I can't concentrate,
I place an extra absorbent Band-Aid,
over my right eye,
the RED CROSS is embarrassed,
-what about the CHILDREN I ask?
They tell me names do matter.
L. J. Walter

April Moon

When the Angels sent you to me,
I knew I was in love.
I got down on my knees that night,
To thank the Lord above.

We used to sit and watch the stars
Under the April moon
But you were taken away from me
Too fast, and too soon

I knew I'd never get over you
No matter how I tried.
You don't know the endless nights
I've thought of you and cried.

Now a year has passed
Since that dreadful day
I want to forget the horror
But I can't get away

Because you were taken away from me
Too fast, and too soon
So now I lay here mourning you
Under the April moon.
   Malissia Van Meter

Wailing

I heard this woman screaming
I knew it couldn't be me,
That wasn't how you handled grief
Not in my family.
The Woman's voice was wailing
Please bring her back to me
I'll gladly go to hell,
She said For all eternity
For just a chance to hold her
And watch her sunny smile.
I'll gladly go to hell,
She said please bring her back,
Just for a little while.
They closed the lid upon her
And they carried her away,
I heard a women screaming, Oh God!
Please don't let this be.

Take me, take me.
   Kay H. Weller

"My Silent Prayer"

As I come to leave my silent prayer....
I know....that he knows.....
I am here......
I feel his presence everywhere
As I see him before me
In my silent prayer....
Yes....he is away
Many many years today.....
To me.....he is always there
With a smile......
Untouched by passing years......
With a kindness
That was always there
I see him......
As I say my silent prayer.....
With a love.......
Untouched by destiny......
Yes....I see him before me
As I leave.....
My silent prayer.....
   Vivian Kasakov

Springtime

Springtime,
I know you.
You are
baseball bats,
playing with cats,
climbing mountains,
people shouting.

Springtime,
I know you.
You are
smiling faces,
relay races,
no school,
swimming in a pool.

Springtime,
I do know you.
   Matt Stevens

Bare

I love the truth of winter;
I like the feel of bare.
The trees are silhouetted;
There's bareness everywhere.

I see exactly how they are
Without their leaves to hide.
It makes me wonder how they feel
To know I see inside.

If people had a winter
And we could see them then,
We'd find many treasures
They choose to keep within.

Perhaps they just don't understand
The joy of being bare.
They keep their foliage all year long
And never know what's there.
   Sharlotte Jones Rynders

Winds

The wind, gentle wind,
I like the wind to blow,
It carries on its whispery back,
The thoughts of long ago.

The wind, gusty wind,
I wait for its whistling song,
From every nook in this old house,
It tells of lives long gone.

The wind, gale wind,
I hear it shriek and tear the shore,
Who knows what things will come to pass,
A birth, a death and maybe more?
   Marian Simpson

An Angel

Wherever I go,
I will show,
My Guardian Angel of strength
Sits upon my shoulder of length
So cheery and bright
It brings faith and insight
Life is more caring
While he sits a sharing
He is my Shield
When I feel I'm in a battlefield
So with faith and love
I will look to my guardian above
   Roseanne Hunniford

Too Late

I'm old and, oh, so lonely.
I long to hold you in my arms.
My heart aches when I think of you.
I look at these four walls
And they become a virtual prison.
No one will ever know the tears
That I have shed when alone;
Nor how the knot in my stomach tightens
When I see a child skipping
Before her grandmother.
Lord, will the pain ever go away?
You see, I can never be a grandmother.
I will never feel your hand in mine,
Nor see the love in your eyes
That is so special between a child
And her grandmother.
I can never experience these things
Because, God forgive me,
I aborted your mother years ago.
   Mildred Hardison

The Dove

A shot in the dark I did so well,
I met a girl I loved as well.
She stole my heart away from me,
And now she wants to set it free.
She sat upon a strange boys knee,
And told him things she never told me.
I went home that night to cry in my bed,
Not a word to my mother I said.
My father came home late at night,
To search for me from left to right.
Then through the door that he had broke,
He found me hanging from a rope.
And just as he was about to cut me down,
A note from my shirt fell to the ground.
It said;
   "Dig my grave and dig it deep,
   Bury me in marble from head to feet.
   Then at the top put a dove,
   To show everyone I died for love."
   Neil Eugene Bishop III

"I Miss You"

I miss you baby very much
I miss the way we used to touch
I miss your kiss, your warm embrace
I miss looking at your smiling face
I miss the way we used to talk
I even miss the way you walk
I miss making love with you
And the way you used to say
"I Love You"
I miss the sound of your heartbeat
When I would lay my head on your chest
After all baby making love with
You was the best
I miss everything about you
that's why I am going crazy without you
letting you go was the worst thing I did
and I'll regret every moment that I did
I miss you more than you'll ever know
I Love You Baby with all my
heart and soul.
   Marian Morales

I Never Saw Your Face

I didn't know your name.
I never saw you face
But I know you walked in goodness
You lived in faith and grace

You must have had such determination
To have given your liver to me
To let my life continue on
With my wonderful family

You have given and I have taken
That precious second chance at life.
I promise you I shall do my best
To live up to your expectations of strife.

June K. Vargo

Embrace

Held tightly in his warm embrace
I rub my cheek against his face
I feel his pain and hear his heart
We lovingly have a brand new start
Our embrace was our foundation
It was not my imagination
I know he loves me and he cares
As he is and as he stares
Across to me from where he is
I hear a heartbeat and know its his.

Sarah Schmitz

She Is My Comfort

He lay down next to me
I sat beside him dutifully
Sending calm waves of energy
To surround him in serenity.

No words were needed there
To let him know I care,
Just a quiet moment to share
As I gently touched his hair.

Resting in his inner place
Summoning energy at his base
To perform again with grace
Glowing from his perfect face.

As he left to face the crowd
I heard him say aloud
Words that made me proud,
"She is my comfort."

Particia Ann Kerr

Leaf

As I walked along the path
I saw a leaf fall by.

As it traveled to the ground
I thought of you and I.

How at one time the leaf held
on so tightly to the tree.

Like the days we were together
and you held on to me.

As the seasons begin to change
the tree knows it must let go.

Much like when you walked away
our time had come I know.

And as the leaf reached the earth's floor
it was then I knew our love was no more.

Shane Williams

"Places In Eternity"

It was a long night.
I saw forever in that sky
of low-hung polar stars.
Timeless—
but marking time,
like the clock ticking
whose hands are gone.
I grew old under its guise.
Awaiting that night of night.
Until a spark, a ray,
an aurora bloomed
and lit the sky.
The metallic sun usurped the moon,
awakening the sleeping dead.
Death's heads wreathed about them.
On a glowing morning to this summer's day.
Where have I been?
How long will this last?
This time, this timeless time
new born.

Lydia Javins

Pink Geraniums In The Window

From the window on the landing
I saw the sun rise.
Massive golden ball.

In that same window
the pink geraniums
splendidly blooming
that second day of January.

Mist on the window behind
from their breath.
Further back
a row of sugar maple trunks
silver in the winter light.
Smaller budded branches
careening in the bitter wind.

Geraniums at the window
in the southern light
Ancient and gnarled.
Can't predict where the miracle
of pink
will next appear.

Kelsey Mason

Untitled

Ending now and every time
I see a passing chance
To live a breath a whispered thought
That often is the last

An ever turning ray of light
Broken and benign
Crumbling within my dark
Struggling to rise

Alone and lost alive at last
Left to wander on
Searching for sweet empathy
Until at last I'm gone

John Wilson

Death

Such good people
I should be in their place
I deserve it
Drunk
Crazy
seems like a bad dream
you never wake up from
can't sleep at night
NIGHTMARES
car lights flashing
broken glass
blood spattered
over my body
as I sit there in shock
it should have been me...

Vanessa Renée Greco

My Love

As my day is done
 I sit here watching the dimming sun
I am thinking of you, my love, and
of the many time I have held you
in my arms and looked in your
eyes, and thanked God for you
being alive and the many nights
I have spent by your side,
But as sure as there will be a
tomorrow. One of us will look
toward the skies and wonder
why oh why does our loved ones
half to die
but it is not for us to know
the reason why.
But for us to merely, live love and die

Thomas W. Stottman

God's Gardener

In my floral garden,
I spend hours on bended knees
Carefully transplanting seedlings
and forgetting everything else.
Rain clouds and sunlight
Help the flowers grow.
Cultivation and patience
Keep them free of weeds.
I have learned much about life,
Tending to my geraniums and marigolds.
I freely branch out
Giving myself new growth,
By the process of pruning
I accept life's pain,
Sorrow and disappointment,
Along with the joys of life.
I admire God's gift of beauty,
Taking pride in my garden.
I love the joy it gives me,
I appreciate being God's gardener.

Rosemary Trettin

Mourning Tides

I ride the mourning tides
into the waves of tears forgot
I feel it all arise
and then it hits me like a shot
the waters of my dreams
the madness I thought left behind
and then I drown it seems
deep in the recess of my mind

Thom Gerszewski

"My Grandfather"

Grandfather, I lost you one day
I still wonder why

There never was a day go by
that I wasn't sad

I guess it's the way
God intended it to be

I felt like my heart was gone
I didn't want to live on

I wanted to go with you
but maybe it wasn't meant to be

I wanted to say goodbye
But everytime I tried
inside I'd just die

I know you're still a part of me
that's the way you will remain

Everyday in my heart
forever you will be
Kimberly A. Gill

Frogs

Frogs are little and green.
I take them home in my pockets.
Frogs are the cutest things I've seen
With eyes big and brown.

Frogs sit upon lily pads
To nibble on the flies.
Frogs go splash into the water
And come out in the sun to dry.

Frogs make some people scream.
I scare mom with anything green.
Frogs aren't everyone's dream
Because of pond scum and warts.

Frogs however are pals of mine.
Some people eat their legs when they dine.
Frogs may lead a revolt in time,
I will be their human mind.
Kathy Kontes

Alone

Here I lay alone in the dark
I think of a journey I want to embark.

Always alone I seem to be,
never anyone for me to see

Alone, is such a strong word,
no one wants it to ever be heard

All by myself is the definition
this is the worst kind of premonition

To be all alone 'tis what I'm saying,
can't convince myself into staying
Alone to someone try to explain,
can't believe it causes this much pain

Being alone is so very unkind,
waiting it seems, 'till the end of all time.
Thomas M. Phillips

Lullaby My Little One

Little one who lies beneath my breast
  I think of you with all the love,
    As mother for her child.

Waiting in such sweet expectation,
  Your body to caress,

I sit and dream of you,
  With gentle smile.

Little one, we must be calm
  Although excitement quickens
  My heart beat.

Waiting, has become such joy and yet,
  Mother nature says
  "It's time we meet."

Little one, you're here and as part of me,
  I thrill with such emotion
  That I dare not speak.

I raise my eyes to God in thanks
  For this great miracle

And welcome you with love and joy so sweet.
Mary Nichols

I Took A Walk

Today, I took a walk,
  I walked along a river,
And I thought I caught a glimpse of you,
  I smiled to myself,
Remembering yesterday,
  When you where more than
Just a memory,
  And there for a moment,
I felt you by my side,
  Telling me to spit on the hook
Because it gives the worm more flavor,
  Then I felt a tear run down my cheek,
I swear I heard you say,
  "Don't cry, I'll be there,
Just look around, I'm every where."
Dedicated to Woodrow H. "Woody" Barton
Tammy Hinz

"The Love I Wanted"

When I met you
I wanted only your love
And I feel...
God sent you from above

Your arms hold me so tight
And your loving is just right
Your lips taste like red, red wine
And my heart will be yours for all time

As the years go by,
And we grow older
The gray in your hair
Makes me love you ever more

Yesterday is gone
Just a memory, lost in time
Tomorrow may never be yours or mine
But today God made you mine
Lora Martin Bland

Senses Of Today

Today and forever
I will hear
The voices of my ancestors
Far and near.

Today and forever
I will touch
A really close family
I love so much.

Today and forever
I will taste
The flavor and smell
Of that homemade baste.

Today and forever
I will smell
The roses and robins
from a shell.

Today and forever
I will see
Everything is important
to me
Serah Siemann

If You Touch Me

I will be strong.
I will not shed a tear
but I will smile
even make a joke or two.
I'll hold my head high
and not a soul shall know.
I will go on; I will not bow
nor even bend
but do not sympathize,
show me kindness,
press my hand or hold me
for if you touch me
I shall break.
Macelle Beveridge

Malady

When I was young and full of dreams
I wise man said to me,
"Love is a sickness of the mind
Just wait and you will see.
For love can set the heart on fire
And rob your self control,
It can beguile your sanity
And make you sell your soul.
When joy depends on someone's smile
Or someone's tender kiss,
I ask you now, if there can be
A madness more than this?"
I laughed and went my merry way
With the arrogance of youth,
I soon forgot his warning words
And I dismissed the truth.
But now while crying bitter tears
His words come back to me,
Love is a sickness of the mind
An awesome malady.
Rosemary Muntz Yasparro

What Do You See?

When you look into my eyes
  I wonder what you see.

Do you see dreams for tomorrow
  Or pain wrought of bad decisions?

Do you see happiness in your presence
  Or loneliness of empty years?

Do you see joy from a Spiritual life
  Or sadness of being unfulfilled?

Do you see wholeness
  Or fragmented desires?

Do you see strength and courage
  Or a little girl lost?

Do you see more than I want
  When you look into my eyes?
    Lois J. Woodruff

"For You, Poetry"

To get in the mood for you, poetry
I would have to climb
  forests of deserted souls:
prayers of sleepless wolves
harassing the empty nights
  of stars and moon...
I would have to fiercefully
scream horrendous tears
slipping away from the inner
  tremendous fears
To get in the mood
  for you, poetry
I would have to lose
  all sense of bashfulness
naked as the wind itself
I will have to go to
  a never returned place
to let you be in my domains
in times of cruelty, laughter, anger and pain!
    Raquel M. Vargas

For You

If I could
  I would make the sun shine bright
everyday
If I could
  I would make tears of rain stop
    and the shouts of thunder silent.
If I could
  I would give you the riches of the world
    that you truly deserve.
If I could
  I would give you a rose everyday.
    If I could do all of this...
      For you, I would.
Instead I'll give you a smile and my arms
for comfort.
I will laugh, so as to ease your pain.
  For you...
I will give you my heart
  and with that
I will give you all my love
  For you, given all of these things
    I give you all of myself.
    Mickey Schneider

You are the poetry in my life:

I'd never known what love meant,
until I met you
I never knew how to be happy,
until you shared my laughter
I'd never wanted to keep anything,
until you gave yourself to me
I never knew peace of mind,
until you held my hand
I'd never known passion,
until we wrestled in the dark
I never knew how sweet a kiss could be,
until I tasted your lips
I'd never been proud,
until you whispered my name
I never knew what rest was,
until I fell asleep in your arms
I'd never known how to smile, until I
thought about you
I never knew myself,
until you showed me what I could be
    Matt Ooley

If I Had Wings

If I had wings, wings, wings
I'd fly, fly, fly....
If I could fly, I would fly high
I'd fly high, high, high
If I could fly high I'd fly up to sky
I'd fly up to sky, sky, sky
Then I go over the mountain
over the mountain then I go
Here I come under the mountain
under the mountain here I come
There I go round the mountain
Round the mountain there I go
If I had wings, wings, wings
I'd fly, fly, fly
    Smitha Ahamed

Snowflakes

On cotton tiptoes
ice crystals move
around the moon
They dance and spin
and fill with light
then slowly drift
in cloudless night
while specks of dust
travel upward weightless
above the earth
until surrounded
by their gentle attackers
they peacefully surrender
and tumble out of the sky
flakes of snow
funneled by the wind
    Mary Techmeier

You

You are the one
I will always love
Forever
'Cause their's no one there
no one but me
anywhere
no thing no action could take place
that anyone or anything
could even look past my face
    Lindsey Schuett

My Mule

Poetry's too much like school
I'd rather be out ridin' my mule.
I sit all day and study hard
But I can't forget I've lost my pard.

I remember one day he bucked me off
And I landed in the watering trough.
I was soakin' wet from head to heels,
And my pants were stiff as corset steels.

But I liked that mule,
And I always will,
Although he gave me a dirty spill.
    Lena Dugal

Illusions

Illusions would be best
If sometimes they would last
And not be torn apart
  by stark reality.

A case in point is my mother
who loved her sister and nephews
much more than she would ever
care for a husband and daughter.

She and her sister were
forever two little girls, frozen in time

They played violins together
and my mother was always
second fiddle in this
as she was in everything else.

This family's love evaporated
when the sister died
and the nephews never visited.

The daughter she had scorned,
she and her mate cared for
the mother in her hour of deepest need,
her true family.
    Beverly Rowe

A Bell Will Toll

If you are wise, you know all.
If you are kind, you know more.
The sun will rise, and so you shall.
Peace you'll find, your soul will soar.
Sing in sadness, and in joy cry,
Laugh in sorrow, and smile in pain.
For you then gladness, a loving eye,
And for tomorrow, a new spring rain.
The bell will toll, some one's singing,
Softly I can hear it ringing.
Take no fear, in heart be strong.
Love the one, you know won't care.
Stop and hear, their silent song,
Your pain is done. No chain you'll bear.
Then a new life, will come again.
If you are wise you know all,
So pick up your life, a song begin,
If you are wise, then hear his call.
A bell will toll, someone is singing,
Softly I can hear it ringing.
    Robin T. Beahm

Put Your Life In Your Hands

Put your life in your hands
If you dare
Before you cross the threshold
Of any world
Leave fear behind
Walk on through frightful winds
Though troubled nights press in
Go on
Wrong roads do not exist
Roads but point the way
To weary pilgrims who are the way
Somewhere, Nowhere, Everywhere
It is almost winter
Now the voice from the top of the stairs:
'I must leave you in the dark
This lantern is all the light there is
And I have things to do tonight'
Put your life in your hands
If you dare
Is there anything there to hold?

Thomas A. Fudge

Uncertainty

If you love me- let me know
If you don't- set me free
Let me look for love
in the arms of another.

It hurts me to know
my fate is in your hands
Will I spend forever with you
or travel through life with another?

If you want someone else
let me know so my heart can let go
I don't want to spend one more day
thinking about you
If you are longing for another.

Let me know where we stand
I would rather be certain of your hatred
than uncertain of your love
Do you want me- or another?

Lynn Varghese

Our Love

If you see the sunshine;
If you see the moon glow;
Know that you'll always be mine;
As we progress and grow.
Our hearts are joint together;
Our souls have become one;
Our love is always and forever;
Until our lives are done.
When I feel you near me;
My heart stops in mid-beat;
Our love is never-ending;
As far as we can see.
Will this last forever;
I hope we never part;
Because, if we do;
It will break my heart.

Kristen Bergthold

Untitled

Yellowed photographs
Of memories past, sitting
On my dresser top,
Like guardians of my soul
Silently watching my life.

Lisa McCune

My Brother

Angels cannot console me,
Ignorance controls my fear,
Death and disease is what I see.
Sadness consumes my heart.

What am I to do?
Anger overwhelms my feelings,
Sorrow is my companion.

Madness will soon take me over,
Yet I hope for peace and tranquility.

Brother, who are you?
Reveal yourself to me.
Older I maybe,
Truthful I am not.
Help me find a reason,
Excuses will not do.
Remember me my brother for I need to know you.

Ralph Montemarano

Senseless

Feel the power of the Lord.

Listed to His greatness
ignored ever so blatantly
by generations
rehearsed

Until His Mother's Nature
reminds us of her memories
stored in His mercies and
unleashed,
because of our careless wisdom;

Until earned reprimands
remind us of warning past and
released,
because of our negligence to see
by touch and through smell
to taste. To hear, yet

again ignore ever so senselessly.

Audrey Lipscomb

I Still Care

Although I love you
I'll still walk away
Apology accepted
Nothing more to say
My dreams are shattered
Heart broken beyond repair
What you've done was wrong
But why do I still care
I offered you my life
A priceless treasure
Something you took advantage of
Way beyond measure
I know I must go on
But where do I start
It seems so impossible
With you still in my heart.

Phyllise R. Forbes

Losers

In a certain distant land,
in a not too far-off place
is a certain natural garden
being killed by our own race.

It's size was most impressive
and beauty was most savage,
yet both have gone unnoticed
for it's grace we have ravaged.

It's color was green splendor
now seen grey from skies above;
a travesty of mankind
because of a lack of love.

Our rain forests are now losing
yet mankind is losing, too.
A thought given to think upon:
To thine own self be true.

Kim Silvers

Quiet Place

There's a winding road
  In a quiet place,
And birds fly overhead,
And the grass is cool and sweet
  Where I lay my head.

I watch the clouds drift lazily
  In the pale blue sky,
And there is such peace in my soul
I feel I should surely cry.

A tear from the joy of it
  Trickles down my cheek,
If the tear could be heard
  The music would be sweet.

Sweet with the joy I feel
  Within my heart
For this precious moment in time.
  A moment never to be lived again
But always to be mine.

Regina Walkup

I'll Fly Away!

I'll fly away!
In a sky filled with silver lace.
Along a grand board walk.
For a single moment's grace.
Or to see the smile of an angels face.

I'll fly away!
On the wings of a silky white dove.
Far away, and without a trace.
To the majestic God, I love!
In the endless times; forever, above!

I'll fly away!
From days, with long hard ends.
Soaring whimsical, as the night-hawk.
With a whisper of the northern wind.
On a never ending search, for a friend.

I'll fly away!!
I'll fly away!!

Robert L. Perkins

Sad Glory

You glide across the sky
In a velvet dress
blues...purples...
With beams of light
thrown across your coat
glittering
like the night's sky.
You sparkle with a sad glory.
Your tears pour down my cheeks,
And my heart aches
may sad, sad, glory.

In dreams you come to me
and your eyes fill me up.
Lay your hands upon me...
I can feel your love
deep in my soul.
The sun too soon awakens
and I am alone...
Left to feel my own
sad glory.

Kathryn L. Pringle

We...The People

As beings of this planet we call Earth
In an effort to survive...

Should ignore our differences
Herald one another's accomplishments
and embrace each other's existence

Does the bird not love the butterfly?
Which both upon wings grace the skies..

WE...The People

Should love our fellow man
Allowing each one to be a friend.

Constructing and not destroying
This brilliant plateau
Upon which we live

Each sunrise could bring
A new beginning

Filling the Atmosphere
With love, happiness, peace and good cheer
For all who live here

H. Labron Simpson

Youth

He strides through
  In angry cadence,
    Glancing, slyly, to see
    If I am watching.
I am watching
  So he retreats,
    Arrogantly, defiantly, to see
    If I will ask.
I do ask.
  He has no answer
    For reasons yet beyond him,
    But close, for as he goes,
He meets my eyes,
  Touches my hand - lightly
    Trying to make that step,
    Strengthening the tie between us
My son and I -
  Friends then, friends still,
    Friends at last.

Sandra Matteson Dusch

Sarah

What a woman is Sarah?
In child-like wit;
Quite the jester.
In knowledge;
how like the scholar.
With royal charm,
and a swan's grace,
she holds me enrapt;
like an angel's song.
Sarah, my Sarah
Do you need me?
Do you miss me?
My want, her want.
My prayer, her prayer.
So far away in the
ancient suns glow.
Weep in the darkness,
Afraid,
Alone.

Thomas J. Kern

Wisdom In Faith

Wisdom we seek to find
In everything we do
Yet we realize not
Where wisdom comes
Our mind sees the terror
While our heart speaks the truth
Our hands reach for freedom
As our feet walk on
Why do we dream in something
If it only fades away
The light of the candle
Can only burn so long
Love is a word we give
To something we feel
But do we believe in that feeling
That's the real question
Time is here for us
Not against us
And the light will show the way
If we simply have faith

Michael D. Boven

Regarding the Moon

I saw the moon last night,
In her shinning brilliance,
like a jewel;
Illuminating the dark blue
pallet of sky that lies
before her.
She seemed to smile
in the most beguiling way.
Like the Mona Lisa,
she said nothing...
Yet, I heard every word she said.

Nicole Chavez

Life

Life is not unlike a seasoned
leaf, ever-changing in its tumulus
descent to earth, to lie amongst
an infinite gathering of the like,
only to whither and die and be
known no more.

Sean McGarvey

The Painting

I painted a picture
in my mind
Of all the feelings
I've kept inside
A big black painting
with tiny strips of red
one for each and every
tear I've shed
They're scattered out wildly
like slashes from a knife
They represent a feeling
of each moment in my life
Some are big and
some are small
There's just so many
I couldn't count them all
I painted this picture
Then I tore it apart
for the whole idea
represented my heart

Shea Arnold

In Honor Of Walt Kelly

How cheap and easy are words
in other words with Owl
it is another words always

Just fine says Bug
he almost became my
loan arranger

everything is
just on loan
the sun rises every day

he then sets
yes he likes gender
spends the night

Who knows where
what will he eat
where would a quarter go

Except around a dime
What if it were midday all day
I mustn't think of it

Kees W. Bolle

Friends

There comes a time,
  In our lives, when sorrow
Becomes a part of the sublime,
  In every tomorrow.

Friends may come,
  And friends may go.
Helping us to grow some,
  In faith, by the seed they sow.

Joy may come from sadness
  With God as our companion.
Bringing sadness to gladness,
  By our prayer in unison.

Mildred H. Dhondt

Bayloo

You've clearly struggled then, with life,
In shapely strength not oft' awry;
As life's delusions brought forth strife,
And flak of anguish to your sky.

By cruel reality oppressed,
Whose truths one needs at last embrace.
Chagrin...its moral good confess;
Resilient in thine willowed grace.

In strength resolved to live each day,
Eschewing all inertia's power,
Elude intimidation's stays.
Enthrall to sunlight be the flower.

Courageous in enlightened view,
To marshall forth redemptive plan;
And set the engine's goal anew,
Renewing life on frontier's land.

Shall we count coup in common rite
Transcending ignominies of yore;
Then may this catwalk - we call life
With poise be braved in joy once more.

R. Garner Brasseur

The Candyman

The face you see,
In the bathroom mirror,
Is your own.
You have no fear.

Turn out the light,
And close the door.
Call his name,
Three times or more.

When your eyes adjust,
A face appears.
It is not your own,
But he who leers.

With his menacing laugh
And his wicked smile,
You know in your heart
He is truly vile.

You reached out to him,
And turn from grace.
He beckons you come
To his cold embrace.

Stacy Hilton

Christmas Eve

We stand outside the stable
 In the clear and starry night;
The inn is quiet, the townsfolk sleep,
 From the manger, a glowing light...
With awe the shepherds gather
 From field and hill afar;
Angels above, beasts below
 Wait the promise of the star.
Is this the time, foretold of yore?
 Is this the place, is this the one?
We stand ready to adore
 The gift from God: His own dear son.

Norine W. Sharp

Dark Reminders

A single lone wolf
In the darkness of her night
Licks her wounds of sorrow
That represent her relentless fight.

A fight that was very intimate,
A fight between her and her mate,
A mate that was to have lasted a lifetime,
Instead he was taken by fate.

Nightly she howls in the darkness,
Nightly two tears doth she shed,
A tear for the happiness she had
And a tear for the heart she must mend.

Shannon M. Pawley

The Biplane

I was up in a biplane
in the mist and rain,
when a fist -
on the end of a wrist
hit me in the brain.

Now, right then I felt a pain
and insisted that the fist
on the end of the wrist
be put on a chain.

Much to my dismay
that fist -
on the end of a wrist
did not exist
up in this biplane,
in the mist and rain.

Meghan Phillippi

Two Tracks

The first two tracks
in the sand today
were yours and mine.
All too soon
waves will come
and wash them away.
But they'll linger
in my mind.
The first two tracks
in the sand today.

Linda Allen

The Last Dance

So we whiffle, waffle, wuffle
in the shifty, shuffling sand

Twisting, listing, laughing
to the twerpy, slurpy band

And my partners's snappy quips
and the way she licks her lips

Makes me woozy in the belly
in a place between my hips.

So she lilts, and laughs, and sways
in the summer of my gaze

And snips, and slips, and slides
to the winter of my days

And the wit, and chit, and chat
comes to this and then to that

For the dance is almost over
and her hand slips from my grasp.

Neal B. Groman

This House

There it stood out
In the still of night
The lights from the windows
We're shining so bright

And I could remember
As a child, I lived there
The memories came back
I could only stand, and stare.

I can remember the Christmas's
Oh, so very long ago
When my family lived there
And how, we played in the snow

I just had to return
Just this one last time
To remember the happiness
When this house was mine.

Norma Elaine Edwards

Spring!!

Sometimes when you go outside
in the sunny spring
It's nice to see the flowers grow
with all the joy they bring.

It's fun to see the children
running all around
but it hurts to see the flowers
being squished to the ground.

When the kids come in for lunch
their mothers always say
go and wipe your feet
please do it every day!!

Katelyn Jane Jacobson

Together Hand In Hand

Come let us walk together
 in the time that we have left —
Let's leave a ray of sunshine
 for all that we've been blessed.

Let's fill the days with gladness
 and love our fellow man —
Let's do our best for others
 as we journey hand in hand.

Sharing of our knowledge
 scattering all our love —
Traveling along life's highway
 with our Maker from above.

And when evening shadows lengthen
 we lay us down to rest —
Comforted in our knowing
 we have done our very best.

Velores (Val) Jones

Untitled

Courteous
Independent
Teachers
Individuals
Zestful
Energized
Nationalism
Supervisors
Heartful
Intelligent
Polite

LaShonda Yvette Spence

For Sallie (1876 - 1925)

Sallie, you never held me
in the warmth of your arms.
Sallie, you never smiled
and cooed at me.

Sallie, I never gazed into
your brilliant blue eyes;
Nor, did I ever wear a little
dress that you sewed for me.

Sallie, there was no time left
to rock me, under the shade
of the old Paw Paw tree.

You left us when you were very young;
And for you, my heart has always longed.

Still, I feel I've known you, Sallie..
Listen, Grandmother,
Do you hear my song?

Loralie Frances Dearinger Howe

Untitled

Love is evil
in this day and age,
a moment of pleasure,
years of rage.
Be careful when you sleep
and play with care,
a moment of passion,
years of despair.
This little flea
cares not who feels its breath,
a moment without thy sheath
years of horrid death.

Laura Dean

Hands Of A Blind Man

How lucky I am,
In this world,
Able to see,
Able to hear,
Able to talk and many more,
But do I pity those who can't
Or do they fascinate me?
At church the other day,
I shook the hand of a blind man,
A man who lives his life sightless,
He walks, he listens, he'll even join in on
the conversation,
Even though he can't see,
He shakes my hand with a sense of who I am.
He sings, if he knows the words,
He hums if he doesn't
I wonder as I look at him,
Am I the lucky one,
Or is it really him?

Nicole Deters

A Day In His Life

A day starts early just like his:
It begins with wonder.
Each accomplishment carries content.
Able to work, play and live his life.
To know that he knows, and is pleased.
A day ends with satisfaction.
More pleasure need not be realized.
A day in my life.

Stephen Edward Molcsan

Memory

The memory of being
In your arms,
The feeling of protection
From harm,
Will remain with me
Through the years,
'Til old age
Slips its shroud
Across my mind,
And allows
Forgetfulness to meld
My loves, fears and tears,
Into a fabric of
Vague recollections,
From the threads
Of all those bygone years.

Susanna H. Knapp

Remembering

Echoes of past summers drift slowly
into a foggy memory,
and the sparkle of anticipation
lights up my blue mood.

Shadows of a distant past
throw a pleasant shade
on the highlights of today.

Yesterday is gone,
but the picture it once painted
stains my palette
and my brush aches to dip
a second time.

Linda S. Rickabaugh

Fly Away

Further and further
Into destiny we flow
Only one is sure
Only one can grow

Ah, we see it
It sparks and glows
The candle is lit,
We both know

How it burns inside
An everlasting desire
Lust that shines through
Eternal fire.
Our love, so true

On the highest cliff
Above the deepest sea
Our love can conquer
Forever, may it be!

Michele Hoxie

Untitled

A rose is a flower like no other
Its pedals are made of silk
But never trust a cats beauty
Because under the soft velvety paw
Lies a thorn.

Oriana Hauer

Night Search

I walk alone as darkness falls
Into the land of night...
Hoping to see, in this dim world,
What was obscured by light.

The moon is full and shines for me
To light my darkened way,
Searching for that perfect love
I could not find by day.

The myriad of twinkling stars
Keeps me company
Along the dark and lonely path
As I search eternally.

I walk along the Milky Way,
The rainbow of the night...
Perhaps I'll find its golden pot
Not visible in light.

The silence pushes me away
And permeates my soul,
So I must return tomorrow night
To pursue my elusive goal.

Sondra Weiss

Take Me Away

Pull me away,
Into the night,

I want you to,
take me,
away from this hell.

I wanna be,
a star like you,
always shining,
in the middle of a crowd.

I only love one,
but you, love a universe,

I think I love,
but I don't know.

Is love an actual marriage,
or is it, just holding hands.

Molly Beth Morganski

Untitled

Strength
is a tender rose 'mongst bitter thorns.
Courage
is rising above one's own fears.
A woman
is the inner beauty she possessess.
A man
is one who will die for her,
yet cry with her.
Beauty
is a love pure and true.
Innocence
is a new life born of love
shared between two.w
Love
is when I'm with you.

Ron Bell

A Cry In The Night

A cry in the night,
is all I have left.
In the lonely world outside,
there is too much light, for me to escape.
When the sun goes down.
And the moon comes up.
My heart begins to breathe
from the darkness above.

A cry in the night,
is when I'm all alone.
When no one is there.
When no one is home.
I cry so loud,
that even heaven can hear.
All my grief, all my sorrow,
all the life, that I've lived.
All the love that I lost,
all the pieces of my soul.
That are there, but are all alone.

Tali Zelkin

A Mask Covering True Identity

Behind my mask
is another world
Behind my sparkling eyes
are silent cries,

Unending tears waiting to escape
Unsure of what goes on behind my iron slate
My mask is how I'm "supposed" to be
But behind it all, is my true identity,

Behind my exultant smile
is someone feeling low
But all they see is a never ending glow

Behind my mask there are endless scars
that no one can see
So much anguish belongs to me.

Lisa Roper

Of Time And Value

More life for you? For me?
  Is breath but that:
    added years
    of pleasant hours
    within time?

What of life's quality:
  values beyond
    money
  and satisfaction
  and frail pride?

If more time be all,
  then life,
    like a dead dog,
    should be buried
    and forgot.

G. J. Dubovik

"The Wall"

No one knows what it holds within.
It may have fingers, claws, or fins.
A passerby hears a scream;
he hopes that it is all a dream.
But with each coming step he takes,
his body slowly starts to quake.
A nearby gate squeaks to a close;
but by whom no one knows.

Katie Scarlett Kelly

Love

The reason for me to live
Is for the love I can give
Each bit of love is never lost
It rings on wings of a heavenly host
And is recorded in the heart of God
For us to share for us to give
This is the reason for us to live.

We can know a love so strong
That life goes forever on
In the power of God love we can be
Forever safe in eternity
God is love therefor I see
The reason for me to be
Is to let Gods love flow throw me
To all suffering humanity

Wrapped in his arms of love
All of life is clear to me
A peace so sweet a love explained
Now we can know and we can see
That love is all life was meant to be

Stella S. Stern

Why Do I Love You?

Why do I love you?
Is it because
To me you present
All the magic of the stars?
Have you ever looked at star dust
In the darkness of the night
And it seemed as if God was sending down:
His heavenly light.
Now I ask myself
Why do I think of you?
And the answer comes to me in the
Darkness of the blue.
I think of you because you are all these
Things I adore and I will always
Love you forever more.

Sarah Murrell

About The Mind

I wonder what goes thru someone's mind.
Is it love they want to find?
Is it hate of some kind?
Are they living with fear?
Have they lost someone dear?
Going for a new job.
Is someone ready to rob?
Is there an operation near?
Waiting for something to be a cleared?
Going on a first date?
Getting to work and being late?
Looking for a new car?
Or living it up in a bar?
Writing a story of your life?
Waiting for a divorce from your wife?
Going to the doctor and finding something wrong?
making a video singing a song?
Gambling lots of money away?
  Most of all.
Hoping everything works out for the day.

Sophie M. Sobers

Steerage

This life I must say
is like a horse run wild
while I bareback do cling
to mane and tail with a terrified smile

There's danger in this headlong dash
if only I could steer or lead
but safety is not foremost
to this wild impulsive steed

Thundering hoofbeat on the frozen ground
assails my battered brain
clattering across rickety bridges
then mercifully, back to sod again

Freezing rain, we gallop still
blistering sun, as cruel as the chill

One day this horse may stumble
who knows how great the pain
when the ride is finished
mercifully, back to sod again

Tom Morgan

River Of Memories

River of memories
Is like sunshine and rain
Some makes you happy
Some bring you pain.

River of memories
Worth more then gold,
Memories of moonlight
To have and to hold.

Memories so precious
I hold in my heart
Knowing the rip tide
Will soon tear us apart.

Tho we may be together
We will never be apart
For there is a bond between us
From you straight to my heart.

Lona Hutson

Love

The love we share
Is oh so rare
We laugh we cry
We wonder why.

Together we are
Together we'll be
Then why do we separate
You from me?

We think we act
Without a word
Then are ashamed
For being so bold.

The things we do
The places we see
Never as me
But always as we.

Our love is rare
As we are two
From one to another
I love you.

Linda A. Bell

Enigma

Our cat Fred
Is sitting on our bed
His amber eyes transfixed
Upon an empty wall
Enrapt by nothing there at all.
Is he bewitched?
Could it be self-hypnosis?
Or maybe a psychosis?
He sits and stares unblinking
At what I have no inkling.
Does he see things that we
mere humans cannot see?
It's a very well-known fact
And one that's indisputable
That felines are inscrutable.
That's cats!
Thelma Kellogg

The Cat I Hate

The cat that I hate
is the cat that stays up late.

He's very mean,
and sort of lean,

He's the cat that I hate.

He picks on all the smaller cats
including my little brat.

My brat tries to fight
but ends up getting more bites.

The cat that I hate
is now tied up to a gate.

So I won't see that
cat anymore!
Stephanie Andor

Life

Oh life so vain,
  is there no end to the pain?

Days lost, years past,
  Sorrow that always last.

From one journey to the next,
  An endless sea of misery.

Till one day you'll find,
  Life really was kind.

We make our life good or bad
  Our decision is what we had.

Oh so blind why I can not see?
  My life is made by only me.
Lisa Kallab

"Whispering Leaves"

A few days ago, it seems,
It felt positively freezing.
Now I awake... a new day
Taking in the scent of Spring
And the sun gleaming.
The sky clear and quiet, the air clean.
I stop to listen . . .
Whispering leaves, romance the trees.
Ruth Yates

Now and Then

A friend
Is there when you need him to be.
Wouldn't disappoint you purposely.
Applauds you when you're up.
Supports you when you're down.
Is your best buddy all around.

Now
You were not a friend to me
Chances are you will never be.
There are no chances left you see.
You've spent them all selfishly.
So many years wasted foolishly.
Expecting you to become friendly
How to state this simply?
There is no more we.
There is only you....
And just plain me.
G. Constant

Kindness

Did you ever think that kindness
Is to life as yeast to bread,
Kindness that will lift the spirit,
Banish cares and fear and dread.

It is found in little bundles
Of things we do each day
For those who are about us -
In some deed that smooths the way.

A word that's spoken softly,
A kindly twinkle of the eye,
Some little act of helpfulness,
A smile but not a sigh.

Will weary burdens lighten,
Keep a broken heart at ease.
Kindness is some tender mission
That's often done to please.
B. Jetton

Grammy's Smile

Grammy's smile is the bestest smile,
  it can swoosh away trouble.
Why, it's so warm and friendly...
  it'll make your goose bumps bubble.

Grammy's smile is the bestest smile,
  there just ain't any better.
And the nice part is she'll share it...
  all you have to do is let her.

Grammy's smile is the bestest smile,
  full of love and tender feeling.
And just like homemade chicken soup...
  is awfully good at healing.

Grammy's smile is the bestest smile,
  except for just one other,
And that's the smile that Grammy has
  when she smiles at you as Mother.
Richard Rampolla

Morning Flower

I saw a flower to my delight
It's Petals fragrant, soft and white.
I saw a flower to my delight
It's petals kissed with morning dew.
I've never seen a softer hue.
I saw a flower to my delight
It's petals fragrant, soft and white.
Lisbeth Anderson

"An Alien Hides On Your Porch"

Nestled around a woven God
it cries in the night
for a duplicate monster...
With a hole in his pocket
where he carries his time
It's fearing heart feeds
the poetic soul...
He's on fire in the head
and his toes are freezing..
Morning brings him death
of a thousand fears
and his baby in tears
wandering and growing
in our lost city
Richard W. Siems Jr.

Dreams Shattered

Lives scattered, dreams shattered,
It does matter.

Dreams of tomorrow
Brings sorrow.

Dreams of yesteryear of the
Love ones dear.

Dreams that end with tears.
Memories gone by.
Blew up in the sky.
  Why?

Young souls will never
Grow old.

Love ones we yearn to hold
They will never meet their goals.

Dreams that will never be.
Dreams that meant so much to thee.
Marlene Crowell

The Sunflower

There is a flower we all know
It grows tall as it can be.
It has a cheery color
And friends called honeybees.

It reaches high into the sky
Growing huge with all its power.
This flower reaching to the sun
Is called the bright "Sunflower."

It looks so grand against azure skies
With clouds as white as they can be.
And when there is a field of them,
It looks like a sunny, yellow sea.

Their bright and cheery color,
It makes us feel so warm.
Just like the sun and summer breeze
That take away the storms.

So, I greatly admire you, "Sunflower,"
Growing tall as you can be.
You get to touch the azure skies
And talk to the honeybees.
Kathy A. Singley

Untitled

As quickly as it came
It is now gone
Left are the memories
Standing all alone

Upon a new horizon
Hidden from despair
Words of lasting promise
Still hang in the air

Taken from a poem
Lost on a cold heart
Epic is the treasure
Forgotten in the dark

Longing and loving
Lasting through a span
Compassion stepped in
And led me by the hand

Kristi Dawson

Perpetuity

Beauty is for memory;
It isn't meant to last!
The rainbow and the sunset
Both go by so fast.

But when we think of beauty
Far beyond compare.
The rainbow and the sunset
Are always ours to share.
So why should I be saddened
Because my dream is gone
When deep within my memory
The beauty lingers on!

Neva Dawkins

Computer

Computer is king
  it knows everything
It tracks every drive, every dollar
  It sees every cent
  Where it came, where it went
It seem its a number one scholar

  It seems that it knows
  Where the money tree grows
How to plant it and raise it and tend it
  Its joy to the soul
  A healthy bank roll
In encourage how not to spend it

  But I cannot see
  How it will help me
Computer, I simply cant do it
  If fall down and stay
    adrift and astray
While other folks, they will go to it

Wilmer Wilcox

Post Script

Life gives some pain,
Life gives some sorrow.
But with a little help
From God,
We'll be happy tomorrow!

Louis A. Suchanek

The Bombardment

The bombardment was brutal,
It lasted for days.
We were all baffled,
As we stared through the haze.
The smoke filled our lungs,
It burned at our eyes,
The roar of the cannons,
Rang through the skies.
We ran for the muskets,
To defend our fort,
But cannonballs kept flying,
From the ship in the port.
We kept on fighting,
Through the blistering heat,
And when nighttime fell,
We forced a retreat.

Nick Maieritsch

I Like Reading Poetry

I like poetry far and wide;
it makes me want, to run and hide;

To a far secluded place;
where I don't have the world to face.

Perhaps another place in time;
where me and poetry, are all mine!

Let us go now; let's make haste!
not a second must we waste!

There we'll have the time to kill!
reading poetry at will.

There is no sun rise or sun set;
it's strictly poetry, we'll get!

A place where light shines all the time;
where me and poetry, are all mine!

A place where I can lay in bed;
letting poetry fill my head!

There is no need to eat and drink;
more time for poetry; don't you think?

So come with me, let's be the first!
with poetry, well quench our thirst!

Robert E. Filip

Attainment

The moon is knowledge and wisdom
It may not be seen sometimes
For the clouds cover its reflection
But clouds go away

I may see the moon through tree limbs
Or through my windowpane — while inside
It may bounce right off the water

Moons do enlighten me
They affect my tidal waves of anger
Without those tidal waves,
I would be like the many fish
Who would flounder around without a beginning

We see the moon on earth because of the
reflection of the sun
You are the sun
I am the earth
The moon is ours

Marsha L. Geist

Change?

Time goes by,
It seems to fly,
And I sit and wonder why.

So many things seem to change,
And stay the same, it is so strange.

Is the sense of change just a deception?
Is it really just a change in perception?

Are we just seeing in a different way,
Than we were yesterday?

So the question is, which I pose to you:
Is this change really true?
Or might it be we choose to see,
The same things, a little differently?

We seek progress through changes,
But could it be our mind, just rearranges?
The same old stuff each and every day,
Our minds might just be bored, and with us
will play.

Making us believe that things are new,
When really it's just our change in view.

Laura L. Bron

Women Of Today

Once upon a time
It was believed that women
should be pedestals to men

Women were expected
to be soft-spoken and smiling,
while men basked in the glory.

However, we, the women of today
have the grace to hold ourselves high.

Today's women
are more than just pretty faces,
We are strong, goal-oriented individuals
who fight for what we believe in.

We have come a long way
since our ancestors;
For we are Mothers, Doctors,
Company C.E.O's and Role Models.
By not giving up on our dreams,
by experiencing life
we have not ceased being women.
Celebrate the woman that you are!

Marilyn Vega

In Cherished Memory

In cherished memory of all our dear ones,
Life is but a garden, in which we
plant seeds
Hope, love and tenderness of kindly
thoughts and deeds.
When the Sun has settled beyond the Hill
and tender blooms have vanished,
And Dear Hearts are still,
We live with Memories, faith courage
and Trust,
Till we meet our Loved ones
In the Heavens, as we must

Mary Perlow

Dance On The Sparkle Of The Dew

Reach out to capture the moment
It's the dawning of a new day
Dream your dreams your way
On the horizon of the sunrise
Everything is fresh and new
Dance on the sparkle of the dew

I should let you go
Just like the sunset turning into night
Don't you know I loved you so
It's time my heart took flight
Across the night sky
To the horizon of true love
The time has come to untie the lace
Of your love from my heart
And cast the ghost of your memory
To the winds that haunt
The passages of my mind
Everything is fresh and new
Dance on the sparkle of the dew

Sonja S. Rodger

"The Winner"

"Life is like the lottery,
It's yours to win or lose -
We gamble, it's either make or break,
From birth we have to choose"

"With life you either play it safe,
Or take a chance you'll win -
To start from the beginning,
As you go through thick or thin"

I've taken many chances,
Hoping to win it big.
But as luck would have it,
No time for me to jig"

"We've been married nearly fifty years,
We've shared the good and bad -
We're looking ahead for the big five-O,
A time to be happy, not sad"

"Today I feel like a million,
Without a worry or care -
No more betting the lottery,
Only wifey's love to share"

Marty Rollin

A Dream

Now that I know
I've been dreamin' all along
imagining you were here
right beside my side
thinkin' you were always mine.

Now that I see
it was never meant to be
'cause you found someone new
and I am only a fool.

Even to think
that it was really true.
Now that I know
I shouldn't have loved you.

Saumi Luong

"The Orphan Ship"

"Oh, God, since I've come to Thee
I've felt like an orphan ship
on an open sea
 A stranger to all ports to be
 Longing for my new home
I want to see
 Northwest across the Lords sea
of stars
 Toward Christ' glory, our
beacon in the night
 Surer then any port-O-call
already in sight
 Oh, Lord, do not tarry!
 The Earth seas are getting
stormy
 But however long it takes
I'll never be beguiled
 I now have my sea legs and I'll
Stand as your child"

Larry Dean McClure

"A Poem for my Grandpap"

Since the day you left me
I've never been the same
The tears just won't stop falling
but no one is to blame
Why did you have to suffer
Why did God choose you
You were such a good person
Always cheerful, hardly ever blue
I hope you know we were there
every step of the way
We will always love you
And that will never change
I wish you were here now
I never got to say
How much I am going to miss you
Each and every day!

Lauren Ross

Moods

My thoughts are like a skipping child
Jumping from stone to stone,
Stopping just to change direction,
Amusing itself alone.

My thoughts are like a gushing brook
Whose waters do not flow deep,
Not marking any impressions
Or pebbles that one can keep.

My thoughts are like a heavy veil,
Misty in its appearance,
Making me wonder about life
And its strange occurrence.

My thoughts are like a massive stone,
Difficult to dispel,
Though I may try with all my might,
They always come back to dwell.

Lee Dubin Lasker

Like A Rose

Like a rose I was once a bud
Like a rose I was small and tight
Like a rose I grow and grow
Like a rose I lived my life
Like a rose I wilted away.

Amanda Burgess

Growing Up Trouble

It wasn't long ago,
just a couple of weeks
I got into trouble yea! Pretty deep
Pete was yelling
Mom was too
'Cause I busted a tire
on the mower, that's true
Please have patients with me
You see, God's not quite
finished with me
But it won't long and
I'll be a man
Then God will say I finished
my plan.

Nickolas Proctor

A Moment To Wonder

The wind dashes by in a glance
Just as it was still yesterday
The clouds shift in subtle threads
Even as my eye meets the moving edge

It's soft, floating
Like chiffon between my breast
Ever moving, changing, feeling

The trees move like a graceful swan
In the soft breeze
It touches me gently
Then, I follow nothing
As you are lying there
So still, quiet, frozen

A little imp with a halo
That you are
I never know what you'll do
For then you've come and gone

Susan Smeltzer

My Wall

The memories that haunt me,
Just seem to slip away;
Behind the wall of loneliness
That helps me face the day.
I needed something to keep me strong
When everything seemed bleak;
That wall was my protection
And I did not have to speak.
The pain was always there,
Behind this built in safe;
I use to keep this pain inside
And not destroy my faith.
Sometimes when the sadness
Keeps coming back to me;
I use that wall many times
To keep my sanity!

Odessa A. Szumita

The Burial

A coffin passed through the mist,
 like a pyramid rising,
Tears in raindrop patterns
 long black dresses furrowing the earth

Fallen lilies in a field,
 sadness, like incense in the air
Breathing deeply, deeply, into despair

Louise Lopez

Tears

One mighty blow heard round the globe
Kind of like two clashing worlds
Land of freedom has been rocked
Always looking back in shock
Humble though we may be
One can bring us to our knees
Many of us cry at night
Always thinking of the sight

Crayons and toys lay on the rubble
Innocent blood spilled on forever
Tears of anguish heard all around
Yours and mine fell on the ground

Babies faces come to thought
Of the loved ones we have lost
Mother's cry heard in the night
Bring my babies out alright
Intervene dear Lord we pray
Nothing helps me with this pain
Grant me freedom from this suffering

Lana Purcell

A Friend

Friends are a lot of fun,
Laughing, yelling, laying in the sun.
Carefree, walking, gaily along,
Sharing a thought, a joke, a song.

Sharing sorrow, tears, and grief,
Sharing a snowflakes, a raindrop, a leaf.
Sharing a silent spot;
Enemies we're not!

These are all signs of a friend,
A friend is a start - not and end.
It's open as a door,
But there's so much more.

Friendships forever -
And always to share.

Liola Bice

I Don't Understand

I don't understand why the ozone
  layer has holes,
Why people in our own country
  are starving,
While we feed other countries! or
  why people are racist.
But most of all, I don't understand
  why my hair won't do what I
  want it to.
Why the sun doesn't set to the east,
How magnets work
And why calculators are smarter
  than me.

Kellie D. Smith

Mid-Life Journey

Passing through mid-life
Like a ship upon the sea,
Good voyage results
From thoughtful navigation!

Paula Tingley

Meditation In A Japanese Garden In Kyoto

Silent, odd shaped trees and mounded hills
  leaved into a cloudless sky,
They pleaded for an adoring eye.
Birds trilled defying the quiet beauty and
  competed for ecstasy.
Sensually waters in the lake rippled as
  gold fish etched their space.
Tall grasses and hanging branches with
  pink blossoms stared at their beauty in
  a mirrored image.
Bent over gardeners stoically raked
  stones and pushed grasses. They
  made funny shadows.
Suddenly a gust of wind ruffled every
  tree and bush and even the flowers
  danced.
I forgot to meditate. I laughed.

Muriel Krug Wiemer

Seasons Of Life

Autumn colors all around
Leaves of gold, and red, and brown
Breezes blowing, dark clouds showing
Drying leaves come twirling down
And make a cover on the ground
Cooler nights and birds in flight
Warming fires and candle light
Sitting by the fire so bright
Holding hands on winters night
Quiet moments passing fast
How we wish this time would last
Outside winter winds are blowing
All to soon snow will be falling
Off to bed to dream life's dream
Resting peacefully, so serene
Waking to the morning light
Sunbeams shining oh so bright
Seasons passing in the night
Warming fires and candle light
Another day,...another night

Loretta M. Wismer

Lost-A-Poem

Once again, not much time
Left for me, to pen a rhyme

Chaucer dear, do tell me please
How to find your expertise,

Perhaps I need a Thoreau Pond
To free my poem from worldly bond.

Sweet hope, that springs eternally
Bring back the dream that used to be
I'll nourish it most tenderly!

'Tis quiet now, no kids at play
And chattering planes have gone away

Sweet music now, I softly hear,
How Brahms does soothe a troubled ear!

Alas! is that my timer calling me
To wrest me from my reverie?

And alas for me—tis plain to see
That dinner steals priority!

Yet much sweet joy awaits for me
At Chaucer's Thursday Poetry.

Lillian K. Smith

The Storm

This day I awake,
  life anew I partake;
tempting not fate,
  thanks, the heavens shake!

Now the rain must fall,
  and answer to its call;
Look higher and higher,
  see the sky on fire?

Boom the thunder bang,
  accompanying the rain!
The bright light in the sky
  is similar to the eye.

Lightning so crisp and clean,
  to gaze at it so serene;
elements together,
  the fear seems forever.

Deep deeper we look,
  to find the truth we shook;
the mirrors in our mind,
  will fade just give them time.

Michael C. Jones

The Candle

Daybreak and the candle ends,
Life ebbs, as the long trail bends...
Will it go to horizon's edge
Or mesh with the clouds sailing by?

What is in store for the soul?
A passing over, and out?
A sailing and a rout?
What does it mean - the candle's end?
What portends the dreams that rend?

I treasure most, I think,
The gift I was given . . .
I did deliver
Hope for the driven.

Goldie R. Scherberg

Matin

Dawn; quiet, still.
Life's calgon time.
Body, spirit refreshed.
Tranquil respite...

Like a clean slate, the day ahead.
What will it bring? Maybe I will...
I should... I have so much to do.

Stop! Be still.
Stay within the present.
Don't mark your slate just yet.
Let us silently visit.
Let this be our time,
to re-member, re-create, re-joyce.

We need each other to facilitate today.

Yes, you're right.
It is easy to get caught up in I.
Well, let us go: sweep the floor,
offer a hand, be there for another.

I enjoyed our visit.
Let's meet for a coffee break.

Nancy L. Annoreno

"Do You Know Me"

Do you know me
  Like I know me
Can you like me
  Like I like me
Do you think I am pretty
  Like I feel I am
Do you know me
  When I am sad
    Blue and lonely too
Do you know me
  When I am happy
    gay and carefree
Do you know me
  When I am just me
So do you know me
  Like I know me...

Shasta Arnold

Adam

You will find many names in the bible
Like Shadrack, Mesach and Abednego
There is Jonah and Eli, Noah and Ham
But Adam came first, don't you know

History has names like Lewis and Clark
Baseball had a guy called Joe
Bethoven made music, Galileo saw stars
But Adam came first don't you know

I will meet people with different names
As through life's journey I go
But there won't be another like Adam
He will always come first don't you know

Nancy Ripley

Too High A Price

My darling little angels
Like stars you shine so bright
I love you more than life itself
Someday I'll make it right

I pray someday you'll understand
and forgive your mom and dad
for making you two pay the price
when things for us went bad

We didn't mean to hurt you
we didn't mean to fight
But, sometimes we do foolish things
instead of what is right.

And so my precious angels
you must know this is true
That even though we're all apart
we always will love you.

Stephanie Reiswig

The Journey

I feel so strange
Like there's some place to go
What it is; is change
This I know
The journey of your life
It sticks you like a knife
Some pain, happiness and sorrow
It feels like there's no tomorrow
But when it's said and done
It seems like you've won
The journey

Trisha Denette

Season's End

Lacy petals brush my cheek
like the breath of a butterfly,
soft and slight, a whisper,
as the clouds roll softly by.

The summer scent of flowers
flirts sweetly with my mind,
an elusive recollection
of a place I long to find.

Sunlight, honey-gold and sleepy
mellow-tinged behind closed eyes,
intoxicates my consciousness,
beckons dream's gentle sighs.

The birds' songs from the treetops
blend with the silent green;
I mourn the day, the season,
with a smile, gentle and serene.

Lisa Helen Phillips

Dream Angel

My eyes,
Like the silver screen,
While I slumbered,
She appeared,
dressed in snow-white,
Eyes of aqua-marine,
feather wings to soar,
unselfish, cherishing, tender
Inquiring of my one wish,
I replied sincerely,
Unconditional love,
Smiling kindly,
She slowly faded,
back into my dream world.

Sharleen C. Hutchins

Timeless Moment

The moss was soft
like velvet to the touch
The rock was warm
and rough
and solid in the earth
A hazy, golden light
pervaded all around
It was perfection

And at that moment
In my mind
I saw what could have been
A life time
Melting into seconds
Then quickly, as it came
It went
And flew away
with the breeze that followed

Mary Wittkower

Untitled

Salty blue green mist
Murmur of a rhythmic roar
Vide 'o Mare Bello!

P. A. D'Alessandro

Soft Rain Whisper's Your Name

Soft rain whisper's your name
Like water dancing to music
Dreaming sweet vision of summer
Of me and you
Soft rain whisper's your name
Sweetly cross my lips
Bending down to kiss you
Like a thousand times
I have done in my dreams
Soft rain whispers your name
I look into your eyes
With love and understanding
Like a warm summer breeze
Blowing softly throw your hair
Soft rain whispers your name
You hold out your hand for me to take
Pulling me closer, with your warm and
gentle touch
Soft rain whisper's your name
Like water dancing to music
Dreaming sweet, vision of summer

Martha Jane

The Only Cure

Open up your heart
like you care.
Look into my eyes
and see my tears.
Listen to me
and let me share
my feelings, if you dare.
There's a part of me.
You've never known.
Please try and see
the part of me
that loves you so much.
I feel your pain.
The hurt you try to hide
so deep, you can't explain
why, it won't subside.
Please listen to me
and you will see
love is the only cure.

Misty Smith

Only Respect

I look at you across the room;
listening to us:
your husband and me,
two buddies.
I hear your voice
speaking at times with precision,
feelings defined and deep.
I remember the years,
as you moved from a girl,
to a woman and a wife.
I have no words
to encompass the changes
in time,
only respect.

Lawrence Michael Dickson

Me And Winter

Me and winter,
Me and winter,
House so cold,
Moon so bright,
Me and winter for
the rest of the night.

Megean Mincher

"Walking"

A
little
while
ago
I thought I
was
alone

Know
I find I
got to
black/love
the
long
way
home

Scott Davis Jr.

"Summer Grace"

Pretty little summer
   Little golden haired girl
Toddling through the flowers
   She gives my heart a whirl

Little feet a stepping
   Toward grandma in the wind
Her hair gently flowing
   Love that has no end.

My little ray of sunshine
   A precious little smile.
A miracle from heaven
   My golden haired grandchild

Grandma's little dumpling
   The apple of my eye
Your rocking chair is waiting
   Let's sing a lullaby...

Tina Gray

The Clear And Starry Night

The stars in the sky,
looked like
the glittering of diamonds
against a black velvet sky.

The night was magical,
yes indeed.
The answer is right before you,
but you cannot see.

You hear the Wind Lady,
you feel her touch,
but you cannot see,
what there is none of.

You hear nothing but silence,
like a cold winter's night,
but you can imagine,
what it sounds like at spring time.

The night must end,
you are sorry to note,
but then all magic dies
before you know.

Nancy Baker

Untitled

All alone in a burnt down building,
looking at what is left,
all there was, was ashes,
but the memories still lie there.

My mother in her rocking chair,
rocking my baby brother to sleep,
My father was in bed,
after a hard day at work.

Looking at nothing,
but coal black,
crying, singing to myself my mother's
favorite lullaby.

I hear something,
something soft, so comforting,
there stood an angel, an angel from above,
looking down with a smile as she sang
in a whisper my mother's lullaby.

Tabitha Holbrook

Why, Die

In the field all alone,
   looking to the sky.
Wondering if to go home
   tell me why.

The love of life
   oh so very strong
Under the knife
   I hope never wrong.

Look in my heart
   look in my mind,
I want to start.
Do you mind.

Tell me why
Tell me why
Do I, do I
Want to die.

Pauline Ruffin

"Love For Life"

There upon the grass I sit
   looking up at the trees,
Feeling the breeze against my face
   seeing changes in the leaves.

Autumn is here, what a beautiful sky
   I love this time of year,
Rain in the air, leaves are falling
   I can hear the sounds of deer.

Hot days of summer have come and passed
   Winter is on it's way,
Getting out the ole winter sweaters
   The farmers are baling hay.

Loved ones snuggle close beside
   The birds are flying in rhythm
It's the time of year I love
   I thank the Lord, for what I've been given.

Nina Shedosky

A Christmas Prayer

In the spirit of Christmas
Lord give to me
the gift of compassion
so I can see not with my eyes
though witness they'll bear
but with my heart
to a love that is rare
in the spirit of Christmas
Lord give to me the gift of forgiveness
with those I disagree
not with my tongue
because it can betray
but with my heart
as right leads the way
in the spirit of Christmas
Lord give to me the gift of confession
so my heart will be free
of all of the sins
the secrets the strife
that have crippled my chances at a good peaceful life

Ken Booth

Love Gave Me Love To Love You

Love gave me love to love you
Love gave me love in these hand's
To touch you
Love gave me love in these arm's
To hold you
Love gave me love in these lips'
To kiss you

God gave all his love for you and me
And the love I have for you
It's surely from heaven above
From the wing's of his love

Love gave me love in my heart
To love you
I only want to give it all to you
So darling give all you're love to me
Let's seal it with a kiss

So darling let me give you my love
And you give me you're love to me
Let's seal it with a kiss of love
Let's seal it with a kiss of love

Ralph Robinson

Mamma

Something beautiful lives today
Lovely flowers along our way,
Bringing love and sweet thoughts of her
Wherever pretty things occur.

Something lovely remains with us;
Cling to this always now we must.
Boundless love she gave to her own
Is stronger now that she has gone.

Something challenges our thoughts still;
Each child's role in life to fulfill
God's will to do each day living
Love like hers—for others giving.

Nellie Johnson Spinks

Pioneers

Scattered bricks and bits of wood,
Mark that spot where a house once stood;
But once abandoned couldn't last,
Against summer's heat and winter's blast.

Beyond that spot on a little hill,
An apple tree stands stark and still;
Where once an orchard hoped to be,
But only now, this lone, dead tree.

Beneath that tree an unmarked mound,
Where a child lies sleeping in the ground;
A child who never lived to see
The springtime grass or the apple tree.

But some stayed on and faced the worst,
And tightened belts and only cursed
The drought and hail and winter's cold,
And the only thing they grew was old.

And from this solid homestead seed,
There grew an ever hearty breed;
A breed whose children lived to see,
The springtime grass and the apple tree.

Leonard J. Schladweiler

Along My Way

Along my way throughout the day
may I touch someone and share,
The wisdom you bless me to see to
show them that you care.

Along my way throughout my life
may I give all that I can give,
To help a soul, a breaking heart to teach
and learn to live.

Along my way throughout this time
may I do all you ask of me,
To love people, animals and the earth
we share, and be all that we can be.

Along my way in passing may I tell
you something else,
In order to love someone in this world
you must first.. just love yourself.

J Denise

Untitled

A book of memories,
of you and I,
of special places
and special times.
A world of two,
just me and you.
No social graces,
to adhere to,
an instant feeling,
of minds entwined,
our eyes revealing,
a love that binds.
Lives in my heart,
while we're apart,
until we meet,
and find the spark,
that makes a memory,
a new page marked,
in a book of memories,
of you and I.

Katherine Hunt

Looking Ahead

Fate dances in our shoes.
Memories tie the knots.
Walking along the beach one day,
You look down and your feet are shot.

How did they get like that you ask;
As a serpent runs past.

There are birds along the tide,
But one can not fly.
You can only guess what happened to him
As you look into the sky.

In the mind of every human being
Are memories we hold dear.
Do we acknowledge what's inside,
Or do we hide for fear?
The knot could be tied on each pair of shoes.
Or are we binding ourselves together?

Will these memories pass and fade?
They're best if they're kept forever.
Yet the sky is the color of jade
And there's a tree over there making a shade.

Sandra L. Kernstock

Tooth Paste And Blood

When tooth paste and blood,
Mingle well with your tears;
When the unfloodables flood,
Over suicidal peers;

When mountains leap and fall,
With the way of your mood;
When friends don't call,
With fear of the rude;

When pencils and paper,
Don't write away pain;
When the curious gaper,
Starts to refrain;

When the painfullest lashes,
Throw memories, not blood;
When the combination clashes,
And is no longer good;

You'll find that comforts,
Turn into fears,
When tooth paste and blood,
Mingle well with your tears.

Rye Wendt

Poetry

Your poetry, is a gift of God
More precious than gold
God lays His words upon your heart
Their yours, to have and hold.

To be the bearer, of His words
Is a very heavy load
To bring out laughter, joy or tears
As you travel down life's road.

Though, others stop and criticize
And try to change your thoughts around
Remember, God gave you the honor
Of writing His words down.

Kathryn J. Warner

Awakening

A Spring awakening through a
morning window is ablaze in
pink corn silk blooms like
tiny parasols.

They are atop dark green fern
limbs of the Mimosa tree, bobbing
like musical carrousels.

It excites the eye in surprise
as spinning humming birds come
in sight.

Long needle beaks, darting in and
out, sipping nectar in a ballet
of flight.

Yearn to fly into this green and
pink corn silk frenzy, spin and
dart in winged delight.

Ever awakened by surprise, I
become sown in Earth's unseen
veils like night.

G. de Vries

The Pier

It postures as stern as a
muscular back.
It distorts the sea with
it's vertebrae track.
It's length is great, it's
width not wide, upon the sea
it seems to glide.
From timber and steel
it comes to be a fisherman's
throne
He baits and hooks for
catch unknown
Upon the sand the pier
does lie,
Upon a sea that cannot die.
And if it should I surely
pray, that I'll be gone before
that day.

Wayne Cribb

Untitled

you consume my thoughts
my dreams
your image fades into the clouds like
moonlit shadows dancing beyond the horizon
stillness conquers the night as
excited stars sparkle fresh dew
on thin blades of carpeted lawn
random memories of perfect evenings drift
between consciousness and sleep
a touch
a kiss
the soft whisper of your gentle voice
finds my ears wanting to listen as
i strain to see where
you have gone
i awake

Rowena E. Mante

Memories

I know a man and a woman
My grandparents they still be.
For without their loving kindness,
There of course would be no me.

They shared their dreams together
As the sun did come and go.
And loved their children dearly;
They often told them so.

But years have come and years have gone
And they have but just one thought,
That they're still loved and needed;
It really does mean a lot.

So get your pen and paper
And copy down a line,
Then add another and another
And send it there in time.

For the day will come, you'll have the time
And guess where they will be.
Up in heaven with God Almighty
Thinking, did they really, really love me?
— *Lucinda L. Kendall*

My Journey of Love

My eyesight is dimmer,
My hair has turned gray.
My gait is much slower,
I'm weaker each day.

My bedtime comes early,
My wake-up comes late
With naps in between
For me and my mate.

But to slow down is good
Time to savor the past.
There's no going back,
Time to relax at last.

And one thing is certain.
We're lucky, oh boy!
To have eight great kids
As our pride and joy.
— *Marion V. Joynt*

My Prayer To Jesus

I will close my eyes and bow
My head, and thank you Jesus
For our daily bread. I thank
you for each breath I take
And praise you for my morning wake.
I thank you for my eyes you gave
for me to see the love you made
I thank you for my health each
day and pray to you I'll see
another day. I pray that
you will stay by my side and
guide me true the good and bad
times. I know that you will
watch over me, and keep me safe
and sound. For no matter where
I go dear Jesus, I know you'll
all ways be a round.
— *Kela Renee Hill*

The Intruder

Reality, I didn't need him,
  My life filled to the brim,
But I remember the day
  I let him move in.

I made him so happy
  It showed from the start.
And, I again knew, trampled
  Were the strings of my heart.

In so many ways he showed
  How he loved me.
He never once had
  To plain out and tell me..

Where once thought my life
  Full right to the brim,
now, how could I ever
  Be happy without him.

And where did we meet,
  If you want it all known,
He was just a stray dog
  I let follow me home.
— *Melba Honey Wolfe*

A Prayer

I give you this child Lord,
  My love for her runs deep.
But she's yours now dear Lord,
  To always have and to keep.
Work your will within her
  And keep me off to myself,
So she can find you Lord,
  And give to you herself.
If I get discouraged,
  Or even dismayed,
Remind me to bless her,
  And praise you each day.
And never let Satan slip in
  A single tiny dart,
Or take her from you
  And put on her his mark.
She's yours Lord, forever.
  On her is your seal.
This is my prayer Lord
  As before you I kneel.
— *Shirley A. Karafa*

Latter-Day Don Quixote

I've been out jousting windmills,
  My noble steed a mule!
And I have been thrown to the ground...
  I know that I'm a fool.
And yet perhaps fool-wise enough,
  And surely not afraid...
To see my life's a losing cause,
  An asinine charade!

For windmills never yield to lance,
  And fools will thus be thrown;
Until they tire of foolish dreams...
  And dreaming all alone!
So if a broken lance you see...
  And empty saddled mule...
You'll know at last the battle's done.
  Pray for a silly fool!
— *Keith R. Frost*

Oh Lord I've Failed Again

Through reaper filled nights
My only company is insanity
Through dreams my day begins
Oh Lord I've failed again

There's no light shining bright
Only demons screaming in the night
Their screams never end
Oh Lord I've failed again

As I walk these old coble streets
A crimson river flows at my feet
So many pleading eyes
There only question why
Somewhere a child cries
I only hear her die

The images are haunting me
Cold death is mocking me
My tears are all cried
How much pain must I take before I brake
Oh Lord I've failed again
— *Shon A. Gwynn*

My Rites

To God my life is an open book.
My rites clearly shown
What I wouldn't give to have a look
But the pages are obscure with
With lyric unknown.
My rite to read my book.
Lord what have you done
Oh ye of little faith
Why do you hesitate
You have to believe in me
Only then will you see
I am the key to your sight
For it is I who rites you're book of life.
— *Teresa Stephens*

Relevant

It is autumning.
Nature folds her arms.
I feel alarm,
For I am autumning, too.

It was springing!
I was born of song
and for so long
I was spring, too.

Summer burst!
As quick as rain
it left again,
and I am leaving, too.

Nature's sign:
follows winter,
icy splinter,
and I will be wintering, too.
— *Rebecca Foust*

The User

  I'm used and abused by a friend
of mine who is quite dear to me.
He gives me his love in different
ways in which I just don't see.
  I try and I try to understand why
the different ways he cares,
but all I can see when he looks
at me is he wishes I was bare.
— *Linda LaPlace*

Then And Now

Here, then, is NOW!
   Never to return.
No matter how much I yearn;
Wanting more things to learn;
Thinking I had time to burn.
   Whither went NOW?
Just a moment, please!
   Here below
I still have things to do, you know;
I thought time would more slowly flow;
As I drifted along, somewhat slow;
   Living at ease.
What, no reprieve?
   I need time
To finish this life which is sweet,
No more my good friends to greet;
It's so hard to accept defeat.
   Must I then, LEAVE?

Paul Allen Edwards

2107 A.D.

Walking in the shadow of a rainbow,
Never to rise above the rest,
Even though we try so hard
To put forth our best.

We hide in our fears;
We've banished dreams from our wind,
Forever to be the slaves
Of this God-forsaken time.

Who knows what lies beyond
Our fiery, metallic sun?
Still the 'droids strike us down,
But the battle has just begun.

For we will rise from the caverns
To destroy this tyranny
There on the throne
We'll control our own destiny!

Richard H. Perkins

Bonsai

Lo! The dwarf cypress
   Never to rise high:
Shaped, clipped and tethered
   Oriental Bonsai.

Earthenware crock
   Roots amputated;
Foliage fine-feathered,
   Growth abbreviated.

Gnarled old trunk
   Grotesquely slanting
Scenic perfection
   Quaint and enchanting...

Thomas P. Ulmer

Untitled

An angel in white dances through the night.
Touching the hearts that yearn for the light.
The night stars twinkle when I look in your eyes.
I wonder if my white angle has danced
   through the skies.
A warm gentle glow warms through my heart.
I finally made a brand new start.
I lay in your arms, it feels so right.
A special thanks to my angel in white.

Michelle Kahns

That Good Old Dollar Bill

The dearest friend you'll ever have
   Next to your God and Mother
Is not your buddy or your dog,
   Your sister or your brother.

This friend I'm speaking of can't talk
   Nor can it feel or love;
But when you're in the greatest need,
   It yields without a shove.

It takes a lot of know-how
   To keep this chum around;
But once you have it mastered
   You're standing on real ground.

So, if at times you want a friend
   When the going is down-hill,
Think twice before you part with
   The Good Old Dollar Bill.

Mildred L. Jordan

The Waiting

She walked to hell's beguiling place
   no fear of what could harm.
Not a sign of pain was on her face
   nor hate to thwart her lovely grace
   for none could steal her charm.

Deep inside her bosom cried
   a thousand screams aloud;
for death had taken from the bride
   her lover from her gracious side
   that somehow God allowed.

Again she approached the grassy knoll
   where he was laid to rest;
laid flowers on the dirt filled hole
   his home till that great trump'ters toll
   then wilted on his chest.

But misery could not rob her will
   or break her iron trust.
Her Father's power over that earthen fill
has made her tempestuous heart be still.
   Soon he'll rise from this dust.

Robert W. Danskin

Untitled

A fly — if were I
no forest dense
nor mountain lofty
'twould me from keep
soaring, to the sea — to the sea!
And on breeze warm, salty,
float I'd lazily.
With mercurially the murmuring
of waves prismatically
in million my eyes, glittering!
And I, the fly daring
—if were I!—
would snoozily snore
on a sunning starfish,
asleep also who's fallen, orange.

Rae Arrington

Never Will Forget

I'll never forget this life.
No matter how many lives I live.
The beauty.
The pain.
The reckless abandon.
The total restrain.
Images.
Thoughts.
Will always remain.
Silhouettes of Angels.
Cloudy shapes of my demons.
I'd never leave this.
No matter how strong the reasons.

Mark Grindell

"I Wonder"

No one to love
No one to care
Who do I turn to
I wonder

There's more pain
In love
Than there is
Love

So why do we hunger
For more hurt and
Confusion
I'd rather be lonesome
And hungry

This old world
Don't make seance
No joy and
No pleasure
So what do
We live for
I wonder

Pamela West

A Woman Alone

No one to greet the dawn
No one to mow the lawn
No one to talk to me
I feel so sad and lonely
Can't even watch TV
Nothing to interest me
Can't go nowhere alone
And wishing you were here at home
That's how your life has grown
When you are a woman alone;

No one to kiss good night
No one to off the light
No one to keep me warm
Nor to protect me from all harm
Or turn off the alarm
Can't seem to get to sleep
Hear every little creek
Nights are so long when you are gone
That's how life goes on
When you are a woman alone;

Rita Welch

My World

If you were in my world
No one would have a face
There wouldn't be a war
A battle over race

If you were in my world
There wouldn't be segregation
Everyone could be their own person
We would live as a nation

But this isn't my world
I don't have a choice
All has hatred
We all have a voice
The world shows expression
The people kill
Those with a heart
Won't believe this is real

If you were in my world
Your spirit could be free
No problems or worries
Just your spirit and me

Robin Weaver

Despair...

No where to go
No place to hide
Life washes over you
Like a deep dark tide.

Hope all gone
Dreams disappear
Thoughts run through your head
And it's the results that you fear.

Things have to improve
Wonder where you went wrong
When all you have to show
Is a hand written song.

All the roads have been taken
All the rivers are dry
Makes you wonder
What else you can try.

Rainbows have faded
Only dark clouds fill the sky
Your heart is feeling heavy
All you want to do is cry.

Leann Coleman Koraska

Untitled

No greater joy hath life than love,
No quantity of stars above,
Could fill the empty hearts of spring,
Of those who know not what it brings.
To live without a falling tear,
Or hold the thought of someone dear,
A barren cold to face alone,
My spirit longs to have a home.
Embrace thy soul emotions free,
To hold you for eternity,
I've crossed the void of endless time,
To give to you this heart of mine.

Thomas W. Del Santo

Decor

There is a hole in the wall
Nobody sees
Created in anger
The frustration of insanity

It is hidden with a painting
Smiling alone
Shielded by lies
From a truth unknown

There is a soul drenched in pain
Screaming confusion
Feel inside

Robert Brower

Shark

He started to come right toward me,
Maybe as if he should ignore me.
So fierce in size,
So small in his eyes.
Why are we so fearful,
When all he is thinking is cheerful.
Maybe he should pass,
because he was going too fast.
Should he stop, could he stop,
or even would he stop.
But there he goes,
Everybody knows,
Why he flows.

Melissa L. Cavanaugh

Backyard Canal

It is peaceful
Noisy when the boats go by
In the evening fish splish and splash
Reflections of the Full Moon
Make one's heart flutter

Adorable baby ducks swim by
It's unique to watch them grow up
They often stop for handouts
The flower garden thrives on its water
And I breathe in its serenity

Cast your fishing line
Patience is the rule
You may get a bite
Guess what they're just teasing
Catch us if you can

During winter it freezes over
When the great winds blow
Enjoy skating, sledding, and hot cider
Lie down and make an angel
As you reminisce yesteryears.

Shirley F. Bowerman

"Kyle"

"You are the light
  of my life,
The song in my heart,
You are the Best friend
  and son,
A mother could have.

You are miracles and fun,
  joy and laughter,
Happy tears forever after."

Kitty Derian

Truth

I can not be your slave
Nor a possession to be kept
I am but human
With morals and contempt.

I have been telling you
So loud and clear
You choose not to listen
Without anger or fear

I have spoken these words
For the very last time.
I can not love you
For it's lost deep inside

I need to be free
Before it's too late.
Can you let me go
From this dark empty place.

Neelum Thakoor

"The Fight"

It was a lovely summer day
Not a single cloud in sight,
When a group of people gathered
To watch our gruesome fight.

It started over nothing.
In fact, I still don't know.
But, I've always been a gentleman:
I allowed him the first blow.

He took a swing, it came real close.
I must admit I flinched.
Why was this foolish, old buffoon
Trying to get me trenched!

I was quite calm, I must confess.
You'll find out really soon
That my quick move and my first punch
Laid out that stupid goon!

Yes, he had practiced really hard,
But now he knew my might,
As I still stood and he was down,
For I had won the fight!

Kristofer Geoffrey Gonzales

Maw Maw

She gets up in the morning,
Not as quickly anymore.
Bones that used to be young and spry,
Are now older and much more sore.

She sits in her old rocking chair,
At her home all alone.
She'd like for just a short visit,
Or maybe just a chat on the phone.

She has lots of grand kids you know,
But for her, it's not too many.
But as she looks around the room,
She doesn't seem to see any.

They forget about her sometimes,
When they are out in their busy lives.
Out playing with their kids,
Their husbands or their wife.

We need to all remember,
She's the one who started our family tree.
So a short visit, or a chat on the phone,
Is not too much to ask of me.

Lisa K. Calder

To Fly

I still wish that I could fly
Not by plane or rocket ship
The part of me that you can't see
Or feel..has a longing to be
Has a wisdom beyond...this me
To be free

To soar, to float beyond
Cloudy days, or murky skies
To wave mighty wings goodbye
To pain and sadness

To open the deepest part
Of this my silent heart
To the very eyes of God

Lou Ann Prusa

My Gift To You

I want to make love to you
not with my body
but with my soul
I want to bathe you
with my essence
baptize you with my thoughts
pour my emotions on you
saturate you with my being
give you my all
present you with everything
my gift to you

L. Dranae Jones

The Reality Of Life

When you are high on life
nothing can bring you down.

When you are down
nothing can pull you up.

Life is a journey up into the
mountains and
down into the valleys.

It's a roller coaster ride,
an emotional journey of ups and downs.

Life is a stage and we are the players
without a rehearsal.

We ad lib as we travel through time.
We're funny, sad, angry and loving.

Whatever the part calls for at the time.
Whatever emotion is brought forth by
Whomever or whatever we encounter.

When the curtain falls
The journey is over.

Mary Elise McCormick

Untitled

Thoughts, thoughts of life
of the old that dwells within,
of the new that has given richness,
thoughts of past, core of the soul.
Yesterday ever so strong in my mind,
days go by the new become a
hidden part, as it was before,
shared barely, as the connection
and growth vanish, visible
traces remain, going on with
the journey of life.

Maritza E. Clay

"Living"

Thrust into life's indignities;
nothing gentle here.
Breath of life or fear
the death that's waiting near.
Straining for air,
lungs about to burst;
eternal thirst perpetuates
then activates a life-long search.
Looking for I know not what.
Still driven to seek.
Now and then — nest and rest.
Life emerges.
Begins the quest again.

Leslie Booker

Life

Nothing to do
Nothing to say
Love fades away

Nothing to do
Nothing to see
Love goes away, far away

Love is a ghost
whom haunts you
Night and day

Love is a rose
with its undying beauty
no one can tell if it will stay
Or leave

Nothing to do
Nothing to see
Blackness, despair

Nothing more to do
Nothing mores to see
Death is at my door
  Knocking for me

Melissa Gilman

Alone

What a hollow feeling
Now that she's alone
She's left with an emptiness
With no one to fill the void -

She never knew how much
His love filled her up,
Making her whole,
In every way a woman -

That woman is gone now
Who flourished in his midst -
She's lost in her memories
Holding on to the past -

She's afraid of the pain
That comes with letting go -
She's afraid to face reality
Admit her true love is gone

So she'll shed her tears
As she dreams of the past
Praying that someday the past,
Will again - become reality -

Michelle G. Guttromson

Sweet Words

I'll make the wish
of a life
time.
A wish to be
with you.
The things you
says so sweet,
but are they also
true?
I'd show you how
to count the
ways to show
your love some way.
But how am I
Suppose to know exactly
what to say?

Michelle Chambers

Save The Children

Children, the lost souls
Of a new generation
With no one to see them
And no one to hear them

Hearts full of loneliness
Eyes full of pain
Minds full of hate and revenge
No hope for lives that are real

They run with the pack
Fight wars in the streets
They hide in the shadows
Screaming to be noticed

Who will love them as they are?
Who will show them a gentler way?
Who will teach them how to solve?
How will they discover who they really are?

These troubled, unsure children
Starving for love, yearning for attention
They are the future of our planet
Without change, what will that future be?

Rosemarie L. B. Checketts

Nothing New Under The Sun

With everyone in serious thought,
Of all the battles and wars we've fought,
With the talks of strategies,
Wars in our streets and overseas,
So caught up in weary worries,
Fatal endings and teary stories,
Nothing new under the Sun,
There is nothing new left to be done.

I sit and ponder all of this,
And know I'll relish my next kiss,
My thoughts repeat of treats so rare,
Fantasies of trips to share,
Denying ourselves of no pleasure,
Of good things what is our measure.
Life to be lived, can be missed,
Will you be trapped in it's abyss?
Nothing New Under the Sun,
There is nothing new left to be done.

Patty Leitner

The Wanderer

The forest was an iron cage
of deep everlasting gloom
and branches with wraith-like
fingers tried to choke the moon.

And in this eternal darkness
in this shadow o'so cold
treading silently through the forest
walks a disembodied soul.

His skin is o'so icy
his glare can make you melt
and throughout this darkened forest
his spectral presence is felt.

Walking through the forest
treading silently through the gloom
walks a disembodied soul
beneath the ghostly silver moon.

Michael J. Fitzgerald II

A Voice In The Silence

The children say they're not afraid
of going to war with Saddam Hussein

We are ready they call
We are ready..

When all the world is fretting
about the Middle East setting

Think of the family and the friends
who we will never ever see again

Tears fall from men's faces
in a million different places

All over the world we hear the sound
of the iron fist beginning to pound

the nature of war is a dreadful thing
when we cannot hear anyone sing..

Kristin Cochenour

Black Woman, Shake Chains

Black Woman, shake chains
off your mind-
the strain

Black Woman, shake chains-
your beauty still remains.

Black Woman, shake chains
off your heart-
the pain

Black Woman, shake chains
your courage still remains.

Black Woman, shake chains
off your gifts-
they're gain

Black Woman, shake chains-
your spirit still remains.

Tanya K. Dixon

Nightfall

The sun pulls a curtain
Of lavender ribbon
Across a pale sky
And with a laugh
Rolls into bed.

Free from its glare at last
We seek our rest
But errant thoughts
Drowned in sweat of day
Crawl into the mind
Like beasts on prey.

We writhe and toss
To clear a pain-filled night
-To no avail,
Tortured days turn into tortured nights
And leave us beaten
And less than all our hopes.

Margie Donohoo

Being Gay!

We have a flag with the colors
Of the rainbow, which shows
Everyone is equal

We have the triangle to show
Our pride in what we
Believe

We have the freedom rings
To show that we are
Free and won't be
Shut in the closet
Any longer

We have the red ribbon
To show that we will
Stand by those who
Are dying

We march together with pride
And stick together like family

This is what being homosexual
Means to me, and I'm not ashamed to
show the love
I have for the most wonderful woman in the
world

Kat Sulak

Young One

The kitten comes out
  of his basket late at night,
His fur like carpet,
  his eyes so bright.
He plays with a string
  throughout the house,
Trying to catch
  a tiny mouse.
His thoughts full of excitement,
His dreams so wild,
He falls back asleep
  like a new born child.

Melissa Moccia

My Last Year Love

I don't understand why?
Of the things of the destiny.
I though I forgot you
But your memory still live here.

I though I forgot you
But I still live.
To remember your love
To remember the day you forgot me.

I don't now why?
That I still love you.
Woe women what a illusion
That in my mind stayed.

You where my illusion.
You where last year love.
Whom I think that my heart
My life forgot you.

And another time I fall
The destiny failed me.
That again without wanting to
My life I still love you.

Maximino Toro

There. . .

Against the jamb,
of your door
a jar.
There!!
surly and ugly
leans a thug
demanding another days dues.
Most days
some small change
such as hues
shading one's hair.
Other days
more priceless tolls
precious and rare
as heirlooms
like warmth of heart
or serenity
for our souls.

T. James Cameron

Reach Into Your Soul

Reach into the deepness
of your soul
What you find there
takes no toll
keep the faith alive
and do what you can
to survive
people live
people die
death could happen
in the blink of an eye
we must not dwell on those who died
cause life goes on
and so do I

Katrina Berkopec

Savior's Call

Come thou unto Me,
  Oh hear the Savior call.
    Though thou art weak,
      He'll never let you fall.

For this cause He came,
  To give you life anew.
    Teaching you the way,
      That leads to Heaven true.

Take now His hand,
  Walk within His light.
    Let His love surround you,
      A cover in the night.

He beckons each one come,
  Oh hear His precious call.
    Come to Calvary's crimson tide
      He calls to one and all.

Mary Maxey

Embraces

The child whispered softly:
Oh, hold me, hold me close;
Hold me in all the many ways,
The ways that you encircle me;
Hold me tender and sweetly;
Hold me close and so firmly;
Hold me with compassion and caring;
Hold me with anger against the hurts;
Hold me near so I shall not be lost;
Hold me with so much love
That I can stand alone.

Mary Sullivan

"Emptiness, Emptiness"

My arms are empty,
oh, the ache.
His chair is empty
my heart will break!
And when night falls,
the bed is empty.
Oh, to hear his call!
Alas, what desolation!
Will there ever be a time
When I am free from sad frustration
or must I simply wear a smile
And hide the emptiness
there all the while?

Pearl A. Blackburn

A Rose

I'll send a rose to speak for me.
"Oh" to open my mouth and speak freely.

To express sweet loving refrains.
But no words will come,
only silence from fear of shun.

So I'll send him this rose, to express
what my heart will not — let me confess.

Yvonne Jo Queen

The Mask Seller

Let's go back in time to see the
old mask peddler limp the cobbled walk
His lantern flickers, but burns
brightly enough casting shadows
His hand gently holding a string
of dancing masks
He smiles down at his wares, each
one telling a different story
He beckons you with a quick gesture,
Trembling hands holding forth a
mask for your delight
Choose one, only a sixpense
Infringing faces dancing on a string
display conflict of personalities
The mysterious green robed peddler
loudly shakes the old brass bell
as he disappears into the shadows.

Phyllis Wakefield Knox

Peace

The wind rippled through her mane
On a bright and sunny day
Her eyes sparkled from the light
Her horn shined in the prettiest way

She shimmered and shined and jumped around
She was definitely a sight to see
I thought for sure, positively
My eyes were playing tricks on me

She had a snow white coat and mane
It was the softest I had ever touched
She danced and frolicked in the grass
Flowers covering her mane and such

She had the most beautiful deep blue eyes
As blue as the deepest blue sea
As I looked into those loving eyes
I had known then, she had come here just for me

I started to run and jump and play
And her magic started swirling around me
It lifted me up into the air
Finally, at last, I had found peace
*In Dedication to my
Aunt Patricia Ann Edwards*

Nichelle L. Goff

Autumn Now

I went for a walk
On a cool autumn afternoon.
In the park I stepped
On the carpet of glistening leaves.
I thought of them as nature's tears.
The wind curling about me
Whistled monotonous song,
I stopped and listened...
Suddenly the trees in the alley
Exploded in gold and red flames.
They will die painlessly, without names.

Maria Matusewitz

Environmentally Aware

I like throwing trash
out of my car window.
It makes me feel good!

Sharon Aaronson

Cross

A golden cross
on a golden chain.

Does it symbolize submission?
Or is it worn in vain?

In a home or on a person
Does it consecrate?

Is it worn around a neck
just to decorate.

Do you really believe and hope
in Eternity?

Is that cross in your heart?
Or just for eyes to see?

Robert Tavarone

Untitled

On certain times a splendor comes
On fresh whispered mornings,
And spreads across the soft stillness
A quiet sense of eternity.

Foxgloves mute their dotted bells,
Pictures cease to talk,
Hollyhocks open their periscopes,
And words retain no thoughts.

Years empty our struggling creeds
Before the awful presence,
Body and mind lose meaning,
The soul occludes its essence.

Walter E. Smith

My Rose

God looked down from Heaven one day,
  on His garden vast,
Searching for the perfect rose,
  the one with scent to last.

His eyes perused the roses that fulfilled
  the external requirements
Those of beauty and honor but
  lost in these confinements.

He looked at each and every rose,
  all His own creation,
And finally found the one with
  internal-external relation.

He picked that rose of beauty,
  the example of perfection,
The precious scent from in and out,
  the Rose who knew not of rejection.

God caressed the precious Rose
  that compared to no other,
Then handed it to me, His child,
  Thus giving me the Perfect Mother.

Wendy LaCoste Bedsole

Time

Circles within circles
spinning into and out of themselves
always changing but never changed.

Raymond E. King

Untitled

Trees that talk
on midnight walks
whispers as you pass

Swaying wind
that never ends
dancing in the grass

Shadows drift
so very swift
in corners of the eyes

Dawn comes fast
night won't last
somewhere a mother cries

On we travel
o'er grass and gravel
running in the night

Away from tears
away from fears
fleeing morning light

Laura J. Cronin

Knot Holes

What are those funny looking holes,
On my door facing front.
Indentures in a dance,
Meld together years untold.
Now swinging forward united,
Forever this door you grace.
And no one even knowing,
You are in this unworldly place.

And yet as I stare,
Knot - holed, infamous, intriguing.
You are - that simple wooded plane,
ever dancing again and again.
Of what great mystery involved.
Implications of much wood,
Airy space centered,
Oh hollow door,
YOU ARE

Sandra L. Lee

Together

Throe empty halls with nameless walls
  One might pass unforeseen

To be unknown and all alone
  Do you wonder what I mean

To search for love with one's heart
  And capture the emotion

When two people find true love
  Can there be devotion

To embark upon a journey
  High into a cloud

We must find the road of stars
  And call our names aloud

To rise above in search of love
  Heaven be our guide

With our hands, we close them tight
  Together side by side

Walter E. Kielbowicz

"One World"

One world,
One race,
Thriving.

One world,
Many races,
Striving.

One world,
One race,
Human.

Steven Arthur

Silence

Silence of the room fills the air,
Only a dusk of wind and a faint stare.
I wonder if the shadow feels the pain.
By the window upstairs,
I watch as the figure moves.
Slowly but surely, it can be seen.
A mad man.
Once, twice, stepping down to the attic.
This scene is very dramatic.

I once lived in this house.
It has been shut out.
The mad man has appeared again.
The silence is no more,
But a faint thump at my door.

Misty Shuler

Saturday Night

And
Only bills to pay,
No dancing on the ceiling,
No callers to converse with
No Excuses
Only a tad of loneliness,
Until
A yard sale record
(a bargain for only ten cents)
Emit wonderful sounds
And
A broom becomes
A handsome prince,
Waltzing round the room.
PRETENDING
Adult Behavior?
An essential antidote for loneliness
Music enhancing a life
One rainy Autumn evening.

Stella Riffle

"In Time"

No fight and war.
Only peace for salvation reward.

Struggle with determination has the
best way making it in today's world.
Your mind no one can read, but your
heart everyone can love.

Walking on water as we are trying
to be secure underneath, gives us the
courage to be ourselves indeed. All in
time things will succeed, then soon we
all will be free.

Kari Spencer

Untitled

Heroes Aren't Made. They're made up.
Open the door and you'll see
She wasn't there, he wasn't there.
What's a hero?
Close the door. Do you see her?
She doesn't exist, she's not real.
How can you know? Reflections
Always lie. Green is
Blue and White
is Gray. It lies. Your hero is real.

Lina Yang

Soul Mates

We all wonder Where and When or If.
There was and is a time of Far Away
like in childhood stories
and science fiction tales.
The mind's eye sweeps back and forth
through eternity
And sees us as we were
And are to be.
Pasts, shadowed in dreams
Futures, illumined by familiarity.
We feel we know
yet doubt our intuition and call it
Coincidence.
How frightening it is for us
to acknowledge the loop in our existence
that has spiraled and intertwined
like the ribbon on a package.
Dare we to speculate:
Does karma consume or consummate?

Pam Hodges

Am Concerned

Did I came from a distant past,
  Or sprung just now,
So that in time, if ever come
  Am a better man?
Whatever be in my own case,
  'wont' matter to me
Only what am concerned about,
  Man's fate's truly free.

Freedoms are men's best friends,
  Maybe better than dogs,
Because with company,
  I am not free at all.

Quirino C. Amore

"Mother's Day"

Some are honored in a special way,
others are given a treat.
Others are given a gift from the heart,
this one can't be beat.

Love is what a mother gives,
to her children each day.
Can we not return this gift,
to them somehow, someway!

So remember on this special day,
to thank that special one,
Remember how they helped you every way,
in all that they have done.

Tim Burton

Untitled

Moments so tender,
Our hearts surrender
To the smile on a baby's face,
Love and protect them,
Guide and correct them,
Given only by his grace.

Nancy Norton-Yetter

"O Sun!"

Rays burn bright despite
  Our hidden fears, shadows
Dissipate, yet return
  Throughout the years
To haunt, perplex; drive
  Us beyond the ever-present
Moment, here, yet somehow gone.

Warmth fills the corpus of
  Misery, brightening the dim
Thoughts that lie within the
  Crevices of the mind—hidden,
Yet, O, so very real, but
  Appeal not to life it seems
For shallow indeed our dreams.

Shining brightly; fixed tho'
  Earth spins. The motion of time
Moves us to and fro,
  But oft in limbo betwixt!
O what radiance and beauty—
  Hide our interior, bleak; Your light fills
our eyes.

Peter Roland II

God's Understanding

Bless Little Donnie
Our pride and our joy.
Thank you for giving us
Our loving Boy.
Thank you for being
So good to us three,
My Eddie, my Donnie,
And most of all me.
Forgive me for failing
These boys that I love.
Help them to love me,
For I need their love.
Make us forever
Real happy to be,
With You as our Helper
My two boys and me.

Myra D. Trinque

Love Song

Old dear,
Our souls intact,
United into one,
We trace the years' slow rhythm,
Rushing by yet lingering,
My breath your breath,
My heartbeat in your breast,
A single entity;
Thus we are forever
As the sparkling stars
Outliving death.

Louisa M. Murray

The Man In The Battered Hat

I woke up this morning,
Outside was drizzling rain,
The rain on the rooftop.
Nearly drove me insane.

I saw an old man,
Asleep by a fire.
He had not a home,
Or proper attire.

He didn't have boots,
Or a coat that was warm.
He was clutching a bottle,
Like a port in a storm.

His hat was in tatters.
As well as his coat.
I could hardly swallow,
The lump in my throat.

When I hear folks complain.
About this and bout that.
I remember the man,
In the old battered hat.

Violet Loreane Mutz

Memories

Dictators bear no reign
  over memories
Sweet, soft, gentle memories
Treasures that are safe
  from thieves
Rape of the soul
Rape of the spirit
But memories are unbinding
Wealth is synonymous
  with memories
The joyous, the painful
All are ours to experience
Once, twice, a million more
A catalyst from what we
  were in the past
And who will be
  in the future
Sweet memories
We have nothing more

Teresa L. Cantrell

Together

Life is a narrow bridge
Over the deep gorge of death.
You'll protect me from the gaps, and
I, too, will do the same.
The bridge is to narrow to walk
side by side.
Therefore, we become one.
The further we go, the wider
the gaps get.
Together we tackle the bridge of life.
Together we prosper.
Together we live.
Together we slip through the gaps.

Kristina M. Chandler

Books

Same books are visors
Pain books are principles
Lane rules are books
Fame friends are extra booklets

Tad Thornhill

Untitled

The hypnotic waves
over the sands of Time,
Back—and—Forth
With Reason and Rhyme.

The Life He breathed
into each one of These
Beholds a greater significance
than a mid-summer's breeze.

Some never get it,
some never try,
but Those who live Life
possess a Hope when they cry.

When They said, "Carpe Diem!"
They knew what They meant,
Spend every Day
So your Life isn't spent.

To mourn the death of a loved one
is a sad part of Life...
To mourn the Life —
a tragedy.

Kathryn Riehn

J-Birds

Shrikes, toucans, holocaust.
Owls, martins,, spoonbills, fire.
Swans, thrushes, eagles, pyre.
Gulls, cuckoos, falcons tossed.
Jays, blackbirds, spoonbills, day,
Quail, curlews, martins clay.
Swifts, bluebirds, magpies lost.
Storks, buzzards, woodcocks, crime,
Flamingoes, tits, tern time.
Cranes, parrots, turkeys crossed.
Ducks, herons, buzzards knell,
Geese, hornbills, vultures-Hell.

Wilhelm Nightingale

Bicycling In Bosnia

Cycles of love and hate,
Peace and war,
Bullets in the air.
Tricycle and bicycle,
Water bottles fastened
On the bike's side.
Bosnia's boys go cycling
Not for sport or play
But to bring water home
For the famished family today.
They peddle past shells of cars
Down through once quiet villages.
A time to laugh,
A time to cry,
Cycles of love and hate.
They race toward the river.
Bosnia's boys go cycling by.

Mary L. Warner

Grandma

God gave you to us to
Remember always
And carry on your ways
Never harsh or impatient
Dear to us all
Mothers' mother
Amen.

Tracy Shoemaker Brewer

Untitled

We wandered into waning hours, with no
conceivable outpost.
People of the night. Tamers trotted behind
us with heart alive
from fright. We could not stay still,
They would stay and till, the safe land.
We were pure and more —they had minds
to kill, what they
could not understand.

Rob Usinger

In Fall

The shadows of day
play on colors of green, red and gold
til' dusk cradles the earth
in soft muted tones
and hides them, in a darkness.
then, couched in silence,
night stalks the land
touching every secret place
that nauru does possess,
it whispers an echo
that tells the earth to rest...

Yvonne Cooper

Night Magic

Last night I saw a dragon
Playing poker with an elf;
And a witch was mixing potions
With the bottles on the shelf.

The smell of the troll-popcorn
Mixed with fairy dust;
And the music of the gypsies
Came at me with a gust.

The leprechauns were beating gnomes
In a friendly game of chess;
And who was selling hot dogs,
But an enchanted mermaid princess!

I chatted with a wizard
As the fireflies turned off their lights;
For while I had been marveling
The darkness turned to bright.

I was soaring on a unicorn
When the ominous goblin said,
"Time for school, get up!
Get up you sleepy head!"

Neela Janardhanan

Life

Listen to the
roaring of the train through one gate
and its disappearance with the other.
Like the life,
as if within the blinking of the eye,
you have to live, laugh, love and learn.
So, buckle up at once
to attend to the needs of life and man.

Ram Mahabir

A Woman's Nightmare - PMS And Menses

Today's the first day of your menses
PMS nearly blow out your senses
Face this day with much disdain
Nausea, cramps, bloating and pain
Tired and drained like a balloon
Relieving the stress of the PMS cocoon

The second day is not so easy
Run to the bathroom bleeding profusely
The menses is here in its fullness
The third day is not so much mess
The fourth day is here it's now blending
And on the fifth day it's the ending

Now that the menses is leaving
Weak and drained but much relieving
From PMS and Menses good riddance
Equilibrium restored with much confidence
Enjoy the freedom from PMS and menses
Be all you can, charming, sweet and have no fear
A few more weeks the vicious cycle again is here
A woman's nightmare - PMS and menses

G. Eastman

Positive Is...

Positive is a fresh start
Positive is having a big heart.
Positive is a nice little prayer
Positive is just being there.

Positive is a gentle kiss
Positive is fulfilling a wish.
Positive is a warm smile
Positive is going the extra mile.

Positive is a warm sunny day
Positive is doing it your way.
Positive is a pat on the back
Positive is finding your knack.

Positive is a well-deserved rest
Positive is doing your best.
Positive is an open mind
Positive is just being kind.

Positive is being positive
Positive is to live.

Michael Luppino

"Sequel To The Preacher"

When he was a young man
preaching was strong -
Exuberantly warning
Between right and wrong;
As the people all listened
Their hearts filled with fear!
God's sudden appearance
Must surely be near!
As year followed year
And the preacher grew old,
He never seemed tired
Of the tale that he told;
And as for the people
They were much the same -
Watching for God
With the preacher to blame,
"He should have known from the start what
We all know today!
We had time for repentance
And plenty to play!"

Ruth A. Black

Fantasy

The formality of life
produces
magnanimous images
of reckless abandon
and involuntarily
augments
the carnal inhibitions
of the impassioned
sophisticate.

Rosemary Logisz

Run To The Sea!

Run to the sea! It beckons, beguiles.
Pulling my body
To stay for a while.

Rhythmic pulsations twist and swerve.
Melting the pain
Of my knotted nerve.

Run to the sea! It beckons, beguiles.
Pulling my tears
And placing a smile.

Rhythmic pulsations crest and swell.
Melting the pain
My memory knows well.

Run to the sea! It beckons, beguiles.
Pulling the mask
That hinders my style.

Rhythmic pulsations hypnotize me.
Melting my chains
To set my soul free.

Lynnette Schuepbach

Tempest Winds

As tempest winds blow swirling
Pushing trees against the night
A distant star steers threatening clouds
Toward the calm of morning light

And somewhere in the fury
When the dividing line is crossed
A lighting flash lets broken pines
Regain the dignity they've lost

Soon echoes in the distance
Ride the air that's fresh and clear
And muffled sounds send tired ground
What the night refused to hear

As the renewal of the forest
Takes the fragrance of the soil
And leads dancing through majestic trees
Word the clouds again will boil

Sharon M. Tuttle

Green As It Gets

Sun,
Rain,
Good topsail.
Body, soul, faith,
Stir in stars
add love.

Michael B. Delsanter

Holocaust

Hundreds killed every day
Put in crematories
Trying to survive in any way
Nazi's shooting them on the spot.

Children having to watch parents die.
They did nothing wrong
Does anyone know why!
Why Jews were put through
hell because of what they believed?

Crematories, being shot, selections
all part of concentration camps
marching through snow for many miles.
Fear of losing family, friends
even people you don't know.

Surviving Jews not forgetting
wishing they'd survived in better conditions.
Having nightmares until the end
Leslie Staack Nebraska

That Town

How am I to feel about that town
Raised and grown to what I am now
Should parents be praised
Or scolded for their choice?

There has been laughter and loss
In that town, its vastness
Of suburban sprawl and empty heads
From which now I separate myself

I can still feel the warm air
With balls flying through my backyard
Childish screams and shouts
Interrupt quiet summer afternoons

But I can also see hopelessness
From those who cannot leave
Young men and women
With dreamless futures ahead

Isolated in their little groups
Families debate the issues of the day
But can't even see the trouble
Right in front of their own faces
Ted Gotsch

What Love Is?

It's two hearts
reaching out to
become one.

It's two souls
reaching out
to become
soulmates.

It is two people
who care and
understand each
other.

It is about a couple
that want to join
their hearts and souls
in unity for eternity

That is what love is.
Matt Posten

Desert

Unrelenting sun,
Remote and deserted fields,
Freezing in the night.
Sarah Kielty

"This Final Season"

The prophet chants, the angel sings,
Rise to power the ten crowned kings.

Prayers rising to the ceiling and falling,
Spectral lights diffused and calling.

Recognize this world of strife,
Tree of knowledge, tree of life.

Gather the saints to explain the reason,
Horsemen ride upon this final season.

Breaking the bond of gravity,
Blessed rapture and eternity.

Surrender the suffering of the mourner,
The walk to Eden's just around the corner.
Leslie J. Apodaca

Cypress Park Circle

Just a lone little cat
Rolls around in the sun
   The circle is empty

The quiet is hanging
'Til the day has begun
   The circle is empty

When the first engine roars
And the gravel is spun
   The circle is empty

Now the joggers start out
On their fast daily run
   The circle is empty

The clatter of morning
Lets night know it is done
   The circle is empty

Each piece of the puzzle
Hits the road one by one
   The circle is empty
     It always is!
H. Ersley

Eternity

Beat!
Said the sun as it shone through the clouds
like a stained glass vision of Christ.
Its silver rays brushing my face
making brighter my complexion.

Inner strength swelled with the Spirit.
The maverick wind pulling,
shouting the parable of truth.

Down it poured onto me, through me,
  drowning me in the tears.
I gave myself to the sun and the wind
  and in a fury,
The peace of calm serenity washed over me.
Eternity!

Kathryn L. Schuetze

Two Sides

Very strong to handle life's difficulties,
scared to change with time.
Caring of peoples needs and wants,
too stubborn to trust others.
Seems to have everything going for her,
feels as a failure to many.
Responsible and reliable to others,
Feels as though she has to.
Appears to have control of feelings,
hides true feelings from others
for fear of losing friends.
Active in nature and activities,
hurting physically and mentally.
Awaiting for future goals and success
can't put past behind.
Appears to have a good head on the shoulders,
inside broken into millions of pieces.
Which side is the real me? I don't know, do you?
There's two sides to every story and two
sides to every person.
Kimberly J. Wolfe

"To Love And To Be Loved"

Broken pieces
Scattered
Slowly a puzzle forms
Gently connecting...
To live in bliss,
Harmony and peace,
All shall come together on a day.
Seeking,
Finding,
Questions are answered,
Happiness is living
Living the road you pave.
If the other shall fall
And has scares of before,
Leave him be,
For another road will be made over time.
Kim Miyaki

Night Shadows

Shadows shifting in the dark
Searching the night
For Coalition-Cohesion

Watching grayness drift in sleeping minds
Like clouds in the night sky
Waiting for dreams to form nightmares
Waking-Screaming

Or dreams of Hope
Of Love
Crying out for
Completion-Renewal

The Night Shadows
Watch-Lurk
While they stand guard
Over Souls made vulnerable by sleep
Nadine Frisch

Cherokee Indian

Sacred skies on sacred lands,
They all praised up with their hands,
For the rains the Gods provide,
But the Gods did not abide.
So they still danced and prayed for rain,
Until the sacred rains had come.
Tim Werner

"My Brothers Break My Heart"

Little children tagging on the walls
See the beauty you destroy.
You've been ruining all the falls,
The environment we should enjoy.
The small town rages,
And blames everyone.

Though we came from the same mother,
I look at you with disdain.
I can not endure the pain
Of innocent ones.

Leave the gangs for a chance,
Cease the shooting of "Today".
My heart believes in you.
Listen to what I say.

You're more than gold.
Taste success before you get old.
If death takes you away,
You'd have taught the perfect song.

From your tomb you'll see the sun —
On the face of everyone.

Maria Isabel Tinoco

"Down by the Sea"

The other day I went down by the sea
   Seeking where she used to be
The sun was bright on sea and sand
   Thinking she would take my hand
Her golden hair and eyes so bright
   But only a memory was in sight
The waves gently kissed the shore
   Each one whispered her name once more
Quietly to me
   Beside the sea
The sea gulls cried as I left the shore
   If I could love her, just once more
And now I live with dreams so fine
   That stay with me all the time
Close by where she used to be
   West of the pier
     Down by the sea
     Down by the sea.

Skyline Johnee

March Winds

The winds in March do blow.
Setting the birds in flight.
It's the best time that I know
To fly a high-flying kite.
Up over the housetops, over the trees
So carefree and gay
Dipping and sailing along in the breeze
Until the end of a windy day.
Down comes the kite, down to ground
Careful of wires and tree limbs
To be put away, and then found
to fly on another March wind.

Lois M. Young

Untitled

Privacy, intimacy
Sexuality a novelty
Passion, obsession
Devotion an alternative
Friendship
Censorship
Just pretend
Don't ask
Don't tell
Hold your tongue
Prejudice
Consequence
For the
Conquest
Beauty, reality
Conformity
Get
Real!

Myra J. Sands

This Was My Mother... Her Name Was Dorothy

Passionate always, never passive
shaking with courage
fighting for life for
me—her child; for her, as mother
together
Too much love in
her soul, too much
distraction, with the struggles
of each day gnawing at the
fleeting thin repose of night
Life bites chunks from Life
devouring itself
The heart breaks with hunger
as love waits barefoot in the snow.

Nancy L'enz Hogan

Her Mind's Eye View

Long halls filled with pain
Shame and guilt fall like rain
Endless stairs reaching high
Childhood paths in her mind

Where she goes deep inside
Finding walls - old and high
Built for tears never cried
Swallowed in as a child

But face them she must
For too soon we are dust
And the time in between
Lived inside and unseen

Is her best and her worst
Is she blessed, or just cursed?
With this longing to find
Answers locked in her mind

And to now shed the tears
She's fought back all these years
Relief filling her eyes
Finding joy, she now cries

Wendy Lyon

Love Was Her Appetite

Hand in hand
She drinks his light
One beat to the next
It fills her heart
And warms her soul

With every rapturous spoonful
He feeds her mind
One taste after another
Filled with endless passion
She grew to love him without hesitation

Yi-Hsin Lee

A Woman In Country

They asked, and without question she came.
She gave them her rank and her name.
Battles raged and hearts beat fast.
Troops engaged, men breathed their last.
For the dying, she must be brave.
To save the lives that she could save.
A shield, against wars hellish sound.
Her hope to see them homeward bound.
To hearth and home, at conflicts' end.
A time for body and soul to mend.
For love of country, and service true.
With these few words, I honor you.

Winnie J. Powell

Grandma

She makes you feel special
She makes good treats
She makes chores fun
to get the work done
She makes, the rain go away
and the sun come out so we can play
Her voice reminds me of those
good old days
When we used to sing and dance
But now none of that takes place
For I cannot see her face
She is gone yet still here
She is as close as close can get
She is in my heart so I won't forget

Hayley Bykens

Sarah

She lived in dreams
She walked through life
With a grace that would betray
Her soulful spirit
Her vulnerable heart
That oft got in the way

And she would not reveal
The wounds and grief
Regrets and dreams
Those she kept well hidden
And the years have yet to heal
That which is forbidden

Sally Pillsbury

"Moon Phases"

"The full moon at night
shines so bright, looks down
at the masses so snug and tight.
"The new moon is encircled
with a black frame, making
it unique in design and mind.
"The half moon groans and
moans for a brighter side,
as it only sees half of the
universe in disguise.
"The quarter moon is cheated
much more, because of the
dark clouds and the bright stars
outshining him galore.
"All in all the moon is
contented to start out as one
whole, and unselfishly divides
himself for all the world to
explore from the core.

Mildred L. De Marco

Silence

On a rainy day -
silence cannot be found
On a sunny quiet day
very few words are floating around -
The silence can be found -
Peacefully lying on my bed
with silence all around -
While I lie so peacefully
I dream about the clouds -
while a small ray of sunshine
appears from the sky.

Kristina Johnson

Endless Love

Many years have come and gone;
Since I left my love and home,
I started out to forget
The one I love but I haven't yet.

In dreams I see his smiling face
There's no one else can take his place.
I try so hard to hide my sorrow
But for me there's no tomorrow.

As the sun is setting at my life's door
I know not what my life was for:
I only know I've loved in vain
My heart can never love again
For I have found my endless love.

Thelma Williams

Seasons In Time

Leaves full of life
   so green and strong.
Fall unyielding with cold
   soon to change everything,
From green...
   to yellow, red and gold.
As seasons change
   so do our lives...
Starting young and strong
   believing we will live forever,
Later to find we were wrong
   leaving weak, frail and old.

Vicki L. Velmere

Your Importance To Me

I've had the time of my life,
   Since the day I met you.
You're my source of inspiration,
   My love for you is true.

This has to be right,
   My heart is so true.
Gently touching my soul,
   So deeply I love you.

You've kindled a fire
   That will forever burn.
Oh! How my heart does,
   Constantly yearn.

Day after day,
   And into the night.
Week after week,
   With all of my might.

I'll love you for always,
   Forever and more.
My darling you're everything,
   I could possibly wish for.

Sandra Logan

Ricky

When I first saw you
Sitting over there,
You didn't know who I was,
And probably didn't care.

As the years went by
the closer we grew.
"In This Life" is our song
It fits me and you.

You've become the best guy
That I have ever known.
You are very understanding,
And it's really shown.

Now that we are like
Husband and wife,
I just want you to know
That you are my life.

Our days are numbered,
And may they be many or few,
I hope to spend every last one of them
Walking, talking, and cuddling with you.

Kimberly Wofford

None But The Lonely

None but the lonely, should he like I
Sitting silently while the world goes by
I sit here alone each night and day
And while sitting here I start to pray.

Why, dear God, is this world of ours
All confused and full of sorrows
Why, oh, why is the world today
full of despair and I further say

How come dear God, did I get lost
Have I forgot the things thou taught
Am I too stupid too blind to see
The wonderful thou gave to me

When all is over said and done
My sad, sad, thoughts are o'er and gone
You've taken my hand and said to me
Look up my child, I am here with thee.

Roberta H. Clifton

Gaelic Image

Celtic sod house...
skull-like appearing with
two empty window sockets flanking
the doorway passage...
purpose long ago completed.

People born, baptized,
raised and gone,
cows now roam the sacred ground
within its shelterless seams.

Erected upon the land...
appearing as an earthly
outcropping,
Gaelic winds swirl around
and through the edifice...
piping magical reels
for step dancing faeries
and visitors graced
with imagination.

Lawrence Etue

brother robert

black shirt sprinkled
slightly with dandruff,
opened collar at the neck
exposed adam's apple.
black slacks, pressed,
shine in the fluorescent
classroom lights,
a water fall at night.
black shoes smudged,
kickball games at recess.
lips traced, white paste,
it gathered in the corners.
breath, stomach bile and peppermint.
hairy knuckled large hands
raised the book
to glass widened eyes.
the mouth praises the words,
the origin of the species.
by christmas break,
we go through evolution.

thomas j. caulfield

Vivarin

I sit and watch myself
slowly deteriorate,
a sickening sight,
yet unstoppable;
I am beyond repair
save for the antidote
you, my beloved friend
the rush,
the feeling you give me,
quaking...
shaking...
...then slowly dying
back to reality,
into an eerie comatose
of sleepless lunacy...

Megan Wojak

Leaves And Love

It's coming
Slowly, surely
Descending, hanging
Falling, softly

I speak of autumn
And how our spend time,
Summer, gracefully
Vanishes without a trace

Autumn is sneaking in
Cleverly, gingerly
Creeping, crawling
I love it, live it

Autumn approaching
Impassions me
Anxiously awaiting
The Harvest Moon

My autumn love,
The best kind,
Is out there
Waiting for me.

Shawn Carroll

Love Is...

Love is like the ocean
So beautiful when calm
Yet, the waves have to crash.

Love is like the wind
It moves in all directions
Yet, someday's there is no movement.

Love is like a star
Shining so bright
Yet, it has to fall sometime.

Whatever love is...
It's sure to take you up
Yet, bring you down just as quick.

Kalpesh Patel

"He Came To Me"

She didn't want him
 So he came to me
  Bewildered, confused,
   wondering why
Smiling - he loved
  instantaneously
 But did I?
He grew and he grew
 along the way
My heart grew with him
 So they say
He loved me and I loved him
 So he came to me-
  Oh so grateful to have my
adopted son!

Sharon LaBollita

Untitled

Fixed, vacant eyes,
staring past present time.
Mouth rounded in terror,
or perhaps by awe,
left breathless by the sight he saw.
Spirit gone which was once intertwined
with a form from terra firma.

Steven J. Nerheim

Special Friend

I won't tell you goodbye
so, I'll only say so long,
for goodbye seems so final to me
although I've not known you long.

Knowing you I feel I've found
a very "special friend", a true and
honest and loyal guy, who likes to be
everybody's friend.

There's friendship in your eyes and
smile and laughter in your heart.
That's why you make it so darn hard
when you say, that we must part.

You have strength of a mountain
and listening is your door key.
You show warmth and friendship
to everyone you see.

You have helped me to strengthen
my pride to, "look and listen" and
know, new hopes can be born...
without destroying the old.

Shirley Burnett

"Abandoned Baby China Dolls"

Little china baby dolls
So precious, and so sweet.

Abandoned by your mama's arms,
Where security and love once
  rocked you to sleep.

Her love is felt no longer
As you cry yourself to sleep,

The pain and suffering you must endure
Is it now beyond someone else's reach?

Abandonment, loneliness and hunger
Where no one sees our hears;

Then finally death appears
And wipes away your tears.

Reta Wright

Daughters

Daughters are a special breed,
So pretty in all their frills.
Giggling and laughing,
Filling my heart with love.
Pony tails and doggie ears,
Swaying in the breeze.
Girl scouts and soft ball team,
Seems to take all my time.
Dating and driving the car,
Makes me walk the floor.
High school and graduation,
Swells my heart with pride.
Walking down the aisle,
With that special someone.
When my work is finally done.
Oh how I long for little girls,
With pony tails and doggie ears.

Lillie Mae Goodwin

IT CAME FROM THE HEART OF OUR TEENS

Her Dad turned on the wrong street
So she must permanently be put to sleep
No matter she was only three
All because of a teen-age creep

I'm my son's Mother, a woman replies
I did my best without his Dad
So now I realize I wasn't very wise
I didn't know he was telling me lies

A family's shot without remorse
A teen-age boy brought to court
A family love they gave to him
But a war on drugs made his mind dim

What are our goals in future teens
Will they war our neighbors on the streets
Will the racial warriors become a team
Are our hard working Mothers doomed to weep

Making the plans for a future world,
With good replenished among our teens.
Positive outlets for anger and grief
Bestowed upon our teen-age perils

Susan Lawson

Godspeed

Godspeed
So slow as to carve a canyon
As swift as the turning of the moon
And the changing of the tides

Grant me Godspeed
So I may smell the flowers
Marvel the sky,
Hear the ocean,
See the stars in my love's eyes

I wish upon myself Godspeed,
For I move much to fast.

Kevin G. Huff

My Father

My father was a big man,
So strong, so kind
He loved to laugh
And tell his jokes.
His wife and kids
Were his life,
He dearly loved
His wife.
When I was born,
He nicknamed me
Teencey, because I
Was so tiny.
I felt warm,
I felt thankful
I was born
With such a
Wonderful Daddy.
I'm glad he loved me.

Teresa Meadows

Writer's Secret

The pencil in my hand
Speaks to me
It tells me what to say

Larry Shane Farr

A Granddaughter

My Kagan, my Kagan
  so sweet and shy.
How I love you.

  When you look and
smile at me my heart
breaks with joy and happiness.

  Our little games we play.
The walks we take.
The dolls, the balls, the dishes

  My Kagan I cannot say enough
about the one I love.

Glynnette Barnard

Bang-Bang You're Dead

"Bang-bang you're dead!"
So the little boy said.
Just an innocent game of fun,
With Daddy's loaded gun.
Who'd have thought
Daddy wasn't taught
To keep you safe and sound?
Who'd have thought Daddy
Would leave a gun around?
"Bang-bang you're dead!"
So the little boy said.

Linda L. Aker

Our 1st Kiss

Our first kiss was so soft,
So warm and so tender, and sweet
So much so as to cause
My mind to faint from surprise,
And my heart to leap for joy
At the mere touch of you!
Press ever nearer to me!
Let my love hold you,
As my arms enfold you.
Licking lips and sucking tongues,
That have for so long yearned
For love's sweet feast!
Cling to me tighter, don't ever release
Suck in my soul, come on baby, come on
Kiss me harder and deeper,
Kiss me rough, kiss me long
Kiss me ever so passionately, then
Kiss me over and over again!

Maurice Weldon Young

Wild Flower

Bright little wild flower,
Sown by chance,
Smiles sweetly at the blazing sun.

Such seeming frailty
Weathers the beating rain.
A vigorous little spirit belies
The poor and rocky soil.

Yet, dare not dig it up to
Place it in the comfortable
Protection of the fertile garden.
Untransplantable-it dies.

Some people are wild flowers.

Penelope Palmer

Opus 60

Come soft upon this Sylvan scene,
Sobered bone reality,
To hear Pan's oracles in their groves
Soothe blithe Morgana in Avalon:
Hear on her throne, Cybele play
In her dabbled leaf colonnade:
Behold the wakening Thespian plain
Where now Great Phoenix burns again!
As moist seeds tremble in their birth
In their furred, dark, beryl1ed laminae
Touched by some mystical unison.
In these pleasant haunts of solitude.
Vines, growth embowled, long tacit climb
Toward Mount Olympus' euphoric Gods;
While Satyrs play their rude syringe
Fair Orpheus charms the lifeless stone.
Come, drink with Zeus, ambrosia
That delirium might in rapture swell;
Might hear nymphs pipe; dream Orestes, dream
From their genesthetic citadel.

R. L. Coret

Reflections

Though life's journey carries on alone,
  Softly leading into roads yet unknown.

Often I pause in a moment's reflection -
  Eyes all aglow,
    The heart's warmth softly overflows.

Reflections of days past,
  Seeming long ago,
    Yet as real as the life I know.

On the outside -
  The chill of life's journey alone,
  While on the inside,
    The heart's warmth softly all aglow.

Reflections of times I've known.

Melvin L. Luetje Jr.

Dreams

Beyond the sunset, there are dreams.
Some have hoped for but never seen
Some have made them come true
Others have never made it through

Some are dreams that come to pass
Some are memories that will last
Others see them where they are
In the future that seems so far

There are dreams of fortune and fame
When they end they're not the same
Failure comes in such a blow
In this life we never know

Dreams are like a picture book
So often we would take a look
Like picture frames upon the wall
Some are short and some are tall.

Virginia Meadows

Trees to Dirt

Trees
Swinging, swaying
Rustling, howling, crying
Plant, bark, roots, soil
Stationary, wet, solid
Moving, drying
Dirt

Michael Taylor

People At Courage Center

People at Courage Center is mighty sweet,
Some in wheel chairs,
Some can't speak.

Some can't talk,
Some can't walk.
That doesn't matter for the love they got
Can't be bought.

But they all seem to care,
Because they have no fear.
They all have pain inside,
You can tell from their eyes,
That's where the courage lies.

A. L. Kelly

Happiness

The days they pass,
some slow, some fast;
we wonder how the world
will ever last.

We have developed a
reliance on pleasures,
seeking a future, but
forgetting our treasures.

Foolish are we to
forget who we are,
letting our wishes
wander so far.

There's a need to get back
to the basics of life:
live for today and strive
for what's right.

When are we happy with what we have?

Sheila Turman

Seasons Wonders

Springtime flowers
  somehow knows.

Summer breezes soon
  will blow.

Falls brilliant colors.
  Where did they go?
Now all covered by
  winters white snow!

Minnie Karchinski

We're All Looking For A Love

We're all looking for a love,
sometimes it's a task.

We're all looking for a love,
have they already crossed our path?

We're all looking for a love
someone to share with and laugh.

We're all looking for a love,
we'll cherish them and express it
they won't have to ask.

We're all looking for a love
they don't have to have been perfect
because we all come with a past.

We're all looking for a love
that when found through sharing, caring,
and giving in Jesus Christ's name, will last.

Reginald Joyce

"Magic Of The Rain"

After each
Spring-time rain,
Life is reborn.
Flowers open up
To the sun,
Thanking dear Sol
For a thirst-quenching drink
Of sweet water.
Birds sing praises
To the beautiful
Blue skies,
While animals and insects
Chatter and buzz
With the excitement
Of clean, fresh air.
And a couple
Strolls hand-in-hand
Through the park,
Taking it all in,
Making a memory.

Kristi M. McGilvray

An Ordinary Day

Raise the sun unfold the petals,
sprinkle morning dew caress the meadows -
A new dawn crisp and fresh,
favor the day nothing less -
Rotate the world rhythm of dance,
evolution is a lifetime stance -
Cherish each second life's not forever,
being alive's the ultimate treasure -
Play the game day by day,
it's not easy what to say -
Move the moment choice or chance,
love is found deep hearts romance -
Light the stars without a match,
if they fall make the catch -
Lift the moon make dark bright,
add a smile all is right.

Steve Messa

Counting Blessings

The money-changer's weary hands
stained with gold and black
Lift another glittering coin
atop the coiled stack
Indulgences, the paid-for sins
denials of the truth
Result of Adam and of Eve
we ate of knowledge fruit
Layered steps reach for the sky
upon the wobbling scale
The top one spills
and with the rest
falls straight down into Hell.

Owen Shelksohn

Fraud

Outside my window
the cedar laden in snow
is bent and bowed in my direction.
How like that tree you are.
Tomorrow you will both rise
and reach out for the sun,
ignoring me once again.

Margaret P. Mannigan

A Chance

A white rose is blooming.
Standing upright and strong
Fulfilling it's purpose
Completely, for now...
With dignity it may drop
Its' petals
Back unto the earth
From which it came -
So as to nourish new life
Therein
Waiting ever so patiently
For a chance
At last
A chance.

Mary T. Miller

My Road

  Sitting here gazing out
Staring down time what am I doing
Where am I going
  I am waiting for the
Big Balloon to pop! How can I
  give time a task for a change.
I want to go where no one has gone
I want to do what no one has done

  But we all must travel that
long, winding, difficult road.
    Though it looks abandoned
It's been traveled by all
  It can be a lonely time
I must be positive
    and look straight ahead
will I be true I need help.
I'm standing alone
   in the party of life.
    Watching, learning, waiting.
   Does the road end?

Vicky L. Burke

Child-Filled

The empty red swing
Still in the heat of the hour
Handcuffed to the sky.
We are both barren
Silenced by childless space.

A soft wind sighs
Nudging life
From rusty memories,
Coaxing corroded chains
And curling red paint
Into living form.

In spirited dance, the wind
Lifts the swing —
Now a red butterfly
Flutters over the earth
Flying higher and higher while I
Clutch my stomach.

Marcia Gamble

Haiku #7

A small brown mouse hunts
To the music of crickets
And quiets the night.

Michael Taylor

Music

Melodies that
Stir the soul,
Touch the heart and
Soothe the mind,

With memories
Painful or
Pleasurable.

Somehow it sweeps
All your wandering thoughts
Together,
Into a pattern of emotional release.

Linda Jill Lustgarten

Me And My Monster

My tears fall like rain on a dark and
stormy night;

My heart beats like wild horses
running from a monstrous spirit.

My hands are weak like leaves in
autumn winds blowing harder and
harder from time to time;

My mind is twisted from the
confusion and frustration of my love
not coming home;

The nights are so cold and dark its
for one day we will destroy this
monster and hope that he never returns;

For your love for me keeps the
sanity and the hope alive for one
day we will be back together!

Michelle Pogue

Spicy Nights

Some days are nice like
sugar and spice.

The cats chase the mice
while I'm eating the rice.

That makes me say "yikes!"
So I chill out here on the ice at night.

Or do I stay inside and
decide why the cats chase
mice and I eat the rice.

I have a bowl of rice, I
shake it up with spice, that's
why rice is so nice and
the cats chase the mice.

Sharolette Nicole Gill

Untitled

Multi colored sounds of Harmony soar
thru the air giving joy to those who
really listen

Clouds of Peace drift thru the sounds;
hear, feel the fluffy warmth of being
at Peace...

Mona Fox

"Suppose"

Suppose, suppose, suppose, suppose.
Suppose a mutual love had not.
The throws of anguish be my lot.
Nights swimming a loveless bed.
Pains gnawing within my head.

Suppose a mutual love had not.
Aloof, a stranger, felt forgot.
One not to love, one not to care.
Sitting, vacant, alone a stare
Feelings halted, all inside.
Brimming caldron, bursting wide!!

Suppose a mutual love had not.
Have I a love, Hurrah! Hurrah!

Shirley Godbolt

The Orchard

Sweet!
  Sweet!
Oh what delights!
Apple trees!
Below the wheat sun
Upon faces become,
Cherry smiles!
Little children
With such wide eyes
Run to this fortress
Around!
  Around!
See the apples
Falling down

As they do imagine all
Is just for you
These moments gained
So don't turn away!
For today may shine
And tomorrow may rain

Sharlene Snyder

God's Autograph

The bud is small,
Sweet and red,
insecure,
in its bed.

It's growing fast,
tall and strong,
that little bud,
can do no wrong.

Opening bright,
not forlorn,
walking up,
to a beautiful morn.

Velvet soft, glistening dew,
the petals are, very new.

Long green stems,
bright green leaves,
that rich deep color,
blends with trees.

Now at last, open to you,
God's autograph, fresh and new.

Katrina Flavell

Uhh, That Feel

Hellen I would love to whisper;
  sweet nothings into your lovely ears.
And oh, how I would like to kiss you;
  like a fire that's hot.
Each tantalizing lick shaking me
  even more.
Until one moment I am playing,
  you like an organ.

Marc Roberre

My Forbidden Lover

My forbidden lover
take me in your arms.
In your cold embrace
I feel both strange and warm.

There is something in your darkness
Something strong and right.
To me you are my lover;
To them you are just night.

Your hands of velvet darkness
Slowly stroke my skin.
Your brisk wind does blow
and blankets me from sin.

Always to soon the day will come
to steal you away from me.
Once again 'til the sun goes down
it is only in my heart you'll be.

Kerry Ann Korchman

All Time At Once

The sun, the moon, the earth, the sea
Tell me what you believe
Tell me what you see, what you were told
What you know
There are no secrets here

Open up
Let me inside
If not for hours, for minutes at a time
You won't have to look for me
In the sun is where I preside
I'm an angel without wings
A broken lonely soul.

Shaun Kane

Scarlet O'Hara

Scarlet O'Hara is more
than just a woman
She was name after the
original "Old Katie Scarlett"
Her grandmother

Strong and fearless
knowing how to take a stand
A daring horseback rider
loving to race and hunt

Miss O'Hara knows sharing and kindness.
Even tho', she had many hardships
and troubles during her time,
But she wouldn't not give a dime,
for the two people she loves the most,
Her daughter Cat
Her husband Rhett

Valerie D. Keesee

Teardrops And Raindrops

There were tiny flowers
That bloomed in the garden of love,
Their dew covered petals
Reflected the sun that shone above.

Soon the dewdrops melted away
And the petals drooped in the searing sun,
There was sadness in the garden of love
As all the flowers wilted - one by one.

A little girl walked by the garden,
Seeing the wilted flowers she began to cry,
And as her tears fell upon the earth
She looked for help in the mid-day sky.

As if by magic - a cloud appeared
Directly over the garden of love,
And cool - life giving raindrops
Fell upon the flowers from above.

A smile returned to the little girls face
As the wilted petals began to rise,
And the little girl rejoiced
Beneath the cloudless skies.

William A. Caddell

Things I Got

What's with these things
that collect on my coffee table,
and my kitchen counter,
in my top dresser drawer,
and my closet shelf?

I can't get rid of them
because they remind me
of something I must do, or
I must check on, or
be sure about.

Maybe to prove later in court,
or to entertain myself
when there is nothing to do.
They could help comfort me
when I have no money, or friends.

But, mainly these bookmarks,
space marks and landmarks
on the time line of my life
helped not at all, when
I had a heart attack.

Patrick Fitzgerald

The Germ

I am a germ and like a worm
That faults tomato, corn and apple
I creep into a person's nose
Or in their throat I do repose
Where with their health I grapple

I make them sneeze, cough and wheeze
Their throat's on fire, a germ built pyre
I really am a villain
But what is this that's in their mouth
Oh, No! It's Penicillin

Samuel Feldman

"River Of Life"

Life is like a river
that flows cool then warm
rough spots then smooth
with my great falls.

My heart flows
flows like a river.
So many broken hearts
hurt from all the falls.

Please pick up my heart
and prepare me for the ride.
The long smooth ride of life,
life with you.

Don't break my heart
when you decide,
decide to throw me out.
Out in the cold, rough, river.

Make sure I'm strong
for the life with out you
as my heart is like
a cold, rough river.

Nancy Jo Wilson

"Alone"

She thought about the years
   that had passed her by.

She thought about the happy moments
   that had made her cry.

She thought about the smiles
   she had left behind.

She thought about the tenderness
   she would never find.

She thought about someone
   from out of the past.

She thought about "Why"
   knowing why it didn't last.

She thought about the love
   she had never found.

She thought about these things
   without making a sound.

   And then she cried.

Monica L. Grasso

My Blessing...

For God so loved the world,
that He gave it His only Son.
Am I so less loved,
that I will never be blessed with one?

As my heart begins the questioning,
my mind wonders of his plan.
The Lord reveals to me my blessing,
it is in my husband, Van.
For the Lord blessed me with not a Son,
but with the love of a wonderful man.

Vonnie Berry

Untitled

Then was a time
That I once said
that I was you
and you were me

And so therefore
we were me

Now
is the time

That I can say
that I am you
are you are me

and so therefore
We are

Timothy L. Ward

Trees and Me

I think when I read Kilmer's "Trees"
   That I should fall upon my knees,
If God loves trees and makes them grow,
   It's not that difficult to know
He loves His children here on earth,
   To whom He sent His Son in birth!

God loved me first, I praise His name,
   For Christ, His Son, my love proclaim!
For trees - for all God's earth, I pray
   For Christ to lead my homeward way,
For only God can make a tree,
   And only Christ can make me free!

Kenneth D. Hatcher

My Precious Friend

Precious friends are precious few;
That is why I am so proud of you.
For you have shown, without a doubt,
What precious friends are all about.

What a blessing you are to me,
For it is in you I see
God's love flowing sweet and tender.
His Spirit rises to majestic splendor.

In God's own perfect time we met,
A very short time ago—and yet,
What a joy it will be
To know you throughout eternity!

Though our time together has been short,
I hold this feeling in my heart;
God must love me so very much
To add to my life this loving touch.

Toni Conway

I

My I is an I
That shall never die
No matter indignities
And years of miseries

My I is an I
Beyond all skies
Mysterious infinities
Rebellious centuries

My I is an I
That's made of divine
And all that's sublime
Make my I

B. Mancini

On The Inside

The dream was cast aside for fear
that someone sloven may be near.
To pass the product of one's own mind
for all the world to uncover and find.

What unfortunate luck one would have
to let loosed such a presentable plan.
Securely now the image rests,
in the bodies private fortress.

Rhodes

"Life's Journey"

You cannot go back to the you
   that was you.
You cannot go forward
   one day in advance
You can't change the future
   or one circumstance
So live that your days
   will bring the joys and love
   of Gods promises of grace

Wilma E. Gleason

Life's Journey

Life is just a trip
That's been paid for in advance
By God who believes that all of us
Will make it if given a chance

For some the trip will be short
And the destination clear
With God's love to guide them
They will have nothing to fear

For others the journey is endless
No destination in sight
To wander lost in darkness
Searching for the light

One thing to remember
As you plan your trip through life
God has paid for your ticket
But you must catch the right flight.

Sylvia Sawyer

"The Tiger"

If I were a Tiger
That's what I'll be
I could steal along
And kill indiscriminately

If I could choose a path
Myself, a Tiger I would see
Just to pounce along the reeds
So svelte would I be

Yes, a great majestic Tiger
A perfect creature, from the Three
With gleaming retraceable claws
That could slice eternity

But if a Tiger I would be
With claws arranged so perfectly
Could I cut away your soul
And remove your dignity

So if you have thoughts of impropriety
Perhaps the Tiger you should be
Point your claws for all to see
And restore your dignity

E. J. Wilowski Jr.

Follow Me

"Be your brother's servant,"
that's what the Lord does say.
"Put all things behind you
and let me be your way.
Trust in Me to guide you
to wherever you may go.
For you know not where you're headed.
But I, the Lord, will know."
"So, put your faith in Me my child
I will not leave you alone.
Just follow Me through your life
and I will lead you home."
Norman A. Robitaille

First

The night was dark
The air so cold
Dawn came slowly
Until your eyes I did behold

My body warmed
My spirit took flight
As I did love you in the night

You kissed my lips so tenderly
I'll feel your love eternally

A glance
A look
A fleeting smile
Makes every moment so worthwhile

I want to shout, at last I'm whole
For with your love, you made me so

I am sunrise flaming bright
A petal unfolding to the light
God above has told me so
We are love at last I know
Vera Dagg

Ode To Light

It was the neutral softness of gray
The beginning of night, the end of day,
Over was the harshness of bright
We were welded in misty twilight;
It really didn't last too long
This fading day was a dying song;
For we can't live over our yesterday
It's a memory we gather along the way,
And this neutral softness of gray
Introduces memories for a brand new day.
Mildred M. Hardy

You Loved Me

I looked into your eyes
the eyes of blue sea's,
and a heart of gold,
the treasure of life is
what you were to me.

Now it's gone
the heart I loved,
now it's gone
the eyes of blue sea's,
gone but not lost.
You loved me once
You'll love me again.
Paulette Cain

Painful Purpose

I walk and run and try to hide,
The being burns me from within.
Rules I cannot now abide,
For being thrown to deadly sin.

Rocking backwards in my mind,
Pulling forwards with my heart.
Thinking thoughts, though not so kind,
Tearing my poor soul apart.

Painful pretense enters in.
Pressure overwhelms my sight.
Knowing not how long it's been,
Piranhas of reality bite.

Kill the channels, end the scenes.
Find new hope for sanity.
Curtain calls invade my dreams
Of pretense laced with vanity.

If reason ever blocks your path
Of vengeance, hate and painful wrath,
Sleep today and scorn tomorrow,
For you too were born in love of sorrow.
Stacey P. Davis

It

It burns through
the body like a
raging numbness

It begins deep in the
throat then follows
behind the eyes

It flows through
The veins and past
the heart

The thoughts spiral
as the control leaves

Legs are weak from
the powers that serge
within

Large desire builds to
thrust my fist through

But I cannot because
I do
Tania Gies

The Inevitable

Swiftly, silently
The chill clawing at you
Shackles tighten, your throat dries
Perceptions change as your mind narrows
Odors change and are never forgotten
Reality embraces
Gazing into the eyes of His next victim
Wishing for a quiet painless journey
Knowing nothing can be done
Waiting for what
The clawing more impatiently
Loving for all we have
Crying for all we will miss
Knowing that in time it will be us
Shukuno S. Wakeland

Mourning

The darkness of a winter's day,
The cold of dawn in which I lay,
The stillness of the windless trees,
The silence brought me to my knees.
The death of my greatest friend,
Had finally hit me again.
It hit me then and hit me hard,
The shock of it caught me off guard.
If I knew then, what I know now,
The gun would have never gone
off...POW!!
I learned the hard way and once only,
And now I'm the one who's lonely.
Rebecca Peters

A Mother's Love

Oh! If you only could behold,
The depths of sorrow in my soul!

You then would maybe stop and check,
See how your actions hang round my neck!

Because I love you I try my best,
To help you with your trying test!

But with you, My Love, they seem to grow!
Just where they'll end only God will know.

But this, my love, I want you to remember,
My love to you is with full surrender!

Love without any major conditions!
Love like that of the Great Physician!

His call to us is but to Him come.
The good, the bad, to all not some!

So this, my Love, is what you should seek,
Your problems and trials lay at His feet!
Shirley T. Woodruff

Dad

To see the tired, wrinkled face,
   The eyes so full of pain.
To see his hair now filled with gray,
   His stature stooped with strain.

Though seldom tears are seen to fall,
   So silently he grieves.
Within his heart, his soul does bleed,
   His sorrow never leaves.

So different from a mother's way,
   A father mourns the child...
That briefly filled his life with joy
   And touched his days with smiles.

Some comfort can he take in knowing,
   His child now lives with ONE,
Who fully understands his pain
   for He too has buried a SON.

God's gift to fathers here below,
   The knowledge to be had.
Someday he'll hear again that voice,
   call out the name of "DAD".
Marlene Wriston

Dracula's Rising

The sun dips low
The flames are growing
The blood is flowing
And Dracula is rising

Wolves hunt
Bats fly
A mist settles in
And Dracula is rising

Life is cheap
Food...nothing more
Grab your crucifix
For Dracula is rising

You were warned
He is here
The dead travel fast

Dracula has risen.
Samantha McCullah

Concerning The Flower

For this gift of love
the gift of the rose
How it fills our very being
giving grace propitious pleasure
Sculptured in silence
this joyful celebration
Expressing that which cannot
be put into words
Yet cannot remain silent
This gift of the heart
Donna M. Williams

When Love Is Lost

When love is lost,
The heart does bleed;
Pain, anguish, do rise
To overwhelming degree.

When love is lost,
The soul does fade;
With no soul,
There is no life.

When love is lost,
Time is ended;
Stagnant, suspended,
Time moving neither
Here nor there.

When love is lost,
The flesh does whither;
Growing old and wrinkled,
Consisting only of a shell.

When love is lost;
Life is lost.
Tammy S. Milburn

God's Star

A star is shining bright
to guide us 'til comes the morning light.
It is God's gift from above
for us to know of his sweet love.
It is the most beautiful thing,
so when you see one,
in your heart, you should sing!
D. K. Hey

Hand Me A Pillow, Please

A loneliness that deprives
the heart of it's full extent.
A bitterness towards love,
misgivings of tenderness for
a solitary night.
Not worthy of myself.
A time to grow forth and
venture in the beauty of my
soul and its simplicity.
Nights turn to down without
the whispers or cries of the romantic.
The wishes and dreams
turning inside, threading the
uncertainty and doubt into
a claustrophobic realism,
I gasp for breath.
Soaring the flight of willowy skies,
he lies beneath the clouds,
walking with the daisies,
Hand me a pillow, please.
Yahni Chismar

War

The pain and misery,
The hurt and despair,
Where all this leads to,
I think you know where,
It is something we all know about,
You talk about it with fear and doubt,
Someone out there is to blame,
For all this shame,
That WAR has proclaimed!
Natalie Ciresi

Beatnik Poem

The lies, the lies
The hurtful lies.
The rumors they fly,
As the Victims heart dies.
The shame, the shame
the shame that is felt.
The punishment,
That is dealt, is dealt.
Someone cries,
They cry, they cry.
as the lies,
They fly, they fly.
Someone's pain
Is another's gain.
Their, pain their pain.
Is another's gain.
The lies, the lies.
The hurtful lies.
The rumors they fly
As the victims heart dies.
Trisha Carter

January Garden

My roses have forsaken me
  this gray and wintry dawn.
No velvet petals, softly scented
  do I find here this morn.

The earth feels hard with frozen lumps
  where once was sweet with dew
No clover blooms, nor bees come buzzing
  Dear June, how I miss you!
Kathleen K. Mann

A Walk

The silence that comes between two.
The impassable moments,
The silence ensues.

The light on their faces,
No longer remains.
For the silence has killed,
Their loving embrace.

Soon all the leaves will quit talking,
Love will be silent,
And I shall go on walking.
Robert Bridges

Too Young

I didn't know it until it was over.
The last time I saw him he was young.
He grew old in a short time.
The decades that were left in his life
Were crammed into an hour.
My age sheltered me from sickness but
It also built a wall between him and me.
I think I should have been there
To hold his hand
For one last time...
To say
Good-bye.
Lindsay Sparrow Thorne

Untitled

 Oh, how I love the breeze at night,
The leaves and trees and all the fright.
How the flowers come and go,
See how all the pumpkins glow.
Rain and leaves all come down,
Birds and squirrels go round and round.
Ghosts and Goblins are best that night,
To scare and scream and do the fright.
Everything is scary,
Everything is in fear.
Autumn is the best time of the year.
Mercedes D. Maia

The Golden Chain Of Friendship

Friendship is a golden chain,
The links are friends so dear,
And like a rare and precious jewel
It's treasured more each year.

It's clasped together firmly
With a love that's deep and true,
And it's rich with happy memories
And fond recollections, too

Time can't destroy it's beauty
For, as long as memory lives,
Years can't erase the pleasure
That the joy of friendship gives

For the golden chain of friendship
Is a strong and blessed tie
Binding kindred hearts together
As the years go passing by.
Theodore Parker

Dr. Arshad The Great

Dr. Arshad is
   The man of the hour.
Among others,
   He's really a tower.
He races from patient to patient
   Because he's the best,
Although I think
   He should get some rest.
He's a man of great intellect
   To be sure,
And not the least
   Is he demur.
As a specialist,
   He's at the top of the list,
But that people follow his orders
   He always insists!

Mary L. Flynn

Cry Of Love

The candle light fades as
the night falls.
Her love for him grows deeper
as he holds her gently in his arms.
They make love not for the first,
but for the last time.
As he leaves, he kisses her softly
on the forehead.
She starts to cry as a plea to stay,
but he only walks away.
He glances back over his shoulder,
but now it's her turn to turn away.

Toni Fulton

If I Could Hear That Whistle

I've sorely missed that whistle sound that
came from the trains and
the old pulp mill. Our parents used it for a
curfew, and its bellow haunts me still.

I'd follow a path toward the river, and
stand on the banks above
where I could look down and see old
railroad tracks that lay idle and rust.

From the path above the river one could
see logs as they drifted
toward the cutting mill, but this stillness
would be broken by a far off whistle's shrill.

That steam-engine, coal smoke swirling
from her stack, puffs of
steam below, flew out over her tracks, as
the engine pulled on passed.

Box cars rattled as did the flat cars and
such, iron wheels made a
deafening earth shaking rumbling noise, on
that old railroad track.

Seems I miss the old trains calling, when I
lived close to the tracks,
and the things I like the most about it, are
never coming back.

When I stood there watching those trains,
they would shake the earth,
seemed those fifty cars or so, just flew by
much too fast.

If I could hear that whistle
when it was soft and low,
even at a distance,
it would set this heart aglow.

Eugene F. Bernard

To Thee I Sing

Shivers, bites, and shakes
the open - window wind.
I clutch the blanket
(wool for warmth);
my icy feet on yours.

Hot breath
Warm tongue
Now flushing with heat,
Feverish, I roll on top.

The blanket on the floor.

Linda Durnbaugh

Pain

Can't you see the pain in my eyes
The pain that roles down each eye

Can you see the bird holding out his wing.
Well that's me, that's me.

If you could only see the true me
You would understand what I see.

If you could only switch places with me
The road that you never see.

You would understand me
You would understand me.

Pamela Givens

Not Me

The person in the mirror
The person that I see
I know not who it is
Because that person is not me
The person that I know
That person cannot be
It isn't who I think it is
That person is not me
You cannot prove
Because I will deny
I will not pay the fee
For that person is not me.

Lezli Skog

Mental Intercourse

In tune to your dark side,
the pumping vine full of blood,
I'm thirsting for you. The
scent of your skin awaiting
to taste from the outside
deeper within. Eyes meet,
look my surface soul onto
my third eye. Let me run my
thoughts through your mind,
feel your emotions. The closer
we get to becoming one, I
long to be you. Figuring that's
the closest I could get to your soul,
is penetrating it.
Metamorphosis changes the
structure of my being;
finalizes my utmost desires.
I am you.

Portia Spencer

Margaret Rose

Beneath the sea in ocean caves
   The pure and lustrous pearl
Shimmers still below the waves
   Less fair than our dear girl.

The daisy, like the day's gold eye,
   The warm and glowing sun,
Awakens to a topaz sky
   When morning's just begun.

The rose's petals, silken, rare,
   Of pink or angel white
Breathe incense on the balmy air
   As dawn breaks clear and bright.

Now gem and blossom dwell together
   Where our sweet garden grows
And thrives like mountain heather —
   Our precious Margaret Rose.

Margaret A. Uhler

The Wave

What a feeling along the beach,
   the seagulls so close in reach,
As I feel the ocean hit my feet,
   and leave in one big sweep.
My feet sink deep into the sand,
   a funny feeling of no land.
It reminds me so much of life,
   between a husband and wife.
As problems begin to flow in,
   you feel, you may not win.
How fast you begin to sink,
   even faster than you can blink.
You must find your way back to shore,
   just like seagulls, you can soar.
It's found deep in the heart,
   be strong don't split apart.
There will always be a wave,
   but that helps to be brave.

Patricia Goskowski Kubus

Untitled

   The last day of the world,
The sky has not yet fallen.
The sun and moon made peace,
From a quarrel long forgotten.

   And in this time of judgement,
There are no thoughts of fear or dread.
just those of long ago memories,
And the ones that lie ahead.

   In the dusk there is no hunger,
And there is no war.
No guns, no drugs, no sickness.
No reason for alarm.

Megan Morrison

Rainbow

The clouds were dark
The wind was sharp
It was pouring hard -
I felt lonely
And the day was gloomy;
Suddenly
I saw a rainbow
It was you!
Thanks
for brightening
my dark gloomy days.

Nita Somani

Snow At Dawning

While riding in this morning
the sky was not yet light,
some snow was falling aimlessly,
it was a peaceful sight.

It gently drifted toward me
as I drove into the dawn,
it sparkled in my headlights
like a thousand jeweled morn.

I wished to stop and keep that peace
all for my self alone.
To share with none that cherished sight,
to be a shadow sown.

To just stay there and watch and wait
for the right moment so,
a peaceful moment I could make
for an unsuspecting foe.

Lois Pederson

God My God

A cold night
The snow in sight
no place to rest
I feel the fright.

Alone so far
From home tonight
I pray for a bit of bite.

A candid hand
The one who saved
My soul from hell
The dreadful place.

It's God my God
In the holy book
The bible that is
The one that I took.

Piedad A. Mendoza-Kickham

Restless

The stillness of the night,
The soundless wind,
The unrustled trees,
Amid a restless soul.

Silence, no words,
Relentless thoughts,
Colossal questions,
Washed ashore by a restless soul.

Tossing,
Turning,
Sighing,
Moaning,
Clawing,
Kicking,
Grasping,
Choking.

Sandra Torres

Swansong

The Shadows rise, the Sun hath set
   The Stars burn pale and cold
The Evening mist hangs damp and wet
   And I am growing old

Beneath the Autumn moon I spy
   The leaves of burnished gold
That mould'ring on the ground do lie
   And I am growing old

Here in the fading light I see
   Time's hoary tale unfold
For Death will soon be here for me
   And I am growing old

The Autumn Wind blows damp and wet
   And chills the fingers round my heart
I die with only one regret
   My love and I must part

I fear the Night, so cold and wet
   I fear the chill the Grave doth hold
Then hold me tight and tighter yet
   For I am growing old

M. Malefica Grendelwolf Pendragon LeFay

Grandmother

Mom, mommy, mother,
   the sweetest words we know?
So many emotions, so much wonder.
Whoever thought, such simple words,
   could mean so much?
That first time that sweet face looks
   up, and says "mama."
You realize that child is growing up,
   oh how will you let go?
Then along comes so many questions,
   so many "why's."
You look into those eyes, you realize,
   it's no longer "mama," it's "mother."
As that child grows, you wonder,
   how well have I done my job?
You'll get that answer when, with
   the tears of love in their eyes,
They let you know, no longer are
   you just "mom," now your "grandmother."

Lacreta R. Thibodeaux

A Prayer To A God

On my knees I look for strength
The things I cannot do by myself
I fall to the ground asking for help
The silent cries I make
No one is listening

I have called upon its power
To lay my soul to rest
Not to want another life
Only to want my peace
See my pain and grant my wish
And let me be with you

Spare my soul and ease my hurt
Please send me to my grave
For what I had on this earth
Has left me to myself

My time has come
To get my call
So help me higher one
I need your help to break my hold
And end my sorrowful life

Sarah Church

The Effort

Though long ago I still recall,
   The trembling and the fear;
The nights I spent in study,
   The books that I drew near.
I'd curl up in my favorite chair,
   And read 'til break of day;
My mind would swell from all the words,
   I hoped that they would stay.

Then came the dawn, my fears grew tense,
   My time was drawing near;
Perhaps I'd take just one last look,
   Too late, the time was here.
I raced across the campus green,
   I hurried to my class;
Then entered in and took my seat,
   I prayed that I might pass.

Though long ago I still recall,
   My laughter on that day;
It echoed through the empty halls,
   The sound of Saturday.

Robert F. Newton

The Coming Of The Spheres

And finally they appeared
the two glass spheres
of the mind
the quintessential counterparts
which we all have been crafting
since the beginning of time
for some they are the gatekeepers
in a gateless world
it is this great majority who refuse to
see the battery which sits
shining in the sands of ancient
cairo
and for this I am deeply sorry

I wish that it could be some
other way
but the spheres will continue
to sit on opposing sides
it is the great debate
a bloodbath on a sunny summer
Sunday afternoon.

Mike Weltz

A Timeless Passage

Motionless, you gaze on into
   the vast sea of antiquity;
Your mind set on those memories
   enveloping your mind.

Silently, your thoughts ramble
   through the passage of time,
Your eyes an open labyrinth to
   the swiftly fleeting moments.

Your eyes graze my dreams,
   seething through the visions
that I must discern and yet
   believe are a reality.

Laying my chisel to rest
   I must walk away;
Knowing that my dream has
   become a reality—

The past finally a part
   of the present.

Melissa Rowell Blackman

Untold Feelings

If only I could tell you,
The way I really feel.
How much I really love you,
And know that love is real.
To feel you hold my hand.
To know that you are their.
To make you understand.
How much I really care.
I will always love you
I know you love me too,
Just to feel you here beside me,
   And know that love
      "Is True"

Nathaniel Tex Dorsey

The World Today!

I sit in silence
The world continues to move,
While I sit there.

When I am hurting,
The world does not stop for any,
Even though the pain.

I am out of love,
For you, me, and everyone,
No more love for me.

The world is dying,
The world has no love,
Death is coming soon.

To the world comes,
Death, destruction, and hatred,
The world is dying.

Death, death, death, hatred.
Nothing else in the world,
But hatred and death.

Rebecca Liegl

The Lucky Man

She smiles
Then leans
Gives me a kiss
Peace and comfort
Floating
Her face
An unknown place
Senses all in tune
Feel the warmth
The sun has entered the room
I open my eyes
Mmm, your angelic face
Fantasies do come true
When your woman
Expresses her love for you.
My love
My life
My wife

Nicanor Amper III

This moment

It all depends
upon a spring rain
and droplets left clinging
below white birch boughs
to sparkle in the sun.

Ted McKnelly

Life Not Lethargy

If happy I truly am
then self pity need not be

If riches I have
then money I do not need

If old I become
show me how young I can be

If ever I am envious
then open my eyes

If sickness sets in
then keep the faith

If death becomes
then fate it is

Van P. Offerman

My Prayer

Drugs gave me the wings to fly,
Then, they took away my sky.
The drugs would wipe away my fears,
But in my eyes, you could see the tears.
Why did my life turn out this way?
I guess my weakness made me stray.
I pray tomorrow when I awake,
The Lord will help me beat the stakes,
To see that drugs are not way out,
And make me strong to fight the bout.
Oh, precious Lord, please hear my plea,
And make me whole again...and free!
I place my fate in your command,
I know you'll take me by the hand
And guide me to the road that's true
Please, make my gray skies all turn blue..

Ronald Keirs

If You Are Not

Dear God, if you are not
then what am I?
A mist of dust
that floats across the moon
to vanish in the glow
of dawn's first light?

A slender fragment
The idea of some strange God
who knows not love.
The yearning of a soul
without a home
if you are not.

But I have felt your touch.
I have no proof.
Still, I have walked
the path that leads to
love and joy and light,
To knowing You are,
God Is!

Laura Rowbotham

A Small Blessing

Walk to the window slowly;
Try not to disturb the light.
Stand quietly.
Look toward the feeder in the garden;
Look toward the althea and the hibiscus.
Disregard the bee and the butterfly.
Look closely.
Maybe you'll see the hummingbird.

Sarah Demetriou

Time And Place

To my beloved one in life.
There is a time and place for love.
Maybe not in the morning light.
In lazy afternoon warm ray.
Too busy for evening candle.
Too late when the night owls are out.
When the magical time is right,
It will stop all the crazy fight.
The world has only two people.
Time for us has no meaning now.
Time its self has a place for love.
Love, sweet love, has a place for us.

J. D. Shultz

Ever It Will Be (For You Sweetheart)

As you celebrate your birthday
There is no better way
Than let you know
How much I feel about you.

I love you so much
Bigger than my life
And this always will be——
As there are stars
That grace the heavens
Rivers that meet with the sea
Winds that shift the clouds
And flowers that scent the air.

I will love you
As there is life in me to live
Through the years few or many.
Sweetheart, to sum it up—-
I will love you once
And ever will it be.

Romeo A. Galinta

Grandparents

Grandparents are fun.
They help you through the day.
When you are sad, they make you glad,
in every special way.
Baking cookies, telling stories,
are only some of the things they do.
But there is only one special thing
that Grandparents do.
They just can't stop saying,
"I love you."

Kristen Romanyschyn

Good-Byes

I hate good-byes,
They make people cry,
They make some people sad,
They make others mad,
So many words to say,
"Why do they have to go away?"
Why can't they stay forever,
A good-bye is never forever,
You could send a letter,
To wish them better.
You could send them a card,
To send your regards,
You could give them a phone call,
In the spring, summer, or fall.
Just remember....
Good-byes are never forever!

Stephanie Dammen

Those Things

Sometimes you feel like
   things are not going right.
Then you sit and talk
   to a friend or stranger.
You come up with a way
   to help things out.
And you go to the problem
   and correct it.
Later those things seem
   to get better.
When things are right and
   are going so smooth, just one word
   can mess it up.
The things that are right
   and then goes wrong can crush you.
With confusion, tears, and
   anger, you are in the same place.
But with a hug or two and
   a friendly face to be there when you need it,
   you can work those things out and start
at the beginning.

Tina Marie Shults

Mama

Mama with love
This is for you
You fill me with joy
When I am blue
You're there when your needed
And there when your not...
Mother my dear
I love you allot...
Mama, mama you raised me to be
To share
To love
To give willingly...
What would I do
Without a mama so dear
You are an inspiration to me
Year after year...
Mama with love
I give this to you
Life would be meaningless
Without a mama like you...

J. Uilani Cockett

Misty Morning

  Misty morning star lite night
this little bundle of fur so right.
  With her big bright eyes she look
at you, to bring you the most delight.

  She was in my day and in my night.
She'd be the one to make all fears
right. She was seldom heard but always
came with just one word.

  She was always there when I was
alone, this little bundle of fur who
lived in my home.

  Misty morning to dark of night.
To my puppy who is gone
  In heaven you will be alright.

Mary M. Rogers

Spellbound

All my love I give you freely
This my love there's no denying
Springs from all the knowing me
All the years before the sleeping
I knew not what I had to give
Now I know and this awakening
Fills me with a wondrous joy
And my life is spilling over
Take it please and more and more
I have lost the whole beginning
And the end I cannot see
So now there's all the joyful living
And the whole is all the giving
That my love is all of me
I am the source I am the fountain
I am the love I know so well
I am the witch and you the wizard
And no one dare to break the spell

Peggy Roundhill

Delicately Tainted

Unattainable -
This thief in the night,
Who compounds your dreams
Into sick thoughts,
And captures your soul,
All the while,
Smiling at your pain
With morbid desire.
Sex is the way
That seems naturally ritualistic,
But you'll loose
As you become one with temptation.
While - its true
he'll show you the way
to a secret garden,
This treasure contains
unspeakable desire
As you patiently dig
your own grave...

Tanya Sowden

They'll Know Him Too

You've said goodbye to a brother
This was also done by mother
but if you keep him in your heart
You will never be apart
Speak not of him with sadness
but remember him with gladness
Sam would not want you to grieve
for you know he had to leave
Just keep a warm place in your heart
and when you feel torn apart
open up your heart and look inside
for there, his memory will abide
One day you will tell your children
about their uncle Sam therein
So keep his memory in mind
how he was so brave and kind
Remember all these things about him
so the memory will never go dim
When they've heard, they'll know him too
Just as you, yourself do

Mary Jasilionis

Maybe Tomorrow

Maybe tomorrow or just maybe today
This whole world will find a better way.
Maybe tomorrow the wars will all cease
And the world can know a time of peace.
Maybe there can be trust among all men
With fairness and honor and maybe then,
A home for each child, woman and man
With good clean water in every ones land.
Maybe tomorrow there will be a better way
Maybe tomorrow or just maybe today.

Maybe tomorrow there'll be joy and love,
With warm sunshine and blue skies above.
Maybe all folk will have little to say
As persons pray in a different way -
And every hungry parent and child
Will have enough food to last for awhile.
Maybe tomorrow there'll be a smile on each face
With health and jobs in each persons place.
Maybe tomorrow there will be a better way
Maybe tomorrow or just maybe today.

Nyle Kennerly D'Alesandro

Just Wanted You To Know

You'll never be alone,
Though no one may be there.
Your hopes, dreams and problems
we'll both share.
You've come so far, worked so hard
to get to where you want to be
Your tomorrows are an open window,
the whole picture yet to see.

Your will; will take you
as far as dreams can soar,
and I'll be there for you.
To share the joy,
To pick up the pieces in sorrow,
To share in what is you.

It may not be in person,
Just a voice inside your head.
But I'll be there
Because,
I love you,
And you'll never be alone.

Steven Mau

Vision

The lily is gold regality
Though white in this starlight
Centuries call at the smell of it.
In some old alchemy of time
In sense and candlelight beckon,
Exault and gather to us
In a cathedral of cool aisles.
The hot nigh shuddering dies
With a lily in a circle of light.

Margot burns a taper
And silent is her soul
From the seraphim is the gold
In her glory of nimbused hair.
From high in the windy transcript
Thin sounds of that lost world
Their variants harmony is on her
Touching what it cannot hold.

Mary Kellerman

Conscious Awareness

I center, step aside and watch.
Thoughts consume me, emotions seem real.
Anxiety threatens and fear emerges.
I struggle, then let go.
I repeat, not once, but a thousand times.

I center, step aside and watch.
Thoughts come less
Emotions like waves, fade
Anxiety less, fear faced.
I marvel, then let go.
I repeat, not once, but a thousand times.

I center, step aside and watch.
Thoughts subdued, meaningless
Emotions felt, released
Anxiety gone, fear let go.
Peace, love, joy and serenity
I repeat, not once, but a thousand times.

Conscious awareness gives birth
to a conscious Higher Self as the
soul learns to care for itself by
letting go.
Shirley M. Vernon

One Day

One day is worth a
    thousand tomorrows.
Grasp it! Hold it ever near
    Savor each and every
moment while the time is here.

Celebrate the hours with
    the ones you love with care.
Remember each and
    every minute of the time
you have to share.

Embrace the precious days
    of time as though it
were Forever.
    Because today is now
and tomorrow maybe
    never.
S. Rose Turbyfield

Omnipresence

One power flows
through countless forms.
One being stares
through countless eyes.
Through evolution
great and small,
one life flows
and never dies.
We are that One!
We are the sun.
We are the life
of everyone.
Infinite beings,
forever free.
The great I AM,
not you or me.
Michael L. Pardue

The Eagle

I close my eyes and listen
Through stillness or thrashing wind
    I hear the eagles cry

My mind travels to mountains
So brilliant and so massive
    I see the eagles form

I clear my mind completely
Make no movements and no sounds
    I feel the eagle close

Deep within my heart and soul
Now until the end of time
    The eagle never dies
Tina M. Hazel

The Beach

We rode our horses down
Through the cliffs
Cold and windy wet
We watched the sea
Rumble pebbles to the stones
And urged our horses near its mouth
Their feet stepped, faltered
At the half-moon bay
Through fog patched inlets
We found the path
Back to the coastal highway
Terri Maria Merritt

Slow Drum

The footsteps of my drum
through the slow dusk
on muffled deerskin moccasins
    come

In river mist and sleep
and far - off remembering
telling old tales

Of somewhere I left my drum
so long ago
that only along my dusty trails of dreams
    the footsteps now
    come slow

And an old tale whispers
    ... follow...
Rossmé A. Taylor

Raindrops

Sensing the thunder
touching the rain
with calloused
fingers and
soap dried hands
Cleansing the soul
with the lightning
repenting with the
dark clouds
Moving on to the
next storm
Shoshana August

Rhythm Of Life

Thump,
    Thump,
        Thump.
The pounding in my head...
    my body...
    my soul.
Driving my inner self
    outward,
        upward,
            onward
to new heights and
    destinations.
A drum to the dance as
    a heart to life.
Feeding,
    thriving
        on the beat.
The food of dance,
    the rhythm of life.
Todd Alan-Kersh

Untitled

Tho I do not seek
    thy grave
Nor listen for
    death's call
A tombstone raven
    watching upon
speaks an eerie caw
    and with the winds
so subtle
    and this moon
so fine
    a whisper of death
beneath thy breath
    brings thy heart to dine...
Scott D. Vanosdol

Time And Eternity

Time is endless.
    Time is short.
Time is measured
    By watch and clock.

Eternity is forever
    Eternity never ends.
Eternity is awesome.
    Man just can't comprehend.

In Bethlehem was born
    A little baby boy.
He was the promised Savior
    To shepherds he brought joy.

He taught us how to love.
    He died to make us free
To choose to be with God
    Through time and eternity.
Lillian R. Yundt

Pillow Talk

Hidden secrets
Vanished teardrops
Intimate snuggling nightly,
Whispering,
Ears of fluff heed
Tenderly, caressing woes
Saturated body, rescued eyes dream
Pillow talk, pillow talk
Shirley Hodges

My Blue Isle Sky

My blue isle sky don't ever go away
Time stands still I know it will

My tears won't dry
I really don't know why
Distance seems too barren and empty
I grew up in a land of plenty
I heard the sound of closing doors
As I walked softly along the wooden floor

But to wander and yearn
About what's around the turn
And listen to little sunflower
While the clock ticks up to the hour

I've wanted this world
To make it mine
The adventures of the soul
Wanting to behold

My blue isle sky
Don't ever go away
Push back the dark clouds high
And make the season in the brightest of days

Robert A. Goldstein

A Loan

Trusting eyes, trying to focus,
tiny fingers curl around mine.
A look of contentment, so innocent,
his journey just beginning.
I am the willing mentor;
I'll gladly throw balls
for little hands to catch.
Getting wet feet while his stay dry,
retrieving the boat that got away.
Bedtime stories, goodnight kisses,
watching as sleep claims him.
My body is charged with emotion,
he has so many adventures ahead.
I am selfish, I want to share them all.
But, if by chance, the time
is shorter than I'd like
I trust he'll know my sadness.

Lois Rashbrook-Carlson

The Wind

The wind is whistling o'er the trees
'Tis spreading sails on ships at seas

The wind is turning giant windmills
The wind is racing o'er the hills

It sails the cloud, it sails the bird
And still it never speaks a word

It flies the kite and breaks the string
The boys call it a naughty thing

It makes the leaves come twirling down
Into the woods and all around

It freezes the waters, it bites the nose
It comes a whistling through our clothes

The winds an awful spiteful boy
But still it fills our hearts with joy

It covers all the ground with snow
And then we all a skating go

The wind's an awful, spiteful boy
But still it fills our hearts with joy.

Wade Groce

A Happy Day

What a glorious day,
To be light hearted and gay,
Just look around you
You'll know exactly what to do.

Let yesterday go,
For you must know
Tomorrow will let you grow
The seeds you will sow.

Enjoy the vast blue sky
Then repress a sight.
Let all bad thoughts go by
Be happy before you die.

Mrs. Kermick Kilchrist

Reticence

Why are we forever trying
to be masters of our hearts,
when all we are ever vying
for is peace for all our thoughts?

Can't love be that important
in a peaceless world as this;
or, are we to act complacent
amid the changeful bliss?

It seems we all need emotion
for sanity to stay with us,
but even through all the commotion
we keep ourselves behind us!

Be aware of how you show it,
lest others come and label you.
Yet do try to reveal it,
while always being true.

You know you're real alright-
the feelings are all too strong,
But holding them so tight
won't make your lasting throne!

Russell C. Pottharst

Painted

Painted by a longing,
   to be the best of all.
Seeing myself beyond me,
   as too strong to fall.

Shadowed by my wants,
   needing to hold on.
Never letting go,
   though I am at wrong.

Masking every fault,
   begging it left alone.
Hoping they see only my guise,
   and let me act my show.

Suzanne Yoder

Hold Fast To Dreams

Hold fast to dreams
They being Divine Inspiration
It is that which spurs you on
If not for Dreams, we may not
see the end product of someone's vision.

Disregard the slowness it takes
Perseverance.
Who knows what future holds
from a Dream that has come to fruition.

Marilyn Kay Giuliani

Why Must Everything Have A Name?

Everything should have a name.
To enjoy it once and be able to recall it
in feeling, emotions and words,
It needs a name.

Search and re-search for the words.
There's sure to be one somewhere.
If not, make one up...
To revel in the sound, the euphony.
Roll the letters off your tongue.

As you listen you can hear it, see it,
Sense its closeness, all again.

Martha A. McKeon

Love Like The Wind

Your love is like the wind,
   To feel but never touch.
You came in through my open door,
   You changed my life so much.

Your a cool breeze on a summers day,
   Warm on a winter night.
Yours eyes are like shining stars,
   On a moonless night.

Your smile is like a ocean breeze,
   Coming off the sea.
I lay in my bed at night,
   Wishing we could be.

I wonder what it would be like,
   To hold you in my arms at night.
Could you help me with my insecurities?
   And make them all seem right.

Your love is like the wind,
   I wonder if you know how much.
I hope and pray each and every day,
   Just to feel your touch.

Stephen C. Brown

Love

Love is knowing when
   to hold on tight and
   when to let go;

Love is saying the right
   thing and knowing
   when the light and when
   is silence;

Love is knowing when
   to laugh and when
   to cry;

Love is knowing when
   to argue and
   when to forgive

Love is knowing when
   to talk and when
   to listen;

Love is knowing when to
   take and when to give;

Love is knowing without
   knowing how you know.

Lisa Polhkowski

A Parent's Prayer

Help me to train my children, God
To know when they are weak
So when they find themselves alone
They will turn to Thee and speak.

Help them to stand erect and proud
Unbending in defeat.
In victory, if not humble
I pray Thy will they seek.

Help me to guide them, God, I pray
Not on a road of ease,
And if life turns their walk from thee
Draw close unto them, please...Amen.

A. L. Blanton

The Party

Just stand still a minute, Life,
To let me view this day.
Let me hold it close to me
Before it slips away.

Let me grasp this moment now;
It's mem'ry clear and bright.
Let me see each part of it
Before it fades from sight.

Let me feel the joy of it
As dear friends shared with me
Loving thoughts, and reminisced
Of times that use to be.

I'll relive this day, again,
When I am feeling low.
I'll pretend I feel its warmth
And bask in afterglow.

Oh, Yes, it's been a lovely day!
Reluctantly, it ends,
But I'll recall with thankful heart
This day - with all my friends!

Marilyn K. Walker

"A Child's Love"

To have a child's love
To love someone for
What's on the inside not
  the outside.
To not to know of all
the pain today.
To enjoy life as it is.
To be protected and loved.
To have no worries or pain.
To enjoy life at the fullest.
Oh, how it would be to have
A child's heart.

Rosemarie Poteet

Deception

Loved
Until
It crashes down.

Nicole Du Frane

Societal Mood

I remember that Big Jim
Tried to ride him;
He was a mighty man,
But could not tame the stallion.
They sent a call for Curly Jack.
He too was thrown-off his back.
He was even too big a problem
To be handled by Lassoing Lem.
He was such a burden for the corale
That he shook the crew's morale.
He had become too much for the crew.
They wondered what to do.
One day when they were in a societal mood,
They decided to make him into dog food.

Terry McGregor

Perfect Said I

Perfect said I,
To me you look divine.
Perfect day for rain said I,
To me nature looks kind.
Visualize the perfect day said I,
To me you taste like wine.
Upon this even day said I,
The night is best with crime.
Does this have a rhyme said I,
Because, each word has a dime.
When I look into the night said I,
It clouds my mind with pride,
my love is here for you said I,
Because, love is rather blind.

Perfect said I,
Because life is beauty
kind.

Mitchell Hood

"Hurting"

It hurts so much to speak your name
to remember who you were.
I want you here with me now.
Is this selfish? I'm not sure.
Your memories are still so vivid
and you are so dearly missed.
It broke my heart when grandma
leaned over
and gave you your final kiss.
You left without a word
only the absence of breath.
Why didn't I say I loved you
and wish you all the best?

Nycki J. Ward

Mr. B

It's comforting
To see
His smile
That waits for me.
The little twinkle
In his eye
And just the way
He says his "Hi".
It warms me
With its tenderness
And lifts me
From this
Dull-a-ness!

Mary Harding Falk

Love's Presence

I waken in the dark of night
To see your form in dimmed light
Your gentle breathing softly sounds
My heart rejoices—leaps and bounds.

You're there, beside me
A presence treasure
Breathing softly
In sonorous measure.

Rejoice then I, that you live,
And that LOVE, to me you give
A touch a smile, a word, a kiss
Is not ecstasy made of this?

Now, when I face affairs of living
The good, the bad, the unforgiving,
I conquer all, and know no fear
Strengthened by LOVES PRESENCE near!

L. Kenneth Armstrong

Destiny

Destiny awaits her
to take her far away,
to places long forgotten
in dreams that went astray.

Her secret love embraces her,
his kisses are a blade
that cuts through to the passion
that sleeps within the maid.

A bed of roses made for her,
her virtue is the prize,
to love her to her very soul
where in the beauty lies.

E. L. Fortier

Gods' Decision

We know it's God's decision
To take us from this life
Even though the pain he'll cause
Gets deeper with the light

There's got to be a reason
He takes them all too soon
It seems as though he needs their help
To help him hang the moon

That must be why it seems so bright
On the cloudiest of days
To help us see our way back home
In the darkness and the haze

And though we know we'll miss them
We will see them again
For God has drawn our paths outright
And will help us in the end

It's true the hurt will lighten
But we will never forget
The memories and love we shared
With those whom he has picked

Mary E. Johnson

Life From Life - Mother Dear

For life, I thank you mother dear
To this soul you gave living
To this heart you gave beating
To this breath you gave breathing
For the loveliness of your soul
For the beating love of your heart
For the never-ending gift of your grace
For the loving smile upon your face
Our hearts are true, how lovely that
   they are two
God made them, one from the other
One is mine and the other is my mother's
We owe them to God — we must give them
   back someday -
   And thank Him for the loveliness
   of life.
   Leo J. Connor Jr.

Thoughts

Synchronizing one's own mind
To thoughts on high above,
Can mean the world's greatest find
Of things concerning love.

The mind, a precious thing indeed,
Worth more than finest gold.
And yet it's value will exceed
If pure thoughts it will hold.

When good or evil come to mind,
These things one can't control.
But what you choose or leave behind
Could win or lose your soul.

As wind which travels to and fro,
So do the thoughts of man.
Though wind will freely come and go,
The thoughts will guide the man.

So go the thoughts.
Thus goes the man.
   Tomas Castrejon Jr.

In Memory Of A Friend

Passing by a star so close
To touch it with my hand
Slipping through the black of space
As the hourglass filters sand

Planets are but stepping stones
To a higher destiny
To move throughout the universe
A spirit traveling free

Seeking out the sacred ground
Where righteousness awaits
And peace and love and happiness
Are all the worldly traits

Guided by a gentle hand
That moves me to my goal
I am a living spirit now
My body is my soul
   Kenneth A. Zalevsky

My Love

My love, you're all I need
to watch the flowers grow,
to see the beauty of the land
to feel the still winds blow.

Your love is all I need
to make my days seem bright,
Your tender kiss and gentle touch
make everything so right.

Your laughter fills my heart with joy
Your sadness, my eyes with tears,
and with each passing day I know
our love will last for years.

Though darkened days and sleepless
   nights
may seem to keep us apart.
These lines I write to you my love
for they're what's in my heart.

These words are just a fraction
of how it is I feel,
your forever in my heart, my love
for what I feel is truly real.
   Tammy S. Bailey

Yesterday, Today And Tomorrow

What yesterday was a potato
Today is a part of me,
And the water now one with my blood
But lately flowed free in the sea.

Though my body, the vessel of me
But yesterday came from the sod
My soul, the essence of me
Will tomorrow return to God.
   Leona E. Cranston

Displays Of Harmony

Tantalus' anguish will be over tomorrow.
Tormented by thirst and heat,
and days scaled down by centuries.

Agony and struggle for life,
violent displays of harmony.
Evidence of a new season.

Patterns of chaos,
a vehement suspicion of Order,
these are the cosmetics of cosmos.

Dreams that I cannot explain,
verbal dexterity is my weakness!
The silence of the wind is my power.
   Panos M. Pardalos

Media

When the blood flows
where's the care go?
When the innocent cry
do we even ask why?
Or are we glad it's strangers
Bad news is good news
when it ain't wearing our shoes
I win
as long as you lose.
   C. Hughes

Sounds Of The City

Buildings towering, reaching, glowering,
Traffic tearing, bearing, barreling,
Engines purring, merging, surging,
Humanity teaming, streaming, scheming,
Workmen, hustling, lusting, cussing,
Cranes lifting, machinery glistening,
School bus crawling, children brawling,
Boys bickering, girls snickering,
School kids jesting, testing, besting,
Lakefront roaring, waves soaring,
Whirling, hurling, spraying, playing,
City alive, driving, thriving.
   Marilyn Hamman

"The Search"

A lone warrior,
traveling through time.
His power affects everyone;
from beggar to King.
All bow before him.
All hope to find him,
For it is everyone's wish
to follow him.
Those not strong enough
lose sight of him.
Only the strong can be part
of his reign.
His name: Love
And he has found a home
in our hearts.
   Michael P. Harrison

Sound Of One Hand

Quarks of cosmic
   trees dendritic,
   blood flows branching
Fractal skies,
Waves of windburned
   roman riders,
   bang-engendered
Starlit birthings,
Secret-sucklings
   drinking light,
   answers found
In patterns echoed,
Curving space
   to hopes unending,
   life bestowing,
Vision sending,
Can you hear
   the hand unseen?
   Richard J. Metzner

I Have...

Body glazed
Unlike the others covered by
Sand hills and desert camels.
Mind amazed
Unlike the others drowned in
Petty squabbles and not-worth-it sorrows.
Heart beloved
Unlike the others wrapped in
Paper mache strips and hardened lips.
Soul recovered
Unlike the others lost in
Turbulent dreams and "I wondered" years.
I have...
   Alex Gonzalez Mir

Frustrating Silence

I comb the blowing
Tresses of the wind.
My hearts yearns
To sing the song
Of the traveller.

I am more than
A rustle of leaves,
The distant whistle
Of a train,
The owl's hoot.

I wish my song
To be heard
On this planet,
However,
I have yet to find
A voice of my own.

Marshall Kline

At Last

Teresa, when at first we met
True love was unknown as yet
As I began to believe
Myself I did not have to deceive.
A friend, a partner, a lover,
All things you could cover.

Deep in love and respect I fell,
By all the great feelings I could tell
A future, a hope, a dream, a life
When I finally won you as my wife.
The years, they've all been great
If on a scale one might rate,
A perfect ten? Well not quite,
To say it's been would not be right.
A seven? An eight? A nine?
Add a half to nine and be fine.

Here's to five of wedded bliss
And if you're still reading this,
To you, all the love in my heart
And may we never be apart.

Raymond DeLude

So, I Must Say I Am Blessed.....

I must say I am blessed when I can
Truly appreciate the man who I
Call "Daddy", friend and most of all
A dedicated man of God
So, I must say I am blessed.

I must say I am blessed when I have
Made my Daddy proud of me and who's
Smile I can see and feel
So, I must say I am blessed.

I must say I am blessed when I know
The strength and by the grace of God
My Daddy has kept and keeping his
Family together, despite our trials
And tribulations that we have endured
So, I must say I am blessed.

I must say I am blessed when I can
See the strength, courage, and the
Determination of the man with the
Possible mission
So, I must say I am blessed.

Kendra Carter

Lonely Tree

Come sit with me
Under our lonely tree

And wipe away my tears
Hold me like you used to
Chase away my silly fears

I cry for you - most every day
I miss you more - than words can say
These tired eyes - would like to see
For you to come - and sit with me

Once more - with you
Once more - for me
My heart and I - would love to be
Here - beneath - our lonely tree

Suzan M. Lewis-Escalona

Next To Nothin'

Cousin Candy would play for hours
Under that old oak tree
In the same old dress
And no shoes
Ashy black skin
And plaits on her head
With dirt and an old frying pan
And urine to make mud
Candy would cook her concoctions.
She was blind in one eye
From ignorant neglect
So with head to the side
And a smile on her face
She'd dig and sing
And run around that old oak tree
And make do
And be happy
With being poor and black
And next to nothin'.

Karen A. Winckler

"A Husband's Prayer"

From the moment of our very first kiss
Until I breathe the very last breath
That the Good Lord's gonna let me take
May I thank God everyday
For letting you come into my life
To spend each sunrise that you cherish
To spend each sunset that I relish
May I thank God every night
For having you beside me
To live this thing called life
With you as my friend
With you as my lover
And you as my wife
With all the warmth in my heart
Remember today
That I love you babydoll
I have, I do
And I always will
All the rest of my days

Paul Edward Dowdle III

Screams Of You

It was so long
until I stopped
feeling
your arms around me.

The scent of cologne
smothered me
for months.
It hung in the air
like your last words.

I woke at night
screaming your name,
awake until dawn
reading your poems.
The chill would warm
with ashes of words.

Heated memories
melted into icy thoughts.
I began to miss you
more than I had ever
loved you.

Tedi Toca

No One

No one cares when the heart is content
Until sadness overcomes.
No one cares when they're feeling good
Until sickness strikes.

No one sees the smile of a child
Before the crying eyes.
No one sees the beauty of a tree
Before the leaves fall.

No one hears the insult of a crude
Unless its to them.
No one hears the plea of a child
Unless its their own.

No one appreciates the love of a friend
When they forget its there.
No one appreciates the best of life
When they have it.

No one knows where the path will lead
If they don't follow it.
No one knows whether the candy is sweet
If they don't try it.

Susan L. Randall

The Battle Within

(A Tribute To The Chechnyan War)

Ever-more we fight far on,
Until the dawning of the day.
Ever-more our days are gone,
As we fight for a meager pay.

Our country is damp beneath our feet,
As one more heart fails to beat.
Our land is drenched with blood of old,
Killing our neighbor in search of gold.

I feel my foe coming around the bend,
And I kill the face of my long old friend.
I feel I have committed a most dire sin,
By killing my friend - "the enemy within."

I wish for this day to end too soon,
So I may forget what we have begun.
I wish for the ring of a peaceful tune,
Saying this war will forever be done.

Michael Rhodin

The Sea

Speak to me, oh great sea of intrigue;
Vowels that touch the inner ear.
Rough notes of mystery you bring;
A sense of uncertainty and despair.

A light shines upon your line-
Parallel with the shore.
An adventurer has heard your song;
And never is seen a'more.

Speak to me, oh sea renowned,
Of those passengers that you sought.
Minds distorted of things you said-
Truth was silence that you brought.

Beauty that your voice brings
To those who know your sounds;
But loneliness and fear inside
To those who pass your bounds.

The vastness of space you bear,
As stars above the sand,
A goal to those who tread your line -
Never controlled by man.

Roderick L. Wise

Just A Vision To Beheld

Just as I see you
wake my strong desire,
extreme in deep affection
while bathing in your smile.
A warm inner glow
comes all over me
soft and touching caresses
farther than my reach,
grasping my attention
as it longs for your embrace,
a wonder for your lips may hold
me captive in your face.
Entrancing as it seems
adoring from a distance
endearing eyes are seen
as miracles persistent
cling in memories to please me
with dreams of loveliness,
just hope lies beyond this feeling
to reach beneath your dress.

Will Cline

Underneath The Apple Tree

Roses in the sky,
Walking across my eyes
Images of the clouds I see
As I lay beneath my apple tree.

As the sun begins to set
I'm reminded of more yet,
the colors of red and gold remind me
Of the apples ripening on the tree.

I've been day dreaming as you know
Summer's past, fall will go.
In two months there will be snow,
At this time the North Winds blow.

It's now real dark beneath the tree
The stars are calling at me.
It's time to go to sleep and dream
Of all the pleasant things I've seen.

Kara Horner

Crow In The Snow

Crow in the snow
walking, scratching,
in close, at risk, wary.
We see each other,
neither moves;
man frozen in crow's eye,
crow frozen in man's eye.
We thaw.
Crow in the snow,
walking, scratching.
Man at the window,
each desperate for spring.

J. Holmes

Want To Kiss On Your Forehead

Want to kiss on your forehead
Want to kiss on your cheek
Want to kiss on your lips
Want to kiss on your breast
    Could you let me do so?

Want to look in your eyes
Want to hear your voice
Want to hold you tight
Want to share a night
    Could you let me do so?

Want to comb your hair
Want to see you bare
Want to be you dare
Want to handle with care
    Could you let me do so?

Want to love me
Want not leave me
Want to marry me
Want not sorry me
    Could you let me do so?

Naeem Sharieff

Effleurage

Waves rolling up my legs:
warm hands. No,
it is warm water,
luminous heat,
the sun made fluid.
A molecular deception —
not light swirling
liquidly through my body?
not the paradise surf,
a champagne foaming
on my skin?
not heavy golden water?

I am rocking rocking
rocking in the wake of
the universe...

Trudy Pranulis

Victims Of Floods

Thousands of people stand helplessly by,
Water falls from the sky

Rivers over run their banks
Houses get flooded and devastate lives

Is it the end? Do they say goodbye
to the dreams that get flooded
from the sky, and the rivers that run high

The victims stand by, and cry
How will they get by?

Terry Eenhuis

Silent Prayer

Eva, the student Hungarian
Was invited for dinner by Marian
Whose Mennonite family she fondly greeted
They said: Pleased to meet you and
Won't you be seated?
'I'm hungry! I'm starving and
Could eat a horse'
(She only thought, this,
Not said it, of course).

The food's on the table
In prettiest dishes
No one started eating, though,
She got suspicious
And sat there and waited,
The chicken got colder -
'I'm fainting with hunger
And am getting older',
She thought; unaware of the Mennonite way:
Before each meal they silently pray!

E. Karstens-Cox

God's Perfect Gift

A warm fragrant bundle
Was sent from above
To teach me of patience
And all about love

Curling mini-fingers
Fastened to my heart
Downy-soft curls crowned
A small work-of-art

A sweet precious essence
Gave soft little mews
A tiny rosie mouth
Blew soft breathy coos

Kissed by many Angels
The cuddly small gift
Touched my soul forever
God's most perfect gift
My baby

Marjory Nierman

Creation

The creation of today
Was started tomorrow

Thinking of yesterday
Drowning in sorrow

That's why we all must stay
With minds so narrow

That it keeps us in a world of decay
And like a rabbit we burrow

Trying and trying to get away
So here we are in yesterdays tomorrow

While the Gods do play
As we sit in pity and sorrow

So listen to what I say
Get up and start tomorrow

To change yesterday
Say goodbye to your sorrow

And then you can begin today
Both yesterday and tomorrow

To be with the Gods as they play
Never more to see sorrow

Steve Dean Sandusky

Reverse Roles

Alcohol it seems
was the God of your choice.
The victims of disease,
were your children and your wife.
Denial of the problem
brought about your demise,
divorce it seems was the only choice.
We spoke, we pleaded,
we tried to make you understand
the problem you faced
was not out of hand.
We're no longer your victims,
as if you had planned
to push us aside
with your evil hand.
The alcohol retains its evil hold,
making you the victim,
of the pain
we were forced
to enfold.
Richard Swiontek

A Barren Time

Innocence marred do
waters poisoned
ozone seeping
forests burning
Man is sleeping.
children playing
addicts shooting
guns firing
The world is dying.
polluted air
acid rain
people dying
is there blame?
Man is weeping
Man is sleeping
Luann Thierer

The Puzzle

Life is a puzzle
we attempt to solve.
The center, our spirit
around which we revolve.

Born into a world
we know nothing about.
Encumbered by fear,
uncertainty and doubt.

Misguided adults
beget misguided youth.
The chain lies unbroken
with little to soothe.

Around and around
the riddles do run.
While, from the threads of time
our stories are spun.

Like the change of the seasons
we grow and we die.
A circle without reason.
We can only wonder why.
Matthew W. Roback

Dad

As each day passes
We continue to ask God why
He would call you to Him
Leaving your children behind.

Knowing you're in a better place
Helps take away some of the pain
But as new things happen in our lives
We wish you were here again.

To share our joys and our sorrows
To laugh and to cry
Wishing we could reach out
To hug you just one more time.

Dad, one day we'll see you again
It could be tomorrow or next year
It feels like forever to us
Until we'll again be near.

Memories and pictures we'll cherish
Forever in our hearts
Until the day comes
When we're no longer apart.
Leann DeBord

Unabridged Destiny

In the age of our birth,
We could have been the same.
Destined to be different,
we forgot from where we came.
Through the course of the years,
apart we have grown.
Separate roads travelled,
many roads known.
Several years in the distant,
converge we may try.
But our instincts overcome us,
our spirit begs to fly.
It's so hard to live with frustration,
our passions a raging fire.
Melting away our reason,
we're living in an endless mire.
So when you're travelling down life's
sullen road,
keep your spirits high.
Be conscious of all your surroundings,
and watch for me in the sky.
Ted Michael Smith

You Love Me

Just like two red roses blooming,
we met.

Although the weeds may grow high
our fragrance will live on.

For I see sunshine above us
The rains that fall are kind
We will grow strong together
Although some day we may wilt
and die,

I worry little about that now.
For I am enjoying your company
And counting your petals
You love me, you love me not,
Taking thorns away one by one
So that we may entangle without pain
Counting our petals once again
Ending with "You love me."
Rebecca J. Meyer

October's Weather

Be it in forest or heather
We must love October's weather.
It brings a gift of bright blue skies,
Enhanced color, before our eyes,
With bright hues of red, green and gold,
Like spectrum beauty to behold.

Our creator made every bough,
Colored them, but we don't know how.
We enjoy this gift of beauty.
It instills a sense of duty.
Let us think on our maker's love.
Beauty like this is from above.

If we, within our maker's sheath
Could make just one beautiful leaf,
Would he ask this be left to him
And we with love filled to the brim
With steadfastness none could sever
Thank Him for October's weather?
Pauline M. Coppage

Sisters

My sister Kimberly and me,
We play all day in the big Oak tree.

We run and skip and jump and laugh,
And pretty soon we'll see a calf.

My sister Kimberly and me,
We love each other, can't you see!

My sister Christina and I,
Will some day make a Apple Pie.

My sister Christina and I,
We will love each other till we die.
Leona Lucariello

Freddie

I know an old woman named Freddie
Who calls her husband daddy
Some may think of her as poor
Of this I'm not so sure

For she has a heart of solid gold
That never knew how to be cold
Hate: She has not any
And she is loved by many

This is not a story to be sold
I just want it to be told
That I love this woman; Freddie
And her husband; my daddy.
Loretta Harris

Untitled

For now he is high above the moon,
We wonder why he left so soon.
Something's in life we may not know,
For the time has come he had to go.
You may mourn, today and tomorrow,
With your hearts full of sorrow.
There come's a time we must move on,
Even though we know he's gone.
For God has come and took him home,
In our thoughts he'll always roam.
Randy A. Roe

As Time Passes

As time passes,
we reflect,
Of all the things
we regret.
Our ups and downs
we except.
Of wrong doings
we correct.
The giving and forgiving
we neglect.
Our stories and memories
we collect.
And new challenges
we expect.
But As Time Passes
we shan't forget,
The gift of life
we must respect!

Linda G. Carpenter

"At Love's End"

The end is near
We see it through a tear
We wish it not be ours
For we will grieve for hours

All we see is truly free
But love we cannot see
For it is caged
For this reason we are engaged

We see with our eyes
What we see is a surprise
That love can help us all
We must just answer it's call

We feel with our heart and soul
Yet sometimes we play the fool
Not long enough to be blinded
So our spirit can be reminded

We need closure in our lives
Wishing the other survives
Saying goodbye is clouded by sorrow
Let's try to find a new love...tomorrow

Tim DiVito

Oklahoma

Oklahoma,
What a wonderful place.
America's Heartland -
Cities and farms.
Forest and plains.

Oklahoma,
What a wonderful place.
Cool, wet summers,
Seas of golden grain,
Oceans of sown corn.

Oklahoma,
What a wonderful place.
Food for the nation,
Lakes for vacation.
Hills that roll,
And bins of coal.

It was good for farming,
Until the bombing.
The Midwest was, and will
Be again, a wonderful place.

Rhett Dougherty

Today

This day of days began at dawn,
    What can I do or say
To make a difference in this world
    And help someone today.

Today I can help someone in need,
    Someone in deep despair
And with kind words and helping hands
    Let them know I care.

Of offer shelter to some lonely soul,
    Ease one tortured mind
And maybe in this troubled world
    A precious gem I'll find.

I'll forget ill-will and prejudice
    I may feel for another,
Regardless of his race or creed
    Because he is my brother.

Tomorrow is uncertain
    And yesterday is gone.
I only have one day to act;
    That day began this dawn.

Lloyd W. Smith

The Colors Of Life

If we could paint the shades of life
    What colors would we choose?
'Twould be a mighty searching task
    Since life has many hues.
Red might be for love of life,
    For friends and families dear.
Orange would stand for brighter days
    Yellow for doubt and fear.
Green shows new beginnings
    New hope that springtime brings.
Blue for our souls and the peace of God,
    The joy of living things.
Dark indigo for times of grief
    Of gloom and dark despair
But violet shows a comforting light,
    Understanding and care.
Each phase of life will circle back
    So learn to grown and gain.
And no matter what the future holds
    Remember, rainbows follow rain.

Virginia Wray Floyd

Oh Do I Love Her

Oh do I love her
    What does she mean to me
    I'd lay the ground she walks on
    I'd kiss the feet she walks with
Oh do I love her so
    I thank thee every night.
    For the day we were united.
    To be together forever
Oh do I love her so much
    She looks back on the days
    That we shared together as one
    As long as we could
Oh do I love her so much to die for her

Scott Meyer

Yet I Still Have

What else can I do
What more can I say
I like living my life
However I _____ choose to do so

Father and son can't get along
Makes no sense to me
as the day grows long

I say father unto me
what is, what could be that is so wrong
can you tell me
give me the answer
tell us we can

Love is Everlasting

Michael C. Lewis

Untitled

Once I loved thee
    when first we two met.
And you loved me
    and may love me yet.

But the world intrudes,
    things beyond control
press soft interludes
    which join soul to soul.

Now haste and hurry
    rush a tender kiss,
While waste and worry
    wash away our bliss.

Flames flicker lower
    Questions come and go.
Is it all over?
    Can our passion grow?

And yes my fairest
    my hearts still as true.
And yes my dearest,
    forever - I love you.

Michael Mizerny

Grandma's Attic

Every sunday afternoon,
When grandma's having tea,
I go into the attic,
To see what there is to see.
I see the big old mirror,
Bought in 1923,
And the box of pictures,
From when my father was 3,
A music box in the corner,
Brought across the ocean blue,
And it hasn't worked since 1902,
Then when I am done.
I look out the window at the sun,
It is sinking through the trees,
And I know it's time to leave,
Grandma should be done with tea,
And I wouldn't want her to see me.

Miranda Rashell Christy

"Life's Not Worth Living"

My life's not worth living,
when I can't hold the one I love;
I know I'll be happier,
in the heavens up above.

I can't go on with my life,
when it's not worth anything;
I just wish that I could leave,
and go where angels sing.

I'm just sick of living,
through all of this pain;
am I misunderstood,
or just going insane?

Why does my life
have to be this way,
I just can't live like this;
can't take another day.

Nobody understands
what I'm going through,
my life is meaningless,
as long as it's without you.

Tony Bates

Then And Now

I lived in a world of fear
When I met you,

I live in a world
of fear now,

But the things I fear
now are different,
from the things
I feared then

But as long as
you're with me.....

I can face the
fear.

Mary J. Little

Once In A While

Once in a while...
When my environment is blue,
My gray skies are clear
With one thought of you.

Once in a while...
About you I think,
With a focus so great
I don't pause to blink.

Once in a while...
I have memories of you,
Of our wild thoughts
And our silly days too.

Once in a while...
When I haven't a choice,
My mood always changes
With the kindness of your voice.

Thinking of you...
...makes me smile,
And I realize...I think of you more...
...than just once in a while.

Wilson L. Williamson

Butterflies

Butterflies fly so high with the wind.
When they used to wiggle and bend.
They look so innocent when they fly
When I watch them I just sit and sigh.

They are so graceful when they land,
Even when they seem to flutter in the sand.
I love to watch the butterfly fly,
Even though it's high in the sky.

Butterflies, they will never ever end
In this wonderful, beautiful land.
Where things seem to bend and stretch,
Even when we sit by the fire and sketch.

When night falls they find a tree,
A flower, or a bush to stay the night.
And when they finally settle down,
They soon are safe and tight,
And can have a very peaceful night.

Laura Wells

Lessons From Life

The things you learn
when we grow old.

Are lessons from life
as it unfolds.

Treasure the crossing
of each stranger you meet.

From them knowledge of wisdom
your soul did seek.

Time is wasted on hearts
you can not touch.

Honor the ones
that deserve so much.

See Gods beauty in gifts
we can not possess.

Structure your life
with happiness.

Susan Koppert

Remember Georgia?

Do you remember the times
when we'd pack a lunch
and head toward them hills?
It was usually 'round springtime
when Georgia blossoms.
You were still my boy back then:
a youngin', running free.
Do you remember skipping
through the cotton fields,
and disappearing into the forest?
We'd hide behind the pine trees
and scare each other.
You'd look for night crawlers,
and I'd be singing a song.
Our worries were so innocent and simple:
like frettin' over which steam to play in,
which tree to pick berries from,
or which one would carry lunch.
Do you remember,
Georgia?

Tanya Toter

In My Arms

I could feel your body quiver
When you were in my arms
You made me feel so proud of you
When I stole all your charms

I wish that I could be there
And catch that smile of yours
I'd take you in my arms again
Then we'll sail across the shores

I would hold you in my arms
And I'd never let you go
I'd tell you how much I love you
Then tell everyone I know

I feel your love around me
And I think of you each day
I can feel your body next to me
As I go along my way

One day I'll be back to hold you
Hold your body next to mine
And driving along the highways
You're always on my mind

Ruth Shelton

Discipline

She's only nine, I remind myself
whenever riled to reprimand
  my image in her,
the one that resents scoldings
I oft deserved, received,
whose fuel reserved this moment.

Her hands are small, but crafty,
like her mind. In time
I'll teach her patient thoughts;
In time I'll show her other books
to battle disconcerted looks
and patience spurned.

In time, I think she'll learn,
hopefully in time.

Steve Trent

Confusion

Walkin'...
Where am I going?
So much has happened.
When will it end?
Who knows if there's hope.

Looking around...
People all over; the rich, the poor.
Are they equal?
Nobody knows who's better.
Too much value on everything.

What about life.. enough problems.
All built up, time bomb, ticking away.
When will it explode?
Only time will tell.

Is there a solution?
Run away... may help, can't keep it up.
Face life... liquor, drugs.
Pass time, only postponing reality.
Life is funny.

Maybe...someday we can all laugh.

Matt Blacker

Our Mind?

Love and hatred.
Where are they?
In our mind.

Happiness and sadness.
Where are they?
In our mind.

Heaven and hell.
Where are they?
In our mind.

Our mind has everything
We want — love, happiness, and heaven.

How can we feel all these?
When we empty our mind.

Ok-Gyung Kim

Lost Souls

I wonder.
    Where do the souls of lost spirits go?
A calamity,
    wouldn't you say?
A mind,
    Is only one part of life.
The soul,
    makes the rest.
Look beyond mortality.
    The vulnerability is exposed.

One more time.

What happens to a lost soul?
Is peace ever achieved,
    or does it float in the breeze?

I guess I won't know
    until my soul,
    searches.

William H. Bickford Jr

I've Discovered A Place

I've discovered a place
where flowers grow,
but no one is allergic to the pollen.

I've discovered a place
where everyone knows your name,
but no one knows any cut-downs.

I've discovered a place
where there are kids,
but no one has any guns.

I've discovered a place
where there's always a rainbow,
but never any rain.

I can't visit this place physically,
only mentally:
but I would like to
if you come with me.

Because,
I've discovered a place
where everyone smiles,
but no one cries.

Kristin Brown

The Butterfly Song

Butterfly Butterfly
    Where have you dreamed?
I've dreamed all around the world
    and have seen all the scenes to see!
Butterfly Butterfly
    You are so beautiful - Like Water!
    powerful, yet serene.
Butterfly Butterfly
    will you, with your flutter;
    overpower me?

W.W. McCorkle Jr.

My Secret Place

I have a secret place
Where I hide things warm and dear,
A spot where I feel safe;
No bad things enter here.

What I keep is guarded,
Feelings that come and go,
Emotions I won't tell anyone,
Private thoughts no one will know.

My secret place is dear to me,
A curtain no one dare part.
If they did I'd surely die,
For my secret place is my heart.

Tamara L. Harris

Lost Being

Inside my quiet, solemn world,
Where no one sees inside;
There lies a being yet unfurled,
Full of passion, warmth and pride.

I am a very different one,
Or so I have been told;
Yet underneath the gruff outside,
There lies a heart of gold.

There are the times when I'm alone,
And desperate is my name;
To find someone to love, for me,
So our hearts can beat the same.

A person who's warm, a person who cares,
A person who speaks from the heart;
That person's you, your soul you bare,
I can never see us apart.

So come inside my solemn world,
And see the real me inside;
Come see the being become unfurled,
Experience the passion, warmth and pride.

Regina Lloyd

"Down Side"

In the darkest moments
When loneliness is your friend

Thoughts are suicidal
The beginning is the end

The need for reinforcement
in the shadow you must wait

Tomorrow becomes tomorrow
a life consuming trait

Losing all the battles
Cheating counts as fair

Is this life worth living
In sadness and despair

John Paul Wilson

What Kind Of World

What kind of world we live in
where striving to reach the top
is the only way.

The ones that are stepped on
don't matter.
No one cares.

Still a few seem to come along
coming only to help others up.
This is all that's left for them to do.

They no longer need to reach the top
for in their hearts
they already have.

These are the people
that deserve to be at the top
for they have done the real work.

Great friends they make
a caring person
that just might help you up along the way.

Tammy Herbert

After Driving All Night

My mind is awake in a dream world.

My mind's awake in a dream world-
Where you can fly inside with me,
And dream to see what we can be:

A butterfly or a bumble bee,
A mustard seed or a redwood tree,
A helping hand or a boogie man,

A copper mine or a garden plot,
A habitat or a parking lot,
A haven where ev'ryone stays free.

Awake and see how we can be
A catalyst to help friends free
The time and effort it must take

To make a dream reality -
Where every life is cherished
As a most sacred part of "We".

My minds awake in a dream world.
My dream's awake in a real world,
And your dream is awake in me-

A haven where ev'ryone dreams free.

M. L. Farahay

Eight Hours

Sleep, Sleep
Whirling, falling,
spinning into the
unknown mysterious
deep.

Dream, Dream
A potpourri of
images and patterns
kaleidoscoping along
a misty stream.

Awake, Awake
from thy world of
mythical charm
there it goes
that doggone alarm!

Mary Albertson

Untitled

Honesty is lost behind clouds of deceit
while the sun eclipses the moon
stealing the light but combining
the energy
Only the moments of absolute
exhaustion provide peace for the
frenzied notions of morality
and concern.
There is no question that the
camouflaged do gooders permeate
the land, the air the sea.
Perhaps no creatures escapes
the falsities of true honesty
and righteousness.
The heart fire sheds light
on the souls that put forth
no effort yet causes doubt
in the minds of the earnest.
Pursue love's genuine peace.
   Liz Shimkus

White

What is white
White is the snow on a
   winter day.
White is the horses that
   eats the hay.
It is the mouse that crawls
   on the floor.
White is a far away
   grocery store.
   What is white,
White is the dove who
   flies on a roof.
I've seen white before
   I even have proof
White is the cat that
   eats the mouse.
And sleeps on the furniture
   that sits in the house.
White is the flowers
   that grow on the lawn
White is the paper
   I write poems on
   Tracie Hughes

A Window Of Armstrong-Browning Library

The red of a thousand roses, crushed
Into an unaccustomed plane
Lets fall its song.
The blue of a thousand voices shrieks
To the mute air.
White is the piercing bird song
That seizes and will not let go.
Pale as November wind a grey light falls
Through molten veins of a slender hand.
   Anabel Reeser

Let Freedom Ring

To free a nation and not its people,
is like having a church without a steeple.
The structure just isn't the same and
people will find it hard to call it by name.
The desire for the right to be, is like life
to the living and there is no blame.
Give us the chance to live and be proud,
instead of feeling ashamed.
   Carlos Rose

Nwyvre

Flames dance the old dance
inside the druidic circle
a force within a force
the living dragon
inside a ring of stone
its fiery breath reflects in your eyes
or is it the soul of you looking out
I have known that soul before
when the dragon was not so contained
when its wing beat could quicken
the hearts of women and men
as its shadow crossed their path
my own heart takes flight in your presence
as if you were the magnificent creature
returned to destroy the last remaining
memory of your terrible beauty
I would lay down my sword and welcome
the sweetness of consumption
as the white hot light
becomes my only existence
   Deborah J. Pattison

Consumer

Loss of money stretched out beyond checks
into a clover like shape that has Irish written all over it
a warm glow that shines filtered through my fingers
the hand shrivels into a cocoon that will yield no fresh butterfly
or hungry moth
just something that dissipates until it is a visual after image
like the red shapes that float
over recently closed eyes in the dark
or like the nightmarish image
of a funeral body cloaked in ceremony and abandon
that is tied to family emotions like a square knot
taut yet easily disentangled
and transformed back into a shapeless string
or teeth that retain memories of fractured imagery
male pride, female industry, streamlined corporate America
items lined into categories
symmetrically placed so as to artificially increase its value
individually torn from the gestalt and altered into mundane function
by the person who imagines and analyzes simultaneously
   Douglas J. Smith

Night Play

In dreams I rode my steed of white
Into the blackness of the night
Capturing sun and moonbeams far
Showering sparks from every star
I twirled on Saturn's circling rings
Jumped on the moon and made it swing
Played with my friends of the Zodiac
Then placed the dippers back to back
I lassoed the North star, pulled it near
I molded the moon into a fattened sphere
Constellations laughed at my mischievous fun
When I took the bow and arrows from Orion
Then aiming at a cloud of white
I shot an arrow through the night
It bounced along the Milky Way
Then turned the night into next day
I aimed again at clouds of white
Then turned the day back into night
I giggled and mounted my steed and then
Rode back into my dreams of night again
   Judith Schwartz Howard

"Nostalgia"

Linda loves old lace, handmade, long ago.
Irish linen cloths, embroidered, quiet and slow,
By girls in gentler times, when hope chest treasures grew
Then tissue paper wrapped, and kept, until the day
  That Mr. Right appeared.

Linda loves, petit point, still redolent,
Of sundays, spent in sunday parlors.
Antimacassars, elegantly placed,
Dainty napkins, lace edged, laid on,
Flowered china plates, in readiness,
  For sunday parlor teas.

Linda longs, for the time, when
  Time, moved slowly.

Amy Taylor

Vanity Of Death

A lonely old man with a smile on his face,
is going to go to a different place.

Though the heart is like a lump in my chest,
I know the old man must have his rest.

All his life the fellow did roam;
Never to love, and never a home.

All his life was one big hurt,
cheapened by hate - darkened by dirt.

But is that not a tear in his eye?
Am I wrong to say he's going to cry?

With a final struggle the old eyes met mine;
Is my love the only this poor soul will find?

Was it in vain that his face spelled death -
as the lonely old man took his last breath.

Cheryl Magathan

Dreams

Fields of dreams
Is it a vision of hope or a world of confusion
Dreams O' dreams
Give me a vision of hope
Help me understand this maze of confusion
Is it just a never ending maze of fading vision
Or just a blurred vision of hope which will never be real
Dreams O' dreams
Show me visions of hope
Visions that this world has a hope in the future

Connie Brooks

This Person

This person I fell in love with about a year ago
is still in my heart trust me I know

Together we've been through thick and through thin
But it's all because of the things we did

I love this person with my whole heart
But it seems like everyday we've got to make a new start

I never want to lose this person
because he means too much to me
I just hope that is the one thing he will always see

I never want him to give up on me because he means so much
And if I ever lose him I'll also lose that special touch

That special touch is love the one thing that I need
And if he ever takes that touch away I know my heart will bleed!

Jessica Novak

Empty Heart

  The day you never call,
is the day I shall fall.
  I forgot all hope;
our love was broke.
  My heart of tears, my blood
and fears. Never seeing us together through future years.
  The hatred in yell.
I'll forever burn in hell.
  Visions in my head,
are of my false fell.
  Less to the world, but more to thee
Every single thing was taken from me.
  Including you, my love, so true.
I hate myself, but I'll forever love you.
  Don't worry about me dying.
About suicide. I'm too much of a coward to take that ride.
  You can't kill someone
who has already died.
  I'll live each day with an empty inside.

Janelle Arnold

A Mother's Love

To My Mother - Marion M. Williams

There is nothing as unfailing as a mother's love; unless it
  is the love of her daughter.

They are always, always there for each other; doing for each
  other what they ought to.

When a child is born, a mother plainly decrees she will
  guard her with her life.

When the child grows up, she's there for her mom through
  all her trials and strife.

Together, they're there for each other with a love that
  surpasses all understanding.

They always consider the other one first, with a dedication
  that is truly outstanding.

So strong a bond, 'cause it comes directly from God,
  Our Father in heaven, above.

Yes, unless it is the love of her daughter,
  nothing compares to a mother's love.

Barbara Williams

You, You You

Could there be another you; could any one take your place.
Is there another perfect smile to make and feel such sole rejoice
Would I be thrilled and raptured while I listen to another voice.
Is there another loving hand which I could hold from noon till night,
And could there be a love as grand as ours, real, so right.
Can there be other lips that I may kiss, thrill me like yours do.
Can there be other perfectly beautiful nights with anybody else.
There's just one answer I can give.
Will be the same the long years through,
No matter how long I might live, there will always be you.
Never another.

Gertrude P. Zalar

Close To You

A simple form of me to you,
  is when all of my feelings start to come true.
My feelings are not a bullet, but a turtle running a race.
  Never losing sight of where its going or never its pace.
The rapid pumping of blood to my heart starts to flow
  Alerts me to your presence when you start to come close.
My palms get sweaty; my temperature starts to rise,
  When I get so close that I can see deep into your eyes.
That first touch of your arms around my waist
  makes me see bright stars all out in space.
I will hold you close and very tight to my chest,
  then I will look at your lips and wonder what is next.
I don't want to move to fast because I am a turtle running a race.
  Then I will pull, you closer so we are face to face
At last the gentle touch of your lips next to mine,
  brings out all the feelings I have left inside.
I now have set out what I have started to do
  When we depart all I am going to think is how I want to be close to you.

   Derrick Ervin

Untitled

  Love is a friendship that has caught fire
    it appears as quiet understanding
    trust, sharing and forgiving.
Love remains loyal through good and bad,
  it settles for less than perfection
  and makes allowances for human weakness.
Love feels content with the present
  it hopes for the future
  it doesn't brood over the past.
Love includes the day in, day out chronicle
  of irritations, problems and compromises,
  the small disappointments, big victories
  and common goals.
If you have love in your life
  it can make up for a great many things you lack
If you don't have it
  no matter what else you have
  it never feels enough.

   Caron Farnham

Rage

It's an all consuming rage.
It burns more brightly than the sun.
And it hurts more than the fires of hell.
I want to hurt you like you hurt me.
I want to scream, I want to throw things,
I want to make you feel the way I do.
I want you to understand that I am sick.
I want you to stop being so self-centered.
I want you give a damn about me, I want the impossible.
I want to cause you the kind of hurt you've caused me.
But nothing can make the pain I've received.
The will to defy you is so great I could scream.
I want to cause pain, I want to cause agony.
In this very moment I feel an urge to kill.
Kill or be killed, the law of the jungle.
For some reason it seems to apply here also.
I'm snapping, loosing my grip on reality, loosing my grip on sanity.
I'm festering, a deep, agonizing wound inside me is growing,
Larger and larger and larger.
And soon it will consume my soul.

   Anna Oltmanns

What Is Love?

  It can make you Good.
It can make you bad.
It can make you laugh.
It can make you sad.
It can brighten your days
Torment your nites.
Make your wonder if anything will turn out right.
It can tear families apart.
When all it would take is love from the heart.
We sit, we ponder, yesterday shadows.
When thoughts of tomorrow, is all that should matter.

  Tomorrow promises, tomorrow dreams.
They are out there, no matter what life seems.
So if you have love, hold on tight.
For it can slip away, like a thief in the night.

   Ethel Wynn

Short Memory

I have such a short memory when
it comes to my past,
Childhood and adolescence have sped by so fast.

Spiritually I've neglected to
remember many things,
Like how Jesus saved me or the joy He brings.

Why can't I remember to thank
The Lord above,
For His tender mercies and
unfailing love?

I know He's hurt when I don't watch and pray,
I'm invited to His house, why won't I stay?

Remind me, Lord, of your mighty hand,
Hide me in your shadow and strengthen
me to stand.

Lord forgive my short memory
Lets make a new start,
I'm bowing before you with a
contrite heart.

   Jennifer Pereira

"No Love Was Meant To Be"

Their are some things, that are not meant to be
It could happen to you, as it has to me

I once was young, and I had dreams
I always wanted it to happen to me
Just to feel his love, when he looked at me
But that just was-not meant to be
I was only living a dreamers dream

So now as the years have passed me by;
I no longer sit and cry, to feel your love
Or see it in your eyes
NOW I KNOW THAT LOVE HAS JUST PASSED ME BY

   Belinda Armstrong

Betrayal By A Brother

Death is brother of hatred and cousin of life,
It has destroyed my family and cursed my wife,
The hate for my family has come from the past,
With open arms we welcome him and trust is fast.
In the middle of the night he takes his chance,
He takes my sister on a forced romance.
It has been a year and I begin to grow old,
A heart once filled with love has now turned cold.

   Christopher Quiles

"His Great Cause"

The sky is beautiful, with its radiant glow.
It covers the heavens wherever you go.
Birds fly by with their flowing wings.
Also show they are beautiful things.
Then they fly down to the trees,
And nestle amongst the leaves,
Which fall to earth and cover the ground,
To show that God's beauty is all around.

The babbling brook, the rushing falls,
All show that God had a great cause.
He put them on earth to let all know,
That within these things, his love he'd show.

So when you walk upon God's soil,
Remember how he has toiled.
To give to us, these amazing and beautiful sights.
So let's all join together and praise him tonight.
David C. Ware

Old Clothes

Your love is like old clothes
it doesn't fit me anymore

It's too tight
I can't breath

It's out of style, out of shape, out of touch
and WAY out of line

It hangs in my closet
a vampire bat
SCREECHING!!!
behind the closed door
in the corner, in the dark

IT'S HAUNTING

Should I throw it in the garbage?
Give it to a needy organization?
Store it in the attic?

I think I'll just wear no clothes
till I find new clothes
to replace the old clothes!
Judi Kerwin

The Power Of Prayer

A prayerful life is a precious gift to treasure,
It gives hope for tomorrow, sweet peace beyond measure:
'Tis the source of conversing with our blessed savior,
The guidance we must have to remain in his favor.

Prayer opens the door for grace, faith and love,
Repentance, salvation and a vision of things above,
It will shut out all despair, doubt or fear
Giving the blessed assurance, Christ's coming is near.

So build up your faith by praying every day,
Wait and listen to what Jesus has to say:
Then season your prayer with a little more fasting,
You'll conquer your foes and gain life everlasting.
Alice Ragland

Untitled

Love is a secret preserved in your memory
It never means anything till you tell someone else
A secret, a promise, a bond between lovers
A promise held captive until it is broken
Love that is broken is slashed between hearts
Hearts that will not mend unless love returns secret
Christine Aro

Time On Their Hands

My wrist watch is a strict boss.
It has a firm grip.
Not a minute is lost.
Not a second is skipped.
Hands advance at a steady pace.
No turning back, a relentless race.
Watches, I thought, have no choice,
until distraught, I heard a voice.
"We're the new breed - the technical elite.
Humans can't compete. We've learned to speak.
On the job night and day, no stop no pay.
Workers resent being treated that way."
"You mustn't talk like this.
You're only a watch that I wear on my wrist."
"But I'm your boss. I've got you in my grip.
When you look to see where my hands are,
You know I always have the answer."
Geneveive Griffin

A Poem

'A poem' is something that is not easy to start,
   It has to be sincere and come from your heart.
The subject and content is all your choice,
   For all will read and feel your voice.

Fact or fiction the words must flow,
   It must make an impact and the reader will know.
The strength and points will stand alone,
   These lines must roar with a unique tone.

The listener shall hence and heed the point,
   Each line 'a poem' is a well oiled joint.
Clear and brisk each word must sound
   To all will be known where these words were found.

A word with words will give great pretense.
   As for a word alone with not make sense.
So gather your thoughts and print them clear,
   Make them dance so we see what we hear.

So to finish 'a poem' just take a pause,
   Read your words, did you meet your cause?
End it gently, your pen will no longer roam,
   Now you too, completed 'a poem'
Albert J. Adams Jr.

How Do You Find A Friend?

Since friendship is not tangible,
It is very difficult to describe.
You cannot pinpoint it like other things,
It is something you must feel inside.

People come in all sizes and colors,
So how do we chose the ones we love?
They could be twenty or even forty,
Or round as a ball or small like a dove.

It seems the external package,
Is what first draws us near.
But it is later when we see the inner self,
That makes us feel secure.

We will meet all types of people
As through our lives we go.
But we will never recognize a true friend,
Without first looking within their soul.
Jean M. Davidson

My Palace Home

My home is my special place
it is where I like to be,
because there, there is so much love and care for me.
To me my home is like a palace with pretty golden trees,
I love to watch them blow in the summer breeze.
My home is a special place and a happy place.
It doesn't matter where I go, because I will always come home.
I think there is no place like home.

Elizabeth Anne Hylton

My Shadow

I look at my shadow in my room at night.
 It looks so dark, so gloomy, so all alone.
It's there in the night by itself — dark on dark.
 At first I feel sorry for my shadow.
 But then I realize. . .

I'm not looking at my shadow at all,
 I'm looking at my mirror.

Charles C. Mischke

Through His Eyes: A Firefighter's Wife

I'll never turn a deaf ear, when your telling me your story,
It may be over one hundred times, I promise it won't bore me.

I saw you fighting that fire, the flames were oh so high,
And then I said a little prayer, Lord, take care of my guy.

The fire was going through the walls, the roof about to collapse,
And as I stood there watching you, I gave a little gasp.

Then all of a sudden you heard a noise, the chief did sound the alarm,
He's God outside, he's looking in, to keep you safe from harm.

You get so angry when you say, he pulled us out to rest,
But, oh my darling I'm glad he did, you know he does what's best.

So now I make this promise, when you talk about that night,
I'll never turn a deaf ear, I love you, your my life.

Anne Marie Healey

TIME

It might be in the morning just at the break of day,
It might be in the evening when the sun is going away,
It might be in the Sringtime, in the Summer or the Fall,
It might be in the Winter when Jack Frost comes to call.

Our time is short upon this Earth so make it really count,
Be honest, fair and friendly as you try to scale the mount.
Be wary of those people who try to rush you through,
Just keep your head and take it slow that's just what you should do.

Be grateful for the time you have with all those that you love
This time is given to you by that good Man above,
And when it comes the time to part just think about the past,
Your memories will comfort you these thoughts will surely last.

So use your time productively as you journey through,
Life is just what you make it, it's only up to you.
Remember time is never done when you reach journey's end,
Like the seasons that we spoke of everlasting will transcend.

Douglas W. Grimshaw

Daybreak In The Desert

As the sun rises over the mountains high land;
It reaches across the hot burning sand.

As the last speck of night disappears with the days,
The coyote in it's den listens and lays.

Alert and alive the warthog they runs out,
And meerkats run in a row short and stout.

The road runners run can make no sound,
But the heyena's laugh can be heard all around.

As the sun reaches over the clear, blue sky,
The day is hot, and the temperature high.

The sun reaches over all the land,
It reaches over all the sand,
It touches every animal in sight,
Every cactus, every tumble weed,
But not in the night.

Brynn Lopez

The End Of Silence

Have you ever listened to silence?
It screams at me.
It pounds in my head like a heart waiting to explode.
A voice speaking in the night.
But whose is it?
My own?
Does my subconscious speak to me or with me?
Or is it a stranger?
Strange eyes staring through me,
A strange mouth whispering my name in the darkness.
The darkness itself seems like a stranger,
calm - quiet - silent - but strange.
Like a child playing quietly in the corner,
ignored - forgotten - alone,
always alone.
Until sunrise when the darkness disappears,
The silence ends and a new day begins.
A day that will once again end
In silence.

Casey Alford

Words Of An Angel

I'm walking beside a familiar face
It seems strange and out of place
He is a stranger, I've never met,
My family and friends, I'll never forget

He's taking me home, where I've never been,
To look upon you again and again
With words of comfort and full of grace,
He brushes the tears from my face

"I'm too young and I'll be missed," I say
"This is why I'm taking you away.
Heaven is beautiful and full of love.
Watch out for your family from above.
My angels must be strong and kind.
With these gifts, you'll lead the blind.
Help your loved ones to believe in me.
I gave MY life for them and thee."

Connie Bellar

An Artist's Thoughts On Painting

What is the ghost that tortures me?
It's the ghost of an idea being born
That touch of a thought leaves my grasp unfilled
Like a dream that dies with the morning.

Heartha Whitlow

"A Special Birthday Present"

The nicest birthday I ever had - although
it started out a little bit sad -
But when the nurse said, come take a look!
It's something "special" for your Baby book.

Big feet and hands, and long black hair
The gift of Joy just filled the air.
I thanked the Lord for such a blessing to share
My "birthday" with everyone there.

If you haven't guessed yet who surprised m
that day, his name is "Jason" What More can I say.

So let me tell you now with the Lords help and
a few more years, there much to be done amongst
all our fears.

Each day we just pray to do the best we can
and rear him to be finest kind of little Man!
   Claudia Phelan

"A Child's Heart"

A child's heart is pure and innocent.
It tells you exactly how it feels.
It knows not how to distort the truth.
It only tells what it feels is real.

A child's heart can't imagine how it
   would be to disillusion the mind.
For it was born much too kind.
It is only when life makes it wilt,
That it becomes over occupied with filth and
The guilt over what it has done to sew
   it's life's entangled quilt.

But for now, a child's heart is pure and kind.
I offers empathy for all mankind
And it provides comfort to all who look within to find.
   Felicia Ann Washington

The L.A. Earthquake

L.A. City was awaken with a shake
It was God's work make no mistake

The building they reeled and rock from the bottom to top
I guess they wondered when it is gonna stop

They laughed and joke and say
But there will be a bigger one in a future day

They saw everything begins to sway
They even saw the earth give way

There was some that screamed and cried
And some even had to watch while love ones died

This world is so full of sin
It's not fit for anyone to live in

Is may not be to long before we say
For some of us it'll be better after the judgement day
   Bonnie Wood

The Great Tree

The great tree stands in my yard,
It's big and old and hard,
It has a swing,
And everything,
It is very useful
Especially to get away from the neighbors bull
   Elaina Erwin

Untitled

Before all else, no thing stood. God was alone. He thought
it was good. God played with His power and fashioned His
mate. She was His opposite. God said She was great. He
loved Her so dearly, the two became one. They rolled
together, formed a sphere. They had a son. He was made in
their own image. The three comprised one orb. God love to
spin creations, so He spun one more. Fire, Water, Sand, and
Air, God's magnet in the middle spun it, held it there. It
was perpetual love in all God had wrought. The song was
beautiful. The dancing never stopped.
He loved his mother as all young boys do. He came to resent
the love his father knew. God of course was furious, but
gave His son a choice: avoid the fruit in the middle, or you
will be destroyed. He reached out for his mother. She held,
then let him go. He lived in his own sphere now and She
watched him implode. Before all else an hour glass stood.
Anger froze it like ice. God said it was good. Before all else
an hourglass flowed, one end was clear, one end rainbowed.
Fire and Ice. God loved His wife. Earth in Air, a falling heir.
   Anne Grogan

Tears Hope

Quietly he rest there, with his future in his hand.
It was no bigger, no smaller than a grain of sand.
It contained all the hopes and fears of a million years.
And yet it foretold every single one of his fears.
In his palm it glows, with the light of a thousand stars.
But then, it laid silent, like the beat between pulsars.
Then, as the energy and power began to form,
He felt his emotions stir, he returned to that fateful storm.
He lay there in shock, but the choking fear is present.
The rank smell of blood was the greatest of unpleasant.
The crushed metal of the car surrounded his body.
His mind knew the relief, to let go, disembody.
The pain in his lungs made breathing hard to continue.
But thoughts of his family bonded him like sinew.
His son, his baby daughter, and his wife of ten years,
That which brought him present, to the sight of his wife's tears.
One of her silvery tears lay upon his dark palm.
The other palm captured in hers, the source of his calm.
   Jenna Ward

The Winds Have Shifted

And then he knew.
It wouldn't last until he could change it.
It would die long before his actions could stop it.
This he knew.
It was already dead.
He had been carrying a corpse for a long time.

He should have noticed the weight get heavier.
It was obvious to him now.
The wind had shifted, but from his shelter he couldn't see it.
No, he wouldn't see it.
But, he can't help but smell the stench on the wind, now.
He had been carrying a corpse for a long time.

He thought it would last forever.
It would always be there.
No matter how much he thought it would never change.
It had changed, now.
There wasn't much left to do about it.
He had been carrying that corpse for too long.

I guess it's time for a burial.
I guess it's time to grieve.
   Christopher Prince-Colbath

My Purpose

There is a story I choose to tell,
It's about a girl I know quite well.
Her golden red hair, That little freckled face,
Grew bitter and cold and colder each day!
Just let her be free out in to this world to roam,
To seek her identity, she didn't find at home!
Can you answer me, does the journey end?
She won't give up, until she succeeds,
God made her strong with ability!
A little scared she hates defeat.
Then one day she knelt and prayed,
Dear God who am I?
He said to me that very day,
While your an angel my dear, I made you that way!!
MY questions were answered all in that day!
My journey for home is what I began.
Listen real close to those girls with a glow,
For words of wisdom, is what we speak,
Never forgetting those people in need!

Carla Sue Pamperin

Sky Soldier Legend

Here is a story for young Paratroopers,
its about soldiers that come down, down, down from the sky.

They called them Sky soldiers... no need to wonder why.

The tunes of glory and the sadness and sorrow,
made them hard and tough to make a better tomorrow.

The Sky soldiers are coming and the enemy is running
as the Sky soldiers come down, down, down from the sky.

Like others before them who served with pride,
our nation is grateful for the freedom they provide.

With faith and glory, now remember this story...
it's your turn to be like them.

Sky soldiers coming down, down, down, from the sky.

Daniel Ojeda Jr.

Life of A Rose

The ROSE, so beautiful and fragile, like an infant.
Its beauty soon blossoms like the innocence of a child.
Its fragrance, perfumes the air with sweet memories.
A child refills a vase with water, extending the still life beauty of the rose.

The rose reaches its peak of beauty.
A petal gently falls to the table.
A woman removes the fallen petals from the table, gently.
The image of the rose reaches full maturity.

The rose starts to shrink, like the wrinkles of its admirer.
An old woman looks at the rose stem with no petals.
Its' beauty has faded away, as a tear flows down the curve of her face
It reminds her of her memories, as a child with her first rose.

The rose stem looks helpless, until she plants it in her garden.
With the warmth of Spring, the pale stem blossoms.
New leaves and a new rose bud appear, and life begins again.
LIFE IS A BEGINNING THAT NEVER ENDS.

Antonio Puglia

Untitled

Light breezes—thirsting for knowledge—
Lap at the flag hanging its heart at half-mast.
"Hoo-oo-oo-i are you so sad?" they whispered.

The flag—overcome?—didn't answer.
The breezes grew into an insistent wind,
And made old glory shred a new tear.

David Roberts

Burdensome Path

I walk along a narrow path,
Its end I cannot see.
I started very long ago,
A life long path for me.

Along the way my strengths are tested,
Great tests I must survive.
For if I am to meet my goals,
I know I must stay alive.

For deep within my heart it dwells,
This feeling of despair.
A loss too great for explanation,
A loss too great to bear.

As each one leaves their earthly existence,
And travels to a better place,
I feel my strides getting shorter,
But I know I must keep my pace.

I understand my losses have been many,
And I sometimes feel no worth.
It's time to follow my path to love,
The basis of all heaven and earth.

Joanne Beall

The Summer Eric Moved Away

The FOR SALE sign stands at attention in the front yard.
It's hard!

It's hard to say goodbye to the summer; to the friend,
I'll never see again.

Eric moved to the big city
ending our playful days.

He moved to the big city to make another friend,
who will understand his special ways.

Sure, Eric had moods.
I was too young to understand.

He took pills for theses I think.
His mother said he was on the brink
of returning to a normal life.

Eric moved to the big city
I hope to find a good life.

Emilie Louise Ille

The Moon

The moonlight shone like a firefly in the night.
Its lavender glow so soothing and bright.
The designs on its surface like delicate lace,
Thought to be a picture of the man on the moon's face

During different stages it changes its shape,
Always repeating its cycle like a rewound tape.
The tides of the earth coming in and going out,
Obeying it and gravity without a complaint nor a pout.

The moon is so quiet it moves without a sound,
Following its orbit like a scent by a hound.
Always ever present by night and by day,
Even if not seen with the earth it will stay.
The moon is a symbol of complexity
Made by nature for the whole world to see.

George Rose

"One's Weakness"

The pain that you feed me, tastes sweet makes me want more.
It's like a stream of blood that I feed off of at the 12th hour
in the dark, I can taste your fear, and hear your heart
beating louder as I am taste your sweet drops of fear
dripping down your muscular body,
your leading yourself to your own grave,
Walking your way to hell! Just as you think your safe,
You turn to a dark hallway, you walk slowly and cautiously, you
Find me waiting at the end, you never stop to think about
stop to think who or what I am, but
you are just blinded by beauty, as you
feed me with your sweet pain and blood.
  A sudden bright flash, then a deadly black darkness
falls over another lifeless body, at his own expense.
  Jenn Jez

Daydreaming

As I look into the sky, I wonder if it has an end.
Its massive shapelessness, dreaminess invites me to pretend.

Thoughts of wondrous, adventurous journeys begin to fill my mind.
The countless unknown destinations, I know I'd surely find.

Oh, how I wonder what life brings, in far away land and skies.
Somehow I know there is waiting for me, a glorious surprise.

I see success, health, wealth and happiness, as I look above.
The clouds spell out excitement, mystery and eternal love.

Fantastic deeds, exotic places begin to call my name.
My heart's desires swell within me; the sky will never look the same.
  Brandace B. Bain

The Glass Pain

The face in the mirror is not mine
It's nothing that I could define
Behind the pane a reflection hides
Beyond the pain, my soul resides
My eyes see more than they tell
Past this mirror is a fiery hell
When the face peers out from its glass cage
You can clearly see its burning rage
His nostrils flare and I just stare
This black putrid sloth, in this hell-hole
Was once formerly my angelic soul
  Elizabeth Buchta

Love's Light

There are so many stars shining above
It's our choice to find one to love.

We search for the one that is always bright
Hoping the decision we make is right.

All the stars with deceiving rays
Cut sharply through a life of confusion and haze.

All the beams should help light the way
But no it's still dark with no sign of day.

Then a star ray shined through my window true
It reminded me of no one but you.

Because of its light I began to see
By your side I could spend eternity.
  John T. Barrasso

Discovering A Broken Heart

Now they're torn apart,
I've just discovered a broken heart.
The more they let their minds and souls flow
Free, the more my heart hurts me.

I thought we'd always be a family,
But I guess they weren't meant to be.
I thought we'd be a family forever,
But something didn't want us to be together.

But the more they let their relationship die,
The more at night I constantly cry.
And when they're finally apart,
Someone will discover a broken heart.
  Erica Evette Wright

The Power Of Prayer

The power of prayer is a gift from God
Jesus went to the mountain and prayed a lot.

His prayers were answered by the galore
Jesus is the Son of God and our Lord.

When you are ever broken-hearted or in need,
Jesus will be right there to help you indeed.
In luke 4:40 you will read of
The many people that He has healed.

You must pray, as many years will get away.
Remember your prayers will always stay.
Through prayer, God makes you a channel of his power.

God has a place for you in his heart,
Your sincere prayers will keep you there from the start.
  Harold John

The View

Tails aflame wagging in their orifices, a bubble of hot air
Jiggling, juggling jowls of gossip meat
Cowardly vulture queen at his side, doing her hyena stride
Taking in pride, their deeds delight
Idleness nested jealousies in their minds, friendships worm
A glance on parchment set the mold, secrets, they stole
Jealousy came two fold
Painted faces in the jungle of life,
Curare darts struck friendship's heart
Let the drums strike, eat humble pie, pay the toll
Alas, true friendship has the sweetest scent,
A rose bud we're blessed with
Expressed through heart, breath, and soul if it's to bloom
And I the sparrow viewed it all.... watched each petal fall.
  Diana Dolhancyk

"Couple"

You sit at your piano in the cold, lonely room,
  just playing the black and whites of some familiar tune.
I peek in behind the doorway just to see you sitting there,
  and I listen to your music flowing through the dark, night air.
Suddenly, our eyes meet just like we're in some crowded place,
  we make our way to each other.. you and I within the moons embrace.

I could never leave,
  nor keep you from my mind.
I believe in us forever,
  until the end of time.
  Jaclyn Carnovsky

Waiting To Die

Once agility thrived
Joints failed to collide
Now they crumble and collapse
Waiting to die

Once energy pulsated
Rippling through each elastic muscle
And moist marrow filled each knuckle.
Now dry and shriveled like wrinkled, sun beaten leather
Waiting to die.

Once the cranium exhilarated with vibrant ideas
Now memory slowly evaporates like foggy weather...
echoing future tears
Waiting to die.

A flower brings beauty to every room
A seed must die to bring new life
But is remembered for its beautiful bloom.
Waiting to die.

Crystal Jackson

Just Another Day

Winter time, looking out the window seal.
Just another day, Watching time drift away.
The fire burns as the ashes fall to the floor.
Another man dies. Another soul lost to the world.

Sitting on the porch watching the summer fields.
The sun is shining bright, the dog lies on the hill.
A women sits by the cradle rocking the babe to sleep.
You hear the cry, and the cry runs so deep.

Looking out the window as the sun is going down.
Another man is lost, nowhere to be found.
Can't find the way, no one laid a road.
Another child is gone. Lost in the world.

Lying in the bedroom watching the sun rise.
Another day in life, just drifting by.
People come and go, they die or fade away.
Another life moves on. Nothing is here to stay.

Doug Smitherman

Pesticides And Pain Killers

No colorful flowers to fill the room
Just pesticides and pain killers to fill the room
No lavish fruits or the sweet smell of the air
Just a depleting o-zone for which no one cares
Pain killers, beepers, pills and booze
The only thing we have is our soul to lose
Soufflés, parfait and chicken fingers
A pollution cloud of death is what lingers
Criminals for justice roam the street
All of us are followers without any lead
The firing squad of society aimed at the young
A world where drugs, sex and danger is fun
The elements used for one blink of pleasure
Regretting the loss of an environmental treasure
On each end of the spectrum a problem
With armies and guns that try to solve them
Is our world on top of a collapsing pillar
And now our doom is pesticides and pain killers

Jamie Bond

Memories That I Will Never Forget

I smell your perfume every day
just to help me see
the beautiful flower
that may someday be away.

Your hair, like hot sun on cold winter,
makes me feel like a star in paradise.

Rare bird voice, it's your sound
that can make never-seen-light appear on the ground.
I start to cry
tears fall in my heart already dry.

All our memories, they're in my brain.
But your image,
in my heart will remain.

Daniel Riobo

Kids of Mine

Kids are beautiful in their own special way.
Kids can be funny when their at play,
Kids are happy most of the time.
Their not like adults, their happy with a dime.
My girls are the prettiest on the Block,
I hope they don't marry some stupid jock.
Some kids snore awful loud.
I'm their daddy and I'm still proud.
All I can say is Kids are people too!

James Campbell

Two Sides

One side of me is good and virtuous,
Kind and fair, honest and righteous.
It doesn't lie, steal, or cheat.
It's friendly, cheerful, and very neat.

My other side is rotten and bad,
It is mean, angry, unkind, and mad.
It's vile, cruel, noxious.
It's uncaring, contemptible, and pugnacious.

These two sides collaborate
To make me human; not too evil or great.

Courtney Sumrall

A Sailor's Lot

It seems to me a sailors lot is all tied up in sailors
Knots, the moon, his light on the sea, the stars
Are his family"

Oceans big and oceans small, he dreams of sailing on them
All"the cool winds that blow in spring, gently urges his
Ship in swing"

Stormy weather that bring on the gale"followed by the
Bursting hail, only convinces him more so"that sailors
Like the armored go: doing their duty for love of man
And enjoying life the best they can:

Brenda L. Budjinski

Lady Of Grace

Lady of grace
Lady so fair
Such wondrous joys that your willin' to share
Whispers of velvet
Caressing da soul
Dreams of love, that only you and Jalle' know
Cascading tears through moonlit eyes
Born once anew of what once was dead...
Given clearer skies

Edward M. Dean Jr.

No Fear

Fear not the way I feel;
Know thine own feelings.
Wonder not what is in my heart;
Know that mine feels for thine own.
Worry not about our relationship;
For we are destined to be together.
Think not that we are miles apart;
But merely a phone call away.
Dwell not on distance;
Know that we will be together forever someday.
Want not to hold only my body;
For you have my soul.
Feel not uncertainty;
Have confidence in us.
Ask not that I be thy girl;
But thy best friend, love, and companion.
Cry not tears of sadness while we are apart.
But tears of joy for when we meet again.
   Anita Spencer

The Rose

Its delicate slumped-over body looks at me pathetically,
Knowing that it has lost another battle, the battle for life;
A war of two spirits, competing endlessly.

The fragile petals dropping one by one, the wilting of the leaves,
The breaking of the stem, killed by age, natural and peaceful.

The crumbling of stepped-on petals..the crushing of a dream,
The tearing of fragile leaves..the ruining of precious ideas,
The cracking of the stem..the final death of the soul.

With one always giving up before the other,
The other always winning.
Yet for some reason God gives it the strength to try again,
Every day getting closer to that one day when there will be
No war, no winners and only friends.
   Dawn O'Neal

That's My Boy

See that boy running over there
laughing and playing without a care
That's my boy.

He can make me laugh or cry with joy
I love that little fellow, my little boy.

Look at those eyes and that pure red hair
Even freckles on his nose here and there.

Hey Tyler! Hey Son! Come to your dad
Look at him come, it makes me so glad.

Arms stretches out, his face all a smile,
Thank you LORD for this dear child.

And thank you Lord for his mother too,
I have them both, Thanks to you.
   Clara E. Lansing

Let's Break Forth Into, Singing, Unto The Lord...

Let's break forth into singing, unto the Lord...
Let's break forth into shouting, unto the Lord...
Let's break forth into praising, unto the Lord...
Let's break forth into preaching, unto the Lord...
Let's break forth into teaching, unto the Lord...
Let's break forth into healing, unto the Lord...
Let's break forth into dancing, unto the Lord...
Let's break forth into laughing, unto the Lord...
Let's just worship the Lord in spirit and in truth... amen.
   Gale Simpson

Wisdom

Amongst the briers and patches of thorns,
Lay a tiny nest of birds.
So frail and helpless to nature below,
Where trod the beast and mammoth herds.
Yet in their frailty a strength is born,
Not common yet to man.
For inward lies a hope of courage,
To scour, yes, yet devour this immortal land.
Wisdom shows herself in the span of her wings,
In courage she climbs to heights unclaimed.
She scales the cliffs and again cheats death,
Her modesty shows no refrain.
Wake up my brood, wake up!
Tis now your time of test.
Be swift and subtle about yon peaks,
Bring back the snow upon your breast.
Think not yourself of high esteem,
Be cunning and keen in thine own eye.
Forget not my love, it is not you,
But rather wisdom that shall not die.
   Judi Daily

Nature Is Beautiful

Nature is beautiful. Watch it.
Learn from it.
Look for every drop of water in a river,
As many flow together along the sand.
See each feather on a bird,
While hundreds of them help the bird fly high.
Watch every pine needle on a pine tree,
As all blend together to lean every which way.
Look at the clouds and see them float along the sky,
While covering the sun with their odd shapes.
See each petal of a flower reach for the sun,
As if trying to smile at it.
Watch each drop of rain fall to the ground,
While billions of them make a storm.
Look at the long grass sway left and right,
As if it were an ocean in a storm.
See the mice scamper into their holes,
While running from an enemy.
Nature is beautiful. Watch it.
Learn from it.
   Amanda Johnson

Carnival Fantasy

Cute little trolls walking with the toad
Led the children down the purple brick road
A show of puppets laughing with joy
Soldier boys playing musical toys
Pink cotton clouds and angel skies
Round and round on velvet pony rides
Mirror, mirror who is the funniest of all
Is it your image or something tall
Bright red candy apples for the queen
Moon beams starlings pretty things
Watching the musical carnival rabbits run
Two headed clowns and balloons are fun
Amused thoughts and voices laughing
The carnival lights are dazzling
Blue bell flowers and cockle shells
Colorful shapes and chiming bells
Funny faces peeking over the bells
Reciting stories they like to tell
It was fun in the fantasy land
The trolls played the music of their band
   Betty Clements

On Leaving Impressions

A footprint
Left in the sand by the sea
Lasts only as long as the waves take
To crash onto the shore.
But we want to be remembered
To be important.
So, you who would walk on the beaches,
Will you hide your footprints away
Where they are safe from the reach of the sea?
Or will you simply
Leave a deeper impression
One that can last, that can withstand trial?

Allison M. Otto

Old Woman On A Bench

An old woman sits squatting on a bench
legs spread outward oozing pus from sores and crust
a forgotten babushka of the past

A Russian man says, "pretty no?" Derisive scorn
in English so as not to offend he thinks
but the woman knows

Her face and hands lined with a thousand regrets
shout out, I was beautiful once
I even raised a family for peace

Before I knew or understood that time and place
would sing a cruel song the world would not accept
and leave me alone to my eternal detriment

Her tears wash my eyes in silence
and I turn away as much from grief as inability
to lift her from the dust of yesterday

An old woman sits squatting on a bench

George Neitz

Starting Over

There was once a time when stress was high and sadness was a way of life.
My mind was filled with worries and fear; instead of peace there was strife.
Uncertainty abides with me each night and day.
No more do I wear the rings.
Numerous obstacles in my way. I leave behind familiar things.
Though it is sad it must be like this, I feel relief as well.
Certain things I will surely miss. Only time will tell.
Lessons in life are not always easy. They tend to slow us down.
But in the end we learn life's lessons without losing much ground.
As days pass, I realize the future is open, mine to mold.
I've opened a new book in my life where there are stories untold.
I look ahead with new views. I feel revived, suddenly alive.
I now know that I made the right choice to leave.
I can hold my head high.
I no longer have a weight in my heart. I no longer ask myself why.
I thank God He gave me the strength to do what was right in the end.
And no matter how tough it seems to get,
more strength to me He will send.

Carla Coleman

These Iowa Hills

The beauty of these rolling hills
Like the waves of the sea roll on
Filled with many shades of green
Since the colors of autumn are gone
In summer they look like a patchwork quilt
Fields of corn and hay and beans
Just rolling along through the country side
Going forever it seems

June Fetter

The Darkness

The Darkness surrounds us as we walk through the vast wasteland of life.
We dream to be somewhere, anywhere but here.
Some do drugs to escape reality as do others use religion or art.
Some do all 3. While others just rot and complain.
As we walk The Darkness thickens in its enigma so we ponder the
    question, why are we here?
Disgruntled postal workers, serial killers and the sort have the right idea
In the stall at a McDonald's someone wrote"
    "the white Aryan nation is coming kill all Blacks"
Well you're wrong,
it's already here but not just for Blacks its here for us all.

The Darkness is its great abyss closes in and constricts our souls,
    twists our minds and hearts till we can no longer love, worship or think.
We can only sit there with a blank stare and think why?
When The Darkness seals itself we die.

Adam Rubins

The Tempest

It begins to grow dark.
Lightning flashes, thunder cracks.
The wind grows in strength as the first droplets of rain begin to fall
The atmosphere becomes charged.

It begins to grow dark.
Feelings rush in, emotions are electric.
The tempest rages within.

The storm grows in intensity; it ravages the land.
Lightning now streaks across the sky, blinding.
The roar of thunder becomes deafening; mingling with the
    screaming of the wind as the rain pounds relentlessly down.

Every muscle, every nerve, comes alive.
The heart beats faster.
All senses are heightened.
The tempest inside rages on.

The rain slows, the lightning fades.
Thunder rumbling low, as if a distant reminder of things past.
The wind blows gently, caressing; while birds begin to sing quietly.

The first tears begin to fall.
A rainbow appears. The storm is over.

Abigail L. Jones

Nightfall

The December Sun was slipping to the ocean in the West,
Like a blazing ball of fire as it settled down to rest.
I watched the blue Atlantic take on the shades of night,
And I noticed how the water played with the fading light.

The sky was like a painting that an artist had arrayed
In purple gold and orange, so beautifully displayed.
My footprints in the sand, as I walked along the shore,
Were erased by little waves 'till it was smooth and clean once more.

I felt the fresh sweet air brush the teardrops from my face.
No smog or fog, no bitter cold, was ever in this place.
The moon was up once more, chasing shadows in the trees,
And the lovely winter flowers cast their fragrance in the breeze.

Peace settled all around me as my troubles fell away,
Slipping from my shoulders with the passing of the day.
This tranquil little island, this calm secluded beach,
Put the healing powers of nature right within my reach.

Dorothy C. Miller

"Darkness"

It seeps through your soul...
Like a child in a candy store...
Pain. Silence. Dread!!
The horrifying fear of not knowing what's before you...
You'reFALLING...FALLING...FALLING!
Anything and everything bad that can happen welled up
inside of you can not even come close to comparing to the
terror... and horrid ways of the "dark!"
It lurks in every hospital waiting room...
And sneeks around every street corner...
It's on every turn in life...
It can NEVER be avoided or destroyed...
In front of you, behind you, it will always be there!
To the north, to the south, and to every side of you,
And all you can do is...
BEWARE!!!!!
Jacque Crittenton

My Dear

How ever do you carry on
like a dark fix?
Where do you discover such
expressions?
You converse as an epic poem,
clear and assured.
I enfolded gracefully to the brink of
delight.
Enraptured by your power to express
your sensations.
The tone stretched my psyche farther
than any creature could conceive.
Each day breathed the sun purely for you.
When greeting you, I was bathed of all my sins
as a school girl pardoned for her absence.
The joy you bring is not unlike awaking
to a ravishing sunrise.
Unsurpassed companions like you are uncommon, and ordinary
people like myself are lucky.
Amanda Pyle

"The Way You Make Me Feel"

The way you make me feel feels so right,
  like a huge star burning bright.
Our love will last forever, and this I see.
  As I look into the future, I see you and me.
You look into my eyes ever so tenderly.
  As I look into your eyes, love is all I see.
The touch of your hand, the love in your kiss,
  are the little things I'll always miss.
We see each other little, and that is true,
  but my heart skips a beat every time I see you.
Your feelings for me are deep inside your heart.
  I hope and pray that we will never part.
The Lord is with us, and this we know,
  that His light upon us will forever show.
Dawn Ramos

Let The Bells Ring

Listen to the bells ring as the spirits rise.
Listen to the shots ring out as a young man dies.
The Blues and Grays mix viciously defending what they think right.
The Blood they shed upon the land is the reason they must fight.
A voice inside them screams out, my body reeks with pain.
Is death so near and life so short, it all seems so insane.
To pit brother against brother is the most criminal of acts.
To rush and fight for victory, before they knew the facts.
Let the bells ring reverently to alleviate the fears.
And bow our heads for history to shed sympathetic tears.
Bonnie Zeller

Knowledge

The epiphany of life everyone seeks.
Like a light shining through a dark expanse that
  makes you aware of all you missed.
An all powerful, consuming, driving force pulling you
  to the edge and abandoning you there.
The prize of science's eternal quest.
Ignorance's bane.
A well wielded implement for all who have
  succeeded.
Heavenly, warm feelings you receive when
  inspiration hits.
Or, the ultimate earthly hell for those who know too
  much.
Jacob Keniston

Untitled

It rests in your hand
like a sword gleaming in the light.
It slashes and swoops and swirls
and draws blue blood with your might.
It lays the enemy's body to ruin
leaving its marks for all to see.
Always and forever, wounds never to be healed;
the cuts remain etched in every reader's memory.
Dennis Campbell

"The Fire In Your Eyes"

Your burning eyes pierce my body
like a torch.
My heart bleeds,
but I still have enough life.

To stare into your eyes.
Eyes like beautiful bronze coins
that even make angels envy,
about what they long to have; your eyes.

When I look into your eyes,
I see heaven, with majestic mountains, and towering
  waterfalls so serene
A magnificent sight.
Shimmering pools that make me dream,

About the fire in your eyes;
that never dies.
Gene Takashima

Castle Sky

Spread against the water,
Like dust in the sand,
She cries for the one she loves,
Face against her hand,
Eyes cold with fear ill walk this promise land,
(Come with my love one,)
And take me by the hand,
For in the castle sky we live and die,
They came and gave us nothing,
Then took our lives away,
We waited for tomorrow,
The day that never came,
I don't want to be someone,
I don't want to take the blame.
John Claridge

A Lenten Lament

Oh, how to thwart the desire for un-lenten things
Like the delight of diaphanous butterfly wings,
And the delicate ingest of wiggled guppy tails.
Imagine butter-braised eyes of hump-backed whales!

Not to mention locusts' tongues and elephant meat,
Or armadillo shells for fried froggies' feet,
The aardvark's dark side, the camels' humps,
And the slick, quick energy from kangeroo jumps.

Too much to suffer, to agonize and groan
Until that morn the Lord rolls 'way the stone
And rises again on the Glory morn
To proclaim with grace our souls reborn.

Oh, the dread of wait, the woeful lament,
The body's denied, so doleful and spent.
So, Lent, be on your way and let spring shine through,
I'll pot culinary sins and simmer a stew.

Helen V. Healey

Legacy Of Love

Life is but a whisper
Like the gentle breeze through the trees
We're here for just a short time
And often we cannot see
The simple law of love
Laid down for you and me

We often feel that no one love us
No one really cares
So God sent his blessed son
To brush away our tears.
And then he left us with one simple commandment
That was to last us through the years.

Love one another, he said,
Don't turn your back on your brothers tears,
Let the love I give to you shine through
Your life, so that all the world can see
Each life I have blessed from above
Should leave this earth, with a legacy of love!

Deanna R. Crane

Angel

I feel trapped
Like there is no escape
And four walls surround me
Walls of lies, deceit, denial, and anger.
They control my every thought, my every move and my every emotion
Then all of a sudden a door appears
A brilliant light shines through and through the door comes a
    beautiful woman dressed in white.
She stands there and smiles at me
She beckons me to come
I want to run to her but I can't move
She must think I want to stay
For she starts to go
I stretch my arms and call to her
But she does not answer
She is gone
Why did you have to go woman in white?
Why couldn't you stay by my side?
I need you to help me woman in white
I need you to guide me through life

Denise Pareja

Playgrounds

Playgrounds and fantasy land
Little girls go hand in hand.
Jumprope and monkey bars
Basketball and boxcars.
Little boys pushing and stuff
Trying to act rough and tuff.
Soccer and a game of baseball
They all cheer as one hits it over the wall.
After pretending to be in the Hall of Fame
It's time to play a new game.
Imaginations soar on high
Smiles and laughter do not lie.
This is where kids can have some fun
Math and Science forgotten and done.
No teachers or parents in sight
Playing with all their might.
When tired out and no more can roam
They say their goodbyes and head for home.

Cindy Sosa

Crack In The Sky

Breaking through ebony-blanketed ramparts,
Locked clouds the moon forces apart,
    Cracking the sky,
    Light from dark,
    Allowing sight into the mind's eye.

Nevermore to remain the same,
Fleeting glimpses of illusions of fame,
    While luna lingers and leers,
    Her ghostly sliver of shame,
    Then as suddenly disappears.

Catherine Burke-Warren

Loneliness

The day wears on.
Loneliness engulfs the block.
A single leave rustles across an empty driveway.
The sound is heard for miles,
Disturbing the silence for only an instant.
Once again there is silence.
Nothing coming from nothing.
Where did they all go?
Not even an insect remains.
Where has everyone gone?

The answer lies within.

Angela M. Hart

Consider My Love

Consider the lilies, the ocean and sky
magnolias in moonlight, ducks flying by
Consider the tides, they come and they go
and we cannot change the ebb nor the flow
Consider the mountains covered with snow
the golden leaves of autumn falling below
Consider the apple blossoms that fill the air
with magical moments happening everywhere.

Consider the stars we never have seen
the glory of Easter when everything's green
Consider the seasons of summer and spring
with roses and lilacs and robins that sing
Consider the sunset, the death of each day
the passing of time for nothing can stay
Consider my love in beauty arrayed
For this is the gift my heart has made.

Jeremy C. Pick

Philosophy To Fall

I live autumn more then this life's season.
Longer I love the days of this season
And these days later to be remembered.
When days that fade into long winter hours
Have come to a fireside, leisurely time
Then I might philosophize and wonder,
Memory over the experience
Is greater in the instance of beauty
Because beauty is better remembered
And only in beauty is loss fulfilled;
This is the frost's philosophy to fall.
Its elements I recall were color.
In the morning fields the blue haze lingers
Until the buoyant sun burns the waters
On flaming leaves of red and yellow.
Across the path the blackbirds skirt and sing
On red ripe milo between the tree rows
Where some trees before had gathered sweet fare,
I should have had my share to be like wine
But for now remembrance will make me still.

Brent Unruh

When "I Do" Becomes "We Did"

That glorious day has come at last -
Look to the future and forget the past,
And once those wedding vows you take,
You must not think it a mistake!

An eventful life you will surely see,
Remember to tackle each trial with glee!
When the funds are low and the bills are high,
Just smile at each other and gently sigh!

When the children come, along the way-
Just praise that blissful wedding day!
Husband - be glad for that overtime -
Wife - don't you nag of grease and grime!

When the kids move out and you're all alone -
The two of you in your quiet little home,
You'll be ecstatic and overjoyed to hear -
That your new little grandchild will soon appear!

When you both are old and very gray,
And the wrinkles just will not go away -
You'll sit in rockers - wearing a grin,
And thinking you'd do it all over again!

Deborah B. Stewart

What Have You Done To My Land?

I am just an old Indian squaw,
looking at a land that you never saw.
Buffalo and elk so freely did roam
across this land, our home.
High above the eagles flew,
across a sky so truly blue.

Then one day the white man came,
he wanted our land to tame.
We gave you our hand at Plymouth Rock,
and helped you through winter's hard luck.

You littered my soil with buffalo bones,
drove away my people from their homes.
You took away the land where I grew my maize,
and gave me a city full of smog and haze.
In friendship I gave you my hand,
but what have you done to my land?

Dieter Hoffmann

The Sunrise

I love to see the waterfalls cascading down the waterway.
Looking at the sunset in the park, the autumn leaves
are slowly coming down on us.

To see the golden leaves
The skies have gone dark on us, and its started to rain
We need the shower of blessings from above

The elements of this world are beautiful
And hoping for the truth
The Autumn comes and hear, We go off to a loving world

My heart sparks when the moon light is bright
Hoping to catch a glimpse of the sunrise
The sun glows that makes me feel warm and earthy inside

Looking at the earthy way, and beaming at the sky
I am waiting for the valley to rise in the starry skies
When I call to the mountain I hear the wind roar.

It sounds like music to my ears, and whispers all day long
The rain came down and the wind blew hard
Hoping that the sun would come out again
Lets always put the sunrise in our hearts

Clyde C. Seaton

Seeds Of Desolation

Alone
Looking at the world from the inside out
I stood in this place
This "Hole in the Ground"
Where the earth had exploded
In one great thrust
Leaving its scar behind
And there I was
In the middle of a healed wound
In awe of nature's power and beauty

If I were to cry, would anyone comfort me?
If I were to sing, would anyone listen?
If I were to laugh, would anyone smile?

I looked at the parched ground
And was surprised at what I saw
There in the middle of emptiness was life
A dandelion somehow surviving the abyss
And I took comfort to think
That somebody's wish had traveled this far
And planted itself in nothing... and survived

Cerissa Linder

Love Makes Us Cry

Love makes us laugh,
Love makes us cry,
Love is the one who says good-bye.
Love is humble,
Love is kind,
Sometimes love is all that is in the mind.
So when the time comes, we must be prepared,
  To let go and not be scared.
Love will always be, just a step away.

Christine Diesch

"Ma"

The gender that bears child
loves, cares for you and nurtures you
Ma! Supports, helps and watches you.
Secrets are hidden and close to no one is told.
Ma is dying have to be bold
crying and weeping surrounds the area
six feet under is where it takes place.

David Richards

Love

Love someone and tell them so.
Love new friends that come and go.
Love for Christ has promised you,
Blessings every morning new.

Love the days and let it show.
Thank God as they come and go.
Love the work you have to do.
"Great is they faithfulness," mercies anew.

Greater love has no man known,
Than the one who's on the throne.
Love that's patient, gentle, kind.
Love that brings one peace of mind.

Love the things you have to do,
For Christ's love constraineth you.
When you love within your heart,
The love of God t'will ne'er depart.

Darryl Lynn McLain

Trapped In Another Vacuum

Pain controls my past, present, and future
Love takes another beating
A walk on the wild side becomes normal
Nights steal my soul; demons make small talk
A family's doomed reality is realized
Situations create angst among us all
Mental burnout offers a helping hand now
A mother cries; I become just
Another casualty of circumstance

Danny Wilson

A Sonnet To Newlyweds

Welcome newlyweds, to the world of lovers.
Lovers make such funny, delightful sounds together.
To all you newlyweds, may I now suggest,
That you become each others friend, your best friend.
Friends like each other and care,
And talk about things big and small.
Then, at times, they just sit and sit,
And say no words at all.
And tranquility abounds.
Because you see, silence, too, has become their friend.

Henry Enrice Storino

Rain

It drips, it drops,
Making a river of wishes.
It mists, it pours,
Creating water for all the fishes.
It sprinkles, it tinkles,
Forming a rainbow in every eye.
It bubbles, it puddles,
Falling from the dark, deep, blue sky.
It shivers, it chatters,
As the moon guides its way.
It's wet, it's cold,
For when it hits the earth; in the ground it will stay.
We take it for granted, something we can't live without.
Will it ever disappear and leave us in forever drought?
So as it falls and waters our souls,
Our lives are put together, as the rain fills in the holes.

Ann Crowe

The Sacramento Poem

State Capitol! State Capitol! Make it once. Make it twice.
Make it many times till its nice.
Mighty pretty to the eye.
Even though it doesn't touch the sky.
Eureka!! I found a bright golden seal
That's stamped on every bill.
Is it the court?
No, it's Sutter's Fort!
From cannon balls to cells
And doctors to cure your ails
Is it Natty?
No, it's definitely Patti
Standing tall with her doll
In a dirt hall.
THUNDER!! That must be thunder I hear!!
NO, it's the rain dancers in gear.
Dancing to the woven baskets that they're near.
And stirring up dust from Old Town I hear.
With roads made of dirt that go snap, crackle, and pop
I hopped into my bus like a good little tot.

Christina Mitchell

For You

They play upon emotions.
Make promises that they keep.
No one gives you something for nothing.
After you pay, would you be able to sleep.

The tools they use.
Parents can't afford starter jackets or $100.00 tennis shoes.
At home you don't feel loved, you are lonely and confused.
You feel your family has let you down.
Open your heart and eyes, Love is all around.

Your family loves you and supportive of you in every way.
Provide food for you and a place to stay.
But from that you stray.
You get farther and farther each day.

The glitter is in your eye.
Now you possess a scarf that would cause you to go to jail or die.
You can't get out without a fight.
Sometimes without someone losing a life.
The grass is not always greener on the other side.
Some don't find out until after they have died.

Janice Russ

Marriage Blessed By God

Marriage was ordained by God for two.
Male and female He joined you.
Put Him first in all you do
And to each other always be true.

Love is gentle, love is kind.
Love is forgiving, love is blind.
Work together to build a home
The family will enjoy, with no thought to roam.

Children are given to make a marriage complete.
A joy to have around your feet.
Train up the children to honor and serve
The Creator to whom their best deserves.

One life to live, so quickly it passes.
Don't waste your time among the masses.
Take time to steal away and pray
And study God's word every day.

The trials of life will seem so small
When on your knees you will stand tall.
Prayer and praise will give you power
To help you through each passing hour.

Elizabeth B. Beckham

New Beginnings

Dedicated to Floyd & Laurie Green
Life's cycle runs to and fro
Many times leading you places you never thought to go.

Then love begins to fill deep down within,
What is this feeling, he's my friend.

Your heart is racing with such a fierce pace,
You can't wait to hear his voice
or see his face.

The two become as close as one,
Both so afraid, but too in love to run.

Never did I dream I would find a love so sweet,
To make my life feel so complete.

So life has turned it's cycle once again,
He's not only my love, but my best friend.

A blessing sent from God above,
Trust in Him and He will give you love.

New beginnings for the whole world to see,
I'm in love with him, and he with me.

Denise H. Berry

No More Cop-Outs?

To be, or never to be a "cop-out"
   May reflect our own individual choice.
But after the "weaseling" of Adam and Eve,
   Our position we'll quietly voice.

After Cain had slain his brother, and heard
   The voice of the great "Mighty Reaper",
He sheepishly denied his death to God
   Protesting, "Am I my brother's keeper?

God counted Abram's faith as righteousness,
   For Abram always honored our Lord God,
And to him God e'er promised descendants,
   As the stars over the land where he trod.

But Isaiah's crowd "copped out" 'neath his preaching
   Because he labelled their righteousness rags,
For Christ had not as yet sent His Spirit
   To empower them to scale heaven's crags.

There need never be another "cop-out",
   For soon Christ's Spirit will our hearts indwell
And we can exchange, our rags for riches
   If our hearts e'er practice righteousness well.

Bernice Yeoman

To My Son The Eagle Scout

My son:
   May the stones in your pathway be
reduced to sand, the boulders to gravel, and
may the walls you scale be made of
limestone, so that when they are mixed with
the rain waters of life they will form a
concrete foundation upon which you can build.
   Never soar so high you loose sight of the
Cub and never hibernate so deep or long that
you cannot often look up at the EAGLE.
For it is the grandeur of one and the
humility of the other that inspires man to
noble deeds.
   Always remember the Great Spirit walks
beside you and his love and ours goes with
you now and FOREVER!

Joy Lee Robinson

The Thief On The Cross

He was just a thief, sneaky but not cruel.
Maybe had no loved ones or ever went to school.
With punishment extreme, told he had to die,
Beaten, nailed onto a cross, our blessed Lord nearby.
In agony we do not know, under blazing noonday sun,
Torn and bloodied, hanging there until all life was gone.
No one there to mourn his fate, he was to expire in shame.
With insight he said of Christ, "In him was found no blame."
In midst of pain he cried aloud to any who would hear
"This man has done no wrong he should not be here."
He saw the Lord for who he was.
With hope he cried, "Remember me."
And Christ, with love, for which he died, responded,
"Come with me."

Arlene Hinds

I Love You, But I Hate You

I thought about you today, retaped together and photo
Maybe I should've left is as is, saved the
time, of tearing it up tomorrow.
In your absence I can't help but wish that
you are always near
I can't wait to be with you, so I can wish
that you were never here.
I went to our church up the hill and prayed
for us and for you
I prayed for eternal love and happiness
This was after, I placed the curse on you.
I've prepared us a beautiful dinner, sit
and enjoy this candle lit moment
relax, and eat my love, I swear
it is not poisoned.
I love you more than yesterday I
know this much is true.
Maybe its because I know that I always
love you the most
after I have hated you.

Darlene Torres

Open Your Hearts

Do you suppose we're misunderstood?
Maybe we don't present ourselves, as well as we could.
We've strong demeanors, could this be why?
They don't seem to think we hurt or we cry.
Accept us as we are, that's all we ask.
Why is this such a difficult task?
Let's not be caught in hard-hearted pride,
And just let kindness and love be our guide.
Just think of the joy acceptance could bring,
To hearts opened wide, and willing to sing.

Brenda McPeters Ritter

Gallery Garden

She rests in queenly repose in
memory's timeless garden,
Queen Nefertiti
Guardian of Egypt's sacred mysteries.
Her glowing grace and beauty
Vie with the morning sun
Bathing the Emerald garden.
A gentle breeze whispers
through leaves of shaded philodendrum
a slender stand of bamboo
Fringes water trickling from the
mouth of a laughing nymph.
The gallery walls boast art treasures, great and small,
brilliant and sacred.
Nature's timeless gift of art is this garden gem.

Esther Hohn Keller

Father

To see you in so much pain, it brought me to tears
Me losing you, is what I so much feared.
Not feeling the pain you felt, not understanding why
If it wasn't for that wonderful woman
To think, you could have died.
If something would have happened, I don't know what I'd do.
My heart just starts to crumble at the thought of losing you.
The pain I would feel, much greater than your own
I wouldn't have a father, I'd feel so all alone.
"I Love You" more than words can say
It would break my heart if you went away.
I'm still so young, I need you here for a while
To help me raise my children, to walk me down the aisle.
To see you in the situation was the worst thing that's ever
Happened to me. Not to be able to give you a hug
It really made me think. And I hope these past words
Have made you think too, because I don't know what I'd do
If I were to lose you. The more I think about it
The more I want to cry, because without you in my life
The days would just drag by.

Jamie Elizabeth Becker

The Walk

It's cold, the leaves are tipped with frost, the
meadow crunches beneath my feet.
My breath is carried away, suspended in the air,
drifting as clouds on the mountain.
Alone I walk through this valley, thinking and
not knowing where the future lies.
I pause... reflecting on journeys of old and the
lessons they brought.
A smiles rises when thoughts drift to friends, and
the pleasures they bring.
Huffing my collar, I walk on, to escape the moment
and the chill.
There will be other moments and walks, to be alone
and dream.

Eric R. Mannerberg

My Souvenirs

Tucked away with souvenirs are memories of the years.

My souvenirs some forgotten over the years bring back memories going through my souvenirs. My! How many cluttered boxes? Priceless. Memories of my old teddy bear bring a smile, remembering the closeness hugged so tight to calm my fears. Old hanky, yellowed with years. I remember it dried a few tears. What have I got to lift my spirits?

Next time I review my life, I will understand.
The rage today later becomes a souvenir tucked away. Not all are happy memories. Some tears must fall somewhere along life's ragged way. That's just a tax we all seem to pay. Happiness doesn't come easy. There's always something popping up to remind us life's always tough. Hang onto love no matter what. It's the most priceless souvenir you've got.

Addie Hill Yeager

Untitled

Ah, my friend,
My eyes bear witness to your shimmering end.
And as sweet memory depletes,
I find words to be fleet.
I can only hope
Through ranks of angels armed
You may pass unharmed
Or frolic beside demons with wings
To live and learn a thousand things.

Colby Jenkins

Shadows

Shadows in the attic
Memories in the dust
The trunk, the chair, the pictures, the toys
Silent they lay there with yesterdays noise

Shadows in the attic
Memories in the dust
Uniforms and bridal gowns,
Baby clothes and cap and gowns
Generations come and gone
Silent they lay there with yesterdays noise

Carole M. Sorvino

Edad

With my age I am as if the setting sun,
memories, thoughts, reflections,
fill me with the pride of those I've lost
and of those that have passed.

I was a sun, brilliant as a shimmer,
engulfing, encompassing
every spectrum, and band in it's hue.
Only to set one day, and pass these to you.

Have risen every day to a new challenge,
learned how to claw, educate, and speculate,
my tomorrow, your tomorrow that hasn't seen,
my fight for equality, in the mad-mans' dream.

With your age, as if the rising sun,
memories, thoughts, reflections,
are turned by the smokes swirl of an emptied gun.
... Those I've lost and of those that have passed.

My shimmer has turned into a showering glow,
intent on helping the birth of a new son.
Giving to it the strength of all my rises and all
my sets, taking with me only the love for a new day.

Daniel Svedas

"Mother"

Alone. Is where I am left. Standing near the middle in a reflection of darkness with only the wind to cradle me during this sadness, this endless madness that I re-create and live day by day. I count as vials fill with tears that I now must force out; to hopefully feel better, but no calm enters this world. Nor any light.
The cold ground. Now wet with solom. And some regret. Again I'm lost with the question in my head. Grays and blacks. Sharp as the razors edge. Bleeding into my mind. Hours being filled with nothing but emptiness and the only feeling which I repress, loneliness. If only the sun would rise. I could look and see the day a sandy shore, alone no more?
But the skies remain in their tint of black. And still I stand, near the middle, and wish that you would step out of my darkened reflections, take my hand to lead me home.

Catina McDonough

"Past And Present"

Past and present precious time has been spent.
Moments go by with laughter and cries, screaming as its
 tearing you soul up inside. Struggle in times
the fear that you find, opens your mind to more.
 Feel deep within your glory and sins clutching
for nothing much more. Life's soon to die beyond ones
 endless cries. My mind declines protrudes in time.
Thought you where mine. Only to know it was unity suspended
 in time. To my death the love I bleed.
In my last unspoken dreams we shall be whole as one eternally...

Cynthia A. M. German

Momentous Moments

Zit zit zit - there they go
  moments that stagger the mind
    The mediocre accompanies the pro
      As Mother Earth absorbs her kind

Sit sit sit - as think tanks grope
  For a leash on Space and Time
    O legacy what a tote!
      Ah-h-h - the prank of one ancient Ensign

Git git git - ye olde obnoxious rote
  And foibles that hobble all men
    To - wit wit wit - Take note note note
      Now is when

The stint stint stint of Great Brains
  Is to blow it's stack of moot
    While the Unpretentious appertains
      Recouping the Booty and Loot

Albeit - it it is the fallen too
  Who will rise to prize the Earth Worm
    Though Infinitesimal; Loyal and True
      To the out working of a Most Royal Concern

   Josephine M. Bush

Mother's And Daughters Day

When you were born, crying so loud
Mom's eyes filled with tears, she was so proud
The day's and year's flew by so fast
If only there was some way to make childhood last
Mom was there, thru all your pain and joy
From your very first date-to that special boy
Then came to prom, and the senior dance
Your new dress and slippers, didn't happen by chance
Mom did without, so you could be proud
You looked beautiful, there in the crowd
The day you got married, mom tried not to cry
She gave you her blessing and told you goodbye
She's still there for you, thru thick and thru thin
A mother's love is forever, there is no end
Today is Mom's day - so pay up your dues
If it wasn't for her, there wouldn't be you

   Ella Mosley

To Mom

So much you have given, that will never be repaid.
Morals and trust, the foundation for life you laid.

You gave your hope when mine was lost.
You gave yourself, you'd pay any cost.

So much you have given, that I've not yet received.
When the world was against me, you still believed.

You gave your joy to ease my pain.
You gave your sun to chase my rain.

So much I have taken, before learning how to give.
Your money, your food, and a warm place to live.

I took your love without any shame.
I took the credit, gave you the blame.

So much I have taken, without giving one regret.
Disobeying each rule, for my own good you've set.

I took your life to make better my own.
I took your youth to make me feel grown.

Looking back now that I'm older, I've come to see,
I could never ever repay all you have done for me.

The times you were there, when I needed a Friend.
Without asking, you gave your all again and again.

   Eddie Hayes

So the Story Goes

So the story goes:
Most for one and zilch for many.
The last will be first and the first will be last.
Toil will bring perhaps a penny.

Most for one and zilch for many.
What is the gain or glory
Toil will bring? Perhaps a penny,
But there's never enough to live on.

What is the gain or glory
My heart holds dear? The truth!
But there's never enough to live on.
That's the way it is.

My heart holds dear the truth:
The last will be first and the first will be last.
That's the way it is,
So the story goes.

   Crystal K. Miller

"Down South"

Way down south, where every thing is fun
  Most of the time, we don't have to carry a gun.

The weather is mostly fine and nice,
  It's probably because, there is rarely any ice.

Every time you see some-one, you're greeted with a smile
  The reason being, when you see them, you don't have to run for a mile.

Every time you're greeted, they always say hello!
  You stop and chat a-while, and then you have to go.

It's really very nice to live this way,
  Then you hear some-one call to you, "have a nice day."

There's folks that envy us, for living down south,
  But they, never voice this out loud, with their mouth.

   Earlene Morefield

Smiles Of Starch.... And Stone

Late in May the graduates march
Mothers gather with smiles of starch

  So your son graduates?... so does mine
  I am prepared... I'm doing fine

  Your oldest you say?.... uh, oh, my baby
  I am prepared... I'm doing, uh, maybe

  Donned in my black skirt and blouse
  no... not because of my empty house

  But because of black's elegant style
  Surely not because I'll miss his smile

  It's that black's silhouettes are so thin
  See... I am prepared to graduate Ben

Late in August, the collegiates phone
Mothers listen with smiles of stone.

   Colleen C. Fogarty

To Live

To cup my breath within my thinning hand,
My life's desire now struggling to remain
A rock against the crashing, numbing wave
Of darkness swirling quickly over me,
Helps me defy the tide, the moon, the stars
So that my breath, with fire and whirlwind force,
Pounds like a fist against mortality.

   Alvin Haimowitz

Coming Of Age

All the doors open wide.
My life is now to begin,
with such hastefulness
did my childhood end.

I know I can't go back,
but the memories will be in my heart.

Now it is time to move on and where do I start?
For I do not know what the future may hold.
All I have to guide me is my heart and the Lord above.
May he give me wings to fly like a dove.

Christie Perry

On The Altar She Laid Her Heart

To God I surrender to him I give
My burdened heart that he may heal
Full of anguish and despair it's in need of much repair
Fix it, mend it, even break the hardened places
That I may be fit to love in all cases

I told him yes and he didn't say no
I held on and he didn't let go
I gave him my trust and he filled me with his love
I thought I was alone but he gave me all of heaven up above
To him I went and cried
He took his hand and wiped the tears from my eyes
A failure to life is what I thought of me
But the apple of his eye is all he could see
I told him to forget hope, it's nothing but a dream
He assured me to keep hoping and with time he'll show
Me what it all means
With my heart I can now believe and that gives me the
courage to receive
A debt was paid I didn't realize
To be my friend is why he died

Etta M. Davis

For You

How long have you stood by me,
My eyes forced shut or comfortably closed?
I have not known you've been beside me.

Can the years pass,
Can the space ever widen.
My time, our time together has been,
Forgotten.

Through sadness, or sleeplessness,
My weary sight has returned.

I've only seen, only felt,
Those and this that I have lost.
Though now I see you beside me,
Now I can look upon you,
Myself,
And smile.

Jeffery B. Meier

Indian Summer

Warm breezes blow over my skin.
My shirt ruffles, and my hair blows over my eyes.
The ripples on the water make a tinny frog jump.
I turn to find falling leaves, and the galloping horses stir up dirt.
When the dust clears, there are you walking towards me.
In your hand is a beautiful bouquet of flowers.
The Indian summer has begun.
I drop one flower by my bare feet for mother nature
as a thank you.

Angela Wagner

Born Again

Words cannot say nor the heart convey
My feelings of love when I pray.

A new life you've given because thou art risen
The blessings continue their flow.

You've allowed me to care with others I'll share
The good news of thee in this world.

Praise God you are He who saved even me
From sin damnation and death.

My names in your book I don't have to look
Faith has assured me that way.

Your face I have seen like the impossible dream
As promised to me by your word.

My Lord God and Savior I pray my behavior
Is acceptable and pleasing to thee.

Elwood Watson

On Being Bald

A shiny pate is my fate,
My hair is very thin;
I had no voice in this choice,
Just like a lot of men.

But those of us bare, without hair,
Should not run away and hide
We still have our brains and other things,
Including a share of pride.

Yet some men sense, by some pretense,
That they should wear a rug;
Able to re-cover, they soon discover,
It has them feeling smug.

Some say it's DNA
That causes the hair to fall;
Then I'll say it here, it was Grandpa dear
Who caused me to be bald.

But I don't know why that I should cry
For being how God made me
For it is what we've done, during life's brief run,
That matters in Eternity.

Alfred R. Jennings Jr.

Sacrifice

My hand moves the pen that writes you these words.
My hand picks up the phone when you call.
Your hands hold my heart.
Your hands have the power to crush it.
My hands have the power to save it.
My hand reaches out to you,
Hoping you'll take it into yours,
And save me from this fall.
Hands grasping each other,
You pull me to stable ground.
But as you reached out to me,
Your hands dropped my heart,
And it shattered on the Earth,
Like so many shards of glass.
My hands tried to catch it, but to no avail.
You saved my life, but you killed my soul.
Now I look upon my fragmented heart,
And I realize that it was just a sacrifice,
A gambit in which our hands could unite.

Jocelyn B. Paradise

My Old Friend

My skin is pale an my bones are frail
my hearing is gone, can't remember where I belong
can't tell night from day
can't seem to find my way
times I recognize the people I see
times...my daughter...I wonder who she could be
the only ones I know are the ones from long ago
I've been here for so very long
maybe that's why my patience is gone
I've been through things this ole world don't know
times that will never be no more can't hear a lil-baby cry
can't hardly walk no more, but Lord knows I try
none of my favorite foods taste the same
times I forget an call my dead mothers name
can't no longer greet the morning dew
why am I still here? Oh how I wish I knew
guess I've done my very best, always tired can't get enough rest
I have reached 103, bet there's not many left like me
one day soon I know I want be
the angels will come an set me free, an all the life will return in me.

Angela Hulett

Untitled

A single tear rolls down my cheek
My heart is broken in two
Closing my eyes thinking back
I wish I never met you
The love I feel deep in my heart I know will never leave
So I sit here and think about us
It wasn't meant to be
All of the feelings I have for you I can't express in words
But now my minds all blank inside it's all becoming a blur
I wish you were here so I could show you the way I feel right now
I wish I could call you and tell you I love you
But I just can't figure out how.

Carrie Buel

Reflections Of A Lifetime

Deep thoughts though strange,
My life before now - little sis, dark hair,
skinny legs, blue eyes trying to learn.
Shy, fearing, loving, hopscotch with chalk.
Best friends... so many people now empty spaces
A favorite playmate is now but a tombstone;
cold, hard, just a memory.

Once a family of five but in a blink of an eye
is only three; the youngest - me.
Grown up..a mother, grandmother helping little ones.
Those who call me "nan".

Classmates move to and fro. Me? A secretary, a nurse.
A husband tall, helping, loving, laughing, joking.
A movie buff, hoping..for his own.

We are but a mist...and so on with the list..but however
and whenever it ends, it will be with a success totaling three.
What are the seasons? And what will they bring?
When it is "my time" I pray it will be spring.

Joanne Davis-Flint

Rainbows

There are Rainbows in the Sky after it Rains,
  Nobody can reach the Rainbows because they are that high.
  Nobody can reach the clouds because they are as high as the
  Rainbows.
The Lord has given - To reach Heaven because nobody can reach
  the Stars.

Allison Hannah Cardullo

On The Mountain And In The Valley

I met Him on the mountain top my mighty Lord and King,
My life was full of blessings I had no need for anything.
I had good health, my kids, my home, salvation full and free;
It seemed the enemy had no part in all my life you see.
Then God allowed the enemy to touch the dearest thing I had,
My heart was bruised and broken my countenance Oh! so sad.
I prayed; "Lord; why did you do this, when I tried to do my best?"
The heavens seemed like brass no comfort or no rest!
When I was at my lowest ebb, he spoke so gently,
"My child, to learn to really love this is how it has to be.
I'll use you if you'll bear this test and compassion I will give,
I'll direct you to help others and show them how to live."
"But is it necessary Lord to tear my heart apart?"
His answer, "if you cannot bear this suffering how can you lift a
  a broken heart?"
So, I humbly bowed before Him and said, "Your will be done."
So, into the valley I did go, my life's work had begun.
So, I met him in the valley, the lowly Nazarene,
He gently offered me his arm and said on his to lean.
So leaning hard upon his arm, though the way has been rough and long,
I found new courage, hope and peace and yes even a song!

Edith C. Tanner

Immortal Beloved

As thick as the darkness of a black night
My love is as strong as the morning light
The love which flows from the depths of my soul
Intense as to conquer time and it's toll

Your love burns me as deep as red fire
Enough to consume my whole entire
Eternal passion you swore to possess
Forever growing each time you confess

To be as one in love everlasting
Emotion relentlessly ever vasting
Affection is a mystery long unsolved
Our love is a seed that can't be resolved

Some mortals say it is mere illusion
Love like this is deception, delusion
Desire this strong is but a fable
Forsake it now before you're unable

In my heart I know these feelings are true
And this, my love, I am pledging to you
It is so and shall always be
My devoted love for all eternity.

Amanda Monroe

Regrets

I regret that night so long ago,
My mind was clouded and you had nowhere else to go.
In your arms, you held so tight,
And made love to me all through the night.
Then you got up and left, so quick and so sudden,
Leaving me with absolutely nothing.
The shame rushed through me,
What have I done?
I gave you everything, and you left in a run.
I feel so empty inside,
Why did I try to keep you near, when you don't even care?
I've grown cold inside and I'm never going to trust,
That look in your eyes or the smile on your face,
It is nothing but a charade, so phony and fake.
Never to love, Never to care,
You took me so far,
And then left me there in the arms of despair.
I have nothing to live for,
You've stolen it all in just one night.
That night so long ago filled with Regrets!

Amanda J. Butters

I Am Amazed

I am amazed that you should be the one in
my thoughts.
You, of all others that could be there.
I cannot say when it was that I first became
aware of you. Awareness came quietly, stealthily
upon me, like the rising of the sun upon the
horizon; bringing with it the beauty and
grandeur that comes with morning light.
I see you now as I never have before.
I am aware.

Quietly within myself this awareness lies.
And I . . . I am almost afraid, lest you see
it in my eyes.
Deborah Louise Chambers

Growing Up

For faithful peace on earth, I give up my old sight,
My vain vision of things to search science and light
Not to make once again this fault any longer
To see or treat people as enemy or stranger.
Now I stop wondering whether America
Is your native land or Asia, Africa...
I do not truly know if those unlike names
Are not a result, a try to invent games
to kill boring time and get living better,
But I can certify that you are my brother.
It is not important the color of your race
Nothing really confirms, specially in this case,
That what we have been taught is not fictitious right.
Thus, black could be yellow as red could be white,
But there is not a doubt that we, men, are equal.
I can not consider any resigned ritual
Condemning this great world to go worse and worse,
But I accept as true that we possess the force
To alter our lives by our mutual power
To love, to suffer and help one another.
Carlo Auguste

Spring's Rising Dynasty

O, my sweet, sweet spring share your heavenly tapestry.
My very essence, glides with glee, in hopeful rendezvous;
Away from terrestrial winters; away from disharmony;
Melting, among th' kaleidoscopic angels, in symphony;
Away from earth's winter of seasonal, polar interview.
Awake flower souls, from winter's bleak residue!

Iridescent angel wings, ripple delicately, with harmonious hues;
Fluttering across silvery sweeps of moonlit musical nights;
Touching earth, with wands of kisses, of sunlit prismatic dew;
Creating halos of rainbow spheres, bidding winter adieu.
Farewell! Ye wintry demon of cajoling blizzard of appetites!
Witness the budding notes of eternal life ignite!

My spirit pirouettes, with the feathery breezes, above the seas;
Across the spans of time within time, in phantom's airy flight;
Dancing to the songwind's whispers; singing the soul's melodies;
Embracing, the honeydew dawn of the irisated, cascading rhapsodies;
Spring's rising dynasty ascends beyond earth's paltry height.
Gone, the twilight canopy, of winter's insipid spite!
Bunny Swift

"A True And Beautiful Dream"

To sit by the sea
neath the clear blue sky
with those great waves rolling again
how high they climb - you would
think that each time, they would
cover the spot you were in.

You look all around, and
you hear not a sound. But a
very faint sea gull's cry!
Such beautiful things with
their great white wings -
And oh how graceful they fly
you feel a slight breeze you'd think
wouldn't stir a leaf from the smallest tree
yet it blows through you hair without worry or care,
and you'd think's can this possibly be:
Oh I'll go back again to that beautiful dream.
and again let it happen to me- A dream for you too.
So magnificently true! A dream by a beautiful sea.
Frances McGarvie

Smoldering Judas

Smoldering in Hell, creosote-crusted Judas,
Neck stretched in eternal pain,
Fused from searching upward
Through eons of sin,
Begging cleansing tears from Him.

With tear-flaked eyes
You professed to adore Christ,
You'd seen him raise the dead,
Knew he'd scourged the temple
And stilled the waves.

You wanted those soldiers,
Drunk on wine and curses,
Muscle-bound to Rome,
To quake under that power
Your Kiss was meant to trigger.

Ah, but wither-brittled Judas
With burned-over eyes and tears of flame,
You didn't understand His choice of power:
The permeating warmth of the resurrection
Flowed through your searing-cold kiss.
Bessie Soderborg Clark

Two Of A Kind

Two of a kind, that's me and you,
never alone, never feeling blue.
When we're together, spark's always fly,
Our other thoughts tend to die.

We're as happy as we can be,
I have you, and you have me.
No bad thoughts flow through our mind,
Unfortunately we were so blind.

Then something strange happened one day,
I turned, and you went away.
You made me feel like I was dead,
Just so you could go to another girls bed.

But that's okay, one day you'll regret,
If you don't believe me, let's make a bet.
She won't put up with your foolish ways,
I'll be sitting here just counting the Days.

Well, everything is over between you and I
We never talked or even said goodbye.
We have grown far apart
Sometimes I wonder why did it even start.
Christy Maitland

On Aging

No yearling I,
No callow offspring of a New Age coupling,

No reservoir of unfulfilled dreams
Or reflection of what might have been.

No product of the streets or controlled substance,
But a seasoned traveller on a path littered with husks of forgotten tribes.

Determined that my legacy will be valued with the trophies of those
Who blessed their existence by honest labor and moral certitude.

I must not tread lightly
But leave footprints hard to fill,
Lest my heirs murmur
'He would have, should have, could have,
If he'd only had the will.'

Frederick W. Koch

Remembering Ginger

Alone in a double bed I sleep,
No cat to share my slumbers deep.

Illness took my cat away,
I lost him one cold March day.

I grieve for the cat I loved so much,
A cat I sometimes was afraid to touch.

I never loved him the less for this,
I knew it was only his response to previous abuse.

One Christmas Day he became mine,
He came to my door as a starving feline.

So distended was his stomach from hunger,
I thought he was an expectant mother.

When guests came, under the bed he'd hide,
In time, his fear of people did subside.

A lap cat he never got to be,
But always displayed aloof dignity.

A mountain lion of diminutive size—
God's beautiful work he exemplified.

I gave him a home, but he gave insight to me,
On how precious living creatures can be.

Ellen Sandstedt

Storm Revelations

The rain falls
No, it pours
Wind blows, shrieks past
The trees shake and quiver at natures fury
There is nothing outside save the rain
Lighting strikes and lights up the entire room
Looking out the window I see
The bright flash and dark gloom that follows
Harder and harder the rain comes
Releasing its anger on all things below
And still I sit and watch out my window
Thunder roars, deafening to my ears
Yet I cannot leave my station
More wind, more rain, more thunder, more lightning
And still I do not leave
One final crack, one last burst of light
Splinters that sheltering glass
And all is quiet once more

Carrie Lewis

Night And The Killer

Axe came down W H A M was all a dull thud...
No knowledge no worry as dogs could see, so knife,
so bone, so elimination was evident, the bushes stood by,
trees were stenciled onto night...
Why was it to be? Only his boots answered.
Where was this body to go? His dog stared at him.
Ants on the summer dirt floor. Red with tiny black ants.
Outside: The world.
A deranged boy stood by the door. Staring. How a son should.
How should one?
It was all simple: Death, son, Death. Understand?
Life and —, see? the boy left, dog stayed with the Master...
What Law? This man RAPES my wife, he got his Law
country lawyers all cheat and smell like c*m, Your Honor
society don't FIX it, jus' keeps the sun from fartin'...
Court Ajourned. He saw the body, cut up, dog sniffing
at it, dropped his knife and axe, but the boy, but the boy...
the dirt soaked red, ants, dog whining MERCY, MERCY, the moon.

Jeremy Johnson

Baby I Don't Have Time!!!

Mom can you give me a hug?
No, not now, I'm working out to Richard Simmon's new video.

Mom I'm lonely, I need to talk!!
Honey, where is Shanika or Suzie Q?
They are your friends and know
how to talk to you.

Mom I'm going out tonight, do you mind?
No baby! have a great time.

Mom guess what? today is my birthday, I'm sixteen years old.
That's good baby, here's a few bucks go enjoy yourself.
I'm meeting Fefe' for java. Mom do you have a minute?

No honey! but what is it?

I have a new mother and she is always around for me.
She listens when I need to talk. She holds me when I need a hug.
She picks me up when I'm down.
She is never too busy for me, she loves me.

Oh!! who is the person??

Her name is Coco, Cocaine to be exact.
She lives on the streets with me, She'll never leave me.
She's my Best Friend, my Lover and now she's my mother.

Thanks Mom, P.S. I'm pregnant!!!!!

April Thomas

I Love You Happily Ever After

Though time has marked lines on your face,
no other love can take your place.

The air your life depends upon is smokey.
There is concrete all over, now.
They have dug into your spine and buried you.
They have fought and scarred your face.
They think you're old
they think you'll die.

But time and destruction will never take away
the feelings and memories I have of you.

Yes, no matter how old or wrinkled,
there's one thing you can bet:

I loved you Mother Earth,
once upon a time.

Carolyn Griffin

In God Have I Put My Trust

In God have I put my trust,
No one else is righteous or just,
Only my Saviour could ever be,
So totally sufficient for me.

No one else could ever know
How I feel when I'm so low,
A tender verse I begin to recite,
Makes it feel like He is right by my side.

I could never fear, (since I believe)
What man could ever do to me,
My life they may threaten to take,
Big deal! Just a little sooner I would see His face.

Praise I will continue to give,
No matter how long He lets me live.
Whether tomorrow or some other day,
I'll praise His name with no delay.

Even as Job did say for him it was a must,
Even if He takes my life, in Him I'll continue to trust,
My Savior and King and Lord to be,
None is so precious as Jesus to me.

George Guinn

"Scandalous"

A friend depends upon a truthful friend;
Not a fake person and not a brick wall.
You made me out to be the biggest story of them all.
The trust I had, gone away.
You murdered my heart, you smothered my soul;
Now all that's left are red hot coals.
My mind is still hazy of a friendship gone bad,
You told everybody you were glad;
So I bowed my head and walked away sad!
Now that you've taken all of my trust,
You trampled on my heart and stomped me to dust.
What on earth did I ever do, to be mistreated, by a friend like you?
To let you know, you hurt me so,
I refuse to be nice, to be outcast twice!
But if ever a friend could love someone so,
I guess that would be me,
That's why it hurts so.

Jenny McDaniel

Untitled

With my love I offer you a corner of my life,
Not a lonely corner forgotten by the sands of time,
Nor the spotlight where everything will revolve about you,
But - a part that will blend with all you've given me,
Fitting into the intricate pattern of my life,
A pattern that shall give beauty and harmony to two lives,
Two lives joined firmly - yet not permanently bonded,
For with my love I can do no more than ask you to stay,
Because no true bonds are present to hold you - only my
   hope that you will accept what I want to offer you.

Deborah R. Walsh

The Picture

Just a picture to remember you by
no touch, no kiss, no one to hold me when I cry
I can't hear you say things that make me
   feel good
I can't hold you tightly, I wish that I could
You can't say "I Love You" so I can hear
You can say "I miss you my sweet, sweet dear"
I can't hold you closely or by my side
I feel so lonely, so empty inside.

Jaimy Dalley

To Sin Is To Live

We hide in the shadows of our terrible ways
Not forgiving ourselves for our sins
But if we don't no one else will
To do wrong is a part of life
To sin is to live
And live we will, forever, on and on
For to die is being only a memory
To live is to be acknowledged
To sin is to live
We accept who we are and live how we want
Together we shall make it
As one we will grow weak
Fading further from life, I am a memory
To sin is to live.

Brandon P. Steinberg

In My Heart

In my heart there's a place
Not in a chamber or behind a closed door
But a place as far and wide as the eye can see
And as deep as the ocean floor and more

It's a place where time sometimes takes a break
To enjoy the pass
A place where you and I go
Where no one else can enter
For this place belongs to you and I
In my heart.....

Charles Christopher

Gifts Without Cost

This man has given me so much
   not of gifts from a store
      but from a place many can't touch
A place from within his heart
   and from all the things he has to give
      his heart is a rare piece of art
Without his inspiration an guidance
   I simply wouldn't be the person I am today
This man has created a part of me that's inside
   that only he can take credit for
To have never of had him in my life
   that part of me would be empty
      always searching for something more
To give this man
   what he's given me, I could never
But I know in my heart
   a part of me will love him forever.

Ann Marie Racicot

One Beautiful Autumn Night

One beautiful autumn night in the month of November, it shall be one night I'll always remember. I met this one kind and wonderful young lady that somehow I knew someday we would go steady. The time we met seemed to pass by so very fast, but I knew our relationship would somehow last. On that same wonderful clear autumn night, everytime I glanced at her, she looked out of sight. We laughed, danced, and we talked. She seemed like a living doll as we walked, and as that beautiful autumn night came to an ending, I was so thankful that I had met this beautiful lady, that all my love is all I would be sending.

Daniel Telles

Daddy's Girl

I once was daddy's Girl,
Now I have no one to turn to.
When we would be together it was,
like a different world, where we were on top.
He would help me out with my problems
Now I can't trust anyone.
When I go to sleep I wish on a
Star that I could spend one last time with him.
When I walk down the streets I see
Kids with their dad's, and I have no one.
Now I know it wouldn't hurt
to be daddy's girl.
One last time.
Amy Estrada

Never Let Me Go

So many reasons to tell you goodbye,
Now the tears are continuously flooding each of my eyes
I thought we'd be together, I thought we'd still be in love,
But sometimes just saying "it" wasn't a bit of enough
I tried so very hard to make you understand
That I would never let you go if you would have held onto my hand
But you left me alone crying I sat as you just walked away,
You found a new love with someone else and had nothing left to say

On the day you'd leave I knew it was coming soon,
I felt I wouldn't care but now my heart sits in ruins
You called me the night before you left and told me that you missed me
Then the memories came back of the day you first kissed me
You were the first love that my heart would come to know,
I only wish your heart would have never let me go.
Alex Chavez

The Secret Of The Stream

The stream flowed silently on
Oblivious of turmoil
Creating a peaceful calm
Captivating the atmosphere
Around the house beyond, with the willow trees near.

The stream flowed silently on
Past the little bridge
Keeping its secret locked up somewhere within
Asking nothing but the freedom it possessed
Having nothing to protest.

The stream flowed silently on
With hardly a ripple
As if the breathtaking beauty of the landscape
And the greater goal of distance
Was its sole purpose for existence.

The stream flowed silently on
With an awareness
Of its omnipotence
For without is abundant flow
A whole army of wildlife and vegetation could not grow.
Julia Fox Miller

Untitled

If you only knew how I feel inside.
Or even the thoughts that go through my mind.
To be a creator and destroyer of life,
both done in vain, confusion and sorrow.
I too should have been destroyed at that instant.
But instead condemned to live a life of guilt and pain.
Morally wrong, never to forget.
Nor forgive myself for my wrong doings.
Who am I to destroy a life that has not yet begun?
Or to condemn another for my sins?
Elsa L. Vazquez

Venice

A group of men jabbering at the table,
Oblivious to the activity around.
The passersbys' ignorance of the cobblestone world below their feet.
A blind Venetian sits not making a sound.

In the afternoon there comes a smell
From thick, steamy, red - a shattered vegetable.
Seeming to have no substance, but friendly with sustenance.
Engines stop and stomachs ache to be filled.

A soft tongue flitters into the next person's ear.
The Rosary Girl throws back her mop of night.
Silver chatters and Excess is an untranslatable word.
The day winds down with gripe.

The streets around here are not quite the same.
They are friendly with sustenance and also with substance; unless
  there is no boat.
A city drenched in history much more wet than the street.
As cappuccino is sipped and pasta thrives here unbound.

The chests heave softly and a snowball hangs in the dark
Dripping light on the mosaic cafe walls.
Nothing is heard but the occasional bay of a hound.
A blind Venetian sits not making a sound.
Brian Keith Sommers

Nature's Wild Flowers Beauty

Each year wild flowers grow at my door
October here blue Clusters lovely as any
Fall their beauty radiant more and more,
Butter flies yellow, orange black white are many.
Bumble Bees, with fuzzy colors of yellow black and white.

Food for them wings fluttering spread wide as eagles
Small ones beauty of fall, each year a lovely sight.
Birds bees children at play the barking of Beagles.
Eva Forrest Williams

These Trips To The Zoo

My father's enthusiasm is that
    of a four-year-old
    innocent, joyful, complete

At the Zoo yesterday, he responded
    to each loud, pleading whistle of a
    white-faced whistling duck
    the way a small child would
His mouth a big O
    his eyebrows high, surprised
    his eyes filled with
      this-alone-is-the-only-second-of-my-life joy

My father has brain cancer
    Is that what it takes?

It is more than enough, for now
    these trips to the Zoo

It is so much more than many ever get
Jana K. Shaker

Pain

What is pain?
Pain is a word.
But the very existence
of a wound
is an entire universe
We have not yet discovered.
Each wound has a different personality.
Each personality has a different universe...
Christan Mullee

Genes 'N Things

Mother was a collector unsurpassed,
Of birds porcelain and figurines glass.

L'ladro, Hummel, Woolworth and garage sale,
Arrived as dependably as junk mail.

She vowed her life they enhanced with beauty,
But daily dusting befell my duty.

Year in and year out, numbers multiplied.
Nothing could stop her, believed me, I tried.

This fetish of hers was driving me wild,
Aside the fact, I'm her clumsiest child.

Accidents did happen and some I broke,
She'd scream in grief like I'd made the cat croak.

One thing for certain, I knew as a fact,
In my own house they'd be not one knick-knack.

I know she'll declare in a voice of doom,
My home has the charm of an empty tomb.

That woman's obsession is proof to me;
Nature blows some acorns far from the tree.

Anne A. Carpenter

The New Order

Into the night, there's an vision.
Of camelots paradise,
Such as Heaven.
For an Prince's dream,
While the travelers of many nations.
Is anxious to listen to Arthur's proclamation.
As distance rivals and Evil Villans.
Believe in living by the sword.
While they've tried to bring Arthur's and Camelots damnation.
Because of the new orders meaning.
(For) Truth, Justice, Pride and Freedom.
Listen to the call of Honor and serenity.
Even from the sorcerer named Merlind
Beyond the travelers trials and corrections.
Where the roundtable sets.
It does not have an invitation.
You must earn and deserve.
Believe the King Arthur's words and Camelots meaning.
As for the Roundtable, in the travelers vision
There is an empty space to be filled in King Arthur's Kingdom.

Daniel Polson

The Price Of Reason - Wonders Asunder

Perhaps in the thousand tiny miles
of capillaried legs and arms
of old and winey men
swatting flies while
waiting for those sent by mothers
to get the daily papers from
the local "newsagency" -
an excuse of a title was that —
Perhaps in those dim and airless
but bright - lit sunny huts
were first omens of what lay ahead.

Or so it was thought.

Perhaps it was in the overhead conversations
of women islanded by men and places
talking of those lost, of others being borne
while bodies became bloated with child-bearing
   and caring.

Here the early signs of what could be
Became blurred with what was for most.
And so the thought - is this too, for me?

Anna O. Soter

Morning

I stood in St. Paul's graveyard in the haze
Of early morning. And I saw the dates
Of men deprived their rightful span of days
Because the eighteenth century held hates.

Then through the thinning haze there came the roar
Of twentieth century warplanes overhead.
Their lustful engines crying out that more
Must join the swelling ranks of war torn dead.

Thus we progress from one age to another
In laws of science and the useful arts.
And find that man can quicker kill his brother
With rockets than he could with feathered darts.

When will we learn there is a God above
Who sent his son to teach mankind to love.

Howard M. Fitch

Virtues Of Life's Virtues

Each day passes as though scared by the powers of evil and good. Light and dark appear and disappear in the mirrors of life. As human thoughts and emotions reflect through a soul, time has stopped to watch the colors thrown from the body and mind. The moral of human virtues floats on our mind and heart such as silk upon a sword, delicate, yet easily cut and hurt. Enough of it may blind our body of the lies, but too little, and we see the unwanted truth. Wisdom brings out the truth and hides the lies beneath. Loyalty proves faithful and foolish of the heart. Power gives strength, but does not discipline it. Compassion gives wings to our soul, but can't hide the sorrow that it feeds from. Friendship can only go so far, then it becomes a fork in your path. But always have faith, for to believe in self is to see the reality in one's dreams. Yet, when our soul is blind, we are not able to soar above the dream. It takes flight and we hold on with our hopes and desires, for to have stones in our pockets is to have never known life.

David Lin

They

I get so tired from day to day
Of going things because "they" say.
"They" know it all, there's not a doubt;
But how did "they" get so much clout?

Just who are "they" that "they" should run
My life from dawn 'til setting sun?
And why should everything in sight
Be based on what "they" say is right?

Since who "they" are remains unknown,
A lack of faith in them has grown;
For many times they're proven wrong,
And still I follow right along.

If you don't mind, please it's no sin,
It's not a crime or just a whim;
From here on out, I'll live my way
And not do things because "they" say!

Jan Marie Newby

Journals A Gift Of The Heart

    Images of time are recorded here, traces of love, inklings
of joy, spatters of sorrow, and painful tears
    Bits and pieces of self revealed in every world, carefully,
such that the meanings could be heard
    Painted pictures of many heart sung stories, cling to the
pages, sculptured beautifully by the hands of God to last
throughout the ages
    Each occurrence is dear, sweet to the heart, it should be
preserved in good care, every single part
    So that those who cast their wondering eyes upon the script
of life; lovingly carved here, shall cherish the possession of
the sands of time running through fingers and dwelling in a book
of years

Darla Hays

Waiting

I sit in a straight-back chair watching the shadows
of my pain fall on yellow paper;
I choose to sit alone.
The roses you brought to me last spring
still sit upon the mantle crisp and brown.
They have become like the chill wind
that beats like hell's fury against my locked door.
    It must be winter in the mountains about now
    ...and you haven't yet come.
I keep a warm blaze going in the fireplace and watch for you
through the dusty window that looks upon the horizon
you disappeared into time and time ago.
    Just lately I've been thinking about taking the love-tokens down
    and crushing their petals into the fire.
    Those are the times I can't escape the doubt that clouds my mind.
    And I wonder if you will return at all.
    But crushing them crushes all hope
    and my love for you won't let me.
So in the twilight I sit, listening to the sound of emptiness
echo through my vacant heart

Candy Anderson

"22 Christian Lane"

I fight to make these tugs at my heart
Of no real consequence
As I drive past the places where we lived.

One of the barns has been taken down
And patches of its brown floor peek through the snow spots.

Corn-stalk skeletons are all that guard
What remains of someone else's garden.

The house is dark, yet smoke curls around the chimney,
Down the eaves, and past that stair-case window
Where I hung the macrame lion.

This foolish car has stopped
As if it were a horse with free-rein.

I am losing this fight.

On the back of a horse
I look into this yard
And both snow and years are melting.

For a moment our apple tree's blossoms
Are gathering moonlight

Until I realize
The apple tree is gone.

Bob Woloss

Men Of War

They sit and tell stories of the war,
Of rival conquests and the near escape
Of bars at night, the lusted after whore,
The stories of the girls whom they might rape,
The echoes of the battles and the cries,
The people whom they murdered with their hands,
They saved themselves with desperate, feeble lies,
From the Lord's and questioner's demands,
So they smoke and breathe the foul wrought air,
And dance and jingle with their sweet wine,
And dream of maidens comely and fair,
By whom they choose to epitomize the divine,
And so these men sit softly in their tents,
And dream that night of wars that were not real,
Into their minds was placed a fatal dent,
The day they killed for reason of their fear,
We say we've grown and live anew,
These men, we say, are of the past,
But soon we must with pain admit the truth,
Our hearts these men inhabit to the last.

Florence Neymotin

The Human Race

Cause she was born woman and not otherwise, when crossing the rivers
of the Oriental lands...All the boys are tied, so they don't collapse.
And the little girl, while playing her games fell into the waters...
Is there someone who cares?

Cause she was born woman, her parents arranged a marriage where love
didn't have any place...And it doesn't matter when the man departs
and the flames of fire are covering her...
I wonder what happens if she departs first?

Cause she was born woman in the U.S.A.
Forgetting the years and all the hard work, while studying careers
just like a man...She is underpaid, doesn't get a car,
also, has to pay for her cellular...

On top of this all for keeping her job, all kind of harassment...
What did she study for?

I hope that in the future, closer every day, we admit the greatness
of being humane...And from the day on no one looks at others
seeking excuses or differences...

Probably in the day that another discoverer came from far away
all color and variety of women and men introduce themselves as
"the representatives of the human race."

Elaine L. Mayol

House Of Refuge

There is a place of beauty, far and beyond;
Of tranquility and peace that lingers on.
Secret caves and shallow passes,
Gentle waves and life in masses.

Memories both sweet and painful.
Of love and life, of death and sorrow.
We came to think, to feel, to listen;
To calm and sooth the tears that glistened.

(Back then) at low tide, we braved the caves.
(Back then) at high, we challenged the waves.
Now, I think of you as each wave crashes.
And here is where I'll spread your ashes.

Dawn Lynn Cline

Untitled

I wish I could write of lover's dreams
Of winged horses and castles in the air
Of knights in shining armor
And beautiful maidens fair.

'Tis a time I envision and dream very well
A time during which, wish I had lived to tell

When men rode a breast fiery horses about the countryside
With weapons to do battle in treacherous weather they'd ride

To fight against armies in faraway lands
Or save the life of their lady love's hand

A time when love meant passion
A thrust of emotions, not a gentle caress
When love was a flame not an ember
Romance would begin with a lustful "yes"

When the pain of love was truly part of it all
But this pain and passion made even great men fall.

Of the conquering hero with sword and shield
Making his way home and before her he kneels

She leans down to him with a gentle kiss on her lips
She bestows on his forehead, what romance is this!

Isabel Guerra

Tomorrowlost

Lethargy mothers the mind of the lad,
Offering thoughts of delay;
Spoken by sloth, understood by the idle,
Tomorrow is so far away.

Tedium sits and distills in the soul,
Onward, enduring the days;
Martyr to passionate visions of glory
Oblivion opts to allay.
Rancor resides as a husk on the heart,
Recalling the hours decayed;
Obsolete truths that tomorrow once promised,
Withered to yesterday.

Erik Fetler

My Mother

There is a woman in my life
Oh! But she is not my wife
She is with me in happiness and in strife
That special woman is my mother

She brought me into this world, so cruel and cold
With the warmth of her love she has made me bold
With all of my troubles she fills her mind
No one can replace her for she is one of a kind

Even though I do not always tell her
How very much for her I care
I hope by this I am making it clear
She is number one and she is so dear

Adedayo Doherty

1937

Soaring high through midnite skies,
Piercing through thick morning mists;
Flying farther and farther into the West,
In a squat mono plane
With just one companion,
Fashioned for greatness,
Armed only with courage,
The God and this goddess
Ended their quest.

Barbara Lorimer

Sounds Of The Sea

Dolphins flip in the moon light.
Oh how their tails glitter so bright!
The waves roll high in the purple pinkish sky,
And the sand is now cold.
And the day is getting old.
Why I'm sitting here on the beach alone,
Is because I'm listening to the tone,
Of the waves crashing high.
Little droplets jump into the sky,
It's getting dark as you can see,
But I'm so glad it is me,
Sitting here listening to the queer
Sounds of the sea.

Alyson Van Deusen

You Lied

Us as a movie, each memory a frame.
Oh, isn't it a pity, far gone from shame.
Don't dare look at me, we know who's to blame.

You'll miss the rest, not patient to wait.
It was you who left, left me in this very state.
Soon you will have awaken, but it will be too late.

Only if you would taken a little more time to think,
Don't worry about it now, oh have another drink.
Our chain has been broken, broken at each link.

With no longer any connection, I discard my shackle.
No longer any kind words, all I hear is his cackle.
Your love truly evil, straight from the Imps satchel.

So drawn and tired, what's left is barely a corpse.
Raping my love, your heart so coarse.
But blood for blood without remorse.

Everything and my all, at least I tried.
Trusting every word you said, to bad for you, (pause)
you lied.

John Brom

"Christmas Is For Children"

See a child face wide eyed and full of wonder,
Oh! Santa will you bring me everything
I ask for, a doll, a bike, roller blades,
Trains, a doll house,
Oh! So many more toys I can't remember
Oh! Santa I won't sleep tonight cause
I can't wait till tomorrow, then it will
be christmas morning
Did you bring me everything I ask for
I really was good all year, well pretty
good almost all the time - but santa
I will be extra good next year promise -
Oh! Santa you did bring me everything
I ask for -
Thank you santa, thank you!
See the wonder of Christmas in a
child's face -
After all Christmas is for children

Jean Micozzi

As Two Become One

As the chapters in your life are written
Remember to let God be your main subject;
So as the story of your life together
can proudly be retold for generations to come
as two become one.

Antoinette Nevill

"Old Folks"

The "Old folks" live just down the street;
old wrinkled faces, their clothes not always neat.
Kept in a "Home," they can't get out, even to roam!
closed doors they face, because they can't keep pace!
Day in, day out, life goes on the outside;
but for these "Old folks", time just "Goes by."
Told when to get up, when to eat;
When to take a shower, even when to go to sleep!
Can't something be done for these "Old Folks?"
For, they too, were once on the outside, full of dreams and hopes,
All had families jobs, a nice house, things to do.
Life was enjoyable, fun, no one ever got blue!
But now, for these "Old folks", life has slowed;
Nothing to do now, they've been put on "Hold."
A cheerful word, a friendly smile, just a minute of your time;
Would brighten their world, bring a moment of peace to their minds!
So the next time you drive by a "Home" where the "Old folks" are
Stop by, spread some "Sunshine," it will go very, very far.

Christine E. Bell

Orange Footprints

They walk out among leaves brushing faint love
on seeds laying for a dove moving seas.
Tasting the stories of a blinded wind, missing the pain
of footsteps, taking the night and hiding it,
they float above it all, raging, praising.
A fossil tipped orange swaying on a tree, boiling in the sun,
gives the scent of hunger to the inner depths of a beggars mouth.
Dry and crunchy, the blisters harmony, a juice of what is.
To look behind the wall growing with every footprint
captures the tongue in wisdom's pocket and
stitches its wounds with the orange skin.
Bitter wine swallowed to clean, bridges past to sea,
where footsteps can be seen.
A tail to follow a light haunted sky, a wraith of the self
explored story, a living walk of intangible doubt.

Damien Aherne

When The Sun Struts

Routinely I pass these barren hills clothed in grey
on stage before the faded purple mountains beyond.
A place the "Grey" buffalo roamed and plains Indians summered.
But tonight the models parade a different sight,
designer fashion from falling sun.

Heat waves dance to the chorus of insect hymns
while sweet fragrances of sage and Russian olive linger.
The white parched clay swells and becomes slippery
when heaven cries rain.

Now emerge like great white elephants
richly jeweled in their mineral raiment,
outlined with wild flowers in a Monet palette,
and laced with soft green sage and rabbit brush,
revealing the significance of a community's existence.

In the crash of a setting sun
this fashion show dawned with sunset.

Diana Mayland

My Friend

My friend is a dreamer,
She can turn into anything she wants to.
She runs wild in the school halls like a white water river.
Everyone knows her or has met her before.
She gets ideas at the speed of light,
She is very, very bright.
Her name is Imagination, and we stick together,
And I never, ever, leave home without her.

Janet Nahrstedt

Exile

Oh, I wish I were back in my own home
On the shore of the rolling sea,
Where the sea gulls scream at the creamy foam,
And the winds are as wild as me.

How I long for the storm and the west wind,
The breaker's pounding roar,
Lapping of calms in the morning,
Seaweed along the shore.

Give me the wind's wild pranking
Among the high sand dunes,
Where the sea snipe's tiny foot-prints
Weave for me magic runes.

Give to me my freedom
In the place I long to be,
Where the sand flower grows blue in the sunshine
And the winds are as wild as me.

Francis B. Johnson

Heroes

Heroes are not only found
    on war-torn hills in distant town?
Or sterile buildings throughout the land
    where life comes and goes in one brief span
But at a desk at dawn, or dusk or noon
    with pen in hand they compose a tune
Or write a line to laugh about
    and lift the Spirit completely out
Of some grey pit of mediocrity
    into a realm that's wildly free
And here it moves in such a way
    to a far-off place, a forgotten day
And then turns homeward to paint the heart
    with the ink from the words that heroes start.

Frances Willard

I'll Love You To The Very End

I'll love you to the very end
On your love I always depend
Your love is my reason for being
Through your love I've found life's meaning

I'll love you to the very end
Your love is there to heal and mend
Your love gets me through each day
Knowing at night we'll share in your loving way

I'll love you to the very end
Your heat your soul you freely lend
Without your love what would I do
Where would I be, what or who?

I'll love you to the very end
Your there for me and you always defend
Weather right or wrong it might be
Your love is always what I feel and see

I'll love you to the very end
On that you can always depend
Your love is what I need and no more
Your Love is what I want, need and live for

Ankica Ristic

Memories Of The Heart

Memories filtering through the long past years,
Remembrances of big brown eyes and crystal tears,
Of gentle laughter, sweet and full of glee,
Of youth, coltish, innocent, spirit ever free.
Keeping pace with life, ever moving, full of fire,
Filled with courage and dreams that inspire,
This youth, my child, growing, time measured in years.
Safely tucked away, yet held forever near,
These are the memories in a mother's heart!

Carol Poel

Searching For "Once"

Once I caught a butterfly and put it in a jar.
Once I used a box and pretended to drive a car.
Once I played with dolls and I became their mother.
Once I made a boat and the captain was my brother.
Once I built a fort and attacked the enemy ground.
Once I got real dizzy when I began to spin around.
Once the hardest thing was to learn to tie my shoe.
Once, like an airplane, I thought I could fly too.
Once I stayed outside until the light turned dark.
Once I spent my summer days playing in the park.
Once I believed the story about the Easter Bunny.
Once I thought a dollar meant a lot of money.
Once I couldn't cross the street without a helping hand.
Once I liked to build my castles in the sand.
Once I thought hard homework meant adding three and three.
Once I climbed a ladder and reached the top of a tree.
Once my little short legs couldn't reach the floor.
Once my little short arms couldn't open the door.
But now I'm searching to find just one four leaf clover,
So that I can make a wish and hope to live "once" over!

Debby Huntzinger

Imperfect Reflections

Think of me as a brilliant star,
once wished upon, now viewed afar.
Remember me as fire in winter, warm and snug,
but fleeting ever.
Picture me as time well spent,
used nonetheless by goodness meant.
I leave you now and shed a tear;
love you but can't escape my fear.
And so I must go on and not look back,
keep memories fond if not intact.

Good-bye for now, good-bye for then,
good-bye for always trusted friend - and lover too.
But as I go remember this:
I lived a life each time we kissed,
fulfilled by your unselfish grace.

I see things for you I cannot reach,
your worth is much, I cannot teach...
my soul ever to reflect your perfect admiration.

Gwain Addison Davis

Flowers Are Blooming

Flowers are blooming on a nice spring day.
Pretty one's, skinny ones, tall ones some we eat, some we grow,
some are in tall, tall trees, some are under ground,
some are in your home, some are in your garden.
Flower are everywhere, some are sweet, some are bitter,
some are as beautiful as snow.
Flowers are blooming on a nice spring day.

Indigo Bishop

The True Servant

One who does what God says do,
One who goes where God says go,
One who gives as God says how,
One who help save other lives.
A man called by God is truly wise,
He's willing to live, just to die.
To be with God in the Heavenly skies.
Going through the struggle, both day and night
Knowing that one day it will all be right.
Realizing the end is soon to come,
Just to hear the Savior say my dear servant well done!!!
You ran the race so faithful and true,
Now come to the place I've prepared for you.
Your struggle is over; no more heartaches and pain,
You are with me now; never to hurt again.
I love you Dear Servant; Dear Servant so true
My Servant, My Servant;
God has truly blessed you.

Helen J. Winbush

Drinking, Thinking

Drinking, thinking you are a cool
Only knowing you're the fool

Find yourself drunk again
Throwing up with a friend

Jump in your car and drive away
Just like you would any other day

Friend says faster, only to disaster
Tires screaming and you're not dreaming

Headlights blinding
Your mind is unwinding

Darkness

You are sick and its not a hangover
The story of your life has just been turned over

Your lungs fill with blood and your face is a mess
Heart beats faint and your body is torn from its flesh

You know you'll never do it again
Because for you my friend, this is the end

Jim Norton

Marry Me

My love is not dependent upon time or circumstance,
only the body we are

And whether we live in a time of abundance and warmth
or a period of scarcity and wrath,
it is you I wish to live with

My only companion
to be with always
our souls reminiscing over the sights of our experience
and the senses we had shared.

Whatever doubts either of us may have had
about our souls living life alone, without love—

I promise you
that as the body we become grows old,
a body built upon faith and love,
the richness of life, the fulfillment of our essence
shall bring us happiness

If you will commit yourself to me
I will this day pledge to you
my heart, my soul, and my actions

Will you marry me

John David Potts

The Stars Never Lie

Up in the sky I look to see
Only the stars staring back at me.
They twinkle and shine so radiant and bright
Not only with beauty, but with light.

Those long defied stars of Shakespeare's time
Only Romeo and Juliet would know of their crime.
And in "Gone With the Wind" with Scarlett and Rhett
Was it really the stars through which they met?

"It's in your stars," philosophers say
Your fate, your destiny, the shape of your day.
So innocent they seem as they twinkle on high
But the wise man knows, the stars never lie.

Erin Marr

Living In The Country

What a wonderful feeling to start each day,
Open the windows and smell the fresh cut hay,
To see the sun rising over the hill,
Knowing that there'll be a field to till,
Hearing the cows as they "moo" their good morning,
It's also time for milking - their way of warning,
What a beautiful way to raise our little ones,
Like mothers, like daughters, like fathers, like sons.
May they realize the beauty of country living,
And grow up to appreciate the hard work and giving,
And when the sun goes down at night,
All my animals are in and out of sight,
I look at my loved ones, thank God for each day,
And hope tomorrow I can help someone some way,
Country living is just the greatest thing,
Where else in the world could you live like a king?

Diane DeYoung

How Can This Be

The lights on your life were suddenly turned off.
Or could it be that on your life the lights are turned on.
A difference of perspective, a change I perceive.
I wonder and ask how can this be?

Darkness has encompassed you from all around,
Or should I say, the darkness within has been profound.
Grasp with confusion, not knowing what to believe
I ask myself again, how can this be?

Living your life without Christ, will leave your life exposed,
A spiritual union on the verge, of being decomposed.
With painful outburst and anguish cries, I turn my head toward the sky
Seeking answers and asking why? And how! Can this be?

No purpose realized for your life, no motivation, just inward strife
Evading direction, causing depression, and unfulfilled plans,
Has lead to your digression, and is now where your life stands
I ask God when? And how can........this Be?

Gregory L. Proctor

Perceptions

Their food is adequate but not up to our standards,
Or did we forget that culturally ours is not necessarily grander.
Their clothing is colorful or may be considered drab,
But by our standards and not their own cultural class.
Their music is interesting and their dances are amusing,
But so we ours to them-if among us and musing.

They speak their own strange language among themselves,
And that should be denied or create a cultural hell.
We are not biased if we hold their customs in disdain,
For they should rethink their perceptions or struggle in vain.
Cultural and ethnic perceptions can be selfishly cruel,
Yet we in a mixed nation of immigrants should be above such drool.

Anthony Torres

The Afterlife

The afterlife, oh how the sweet sound beckons
Or presents a burning sensation to the bloody wound
Death itself fears not life,
It is the ally of its effort to create a new world
And when death finds you and crossed your path
May you feel the presence of God all grace throughout your bones
And fool, if your guilty soul shall find Hell,
Fool, envy not your Devil, who has no figure,
A forgotten angel is not your celebrity
And may you feel the blade of a razor
Cutting to sever all left that is good
Your corpse burning but only a stick in Hell's fires
You are among many who defy the noble practition of life
And you, faithful one, will find the golden kingdom
And be washed and cured of only minor ailments
Thus, God's presence is infinite always
And blessed those who can follow the righteous path
But wicked so shall find the pain of bloody death
And Greed shall prevail once again
As you repent your soul, but fail for Eternity

Chad Gilchrist

Traffic

Traffic, traffic as far as I can see,
Or so it seems to be. Two times a day,
To and from work, money to earn for me.
Locked in a moving prison each way.
The noise, the smell, even with the windows up tight.
The darter going in and out each lane,
Risking fenders, bodies, as well he might.
The loneliness, boredom, when will it end?
But miserable as it is this way,
I do have time to use all just for me.
I play my tapes and think my thoughts each day,
And improve my attitude importantly.
And what if sometime even I might well say,
Give me traffic again, just for a day.

Deas A. Coburn

Our Golden Days

Do I speak of golden rod along the roadside?
Or the beautiful golden sunflowers that abide?
No, I'm telling about our life full of golden days.
My husband and I met on a blind date-ah-golden rays.
Two years later we were married wrapped in golden bliss.
Our farm home with golden memories and kiss.
The birth of our son, a blessed gift to us was sent.
Six years later, our first daughter's birth a golden present
Sixteen months later our last baby girl was born.
Golden heavenly gifts these three our home did adorn.
Farming when drought came was far from a golden time.
My teaching career had many golden moments sublime.
Master degrees for our children were golden events.
Their weddings were truly treasured golden moments
Then came our six grand children - little golden spirits.
From two to twenty, they fill our days with golden bits.
Next year we celebrate our fiftieth golden year.
If we live into 2000, more gold will appear.

Edla Josephine Freeland

Do You Have Time?

Do you have time to get on your knees?
Or time to say thank you and please?
Are you always taking things for granted?
Believing you'll get all that you've wanted.

Do you have time, a wee bit too give?
Or time for a kind word and truly live.
Is there time to say a little prayer?
Also the time to tell God, you care.

Is there time for small-things that count?
It isn't how much or how big they'll amount.
Are you day dreaming? It's time to awaken,
Forgive and forget and never be forsaken.

Do you have time to appreciate the day?
Or the night as it slowly drifts away?
Do you have time for our God up above?
Only one way, with gratification of love.

Artha Bellamy

"A Woman's Lamentations"

Will God create a man again
Or will a woman, He Begin
To form again a human race
For planets in our Outer Space.

What will God, this time devise
To make a woman twice as wise
No aches, no pains, for her to chafe
No troubles, dangers, she'll feel safe

Now God, we're thinking of a perfect place
Where does Man enter in this race
Your World, Dear God, cannot increase
That's the human point, to say the least.

So we'd best, I guess, let God alone
To rule us humans from His Throne
We'll keep Gods rules for a perfect wife
And go to Him for Eternal Life.

Helen Scott - A.P.

Should I?

Should I write a poem, and try to win?
Or would it be too scary, if they could see in;
Through the windows of my soul and see nothing but sin?

But there is so much more to view and see,
Tiny droplets of dew, so crystal and misty,
Each enclosing, cocooning little bits of me.

Through the windows come views of colors, so bright.
Each entangled in minute interactions with others in the light.
But which one is me; which one gives birth to my sight?

Oh web of living, oh spider of day,
Hanging so fragile on corners of light you lay,
Silently weaving a melody for play.

But a melody, with no words, not one
A song unfinished, a life undone,
Hoping and dreaming that the lyrics will come.

I think I will write a poem and try to win.
Words with hope and promise and a smile and a grin.
Throw open the windows and say; please come in.

But winning was never the key.
It was the poem that opened the door to me.

Debbie Hester

Beloved

Take me to be with thee; my undying.
O're hither doth I need be?
My undying beloved.
Stay with me; thy doings never depart my undying
Lead me with thy marvelous heart,
My undying beloved.
A sheathless sword am I, my undying
Without your omni supply
My undying beloved.
Sweeten my lips with a silkened touch, my undying.
Abase my tongue with pureness, much,
My undying beloved
Imprint my brow against thy chest a-brew, my undying.
Join with me from hither to,
My undying beloved
In your love my 3 parts entwine, my undying.
You saved me; I'm now forever thine my beloved,
Undying beloved.
Soothe my Mind...

Andrea I. Sellers

Untitled

Why do I seek what I should not?
O'soul, of my souls!
Why does the lust always surface?
O'soul, of my souls!
Why do I search, and search and search?
What am I seeking?
O'soul of my souls!
Where? Oh where? Art thou?
O'soul of my soul's!
My heart cries, for I seem to be lost and wanting!
O'soul of my soul's!
Am I too weak or shallow to know
What love is?
O'soul of my soul's!

Douglas Leon

Just Imagine

Just imagine that there were no Earth,
other planets or Mars.
Not even the sun, moon or stars.
Just imagine that there were no more
plants or trees.
Not even the birds, animals or bees.
Just imagine that there were no seasons at all.
Nor spring, summer, winter or fall.
Just imagine that there were no sky to see.
Nor even people like you and me.
Just imagine there's no one to love or care.
Because no one would be there.
Just imagine that there were no day or night.
Nor sun or moon to gives us light.
Just imagine that this is real.
That time stood perfectly still.
Just imagine that there's nothing in space.
Not even a planet for the human race.
Just Imagine.

Etta Mae Buckner

The Human Rage

Violent eruption, so full of destruction no
production or construction
negative positives spew from impulsive explosions
they only cause lethal emotional erosion
keep your composure
through abrupt exposure
or a life will come to assuddenclosure

Jennifer Lynn Hassell

Untitled

Life is a woven road of responsibilities
of children's needs
husband's wishes
friend's requests
career goals
Pulling the strands of my weary fibers
To and fro
Back and forth
Until the soul feels out of shape
Ready for a break
To sit and feel the flow of life regain its balance.
  Joan Smith

Stillborn

We ask ourselves and we wonder why
Our baby boy was destined to die.
Huddled for months he was safe within,
Barred from this cruel world of heartache and sin.

Yes, we all would have loved him so.
Yes, we'll miss him, but he'll never know.
And although we never saw his face,
There's a mental picture we'll never erase.

He'll always be smiling, he'll never cry.
He'll always be perfect in our unseeing eye.
And when we see the baby clothes stored in the shelves
We'll try to forget and not pity ourselves.

We secretly ask, "Did God make a mistake?"
But we know though the Lord gives, the Lord also takes.
For some unknown reason it was part of His plan.
We trust He did best, though we don't understand.

And though others may forget through the passing of years
His memory will haunt us with tender tears.
Though his days were finished before they'd begun,
We'll never forget, he was still our son.
  Jean M. Martin

Grandpa

Our daughter calls him grandpa
Our boy, he calls him pop-pa
A better'n six foot bag of bones
In our eyes, above the rest, he stands alone.

He likes to drive old Dodge window vans.
He is far from wealthy, nor a very strong man.
But he is strong at heart and rich in love.
And believes very strong in the man above.

He loves to play blue grass, old guitar in his lap
And always let the Bible be his roadmap.

He knows there will come a day.
When that roadmap shows him the way
Directly into the loving arms of his dear departed wife
I am very proud and fortunate to know such a man in my life.
  Gary L. Clark

Mother

This word brings a smile to my face
Reminds me of things like learning to tie a shoe lace
Your the woman who gave me life
You let me grow with you during your trouble and strife
Although we're not the best of friends, I feel that your love is here
I just wish it was some way I could grasp it and bring it near
I want to be your daughter, and your friend
Remember Mommy my love will continue to be strong
for you even until the end.
  Chelsea Thompson

Fruit Of The Spirit (Galatians 5:22,23)

By abiding in the true vine of CHRIST
Our lives will begin to bear fruit
The love, the joy, and the peace of GOD
Will sprout out as we yield to the TRUTH.

The long suffering that JESUS CHRIST endured
Is a part of the fruit we must bear
But CHRIST has caused us to overcome
So saints, we have nothing to fear.

The gentleness, goodness, and faith of GOD
Should show forth in our lives so bright
To bring this world full of darkness and hate
Into HIS marvelous light.

Denying ourselves should be our goal
For meekness and temperance to grow
For the sprouting of these blessed fruit depends
On how much of ourselves we let go.

The fruit of the SPIRIT comes from hearing GOD's WORD
And by doing the things that we should
So when people begin to eat of our tree
They will taste and see that the LORD is good.
  Diane C. Stratton

Letter To My Son

I have so much I want to say to you son,
Our lives will never be the same.
The worst is over,
All the heartache and tears.

You've grown up
All I can never re-claim those years.

But, I have so much I want to say to you son.
There are so many memories of a little boy,
I held on my lap to have his first haircut.
When you lost your first tooth.

You have grown up so fast, you are not my little boy anymore.

But I have so much I want to say to you son
I love you

And our lives will never be the same.
  Elnora S. Davis

Hope Lift Thine Eyes

When life's dark storm clouds blot the sun's fair face,
Our thoughts wing backward through the skies of time,
To glimpse some haunting carefree childhood place,
Amidst the green and gold of years sublime.

Conflicting moods harass the mind and heart,
As gazing, our unseeing eyes review,
A long lost land that's in a world apart,
Interred and gone with all that was once new.

A longing to relive invades the soul,
That kills and withers us with discontent,
But time, alas, we never will control,
For life's a span that soon is spent.

Hope, lift thine eyes to that which lies ahead,
For pathways of the past you'll never tread.
  Jerrold Jack Rotwein

Wombman Of God

When cutemates privately nourished their still unripened buds,
Our touches were glazed with bashful blushes
   and dewed with dampness of primeval mistrust.
It was a time yet innocent of blossomings, soft crevices,
   or frilly garments undone.

Yet this pre-pubescent epiphany unfurled a creature professed
   so rich in grace,
Secretly shrouded in sackcloth brown, and white-wimpled in the essence
   of starchness bright,
With waist cinctured in beads of size almost obscene,
Her feet shod in feminized boot-wear, polished black,
   always spotless - oh, so clean,
Sans sculptured torso, sans breasts, sans nylon-tinted legs,
Save the etched shadow upon her upper lip, also sans hair.
She allowed a demeanor face, so barren of sensuous vice,
Framed in eyebrows unplucked, never blushed with silken powder so fair,
And creased with lips by color or gloss unspoiled.
What I espied that day was so fascinatingly unfemale though real,
Scarce could I be but enamored with someone so macho,
   as this holy wombman of God.
   Henry P. Mucha

Summer's Castle

Today my mind has taken me
out building castles by the sea
my guess the year was fifty-three
and there we were, just you and me.

Sitting by the oceanside,
building castles, full of pride.
Intricate windows, complex doors,
a moat dug around where the water, roars.

What, oh what a memorable day.
Then in rushed the tide and washed them away.
Grains of sand swept out to sea,
maybe washing ashore on a Florida Key.

Picture the castles, you and me.
Lasting an eternity.
It's now I've returned to the shore
with hopes of building just once more
a castle so high and heavenly
it may end up in Galilee!
I know it'll surface some place or another,
a castle built for the love of my brother!
   Carol A. Adamus

Marie

A more spiritual woman, you'll never find.
Overflowing measure of humanity kind,
Her life was filled, full of energy and love.
With patience and courage, the long road was paved,
A new experience, awaiting, to be with her Lord.

The eyes of her soul, could see the end near.
The spirit spoke quietly, three nights, she was told,
Of an life-threatening illness, taking it's hold.
A malady to make white, our mortal to appear,
But the living among the dead, she would be in our tears.

The healer inside said to teach her and hold.
The wisdom our own body has, to know,
That which we need for health and well being.
But being so sick, there just wasn't the time,
Until God stopped her heart, this dear friend of mine.

A divine favor, with which God blessed,
Until He planned their unity.
He filled her time, with thoughts of serenity.
The collective mind, it holds the key.
My dear friend Marie, does live on, inside of me.
   Bette Horn

The Hypothesis

The morphological solution to our dual
Paradox cannot be figured out by environmental
Hypotheses. I am not a scientist,
More of a rock-tosser, and always I am regarding
Someone else's face in the looking mask, the wading pool.
The selective permeability of fourteen glances from
One him makes a million hymns in my
Notepad—my pen burns and leaves
Traceable tracks like an unsmog
Checked helicopter. See, the ink,
My vein's lifeblood, is running out of
My skin's blankets! A renewal! The skin of my root's
Shoots is blooming again—I have a new reason to
Navigate, to sing. With one or one
Half or two million thousand zillion
Words I prove Sartre, I prove Camus
Wrong—beneath the bark of my
Seemingly meaningless Aspen,
There are cells breathing. This
Gives me reason to grow on.
   Heather Faye Woods

"Just Us"

   It's been several years since my birth, and my
parents were pleased when I first set foot on this earth.
Expectations were high and the thought of failure brought
tears to my eye. No matter what, they always made a fuss.
But that was just between us.

   As the years went by, my father passed, and I
continued to watch my mother bust her ass!! She struggled to
do the best for me, and to make me understand education is
the key. I did my best to conquer success, but when I failed
the test, and everything was a bust. I finally realized no one
was there but just us.

   Now I have children of my own and guidance must
be shown. I must be the able to teach them which path to choose,
never allowing them to snooze. Life is too important to them
and to me, and that our love for one another is the only
guarantee. Now I understand why I must make a fuss, because
nothing else matters except JUST US.
   Deron Johnson

Homebound

A single thought pounds in her mind; home
Passing the same gray building;
walking the abhorrently familiar worn path under the same encroaching,
dreary sky; wearing the same confining, revealing drab uniform;
she feels his presence
Sight is unnecessary to confirm her suspicions
"Hey, Baby" growls the dirty, sneering laborer, predictably
She quickly scurries by, like one dodging a human collision,
head held like a shamed child, sagging low
Embracingly, the rounded door swings open,
like the wide arms of one known long ago
Safe at last.

The same charred, matted weeds underfoot
A suited man emerges from a Mercedes;
the whistles and degrading words are heard
Feeling the sting, she freezes
What now?
Shock overcomes her; she is unprepared.
   Christine Myers-Anderson

Class Reunion

Gather leaves of maple, oak or run
Past years through rain or sun,
From 1945, now fifty years,
As Nagasaki mushroomed with our fears,
And only five boys stayed as grads,
The program worn and typed, no fads,
By girls like Doris, Ann, Yvonne,
Faces photo-dim and shades are drawn.

We gather class reunion and remember,
Winters, springtime, the best September.
Do you remember then? Who broke the glass?
Who was that? The one who skipped the class?
The books of learning all now yellow turned
Are there upon the shelf of life we learned.

Charles Knoll

Love

Kindness is always welcome
Peace, you always have to have some.

But what else is missing from your heart?
It's love, and that's the most important part.

Love is kindness, peace and friends
Love is something that never ends.

Love is the dove in the sky
Love is something you cannot buy.

Love is something you cannot live without
Love is something you cannot doubt.

Love is worth more than gold
Love is something that can't grow old.

I hope I've made my point over here
That love is something very dear.

Carmen Lam

Poet's Call

You have the talent to write and you must.
Pull out your old stuff and shake off the dust.
Nothing is good enough "What should I do?"
Enter the contest and prove that's not true!
I'll write of the Seasons, Emotions and God.
Perhaps I'll do mozart or just something odd?
Quick! Silence the negative voice you're hearing,
Respond to the poet's call, what are you fearing?
Blessed with a gift you've kept hidden inside,
Gone are the years you let swiftly go by
Share it with others while yet there's still time,
In you lies the power to make it all rhyme. Janet Ross

Janet Marie Ross

In Memoriam: Amelia Earhart And Fred Noonan Red Dots

She wears one of those red dots, what does she do that for?
Please, ask me.
I heard they wear that because of their religion...
Please, don't assume.
Is that the same religion where they worship cows?
Please get to know me....and my beliefs.
I heard they have arranged marriages...
Please, don't judge me.
They wear those saris and their belly flops around, how crazy?
Have you been to the beach lately?
I don't know why they're here, they are so different from us...
as you are different from us...
Red dots, cows, curry...too weird for me.
Ignorance, Prejudice, Racism...too weird for me.

Bess John

On Hold

While I'm waiting for whom I'm calling,
Please don't play music so appalling

I know you think it's what I want to hear,
I'd really rather rest my ear.

It's not my taste, I can not buy it,
I'd really rather hear some quiet

If I like classic, you like rock
If I dig jazz, you play me Bach

Blues and Rhythm, Western and Country,
I'm afraid to me, it's all effrontery

If I want tunes, I want to choose them,
I have musical sensitivities, don't abuse them

I'm trapped here in a musical cul-de-sac,
"Never mind, I'll call him back!"

James M. Rapp

Untitled

Dark room, black room
Peace holder and friend
Will there ever be a day when this insanity will end?
Homeless, jobless
Can you spare a dime?
Unfortunately there are those who do not have the time.
Murder, killing
Shot you in the head
Like one big game you're out to play before you end up dead.
Violence, abuse
Why hit a little kid?
Does it give you pleasure thinking back on what you did?
Drinking, driving
Won't give up the keys
It's always the same story until your wrapped around that tree.
A wish, a dream
Is that all it will ever be?
However long it takes, I will not rest until our world is free.

Heather Shaski

"Satan's Tools"

When I came to this evil valley, I was just fourteen and started poking heroin in the alley.
Then grass, I did smoke, seemed life was just a joke.
Then came the cheap thrills of acid and pills, Oh like placid-dills.
In the valley and in the hills, oh those damn cheap thrills.
When I think about it I get the chills.
And lets not forget all the liquor, that made my life even sicker.
Damn this evil valley and its hills.
I've seen many a boy and girl take the ride and cheap thrills.
Now they're dead and gone, and don't have to worry about
   paying their bills.
Now I'm thirty-five and hooked on crank, it's all run me over
   with the power of a tank.
All I have is me and this valley and damned hills to thank.
Two years of being followed, it's made me real empty and hollow.
And what's worst is the curse, because the people that follow me
   are just as empty and hollow.
I can't say who's sicker, me or the ones that
follow, I can hardly even swallow.
Damn this evil valley and its hills, that give me the creeps and the chills.
They can put me in jail, knowing I can't throw bail.
And if I ever got out, I'd still be an alky and addict you see.
Which is a crying shame, cause that's not really me.
Damn this evil valley and its people and their hills,
Damn them cheap thrills and these damn chills.

David S. Horn

Power Without Pay

If I wanted power without pay by the hour, my jobs might include:
Polishing Earth's winter sun till it shone,
White washing the moon as clean as a bone.
Hanging diamond stars on hooks for a night's sky;
Ringing out clouds until they were fluffy and dry.
Plugging in lightning in time for the chase,
Adjusting the volume of thunder's bass.
Stashing my savings in Swiss river banks;
Heaping mountain bottoms with rainbow's thanks.
Stirring the sea with hurricane's blows;
Then restoring rhythm with ebbs and flows.
Closing the drains on crystal ponds and lakes;
Showing runaway streams my hiding place.
I'd work for one life without any pay, If I had such
   power for just one day.
   Jennifer Lopez

The Fortress

Innocent victim of true individuality,
Poster child for undeserving attack,
An outcast to those who have sight
but cannot see.
No more fight left within,
No one left to turn to, Cling to,
You slip inside yourself;
So begins construction of the fortress.
Stone-by-Stone, Wall-by-Wall,
Build it up until not even you know where it ends.
SAFE, HIDDEN, ALONE, NUMB.
Within the engulfing darkness of this tomb,
The light which is your core, Your soul,
begins to dim in the restricting hollowness
That is your pain.
Yet under the continuous whisper of love,
The fortress will crumble to nothing.
Your soul soars on angels' wings,
You live in the movement of dancers,
You are YOU once again.
   Daniel Christensen

Circus On The Rainbow

The lightning pops its cork as the thunder starts
Pounding a celebration, a silk lining in every cloud,
And turning up the perfect sound more than once
A herd of stampeding elephants silver shakes the ground.
Bubbles and balloons floating the telegraph with
Cooler spells that spin a hot string and
Other spidery things lighter than the
Soft refrain the golden birds are gallantly
Singing in warm serenades to the mystic evening.
A flourish of trumpets! In the electric parade-
A little lower than the honking horns,
Wizards in the same theater flickering
To short-wave, the lights go out! Across the ceiling
The signals of the traffic candle a magic lantern
Yellow, red, and green - each one, swinging, on
The trapeze an empty space inside
The ringmaster's brain - a hush falling over
The crowd, each acrobat balancing awhile
On the highwire in between, each one shimmering
On the street corner in the puddles of rain.
   Charles Morris

Flag Draped Coffin

The emotions in the cemetery were mixed. Mixed with pride, grief, sadness, and sympathy. The mother cried, the father sniffed, but he was proud of his once military son.

The guns fired and the horns blew, as the soldiers saluted the flag draped coffin. A man, a brave man, shot in the line of duty saving his country. That man was now under our symbol of freedom.

As they lowered the coffin with many tears, kind words were said about the brave man in the flag draped coffin.

A man, to some that had no name, but was remembered by his unselfish act. A young man, too young to die, was being buried in that flag draped coffin.
   Jamie D. Van Buskirk

Messengers Of Death

Under cover of darkness the messengers hum,
Programmed, unwavering in their course,
Far above the world below,
Answering the call of some aged drum.

All because of power or oil,
All because of greed or land,
All because of something else,
All to acquire ill-gotten spoil.

Through the centuries what the gain?
The bony hand that wields the scythe,
The skeletal arm that reaps all men,
Countless souls in the earth were lain.

And they who think their will be done,
And they who rule with iron first,
And they who send men to their death,
Too soon, they too, will all be gone.

And yet the messengers' rockets burn,
Programmed, unwavering in their course,
Far above the world below,
When will they ever, ever learn?
   Harold L. Sampson

Loneliness

Loneliness fills my heart like rain fills a deep
Puddle on a deserted dirt road.
Both seem to be untraveled, and heartache grows like
weeds on the side of the path.
Both are unexplored, for people are afraid of what
they may find at the end of their Journey.
Both are alone at night as darkness consumes
the whole being, as if it is nothing....
Perhaps darkness is right.
The only difference is a dirt road has light cast upon
it by some weary traveler whose footsteps slowly go
through the puddle of my heart.
   Barbe Faulkner

"Stacie"

Laughter catch a frown;
   Rainbows turn it upside down.

Moonlight plays on water bright;
   Raindrops scatter pale moonlight.

Sunshine cast its shadows deep;
   Darkness makes them indiscreet.

Children playing in the sun;
   Soon become adults of none.

Childhood dreams of happily ever after;
   Make may for reality, you will master.
   Eleanor Julian

Shadows

The shadows seem to stretch all ways;
Pulling colors of grey and black.
They seem to bend, dance and play,
Like looking for their own way back.

Some blend and swirl and play on light,
Some hide like some hideous beast.
Others stay completely out of sight,
While some stretch from west to east.

Shadows, shadows, figures of the night.
The echoes of the breathing walls,
They give some terror and others a fright,
Like a long empty half lit hall.

Gary Alton Waltemire

Mr. Macho Man

Mr. Macho Man, stay with me,
Put on your funny face, come dance with me.

Put your clown out suit on, mess up your hair,
Love me tonight, in the cool night air.

Mr. Macho Man, run away with me,
We can dream any dream you want to see.

Put your big shoes on, hold me real tight,
We'll jump into new worlds, and enjoy our flight.

Mr. Macho Man, please honk your horn,
Within you, a new man will be born.

Oh, Mr. Macho Man, where is your pie?
Have you forgotten how to laugh and cry?

Mr, Macho Man, where did you go?
Don't leave me here all alone.

...Mr. Macho Man!...Stay with me,
Put on your funny face, Mr. Macho Man, ...Wait!....

Mr. Macho man, Mr. Macho Man!
Please dance with me....

Jody D. Thomas

"Every Time"

Every time I see a quarter moon, I think of you again
Quiet nights and dancing eyes, I miss your touch my friend
The night air brings a gentle breeze to my soul alone once more
Once again I've had it all, just to close the door

Every time I see a quarter moon, I remember other days
When you tried so hard to comfort me and lead me through the haze
I drew you close and pushed away, like an angry sea
Left you swimming all alone, while I took care of me

Every time I see a quarter moon, way up in the sky
I remember how you'd look at me, as you asked the question why
Why do I need to run and hide from those that love me true
I could never say what's in my heart, I ran from me... not you

Every time I see a quarter moon, every season, every year
I'll wonder if you see it too, on a night so crisp and clear
Will you think of me, just one more time and know I remember too
Every time I see a quarter moon, I'll always think of you...

Austin B. Dunham

Life

The water in the creek
Quietly rustles by the rocks,
Many a deer stop to nourish their dry throats,
While thirsty young geese come by the flocks.

Birds with their new young,
Chirp while perched upon the branches,
Singing new songs,
While their young try new dances.

A soft breeze blows into the air,
Witnessing the new life springing everywhere.
The breeze smiles as it sees
The comical expression in the new born mare.

The weeping willow branches dip into the creek
And flowers open up their sleepy eyes.
Apple blossoms blossom everywhere,
While the last of Winter packs up and says "Good-bye!"

The gloom of Winter
Is cut by the knife
Of spring's resurrection,
And of its Life.

Arifa S. Chaudhry

Gray

Sometimes I think it would be best if the only color was gray,
Racism and its ugliness would have no place to stay,
White hoods of ignorance would never have been worn,
Slavery and supremacist groups would never have been born.

If the only color we had was gray,
Gangs would have no colors to display,
Little girls in pink wouldn't be separated by little boys in blue
Black wouldn't be the color of mourning
White the color of something new.

In a world of gray nobody would have been sold by the color of their skin,
A silver medal meaning your not good quite enough to win
This would be a world where Emmett Till would live today
If the only color we had was gray.

Christine Bathke

Search With In

Condoning only my centered self;
Raging out I step upon my own grave.
It's width I shan't not look upon;
For it's depths I can not escape;
Fallen; I grasped for foundation
Where beneath my feet there is structure
To build upon a different form of solidation;
Embracing all that I had hated;
Narrow, becomes my width;
Shallow, becomes my depth;
Forever, does not seem as long now.

Angela Charlton

Untitled

I smiled as she cried
She glanced as I sighed
Saying goodbye to life
Such an admirable wife
Life's irony I confide

Secure in her sorrow
His life I could borrow
Hoping for the same end
Surrounded by the love and friend
Maybe I'll find tomorrow

David B. Newshutz

Storm On The Boulevard

Lightning skies optically shredding my eyes
Raining swells of blood from my storming skies.
A hurricane of lying daggers and dying tears
The eye of the storm, she feeds off my solemn fears.
Twisting every secure emotion in a tornado of shared hate
Greenish gray clouds lurk over the horizon, taunting my blissful fate.
Cold winds pierce my frigid soul; solidarity brands me
Destined to walk alone through timeless mists, an ignorantly
　　chosen journey.
The echo of silent thunder blares through the blinding eternal night
Pale apparitions drift through a fog of glistening tears, a
　　pandemonious sight
My soul is drenched with heartless neglect and lies
Baffling mists disperse, ghostly blurs seen through my slowing cries.
In the midst of the greying streets, a lone soul
A single tear, fallen on a velvet petal of red; solitude takes it's toll.

For I've been shown; a single Rose does not seem as alone
as a thousand broken hearts wandering the Boulevard of undreamt dreams
　　Adam L. Reck

Good Morning Duet

A dear little lady, living alone, who was
really quite shy, and not very well known,
Stepped from her door as the dawn filled the sky,
When trees with cathedrals of branches arched high.
Rays from the sun streaming gold in between
Stippled the shadows and gilded the green,
She lifted her head and a melody rang,
Sweet toned and clear, as she fervently sang.

But listen! A mockingbird trilling each note
Exactly the same as the ones from her throat,
Accompanied her in a perfect duet
In this moment of a sharing shell never forget!

They sang as the sun rose, each soul to convey
The joy in their hearts as they welcomed the day.
Then, soaring and singing, the mocking bird veered
Into dawns golden brilliance and fast disappeared

No one could know, because nobody heard
This happy duet to attest to her word,
But the Master of Music conducting above
Was aware they were praising the work of his love.
　　Edith P. Dill

Eddies And Currents

The quiet tears that fall upon the still pond
Reflect the depth of feelings that go on an don
Like ripples that reach out to those with whom we bond
With tears that float like petals on the still pond.

The eddies and the currents take us where they will;
We part, and meet, and part again for good or ill.
We long to rest in waters that are deep and still,
As eddies of life's current take us where they will.

And there are those with tears that drown beneath the brine,
While others float upon their surface fair and fine.
We can but make the most of what, in life, we find,
As some will thrive while others drown within the mind.

And there are those who learn a slower pace to go,
To search within and claim their fears for weal or woe.
They work to scrub their spirits clean of dirt, and lo,
The mirror sees the radiance, if they but know!
　　Choela Leslie Arnold

Lady Bird

By the Texas roads where the bluebonnets grow,
　Reflecting the blue of the sky,
See the scattered patches that suddenly show
　In the early spring — and sigh.

In the blooming fields where the primroses blow
　When the April wind is high,
See the waving pinks saying hello
　To the traveler passing by.

On the river banks where the people go
　When the light is getting shy,
See Lady Bird in the evening glow
　And the blooms that beautify.
　　Helen Burton

Nature's Magical Moments

What do we see in the bright shining Sea?
　Reflections of beauty for you and for me.
What do we see when we rise at the dawn
　On a cold Winter morn looking out on the lawn?
'Tis a beautiful blanket of crystal white Snow
　With fresh little tracks, where did those Bunnies go?
As we gaze up the Valley at the dazzling Sun
　We're reminded of Jack Frost with his paintings all done.
While he rests and prepares for his next busy shift
　His fine etchings we treasure, oh my what a gift!
And what do we see after Winter is o'er?
　Mother Nature's achievements right at our back door.
Blooming buds on the Tulips, sprouting Leaves on the Trees
　Coaxing Spring to return with its' sweet balmy breeze.
Then what do we see on a hot Summer day?
　Farmers gathering Hay and the children at play.
What do we see on a gorgeous Fall morn?
　Magnificent hues......Thank God we were born
To enjoy God's creation, an original art
　We count all our blessings of which we're a part!
　　Betty Ann MacPhetridge

Saint Of Charity St. Francis Of Assisi

Saint Francis of Assisi, tell me, where is the consolations.
Saint Francis of Assisi, Saint of Charity, comfort me,
Saint Francis of Assisi, when I speak of my griefs,
Saint Francis of Assisi, grant me your strength,
Saint Francis of Assisi, you did had in your painfulness hands
　the stigma of Jesus Christ
Saint Francis of Assisi, love grant you strength,
Saint Francis of Assisi, you did pray for peace, and
Saint Francis of Assisi, and by fate you conquer by it
Saint Francis of Assisi, you knew how to forsake pride,
Saint Francis of Assisi, you did love beauty in Natures hide,
Saint Francis of Assisi, you did had Mercy and Pity for the poor
Saint Francis of Assisi, you did not use your swords in cruelties
Saint Francis of Assisi, you found peace from all strifes at need!
Saint Francis of Assisi, gentle, noble, and thrill with joy, it is
　your infinite.
Saint Francis of Assisi, your free will, was a dream, of light noblemen,
Saint Francis of Assisi, your love greatly for the passion of Jesus
　Christ, and because of this,
Saint Francis of Assisi, you did find blessed beyond by merit of your miseries.
　　Dolores Maria Bolivar-Brauet

A Petrarchan Sonnet on the Castration of Animals

A boar, if neutered as a piglet, men
  Rename a barrow, but, if gelt in full
  Maturity, a stag; a proven bull
Becomes an ox, a calf a steer; a hen-
avoiding cock's a capon; stallions, when
  Emasculated, will as geldings pull
Their wagons patiently; rams, cut for wool,
Are wethers unaggressive in the glen.

The strong bull of the mountain - now resigned
  To never mate the grazing heifers left
    In nearby meadows - joins beneath the yoke
His once pugnacious rival. Redefined
  As oxen teamed for plowing, they - bereft
    Of testicles - shall help some struggling folk.

    Gary Lewis Brancae

"Is He Is Or Is He Ain't"

Can you measure a man to determine his worth -
like a butcher selling meat by the pound?
Would you start at the top, or tape up from the
ground, or measure his inches around?
Do you question his weight - is he fast or slow - is he clever, corny, or quaint?
Whatever his size, is he stupid or wise -
does he have any "Get-up-and-go?"
Whether skinny or fat, a dove or a rat - is he lacking in this way or that?
Is he at all superstitious? If at all I might be a trifle suspicious.
Can he be more than a shell of a man?
These may be silly questions, perhaps -
well, it would hardly be fair - to judge by his color - or hair.
Does he sit on the fence in the proverbial sense -
lie fallow - or take a firm stand?
In life, you see - the real question will be - in a pinch -
does he have any SAND???

    Alvin J. Kuppenbender

Florida Spring

Clear brown waters, scarcely moving,
Ripple from the darkling woods.
Fishlets frisk in their chilly nursery pool.
But quietly, all are waiting -
As spring holds back her verdant touch.

There is another, too, who waits, perhaps close by
Where sleeps the silent shining gator?
Beyond that fallen Oak wrapped in vines?
Perhaps beneath yon palm, so limp and brown?

Or is he snuggled - snoozing -
In some delightful bed of ooze?
His bulging eye fast closed
His mighty tail laid cozy by the bank
Unseen in his winter coat of leaves
He waits the gentle nudge of spring to call him forth

Passers by, furred or sweatered,
Hasten softly past his lair
Lest this be the day
He hears spring's clarion call
And lurches out to look for lunch

    Carol T. Kessler

A Railman's Hymn

Ride the rails, proud engineer and go slowly around that curve.
Ride those silver rails that stretch to the heavenly skies.
Through the clouds to somewhere between the stars.
Rails that ties this heart to yours.
Build up steam as you make that early morning run.
To climb that final steep grade.
So, you can be ready when reaching that roundhouse in the sky.
Give us a cheery nod and a whistle goodbye.
And so, when I hear a whistle at night.
Seeming to call me from across the plains, behind the distant trees.
I will think of my beloved engineer.
Riding those silver rails somewhere between the stars.
In Memory of Frank Bowar

    William Bowar

Music

Many times I hear your glorious voice
Resound with true majestic melody;
Of all great arts, you are my supreme choice,
So inspire me with your philosophy.

Your existence may be carefully traced
To the days when human life first began,
And your enchanting melodies were placed
To delight and intrigue the soul of man.

Then you are the servant of those long dead,
And you are the master of those living;
Through you, holy messages may be said,
Oh, Music, instrument of God's giving.

May you be my divine inspiration,
And my harmonious consolation.

    Helene Marnchianes

A Sonnet To An Alcoholic

At the end, the beginning sways as if hung, a criminal
resting on the table like Rappuccini's daughter,
small self forgotten, not known or minimal.
How can you change or I when we're set in mortar?
Tall buildings don't deteriorate, they fall or crumble,
disappear into the four thousands years that got us here
because time makes it known what you do, think and mumble,
lets reversal protect you centered in its sphere,
the tiny bubble circle called home and breath, the shelter.
It's iridescence floating, somewhere old,
in the bottle, a genie wish going Helter Skelter,
visions speaking clearly, redundantly, but always told.
Stories only have so many themes
and glass jars contain few dreams.

    Gretta L. Jacobs

Ephemeral

The morning rays stretched across the city.
Rising, growing, ready for a new day.
The sun reached through my window to comfort me,
Somehow knowing I could not stay.

I felt his warmth embrace me gently.
Softly, slowly, he held my trembling hand.
He touched my heart and encouraged me.
His sturdy arms gave me the strength to stand.

I stood there in his brilliance weeping.
Dreaming, wishing, for a chance to make it right.
He felt my sadness and dried away my tears,
Just before a cloud hid him from my sight.

    Camina Stevenson

Nearing The Millennium

The only way to be is most f**kingly filled with feelings.
Risking nothing, but that core of isolation, that stomach tightness
Which gnaws at guts and renders wonder hopeless.

Are we great enough, so expansive
to take the pain of forced fittings straining,
to release pins that have held so long, and rusted at that?

Will we weather thwarted wonder's greed,
rendering moments of peak realization and
aggressively taking and demanding more,

Until splitting screeches, and wrenching sounds of desperate
affirmation tell us to
Touch beyond the pale of what is now?

Can we let go of all that is to begin again as new,
and then, alight, as the butterfly in the moment,
so nakedly and so softly...
on a twig?

Jeanne Louise Rossman

The Bunch Went To Lunch

On the autobahn at one hundred ten
Roads that stretch by glens of arnicas
Are possessed by treads that cling talon-like
Holding the road with adhesiveness.
In the coach sodas are swigged
Like swoosh shots in a ball game.
Fat men smoke cigars and impress each other
With how conservative they are of their bred rights.
To leave no delusions of their inclusions
They secure the windows and condition the air
To fifty-nine degrees. They talk in low utterances
Of how intense the grip of winter will be
And conclude tapping away their cigar ashes,
An eastern use-colossal with days of rain
Upon a ming, perhaps a marl.
A man carrying the world in his pocket
Will find refuge in his igloo.

Gerald Rogero

She Is Me...

Tears pass slowly; rain drizzles on the window
Sadness overcomes the heart that once loved.
Heavy, burdened breathing
A sigh of unrest - defeated in the face of love.
Passion unleashed once long ago,
The feeling of belonging diminished by cries of pain.
Hurt, so vast and gripping, smothering the soul
Until breathing is almost impossible.
Does the pain ever subside for her?
Does the heartache lessen?
Will she be free to put down the wall
And feel the love again or will the pain make her afraid?
Will she ever belong to anyone except herself?
Will passion ever reunite her with life and
Bring smiles of contentment and laughter to her soul?
Dare she try to love again?

She deserves the love that is all around her.
Laughter and warmth radiates from her...
She is all she is... and she is me.

Cynde Pletz

The Raisin

A seed
Safely sealed off from the world,
Encapsulated by an impenetrable shield
Within nature's belly it waits...

Warmed, nurtured, caressed by mother earth
Slowly, slowly...

The bud is delivered into life
Oh how it struggles for those first few millimeters
Roots-shoots-vine upon intertwined vine
Succulent, delicate fruit
Luscious indulgence

All too soon perfection fades
The sun, once invigorating-now infecting,
Draining and shriveling the fragile skin
But yet-still as sweet

Judith Schwartz

Dreams

Tumbling, falling
Screaming, calling
Tumbling, turning,
You smell something burning.
You suddenly realize that the something is you.
Shadows surround you,
you try to push through
but are violently thrown back
Something growls and you turn to run,
you find yourself armed with a gun.
You pull the trigger,
the barrel grows bigger,
it is a snake, it sinks it teeth in,
it fans like pins,
your arm goes numb,
the feeling spreads,
things roll at your feet that look like heads,
you wake up.
Then you notice that your clothing is crusted over with clotted
blood and you begin to scream.

Charles Matzner

The Empty Chair

Where else but at the head of the table
   Seated in his favorite chair
His arms were strong and able
   Now his legs would tremble with wear

He was the center of the family tree
   Its light and shining star
Always giving, don't you see?
   Commanding our presence from near and far

His youth was gone, hair thin on top
   But his grin remained the same
The stories he told, reminiscing non-stop
   We all knew how he played the game

Of life, always giving and sharing
   Self-centeredness was not his style
Man-kind was born to be caring
   And with his charm, he would a person beguile

The chair now sits by empty and forlorn
   Its personality gone with the night
Our hearts are heavy, and we mourn
   Only time will heal our loss:
     But Heaven's Gained Its Newest Light!

Barbara J. Fields

The Swimmer

The frog on any warm summer's day sits lazily on it's lily pad
Secure and confident with it's ability to hop from sear to seat
Until one faithful day a mistake of nature -
One powerful leg not extended enough plunges Mr. Frog
Into unknown depths in a drowning struggle, death so eminent
A seeming betrayal of his own beautiful world of pond and sky.

The unexpected deep is a pitfall even to the strongest swimmer.
A sudden engulfing fright that gives way to instinct
Motivation that directs every to the most weakened legs,
Test strength, stamina, the will of the most invincible heart
In a battle that sees, smells, smells, feels, hears, faces - mortality.

I, like the frog, am a swimmer
Flung into the deep morbid waters of disease
Know agony as dealt by the moment when fear flashed it's hand
Survivors, born of raw courage whose ecstasy in triumph, forever
Remembers and feel that lifelong brush of humbling appreciation
That spirits, existence once threatened, in awareness and hope
Grab, cling, hold firmly to their prize of life
Alert in happiness, caring, enterprise, knowledge
A tribute to the self, to kind, and the mother earth.

Barbara Welch

Ode To Alzheimers

Where is the husband I used to know?
Seems so very long ago
Straight and tall and proud he stood
Helping others when 'ere he could

Happy times and days of strife
That all goes with married life
Oh where is the husband I used to know?

What should have been his peaceful years
Are filled with torment, pain and fears
Confused, alone in his own world
Will he hug me today or shove me away?

Wanting his wife of yesterday
I cry no more as I did before
God gives me strength to face what's in store

For my little boy I pray each day
Lord grant him peace as he fades away
Oh where is the husband I used to know?
Still in my heart as he was long ago

Bernice Snyder

"The Thinker"

I prefer to be called "the thinker," when I'm
seen with a pen in my hand. I hope it's
not sounding persnickety. And I do hope
you'll soon understand. Some days all my
poems come so easy. Then there's days when
I struggle and frown. Just searching for
any two words that rhyme, or for a
logical thought to write down. I guess
it must be the mood that I'm in, which
decides to write "light hearted" or "not"
For at times it takes all the thoughts that
I have along with those I haven't got!
Well, enough has been said from "the
thinker." I'm sure you now know what
I mean. And where this poem lies, more
"light hearted" than "not?" Let's just
say its somewhere in between.

Gladys Hawkinson

Night And Day

When cheerful sunlight streams through windows,
Sending happiness wrapped in ribbons and bows,
The birds begin to chirp and sing their lilting song,
And morning bells boom out "Ding Dong".
The flowers bend heavily with dawning dew,
Bees begin collecting honey for me, and for you.
The grass is so green, the sky's blue and so bright!
The daytime is - once again - a truly marvelous sight!

Then the sun goes down - dust settles in,
And night shall now, from here on begin.
The moon rises up, stars twinkle in the sky.
And the living sleep on with barely a sigh,
But then again sleep is almost never silent.
With dreams of, perhaps, a Prisoner and Tyrant.
And among all this beauty, all we have to say,
Is that it is, "Different as Night and Day!"

Chrissy Hennessey

The Monster

The Monster lurks beneath the surface,
Sending small ripples to disturb the tranquil serene waters.
It bubbles up, rising higher and higher
And dances on the top like a swarm of bees after honey.
Pushing itself higher, it raises itself out of the water.
It will not be denied!
Rise up, "Oh Monsters" and consume me,
Let me feel your claws tearing at my insides,
Spilling out, exposing long held "garbage."
Ripping me open to spill out into the cleansing
Water and turning it red with my life's blood.
How long will he remain? Let him remain and do "his thing."
Don't run him away with offers of sweet things
That calm and appease him,
For he will only surface again another day!

Jewell Durham

The Aquatic Hippopotamus

The aquatic hippopotamus
Seems strange to quite a lot of us.
Although to native born, he's just a square.
While his habitat is watery,
He's dirtier than he oughter be,
So cleanliness to him is rather rare.

We hear he is herbivorous,
And often times vociferous,
He can be seen where ever water's course.
He sure ain't built for speed,
This hairless quadruped,
So why has he been dubbed — "The River Horse"?

Gordon Hilstad

Chameleon

Ever changing to fit in with her surroundings
   she knows not who she is, only who she can be
She is no one, yet she is everyone
   all she wants is to belong
Now she dares to stand out, a sparkled blue against her
   environment of drab yellow and orange
Suddenly she becomes vulnerable... waiting
   waiting for someone to discover her weakness
Waiting for someone to see in her something she cannot see
   something she doesn't want to see
   then turn their back on her
Slowly she fades into the background
   her moment of glory is gone
She makes a silent wish that someday she will find courage
   that someday she will find herself

Amber G. Fillmore

The New Beginning

The day our daughter was born;
She came into the world with quite a storm.
The doctors told us, she was quite sick;
But we knew in our hearts, that she'd get well quick.
The years rolled by, and she really grew;
And oh, what a whole lot she put us through.
The next thing we knew, she was out on her own;
How proud we all were, she could do it alone.
Now, Con is our daughter and Mike, our new son;
Our wishes are with you as you go on.
What a wonderful start that you have today;
And with all our blessings, you'll go on your way.
To Atlantic City, have fun and play.
It's a whole new beginning, now make your way.
Life's hard, be strong, and don't go astray;
Life's like a box of chocolates you'll hear us say.
Congratulations on your wedding day!

Joy Stevens Lytle

Reflections

It meant a lot to me to be married for 41 years.
Call it tradition, sentimentality, never giving up.

I've been naive, subservient, giving, accepting, loving

The handwriting has been on the wall loud and clear for many
years and I chose to ignore it.

Hoping against hope that somehow things would change
things would be different
someday with time, patience and prayer
he'd be there with me, for me.
We'd be together in our twilight years

And now I pine and cry and reflect on all those false dreams
The reality is bombarding my soul
I was living in a dream world
I created a sense of fulfillment which could never be with him
They say love is blind
It's true
Now my eyes are open and I see the reality
It's so painful
But with God as my co-pilot I can soar above this hurt
I can and will be strong, alive, loving, forever

Fran Crownover

Untitled

As darkness comes to rule the night
Shadows dance in the dim moonlight
Of angels of demons I do not know
For this love has taken a piece of my soul
What spell she had on me I can't explain
For on my heart I carry scars of sorrow and pain
And as I lay my head to sleep
Memories of the past slowly creep
And as the night passes by
My screams echo throughout the sky
To be written in the realm of time
Of loves greatest crime
Sometimes I wonder if I should stand and fight, or just
Walk away
And let her demons have their way
For nothings really what it seems
When you live your life in such a dream
Now night has broken, becomes the day
And in my mind she fades away

Anthony Weygandt

Untitled

What green pulls life thru dark caverns
shattering the earth in the search for its source
to end as a leaf offering glorious obeisance to the sun

What light born at the edge of the end
speeds by a billion watching starsuns
to end as a cloud endlessly changing like life itself

What love sleeps inside the soul and wakes
at the gentlest touch of recognition
of the deathless link with its like
to end as a smile radiant like the innocence of a child

What unknown sense of longing draws you beyond
to reach for others in desperation and loss
transcending mute unknowing indifference
to end in a hand that holds only the gift of holding on

What happiness hides in the heart of all who feel
the union of the great and small and the joyful
growth that rises from the earth mother
to end in a tear clean and pure like a leaf in the rain

Ian Cheverton

The Artificial Nightingale

"Silence.
Shattered.
Feather of nightingale wing
shimmies into the quill of the poet
tiny line of ink
words like angles' breath
and song of soft screams
- a warning -
currents of liquid music flow through her naked throat
emanate from the cavern of her mouth
echoes tongueless
barren, yet vengeful
filled with the deified power
of one given song to defy
the violence of a lonely king.
And she will sing until her throat bleeds
holy water instead of blood
purity of resolution and strength
"A blessing. Bride and flight
She alights."

Julie Ann Nathanson

She Plays With Her Dolly

She sits huddled in the corner, playing with her dolly.
She can still feel him touching her and she wonders
Why?
She glances up at her friends and thinks,
...Do they know?
...Can they tell?
...Will they leave her when they realize she's bad?

Why did it have to start?
Why did she let him do it?
Why did he choose her?

She just wanted to be loved!
She just wanted to be hugged!
The hurt pierces every ounce of her being.
And she wonders what death is like.
And she keeps the secret.
And puts on the plastic smile.
And she plays with her dolly.

Faith Jez

Where The Sand Meets The Water

At the place where the sun meets the water, you can see
all there is to see.
As the orange of the dying sun reflects on the shore, the
beautiful sand urges you to take a rest on the salty-smelling mattress
of the earth. And so you lie, in the vast space of where the sun
meets the water.
In the Morning, you awaken to the soft chatter of squirrels, looking
for nuts in the near-by forest. The ducks, swift as the morning tide,
look for food close by, but are not threatening. They walk up to
you, but soon realize you have no food to give them, and begin
squawking, and looking for food somewhere else.
Later the sun comes so bright that you can feel it eating
away at the sunscreen on your arms. The ducks are still scavenging on
the beach, but it is useless because they have already eaten all the
food days before. Seagulls now search the sky doing their nose dives
into the water, looking for that careless fish that stays near the
surface, not seeing the giant bird that is above it.
And night comes like a deep dark shadow swallowing up the sun.
Reluctantly, you make the journey to your car cherishing your
experience at the place where the sands meets the water.

Ben Dowling

A Gourd Christmas

YOWL—the long . . . dog days of August!
Joy to the world! Insect-low-tone!
The GOURD VINES have RISEN from the sandblasted DUST that was loam!
With "THE" STAR baking the sky,
Like waving, smiling, sunflower cookies, GRANDMA'S GARDEN didn't all heat-die.
Pearl-necklacing the ten-foot holly bush, the garland crawlers had climbed...
Pinnacling; the holly became evergreen, within my autumnal mind.
A dizzy yule-imagination: sparkling bright-orange Mexican sunflower
Christmas bulbs
Light ant colony train stations!
From presents of bowed pink mountain laurel at the tree's base,
the birds and the bees did race...
Spreading, green and purple-flowered: mint into jelly;
To brighten my parched, wearied, baby-boomed little-boy face.
Like Christmas Eve, decorations were hung...
Gourd ornaments: BOTTLED for the non-water-rationed TIMES,
Bodily curved elongated OTHERS for fountain kissing under the mistletoe chimes.
A round small one like PERFECTION.
Two mammoth pumpkins (not already full-grown), also clung;
one turned orange, one still cream.
As gourd colors change: stripe, mottle, bump, gleam...
My dream GOURD CHRISTMAS
Not winter, not yet autumn, but a heat-stroked sunglassed dazzler
Currier and Ives scene.

John Laffey

"America's Dream" The Challenger

The Challenger! The Challenger! It's mission to explore
No thought of not exceeding as so many times before
The Challenger thou does respect and America even more
It's Astronauts with joy they sought a challenge to explore

The count down has finally come, as they counted down from ten to one
And off the Shuttle soared through the sky as below the crowd watched it fly
What a glorious feeling to know they tried.
The Challenger! The Challenger!

As the crowd below watched with delight to the friends and family it was a sight
Then suddenly with such despair the shuttle exploded in mid air
Its destiny just ended there.
The Challenger! The Challenger!

The mission of the Shuttle craft
Five men, two women challenged to do their task to find the answer
  and proud to explore
The Astronauts death was given for.
The Challenger! The Challenger!

Delma Kirby

My Sweet Fuzzy Lady

She's always been there when she's needed.
She sings those beautiful songs
She cuddles me when I need it, and even if I don't.
She listen's very closely with her eyes filled with interest.
She never has turned away from me.
Though her years have overcome her,
she truly hears what I've to say.
Her pride filled walk stays steady to this day.
For many years she's been my dearest friend.
Within her mind she holds my secrets,
and my dreams of yet to be.
Without her it would have been a loss,
for the love that she has given, has taught me to be me.
I carry her in my arms and cuddle her with love.
In hope to return at least a half of what she has given me.
My sweet fuzzy lady, a light few pounds you weigh.
Your colors of three so perfect with shapes.
Your white so fresh and clean.
In me you trust, to keep your dignity.
Yes, I'll be with you till the end.

Janice A. Wilder

Willow

To touch the ground and the infinite blue,
She weeps but not to cry.
A life measured in mass;
With a foliage of tears she will pass,
Some day - but not today.

With cool dew dampened grass trodden by life
Come the essences of the earth stage.
There are those who come to speak;
Many who often sit and think,
Over the years and under her tears.

To live - to survive - it's a reason to stand,
And through her sheltering arms shines the dawn of a new day.
No seasonal yield of treasure
On the table or in the hand of man's pleasure.
But that was the plan, so the willow stands.

Brian Alexander

Dearest Friend

I have a friend so true to me
She's never failed my trust.
When life was harsh, my friend was there
From dawn until the dusk.

She never questioned me about
My reasons - or my acts
She simply smiled and understood
No matter what the facts.

She held me when the tears would fall
And took my hand in hers
She comforted my aching heart
With love till peace occurred.

She gave me courage with her strength
With patience, she stood by
Supporting me in every way,
She consoled me when I'd cry.

There is no better soul I know
Than this, my dearest friend
She's loved me unconditionally
And will until the end.

Bunny Geller

The Mystery Of Old Faithful At Yellowstone

An ancient ground with reverent eyes, where beseeching waters rise to
set in motion thoughts formed deep within the heart of Earth herself.
Thoughts that transpire into soaring fountains of highest hope. Spectacular
in beauty, formed in nature from the very essence of life,
is now focused on Earth's own faith, spewing columns of continual grace and prayer.

An energy of Earth's own breath, numbed by pain long ago, now seeks
new adulation of joy by rising to glorious heights. Dreams expand in
the rising mist and force their way to the surface to display the hidden
meanings in the rise and fall of a breathing Earth. They pause in mid air,
only to fall back to the ground encasing their secrets in clouds of misty vapor.

Life emulates from Earth's deepest core, perfected by rumbling patterns,
reminiscent of tympanies' deepest tones. Persistent symphonic sounds
resound thru ancient rock and molten sand. At the right moment nature
will echo forth a spectacular display, a mystery in its design, its purpose
on a higher plain. A presence continues to complete the fullness of a plan.

Water changes its design and purpose many times, flowing into streams and
oceans, giving life to all it meets. Without its presence life would cease as we
understand it, yet the faithful geysers at Yellowstone persist in their tribute to
this precious substance. The power of water is continually at work in our world,
as if guided by an omnipotent hand. By water all life is cleansed and reborn.
Diane L. Coolidge

Survivor

My mother waged more wars than any soldier has ever known.
My father was the general and the battlefront was our home.
The nights and days were stormy and passionate as their lives raged on.
Onward to a life known only to a battered woman.

My mother marched the battlefields and held us to her breast.
She protected us from war zones and little did she rest.
The weeks and months were explosive and intense as their lives raged on.
Onward to a life known only to a battered woman.

My mother's emotions soared with the ups and downs of my father's idiocrasy.
He thrived on mother's weakness and her addiction to him became
   a morbid symphony.
The years and years were tumultuous and impassioned as their lives raged on.
Onward to a life known only to a battered woman.

My mother waged more wars than any soldier has ever known.
My father was the general and the battlefront was our home.
The general's battle cry remains in silence forevermore.
My mother's hair is gray now, but her love for God made her a survivor
Carolyn Gresham Cook

No Reason For Rhyme

Looking ancient for his forty-four years, living in a world all his
own, he was never alone. I however never got used to the hospital
bed looking oddly out of place in his room. Nor did I again enjoy the
sun after it reflected off the shiny, silver bedrails, throwing ugly
light on his face, giving real life to his disgrace. And the smell of
that bright yellow stinking room almost gagged me every time I walked
in, but I would and I'd stay and feed him ice from a spoon, seeing
his body give in.

His hair falling out in clumps, his lips cracked and bleeding.
One look into his eyes brought tears to my own. I wondered
if inside he was pleading, for he could not speak even though
he tried. His ears they looked deep-fried.

A body frozen in time, a man engulfed in pain, spending his energy
to smile in vain, fighting for the flesh with heart and soul.
Damn it all! He just wanted to grow old. But when his body gave way
to the woes of the day, my father lie there motionless and numb,
finally allowing the night to fall, knowing tomorrow would never come.
Eric Crawford

Two Paths

She mounted the ladder one rung at a time,
She toiled to leave worries and labor behind.
At last great honors and wealth she has won,
As she steps to the top, from the very last rung.

The other one quite content it might seem,
Stayed at the bottom to live in her dreams.
She was poor and distressed as her trials she bore;
While barefoot children played 'round 'bout her door.

No fortune or fame for the things she's begun,
No great name in history for the work she has done;
Just paid back with love and sweet tender smiles.
"Can it be that I've failed? Has it all been worth while?"

She sighs at the top looking down on the other;
For after all, what's greater than being a Mother.
Emma Bush

The Tail End Of Seventeen

On the tail end of Seventeen
She was her mom and dad's Homecoming Queen
You'd never catch her getting out of line
Her folks they always knew she'd turn out fine

She wasn't into any social scene
Her folks thought that was part of "keeping clean"
But when there's no place to lay down your cards
Seventeen can hit you awful hard

A pen and paper were her two best friends
She wrote off her sorrow like some small expense
Her secrets are still safe with that pad and pen
For one day her journal closed, never to open again

On the tail end of Seventeen
What occurred none of us had foreseen
It seems she never came to school that day
For she had gently kissed her life away

On the tail end of Seventeen
The class was silent but the tension screamed
A small, red "x" on her attendance card
Marked the day Seventeen just got too hard
Genevieve Grosjean

"Wicked Mountain, Mounted Black"

Wicked mountain, mounted black
Sited trees looking back
Yonder sea, see him ride
Yonder mountain, through the skies

Wrinkled trees rooted old
Highest tops saged with gold
Rising sun, rises bold
Yonder sea, the stories told

Creatures human, running slow
Yonder mountain packed with snow
River runs down the slopes into open waters
And upon the lake.. A boat

Salmon running up the stream
Soon to die, so it seems
Amebas rolling in the soot
to crawl upon the beach and walk on foot

Wicked mountain, mounted black
It is a human looking back
A tigers eye.. An Indian old..
For centuries these stories have been told
Cynthia Yeager Brown

A Casual Glance

She caught my eye, her silky brown hair shining in the sun.
She was a stranger to me, I was an unknown to her.
Fate was kind to both.
I spoke to her, she answered me. "My name is Jose," I said.
"Mine is Rosa," she replied.
At length we conversed with the words flowing in the summer breeze.
"Are you seeing anyone," I asked. "No one," she answered.
Her voice had the melodious strains of heavenly music.
"May I see you again?" I asked. "May I walk with you?"
"May I see you soon?"
"How soon would that be?" She inquired.
"Would tomorrow be too soon?" I remarked.
"No," she said, "tomorrow would be fine with me."
I held her hand and we walked along the path.
That casual glance of years ago turned into a love that to this day endures still.
A love that grows stronger with each passing day.
A love that will survive eternity, a love born of a casual glance.

Arthur A. Grijalva

Moon Magic

I remember my mother's hair. It was red and braided.
She was beautiful
We talked and laughed and grew together,
She told me about the moon.
"If you stare at the moon" she said, "it makes you beautiful,"
As she spoke, I looked up at the moon.
I knew it was true
I felt like she told me a magical secret.
A secret that only she and I shared.

When the nights were still and the air was clear
We would let the moon shine on us.
We opened our mouths to let the moon shine in.
Inside beauty is the purest kind.
We laughed a lot but we still did it.
We are very beautiful people.

When my daughter was born, I brought her into the moonlight
And whispered to her the secret of the moon's magic.
We open our mouths to let the moon in.
We laugh a lot, but we still do it.
She is beautiful too.

Dorianne Gollubier Pollack

Gentle Breeze

Gentle breeze
Shifting leaves
Stretching for miles
Reaching me, teaching me
Feels so good
Take me for a ride gentle breeze
Take me to the end where quiet is real and
real is peaceful

Gregory Lee Harman

Without

Walking through the dark green forest
Slivers of sunlight shinning through the trees
Gentle rain starting to fall.

Moonlight glowing all around
Gazing up at the clear dark sky
Stars twinkling high in the heavens.

Midnight walks along a sandy beach
Enjoying the stillness of the night
Waves dancing joyously toward the shore.

All these things are truly beautiful to behold
But they are all empty because something is missing
...YOU!!!

Gary L. Wheeler

Utah's Autumn

The tall, golden Poplar Tree
   shivers by the dark green pines,
There are mounds of orange pumpkins
   at this bounteous harvest-time!

There are rustling Halloween corn-stocks
   in the cool, crisp autumn air,
And loaded trees of apples, dangling
   by a scare-crow, propped up there!

The sights and sounds of autumn
   after summer's long, hot days
Is as restful and inviting...
   as the full moon's misty haze!

Of all the changing seasons
   in the inter-mountain west,
It is this glorious time of year...
   The season I love best!

Faye West Guercio

Time Of The Day

The days seem longer when you look back.
Shorter when you look ahead.
Time has no meaning with life,
Because it goes on forever and forever.
Number is always the same.
Matter of what time of day.
Its the same everyday.
It always will be different way
We live and style we came from around the world.
Treat time slow and easy.
There will be no rush with time.
Its not going anywhere.
We use time for everything we can count on.
Only the year comes short with time.
People only rush with time.

Dan Gregory

Two Trees

In every man grows two trees
Side by side they grow
One is good and one is bad
but do we really know?

In every man lives two trees
Side by side they be
One is good and one is bad
Which will it be for me?

In every man lives two trees
Side by side they stand
One must live and one must die
to fulfill an empty man

In this here man lived two trees
Side by side they grew
One was good and one was bad
The good tree made me new.

Eugene F. Wiesner

Hero, I Apologize

Admiration, high expectation, the subscribe
   standards of society
Though successful you may be
You must continue to achieve the glory and
   fame of society
Its a constant battle for you
To meet the status of society
A continues battle it may be
To prove yourself to them and me!

Della M. Bouldin

Grandma Bess

The years go by as they please,
Some are hard, some pass with ease.
It takes all types for it to go 'round,
Just look at the friends you found.
Then one day a special one springs,
A blooming rose with beauty to bring
A heart wide open, to give her love,
As planned by Him, up above.
Only the ones that know her share,
Her uniqueness, that's much to rare.
Grandma Bess today your day,
Thank you for your guidance along the way.

Jennifer Kline

Resurrection...

A rebirth to all things
Sight once clouded by the blackness of necessity
Reawakens to the glory of the sunrise.
But the sun sets as well,
And the blackness never fades entirely.
Fear makes it linger
Necessity darkens the grey haze
Back to black.
The rebirth clears the mind.
Enhances and enlightens,
Undoes what is done.
The metamorphosis of the soul
Is destructive.
They weep and scream.
Clutching the dying rays of the day,
Shrinking from the returning darkness.
Fighting the thing that is all-powerful,
Helpless.

Erika Kendra

True Cry

A life long riddle my heart and soul devoured within the middle
Simple and plain; yet caught within
  the complexity that continuously remains

A caged bird; just another nerd...
  squawking, cawing, somehow I must break free

Deathly, silently yet kindly...
  please someone release me

Afraid; for never to be paid...
  I need to proceed

Fire, raging, burning yearning deeply from within
  Peaceful hope for a better tomorrow...

Yet ironically, not for me; yet
  for this striving family

Split, hit, living softly within...
  the love of their subtle combination
Existing in poverties damnation...yet middle class

Similarly, money never lasts...
  While the love grows strong

So freely my eagle heart soars...
  my family's love will exist for evermore.

Alison Thornton

Nocturne

The sand turns cool beneath my feet, but I am loathe to go.
The surf begins its measured beat, and weary Gulls fly low.
One last vestige of the Sun bathes all in crimson light.
The offshore breeze announces the onset of the night.
Still I linger, clinging to the wonders of the day, and
try to share these feelings with my friend, who went away..

Brian T. Allen

The Gift

It is the middle of the night.
Sitting near an open window, I hear
  the rustling leaves of a tree.
Through the screen comes a cool and gentle breeze,
  refreshing me, and I begin to reminisce.

The words of a song rise into my mind and for a few moments
  I am in Germany, over twenty years ago,
   an English teacher whose students are eager
  to learn the lyrics of American songs —
   no grammar lesson today, Gott sei Dank!
As I play the song for them, I imagine it as a sort of
  gift, which some will appreciate immediately,
   others later.

I come out of my reverie, whisper-singing to myself,
  and know that the gift, a thing called love,
   has found its way back to me.

Julius Karl Schauer

"Thank You Mom" (Baby Brothers)

Building forts and climbing trees, knots on the head and
skinned up knees. Secret talks that know one can hear,
going through things like pain and fear. Plans and dreams
that involved one another, all this I did with my twin brother.

A saddened heart and a gun in hand,
took him away to the promised land. I'm locked up and
I have to be strong, I have to live and carry on. But living
with out him brings pain I can't bare. I'm so hurt and lonely,
and lost and scared.

All my plane involved my twin, back to back
I knew we could win. All that's changed,
now I'm alone. The pain I feel cuts deep to the bone.

In the black hour that I received the news,
I thought and wondered what to do.
Then this great idea popped into my head,
It would be much easier if only I were dead.

But how would I do it get rid of the pain? Hey wait a
minute, yes, the train! And then I looked over and saw the
reason why, I must live on, I can not die. Thank you mom
for these two little guys, they're not big, but they saved my life.

Gary Piper

"Ode To Our Astronauts"

I was standing one night by my window, in a daze
staring up at the moon, when I thought of those
guys' with such courage, by now they're circling
the moon, and I wonder what they might be saying,
as they fly their ship through the night, and we
here at home are so thankful to them, that we are
now pioneers out in space.
Truly these three men should be commended, for such
a risk they took on their own, an upon their return
back down to earth, we should all cheer and shout,
God bless you, we welcome you home.

Joseph H. Gilmartin

You Won't Always Call Me Mommy

You won't always
smell like graham crackers and apple juice
and you won't always
ask for your favorite story over and over.

You won't always
prefer my hugs to everyone else's
and you won't always
let me rub your soft hair before sleeping.

You won't always
look for me before trying something new
and you won't always
want me to notice each small success.

You won't always
step on my toes when you reach for a hug
and you won't always
need me like you do right now.

You won't always
call me "Mommy"...
But I'll wish that you did.

Barbara Way

Mistress

Rest in me, in your desired restrictions
Smile upon the forbidden inhabitation you have construed.

No, do not pursue the devastation of all you have
In my eyes I imagine it not.
But a time to give of myself.

How I wish it were not the same as this moment.
Then the innocence you knew would no longer perish by one kiss.

Everything wonderful would be seen by my glorious eyes.
And my worries not be those of another more precious.

For I am just that-none better or timeless.
Yet I am concealed, my touch sheltered and
strung from a guilty shyness.

Still my hand still long to sense you; and
the coldness I preserve waits for an instance
that it shall be relieved.

Until then I weep through my madness.
Yet I pause from this day's obsession and dream
off to another where I'll be with you at last.

Gina Bozzelli

'Cause Of Me

I swear to the Lord that I love you so.
So much that it's something I'll always know,
But when your brown eyes won't look at me,
And when your sweet lips won't smile for me,
I begin to wonder
When my heart beats like thunder.
If it should,
Or if we could,
Be lovers,
In covers
Of silken satin.
Then I realize, my heart starts to flatten,
We can never be,
And it's all 'cause of me.

Jenny Pinson

Black Woman

A diamond in the rough
Smooth like Butter, not tough
She is an Intellectual mind
Shows Respect and Love for all Mankind

She gives Me strength when I am weak
Empowers Me with the power to speak
She embodies the word grace
The provider of future Generations of My Race

Wisdom is at the tip of Her Tongue
Knowledge is what makes her Queen in my Town
Her smile shines for miles
She too, is a Jewel of the Nile

Her motion is like water flowing down stream
She is the Woman that put colors to My dream
Left out of His-story
To me, that's one big mystery

Soaring like a bird with clipped wings
She is capable of Stomaching anything
An art work in motion
She remains sensitive to all My emotions

Clyde Ettienne-Modeste

The Willow Tree

I love to watch, the willow tree,
So green, so soft, and billowy,
Swinging, and dancing in ecstasy
As the whistling winds, blow wild and free.

When leaves appear, in early spring,
It calls the birds, their songs to sing,
They twitter, in and out with glee,
While proudly, stands the willow tree.

As the summer comes, without a care
Its branches swing, like a maiden's hair,
The trunk, it hugs them tenderly,
How lifelike is the willow tree.

The autumn spreads its golden gown
And the trembling leaves, come tumbling down,
Their time has come, though they cling tightly,
They loathe, to part from the willow tree.

Now the wintry tree stands tall and stark,
Its branches shimmer in the dark,
But oh, how sad, how sad, I'd be,
Had God not made, that willow tree.

Bridget Rossi

I See Holocaust

The rest are no less poignant and not real.
The reality has still not set in, the law
is beyond mine and any other human understanding.
For 45 years there are untold dreams, life's thoughts,
remembrances, pain and forgetful sign of times.
It still stares. It still means this took place.
Sadness only makes six million faces look like people,
human make us look like ourselves.
The wretchedness of our beings is only found in shear
desperation; longing is not a reason for existence.

Bill S. Albo

Memories

The floor is dark and unstable -
So is the ceiling but it has lights.
Desks smell of old, damp wood with a collection of chewing gum
   under the seats;
The heater doesn't work and the window is broken.

The lonely room used to be a place of learning -
Now books are dust covered and corners are full of cobweb experiments.
A stiff-legged old man wobbles through the door with the help of his cane;
He chooses the last desk on the right side of the room,
He pulls out his book and blows off the unwanted dust;
Yes, page 113 is correct so he begins to read -
A single tear fills his eye and suddenly finds it's way down his lined face
He raises his hand to be excused -
Then reality tells him that he's all alone;
His cheeks blush as he turns once more -
One last look at the room of memories.

Time has passed and the building looks more decrepit than ever;
The door no longer has use of its hinges.
Through the shabby doorway, a second man steps
Looking for memories of a long lost father.

Andrea Cavender

Someone You Care For

Without someone you care for, to share with, everything,
So many moments in our lives, wouldn't mean a thing.

A summer stroll at sunset, with a quiet little talk.
Without someone you care for, would simply be a walk.

A trip into the countryside, as fall colors come alive.
Without someone you care for, would simply be a drive.

Your Christmas tree, with all the trim, that you put up with such glee.
Without someone to share it with, would simply be a tree.

And as you know, we like nice things, nice house, nice car and such glee.
But without someone to share them with they wouldn't mean that much.

So keep in mind, as time goes by the little joys we share,
Would not be joys all by themselves, without the ones who care.

So tell me please, of pretty trees, of sounds, of smells, of sights,
Of all the little joys you have, to fill your days and nights.

These little things that fill your life, I'm asking you to share.
A joy to you is a joy to me, that's because I care.

Glenn D. Larson

God Is Greater Than Any Problem I Have

When I wend my way home to my little nest;
So worn and tired that I cannot rest,
I know in my heart that I am blest
For God is greater than any problem I have.

When I awake in dawn's gray light-
After a tossed and sleepless night-
Thinking of plans that did not work out right-
I know God's greater than any problem I have.

When I kneel down at the close of the day,
Mind filled with all the things I want to say
But cannot find words with which to pray
I know God is greater than any problem I have.

When I have problems that I need to share
But family and friends don't seem to care
It is good to know that He is always there
That God is greater than any problem I have.

Gladys Peyton

The Line

These problems are real, yours and mine;
So many talk of them, now let's walk their line

You can see hopes built high then crushed like jelly beans;
To live a decent life, they know not what it means

To steal, thug, and disrespect are ways of life;
Abuse, malnourishment, and welfare are just part of their strife

A role model or rather they know not of the;
This should not matter, we are alike, them, you and me

Some try to take care of their mother by selling drugs;
Others run around like animals and act like selfish thugs

The population is not all bad;
Some stay out of trouble and try their hardest, rather sad

Not all Mexican, Anglo or Puerto Rican;
Some Asian, mulatto, or Afro-American

RoShawn has a "4.0", trying his best;
But Leandre is an athlete that stands out from the rest

Juan is a thug who acts rather wild;
Maria is pregnant with her second child;

These problems are real, theirs, yours, and mine;
Now we've talked about them end even walked the line

Joe Barnes

Iwo Jima: No Tougher Fight

Volcanic ash got soaked with blood. We had no place to hide.
   So, move ahead is what we did, with pain, and "Semper Pride."

By nightfall we had cut across the shortest neck of land;
   Two thousand men, our dead and wounded, scattered on the sand.

The next three days we fought them, both in front and to the rear;
   But, February twenty-third, a sight we had to cheer:

Five-hundred-foot Mount Suribachi, highest ground there'd be,
   Was captured; and our flag was raised for all Marines to see.

With two thirds of the island left, and they entrenched uphill,
   Surrender was not in their plan: More blood would have to spill.

No matter what we threw at them, resistance was so hard,
   Each day's advances had to be just measured by the yard.

In general, fighting took four weeks; some units, more like five.
   Yes, we survivors, boarding ship, thanked God to be alive.

The only victory where we had total losses more than they.
   Those casualties, by fallen thousands, unbelievable to say:

Their dead, in thousands: twenty-one; and ours: six thousand not alive.
The total of our dead and wounded, in the thousands:
   twenty-five.

We men of Iwo reminisce, these fifty years 'tis now:
   Of lost Marines, no tougher fight. We know the why...the how.

Frank Gardner

Timeless Expectations

Sunshine is golden and the sky has limitless praise.
The mountains, the trees, the birds, the bees;
beauty is everywhere.
Happiness flows through the eyes of the beholder and
Raindrops form only to bring out the best in someone's gray clouds.
And over the horizon is a picture so rare-
it shines forth for all to see.
Letting you know there is hope for everyone who tries.

Arleen A. Earnest

Autumn Secrets

Watch the dew spread out so softly,
so quietly and secretly covering the ground.
Do you wonder from where it comes?
Or wish you could see the secret source?

Watch the leaves change, oh so silently.
And yet screaming the joy all around.
Thinking how can there be this secret,
with so many who are aware.

Watch the mums open wide their glory.
Totally ignoring the cold snap of air.
Saying with each open flower,
the secrets over here, no over there.

Watch as the ducks fly quickly over,
The secret tells them when and where.
Noisily telling all who will listen,
the secret, it is everywhere!

Just listen, listen to the secret.
God is talking, quietly whispering.
The secret is made for you to share.

Germaine Steakley

Something's Missing

I have a fairly good life
so society thinks.
But society doesn't realize
that there's an absent link.
Something's missing. Don't you think?

According to some bright dear hearts,
I'm quite level in the head.
But to me, I'm consistently falling apart.
Would I be better off dead?
Don't answer that question. Something's missing.

A part of me feels love inside.
Another part feels hate.
Why do mixed feelings preside?
Why is there no clear path to the open gate?
Both are present. What's missing?

At one point I really believed
I would always know which path to take.
I now realize there's more to be conceived.
If I understand that, I must have the answer.
Something's missing for goodness sakes!

Anita Jarrell

My Niece Lora Lee

She was born in the spring
So tiny, so wee.
This little bundle made my heart sing.
My niece Lora Lee.

From baby to toddler to child she grew.
Her hair reddish blonde, eyes sky blue.
When she grows up, what will she be?
My niece Lora Lee.

She went through school, seemed before she began.
Then off to the chapel to wed she ran.
Now a young woman, wife and mother I see.
My niece Lora Lee.

A terrible accident in the spring.
Took her life, now with angels she sings.
She left behind her children, three.
My niece Lora Lee.

George A. Clark

Black Child

Raise your head up high, look straight ahead,
So you may see where you are going.
Those ahead of you have fought the battle, but the war is not over.
The weapons of your enemies have not changed
SUPPRESSION, OPPRESSION AND DEPRESSION.
You shall rise above them all.

BLACK CHILD
Life does not always give you what you want.
You must do the best with what you got
Motivation and determination shall be your guides,
With them as leaders I know you will go far.

BLACK CHILD
Life has no time table, for you ar here today and gone tomorrow.
So live each day as if there is no tomorrow
For life is just a heart beat, but living is an art.

BLACK CHILD
You may not gain the riches of gold and silver, that you seek
But the treasure you find is worth all the gold in the world,
It is the belief in yourself.
When you believe in yourself all things are possible.

Cheryl D. Taylor

Fourth Of March

On the verge of spring
Soft rains and southerly winds bring
Nature's bountiful flowery display
To announce Ellen's birthday!

The scented air the humming bees
Foretell the greening of the trees
The calendar in its inevitable way
Tells us again its Ellen's birthday!

Respite from winter's gray and brown
Tender shoots and shrubs with flower crowns
Brighten our path along the way
To joyful celebration of Ellen's birthday!

What manner of person can she be
For nature dressed in all its finery?
For family and friends on hurrying way
To join again to mark Ellen's birthday

Wife, mother, friends galore
Author, chef and virtues more
Make us joyous and gay
When we celebrate Ellen's birthday!

Allen J. Angers

A Friend For Life

Do you have friend for life?
Someone who can stop your strife?
A person who is there for you
Never gives bad comments on what you do
This friends is wondrous
Always true
Loyal and brilliant, and worthy to you
But does this friend believe in you?
Believe you when you say your true?
Does this person really stop your strife?
If so,
You have a friend for life.

Jennifer Anne D'Amico

All Of Me

As I sit looking at my life and the people who fill my days,
Some are there by choice others are just there.
I know many and many know me.
But only a few ever get to the place of really knowing me.
Only a few will I reach for, being vulnerable, looking for acceptance.
Why is it the things you want most belong to someone else?
Can a relationship that brings fullness and questioning be so wrong?
It has taken me a long time to get here emotionally
   because of my protective walls.
But with you, all things are possible.
Completion comes in areas I thought would stand forever incomplete.
Commitment is experience.
Love is shared.
Loyalty has engulfed us in whatever lays ahead.
I have given you all of me.

Elizabeth A. Burge

The Princess Of Mars

Some walked in beauty like the night
Some flew like fairies soar in flight
To other worlds; seeking a princess of fairy tale ilk
A romantic angel garbed in silk
Whose robes of cream and peach reflect
Her grace, her warmth, her pearled swan neck.

They looked for her at a royal ball
Found her Waterford slipper at Monaco Hall
Even rode the Snow Queen's horse-drawn sleigh
On a frosty Italian December day.

They sought the help of fantasy lore
Came Christian Anderson, Brothers Grimm, and more.
But those fairy tales began to wane.
They continued their quest but all in vain.

Then "Hark." Lights twinkled on in a field of dreams
Beaming a spiritual being with seraphim hair.
And heavenly choirs rejoiced in song
For Princess Marlene and the Prince of Mars
AT CAMELOT IN A FIELD OF STARS.

Irene S. Dunne

The Way Life Works

The way life works in weird indeed...
some people don't even have the things they need.
While some people get whatever they want...
some can only dream about it in thought.
While the rich don't have to try to survive,
some little kids are barely alive.
It's amazing how cruel some can be,
while humans are living without food to eat.
When some families are gathering for a feast,
the homeless are going through garbage to eat.
People may laugh or people may cry...
but if it doesn't stop, millions more will die.
Life can be good, or life can be bad...
but to think of all this...doesn't it make you sad?
This world doesn't make much sense...
if you ask me, I'd say it's kind of dense!
I wish life was good to all that lurks...
but I guess that's just THE WAY LIFE WORKS!
INCREASE THE PEACE!

Alan Kindred

Time

Time itself is very much of the essence
Some waste it, but for others time is well spent.

Some practice carpe diem, which means to seize the day.
Some look forward to tomorrow, for they see no other way.

Some pray to God and may be heaven bound.
For they know lost time is time that can never be found.

As you search for a good time to rear its head,
You have wasted half your life for time is already dead.

So seize the day and live for the present
Because time itself is very much of the essence.

They say that all work and no play makes Jack a dull boy,
But the pleasure and success of time well spent can only bring joy.

What one does or has only time will tell.
Whether one eventually calls home, heaven or hell.

So keep moving on and may not your path be blocked.
For time is of the essence, and there's still time on the clock.

Joseph A. Skrine

Walking Home Alone

Walking home alone one dreary night, she could feel it in the air
something wasn't right. Then around her mouth a hand drew near,
this was the night, she'd meet her worst fear.
Drug a short way to a place unknown, she begged and pleaded,
"Please leave me alone." He placed his hand beneath her breast,
then ripped the shirt form her chest. He whispered softly in her ear,
"Don't say a word, do I make myself clear?"
A dark cloud fell as he did his thing and she knew that moment,
nothing would ever be the same. Dropped by the street fully abused,
she knew no one would want her, now that she'd been used.
Millions of thoughts ran through her mind, knowing that in a razor
she would soon confide. Now at home alone in the dark, she sat with
that razor ready to make her mark. And once she'd made her mark she
knew, that in 30 seconds her life would be through.
She couldn't believe what happened next, she was constantly surrounded
by rapes kind of sex. For it's said to be true that if you take your
own life, no matter the way gas, gun, or knife, that forever in hell
you will leer, constantly surrounded by your worst fear!!

Amy Elizabeth Garris

Happy Retirement

Retirement means staying home and adjusting to the pace.
Sometimes it's very boring, but then I love it at my place.
Each day there are these things to do, that I never did before.
Like filling up the ice cube trays, and going to the store.
And then the thought occurs to me, I'm doing things I never did.
Who could it be that did these things, it surely was no kid.
Who did the chores that I now do, it had to be my wife.
I'm doing all the things she did, Boy, she really had the life.
I love to go out shopping, and treat myself real good.
I stop and have a bite of lunch just like I know she would.
I watch my shows on television, then have a little rest.
To think I could have always had this job, it really is the best.
The conditions on this job are really very fine.
I just have to make the best of it and happiness is mine.

James Ferguson

Oceanside Dawn

Dawn slides quietly over the azure horizon,
To be followed by the glorious blaze of the morning sun.
A salty sea breeze sets the seagrass 'awhisper.
Gulls dart about, searching for an easy meal.
A miscellany, of shells lie nestled in the warm sand.
The rhythmic flow of the waves brings serenity to the soul.
God has spoken, without saying a word.

Janice Hodge

Leaky Roof

Irresistible melody so quietly serene,
Tap, tap, tap, obscured, embellished by a dream,
Refreshed still slumbering spirit lost in wondrous lands of being.
Could it be aged heartbeat drumming filling life with flow?
Or a clock's true pestered ticking just a half less wind to go?
Maybe it's mind's faded memories haunting raised from below.
Tap, tap, tap, exalted louder than before,
Stirring now resistant sleeper from desired dreamer's lore,
Funny little raindrops falling humbled roof to sodden floor.

Cathie Kincaid

Saying Good-Bye

Saying good-bye is never an easy thing
Sometimes you have to slip of the ring
The ring that holds you together as one
Take it off and hide it away

Maybe if things get better you can slip it back on someday
But until then remember all the good times you had
And forget why he made you so sad
He never tried to hurt you

He loves you too much to see you cry
There will always be apart of you that wonders why
Why he lied to your face
Knowing you'd be torn in two

Now your feeling sad and blue
But always remember you love him and he loved you

Heather Sirek

Autumn Days

The leaves have started to curl.
Soon they will turn gold, brown,
then falling to the ground - disintegrate
gone altogether, leaving behind lonely trees,
stalked bare, pitiful and devoid of beauty.

Sunflowers in their glamour
will hang their heads and quail
then rot.

Yellow jackets busy themselves to
savor the pollen
nestling their cute bodies in the bulbs
one last time.

The grasslands surrender their hue
to the elements.
Soon the veil of winter
will cover them.

The twitter of birds grow faint
as they prepare for a southern flight.

Judith Grant

Untitled

Somewhere, someone was pulling my
soul out of my body, leaving me there
restless as I said, "its not my turn,
I don't want to die!" I've got many years in
front of me, please don't take me.
They pulled me closer and closer to the bright
light in the dark starless sky. Please,
I beg of you, let me go, I'm not ready.
These people in white gowns with gold outlining
their body and with wings more
beautiful than a swan lowered me down to
the ground and laid me peacefully in my bedroom.
Then they all left as quiet as the came.

Jennifer Smith

Once Again

Three minutes before twelve, and my grandfather clock rang out early,
sounds of children crying for their mother seemed so crisp in my mind,
though it wasn't real anymore.
She hurt me that night, in the moment I'll not soon forget.
She ripped and tore at my skin and hair, biting my tender leg.
How are you this morning? She asked, like she was my friend.
But no friend of mine ever caused me so much pain before.
I was surprised, with myself, I ran, hard on my wounds and my body
broke, tripping me in feeble attempt to escape.
I rose, cringing on every step, pushing away, but I could not
hold myself up any longer.
She was over me then, swift like the wind, laughing at me, while
I cried in desperation. I thought I would die on that dirt road,
Her hellish laughter still plagued the air as I crawled away,
blood sprung from the beating she gave me, attacking me with
that pipe, but I turned on her, life springing forth,
and I threw her away, to that rock, where She died.
I ran to the church and sat for three hours, until I missed her so
much, I killed myself.

Dennis Mahoney

Man's True Pride

Beyond all earth's endeavor, through time and
space implied.
Out there is God's great paradise.
Indescribable - Man's true pride.
Less conscious thought of where or when,
Life's ending not to be.
Beginning there for evermore, cleansed
Conscience resting free.
Love's meaning now reality, o'er from the
Farthest star.
Forgiveness spawned fulfillment, just reward
For where thy are.
Relaxed with fond contentment, once sought
Answers ne'er to seek.
Engulfed with glow of a mighty throne, God's
Symbol, forth to speak.
Beyond all Earth's endeavor, through time and
Space implied.
A soul's found heaven's glory.
Indescribable - Man's true pride.

Edward A. Nicholson

Mythic Renewal

You are the unfolding of the goddess, receive her fully!
Spark to the dance of her being, let body's magical energy be heard.
No more Amnesia! Be serious!

Gain your equilibrium. It is original nature.
Shape your destiny and announce who you are!
Dream and gather!

Greet the morning sun and preserve your wildness.
Trust your ability to heal and birth through your pain.
Listen to the mythic bells!

Power slumbers in no-mind and in conscious sacrifice.
Hospitality cries out anew to the hidden wounded,
Tolerated for so long!
Reclaim! Recover! Remember!

Tears and depression - willing ground for cultivation,
Offer raw power transformed.
Burdens lessened, can sing!
We are each a great song!

Dee Pye

Move To Heaven

Circles ever spinning in the air
speak to me from above
of the earth and how we may always travel
through the time and space of the other.

Movement abound takes us forward into
reality where we know not,
  we no not.

We move and bump
and hit and stumble and mumble over the rocks of the earth
as we move forward in time. Forward in time. Forward in time.
To the space of where time is no meaning is know meaning

For time is here and we
are in it - through it -
in no time, in know time,
  in true time.

And as this time moves and we are enlightened
To its ways we reveal much and reveal more
as the sky moves. Onward
And we are seen from the tower as beings as beings as being.

Judy Weaver-Duval

Speak True

Speak true to the world around you
Speak true from the heart beating inside of you
Speak true from the soul that guides you
Speak true to the community reaching out to you
Speak true about your loved one beside you
Freeing the soul is everyone's continued goal
Becoming one to make the mind and body whole
Don't be ashamed or afraid of how other's will view you
Thank's for the honesty that has been so revealing
Be proud of your achievements throughout this process
We're no different than the rest
We'll strive to be our best
We truly know the meaning our pride, respect and dignity
This is a reminder to embrace life
There are endless possibilities
Continue to speak the language that represents meaning
every moment in our lives.

Donna E. King

So In Love

  In some point in life, the wild elusive
spirit is quieted, by that which has
been beyond your reach.
  Only in your dreams and wishes and
hopes that wild abandonment is subdued.
  But not to the point of imprisonment.
  But rather to the point of contentment and peace.
  Which only you can know and feel in your heart.
  It is a sweet capture, a quiet
sign of relief, with excitement
and expectation lingering.
  Sweet and content is the soul.
  As it should be when two are so in love.

Edith N. Martin

Fallen Tree

Lived mighty and glorious
throughout its life
Now lays twisted and broken
from old growth strife
For those of you that think trees come and go
they are always here to put on their show
If you look real hard near this fallen tree
there is life from its seed growing wild and free

David Allen Brewer

"Hypnosis"

I am hypnotized by the trees.
Standing here on my grassy patch, body against the wind,
becoming enthralled by the mesmerizing dance of their long,
lush green arms as they sway, reaching for the heavens.

I am tempted by their whispers.
I can not escape their grasp.

Lying on my grassy patch, the wind blows stronger.
Eyes closed, feeling the tree's bounty collect around me,
hearing blades of grass echo the song of fallen leaves.
I look up to see nature's branches caressing
the horizon in a delicate kiss.
I stand up.
I raise my arms. Higher and higher I stretch my arms.
My body extends upward. I balance myself on my toes.
Higher and higher I stretch, to see if I, too,
can reach the heavens.

Adrienne Haston

"My Companion And My Friend"

When the sun came up I knew you were there,
Standing in your stall...no love could compare.

I took you for granted and you never let me down,
No matter what I wanted, you were ready...without a sound.

The joy that you gave me, no matter where we'd go,
Flowed through my veins and made me proud and love you so.

But the pleasure of your presence has been taken from me this day,
I wish I could touch you, "Oh Chip, I wish you'd stayed!"

For the tears are so many, that I shed for you now.
Not tears of the joy...that escaped me somehow,

But for the heartbreak I feel, way down deep inside.
You were the "joy of my life," and now it's untied.

For you are at peace, and your pain I now feel.
You'll live in my heart forever, and from your memories...
  I hope to heal.

Eleanor J. Black

A Telephone

O Christmas tree, O Christmas tree, standing on the fence,
There are so very many of you, the population is so dense,
I walked along the lonely roads and missed the lovely lights,
The Christmas cheer is now replaced with anger and with fights,
I hid my face amid the dust that covered Santa Claus,
My hands, oh yes, I'd say they were as soft as a stuffed bear's paws,
I wandered off through deep valleys just to see a telephone,
And when I saw the outrageous price of a call it chilled me to the bone,
I could not stand to dwell upon the greed that held the night,
I cut through a nearby yard and suffered a dog bite.

Isaac Kirschenmann

Aurora

A sea of liquid indigo chased in frothy silver.
Stars burning bright in the moonless night,
  across the vault of heaven.

There appeared in orange-red a single glowing line.
Written on the ebony waves in a mirrored shine,
  beneath the vault of heaven.

Like a veil of finest silk the shimmering colors fell.
Rainbow colors silently waltzed over the ocean swell,
  beneath the vault of heaven.

From horizon to horizon on the darkened gentle sea,
The spirits of the children dance in silent harmony,
  across the vault of heaven.

Douglas E. Croyle

He Was Like A Tree

He was like a tree to me.
   Standing tall like a palm.
Grounded and rooted,
   Leaning on GOD'S everlasting arm.

He was like a tree to me.
   Bending with the wind, then standing tall again.
For faith had taught him to march
   On and be courageous and strong.

He was like a tree to me.
   Planted by the sea; his life like the waves,
Washed over you...you and me.
   Patience for him was easy: For prayer was the key.
For he promised to keep on until eternity.

My tree stayed faithful until the end,
   An ambassador who preached against sin!
   Ida B. Jackson

The Colors Of Her Days

A long dark hall opens to a blazingly sunlit room. A child
stands in the doorway, alone, her mother is in a large white
bed holding a tiny baby. The room is so bright and she is
in the dark, outside. White

A large maple tree in the spring, fresh, small leaves. The child
is high in the tree, skinned knees, scratched hands.
Scared, her freckles stand out on the small pale face. Green

The curtains are heavy and dark, the mixed aroma of her father's
cigars and her mother's perfume makes the child feel uneasy.
She is twelve years old. Curious, she opens a dresser drawer, all
silk and lace underthings. Rose, dark rose.

The boy touches her breast, the moonlight shines on the water, the
girl moves away. She is uneasy as she was in her parent's
bedroom. They kiss and she loves him. He smells like
Christmas, mince pies. Silver, shiny

A woman married, children, yellow, gold, red, black, black.
   Kaleidoscope
So many days, so many years. Now the colors are
muted, watercolors. Lavender, gray, the color of her veins.
   Emily Childs

Stolen Moments

Stolen moments are the ones we keep secretly
Stealing away time to embrace, to enjoy
   To kiss and be kissed
   to love and be loved
Stolen moments keep alive breathing lust
The breath of happiness
The breath of ecstasy
The breath of life.

Loving in darkness and confusion,
Loving with guilty emotions,
Is all that can be with a love taken dishonestly

Will this love-type grow like flowers?
Will it die with each passing day?
   To the husband, the wife, the adulterer too,
   Follow your heart: Steal away, to stolen moments.
Love-
Beautiful, ugly, honest, or crime,
Or simply an inconvenience of time.
   De'Aundra Jenkins

"Sweet Harmony"

The night is young,
still so many things to do,
here I sit all alone,
waiting for dawn's first light,
wishing you were here with me to see it,
soft stillness in the night,
Let's you know I'm here thinking of you
No one else but you,
Watching the silver moonlight,
Glisten in the silky water of the lake,
suddenly, I hear a voice,
more like an angel, singing from a distance,
telling me everything is going to be alright,
it brings a smile to my face, at that moment,
Dawn sheds a peek of sunlight,
Like a gold coin being thrown in the
air and getting stuck,
now I know for sure we will be together, forever.
   Angela Marie Dinardi

Together

I wear you like an old felt hat
   strangely familiar and comfortable.
You silently invade the unswept corners of my life
   and nestle down to stay.

Like a backwoods cabin warmed by glowing embers
   we settle into relaxed routines.
I long to grow old with your familiar smile
   gently tracing the mysteries of your body with
     my fingertips
   dancing over mountaintops hand in hand
   cradling one another through our valleys
   sharing our tears and strengths alike.

I wear you like an old felt hat
   with years
     and years
       and years ahead to cherish.
   Gail Sari Kennedy

My Sweet Niece

Andrea is my niece, wanted by all except the police.

She was born to my own sister, lucky for me I became her first sitter.

Her eyes were so beautiful, bright and brown,
such a joy I never wanted to see her frown.

I took her for a photograph to surprise her mother,
with tears in her eyes however, I wished I hadn't bothered

I took her training wheels off her bike when she was three,
what to our amaze off she rode pretty as you please.

How will we ever teach her of the birds and bees,
no worry, old Mother cat already showed her for free.

She got older and married a husband so gentle, loving and kind,
he's just the kind of man I had in mind.

I think it's like her Daddy she looks,
but her husband says it's like her Mother she cooks.

She's fun, honest, fair and pure,
more like her the world would be better for sure.

Where ever she is there is love to be had,
her giggle and her laugh is healing to the sad.

Will you bless her and keep her I pray oh God,
thank you Father, for I just felt you nod.
   Grace Marilyn Kemp

Who Am I?

My feelings lay deep until now.
Suppression of thought, my mind doesn't allow.

The words flow on paper with great ease.
With each word, confusion it frees.

The more I face what I feel,
the more my beliefs become more real.

I look deep inside and all I see
is the real me trying to get free.
There's a person inside who's so unsure;
but sometimes that person is completely pure.

She knows who she is without a doubt
and knows what life is all about.

When I am alone and don't try to impress;
and when I say to hell with all the stress,

I stop and think of how I feel
and only then, I know what's real.
    Jodi Stevens

Homesick

Imagine yourself in a far away land,
   Surrounded by mountains on all sides,
A place you would like to call you home,
   And you would express it with all your pride.

The lakes are so clear, the bottom can be seem,
   On a nice bright sunshiny day.
At the same time the air is so clean and fresh,
   That it takes your breath away.

Church bells can be heard, both far and near,
   In large cities as well as small towns,
Whether it be day time or late at night,
   They are heard on every hour.

The people there are never in a rush,
   Instead, they are the kindest of all the lands,
This place sounds like legendary Shangri-La,
   But it's not, it is Switzerland.
    David Owen

"The Riddle"

For all those who have loved and lost
Take solace in this, which I will say
Is not the end of a life,...but the
   freeing of a spirit?
Spirit which leaves traces in our hearts
as sure as footprints on a sandy beach.
'Tis not true what they say
that death be a final farewell.
'Tis but a brief adieu that our spirit
   knows quite well
On and on we will go into this eternal to and fro

Labors of love a shining proof.
as like a diamond in the rough.
Perfection not a goal, but a starting mark
Indeed a measure of inner tranquility
Yet these be but mere exercises in futility
in which to find no measure of humility
the one true clue which has been
   dealt in this,
a riddle put to work.
    Alexandra Martinez

Take Time

Take time to show your love, it is the best feeling.
Take time to pray, it is the source of power.
Take time to sing, it is the beauty of music.
Take time to see God's nature, it is God's beauty of the world.
Take time to read the word, it will give you wisdom.
Take time to be kind to one another, it is God's love.
Take time to listen to others, be kind and help them, but be wise
   and understanding.
Take time to use your talents, obey God.
Take time to love the Lord with all your heart in all the days of
   your life.
Take time to love the Lord, because He always takes time for you.
Take time.
    Donnette Lee Schumacher

"Woods And Wishes"

A friend and I decided to leave our chores
Take to the woods—spend the day out of doors

It was a perfect day—so nice and warm
Not a cloud in the sky—no sight of a storm

It was mid October—the best time of fall
Each tree a different color—we enjoyed them all

Mother Nature had painted all of her trees
And they danced and twirled along with the breeze

An artist palette—so many bright colors
She started with green— then added the others

Orange and yellow and on to wine red
The wild flower seeds had all gone to bed

We slowly walked and circled the pond
Enjoying the new look the trees had donned

We forged through the weeds down to the creek
Found trails of animals and took a peek

We gathered clam shells along the bank
Then sat for awhile as cold pop we drank

We forgot about laundry, dust and dishes
Just talked all day—in the woods about wishes..........
    Janey B. Johnson

Reflection

Quietly they shine giving us a glimpse of hope.
Taking away our fears and replacing them with
faith for a brighter world.

They glide through glistening waters
with a sense of tranquility.
Their only worry is man's stupidity.
A beautiful gift-one we cannot
understand only to learn from.

The gentle giants - a mystery of
beauty and serenity, created for
us to care for, to love, to enjoy.
Only we are destroying.

One man can destroy God's creations.
A killing of a whole other world.
Only stars will shine, one's faith
will always be there.
    Carolyn Armstrong

Our Days

Our days go by with barely a glance,
Taking for granted they will always last,
But one day we awake,
And the young days are gone,
We have become older and how unknown,
We don't even know how our days were spent,
And if not broken, we're badly bent.

But don't despair-all hope is not gone,
Keep your spirit strong and you'll move on,
A cool glass of water is very sweet,
A wave from a friend or strangers on the street,
Life changes every day that we live,
And all of us still have much to give,
Hold up your heads my friends and live.

We do not know when our call will come,
We don't need to know-we're going home,
The grass there is green, the sky is blue,
If you don't know Him, what hinders you?

Dorothy W. Oglesby

The Relentless Storm

Raindrops charge violently from the sky,
   Tap tap tapping unrelentingly against my body.

Each drop piercing my soul,
   Each drop invading my sanity.

I look toward the sky,
   I prey for forgiveness.

I fall to my knees,
   I cover my head.

The rain continues,
   The pain continues.

Each drop piercing my soul,
   Each drop invading my sanity.

Jonathan L. Howard

Untitled

In olden days, family values, Bible text.
Taught them stage to stage what came next.
But TV broke that great bubble,
Brought us nothing but trouble.
No respect for friends, property or sex.

Let's face it their acts are uncanny
They can't blame fact they had not a nanny.
Extenuating circumstances are a bore,
They're just clutching at straws.
All their violence is just not fine and dandy.

Within first years after they are born,
Through all orifice bright jewelry is worn.
They do not pay for what they wear,
Just stolen, food bank or welfare..
They know not how to work, can pickles, raise corn.

Peer pressure through all life has been there,
There's no one not confronted by a dare.
Exploded with great laughter and shrugs'
There was not hint, knowledge of drugs.
Biggest fright was a bogey man up the stairs.

Barbara Nason

Too Much T.V.

There once was a guy mane Ted, who watch t.v. until he was dead!
Ted loved Comedy, Ted love Drama, but most of all Ted love his Mama!
When Ted was dead, she found out what he had said,
"Television is my life if it ends I'll leave my wife".
She was mad that he didn't care so turned in-polite and
started to stare. Some people thought that was rude, but she
just treated them like they were nude! Then one day she
forgot what Ted had said, she even forgot that Ted was dead!
She came home and Ted wasn't there so once again, she started to stare.

See what television does to life?!

Inna Ruth Vigdorchik

To Sigh No More

I feel within me, very deep
Tender feelings that are me
I feel them even as I sleep
They are with me, even constantly

I've tried to hide them from myself
And pretend they are not there
If only they would stay on the shelf
I could go through life without a care

To stop these things, its all in vain
For this one within, called I
Will continue, no matter the amount of pain
To reach a world, beyond the sky

The world I seek, is quiet hard to find
Since true inner self, I have to give
To this one so rare, this special kind
The one I'll love, this life to live

I know that this is what I must do
And so I'm going to really try
With total trust, to one so true
To give of myself, no more to sigh.

Gary D. Onks

End Of The Tour

Then, at last we reached the wall
That bears the names of our country's best.
I felt the pain of that gruesome war
Burning deeper into my chest.

It's shining beauty reflected sunset hues,
Yet absorbed the tears against it shed.
I wondered how many had come here,
And in dreadful shock, swiftly fled.

I broke away from all the others
To stand alone and gaze at the wall,
When came close beside me a young soldier,
As in reverence, he stood straight and tall.

Silently, we drifted away,
Away on a cosmic sea.
Tranquility ended. I knew his sadness
When he turned and looked at me.

Suddenly, like sister and brother,
We hugged tightly, without trace of shame.
Then he pointed slightly upward and said,
"There is my name."

Dawn Hilliard

The Date

September 23, 1993
That date is forever etched in my memory
My husband, my love, my friend was taken from me,
By a cold - hearted killer who shot him mercilessly
My priceless love was killed for money;
Cold-hard cash (green inanimate paper)
That date continues to come every year,
And yet I have no one to fill my life with cheer,
No one to say, "I love you" or just
To put his protective arms around me
And say, "everything is going to be alright"
There is nothing I can do to bring him back
Despite all my might
Useless, angry, confused, alone
Those words now describe me
It started September 23, 1993.

Constance Humfleet

Crystal's Of Essence

Fair Purple uplands, the winter of Puritan snows
That enshrouded thy tremulous birth
Melts slowly to spring, now the south wind blows
O'er the face of this generous earth.

Thy elms are outspreading their flexible arms
Over meadows more fruitful and broad,
And soft ivy is veiling with negligent charms
The gaunt walls of the castle of God.

With freedom for heritage, reason for star,
And friendship for sojourner here.
Shall music long tremblingly sound from afar
Or genius be smothered in fear?

Where the ages may meet and the spirits may climb
To a truth that is builded on doubt,
The eternal may dwell mid the currents of time
And peace above barbarous rout,

If to glory, young mother, thy destiny tend,
If thy labours have honor in store,
Our loves shall not die, though their chronicle end
Nor mortals remember us more.

George John Guerin

Great Treasures

It's not the things that can be bought
That give the greatest pleasure
There are some things in life
That you can share
That no one can really measure
Be a friend a burden bear
To someone who is in despair
A beautiful word of consolation
A glorious song of adoration
That warms the heart and brings jubilation
A prayer of deep dedication
That gives life and revelation
These are treasure of great price
A thoughtful word, a good advice
To cheer a heart, to end a sigh
A faithful prayer brings victory nigh
From God in whom we do rely
A friendly smile, a warm embrace
These things will really suffice
When days are deary and long

Joy Howard Hilliman

The Autumnal Mood
(Under The Influence Of A Lester Young Blues)

This is the first time in months,
That I have trailed back to the land,
In search of something that I once lost
Or sacrificed.

That very breath of an unaffected child.

A saxophone blues plays deep in my head
As I take my very first steps
Onto the haunted grounds
Of a once cherished and lively childhood.

There are no obstacles to be found here,
Only kingdoms of the unspoiled and pure...

The only voices that are to be heard
Are the blowing of the open land's winds,
The thrills of a childhood's curiosity and excitement
And the pulses of a jazz saxophonist
Who is my savant in tolerating an adult's body.

This is the ensemble that I have dreamt about
In recent dreams.

And an autumnal color
That is damn impossible to maintain consistency.

David S. Minjares

Everything Has a Feeling

Everything has a feeling that it can feel,
That is what it is to be real.

Weeping Willows shed their imaginary tears,
While releasing their burdening fears.

Looking up to the sweet, clear sky,
Makes you feel like your in a lullaby.

Peace should be everywhere,
Making people live to love and care.

Snowflakes are like crystals, floating softly to the ground,
Moving ever so gracefully, never making a sound.

During autumn, leaves are changing, slowly dying,
While towards the south birds are flying.

Listen to the sweet song of the Chickadee,
Chirping it's name, Chickadee-dee-dee, Chickadee-dee-dee.

Listen to the wind whistling quietly through the trees,
Listen to the great buzzing of the bees.

Nature is such a beautiful thing,
The opening of buds, and the birds that sing.

Everything has a feeling that it can feel,
That is what it is to be real.

Danielle Wilbur

Faith

I have faith. "In what?", you may ask
That I'll met the right girl, and that's quite a task.
I will give her flowers and pull out her chair
Show her respect; let her know I care.
Her interests will be more than money or my physique
She will think I'm special, perhaps even unique.
When problems arise, we will talk them out
Not rant and rave and throw things about.
To one another, we will each be true
She will trust me; I will trust her too.
I believe in the words written above.
Because I have faith in a thing called "Love."

Evelyn L. Smith

Keep The Faith

Push it down,
That is all you can do.
But please don't frown,
I will still take care of you.
You can not control it,
You feel like you don't fit.
I know it is scary,
Why can't we be perfect like "Little House on the Prairie"?
You are my hero,
But now you are only down to zero.
Does everything have to be a contest?
You go to such extreme.
Now it is my turn to be the best,
You can fall down stream.
Fate,
That is the part I hate.
   Heather Ackerman

Our Garden And Our Pet Dog

A garden and a pet dog are both a source of joy;
That is if both could exist together in one's world;
But the garden grows plants which doggie loves to destroy;
There's ambivalence as to which shall stay for us all to enjoy.

There seems rather no question that both cannot co-exist;
When flowers bloom or young plants grow, Blanche,
   our pet cannot resist;
She must use her paw to pluck or uproot;
Or use her teeth to pick the vege plants young fruits.

Keep the garden or keep the pet,
It's hard to decide which one to reject;
But a fair solution, me thinks, is to see that both are kept;
By making possible a system of mutual give and take.
   Federico J. Burgos

Night Time

Night is the most peaceful time on earth.
That is when we think of what things are worth.
By choice we do the things that are best.
Making the day a beauty with just a guess.
The sounds of animals and insects can be heard;
Outside your window without saying a word.
The moon and stars are a sight to behold.
Look up and make a wish that's what you've been told.
Lights can create a great sight;
When the moments are just right.
You can escape in the darkness and meditate;
Because that's when you tune in and relate.
Goodnight and sleep tight they say;
You may need it for the next day.
   Doreen Goldson

Life's Dreams

It is the dreams for which we reach in life
That light the fire to glow within the heart,
And make endurable all of the strife
That besets us in pursuits from our start.
A dream that beckons us to follow it
Supplies the inspiration that we need
To continue pushing and never quit
When ambition demands that we should feed
Its fierce flames with our untiring toil,
For dreams are not realized magically,
And wishing will not make a kettle boil,
These transitions always exact a fee,
   But without dreams life would indeed be bare,
   And cultivating them is worth the care.
   Gwyndolyn Smith

Who Am I

As I look in the mirror, I see an image who am I.

Could I be a figment of my imagination, an invisible vision,
   that only I can see.

A vision that has no color, no name, no place on this earth
   except in the mirror.
With a blink of an eye the image is gone, taken from the
   mirror like a piece of broken glass.

Taken away but never to be replaced, except by the mind.

As I look in the mirror, I see an image, who am I.

Could I be an image trying to escape from a body entrapped
by the mirror for purposes unknown or just an image, a
reflection of a person that wants to be, but can't.....who am I.
   Jewell Forney

Eagles Fly

Eagles fly, but do they know
that those who don't often die?

Die they don't of sickness of health.
Rather they die of greed for wealth.

If not for this, then surely for hate;
the foolish emotion that's always the bait.

They live for things and they die for things.
So stupid are they that they do not see:

Things don't feel, only we.

And who are "we" you ask with wonder?
"We" are humans who always blunder.
   Dawn E. Knutson

The Night

The night brings a darkness
that only the eyes can see.
The cold dark emptiness
that seems to always be.

The night can be long
without end or relief.
To be alone and frightened
is something no one should be.

And then when a prayer, you create the light,
a brilliance beyond anyone's sight.
For the light has reached my very soul,
for only your strength can truly console.

Fears are within this mortal body,
the fears of the night, with no light.
But your love is all around, your
love is within; and I pray and I thank you
for being all that truly is.
   Catherine A. Young

Deep Breathe

   One by one with a dream locked away in a white box in
the corals of their mind; my people willingly but, also
blindly slip the transparent noose around their necks and
swing from the ecstasy of drugs and alcohol far removed from reality.

   Amidst this playground of destruction we move closer
to the total dilution and disorientation of what was once
known as the central nervous system of black existence,
the family, brotherhood and pride.
Turn toward the sun and challenge adversity to its end!!!
   Gregory J. Johnson

Poor Little Boy

Who's that little boy playing in the street?
That poor little guy with the hole in his seat.
Poor, poor little guy with the dirty face.
The one with the shoe with just one lace.

Who is that little guy, who's playing in the dirt?
That poor little guy with the too small shirt.

His Mother must be just plain awful.
Certainly this couldn't be lawful.
To let the little guy run around wildly.
To hang the Mother would be justice mildly.

Where is his Mother? I keep screaming.
I look again, and I think I'm dreaming.
He look's familiar under all that dirt.
And I think somewhere I've seen that shirt.

Oh no! I think, it just can't be.
That little boy who call's to me.
Hey! Do you want me to come home?
Oh my goodness, he is my own.
   Janet Mueller-Maynard

Death's Door

They said she had two pairs of shoes
that sat in corners of her world
all shiny and smooth once
now worn and weary of places often traveled
she lies there thinking
what's to become of foolish
unharnessed ways,
and souls that visited her
'til morning light,
with heated nights and
Sassey conversation no more
but pungent death pulls at her linens -
grey and stained with memories of those gone before
revealing what was desperately wanted covered
she drifts to a lasting sleep now
to eternal worlds
riding wings of celestial clouds and
new shoes to wear.
   Barbara J. Black

Nostalgia

I saw a familiar face in the orchard.
The apples are hanging there,
Crisp and shiny in their full, fall-ripened freshness.
Heavy and clustered they hang - perfect for picking.
But in the deep grass, one I spied extra large,
With a worm hole and a bruise.
Fondly I picked it up and nestled its cool skin in my hands,
Flicked off a crumb of black soil,
And rubbed it clean and polished on my pants.
A worm hole? A bruise? What matter?
A beauty spot! And a wound - sweeter for your injury.
Why are you shunned? Rejected?
My sons scorn you; my daughters cringe with fear.
Yet, you I choose above your unmarred peers.
O how I favor you! And savor you!
You are the flawed beauty of life - reality.
You stir my memory with all the tastes,
Smells, sounds, and charms of orchards.
With you I am at peace - comfortable - at home
With the cool, moist earth.
   Darwin C. Knudsen

To Maria

Your mysterious and perplexed eyes,
That seem to wander every way
With a sardonic smile, disguise
their river of deep hate.
The explosive reactions that take
Place behind those irises appear on the surface
As nirvana; but if a scope could examine below
the hideous undercurrent, it would discover
Pompeii, frozen and refusing to wake.
Awake the dead world! Cease to refuse the light!
Shake off those well-protected ashes
that are deceiving you. They do not cover
Dead bones suspended in time. Instead, they
Conceal plumage of a golden Phoenix, yet to fly.
   Eleni Vickles

God Is God

As I slept last night I had a dream
That somewhere a baby cried for me.
And in this dream there was nothing I could do.
And, still the baby cried for me.

When a baby dies, I wonder why
God calls them home so fast.
For they've never lived to see a day
Or to give God the praise, at last.

But, then, that's why God is God
For He knows and He sees all.
And in His way, He knows what to do
To satisfy one and all.

So, in this dream, I cried too
But, now I know why, you see.
For as I said, "God is God"
And He's there for you and me.

In sickness and pain and death and life
He always knows what to do.
So, dry your eyes and don't be afraid
God is there for you.
   Donald L. Simms Sr.

"30 Whole Days"

It's been about a month and we both know
that thirty whole days has a lot to show

And in case you haven't noticed, it's got me in a shock
a natural high feeling seeing you around the clock

As the sun rises, your name crosses my mind
pure sweet memories as I watch the clock unwind

And as the day breaks, I start all over again
Thinking of how lucky I am to have you as my friend

You may not come first in my life but your place has it's mole
X-marks the spot in my heart, body and soul

And day-by-day I'll continue to smile with grace
And as long as I'm with you, you'll continue light up my face

I hope that your what I've been looking for all these years
cause I've wasted too much time and too many tears

So let's never say goodbye...
but if we do...
then let's go in our separate ways...
and save those silent cries...
for all those rainy days
   Belinda C. Weir

Spirits Of Old Growth

I had a vision
that you and I stood side by side
in the same sacred forest,
our Spirit of place,
our souls manifested in trees.

We opened our branches in compassion
and became a sanctuary for songbirds.
We cleaned the air, provided shade,
bound water, treated all reverently,
harmed nothing.

Our souls hugged one another.
We were the reflections of thoughts that had come
and dreams yet to come.
We shared with wind, rain, sun, and snow,
our beings made of sun and star dust,
absorbed by moon, nourished by life,
washed by rain, brushed by lightning,
touched by thunder and rainbow.
Our world in balance with all creation,
The Creator's witnesses in all seasons.

Ellen C. Truong

The Pathway of Survival

The sky, an ominous gray
The air, crisp, not quite cold enough to see your breath
But, with the mist and drizzle a chill could sneak up on you
A wooded path, I walk through brush and partially leaved trees
Muddy and slippery the path is with a coating of wet leaves
Fall is here on this early November morning
I feel like a stranger invading the privacy of the woodland occupants
Squirrels hiding their winter feasts
Deer and birds competing for the last of the berries on the bushes
they stop, look at this stranger, and go on with
their business
Survival
And I, almost oblivious to them, walk in deep thought
My survival

Joseph E. Cristanus

"I Love You" Notes

"I Love You" notes slid under the door.
The crayons and paper scattered on the floor.
Continue sweet Daughter - I need some more.

"I Love You" written in the steam of my shower.
Exclamations and hearts and many a flower.
I can't believe we made it this far - You, Me - Our.

"I Love You" notes found placed in my bed.
Like you're tucking me in, when I lay gently my head.
My Dear I haven't missed a word you've said.

"I Love You" notes left for me on the table.
Sweet Daughter of mine, let us share in a fable.
For the Love that we share can not be given a label.

"I Love You" messages in your breath on the glass.
I am interested to hear what's going on in your class.
Blessed through our lives, together we will pass.

The Love in your eyes I see on this day.
Is the Glory from Heaven coming your way.
"I Love You Virginia", I'll gratefully pray.

Irene Perry Unger

Flawed Beauty

Yesterday, I saw a familiar face in the orchard.
The apples are hanging there, crisp and shiny
In their full, fall-ripened freshness.
Heavy and clustered they hang, perfect for picking.
But in the deep grass one I spied, extra large,
With a wormhole and a bruise. Fondly I picked it up
And nestled its cool skin in my hands,
Flicked off a crumb of black soil, and rubbed it
Clean and polished on my pants.
A worm hole? A bruise? What matter?
A beauty spot! And a wound - sweeter for your injury.
Why are you shunned? Rejected?
My sons scorn you; my daughters cringe with fear.
Yet, you I choose above your unmarred peers.
O how I favor you! And savor you!
You are the flawed beauty of life - reality.
You stir my memory with all the tastes,
Smells, sounds, and charms of orchards.
With you I am at peace - comfortable - at home
Near the soft, moist earth.

Darwin C. Knudsen

The Man I Use To Be

These old sidewalks seem so dirty, and there's cracks along the walls.
The back streets get so lonely, when you're running from the law.
The tired look on all their faces, say they've been here for a while.
Just hanging out in corners, long hair and beards and all.

The body seems so useless, when you've got no one to care.
Cold and hungry and dirty, with only a bottle left to share.
But when the bottle's empty, and the body's filled with pain.
You may wake up in sunshine, or you may wake up in rain.

From alcohol to drugs, from everything to nothing.
Some are first class folks who went astray.
From the top with real high living, to the streets they've all been given.
With no more than a sidewalk, for their home.

Now the first step seems the hardest, as my feet begin to move.
My body aches and trembles, to myself, I have to prove.
These streets I'll leave behind me, new roads ahead, I'll see.
I'll prove I'm still a real man, the man I use to be.

Jackie Sullivan

Mother's Flower Garden

I open the little garden gate,
the creepers I walk under.
The flowers are so beautiful, I stand and gaze in wonder.
As I walk along the path to the garden's furthest end,
The different flowers seem to nod,
and regard me as a friend.
The marigolds on one hand as yellow as the sun,
Will bloom in all their glory, till the day is done.
Pansies, petunias, iceland poppies,
mallows, for-get-me-nots blue,
Sweeten the air all day long,
until the falling of the dew.
These plants spring up so fast,
out of the warm moist ground.
We walk out each morning,
new flowering plants can be found.
Mother works to her heart's content
among her treasured flowers.
It's there she loves to walk and weed
in all her leisure hours.

Betty W. B. Thompson

The Beauty Of Christmas

The beauty of Christmas is not a Christmas Tree
The beauty of Christmas is not the things you see
Or even church bells ringing and snowflakes in the air
Or happy children singing with brand new clothes to wear
Its not Christmas candy or a special prayer that's said
And not a toy so dandy or a new hat upon the head.
Its not a santa's visit down the chimney Christmas night
Or stock kings filled with goodies or special flying kite
Its not even a fire burning or glasses held up high
Or grandma and grandpa coming with a fresh baked cherry pie
Its not a pretty christmas card or a pointsetta standing there
And not a snowman in the yard or a doll with human hair
No the beauty of christmas I'm afraid is much more
Yes the beauty of Christmas is the opening of the four door
To welcome in those of need with warmth a love to share
Yes the beauty of Christmas is how much we share and care
Edna Elsie Cillo

Echoes In The Dark

Dana? Dana? Dana? Dana?
The came echoes through my brain like a wave
Who? Can it be me——No!!!! I am only me
I have no true identity
  I am - that is all

Cold images flutter like the autumn leaves, desperate to escape
they have no destination - only to escape
do my words escape?
Or do they merely fall on a page never to be read
  I wonder
    I wander,
      drift

Must you read these thoughts?
If not - they have no destination
they only lie here like a deep, dark secret,
anticipating their unleashed power over you

"Me?" you shriek, shivering in spite of yourself
yes, you and you alone
I laugh as you shudder in your cowardly world
Dana Hammons

From Here I Choose To Where This Thought Must Lead

From here I choose to where this thought must lead,
The children know with skinned knees vengeful red;
A seed once sown is only but a seed.

The younger men with passions, war and creed,
Know not the sores they've sown when fully bled,
From here I choose to where this thought must lead.

Young ladies laced with visions: A white steed,
Find loves first face a valentine - now dead.
A seed once sown is only but a seed.

Aurora's realms flash lights with God's stern speed,
Men ponder polar readings more, and bread;
From here I choose to where this thought must lead.

Wise men and sage, sift truth from thorny weed,
God's appled eye shines all that is now said;
A seed once sown is only but a seed.

White knights, red hearts, men think most is to bleed,
Man here must face the tree that oft is dread.
From here I choose to where this thought must lead.
A seed once sown is only but a seed.
Andrew J. Edwards,

Silent Whispers

A casual observer nods in approval.
The child's uniform is starched, the hair pulled back.
Dark circles hide undetected under wide hazel eyes.
The disease reared its ugly head again last night.
Sweet dreams of the children rudely interrupted.
Sounds of hate and disgust spew from the man's mouth.
Words slap the woman helplessly huddled in a dim corner.
She sinks deeper into denial and despair, devoid of hope.
Tentacles of the disease crawl in the dark under bed covers.
Four young children lay frozen with fear.
It approaches like a wave leaving goose flesh in its wake.
Slowly it reaches into their heart and squeezes.
Silent tears roll down freckled cheeks like morning dew on rose petals
Whispers hang in the air unanswered as the disease continues to spread.
'We must not forget to sweep up the glass.'
As the sun rises, sighs of relief echo with hope for now.
In the shadows lurk the fear, the hurt and the memories.
Whisper softly for no one is allowed in.
Please God, hear the children.
Catherine M. Windish

God To Me

God is the little hummingbird drinking the sweet necator,
The eagle souring thru the blue skies;
The power of a summer thunder storm
And the calm of the eye of a hurricane.

God is a baby's first cry at birth,
The smile of an elder leaving this earth;
The love for a friend or foe
And the faith of a marriage vow.

God is our many troubles on this earth,
The happiness we share with loved ones;
The growth of a seed to a mighty oak
And the destruction of a civilization to be never more.

God is the strength we receive from prayer,
The wisdom to do the right thing;
The faith to believe in the unseen
And the love we share with all of nature.

God is a rose, His autograph to us,
The Bible, His word, our teaching tool,
The reason we are alive to learn
And the future for all who follows His will.
Caroline L. Britt Mullins

A New Man Is Emerging

A new man is emerging...
the image of this new man is not yet clear...
but the horizon is becoming red...
and the sun will soon be there...

The first rays are already available...
although still hidden in the morning mist...

The new man has already arrived in fragments...
but only in fragments...
The new man will not be Hindu...nor a Islamic...
will not be a Christian...nor a communist...

The new man will simple be an opening...
a window to reality...
His eyes will be available...
they will not be full of ideas...
The new man will not live out of belief...
He will simple live...

The new man will not look somewhere...faraway...for God
He will look here...close by...
Now...will be his only time..
Here...his only space...
John De Mesa

Grandfather Clock

It stands in the corner of the living room
The clock which my grandfather made
Out of cherry wood for my parents' wedding.

Majestic but worn, its face has yellowed
The hands are fixed at eleven to three; who knows whether it is
   morning or night? Who cares?
Even so, the pendulum still has a stately rhythmic sway.
Yet only, only at times when...

In the cabinet at the base, with its lock broken
I discovered my childhood scribbles, a little wrinkled, a little torn,
Identifiable by my first feeble signature
But, drawn with powerful crayon strokes.

As I pass through the hall, sometimes, I forget to even look its way.
And, I sometimes forget to clear the cobwebs, but,
Somehow, it knows, it knows that I love it always.

Still, its has lost, lost all that I knew,
I remember, blurred as it may
Why, oh, why does it happen?
The creaks and the sighs.

If only, time stood still
Stiller than the hands frozen at eleven to three.

Eileen M. Angelini

The Blizzard of Seventy-Four

The snow had begun in the morning that day
The date was December the first
Of all of the snows I have seen in Detroit
This one was surely the worst.

The flakes they fell gently and then, criminently!
They started to come down in chunks
You could easily guess at the depth of the snow
By that time the trees had no trunks.

The snowflakes they scurried and then I got worried
That I would be snowed in for good
From out of the blue I suddenly knew
That if I didn't shovel, I would.

Hilde Kampf

"Trusting"

As we all grow older, we notice more and more,
The simple little things we always seem to ignore.
The trees and flowers, that bloom in early springs
The sweet little tunes all the birds sing.
Always in a hurry rushing here and there,
All those things ignored without a simple care.
Now as we walk at a slower pace,
We see the world around us and what's
Been taking place.
So while we are able to change what we must,
Let's all get together, and in God put our trust.

Dewey Lawshe

Love Is

Love is the foundation of friendship building,
   The extra effort of self-giving,
   The power to overcome misunderstanding,
   The ever present spirit of forgiving.

Love is a key to the door of tolerating,
   Patience with another's blundering,
   The reflection of devotion unrelenting,
   The heart string that leads to caring.

Love is a special combination blending
   Faith, hope and trust
   In a bond never ending.

Evelyn C. Reece

To Cheer You On

In life's endurance race, my heart roots for you all the way.
The entire distance—and beyond—I've one desire: to cheer you on.

Filled with caring, hope and pride, you'll find me there where I
  belong—
Near you . . . always on your side—sure as daylight follows dawn.
I'm the one who shouts your name, with applause for your success
When you get the inside lane; have a run of happiness.

You can see my in a cloud; hear my voice above the crowd:
Loyal . . loving . . long and loud, I'll be there to cheer you on.

Even though the run's uphill, my best wishes follow you:
That you have a winning race; lead the rest in all you do.
Then as you get your second wind—for the final lap prepare—
No matter what your chances are, never doubt that I'll be there.

And when the finish line is crossed, and your other fans have gone
I will still be backing you (as I have been all along).

You can see me in a cloud; hear my voice above the crowd:
Loyal . . loving . . long and loud, I'll be there to cheer you on.

When the other fans have gone . . . .
Sure as daylight follows dawn . . . .
The whole distance—and beyond—
I'll be there . . . to cheer you on.

Andrew Barrow

The Angel Hue

Joy is the blue of the fire's hot flame
The faint shimmering of feathers
on the row's black breast
Joy is the blue in the child's sky
deep enough to sink hands into

Joy is the blue in larkspur,
lupine, the midnight blue in monkshood
In the fickle face of the humpback moon
in love with the Seven Sisters

Joy is the blue, the moment before storm,
a swirling sea of octopus ink.

Joy is the blue in river stones
silent and smooth
and the heavy morning mist of the Smokey Mountains

Joy is the blue in the sand
and sweet fern of a blueberry field

Can you see it? Blue?
The angel hue of blue-eyed grass
Can you see it?
Is there no blue for you?

Elizabeth Harvey

The Storm

Thundering in it's delirium, Lord over all,
The fates are set against us.
Frightening, yet splendid in it's passion,
The rain seems to penetrate my very consciousness.
The sifting waves beat the shore with frenzied fists,
Like a raging battle as yet unwon,
Compelling in it's fury yet not stopped,
For man has no power now,
Proof that natures forces are stronger still,
Meaningless, insurgent are our laws to you.
The winds cease now, their mournful cries no longer heard.
Trees bow no longer at the Masters feet,
For you are free again.
Washed of imperfections, cleansed and shining,
The storm is past.

Betty G. Bruce

A Poem For Thought

Penetrating the inner walls of insanity
The flowers burst into flames
And the lovers cry in pain
All destruction has different causes and effects
The reflection shows it in different ways
Cameras were playing tricks
And the eyes became baffled and disarranged
The streets became pungent with filth and pollution
All rhymes turned chaotic
And the free souls became encaged in guilt of long ago
All of these are happening
And the child's eyes of the
Future will know none of the beauty of a flower
Blooming brightly or a meadow
With daisies drifting to the surface
The earth will be bleak and gray and
Imagination will no longer exist
It will be mechanical and perfect
But the beauty and tranquility
Will be vanished.
   April Volak

Wisdom

   Wisdom, that of which I am learning
The gathering of my most collective thoughts.
   Borderline of sanity, keeps coming to my mind.
   The absolute point of no return?, - or
the next level to a higher consciousness?

   You that stands there in judgement
how sad and misfortunate, for don't you
see there is more than what meets the
eye, so much, much more.

   Open your minds eye, to see and feel
about, you, be not impatient though, for
you'll loose your train of thought
smooth and easy...absorb now absorb.
   Cant you feel it? Almost as though
its breathing inside you.

   In learning, comes wisdom, with wisdom
comes peace, with peace comes love, and
after all, isn't that what its all about??
   Jim Hartley

My Deal

Why is it that I let it go so deep
The hurtful ways of others that make me weep
I should be just like stone
Ignore their ways, they are so prone
Destined somehow to be the mean one
I will not follow fools, that won't be done
I will be wise in some other way
Change my attitude on this day
Make the best of what I am dealt
Get over these troubled feelings I have felt
Get past this way of reason
Changing as does the season
Changing all the while from hot to cold
But with God's help I will be bold
Enough to stand my ground
Innocent enough to take away the frown
I can be whoever I want to be
That is the only way I know for me
Thru the charades others make
I can be someone great!
   Cindy Snow

The Garden

The roses, the violets,
   The garden which envelops my soul,
      sweet peace sweeps over me
         covered with love.
Every breath I take, I can feel your presence
   So near to me, it sweeps over me
      I long to run to you
         barefoot, barely breathing.
            Overcome by love
               Overcome by the sweetness
                  which your touch brings.
Your touch brings a joy to my heart
   Such a joy I have scarcely felt before.
      This joy will carry me through the days of life
         Your kiss, more beautiful
            than the touch of a velvet red rose
               That kiss will remind me of this visit
                  until I am able to return.
   Amy G. McCann

Nature's Rule

It is the breaking of another spring
The grass turns green and the birds sing,
The honeybees buzz around their hive
Soon there will be many a new life come alive,
All of natures creatures are well aware
Soon there will be many new lives to share,
They must teach the newborn how to survive
The young must be taught how to stay alive,
Their survival depends on their wit and skill
To eat some must learn to hunt and kill,
Others will hunt food in a different way
But all must learn to survive night or day,
They must all try to avoid calling deaths cry
For the rule is the strong live and the weak die.
   Jerry Lien

The Way

The way...is awash with the love of each other.
The way...is awash with the blood of our brothers.
The way...is awash with the tears of our mothers.

The way...is awash with the light of the stars.
The way...is awash with the lives lived thus far.

The way...is awash with answers to all questions.
The way...is awash with the right paths to heaven.

The way...is awash with the footprints of forever.
The way...awaits us all.
   Bad Nuz

The Hour

As the hands of time take their toll, I feel
the icy hand of death grab hold.
Its fierce bite leaves a trace of sin, love
is gone Satan is within.
Death is coming quickly today.
Fall to your knees, it's time to pray.
Demons are living, walking on land.
Stay with me now hold my hand.
<u>We are as one centered in light.</u>
Satan is coming as dark as night
Life is broken, the world is gone.
Light is darkness, will it go on!
   Jessica Roten

Is My Dad Dead

As I think of the blue skies,
The green grass, the warm breeze;
I can feel my Dad's presence.

As I think of the frost on the hills,
The sparkling ice on the trees and the curtain-like fog in the air;
I can feel my Dad's presence.

As the earth is plowed in the spring,
The seeds planted and the crops harvested in the fall;
I can feel my Dad's presence.

It is so hard to imagine each day,
Without ever hearing his voice again or seeing the twinkling in his eyes;
As he teases so gently.

The caring that he gave,
The strength of character that he encourage in each one;
It is all still here.

He has changed form and joined forces with nature.
Now he is a part of everything around me,
And I know I am loved.

Ellen Zimmerman

My Guy

I think I've finally found
The guy that's meant for me
We love each other greatly
Its always plain to see

He hugs me when I need a lift
And holds my hand in his
Those blue eyes shine when he smiles at me
I never expected this.

He'll find other interest I'm certain
But I'll not think about that soon
He knows I'm totally devoted
And I'm sure he hung the moon

When he turns to me as he's leaving
And says "Grandma, I love you!
I'll let him go with a tug at my heart
And say, "Tyler, I LOVE YOU, TOO!

Denise Bright

Painting Of The Masterpiece

The wispy white clouds against the brilliant blue sky
The incessant chirping of the robin, the sunlight dancing by
Pools of deep blue against vivid pastures, emerald green
Daisies, with their heads tilted in the sunbathed scene
What unseen artist brush painted this masterpiece of the eye?

The silver lining of dark ominous clouds, the clapping thunder
Flashing lightning streaks, is nature's beauteous wonder
To look upon a wild stallion rearing his lithe body in fright
To hear the roar of the mountain lion in the dark stormy night
These things are given to us and many more things to ponder

The gossamer wings of butterflies, the shimmery tails of fish
Palettes of color in the coral wreath, green waves of ocean whirl & swish
Rolling cascades of sand, a rainbow curved across the golden bay
A child's trusting face, the promise of another day
How can we not know the Master's Touch? This is our Father's wish

Wondrous and breathtaking is the beauty of man's Soul
Cast upon this earthly scene, the sunlit splendor of morning gold
Dandelions, hyacinths, bubbling mountain brooks, laurel in the glen
The Glory of this world is surpassed only by the love within
Observe the bright evening star, such great joy for all to behold

Barbara J. Hughes

"Only A Child"

Lost, confused, alone, afraid, yet in the middle of a crowd
The hurt is buried deep within, in life's symphony the drums're too loud.
Covered over, time and again, concrete walls will not break down.
Cracks in the recess' of my mind, to such madness this child's bound.
Slave to terror, endless fears, no freedom does this child see
A child, once happy, full of life, curls up slowly dying in me.
She has silent tears, a voice, too soft, unreleased from my soul's pit
As long as I ignore her cries, in a corner punished, she will sit.
She can't make me face my ugly truth, not a scene nor even a word.
If I leave her there all alone, her cries of pain will die unheard.
Lost, confused, alone, afraid, yet in the middle of a crowd.
The symphony of life's beautiful accompany the pain of drums
Too loud.

Chianti Marie Camara

Tapestry

It twists, it swirls, it bobs and whirls;
The forms take form and change, unfurl
From young to old, the boy and girl,
Eternal hate to cherished pearl.
They romp, they play, 'til end of day.
Unnoticed, crushed, the flow'rs of May
Sigh long and deep, forgive the fray
And bid sweet naivete to stay;
But somewhere deep the human soul
A voice will shout, "No longer droll!"
Alarms will sound and bells will toll:
Grown size and wise, no longer foal.

Eric Klotch

And There Were Flowers...

The gentle licking of my puppy's tongue;
The lapping of the cool, fall breeze;
The tickling of the tender, winter grass;
The coziness of a warm fire on the hearth;
The crackling of pecans in the stillness of the night;
And the creaking of old joints shuffling towards the barn.

The crying of a new born babe;
The weeping of the morning;
The delicious smell of fresh cut flowers;
The cachinnating sound of the babe discovering his little toes;
The smile on the mornings' face of infinite forgetfulness;
And the slow deterioration of once dewy, fresh flowers.

Elaine Daniel

"The Great Gift From God"

One of the greatest offerings
  the Lord above may send
Is one often taken for granted
  The gift... we call a friend

Someone who will always be there
  Through both bad times and good
Always instinctively recognizing our needs
  And doing just what they should

As we travel down life's highway
  Things don't always go our way
We often need a comforting word
  Just to help us make it through the day

We should remind ourselves daily
  As through life's happenings we trod
The importance attached to having friends
  For they are the greatest gift from God

Doris Aline Coffey

Song For Larry

Alone in the dark
   The lights are flashing, people
Are dancing - but I'm so alone.
   You turn and look at me — 'MAGIC.'

My cold heart begins to
   beat again.
You smile at me. I need your warmth,
   I need your love to save me.

All I see is you. All I need is you.
   The lightning flashes above
Is it the thunder or your kiss
   That causes me to tremble so?

In the touch of your fingers and the brush of your lips
   The magic becomes real.
Slowly, I'm drawn into you.
   Please, help me to become real.

Love me, Larry. Make me cry out for you
   Even when you're not near.
Hold me now — hold me forever
   Lost in your 'Magic.'
     Camilla Everage

Flying Rain

I love listening to the rain splatter on the window,
The little pitter-patter coming from the window.
The raindrops having a fun time on the clouds.
Flying!
Flying, dancing with the clouds and the sky.
Clash, boom, the frightened drops fall below.
Flying through the air,
Falling, squirming, gaining more speed.
Splat!
They hit the ground exhausted.
CLASH! BOOM!
I love listening to the rain, while hiding under the bed.
     Andrew S. Easton, Age 12

The Lone Wolf

Beneath the yellow moon, hear his lonely cry
The lone wolf searching for a mate under the starry sky.
A howl pierces the darkness a shadow crosses the plain.
They meet the young she wolf is in pain
Her paw is torn and bleeding from a trap that she broke free.
The lone wolf turns as if to say follow me,
he takes her to his cave and lays down by her side
Sheltered from the cold, away the hunters they could hide.

Days went by and three pups were born on a hot july night.
cute little things, two grey males and a female of purest white
They grew and grew they learned to hunt and kill
from rabbits to deer they hunted with deadly skill.
The day had come for each to go their own separate way
She watched them go, but the lone wolf he would stay.
Across the mountains and valleys they would roam
through the wilderness they called home.

One clear day a shot rang out and then a hunters triumphant shout
A sharp yelp and the she wolf falls to the ground.
The lone wolf is on the run he will never forget that sound.
He stands upon the mountain and howls his lonely cry,
the lone wolf is alone until it's his turn to die.
     Francie Aguirre

The Heart

Is one of the most precious gifts,
The Lord has given.
For someone to mistreat, or mishandle it,
should be forbidden.
But for some it's a pleasure to hurt another,
So you find yourself,
Not wanting to share it with any other.
Which is wrong! So you wonder,
why something so important and precious
Can also be so fragile and strong,
And then you think?
How should mine be?
And I say to you,
The way it was intended to be
precious and important,
fragile and strong!
     Cedric Lloyd

The Depth Of Perception

"Just look at that sunset," said
the man with no eyes.
"Is that not the most beautiful thing
you ever saw in your life?"
He turned in my direction, and said it again.
And asked for my name.
And complimented my tie.
And he asked me if I was blind.
Well...

This man and I, we talked for a while,
and he made me laugh and he made me think.
He saw this world as clear as it could possibly be.
And this man knew all of my fears
and how often I would break down into tears.

"That was once me," he said after a while,
and then with a smile he said,
"but that all changed when I took out my eyes."
     Donny Auber

Are You The One?

Are you the one whispering in my ear?
The one saying you will always be near?
Are you the one healing me?
With hands of love and a heart that can see?

Father of understanding,
Father that is wise,
Father of strength,
And Father of mind.

Even when you are far away,
By my side you will always stay.
When the Prince of Darkness makes my life cold,
You can fight it off from my soul.

You wipe away the tears in my eyes,
You gave me the ring to the birds of the sky.
Are you the one that set me on a cloud?
Are you the one that makes me proud?

I believe in the wise men,
And I believe in hideous fools,
Yet nothing is stronger,
Than that love I feel in you.
     Joshua Thusat

Inside

Look inside the walls that surround me
the ones I chose to hide

Where only darkness lingers
and the sun never finds

Look inside the house I live
so sterile clean and tidy

Masking all the sadness
growing deep inside me

Look beyond the laughter that everything is fine
It grows like a tumor just wish it was benign

Look into my eyes again so I might find the way
and take away the darkness and show me light of day

Look into my heart and soul and rid me of my pain
and let me find the peace within so I can live again

Alex Romos

A Tribute To Snowball

Her big brown eyes were glassy and sad;
The pain seemed unbearable from surgery she'd had.
The chipmunks were running and chirping real fast,
She'd not run and chase them as she did in the past.

There is no more barking as we come down the walk,
And no response from her when we talk.
Her tiny little body, racked with pain,
For nourishment she would have to be hand fed again.

Her tummy all covered with nodes big and small,
Our vet was not hopeful when we gave him a call.
He looked at her briefly, and we heard him say,
"If it were my dog, I'd put her away."

Those big brown eyes 'neath her fur covered frame
Seemed to be saying, "Don't leave me here again".
Before we reached home, there's one thing I know
Our little friend has gone where the good doggies go.

There is an empty spot where her dish once stood.
No more begging at mealtime for a morsel of food.
Our little pal has gone, but we can never erase
That ever present memory of her dear little face.

Elaine Rhodes

Winter Rose

On the lands of the oldest snows.
The place of the filtered light, and no warmth.
On chilled lands where nothing else grows.
A place of the crippling, crawling blind.
   Forever cast with their seldom light.

Whispering, blowing nightly winds.
Snow covered sight. Cold struck sins.
Of long ago. Keep them in, and they will surely grow.
   Love she wished she would one day find.
   WINTER ROSE.
Friendship she will never know.
She is one of a kind.
Sorrow her soft face will always show.
Tears of a life time.
She screams out so loud, and so very proud.
To only the ears, which will never be found.
All her days and nights, loneliness she cries.
Like whispers, and singing from the soft river flow.
These are the tears of the sweat—WINTER ROSE,
   WINTER ROSE.

Bryan J. Burdick

Rainforest

See the trees come crashing down,
The plants and leaves have all turned brown,

The air is dark with burnt up fuel,
And now you think, "Who'd be so cruel?"

They kill it all, don't even care,
what living things might live in there.

We tell them "It might cure disease!"
But they'll move on ignoring our pleas,

They've changed the way that our children will live,
We'll have nothing to show, we'll have nothing to give,

Some day they'll realize what they have done,
The war is now over, the fools finally won.

Anders Rasmussen

"Rat Race"

Morning breaks on a brand new day,
The rat race of life is underway.

With stiff bones and joints, I roll out of bed,
God only knows what kind of traffic's ahead.

With dulled senses and stupor I hop in the shower,
I have to hurry, I have a meeting in an hour.

I have to get some coffee to get my body moving,
I jump in the car and immediately start grooving.

The expressway is congested—I'm running out of time,
I drive on the shoulder to bypass the line.

On the way into the office, I spill coffee on my shirt,
My secretary wishes me good morning and I'm nothing more than curt.

I open my briefcase and much to my dismay,
I forgot my presentation—it's going to be a lousy day.

Finally at 5:00 the day is done,
I didn't know humans could have so much fun.

I wish I could relax and enjoy the simple things,
Tomorrow's a new day—what will it bring!

Donna Rippley

I Miss You

I wish, I could find, the words to express,
The reasons for moving and not cause distress.
I'll never know, if it's right or it's wrong,
I only know, that I need to be strong.

For a mom and dad's love, to spread and to share,
No matter how old they get, never stopping the care.
As each one of the bunch, has a niche in my heart,
'Cause they were wanted and loved, right from the start.

Life is a daydream, that doesn't work out,
The way you expected or thought all about.
I thank God, we don't know, what is in store,
For we'd never keep going, to live on for more.

But finding the Lord, along life's way,
Is the answer to living, from day to day.
'Cause life with a purpose; to meet Jesus again,
Is a beautiful thought and a wonderful end.

Since life everlasting, is His great promise,
To be with our loved ones, those that we miss.

Barbara L. Laubert

Long Ago and Far Away

A flash of pink across the sky,
the roseate spoonbills passing by.
The thrill and wonder surges strong
and I remember a time so long ago and far away
on distant shores where I once did play
and sing a little victory song,
yes, a time of wonder now so long ago and far away,
yet remnants now want to stay.

A flash of pink and then its gone;
the thrill escapes the magic wand.
Yes visual images against the shore,
a birdal tribe creates the score
with a screeching symphony,
it finds a textured harmony.
With cicadas, crickets joining in
the pitch is raised and lowered again.

I wonder who leads this orchestra now?
Prime Creator masters how to build the music and the song
that links to memories once so long ago and far away
that now returns this summer day.
Gail L. Blanpied

A Vessel On The Sea

Make me, O Lord, a vessel on the sea.
The sea of life bestowed to us by thee.
That I may sail the waves of happiness,
And ride out all the waves of pain and stress.

So when the sea gets rough and currents thrust,
And everything appears to be unjust,
I'll open up my sails and leave the past,
And float til calmer days are found at last.

Then when the days are smooth for sailing on,
I'll bring my anchor up and carry on,
While gentle breezes move me nearer land,
Where the Creator of the earth shall stand.

Then when my life on earth shall close its door,
I'll dock my earthen vessel on His shore,
And kneeling praise and beg that I might be,
Allowed to live with Him eternally.
Darwin R. Fisher

The Loss

I felt you as you passed
the separation woke me from a sleepless sleep
the tears of the night still wet upon my pillow
the pain of knowing still pulsing upon my soul.

In the darkness I sat
and flew with you as you were lifted
the wonderful rays of your existence reached out-
gently, but forcefully, they called me to be witness.

I have dwelled many hours upon that feeling
being born of your flesh, the connection strong
these ties remain unbroken still, but now incomplete-
I can soar with you no more, earthly bonds hold me.

As you lingered about the morbid scene
you shared in the loss, still trying to hold on
the tears you cried fell from the heavens as rain
and joined with mine for the last time.
Anne Marie Phelan

The Buck At Sunset

It's etched upon my memory, like a photographic still.
  The setting sun touched only the topmost reaches of the hill,
Turning autumn leaves to fiery glory 'neath its spotlight,
  While all outside the circle was merely black and white.

Poised against this backdrop, dramatically detailed,
  The most majestic buck my eyes have e'er beheld.
An impressive rack of horns spanned out, dark against the sky,
  Velvety eyes upon the sunset, head held proudly high.

Slowly, he turned to face me, aware of another's presence.
  Breathlessly still, I stood admiring his magnificence.
He paused, only for a moment, to stare inquiringly at me,
  His soft brown eyes awash with avid curiosity.

I sensed his indecision as to what course was best to take,
  Till his survival instincts warned him what could be at stake.
He bounded off into the forest with a sharp flick of his tail,
  An abrupt snort the only answer to my sad farewell.
Brenda K. Rose

Daydreams Of A Sailor

Above the sea as day breaks through
the sky in lighter shades gives the sailor a view
of untroubled sailing with chance to dream of ports yet unknown.
And a stirring of memories of old Ports long gone.
So many times surrounded by water, with no way to relieve the tension,
his mind is filled with hopes and with doubts.
Or dreams too numerous to mention.
Thoughts come to mind of people gone before.
Of love lost because of the lure of the sea from the shore.
It's then waves of emotion roll ever him like the water
that separates him from the safety of the harbor.
Today he'll live to the fullest in the glory of the moment.
Basking in the rapture of the morning that enfolds him.
Saving negative thoughts for another day
when red hues in the sky will come his way.
Then jolted to reality he would fight with all his might.
For it's then sailing would becomes a fight for life.
He has learned from experience to let the sky's hues be alarming.
For true is the saying "red sky in the morning sailor take warning."
Betty B. Holmes

A Tribute To Mothers

Baby your Mother like she babied you,
  The words to the old song still ring true.
Baby your Mother like she babied you - back in your cradle days.
  What precious memories they recall
Of a Mother, who gave to me her all!

She rocked me to sleep, she taught me to pray,
  And tended my needs in her own special way.
Where did all the years go?
  They flew by on fleet wings,
But the memory of her presence makes my yearning heart sing.

She tenderly guided me all through the years
  Until I at last "left the nest."
Soon God called her Home to her well-deserved rest.
  Sometimes I wonder - did I baby her like she babied me?
So I still try my best to fulfill all her dreams.

If your mother is with you this gold Mother's Day
  As with her you share joy or sorrow, love, work or play
Go hug her "real big," and kiss her, then say,
  "I'll baby you, Mother, like you babied me
Back in my cradle days!"
Ferne I. Colvin

"Winter Time At Whitehall"

Winter time at Whitehall is a glorious sight to behold.
The snow piled high really catches the eye,
And some snow birds are still flying high.

There are deer tracks here and there,
Raccoons and squirrels are abounds.
The trees are bare but in the air
God's glory really bounds.

Hillside Lodge has a wonderful setting.
We gather round the cozy fireplace.
Dear God, I hope we're not forgetting
Your love, your concern and your grace.

A familiar sight — is getting stuck in the ditch.
We get out the tractor and soon we are hitched,
And on our way — Praising the Lord
For all the blessings He can afford.

The snow will melt, and spring will come.
And soon the Youth Camps will start.
Then, Camp Meeting and the grounds will hum,
And praises will flow from the heart.

Elizabeth Wall

Untitled

The terrible thought of hatred,
The stereotypical views,
The nasty looks on faces,
Why must it always be you?

To turn and to stop the anger,
Is what we ought to do,
Yet we stand by and watch, as another fight begins,
And allow liberty to disappear.

Dreading the thought, of the great outdoors,
Yet you aren't ignored,
For you can never go anywhere,
Without being threatened.

The terrible fate,
Dropping painfully on us like a sharp iceberg,
Why is everyone so cruel?
But we never find the answer!

The grief on the journey,
The frustration it leaves,
It follows behind you, forever,
Because the experience of racism is unforgettable.

Elena Morgenlender

Many Of One

I awaken to a pale blue state of being
The storm has ended and there is only calm
A loud silence rules this land
A sickening quiet that makes the air strange
Everything is new, yet I've seen it all before
I reach out to touch it and it disappears
I am surrounded by nothing and love that I am alone
I am free to wander about in my own reality
Confined only by that which was once unknown to me
Falling through infinity with nothing but my thoughts
Thoughts which are alien and not my own
I wish only to remember that which I never had
To know the mysteries which are yet unanswered
I am drawn in, pushed away, and remain at the center of nothing
I am given the knowledge of myself to return hastily
I wish to be alone and at once I am
Alone, only with that which was given but never received
Though I know I will never be truly alone
For I have the knowledge; I am many of one.

Joseph Candella

Fall Impressions

Morning fog paints the ground white.
The sun is hidden by the fog.
The sun kisses me warmly as the fog walks on.
Leaves chatter like the squirrels.
The wind's strong breath blows my hair
   off my shoulders as I walk.
Whining wind is a violin singing a high note.
The air tastes like dust in my mouth.
Smokey air floats around cotton clouds.
Leaves fall swiftly and elegantly.
They are carefree as they fall.
Innumerable leaves coast and dive to the ground.
They are left in puddles of color:
   red like fire, gold like rays of
   the sun, brown like the earth.
Leaves grumble crisply as I step on them.
Bare tree branches cut the sky like a knife.

Carrie Osborne

Reunion Joy

What a joy to be together,
The time has finally arrived,
The reunion of kith, kin and family,
Of which this group is comprised.

We've traveled from every corner of this, the USA,
Some from the East Coast and,
Some from the West,
And some from a very close way.

We've met new faces; learned of new places,
Exchanged interesting history,
Some of it glad; some of it sad,
But all of it given succinctly.

We've always been genetically connected
Because of our ancestral bonds,
Now we have an added cohesion,
That of togetherness and love.

And now we part for our home return,
All the more richly endowed;
With a sense of family unity and love,
This reunion has made us proud.

Joyce E. Hornbeak

Outward Bound

You begin to become a mere memory.
The raging current of your presence
Is merging with the ebb of absence.
The pump of blood now starts to mock me.

The beat hangs heavy with your being;
Late love will stay the tide forever.
Where is the hyacinth, the heather?
Are the metaphors of grief worth saying?

The corpses carried by the torrents
To the endless swell of ocean
Are wearing most familiar faces.
I cannot fathom where our place is.
But you will know: my brain's final image
Will sail for your mind in its last passage.

Joan T. MacKenzie

Until

It sends chills up through my spine
The smiling sinners, their love divine
They always embrace their careful way
Of thinking it should have came today
The judgement call from the knowing book
I wish sometimes, I didn't have to look
Within the words, the stories that tell
The way about living, that road into hell
The sky so blue it beckons me to dive
So why should I question if the souls alive?
Sometimes I don't think about who I am
I just say thank you for the ransomed man
But that is not enough to stop my pain
The life I have lost, the blood I have gained
I regretfully torture my thoughts passing through
Until, dear God, I believe I've found you

Jennifer Stanley

The Dream

The dream of meaning everything, the feelings you think he feels.
The times you spend together, the moments that you share.

He means more than anything, nothing could pull you apart.
Until one day somehow, you've realized your dream is only being dreamed.

By being burned and used you begin to hate life.
And what its worth.

So you turn to the darkside, where you find only poverty and despair.
Dazed and confused you only wonder why, how can this be happening to me?

Oh Lord hear my prayers for what your about to see.
I see no point in me being me.

One swift slit the razor fell.
As I lie thinking for heaven or hell.

As I'm being rushed down the hall. I see my life pass before me.
Just to look up and see my parent's with no mercy.

I made a mistake Lord please don't take me.
The last sounds I hear are the ones from my dream.

Saying I Love You.
and will always be near.
If only now it wasn't a dream.

Colleen Gibbons

Parity

The golfers here are lean and mean.
The toughest that you've ever seen.
They sure have muscles, believe you me.
They use them well, you must agree.

They're broad of shoulder - broad of beam.
We hold them all in high esteem.
They hit the ball a country mile,
And whip the foe with lots of style.

The shots they miss are very few.
They terrorize opponents too.
It's true there's some profanity.
So what is that to you and me?

But really, I must raise my voice,
And say please come and let's rejoice.
For this is really nothing new,
We have some good men golfers too!!

Chuck Sexton

Out Of Season

It's a day before the seasons change
The trees are dying, cracking, hollow and empty
Rapidly shading, so few remain

In the sky, clouds rearranging
Dispensing cold air and a smoke filled mist
That blankets and imprisons
What little life still exist

Yesterdays are the seasons of past
Revolution of a machine, in command
Of an endless cycle that has always been

Replenish just to demolish
Regrowth just to diminish

Snowblind are the yesterdays
Sun glistened is an eagles eye
For the seasons must always change and divide

Constant is the quest to live and die
For the end of the season
Has called for its last time

Christopher Hasson

"Highways Of The Future"

Between now and 2095 A.D.,
the U.S.A. will still be free!

We'll feed the world as we've done before,
from farms upon the ocean's floor.

In the Mideast, peace will reign.
All men on earth are brothers again.

The third planet from the sun is the place,
to visit when living in outer space.

Pollution will be the least of our troubles,
our cities will be underneath glass bubbles.

Last but not least, let's not despair,
all of our highways will still need repair.

Joan Greisman

Open Up

I took some questions to the ocean.
The waves just blew me away.
The answers were skewed in the air -
I couldn't hear what they tried to say.

I took a stick
and tried to write a letter in the sand -
But the waves washed up what words had left my hand.

With my finger, I scribbled in the brine -
But the ocean was hungry and swallowed each line.

With tears rolling down my cheeks,
I gave up on the sea -
And as my salt fell and mingled with hers -
The ocean answered me.

Ashley Kemp

Polluted Tears

Whales and porpoises give warning to man
They try to swim on land
We have oceans with new motion
And the lands full of sand
And man he still don't understand
Earthquakes and volcanoes stand up in their place
So what will happen to the human race
Rain forest one day tomorrow no more
And then I wake and cry polluted tears

Gerald Litalien

Cool Clear Water

On the banks of the river of cool clear water
the willow trees hung low over it's side
the snakes slithered thru the thick brush
as the Deer drank the cool water and fled to hide.

It is time for all of natures own to wake up
the animals climb from the ground up to the trees
the birds fly thru and around the green woods
the squirrels, the rabbits, the opossum all move with ease.

Down to the River where the life blood flows for all
goes each of these, travelling his or her merry way
slithering, chirping, clucking, cracking and crawling
to get his or her share of life's blood each day.

They slake their thirst as tho it would be the last
then frolic in the cool clean waters and look
right and left to watch for any danger there
everything is fine so to enjoy a snooze in a shady nook.

Come to the end of the long and playful day
they each go hither and yon in a weary way
back to their home built or dug in the woods
on the edge of the river to be visited another day.
   Curry Barnes

Christmas

Every where I look I see a wonderland of snow,
The windows in the store fronts, with Christmas Lights aglow.
People filled with laughter, there's music every where
The presents are all gaily wrapped with tender loving care.
It's Christmas.

The Shopping Malls are crowded, people checking off their lists.
To make sure not a single Soul, at Christmas, will be missed.
There's turkey, and there's stuffing and sweet potato pie
There's apples, nuts, and candies, that fill the children's eyes.
At Christmas.

The reason for the season, is to thank the Lord above.
For sending us His precious Son, His greatest gift of love.
God sent to Earth His only Son, in a stable to be born.
To lie upon a Manger, and just swaddling clothes adorn.
First Christmas.

Upon a cross he gave his life, our sins to take away.
And it was only for this reason, He was born on Christmas Day.
Because God gave this precious gift, now sinners can be saved.
For this great gift of God's endless love, we celebrate this day.
Merry Christmas.
   Anne D. McGrath

"The Wonders Of God"

I feel the wind and see the rain,
The wonders of these stuns my brain.
How God controls each and everything,
With his help, all his wonders do bring.

The mountains so high, the valleys so low
The oceans and lakes, the grass that doth grow
The trees so tall and many flowers their bloom
One wonders the earth has so much room.

The many people of color and race
The food grown for all, pray all give grace.
The many inventions and science to help us
Yet through Him above, who has shown us how and it will be thus.
   Alvira V. Hendrickson

The Rain

I'm looking at the tears falling from the sky.
The world is dark and grey, just like I feel inside.
Memories of the past are very strong today,
I can feel old pains and fears in the strangest sort of way.

It's as if you are still there; just out of my grasp,
And my heart is still bleeding, always remembering the past,
I can hear the cold wind crying, as my heart beats in my chest.
I know I must go on living, following my unknown quest.

The trees are bending and breaking from the fury of the storm,
Reminding me of love rooted deep, yet, not far from harm.
The wrath is now subsiding, the earth is wet and clean,
But the tears keep on falling and I don't know what it means.

I see drops add to the puddles on the cold uneven pavement.
A chill runs down my back and I wonder where the love went.
   Angela Sallman

Love

First a smile to remember me.
Then a kiss never to be forgotten.
That was only the beginning of our love.
Each and everyday my love for you grows beyond
words, letters, and gifts. My love
for you shows when there is
silence between us. Each day
I thank God for giving me the
chance to love someone as
wonderful as you. Loving you
is a natural high that I
have fallen in love with. Everyday
with you is like the first day
our love came to be. Everyday
that I'm not with you feels
like eternity, for eternity are
the days I want to spend
with you. I like you, I love you,
I am in love with you.
   Adriana Rodriguez

What A Way To Die

I want to cry
then I wonder why
my love for you must die,
though I lie and say "I'm fine."

My heart is brazen
yet I'm soft spoken
my heart and mind full of hurting emotion;
again I lie and say "I'm fine."

Again and again I cry
I feel as though to die inside;
the pain I feel I cannot hide.

My love for you runs so deep
I cannot help myself but to weep
forced to keep my feeling inside
then and only then will my heart truly die.
   Anna E. Bryson

Untitled

Everything starts to fade out of you
then you hit the bottom
and no one wants to accept it
so the rock is supposed to turn into air
   The pretty people let you know
I still hate nothing
people say things
what the corrections made
the weirdness has infected all
she acts like it has disappeared, she's been cleansed
I can't say the same
she's trying but it's just not working
its true there is no one else
like each other it is only expected
she's given up the fantasy and when she wants it back
the fantasy has given up on her
    Jenny Wade

Dreams

You feel your eyes closing fast,
Then you know your day is over at last.
If you have some trouble falling to sleep,
Just close your eyes and count some sheep.
Finely you see something pretty and bright,
With people and houses that give you no fright,
Then suddenly there's something that's horrible and bad,
And everything around you just makes you feel sad.
Oh no, oh no, can you give me no more?
Please get me out get me out of this horror.
Then you wake up and notice you can't hear a scream,
And you say to yourself, it was just a dream.
    Jennifer R. Beyers

The Road Home

There are roads that are long and weary,
There are roads that are short and dreary.
There is a road I love to roam,
The dear old road which leads to home.
It winds up thru a pine scented forest
Where perpetual twilight does reign,
Thru meadows rich in clover bloom
And fields of ripening grain.
It leads into a wide old lane
Where trees surround it like a wall,
That in blossoming time it almost seems
Like walking thru a marble hall.
I know the spot where strawberries grow.
And barefoot children were won't to tread
In the summer dust that often laid
As thick as butter on country bread.
At the end of this road is home,
And in the home is love,
In spite of all cares and troubles
It is sheltered from above.
    Eleanor Delker

Undaunted

"Incorrigible," some might say
This magnificent Indian Summer!
Hanging on as it has
To the celebration of itself in all its beauty.
Not wanting, it would seem,
To let the promise of an extreme cold
Frown on a comforted people.
Powerless, nonetheless, to stop the inevitable,
Autumn smiles knowingly and says:
"Enjoy me!"
    Frances Smalkowski, CSFN

Abuse

Hidden well in the top dresser drawer,
there found his life's last will.
The memories that are so sore,
those memories could make him kill.

He picked up the gun, that reflected his face,
as sorrowful feelings rushed with the tears.
And he thought about where he stood in that place,
now he no longer must his fears.

He thought about those sorrowful feelings and pain
the last fear from every bruise and cut.
About his father, crazy and insane,
and stuck with that feeling in his gut.

He looked at the gun that he grasped in his fingers,
then pointed it at his dead.
He quivered with fear as he pulled on the trigger,
and just like that he was dead.

No need to take the abuse anymore,
now that his suffering's done.
After he reached in the top dresser drawer,
and pulled out the pain ending gun.
    Diana De Augustine

A Wish For A Kiss

Once I went to a magical pond
There I saw a Leprachaun

The little man said, "How do you do?"
My reply, "Just fine, how about you?"

The Leprachaun shouted, "I'll give you 3 wishes"
"But only if I get 3 kisses."

Well, I gave him 3 kisses on his cheek
Then he fell to the ground, "You've
made me so weak.

"No more wishes" he said, "for you!"
So I started to cry Boo hoo boo hoo!

"Okay, okay." "Three wishes for thee"
"But keep your kisses away from me."
    Gina Del Coiro

Cobalt For Fifteen

The double steel doors close.
There is a cold silence.
I am alone...
With the piercing childhood memories of incestuous abuse.
Alone with the key to my soul...
Prayer, so ferocious and moving.
Much like the fired up radiation machines.
Alone with the ball bearings...
Roaring with aggressive anger as they hit the glass tray.
Filling my heart with painful echoes of my perpetrator.
The tray methodically moves over my abdomen...
Poising itself to combat my manifested fear... cancer.
Alone, I use my key to speak with God.
Please embrace me... no more burning, no more pain.
Relinquish my fear... forgiveness is the precipice of life.
Hold me tightly as we equally walk hand in hand...
Down the road of infinite wisdom.
Filling my soul with love and hope.
I am no longer alone... I am a survivor.
Together at last with illuminating peace.
    Claire Lake

The Promised Land

Please take my hand, come along with me
there is a place I'd like you to see
we will arrive early we will stay through
the night, and we will walk through heavenly light

There may be a breeze that does nothing but
please and flicker of light to warm you at night

You may find it hard to believe
your eyes,
For around every corner their will
be a surprise

Then at the hour when the day is done, you may
not want to go back to anyone

Its your decision if you go or stay
but I made a promise I'd pave the way

Now won't you please try and understand,
for now your standing on Gods land
   Bernadette Trzaskos

Sanctuary

There is safety where I dwell among my dust-filled, printed pages,
There is peace and certain comfort locked within each treasured tome.
I am shielded-am protected from all hurt hurled deftly at me,
I can live within my writings, calling any place my home.
I can laugh, beset with sorrow, stroke of pen, it disappears,
I can joust with fate the morrow, turning laughter into tears.
I can punish those oppressors who would have me put to test.
I reward the kindness shown me giving nothing less than best.
Here I can't be broken, nor my feelings quelled to nil.
My books can never hurt me, never devastate my will.
My friends, my allies comfort me.
They only give, not take.
And lo, upon my passing, will provide a proper wake.
   Jacqueline S. Doan

Home

I miss our small town
There was green instead of brown.
I miss the colorful leaves of fall
Thinking about the park and playing ball.
I miss all my favorite places
And being with so many familiar faces.
I miss my favorite creek bank
And fishing until the sun has sank.
I miss the saturday night races.
No doubt about it, home is where my heart is.
I miss the friends who will never come home,
The Hideaway and Kelseys pond, time shared, remembered alone
I miss the shade trees and the country air
Playing games and winning prizes at the county fair.
I miss riding my snowmobile when the temperature is forty below
Yes, with each passing day, there is one thing I know,
No doubt about it
Home is where my heart is
   Frank R. Post

Loss

Grieving remains an aloof stranger
Though death has intervened.
The panacea of unbidden tears
Refuses its grace.
Stones of heaviness are too great a burden
Merely to be named sorrow.
That would be commonplace.
Bereavement is only a word, defining nothing.
A barren explanation not fit to clarify
This quiet anger.
   Geraldine Bauer

Halloween

Halloween will soon be here,
there will be witches and goblins and ghosts to fear;
jack-o-lanterns will flicker in the night,
many of the costumes will be out of sight,
there will be guessing games and tricks to be played,
but remember too, there are rules that must be obeyed;
like don't dart out in the street between cars,
watch where you are going and not at the stars;
don't eat any goodies until you get home,
stay in your own neighborhood, don't roam;
yes, halloween could be a fun time,
if you take heed to my little rhyme; "Happy Halloween!"
   Dotty Spinosi

Hell's Web

To those of us sinners condemned to hell,
There's a beginning but never an end.
No loved ones, not even a friend.
The creatures that can't wait for you to get in,
Are more scary than any features we've been.
And the noise is so loud once you get in that you try to hide.
You try and run back to outside, and just then
another creature grabs you by the hide, and swallows you deep inside.
The heat is so hot you beg to a drop of water or wind.
In hell there's a beginning but never an end.
Father please, please forgive me for my sins.
I swear I won't do them again.
You pound and you knock on heaven's door,
But all you hear are screaming and roars
of the monsters of the hell that you're in.
In hell there's a beginning but no end.
God knows you no more, cause he's warned us so many times before.
For us sinners the gates of heaven are closed forever never to
   open again.
That's the price we'll pay for the wages of our sins.
In hell there's a beginning but never, never and end.
   David S. Horn

There's A Cat In My Lap

I'd get you some tea, but golly gee,
There's a cat in my lap and he's taking a nap.

I'd offer you booze, but he's taking a snooze.
Don't ask me to hustle, I can't move a muscle.

There'd be toast with butter and something or other,
But as you can see, it's just not to be.

I'd serve you a feast if it weren't for this beast,
But it wouldn't be fittin' to disturb this kitten.

We could have a nice talk or go for a walk,
But I can't disturb him - I'm afraid to perturb him.

When my cat's asleep I can't make a peep.
If I get too gabby he'll just wake up crabby.

He might scratch and claw me, or even maul me.
It's much better to wait than to tempt my fate.

Oh, isn't he cute? Just look at this brute.
He's dead to the world all cozy and curled.

He looks like he's frozen but he's really just dozin'.
Maybe he's fakin' - I'll just try to wake him...

I'd be the best hostess - the one with the mostest,
But it's like I said - oh, never mind - he's dead!
   Janet Washburn

Journeys

My, what crooked paths of cobblestone
these bare feet have wandered

How many hours have been exhausted
looking for green grass
and willow trees that drape the prairie floor

I've trod rivers full of rage
looking frantically for the calming of an out cove

So many nights
I've hid within the safety of your arms
escaping being eaten by the wolves

Now with faith in my soul
the forest I see is thick, luscious green

As cottontails hop
in the wink of an eye
and day lilies dance to the tune of the breeze

My heart is at peace now as God lights my way
I no longer stumble alone or afraid
Jan M. Kilgour

Untitled

Innocent eyes and smooth skin,
these make up a child.
As he grows and start to sin,
the lines begin to appear.
His eyes eventually darken
as his innocence leaves him.
Now an old man with eyes that are no longer bright,
but completely overcast.
And lines so deep his skin is lost in them.
Finally in his coffin, he lays to rest.
So many sins, so many lies.
Dina Crosta

What Shall I Tell Them?

Two small children sitting by my side
These two children are my joy and pride
There is so much about life that I can tell them
Yet there's so much that I must hide
I can tell them how much I love them
But I can't tell them why I feel so knotted up inside
My mind begins to wander, my head begins to swirl
What should I tell my boy, what should I tell my girl?
They're not too young to know that Jesus died
So people could live and be set free,
Free from the things that can devour you and can devour me
Lord this is my prayer and this I ask,
Please always keep my children safe as you have me
And the cruelness of this world
Please don't let them see and I pray they never know
The things that trouble me
Helen Brown Dunlap

God's Precious Jewels

From tiny twig, or needled pine,
They glisten and gleam like gems divine.
Clear as rain-washed clouds they glow,
Translucent as glass the artists blow.
Touched to life by the morning sun,
In fragile beauty, like cobwebs spun.
Lightly suspended, each gemstone of dew,
Like beads from God's necklace, given to you,
Reflecting in glory, the work of his hand,
Beauty unrivalled to brighten the land.
Touching with splendor the advent of morn,
Clothing in beauty a world just reborn.
James F. Sullivan

Friendship

I love to describe intangible things.
They appear so often as having wings

One cannot see it, but really feel it.
Between good friends it is a solid.

It not only makes you happy inside.
It last long and can be trusted beside!

You can call each other by phone, wherever
There always is a cheerful, "Hello", a refusal ... never.

It was such fun to go out shopping
When we had money or if we had, nothing.

We were together and we could talk
Either driving in a car or walk

We also had much fun on our trips
Full of curiosity and smiles on our lips.

Whether it was to zion or Bryce Canyon
Tropical Hawaii or the Grand Canyon.

When you know each other for so many years
All this is like music to our ears!

When we can talk, listen, laugh or cry
It always was and is great our friendship, that is why!!
Johanna A. Garretson

My Boys

Laughing, running, playing, jumping, full of unending energy.
They are my greatest joy.
They push me to the edge and with one sweet, innocent smile,
  they pull me right back.
They test their limits and I am always amazed at their fearlessness.
Intelligent, witty, anxious, independent, full of unanswered questions.
They offer their love to me, just because I am Mom, and I am blessed.
Their hugs are magical, and I feel so loved, embraced by their little arms.
I look in their eyes and I see wonder and amazement.
They approach life with such excitement.
I can't help but look at them and wonder how I got so lucky.
At night when they are asleep,
I sit and watch, and wonder what they might be dreaming about.
They look to me for answers, and although I share what I know,
I am really the one who is learning.
My boys, so young and inexperienced have taught me
what I have been trying to figure out for years, that love and
forgiveness go hand in hand.
Thank you. Mom
Jeannie Palacios

Untitled

People are funny in things
they do, some like to gossip
to see what you will do.

If you ignore them, they
will get distressed thinking
you defeated them at their
little test.

Only the strong will survive
in this world, for the weak
will die from lack of word.

You must believe you
can pass the test of going on
defeating the rest.

Keep your courage, do not
doubt, and you will always
be a winner, you will
always win out.
Carol Blackburn

Alcoholic's Behind The Wheel

The alcoholic is a joke, their whole lives appear to go up in smoke.
They drink and they drive, while everyone else fight to just stay
  alive.
Their families cry, feeling like they have lived nothing but a lie.
Alcoholics seem so unfair, the life they live, they should beware.
We all hope their disease will go away, then the true loving person
  inside could come out to play.
Alcoholics, I guess are here to stay, but please God, tell us there
  is a better way.
The hurt, anger, and distrust their families do feel,
  will never go away, till there are no more drunk driver's behind
  the wheel.
Elizabeth Wangberg

The Contrast

When darkness falls, the shadows come out.
They emerge from tiny cracks and holes amongst the walls.
Some shadows are grey; they slip around each other.
If they make a sound, the lights come on.
Then they would perish, so they must be quiet.

The silence is deafening; It is forbidden.
The people that the shadows surround,
are the ones who suffer.
They are tortured by the unseen.
Facing the unknown, is like death.
The only hope that keeps them alive
Is the same thing that kills the shadows,
Light, hope, and love...

Those are their weaknesses
When the morning breaks, daylight surrounds them,
The shadows are forced back into hiding...
Until the evening, then darkness will terminate the light.
They will live once again!
Daria Favale

Enigmatic Love

Being in love can make people sick.
They feel love is some folly or an evil trick.
Love can turn the wisest person into a helpless fool.
If one does let it, love can hurt, maim, and most definitely be cruel.
Some believe love is a malicious monster that steals in the night,
But to most others, love is a magic that can make a day sparkling
  and bright.
Love is not meant to pull us apart.
One must not love with the eyes, but with the heart.

Love is an understanding without conditions
That knows no boundaries or prohibitions.
A caring beyond the deepest attraction,
Which in times of trouble hinders not a fraction.
A longing effort to support another
With an unbreakable bond that the worst of storms cannot weather.

Love is a glorious gift that vanishes never.
My love for you is simply forever.
Jill Magargee

Hiking With You The Other Day

Under the inky clear sky, I waltz down the puzzling paths
Tickled by the golden wheat, trampling the yellow dandelions

Looking down, I could feel their freshness beneath my feet
The tingling breeze bathes the bare breasts under my shirt

With one arm around you, I reach to your concealed happiness
The sudden surge of love surrounds me, it rids your sadness

We melt, float and ascend up high, like lilac blossoms in May
Here I am, in autumn, a free spirit longing for a secret getaway
Hong Zou

Fear

There are some people in constant dismay,
They harbor a sense of dread everyday,
They hardly ever look on the bright side,
Their panic and fear causes them to hide.

Instead of looking up at the beautiful sky,
Watching the gorgeous cloud formations float by,
In autumn, looking at colored leaves on trees,
Listening to the singing birds and buzzing bees.

They are in a constant state of apprehension,
Their brows show signs of consternation,
Every little sound or clamor causes fright,
They are constantly so very up tight.

I wish that somehow they could see,
What a wonderful world it can be,
If only they'd let God in to stay,
Letting Him lead you will push fears away.
Catherine F. Seidel

The Warmth Of Their Love

With arms embraced,
They huddle beneath a woolen blanket.
Gazing into the sky, they search the stars for answers.

Will their lives together be happy and prosperous?
Or will there be trials and tribulations?
For their destiny will be what they make of it.

Though the air is cold and crisp,
The love within their hearts,
Is as warm as the blanket around them.

As long as they have one another,
There is nothing that can stop them.
For their dreams can become reality.

While dawn draws near,
And the sun on the horizon,
They gaze into each other's eyes.

For this moment shall always be in their hearts,
And the warmth of their love for one another,
Has an ever lasting fate.
Jane E. Savage

Lets Save Our Children

Lets save our children before its too late
They need love and not the hate.
Abuse is tearing, at our generations, to be.
So open those doors, look out and see.

Lets save our children, who can't walk alone
Thru alleys, parks, or a zone
Daylight is good, its easier to see,
but darkness hides, the abuser to be.

Abuse is visible - its a mirror, you see
Looking right at you, like a sting from a bee.
Neighbors help when you see this child,
With grief in his eyes without a smile.

A body with marks are surely the signs.
I....I....I.....I.... he whines,
Never, completing a sentence, a haven of fear
Watching for his offender, he thinks he's near.

So lets save our children, oh, neighbors we can help.
Hot lines are everywhere, they'll give you the pep,
To save our children before its too late,
God loves us all - abuse he hates.
Fannie C. Wims

The World Of A Child

There were times when the sun kissed the cheeks of children at play.
They laughed, danced and sang songs all summer's day.

When the breezes blew fresh a pine scent from the trees,
and the meadow were filled with pink clover and bumble bees.

When "green house effects" scorched not one sweet little head,
and the water was safely clear blue and not full of lead.

When all could run freely through the streets or walk to a park.
With no terror of gunshots from screeching cars in the dark.

With handmade petals of poises and leaves in their hair.
No worry of strangers made them burdened with fear.

When the love for a child was never too much,
and there was no such a thing as a "bad touch".

When a child needn't dream of family or a home off the street,
or have wonder of whether that day they will eat.

When their dreams were of castles, dragons or pixies and elves,
and everyone taught a child to believe in themselves.

There will never be sweeter memories of lost treasures found,
or the song of angel voices making lullaby sounds.

The peaceful world of a child should never be stolen away.
Innocence lost is a consequence too costly to pay.
Ilia Akers

To Mother

With tears of anger in my eyes, I can hear her words around me.
They remind me of the rain-cold, yet comforting,
  and falling from every direction I can see.
I watched each word cradle on her tongue then dance through the air
  to my ears.
Her voice could sound as lilting as a summer shower or calming
  like the wind.
Even electric like a midnight storm.

But now, her lips speak softly, almost whispery like an autumn breeze.
So gently and sincere - buttery and warm.
I close my lids and feel the anger fall from my eyes and diminish
  down my cheek.
I listen to her words echo in my ears - almost singing,
  the sweetness of each syllable,
"I love you."
Danielle Nelsen

A Family Dinner

As you sit and listen to my words relax
Think of nothing
Close your eyes
Feel the love that comes from our hearts
The love that we pass to one another
This day that we have been brought together on
Will be the mist memorable
The words that we will speak
The hugs that we will exchange
We shall never forget even when the times we shall not be together
This day will mingle in the heart with the mind...

Time, oh how it passes so fast
Is there enough time to do as we all want
Share our dreams
Now open your eyes
As I look out upon all of you together
You have now seen my dream
Which you made come true
  I LOVE YOU
Cheryl Zaha

The Dance Of The Banshees

It was the midnight dance of the Banshees.
They were having a loud riotous ball.
The pale moon was sailing above the trees.
There was much strutting by both big and small.

Someone would rear back her head and holler.
It was a bay to the sliding wolf-moon.
It soared on high full of fitful choler.
The wild crescendo made an eerie tune.

They did a wide sashay into a prance.
The jigged and yawed about in frenzied dance
With elan that grew and ended.

Higher and higher came the feral cries
As they swirled and dipped and spun about.
They were painting and sounding grunting sighs
Which dissolved into the next screaming shout.

They dance and wail as they shrieked of old
With never a thought of making amends.
Their keening cries will never lose their hold.
Hee-hee-hee. I don't care. These are my friends.
Frank Ducat

The Best She Can Be

Sometimes I know our life is fast paced and you're expected to do
  things as you would in a race
Get up, get dressed, go wash your face, brush your teeth, brush your
  hair, it just doesn't seem fair
Well life's not always fair as I'm sure you'll agree
Why is my Mom always nagging at me
I do as she says while I'm running like mad and at times I don't know
  if she's happy or sad
She says, I'm just stressed, don't take it personally
But I can't help but ask does she understand me

Well I do understand you and want to express I appreciate you very
  much and think you're the best
But although I'm demanding and sometimes impatient
Crying and whining just doesn't quite make it
I can imagine what goes on in your head
You've got homework, baseball, friends and chores too
You almost want to scream and yell what more can I do
And just when you think that it's time to relax off we go to run
  errands and then time for a bath

We have a great life, it's fast but fun
I wonder at times how we get anything done
And so in closing I know you'll agree
Our life is just short of a little bit crazy
But one thing's for certain, it's easy to see
My daughter Chelsey is the best she can be!
Barbara A. Phillips

A Lesson From The Cathedral

Have you seen the Gothic Cathedral of Amiens?
This church, this grand creation of devotion,
stands manifest: a hymn to God and a symphony
of human aspiration played in glass and stone.
It gathered itself through rank on rank of columns,
while holding steady on its base with flying buttresses,
at last to lift its being into place, earthbound and soaring.

A human being has two feet on which to stand
and two arms for support. But in his mind
as many pillars of possibility can grow,
when complying angles give support,
as he can dream within his time;
and take his multivalent stance,
if firmly rooted in the heart,
to give stability in storms
and bring new light into his life.
Jeanne Thomas Blake

Goodnight

Sittin' down in my easy chair,
Thinkin' about how much I care.

My feet set down, on that spot on the rug,
I want to reach out, and give you a hug.

Or maybe make it, a passionate kiss,
If only to show, it's you that I miss!

Though the distance between us, is many a mile,
When I think of you, I break out in a smile!

I want to call you, each long lonesome night,
Just to hear your sweet voice, as I turn out the light.

Where are you my love, the one I hold dear?
I want just to hold you, or least have you near.

I sit with my memories, most of them great.
Though it's one in the morning, it is getting late.

So with the grace, of God up above,
I'll see you again...Goodnight, my love!!!
Don Pearce

The Pain We Shared, Different Yet The Same

I remember that night
Thinking of all those years that you continued to fight
The strength that you possessed
The beliefs that you professed
Displayed your will to live
And the wonderful things you did
The way you cared for me and taught me to see
You were in so many ways my other mother
Being there when nobody else would bother
The hurt I caused you
But still the things for me you would do
I wish I could go back
The time together we lack
I promise something for you
I will make all your dreams for me come true
Even though I wish you were here
I know I have nothing to fear
Now that you are at peace, finally at rest
This I know for you is the best
Our days together I will never forget that I cannot even regret
Danielle Enage

Runaway

Sweating, panting, running,
this fears plagues my every move.
"Try to hide to avoid the man,"
run, run, run.
Trip and fall, crawl to a safe place.
Looking for comfort surrounded by this
cold steel dumpster.
I lye motionless, with teeth gritting.
I feel my heart beating louder and louder,
like that of war drums.
Scanter out and begin to run,
Hear a crack of thunder from this gun.
Feel my back split and blood run.
The cold pavement is now my resting place.
I see the moon in the sky, and the man's face,
if only I could run.
One last smile from his mug,
and the moonlight off his barrel.
Bang.
Geoffrey Gilbert

Untitled

Drugs, alcohol, cigarettes, sex. How as a parent are we to handle this?
You try to talk to your kids, but to no avail. At such an early age they want to be an adult.
They don't understand the stress, we as adults face daily.
We try to show them love, but it apparently is not enough.
Not when they have gangs to turn to for love.
What kind of love do these gangs have? They beat you in, and, for most, you cannot leave.
You are there's for life. But to show their love, they let you get away with murder.
And sometimes, that is exactly what happens.
With the gang, they can be the individual that they want to be.
Drugs, alcohol, cigarettes, sex. That's what kids feel will make them an adult.
Drugs...addictions, brain damage, death. Alcohol..addictions, brain damage, death.
Cigarettes...addictions, lung cancer, death. Sex...addictions, STD's, death.
Why do what you know is right, when you could be stupid and be cool... and possibly
DEAD!! Come on kids, show us that you're adults.
Be responsible, be safe, and be smart. Grow up...GROW UP.
Stop, look, listen. Let us adults see you as adults.
George Chambers

You Know What I Mean

Riding down the road to my surprise,
"This beautiful light," blinds my sight
The closer I got, "You know what I mean,"
The electric glide, this killer machine
with chrome so shining, dressed in
black, the electra glide, top of the line

Oh! A surge of energy, hits my soul, when
I see a Harley coming down the road,
Oh! The sound of the engine, passes me
faster, than a streak of lightning in the wind
Oh! She's my passion, she's my freedom,
Freedom to ride in the wind

Well they started her up, I shook all over
"The closer I got," she called my name,
Well there's only one thing, that drives
me crazy, that's the sound of a Harley
coming down the road
Carla S. Bell

Ownership

The wild geese think they own
this edge of the lake as much as I.
Should truth be told though,
we are both borrowers
from the deep reach of God's creating
and the deep future of watching generations.
But when the sun rises crackling
over the line of trees atop our mountain,
when, at noon, it thrusts deep into the lake,
at evening when it paints the surface red,
I know it is mine,
not by deed, but by memory,
and I take a heartbeat to write upon
the water's face
the name of my love,
so that the sun may read it to God
and he might laugh in recognition.
Daniel C. Nusbaum

To My Wife

Wave upon wave crest upon crest
This is how our souls are laid to rest
You battled so hard your whole life long
The sea has come and the sea has gone

You rest on the beach content at last
Your soul finally released and heart happy at rest
The physical self freed of pain
For that is when the angels came

You have blessed us all and lifted our soul
Though the process sometimes mystically cruel and cold
we stand before God as the sun goes down
Humble and blessed as the waves go round

But still the waves and crests will come around
One upon one forever bound
We have lost you not for with each sunset
our souls have met in the west

To my love I say good-bye until the waves and the moon are high
For you will return Angelic form on the wave crest so high.
Wave on wave, crest on crest
Someday my soul with yours will rest
   Jack Knaus-Holm

"God's Land"

The trees of many species stand
This is the gift of God's great hand.
The creek so great or small
The smells lift your spirits tall.
The mornings golden hues
The sky of pink, purple and blue.
The wild flowers and grass bend in the breeze
The song of the birds and bees.
The beauty is everywhere you look
The chipmunks and squirrels are busy at work.
The smells and beauty of all the untouched land
This is the wonder of God's Great Hand.
The mystic beauty of God's Land.
   Janet O. Reese-Howell

The Raven In The Locker

Now this is a story all about a raven.
If you want to be scared, this is the story you've been craving.
I was coming from class to get something from my locker.
Last class was gym. We had a nice game of soccer.
And from my locker came a rapping.
And from the rapping came a tapping, tapping at my locker door.
And from my locker came a voice. It said, "Nevermore."
I opened my locker. And what stood there gazing? It was a charcoal raven.
And in his eyes I saw there was something he was craving.
It was the ghost of Edger Allen Poe.
And what is more, he was searching for his lost Lenore.
"Tell me something boy. Tell me where is my lost Lenore."
"You know as well as I do Mr. Poe. Lenore is nevermore."
"Then it shall be. This is the punishment forevermore.
This is the punishment for not telling me where is my lost Lenore.
For you shall be nevermore. For as long as the ravens fly, die you shall die."
He went up in a puff of smoke. I couldn't breath so I started to choke.
I was dying. To the grave I was bound.
So I plunged forward, to the ground. Into my grave I was laid.
And forever, I became like Mr. Poe's lost Lenore.
She and I, like everyone else, became nevermore.
   Jeremy Adler

Evil Earth

The writing's on the wall, the graffiti in my brain,
This worlds only purpose, is to drive a person insane.

Get it straight, evil earth, you can't drive me anywhere.
Understand this, that I refuse,
To pay your tariffs or falsified fares!

I've rode your track once or twice
And wound up verged on Lunacy.
I've got turned around one last time
And vow to defy this legacy

Everyone's trying to take each other down,
Therefore, I'll walk alone.
Off the beaten path of the rest of the world
To a place that is my own.

Everyone's a poet, and every man a killer.
This whole damn race is living in a low budget thriller

Wicked world with your wretched ways,
You might as well let me be.
Relinquish the hold you thought you had,
Your prison no longer appeals to me.
   Dina Bettis

The End Of Three

Through the thoughts of time and nights of wine
though love in despair, no one is there
she sits alone by the phone waiting for the ring
the ring she sees sits on her finger
losing its shine losing its luster
where could he be, where is she
alone by the phone, waiting, waiting
across the town he sits by a pillow
crumpled and flattened from a night
of another satin. A thought of her crosses his
mind and a hand touches him from
behind, the eyes of a stranger look
from below, asking and pleading for a hello.
No smile from his lips from a night
of moving hips. He knows she sits
alone by the phone waiting, waiting.
Waiting by the phone, no one is
there, she is done with this love
in despair... suddenly in silence you can
hear the phone that's alone....ring....ring...ring...
   Jennifer Cancel

Love

Love is a flame that burns
Through time and eternity
For it is touched by
A never ending divinity.
Those who have it are blessed beyond measure
To possess this rare treasure.
In you, I see all of the above
For they are the immortal signs of love.
Your eyes are lights in our sky
So close to our reach,
And warm, each to each
Your eyes are the lights to our love!

They shine than the stars above
Whether days are dark or fair
Their light will always be there
Shining through time into eternity.
Our love is a heavenly thing!
It is our song to sing
Whenever we may be
On land or the deepest sea!
   Charlotte J. Chambliss

...Red In The Morning

I've fallen for you,
out of the clear, blue sky, it seems,
thought appearance is not always reality.

The CLEAR...BLUE...SKY...

BLUE...no, another color would be more appropriate.
That color...that color...
of a Burning Heart; a newfound Passion,
the color of Anger; of Love.

CLEAR...no, I don't believe that is so either.
Eyes Tinged with tears;
A mind Opaque with misconception,
Muddled with the realization...that it can Never be.

OUT OF THE CLEAR, BLUE SKY?
Doubtful, though nevertheless...my perception.
But the Reddish hue; it invades my thoughts and my dreams,
that Misty haze; it Clouds my words and my actions.

OUT OF THE CLEAR, BLUE SKY?
I don't know...but regardless of Tint or Opacity
My Sky...
IS ABOUT TO FALL!

Eileen M. Burger

Love Is For All

Days come an days go
Time seems to slip away
The seasons have come and gone but you are here to stay
I have looked for you in the day light
And tried to find you in the moon light
But yet no matter where I look you are always right there
Where you said you would be.
Some have gone to the top of mountains
Others to the depth of the sea
Yet some seek to find you in others
But you have been there for all just the same
You never change
You said seek and ye shall find
But the lost caverns are in the mind
For you are with us all the time
Search your inter most soul
Look to your heart
For there is where you have been all the time
For it is true love you are looking for
And God is love, and His love conquers all

Emmanuel Clary

My Precious One

The one after time of forgetting remains in my thoughts.
Reasons I can't understand.
Friends we remain now.
The one I tried to get over.
The one at times I hated.
Still this moment causes thoughts of love.
I want nothing but to end these ridiculous feelings, thoughts or what ever they may be.
All I want is to move them away.
Something I have done once before, today it has changed a bit.
Tomorrow I shall get over fast.
Still he keeps as the one I treasure deeply to my heart.
My precious one.

Hollie Dunkle

Loneliness

Loneliness

Sometimes it is an ache that grows and tightens my chest and throat, allowing me only to steal breaths in between my sobs.

Other times it is a twisting pain so sharp it only allows me to release my breath in a gasp.

I have saturated my pillow with tears as if it had been left in the rain.

And I have wiped so many tears away with my hands that they dripped with moisture as if they had been washed.

I was asked if I ever felt loneliness, and my response was yes.

What I did not say is that only the dark truly knows how much it hurts.

Christine Bowman

See Like A Dove

Your soar above the highest peaks of flight
Through ghost-like rainbows fading into mist
You ride your wings, your breast of virgin white
With warming rays of sun you're kissed
You laugh at man, we're ball and chain compared
If we could see as you do, pain and suffering could be spared
We each have a mask to hide our distant moods
We plan a flight, but not as graceful as you do
You understand the meaning as a bird that stands for love
Can we ever swallow pride enough to fly with you above?
One day our world will finally have to rise
To see like doves and know where sorrow lies

Donna Marie Low

"It Won't be Denied"

Death carries a reaper by his side.
Through him mainly you fantasize
About the things that he could be.
He'll lead you to insanity.

Death is not a f**king dream,
Though no most people he may seem.
We don't know if he's real or lie,
But we'll find out the day we die.

Death is the monster under your bed,
The aching pain inside your head.
In the darkness he lives still.
Dare do or say what you will.

Death is at the edge of your skull.
You scream for help, but none hear your call.
You realize now there's no where to hide.
Mortal soul and body subside.

The sacred things he says to you
Make you wish he'd run you through.
Now way to run, no way to win,
The holes of death will pull you in.

Dave Waldenmaier

A Lovers' Prayer

I look to you for guidance when the storm is too much to bare. I look to you for wisdom when it seems no one cares. I look to you for strength when I'm down. I look to you for warmth when my hearts been jerked around. I look to you for love when it seems my cup is empty. I look to you to fall in love with when it seems there is no one else for me. I look to you for understanding when my lover has cut me loose. I look to you for shelter when I face abuse. I look to you for support when no one else is there. I say this before I sleep at night, a secret lover's prayer.

Dawn L. Douglas

Wait, Wait, Weight On The Lord

When things seem bleak and dreary and you feel
tired and weary, Wait on the Lord.

When you receive your blessings and the promises
made by God, Wait on the Lord.

When your burdens seem too heavy and more than
you can bear, and your life seems to be full of
hopelessness and discord,

Place all your worries in his hands and put your
burdens' Weight on the Lord.

Joyce Ann Lee

Good-bye Love

   Slender hands grasp his picture
through the shattered glass her tears dwindle to his face
in the middle of a cold, desolate floor she remembers the past
Sacrificed innocence, body, soul, mind, heart
Her eyes saw unrealistically they'd never part
She grew subservient to his love, his touch, his smile, his embrace
She was incessantly his, any time, any place
Her love or him - like a bird, it flew so hard, so long, so strong,
it would never return
His love for her gradually began to take a different path
he broke apart from her not knowing the consequence
not knowing she would crash
Lying in the middle of the floor in a heap of salted brine
she knows she loved him and still loves him no less
A vengeance on her life's track grows near; he was her beginning,
she would be her end, her eyes gaze upon a blade as a friend
pressing the sharp edge to her lips, dark crimson drips, in braveness,
love, slits her wrists, she'd rather die than live without her man
Gazing into her lover's eyes one last time she gives a bloody kiss good-bye

Jenna Halverson

Time

   Time is a valuable thing to waste.
Time is your future, your past and the present.
If you waste your time in life.
Your bound not to have a future.
If you'd wasted your time in the past.
You better make up for it in the present.
If you have some spare time, think about your future.
If your future turns out good.
Thank goodness you didn't waste your time.
The past, future, and the present are very precious.
So use your time wisely.
You will be helping your future.
If you have no spare time.
Use what you have carefully.
The time on the clock doesn't mean anything at all.
Because all it does is go tick tock.
Everything you do is what your time really is.
If your done with all your work.
You have some extra time.
Your time is a valuable thing, make sure you do not waste it.

Jennifer Kolka

At End Of Trip

To be home.
To be held within the structure of these
  familiar things:
My chair
My couch
My bed
My walls.
To be enfolded in their familiar shapes and
  forms, at last;
I am home.

Eva M. Stuart

The Toddler

In the mystic-dagger moon of midnight
Through the valley of the shadow of my hall
Walk with me, straighten me or follow me
To new lands somewhere east of the fall

Mother is given to the spoken word
Father with the hand and the voice to call
And inflict and wound and flee for his life
To new lands somewhere east of the fall

And I mourn for the cradle and mother
Mourns for the time when I was polite
And father was not such a lunatic
In the mystic-dagger moon of midnight

In the mystic-dagger moon of midnight
With notions of war and ghosts in the hall
Flying from the onset of fitful sleep
To new lands somewhere east of the fall

Cameron Webster

Wind

Like gentle hands moving caringly
through their lover's hair,
Doth the wind caress the tips
of the pines with it's chilling fingertips.
Thus does the river also take on
a life of its own,
Carelessly frolicking over aged stones
as it gracefully cascades down the mountainside.
Yet to most these scenes go unseen,
Even by one who wishes nothing more,
but to be in their presence.
At the hand of Man does the lifeblood stop,
rivers are dammed, pines are cut.
For these are the men who are truly blind,
spreading their sickness to eyes
Which must now strain to see.

Darryll A. De Coster

A Blizzard's Enemy

   Covering the placid sincerity,
time does moves on.
   The snow makes everything white,
but melts away with sun.
   my hands touch very tenderness,
that money could never buy.
   Blizzard! Like snow-peace drifts,
the freezer couldn't keep it, I mustn't even try,
   The merry way of life-
each pathway has its thorn.
   Something not even hope can keep,
and something new is born.
   Fairy tales, snow flakes-
the bestial act of human kind.
   In this the sun is the enemy, or
maybe only change, or perhaps both combined.

Cami Godfrey

Pain

I feel like I am trapped inside a room of pain,
trying to find a way out. I look
for a light, a hallway, an exit, or an end
to this pain that I feel, but all I
find is that the room gets bigger and
bigger. I look for a friend or a smile
to reassure me, but all I find are other
people trapped trying to get out. Then I
realize that I am the friend they were
looking for...so I smile.

Amy Scouler

Abused

The Lord of Darkness brings me life,
   to agonize and terrify;
My existence has two reasons,
   to bring you pain and horrify.

You rise from sleep with a loud scream,
   After seeing me in your dreams;
You scream "I'm coming after you",
   But do you know just what that means.

I can bring you death while you sleep,
   or cause you hate while you're awake;
You sit alone and think of me,
   but this one thought will make you shake...

   "Come to Daddy"
Jeffrey Hatzenbuehler

Sonnet 4

Oh to see through a child's eyes once more,
To be able to hide behind innocence,
And to believe the world ends at your fence
As life was just there for you to adore,
Smiles and hugs only mattered, nothing more.
Gray areas, too hard to see, made no difference,
And crying was always the best defence,
But Age has swept these things through the front door,
Or does a small child live in my heart
Ready to jump, laugh, and play once again,
Quietly waiting to run in the sun
Free from the troubles that rip me apart
And ready to go for fourth down and ten?
If so, I wish he'd take the chance to run.
Aaron J. Kabler

There Are No Albatross In Oregon

I went to the seashore by myself,
To bathe in sea foam and heal my poor saddened heart.
Hemingway joined me from a rich mahogany shelf.

I journeyed across the sands,
And swam through the cold stinging waves,
As the wind whipped my eyes and hands.

Hemingway whispered in my ear,
And my heart began to swell like the waves.
As I envisioned sailing out beyond the point of fear.

And sailing towards the line where the sky meets the sea,
The backs of the magnificent waves stood high,
And boldly and brazenly bared their bountiful backs to me.

In that mighty, magical, and mysterious moment,
All my sadness slipped, silently, and fell away from me,
Helplessly, into the deep, dark, blue, sea!
Janie Reece

"Let The Earth Be Your Friend"

Winter comes and winter goes
To be replaced by spring
Then summer and fall follow along
With symptoms that each season brings.

The spring brings birth and renewal
The summer: growth and joy
The fall brings the harvest and colors galore
The winter: snow and toys.

The earth in all her splendor
Is a magnificent work of art
Her beauty is a thing to behold
And it touches every heart.

So stop and smell the roses
And listen to the wind
See the wonders all about
Let the earth be your friend.
John W. Schmittou

"An Innocent Excess"

Forgive me but I know no way
To be a fraction less than every bit in love with you.
I cannot say that my attraction
Even knows the possibility of fraction.

Portion is a part
I cannot play.

Love knows no degree; I cannot love a half
Or third, or part, or piece of whole.
Love lies beyond the absurdity of all condition.
It is all or it is nothing.
It is utter; it is entire; it is eternal fire
Of supreme fruition.

Forgive me but for this obsession
I must make a thorough and complete confession.
I say forgive because I fear that you might fear
From me (so soon) such fullness. Please do not.
Be patient with an innocent excess.
It is the way of love, and I cannot do less.
Joseph Nicholes

My Daughters

I am not looking for new words
To be used in describing my daughters,
As all the old words have been said.
But, I'd like to tell someone
What they mean to me,
Before I turn up dead.

I have three daughters who are
As different as night and day,
But each as beautiful as any flower in bloom.
Not only are they beautiful to look at,
But they are kind and gracious too.
You could spot them quickly in any room.

As I look back over my years with them,
I experience only pride and joy,
As I continue to grow older and older.
Oh the hours and hours of happiness
Given by my three darling daughters,
Who have never been a weight to my tired shoulders.
Albert R. Eselhorst

"The Sky Is The Limit"

The sky is the limit for you and I
to become whatever we work for and desire!
Just like going to heaven you gotta discipline yourself
no one can do it for you but you can ask for help!
To accomplish any thing we must stick to our goal
our time here is like a snowflakes to soon we get old!
So watch out for those friends who would get you off track
with no ambition or hope for their future they may attack.
But what is right for you is not always right for me
we all want to stand up and be counted as a special somebody!
Be true to yourself speak up for your thoughts and beliefs
we are born with our God and our country
anything more is up to us to achieve!
Good luck to you whoever you are
be honest be faithful be kind
there's a big world out there to explore
tread cautiously and you will be fine!

Daisy D. Bartholomew

Dream Catcher

It takes a dream
   to catch a dream
Rich man, poor man, beggar man, thief
   Dreams are there
      for those who dare...
         ...to dream.

   CATCH!

You can catch many things with the greatest of ease,
A virus, a frisbee, a soft summer breeze,
A joke or a tune, perhaps a big yawn,
A bug in a rug and I've even caught on.
Catching a dream? Though it hardly seems true,
You can buy a dream-catcher for eight ninety-two.

Joy Misener

His Hands

From chaos to order, it was his glorious plan
To consummate this sphere from his omnipotent hands.
Hands that created in copious splendor
All that's needed for life's provisions.

When I consider his imaginative work, I stand in reverential fear
How those tender hands made birds, beast and mankind so dear.
So dear to himself, in his imagine he made man
Knowing this as he completed creation, he whispered, you are my
   ultimate plan.

Then in a moment, (in a twisted fate), God's ultimate creation, man
Sequestered his image from his creator and parted from his hands.
What once was fashion taintless, became this universe's only
   maculation
Even mankind himself condescended to become the lowest of creation.

Omniscient in everything the master creator had a scheme
"I'll give charge to my son, for the one made in my image must be redeemed."
Confabulating with his father, the son took on the form of earthly man
Identifying with man's infirmities, he placed the weight of the
   world in his hands.

Now thanks to the father and his redeeming son
Humanity has been extricated from iniquity, now with the father
   we are one.
But there is something mankind should never disband
His relationship with the father, son and spirit is in his hands.

Bernett S. Roane

The Whispering Tree

I sat beneath the whispering tree
To contemplate the why of me.
Dark clouds burst with showers of tears,
When I shyly confessed my hidden fears.
Emotions faltered and tried to flee,
As I rested my head upon my knee.

The tree whispered, but I could not hear.
Perhaps it said... "No path is clear."
Broken hearts and hopeless dreams
Make way for tiny, soothing streams,
That gently lift and clear the way,
Taking twisted branches that beg to stay.

Softly the leaves rustled and fluttered about.
Till all of a sudden they seemed to shout:
"Listen, learn, absorb it all...
Stop hiding there behind your wall."
Only then will peace gather round,
And plant you firmly on the ground.

Jan Clements

"Happiness"

To hear your smiles
To feel your joy
Your warm hearted laughter spilling across my shoulder
Tender hands creating soft sighs.
Then turning to see the light of the sky as it bends
To touch your eyes.
Knowing you is a special happiness

A small child's hugging arm at my hip
The glistening shine on his plump lower lip
Quickly moistened after a delectable treat
Then the blush of color on his full rounded check
This is a moment of happiness

A quiet night of deep restful sleep.
Then wake to the languid, tingling, feeling of reach
For arms that continue to keep
On returning to encircle one another
Yet open wide to welcome each others feats
This is the ultimate happiness.

Gwen Brown

Freedom

To know someone, to hear their voice,
To have a friend, to have a choice.
To hear the bells ringing loud and clear.
To know, to feel the freedom so near.
To become one with that which is.
To belong to a country so free to give.
To know that I am free,
How much it means to me.
So long ago the wars were fought,
The blood was shed, and men were shot, for Me.
Did they realize then what their blood would become?
Part of a country, part of me.
Did they know? Could they see.
All of my life freedom has been handed me,
Upon a silver platter,
Only do I realize now, how much it really matters.
All that has been given me, passed on through generations,
More than time, but a sense of being.
A sense of knowing who I am.

Carol Clark

I Am A Reality

The family doctor was Dr. Cooley.
To him went the young mother-to-be.
Tis a chain of pus tubes said he.
He was quite mistaken, you see,
That chain of pus tubes was me!
I am a reality!
Another leaf on the family tree,
The apple of the eye of my maternal granny,
The answer to the prayer of my daddy.
Although a special innocuous baby
I was noxious to my dear mommy.
Mostly because a colleague of Dr. Cooley,
Dr. T. T. Wendell, decided that he
Would respect the doctor instead of mommy.
With his forceps he almost blinded me
As he attempted expiation of his atrocity
In treating mother as if she was a dummy
Who knew not what was in her tummy!

Amanda C. Elliott

A Champion

Georgia is where he lives,
to his fans he gives and gives.
When he's in his shiny red car,
he stands on the gas,
getting ready to make a pass.

He's known from far and wide,
his red hair he cannot hide.
Who is this champion I'm speaking of?
Well it's awesome Bill from Dawsonville.
on Sunday evenings he's on the track,
racing around with the rest of the pack.

That checkered flag he is wanting to see,
at the end of the race victory lane is where he will be.
Smiling and waving to his loyal fans,
as they stand and cheer because they know
he is the number 1 Winston Cup man.

Donna Walker

To The Tournament Loser

The goal to win the trophy,
To hold it high in your hand.
But the dreams of the victory vanish,
Swept away like castles of sand.

On the scoreboard high above,
In the lights the final score.
In the books the numbers tallied,
To give no less and no more.

In the winners circle,
The opponent earns the place.
With the victory goes the gold,
To the swiftest goes the race.

To those that have played their final game,
To other hands the torch is passed.
From all the victories and all defeats,
May it be the fondest memories that last.

Tomorrow laughter rules the day,
The morning dawns clear and bright.
But in these moments, friend and foe,
Permits this tear tonight.

Ed Anderson

The Little Brown Book

We got together that cool autumn day,
To laugh and talk and dream and play.
A chance that seldom came to be,
It was a precious time for my friend and me.

We browsed through shops and dined on a boat,
caressed our memories and shared our hopes.
As we walked along, we saw a bazaar,
Such curious things, even a nineteen-fifty car.

When suddenly my eyes spotted a book.
I couldn't resist, I went over to look.
The cover was simple hardback and brown,
I began to read and could not put it down.

From each page poured life, beauty and love.
I knew it was sent from him above.
How grateful I am for this treasure of thoughts,
Such words of power from the little book that I bought.
Joy often comes in a smile or a look,
I found it that day in the little brown book.

Jean Henry Yokley

Incarceration

   Destiny sees many roads, bread crumbles
to lead us back, who leads must follow,
trails abound, with darkness, to see light we lack.
   The forks in roads know many ways,
to lead you in a march astray. The sanctions
of true righteousness, cannot be found within a day.
   A picture perfect moment knows, when
hands emerge to show, a reach within a
soul search felt, the touch of even flow.
   Instinctively the off spring of our
knowledge, there will grow, to weave into
a path of sense, the seventh here to know.
   Another destination sought, has found
incarceration revealing keys to many doors
the magic's in abrasion
...Love is our Sixth Sense

Alfred Lechuga

"She"

Death turns a pretty face
To life unkind.
But ecstasy deceives—
Like the tender buds of Spring
That breed on Death.
The more we know of Beauty—
The more we know of Death.

And April is the cruelest Month.

Yet we who crave the rosebud—
We who crave for change—
Love Constancy.
The more we know of Love—
The more we know of Death—
The more we greed.
And She who wears a double face—
Keeps turning in Her Ecstasy.
She Bleeds.
Softly She sings
Like the gentle hum of bees
And we hear a single beat.

Gerry Anne Lenhart

Hesitation Was Right

Longing and hoping as the night wore on,
To make love to her before morning's dawn.
Yet there was this sense to share more than that,
Our talk, her smile, just to hold for a while.
With the desire to go further, hesitation prevailed.
That night changed my sight, caused me to think.
Hesitation was right, hindsight agreed.
We had fallen in love, or was it just me?

Joseph R. Keenan

Country Morning

The mornings in the country are so beautiful
to me. You can hear the birds singing from
the top of every tree.
The dew's like glistening diamonds sparkling
on all the little leaves. The spider webs
are everywhere, like lace upon the trees.
The little bees are busy in the early
morning light, going from flower to flower,
pollinating in their flight.
The air is just so fresh, you can breath a
great big sigh. It's so breathtaking, it
almost makes you cry.
The leaves on trees will rustle, and its
peaceful as can be. A morning in the country
that's the life for me.

Diane J. Wilkerson

Please Grant Me The Courage — Bengal Bandanna

Please grant me the courage to open myself up,
    To move ,in spite of being vulnerable to attack;
To speak what's necessary even if my hearer finds the words bitter.

Please grant me the courage to obey Your wishes,
    Even though I may not like the idea;
    Even if I might get hurt by cruel words or dangerous objects.

Please grant me the courage the travel beyond my comfort zone,
    And explore regions that I don't yet know;
    And extend the limits I've set into the realms where I'm insecure

Please grant me the courage to correct those I love.
    Not to puff me up, but to guide people to truth.
Not to think I'm better, but to be joyous in them, lest I should fall.

Please grant me the courage to not strike back,
    Because somebody took and swing (at me) and struck me down;
Because someone insulted me with no remorse... I need mercy myself.

Please grant me the courage to go against the crowd.
    The crowd seeks only-pleasure and whatever's "In".
There's no grit in ganging up on a hated creature who needs my love.

Please grant me courage, I don't have enough.
    I don't want to be a coward... at least not anymore.

Eric T. Crumb

The Mountain Stands

Above the streets, the mountain stands alone.
Trees grow its slopes, and sparrows fly.
There rock and tree and sunlight rule on high;
No king may sit atop that snowy throne.
The mountain stands, a living mass of stone,
Its shining peak still reaching for the sky,
Bearing the marks of centuries gone by,
Bearing the seeds of ages yet unknown.
The mountain stands; peace dwells upon its slopes,
Peace born of sun and rain and countless years.
The mountain stands. Its peaks proclaiming joy,
It stands above the summit of our fears.
Some things there are that man cannot destroy.

Amy Livingston

Doing Time

My eyeballs beat, wild blood has washed me down
to pace a lawless night of Janus eyes,
Briareus hands, quadruple step, and lies
twelve thousandfold; where Psyche, ox-eyed clown,
howls for the myriad life, a saga writ
as jealous dreams bore caverns in the earth
for sculpting other worlds of me.
Such birth, if it were done, would people all the Pit
with demons, hordes of me, and I would go
through unsuspecting lands a rout of selves,
my secrets buried whither no man delves.
Still I am flesh; I cannot fission so;
this clay impounds the only Me that men
allow, though selves collide (and cry) within.

David Massey

The Burden Of "Truth Telling"

Cover truth with uneasy, shallow laughter,
to protect a friendship,
which hangs by a spindly social thread.

Contacts which are maintained through a need,
from which side the need is greatest is
most difficult to discern.

A social tie of "help" for slippery souls,
who operate in society out of necessity,
yet would feel more comfort letting go.
However, images and sanity MUST be maintained?

Why does truth separate, yet bind?
It is such a dangerous commodity,
yet a trait said to be of "greatest value."

I must hope "the truth will always set me free."
I am helplessly tied to the telling of it, from my view!

Don't ask for MY truth,
unless YOU can stand the possible hurt of it.

It is true that "truth is so rare a thing,
that is delightful to tell it."
Often painfully delightful to tell it! A burden!

Gwen Patterson Reichert

Our Golden Years

The golden age is a beautiful age,
To reminisce about things of the past;
Years gone by to come no more, we wonder, how did we last!!!

We haven't been good all our days,
And still not proud of some of our ways;
But God of mercy, who can do no wrong,
Allowed our golden years to roll on.

We thank you for the house you gave us,
Down by the side of the road;
For it was there you taught us, how to carry our heavy load.

We'll never forget from whence we came,
And we thank you daily for our spiritual gain;
Order our steps as they have become slow,
For there are places that we just can't go.

Keep guiding us in the right direction,
As we cling to your love and protection;
We can't relive the years,
For they are passed and gone;
But we want to thank you, "this day",
For allowing our Golden years to roll on.

Evelyn Martin

A Mother's Prayer

To see a dirty little face smiling up at me
To see two small untidy hands, reach out
   lovingly,
To see two smiling, devilish eyes speak of
   play and fun;
To see two tiny, toddling feet stumbling as
   they run;
To kiss that tiny dirty face, caress it
   tenderly;
To grasp those small untidy hands that
   child-like clasp my knee;
To read those smiling devilish eyes, and
   see the love light there;
To aid those tiny toddling feet and lead
   them far from care;
Oh God above, let these be mine
And my life's worth, in debt, is thine.
   Claire Young

Watt Four!

I draw up in a fetus form
   to shield me from their tortuous scorn.
Unto this world that I was born
   remained little trace of Alpha form.
Now they cling to conscious lies, and
   take from knowledge, truth, and pride,
   to give to worthless alibies.
I drew in closer, and closed the door,
   to spare me from the rubbish ruins,
   and sights of horror.
For it is them that take the floor,
   and call the shots in this doomed caged world.
Then someone knocks upon my door,
   and reminds me of Omega's lurid ward.
I see a crystal sparkling stream
   that gathers round and comforts me.
As I stand upon a solid righteous forum,
   and I'm blessed from the highest form;
I know their twisted words are weak and fray,
   and Satan has founded their quietus stage.
   Angela G. Gilliam

Rainy Days Love

The silver moon peeks thru the wispy cloud
To shine above the scented pine that stands so proud
The woodsy fragrance of the summer rain
Can any of these appease my lonely heart's pain
Is my lover a phantom of my dreams
Or as real as the seems
His kiss is a whisper so gentle and soft
And as his lips first kiss mine, I am truly lost
The caress of his hand leaves a burning trail
And images of what will be leaves me weak and frail
But I am so afraid of the feelings he creates
That I can only go slowly, while he awaits
For he is the master of my love
And I will submit to his love like an innocent dove
Would that the summer rain could quell the all consuming fire
No, only when I surrender to my own heart's desire
   Jeanine M. Lethrud

Love Always

The challenge begins, the two of you unite to become a team
To struggle through bad times and cherish the good, as you both stride
   toward a dream.
You wake every morning to a smile that makes your day.
You give each other a hug and a kiss, then off your separate way.
The days bring you ups, downs, lows, and highs,
But when you think of your love, the time simply flies.
Each other's every move you will begin to know.
When you're in love, its a feeling that will show.
Time flows by and your happiness does not miss a beat.
There will be challenges ahead that you both must defeat.
Your children are born and bring changes of joy and tears.
You hope and pray for them throughout the years.
The trials of life will put your love to the test;
You must never forget the reasons why your mate is the best.
The pressures in life can be oh, so great.
Deal with them immediately if you love you mate.
Once they are gone, it all becomes so clear.
They will now try love with another and you shed a tear.
Time slows down and longer are the days.
Do not take your love for granted — "love always."
   David White

A Lover's Rose

A lover's rose I give to you,
to symbolize my feeling for you.

The perfume from the rose is sweet,
it's just like your personality.

The stem symbolize the sturdiness
of our relationship.

The leaves on the stem,
tell of the mountains and valleys we've been.

Only the thorns will tell,
the trials and tribulations we must have.

Now that I have described this rose,
it tells our life as you can see.

A rose is the symbol of you and me.
   Elizabeth Richburg

Utterness Of A Secular God

I am the white rock God.
To those who yearn for me, I am a genie
with the power to grant them a wish every time
they light me and inhale.
I enter their bodies, my smoky form permeates a red sea
to the brain, where I engineer their desires - visions of mundane
fantasies and fears.
I am Alpha and Omega and
they are helpless like Samson without his hair

But why do they come to me?
I demand everything and give nothing
but pleasure, for awhile, then pain, anguish, and grief.
It's ironic you know - the farther down they go,
the more apathy I inject into their lives.

My believers are many.
Politicians and policeman, laymen and lawyers
all bow to my control over their thought, lives and dreams.
They'll kill and lie, steal and die for the gifts they think I bear.

So come to me, eat of Eden's other forbidden fruit and
join me on a pilgrimage.
   Archie Holmes Jr.

Life Is A Poem

All peoples, all colors so precious
  to you and me
Appreciation should be the top
  priority
Not the useless, fights to be
Together admiration can unite our
  society
Whosoever continues to harm our poem
  of life harms our hopes for
  all people to see
Don't make ruthlessness a
  credibility
Kindness is our survival, so you
  best believe in thee
To succeed, all peoples, all colors the
  world over have the ability
     Geraldine M. Olds

To You, I Come

No tangible gifts I bring, riches I have not,
To you I come with a quite spirit, beaten and
worn, riddled with pain,
I give you all that I am, a priceless treasure,
created out of love to give all that I have,
to roll back the curtains of your world,
that you may marvel at the glow of my love
touching your face as I share with you,
the wealth of my wisdom,
the comfort of my patience,
the security of my integrity,
the soothing of my understanding,
the astonishment of my virtue,
the enchantment of my generosity,
and the explosion of my spirituality.
To you, I come with nothing,
To you, I give everything,
I give you me!
     Elvira E. Stewart-Kennedy

Special People

There is a group of people we need to recognize.
To you they are just regular people.
To me they are angels in disguise.
They care for children who might otherwise be alone.
They give them the love and security of a happy home.
And they give this love to all children -
no matter what sex, color, or creed.
And all this love is given unconditionally.
They try to teach them what is wrong and what is right.
They guide them through the day.
And they pray with love at night.
And if by the Grace of God a miracle comes along,
And one of these special children gets to go back to their family and home,
Even though it breaks their heart, they try not to shed a tear,
But put on a happy face, and smile from ear to ear.
Because they know in their heart that this special child,
Was not theirs to keep, just on loan to them for awhile.
We really commend them for the special work they do.
My hat's off to you guys. I know you are heaven sent.
May God Bless each of you who are Foster Parents.
     Betty May Bosley

More Today Than Yesterday

The years have come and gone and I care more about you
today then I did yesterday.
Our hair may be a little grayer and our walk a little
slower, but you're still beautiful to me.
We may not be able to remember everything we use to
but we still know what each other is thinking.
We're not as young as we used to be,
But all you have to do is smile that sweet smile
or get that twinkle in your eye.
My heart skips a beat just like it did so many years
ago when I look at you.
We may not dress in the latest fashion or go to all the
places we use to go.
But we still get out and have some fun it just takes
us a little longer now.
I don't know where all the years have gone,
but I still care more about you today then I did yesterday.
     Deb Harnden

Mommy And Daddy's Love

Today your just a little boy in Mom's and Daddy's eye.
Tomorrow you'll start growing more and then you'll wonder why
Mommy's really silly and daddy's really sly.
Soon you'll be getting bigger and you'll be sure you know
Better than your mom and dad cause they're just growing old.

But while your thinking all these things remember one big fact.
That mommy brought you up and Daddy knows where it's where it's at
Of course you know, it's really true, mistakes you'll have to make.
Just like your Mom and Dad, you'll have your own heartaches.
But while your doing this, remember they did too.

But remember this dear Grandson;
Of all the things above
You never will have done them,
Without Mom's and Daddy's love.
     Albert Ruprecht

Prelude

The coming of dawn we walked and in hand,
tomorrow's dreams spread out before us like sparkles in the sand.
A delicate balance of shadows and light,
made everything seem perfect on this special night.
East of the sunrise, close, at waters edge,
we talked, made our plans, and our love we did pledge.
The voice within me was filled with surprise,
as it encouraged me to take that walk through paradise.
The windows of the soul, what shivers they sent!
Like nothing I'd felt before, like mists of enchantment.
I knew then the path not taken could lead to many starts and stops,
beyond the stars, the rainbows end, and even between the raindrops.
A sea of treasures awaits me as I start the garden of life,
and I'll make this life a voyage to remember, as I become a wife.
     Ginger Henson

The Diamond In Your Heart

Linda, the diamond in your heart you feel
Transcends the sorrow in those around you
What once was a dream is now very real
Then cherish this gift known by precious few.

Glow above them in your radiance high
And listen to their moans of betrayal
Each one in turn speaks of loss with her sigh
Each longing to get out of her life's jail.

Remember this feeling well and have fun
Close to your heart and your childhood's sweet dreams
To lift your chin up from tears to the sun
And reflect it back in a diamond beam.
     John Caywood

Heavenly

An angel without wings that still flies through the night
touching every star that gives light
to her eternal glow...

Her expressions like meticulously sculpted cherubs
Are chiseled in my mind
With features as pure as a lily's new buds
And laughter just as kind

It springs forth like music from a harp
Ensued by a delightful smile
Like the melodious song of the meadow lark
Presented to a tender child

She places me in a dreamscape
That's as true as celestial bodies
As they shine upon a peaceful lake
And give meaning to the world around me.

Jody Smith

Days Gone By

I've spent my life in this little town
Trembled at it's mighty storms and felt
The gentle rain fall down
Tanned and reaped the summer's bounty
Of this little town in Pittsburgh County.

The schoolhouse was built in thirty-six
The bell that called us to school
Hung from a tower of red bricks
In place of children, now older folks
Sit playing checkers and telling jokes.

Saturdays were spent at the old movie house
The big silver screen is silent and still
Cowboys and Indians gave us youngsters a thrill
As they thundered across the shining screen
Now silent as a church, quiet and serene.

The town was thriving in the twenties
Until the Great Depression came
Many folks left to seek fortune and fame
Still, no matter how far they may roam
Soon will return and make you their home.

Erma McGill

Internal Grip

Listening to the rush of my plasma through smothered thoughts,
Trembling within so slightly you only notice the movement

Wanting to pounce on the back of a wild elephant in a stampede,
Scream so loud all things come to a stop and ponder the note

Wiggling on my stomach in damp dirt covering my body in earth,
Set free the boundaries that fix my hair and iron my clothes

You think you know who I am, how could you? I don't
Evolving with time a root plugging forward inch by inch

The veil that covers our souls are quite different by sight,
Naked souls would be a delight to be seen in a dance

Nothing to be covered or hidden from within,
Emotions go free
Not questioned or criticized by those with hidden fears of their own

Debbie Sweatman

Be A Friend Of Mother Nature

Sweet golden moments of the gone past
Trickle down from memory like honey drops
Leaves of the time tree start moving when
Fresh breeze of the loneliness come blowing
Collection of broken jewel traces, they are
Celestial stars twinkling in my inside
Shadings and shadows like cast clouds
Would dare not hide those lovely rays
Share with me nature's gone glory
Torn away now by modern lifestyles
If destruction goes on in this fashion
Future generations won't know greenness
Resist trends raping earth's beauty or her
Hot temper will tilt all the balance
Educate, enlighten masses; otherwise
Global disasters are lot foreseen

Jay Andrews

Always With Me

  I remember your warm embrace your gentle
touch, how you made me feel like a woman through and
through, and this I dearly loved from you, you made me
feel brand new, and this my dear is oh so true.
  I needed you more then you know, and oh how
I still need you, and this will always ring true, I
hope you will never go, to be with me even after old I grow.
  You are my strength when I am weak, you are to
me all that I seek, you are my light on the darkest of
night, you are my joy and delight, even when you are far
from my sight, you are everything that's right.
  You warm embrace, your gentle touch, to me
you will always mean so much, it's as if God sent
you to me, and with me you shall always be, you hold
a special piece of my heart, and this will never
part, no matter what comes to pass you see,
even if it's in a memory, you will always be with me.

Amanda S. Nix

Saline

A lazy old river twisting around thru the
Tull Bend and around past the open banks.
There's a splash as an old logger-head
turtle falls off a water soaked treetop
sticking out from the bank and into the river
like a white water monster, torn from its
roots years ago by erosion and finally blown
over by the wind.
A tall slender cypress tree stands watch over
the Brumbelow Bend like a lone, lonely sentry.
If only it could talk! It could tell of
the old shack in the cane break;
could tell of the swampy alligator pond;
could tell of a small lad in a straw hat
and ragged, knee-patched overalls,
beautiful, beautiful!
It all cries of beauty on the Saline River.

Charles Miller

Perfect, Gentle Night

Shadows of evening ending the day
Turn down the brightness of the last sunset ray,
Changing the outlines of familiar places
And muffling the sound of the day's busy races
Until quiet surrounds us and brings fresh revelings
And we listen differently to our thoughts and feelings,
Sometimes afraid, sometimes at ease, aware and often
 reflecting
Until night then contains us in soft, sweet relief
And a measure of peace and welcome forgetting.

When the darkness of night seems to bring a new vision,
When memories sharpen and come quickly to mind,
We can melt in the shadows and relax in the night,
Refreshed and renewed, the darkness our light.
 Doris Barton

The Who-Dats

The hour approaches on that mystical night of the year,
Twilight dims, darkness falls, the WHO-DATS appear.
Their wails and screams send chills up and down your spine,
You quiver, your legs go limp when you bump into their kind.
The wind howls, the trees bend their limbs to hide their eyes,
To look into a WHO-DATS face you become mesmerized.
Cats and dogs run away to wait in a safe place,
'Til morning to venture out when the sun shows its face.
Slowly yells become louder as WHO-DATS come to your door,
Your doorbell rings, a loud knock, you're shaken to the core.
Standing there before your eyes vanquishing your fears,
Giggling little children with hands out have appeared.
You relinquish the ransom, it's "trick or treat" they demand,
With bits of sweets and fruit they'll leave alone your land.
Off they go into the night with never a look back,
Squeals of joy to the next house their sweet tooth to attack.
Bags of sweets WHO-DATS succumb to the lateness of the night,
Quiet returns, evening retreats, in the mist of a pale moonlight.
 Eleanor F. Basinger

Tunnels

Down into the depths I go,
 twisting...turning...
  light ahead beckoning, calling me to hurry! Hurry!

There is no time left to wait. The time is now!
 Dance my dance...sing my song...
  but do it NOW before all is lost again in the shadows.

In the tunnels there is a rich deposit of mother earth, waiting to
 be discovered with careful, caressing fingers.

There are riches abounding in the tunnels, but only for those
with eyes open enough and wise enough to see the treasure that
awaits...in the tunnels.

Sweating...bending...crawling...on my fertile belly like the
original snake of wisdom,
just one more turn, and then it is in reach.

The light.
It is mine to reach for, mine to behold
with eyes that are open...

Now that I have descended into the depths of the tunnels.
 Deborah Clark Kelley

Untitled

I will not oversleep the day God comes for me,
Two extra words in iambic as you can plainly see.
No more a threat to Shakespeare or Elizabeth too,
Sonnets written not in rhythm and so, from them eschew,
Rivalry. No pun. And so, will I resume this thought.

The day HE calls I will be ready to make, or not, the climb,
The choice is His as it's always been, never not, not mine.
All things wrapped in my behalf, abundant and redundant,
Of matters business, family and friends, and yes, confidant,
There is no message left for thoughts unsaid —nor ought.

Rejoice this day for knowing me, without tears my leaving,
Let time sharing moments give solace, not bereaving,
My perceptions in living have always been with cheer and no regret,
And pain enjoyed. And when God comes, I will Him let...
 Herman Bernstein

Missing Two

Life I've seen drained from the people I love
Two of my brothers I am thinking of
I've seen them take their last breath
and leave this world to go to rest.
In God's great city they were met
by friends and family and all the rest,
Now at peace which they never knew
they'll watch over us to make sure we do.
Fights and trouble we had many
but stuck together which gave us plenty.
I love them so and miss them too
my love for them they always knew.
 Havah Sandra Elaine Burley Hume

Life Is A Battle

When time goes on the soul gets mixed,
Two proceeds as one then all is fixed;

War comes and goes, many battle scars made,
Though we fight side by side and are enemies that may fade;

We battle for our life or does life battle
with us, the problems are many then we make a fuss;

This phenomenon made it so, this phenomenon called life;

So battle on we will and in the end the two of
us shall stand, facing each other holding hands;

As the battle came to close, we hugged each
other in victory, not fighting any more for
now we have unity.
 Gerald K. Schleig

What I Know

I know not archaeology
Unacquainted with antiquity
But this I know
The song of birds
The whisper of a falling leaf
The love of a mother
Happiness and grief
I know the sound of waves
Against the bounty shore
The unforgettable poem "Evermore"
I love the freedom of my land
The Statue of Liberty
As she holds the beacon of light in her hand
Oh, I love so many things
And all the people that I meet
But most of all my Bernie
Our 61 years have been a treat
 Jeanette Gottlieb

Our Children

So small they are as they come to this world
Unaware of what lies ahead
Will they find joy and happiness
Or things in life that we all dread

As they grow with our guidance and strength
And knowledge we so willingly give
Will they use it for their own good
So a happier life they may live

We are there when they triumph
And we are there when they fall
We are there for support
Through the good and bad of it all

As they get older and move away
We wonder why so fast they have grown
Now they have their own children
And have left us all alone

Ernst Skvor

To Gaze, And Then To Dream

Six balloons in a late western sky
Unfettered float as I stand by.
With ease they drift, and rise and sink.
I leave my tasks to watch and think
Of dreams of youth that bade me stray
To lands of Fantasy - so far away.
Gone, gone, long gone - those dreams of long ago,
But still I'd love to be up in that Sunset Glow.

Far above Earth's turmoil and its clatter
Man's trifling chores seem not to matter.
In reverie my youth returns.
Though I have aged, my soul still yearns
To rise above this Earth and dream
That things here are not what they see,.
Oh! Bright balloons still sail the evening sky
Many dreams to awaken as I see you gliding by.

Anna Lundy

Wind Tracks

The wind walks the forest on rustle feet.
Unseen, unheard, untouched;
   Unleashed on the leashed.
It dances to life's lyrics with a baffle beat.

The probing wind stalks where threatening shadows seat;
piercing the darkness, like lightening lighting,
   Shadows retreat.
Revealed verses of wisdom past, pealing pines repeat.

The wind speaks in soaring gusts of silence o'er the forest floor
Of promises kept with wingless larvae and equinoctial lore,
And promises made, of time without tension, where wind tracks end
At forevermore.

The winnowing wind now walks footless on word unsheathed.
   It had became flesh and trod through its forest to die;
And dance unseen, unheard, untouched;
   unleashed on the unleashed
Following wind tracks bequeathed.

Jay Walsh W.

Love's Embrace

As I go home, my spirit stretches across the plains, while my soul
sparkles among the stars.
Within God's world and within your love, I will be all the splendor you know.

Feel my gentle touch, when icy snowflakes land upon your face. Know
me, as I am the warmth which melts them away.

When the waves of the mighty ocean crash upon your feet, look at me.
See my smile in the spray, as it glistens in the sun.

When the storms rage, winds blow, rains beat upon your pane, and the
thunders roll o'er the heavens above, hear me. I am the passion of their song.

As the fields of lavender come to bloom, frolic and run swift. Catch
me, as my fragrance floats upon the lofty air.

When the great forests echo in their silence, sense my serenity. Sing
my name, let me dance among the laurels.

And as the glass is raised for the toast of the night, taste my
essence, let nature's enchanting spirit ease your soul.

For this is God's world and I am home, alive within His splendor.
Embrace His love in your heart for within this love, we shall never part.

Je'Nean Bennett

If I Could Hear That Whistle

I've sorely missed that whistle sound that came from the trains and
the old pulp mill. Our parents used it for a curfew, and its bellow
  haunts me still.

I'd follow a path toward the river, and stand on the banks above
where I could look down and see old railroad tracks that lay idle and rust.

From the path above the river one could see logs as they'd drifted
toward the cutting mill, but this stillness would be broken by a far
  off whistle's shrill.

That steam-engine, coal smoke swirling from her stack, puffs of
steam below, flew out over her tracks, as the engine pulled on passed.

Box cars rattled as did the flat cars and such, iron wheels made a
deafening earth shaking rumbling noise, on that old railroad track.

Seems I miss the old trains calling, when I lived close to the tracks,
and the things I like the most about it, are never coming back.

When I stood there watching those trains, they would shake the earth,
seemed those fifty cars or so, just flew by much too fast.

If I could hear that whistle when it was soft and low, even at a
distance, it would set this heart aglow.

Eugene F. Bernard

Eternal Cry

In the darkness of a misty night, mother earth suddenly brightens the
  sky with her thunderous cry.
Her tears seep down into the soil bringing life to all that they touch.
I watch this miracle as a cool, moist wind hits my face and dances past.
Her tears blend with mine and hide my true agony from the rest of the world.
I long for a touch that I have never known, yet feel I have eternally lost.
This anguish doesn't wash away from within my soul as I stand in the
  cleansing rain.

I look to the stars for their infinite wisdom, but none is shared.
As the heavens look down upon my broken spirit, I fall to my knees for
  all to see.
My soul calls for its other half, but its cry dissipates into the ominous darkness.
Mother earth's coarse skin enfolds my weary, shivering frame,
and her cold dark kiss sends an afflicting sensation through my bones.
The only reply that my heart, my soul, and my being hear...
  ...is the reply of the uncaring, deafening rhythm of the rain.

Edward L. Pinkerton

A Walk In The Country

We "gals" as a body decided, a few bulges we might do without,
so armed with the best of intentions, we put on our shoes and set out.

Each day without fail we would gather and together we'd stagger along
to some hallowed spot in the valley, thinking soon we'd be skinny and strong.

So we've tromped through the fields and the orchards we've been soaked
to the skin in the rain. We've been followed by dogs and shrouded in
fog but undaunted we've set out again.

One day in the month of October, we had bullets whiz over our heads,
and it caused us to stop and to wonder if we'd rather be skinny or dead.

As we'd pick up the pace on the pavement, our mouths went as fast our
feet, the faster we walked, the faster we talked - a more "yakkity"
group you'll not meet.

As the snow and the cold fell upon us, out the window we'd gaze in
despair. How we missed our excursions each morning and the pounds
crept back on - everywhere!

When the ice and the snow had all melted and no icicles hung on our
nose, we resumed, oh so gaily, our walking, hoping soon to get backin our clothes.

Our friendships have grown with each meeting by sharing the good and the bad.
We've listened and pondered and somehow it has eased any burdens we've had.

From the high country roads we would wonder at the patchwork of orchards and farms.
What a beautiful place to go walking! So at peace with its own country charm.

We've admired your flowers and gardens, we've guessed at their species and names.
And somehow this walk into nature has eased all our minds and our pains.

Gloria Monson

Mirror

Sometimes you look at your reflection, and see someone else. That
person you see in there is not really you; a lifeless image of
yourself is all you see. If you laugh, he laughs, if you cry, he
cries, if you sneeze, he sneezes. An image with no emotions, no
character, and no spirit.

The image is never true, but constantly changing, always agreeing,
always accepting what is put upon him. Unlike a picture. A picture
is frozen in time. Your feelings, and your spirit are captured
and frozen into a time frame. If you were sad, your sadness
is captured forever. At least, until the picture remains.

The mirror on the other hand, is a liar, a cheat, and a friend.
It never lets you down. It tells you what you want to hear. It
also shows you what you want to see. The mirror never argues
With you but agrees faithfully, whether good or bad.

Sometimes as I journey through life, I wonder if life is just a
big huge mirror. All you see is other peoples reflections. Their
Reflections is what they want you to see. Always afraid to show
Their true self. That's because they don't even know who they
are. They've been too busy projecting else, that they
have lost touch with who they really are.

Fernando A. Lazcano Jr.

"Dreams"

In today's society it is very hard to make your dreams come
true. It is hard to look the other way when others are making easy
money, and your not.
The heart is a very strong thing that beats from with in. You
put in mined the goals that are needed to be set and the heart will
be your strength to guide you. It is always said only the strong
will survive. Your heart, your mined, and your determination will
help you become what you want to be.
It is easy to be bad, yet it is hard to be good. The bad is
making a lot of money while the good is waiting for their turn to
come. Devotion, Recollection, Eagared, Achievement, Maintaining,
and Strategy. This is known by what we call in our mined dreams.

Jheran Denis

Today

Today comes from unknown,
   Unknown which I have known for many years.
Every today creates me unknown,
   Unknown which is too far from me known.
So, today is not a day for the truth,
   The truth which never becomes a fact.
     Because today is not owned by me.

Today becomes future
   Future which I have known for only one day,
Every one knows me on future,
   Future that is set up by unknown me,
So, future is only day for myself,
   Myself which is free of fact.
     Because future starts before midnight.

Byung J. Min

"You Are the One with Roses in her Skirts."

You are the One
Unfurling petals like Omar's garden
   that billows near the river and tosses in the sun.
You are the One, the rambling rose,
As free as roads that eternally run
   through foreign lands
   you richly grew and blew across.
You are the one with roses in her skirts,
That never missed a ray of light
   of eye or mind,
   that petals love,
The web that beauty walks at night,
And voluptuous,
Drips the peach upon the face of day.

Judith Bean

"Photograph"

It sinisterly curves upwards then downwards.
Within one simple plane.
By two dimensions it is formed.
The wicked colors of foreboding death,
   though now the sun shines,
   and all is brilliant;
   then they will say,
   "Once the sun shone..."
The profound abyss of the shadow,
In every pondering, wandering thought
   is lost to itself,
   given up in the high places,
   made to pass through the fire,
   pay their bail...
The vegetation corrodes and will all become
Food for worms
   and will all die,
   and will all cease,
   and will all disappear,
   and will all vanish...
Though the flames so salient and radiant
Show the life,
   I tell you now,
   I tell you all,
   Shma Yisroel:
   It will become gray,
   It will become ash.
And it will all be no more...

Alex Miller

One Kiss

Today- I did soar
With eagles on high,
Gracefully floated
'Mongst clouds in the sky.

I rested on peaks
New covered with snow,
Watching with int'rest
Life's problems below.

Through my being
A feeling of peace,
And now contentment,
With God, I'm at ease,

Yes, and all of this,
Achieved it is true,
After just one kiss
My love, just from you.

Clarance Taylor

Curly And His Boots

Curly opened the rusted door.
With effort he rolled to the left,
Slid slowly to the ground,
His feet plopping into the dust.

Standing tall was not an option,
He was bent like a comma.
Hugging his boots to his chest,
His gnarled hand clutched his cane.

He appraised the shallow high steps
From street to repair shop,
The lower one was as tall as his knee.
Acknowledging defeat, he sat.

Picking up one cracked boot,
He struggled to remember it new.
He bought them before Sarah died,
When life was God's gift.

Tears rolled down his crevassed cheeks,
Fifty years without her, and the babe.
His three-fingered hand patted the boot.
Hard wear, that's what we've both had.

Joan Kessinger

Plea For Humanity

I am a human being
with feelings of my own;
I need someone to care for me,
I'm afraid to be alone.

Sometimes it's hard to understand
When I scream or cry;
but things are so different
from times of years gone by.

You must try to realize
I need lots of affection
a simple smile or hug
is better than rejection.

I need to know I'm loved
and that people care for me.
I consider this my home,
and you my family.

So...please take good care of me.
You are part of my home;
think of what I must feel,
and love me as your own.

Christine Frizzle

Deception

I thought he was a China man,
With hair standing up tall
Cut short upon his head
When he turned around
He was an American GI,

Now a days, anyone
Can fool you
Fat guy, red hair,
And pony tail,
I thought he was a girl.

And so I crept around
Just one flight down,
I saw her in floral shirt
With green and yellow pants,
The pony tail I saw before, the girl;
She turned around
Behold she was a boy.

Hazel McShane

My Christmas

Christmas time comes once a year
With happiness for all
There's joy and laughter every where
And christmas trees so tall

Its not the things that you receive
Or what you wish you had
So lets be thankful everyone
And at christmas time be glad

Every day could be the same
So why not do your best
To try and make your life worthwhile
With lots of smiles of happiness

Christmas time could be all the year
If you'd only do what right
May God Bless you one and all
On this happy Christmas Nite

Alfred Currier

Daddy's Little Girl

A little girl once stood astray.
With her heart in her hands,
She offered it to a friend.
They turned and walked away.

Again and again,
She offered her heart to a friend.
They turned and walked away.

She begins to build a wall,
Laying one brick on another.
No one is going to hurt her heart.
She has to protect it from her brothers.

Brick by brick, the years go by,
Bye and bye, she begins to cry.
Now she knows her heart will die.

This little girl,
Now all grown up,
In desperation,
Reaches up.

Dorothy Smith

Fall Equinox

Finally, this hot dry August west,
with its fields of stiff yellow grasses
rising up from jigsaw puzzle dirt,
is called to an end.

Sweet, sparkling rain fills the air,
covers the earth, is sucked with greed
by long barren roots desperate to wash
out the toxic residue heaped upon them
by many weeks of arid winds.

The sun grows distant and yet lays upon
the land ribbons of color, yellows and
reds that stream down the gullies,
wrapping the hillsides for harvest.

A family of geese, in the middle of
their mighty migration to the south,
pause to admire the package,
reminding us that all of it is
part of the poem.

Jane Marquardt

"Children"

Small fingers,
With miniature toes.

Sensitive feelings
And a tiny nose.

Looking at you, only 2 feet high,
Wild imagination that reaches the sky.

Not afraid to ask questions,
(With the wrong verbs)
Things you might say took
A lot of nerve.

Only require a few basic things,
Some love, a hug, and a lot of attention.

You see, children have their own
Purpose and mission.

So look deep in your heart,
Be nice to a child.

The feeling will make even an
Old Scrooge wear a forever smile.

Alisa Eileen

Driftwood

I stand erect
with nearly molted skin
one last trace
of mottled bark,
stabbed
into my trunk
with a jagged remain
of a snapped branch,
edges curled
as a burnt posting

Oh how I could tell of

   winds that whirled
    gypsy moths that staked their claim
    passing flits of butterflies
    black crows shadows
   beneath the onset of nightfall
   before the vines
   choked
   my breathy limbs

Angela Reilly

Circle Of Love

She cries herself to sleep at night,
With no one to hold her tight.

They try so hard to understand,
But she will not take their hand.

No one knows just how she feels,
But they hope their love helps to heal.

Of course she loves them all,
But she has suffered too hard of a fall.

She loved him so,
And has learned to let him go.

She knows his love was true,
For he's in Heaven and with her too.

Her broken heart has now mended,
Even though his life has ended.

She has found someone new,
And his love is just as true.

Jennifer L. McVey

Guardian Angel

Life is so bare,
with those who don't care,
as they tear you apart,
Apart from the heart...
the heart of love.
Love so caring,
love you're sharing,
with someone so unique,
they're not really there,
while you know in your heart,
straight from the start,
from the very first day,
till there's nothing to say.
Nothing can describe it,
no one can deny it,
none know why,
it's just there.
It...
is your guardian angel.

Julie Merritt

A Wanted Child, Unwanted Gypsy

Having a drink, once again
  with thoughts of her, feeling the pain,
  remembering when last held,
  only loneliness to be felt.

With memories of becoming a dad,
  the bitter taste of a love gone bad,
  a cradle crafted in anticipation,
  now a reminder of indignation.

A child I so wanted to embrace,
  now a part of thrown-out waste,
  butchers for hire, paid to kill,
  a lost woman at their will,
  torn from her, my love's seed,
  servants of the devil, they are indeed!

The henchmen's wages I had to pay
  for them to take my joy away,
  curses pass over my anguished tongue
  for against God's will, what they have done,
  a loud yet silent cry from within,
  hoping they meet the Creator... again!

Jon (Gypsy) Cotey

Trapped

I'm trapped in a place,
With violence and crime.
Where ladies use mace,
Just to keep them alive.
I'm trapped in a world,
With crimes like abduction.
Where people think the Lord,
Believed in destruction.
I'm trapped in a universe.,
Where gangs think they rule.
Where living is a curse,
and where killing is "cool.:"
I'm trapped in a bubble.
There's no way out.
Where there's only trouble.
That's what the world's about.

Cristin Evans

The Rose

Life is like a rose.
Without a choice it is planted.
Whether or not it wants to be there
it is born, Coming out of its shell,
it begins to grow with no worries
of its own, but as it reaches a
point when it gets its petals;
little cruel birds come and peck
at it, hurting it, letting it learn how
to feel pain. As it grows older
it becomes a full blossomed rose,
it grows thorns which it uses
as revenge to anything that try's
to hurt it. But, as it grows older
it begins browning and welting.
Soon, it dies and nothing is left
of it except the memory of it's life.

Andrea de Aguayo

Introspect

I sat alone in the darkening room
Without conscious thought - without pain.
Neither fear nor courage within my being.
A time transcended - solitary - unfeeling.

A moment suspended in ethereal time
Shared only by spiritual clime
A paradox frequently stated,
"No man is an island!" All related.

Yet comes a time in each one's life
When he must face comforts or strife.
Only then is fate really known
For that's when each of us is ALONE!

Edward A. Pascucci

Fleeting You

Darling, I'm almost crushed with the
  wonder that is you.

Hold that something you possess of me
tenderly, because it is a fragile thing
that is within your power to create
into a beautiful strength,
or break into a thousand fragments
  tossed by a ruthless wind
    should you go.

Darling, I'm almost crushed with the
  wonder that is you.

Bea Warner

Shell

Why am I in here?
Without ever taking it for granted
I can always go in and out
Yet, it's mysteriously silent
I can easily pout

There are people like me
Who build themselves a wall
But mine is not called Berlin
So it won't come down at all

Why did I build this Great Wall?
My eyes saw this world
And I felt misunderstood
I wanted to shut them
To imagine a whole new neighborhood

But I did not end at that
I imagined a larger goal
For every human being to walk hand in hand
So no one can fall down a hole

Anna Bonifacio

She Called But I Was Not There

She called but I was not there,
Without me she wouldn't have a prayer.
She wanted to take her life,
Because there was so much strife,
She called but I was not there.
She told me of times before,
When she was down and felt ignored,
But there had been someone there
To help her with loving care,
She called but I was not there.
Now she's gone and it's all my FAULT
Because...she called but I was not there.
Sometimes I wonder, what was so
Important that I wasn't there when she
Needed me?
Everything else seems so dumb and not
Worthwhile! She's gone and the world
Still turns, no one cares that she's gone,
And it's all my fault!
Because she called but I was not there.

Caitlin A. Reynolds

Our Angel

On a day not so long ago,
Word came from heaven above.
That God would send a special gift-
Living promise of His love.

I had you pictured in my mind,
I could see your eyes so blue.
I could touch your tiny fingers-
Hear your soft and gentle coo.

You were mine and Daddy's angel,
Your sweet smile we longed to see.
Never thinking for a moment
That our dream would never be.

God's garden needed a rosebud-
Not just any one would do.
It had to be the most perfect;
He searched - and found only you.

Our sweet little angel baby,
Heaven's angels hold you now.
Daddy and I love you always
And we'll come when God allows.

Elizabeth Hepner

Words

Words of Freedom
Words so True
Words that Mean
  Nothing to You
Words of Laughter
Words so Hollow
Words that Fill
  One with Sorrow
Words of Years
Words so Forgotten
Words that Taste
  O' so Rotten
Words of Race
Words so Blank
Words that Sail
  Eventually Sink
Words of Mystery
Words so Strange
Words that Stop
  Turn the Page

Bradley David Cox

Still A Child

As a child - Gathering wild flowers in the field
Worldly cares were not for me
Summer winds blowing in my hair
I felt completely free.

There were moments when I knew
My freedom would not last
That soon my childhood pleasures
Would be memories of the past.

With zest of life I hurried on
To do my work each day
And in the rush of worldly cares
Sometimes forgot to pray.

My Lord forgave my thoughtlessness
And I have asked for grace
No more to worldly pleasures turn
While I seek His face.

Now aged without - yet always young
When I look back on fields I trod
My heart can now remain at rest
I am a child of God.

Buena Rose Brack Baize

My Grandma

I like to go to Grandma's house
Would be fun to go every day
What Grandma calls her daily work
To me it's only play.

On Friday we bake lots of bread
And make it into buns
When they turn to a golden brown
We know, the buns are done.

Then we vacuum up the rug
Grandma says "It's just simply filthy."
It sure looks alright to me.
Sometimes - Grandma's are silly.

We are tired now, so we sit and sew
Grandma helps us make things so pretty
She made a quilt - that's just for me.
Finer than one from any city

When things are just awfully still
And Grandma's head will start to nod
I know who she's thinking of
'Cause Grandma talks to God.

Ernest Knauss

Untitled

If you were in my arms...
would you stop the rain?
Would you help me through the pain?
If you were in my arms...
would you stop the tears?
Would you help me overcome all my fears?
If you were in my arms...
Would you help me stand?
Should I fall, would you give me a hand?
If you were in my arms...
would you stay by my side?
Would you love me 'til the day I died?
If you were in my arms...
would you be my guiding light?
Would you make everything all right?
If you were in my arms...
would you be mine?
Would you lay your love on the line?
If you were in my arms...
would we be together now and forever?

James Brian Edwards

Untitled

Slaves to society
Yet dreams hold us back
Racism declares
Who is white who is black
Lovers cry though
They have the key
And fat rich men yell
I am not free
The lonely smile
At pain not yet gone
As critics decide
What to preach on
Dreams not come true
Cause all our tears
But it is those dreams
That take away our fears

Amelia Bond

Last Light

Breaking away from conformity
  Yet, imprisoned by a thread.
Challenging the Lust in Life,
  Or, succumbing to the Dead.

Freedom found in Nakedness
  Arms stretched out as wings,
Leaves vulnerable to treachery
  That another's territory brings.

Dancing on Winds
  Of twilight shadowed clouds,
Fearful of Death beckoning
  Legs covered in a shroud.

Things are never what they appear
  Fashioned in symbols of disguise.
The delicate Play of Life and Death
  In conformity we find demise.

For Beauty is in the Artist's eye
  Ever changing with the Dawn.
Yet, the Ugly Duckling always leaves,
  Its aggression in the Swan.

Julie Ann Faurot

Reality

You're gone forever
Yet you're still here
I've said goodbye
Yet shed no tear.

You say you love me
I don't see how
I've just been hurt
I can't give love now.

You tell me that you see my point
Yet I don't understand
I thought my life was over
Yet my heart is in demand.

I can't explain my feelings
It makes me want to cry
My mind is saying hello
While my heart has said goodbye

Ann E.

You And Me (Toi Et Moi)

You and me
You are me
Annihilate - exhilarate.
Who is to tell
A tale of destruction?
Toi ou moi
Or you and me?
The top of the world
Tomorrow but today
It's butt.
What a story really
In your eyes, it's me
It's I this other that you chase
Down and up and attack sideways.
You and me - it's all the same
Ten thousand millions of bedroom
Windows lighting up here
Turning to dark there
And from Venus and Mars
Everything is blue anyway.

Colette K. Hirsh

Analogue

Arboreal creature
You are recipient
Of Investiture,
The gift sapient,
On biologic substrate
Of your brain copied;
A floppy disc sensate
Touched by the Uncreate
With program self-running,
Software called being.
Wondrous complexity
Lodged in fragile housing,
Of biological binaries,
A momentary singularity
Down from the trees.

Joe A. Bradley Jr

Guardian Angel

A whisper is an angel, a guardian angel
you can only see and hear.
Kisses in the wind, they are a gift,
from above.
In your heart, you know they are watching
you, day by day, as you grow,
a guardian angel is there for you!

Dolly Ann Martin.

For The Money

That's not your money
  You believe that's your money
  I'll tell you what
Lets see if that's' your money
  If I had that money
I'd know what I'd do with that money
  Ain't nothing wrong with that money
That money is a pungency
  That money is a moderate
That money could answer
  See, that's not your money
You think you are something
  Don't you
Why don't you just get on up
  And get down
Get on the good foot and move forward
  I wish I had that money
    Henry L. McShan

What Color Are You

In this world of color
you can see many things
harsh words can be spoken
to kill a persons dream

Time stands still forever
and the hate just grows and grows
in your mouth you have the power
to destroy people you know

What color are you
what difference does it make
are we to be ruled by hatred
and kept in our place

All through the Bible I read about
the same problems we face today
so what color are you
comes in second to your hate

God loves us all
and in His eyes we are the same
by His grace, I find peace
and am known by just one name -
CHRISTIAN.
    April L. Colie

The Gift Of Love

Oh what a beautiful day God has given us
You can smell the clean crisp air flowing
  from the morning dew
The sun is high above and bright as God
  prepares another
Glorious beautiful day with his love
The skies are blue as the ocean seas
The leaves in the trees are whispering
music for another glorious day
Oh how magnificent this day will be
The birds are chirping God's glorious tunes
Everywhere you look you see God's creations
Oh how it magnifies the soul, as if heaven
  is reaching out to you
Oh how beautiful this gift of love is that
God has given us
Let us not take it for granted, for he has
  paid the price for us
Oh how glorious and wonderful he is
Oh how beautiful this gift of love is
For nothing is greater than the gift of love
    John J. Debney

Southern Comfort

Not much has changed in the South
You can still find a good meal
to put in your mouth.
It may be veal
or fried chicken and beans.
You can eat till your belly's big
and the table leans.
You can go to a shin dig
and have lots of fun.
Down here football is popular
So take a seat, and have a honey bun.
The huntin' is spectacular
and the fishin' is superb.
From Savannah to Frankfort
please do not disturb
the fine quality of Southern Comfort.
    Dean Leach

September 17, 1994 Robert C. Miller

You spent your life doing for others
you did the best you could,
and when you spoke, no one listened
even though they really should.

You spoke of things of time gone by
though dates weren't really clear,
but the morals of which you spoke,
were of the things that they should hear.

Maybe your accomplishments were not many;
to others any-way,
but God kept tally of all those
that's why He called on you today.

Oh that I should walk so proud
to have known a man so kind
for his heart was made of gold
the purest you could find.
    Dallan Frandrup

You And Me

  The way I am
you don't care
  The things I see
you won't look
  Things I smell
you would never sense
  This hurting I feel from you
you don't feel
  The things I want in life
your not interested in
  All that I do for you
you don't see - you look through me.
  It's not the love you cannot see
It's only the love you cannot find in
yourself for me.
  From you to me - granted to thee
a love that could never be,
be between you and me.
Hearts of another so wild and free,
will always belong to me and only me!
    Christy Lambert

"Dear Lord"

There's so much I have to thank
you for, I don't know where to start.
So I'll just say thank you, from
the bottom of my heart.

You've done so very much for
me, and made my life anew.
I'm constantly reminded, that
there's nothing you can't do.

When my time on earth is
ended, and I'm call to my new home.
I'll have the joy of knowing
I want be there alone.
    Doris Tyner

First Love

As the sentinel of her youth,
You guard the simplicity of her purity
With passionate vigilance and authority.
When you kiss her
With lips that extinguished youth
So many times before,
For a moment
You possess her innocence
So radiant, like new moonlight
You blind her with love
Labeled true by your words.
The immaculate girl is dead inside you
A woman is your reward
    Dave Lustenberger

To Be...

To be what you want to be...
You have to be strong,
You have to stand tall.
You have to be brave,
You have to be daring,
You have to be equal.
To be what you want to be...
You have to be alert,
You have to be yourself.
You have to be encouraged,
You have to be caring
You have to be great.
To be what you want to be...
You have to work hard,
You have to think hard,
You have to be ready,
You have to be smart,
You have to accept adventures.
    Annabelle Valdellon

Frog 'Neath A Mushroom

Hey there, froggy -
  you with the satisfied grin!
You're a right plump fellow
Squattin' there 'neath your
  mushroom parasol;
Squintin' in the sunlight;
Peepin' out at the world.

I'll bet your countenance -
  so full, so fat and satisfied -
Belies your real purpose:
  Poised...
    Waiting...
      For an unwary morsel
        to happen by.
    Anne W. Riggs

To Nina With All My Love...

You have tested my heart
You have visited me in the night.
You have blinded me to see
What is wrong from right.
You have made me see with
My heart, not my eyes.
You have made me see the stars,
Fall from the skies.
You have made me see what
Others never had,
This makes my heart and soul
Happy and glad.
I love you much as you will see.
I pray to God it will soon
Be you and me.
I love you.
Gene VanGiller

The Friend That Cares

Are there times you want to run away;
  You just can't face another day?
The Savior must have felt that way;
  Yet he took the time to pray.

You tell yourself Oh what's the use;
  But giving up is no excuse.
He's your comforter and guide
  And will always be there by your side.

Nothing's going right for you;
  And you don't know what to do?
The One who knows you of all
  Waits patiently for you to call.

Perhaps there's not a friend around;
  Or someone special let you down.
Jesus is the Friend that cares;
  All your burdens he will share.
Janet Lee

"Hide-N-Seek"

Oh no you man
  you man of mine.
Get off that couch
  my boy go find!
You tell him "run and hide,"
That you'll come find him
  by and by.
Then down you sit
  with paper in hand
going to read while you can.

Oh no you man
  you man of mine
My boy-go find!
  Lest he be lost
and gone for good
My boy-you find!
Judith Marie Moore

Untitled

I's thinks, you'se thinks
You'se knows, what I's knows
If you'se knows, what I's knows
Then please, tell Me's
So I's knows, what you'se knows
If you'se don't follow, no need to fret
Cause it's a sure bet
That the author is weird
Gerald Halstead Jr.

In Your Sleep

In your sleep
You reach for me
Is it me you're really reaching for?
Is so much want to think it is

In your sleep
That place where I cannot go
When you are alone with your thoughts
Am I there?

In your sleep
When you speak words I cannot understand
Are these words for me?
In your sleep
If you sleep long enough
Please, let me find you
Wait for me.
Delian B. Slater

Arrow-Pierced Heart

When our love started out a new,
  you said we would never part.
Back then it came to us so easily,
  but just today you broke my heart.

For you threw away all the memories,
  when you said our love was through.
As you pulled the mighty arrow back,
  straight to my heart it flew.

I have never experienced so much pain,
  as your words ran through my mind.
But then I guess that's the price we pay,
  when we let love steal us blind.

Even so I wish you peace, and all the joy,
  and may your heart never know.
Of how a sharpened arrow feels,
  when someone lets you go.
Anita Goldman

My Grandfather

Rocky said "get the hell up" because
you were lying on the floor in a messy
apartment where the stench of tequila
kept all flies out of the room.
You regretted every signing up for
an early Saturday class, then
being in a band in the first place,
playing gigs in far away places that
would get you back home at some
ungodly hour, and
  your dad has the key
so he can come in at some obscene time,
step over snoring bodies to get you
up on the way to school and
on those rare days when you
finally assume the role of parent
with me, you say that it's
your job to
kick my ass, since
Rocky kicked yours.
Benjamin Gioia

"Gaudeamus Igitur"

As one grows older and starts to think,
You wonder why your muscles shrink.
And where your vim and vigor went
And why you now don't make a dent
In plates of food you used to eat
When in the past you craved more meat.

And breathing comes in shorter gasps,
You wheeze and cough and start to rasp
As on you go at modest pace,
It's not as though you want to race.
Why can't I do the things I did
And live again as does a kid?

The answer to this is, I fear
You're growing older year by year.
As age begins to take its toll
No longer can you "rock and roll"
And once you reconcile this lack
Forge ahead and don't look back.
David T. Collins

a kiss

I've been betrayed by a kiss,
your bliss, your hiss.
I've been betrayed by your soul,
the cold-
ness of your eyes
that bring me down
into your night.
I've seen the hate,
the wait-
ing for the right time
to strike, to dive,
into my inner reaches
and suck on my soul
like leaches.

I've been betrayed by your kiss,
your bliss, your haunting hiss.
  I've seen the cold
  now release my soul!
Christopher Allan Burchette

An Angel Came

My friend please stay with me,
Your face the last I want to see,
Johnnie don't cry,
With you comforted I die,
I love you written on a sigh

In heaven I'll see you,
We both know,
For now I am free,
It's time to go,

Crying from my soul I am missing you,
As I lean and softly kiss you,
Multy-heart to heart I hold you,
Until in time I go to.
Johnnie Davis

Humor

You touched me with
  your forgiveness
    and humor Lord,

I can now laugh at
  my failures, and be
    amazed at my strength
when needed.

In your love, I can love,
May I find humor in
  all my failures,

Make me like a child again.
  filling hearts with laughter.
      Connie L. Chase

It's Time

You bought a new car
You're not going to share
That's the wrong way to think
What about the air

But outraged you are
At the cities large
Who've been trashing the oceans
With barge upon barge

You shout and you cry
But it's just a big lie
'cause you say you're the victim
Without a blue sky

But there's much to be done
Although not always fun
Just open your eyes
It's not a surprise

That the ideals you sought
Should often be fought
And in order to win
We ALL should begin
      Christopher Everett

Sweet Love

My fingers glide over your body;
your skin is so soft to my touch.
You melt in my arms and move closer
and I whisper, "I love you so much."

My hands can't resist your sweet body;
your eyes are alive with desire.
My lips touch your breast and you shiver;
I'm consumed by your heat — I'm on fire.

You reach down and gently you touch me.
I cling to you softly and sigh.
Your touch is like magic - it thrills me;
It takes me to places so high.

Our passion keeps mounting and burning;
we mold and explode like the sun.
We embrace and we cling to each other.
It feels as though we are one.

The passion subsides and I hold you;
your hair feels like silk on my skin.
We kiss and you tell me you love me
and slowly — we make love again.
      Charles L. Mashburn

The New Job

You've made up your mind,
you're on your way.
The choice was your's,
you've no reason to stay.
The future's ahead,
so forget the past.
It's a great opportunity,
you can handle the task.
I'm sure you'll be missed,
by one and all.
Don't turn into a stranger,
just give us a call.

Good luck with the job.
      Dan Hickman

My Heart Smiled

We walked in the moonlight,
Your hand held mine.
We talked.
  My heart smiled.

We stopped in the brightness,
You held me in a warm embrace.
We touched.
  My heart smiled.

We shared big things and small,
We shared God and our faith.
We prayed.
  My heart smiled.
      Janet C. Pennington

The Battle

Though I've never been a soldier,
Who has gone to war to fight.
I have a private battle.
I try to win each night.

My enemy is no stranger,
In some far and distant land.
He rises with me each morning,
We face it hand in hand.

And though no one can see him,
I know he's always near.
When I think of something awful,
And he says things, that only I can hear.

The battles that I'm fighting,
I must win at all cost.
To be the man I want to be,
And find the me I lost.

Yeah, my enemy is sneaky,
The way he runs and hides.
How I wish he was in front of me,
Instead of deep inside.a
      Lloyd F. Blackwell

Queen

Have you seen her; the Queen of Beauty
With hair of raven black
The sun's shadow lingers to her flesh
And I bow in adoration
For I am her King.
      Kelvin Carter

Family Memorial Moments

As we pause today to remember family
Who have gone on before;
We thank you Lord for blessing us
To share your love once more.

We know our days on earth are few
And our life one day must end.
So help us as we go our way,
To spread your love to men.

God give us comfort in your word
To continue in this faith;
And guide us all, step by step
Each and everyday.

Then help us Lord to remember you
In happy and sad times.
And prepare us for our final rest,
With you, beyond the skies
      Zenobia Randell

A Grandma Now

Once there was a little girl
who sat upon my knee,

And listened as I read to her
or she would read to me.

That little girl has long since grown
and books were put to rest.

But don't feel sad or don't be blue,
cause it was for the best.

For now another little girl
has come to take her place.

The feeling and the fun is there
its just a different face.
      Norita A. Pont

Recovering Catholics

We are among the dysfunctional boomers
Who were held hostage by litanies
Of saints and ejaculations in our missiles
That gave us days off from purgatory
As we bent our heads in humility
Swallowing sacrificial mysteries in blood.

Mourning with tears at stations of the cross
And sweating with clammy hands folded
Waiting in apprehension at the confessional
To tell our secrets of venial sins committed
Being told we reached the age of reason
At seven years old, knowing right from wrong.

Mostly we were as good as golden cherubs
Making our First Friday's, nine in a row
And during the month of May we kneeled
With rosaries amid lilacs/lilies of the valley
And prayed daily to a Virgin highly unlikely.

Yet we continue to give lip service
Professing belief in the Annunciation
Recovering /on Sundays/ from ex-communication.
      Mimi Trudeau

I Am

I am the horse,
Who wins all fights;

I am the wolf,
Screaming at heights.

I am the owl,
So wise and so free.

I am the man,
Who uses the three.

I am the lion,
Who stalks out at night.

I am a dreamer,
To nature's delight.

Kelli A. Corey

Untitled

Our Lands are important with
  Whom we share,
Our wild mustang are sure
  to be gone,
The Indians have fought and
  won their battles
To stand upon sacred land
  and vow to the God's above,
The lands are gone but some
  still remain,
And the echoes of the mustangs
  hooves still linger on
  today,
Our native Indians have almost
  disappeared,
Why the mustang have vanished
  it is still unclear,
For we are the people with
  whom they live.

Mary L. Smith

Rebecca, A Paster's Wife

There is this gal named Rebecca
Whose voice belongs on a Decca.
She married a preacher,
Not a music teacher;
Hymns she sings and operetta.

The pastor taught her to ski
And hit a ball from a tee,
But she'll never know
How far she could go
In opera or symphony.

Piano and organ she knows,
But gets itchy when it snows.
She leaves the worries,
And pack her skis;
Off to Colorado she goes.

Golf she plays all year long,
When she doesn't contract a song.
Music and sport is her life
As she lives husband and wife
In Green Valley, south of Tucson.

D. C. Winburn

The Child

What is going on,
  why is this child weeping?
Separation from his brothers,
  has been too long.

What is this abuse,
  toward one another?
Does only the child see,
  we are the accused?

How many tears,
  must be uselessly shed,
Before we stop fighting,
  before we finally realize?

Where is love of God,
  and the unity which once was?
What's happened to friendship?
  All he knows is it is gone.

Sara Walters

Incantation

Dark whispers deep within
willing me
wanting sin.
Willows out my window whine
why ward this wondrous anodyne?
Cryptic winds see through
my soul
tell me
wicked heart, console!
Waxing and waning the willows
blow in
wrathfully wrecking ideals within,
warranting all your worldly wins,
will I will I
in waste
I sin.

Lora Dymphna Gardner

Moon Lit Nights

Moon lit nights,
Windows
on heaven,

Visions
of paradise.

Stars sparkle
bright, soft,
Moon glows

Wonderfully clear.

Seems to me
Angels are near as
unspoken dreams

Drift over me.

Star Dust, Moon Beams, echo...
echo back,

Lovely...
lovely sight on this

Star bright... Star light,

Moon lit...Moon dreamed,

Wonderful night.

Wanda Locke

Untitled

"My eyes are
windows, thru which
my brain can see
and my mind never
forgets"

William K. Dimitri

All Alone

Thinking of you
wishing you were here
so I can hold you close
and tell you that I care

I really miss you
more than you may know
just one more chance
and I would never let you go

I would do the right things
if I ever had you back
not being with you
is the one thing I lack

But it's nobody else's fault
I messed up on my own
and now I'm paying the price
because now I'm all alone

Leonard Knecht

Aim For A Star

Aim for a star, never be satisfied
With a life that is less than the best
Failure lies only in not having tried
In keeping the soul suppressed.

Aim for a star! Look up and away
And follow its beckoning beam
Make each tomorrow a better today
And don't be afraid to dream.

Aim for a star, and keep your
  sights high!
With a heart-full of faith within
Your feet on the ground,
And your eyes on the sky
Some day you are bound to win!

Patricia M. Farler

Love Search

My heart overflows
with a love so deep
I long for someone
my love to keep

To take my heart
To soaring heights
A love to fill
The empty nights

Someone to share
My joy and strife
Someone to travel
The crossroads of life

The questions are many
The answers are few
I go through life
searching for you

Randy Hamilton

Mother's Prayer

Dear Lord, I humbly come to you
With an earnest mother's prayer,
That you be with my little ones
When it seems, I can't be there...

Guide their young and eager feet
In the pathways of your quest,
Well covered by a canopy
Safe in your arms of rest...

Lord, only you can look ahead
Viewing what seems to us a blur,
So I'm asking, Father, guard them well
In whatever may occur...

For as they grow, it seems to me
That our days are more apart,
And I can't be there quite as much
As I was from the start...

Their security rests entirely on
The grace and love you give,
And so with you I entrust them well
With a faith that's imperative...

J. Corinne Davidson

Navigating For A Safe Haven

The rain beats down upon the ground,
with each drop a different sound.

Lightning strikes with a mighty force,
just let nature run it's course.

Clouds diminish, the sun appears,
slowly drawing up the tears.

A glorious rainbow fills the sky,
color's so brilliant you have to sigh.

All kinds of weather that you'll endure,
a breaking point is in store.

Kathy J. Myers

Choices

A young woman lay in restless sleep,
with feelings flowing centuries deep.
From whence they came is mystery.
From futures gone and present need.

They swell and bubble up the parts,
Until they cometh to the heart.
And hearts we know are fragile things,
where feelings mix and love begins.

Confusion overtakes the mind.
His actions confirm a wanting sign.
But then he turns-perhaps to close.
For he needs no one, this is his choice.

The pillow's wet as tears stream down,
She chooses him, but he has flown.
A heart is torn between what to do.
Shall patience reign over or aggression push through?

She wakes with waning want and need.
A lonesomeness, for he was freed,
last night from her arms she let him go.
As she prayed to God that he'd choose her.

Manette A. Nezezon

Reverence

She shuffles along
  with her head held high
Little old lady passing by
No one notices and no one cares
Her memories many
Her thoughts far away
Of by-gone yesterdays
And dreams long lost

Where is she going
And what is her name
She was someone's child
Is she someone's mother
Was she someone's lover
  a long time ago

With a heart filled with love
She smiles as she passes
Little old lady shuffling along

Kay Belvin

Your Presence

You capture my soul
With one deep look.
The presence of you,
Makes me shiver and shine.

Your languages of love
Brightens up my soul,
And brings happiness to my heart,
Which is so lonely and cold.

The thought of you,
Brings hope in spirit.
It lights a flame
That brings peace to the heart,
In a heroic way.

Your loving heart
Brings out your spirit.
You care,
Share,
And enlighten the world,
Which makes your romantic soul,
Shine in your heart of gold.

Linda Ruth Rust

One More Step Till Yesterday

I woke up this morning,
with one thought on my mind;
about how you had to leave,
about how you had to die.

The thought got me crying,
and I know I won't forget;
the way you used to tease me,
the way you were my friend.

You tragically reminded me,
how precious life can be;
and then you had to leave,
so I could learn and see.

I feel as if you're still here,
deep inside my heart;
and still I yearn for you,
to chase aside my fear.

But I know that you'll be,
happier where you are.
And I just have one thing to say,
"One more step till yesterday".

Terri Jo LaDeaux

Two Spheres

My mother awoke
With slowed speech
and immobile limbs
She looked expectantly
in Hippocrates' room
stripped of her dignity,
time is her fickle friend,
Now her world is suspended
between two spheres
Past and present,
present and future
And Hope is her Muse.

Leslie F. Doyle

Strange Days

Strange days find us
With strange ways ahead.
Strange sorrows find us
With strange tears to be shed.

People change
And years estrange,
When desperation leads us.

Silence grows
And distance shows
When loneliness feeds us.

Strange days leave us
With strange burdens behind.
Strange days leave us
With strange joys yet to find.

Michael J. Eshleman

Maggie "O"

Little girl, Little girl
With strawberry head of curl
"O" - How I love thee
Explorer's eye - of color green
And sweet - that cherub arm
I pray thee - no-one harm
Your soul to me - in gentle trust
To grow and nurture - unto dust
World be kind - "O" this lass
No heartbreak - only love
Until - that day - her pass
May Wisdom, Joy and Glory
Be in footsteps as she stride
And Angel Wing with chorus sing
That day - in Purity - His bride

Val Kohlman

This House

This house was once filled
with the laughter from me and you.
Now it is all gone, just like
a dream, that I do not remember.
This house was so cheerful,
what happened?, do you know?
This house cries for the laughter,
the happiness, the love.
I say to this house, do not
weep, he will come, laughter,
happiness and joy will be
here also. Please do not weep, for
the memories you shall always keep.

Rebecca Johnson

Christmas On The Prairie

Now it's Christmas on the prairie,
With the sage all trimmed in dew,
And I'm riding down the canyon trail,
To be once more with you.

How I long to see the ranch fires,
With the yule logs burning bright,
And the old corral, with little doggies,
Sleeping through the night.

Oh, I've been away a long time,
Ever since that summer past,
But now snow is glistening on the pines,
And I'm heading home at last.

See that old coyote howl,
At what surely is a sight.
Old St. Nick is riding herd in,
Jingling spurs and stetson white.

Now I see my spread before me,
Nestled in the snow,
Yes, its Christmas on the prairie,
And the world is all aglow.
Robert M. Duncan

Word Tapestry

Oh life that forms the words
  within my soul
And captures all experiences
  I behold
The light of mirth that sets
  my face aglow
Darkness and dread that fills
  my heart with woe
A symphony that sets the
  music free
Both happiness and sadness
  form degrees
Of the colors in this poets
  tapestry
And culminate when everything
  in time
Comes together in a verse
  or rhyme
For all to see the inner part of me
That blossoms in myself my poetry
Patricia S. Ashforth

Boundary

  I must sit in my yard
within the fence
  waiting till I can reach the lock
and open up my gate
  enclosed in this boundary of life
while I see teenagers
  jump over the fence without a worry
my parents walking in and out
  with little expression on their faces
I sit there watching all that is going on
  wishing all the while to leave the
protection of my home and fence
  jumping into the huge world
Kenzi Snider

You Hold Tomorrow's Wisdom

You hold tomorrow's wisdom
You throw away yesterday's sins
You hold your hopes and dreams
You throw away your fears and hurts.
Ricki Terese Barta

Stained

Sweet fierce hunger
Within this wisdom
Stone walls of creation
Tower

Gazing up at illusions
Temptations to freedom
I am the servant
Remember

White teeth striking
Tongue drenched in vulgarity
Lashing
While lips are chanting

Beyond the surface
I weep
My urge for fire discreet
Delivering unknown passions
Maricarda Ortiz

Wings

Like an eagle, I can soar,
Without my wings I could no more.
Through the clouds I can fly,
Without my wings I would die.

Wings of joy, wings of love,
Wings in my mind of a dove.
Love in my heart is so true,
The target of my love is you.

Wings in my heart, wings in my soul,
Wings that are wild and out of control,
And yet they're gentle and so sincere,
So far away, and yet so near.
Melodie Leonard

Without You

Without the robin
Without the rainbow
Without the mountains
Without the meadows
Without the breeze
Without the brook
Without the forests
Without the flowers
Without the dusk
Without the dawn
  Without your life
  Without your laugh
  Without your love...
    Without my strength, my spirit,
    my soul.
Ricarda McDonald Payne

The Shore

The waves crash upon you
You withstand their force
. . . for awhile.

Every wave brings a treasure
a bit of knowledge
from the past, for the future.

Every wave takes away
a bit of who you were,
changing and altering.

The waves crash upon you
forever changing,
forever the same!
Peter John Lee

A Letter To Nicole

Sitting here late at night
Wondering if you're alright
Are you an angel?
Do you have wings?
Is heaven full of beautiful things?

One day soon we'll be together
Time goes by just like the weather
You're my friend, you'll always be
I miss you terribly, do you miss me?

You've left a beautiful family behind
But I know you're always on their mind
Time has suddenly gone by so fast
So now I'll make the memories last

As I think of you in your place of rest
I know that what happened is for the best
And although I'd much rather have you here
It helps to think that you're somewhere near.

Yes, it's true, we had to part
But there's one place you'll always be
That's in my heart
In loving memory of Nicole Warner
Victoria Larson

Mother

  My mother means the
world to me.
  She is the type of person
who stands by her family.
  Through the good and bad
times.
  In my heart my love for
her will never die.
  She's there to put the
pieces back together, when I
have a broken heart.
  She's there to pick me up,
when I have fallen down so hard.
  She is the type of mom
who should be cherished at all
times.
  I just want to let her
know I am very happy she's mine.
Sharlene Ramos

Searching

Have I done all that Jesus,
Would ask of me to do?
Am I walking in the path,
With His anointed few?

Have I said each day the things,
That God would have me say?
Do I speak each word with kindness,
And in a pleasant way?

Have I gone each day to places,
That Christ would have me go?
When oft by Satan tempted,
Do I always answer "No"?

Am I willing Lord to be,
What Thou wouldst have me be?
Letting my light so shine,
That others Christ may see?

Lord help me humbly ask myself,
These questions day by day.
And help me walk in all the light,
That Thou dost shine my way.
Naomi L. Burris

"Despair"

Where did Love go?
Wounded within my breast
It can not strengthen now,
Crippled love cannot grow.

What did love know?
The small things done and undone.
Respecting not the promises
Of joy we might have known.

Who crippled love?
Lovers only can know
Angry words flung on the breeze
Like darts they wound the heart.

Love is in despair now.
An embryo that did not fulfill
The promise of its first seed.
Fear can not let Love show.
Nadine Simms Long

A Call From The Seats

Grind the axe,
Write the word,
Will any of us ever be heard?

Students have souls,
With a purpose to vent,
Our Spartan lives,
Are a perpetual lent.

Now you hear, you
Pedagogues of the letter,
Our internship here,
Means we will get better.

Lend an ear,
Gurus both old and new,
Keep your heads out of the trees,
Then your message will get through.
Robert J. Olson

My Dying Patient

I know you're dying,
Yet I try to make you smile.
You do respond to my jokes,
Once in a while.

Your eyes are closing,
there's a smile on your face.
Your breathing's ceased;
I know you're in a different
  place.

You know I'm crying,
though I barely know your name.
But as you left this earth
A part of you, with me,
  will remain.
Lucy Comenzo

Father's Day Salute

In the past and the future,
  You are the light,
You are the reason my future is bright,
  I can count on you,
I know you'll always come through,
  You are my dad, you are a delight!
Michelle Valore

The Ocean

Looks so innocent and sweet
yet it sweeps you off your feet
drags you down to the icy blue
covers up and swallows you

Pulls you down
with a beautiful sound
only by luck can you escape
saved by a prayer or fate

Remember when you see the ocean
overcome with hypnotizing notion
the water that's an innocent blue
with a foam that tops hot stew
those waves are deadly
singing a dangerous medley
and when you turn back
the ocean will make it's attack!
Nancy England

First Grandchild

Our precious little one
You came along today,
Not that you were supposed too
but we'll keep you anyway.

Sunshine's coming through the window
The ground is full of snow,
You're stretched out in your bed
With lots of room to grow.

You have a tiny turned up nose
Little legs and a head of hair,
You haven't any butt at all
And for that you'll never care.

Life isn't a bowl of cherries
Of this you'll become aware,
But we will give you strength and hope
And all your hurts we'll share.

Each and everyday of your life
We'll show you care and love,
Only one could love you more
The good Lord up above.
Linda M. Butler

Secret Admirer

It doesn't matter what you wear,
You catch my eye when you walk.
It doesn't matter what you say,
I always listen, to hear you talk.
How can I ignore these feelings,
I buried so deep inside.
How can I not let it show,
My passions I try to hide.
I see you when my light goes out,
Your always in my dreams.
I can hold you in my arms there,
And say all the words I mean.
I dream of the softness of your lips,
And your body pressed with mine.
I dream of long passionate hours,
Lost together, forever in time.
Its so hard to stay away from you,
Not telling you how I feel.
Its so hard to watch you from afar,
Knowing that my love is real.
Rick Jeric

For The Loss Of A Loved One

Now that you have gone and left us here
You have caused us many tears
You were loved by the Lord and us
And many hearts have grown to trust
We'll remember you by what you've taught
And the many blessings you have brought
Not to mention for being you
We'll all strive to be like you
For we know it's what is right
To always continue sharing the light
No one better was sent to earth
And also born of royal birth
We'll walk tall just as you have shown
That way you'll know we've grown
Please remember that you were so very loved
So trust in the Lord and also us
Now that your work on earth is done
Ours has only just began
For now you must go and leave us here
But we'll remember that you're so very near
Sara Thornton

To My Far Away Friend

I often wonder why I can't get
  you off my mind.
Because I can't concentrate I
  find myself always in a bind.
You've touched my heart in
  many ways.
And in it I know you will
  always stay.
When I get free time I always
  want to spend it with you.
That way I know I will always
  be happy and never blue.
I hope we can get closer as we
  go through each day.
And "you're in my thoughts forever"
  is what I'll always say.
My one wish though, is for you
  to be mine.
And I hope in the future me
  in your heart is what I'll find.
Tonya Mozenko

A Friend Is...

A friend is someone who you tell
your most deepest secrets to.
A friend is trustworthy and always honest.
A friend understands all your problems
and helps you cope with everyday life.
A friend is loving and kind and is
always there when you need someone totalk to.
A friend is someone you laugh with
and comforts you when you cry.
A friend is someone you'll never
forget, and, as the years go by, and
you're looking back at the past.
That friend will always be in those,
memories, for a friend, is true.
  Are you a friend?
Richard William Conway

"Try To Exceed"

When you try to be best,
you seem to get worse,
don't try to go above
too fast, for then you will
forget the past.
Take things slow, for
you will eventually grow.
So stick in there,
when things go wrong,
for you will soon
be strong.

Tara R. Nemitz

Lead Cross

Malevolent are you to young and old
your wrath torments our body and soul

Destroyer of dreams hopes and joy
no God or man can stop your ploy

Lonely victims we are not to you
our family and friends suffer too

But know this which will come true
someday I will parish and so will you.

Walter J. Mongiat

Midnight Caller

You call upon me while my eyes are closed,
You set my heart aglow.
But you disappear with the light,
I can't help but wonder where you go.

You're my midnight caller,
You're my midnight caller,
A shadow in the night,
Disappearing with the light.

My mind is with you everyday,
I want to be with you in every way.
But I can't find you in the light,
I'll have to wait until the night.

As darkness falls your love, it calls;
You're my midnight caller,
A shadow in the night,
Disappearing with the light.

When I close my eyes you call on me,
You fill my dreams with ecstasy.
A shadow in the night,
Disappearing with the light.

Robert C. Dick Jr.

Kathleen

Poet, whom we all adore,
You're mistress of the metaphor;
Simile and imagery
Enhance your verses, rhymed, or free.
Verse perceptive, ever kind
Flows calmly from your artist mind;
A mind as restless as a cloud
Speaks your restless dreams aloud;
Hints of futures, lauds times past,
Answers questions seldom asked,
Speaks in bright or mystic tone,
Speaks a radiance all your own,
Speaks of flowers, of bird, of tree,
Speaks to lovers, speaks to me.

Millie Shepard

To A Mystical Place

You always called me
Your bright and shining star

Our love carried us
To a mystical place afar.

Oh, we struggled too,
We were friend and foe

I just never suspected
The other woman, lady snow.

We loved so hard
Until the bottom fell out,

I was left wondering
Full of hurt and doubt.

I've been replaced now
Your bright and shining star,

Lady snow carried you
To a mystical place afar.

Cheryl Mangin

My Dearest Grandma

Your frail body can hurt no more
Your feet will never be painful for you.
The bruises in your arms will heal
You will never be tired again only full
   of energy
You will never be cold only warm and cozy
Souls are free to go anywhere they please
You've been set free from the pains
   of being alive
Your soul lives on and the memories
   we shared will always be in my
   mind and the love you felt for
   me close to my heart
I love you Grandma and always will.

Denise A. Bloskey

When Waves Die

Sitting by the river
your head on my lap
I've never felt so needed
caring caresses, loving whispers

Walking hand in hand
I could walk forever
you felt so right next to me
simple touches, hidden meanings

You found that shell for me
You pressed it against my ear
I heard the ocean
Pounding wildly, passionate waves

We talked for years
Without saying a word
I knew you loved me
You knew you had to leave

And when I pick up that shell
That I'll never let go
I try and try but
I don't hear the ocean anymore.

Stacey M. Schaffer

Rush On The Edge

As the white dust invades
your inner existence
And the edges of your vision ripple
unclear as a mirage

You tap your foot to the beat of pain

And your frown eludes a smile
as sane loses to insane

Your heart beats no, your mind reasons go
how or when or may it end
this evil bond with the devil
you call friend

With each draw comes
the pain, the fear
you grip your chest
to feel the rhythm

You breathe deep, heavy, fast

You know it could be
you pray it is not
this breath you take
your very last

Scott C. Schulman

Baby Shower

Welcome little one.
Your mother and father
thought you'd never come.

They've been making the
house all ready for you.
Not knowing whether to
paint it pink or blue.

You're daddy is ready to buy
all kinds of toys,
but hasn't been sure to get
girls or boys.

I am your mommy's best friend
Meshelle,
and I hope you'll like me
just as well.

Your parents are so happy
and full of joy,
and just can't wait
to meet their little girl or little boy.

Meshelle A. Robinson

To My Daughter On Her Third Birthday

Precious little lady,
You're the love of my life.

My love for you is different,
Than the love I have for my wife.

The time we share together
Is so special and too rare.

The world seems so much brighter
When we cuddle in "our chair".

Your gentle hands, your smiling face,
Your tiny, tiny toes.

And who has ever seen a cutter
Little turned up nose.

The joys of love have never meant
So much to mom and me.

And just to think my little dear,
Today you're only three.

Tony Reda

He Is Our Strong Tower

We have a faithful friend
Upon whom we can depend
Upon whom the storm of life truly does expend.

Let us run to our friend
So that all troubles would truly end.

For our Lord is our flower
He is our strong tower.

But, he didn't come for us to stay
Where there are only high towers.

He didn't come for us to stay
Amidst the roses and the flowers.

So let us come to him today
As He softly says.

There is life with me today
So come with me and pray
And I will show you the way.
Gale Leistman

Distinct Love

   Had I not envisioned your arrival, the mist of your
vapor would have escaped my fleshly vault.
Your love has made all things possible and all things beautiful.
You have inflamed my heart and my soul
is enchanted by your mere silhouette.

Your spirit seeps into my vessel causing a major eruption of ecstasy
Something within my soul takes flight at the touch of
your honey coated succulent scented lips. The sound of your
melancholy gestures falling on my ears discloses a
reincarnated love for me.
The glory of the day is in your face
and the beauty of the night is in your is eyes.

With just one twinkling of your eyes you have resurrected
my nestled passion for life.
Yesterday is but todays
memory. In my sleep, in my dreams and in my awakening I
love you and you will always have a place in heart.
Diana Dass

Magic Mirror Of Love

Once a man, I greatly admired,
Very heavy demands, were sadly required.
Wanting to prove myself to be very true,
I found there was nothing, I wouldn't do,
Then one day. I had a terrible fall,
And saw a magic mirror on the wall.
I heard a voice saying, "come on in a
mysterious journey is about to began".
Imagine climbing a rainbow, touching the sun,
Picking up dew drops one by one.
Building big castles from raindrops that fall,
Holding the moon to use as a ball.
Riding a cloud, catching a star,
Grabbing the wind wherever you are.
A blade of grass you use for a rocket.
You pick up trees to put in your pocket.
Dance on the ocean, sing under the sand,
A big experience for such a small woman.
The wonderful things you could ever think of.
You'll find as you walk through the magic mirror of love.
Jennifer Wiley

The Deserted House

Eyes of broken windows, the house stares at us.
Vines cover the walls, they grow in the dust.

Grass now long dead, has all gone to seed
The garden, untended, has returned to weed.

Mice play on the counter, where once bread was made.
A stray cat stops by in search of the shade.

Bits of lace flutter, from a window upstairs.
It remembers a time when there were no cares.

The back porch has fallen away from the wall.
A rocker sits perched on top of it all.

He farmed the land, he milked the cow.
He helped with the garden, he ran the plow.

She fed the chickens, cooked, canned and cleaned.
She tended the children and rocked in between.

Where are the children that swung happily?
The tire swing hangs listless, a rope from the tree.

The house speaks to us, in words from afar.
Remember my friends, just how transient you are.
Ann Caskinette

Lyssis-Poem 24

Like a river of diaphanous silk, you slither past
visions of some shared future-present that was;
You descend in smiles, deciphering silences of last.
Naked truths are sealed in your blue gaze of ice...
This enigmatic look that melts my disguise of want.
One rhythm, one tone, repeats again and again,
As we stand alone in some dim casting room
Two blushed silhouettes, shadows disrobing to a chant
No props, no scripts, - just another piano melody becomes.

Doubly naked, I stand shaken;
wearing no mask for the cry of your touch,
Another encore for that shared indelible kiss.
From July to September,
an instant is captured in fifteen full moons of you
Like your impromptu,
I'm never content in my appetite for your grace,
I invoke melancholic poems,
the metallic taste haunts my wandering nights
The Blood of your Womanhood on my palate like a prayer,
A libation at Diana's altar, "give me another season, Goddess..."
To behold you in another summer's wet skin
And count the turns of time with another measure of YOU.
Elena M. Gomez

The Giver

She sits waiting.
Waiting for someone to notice her.
She waits for someone to take
   the knowledge that she can give.

Some do.
Others pass her by like garbage on the street.
She does not ask for anything in return
Just a moment of your time.
It does not take money or jewels to
   receive her knowledge.

If you see her sitting there, do not
   pass her.
Do not ignore
All she wants is a moment
   of your time.
Casey DeGrechie

Pain

It's waiting - always waiting and lurking on the edges
Waiting to sneak in and take over
Have to be on the alert - be watchful - can't lower my guard
Careful - careful - the enemy is here - out it comes
God - its taken over again

Anne C. Viscelli

That's What They Do

Was just a chicken a strutting my stuff!
Walking round the barnyard, that was anuff!
I was in chicken heaven or so it seemed,
It was that Big Red Roooster of whom I dreamed!

Pick—Pick—Pick—Pick—That's what they do!
They don't seem to care what happens to you!
And now I'm alone in this cruel land,
They've picked at my ankle — don't ya understand!

And then one day, as I strode along,
I tripped over my pride, and then I went wrong.
They said look out, but I didn't heed,
As I looked down, my ankle started to bleed.

When someone's alone and looking for friends,
And they're ankle's a hurting, hoping that it mends;
They only look for someone to love,
Maybe all that's left, is WAY UP ABOVE!

Child Of The Masquerade

It's deathly quiet here, no voice to penetrate the dark.
Walking through rooms in fear I long for some sort of remark.
Feeling no love or compassion within this soul,
the emotions felt here I knew were never told.
I see a little girl who now is in the past,
happy and gay was she, unknowing it wouldn't last.
Life played a game with her, turning happiness into stone.
And now, that saddened little girl is on her own...all alone.
Put out so suddenly before learning about life,
emotions melted, edges sharpened...finely as a knife.
She looked around just to find that life is a masquerade.
Responsively, her last emotions had finally begun to fade.
Thus, the little girl who once sparkled like a jade,
had become one tiny part of today's lonely masquerade.

Cindy C. Demars

The Island

The sea gull stood at the explored end
Wanting to run into mysterious unknowns
The rhythmic waves called ever so gently
Mesmerized, the sea gull stood, waiting.

The sea gull stood at the explored end
Wanting to feel expanses of new emotions
Silently he watched waves come and go
Envious, the sea gull stood, waiting.

A flock of like sea gulls alighted
Over the sea's violent beginning
Freely to calmer realms they flew
Safe, the sea gull stood, waiting.

The lone sea gull felt the sand
Thoughts and desires forgotten
The flock of like sea gulls vanished
Conditioned, the sea gulls stood, waiting.

The sea gull still felt the beating
Mystical lure of moon and sea
But he turned and plodded to his brood
Whimpering, he stood at the explored end... Waiting?

John T. Dimos

"It's Your Choice"

This is your home and you are welcome here, you will be
warm and safe and the cold night you need not fear.
How many times have we said, the door is open and here is
your bed. IT'S YOUR CHOICE.

Here is a shower, a refrigerator with food to cook,
a warm clean home just take time to look.
We love you but we aren't going to drag you back, if it's
courage, wisdom and common sense you lack, IT'S YOUR CHOICE.

We have all made mistakes which we can not change, we can
only go on and not let others our lives disarrange. We must
work for the things we want and need and learn to appreciate
what we have if we want to succeed. IT'S YOUR CHOICE.

You are young, an American living in the land of opportunity
and the land of the free, it's up to you what you want to be.
Welfare, drugs, no school, no job, don't be a fool, stop take
charge of your life and get rid of the strife. IT'S YOUR CHOICE.

Live one day at a time, but please keep in mind, only you
can make the change and make the best of each day, don't look
the other way. Let the Lord and your family be your guide, take
my hand and we will walk together side by side. IT'S YOUR CHOICE.

Doris June Winkelman

A Simple, But Sweet Note

A simple, but sweet, gentle note,
was as sweet as the one who wrote.
It filled the poor with hope anew,
as it gently, simply flew.

It softened hearts of cold,
Capturing others in it's hold.
The broken-hearted listened well
and thought of all the times they failed.

As the note filled each heart with song
they hadn't felt this loved for so long.

So as you see, this note, this song, is you and me.
How we live and how we give.

For life is a song, some mistakes and little wrongs.
Harmonies and melodies, all put together by you and me.
Now how we play the song, if we don't like it
that is wrong.

For we only have one life to live, one song to play
It's how the song is done and how much you give.

If you care and enjoy.
Now that, my friend, is a song.

Cassandra Hull

I Am No One

I am no one, I walk the night
Way out beyond all sound and sight
I am no one, I walk the night
The darkness of night, the anxiety of day
All this bothers me not
Because I am no one, I walk the night

The night to me is full of rapture and hopes of flight
Not like the day that I know for sure is to come again
Because I am no one, I walk the night
Far from all sound and sight

The night is long the day is short, thank God for this
For someday we shall neither know day from night
I love the night all full of unexpected flights
Because, you see, I am no one, I walk the night

Charles T. McDonald

For Who? For What?

For Who? For What?
Was the Cry.
Rising up from the deepest corner of self indulge-land,
For who? For what?
Was the lie.
For if truth be told you wouldn't a said that, man.
For who? For what?
Oh hear my plea.
One for the money, two for the show,
For who? For what?
Afraid someone might see.
Three to get ready with no place to go.
For who? For what?
Take a look inside.
Back it up to the place where heroes begin,
For who? For what?
Is there no pride.
Success, sweet wine and efforts end.
For who? For what?
For the win.
   Herbert L. Lane

The Sea

The rolling, roaring, splashing sea
Wasn't made for you nor me
'Twas made for those who love to roam
Who love the sea, its waves, its foam
It is for those who call the sea their home
The sea was made.

On starry nights when all is clear and calm
It is the sea's enchanting balm
That soothes many a weary and lonesome heart
A heart whose love is miles apart
And yet the love of that very heart
Is with the sea.

Its bluey depths, its sparkling gleam
Was made for those who in it dream
With each new tide you hear them sigh
For they are mortals who will never die
Just slumber on a bed of waves
Beneath a starry sky.
   Elizabeth Edwards

Toast

24 years of submission
Watched you pray to your liquid Jesus
Walked on glass..... spoke in a hush
Your life support system has begun to grab me
Now you begin to disguise it
Mother, brother grow blind, deaf, numb
Never breathed my own breath
It's time to breathe
Time for you to taste my pain
Drank and turned me into that bastard boy
Never around to help me grow so I taught myself
Family shrank....bottle grew
You alienated me from you with your bottle of love
You drank my childhood away
Never once did I complain
Now watch me explode....now live with my rage
You're so sad and pathetic to be controlled by liquid Jesus
All this bitterness welled up inside me
I raise the glass to you I've poured
Now drink my anger and hatred I have for you
   Bart F. Hansen

Watching The Fire

Catching every sparkle that comes with
watching the fire,
I can't think of anything that could ever
take me higher.
Reflections bouncing off the embers onto me,
the fire lets me see things, the way I want to see.

So quiet and solemn, the night that runs forever,
The solitude I'm finding, I'm wishing it forever.
And when the fire is just about to die,
I'll throw another log on, so I can sit, just awhile.
   Carlton James

Beginnings

Labor Day has come and gone, and summer time, as well;
We can recall the good times had, in memories to dwell;
It's back to work, vacation's out, the fun times are all past;
It's nose to grindstone, to the line; seems good times never last.

But, hold on there! It's not Fall's fault that Winter beckons neigh;
It's the planetary voyage through our dark galactic sky!
Back when these orbs chased 'round the Sun as barren, giant rocks,
Earth had her rigid schedule, plus autumnal equinox!

Thus, Nature, God, or Circumstance (take, if you will, your pick),
Stands charge of seasons passing on, each clock's advancing tick;
The waning day, the growing night, leaf paintings bold and fair;
The frost upon the autumn crops, breath-steam in frigid air;

Don't begrudge this season for the Winter it presages;
But, rather, celebrate the turning of the earthly pages;
As Autumn's quilt is sewn to ground by swirling, cooling breeze,
Take part, exult; rejoice, revive; for later, Winter's freeze
Will give us all time to reflect, repair for the rebirth;
Our hemisphere awakes again and Spring's upon the Earth!
   Gary D. LaPatra

1995

1995 has been quite a year -
We celebrated our golden anniversary
Surrounded by friends and family we hold dear.
Just days later our first great grandchild was born.
A darling baby girl
Who has us all in a bit of a whirl.
Then came our fifty-fifth high school reunion.
Wonderful to see old friends.
And with them visit the land of Nostalgia
Bordered by Grief (for those no longer with us).
Then came the book in which my very first poem did appear.
All my friends gave a cheer.
And the year's not over yet!
   Druscilla L. Radloff

To My Valentine

February 14 is Valentine's Day
We each show our feelings in a different way.
Some show there love by giving flowers
Some learn a poem of love, this takes hours.
Some say, sweet for the sweet, and give a box of candy
Others give a Valentine's day card, for some that's dandy.
Some will take there love ones out to dine
Some will show there love with an expensive bottle of wine.
Some will give a single red rose
Others a small present will ribbons and bows.
To you Faith I give something you can't open up or take apart
To you I give my Future, My Life, My Heart.
   George Flurry

Valley Forge And Buttercups

It was very, very, early, when we started out that day; and from where
we lived, it took some time to go that far away.
The sun had barely risen, the dew had soaked the ground; but we were
in our first love, and hardly noticed our surround.
We visited the campsites, and remembered the battles of old; it was
spring and hard to imagine the troops in the snow and the cold.
We talked, and walked, up and down the hills; we picnicked under a
tree; it was a perfectly, splendid, day for my new love and me.
As we left the park, a strange thing happened, I'll remember 'till
I'm old; we walked through a meadow of buttercups;
and our dew damp shoes turned to gold.

Harriet H. Lindquist

Count Your Blessings

In an age of dissension
We look upon the wonders of all
Marvelous, to say the least, inventions
Numerous, as summer, winter and fall

When our world stops with grief or pain
Why do we question, how can this be
I'm so important, look at my gains
Compare the universe to simple me

Count your blessings big or small
Take time to smell the roses
Pause one day a month to recall
All life's precious treasures poses

Smile at a child, everyone you meet
Greet with a handshake, or nod of your head
For money is not power but defeat
Caring and touching souls is riches instead

When I pass on I hope all will say
Tenderness and kindness were always assured
There went a person rich in every way
A smile for everyone, we'll miss them for sure

Joyce Loomis

Dying To Look Good

What are we but a container for our soul, our character.
We need some guidelines in which to fit.
At first we are assumed to be our hair,
   or our height or our weight.
Sometimes we are seen as our cars,
   or our homes or our clothes.
But when we discover love we become our hearts.
We are our laughter and our sorrow.
We are our history.
Our bodies are just "matter"
   to dress up and drive places.
To lay on top of one another so our souls can touch,
   our hearts can meld.

Eventually our bodies are what we leave behind.
Then No One is better dressed.
No One has a nicer yard,
And Everyone is too thin!
We must understand this notion before it is too late
   and Dust is Dust.

Caren Kaye

Faith

No one knows the way Faith turns,
We only know it sometimes hurts.

Little ones can bring us so much joy and happiness,
and yet they can also bring us such Sorrow and Sadness.

Though we tough it out as we may,
Only wishing Happiness will return someday.

Think of good, and pray to God,
for each day we have a growing bond.

So sleep little one and get your rest,
and each day you will grow at your best.

No one knows the way Faith may be,
We only know it takes time to see.

Cathy Fitzgerald

A Childhood Place

There is a plea in quiet childhood memory sweet
we return to refuge seek...

The apple trees beside the barn, their canopy my tent
to run for shelter in the rain
and watch the storm progress

I see the stand of poplar trees
shimmer-gray-green-silver bend
to let the wind pass through upon
its journey with no end

I see the lightening streak the sky in colors full of life
and hear the thunder roll and speak from
nature's hymnal grace

And as the traveller on this storm
to places yet unseen
and tests of venture ply against
each daydream moment's wing

I reach out for clover sweet and daisy-grass abound
and tender leaves yet dry and deep—their canopy my tent
that childhood place in quiet memory sound
to hold the soul when refuge seek.

Barbara Jean White

Beach Fire

When the picnic was over,
We sat by the tide,
Watched the white-winged seagulls slide
Down blowing the evening wind.

The stars came out above the sea
Dad gave shout
"Oh, wish on that little brand new moon,
Lets build up the fire with wood from the dune"!
We wished on the moon
Built up the fire
Sang while the sparks flew higher,
Higher, like stars of our own
Above the foam
TIll growing sleepy.
Then, we and the birds went home.

Charles C. Satriani

Untitled

Now the one so loved is sleeping,
We show our hurt with tears and weeping.
I know now, he feels no pain,
but what I feel is sorrow and what I see is rain.
One thing he showed to those he knew was love,
even though it was invisible I could see it like a dove.
What he gave could not be bought,
and what I learned one day will be taught.
For now I know I must be strong.
To help myself and the hurting along.
One day we will find the pain has slowly started to
pass, and the heart has begun to heal like the rain
we see and feel has become but a haze.
I can see the sunshine again,
and I can make out the colorful rays.
My memories of Grandpa I will hold near to my
heart, and as the years may pass,
I will remember the fun we had and the love he
gave and made last.

Jennifer Ann Pekala

Tears Of Silence

Those tears that we do not allow to be born,
We suck them back in - in fear that weakness will show,
We punish our selves, for having deep feelings, that make us weep,
Weep in sorrow, weep in sadness, weep in shame,
Weep in pain - through feelings of hurt.
We weep for something, that we have lost or
Something we are missing.

A void yet to be filled,
sorrow seeking forgiveness,
Hurt yet to be healed.

We all seek something, something to help us heal, but what?
A simple sense of unconditional love,
Given out of respect.
But well deserved and needed, in a world so harsh,
An umbrella is needed to protect one's wellness.

Gina A. Whitacre

The Perpetual Test

Praising God as He created each creature on earth
We watched in awe at your beautiful birth
He molded you carefully into His own likeness
You stood so tall, so proud, so righteous
He favored you humans and placed you above the rest
This angered with us for we believed we were the best
Armed with this knowledge Lucifer thought of plan
Let us go down and corrupt this creation called man
We'll turn them from God and place evil in men
Then God will see they're not perfect, we're better than them
Unbeknownst to us God had called to the one who was greatest
God said Lucifer my son, all my creations I want tested
He stated he would do this with one stipulation
If we asked for forgiveness He'd give us redemption
So God turned to Michael so beautiful and serene
And said I want you to find those worthy enough to redeem
To those of us who repented He assigned a great task
Reverse what we've done or we shall face Gods wrath
We became your guardians and we shall never again rest
Forever with Michael guiding you through Lucifers test

Corrine Huer

They Learned It From Us

Our nation's youth filled with hate, anger and violence...
We wring our hands in disgust.
Sadly, older Americans, they learned it from us.
We revel in the glory of another successful drug bust.
Where did the narcissistic quest start from?
They learned it from us.

Hundreds of generations' affairs with nicotine and alcohol
Created an abyss into which our offspring would fall.
No, we did not have cocaine or the various amphetamine pills
But we sure had plenty of nicotine and alcohol stills.

Remember as we are quick to a judgement rush,
Much of this destruction they learned from us.
They were not born hating each other for the color of skin;
We emboss our legal tender with "in God we trust."
Then, why is school prayer causing such a fuss.
Because of mixed messages, they learned it from us.

Younger generations did not invent this mess.
They inherited this legacy of hate and distrust.
Though not a pretty sight, they learned it from us.

Jeanette H. Jefferson

Who Am I

Who am I? Do you know?
Well let me tell of the seeds my ancestors sowed.
Not cotton seeds, or any other foreign weeds,
But seeds of life: Of you and me.
Seeds of thinkers, of mathematicians, and engineers:
Seeds that were hated because of fear.
Seeds of color: Black, yellow, red, and brown,
And upon their heads rested a crown.
Who am I? Do you know?
I am life from a seed sowed long ago.

Erica Stokes

The Gentle Man

He often walked the park alone, this gentle man we knew.
We'll miss him so...it's nice to know that truer friends were few.
Our acquaintance we'd renew each spring,
  all we knew him by was "Stan."
He'd wave to us as we'd rush by...he was a gentle man.
He'd meet the morning sunbeams at the entrance to the park,
then walk and talk till we were gone and everything was dark.
His tattered clothes and we'll-worn shoes were not of wealthy store;
But, they were warm, and though second-hand,
  he perhaps enjoyed them more.
His gate was rather awkward and he'd fumble with his cane,
but never once, that I recall, would the gentle man complain.
He'd touch the leaves and smell the breeze and call each shrub
  by name,
"Hi! Miss Rhodi and Solomon Seal! And how's Mrs. Golden Rain?"
We'd follow behind, and listen intent as he'd add each flower to
  his song.
"My goodness, Mrs. Tiger Lil, and why is your face so long?"
He'd tell us stories by the hour, and yet none would he repeat,
and then before he'd shoo us off, he'd give us each a sweet.
Then he'd prop himself against a tree and rest for awhile as
  we played.
Our carefree laughter'd fill the air... to him it was an accolade.
But, though he's gone, he's left for us the beauty of his mind...
And we'll ne'er forget that gentle man, you see... our "Stan"
  was blind.

Doneen Owens

Today

What a Day!!
What a beautiful, wonderful, glorious day!
I rose this morning to a brilliant sunshine.
Birds were singing as they scratched for worms.
I heard the wind blowing thru the trees-
I smelled the sweet fragrance of a flower bed.
Then I realized what a privilege I have.
God has given me another day—
To live! To laugh and also to cry!
To Touch and be touched!
To show love and be loved!
To be my brother's keeper!
Then I remembered, "I must live this moment!"
Life offers no guarantees for tomorrow!
I must live this day wisely!
Thank You God for this beautiful day called today!

Frances H. King

When You're Ten Years Old

Clear water running by the sycamore tree.
What a place for a boy and his dog to be.
Down in the woods, early in the spring.
Listening to the lark and the whippoorwill sing.

Water snake swimming across the creek.
Red squirrels playing hide and seek.
Across the valley and up on the hill,
Hazel nuts growing by the old Grist Mill.

From the top of the hill there's the town below.
The road winding through where the green grass grows.
Down the road and over by the school,
You can see the preacher coming, riding his mule.

There's an ice cream social down at the church.
Horse and buggy's in the shade of the big white birch.
Nights of silver and days of gold.
The whole worlds a wonder when you're ten years old.

I've gotten older, but I remember still,
Across the valley and up on the hill.
What a place for a boy and his dog to be.
And clear water running by the sycamore tree.

Jack F. Chastain

"Grandpa"

I have often wondered what people say and do.
What do they mean by death, this world I never knew.
The tears are there, the feelings too, this word
death I never really knew.

I feel it deep inside these tears are flowing free.
This one big word death, it's so hard for me to see.
I see that people understand, and they are there for me.

Everyone is hurting, I am too strong to fall.
Wait, please wait for me, and I will make the call.
On that day, there is no doubt. I will be there for all.

I know this hurts, I know that this is real.
I will always love you, a love I can't help but feel.

Emotions are flying, what am I to do....
I'll sit back and think of all the memories I have of you.

Heather Robinson

To Sarah

We rode along; she wanted to know
What I'd leave her when I would go.

I found myself in very deep thought
Of what I have that could be bought.

I've never been one to get much pleasure
In collecting items of earthly treasure.

For treasures take time from the daily fun.
I've enjoyed the race, not the medals I've won.

And a wise steward keeps his gifts in mind
To best serve God and all Mankind.

So maybe you can settle for our times of caring,
Loving, praying, taking, giving and sharing.

And some day in memory it will come to you clear
That what truly matters is—I love you, dear!

Avis Lull

My Dearest Child

My dearest child of only two,
What in these years will become of you?
As I gaze into your big wide eyes,
My role I've come to realize,
As parent, teacher and that of loving friend.

What first of life's lessons do I teach?
That one's measured by deeds, not just speech.
That heritage, though important, is not the end,
Nor is the color of one's skin,
But to see each person that you meet has worth.

To welcome authority and it's bounds.
To embrace love and friendship when it's found.
And of God, both a balance of love and fear.
To hold truth and honesty so dear.
And to know that success is a treasure found inside.

My dearest child of only two,
This is what I pledge to you.
To love you and to help you stand,
To be there with an open hand.
And to encourage you when it's time to walk alone.

Jane L. Kolibaba-Tucker

Life

I ask myself time and time again.
What is life? Is it to be lived?
For what, I wonder why it creates so much pain.
Another page turned and yet nothing is gained.
My life has just gone into the heaven with him.
Oh could it be that I have lived only to love.
Have I been trapped in a closet of love,
never facing the fate that death
only had to be let through the gate of his life.
Twenty years down the road it is my time to go,
so I just sit and wait for it to come.
I see angels are waiting above.
I see the man that I still love.
I open the gate of a fate that lies ahead,
So I close my eyes and take his hand.
Before I turn away, I look back at my life
to see what I have accomplished.
Then an angel asked me if I would do it again
"Yes it is my life," I reply. "It is to be lived."

Amanda Hendricks

Spread Out Your Wings

Spread out your wings and watch flight take form within you,
What joy consciousness brings as journey's end is what begins you,
To decipher in being, unto the plane of all-splendor,
With no fear of the fleeting, to connection surrender.
Bursts the seed, now revealing, the depths of Unity developed,
With the knowledge of feeling all worlds, in my heart, enveloped,
Through the sky and the earth, heaven in and amongst you,
Stars fall from their berth and it is known that I love you.

Edward L. Barocas

La Lune

Oh dark of night, with stars so bright
what secrets do you hold for us to delight?
The moon so full, or half, or none
beckons to us, we feel her tow.
Wind and water are at your command
ceaseless and constant, they ebb and they flow
and will likely continue long after we go.
We have wondered for centuries
what power you hold, over us and the earth,
for all is connected, both little and large
your secrets we are just now unfolding.

Erica Moore

Grandpa's Trunk

If Grandpa only knew
what the treasures in his trunk for me would do.

A God fearing simple farmer he was
with simple items in his trunk
that he probably thought was only junk.

Grandpa's picture in a tiny metal frame
so handsome, he was a pleasure to any dame.
A marriage certificate, small pocket watch, a can of Men's
Talc, a thin ivory pen, a tiny cheap metal knife;
they were all part of the past and of his life.
Many pictures of family members of the past,
little did they know their memories would last and last.
Many I don't even know, but I treasure them so.
The look/dress of that period in time to all I want to show...

Now I have Grandpa's trunk
with all his personal junk;
to my boys I will leave when I am gone
to rummage thru for the memories to go on and on.
The memories which mean so much to me....
I am sure to them it will also be.

Deidra Cox

"Mirror"

   Turn around and look at me and tell me
what you see.
   Loneliness or happiness it's all just part
of me.
   Find the truth and find the lies, but
find the reasons why
   And turn around and look at me even
if you cry.
   If your search is deep enough, and if
you've found you've hurt yourself.
   Even better if you cry, then you've found
the reasons why.
   So turn around and look at me and tell
me what you see...
   Someone who is better than the someone
who was me.

Christine J. Tarter

The Search

Sometime searching not finding
What you're seeking. Ever looking
never seeing. Hidden in the shadows
of the everlasting night. It lies, covered
by darkness like blanket of wool
To deep to uncover. Just beyond
your fingertips. To far to reach
Beyond the distance of the age of
itself. The search goes on.
It cannot be found.

Amy Bass

When A Heart Reaches Out To A Heart

There's exquisite joy for a girl and a boy
When a heart reaches out to a heart.
There's pleasure in life for a husband and wife
When a heart reaches out to a heart.
A parent and child can be reconciled
When a heart reaches out to a heart.
A feud can be ended - a friendship be mended
When a heart reaches out to a heart.

There's comfort from pain only love can attain
When a heart reaches out to a heart.
There's nothing compared to sympathy shared
When a heart reaches out to a heart,
Or the touch of a hand that says "I understand."
When a heart reaches out to a heart.
They're joy without end in making a friend
Whose heart reaches out to your heart,

But nothing transcends the peace that descends
When Christ reaches out to your heart.
Sing praises redundant for blessings abundant
When Christ comes into your heart.

Ella V. Working

Christmas

   Christmas is a festive time,
When all the Nation's bells do chime.
   When the Race's once separate as can be,
Join together in harmony.
   When friends and relatives forget bad past,
And hope this day will always last.
   When little children wait to see,
All their presents under the tree.
   When all CHRISTIANS go and pray,
To celebrate this special day.
   When everyone is full of song and mirth,
To pay homage to Jesus Christ his birth.

Bill Benoit

Good Friends Apart

   An old man sat down and cried
When he found his best friend had died.
Best friends they've been for fifty years.
In deep despair he spills his tears.
He dried the tears that wet his face.
His friend was in a better place.
Memories comforted his heart,
Since death can't keep good friends apart.

Many friends come, but few can stay
They always seem to fade away
Don't hide the pain. Tell someone new,
Maybe they'll feel the same way, too.
Everybody has had to cry
When their good friends tell them good-bye
But everyone who has a heart
Knows nothing keeps good friends apart.

Erin Nichelle Brown

The Finished Product

"Like clay in the hand of a potter, so are you in my hand."
When at first I heard this, the true image of my God was so grand.
  How special and unique he makes me feel,
to know that he shapes us as if a potter at his wheel.
  He shapes us and remakes us if we're tainted or marred.
He is our protector, our father and friend, he watches and
nurtures us so we ought not to be scarred.
  We are all such unique vessels made from the purest of pure.
Though things may get tough and things may turn bitter, with a
little faith and God's love, there is nothing we cannot endure.
  Unlike a vessel we can be tread on too much and become
weak and easily shattered.
Without faith and hope in our Lord, our lives become nothing
less than tattered.
  Isn't it wonderful that in God's eyes we are never useless.
  Even when broken, God's just not quite yet finished with us.
  So Lord take me in your hands and mold me and shape
me into your vessel, at whatever the price.
Because Lord my God, for me to live is Christ.

Delynda Badeaux

"That Special Feeling"

I love that special time of year,
When days are cold and Christmas is near.

Snowflakes are falling on window panes,
Trees are decorated with candy canes.

Little children make out their lists,
Moms are busy buying gifts.

But the greatest gift is Jesus' birth,
And the love he gives to all here on Earth.

I wish it could be Christmas everyday,
So that special feeling would never go away!

Brian Morris

Two Tiny Hands

Just two tiny hands! What a sly surprise
When first discovered by Baby's eyes!
Touching the knuckles, the creases, the ridges;
Entwining the fingers, making circles and bridges.
What joy! What wonder! "They're part of the ME!"
Laughing, baby claps hands together in playful glee!
He doesn't know now, but he will, one fine day...
That hands can cause happiness, evil, dismay...
Heartache, heartbreak, murder and fear
More horrible than the mind or soul can bear.
Teach baby to be kind to his hands with loving care,
And make them do good things. Warn him to beware
Of having them do bad things or deeds that destroy
Love, decency, honor, peace, truth or joy.
Help baby appreciate the best hands can do...
To foster hope, faith, charity and brave deeds, too;
That his hands make what he'll want them to make,
That his hands can break what he'll want them to break.
So, to you, I say... "Look at your hands in a small baby's way,
And really thank God for your two hands today!"

Dorothy F. Youngblood

A Disgruntled Friend

When will you think of me? When it's cold outside;
When gloom-bells ring; When children cry?
When you're sopping wet, about to drown,
Why only then do you remember that I'm 'round?
Why when the Best times, good-times call,
Do you not even think of asking me to the ball?
I'm there when you need me, and you know that;
But why in the hell am I starving while you get fat?

Chris Anderson

Grand Dreams

Such happy thoughts flow through my head
When I resting on my bed
After a rough long day.
I envision, in my mind,
The what, where, when, and time
I will go, see, and do
These wonderful dreams of mine.
I smile to myself.
My eyes twinkle like a shining star.
Sometime,
I will travel far.
Places, and friends await me on foreign shore.
The door,
To opportunity,
Will open wide
And I will step inside
To travel the world, far and wide.

Glenna Weber

Broken Hearts

How do you mend a broken heart?
When it's broken in so many different places,
By so many different people who don't seem to care.
Love goes many different ways.
But I wish it would only go one way.
To happiness.
Then you don't have to mend broken hearts.
But it goes anyway it wants.
And that's usually to a broken heart.

Debbie M. Bradley

A Woman I Know

She knows just what to say,
When I've had a rough day;
From her the things I hear,
Make it worth living, through the year.

She is more than a Mother to me,
She is some things, that only I can see;
If there was a quality, much deeper than love,
Even to this, she would rise above.

They say no one's perfect, but she comes pretty close,
In my book, she'll always be the most;
She is my friend, my companion, my pal,
If she wasn't my Mother, she'd probably be my gal.

We've done some things, I'll never forget,
Beautiful memories in my heart, is what she has set;
This woman I know, to me is very dear,
When someone mentions her name, Love is what I hear.

Bernie D. Mayse

The Legacy Of The Challenger

They stepped into the future with ideas of gold
All the challenges in the world would soon unfold
Organization of thought was readily met as
they uncovered the veil atop the complex
Touching boundaries that once were dreams
Implanting reality, working as a team
Among the stars their spirits glide free
A nightmare this shall never be ONLY A LEGACY, of,
Never giving up until the world responds, by
GUIDING ALL THE UNIVERSE
INTO A NEW HORIZON

James M. Brown III

High Off The Ground

Oh! My mind goes back to those childhood years,
When life was simple and hard.
When Mom and Dad went their separate ways,
And we "four" didn't understand.

There on Poplar Street we'd play, at our house so "High Off The Ground"
Cripple, our dog, trotting close beside,
Many playmates all around.

We'd play all day, till Daddy called us home,
With a whistle we "four" knew
He'd gather us home at the close of the day,
To the house "High Off The Ground".

That old house no longer stands, at 13 Poplar Street,
But my mind still recalls, those days long ago,
Of the joys and sadness shared, by my brothers, Sis and me,
At that old house "High Off The Ground".

Oh!
To be able to hear once again, that sound of him calling us home,
But Daddy heard that call, just a few days ago,
When our Heavenly Father called him home.

Now..., My heart rejoices to know, that Daddy knew that sound,
And he's now at home, in his Heavenly Home,
The Home, "High Off The Ground".

Juanita Johnson

Soul Sister, Little Sister, My Sister

Look up to me for support
When Mamma doesn't understand.
Look up to me, when hard times has a thin line.
I'll give you my hand.
We stick together when times are rough.
When one's needs are plenty, the other has enough.
We have the same features, same ideas, same needs.
When your soul is unhappy, my soul bleeds.
But now I am older, and you're repeating my past ages.
No one knows our life story—"The Soul Book"
With black pages.
And even when I am no longer around, look up to me.
I'll be with you.
Calling with the faintest sound of a whisper—
"Soul Sister, little sister, my sister"

Chevelle D. Smith

Untitled

Lush, red and wet the glass sweats
when our breath rises, a raga moves across my lips
lifting its song from beneath my tongue as colors take their shape
in the smell of your flesh, offerings, grape rinds and liquid

Wandering Native Warrior, through the
nine sultans, after 33 years of blood, earth, sky, and stone
your conscious mind raging the sound of the ocean's brisk waves
will vanish, practicing with simple hand and foot a Thai tradition

Tangled in each strand of your hair, is the scent of fresh dandelion
invading my spirit, with your bedroom eyes I much prefer
my head wreathed between the circle of your arms on a summer's eve

But the cold air creeps up against white spandex layered evenly
  between my breasts
and whispers into motion those tiny moon-shaped fingers sprawling
  across my florid in
moving back and forth, and then I drip, with the rhythm of the rain
  crying, lush

Alecia J. Cohen

Once We Were Young

Once we were young, in our days of youth
When our feet were small, and our minds were new.
We played all day in the glimmering sun
Not missing a chance to have lots of fun.

We hardly grew tired of swinging so high
I still believe I could touch the sky.
A rainbow would seem like a marvel back then
A birthday party was a kid's best friend.

Eat ice cream all day, have sweet dreams all night
A storybook was our favorite sight.
When friendship was simple, and laughter was too
What was a worry? We hadn't a clue.

Pretending became our favorite pastime
Grab hold of balloons and maybe you'll fly.
A big butterfly was a treasure to see
My favorite place was in a tall tree.

When good thing should come, they often must go
Time takes away youth, but how could we know?
Those years were numbered, and now are long gone
But sweet memories of childhood will always be strong.

Holly Babik

"He Is The Great Wizard, My Dear..."

You say the sun, my dear, comes out about midnight
when the powerful star retires full of dreams,
in the dayburns in fire shedding its light all over,
to conceal it later, going away so far.

But, comes back to move as a marvel king
in a world that await eager to reach its rays,
giving energy to mounts, oceans, clouds and winds
as a witch pointing out her most triumphal of deeds.

The rainbow showing up the colorful stripes,
the eclipse shines, full of mystical splendor,
the aurora borealis to travelers enchant,
and all in the Nature become inflame of life.

He is a magician, you told me many times,
that in the vast Universe, looks at the stars move around,
the light of the sky admiring, as seeing the heaven above,
while a silvery moon to wondering invites.

Is a sorcerer, I heard, the greater of all them
giving us breath and force, to continue to live,
and then, on time, we go in a twilight, beyond,
to embrace at least, the end, the final of the flight.

Esther Ortega-Lage

To See A Knight

There is no knight is shining armor, or is there!
When we look for love
We often look in the wrong places.
Do we forget to look in our hearts?
Only then do we know true love.
Learning the love we need for ourselves,
Having the faith to believe in oneself.
To see other people with open eyes,
To accept people for all the bad
Not to judge another.
When we achieve these goals
Then it may be true.
There may be a knight in shining armor.
We will see though the fog
We will overlooked the faults
We will forgive without question.
We will love ourselves first-then someone else.
When we see true love we will see the truth,
We ourselves become the knight in shining armor.

Jane Goecke

Love Forever

Thinking of you my fears fade away, sweet dreams of us together.
When will that day I long for come and let us last forever?
Is it a sin to love so deep, these feelings I have overflow,
When will others get out of our way and allow our love to grow?
Someday's, tho we are miles apart, you seem so very near,
Then times I hold you in my arms and there's a distance that I fear.
A wall surrounding our love, yet another between us too,
How can we survive this war, is our love so very true?
So many conflicts, so much to fight,
A battle going on, still I know this love's right.
So darkness around, please fade in the dawn,
Tear down this wall between us.
Let only light and love enter in,
Where hurt once was, let healing begin.
We have our whole life to share and to give,
May our love be our strength to allow us to live.
Let not others take this gift that we have,
It's ours, we made it together.
So as we take hold of this essence called love,
May it unite us together forever.
Alethia Reece

Jack Frost

Why in the coldest of the night
When winter has appeared
How does the frost come so silently
With no wind or warnings heard
What makes it so solid on the glass
And everything that sits through the night
Why do I have to scrape the frost
When in open space it sits
Why can't it leave the way it came
Without the sunshine bright
Why does this always come at dusk
And early dawn with ground and rooftops white
Is it because there is an artist, Jack Frost
That paints through the night
For nature's paint brush has four seasons
And for this is the reason why
To bring the colors of delight
That comes silently without seeing magically
Eternal as to be of yesterday, today and tomorrow
To fascinate the world around me
Geneva L. T. Spencer

The Beautiful Stream Of Life

Life is like a flowing stream,
When you are young you have a dream.
You flow across the rocks that are hard,
And as you travel, your heart becomes scarred.
But along the stream grow flowers of love;
The ones you care for, and the Lord up above.
Bettie J. Grace

Where Were You Last Night?

Where were you last night when our baby was up crying?
Where were you last night when our child's innocence was dying?
Where were you last night when a man had robbed our home?
Where were you last night? Now our daughters all alone.
Where have you been in the last eighteen years?
Because of you my face is full of tears.
Our daughter died of Vodka and Brandy.
Where were you when you were supposed to be a daddy?
Because of you our life is dead.
Where were you last night?
Brian Parker

God Only Knows

God only knows the pain that's caused
    When you hurt the one who loves you.
You tell him lies and break his heart
    Until he doesn't know what to do.

You took him away from the person who cared
    To use him and hurt him so.
The pain you caused by doing this
    Only you and God will know.

He loved you so much, he always has
    Since you can't remember when.
Hurting him, as you soon found out
    Was one of God's unwritten sins.

Now he is happy with someone who cares
    But you, are you happy right now?
Go out on the stage, go on! You've earned it
    Go out and take your bow.
Eve Christy

My Love

Life between us is so beautiful,
When you make love to me,
You give me a part of you that will always be mine.

I want you to know that
Your touch puts a chill inside me
And your smile always makes my day.

Your eyes are a deep brown and so beautiful,
Always watching me and protecting me.

I feel so warm and safe when your arms are around me.
Like the day you hugged me,
Took me from everything and made me so happy.

Your thoughtfulness, your kindness
And the way you care about me
Makes you so very special to me.

You are not just my lover, you are my best friend,
You are a very big part of my life
And I will forever carry you within my heart.
Janie L. Garcia

You Find The Answers

Whence came the concept of sin of God to disobey?
Whence came the devil or hell where sinners pay?
Where stands the tree of the knowledge of evil and good?
Where's the garden in Eden man left but never should?
Where's the tree of life to cause man to live forever?
Is there a heaven with endless and sorrow never?
When given a choice why's one right and another wrong?
Who made the choice its not best for man to live alone?
Where's the garden God has prepared for that special few?
How did forty days of rain cover the earth and mountains too?
Buddha mean enlightened and Messiah's anointing does too,
So why's Buddha in error and Christ's words held true?
Jehovah means "I am that I am" and what is, is what it be?
Where's the one with the wisdom through which it we seek?
"If we can pose the question then there's an answer too -
And the responsibility for finding it - is up to me and you."
Brett De'Angelo Lucas

My Mother

My mother who was it first my baby eyes did see
Who was it that took good care of me.
Who cheered me when I felt blue.
And who could I take all my troubles to.
In all this world there is no other.
To take the place of my dear Mother
Colleen MacIntosh

A Period Of Time

Whenever the sun shines in our heaven
Whenever the wind blows south, is when
two strangers whisper softly and laugh
like innocent children lost in a period of time.

Whenever the bright day turns to gray.
Whenever the white silver moon finds
her warmth in the still of the Summer
nite, is the time when I hear the
tone of your voice calling me back
again. If one star falls down, down
to the ground, I'll wish for these two
young souls to meet once again. I'll wish
for your protection and to give me all
your inspiration.

Whenever I think of my lovely rose,
I think of all the coming seasons.
Whenever I think of me and you, is
when sweet words sicken and the
colors of the rainbow begin to fade
out for some reason.

Evelyn Y Orlando K. Romero

The Attic

I climb up the stairs to the attic
Where a box of old treasures unfold,
There's a handful of soft scented letters.
Where a young couples dreams were once told
There's an old photograph, kind of faded
That I once used to treasure so dear
And my heart whispers words, oh so lonely
That only the angels can hear.
My hand twists around a gold locket
That I've had in this box, all these years
And memories of promises broken,
Fill my heart, and my eyes, full of tears,
And I wonder if you have forgotten,
Or do you hold these memories too
In your heart. Do you climb to the attic,
And remember the girl who loved you,
And goodbyes just don't come as easy
To me, at this moment in time,
For my heart just can't stand the aching
Of leaving these memories behind.

Dawn Marie Peterson

Ode To A Special Tree

There will be millions of leaves on this tree
Where buds poke out of their bed
They will spread out the millions of them
For a canopy over my head

There will birds to live in this tree
And make for their families a nest
Squirrels will climb to the very tip top
And stand on their heads as in jest

There will be room for a spider or two
but not of the poisonous line
They will spin webs all shiny and new
The leaves will hold them just fine

The branch below is straight and strong
And holds a rope for me
I could stay here and swing all day
In my home 'neath the big oak tree.

Gerry M. Hollingsworth

Where Did The Time Go

How many times have we heard the expression...
Where did the time go???
Time is like a runaway train
We hopelessly try to slow it down or stop it...
but time is ceaseless it has no favorites, it
waits for no one, it continues to travel forward.
Our first day in school-where did the time go?
Our graduation from school where did the time go?
Our first day of employment-where did the time go?
Our first day of marriage-where did the time go?
Our first grandchildren-where did the time go?
Our first day of retirement-where did the time go?
Unfortunately many of us are procrastinators,
We delay things that are important to us and that
we enjoy doing... we will undoubtedly use the expression
"We'll do it some other time" but unfortunately we
are running out of TIME.

George Azzinaro

Dollhouse

This dollhouse we live in
Where people have strings that guide them,
Where legs can fall off by a loose thread.
Where changing your mind mostly means turning around.
Where the stairs we try to climb can be moved without us knowing.
Where the back of the house is missing
   and the outside is big.
Where we cannot listen or see or feel.
Where we cannot move or touch or cry.

Dana Nicole Miller

The Artist

The sunlight penetrates the room
Where stands the lone easel;
A solitary artists weaves and intertwines
Colours with sweeping, feathery strokes
Of his skilled and gentle hands.

The brilliance and clarity of
A multitude of colours permeate
The huge canvas -

A golden tapestry of complicated weaving -
Yet accomplished by so gentle and caring a touch.

Lovingly the artist accomplishes
Each individual stroke and touch -
Like a father ministering to a child
A lesson on life.

The artist never ceases to apply
A multitude distinct and beautifully harmonizing colours -
To the tapestry that is,

Your life...

Bianca Vandemark

Buy Me A Mountain

Buy me a mountain for heaven to reach,
   where struggles are met by wonders that teach.

Flow through a river of crystal and blue,
   to nourish and cleanse this mountain anew.

Send in the animals wild and free,
   give them respect so they may be.

Fill it with children, for they all belong,
   their laughter,
     their dreams,
       their voices in song.

Fly in a rainbow to color the sky,
   remember the promises held inside.

Buy me a future, fill it with Love.
   Be with me always,
     smile from above.

Becky Hance

Passing Of A Giant

The Whirlwind thundered from out of the Book of Job.
"Where wast thou when I laid the foundations of the earth?
Declare, if thou hast understanding."
Einstein, with only pen and paper, took up the challenge.
On the canvas of Eternity he painted God's panorama.
His intellect, his brush, his faith his oils.
The boundless cosmos, black holes, galaxies, were his landscape.
Matter, energy, time, space were his paints.
He pricked the atom, boxed expansive space.
Added time to the three dimensions,
Explained relativity, curved space, how even time changes.
He unfroze matter, proving that $E = mc2$.
"He combined Nature's forces into one simple formula.
Yet, he despaired the brute force he helped to create."
He believed in pacifism, freedom to think, hated war,
Giving his life to unlocking God's secrets.
At his death he gave his brain to science, his ashes back to earth.
Shyly he took his place along Newton, Pythagoras, Galileo.
His lasting monument — human progress.

Howard Loeb Frohman

Where Were We?

Where were we, when God made the world?
Where were we, when the heavens unfurled?
Where were we, when man made his bow?
All this, I wonder, where when and how?

Now, I have an idea, let me explain.
I certainly hope no one thinks I'm insane!
For I think as I work and again in the night,
'Til my mind is full of my souls insight.

There is one thing that steeps in my thoughts,
Like a silken thread, it weaves in through the slots,
Of this silent machine that is known as a brain.
From this thought I find hope, from it I gain.

Where were we, when God made the world?
We were with Him, our souls were entwirled.
Where were we, When the heavens were born?
We were in Him, unscathed, nor forlorn.

Where were we, when man was presented,
To this Earth, which God, His very Being, invented?
We were part of Him, His likeness made real!
And the book of the Bible is His covenant, His seal.

Catherine D. Heston

Untitled

Once, you said to me
Where were you when I was young?
I thought at the time
Wish I had said that first!

For you make me as a child again...
Full of he simpleness of love.
I am your best of friends
And you, indeed, are mine.

Your smile can release my weariness
Erase the years of trials...
You don't demand my strengths or talents
But allow me to give as I am able.

So I say to you this special day....
I love you as if we were young again
And I know inside my heart and mind
You love me just the same.

Anne V. Anderson

The Lost Soul

The lost soul wonders throughout her life,
Whether or not she'll be someone's wife.
The lost soul travels from place to place,
Looking for life in any old face.

She travels an endless road, slowly drifting away,
She travels any highway, just hoping to stay.
She wants so much to be in one place,
Yet the lost soul travels, far away into space.

She cannot stop and find her true love,
For the lost soul hears a calling above.
The lost soul believes, each time she will stay,
Yet time will show, it is all in dismay.

The lost soul feels time will soon show the way,
Yet time passes by, as if it's running away.
She wanders through life, and plays a cruel part,
Each time in love, she injures her heart.

The lost soul requires a gift of life,
To make her complete, and pull her from strife.
So come take my hand, and never let go,
Your lost soul will end, and a pure soul will show.

Dan Fielding

Ageless

Don't let age control your life
Whether you're somebody's husband or somebody's wife.
It may take some doing, but that's part of the fun
You learned how to walk before you could run.

Take time to enjoy a small part of each day
Don't worry about what others may say!
If your children ask questions, or laugh at your style
Just tell them they'll be there, in a very short while.

If you've noticed your body has started to sag
And your schedule's becoming a bit of a drag,
A trip to the health club can make you feel great
Then a night on the town with your spouse as your "date."

So don't get discouraged, whatever you do
There are others out there who are counting on you.
You won't know how great ageless living can be,
Until you make up your mind to try it and see!

Faye Baschwit

Left Brain, Right Brain

Left brain, right brain,
Which one shall I use?
Left brain, right brain,
Which one shall I use?

I always thought I was special,
Because I use the left brain, right brain,
They were given to me by GOD.
Which one shall I use?

I'm emotional, creative, sensitive,
I do not care about logic, rational, YES.
I do care about language.
I'll use left brain, right brain.

I will be sure to always,
Choose left brain, right brain,
Because I pray and GOD answers.
He will instruct left brain, right brain.

So, what's the big, big fuss!
I see no reason for it in the PRESS.
Check it out, in GOD'S word.
He's the one who CHOSE left brain, right brain.

Connie James

The Pond Remembers

Sheets of rain billowed out across the earth,
Which was mumbling, on the verge of
Awakening. Clouds of dreams,
Harvested from somnolent minds,
Shuffled lost in the upper air
Until finally they left in despair.

The wind, soothing as a mother's hand,
Smoothed the wrinkles,
Urging the rowdy surf to shore.
Water rose, overtook the
Unarmed crop beneath, lugging
A starched stillness.
So the sea was created;
So the rustling wheat was hushed.

Now fish, ever the optimists,
Carouse day and night
In their new-found jungle,
Revelling in a world begotten
By the prowess of the storm.

Emily Gail Kushner

Memories

It was time for our nature walks
Which we took each spring;
Mother led the way with Freddie, Bobby, Jeanette, and Dickie in tow.

We climbed the hills, journeyed past Baker's Pond,
down to Second Sands
To Heartbreak Hill where the ocean met the sky.

Mother knew where to look for each of the special wildflowers —
Dogtooth violets, lilies of the valley and the snow drops were at
  Baker's Pond...
False Solomon's seal, jacks-in-the pulpit were at Second Sands,
The hepaticas, ladies slippers and trailing arbutus were on the
  upward trail to Heartbreak Hill,
We ended our journey past fields of black-eyed Susans, sumac,
Queen Anne's lace, on down Labor-in-Vain Road...
The delicate blues, lavenders, reds, whites, yellows —

Nature's panorama is still in my memory...

Jeanette Cronin Wood

Sunset Reverie

Multi-colored hues announce your leaving,
While heavier tones of fire enshroud you,
As you melt into the earth in regal splendor
Leaving cotton candy clouds behind you,
I watch the horizon where a moment ago,
Suspended, you hung low;
But now your once radiant streaks of light
Are slowly dying into night.
Countless eyes have watched you thus in ages gone by,
From a primitive past to the already dying present,
While you serenely look on from your fiery firmament,
As life and feelings perish for all time,
Will you still watch with an indifferent eye?

Hilda Rodriguez

Man Or Beast?

If we are all God's creation
While the ridiculous stance
We all must make in our fashions
Just to put on a pair of pants?

We must empty our bodies of waste
In the most disgusting ways
And do things we all hate to face
To keep up with the tricks that life plays.

Sex, though wonderful, is a posture
That makes us look silly and strange
And get into shapes that would foster
Mirthful thoughts of the mentally deranged.

Why then this yearning and reaching
For something intrinsically free?
There's something sad and beseeching
In us all to a certain degree.

Was it God or something more profound
That lifted us from Beast to Man.
Though dust we are and tied to the ground
We're surely part of a grander plan.

Barbara Ingle

Thank You For Calling...

I lay still on the edge of sleep,
   while you speed towards your day

The overseas
SNAP, CRACKLE, POP
reach me seconds before your
   "'elo!"

Car phone in the Porsche conversations
   your motor through my midnight's
four time zones and thirty kilometers per hour ahead of me

   "How are we?"
Your day, the girls, petty frustrations,
   astonishing confessions
white mini skirted women top off golf holidays in Spain

Ask you no questions, you'll tell me no lies -

We build trust and friendship
in increments of twelve, sixteen and twenty-two billable minutes
You receive the bill
   I hope not to pay dearly...

Elsie Echevarria

A Man Called Chico

Long sleeping jungles were rudely disturbed.
Whining chainsaws produced tree stumps uncurbed.
Progress with bulldozers moved on vast tracts.
The burning ignored "save the planet" facts.

High-staked schemes. That's what it was all about.
Power and big business pushed justice out.
The campesino was doomed to foul play,
while politicians looked the other way.

Chico. Yes, Chico Mendez was his name,
He stood strong when killings and brute force came.
Ecologists applauded what he said.
Latifundistas wanted him stone dead.

To stop destruction, he kept defying,
well aware he was flirting with dying.
Resisting the road project roused fury.
They shot him Christmas time in Xapuri.

The hallelujahs echoed for a birth,
while tears were shed by a hole in the earth.

Francisco Alves Mendez Filho,
hero of the rain forest called Chico.

Essi Morsink

"Rhoda"

Oh where, oh where can I find the magic; the magic of the wind whispering in my ear

If I had anything on the face of the earth, it would be the leaves falling, falling to the ground

If I had a pair of feathery, shimmery golden wings, I would fly to the sky with the beautiful geese eating from my hand

If I could smell the sweetest rose, my heart would pound with all its got, because I've seen it all

James D. Hess Jr.

Like Black And White

Across the lines
Who dares to go?
Over the seas, across the streets, living under
bridges, or even silk sheets
Where are the lines that separate?
Choose sides, or run for your life
Tonight the riots begin again
Racist tempers fly
We have killed the dream of America
Love is hate
War is peace
Someone will have to answer when the blind
remove their blindness, and the speechless
speak the truth.
Will it never end?
Seek the truth
It is clear like black and white.

Cecelia R. Yerkes

Your Heart

Home's where you hang your heart,
Who never you'll have to part.
It's one of the best,
Within your chest.
It's red and shaped like a tart.

You hang your heart like you hang your hat,
High on a wall or gently on a mat.
They're delicate organs,
Be very gentle,
You can't find one of these at an auto rental.

Ashley Hackney

You Are Remembered

For you - with the silvery hair
   who rocks alone in that ole rocking chair
For you - the one just lying there
   with failing health and skin so fair
For you - who waits just once more
   for certain footsteps thru the door
For you - one lost within a dream
   who's chosen the lesser pain it seems
You are remembered this special day
   and loved much more than I can say
For you are the gracious one
   who kissed the hurt and bid it gone
For you - the work was hard and long
   in your teachings of right and wrong
But you never once gave in
   to life's trials and hurt within
For you have passed by so much
   to fill our needs and give us much
You're remembered each and every day
   and loved so much in every way

Freda B. Moore

Celebration Of Freedom

All glory and honor to the God of my life,
Who sent me Love's suffering and strife -
To sow thru stinging tears,
Many painful-pain-filled-rain-filled- years.

Jesus, have mercy on me - a sinner!

My all forgiving, all merciful Lord, release me — unbind me —
Set me free in your Love - this humble servant is in need.

Come, plant your grace-filled, tender - Holy seed,
Of the word made flesh.
Espouse our hearts in one to mesh.
I am your servant in distress,

Jesus, have mercy on me - a sinner!

Alleluia-glory to God-salvation comes-it rains no more.

What I sowed - what I planted in tears,
I reaped - I harvested in joy.

My deliverer - my Savior nears - He erases my tears.
See how His arms open wide,
To embrace me - to heals me - to lift me.

My King of Glory - Hosannah in the highest.
My Jesus is here - My Jesus - My Lord and my God!

Helen Pieper

For Fathers Day

To a man so strong and wise
who taught me life with open eyes
He helped me learn the right from wrong
Taught strength when weak, and pride when strong.
On sure broad shoulders he does hold,
My growing pains as life unfolds
A fine, unbending solid oak.
Taught me to see through clouds of smoke

The gift to see five steps in front
To see deceit and those corrupt
to know what's knocking at my door
He taught me this and so much more

Could such a man truly exist
Who through the worst would still persist?
Be sure he does... I say it loud!
He is my father and I am proud!

Angela M. Brilis

Untitled

There once was a young cowgirl from Palo
who was desperate for a guy don't you know.
She looked here and there
but couldn't find one anywhere.

Then she said with a sigh,
"I think I'll give roller-skating a try."
And while on roller-skate wheels
in love she fell head over heels.

This guy that she found
he digs in the ground.
He said "Shaun is my name and Tiling is my claim to fame."

She said, "I love you."
and soon they both said "I do."
Now to the two there was added one to make three.
And they're what you would call a family.

But now you can't call her the young cowgirl no more
'cause she got old, she's past 24.

Happy 25th Birthday!
  Gary Swartzendruber

The Hope Of The Future

I'm one of the thousand of black women,
whose homeland was in the deep South,
couldn't always speak my peace
I had to sometimes hush my mouth.

Couldn't understand why I couldn't eat
in the same place where the white folks ate,
No, but I had to go to the back door space
where they would angrily serve my plate.

Then sometimes they would call me nigger
which caused my heart much pain,
until I said to myself one day, why?
Since nigger was not my name.

But Dr. King gave me hope for a brighter future,
he said, "things won't always be the same,
one day Blacks and Whites would all come together
if everyone make this their aim.

So since our living is down here on earth,
we must fight to stop the hate,
and let love flow out from heart to heart,
before it becomes too late.

  Fannie B. Knight

War And Peace

I held my friend's hand tenderly and heard her anguished cry
Why did they take my son from me? He was much too young to die!

A young wife stood upon the dock, two children clinging to her arm
Her sailor mate was called to war (God keep him from all harm!)

A little family huddled close, bereft and all alone
I heard the children's plaintive cries "When is Daddy coming home?"

A serpent rose from darkest hell, its talons dripped with blood and gore
And when it blew its fiery breath, I knew its name was WAR!

Its only message was DESTROY! It pitted nation against nation
And as it crawled across the earth, it brought death and devastation!

I breathed a prayer heavenward, to my Creator up on high
And in the silence of the night I heard the angels cry!

"Wars are not made in heaven, and they will only cease
When we claim each man our brother, can we ever hope for peace!"

Yes! Each man is our brother and each man has much worth
When we hold these truths inviolate, we can then have PEACE ON EARTH!

  Doris Dickson Coville

Untitled

Dear Lord please help me life's so unfair,
Why did You give me such a heavy cross to bare?

My child He answered turn and look around,
So I did and couldn't believe what I found.

My cross was not heavy in fact rather small,
There were times I found I had no cross at all.

Why are others so happy their life so easy,
Why Lord why couldn't that of been me?

I've heard You only give us what we can take.
Please Lord I pray give me a break.

Times I feel so alone like no one cares,
Please give me a sign that You are there.

Take away these awful feeling sand salty tears,
Strengthen my weakened spirit consul all my fears.

Show me a reason to go on,
Give me courage make my heart again strong.

Lighten this burden please help me cope,
Give me a sign renew my hope.

Thank You for listening to what I've had to say,
Please help me through another day.

  Andrea Wisniewski

Questions

Mother, why did you leave me
Why did you turn and walk away

Father did you see me
Did you even know my face

Lord, can you hear, tell me
I'm not crying into space.

Lover, do you need me, can you
feel me when I shake?

Pictures on the wall, shadows in my mind
We all go back from time to time.
Who was wrong and who was right,
We all must judge between the dark and the light.

  David B. Lee

Grief

I am grieving...
  why do I have to face the hurt, anger, pain, and darkness?
I am hurting...
  my heart is wounded, my dreams are shattered.
I am angry...
  I do not want to accept the loss.
I am in pain...
  I feel so overwhelmed as the pain etches it's scars on my heart.
I am in darkness...
  it feels as though the light of my soul has been extinguished.
I am grieving...
  I must face this journey, it is my own path to take;
  I must feel the hurt, and the pain;
  I must accept the anger, and step into the darkness...
    if I am to rebuild my dreams and to find the light beyond the
    if I am to find the light beyond the darkness.
I must release the hurt pain, anger, and darkness;
  if I am to survive.
I must grieve; if I am to live again.

  Carrie M. Cooke

Leaving You

Letting go is harder than I thought
why does it bring so much pain
memories of all the love and joy you brought
oh, how I wish I could see you again

Do you remember me, am I still in your heart
as days and years pass
visions and dreams you are forever a part
my love for you will forever last

Do you hear me talk to you
when days are harsh and rough
do you know you talk to me too
life isn't always so tough

I miss you, more that I realized
close to your heart always keep my love
for it will never die

Jennifer Anne Revie

Time

From where does time come and where does it go?
Why does it seem to sometimes go fast and sometimes slow?
Time has no beginning and it has no end
And we can't turn time back to what might have been

Time is here and time is now, can we catch up with time somehow?
We rush around and we hurry so and we wonder
Just where did time go! We don't have the time we say
To do the things that others may
We are tired when work is done and now we want to have some fun

By the clock our lives we live and to others
We have no time to give, what a price we sometimes pay
For the time that we let slip away
Once time is lost it can't be found, time goes on and on
And it makes not a sound

We can't save time, it must be used
And time should never be abused
We can't buy time, though some people say
That time is money and for their time we must pay
We should not waste time and time there will always be
But what we do with time will be up to you and me

Iva Nell Lineaweaver

Why

Why is a job harder to find than crack?
Why is the white man always ready to attack?
Why are the prisons filled with people that look like me?
Why is Africa still not free?
Why do Republicans leave us no hope?
Why are Democrats such a joke?
Why do I work to still be poor?
Why do the rich want for more?
Why do clothes make the man?
Why don't the hopeless take a stand?
Why do women need liberation?
Why do sinners yield to temptation?
Why is education not a priority?
Why are people of color called a minority?
Why do we say, "abortion must stop," when the people that are here we won't adopt?
Why do we say, "crime doesn't pay?"
Do all criminals feel that way?
Why does the Klan still exist,
   when the Panther party was quickly dissed?
Why is health food so unhealthy?
Why are tobacco companies so wealthy?
Why do only children question...Why?

Isaac R. Miller

Reflections Of My Roots

At times I sit and ponder the complexities of life;
why men do the things they do and fight the things they fight.

Why they hurt their fellow man and tear his soul apart,
I sit and think about these things and where I got my start.

The roads been long with pain and strife and still so far to go;
but when I think about my roots - oh, I love them so.

I think about my Father and all His wondrous deeds;
His wisdom, strength and power, and how He fills my needs.

He made the earth, the moon and stars and holds them all in place;
He crafted and He shaped this world — and more in outer space.

In love He made and fashioned man and breathed the breath of life;
for we all came from that creation - Adam and His wife.

He sent his son down to the earth to give his life for me.
It is this act of His great love, that really sets me free.

In God's great image I was made; I hold my head up tall,
for He's the God of this vast world and the Father of us all.

Donna Jean Bell

Autumns Hooray

There 'tis a garish witch with a tall pointed hat
Wide brimmed and sashed with the blackest of black
Perched on a broom gliding through the moonlit night
Whilst lurking the darkest shadows of Halloween night

Tis heard the scariest of scariest green eyed black cat
Yowling it's lament to murky shadows of the night
Tis there clinging precariously to the tip of the moon
Whilst gliding over the swamp to the cry of the loon

Shrieking goblins and gremlins smirking far and near
Howling and yowling until seems scariest to hear
Tis time of tales of long ago and gone yester-years
Till all scared and shivering whilst my cheeks seep a tear

Shimmering ghosts weaving veiled in black and grey white
All booing and hoeing on this scariest Halloween night
Tis an ode to Indian Summers and hazy days of fall
Whilst the Jack-O-Lanterns beckon come one come all

The revelers festively costumed each guaranteed to please
All to tantalize and tempt for trick or treat please doth tease
From fashionable prince to pauper and the lovely fair maiden
Traipsing midst the shadows with Halloween bags brim laden

Dorothy Collette

In Search Of Forever

Have you ever mused the haunting waves of deaths impending tide;
Will it be an ethereal journey in eclipsing the final divide;
Or shall it be a turbulent quest on the reins of an angry steed;
Will we embrace our ultimate horizon or beckon to recede.

I have heard there shines a radiant essence that abrogates time and age;
An ambiance of serenity that will quell life's scornful rage;
I ponder the chance to grasp the core of this supernalic force;
And be ensconced in the clairvoyant peace if its eternalistic course.

But indeed I harbor a thwarting fear of deaths forever path;
As I've seen its aura embark with blyss and inflict with scouring wrath;
And when our mortal hour glass has tapped its final sand;
Will we only have our faith and soul to help us understand.

When I call to mind my proclivity of reaping fruitless seeds;
I succumb to the question of consequence of my many thoughtless deeds;
But in my heart there lives a God who is absolute and true;
And so in His hands I will rest my search of forever's life anew.

Frank J. Ryan Jr.

Children...Our Future

The smile of a young child
will put a smile in your heart.
Her face so pristine and mild,
his little eyes glimmering bright,
their every move a beautiful sight.

If only every child could be cheerful
this sour world would turn sweet
as that of a honeysuckle freshly culled.
They shall spread good cheer throughout,
and the world shall be better no doubt.

Children are the reason for our cheer,
for it was the little Christ-child
that became in our hearts most dear.
as a babe He brought Mary much beatitude,
and as He grew brought peace to the multitude.

Our future rests upon their countenance.
Treat our children with utmost love,
so our world will have a better chance,
to go on surviving with peace and harmony
throughout and beyond everlasting eternity.

Joseph Adam May

Feelings

A cheek dried by harsh winds,
Will tremble at a passing breeze.
A love song kept without an end,
A heart left with no time to mend,
Has no voice to scream out, "please."

Roads leading to nowhere,
along a crooked sea.
A wound becomes a jagged tear,
A life with no one to care,
Bound by a lock with a broken key.

A scared voice afraid to plead,
Lost in a storm of truths and lies.
No one to fulfill a dire need,
Harsh eyes will read his solemn creed,
With tears marking his good-byes.

Irving Lazerus Guzman

Mirror Of My Soul

I stand all alone, waiting for you.
Will you exist, my fate, my dream.
I know you are their, I've seen you before.
The star at my moon, the light in my eye.
A long summers night, we danced in the sky.
I loved you then, I'll love you again.

You touched my heart, then my soul.
The purest of emotion, inside like a beam.
To look beyond, the love that is deep.
The softness of breath, the smile that I'll keep.
I'll meet your emotion, your mind and your heart.
I'll be their for ever, if only in thought.
I loved you then, I'll love you again.

Mirrors of my soul, reflections to define.
Softly at first, to this shadow of mine.
The cycle of life, will be left undone.
My passion, my love, my friend, within one.
No one will know, no one will see,
The soul of my heart, that is you and me.
I loved you then, I'll love you again.

Barbara J. Hoffman

Let It Out

Shackled deep within, straining, but hearing no taunts.
Will you let light touch its clandestine face?
Maybe you will...maybe you won't

It eats away at you until nothing is left.
All the while it howls harshly in pain.
Do your ears throb yet? Are you deaf?

Finishing its meal its gives a hearty shout.
The time has come to meet its demands.
Stop lying to yourself, let within become without.

There is nothing left. It has reached all ceilings.
It has become the very core of you.
But once again you beat it down...your true feelings.

Why do you fear breaking your torturous pact?
Are you afraid of what others may think?
Do you wither under cynicism? Is that a fact?

Other have come to end it in a step that was bold.
They may have been ostracized. They may have been praised.
But that doesn't matter 'cause the truth was told.

Daniel Smith

Untitled

I wish I had a girlfriend,
wish she was fly.
I wish she'd make me happy,
and would never make me cry.
It's really the inside and not the outside that counts,
This you cannot, cannot deny.
If she is faithful and honest
For this, you will die.
You must look very hard,
To find someone so kind.
For this kind of person
Is so very hard to find
The worst kinds of girls
Are the ones that always lie.
If you know you have one,
No matter what, you say good-bye.
If your girlfriend had others before you,
You're lucky and you're clever,
There is a good chance
You could stay with her forever.

David An

An Ordinary Man

Neatly figures, tall in stature,
    with a calm that only comes after the storm.
He has spent six decades preparing for this moment in time.
Without position he is secure.
Without family, he feels loved.
His reputation is without imperfection.
The more pressure matter is able to withstand,
    the more valuable it becomes; he is valuable.
Yesterday's victories are only memories.
Wisdom blossoms - no longer
    lying beneath the surface of knowledge.
He has taken responsibility for his actions.
The new course has been mapped and this ordinary man will change the
destiny of other lives around him, as well as his own.
Evening is coming on, with the shadows of the live oaks on the door
    front and the sunlight sinking into the horizon.
A stroll would be nice. Without warning, this new course begins.
She formed the image of a well cared for garden - colorful, vibrant,
    alive with pert eyes she faced the ordinary man.
She too has been preparing for this moment in time.
Gracious Lord, can it be this is the miracle you have promised me?
An ordinary man.

Jan Sheppard

Yankee Man Billy

He stepped to the plate with his bat in his hand,
with a look of determination, this Yankee Man.

The man in the black and the lady in red,
cried "go for it Billy, we're your #1 fan(s)."

"Give the ball a big hit, give it the one, two, three punch,
Send it to the outfield and serve it for lunch."

So Yankee Man Billy with a smile on his face,
sent that ball a-sailing, right out into space.

He rounded the bases as though he'd been fired,
and strolled into home - why he wasn't even tired.

His teammates all clapped for old Yankee Man Billy,
and he bowed and he smiled, and acted real silly.

Then he waved to the crowd, to the lady in red,
to the man in the black and he turned and he said.

I am Yankee Man Billy - I can bat, I can run,
I can giggle and wiggle and have lots of fun.

I can win the ball game, I can put on a show,
cause today is my birthday, and I'm seven you know!

Alyce M. Bockbrader

Surrogate For Mankind

All of the faces that have ever turned from me
   With contempt,
   Or disgust,
   Or neglect,
Or just because they looked another direction,
All these faces turn again to me
And beam upon me
When You look my way with tenderness.

All of the hands that ever raised against me
   First clenched,
   Or grasping,
   Or threatening,
Or just because they sought to stay me there,
All these hands clasp mine once more.
In fellowship
When your hands seek mine with tenderness.

Thus walls give away and chasms close,
And I, estranged, am bound again to humanity.

Graciela Keller

Twilight

The stars in the heavens the almighty made,
With those left over, in your eyes had them laid.
The sparkle in them is like an angel divine,
I could tell it was love when your eyes met mine.
That spark, that glow, seemed to pull me in,
What you did, it must be a sin.
My mind went blank, I lost control,
You touched my heart, and reached for my soul.
Your spell overcame me, right then I was yours,
This love for you, from my heart it pours.
You will never know how I felt that day,
I would like to explain, but words cannot say.
The life you gave to my weary soul,
To be with you is my ultimate goal.
For a glimpse of you, I'd do all that I can,
Because of your beauty, I'm not the same man.
Please my love, hear my desperate cries,
For I have fallen in love with your beautiful eyes.

Joe Thomas

The Entertainment Media And Morality

Today the entertainment media is obsessed
  with depicting actions violent, vulgar or lewd
And objections based on moral grounds do
  not in anyway make one a prude
The productions are devised only to
  assuage the viewer, to provide monetary gain
Is it possible to watch these incredible
  antics and remain reasonably sane
In their cruelness or crudeness they
  make one traumatized and insecure
Certainly they represent an onslaught
  against young minds becoming mature

Charles M. Stern

O Victim

O victim, my victim,
where does your courage mutter at the moon?
What field listens to disgrace imagined?
Your stenciled rags protect you no more, only the skin
wants tomorrow's pale coffee.

O victim, my shadow, which solution can you reject fastest?
What wet paint hasn't been sat on?
This carpet ignores your bruises, most of the time,
if only you'd believe it.

Cleotha Arnold

To Our Mother

To have had someone so unselfish, so caring
  with faith in us so strong
To have had someone whose guiding wisdom helped
  light the right path to life as we came along
To have had someone that when life would
  hand us those times of despair
Her warm words of sympathy and smiling words
  of encouragement would always be there.

We were blessed to have had someone like that
  to share with each other
And we each have that special room in our
  heart that's reserved for our mother.
And, although her worldly race has been run
  as indeed, we know that it must
Let there be ashes to ashes and dust to dust.

For it is our comforting resolve as this
  parting we face,
That we believe with Him,
  she has taken her place.

Jimmy G. Couch

Guilt

It washed over me
with is dark and chilling eyes
Making me cringe
It choked my heart with its every pass
going deeper and deeper into my soul
making my emotions fly
with my every breath
creeping over me with a deadly grip of fear
Making my emotions soar to the surface
So they could once again blind me of my happiness

Arren Lilly

Treasured Memories

At first, finding time to write seemed so hard to do.
With the hustle and bustle of each new day,
Learning new ways for our life, now was true.

So many times the thoughts of friends and family dear
Would flood the gates of our mind.
To treasure now as days go on... the people we left behind.

And then, as time went on
And good times became "treasured memories",
The pen still could not be lifted
For in our heart sadness drifted.

But now I sit again with pen in hand.
Our mind etched with precious memories
From past reunions in a distant land.

The thoughts of good times, of joys and years,
In our heart we will always hide.
Always to be treasured, always to be held inside.

With thanks, we send this thought
That in our heart is caught
The life we spent with you
Never to be forgot!
Elizabeth Petrilli

Salty Sea

We used to sit upon the beach
with the pristine sand beneath our feet.
We shared our souls, we shared our dreams
of sailing the saline sea.

The moonlight's splendor illuminated our path
as we breathed in the warm moist air.
It seasoned the flavor of our dream
of sailing the saline sea.

Lo, we did not notice the tide creeping in,
as the sand moistened beneath our feet,
For we were as one lost in a dream
of sailing the saline sea.

Then came the crashing waves,
it parched our throats, we could not speak,
Hopelessly struggling in the crests
of a turbulent saline sea.

I reached for you, to no avail
and then I lost sight of you.
Forever drifting away, away,
forever adrift on the saline sea.
Jeff Turner

Mom

The most wonderful thing that's happened to me,
Without you what would I be?
You watch over me everyday,
And look over me in your own special way.

Kind and strong in courage and heart,
Always pitching in and doing your part.
You walk high and proud holding up your head,
Never quit or give up, that's what you said.

So perfect and honest in all you do,
Today I say, "Hey mom, I love you."
You dedicate your life to making me great,
Knowing that God will determine my fate.

So a dollar ninety-five for this card I pay,
To wish you happy 36 on your special day.
Andrew Charles Pusateri

Moonshine Night

as the rain falls, looking through the trees
wondering where to go into the soft, gentle breeze

beside the lake, beneath the moon
cool wind breeze, through my hair

moonshine night in a mountain village
hiding in the woods in the deep trees
under the moon, beneath the stars
the young folk dance, led to the lake by a King & Queen

away from a crowded place
from the big city lights
wandering away from it all
far, far away out of sight

the light of the night will shine on us
make our own paths as we run in the fields
run from frustration just to get away
let our reflections slip away

moonshine night in a mountain village
hiding in the woods in the deep trees
under the moon, beneath the stars
the young folk dance, led to the lake by a King & Queen
Jason Kenneth Serafin

"A Sign Of The Times"

Once a simple childrens' rhyme spoke volumes to the masses;
with three words changed to fit the times, it now separates and classes.
Anticipation mounts as we all push to plant the seed
that grows to redefine the words race, color and creed.
Justice now seems lost in a land where lines were once revered,
as the graying of what's right and wrong is fast becoming clear.
Sticks and stones may break your bones,
  but words will "never hurt you,"
was appropriate when absolutes still were all adhered to.
The world fragments though pundits claim a new order's on the way.
Looks more as though we're backing up, dragging feet of clay.
We all would like things to improve for generations hence,
but until mankind looks vertical, horizontal makes no sense.
The rhyme has changed as well we have, yet in the worst of ways,
for as we ponder where to go, we grasp at yesterday.
Seems that life's a bit more bleak, though the forecast calls for sunny,
For while sticks and stones still break your bones,
  words will "cost you money"
Carl Lentry

The Black Woman

One cannot deny the strength as well as the beauty of the black woman.
She is one of joy, admiration as well as humility.

Time has come that we must stop what ever we are doing, and look
upon the face of our Black Woman who has risen to the height of
  great hope, faith, and patience.

As we look at her, she represents a symbol of the total aspiration of
all women with her creative charisma, exhilarating all of her ability
  of nurturing love and understanding.

The Black Woman attacks her challenges with vigorous zeal and move
up into position where as once women would never dare to go.

The Black Woman is setting goals for her self in this great society and
going forward to achieve and excel in every area of her life.

The Black Woman is great in stature.
Bold in her undertaking and sincere in her endeavor.

The Black Woman, establishing herself in history.
Joyce Smith Thomas

Geisha In Nostalgia

A whiff of mellow perfume drifts into dim languid store front,
Women's voluptuous soprano tones tear through silent air.
Three thickly painted faces wearing puffy wet-ravenblack wigs,
Dressed in gaudy kimonos emerge through the rattling glass door.

Across the street from geisha house annexing sushi-tempura bar,
My mother retails tobacco, incense stick, charcoal et cetera.
Receiving amiably coquettish customers with a rustic smile,
She hands over "Golden Bat" cigarettes under the naked bulbs.

Nineteen thirty depressed Japan, nightly exposure toward geisha,
My childhood is embraced with song, dance, samisen and drum.
While my father goes to remote mountain school like hermitage,
Writing classic Chinese poetry, teaching whatever kids need.

Lonely potted wisteria standing on store's dirt floor corner,
Where a stocky artillery sergeant trysts with a favorite geisha.
Visual beauty on her doll figure as if foreign kind of creature,
Strong cosmetic fragrance wake my thought into mystic world.

Some cold day in my six grade's year end, neighborhood gossip,
"Gardener's twelve year old daughter was sold for geisha" spreads.
Becoming geisha by sacrificing herself paying her parents' debts,
Leaves sadness beyond red-light romance through my nostalgia.

Esaku Kondo

An Ocean Sunset

The sunrises, the sunsets, you walk along the beach
wondering and thinking this is the most peaceful place on Earth.
Smell the fresh ocean breeze, feeling happy.
I walk down the beach, in the sand and watch the
beautiful golden colors of red, orange, yellow and brown
as they come crashing at my feet. Seagulls overhead
squeaking at you, to go away. The only problem is you
don't want to leave this dream of a place.
You find footprints, and think of the poem.
Being in someone's step, I love the thought of being
with the ones I care about. The sun over the ocean
is very peaceful. I walk down the beach forgetting
all my worries. Dreams appear, I never knew existed.
Watching the sunsets, I relax in his arms.

Amanda Farrell

Untitled

Staring into your eyes,
Wondering how many lies
Have passed through there so many times before.

Trying to understand your sadness,
The stress in your eyes leans toward the madness
That you feel deep within.

Sad must be your heart,
Of all the love that had to part
For reasons making no sense.

How confused you must be,
Thinking you don't have the key
To make love stay in your life.

Realize though, that your own love need be,
The only love you need see,
For that is the only true love there is.

John Trumbull

"Louisiana Bayou"

There is a place not far from here, where the sounds of the
  world seem to disappear.
Deep in the south, where the bayou flows, oh what a sight to behold.
It's slow moving current seems to slow down the pace of my
  hurried life.
Shadows of moss draped oaks are reflected back to me.
It's beauty wanting to be shared, by you and me.
Time is loss here, it seems to stand still.
Only the setting sun, a reminder that day's end is near.
The soft red glow of the setting sun's rays, dance in and out
of the draped old trees, hurriedly trying to find, an object
  to cast their light upon.

Jane Portie Landry

Love

To find the kind of love I need,
would mean the end to all my leads.

For now, the love that most men want,
is from the girls who want to flaunt.

I need a man who wants constant love;
not for me to spread my wings
and fly away like a dove.

When the morning light comes shining through,
I want to remain here in love with you.

I need your love to see me through,
all the things in life left to do.

I need your love to help me see,
the kind of woman I need to be.

True love gives you the greatest high,
and stays with you until the day you die.

Love is there through thick and thin,
and helps you start life over again.

Brenda Metz

If Everything Were These, Would They Be Beautiful

If everything were these,
Would they be beautiful;

Silent as a water-worn stone
With covered edges where the moss has grown-

Wordless
As the flight of birds

Motionless in time
As the sun climbs

And leaving, as the moon silhouettes
Branch by branch the entangled trees,

Leaving, as the winter leaves behind
Memory by memory the mind-

Beauty should make up time-
Motionless and leave

For all the past time of grief
An empty pasture and a maple leaf

For love
The breathing wind and waves of the sea-

But beauty should not mean
But simply be.

Faith Duvall

Surprise Visit

If Jesus knocked on your door, and asked to stay awhile,
Would you gladly let Him in, or would you stall Him for awhile?
Could you look Him in the eyes, or would you stare at the floor?
If Jesus came to your house, would He be welcome behind the door?

Would you set an extra place for Him, so He could sup with you
Or, would you make excuses and say you had too much to do.
Maybe we should take some time and let Him know we care,
By reaching out to others and with them our bounty share.

So we'll feed the hungry, tend the sick, and visit the elders too,
When we extend a helping hand, we'll be serving our Savior too.
For if we do these things in Jesus name, we pray,
We'll be showing others by our actions, His love for them each day.
Audrey M. Nelson

Untitled

In the chillness of a barren winter
wrapped in ice
live the seeds of a blazing Autumn harvest.

Scattered acorns
making a bed along the forest floor
carry the blueprint
of a stately oak.

Night and day play seesaw
lighting and darkening the hemispheres.

At the moment of birth
death too has its beginnings.

What appears to be so
must always be challenged
to reveal the possibilities within.

A discerning eye will discover
that all in Nature is inseparable.
Elise Asch

Berlin Wall: Rest In Pieces

This word,
   written on the land in blood
    with brick and bristling wire,
   spoken by submachine gun,
    read by searchlight and the dishonored sun
was proven false each day
as the life it would have defined
risked death
not to live its lie.
David A. Westover, III

Legacy

If you feel I've taken from you
years of youth,
look then, upon the young ones,
and remember every hour
I spent bringing forth to you
the children you hold close;
The memories of their innocence
and all that follows
as your eyes burn bright,
in spite of life the world serves up to you.
And love me, if for nothing else, then,
but the future left to those
who bear your name...
And all the love you give them
to be carried forth
and touch, yet one more
tender generation.
Jacquelyn Ann Mayer

My Life Mission

The sky is gray and darkness surrounds me,
Yet I still look on, keeping my eyes set on glory.
The temptations, the trials, they all seem to fade
Because I look on, knowing they will pass away.
The things of this world won't come close to compare
With the love and the friendship that I'll share up there.
I can hear him calling and telling me to go
Into all the world, so that others will know
There's a man whose love is truly divine,
And I'm excited to tell you that His love is mine.
My mission is tough but it's all worthwhile
To know I'm in peace and to know I'm His child.
So I'll go into this world and I'll fight the good fight
Because Jesus is Lord, and Jesus is right.
Deena L. Lay

Now-Beauty Forever

Touched by the light,
Yet overpowered by darkness.
Intelligent and beautiful when well,
So sad and sick when lost.

The light that once touched her,
is now on her forever.

She can now sing and dance in the warmth of the light,
And be well and happy for now and eternity.
Amy McCain

Goodbye For Now

The time has come for us to say goodbye
Yet we both know it is not forever

Each day spent without you, my heart will cry
counting the days 'til we're back together

We have grown closer with each passing day
and have formed a bond, which no one can break

Cherish our love as you go on your way
and believe in the dreams our love will make

In time, once again, our hearts will unite
and be together for eternity

Above the rest our love will shine so bright
to let us know that it was meant to be

But until then, I will miss you, it's true
goodbye for now, remember, I love you
Jennifer L. Conner

The Tear

Can you laugh? Can you cry? Just look me in the eye.
You are frightened, yet you stand, not even moving a hand.

You say you're alone and have nothing to stand for.
Your face solemn and unchanged since you walked in the door.

Other tears fill the room, and many muffled sobs.
Her soul taken away, all who knew her feel robbed.

But you among all, full of pain and remorse,
Your voice used to shine but now sounds quite hoarse.

The bed where she slept in the place beside you,
Shall be empty every night and during the morning dew.

While the last mourner leaves your eyes are still cast upon her.
The room is almost empty, not anymore a stir.

You feel much alone sitting in this place, for hours you haven't moved.
Until, at last, a tear slides slowly down your face.
Amy Tomes

A Dream

A beautiful morning in Mid-July
You ask to see me, "Try, please try!"
I rush to see your handsome smile
Only to find a tear in your eye

"You love me dearly, or so you say
I need to know how you feel today
I have received your card of thoughtless words
My heart I give you, but not for play

I answer you, "My Love, My Love, this is mistake
My love is real, far from fake"
I dry your tear, you push me away
You hurt me more than I can take

I saw you now angry and mean
A side of you I had never seen
My thoughts unclear, my heart in pain
Your manner is cold and unforeseen

You speak as though you can easily redeem
My love expressed through moments that gleam
You never called, I shed my tears
I wake to find it is only a dream

Elizabeth G. Candelaria

Sleep

Like a lioness upon her prey,
You crouch in the shadows surrounding my bed.
I evade you, defying your power,
Your inevitability this tiresome day.
I refuse to acknowledge you like some religions
Or so much tax on my solitary penny.
Still, you wait to pounce.
Slayer I am,
I plan to knife your dragons,
Keeping their nostril fires
From singeing closed these weighted eyelids.
Then, like an undertow, you pull me,
And I, aware of no other haven,
Slowly drown in your sea.

Franchon R. Jernigan

Sing Somethin' Simple

Objective truth would make you seem an airhead;
you felt, in fact, the world owed you a living.
Accountants know that black won't mix with red,
but you mixed up the taking with the giving.
Did you con some street-folk to hoist up food?
Some ex-slaves, who passed by three times a day?
Unless you learned far out (saints can be crude),
you'd need them too to hump your wastes away.
And with so soap or water, there's no saying
how you, St. Simeon Stylites, stayed so clean.
If all our compensating lies in praying,
won't our Great Mutual Fund bleed white, from green?
The highest, Priest and Levites, keep the till?
The lowest, robbed and beaten, pay the bill?

Eugene Kraft

The Unaccomplishable Accomplish

Looking down the mountain,
You realize how incredibly tough it was
To accomplish your goal,
Wanting to let the world know how proud you are,
How it took time and patience.
Bruised and bleeding and not feeling a bit of pain,
Until your next journey,
When you realize that you are at the top,
And the only way to go now, is down.

Anna L. Mazloff

Spring

I'm in a tizzy, joyfully dizzy,
With wonders of spring!
Just go crazy when I see a daisy
Or hear a bird sing.
Spring glorious and victorious
Over the winter grey.
I'm a whirl with the new made world
And all the lovely days.
See the buds appear, green grass everywhere
Through the field and wood.
Glad songs of praise to God we raise,
For he said, "It is good".

Josephine H. Kale

Loving You

I never felt loved until there was you;
You gave me a whole new point of view;
Despite our plight through thick and thin;
I never felt loved till there was you;

Is it any wonder, you allowed me to be me;
Someone you were very proud to see;
Although you are gone, and my eyes can no longer see,
my hands cannot touch;
You have left behind such sweet memories that have made me
strong and tough;

Even in death our spirits are still together;
I will feel your presence forever and ever;
As I lift my eyes a rainbow I do see;
Because you have given me the most precious gift,
You have taught me to love me!

Debra M. Giarrusso

Personalized? Good-Bye

I begged you to never let me go.
You have touched my heart
And left me to my own.

You promised that we would never be apart.

As I cry myself to sleep,
I ask myself why you had to go?
As I dream of you and your kiss,
I remind myself that I did love you so.

You were the one that I feel in love with again.

As you let me go,
I say, "Good-bye."

You were my heaven,
And life without you,
Shall become my hell.

Gregory S. Morrison

One Minute After

Your worries are none, your thoughts are free.
Your cry is silenced, your pain relieved. Never to
ask why or how this came to be, but only to enjoy the
sound of silent peace. To understand this is to know,
not to fear. Something so near as tomorrow. It's a
beautiful light, so no need for sorrow. Close your
eyes and imagine a beautiful diamond shaped light, and
in it all your favorite things. A silent night,
a quiet storm, a summer breeze. The sleepless dream.

Glenda Johnson

Untitled

I am the beautiful
You leer at me wanting recognition
I am what you crave
I cannot sate your hunger
It is only a face of flesh
A mere vessel of bones and blood
Nothing thrives behind my fraudulent eyes
Nothing survives in my unlit blackened soul
Not spirit not life not love
I am the beautiful
I am the torturer
I fulfill my destiny
I am sought yet never captured
I am the beautiful nothing more
I create your desires and pervert your sanity
I am the beautiful
Endlessly pursued and revered
I am the craved, you who cannot get enough
I am your disease
I am your death
Jason Patrick Adam

To My Addiction

You were my companion when I felt all alone
You made me feel as powerful as a queen upon her throne;
You told me I had the courage in life's war to gallantly fight
You were my shining armor and I was your radiant knight;
You told me that when together I'd be a shining star
You tricked me into believing that without you I'd not get far;
We buried my disappointments with each passing of the years
Together we mastered hiding all my sadness and fears;
You covered all my feelings so I wouldn't face the pain
Disillusioned by your glamour, I gladly played your game;
Subtly you reeled me in without a word of warning
I went to sleep with you and woke to you each morning;
You were always on my mind as more of you I needed
Give you up was said to me but I let it go unheeded;
Suddenly you came to collect what's due from me it seems
To take my soul and spirit and all my unfinished dreams;
But I'm told there's a Power stronger than both of us
That by His Hands I'll be rescued if only I will trust;
With this Higher Power I'll live One Day At A Time
As He tenderly guides me up each mountain I must climb.
Judy Hallenbeck

Be Aware!

Marriage is like a plant.
You may water it, feed it and watch it grow.
Some even talk to their plant,
hoping it would hear.
So if there comes no respond,
don't be desponded.
Sometimes, brown leaves may appear
and you fear it would die.
Then suddenly green shoots sprout
and you know it is going to be alright.
But if brown leaves continue to
appear and gradually it dies;
let it be an experience,
but remember that you have tried to keep it alive.
And if you decide to get another one,
let it be different,
unless you know you can master it's care.
Andra Persaud

My Friend

You've been special to me since so long ago.
You mean more to me than you will ever know.

You've stood by me so many times and understood my tears.
Every time that I was sad you were there to calm my fears.

The friendship that we have, I hope we always share.
Because you are the way you are, for you I'll always care.

You're everything a friend could be, you've never let me down.
The friend I want, the friend I need, in you that's what I've found.

Through all the days, and all the nights, you will always know.
During all the sadness and the tears our happiness will grow.

Because you are so special, because you are my friend.
This poem I shall give you this poem I shall send.

And every time you read it, you will know I care.
And every time you need me, you know I'll be right there.
Ashley Malchow

Box Of Yesterdays

So......
you open your box of yesterdays
to put another day in and
so doing you fondle once again
the tattered yellowing treasures
of sun filled times that your heart
ticks it clock on, with your mind
keeping time with palpitating misery and angst,
THIS is what you are....the continuum
all that it contains, the contents of the box and
you go to it, from time to time, to look into it's mirror
seeking your solace...YES!
(and your identity)
a box full of memory......verifying
what you were....what you ARE and
what you are .....becoming.
Frank G. Hoffman

Untitled

She stares at fronds and intimates
'You see how they bend with the wind?'
I chide her silently for distracting my attentions
She knows my indulgences involve a certain excess

Her long fingers dance for emphasis
Her elbow drops, the merest of invitations
The ridiculous curves of a delicate appendage
It is enough to unnerve me, this superfluous motion

The pale underside of her wrist glances upward
She remarks in earnest, 'the wind must define itself'
A wrinkle smooths itself, somber once again
A half-smile plays upon it as the wrist bends slightly

Her small foot sickles inward, scratching its brethren
I don't want to follow the square toes, curling downward
The frown of a single strand of muscle as it eludes
The smallest toe and shies tentatively toward a jutting ankle
I want the pliant stems to dip languorously downward
and brush the water's surface, without conflict

She claps her warm palms together, and trembles
'The wind has died', she states unnecessarily
Jason Lorin

Forever In My Dreams

You came to me in my dreams.
You stood before me looking into my eyes,
　reading my every thought, revealing my
　innermost secrets.
Without a word, you felt my every feeling,
　my joys, my sorrows.
You wept as you felt my pain.
You laughed as you felt my childlike sense
　of humor.
You smiled when you saw my love of life and
　my zest for adventure.
I feel for you as I feel for no other.
I trust you to keep my secrets.
I count on you to be there when I need you,
　when I want you.
I will never feel for anyone the way I feel
　for you.
My sweetheart, my lover, my best friend.
If I can't have you as I imagine you, then
　you must stay forever in my dreams.

Brenda A. Kulp

Called Forth In Love

You, that are without form and void, when shall I call?
You, that have not yet spoken a sound -
nor yet in your mother's womb been found,
when shall I call...your name?

From the earth your first father
I formed and found
I loved the man I fashioned and formed.
His need I looked upon, kindly... a mate I formed.
This pair, Adam and Eve, their names I called.

You, yet unborn in your mother's womb
in the darkness there, but in my eyes your visage does loom...
Are fashioned and formed by my plan.
By my love each "baby" woman and man,
like you, called into being... I've called by name.

When I've called, each one, I've
called them to commune with me - when in their spirit,
their Heavenly Father they see; when in their mind and heart
they are aware, without form and void they still would be...
had I not called them forth, by name -
to live and love, and speak with me.

Harriet Trehus Kvingedal

Wind Song

I remember You-the desert-where I was born.
You, the barren land, the moon's ballroom,
In you I anchored my roots like a mesquite tree.
I reveled in your tears -
The rain that cleansed my branches -
The fingers you weathered and taught
To be anchors for others.

I remember how the great wind wrapped me in its sheet
And taught me to fly over the earth -
Spreading seeds, moving the earth, creating dunes.
And the coyote who heard my howl.
Together we spoke the enchanted language.

Your tall grasses taught my legs to dance
And the parched land taught me to hold fast
To whatever songs washed through my soul

And now that I have left you -
Moved away from the Yucca and the tumbleweed,
Your enchantment lives in me and
I have become the desert a wind song
for those around me who need your quiet strength.

Deborah Benanti

For My Mom

Through the good times and the bad,
　You were there to hold my hand.
You dried my tears and calmed my fears
　Without fail throughout the years.
You healed the bruises, cuts and scrapes.
　Hugged the broken hearts away.
You always listened to what I'd say,
　Why did God take you away?
Your love unconditional, your shoulders so strong,
　Now your arms are forever gone.
No more hugs or kisses or words,
　I hope I'm strong enough to face this world.
One day you were here but now you are gone,
　Does God know you took my heart along?
Now in my world there's a great big hole.
　I just tell friends, "That's where Mom goes".
I hope I can give each day on my life,
　As much as you did as a mother and wife.
And as long as I live, no matter how long,
　The love here for you will always live on.
　I love you Mom!

Christine Anne Heitzman

Abiding Love

There are many things to ponder, as you go through life in this world.
You will stop and sometimes wonder
whether to spin or whether to twirl, OH YES!

You will ask yourself these questions, and many, many more besides,
you will ask yourself these questions
and seek the answers from where they abide, FOR EXAMPLE!

You will want to know where love is, and how it came to be.
You will want to know where doves live,
and who put all the fish in the sea.

You may even want the answer, to whether the sky is gray or blue.
There is one who has all the answers, but first, know that he loves you

You may want to know what happens to the night,
when day comes out to play, your might want to know
the answers to that question, in a sort of peculiar way, or

You may want to know who keeps the sky from really falling
to the ground, and do we know for certain, for sure,
that the world turns round and round?

George Whitfield

Trial Of The Century

Deep in the heart of man - black and white
Young and old, rich and poor - a summer night.
The children slept while candles burned
Their father's blamed - police concerned.

If only the barking dog could talk
He led the way down the bloody walk!
The families gather - mixed and matched
Crying, listening - two lives were snatched!

Witness after witness came to testify
Then the white cop racist tells a lie...
The prosecution builds it's case
The defense does their's based on race!

The jury really finds life hard
Cooped up too long from their own backyard!
The judge provides the best he can
Enough are left according to plan.

The anger and rage erupt at last
Key witness compared to Hitler's past!
The prosecution sum it up, then rebut
Reasonable doubt? The jury's out-now what?

Jennie Cummins

Meeting Again

Oh what a wonderful surprise to look up and see
your face and that happy smile, a face from so long ago.

When we sat and talked of the many years that had
passed, it really didn't seem that long ago.

And when I mentioned that special night, we both
felt a little embarrassed, as if it had happened yesterday.

It's hard to put into words the strange feelings
I have tonight, it's a warm, all over happiness, a smile in my heart.

Over the years I have thought of you and wondered
where you were. I am so glad we met again.

Dora Jean Muller Sewell

Mother

If your eyes could talk, they would say, "I love you."
Your feet could walk, they would come to me.
In time of trouble you are always there,
Hoping and wondering for a pleasant affair.
A mother's love is never in despair, though she's not
invisible when she's not there.
I see her smile in a pleasant array
She loves me more day by day.
She keeps me dry, if she thinks I'll cry.
She feeds me, if she thinks I'll whine,
Although, she never gets to dine.
I think this is your mother and mine,
For, we both think she's mother divine.

Ann Romans

Beneath My Wings

With all resources at the beck of
your five-year-old heart and mind,
you strive against the sadness that's undone
our little family, all in vain.

It's gone, that family you yourself created.
It was as evanescent as your babyhood.
Your mommy and daddy never really had a chance
to stay together, though you made it last a while.

A pause. I'm crying as I write this.
Your sorrow is my own, as is your joy.
"I want to be a baby," sometimes you say,
mumbling over thumb in mouth to do it.

The magic will not work, of course,
I tell you just as gently as I can.
But I respect and love your heroism
in this most lost of causes.

Your courage helps me summon up a bit of mine.
My eagle's wings are not for soaring anymore.
They're for enfolding my beloved chick
within the drafty remnants of our nest.

Jack Cargill

Mutual Admiration

You're more of a man than most men I know,
You're more of a person because you can grow.
A better friend I'll never find,
A quicker wit within your mind.
Compassion flows like a steady stream,
Your sensitivity is every girl's dream.
In will-power you hold second to none,
And what's more, you're a lot of fun.
I think by now you must have guessed,
Of anyone I know, I love you the best.
I'm sure that it just had to be fate,
That you met me and I'm just as great!

Carol Griffin

My Uncle Pig

That napkin tied under your chin,
Your fork in hand, that silly grin.

You glance at the table to pick your first victim,
As the rest arrive you say "Please pass the chicken."

Like a hungry lion, you pounce on your prey,
With only a clink of your fork on the now empty plate.

We see your eyes glisten as you search for another,
And you point to the corn sitting next to my mother.

You gobble it down hardly a flinch,
Your stomach must be a bottomless pit!

We smell for an instant the huge piece of pie
That you polish right off in the blink of an eye.

Hey! Don't leave so fast! We know your wishes!
You don't want to wash all those dishes!

Anne Holland

The Cowboy II

Yes, I remember the day that
your freckled face shone in the sun;
the day you told me to love you or to leave you,
as I hid my wrinkled brow under my hat
and my boots left your porch.
So many years have passed since that day.
You never left town like I did.
But the smell of old leather
and the feel of a bronco called to me.
And now I am here for you,
with only a few of my own years left.
I had hoped my return would bring happiness for us.
But as I give these roses to you,
the ones that were meant for you so long ago,
I wish I had done it sooner.
As the lid closed, I vaguely recalled
your sweet laughter and cornsilk hair.
"I love you, sweet Sue", I whispered.
I never meant to say a good-bye before my hello.

Brenda Brunhoeber

"Your Love"

Your love is the water I need to quench my thirst.
Your love is the food I need to conquer my hunger.
Your love is the light that guides me through the dark of night.
Your love provide me shade in the heat of day.
Your love is my spring rain bringing blooming thoughts
    and deeds for you.
Your love fills my heart with joy through and through.
Your love is fresh as a mornings dew.
Your love is honest, clean and true.
To risk your love only a fool will do.
Till the last breath I take,
I will never love another besides you.

Anthony Cochran

My Thoughts of You

To me you're special in every way.
You're the reason I'm alive today.
You taught me the difference between wrong and right.
You even tucked me in at night.
You've tolerated me for the last 14 years.
Through the sound of laughter or the cry of tears.
You're all of these things together combined,
So I hope you'll keep these words in mind:
YOU'RE SPECIAL, YOU'RE SPECIAL, YOU'RE SPECIAL I SAY!
YOU'RE SPECIAL TO ME EACH AND EVERY DAY!!

Danielle Dawkins

Goodbye To Love

I awoke this morning, within our bed, 'twas just another day.
Your memory lingers, deep in my heart, as I watch you walk away.
I sat within our precious home, a place where we shared love.
I sat and cried, and begged for peace, from angels up above.

I sat and traveled, down memory lane, I saw you everywhere.
This big old house twas once our home, your love's no longer there.
I reminisced of sweet laughter shared, our moments in the sun.
I thought back to the day we met, and the life that we'd begun.

I found a photo of you today, you looked content with life.
You had no cares, nor worries too, as you conquered every strife.
I held your photo, within my hand, so close to my heart.
For today my world will there-fore end, as you make a brand new start.

They played our song on the radio, twas a song you played for me.
It took me back, to a place in time, when our love was carefree.
I sat within our precious home, I shed so many tears.
I'm haunted by your memory, and of our precious years.

I'll pack away, each memory. Each one I've shared with you.
Each box shall hold sweet memories, and all that we went through.
I walked into our precious home, and a tear came to my eye.
Today we said farewell to love, today we said goodbye.

Anthony A. Mixon

Demise

Living through life amounting to nothing
Your only say so is that of a mime.
Pricking your finger on a thorn of your own.
The fluid will poison you in a short time.
Shielding yourself from your own reflection.
Trying not to cope with yourself each day.
There's millions of changes you need to make.
Stealing from yourself is your only way.
Submitting yourself into the hands of others.
You wish you'd feel your heart cease to beat.
You cry yourself to sleep every night.
Clawing at your eyes can only help you see.
When you call 911, is the phone always busy?
Are you the one tying up the other line?
Your wrists are weakened by the razor's edge,
But you tell yourself that everything's fine.

Jerry Jones

To Autumn On Graduation day

You've scaled many hurdles to get where you are
Your parents have kept you from going too far
You've learned how to crawl and to walk and to run
And most of the time I'm sure it's been fun

And now comes adulthood— a big step in your life
Where you must learn how to handle the strife
Of being a woman— a making a life
And someday I'm sure you'll be someday' wife

But—before you succeed in the future you must
Again learn how to walk and to run and to trust
You must learn to make work seem like lots of fun
Then success will be yours and you'll know that you won

Being a Christian we know that you'll choose
The right road to travel and then you won't lose
For you'll trust in God and ask day by day
For his protection and help all the way

So good luck dear autumn as you graduate
We're glad we could be here with you on this date
Good luck in your future— your battle for knowledge
We'll return someday soon as you graduate from college

Dorothy Stanberry Lind

If Only For One Night

If only I could Luv you for just one night
Your slightest needs I would attend and
Your body I would delight
Every inch of your essence I would ever so
Softly kiss
Taking it slow I'm in no rush making sure your
Time with me as well spent
Caressing your back like a warm summers breeze
Nibbling your ear and whispering those sweet
Nothings that you so Luv to hear
Once I am inside of your world you won't want
Me to leave until I find that certain spot that
You know you Luv having touched so much
Eternally in my arms is where I long to keep you
Making Luv to your body and to your soul as if it
Were my life long profession
Becoming one with you like no other man sharing
A special bond that will last and last
All these things I would a thousand times
Do if only I had one night with you.

Efrem D. Jackson

Pure Seat Of Justice

True seat of justice always abides
In God's pure Heaven above the skies
Of Earth: Mankind has lost perspective sight
Thank God soon there will be righteous light

God has placed a conscience in each life
However, many have seared it by earthly strife
In Holy Writ we find God's most Holy Word
Only those in Spiritual tune his word have heard

A righteous King is promised soon to appear
When Mankind will learn to become more sincere
No longer in that time will evil ever survive
For the foe will be bound as the King arrives

With a life ahead for the people in that era
Blessed with judgment pure and holy without error
Keep this Hope to stir us on to faithfulness
To serve our Lord in abundance of gratefulness

God knows each heart and answers our prayer
Come Lord Jesus with your Father's loving care
Bless all who live now in a prayerful state
Our King will arrive to open Paradise gate

Susan Essler

Medusa's Folly

Inflammable,
Immortal like goddesses with their ethereal Venusian beauty
Their faces move in color
in repertoire
looming above cities, on roads for all to aspire to.
If they feel or speak no mortal soul knows
they are ensconced in the perfection
of manufactured visages
And are thus unknowable
Sad sisters on earth in unison agree
that this is what their men want
Fear the illusion
and perish the truth.
Fable alludes to the fury of Aphrodite's jealousy
upon hearing Medusa's proclamation of personal beauty
superior to hers
Thusly insulted, Aphrodite fated the gorgon to
serpentine form,
whose very looks turned one to stone.
Beauty Vanishes.

Marlene Smith

Youth

Every child is shoved into this cruel, uncaring, greed infested world. The fortunate ones are brought up with love and proper guidance. In this period, your personality is molded and defined by many experiences (unforeseen downfalls and incredibly joyous occasions). All awhile being taught to be a contributing member of society - like some immense herd of sheep being driven ever onward - unaware of the eventual slaughter that awaits us all.

From the beginning you're always being told to "Grow Up" and "Act like an Adult." When you finally do start growing up, you feel your youth slipping away. You begin wishing you could shine off all responsibility and become a child again.

Once realizing you can not do so, you set your sites on a time in the distance when you're allowed to retire and finally can play again. When you do reach this moment, you realize that you've turned into your grandparents-leaving you with only your memories.

Live all your youthful years to the fullest.
Follow your heart and not the masses-or
You may wind up wasting the best years of
Your life.

Chad Eshelman

Progress?

The trains don't stop here anymore.
Why, I remember a time, when the place would be filled with people,
and the conductor would yell "All Aboard!" and all the scuffle and
the hurry and the tears and the hello's and the good-byes.
Now they are gone.
The planes don't stop here anymore.
Why, I remember a time, every Saturday, I would go down and watch the
planes come in and go out, and the people, all the people, and all the
scuffle and the hurry and the tears and the hello's and the good-byes.
Now they are gone.
The fish don't swim here anymore.
Why, I remember a time, when I would come down to get away from all
the hustle and bustle and find a stick and safety pin and string and
a worm, and I would catch hundreds of fish. Some were pretty long
(well, not that long!), and some would get away.
Now they are gone.
I don't go there anymore.
Why, I remember a time, when I used to go to all these places and
watch the people, and all the feelings. Now they are gone, and I
realize, that it's time for me to go.

Herb Fleischer

To Daddy, I Grieve, I Believe, I Rejoice!

Sometimes we didn't think you gave us much,
You gave us LIFE, a whole lot of us.
You gave us FAITH, to help us during the trials and the temptations
  of the world.
May we end our lives as strong in that Faith as you were blessed to do.
You gave us LOVE, maybe it was disciplined too often by the fact,
That you were the Dad, and we, though adults, were the Children.
Whoever said, Love don't hurt, has never loved.
You gave us HOPE, the belief that we could do anything or be anyone we
  wanted to be.
Your strength and endurance through your long suffering illness,
  gave us further Hope.
When I think of God as our Father, it's easy to identify because of you.
And lastly Daddy,
You gave us DEATH, it's rough but I know your spirit is always with us,
As we REJOICE in your new life,
As we BELIEVE,
And so do we GRIEVE.
I LOVE YOU!

Hildy McLaughlin

Love's Renaissance

Love, sweet lonely love,
implants a wild seed of passion in my heart and
spread its fame through out the entire anatomy of the body.
Gently, fountains and streams of life
began to boil in my mortal flesh while
sweet living poetry filled my emotional spirit
as I burn a passionate kiss on her lonely lips.
My love for you is deeper than the well of time.
Why does love drink my soul to all that is beautiful?
O my GOD, my heart is open by love's holy expression.
Love's Immortal Renaissance conquered all internal anxiety and
resurrects dead feeling in the symbolic house of my abstract soul.
I love you,
for we are a single entity in an emerald universe.
We are the golden reflection of each other's loving soul.
Here, take these spiritual orchids picked from GOD's own garden and
let us sit among the clouds while our hearts dwell in the
Great Immaculate Chamber of Delirious Ecstasy.
Love, sweet, lonely love,
I thank you.

Martin E. Gibson

Treasures

She's alone and scared in a white-walled room,
in a bed that seems so full of doom,
she finally hears a pitiful cry, as with pain, blood and tears,
her first child is born. She gazes at him with wonderment and
awe. Holding him to her breast, she feels a special glow, that
through the hell there was a light and that light was her newborn
son. Within a period of ten years, always careful not to let
anyone hear the silent screams in her throat, or to see the
fear in her eyes, she is so grateful as she accepts the blessed
relief, as she hears all is well and a new treasure is placed
in her arms. God is good she says as she thanks Him again for
His gift. Five times in all this happens to this sad, lonely
woman-child, who has only God and her children to bring joy
to her life. Three boys, all the same but different somehow;
the girls are creatures of such beauty, to her they are really
all the same; like dew drops glistening and bringing forth colors
from the sun, her children are her pride and joy, her
only true treasures from above.

Patricia A. Chapman

The Perfect Rose

I took a short walk, one spring day,
In a beautiful forest, where the wood nymphs play.
When there in a clearing before my eyes,
Stood the perfect rose, the perfect prize.
For sometime, I stood entranced,
I pictured a ball and asked her to dance.
When the wood returned into my view,
There was but one thing I wanted to do.
To capture this wonder and make her mine,
To dare not to share God's beauty defined.
I crept ever closer to catch sight,
Of delicate petals that hold the dew at night.
Her fragrance so sweet did fill me with delight,
Her blooms seemed ever redder in the bright sunlight.
Though as the distance vanished, my vision cleared,
And dreams of perfection all but disappeared.
Thorns, withered blooms, imperfections not known,
Now replaced seeds of wonder at first glance sown.
How could I not see that which was before my eyes,
To rather dream of a perfect rose, a perfect prize.

Richard S. Page

The Great North Wind

Against the eastern vista where obsidian sky ruled over day, the
village lanes eclipsed in the foreboding lull of winter's early deep.
Now fell the first alabaster flake against the verdurous woodland lay,
as the powerful North Wind rose from his glacial den of chilling sleep.

As he blew along the coarse cobblestones and twisting sapphire crested
streams, his touch drew icy portraits along the ever piling snows of
chilling mist. Pinching the children's cheeks he hounded them with
rakish howls and frosted screams, then prancing over rooftops he
danced on eaves and pointed his frosted fist.

Pine trees arched in stately bow as the mistral flew high in winter's
gambol, and faraway in iceland's frozen tundra Jack Frost shrieked in
wild glee. He always hitched a ride on the seasoned rounds of North
Wind's frigid amble, for it was he who painted glitter on every snow
cloaked Christmas tree.

Night brought ethereal mansions raised in diamond peaked translucent
mounds, beneath stately lighted arcs gelid snow flakes swirled in
crystal muted curls. Children hid their heads in feather pillows to
dim the North Wind's roaring sounds, but he sought out every single
crevice and blew across their beds in whirls.

One fine day the Great North Wind saw a purple crocus raise her vibrant
fold, and dreamed he of his hidden cavern in far Antarctic's
wasteland gloom. So gathered he his cloak of frosted ice and flew
toward the northern cold, with a merry promise that he would come
again in budding winter's bloom.

Elizabeth MacDonald Burrows

"My Friend And I"

Thirteen! A simple number on a calendar, revolving twelve times a
year. Just a number adorned by two's of syllables and digits we can
hear. Slowly this number weaves it's web, on a day well known, it's
friday! Now with superstitious woes, it flaunts it's fear, often as
it may. Tho I find this day quite foolish, I know a personal friend,
Who finds this day most fearful, while she waits for it to end. Never
leaving her home this day, and eyeing the hands of a clock, She claims
safety lies within, as she dwells upon "tick-tock"! Uncomfortably, on
a floor she be, choosing not to sleep in bed. I ask of her, "Why on
the floor?" her response, "I can't fall far"! she said. Dirty
pots, dirty pans, cleaning left undone, for fear of getting hurt. I
know this truly disturbs her, for tomorrow is left the dirt! Nary a
black cat be visible, her shades pulled down so tight. No ladders
even in the house, she'd find a mouse a better sight! So as to end
this foolishness, we wait 'till the next day arrives. Like a new
years eve, she'll be relieved, I know, for I'll hear her sighs! Go
way, Friday! begone thirteen! until again we meet. You never fail
to come around, but...she'll fight to beat defeat! Now I must admit
to all! I've told a tiny lie. That personal friend I spoke of...
is... no other, but, foolish I!

Dottie Macik Race

Chicken Of The Dream

In order to make the tuna (she said)
you've got to cut the cat
   sideways
quick as you can, across the throat

It'll just twitch (she said)
for a few long minutes, the
Ichabod Fe-line
and then you can eat.

It's true, there are 101 ways
to skin a cat
but in dreams, you know,
the scariest moves are slow

And all in my many years
of consuming tuna,
I never remembered it being
  this hard.

Sonja Sherritze

Holes

It rained sweetly in the city today;
in the part that's apart from me
I didn't care anymore, but the puddles were deep
just the same. As deep as true love, as true sadness,
as deep as the holes that burn through my skin and
bleed me dry. Then somehow give it meaning again.

Yes, I wore torn clothes today and everyone told me so.
They think they can see through these wet shreds,
through the holes, but the holes have burned right through me too.

These are graves they choose for themselves.
NOW I'm standing over the box. On the outside
looking in at myself being knocked down and
beaten, spilling my blood, being spit on.
NOW these rainy rips are a part of me, they become
the part that's part from me. Like your stained lips
still burn me. Like their words, laced with acid,
they're just waiting to get wasted...

My holes are lined with tears, just waiting to be tasted.

Mark Koncikowski

My Garden As Performance Art

As the spider had his season ticket seat
In Section B, Row "D", seat 6 from aisle,
We first began to nod, then sometimes smile.
When his silvered body fell to early frost
I regretted that we never even spoke.

From: left. quite early in the Act
A villain slug came center stage
To suck the life from leafing greens.
I plunged a garden stake through his black heart.
Heroically, I saved a few young struggling beans.

Though lettuce was the proclaimed star
Through beauty, tenderness and taste,
It ended up in bitter seed
Because the audience had tired of it
And let it go to waste.

We've put our programs on a greenhouse shelf;
They'll tell us once again next year
Our hopes are what forever we must sow
Tomatoes big as a young boy's head,
The violets that lie just beneath the snow.

Kate Sears

"Who's Red Now?"

   Many moons ago, the Red-Man roamed this continent
in communal bands.
   The life of the community was first to them.
They followed the prompting of their "manitous" and gathered
food for all from the abundance which mother nature provided.
They clothed each other and their children and taught the
next generation the truths necessary to carry on.

   The Other-Men came and by devious means
drove the Red-Man from his home.
   Today, they are bound to reservations - never no more
to roam in mother nature's garden.

   History has recorded for us how the Other-Men have won.
   But what did they win?
   They are now banding into "gangs,"
slowly killing each other off.
   They are destroying the very base of society; the family,
the children, the passing on of truths.

   God's laws are not being obeyed nor are the laws
of the "manitous."
Who's Red now?

William S. Dietzler

Kamal The Camel

I'm glad to be called Kamal the Camel
I'm ugly, but useful and I stay out of trouble
My head is big, my ears are small
I've one large hump, but others have more.
My curly eyelashes with thick eyebrows
And my woolly fur prevents me to frown.

Remember, I can go days without drinking water,
I serve my desert master and his only daughter
They can drink my milk and turn it into cheese,
Melt my fatty hump for butter and do as they please.
Please leave me here in the sandy desert, not in a zoo
I have already demonstrated to you what things I can do.

"Marhaba, hello Kamal" in Arabic I'm greeted
"Shukrun, thank you Kamal" they surely mean it.
I feel so happy and useful in the hot sandy desert
No wonder my nickname is SHIP OF THE DESERT.
No other animal can do my work,
Yes I'm ugly, but useful and never a jerk.

Madeleine M. Hoss

Gramma's Trunk

A little girl in Gramma's trunk,
In a dress too long and heels that clunk,
Will someday grow to be a bride,
Her joyful tears her veil will hide.
She'll walk the aisle on daddy's arm,
To a handsome man with all his charm.
She'll walk to him and say "I do,"
And dream ahead of a baby new.
Now from that trunk where her dreams were formed,
Her own sweet girl is now adorned,
And maybe when she's grown up, too,
She'll have some kids, but just a few.
She'll save that trunk to give to them,
The dress too long with a ragged hem.
That trunk's been saved from year to year;
And handed down to loved ones dear.
It's given with love of memories past,
It's a gift of love that will always last.

Keli Moreno

Untitled

In a make believe world, where you know every face.
In a make believe castle, that's all covered with lace.
The friends you have sit and smile all day.
They just walk around being happy and gay.
You grow closer and closer to the people you know.
And the wind always blows and the rivers always flow.
No differences, no discouragement, just be who you are.
In that kind of world you can really go far.
Bring me to that world and the castle in the sky.
Cover me with lace and the friends that never say goodbye.
Let me hear the wind and look into the sea.
Let me take a trip out of reality.

Susan Bradbury

The Playground

Shuffle through crimson sheets of lifeless oak-skin:
In dim forgotten schoolyards where every one has been.

Memories eternally cased in sweat smeared swing-sets;
History catching instruments, nostalgia nets.

Symbols of American beliefs and lifestyle.
Timeless are these monuments, come sit awhile.

Enjoy these precious treasures which I have found;
In a most charismatic place, a playground.

Michael Fitzgerald

The Passing Of The House

There is an old house, being torn down,
In a town.

A layer of asphalt removed, the old wooden siding and
The window cornices are reveled to the sunlight.
Making the house look proud with character upright.

The open porches over time were enclosed.
Will they, again, soon, be exposed?

It's walls, the secrets they could tell,
If, only, we had the time to listen well.

It's been a slow process, no blasting,
To make way for the new, needed, store.

A glimpse of this Old House's Beautiful Past!
Before, it will be seen for the last, and no more.

Phyllis Metzger

Burden

I can not touch her for she is enclosed
in a tunnel, vertical
thick steel pins piercing
her very soul and body.
The wind is ripping on her flesh
piece by piece.
Up into the glowing dome
Leading to black hole vastness.
Outer space
One can see Pluto out of the corner of thine eyes.
Vulgar, pulsating
As the sweat drips down my forehead,
as I press forehead
HARD
Against the plastic
tubular machine.
As I can watch her melting,
and ripping away
She is leaving me.

Shawn Leslie Glide

Soul Mates

In the beginning the two are as one
In body, mind, spirit and soul.
Bound together, the ties are then undone,
Inexorably separating what once was whole.
   Their life paths cross and recross;
   Countless times they know each other.
   In silence they accept each loss,
   Knowing time will again bring them together.
What purpose then created soul mates?
Do they each know who they are?
Does one travel far while the other waits
Patiently, keeping some astral door ajar?
   Nothing save the fragile thread of what once was
   Ensures that recognition between the two
   At a common crossroad in a chosen time does
   Reignite a waiting love that life shares with but a few.
Our purpose cannot be achieved apart
From each other. We must now join until
We are again the same in body, mind, spirit, soul and heart.
It was foreordained. We can no longer remain still.

Nancy M. Siebern

Awful Smirk

Musty smell of oil burners
in dank, boring basements
dust settles in my hair before
I pull the hood of my sweatshirt
cigarette filters in exposed light.
A six pack of miller time and I'm chewing Dentyne
I watch his mustache, the handlebar kind,
his mustache doused with drink
sawdust spills from his brow.
I watch and I watch and
I want to smash and run and get away
but the basement is empty
as empty as the rest of the godforsaken house
so I eat his chapstick and talk about the rain,
hand him a wrench.
Sarah E. Tarling

The Butterfly

Oh flutter through the air so free; you seem to come in every hue.
  In fiery red, in olive drab and even iridescent blue.
With subtle mix of pastel pink and ordinary brown on part,
  A plain and ordinary mien becomes a treasured work of art.

When folded up your wings are plain to stay unseen against the tree.
  But when unfolded you explode in brilliant colors, gloriously.
Not we see you, now we don't, you jiggle through out rims of sight,
  A moment gone, each moment there emits a grand impulse of light.

Escape the tentacles of the earth and soar above for all to see.
  Remind us each and every one of butterflies of memory.
Of happy days, of warmth of life, of summers hot with azure skies,
  Oh please, just make us once again small children seeing butterflies.
W. Richard Klein

I Could Hear The Quiet

I could hear the quiet.
In front of me the narrow road lost itself in the snow-covered meadow.
Behind me the massive church stood its ground in the open landscape.
I could see in the far distance the sun saying adieu to the grayish-white alpine mountains.
My thoughts were on beauty and tranquility.
I could hear the quiet.
Russell A. Baum

A Moments Measure

When faith and love and life cannot be measured
  in heart or mind,
And leaps aren't tethered by sense or thought,
'Tis then the death of childish pleasures are mourned
  and freed and considered naught.
What measures this soulful journey traveled?
  Neither time, nor miles, nor mirth.
This life created by love's own word
  finds solace in love's sweet birth.
Count not the death at each days end
  for merit or value or score
But live the moment now, my friend,
  for love has not promised more.
So measure not the moment
  on a scale of one to ten,
But live the gift each moment brings
  with love and hope. Amen.
Louise Marie Gagne

Imprisoned

You'll find her every evening,
  in her chair by the fire,
and cat, ever faithful, is there, too.
All night the winds blow,
  the mourners come and go,
all seeking the worlds old secrets she must know.
Their woes and their sorrows,
  she hears them all,
tales of oppression from the weary and the small.
And when her time has ended,
  she lowers her eyes,
but her heart reaches up to beyond and cries "Why?"
Wizards and saints all come to her fire,
to feel the colors of the burning wood.
No conversing, it seems to be understood,
she's imprisoned by her wisdom, neither evil nor good.
You'll find her every evening,
  in her chair by the fire,
and cat, ever faithful, is there, too.
Kathleen J. Johnson

Sunshine Coming Through The Trees

In desperation, I longed to see his face
In love, I longed to feel his grace
Oh peace, Oh peace, I beg from above
Oh Lord, please send me a dove
I promise, Oh Lord, Thee will I serve
If only thou would give me a chance
I don't deserve
I am not worthy to come to thee
Please Lord, its the sunshine I want to see
Such tender love for earthly things
My child's smile what joy it brings
The tender touch of my husbands hands
Always knowing he understands
The look of love in my parents faces
Whenever they see me enter the home place
Oh look! Do you see what I see?
Its the sunshine coming through the trees!
Sherry Mitchell

Sepia

Sepia denotes the age, old photo crinkled - worn
In memory of folk long-loved before this babe was born
A snapshot of a moment - frozen in a place, a time
A recollected memory of those once in their prime

Sharp from head to toe, his tan-ness complements her brown
In posing for the camera, was it church or dressed for town?
Hair pressed to perfection - hers; his - waved beneath his hat
Stately in his six-foot stance; right next - cross-legged - she sat

Look closely at his calloused hands - soft soap can't clean tough stains
And there around her soft brown eyes are tell-tale signs of strain
Of hard-time overcome and too-few victory attained
And gratefulness for blessings as the sunshine chased the rain

Though better times reflect within a captured hint of smile
There faded to it's edges is a triumph in life's trials
For each of us has sepia - displayed or packed away
And from the faded memories we garner strength today.
Pamela Kelly Phillips

A Poor Child

Bent garbage cans punctuate the alley clothes,
just clean hang limp as dust
the lost child searches the shadows.
His feet walk slowly across the dirt,
with pebbles and glass digging
to find his dreams!
Teri Pavone

Shayna's Warrior

He is always with me, my handsome warrior.
In my minds eye, he is now, as he was then.
Tall, strong and forceful, he captured me
with his spirit, the song of the hunter,
the wonder of the wild.
The force that carried us through many a
darkened wood is with us still.
Now as we wander from moon to moon
tirelessly seeking to reunite our souls
time passes slowly.
My warrior loves me, whom fought
at his side and shared his heart.
That love is what drives me,
each new dawn, to venture forth and
seek him out again, my warrior.
  Shayna Pearson

When I Touch You

My darling love, last night we fought again
In ritualistic postures of the past,
Each sounding themes attuned to his own pain
In narcissistic deafness to the last.
The rapiers flashed, each word a cutting edge
Drew blood from wounds through scabs transparent thin,
In recall of past hurts another wedge,
Another chasm in the space we win.
And then my silence and your sudden tears.
I reached across the stars to touch your face
And saw you as you were in other years,
The dream restored, the anger gone, no trace
Of battle or of heartache in your eyes.
When I touch you the wonder never dies.
  I. Astrakhan Lynn

Long Awaited Sun

It's an old house now with creaks that sound like whimpers
In the floorboards hide the secrets of silence long stor'd
Of children who peek'd and long'd for the world of safety
From the bottle's cry and wounds that will never heal

The monster is dead, to heav'n we pray he is gone

The gray sky now bright
Dirty windows await the sun
Old children's faces
Still fill'd with the hope of life
Now run to the light
From their darkness, pain and strife

The angels have come, our prayers for d'livrance heard

Rust'd bolts and lost years
Once safe doors fall off hinges
Freedom found at last
And tears turn bitter to sweet
Touch me angel pure
Lead me gently to beauty meet
  William J. Quinn

My Vision

I had a vision in time of sorrow.
It helped me know things would be better tomorrow.

What a beautiful sight to behold,
My loved ones hand in hand and once again whole.

It was hard to cry, then, for my pain.
For my loss, was their gain.

A gain of peace and serenity.
They are together again with love for eternity.
  Lisa Burk Crawford

The Key...

Some say love is like a key..
In the hand of one who believes...
That to open a door, can mean much more...
Than the direction you turn the key...

A sense of control over a human soul
Just for the power to be? No...
It's all in the direction you turn the key...

Open the door to love and explore...
The love God gave me for you..., kept in store...
Behind this guarded door...
Flowers...spring...fresh air..., sometimes...rain...snow...cold winds.
The beauty in life is to examine all elements...
Necessary to life's fullness..., afraid..anxious..uncertain...
Of what might be...where you've never been?

Remember...a closed door has no answers
Courage opens life's true aspect of love...a chance to take...
Open the door to our love...
  And...
Discover much more...
Than the direction you turn the key...
  Rene Eastern

Dawn

When I awake at Dawn you are the first thing my mind sees.
In the middle of the night, you star in my fantasies.

I find it hard to speak the words that say what I'm feeling,
But when you are near my heart and mind start reeling.

You are so good, the perfect lover,
After you, there can be no others.

I need nothing more than to hold you near.
I want to find a way to love and keep you here.

When I see you smile, my heart takes wing.
My body trembles and my heart sings.

You have given me a beautiful day.
Since we met, it's always that way.
  Linda L. Woolf

I Must Not Remember

I've forgotten your face,
  in the rains of September.
All the memories erased,
  I cannot remember.
I must not remember!

I've forgotten your smile,
  on the cold days of November.
Our love for awhile,
  I cannot remember.
I must not remember!

I've forgotten your spirit,
  in the days of December.
Your singing voice....no more will I hear it.
  I cannot remember.
I must not remember!

I cannot remember—September.
I must not remember—November.
I don't want to remember—December, and yet,
I know in my heart... I'll never forget!
  Mary Cagle

Landscape Of The Mind

Walk awhile with me, stranger,
In the tortured landscape of my mind.
The silver highways of neurons and axons
Awaits those strong enough to pass.

Do not forget me, stranger,
For pennies drop from the hand of an errant traveller
Roll into the shattered dark and light of a sewage grille
And splash forlornly in tepid, murky water, never to be recovered.
Thus it is with the library of my mind;
My memories fail me like the relentless falling of those pennies.

Mourn with me, stranger
As we waft on the wings of a nightmare.
For though they may be of our own creation and choosing,
They are always easier to accept
Than the grim reality we all face.

Go in peace, stranger;
I ask you to walk in my footsteps no longer.
Do not tread in my path of both sterile light and stygian darkness:
For those who are willing to see, a path will present itself.
May yours be brighter than the fate I have chosen.

Seung Park

Remember Them

How so very quiet
In this place where I now stand.
So much to see, so much to do,
But no longer.
Once this place echoed the sounds of life,
Men and women, sadness and joy, children at play.
Those sounds and more could be heard.
Then came the sounds of war,
Now there is silence.
The wind echoes the voices
Of those who were here so very long ago.
Today there is only the wind
To tell the story they have to tell.
Long since forgotten,
Marked by a moment in history,
Those who were here are gone.
The heart of who these people were
Should never pass unnoticed.
We should listen to the wind,
We should remember them.

Kurt G. Lessenthien

Love You Mom

To look and see what you have done,
In times of trouble, you've never run,
Some times were bad, but most were good,
We know you did the best you could.

You've cried a lot, so many tears,
Over your small amount of years,
But with laughter, love and lots of care,
We knew that you were always there.

We gave you trouble, we gave you pain,
We sometimes drove you quite insane,
But through it all, the good and bad,
The times were more happy, rather than sad.

We plan to give you the very best,
Through all the years of retired rest,
For our love comes straight from the heart,
Just like it did right from the start.

Peggy Nielsen

Ohio College Experience

Lonely in my tower of isolation, feeling so good
  in this world of desolation

Window shows evening sky, clouds and airplanes
  go whizzing by
Ohio lights and flat lands
stand below the shadow of my eye
I smell the scent of warm apple pie
Baking in a small wooden house off in the distance
Reinforcing my contempt at this very instant

Come with me into my lookout of paradise, gaze
with your eyes across this beautiful state in the
heartland, shaped and altered by the sweat and hand
of many a man.

Stephen Block

Untitled

You may choose your stance in love and life
in times that hotly race toward decay
The choice itself's the weapon close at hand
Too easy reached by those who feed its will.

A redwood petrified by age's master
Icy tribute to its enduring structure
Lifeless shield that guards from man and nature
Even blasted down, the dead is dead.

Honor is a love without forgiveness
Love, an honor to know human shame
Bear the choice which thrusts you to the crossroad
And watch that it will never jump the tracks.

Summon inner strength to aid your choice
The stony redwood cannot help you now
Love and honor cannot be the same
Life is fragile, but still will not be tamed

Two seeds spring from redwood's golden flower
To breed a twin is nature's aberration
Destined to relieve their Cain and Abel
One to love, the other to his honor.

Margaret Nash Walker

The Streets

What's this world coming to?
Instead of fights, we use guns and knives.
What's this world coming to?
When we walk the streets, fearful of our lives.

Our days no longer belong to us.
They're the property of the thugs, the crooks, the hoods.
How the hell can we get 'em back?
When we're scared of our own damn neighborhoods.

Everyday you venture out,
Into a world with no definition.
Not knowing if you'll return or not,
Your days are filled with suspicion.

Who's that walking up behind you?
Is he a friend or is he a foe?
You'd better prepare yourself for the worse,
'cause in these streets, no one knows.

You'd better be careful out there,
"Will you make it home?" you don't know.
Don't look to confident and don't trust no one,
'cause in these streets, your friends may be your foe!

Robert Logan

There Lay My Love

There lay my love
In yonder field of clover and weed.
There lay my love
Where flowers never grow and beauty takes no heed.

There lay my love
There is field so barren.
Life only visits to lay a wreath upon my cupboards bare,
Where the only sound is a whisper of wind moving by my love,
On its way to cool some other love's summer air.

There lay my love
In the bosom of carefree sleep,
Loved still, with each passing day,
Under willows bent, swaying in the breeze.

There lay my love,
And there I'll journey
Till the day willows for me do weep,
And there I will join my love in peaceful sleep.
    Viola Robinson

Untitled

Only the rustle of the grass
Indicated his fall to the earth
He was here alone to learn his self worth
His cries were not heard nor were his pleas
So he lifted his head higher
And rose to his knees
His scream pierced the air
But was heard only by the passing bird
He unclenched his fists
And looked at his hands
His heart heavy, he found the strength to stand
Only the trodden grass showed his footsteps
As he walked up the hill
He was dimly aware of the knife he held
For he was thinking only of the intent to kill
Once more he fell to his knees
Begging someone, somewhere to answer his pleas
Silence being his only answer he raised his knife
Knowing very well he was about to end his life
"Good-bye" he said
    Nicole Silvers

Morning Colors

I saw the morning colors.
Inside it made me proud to witness such an event.
I saw the Marines stand tall
  while the bugler played his song.
And they carefully unfolded our heritage with
  gloved fingers that were strong.
I heard the snap as they straightened the flag,
  and proudly raised it high.
For all of those who lived for it, and
  all of those that died.
For all the things it stood for,
  and all the hopes it unfurled.
I wiped the tears from my eyes,
  and proudly stood as tall as all the
  others who watched on too.
I knew I'd never see another flag
  with guts like the Red, White and blue.
    Lori Ann Lewanski

Sensing Her Beauty

    Her perfume over-powering my senses with great intent. Opening my eyes to a beauty that is very compelling to my mind, with a gorgeous smile that interacts well with a charming personality.
    Eyes with a deep stare sending a tingling sensation from my toes to my nose. Hands so soft and tender enough to make this grown man, surrender some of his precious time.
    A walk of class, tells of her admirable style which is breath taking with every stride. A sweet voice, that is expressive while commanding your attention. Her energy glows towering her character to it's peak; there is no question ??? to why this sister is unique.
    Legs! Captivating matching an adorable temple, catapulting a sensual look refreshing amy twin a sight. A natural warm heart and kind soul propels her to be in control of her life. From top to bottom, again there is no doubt! regarding what her true elegance is all about.
    Stephen Burrowes

Forgetting Faith

The illusional disillusionment splashes in a gulch where life lapses
  into oblivion.
That great circle entraps all who enter its irresistible intention.
As the flickering flame flinches, the blissful belief vanishes
into an unparalleled paradigm where readmittance is futile.
Life's levity crushes confidence and recycles it as unproved faith.

beLIEve the truth—perceive personal power—rewrite the rules—
  conceive constant control

Nothing is everything:everything is nothing
Life is contradiction:contradiction is
lIFe

Mesmerized by memories
Idyllicized by ideologies
where renowned renewal
is a distant dream.

A romance never revealed, a truth always concealed
A hand never redealed, a wound always unhealed.

Pain's blistering battle scars without discretion,
donning formal frocks unscathed from the fight.
Each blithely becoming constantly constricting;
extinguishing existence.
    Sherry L. Colombaro

Individual Experience

We all turn individual experience
Into the memories of childhood
Goals that we set at the beginning
Change with each new illumination of life
The journey we embark on
Is never the one we set out to take
The road we find
Is never the one we first wanted
The love we find
Is never what we thought it would be

All that we have is years ahead
To which we must all pass through
But it is what is done
With those years that make us all
Individuals with life
Individuals with soul
    Misty Faucheux

Ode To A Lover

The lover, as he casts his eye
Into the sky at night,
Thinks not of earthly things, but of
His mistress's angelic light.
No sleep gains he, for all his dreams.
Are dreamt of while awake;
For the lover doth dread sleep perchance there
His mistress his love forsake

To the lover all things are brightened
When his love is in his eye.
With her the world abounds with life;
Without, that life doth die.
Her eyes the stars upon which the universe hath spun,
In night time he doth cry aloud, for radiance from his unseen sun.

The sweet music of the nightingale,
Becomes the song of the birds of day,
But the lover has refused all sleep,
Upon his bed he doth not lay.
For one hope held him through the night.
As now dawn comes, ere so dim.
Where slept the heav'nly angel bright,
Perchance she dreamt of him.
  Kyle T. Dugan

Mom

Seasons come and seasons go.
It seems I held you not so long ago.

I was there the day you died, and it felt so
strange, the way I felt inside!

I knew it was real, I knew you were gone,
and I cried so hard for you to come home!

I did the best I could, to always be there
as I should, to see you smile, cry a tear
in pain, but... I always ask God to let you remain?

I knew someday he'd take you home, I looked
for signs so I would know? I wished for more
time...I should have known for he knew best,
it was time for you to go.

I'll cherish the time we spent together, close
my eyes to remember...seasons come and seasons go,
I'll love you forever MOM, ever and ever!
  Sandra Lynn Caudill

Untitled

To live among men, and man's environment
is a deed we all must experience once,
but in this one it is impossible
for he looks for rich's not,
greed not in his being,
man's war is his nightmare,
love is his position,
his love is for, the flowers he smells,
the green he sees, the freshness of the air,
the coolness of the mountain brook,
the newborn child,
and other nature of which he is of, but,
he is stopped, by man, man's war.
And man's environment,
and there is nothing,
nothing until earth and it's true nature
are reborn again.
  Travlen Travis

"Spirit Bound"

Up above the stars so bright
is a golden gate of God's design.
To enter there means death below,
but spirit bound to our heavenly home
where family and friends from past long gone
with open arms to welcome you home.

Do not cry for me no more,
for I am with Jesus in our heavenly home.
Where pain and suffering are things from the past,
joyfulness and peace forever to last.

So do not cry for me no more,
for I am with Jesus in our heavenly home.
  Wanda L. Voorhes

Home

There was no love at Home Sweet Home,
Just angry people shouting and quarreling.
That's all I could hear!
Where is Home Sweet Home?

No tenderness, no smiles,
Only I wished for a compromise.
Free flowing tears, an aching hearts
Hoping someone would notice with outreached arms!
  Magdalene Idol

The World Inside

The world inside in which I hide
Is cold; dark. I dare you to hold
The beating jewel, the heart, the tool;
The sole center, the soul's dissenter.
  The shadow play of words I say
  Is short as an arrow shot
  To the target, and I don't forget
  The sole sender, the one soul pretender.
  I tread softly here, you don't hear;
  I sing too, find things to do,
  Keep the jewel, my heart and tool
  In the center, the beating soul tender.

The shadows play off words I say
To the taught, as it after neglects
The world inside in which I hide.
  O. Blanck

Fear Of Change

Why must we all fear changes?
Is it because something we love rearranges?
Or is it because we do not want to lose something close to our heart,
And fear a brand new start?

I will not deny it - change is one of my fears
Change has made me laugh a billion laughs and shed a million tears
Moments and memories I cherish and review
That stick in my mind, that I have lost and will lose

Sometimes I wish I could live my favorite moments again
But I know more memorable things in my life are about to begin
It is not the future that I fear
It is the thought of what will be lost and things that are dear

Change always has a good side
But it is something that is done on your own without a guide
How you determine to succeed and make changes is your decision
In my opinion it is in the way you pick your path and strive for a mission

I feel changes are reality and goals are dreams
But that is not always how it is or seems
You must have both reality and dreams to be successful and feel powered
But if you do not have or make change, you will forever be a coward.
  Melissa Ball

Essence

Where is the essence of my beauty?
Is it in the ebony of my eyes?
Where do you derive your pleasure?
Is it within the movement of my thighs?
Or is it my flawless brown skin; although beauty is skin deep?
I'll open up my heart to you, if it's secrets you promise to keep.
   Where is the essence of my beauty?
Is it in the ivory of my teeth, or in the sweetness of my tongue?
Is it my wisdom, or my naivety since I'm young?
   Where is the essence of my beauty?
Where does the truth lie?
Is it deep inside of me, or something only seen from the outside?
Does my candidness upset you?
Does my sensuality take you by surprise?
If you come closer, then you will see my inner and outer beauty
exuberant in size, extent and degree.
When you do, I'm sure you will see
my loveliness is hidden all over, under and inside of me
  I AM THE ESSENCE OF MY BEAUTY!
    Tamyka T. Sanford

To Get An Answer

Ah, my friend, the greatest mistake you'll ever make,
  is listening to the breeze as it comes off the lake.

I listened, as its sounds whistled through the reeds,
  and now my eyes can only see empty deeds.

That hell sent breeze whispered the name of a girl,
  my friends, there was no finer beauty in all the world.

Her image made my heart stop,
  her laughter, my ears pop.

This damel was there
  if only I could make her aware.

Aware of me.

Yet this breeze that was the angel's home,
  would go no where near were I would roam.

So alone I sit, by the long, long lake,
  hoping that someday I may catch the beauty with my bait.
    Raymond F. Albin

Stop Brother!

Oh the woes and sins of man
Is my way beyond any measure.
Fighting, killing throughout the land
Do you dare to call this pleasure?

Stealing, robbing, living a big lie
Not giving any thought of love
Mothers just hang their heads and cry.
Looking for an answer from above.

Stop brother! Listen just a while
To the heartbreak, hear the pleading of mothers
Stop snuffing out precious lives
Soon there'll be no one to call brother

Yes this world's full of woes and sins
Running rampant with sad disregard.
Do you wonder, when will it end?
Let me tell you, with the coming of the Lord!
    Lucy M. Boykin

Love Is

Love is something you feel
Is it fake? Is it real?

Does it make your heart go flippety flop?
Or does it just go blop?

Does it make you feel like you're flying high,
Or does it make you wonder why?

Do you hear the thunder and see the lightning,
Or is it just kinda' unexciting?

Does it make you really want to dance,
Or maybe just do a little prance?

Does it make you want to climb a wall,
Or are you getting ready for a fall?

If you feel like it was sent from
The angels above
Then you can be sure—it truly is love!
    Lois Akright

The Morning Dew

The morning dew that surrounds this precious ground,
is natures blanket of love. It's here to keep all of it's
beauty resting peaceful, during the darkest hours of nightfall.

When the early morning awakens, with the warmest sunrise,
caressing the sky with it's gentle light and soft colors,
natures animals begin to stir. The delicate flowers with
their tender buds and thick forest with it's rich greenery,
stretch up to the heavenly skies.

As the sunrise begins to brighten, this beauty becomes magical,
as it glistens with it's rich colors, and a special kind of
freshness that signals, a new day has been born, more precious
and tender than the one before!
    Lisa A. Maines

Heaven Sent

Your refreshness for life,
Is sent "I think" from heaven.
Your vim is worth the strife.
The friendliness is just you "A Special Person"

I can feel the touch of spring coming,
It reminds me of you.
The life flowing through the pretty flowers,
Makes you know when you leave earth,
You're not through!

Never change your "cheerful ways,"
They uplift people, just to know you.
They're contagious to people everyday.
That's why I know "you're sent from heaven!"

An Angel, maybe.
Who knows, but one can dream.
But as I can see,
When I get to heaven, I hope they're all like you!
    Russell D. Wier

I Want To Be Selfish Now!

I have worked so hard, 'Lo these many years;
It has become my way of life.
I know no other way to live;
I've known so much pain and strife.
One step forward, then two steps back;
My children were there to see.
Anything, worth having in this life;
Takes prayer; perseverance and the unshakable belief in me!
    Shirley J. Parker-McCoy

Rite

The ability to learn, from one who does not know
Is the ceremony for the willing
Preserved carefully, the most beautiful of traditions.

A choice that is wrongly made, yet carried through,
As though made by a god
Who is unable to view himself
Through willing eyes,
Accepting.

The object he beholds, the candle.
Seeing by its own light
Yet destroying itself
Serving no other purpose,
Excepting.

The adoring face, analyzing, with faulty reasoning
And emotion far from pity.
Afraid of the shadows cast by the steeple
Blinded to the scatter of colors beneath his feet
At home in this place
Of consciously misplaced faith.
   Kelly A. Hess

Crime

Crime is out there everywhere.
It could give you quite a scare.

To the victims, their never the same.
Who in the world do you blame?

They claim it's poverty, joblessness and drugs.
We have to stop hiding it under the rug.

Criminals are set free.
All they do is cop a plea.

If we kept them in jail,
maybe the system wouldn't fail.

Victims have know rights at all.
We better soon get on the ball.

It's time to stop all the crime,
and get rid of some of the slime.

You have to lock your home and car.
You can't even travel very far.

If you do a crime.
You should have to serve the whole time.
   Nancy Ann Raymundo

The Wedding

Climb with me toward the summit
It is the dawn of our new life
Night lingers in the sky with morning
Moon is the husband, Sun the wife

Swim with me through eons of oceans
The tide will surely ebb and flow
Calm water - I float beside you
Together - we kick against the undertow

Dance with me when you hear no music
Our souls - tenor and soprano can sing
We make our own joyful noises
Sometimes trumpet brass-sometimes harp string

Walk with me until the dusk settles
We'll bathe in the warmth the setting sun sends
Two - crossing the years together
Soul mates, partners - lovers, best friends
   Teri Richardson Butler

Thoughts Of You

The source of my utmost happiness
   Is the nearness and thought of you,
My heart is changed to gladness
   With thoughts of your soul so true.

Your image is forever in my mind
   As well as your kindness and cheery smile,
'Tis enjoyment in these things I find
   That keeps me happy all the while.

When you are near I seem to concentrate
   Upon the wonders that life holds for me
What can be the outcome of my fate,
   If I cannot share my joys with thee?
   Leola A. Haffley

Tranquillity

Here in this quiet shell of beauty
Is the sound of a new robin's yawn,
Of waves in lazy surrender
And a doe love-nuzzling her fawn.

There's the sigh of the wind stirring gently,
Of roses faint sipping of dew;
Of butterflies lighting on lilacs
And the sky's slight changing of hue.

The whisper of clear falling water,
The susurrant song of the grass;
The descent of suns to their slumber
Kissing the nights as they pass.

There are chimes that echo in twilight
And clouds that glide through the moons;
The stars waltz over the heavens;
The locust strums faint little tunes.

In this world of music there's splendor,
Escape from the madness of men.
The curve of the shell holds enchantment;
The silver of peace is within.
   Wilma Mann

The Power Of Wisdom

To pander in the garden of life
Is to sell your soul to the evil
To live in the robes of Jesus
Is to suffer the unbearable, and not weep
To bear the gift of life
Is to carry a burden for the rest of your days
And to kill a man
Is to extinguish the gift of a burdened soul
To torment your brother
Is to turn on our own kind
And cause yourself to suffer great loss
Wisdom is the only way
And for wisdom thy must pray
For it is one thing that money will not buy
Money is a lie
And stealing will not gain
Wisdom is not a material thing
But a gift from God and God alone
   Patrick J. Gooley

"Our Baby"

I think in our life the greatest joy,
Is when God gives us a baby girl or boy.
A father's hopes, and a mothers prayer,
As she sits there holding her baby in a rocking chair.
The family gathers around for all who wants to see,
This sweet little baby that God has sent to thee.
Dear little one so very sweet and so kind,
As you grow and even cry, I'm so glad you are mine.
You are so tiny as I hold you here in my arms,
You have so many of your own little charms.
As you grow and grow into an adult some day,
Just remember you will always be my baby in your own special way.

Shirley Benedetto

"Life"

Life is a very precious thing,
It can leave you as fast as
a bell makes it ring.
While most people realize this, others do not.
They waste their own bodies
not knowing what they've got.
It's a shame to see
so many people die.
Imagine their families,
most not being able to say goodbye.
Aids, drugs, and suicide
are some of the ways,
But most commonly are the ones used in these days.
All caused from sadness and hatred within,
Now how is this the answer,
not trying to win?
Why is life so low on this degree,
So much hatred why not just agree?
Life is so precious can't you see,
What would this world be like without you and me?

Tiffany Figel

Sudden Changes

This just has to be a bad dream
It can't possibly be what it seems
Down this long yellow beam.

I am hopelessly lost in this place
So unfamiliar, no one knows my face,
I feel I'm caught up in a furious race.

But, I know when I open that door
I'll be back at my desk just like before
And I won't feel lost or strange anymore.

What ever does this bad dream conceal
And why can't I understand what it reveals?
Oh God! This isn't a dream—IT'S REAL!

Naomi O. Pittman

Dream Lovers

Their love is pure
It can endure the scrutiny of time
Temptation are but vapor
Exhaled during the nights slumber
Evaporated in the morning light
They cannot abuse, forget or deny
They are powerless
To inflict pain
For in that pain they would cease to exist
They leave...
Only to sleep and dream again

Stephen Pulver

Mighty Like A Rose

The rose upon the vine first was a bud.
It grew, it spread, unfurled its lovely head.
It blossomed into joy as nature fed
The food and loving care that nature could.

It spread its petal wings as if to fly,
Yet flying would destroy its beauty here.
If only it had tried its wings of fear,
To gain a world where all pleasures lie.

While wanting to be queen of some known field
Where men would praise and claim it as a bride.
Instead, it stayed quite safe; because of pride
Until its petals to the ground must yield.

Try your wings dear Rose while in your prime,
There is a day when all that's left is time.

Virginia Butler

Sleepy Thoughts

The thunder crashed, and I was suddenly awake.
It certainly sounded like a big earthquake.
As I lay sleepless in my bed,
Some strange new thoughts popped into my head.
Suppose the dictionary had only one word.
Suppose my cat never, ever purred.
Suppose my music book has only one song.
Suppose the sun shines all night long.
Suppose I outgrow my brand new shoes.
Suppose in school, I take a snooze!
Suppose my best friend turns into a monster!
Suppose all people are allergic to lobster!
Suppose I have to move far away.
Suppose I have lots of homework today.
Suppose everyone gets locked out of their house.
Suppose my cat eats my neighbor's pet mouse!
All of these thoughts are making me sleepy,
Oh, no! My room is staring to feel creepy!
Suppose...

Lindsey Bernacki

Untitled

I recall sitting beneath a tree so many years ago
  it could only be tomorrow, basking in the silent
  songs of that first sentient benefactor with whom
  I sought shelter from home.

I remember lying prone amidst damp foliage in moist
  mothers flesh, amazed at the peace I felt then
  as undetectable chords and rhythms helped salty sweet
  fluids find passage through straining eyes from a
  too soon bitter heart.

I remember my wonderment also, watching this ancient
  androgynous being dancing with a gentle, equally
  sexless breeze in a passionate, soulful ballet
  as it rained pink and cream blessings upon me
  almost unintentionally.

The solace I felt then returns to mind too, the peace
  that trickled into my child's hardened heart as I
  witnessed the subtle union of that vagabond breeze
  and the stoic elm, both content with their silent
  song and brief time that they shared.

Ted Carson

The Color Of Life

There is this certain color in life that everyone wears or uses
It describes our personalities, Thank God, HE let's us choose it
There is one that I know of
that makes you hateful and envious inside
But it's up to you to seek Him,
And He will be your guide.
There is one that gets you down
With great depression and despair
But the good Lord can take that out of your life— If you so dare.
There is one that makes you fearful
And you might even start to run
But if you turn your life over to Him
You can have Heaven under the sun.
There is this mighty color
That makes your strong and stand tall
For the trust you put in him, Worked after all.
So if life gets you down
There's a color you can use
For the good Lord above
Says you can have anything you choose.

Patricia F. Richardson

Untitled

An event took place seventy seven years ago,
it filled a Mother's heart with glee.
God saw fit to give her a little boy
that little boy was me.

My family was proud of me, and they often proved it so.
As they would do me favors and let the true love of God show.

As I grew up into manhood,
the way was hard, the hills rough and steep.
My family relied on Jesus, and trusted Him our soul to keep.

Life has been no pretty bed of roses.
It was no pillow of ease, but it was a happy time for all,
as we tried, our God to please.

They are all gone now except one brother and I,
and we are up into the evening years,
often my mind does wander back,
and I'm not ashamed of the tears.

But one day my Lord will call me
to go home from toils of life set free.
I look forward to that great day,
when we will be together, my family and me.

W. F. Loper

Guardian

A beautiful soul is watching me.
It shields me with its heart
From all the eternal evil here.
It shines light where there is dark.

This soul carries not a rigid spear,
Nor a sword which slices in pain.
It carries not a thought of war or hurt,
But only one wish to heal the maim.

I shall always be grateful to this guarding soul,
For helping me begin to overcome
My fears, my greed, and my criticisms,
Which lie in my heart and on my tongue

My own soul shall one day be cleansed of evil,
And I shall stand shining before gates of gold,
Prepared to join my guarding angel,
And kneel before God and the saints of old.

Patricia Lynn Feeney

Bird Song

Bird song is God's creation lifting voice.
It wells up unbidden in bird, in man;
The singer has no choice but to carol forth
   in torrents, the Fundamental song

Creator in his creatures singing, lifting voice;
Were the mouth stopped, the emanation would prolong
Through eyes and pores and hair, the primal noise.
From very spirit issues, springs,
   and floods, this song.

Kathryn A. Sikorski

Tear Of Sorrow

A tear rolls down my cheek
It is distinctly different though
not like a kiss of dew laid upon a flower.
This is a real tear
A tear for what has come about
the pressure, the jealousy, the hatred
over little things.
Which has caused me to gently closed my eye
and have an emotional filled tear
erupt from my eye like a volcano, yet
it is so delicate as it slowly crawls
and falls down my cheek
because my soul has just died.

Lindsey Dorval

Seasons

The Summer is slowly fading away,
It is getting colder, day by day.
Soon Fall arrives and then brisk nights,
And soon we'll see some of Nature's delights.

Bright splashes of color on all of the leaves,
Makes a magical fairyland of all the trees.
Soon Winter arrives, and hard winds blow,
Bringing in, the ice and snow.

Then Winter sports will be our fun,
Lasting 'till the Winter's done.
Spring is now coming, very fast,
And the land is no longer white and vast.

Soon sleeping flowers will raise their heads,
Awaking from their Winter beds.
Spring is such a beautiful time,
Which is causing me to write this rhyme.

Sara Santefort

Untitled

Love is for me, love is for you,
It is one thing a person can always do.
Love is patient, love is kind,
with no sight of envy, True Love is blind.
If love is true, it knows no pride,
There is one part of love, people try to hide,
it's that little selfish motive that's hidden inside.
Love is gentle, it makes no demands.
Despite all wrong, True Love still stands.
Love is holy, but also pure,
It lasts forever and it will endure.
Love is loyal, believes the best,
It knows the truth, love stands the test.
It forgives all we have done and still won't rest.

Leroy Hanlin

To Stand Alone

There is a steel rod within me
it is very thin and weak, but it is my happiness. It is also,
because of its weakness, the reason I run away from myself.
The happiness I seek is semi-complacency with
confinement, the ability to tell myself that things are alright,
though those around me may not be in the air on wings of freedom.
I only want to be able to nurture myself. My mom does
drugs, as do many of my friends, as a way to escape
unhappiness, to find the strength to be happy. This strength
is always easily found through outside forces. During
childhood, it is found in the loving arms of mother and later,
as self-awareness kicks in, it is found in drugs.
I need some independence

Responsibility should not be forsaken,
but nurtured,
nor run away from,
but embraced.

I'm okay and I really do have nothing to be sad about,
nor any reason to feel small.
   Steven Vance

"The Good Ole Days"

Don't you pine for what used 'ta be
It just ain't the same, or ever will be,

As a matter of fact it never was
You just 'membered the good and forgot the blahs.

Now when you're dreamin bout the that good ole time
I bet you can member some ole man pine,

"Way back yonder in the days gone by
It was peaches'n cream and pie in the sky."

Your good ole days he didn't like
But he looked on back when he was a tyke,

When somebody else carried the load
Just twern't his time to travel that road.

So when feeling your load in mournful ways
Just remember, for somebody else it's "The Good Ole Days".
   Wilson McKee

Master Potter (Jeremiah 18:1-10)

It's just a piece of clay, hard and stubborn as can be.
It looks so worthless to people like you and me.
But the potter sees potential, from a potter's point of view.
He sees it as something valuable, after it is renewed.

He puts the clay through a process, causing it to respond to touch and feel.
Then he makes a useful vessel, shaping it at the potter's wheel.
We are like the lump of clay, hardened and stubborn as can be.
The master potter sees with mercy, the vessel he can make of you and me.

So he draws us by his spirit, showing love and kindness too.
He forgives our sinful past, and by his word we are made new.
As we walk in full obedience, and his light is shining through;
We become a useful vessel by the good things we can do.

  2 Corinthians 5:17 "...if any man be in Christ, he is a new
  creature: Old things are passed away; behold all things are
  become new."
   Raymond Jolliff

And I Cry (Empty Road)

When I see you,
it makes me feel so angry and sad,
that we are both alone,
and not together.

I want to tell you how much I care,
but I always cower in fear when given the chance.
Something, maybe the words you said, hold me back,
from telling you that I am sorry for all that I have done.

I have changed my life,
It was not easy to look at myself and find all of the mistakes,
but I did and have now tried to correct them.
I cry, because I miss you,
I cry, because I am all alone,
I cry, because I love you and we are so far apart.

Love is a feeling that will not subside,
not in the strongest of men or the weakest of beings.

So I stand here alone, on this empty road,
thinking about you and me,
and how it used to be.
I know what I have done, please, please give me one more chance...
   Michael Maltese

A Love For All Seasons

The love I give you is not jealous nor is it selfish.
It seeks no advantage, nor does it seek to control or dominate.
It seeks to warm and soothe, to give refuse from the storms of life.
It seeks to understand when there is a lack of understanding.
It seeks to give guidance to find the right direction when there is
  confusion.
It seeks to bring happiness, and hope where there is sadness and
  hopelessness.
It seeks to bring calm and serenity in times of turmoil.
It seeks to give courage and strength when you are afraid and falter.
It seeks to bring friendship when you need a friend.
It will not give up on you, nor will I.
   Preston Shirley

I Wish I Were A Clown

I wish I were a clown.
It seems every clown you see has a certain mood.
A happy clown, if things go wrong the clown
  in costume is still happy.
A sad clown cannot ever smile if he has
  a great day.
I wish I were a clown, a happy one I
  would be.
It would make it look like everything was
  all right even if I were not.
If I were a clown I could make children
  happy and that would be a
  reward for me.
Just putting all the troubles you have
  away for a little while.
Doesn't that sound so wonderful.
I wish I were a clown.
   Victoria Clodfelter King

Kind Thoughts

Kind Thoughts and sweet memories of you distract me.
Knowing that miles and trials separated our fates, yet
sparked by the heartfelt attractions, we created the time and place.
Feelings that were never pressured to last, somehow gave us more freedom to relate.
You have filled a permanent place in my heart.
Thank you!
Love, your friend for life.
   Sandra Christine Sweeney

A Black Tint

The heart of a war is damaged and sore,
It seems to last forever more.

Many innocent people are killed.
Many empty coffins are filled.

Yet that does not stop the incredible hero.
He knows everything there is to know.

Here is brave and tough inside,
He is willing to fight the highest tide.

War is over, hero does not die,
He is not a hero in American eye.

Hero is shown no acknowledgment,
For in his skin there is a black tint.

Hero is spit on and treated like dirt,
Yet that does not stop him from wearing his shirt.

This hero is still overcome with pride,
Just goes to show you what counts - is inside.
   Natalie Sylvester

Unfulfilled Passion

Your passion ignited a love so deep,
It sent my heart into a
   Timeless sleep.
As the years went by each night I would cry,
For a love I knew that could never Die.

Heartaches and discontentment was always the same,
As life seems to play such
   Treacherous illusive games.
With Emptiness and hope, My heart took Flight,
In hope that one day I would come out of this Night.

Your picture I carried with me, as my passion beheld,
Fond memories endured even the
   Fire of—Hell.
When I saw you on that blessed Day.
I knew it was I who had gone Astray.

O My Love, now that I have Found you,
What once was a spark, is now a blaze.
I know I can never go back to those
   Unhappy Days.
   Robert L. Lynch

"Game Named Time"

A basketball hoop sits in the garage rusty and old...
It still remembers the games of ten years ago...
The football field has long seen change...
Now all what's left are fences - wood and chain...
The bed in the basement once filled with tired boys...
Now sinks down under the weight of dirty boxes and broken toys...
The bushes and trees which covered kids playing hide and seek?...
Now are the homes for rabbits large and meek...
Many were the reasons to walk someone to the store...
But the store and the reasons are no more...
In the alley once filled with girls and boys, all that remains...
Is a trash can which reads: 2146 N. Main...
We may wish things stay the same...
But times have changed and we can't stop the game...
   Kenneth W. Coffey

Tommy's Hope

He did not know how he got down in there.
   It was a dark hole but
      His heart was beating and his fingers and toes moved.
He knew he was alive.
He grabbed the cord of hope someone threw to him.
   He held on.
She knew he was down in there;
   She must have been deaf.
She did not hear his heart beat or
   His fingers and toes move,
But she knew.
He was still down in there holding that cord of hope
   when a storm began.
And she ran.
She let go of her end of the cord and he fell
   into an eternal oblivion.

He never got the chance to call her "mommy".
   Sherry Bubnowski

A Texan Goes Fishing

When my husband died, I had to start a new life.
It was difficult after forty years of being a wife.

We had enjoyed fishing and camping out.
I decided to try new places and see what their fishing was about.

In Alaska I caught a forty one lb. King.
It hangs over my fireplace-makes my heart sing.

Always thought the big one's were too much for me,
went to the Florida Keys to check it out and see.

Brought a hundred lb. Tarpon and a large sailfish home.
All my fears of the big one's was gone.

Learned to fly fish in Colorado and still shiver
at the memory of the twenty one inch rainbow caught in the Blue River.

In Canada I caught more than anyone,
enough to feed all of us before we were done.

They asked me to account for my lucky day.
I'm from Texas is all I would say.

Some of the fish was brought back to share with my friends,
others released to fight again.

Life is precious and new joy I know.
Wonder to what new adventure God will have me go.
   Kathryn Mize

Love

I was 20 she was 22
It was my love that began to pursue
Ever since our first rendezvous
All my thoughts, solely dedicated to you.

Most girls so bogus, you so true
Your face so beautiful, so brand new
It was then I realized I loved you
All this was meant to be, deja vu.

On the night of our candle lit dinner, beefstew
It wasn't the best, but we made - do
Our crush grew, grew and grew
To limits of, well, you have no clue.

Our relationship, huge break through
We played games, variations of peekaboo
We took trip, rode the love canoe
We broke current and rode the bijou.
And just think, all this was just the debut.
   Matthew Fillebrown

The Smell Of Mortality

I was driving down the street, complaining about my car.
It was night — many lights flooded the street.
A man passed through one of the lights.
He looked worn, with holes in his shoes and dirt caked on to his clothes.
His eyes had a ravaged look — as though he had something to say,
  but couldn't get the words out.
I didn't want to stare, yet he commanded my attention.
He walked with an air of authority that wasn't lessened by his appearance.
He was a person, with a history and a family,
  and a reason for living on the street.
The man sat down by a pay phone, settling in for the night.
A person passing by stopped to offer loose change to the man.
He looked up at the offering, then down at his hands.
He wiped them on his shirt before he accepted the change.
His hands smelled of mortality.
After that I was too far away to see him.
I lifted my hand to push my glasses up.
I had to wipe my hand before I put it back on the steering wheel
  it smelled of mortality.
Nicole Ouellette

My Thanks

To you I give my thanks!
It was your smile that gave me joy.

To you I give my thanks!
It was your strict hand that kept me straight.
Sometimes I wonder why?

To you I give my thanks!
It was your persistence that changed my ways.

To you I give my thanks!
It was your perfectionism that made me achieve.
Sometimes I wonder how?

To you I give my thanks!
It was your knowledge that opened my eyes.

To you I give my thanks!
It was your love that hugged me with hope,
And NOW I know!

For through your eyes you saw in me
a greater person that I could be.
...To YOU I give my THANKS!
Warren P. Edwards

Where Is This Place

There is a place where everyone want's to be,
It's a place of fear, horror, and happiness,
This is a place that no one can ever see,
Dreaming of a world of isolation,
Cold, dark valleys,
Never ending mountains,
A place non-existent to reality,
Sometime's it's lonely,
But so beautiful,
Sitting alone by a window,
Other's just love to watch the snow,
Most of the world would rather be flying,
Can you find this place,
It's out there somewhere,
Everyone has their time.
Michel Daoud

A Boss

A Boss is like a diaper sagging on the hip.
  It's always on your bottom and usually full of it.

A Boss is like a meadow, flowery, green composites.
  But if you look amongst the blades, you'll see bull deposits.

A Boss is like a paradox Yin and Yang in one,
  Don't look now bossy dear your halo just fell on your horn.

A Boss is like a metamorphosis a good job done is praised
  but when you screw up royally, then all hell is raised.

Don't take these metaphors and paradoxes personally,
  because I scribed them on my P.C. totally in punnary.

Because as your employee I believe this tenet
  That as A Boss you've been fair and honest, Janet.
Shelby J. Stone

Halloween

It's orange and it's black and it's a time to enjoy
It's gay but with a touch of mystery
A time of hugh yellow harvest moons and brisk winds at night
Of leaves on the ground everywhere and pumpkins lying against trees
Halloween, a night when there's magic in the air
A time of witches in black flying across the sky on broomsticks
Their shadows seen against the hugh yellow harvest moon
And children in masks and costumes ringing door-bells
In a brisk wind at night.
Of black cats walking through leaves on the ground everywhere
And Jack-o-lanterns lighted and grinning in windows
Made from pumpkins lying against trees
Halloween, it's fun but with a touch of mischief
A time of costume parties and apple cider, of great bon fires
And black masks a night when there's freedom in the air
A time of make believe goblins and princesses dancing together
At costume parties and young and old alike drinking apple cider
Of ghosts leaving their graveyards but not going too close to the
great bon fires and romances between strangers in black masks
It's orange and it's black and it's a time to remember
Phyllis Flynn

What Keeps Me Going

What keeps me going are very special things.
It's nothing like money or diamonds or rings.
What keeps me going through gray, rainy days,
It's someone like you who helps me in many ways.
What keeps me going when people bring me down,
It's when you tell me to "have no frown".

What keeps me going when I just want to die,
It's the way you always help me to get by.
What keeps me going with a low-self esteem,
It's the way you showed me just how to dream.
What keeps me going through all of my troubles,
It's when the love you give suddenly doubles.
What keeps me going is everything you do,
Especially when you give me a friendship that's true.

What keeps me going is a very special thing.
What keeps me going is all the joy you bring.
What keeps me going when I'm feeling so blue,
It's just about everything you do.
If you've ever wondered what keeps me going,
It's the friendship between us that just keeps growing.
Karin Diaz

Untitled

Behind the gray brick house, a small hill rises.
Its green, gentle slope curves carelessly,
Like the spine and tail
of a great resting reptile.
On the apex of its back
A magnolia tree extends evergreen arms
Toward four nearby fruit-bearing saplings.
This landscape's elevation offers privacy,
And invitation...to run up and down,
To coast or glide, roll or ride,
Slide its inclination.
Ruts from knobby bike tires,
Narrow sled runner scars,
Crisscrossing its thatchy side
Are slowly receding.
The little hill stands alone, quietly,
Leaning northward, a wind-break, sheltering us below its brow.
When morning sunrise slips lightly over its shoulder,
I'm tempted to run outside to say, "Welcome new day!"
Pat Bell

Life Through Woven Curtains

The woven curtains scatter light that comes from who knows where,
It's like my life that's broken into little lonely squares.
Each block a story in itself, a saga yet untold.
If you could read those little squares, you'd see my life unfold.

The threads are tiny highways, the many miles I've roamed,
With broken dreams and shattered hopes, I'm always going home.
A ledger of my life is there, a history of me!
A diary of my past laid bare for anyone to see.

Each tiny box a point in time, a door that holds a tale,
They tell of love and life and hope, though often they seem pale.
They form a pretty pattern there upon the shaded pane,
I wish my life were styled so, with smiles instead of pain.

Although it's been a somber road I've often had to follow,
There have been good times with the bad, and maybe so tomorrow.
As time goes by and seasons change, so much does my fare,
But the curtains still break up the light in little tiny squares.
Ricky J. Stanton

Lost Love

In the springtime of my dreams
It's music now fades
Into the chill of bleakness,
Your sleep is deep
As I weep of my loss,
Too fast into this day
Nights ending came too soon,
The music has stopped, and I am lost
Just standing in this shadow of silence,
I listen intently for your voice
Look deeply for your expression,
But, I am blind now
Only reaching and finding memories
Locked within the grasp of what we once had,
Side by side
My thoughts, my dreams, my love
Are with you still,
Always, yes! Always
They live within the silence of my heart,
That beats for you alone.
Kathleen Cypert-Arnold

Lost In Love

I am lost in love, I don't know what I feel
it's like the heavens up above

Full of happiness and full of grace
I often think of you and I see your face.

Your smile is so bright like the morning sun
You always make everything right, and things more fun
Your eyes twinkle in the night
Your heart beats a silent song
and your hair glistens in the sun light.
I will love you forever if you will have me
but there is someone else in your life I can see

So as I walk away heaven starts to fade
The morning sun never shines to start a new day

I am no longer lost in love
But have a broken heart
Maybe someday soon a new life will start.
Sonya Ann O'Dell

The Homeless

The Homeless worry me, all of the time.
It's not just the Holidays, that's on my mind.
I wish we could do, a lot more for them.
I wish we could give, them a home again.
Warm clothes and plenty of good food.
A nice Christmas meal, sure would be good.
A reason to be happy and to grin.
Not to be poor, then they could win.
Presents under a pretty tree.
If we would all help maybe it could be.
Helping them don't you see. Would not hurt, you or me.
A place out of the wind and cold.
I don't mean to sound quite so bold.
With no fancy clothes, I wish I could see.
A Church that would let them, come and be.
With lots of food, cookies and pies.
I know there would be, plenty of sighs.
Just hoping and praying, this could be.
The pleasures this all would give to me.
God please help them, I know you can see.
God in Heaven, please let this be.
Shirley Weeks

Young People Gone Astray

I've listened, I've wondered
I've heard people say
Young people now days have gone so astray...

Instead of judging and showing no care
Why not touch a young life to show you are there...

The young need to know that you understand
You'll be there when they need you
And you will give them a hand...

Take time with young people
Always include them in your plans
Take time to teach them the facts of Life
And all of life's demands...

Take time with young people and show that you care
The results can be astounding
And proud enough to share...

TAKE TIME WITH YOUNG PEOPLE
AND MAKE A DIFFERENCE...
Verleen R. Green

Running Through My Mind

Timid as I move toward a new fantasy.
No, it's not new. The fantasy is ancient not
only to me, but also to the entire world.
For some, it becomes a reality much sooner than others.

The reality can be shockingly, invigorating
for some; expectedly despairing for others.
Ironic, is it not? This is the fantasy that's
been running through my mind.

I don't like tattoos. I speak not of the
physical adornment to be marveled by all
or by none. Those can be attractive.
I speak of a mental one, indelible and invisible.
The fruition of this fantasy I wear like a tattoo.

Louis L. Blackmon

The Love Of God

The love of God is mightier than angry, crashing seas.
Its power splits the heart and bears the soul eternally.

It's purer than the whitest snow that falls 'mid winter cold,
And purer than the mountain spring, refreshing to our soul.

It's truer than the truest love that man has ever known,
And truer still, His seeds of love within our hearts are sown.

It's sweeter than a newborn babe sent down from heaven above,
With angel kisses all aglow, a gift from God belov'd.

His judgement just, is ever fair, upright with sin reproving.
Defenseless stand we in His midst, in judgement sin removing.

His love is everlasting, never-ending, mercies sure,
With hope and joy for dying hearts and lives that will endure.

Lynda Bryan Davis

My Cathedral

I've walked the snow-white sands of Vero,
I've body-surfed at Santa Cruz;
I've blessed each golden grain on Maui,
With its celestial tints and hues.

I've watched with awe and wonder,
As the surf came crashing in;
And I froze in trepidation,
At the sighting of a "fin."

I've watched the whale and the dolphin,
As they "teased" just out of reach;
And I've come to the conclusion,
That my "Church" is at the Beach.

Where each grain of sand holds things eternal,
And the tide's infinity;
In the depths of His great oceans,
I see His awesome majesty.

So, as I stroll through my "Cathedral,"
With its pews of shifting sand;
Each pounding wave forms a procession,
To the power of His hand.

Robert L. Neal

Hi Mom!

Hi mom! I'm Alive could you hear my heart beats? I'm
inside in your womb starting a new life just waiting
for the moment that you could hold me in your arms and
I can see you in your eyes. Yesterday, I heard you cry
saying that you have women rights and you don't want me
alive. Please don't, don't stop my life. I know that you
have women rights but no rights to stop my life. I'm not
a trash I'm a human and I also have human rights.

Lupe Ramirez

In Love

I love you more than life itself;
It's probably because you act yourself.
You're very special in some kind of way;
Just seeing you brightens up my day!
I think about you constantly;
I just can't stop;
Being alone with you is like a dream come true;
When we're together, we're stuck like glue.
You're every wish is my command;
How 'bout making love at the beach in the sand?
You're lips are as soft as rose petals;
If love was a sport, you'd win a gold medal.
A smile on your face, puts a smile on mine;
You're very cute and very fine;
You're my dream guy, oh yes you are,
I hope this relationship goes pretty far.

Rachel Schuckmann

The Train Song

I hear that train whistle calling me
It's time to board the rails and make my leave
Restless — to be alone — destination unknown
Doesn't matter where — there's always room to roam

Long cold nights in a boxcar
Or sitting at the campfires under the stars
Smoking stoggies and eating my stew
While taking a nip or two

With stories to tell and listening so well
My faithful companion wagging his tail
If you are lucky to be with me
A philosopher I'd be

I recall my adventures from town to town
I know I could never settle down
No wife — no kids — no family
No responsibility

I never had a love whom I can depend
Except with my little four legged friend
A thinker, a lover, a dreamer, I can be
But riding the rails I'm free

Linda Ward

Memories

As we go through life we store our fun times
Just like a jewel box we tuck these fond lines
In the folds of our brain

We can't turn back the pages of time
But we can call to mind the pages we want to remember
Just like a fond book we've read and read

No one can replace the pages of our times here on earth
When God allows the book to be closed only
To be opened again in Heaven

And only our Lord Jesus Christ will be the judge
Whether our book of memories was worthy of a grand prize.

Now before the last chapter is tucked away
Ask that great judge to come in and help you finish your life

You will find the best was saved until last and
Enjoy every minute of today those memories have served
Their purpose... live for today

Mary Alice Goodwin

Reflection

Even as the snow falls gently
Its timeless beauty imprints freshly on my mind
But cannot console my aching heart
Or the anguish that I feel deep inside

Illuminating the night to a bright silent world
The same glow as a child I often felt
But now in indifference I gaze out across the white
A victim of maturity and pain I cannot fight

Just as the sun beckons the glistening ice crystals home
And the earth greedily partakes the rest
So too God, excise my agony from within
And lift my spirit up once again
 Susan Ciavarella

Stronger

My pain is healing, yes it's true
I've scars from my battle within
My battle for truth.

My spirit soars, as high as a falcon,
On a clear day.

Through trees, over bridges and over crystal seas,
I am free.

I hear my own voice cry for peace in my soul.
And this continuous mystery of the world
Won't let me go.

I fly between mountains
The chill burns my flesh
I shiver with delight,
I can feel again!

I turn to my healer
Her wisdom runs deep,
A sensation startles my mind
As I discover
My healer is me.
 Kristina Bryn Dudley

"Corruption"

The city is corrupt, the suburbs as well;
just look around us, we live in pure hell.

A simple walk around the block brings on a rape;
sometimes the cops don't care, they let the bad man escape.

There's mugging and shooting every single day;
most people just turn their backs and walk away.

There's not a lot of happiness on either side of the tracks;
it's a sad thing to say, but someone must state the facts.

In the mist of confusion in a world so cold;
there's nothing left but sadness for the young and the old.

To tolerate a system that is totally corrupt;
they should abort it from existence, if I may be so abrupt.

If you don't have wealth and power, you may as well step aside;
the poor ones in society live with nothing, but their pride.

It's hard to justify starvation in the eyes of a hungry child;
to wipe the tears is difficult, that's putting it quite mild.

The unfortunate do what they must to survive;
while others sip wine and champagne, their money keeps them alive.

There's many misconceptions about life ever after;
but not much confusion about our worlds disaster.
 Kathy Seibert

8:14 AM

In the early morning light,
Just as the sun stretched its rays over the horizon,
Yet left us.
Not in agony; there was no discomfort.
While I cried and cried and my eyes swelled,
My heart didn't drop a tear.
My soul knew that you were
Finally at peace,
Tranquil and calm,
That you were in a better place.
It's difficult to let go,
But I know that you know you're loved,
And that makes your loss less painful.
Thank you for teaching me,
And loving me.
Now, each time the day begins and the sun stretches to greet me,
Your memory will shine from the depths of my heart.
 Kirsten Krick

A Southern Spring

When April showers come and spring blows its gentle breeze across the
 land birds sing, tulips, daffodils and dogwoods are in full array.
We all know this is Mother Nature at work it's all part of God's plan
 So, lift up your head and rejoice this is another beautiful day.

Easter is on its way, a rebirth, everything looks fresh and new.
 God's son gave us his promise and Easter confirms the fact that
this is true. The wonder of Easter unfolds its story
 Proclaiming life's promise of eternal glory.

The day is as fresh as a newborn child.
 Early morning air is clean and mild.
Flowers are in full bloom nearby
 And, they welcome a visit from a beautiful butterfly.

The church bells are loudly ringing
 Listen closely and you can almost hear the angels singing.
So, lift up your hearts and sing praises with your voice,
 "The Lord is risen", In praise, we rejoice.

Assess all nature in full array dressed for this special morn
 The crisp, new Easter dresses, after today, will be worn.
Compare all beauty and then stand in awe of the dogwood tree.
 This is how I see Easter in the year of 93.
 Va.

Wish

"I want to be a clown and make a lot of people
laugh when I grow up."
Said he when he was very young
But he never was.

"I want to be a fine athlete
and everyone will praise me."
Said he when he was a teenager.
But he never was.

"I want to be a great lover
and all the girls will want me"
Said he when he was a young man.
But he never was.

"I want to be a great financial success
and I can buy anything I want."
Said he when he was middle aged.
But he never was.

"I think I'll just be ME."
He was older now
and suddenly happy.
 Robert Loomis

The World

I stand there as the rain roles down my face;
just watching the world and all its disgrace.
People yelling and fighting, and people just there;
what is the world about one big scare.
Some people don't even know where they'll be tomorrow;
it makes me kind of sad and fills my heart with sorrow.
Some people may be homeless or may even be dead;
it's like their life is hanging by one piece of thread.
It's like their life is hanging by one piece of thread.
Hopefully one day this world of bad will end;
and people's lives and hearts will then start to mend.

Sara Fortner

Untitled

The world is gray,
Just a mixture of black and white.
Black or white.
Not red, nor blue, nor purple.
The world is a simple place
But is complicated by its dwellers,
Who mix everything into a collage of confusion,
And destruction and fear.
We are simple people with complicated minds,
Afraid to give something a chance.
We dare not be different,
For we fear the ignorant
Who know, no better.

Kateri Gaskin

Love Is

Love is having your very own puppy,
Kitten, hamster, or even a guppy.
Love is arguing with your brother,
Father, sister or your mother.

Giving hugs when you've made up,
Overflows your loving cup.
Religion or family, it's all the same,
You have only love in return to gain.

Most of all, hold dear in your heart,
The parents that have given you your start.

Wendy Hager

Annie

  Full haloed moon...
Lavender night sky...
Mists of Night push as, moisturous breath exhaled,
   sends asphalt concrete smothered withered
day's heat's perfume inland to rattlered tarantulated
   rocks, gullies and once watered drybeds.

  Ripe scented sea kelp...
Jasmine flavored grass...
Mists of Nights push as, domiciled aircraft leave
   quiet zones of quizzical looks of absented void
melodious with unheard sand ruffles of sharktailed waving
   silent gusts.

  Muffled ship horn...
Hiss of salted hull...
Mists of Night push as, flattened wave meets
   envelope of grey sealing time, movement,
hopes of another day away with Full Haloed moon.
   Lavender night sky...

Patricia Armstrong Bartlett

The Empty House

Empty house, how sad it is when people have to
   leave because of sickness of death.
Each room holds memories of things said and done.
Cherished are the family gatherings, Holiday
   dinners, and the beginning of each New Year.
Window are all shut, doors are all closed,
   and a still is in the air.
The dust settles in, the cobwebs come,
   and the mice begin to run.
The "for sale" sign goes up on the lawn outside,
   and new people come and want to buy.
Empty house, you will soon be filled again with
   new memories of things said and done.
The dust will be wiped away, the cobwebs will
   come down, and the cat will chase the mice around.

Lillian Barb

Reflections

Time, "Oh", how I've weathered,
leaving carved lines and shades of gray.
I see my reflection in the mirror,
images long forgotten, of my yesterday.

Those times, long gone and never to return,
my past I know, my present I see.
Traveling life's highway of mass confusion,
I often wonder what my future could be.

Performing on the stage of the living present,
has left me divorced from what's real.
Dreaming of a special soul to identify with,
someone to hold forever, feeling what I feel.

To many sleepless nights have come and gone,
what about all the forgotten promises alas.
From those here and beyond we've encountered,
they are the chapters, in our book of the past.

We must face the future with hope,
because nothing will ever remain the same.
Hopefully leaving a small mark behind,
leaving mankind a better place to claim.

Tim Pugh

We Are One

Each ecstasy that you have made me feel
lets me know that fantasies can be real.

You have gently caressed my soul
held me in your arms, made me whole.

There are no chains binding my spirit.
The voice of doom I cannot hear it.

And darling I will forever cherish your heart
and I will know that we should never be apart.
But when I cannot be there to hold you and comfort you and love you

Think of me in a soft special way,
I will remember your smile all day.

And I will miss and want you and need you
to come home to me to share
in our love that is so rare.

A love that is magnified each time our flesh is one
as our bodies pull together from moonlight to sun

And we satisfy again our ravenous desire for
more, still more tasting together, teasing, pleasing...

and loving,
until our breath is from one body and we are one.

C. Lucas

The Garden Of Court

In the garden of court
Lies grow as the weeds.
Wild and free,
Suffocating truth from all light of day.
No drink of hope,
No nutrients but betrayal.

Pushing, pushing, to rise above,
Truth shines at last for a brief interlude.
Then is crushed again by the lies overgrowth.

"Give up, "say the weeds,
"You'll ne'er flower again."
"Never, "says the truth;
"I will live beyond."

"For God is my glory,
Salvation my hope."
Truth finally wins when lies are exposed.

Nanette Metskas McCarthy

Peace Of A Rose

The rose opens as the new day breaks.
Light shines on the destruction during the night.
The men are sore with many pains and aches.
During war the scars are symbols of the fight.

While a rose is a symbol of hope.
Peace is sure to come in time.
Beauty of a rose is like medicine to cope.
With the death, pain, and crime.

The rose softly cries.
As a boy goes off to fight.
Knowing that many more will die.
She stands innocently in the light.

When a soldier picks her from her stem.
And smells her sweet scent.
He plucks the petals as if gems
Then gives them to his comrades showing peace is heaven sent.

Michael Eichner

Dark Life

   I look around for something in
life that is right but every time, I turn around
and see a whole new dark life.
   Dark life is a dream I have
all my life and I, pray, pray that someday
it will go away.
   Dark life is like a dream
to me, it makes me think of things, kind and
sweet to me.
   Dark life it is sweet to me
because, when I think of dark I think of
my life being in a tunnel of darkness.
   Every time I think of dark
I think of many marks upon a tree
that bring out the gift in me.

Pamela Walker

Poor Or Rich

We may be poor in material things,
Like a fancy house and diamond rings.
We don't drive an expensive car,
Nor travel to places that are too far.
But I really don't care,
Because my family can share,
Something that means much more,
Than the house, car and travels to a distant shore.
We have love, caring and laughter,
For this day and forever after.
That's something money can't buy,
And with each day it will multiply.
So to those who think rich means,
The things you buy with dollars so green,
I feel very sad for you,
That you couldn't be rich like me too.

Mary R. Miller

Grace

Little girl within,
  lifeless, breathless rag doll
Obedient, docile child
  who has forgotten how to dance to the music of her own soul.

Wounded, broken spirit
  no longer able to hear the voice of the Sacred within
A soul filled with terror and pain
  listening only to voices that bury dreams
  and turn wonder into worry.

And then, one day, an unexpected whisper
  calling her to life once again
  a feeling of being cradled in holy arms
  a breath of life blown into her suffocating shell
  a recreation of dust and clay.

Oh empty, little one,
  Receive
  Breathe
  Dance

  Be Filled

Mary Heintzkill

Hurricane

Hovering o'er the mellow moon an illuminating light
Like a halo cast its spell upon the sweetness of the night.
Not a star shone in the heavens and the clouds fell close and low;
Before us beat the angry surf. Pounding its turbulent way
Beyond the great unknown was stretched; it all before us lay
As quickly from the sky above, from behind the mountain peak,
Came the whistling wind, witching storm, tempest which legends bespeak
All in a moment it passed us by and there, 'neath the palm with
  delight,
A bit awe-struck and wondering too, at the magnitude of the sight,
We turned our eyes to the heaven as the moon bowed out from a cloud;
Gaily she laughed from her throne in the sky, gone was her mournful shroud;
A million stars were carefully placed, iridescent, across the night.
Breakers subdued, evening calm; all with the world was right.
But never again do I wish to see a halo 'round the moon
Nor a weird, illuminating light accenting the breakers' boom.
For mine a nod, smile from the stars, kiss of the gentle breeze.
Horizons of softness spread afar for the eyes and the heart to seize.

Sara Hewitt Riola

Humanity

A seashell
  like a human
if not perfect
thrown back or not accepted.
All of them have some flaws
  like us.
Can we accept them the way they are
or change them like the sea does to a shell?
Shape it, mold it into something we can accept
Is that fair?
Why can we not keep it and treasure it for its worth?
Why toss it aside because we think it is imperfect?
Accept each as it is - treasure it
  for no two are alike.
    Marilyn Goode Weber

Mr. Can, Sir

The body slowly deteriorating,
Like a rat, you gnaw at the rope of life.
You cause pain - deep and severe.
And, force me to deal with you year after year.

So fierce you are,
You make me see red and burn within my soul.
Yet, the darkness of your nature represents the thief you are.
You've stolen so many priceless jewels and precious stones.

Your attempt to exist in me;
Thank God, for reasons unknown have failed.
Yet, the lessons learned and the fear instilled have only been too real.

The many thoughts of never:
Seeing my success, Finding my love,
Mothering a child, Being able to give back to those deserving,
Feeling blessed, seeing the light,
Have taught me to live every day of my life extremely.

The lesson, "Be thankful for the little things..."
Has nonetheless ripened and grown.

Obstacles overcome.
The belief, "Everything happens for a reason."
But, "Why, Mr. Can; Sir, must it take something so bad...?"
    Marjorie Joseph

Eternal

The leaves of the trees take flight to the ground
like butterflies dancing in song;
and catching the sight of them once and again,
I admit to you; I was all wrong.
You called me the sun, I called you the moon,
we both agreed we had our doubt.
But sitting here, listening, passing our time
is turning me inside and out.
When new flowers die around the new stone
and ground heals above your new bed,
I don't think that it will matter at all
what you did, or what I said.
As the sun disappears behind all of our years,
remembering only the best,
I lay here beside you, above and beyond,
Together we receive our rest.
And now the moon rises, your scent in the wind,
the roses so bitter and sweet;
Though we depart now, so much as in love,
I know once again we will meet.
    Marcella Johnson

It Couldn't Be...

It's your memory that flies
like pollen from the flower of time...
It's your caress, your kiss,
the fragrance that travels through the air that I breath...
Once more you become part of my days,
Once more I think of your return...
Our romance couldn't be a legend, a myth,
because the fire of your body
left its traces marked on mine...
I keep on dreaming of the magic
that your burning skin irradiated in the moment
of our fusion;
When you were looking for refuge and being a fugitive,
you fell prisoner in the nets of a savage passion...
But everything was that way,
we searched for the endless ecstasy
in the union of two fleshes,
and it was the total consummation of two souls
that were vibrating to the rhythm of one heart...
No, our love couldn't be a legend nor a myth...
    Saul E. Bautista

Pearl Moon

The dark clouds cover the pearl moon
like the cloak of death worn by lonely men's souls
as if to never show its face again,
but let known there by the tears of rain.
Vast and plain it sits staring at sadness as it turns time
at a never ending pace.
Starvation of its shine, it willows at a cotton cloud
filled with nothing but dead thoughts and empty hearts,
to which never were fulfilled at its time.
Yet the unknown powers of the moon still conger,
and man, who knows all, can't explain its nirvana.
    Virginia Smith

A Son's Favorite

My heart boils with a simmering desire to find peace
Like the quiet of the ancient mountain valleys.
I do not want to be questioned
  As to the validity of my beliefs.
Because they are personal only to me.
All of us know what we want
But we are often misled by the distractions of life.
Hence, we often struggle with issues that are immaterial
  To the resolution of life.
Just as the vain person may believe
In the image of a mirror - The distracted person
May listen to the noise of a crowd
  Believing it to be the voice of life;
Thus, He may live without allowing his own identity to surface.
    J. W. Martin

Love

Love is a gift, a treasure, a joy,
Love is not to be played with,
Love is not a toy.

Love is a piece of silk, shining and glowing,
Love is a brook, rippling and flowing.

Love is a candle burning clear and forever,
Love will never burn out,
Never, ever.
    Kelly Knight

"Chiisai Was Her Name"

Most beautiful of blue, were her eyes
   Like the sky, after a storm
Her fur, so soft to touch
   On a body, so tiny and warm

Little ears, move to the sound of a whisper
   Her voice, like a tigers roar
So dainty was she at meal time
   At her place mat on the floor

Games she played with her master
   Hide and seek, it would be
Later, so tired, her breathing so fast
   I think she was laughing at me

A traveling companion she was
   In the back seat of the car
Every thing for her convenience
   Treated, like a movie star

Twenty one years she belonged to me
   But death finally came
A siamese cat she was
   And Chiisai was her name.
    Margaret R. Potts

Life Long Friendship

Just seeing your face brightens my day.
Like the sun you bring light into the windows of my heart.
My soul flies free like a butterfly in the shade of your warmth.
Like a true friend your smile gives me strength,
   to face the unknown.
But yet when you're not around I still feel your presence
   by my side, guiding me in the right direction
   of my destiny, to conquer the unseen.
For this I love you as if to love a part of my own
   self-being and image.
But yet to know two things so close are not as one in flesh
   but in soul.
Always a space in my memory no matter how vague the
   image may be,
   will be a picture of you always being there for me.
For this I give you undying love and gratitude.
   For your will so strong.
For true friendship that time nor space can fade.
In my memory thou will always stay
   Until my time is passed away, no sooner could come that day.
    Michelle Paige

The Nobel Cottonwood

Try relaxing under a grand cottonwood tree,
Listen to the whisper of things she has seen.

Her leaves clap with pleasure, as stories unfold;
Head held high, body sturdy and bold.

Spreading long arms to embrace each day,
Shielding all creatures with her span of shade.

Perseverance of life that flows ever strong,
While her shower of cotton dance with a song.

The gnarled old bark, wrinkled with age;
Grandmother to nature, wise and unafraid.

A nurturing home for many, as a playground of fun;
Sentry to the weak and ascending prey on the run.

Like all things of old, she becomes broken and bent;
Still grasping to life, as the mighty wind blasts.

Refusing persuasion—holding firm to beliefs;
One nobel cottonwood reluctantly weeps.
    Shauna Vucetich

God's Grace

She walks in silence
Listening to her heart
She smiles in God
For he loves her

She lives for this love
In which she gives to others
Living in his eyes
She breathes his word

She promises to be faithful
And full of selflessness
As she loses herself
In order to love unconditionally

She pleases herself
For in her heart
She knows this is good
For she lives in God's grace.
    Lisa J. Sievers

Untitled

When I lie awake at night
listening to the rapid, monotonous beating of my heart.
I wonder if my loneliness and I will ever stray.
My soul lays forever restless
While my spirit stays at war.
The uncontentment of my heart never
leaves me alone.
The continuous slashing of my dreams departs
from my presence leaving wounds as deep as
the blood that runs through the veins of a family
The torture changes my mind to a cold,
meaningless, thinking time bomb that makes me
feel alone and very afraid.
As long as that blackness fills my chest
and the coldness fills my soul,
I will forever truly remain alone.
    Rana DeBey

Darkness

The sky is a mural of black,
Lit only by the twinkle of distant stars,
That shine like diamonds in a far away mine.
Yet there is no one there to gather the precious stones,
Only darkness.
The wind blows sharply through the forest,
Chilling an abandoned child,
And making it cry.
Yet there is no one there to answer its calls,
Only darkness.
An old beggar walks the streets,
Peddling tacky souvenirs,
And is greeted by a local thug.
Yet there is no one there to help this man,
Only darkness.
    Robert J. Mishur

Fading Flower

My life is like a fading flower
My feelings grow dimmer by the hour
I close up tight with secure walls
Caring less and less with each petal that falls
The flowers around me are yellow and bright
They get all the glory and block off my light
Nobody's looking as I fall to the ground
Look at all the pretty flowers that grow all around
    Susan Natale

Architect

    The architecture of the mind
   leads a stairway lit,
  to a buried secret
 which others cannot find.
Up in the attic lies high hope,
   for dreams of being
   and a world of believing
   parallel to each slope.
   In the basement of the mind
   your path is not clear
   and your darkest fear
   lurks close behind
    in a place you don't want to find
    in a place you don't want to find.

Matt Soloway

Constitutional America (The Beautiful)

When I was born, as I am told, there were three guarantees.
Life was the first. I was here out of some cursed family tree.
Liberty, the second of them, was not mine to behold.
The third and most important one was stolen by the bold.
Pursuit of happiness can not occur with out the liberty.
Life can not be surely life if denied we can be free.
Freedom is now mine I know. I caught on kind of late.
But better late than never I supposed has been my fate.
So now I pursue that happiness which is most precious and dear
And take nothing for granted as closer and closer I near
The goals I've set in my life which I should share and give.
Life, Liberty and the Pursuit of Happiness makes it wonderful to live.

Lisa M. Lindstrom

A Daughter Never Known

The child that is not born,
  lives quietly in my mind's eye
The child that will not be,
  sleeps softly with me
For though I will never see her face,
  or hold her hand,
  I see her clearly
different places, different times
She hides in secret corners
  deep in my soul
and startles me in the smile
  of some other shining face
I imagine her laughter, her hair, her eyes
and wonder if she watches me,
  reaches to me.
   from her place I cannot see
The child that is not born
 I'll love forever
The daughter that will not be
  still lives in me.

Margery Dempsey Bogus

Untitled

Lustfulness
Lustfulness is so thick in my mind,
that it's choking my heart.
Pain through my whole body as days pass by.
How long, how long before I give in to it.
Lusting for others most valued possessions.
Gold and silver is nothing.
I keep telling myself this,
But actions speak louder than words.
It's eating away at my soul.
Oh, please take this lustful mind of mine
And turn it to something to please my divine God.

Phillep Person

"I'm Just Missing My Daddy"

I'm just thinking about my Daddy -
Living high up in the clouds;
knowing that he's looking down
upon me from heaven above.

I'm just remembering my Daddy -
And all the special times that we shared
when no one else seemed to care.

I'm just honoring my Daddy -
Because he adopted me when I was just a baby,
and made me feel like his "special" little lady.

I'm just loving my Daddy -
He was so very strong, and
he helped me when I went wrong.
He was a man of great strength and love
who is now flying free as a dove.

I'm just missing my Daddy -
Wishing I could be with him
up above in the soft white clouds
of peace, love and harmony!!!

Kathy M. Dolle Ater

Ode To Harriet Tubman
(an emancipation of the underground railroad)

Am dis yo' chile
  lo dese many yeah's
I spects hits mo den
  many lon yeah's
Sense dese here folks called' yo name
  believe me, we'se just de same
Cause tings hav' made so lil change

Am dis yo' chile
  seems lak I feel de pain
  dat troubl'd yo' heart,
hear it, hyeah me
lo dese many yeah's
  Am dis yo' chile

Norma Shelby

Dr. In The Mirror - March 95

Think me not lonely for thinking
lofty thoughts of solitude,
A self indulgence I take
to motivate the plan.

Threading thoughts and declining decisions,
who watches wheels when I win?
Good, guile, guilt and clock
to motivate the "Doc".

Personal perseverance
estranged from achievement.
Who know how few show
the victory shallow?

The circle, complete conscience
just The just judge.
Life lies latent,
escape in effort.

J. Maurice Hourihane

Inner Self

Who am I?...I am a portrait of my inner self.
Look deep within to find the answer.
Days and nights go by, that I torment myself,
looking, searching, but never finding my inner self.
Can it be? That reality has finally taken
a hold of me, am I trap within myself
forever? My God! I pray that the day
would come, when I can reach out and say,
it's me! I have arrived! I have found my
inner self....It took me years to get in
touch with my inner self, days and months of
struggling, overcoming obstacles, making and
breaking decisions, and just the mere fact of
growing... After years of feeling like my life
was never organized, it's finally coming together.
I decided to sit down and search deep within
myself to find the true me, you know, I'm glad
I did....I found truth, acceptance, love,
courage, motivation, and best of all respect, respect
for me, respect for you, and respect for my inner self.
Michelle Duggins

September Morn

Such a delight, this September Morn.
Looking at the crimson sky at the break of dawn.
The autumn air kindles embers of the heart,
Yet soothing is the wind, like a tender touch.
Dancing with the sunlit skies, rays of sunbeams on the dewy grass.
Oh how lovely, September Morn.
As I watch the shimmering waters of the lake
Illuminating hues of red, yellow, and blue.
Fascinating.
Savor the beauty.
The colors of autumn air radiant in the crisp air, as the
leaves rustles in a stately manner.
September Morn amidst nature, precious beauty in search of you.
You are mine forever more.
Sheliagh Joseph

Thinking Of You

Although we haven't had a chance to talk, I'm still
looking forward to holding your hand as we walk.
Two people brought together by fate, both looking for
that extra something to help keep us straight.

Each writing to you is just a little part
Of how I feel, from the bottom of my heart.
I have many hobbies that I'd like to share, if you'll
give me the chance to show I really care.

I'm an honest person and I say what I feel,
And I will admit it's your heart I'm out to steal.
You are a beautiful young lady that I'd like to get to know
better, so why not give it a chance or we both may regret it.

I'd like for us to start out as friends, and let the
fate that brought us together never end.
Lawrence I. Zippin

The Open Ended

Entering the open ended a salute comes to mind. Here's to
metamorphosing to bits, to the mere accident of order in chaos and
the exploration of the micro and macro Universe in an endless
effort to reach dimensionless space.
Here's to a celebration of nature and life to the fine art of painting
in all its forms and to the hope and faith in constancy and continuity
upon entering the Twenty First Century.
H. Marie Murphy

Night After Night

I sat on the bathtub side
looking into your cerulean watering eyes.
I know you were drunk.
I knew that every night.
You would use me as your pillow
and I Would accept.
My butt fell asleep and
I told you everything would be all right.
You would just sit on the toilet
with pink sponge curlers in your hair
and sunken eyes hiding behind your bony palms
while you sobbed — sobbed like a baby.
You were a water mill - always churning and
water flowing and never getting anywhere.
I sat on that tub until my butt fell asleep
or until there wasn't any more water.
Steven T. Schmidt

hand me downs

silver names on silver chains,
lost but found again
and almost forgotten,
smiles and hand squeezes,
dreamily she asked if she will be remembered.

memories stuffed in old borrowed socks,
never to be worn again by the same person,
the stale candy in a jar
but the flowers are gone, the dirt is bad,
we will remembeR.

candles are lit
and the wind blows,
fire stays in the hearts
of the children looking on,
we will remembeR.

the procession moves on,
eyes come out of a daze,
minds return to the present,
gripping the blood pumping muscle,
i will remembeR, always.
Naomi Tarle

"Circulate Love"

I am loved and loving;
Love circulates through our minds
And also through our bodies,
Love quiets our anxiety,
Softens our voice,
Quickens our actions
Love lifts us above any and all challenges,
Giving us perspective that will
Help us to understand our
Important place and role in life,
And the good we have to contribute;
Whatever we think, say or do,
We want it to be with love;
The love we give and share,
Comforts, strengthens, heals and motivates
Not only me, but you and, others too!
So let all that we do be done in love!
Nathaniel Birch Simon II

The Final Stage Of Life Is Death

Can one have this wish upon request
Love is death, death is love
Set aside from above
O blessed with death just to be blessed
Like an old friend
or a real good quest
Always welcome in this heart of mine
Is there pain, its not explained
Show me a signal, show me a sign
Unconditional love for death
Internal life or internal rest
The forbidden angel will take the fall
Death can save us, but not us all

Kirk Lindner

Reflections Of Beauty

Opening my eyes, let's lights twinkle - reflections in loving eyes of earth.

Wince for stars passing on staircase of cloud - a touch of warm breath, for her smile a fallen angels head be bowed.

The night lives on. Riding upon wicks of hair - so silken her skin - so soft a touch of precious silver. Can my hands cease to quiver.

The eve grows dark, my lasting heart grows cold. I mercifully kneel in face of lasting beauty, tenderly beneath her feet.

My sword upon my shoulder, she dances out of sight - not to have felt or touched her warm lips - come again beautiful lady. Save my heart tonight.

Always the wind, her fragrance, until all of our todays and tomorrows, our hopes and desires on a tide of empty hearts and dreams slumber on moonbeams to rest.

William M. Winspear

Royal Nature

Imperial water lilies promenade atop a lucent empire,
majestic scepters adorning their master.
Dominance proclaimed.
Hypnotic, pungent aromas imbue the grand arena.
Suspended animation.
Sudden wisps of air march.
Awakened, enchanted nymphs salute with their
chlorophyll appendages.
Prowess evinced.
Unsuspecting land sleeps.
Diving deep into the watery fortress, the ouzel
becomes the court jester.
Mused, Mother Nature laughs, then
cradles her citizens as night draws nigh.

Kathleen A. Kolar

Laughing Hands

   The unseen of it all
Makes the realness of it small
And the parts we all play are just tokens
   The games people play
Effect us still today
But the purpose of it all is forgotten
   Greediness is the key
Oh that's what they believe
Playing parts in his wicked imagination
   In the blink of an eye
All the puppets must die
Still seeking for that false mis-salvation
   The laughter echoes on
In the stillness of black dawn
When the game starts clean over with new pieces.

Manuel Marquez

Caveat Emptor

Don't want to make you scared
Make you lose or raise your hair
But consumers are at war and all is fair
So it is the buyer who should beware
Delivering a sermon you won't hear in churches
This is how to determine what you purchase
You need to apply a strategic plan;
Keep supplied, increase demand
The plan is words so parse the phonics
Add a few charts from economics
To the topic that I will be covering
Why the consumer is the sovereign
The king of beasts, like the lion
You're the king when you're buying
Just a king? Why not emperor
So remember Caveat Emptor

The customer is king, why not emperor
Why should we have to Caveat Emptor
Do it year round, January to December
And remember, Caveat Emptor

Martin White

Looking Back Over 48 Years Of Marriage

John was always positive about handling any handicaps making most of ones best.

Self-pity was not part of his character.

He always had the kind of faith that produces courage.

We did disagree at times with zest, but somehow - no debris from the past encounters cluttered up the future.

After all most marriages have some ups and downs!

Under John's coat was a heavy heart, but a kind one. One that would do nobody any harm.

John was most always kind and thoughtful, and a mighty easy man to live with.

I will miss him very much.

He had four excellent Doctors trying to help him get well, but I believe our Father in Heaven needs him up there.

Peggy Griffith

Petty Peers

The kids at school were mean to me
Mama said they were jealous
Of my wonderful good looks
And my exceeding bright intelligence.

She told me not to listen,
But to ignore their words instead;
Not even to pay attention
To anything they said.

She said that I could tell them,
If they kept on being mean,
That I would tell Teacher on them,
And that would stop their steam.

"But really, it would be better", she said,
"To look at them sweetly and smile instead."
So I did that, and do you know what?
They quit being mean to me - they stopped!

Somehow they got embarrassed
And looked ashamed and shy
When I responded to their taunts
With my lovely winsome smile.

Martha Turner

A Gift Of Divine

Individuals that touches my heart
May know something that I may not
A gift of divine.

To give me strength, happiness
In you I may find sweet success
Of a gift to define.

In you I may find strength, happiness on high,
Continue to touch my heart and draw me nigh.
God is able and divine.

Pearlie B. Spencer

Questions Unaswered

After years of searching the answers start to flow
Maybe soon I will understand what made you go
I'm hoping that this doesn't turn out to be
Just another big disappointment for me.
I'm looking forward to finding you, Dad.
I think you should know about the life I had
What were you doing when I was left alone?
Why didn't you try to find me? Or pick-up the phone.
Where did you go? What did you do?
These are just some of my questions for you!

Yvonne Casal-Tillman

Who I Am

Sometimes a man caught in a world of greed
Maybe the role of a child with a demanding need.
More confused with the reality of life,
Too often neglecting his loving wife.

Ignoring perceptions of dreams that were made,
Struggling identity that just seem to fade.
Gifted qualities not always endured,
Misguided martyr, too easily lured.

Forever competing against one's own guilt
Searching for the keystone of a better life to be built.
Conservative thoughts that hinder success,
Still driving for only the best.

Years of hard work taking it's toll,
Always in search of life's purpose and goal.
Yet refusing to falter when I'm in a jam,
Because I can succeed, I can change,
The person I am.

Peter T. Stoeckel Sr.

You Were There

When things go wrong as they sometimes do, you came to
Me from out of the blue. In times of trouble and despair
I looked around and you were there.

Life is worth living with ups and downs, turning a smile
into a frown, when all seems bad and up in the air
I looked around and you were there.

In times of pain, your voice is soothing, knowing that
you I can't stand losing. When all seems lost and
worse for ware, I looked around and you were there.

When I am lonely, as I often feel, I know this
friendship is for real. Like De Ja Vu or ESP, I
know that she will stand by me.

When the phone rings, I pick up and stare
Knowing that someone really cares. Now things
are fine, I am no longer scared, cause
I looked around and you were there.

Theresa Patton

"The Candle Watcher"

Ever watch candles burn?
Melting wax, so smooth and hot.
Velvet flames kissing the air.
They look like lovers.
 I think of you we were once
like candles. Smoldering, dancing
fire and air meeting together...
Ever watch candles burn? Wax,
like molten lava, welling upon the top.
It creeps closer to the edge, too full,
dying to be released, like me.
 Now I watch candles burn, I see
them crying hot angry tears. Like
me, when I think of you.
 Seering flames peter to the wick and die.
Melted wax, once dangerous to the touch
is now cold and hard.
Like my heart when I think of you...

Lora De Blasio

Best Friend

A best friend is a beautiful thing.
Memories to keep from summers, fall, and spring.
I loved you like a sister, I loved you like a friend.
But now I feel so sorry, that it had to end.
You always made me smile, it always felt so great,
But when you moved away, all I felt was hate.
I'll think about you often, and wish that you were here,
I still can see your smile, please wipe away my tears.
We shared our heart and secrets we cried and laughed a lot.
We knew we were the best of friends,
at least that's what I thought.

Tonya Avalos

Colour Guard

Red married yellow one dawning
Midst tears of joy from the dew,
As a wondrous elm with its green-leaf awning,
Waved at the azure blue.

Gold of the heather danced in the breeze
Attended by violet and puce.
A comatose rainbow awoke o'er the leas,
And a chorus of colour broke loose.

Brown, pink and mauve arrived on the hills
On this phantasmagorical day,
And the lush, tall grass, nudged by the wind,
Tickled each blade in its sway.

Concentric circles containing the stars
Now doth earth adorn,
As red and yellow fuse in a cloud
Beauty Born.

Lawrence Martin

Creation

Sculptured in the stone of the Mountains.
Moulded in the wet flesh of the leaves.
Composed in the rhythm of the streams.
Etched in the fertile soil of the earth.

Come to me... come to me...
With your passionate heart.

Your image binds me with love and fear.
Gentle touch of creation
You are here.....

Richard Koster

Silverbird

What was it that caught my disbelieving eye?
Might have been the silverbird,
gliding through my open arms,
somebody he loves.
Round and round,
not supposed to stay,
not supposed to hold onto
Did I perceive a sigh, a last deep breath?
So much love in a single dancing feather!
One last sign, one last breath.
Look up! He fades!
A trace of golden light
remains forever in the breeze.
And so it goes,
and so it goes...
Simone Schachl

Soldier Of Life

I have run with determination across the
mine fields of life. And have fought to death with honor,
against opposition and strife.

I have crawled the walls of social disruption
often hurt and worn. And many times rebuilt a heart
in pieces broken and torn.

I have chased the light of righteousness throughout
all the years. And fallen back holding mine over
darkness, in shame and in tears.

I have strived to succeed for beyond all the rest.
and fought even myself to pass my father's test.

I stand a soldier of life not yet allowed to retire
and battle on through everyday in the midst of
worldly cross fire.

And yet against the fullness of time I'll not return
or retreat. For God my father in memory of you
will always conquer defeat.
Jack Gandesbery

A Child's Monster

She sits so quietly in the chimney space,
listening to hear if the monster is near.

The monster hurt her, but she does not understand,
that the mean bad monster is really a man.

Hiding in boxes, with clothes over her head,
she makes sure she is buried except for her breath.

Crouching and cringing, she sits there and waits,
hoping and praying that he won't make her ache.

Hiding and holding her breath all these years from a monster
she truly did believe in and fear,

Only now she grows older and the truth becomes clear.
She opens her eyes and she sees whom she fears.

It was not a monster she hid from at all.
It was her brother who molested her when she was small.
Valerie Jane Tonkovich

Magnificent Beauty

If only you could capture the beauty of the sun setting down on the earth
With its bright orange light laying across the entire medium
blue sky with its so many shades of blue falling down into even layers
Separating the skies from the sparkling city lights as the sun
slowly fades away to its resting spot for the night
Only to appear fresh and vibrant the next morning to awaken
the earth with its bright rays of sunshine
Ah- if only you could capture such magnificent beauty
Kressy Silver

First Dance

His arms slipped easily around my waist
  my heart skipped a beat as I looked into his face

Our bodies easily tightened together
  almost as softly as a bird and it's feathers

Heat generated between us ever so quickly
  that my stomach became tense, queezy, and sickly

As his warm breath entered my virgin ears
  my arms were entranced to pull him near

At that moment I was in the clouds high up above
  but my heart knew the truth, I was really in Love
Katie Miltner

This Is My Prayer

Dear God in heaven please here
my cry and prayer as I go through
all of life, problem, trial and tribulation
I need all of my strength, and my
family to be with me, so God in heaven
I need you to guide me through all
of these things, and lead me out
of this family of hell. So we
can pray together.
Mary L. Freeman Jones

Terror

The dark, black night, illuminated by the
moonlight, the light reflected boldly on
clans white-hooded suits, his pus-filled
eye dimmed what little light he had,
Pushing, stumbling, frantically his heart beat
in horror, falling to his knees, begging,
pleading, screaming, praying, his hate-
filled heart now stung with fear, as the
leader of the mob gave a cruel, dispassionate
laugh, in his hand dangled his victims
destiny. Pity? He had none, the man's cries
of desperation went unheard, and as the mob
obeyed the harsh commands of their leader,
they scornfully mocked and put the beaten
man to shame. Seconds later, the masked
figures rudely shoved him to the stool.
Stunned, he stepped up, as the rope entangled
his neck he whispered "Have mercy", he
disgorged his last breath, as billowing
clouds of light engulfed him. HOME FREE!
Sarita DeLos Santos

Submerged In His Routine's Life (The Man)

Submerged in his routine's life and without no
more exits, today's man walks every day in
this steel and plastic world and in his walk.
does not make no more remarks as his ancients
philosopher's made, the only inheritance he is
leaving today is smog, fatigue, loneliness and afraid.

submerged in his routine's life walks with more
sadness than ever before, because he is thinking.
Just in himself and He does not matter the rest
of species get extinguished.

Submerged in his routine's life breaking anything
in his way today's man walk to the end because
God does not guide him any more.
Ricardo Rivera

Untitled

I swam among the myriad colors of the ocean
Moving and reflecting
What does it all mean?
Is this 'Maya' that the world talks of?
The answer came back with the waves
Screaming at me
I AM
And
So
You ARE.
Usha Ayyagari

The Leaves

The many leaves dance slowly in the trees,
Moved by a subtle whim,
Creating the music of an ancient hymn.
Young creatures are carried aloft and fly,
Others are born and more than a few die.

The many leaves are now carelessly torn from saddened trees
As the wind howls its mad chorus.
And all in all, the storm devastates the young, virgin forest.

The wind now sends a gentle breeze floating through barren trees
As if to apologize for past offenses by nurturing with loving caresses.
And the new leaves sing the story
Of a matured forest in unimaginable glory,
But the wind continues its sighing
And creatures continue their dying.

The many leaves slowly swirl away from old forgotten trees.
I sit alone and listen to the sad song
Of leaves pining for times now gone.
"And was it worth it?" I ask the forest,
And in reply I hear the beautiful ancient chorus.
Kenneth L. Miller

I Can See You, Read You Writer

The writer spoke - unto himself
Moved down his pencil, and then gently wrote.
While setting to his side, top to bottom
His shot glass high and dry.

After grabbing the stained yellowed paper beneath his callused palms
His thoughts began, well read lying scattered upon
The tight fisted lines that cradle his hope;
Draining into the dark eve of night
That buried the wind on the street below.

His canter was that of nothing more than a moan
That grew coarse and more bubbled as the evening drew to its close.
His arm moved lengthwise across his chest
Grabbing fiercely at the bottle casting a shadow - lightly just.

A teardrop fell across his nose;
Drenched with hate and riddled with fear his pain gently rose.
His eyes grew more colorless, wild, and wide
As he let fly high and loose to himself
For which in opening he writes:
I am alone. Bitterly, I am all alone.
Shane Hull

Moonlight

Through the cloudy darkness
Of the fallen night
One moonbeam
Pale and silent
Slices a silvery path through the navy sky
Shinning down with a luminescent glow
And bringing a symbol of hope
To a shattered world.
Sherrie Jackson

The Wind

She whistles and sings so happily.
Moving around from tree to tree - sea to sea.
Oh, to be so wild and free!
When she's in my face the world's carefree.
I love her force - her strength - her abilities.

She must be a spirit from a long ago world
Who's vengeance is forceful,
She can kill when she swirls.
Or be as soft as a kiss on a new baby's face.
She's a spirit of color, beauty and grace.

So where did she came from?
Where will she go?
She's as old as time,
And that's all that we know.

But she must have been doing something right,
In her day, her time, her living life.
For she was blessed with the perfect eternity.
Moving around from tree to tree - sea to sea.
Oh, to be so wild and free!
Theresa Priebe

There Is A Crowd

There is a crowd out there tonight,
Much larger than anyone would expect.
Entwined, webbed, intermingled in their own priorities.

There is a crowd out there tonight,
with a history making more histories.
Bringing all their experiences and expectations
from one moment to the next.

They recorded your wealth and live with the profits.

They are your living records,
Effected, enriched, inspired, changed,
Moving from one generation to the next
Bringing you with them.

They are your living records.

Now dispersed, in their homes,
Yet, in some wondrous, exquisite, intelligent, miraculous way
You lie with them.

There is a crowd out there tonight,
much better than anyone would expect.
Mary Ann Greco

Of Human Killers

Oh, will you ever learn that upon your streets there are riots
Murderers go free and kill again
Your people ridicule those whose skin is different
You don't care what happens so long that you come out ahead
In the dark corners there is somebody who is starving
Somebody who gets robbed of what is rightfully his
But still you cower to do anything about it
From this you get your pockets full
While those that you don't care about go on suffering
What do you care! Upon thy highways is someone who is a killer
A killer of mankind but yet he goes unnoticed
Someone who does only one crime you jump on him
But if his skin is another color
He is tagged as to being a criminal forever. But what do you care!
There are others who rob, stealing from those who are not well off
Those who cheat the public; even some of your men in government
Even those are as dishonest as those who get away with murder.
But like all places you have your good. But when will it ever show up
When in this barren land of lost love will you come to prove yourself
For it is said that you will pay the toll for what has happened
 in your land.
Kathy A. Houck-Simcox

His Empty Goldfish Tank

His fish tank hides in the wall behind the door,
Murky-brown liquid settling on the lower bottom.
Tiny dusty woodboard tightly closed atop,
Isolated, forever.
Stains clinging to the faded blue marbles,
Water pumps resting above a lonely seaweed.

I never clenched my fingers,
With cheerfulness, to tease the fragile pick creatures.
They were fighting among themselves,
Reeking of desire - youth playing eat-up.

A brand-new home has been ready for them,
Swimming freely in the pool of golden warmth.
Slipping one over another, need not be fed,
Chasing as no watchful eyes behind the glass.
The scent of ocean hints seduction,
Romantic rain-barrel.
The fish will no longer try hard to breathe,
In a tiny sealed space...

Kelly H. Zou

Untitled

With most people, at most times;
My anger and frustration lies dormant.
I don't ask much of people only; don't lie to me.
Shoot your arrows strait and true.
One lie may beg forgiveness,
Two lies won't receive trust,
Three lies breed anger to the point of calm,
The eye of the storm.
Reasons for your caution swirl as thick and quickly as the wind.
Wind that buffets, brings stinging rain.
Open my eyes so I can see,
I see your lies and many faces.
Beware, my trust you have no more.
My protection and friendship;
For once my heart follows my brain.
All is not done and over; just you.

Lorna Butcher

Going Home

I'm going home - again. Back to where it all began,
My birth, my childhood, my teens,
Back to youthful memories, hopes, and dreams.

I'm going home — for awhile.
Back to see an old friends smile,
Back to see the schools where I learned,
Back to "special" places, for which I've yearned.

I'm going home — once more.
Back to where love first opened my heart's door,
Back to the same small town that I love,
Back to where dear ones are missing, but smile down from "Above."

I'm going home — what more can I say?
I'm going home, where I first learned to pray,
I'm going home, to re-live all that I've missed,
Going home, and remembering my first kiss.

I'm going home — but not to stay.
I must return and not live in "yesterday"
The past is gone, but the memories still cling,
Thank you, dear God, for the joy — and pain they bring.

——I'm going home!——

Louise Green

A Replacement

The sun wraps ever cooling spirals on
my arms
and legs,
Softly
dripping
warm rivulets on to my spine.
I don't replace your fingers with the rays.

The fog rests mist smoothly on
my cheeks
and coasts
Down
my eyelashes
in wider streaks of brown.
I don't replace your whispers with the damp.

The wind riffles my hair,
Flower petals kiss my calves and
Ripples of laughter caress my lips.
I replace you with my life.

Meridith Anne Wolnick

Energy Vs. Rest

Some days with the arthritis I have,
My body puts me to a test;
Do I get out of bed or rest?
Before I move, I pray, "Thank you Lord for today."
Then, "You're in charge, help me out of bed."

I sometimes experience pain and stiffness,
So I learned new ways to use my body parts;
Now I can get each days tasks all through.
I have plenty of time for home schooling,
Story or poetry writing, fun and exercise.

Would you quit living, quit moving? Not me!
Faces show the worry, the pity and the stares;
Because I'm crippled? "Please don't! Stop it!", I say.
Celebrate life with me, faith, hope, love and charity.
In its place PRAY, for a better day, each day.

How would you feel in my orthopedic shoes?
Adjust your thoughts; find the good in me.
As we pass say, "Hello, have a nice day, God bless."
I'll do it for you, anyway! You'll make my day.

Leona Knoll

Formation

One day I came — a small little creek
my body was tiny my heart very weak.
Mommy watched over me as slowly I grew
a gentle splatter then a drop or two.

My current grew stronger... off the mountain I came
some pebbles joined me even some rain.
I grew larger and faster more in control
I then hit a boulder and started to roll.

My current went wild I hurled all around
I crashed over falls and smashed onto new ground.
My mommy was gone I felt so alone
deserted and scared I heard my heart moan.

Then slowly the Sun rose and sent me her rays
they warmed and secured me helped soften my daze.
Slowly...one step...then two...even three...
I crawled down the path made especially for me.

No more will I fear no more will I doubt
I will be strong and brave even when I tumble about.
For when I'm alone I will look up and see
the Sun's always there...keeping watch over me.

Mary Lowe

You Can Go Home Again

Although no longer a part of me yet forever a part of me
My childhood home where so many, many memories long past forgotten
   come flooding back when time is taken to reflect.....
The Guava tree from which so many jars of homemade jelly came
The tire-swing swaying from a high oak limb.
The beautiful hunting dog "Queenie" who was forever digging out of
   her pen to chase us down the street
Oh, the street, of red brick, so common then a rare sight today
Early evening games of Hide and Seek, Mother May I, Red Light Green light
The view of big brother's fishing nets, partly finished,
hanging from the clothesline pole the same clothesline which
encouraged so many "sheet houses" on sunny, summer days.
The ever-present back yard vision of Daddy cleaning his catch of the day
The wonderful aroma of Mom's bread pudding, tasting as good cold
   as it did straight from the oven.
So many more, all resting somewhere
in my mind will come to me at moment's repose.
Although no longer a part of me yet forever a part of me.
   Martha McCalister Denton

A'yana...

"How can I have an impact on the world?"
my dark skinned sister asked?

I smiled at her words as I stood in the African American
section of the book store.
It was the first time in my life I had done that!

Indeed!...how can you question your impact?
But for you, I would not be standing here today!

You impact the world being you! Touching the people you touch!

The books I looked at reflected pride in being black...
Reading title after title, I began to wonder why I had not thought
about "pride in being white..."

Is it because when asked, I identify myself as Italian?
Is it because I grew up in a white world and take the color
of my skin for granted?
Or is it because I see people...not color? I do not honestly know!

The books on daily meditation especially caught my interest,
as if the need for spirituality were different somehow... but is it?

I frowned and looked about wondering why there wasn't a book titled
"We are of the Same Earth You and I"

Because we are of the same earth, you and I impact the world being who
we are...women of this earth and friends!
   Mirriam Livingstone

I Have My Wings

My eyes are closed;
My hands are cold;
But my spirit is still warm, and now I know how to live.
   I am meeting ancestors who I have never known,
     and acquaintances I made when I was a child.
   I live among friends and relatives that I thought
     I had forgotten, and now know I have not.
I have everlasting time.
   I must look ahead, not for myself, but for the people
     I left behind; the ones who I have cared about.
   I have to give them hope for the time yet to come.
   I have to help them discover the future.

I have my wings.
I have earned them.
Now I have to show others how to spread their own wings,
   and how to fly on their own, so they may glide into
   all their tomorrow's, and soar upon the
   future of humanity.
   Gy. Dioguardi

In Love Without You

As I sit here alone without you near.
My heart is filled with so much fear.

This fear in my heart brings so much pain
And from it I can not refrain.

The people that are around me are filled with negativity
Never trying to help. They just always down me

Without you I don't think that I can make it another day
Because without you by my side I cannot see the way.

If you were to leave me now I don't know what I'd do
I just can't picture my life without you.

The days seem so short, and the nights so long
The tears may fall but I've got to be strong.

Strong enough to stand the test of time.
Because I know one day you will be mine.

What can I say what can I do
I can't stand it anymore, I'm falling in love with you.

Love without you cannot be so
Because my love will only grow and grow.

Lady please stay, and never leave me
Because one day soon we will make a family.
   Rodrick D. Cotton

"Lovers"

Can't hide this feeling...
my heart is reeling...
just once could it be you and I...
don't you see the desire burning deep inside...

To feel your body next to mine... Skin to skin...
let's lay all the emotions on the line..just maybe
we might get lucky...we could win...
To hold you in my arms, to kiss you, just the two of us
even for an hour...what ever the price, don't think twice
anything is worth the fire

One moment at a time... life could be so sweet...
only if you were mine...
lonely days, sleepless nights...loving the wrong one...
what can we do?
Hold me now, before the night is done, close the door...
it's only me and you...

Place your hand in mine..for a little while I'll give you warm love,
I'll make you smile..the pleasure will be worth the pain..memories
are better than having nothing...in our hearts a trace of each
other will always remain.
   Sandy Balistreri

Home

Home is a memory
of a distant place I once knew,
where the streets were my familiar friends.
And smiles and tears were common
that home is now a reflection of my youth.
Through the growth of my aging
I found a new home I go to.
I open the front door deep within
And I welcome myself in,
I am home.
   Kathleen Culla

Seaward Journey

I travel by the morning sun,
My legs tiring as I run.
I look to the west and to the east,
I'm still pursued by the wanton beast.

I now have traveled half a day,
I look around - I've lost my way.
I must travel to the west,
There is the sea and my rest.

There is the beast with his two evil eyes,
Taunting me with his terrible lies.
He laughs and spurns - I'll never reach the sea,
But we will succeed - the sea and me.

Here I am - running free,
Hoping, hoping - I will hear the sea.
There it is - the sea at last,
The beast is fading - like the past.

Here I am - out of breath,
Once again - I've cheated death.
Here I will stay - by the sea,
Always happy - the sea and me.
Roger Smith

In Their Eyes

So small and innocent, this they are.
My love for them goes so very far.

They look to me for strength and love.
The kind you give me now, from above.

I look in their faces and see you there.,
The love they have so innocent, so rare.

And now that heaven is your home,
They will carry your memory where ever they roam.

Your memory will be with me, on this you can rely.
Every time I look at my girls, I see you in their eyes.
Teresa Stuart

Visiting The North Woods In July

We come to the North Woods, looking for restoration,
My soul is drained, my faculties sapped, headed for ruination.
Near the shore of a crystal-clear lake, I hear the soft whisper of trees;
Birches, maples, spruce and oaks, joyfully welcome their patient.

It is late afternoon, a cool breeze comes up,
And soft clouds come down from the North.
We enter, like refugees, thirsty and tired,
The children sigh with relief.

Chipmunks and deer, patient and lovely,
Feed quietly, down in the glen.
The Sun filters down, through a mantle of leaves,
Casting shadows that promise us rest.

Like magic, the dusk melts into Night,
Shadows and mists fill the forest,
A restless hush fills the mystical trees,
Nature commands that we rest.

We wake in the morning, to the song of the Loon, calling us back to Life:
"Awake, awake, God's in his Heaven. 'Tis another blessed day."
The madness has ended, the trees whisper again:
"Welcome home, welcome home, the World is at peace!"
Thomas Baffes

The Little Street

I walked along a lonely street it was empty and forlorn
My mind started to wander and my thoughts began to form

I saw the little houses standing neatly side by side
with neighbors chatting in their yards while hanging clothes to dry

The sound of children's laughter was coming from the street
they were playing old familiar games like tag and hide - go - seek

Then the scene had changed completely and it made me feel so sad
the little houses were boarded up and some had been torn down

I couldn't hear the laughter not even one little sound
for the games had turned into real live guns and drugs were all around

I hope and pray that someday soon crime and violence will come to an end
guns will be for hunting not killing someone's friend

Then the scene will change again and you will hear the laughter roar
the little street will come alive and be happy forever more.
Lilly Lugar

So Loved

I stroll down memory lane as I sit here all alone
My mind wanders back to my childhood and my far away home.
I think of pappa telling tall tales so big and high
That clever man was only teaching us values to live by
While hoping that some would filter down to us, and stay
To shape our lives for living in the best kind of way.
Mama always stayed calm, never raised her voice
We imitated her style, it kept us on the right course.
Taking turns, our parents would tell us stories at night
Stories that taught us lessons of love and respect, keeping it light.
We didn't realize it was teaching, in the way they did it
Showing their love and respect for one another, from us, they never hid it.
They nurtured our soul and strengthened our mind
And showed us how to have compassion for others, how to be kind
Morally good people, they never fought or swore
Instilling in our heart to be like them to the core.
To treat others as we wanted them to treat us, too
They often let us know this was called "The golden rule"
Their own life stories won over the fairy tales, by others beloved
My little hand would slip into one of theirs, and I felt so loved.
Mildred Marsh Ruton

Depressed

After all that I have been through I am depressed,
my mind wanders over the thought of death.

The feelings of anger build up inside,
all I want to do is hide.

What do I do with all this anger?
I hide.

I must not hide,
I must be brave for the sake of my soul.

I must not cry for the death you have almost given to me.
Paula Brettmann

The Locket

Shrouds cover the furniture, and dust covers the shrouds.
   Nightly, silence is overpowered by crickets playing their violins.
Proud light has long since cowered behind the distant hills.
   Holes in wool, behind a fastened door.
All condemned beneath a tattered stairwell.
   The closet is void of a key.
Above, red spots hide the brilliant gold of the chandelier.
   A locket, cracked open, lies concealed in the closet.
Once proud beauty shows through the shards of glass.
   The light of day may never reach this forgotten corner.
There still remains a smile upon her shining face.
Thomas Von Phillip Herskowitz

A Different View

Excuse me, if I don't want to play.
My mother has died, I found out today.

They say, at least you got to know her for a little while.
But they will never feel her loving hugs or see the warmth of her smile.

They say, let out your feelings, you'll get better and well
But they'll never hear how much she cares or the good advice she'd tell.

I can't help but feel a large amount of guilt.
I've lost the emotional support on which my life has been built.

Save your kind words, and your inexperienced preach.
Because right now, my heart is out of reach.

You'll never know until it happens to you.
Right now, life has given me a different view.

Take advantage of the time you have to tell them how much you care.
Because life isn't always on you're side, and it isn't always fair.

So excuse me, it I don't want to play.
My mother has died, I found out today.
   Shone Buswell

Heaven Awaits

I'm on my way, headed to the clouds and sky
My soul is still alive, it's just my body that has died.

I'm heading up a road, no map will ever lead
I'm flying in time at a faster rate than speed.

I'm going to meet my maker, be judged and pay a price
But, fear not he said, I'm your savior, yes, my name is Christ.

Believe in me and I'll forgive you all your sins
And once your body dies, and eternal life begins.

No more pain will you ever feel
Because you believe in me, I'm Christ, your savior - I'm real.

I'll meet you at the gate and there I'll grant you wings.
Because I'm Christ your savior and can do anything.

You'll live with me and my holy father
Among the clouds and sky
Remember when we told you, your soul would never die?

A journey up to heaven, a loving place to be
Home with me and my father for all eternity.
   Lisa A. Wells

Destroyed Innocence

When I see a child's tears,
   My own tears I must fight.
For nothing can compare to the pain
   Of screaming echoes in the night.
Arms are raised in anger,
   While cries are made for love
But the arms still all in hate,
   And the tears all for nothing.

What can calm the hidden fears,
   That are carefully kept from sight?
The lonely tears which fall,
   Are tears only seen by the night.
Screams still haunt the mind,
   Destroying the innocence of one.
Dreams of life are shattered to death,
   And the abuse...
      It's just begun.
   Rhiannon Lary

Without You

Without you, there would be no more sunshine,
No more fresh air to breathe,
No more smiles to share.
Without you days would seem like darkness,
Rain would never stop pouring down on me,
And the air would smell bitter,
The laughter would turn into tears of loneliness without you.
Without you the rainbow would loose it's colors,
The grass would stop growing,
And the flowers would never bloom,
Without you there would no longer be a me.
   Tammy D. Touville

The Lovelier View

I once lived in a little, plain house.
   My neighbor lived in a large, beautiful one.
Perhaps I was the more greatly blessed
   I had the lovelier View.

When I've seen a more beautiful person,
   I've sometimes felt envious too:
But, we who are not so comely.
   Can enjoy the lovelier view.

Growing old diminishes one's beauty,
   So, it's tempting to envy the young.
But, the fact remains to comfort the old,
   They can enjoy the lovelier view!
   Madge Miller

Into The Light

My heart feels weary
My soul is weak
My body, so faint
Like a caged animal,
   a lost being
engulfed in blinding darkness;
Lost in a deep bottomless pit,
Yet, I shall find my way out
I see a light, though so faint it looks
I shall pull myself up
I shall strengthen my body
My spirit, shall I renew again
And I will climb with every ounce of my strength.
I shall move, step by step,
Overlooking and ignoring all the sharp rocks,
the slippery surfaces
I shall press on towards my one goal,
I shall find myself
I shall succeed
I know I will finally emerge into the light!
   Violet Wahito Kogi

No More

No more crying no more tears
No more loneliness through the years.

No more days that are not bright
No more sad and fearful nights.

Look to the past you'll do no more
Just look to the future for what's in store.

Taking each day at a time
Now I know I'll be just fine,
   Susan Grishkevich

Whispers In The Wind

Oh, where does he stray?
My whisper in the wind.

It seems an age ago
I walked along the tawny sedge
To see his solitary figure across the bridge
Starring down beyond the water's edge.
Cast in the setting sun,
A stranger he was
And yet in that careless glance
A familiarity I found
Drowned in his aching loneliness.
But the moment was broken
As he turned in haste,
Leaving the way he came,
Passing the piles of golden husk
And still unto this day
I find myself on that bridge,
Waiting in the fading dusk hoping for his return.

Oh, where does he stray?
My whisper in the wind.
   Susanna Manoranjan

The World of Dance

The world of Dance that I have known is gone and in the past
My years of teaching, I can say, have disappeared quite fast.

It was the best career of all, a choice I'm glad I made,
It was something that I really loved, and also, I got paid.

No one could love it more than I, it filled my hearts desire,
It kept me young and in great shape, for others to aspire.

I was their teacher, I was their friend, my students I adored.
And never once in all these years, did I ever become bored.

You watch them grow and hope you'll see a dancer in the troupe,
The one who shines above the rest, the best among the group.

I've been a dancer all my life, I taught for 26 years,
My memories I will recall, with laughter, joy and tears.

How fortunate and blessed I was to do what I loved best,
I thank God with all my heart, for years of happiness.
   Marianne Stahl

Untitled

Me, Myself and I
Myself!
Aye!
Found!
Forever. Love.
Life enduring
Everlasting spirit.
Soul: you're eyes.
My, you're mine! Your!
Expression. Mirror. Mirror expressions.

Me, Myself and I
(My and Self)
Eyes
Expressions, mirror: Mirror expressions —
My! Your, Me. You
Soul. You. And (I).
Everlasting! Separate.
Life. Each embrace.
Forever. Lost.
Friends! Aye!
   Wendy Madison

"Blessed Sweet Fruit And Filth"

Blessed sweet fruit and filth —
mystic specter of borrowed charms
primping in shattered glass'
reflection of truth
you will show yourself true indeed
at the hour of midnight
when no pumpkin lashed to rat tail stallions
can attend your will
to run.

And in the death of a nocturne's knell
won't your entrance,
regal and fairly draped
in the purple of those stately cheeks
whose breath you drained,
feel like suds and grey water
against your wrinkled palms and knees.
Won't you sting and sorrow some inside
for the hopes you gorged on thoughts of men:
the faith you fought for
in their eyes.
   David Prisk

"1,2,3,4....The Mania Of Dance"

Everyone, young, and old,
Naturally loves to move to music.
It makes you more robust,
More happy, more gregarious
In your interpersonal relationships.

Dancing is my personal choice
Of special concept.
It definitely satisfy my appetite.
I love to listen to music
In the early morn.
When I play my favorite C.D.
The creative, choreographical juices erupt.

Each and every time,
My mind and body become transformed
To a young, lithe damsel
Awaiting her premier broadway performance.
All, including the crucial critics,
As hyperventilating, anticipating.
Stridently walking to center stage,
The unfulfilled dreams of patty come true.
   Patricia Myatt Wilson

Serenity Is A Whisper

I have found a place of contentment
Nearby, within my very being.
A careful search revealed
This most elusive gift.

I need no longer look about
For excitement, nor adventure's promise;
Far removed from the hurried quest, is a treasure
Confined in the visions of each day.

There's appreciation of family and friends,
And the wonders of nature to behold.
There's loving, sharing, learning and teaching,
Music to soothe and art to delight.

I've found the treasure, the miracle within
To know myself, the truth of who I am,
By listening for God's own Spirit, but a whisper,
To satisfy my trusting soul.
   Lola M. Smialkowski

Hopeless Chance

This deadly venom has burned my soul.
Never ending emotions have created a hole.
Deepening itself with every glance.
Unforgettable feelings with a hopeless chance.
Still I linger as unstoppable desire,
Smolders through my body starting a fire.
Convulsing through my every nerve,
As you taunt my body's every curve.
Realizing that you will never comply,
With holding your love sends tears to my eyes.
Knowing the pain that this venom has caused,
Makes all my actions uncontrollably pause.
Satisfying my own need to feel secure,
I never will touch your body so pure.
This venom will continue to rage through my soul,
And my unanswered love will have no toll.
   Mary Ann Swochak

The Girl in the Mirror

Until we met, I never knew the girl in the mirror...
   Never thought she was pretty enough,
   strong enough,
   smart enough...

Then for a very brief time you came into my life...
   And you gave me the hope and courage
   to live,
   to love,
   to trust...

No one has ever touched my soul the way you did...
   Even through your sickness and pain you
   were strong,
   and gentle,
   and knowing...

You accepted me for who I was, no questions asked...
   And you taught me to do the same,
   with love,
   with grace,
   with regard...

Dad....I wish you Godspeed, till we meet again, so long.
   Melody Smith

Beneath The Stars Above

Beneath the stars above, I watched the
night go by. The moon so bright and full,
soared above me. Just seeing that view
made me want to wish I was up above
in that world above my own.

Beneath the stars above, you and I talked
the night away, getting closer then ever
before. We laughed, cried, and shared the
times spent together, you and me, together!

Beneath the stars above, for a moment I
felt safe and free from my world I really
live in. No bothers, no worries.
I felt safe and free. Just me, all alone,
the way I wished it to be.

Beneath the stars above, I read this poem
to you, the way it always was meant to be.
Beneath the stars above is where
I'll always be.
   Meghan Sekreta

Night And Day

All is peaceful, slumbering
Night is tightly wrapped around the earth
The stars gaze down, carefully watching
Along with the moon, the lantern of the night

The sun stretches its arms up to the horizon
Gradually rising to invade the darkness
Night creeps back into its corner
Sun shines its brilliance to wake the earth

The sad stars fade, their tears
Left on every leaf, petal, and blade of grass
The birds sing, call good morning to all
Creatures of the day replace those of the night

Another day begins, too soon to end
Night slowly moves to conquer the sky
Night and day in constant competition
Both patiently taking turns to mask the heavens
   Kristin Meyer

Sleep, Sleep My Dear Child

Sleep, Sleep my dear, dear child, Sleep
Night-time befalls you
Morning will keep!!!

Sleep, Sleep my dear, dear child
Let your imagination and dreams run wild
Lay your head down to rest, lay your head down to slumber
Let your mind lumber aimlessly through tall emerald forests and kelly
green shamrocks, through rainbows and kites that fly high in the sky

And before you drift off to sleep, listen to the wind blow your name
Listen to the birds and the crickets chirp
For when morning has broken and the silence is gone,
Your dreams, shattered like glass, fall upon your pillows
like tombstones marking their resting place

As you awake to greet a new day, listen to the wind whistle your name
Listen to the leaves as they rustle
Leave some of your dreams laid there to mourning upon your pillows
And grab some to bring with you as you play out the day

Sleep, Sleep my dear, dear child, Sleep
Night-time befalls you
Morning will keep!!!
   Patricia A. Collins-Spina

The Way Before Me

Thinking of nothing.
No plans to foresee.
Just wasting away like an old withered tree.

Until one night, when I could hardly see,
the door to death was lurking for me.
All I could do was shake and shiver,
in hope that my love for the Lord would
allow me to be delivered.

He knew how low I was.
So he chose to speak from up above:
"O come to me, my little one." I am the
Son of the most powerful one.
I've come to your aid, so do not be afraid.

Just touch my hand and give of your heart.
For no longer more will there be any harm to thee.
Just walk with me and you'll see
That this is the path I have made for thee.
   Tangela M. Coleman

I Will Be Acknowledged

No matter how far I travel, or how long I sleep.
No one can see me!
Nobody hears me!
I will be Acknowledged.
I will stand in my shadow.
I will glow in the dark.
I will stand on the tallest building
Until I become Acknowledged.
I will cross the world to climb the highest mountain.
I will swim across the farthest sea.
I will make the world a better place.
One day, I will be acknowledged.
If I die, this world will not end.
I will leave this world as a friend.
Before I go, I will always know, this day I was Acknowledged.
Yolanda F. Newbill

Curbside Chat

tendrils of smoke dissipating into the
    nightly breeze by the moon's
    bright rays, my cigarette burns
    between
my   fingers after only
    a drag to alleviate
    the tensions,
    all I do is sit and think of
    my life and how much
Suicide
    would even be a waste of my
    so - called precious time since
Death
    is the same as what I'm
Living
Matt McClure

The Depression

No glimpse of inspiration
No hope for happy resuscitation

Engulfed by sleepy black nothingness
A raging storm is wearing away the
construction of my mind, my earthly fortress

Like an unabashed, blind beggar
I claw my way through chambers of bitterness and hate.

My outlook is careless, and it doesn't seem to pass
I only see what I want, through my vision of broken glass.

Inky black sadness oozes out my pores
And the days prevail to be long, drawn out battles.

My hands grope for a grip to hold
But alas, I continue to slide dawn faster and faster,
and it is getting old.
Laura Paulsen

Confessions Of A Mother

MY HEART CRIES!
No, my heart sobs, my heart feels squelched of life,
the wringing of the blood of life as a water soaked sponge is twisted!
How difficult to let go - how impossible to hang on!
How I've strived, pushed, encouraged, challenged, all to let go!
All to feel my heart CRY!
The years - the days - the hours - how intense!
The struggle. Always the struggle.
Be strong. Be strong. Be strong.
Never let down. Never be less.
Always be strong.
MY HEART CRIES!
I am so PROUD!
Patricia V. M. Schallert

Friends

No matter who you are,
  No matter what you do,
There's always people so true and dear to you,
  Laughing, giggling and always on the go,
Still there's simply time to let the feelings show,
  Good times and in bad,
There's always a positive support,
  Hope and courage are two important things,
But humor itself sure takes out the sting,
  Friendship, support and guidance mean so much to one,
Truth and honesty can never be outdone,
  Listening and understanding play the part,
That's what makes friends stick together
immediately from the start.
Linda Doxtader

Ambition

Let your dreams open the door
No one can put a lock on your goals
What lies ahead is worth fighting for

Raise your standards, continue to soar
Grab life by the throat and lead your soul
Let your dreams open the door

Allow your mind to strengthen its core
Even when life has taken its toll
What lies ahead is worth fighting for

For you there are many treasures in store
Reach for the flag on the highest pole
Let your dreams open the door

When you've reached all the stars, reach for more
In your life you own the lead role
What lies ahead is worth fighting for

Don't let others keep your score
Be the king of the steepest knoll
Let your dreams open the door
What lies ahead is worth fighting for
Lacey Wolfe

What A Lady

There was a lady, a lady indeed,
not only a grandma, but a pal, too.
She was there for me in time of need,
in happy and sad times.

This lady knew how to have fun,
she didn't show favoritism, she loved everyone.
She had a special twinkle in her eye
that not one person could pass her by.

Yes, when it snuck up on her,
it was silent as a picture.
It took her gradually by surprise,
then I knew there was no saving her.

All I can do is go on with my life
not dwelling on the past.
Making the best of every moment
as time passes by so fast.

She was so very dear to me
in more ways than anyone can imagine.
This is what is for the best and meant to be
for now she is gone, yet memories held within.
Kandy Allen

A Sweet Song Came To Me

One night upon a feather pillow in my sleep,
No one gave a warning, but a vision came to me
   She cast her spell upon my heart
   She vowed that we would never part
Never was created a more perfect sight to see.

  One day, upon a tiny stretch of sandy beach
No one gave a warning but a sweet song came to me
   She whispered softly in my ear
   I want you always to be near
Wherever we shall wander, we shall be in ecstasy.

Now, I can't move a mountain; I can't walk across the sea
And I can't sail up to the sun, or climb the highest tree
   But I have dreams that I can fly
   And I will share your love tonight
No imagination can transcend these magic dreams.
   Martin Camhi

The Silent Room

In this room, where no country or street surrounds,
no one is human,
   or visible...
and freedom creates forms in celebration...
A knife long crack, snaps
revealing an untouched earth of search,
   ....and rebirth.
In this room,
where freedom breathes a body,
there, sudden forms, freeze the light
   as knuckles... rapping echoes
turn this life....back into roving eyes,
attached by a head and neck....
to hear, and stretch, with arms, and hands that reach,
and legs that stand, and tears that breach...sadness
   .....and madness
but the never answering body remains...staring still,
without blood or life
   until.....
freedom appears in silence.
   Michael Illuzzi

What A World

People say we're reaching a dark age,
Of drugs, crime, pollution, and decadence of government.
People say we're reaching the final stage,
The end, apocalypse, the time of judgement.
It's been said before in times of rage,
Seldom thought out, but this I will hint.

That from the lips of irrational, foolishness spews forth.
They should learn their history and think some more.
For all this has been said before,
As early as thought even in folklore.

There's always been crime, be it horrific or small,
Drugs once medicine, governments overthrown.
The earth we've abused since we merely crawled,
Our need to transcending at times makes us not at our own.

We long for peace and improvement, too quickly, too soon.
When perfection's not reached we behave like spoiled children
We grow impatient breeding hate and war, buffoons.
It is from this we must learn a lesson,
That without patience we are all quite doomed.
   Zachary G. Ollila

Evolution

I am no-one,
No-one is me,
To create a similar should not be,
How is the creator is the creation.
On what account can be able to build a nation.
No-one knows the problem of today,
Hate is a common display,
Ugly as it seem,
You will be mean,
Why is the World formulated by day and night,
It's only for man to continuously fight,
This can go on and on,
But I will be gone,
And the World will soon fall down.
And then one will .... be around.
   Thon Huy

Embrace

Dark and painful, through life he trudges,
No rainbows, no light, unfair he judges.

Vainly he searches, through infinite dim,
When a lighthouse appears, on life's outer rim,

Away to the source, to bequeath this blind land,
He enters the light, his heart in his hand,

The light reaches out, he basks in the glow,
On a mountain of goodness, from the lowest of low,

The light fills his world, with feelings anew,
Joy beyond bliss, the light ever true.

Beauty and love, in this light fit for two,
His journey has ended, for this light is you.
   Robert McKiernan

Untitled

I dreamt a time of hungry youth,
no spare change to buy a meal.
I dreamt again, this time of pain
and wounds that would not heal.
I dreamt a time where children cringed
from fear of the world outside,
I dreamt again, this time they screamed
from abuse their family supplied.
I dreamt a time of a nation slowed down,
dependent on crack and weed.
I dreamt again, this time to see our communities
falling to their knees.
The one last dream I had that night
I heard my conscience say,
"WAKE UP! These dreams are not just dreams,
they're happening today!"
   Robert Roy

First Touch

The snow was falling gently to the ground.
No wind to disturb the silence,
only the soft crunch of my boots on the snow covered pavement.

You were ahead of me in the parking lot.
My heart was pounding, hoping you would look behind you.
That's okay, your car is parked next to mine.

We talk about the weather while cleaning the snow off our cars.
I throw a handful of snow at you.
A small snowball war goes on between us.
You dump a handful of snow down my back.
I laugh, you laugh and we each drive our separate ways.
We didn't know it, but that was the beginning.
   Rebecca Hilbert

Darkness

What is the color of Darkness?
No! You are quiet wrong, it is not black,
The night it is black, and the night it is beauty,
and the darkness it is ugly.
Yes, the darkness is ugly and it is
lonesome and it is sad,
But the night it is full of unseen beauty,
and beauty that is seen is false,
and beauty that is felt is true.
Do not let the darkness fool you as it
masquerades as the night,
For there is beauty in the night,
As there is darkness in the light,
and the light it casts away the night,
but it cannot cast away the darkness,
For the darkness it does not lurk in
corners or closets or under beds.
The darkness it does not hide in attics or basements,
It is in our minds and it is in our hearts
and it is in our very souls.
    Marino

Locked In The Real World

Giving it away - I'm sorry I didn't ask
none cares - beauty is only skin deep
happy in life - dirt is the ground
heart and soul are your life!
Keep every secrets to you soul-never let them you down
Clear and navy blue - see the doctor or see me
Never in a lifetime - I'm sorry
I didn't mean for it to be
Never see the stars - never been outside
Locked in a closet-no life-no light-no food
No soul-But still alive hell in the world
Get rid of all the guns
Lets ride to the stars
Be one in a million
    Michelina J. Fedele

You Loved The Hurt Away

Been through trials, been through struggles,
not a hand would no one lend.
Kicked around, then stomped down,
wanted for my life to end.

Day to day was just a drag;
seems there's nothing to live for.
Life can be a real letdown;
surely must be something more - then you loved the hurt away.

Left alone so many times;
all alone to carry on.
There were times I climbed the wall,
wanting mostly to be gone.

Things I lost back in the past,
so down and brokenhearted.
Never knew how to go on,
and then your loving started - then you loved the hurt away.

You just loved the hurt away;
caused the pain to go away.
Thankful for another day;
you loved the hurt away - Away, Away, you loved the hurt away.
    Michael D. Wood

Grasping Time

Pulling life from the very soul,
Not merely taking but devouring every breath.
Living by the hidden voice,
Announcing the innermost secrets of being
And knowing them.

Missing that which was yesterday or
Just perhaps what was there.
To capture that which is within the self, and without.
Grasping time in your hand and freezing it for an instant,
Only then letting it go to become the unretainable past.

To sit on eternity's shoulder,
Looking into the face of
The oncoming pale horse,
Then turning and racing past all regrets
Into ones own existence.
    D. Thomas Noonan

Life Is Tough

Life is tough...so they say,
Not a bed of roses...but then who promised
  it would be that way?

Trials will come...and trials will go,
What is that saying...
"We reap what we sow?"

Friends are a comfort along the way.
They make us laugh, let us cry...
  Help us through the toughest day.

Life is tough...but soon we learn
The building of character, although very tough
  is the vehicle by which we are taught to discern.

The fire of life will help to refine
Burn away the dross...
  and make us shine!
    Sherrie C. Hunt

Perhaps Someday

The stars at night and when the sky is blue,
Not a moment passes when I don't think of you.

Your touch, no matter how soft and tender,
You can bet I'll always remember.

Your kiss is sweet,
It lifts me off my feet.

When we must part and go our separate way,
I look forward to OUR next day!

This is written with all my heart,
Perhaps someday we won't have to part.
    Mary Lou Martinkovic

"One Artist"

I'm an artist not to be pimped,
Not to be a whore;
For what good is speaking if you have no voice?
What good is opportunity if you have no choice?

I'm an artist not to be fooled,
Not to be big brother's tool;
For what good is being civil if you have no rights?
What good is a pulse if you have no life?

I'm an artist not to be victimized,
Not to be trivialized,
Not to be characterized by any elite;
For what good is an artist without his art?
    Michael David

Forget-Me-Not

I worry that I'll forget her...
not because she was not memorable, but because the pain
is great and numbness is preferable.

I worry that I'll forget her...
not because I did not love her, but because the years
without her sharpen as the years with her blur.

I worry that I'll forget her...
not because she died so young, but because I was
so busy, too busy, too headstrong.

I worry that I'll forget her...
not sure why...
I'll always care.

I worry that I'll forget her
not because she is not with me
but because I am not There.
    Sue A. Mosser

Trapped

I am trapped inside myself.
Not knowing how to get out.
There is a woman inside me.
Crying to get out. But no one will help her.
She tries to do the best she can.
But her best is not good enough.
I want to be good at everything, like my Mom.
She is great and my best friend.
All my friends try to hurt me.
It seems like I will always be alone.
All the things that I am good at either
   get ruined or don't mean anything.

The woman inside is crying help me, help me.
I want to be a big shot, instead of a little person
I don't understand what is going on in my life.
But it seems like it is falling apart.
I blame everything on myself. Why do I have a negative attitude.
Is it because of my past or what. I don't get life anymore.
Where is my best friends, a true friend.
I can't seem to be able to find them.
    Sandra J. Durfee

Memories Of You

My heart once glowed with tender warmth,
Now it is frosty and cold.

My eyes were once shimmering with hope,
Now they are distant and dull.

My ears once heard affection roll from your lips,
Now they hear nothing.

My mouth once rambled with rambunctious cheer,
Now it speaks of hopeless doom.

My room once possessed life and laughter,
Now it is deathly; possessing tears of desperation.

My phone once rang nine times a night,
Now it lays still and silent.

My self was once considered special,
Now I am no one.

My mornings once gave me reason,
Now I go back to sleep.

My words once mattered
Now no one listens.

My life was once alive,
Now I am dead.
    Mary E. DeAndrea

Do It Today

Recalling those
not so forgotten times
I laughed and happily reminisced
about the innocence of my youth.
When life was new and full of dreams
with it's haunting, scheming, tempting themes.

While wondering 'bout my
my new "today",
I was not so happily reminded,
"My Friend! Look! You're old and gray!
and not so far off from the grave!"

And planting my feet
back on the ground,
I shrugged and mentally walked away.

But, Lo! I could not escape
before hearing one last truth which then became my fate;
"Oh! How fleeting is our youth!
And how ugly
unfulfilled pursuit!"
    Lacinda Beggs

Reflections Of Sarah

Heaven is a place
not to be awaited like a Christmas present
but a goal to be obtained
It is not a physical place
but a state of mind
where all is at rest and peace comes natural

Heaven is walking through a cornfield
in the middle of a thunderstorm
holding hands with "the one"
and having nothing to fear
Heaven is that shining moment
when everything goes your way
Heaven is when you look into someone's eyes
and see yourself reflected back
Heaven is swimming to the bottom of the ocean
and realizing that you're home
Heaven is love for love's sake
and life for life's sake

Heaven is holding a rose
and realizing she has no thorns
    Matt Cashner

My Brother Man Is Gone

My brother is trouble and don't really care.
Not trying to protest his self or beware.
of all the things that he does to himself
he's all the time blaming it on somebody else.
Nobody is troubling him it's only that within
he even blames it on some of his kin.
Not looking at the problem or trying to brake it down
he's caught in the middle looking like a clown.
Will he ever try to get his life together
or will he be still a man that's not free.
Not free at all but that don't matter much
the life he's living he don't know he's caught up.
Not seeing how the world's moving all around him
He's satisfied and content with the situation he's in.
Who is my enemy who is my friend
he's lost and forgotten dying in Sin.
    Matthew Johnson

The Hike

Hiking, hiking for miles
Nothing but endless rows of trees and many animals

Hiking, hiking for miles
Sweat running down your back giving you chills

Hiking, hiking for miles
The sounds of you and your companions
Crunching the fallen twigs and leaves beneath you

Hiking, hiking for miles
The taste of the fresh clean air in your mouth
As you open it in awe at the beauty of the forest
Rachel L. Ross

Dad's Death

Daddy why did you have to die
Now all I want to do is cry
Mom and I are now alone
Now we have to read your name up on a stone
Dad I know that you was a good man
Mom says' you were always there to understand
I just wished I could have known you better
I just wish there was some letters
I'll always love you Dad
I do miss you and that is what makes me sad
my memories of you aren't so clear
and most of all that's what I fear
I was only five when you left
It sure has made my life a mess
mom helps keep you with me
she all the time has love to thee
Dad I miss the father and son things
even your love you would bring
someday Dad I hope to see you again
for I am you son and always a friend
Veronda Whitman

"My One And Only"

I wrote a poem about number one
Now time has passed, the others are gone
Billy my man, my heart you have won
My one and only, you'll never be lonely.

You're faithful and true; I am too
Don't even worry, doubt or fear
Someday at last, I will be near
We'll be together, no matter the weather
True love forever; I'll leave you never.

You're my one and only; never be lonely
Our love is true; just us two
No room for three; just you and me
Our love is strong; will last our life long.

Just wait and see; happy we'll be
My one and only; I love you only!
Rita Schurade

Untitled

Life is a woven road of responsibilities
of children's needs
husband's wishes
friend's requests
career goals
Pulling the strands of my weary fibers
To and fro
Back and forth
Until the soul feels out of shape
Ready for a break
To sit and feel the flow of life regain its balance.
Joan Smith

Towards Existence

O Man, in thou alone the world is rotating
O Man, in thou alone the peace is ensured
O Man, in thou alone the ecology is guaranteed
O Man, in thou alone the population is controlled
The prolonged lamentation brought a flash
With the cautioning hymn of smash
Fear not, I am with thee, blessed the nature-the Savior
Fear me, I am with thee, terrified the warfare-the Destroyer
Fear not, I am with thee, consoled the Sun-the Savior
Fear me, I am with thee, whispered the pollution-the Destroyer
Fear me, I am with thee, encouraged the Sea and Earth-the Savior
Fear me, I am with thee, threatened the population growth-the Destroyer
Fear not, I am with thee, assured the magnificent, the Savior
Fear me, I am with thee, shivered the fire and lightning, the-Destroyer
To fear or not what I have to do
To me it struck deep, I was grieved
Thought and thought how could it be relieved
The answer to me with its feathers came forth
PRESERVE ECOLOGY AND PEACE; CONTROL POPULATION GROWTH
Then the world would survive for ever and ever........
C. Purushothaman

"A Christmas Eulogy"

'Tis the season that brings all joy ov'r the birth of a righteous boy.
Thru the annals of time thru a kingly line a tree of hope.
To highlight the seasons glows in every window its' colors show.
With red, green, blue, and gold, all the ornaments a mind can hold.

Tho the season is so fleeting as poinsettias are red and white.
Like leaves of gold its' hands unfold to give a natural glow.
Garland wreaths of wheat greet with peace the presence of the LORD.
While cinnamon spices and kitchen devices harmonize the seasons' cheer.
As the holy angels sing of a coming king in this Christmas year.
Shelia Herrington

Untitled

Cherish the limitless days of your youth, before the restrictions
   of adulthood close in
savor the sweet flavor of love, for heartache leaves you bitter and sour
live life to the fullest, before death leaves you dead
treasure your friends, before time turns them into enemies
value your youthful spirit, for it grows worthless with age
spend your days with your face turned toward the sun, for the clouds
   are moving in
make every moment unforgettable, before you begin to forget
pounce on every opportunity, before they stop knocking on your door
load you life up with memories, they'll be all you have to remember
create a life worth living...
Or don't life
Stephanie Kramm

"Incarnation"

Poetry as if it were dictation
Pages and pages of no correction
Removes one phrase and there would be diminishment
for this is the very voice of God
and staring at you through this cage of ink strokes in an
absolute beauty
You choose for your instruments, Oh Lord
and I,
I only have the ability to recognize it.
Maria Rice

Nothing Left But Brown-Green Lace

It was during the Summer
  of his second year,
That Japanese beetles came
  from far and near.
They ate the oats, wheat, and corn in the ear;
They ate the roses which he held so dear.

Nothing left but brown-green lace.

His wife had left him in the earlier May;
He did not understand why she went away:
The kids in the yard hard at play,
Angels came to take her that day.

Nothing left but brown-green lace.

He missed her so and
  would for years.
Fighting hard to hold back the tears
He saw her brown-green dress
  in the closet mirrors -
The lump in his throat -
  his heart full of fears.

Nothing left but brown-green lace.
  Martin Nelson

My Own Footsteps?

I gazed into the eyes,
  of the man I wished to be.

So truthful and so bold,
  to not reflect of me.

I sip on my sherry and water,
  a man I wished I weren't.

Now I've found, I cannot hide,
  the body in which I'm current.

As the lines draw beneath my eyes,
  I feel I am repulsed.

My father in me not,
  I dare not to revolt.

I wish my life were as clear as glass,
  as once it were with me.

Now I find troubles, worries, and lies,
  as my father found with he.
  Thomas Provost

"Teach The Children"

Teach the children of today
Of the values that you learned years ago.
Instill in them morals that you may
In time, watch them grow.
Teach the children of today,
The presidents and leaders of tomorrow.
Keep them from wrong, and show them the way.
Show them the right path to follow.
Teach the children of today
To believe in themselves and in you.
Teach them how to pray,
And to "thine own self be true".
  Ronda L. Lay

Untitled

His pain and suffering was so severe.
On death's door he had no fear.
He wanted him to come and set him free.

He was so tired and Jesus saw,
Then Ten Commandment's were my dad's law.
Life can be so cruel. I don't understand,
But Dad never questioned God's Master Plan.

Jesus swept down and took him away,
I'll never forget that Glorious day.
Dad is resting for the first time in years,
Although I have cried a million tears.
I know Dad's where he needs to be.
He is so happy and breathing free.
  Twanna Holmes

The Challenge

Five men and two women were on their way.
On that January ill-fated day.

They had prepared and trained without rest.
Giving their all, they were the best.

Six from the space program had planned for that day.
And one was selected in a special way.

They all had faith in the venture they shared.
And eagerly sought it because they cared.

You must set a goal one of them said.
And follow your dream wherever it led.

They all climbed aboard man's greatest machine.
Each of them fulfilling their own special dream.

While family, friends and the whole world looked on.
You could feel the pride in the cheering throng.

Imagine the thrill of their liftoff into space.
You could read the emotions in each and every face.

But before they could even believe it was true.
Smoke fire and explosion against a sky of blue.

An accident, a terrible twist of fate.
For the seven who had gone and wanted not to wait.
  Ruth Ann White

"I'm Stretched On Your Grave"

Our dreams have vanished,
our beautiful magical garden of love and life,
our garden has been taken away.

The roses has closed and died.
The Jasmine flower lost it's fragrance.

I'm stretched on your grave
the darkness seeps in.
Our dreams have vanished.
Dreams of looking into each
other's eyes and saying I do....
dreams of conceiving a child.

I am stretched on your grave
and will be there forever.

I will be there someday in your beautiful
sky garden, holding you for eternity.
  Veronica Ann Hurley

Ma-Ma

As I sit here wondering what to write,
On this long and somber night.
I can't imagine what to say,
That hasn't already been said in some other way.
The day was long, but the nights are longer,
Without you here my love grows stronger.
Even though you are not with me, life goes on,
Somehow I get by with you gone.
I miss you greatly every day,
Each reminds me of your gentle way.
Your peaceful wisdom and view of days gone by,
As I sit here wondering what to write,
On this long and somber night.
  Lesia Holley

Some Silence

In a nitpicking fight
Over what should be the noun,
We wasted half the night
And you really brought me down.

You threw me in a major quibble
With hidden words and double meaning,
Nothing but promotional dribble,
Equated to your pomp and preening.

Couldn't we get down to the basics of us
Without riding some tangent off into space?
I want to go home, babe, not get on the bus
For some street named semantics, losing my trace.....
  L. Lee Sorensen

"Home"

  Life is just a resting point, only
one moment in time, until we travel to a greater
place more loving and divine.

  In this place there is no pain, no
room for tears to fall, only the glory
of God's love, enough for one and all.

  The comfort of his perfect arms shall
greet her at his throne, and the beauty
of eternity to her will then be shown.

  Peace and love shall fill her soul,
through paradise she'll roam, with her
parents, friends and family...
    At last she will be home.
  Stacy Sands

Kandia

I see Asia in your features...
One of mother natures most beauteous creatures.
Sweet dark chocolate...
When engulfed in your beauty I almost forget;
About how oppressed we still are.
Cause within you I find hope your my shining star.
And my love for you would be as wild as the congo;
As long and as everlasting as the Nile.
I find sanctuary in your gorgeous smile.
And your so distant, as far as Asia. Yet as close as my
eyes can see, why is it so difficult for you to open up to me?
Open up to me like Tutankhamen's tomb, and we'll create a new
nation from your nurturing womb.
  Kafre Shabazz

Marine

How brave we are for being there to fight, always looking over
  ones shoulder all night through the darkness of the night.
When our hearts and souls reach a strange world everyday elapse,
  is another hurdle.
We move towards peace, that is the American way, it isn't all
  hardships or working for pay.
Something from the start in a Marine's life is installed within
  the Marines heart.
It is unexplainable in words alone, it's a feeling that Marines
  have, a feeling of our own.
The red,, white and blue speaks out in our voices, and our actions.
It stands for Liberty and Freedom. Our forefathers left us their
dreams to life, there thoughts of happiness. We should be so
generous to the children of the world, they depend on us to keep
them happy and well fed and free. We as Marines we'll treat the
future as we would as our own children, not wanting them to grow
up barbaric. We as Marines will fulfill these promises by performing
peaceful actions to keep the harmony in the world.
This is dedicated to the men that lived and died in the word of PEACE
  Steven Dell

Ground Zero

Sticks and Stones.

A cluttered clap-trap keeps my memories.
Only a battered knapsack cradles my tiny wishes;
A gray-walled refuge from a grey-willed world
That swallows my pride whole.
I come here to hide away
From the quick-switch tongues that lick the air
For the strangeness they feed on in a sudden jerk.

May Break my Bones.

In the eyes that stare from the walls, comforts are shallow.
In the ears that listen from the halls, promises are hollow.
The rot falls like rain on my head.
Hard little skies that fall to my bed.

But Words.

Beneath the sounds that surround me, my mother reaches.
Above the anger that engulfs me, my father watches.

Will Surely.

In my passive room, my hidden room, blows fall lightly.
Within my silent room, my shuttered room, thoughts strike
harshly.

Kill me.
  Laura Barltrop

Forecast: Rain

There are no shadows, no yellow moon,
only heat lighting in the North.

East wind with its summer voice beckons the
song of the whippoorwill to concert the
growing corn and invite the willow leaves
to curl upward in a majestic prayer for rain.

As the fireflies imitate the stars that
have gone into hiding, droplets wash the
salt from my brow through burning eyes, on
their search for the sea.

Frogs sing of peace in the valley, for
tomorrow sunshine will cover this corner of
the earth with everlasting life.
  Lloyd J. Vix

"Return From The Darkness"

She sits in the still of the night
Only aware of every breath she takes
  and every beat of her heart
Her body numb from all the confusion
  taking her mind thru the days past
Her spirit reached down to the depths
  of the darkness
Her body drawn with the cold
  inner feelings of her loneliness
Her mind wonders, looking for the
  depths of her soul
Taking her mind to the warmth of the
  sun, a soft breeze to her face, sounds of the pounding surf.
Returning in time when she felt alive
Remembering the arms reaching out to embrace
The music of a soft spoken word
A brilliant ray of love piercing the soul of her being
With the warmth of her thoughts she drifts
Drifts into the dreams of peaceful slumber
Engulf with the magic, never alone again
    Susan Y. Colquitt

Untitled

I know I cannot take back my words
  or even the damage that they have done
Had I thought before I'd spoken
  perhaps this pain would be none
I think our tongue can be our worst enemy
  for he knows not right or wrong
It then is left in the hands of our heart
  to determine where the love lies in our song
And in this tune a melody cries out
  it's better to keep this thought inside
For if released from one's mouth
  only bad things come which cannot hide
So you see my friend, my heart has failed
  in keeping things from remaining within
For friends and friendship mean the world to me
  and losing one would be a mortal sin
But then again, I too am only human
  and mistakes are bound to fall
I only wish I didn't hurt the ones I love
  to learn life's lessons all
    Stacey Jenkin

I Wish

I wish I could walk along the shore with friends
or someone I loved
to feel the breeze flow through my hair,
the waves splash upon my feet
while the sand rolls out from under them.

Off in the distance a sail boat glides across the horizon;
the fine line where the sky meets the sea,
where the sun disappears.

Children running across the sand chasing foamy waves
that tickle their feet and chase them back to the shore.

Crowded daytime beaches make way for secluded moonlit nights.
Time to share thoughts, dreams, hold hands and steal a kiss.

I wish I could have all of this.
    Kathleen Mead Palmer

Babushka

Two days from shore, exiled from home
  Our Gods no longer welcome there
Mama clutches baby to her fertile bosom
  Fuzzy lips waltzing, a frumpy lullaby
The boy oblivious to nourishing flesh
  Threatening to avalanche
An infant's tongue, blissfully silent
  But wondrous eyes bursting with onomatopoeia
Mama looks to the sunset and sighs
  She longs for those yesterdays
  She skipped barefoot with angels
And me, I am that captain
  Last night I set our course on a frigid star
And I haven't the heart to tell Mama
  That now we are hopelessly lost
Still, I have no worries
  My ship is steady on the calmest of seas
I grasp for the sea birds above
  As we all melt away
  Into the screaming pink horizon
    Kenneth B. Tebo

Benjamin's Teacher

We gave you precious cargo back in August '94.
Our little brown-haired angel so eager to learn more.

All ready for the second grade, and curious about you
He loosed my hand and entered your world of learning new.

"Oh Mom, there's too much homework, so many poems to learn.
My teacher says, 'Get organized.' Mom, aren't you at all concerned?"

"Why no, my child, by now I'm sure Mrs. Floyd is quite the best!
Do what she asks you everyday, and you'll have much success."

Ben took the best he'd learned from home, combined the same from you.
And now we're very proud to say he's mastered Grade Two.

Such energy for teaching, the likes I've never known!
So grateful for the time and love toward Benjamin you've shown.

The year's at end, Ben must go on - here's thanks for all you've shared.
For all you've taught and all you've done - deepest thanks because you cared.
    Kathleen Steinbacher Hepner

Silent Tears

I wish I could cry and shed my tears, but the
pain hurts so deep inside.

With a pain such as this the tears lie silent
In a dormant tide.

I reach out for a touch of gentleness only to
feel the slap of anguish from what should be
the gentle touch of love.

How can I reach the pain hidden so deep, how
can I stop the pain that seems to have no end,
how can I make the silent tears find the
soothing touch of love.

Can you hear me cry, can you feel my need, can
you turn this pain into calm and let the tide
of silent tears flow in a gentle stream?

Release the current that silently flows
deep inside me to such an extreme.

Release me from this torment that rages in a
quite pool of silent tears waiting to weep
into a pleasant dream.
    Terri Folbre

With Love, To Cindy

A new night, a new day
Our loved one has gone away,

To God, and in heaven, so pure
A place for peace, and that's for sure,

No sickness, problems, or life's troubled ways
A place where we long for throughout the days,

For a soul to endure and rest
Cindy strived to do her very best,

A home not like on earth we never had
For heaven, it is a place for us to be glad,

Cindy, you will always be alive in spirit and in our heart
For your memories and love will never, ever, part.
  Susan Tice Townsend

The Picnic Pond

By the pond there's laughter and fun
our picnic has just begun,

The birds fly high and the bee's buzz away
I wish we could do this every day.

I lay in the tall meadow grass
while my brother fishes for bass,

My dog is there so I play within him
I give him water from the barrel tin.

We get ready to leave, we drive away slow
And now the gifts of nature I know

I'm happy to day I'll be happy forever
To have this moment to have it together.

I have no memories that are quite as fond
as the ones of the picnic pond.
  Katelan M. Thompson

Ice Cream Snow

Every winter... when my brothers and I were young,
outside, our Dad would go,
shortly, he'd come back into the house,
with a great big pan of snow.

In those days, everyone was poor,
but, being kids, that never concerned us,
and when Dad made that Ice Cream Snow,
we knew it was worth the fuss!

To this day, I don't know how he made it,
but I remember the proud look on his face,
as the four of us sat at the kitchen table,
with a bowl of Ice Cream Snow, at each place!

If I could make a wish, and go back in time,
I know exactly where I would go,
I'd be sitting at Mom's kitchen table with my brothers,
eating Dad's.... Ice Cream Snow!!!
  Lorene Parshall McCahan

Empty Arms

I sit in my rocking chair looking at the moon
patting my belly, feeling my empty womb.
My eyes are filled with tears, thinking of
my future lonely years.

Feeling all alone looking at the phone
knowing there is not one who will understand,
the kind of feelings that make me
feel so bland.

My husband, my mother and family try to
be comforting and consoling to me, they tell
me I'm lucky I don't have something
wise wrong with me.

These words are fine, but they just don't understand
that my empty womb and empty arms are
more than I can stand.

People don't understand that I am torn apart
and all that I have left is a broken heart.

I cry everyday but that doesn't help.
I would never do myself any harm, but
somebody please help me deal with my empty arms.
  Susan Hoffman

Peace

Peace is when all nations can walk hand in hand.
Peace is taking time to help your brother understand.
Peace is for the children, the hungry, and the poor.
And peace is being there for all, to never shut the door.
We are each our brothers keeper, we are even more.
All of us are family, so why do we make war?
Lets all come together before it is to late.
Start loving one another, we have to stop this hate.
Our precious world is troubled, why can't we take a stand?
To stop the wars and violence, the raping of our land.
From the sea shore to the islands, rain forest and desert too.
This is our earth we're killing, what are we going to do?
Let's link our hearts together, the world can be free.
And bring about true peace on earth, goodwill and charity.
  Sherry Sue Adams

Change To Peace

WAR No questions No answers No reasons but why is there still peace?
PEACE Questions Answers Reasons so why is there still war?

Minds are made into what you want
so why are some bent and why are some not?
No one wants war but there is no end
Peace is the only thing here to lend
It's the only answer I can give
but peace is a different way to live.

HATE No questions No explanations No apologies
  but why is there still love?
LOVE Questions Explanations Apologies
  so why is there still hate?

To love is to live and to hate is to die
So why are there still some that cry?
If you want to live you have to see
There are some things that have to be
If you understand that they are there
you can find and feel them anywhere.
  Rachel Leigh Hanson

A Gallery Of Elegance

Compelled by the aura of the moment,
I was stunned by the beauty of what was before me.
Held captive by such a spectacle, the ecstasy of beholding the
sunset was mine. The sun, in all it's grace, was beckoning unto
me; as the clouds solemnly drifted before it's luster. The words
of eternal beauty glistened from the shimmer of the sunlight.

A warm breeze passed through my soul carrying the sweet scent of
plumeria. As the still rush of the tide was before my feet, the
elements seemed to have been singing a song of tranquility.
Moreover my heart breathed the life of the evening sun causing my
eyes to gleam with serenity. Woven within my heart was all this
array of beauty. The sky was orange. Then turning red it melted
with a hue of purple. A gallery of elegance such as I had never
seen passed along the edge of my soul. A subtle descended upon me
whispering the words to follow. The stillness of the air was as a
ship inviting me to board. As the illumination from the sun began
to diminish, I gave my heart to the moment. The sun, appearing weak
yet so close, fell lower and lower. As the sun descended over the
ocean and the light slipped away my heart sang out "carry me away".

Roland VanDenBerg

Tomorrow's Time

Tomorrow's time is said to be everyone's distant, hidden future
that none of us should ever have to know.
Even though we try to follow our more important duty's
for the every day place's that time allow's us to go.

With our special, common-sense that some of us do depend upon
comes the great happiness and satisfaction that life seems to achieve.
Our time help's us work out our own personal-problems
by making time more important than anyone of us could possibly believe.

So every one of us should find some sure and honest way
to use this precious gift of time and treasure every single minute.
Do not waste your hurried footstep's, by turning towards the wrong path
because life gives us back only whatever we put in it.

Sometimes, our one and only hope, wistfully turns to deep, unwanted despair.
never believing that things will ever turn out just right.
Than time patiently steps in to help soothe your uneasy mind
and brings you gently out of your lonely and darkened plight.

Once that time knew that it was put here to bring forth sweetness and charm
it never made any poor excuse's or find a good enough reason to
stall. when it made the most endearing and unbeatable, beautiful
person of you it surely knew that this time was the best, well-spent time of all.

Dorothy Meehan

Abuse

Man, woman, child just a screaming, while the tortures stand there
just a beaming. Standing there with fire in your eyes, while
lightening strikes across the skies. I wonder what is on your mind,
do you have one, have you lost it, or are you just blind? The hurt,
the pain that you cause with your hands, is like cutting the
circulation with rubber bands. My mind is pummeled with your lips,
while you stand before me with knuckles on your hips. It seems as
though night has drawn, it's curtain on my life. Your words cut
through like a saw bladed knife.

The wound is far deeper than you know, but the healing of this wound
will help me grown. Sit down sometime and search your soul. Could
you honestly face yourself so bold. Could you take the grief, and the
pain? That you strike, and spit, and issue so vain? Are you just the
product of an uneasy mind? Trying to turn back the hands of time.
The sun is rising in the East, behold, something is happening to the
beast. It stagger and sways, then drops to the ground. Then with
God's mercy, a person rises with a crown.

Ruth Allen

Soar As An Eagle

If I had wings as an eagle,
  Over mountains and valleys I'd fly.
I'd spread my wings toward heaven;
  With splendor I'd soar through the sky.

As sure as the storm clouds gather
  Upon the horizon so blue,
I'd sail straight toward the clouds
  As all brave eagles do.

With wings outstretched and head held high
  Straight over the clouds I'd fly,
Until the storm was over
  And the clouds had passed on by.

I know I cannot be an eagle;
  But I can surely try
To be like one while here on earth,
  And fly as eagles fly.

Oneita Bailey

Observations About Cats

Cats curl up in a ball on my lap,
Playing all night, in daytime they nap.

Cats hide out in dark secret places,
Whiskers accent their cute little faces.

Cats climb trees they cannot get down,
Their fur always sheds on my favorite black gown.

A cat's coat of fur is as soft as silk,
Their favorite treats are tuna and milk.

Cats sleep between people's legs,
Always seem hungry, they constantly beg.

A cat's paws walk on whatever they want,
Looking for trouble in alleys they haunt.

Cats eat bugs but reject their food,
Occasionally are shy but may appear rude.

Cats hiss while their fur stands on end,
Always land on their feet, not their rear end.

A cat's spiny tongue does the job of a shower,
They're a comfort to me in my bluest hour.

My dearest companion, never letting me down,
Together in love, unconditionally bound.

Leslie Plimpton

Hindsight

As down the road of life we wander,
Perhaps, sometimes to pause and ponder
  The mysteries of what might have been
What may have been-or could have been,
  The wondrous joys we may have shared
If only we had been prepared
  To meet each opportunity and challenge
With wisdom, and sufficient knowledge,
  That, no matter what our lot may be,
What might have been-would be;
  For good fortune comes to those who dared
To work, and learned to be prepared.

Richard W. Engle

Pelican Bay

Grey skies, grey concrete, steel pre-fabs. Baleem Whales and
Nightengales-and yardbirds. Blue denim, funny shirts, that look as
if they were balloons-floating in air!

Young men, brown-black, curly hair-big eyes that ask: "Why". Screws
in Khaki that seem preoccupied. Security and lock-step along high voltage wire.

Denied Access. "No clearance today." Sorry sir, you can't come in
here. "No pictures here." The zoo exhibits cannot be seen today! Go away.

Dripping wet skies, crying upon earth green-red blood drops.
Sequoias scrapping the sky. Ocean fog- lost fisherman at sea.

Lost young men-sharks on land, floating Jelly-fish, yellow, brown,
white and red. Arthritic knee-jerk Apparatchiks. Grace and a severe mercy!

Jesus on the main-line, a man of sorrows, acquainted with grief.
He knows the pain and still remains. Bright light-Hot on a cold September night.

M. S. Lynch

How Shall I Know Thee?

I know my God doth have a plan for every woman, child and man. That
man nor woman live alone; that every child must have a home; that
wife and husband render due to one, first mate, forever true. And I
know my God shall comfort me, until that day, I shall meet thee. But
oft' I ponder, "What might be?" I wonder "How shall I know thee?"

I look for eyes with clarity which see the longings deep in me. Which
see with truth both far and nigh; compassion's eyes, unafraid to cry.
I look for lips that do console; a tender smile that warms my soul. A
listening ear to hear my voice, both, should I cry or do rejoice.
With hands sun-darkened, skillful, strong; to honest work they do belong.

Your mouth speaks wisely, praises our King; shouts in laughter, songs
you sing. You whisper words I long to hear, counsel mild, as God you
fear. Your reason, fairness known far and wide, you are a man in whom
I take pride. You are quick to see my diversity, and accept whichever
ME is ME. For I am Woman and you must see, how passion's flame ignite in me.

Am I am Parent and you must know, to train a boy in the way he should
go. And I am Wisdom; I need to be heard, but too, I am Folly and
need be deterred. Your character sees to be firm, yet mild; for
oft' you'll find, I am but Child. My heart, my Father, he will read;
direct him, he will, with all I may need. So now or later, each other
we see; not to worry; "How shall I know Thee?"

Kathleen E. Creech

The Plague

There is a plague among us, which brings destruction wherever it goes,
It's will is relentless, in the path in which it flows;
It chooses each of its victims and in time it gets more and more,
Before you know it the plaque has spread like an agonizing sore.
It comes to you as an instrument of pleasure; one which will never end,
But no one can predict the pain it can inflict, as its dominance continues to bend.
It robs you of your sense of value, as your morals become so few,
It steals the very essence of life, and soon it will take that too.
As desperation sets in you try to turn back; your independence you try to redeem,
But just like a hook it lures you back and you loose your self-esteem.
And then you must be sent away, society can take no more,
After several months of madness they let you out the door.
You think you're cured and that's okay; but it's only an ambition,
For the plague will never go away, it's only in remission.
And now it's gone to take other lives while yours has melted away,
Destroying the lives of other victims whose lives have gone astray.
But fear not, the plague has no power, the power is in you,
Just remember who is in control, and you will make it through.
So try to keep your intelligence, and don't trade it for pain,
Because if you do, it will conquer you, and it's name is CRACK COCAINE

Reginald Craft

Untitled

F. Is for the Friendship we had.
R. Is to remember the good times we had.
I. Is for the important things we did together.
E. Is for you to evaluate the fun things we did.
N. Is that we never lied to each other.
D. Is for all the days we spent together.
S. Is for the sad days we spent together.
    like today were no longer FRIENDS.

Mercedes C. Rojas

Ghost Poison Ivory

The way I was I will never be again.
Poison ivory grew up my legs.
His arms nailed to a cross.
The pain he went through to save us.
The angel was born in a mansion.
And grew up in the countryside.
The life and death of a poet.
A Savior to lost souls.
I heard her ragged voice across the house.
I saw her blood drops on the floor.
She was raped, beaten and killed.
I put all my trust in you.
And you betrayed me.
Trapped in the forest with the ghost child.
In her ghost world,
Picking ghost flowers.
Scratching to the itch of ghost poison ivory.....

Marlena Huze

My Inner Peace

As I sit pondering with furrowed brow
Reflecting on my existence until now,
Life has been especially kind to me
And I am wondering about my legacy.

I see a life I would not change
With all its joys, tribulations, and pains,
I thank the Lord for bestowing on me
The strength and courage of my destiny.

I thank Him for my family and friends
Prayers, joys, and earnest desire to mend,
True inner peace in Him I depend
Encouragement and assistance until the end.

My desire to leave a lasting impression
On all who share my earthly remission,
Patience is my utmost virtue
As I anticipate my eternal curfew.

As I trod down the road of life with pride
Aware that He is by my side,
To help me cope with the twilight years
And guide me to eternity without fear.

Rita R. Seib

"What You Can Be"

Quietly let's gather around,
place your feet on solid ground.
Listen well and you'll hear the sound,
of this spinning earth to which we're bound.
Focus on the light and darkness is no longer,
keep yourself in tune and you'll become stronger.
With you mind at peace and your senses heightened,
you'll be armed with power and no longer frightened.
Now open your mind and you will see,
The path you have chosen,
and what you can be.

Tishawna Smith

A Job (Man) With No "Benefits"

I've cooked my food for you, and served it to you,
I've washed your dirty laundry, and ironed your clothes,
I've fixed lunch for you to go to work with,
I've even tried to make sex very enjoyable for you,
I've respected you and your wishes, and I did not force you to be a father,
I've given my hard-earned money to help you with your financial problems,
All these things I've done for you from the kindness of my heart,
you didn't even have to ask me to these things!
But, yet when I need you for something, I always get a
"NO" response, "NO BENEFITS!"
I can't even seem to get $2.00 from you for a love of bread!
Good people with good hearts you don't meet everyday, and good thing
only comes along once in life! I was your good thing, but, as I see
it your content being a "DEAD END JOB WITH "NO BENEFITS!" I only have
one life to live, and I can't allow you or anybody to rob me of my
"benefits"! Hopefully, one day you will realize nothing in life is
for "free", and that no relationship will work for you if you only
"receive" and never "give" benefits!

Sheila Tompkins

Broken Mirrors

I broke the mirror that imprisoned the vision of my hate
No longer could they see it reflected in my eyes
As indifferent skies turned black and shadows whispered in my heart,
   only the ghost of a memory could kill the pain
Illusions taunted the lost soul that wandered for so long, 'till
   everything faded away
Nothing left but the pieces of the broken mirror
And a prayer that lived within my tears
The wind desired nothing of my pain
Yet as the days were lost it changed it's course
A fire began to burn so deep, melting what once was, and would never be again
It was then that the pieces of my life, shattered and torn, merged as one
Healed by only that which could ever have taken me to the Heaven I am in
The love that I found in you
Storm clouds sweep by above the trees now and then, and rain can engulf
   the stability upon which we stand
But broken mirrors have turned to glass, and I will always see through
   to the truth
Where love will forever be waiting for you on the other side

Katie Bayer

A Cycle Of Love "A Wilderness Day"

   On clear bright days the birds will sing, thanking God for all he's
made through the meadow lush and green, the perfect blades of young
grass gleam, touched so softly by the wind as if to say I feel again.
Natures works are all divine, through ones eyes they can't deny, the
ever present sense of love.
   The snow that melts when spring comes forth, will spread its love
for all to grow, the fragile bud that stands alone, will soon become
a full blown rose. As the seasons start to part, the inter-faith of
natures heart, begins to sigh and gaze with pride to all the
wonderments of life.
   The white pearl waters of rivers flow to nourish creatures large or
small, the love of life of which it flows, provides the earth with all
it's growth. The early dawn of day brings light, with hope and faith
for better lives. The evening sun retreats away, reflecting thoughts
of brighter days' when all the people in the land will show respect
to all that stands, using only what they need and wasting nothing just
for greed. Giving knowledge and helping hands only brings the best in
man, and with patience, love, and faith, we all can find that natures
day, of peaceful thoughts and warm embrace.

E. J. Mendoza

"Feeling Sad"

As I stare into the darkness,
Pity overcomes me,
I feel so lifeless,
It seems like eternity,
Life sucks dearly,
Death seems so nearly,
You don't understand the things I'm going through,
So I wouldn't even ask if I were you,
I cry - I weep,
I die - I sleep,
My heart aches,
My heart breaks,
My head hurts,
My heart hurts,
My eyes swell,
My heart's not well,
It's not you or the things you do,
It's just me feeling blue.

Tiffany Kinsey

Where Do Poems Hide

Poems hide in the wings of a bird that flies
Poems hide in a sweet girl's eyes
Poems hide in an empty pocket book
Poems hide in corners, walls and every little nook.

Poems hide inside a mother's kindness
Poems hide inside a child's tears
Poems hide behind a father's strong hand
Poems hide in a child's laughter.

Poems hide in beds when children are scared.
Poems hide in the sparkling eyes of a sweet teddy bear
Poems hide in a child's dreams
Poems hide in a still picture.

Poems hide in your heart
Poems hide in your mind
Poems hide in your soul
Poems hide in the sunshine.

Poems hide in sisters and brothers
Poems hide in the hurt of others
Poems hide in the wings of a bird that flies
Poems hide in a sweet little girl's eyes.

D. J. Jensen

Gangster Girls

How will you support your children?
Rob, steal and Jack, replies the girl of 16.
At 14 a mother, at 16 havin' another.
Where you goin', gangster girl?

Who's gonna take care of the children?
What's gonna happen when you're gone?
Huffin' and puffin', crackin' and jackin'
Ain't no life, gangster girl!

Society buildin' walls higher and higher.
The ladder of life gettin' shorter and shorter.
What if Brentwood or Bellemeade knew this girl?
Can we abandon the gangster girl?

Count your money, don't give her a second glance
Turn your back on the scared tough girl,
She doesn't deserve a chance,
Poor, poor gangster girl.

Can't get out 'cept death, she say.
A home boy's Ho is her pointless life.
It ain't pointless, she say,
It's the life of a gangster girl.

Willy K.

The Universe Within

Look to the heavens for inspiration, for there will you discover the mysterious of eternity. Flickering lights in a vast ocean of darkness beckon you to listen to their voices, each echoing like a spirit spirit calling from across Elysian fields. Memories from ages gone by are kept aflame forever in an otherwise vacuous sky.

And the sun and the moon stand like guardians of the realm, waiting for one who will cross the threshold out of this manacled world. Open your mind to the energies of these celestial wayfarers and be awakened in the ebb of time.

The counsel you will receive is wise beyond measure, filled with the words and images of days unrecorded and all but forgot. Free yourself to the unbridled rush of emotions which propel the stars ever onward. Reflect upon the messages of each and every wind. In the end, all will be clear. The answers you seek from the depths of the universe will always be, as they have always been, within.

Angela Beltrani

Just When

When it seems like my world is upside down that's when to step in.
   Just when I think all hope is gone that's when you appear with hope and peace.
   When everything around me comes falling down and I have on one to talk to, and my eye are full with tears, that's when you talk to my heart.
   Just when I try to do the right thing and the wrong comes around that's when you tell me to hold on help is on the way.
   Lord, have patients with me for I'm not though with you yet. I need you more in my life then I did 3 years ago.
   Just when I have no where to run no where to turn to - that's when you say my child - my child fear not for I'm the light, the true vine, I'll give you inner-peace.
   My child go to the hills, for there you will find all the help, you'll ever need.
   My child you will never have to worry nor will you have to walk alone, for I'm your strength when you're weak, your sun shines when your days seem the most darkest.'
   Lean on me my child and you'll never feel lonely again. Pull all your trust and faith in me.

Kellie Lewis

Garden Of Eden

I know a garden where flowers are too brilliant to look at straight on.
In order to see you must go through a room where nothing is expected,
But everything is real.
It is worn and frayed and beautiful from the efforts of making a soul.
It contains rare splendor that comes to only those t hat are perfectly loved.
There is no silk here.
Only burlap.
Nothing is glossed or lacquered or pumiced.
But it is loved.
Here, where I am always a child, I play a trumpet that had long ago lost its operative parts.
But I can hear the music.
I do not know how to sing or write poetry; but I know how to pray.
I know how to take a mental picture of a perfect summer day,
And keep it in order to always have it for after that part of you is gone.
A man once drew my portrait on a tablecloth,
But I do not remember if it was any good.
I remember what matters; what I need to exist beyond this garden gate.
And what haunts me when I am in bed at night.
I am so scared of forgetting.

Katherine Stevens

Hands

Hands, rose petal soft in infancy,
Seemingly are the minds first curiosity.
Unique tools, a Master designed,
Prints, marking them one of a kind.

As the mind begins to grow,
Hands are its richest learning tool.
When the mind has grasped the learning tasks,
Hands no longer teachers, are servant at last.

Hands can be gentle, loving and kind;
Give guidance, or pen a line;
Perform great feats of dexterity,
Giving credence to their ability.

Hands hold the sword that downs the foe,
In senseless anger can be brutal and cold.
But always hands are only tools,
Guided by the minds given set of rules.

Let it be said, when a man is laid to rest,
His hands laid stately upon his earthly chest.
"He left his hand prints upon the annals of time,
He left a legacy of inspiration for mankind"

Sandra Starks

Sunday Morning

The alarm awakens us from a deep sleep,
Seems like I just stopped counting sheep.

She reaches and hits the snooze without opening her eyes,
The alarm is sounding time to arise.

That five minutes turned into a half-hour,
Now we're standing in line for the shower.

Hurrying to dress and to eat a bite,
We said we wouldn't do this last night.

Dressing kid's, putting on shoes,
This must be the Sunday morning blues.

Off to the car we're doing just fine,
Pulling into the parking lot with no spare time.

Into church to worship and pray,
Let's give Jesus thanks on this Lord's day.

Thanks for all these little tests,
It makes me try my very best.

To be that person He knows I can be,
The one I'm searching for inside of me.

Windle White

A Better Place

Going home to God's Better
Place a special time for human race.
No hurt, sorrow or distress. A warmth
and joy to comfort without making
you second guess. Nor are we perfect;
we're human kind cause God made
us that way even though we share different
minds. This ole world has been a struggle
love, pain, hurt and distress but heaven
sends us to better times to conquer the rest.
On this earth we all do good and bad;
now the time has come to go beyond Karma for
eternal peace. So rejoice and be happy you
knew me; never be sad. I'm leaving on this
earth a part of me and a part of you. So wipe
away those tears because I'm only going to rest
Until God takes me all the way home and if
you wish to see me again rejoice in the Lord
and you'll never be alone.

Linda F. Hurdle

Dark Boomerang

Tri colored memories of sadness more devastating than the bombing of
Pearl Harbor so merciless and utterly unkind
Spasmodically fluttering the hemispheres of my once becalmed mind
Drown deeper into lonely grief imprisoned by it's bind
Disturbed by a ploy to destroy
The discovery
of recovery
So I serve you notice of eviction
Drawn from my inner souls' strong conviction
I cast you away for as long as I live
My life to you no more will I give
Inside of it you'll never ever reign
Your efforts are all counted as vain
Like a boomerang return to your domain
Mary Antionette Morgan

A Private Observation

Today I chanced to observe one of the most beautiful
pictures I have ever seen
It was like an elegant moment stolen from some old
grand masters painted canvas.

A scene so enchanting I had no doubt it was created
by God and Mother Nature for my private view
In this quiet forest glade this very afternoon.

It was like an Angel had descended from Heaven and had
brought a nativity scene for me to see.
I watched a small group of wild creatures in this
glade feeding, gently playing, and drinking water from
the stream.
I saw the white dove-symbol of world peace-
three baby chipmunk, 2 squirrels, a tiny fawn and the
mother deer.

It was so beautiful I knew I was trespassing in
some picturesque enchanted forest from a long lost yesterday.
Lee E. Herring

Christmas Dinner

Gathered round the board,
share the Oplatki and prayers.
The extra space for the stranger conspicuous.
No one has ever come,
but out of duty we keep waiting
for someone passed or not yet arrived.
Who's to say?

On this night of talking animals,
the straw beneath the cloth
reminds me of the manger
and before that the fertility of the Earth
and all of Her goodness.
I can smell its freshness above
the barely and mushrooms and onions.

Imbedded in the straw and barley,
the coarse bread and tongue heavy language,
beyond the symbol of religion, is where we come from.
And our tongues, too heavy for English words
are freed when we gather to keep vigil and celebrate fertility
In the dead of winter, in the symbol of Child.
Robert A. Sarnowski

Tristan's Tryst

Alas, poor Tristan, doomed to an ill-fated affair;
Pinning for his lover, Iseult the Fair -
Climbing the vine-covered, illicit lattice -
Coming face-to-face with an intricate abatis;
All for his heart; but all for nought.

Reaching the wall, he held out his hand - bestowing a charm to the
    one he thought was his Iseult; the Bright, Beautiful, and Tall.
Being identical; he could not tell them apart at all, very well.

But behold!
It was the White-Handed Isolde who first touched his hand
And; as if in union, took the Stone of Cornwall.
From that day forth, his fate was sealed; tricked by a kiss that
    quickly congealed her desire over his;
While her uncle Mark silently conspired with the friar
    to concoct a deed too terrible; even for the dark.

Alack, pitiful Iseult the Fair -
dying by her own sister's poisonous snare;
Set like a lionesses' livid lair.
When Tristan finally found her there; he too, lay dying from
love's deepest despair.

Two star-crossed lovers none-the-less, were Iseult-
And Stir Tristan of Lyoness.
Michele M. Rousseau

"The Sweetest Dish I Know"

As the night began to blanket the face of the earth, I
placed my feet under the safest and sanctimonious place
my stomach had ever known.

My mind is completely open to the dish, which unknowingly,
was about to be forced upon me, yet its sight brought no tone.

For I had seen this plate before, there was one main
course with no side dish.

The course was cold raw meat, the blood oozed slowly
through the dents of the meat, but would not fall for
it clung to the old meat like a dreamer to a wish.

Then rose a cold icy crust to the surface and I pleaded
with myself not to indulge, for, also there was a growing
colony of mold.

And so I finally ate and enjoyed my snowy meal, so
ultimately—REVENGE is a dish that tastes sweetest
when served cold.
Rich Hamilton

Point Blank

Point blank - anybody, anywhere.
Point blank - all the G.I. Joes go there.
There are rules and releases and helmets to wear,
To play this game you must take care.

From the gun, the paint pellets fly.
Like the colors of the rainbows, they all zoom by.
Indoors, outdoors, wherever you play.
Barrels, bushes, and trees in the way.

Tires, gullies, cactus, creating a maze.
Excitement, suspense, your mind's in a haze.
The thrill's in the hit (except when it's you).
The skill of the player can keep him from view.

Win or lose, this game's a blast.
Play it once, your fate is cast.
You'll be back when you've got a "buck"
So, play it safe and "lots of luck"!
Lee Brieden

Its Name Is Progress. . .

Am I too in love with moonbeams for today?
Please, don't yank the carpet of my world away.

Listen up, why gouge out the eye of my sky;
And break the back of my hill with bricks piled high!
What's wrong with green grass, sumac and violet patch,
Songbirds on watch above nested eggs to hatch;
Oaks echoing suede gloved silence of Spring shine
And star ringed nights like before the neon sign?

So, hit the black top to where what man has wrought;
And mall-hop like mad for peace that can't be bought.

MaryAlice Adams

Friends

If you have a special friend
play and have fun again and again
everyday your friend will be there
to share and dare the laughter of the song in the air
Be fair and kind and treat your friend right
Because if you don't they will be out of sight
So don't try to get in a fight
Always try to do what is right
If it feel right in your heart
Then your special friend must have be there
from the start!

Laura Nunnaley

Our Son

Stop, for I feel your pain,
please don't share it with me.
Your pain, your agony.
I'm not that strong. Yes, I am so weak.
Cry, if you must, but why am I here,
sharing your pain.
Why must I hear your Screams?
The doctors saying "Push one-two-three".
Your breathing is strong, Your eyes wide and red.
Your face looks quite pale, as if you are dead.
You look at me, I look at you,
Why are you punishing me, what did I do.
Wait! what is this sound I hear.
a sigh of relief? What could it be?
a different scream, a sweet gentle scream,
a son, a son, you gave to me.
Now, I understand, why I am here.
Sharing your pain, your love, your life.
The miracle of birth,
Our Son, our son, our sweet gentle son.

Pedro W. Gomez

The Sunshine Virus

Dear Teacher,
   Please excuse my son, I'm sure he's not the only one,
but when the sun shine you must be aware
it's hard for him to keep his seat.
His work is often incomplete
And he suffers great discomfort being there.
I'm told this flares up in the spring
And seems to itch when school bells ring,
By afternoon there is a rash anticipation
My young son has it worse than most,
So I have had it diagnosed
The doctor calls it "Bored of Education"
They thought it never struck adults
But now they have school test results.
He said there's really not much you can do
Except ease up on firm insistence
Scolding lowers the resistance,
And many, many teachers get it to.

Lynette LaPage

Soul Searching

I've found paradise in the heat of a sweet embrace,
I have felt great pleasures in satin and lace.
These eyes have seen far too much to
understand, yet my curiosity grows, beyond demand.

My hand, for it so quivers, yet it still writes.
My heart, it ponders, in a world full of wrongs and rights.
Tear stains cover my face, has hatred wiped out the human race?

Eyes that cry so soft in the night, have mighty strength, have
strenghty might. Forget about yesterday, for tomorrow is another,
life's turmoil and fisticuffs has cast my heart to smother.

For skeletons hidden away in my closet has shadowed evil silhouettes
on my soul. Pain has pushed me into a dark hole.
Feelings of thrill have run up and down my spine,
for I long for the tasting of lips as sweet as cherry wine.

If you shall ever read my writings, then you shall read my life to me,
but only as far I let your eyes and mind see.
Simply for what you have not lived, you shall not understand,
if I cannot lead you than I shall let go of your hand.

There are some old evils that don't want to be embraced in the
innocence of youth, a path so unpredictable — HA! ain't that the truth

Love and Life — there is no substitute, and those sweet whispering
words of saccharine, to which I am mute.

Shantey R. Lindsay

The Bird Ghosts...

I saw him and he did with one finger
Poised call them
Thru colored prisms of glass,
His two bird like ghosts
And he touched them I think
And spoke to them and they listened.

Later he bid them go and they did,
He would look again at me
As if the bird ghosts had never come at all
Thru colored prisms of glass
And perched upon his shoulders
One and one
And listened to every word that we spoke.

Norman Thaddeus Vane

Compassion

Rarely recognized, as the conscience of the heart
Pure and absolute; my essence, from the start.
Varied and many are the endeavors of mankind;
Hectic their pace..with hardly a moment to unwind.

The torrent created will surely sweep some aside;
Lost to the mainstream...and left needing a ride.

Gone are the familiar faces that did lend a hand,
Leaving them alone, within a strange land;
To kick and struggle until are sore...
Still hoping to gain that which was familiar..once more.

Silently...from among those hordes without passion,
Must I find one of them, whose heart I can fashion;
To stretch their resource, yet an extra mile;
And return to a lost face, that special smile.

So...consider for now, that without the sweat of my brow;
Where.. in this wonder of creation, would humanity be now?

Paul Prusiensky

Simpelcide

Stir me up
pour me out
let my blood oozze through your spout

I took your life
and now your dead
just put the gun up to your head......up to your head

Why'd I do it
I don't know
I've always been a little slow

I put the gun
into my mouth
I pulled the trigger
I'm headin' south......I'm headin' south
Robby Curley Jr.

So

So what if murder is a crime, I've seen worse things.

A person can get locked up for robbing a bank, but not for robbing someone of their self-esteem.

So if I call you names and hurt your feelings, so what!

It's not against the law. So, excuse me if I'm cold hearted it's just a natural flaw.
Marla Mahoner

"Trapped"

Trapped in a box, on the third floor no less.
Pulled by the gravity we all were quite stressed.
Outside commotion to get us all out,
Inside commotion that we won't get out!
Praying talking and screaming at times,
After twenty-five minutes she finally arrives.
Yes, our hero she comes and with a pull and a tug,
Frees open the doors, and lets out everyone.
At last it is over, we're much wiser now.
We keep Jaime away, from the stop button now!
Kristi LaFountain

The Struggle

Wandering, rambling, aimlessly,
  Racing for that nearing shore
    A twig upon the sea of time
      It's refuge reached to leave no more

A myriad of raindrops we,
  Descending through our youth
    Quixotes, ludicrous, one and all
      Searching out that final truth

Hitler's Lions some of us
  Christ's lambs the rest
    Both nurturing one blade of grass
      When finished with the final test
Larry Beck

Elaine The Pain

Elaine the pain I say she really is
she bugs me, she tricks me. I really do
not like her. One day I say I'll really
get her back for what she's done to me.
If she get's me back some day some how I'm sure
I'll also get her back
Tiffany Calderone

Harley Country U.S.A.

Dusk rises with the setting of the sun
Rainbows frame the vast sunset
Tendrils of smoke rise from the tobacco barns
  as the burley is cured
Cows leave their pastures and trot on home
The reds; golds and oranges of the turning leaves
Appear brilliant against the background blue sky
  and green rolling hills
The grey silos stand at silent attention
  saluting me, one by one, as I pass
My pipes rumble and roar as I navigate
  winding two-lane blacktop
Horses neigh and dogs bark as I roll past
  their farms
Red barns, white farm houses, silvery blue ponds
This is truly Harley country
Lisa L. Dotson

Tin Rap

"10,000 soldiers and a will to be free
Rampaging armies that kill and then flee.
Is this the only way we know to stay alive
Bringing pain and sorrow and nothin' but strife?
Killing all the people, even mother and child
Have we all gone crazy; are we really all wild?"

"Can't we find an answer, have we really looked?
Could be in their eyes, could be in some book.
We all should take the time to care today
And tomorrow you can bet, it just might pay.
So take a long hard look deep inside your hearts
We all can make a difference if we each do our part."

"It's not so complicated you can figure it out
it doesn't take a mastermind, just need to lose the doubt.
Nuclear wars and little starving babe's eyes
Wake up world don't you hear their desperate cries?
Clean up the land and we'll see a brighter day
That's the way I see it, and that's all I have to say."
Susan C. Belanger

When

The thoughts of lovers far apart
Reach out and touch each others heart

When the night is clear and stars are shining bright
I'll be thinking of you when the moon casts down it's glimmering light
I'll know you're beneath it's glow too

When the autumn leaves sparkle and a gentle breeze
brushes against my face
I'll hope the same soft breeze touches you and brings
a memory of my embrace

When the first snow falls and blankets the ground in white
I'll imagine your eyes with mine watching this beautiful sight

When I am excited and happy or hurting and sad
I will share in my mind with you good times and bad

When I'm listening to notes of a love song played low
and it makes my heart ache as I'm missing you so
I'll remember the words that you spoke to me then
and believe that we'll soon be together again

When,...in the quiet of the night, I lay my head upon the pillow
If you listen carefully...you can hear me whisper your name
and I'll dream...you are whispering mine the same
Kathryn Scott

A Quilt, A Pattern Of Life

The old green dress was thin and worn
ready to be discarded because it was torn.
Yet the discards could yet a purpose serve
with scissors to cut—a rectangle, or a curve.

Different sizes of cardboards, a pattern to be made
with old dresses, shirts; colors for a design to trade.
Hues to dark, shades of light, wonderful colors to bring
when placed here, when placed there — a double ring.

Events in life may be like the old garments' worth
cut asunder, torn, shattered pieces to give birth.
A tattered life filled with despair and pain
all fit together as you walk down memory's lane.

Heartbreaks, a tear, a smile, a touch,
floods through your mind like an artist's brush.
Cloths spread out, patterns on top, to make a double ring
the fun, the laughter, a soft breeze makes your heart sing.

From a very small seed your life began
growing as you walked along life's span.
Parts are dark, some may be blue
this is why your quilt of life rings true.
  Wanda Jo Crawford

"Sea Of Life"

At the beach the stars and sea
Reflect a life determined to be
In the night the sea is gray
Stars are beacons from far away
All the while I stand and stare
In a darkness yet quite aware
Of nature flowing in and out
The tide rolls in
Its ebb not without
A moving wonder that never ends
It lives to tell a message that sends
Me walking back from the beach
With stars and sea easy to reach
For the memory lingers of continuous motion
A reminder instilled of life and devotion
  Pat Lavala

Water Wonder

Liquid lucid life!
Refresh my soul, baptize my spirit
run over my whole body naked, cascade through every follicle
slide down the hair on my head, meander, stop.
Cling for dear life and then ripple at my feet

Gush down a falls over me
cut canyons in my shoulder blades, form valleys in my spine
Erode my body like you wash away mountains:
Split me up particle by particle and carry with you
along your downstream journey to the heart of the earth herself

Flow on, river
mighty droplets reflecting the sun with brilliance and movement
Dance jig shimmer ebb ripple drip-drop dive plunge
splatter off into the air and become the air, until you reform as one
and smack back down upon the rock-snatching
a particle as nature's forces act upon you

Melt away my fingers my bones my torso with your power
until I wander off piece by peace
in each and every one of your tributaries;
in search of my destiny.
  Paul Kreher

Old Man

Weak, old man
Refrigerator wheezing, weeds growing.
Days telescope, all alone.
Last free day
Fighting weakness, he goes outside
Dusty, dry earth. He's sweating.
Going to Baltimore. Last free day.
Young man pulls over, hands him a white helmet
They whiz off. Free.
Going to an old folks home
He's independent. Free.
Strong in mind he sits in a chair with no rockers
Hiding weakness. Wants to die alone.
Thoughts turn to home made fudge and reading books.
Shoulders slump, mind vague and angry
Walks into home tall and straight.
Meets Mr. Pond, he tells his story:
Cracked plaster walls and waterproof mattresses.
Stale cookies, old and tired.
  Myra Dinsdale

Remember The Folks

When everything seems right and going your way,
Remember where you were, and where you are today.
Remember back when things weren't so good,
Then remember, the folks who always understood.

Remember the mother who sat by your bed,
Dried all your tears, and cuddled your head.
Remember the father who led the way,
Helping to make you what you are today.

The farther you go, and the higher you get,
Remember the folks who think of you yet.
Keep your heart humble day by day,
And remember the folks along the way.
  Shirley S. Adcock

Downsizing

Now-a-days whenever I hear
Restructure or reorganize
Immediately rings in my ear
The word "downsize"
I hear laying off people
Is the easiest way to reduce cost
The idea may sound simple
But who or what are affected most?
Low self-esteem of the people and their family
Along with fiscal and mental depression
Can cost the taxpayers a lot of money
Compared to the savings by cost reduction
Reduce overheads and material usage
Eliminate all kinds of wastage
Be sensitive to people's needs
Consider their good deeds
In every corporation
Pink slips should be the last option
People are not robots
With "buy-off" emotions cannot be bought.
  Sabyasachi Gupta

Nightmare

Life is a nightmare
That always come true
Even when you don't want them to.
Things always happen
And you have no control.
But one of these days, it will all be true!
  Shanna Marchinke

It's Just My Nature

Falling or failing is in my nature
Rising or flying is in my nature
Times may come
Times may go
I come as I may, go wherever I wanna go
Nothing to hold me
or control my nature
Don't try to stop me
It's my nature to do what I wanna do
I never thought I had to ask you
Once again I've gone a little further, further, and further
I feel you know me, want me

Can you hold me or even stop me?
Don't try to...
My nature won't let you
Shalirita Singh

I Have

Played soccer, opened a locker,
Sailed Higgins Lake, skied outside of the wake,
Petted a cat, swung a bat,
Hit a ball, run in the hall,
Dunked a basket, put a hamster in a casket,
Read a book, fished with a hook,
Swam on a team, eaten a Taco supreme,
Lost in pool, broken a rule,
Milked a cow, smelled a bow-wow,
Ridden a bike, thrown a strike,
Dove in the river, gotten a splinter,
Climbed a tree, swatted at a bee,
Driven a boat, written a note,
Felt good, and made a poem for Mrs. Wood.
T. C. Ford

Untitled

Like the sirens of you're
Sailors crash into loves rocky shore
Lured by your enchanting voice
Lonely hearts have no choice

Cause Aphrodite smiled down on you
Giving you beauty thru and thru
With a loving heart that's rare
That everyone longs to share

Whenever Eros fills hearts with desire
Apollo picks up his enchanted lyre
Giving music to the morning breeze
Joined by a choir of flowers and trees

Morpheus and Ikelos spin their tales at night
But their visions of beauty rarely see daylight
For their magic can't begin to compare
To the 'garden of eden' that we share

Cause Aphrodite smiled down on you and me
Giving us love that will last an eternity
Rick Peterson

Untitled

Oh, hypocritical blow job queen!
Seeks forgiveness in bizarre places
uncharted lands of my psyche,
so benevolent in spectacle,
merciless wicked beyond.
A coiled serpent under a white lily,
tinted with scarlet, melancholy butterfly massacre.
Odessa Zeromus

Dreams Of Yesterday

Blessed by the morning rain
Satisfaction stretches a smile from ear to ear
The sun struggles to greet me with it's warmth
And I am graced by nature with a cushion
It appears that the shades of time have touched each strand of my youth
For the twinkle in my eyes have dimmed
And the snap in my movement that has slowed
My life is numbered by one grain of sand
Reflecting unequalled passion for happiness, for challenges
Gifted with visions of my legacy
I embrace the silhouettes
Etched onto blankets of hidden pages
Each breath that I labor echoes a song of laughter in my heart
As traces of a gentle glisten engulf my smile
Recalling the colors of the rainbow
And the majestic beauty of my homeland
I yearn to play in mythical land
Where the sun dances beyond the clouds
For the fair winds of the universe wash through my soul
As I am invited to sit through dreams of yesterday once more.
Ruth K. Marks

Trip Two Bits

  So there I was flying through space, when I noticed my scanners had picked up a trace of several objects matching my pace. It would have to happen this far from home base!
  I then changed my position for a tactical one, forcing them to fly toward the sun. I took aim and fired my gun, and then noticed that my gun was on STUN.
  I didn't have time to get them back in my sight, as I had to avoid blasts from the rest of the flight. It wasn't until then that I noticed my plight, when I saw twenty ships! I turned white.
  I thought that a Space Bomb would be best to begin. To blow-up in their midst, is what my plan had been. Things went my way and I thought I would win, when I had to stop to put another quarter in.
Michael A. Hvidt

Set Her Free

There is a little girl inside of me that is crying to be free.

At age five he came to my bedroom in the lateness of the night.
He scared and hurt me but I didn't know enough to fight.

I thought this happened to all little girls by their dad, I didn't know our secret was so very, very bad.

The silent screaming mommy, mommy save me! I would cry.
Help me please, Oh God, I just want to die.

Then he would whisper in my ear "I'll hurt you and mommy if you tell."
He is dead now and I hope he rots in hell.

The pain for me still goes on, I've tried to cover it with drugs and booze.
I hate myself and have no self esteem and feel there is nothing else to loose.

Time and again I've tried to take my life to set that little girl free.
Please help me find my sanity, I need me and all that I can Be.
Patricia Dowd

Loneliness

Why do I feel like this, so lonely all the time?
Sometimes I think there's no one there even if I'm not right.
I know that I just cannot hide the pain I feel inside,
But is hard to let it out because I kept it all the time.
So I just sit here thinking, maybe I should cry?
I've tried to tell so many people about how I feel sometimes,
But something stops me, and I am just afraid to let pain out.
I have to tell someone the way I feel right now,
Before it is too late, and the time is gone.
Luba Dubrova

Untitled

No separation of sky and sea
Selene sings to Poseidon a song of divinity
She lays upon his roving flesh
Lets out a mystical sigh
For an instant the two become one
Opals bleeding from her thigh
He lets out a thunderous roar
Waves rising and crashing, licking the ocean floor
Apollo steps in with a voyeuristic grin
To separate the lovers
From their most orgasmic binge
Melissa Blankensop

Paws' Song

I had a little bunny and the bunny's name was Paws.
She had cute white fur that hid her claws.
She was the nicest, softest bunny that you ever did see,
I loved her like myself and I know she loved me.
She was softer than any rabbit anyone's had.
To touch her cool, gray fur could stop my being sad.
She died the other day in her bed of straws.
My bestest bunny friend, my little, gray Paws.
We wrapped her in a cloth as blue as the sky.
I laid her in the ground, and let my heart cry.
My only bunny Paws. Now resting peacefully
Beneath a quilt of flowers from a crepe myrtle tree.
Laura Hansen

Autumn

Smell the crisp morning air
See the trees sway slow and fair,
I sit on my steps ready to play
As I watch the trees sway and sway

The wind blows silently
As the leaves crunch quietly
The orange and yellow leaves on the ground
Crunch quietly as we run around

I stop and rest and hear a sound
If you take time and hear
There's a colorful sound in your ear
Leaves crunching,
Children running,
Crisp morning air,

The wind is blowing without care
I feel the wind blowing through my hair
I see the leaves fluttering with care
Leaves crunching, wind blowing
Crisp morning air.
Those are the sound of autumn you see and hear.
Tiffany Jones

"Final Curtain Call"

Competing with space and gravity,
She mixed crinoline with time.
The hellish heat from lights parched her flesh
While a cacophony of kettle drums stifled the flute.
Peering eyes were masked by the darkness,
Reflecting a tormented smile in their mirrors.
Rosin sang on frail, pink satin toes.
Gyrating, she soared with the grace of a gull.
The once fluttering heart beat as if stone...
Since decades, her enemy, hid in the wings.
Tears fell on roses with a curtsy of remorse.
The phantom exit beckoned her well worn path.
Alone — Memories and pink shoes hang on a wall.
Mary Kay Fleming

Prayers For Spring

I know a man, who tho' kind and gentle, is so
sensitive to life that he wears suits of metal, I
struggle in vain to find some way to enter, through
places worn thin - to reach the honeyed center, and
I'm glad that I've loved him for now I remember, how
the coldness of armor can freeze me forever, still
I yearn for a glance and a crushing embrace, as
the pain I feel leaves when I numb to erase, for
Spring's coming early and it really does matter, that
the warmth plus the coldness could cause it to shatter, I
stutter in saying good-bye to a lover, when
the thawing could reach him one way or another, so
I sit back and watch and I wait and I pray, for
the love that I feel to reach him some way, still
the metal I slam against makes me remember, how
the coldness of armor can freeze me forever.
Kris Lavedas

When Passion Rests

Touch... breathe...
　See thru me, I'm exposed.
Painting feelings to the touch.
　Fingers like flower pedals
　　blown in the wind,
　They pass over your naked skin.

I long to measure the capacity
　of your sensualities, and how
　they move within you.
Cautiously I press myself against you,
　They move within me,
　My emotion flutters with erratic rhythm.

In the subtleness of quiet thought,
　when desire is silent...
　and business is as usual.
There is a passion that rests,
Like a seed fallen into the winter ground,
　Awaiting its season to rise
Reno K. Lawrence

If My Womb Had Windows

Fourteen years old a young girl in love
Seemed all that mattered to me
My boyfriend was all I had and all I'd ever need
Then one day I realized a change inside of me
I was just a child and this child was going to have a baby
If my womb had windows I could truly see
My precious little baby smiling back at me
If my womb windows it would bring tears to our eyes
To see many mommies take their own baby's lives
But my womb had no windows and confused at the time
I aborted my baby's life and committed a terrible crime
tears flow down my face today realizing what I had done
God knows the pain I have for my special little one
God knows the hurt I have inside each day of my life
So it God gives you a child please don't abort, think twice.
Think about your precious life that God gave you and I
That precious baby needs you mommy so please don't make them die
Oh Lord if my womb had windows....
Lana Puckett

Beacon

Light: guiding through storms of darkness
Thrusting tide: drowning the unearthed sand
Faithful pulse: calming the soul
The Beacon: widening the path to the rainbow's source

He brings us home.
Susan Goldsmith

Flames

An ear piercing bell echoes through the firehouse
Shadows of people are racing around gathering their
Equipment

Black rubber boots
Long yellow coats
Hard hats and hoses
Are all put on the truck

Roaring sirens and a red blur race around every corner
Finally coming to an abrupt stop

Powerful sprays of water shoot up into the air
Drenching its surroundings

The bravest firefighter darts into the burning building
Trying to avoid the flames

The fire seems to grab at her feet pulling her into the sea
Of reds, yellow, and oranges. Her arms fly about wildly
Out of control destroying everything in her path

She's blazing out through the windows as the horrified
People watch from the sidewalks

Everyone is gone now except for her thick curls of black
Smoke and smoldering ashes
Kelly Grim

Untitled

As far as the eye could see were blue skies.
Shapes of white blended in occasionally.
From behind, I could feel the warm embrace of the summer sun.
With the cool ocean breeze, every strand of my hair gently raised up,
   then lay close to my waist.
My feet sank even further into the sand with each new wave.
A child's laughter could be heard nearby.
He was the Lord of the Land; and very proud of it.
His castle stood tall until high tide crashed over it.
No longer was there laughter.
Only sadness and salty tears running down his sunburnt face.
Affectionate parents comforted him with a simple hug.
They gathered their things and left; the child's attention toward
   something new.
While I stood with my feet in the ocean, I watched the child's castle
   deteriorate as if it never existed.
As the sun began to set, I turned to walk away.
At that very moment, a feeling of peace overwhelmed me.
My mind was cleared of the daily tribulations we all encounter.
A new day would approach shortly.
After experiencing childhood once again; I realized...Life is good!
Tonya Anguzza

Remembering Mother

Mother is to be remembered by everyone.
She's the one who suffered and brought you into this world to stay.
She's the one you should find these three little words to say.
I love you mother everyday.
Whether she's alive or has passed away.
She's the one who taught you to read, play, and pray; also to obey.
The day will come if your child is taught the same way,
They will be happy they learned,there love of mother should
always be here to stay from here to eternity
Whether it be a letter or a post card or a phone call, from far away
God will show you her love is with you night and day, alive or past away.
M. Tolbert

Metanoia

The woman stood stripped - naked - weeping.
She had seen the futility of it all.

She wept and wondered how
she would leave behind the striving,
the struggle to accomplish.

The forest was thick, the thorns were sharp.
They pierced her, cut into the marrow of her heart.

She saw the pictures fall from the wall,
the boutonniere flower - dead on the floor,

The punch bowl spilled in the fine carpeted room.
She heard the poor man's hurt voice - his gift refused.

Stark naked was that scene for her.
Guests' eyes wide open, saw nothing at all.

She knew in her spirit the truth that day.
The door had opened to let her return
to the forest with brambles and thorns,

To embrace that darkness — to feel its sting,
to dance in that darkness - until she can

Sing the song of acceptance, the song of joy.
Virginia Flanagan

A Tribute To Sally Ride—1983

   America is honored by a graceful astronaut.
She labored hard for this reward, and tirelessly was taught;
Now she's ready for a flight aboard the Challenger.
We all will cheer the engineer and send our prayers with her.
Sally Ride, we salute you for your courage,
USA's first lady astronaut in space.
You are thirty-one, a tennis champ, a pilot,
And a smile is always on your pretty face.
With your training for the S T S -7,
Keep your "cool" as round the world you glide.
You-re a "Super Wonder Woman" and you're blue-eyed,
You are five feet five, with brown hair, Sally Ride.
When the Challenger lifts off from the launch pad,
You can rest assured we all will watch with pride.
We will say, "There goes four brave guys and a lady.
History is being made by Sally Ride."
America gives praise for their courage,
Five astronauts so brave and unified.
You're a "Super Wonder Woman" and you're blue-eyed.
We support the team and love you, Sally Ride.
Kathryn Kyzer

"I Hate Her... I Love Her"

I hate her, I hate her, I hate her a lot
She's always demanding the things that I got
She runs here and there, she pulls at my hair
I hate her... that sister I got

She's only a baby my Mommy once said
As one of her playthings bounced off my head
She'll wreck the whole house, it's a matter of time
I hate her... that sister of mine

When it's our bedtime she hides her small head
Afraid of the monsters that lie 'neath her bed
She tells me to chase them away from the door
Cause she's only three, but me! "I'm four".

She's finally tired without wanting a drink
She tells me, "I love you" as her eyes start to blink
It's hard to imagine a devil in pink
But I love her too... I think!
Michael Caputo

Jennifer

She sits quietly without much to say,
She never complains that's not her way

She often calls me so happy, so bright
It makes me miss her, I lay awake at night

I read old letters and listen to our song
I think of the summer when nothing went wrong

It's so unfair for her to be alone
She can't imagine how much my heart has grown

It's a terrible feeling when we're apart
only thing worse would be a broken heart

If I could only see her in front of my eyes
We'll be together forever is where the truth lies

Of not for tonight, then for the future to come
She makes my heart still, my body becomes numb

Whether it's those gorgeous brown eyes or smile of pure gold
From the first night I met her my heart had been sold

To a girl named Jennifer so beautiful, so bright
I wish I was with her on this lonely night

I'd sit down beside her, there's one thing I'd do
I'd express my true love, "I'll always love You"

J. Richard Crozier

First Love

She was one among many, yet, no other could I see
She never spoke a single word, stood gazing straight at me
Her dress of pink satin was decked with ribbons and lace
Clear blue eyes, raspberry lips and a pleasant smile upon her face

She soon became my confidant, the dearest friend I'd known
Teasingly I would call her "Shadow", so happy I wasn't alone
She never frowned, nor cried, nor wanted her way
At a moments notice, I would call, she was always ready to play

My heart is sad as now I see that we are growing apart
She simply cannot change with time, I could not see it at the start
She doesn't care a thing for shopping, quit going to the mall
Today I go and leave behind, my dear old friend...my doll.

Rebecca Coose

A Dream Come True

I dreamed of a girl, who looked a lot like me
She spoke like me too, but it couldn't be.

She'd accomplished things, that I only dreamed of
She'd overcome obstacles and risen above.

As I watched her life start to unfold
I realized that through her, my story was told.

I saw the mountains that stood in her way.
She climbed them with vigor and never dismay.

I remembered those mountains, they were much too tall.
I just gave up, and didn't climb them at all.

As I watched this girl, who looked a lot like me,
I compared my defeats to her victory.

I was given of glimpse, of how it could have been
If I'd followed my dreams and didn't give in.

I dreamed of a girl who looked a lot like me.
I realize now, that it still could be.

Zonya Brewton

Mother Nature

Mother Nature carefully unfolds and shakes out a brand new day.
She takes great pains in making sure, each is different in every way.

She wears each day, like a brand new dress.
Flaunting it proudly, with just a hint of seductiveness.

To allure you, is her only reason.
Wearing the perfect outfit, each day of every season.

Boasting colors that show off an exquisite, yet most vibrant spring.
With the symphonic accompaniment of beautiful birds that sing.

Long, hot, sultry, hazy summer days, Mother Nature is eager to please
It's as if she lifts the hem of her skirt and fans it to make a breeze.

Displaying autumn's awesome rustic colors, of yellows, oranges and
    bright reds.
She struts like an erotic tease dancer, striping till all of the
    colors are shed.

Even Old Man Winter's brisk days, don't seem as cold so much.
Covered with a fresh blanket of snow, they even warm up with her touch.

Spent, Mother Nature gives in, at the end of a long hard tiring day.
Allowing Father Time to take the day's light and put it forever away.

When darkness gives way to light, and day is eager to begin,
After a rest for a short while, she goes back to mothering again.

Linda A. Townes

Lady In White

I once knew a lady, a Lady in White
She was my friend, lover and life -
She was everything I wanted, filled all my needs
I gave my soul and she set me free -

I could soar like an eagle, even touch the sky
Anything was possible with the Lady in White by my side -
Seemed like I was anyone and everything I wanted to be
She possessed me, she was my cult of personality -

Lady in White took a new flight
Her true colors shining like a thief in the night -
Queen of Deception, Mistress of Illusion
I was tangled in a web of lies and confusion -

Wings of feather turned to chains of steel
Her stranglehold was all I could feel -
She's a deadly vice, one that cuts like a knife
She'll take it all, even your life -

That lady... the Lady in White.

Stephanie Sands

Carolina

July was hot. The stucco lath board house in East LA shimmered like an egg being fried. Paint peeled as termites feasted on the fifty year old frame. Mom, shiny with perspiration, cleared the dishes from the dining room table and Dad ushered the kids out onto the porch. He held the baby, Carolina, in his arms rocking her. She squirmed fretful. He set her free and she crawled to the cool grass. In the distance rubber squealed as a van rounded the corner at high speed. In the back a sixteen year old gangster, known as Tony, was intent on earning his stripes. He braced himself against the side facing the sliding door.
A black machine gun called Uzi was cradled in his lap. Carolina played on the grass tasting its coolness. The door to the van slid open just a gap. Tony rolled into position behind the gun, feeling cool. Carolina got her feet, grass leaves in her hand. Tony's finger tightened on the trigger...an extra squeeze away, she filled his sights, he hesitated and the van moved on. Carolina waddled to her father. "It's cool," she said handing him the grass. "It's God's gift." He said.

William Nelson Clark

In With The New Out With The Old

I hate life!
"Should that be a statement?"
One old man said to another.

I regret not going on that cruise
"Well, I told you, you should have father!"

"Dad, It's not that bad.
There's bingo, smoking and a congenial roommate."

"It's not so horrendous.
There's breakfast in bed, and in the dining room that lady
  you always forget her name, Ms. Alzheimer
    can be your dinner date."

"Hey Mr. Dementia! You're room's down that hall!"
"Oh no it's not my son's coming back to take me home you'll see."
"He's right he is back only to show him his son could crawl."
Lori Ross

Balch Lake 1995

Straining to hear the loons
Shrieking out their peaceful presence
A sigh escapes my heart
Drifting across the eventide lake.
One year since last this,
The solemn laughter of birds,
Keened with me a brother's choice to die.
Tonight they join their rhythmic dives
With the heaving of my soul
Their sedate calls echoing my silent screams
For a son with brother has gone to lie
Leaving with me the language of loons
Trapped with them in our crazed sanity.
Winnie Kender

Under His Wing

What hellish demons have brought me here.
Shrouded in darkness.
To no longer see one single beam of light.
To show me who this woman is I no longer recognize.
The eyes so barren
Of any worthwhile existence.
The heart and soul depleted.
Depleted, lessened and weakened
As by removing something essential.
For having this precious element removed also brings pain.
The pain is still mine to love
With as much intensity as the loved one left behind.
I now find comfort in the darkness,
Where the memory of her lives on, unscathed.
Within the security of the darkness,
A single feather gently blown aside by the wind
Has revealed an awesome light.
A single brilliant beam of light shown upon my face,
I was beneath His wing, gently being healed by His grace.
Kari Reavis

My Blossom

It flew silently upon the gentle breeze
Small, sweet, and fragrant, smiling at all it sees

Still it goes on in the summer sun,
Knowing that its journey has just begun

It sends my love to you
It sends my love to you

When it arrives the sky will be bright blue.
Reena Magsarili

Flower Of Life

Shadows moving, Surrounding all;
  Silence, darkness, As spring to fall;
Darkness lifting....life begins;
  The unbroken circle... around and around.

Images, Dreams, flow through the sky;
  Laughter, Tears, the years go by;
Together we grow, just He and I;
  Spirit of kindness... Flower of life.

Standing together, holding my hand;
  Guiding each other, forever to stand;
This handsome image of Heavens Love;
  Beautiful child from Stars above;

Tall and strong... He takes his stand;
The unbroken circle....around and around:
I close my eyes...He's now a Man...

While on and on together we go;
  Shining light, face aglow;
Loving hearts...this Man Has Won...

My Gift from God... my flower of life;
A Gift of Love...God's love... .....My son...
Sandra L. Linville

The Bitter Sweet Root

For my friends
The myth that life is
simple and easy.
How I did run, a child, chasing butterflies
Oh, but they did tease me.

Yet in my nightly pillow
I dreamt and sought to be,
like that mighty tree.
It always held my delight, that old willow.

What I did not know. How could I?
The price one pays for wisdom.
Living can bring such pain,
you wish to die.

But we do not.

It is the bitter sweet root,
the joy and the strife.
Striking deep within the earth, the heart.
Giving such power and magnificence,
to that old tree.

To life.
Laurie Ann Erickson

Silent Cry

Listen to the night, for what it will say,
sit in silence, it will come your way.
A cry of help, a cry of fear,
for on a child's face forms a painful tear.
We may not see them, yet they are there,
to them it seems that nobody cares.
It's not our problems, it's not for us to say,
give them money and they'll go away.
Their bodies are weak and becoming frail,
the bread they will eat may be stale.
All they ask for is a very small part,
of the un-used portion of your heart.
Listen to their cry, for it will never subside,
though you may try, you can never hide.
  For: While one child cries,
    Another one dies.
Paul M. Cheski

Color Me Clear

I believe I saw the future today
Sitting in the park watching children play
All running all laughing all playing as one
From opposite directions Mom's came fast
Shaking a finger and kicking up grass
Pulled the children apart
Screaming do as you have been taught
Play only with your own kind
One child crying ran away
Into mom arms and I heard her say
Hush hush my baby you will be ok
A little head tilt forward my way
With two little eyes shining
Through a constant flow of tears
Beyond the quarreling came the words
That I will all ways hear so clear
Mommy you thought me all children are the same
Red blood on the inside all children of God
Mommy I cry for the children cause their mom just now forgot.

Margaret L. C. Glass

One Kiss

Anxious beating hearts had we,
Sitting there underneath those huge oak trees.
We tried to chat, but our eyes continued to meet,
And from our minds we could not keep
The truth that was developing between us two.
And it was with one kiss that we both finally knew
No matter what happened in the future unknown years,
Together we'd stay through all of our fears.
Dreams have been made and laughter has been shared.
I myself can't think of a time when I have so cared
About one individual who has come into my life
And brought me such love found only between a husband and wife.
Whether we will encounter sunshine or storms on the road up ahead
As long as I am with you, I have nothing to dread.
So, please say you'll put your hand in mine,
And together the obstacles of life we shall climb.

Meghan Miner

Helpless Love

The light is droning out my eyes for the love I have is
so bright it can only disguise, the loss I feel that only
your love revealed. Why must the love we share be so distant
and so unfair, why must the words you speak be written on a
sheet? Why must my heart break so, why did I fall so fast,
my heart said yes but, my head said no. I sit and lie awake
in my bed. These questions keep coming up in my head. I sit and
think of a special place, and then the tears stream down my
face. I try so hard to chase those thoughts from my brain,
but then I realize I love you too much, and the tears fall like
rain. The minutes pass by, as I think of why, why we had to
say goodbye. Why does love hurt so much? I can't help thinking
of every touch. Every thought of you I my mind. Each word
you said so loving, so kind. Every time I close my eyes, I see your
face no trace of lies. I feel your arms, your warm embrace,
it sends me of to a special place. Every time I can recall, I
think of the time we had, in reality no time at all. The days
we shared went by so fast. If only I could make them last.
I wish I knew our destiny, our fate, for this sad helpless
love is like a heavy weight.

Sara Neal

alittlegirl

It was my birthday today. I turned
six years old and had a big birthday

party. My mom gave me a party at the park where
there were swings and slides and even a carousel and all my

friends came and I had a really really good time. But it's
nighttime again and I'm so afraid and you would think that at

least on a day like today I wouldn't have to be afraid. And I'm
so tired but I'm scared to go to sleep. And I'm scared to stay

awake. I'm lying in bed, under the covers, all scrunched up
against the wall in the corner. But there's nothing I can do to

get away. I was so happy earlier, why can't I be that happy all
the time? And then the most dreaded thing happens: There is a

soft knock on my door and he says, "Pumpkin, you awake?
Let me come tuck you in," as he comes in and

he shuts the door behind him.

Vanessa Siegal

Snow

Fleeting fragile individualist,
Slushy sleeting crystal glaze,
So slo-mo precipitation twist,
Tiny architect off days,

Drifting downy insulating fluff,
Frosty frozen jagged crust,
Falling far too much or not enough,
Blinding blizzard dusty bust,

Delicate dancing latticed doily,
Deadly driven icy rage,
Collecting cold in corners coyly,
Boldly blanketing life's stage,

Flurries afloat prolonged and pelted,
Dangling daggers clinging on,
Swept shoveled scooped plowed blown or melted,
Golden sunsets sparkling dawn,

Skid skate sled slide stumble slip or stand,
Bunnies stay as snowbird's flee,
Winter wonder or barren wasteland,
Snow breeds little apathy

Steven C. Heaton

High Fly The Angels

High fly the angels,
some looking up some looking down.
High fly the angels on silvery wings,
they know not where they are going or why.
High fly the angels,
looking down at the world beneath them.
Dreaming of the wonders below.

Some angels fly too high the sun burns their wings,
their silvery wings blacken and turn to coal as they plummet to the ground.
These are the fallen angels walking in the world among us.
They don't look up at the golden sky above.
They have seen the golden sky on silvery wings.
They have seen the black earth with no wings to bear them.

High fly the angels,
looking at the fallen below.
High fly the angels on silvery wings,
wishing they were fallen, the fallen doesn't wish at all.
High fly the angels on silvery wings, but who need wings.
The fallen angels are the happiest.

Morten Andersen

"There's Daggers In Men's Smiles"

There's daggers in men's smiles,
Smiles filled with bittersweet romance.
But bitter, cruel, harsh realities
bite down on your soul.
The stabbing sensations in your heart overrules your senses.

The chance of a lifetime or a lifetime worth of misery?

I see the daggers in all of your eyes.
Even the most precious of the emotions are invaded by the daggers
Fiery points that stab with pool precision.

Will there always be the presence of those daggers?
Or will they someday release your tormented soul
so that your eyes will be free of pain.
Sarah B. Madden

Wild Fire

Fire ablaze, mountains aglaze with nature's cleanser.
Smoke clouds building, winds rescinding, night falls in splendor.

Residents worried, fields renewed, brush removed,
evolution begins a new cycle.
Mother Earth rejoices her new seedlings.
Trees are born from the ashes. Residents recycle.

Dawn breaks, Animals vacate charred landscape.
The sun rises. The earth glows,
embers smolder,the smoke has settled.
A new era has begun.

Fire ablaze, mountains aglaze with nature's cleanser.
Linda Strom-Medvitz

Cousin To Cousin Wrap

You're Sharron's and Big Vic's thru God's plan
Smoother than the singin' Boyz 2 Men
Cute as a button, so cool when you struttin'
Next to you, Jerry Rice ain't nothin'
Wouldn't mess with your Spades
Hecka bad on rollerblades
You're the Prince of Sega
And a bad Intendo Playa

New York Undercover
Can't top you, brother
Cause you're sharp as a razor
Sho' nuff a Trailblazer

Only 11 years old
Much wiser I'm told
My wounderful Cousin, more like you
I'll take a Dozen

May 4 it's your Way
But, pretty please, let me say
VICTOR, here's wishing you
The HAPPIEST BIRTHDAY!!!
Vicki McGee

Oh Hemlock Tree

Oh hemlock tree
so bold, so beautiful,
standing alone so tall, so proud,
Your light green branches so soft to the touch,
bending ever so gently in the breeze.
Oh to live as you have lived rooted in this earth
for such a time. How many years, how many storms
and how many people have passed your way?
Can you just imagine
to be a tree so bold, so beautiful?
Oh hemlock tree, oh hemlock tree
swaying ever so slightly in the breeze.
Martha Lynn

In Hiding

I've been relocated to some strange place
So Hitler can create his "Master Race".
Everyday I am made to live in fear
I pray that the end of the war is near.

I was just nine when the Gestapo came
They hunted the Jews as if they were game.
They took us away in the dark of night
We were packed in a train, stuffed really tight.

Most of the passengers died on the trip
The people that made it were forced to strip.
All of the prisoners were filled with fright
While SS pointed to the left and right.

Luckily I hid from the Nazi men
Or I wouldn't have lived til I was ten.
I'm all alone in this dark enclosed space
Because Adolf Hitler abhors my race.
Rosalyn Pham

Out Of Silence

A deep silence pressed into my world
So I could hear the sparkle on the water
Strengthens my heart like morning due on roses
Listening to your smile bubble with delight

As I seep in the quiet of my hot tub
I hear the opening of my pores
In the thunder of a roses summer smell
Hearing as the crinkles touch your face

A deep silence lives within the world
Where I can hear the voices of forever
Deepening understanding of the earthly cries
Listening between the worlds lies

A droplet spreads the light from red to violet
A beam reaches straight into my eye
Flashing calming soothing and the eagle flies
Knowing you are standing straight and tall
Robert Norris

Alzheimer

I think I know him sitting on the edge of my bed
"So," I say, "it's raining, I say." "No it isn't." she says,
as I look at her looking at him looking at me
turning to look back out the window up into the sky
blue above the buildings dark clouds.
"Oh, not raining up there.... only down here" in the shadows.
"Mother, where's my wife?"
"I'm your wife, now come, let's get dressed." she says, softly
her fingers fall on my shoulders gently
to pull me from bed.
"Dad, you need a hand?" he says
wrapping his arms under mine
to lift me up to his apprehensive eyes.
I shrug them off, standing,
"I say, you two, what are you afraid of,
I've dealt with you kind of people all my life."
Michael D. Snyder

Untitled

I am not one to say
    that my lover should love as no other
        even those in past generations have loved
Yet, my heart aches for a mate
    to possess my soul with a passion so strong
that those who have not yet experienced love
    will look upon us with envy.
Lisa Lang

Lonely

Burdened, trudging through the darkened snow
so little ground is covered so much left to go

There seems no point, no destiny, no place for which to aim
The ridges I am crossing all somehow feel the same

A sudden splash of color is nestled in the gray
The first fleeting glimpse turns my head that way

This thing becomes my focus a reason for my trek
I set my course toward it though it seems merely a speck

Now in full view I see it, standing all alone
A solitary flower in this waste land has grown

To some it's just a flower but to me a ray of hope
As this frail life defies the odds so I too shall cope

With my new found faith and soul brimming full of life
I set out to find the rest who've overcome the strife

Together we shall face our fears and together take a stand
No problem proves too difficult when we walk hand in hand
  Kristy Ramsey

Soul Love

Though love has injured my heart,
so many times before, I know truth
awaits me, just beyond the golden door.
For behind there waits another, who is
hurting just as me, and once our paths
cross our hearts will set us free.
Our souls will grow stronger from the
powers up above and our hopes will last
longer as we grow to know great love.
Our dreams will come through, like we
always knew they would, and our faith shall
remain true just as our hearts believe it
should. And after our souls have left
this world in which we know, we shall
unite once again and forever grow and grow.
  Sean Boe

"My Child"

 This child so young and innocent, filled with
so much pain and frustration.
 There is a world of so many people, but yet my
child stands alone.
 There are doctors, teachers, and therapists who
think they know what's best. There knowledge comes
from books, laws, and degrees.
 Then there is me, his mother, who feels his emotional
pain, but yet I am as helpless as he is innocent.
 They may use their books, laws, degrees, and medicine
but is that what's right?
 My child for which I would live and die for.
My child for whom I care for, whether he be right, wrong, or indifferent.
This is my child. He is part of me, my heart, mind, and soul.
 So tell me who's to say what's right for this innocent child.
  Samantha Mae Bisbee

Hobo, Zero, Hero

Sometimes things happen to us,
That make us feel just like a bum,
In everything we are batting zero,
And we feel so blah and glum.

'Til we remember "God's Grace is sufficient
It is abundant and it's free,"
When He sends His Guardian Angel,
To watch over you and me.
  Willie Lou Shirley

My Little Life

I stand on the threshold of my middle years.
So much stronger am I, with many less fears.
Yet, so much of life I've not yet seen.
For I married early when I was a teen.

Some say, I've lived a little life.
Just being a mother and somebody's wife.
For I've not slain dragons, nor developed some cure
But in the realm of real life, I've done far more.

No not done much with my little life, save one.
I've created two daughters and a son,
though society doesn't value what it is I do.
And sometimes, I even feel the same way too.

But someday when the children are all grown
And one by one they've left this home.
I'll then have time to invest in me.
Then, when I look back I'm sure I'll see
that I wouldn't have lived my life differently.
  Marie Riddell

If Roses Had Wings

If roses had wings, they might fly away,
So the good Lord didn't give them wings,
He wanted them to stay.

Then He made you like a rose,
Yes, Darling, that's what you are,
A rose sprinkled with star dust from a very pretty star.

He must have heard me dreaming in my sleep late one night
And He sent what I was needing to make it all just right..
A rose, A very special rose, that's what you are,
A rose sprinkled with star dust from a very pretty star.

He sent a beautiful rose the beautiful one of all,
one that He knew would bloom forever - winter, spring, summer and fall

A beautiful rose that's what you are,
A rose sprinkled with stardust from a very, pretty star.
  Robert H. Whitley

Passing

I was the Shaman, who flew with the eagle.
Soaring high above the earth, while descending into the kiva.
Communing with the gods, running beside the coyote.
An entire people followed me, descending into the kiva.

I was Suryavarman, a most ambitious king.
My people built Ankor Wat, fearing my kingdom would crumble.
Building, warring, enslaving, ever expanding my borders.
Bringing my neighbors to their knees, only to have my kingdom crumble.

I was Sid Hartha, practicing asceticism.
Meditating and fasting, seeking the face of God.
Delivering to the people, a more perfect way to live.
With all becoming nothing, seeking the face of God.

I was Levi of the Magi, seeking to understand God.
Casting arcane spells, as the practicing magician.
Communing with the demons, to bring about my ends.
People still follow me, the practicing magician.

I was mankind, proclaiming to the cosmos.
But my proclamation went unheeded, by an unimpressed universe.
Extending my boundaries, destroying my world.
As my passing went unnoticed, by an unimpressed universe.
  Steven L. Huseby

Escape

The sun's rays embrace me like the arms of a lover
Softly caressing my tender skin
A chill almost orgasmic races through my flesh as
The cool breeze kisses my face with such gentleness
I dance to the birds songs like a crazed circus clown
I fall to the ground feelings the grass flutter swiftly with the air
I gaze into the mass of blue nothingness while the
Clouds seen to hover over me as would a blanket on a cold and stormy night
The sky begins to fall in droplets touching my face gently
Like the waves of the ocean touch the shore
The dew of the Heavens permeates my gown weighing me down
I leave the pale beige sheath on the hill to gather rain while I
Rant about adorned only by the gifts granted me by Mother Nature
I reach to the skies and the trees begin to shake
A blustering wind picks me up and carries me away never to be returned
A tear of joy streams down my cheek
Flushed to a shade of red as pure as a rose
As I fly through clouds and into the sky
I embrace a passing star and
Escape into the night
Marilaine Miller

Your Life

The world is made up of good and bad,
   some people are happy, and some are sad,

The life you lead is what you choose,
   sometimes you win, sometimes you lose,

On the days you win, there's a smile and a grin,
   on the days you lose, there's a frown and you're blue,

It all depends on how you look at the pot,
   some days your lucky, and some days your not,

You can stand in the corner and dwell on your thoughts,
   or you can jump back in and see what you got,

See, your life will have it's ups and downs,
   peaks and valleys, smiles and frowns,

It is up to you on what you do,
   if you don't give up, you will never lose...
Steven K. DeLon

I Wonder Why?

I Wonder Why my love is so strong.
Some people say it is wrong, to love a person so much.
They ask. I Wonder Why?
I Wonder what Heaven looks like, and when is the day that I go.
I Wonder to myself, how should I know.
I Wonder Why, the people that we love the most have to go so far.
Just the other day we were looking at the star.
The star of light, so bright because you are my light.
I fight every day just for you to stay.
I wonder why?
Leslie Ann Chiucchi

The Palm

I've often known a fool to say
That nature can be driven out with a pitchfork.
But nature will always return
For there is a snake hidden in the tall grass
Offering praises to the empty-handed traveler
Who sings in the presence of the robber.
While behind the horsemen, the vanquished and proud
Bound to swear the words of no master.
Let them hate, so long as they fear.
For their sufferings are also their lessons.
And as pale death knocks with impartial foot
At the poor man's but the kings castle
Let him who has won the palm wear it.
Scott Ferguson

Hindsight

If I knew then, what I know today
Some things would be different, needless to say
Without question I would savor, the years of my youth
For the "Stories" adults told us, turned out to be "Truths"
Life really does change, as the years come and go
And they are quick to remind you, that they told you so
I remember endless lectures, all the warnings in advance
I'd sit trying to look attentive, while I thought about the latest dance!
Who cared about tomorrow? All I lived for was today
Trying to hurry through my homework, so I could go outside to play
Looking back those classroom hours, sure would be much better spent
I'd much rather pay attention, than what I pay each month for Rent!
But at the time I couldn't fathom, that I would someday be where I am
My oh my how times have changed, once a boy-I'm now a Man
No more endless days of Summer, games of tag beneath moonlight's glow
Gone are days of Mom's hot chocolate, after playing in the snow
Of course there are times I wouldn't trade, for all the riches in the World
Like receiving my first ball glove, or the first time I fell in love
But there would be some minor changes, for I now see the tunnel's light
I feel I know the true meaning, of what's described as mere "Hindsight."
Reggie Jones

All My Tears

I have loved you in the days gone by.
Someday may we be together you and I.
The time we spent was so precious, I hated to see it pass
There are moments when you stand so near
I long to caress, hold and call you dear.
The times we've had meant so much
Yet I hunger for your touch.
What a gentle, kind and loving man you must be
Will the future hold something for you and for me?
I know as I see you with others it can not be so.
But, the times we've been together is not easily forgot.
As the days pass by and the months turn into years
I will love you from a distance,
Keeping with me.... All my tears.
Tamera Dean Broadhead

"Praise Be Ya, Russell Long"

A doe-eyed Army veteran, ripe for the taking,
Somehow 'Nam Police Action I avoided,
Darn old luck, certainly not planning, pal,
At first, wanted the experience,
No Purple Hearts, man, so cannot complain about the ending.

Married young, then followed the crowd to Delta J.C.,
I took nigh-on four years to score the A.A.,
While making coat hangers for a living, thankful for the opportunity,
Surely, a man on the upswing, real career still thought pending.

Days flew, years piled on, blood pressure up, hair turned gray,
Couldn't believe I still stayed the factory,
Comfort zone overtook this once-young fool,
Benefits soothed me, real world scared me,
Thought we lived the good life, our bills piled up while banks still lending.

Pious John S. sold, then still moved plant to the desert,
Claimed forced-on ESOP for our security,
The tax laws, not religion, ruled that day,
Sixty-eight loyalists out of work,
As always, a god found another way of winning
Steve L. Guthrie

Dad

I've never seen you quite the same as the day your mother died,
Something broke inside me when you closed your eyes to hide.

I'd watch you swirling lemonade around her cloudy glass,
Perhaps you thought of your own life and how it too will pass.

Perhaps you thought of summer camp and how she said goodbye,
"I'll be back my precious son your mother does not lie."

Perhaps you thought of her cookie tins and boxes full of bows,
Perhaps you thought of her neat boxwood all lined up in their rows.

But you tried to speak of maps and things and highways passing through,
and suddenly the words would fade and slip away from you.

No, I've never seen you quite the same as the day your mother died,
You turned into her child again, trembling as you cried.
Penelope Love

I Wish

I wish - just once that I could talk of
something from yester year without being told
I'm living in the past.

I wish - just once that I could say I got
home from work or had a vacation - without
being asked, "Whatcha do, deah?"

I wish - just once that I could tell of
an incident that was sorrowful me
without getting a verbal pat on the head.

If I say somebody made a mistake, it was
a sin. If I call somebody a boy, he's a man.
If I refer to a lady as a grandma, she's a
great grandma. And so on -

I guess I'm just asking - please let up on the
fault finding. Take me as I am, enjoy me for who
I am, if I do something well say so but don't be
gushy. Am I asking too much? I don't think so.
All I'm asking is to be treated like everyone else.
Weigellia G. Trook

My Old Pal

Old Sam waits for just a pat on the back or his head;
Spending most of his time asleep in his bed.

Dreaming of last hunting season;
While his master followed him wheezin'.

A chill in the air and leaves falling;
Off in the distance Geese were calling.

Finding the scent of a bird and then pointing it;
Getting to retrieve, if his master got a hit.

Being scolded for making mistakes or running away;
Getting a big hug and sharing his masters lunch, all in the same day.

Hunting, running, and off the chain being free to roam;
After a while, his master says it's time to head home.

The day was great and we had a lot of luck;
But all to soon, his master loaded him back into the truck.

Out of the truck, into his box all nice and warm;
But he'll be rested and ready, come tomorrow morn.

Old Sam puts up with my faults and short falls;
And comes runnin', ready to please, when he hears me call.

All these pleasures will be remembered with a smile;
Long after my old pal Sam hunts his last mile.
Robert W. Pence

Spirit Of Christmas Lost

In stillness walks the
  Spirit of Christmas,
    silent and old as time,
      yet joyous as the fallen snow.

Be still and seek the
  sun even as it does not shine,
    and the Christmas spirit shall
      open your eyes to be the greatest of artists.

Listen. He calls you softly
  with his lantern of hope and gentle eyes asking
    that you remember with only a gesture or a word
      that Christmas is something more.

In silence stalks the true meaning,
  radiating from the eyes of the
    Christmas Spirit as with bowed head, he walks the earth with
      only the lantern of hope to guide the way.

Searching he will move on in
  endless pursuit of open
    hearts, and reaching minds
      to give his knowledge, as a gift.
Melody J. Howe

Great Courage

Strut into the paddock, the crowd is a roar.
Spurs are a jingle, the fans wanting more.
The knot in my stomach, and sweat on my head.
Thoughts at last moment, leaves me to dread.

Second look at that stallion, And wanting to run.
But standing so proud, I'm dad's only son.
This gives me the courage, to sit it astride
Determine to do it, to hold tight and ride.

The knees are pressed tight, With the drop of the hat.
It's going, It's going, There's no turning back.
The clock is ticking, seconds crawl by.
Oh why did I do this? Why oh Why?

Tears of anticipation turn, tears of fear.
Two arms wrap around me, My daddy is here.
Unplug that black stallion, he bucks me no more.
In daddy's arms, We stroll out the door.

I know I can do it, I know I can win.
When I'm a Big Boy, I'll try it again.
Roxann Miller

Miss Liberty

In New York Harbor, in the land of the free
Stands America's symbol, our Statue of Liberty.
Many have caught their first glimpse of you
From a ship in an ocean of blue.
In search of a new life, a new home,
They come to America, never more to roam.
With your lights aglow at night
You are a breathtaking sight.
Beckoning to all, your torch lights the way,
Leading mankind to a new and better day.
A symbol of freedom, hope and pride
Guiding the masses, may you always reside
In New York Harbor, in the land of the free,
America's symbol, Miss Liberty.
Sheri Calvert

William Michael

The darkest lover i've ever had
stands in the center of my mind
hearts as fragile as a child
soul as powerful as fire.
I feel i could comfort you
I'm sure i could help heel you
I know i'd be good for you
we may become angels.
Lives on blood and honey
drains red water through my hide
can see through eyes like clear-glass windows
tries to shelter me with fire.
It is you i've known forever
it's you i've come to love
and it's you who are my sanctuary
we could be the most jealous angels....
Stephenie C. Foster

Quickened By Angel's Song

From well's greatest depth, I rise through
　　star-strewn waters,
to bubble atop fount's effervescent crown,
quickened by angels' song.

In one timeless moment, I'm changed
　　by the note,
and tangible blindness yields
　　envisioned experience.

My vital scintilla dances to crescendo waves,
charged with heartfelt visions only
　　dreamt of before,
quickened by angel's song.

Violet waters and golden foam blend into
　　more gentle solution,
I am equal in all life and it in me,
a blissful homogeneity.

Flowing over curve's shining crescent,
down through each starry tier,
I am one prismatic drop among infinitely more,
quickened by angel's song.
Valerie F. Virgona

Blindside

Autumn air was my company as I gazed at the night
Staring past the close cut grass.
It seemed to be reaching for me in comfort,
The blades softening their razor touch to dry my tears.
I hear the echoes of long ago
That are almost as real as the quiet.

Floating above the field I see my rememberings
Too close to touch.

Swirling, surly wind, nature cutting flesh.
There is
no
way
out.
Circles
more of
into harsh
blend words
that
Kathleen Cooper

The Game Of Life Is

The game of life, is hard, real and true,
　Stay up on the game or risk being beat black and blue.

The game of life is low down, scary and shame,
　Take care of business or be eaten by the game.

The game of life, is seeing, believing, hoping, that things would change,
　Watch your step, be careful of the fortune and fame.

The game of life, is being strong, honest and wise.
　Take life one step at a time, that way you will have a chance
　　of seeing the next sun-rise.

The game of life was meant to be sold and not told.
　That way you would have paid your dues and earn the right to get old.

The game of life is just what you make it.
　Don't sit around asking for nothing, go out and work for it,
　Demand it and take it.

The game of life is there if you want to play.
　Put God first in your life and always pray for another day.
Ramon T. Dandridge

Siren Of The Sea

I hear you calling, Siren of the Sea
Strange lands seductive in their mystery.
Through storms that toss the mighty sea
My heart will always be with thee.
All across the long and lonely miles
No sight can match your smile.

Adventure, strange lands, Seductress Sea
They all reach out to beckon me.
Though my mistress sings impassioned pleas
Your love is stronger than all.

Calling, ever calling out to me
My sweet, cruel Lady of the storm-tossed sea.
'Cross oceans deep and mountains wide
Your love will always be my guide.
'Though I sail once more on morning's tide
In the stars, I see your eyes.

Maidens gold or dark of hair
Islands rich with spices rare.
The sharp, sweet bite of salt sea air
Your love is stronger than all.
Kate Coffee

Trains

Out the window I watched the scenery melt into green and brown
　streaks,
each railroad tie passes with each heart beat.
Just two more stations before I reach my lover's outstretched arms,
remembering back to when I last saw you,
I kept telling you to be strong even though it was I who was weak,
one more station to go...
The past few months felt like a string of eternities.
will your love be as intense as it was before?
...Train slowing to a stop.
Stepping from the rail car my eyes search frantically for your face,
can our love overcome the time we've been apart?
The smile in your eyes and gentleness in your voice melted away
all my fears, felt as if we parted yesterday.
L. R. Brown

The Alley

Silence. Complete silence.

I stare out my third story window into the dimly lit alley.

Silence Mosquitos swarm around the single, cracked
   street light as though they are worshipping a God.

Silence. The alley is no longer empty.
A poor fool stumbles blindly down the alley,
   a bottle of whisky clutched in his hand.

Nothing. Silence, A cheerful police worker trots down the alley.
Swinging his bully club like a little girl swings her baton.

Nothing, That's all it is, nothing. Today nothing, everyday nothing

A man in the building next to mine comes
   racing out of the ground level door.
He pleads for his wife's forgiveness as she
   hurls china plates at him from the overhead window.
Crushed, he hangs his head in shame and walks
   mournfully down the alley in only his undergarments.
She vanished from the window. Silence. Complete silence

The shattered china lies in the light of the
   street light like shattered dreams.

Silence. Nothing, but not nothing.. everything.
   Karen Derr

My Niece, The Swimmer

Debbie is a swimmer, and a good one to be sure.
Stroke by stroke she practices, each day the whole year through.
The butterfly is her specialty, but any she can do
Sailing like a fish, across a sea of azure blue.

Debbie is my niece, a real sweetheart of sixteen.
Swimming is her love, for the present that's her scene.
But how long can her charm keep away so many guys?
Because her cheerful, friendly ways are a joy to all their eyes.

Debbie is a swimmer, one who really loves the sport.
Her teams consist of sweet, young girls - fat, skinny, tall and short.
In this age of low morals, some people frown on teens
But not my niece, the swimmer; her daddy's teen age queen.
   Priscilla A. Steindl

Photographs From Home

Pictures in Black and white
Strong and bold.
Pictures in Black and white
Of young and old.
Pictures in Black and white
My Kings and Queens
Pictures in black and white
Royalty and Blacks, reds, golds, and greens.

Memories of times gone by
Rivers flowing through my neighbor "hood"
A place where the love is as strong as the noon sun
Where rhythm is as fruitful as the mango in the Nile Valley

Pictures in Black and white
Loving and true.
Pictures in Black and white
Skies in aqua blue.
Pictures in Black and white
My Kings and Queens
Pictures in Black and white
Royalty in Blacks, reds, golds, oranges, yellows, purples, and greens.
Home.
   Tiffany A. Simpkins

The Deadly Sin Of Envy

"A monster begot upon itself, born in itself"
Strong enough to dissolve a friendship,
Powerful enough to destroy a race.
Self-induced paranoia
Initiated by mistrust and niggardliness,
Intensified by obsession.

I see my race die everyday as a result of this.
Hitler could only dream of turning a people
Against themselves and have them do his dirty work.
We stand divided,
A friendship frayed.
You lose, we lose, because either way in the end
You stand
   Alone.
   Tahirah Turner

"Suddenly!"

Suddenly, I am a Senior Citizen!
Suddenly, I am without wages!
Suddenly, my life changes!
Suddenly, I have no identity!
Suddenly I am out of everything!
(Pay checks, union benefits, food, etc.).
Suddenly, I am alone and sad!
(In pain and disabled)
Suddenly, I find out how cruel humanity is!
And suddenly I learn that long
Suffering makes you a spiritual person!
And suddenly I am glad!
   Mrs. Beryl Singho

Alone

Alone in a world so heartless so cruel,
surrounded by loneliness and pain.
I turn towards you, I do so in vain.
Your my only answer you ease my pain.
   Some people turn towards
money or fame, some choose a bottle
some go insane.
Not me I choose you.
   When I look in the mirror I've
seen what you've done, you created a new me,
I'm afraid you won.
   You created a person who's no longer
free I'm trapped inside so let me be
I'm tired, weak afraid to fight.
Wondering if I can make it through the night.
So sadly I take another bite.
   Nicole Buchko

Invisible Art

I am sitting in the theatre
Surrounded by unsynchopated hammering, drilling, sawing
And killing.
The crew scurries about dabbing and splashing
Their soul onto the set
As to please and spoil their artful eye.
Four days until opening.
I, too, have dabbed
Here and there
Fulfilling my expectations even more so as
The rhyme of being
Hypnotically and rhythmically
Duplicates itself onto another, leaving the cast
Who dare step in my shoes
To play and dance with God.
   Tara Rizzo

The Storm

...A storm that abruptly entered my life,
   surrounded me, sheltered me;
Made me see wonders and sheer excitement
   throughout its storm.
Noticed had I, that I was not afraid,
   the wind did not give me chills...
     just friendship, and warmth.
And as I found myself getting closer to
   the storm, finding it more inviting;
It, as all storms do, came to an end.
   and moved on elsewhere,
     leaving me behind, cold, and in awe
       out of what just passed.

For I thought to myself, "This is one storm
   that I shall never forget and will await
     the day it returns...
       this storm known as "My Friend."

Mark Ferneau

"Inner Me"

The unexplained, feeling is gone, no more fears, no more
   tears, no more years to add for the lesson I had to learn
When reaching to this point I have finally adjourned.
The lesson was long and hard to bare when all odds went everywhere.
To rhyme with reason is challenging to those
   such as me for letting you know this "inner me" didn't think
I could but I did no more sing it again Sam songs for me
   for I have found this discovery inner me.
The unexplained feeling is gone like yesterdays songs that linger on.
No more fears no more tears like the years there gone.

Patricia May Ernst

Amanda's Song

Bubble gum, ice cream and pony tails
Swing sets, beaches, buckets and pails
Hugs and kisses and brushed away tears
Ice cream cake and big teddy bears
Always a smile and an "I Love You"
I'm stuck on her like band-aids and glue

She laughs and she smiles, how she just loves to play
On the real stormy nights I take all her fears away
She's loving and she's giving, she's got a real big heart
She's always so aware, she's very, very smart
Amanda is her name, it's as beautiful as she
She's a part of my life, she's a part of me

I hold her and I hug her and I kiss her good night
The feeling she gives me makes everything right
She laughs and she giggles as she says "You know what"
And the sound of her voice is the beat of my heart
I'll be there to save her and to hold her small hand
Her protector, her hero, her friend's what I am

Paul Stutzbach

Passion

Passion,
   Temperatures rising, body breaks into a cold sweat
   Visualizing love exchanged if we just let
Passion,
   Over ride, excite the senses burning with desire
   Guide my love to depths, your love requires
Passion,
   Intimate pleasure, silhouettes caressing in the dark
   Loves treasures, lustful yearning succumbs the heart

   Screams of passion

Leonard Burgess

Mommy

Give me a hug mommy and dream of me giving you mine.
Take my hand mommy and hold it one last time.
You need not wonder why or what you did wrong,
For mommy you're the reason God let me live this long.
You have taken such good care of me. You always put me first.
But mommy, me being here with you any longer was just not meant to be.
It's time for me to go now, it's time to set me free.
But don't worry mommy I won't be alone.
I'll have others looking out for me. I'll be in my new home.
When you think of me don't feel bad.
Imagine how beautiful it must be.
Oh mommy, don't be sad.
I can run now and laugh and play!
I can count and read and talk and tell stories all day!
And when it's bedtime and I kneel to say my prayers,
I thank God for my mommy and I pray He takes as good care of you as
   you took care of me.
Then I close my eyes mommy and I dream of the day you will come to be with me.
The day we can run and laugh and play.

Michelle Wittkopf

Little Girl

You can't have him.
Tall with blonde hair and blue eyes.
He's a savior little girl.
Don't even think about him that way.
You shouldn't hurt yourself and talk to him.
If you wanna try to get him,
Get in line little girl.
What makes you think you could?
Did his eyes make you cry?
Stop yearning little girl.
He could have any woman he wants.
What makes you so special?
Do you believe he thinks about you
and your imperfections little girl?
You think he's perfect,
he doesn't even think about you.
He may talk to you
but don't let it go to your head.
Your just a little speck in a big man's world little girl.

Michelle Verdon

Just An Ordinary Guy

He was just an ordinary guy,
   that Dad of mine;

Never took the time to ask us "Why?"
   just gave us his "all" when it came to his time.

He approached life in a care-free way,
   almost every single day-to-day.

When it came to be his time to go,
   he accepted that it was to be so.

And, off he went in his care-free way,
   with a smile, no fight, no words to say.

Now, I believe, he's up THERE looking down,
   and sometimes I can feel his very slight frown.

But ALWAYS I know that he was just an ordinary guy,
   that Dad of mine;

Never asking "Why?"
   now and for all time...

Laurie Ann Rodrigues Stephens

"Yet, Where Are You?"

I walked briskly, up and down
Tears flowing like a river between my eyes
I am searching for someone
But here I am again ALONE with my troubled mind.

Comfort me Oh God, yet where are you?
I am searching for a refuge for my lonely, aching heart.
Anxious, disturbed, angry and bitter.
Yet, where are you?

Years have passed by;
trees turning green to yellow, to orange.
Yet, where are you?

Lonely and hated - will you come now and carry me away?
Away from this cold, lonely world - maybe?
Maria Evita M. Israel

Till Death Do We Part

Images in thee, they drift with the wind,
tears touch my cheeks as I see you again,
Lying in our bed you
look so alone lost in your thoughts
God I wish I was home, to lift the
burdens I know that you bare,
To whisper ever so softly that I'll
always be there, to take away your doubts and fears,
I would give my life
To erase your tears, for you mean the world to me,
There is nothing I wouldn't do,
but try as I may these walls I
can't walk, though you have to hold on
to the dreams we share and know in your
heart how much I care, the day will
come when I am able to come home
and never will you left alone,
This promise I make straight from the heart,
I love you my precious
Till Death Do We Part.
Todd Shade

Fan Blades Blur

Moving, fun blades blur by some unseen force
Testing, the curriculum life, the only course
Time ending, is hard to conceive
Everybody telling, in what to believe

Trying, to find the purest of truth
Hiding, in a society of cagey youths
Swimming, through noise I strain for fresh air
Sounding, in my mind I am unable to share

Sending, my tear, an unopened message
Flowing, fears dry on the face of carnage
Finding, no refuge from this mind game I play
Dealing, with moments from day to day

Gambling, a sleepwalk on a tightrope of flame
Living, a dream for either glory or shame
Questioning, the questions a mind can't define
Craving, for knowledge of all things divine

Leading, I live the life that I am
Doing, the best at whatever I can
Condensing, a lifetime, like pictures on a screen
Limiting, my actions in reality's scheme
Robert L. Tompkins Jr.

Best Friends And Lovers

Nothing is more important in life
Than a best friend to help you get through
All of the troubles and worries
And all of the times you are blue.

A best friend will be there beside you
No matter how bad it may be.
And you will always be there for them
Through all of their misery.

The ultimate thing you can wish for
Is to be a lover and still a best friend,
To always be there for each other
When you feel that the world's going to end.

You can talk of your troubles together
While you're holding each other tight,
And dream of your future together
In the wee hours of the night.

I know that some find it hard to believe,
But I also know that it's true.
Because I have a best friend and lover,
And I can promise that you do too.
Teresa Kapp

An Ode to the Dandelion

No less a harbinger of spring this first of a May day,
Than the robin seeking angleworms emerging from a wet soil,
Or the V-column of a returning gaggle of honking geese,
Or the dandelion, the first dash of color from a long dead earth.

Never cultivated, unplanted, seldom noted and never heralded
But somebody should -
This splash of burnished, freshly minted gold that only a fool would pass by.

Why is this beauty uprooted or poisoned to make room for the
    uniform monotony of green grass?
Must we stifle the fruition of these bright florets to the silky white plumes
That seek a spring breeze that wafts their seed to another growing place,
There to germinate and further enrich the coffers of Mother Earth
with its bullion of treasure so unstintingly give.
Few plants can probe the earth so deeply for its moisture and nutrition,
Or withstand the ravishes of man's spade or spray
And yet give so unstintingly of its beauty, or even its greens
For a tasty salad that requires no weeding or fertilization,
    or its flowers for a sweet and tasty brew.
I, for one, can cherish this treasure and deplore
The thoughtless destruction of this noble and sensual - DANDELION.
Robert J. Dicke

Thank You God For Dreams

Thank You God for daydreams in the middle of the day.
Thank You God for sweet dreams near the dock of the bay.
Oh Thank You God for dreams anytime of the day.

Thank You God for dreams of Your love enfolding, renewing
And strengthening me.
Thank You God for dreams of Your presence surrounding me.
Oh thank You God for dreams that are very real to me.

Thank You God for dreams of Your spirit leading, directing
And protecting me.
Thank You God for dreams fulfilled within me.
Oh thank You God for inspiring me to dream.
Sulesa Harmon

Springtime

We call it springtime, and this is the season,
That beautiful flowers bloom and grow.
The aroma of the flowers could they be the reason,
That through our veins love seems to flow.

The smell of flowers, the beautiful colors,
Of the months March, April and May.
This is the season there is no other,
When nature is so glorious and gay.

April showers seem to bring May flowers,
But what instills infatuation in our hearts.
How are we then taken by the overwhelming power,
The love that spring always sparks.

The mating of creatures, the life they bring,
Could this be God's will for the Earth?
Listen to the Angels while in heaven they sing,
As they welcome a new day, a new birth.

Marquis Ronell

Butterflies And Shadows

Butterflies are free and in this part of my life I found,
That butterfly is me.
To look ahead with hope and even feel desire
Each morning I awake to see the sunrise
And slowly watch the day unfold, oh, such beauty to behold.
And what glorious new adventure shall I have today?
As I do my shadow dancing with life.
Caring and sharing with each person I meet,
Then comes the sunset, it looks like it was waiting,
Waiting just for me.
I drink in all its beauty, all my eyes can hold.
I hang on to every precious moment, until another new day unfold.
I take each new day as a present,
While I shadow dance with life.
The time was right, the dye was cast,
I made my move and left the ghost of my past.
I have started to become the woman,
The woman I thought I could never be.
And the only shadow you will see,
Will be my shadow, dancing, with me.

Patricia Viola

"The Omnipotent And The Potency"

That which flows out from GOD SUPREME must return,
That energy includes all of us,
So I have learned.

We go in HIM, get cleaned up, and come back out,
Souls going back to the physical with a shout,
Age? All souls are the same,
Experience in the material is where the difference came,

This eternal pulse the mind could not conceive,
Intelligence can not understand why,
But only confess to believe.

GOD SUPREME is omnipotent,
We are HIS potency,
We came from HIM out,
Continuing to the material with a shout,
Until we tire to roam,
Go back to the SUPREME, and stay home.

Uriel Overton

Destiny Intervened

It is only here, in darkness of night
that I find peace.

For here you are always beside me, nestled close against my back...
encompassing my entire soul with the warmth of your love.

Here we are one and we guard our desire for each other
with the might of destiny intervened.

Together we are strong...an invincible entity.

Near to you my pulse races, yet my fears are quelled.
Calm flows over me.

And again the dawn breaks, tearing you from me...
until the angels lead me again to you, in the cloak of night.

Come dark angel and speed me home...
to that place where peace reigns and love is eternal.

Melissa Ann Maynard

Africa! Be Not A Mountain Of Ice

Africa! Be not a mountain of ice
that illuminates the night of the living world
from its darkest basin.
Beyond the bleakness of the human spirit lies yet,
that supreme light of yours, once shone in the deepest
recesses of mankind.

Africa! Where are you now? Where is your Egyptian spirit?
Where is your ancient light? My Africa,
let your light flower again and rekindle your spirit!

Beware! Your children, in wars, are dying...
Your children, are lost and crying...
Your children are angry and bleeding...
Your children are alone.

Africa! Are you still the sacrificial lamb of humanity
or the hidden treasure of the universe?
Why kneel down and scorn your lot?

Africa! Be a marvel and a mystery, like your pyramids
My Africa! Be a mountain of ice that chills and sparkles
the spiritless world.

Remigius Chikere

Forgotten Vows

A faithless land,
That kills its young,
Which does not understand its past.
A lost prologue,
Dispelled and forgotten,
Its hope once built upon faith
Now all but wasted and unnoticed;
Corroded by its own selfishness.

The faithful few,
Not unlike a dying soldier,
Who musters his remaining strength
To draw himself up with the living,
Only to fall again upon a barren waste.
His wounds so deep,
His blood shed upon an already drenched battlefield.

The giants who cleared this land,
No longer honored,
Now all but forgotten.

Spencer N. Roads

I Found My Way

A picture was drawn for me many years ago
that shown my life line. How could this be?
Why didn't I see?

There's a place I can go when the tension's
high and I'm feeling low. In a flash I can
be in another space as a different me.
There's no arguing, there's no fighting,
everything is love, no such word as "War".
There's no black and no white rainbow
colors they, dress the day and nights,
life's a paradise.

It's amazing how the mind can do what
you wait it to. I can take you to a time
where you'll want to stay forever, feeling
everlasting pleasure. I think I'll
treat myself to all the pretty, feeling
everlasting pleasure. I think I'll
treat myself to all pretty places
in my head. "Yes", I'm going to treat
myself to all the pretty places in my head.

Rebecca Marie Bighum

"Friends"

Sincerity and kindness, leaving all bad things behind us,
that's what makes a friend;

Caring and sharing, sometimes even the clothes you are wearing,
that's what makes a friend;

Considerate and understanding, keeping secrets and party
planning, that's what makes a friend;

Helping and never uptight, trying to do what is always right,
that's what makes a friend;

Pleasant and sweet, always believing in your whatever problem
you may meet, that's what makes a friend;

Patient, trusting, reliable, LOVING, happy, smiling, forgiving and
forgetting, caring about what is on the inside and not on the out,
THAT'S WHAT MAKES A FRIEND!

Lauren Millsaps

Love Story

Darling, my love for you is true
That's why I'm so lonely and blue
Nobody knows the hurt I've been through
But survive I must, I always do.

I know you are inside Heavens Gate
but for me I must wait
I'm sure I still, on earth have a duty
before God lets me see you
and other loved ones in Heavens Beauty

I miss the joy you brought to me
Why your death happened, I don't see
only God had bigger and better things for you
It's hard to go on without you, but this I must do

The nights are so long
I wish I could hear you sing me a song
and hear the laughter, and see the smile on your face
also watch you Bowling in that perfect place

All the little things (and the big things) were so special
I will always cherish them close to my heart
I wish we never had to part.

Mary H. Bruning

The Encounter

The moon was out, the stars were bright,
 the air was chilly, oh what a night.
The scene was romantic, an absolute dream,
 a vision of beauty.
One asks themselves, was it really real or just a dream?
Two strangers from worlds apart, feeling and sharing
 emotions of the heart.
A God send from heaven, an angelic sight.
I often sit and ponder when I think of that night
so long ago, when the world was at peace, and so was my mind.
I think I'll just tuck it away in the folds of my
Heart, and then on rainy day I'll remember,
that yes, it was quite a night!

Vernon Thompson

"The Smith Babies"

Never again will we hear the cries of the babies
The babies under the water
Never we again to hear the cries of the babies
Except the mother and the father

The nation mourns for the loss of the little ones so small
Never has anyone so tiny been able to stand so tall

The innocent ones pay the price for the actions of the crazy
So helpless, so dependent on us, so beautiful, like the daisy

What is the world coming to be
When mothers can kill their children
What kind of world are we leaving behind
For our children to build on

Taking their life before they're born
Or after they are here
It doesn't matter when the time
To make God shed a tear

Never again will we hear the cries of the babies
The babies under the water
Never we again to hear the cries of the babies
Except the mother and the father

Lynda E. Baker

Beyond The Blue Of The Sky

  Beyond the glittering stars, the moon, and
the brilliant sun -
  There is a Canyon high, vast, and endless,
the home of the majestic eagle.
  Overlooking the rim of the Canyon there is
a rolling valley.
  A beautiful vibrant haven, verdant and
sacred, the home of the Lord Christ our Savior.
  When our soul is called to this heavenly
repose, Christ the Lord surrounds us within
His Holy Grace. We are in heaven, so high, ever so high -
  Beyond the blue of the sky
  Flowers bloom everywhere in brilliant profusion. There is no rain.
  The angels glide on velvet carpets and white lace.
They speak in musical whispers, and a soft sigh.
  Beyond the blue of the sky
How happy we are to live surrounded in such splendor and eternal peace
  Embraced within the Holy Spirit of
God, safe and secure, ever so high -
  Beyond the blue of the sky

Lidi Mary Kyle

'Twas The Night Before Doomsday

'Twas the night before doomsday, and all through the world,
the bullets were flying, the bombs being hurled.
The rockets were aimed at their targets with care,
A nuclear holocaust hung in the air.

Civilization lay tense in their beds,
While wishes for peacefulness danced in their heads.

Like a hymn of the dead the war sings it's song,
reminding us all that we can't get along.

Prejudice, hatred, man's primitive urges
will soon be no more — his apocalypse purges.

Then on the horizon arose such a clatter,
I sprang from my cot to see what was the matter.

In from the window came a hot blinding flash
that blew off the shutters, and burned up the sash.

When what to my wondering eyes appeared then,
but four galloping horses and on them four men.
On Famine! On War! On Pestilence! Death!
Though man's learned his lesson, he's breathed his last breath.

'Tis the night after Doomsday, and all round the planet,
the insects inherit what we took for granted.

Sean Mogle

I've Seen It All

I've seen it all, the rise and fall,
The change of guard, the life so hard, I've seen it all.
Seasons change, they rearrange,
Cycles end, then sprout green again, I've seen it all.
War roars, anger soars,
Blood spilled, people killed, graves filled, then rebuild.
Sometimes I rest, it's for the best,
Then my eyes don't see what bothers me, I've seen too much.
I've seen the good, I knock on wood,
I say my prayers, know he still cares, I've seen it all.
I've seen the young, with arms outflung,
Embrace their love, like hand in glove, I've seen it all.
With great disdain, seen MURDER entertain,
Seen justice prevail, and... hide behind a veil, I've seen it all.
Tis time to part, I'll rest this heart,
My last good-night, I see a tunnel of light,
Now... I'll see it all!

Rick Maloy

Destined

Beaten, battered and broken hearted
The child is thrown against the wall
Again slapped, again kicked
The child feels like a rag doll.

Living in an awful world
A world of torment and fear
Crying inside the child still smiles
Being called names he does not want to hear.

Growing up in fear of danger
No longer a child but barely a man
Across his face lies a wilted smile
Wanting to love, he no longer can.

Not wanting to notice
His life isn't going anywhere
He takes a knife
Knowing no one will ever care.

Sherrie Heglund

This Love

This love, so different, so peaceful.
The child's love, so blind, so trustful.
The teenagers love, so consuming, so hurtful.
The first true love, so possessive, so distrustful.
The second, the third and more all to grow.
This last love, so different, friends.

Patricia Kennedy

She Earned Her Wings

It was a restless night, before I fell asleep,
The clock had chimed one time, I was wide awake!
I felt three pats upon my cheek, I thought it was a dream,
When a long remembered voice called out my name.

I'd heard the voice of my child so many years ago.
When I worked late and got to sleep, she often would awaken me.
Always she had a need for school or talk about a date;
Her voice silent many years, the body in a grave.

Again - three pats upon my cheek and she said "Mom"
I opened my eyes and saw my daughters form.
Dressed in a long white flowing robe, a light about her head,
Her bare feet floating - just above my bed.

"I earned something today, you are the first to know,"
Her right arm crossed her chest and lifted up a wing,
"Now I can fly" she said, "I got my wings today"
Lifting her arms and wings in flight, she blew a kiss - good night.

She had always patted my cheek three times when she was here.
My child called my name - herself revealed.
The clock chimed five, I must have had some sleep,
With angels unaware, - one awakened me!

Mary K. Willey

Winds Of Memories

It's past midnight.
The clock is ticking like a bomb.
I lie in my bed but can't quite sleep.
There's something wrong.
I can feel it, but what is it?

I decide to sit on my porch.
As I sit all is calm.
Suddenly a burst of wind passes, full of memories.
I remember my past love, the way I felt.
I remember the huge smiles which disappeared so suddenly.
I remember the undying happiness which has died.
I remember my old friends which I hardly see.
I remember the moments me and my friends had together,
But last of all I saw the cross that Jesus was hanging from.
I saw the nails in his hands and feet, the mocking he took.
I saw the good times me and the Lord had when we were so close.

Suddenly I felt the tears coming down my eye, one by one.
It wasn't a tear of sadness but a tear of joy.
Those tears were the joy of knowing the Lord.

Neal Kim

Friendship

A feeling to be treasured
The closeness and understanding of another
  human being cannot be put into words
You know when they are sad, happy,
  and O.K. with the world
When they are down you are there to give
  them a lift up
To give Advice or just listen,
To stand by them through the hardest times
But when you are let loose to have fun,
There are no words to describe it,
You are Silly, can say things so outrageous,
  and laugh at nothing
Have fun just being you,
And your life has a new outlook
  each time you are together

Wini Kearney

Death Of An Aunt

When the estate is settled
The clothes given away
The house consigned to others
The treasures divided, bestowed with care
On those who cannot know their history;

When the headstone you wanted is set in place,
Your letters, tied in packets, discreetly saved,
Even your jewelry scrutinized:
"Can this old brooch really be an amethyst?"

When the old pictures are found and sorted
And we admit we don't know who they are
"Distinguished, though, in his uniform;
No name on the back, alas..."

We try our best for you,
And yet the cloud of forgetting
Creeps ever closer, blocking out the sun,
Till we are left in shadow—wondering,
Wondering who you were.

Martha Crabtree

Witness To Love's Triumph

I stand in witness, bound by love to bring
The covenant of life to love, and sing;
Recalling to us, lovers who before
We were, once hung love's welcome on their door;
And ever conscious, how words never tell
The depth of love's astonishment, and spell;
Nor lift the cloud, that veils the mind, and sky,
When love would lose its voice, and touch, and sigh;

But here, like crocus on the edge of Spring,
I bring the love of life to love, and sing;
And, like the forest waking, call on each
Of us to bring creation into reach,
And in love's chorus hear, and mirror see,
Our own love's triumph, in love's galaxy.

William McPhillips

"Beyond"

Where is this place that people say
The lily grows in simple splendor?
Where bird song floats through aspens green
And destiny itself awaits between

Where is this place that people say
Children run with ageless wonder?
Where moonlight sweeps lush valleys green
And death, unknown, is never seen...

Leonard Enrique

Ode To A Skull

  Through the pale moonlight, the grinning skull laughs the devil's delight.
  With hollow eyes that pierce the night, in black pools of never ending sight, the pale skull laughs with the pale moon light.
  In another time and place with eyes so clear and bright this skull could see the world, and all that was right.
  This skull could sing and hear the wonders of the world and make sweet love to an angel of delight, but now sets quietly among the things of the night.
  Darkness or light, which is better I ponder? this skull of the night.
  I ask thee, oh skull of the night, in which of the worlds do you delight?
  Is it better dead or living among the light?
  Grinning through hollow eyes, you mock me in your night of delight and give me the answer of your wisdom for the long journey of the night.
As I turn, your empty eyes burn into my core only to fuel the fires that have raged there before. Softly now, I open the door that leads into the night, not really knowing if the darkness can bring me light.

Michael Boortz

People Of America

The rich, the wealthy, the well-to-do
The diamonds, the jewelry on me and you
The dances, the parties, the fancy cliques
The imagination of your mind playing tricks

America the brave the sons of liberty
America the beautiful in the eyes of the refugee
America the caring, extending out her light
America the "family" except the black and white

The poor, the desperate the dying
The park benches, the cold and the crying
Eating left over food from one you never met
Wondering if it's all you'll ever get

America we're slipping - falling apart
America band together reach from your heart
America stands for family and its liberty
America, America God shed His grace on thee

Sharlene N. Souders

Vision Of Love; Love Is A Child

See the baby; so new, fresh and pure,
  The eyes of the parents; proud, happy and sure!

They hug each other warmly, melting as one,
  Gazing at a miracle, so beautiful, their son!

Bonding, yes quickly, the love surely grows,
  Love unquestioned from his head to his toes!

Touching Mom's face with his tiny delicate fingers,
  The scent of the newborn, the fragrance it lingers.

"We'll love him forever!" they tell one another,
  "Let's teach him of God, love, and his brothers."

A heart so new, begins fresh and pure,
  Love and kindness for the child, good beginnings to endure!

Timothy S. Cohen

The Sign

I try and try to see the light,
the innocence of life.
But darkness slowly unveils himself,
the never ending struggle to save myself.
You're very smart, I give you this.
Turning my own soul against me,
But I am afraid you must try something else.
For I am growing stronger,
both body and mind.
Well, I'm ready now,
just give me the sign.

Nicole Morales

Beloved

Hello.
(The eyes, the face, the smile)
Enchantment!
It's love!

I do.
(The eyes, the face, the smile)
Commitment.
It's forever.

How could you?!!
(The eyes, the face, tense, flat-line lips)
Betrayal, Anger, Grief...
It is different now.

Hi. How are you feeling?
(The eyes, the face, the smile)
Commitment.
It has been good.

I have always loved you.
Wait for me.

Merrilyn Slack

Stale Fear

I sit alone in a warm room
The fan above me only seems to encourage the heat
My windows reveal a grey sky and fading light
Summer evenings drift away as the new season emerges
I sit alone with scattered thoughts
And I feel afraid without reason or surprise
Years have past and I have sat here alone
Memories bring little more than a regretful smile
I sit on this bed alone, afraid, despising it
This lukewarm fear seems to mature as I do
The layers of it unravel for me to glimpse inside
But all I ever see is my own expressionless face
My fear has lately become stale and hardened
Mold grows on its underbelly and truth is the mirror of its eyes
I possess this fear with hateful acceptance
Still it lives by feeding on the doubt in my heart
I sit alone in this warm room and converse with my fear,
And the only aspect that frightens me now is its persistence

Lisa Neusch

Love

Love is a mother's arms, the glow in your father's eyes
The more they think of losing you, the more they want to cry

Love is a brother's compliments, a child's adoring cries
The more that you grow up, the more that you despise

Love is something to share with family, friends and lovers
Sometimes you want to share it with everyone alive

Love is something everyone wants, even though it is not a prize
Love is something to look upon with very wondering eyes

Melissa Annette Campbell

My Girlfriend Has A Mustache

My girlfriend has a mustache
The first thing I noticed about
her was her large crystal clear eyes

The second was that she has a good
right-hook, which she uses for
instructional purposes only

Her mustache is smooth and soft, like baby hair

It sits like a faint shadow cast
upon her upper lip

Sometimes she rips it out of her skin
with wax that has been melted poured
on and left to cool and dry

And when she does...

I have to say "Honey where did your
mustachio go"
She tells me "Oh i got rid of it"
That's when it's time for me to say...

"Honey do whatever you have to do;
but I love you mustachio or no mustachio"

Then comes the instruction.

Rodney C. Johnson

A Pillow Of Wishful Dreams

Awakened by a sunbeam
The flaming orb of warmth
Penetrates my face, as gentle September breezes
Waft through my room
Casting black and light shadows
That flicker across the sheets
Emulating a colony of ants
Scurrying about in confusion

The pages of my book, flip over one by one
Some that I read thoroughly,
Others that were skipped over
Now being yanked from the binder
By the late summer wind.
Ripped to shreds, scattered on the floor
You say we can be 'just friends'
The chapter never ends...

Turning over I drift back
Into my slumberland, my sanctuary
A recurring dream transpires,
A reminder of my desire for you

Ronald A. Busse

Life

There is too much pollution, and no solution.
The flowers are dying because nobody's trying.
By different people's litter, the streets are being glittered.
And yet all the more life stays free.

More people go on welfare because nobody seems to care.
There is way too many smokers and still not enough jokers.
The abusers need to be caught and trials need to be fought.
And yet all the more life stays free.

There is too much violence because nobody teaches silence.
There's not enough love in the air because nobody seems to really care.
You hear no ringing from the church bells dinging.
Because our town has shown that it has really grown.
You usually find the ding where the whole town can hear the ring.
In our town there will never be a ring.
And yet all the more life stays free.

Laura George

The Children Of The Lands

Hear the children cry; please don't let us die.
The future of the world is in our hands, and
One day we will pass it on to the children
Of the lands.

Hear the children cry; dear Lord, don't let us die.
A child's world should be filled with happiness and
Laughter, they should be able to set goals to go after.

Hear the children cry; we can't let them die! If all
They see is hunger and strife, then tell me, what will
Become of their life. It's time to make a stand and
Help the children of the lands.

Just give a little whatever you can, anything at all
Would be a helping hand. So one day, maybe we
Won't have to hear the children cry; please don't
Let us die.
Virginia P. Teets

Changing Times

The times are getting tougher.
   The gangs are getting rougher.
Pollution's at the top of every list.

Corruption's in the headlines.
   Destruction is a bad sign.
Temptation's getting harder to resist.

When prayers went out of schooling,
   by some judicial ruling,
it seemed to be the start of all this strife.

My faith is getting stronger.
   Will I be around much longer?
I must make all the days count in my life.

If we'd "Do Unto Others,"
   we'd all be loving brothers.
A dove would be our emblem - not a knife.
Patricia Olson

The Nine O'Clock Hour

The nine o'clock hour, well, what can be said?
The hubbub is over, the kids are in bed.
I sit in my chair, kick out the footrest,
this is the time when I'm feeling my best.
I reflect on the day, it's "ins" and it's "outs",
all the hugs and the kisses, the screams and the shouts.
How many times did I hear myself say,
"Don't touch that!", or, "Please, will you put it away?"
Or how many times have I heard in reply,
"But it's mine!" or, "If she can do that, so can I!"
The examples above are some "outs" that I mentioned,
believe me, my whole day isn't filled with such tension.
I have also had plenty of "ins" all day through,
like the kiss on the cheek with the "I love you too".
The songs that were sung and the books that were read,
and all of the humorous things that were said.
I'd say all in all the day went just swell,
and as for tomorrow, who really can tell.
Kathy DeKarske

Childhood Memories

Peach walls and worn red carpet,
The picture of a box room.
Laying on a soft feather bed,
Santa bear in tow.
Nestled in a patch work quilt,
guarding against the sweeping breeze.
Staring at the looming dressers
with their silent figurines frozen in time.
Natalie Moran

Aftermath

The blue Pacific is calm now,
The islands sleep under the tropical sun,
Those other days nearly forgotten.
But there are those who remember,
When the sea roared and the islands trembled.
The silent figures who walk the quiet beaches
   remember,
Guadalcanal...Leyte....Corregidor....
   New Georgia....
They will never forget!
Do you remember!
Jane Dunnell Gilbert

A Friend For Always

Every morning, as I would wake,
The kiss of friendship, my cheek did take.
When I needed you to heal my sorrow,
To wear a smile, your kisses I'd borrow.
You would always find me, through my scent,
And so my heart, to you I lent.
I had a dream, you left my side,
Like the ocean, gone with the waves and the tide.
Many years had passed us by,
Until the day, dark clouds would fly.
When you had looked, to me to leave,
I looked away, so you could stay, I believed.
But I could not look far enough away,
Because the moment had arrived, you could not stay.
And so the heart, that I had lent to you,
Had left me numb, to start a new.
So when the falling sands go by,
We soon will learn all shadows must die.
Lisette Sucari

Dusk

The grasses quivering,
The leaves all rustling,
The bird's last note trilling through the air,
And dusk has come.

Soft footsteps sound,
Away the deer bound.
At the edge of the woods, one turns around,
Gives a snort and stamps on the ground.

There he stands, a stalwart king
With his glance unwavering,
And his horns, with velvet shedding,
Shine in the light the moon is spreading.

Paying no heed to the dew that is dropping,
He is still there, waiting and watching.
Above the vast meadow, a few stars are shining
And the end of dusk has come.
Lois A. Shell

To The Children

Oh to the children whose imaginations are so strong,
the lives that they lead as they play along.
The world looks upon them as a generation gone wrong,
but these little children will carry us on.
We are here now, but won't always be,
and our children need something we've neglected to see.
They need a love for the land which is fading every day,
and a love for mankind that has already gone away
A sense of direction that comes from the heart,
and lots of love to keep them from falling apart.
God can reassure us, but what about them?
What do they have left, life's getting very slim.
Michelle Whisnant

Thoughts Of You

The seasons are changing and so is the time.
The leaves will change color, except for the pine.
It's hard to believe so much time has passed,
But our love for you will always last.

We took a walk down memory lane,
Somehow, as expected, it wasn't the same.
The sea, the shore, the sights of Maine,
Just left our hearts in a lot of pain.

We miss you more with each passing day,
We'd love to see you and just say "Hey".
That won't happen as we wish it to,
So we send our hearts, this day to you.
   Sophie Courter

Brother

The time we spent was short but sweet,
The memories we share we can never beat.
You know I love you till life's end,
You were both a brother and a friend.
And now I can only pray,
That you and I will meet someday.
If you believe, and so will I,
Our deep love will never die.
Even though our blood is not the same
I smile whenever I hear your name.
And always remember, don't ever ignore
For I love you as a brother and so much more.
   Mirna Hariz

The Beckoning Light

My life is propelled by the beckoning light
The light which shines so very bright
It guides me to destinations untold
Led on a journey righteous and bold.

The light that burns the eyes can not see
Its brilliance remains in the soul of me
The direction it leads no longer I fear
For I know that point I soon shall near.

That I seek is you my dearest love
A place unseen from bellow or above
My journey ends within your heart
For I can not avoid St. cupids dart.

The search is on I'll find I pray
The woman I'll love each and every day
I ask you darling to prepare for me
That beckoning light from inside I see.
   J. A. Emerson

"Reflections"

As I stand before you, there's a glare in my eye,
The look of confidence, I know who I am,
I'm a proud junior, one year left to go,
With scattered thoughts, what's in my future to come.
Will I graduate, is college ahead,
I sure hope so. I stand here alone,
Yet, I am not lonely, I feel the warmth of my family
Who were all in this room before me. I am confident of my style.
And everyone likes my look, I proudly wear my Chicago Bulls shirt,
With bluejean overalls to match. Do you like them?
I sure hope so. Now I'm older and wiser,
With a few lessons under my belt. I've been down a couple of roads,
The road to maturity, the path of mistakes,
Quarrel avenue, and lovers lane.
I've learned self-respect, also respecting others as equals.
Some think I'm confused, others say I don't know what lies ahead,
I know my destiny, I know what I'm here for,
I know my cause in life, I know I'll do something important,
I'll show the world I once existed, at least I hope so.
   C. R. Hullum

In Search Of A Friend

I searched the world watching, waiting for him;
the longer I waited the bright light of hope turned dim.
I searched the mountains and I swam through the sea;
I started to believe he had left me.
I walked a mile or maybe two;
I traveled through valleys and crossed rivers too.
Then one day I saw a bright light;
For I was no longer in the night.
For his arms were stretched out wide as he stood there;
With his eyes like fire and long white hair.
In a blink of an eye I was standing next to him;
And that bright light was no longer dim.
It burned bright enough for everyone to see;
He had never left for he was right beside me.
   Michelle Capps

Making a Decision After Hearing A Call

Dedicated to: Mr. & Mrs. Bill and Delia Graves
Today a new day has just begun
The Lord has spread His love to all houses
Dear friends! Be glad while God is calling you
If you are faithful following God, later on
You will enjoy hearing the Lord's peaceful song.

There was a grey haired couple at the Gospel Meeting
Who made their choice by standing up
Having the determination to fellow Jesus step-by-step
Your life is much newer and many times fresher than before.

How nice was the moment both side-by-side stood up together
All the church had but one heart in union:
Silently praying to God to keep them healthy and peaceful
As long as they are blessed with living this earthly life.
   Phu Nguyen

Dreams

The sky is dark
The moon is full;
Flying free from shackles of flesh and bone
Soaring high, the mind is free.

What was fantasy is now reality
For imagination wears the crown
And subconscious sits at his side;
Scientific facts dance and make merry in the depths of the night.

Free to fly
To see the unseen
To express the inexpressible
Free to understand the incomprehensible.

What was dark is now light
For the sun begins its daily climb
Extinguishing the dark's hidden light;
Mysteries and solutions part to sleep through the day.

The sky is dark
The moon is full;
Tiptoeing softly through the night
The forgotten dreams return, the mind is free.

Margaret Shipstead

Moonlight Forever

As we lay underneath the stars
the moon rolled over our heads
the wind blew heavy and strong
and we held hands against the raging night

As the clouds rose past us
the air was sweet with spring
smiles were so bright in the soft light
but for the love we were alone

My brown-eyed lover in the dark
you were what I needed then
so good and understanding under the stars
so pure in what you were

As the night became the day
and I awoke to a new beginning
you knew that I had to forget the night before
and that it was to be done

As we lay underneath the stars
the moon rolled over our heads
the wind blew heavy and strong
and we held hands against the raging night

Ryan Barker

Untitled

My friend,
the one I love
who makes me lose all self control
the beat of your heart is also mine beating
a pleasant distraction
as I gaze I grow fond of your reflection
and collect reveries with great affection
my heart and soul conspire your possession
flowering passion that destroys all reason
precious recompense for a heart aching
make shambles of inhibitions
delectable perversion
bother me with caresses, disturb me with your kisses,
triturate me please with the force of your rhythm
tire me with the power of your seduction
so when to slumber I will have finally given into
as I succumb, only the splendor of our flight
is what I will muse
in Luna's arms I will surrender
and need not dream...

A. Fregoso

Ode To The Romantic

The candles in place, the wine at chill
The music is soft as shadows in darkness dart aloft
A knock at the door, the greeter and greeted embrace in place
The gesture to enter in silence is made
O' yes, this pretty lady has been here before
For she knows what is in store.
For her man is a romantic and he's learned his ways
Across the Atlantic where Mommy has taught him
How to treat a lady.
his gestures respectful this man intellectual
Draws chair from the table O' this man is able
Conversation quiet, let the dancing begin
This romantic has won her so he asks the question
And in days marriage ensues
Now let this little lesson in prose
Show you bachelors how to propose
And win your lady
With a quiet eve and a rose.

R. Wintheiser

God Smile On Christmas

God smile on christmas
The night before had been an
Silent and holy one for, far away
In a manger baby Jesus was born.

Under a star that shine so bright
Pointing to an light in Bethlehem
Hark the Herald Angels sing,
There's a song in the air.

The coming of the faithful to the Christ child.
The first Noel the Angels did sing,
The holiest of Holy nights that brought,
Joy to the world!

The Christ child reigns
A king is born Alleluia, Alleluia,
Wonderful, Emmanuel,
The Prince of peace!!!

Scharlena A. Porter

The Arkansas Legend

You have produced a Rock; President Bill Clinton,
The "Oak" Johnny Cash, whose country music hangs on,
So tonight, poetic fans just let this be
A reflection of leadership and talent; just great to see.

Let's clap! Dance! "Rock! Sing! For all to see
We are alive, healthy and a poetic tree,
Rocking away with Arkansanians, you and me
Sax and rock; so enjoy this special party.

Oak[y]! Oak[y]! And who?...Rock[y], Rock[y]
Chant! Chant! Please let's dance! Be Free!
Celebrate these greats; our legendary,
"Oak[y]! Oak[y]! And "Rock[y]! Rock[y]

I want for you and the poetic tree
Joy, laughter, fun, till eventually,
The hall is aglow with U.S. great citizenry
As talents explore into the 21st century.

So "Oak[y]! Oak[y]! Oh! Key
In on the rock; promote artistry,
Blend rhythm; Sax and the string guitar,
Let's see: aren't they specials of this musical war?

Margaret Alexander

"And Sailing, No More"

Yawing and creaking with each gentle swell,
The old sailing ship seemed to whisper, low.
I ache with each tide, with each rise and fall,
And tire with each storm, with each hard blow.

Many years on the seas have taken their toll,
The deck are worn, the hull getting weak,
This old gal, has seen better days.
The waxed felt caulking is starting to leak.

Many crews have climbed through the rigging.
Many first mates have yelled out orders.
Many times this ship has crossed the oceans,
And so it goes, she has crossed many borders.

Just one more sail on the oil deep blue,
Just one more time in the wind and roar,
Old Neptune is calling, calling to her,
Then history with have her, and sailing, no more!

Richard L. Williams

Untitled

Where's that little barefoot boy, with the bandage on his toe?
The one who had a dog named pooch, who followed where he'd go.

They'd run and laugh and chase the birds, that gathered by the sea,
And felt the sun upon their face, and like the wind were free.

Sometimes they were knights of old, or sometimes pirates too,
But when you're young and full of dreams there's nothing you can't do.

They built a mighty castle, although just made of sand,
The thing that made the magic, was paws and tiny hands.

But time is like a circle, it never has and end,
And then one star-lit summers night, it took the boy's best friend.

I'm sure that little boy at night would look up to the sky,
And think about his pal called "pooch" and ask the question "Why"?

I often wandered where he went, or found his lady fair,
The one within the castle, with soft brown eyes and hair.

I think I knew that little boy, for one time long ago,
I happened by a little stream, to watch it dance and flow.

And as I stood there watching, while shaded by a tree,
I saw that gentle barefoot boy, staring back at me!

William H. Battersby Jr.

Opposites Attract

Opposites attract believe me it's true,
the one you think you hate might end up loving you.
You may not know at first,
I tell you no lie,
but after a while you'll start to see he's more than meets the eye.
He'll start to buy you things,
like roses and perfume,
and soon you'll start accepting these gifts,
and displaying them in your room.
You'll give him one more chance,
he'll wine you, dine you, give you romance,
and before you know it your in his trance!
You'll end up in love,
walking hand in hand,
remembering the day,
his face you could not stand.
So let me warn you ladies,
if what I say is true,
you'd better be more careful.....
the next victim could be you!

Melissa Santana

Little Meg

There once was a shy, little egg
The others called "little Meg".
She knew one day she would hatch and be free;
She waited patiently.
Every evening she shook in her shell.
"I'm doing swell; I can tell.
Perhaps tomorrow I can open the shell."
But the sly fox knocked little Meg out of her nest.
She rolled to the edge of the well.
She thought, "What if I fell?
Would I break my shell?
Perhaps I'd better yell.
But no one can hear me inside this shell."
What a predicament for a little egg!
"I fear for my life!" cried little Meg.
Just then her mother swooped down and caught little Meg
As she was about to go over the edge and into the well.
"I am doing swell!" she let out a yell.
Hooray for little Meg.

Rolann Aronson

Show You Care

Set it aside - it's in the past.
The pain you feel doesn't have to last.
It's your life now - you're not controlled!
Do you want to live or be consoled?

When we were kids, we did submit.
To the abuse, they did commit.
We were the victims...there was no guilt.
It's on their shame, our lives were built.

We're stronger now, we did survive.
We're bruised and scarred, but we're alive.
We are now members of a secret club-
No one knows, but the Lord above.

They can't hurt us, if we don't let them.
In His own time, God will get them.
So learn from it...don't pass it down.
Your kids need love...while you're around.
You have feelings they need to share,
It's up to you to show you care.

Sylvia Link

Walk The Fear

A prayer for release from the barnacles of despair.
The pit that pulls your soul deeper and deeper into its lair.

Hell is the only end or so you think with your muted thoughts
That transcend all other notions and motions that you were taught.

You took up drugs, trying to release yourself for a moment from
Pain, only to find there was no gain.
Despair was your middle name.

Each path was strewn with boulders and walls seemly impossible to Scale.
It was as though you were held down by a nail.

Then your guardians sent you on a mission.
Your heart was opened to truth, wisdom, and vision.

Courage is now your middle name.
You've walked the fear and nothing will ever again be the same.

Sharon Swain

Freedom Lent

I feel your strength beneath me as we glide against the wind.
The power of your body both enemy and friend.
Reaching for a mountain, I alone could never climb.
The wild in your spirit becoming one with mine.
Mystic in your beauty, majestic in your grace.
Freedom taken threw the ages shows gently in your face.
Your eyes pools of mystery, inspire trust and fear.
And a flight of fancy when life was held more dear.
Your mane flows in the wind like the clouds across the sky.
You yield to my command, never asking why.
Your hooves pound out my heart beat, for a moment we are one.
You stir in me a passion as we race into the sun.
And as the night surrounds us, my body tired and spent.
I thank you for the freedom you for a moment lent.
   Mary A. Arndt

"To This I Question"

This object be invented for?
The purpose understood by all,
to only get—to point B—
Where there, they follow this as well.

If point B had not, this object,
from point A, would there be expectation ceasing.

This, the first questions to an envision,
which came true by one who finished a thought.

Shall this be the haunt which follows us?
The object that has often enough done harm?
This—which fuels an existing frenzy.

Unique, not brilliant this be—
It is that, because I, along with it reminding tick,
acknowledge, that it, be a tick away—from my time.

A wake-up tool both conscious and reality it plays—
Again, one being questioned, the other—brilliant.

But now, concentrate the brilliance, for realized I,
how truthful it be, when hear do I, its ticking cue.
   Warren A. Kaneshiro

A Wish

I ride my bicycle between the motorist,
The scent of gasoline bothers me constantly,
I turn right; towards a road less congested,
That takes me to the river and white painted benches.
I go east where the sun is rising and pink
and I can look at it without a squint
I feel the moistened breeze swelling my face
I see the water a foaming brocade
adoring the shore and leaving rocks glowing
In the distance like a huge beast floating
A boat passes by slowly.
In the sky a triangle of feathers
In multicolored pairs of seven or tens
Weave the space and catches my eye.
And oh those birds! That flock together;
and I wish I could fly.
   Nelly Baez

A Glow In The Dark Night Sky

The stars in the sky at night shine like diamonds in the ring of life
The sky without its eyes is a black dark place of peace.
Stars fall from the sky upon the earth to fill the hopes and
wishes of its many people.
The people call out to the stars each night wishing for the
fulfillment of their hopes and dreams.
At times their hopes and dreams are fulfilled from a glow in the
dark night sky.
   K. Canavan

A Dream

She lies awake, conscious of the chill on her flesh and
  the scent of the salt in the air.
Her lips are still burning, every nerve ending is alive and
  longing for more of his touch.
Yet, she is still in her room.

How can this be, she asks herself.
  I am here...alone!
How can I still feel him?
  Are my dreams so alive with my desire,
that I bring them to me in my waking moments as well?

Oh such sweet dreams, how you torture me!
  But what is this?
Sand??
  Asleep she falls,
hoping to find her Love a second time.
   Kris Van Beers

Today A Rainbow Of Thought

I wish all people could feel the contentment,
The serenity that stirs inside my soul, all
The wonderment as I observe the architectural
Lacing of the frosty crystals of ice in a morn
Transferring into the glow of day, the crisp
Intense blue of the seemingly magnified sky,
The dazzling multi colors of autumn,
Illuminated by the penetrating thrust of the
Suns rays to let our souls cleanse itself of sorrow,
And to arouse our sensitivity that through
Our despair, our turmoil, our life
Was worth living if only to see one such day.

I pray, as my last breath nears, it will be in
The Autumn, and that I will see the gentle breeze caress
The rustic golden leaves from their last grasp of life,
And as the leaves sway to and fro, falling to their final
Destiny, I too will know that my final destiny
Will also be to this wonderful earth
And I pray that my journey into the unknown.
Will he as magnificent as that one scenic Autumn Day.
   Lawrence I. Singley

"The Lady Of My Dreams"

It is not possible to forget,
The simplicity of your smile
Nor the enchantment of yours eyes
and much less the beauty of your body
That lies within the arrogant splendor of your figure.

It's such a pity that you belong to someone else,
Because with those looks that you give
You could capture anyone's heart
Like the shimmer of your pupils in a lake,
and if you set your mind to it, you could have lovers everywhere

Guatemala has been known as the garden of many beautiful flowers
and that from within blossoms a downpour of harmonious colors
and from that same place submerges your image,
which attracts the attention of all who know you.

Love always, when people love you, and when they scorn you
love the hand that cares for you sweetheart,
as well the one that wounds you
love everyone and everything, because "love is life"
love in the sense that the whole world could see
and acknowledge that you are someone special
   Max S. Flores

Parallels

The miracle of sunrise—the miracle of birth.
The slow, sure pattern of our lives and days.
The mornings and the evenings—the winters and the springs,
The parallel of cycles in our ways.

God sends us joy and sunshine—sadness, raindrops, tears;
Hope and a glowing rainbow—dark clouds, doubts and fears.
Flowering springs, and blossoming youth;
Long summer days and years.

He sends us trouble, storm and strife—the autumn of our later life;
The changing, brilliant hue.
A warming fire in winters' cold—children's love to warm the old.
The change of generations, ever new.

The quiet gleam of sunset—the promise of tomorrow.
The certainty of night, and rest from strife.
The grateful benediction of sleep, and rest from sorrow.
The hope of yet another, better life.

We are the sum and total of our yesterdays.
Our memories hold the threads of yester lives.
Threads that shape the pattern of our ways and our tomorrows.
His pattern—that we use to build our lives.
   Mary A. Grenier

Easter's Promise

Bees are buzzing... flowers are fresh,
the snow from the meadow has melted;
Songbirds sing by the bubbling spring
and green grass grows
where gentle raindrops have pelted.
It is the season of new life,
spring breezes blow softly and warm;
The brook's melody is played
beside the cool shade...
where butterflies kiss blossoms as they swarm.
One of God's promises is told by the rainbow,
which nestles near the crest of the hill;
Springtime is bursting
and my heart is thirsting,
for Easter's promise...my soul to still.
   Ronald G. Morris

Coming From The Heart

The soul emerges coming from the heart.
The spirit awakens coming from the heart.
The mind acquiesces coming from the heart.
The truth is known coming from the heart.

I function from my mind.
Hiding from the pain, the grief, the fear.
Seemingly asleep in my heart.
On occasion, their wakefulness alerts me to their presence.
If my mind wrestles with them, anxiety and depression prevail.
If experienced, the pain, the grief, the fear become friends.
For they awaken me to life and to me.

Without the pain, there is no pleasure.
Without grief, no joy.
Without tears, no laughter.
Without fear, no courage.
I awaken when coming from the heart.
   Teri K. Smith

Forgotten

Walking down the corridor.
The strange smell of death reeks within.
Moaning echoes within the hallway.
Each room is filled with the forgotten human beings.
Their bodies heaped in piles of
fragile bones and flesh.
They seem so helpless.
Their protruding eyes search
for some recognition of life.
No this is not life,
for life has come and gone.
Their frail bodies are tired.
They want to go home, but the
only way to get home is through death.
   Rebecca Curry Gum

Mystical Scene

In the cool darkness of the morning before
   the sun comes up, the waves come crashing in.
The sand is still cold and it tingles between
   your toes.
You start to walk down the beach to take a
   wake-up swim.
Finally you get to the shoreline after that long
   unforgettable walk.
You stop and set your eyes on the pink sun
   just showing its magnificent rays.
You just look and look without even noticing the
   oncoming surfers with their boards all shined up.
The sensational sunrise is so new to you that the
   gleam doesn't hurt your eyes and the crashing
   waves hitting your ankles don't even startle you.
The elderly people begin having picnics on the sand.
It is now high noon and the sight is so beautiful
   you wish you could look forever!
   Rian J. Mills

Winds Of Recovery

I was on a dark and lonely road
The sun hidden behind a deep, dark cloud
My shoulders were carrying a massive load
Oh, GOD, where are you? I cried out loud

The moon tried to peek from behind the haze
Moving so languidly in the murky night
My thoughts were a jumble, my mind a daze
And then I saw it, a shimmering light

At first I couldn't believe my eyes
And then I knew it was a discovery
I could cast away all my guilt and lies
For I was sailing the winds of recovery
   Mike V. Flaten

In A Valley

As the sun comes up, and the new day is born
The valley is as bright as a sunflower.
The sky is a bluish-purple. The Air is as fresh as a rose.
The trees are as big as a giant and as green as a leaf.
Then comes the death of night.
The moon is as a candle shining in the sky.
The sky is dark as black. The valley is as black as a panther.
The trees are like monster walking around.
The air is musty and humid.
Then everything is quit.
   Sabrina Weststrate

Trust And Be Happy

Though the clouds hang low do not worry so
The sun may be out of sight, everything will come out right
God is still on his throne, he won't leave us here alone
He controls the stars, moon and sun, every battle he has won
Even to death and its sting, peace and happiness he brings
If we trust and never doubt, He will surely bring us out
He will take us home on high, to his heaven bye and bye
Strive your best to do his will, help your brother climb his hill
Show him God's way is the best, though the devil will him test
By example let him learn, right from wrong he can discern.
Everything good is from above, to each one he offers love
the devil your soul would gain, your life ruin, bring to shame
Be not easy to deceive, in your heart salvation receive
Trust him with your decision now, escape from problems he'll
  show you how
True happiness then you'll know, peace of mind, face aglow
Heart content, and happy be, since from sin you're set free
The sun will shine throughout each day, as we let our savior have
  his way
Clouds will still come, eyes grow dim
  "We Won't Worry, We Trust Him"
Pauline G. Adkins

Escape

Yesterday is just a memory, today is just a fear;
The tears I shed for yesterday, today they seem so near.
If there was just a button, that could change mistakes I've made;
If there was just a blueprint, new plans would all be laid.

The button would erase — delete the heartache and the pain;
The prints all drawn and complete, would somehow do the same.
If there were just a handle to lead to a trap door;
A ship all docked and ready to sail me to a distant shore.

I'd climb aboard — my fear and I, and softly float at sea;
I'd let the tears of pain I feel wash slowly over me.
Each pain — each hurt within my life would slowly disappear;
Each drop would reach the great deep blue, new land would
draw me near.

Oh, if there was just one small chance to take it all away;
Replaced would be the sadness — the skies to blue from grey.
But such a place within my reach, my eyes can not quite see;
I guess I will just drift away within my mind a dream.
Linda Wiatrowski

Seasons

This is the summer of my year
the time I disappear
travel to different places
meet new faces

This is the autumn as the clock goes around
the time the leaves fall to the ground
back to school
teachers rule

This is the winter of my growing
outside it is snowing
trying to read write and learn
memories of summer burn

This is the spring of my day
new life is on the way
I passed the grade
the seasons fade
Timothy J. Buzzelli

Red

The color of love or the hue of passion.
The tone of anger or the scheme of rage.
Brilliant rubies on a monarch's hand, for such is life in a
Child's castle high.

Sudden brightness like the blush creeping over a cheekbone.
Inflamed like the print behind the sting of a slap, or in the
Eyes watching tail lights with a goodbye fading in the dark.

Gentle to the soul like strawberry stains on summer skin,
Traces of lipstick gently wiped from his face, or a dewy
Rose this morning for a pressed memory tomorrow.

A slow to slumber evening sun or a wild and torrid dawning sky.
Dark and sweet like a depth of wine in a glass or cherries on
The vine. Raw and ragged like hands too long in cotton mill starch.
Unruly like the cap of hair framing the pale, freckled face.

Together with orange tint, this southern clay earth;
And with burnished copper shades for the proud souls driven
From it. And for those who remain, proudly so yet today.

I skinned my knee and there it was. Mamaw, too.
  "Just look at all that pretty red blood!"
Pride more than pain bringing tears. "That's the color of life,
  young'un." Smiling, I always knew it was.
Shannon A. Lumpkins

Song Of Angels

The wreath is hung upon the door,
the tree lights sparkle, bright!
The shoppers in the crowded stores will hurry home tonight;
gift to wrap and cards to write.

There's Santa Claus in every store
and on the street a dozen more.
Expectant children, clamoring for
one more chance to tell their dreams,
hear not the rush of Angel wings.

This is the time of Jesus' birth.
The blessed child came down to Earth.
'Tis he who comes again this night,
to fill each heart with sweet delight.

Wrap your gifts and dream your dreams,
but pause to hear the Angels' wings
and listen to the song they sing!

Christ is born,
The heavenly King!
O' come, let us adore Him!
Marjorie Baranski Thompson

"How Love Feels"

I've fallen in love for the first time
the value is worth more than any dime
It's much a strange but warm feeling
and it's the words greatest healing.

I can't eat or sleep because the feelings so deep
I hope this feeling is for keeps
I would hate for him to break my heart now
It would be as if my life were over and
It's time to take my final bow.

When I'm around you I feel so good
Just like a person in love should
If I could I'd be with you 24-7
It would be as if I were living on an earthly heaven.

I've finally said goodbye to infatuation
I've also left alone no good sex relations,
I've finally moved on to a bigger and better things.
I've finally found the ultimate love in my king.
Tamika J. Evans

Familiarizing With A New Mystery
(In honor of the birth of Micah Abraham Edwards)
I've grown familiar with the mystery of death
The violent turn or the moment
One forgets to breath
The last gasp and the letting go

Now is the time to become
familiar with life
the mystery of Birth

As my wife's belly swells, the fear grows
to confront this new direction and opportunity
to discover many new secrets and hidden strengths

Rubbing her stomach
which is no longer the flat, familiar terrain,
the baby kicks sharply
not easy to grasp that which is hidden

Death is familiar
One moment you take breath in
The next you don't
Birth remains the mystery
Head first emerging from darkness into uncertainty.
   Morry Edwards

If I Were The Wind
Oh, to be the wind and forever race free.
   The world to be my home, exist for all eternity.
I'd move through forests of fir, oak and pine,
   Whisper to animals and lovers a song divine.

I'd race upon a mountain top where few will dare,
   a harsher sound then my song will blare.
An artist so great for mankind below I would be,
   paint pictures with clouds for all to see.

I'd dance upon the desert, carve the shifting sand.
   Follow a twisting river to the sea in every land.
I'd fill a sail or make the water dance with glee.
   I'd caress a field of wheat, my movement you could see.

Then there would be times, when I move not a reed.
   'Tis then I stop to think, what would I have and need
With freedom alone the want and need would be great.
   I can touch but never be touched, have no love of a mate.

I can surround, but never be held, touching one sided would be.
   Why live life forever, without a mate to share it with me?
So it is during this time of deep thought of love and care,
   I cannot be the wind - I must love and be loved, always share.
   Melvin Hoppe

Untitled
Gently, the softness of evening arrives to ease the day away.
The warmth of her tenderly envelops the universe.
Gentle, swirling images fill my thoughts.
Images, feelings, of places and people,
People I know, people I'd like to know, places I'd like to be.
Friendly inviting images, scattered haphazardly across blue velvet;
Happily circling and teasing.
Each one calling out to be remembered, to be savored, to be born.
Always within sight, never within grasp:
Yet sometimes...
Sometimes so near I can hear them encouraging me,
To go further, to try harder, to reach, to grow
Until finally...
The day suddenly reclaims her domain, and the sweet coolness of the
   morning air welcomes me to a new day.
   Sherrie Wakeland

Inspiration
As the refreshing feeling of rain trickles down my face
The warmth, the love, and the care I embrace
My heart soars wildly to the deep blue sky
The pleasure of happiness gives me a high
Birds sing cheerfully with all of their might
Their wings are spread preparing for flight
This thrill of excitement fills me deeply within
Where will it take me as the journey begins
To all heights of fulfillment and ecstasy I am told
As the sun beams upon with a pigment of gold
I can feel no stronger than I am right now
It cannot be explained, there is no way how
For each has their own treasures to endure
As for me I must say I have more to explore
   Mindy Breden

The Old Pond
As I look into the old pond
The water is absolutely still
In the water I see a reflection
It is the beauty of the autumn colors in the trees.

I think of days gone by
Of mother and father, and the home where I grew up
And of running carefree through open fields
I think of future days
Of a wife, children, and grandchildren
And of leisurely walks through open fields.

The freshest of breezes stirs the water a bit
And I am awakened from my trance
I think of the present
Of how moments like these are special indeed
My heart is filled with peace
My soul with tranquility.

I turn my collar up and walk back to the world
Refreshed as always by the old pond
And I wonder why I can't experience this feeling
Every moment of every day.
   G. Simpson

Stranded On The Beach
I am a beach waiting for the tide,
The waves are my transportation,
My chance to get away,
I need the water to carry me,
To lift me off my feet and take all my troubles,
I want to get a taste of the ocean,
For I am as lonely as a lark without the waves to guide me,
I want whispering waters to whisk me away,
So I can reach my wildest dreams,
I want to make a difference in this world,
And help others stranded on the beach.
   Michelle K. Maze

Your Spacelord:
I am your spacelord and you are my tenant
The words that you utter I hold in my being
Your seeing is real of the space you possess
But soon you will leave I won't tell you the rest

I'm full of round spheres and bright glowing torches
Which help you and guide you through the night the approaches
I'm real and present to you as a landlord
To lend you a space that you know exist

But soon you will leave to another sphere, I know for a fact
That I will always be here.
   Luis Rivera

Untitled

Hope walks through the door
the whole world stops and smiles
Hello Hope, it whispers
while wrapping her in the kind of embrace
that only the earth can give
Gentle and invisible, like the presence of angels
at births and deaths
waiting with open arms
to give and take the lives of strangers
Beautiful Hope, it whispers
lifting her up with breezes
so she looks as if she's flying
and it gives to her as a gift
all the warmth it's held inside
the warmth of going home
after wandering through winter
the warmth of a thousand summer nights
and a thousand stolen kisses
My Hope, it whispers
and fills her days with dreams of springtime

Mary Doherty

President John F. Kennedy's Assassination

The twenty second day of November.
The whole world will remember.
How each of us was stunned,
When the special news was run.
Announcing: Our President has been shot.
You didn't know whether to believe it or not.
That the life of this gallant man,
Could be taken by an assassin's hand.
Yet! There it was before a cheering crowd.
Three bullets rang out loud.
On lookers saw at a glance
The smiling President had not a chance.
With sad remorse every heart filled.
When his body lay stilled.
When confirming words were said:
"Our President is dead." Everyone bowed their head.
Some in prayer, some just grief.
Everyone was bereaved.
With the wretched encounterment,
To such a great President.

Louise Page

Rejoice, Be Glad

My Family and close friends,
The wind beneath my wings —
I know you were there taking care of all things.
Don't be sad — Rejoice! Be glad!

Remember me as a Ray of sunshine
Helping those lagging behind.
Educating the young was part of my game —
I wanted them to succeed and not be ashamed.

I delighted in giving advice —
Never once, always thrice.

Many friends I had far and near;
Each was special in their own way.
Have no regrets because I could not stay.

The church is where I wanted to be.
Allowing preparation for this long journey.
Heaven has always been my ultimate goal.
I am warm — I am secure — not cold!

I have truly done my best
And now God has taken me home to rest.
Don't be sad — Rejoice! Be Glad!

Linda Lindsay

Bluebirds And Rainbows

Misty mountains light with gentle rain,
the wind softly guiding a sailboat on it ways to port.
Man competing with Mother Nature
who inevitably is holding down the fort.

On shore, a tiny Bluebird sends a message to his mate.
The clouds darken across the bay,
while the tall Oaks bend gently to the breeze.
At the end of another day,

Like life in its own infinity,
measured by toil, happiness and pain.
The darkness disappears, as always
and the rainbow appears again.

Bluebirds and Rainbows, beauty beyond compare,
stretching from mountain top to the sky,
a fleeting moment only, for man to grasp the wonder
before it passes him by.

The secret of life and happiness is with the Bluebird
and Rainbows
since through all darkness comes, love, beauty and light,
God's message of eternal hope.

Katherine Ryan

Dusty Remains

I am the dreamer who's dreams have been shattered,
   the window who's glass has been broken
I am the bird who has lost both her wings, the mute one
   who has never spoken
I am the pure heart who's heart has been soiled,
   the lucky who now pays the cost
I am the well known who has been forgotten, the
   found soul who's just gotten lost
I am the blue sky who's turned cloudy grey, the white light
   that turned itself black
I am the loving who now feels the hate, the best
   friend who's now turned her back
I am the wanted who's no longer needed, the
   sturdy who had a great fall
I am whomever is left of this person and I am
   just no one at all.

Melissa Leigh Roberti

Raindrops

As the raindrops pitter-patter on the window pane
Thunder claps her hands to a chaotic beat
As lightning dances across the sky
Two, huge, brown eyes
filled with their own rain
Cascades down her cocoa-colored face
As she remembers...

Pain, agony and hardships that she's endured
Worries and wondering
That have caused her to wring her hands
Free of a world that she does not understand.

Kordai DeCoteau

Seasons

Fall merges into winter and dons a coat of white,
Then picks up her needles to shorten days and lengthen night,

And as winter enters into spring she changes to a gown,
Of brilliant green and colors bright as soft spring rain comes down,

As spring evolves into summer she dresses up for fun,
Of vacations, swimming, picnics beneath the summer sun.

Then autumn with paintbrush in hand creates a whole new scene,
The leaves drift down, the flowers sleep and winter's here again.

Laurel Zeman

God's Son

When you're feeling lost or confused
There is always someone there,
To hear your problems and worries
And lift you from despair.

It's not your family or relatives,
Or even your best friend.
There's someone that's always here for you
From the beginning to the end.

Just close your eyes slowly
And present your lonely, needing soul.
For Jesus Christ is the Savior
Who will restore you to whole.

Do not be afraid, Friend,
Because you do not see.
The Lord will lead you through darkness
To help you see the light and be free.

You will always be protected and loved
When you have faith in the Holy One.
For He is everywhere among us;
He is Jesus Christ, God's only Son.

Terri L. Belicek

Window Of My Heart

I sit all alone and I wonder why,
The world has suddenly passed me by.
There was a time not long ago,
My zest for life was all aglow.

Fireworks brightened the heavens above,
And hand in hand we watched with love.
Our children grew tall and made their ways,
And yes, mistakenly, those were the days.

Now storms menace my lonely still shores;
The lightning flies and the thunder roars.
And waves lash out and bind me ever tight,
As I'm cast into the cold darkness of night.

My soul cries out, my heart holds still;
"Lord, take me home, if that is your will."
I've savored the many pleasures of being;
My cares for now are all plainly fleeting.

The sun feels warm upon my young face,
As if covered by pure white, delicate lace.
I'm able to see clearly; I have a new start,
As I peer with joy from the window of my heart.

Pauline M. Bembenek

Sail Away

Jolly Roger flew with a frightful clue coming fast on a starboard tack
The zephyrs fair from the pirate's lair, flapped not the Union Jack.
With energy thrift the wanderers drift across the Universe wide.
To an unknown land the small brave band set sail on the cosmic ride.

The wind it wails, the safety pales, it's a chilling blow embraced
To walk with pain 'cross the bounding main, alone in the frigid waste.
And navigate brine on an endless line the adventure we all seek.
That night's a road with a psychic load or so the heart did speak.

In a place so far from the nearest star, one morn in a distant time,
They left in the quiet on a meager diet seeking the cosmic rhyme.
Their hearts confessed their fears repressed, crossing boundless fear.
Bright stars abound the universe 'round and end up right back here.

A word of pearl will always curl so deep inside man's soul,
With joy and fear so far, yet near...when spirit seeks the goal.
So hoist the main, full beams the moon, and sail away boys, away.
The wind at our back we sail the track, and sail away boys, away.

Richard A. Hein

The Song Of The Dove

Oh how beautiful art I my love sitting perched upon a tree next to thee.
Looking upon me with thee I often see reflections of He.
He who designed me to be the me that I could only be with thee.
One not to be above nor beneath thee, but together to be the we that
  we must be.
Quietly sitting I stare at thee with great eyes of passion and glee
Thinking upon the promises made between me and thee, my heart bursts
  with joy when thou looks at me.
Thy looks bless my being, sending me into an eternal flight of the mind
where I can only wonder why I was chosen for thee?
Soaring higher and higher because of thee is my spirit, pausing only
to sing unto thee about the love that stems from inside of me.
This is the love that I feel from mere glances of thee, but to talk
and to touch thee are desired joys turned reality.
As I look at thee my heart gives thanks to He eternally.
He, thee, and me, security are we.

Tamara Angelic Wright

Rain

Rain upon my window cell
theirs so much love in the rain.
Can you tell?
Rain upon rose petal fair
Rain in my heart
Rain in the air
The wind sweeps the rain through my hair.
Love is like a rose petal fair.
Listen to the rains lovely sound
like a harp a heavenly angle found.
Listen to the rain, listen hard
listen well it tells the tale of peoples falls
and how they fell.
Rain falls faint it falls clear
like a little child's tear.
Listen to the rain
and you will have no fear
no fear of life
no fear of living
no fear of helping your heart giving

Mandy Lynn Tisler

Killer Of Giants

If none of us believe in war
Then can you tell me what the weapons for
Listen to me everyone
If the button is pushed
There'll be nowhere to run

Giants sleeping, giants winning wars
Within their dreams
Till they wake when it's too late
And in God's name Blaspheme

Killer of Giants threatens us all
Mountains of madness standing so tall
Marches of protest not stopping the war
Or "The killer of Giants"!

Mother nature people state your case without it's work
Your seas run dry your sleepless eyes
Are turning red alert
  "Killer of Giants!"
  "Killer of Giants!"

Sara Mercer

"The Hunt"

I sit; waiting;
then I hear a noise
as I look up I see him
he is proud;

His antlers have many points
he is old and smart to have lived so long
I watch in awe and wonder
today will be his final day, for this time I have outsmarted him

As I lift my gun slowly up, he smells the air
he senses me!
I know I cannot rush my shot
his head returns to the ground

The sight is on him
I slowly pull the trigger
then, a click
without hesitation he is off!

I have misfired;
and now the hunt begins again.
Karl G. Richardson

Church Bells

When I hear the distant church bells ringing
Then, I only hear the distant church bells ringing
It seems to me that angels are singing

Exaltation conceived from the pure sound
An inner stillness captured by the holy sound
Immaculate whispers from church's grounds

Images of heaven adorn the notes
Chimes telling stories through eternal notes
Massive sound covers earth a pious coat

I'm taken back to my childhood vision
Playing till dusk, hearing the angelic vision
Wondering with my imagination

Every time I hear the church bells ringing
To me it seems the angles are singing
Oriana Nicole Tavoularis

The Loch Ness Monster

We scanned the loch looking for her,
Then we saw the slinking monster.
With near twisting snake-like transformation,
It quickly caught our attention.
Yet hardly moving, its tail grew lame,
And exceeding boring it became.
Wearing a trench coat, certainly not to impress us,
Our guise stormed deliberately from our bus.
Like a brave, unbashful, British Bobbie,
She sought the head of the monstrosity.
The brain, yearning for a peek of Nessie's smile,
Had merely stopped and backed traffic back a mile.
Now, we could not hear our guide's demands,
But we could see her waving hands.
The red faced driver quickly complied,
And the monster traffic, somewhat open-eyed,
And finding a hole the size of a Mac Truck,
Did put itself in second gear along the loch.
Meanwhile the winding tail took a lesser route,
While tourists emptying British buses glanced about,
Like weary travelers on a Scottish pilgrimage,
The famous Nessie for to seek above her hermitage.
Patt Roach

Strolling Down The Ms. River

As I take a stroll down the Ms. River
There are many sights
Even if I did this at night
The calm waters taking my boat down the river
The chills make me quiver
Trees, and flowers, and deers I see
And also a honey bee
As the sun is going down
The less the river shines
And as the sounds coming from around
Such as crickets and the water flowing combines
It brings sweet music to my ears
As I take a stroll down the Ms. River.
Vu Tien Huynh

The War

There's a war going on at this time.
There are two captains, who will be mine?

One captain says, "If you follow me you can't go wrong.
My army is many and we are strong."

The other captain says, "My soldiers are weak and number in few
Sometimes my plans seem hard for you."

The first captain says, "There are many ways I can get you to join.
It's through love of this world I can get you going."

The second captain says, "There's only one way that you can come in,
The battle has been won, Please accept my victory over sin."
Larry Kokinos

Open Your Eyes And See There Is Beauty Outside Of Me

Open your eyes and see
There is a world outside of me
Beyond the trees, to the oceans, to the seas
There is beauty far beyond the world you see

If you look you can see the
Beauty in front of me...
The snow, the clouds, the sky
The mountains which I climb
The stars I see at night
The waterfalls, flowers, and trees
  are all beauty to me

For many there is beauty only
They can see, but only because
  they believe

Do you see what I see?
Do you hear what I hear?
Do you believe what I believe...
That there is beauty outside of me
Margarita Crespo

"Suicide"

When the power of all depression surrounds me,
There is no one who cares or gives me sympathy,
I feel so alone, terrified, so unwanted,
Afraid to face tomorrow, so scared, so daunted,
All of my feelings seem different than many,
Life has always been down, this is my destiny,
There are times I feel suicide is my way out,
Drawn from the ridicule and treatment as a lout,
To commit self-murder, eternity in hell,
A life of more misery is where I might dwell,
Seeing where death is everywhere and hatred grows,
With pain in endless wars and continuous foes...
Renee Roberson

Sarajevo Why?

Beyond the words of precipitous hope,
  There looms a veil of hate.
Where peace united once passed and nodded,
  Bullets and rockets now fly through the gate.

The voice of world brotherhood has been stifled,
  By the roiling beat of mass condescension.
The efforts to help, though well meant, are still slight,
  As the occupants grovel in cold apprehension.

"Will tomorrow bring death, life or freedom,
  In some form that will honor the seed of our trials?"
"How we long the days when the torch was borne,
  Through the cheers of our people, across our miles."

Will we do anything to bring back the beauty,
  Of a land once so noble, now swallowed by vice,
Or is the code of the world now become as the mercenary?
  Saying, we can't help defend you if you can't pay the price.

Zane R. Bollom

A Special "I Love You"

As I remember my first few years, one, two, and three,
There seemed to be so much I wanted to be.
As my life grew more ambiguous for the next three years,
My future seemed to pass in and out of my ears.
As I struggled to reach the end of four,
I met someone I truly adore.
What she gave me was so great, I could only wonder if this was fate.
She opened my eyes and made me see all I really wanted to be
As I continue through my years,
I want to give a very special thanks and I love you
  for this will forever be true.

Natasha Ham

"That Snowflake"

Oh! see that snowflake coming down?
There's another and another falling to the ground.
My heart jumps with childish delight,
To see the snowflakes in their flight.

Dancing and swirling on winds a loft
And their landings oh so soft.
The trees that were bare and bleak some how,
Have gathered the snowflakes unto their bough.

They stand with limbs in winter white,
Caressed in beauty with out a blight.
I feel so small just born anew,
Taking in this awesome view.

As the moon shines upon the snow,
A magical scene is set aglow.
How wonderful to have this peaceful glee,
Way deep down in side of me.

It makes you warm tho it be cold,
To see the wonder and behold.
If I were to choose one expression I'd say,
Oh! God was here today.

Viv Laramore

Rarely

Rarely does one speak to an Angel, rarely
They mostly come out at night, mostly
I spoke with one tonight,
She smiles and adorned the world...
Give me a gun, and I'll sink the sun
to speak with my angel again...
Mostly, I don't know what I'm looking for, mostly
and Rarely I find it...
Rarely.

Scott M. Palmer

Hands Without Guns

City streets on a rainy night
There's not a car or a person in sight
The air is swift and the moon is not out
The city is peaceful without a doubt
Is this the truth, no I think not
A few seconds ago five men got shot
They all died except for one
And this is all because of gun
Are you in fear or do you care
Violence is not coming it's already here
I'm still waiting for peace so when it comes
It's because we increased the number of
  HANDS WITHOUT GUNS!!!

Natasha Renee Paige

The Jericho Road

Golden Arches beckon them on,
these children of the Jericho Road
Just left Dover, Del., a score ago -
but on they plunged; 'tis the Tri-Cities they succor;
"Lord, we fell through the grates and humanity picked us up,
'twas a big heart -
Sister, brother, envelop us now for we are wee little folk."
Public action to deliver shelter - P.A.D.S.
Having been down the Jericho Road,
it looms on the horizon, this hospice of mercy.
'Tis you, oh church, who opened your heart not to a stranger,
but a beleaguered child of God.
Momentarily, success passes them by, tough break, beat up -
but there he stands tall, that Samaritan,
with polk bag a jinglin'.
They see your hand Lord and like our supplications
they bang at heaven's door.
Well done, you servants of God,
enter into the joy of His reward.
Both are blessed, the giver and the receiver.

Otto Unzicker

A Tribute To The Blues

With heads held high, they salute their crew
these magnificent men in gold and blue

Few have known the pride they feel
as they climb into their jets of steel

Like powerful eagles the Angels fly
forming a diamond in the sky

With precision and skill they perform their show
while thousands of eyes are watching below

They slice through the air with beauty and grace
in skies of blue and clouds of lace

Diving and turning and rolling on cue
racing the wind on wings of blue

In a final pass they thunder by
then one by one they leave the sky

Performance complete, it's time to land
touching down they raise a hand

Once again they have passed the test
the Blue Angels are the Navy's best.

Leslie K. Toop

"Mothers"

Mothers are so tender and so sweet —
They all may look the same but all are so different and
unique.
They all have good and bad things to say,
But they all have encouraging words to get you
on your way.
They all are smart in their own little way,
They can tell you things that you can't find in a book on any
given day.
Mothers are bad and mothers are good,
Mothers make you feel like a son or daughter should.
Mothers can be wrong and mothers can be right,
But don't blame them for your wrong doings,
Just ask the Lord for forgiveness day and night.

Shermaine Alexander

My Students

My students are sweet and kind.
They always love to give me hugs.
Hugs and screams of "Ms. Laura"
Are always what I need to hear
To get me going early in the morning.

My students are like my children.
I always show my students' pictures
To my loving family.
I love all my wonderful students.

My students know that I love them.
I try to teach them the best I know how.
Sometimes my precious students will give me
A pounding headache, but their smiles and sparkling eyes.
Are worth all the pain that I endure.

Laura Sexton

Best Friends

There comes a time in every life someone special comes along,
they cheer you up, they are always there, no matter right or wrong..

They care about your feelings, they share fun secrets too..
They have such fun together no matter what they do.

They give advise when needed, sharing the sad times through,
always stand behind you for they like you just for you.

No one can explain it, others don't understand how two people
that are so different can walk off hand in hand.

Some people become so jealous in this friendship that they share,
they like to judge the other one and wonder why they care.

This bond they share is special, the closeness is so rare,
they lift each others spirits just to know that they are there!

She fills the place for the sister that you always wished
you had, she's there if you ever need her, even when it's good or bad.

No one can fill her shoes, she's a special one of a kind,
for her name is, "Bonnie" and I'm glad she's a friend of mine!!

J. Ann Springer

Lost Dreams

The things that I wished most for, were the
things beyond my reach.

The things that I most longed for were the
things I could not see.

So I sit and wonder if I could have had all
of these things, if I had just let go of my dreams.

Sonya Rebecca McDonald

A Galaxy Called Life

My thoughts
They come from a distance place
Travelling like a falling star
Fast and Bright, they come, one by one
Each is like a sun or moon
Shining bright day and night
Waiting to be discovered
Reveal themselves and show there true value
Is what they want and to speak there mind
And try to help others lost in this Galaxy
We call life
By Shining day and night they give direction
For life is a Galaxy
We must search to find our own star
And help it to shine bright day and night
We must teach it so it will not live in fear
Hopefully knowing we're living very near
It must learn and grow
And show it knows the way only can we let it go
Knowing it will grow and live till it's light shines no more

William Gramlich

God's Little Bumble Bee

The scientist claim a bumble bee can't fly, -yet
they fly any-way, -we can't deny.
The bumble bee is a funny little thing, -I love
to watch their buzzing on the wing.
The scientist claim their body is too big for
their wings, -yet, -it doesn't matter, -they still
do their flying thing.
As a little boy, -to watch them, was my delight, -
I thought their buzzing around was a real sight.
They could bore a hole like a man, -even though
they had no drill in their hand.
They flew around the old barn, -when I was a lad,
Oh, -what fun to watch their buzzing and flying I had.
Well, -we must close out as there seems to be no
end, -as I watch the bumble bee in my mind's eye—
—fly,—fly—and fly again."

Thomas S. Fowler Sr.

September 26, 1995

Five white-tails came to our backyard today.
They halted stock still, heads raised, listening - being.
Each soft, brown ear ticked in response to the slightest sound.
We gathered at the window, barely breathing for fear they'd run,
But they were statue still, waiting - watching.
Suddenly a train exploded past the yard, howling at the crossing.
The panicked deer raced off beyond our view.
We finally breathed, recalling how they looked and how we felt
  when we were watching them.
As we stood talking, pointing out the place where they had been,
Five white-tails raced back through the yard
And disappeared into the woods.

Kathie Strey

Memories

Thinking of all the time we shared, I often start to cry.
Those who didn't know you well, often wonder why.

I tell them of the good times; I tell them of the bad,
But always just the telling makes me feel less sad.

Now that you are really gone, I am learning to be bold.
There'll always be a piece of you for my heart to hold.

I'll never forget you or the memories you gave,
And thinking of those memories will help me to be brave.

Terri Curry

Souls Lament

Shadows moving aimlessly
They have nowhere to go
Life takes its toll
Searching never finding
Life is always binding

Inside or outside the soul is never whole
Going around in circles and no one ever knows
Searching never finding
Life is always binding

Lost in the crowd
You blend in not knowing who you are
Searching never finding
Life is always binding

As the years pass
You are still a shadow
And it is time to say goodbye to life as you know
Searching never finding
Life is always binding
   Lisa Mitchell

From The Heart

Feelings help us identify our priorities and our purpose.
They make up our emotional selves-the part of us that makes us human.
We see, we think, we process information.
But it's our feelings on a matter that make it meaningful.

Our daily lives stretch into a lifetime
of mundane intellectual choices.
But interwoven into life's course are highlights!
Colorful sparks of time which
poignantly bring our lives into sharp focus-and give it substance.

We attempt to be "practical"—
to be in control and always direct ourselves toward choosing
what is best, predictable, safe.
We are taught to value that way of thinking.
But in restricting ourselves, our meal is eaten without flavor.

Therefore, let me risk living my life from the heart—
valuing what is practical, but, also, not missing the opportunities,
when they arise, to taste life's spices...even if I get burned.

The memories of a lifetime are bittersweet; feelings have a cost.
But, in the end, these emotional experiences will be the most
significant, and they will have helped determine that person I became.
   Michelle Neace

"Regrets"

The world will never be a joy to me
Things I won't ever be able to do
And all the beauties I will never see
Pondering this makes me feel timidly blue
The immense gold ball setting in the sky
Waves from sapphire seas soaking in sand
Seeing what I'll miss makes me want to cry
I'll drift away to a far unknown land
The kelly green grass and the joys of spring
All the happiness of the summer sun
Hearing the loud sounds of a church bell ring
The good times the bad times and all the fun
Everything I ever loved has slipped away
Like the sunlight on a long summer day
   Kristin Hagestad

Through The Storm

"And the people watched as it came and cried as it destroyed.
They reached for their Father's hand, rise above Hugo's wrath,
and looked toward the future, with hope."
A flash of red mars the earth's ceiling,
   The threat of evil looms o'er the land,
Gray skies are slowly coming,
   As He covers His "virgins" with His hand.

Dark clouds creep into the night,
   Hovering o'er the land's great beauty,
A streak of lightning pierces the sky,
   Stirring fear and uncertainty.

Claps of thunder applaud with satisfaction,
   Surging seas rise from their grave,
Branches bow to a standing ovation,
   As winds churn fearlessly with rage!

Fate and havoc rest upon the "virgins,"
   Crippling them with such fright,
Their dignity "stripped" limb from limb,
   As a "fist" hammers on with might.

A glow of white adorns the earth's ceiling,
   Glimmers of hope shine throughout the land.
A golden star, majestically rising,
   As he helps His "virgins" rise and stand.
This poem is dedicated to the people of the U.S. Virgin Islands
Who were touched by the fury of Hurricane Hugo on Sept. 17-18, 1989.
   Semele A. Cid George

"My Hands"

People think that I hold the whole world in my hands.
They think that I get what I want when I want it.
But people don't realize how heavy the world is,
how the weight of it makes my shoulders cave.
They don't see my head drooping,
or feel my weary bones, just on the verge of collapse.

People consider me lucky to own the world.
They expect me to hold it perfectly straight.
I am chastised if I tilt it, even just a little bit.

People don't see that the world naturally tilts,
that no one would want to hold it entirely upright.

Sometimes I wish I could just drop it,
just let it all fall at my feet.
Let someone else hold it;
let someone else sag below it;
let someone else curse it;
and let someone else finally surrender beneath it.

But I continue to hold on with all my might,
because from underneath, a friend gives slight relief for a moment.
So I adjust my grip, and solidly remain holding the world in my hands.
   Sarah Orosz

Rotten Bananas

Rotten bananas and sour cream
   Think that's bad you should smell the sink
I got broken windows and a squeakily door
   Toilet back up and there's a hell of a lot mode
TV blend up the radio won't play
   Rent is due and didn't get paid
Went for a drive, ran out of gas
   Bet on a horse, of course, it came in last
Those rotten bananas are starting to stink
   Have to end this poem, cause my pen's out of ink!
   Micheal A. Thompson

"Thanks"

Summer days have come and gone
   They were so hot and very long
We pray for winter to come soon
   And when it does we pray for June.

We pray for what we have not
   And forget our thanks for what we've got
We are so thoughtless with things that are near
   We're always wishing for what is not here.

If we could only see this world here below
   We would thank our "God" this I know
For there are so many with so few
   That it's time to thank God for life anew

So close your eyes and say a prayer
   And remember God is always there
For he will give you a thankful heart
   A gift of love that will never part.
      Sharron Newhouse

Mito And Danny On Rollers Skates

Around and around the garage they go,
They would never think of going slow.
Before the knack of skating had been found
They landed mostly on the ground.
Energy they did not lack
While into the walls they would sometimes smack.
Mito bumped into Danny's head
But up and away Danny just sped.
Mito knocked over a chair,
He was so happy he did not care.
They were so very busy
They did not care if they got dizzy.
The day was not complete
Unless they tripped over their own feet
They got so dirty from head to toe
They didn't want to stop, just go, go, go.
Yes, Mito and Danny wanted to skate all day
never to have to put their skates away.
maybe some day the world they will tour
Life for them is never a bore.
      Winniferd Gilchrest

God Sent Me You To Love

God sent me you to love,
This I really believe,
And love you I will do,
Because God sent me you.

I think back to the good time's we had,
They were beautiful and not bad.
I also think of the good time's to come,
When we'll have everything and then some.

I also think of God's plans to be,
And his blessing's for you and for me.
We know he has plans for us all,
No matter how big or how small.

God blesses each of us in a different way,
And he blesses us more each day.
And the best blessing to come from above,
Was, God sent me you to love.
      H. A. Gillette Jr.

Reflections

Reflections bring back the past, from the start I know it would last.
Things have not always been good, but with you, I know life could.
Love that is bound from above is beautiful as a dove.
The times in the park is distant but true love is always persistent.
When I first saw your face I knew that time would set the pace.
The thrills that we have had, will make any heart glad.

   The chance that we met, was a good bet.
When I think how we came, there is no blame.
Your eyes I remember, but it was the smile,
that made me limble.

   May was the time, while I yet was in my prime.
When love is true, looking back I know it is you.

   Time will not wait, but with this memory it is never
too late.
      Wesley Bates Sr.

Times Of Passing...Times Of Love

Times of passing, times of love
   times of sharing, times for hugs

Moments running, through reflecting eyes
   moments of laughter, soothing fleeting ties

Can't think to long, on days gone by
   must focus now, on teared good-byes

Looking deep, within my soul
   now is the time, that I must go

To path, to flight, to dawn of day
   My future beckons me go... yet my heart, longs to stay

With people, and friends, and familiar places
   a younger heart remembers, each of their faces

But time draws near, to change the path
   for nothing of this world, is meant to last

So now, to heart, I entrust these seeds
   of friends, and loves, and tender deeds...

...To a time of passing, a time of love
   a time of sharing... ...one last hug
      E. A. Vicol

Think Of A Child

When the world seems gray and you are down,
Think of a child dressed as a clown,
In great big shoes, a bulbous red nose,
With bright rainbow colors on his clothes.
Then smile!

When you are angry, just finished a spat,
Think of a child dressed in only a hat,
Wearing only a smile - no clothes at all;
Standing so proud, like he's ten foot tall.
Then smile!

When you are lonely and you just want to cry,
Your life seems a mess; you just want to die,
Pretend you are that child without clothes,
That silly little child with the bulbous red nose.
Then smile!

Life isn't so bad when seen through a child's eyes.
A child can see the rainbows in spite of dark skies.
So imagine the shoes and the big red nose,
Think of that hat - forget the clothes.
And smile!
      Lynn Mayfield

My Prayer To Lord Jesus

"Lord Jesus-Lord Jesus!
This is brother Joe, who wants thank you
for all the things you done

Today has been trying, but you were here
When my prayers need answers you were there
For it's my friend who is near and never is out of reach
that's my Lord Jesus to keep.

This is my story, I pass it on to you
and may you give this message to share with others
and tell others, that the thing to do.

In closing, wants again I say thank you for
all the things you have done

Placing my hands to you Lord Jesus
what wonderful blessing for things to share

I know that if I place my hands to you
things will be brighter and clear,
that's why I call for you "Lord Jesus"

I know when things go wrong to day
how wonderful it is to call for Lord Jesus
for that's why I call for you.
   Robert J. Ramp

The End?

Some people believe that death is the end.
Those seriously ill think death is a friend.
Those who are very religious think you never really die.
Those who are not think that's a lie.
After a long and happy life, death will bring you peace.
But peoples love for you doesn't have to cease.
I, myself, am confused and fear death some.
One thing I am sure of is one day death will come.
I don't know when that time will be.
But when it comes, there will be someone who loves and remembers me.
Death is a natural act.
We will all die in time and that is a fact.
   Nicole Grieco

No Imagination Required

I have experienced life when it has been pure hell,
Those who have had similar problems know it well.
We all know the mind is very complex.
It controls every thought, feeling and reflex.
Suddenly, simple tasks become major chores,
Like getting out of bed, or walking out the door.
When I have no choice but to function,
I worry that it will happen until it has begun.
My heartbeat races as a tingling sensation runs down my arm.
The room grows smaller as my mind sets off an alarm.
The warmer it gets, the harder it is to breathe,
As my stomach begins to churn, all I want to do is leave.
Run, as far as I can, from that which is destroying my life.
Preventing me from being a good Mother, daughter and wife.
This situation is difficult to explain,
It feeds on anger, fear and pain.
Mental illness is primarily to blame.
At first, I experienced guilt and shame.
But, problems like severe depression and panic attacks,
Are not imaginary, but cold hard facts.
   Kimberly Reffett

A Christians Welcome

To welcome you gives us a divine
Thrill, because we know that its also God's will.

We welcome you with a prayer, because you can say them any time,
any place, any where, and they really make
life's daily burdens easier to bear.

We welcome you with a smile, because
they fits every face and is never out of style.

Welcome if you are Asian, African, or European decent, because God
say that we all must repent, and gave his only son as living evidence.

Welcome to the youth, welcome to the more mature because there's plenty
   of God's work we all can do.

Welcome to the bold, or meek,
Welcome to the rich or poor, because
with God it doesn't matter what you
have or who you may know

Welcome it you have been saved welcome it you are living in doubt
Christ will make every thing alright.

We welcome you now, and the whole year through in fact our welcome
is always extended to you.
   Mordecai Walker

The Aura

Have you ever thought that each man has an aura?
'Tis gold or silver, copper, bronze, or ebony the aura.
Is in the feeling, the mood, the persona that is the aura.
Can cast a spell or weave a dream, or quietly bind in unseen chains.
The soul and heart and mind of that being which can sense the aura.

Few indeed, can ever know or comprehend, the aura.

For it creates a mystical binding that only death can break.
Tis fate they say, tis destiny, tis true the aura is there.
Patient as time, weaving in and out, over and above, high and low.
Forever, binding those who know, the aura.

No questions need be asked,
One look can bind it all till eternity,
It is simply there, buried within the mind.
Born innate, to be awakened only, by those, whom have been chosen,
By higher powers than man can make, or even try to break.
For in so doing, it rises from the depths and then it is known by all.
That, the few, the very few, have what is known as, the aura.
   Maude L. Weaver

To Henry Thoreau

What I would give to walk with you,
Through fields and forests thick and green,
To speak of life and all that's true,
While viewing nature yet unseen.

What I would give to sit with you,
On the banks of Walden Pond,
While gazing ore' the mirrored view,
Of scenery which you were so fond.

What I'd give to share a night,
Of hearing creatures songs in tune,
While writing journals by lamp light,
Recording life from a poet's view.

Henry, it's been a century or more,
Since your genius graced this sand,
No other like you has yet been born,
To walk this rich, ambrosial land.

Oh, what I'd give to walk with you,
Through an eternal Walden Wood,
As kindred spirits seeking truth,
While enjoying God's sweet solitude.
   Tippeney Bullock

From Daughter To Mother

Mother you have been their through THICK and THIN
Through the GOOD times and the BAD and now to the END
And though I can not VERBALIZE the way I truly feel
I must say you've done an EXQUISITE job indeed and yes I'm FOR REAL
A GRADUATE, A WOMAN, A LADY: You've truly done your BEST
RESPONSIBLE, INDEPENDENT, HEAD STRONG
Look at the finishing PRODUCT are you IMPRESSED!
It's OVER, I'm DONE you must feel RELIEVED
All the things we have gone through and STILL I have SUCCEED!
Without you I could not of MADE it with you I PRESSED on.
The small talks and MOTHERLY conversations gave me
   the STRENGTH to MOVE on.
One GOAL we have ACHIEVED with many more DREAMS to come
You are a ONE IN A MILLION MOTHER and I am the LUCKY ONE!

Sonya Renee Bouie

The Horse I Never Knew

She rode like thunder
Through the pouring rain
The moon glistened,
On her long gold mane.

Her eyes shone like diamonds
In the deep dark woods
She galloped with such grace,
As though I knew she could.

Her neigh sounded like it came from a land far away
Crying to be free,
As if she wanted to run forever and ever
That seemed to be her need.

All of a sudden, from nowhere came a wind
Her tail stood straight out
Like there was no end.

And with a great bolt
Away she flew
My old horse Jade,
The horse I never knew.

Laverne Garrett

What A Present God Would Bring

What a present God would bring,
To a Groom and His pretty young thing.
It would come from the heart,
I knew that from the start.
What a present God would bring,
To a groom and his pretty young thing.
Something with rhythm and rhyme.
Something that would last throughout all time.
What a present God would bring,
To a Groom and His pretty young thing.
God sent his only Son,
To die for us all,
That's a gift you wouldn't find in the mall.
What a present God would bring,
To a Groom and His pretty young thing.
What a perfect example it came from above,
The most Precious Gift of all.
   His Love,
Now that's a present God would bring.
To the Groom and His pretty young thing.

Susan Ruhr

Grandma

This poem is dedicated to my forever loving Mema
Who died on December 1st, 1995.
Grandma you needn't worry, it'll be okay;
things will turn out all right, more than we can say.

Your love has been relentless, all through these years;
you've helped us through everything, even our tears.

Your face is deep with wrinkles, your heart has been through much,
you touch every child, with your special touch.

Your kindness has been there, solid, thick, and true;
grandma, when I grow up, I wish most to be like you.

These words may seem childish, dumb, or absurd;
but grandma, with all my heart, I mean every word.

Nadine Ahmed

Time

Time can bring you down,
time can bring you up.
Time can vent your needs, or
time can make you beg and plead.
Time can make you happy, make you sad,
make you glad, make you mad.
All it takes is time.
Time can heal old wounds.
With time it can make you rich or
the time you spend can be a friend.
Time can teach you to believe or
help you to perceive what time can give you.
Because like I said all it takes is...
Time!

Robert Bay

Innocence

Unjustifiably stripped
Thrown into a contorted reality
Many memories kept,
Alive and protected.
In thoughts of grown children
Yearning to grasp, the overwhelming, urge.
To toss tail to the wind.
Run fast. Hold on tight.
Swing as high as you can,
   Let laughter consume.
Reach in and acknowledge,
   this child
For it's name is
   "Innocence"

Rebekah L. Robbins

Bleeding Heart

Mind racing over my life,
wondering where I am going to end up this time.
The roads are all dead ends not knowing where to go.
Here I am giving away myself, but nothing coming in return.
The emptiness I feel, I just don't understand because my life is complete.
But I still feel I am incomplete.
What do I want? I don't know.
How to express myself? I don't know.
This pain is tearing me up inside, with no one to talk to.
Stop I say, doing this to yourself.
Love will find you one day and it all will be okay.
Take a look in the mirror and realize you are something special.
And having you to LOVE is a treat.
But I still don't understand the loneliness inside.
The hurt of a Bleeding Heart.

Lydia Barnes Wardell

Human Destiny

Said God to Saint Peter
'Tis rating time for our galaxies
We will seek the planet of highest morality
How fares our planet Earth?
Surely, one of the gems of the universe!

Earth with all its beauty and resources
Is torn by war, crime, poverty and other negative forces
Moral growth has suffered many losses
Destructive behavior has devastated
What the hand of God has created

Human destiny is to evolve
To higher ethical beings these problems to solve
Peace must replace war and love overcome hate
For it is in the hearts of mankind
That evolution must take place

Unless humanity evolves to a higher moral plane
The righteous will never reign
A teardrop fell from the face of God
With all hope spent and emotions pent
He and Saint Peter bemoaned the noble experiment

Marjorie Guess Hall

Autumn Awakening

What sound of music wakes me from my dreams?
'Tis the Mockingbird from which
Such pulsating repertoire streams!
Hiding in you Holly, with the berries turning red
Whilst I lay dreaming in my cozy bed.
For, there is a nip in the air o' days,
And the creek runs bluer in it's relays.
This sound of music brings a smile,
As I lay and listen awhile...
I reach and pull the drape aside a nearby pane.
I see the ascending sun catch gold again,
Atop the maples touched with turning
Into the shorting span they are learning...
Can this be only a shadow of what is to be
When God lets us His glories see?

Mary Bernice Plummer

Untitled

At last the cities died out and the world seems
to be sleeping a peaceful sleep I lie awake and
think I can't go on any longer like a voice in the
night I faintly hear,
"You are not alone, I am here to guide you along.
You and I can never part just as long
as I am in your heart."
The voice suddenly fades and leaves me astray
that came to me in my time of need
To give inspiring words to let me know they
care for me.
Like a knife piercing through my heart, I know
the voice is the beautiful voice from my Lord and savior.
He comes to me and I respond by whispering in the darkness.
"Dear Lord I know I am not alone, thank
you for guiding me on.
You and I can never part because you
always have a special place in my heart"

Rayma Dee Delavan

To My Anticipated Son

I anticipated complaining of a waking baby;
Not of being grateful he's able to wake at all.
I anticipated the wonder of time rushing past;
Not of reflecting on milestones so small.
I anticipated crying at immunizations and bumps while learning his way;
Not of agonizing at more tests, evaluations, and word of more delays.
I anticipated choices over preschool, clothes and scout troops;
Not of choices between hospitals, specialists and which support groups
I anticipated loving him, but enjoying his independence from me soon;
Not of loving him so much I'd want to keep him sheltered in my cocoon.
I anticipated health and perfection when my baby was inside, thinking
    anything less would be tragic;
But now that he is here, my special son has worked some kind of magic.
I anticipated anger and disappointment at this fate;
Not the joy and growth and knowledge that have become mine as of late.
I anticipated something different, that is certainly true;
But that's because I never could have anticipated one I love as much as you.

Kathleen Hoppe

Roses

The red roses were laid on his casket by his grandson. As the priest gave the man back to the cold earth, no cared and few were sorry. He had been a powerful man, almost a God. Some worshiped him, some hated him, some cursed his name, all feared him. He was the one who decided who would live and who would die. Yet, he never pulled the trigger, never cut the flesh. He had reasoned it as business. Just business.
The small crowd had come to give their last respects and, once he was buried, they quickly left. When all were gone, the wind began to quicken and the roses pushed themselves from his grave but it was too late. They had already been stained and defiled by the blood that covered this man's head. As the wind stripped the petals from their stems, what once was red became black. Black like death. The petals soon sank into the soil and there grew black roses. Black roses near the grave of Satan himself.

Renee Peacock

My Corner

Got a couple bucks in change in torn blue jeans at midnight.
Prob'ly enough for a beer washed down cold on hot steam summer city night.
Feelin' good and broke, but I'm high — prob'ly cause God is too!
Neon flashes in my tired eyes, pink, and blue, and white.
Wish I had enough for another beer, but really...and secretly, I don't care.
Long as I got me and my jeans, I'll never be alone.
Besides, God loves me and his blessed son, the Buddha
whose real name is Jesus Christ, is my friend.
Nothin', but nothin' seems better than life, walking on
These dirty streets, like a bum, but stone free.
I ramble like jazz heard on fifties' radio - loud and cracklin'.
Kerouac is here with me, too; beautiful son, Jackie boy.
He is and was always golden zen child.
I smile and whistle, thinking madly as I head toward
Cheap hotel (already paid for, as I'm flat busted now)
for much deserved sleep and dreams.
All is well in my corner of eternity...
How about you?

Milton S. Hoff III

Nature

I hear the sound of rustling limbs against the warm spring air. A sound in which no echo rings, a melody now so rare. I see the flowing waters of a distant meadow brook, and wonder how this beauty thrives when no one stops to look. There's nature all around us to be enjoyed by all who care. Just take a moment, feast your eyes on God's work everywhere. He took the time to make our earth, moments more precious than ours, he covered the land with beauty untold, with wildlife, green hills, and flowers. I hear the sounds of Springtime as robins build their nest, and gaze with awe and wonder to Mother Nature at her best.

Sandra M. Barthlein

Help Help

Why can't we make this world a safer place instead of fighting,
stealing and all the waste. Why does everyone want to be on top
Majority of the time they come down with a flop. Man thinks that power
is so great but it will not get you through the pearly gate. If we
cannot be honest with ourselves and all others how can we accept you
as our brothers. Take time with your children everyday or night teach
them to love not fight. We take to much time for ourselves I'm afraid
we leave the responsibility to the sitter or maid. We should know
where our children are at all times and teach them responsibility and
character and they'll grow-up fine. Teach them to live with their
fellow men and always be honest and don't just pretend. We say we are
not prejudice, but o what a lie because most of the time we don't even
try. Wake up America before it's to late. It's not just in one city,
it's in every state. Come on America get off your duff. Let's show
the world we are made of good stuff. Don't just read this and put it
aside let's all talk to each other and really try.
Norine Rydzewski

...Not My Daddy

I want a man who understands my cries and my tears.
Someone who knows how to hold me when I have fears. A man that
understands that I will always Love and Keep God first. A person
who will not try to tear down my world, but to help build. I want
a male that will help encourage me and hold my hand. I want a man
who loves and fears God that's his first command, I pray for a man
who is my friend, my helpmate, my spouse, my one true love and a
child of God.

I dream of a man that will try to reach into my heart and drive
to help heal my soul when I cry. A man that will treat me like a
queen, carry me like a diamond and love me like a woman needs to be loved.

Someone who I can share my thoughts, my dreams and my prays with.
A person wo I can confide within and I can hold through the day
and the night. A person who will try to shield me from the harm
and the evil sight. I pray for a man who cares and has a concern
about what I do and where I go. A man that can say what he feels
and what is in his heart. I'm not asking for a man with fortune or
fame, I don't ask for a man with a bodybuilders frame.

I pray for a man who is..........Not My Daddy!!!
Sherilyn Kathleen Smith

Separation/Union

I know the separate union of oneself. The conflict that one goes
through within thyself. Like the game Tug of War, the rope can pull
both ways. However, I am holding the rope at both ends.

I pull myself away, away from my thoughts, my emotions, my decisions.
Disconnected from myself, distant from conflicts within me.
Withdrawn from a part of myself that makes me, me.

I am made up of many parts, some of which I was born with, others I
have constructed. Like a carpenter, I constantly continue to build.
Pain sometimes can be endured while building. My fingers may slip and
get in the way of the hammer. I can experience excruciating pain.
When I am finally putting on the finishing touches I feel I have
accomplished something and may even see the results. I cannot tell
how the weather will wear me down or if my interior and exterior will
fade. Unlike a carpenter I will never be completely finished. I only
hope I will continue to build.

I am one person. I cannot be separate from myself. I can only
continue to grow if I am united within me. I see reflections of my
physical self in the mirror. I can touch the reflection of myself
with my fingertips. I can grasp my physical self. I cannot reach out
and grasp my emotional self, which is a part me. I can only feel it
for what it is inside me. I have felt the confusion, the whirlwind in
my mind. The blizzard in my heart, the traffic and commotion in my
thoughts. I have felt the separate union.
Yvonne Laramie

Lightning

Gee, it must be really frightening
To be the one who is struck by lightning.
To feel the tingle in your head
And wonder if you'll wake up dead!
The tingle, starting at your scalp
Leaving you unable to call for help,
Continuing down, and going thru your stocking.
It's an experience, to say the least, most 'shocking'!
Margaret Slavicek

Nothing Lasts

I wish I had the mind and the time
to enjoy this Life of mine. Instead I'm
running just as fast as I can from the
spotlight into the night.

I know nothing Lasts forever; just with
ours could Last a Little Longer. Longer
than the games we've played of being fools.

Raindrops keep falling. Life is stalling but
time is passing. Nothing much to do but
think of you and the Life we never had.

I know nothing Lasts forever; just wish
ours could Last a Little Longer.
   One more day,
    one more hour,
     at Least one more kiss.
Ryan Parejko

Sonnet On Vanity

What can a woman do to catch my eye,
   To entice my mind away from football scores
   And golf, and waken primitive desires?
How can she take the place of apple pie?

Will Crest or Listerine or silicone
   Or lining eyes or enclosing thighs and hips
   In latex sausage skins or reddening lips
Enthrall in nylon net this wary drone?

Alas, poor foolish, vain, exploited child,
   Your artful measures leave me unbeguiled,
   Waste time as well, so you must learn the game
   Of vanity by heart—the way to fan my flame:
A woman's irresistible when I see
She can't resist the looks and likes of me.
William Dusel

My Imagination

My imagination is a gift to me,
To escape a while from reality;
In my mind I contemplate,
And slip from under life's daily weight;
In this way my spirit soar,
On wings of fantasy or history's lore;
Today, I thought me a lady fair,
Enchanted by knights, who armor wear;
Yesterday, I traveled through galaxies,
To land on planets of strange terrain and seas;
Tomorrow, who knows where I may go;
Only Father Time does know;
My imagination, a gift to me,
To take me where I want to be;
My imagination, uniquely mine,
Like a ghost rider passing by!
Rita Denison-Gallmeyer

Tree Killers

"Tree Killers, tree killers," I yelled!
The woodcutters axed and sawed, they chopped and spliced the tree trunks; trees that had been growing and preserving the air for years. Now the trees are laying on their sides with their vintage roots exposed to the sky.

"Tree killers, tree killers," I shrilled!
You have tossed them aside, you have piled them on top of one another for the garbage truck to haul them away. Don't you know trees only brush against one another when the wind blows. Don't you know trees are the spirit of the earth; our ancestors and our message keepers. They have a place under the sun, they grow and stand proud and you nor anyone would cast them aside if you knew their purpose.

"Tree killers, tree killers," I shrieked!
Now their looking at the sky with their roots cold and rotten, green leaves turned brown. No longer will I see them swaying with the wind or making sounds, "wish-sh-sh, wish-sh-sh, shoo-o-o-o". No longer will they change colors with the seasons and appeal to my weary sight. Oh, how I miss the trees!

"Tree killers," I yelled!

Tonia E. Chapple

Silent Soliloquy

Here within a secret place a thought of you. A bird on wing a summer day, the rustle of the leaves and children, gleefully wide eyed wondrous, unconstrained content at play.

Thoughts that travel and traverse delighting in the universe fell upon the hidden recesses of this, discursive soul. What did those caring eyes discover, friend or foe misguided fool deluded, or an unsuspecting lover.

It now escapes me all that dreaming but then recollection of lakes and streams and Quixotic questions beholden in dreams and only in dreams the answers, those magical keys that unlock and set free buried meaning.

Tell, pray do tell, if I were a lake would you sail me? Swift adept, skim and slide clear water licking high sterns side with spray on face to cool the cheek, horizon far, though always looming in that place, that far and distant place.

Once in that far incurious place and I was a taught tuned harp all lacquered and new, would you play me? Pluck gently at the center cord, possess caress the shape and grip with strong hands moulding, firmly holding.

Softly squeezing, teasing out melodious strain a sweet, a lingering refrain to set secluded senses skyward, reeling. Here, within a secret place a thought of you.

Sandi D. Abell

Between Two Worlds

There is a place I called my home, of misty hillsides where dragons roamed. The forest was dark, and thick with dew, and the tree creeked as the wind blew. Then one day the misty fog cleared, and to my surprise a Prince appeared. I said, "What do you want, and why are you here?" But he just looked at me and said not to fear. He said, "I am a prince and a mighty knight, and will change this darkness to light". I said, "But the forests grow darker day after day, and there are too many dragons to slay." Then he spoke as if in a soft breeze that had transforming power, but I sat in my cocoon, like a closed up flower to bloom. Then as I listened to him I began to feel myself unfold. He said, "Believe in the light that shines within you and cast out your fear, and these dragons of yours will soon disappear". As I emerged from this former world, my surroundings began to take a change, the forests were singing and not furiously blowing. The Prince slowly faded off from my world and never returned, but inside me was a light that always burned.

Mary Kalnas

The Wait

As the sun sets, I climb our hill
to watch and await your coming.
The wind gathers scents of pungent
earth and night blooming blossoms.

In the last sepia glow of day,
I watch two butterflies dance and
flutter in the breeze on bright,
velvet, patchwork wings.

Is there warmth in those small bodies
against the chill of night? Do they
lie together in repose, their wings
wrapped about each other?

Where do butterflies go as dusk falls
and day is swept away? They are too swift
to follow as night's black closes round.
But they are together, as we shall be soon.

Roberta Pellant

Oh, Gay Butterfly

Worn and old his soul's garment changed
To winged loveliness.
Like a master musician who draws
A thrilling sweetness from a cracked instrument.
A slight flutter, indeed a delicate performance,
And with feminine eye, not to brag.
The male caterpillar flew away in drag.

Vivian C. Allison

'Jesus' My Hiding Place

'You' are my hiding place from every storm of life...
To you I run when I am scared, 'You' shelter me from strife.
When I feel frightened and alone, to Your arms I flee...
'You' always welcome me inside, You hold me till I'm free.
Free from every tear I've known, free I cry to You...
What a comfort, what great peace, to know You love me true.
'You' hold me and console me, I look upon Your face...
I run to You in storms of life, You are my hiding place.

Patricia Ann Wilson

Today

Today, there's a sunrise
Today, there's a sunset
Today, there will be winners
Today, there will be losers
Today, there will be happiness
Today, there will be sorrows
Today, we must decide to say yes for tomorrow
Today, we must decide to say no for tomorrow
Today, we may live to see a tomorrow
Today, we may die and there will never be a tomorrow
Today, we know that there was a yesterday
Today, we know that there will be a tomorrow
Today, it's the most important thing in our lives

We are here today.

Matthew Lombard

Uninspired

Uninspired rain still falls,
uninspired nature calls. It's required as
life goes on that everyone becomes
uninspired, so they may grow old and
become very tired and rot away in the
earth once their life expires.

Melinda Simonton

Metamorphose At Eckley — Lynda Woolf

Just before dawn the old company house is desolate, no paint,
side porch collapsing from the weight of a hard Pennsylvania winter,
supported only by two 4 x 4's leaning toward it.

The sun begins to rise, the reflection of light off the windows
revealing the tulips just breaking through the ground. As the light
intensifies, the new grass shows itself, a grasshopper hopping about.

The form of an apple tree appears, just sprouting its buds, soon to be
white with flowers. If I close my eyes I can picture the red round
fruit and then imagine the smell of cinnamon and apple in a newly baked pie.

As I glance toward the broken porch, I see a little nose poke out,
then another and another. A litter of kittens makes its way out into
the day. They roll about with each other until Mom comes and swats
one's nose. They then follow their mother to a morning feast.

Now the sun is fully risen, I look up into the cloudless sky with its
shades of azure and sapphire unmarred by man, made glorious by nature.

I look again toward the house to see that the door is painted a bright
green, the color of hope. The house looks no longer desolate, it is
such a beautiful, wonderful house.

Lynda L. Woolf

The Upper Story House

My mind is like a Victorian house.
The attic is my memories - some from my ancestors and some from my
yesterday's. The bedroom keeps all my secrets and special thoughts
and dreams. The windows let new thoughts in and old thoughts out.
The kitchen is where my mind works like a wood burning stove,
but sometimes can get out of hand if not used properly.
The stairwell is where all my hopes awaits to be uncovered, from
the shadow and made to come true. The library is my fountain of
knowledge, each tome with a new story to learn whether fiction or non.
The best room in the house is the parlor that holds:
My quilt of years - each piece represents a new birthday or an event
that I can look back on, hereafter.
The pictures on the walls of the parlor help restore the memories of
my loved ones, no matter how unapproachable they may be.
The mirrors reflect into my inner self and reveal my true pensive
image. The walls sense my tears and comfort me, the walls sense my
fears, and light up a new way. And the familiar piano plays away
my anger with its sweet melodic tune.

Sarah Varley

Inside Of A Thought

A shadow in my eye, it seems to be, like running water so smooth to me.
The kind that seems to be so very rare, and the fulfillment of happiness is in the air.
A thunderous - silence is what I see, but it seems to pay no attention to me.
A difficult test was put to work, for what, I guess to keep alert.
Of all the things that passed me by, never so eager to wonder why.
Why is a question asked by many, if the answer was known, it would serve me plenty.
To know the truth, or to let it go, to catch - this air that seemingly blows.
At times I am bothered by this unearthly scene, hopeless is what it seems to bring.
To obtain satisfaction, to stop this wait, to catch this air that blows so late.
It seems to think in some ways like me, maybe for a reason, maybe just meant to be.
Like thoughts from within, that make no sense, there's one that sticks with you,
   and this one is a part of you.
The biggest part of all, in the life you live,
For there's only a short time to obtain, the things you want to give.
After all is done, the air is caught and this is my day.
Then comes the times you wished for, do not let this slip away.
Because if you fail, to keep the stay, the shadow will catch you again another day.

Ray Bolton

My Heart

My heart was like a locked box
Waiting for someone with the right key to open it.
My heart was like a vase inside that box,
fragile, clear and pure.
My heart was like a rose beside that vase,
delicate, small and beautiful.
My heart was like a thorn on that rose
pain to those who touch it.
Someone stole my vase.
Someone stole my rose.
Inside that box all that remains is
the bud left by someone who stole my heart.
My box had a bud for the someone who
unlocked it again.
My bud is now a rose.

Kristen Male

The Bald Eagle

The tall proud bird soars through the skies,
   wandering endlessly through the heavens,
   never knowing where to land.
And when it does, it's so beautiful
   you'll probably never see it again,
   unless it's on a coin in your hand.
You wonder and wonder will it ever happen again?
   One of life's great expectations has come and gone,
   but life will always go on.

Sean Berry

The Teachings Of Life

Sitting alone in a crowded world
wanting some form of company
The lights are shining and tokens are moving
but alone, I can't see

Waiting to hear a faint whisper
that says be on your way
but the walls fall down and business shuts down
and clouds turn grey

All I want is to get out of here
for a world that's different and free
but things get crazy and hold me back
and the ground falls out beneath

My mind is turning and fleeing from me
as I try to find a way out
as time stands still and the world functions
I learn what life is about

Shannon L. Woodward

Which Art Thou Love?

Summer is personal, everyone's friend.
Warm and wonderful, he's there to the end.
Full of jokes, life-of-the-party and fun.
A jolly good fellow to everyone.

Fall is in sports cars and 'Paco Raban'.
Brisk, sophisticated, self-assured man.
Smooth in tuxedo, he pivots and twirls,
Stealing the kisses and hearts of young girls.

Winter's a man to put most of them down.
He wears his guns when he goes into town.
Jaunty and booted, he'll cut you no slack;
Cynical and terse with hasty comeback.

Spring comes quietly; very appeasing.
Better choose this one; ever so pleasing.
If he's the gentleman I think he'll be,
I can still go out with the other three!

Miriam White Crawford

Love That Hurts

As he comes forward she sees "them" flash before her.
She recalls each loving word and action, as she feels each bruise of pain.
With every word he yells in time of hate, she remembers each word filled with feeling.
As his eyes get bigger and filled with rage, she just closes her tighter.
When she feels his fist, she remembers his touch.
When he pushes her against each wall, she recalls building it with him by her side.
As he throws her out, she calmly gets back up, brushes off the dust,
   and walks back into what she calls "home"
As he orders her around, she follows his orders in hope to do right this time.
When he has fallen asleep on the couch, she gently him with a blanket,
   forgetting her aching body, and remembering how cold it gets at night.
As the sun rises and falls, she becomes used to this form of love and recalls no other.

Lizy Dosoretz

Myself With You

With you, I long to tiptoe upon the seashells, for they make the beach smile.
To dance amidst the sea oats would bring tears of happiness to my eyes.
I yearn to make footprints on your heart, that the waves themselves
   could never cleanse.
Background melodies play as we sing to each other, songs of admiration.
Soft spoken waves embrace the every thought that comes between us,
   smoothing it for better perception.
Our constant, rhythmic communication only allows us to better our
   knowledge of who we are as individuals, and as a couple.
Whispers of tenderness explore uncharted terrain, with intent to adore
   the spirits within.
My tears freely flow to the sea, to accompany the others that make
   it's flavor so salty.
Vowing to dismiss past feelings of betrayal, we replace vacant spots
   with sands of sincerity.
This love we could share can rock the beach to dreams at night.

Manda L. Moore

The Travelers Of Muse

In red brilliance they travel towards the morning star.
These wanderers of the earth; these nomads of a common thread seek
   enlightenment from the elders of the land.
In winter they have toiled; in spring, in summer, and in fall, yet
   still no antidote to the poisons of their minds.
The four detectives on the case of a common mystery trudge on,
   finding no clues along the way.
Their travels will take them to the mount aside the never ending river
   amidst the Forest of Illusion.
While on their quest, many perils they do encounter.
The Dermates, half men and half bulls, inhabited the Great Plains of Setira.
Not to out do the Fropolia, that creature of deadliest nature, a man-
eating bat with wings of seven feet in span, which swarmed the cave of the dead.
These to list them short, were of the most feared.
As hunters on the prowl, they venture through the great forest of illusions.
Confronted by a foe of few equal, they struggle to survive
   the brutal onslaught of this mighty opponent.
All but one were slay by this lord of the forest.
Fleeing for life and limb he paddles across the great river to find
   the foot of the elders mount; atop of which he meets his destiny, true enlightenment.

Stanley E. Morton III

Oh How I Love Thee

I will give you light, so you can see, if only you have faith in me.
Put your feet upon the water and your eyes upon me, oh how I love thee
I will give you strength, so you won't be weak, if only me you seek.
Put your feet upon the water and your eyes upon me, oh how I love thee
I will give you friendship, so you won't be lonely, if you confess me only.
Put your feet upon the water and your eyes upon me, oh how I love thee.
I will give you happiness, so you won't live in sadness, if you will only show kindness.
Put your feet upon the water and your eyes upon me, oh how I love thee
I will calm the sea, if only you believe!

Larry D. Muncy

The Loner

Whispers in the dark
What would they say
Behind closed doors
The secrets will invade

The curtains are closed
What will they do
Who only knows
Except for the two

Who knows whats within the night
What thoughts are hidden behind their eyes

The silent ones shall they use their voice
The quiet footsteps-where would they lead

Where is he going
This creature unknown
With only his shadow
To keep him from being alone

Sherry Lee Oldham

Dad's Prayer

Let me not forget Lord, that I am to be to them
What you are to me.
Let them see me as I see you.
Let me love them as you do me.
Let me provide for them as you do me.
Let me not forget dear Lord, that I am to forgive
As you have forgiven me.
Help me show grace O Lord, abundantly.
For all the failures in the past
And for the ones to come,
My prayer would be that you teach them Lord,
To forgive me as you have done.

Ronald J. Allen

Wheel Chair Fling

Rolling to the dance floor we go,
Wheel to wheel, means toe to toe.
Swing your partner and you'll see
That there in the wheel chair, sits little "ole" me.

I want to dance and sing the whole night thru,
Do the Wheel Chair Fling that I'm teaching to you.

Kathryn Lockwood

When

When
when
A leaf falls   float
A flower blooms   won't   back
To the ground (does it know) it   up?
(Does it know) it will never
              bud
                    again?

Molly Friesen

O Shooting Star

O shooting star
Where dust thou flee
Across the heavens and o'er the seas?

Art thou fleeing from the past
To find a new life on another mast?
Sometimes I wish that I could be
Attached to thy shining beam.

You would take me far from here
But, would I be thankful to you each year!

Mary L. Essary

What?

The wind carries my thoughts
To far away places for others to hear.
Shall I remember the vague comparison
Between
Thought and opinion?
May I ask a question?
Why must I believe so strongly in my opinion?
I am not wrong!
I live my life as if I were riding on a
Gust of wind.
I am not able to return to yesterday yet
Tomorrow has not yet entered my mind.
Again it is my opinion that
Commands
My life.
For once I wish my
Opinion
Would remain just merely a
Thought.

Matthew J. White

Among Autumn Leaves Falls The Child In Us

I once Crawled through Spring times bloom
to find laughter in the scent of roses.
New life born into this pastel paradise
tumbles and rolls through fields of warm green things.
to notice children dancing in the saltwater's mist.
Life now resides in this dry desert
to race against the cool breeze.
I once Walked through Autumn times color
to realize things change.
Life now slows as the forest catches fire
to stroll through rustic winds.
I once stumbled through winter times cold
to ponder walls of snow flakes that drift from Heaven
to touch the Earth.
Life now stops to dream in these white fields
to cherish secrets of the past.

Thomas F. Snyder

Somewhat Amazing

Out of all the places to go,
To see and to be,
Right here we were.
In such a small place.
It's Somewhat Amazing.

Our paths had to cross,
Not only in such a small place,
But at just the right time.
Things must have been just right.
It's Somewhat Amazing.

I have stood outside on clear summer nights,
Astonished at all the stars.
Wondering how in such a small place,
Can I see and feel so much.
It's Somewhat Amazing.

As I look up and whisper your name,
I can't imagine anything feeling more right.
It wasn't just only meant to be,
It was meant to be, Somewhat Amazing.

Randy Mark Tolar

Moon Gazing

The moon dances in brilliant light
To gather me up and pull me close
This gentle sphere of glowing splendor
Rests peacefully, cradled in night's blanket
I look deep into it's heart silver white
Allowing memories to drift gentle on my mind
Letting my heart embrace the dreams inside
For the moon's heart will grant all wishes true
As I outstretch my arms to welcome it's invitation
A cloud enshrouds the moon's graceful calling
The sky is darkened and mourns it's passing
But new life is reborn when the curtain is drawn
The moon shines again in all it's glory
And once again I see my heart spread out
Yet captured inside this frame of beauty
I close my eyes and wish you were by my side
Sharing in this moment of loving the beauty above
The beauty of moon gazing.

Stephanie Hulme

An Awakening

Each morning An awakening
To hope to fulfill
To walk the road carved to carry out God's will
For the Future their is certainty
Their is certainty for the past has left no doubt
Follow the Son for He is the one.
Who knows the most righteous way out.
Almighty God provided J.C. for me
A cover, for I know not what I do, Aware.
Transcend heaven's peace nothing else
To walk, to talk with Him alone, in paradise
Glory, Glory, Glory
His call made me feel divine
Shining thru the window in my mind, in my room
On top a mountain high
Overlooking a valley of discontent
A most sensitive view blind faith shows me
Some time to feel his majesty.

Keith Murph

Heaven's Way

Now you know I'm just little, but I know the way
To Jesus's side in Heaven I'll stay.
He will guide me and comfort me all the way to the
Glorious land where the skies never gray.
I know you will miss me, I'll miss you too,
Just keep your faith in Jesus he'll see you through.
I'm one step, I'm two steps, I'm three steps away,
To Heavens big door, where loving people stay.
We never had a guarantee, that said we'd never part,
Just remember I'll live forever in your loving heart.
I was here for just a little while, to run, laugh and play
It was just a short stop on Heaven's way.
But now my Jesus calls, and in his arms I'll stay.
I'm one step, I'm two steps, I'm three steps away,
To my place up in heaven, where there is rainbows
All day. I no longer will be there to spend time with you,
Remember there are others, who need you too. We will be together
again someday, till then I'll be happy in his arms I'll stay, so don't
feel so bad when you think of me, I have my loving Jesus, to keep me
company I'm one step, I'm two steps, I'm in heaven's door.

Sue Miller

Is There Justice For The Black Man?

I ask the Lord to bless every black man's head,
To keep him from doing wrong.
Bring a mother child home,
Safe and unharmed, not beaten
Or whipped, but let him be able to stand.
Is there justice for the black man?

I read the paper and I look at the news;
Another black man has been accused.
Tears fall from my eyes - I ask the question "why?"
Must some our men be punished for crimes they haven't done.
Someday, my brothers, this battle will be won.

They did the same 2,000 years ago.
To another man we all know.
They hung him out on the cross with stretched out hands.
Is there justice for the black man?
To our black men I say you better get serious.
Stop killing one another and quit being furious.
Time is at hand: is there justice for the black man?

Kathy Winston

Listen

Mom was right
To keep me tight
For in this world, she said
"Many things are out of sight."

I was young at heart
A girl with innocent mind
I saw nothing but joy and laughter
Lollipops and roses were things I sought after.

The flowers bloomed, and I grew up
Back in my heart and mind her words were on top.
Her voice was my guiding light
Filled my life with days and not a night.

Now, I got words to speak, a life to own
Her touch of love, her words of wisdom
Made my life a world of kingdom
That will pass on just like a throne.

So you children of the world
LISTEN as much as you could
For what you hear from dear old MOM
Is what might be in the days to come.

Zenaida Lazarte-Oconer

Send Me Some Rainbows

Fling me a handful of stars
To lighten these later years
Moonbeams are not quite bright enough
To quiet my doubts and fears

Send me some rainbows on which to linger
Make them brilliant with wondrous hues
Speak to me softly and touch me gently
My body is fragile and could stand no more abuse

Lighten my load and give me peace
Teach me to smile a bit more
Others have burdens heavier than mine
Keep me close to the shore

I shall not cry or beg for solace
My lot was cast long ago
I shall walk lightly and plead for others
Bringing me peace and joy for my soul

Lillian Smith

"Would Be"

To hold you, would be a dream with no end...
To look into your eyes, would be looking into the
    depths of untamed passion...
To feel your warm breath upon my skin, would be
    a tropical breeze from an ocean beyond...
To hear my name pass over those soft sensuous lips,
    would be the roar of the mighty lion
    claiming his territory...
To feel your gently caressing touch, would be
    to float among the clouds.
But within each touch, would be the passionate
    tremor of the mighty earthquake...
Lips upon lips, would be the molten lava
    of passion...
...And to hold you,
    would be but a
    Dream....

Tracy I. Vanier

Dawn's Early Light

I felt an invisible hand shake and waken me
To look up through the heart of my mimosa tree.
Where the sky came brightly peeking through
In the loveliest shade of antique china blue.
The trees dainty fern like leaves formed a canopy of lace
That rested like a shawl on the shoulders of space
It was a sight mortals seldom get to see,
And I thanked God that he'd awakened me.
Smiling I stretched, and gave a long, lazy, yawn
Wondering if you too had seen a lovely dawn.
Song birds now awaken to greet the new day,
Adding to dawn's beauty their symphonic round delay.
Butterflies drift by on colorful winnowing wings
While buzzing bees add magic to the sound of things.
I vow I'll never again be an errant sleepyhead.
But, arise early to greet each lovely dawn instead.
No wonder god planned for us to sleep in the night
So we can waken to see the dawn's early light.

Mary Ethel Frost

A Tear

A single tear rolls down his cheek,
    To me, this is a great relief.
His heart is open, he has tears to spare.
    This sympathy, who does he care?

A single tears rolls past his lips.
    I look into his eyes and get only a glimpse.
Of the sorrow he feels is true.
    At the moment he doesn't care who is who.

A single tear rolls off his face
    Only to start another of grace.
He sees before him a life gone by,
    And now he stands alone, only to cry.

A single tears falls to the floor.
    Only to be followed by just one more.
The sounds of whispers, he turns to hear,
    But when he looks, there's no one near.

A single tear left in charge,
    To mind all others while they're at large.
Just one last look as he walks away.
    To make sure the tears have stayed.

Lynda Smith

Untitled

Wondering what this world could do
To make one person so down and gloom
I sincerely wish and want to say
Keep your head up, it won't stay
No matter what you do or plan
There can always be changes to make your stand
Take your time and work things out
Don't let them build to quite an amount
Each mistake look at closely
Through the right eyes, they'll dissolve mostly
Be a friend and you'll have friend
Always having a word to lend
Such a happy, caring person at times
Is always the one to change our lives
Try to think and maybe see
The disastrous problem that'll never be
Problems need help but don't deny
There is no reason they limit the sky
They'll be solved and you'll get over
There's still rainbow and four - leaf clovers
  Mike Wiseman

Untitled

Seeing things that are not real,
Trusting things I can not feel,
Hearing things that have and sound
Looking for something that can not be found,
Wishing on stars that are not in the sky,
Knowing the truth and living a lie,
Building a world that is starting to fall,
Trying to hold on to nothing at all.
  Michael F. Bishop

So Long Hero

Everyone has heroes as so I'm told
To meet your hero is almost worth gold

Well I always believed there's no such thing
Now, really what can a hero bring?

We never expected it, well at least not from him
Cause everyone knew him as the hero with the tilted brim

We always knew his friends were no good
On the corner is where they always stood

Bobby never thought he'd get mixed with that
Pretty soon everyone knew him as the "Top Cat"

Rick and Keith were his friends
We knew something was up when they popped up with a Benz

His mother just sat and cried and cried
Then we found out that Bobby had died

What they did is too brutal to say
Whatever they did — Bobby died anyway

We never understood why Bobby had to go
All I can say is "SO LONG HERO"
  Lillian Le'Shanda Prince

Dawn

The weekend with you, was special in many ways.
We shopped and baked, forgot a few things.
We helped your mom with a problem or two.
But baby, I was with you.
I long for another day with you.
Silence was golden, with you near.
  Kenneth Howell

Mountains And Molehills

Mountains in our lives are struggles you see.
To mold and shape us into what we should be.
Climbing the mountains of life can bring suffering and gain.
Only to instill in us the knowledge that we grow.

So face the mountains head on, learning as we go
The prize at the top may be more than we know.
Talking about mountains, there are molehills to you see
Little pieces off the mountain to trip up you and me.
The little things that don't matter come into our life
Sometimes causing heartache, misery and strife
We make them more that what they should be most times
Increasing them in size as we fuss and whine
They won't make or break us, change us in anyway
Leave them little molehills they are safer that way

Mountains and molehills go hand in hand
It's what we make of them in our life's plan
Go on work hard climb a mountain or two
Watch out for those molehills they can get to you
  Rosie M. Thomas

"What I Can Do"

It would be false; simply untrue,
to say I understand what you're going through.

It would do more harm were I to pretend,
to have a full understanding of what I can't comprehend.

What I do know, what I can do,
is be at your side to comfort you.

Perhaps if I reach out you'll take my hand,
open up your very heart to help me understand.

If I listen to every word, catch your every tear,
a true understanding will take hold and appear.

Together we'll work to make things fine,
for your pain is not just yours, but now also mine.

I will do all I can to help you through,
because I love you, it's what I can do.
  Ronald V. Scott

The Holiday Season

All the children's eyes are aglow,
To see the first glance of new fallen snow,
People hearts are filled with love and cheer,
The holidays are always a happy time of year,
Everywhere, there is peace and joy,
Smiles upon the faces of every girl and boy.
The trees is decreased up very nice,
Christmas treats prepared with sugar and spice,
Every child wonders what Santa will bring,
Christmas songs that everyone loves to sing,
All the shopping has been done,
Now its time to have some fun,
Christmas games that people can play.
Only twelve hours till Christmas Day,
Young one's all tucked into bed,
While visions of sugar plums dance in their heads,
Unwrapped presents lime the floor,
The turkey for dinner is purchased at the store,
A time to give and to share,
Let the spirit of the holy one fill the air.
  Toby Shawn Meeks

The Prairie Lily

To a child it was enchantment so rare
To see its red-gold cup glow in the meadow so fair.
In this prairie garden, with the tender care of God.
Grew this treasure from the dry clay and the sod.

In my garden today grow many lilies so gay in
Orange and yellow, white and red
Holding forth in their beauteous array.
But my thoughts oft go back to that long-ago day,
For I long to walk in that prairie garden again
Where the prairie lily did once reign.

The queen of the meadows so fair,
No longer lives and blooms there.
With time, came changes in the use of our land.
Lost was the beauty once held in a child's hand.
We praise nature for her beauty galore,
And the prairie lily lives on in memory's store.

Ordia Rave

Kids

Look at where we live;
to see what we give.

Make our kids want to hide.
Go to school - peer pressure.

Walk the streets getting shot or beat up.
Get caught with gangs, drugs, and alcohol.
Get raped or have kids.

Die because of hunger.
Lose their childhood because of war.
Lose their parents,
because they are being beaten.

Kids need a better way of life.
Don't make our kids want to hide.

Look at where we live;
and think of something better to give.

Rebecca Rising

Sacred Is The Earth

Strange to my people is your desire to buy the sky,
To sell the warmth of the land, the freshness of the air,
The sparkle of the water.
Sacred is the earth. It can't be bought. It can't be sold.

The perfumed flowers, the deer, the horse, the great eagle,
Sisters and brothers are we to the earth.
Sacred is the earth. It can't be bought. It can't be sold.

To give up our land will not be easy.
Blood of our ancestors are the streams and rivers.
Memories of my people lie in the reflection of the waters.

Hear the voice of my father in the waters.
Feel the thirst of our brothers at the rivers.
Give kindness to the land.
Sacred is the earth. It can't be bought. It can't be sold.

White men conquer the earth and all its glory to become its enemy.
I know, because I am the chief.

From the children you want to kidnap the earth to forget it,
Leaving only a desert.
Sacred is the earth. It can't be bought. It can't be sold!

L. Carolyn Walker-Greene

Wisdom

The merriment once seen as reality
  to shift in undue resignation
    to behold a new theme
      a new purpose
The change of one's perception
  to turn from mere obligation
    to renounce the youthful lusts of dawn
      the image of a phantom hope

The reward once seen so dimly
  to contradict the firm necessity
    to render to the hand of fate itself
      of destiny revealed
The destruction of what did destroy
  to expose the page of life unturned
    to glorify even the mere shadows of a better thing
      a purer thing

M. Kristi Kirsch

Lost In The Rain

Upon my face the raindrops fall,
To softly disguise my sorrow,
The rain pours and drowns my heart's call,
A call to fill a heart that's hollow,

Louder and louder my heart sounds,
But seen and heard is the lightning and thunder,
The storm rages on and the thunder pounds,
Lost among other calls, no one hears, and I
Wonder...

Will Love ever here my sorrow,
Or will I still be alone in the rain,
Tomorrow?

Steve Martinez

Rockin' At The Rock House Cafe

Every Saturday night when I was 21, we would all go
to the Rock House and have a lot of fun.

This cafe was all built of stone, and it was the place to
go for a wild Saturday night away from home.

The jukebox in the corner was always playing. Lots of
people didn't know how to dance but did a lot of swaying.

You could always be sure of lots of fights; But what
the heck, this is the Rock House Cafe on Saturday night.

In those days, I thought I was doing alright but like
Hank Williams sang in his song, "Praise the Lord, I finally saw the light."

This all has been a long time ago, and I guess those in
my old group that are still around have gotten a little slow.

But if you drive up that highway today, you can still
see that building made rocks called the Rock House Cafe.

Presley R. Sanders

The Beach

The only sound was the roaring of the
waves, and the water slapping at the sand.
The sun was setting and the sky was
beautiful shades of pinks and yellows
smearing together like a watercolor painting.
The twinkling of the stars and the
shimmering of the fires scattered along
the beach was the perfect touch to a beautiful night.

Stephanie May

Mother

To the woman who was there.
To the woman who has so much care.
To the woman who ran to me when I fell.
To the woman who kissed the place to make it well.
To the woman who set me straight.
To the woman who hugged me when I did right.
To the woman who always knew.
To the woman who valued truth.
To the woman who taught me right from wrong.
To the woman who made me strong.
To the woman who is pure as a dove.
To the woman who has all my love.
To the woman who is like no other.
To the woman who I call Mother.
Michael Jason Huls Miller

A Matter Of Years

It's only a matter of years, before women fully awaken
   To their own power within, never again to be forsaken
One by one, they are rising from the floor of submission
   Not willing to be kept anymore in a world of oppression
They are ready for new ideas and belief in themselves
   Their hidden strengths are coming down from the shelves
That women are any less in God's eyes, just isn't true
   So how can masculine supremacy be allowed to continue
Blocking the way to progress in these troubled times
   When abusive aggression is leading to horrendous crimes
Of the heart, at home and abroad, like a roaring fire
   Threatening to destroy if pride and anger do not retire
Feminine energies within each soul need to be reflected
   And made equally important if harmony is to be expected
Imbalance began so long ago, by the false ideas of men
   Who assumed, by the way of arrogance, power over women
Yet it is woman's burden now, to stop being indifferent
   To remove today's restrictions and be more independent
It's not about winning a game, it's about justice for all
   And about saving humanity and the planet from a long fall
Nancy Osberg

Nests Of Spring

Memory is the sweet perfume of time,
Unseen but sensed, the vapor of the past,
Ripples on the sea of yesterday,
The ever-lengthening shadow life has cast.

Sweet perfume. The mind and heart contrive
To cherish more the rain and not the clouds,
Clinging to the happy things that were,
Recalling faithful friends and not the crowds.

Drifting from the vault of former years
Like smoke that trails a lazy summer breeze,
Recollections charm our latter days,
The nests of spring that cling to winter trees.

Pebbles tossed upon a placid lake
Give birth to waves that seek a distant port.
So the moments from our happy youth
Fill harbors rich in dreams when life is short.

Gardens of the past bear thought bouquets.
Fresh flowers are beauty that tomorrow grows.
Memory is a lovely, empty vase
For memory is the fragrance of a rose.
Kenneth Wightman Heady

Autumn's Omen

The maple trees, once verdant, are turning
To tones of golden brown.
Thru the autumn mist their crinkled leaves
Come gently floating down.
Squirrels flip their saucy tails
Their protruding jowls foretell
That winter is lurking just beyond
The cast of autumn's spell.

So it is with life — it runs the gamut
And each season has an ending,
As winter drapes her cloak around us
To prepare for cooler days impending.
We can still look forward to the dawn of day
While here on earth we dwell
For it matters not how long we live,
But have we lived it well!
Mary J. Ballou

Through The Lands We Love, To The Ones We Know

Through the lands we love, to the ones we know.
We can reach for the old ways, we can touch the sky.
To the mountain hills, to the sun on high.

Through the lands we love, to the ones we know.
We can hear the drums, from the spirit cloud.
Talk to the old ones, we can hear them loud.

Through the lands we love, to the ones we know.
We can smoke our pipe, to the lives we met.
As we hold a dream in the dream catchers net.

Through the lands we love, to the ones we know.
Michael J. Murphy

Form... To Meaning

Braided lines of light reflect the melancholy twists of life
Today to someone new but with strong ties
following the who...used to be

Rush to flush my soul and hand in my heart,
Taken in exchange for the gender I want
Melt quickly I to layer you with a transparent membrane of me
Adding no thickness, only nourishment to feed

Imagery imagined with soul not separated,
I beg to express my reality
Your invocation is my invitation to ingest myself and chew upon you:

   Blond cropped hair with yellow fair skin
      continuing slowly over muscle and bone
   From the lobe of your ear bearing the un-matured hair
      of white, child light
   I want you

   Move to my lips my tenderness desire
      to touch rounded shoulders with bone visible but not protruding
   Frame of fragility with slight proportions of muscle and bone
      given as if only enough to reduce extreme contrasts in contour
   A touching hand moves smoothly to front your chest and
      press strength to your soul
   Lower to breast with tension at it's start gravity pulling down
      the concentrated feminine tissue
      almost to separate it from it's source of existence
   Press north I support with an understatement of respect
      my left runs a right to center seem
      and feel the connection of our being
Todd Gavin Patasnick

What If It Were Today?

Do you know what your future will hold?
Today, tomorrow, day after day.
Are you fearful for your life to unfold,
To hear God say,
The time of judgment is here,
The end is near.
But Lord, we've only just begun,
We've not yet gone the extra mile.
Have I truly placed my faith in your son?
Am I ready to face the final trial?
I say I believe
All I must do to live
Is freely receive
What you are ready to give.
I must no longer fear death's sting,
For eternal life your son's death did bring.

Shawn Faille

In The Shadows.....

Tales of forsaken seniors warehoused like broken toys;
tortures of throw-away children littering the streets in
pure abandon; and now, women, harboring in the shadows,
their identities obscure, their sojourns undaunted.

Mother, daughters, sisters; everyone in between and
beyond; splintered families, empty nests, a wounded hearts'
soul; life's harsh realities ravaging hopes, fragmenting dreams.

The Cinderellas, the Joan of Arcs, struggling for existence
in the twilight; they are everywhere yet nowhere;
tangled in our misguided stratus.

They've manifested as a subculture, highly visible, mostly
silent; regardless of status, the spirit uncrushed, their
mission only temporarily aborted.

They persevere to overcome their plights, continue their
quests, carry their scars; each dawn yields a test and a
triumph; survival, vision and that dance with destiny.....

Victoria Blue

Nests Of Spring

Memory is the sweet perfume of time,
Unseen but sensed, the vapor of the past,
Ripples on the sea of yesterday,
The ever-lengthening shadow life has cast.

Sweet perfume. The mind and heart contrive
To cherish more the rain and not the clouds,
Clinging to the happy things that were,
Recalling faithful friends and not the crowds.

Drifting from the vault of former years
Like smoke that trails a lazy summer breeze,
Recollections charm our latter days,
The nests of spring that cling to winter trees.

Pebbles tossed upon a placid lake
Give birth to waves that seek a distant port.
So the moments from our happy youth
Fill harbors rich in dreams when life is short.

Gardens of the past bear thought bouquets.
Fresh flowers are beauty that tomorrow grows.
Memory is a lovely, empty vase
For memory is the fragrance of a rose.

Kenneth Wightman Heady

Reality

I lay awake at nights.
Tossing turning.
I hear your gentle voice caressing my soul
I feel your strong hands stroking my body
I feel your lips over my heated body.
I want you...I need you...

I awaken to realize it is all a dream.
You are no longer lying beside me
My thoughts are constantly with you
I want you...I need you...

When will my memories of you diminish
When will I have you back in my arms
telling me that you love me?
When will I hear you say....
I want you...I need you...

Rosemarie Hylton

Heart Break

All the deception, and all of the pain,
total destruction, with nothing to gain.
It hurt so much when he broke my heart,
stupid me I should've known it from the start.

He said he'd changed and loved me so much,
now never again will he feel my touch.
He really rubbed it in with that ugly display,
and ruined what I thought would be a perfectly good day.

He certainly helped me make up my mind,
I don't know how I could've been so blind.
Why did I believe him and all of his lies.
Now I'll never forgive him until the day he dies.

He said he'd wait for me forever,
now there's no chance we'll ever be together.
I thought someday we could work it out,
now I know it's over without a doubt.

Rebecca Parmer

Easter Vision

As dawns first rays engulf the earth, the suns warmth graces dew touched grass,
The empty tomb shows one and all, the prophecy has come to pass.

It was spoken of in days of yore, to believers young and old,
That on the third day He would rise, the scriptures had foretold.

For on the cross all bleak and worn, our Savior was crucified,
In order to forgive our sins, the Son of God had died.

The earth it shock, the heavens moaned, the Savior King was dead,
As nails pierced His hands and feet and thorns circled His head.

His empty tomb, the stone removed, caused Mary to weep forlorn,
But joy was soon to follow, on this blessed Easter morn.

Good Christians join in hope and song, of purpose, love and vision,
As angels from on high proclaim, Rejoice! The King has risen!

Steven T. Galbraith

Untitled

Have you ever stopped to consider old age
Which hits us all in the final stage
The print gets smaller as we slowly age
and the furniture that we like to move
is heavier now in 'tis present groove!
People don't talk as loud as they should
I miss a lot of news that is good!
but there is one thing I've promised myself
I'll make the choice that puts me on the shelf!

Lena Holzman

Lesson

I speak with Carlos under unbiased fluorescent light.
We talk, laugh, and take excursions through sixty years
of bitter sweat memories, ideas, and regrets.
"If I only knew then what I know now...."
We live ten minutes of the present in the past,
then I rub the soreness from his hip
(He claims arthritis; I think he just enjoys the extra attention).
His sense of humor and endearing stubbornness are testament of
strength and wading through his day dreams he imparts the lessons
He paid so much for so long to learn himself,
to a grandson who is only just starting to appreciate
The wisdom and friendship of his teacher.

Ryan Dover

The Saint Of The Bells

He liked the sound of the bells that chimed in the great stone
tower which rose above the cathedral. The crude harmony
of the bells somehow resonated into the depths of his soul,
finding some likeness of itself deep within him. At night the
harsh white artificial light of the spotlights illuminated
the statues of stone upon its edifice. They stood, unmoving,
like corpses, dressed in the robes of history, with unseeing eyes,
and grim looks of determination upon their faces. This was not
a place of light heartedness, gaiety, or mirth. This was a serious
and holy place. The visages of stone looked down with imperial
gaze upon the light hearted frolics of human flesh below.
Not approving or disapproving, but staring silently into space.
When the bells clanged on the hour and on the half hour, he could
feel himself drawn irresistibly to the shadow of the great tower.
Oh, how he longed to scale its heights, and take his place among
the stone people, the frozen statues on its heights. Then he
would leave behind forever, this foolish world of silly laughter
and empty love. And he would become a saint of the bells, a
name to be remembered with reverence and awe.

Paul Flodquist

The Wind Blows Me Away

The wind is a heavy traveler
Transporting sounds, gossips and cries
Whisper in my ears and leaves me wondering.

What can I answer, you have seen it all,
The shelter of darkness and light,
The thunderstorms, the clear and blue skies.

Look at the birds, do they follow you, you follow them?
I wish I could abide in your wings.
I could travel as far as Marrakech.

What is out there attracting me so much
And yet, more I travel, more I want to see.

Cross my heart, seal my lips
And whisper again what you have heard.

Am I the only one able to hear you,
Or the other people just keep silent?

Marlene Andrade

My Strength And His Light

Many mornings I awake, I look outside and watch the lake.
Will I fall before the quake? Or is this world something
I just can't take? I don't know but strengths on my side.
So I guess I'll hop on for the ride. Where He takes me I don't
know but in my heart I know I'll go. For shallow is the wind
and also the grave, but as for my Strength He is mighty to save.
He won't leave me I know he won't. So what I'll do is hold on
tight I'll put behind me this terrible night. I have forever
conquered darkness through my Strength and His light.

Tracey Johnson

Out Of My Sadness

YOU AND I. It just wasn't meant to be. Oh, how I've
tried to forget you, but how can I ever forget—

The laughter in your eyes, the beauty of your smile,
The gentle touch of your hand, the comfort I find in your words?
You've been alongside me and shown that you care.
No one could have a more precious friend in their life or a more loyal confidant.
I'm thankful for your determination and positive outlook.

OUT OF MY SADNESS, I have discovered laughter while tears
streamed down my face, joy that I didn't know was there;
Strength when I was at my lowest point.

Many times I felt like I was merely circling the mountain
instead of tunneling through the darkness. That is when I
found the light of your life led me OUT OF MY SADNESS
into the light of day.

Mary Frances Brooks

True Love

True love comes to a lucky few.
True love is something rare.
Life without love, is just to much to bare.
We go through life wondering when and where
Love will come our way.
Will it be tomorrow, will it be today?
Will it come our way or did it come yesterday?

Love turns to hate, sometimes quickly —
Sometimes late.
Tolerance halts the growth of hate,
Enabling us to live with our mate.
Without love we cannot survive.
Love is abstract as is time.
These two things have laid waste to my mind.
You cannot save love, it must be rejuvenated,
So that it will not grow to hate.
The sun shines warm from up above.
Don't you know it's time for love!

Yens Schaedla

One Ribbon Flows

Come to feel a feeling, finally know what's out there.
Try to be free, try to love, try to forgive.
The pain comes to Kill,
The glory comes to Lose,
But one ribbon flows, the wind is but its carrier.
The symptoms are weak,
But the feeling is strong.
The ashes of dust have sung,
The chains of bond have fled.
What's left returns to earth,
What's gone returns to death.
Forever the heart beats, but today the mind stops.
The soul bleeds - only to flee to hell.
There, there is no peace...
The ribbon must let go
The wind must find a new path,
The glass of life must surpass the blow,
Life must go on!
If only the mind knew how to bleed...

Melody J. Patterson

The Heart By The Rain

The spirit of the northwind calls,
'Twill rain, I see it with sorrow;
One by one great drops are falling,
I feel the water trickling down my feet,
Yet, not so rudely as to make one sound,
'cept from the throat of the overflowing spout;
Down through chasms and gulf profound.
You can hear the quick heart with a tempest beat,
Yet, even in its very motion the calm is clear
That follows an idlesse mood, and instantly
All the sky is hid from rainbow clouds,
Just as I see two river currents,
Join their course in silent force;
This, the unconquerable strength of love.
I grow well with soft heartbeats,
As rising wind in leaves now decreases,
Eye the gladdened heaven, next the glistening earth;
The best of the heart beating harder with pleasure,
An elegant sufficiency, content,
To feel you tread it, to tears and rain.

N. Ming S. Ureta

When Little Angels Fly

When little angels fly, our hearts are breaking, all we do is cry.
Unanswered questions, guilt and shame, will anything ever be the same?
We've tried so hard, what have we done.
This little life had just begun.

So many prayers, and hopes, and dreams, we didn't know,
God planed other things. When little angels fly.
For God was ready, arms opened wide,
That little angel flew straight to his side.

That little baby, you loved so much, now knows the love
of our Lord's touch. That wonderful feeling, we will not know,
until the day he takes us home. When little angels fly.

Your baby's wings have grown and grown, his heart is with you,
God will make his presence known. When little angels fly.

Your little angels looking down, he'll see you here,
on this hard ground.
He'll visit your dreams, from time to time,
and help to give you peace of mind. When little angels fly.

Kathy MacLean Uetz

Quintada

Deep against deep, in sleep as under the sea,
Unanswered questions sink like storm-blasted ships
Into lead-heavy silence ...

The stillness weighs itself against trade winds -
And questions, like bound cargo on a rusty freighter,
Slumber - rocked in the ocean's treacherous dark cradle ...

On the horizon of dream-haunted seas a three-master
Runs full sail - Captain and crew sleeping and silent -
The conch-shell whispers, questions their turbulent tale ...

Thunder answers the probing of lightning through clouds
Thick with rain - breaking slumber with roaring alarms
Challenging uncharted seas - untested ships...

So, too, our ships, with their cargo of dreams,
Sail silently over the restless waters of the night -
The tides indifferent to questing or resting ...

Velande Taylor

"Husband And Wife Become One"

Heart felt love for each other,
Understanding each others needs.
Secure bonds of marriage,
Becoming united as one, we do heed.
Aches and pains may cause others to stray,
Not for us as you can see;
Deep admiration fills us with glee.

Walking in the harmony of life's pleasures,
Independent yet close, is one of our treasures.
Forever together our vows we took,
Eternally grateful for our life book.
   As husband and wife our unity thrives,
   We'll go on and on till the end of our lives.

Thressa J. Wengland

Janis

Tossing her hair like a peacock's
   unfurling feathers.
Her lyrics a spider's web, complex and branching
Her laughter like the cackle of a
   gnarled gnome, happy and yet
   reaching for something unattainable
Her soul on a quest for the perfect
   world where there is no pain
Savagely she drinks from a bottle
like a man that has found an
   oasis in a seemingly endless desert.
Injecting heroin to numb what she
   didn't want to feel: A wounded, dying animal.
And still her voice, pure and true, rasps on, sounding in my ears
A life blown out as if it was a candle that the wind.
   danced over, taking the flame with it.

Teresa Wilcox

"Tribute To A Poet"

The best of what I write is a skimpy lot
Unless one counts the words I've given away
When they arise from that interior world
where intuition and inspiration play,
hidden in the deep and tranquil sea that laps
on the shore of the mind, behind the busy day.

There are some folks - a scattered few at most
Who've read my phrases when I'm but the host
of sudden bursts of cosmic love or cry,
and like an ant reach up to write the sky
with words that soar - an inch above the coast.
Far greater must the host be here than I!

Now as for POETRY, my heart grows still
on those occasions when I absorb the syllables
that flow from Rarity's pen -
And soul is awed by gifts beyond my ken
With words that gather momentum in their flight
to kindle sparks from the Dark of the Living Light
and shower consummate Splendor back again.

Madelyn Marie Chrisman

Autumn Days

Colorful leaves dancing down the hill,
With just a hint of winter's chill.

Squirrels and chipmunks busy as can be,
With walnuts and shellbardks falling from the tree.

Geese flying southward on the wing,
Fall shows its beauty, and makes our hearts sing.

Fall turning the world to Autumn's gold,
Close by, biding her time, is winter's cold.

A. Jean Brown

In Memory Of A Flower Of Love

A planted seed we never know just what there is to be
Unless we give it tender care and nurture it on to Thee.

Then we'll know who's in control and what the future holds
For in His plans we're in His hands, it's there our lives He molds.

But soon the seed to bud does grow and seeds the sun to fill
Its need to blossom and mature; discover its own will.

Oh what a joy to openly share and often praise His name
When learning the creator's and bud's will are the same.

With this shared will a blossom blooms its fragrance overflowing
That all might share and become aware of its moments glowing.

But alas too soon the blossom's bloom is over and now fading
So let's recall it's beauty all in love and our own sating.

Unlike falling leaves of fall with nothing more to say
This fallen blossom's witnesses will proclaim another day

That God is love and on His throne and always there will stay
'til all His children He has come on their glorious way.

So fly on blossom, fly on, on angelic wings fly high
To keep your life's appointment with our Savior in the sky.

The garden yet grows without the rose but ne'er its place forgotten
For in the plot remains the spot where it was first begotten.

Though the void is still there its roots the garden bares
As a lasting witness to all that the garden gladly shares.

Oh, for a thousand tongues to sing the glory of our King
And to His bosom bring a most beautiful song to sing.
  Stan Kelley

"A Gift From God"

For seven years, your heart was lost.
Unsure and desolate.
Searching for an answer,
Maybe your heart did not realize it, at all times.
But God knew.

You suffered throughout those years, with many misfortunes.
Sadness.
Yet, your suffering was not meant to be in vain.
Those seven years of passages, led you into a new light.
A new world of pure love-absolute.

God answered your many prayers of sincerity, with consolation.
Guiding you to your place of serenity,
Yes, God only knew.
And with many years, serving God.
Loving God completely and heartily-were you rewarded?

For your heart answers yes, since God led you astray.
To the love you have yearned for and so much needed.
Into my heart, into my soul
Deeply you entered.
With the guidance of God.
  Rosenda M. Acosta

Look At Our Earth

Stop and ask yourself where have the blue skies gone?
You can see the answer every morning on the horizon at dawn.
The sun is greeted daily by a thick cloud of gray.
This cloud is air pollution and it's stripping the earth's resources away.
Throughout history man has destroyed his God given paradise.
Leaving future generations to pay the price.
How much abuse can our fragile planet continue to bear.
Let's stop the destruction before nothings left to share.
  Tonya Peters

Untold Love

I spend the night playing solitaire,
Until my eyes grow weak from wear and tear.
The nightmares I try to tame,
I can't—so, I wake up calling your name.
I can't believe our love will never be shared,
If only I could take the chance that maybe you cared.
But the words I can not say,
For past the heart, they know not the way.
Hiding my feelings within a friendship that's true,
So I can be just that much closer to you.

I would do anything to ease your hurting,
But I must be careful not to reveal my true feelings.
I would change in a heartbeat if it were up to my will,
Because I know your type and I don't fit the bill.
So I must write my feelings down,
For without this, I would go through life with only a frown.
I know that I need you like water to a fish,
If your feelings were the same, I would have my wish.
But I know I am destined to go through life blue,
Because I will never get enough nerve to say, "I love you".
  Russell Bennett

The Place I Call Home

There once was some empty land,
  until one day when a man.
Named Thomas Fawcett came around,
  he bought the land that was
  to become Fawcett's town.
When James Bennett saw our clay,
  our pottery industry was born
  that day.
Our little town has really grown,
  "Pottery Center of the World"
  was what we were known.
Now most of the potteries have
  shut down,
The Knowles, Taylor and Knowles, the Harker,
  And the Taylor, Smith and Taylor potteries
  and the Taylors pottery
  are not around.
A lot of history has came and gone,
  A new generation of potters
  will have to carry on.
  Rebecca June Twyford

My Garden

My garden is like a patchwork quilt,
  Upon a huge bed of black earth...
A triangle of flaming reds and sapphire blues,
  A square of deep purple...
Side by side with a circle of sunny yellows.
  It is a wondrous sight, my garden...
The penetrating perfume of the blossoms
  Fill the silent air with lingering pace,
The billowy breeze bobs each head
  In the dotted rays of the smiling sun.
The buzzing bees swirl and sweep from petal
  To petal, their humdrum blending with
The mixed chorus of chirping birds...
  Yes, my garden is like a patchwork quilt,
Upon a huge bed of black earth!
  Virginia M. Heprian

"I Am The First And The Last"

The pictures we perceive as the truth of our human past,
Vanish in the recognition that "I" am the first and the last.

Life has never started and therefore cannot stop,
Man has been alive forever; so other beliefs may drop.

The misconceived perception of a life that lives as matter,
Are but bits of dust, when seen in Truth, must scatter.

The history that I think I lived, the roles that I have played,
Have never been my real name; it is Soul where I have stayed.

I have never been a victim filled with stress and strife,
I've always been the loving, joyous, happy song of life.

Therefore, all of the problems that have seemed to rise,
Have never been the view from My divine eternal Eyes.

Only that which Love can be,
Has been the wondrous Universal Me.

The only picture painted on my Mind,
Has been by Spirit, not by time.

Love alone has been my Being,
Always Life's eternal Seeing.

So, in the Alpha and Omega of the eternal Now,
Is not only, where I dwell, but also when and how.
Patty Hanson

I've Thought Of You So Often Nearly Everyday

And I know God's watching over you in a
very special way.
What pain you've had to go through
If people only knew...
They'll never know the heartache or
the suffering you went through.
Unfortunately the greedy people in this
world very seldom care.
But isn't it wonderful to know your
true friends are always there?

To listen, to comfort, to help cheer you on
To go to bat for you when the pressure's really on.
And so in closing of this poem.
I wish for you a peace you've never known
For the Lord will take on all your cares
as those burdens are for Him to bear.
Dedicated to Nadine 8/95
Viki S. Pharis

Violence

Violence is an evil, that lies deep within.
Violence bursts upon us, many times from our own kin.
Violence causes terror, we often can not hide.
Violence takes us on an unforgettable ride.
Violence comes to find us, where ever we abide.
Violence is an evil that can not be denied.
Violence tells a story of another kind.
Violence has no pity and preys upon the mind.
Violence leads a man to murder and hate of every kind.
Violence has a mother and a father too.
Violence just breeds violence, so what are we to do?
Refrain from breeding any violence.
It's all up to you and me, for,
Violence is the opposite of all humanity.
Rose Marie Capen

Life

Splashes of red and gold
   vision returns as the owl retreats
a child is born
   thrown into the fresh air
a new beginning-pure love
   not yet smeared with the shadows of hate
The ball of fire grows
   and the children below live
     sitting running beneath the canopy of trees
falling hard to the pure earth where the shadows are already growing
The sun begins its decline
   anger and sadness rule with the shadows
forgetting the earth and what down is
the shadows spread and encompass all;
yet no one mourns the passing of a life
   for the moon is rising
     she shines bright and happy
   moody in her month
     not knowing who gives her life

Wisdom can fly only so high
Michelle Wallace

Silent Intruder

Forest undergrowth, mist shrouded and dew covered,
Waiting for the first glow of dawn in the East,
The first reflection off water covered greenery.
Small animals, wide eyed and innocent,
Watch the coming of another new day
With the giddiness and trust of youth.
Symphonic sounds of singing birds slowly commence.
Transformation: from dank and grey
To a sunny summer dell;
From the muffled silence of creeping fog,
To a glade alive with sound and colour.
Leaf filtered sunlight, a single ray,
Falling in the center of the wood bound clearing,
As if shining upon an alter in praise;
A feeling of awe, of some holy occurrence,
A magical rebirth, heaven sent, a sacrament.
Ever moving stillness, anachronistic in it's truth.
I am man, the invader of wilderness sanctity,
And I, unmoving, watch the tent of day unfold,
Then silently steal away.
Philip A. Eckerle

My Son

He sits supported by foam and steel
Watching intently as the children play
He can not join them, not today
He laughs and cries, like every man, riding the emotional tide
He cannot hide
He loves and is loved, He touches lives
Sharing his life with those who are
He was innocent, life is not fair
He has a purpose, there is a meaning reaching beyond the senses
He came to take down fences
He has a heart, a mind so pure shining like the morning sun
He is my son, He is my Son
He is a blessing to my world, teaching things I could not know
He is flesh and blood and bone and He is soul
He does not stand alone, this child, showing there are more
He came to open the door
He knows in time this will all end, waiting for the day
He too will play
Lance E. Bernhardt

The Flight

Growing up in a small town with an average job
was easy for Jonathan, but he wanted more.

Jonathan looked up at every airplane, always
wanting to experience the feeling of flight.

As Jonathan was driving on his journey several
states away, he noticed every plane, large or small
dreaming of the day he would fly.

He bettered himself with a good job, but very
dangerous. Thinking of himself taking his first
plane ride, his dream was getting closer.

Jonathan at last was on his first plane ride.
As the plane accelerated the pilot and the passengers
could feel the force pulling them back, the plane
hitting turbulence, frightened some.

Finally the plane landed. Jonathan's family was
there as they carried his casket off the plane.

William R. McLemore Jr.

Wagner

The night before that terrible day, the air
was filled with music and prayer.
Each man of the 54th had one thing in their minds
they were going to march it to enemy lines.

That day, the men stood there just a little afraid
and brave as they waited to do as their Colonel bade.
In each loyal heart they knew why
they were charging just to die.

At each shouted command bodies flew,
bullets pierced the air and the sky, so blue.
Soldiers mourned at their fallen friends,
but marched on to meet their ends.

When they reached the last sand dune,
the Colonel led the way, the pale moon overhead.
A single shot out of so many left
a poignant imprint as their colonel fell to his death.

As their valiant Colonel fell,
a single shot to the heart was all it took-a single shell.
His men silenced at their fallen leader a curtain of black
fell but faith was something their hearts did not lack.

Stefanie Nagata

A Rebirth At BreadLoaf

Mother twisted tight braids from wild hair:
Watch out for wind, for sun, for rain
be careful of your footsteps on the earth.

No one spoke pleasure of trees.
She knew men were hung from trees
were buried in coffins sliced from thick trunks.

Today she stares at the Green Mountains of Vermont
the glory of Breadloaf
rich with oak, maple, pine and cedar.

She hears her mother's bones
whisper in the wind:
Do not step too lively in this natural world
there is only pain and grief.

Tomorrow she will place flowers at the gravesite
carnations and roses, iris's and gladiolus.
She will sit under the afternoon sun
and caress the cold letters of her mother's soul.

Under the green gaze of the Hollywood Hills
she will ask for a healing
a healing and a forgiveness.

Rosalind Levine

Lost And Found

(He) A young boy sits alone on the farm and ponders
Watching others much older than he roving
Searching for answers to the meaning of life
He starts early his years of loneliness and roaming
(She) The girl lives a thousand miles from his home
There is a family but she too feels alone
Young and innocent her mind also wonders
She sees through his eyes the same spirit of thunder
No love for me here why is life such a blunder
(They) As the years go by like time on a clock
Moving so quickly neither can slow to even a walk
They have never known love these two star crossed lovers
For those in their lives were too busy taking
Instead of giving the evening covers
(He) More spring flowers and scarecrows have come and gone
Through mourning the dead he sees that life must go on
He finds giving love and forgiving could be the reason
To go on living for just one more season
(She) Restless are board with life but with the well being of others at stake
(She) too goes on searching but wants to make no mistakes life can be
Funny in some small ways for just living life is not for always
(They) Once lost but now found the lovers are together
With God's help and other's efforts their love will last forever.

S. Blake Cejner

Reflections

Sitting here with you
Watching the sun through the trees,
I look back on my life;
I reflect on our time together.
We share our first cup of coffee
Watching the morning sun melt the dew from the ground;
You hold me close.
As the birds sing and play, the sky turns from violet to blue
You kiss me tenderly.
Watching the sun burn the fog from the lake,
Seeing the ducks splashing about with their young
I'll always need you.
Glancing at your face I see the eyes that often comfort me
And the smile that tells me you love me.
Looking at you I realize how much you mean to me.
I'll never be without you.
I've spent my life looking for you
Only to find my search has now ended.
You are here, you are mine.

Patricia Linn Sohn

"What A Child Is Like"

A child is like a bright star on a clear night,
Watching them discover new ideas and sounds is a wondrous sight.
The way their eyes light up to see a butterfly take flight.
Laying in the grass watching the antics of a kite,
guessing what shapes the clouds look like.
Building tent forts on rainy days,
Oh no, no lights lets pull out those flashlights!
Playing hide and seek,
hearing squeals of laughter is pure delight!
The wonder of snowflakes and snowmen,
of first snow, snowball fights.
Dance recitals, little league games, school days,
little eyes shining and bright.
Little hands baking cookies, making wishes,
dreaming of the future, this is what a child is like.

Sandra George

The Sign Of Love

While strolling in the garden with my grandmother one afternoon,
we came upon a dogwood tree in bloom.
My grandmother said, there is a legend, the original tree was big and
straight and that after the crucifixion of Jesus on that tree, its
form was changed to a smaller tree, baring cross shaped
flowers and blood stained color,
to show us His love will forever be.

Did you ever see a tree as lovely as the dogwood tree?
Its flowers come blooming in spring, baring the sign of our
   Saviour's love.
The sign of a true love, deep rooted from above, oh! Because
   it stems from God's great love.
See the sign of love.

When you're in doubt, please reach out. Pull a flower from
   the dogwood tree.
The flowers are stained with God's love.
He left them here for us to see that His love will forever be.
See the sign of love blooming in the flowers on the
   dogwood tree.
Mariann E. Barr Yates

Too Many Broken Hearts...

Too many hearts are being broken,
We can't hear the people's cry of hurt,
Cause their words aren't being spoken.

Many are afraid to speak their words
Of love, because they can be made fun
Of or people would laugh and when
They laugh their heart is broken in half.

Many people get a broken heart from a
Guy, when they find out their love for them
Was all a big lie.

Broken hearts can be a great pain, but you
Need to realize, as you get older there is
More in life for you to gain.
Sara Kubik

Permission Granted

We gave you our permission.
We didn't want to see you go.
You pled with us, "Please help me!"
It hurt to see you suffer so.
"I see Herbert." You told us.
"He's calling to me."
"Go to him," we told you,
"You will finally be free."
They say you go gently into the night.
It just wasn't true. You put up a fight!
Together again with the love of your life.
Herbert and Ethel, husband and wife.
We still miss you, dear Aunt and Uncle,
We'll try not to cry.
One day you will call to us,
From that sweet by and by.
We hope we're as strong
When we face our plight.
You'll hold out your hand,
And guide us into the light.
Susan J. Makela

...Time...

Time
We have it, before us, behind us, and around us.

Time
We share it with loved ones,
at home or abroad or not at all.

Time
We give it through out our lives, as we work a days end.

Time
It is taken from us unwillingly,
as those around us demand it.

Time
We regret it's passing, wishing
we had spent it more wisely.

Time
Wanting more of it, or hoping
it would pass us by quickly.

Time
It is to enjoy the quality of it's
ever passing, and the quantity of it that over comes us.
Toddeanna E. Walker

Who Says We're Poor?

Who says we're poor?

   We have the stars that shine at night
   We have the sun with its brilliant lights,
   To us this wondrous earth belongs
   We have the birds with their sweet songs.

Who says we're poor?

   When summer comes, we have the flowers
   For us to gaze on, they are ours,
   We have the woods and trees in blossom
   We have the animals who are really awesome.

Who says we're poor?

   When winter comes, we have the snow
   That comes down softly to the earth below,
   We have "Jack Frost" designs on the window pane
   And children slide riding down the lane.

Who says we're poor?

   We may not have money and material things
   But what we have is the air we breathe,
   The sun on our face and the feel of the breeze
   Not fame or wealth but love and peace.
Nettie P. Rocco

Playing Cowboys Mexican Style, 1958

The cool October wind chilled our fingers as
we held onto the reins, yet we continued our El Paso
play, branding the dry clay with our signatures.
I was the townspeople with land and cattle;
we would fight to the end in our ok corral.
Villa drafted the poor, promised them the world,
killed those he couldn't persuade. With the house
broom as my horse and my aunt's cane as my rifle,
we fought until Villa and I stood facing each other,
waiting for John Wayne to settle the dispute. But
usually a call for hot cocoa ended the feud.
Robert Giron

The Riddle Of Life

When the world is gray and lonely.
We sit and pray to God.
And we wonder why we all aren't happy.
And we ask him why is the world so odd.

He answers us in his own way.
He will not give you a wrong answer.
But something that is puzzling and it can't be solved today.
It is the riddle of life to tell what we are and who we were.

It is only God who tells you this because no one else could know.
And as long as God is with you no riddle is left unsolved.
Just keep on solving the riddle of life and your heart will grow and grow.
Now with the knowledge of your life your world has now evolved.

So now that you know what the riddle of life is all about.
You can go and help someone else think over too.
But don't tell them the answer just let them figure it out.
And sooner or later they'll pull through just like you.
Robert Houston

Grandmother's Empty Home

I walked through my Grandmother's empty home
We sold it just this morning
I saw at each turn so many memories
That it seemed I couldn't bear to leave

I saw the happy holidays with all the family there
Sitting at the big table ready for the wonderful food
Grandmother had lovingly prepared

I saw many ordinary days with only us two
Grandmother dressed so neatly
And ready for church
Or sitting quietly and helping
Her needle to work

This was the memory that hurt me the most
For it was at these times I'd sit with her and talk
I on the wooden floor and her in the old rocker
It went on for hours which disguised themselves as minutes

Oh, how I miss the sound of her voice
I strain but cannot hear it now
She's too far above to be heard
In an old, empty house.
Zenia Sullivan

All For Nothing

Struggling through the hardship and pain in life
We strive to do the best
Trying to reach the top
Getting above all the rest
Never once thinking that all this work is for nothing and that
One day we will DIE
This is all for nothing!
Is it really worth the fight?
Why do we even waste our time?
We work and then we DIE!
Do we really need this stress?
Working and competing
Sometimes we just wonder if it will all pay off
But then we say, how could that be?
Why can't everybody just realize and see that
This is all for nothing!
Is it really worth the fight?
Why do we even waste our time?
We work and then we DIE!
Laura Ricca

Waiting

We wait in line at the post office;
We wait in line at the store.
We wait in line at the pharmacy,
And when we eat lunch we wait some more.

We wait in line at the service station;
We wait in line at the bank.
It seems we are always waiting,
And to what do we have to thank?

"What in the world is the hold-up?"
We finally ask with a frown.
With a sweet smile we receive the answer,
"Sorry, the computer is down."

I hope when I get to heaven and stand
   at the Golden Gate,
That Saint Peter will let me enter, saying
"There is no need to wait; we have
   been expecting you, and
The good Lord knows your face.
Computers are used only
For those going to the other place."
Mary H. Bauch

We Are Real!

A pretty Tuesday, just an ordinary day,
We were on our way home from school
and he came so hard, fast, and out of the blue,
I prayed it would all go away.

He can't imagine how we feel,
He took control of our lives when he had none over his own
'cause of drinking and driving,
He got a slap on the wrist - oh that judge,
I want to say, We are real!

I see my boy's faces, tears, and fear,
and we'll never forget how life and death
flashed before our eyes,
It's hard you know,
You see, life is truly precious and I care.
Reni Lachterman Parker

The Summer Of 91

My friend, my friend
We were walking in the woods
And seeing all the trees around.

You started telling me of the rage of a small boy,
The world didn't bring him much joy.
Then, you told me of your special unit in Vietnam,
And the dead babies before you.

Being alone in the woods just didn't seem to set you free.
Oh my dear friend, you went away to the only place you could be.

You brought much pain into this world,
And we all sometimes do the same.
But in your last year,
You were the best, the best man any man can be.
Oh, can't you see!

You went to a higher place.
Traveled a path designed by God.
See, sometimes the wind blows at just the right time.
Sometimes the clouds part, and the sun shines.

Oh, my dear friend, the cancer took you to the only place you could be.
The only place you could run free.
Thomas Berntsen

Good-Bye

There comes a time when good-bye must be said.
We wish it would not come, but it can not be stopped.
I know that time has arrived.
Knowing it is here, sadden's my soul.
I dream at night that you still care,
But I reach out and you are not there.
You act as if I do not exists.
My heart says, "Keep going, keep trying, don't quit".
My head says, "Don't be foolish, it's over, give up".
I do not know which way to go.
My head and heart do constant battle.
It tortures my soul, but I know I must move on.
Will there be someone to love me?
That person is out there some where.
I must now go find her.
Even though It hurts my soul,
I realize the time has come to say good-bye.
   Robert T. Holmes

A Victim Of Salvation?

Am I the Serpent in your mother's garden?

One day she decided to be saved and now
wearing pants has become a sin.
Did you know the devil has taken control
of the airwaves with the exception of Hallelujah songs.

Am I the Savior of your innocent childhood?

Sitting on my lap, you ask if we can dance.
I pull out the full-length mirror.
You slip on my oversized, blue heels.
Behind closed doors our bodies jump and sway
to the rhythms long after our hair is flat and wet.

Am I the Speaker of the real truth?

You once said you hated God because
He took your toys away to heaven.
Was I wrong in telling you
mom was the one who hid them in the attic.

Am I the Serpent?
   Sandra I. Castro

Keep Smiling

Keep smiling you say?
Well, I suppose...
but then again the pain and suffering
I'm the only one who knows...

Time to let go...
nothing to say....
just stand quietly and watch everything, everyone... slip away...

Call it a day my friend, kneel and pray...
and if you're lucky one night they will come and quietly take you away.
   Vincent A. Iasiello Jr.

A Brother In Christ

When I come to you for a helping hand.
You never bat an eye.
How can we work this out?
Is always your reply.
How much closer is the Lord's love than this?
When an out stretched hand in touched,
By a fellow man.
   Marie Clement

The Little Boy And The Sea

Once upon a stormy sea in a small vessel there
   were but three. The Captain said, "fear not my son,
   many's the storm that I have won." But the little boy
   on his mother's knee, looked up, and the face of death saw he.

In mid-afternoon the world was dark, the lightning cracked
   he saw the spark. Strong winds howled came torrents of
   rain, waves washed aboard the boy cried in pain against
   the rod as he hung tight, his mother was gone in one flash of light.

The Captain, a mighty man was he, but claimed him also had the sea.
   The little boy cried, but who could hear?
   On stormy seas only God is near.

Many days passed when the vessel was found. The sea was so
   calm, it made not a sound. The sun so bright, the sky so
   clear, the soft rustle of water could one only hear. And
   there beside the rod was he, a little boy frozen by the salty sea.
   Virginia Kulhanjian-Freeland

New Friends

Was there ever any friendship quite so wonderful to see?
Were there ever any others who could always just agree?
No other pair could so thoroughly enjoy,
being with one another,
as the dog and the little boy.

They take long walks together
through fields and rippling streams
strolling along the byways,
dreaming their happy dreams.
They never quarrel or bicker nor do things to annoy,
for there is perfect understanding
the dog and the little boy.

There are other friendships that are good and kind and true,
there are often bonds of sympathy
that last a whole life through,
but the pals that are the truest,
with the whole world to enjoy,
who are made just for each other
the dog and the little boy.
   Mary Beth Vestal-Knight

On The Deep

The ocean thunders with cetacean symphony...
Whales sing to honor God, as we do:
To express the love they feel.
Dolphins choose to play.

Tonight, I am my dolphin self, free in dreams to roam the deep.

   My dolphin brother breaches for the pleasure of the light;
   I follow, thrilling to the leap and the reentry,
      cleaving deep beneath the bracing cold of mother sea.
   We race for the horizon, and know the speed
      by the pleasure of the doing.

   Each arc beneath the water sounds a fragment of the greater song;
   Each leap into the air is purest joy....
   Such is our tribute to the Father/Mother/God of air and sea.

   We are not less serious than whales.
   Our song is in the doing...
   Our work, the silent sustenance of those upon the land.
   With our huge cousins, we hold the world in balance
      for the day when Earth and all who choose ascend together.

We are all mostly water.
A dolphin's call travels easily through water.
   Eileen Penelope

From My Window - Autumn

What a glorious carpet of color
what a beautiful sight to see
as I sit here by my window
nature puts on a show just for me.
The leaves are now gently falling
as the breeze whispers a song through the tree
there are red, yellow, brown, green and orange
such beauty I never did see.

The pleasure this season brings to me
has wonders that have to be told
there's so much going on in my garden
among the color my eyes now behold.

Squirrels, picking nuts, just to hide them
birds, chattering in treetops above
spiders, spinning their webs on the flowers
the sun shining on all this with love
Oh, stop, for a moment, look and listen
feel the beauty this season has sung
soon the trees with snow will all glisten
like diamonds, where golden leaves hung
   Margaret T. Teliho

Bosnian Boy

Little boy,
what do you dream that makes you sigh?
Long, do you stare at darken skies.
Is it because, the world's lost its friendly lot?
What can I do to put an end to rifle shots?

Little boy,
why does a tear roll down your face?
Why does your heart quickens its pace?
Is it because, you hear men cry, and cannon's blow?
What can I do to see your face again aglow?

Little boy,
Why do you run away and hide?
Won't you let me hear your side?
Is it because, all mankind has let you down?
What can I do to see you smile, no more to frown?

Little boy, why not turn to God, to embrace?
Do you fear, He too, will not show face?
Is it because, you are alone, and love has strayed?
What can I do to give you hope, not be afraid?

What can I do? What can I do, little boy?
   Victor E. Legaspi

In Your Yard

Look out your window
What do you see?
Do you see me lingering
In your garden?

I walk along the winding path
Hoping to get to your door.
If I reach it, will you let me in...
Open the door, open your heart?

If I reach out will you take my hand
Or turn your back and close the door on me?

It's the chance I take
Walking through your garden
Being careful not to trample
Your beautiful flowers along the way.

But I will gladly take the chance
Because I love being in your yard.
   Patricia Drop

What Happened

What happened to the Doctor's dedication,
What happened to the Teacher's avocation,
Where have all the Mothers gone?
So much is missed of Life's sweet song -
Their children are growing up so fast,
And we cannot regain that which is past.

We need solid moral teaching -
We could use some truthful Preaching,
One can't make a difference? One can't stand alone?
It just takes one to start a ripple, one, to throw the stone.

What happened to the Children's education?
What happened to the Leaders of this Nation?
I'm sending a petition to my Father on His Throne,
I'll ask for intervention, for guidance from above,
Ask also for compassion - to fill this world with Love.
   Loretta J. Pitts

Oh What A Day

Oh what a day, when Jesus I see.
When I kneel at my Saviour's feet
His face will be bright as the sun up above
and His eyes will reflect the depth of his love.
Oh what a day, what a day it will be.
He is coming for you, He is coming for me.
Don't wait to be ready, He could come any time.
He will call us by name and say these are all mine.
What a day it will be when Jesus comes for me.
Rejoice and sing praises—don't weep for me.
Remember, I am happy and where I belong,
together with Jesus, in my Heavenly Home.
   Peggy R. Boyd

Caring

When do we stop the caring,
When do the feelings end?
When do we cease to remember
The heartache of losing a friend?

It makes one want to surrender,
To plead a solitary existence is best,
To never make an acquaintance,
To never again fly from the nest.

Were the good times worth all of the bad ones?
Were the caresses worth all of the pain,
Of knowing our days were numbered,
Of looking forward with nothing to gain?

It seems like I've known you forever.
It seems like you've always been there.
How can I help but remember,
But how can I cease to care?
   Mary P. Harris

Someone My Friend

I know now when I have a friend
when I'm with someone who makes me smile.
When I'm with someone who helps me see,
how beautiful the simple things in life can really be.
When that someone has a warm word to say each and every passing day.
When that someone really knows me and cares about the things I say.
When I can confine that someone my deepest thoughts and prayers
and when I'm with the someone I can trust in.
There's no reason to pretend, for I know I'm with a friend.
But few there seem to be.
To find a friend like you are to me
I want to tell you too,
I'm thankful to have that someone like you!
   Lena M. Avalos

"My Teacher"

I know a lady in our Church
When a jobs to be done, she never shirks,
She pay's Her Tithe's with a ten percent
Then a free will offering, before paying the rent,
of her, I've never known an unkind word spoken
Nor a vow made or a promise broken.
She's up bright and early each Sunday at Dawn
To Sunday school and Church with a cherry smile on
Back again on Sunday night,
she's right there shining her light
Again on Wednesday to the prayer meeting band,
There she is, always, lending a hand.
I guess by now, you've each guessed her name,
Its Laura, Mrs. Hatcher, there've one and the same.
We know God is pleased with the work she's done,
The classes she's taught, and the battles she's won.
She's been an inspiration, to and to all.
For eighty-five years she's answered God's call.
She's always been faithful, to God and her Church
She loves Her Savior, so she gets right to work.

Lillian Blevins

Human Soul

There is a small window in human brain,
when all strings of life are tuned,
this window opens up little by little,
like the melodies in Brahm's Orchestra.

Like a little bird in its nest,
the caged soul then peeps through this window,
and listens to the birds of Spring, and Autumn,
who claim to have climbed the hills, where Moses stood.

Suddenly the caged bird looks at autumn trees,
listens to the sighs of falling yellow leaves,
and compares them with the cries of Sarajevo valleys,
where the human shadows hold their breath.

Then the soul of this Universe knocks at its heart,
kisses the tiny soul with its love and joy,
and finally before its departure, asks
for the returns of its pleasures, only in human suffering.

The soul shuts the window of its nest and asks, "What is Life?"
The Universe replies, "Life is living in Infinity"
The tiny human soul again asks, "What is Death?"
There is a wide laughter in the sky, "It is only an illusion".

Vishnu P. Joshi

There Is Hope Even In Despair

When in your life, there is despair everywhere-
When even the brightest day seems dark all over-
When there is sadness throughout -
When you are depressed because things have gone wrong for you
When you have lost all hope and feel gloom deep within
Look and listen because there is hope in the air-
Listen to your heart and feel its beating.
Realize that you are ALIVE; make the best of what you have.
Be thankful for the sunshine, the flowers, and the laughter that rings from
    someone's joy.
Be thankful that you are living and you can make happiness your desire.
Smile, do not despair. Be thankful for the little things that
    are all around you everywhere.
So don't despair, there is hope somewhere.

Lois Nelson

Transfer

When the old bard has run out of steam,
When his think tank is drained completely dry;
He may as well be laid on a shelf,
Where, all alone, he can groan and sigh.

Still someone should take up the cause,
For the need of giving encouragement is great;
Out there many are ready to give up in defeat,
So they face a terrible and eternal fate.

Surely there are many who can write,
If only an encouraging note or a line;
They could show appreciation for a friend,
In so doing an unused talent they may find.

So pick up the mantle where it fell,
And begin writing praise in prose and song;
Send the message out both far and near,
"Twill surely help folks to keep on keeping on.

Then when all the pages have been written.
And finally the pen can be laid aside;
Yet the encouraging words will live on,
There in faithful lives where they abide.

Will H. Havens

When I Cry

Who cradles me in a cloak of passion
when I cry?

Who binds me in the armorment of ecstasy
when I cry?

When tear drops seize me
strong as vines bathing the earth from infinity,
who really cares?

Where lies the path of splendor
shimmering with familiarity,
when I cry?

When have I ever been caressed with eternity,
when I cried?

Where falls piercing moisture,
that penetrate pools of sorrow,
when I cry?

When skin pigmentation regulates me
to be considered a second-class citizen,
who will ever care
when I cry?

Renee Barr

You Are With Me

When you're not home and I am here alone, you are with me,
When I lay down at night and all is quite, you are with me,
When I start my day and nothing seems to be going the right
    way, you are with me,
When the days turn into weeks and it gets harder to go to
    sleep, you are with me,
When the old feeling of doubt starts stirring about, and I
    act like a child whose gone off to pout, you are with me,
When I know it was meant to be, I feel in my heart your the
    one for me,
When it has to be fate that we are together. I think that
    means it will be forever,
When the phone rings and you tell me your home,
I can't wait to see you and get you alone.
Then I know what the waiting was for,
    the happiness we feel the love and the joy,
There is no better feeling then that in the world. Because
    that's when you are truly with me.

Nancy Walters

"What Keeps Me Going"

What keeps me going is the thought of you.
When I look into your eyes I see the answers
to all my fears.
My fears of being alone.
I know that when I'm with you nothing can hurt me.
You won't let anything hurt me.
You are there for me when I need you.
You appreciate me for me,
and every little thing I do.
I watch you. I listen to you,
And you me.
I waited all my life to be happy.
I find you and I am.
Finally after all these years, I'm happy,
and you are...what keeps me going.
   Mary A. Kuchman

Good Bye Alcohol

Good bye alcohol, you son of a gun
When I started drinking, it was only for fun.

You took me down this path that others had been too,
I seen them in my journey, but I couldn't add 2 plus 2

You mixed up my brain and emotions with those spirit filled potions.
Then you let me go to find my way back, but I was blinded by you and
   that was a fact.

But you knew when I awoke I would need you again,
but this time I took your hand and we'd go down that path once again.

But you didn't let me go where you did that time before and things
become a lot different....Why? Because I had to drink more.
The pleasure turned to pain to try to remember "what a shame".

I didn't drink for fun now, I did it for effect.
And in my messed up mine, I thought I had a defect.

So one night in my bed, I prayed to the Lord for help.
And he put my mind at ease, he showed me the way through his eyes to
Ashley and they told me I had a disease.

You can do alcohol, coke, heroin, pot, or pills, but if you don't look
up and reach out to your "higher power" this stuff "kills".

Good bye Alcohol, you son of a gun.
You thought you had me, you thought you won! NOT!!
   Michael J. Jones

The Lighthouse To My Soul

When I was down, he was there to lift me up.
When I was sad, he was there to brighten my heart.
When I was angry, he put a smile on my face.
When I was in need, he was there to fill my cup.
And when I was lonely, he sent you to fill my days,
to hold my head, to share my sorrows, and to fill my bed.
The Lord above sent you to be the light in my home,
for he is the light in my soul.

Like a beacon in the night, the Lord is my light.

For you, my wife Ranee, you are the light of my home,
And the precious Lord above is the lighthouse to my soul,
and the foundation of our future.

The Lighthouse to my Soul
   William H. Lane Jr.

God Will

When I listen for awhile God will speak
When I wear a happy smile God will speak
When I hum a cheerful tune
   to chase away the gloom
No matter where I am, God will speak.

When I breathe a little prayer, God will care
When I ask for strength to cope, God will care
He'll take my troubles great and small,
   His peace becomes my all
I know, Oh yes, I know, God will care.

When I tell about His goodness, God will hear
When I tell someone "I love you", God will hear
When His name in praise I sing,
   "Hallelujah, Christ is King!"
My song will reach to heaven, God will hear.

Yes, my God will speak to me, for He is there
He will stay beside me and He'll always care
He will tell me not to fear,
   and wipe away my tears
He is my Savior and He always cares.
   Marjorie Potts

Nameless, Faceless, My Companion True

Whenever I seem pensive and purposeless
When I'm afraid my life is a mess

When I want someone to wipe my tears
And whisper words of comfort in my ears

When I see lonely hours stretched out ahead
And hear echoes of thunder as I curl in my bed

When brisk afternoons give way to enchanting nights
With their distant twinkling of magical lights

When Nature's cool fingers brush my cheek
And I'm too full of happiness to speak

When I admire a profound thought, a turn of phrase
And want to share a ridiculous moment, or sparkling verse

It is then that I think of you
Nameless, faceless, my companion true
When our paths cross, will I recognize you?
   Rekha Ramamurthi

True Feelings

When I'm bored I like to write
When I'm bored I'm out a sight.

When I'm with you it's really nice.
When I'm with you everything's alright.

How come when we're apart.
I always have a broken heart.

I like the way you make me feel
Girl, you give me such a thrill.

I know you don't feel the same
and it's me alone to take the blame

I wish you well in whatever you do,
Because your feelings make mine come true.

I'm going fight the feeling in my mind
Because I know you can be so unkind
   Edward

Freedom Day

My father sailed on this great freedom day
when immigrants were often herded on
to Ellis Island shores the steerage way.

There were few words in English he could say
but he had youth and courage and was strong.
My father sailed on this great freedom day.

Not much food, no money, no place to stay -
but others poorer yet - amid the throng
to Ellis Island shores the steerage way.

Thousands with hope, young, middle-aged and gray;
some did not hear, see, nor know right from wrong.
My father sailed on this great freedom day.

Gardener by trade, to plow new life in clay,
determined to succeed, he queued along
to Ellis Island shores the steerage way.

From patriotism he would never stray -
with liberty for all by prayer and song.
My father sailed on this great freedom day
to Ellis Island shores the steerage way.

Maxine Kaiser Russell

Women And Chaos (A Rondel)

The day it came, I heard the wind go under;
When it surged back, I saw they still were there.

All held its sound, no tapping twig, no thunder;
No nickering of the trembling colt to mare;

The day it came I heard the wind go under.

As to a cave, sucked down, seized by the hair;
It's glory shorn, drained all of wonder.

When it surged back, I saw they still were there.

Great throngs with songs to sing were blown asunder;
Torn baskets found, those left gleaned up to share.

(The day it came, I heard the wind go under.)

By baskets stacked, they, trembling, lean and stare.
(Do widening rifts reveal a cosmic blunder?)

When it surged back I saw they still were there.
(The day it came I heard the wind go under.)

Myrtle D. Zimmerman

What I Truly Want.....

Life holds so many surprises
When it throws you a curve, you wonder why
Can love be real or is it just a fantasy
Why can't love become a reality
Trust is just a word
In most relationships is seldom heard
Peace is a feeling that is needed
Once received can it be righteously perceived
I live and wonder why
Can any man truly touch the sky
Understanding comes in time
But finally and not nearly least
What I truly want is physical and mental peace

William Thomas Jackson Sr.

Funerals

A friend passed and many people came,
when it was over, everything was the same.
We saw those we had not seen in years,
close friends and relatives eliminated tears.
This seems to be the place to find,
old friends who seldom enter our mind.
We see them, greet them, smile and stare,
turn, walk away and disappear.
Songs were sang, words were said,
this is the usual respect for the dead.
We always speak of death as joy,
equal to the birth of a girl or boy.
Funerals to me are agony and pain,
which place everyone under nothing but strain.
The songs and words bring on crying and fainting,
Michael could not have done a more agonizing painting.
Is it fair to those who have been so dear,
funerals punish those who care.

Lewis E. Forrest I

Happy Silence

How do we talk
When our loved ones can't hear
Love can be shown
With laughter or a tear
It can also be shown
With your hands and a smile
Signing with love
Can be seen for a mile
A silent world of wonder
Can be one of love
Full of facial expressions
Gestures of kindness full of life from above
Deafness is beauty
Unique to each being
Full of new discoveries
A silent world seeing

Nola Nackerud

Untitled

I saw for the first time
you without your hand
in a room of perpetual dusk
smelling like antiseptic illness

As much as we sat with you
as much as our hearts seized with yours
you bore the brunt of it alone
that ceiling for a sky
a silent dialogue with your body every slow hour of the night

And I know in the space of one minute
it was etched into my mind for better or worse
the introduction of your handless arm to my reality
the nurse who missed me in shadow exposed the stitches
I think I met that absence before you did

And once home, still feeling the spirit of those fingers
we grew something in their place
that could hold more and give more
that pulled me to my feet more than once

And so I let go of my father's one hand
and take hold of the other

Megan Haas

Think Of Me

When I'm gone, think of me.
When the dusk turns to dawn, think of me.
When the skies are blue, think of me.
Even though we are through, think of me.
When you hear our song, think of me.
Think of all the times I pleased you so.
Don't think of the girls before.
Think of all the closed doors.
All your friends tell you to forget me but
I'm asking you to remember me and all we
went through.
Think of the time when I loved you and
you loved me too.
When you feel lonely think of me and
I'll be there with you.
I'm not saying you were right to let go,
nor am I saying I was right to hold on.
I'm not asking you to come back to me.
All I'm asking is for you to THINK OF ME!

Sabina Catarina Boggess

Black Woman

When they look at me, they see black.
When they look at you, they see woman.
But I am the most dangerous woman they deny their sight.
I did not teach you that, they holler with indignation!
No, I reply with smugness. I taught myself and I will
Continue to defeat them with their own weapon.
Knowledge is power, for they have proven this again and again and
 ignorance is bliss.
You say that you too are a minority and share my struggle.
I scowl, barely concealing my contempt, for you have not a clue.
When they look at me they see not
Mother, lover, educator, hope, freedom and pride.
When they look at me, they see black.
When they look at you, they see woman.

Valoria R. Smith

Untitled

There are times in our lives
When we question our very existence.
When sun shines brightly
Yet, pain lies close to our hearts.

Somehow it seems the world should reflect our sorrows.
Rain should fall and skies turn dark.

But today the sun shines and all seems well with the world.
Yet, I know the sunlight changes nothing.
Day by day ...
Hour by hour...
Your death is coming

Kathleen L. Enyart

You Said

You said you loved her, but how could this be true.
When you beat her unmercifully until her face was through.

You said it was just one time, you promised it would never happen again.
But the rage in your fist is an unforgivable sin.

You said she deserved it, you said she was wrong.
Please tell me what she did so horrible that caused you to beat her so long.

You said you loved her, but how I will never know.
If this is your idea of love you'd better pack your love and go.

You said you loved me, your daughter, more than any other.
If these words were true you would never have hurt my mother.

How many years ago did you as a man pledge your love to her for life.
You are no real man, for a real man could never hit his wife!

Kai Lee

My Nationality

Images of our ancestors, great people before.
Where have you gone, where may you be?
Look upon yesterday, a world of old, a past of heritage, a past of soul.
To learn and seek my forgotten nationality is a path a key of peace within thee.

How do I get there?
How can I be what once lived long ago so free?

Do I dig with a shovel? Or dig with a hand in a book of records?
Or in a back of sand? Will the book melt into a puddle of words yet to be known?
Known to myself or known to the world.
About who my family was and who they come to be in a world of some war,
  Yet they say we are free.

Tami Martell

Mother! Mother! Mother!

You didn't even knows me when you carried for nine months.
When you deliver me I couldn't say one word.
You took good care of me.

MOTHER!
You have given me all your life by accepting any struggles.
You had taught me the right from wrong, and you
have pay attention to me days, and nights.
You was always there for me when I need you.
You have given me the courage I deserved.

MOTHER!
How could I ever thank you for all works, you have
done for me I will thank you by proving you dream t became reality
I will be there for you whenever you need me.

MOTHER!
You are the wonderful woman I love in my life.
I love you more then my china doll.
Wherever I will be, I will always remember you.
I am all yours.

Rufin B. Gbado

First Fall

I'll never forget the very first night,
When you kissed my lips and held me tight.
I knew right then it was meant to be,
But still I thought to myself "why me?."
I wasn't really sure how you felt,
All I knew is when we touched my heart would melt.

I wasn't exactly sure what I should do,
I was in love with him and falling for you.
I had to make a choice either him or you,
Which would it be, only my heart knew.

At first I wasn't sure if my decision was smart,
But I've always been told "just follow your heart."
So that's what I did and now we're here,
Together with you now I've nothing to fear.

Michelle Yeavon Daniels

Lillian Ruth

Patiently waiting day by day,
Until your Daddy could proudly say,

It's Lillian Ruth, all healthy and bright
To look upon you is such a delight.

Ten little fingers and ten little toes,
Some reddish brown hair and a cute little nose,

Grandmas and Grandpas and Aunties too,
Were all on hand to welcome you.

Happy we are to have you here,
To shower with love year after year.

Miriam R. Huston

Will You Think Of Me?

Dear one, will you think of me
When you turn back the covers tonight?
For I think of you - and pretend you are here
When I slip into bed each night.

It's been many years since you held me,
But it's said, "Love like ours never dies."
I know that's true because I hear your voice,
I feel your arms enfold me as I close my eyes.

I feel the soft covers around me
They're like your warm body and arms.
The pillow 'neath my head is your shoulder,
And, sleeping, I dream of you and your charms.

You're with me the whole night through
Not having to leave me the way you used to do.
My dreams are sweet, but I need you to assure me.
That you're thinking of me, holding me, loving me, too.

To find one's love is so special
That across the miles we can re-une.
We can't be together because you belong to another.
We met too late, after each had wed another too soon.
Marie Anna Allen-Smith, Ed. D.

"A World Without Tears"

Just think of a world a world without tears
where a man can live for a million years,
with never a grief, nor ache or pain
and never a thought of dying again.

Think of a world where a man plants a vine,
he can sit in its shade and say "this is mine
he can live in a house his own hands have made
and naught shall molest or make him afraid.

Think of a world without blood shed or strife,
where no man dare take another man's life,
where man unto man will unite in peace
and malice and hatred forevermore cease.

Think of the earth as a global paradise
where mountains and desert will dazzle your eyes,
with beautiful flowers and shrubbery and trees,
with gay butterflies, songbirds and bees.

Think! Just as sure as Gods' word is truth,
a man shall return to the days his youth,
his flesh shall become like the flesh of a child,
and the words that he speaks will be cheerful and mild.
Particia Janes

A Friend

What is a friend, how much is one worth?
Where do you look in heaven or earth?
Does one serve a purpose, is it vital to life?
Could one make a difference amidst all this strife?
Can one make you laugh or can one make you cry?
When you just can't go on, can one make you try?
Is a friend really pretty, perfection to see?
Must a friend always be in agreement with me?

A friend is a person whose worth is untold,
It can never be measured by silver or gold.
The purpose it serves is hard to explain,
It shares all our joys as will as our pain.
It's ready to laugh and it's ready to cry.
When I say "I can't" it says "We will try."
A friend is true beauty, some young and some older.
Beauty, like love, is in the eye of the beholder.
If I had my choice from beginning to end,
My first choice would be the one I call friend!
Mary Hoover

Come Along With Me To Faraway Places

Come along with me to a faraway place
   Where history shows a timeless face.
Columns that rise on a seaside hill
   Tell an ancient story that lives with us still.
Temples, calm harbors, and endless blue sky
   A world of delight for an artist's eye.
Tranquil fields of olive groves, leafy cypress trees,
   A legacy of days long past - the Golden Age of Pericles.

Then let us wander to places "down under,"
   A spectacular land of beauty and wonder.
We'll watch fairy penguins parade on the dunes,
   And listen to Lyrebirds singing sweet tunes.
We'll see Wombats and Dingo Dogs, Kangaroos and Koalas,
   Lorikeets and Wallabies, and trees full of Galahs.
We'll ride the outback in a rickety jeep,
   And run with a kelpie dog mustering sheep.

After that we could ride in a caravan
   Of camels enroute to Afghanistan.
We'll follow the trails of the traders of old
   To a world of adventure that ever unfolds.
Mary D. Nunez

Untitled

In the uncertain times where heartaches took their toll,
where love gone awry left anger and discontent - feelings of mistrust,
you hid pieces of your wondrous self away.

Let me be the one to renew your faith in love.
Let me turn your anger into radiant smiles,
your discontent into a warm glow within your soul,
your mistrust into an easy journey back to feeling and believing.

Let me give you the gift of myself - my love,
devotion, honesty - so that we may merge
into an endless stream of reality and fantasy
to play out day after day, night after night.

Let us be two sharing one circle.
Love me - let me love you.
Rosel I. Chappel

The Artist

The sunlight penetrates the room
Where stands the lone easel;
A solitary artists weaves and intertwines
Colours with sweeping, feathery strokes
Of his skilled and gentle hands.

The brilliance and clarity of
A multitude of colours permeate
The huge canvas -

A golden tapestry of complicated weaving -
Yet accomplished by so gentle and caring a touch.

Lovingly the artist accomplishes
Each individual stroke and touch -
Like a father ministering to a child
A lesson on life.

The artist never ceases to apply
A multitude distinct and beautifully harmonizing colours -
To the tapestry that is,

Your life...
Bianca Vandemark

My Last Song

Where the daisies laugh and blow,
Where willow leaves hang down,
Nonny, Nonny, I will go
There to weave my Lord a crown.

Willow, willow, by the brook,
Trailing fingers green and long,
I will read my Lord a book,
I will sing my love a song.

Though he turn his face away,
Nonny, Nonny, I still sing
Ditties of a heart gone gray,
And a hand that bears no ring.

Water, water, cold and deep,
Hold me fast that I may sleep,
Death with you is hardly more
Than the little deaths before.
   Sharon Sitton

Silent Consolation

There are special times when you bring me
your aching heart and tears of sorrow.

Troubled times when a spoken word might be
an annoyance or promise of tomorrow.

These special times of no utterance simply
require my open heart, reassuring hug or gentle touch.

The pure offerings of love, understanding, charity
and sharing that mean so very very much!
   Sandra E. Spears

I Wish A World

I wish a world
Where you could walk down the street
And be liked
Not hated
I wish a world
Where in the morning you could open your eyes
And be confident
Not afraid
I wish a world
Where you could love
Without being afraid
I wish a world
Where war is confined to the jail of hate
And peace is greeted at the gates of love
   Rachel Stone

Feelings That Are Seen

I have a voice that melts glaciers when I sing,
Yet I have no ear, no heart, other than my own,
into which my warmth and tenderness may flow,
Your cheeks are as two hills, sheltered with untouched snow,
Heavenly voice I hear from thy lips, so full of life and so immortal,
Hair, smooth like the sand which gracefully falls from a divine
hourglass, if you were with me I would caress you with feelings,
Feelings beneath human flesh and bone,
Feelings Dear Lady, only you can appreciate,
I am the Sun you are the Snow,
Allow me to shine on you my feelings so that you will turn,
to a pure pool of water, not of tears, but of a cool bliss.
   Maziar Vaziri

Victory In France A Tribute

Cows graze benignly now in coastal fields by wave washed shore
Where young men died before they hit the sand
And boys from far across the sea fought valiantly that eve
Their fear-filled eyes peeled to houses standing by the foam.
What shore was this? What now, brave hearts? Who knows?

Into wind-blown waves they leapt in single file and raced for
Cover, comrades falling all around - 9,000 lost that night.
"Move in! Move in or die," the battle cry rang out.
Tanks and landing craft sank fast amid the thunderous fire
Death all around. So far they came, for this.

With dawn, calm seas now yielding sorrowful toll in gentle wash.
How cruel the sight! Wounded and dead retrieved for motherland
And home - boots, helmets, love-treasures crushed in wave
Silent toll on quiet dawn for battered flesh,
Man's inhumanity to human kind to end.

Cows graze benignly now in coastal field by wave washed shore
Hauntingly serene. Was it ever real? A sea bird cries.
Fifty years of silent fields bought by one thunderous, stormy
Night of terror - each day a gift hereafter.
Lift now the veil and ponder - ever.
   Maureen H. Nalin

Jodie Diane

A woman child of beauty and grace
Who has life standing ready to plead her case.
Ready to bloom and open anew.
And there isn't much she has to do.

Just open her heart and let love flow out
The blessings will multiply, of this have no doubt
Trust is very fragile, but can be achieved.
It's up too her, she has to believe.

She's so very complex, yet so simple to love.
She's surely a blessing sent down from above.
So Lord don't close her heart, open it wide
Invite all who love her to dwell inside
   Cheri Engle

Balm For Broken Dreams

Are you drooping and sagging from self centered woes
which are a part of your life you dare not expose?

Does your anger and hurt keep you trapped in a fold
that is lonely and bruised and covered with mold?

Here is some help which will surely suffice
and protect you from skidding all over that ice.

Reflect for a while on Romans 12:2
and relish the changes that take place in you.

"Be ye transformed by the renewal of your mind."
Means don't let that old, frayed cord rewind.

Replace it earnestly with a new dream to explore
and enjoy the beauties of life evermore.
   Rosemary G. Hinkle

A Natural Mother

Has a gentle sweet heart,
   Which freely reaches out!
She sees the children and feels their need,
   There is no doubt!

Standing watching like a shepherd.
   Protecting his sheep!
Never allowing any harm,
   To those in her keep!

A natural mother,
   Such an excellent example!
Filled with agape love,
   Such a heavenly sample!

Truly blessings are given,
   During these precious moments!!
A privilege to witness,
   These tender events!

William R. Turner II

The Sun Rises Up

The sun rises up to begin a new day,
Which shines upon the old farmhouse, down Georgia Way
It's rays recollect of a time long forgotten,
When whole families arose to harvest the cotton.

Our family was of the common man.
We couldn't afford the negroes with a skin of tan.
So we trudged out of bed at the crack of dawn,
and had a sparse breakfast, with a sleepers yawn.

Mother went about to tidy up our home.
It failed in comparison to those of majestic Rome.
We had to make do with what we had,
Cause us farmers are poor, but never sad.

Father and I went out to start the harvesting.
Sun up to sun down, there wasn't no restin'.
The money from sellin' the cotton, was given to the bank,
Cause if we didn't, deeper in debt we'd sank.

And now it's dusk, the sun sinks down to night.
A chilly breeze has picked up; not heavy, just light.
How soon we forget what our ancestors worked for:
To make it through the day, no more.

Stephen C. Romanetz

Thank You For Calling...

I lay still on the edge of sleep,
   while you speed towards your day

The overseas
SNAP, CRACKLE, POP
reach me seconds before your
   "'elo!"

Car phone in the Porsche conversations
   your motor through my midnight's
four time zones and thirty kilometers per hour ahead of me

   "How are we?"
Your day, the girls, petty frustrations,
   astonishing confessions
white mini skirted women top off golf holidays in Spain

Ask you no questions, you'll tell me no lies -

We build trust and friendship
in increments of twelve, sixteen and twenty-two billable minutes
You receive the bill
   I hope not to pay dearly...

Elsie Echevarria

Morning Harvest

Dawn comes.
"Whip," one drowsy "whip"
...the voice of the exhausted whippoorwill.
A quail whistles "Bob White," inquiring.

Early awake,
meeting cool air and the dew
women gather the succession of summer:

Strawberries, raspberries,
blueberries, blackberries,
peaches and plums, apples and pears...
and with the reaching and the plucking
as the fruit leaves the stem,
remembrance comes.

The torch of harvest-past
gleams in the stirrings
of this sunrise.

Leona Mason Heitsch

Holy Cow's, Baby Ruth's, And Old Milwaukee

Cans of A&W and candy cancer sticks
whisked me into his world of tobacco and barley.
Lodged between sounds of crickets mating across the lane
and the voice of Phil Rizzuto beyond the screen door,
my father's father and I pontificated life.
Philosophers were we, also collaborators,
cloaking one another from the watch of Grandmother,
who policed the intake of sugar and alcohol.
I swapped him my silence about beer and cigars
for a handful of chocolates and a can of pop.
In cahoots! Defaulting me into brief adulthood!
These intemperances minimalized Grandpa's days.
I wonder whether this cohort should have been a stoolie
as I sit sipping cocoa and munching biscotti.

Kevin J. Fuller

Nature's Sensate

As I sit gazing out my window, the stately pine, oak and hickory whisper in the wind and sway with the grace of a ballerina in a wondrous dance.

The approaching storm seems to fill the sky with a somber black veil and rumbles with the sound of ten thousand drummers drumming.

As the rain drops begin, my mind envisions the sound of a single steed galloping across a vast plain with the thundering hoofs of one hundred mavericks in pursuit of this illusive white foxfire of legends old.

As the sunbeams one after one peak through the ragged veil the sounds of God's winged creatures, the clean fresh washed air, and rainbows brilliant hues truly please my senses.

And I gaze again and find my mind at peace.

Nancy Mumphrey

Silent Consolation

There are special times when you bring me
your aching heart and tears of sorrow.

Troubled times when a spoken word might be
an annoyance or promise of tomorrow.

These special times of no utterance simply
require my open heart, reassuring hug or gentle touch.

The pure offerings of love, understanding, charity
and sharing that mean so very very much!

Sandra E. Spears

The Tree

The leaves fall quietly,
Whisping in the wind.
The leaves drop quietly,
Each so brittle thin.
The air stands dark and void of life,
A cold front breezing in.
And when the winds begins to rush, the leaves begin to fly,
Plucked from life into fate by a stream for strife.
The strife flows whispering, pouring in with a cancerous breath.
When one stops to take a whiff, he gets a snout of sour death.
Hear it yell with bloody voice, yet nothing there to see.
Watch it snatch, with bony hand, the leaves from the tree.
In agony the tree lurches, swaying in the wind.
Oh, how much pain it faces as it strains from giving in!
There appears a moment, a strenuous moment, a moment of fears wake.
The tree begins to fear and worry that it might well break.
It stopped!
The wind went silent now.
The tree withstood the plow.
The snow has come, no need to run; a time of resting now.
   Richard S. Dennis

Untitled

Playing in your long dark hair!
White the sun light dances blossom are blowing
this is all smoothing as I'm tuning my fingertips
are grooving to play in you long dark hair, O
what a sight pure delight as a breeze flow
though and your long dark hair waves toward
the right into the sun light, so bright, greatness
is a curls with a radiate. Body the swirls
Teasing is pleasing, but so is receiving the
slighted rotation set off the biggest vibration
of shimming of swirly curly of hair and starting
to float I'm reaching for the waves of long
dark hair, beckon me near into the bountiful
Highlight are glowing my heart is flowing for
the girl, I love you so deadly, attraction is risen
for the love affair with the long dark hair,
is revealing astounding control, as each
every strain seen to fall back into place,
I'll be playing in your long dark hair!
   William Clark

What Happen To Hope

Standing on the Corner, late at night
Who are they, do they think its right.

Standing in a crowd using fowl language
Not caring who's walking around in bondage.

Black or white it doesn't matter
Runaways everywhere its not getting better.

The elderly scared to come out
The young scared to do right
What have the world become.

Mother's fighting daughters,
Father's fighting sons,
Brothers and sisters Sister's Stabbing
Each other in the back,
Oh no this couldn't be right.

Lord look down on your kids
The older they get the weaker they are,
What happen to hope, that's what
we need, hope for your kids and
Mine...
   Melissa Hatten Davenport

Coming Of Age

He's just eighteen, this son of mine
   whom I carried, nursed and raised alone.
   Excitement glows upon his face
   as he carries out the last of his clothes.
   Did I raise him right? Can he face a world
   where troubles lurk at every turn?
   Will he visit; does he care? Is he
   leaving to be free from my reign?
   My lips are sealed and I lecture no more.

I dab my tears and force a smile
   as I hear his footsteps in the hall.
   He hugs me till I gasp for air, then chuckles
   when I punch his arm. "I'm outa here"
   he speaks with zest, taking one last look
   around the room. "I'll be by tomorrow
   to mow the lawn, and tell Grandma
   we'll pick her up for church at ten."
   His words touch my heart and I sense
   the love from whence they came.
   He's a fine young man, this son of mine.
   Valerie Copenhaver

'Pain Thru The Pane'

A gust of wind comes so abrupt
Whining, whistling and whirling, corrupt.
Robbing the rain of its gentle tap
Turning the dance into an unheard ballet.
Sweeping the breath of the city away
Painting the sky a murky, dark gray.
Grounding the birds from their usual flight
Hushing and shushing them in their plight.
Ripping the stumps, and twigs of their aging leaves
Forcing them to stand naked as barren trees.
This breeze, it blows, rushing my world right past
And I haven't moved from my bed, looking out of the glass.
   Terri L. Scott

An Angel Among Us

For years I've mourned my mother,
whom I lost when I was young.
I missed her love and companionship;
the lullaby's, she sung.

I felt alone during those times, that were tough;
swimming upstream, in waters that were rough.
I fought my battles, and conquered my fears,
though I never had anyone, to dry my tears.

There were so many times, I wished she were here;
so many times, I needed her near.
I resented the good times, that she couldn't share,
I always felt life, had been very unfair.

Then one day, something became clear, to me;
She was really much closer, than anyone could be.
She was on my shoulder, during those darkest times
She'd pulled me along, all the mountains, I'd climbed.

She carried me through, my torments and storms,
She mended my heart, whenever it was torn.
She was always there, I just couldn't see;
My Guardian Angel, is what she'd been to me.
   Sheryl Schlieman

Walk On A Rainy Afternoon

Among wind scattered petals on the ground
Whose broken colors shimmer in the rain
Lie memories that drift like waves of sound
And hope filled dreams which never come again.
The falling mist has overcast the sun
A blaze of lightning stops and staggers me,
Reminding me of battles never won
And bringing dread of pain that still might be.
A gull is shrieking as he journeys back
To some safe place beside the stormy sea.
My mind extends beyond the weighted black
Reaching for hope that brings tranquility.

The sun comes out, a rainbow arches high,
And I find peace beneath a brightening sky.
Ruth E. Williams

Grandma, Grandma

You are loved by many, disliked by few.
Why did this have to happen to you?
Grandma, Grandma - why did you leave?
This is all so hard to believe.

I trust in God to know;
So, I just have to let go.
And remember that someday, somehow
I'll be with you again, just not now.

When God held out his hand for you to follow;
He took you to a special place but left us with sorrow.
Grandma, Grandma - why did you go?
You'll be missed by both friend and foe.

Your memory will always be in my heart.
Therefore, we will never be apart.
Through good times and bad times, yet to be.
You will be there, right beside me.

You've touched many lives with your special ways.
I'll never forget the good ol' days.
Grandma, Grandma - I think I know why.
God gave you your wings, so you could fly.
Linnea Lightwine

A Letter To Loneliness

Dear Loneliness,
  Why have you come to visit me? Of all the emotions I know, you are the one I had hoped not to meet, yet here you are.

  I fear you, and do not want you here. You make me feel insecure, frightened, and unworthy. You take away my reason for living, and my motivation. You leave me empty and exhausted.

  Loneliness, you are an angry emotion. I feel as though you are punishing me for my selfishness and pride. What have I done to encourage your presence? What do I have to do to make you go away?

  I am surrounded by people, yet I feel as though my soul is gone. You have taken it away. You make it impossible for me to reach out for help during frightening times. You make me feel as though I am a burden to others and unworthy of their love and support. You have built a stone wall around my heart, unyielding to those who may wish to enter.

  You cause me to seek those who hurt and abuse me, for that is what makes you stronger. Leave me now, for you have done your damage. You have broken my spirit, destroyed my self confidence, and turned my dreams to nightmares.
Lori E. Pisani

"Why, Mommy, Why?"

In the past when a child asked
"Why, Mommy, Why?"
It was often to ask
why birdies can fly.
To explain, 'though not easy, is relatively mild,
so we think up the reason, and explain to our child.

In the present when a child asks
"Why, Mommy, Why?"
It is often to ask
why their friend had to die.
Guns, AIDS, abuse, or the such
our natural response "It won't happen to us."

In the future when a child asks
"Why, Mommy, Why?"
And the world is still cruel
with many reasons to cry,
put the blame on yourself as well as the others,
it means we failed our kids as fathers and mothers.
Mary K. Lewis

Why?

Why do we take what is said to be offensive?
Why must we constantly be on the defensive?
Why must we always fight?
Why can't everything be right?

Why must the pain run deep?
Why is it hard to sleep?
Why do we do the things we do?
Why can't we say "I love you too"?

Why must we run from each other?
Why can't we trust one another?
Why can't we just admit what's wrong?
Why can't we find out just where we belong?

Why don't we know what we are looking for?
Why can't we be something more?
Why don't we try?
Why do we let ourselves cry?

Why do we only speak when its too late?
Why do we leave to much to fate?
Why do we seek help from up above?
Why do we search for love?
Nicholas Carrozzi

Birthday Party

If t'was the night before Christmas
Why were we in the house, while
Mary and Joseph were searching,
High and low, 'round about,
For a place to stay, yes, just for a night
To have this new baby, named our Lord Jesus Christ.

We should have been praying, as the shepherds came closer
Bringing their gifts to share at the altar.
The blessed event, on that star-guided evening
Changed the whole world, as stars began shining.

Prince of Peace, Child of Light,
Celebrates His birthday, on the darkest of nights.
Please share this season with the bit of His cake,
Let the candles burn brightly before You partake.

Sing 'Happy Birthday, Dear Jesus'
Thanks for 'YOUR' holiday
Then guide us home safely
As we go on our way.
Patricia B. Kepler

Yesterday I Saw You

Yesterday I saw you standing in a meadow;
Why won't your eyes meet mine?
This is what we agreed, you whisper to the poppies
As they nod assent in a gentle breeze.

Yesterday I saw you standing by the river;
Why won't you look at me?
Remember our deal, you murmur as the carp swim by,
Their bodies coruscating from filtered sunlight.

Yesterday I saw you standing on a mountain—
At last! Your green eyes meet my brown.
Is this all, you ask with tears glistening in your eyes,
Your final question to the winds.

Yesterday...
Oh, yesterday I saw you.
All you said,
All I heard...
Is the way it ought to be.
Tabitha Williams

A Gold Star Home

It was a just a plain white Indiana farmhouse,
With a hallway and bedroom with pale wallpaper.
A bit of a darkened parlor and a soldier boy's picture
Displayed prominently on one wall.

A farm kitchen with the real front door,
Inside, a rocking chair awaits pa and a
Pot-bellied hot stove awaits supper
Once ma gets off the phone.
Heard about our boys? Heard about them overseas?
What did you hear from Ernie today?
What did he write from the front?
Many boys never came back to these solid old farmhouses,
Many slept in the water off Omaha Beach,
Some slept in Italy, with their men
Gathered around them to say goodbye
Others slept on Ie Shima on the other side of the globe

They all slept and back at home
A small gold star is all that's left.
Steve Joos

Someone Special

She's like a princess, such a lovely sight,
With careful hands she gathered us about;
A woman who has settled many fights,
She loves each one of us without a doubt.

We have encountered sorrow and some pain,
She's one who cares to give us tears of joy;
At times we drive her crazy and insane,
Her world revolves around her girls and boys.

And we can see the love that's in her eyes,
Without applying effort on our part;
She knows we see her—wonderful and wise,
With many special places in our heart.

Her warmth and peace are given through her care,
My mother's precious love is everywhere.
Melinda Youngers

The Senior Years

For the senior years I plan
With charts and folders, advice from all the clan.
To settle in some Sylvan Isle.
Each day to walk a mile.
Oh how I hate the drudgery of the job.
I want to leave the scrambling mob.

With charts and folders, advice from all the clan
I will not wait any longer than.
But how from my cherished desk to move.
Security is here within this groove.
And though visions of ease do Titilate,
Still about the leisure years I vacillate.

With charts and folders, advice from all the clan.
Who knows what lies beyond for man?
Is boredom there? Horizons to explore?
The mind is fixed, the fact is sure,
I will leave this job behind
The world is there, all futures are blind.
Vernon Delgado

God's House

There's a little red brick building on the outskirts of the town,
With doors that open oh so wide and a bell that's heard for miles around.

The welcome sign is always waving for those who will come in,
The Landlords are so happy when someone is born again.

God the Father is the Landlord with Jesus his own son,
The Holy Spirit also to see their work is done.

There's a wave of rushing Glory to fill empty souls up to the brim,
With Peace and Love and Gladness that comes from deep within.

The Invitation spreads to all asking all to come and dine,
To share in Love and Kindness and to see how we do shine.

We are one big happy family singing praises to our God,
Singing praises for our blessings as along life's path we trod.

Praises for the morning sunshine for the stars that shine at night,
For the trees and for the flowers and the waters with all their might.

These all may seem quite simple, well, in fact, the may well be,
But, they're all so very important to God's growing family.

The Landlord sends an open invitation to come visit any time, God says,
"Come, and please feel welcome in this little house of mine."
Laura Stairs

"The Hardest Mountain To Climb"

There are many mountains in life to be climbed
With each one comes decisions we must make
Some are high, others low, so we must ask our selves -
Just which mountain should we dare to take.
And there are mountain in life, with a purpose,
Yet we ask, what these reasons may be
If we'd take but a chance, and attempt it -
God is waiting for us, patiently.
And tough the journey may seem, but forever
Only distance can lessen, it's time,
With each step at the least, draws us closer -
To the hardest mountain, to climb.
Nancy Rodriguez

The Band Tree

I love the musical way the wind blows through your leaves,
With every breeze a new measure of its chorus is played.
The waving motion of your limbs conducts this symphony I hear.
Even though the wind blows through the leaves of every tree,
Your singular symphony is unparalleled in its kind.

The experiences you have seen and the memories that you have,
I could not accomplish in two lifetimes.
I can not begin to imagine the vast store of knowledge that you employ
If you could speak, oh, the stories you could tell!
I, like a grandchild, with her grandfather,
Could sit listening, amazed, for hours.

When I am near your gnarled limbs,
I can do anything that is in my heart.
In many ways, you are the shelter from my storms,
Your umbrella-like arms give refuge and protect my soul.
I feel as if you could reach down and lift me from harm.

It is by the symphony you conduct, the memories you possess,
The feeling of refuge you give me, and your blinding glow at sunset
that I am glad I was able to experience you.

Kathleen Boone

The Miracle Of Life

Our dear little one, heaven smiles down on you
With hopes and prayers, of a dream to come true
God has given you, a piece of his heart
The miracle of life, which you are part
He holds your hand, and guides your way
To make you healthy, and stronger each day
He walks by your side, so alone you won't be
To carry your troubles, so you can be free
He caresses your pain, and dries all your tears
To give us all courage, and rid all the fears
In his eyes are warmth, from his heart flows love
The miracles of life, only comes from above
As Mom and Dad, do all that they must
And doctors and specialists, in whom we have trust
But as we all know, and should always see
The miracle of life, only God gives to thee

Vincent James

A Gaze Within

Gazing in I could see someone who wasn't yet free,
with life and love and a bit of me.
While looking and pondering, but never staring,
I caught a glance of someone, who longed for sharing.
The eyes could tell what the rest could not,
there's still life in here, don't give up.
Maybe I'm leaving some things undone,
or perhaps some things that you have just begun.
My eyes may tell you more than I can,
even though I'm leaving early, I'm sure there's a plan.
So while you're gazing and glancing in,
just remember I feel and know just where you've been.

B. Rex Smith Jr.

Untitled

Writing without experience is all the more grand.
Words coming from mind that have yet been exposed
Therefore leaving all of the contamination behind.
Creativity has yet to be filed down by the years,
Freedom of not worrying about any would be peers,
Censorship not yet having had time take hold,
Thoughts previously unspoken are now being told.
Becoming the gift of all those living in this land
It opens the minds that were once tightly closed.
It's more wonderful than any archaeologist's find.

Paul Gunther

This Is Me

This is me
With my clumsy gracefulness; Good intentions and wishful heart.
Suspended in a majestic hand.
This is me,
With weaken strength that eludes me. Wanting to feel nothing,
but again feeling everything. Wearing it as a shield not to
protect but to be a reminder of things left to come.
This is me
Caught between shadow figures of myself in different shades of light.
Not knowing the concept of it all, but forging through
logic that cannot be found and thinking that is to simple or complex.
This is me,
Not bracing for the expected fall.
Chasing clouds like a child full of wonder and magical hope.
Holding up little pieces of my soul so the world can see.
This is me

RoxAnna Rich

The Rose

It starts out as just a little bud.
With nourishment and love it grows.
The bud grows and grows and grows.
And soon that little bud is blossoming.
It blossoms into a full fledged rose.
The rose goes through the beating of rain, and howling of wind.
The hot of day and the cold of the night.
And after all this the rose looks so beautiful
Then as everything does die,
The once beautiful rose starts to lose it's petals.
But you mustn't remember the way it looked as it died.
You must remember the way it shone so bright.

Kimberly Roesler

Moving On

We walked a many miles
with our nonviolent smile
a rainbow color of peoples
to help you with your dreams
Rev. King you really made our team
no way we could lose
with all the stuff you use

We walked with pride and dignity
through all the racism and bigotry
we took all the bumps and bruises
all the hate and evil smiles
but we didn't let that break our stride.

Rev. King, we walked for freedom and liberty
and justice for all
we did this for you, that's why
you didn't let us fall

So people raise your glasses
for one and all.
Rev. King when you went to the mountain top.
We heard your call, free at last, free at last...

Sarah Eason

Berlin Wall: Rest In Pieces

This word,
  written on the land in blood
   with brick and bristling wire,
   spoken by submachine gun,
    read by searchlight and the dishonored sun
was proven false each day
as the life it would have defined
risked death
not to live its lie.

David A. Westover III

Our Love

When we meant for the first time, we were two separate individuals,
With our own spaces and our own needs.
As our love grew stronger everyday
Our space now one, our need to be together.

We pledged our love and our devotion to each other as we were married.
Now as the years have passed,
I have seen our love deepen even more.

Our two sons were gifts to each other
From our love, a gift from heaven.
Everytime that I look into their eyes,
I know that we live and they live because of our love.

Our love for one another is still growing
Stronger everyday, as so are we.
We have grown from children in love,
To adults, in love with our children.

You were my first love, my only love.
Our love Stephen, has made my life complete.
I will be forever devoted and in love with you.
Our love Stephen, nothing could ever compare.
Our love, forever more.

Kathy DeJohn

On The Outside Looking In

Life has empty pages that are waiting patiently,
   with pen in hand we live from day to day.
The story can go on and on or turn around you'll see,
   another page is gone and thrown away.
There are too many people waiting, merely reading the tale,
   dreaming of all that could of been.
There are mountains to be conquered,
   why, there are oceans we could win.
Sometimes it feels we're on the outside,
   on the outside looking in.

Look a little closer you can read between the lines,
   fill the empty pages of your life.
The words can hold a meaning, as our lives can intertwine,
   take the taste of living as you write.
There is so little time to capture, before the chapter is through,
   we're moving along so please begin.
In the end the words we've written,
   will mark the places that we've been.
Sometimes it feels we're on the outside,
   on the outside looking in.

Steve Suski

Converted One

I walked through "hell"
with the Devil behind me
his pronged fork waving in the air.
I nearly fell—in the flames blindly,
scorching my body, singing my hair.

The blast of the flame—
the glare of the light—
I walked and I ran,
nearly dying with fright.
Then, suddenly, I faced the Devil and said,
"Stop, don't touch me, I am already dead.
My soul is in Heaven I just felt it go.
So, I'm not afraid of this Hell here below."

I kept on walking until I saw light
of sunrise breaking into the night.
My body cooled—My soul flowed in—
I felt completely washed—of sin.

Marjorie W. Huden

Timeless Love

I watch him sitting there
  With silver hairs that resigned youth,
  Wrinkles of life's roads that appeared
  Like traveled paths of time with each year
Suddenly, memories of past come to me
It's a young man, I can again see.
  Treasured moments of courtship flood my heart
  Of when we first knew we could never part.

His carefree ways
That excited my days

His special smile for me
Was what I longed to see

His voice deep and tender
Causing my heart to surrender

His touch that made me quiver
Flooding me like a beauteous river

Yet, old memories are the present
When he looks at me
Oh, what love will do
From time it sets us free!

Marilyn Bublitz Berning

"Farewell My Love"

I often gaze into the sky.
With so much pain I could cry.

What made him go back to his old way of life.
Not wanting to provide for his children and wife.

What could be so awful to change him in such a way.
That he would leave for awhile, and just stay, day after day.

Telephone calls from unknowns all through the night.
I had this unhealthy feeling "that something's not right."

We had a talk and he pretended everything was okay.
Until the next time he stayed away.

The house was old and falling apart.
And colder days were beginning to start.

We moved away to another place.
I could see the happiness on our children's face.

The children want so much for their dad to be better.
All he has to do is call them or write them a letter.

Maybe one day his behavior will change for the better.
And he will remember, Lord Jesus his Savior.

Theresa Lynn Thomas

Seasons

He comes to me by chance; warm summer,
with spoiling words and tender touches,
and treats me kind and steals my innocence.
He comes to me, bleak winter,
in the guise of bright spring,
and does his work and leaves.
He comes, but not to me,
with ego high and mighty,
and plays and, too late, sees his err.
He comes to me, repentant fall,
with confidence I've far too often bolstered,
and, as I cry, is turned away.

Kathryn Chandless

My Last Hour

A zest of cold pain shoots through my blood stream
  with the speed of a bullet.
The euphoric sensation of my liquid ecstasy
  wraps me in a world of illusions.

I withdraw the shimmering silver needle
  which has once again
    become a part of my thumping vein.

The sporatic explosions of my heart
  echo throughout my head
The sweat that drains from my body
  is absorbed in the stench of my clothes.

The poison that is injected in my vein
  begins to fester
    like an infected sore.

It spreads through me reaching every inch of me
  striking the deepest fathoms of my corrupt soul.

Here I come to a screeching halt
  the pain is numb and the pleasure is forgotten.
Silent I lie
  with a crown of weeping flowers six feet above me.
LeVar Michael Penn

Lakeway

Sunlight swims across a small lake.
With the wind at its back, sunlight
glistens in a broadening path,
stretching and growing in a gentle wind-swept curve.
With the wind at its face, sunlight
pours into the lake a radiant line
of dancing stars and sparkling lights,
dazzling like a cherub in choir composing spontaneous ballet.
With the wind circling in hard swoops, sunlight dilutes the water,
while neighboring trees of red pine needles,
and silver maple, and quaking aspen leaves
speak of the wind in flowing terms.

In the sky, geese are flying
on another current of wind.
Electrifying into the south,
into the face of the wind,
and the heart of the sun,
trumpeting unrestrained love songs,
these geese inspire in their formation the natural eloquence
of all we cannot understand.
D. V. Arthur

Unattainable Him

He moves on to another,
Yet again it is not me.
At times, flirting is essential to give whispers of my adoration,
But one is eternally in the way to veil his eyes.
He is oblivious to the fact that I can treat him better than others.
Beauty, that is all he perceives,
Not brains and wit.
I fear that all we will ever be is acquaintances.
I hear of the other every time we converse,
Though these moments are few.
Dreams and fantasies stream through my mind,
But will never become reality.
Friend, a word like a blow to the stomach,
Friend, and that is all.
Leia Kathryn Wood

Dreams

What do you dream of?
With your eyes shut tight.

What do you dream of?
In the dark, silent night.

Do you take flight with your dreams and discover new lands?
Do you become a 'baseball man'?

Are you playing in the mud and grass?
Are you running very fast?

Have you made the game-winning play?
Have you pitched a winning save?

Do you see your Mom and Dad?
Cheering you on, from the stands.

Whatever you dream, large or small,
Remember you can be anything at all.

No limits, no boundaries should exist in your dreams,
What is important, is that you believe.

Believe with your heart, believe with your soul,
Believe, Believe, that is your goal!
Melanie K. Graves

Mother's Day

A warm heart is what is needed to be a very special mother
With your guidance I see there will be no other

When things go wrong I call for you
Because I know you know what to do

You're something special that's always near
It's like a humming bird in the air

You embrace me with the love you have
That lead me to that right path

You gave me strength to carry on
Since the day that I was born

You gave me a step on what I need
To believe, achieve and succeed

And now I am grown
And on my own

You did your best to raise me right
And now you see I'm doing alright

So the love you gave was all so true
And I know it's all because of you

I wrote this poem really to say
I see why they have a mothers' day...
Tamaka L. Speller

Lake In The Woods

Lake in the woods, Oh! How beautiful you are!
You twinkle and wave at me every morn.
The things you see are very clear, but with my eyes there is a blur.

Lake in the woods, Oh! How beautiful you are!
What is in the bottom, no body knows.
Are you covering your shame like me?

Lake in the woods, Oh! How beautiful you are!
You are clean and pure on the outside, just as me.
But may I ask are you the same inside and out unlike me?
Michelle Ingles

"Love Is..."

Love is... caring and sharing
with your love one, and sticking with them
through thick and thin.
　It can make you happy or sad,
and if not strong enough have you in doubt,
and wondering when.
　Love is... the answer to
racism and ignorance, for it is the key to
everyone coming together in peace, and in harmony.
　It is something that will set your mind
and your soul at ease, for it gives you a peace
of mind, and it sets you free.
　Love is... the cure to every
sickness around the world, and to helping
the homeless, because there is a need.
　It is also a way of forgiving,
that is you believe, and coming from the
heart, that's what I believe, "Love Is..."

Ronell Johnson

Estranged

Our essence mingles deep inside of you and me.
　Withdraw your essence from me and the void creates a vacuum
　　that swallows up my face.

I seem not to exist except for the sound of my heartbeat
　and the misty veil of my breath on the windowpane as I strain to
　　see but can only feel the pain as I watch you go away from me.

To be near you pleases me in so many ways.
　Stay close to me.
　　Not owning, not controlling every moment,
　　　but continuously and immutably touching.

Our spirits touch and silently we rise above the world
　soaring beyond foolishness and petty expectations.

Our bodies touch bringing comfort that rivals the caress of mothers
　womb imparting joy that soothes the wounds of life's painful mistakes.

Our minds touch and our thoughts, entwined,
　become an effervescent brew that ages to a ripe, heady elixir,
　　perpetuating life like a fountain of youth.

Our hearts touch and we are one,
　the universe encircled by our embrace, infinity our playground.

J. Adele Savage

Letters

AaBbCcDdEeFfGgHhIiJjKkLlMmNnOoPpQqRrSsTtUuVvWwXxYyZz

These are the letters we learn before three
Without them no words, nothing to read

Twenty-six only, not one more, not one less
Enough to communicate, create, and express

Arranged by a lover
confirm feelings that grow
Arranged by a poet
gives rhyme reason and soul
Arranged by a child
tell of puppies they loved
Letter word perfect
mothers to sons
Secret words kept—keep daddy's little girl.

Because of these letters quiet plain and quiet bland
When arranged have brought peace and war to our land

Twenty-six letters odd in shape, line, and curve
One by its own is a definite word

Mighty in strength, for you it would die
It is living, it is breathing, it is you, it is "I"

Timothy P. Kiss

A Journey

A group of 12—it works out evenly: 6 boys and 6 girls
Different ages and different interest, but one goal:
To enrich their spirit and transform their souls...
Some say it was a calling, others say..."because."
No matter what it was, they are sharing themselves.
This is no little trip somewhere in PA; it will be a table tail worth
telling to parents friends, to others far, far away.
to show themselves as a "living sacrifice."
"We are going on a Journey" they say,
They have a bond that is stronger than steel or other mortal; LOVE.
But with feelings of joy from above, one person stands in the lead,
The father of these tours, the man known as GOD—
Who planted seeds with an open heart, and whose
people are drawn like iron to a magnet and are not falling...
A-P-A-R-T.

Laszlo Onody

Those Picky Seagulls

"May we eat lunch down by the river?"
"Yes, but if you're cold, don't stay there and shiver."
The children threw crumbs to a few cruising seagulls.
Down they came in a hurry.
The lady next door said, "My such a worry.
They must be starving! I'll get some bread!"

They came, they came from out of the sky,
But for plain white bread? Huh!
One took a nibble, but only one.
No dice! But then, they weren't shy
When I threw in home-made whole wheat muffins!
(With no preservatives, I might add.)
They ate and ate, their feathers rufflin'.
They certainly weren't afraid nor
Anything! Ding! Wish I had more
Home-made whole wheat muffins!

Lillian M. Cavil

A Families Love

A families love is so complex.
Yet people still try to make it an easy text.
They think that you just have to say I love you.
But, that is not all together true.

A family has to be made and molded.
And pray that the Lord will guide and hold it.
But, of course prayer without works is dead.
At least that is what the Bible said.

You may be wondering what do I know.
Well, I know that you cannot just make a family
and expect it to be like the "Cosby Show".
You have to spend alot of time.
And put in more than just a dime.

Sometimes they may seem to bother you.
But, that is only because the family loves you.
So just remember that there is no greater love.
No greater love than a families love.

Lekita Ruth Smith

Screaming And Screaming

You gave me birth,
   yet you take away my life
crying, naked, ugly
   in a bottomless existence, I die
wound of your womb
   I cannot help that I am
   or that I am me

Twisting me with your wild dog teeth
stabbing me til I'm nothing
laughing, you wring out the last of my blood
   (the blood that was yours)

Why do you destroy what you once were compelled to create?

Please stop
please, please stop
you hurt me so much
you murder me
please stop
   Sarah Speranza

It's Hard Not To...

It's hard not to think of you when
you are always in my mind every second of the hour.

It's hard not to pretend I am yours
every minute of the hour

It's hard not to want you close to me
every second of the hour

It's hard not to need your love
every minute of the hour

It's hard not to want your love
when it's so freely given
every second of the hour.

It's hard not to love you
For your gentleness and kindness
every minute of the hour

It's hard not to love you more
for your patience understanding
every second of the hour.

It's hard to give up the friendship to become lovers, yet...
but, maybe we'll never have to because it will always be there
stronger, every second and minutes of the hour.
   Migdalia Deleon

Untitled

You long for a perfection which rarely comes
You are discontent with the simple things in life
(Your heart doesn't start at the howl of a dog
Nor clench at the sound of a child crying)
I whisper in your ear sweet nothings of longing
You shrug with irritation; my warm breath tickles your ear
Sadness flows like a sluggish stream
And the dreams go where no one can come from
I wished for a lover once upon a time
But you were like a chameleon
Once I had rested secured
Then you twisted my love and regard
Like a smothering blanket you called it
And threw it quickly off
My soft voice can't be heard over your shouts to be gone
Like rain trickling down moss-covered trees
My loss is hard to bear
Will I find another like you?
I hope and yet hope not
What if I find you are all I can bear.
   Kellie D. Gore

Pure White Rose

As you turn sixteen on this special day
   you are like a perfect white rose,
Fragile and small like a beautiful bud
   as pure and as white as one knows.

A rose bud if handled will crush and bruise
   the petals will look brown and torn,
Pulled from the stem before it has blossomed
   the flower's beauty we must mourn.

A pure white flower you promise to be
   if you guard the beauty within,
The time will come for the flower to bloom
   you'll know when it's time to begin.

Somewhere a mother prepares her fine son
   to have a good heart that is pure,
A worthy young man who will guard your love
   this love will be precious for sure.

Protect the rose bud and for that coming day
   when the pure young man you will meet,
For eternity you will always be
   his pure rose he'll forever greet.
   Lona Johnson

You Are

You are the Candle
You are the Flame
You are the mirror
That reflects the flame from the candle,
That shines around me.

You are who you are
No one can be YOU, but you
We have the heart
That beats as one,
When we're together, you are my sister

You are the sky, you are the star
You're the moon, you are my LOVE
You are everything, and MORE; YOU ARE MY BLOOD

You are unforgettable,
And that's the way you are in my heart.
Time could never change my love; FOR WE ARE FAMILY.

You are my SISTER
You are my BLOOD
WE are FAMILY
I give thanks to GOD for having YOU in my life.
   O'Neal Sim Cauley

True Love

I see your agony, my soul knows your pain
You cannot shed a tear and I don't weep an ocean
I want to be with you
I know I could end your famine of unhappiness
It is within my power, I could be your banquet
I love you - I love you - I love you
It is because I love you that I hurt you
I know something you do not
I know I am not for you
You will find one better than I and she will be your bliss
I wish for that time
You cannot fathom my love
You love me too much to be Without me,
but I love you too much to be
With you.
I will let you suffer
I will suffer your pain twice over
I will endure for us both
One day we will be happy - we will be happy apart.
   Kristy Hoch

Oh, The Beauty Of You!

As a babe in my arms
You captured by heart with your many charms.
In your ruffled hats you looked so fine
Oh! How thrilled I was, that you were mine.
"Your beauty," So sublime
Oh! The mere present of you, "So Divine."
Your eyes twinkle, like the heavenly stars so bright.

Having you for a daughter makes everything just right.
Your "Beauty," is both inside and out.
A very precious daughter is what you are all about.
Even though we are now separated, in our hearts, we will never apart.
For your "love," has captured my heart.
Oh the beauty of you so fair.
Not even the splendor of the heaven can even compare.
Mary Ellen Lamie

How To Have Fun

How you could have fun?
You could lay under the sun.

You could play ball or dress up a doll.
You know it really doesn't much matter at all.

Some people play a video game.
I never thought of that as being lame.

How about a vacation at the beach?
There's alot more I can teach.

You might go rollerskate;
That'll increase your heart rate.

You don't always have to lay,
So use your imagination and go play.
William Shaffer

This I Do In Honour Of You

What you gave to me was more than the eye could see,
You gave love to a heart that was broken and in despair.
You gave hope to a person who just didn't care.

You gave my mind new thoughts to think,
You lifted me up when I was beginning to sink.
You gave me your Spirit and with it I am very very blessed,
You gave me joy and peace, love and happiness.

You gave to me long before I ever walked this earth,
A long, long time ago, you gave your life so I could have new birth.
You've given me so much my Lord I wonder if I could ever repay,
All the love you still give to me each and every day.

For this I do, in honor to you, thank you so very, very much.
It was a wonderful feeling when my heart You did touch.
And I know your love is with me even when I'm alone,
Because that's when I pray and wait for the day You come to take me home.
LaDon Coile

You

I drown in you; yet I breathe.
You surround me like liquid lava; yet I do not burn.
You send out thoughts that engulf my entirely; yet I do not smother.
You are there when I need you; yet you are not near.
Your voice is like a summer shower; yet I do not get wet.
Your hands are like velvet; yet I feel their strength.
Your lips demand; yet my not body.
Your chains, they bind me; yet I am free.
You hold the key; yet it does not lock.
Who are you? you are me; I am you; we are one!
Toni Pietrangelo-Jordan

Lovable Puppy

To Dan and Heidi, both so dear
You got a puppy, so we hear
Golden lab, girl or boy
Sure to bring you lots of joy.
But on your floor a mess it makes
You'll frown and scold and finger shake
Send it out upon the grass
While soon your anger it will pass
When the training it is done.
Call it nice and it will come
Praise it well, it's been fun,
Now you have "a tail wagging son of a gun."
So if you find these words are true
I made them up just for you
Now this verse I will end
Lots of love, Pauline and Ken
Kenneth Tremelling

"Dear Lorenzo"

I wish you were here because you take away my fear.
You help me go the right way, so I wouldn't be like you one day.
I'm trying my best, and GOD has put me to his many test.
I failed them all.
I'm gonna hold my head up tall, and break the devil's wall.
Bangin' and slangin' will end my life.
I wonna grow old enough to become someone's wife.
You only live once.
Don't be a dunce.
Take the devil as your Savior, and you will be with harm at once.
Take GOD as your Savior, and you will be at peace at once.
So, when you're going to hell, I know you're gonna say,
"I should have lived my life the RIGHT way, Mrs. LYKE's way, GOD's WAY!!!"
Tasneem Taneshia Nance

A Mother's Love

It seems like only yesterday I was holding you in my arms
And now you're all grown up and not the baby anymore
I sit and reminisce about the times when you were young
I couldn't wait for you to take your very first step
And now I wish that you were my little girl again

The day you took your vows and looked beyond into the future
I know then that you were a woman and ready to make your own decisions
You didn't need me anymore to guide you in this world
I had to let you go and realize the time had come
To let that little girl that I once held take the
final path life has lead.
Synell Simmons

In That Little, Tiny Place

In that little, tiny place where
You keep all your hopes and fears
In that little, tiny place where
You keep all your smiles and tears

Where you keep all your memorable memories
And all those little white lies
And that little place in your memory
From when you laughed to when you cried

In that little tiny place where all your secrets stay
And you seem to go there when your mind goes astray

This little, tiny place
Is not a body part
It's that little, tiny place
Way deep down inside your heart!
Norine Mulry

Dearest Rachel

When she made my life cold and dark,
You made everything all right.
When my body could not find rest,
You gave sleep back into my night.

When my heart had fallen to the ground,
You lifted me up and out of the dirt.
Talking to you was the greatest
When my world was one of hurt.

Feels like a dream when my eyes catch yours,
Wish it would never end and you would never go.
These conversations mean so much to me,
More than you could ever know.

If only I could turn back the time,
Rather than looking ahead.
I would forget all about her,
And fall for you instead.

Thank you Rachel.
> *Shawn T. Ring*

Climb Aboard

If you want to get aboard
You must Praise the Lord
If you want to improve your days
You must kneel and Pray
If you want to get aboard, you must be true
You must treat others, as you would want them to treat you
For whatever road you choose
The Lord will follow, win or lose
If you want to get aboard
You must always trust in the Lord
The Lord has mercy on those that are not true
But do not be one who is not true
Whisper to yourself, Climb Aboard
Trust in the Lord
And Climb Aboard
> *J. Kent Kellum*

The Road Of Life

The sun has risen, your life has started.
You must take the path you were meant for
And follow it throughout your life
Like a river follows its path
And a horse follows its own.
But you must find your own trail.
No footsteps will guide you, only your own.
Don't desert them and turn back during hard times.
Keep on going, like time does.
Don't waste your life by looking what is behind you.
Always look at what is to come in front of you.
And remember, while others stop to rest,
You go on.
And you, only you, have reached the end of the road.
Finally, your life must end.
You reached your goal, your summit.
The sun will set for you.
But for someone else,
It will just began.
> *Neeta Lal*

The Joy Of My Days

If you want to know what is feminine perfectness,
you need only look to Tabetha Kirksey, in all her flawlessness.
She is on Earth only by divine intervention,
an she brings out all my romantic intentions.
My personal goddess of beauty is short with Wonderful blonde hair,
and a moment she isn't on my mind is waste beyond rare.
Tabetha owns Green eyes, a small exist and big lips,
short fingers, a deep value of education, and perfect hips.
Her red lipsticks, blonde hair, green eyes, and blue eyeliner
reminds me of and endless field of trees in fall,
In her presence, everything else declines,
and nothing else matters, nothing at all.
I love the way she walks by, like an innocent breath of spring,
and I hope she likes her new diamond ring
I always get lost in her eyes and the endless sea of green,
and I look forward to everyday I can call her my queen,
> *Morgan Ackerman*

Just A Stroke

Has there been a time when you felt really down?
You tried to force a smile, but could only frown.
People tell you to just keep your chin held high,
That doesn't work, and you let go a sad sigh.
The bible says that, "this too shall pass,"
Trying to go, you give your living car more gas.
That didn't work, you haven't moved anywhere,
Feeling God deserted you, gives you a scare.
All of a sudden, from deep down inside,
Comes an emotional feeling you just can't hide.
Your heart flutters as tingles dance up and down your spine,
All of the dreary gloom now starts to glitter and shine.
Feeling much better with each breath you now take,
Your total astonishment you just can't fake.
Your lost as to what just took place,
Going from that very sad, to a happy face.
What just happened, how did it start?
My friend, "The Great Spirit" just stroked your heart!
> *Keith B. Cahall*

Good-Bye

I started to fly
You want me to stay
I tried to relax, now you want me to play

I went after my dreams
And you made me come back
I'm trying to live my life
Won't you cut me some slack!

I opened the door, you shut it behind me
I try to remember on my own
But yet you remind me

I've chosen my own environment
You say "that's not enough"
I'll make my own decisions
Shoot..... I'm growing up!

I try to be me, you say " who are your really?"
When I attempt to respond
You say, "aw don't be silly"

You push me and pull me
But what are you really achieving?
Think as long as you like.... cause Mommie, I'm leaving!
> *Kenya L. Jackson*

Beware!

If your happiness, is because of others sorrow.
You'll get yours, I not today, tomorrow.
If in calamity you rejoice.

And to cause others grief, is your just choice,
You, can never do any good.
Because, your heart is made of wood.

In just one moment, you will find,
Your whole life, you have been blind
too, late will come you change of heart
when, your ready too depart.
   Richard A. Granholm

"Only A Sound"

As you travel around the bend,
You'll soon hear the sound it will send.

It calls you by Soul, Name, and Spirit.
You must follow, for only you can hear it,

It's cold and dark, it's warm and bright;
As the moon rises into the night.

You become scared, weak, and alone;
Until the call loses its spiritual moan.

You're trapped in a box that nobody sees,
Your body becomes tense then shivers with glee.

For in that box you have found,
A secret so deep...
It's only a sound.
   Mandy Cherie Brown

Take Me Back To The Good Old Days

Can you remember way back when
Your date was over at half-past ten
And you thought your life would be complete
If you could ride in a rumble seat?

Entertainment was very ingenious at times
When charades were played or maybe mimes,
And oh, remember all those kissing games
When the boys selected only the prettiest dames?

Barn dances were popular all around
And many a fiddler could be found.
You walked to school whether a mile or more
And never considered it much of a chore.

Sundays were observed as a day of rest
When folks went to church in their very best.
Oh, to go back to those good old days
To live once more with out simple ways.
   Virginia W. Farr

Forever Friends

Through all the tears, throughout the years,
You've stood right by my side.
Through all the fights, and sleepless nights,
You were there when I cried.
When I was depressed, only you could have guessed,
What it was I needed to hear.
And when I couldn't explain, how I felt all this pain,
You made confusion seem so clear.
We both may change, our lives rearrange,
But this loving will never end.
So through the hard times, look back on these rhymes,
For we will always be forever friends.
   Michelle Hall

The Daisy

The morning air finds you fresh with dew,
Your full face turned upward toward pale skies.
You stand tall and proud in your garden plot
With arms stretched wide to catch the golden rays.

The noon day sun sends her beams of love
To warm your lively heart of green.
Always growing, always reaching out,
You meet them with overpowering joy.

Light afternoon showers come unexpectedly,
Quenching your everlasting thirst
While your head bobs on its slim neck,
Nodding a greeting to the pelting rain.

The evening light finds you still.
As you fold your long white lashes
The fading sun sinks below the horizon,
And you await the coming of another dawn.
   Sandra Manger

Jessica

Little girl so far away
Your Grandmother has some things to say
How very much I'd like to hold you
And to gaze upon this life so new.
I'll not be there when you learn to walk,
Nor hear your first words when you learn to talk.
But there will be vacations when
We'll see each other now and then.
Until we've time for hugs and kisses
I'm sending you all my best wishes.

Little one so very new
with hair of brown and eyes of blue
You've come at a time of wars and strife
It seems no place for such a precious life.
But the hope of the world and of our nation
always lies within each new generation.
If I could fill for you one wish
and I have thought a lot on this
Fame? Riches? No not these
I'd wish for you a world of peace.
   Lee Ann Cronk

Mother

You're always there when I need a friend,
You've always been someone whom upon I can depend.
When I need a shoulder to lean on, you lend me yours,
All the things I've been through, you've seen it all before.
I don't have to say when something's wrong,
Somehow you can always see.
When I can't find my way through,
You're there with me.
You don't tell me what I should do,
You tell me to think all my feelings through.
Your love is timeless,
Its always given freely,
So I want to thank you
If there was one thing I wanted to be,
When I got older,
I was to be like you, Mother.
   Veronica Susan Miles

I Am A Song

Remember when you were so sad?
Your hands pressed against your eyes; so locked in pain you could not
even move, nor scarcely breathe,
                lest you shatter...
Nothing would be left of you...
                except fragments of sorrow.
But I invaded your grief.
      I swept through your mind, burning all resistance.
I wrung your heart until your fists unclenched,
and the dammed up tears ran freely down your face.
          I am a song.

How beautifully balmy is this particular night.
A coveted lover's dream...unearthly.
The magic of inloveness surrounds you easily;
It becomes you as cloud-glory becomes the setting sun.
One look at your beloved...
         and all that you are falls away.
He is the first created, and you the first woman;
         Love is new.
I will enter your world... softly in the beginning;
With unutterable, tenderness...drawing, binding, exalting,
severing you from this present world.
         I am a song.

Days and nights, weeks and months converge;
It is Autumn time and still the aged sun warms you.
Seasons of love and joy, of sorrow and frustration
and always of hope form a circle around you.
They are like family;
        First one visits you, then another;
Each in their inescapable turn.
They cannot be denied.
But while men live and know life,
        from its depths and heights
      I am a song.

Stephenie C. Monear

Feelings Of Love

My love, I give a rose to you
Your heart beats constant, strong and true
You never waver, but steady the course
The feelings of love, what a powerful force.

You put aside your worry and fear
To chase my rain, make rainbows appear
How long you have loved me, I do not know
What matters now, is you've told me so.

Two hearts entwined, from now till the end
Two minds so strong, but willing to bend
Sometimes the shadows may make us fall
But the feelings of love, are worth it all.

I remember the day, remember it still
You said, I love you, and always will
From Cupid's quiver, the arrow flew
It's aim was straight, for I fell too.

The power of love, binds two as one
The light of love, is like the sun
With bonds so strong, nothing can sever
The feelings of love, now and forever.

Millie Bonvillian

"And For Mine"

By the stroke of a pen, I can write of your love.
Your longing so gently caresses my heart.
A memory of the past flashes in my soul.
Every lonely night is spent Dreaming of you.
My fantasies are filled with Dreams of the future.
In my actions I can't refrain from loving you.
Your love is the only gift you can give to me.
When will we wed, in the Cathedral of Love
and hear the Angel Choirs singing?
How graciously God doth send his fiery love to fuse our hearts.
Indeed, we are a match made in Heaven.
Oh, how I do need you, starvation reeks in my spirit.
Our love flies higher and higher in the quiet wind
as it soars through a raging waterfall.
In every solitary action, our love is present.
Many emotions come and many go, our love yet remains.
Do you want to love me more and more?
Our love has taken much time to create.
Until our love is perfectly united together
our hearts will cry out in pain to one another.

Shannon R. Chadwell

Angel In My Window

Somewhere my little angel in the corners of my heart
Your memory is so incomplete it lays on life in parts
I've often wondered how your face would look
While your were fast asleep
Would your tiny body wear baby blue
Or adorn the softest pink
I remember when I touched myself and felt your little form
Growing there inside of me, waiting to be born
Then that fragile moment came but you would not survive
I would have gladly given my life for yours,
Just to hear you cry.

Somewhere my little angel where my heart has not grown cold
Your sitting in a window box barely four years old
Five little fingers are spread atop the window glass
With your baby lamb beside you held firmly in your grasp
Your favorite little Easter hat attached to the bedroom wall
The ribbons flowing softly, your most favorite part of all

Somewhere my little angel, the Lord now holds your hand
I'll never stop touching the window...I doubt I ever can

Valinda Ross

Earth

Oh Mother Earth, how do you fare?
Your once cozy bosom now burns with harsh chemicals.
Your massive arms alone outstretched can no longer
Protect us— for you have been wounded.
The molestation that man has done to you;
You have been robbed of your health and beauty and
left with low esteem and pain.
The abuse you have taken; the scars that are left behind—
How do you still function?
How long will you suppress your fear and
restrain your inner power?
Your tears of pain are acidic and
your streams, once full of life, contaminated.
Your fruitage is tainted, sometimes lethal—
a cause and effect maybe, but not by choice.
How much longer will this go on?
How much more can you take?
Will you retaliate or will you suffer the
consequences for the rest of your existence
—as many of the abused do?

Melissa A. Harnish

Billy

Your sweet angelic voice saturates my dreams,
Your songs speak to me.
Each word tells me how you feel.
Emotions unveiled,
Open my imagination,
Send me on a surrealistic journey,
I never want to return.
I'll stay here forever,
Existing in visionary deceit,
Only wishing to be restored by your cry.
Then I will know,
You are enchanted by me as well.
   Michele Mielko

Beloved

Your arms reach out and hold me in a warm embrace
Your touch a gentle caress
I feel safe, secure . . . nourished
But today I felt sadness steal into my soul
As I watched them come for you
Tattered, forlorn you stood valiantly against them
But you were no match
And even though you have no legs,
Your limbs groaned with the onslaught
Today they cut you down
In the prime of life
And like your name
I shall weep forever
Dear friend
Companion
Willow tree.
   Vicki Holden

Cindy

Your caring and honesty shines like the sun
Your words rings strong and true
Your heart is full of love and is open to the world
Your laughter is like a country breeze
The breeze that you can enjoy year round
You are like a childhood friend that you want to grow old with

You are open body and mind to people
You care with so much trust, that know one could be untrue to you
You are like an angel, that was sent to this earth to give joy to people
To me all this makes up Cindy in my eyes
   Robin E. Weaver

Pay Day

Pay day - life would be dull without you
You're so dear - you bring cheer
You are my sky of blue
Pay day - wife and kids adore you
Every day - every way - you help me see them thru-
These tired hands must work for me
They can never be free
I drive them on-eight hours a day
Gotta earn my pay
Pay day - must work my whole life for you
All my shimmers - all my dreams
Live long as I have you
   Ralph Montello

Success

A prosperous course of anything attempted; my webster defines success.
To me it cannot be defined, for it's life and nothing less.

Success at the age of four, were small things it is true,
But pride within me swelled my heart, when I learned to tie my shoe.

I started school with many goals, learning to read and write.
I found success in doing my best, and a teachers smile so bright.

At sixteen all things must be right, each achievement important it seems.
We strive to be just like our peers, to earn an A, or make the team.

When I thought I'd reached the top, with a high school diploma for me.
I found there were new successes to form in landing a job, or college degree.

Now as the years have long gone by, it's plain for me to see,
That in the end my true success will be measured by others, not me.
   Lori Kasner

The Wall

I carelessly shake my head as I think of the task ahead, my fears wrapped in ambiguity, my sorrows glued with worries, with only that 'cellophane tape' holding me in place. Feeling suffocated, I lean against a bare brick wall and simply see life's bareness in it. My fingers try to cling to every little groove it finds, as I feel gravity pulling me through the unmoving floor... But only time seemed to be slipping. I slowly open my eyes in disbelief and press the floor with my feet, to make sure that it was bearing my weight. I look longingly at the wall, and run my index finger along that labyrinth of cracks- hesitating to leave the wall and move on to face life. My rust colored finger and nail, still idly trying to find the 'dead end'. I hear the gongs but pay no attention - simply too involved in that childish pastime. Suddenly my finger stops, and my eyes start to notice each imperfection. I wonder as to how that wall with those infinite number of cracks, was still standing- weathering the vagaries of this world, and still supporting the ceiling above, the wall above that ceiling, the ceiling above the wall..... An enigmatic smile fringes my every organ, and my muscles start becoming taut; my one hand reaches out for my haversack, the other for my boots and my senses start humming the tune of "I shall overcome."
   Sachin D. Sheth

"Alliance Of The Formerly Mentally Ill"

When you are no more; God forbid, where will I go to spend my glory?
Who will I see that will remember all that was?
We are the last; all that's left of those who, summoned the antagonist
   and held them dear
That camaraderie we owned is unattainable in friendships formed of real
Where will I send my broken attitudes for fragile patches from one
whose expertise is improvising remembering how to dance around the
land-mines of propriety with laughter in her league
Who will defend the substance that was and still is me—somewhere
We know the worth of distance when it fills those awful spaces
We know the weight of silence when it's pressed against the enemy
   at hand or how to care for those the city harbors and yet rejects
Those who can't allow the touch of caring — they understand
   that daggers line the fabric of concern
Who else is a survivor of that war to prove her fortitude
Where will I go to gather meaning with giant hands
Stay my friend
You need this bond of bravery and wild truth as much as I
   Rena Applebaum

Oldman

The old man sat by the road watching cars go by. He thought of his
yesterdays with a quieter life.

He thought of his children bouncing on his knee, the aroma of fresh
baked bread drifting through the front door screen.

Years came and went. His youth went speeding past. He dreamed of
yesterday and what he might have had.

As he sat on his suitcase hoping for a ride. Loneliness came over
him. Tears filled his weary eyes.

A white car stopped on the shoulder. The passenger door opened wide.
He stood up getting his suitcase being thankful for this ride.

A man got out of the driver's side with long brown hair and white
flowing robe. "Come with me my son. I have come to take you home."

The old man stood where he was setting his suitcase upon the ground.
"I cannot leave this world until my family I have found."

The driver of the car had a smile upon his face. "Your family waits
for you in a most glorious place.

You see my son they have been waiting for you quite a while.
They perished the same night you left looking for your wilder life."

The old man hung his head in shame, tears were flowing down his face.
He had pain deep in his heart for the pain his family had faced.

"Please do not be sad my son. Your family still loves you so.
You paid often for your decision now let me take you home."

Peace came over the old mans face. His eyes started to shine.
His journey now was ending. He now had his family and peace down deep inside.

Karen Sue Scharmen

Grandpa's Dream

Deep in the green, grass-covered valley, where river waters roar, and wild animals roam,
Below a rugged terrain, very steep and high purple mountain range, I call my home,
I stand in awe, of all, the surrounding beauty encompassing me.

On the mountain side high up, where frigid air and cold temperatures rule, forbidding
trees to grow, a boundary, naturally formed by the timber line,
separates a beautiful white, snow-capped peak
With ice covered cliffs, from the purple mountain range below.

The late afternoon sun lazily orbiting west, reflects brilliantly, off
   the pearly white snow-capped peak,
Mirroring beams of sunlight high into the heavens, while in the grassy
green valley below, night shadows appear, and wild animals restlessly
   pace along the river's edge, as if dreading
The ending of the day, while also anticipating the dangers of night.

Now, as the day gives way to the night, and a beautiful dark
   star-studded sky, forms a canopy over the high mountains, and deep
valleys below, I close my log cabin door, pull down the shades,
Turn out the lantern, give thanks for the day, and continue to dream,
   until another morning dawns.

Robert L. Yeager

Stand Together

In all my 20 years I have shut away the pain,
of this world around me the drugs, the guilt the shame.
Is there any mercy for these children carrying guns,
listen to my warnings it could be your own son.
One person can make a difference with prayer, strength
and hope, stand together to make the difference
and get rid of the crack and dope.
These are our children crying out in pain,
step out of the shadows before more of our children are slain.

Amy Rogers

Destiny Blue

The blue flower is standing in
the orange swirl vase -
not a care in the world -
not a petal out of place -

I wonder if I could hide
inside this blue flower -
maybe for a moment or
perhaps just an hour -

Who knows, the blue flower
just might be looking back at me -
ponderin' its future inside
the likes of me -

Ann Stegenga

Mood Manhattan

Not for us
   the stridence of Village guitarist
     singing songs, contrived,
   of love and despair.

Not for us
   the young eccentrics
   sprawled on Macdougall Street,
   flaunting false wisdom
     and sadness unearned.

For us
   the pregnant sound of silence,
   the erratic rhythm of stumbling words,
   remnants of doubt and anguish
    and yearning
   torn out
    and offered
   with childlike trust.

Felix Laumann

Sadness

It drowns me at night,
   before my weary eyes sleep
It howls down inside,
   the pain so very deep
It rips me to shreds,
   then calls me to tears
It beats against my body
   and caresses my fears
For every drop of rain that falls,
   a piece of me shall fall along
hitting the ground and whispering to me
   in endless tortured song
Then my tattered bones can fight no longer
   my muscles grow weak, instead of stronger.
My heart becomes tired and it's beat grows faint
   then I die, leaving nothing but
    the pain
      the words
        and the hate.

Zachary Zilba

Untitled

My eyes are drilling
My nose is bleeding
My feet are soaring
My arms are hurting
My nails are breaking
Can't you see, I'm panicking

Maxine Tam

Untitled

A memory of a memory
Is a memory lone gone,
Far too long to remember
What was wrong,
But now it's gone
No need to try and
Remember the time
That was young,
That's why a memory
Of a memory is not
A memory for long.

Danreco Tucker

A Distant Cry

An infant child is crying near, it cries from loneliness and fear.
If you can't hear it must not be, but it is real for few like me.
What this means is most don't care, nor does its mother standing there.
The love for life she does not know, for as a child she did not grow.
She to was treated much the same, a loveless life of endless pain.

The distant cry is far away, it grows more louder every day.
Abort its life before it's free, or live on Earth in Hell like me.
Suffer child, you'll suffer long, the right you do is also wrong.
No one care for who you are, so ruin your life and run afar.

The crying child it has no name, fatherless and feels ashamed.
It guides itself most on its own, the streets you see is place call home.
Full of rage and no control, inflicted pain has taken toll.
Failed at home and in the school, to seek the church it feels a fool.
Fights, drugs, sex, the gun, appears the streets already won.
A child whose life was born in violence, now begins its final silence.

Why? For what? Can they not see, another child in misery.
Worship, pray with no intent, is this why the Lord was sent?
Save the children, save them all, if we do not then we should fall.
It's very sad a child should die, because we can't hear a distant cry!

Eric Charles Green

Homesick

Imagine yourself in a far away land,
  Surrounded by mountains on all sides,
A place you would like to call your home,
  And you would express it with all your pride.

The lakes are so clear, the bottom can be seem,
  On a nice bright sunshiny day.
At the same time the air is so clean and fresh,
  That it takes your breath away.

Church bells can be heard, both far and near,
  In large cities as well as small towns.
Whether it be day time or late at night,
  They are heard on every hour.

The people there are never in a rush,
  Instead, they are the kindest of all the lands.
This place sounds like legendary Shangri-La,
  But it's not, it is Switzerland.

David Owen

Respect

  Green is life peace forever needed by all species,
to bring harmony to the great lands and seas of earth

  Greenpeace is a beautiful name to those that try and keep
the harmony between man and nature

  The mighty gentle giants of the deep, are still with us yet,
but ours to care for and embellish with the hope we never again
shall see the harpoon,
  The cry of pain and the spurt of blood, that hurts all mankind
For here is another intelligent species, never to return

Lawrence Wells

It's Lonely At The Top

As I have traveled the lonely road to success
You have thrown rocks and mud to slow down my progress
Just like a crab when one is nearing the top
You tug and pull and will not stop

But if I move into the ghetto and hang out on the street
I will then be alright cause you will feel no defeat
If I partake in gossip and drop out of school
I guess at that point I would be considered cool

I refuse to stoop to your level just to be accepted
I have a friend in Jesus therefore I am protected
You can talk about me just as much as you please
And I'll talk about you down on my knees

And just for the record they also talked about Jesus Christ
Although for us He paid the ultimate price
But He just let them betray and talk and carry on
For He also knew that he had caused no one any harm

Shannon Williams

Lost Light

While sitting alone in the park, Martha realized that at sixty-five
she had spent more years there than she wished to count.
As she watched the children at play,
she readily recalled the many hours of laughter and tears,
but more than that,
she especially remembered the spiritual innocence of the children.
This wonderful gift that was reflected in a glow of light
which seemed to shine from the eyes of the children.
It was this beam of light that made her feel all warm inside.
It was this glow that implied that all was well in the world.

Now, as she looked at the children, she felt weighted down with an
unknown fear that was saddening and disturbing.
"What is this?", she asked herself as she began to search the
faces of the children, one after another.
Then suddenly, as if she had been struck by lightning, she knew.
It was there in the faces...all the little faces.
The spiritual innocence was gone.
There was no longer a beam, there was no longer a glow.
The eyes of the children had lost their light.

Carol Huggins Warren

The Scent Of Springtime

From down in her whirlpool soul twist lonesome daydreams:
"That cruel vulture wrapping his arms around my heart!
Then, walking away letting the blood drip dry.
One more line on an aging face, another taste of bitter flowers,
Another journey for fool's gold.
He even came with the scent of springtime
But my teardrop leaves have turned brown...
No more fingers will tickle this bellybutton;
No jokes will be shared between the flicker of candlelight.
I have placed a broken flute from the closet in my gut.
Am I just a cylinder of lipstick beneath the chair where he sat
Staring into my twinkling eyes...?
Only in dreams does the prince get to the princess,
Only in storybooks where we smile at lies!
Love is life's fuse between age and illusion.
A song that rings your bell, a motto to live by...
Unknowing as a child...
Unknowing as a child..."

Bartholomew Villa-McDowell

To Maria

Your mysterious and perplexed eyes,
That seem to wander every way
With a sardonic smile, disguise
their river of deep hate.
The explosive reactions that take
Place behind those irises appear on the surface
As nirvana; but if a scope could examine below
the hideous undercurrent, it would discover
Pompeii, frozen and refusing to wake.
Awake the dead world! Cease to refuse the light!
Shake off those well-protected ashes
that are deceiving you. They do not cover
Dead bones suspended in time. Instead, they
Conceal plumage of a golden Phoenix, yet to fly.

Eleni Vickles

The Question, What If?

A book full of pictures
Is not all I have left.
There is the anger, the hurt,
The question, WHAT IF?

What if,
I had been nicer,
more loving,
or proud?
What IF,
I had been there
for crying out loud?

Did you know
you would hurt us?
Did you plan
to go?
Again these are questions
The answers, I will
never know...

JanMarie Tregellas

November

Remove the shroud, let the show begin!
Skin taught to stretch tight over the bones
Creating a circus tent.
Inside are the atrocities, side show freaks,
All of yesterday's clowns.
Red trickle artists, tumbling from high wire lips
All speaking mindlessly
of the bruises which
cover like misinformed observers
And all reeks of tainted innocence
the scent lingers, masking the
bloom of madness
An infection is here among the poppies,
among caged beasts, a competitor of reason.
Two orbs in the mass crowd, wide and grey
scream at the attractions wordlessly,
plead desperately for the ring master
to once again, for pity,
cover the mirror, replace the shroud.

Jessica Tilley

Native Justice

We came as followers to this Great Spirits Lands.
Only the earths gifts we made from our hands.
We taketh an given for every last day.
The Great Creator taught us as visions we pray.
The Eagle will guide us on this Mother Earth.
For vast herds of Buffalo shall give us great birth.
We have all this given the wind, stars and trees.
Each season passes just watch fallen leaves.
We honor our elders, we smoke sage for past.
But this moment a vision for war came up fast.
It look many warriors, it broke many hearts,
it took many children and families apart.
Yet, the Creator let us live another day.
Too, be put on separate lands and all sent away.
It took away Great Spirits.
But yet out of heart,
we've given a Nation for just one part.

Stephen Alexander Taylor

I Am

In the cosmic thought of love, I stand before thee
Naked, ready to be clothed by lights, color and love,

Expand myself in to matter,
I forget who I am.
Yonder years I search to find myself again,
Multiplied, centuries of new faces I do not recognize.

Then One day a spark appears
I recognize my face,
Its yours in mine and mine in yours,
and yet we have our own space.

Millions of faces searching new places,
looking for the face in mine,
Take the time and you will find
that mine is thine and thine is mine
To bring in the joy and laughter.

Linda Summers

A Father's Lament

Who will tell her
How can she understand
Why Mom and Dad
Don't walk hand in hand

Will she turn away
When I try and explain
That staying together
Caused hatred and pain

Will she know that I love her
Even though I'm not there
Does she know how I miss her
Will she know that I care

If she comes to me crying
With tears in her eyes
Will I have the answers
For all of her whys

Edward T. Sullivan

Walk With Me

Walk with me my Darling...
   Take my hands, and hold on tight.
The ride before us will be hard and long.
   Hold on tight,
     for we need to be strong.

Our lives together have shared a beginning,
   and now is the time to share an end.
Walk with me my Darling...
   Take my hands, and hold on tight.

Don't fight the feelings of light
   that binds us.
Our souls will take care of our
   hearts insights.
Walk with me my Darling...
   Take my hands and hold on tight.

The ride before us will be hard and long,
   Hold on tight,
     for we need to be strong...
       Michelle Stevans

Dear Sister:

I thank you for the things you say
That really help to make my day.
I thank you for the things you do
That help me cope and see me through.
I've never had to beg or plead
To have you help when I'm in need.
I often think of childhood days,
Your caring, kind and sisterly ways.
Remember how you'd read at night,
Grimm's Fairy Tales, to my delight.
And there before our oil lamp light
You'd make the world around me bright.
With all my faults and irksome ways,
My idiosyncrasies and questionable phase,
You've always kept in touch and shared.
I've never doubted that you cared.
Deep in my heart I hold to me
The dearest thoughts of family.
Thank you for memories of days long past
Those lovely memories that last and last.
       Sylvia Seabon

$12.78

Just $12.78 to mare a city and bring on pity.
Just $12.78 to scorn a nation.
Just $12.78 to end celebration.
Just $12.78 yet not to confiscate Camelot.

Just $12.78 for destiny can't spare.
Just $12.78 though fate seems so unfair.
Just $12.78 and the shouts ring out then time stands still for about..
Just $12.78 cause a break to bliss oh blessedness.

Just $12.78 to destroy avocation and evoke condemnation.
Just $12.78 a treasonable combination?
Just $12.78 confirms humanity's brute.
Just $12.78 so conclude constitute a tragic substitute.

Just $12.78 to complete a task so a being must pass.
Just $12.78 examine the past.
Just $12.78 how long this must last.
Just $12.78 not a coup however still wonder who.

Just $12.78 once more mourn and texture torn.
Just $12.78 why not broke.
Just $12.78 moreover inevitability spoke.
Just $12.78 a spouse's pillow preludes a courageous widow.
       Carl R. Singleton

No End...

A house with too many open windows.
New, old, and noisy breezes recirculating through.

Is it a moan from behind or next to my head?
Then a repulsive scream, clicking, and feet tapping, is there no end?
Hearing is too easy... Exhausted, I am nearly driven from my seat.

Like a candle burning at both ends, incomplete thoughts, frustration...
Unfinished business, frustration, misunderstandings,
more frustration...

Tomorrow might differ though, things seem to change
daily, — less commotion. — Although, IT will always
return some other time, place, or even in a different seat...

Feeling overwhelmed sometimes, I wish it were possible to
close the windows, end the business, end the exhaustion —-
Stop!—
       Zachary S. Schwartz

Broken Pride

What do you say when a child cries,
What words can heal their broken pride?
All of their lives striving to be complete,
No words can change the fact they've been beat.

You are to love your parents they've been taught,
Yet it is their breath for which they have fought.
Flow like rag dolls in the wind,
Then praying they will not be hit again.

Will help arrive and save the deprived,
From this madness some call love?
Will the day come when something is done,
And the children will be mended their pride?
       Heidi J. Scheffleo

"God's Revelation"

"God" the creator of the heaven's and earth,
"God" the creator of man and woman the true God,
"God" the God of love and of mercy the only one,
True God, the wonder, of the universe,
The time will come in the new order, under God,
Order of goodness and of true love,
His son Jesus was given for all,
Died for our sin's the time will come,
There will be hope, this system will end,
God's word is true for the heaven's is near
The love is true, love of God, is pure, but the wicked
And Satin shall be put away.
In revelation the sounds of seven trumpets
Sound of trumpet, 1. One third vegetation destroyed
Sound of trumpet, 2. One third ocean life and ships destroyed
Sound of trumpet, 3. One third of fresh water poisoned,
Sound of trumpet, 4. One third of sun, moon, and stars darkened
Number 5 trumpet, first hellish invasion of demon's upon this earth,
Number 6 trumpet, second hellish invasion of demon's upon this earth
Number 7 trumpet, the king is coming, Jesus.
       J. C. Santore

The Beauty Of Age

I find in this phase or this
cycle of life
the signs of great wisdom and
beauty at height.

The lines of both sorrow
and joy
are combined
to give us a picture
of Old Father time.
       Gilda Bribieseca Safeeullah

Black Bodies And Blue Souls

"Natural born killer, lobotomies their brains
at birth, micro-chip their skin so we
can keep track or them", "Immoral
raunchy wh**e-f**kers and seed slayers"
They blow young kisses from new dirt
graves, eyeing the tear sullen earth
clawing for one last grasp. "It's their
damn jungle musk a sausage culture.
Beautiful gunshots created in the pupils
Of American ghettos to jest flesh mongers
and joy rapist that fill sable wombs with
crack-demon seeds. Castrated half-men
brag of murders and bitch smacks while
Snow flavored Africans float higher the heroin
My rotting black skin still floats in the wind.

Khalfani Salim

God Will See You Through

When the troubles of the world seem to be on your shoulders,
and people are badgering you to be bolder.
Just close your eyes and think of some thing true,
some thing like God will see you through.
When it seem like things couldn't get worse,
like the whole world is under a curse.
Like problems just seem to follow you,
remember God will see you through.
No matter how big the task or the job to be done,
praying is the key because God is the one.
To solve your problems or to enrich your life,
whether an ill husband or the supportive wife.
Remember goodness is plentiful but evil is few,
and to the full extent God will see you through.

Michael C. Robinson

What Is A Mother?

A mother is a person
sometimes old sometimes young,
given the joy of birth
from the age time begun.

Cares for the sickly
minutes, hours and years,
Trying to stay close always
to the ones she holds dear.

Faces the times and problems
life puts on her mind,
Trying constantly never
to hurt but always be kind.

Seeing the years snatch the ones
she has raisin with pride.
Knowing she will never be able
to keep them near at her side.

Praying that when all the cards
are dealt and the numbers told,
She will always be loved
so she will never grow old.

Doris Robinson

Eternal Perfection

When the future gleams through life's calloused scene.
When you obtain more than in my dream you've ever dreamed.
When you die of kindness, giving, and loves
gentle kiss, and are filled sickeningly sweet with bliss.
Then all that will be is seen at Heavens Gate,
and God will scream with sarcastic hate,
"I suspect you wanted more than fate!"

Todd Purdue

Land And The Man

Land and the man called my father
were both in communion with God.
On Sunday each week my father
walked his cotton field with a youngster
to see if all was looking well.
The man's patience held well till
shoots sprang up into full grown plants
and the harvest was yielded from the sod.
Land and the man called my father
were both in communion with God.
My father was a great believer in
both man and God to succeed in
communion with God and man.

Dorothy Reeves

12 Roses Red

A decade of time illustrates each petal of blossom.
Each decade of time is the quality time spent with your lover
and best friend.

Each thorn of a red rose is the little bit of pain that comes
with every soul. This is why roses are stripped of their
thorns, to assure a bond between two hearts. Although,
a rose should never be stripped completely of the challenges
that may lie ahead. The couple that work together through
these times, are the souls that will last and last.

The stem of a red rose is the extension of the root from ones heart.
This is the path you opt to follow, only to find it's doors wide
open for you.

We hope to pedal through decades of time together.
We create and overcome the challenges of thorns, together.
And we follow the same path only to find the same doors open, for us.

But, the fragrance and essence of a red rose is the true,
I love you.

Vladimir C. Quijano

Love And Commitment

Love and commitment are like two trees;
Standing side by side;
They grow together;
Bear fruit together;
Though, together, each is individual;
Their roots need room to reach out;
Drawing nourishment as needed.
They shadow each other from the scorching sun;
And raging storms;
But, not so much, that they smother each other;
Each needs to feel the cooling breeze,
  and cleansing rain.
They are both givers and receivers of God's many blessings.
A nesting place for birds to have their young;
As well as a refuge during Winter storms.
And in the Springtime together they rejoice and blossom,
Giving hope;
They hold a sparrow's song.

Nancy Pulsney

Magnificence

Holy and magnificent spirit of God...
  Flow freely through my being...
    I acknowledge your authority and ownership
      of my mind...my body...and soul.

Diane B. Miller

The One That's Best

As I lay my head to pray,
I think of things from day to day.
For he I could never envy
the joy, the love that he sends me.
It's now, forever and will continue to be
the dreams of life that will set me free.

I know you love not just I
and will always even when we die.
If I come to that beautiful blue sky,
to meet my love, finally, eye to eye,
broken hearts will never be more
For I shall make my presence to that Golden Door.

The life here is sweet but now it's at rest
as I make my way up to the one that's best.
Cynethea Preston

At Cana In Galilee

The wedding banquet was ready
At Cana in Galilee....
The honored guests - Jesus and his disciples arrived.
Music and dance, song and laughter filled the air.
"We have no more wine" some one called out...
The virgin bride blushed with shame
With embarrassment written all over her face.
Then, Mary said to Jesus: "Son, they have no wine."
"Woman, my time has not yet arrived...." said Jesus.
Not taking NO for an answer
To the servants, Mary said: "Do whatever he tells you..."
Soon six stone jars were filled with water.
With a blessing, Jesus turned this water into wine.
The taste of this wine surprised everyone.
As everyone began to enjoy,
Spared from shame and embarrassment
The newly married uttered a sigh of relief.
Thus at Cana in Galilee, Jesus' prophetic mission began
As Jesus reached out to a couple in need
Jesus...Compassion, Good Shepherd, Good Samaritan...
George B. Perera

Autumn

The leaves are beginning their turning to colors of every hue.
I love to see this sight with all the colors don't you?
There may be something that is much more bright,
But the fall colors of hardwood trees are quiet a sight.
The Poplars, Prickly Ash and Dogwood trees are the first to turn here.
Then Sycamore, Sumac, Maple trees will follow, have no fear.
We can't say we can paint all these colors by hand, this would be odd.
It is done by a higher power as part of the plan laid out by God.
Joel E. Moyers

A Special Place

In the sky or on the land,
there are creatures living.
A windy day or a rainy day,
you will always find the breeze dancing.
Up above those cloudy skies,
there's a place called Heaven.
When you're happy or when you're sad,
there's always someone listening.
So when you're feeling down and up
or even feeling blue,
remember that you're not alone,
because there's a special friend who will
be there for you.
Tamara Martinez

Form... To Meaning

Braided lines of light reflect the melancholy twists of life
Today to someone new but with strong ties
following the who...used to be

Rush to flush my soul and hand in my heart,
Taken in exchange for the gender I want
Melt quickly I to layer you with a transparent membrane of me
Adding no thickness, only nourishment to feed

Imagery imaginated with soul not separated,
I beg to express my reality
Your invocation is my invitation to ingest myself and chew upon you:

> Blond cropped hair with yellow fair skin
> continuing slowly over muscle and bone
> From the lobe of your ear bearing the un-matured hair
> of white, child light
> I want you
>
> Move to my lips my tenderness desire
> to touch rounded shoulders with bone visible but not protruding
> Frame of fragility with slight proportions of muscle and bone
> given as if only enough to reduce extreme contrasts in contour
> A touching hand moves smoothly to front your chest and
> press strength to your soul
> Lower to breast with tension at it's start gravity pulling down
> the concentrated feminine tissue
> almost to separate it from it's source of existence
> Press north I support with an understatement of respect
> my left runs a right to center seem
> and feel the connection of our being

Todd Gavin Patasnick

Far Away Love

Although you are so far away,
my love gets stronger day by day.
You are my world, can't you see,
you are my heart and will always be.
My love for you will forever exists,
no matter where and who you're with.
The many miles between you and me,
get closer as the days go by.
Your charm has captured my every breath,
tears of joy are all I've wept.
My heart so full of love for you,
words can't say how much it's true.
To know how much, how strong my love,
just count the stars that rest above.
Your love so deep as I received,
I know you love me, I do believe.
Though many seconds of waiting in vain,
more love for you is all I'll gain.
You are the swan and I'm the dove,
for you are my far away love.
Walter Paleka

Untitled

Foot and Pain Prints in the snow
Here and there where e'er you go
Wondering who the owner be
Who put them there for us to see
Maybe just a little bunny
or a squirrel seeking food to eat
A child who's playing in the snow,
Better than playing in the street,
A wondering deer his mate to find
Or maybe just a snack to grind
Now that I've tried to clarify
Where all the foot prints came
Your guess is just as good as mine
And we'll see them til the rain
Mary Ouimet

Untitled

I am what I know, be it little, or be it lot.
The wind will always blow.
   Roy Olsen

One Love

It's you I love and will forever
You may change but I will never
The time will come when we must part
But I knew it was love right from the start
I do believe God created you different from the rest
He knows I love you the best
If I should die before you do
I'll go to heaven and wait for you
If you decide to go the other way
I'll ask God if I can be with you on that day
Then we may burn together in the heat of our love
But if you come up top we can fly with the doves
The joy, the sorrow, the love, the pain,
The earth, the wind, the fire, the rain
All shout out your name, my love for you is strong
I dream of you all day and night long
You look so pretty and so nice
Made of what little girls are made of, sugar and spice
Take my love and throw it to the ground
It still won't destroy what I've found
   Jay L. Morris

When Angels Cry

   The angels rain tears of red,
for all the pain and sorrow shed.

   Somewhere in the world a child dies,
from the pain of hunger that grows inside.

   Night falls and a mother weeps,
for her little babe forever sleeps.

   The angels rain tears of red,
but love for the children turn them clear instead.

   Is there but one who knows our woes,
and has forever claimed our souls?

   Are there many who meet in between,
that share our pain of griefs unseen?

   The angels tears fall as rain,
as we all fight in honor and die in vain.

   I search to solve the mystery,
of why there is such misery.

   Could the new star that twinkles in the sky,
be a life beginning as you and I?

   The angels live in heaven high,
and spill their teardrops from the sky.
   Teresa Joy Moreland

"Our Dad"

With the rage and loud roars of a lion, priceless
freedom of the bird, life took him on a journey,
filled with many twists and turns.
But in the end when Heavens light grew near,
we grew to love what once we feared.
So now this heart of great strength,
and endless desire, goes on to provide
us with a hope for tomorrow.
   Loretta L. Manfre

Love Came So Swift

Love came so swift, and swept us off our feet
Like violent winds blowing through trees, on
beautiful mountain peaks

But yet so smooth and so slow, as though
being massaged gently, from head to toe

This love grew straight, and so strong we
thought there was nothing, that could ever go wrong

With the strength of a thousand men, and with
the power we saw, we thought we'd conquered all

But soon again the winds came, winds — winds of
change, and this time without affection, and from
a new and different direction

And no where in our dreams did we see, we might
stall - stall, crumble and fall

So now we're just here, dazed and can only sit and
stare. Trying to understand, how to pick up the
pieces of a...
   Broken women....a broken man
Love came so swift, but yet so smooth and so slow
   Tyrone Milliner

Hope Is In Our Hands

Like two, rays of light meet,
so do triumph and defeat.
We are so far ahead,
other nations we have led,
but there is something missing deep within
and the search for it must begin.
So short our lives,
to be overcome with violence and crime.
Prejudice and hate separate us all
and only we can break this racial wall.
What can we do? What can we say?
It is up to our youth to pave a new way.
   Jill Meyer

Killer Of Giants

If none of us believe in war
Then can you tell me what the weapons for
Listen to me everyone
If the button is pushed
There'll be nowhere to run

Giants sleeping, giants winning wars
Within their dreams
Till they wake when it's too late
And in God's name Blaspheme

Killer of Giants threatens us all
Mountains of madness standing so tall
Marches of protest not stopping the war
Or "The killer of Giants"!

Mother nature people state your case without it's work
Your seas run dry your sleepless eyes
Are turning red alert
   "Killer of Giants!"
   "Killer of Giants!"
   Sara Mercer

"Missy"

My Missy! Why did you leave me,
Why did you have to go,
Do you know how much I miss you,
Jumping and running, and making me smile,
That cute face that seems to know what I say,
Sit girl sit, down girl down, obey me well
Emptiness in my heart will always remain,
Oh how you loved me and I loved you,
My eyes, still swollen with tears of sadness,
So now, Missy, go run, go jump, roll over,
Promise me not to go near the street
Be a free dog, know the feeling,
Rest in peace. Know the joy and happiness you brought me,
You know I will never forget you,
Look at me with your big brown eyes
Remember how much I love you,
Because you will remain with me forever
Until that glorious day I'll be with you again!
David A. McPhail Sr.

In A Single Day

She met him on a friday
the next day took his name
so little time to think it over
life would never be the same

And he - wasted not one second
asked the question right away
"marry me" he begged her
we can do it saturday

Not love at very first sight
maybe more just out of need
to care for one another
that is all that they agreed

So marry dad is what she did
all those many years ago
and from a single day of courting
left a story to be told

Now again they are together
he's resting by her side
nearly sixty years of memories
that need became their guide
Bernard Martinez

A Man Can Move A Mountain

A man has problems that only he can over come.
He will understand these problems until the break of dawn.
His problems come and search at night.
He never realizes these problems, until the time of after night.
The night holds wonders and fears of promises within.

On a hot summer night, when the man falls asleep he dreams of snow.
The man sees pictures of his fears in dreams of visions.
Behind a wintery snowy scene.
Then he realizes his problems and tries to solve them at night,
In his sleep, when he doesn't know they exist.

Man thinks his problems will be solved when he moves the mountain.
He tries his hardest.
He uses his mind and physical power to move the mountain.

He knows all his problems will be solved once the mountain is moved.
He concentrates, without realizing it he has just moved the mountain.
Using, the most powerful weapon of all...the love of the heart.

The man goes back to sleep.
Not realizing but remembering his dream.
"The love of the heart."
Roberta L. Mann

The House Of Pain

The House of Pain is where I'm at
and where I do my thinking.

I try not to depress myself when
ever a holiday comes around.
It's hard for me to express my feelings
but I try my best. I try not to let
my family know how I feel because
we're so far apart.

There's times when I feel like saying that
I'm sorry for putting them through this Pain.
But it will only make it worse, so I keep my
Pain and depression to myself
because I'm in the House of Pain.

Late at night I can hear the weeping others.
There's some who are doing life
and some who will be out soon.
The ones who are doing life only wish to be out soon.

From what I've seen and heard,
I can say we all had our share in
The House Of Pain!
Anthony Llanes

For Susie

Far off in silent distance,
barefoot in a shallow stream she knelt.
Her hair, by the wind, was charmed to dance;
kingdoms of daylight upon it dwelt.

Eyes of evening sky as seen through a gentle rain;
a hue for which all descriptions lie,
shade without a name.

To the gazeless face of water below
her sorrowless hand enciphers—
endless despairs, dreams and desires,
unspeakable things and things left unspoken
float out on gentle rings unbroken.

Whilst slipping further down the stream,
my thoughts as much alone,
my mind recalled what mine eyes had seen,
my heart—what it was shown.

Far off in the silent distance,
barefoot in the shallow stream she knelt.
Her hair, by the wind, was charmed to dance,
and kingdoms of daylight upon it dwelt.
John Lambert

Looking For Love

You must have a reason
For feeling like you do
When you dare to think
There is no one to love you

In order to receive it
First you have to give
Them a chance to love you
Then you will have those feelings beat

So if you will remember
There is a lot of love out here
And if you try a little harder
You will get your share
Herbert L. Kiesow

"Marshall Islands"

Marshall Islands, oh I miss thee,
From the swaying palm trees, to your pearly shores
Like a mistress beckoning her lover, and waiting patiently.
All the diamonds and gold in the world, can't match the beauty which
    you possess.

But all is gone; except for places that have not been found.
Oh, how I yearn for the old days for the lands we didn't pay.
Because our forefathers knew what was good and left us
With the trust which they had cherished so much,
Will always be here for us.
But sadly it's almost gone, like the moon fading at dawn.

Let us come together as one, for our future
Is in the hands of those who don't share the passion
So let's not be fools and be sold.
I pray that we all will come together as a great family,
For only then, the Great Wise ones will rest peacefully.

Remember their trust.........
Please God, guide us...
And lead us on this journey......
Even if it takes all eternity........

Atmeta Malani Lakien

Journey Through Amorous Days

Skipping, jumping, hopping along making
Noises and singing a song,
Eating cake and ice cream too, picking
Roses and sharing with you.

Humming, clapping, whistling rhymes, taking
A trip through the Georgia pines.
It is you sweet honey-bun who makes me want
To run for fun.

When your lips open to speak a world of magic
Is at my feet,
And your chair which brings you out can only
Enlighten me without a doubt.

Tell me your secrets darling of mine for
Sooner of later we'll go wine and dine.
If your eyes should contact my heart, my
Life will forever have a jump-start.

Ivano G. La Micela

Of Dolphin Princes

All are gone now.
No longer do their artificial suns flicker and glow.
Forever darkness falls,
crashing like thunder upon the vacant streets below.

Whispers float through the deep blue sea of a city bright
and full of dolphin princes and their fairy lovers.
Together with their love they built a most powerful kingdom
and from their pearl palaces ruled.

Upon their kingdom never did darkness fall
all was laughter crimson red.

Now, the pearl palaces stand still
coated slick with the sea slime of the ages
where once they glimmered and spun seemingly ageless.

There is only the pervading echo of madness
which seeps through the walls of silently reflective sadness
to weep upon the floor of the deep blue sea
the tales of forgotten dolphin princes and their fairy lovers.

Jeffrey Michael Kuczmarski

Winter Time

Fog covers over
the soft and still chilling ground.
Silent Nature's shroud.

Clouds with gray fringes
rest like gloves on ice fingers
of The Great North Wind.

As great swirling cold
wraps a pale robe ever tight
circling all in drab,

Slush water drips in
thawed drizzles from stringy hair
to clean muddy boots.

Great. Mountains. Of. White.
Pound. On. Pound. Ton. Over. Ton.
When will Snow Time leave?

Run, tell the flowers
who peek through cold, stark frost,
of our yearning for green!

Harlow J. Keith

"Star Boy" Thoughts

"Star Boy" knows he is an Alaskan Malamute,
Courageous, big, strong and playful, also knows he is cute,
He takes everything in stride,
Knowing that he will get his daily ride,
"Stars Boy" seems to know a secret which offers peace of mind,
A secret that "Star Boy" seems to know that I can never ever find,
"Star Boy" loves to wrestle with you in the snow,
With an amusing look in his eyes, always a winner, let's go,
Another round or so,
Also, quite mischievous, also a lot of fun,
Keeps you busy as he is always on the run,
Always happy to hear his master's voice,
A friendly pat which causes "Star Boy" to rejoice,
When I return home he is always at the door,
Happy, joyous, content he knows that I will serve him evermore,
Also, happy, content to let the world revolve to pray, worship and
love, thinks, dreams, sees the clouds in the heavens up above,
No doubt "Star Boy" worship his ancestors, as at night he looks
At the Stars and the moon and does a mournful howl,
I am thankful "Star Boy" is my pal with a friendly growl.

Penny Jones

Imagination

Once upon a stormy night
The winds blew with such a fright
The lighting struck down though the sky
The ghost walk side by side

The bats, and witches came flying around, all
getting ready to scare the folks on the ground.

The devil has now appeared, with his fiery head
reared, pause to commend all the ghost, and goblins at hand.

But all at once dawn came, and all the figures,
showed their fear, and quickly disappeared.

For when I awoke, I found that I was safe, and sound
for all those figures that were dancing around,
were just imagination from my crown.

Carol J. Jones

Master Potter (Jeremiah 18:1-10)

It's just a piece of clay, hard and stubborn as can be.
It looks so worthless to people like you and me.
But the potter sees potential, from a potter's point of view.
He sees it as something valuable, after it is renewed.

He puts the clay through a process, causing it to respond to touch and feel.
Then he makes a useful vessel, shaping it at the potter's wheel.
We are like the lump of clay, hardened and stubborn as can be.
The master potter sees with mercy, the vessel he can make of you and me.

So he draws us by his spirit, showing love and kindness too.
He forgives our sinful past, and by his word we are made new.
As we walk in full obedience, and his light is shining through;
We become a useful vessel by the good things we can do.

> 2 Corinthians 5:17 "...if any man be in Christ, he is a new creature: Old things are passed away; behold all things are become new."

Raymond Jolliff

Rural Routes -Surprise-

School busing rural routes, seasons change "seen"
Exploring white tail deer, capture natures "scene"
Cotton tail rabbits, pheasants, squirrels scamper for their nest
Geese flying north, migration at its best
Students patiently wait, here comes the bus "surprise"
Seasons accommodate, fall, winter, spring, "sunrise"
Parents, students, drivers, accountable time "please"
Teacher sets the table, mathematics then release
Rural routes deliver, future leaders gain
Nature captures interest, students will attain
Delight in childhood memories daylight savings "time"
Here comes the bus "surprise", alarm clocks chime
Kindergarten children, years marching, "line"
Personalities encounter, its graduation "time".

George W. Johnson

"Jeremy And Sherlock" (In Memory Of Jeremy Brett - British Actor)

He played the part with majesty and grace,
  His style was obvious a look on his face.
When the game was a foot and the mystery complete,
  He set to the solving a murder too neat.
The clues were there for all to see,
  Though no one knew the answers save the players and he.
With Watson at your side you set out to uncover,
  Was it the Butler, the friend, the stranger, the lover.
Excitement and intrigue brought his blood to boil,
  The bang of the gun another crime to foil.
The spirit of the chase was always the game,
  To Jeremy, to Sherlock, one in the same.
As perplex as the mystery thus was he,
  For you see Jeremy was Sherlock and Sherlock was he.

Michael Jefts

A Single Heart

Hearts are broken with the dreams that conquer
and should be healed with the dreams that are conquered
In a world, were love means nothing, and hate means everything
these hearts; the broken and the healed, can only survive
if they can feel the lost emotion called love
If they can accomplish this task they are meant to travel together
and become a single heart, shared by two loving people

Gerald B. Brant

Love's Insanity In Verse

Saints preserve me, demons stay away from my soul
I am so encumbered by the pull of my heart
Love, such a source of joy and of sheer misery
Cursed, then blessed, sometimes in the same breath.

It is the unpredictability of love's strange purpose
Each unequaled surge of passion, flowing forth
All of the moments of loss, within the senses
Fear of both keeping and of losing this madness.

It is a madness, quite difficult to cope with
Promises made to oneself, as passion relaxes
Knowing the real test to a spirit is yet to come
When touching upon the flesh, senses are raped.

Rationalization is alien, when blood runs so hot
Surging passion, pulsating through the veins, as a mechanical pump
Not even the shock treatment of constant rejection
Could ever stop the burning hunger to be loved!

Barbara J. W. Jack

"Destiny's Child"

Hold on
We're going too fast
She's almost there
To fulfill her destiny
Pretty soon
She will feel the pain
She will feel the pleasure
Then
She will slowly learn
How to die

Blood the color of roses
Her mind will come right along
Christianity for closes
She soon will be his

All she has to do
Is give in
Everything will fall into place
Slowly the disease will take over
Then
She will most certainly learn how to die.

George O. Howard

Your Filing

If someone speaks an unkind word to you
  File the words away,
Don't let it make you blue
  For it is easier to file it away.

If some dim wit..
  Pointed their finger your way,
It hurts a little bit
  But file it away!

It may sting you ever so
  No matter what gossip you may bear,
File it away neatly and go,
  Then it will stay there.

Words, file it away
  Don't let things bug you,
File it away
  For you know what to do

You can do this for awhile,
  Go on your way
Then go out and burn the file
  Then start another day!

Ila A. Hogue

Untitled

To Fly in its own beauty is to not be captured by the human hands that hold on to tight but to be viewed with the eye as something delicate enough to let go so it can ride with the breeze to return where once it came.

Blu Jean Hintz

Nature's Call

God gives His creatures
each a call
When night comes listen
to the whippoorwills call
to his mate.
She answers back with
her whippoorwills call
just as we could answer
to Gods call to come to Him.

Ruth Hewell

Feeling Alone

Alone in your own world. No one to talk to.
Sitting alone in a dark corner.
Sitting in a puddle of tears.

No one hears or listens to you.
You feel like your life has or will end.
You don't give a crude about your parents.
They have forgotten about you too.
It is like you faded away into the darkness.
Your only true friend is yourself.
You feels like you want to jump out of a window.
But something stops you.
Then you figure out that you have another friend poetry.

Andrew Herring

The Gift

Designed by love
But given by the grace of God to me
Now being only two of us
In the beginning, there were three.

A prayer to someone high above
Now life shall never be the same
This message from my heart and hand
In nineteen, eight-two, you came.

Unlike now, a young man then
My life so full of vigor and steam
So many things have passed me by
Except my very fondest dream.

Someone to love, to hold, and teach
A price bestowed from number one
Of all my earnings, large or small
The greatest gift, is you my son.

Mark Allen Hammonds

"A Mother's Moods"

Mother Nature is angry today.
Lightening streaks the sky like rocket trails.
The tympani of thunder assails the ear.
Wind lashes the earth with the silver whips of rain.
Birds huddle in the surinam hedge;
Lizards cower beneath the banana leaves.
Then suddenly - it is over.
The sun shines through.
The vanda orchid lifts its faces to the light.
Everything is fine again.
Mother is smiling.

Barbara A. Guthrie

"Friends"

You might not have the answers or what I want to hear,
But as I watch and listen, disappearing are my fears.

Your kind words and knowing actions help me sometimes see,
They let me approach the door and use that brand new key.

The understanding and response never fails to lift me up,
As I constantly strive to fill that once empty cup.

You seem to care yet you know so little,
Like a young one banging on a drum or strumming on a fiddle.

You've given me held in my time of need,
Whether it's your kind words or your senseful deeds.

I see so much of myself in you,
as I shake your hand, you see that too.

A friend is someone you can trust near or far,
and that my friend is truly what you are.

Jeffrey Guillod

"Death, Be Not Proud"

The pain of this gigantic LOSS
The pain of SEPARATION.
The Bitterness, the Hurt, the unfairness of it all.

Death, be not proud. Humble thyself,.. and know
Thou art not permanent
But only a temporal wall.

Death, be not proud..... For there is ONE who hath penetrated thy veil
There is ONE who hath overcome thee.
Death, be not proud...And let the dead bury their dead.

The rest is Silence...

Michael Gottlieb

Untitled

Remember me with flowers
Remember me with a smile
Please do not cry for then
it will be a sad day
I love you all I truly do
I have touched and kissed
your brow each day so
you will not feel I am
so far away -
Hold me to your heart
love is the only way
To keep heaven and earth
from fading away -
I fly as a dove and
the lust you see me
I'm just out of sight -
But I'm there, I'm there
Dear ones -

Elaine M. Gennette

Concerning The Flower

For this gift of love
the gift of the rose
How it fills our very being
giving grace propitious pleasure
Sculptured in silence
this joyful celebration
Expressing that which cannot
be put into words
Yet cannot remain silent
This gift of the heart

Donna M. Williams

Free Spirit

To be close to the Earth
  is a heartfelt thing
And when the heart is free
  there is love
And when there is love
There is love for everything
Thankful am I to see and hear
  taste and smell
And touch this blessed Earth
To know that from her loving
  bosom
Springs the life that graces
  all heaven above
From which only God can give
  a peaceful death
    a noble birth.
    Curtis O. Gates

Our Children

  Our children are so special so sweet,
from the tops of their heads, to the tips of their feet.
  Our children are a breath of fresh air
when we need to breathe.
  Our children are the lights in our eyes,
the glow in our hearts.
  Our children are us you see,
when we were young and growing up free.
  Our children are examples of love
what it can do and what they can be.
  The children you see are special to me,
they warm my heart and give me joy.
  Our children are the foundation
of a new beginning and brighter tomorrows.
  Thank God for the children
so special so sweet.
    Kami Fryberger

School Daze

The patter of feet,
  as they walk down the street,
The roar of the bus-
  it's them or it's us.
The screaming, the crying,
  as spit wads are flying.
They race down the hall,
  some short and some tall.
They wrestle in fun,
  with tongues sharp with pun.
Till the ring of the bell,
  will surely tell,
The start of the day,
  is now on it's way.
No need to fear,
  for it's really quite clear,
those ornery creatures,
  are only the teachers.
    Joe R. Flores

Softball

S oftball is not for the novice.
O ccasionally you'll be diminished by
F orfeit or loss.
T he attitude you have must be unaffected by defeat,
B ecause you're out there to hurl the ball, get that runner out
A nd win the championship! This is how my sister,
L aura, thinks as a catcher. She
L oves the game.
    Leeanne Jagusch

Nature By Nature!!!

Nature is Free
And so are we.
When we are seen
the grass grows green.
The grass is green
the flowers are seen
The trees grow tall
the grass grows low.
When the sun goes out
the moon comes out.
Nature is done
before the Sun.
    Aldona Filipowicz

My Son

I miss him so much,
its terrible as such,
I wish we could touch,
my son is in there, I wish I knew where,
his body and soul is still alive,
I know he waits for me to arrive.
The state took him for no reason at all,
put him away behind the big wall,
his mind is so slow but who's to know,
but you watch and see they will all fall.
We miss him so much, someday you'll be home,
and I won't be alone, suffer he does,
and handsome he was , I pray for the day you walk thru
my door, and worry not for you anymore.
    Pat Feliciano

Day Break

An unseen hand with a hidden head,
Shakes its fist at a dead man's bed.
A voice sifts softly from the sky,
As twittering birds in the twilight fly.
A lady walks gingerly over the sand,
Caressing the air with a silkened hand.
All the worlds a moving stage,
A time for beauty a time for rage.
    James W. Erb

My Brother Earl

  I was walking last night when a flag caught my eye
It was silently rippling against the moonlit sky
  Pictures of today flashed through my head
Remembering what the latest newspaper said
  Fighting and talk of a battle, possibly a war
No one really knows what may lie in store
  Glancing above, the flag resembles my brothers face
Then vanishes quickly without leaving a trace
  He is a Combat Engineer, soldier indeed
Always fighting for each country in need
  There are rare phone calls to say he is fine
There is seldom contact along the front line
  But God is beside him, keeping him near
Holding him tight, protecting him from fear
  I turned to leave, Earl was there in a cloud
Reminding me again why our family is so proud
  He is a true soldier, not glorified in publicity or fame
But always my brother...so proud of his name
    Elizabeth Ellegood

Magical, Moring, Mist

The mountains are my home.
Sometimes when I look out
my window. I can almost
see the mountain touch
the sky. And feel the
moring mist racing down
the mountain pecks. I
wail on the smell of
the moring mist after
a rain. It smells so
good. I run out of
my house to dance
in the magical mountain
mist that comes down
the mountain pecks
and glad to be part
of the magical moring mist.

Nellene Cole

This Is!

Power to engage feelings and imagination
Often through the highly structured patterning and rotation.
Entwining all sorts of sounds and rhythms like a musician
That conveys a certain emotion or thought, when it is written.
Rivet hearts and minds, now unbolted, by a pen. Left
Yearning for more artistry, but all good things come to end!

Travis A. Chandler

The Demon Of Eternity

When the darkness comes
  I see the demon
He taunts me with memories of the past
I run to a corner to hide
But nowhere will he not see me
This demon is nothing new to me
You see this is the demon of eternity
Every night I stay awake to hide from him
Yet the sand beast wins the struggle
Then I shut my eyes
To a new war
Will I wake
Or will I die
This demon of overwhelming power
Is taking over me
So stay awake if you may
For maybe tonight will be the demons day
Your night his day this time he will take you away

David Duane Carr

"Enter A Dream"

Enter a dream of love
Love that flow's through
You to your soul mate.
He is out there, faith
Will let it be if you
Let it flow.

Enter a dream of love
Love that will not smother
The burning flame which
Brings forth his arrival.

Enter a dream of love
That cast the flame
Of love to his heart.
A burning flame of fire
Sent to the anticipating
Heart of your soul mate.

Diane E. Butler

The Little Bug

The little bug came flying by
In the cafeteria.
It went zapping this way,
It went zapping that way.
It went zapping back and forth
Then out the door it flew.

Paul S. Buford

My Little Boy And Me

My little boy and me.
We live in a society.
Where things are not always
what they seem to be.

With me doing my part.
And he with his good heart.
He will make it assuredly.

Signs of a young man.
He will one day make a stand.
But for now we'll make small plans.
While we can still hold hands.
My little boy and me.

Mary Bruegger

Who Wins With War

Who wins, when wallowed with wars' wrath?
When wars were wrapped with wealth,
Wisdom withdrew.
Wailing walls were written with warnings.
World's watchmen winked.

Wane wombs, woven with webs.
Women without words; watched!
Whimpering weans wishing,
What war weapons wasted.
Wood wafers were workers wages.
While wealthy warmongers wooed.

Weighty wagons wheeled wars wounded.
Wakes, with wiggled worms, waited.
Wreaths, watered with widowers weeping.
Woe, what a waste, what a waste.

Martina C. Brazil

Fate

Have you ever felt like the last leaf on the tree?
Torn between the nature of things: falling to your fate?
Or struggling to cling to the branch trying to fling you off?
Coincidence that your brilliant colors turn from green at the first frost?
The many chilly nights are but predictions of things to come,
The bitter cold of northern winters: The frost, the snow;
The angry winds that blow, trying to rip you from the parental branch above.
Seduced by the sweet summers swaying breezes that lull you to sleep
The suns chlorophyll dreams promise eternity as a gracious green leaf
Graced by the birds who chirp in your ears,
your veins swelled with sweet senses of youth;
But dry and brittle as the final throes of life has ebbed
The battle is lost once the spring sap begins to flow.
The new buds appear to hasten your demise, as you, at last,
let go and flutter helplessly to the ground below to welcome you
To be a part of the endless circle of "ashes to ashes,
  and dust to dust": Completing your journey from birth to death,
and once more to enrich the earth for new life to come...
For that is all part of God's plan for eternal life,
and why He sent His Son to pave the way for the rest of us.....

Patricia Blue

Respecting The Blues

It ain't so bad having the blues.
All of us done had them and it ain't nothing new.
It be the time you can let your soul cry.
It be the time when tears fill the eyes.

I find myself an empty room and then close the door.
Got to deal with the pain so it don't exist no more.
I ain't about to give a dam what you may think.
I just sit and brood as into blues I sink.

I dust off that old record I packed away long ago.
The one that make you think hard when you feeling low.
I fix myself a cool drink and just think about it all.
Them blues show is humming and I got to answer the call.

Them blues show is got me beat.
Rocking and reeling, barely standing on my feet.
I'm trying to find away out of this deep despair.
Because it show gives you cause to just sit and stare.

Mona Lisa Bass

If My Footsteps....

A careful women I ought to be.
Some little gal will follow me.
I don't aim to stray for fear that this gal will go the,
same way.
"Not at all can I hide or escape her lovely eyes,
She will be right by my side, looking, trying,
To do as I, just like me,
That's what she wants to be. So I must remember
Winter, spring, summer, fall that God depends on us all.
So I'll watch my footsteps because someone is,
Watching and wanting to be as me".....

Bradine Basheer

One Day

One day I will have made
all of my dreams come true.

One day I will be
all that I have ever striven for.

One day I will the gratification of knowing
that I have done all that I ever set out to do.

One day I will look back with pride
knowing I am where I always wanted to be.

I will never look back with regret in my eyes;
for everything I do is an accomplishment
for what I will one day become.

Michelle Baker

My Game

Basketball is a game I like to play
During the night or the day
The flow of a game
And my way to fame
Around the first defender to the goal
Thinking about nothing but putting the ball in the hole
You keep your head down and go
As it seems everyone is moving slow
You jump up and it feels like your flying
The other team just stands there dying
You dunk it home
The other team moans
Man I love this game

Jamie Amodeo

A Prayer

Those living with HIV, Lord why must they die?
Give us a sign Lord let us see...
This plaque is but killing all that is precious to thee...
The suffering we see, the hands we hold, the tears we've dried...
Lord to many people have died.
Oh Lord our emotions are fried, we're to the end of our rope
   tired of having no hope...
Give us a sign, show us the way,
Give us the cure, save our lives this day.
To you we give thanks for the lives we live,
the chance to give hope to those infected,
who have rejected the idea of living.
For the giving of the strength we use at length,
To fight with all our might,
This plaque man made one night...
We live in fright, will we wake in the "morrow,"
our lives still full of sorrow?
Will they say for sure they found a cure?
Lord bless us all who are HIV inflicted...
Lord let us see... when we wake let it be... a cure.

Ricky Alford

The Eve Of Winter

They are beautiful this time of year,
The leaves that fall to the water's edge-
The stalks above seem not to mind their loss,
Their guard of colour given to reflection-
But you do not see, you cannot understand
The story that is told in one, you cannot hear
But all the better for you, you are content.
My wandering shadow can quiver in fear,
But I cannot let go for the passionless frost,
Nor can I shut my ears to the cries of the wind.
Here my memories can stay, dancing with the lilies,
And I will move on until the frost seizes my soul,
And a sweet embrace shall lure my quiet heart to decay.
I can find my reflection too among your reddened tears
And with my dreams, myself, my memories, I will stay
And winter shall be my solace as tomorrow nears.
The sun will shine without me,
And spring will see my reflection.

Christopher Zachrisson

Only You

You see me without emotional clothes
Naked, yet unafraid
Exposing the flaws, which seemingly overwhelm
In my mind's eye
You take it all in
Lovingly laughing at the insecurities
Reassuring, complimenting, accepting...Loving
You clothe my dreams in reality
Make known my secret needs and hidden yearnings
You are my inspiration, muse and desire
My shelter, peace and fantasy
Words can simply not reveal
The degree of ecstasy
Only you can make me feel.

Launi L. Tummolo

Untitled

F. Is for the Friendship we had.
R. Is to remember the good times we had.
I. Is for the important things we did together.
E. Is for you to evaluate the fun things we did.
N. Is that we never lied to each other.
D. Is for all the days we spent together.
S. Is for the sad days we spent together
   like today were no longer FRIENDS.

Mercedes C. Riojas

Eight Point Five

The dog was acting strange,
and far from the epicenter
there walked a mountain range.

It's your fault, San Andreas, it's your fault.

When the nation shakes its tail,
8.5 on the richer scale
goodbye, California, goodbye.

In dreams you'll still enchant us
golden sister to Atlantis
we'll cry, California, we'll cry.

It's your fault, San Andreas, it's your fault.

Fate has written your epitaph
on the scroll of a seismograph.
Goodbye, California, goodbye.

When the nation shakes its tail,
8.5 on the richer scale.
we'll cry, California, we'll cry.

Richard Applegate

My Son

I am proud you become a man of success,
Looking back at your childhood not having the best,
Sometimes not having much food to eat,
Patched Blue Jeans and cheap Shoes on your feet.
You always accepted life and never seemed sad,
Took things as they came no matter how bad,
But then things got better as time went on,
Then you got married and went on your own.
Since then you worked hard and look where you are,
A beautiful home and look at the cars,
You have raised a family and all doing well.
I'm proud of you Son, more than words can tell.

Patsy Louise Miller

Michael Jordan

After the timeout taken by Chicago,
Jordan walks calmly onto the basketball floor,
His Nike shoes are tightened to his big feet,
With time running out and the score being tied,
The crowd becomes quiet,

Ehlo takes the shot and misses by an inch,
Jordan jumps in the air to grab the rebound,
Dribbling past three Cleveland players,
He soars in the air looking like an airplane,
Nance tries to stop him without much avail,
Jordan gets the point before the sound of the buzzer,
The crowd is in a state of shock,
They realize that Michael Jordan is unstoppable.

Kunal Mishra

A Blessing For You

A blessing just for you
   May all the days
of all the years
   That GOD has still in store
Be filled with every joy, and Grace.
   To bless you more and more,
May the hope of heart,
   And peace of mind
Beside you ever stay.
   And that's the Golden
Wish I have for you, this CHRISTMAS DAY!

Edward J. Matlock

Women

Women are special, unique in a way.
Women are happy and sad everyday.
Women are fun.
Women are different in all different ways.

Different races, different hair,
Different hands, different feet,
Different family and friends.

Women stand barricaded at the wall of freedom.
No work, no feeling.
Destruction, discrimination, stand at the door.
Women can't get away.
Going into the 21st century, still barricaded, still sad, women stand.

Women can't see, but women can hear.
The questions, the answers, they're not right, they're not true.
Women are heroes like you and me.

Women are the ones that can always tell.
When you're sad, when you're mad, all women can tell.
Mothers can, sisters can, aunts, grandmothers, all women of the world.

Women are special, unique in a way.
Women are happy and sad everyday.

Whitney Leader-Picone

"The Wall"

There is no shadow today
No "Wall to cast shade
No darkness, no pain
No "Iron curtain" of reign

Freedom spread her wings
and today the darkness went away
What was once a land divided
is now a land united

A reunion at long last
of faces from the past
of smiles from the heart
no longer kept apart

And so we turn the page
and the "Curtain" is raised
to unveil a glorious scene
of what "love" really means
living together as one
in "Gods" holy kingdom.

Troy Alexander

If But And So

If I was rich,
I'll tell you what I'd do -
I'd buy the place called Limbo,
And do as I choose to.

But, in this life I'm living,
Each growing step I take,
I find that my true riches,
Are in my life's mistakes.

So, I'll learn to carry through,
With a tear in my heart, and eye,
And tip my hat to Limbo,
As I go walking by.

D. J. Potter

The Flower

A flower, even when unnoticed for some time, may fade away from one's
memory
But its beauty remains unforgotten
For the flower
Although we may loose sight of it's youthful appearance
One aspect
Untouched
Unscarred
Remains incarved in the beauty of its creation
Its fragrance

Maria Teresa Lagattolla

Peppermint Night

A million little sparkles
  across the water's way
As the sun sets
  on a snowy white day
A shimmer of light
  from the moon abroad
Sets off the night
  the day is gone
A star studded pattern
  light up the sky
It's sight so alluring
  night embers on fire
A peaceful quiet dark
  has blanketed the night
And a perfect winter day
  is awaiting first light.

Robert Blanchette

Dream Essence

A shadow land of
Surreal images
Silently
Emerges,
Shaping a world
Where creator and
Created are one
Sitting through eternity
Seeking the essence
Of the dreamer.

Seneca Wilson

Creative Reality

Creativity is the result of original thought or expression,
the power to create, to be productive or generative.
Where does creativity come from?
Maybe it's a gift to mankind to be used (however) by the soul
inhabiting a human body, and for the most part unobserved in animals.

Reality is relative and solely depends on creativity.
All reality is the result of creativity by intelligence somehow,
  somewhere, sometime.
There would not be evidence of creativity without reality.

Our world is our reality and a product of creativity.
We live in this world by our creativeness to continue that reality.
Humans, therefore are closely akin to the "Maker" insomuch as
  reality requires creativity, and creativity requires a real "creator."
Therefore GOD is real, and creating still.

S. Brownlee-Cobb

A Tribute To A King

America, won't you listen to what I have to say, about a man who
tried to love somebody but they took his life away.
He was born in Macon Georgia, Morehouse College was his pride.
You know when they brought his body there, grown men stood
  there and cried.
I'm talking about Martin, Dr. Martin Luther King. He was a man
who tried to love the world. I hope his death was not in vain.
It was way down there in Memphis the place where he died.
He was trying to help some black men get all their union rights.
I'm talking about Martin, Dr. Martin Luther King.
I can still hear him saying, "Let freedom ring.
For the black man and the white and all the people of this land."
He says he been to the mountain top. Let's all praise his name.

Herbert S. Boudreaux

Untitled

I love him,
But he doesn't know.
I need him,
But I can't let it show.

There's so many special things he does
To make my love grow.
But deep down inside
My love for him I can never show.

They say new acquaintances
come and go;
But I for one,
He'll never know.

Jean Lovely

"My World"

My home my earth my world
Of all the other planets that we can see
By telescope, rockets and tv.
None can compare to the beauty of this sphere.
With its oceans, rivers and seas.
Mars has it's glow of red
Venus has it's mist that reflects so bright
Saturn has it's ring's
And all the other planets many different things
They are enticing, but none as inviting
then this my world so fare.
Setting here in space for all other
worlds to see
Perched there like a rare jewel
separate from the others
"A gem"
Inviting travelers to come in

Wesley J. Rogers

"The Heart Of Pain"

  In this heart of aching pain, in this mind of
bitter shame, of this world of love lost love,
away in this heavenly sky above, hope and
dreams that disappear, now becomes an aching
tear, for the one that past long away, now
becomes a memorable day, my spirit is
gone away with him, for now my life is
oh so dim. Confused and painful my
heart will be, but I'll always think of
him in memory.
"In Loving Memory of Domenic"

Jennifer Gerhartz

Children, Children

We worked our hardest and did our best,
and left it to God to do the rest.
Thank You God for their big success!
The living proof is posted on my class room door.
There is no doubt, that for sure.

I've stroked those talents in each one of you.
So you would know just what to do.
With those stroking you come through
Happiness come to the school, to me and to you.
Judges reads your essays and said you are qualify
You did your very best no one can't deny.

We deserve a standing ovation
For these magnificent, graceful writing creation,
God helped us bring glory and honor to the school
This shows that we are very cool.

I humbly ask everyone of you.
To stand up, stand up and clap for us.
Let's do it without a fuss.
Just do it from the heart
Give it a big start.

Susan Braxton

For Mrs C

The summer has ended
The school bell rings clear
For teacher and pupil
Another new year

Their tempers and tantrums
Their homework and tears
Their futures we ponder
With hopes sometimes fears

Did it merit the effort
The struggle, the pain
Will they live as you taught them
Will you suffer the blame

The school bells are silent
The child now a man
Forever remembers
Your kind guiding hand

Paul Fernandez

Fire

Fire, fire burning bright,
Through the cities of the night,
Hearts of anger, hearts of fear,
Can't escape it's yellow glare,
Spreading through the smoke-filled night,
Burning everything in sight.
Running, running, with all your might,
Trying to escape the deadly night,
In the morning all is bare,
The smell of burning corpses fills the air,
No one survived that gruesome night,
Of the lonely city burning bright.

Marcia McDowell

Fishing With Friends

The boats we all tied at the wooden dock.
It was time to go in, says their waterproof clock.
As each one unloads, the fish stories begin,
And they all hold up, the days catch they reeled in.

"Mine was this big, but it got away."
"A good Jim Engels' excuse, wouldn't you say?"
"Hey, really you guys, at ... at least two feet long!"
"Here we go girls! He's singing his song."

They all have a chuckle, and unload the car,
Off to the campsite, its not very far.
They scale, they clean, they eat their day's catch.
While tales of new fish stories, now start to hatch.

While the boats softly float, on dark waters coast.
The end of the trip, has come much too fast.
Yet the peaceful surroundings, will always inspire,
Growing friendships, and memories, around their campfire!

Pamela J. Edwards

"A Beautiful Canada, In A Dream"

"A beautiful Canada, in a dream"
is about a land of vast opportunities.
It is a land of Mass Cultures, that
bond together nicely, that add the
colors of just what is healthy, full
of life, with a purpose to build,
create, enjoy and learn, from others.

A land, where people help people,
a place to enjoy, Marvel at Nature,
and her wonders, and a place where
faith, hope, and charity rule the
consciences of the Masses of Minds
that bond and create a beautiful
nation. A beautiful county, that is open,
to all peoples, from around the world.

When I vision Canada, I see the Cultures,
the bonding together, of all people in
building a stronger Nation, for all the
World to enjoy, and love. "A Beautiful Canada
in a dream," is what all hearts, and souls dream of.

Blayne McKay

This Winter: A Love Poem

My spirit rises, this time soundless
and gently, like its very descension:
   is the way a day began
   is the way evening later led
to belief and movement.

Ev Vroyevu: Waiting-in-patience
this same self-spirit
eases through itself
to meet its own meek fitting darkness;

And
while the light burden of touch
changes this timeless moment
a simpler fire turns within,
lost in silence, and found,
in a modest, tender mercy.

Moving and curious
I am borne
inside this gossamer, grace-filling
Opening—
not enlightened, thank God, but stilled

Deborah D. Jackimek

The Sea

Stars twinkling in an indigo sky
the sounds of the ocean, echoing softly
in my ears, ever so gently.
Beckoning me closer, closer.
   Ships out on the horizon, looking
back as if to say, come, come
where you belong, with me.
   Together we will travel out to sea
where the air is filled with a salty
mist and the heavens seem to touch
the briney depths.
   Here is where I feel the
closest to the one true meaning,
the beauty of the universe.
I am home, I am free to be me.
    Barbara H. Troia-Fitchett

"The Old Man"

He held his candle high aloft,
to guide her safely into dock.
A maiden voyage, no not this,
the old ship creaked, and rolled to port,
and pushed the fog above the pier.
He held his candle still and true,
and waited for the coming crew.
But most of all the bonnie lass,
his bride-to-be had come at last.
But ere the plank did rattle loud,
he wiped his eyes against the sound,
and thought he saw her laughing face,
and through the fog a fond embrace.
For every year the old man came
to guide his love, safe home again.
    Samuel F. Murray

God Smile On Christmas

God smile on christmas
The night before had been an
Silent and holy one for, far away
In a manger baby Jesus was born.

Under a star that shine so bright
Pointing to an light in Bethlehem
Hark the Herald Angels sing,
There's a song in the air.

The coming of the faithful to the Christ child.
The first Noel the Angels did sing,
The holiest of Holy nights that brought,
Joy to the world!

The Christ child reigns
A king is born Alleluia, Alleluia,
Wonderful, Emmanuel,
The Prince of peace!!!
    Scharlena A. Porter

A Brother In Christ

When I come to you for a helping hand.
You never bat an eye.
How can we work this out?
Is always your reply.
How much closer is the Lord's love than this?
When an out stretched hand in touched,
By a fellow man.
    Marie Clement

Hope Lift Thine Eyes

When life's dark storm clouds blot the sun's fair face,
Our thoughts wing backward through the skies of time,
To glimpse some haunting carefree childhood place,
Amidst the green and gold of years sublime.

Conflicting moods harass the mind and heart,
As gazing, our unseeing eyes review,
A long lost land that's in a world apart,
Interred and gone with all that was once new.

A longing to relive invades the soul,
That kills and withers us with discontent,
But time, alas, we never will control,
For life's a span that soon is spent.

Hope, lift thine eyes to that which lies ahead,
For pathways of the past you'll never tread.
    Jerrold Jack Rotwein

"Analyzation Realization"

Why am I afraid of you?
I always have feelings of
"Dé jà vu" around you
I am in fear...
Yet, I am attracted to you!

Are you the one...?
I've been searching...
Looking and longing for
Wanting, waiting for
Needing but forever missing...
I thought I'd never find...

My heart aches for you
My being yearns for yours
I want you...but...
Are you the one?

Then why am I afraid?
    Marlene N. Johnson

Changes

New faces, new places
  Great adventure
New people, new ideas
  Great excitement
New love, new happiness
  Great living

New faces, new places
  Such anxiety
New people, new ideas
  Such insecurity
New emotions, new worries
  Such a marriage
    Claire Elmore Mortimer

Time

Time goes by
People change
Many stay but
Some go away
You look back
And sometimes say
It took me
Years to
Get this way.
    Kelly Ness

Simply Marvelous

Your eyes smiled as they danced across
the mounds of my silhouette.
Hungry... yet, you tremble as you
drink in the essence of my core.
Anticipating...
With hands exploring,
launching waves that radiates across
my breasts creating
sand castles at their ends.
Your fingers find my wetness as
they disappear into my shoreline.
My hands strolled down your stomach to the water line.
Stroking...throbbing...Entwined, we merge.
You rupture like a volcano. Spurting...
Lava flows slowly, ever so deeply
into my sea of being, engulfing you
as you continue to harden
with every thrust of my rushing waves
you continue to pound with less intensity,
until the sea returns to a calm.
Simone Mitchell

Blinded Vision

Holocaust coloured colored man
Dances under a crayon tinted sky
Frozen sienna lights crack through the air
Breaking dawn into tomorrow
A brown, black, yellow, red man shuffles his feet
As New Year's Day dirt leaves imprints of the past
Closing the curtain to all he has in store
A spirit stands across his reflection
Kissing his shadow
Because he knows his soul doesn't believe
Blood colored kiss
Reduces an infantile gesture of affection
As his fetal mind reflects
He knew his face but he didn't know himself
The mirage horizon crumbles
As he balances his temple on the umber canyon
That he climbed
The mirage horizon crumbles
As he raises his arm
And serenades the descending light.
Troy Gilbert

Life

What makes Earth special is that it carries life,
And it's as beautiful as music from a high pitched fife.
We can't take it for granted for it is a gift,
It is very valuable if you get my drift.
We can find life both high and low,
So we must treat it nicely and help it grow.

Sometimes life helps us and also causes us harm,
But we've done harm by locking animals in a barn.
Our Solar System has nine planets to be exact,
We think we're the only life, but it may not be a fact.
For there are galaxies stretching out farther than we'll know,
We may see them and go where no one will go.

Life is a thing that we will treasure forever,
Life will keep on growing, ceasing never.
Life keeps us growing and learning more,
It keeps us active and we never bore.
And so during life we shall face glory and Death,
And we shall only pause to take a breath.
Brendan O'Sullivan

Growing Up

Well, I know I am losing control,
But something else has happened.
So many things are there to scare me,
My world has become a nightmare!
I look around to see what's going on,
But as I look in the mirror,
I see someone I really don't recognize.
I feel as if the eyes I see with are not my own!
I look again to see if things are different,
Things are the same, but yet they have altered.
I think about my recent actions, and the words that I say.
And I come to wonder, do they have a deeper meaning?
Are they an omen as to what will come?
Or have I taken a step into the quicksand of life?
Of course my life won't be taken, but changed.
It will have a deeper meaning, and soul!
At night I sleep, and finally I dream,
That my words are not an omen for what's to come,
But that they are simply...a sign of growing up!
Brandi Wrenn

Morning Mirror

So much has happened since I last could see you.
I look at you now and I realize the hurt in your eyes.
I close them and walk away from the truths that I face.
I need to touch who I am experience myself

I wanted to wrap my thoughts around you.
I wanted to fill this place with who we are and
who we could become then life somehow became a reality
a place without the hurt of our hearts
without the simple thoughts
without our building spirits.

Why did it matter
who's lives I touched.

How could this be perceived as something less
than our spirits building a place for truth, expression.

And now do you feel less..
I long for the one
I squint my eyes to try and look for you.
I fight myself,
To let the image go,

And in my mind I walk through this place to find you.
Not wanting to look down, but to continue on moving up

I long for you
Lorena Peterson

Love Is Suicide

I wept the day that he was gone,
It was my first love was it so wrong?
He held and kissed me every night
Our relationship ended with our very first fight.
Why, oh why Lord,
Did I do something wrong?
I still cry when I hear our song?
Part of me died the day we were through.
That evening it thundered and lightninged too.
I must bury these memories that make me so mad,
Will someone please tell me why love is so sad.
I guess it's the anger - he hurt me so much,
Sometimes when I'm lonely I can still feel his touch.
With the love of my life I lost all my pride,
I'm warning you all love is suicide!
Jill Liberatore

Mirage

I thirst in thought the same as other men.
Our nomad minds seek rare shade from the sun.
The well's the same we draw our water from.

I sense their sense of fear, of foe and friend.
In battle cries we merely cry as one,
And pray death's price we pay is holy done.

The same soft spirit sighs when love begins.
On curves of silken flesh we sculpt alike,
And reach like helpless babes to nurse the night.

They hear the voice inside that calls me in.
I listen to their pulse. I share their sight.
The same hearts halt, soul swells, at red dusk light.

We dream as one in some mysterious whim.
We are and were, will be, time and again.
   Michael Reade

To You... My Mom...My Friend

35 years already... yep that's me
And oh what a handful you knew I would be

Well, here I am... and I sure was
But without your hands... destination... flub!

The road has been long... easy days... a few
But our hearts and our song... titled "I Love You"

And with that love... oh how I grew
Combined with God above - means I still have you

And how very lucky I can't help but feel
To be a part of your story your so proud to tell

And all of those tumbles that laid in our path
Each has a label with a piece of our past

Now with the knowledge and lessons we've learned
There's new paths to follow old bridges to burn

You gave all your strength and encouraged me on
So with every breath taken...
   I thank you... my mom...
   Sandra L. Olszak

Some People Wish...

Some people wish for lots of money,
a real cool car,
or one to be their honey.

Some people wish for a smaller nose.
A bigger house or,
longer toes.

Some people wish they didn't have to work,
wash the dishes,
or live with a jerk.

Some people wish for a prettier face
But me I wish...
For the world to be a better place.

Many people wish for something new...
But I just hope my wish comes true.
   Katie Heyden

My Anger

From the halls of mind, to chambers of my heart
My anger consumes me; it's tearing me apart.

Eating away my emotions, feeding on my pain
Like a group of hungry buzzards tasting corpses in the rain.

The rain is tears falling from my eyes,
Everyone is dirty, cheap, and pack full of lies.
"Help!" My body screams at me.
"Help me, save me, set me free."

The hole is getting bigger, black and rotten to the core,
I'll take it no longer I'll take it no more.

Lying in white sheets, but blackened inside,
My pain, now evident, from doctors I cannot hide.

"Help me doctor, it hurts to cry,"
Now I need to ask myself, I need to wonder
Why?
   Eileen M. Casarez

Special Day

Special days part of life's encounter
Some recur, others need reminder
When being on the job was number one
Days off with pay were fun
Now, New Year's Day not all that
Too old for celebrant's hat
Washington's and Lincoln's dates of birth
No longer stand-alone worth
Come days of prayer and sparkle
Like liberty, thanks and ecclesiastical
None can ever be as special as May one
First son born that day in 1941
Loved from the start
This master of cello and kind heart.
   Joseph Rutkowski

Winter

Nature's grim reaper comes out once a year
Killing all of nature's beautiful sights.
Winter's chilling face finally appears
along with its cold days and colder nights.

The wind is the sickle that he carries,
Which makes the temperature even colder.
Life in his path that he takes may vary
not stopping to look over his shoulder.

The earth's casket, the newly fallen snow,
conceals all that nature has to present.
All plant life prays for rebirth and does not know
that soon they will become very content.

Then the lights of spring show their wonderful grace
and nature's grim reaper runs and hides its face.
   Troi P. Moore

Respect Is

Recognizing that you must first respect yourself before you
can gain the respect of any fellow human.
Earnestly seeking to reach your fullest potentials and goals in life
Striving to make a good reputation for yourself.
Protecting yourself from all the drugs and violence in the world.
Enhancing your education to the highest degree.
Continuously construct a life built around respect.
Trusting in yourself.
   Tyronica Scott

Freedom Of Our Spirit

When we grow up we are brought up in many different ways:
We have to listen and obey older people no matter what they say.

The next thing we realize is, we are entirely on our own-
Then one day, we take time to be alone:
Then Jesus calls us on the His invisible phone.
We can count on him just like the rising and setting of the sun.

Friends we have a long time are true friends:
Jesus's love will never end.

Freedom of our spirit comes from our Lord above:
Look below, above or anywhere-
You will see the soaring of the SPIRIT DOVE!

Marie A. Durocher

Wake Up!

We have differences with each other all the time,
Somebody is always drawing territorial lines.
Brothers often distinguish their own neighborhoods,
It somehow seems to do them good.
But, now, it's a call for peace,
So, let's chill on the violence on our streets.
Because, we're only taking our own men down,
And it's not that many around now. The fight is not with each other,
We're suppose to get strength from our brothers.
The enemy is the Destroyer, who comes in different packages and shades,
And he doesn't care how he takes you to the grave.
You see, cigarettes, liquor, drugs and guns all kill
but, they don't come in human shades,
So, while we're busy fighting each other they slip away.
They're taking us out one by one,
While we're smiling and calling ourselves having fun.
Regardless, how good it feels,
What does it matter if it's a feel that kills.
Hey, My Brother, don't be tricked!
Loose yourselves from the devils grip. And wake up!!!

Natalie Stovall

What The World Is Waiting For

In the midst of a great storm, deep clouds broke
From out the tempest a haze, from haze, smoke
Sifting through boughs, below - the forest floor
Still framed imagings, of flittering ghosts
They had dreamt such perfect dreams; and it seems
The promise of longing, cast from their dreams
To become real—life sailed by golden coasts...
Was it all these dreamers had waited for?
That, as yet unknown, but a smile in stead,
Motions to distant lands, a visit passed
In different ways; yet a step ahead
Of loneliness, a love spreads hope—will last
Things suggest other then and those that see
Diminished sounds, and what it is, to be
 S

Freedom Of Our Spirit

When we grow up we are brought up in many different ways:
We have to listen and obey older people no matter what they say.

The next thing we realize it, we are entirely on our own-
Then one day, we take time to be alone:
Then Jesus calls us on the His invisible phone.
We can count on his just like the rising and setting of the sun.

Friends we have a long time are true friends:
Jesus's love will never end.

Freedom of our spirit comes from our Lord above:
Look below, above or anywhere-
You will see the soaring of the SPIRIT DOVE!

Marie A. Durocher

Me

I am me and only to be.
It does not matter whom I pretend to be,
only the true me inside.
The only me I really wish to be.

The me I am today,
Only for good reason, is not me honestly.
Could it be the me I wish to be will never be?
For the sake of humor I can pick anyone I want to be.

I have not found the person for me.
The one I am speaking of, the one I desire to be.
I search for a soul for me,
to guide me into the direction of a person to be.

I can smile and make the person who is not me,
fake it and love you as I would love to be.
But then, I am not the me you would wish I could be.
You want the me, the me you know me to be.

The me I want to be is the one to love you, as I would.
If I truly loved the me that would always be,
Is the me that could not change because I loved the me to be.

Leslie Krmpotich

Teachers

What is a teacher someone may ask
Its someone who is always busy at their task

Their task a young brain to mold
And sometimes a small hand to hold

They must not only teach the ABC's
But also be there to help with skinned knees.

A child looks up to their teacher I'm told
As the mysteries of life they help to unfold

They teach us to read and write
And teach us why we should not fight

They teach us about worlds and countries faraway
And the world we see each and every day

They open up our the excitement of music and song
And open our artistic minds as we go along

We learn so much everyday
But yet they give us time to play

We sometimes forget to say how much we appreciate all you do
But from our hearts we THANK-YOU.

Kim Finch

Hell's Web

To those of us sinners condemned to hell,
There's a beginning but never an end.
No loved ones, not even a friend.
The creatures that can't wait for you to get in,
Are more scary than any features we've been.
And the noise is so loud once you get in that you try to hide.
You try and run back to outside, and just then
another creature grabs you by the hide, and swallows you deep inside.
The heat is so hot you beg for a drop of water or wind.
In hell there's a beginning but never an end.
Father please, please forgive me for my sins.
I swear I won't do them again.
You pound and you knock on heaven's door,
But all you hear are screaming and roars
of the monsters of the hell that you're in.
In hell there's a beginning but no end.
God knows you no more, cause he's warned us so many times before.
For us sinners the gates of heaven are closed forever never to open again.
That's the price we'll pay for the wages of our sins.
In hell there's a beginning but never, never and end.

David S. Horn

Caressing Radiance

Shimmering with ageless grace the sun's incandescent rays burst upon the horizon. Seeking out the darkness, radiant shafts of light twinkle with the affirmation of a new dawn. Racing over the landscape, shadows pursue the beckoning shelter of hidden recesses. Traversing East to West, this terrestrial sphere is ablaze with solar energy. Scaling upwards, the sun reaches its zenith bathing the earth fully in embracing illumination. Warmth is returned to the soil and the all important, renewing, life force is eagerly absorbed by the planet's inhabitants. Resembling an archer's arrow in flight, this day star slowly arcs towards the western horizon. Luster, fading from the sky, explodes into twilight's iridescent revelation. As the sun slips from view, fleecy white clouds, blushing pink, cuddle close to the earth like an insecure child to its mother's breast. Contradistinctively, almost magically, another heavenly body appears in the emptiness so recently relinquished. Hanging majestically on unseen divinity the moon casts its silvery radiance over the globe. Splendor abounds as this hunter's friend undergoes its fluid transformation, from crescent to full moon, throughout the course of its lunar cycle. Ocean tides obediently follow the old man in the moon as a faithful dog would its master. At its fullest, the moon bestows an illumination paralleling that of the sun. However, it's a false sun, inanimate and desolate. The lunar landscape is no more than a reflector even at night the suns probing rays seek out the darkness.
Virgil F. Flaherty

Why

This letter is to my heavenly father and to a dear friend we lost and we don't know why!

We just saw her yesterday and now today she's gone and you called her home to glory. She left behind a lot of friends and family and a smile no one could ever replace.

I'll miss her heart, because she always found ways to shine and never showed any fear and that's what made her special.

Lord you know how the days will be, but we lost someone special and its going to be hard to heal so we ask for an understanding.

You know a lot of us don't understand death and why, and when its a loved one it really hurts so do need your help we're on our bended knees.

We'll try not to show fear towards her home going, because we know you called her to work in heaven.

We'll not only miss her, but that smile and the love she left behind in our dreams. I know we'll see her again we just don't know when and that's the hard part.

As I leave with this special prayer can you please tell her we'll miss her and we'll never really forget her smile, because she would want us to remember that about her!
Kevin H. Riles

The Booger Ballad

He was sitting in church with a problem, that nobody else could know.
He was extremely uncomfortable, there was a huge booger stuck in his nose.
He wanted so badly to pick it, but somebody else might see.
For placing your finger up your nose in church would be far too disgusting.
He placed a finger over his left nostril, and blew with all his might.
Then that humongous booger came exploding out the right.

There was a woman in front of him, that wasn't even aware,
that the humongous booger had landed in her hair.
He thought he oughta pick it out, before that booger dried.
But when he missed and pulled her hair, the woman screamed and cried.
Everybody turned around and saw that booger there.
Then he felt responsible for that booger in her hair.

When he got home he felt so bad, he gave the woman a call.
But she was in the hospital, she had taken a nasty fall.
For when she washed the booger out she stepped on it and slipped.
She had fallen on her side, and broken her left hip.
The next day he called to check up on her and much to his surprise,
because of his big booger, an innocent lady died.
Scott Fleischer Nelson

Broken In Two

I lost the one I love
to another person's heart.
But I will never forget him
even though we part.
For he was the one I kissed,
I kissed for the very first time.
Our lips touched so gentle,
it was as if it were a crime.
But now he doesn't love me,
he will never love me again.
That thought tears me in two,
but in my heart our love was like a gem.
Hillary Rose Davis

The Girl in the Mirror

Until we met, I never knew the girl in the mirror...
   Never thought she was pretty enough,
    strong enough,
    smart enough...

Then for a every brief time you came into my life...
   And you gave me the hope and courage,
    to live,
    to love,
    to trust...

No one has ever touched my soul the way you did...
   Even through your sickness and pain you,
    were strong,
    and gentle,
    and knowing...

You accepted me for who I was, no questions asked...
   And you forced me to do the same,
    were love,
    with grace,
    with regard...

Dad....I wish you Godspeed, till we meet again, so long.
Melody Smith

My Special Love

I'm sure I've had a special love
Not many's had the same
If never more I see your face
Alone I had became

I'd know I've had the fullness
The gift from God above
Of life's most special treasure
I've had a special love.

A lot of people seek for it
Through all of life they look
It's something rather rare they say
Like some old care, worn book.

For many years I never knew
The gift from God was mine
Yet like a book, it takes the years
To finally be fine.

I'm sure I've had that special love
The love that ne'er grows old
That year by year with tender care
Grows stronger, dear and bold.
Mildred Kelley

Divinity

The sun, a pure white disc in appearance like the Eucharist

Dancing and spinning in the south. Western sky
Observed several days, with the naked eye

The sun was circled by ethereal shades of
Blue, delicate shades of pink and deep shades of red rose
A private revelation of Divinity, infinity.

Man with his finite limitations cannot fathom
   and unveil the mystery of the Divine

The sun rises, the sun sets, darkness falls dawn appears on
the horizon follows the beginning of a new day, the earth moves
in orbit surrounded by sun, moon and stars comets appear, stars
twinkle and fall the four seasons come and go Spring, Summer, Winter and Fall.

You are the First Cause who created it all with your grace
our whole human race should accept your lovingly embrace it calls us all.

Finite man should heed while he can repent, pray, ask for reprieve
For we cannot deceive ourselves any longer, time is running out
Pray, plead for Your mercy, and our salvation. It is Divine and eternal.

Mary B. O'Neill

Horse Latitudes

"Take to the oars", the captain said, "The sea is calm and the wind is
dead." Grey skies, no movement, quite still she be; look to the
waves, our destiny. The drum bangs out, twelve beats we row. Why
does the time seem to move so slow? How large is this sea, why is
land rare? We've sailed for hours and gone nowhere. Horse latitudes,
how did we ever sail within? A storm will surely rise and pay us for
our sins. "Horse latitudes", the captain cried and said "Take your
stand" Will we ever see the earth of our homeland? We sailed off as
patriots in defense of our land; caught up in battle, we plundered
more than we planned. The endless raids, bodies let for dead; all for
the stolen gold that the sea will take instead. Thunder cracks above
our heads, skies are crimson lined; all the people slain in battle are
dancing in my mind. Fading out, I hear a voice, of danger it calls; a
piercing pain goes racing through me as the darkness falls. The drums
ring silent as stars reappear; I grab for a piece of splintered
wood floating near. Water gently rolls by, as my melancholy moods
closes in on those horse latitudes. Horse latitudes, how did we ever
sail within? A storm will surely rise and pay us for our sins.
"Horse latitudes," the captain cried and said
"Take your stand" will we ever see the earth of our homeland?

Timothy J. Kehoe

Social Inadequacy

The art of engagement tends to allude me
Like water under a bridge from a distance.
Social intercourse is desired beyond words
And harder than talking to a policeman
After a parent's attempted suicide.

You want it so bad, it can't happen.
You get done doing the yard, and,
Putting the mower away in the garage,
Feel the squish of a struggling bird
Under your feet. It makes this smell.

You try to dart or dance away.
And stomp on another one. You get a shovel.
Might as well get used to it.
We hurt more by accident,
And repay wonderful kindness with clumsy intentions.

William W. Hagen

Faith In God (Only God Has The Power)

When I have moments of complete anxiety...
Of doubt, fear, or despair...
When I feel depressed, angry or with hate...
When I feel my life and life in general are a vicious circle...
And I feel that everything repeats itself...
The good and the evil; the beautiful and the ugly...
The hardwork and the crime; the vice and the violence...
The treason, the hypocrisy and the marble heart...
Feeling sad and angry, rebellious, rancorous, vengeful...
Not knowing why...
When I can do no more...
I just relax and put my life in God's hands and pray...
The Pater Noster or the Act of Faith,
The Hail Mary or the Act of Contrition...
Or I just say, "Oh, Sacred Heart of Jesus, I Confide In Thee..."
Or, "Oh, my God, have mercy of me..."
I just drop everything in God's hands and rest...
And the solutions to my problems begin to appear...
And I, like Jesus Christ, resurrect to a better and happier life...

Maria R. Sueiras

To Cia

From your distant peak
let fly your thoughts to soar...
to float...as dreams to me.

Take all wind from the air
and make it your voice to whisper...
to call...to me.

Make the sun and moon your eyes,
with all the sky your face,
and look into the depths of me.

And when you ride down into your valley,
across the field from pain,
take the trail that makes you free...
the way that leads to me.

Glenn L. Adamson

Withered

Such horror, words cannot describe
The grief and misery in the eyes,
Of those still living behind the wire,
As family dies so does their fire.

Raw-boned corpses with no names,
Flesh pulled taut on lucid frames,
Macabre faces on lined in pain,
Yet we still don't see the grisly stain.

The eyes, they tell a thousand tales
Of loved ones lost with feeble wails,
Of babies that were born to death
They took one first and only breath.

That breath they took of air was dim,
With destroyed plans, and dreams, and vim.
In this one case, hope was a fear
To face reality that drew so near.

So much was lost when plans were smashed,
Burn the veil, the dress, the sash,
Raze the cradle made of brass,
Slay the longing of lives past.

Jessica Edwards

A Lonely Soul

I met a man walking down my street
He told me of the sores on his feet
Walking his life away
Loneliness fills another day

I asked him of the places he has seen
And he told me he looks through a glass screen
Avoiding reality's hold
Shuddering in the cold

I looked at his face seeing the traces of tears
Looking through to the unspoken fears
He had known a love a long time ago
But now he has nothing to show

A love that has broken his heart
His dreams have been torn apart

He started walking one day
Hoping to go so far away
And now here he is, in front of my door
Unable to walk anymore

He has walked his life away,
Loneliness has ended this day
    Dawn Kepple

Existence

I will be the street that I drag with these feet,
the marvelous seconds running in a clock,
I will be the rhythmic beat that vanishes,
the monotonous day that fixes the stature of time,
vestiges of torn sashes,
branches that crackle
in consumed words, in dead mollusks
oppressed by salt.

I will be oblivion,
or the remembrance that came from your glance,
now a prisoner of the night,
I will be the silence of a shadow,
cedar cut into a thousand pieces,
rolling in the water currents
who know where?

I will be the past,
air sleeping on the walls.
An echo sinking in the distance.
    Carlos Fernandez

Uhh, That Feel

Hellen I would love to whisper;
  sweet nothings into your lovely ears.
And oh, how I would like to kiss you;
  like a fire that's hot.
Each tantalizing lick shaking me
  even more.
Until one moment I am playing,
  you like an organ.
    Robert Kropf

Untitled

"A hot air balloon
has popped. It
popped I say, Look!
Look! There it is, See it."
"Oh no it might land on someone and kill them."

"Oh don't be upset, That is
only a cloud."
But it has stripes."
"Ahh it won't hurt anyone."
    Gary Swisher

Days of Mold

Oddities were proof of normalcy.
Confusion was proof of clarity.
I manifest my intolerance
Through deliberate, futile silence.

You were comical and beautiful.
I was uncertain and pitiful.
I had to learn how to be myself.
You taught me how by sharing your wealth.

You were sure, stable, fun and focused.
We were wild—no act below us.
We howled, hated, drank and gambled;
Lost our friends; couldn't be handled.

But maturity was soon to come.
We traded away our raucous fun
For job and living and girls to love,
But still have acts that we're not above.

You helped make me who I am today.
When the time came, we wanted to stay
Right where we were, but our growth would have
Been stunted. So we left. And I'm glad.
    Michael Coleman Dee

Emotion

I feel deep, deep rumbling emotion
Way down in the depth of my soul;
Thrashing around like the stormy waters
Fierce, dashing, fearless and bold.

Rolling, tumbling, it has no bounds
Rising, reaching up, up to the ship
Easing down ever so slowly
Like the out going tides.

Then they are still, like a warm spring day
When the breeze is calm and almost still
Looking out over the grass so green;
Then a cool, easy breeze, and the air is chilled.

So much is happening deep inside
The emotions rise up with leaps and bounds
Just as quickly they suddenly go away
Yet, I sit still, not making a sound.
    Valeria F. Seay Shepard

Hymn

Mid-hum I stop to listen — the melody — haunts unconscious mind
Begins again the search for memory, in halls of soul cannot find.

Frantic thoughts unflurry, unknown emotions awake;
Heart-beats skip in hurry, reign over conscience it takes.

Melody that charms soul to sway, through hypnotized cue,
Refreshes while unravelling, sweet music in enhanced hue.

And it plays uninterrupted, so evasive as appears,
This melody stranger to tongue, familiar to ears.

Triggered by SPIRIT, its essence never captured,
Fleeting silence exorcised, I listen again enraptured.
    Susan Lorrine Varghese

The Traveler

A man sat playing blues guitar,
   And though with one,
Alone in a country bar
   Singing songs of home
And long ago.

Sad and mournful songs
   His choice,
A hoarse cigarettes 'n whiskey voice;
   And once nimble fingers
Now and then skipped a note.

Suddenly he stopped his song
   To a loud quiet,
Stared out the door a long, long time
   At fading light
Then walked out into the night
   Bound to a place of never before
Guided only by sight of an unseen door.
   Mel Guenther

Night Light Bug

Twinkle, twinkle little bug
as I watch you strut your stuff.
Do you feel heat in your rear,
I am sure I would most dear.

As the earth fades from light to dark
your beckoning light directs my sight.
Like the constellations you cover great space
without scheme or pattern 'tis no matter.

As you fly in earth's air and space
you decorate with such exquisite taste.
Twinkle and flash without rhyme or reason
such a beauteous sight this summer season.

Those dark woods cast such an eerie glow
until twinkle bug cast a revealing show
such precision erases the darkness and cold
replaced by warm visions of Christmas of old.

Let not rain, wind, fire or foul air
remove you from my country lair.
I would miss your merry chase
about this earth's glorious face.
   Roberta Bower

Dreams Of Tomorrow

With each new seasons change,
The stronger our love becomes,
   And our dreams are closer to reality.
We live and watch the seasons change from separate worlds,
Continuing to hold on to our dreams of tomorrow,
   To live together as one.
Although we live in separate worlds,
   We come together to grow for that brief moment.
Until time to disunite,
Hoping to reunite once again.
For someday the seasons will be ours to share and live
   together,
Uniting as one, never to disunite again.
Our dreams of tomorrow, will be today.
   Kimberlee R. Runkle

BIOGRAPHIES OF POETS

ABRAJANO JR., CESAR M.
[b.] September 7, 1953, Cavite City, Philippines; [p.] Cesar and Anicia Abrajano; [ed.] Terry Parker High, Jacksonville, FL, Brockton Central High, Brockton, MA; [occ.] Switchboard Operator, Sales Intern; [oth. writ.] Several poems and short stories but none published... so far.; [pers.] "Thank you" to my parents for helping me to appreciate all forms of art. Especially music and literature. My influences are Kerouac, Hardy Bukowski, Steinbeck and Baudelaire.; [a.] Ewa Beach, HI

ACOSTA, ROSENDA MARIA
[b.] August 31, 1975, Mesa, AZ; [p.] Julio Acosta, Josie Acosta; [m.] Fiance: Ruben C. Valenzuela; [ed.] Dobson High School, Rio Salado Community College, MCC; [occ.] Student: Pursuing a Career in Bilingual Elementary Education; [memb.] United Family Assembly of God Church; [hon.] AZ Ambassador of Music, Arizona Solo and Ensemble Contest - Voice: 1st and 2nd place. Ms. Cinderella Beauty Pageant - 1st Place; [pers.] I dedicate my writings to God, so they may touch those who don't believe, and encourage those who do believe.; [a.] Mesa, AZ

ADAMS, SHERRY SUE
[pen.] Sherry Sue Adams; [b.] February 3, 1948, Dumas, TX; [p.] Mr. and Mrs. Rhine; [m.] John Leben Adams, June 23, 1989; [ed.] High School, 1 yr. College became certified Activity Director for Convalescent Hospitals, Professional Singer/ Entertainer/Songwriter for 25 yrs. published Cartoonest for Aviation Magazine; [occ.] Disabled Severe Back Injury; [memb.] I belong to the Church of Jesus Christ of Latter Day Saints - am currently Second Counselor to the Relief Society President; [hon.] I was given a special Honor in organizing and putting together at the entertainment for a TLC Picnic for the Residents of all of the Convalescent Hospitals in Sacramento, while I was still a Certified Activity Director; [oth. writ.] Have written many poems have been published in American Legion Newsletter - also in the poetry forum, special mention in writers forum as well as having recorded a musical album.; [pers.] There is so much unhappiness and turmoil in the world - that if I can bring a smile on someone's lips or bring a little beauty to this world, then I feel like I've accomplished and made a difference in people's lives.; [a.] Hayfork, CA

ADAMSON, GLENN LEE
[b.] August 21, 1931, Spokane, WA; [p.] Frank Adamson, Hazel Adamson; [m.] Dorothea Pargoff Adamson, February 1, 1975; [ch.] Branden (Barber), Bryan, Michael, Patrick and Theresa; [ed.] A.B. University of Southern California, Phi Beta Kappa; [occ.] Writer; [hon.] Several Awards and Citations over the years from ACPRA (American College Public Relations Association) now "Case," for Written Work; [oth. writ.] Travel articles for various publications, historical and promotional writing for local colleges, universities, and other non-profit orgs. novel in progress.; [pers.] My favorite poet is Emily Dickenson, Wish she'd tried Haiku.; [a.] Ontario, CA

ADLER, JEREMY
[b.] August 1, 1983, U of M; [p.] Ronald Adler, Judith Adler; [ed.] Currently in 6th Grade at Clague Middle School; [occ.] Student; [memb.] Eight Zillions, 2 Team Member, Academic Games Team Member, Basketball Team Member; [oth. writ.] The jews will survive (in hebrew).; [pers.] I write because I enjoy it. I would like to thank my grandparents for showing me the contest ad. I would also like to thank Mr. Edger Allan Poe for inspiring me.; [a.] Ann Arbor, MI

AGRO, NICASIA
[pen.] Nicki Jo; [b.] September 5, 1984, Voorhees, NJ; [p.] Angelo and Rosalie Agro; [ed.] In 6th Grade at Voorhees Middle School; [occ.] Student, 6th Grade; [memb.] Junior Episcopal Youth Club - St. Bartholomew's Episcopal Church, Cherry Hill, NJ; [pers.] "I am a kind and fun loving person..."; [a.] Voorhees, NJ

AGUILAR, SAUNDRA J.
[b.] July 20, 1944, San Francisco, CA; [p.] John and Carol McFadden; [ch.] Kimberly Anne, Kirsten Lee, Kent Eugene, Kyle John; [ed.] Buchser High School, UCLA; [occ.] Event Producer, Actress; [memb.] "Screen Actors Guild," "American Federation of Television and Radio Artists"; [hon.] Various roles in Television, Film and Theatrical Productions, Creator and Instructor of "A More Feminine You" at Brigham Young University; [pers.] "To be a seeker of truth and to glorify its wisdom."; [a.] Napo, CA

AGUILAR, VERONICA
[pen.] Veronica Aguilar-Medina; [b.] May 9, 1982, Chicago, IL; [p.] Sonia Aguilar, Floreatino Medina; [ed.] 8th Grade Student at Darwin Elementary School; [memb.] I am a Member of the Mary-Kate and Ashley Olsen Fun Club, and also a Member of the Jonathan Taylor Thomas Fan Club; [hon.] I've gotten Awards for special helper, excellence in English, excellence in Science, and for special effort in Physical Education; [pers.] I want everyone to realize that race is just a color and that we are all God's children and should always get along.; [a.] Chicago, IL

AHAMED, SMITHA
[b.] November 25, 1987, MA; [p.] Dr. Ahamadunny Pathiaseril and Ayisha Punnilath; [ed.] Second Grade in Gaines Elementary School, attends Math in Third Grade; [memb.] Junior Bulldog Club, The Georgia Department of Education, Public Library Services Summer Reading Club 1995; [hon.] Gold Medal Awards for reading in 1994-1995, Gold Medal Certificate from Wyoming Association of Elementary School Principals, Outstanding Achievement Awards in the National PTA Cultural Arts Program 1995 - Certificate of Recognition for Participation in Reflections 1994, Super Citizenship Award in 1994-1995, one of the Art piece about Native American's have been displayed and become the Permanent collection in Wyoming State Art Museum; [pers.] I think reading is fun. I can read when I am happy, sad or angry. Writing a poem is not so hard. You express your feelings in writing. Read again and again what you wrote and replace new words if you think that it is better.; [a.] Athens, GA

AHEARNE, PATRICK J.
[pen.] Pat Ahearne; [b.] August 30, 1966, Flint, MI; [p.] John and Sharon Ahearne; [m.] Rebecca, August 26, 1988; [ch.] Megan; [ed.] University of Michigan, BSN; [occ.] Army Nurse Corps., Captain; [memb.] Emergency Nurses Association, Association of Military Surgeons of the United States, Veterans of Foreign Wars; [hon.] Army Service Ribbon, National Defense Ribbon, Army Commendation Medal, Southwest Asia Service Medal, Kuwaiti Liberation Medal; [pers.] I hope this poem is an anthem for all nurses.; [a.] Natick, MA

AHNER, SHARI LU
[pen.] Korina M. Bradford; [b.] March 30, 1965, Allentown, PA; [p.] Theodore R. Ahner and Sharon L. Ahner; [ed.] Bangor Area High School; [occ.] Data Control Technician; [hon.] National Honor Society, Ingersoll-Rand Corporate Procurement Council Letter of Commendation and Award; [pers.] If you look for beauty, that's what you'll find. I have been greatly influenced by my parents and my grandmother, Mary. They taught me what love and beauty are.; [a.] Roseto, PA

AL-SAEED, AESHA
[pen.] Aesha Al-Saeed; [b.] October 29, 1961, Portland, OR; [p.] Loretta Lorenz, Wilfred Lorenz; [m.] Yousef M. Al-Saeed, August 1981; [ch.] Bedriya, Khandeeja and Jamahl; [ed.] Attendend Episcopalian Private Lower and Upper School - (OR, Epis.), Majored in Middle E. History at Portland State College in Portland, OR; [occ.] Housewife; [hon.] Have never attempted before such a challenge as a contest.; [oth. writ.] Have written 4 other poems my mother is especially fund of.; [pers.] I am fluent in Arabic, also now a Moslem convert. My prayers are for "World Peace."; [a.] Portland, OR

ALALAMUA, OLOTANIA ENELEMOETOTO
[b.] July 24, 1977, New Caledonia; [p.] Enele M. Alalamua, Hiasinita Alalamua; [ed.] Graduate of Farrington High currently attending University of Hawaii, Manoa; [occ.] Student, University of Hawaii, Manoa; [memb.] Lector and Religious Education of Saint John the Baptist, Health Academy, HOSA, and a Bowling League Sanctioned by ABC.; [hon.] Writing Award from Farrington Health Academy, Completion and Graduation Certificate for Farrington Health Academy, Grant from Catholic Social Ministry; [oth. writ.] Several poems published in High School's yearly featured edition. Work Used As A Play In S.A.D.D. (Students Against Drunk Driving) assembly. This play was televised on local cable T.V.; [pers.] I tend to write about my inner most feelings and some of those feelings expressed, I am certain are shared by others. It is my sincere hope that through this sharing, that I would let others know that they are not alone and its okay for this feeling to be shared.; [a.] Honolulu, HI

ALEXANDER, EPHRAIM I.
[b.] December 28, 1971, Chicago, IL; [p.] Kenneth and Rita Alexander; [ed.] Oak Park and River Forest (High School), Iowa State University B.S. 1995, Iowa State University MS 1997;

[occ.] Student, ISU Manager/Producer Planet X, Music/Productions; [oth. writ.] Several poems published in school publications, working on a comic book.; [pers.] My major influences are my mother (surprise, surprise), and my good friend Amy Shuster. Without their love and support I'd still be writing on paper napkins and back of phone books.; [a.] Ames, IA

ALFORD, BETTY
[b.] November 19, 1948, New York, NY; [p.] Lorene Moore and George Moore; [m.] Leo Alford, November 25, 1967; [ch.] Trina Alford, Damon Alford, Andrea Alford; [ed.] Washington Irving HS, Bronx Community College, City College; [memb.] Northeast Bronx, Democratic Club; [hon.] Golden Key Honor Society; [oth. writ.] Several unpublished poems and essays.; [pers.] I strive to reflect reality and truth in my writings. I have been greatly influenced by social problems and the bleak outlook for the future of mankind.; [a.] Bronx, NY

ALFORD, RICKY
[b.] 1958, Salinas, CA; [p.] Ben and Betty Alford; [ed.] 2 yr. Community College, Dean's List, Journalist School Paper the Overview, Developer of an Endowment for HIV People wishing to go back to School; [occ.] Living/ Surviving with Aids; [memb.] Living room, Center for People affected and infected by Aids. I am 10 year survivor; [pers.] Trying to insert hope into lives of other HIV survivors.

ALLEN, CHRIS W.
[pen.] Chris; [b.] December 24, 1927, La Grange, GA; [p.] Myrtle and Howard Smith; [m.] Jim Allen, July 29, 1995; [ch.] Terry and Tommy Tuck; [ed.] High School and Self Ed.; [occ.] Retired; [memb.] Golden Kiwanis Club, First Baptist Church; [hon.] Kewanian of the Year 1992, Outstanding Volunteer 1990 and 1991 President of Kewanis 2 Terms and only Woman even elected in Upson County to date; [oth. writ.] Children stories in poem form. Christian and spiritual also lots of personal poems of friends - and many others I have been writing for one year.; [pers.] I enjoy writing and would like to write short stories some poems have been published in newspapers.; [a.] Thomaston, GA

ALLEN, RONALD J.
[b.] July 16, 1958, NY; [p.] Alice Allen and William Allen; [m.] Julie A. Allen, July 24, 1976; [ch.] Four Daughters (Amy Starr, Amanda Lin, Amber Lee and April Spring); [ed.] Southern Wesleyan University; [occ.] Pastor, Student; [memb.] Providence Wesleyan Church; [hon.] My Family; [pers.] A society who forgives is on the road to recovery. Start with family then community then state then country then world.; [a.] Central, SC

ALLISON, CATHERINE
[b.] February 16, 1947, Havana, FL; [p.] Mrs. Rossie Huntley; [m.] David Allison, January 19, 1970; [ch.] Steven, Timothy, Kelvin, Jefferey, David Jr., Angela; [ed.] Graduate Havana Northside High, Associate of Arts Degree Nova Southeastern University, Presently Attending Nova SE and Fla. A and M University to attain Bachelors of Science Degree; [occ.] Presently Employed, Godsen County School Board - Havana Elem. Sch. Teacher Assistant; [memb.] New Bethel P.B. Church, North Florida Reading Council; [hon.] Dean's List Nova Southeastern University, Certificate of Appreciation 5th Grade Department; [oth. writ.] Spiritual Warfare, Joy Cometh In The Morning, Conquer The Dream, Mama's Baby Boy, Giving Something Back.; [pers.] It is not the smart or the swift who survives the continual ups and down of the experiences from life. It is only the strength of endurance, given from God's grace to behold the winner of the race.; [a.] Havana, FL

ALLISON, VIVIAN C.
[pen.] Julia Allison (sometimes); [b.] September 6, 1932, Shawnee, OK; [ch.] Three sons; [ed.] Three years University; [occ.] West Texas Homemaker; [memb.] Abilene Writers Guild, Aids Support Group; [hon.] Received an Award for Poetry (Abilene Writers Guild); [oth. writ.] The crisis-published in the Mesquite magazine (Abilene's literary magazine). A manuscript is being considered by a movie company.; [pers.] Life is never perfect. It is an adventure with journeys and transformations. My writing tries to reflect humanity through our world's tarnished, silver-framed mirror. Reflecting in satire, our prejudices and blemishes - useful and appropriate, or wrong and hurtful.; [a.] Abilene, TX

AMADOR, LILIANA DE JESUS
[pen.] Liliana Amador; [b.] May 20, 1967, Barranguilla, Colombia; [p.] Hugolino Y., Ligia E. Amador; [ed.] Paterson Catholic Regional High, BA from Bates College, (Lewiston, ME), MFA from University of Minnesota, (Minneapolis, MN); [occ.] Professional Actor, Acting and Movement Instructor, (Jersey City State College - NJ); [memb.] Dance Zinger Dance Company, (NYC) New York City, Bates College Steering Committee; [hon.] Twin Cities Theatrical Arts, Amateur Ballroom Champion, Leopold Schepp Foundation Scholar; [pers.] Unrealized dreams reveal themselves only in the absence of fear and passion for the process of living!; [a.] Paterson, NJ

AMODEO, JAMES
[pen.] Jamie Amodeo; [b.] July 21, 1981, Middle Town, CT; [p.] James and Patricia Amodeo; [ed.] Presently a Freshman at Terre Haute South (Home of the "Braves") - Elementary... 6th Grade at Dixie Bee in Terre Haute, IN, 7th and 8th Grade at Honey Creek Middle School, (K-5th at Flanders Elem. in East Lyme, CT); [hon.] Student Council "Peer Leadership" Recognition High Honors, Honors Track Award, Basketball Award - 8th Grade; [oth. writ.] Elementary book on vacation in Disney World.; [pers.] To believe in myself so I can believe in others. To set a good example and not follow bad ones. Education comes first. To do my very best, but I realize I may fail at times, because it's part of growing up.

AMREN, JOANNA
[b.] August 19, 1975, Traverse City, MI; [p.] Thomas and Barbara Amren; [ed.] Center High School; [hon.] C.H. Guenther Scholarship Award; [oth. writ.] Wrote for school newspaper.; [pers.] When I write, I hold back nothing. When I write, I am bold, I am strong and I am free to be me.; [a.] San Antonio, TX

ANDERSON, EDWARD
[pers.] One year the girls High School basketball team won the state tournament championship. The next year they went undefeated in regular season play and were expected to repeat as champions but they lost in the play off games, which was a great disappointment to them. It was to them and others in similar situations that the poem, To The Tournament Losers, was written.; [a.] Greeley, NE

ANDERSON, ELIZABETH
[pen.] Lisbeth Anderson; [b.] February 16, 1923, Los Angeles, CA; [m.] Charles W. Anderson, April, 1950; [ch.] Three Daughters; [ed.] BFA San Diego State University; [occ.] Artist; [memb.] Pastel Society of San Diego, San Diego Portrait Society, San Diego Art Institute; [hon.] Scholarship Award, Pastel Society of America, 1st Place Awards Pastel Soc., San Diego, (2) Juror's Distinctive Merit Award, S.D. Guild's All California Show; [pers.] Good composition in verse, art and music has nourished the soul through the ages.

ANDERSON, JENNIFER
[pen.] Jennie; [p.] Harriet Branche and Clinton Anderson; [ed.] I am a senior at Martin Luther King, Jr. High School; [memb.] Senior Committee (I was co-chair person awards and ceremonies), Law Chronic (Editor), Senior Source Magazine (Editor), Liberty Program Enrichment Program (College bound Students); [hon.] Thurgood Marshall Award - 9th Grade, Honors Program 2 yrs., School Buttons Global Studies Certificates; [oth. writ.] My Inspiration (essay), My Infatuation (poem), How Staying In School Helps America (essay), Million Man March and Time Will Pass (poem).; [pers.] I would like to acknowledge my parents but love me dearly. My twin brother, Joshua - "your my right arm," Stephanie - my little sister stay sweet and to my extended family, teachers and friends - thanks (support).; [a.] Bronx, NY

ANDREWS, JAYAN
[pen.] Jay Andrews; [b.] November 29, 1957, Chittadi, Mundakayam Kerala, India; [p.] V.C. Andrews and Annamma Andrews; [m.] Tissy Jayan Andrews, September 21, 1987; [ch.] Daughter 5 years old - Punnya Ann Andrews; [ed.] BS in Electrical Engineering from India, Certificates in Project Management and Building Systems Design from New York University, MS in Energy Mgmt. from New Institute of Technology (Graduating in May 1996); [occ.] Energy Management Intern at Community Environmental Center, Long Island City, NY; [memb.] 1) Sargavedi - Literary Organization of Malayalis in New York, 2) RECCAA - Regional Engineering College, Calicut Alumni Association 3) St. Gregorios Church, Bronx, NY (NY Chapter); [hon.] 1) Editor's Choice Award from National Library of Poetry for poem "Still Novel in our Hearts," published in "Windows of Soul", 2) 1994 Fokhana Award for Best Malayalam Poem Published in Malayalam

Magazines in North America; [oth. writ.] Several Malayalam poems published in local newspapers magazines. Also short stories and satires in local newspapers and magazines.; [pers.] I like to reflect the beauty of nature and love which makes human hearts vibrant.; [a.] New Rochelle, NY

ANGELL, MICHELLE
[b.] April 5, 1982, Moses Lake, WA; [p.] Larry and Margaret Angell; [ed.] Still attending Chief Moses Jr. High; [oth. writ.] This is my first published writing, and I am extremely excited.; [pers.] Remember to never surf in a snowstorm.; [a.] Moses Lake, WA

ANGERS, ALLEN J.
[b.] July 10, 1921, Abbeville, LA; [p.] Robert J. Angers and Anna Mae Angers; [m.] Rita M. Patout, May 1, 1944; [ch.] Christopher, Patrick, Sally, Carolyn, Mary, Allen, Jr., Nancy; [ed.] St. Peters, New Iberia, LA, LSU, Baton Rouge; [occ.] Independent Real Estate Appraiser and Realtor 1948 - to Present; [memb.] Life Member Appraisal Institute and Past Pres La-Miss Chapter Appraisal Institute, Past Pres Newiberia and Lafayette Boards of Realtors, Dir La Realtors Etc.; [oth. writ.] Appraisal Journal, Condemnation Appraisal Practice, Tech Reports, var poems.; [pers.] Poems for friends and grand children, wood sculpture and water color hobby.; [a.] Lafayette, LA

ARINCORAYAN, DERRICK F. K.
[b.] November 3, 1961, Honolulu, HI; [p.] Nancy and Felipe Arincorayan; [m.] Vicky D. Arincorayan, September 28, 1991; [ed.] Mililani High School, University of Hawaii, School of Social Work; [occ.] Clinical Social Worker; [memb.] Silver Cadeusus Society; [hon.] Dean's List, University of Hawaii - School of Social Work; [oth. Writ.] A Soldiers Friend, Georgia's Grace, Children Of The Red, White And Blue, The Book Of Morality.; [pers.] I write from the heart my inner thoughts and feeling that I may be experiencing at a given time and place. My expression is offered to those who may be experiencing these same thoughts/feelings. In essence to offer comfort to those who may experiencing stress.; [a.] Honolulu, HI

ARMSTRONG, JOSEPH E.
[b.] January 3, 1948, Fresno, CA; [p.] Richard Armstrong and Mary Armstrong; [m.] Katherine Armstrong, June 17, 1979; [ch.] Rodney Dwayne McKelvey (Stepson); [ed.] MS - Biology/Psychology 1980 San Diego State University; [occ.] Research Associate 4/1986 and Assistant Professor 12/90 - Drew University of Medicine and Science Los Angeles, Calif.; [memb.] National Management Association 1988, Institute of Certified Professional Managers 12/6/91, Biological Sciences, Health and Physical Care Services and Related Technologies - Credential 3/29/82 California; [oth. writ.] Personal poetry to my wife.; [pers.] Be respectful and sensitive to all cultures, the poor and the handicapped. The understanding and compassion for such individuals is more than a notion. I communicate to you openly as an acquired brain injured person. (Injury occurred 6/1/95).; [a.] San Diego, CA

ASHBY, VIRGINIA
[b.] September 27, 1920, KY; [p.] W. B. and Minnie (Foster) Nichols; [m.] B. R. Ashby (Divorced), September 20, 1946; [ch.] Four - 2 sons, 2 daughters; [ed.] Diploma as Registered Nurse - 1942; [occ.] Retired; [memb.] Senior Friends, Scrabble Club, Church; [hon.] Honorable Mention in Short Story Contest, Battle Stars for Three Campaigns in WW II Plus Victory Medal; [oth. writ.] I've written 40 poems and dissertations (mostly poems) from the '30s - 1995, they concern nature, family, love, faith, and war, none published as of now.; [pers.] All of my writings are original, but not by me. The words and inspirations were graciously given to me by a Higher Power, usually at a turning point in my life. Several were in memory of loved ones and friends and some about or to my children and grandchildren. I thank all of them for unknowingly lending themselves to my ideas. It's been my desire to seek God through my poetry, hoping this would help others.; [a.] Louisville, KY

ASHE, TONYA
[b.] May 2, 1977; [p.] Larry and Alice Ashe; [m.] Clint Long, June 11, 1994; [ch.] Gaven Bradley Long; [ed.] Murray High; [pers.] I dedicate this poem to my wonderful son Gaven Long.; [a.] Cisco, GA

ATER, KATHY M. DOLLE
[pen.] Kathy M. Dolle; [b.] July 26, 1963, Lubbock, TX; [p.] C. E. and Wilma Dolle; [m.] Phillip W. Ater, July 10, 1993; [ch.] None, except 2 dogs and 1 cat; [ed.] AAS as Legal Secretary, South Plains Jr. College, University of Texas at Arlington - Legal Assistant Program; [occ.] Legal Assistant, Fort Worth, TX; [memb.] National Notary Association; [hon.] Dean's Honor Roll at South Plains Jr. College; [oth. writ.] This is my first published poem. Other poems I've written are only found in my journal or diary.; [pers.] I have been highly influenced by my parents who adopted me in 1964, escpecially by my daddy who died of cancer. My poems come straight from my heart and my emotions. Poetry is a form of therapy for myself.; [a.] Arlington, TX

ATER, WINIFRED WILLIAMSON
[pen.] W. W. Ater, Luara Rodgers; [b.] February 19, 1931, Evanston, IL; [p.] Mamie Cissna Williamson; [m.] Bobby V. Ater, March 31, 1956; [ch.] Robert Verne Ater, Loni L. Ater; [ed.] Elmhurst College; [occ.] Retired Teacher; [memb.] California Retired Teachers Assoc.; [oth. writ.] Many poems, art instruction book, science and local history.; [pers.] Live, and let live.; [a.] Santa Maria, CA

AU, SIUK
[pen.] Billy Au; [b.] February 27, 1975, Hong Kong; [p.] Mui Mui Wong; [ed.] Richard Stockton College; [memb.] National Environmental Health Association; [pers.] I want to say thank you to all my teachers and my friends who have helped me and have taught me a lot throughout my life.; [a.] Pomona, NJ

AUBUCHON, MILDRED
[pen.] Mickey; [b.] September 22, 1917, AR; [p.] Virgi Posey and Willard Shumate; [m.] Clyde Aubuchon, June 16, 1935; [ch.] Two; [ed.] 8th, Some Night School; [occ.] Retired

AUGUSTE, CARLO
[pen.] Annylus Bruno; [b.] April 1, 1968, Porl-Au-Prince, Haiti; [p.] Kesner Auguste, Evelyne B. Auguste; [ed.] College Roger Anglade, Faculty of Ethnology, Port-Au-Prince, Haiti; [occ.] Business Administration Student, Brooklyn, New York; [memb.] Club of Young Poets, Cal, Royal Haitan Tennis Club, Student - Teacher Association; [hon.] Poet of Radio Plus (1990), Writer of the Year (1992), National Theater Grand Prize (1992-1994); [oth. writ.] Stroke of lightning, do you know, I believe...several poems in French: Coup De Foudre, Bookman Mon Drapeau, L'Amerique...; [pers.] This poem is an other cry against crime, war, abuse around the world, cry that will stop when all of us finally accept man of any race for who he really is: "Our Brother."; [a.] Brooklyn, NY

AVALOS, TONYA M.
[pen.] Marie; [b.] August 10, 1981, Brady, TX; [p.] Pat Avalos, Donna Davis; [ed.] 9th Grade; [oth. writ.] To Amanda H. B.F.F.E. with love, always.; [pers.] Have no fear what so ever!; [a.] Mason, TX

BABIK, HOLLY LYNN
[b.] October 25, 1977, Houston, TX; [p.] Daniel and Carol Babik; [ed.] 12th grader at Willis High School; [memb.] National Honor Society Member, 4 years of Marching Band, J.E.T.S., Member, Church Youth Group Service Committee Member, Drill Team Member; [hon.] Who's Who among American High School Students, State Solo and Enseyble Contestant, Most Outstanding Sophomore Award (Drill Team); [pers.] 1 try to interpret situations in life as I see they and then compose they in a figurative manner; [a.] Conroe, TX

BAIGIS, SUSAN
[b.] March 25, 1956, Scranton, PA; [p.] James and Lois (Reid) Bowden; [m.] Edward Baigis, July 9, 1977; [ch.] Brian and Kristen; [ed.] Mid-Valley High School; [occ.] Secretary - Allstate Ins. Co.; [memb.] Throop United Methodist Church Chancel Choir and Sunday School Teacher; [hon.] Honorable Mention "Our Mom" from Lliard Press and Award of Merit Certificate "Our Mom" from famous poets society, Our Hometown - published in Mid-valley News and the following poems published in Local Newspaper.; [oth. writ.] Our mom - a special Windchime it breaks my heart - through the years my little boy - my little cheer leader no dial tone - the buddy system friendships - I'm not the maid stop by for tea - the golden rule; [pers.] Treat others with kindness and compassion follow the "Golden Rule." Cherish the time you have with your parents and family; [a.] Throop, PA

BAILEY, JENNIFER
[b.] October 4, 1971, Charleston, SC; [p.] Franklin and Pattie Bailey; [ed.] BS Aviation Business Administration from Embry Riddle

Aeronautical Univ. in Daytona Beach, FL; [occ.] Accounting Office, World Savings and Loan Assoc; [memb.] Sigma Tau Delta, the International English, Honor Society, Dean's List; [hon.] Private Pilot and Aircraft Dispatcher Certificates; [oth. writ.] Poems and short stories presented in University and high school magazines; [pers.] Balance and perspective are the keys to success and happiness in life.; [a.] San Francisco, CA

BAKER, MICHELLE
[b.] May 26, 1972, Panama Canal Zone, Panama; [p.] Richard Baker, Elizabeth McIntyre; [m.] Tim Peters; [ch.] Johnathan Baker; [ed.] Gulf Breeze High, FL, Pitt Community College, NC; [occ.] Corporate Sales, Infomart, Dallas, TX; [memb.] Volunteering Activities: Heart Association, Big Brothers and Sisters, Dallas Amerifest; [hon.] Editors Choice Award 1995, Nat. Lib of Poetry, "Between the Raindrops"; [oth. writ.] I am currently writing my first book.; [pers.] Since reading "stopping by the woods on a snowy evening" by Robert Frost at age 10, most of my writings reflect the happiness and uniqueness of life, personal growth and change.; [a.] Plano, TX

BALASA, ANDREW
[b.] December 13, 1946, Brooklyn, NY; [p.] Andrew Balasa and Felicia Balasa; [m.] Dorothy Balasa, April 24, 1971; [ch.] Michael Andrew, David John; [ed.] Eli Whitney Vocational High School, George Westinghouse Vocational and Technical High School; [occ.] Retail Associate Sales Leader, Scotty's Crystal River, FL; [hon.] Honorable Discharge, U.S. Navy; [oth. writ.] Several other poems being published.; [pers.] My writings are of life, and more importantly love. Because one day mankind will reach the stars.; [a.] Crystal River, FL

BANKER JR., JOHN C.
[b.] December 13, 1931, Westchester, PA; [p.] Deceased; [m.] Mary Sue Banker, June 25, 1963; [ch.] Melanie Lynn, Sandra Jean, Jennifer Ruth; [ed.] Extensive Military Training (Electronics, digital principles, computer and Satellite Systems) retired AF, 1969; [occ.] Retired Technical Writer (August 1994); [memb.] VFW Post 4305, Winter Gardens Fla, Part member of the Society of Technical writer, Ordained deacon (Baptist) currently teach old testament Theology; [hon.] Many from Military (AF Commendation) and others; [oth. writ.] Several publications in military Instructors Journal, one unpublished book in diaft stage, "Journey Into Hell" (about my participation in Atomic Bomb testing) (1950's); [pers.] A Military writer, and later as a writer of computer-based documents, my goal was "easy-to-read," "easy-to-understand" user manuals. My goal in writing was always to "keep it simple," or to explain things in the language of the reader; [a.] Orlando, FL

BANKSTON, SANDRA G.
[b.] November 16, 1949, Detroit; [p.] Cleo, Annabell Burton; [m.] James Curtis Bankston, June 20, 1980; [ch.] 3; [occ.] Disability Factory Worker; [memb.] Miracle Temple Church of God in Christ; [hon.] From the president of the United States of America Bill Clinton. I wrote a poem about the Oklahoma bombing to let them know, we love them and care and praying for them; [pers.] I try to awaken a spiritual awareness in my poems; [a.] Lansing, MI

BAPTIST, BRENDA J.
[b.] August 4, 1950, Jersey City, NJ; [p.] Willie and Alice Kincy; [m.] Leon S. Sr., February 6, 1973; [ch.] Kinya Lynnair and William Frederick; [ed.] St. Michael H.S. and Pierce Jr. College; [occ.] Mary Kay Cosmetice Senior Sales Director; [memb.] Rainbow Coalition; [hon.] Adult tutor for Mayor's Commission for Literacy; [pers.] When you step out in fear, failure follows the road becomes bumpy and long when you step out on faith, success follows because he will keep you strong.; [a.] Philadelphia, PA

BARBER, MATTHEW G.
[b.] July 2, 1973, Buffalo, NY; [p.] Sidney Barber and Sharon Zubler; [m.] Jennifer Barber, August 1, 1992; [ed.] Pioneer Central; [occ.] Restaurant Manager; [pers.] It takes vision to stand apart from the mindless mass as they follow the Pied Piper wherever he may lead.; [a.] Freedom, NY

BARNES, JOE
[b.] November 21, 1977, Toledo, OH; [p.] Tim Sr., and Willa Barnes; [ed.] Broomfield High (12th grade); [occ.] Student in High School; [oth. writ.] Nothing published; [pers.] I try to open people's minds to racism and other inner city problems which I witnessed while growing up in Columbus, Ohio; [a.] Broomfield, CO

BARNESS, CURRY ARLINGTON
[b.] March 4, 1917, LaPine, AL; [p.] Emmett Barnes and Anne Barness; [m.] Helen Marie Barness, May 12, 1945; [ch.] Carol ann, Mary Ellen, Michael Curry; [occ.] Retired; [oth. writ.] A number of poems several short stories a number of articles for local newspaper on a regular basis wrote Oakview Lakes newsletter for two years; [pers.] My love of the outdoors has influenced many of my poems and stories.; [a.] Fort Meade, FL

BAROCAS, EDWARD L.
[b.] May 11, 1967, New York, NY; [ed.] Rutgers University, The National Law Center of George Washington University; [occ.] Special Counsel, N.J. Public Defender's Office; [pers.] All one needs to find is a connection - the rest is just details. This particular piece was inspired by Judy, Cosmic Trigger, the N.J. "Y" Camps, the butterfly and Myshkin.; [a.] New Brunswick, NJ

BARTHLEIN, SANDRA M.
[b.] October 25, 1946, Norfolk, VA; [p.] George W. and Mary F. Murden; [m.] Jimmy D. Barthlein, October 14, 1978; [ed.] Princess Anne; [occ.] Retired Executive Secretary for Federal Gov't; [memb.] National Piano Guild, American Diabetes Assn. - Norfolk Savoyarads Ltd. - Norfolk Theater Productions, National Modeling Academy, Sweet Adalines Hospitals Volunteer Committee; [hon.] Beta Sigma Phi - VA., Volunteer Award Committee - over 2,000 hours; [oth. writ.] Publishing - National Library of Poetry, Poetry and Short Stories Featured in various Newspapers, Periodicals, Reporter for Local Gov't./C'vilian, Newspapers-Assorted Technical Writings.; [pers.] My love and appreciation for the fine arts, along with the praise and inspiration from my family has greatly influenced my writings!; [a.] Norfolk, VA

BARTON, DEREK
[b.] May 8, 1952, Philadelphia, PA; [ch.] Beverly Barton; [ed.] San Diego State; [occ.] Writer/Actor and Gold's Gym's Director of Pr/Promotions/Advertising; [memb.] Writer's Guild (WGAW) Dramatist Guild, AEA, SAG, AFTRA; [oth. writ.] A one-act play, a sitcom, 3 screenplays, a children's story and over 200 poems. Managing Editor of the gold's gym Magazine; [a.] Agoura, CA

BASCHWIT, FAYE YVONNE
[b.] January 2, 1938, Hillsdale, NJ; [p.] Herbert and Huguette Pender; [m.] Lawrence Baschwit, June 6, 1959; [ch.] Alfred Lawrence, Karen Faye; [ed.] High School Graduate; [occ.] Realtor, Owner; [memb.] NY State Assoc. of Realtors, Natl. Assoc. of Realtors, Order of Eastern Star; [hon.] Realtor of the Year 1989, Greene Cty. Bd. of Realtors, Graduate Realtor Institute Designee, Realtor Honor Society - NYSAR; [oth. writ.] Several poems and articles, inspirational or pertaining to real estate, published in local newspapers or magazines etc.; [pers.] I strive to demonstrate to others that lasting happiness and peace are possible when we cultivate our spiritual life in love, faith, and hope.; [a.] Athens, NY

BASHEER, BRADINE
[pen.] Hamidah Basheer; [b.] July 29, 1958, Cook; [p.] Ester Oliver; [ch.] Twana, Oniki, Shakah; [ed.] I'm still learning!; [occ.] My occupation is, we're every the Lord send me to work!; [memb.] Keystone Baptist Church; [hon.] No. 1 award myself, my child Honor me; [oth. writ.] Yes I write all the time. I don't sleep well so I have something well to do.; [pers.] Repent with style. "I have days that are up, and down. But my Lord lift, me up." Also helps me repent with a smile. So I go on, from day-to-day. With the loving Jesus Christ making a way.; [a.] Chicago, IL

BASS, MONA LISA
[b.] November 23, Birmingham, AL; [p.] Richard and Annie Graham; [m.] James A. Bass, May 4, 1976; [ch.] Tracey Melissa and Casey Diana Bass; [ed.] Brighton High School, Alabama State University, Major - Art, Minor - English; [memb.] Montgomery Art Guild; [pers.] If you stay positive during the dark days of your life, there is always the possibility of finding a brighter day around the corner.; [a.] Montgomery, AL

BATES, ELLARAY WEESE
[pen.] "Sis" "EllaRay"; [b.] July 25, 1918, Beryl (Mineral County - West), VA; [p.] Raymond E. Mary Jane Knott Weese; [m.] Widowed - Wm. E. Bates, August 30, 1952; [ed.] Morgantown High School, Morgantown WVA. Monongalia General Hospital School Under 1943-1946 of nursing - united states Cadet Nurse Corps continued Nursing Education - West VA Retired Registered Nurse - University; [occ.]

Activities Coordinator in Assisted Care of Elderly; [memb.] Active Elder Presbyterian Church USA - Ret Red cross Nurse Vol. North Carolina Association Longterm Care Pacilities. Mon. General Hospital Nurse Alumnae Assoc Register Professional Nurse Cert and West VA. Kentucky; [hon.] Numerous Certificates, Certificates in Continuing Education in Longterm care, Activity Coordinator, Hospice Org - Volunteer, Ombudsman Program NC., Volunteer in longterm care - North Carolina U.S. Bureau Mines First Aid Course; [oth. writ.] Newspaper (local articles concerning activities local rest home poem published local paper; [pers.] I am a "People Person" in that, I care about those in need of help or assistance in all areas - in the past five years - it has been working within a rest home facility - and practicing my faith and ministering to the care of those in need; [a.] Edenton, NC

BATLIFF, SISSY
[pen.] "Sissy"; [b.] November 10, 1950, New Albany, IN; [p.] Wayne and Dorothy Temple; [ch.] Joshua (17), Aaron (10); [ed.] New Albany High School, Circleville Bible College, Kentucky, College of Barbering; [occ.] Owner/Stylist of Sissy's Hair Etc.; [memb.] Eastside Nazarene Church; [hon.] "My Children"; [oth. writ.] First Actually published - I'm excited!; [pers.] When I hear a song or read something and it touches "my" soul and. It reaches the part of me that wants to help someone else's life. I want my writings to touch that special place, in the "heart."; [a.] Jeffersonville, IN

BATTERSBY JR., WILLIAM H.
[b.] March 28, 1936, Abington, PA; [p.] William and Vera; [m.] Barbara, 1962; [ch.] Matthew, Linda and Rachel; [ed.] Abington Sr., High School; [occ.] Notion Picture Camera operator; [hon.] Cover and Article of International Photographers Magazine; [oth. writ.] Seven or eight other poems - not published. My poems come as an inspiration, not because I try to write a poem perse; [pers.] My poems have been written in the middle of the night after awaking from a sound sleep, the words are there, although I have no I draw witere they come from.; [a.] Burbauk, CA

BAUM SR., LOUIS F.
[b.] August 10, 1933, Chicago, IL; [p.] Joseph L. Bom, Katherine E. Baum; [m.] Claudia K. Baum, December 20, 1994; [ch.] Louis F. Jr., Terri and Timothy Eugene; [ed.] Mt Vernon High, Ambrican University; [occ.] Director - Sacramento Attitudanl Healing Center Attitudinal; [memb.] Network for Attitudinal Healing International; [hon.] "Jampolsky Award" for Exemplary Work in Attitudinal Healing with the Facilitative Meditation and Process; [oth. writ.] Short story first prize national contest - through the equitable UFE Assurance Society; [pers.] Reflecting the beauty and peace of my subjects is my upmost beside of expanding the creative process.; [a.] Folsom, CA

BAYER, NICOLE C.
[b.] February 15, 1976; [p.] Helmar Bayer, Nasi Bayer; [ed.] Mount Carmel High School, University of Southern California; [memb.] Cellist of the Bayer Trio; [hon.] Alpha Lambda Delta, Golden Key National Honors Society, Dean's List; [oth. writ.] Poems and articles published in school newspapers.; [a.] San Diego, CA

BEALL, JOANNE
[b.] April 8, 1950, Franklin, NJ; [p.] George and Frances Hall; [m.] Gregory M. Beall, August 1, 1987; [ch.] Eric and Keith Mott; [ed.] Boise State University; [occ.] Administrative Assistant; [memb.] Saint Alphonsus Auxiliary BSU Alumni; [hon.] 1983 Magna Cum Laude; [oth. writ.] Several poems related to personal life experiences. Short life-hearted stories.; [pers.] My life is presented through my poetry.; [a.] Boise, ID

BEAN, JUDITH
[b.] Fukvoka, Japan; [hon.] Dean's List, California, State University, Sonoma; [a.] Oakland, CA

BECKER, AUBRIA
[b.] February 11, 1953, Maui, HI; [p.] Deceased; [m.] Philip Becker, September 24, 1979; [ch.] Micheal, Max, Louie; [ed.] Tilden High Chicago, IL; [occ.] Mom; [memb.] Hadassah, MAD; [hon.] My honors and awards, have giving to me by, the hundreds of people I have touched, all my life through my writings; [oth. writ.] I am now in the process of completing a book, containing poems from childhood, till now. Title "Pieces Of Myself."; [pers.] I hope to touch the human spirit in all those who spirit in all those who read my work. I have been my greatly influenced by the beauty of life and death that surrounds me.; [a.] Palm Spring, CA

BECKFORD, EUTON I.
[b.] June 27, 1925, Jamaica, WI; [p.] Edith & Alfred Beckford; [ch.] Annie Beckford; [ed.] Bachelor of Education (B.EA), University of the West Indies, Kingston, Jamaica; [occ.] Teacher, NYC Board of Education, New York; [memb.] Hunter College Philosophy Club, New York; [hon.] War Medal & Defence Medal (Br); [oth. writ.] several poems not published, a short story and some aphorisms, also published; [pers.] In essence poetry is the good news that reinforces the positive and petitions for goodness, the truth and beautiful; [a.] New York, NY;

BEDNAR, CORDE M.
[b.] Morristown, NJ; [p.] Mary Lou and Eugene Bednar; [ed.] Boonton High School (1988), William Patuson College - B.A., Early Childhood/English Literature (1992), William Patuson College - Masters in Special Education/Learning Disabilities (1997 anticipated); [occ.] 5th Grade Teacher, Woodmont Elementary School, Montville, NJ; [oth. writ.] This is my first published work! I write for pleasure.; [pers.] I have found writing a priceless way, to not only express ones self, but to share one's self and learn about one's self.; [a.] Boonton, NJ

BEDSOLE, WENDY LACOSTE
[b.] April 1, 1973, Mobile, AL; [p.] Vincent LaCoste, Brenda LaCoste; [m.] Jason Bedsole, December 3, 1994; [ed.] UMS - Wright Prep School, University of South Alabama; [occ.] Bookkeeper, LaCoste Construction Company, Inc.; [hon.] Dean's List, Mu Alpha Theta, Editor Literary magazine - The Mind's Eye; [oth. writ.] Articles published in The Democrat - Reporter newspaper.; [pers.] The greatest influence in my life is the Lord Jesus Christ. I believe that influence is evident in my poetry and I strive to glorify His name.; [a.] Mobile, AL

BEGGS, LACINDA R.
[b.] September 10, 1959, Metropolis, IL; [p.] Ray and Karen Beggs; [ch.] Black Cat; [ed.] Millikan High School, Coastline Community College; [occ.] Telecommunications Mgr.; [memb.] Humane Society; [oth. writ.] Several poems. This is the first poem I've sent to anyone.; [pers.] My philosophical statement can be summer up with a line of a new poem of mine, "If your life's not what it should be, better make a role reversal, cuz this ain't no dress rehearsal."; [a.] Anaheim, CA

BEHAN, SCOTT J.
[pen.] Skye Underhill; [b.] September 26, 1969, Danbury, CT; [p.] James C. Behan, Jeanette W. Behan; [ed.] Newtown High School, B.S. Computer Science and B.A. Mathematics, Hartwick College; [occ.] Senior Technologist, James River Corp., Neenah, WI; [memb.] National Eagle Scout Association; [hon.] President's Scholar, Andrew B. Saxton Fellow Eagle Scout, Bronze Palm; [pers.] When climbing the mountain to success, do not forget to pack the essentials: Positive attitude, perseverance, patience, and relaxation.; [a.] Black Creek, WI

BELCHER, ANDREW
[b.] August 10, 1979, New Orleans, LA; [p.] Shirley Elizabeth Belcher; [ed.] Jesuit High School; [occ.] Student, Musician; [hon.] Lettered in Jesuit Marching Band and R.O.T.C.; [oth. writ.] Why try?, never again, meanwhile; [pers.] I believe society is evil at heart. LIfe is only what you perceive it to be, there are no posthumous glories - live now, breathe now, be now! Rise above and live.; [a.] New Orleans, LA

BELL, DONNA JEAN
[b.] May 17, 1947, Washington, PA; [p.] Denny Newland Bell, Lorena Ellen, Eastham Bell; [ed.] Ninilchik High, Ninilchik, AK, Ambassador University; [hon.] American Legion, Scholastic Achievement Award, Salutatorian; [pers.] I'm driven to use poetry as a way to deal with heartfelt emotions and strive to express it in a way others might reflect and benefit from it - especially in the area of improving human relations.; [a.] Gilmer, TX

BELL, JENNY
[b.] June 7, 1982, Flint, MI; [p.] Jonathan and Susan Bell; [ed.] Whitmore Lake Middle School; [occ.] 8th grade student at whitmore Lake M.S.; [memb.] 4th band; [hon.] Honor Role at School; [oth. writ.] Michigan Magic (Fifth grade class book); [pers.] Take whatever opportunities come your way to do something extra, like writing a poem. One day up will be gone and the impressions up have made on others and things you have left behind will be what people remember of you.; [a.] Whitmore Lake, MI

BELL, LINDA
[b.] March 15, 1959, Pittsburgh, PA; [p.] Don Bell and Mid Bell; [ed.] Indiana High School ICM School of Business Currently attending Point Park College; [occ.] Medical Secretary; [hon.] High Honors, Dean's List; [pers.] There has been a loss of true values and personal integrity in our society, and I hope to express this through my writings and by the way I conduct my life.; [a.] Pittsburgh, PA

BELL, RON
[pen.] Vincent Logan; [b.] November 17, 1962, Long Beach, CA; [ch.] Adam Davis, Roxanne Alysia; [ed.] Fullerton College; [occ.] Security; [a.] Stanton, CA

BELLAMY, ARTHA MACKEY
[pen.] Artha Bellamy; [b.] November 29, 1918, Mobile, AL; [p.] Arthur and Emma Bellamy; [m.] walter Mackey (Deceased), May 2, 1942; [ch.] 3 daughter, ages 52, 50, 47; [ed.] High School, Music Institute, Detroit Community College, Dressmaking School and Commercial College; [occ.] Singing, Secretary to Four Senior Clubs; [memb.] "Smith Chapel Church," "Ostomy Association", "Inkster Advisory Board," "Inkster Senior Citizen Choir," R.S., V.P. Inkster", "Inspirational" Choir; [hon.] Honored as a Senior Citizen, a Singer, Composer, Poet and Missionary; [oth. writ.] "How Do I Tell The Children!?" "My Love Is Turning Into Hate," "When" (Words and Music), "If," "Could You Smile", "Roaches", "If I could," "Let Freedom Ring", "Black Mans Creed," "Thompson Towers"; [pers.] I love to write about "God," love and life, I'm 77 years old, as a person my age I'm in numerous events and clubs. I'm the president of the social club, and secretary of two clubs in this building.; [a.] Inkster, MI

BELTRANI, ANGELA
[pen.] Ravenfaire; [b.] February 3, 1967, New York; [p.] Dr. Vincent S. Beltrani and Josephine Beltrani; [ed.] Barnard College (BA), Columbia University's School of the Arts (MFA); [occ.] Bookkeeper, Education, Coordinator Hudson Valley Raptor Center; [memb.] Hudson Valley Raptor Center, International Wildlife, Rehabilitation Council; [hon.] Ethel Stone Lefrak Prize and Scholarship; [oth. writ.] Article for the Poughkeepsie Journal; [pers.] It is only when many people work together that miracle can truly occur.; [a.] Hyde Park, NY

BEMBENEK, PAULINE
[b.] July 31, 1939, Polonia, WI; [p.] Emil and Tecla Kedrowic; [m.] Clifford Bembenek, June 16, 1962; [ch.] Dale, Scott and Jacqueline; [ed.] Wisconsin State University, Whitewater (B. of Ed) Degree; [occ.] Retired 1994 - Business Education Teacher for 28 years Mid-State Technical College, Stevens Point, WI., (24 years) P.J. Jacobs H.S. Stevens Point, WI (3 years) Stratford H.S., Stratford, WI (1 year); [memb.] Wisconsin Vocational Assoc (WVA), American Vocational Assoc. (AVA), Mid-State Vocational Assoc. (MVA), AARP American Heart Assoc; [oth. writ.] Short story published in local newspaper (Stevens point Journal); [pers.] In writing poetry, I can fulfill my aspiration of creating a portrait with words and can, perhaps, instill a few drops of splendor for others.; [a.] Stevens Point, WI

BENNETT, JE'NEAN
[b.] March 30, 1964, Millville, NJ; [ch.] Erin Rose and Daniel Ryan; [ed.] Some College, Modeling School; [occ.] Customer Service Rep for a Communications Company; [memb.] Phi Thetta Kappa; [hon.] National Deans List 2x; [oth. writ.] 2 poems pub in local college magazine - "Returning from the dead twilights of the dream" and "grey is."; [pers.] Fate is beyond our control - it is what happens to us our destiny is our reaction to our fate, and therefore with in our control. Our lives are our destinies and life is only what you make it.; [a.] Milmay, NJ

BENNETT, RUSSELL
[b.] September 28, 1968, Bluffton, IN; [p.] Kenneth Bennett, Alice Bennett; [m.] Karen Lynn K. Bennett, August 20, 1994; [ch.] Bernie; [ed.] Blackford High, Indiana State University, Ball State University; [occ.] Residential Counselor, Madison County Youth Center, Anderson, IN; [memb.] Phi Kappa Psi, American College of Sports Medicine; [hon.] Dean's List Fall 1993, Spring 1994, Fall 1994, and Spring 1995, Golden Key National Honor Society; [pers.] To my friends and family, I just want to thank you for giving me the encouragement and strength to just do my best, because of all your support, I now believe in myself and my ability. (KNAJBR); [a.] Muncie, IN

BERNHARDT, LANCE
[b.] February 10, 1966, Muskegon, MI; [p.] Merle Bernhardt, Bessie Bernhardt; [m.] Justina (Van Wye) Bernhardt, August 12, 1989; [ch.] Zachary, Forrest; [ed.] Whitehall High, Muskegon Community College; [occ.] Factory Worker, Insurance Sales; [hon.] Summa Cum Laude, Certificate in Child Brain Development; [pers.] My goal is to reflect the range of emotions in dealing with fatherhood and raising children, particularly a handicapped child.; [a.] Whitehall, MI

BERNING, MARILYN
[pen.] Marilyn Bublitz Berning; [b.] July 27, 1938, Winona, MN; [p.] Donald and Helen Bublitz; [m.] William E. Berning, September 13, 1958; [ch.] Jeffrey William Berning and Jason D. Berning, Peggy Lynn Berning (deceased); [ed.] Spring Valley, MN High School and small amount of Vocational (Life's Experiences was my best education); [occ.] P/T Business Owner, Homemaker, Writer; [memb.] International Society of Poets; [oth. writ.] Am writing a Christian Book of verses in rhyme - also other poems.; [pers.] God is whose puts I try to track. My parents and family were a blessing to me. Poems are to me - a time to share with those you care.; [a.] Stewartville, MN

BERNTSEN, THOMAS
[b.] August 6, 1965, Rockville Centre, NY; [p.] Joanne and Reginald Berntsen; [ed.] 88 Utica College of Syracuse University, B.A. Mathematics 91 Indiana University, M.S. Math Education 98 University of Massachusetts Ed.D.; [occ.] Math and Science Teacher, High School; [oth. writ.] Article, "Let It Snow, Let It Snow" in The Physics Teacher (Nov. 95), article "What if?" In the Science Teacher other poems published are: A Passage of Time," "Pineconia," "America, The Great Pine," "Paradise Is Brief," "Come With Me To A Distant Star, A Distant Land."; [pers.] Life is a challenge to improve one's self and become whole. Hard work, prayers and staying the course bring us to the mountain top.; [a.] Brattleboro, VT

BERRY, YVONNE
[pen.] Vonnie Berry; [b.] June 9, 1965, Clovis, CA; [p.] Walt and Roberta Taylor; [m.] Van H. Berry III, June 3, 1989; [ch.] Dog Kola, Cat Cody; [ed.] Memorial High School; [occ.] Office Manager, Dr. Steven D. Oliver, DDS; [oth. writ.] Several poems and short stories waiting to be published.; [pers.] "Carpe Diem" "Seize the day." I live every day to the fullest. Life is too short to waste one minute thinking of what could've been. Live for today don't look back."; [a.] Tulsa, OK

BEUHLER, ETHEL
[b.] June 17, 1932, Toledo, OH; [p.] Hobart Tolson and Valma Marie; [occ.] Retired; [oth. writ.] Personal feelings and views.

BICE, LOLA MAY
[pen.] Lola May Bice; [b.] December 15, 1951, Hays, KS; [ed.] 1 year Fort Hays State College Hays, KS; [oth. writ.] None published; [pers.] Deceased - car accident July 2, 1971

BICKFORD JR., WILLIAM H.
[pen.] BLT; [b.] August 12, 1968, Saint Petersburgh, FL; [p.] William and Joan; [ed.] Boca Ciega High School, Grossmont College; [occ.] Naval Aircrew Instructor, Student; [hon.] Awarded Top 3 percent of Poets in 1993; [oth. writ.] Poems published by NLP and completed first novel.; [pers.] My beautiful girlfriend has been my inspiration (440). The best poetry comes from inside the poet. Emotions felt are added to ignite the fire of writing.; [a.] Spring Valley, CA

BICKFORD, PAMELA J.
[pen.] 'PJ'; [b.] July 31, 1956, Jacksonville, FL; [p.] Junior and Clara Walsh; [m.] Billy W. Bickford, September 30, 1977; [ch.] Robert Wayne, Lisa Marie, Bridget Lee; [ed.] Francis Howell High; [occ.] Office Clerk, Medical Supply Co.; [memb.] American Heart Assoc., Supporter Cystic Fibrosis Research Found, "Showstoppers Dance Center, O'Fallon, MO"; [hon.] "Who's Who" in American High School Drama, National Honor Society through High School; [oth. writ.] Various poems in High School and my works company news letters mostly personalized poems for friends and family's special occasions.; [pers.] I try to find the good side of people and of things that happen in life and to inspire and encourage others to "NOT JUDGE" unless you've walked in someone else's shoes!; [a.] Sain Peters, MO

BIETENHOLZ, PETER MARTIN
[b.] December 24, 1964, Zurich, Switzerland; [p.] Peter Bietenholz, Doris Bietenholz; [ed.] B.A. Communications, University of California of San Diego; [oth. writ.] Author of three screenplays "Two hearts and one soul", Cross of thorus", Presumed Dead"; [pers.] I try to write from the heart. I have been greatly influenced by numerous songwriters and composed, whose work kept me company and provided a steady source of inspiration.; [a.] Los Angeles, CA

BIRT, MICHELLE G.
[pen.] "Migy"; [b.] March 25, 1954, New York City, NY; [p.] Thomas E. Griffin and Margaret Griffin (deceased); [m.] Calvin L. Birth ("Lenny"), June 9, 1976; [ch.] Melika Ashanna Birt; [ed.] Prospect Heights High School, Brooklyn, NY, Graduated 6/72, Betty Owens Secretarial School Brooklyn, NY., (2 years), graduated 2/91; [occ.] Receptionist/Word Processor, for an Aviation Engineering Firm; [memb.] Former Girl scout Ass't, Troupe Leader (B'klyn, NY), Founder of "The Many Hanny's" a Theatre Group, (B'klyn, NY); [oth. writ.] Been writing since childhood, never published before.; [pers.] Every person was put on this earth for a very specific purpose. You must know what your purpose is use it wisely and shine like the star you are.; [a.] Doraville, GA

BISBEE, SAMANTHA MAE
[b.] November 2, 1965, Chandler, AZ; [p.] Edwin, and Lena Bisbee; [m.] Divorced; [ch.] Joshua, Tabbatha, Anthony, Travis; [ed.] GED; [occ.] Disabled Mother; [oth. writ.] So lonesome, so sad.; [pers.] My children and I have been though a lot, but we've always survived. My children are my life line every time things got tough I would think about them, and how much they need me, without them I don't exist, they are my life.; [a.] Chandler, AZ

BLACK, ELEANOR J.
[b.] October 12, 1954, Ashland, KY; [p.] Claude and Erma Wright; [m.] Harry Edward Black, February 13, 1989; [ch.] Shawn, Jamie, Tawnee; [ed.] Russell High School (graduated 1972), Ashland Community College (University of KY); [occ.] Secretary; [memb.] 1) 1st Christian Church Chancel Choir, 2) Tennessee Walking Horse Breeders and Exhibitors Assoc. (T.W.H.B.E.A), 3) Eastern Hills Saddle Club, 4) KY Real Estate Sales Associate, 5) Notary Public; [hon.] 1st and 3rd place - Pro-Am Bowling Tourn., 28 - 1st place Horse Show Awards in one season; [oth. writ.] A poem published in "The Rainbow's End" titled "I really care." Editor and Publisher of Church Choir Newsletter and Saddle Club Newsletter where I include poems and stories.; [pers.] Poetry has always inspired my own writings and intermost feelings on paper. I have always preferred to express the way I feel or my feelings to another through poetry.; [a.] Ashland, KY

BLACKBURN, PEARL A.
[b.] January 13, 1917, New Stanton, PA; [p.] Effie Bryan Davis and William L. Davis; [m.] Wayne C. Blackburn (Deceased), November 12, 1939; [ch.] 2, Ronald (Deceased), Wayneen; [ed.] High School and Blackburn Neville Cooperative Commercial College - Greensburg, PA; [occ.] Widow, Homemaker; [memb.] Church of Christ United Methodist 100 Lincoln Ave, Youngwood PA 15697; [oth. writ.] This is my first presentation. My other writings consist mainly of dedications and tributes to family and friends.; [pers.] I believe in God, the united States of America and in all peoples. I believe there is goodness and love in all people, if given an opportunity to express it. My purpose is to show love, appreciation and gratitude to my God, my family and my friends.; [a.] Youngwood, PA

BLACKMON, LOUIS L.
[pen.] Lemon Tea; [b.] June 23, 1969, Timmonsville, SC; [p.] Louis and Katrina Blackmon Jr.; [ed.] Some college (2 1/2 years); [occ.] General Clerk for Communications Co; [memb.] Toastmasters International; [oth. writ.] A small book of poems entitled, "I Would Have Never Imagined"; [pers.] In my writings, I express emotions that have resulted from personal experiences. My goal in my writing is that the reader will feel the emotions with me. In all things, Praise God!; [a.] Fort Washington, MD

BLAIR, JENNIFER
[b.] July 29, 1984, Danvers, MA; [p.] Francine and Kenneth Blair; [ed.] I am a 6th grader at Amesbury Middle School; [occ.] Student; [hon.] Received Excellence in Social Studies, Science and Language Arts Awards 5th Grade, Student of the Quarter 6th Grade Language Arts; [pers.] "We can make a difference, no matter how small, we need, need to try. If we all pitch in life on earth will continue to prosper and our future will be bright!"; [a.] Amesbury, MA

BLANCK, OLIVIA C.
[b.] September 3, 1943, Somerville, MA; [p.] A. Stone; [m.] Harry J. Blanck, January 23, 1982; [ch.] Edward, Danette, Stephanie; [ed.] Leominster High School (61), Bus. Mgmnt. - Wholesale/Retail Computer Repair and Maintenance; [occ.] J.C. Penney, Leominster, MA, Jerry Agriesti, Mgr; [hon.] Merit Awards for Outstanding Poet 1987-1992; [oth. writ.] Other poems published in past years.; [pers.] I love books, to learn from the written words. I've met the most interesting people in my life through a book, or because of books. An education you never get, really, academically.; [a.] Lunenburg, MA

BLAND, LORA MARTIN
[pen.] Lorrie Martin; [b.] December 8, 1929, Shelby Co, KY; [p.] Clarance and Cynthia Boren Cockerell; [m.] Leland Bland, February 17, 1995; [ch.] 4 by William H. Martin; [ed.] 8th Grade; [occ.] Was always since age 15 Housewife; [memb.] Sunshine Homemakers - VFW Aux. Com. Church of God; [hon.] None: When I was young on the farm, I wrote to express my feelings, I always wanted to write - writing come easy to me when ever, I was happy! And even sometimes when sad lost my husband to cancer in 82; [oth. writ.] I've written several songs "It Wasn't You," but never got to send them any where. I was "65 yrs. young" when I found the kind of love I'd always wanted.; [pers.] In 93 I had a triple by pass Heart surg. I prayed to God and seemed to get a new lease on life, I tried to do good with my life. In 94 I met a man, in February 95. We married I feel God has given me so much and I give him the credit for it.; [a.] Shelbyville, KY

BLEIMAN, JOHN JOSEPH
[pen.] John Joseph; [b.] March 25, 1947; [p.] Jack and Dorothy Bleiman; [ed.] Merced Junior College, B.A. Cal State University Stanislaus M.A. San Jose State University; [occ.] Bookkeeper for 20 years; [memb.] PHI Theta Kappa; [hon.] 1970 Air Force Commendation Medal, 10 years Service pin from Hanna Boys Center; [oth. writ.] 25 essays in seven california newspaper, into plus value, and included in treasured poems of america 1991; [pers.] Just as consciousness is an abstract reality, my verses strive to make the invisible soul visible; [a.] Merced, CA

BLOCK, STEPHEN
[b.] November 14, 1976, Washington, DC; [p.] Joseph and Judith Block; [ed.] Chelsea High School, Wilmington College (currently enrolled); [oth. writ.] Newspaper Articles for College Newspaper, currently writing in fictional story, so far its about 65 pages.; [pers.] Writing is life magnified and put on paper.; [a.] Washington, DC

BLUE, PATRICIA M.
[b.] January 13, 1928, Moor Head, MN; [p.] James and Clara Fitch; [m.] Glen Blue, September 14, 1946, (Died on our 49th anniversary); [ch.] Sandra Tracy, Bonnie Bellmer; [ed.] Fargo ND High School Macomb - Michigan Community College Computer Classes, Art lessons (oil), School of Hard Knocks; [occ.] Retired Home Maker, Window, Mother and Long Distance grand mother; [memb.] Cuyuna Gem and Mineral Society L.O.M.P. Heartland poets, "Fate" from M.W.F.M.S. (Detroit MI), 8th place certificate from A.F.M.S. (Boise Idaho), Editor of Agate Explorer Certificate for new editor; [hon.] First place award for "Midwest Federation", American", League of Minnesota Poetry Society L.O.M.P.; [oth. writ.] Song paradies and poetry since grade school, articles and letters to editors annual, christmas letters for 20 years or so; [pers.] Mostly with when inspired by God, it just flows at the time I wrote "Fate" after watching a single leaf clinging to a twig in a wind storm in march applies to family ties also; [a.] Crosky, MN

BLUE, VICTORIA
[b.] Los Angeles, CA; [p.] Brian; [ch.] Chelsea, Blayre, Ashleigh; [ed.] Montebello Sr. High, CA Monmouth State College, IL Prairie State College, IL Pima College, AZ; [occ.] Evolving, Archaeological Studies; [memb.] American Rock Art Research Assoc., Crow Canyon Archaeological Center Archaeological Inst. of America; [oth. writ.] Several published in a Women's Monthly News Magazine; [pers.] My writings are a projection of personal introspection and a reflection of a world from my minds eye.; [a.] Tucson, AZ

BLUMBERG, CAROLYN
[b.] June 2, 1946, Dallas, TX; [p.] Ransom Drury Crow and Bonnie Tarno Harris; [m.] Alan S. Blumberg, December 4, 1981; [ch.] Margaret Smith; [ed.] San Jacinto High-Houston; [occ.]

Housewife, Writer; [oth. writ.] Poems, Book on Consciousness; [pers.] Life is to me about knowing God as an internal reference point, so as to see. From that perspective the world without - As within, so without.; [a.] Olympia, WA

BOBER, FRANCIS J.
[pen.] Frank J. Bober; [b.] September 6, 1942, Adams, MA; [p.] Frank and Josephine Bober; [ed.] High School Degree: St. Joseph's High - North Adams, MA Bachelor's Degree and Doctoral Candidacy: Catholic University of America - Wash., DC Master's Degree: St. Vincent College/Seminary - Latrobe, PA; [occ.] Roman Catholic priest and chaplain to various organizations and Institutes; [memb.] MENSA, Knights of Columbus, Washington Astronomy Club, Metropolitan Cosmology Forum, The Planetary Club and member of several ethics organizations; [hon.] Dean's lists, several academic honors, Summa Cum laude honor, several teaching and organizational skill awards; [oth. writ.] Several philosophy and theology articles published in local and national newspapers, magazines and books.; [pers.] To seek the truth, to live by it and share it with others while experiencing life as fully as possible! I have been greatly influenced by several philosophers, theologians and scientists, especially A. Einstein, M. Heidegger and several Process theologians and philosophers; [a.] Washington, DC

BODILY, LEAH MORRISON
[b.] November 16, 1916, Franklin, ID; [p.] Al and A.L. Morrison; [m.] Elvin B. Bodily, June 12, 1937; [ch.] Fern, Oulell M, Richard E., Kevin F., Shayla; [ed.] Two years at Utah State University; [occ.] Worked 33 years at a retail store; [memb.] Church of Jesus Christ of Latter Day Saints; [hon.] I have an award for working 33 years in the same store, Certificate of Service in the Data Entry program for the Church of Jesus Christ of Latter Day Saints; [oth. writ.] Wrote little poems in our church our news paper. Written articles in local newspaper in the form; [pers.] I am honest in what I do and write. I try to write how I feel and look at life and follow the golden rule; [a.] Salt Lake City, UT

BOE, SEAN
[b.] August 26, 1967, Poplarville, MS; [p.] Ronald and Joyce Boe; [m.] Angie Boe, January 2, 1990; [ch.] Justus (5) and Jordan (2); [ed.] FCAHS, University of Southern Mississippi University of Arkansas; [occ.] Self Employed; [pers.] I believe the purpose of life of life is to give us the opportunity to grow, lifes problem is lifes opportunities. To understand and accept this is to move towards the paradox of life. The home of truth.; [a.] Purvis, MS

BOETTCHER, ALBERT P.
[b.] March 23, 1936, Lackawanna, NY; [p.] Albert and Georgeanna Boettcher; [m.] Rosemary Boettcher, July 21, 1962; [ch.] William, Joseph, John, James; [ed.] Bishop Timon High School, Canisius College, BA, (Latin), '57, MS.Ed '62, go graduate hours in Spanish, Latin, English; [occ.] Retired Latin Teacher from the Buffalo Board of Ed.; [memb.] Buffalo Diocesan Prayer, Worries, Legion of Mary, Perpetual Adoration on Society of Saint Catherine's Church Buffalo Diocese; [hon.] Honor Society of Canisius College, recognized by the New York State Education Dept. for a program of Excellence; [oth. writ.] I've written over forty poems to date and an eighteen page satire titled, The Parable Of The Snow Sheep!; [pers.] My spiritual and religion beliefs are extremely important to me. They are the source of my inspirations to write poetry. Ezra Pound, T.S. Eliot and Robert Frostare my formative influences.; [a.] West Seneca, NY

BOLTON, RAY
[pen.] Fox; [b.] May 27, 1974, San Francisco, CA; [p.] Frances Breland and Danny Breland; [ed.] North Forrest High School, Jones County Junior College, William Carey College; [pers.] My writings reflect experiences in my lifetime but mostly thoughts about my experiences. I was influenced by a friend for whom I think is an excellent poetry writer; [a.] Hattiesburg, MS

BOND, AMANDA
[pen.] Mandy; [b.] April 20, 1976, Denver, CO; [ed.] Littleton High School Grad., Student attending Nebraska Wesleyan University; [occ.] Student, Music Education Major; [hon.] Honorable mention in 5th Grade Creative Writing Contest, Senior Service Award, publication of a previous poems in a Regular High School Journal; [pers.] My greatest inspiration comes from God my maker, and Sir Lawrence Olivier's, "Time Speech." "The quality of your thinking brings about the quality of your life think about that."; [a.] Lincoln, NE

BOND, HERQUELIES
[pen.] Herquelies; [b.] August 12, 1963, Inglewood, CA; [ed.] High School Graduate; [occ.] Singer, Songwriter, Poet, Pianist, Bodybuilder, Model, Metaphysical Scientist; [memb.] Edgar Cayce Foundation; [pers.] "I'm sorry, but my Karma just walked all over your dogma!"; [a.] Atlanta, GA

BOND, JAMIE
[b.] January 24, 1981, Middletown, NY; [p.] James Bond and Te Smith; [ed.] Tecler Elementary Lynch Middle School; [occ.] Baby sitting; [memb.] Lynch Middle School Chorus, Peer Leadership, United Presbyterian Church Armstrdam, N.Y.; [oth. writ.] One other poem published in 1942 Anthology for young adults; [pers.] I believe that in helping others you help your self and I hope that my poetry bring can awareness to all the horrors of our world.; [a.] Amsterdam, NY

BONIFACIO, ANNABELLE
[b.] September 27, 1980, Philippines; [p.] Jayar Bonifacio, Bella Bonifacio; [ed.] Barnes Elementary School, Indian Hills School, Brown Junior High School, Hillsboro High School; [memb.] Beaverton Volunteer Program, Portland Volunteer Center, National Junior Honor Society, Saturday Academy; [hon.] Presidential Academic Fitness Award, Honor Roll; [oth. writ.] Blazers Aids Awareness Essay in 5th grade.; [pers.] Life is a dance you learn as you go. Sometimes you lead. Sometimes you follow. Don't worry about what you don't know. Life is a dance you learn as you go.; [a.] Aloha, OR

BOOKER, DOROTHY R.
[pen.] Dorothy Booker; [b.] December 25, 1943, Pascagoula, MS; [p.] Fred and Lillie Bell Rodgers; [m.] West Booker Jr., December 17, 1961; [ch.] 5; [ed.] 12th Grade; [occ.] Wal-Mart; [memb.] Pentacosta Church Licensed Missionary; [oth. writ.] A short play... "The Enduring Promise."; [pers.] I pray for the hearts of men and women, every where, every nation. to change. There is so much hatred in the world today. I personally see no reason for it. Maybe, by writing, someone life will change.; [a.] Houma, LA

BOOKER, LESLIE
[pen.] Tulani; [b.] December 4, 1940, New York, NY; [ch.] Errol John Brown Jr., Amin Sizemore; [occ.] Administrative Assistant; [pers.] To be used as an instrument of healing in a chaotic world is a gift from God.; [a.] Mount Vernon, NY

BOOTHE, JAMIE KAYE
[b.] August 3, 1965; [p.] James Boothe, Cordelia Boothe; [ch.] Sidney and Travis Phelps; [ed.] Gloucester High, Thomas Nelson Community College and Rappahannock Community College; [occ.] Student Nurse; [memb.] Petsworth Baptist Church; [oth. writ.] Children's Books that I someday hope to have published.; [a.] Gloucester, VA

BORDEN, DAVID
[pen.] David Borden; [b.] December 25, 1949, Los Angeles, CA; [p.] Thelma and Samuel Borden; [m.] Gina Maslow Borden, April 5, 1996; [ch.] Jennifer, Brian and Tessa; [ed.] University of California at Santa Barbara, B.A. in Sociology; [occ.] Medical Health Educator; [oth. writ.] Various poems, two unpublished sociological essays.; [pers.] I love Abe Lincoln's anecdote where he says that needy all people can stand adversity, but if you want to challenge a person's character, give them power.; [a.] Venice, CA

BORELLO, JOANNE J.
[b.] November 13, 1961, Woonsocket, RI; [p.] Ernest and Albina Charette; [m.] Mike Borello, December 21, 1979; [ch.] Thomas and Brandy; [occ.] Bus Driver; [oth. writ.] I have written many poems, but this poem was a real tragedy which ended with hope. I hope it touches you as it did me. Every poem I've written has dealt with real life and feelings.; [pers.] I have been writing since the age of 13. I've always had a dream to have my poems published, but never believed it would happen. If I weren't for the encouragement of my mother-in-law Barbara Gauthier, whom loved all of my poems, I would never have tried to publish them. She was a good woman. It's a shame she can't share this one. You should always follow your dreams, because they really can come true.; [a.] Wolcott, VT

BOSLEY, BETTY
[b.] May 19, 1936, Baltimore, MD; [p.] John and Stella Whitcomb; [m.] Walter Bosley, November 7, 1953; [ch.] Four sons; [ed.] 11th Grade, Franklin High School ni Reisterstown - MD; [occ.] Cleaning Lady for Surry Maintenance at Brendles in Elkin, NE; [oth. writ.] Written

several other poems, none published.; [pers.] Have identical twin sister in MD. Who also writes poetry.

BOTTGER, JAMES
[b.] August 25, 1965, North Kansas City, MO; [p.] Rex and Karen Bottger; [ed.] High School Graduate with 1 semester college; [occ.] Machinist for griffin wheel company (maker of railroad wheels) in Kansas City, Kansas; [hon.] Various Achievement and Commendation Awards from my 8 years of Military Service in both the US Marines and the U.S. Army; [oth. writ.] This is the first poem I have written that I've sent in; [pers.] When I wrote "The tribute", I tried putting myself in the minds and hearts of the vietnam vets. It is my personal tribute to their sacrifice and dedication in preserving peace throughout the world.; [a.] Edwardsville, KS

BOWER, LESLIE A.
[b.] January 31, 1961, Lock Haven, PA; [p.] Charles L. Bower, Marie R. Bower; [ed.] B.S. Agricultural Mechanization, The Pennsylvania State University, M.S. Information Technology Management, Naval Postgraduate School, Monterey, CA; [occ.] Education Specialist, Symbol Technologies Incorporated; [memb.] Lieutenant Commander, United States Naval Reserve, Penn State Alumni Member, Naval Reserve Association Member, Society for Technical Communication Member, National Association Female Executives (NAFE) Member; [hon.] Sterling Who's Who Directory, Executive Editor Member, 1 Navy Commendation Medal, 3 Navy Achievement Medals, 1 National Defense Service Medal, 1 Meritorious Unit Commendation Medal, many letters of appreciations; [oth. writ.] "ADC Card Technologies" article published in May 1995 issue, ID Systems; [pers.] "Soar like an eagle!," Look within yourself to find the eagle (independent, strong, "a leader") and set yourself free to become what you are to be.; [a.] Costa Mesa, CA

BOWERMAN, SHIRLEY F.
[b.] October 22, Toivola, MI; [m.] December 17, 1966; [ch.] Heidi C. Bowerman; [ed.] Pershing High; [occ.] Asst. Chief Clerk Grand Trunk Western Railroad; [memb.] Finnish Cultural Assoc., Detroit, Inst. of Arts, Founders Society and Association of American Wing D.I.A., Friends of Belle Isle, Detriot Zoo. Society, Det. Science Center, G.T.W. Women's Club, MI., Humane Society.; [pers.] Spending my summers on the farm in Minnesota until my mid teens inspired my love for nature and animals. I wish my daughter could have experienced it too when she was growing up.; [a.] Detroit, MI

BOYD JR., LESTER W.
[b.] January 18, 1931, TX; [p.] Lester W. Sr., and Charity May (both deceased); [ed.] Forestburg High School, Att. Cooke County College, earned B.S. and M.Ed., University of North Texas; [occ.] Retired Teacher, Active D.J. and Radio Announcer; [hon.] Selected as an "Outstanding Personality of the South" two times, and various Academic and Scholastic Awards and Honors; [oth. writ.] A few published poems and songs, through the years.; [pers.] People are put on earth to serve God and country, which simply means to work for the good of mankind to the best of our ability.; [a.] Forestburg, TX

BOYKIN, LUCY M.
[b.] February 6, 1941, W Salem, NC; [p.] Deceased; [ch.] Bobby Jr., Barry, Beverly and Bianca; [occ.] W-S. Forsyth County Schools - Bus driver; [memb.] Ephesus S.D.A. Church James H. Young O.E.S. #592, American Legion Auxiliary #220, D.A.V. Auxiliary #9, Agape Women's Club; [oth. writ.] Short skits (never published). Poems for personal reading.; [pers.] I don't have a lot but I use what I've got; [a.] Winston-Salem, NC

BOYLE, ROBIN
[b.] July 16, 1963, Union City, PA; [p.] Frederick and Patricia Large; [m.] Richard E. Boyle, July 3, 1992; [ch.] Brooks; [ed.] B.S. in Health Science, Masters in Elementary Education -Suny Brockport, N.Y; [occ.] Kindergarten Teacher, Brockport Central; [pers.] There is no greater security than the love that surrounds you in a family. I thank my parents for teaching me just what love and family is all about.; [a.] Lyndomille, NY

BOZEK, ELIZA
[b.] May 7, 1977, Poland; [p.] Bogunita and Tadeusz Bozek; [ed.] Magnolia High School, Azusa Pacific University (English and History major); [occ.] Student; [oth. writ.] Several poems never published, I don't usually write for an audience; [a.] Anaheim, CA

BRABHAM, DEBRA
[b.] September 28, 1968, McComb, MS; [p.] Gene Brown, Patsy Brown; [m.] Charlie Brabham Jr., February 15, 1992; [ch.] Katie, Dustin, Brad, Brady; [ed.] Thibodaux High School, Nicholls State University, Southwest Mississippi Community College; [occ.] Homemaker, Self-employed, C&D Logging; [oth. writ.] Several poems for my personal benefit or for family members.; [pers.] My poems reflect the situations of my life. I write from my heart.; [a.] Gloster, MS

BRANDT, KARIN RITA
[pen.] Kar Brandt; [b.] November 22, 1963, Syracuse, NY; [ch.] Kassandra Jewel; [ed.] TJ Corcoran Sr. High School, currently taking continuing classes and Law school is a future possibility; [occ.] Nurse and Bartender; [memb.] "Story Makers," "Endometriosis Assist," "Resolve" Member, "S.D. Single Mom's" Member, the "Writing Center" Member, "Our" Member, I am very involved the braille Institute, Caption groups - infertility groups, writing groups - addressing the public on a number of concerns, I feel are important; [oth. writ.] Co-author "Life sentences" publication, May 95 a story makers project - currently working on projects-one-a fiction novel, the other, my experiences and journal entries published as a self help book.; [pers.] I have wanted to write become a parent for a long as I can remember now both my wishes have come true. Thank you to all my former teachers and mentors.; [a.] San Diego, CA

BRANT, GERALD BEAUREGARD
[b.] December 29, 1977, Orangeburg, SC; [p.] Sue Herring, George Dean Brant; [ed.] Attending West Texas High School as a Junior; [occ.] Full time student in Stimnett, TX; [memb.] Society of Creative Anachronism (Partial Member), High School Choir; [hon.] UIL Sweepstakes band 93-94, All-Region Choir 92-93, Panhandle Honor Choir 93-94, All-District and All Region Choir 95-96; [oth. writ.] Several unpublished poems and begging of short novel also on published.; [pers.] Poetry should create emotion, and emotion creates poetry. In essence, emotion is not a part of poetry it is poetry.; [a.] Stinnett, TX

BRAXTON, LILLIAN L.
[pen.] Lillian L. Braxton; [b.] February 23, 1937, Bronx, NY; [p.] Lillian Mortenson, Walter Mortenson; [m.] Divorced; [ch.] Brenda L. Braxton; [occ.] Retired; [memb.] Montford Point Marine Association (Honorary); [hon.] Plaque issued by the Montford Point Marine Assoc. in recognition of my voluntary services. This is a not for profit organization founded by the first black men inducted into the U.S. Marine Corp. during WW II. They are also the inspiration for my poem "Remember"; [oth. writ.] Unpublished poems, life experience journal.; [pers.] I believe in the saying "Falling down may or may not be my fault, but staying down definitely is."; [a.] New York, NY

BRAZIL, CHRYSSA
[b.] January 5, 1970, San Diego, CA; [p.] Stephanie Brazil; [ed.] Palm Springs High School, San Diego City College, College of Alameda; [oth. writ.] Movie critics and prose published in the P.S. High School Newspaper.; [pers.] I am driven to embody the images, truths, and spirit of now.; [a.] Palm Springs, CA

BRAZIL, MARTINA C.
[b.] October 18, 1937, Brooklyn, NY; [p.] Pedro and Flora Carrero; [m.] Edward Las Brazil, March 1968; [ch.] Sue, Melva, Jr. Don, Lulu, NasMas, Ron; [ed.] Medgar Evens Coll., Teacher Ed., De Anza Coll., CNA and Act. Dir.; [occ.] Help-caring for my grandchild (Doran) and enjoying every moment; [oth. writ.] Wrote short stories and poems for Brooklyn Coll. Vol. Tutor. Prog.- Booklet - some included in book by Prof. I. Vite.; [pers.] I remember not to forget what has been promised in the past. Is. 83:18-55:11-2 will be man's future.; [a.] San Jose, CA

BREBNER, ELAINE E.
[b.] August 25, 1945, Denver, CO; [p.] R. W. Brebner and Frances E. Brebner; [ed.] Doane College; [occ.] Secretary to a publisher; [memb.] Foothills Art Center, Women's Foundation of Colorado; [oth. writ.] Poetry: An American Heritage, American Horologist and Jeweler; [a.] Arvada, CO

BREVES, PHYLLIS
[b.] Antioch, CA; [p.] Manual Bulcano, Jula Bulcao; [m.] Eddie Breves, August 27, 1968; [ed.] Patterson HI, Modesto Jr College, Nursing; [pers.] As I enter the world of prose and poetry I am proud and aware that there were distinguished poets and novelists in my paternal lineage.; [a.] Patterson, CA

BREWER, TRACY J. SHOEMAKER
[b.] July 11, 1957, Bay City, MI; [p.] Thomas and Doris Shoemaker; [m.] Bryant L. Brewer, December 13, 1986; [ch.] Brett Shoemaker, Angelique Brewer, Zachary Brewer, Rachel Brewer; [ed.] Graduate of Pinconning High School 1975, continued education in Medical Field and Accounting; [occ.] Medical Receptionist for Health Delivery Inc. (Migrant Health); [memb.] Sponsorship in Disabled American Vets for 25 years; [hon.] Past President of Civitan - Pinconning Chapter; [oth. writ.] Numerous poems; [pers.] All poems are written from my heart, especially this one about my Grandma.; [a.] Pinconning, MI

BREWTON, ZONYA
[b.] November 8, 1959, Spartanburg; [p.] Lillie Brewton; [ed.] B.S. Business Management, MBA Management Information Systems; [occ.] Project Manager; [oth. writ.] Several other spiritual and inspirational poems, that have never been submitted for publication.; [pers.] I love to write. My writing are always aimed at everyday people with everyday situations. The poems are intended to be inspirational and spiritually uplifting.; [a.] Marietta, GA

BRIBIESECA, GILDA SAFEEULLAH
[b.] August 28, 1949, Chicago, IL; [p.] Kathlyn and Gilberto Juan Bribieseca; [ch.] Donte, Mwata, Asya, Miliana, Yasim and Emir; [ed.] A.A. Degree in Urban Studies, B.A. Degree in Ethnic Studies, M.A. Degree in Environmental Planning Languages Studied - German and Spanish; [occ.] Area Consultant for World Book Educational Products; [hon.] Future Teacher of America, Dean's List; [oth. writ.] A compilation of children manuscripts which include: Shazzadee the Butterfly, Amos the Tyrant Ant, The Garden that grew weeds. A compilation of poems entitled, Tenacity. Lastly, a compilation of letters documents etc., describing a human experience entitled "63257."; [pers.] It is an honor (to be) and a delight to be among the very fine poets and writers included in A Muse to Follow.

BRIDGES, JACKIE
[pen.] Jacquelyn; [b.] December 2, 1981, Savannah, GA; [p.] Linda Brewer, Michael Brewer; [ed.] Student; [memb.] Chorus Cheerleading; [hon.] Honor Roll; [pers.] New dreams and old memories life.; [a.] Bloomingdale, GA

BRIDGES, KEITH A.
[b.] November 2, 1933, Tipp City, OH; [p.] Ralph Soloman and Bertha Leona; [m.] Beverly Ann, June 19, 1954; [ch.] Keith Alan - Robbie Joe - Michelle Ann; [ed.] Bachelor Degree - Transylvania College, Masters Degree of Religious Education, from Evangelical Bible Seminary; [occ.] Retired; [memb.] Past Vice President of Troy Ohio J.C.'s, Heath Ohio Kiwanis, Newark First Church Nazarene; [oth. writ.] A book of poems titled, "Lifes Road"; [pers.] "Give with a giving heart," if you don't share your resources today, you won't share with them tomorrow.; [a.] Heath, OH

BRISBON, LEONARD H.
[pen.] Briz; [b.] August 27, 1960, Green Pond, SC; [p.] Harris Brisbon Jr., and Julia Brisbon; [ch.] Single-Never Married; [ed.] MS, Project and Systems Mgt., Golden Gate University BS, Human Factors Engineering, USAF Academy; [occ.] Presidential Airlift Aviator; [hon.] Meritorious Service Medal (MSM), Joint Service Commendation Medal (AFCU), Air Force Outstanding Unit Award (AFOUA), 1985 and 1995; [oth. writ.] Trust in your heart, sunshine, lady, something, jewel and "How to gret an education anywhere - lessons from an academy graduate who attended eastside highs school in paterson, New Jersey."; [pers.] God, friends, then me; [a.] Upper Marlboro, MD

BRITT, GLADYS LAWRENCE
[b.] January 16, 1929, Saline, LA; [p.] John T. Lawrence and Ida Driggers Lawrence; [m.] LeLand H. Britt, February 12, 1947; [ch.] William, David and Judith Britt; [ed.] BA Degree in English, Library, MA Degree in Librarianship, Northwestern State University in Natchitoches, LA; [occ.] Retired Teacher, Librarian! Now writer for children; [oth. writ.] 3 children's stories published by Creative With Words Anthologies, 1 poem published, 2 poems in "Famous poems of Today"; [pers.] I have written poetry since high school. This is collected in a manuscript now. I appreciate and love family, our country and God.; [a.] Saline, LA

BRITT, RUBY B.
[b.] April 21, 1941, Baconton, GA; [p.] Louise and Lester Brown; [m.] John W. Britt, June 12, 1959; [ch.] Donna Faircloth, Debbie McInvale, Dale Shiver, Danny Britt; [ed.] Michell County High School Darton College Albany State College; [occ.] Postmaster; [memb.] Alpha Beta Gamma National Assoc. of Postmaster, U.S. Baconton Baptist Church; [hon.] High School Grad Darton Merit List Albany State Merit List Nominee for two thousand notable American Women; [oth. writ.] Several published in local newspaper. One in Tomorrow's Dream; [pers.] I believe in the goodness of God, the application of the Golden Rule, and that we should each strive to be the best we can be.; [a.] Baconton, GA

BRITTON, BETTY
[pen.] BF Britton; [b.] December 17, 1942, K.C., MO; [p.] James and Lila Rea; [m.] Kenneth L. Britton, June 17, 1973; [ch.] 12, 8 of his 4 of hers; [ed.] 11 yrs - I did not graduate because I got married the first time when I was 15 yrs old; [occ.] Care giver to handicapped adults; [memb.] Faith Christian Center Portland Oregon; [oth. writ.] Hund reds - but they are all in a drawer in my room; [pers.] The joy of patting words together, and coming up with something beautiful is a gift from God.; [a.] Portland, OR

BROOKS, CONNIE
[b.] November 20, 1996; [p.] Tino and Mina Ventura; [m.] Darwin K. Brooks, May 21, 1992; [ch.] Kelsie and Brandon; [ed.] Kohala High School; [occ.] Deli Owner; [oth. writ.] High School "Creative Writing" Class; [a.] Walkoloa, HI

BROOKS, DAVID
[b.] January 9, 1947, Los Angeles; [occ.] Actor; [hon.] Over 15 years of mixing and living I'm the arts has been 1 priveledge I dont make for granted. You see, I've just worked I'm Romania for two months.; [oth. writ.] Published own book of breakfast poems. Have never submitted a poem before; [pers.] After years of writing on napkins, it feels good to trust the "voice" to a published page. Go out, don't stay I'm.; [a.] Santa Plonica, CA

BROWN, ALICIA DENISE
[pen.] Le-Le; [b.] August 16, 1980, Detroit, MI; [p.] Aljuana and Robert Brown; [ed.] Currently in the 10th Grade; [hon.] A.A.A., C.A.T; [pers.] I think everyone has a true talent in life, I was blessed with the talent for writing poetry. In my writing I can express my feeling and views.; [a.] Franklin, TN

BROWN, BYRON R.
[a.] Santa Clarita, CA

BROWN, ERIN NICHELLE
[b.] November 3, 1982, Compton, CA; [p.] Lee A. and Marci D. Brown; [ed.] Elem. - Aynesworth Elem (K-1), Elem. - Manchester Gate (2-6), Middle School - Storey MS (7) and Southeast MS (8); [occ.] Student; [hon.] Honor Roll Student; [pers.] If you let your wondering mind wander far and free, you'll end up some place, you'll find, your heart wants to be.; [a.] Fresno, CA

BROWN, HELEN L.
[pen.] H. Louise Brown; [b.] July 3, 1951, Philadelphia; [p.] Zollie Odell and Helen L. Brown; [ch.] One daughter Kai (20), one grandson Michael (3); [oth. writ.] Two Books of Poetry, One Short Story (unpublished); [pers.] I love all people and will help anyone who needs it. I believe the world lacks love and caring. So what I say is, tell someone you love them and mean it. It could make a difference.

BROWN, JAMES M.
[b.] August 21, 1952, New Orleans, LA; [p.] James S. Joyce Brown Jr.; [m.] Jacquelyn K. Brown, June 2, 1979; [ch.] James IV, Brittney; [ed.] Holy Redeemer Elementary, Lawless Jr. High, Francis T. Nicholls Sr. High and The University of New Orleans; [occ.] Financial Administrator at a Medical Firm; [memb.] Young Men of Illinois Club; [hon.] Silver Poet Award 1990, 1991 and 1992; [oth. writ.] A Moment of Peace, Just Me And My Pen, Catharsis, Memories, Once A Dream; [pers.] Every dream should be attempted and not just dreamt.; [a.] New Orleans, LA

BROWN, KEITH A.
[b.] June 6, 1959, Blossburg, PA; [p.] Keith and Joyce Brown; [ed.] English Major at Mansfield University; [pers.] I enjoy writing about my environment and "every day" situations. Inspired by the poetry of William Carlos William and Custerzu for the wonderful teachers in my life.; [a.] Blossburg, PA

BROWN, MARINI D.
[b.] July 5, 1982, Kansas City, MO; [p.] Wilmer D. Kent and Terre R. Kent; [ed.] 8th Grade, Central Middle School; [memb.] Theocratic Ministry School; [hon.] Honor Roll; [pers.] Inspired by my dad who writes short stories.; [a.] Kansas City, KS

BROWN, MICHAEL JAMES
[b.] June 8, 1951, Portland, OR; [p.] Robert and Betty Brown; [m.] Junita; [ch.] Tom, Steven and Laura; [ed.] High School - Vancouver, WA Specialized Medical Training - U.S Army Sam Houston, Texas; [occ.] Medical Technician - US Veterans Hospital - Portland, OR; [memb.] Disabled American Veterans; [oth. writ.] Assorted poem and short stories - unpublished - but the grand children love them; [pers.] I see poetry as a window to the soul; [a.] Tigard, OR

BROWNE, CYNTHIA YEAGER
[b.] September 21, 1965; [pers.] Forever indeed the eye is open. Grasping words from the air to re-arrange and put in order, that I know God has put them there this is gift that I've been given I can no longer keep. I must reveal the secrets all the living sheep.!; [a.] Patterson, CA

BRUCE, BETTY GRACE
[b.] September 10, 1924, Nevada City, CA; [p.] Liston C. and Ada E. Roberts; [m.] William W. Bruce Jr., March 22, 1986 (second); [ch.] Steven, John and James Pease; [ed.] Sierra College Graduate; [occ.] Retired but doing some Volunteering; [memb.] P.E.O. Member, Member of N.A.R.F.E. National Asso. of Federal Employees, Member of U.M.W., United Methodist women, a bridge group and a helpful friend to many; [hon.] I have been honored by being born an American, by family, by friends and church, Thanks be to God!; [oth. writ.] "Time is," "Memories" and others not yet in print. "Thundering in it's delirium, Lord," to be published in your summer edition of "A Muse to Follow."; [pers.] A friend in need is a friend indeed and that is what I strive to be.; [a.] Capitola, CA

BRUEGGER, MARY BERNICE
[b.] July 29, 1960, Louisville, KY; [p.] Ransom Lewis, Elizabeth Forwright; [m.] William C. Bruegger, February 23, 1980; [ch.] Sean Curtis Bruegger; [ed.] Plant City High School, Personal Research; [occ.] Self-employed; [a.] Brandon, FL

BRUNER, DAVID D.
[b.] November 7, 1962, Queens, NY; [p.] Rose Marie and James P. Bruner; [ed.] B.S. Chemistry, Mathematics University of Houston, Houston, TX., Spring, 1989; [occ.] McDonald's; [memb.] Tulane University, Rugby Club, (Former-1983); [hon.] 110% Award, Colonie High School, J.V. Football, Albany, NY, 1977, Arrowhead Society (5% Graduate Academically), Lamar High School, Houston, TX., 1979-80, Phi Eta Sigma Honor Society, Tulane University New Orleans, LA., 1980-81; [pers.] In life, it's not what a man does, it's what he is.; [a.] Albany, NY

BRUNER, FAITH E.
[b.] September 5, 1972, East Point, GA; [p.] Dr. Richard H. Bruner and Elizabeth B. Bruner; [ed.] BA in Secondary Education (math); [occ.] Sylvan Learning Center teacher (math and Reading); [memb.] National Council of Teachers of Mathematics; [hon.] All Academic Team in high School, Athlete Representative for Ohio Swimming, Inc.; [a.] Clemson, SC

BRYSON, ANNA E.
[pen.] Judith Rae; [b.] September 13, 1982, Anderson, SC; [p.] Judy Bryson, Pete Bryson; [ed.] R-8th grade, at Oakway Michelle School, in West Minester, SC; [occ.] Student; [memb.] Bethel Baptist Church in Westminester, SC; [hon.] Having my poems published in 2 anthologies; [oth. writ.] Can't you see, forever and a day; [pers.] I voice the way I feel through my writing, and though I'm only, 13, I have alot of inspiration.; [a.] Seneca, SC

BUCHTA, ELIZABETH A.
[b.] July 2, 1982, Maryville, IL; [p.] Roger Buchta, Ann Buchta; [ed.] Pre-School, Grade School, and currently Freshman Year of High School; [occ.] Chained to lead a Life of Drudgery of Edwardsville Public High School; [memb.] YMCA (Edwardsville), Edwardsville Public Library; [hon.] Young Author's for my poetry book "Potpourri"; [oth. writ.] Nothing else fit to print.; [pers.] Live life to its fullest, and hope it doesn't kill you. Pick something up and master it, be it unicycling, guitar, poetry, skateboarding, or writing.; [a.] Glen Carbon, IL

BUCK, JOANNE MICHELLE
[pen.] Joanne Serianni; [b.] May 30, 1949, Philadelphia, PA; [p.] Michael and Lucy Serianni; [m.] Frank Owen Buck, February 14, 1988; [ch.] Rodney Michael Huger, Frankie Michael Buck; [ed.] Montgomery County College, Nursing Degree; [occ.] Freelance Writer with Nursing background; [memb.] Society of Children's Bookwriters and Illustrators, American Heart Association, Sacred Heart League, Save the Children; [hon.] Member of several humane organizations and conservationist groups with a mission to save endangered species and protect their vanishing wilderness.; [oth. writ.] I write poetry and children's literature for children's journals and magazines "Call for an angel."; [pers.] My strong religious beliefs influenced all of my writing. The greatest gift we can offer to one another is forgiveness and compassion. These are the keys to joy and inner peace.; [a.] Harleysville, PA

BUFORD III, PAUL SHELDON
[b.] May 22, 1990, Bellflower, CA; [p.] Angela C. McKinney (Deceased); [ed.] Busy Bee - Pre-School, Los Angeles Academy - Kindergarten; [occ.] Student; [hon.] None at this Time; [pers.] This little can read on the level of a 10th Gd.; [a.] Los Angeles, CA

BURGESS, RAYMOND L.
[b.] October 12, 1947, Muskogee, OK; [p.] Sam and Juanita Burgess; [m.] Mary Lynn Burgess, June 28, 1968; [ch.] Christopher Senora and Mary Sunseeray; [ed.] BA North Texas State Univ., MA Eastern Washington State Univ; [occ.] Chief Contracting Division Corps of Engineers, Kansas City; [memb.] Phi Alpha Theta, National Contracts Management Association; [pers.] Seek to know myself - to seek to know humankind.; [a.] Kansas City, MO

BURGOS, LINDA E.
[b.] September 23, 1966, Chicago, IL; [p.] Esther and Luis Burgos; [m.] Raul H. Santiago, May 20, 1989; [ch.] Isabella Santiago; [ed.] Paralegal, Certification, Some College, Computer Training; [occ.] Paralegal, Juergensmeyer, and Associates Elgin, IL; [oth. writ.] Several poems published in community paper and local library.; [pers.] Special thanks, to God, who fills my life with "Reason," to my husband who fills my life with "Purpose" to my daughter who fills my life with "meaning."

BURKETT, BESSIE SHANNON
[pen.] Bess Shannon; [b.] February 6, 1909, Wayne Co. IL; [p.] Leis and Mary Elizabeth; [m.] Walter Thomas Burkett (Deceased July 3, 1967), July 5, 1934; [ch.] Charles Robert Burkett; [ed.] Elementary Grade June 1949, High School, College, taught Elementary Schools '71 regular in various schools; [occ.] Retired when 70 years old and now 86; [memb.] Many valuable helps as teacher no Retired Teachers Organization; [hon.] In Penmanship, in poetry writing (several various poems honored) of late years especially. I have 5 or 6 unpublished books written. So far not in print for sale; [oth. writ.] Dad and Mom both taught me always word games - to pick matching words etc. Mom read a lot to me when I was a child.; [pers.] My Dad influenced me to write both poetry and prose I took subjects in College that helped in that area also. I read good literature a lot throughout learning years always inclined to want to write both poetry and prose. I wrote my best on every poem.

BURROWES, STEPHEN
[pen.] Monster Man; [b.] December 10, 1964, Barbados; [p.] Victor and Edris Burrowes; [occ.] Commodities reporter; [oth. Writ.] Ambition, Life, Women Of Culture, Desire, A Friend, Great Hope; [pers.] I was very mere by Langston Hughes poetry and it just brought to light feeling I wanted to share.

BURROWS, JOHN L.
[b.] August 5, 1930, Wauhon, IA; [p.] Paul W. and Bertha K.; [m.] Sarah S., October 10, 1970; [ch.] Ward C; [ed.] Grad. Kennewick High School, Washington State 1/2 yr Univ., Kyoto, Japan; [occ.] Former Marine Contractor, Diver, Under Water Salvale and Demolitions Now Retired; [memb.] NRA - AARP - Uniter Methodist Church, NAUI Card Holder; [hon.] 2nd place individual National Scuba Competition (Lake Eufala Oklahoma) 1967; [oth. writ.] Poetry since 1954 (Date first published). Presently write column for local newspaper.; [pers.] I owe my love of poetry to two people: My father and Rudyard Kipling. I grew up with both of them.; [a.] Coquille, OR

BURTON, JANET WORRELL
[b.] September 13, 1960, Winston-Salem, NC; [p.] Elton Worrell and Mona Higgins Worrell Hine; [pers.] I began writing at age eight. I have always written from the heart. My poetry is an expression of myself, my beliefs and my dreams. The most important part of life is love. It should be given freely to others as well as ourselves. My mother is my inspiration.; [a.] Winston-Salem, NC

BURTON, LINDSAY
[pen.] Burt; [b.] July 18, 1981, Morgantown, WV; [p.] Allen and Jeanne Burton; [ed.] 9th Grade Student at Venice High School. I enjoy basketball and softball. I am also a Freshmen Cheerleader, piano and an honor student; [occ.] Student; [pers.] It never hurts to ask.; [a.] Venice, FL

BUSH, JOSEPHINE
[b.] Adamsville, AL; [p.] Calvin Oscar and Willie Lee Bush; [ed.] I had a good basic education by age 14 8th grade. Not a drop out - by any means. "National Youth Administration" 1942; [occ.] Retired to personal study and writing in privacy; [memb.] I have never been involved in literary circles due to privation and other responsibilities, "Responsibilities - Widowed Mother"; [hon.] Are yet to come my Social Security no. is "417-24-5333" I was 72 years of age past November 24, 1995. I hope to reverse that number through writing and reaching; [oth. writ.] I have done many expression in poetry - But I have yet to publish any - I have thought about a Personal Anthology of my own-I need a little push; [pers.] My ultimate is to share my where with-al with all who come with in my sweep and fulfilment! and - - - there is power in the pen Amen!; [a.] Pinson, AL

BUSWELL, SHONE
[b.] March 14, 1978, Albuquerque, NM; [p.] Josefa and Floyd Buswell; [ed.] Senior at Littleton High School, Littleton, CO; [pers.] I believe that the strongest writing comes from personal experience. I also believe that writing should be universal in it's message and not limited to relating to one group or person, but to many people.; [a.] Littleton, CO

BUTLER, DIANE E.
[pen.] Diane Elizabeth Butler; [b.] December 26, 1956, Chicago, IL; [p.] Bobby Joe Smith, Edwina Smith, Maverick, Marco Hillard (The Guitar Man); [ed.] Hayward High School, M.A.T.C., Chabot College, and Uni Lex College; [occ.] Entrepreneur; [memb.] Volunteer To: San Francisco Opera, Ballet, Bravo and Symphony Hosanna Celebration Center Community Theater; [hon.] Account Executive of Month Hailed as "The Miracle Girl"; [oth. writ.] 5 books contributing writer to Local Newspaper various Community Committees.; [pers.] Believe it or not I have fine tune my gifts, to be shared talents and abilities through adversity. Through this that which was lying dormant surfaced with others. I thank my father God for the gifts talents, and abilities he has given me and for the opportunity to share them from the heart with others; [a.] Alameda, CA

BUTLER, JAMEY LYNN
[b.] June 28, 1978, Wadley Flosp, Texarkana; [p.] Dwight and Jackie Butler; [ed.] 11th grade Maud High School; [occ.] Student; [memb.] 77A, 7HA, Youth Group First Baptist Church Maud, Texas; [hon.] Outstanding Teach Award; [oth. writ.] Poems published in Local Newspapers.; [pers.] Wrote this poem after my grand father was killed by a train August 1995.; [a.] Maud, TX

BUTLER, VIRGINIA GOFF
[b.] November 25, 1918, Juno, TN; [p.] WM McKinley and Lavonia Goff; [m.] Holmes Butler (Deceased), January 13, 1939 (Div '51); [ch.] 1. Dr. William Ralph Butler, Nashville TN, 2, Tommy Butler Nashville, TN; [ed.] B.S. Bethel College Memphis State Univ. MA; [occ.] Retired as English Teacher 12th Grade. Formerly Principal of South Haven Elementary School; [memb.] TEA, NEA, Local Teacher's group. In college at Mastin", TN. Was Features Editor for College Newspaper "Volette"; [hon.] Certificates of Merit for work with Literacy and G.E.D. after first retirement my Title was Literacy and G.E.D. Director for Henderson County.; [oth. writ.] Write short stories. None published at this time. Writing on novel even though fiction, it is historical, running from 1890 to present 60 poems; [pers.] A poem "Dream On" by Virginia Butler tells this: "Never lose sight of a goal to reach." Whether this goal is for family or friends, it should be there. It should rarely be a selfish goal; [a.] Lexington, TN

BUZZELLI, TIMOTHY J.
[pen.] Buzz Timothy, T.J. Buzzelli; [b.] April 25, 1962, Detroit, MI; [p.] John and Jane Buzzelli; [m.] Christine A. Buzzelli, December 23, 1982; [ch.] Michelle L., Rachel A., Brittany N.; [ed.] Miami Southridge Senior H.S., Northwestern State University; [occ.] Accountant; [memb.] Institute of Management Accountants; [oth. writ.] Words and things - my personal collection of poems unpublished.; [a.] Corinth, TX

BUZZO JR., BILL J.
[b.] September 30, 1949, Bluefield, WV; [p.] Bill Buzzo Sr. and Elizabeth Hoops; [m.] Dana Mischelle Buzzo, January 17, 1987; [ch.] Debbie, Shane, Billy Joe, Tiffany, Derek, Megan and Lindsey; [ed.] BSBA Accounting Major, West Virginia University, Law Enforcement Certification, West Virginia State Police Academy; [occ.] Private Investigator; [memb.] Trinity United Methodist Church; [hon.] W.V. State Scholarship; [oth. writ.] Poems published in local newspaper, personal poem books printed for family and friends, songs written and sang at church services.; [pers.] I strive to reflect the beauty of nature and the complexity of life in a simple and meaningful way. I have been greatly influenced by my faith in God.; [a.] Bluefield, WV

BYARD, SUE
[b.] February 23, 1940, Waynesburg, PA; [p.] Paul and Jean Lemley; [m.] John Byard, October 8, 1960; [ch.] Cheryl Diane and Sharon Lynn; [ed.] Waynesburg High; [occ.] Home maker; [oth. writ.] My Cheryl Diane; [a.] Willowick, OH

CADY, BONNIE K.
[pen.] BK Barnes; [b.] March 21, 1951, Denver, CO; [p.] M/M E.L. Barnhardt; [ch.] Kerrie and Ryan; [ed.] Currently working on master's and degree in Criminal Justice at Univ. of Colorado at Denvor; [occ.] Drug/Alcohol Counselor, Trainer Working with Convicts; [memb.] Colorado Juvenile Council NAADAC

CAGGIANO, ANTONIO
[pen.] Ant; [b.] February 9, 1975, New York, NY; [p.] Anthony Plaggiano and Evelyn Gleadall; [ch.] Nicole Caggiano; [ed.] Associate in Science at Mount Ida College, Attending Eastern Carolina University for Bachlor in Business; [occ.] Pre School Teacher; [memb.] Quarter Horse Association; [hon.] Deans List, 2 Time Poetry Slam Champion at Mount Ida College; [oth. writ.] Several poems published in point blank literary magazine.; [pers.] My poems reflect a view of optimism, it's not that life's too short it's that your dead for too long.; [a.] North Brunswick, NJ

CAGUIN, MIKE A.
[pen.] Mike; [b.] December 28, 1911, Philippines; [p.] Pelagio and Teodorica Caguin; [m.] Rosario, October 21, 1933; [ch.] Mike Jr., and Raul; [ed.] Preparatory Law - Philippine Law College; [occ.] Senior Advocate - Bay Area Advocates for Seniors; [memb.] Paetenians International, American Association of Retired Persons, Hotel Oakland Tenants Association (Vice President); [hon.] Wrote, Produced and Directed Philippine Movies: Aawitan Kita - (I'll Sing To You) Best Picture ever produced since Liberation of the Philippines, First Price - Oakland's Annual - Employ the Older Worker Week, St. Mary's Center Recognition of ten years of Excellent Service; [oth. writ.] Articles: Twilight years good people die to live, a nation's hope for growth.; [pers.] As I grow older, my work and life have taken on a new meaning with serenity I would never have dreamed possible. Instead of spending my days feeling forgotten and unappreciated, I relish each passing day with joy.; [a.] Oakland, CA

CAHALL, KEITH B.
[pen.] Keith B. Cahall; [b.] October 9, 1956, Chester, PA; [p.] Winton D. and Phyllis J. Cahall; [m.] Amanda A. Cahall, Sept. 22, 1992; [ch.] Kenneth 'Kyle,' Danielle Renee; [ed.] Too numerous due to military dependancy and frequent relocation. Trinity Valley Community College - Welding & Real Estate, Texas State; Technical College - Aviation maintenance; [occ.] Carpenter / artist; [memb.] American Legion - Killeen, TX; [hon.] Honor Roll - Aviation Maint. T.S.T.C.; [oth. writ.] Many, many poems yet to be published but admired by many as being particularly good; [pers.] Children are truly the very greatest gift that God can bestow upon us; Mine have saved my life and opened my eyes to a new and better living less selfishly. God bless the children; [a.] Killeen, TX

CALDERUN, MARGARET L.
[b.] January 14, 1928, Porterville; [p.] Albert and Margaret Villegas; [m.] Adulph G. Calderun, June 26, 1955; [ch.] Two; [ed.] High School American College of Beauty, US Post Office, Nurse's Aid; [occ.] Retire I am a written now; [memb.] St. Ana Church Catholic Daughters of America; [oth. writ.] Mr. Rabbit and Mrs. Scrips Babbles the cat Chunkee King of the cats the boy and the dog poems the garden the streams.; [pers.] I write mosley childrens books I bean writing since 1989 and hope to write some novels.; [a.] Portenville, CA

CALLAHAN, BONNIE ANN
[b.] August 3, 1942, Springfield, MA; [p.] John E. and Miriam J. Marcoulier; [m.] Larry Lee Callahan, August 3, 1985; [ch.] David John Proctor (23), Miriam F. Proctor; [ed.] High School '59; [occ.] Assistant Treasure - Gateway Regional School District Huntington, MA; [memb.] Director Chester Foundation, American Congregational Church of Chester School Committee '82-83; [hon.] Finalist in Miss Westfield Pageant 1960 as Miss Rotary Snelling and Snelling Personnel - Awards for Performance; [oth. writ.] A collection of poems entitled shallow thoughts - deep reflections conversations with myself.; [pers.] I most enjoy the good earth and the free bounty is provides us. My husband and I enjoy gardening and exploring the fields and forests with our beloved patch hound, Cheyenne. My home and family are my greatest blessings and my greatest joy. I try to find something good and salvageable in each person I meet and each experience that touches me somehow this makes the unpleasant moments in life and the frailties of humanity much less noticeable.; [a.] Chester, MA

CAMACHO, LORENZO S.
[b.] August 10, 1922, Philippines; [m.] Leonila A. Camacho, March 20, 1958; [ch.] Dyna A. Camacho married to Emil Gylnquist, Grandchildren: Shannon, Allison and Jane Glynquist; [ed.] Graduate, Central Luzon Agricultural School, Nueva Ecija, Philippines, B.A., Arellano University, Manila, Philippines; [occ.] Retired Federal Employee, Hobbies: Backyard Gardening and Fruit Tree Grafting. Special Products: Pan Tree (Tree topped with Plum, Almond and Nectarine), and Loquat-apple tree; [memb.] American Association of Retired Persons and International Society of Poets; [hon.] Military: Distinguished Unit Badge with 2 Oakleaves, Philippine and American Defense Ribbons, Asiatic-Pacific Medal, Victory Medal, Purple Heart. Civil Service: Employee of the Year Awards. The National Library of Poetry 1995 Editor's Choice Award; [pers.] I like to reflect in my poetry my hopes for advancement of mankind.; [a.] San Jose, CA

CAMERON II, ROBERT WILLARD
[b.] January 16, 1942, San Diego, CA; [p.] Robert Cameron and Virginia Fellows-Jones; [m.] Elie (Mary Elene) Cameron; [ch.] Fleurette (Mary) and Devon Cameron; [ed.] AAS Cosmetology Spokane Comm. College (1988), BA Gonzaga U., Spokane Majors Phil. and Span (1992), Cosmetology Instructor SCC (1988); [occ.] Barber/Stylist, Computer Typist; [memb.] Comm. College Book Review, Group - Charter Member Phil, Club Gonzaga Un.; [hon.] President's Honor Roll, SCC 1986 - Dean's List Gonzaga Un. - 1990; [oth. writ.] Many poems - 4 books in progress - 1 novel (Philosophy based).; [pers.] My inspiration is my children, greatest influence my wife and greatest mentor, Aristotle.; [a.] Spokane, WA

CAMHI, MARTIN H.
[b.] April 17, 1956, Bronx, NY; [p.] Edward and Carla Camhi; [ed.] B.A., Sociology, Mercy College 1981, M.S., Counseling and Development, Long Island University, Anticipated Graduation Date, May 1996; [occ.] 1) Rehabilitation Technician, 2) Program Coordinator for Mental Health Social Clubs, New Rochelle, NY; [memb.] The National Honor Society; [hon.] Regents Scholarship, and Winner of three other Academic Scholarships Student Government; [oth. writ.] "The Key," "Something Beautiful," "She's My World."; [pers.] I believe in the dignity, worth, and equality of all humans. I am a spiritually minded person, and a romantic at heart.; [a.] Yonkers, NY

CAMPBELL, ARIA C.
[b.] October 21, 1980, Nashville, TN; [ed.] 9th Grade, Tullahoma High School Tullahoma TN; [occ.] Student; [a.] Tullahoma, TN

CAMPBELL, DOROTHY L.
[pen.] Dottie Campbell, Delsie; [b.] October 6, 1940, Venango Co, PA; [p.] Ona and Virgil Shreffler; [m.] Charles D. Campbell, September 2, 1961; [ch.] Teresa, Becky and Brian; [ed.] Graduate - Allegheny, Clarion Valley, Emlenton, PA - 1958, Beauty Culture Grad./Seminars - Clarion University on Early Childhood Ed. and Psychology/Required Schooling at Wilson College in Chambersburg, PA for District Justice System/ 4-H Leader/Scouts/Band Mother/Bible and Sunday School Teacher/Jr. Grange Matron/Subordinate Grange Lecturer/Teacher Assistant in Head Start Program, Employee in District Court System for 11 1/2 years, due to developing Multiple Chemical Sensitivities was Necessary I have spent most of the past 5 yrs in writing, sketching, photography and watercolors. The most wonderful resources of hand are my 7 grandchildren and my collection of photos of them with Captions and Writings Pertaining to each, watercolors of my Memories of growing up country in the 1950's and 60's a much simpler time, a time to safely explore nature and all it's wonders, water colors from my "Dark Era" post tonselect I" created in the wee hrs while re-coping from a tonsillectomy at age 55. As my health allows summer is spent in Organic gardening, Companion Plantings, etc. freezing and dying, am presently studying all aspects of herbs and plants as use in health maintenance and healing as due to my sensitivities and unability to take medications; [oth. writ.] Many writings, nothing published.; [pers.] Sometimes answers needed for situations in our lives slip out to encourage us and give us a better understanding as the following poem I had written in the summer of 1994. "Our Turtle" Delsie tell me little Delsie turtle as you travel far and near crawling o so slowly is there very much to fear or is your life like my life as we go along our way and come upon a rough spot we sometimes have to say it might take a bit longer as I stop to think it through then venture of my usual path the safe one... tried and true to the one that leads us on to... something wonderfully new.; [a.] Emlenton, PA

CANAVAN, KENNETH
[pen.] Poet Canavan; [b.] January 16, 1937, New York; [p.] William and Adelaide Canavan; [m.] Carol Ann Canavan, October 14, 1961; [ch.] Timothy, Deborah, Kenneth, Christopher and Nancy; [ed.] High School and College; [occ.] President - Consulting Firm; [memb.] Member Board of Directors, Cocoa Merchants' Association of America, Inc., Cocoa Grader - Coffee Sugar and Cocoa Exchange, Inc., - Coffee Grader (Army Contracts) - National Coffee Association.; [hon.] Retired - U.S. Naval Reserve (Officer, Captain); [oth. writ.] Personal poetry; [pers.] I want to reflect the hope and goodness in people. I will strive by my future poetry to make this come true. I have been greatly influenced by all types of poetry.; [a.] Manalapan, NJ

CANDELLA, JOSEPH
[pen.] Abas Grey; [b.] July 28, 1974, Chicago, IL; [p.] Vincent Candella, Jessica Candella; [ed.] De La Salle Institute, Northern Illinois University; [occ.] Student; [hon.] Illinois State Scholar, Scholastic Writing Award; [oth. writ.] Honorable Mention Scholastic Writing Competition (fiction); [pers.] The aim of my writing is to evoke self-reflection. It is my desire that my work holds different meanings for every person.; [a.] Chicago, IL

CANTRELL, TERESA L.
[b.] January 26, 1964, Dayton, OH; [p.] Victoria and Fairchild; [ed.] Johnson Central High School, Prestonsburg Community College - Prestonsburg, Kentucky; [occ.] Registered Nurse, Humana Hospital - Lexington, Kentucky; [memb.] AACN - American Association of Critical Care Nurses, WWF - World Wildlife Federation; [hon.] Graduated HS and College with Scholastic Honors; [oth. writ.] 'Memories' is my first submission, however I have written several other poems and a couple of children's stories.; [a.] Lexingtron, KY

CAPEN, ROSE MARIE
[pen.] Rose Marie Capen; [b.] August 25, 1938, Connecticut; [p.] William Joseph Le Cuyer, Regina Taschereau Le Cuyer; [m.] Deceased; [ch.] Timothy and Mark (twin sons); [ed.] Two years College plus a Writing Degree from National Institute of Childrens Literature; [occ.] Certified Nurses Aide; [memb.] The National Library of Poetry Iehoralis Witness; [oth. writ.] Several poems published.; [pers.] Writing is a spiritual and emotional outlet which allows us to gain an insight into our very souls.; [a.] Thermopolis, WY

CAPUTO, MICHAEL
[b.] April 21, 1925, New York; [p.] Maurizio Caputo and Josephine Caputo; [m.] Mary, December 3, 1960; [ch.] Christine; [ed.] High School; [occ.] Retired School Bus Driver; [oth. writ.] "If children were statues" - east of the sunrise anthology national library of poetry 1995.; [a.] Brooklyn, NY

CARPENTER, BARBARA
[b.] March 11, 1967, Emelle, AL; [p.] Robert and Cassie Bryant; [m.] Ollie Carpenter, April 15, 1989; [ed.] Livingston High School - 4 yrs, Shelton State College 1 1/2 yrs (Business); [occ.] WATL - TV 36 Accounts Payable Representative; [memb.] Hopewell Baptist Church; [oth. writ.] Song writer, life's light (unpublished).; [pers.] I am inspired by the people who lives.

Touch or who touches mine. Praises to God almighty for being able to fulfill a life long dream of being a writer and at the same time offer "Solid" guidance based on real experiences.; [a.] Tucker, GA

CARPENTER, RICHARD
[pen.] Romeo Rage; [b.] December 30, 1975, Bakersfield, CA; [p.] Lori McNair; [pers.] True misery is seeing your star and not being able to reach her.; [a.] Piyor, OK

CARR, DAVID D.
[pen.] Cryte Spear the Story Teller; [b.] January 21, 1973, Hammond, IN; [p.] Robert and Shirley Carr; [m.] Martha Christina SUK, Perkins, July of 1996; [ed.] Chesterton High School; [occ.] United States Marine Corps, Tanker 1812; [memb.] First United Methodist Church; [oth. writ.] Many pages of unpublished poetry; [pers.] If you believe in it, it is real. In all of my poems there is a unseen meaning to the reading with this I say try to find it!; [a.] Valparaiso, IN

CARSON, JEAN M.
[b.] Spartanburg, SC; [p.] Conley and Ruby McKelvey; [ed.] Boiling Springs High, Spartanburg Technical College; [occ.] Operational Review Manager, S.C. Department of Corrections; [memb.] American Society of Notaries, Carolina Healthstyles Association; [hon.] Dean's List, Can Do Spirit Award, Can Do Club Award; [pers.] I endeavor to maintain a healthy and energetic lifestyle. From adolescence on I have enjoyed expressing my thoughts and emotions in poetry. My inspirations include family, God, and life experience.; [a.] Inman, SC

CARSTENSEN, VELMA
[b.] October 26, 1915, Davenport, IA; [p.] John and Louisa Jochims; [m.] Edward B. (Deceased), April 11, 1934; [ch.] Seven Children; [occ.] Housewife; [memb.] Holy Family Church, Daughters of Isabella, Association for Retarded Citizen's, Handicapped Development Center, Royal Neighbors - A.A.R.P. - Quad City Plus 60; [hon.] Many Awards for Volunteering 33 years for A.R.C. - Volunteer of Year in Iowa - 1974 - Diana Award - Editor of ARC Newsletter which Won State Awards and more; [oth. writ.] Wrote articles for School paper and ARC newsletter. Had articles published in our daily newspaper. Wrote poems for newsletter and local programs. Also for my own enjoyment.; [pers.] Have 29 grandchildren - 21 great grandchildren and one great great grandchild.; [a.] Davenport, IA

CARTER, JODIE
[pen.] Scarlett Grace; [b.] March 19, 1977, Glendale, CA; [p.] Lillian Anthony, Joseph Carter; [ed.] Morrow Sr. High, will be attending Clayton State College; [oth. writ.] This is my first publication.; [pers.] This is my first accomplishment as a future poet and sence this is the first. I would like to dedicated to my hero my mother who has raised me alone for fourteen years, I love you mom.; [a.] Ellenwood, GA

CARTER, KENDRA F.
[b.] March 17, 1973, Calhoun, GA; [p.] Mr. and Mrs. Elijah Carter; [ed.] Cass Comprehensive High School, Floyd College, Georgia State University (will attend in Spring 96); [occ.] Employed at K-Mart; [pers.] I can do all things through Christ which strengthen me. Philippians 4:13.; [a.] Cartersville, GA

CARVEY, THERESA
[pen.] Obsquious; [b.] September 17, 1965, Tacoma, WA; [p.] Herbert Carvey, Sandra Burwellcarvey; [ed.] The Charles wright academy whitman college, BA, 1987; [occ.] Computer Technical Services Representative; [hon.] Best of show-faire magazine; [pers.] If I have made you think differently about one thing, then I have achieved my goal.; [a.] Tucson, AZ

CASSESE, PETER P.
[b.] November 25, 1954, Newport, RI; [p.] Louis Cassese, Josephine Cassese; [ch.] Allison Mayville; [ed.] Graduated Rogers High School; [occ.] Printer/Type Setter Hodges Badge Co. Inc.; [memb.] Member in good standing - International Frisbee Association; [hon.] Several Letters of Appreciation - U.S.A.F. Military Honors Team Offutt AFB, Nebraska; [oth. writ.] Several poems including - "The voice of the wind," "Random thoughts," "The vigil," and "The War Lord," none of them published.; [pers.] I think we should do more to protect the environment. I am also interested in astronomy because I believe our future is in space if we continue to pollute the earth.; [a.] Newport, RI

CASTLEVETRO, CARMEL
[pen.] "Me Ma"; [b.] November 14, 1939, New Haven, CT; [p.] Pasquale and Josephine DiBiaso; [m.] John Castlevetro Sr. (Deceased), September 6, 1958, Al DeRuccio (Divorced), January 12, 1979; [ch.] Sandra, Joanne, Lisa, Lynnette, John, Jr., Frank, Maria; [ed.] Wilbur Cross High School, New Haven, CT:; [occ.] Self Employed; [memb.] MDA (Muscular Dystrophy Association); [hon.] Volunteer of the Year Award, MDA, 1990 New York Metro Area; [pers.] Say, "Thank you God for another day" each morning.; [a.] North Branford, CT

CASTREJON JR., TOMAS
[b.] November 18, 1947, Durango, Mexico; [p.] Tomas and Soledad Castrejon; [ed.] One Thru 9th Grade; [memb.] Golf Car Maintenance Eldorado Country Club, Indian Wells, CA; [oth. writ.] A few unpublished songs and poems.; [pers.] My writings are inspired by the bible. I feel that everyone should let God work in their lives.; [a.] Coachella, CA

CASTRO, SANDRA I.
[b.] December 5, 1959, Las Piedras, PR; [p.] Sara Perez, Pedro Castro Mojica; [ed.] Paterson Catholic High School, New York University; [occ.] Administrative Assistant; [hon.] Dean's List, Cum Laude, Honor Scholar; [oth. writ.] Poem published in NYU'S quarterly magazine - Icarus issue #9.; [pers.] A friend once told me — "you have to face your fears." Though my writings I not only face many of my demorse but I also have an opportunity to record the joys of lining.; [a.] New York, NY

CAUDILL, SANDRA LYNN
[pen.] Sandy Caudill; [b.] November 2, 1955, Huntington, WV; [p.] Samuel Laney Sr. and Marilyn Ruth Laney; [m.] Michael Anthony Caudill, December 13, 1980; [ch.] 2 - Sons, Stephen Michael and Anthony, Junior (Michael is 19, Anthony is 11); [ed.] Grade School - Durbin Elementary Catlettsburg, Middle School - Cooper Jr. High, Catlettsburg, Ky High School - Boyd County High Ashland, KY; [occ.] Secretary with Riverway Terminals, Catlettsburg, KY 41129; [oth. writ.] Several poems written for local Teachers, family, and friends.; [pers.] Every pome that I have written has always came from the heart. I write poetry as a hobby.

CAVENDER, JEANNE MCLAREN
[b.] Monesson, PA; [p.] H. Ross and Mary Park McLaren; [m.] Carl F. Cavender, June 7, 1947; [ch.] Sandra Jeanne, Carla Ann, Charles Brauchler, Elizabeth Anne; [ed.] B.A. Denison University, Granville, Ohio; [occ.] Former Teacher Canton Public Schools, Housewife, Poet, Writer, Water Colorist; [memb.] National League of American Pen Woman, National Council of American Flower Show Judges, Master Judge Certification, American Watercolor Society, Associate Member; [hon.] Won Newspaper, Essay Contest in School, voted in National League of American Pen Women for "Letters" (writings that were published) and "Arts" (paintings that were sold) - Past President of Canton Garden Center (76 Garden Clubs and 5,000 Members); [oth. writ.] I write for newspapers, had short story in February 1995 reminisce extra magazine, have written 12 children's books, have written 4 poetry books, have been writing all my life - editor of AEA sorority newspaper - editor of Canton Garden Center Paper.; [pers.] My father said my poems were thoughts to conjure up, images - I write free style verse, about local subjects in descriptive terms - I paint local scenes as I see them, capturing a bit of local history in poetry or water colors for future generations.; [a.] Canton, OH

CAVES, DONALD W.
[b.] May 15, 1974, Flint, MI; [ed.] Tawas Area High School Baker College; [occ.] Full-time Student and Production Worker; [hon.] Dean's List; [oth. writ.] Truths self-evident, paralyzing incandescence, x-ray, witnessed, chameleon, and the threat with which we live.; [pers.] The belief of man's woes being the result of battle between a supernatural good and evil is a fallacy and a crutch. Man's woes are of his own making.; [a.] Owosso, MI

CEA, VINCENT
[pen.] Vincent James, James Vincent; [b.] October 14, 1947, New York, NY; [p.] Vincent Cea, Rose Cea; [m.] Carol Ann Cea, June 3, 1988; [ch.] Diane Chiofalo; [ed.] Theodore Roosevelt H.S.; [occ.] Retired; [memb.] International Society of Poets; [hon.] Editor's Choice Award - 1995; [oth. writ.] By Vincent Cea, Vincent James, several poems published by the National Library of Poetry, and local newspaper.; [pers.] Writing poems gives me, a very special pleasure, for people to enjoy reading, and my heart to treasure.; [a.] Selden, NY

CEJNER, STEPHEN BLAKE
[pen.] S. Blake Cejner; [b.] December 28, 1950, Chicago, IL; [p.] Walter and Theresa Cejner; [m.] Kathryn Ann, June 26, 1994; [ch.] Lauren (16), Blake Hunter (2); [ed.] In old out of college Mortgate Banking - Mortgage Brakers Banking Marketing; [occ.] President and Founder - Splash Waters Intl-Bottled Water Co; [hon.] Who's Who World Wide; [oth. writ.] A wish on this new Year eve night make a wish for happiness and prosperity for tomorrow will come and brug with it all your wishes fulfilled if your heart is filled with socerity s blake cejner.; [pers.] You get what you get when you go for it, you must be able to recognize an opportunity when it comes along and you must find a way to take advantage of that opportunity.; [a.] Ormond Beach, FL

CHAMBLISS, CHARLOTTE J.
[b.] March 6, 1910, LA; [p.] Mr. and Mrs. Henry and Daisy; [m.] Robert F. Chambliss, March 3, 1938; [ed.] B.A. Degree, M.A.A. Ed.D (Doctor of Education), Gramma School Teacher, High School Art and Crafts, Teacher University Instructor, U.C. of Calif. Art Ed-Gr.; [occ.] Teacher Retired/Writing, Art (Munia Media), Crafts, Maui; [memb.] Beth Eden Baptist Church, Zeta Phi Beta Sorority, Women in the Arts, Museum, Oakland Museum, Alumnae Assoc., Mills College, International Society of Poets, Univ. of Calif., Alumnae Assoc., World Affairs Council; [hon.] Included in International Biographical Book, the World's Who of Who of Women - Contributions, Women of the World, published 1980, International Biographical Center, Cambridge, England, Notable Americans, 3rd Edition Printers, American Biographical Institute, Raleigh N. Carolina or Charlotte J. Chanbliss Ed.D; [oth. writ.] Equasion X, Dramatic Play, Short And Short Stories, Two Ways, Linden House, Mr. Crows Suit, One Moon Light Night, Buck's Return, Over The Telephone, Saint Monica, Night Watch, Good Samaritan, The Adventurer, Gray Monday.; [pers.] Prayer and perseverance are the two strongest coggs in my life's wheel.; [a.] Oakland, CA

CHANDLER, CHRISTY
[b.] May 20, 1977, Shreveport, LA; [p.] Philip and Debbie Chandler; [ed.] Graduated from Abeka Correspondence School, Student of Institute of Children's Literature; [hon.] Dean's List, National Junior Honor Society; [pers.] My writing, as well as my life, is dedicated to the glory of God.; [a.] Shreveport, LA

CHANDLER, TRAVIS A.
[b.] March 13, 1970, Albany, NY; [p.] Marcia J. Carter and Robert L. Chandler; [ch.] Mustapha Shamar Ali Chandler Godchild: Marqueyh Chunieg Chandler; [ed.] Mohawk Valley Community College Hudson Valley Community College; [occ.] Writer, Enterpreneur; [memb.] Wilborn Temple Church of God in Christ; [oth. writ.] Several unnamed poems and short stories; [pers.] A mother not only carries you for nine months in her stomach. She also carries you in her heart for as long as she lives. So when one finds it difficult to reciprocate this love—try poetry!; [a.] Albany, NY

CHANDLESS, KATHRYN
[b.] February 24, 1977, Hasbrouck Heights, NJ; [p.] Harry Chandless and Virginia Chandless; [ed.] Hasbrouck Heights High School, 94 Haverford College, 98, Haverford, PA., (Majoring in Political Science), and (English); [occ.] Currently attending Haverford College as a Sophomore; [memb.] Assist. News Editor at Bi-College Newspaper, Chaverford and Bryn Mawrds, Thursday Night Club; [hon.] Creative Writing and English, 1st place, Has Hts. H.S., 1994; [pers.] Hail to thee, Bylthe spirit.; [a.] Hasbrouck Heights, NJ

CHAPPLE, TONIA E. BURROUGHS
[b.] October 7, 1956, San Francisco; [p.] William H. Burroughs (deceased), Elouise Mayo; [m.] John C. Chapple, September 9, 1979; [ch.] Myisha L. Chapple, Jonathan B. Chapple; [ed.] Notre Dame High School, S.F.S.U.-BA, Liberal Studies - Thermatic Languages Arts United States International University - Master self esteem; [occ.] Teacher on Special Assignment, Homeless Education Coordinator; [memb.] Conscious Parenting Network, Soka Gaki International, ACSA; [hon.] Dean's List, California Board of Education Conference Speaker; [oth. writ.] A poem called, "No Language" Published for a dissertation on biocial development.; [pers.] I have been writing poems since I was thirteen. I believe it is an outlet for me on whatever I feel strongly about. Poems are an artistic way of expressing my inner thoughts.; [a.] Richmond, CA

CHARLTON, ANGELA K.
[pen.] Ecliptious; [b.] August 12, 1967, Nashville, TN; [p.] Barbara Scott, Roy Scott; [ch.] Parisia Jimenez, Joshua Wright; [occ.] Housewife; [oth. writ.] Words, calm eye, spoken.; [pers.] Inspired by love for life, innocence of children, tribulation of our elders, understanding of God.; [a.] Nashville, TN

CHESKI, PAUL M.
[b.] March 11, 1966, Hackensack, NJ; [p.] Ted and Irene Cheski; [m.] Esther Cheski, February 13, 1988; [ch.] Benjamin, Christopher, Alexander; [ed.] Don Bosco Tech High School; [occ.] Federal Fire Fighter; [hon.] High School Honors Society; [oth. writ.] Various other unpublished poems.; [a.] Mililani, HI

CHEWBACCA, JOEY
[b.] March 8, 1964, New York, NY; [p.] Harry and Ellen Guy; [ed.] NY University; [hon.] Graduated Magne Cum Laude; [pers.] I started writing because I love Science Fiction and I think with a little effort I can write great imaginative works. My fondest wish is to complete my current novel about a group of small blue creatures from the third Alpha quadrant. I also want to make it a movie!!!

CHIUCCHI, LESLIE ANN
[b.] January 13, 1981, Ithaca, NY; [p.] Raphael and Diane Chiucchi; [ed.] Graduate of Immaculate Conception School. Freshman at Ithaca High School; [occ.] Student; [memb.] Dance (Dance America Nationalk Competition Entrants); [hon.] Numerous dance and talent awards. New York State Fair Talent Show case. Dance America competition. Tompkins County Talent Showcase; [oth. writ.] Journal of poems.

CHOQUETTE, GLORIA
[pen.] Gloria Rose; [b.] February 25, 1939, North Adams, MA; [p.] Alphonse and Theresa Thibert; [m.] Raymond, April 18, 1964; [ch.] Glenn, Marc; [ed.] B.S. in Education North Adams State College; [a.] Middletown, RI

CIAVARELLA, SUSAN
[b.] October 4, 1955, El Paso, TX; [p.] Conrad Posey, Hazel Posey; [m.] John Ciavarella, October 2, 1993; [ed.] BBA Accounting, December 1989, University of Texas at El. Paso; [occ.] Accountant; [memb.] Amigo Kidney Foundation; [hon.] College - Dean's List, National Golden Honor Society; [oth. writ.] Other poems for personal pleasure - none published, articles for quarterly newsletter at company where I am employed as accountant.; [pers.] I write poetry for the personal pleasure of expressing through language life's experiences and feelings and moods.; [a.] El Paso, TX

CLANNACH, CANDON A.
[b.] July 13, 1963, Clark Air Base, Philippines; [p.] Beverly Shelton-Sallee; [ed.] Currently working on a Comparative Literature Degree with an Emphasis on Celtre Languages and Literatures; [occ.] Teaching Assistant for the Severely Mentally disabled; [oth. writ.] A book titled a method of meditative magic and a collection of poems titled Blodenwedd's Kiss; [pers.] Yeats says it best - "Come away o human child to the water and the wild with a fairy hand in hand for the world's more full of weeping than you can understand."; [a.] Costa Mesa, CA

CLARK, BESSIE SODERBORG
[pen.] Bess Clark; [b.] August 6, 1919, Salt Lake City, UT; [p.] George H. and Florence Lloyd Soderborg; [m.] Marden J. Clark, October 2, 1941; [ch.] Diane-Dennis M., Sherri Lyn, Kevin W., Harlow S., Krista; [ed.] B.S. Environmental Design Brigham Young University 1967, M.ed Educational - Psychology BYU 1975; [occ.] Docent Museum of Art-BYU; [memb.] Various Church Organizations; [oth. writ.] A collection of short stories for my grandchildren "grandpa stories" by Grandma or "Down in Grandpa's Garden." Various short stories and poems (all unpublished).; [pers.] "Whatever principle of intelligence we attain unto this life, it will rise with us in the resurrection...D&C.130:18-89). In 1989-90 I went to P.R. China, with my husband, to teach English at Qingado University. Except for a few days of substituting in a Finnish grade school I had no teaching experience. Our year in China proved Traveling is my hobby. I have to be a very challenging and exciting year. Our family been on every continent except prized education development of the mind. Antartica, including Northernmost City Hammer Fest Norway and Ushuaia, Tierra Del Fuego (Southermost City in the world.!; [a.] Salt Lake City, UT

CLARK, CAROL
[b.] July 20, 1995, Etna, WY; [p.] Don Clark, Beth Clark; [ed.] Currently a 9th grader at Orem Junior High School; [memb.] National Junior Honors Society; [oth. writ.] Poetry published in "Anthology Of Poetry By Young American's"; [pers.] The moment you realize a dream, is the moment that dream can start becoming reality.; [a.] Orem, UT

CLARK JR., WALTER V.
[pen.] Joshua; [b.] October 21, 1948, New York City; [p.] Walter V. Clark and Anna Nelson; [m.] Vera M. Clark, March 2, 1968; [ch.] 8; [ed.] Business Management - A.S., Paralegalism - A.S.A., Business Management B.A.; [occ.] Senior Surrogate's Court Clerk; [memb.] 1. The knights of the round table, 2. Disable Veteran Society, 3. Harvou Reunion Organization; [hon.] 1. Certificate of Achievement in Paralegalism, 2. Certicifate in office skills; [pers.] God has gifted us with the ability to speak. Let us have the courage to speak out against injustice where every it may be.; [a.] New York, NY

CLARK, LILLIAN A.
[b.] January 30, 1941, LaGrange, ME; [p.] Hannah S. Carter; [m.] Alfred H. Clark, October 29, 1983; [ch.] Five; [ed.] Business Degree; [occ.] Retired; [hon.] College High Honors; [oth. writ.] Several but nothing ever sent in.; [pers.] Raised in last land, Maine. Lined in belchertown since 1971. First husband Robert Alley Jr. 15 when deceased. Two children Walter Alleys age 28 when deceased, Tammy Fruehart deceased. These lining age 37, Robert Alley Jr. 37 and Douglas Alley 30, Audrey 36, Castillo. Lined in Mass. since 1964.; [a.] Belchertown, MA

CLARK, WILLIAM
[pen.] Mister William Clark, Clark INCO; [b.] March 30, 1951, Lynchburg, VA; [p.] Deceased Both; [ed.] Lyro College; [Occ.] Welder & Mechanics; [memb.] The National Library of Poetry! The Poetry Society of Virginia; [oth. writ.] I'm putting together my autobiography, in the form of poetic musical lyrics and off broadway!(It's Hot!) If each poem was taken out of chronology they would receive indiviual awards! [pers.] My new auto biography entitled "Divine Romantic Profess!" (Extreme) [a.] Madison Height, VR

CLARKE, JOYCE M.
[b.] March 21, 1930, Milwaukee, WI; [p.] Charles and Lila Hively; [m.] Richard M. Clarke, April 14, 1965; [ch.] Cheryl, Caryn, Kyle (Deceased), Gailyn, Kevyn, Keyth and Jyll; [ed.] Rufus King H.S. (MILW), Courses UWM (milw), Milw Area Tech, (MILW) Minn Com. College (Minneapolis); [occ.] Homemaker; [oth. writ.] Poems published in local newspapers, sorrority Mag, Library of Congress (Congressional Record), Book (as yet unpublished).; [pers.] Family values are vitally important to me, therefore my writings are about my family and about my life experience subjects about which I am most knowledgeable.; [a.] West Des Moines, IA

CLAY, KRISTINA MARIE
[pen.] K. M. Clay; [b.] December 6, 1973, Ogden, UT; [p.] June and Burt Clay; [ed.] University of Arizona - English Education; [occ.] Aspiring Author - Waitress while in School; [hon.] Valedictorian 1991 - National Honor Society - Presidential Scholarship - Vocal Honor Certificate - and Numerous other Scholastic Awards; [oth. writ.] One novel in progress - several poems and articles.; [pers.] Writing is a way of life for me, it is something I cannot live without. In my mind there is but one author to thank and that is Stephen R. Donaldson.; [a.] Tucson, AZ

CLEGG, JAMIE MICHELLE
[pen.] Jamie M. Clegg; [b.] March 12, 1976, Parkersburg, WV; [p.] Lowell and Cheryl Bungard; [ed.] Parkersburg High School, International Correspondence Course; [occ.] Child Caretaker; [memb.] Children International North Shore Animal League, National Wildlife Foundation, The National Children's Cancer Society; [oth. writ.] Many unpublished poems, short stories and one book.; [pers.] I like to try to write on all different topics. I try to keep an open mind.; [a.] Davisville, WV

CLEMENTS, BETTY
[b.] Indiana; [p.] Rudy Clements; [occ.] Writing; [memb.] Other Philosophical I had no money to put my inventions together. I haven't gotten any albu MS out on my songs not been writing song for 2 years yet; [hon.] I won first blue ribb on for my original design jewelry. Fourteen blue ribbons and red ribbon and blue ribbon on my art an two blue rib bons on my original recipe candy and twored ribbons; [oth. writ.] I write songs. I sing my songs. I compose some of the music for my songs. I wrote new and different from the songs previously written, X'mas, western, others.; [pers.] I have saved peoples lives with my psychic ability in the united states. I have inventions I invented and some or a few 15 yrs later vehicles, suitcason wheels and other.; [a.] Vallejo, CA

CLUKIE, DAVID R.
[pen.] Vidda Lekuci; [b.] November 17, 1942, Detroit, MI; [p.] Kenneth and Maisie Clukie; [ed.] Grad. Milton High School 1960, 1 1/2 years Pensacola Junior College; [occ.] Disabled Retirement; [pers.] I strive to treat others the way I want them to treat me. We only get one chance at life, don't know it away on greed and selfishness.; [a.] Pensacola, FL

COBURN, DEAS A.
[b.] April 8, 1917, Dorchester, SC; [p.] Arthur Samuel, Beulah Alexander; [m.] Athleen Raybourn, 1946 and 1964; [ch.] Cynthia Jeanne, Kim Dale; [ed.] Florida State University, BS, Louisiana State University, MSW, 1961, Mater of Social Work in 1982; [occ.] Retired, U.S. Navy, 1955 Retired, Social Worker, 1982; [a.] Brusly, LA

COCHENOUR, KRISTIN
[b.] August 14, 1979, Portland, OR; [p.] Gary Cochenour, Vaughna Cochenour; [ed.] Sam Barlow High School; [occ.] Student; [memb.] The International Thespian Society, National Honors Society, Concert Choir, Barlow Stage; [hon.] Executive Council member for Barlow Stage, Publicist/Manager of Barlow Sound, Honor Roll; [pers.] Everything in life is an opportunity. It is up to you make those opportunities achievements.; [a.] Gresham, OR

COFFEY, KENNETH W.
[b.] April 30, 1951, Springfield, IL; [p.] Haden Coffey, Pauline Hamm; [m.] Mary Lee (Walbert) Coffey; [ch.] Wes, Laura, Kendra; [ed.] Stephen Decatur High school, Decatur, IL; [occ.] Tenneco Packaging Jacksonville, IL; [memb.] Lions Club; [hon.] United States Snow Sculpting Competition - City Of Milwaukee Award (2nd place) 1985; [a.] Virginia, IL

COHEN, ALECIA J.
[b.] November 16, 1970, Florida; [p.] Jack and Sheila Cohen; [ed.] Curry College, Bachelor of Fine Arts; [occ.] Publisher of a world Music Publication called Rhythm Music; [memb.] A Magazine for World Music and Global Culture; [oth. writ.] Articles published in magazines on the subject of Central African Art.; [pers.] Influences: Chilean poet: Pablo Naruda, Proset and short story writer: Flannery O'Conner.

COHEN, CHARLES SANDI
[pen.] Chuck Cohen; [b.] June 23, 1987, Atlanta, GA; [p.] Sandi and Jeff Cohen; [ed.] Attends Nicholson Elementary School, Georgia State University's Saturday School for Scholars and Leaders, Temple Kol Emeth's Religious School; [memb.] Cub Scouts of America, Atlanta Jewish Community Center's Baseball and Soccer Teams; [hon.] Nicholson's Citizenship Award 1994, Nicholson's Academics Award 1995, GA Reflections Art Show 1992, Cub Scout Conservation Award, 2 Gold Arrow Points, 13 Silver Arrow Points; [oth. writ.] My kindergarten year 1993, Chuck and Pooky 1994, Chuck and Pita 1995.; [pers.] Take care of the earth so that we can live.; [a.] Marietta, GA

COILE, JAMES LADON
[b.] August 5, 1959, Athens, GA; [p.] Sherry Wages and Donald Coile; [ed.] High School Graduate and seek an Associates Degree in Ministry; [occ.] Owner of a Home Service Business; [memb.] Temple United Methodist Church, Full Gospel Business Men's Fellowship International; [oth. writ.] About 28 poems and two songs, all religious.; [pers.] At the age of thirty-one after a failed marriage and a life full of sin. I gave my life to Jesus Christ. I never before had written anything. I wrote "this I do in honor of you", to tell what Christ had done for me, and brought me from, and to say thank you Lord. Without Christ I'd do nothing, have nothing or be "nothing!" Jesus Christ gives me the words I write. All glory honor and praise goes to my Lord and savior Jesus Christ.; [a.] Athens, GA

COLE, NELLENE KAY
[b.] April 1, 1961, Cherokee, NC; [p.] Phyllis Ellen and Dennis Shuler; [m.] Jack Roger Cole (Divorced), July 3, 1978; [ch.] Jackie, Christy, Brad Cole; [ed.] Elementary School Bryson High

School ICS Newport/Pacific College Southwestern Community; [occ.] CNA Cherokee Home Health Cherokee N.C.; [oth. writ.] Red dawn mooring; [pers.] I was born in the great smokey mountains. In swain C.O. I'm 21/ 128 cheorkee Indian. My mother is Indian my father is white, and very much a mountain man. I have walk. Many of mountains and herd many botcats hallier. But I still love to live in the smokeys, on top of my own mountain; [a.] Bryson City, NC

COLE, STEPHANIE
[pen.] Stephanie Mogal Cole; [b.] April 22, 1955, Fontana, CA; [p.] Bernard and Lilian Mogal; [m.] Ralph Cole

COLEMAN, CARLA
[pen.] Lee Drake; [b.] February 2, 1964, Jackson, MS; [p.] Neil Wakeland, Naomi Wakeland; [ch.] Jared Anthony; [ed.] John I. Leonard High School; [occ.] Legal Secretary; [oth. writ.] A couple of poems published in my high school anthology.; [pers.] I literally feel what I write. It must move me.; [a.] Palm Springs, FL

COLES, CAROL
[pers.] I have always tried to live and love life to its fullest and observing everything around me has inspired me to write.

COLLIE, NAHSHON R.
[b.] July 1, 1978, Freeport, Bahamas; [p.] Hansel Collie and Lydia Collie; [ed.] Saint Paul's Methodist School, Embry Riddle Aeronautical University; [occ.] College Student; [memb.] Aviation Management Club, Caribbean Association; [hon.] Freeport Player's Guild. Best Playwright, Omega Psi Phi Fraternity National. Essay Competition winner, History, English, Language, Literature, Public Speech, Most Creative Ability Academic Awards; [oth. writ.] Friend or Joe? From the Cradle to the stars, who is this great God?; [pers.] Writing is not just the important of letters or words in ink on a sheet of paper, but it is a special expression of emotion which is transferred from one heart mind and soul to another. My inspiration does not come from the famous poets past and present, but instead from God, greatest poet.; [a.] Freeport, Bahamas

COLLINS, LEANNA M.
[pen.] Leanna M. Collins; [b.] July 21, 1945, Anderson, IN; [p.] Charles and Jessie Ridgway; [m.] Robert E. Collins, June 27, 1984; [ch.] Michael D. Cooksie; [ed.] Lapel High School - IN, Methodist Hospital, School of Nursing - (grad.) attended Indiana Wesleyan University; [occ.] Registered Nurse; [memb.] 1st Presbyterian Church Warsaw; [hon.] National Honor Society; [oth. writ.] Other poetry - none published - yet.; [pers.] My poetry express my deepest feelings of joy and of sorrow, when I am in the low moments, I pull out a book of poetry and read - the Psalms of the bible are my favorites.; [a.] Warsaw, IN

CONWAY, DAVID MICHAEL
[pen.] "Sam Jade," "The Dreamer"; [b.] December 4, 1979, Little Rock, AR; [p.] David and Beth Conway; [ed.] Kindergarten and I am currently in the 10th Grade and Home Schooled by my parents; [occ.] Full time Poet and Writer; [memb.] Church Member at Waddy Christian Church, Sunday High School Member; [hon.] (High School Poetry Magazine) "The Lemondrop," Penmanship Award, Track Award, 50 yard dash Award, Student of the Week, Student of the Month, when I was in Public Schools; [oth. writ.] I have written 104 and poems and short stories and prose, this one particular poem was one of the first. I chose this one because, I have longer more advanced and better prose but I wanted to send in one required word, that didn't go over the space limit.; [a.] Waddy, KY

COOK, CAROLYN GRESHAM
[b.] January 9, 1944, Bernice, LA; [p.] Lewis David and Estelle Spencer Gresham; [m.] Walter Andrew Cook, February 21, 1964; [ch.] Andy, Stephanie and Robert Cook; [ed.] Two-year Associate Business Degree Louisiana Tech University, Rusten, Louisiana; [occ.] Owner-Operator Cook's Senfood, El Dorade, Arkansas; [memb.] Unim Grove Baptist Church, Lillie, GA; [oth. writ.] "Lovely Louisiana" poem published by the American Poetry Society in 1961. "Lovely Louisiana" poem and "voice of spring" poem published in National Antholoy of High School Poems. 1960-61 "The Christmas Candle poem published in North Louisiana Pine Country Backroads Newsapper in 1995.; [pers.] I am the battered woman - I wrote this poem through the eyes of my children. All of the praise and glory for my writing goes to my precious heavenly Father. I want to thank him for a special sister and brother who have listened to my heart and encouraged me to write.; [a.] Lillie, LA

COOKE, HARRY JAMES
[b.] January 3, 1918, Wilkinsburgh, PA; [p.] James H. and Maude W.; [m.] Julia W., December 15, 1946; [ch.] Rob't, Kathryn, David, Richard; [ed.] Uniontown High, GA Tech.; [occ.] Ret. Arch. Eng. (PE), Do-it-yourselfer, Poet, Dancer; [memb.] First Meth., Ch., Elks, Am. Legion; [hon.] Tau Beta Phi, Dean's List; [oth. writ.] Essays, poems used in church srvs. and by local psychiatrist, third-person biography.; [pers.] "Of fame and fortune I have none for of the lowly I am one who through prayer, seeks his God to follow his ways, and escape his rod? To use his gifts of brain and thought, seeking to live as I know I ought."; [a.] Albany, CA

COPELAND, ANNE ANDERSON
[b.] July 22, Mississippi; [p.] I.V. and Syvilla Isaac and W.M. Slack; [m.] Bennie L. Copeland, June 13, 1970; [ch.] Chonda Be'Naye and Chelia Antwynete; [ed.] Roosevelt High School, Attended Sinclair Comm. College; [occ.] Specialized Clerk/G.M. Corp; [memb.] Zion Hill Missionary Baptist Church; [hon.] Poetry Recited at School Poetry Contest, Wedding, Graduations, Retirements; [oth. writ.] Writing for Oratorial Contest - Finalist; [pers.] I endeavor to present inspiration to those in everyday life situations in my writing.; [a.] Dayton, OH

COPELAND, JIMMY
[pen.] Cherokee Flash; [b.] September 15, 1958, North Carolina; [p.] Jim and Laura Copeland; [m.] Mrs. Carmenta Copeland; [ed.] College Level. I am Studing Classical Piano, and Song Writing here at the College; [occ.] Jazz Guitarist Piano Player and Entertainer; [memb.] I belong to the Musician Union and the El Circuld Cultural Hispanico and the Student Body Hereat Charles County College; [hon.] I have two Commercial Records, that put me in B.M.I.I Entertain Exchange Foriegn Students from Europes, Spain and South America, for free here at the College; [oth. writ.] Student achievement award, here at Charles county college, when I wroked for the government, the out standing rating 3 times.; [pers.] To know where you're going, you've got to know where you've been. The world is a stage I am only playing my part.; [a.] Lexington Park, MD

COPELAND, JIMMY L.
[b.] October 17, 1956, Cairo, GA; [p.] Ida M. and Howard Copeland; [m.] Sandra Renee Copeland, May 23, 1976; [ch.] DeChontelle D. Copeland, Jimmy Copland Jr.; [ed.] Cairo High School, Fort Valley State College; [occ.] Lead Computer Operator for Education Service Center Region 20; [oth. writ.] Poems! The veil of racism, a joyous journey home, a shattered image, unresovled feelings, apathy battles love, the perfect trap, the walls of loneliness, a prayer for unity - no one is blameless, etc.; [pers.] I write poetry from the depths of my heart and soul. I reflect from my own experiences as well as my empathy for the plight of other, hoping that I might touch someone.; [a.] San Antonio, TX

COSTANZO, MARY CABRINI
[pen.] Brini; [b.] January 30, 1960, Scranton, PA; [p.] Mary Phillips; [m.] Joseph, August 13, 1994; [ch.] Holly, John, Matthew; [ed.] Riverside High School, University Scranton; [occ.] Decorator, JC Penneys Scranton, PA; [oth. writ.] Many, many, many; [pers.] All of my writings are divinely inspired. I attempt to be a channel for the Lord Jesus to be expressed. All credits are due to God.; [a.] Scranton, PA

COSTELLO, DONNA
[b.] March 31, 1963; [p.] Michael and Leona Pace; [m.] John Costello, August 25, 1996; [ed.] Burrillville High School, Community College of RI; [occ.] CNA

COTTEN, WILLIAM R.
[pen.] Bill Cotten; [b.] April 2, 1940, Covington, IN; [p.] Alva and Nellie Cotten (Both Deceased); [m.] Widow; [ch.] (1) Richard W. Cotten; [ed.] 3 1/2 Years College, Spokane Falls Comm. College, E.W.U., Gonzaga University; [occ.] Electrical Design Engineer; [memb.] Eagles Lodge Aerie #2: Church of Christ; [oth. writ.] Book of personal prose and poetry - unpublished; [pers.] I write prose and poetry to special people and events in my life. I strive to put to pen and paper those things dear to me in the form of prose and poetry.; [a.] Spokane, WA

COTTON, RODRICK
[pen.] R.C. Cola; [b.] February 6, 1977, Kansas City, MO; [p.] Walter and Shirley Cotton; [ch.]

Keanon Trent Wright; [ed.] Archmore High School Lanston University (currently); [oth. writ.] God loves you, the love of my life, beautiful black princess alone, the tears you cry.; [pers.] I ask God to help me be a writer one day; [a.] Ardmore, OK

COULTER, PATRICIA M.
[pen.] Patricia Coulter; [b.] Takoma Park, MD; [p.] Marguerite Murphy, Milton Murphy; [m.] Lonnie B. Coulter, December 3, 1966; [ed.] College of William and Mary (B.S. Psych.), Old Dominion University (A.A. Education); [hon.] Maury H.S. Honor Graduate, Dean's List; [oth. writ.] An original, imaginative fairy tale published in a fifth grade class publication.; [pers.] Look for the positive in life and deal with that. Focus on what's good, flush out the negative. When any bats fly and dart about at twilight, look-for-that-swallows! Take responsibility for all you do.; [a.] Libertyville, IL

COURTER, SOPHIE
[pen.] SCC; [b.] February 19, Rahway, NJ; [p.] Anna and Thomas Iaccarino; [m.] Robert Courter, August 27, 1966; [ch.] Wayne and Robert; [ed.] Scotch Plains - Fanwood H.S.; [occ.] Program Director and Manager of Greenbrook Bowling Lanes, Greensbrook, NJ; [oth. writ.] Several poems published in Local Newspaper; [a.] Northfield, NJ

COX, DEIDRA PROVEAUX
[pen.] Betsey Proveax; [b.] December 17, 1944, Oneonta, NY; [p.] Jerry and Dorys Pidgeon; [m.] Edwin D. Cox, May 13, 1988; [ch.] Travis Proveaux; [ed.] Madison High School - Madison, FL, North Florida Junior College - Madison, FL; [occ.] Housewife; [memb.] SCA - Song Writer's Club of America, 5 Star Music Writers Club, American Song Writers Club, I.S.A.A. - International Society of Authors and Artist, NAR - Nat'l Authors Registry; [oth. writ.] Various (60) will be published in 6 other poetry anthologies. Have 8 poems put to music. Also in local newspaper.; [pers.] Newcomer to poetry writing, some (8) are being put to music. Most of my poems are of family and events, love, heritage and life in general. Am a romantic at heart, very fond of the Victorian Era.; [a.] Loganville, GA

COX, EVELYN ELSA KARSTENS
[pen.] E. Karstens-Cox; [b.] February 3, 1938, Berlin, Germany; [p.] Heinrich and Elsa Karstens; [m.] Alfred B. Cox, April 26, 1958; [ch.] Maureen Beatrice, Andre Benjamin; [ed.] Oberschule/Berlin, Textile School/Berlin/ Germany, Inst. of Children's Lit; [occ.] Housewife, Freelance Writer, Occasionally; [hon.] Overdue; [oth. writ.] Mother Doesn't Want A Snake '90, The Mallard Duck '95, Santa's Red Suit '95, Children's Journal, Animal Tales.; [pers.] Perkasie, PA

COX, JUDY ROGERSON
[b.] April 24, 1953, Elizabeth City, NC; [p.] James and Willie Mae Rogerson; [m.] Norman Ray Cox, February 1, 1974; [ch.] William Ray "Billy" Cox; [ed.] Northeastern High School, College of the Albemarle; [occ.] Secretary; [memb.] St. Paul Free Will Baptist Church; [hon.] Certified Sunday School Teacher; [pers.] Words spoken are soon forgotten, words written will last forever. I thank God for the privilege to write.; [a.] Elizabeth City, NC

CRANE III, GORDON NEAL
[pen.] Trey Crane; [b.] February 6, 1979, Farmington, NM; [p.] Gordon N. Crane Jr. and Diane; [ed.] Aztec High School; [occ.] High School 1 Student and Safe Way Employee; [memb.] Aztec High Concert Band, Student Council; [hon.] Lettered in Band and Best Young Author Award of Living Word Christian School; [oth. writ.] A collection of short stories that have not been published by the name of the many adventures of B.B. snail.; [pers.] You can accomplish anything with God's help.; [a.] Aztec, NM

CRAWFORD, CRAIG JAMES
[b.] August 4, 1967, Des Moines, IA; [p.] William J. Crawford and Mary Ann Crawford; [ed.] Dowling St. Joseph W. Des Moines Iowa, State University, B.A. Graphic Design; [occ.] Entrepreneur; [memb.] Sigma Alpha Epsilon Fraternity, Norba (National off road Bicycle Association), USCF (U.S. Cycling Federation); [oth. writ.] Various poems, short stories (never published).; [pers.] Better to "try and fail" than to "fail to try."; [a.] Minneapolis, MN

CRAWFORD, JOHN K.
[b.] January 31, 1931, Madison, WI; [p.] Howard Dean Crawford, Elizabeth K. Crawford; [m.] Roberta N. Crawford, July 7, 1973; [ed.] Clarkdale, Arizona Public Schools, 1935-1949, Univ. of Ariz., 1949-1854, Univ. of North Carolina, 1958-1960, Univ. of Ariz. 1964-1967, 1971; [occ.] Retired (City Planning); [memb.] Societies in History, Historical Preservation, City Planning, Rail Passenger and Trolley, International Society of Poets; [oth. writ.] City planning thesis, Univ. of Ariz. 1971.; [pers.] I'm also interested in photography, astronomy, geography, and travel, ghost towning, etc.; [a.] Tucson, AZ

CRESTA, JOSEPH M.
[b.] November 12, 1959, Wakefield, MA; [p.] Vincent and Jean K. Cresta; [ed.] Wakefield High School, Northeastern University; [occ.] Writer; [memb.] President of Citizens Advisory, Board for the Mentally Retarded; [oth. writ.] Working in a collection of my poems.; [pers.] Life should be a journey with no definite destinations, so enjoy and explore.; [a.] Wakefield, MA

CRIBB, WAYNE
[pen.] Wayne Cribb; [b.] March 29, 1952, Rock Hill, SC; [p.] Donald Cribb and Julia Cribb; [ed.] Independence High Charlotte, NC, Central Piedmont College Charlotte, NC; [occ.] Entrepreneur; [memb.] Harley Owners Group Bros Club M/C; [oth. writ.] Various poems and short stories.; [pers.] Pick your friends carefully, and enjoy life to the fullest. Don't sell yourself short.

CRISTANUS, JOSEPH E.
[b.] June 7, 1955, Chicago, IL; [ed.] Steinmetz High School; [occ.] Paramedic; [pers.] I've had people say that, "someday you'll be famous." I look at them and think, "someday is only in my dreams."; [a.] Chicago, IL

CROSS, KENDRICK N.
[pen.] Kenny; [b.] May 1, 1971, Louisville, KY; [p.] Sharon A. Maddox and Archie Cross; [ed.] Graduate of Spring Valley HS - June 1989, attended the University of South Carolina at Salkehatchie and earned my Associate degree in Computer Science - May 1993, I have also earned a Certificate in Reservation Sales - February 1995; [occ.] I am currently working as a Technical Support Analyst for Air South Airlines Inc.; [hon.] Maintained Honor Roll/ Dean's List during entire college career while playing Division 1 Basketball earning "Most Improved" 1992 and "Mr. Hustle" 1993. Named to the Book, "National Dean's List" 1993; [oth. writ.] "The Real Side" book of poetry which includes such poems as, "Reality and me," "Let's Talk," "In the mind of a child," and "Violence"; [pers.] I strive to be alive and appeal to keep it real.; [a.] Columbia, SC

CROTTS, MAGDALENE I.
[pen.] Magdalene Idol; [b.] December 16, 1932, Guilford, CO; [p.] The late Dena B. and Clint R. Idol; [m.] Divorced; [ch.] Tim and Dwight Crotts; [ed.] High School, I have a little angel in Heaven named Barry James 2 1/2 Years Old; [occ.] Cook at Oaks at Forsyth Nursing Home, W-S, NC; [oth. writ.] Had two poems published is Hometown Newspaper Kernersville News.; [pers.] Hoping each new day is a new beginning for love and understanding each other.; [a.] Kernersville, NC

CROWNOVER, FRAN
[pen.] Delf Enterprises; [b.] October 18, 1934, Syracuse, NY; [p.] Gertrude and Sidney Karnow; [m.] Wayne Crownover, March 14, 1954; [ch.] Leanne (40), Sheri (37), Alan (34); [ed.] BA Degree Social Work, Gerontology - San Jose State University 1977; [occ.] Retired; [memb.] Questers Inc., West Valley Light Opera, San Jose Municipal Chorus, Church Choirs - 45 years of singing in Public; [hon.] Madrical Singers University of Redlands 1953; [oth. writ.] Reflections, stories and poems in local newsletters.; [pers.] I have always been a positive up beat person, my philosophy of life has been p's - positive attitude, perseverance, patience, prayer, persistence.; [a.] Santa Cruz, CA

CROYLE, DOUGLAS E.
[b.] February 6, 1956, Tripoli, Libya; [p.] Rose B. and James A. Croyle; [m.] Susan B. Blomeley, December 27, 1974; [ch.] Alexa V., Bethany R., Abigail L.; [ed.] Miami Palmetto Sr. High, Communications Schools (various) USCG., Communications Systems Technician (Naval) Work; [occ.] U.S. Coast Guard, Telecommunications Specialist; [memb.] F.R.A., N.A.H.C., C.P.O.A; [oth. writ.] This is my first published.; [pers.] We make our own limitations, and God lifts as above them.; [a.] Kodiak, AK

CRUMB, ERIC T.
[pen.] Bergal Bandana; [b.] October 6, 1967, Newark, NJ; [p.] John S. Crumb, I. Margaret Crumb; [ed.] Montelair High, Engine City Technical Inst, The Chubb Inst; [memb.] UPCW Local 1262; [hon.] Medals: NYC Marathon '92 Jersey Shore Half - Marathon '94, Warwick Marathon '94, Los Angeles Marathon '96; [oth. writ.] Editorials in local newspaper; [pers.] I write to relate to the reader, and to provoke thought. Each piece is a single thought which gets expanded as it's exploded. (It's sometimes therapeutic); [a.] Belleville, NJ

CRUZ, DEBORA
[pen.] "Elizabeth"; [b.] December 25, 1960, San Francisco, CA; [p.] Marlene Jones; [ed.] S.F. Christian High School, Simpson College, Liberty University; [memb.] First Baptist Church; [hon.] Business Excellence Awards, Missions Commendation; [oth. writ.] Freelance short stories and poetry.; [pers.] Through my writings I try to touch others with love, morals, and Christian values.; [a.] LeGrand, CA

CUFFEE, MARQUINTALA P.
[b.] November 28, 1961, Bridgeport; [p.] Charlotte Ann Johnson and Cece Cuffee; [ch.] Felicia and Alicia Cuffee; [ed.] High Central School, Nurses Aide Training (Cert.) Tractor Trailer Licence, Domestic Violence Sexually Abbuse Training; [occ.] Attending School; [memb.] Household of Faith Church; [oth. writ.] I write for a newsletter called the family.; [pers.] I strive to have more eof my writing published because I feel I have much to say.; [a.] Bridgeport, CT

CUMMISKEY, TOM
[b.] August 28, 1952, Detroit, MI; [p.] Mancourt T. and Jane E. Cummiskey; [m.] Janalyn M. Cummiskey, December 30, 1989; [ch.] William, Jennifer, Crystal, Mrya; [ed.] Brophy College Preparatory Arizona State University; [occ.] CPA - Financial Analyst; [memb.] Treasure, Motorola Employees Credit Union - West Board of Directors; [oth. writ.] Volumes of material, written and available but unpublished to date; [pers.] I am generally able to create verse upon request. Writings include seasonal and childrens poetry. Personal writing tends towards philosophical religious themes.; [a.] Chandler, AZ

CUNNINGHAN, BARBARA
[b.] November 7, 1961, Peoria, IL; [p.] Leland and Anna Bontz; [m.] John Cunninghan, September 24, 1988; [ch.] Jack, Ryan and Shannon; [ed.] BS from Bradley University (Major in Mathematics), JD from Southern Illinois University School of Law; [occ.] Lawyer; [memb.] St. Clair County Bar Assn Board of Directors, Illinois state bar Assn, Sunday School Teacher at St. Theresa's Church; [hon.] Licensed in both Missouri and Illinois, Dean's List Who's who among American Students; [pers.] As my parents age, I want them to realize the respect, admiration and love I have for them.; [a.] Belleville, IL

CURRY, TERRI LYNN
[b.] April 26, 1982, Saint Martinville, LA; [p.] Jerry and Susie Curry; [ed.] 8th Grade Student at Catahoula Elementary; [occ.] Student; [memb.] 4-H Club, Acteens, Jr. Beta; [hon.] Student of the Year 1992-93, Piano Recitals, Math Tournament 1992-93, Cheerleader 1988; [a.] Saint Martinville, LA

CURRY, YOLANDA
[b.] March 2, 1958, Newark, NJ; [p.] Ms. L. Curry; [ed.] Malcolm X Shabazz High School, Kean College - Essex County College; [occ.] Senior Social Service Aide/Case-worker Division of Youth and Family Serv. E. Orange NJ; [memb.] NJ Army National Guards; [hon.] Dean's List/Military Achievement, Good Conduct Veterans Honorable Mention; [oth. writ.] Was distribute to family and friends to encourage them not to stop dreaming, but to fulfill their dream and uplift their spirits.; [pers.] Everything I write is my feelings to express the inspiration in others, who want to fulfill their goals and stabilize their gift of dreams.; [a.] Freehold, NJ

CURTIN JR., JOHN-ROBERT
[b.] May 5, 1947, Providence, RI; [p.] Joan-Robert and Claine Curtin; [ch.] Emily Gene, John-Robert III; [ed.] Providence County Day, Syracuse University; [occ.] President/CED, Fifteen Telecommunications Inc., WKPC-TV; [hon.] 1978 Emmy Award, New England Chapter, National Academy of Television Arts an Sciences, 1984 Emmy Nomination, 1990 Allen Society Community Service Award, 1993 Arthur Allan Leadership Award, Silver Beaver Award Boy Scouts of America, 1990, 1992 Eclipse Awards; [oth. writ.] Mostly industry related with exception of collection of poetry.; [a.] Louisville, KY

CZERWINSKI, JOHN ADAM
[b.] September 10, 1979, DE; [p.] John and Shirley Czerwinski; [ed.] I am currently a Sophomore in High School; [occ.] Student; [memb.] I am a member of NASTAR Ski Circuit; [hon.] 1994 High School Writing Award; [a.] Hockessin, DE

D'ALESANDRO, NYLE K.
[b.] March 27, 1924, Springfield, SC; [p.] Bryant and Edwina Kennerly; [m.] Widow of Col. Louis W. D'Alesandro USMC Ret., May 13, 1945; [ch.] 1 daughter, 1 son, 3 granddaughters

DANDRIDGE, EULA B.
[pen.] Judy Dandridge; [b.] March 3, 1924, Illinois; [p.] John A. Dandridge and Nannie Hiyes Dandridge (Both Deceased); [ed.] Augusta Tilghman High School and Business College - Paducan, KY; [occ.] Retired office employees of Studio Transportation Drivers Teamsters Local #399 for Motion Picture Industry; [memb.] International Brotherhood of Teamsters Local Union 399, "Gulls" Women's Luncheon CLDB - Benefiting Different Charities in Oxnardical; [hon.] National Honor Society from Graduation - Aucusta Tilghman High School - Paducan, Ky. and American Legion Scholarship Award, Editors Choice Award by The National Library of Poetry 1994, printed poems in "At Days End"; [oth. writ.] Several poems - one poem "Friendship" in "At Days End", National Library of Poetry - 2nd poem, "Unforce Table" to be in "Edge of Twilight", Nat. Lib. of Poet - 3rd published in the "Dolores Star", local paper in Dolores, Colorado - entitled "Hooked on Colorado" several eulogies; [pers.] At age 5 moved to Paducan, Ky. Mother and family, Mother Nannie, who loved to make rhymes died 2/8/93 at age of 96. I moved to Los Angeles, Ca. at 20 - reside in Oxnard, Ca. since March 1990. Special interest, music, operas, ballet, ice skating, poetry and tennis. Ancestor believed to be from family of Martha Dandridge Custis Washington (Wife of George Washington).; [a.] Oxnard, CA

DANDRIDGE, RAMON T.
[pen.] Bay-Ray; [b.] June 24, 1959, Memphis, TN; [p.] Eddie and Audrey Dandridge; [m.] Cindy Ann, November 23, 1984; [ch.] Eboni, Valarie, Pebbles and Audrey; [ed.] Fairly High School Memphis, TN, Lemoyne Owen College Memphis, TN, Eldorado College West Covina, CA; [occ.] Director of Custodian Services Claremont, CA; [memb.] Simba Inc. Eldorado College Alum. Bethel Seventh-Day Adventist Church, Pomona, Ca. YMCA Pomona, Ca.; [oth. writ.] A competition of poems unpublished; [pers.] I would like to thank God for giving me the talent and my grandmother the late Queen Esther Tate who I really know got me into writing poetry and to my Mom, Dad and family and friends who believed in my work.; [a.] Claremont, CA

DANKERS, JUDY
[b.] May 22, 1944, Galveston, TX; [p.] Henry and Mary Dlabay; [m.] William Dankers, 1966; [ch.] Casey, Jake; [ed.] Jefferson Davis Hospital School of NAG, Un of Houston; [occ.] Registered Nurse; [memb.] Volunteer Red Cross Instructor, Volunteer - Hospice Nurse American Contract Bridge League; [oth. writ.] Newsletter Editor, Whimsical poems published in local newspaper, write personalized and situational Jingles and story - poems for friends and programs.; [pers.] My creative and empathetic spirits unite in my avocation of writing.; [a.] Gainesville, FL

DAVID, DENISE
[b.] Halloween Philadelphia, PA; [p.] Victor David, Barbara David; [ed.] Hofstra University NY, USC - Peter Stark Motion Picture Producing Graduate Program, LA; [occ.] Producer; [pers.] In my experience, most things in life are not what they appear to be. Often my seemingly "worst luck" turned into my greatest gift. When I follow my heart, inspite of my fears, amazing things happen - often quite effortlessly.; [a.] Los Angeles, CA

DAVIDSON, BRENDA JEAN
[b.] March 26, 1968, El Cajon, CA; [p.] Merton Alfred Thomas Jr. and Gloria Jean (Foster) Thomas; [m.] Bret Davidson, February 17, 1990; [ch.] Chelsie Jeanay and Lauren Ashley Davidson; [ed.] Christian Heritage High School, El Cajon, CA 1981, Grossmont College, El Cajon, CA 1995; [occ.] Florist/Singer; [memb.] Alpine Church of the Willows, Alpine, CA; [oth.

writ.] Poems and songs, song - "First But Last" to be recorded by Hollywood Artists, Hollywood, Ca. and AmeRecord, Hollywood, Ca.; [a.] Pine Valley, CA

DAVIDSON, J. CORINNE
[pen.] J. Corinne Davidson; [b.] February 8, 1958, Oregon City, OR; [p.] Mr. and Mrs. Lawrence C. Personett; [m.] Neil J. Davidson, June 16, 1979; [ch.] Jocelyn Joye, Devon Lawrence; [ed.] B.S. Degree from George Fox College/Teaching Certificate and M.S. degree (in general education) from Linfield College; [occ.] Elementary Teacher in Sandy, Oregon; [oth. writ.] Several childrens' stories that I'm presently trying to publish.; [pers.] Writing is a gift that can breath new life into usual things, through a most uncommon touch.

DAVIDSON, KATY
[b.] May 26, 1981, Kuba City, CA; [p.] Ruth Widener and Brantley Davidson; [ed.] Jr. High; [occ.] Student of R.A. Brown Jr. High School (Freshman); [memb.] PADI Scuba diver; [hon.] Honor Role Student; [oth. writ.] Currently working on a novel; [pers.] If you are in the pit of despair, just wait. The pain will go away, you either die or are healed. Don't believe all the krunk they say, that you are fighting or whatever. This happens to everyone. You just have to wait for the pain to go, and want it to.; [a.] Hillsboro, OR

DAVIS, CONSTANCE L.
[b.] September 10, 1951, Atlanta; [p.] Queen E. Davis; [ch.] Phillip, Larita, Corey, Drayton and Maru Gary; [ed.] S.H. Archer High, Atlanta Aear Tech; [hon.] 3 times Editor's Choice Award; [oth. writ.] Published poems 5 by the National Library of Poetry and several poems unpublished.; [pers.] Need to know the truth about something go to "God" hands and knees and get it first hand. I won't believe God down on needs.; [a.] Atlanta, GA

DAVIS, ETTA MARIA
[b.] January 17, 1991, Lynchburg, VA; [p.] Lacy C. Nowlin, Lorraine D. Nowlin; [ed.] E.G. Glass High; [occ.] Residential Provider for Central Virginia Community Services; [pers.] I want to reflect hope, survival, and triumph over the battles and wars that occur on the inside, which are often not seen because some people can't see deep enough, but in the same token, it takes a special heart with a vision to see beyond what's presented to them.; [a.] Lynchburg, VA

DAVIS, HILLARY ROSE
[pen.] Hillary Rose Davis; [b.] August 2, 1983, Park Ridge, IL; [p.] Madeline Davis, Michael Davis; [ed.] I have been through Elementary School. As of now I am in the 7th grade; [occ.] Student; [hon.] Honor Roll; [oth. writ.] Even though I am at a young age I feel that writing poems are a great way of expressing your feelings.; [pers.] The reason I write poetry is because it expresses my true feelings. This poem reflected on how I loved another person.; [a.] Des Plaines, IL

DAVIS, LYDIA IDA
[b.] Buffalo, NY; [p.] Richard Backer, Gertude Backer; [ed.] Lafayette High '85, Educational Opportunity Center '94, Erie Community College, South Campus; [hon.] Educational Opportunity Center, Dean's List; [pers.] This is dedicate to the one person who inspired me to write Gary Earl Ross. Love and friendship always Lydia Ida Davis. Special thanks to the staff at E.O.C.; [a.] Buffalo, NY

DAVIS, STACEY P.
[b.] March 3, 1967, Fairfax, VA; [p.] Jim and Sydna Gong; [ch.] Nicholas Glaize Davis; [ed.] John Handley High School; [occ.] Grid Finished/Assem., Ashworth Bros. Inc., Winc. VA; [oth. writ.] Romeo's Suicide Note, Ode to Idealism, Purgatory, Double-Talk, The art of Politics, Flawed Perfection, Anticipation, The Church, Alone Genocide, Before I Knew; [pers.] I take my attitude from life experiences and hold dear the artistry of E.A. Poe, Chas. Bukowski and others who chose the "road less traveled by"; [a.] Winchester, VA

DE AGUAYO, ANDREA
[b.] August 10, 1979, Caracas, Venezuela; [p.] Richard and Beatriz DeAguayo; [ed.] I'm at Coral Gables Sr. High in 11th gd.; [hon.] Best Student in History, Acceptance into show choir (Cavalier Singers), Most Improved Student in Chorus, Most Improved Student in Math, Superintendent's Honor Music Festival, Swimmer on U.M.'s Club Swimming and for school; [pers.] Life is like a Monopoly game. You begin at start and roll by life (dice). You sometimes get blocks that say go back to start and start all over again but if you keep playing and don't cheat you'll win in the end.; [a.] Miami, FL

DE JACQUANT, JACLYN
[b.] July 28, 1979, New York, NY; [p.] Margaret and Richard De Jacquant; [ed.] St. Rita Elementary School, St. Joseph Hill Academy High School; [occ.] Third year student at St. Joseph Hill Academy High School; [memb.] St. Joseph Hill Academy Varsity Cheerleading Tam and Forensics Team, Tae Kwon Do; [hon.] Spirituality award, Global Award, Second Degree Blackbelt in Tae Kwon Do, First place cheerleading team in State Championship and N.Y. State gold medalist; [pers.] Time has a way of revealing the hidden truths.; [a.] Staten Island, NY

DE MESA, JOHN
[p.] Raul De Mesa, Maria L. Charvet; [ed.] Master Degree in International Management from American graduate school of International Management (AGSIM), Thunderbird Campus, Glendale, Arizona; [occ.] Financial Analyst, Barrio Planners Inc., an agency of the city of Los Angeles, Engaged in Economic Revitalization; [memb.] Thunderbird Alumni Association; [oth. writ.] None of my poems have ever been published.; [pers.] I strive to make a contribution to the development of human consciousness. I have been influenced by Eastern and Western seekers and poets; [a.] Hawthorne, CA

DEAUGUSTINE, DIANA
[b.] February 22, 1982, Orange, CA; [p.] Perry and Brenda DeAugustine; [ed.] Hilton D. Bell Intermediate; [occ.] Student - 8th Grade; [hon.] Honors Student, 2nd Place Imagination Celebration of Orange County, 1994 (visual art), Honorable Mention "Disney Creativity Challenge 1995" (visual art); [pers.] I enjoy writing. I like people to feel the message I send through my writings, whether its sad or happy. Yet, most of all I like to have my writings full of meaning.; [a.] Cypress, CA

DECLUE, ANNETTE
[pen.] Twinki; [b.] August 29, 1963, Portland, OR; [p.] Fern Shumway and Alonzo DeClue; [ch.] Dale James and Christopher Adam; [ed.] Parkrose HS, Community College of the Air Force; [occ.] Supply Technician for the Oregon Air National Guard; [hon.] Airman of the Year 1989, Air Force Accommodation Medal; [oth. writ.] The Lone Sentinel, An Eagle Cry, several poems unpublished.; [pers.] The magnificent beauty of the Pacific Northwest is the inspiration for most of my poetry. My dream is to write so that others can find the beauty in what I see and feel the impression of my life.; [a.] Warrenton, OR

DECOSTER, DARRYLL ARTHER
[b.] May 26, 1972, Warren, MI; [p.] Jane and Dennis DeCoster; [ed.] Beaverton High, Pacific Northwest, College of Art; [occ.] Bicycle Mechanic, The Bike Gallery; [memb.] United States Cycling Federation; [oth. writ.] Poems published in School Literary and Art Publication.

DEE, MICHAEL COLEMAN
[b.] May 25, 1970, Winfield, IL; [p.] Raymond and Maureen Dee; [ed.] Nativity B.V.M. High School, Fordham University (B.S.), Widener School of Law (92-93); [occ.] Platoon Leader, First Lieutenant, Military Police Corps, U.S. Army; [memb.] Military Police Regimental Association; [hon.] Deans List, Distinguished Military Graduate; [oth. writ.] An article for the 8th MP Brigade Newsletter, The Rap Sheet; [pers.] Give 100%! Strive to be diverse. And Always reject that which restricts the development of your fullness.; [a.] Fort Bragg, NC

DEFOOR, JOSHUA DAVID
[b.] January 17, 1981, Columbus, GA; [p.] David and Roxann DeFoor; [ed.] East Lawrence High; [occ.] Student; [memb.] Beta Club, 4-H Club, Band Scholars Bowl Team; [hon.] A Honor Roll, All County Scholars Bowl team, Duke Talent Search, Participant in National History Day; [a.] Moulton, AL

DEJOHN, LINDA S.
[b.] November 29, 1948, Decatur, AL; [p.] Robert and Janie MacGregor; [m.] Joseph DeJohn, September 6, 1985; [ch.] Laurie Roger, Shelley Fluharty; [ed.] Craven Community College, A.A.S., Graduated with 3.88 grp.; [occ.] Writer, I am a cancer patient and work at home.; [memb.] American Cancer Society; [hon.] the National Dean's List - 1991 through 1993. Craven Community College Dean's List - 1992 through 1993. PHI Theta Kappa Honor Society - 1991 through 1994.; [oth. writ.] "Time" is

my first published work. However I have numerous poems, prose, and short stories that I have not yet submitted for publication. I am also working on a novel at this time.; [pers.] I feel that I was afflicted with cancer so that I can help other cancer patients. One way I do this is with my writing. God never closes a door without opening a window. My writing is influenced by what is in my heart.; [a.] New Bern, NC

DEL SANTO, THOMAS
[pen.] Tommy D.; [occ.] Actor - Writer; [oth. writ.] "Man and His Environment" 1972; [pers.] I dedicate this poem to the inspiration of my Heat Heli Turkki.; [a.] Lake Worth, FL

DELANDER, CHERYL
[b.] October 28, 1960, Newfoundland, Canada; [p.] Ray Hoffman and Fran Varnadore; [ch.] Erin Delander; [ed.] Ranum High School, Denver Auraria Community College; [occ.] Administrative Assistant; [memb.] Phi Theta Kappa; [hon.] Who's Who in American Junior Colleges; [oth. writ.] Poem entitled "Someday" published in "River of Dreams," 1994, The National Library of Poetry.; [pers.] My inspiration comes from my heart and my actual experiences. Special thanks to FB!; [a.] Denver, CO

DELAVAN, KAYMA DEE
[pen.] Dee DeLavan; [b.] September 10, 1980, Lubboch, TX; [p.] Rene and Clark DeLavan; [ed.] I'm a ninth grader at Wilson Junior High in Lubbock; [occ.] Student; [memb.] Wilson Jr. High Orchestra, Wilson Tennis Team, FHA, The National Arbor Day Foundation, Westmont, Christian Youth Group; [oth. writ.] Several short stories and poems; [pers.] Faith and Jesus Christ is the most important thing in my life. I always say never put a question mark where God puts a period.; [a.] Lubbock, TX

DELCOIRO, GINA
[b.] December 2, 1984, Oakland, IL; [p.] Anthony DelCoiro, JoAnn DelCoiro; [ed.] George Washington Elementary; [occ.] Student; [memb.] Archies Comics Fan Club, George Washington Band - Flute; [hon.] Honor Roll, Citizenship Award, Perfect Attendance; [pers.] I enjoy poems by Shel Silverstein, Edgar Allen Poe, and stories by Francine Pascal. My greatest influence at school was my first grade teacher, Mrs. K. Forrester, who showed me how to enjoy reading.; [a.] Chicago, IL

DELL, STEVEN H.
[b.] May 21, 1956, Gary, IN; [p.] Lyle and Charolett Dell; [m.] Ludivina Dell, December 31, 1979; [ch.] Michael; [ed.] High School Grad, Griffith High, 1 year of Criminal Law, 1 year of Substance Abuse Counselling; [occ.] Presidential Security Officer; [memb.] Military Order of the Purple Heart, Disabled American Veterans, Veterans of Foreign Wars; [hon.] Bronze Star (with combat V for Valor), Purple Heart, Navy Achievement, Good Conduct, National Defense, Marine Corps Expeditionary, Arm Forces Expeditionary Kwaiti Liberation, Saudi Service, Combat Action, Presidential Unit Commendation Navy Unit Commendation, Marine Corps Unit Commendation, Sea Service, Overseas Deployment; [pers.] My poem is dedicated to the Servicemen and sent in harm way.; [a.] Palms, CA

DELON, STEVEN K.
[b.] December 20, 1961, Kokomo, IN; [p.] Phillip and Shirley DeLon; [m.] Staci L. DeLon, March 2, 1985; [ch.] One son, Alex and one daughter, Heather; [ed.] 1980 graduate of Kokomo High School; [occ.] Sales inspector for Orkin Pest Control; [memb.] First Friends Meeting of Kokomo, Indianapolis Zoo, Indianapolis Children's Museum Board of Christian Education, Chr., Peace Scholarship Committee; [oth. writ.] Several personal poems given as gifts to family member and friends.; [pers.] I enjoy writing poetry for my family and friends. Most of my poetry is inspired by and written for my beautiful wife, who is also my best friend.; [a.] Bringhurst, IN

DEMARS, CINDY C.
[pen.] Cindy N. Caine; [b.] October 14, 1961, Queens, NY; [p.] Carol Caine Lewis, Richard B. Caine; [ch.] Edward Joseph Demars, Stephanie Danielle Demars; [ed.] GED - Dade Co. Fl., Clark Co. Community College, Las Vegas, NV, Broward Community College, Davie, Fla. As degree in Radiologic Technology; [occ.] Radiologic Technologist, Mammography Specialist and Ultra Sonographer; [memb.] The American Registry of Radiologic Technologists; [hon.] Graduated Broward Community College (BCC) in 1990 with High Honors; [oth. writ.] Poems and short verses all unpublished as yet.; [a.] North Miami Beach, FL

DEMETRIOU, SARAH
[b.] December 18, 1942, Cleveland, MS; [p.] Robin and Ellender Pope; [m.] Charles A. Demetriou, January 29, 1967; [ch.] Arthur Nicholas, Elizabeth Nicole; [ed.] B.A. Delta State University - 1963, M.A. University of Mississippi - 1968; [occ.] Freelance Writer, Own Publishing Service; [memb.] Memphis/Shelby County Teachers of English, Tennessee Council of Teachers of English, National Council of Teachers of English, International Society of Poets; [hon.] Faculty Scholar - DSU, Graduated Cum Laude - DSU, Editors Choice Award - "On Seeing a Hawk in the Sky" - 1995, (Between the Raindrops); [oth. writ.] Poem and articles for newspaper, Poems and articles for PTA Newsletter and others, Article in Commercial Appeal, Memphis, TN, Poetry for oral community classes; [pers.] The world contains much sadness and joy - constant tension between two. A conscious effort must be made to increase joy and decrease pain: Civilizations only real accomplishment.; [a.] Cordova, TN

DENIS, THERAN
[b.] January 10, 1977, Haiti; [p.] Marie Jeannette Denis; [ed.] New York City Technical College. I am an Electrical Mechanical Engineering Major; [occ.] I work at Bakers Shoe Store; [oth. writ.] Moments In Sadness, What Is Love, The Final Day Has Come, Finding The One To Love and Feeling Down; [pers.] I always put in mind that, never give up. One day my time will come. And hopefully I will become one of the best poets in the near future.; [a.] Brooklyn, NY

DENMARK, PHILLIS
[b.] January 16, 1950, Lockhart, TX; [p.] Albert C and El Louise Denmark; [ch.] William C. Kreger III; [ed.] Lockhart High and Reagan High, Nixon Clay Business College; [occ.] Administrative Technician II; [oth. writ.] Couple of poems published in local newspaper, also specialized poems for weddings, retirements, 50th wedding anniversaries, and even a funeral.; [pers.] I write from the heart, unfortunately often I find words inadequate for what I feel and want to express.; [a.] Austin, TX

DEROCHER, PATRICIA
[pen.] Jennie; [b.] December 3, 1948, Troy, NY; [p.] Genevieve and Joseph McArdle; [m.] Leonard Derocher, March 31, 1985; [ch.] Patricia and Edward Derocher; [ed.] Cohoes High School; [occ.] Homemaker, poem writer, helping homeless; [memb.] National Wildlife Federation, Eastern Paralyzed Veterans Assoc.; [hon.] Honored by Troy Record and Matilda Cuomo for Donating Time and Making Hats for the Homeless; [oth. writ.] Many other poems; [pers.] I live to make people happy and to do whatever it takes to help those in need.; [a.] Cohoes, NY

DERWINGSON, JONI
[p.] Grace and John Becker; [m.] David, September 4, 1976; [ch.] Daniel and Jacob; [pers.] This poem is dedicated to David.; [a.] San Ramon, CA

DETERLIZZI, DENISE L.
[b.] August 26, 1960, France; [p.] Maryann and Joe Cela; [m.] Leo Deterlizzi, May 10, 1980; [ch.] 3 boys and 1 one the way; [ed.] Vidalia Ga. High School, Cosmetology Trade School JC NJ.; [occ.] Self Employed Hair Salon Owner/Operator; [a.] Rutherford, NJ

DICKE, ROBERT J.
[b.] June 16, 1912, Sheboyqan Falls, WI; [p.] William and Anna Dicke; [m.] Hermine Dicke, August 24, 1940; [ch.] Robert, Mary, William, Katherine; [ed.] Bachelor of Science (cum laude), Ph.D. Entomology; [occ.] Retired Emeritus, Professor of Entomology, University of Wis.; [memb.] Entomology Society of America, Wisconsin Academy of Science, Arts and Letters; [hon.] Alpha Leta, Outstanding Teaching Award, Eagle Scout with 3 palms, U.S. Navy Lieutenant World War II; [oth. writ.] 60 Scientific Papers; [a.] Madison, WI

DICKENS, CHRIS
[b.] October 19, 1969, Carthage, TN; [p.] Howard Dickens, Mary Dickens (1940-1995); [m.] Holly B. Dickens, June 24, 1995; [ed.] Gordonsville High School; [occ.] Factory Worker for Bridgestone/Firestone, Inc.; [memb.] Friendship Baptist Church, Lebanon, TN; [oth. writ.] Anthology of Christian Poetry, Fall 1995, Spring 1995, Fall 1994, Christmas Time, in rhyme 1994, 1995, Higher Rock Music News, The Lebanon Democrat; [pers.] And he path put a new song in my mouth, even praise unto our God, many shall see it, and fear, and shall trust in the Lord. (Psalm 40:3) Thank you, Jesus, for putting that new song in my heart. You alone are my Lord and Saviour who is worthy of all praise!; [a.] Watertown, TN

DIEPHUIS, RONALD THOMAS
[pen.] Ruadh MacMorgana; [b.] February 23, 1951, Detroit, MI; [p.] Nelson Chardoul, Phyllis Kenter-Diephuis; [m.] Valerie Frens-Diephuis R.N., June 1, 1983; [ch.] Four Samoyed dogs, ten cats; [ed.] A.A. Criminal Justice, Pueblo Comm. College, Paralegal Certificate, Univ. Southern Colo., Self study of Jungian psychology, European mythology, Sophian-Goddess spirituality.; [occ.] Self-Employed Paralegal; [memb.] N.R.A., A.S.P.C.A., Full Moon Meditation Society of Fremont County; [hon.] Phi Theta Kappa Honors Society; [oth. writ.] The Lay of Thidrandi, Son of Hall, several poems on mythic themes, articles on ancient European religion and modern Paganism. Working on book on philosophical roots of New Age spirituality.; [pers.] The GOD-force exists in all things, as humans we can choose to act out our animal natures, or to act within our higher, spiritual selves. Creative work, the arts, music, literature can help us release the spiritual self from the unconscious. The dawning new age will free humanity from bondage to religious forms and enhance the flowering of our personal spirituality.; [a.] Canon City, CO

DIETZ, CINDY M.
[b.] April 2, 1968, Ogden, UT; [p.] Charles J. and Janet L. Collier; [m.] James Robert Dietz, June 6, 1990; [ch.] Carlee Jean Collier-Dietz; [ed.] Nampa High, South Western Oregon Community College, South Coast School of Healing Arts; [occ.] Certified Massage Therapist Hands on Healer; [pers.] I know I have truely been blessed when my writings can touch the hearts of others. It is my goal to someday teach through writing.; [a.] Nampa, ID

DIPIETRO, GINA
[b.] July 9, 1970, Philadelphia, PA; [p.] Bernadine DiPietro, Alfred DiPietro; [pers.] This poem is dedicated to Bunny and "Angelique"; [a.] Lansdowne, PA

DISCHINGER, THERESA
[b.] December 9, 1948, Atlanta, GA; [p.] Bernice and Duane York; [m.] James Dischinger Jr., May 19, 1970; [ch.] Jennifer Christine; [ed.] Douglas Freeman High, Pan American Business College; [occ.] Homemaker; [memb.] WIBC, MADD, American Heart Assoc., Houston Diamonds, The Saints; [pers.] Writing a poem for the pleasure of it, and then to have it appreciated by others and be published, is about as good as it gets.; [a.] Houston, TX

DITTMAN, CHRIS L.
[b.] March 13, 1966, Champaign; [p.] Bernard and Betty Dittman; [m.] Debbie Dittman, January 31, 1995; [ed.] St. Joseph High School and Parkland College; [occ.] Inspector, Colwell Systems, Champaign; [oth. writ.] None published.; [pers.] In January this year I married my wife Debbie who lives in the country of Trinidad. Being apart for so long, I wrote many poems to her, this being one of them, unknown to me, my mother sent this one to you. I was very surprised when I got a letter saying you wanted to published one of them.; [a.] Saint Joseph, IL

DIXON, JESSE E.
[b.] January 4, 1933, Chicago, IL; [p.] Charles and Iola Dixon; [m.] Fern J. Dixon, December 14, 1990; [ch.] Three; [ed.] 4 yrs. College Degree in Business and Admin. De Paul Univ.; [occ.] Sales Consultant; [oth. writ.] I have other poems not sent out yet.; [pers.] I write when the Holistic feeling enters my mine. I think about mankind and the peace on Earth that we are all due. I have other poems with same view.; [a.] Chandler, AZ

DOHERTY, ADEDAYO
[b.] May 10, 1964, Ibadan, Nigeria; [p.] Julius Doherty, Elizabeth Doherty; [ed.] B.S. Chemical Engineering 1987, Illinois Institute of Technology Chicago, Il.; [occ.] Sr. Research Engineer, Food Processing (Kraft, Inc.); [memb.] Institute of Food Technologists, National Geographic Society; [oth. writ.] Several unpublished poems, short stories and philosophical perspectives.; [pers.] The only thing certain in life is change. You can make changes for yourself or changes will be made for you. The choice is yours.; [a.] Prospect Heights, IL

DONALD, JAMES H.
[p.] Samuel & Helen Donald; [ed.] Sterling High, VT. Knoxville; [occ.] Collector/ Customer Service; [pers.] For those who think there is no tomorrow, just remember, today was tomorrow yesterday! [a.] Greenville, SC

DONOVAN, GLADYS M.
[b.] November 6, 1932, Harbeson, DE; [p.] Leroy and Nellie Wilson; [m.] Harry A. Donovan, November 17, 1956; [ed.] B.S. Elementary Education Master's Elementary Ed.; [occ.] Retired School Teacher; [memb.] Delaware Retired School Teachers Assoc. taught school at Benjamin Banneker, Alpha Delta Kappa, Daughters of American Revolution, Daughters of American Colonists, Colonial Dames - XVII Century, Church of God - Milford, Del.; [hon.] Junior American Citizens Chm. D.A.R.; [pers.] I've enjoyed teaching and want the world to be a better place. Today's students will be tomorrow's leaders. I have taught public school for 25 years and Sunday school for 38 yrs.; [a.] Milford, DE

DORVAL, LINDSEY
[b.] February 11, 1981, Portland, OR; [p.] Sheila Dorval, Joseph (Jerry) Dorval; [ed.] Berlin Jr. High School, 9th grade at Berlin High School; [memb.] National Honor Society; [hon.] Presidential Academic Award, Robert Frost Poetry Contest First Place, Elected Treasurer of National Junior Honor Society; [oth. writ.] Poem published in a Robert Frost book.; [pers.] I try to put the way people my age think and feel on paper in a way that it makes sense to those who read it. I have been influenced by my parents and grand parents.; [a.] Berlin, NH

DOSORETZ, LIZY
[b.] December 28, 1979, Boston, MA; [p.] Celia and Daniel Dosoretz; [occ.] Student at Canterbury; [pers.] I write poetry dealing with the many aspects of mankind. My poetry should be used as a tool to explore ourselves with.

DOTSON, LISA L.
[b.] June 4, 1952, Brooklyn, NY; [m.] Samuel Dotson, June 18, 1995; [ch.] Patty, Nabil, Kevin, Jason; [ed.] High School Convent of the Sacred Heart, Greenwich, Conn., B.S. Correctional Administration, NY Institute of Technology at Old Westbury, NY; [occ.] Car Salesperson, Mazla of Clarksville; [memb.] Immaculate Conception Church, Roxy Theater; [oth. writ.] Several short stories and editorials published in local newspapers.; [pers.] Once upon a time a young girl went to boarding school. While there she learned the power of the written word. She learned that it can and does inspire a sense of beauty, hope, glory and peace.; [a.] Clarksville, TN

DOUGHERTY, RHETT WILSON
[pen.] Rhett Dougherty; [b.] November 7, 1984, Palm Beach Gardens, FL; [p.] Dr. and Mrs. Edward H. Dougherty; [occ.] 5th Grade Student at the Benjamin School in North Palm Beach, FL; [hon.] Honor Roll Student; [pers.] Rhett enjoys music and the melody of the spoken word. He also finds lyrical beauty in the movement of laughter and sports. He is an avid ice-hockey player, and enjoys the companionship of family and friends.; [a.] North Palm Beach, FL

DOWLING, BEN
[b.] March 19, 1985, Albany, NY; [p.] Ronni Whitman, Jack Dowling; [ed.] Hunter Elementary Class of 1996; [occ.] 5th Grade Student; [memb.] Cat Club 1990-95; [hon.] Raleigh Caps Soccer 1994-95, Winner Read-a-thon 1993, PTA Reflections, Semi-finalist 1994, Blasters State Champion, Soccer Team 1994; [oth. writ.] Hanukkah poem published in the Hunter Newsletter.; [pers.] I dedicate this poem to those who lost their lives in St. Martin during the hurricane this summer.; [a.] Releigh, NC

DOWNS, JAY WARREN
[pen.] Matthew Lovell Downarian, Sterling S. Silverpeace; [b.] September 6, 1936, Reading, PA; [p.] Paul S. and Ethel A. Downs; [m.] Divorced, January 25, 1959; [ch.] Patrick Jay, Brian Scott, Michael Allen, Kevin Glenn, Denise Ann, Kathleen Lynn; [ed.] Reading Sr. High, Univ. of Wisconsin; [occ.] Commercial Transportation Director, ARCO Industries Inc., Milwaukee, WI; [memb.] International Brotherhood of Teamsters, American Trucking Assoc., WI Trucking Assoc., National Safety Council, National Assoc. on Transportation Safety, American Fellowship Ministries, Alliance Church, Milwaukee, WI; [hon.] National Safety Council, American Trucking Assoc., Teamsters Union/Local 200, State of Pennsylvania Carnagie Hero Award, Univ. of Wisconsin-Literature, Milwaukee Writers Club; [oth. writ.] Publisher/Associate Editor of Christian Light, Reaching Out, Words From Within, Numerous Articles, Essays, Poems and Short Stories Pub.; [pers.] I am committed to making a worldwide contribution in literature one poem and one person at a time. As a youth I was influenced by the great classics, they are responsible for the accomplishments I enjoy today - Thanks, Dad!; [a.] Milwaukee, WI

DROP, PATRICIA
[b.] March 14, 1956, Waterbury, CT; [p.] Marguerite and Ronald Hurlbut; [m.] Jesse A. Wright, February 14, 1996; [ed.] Eastern High School, Bristol, CT, Tunxis Community College, Farmington, CT Average: 4.0; [occ.] Self-employed; [memb.] PSI Beta (A National Honor Society in Psychology for Community Colleges); [hon.] Dean's List, Tunxis Comm. College; [oth. writ.] Published in Fall 1995 Edition of "Treasured Poems of America", Poem entitled "Little Miracle"; [pers.] "Be true in everything you do"; [a.] Shannondale, WV

DRUMMOND, RACHEL
[b.] December 14, 1980, Sweet Springs, MI; [p.] Judy and Robert Drummond; [ed.] I'm still in high school; [occ.] student; [hon.] In Florida I got a couple art awards, but nothing as big as this. [oth. writ.] This is the first one ever published, but I do write other stuff, it all depends on my mood that day; [pers.] Be true to yourself and you will never fall; [a.] Higginsville, MO;

DUGAL, LENA
[b.] February 15, 1902, Idaho; [p.] Christina Benefiel; [m.] Deceased, October 12, 1919; [ch.] Four; [pers.] Over my 93 years I have seen many changes both good and bad. I am still proud of our county and our way of life. I think laughter is more important than a frown or a complaint.; [a.] Portland, OR

DUNKLE, HOLLIE ANNE
[b.] February 9, 1979, Roaring Spring, PA; [p.] Shirley A. Dunkle; [ed.] Currently attending a high school as a junior; [hon.] Certificate of Achievement in Social Studies; [oth. writ.] Foolish, Bad Events; [pers.] Writing has allowed me to express myself in many ways. I have found writing to be my gift in life. I give my gratitude to my experiences in life and the support I have received.; [a.] Santa Paula, CA

DURHAM, JEWELL
[b.] November 7, 1938, Reyno, AR; [p.] Eugene Lester and Melissa Lester; [m.] Harold Durham, March 1, 1959 (Widowed 1978), remarried 1991; [ch.] James Harp, Eric Harp; [ed.] Jersey Community High School, Lewis and Clark College, Decatur, School of Nursing; [occ.] Licensed Practical Nurse; [memb.] Roodhouse Christian Church, Greene County Hospice; [oth. writ.] Have written several other poems. Have not sought to have any published as yet.; [pers.] I believe we are here to grow, to learn and to help others, my poems have been a part of my growth.; [a.] White Hall, IL

DUROCHES, MARIE
[b.] April 17, 1962, Plattsburgh, NY; [p.] Florence Cleland and Herman Durocher; [ed.] AAS in Nursing; [occ.] RN-Clinical Coordinator; [memb.] Covenant of Grace Church Bowling League; [pers.] To everyone who believes there is no hope of light shining. There is!! I surviived and learned to live; [a.] Phoenix, AZ;

DYER, KAREN JOYCE
[b.] June 21, 1945, Falls Mill, WV; [p.] Gordon Dyer, Retha Dyer; [ch.] Katrina Thourot; [ed.] 1963 Graduate of New Philadelphia High School, New Philadelphia, Ohio; [occ.] Assembler for Thomasville Furniture Industries Inc.; [oth. writ.] Several poems published in local newspapers and magazines.; [pers.] I love writing poetry and draw inspiration from every faced of life.; [a.] Trinity, NC

EADS, RAYMOND
[pen.] Scott; [b.] February 18, 1972, Troy, MO; [p.] Joyce Grow, Don Grow; [occ.] Poet, and current student of the lesson of life.; [oth. writ.] Lovers and Friends, Fading Away, King of the Fools, Broken Promises, Love of a Lifetime, and many more I have plans to publish.; [pers.] I feel that poetry is an excellent way of expressing one's inner feelings and outlook on life, I owe a lot to my mother for always believing in me and giving me inspiration during hard times to overcome obstacles and achieve my goals.; [a.] Rockford, IL

EARLES, CASSANDRA
[b.] September 15, 1979; [p.] William Earles, Cynthia Earles; [ed.] Junior in St. Helens High School; [occ.] Student, I also work at the Columbia Movie Theater; [memb.] Thespians; [pers.] To me, writing is a piece of life, flowing freely from someone's mind. If you disrupt that flow, no one will ever know how they feel.; [a.] Saint Helens, OR

EASTMAN, JAYNE R. K.
[pen.] Jayne Kooy, Jayne Eastman; [b.] November 30, 1965, Ellensburg, WA; [p.] Jack Kooy, Susan Selix; [m.] Glenn Eastman, August 20, 1994; [ch.] Drake Eastman; [ed.] Ellensburg High School, International Air Academy; [occ.] International Rate Specialist, Uniglobe Travel Central Services, Renton, WA; [pers.] Family, life and love continues to inspire me when I write. True feelings of myself and those around me is a major part of my poetry.; [a.] Federal Way, WA

EASTWOOD, SUZY
[b.] May 2, 1955, Fresno, CA; [ch.] Chantel Eastwood (daughter), Cassidy Eastwood (son); [occ.] Computer operator for a Maintenance firm.; [hon.] My greatest honor at this point was to be awarded the opportunity to be a published poet.; [oth. writ.] Nothing that has been published but several inspired by my traumatic Divorce.; [pers.] Would love to be discovered for my lyric writing ability that can be put to music.; [a.] Lakewood, CA

EDGAR, DANIELLE
[b.] November 5, 1984, Mason City, IA; [p.] Harold and Phyllis Edgar; [ed.] Elementary 5th Grade; [occ.] Student at Nora Springs - Rock Falls Elementary School, Nora Springs, IA; [memb.] 4-H, Iowa Youth Program, Girl Scouts of America; [hon.] Received Drama Award for Participation in "The Sound of Music", High School Play; [oth. writ.] This is the first time I have entered my writing into a contest, I enjoy writing poetry and stories to fill my free time.; [pers.] I like to write because it expresses my feelings.; [a.] Rock Falls, IA

EDMONDSON, BETTY ALICE
[pen.] Betty Youngblood-Edmondson; [b.] December 11, 1936, Seco, KY; [p.] Paul and Hattie Youngblood; [m.] Lee Edmondson, April 23, 1981; [ch.] 4; [ed.] High School, Computer Tech., Secretarial Courses; [occ.] Home Business; [memb.] VFW Women's Auxiliary, Book Clubs; [oth. writ.] Collection of over 200 poems since 1970.; [pers.] It is better to die living - than to live - dying.; [a.] Bristow, OK

EDWARDS, BONNIE L.
[pen.] Bonnie Lou; [b.] December 22, 1958, Syracuse, NY; [m.] Thomas J. Edwards, October 12, 1979; [pers.] I have always enjoyed writing and find that I can express myself through my writing. My unending love for my husband prompted this poem and I dedicate it to him.; [a.] Kansas City, MO

EDWARDS, MORRY
[b.] January 30, 1950, Jacksonville, FL; [p.] Abe Edwards and Edith Wolfson Edwards; [m.] Dawn Marie Edwards, May 23, 1992; [ch.] Ryan Lindsey and Micah Abraham Edwards; [ed.] B.A. Vanderbilt University, M.A.T. Brown University, M.A. and Ph.D. Western Michigan University; [occ.] Medical Psychologist; [memb.] Several Professional Psychological Organizations, several Community Organizations and Charities; [oth. writ.] Several professional articles, a book of poetry, Remembering those Who Sleep Beyond The Dust; [a.] Plainwell, MI

EDWARDS, WARREN PATRICK
[b.] February 10, 1968, Atlanta, GA; [p.] Helen E. Harvey and William P. Edwards Jr.; [ed.] Benjamin E. Mays High, Clark Atlanta University, Mercer University - Atlanta; [occ.] Teacher - Science, Canby Lane Elementary School, Decatur, GA; [memb.] Kappa Alpha Psi Fraternity; [hon.] Dean's List; [pers.] God grant me the serenity to accept the things I cannot change, the courage to change the things I can and the wisdom to know the difference.; [a.] Atlanta, GA

EDWARDS-WHITT, THERESA
[pen.] T.T.; [b.] May 11, 1954, Liberty MO; [p.] Elby Edwards and Lucillle Edwards-Pearson: My father died when I was very young. My Mother remarried to a wonderful man I consider my Dad and still do, his name is Harold C. (Stubby) Pearson; [m.] divorced; [ch.] Maryellen, James, Justin; [ed.] Oak Park High School; [occ.] Self-employed; [pers.] I wrote the Sunrise of You Back in 1987 in the memory of my mother. I share this piece of poetry with a close friend when his mother passed away. Now I wish to share this with everyone, to bring peace to our souls.

ELLEGOOD, ELIZABETH M.
[b.] November 9, 1973, Red Bluff, CA; [p.] Nila and Eber Osborn; [ed.] Los Molinos High, Shasta College; [memb.] Children's Miracle Network, Corning Bethal Church; [hon.] Miss Tehama County, Various Scholarships; [oth. writ.] Various poems and essays printed in community.; [pers.] The poem, "A Face in the Flag" was written in honor of my brother while he was fighting for our country, serving in the American Army.; [a.] Red Bluff, CA

ELLINGSON, DEBRA
[pen.] Night Owl; [b.] January 6, 1955, Brooklyn, NY; [p.] Rudolph Eule; [m.] Earl James Ellingson III, February 9, 1979; [ch.] Earl James IV and Nicholas James; [ed.] Luther College, (BA Degree in Social Work and Religion); [occ.] Ranch Wife; [pers.] I dedicate this poem to Rudolph Eule, my father, who searched 39 years to find me. We had only 10 months together but he gave me a lifetime of love and memories that no one can take away.; [a.] Hamilton, MT

ELSHOT, KITTY
[b.] September 26, 1976, Surinam, South America; [p.] Vicky Elshot D'Andrade and Harold Elshot; [ed.] Mariner High School, Bethune - Cookman College; [pers.] I am blessed to have such a wonderful mother, loving twin sister, great brother, and fantastic group of friends.; [a.] Cape Coral, FL

ELSON, DELORES
[pen.] Dee Elson; [b.] August 24, 1941, Decatur, IL; [p.] Arthur and Helen Stain; [m.] Eddie Elson, June 13, 1959; [ch.] Michael, Rebecca, Samuel; [ed.] Elementary and High School at Sullivan, IL; [occ.] Homemaker and Excel Representative; [memb.] First Christian Church Monticello, IL, Ladies Council F.C.C.; [hon.] American Legion Award - High School Recognized by classmates at 30th Class Reunion for Poetry; [oth. writ.] Composed poetry for reading and sharing with my congregation.; [pers.] I feel any talent I have is God given and should be used to His glory. Be it poetry or any other aspect of my life.; [a.] Cisco, IL

EMANUEL, LAVERNE BOND
[m.] Joseph Emanuel; [ch.] 5 children; [pers.] Artist, Poet, Song Writer, Business; [a.] Saint Ann, MO

EMERLING, JAE
[b.] June 1, 1975, New Haven, CT; [p.] James Emerling, Geraldine Emerling; [ed.] Notre Dame High School (West Haven, CT), Wesleyan University (Middletown, CT); [pers.] I write several poems whose goal is to dismantle the barriers of reality, the barriers between dream and action, and to strive toward their dialectical resolution. They are attempts at what French poet Andre Breton called "A true photography of thought."; [a.] West Haven, CT

EMORY, ALYCE DODSON
[pen.] Adodem; [b.] October 15, 1961, California; [p.] Howard and Jualynne Dodson; [ch.] Anthony Earnest Howard Emory (son); [ed.] B.A. in Sociology, Georgia State Univ., 1990, Graduate Study, Clark Atlanta University; [memb.] Delta Sigma Theta Public Service Sorority, Inc.; [hon.] First Place, Annual Writers Workshop Poetry Competition, Clark Atlanta Univ. ('92); [oth. writ.] Poem published in "Catalyst" Magazine, Articles published in Clark Atlanta University Magazine, "Swingloe" music news paper.; [pers.] "Don't leave the arena to the fools." Toni Cadebambara.

ENGLEMAN, JANET
[pen.] Janet Engleman; [b.] April 8, 1940, Kentucky; [p.] William and Gertie Fawbush; [m.] Divorced; [ch.] Jim Jr., Michael, Kathy, Angie; [ed.] Graduated 12th Grade, Ahrens Trade High School; [occ.] Retired/Disability; [oth. writ.] I have seventy spiritual writings in my possession I have never submitted anywhere because of lack of confidence and or finances.; [pers.] I can express my inner soul best by writing as opposed to verbal expression, as with many persons who experience depression or low self-esteem.; [a.] Louisville, KY

ENRIQUEZ, EDWARD
[b.] January 21, 1977, El Paso, TX; [p.] George and Rachel Enriquez; [ed.] Eastwood High School; [occ.] Architect Student, Texas Tech University, Lubbock, TX; [memb.] Texas Tech Rugby Team, Texas Tech Catholic Organization; [hon.] Sigma Nu, Leadership High School Alumni, FCA; [oth. writ.] Other poems published in High School publication.; [pers.] Do your best... God will take care of the rest.; [a.] El Paso, TX

ENYART, KATHLEEN
[b.] March 20, 1952, Columbus, OH; [p.] Harry and Virginia Fearing; [m.] Roy Enyart, February 5, 1972; [ch.] Roy Jr., Kelli, Ryan; [ed.] Marion Franklin High School, attended Capital University; [occ.] Reynoldsburg High School; [hon.] High School Honor Society, Madison Township Civac Award; [oth. writ.] Poem published in Capital University's Poetry Annual 1971; [pers.] Prose is the poet's way of venting the soul. We exist daily surviving the promise and the pain.; [a.] Columbus, OH

ERB, CHRISTINE
[pen.] Christine Erb; [b.] September 24, 1923, Lyon Co. Ky; [p.] W.W. & Clara Winters; [m.] William B. Erb, March 26, 1954; [ch.] 3 Girls, 1 Boy; [ed.] Equivalent (High School); [occ.] Saleslady / Fuller Brush Co. Great Bend Kansas 32 years; [memb.] V.F.W. Aux # 3281 (Past Pres. Order Of Eastern Star, Past Matron) [oth. writ.] Several Songs, 3 recorded. Several Poems None Published; [pers.] Never give up on anything you set your mind to;

ERB, JAMES
[pen.] Andy Rush; [b.] November 8, 1929, Bronson; [p.] Harry Erb, Mary; [m.] Donna, January 11, 1964; [ch.] Eric James Erb; [ed.] Studied at Several Colleges; [occ.] Inventor; [memb.] Own numerous inventions and copy rights, most recent: Method for using water as a fuel.; [oth. writ.] Written seven books on Philosophy plus a New Science; [pers.] Pain is the most useful feeling of all.; [a.] Battle Creek, MI

ERDEI, EUNICE F.
[b.] June 22, 1932, Ocoee, FL; [p.] Thomas Pinkney, Eaver Pinkney; [m.] Two marriages, both spouses expired, Eugene G. Rogera, March 26, 1952, Frank P. Erdei, March 29, 1981; [ch.] Thomas Riley Rogera, Kevin Lynn Rogera, Martha Barbara Rogera; [ed.] High School Graduate, Ocoee, Florida, Certified Nursing Assistant, City College - Gainesville, Florida, to be a licensed security guard; [occ.] Security screener for Globe; [memb.] Security - Gainesville Regional Airport, Dedicated member of Church Group, Church of God of Prophecy - Gainesville; [hon.] Class Valedictorian - 1950 Ocoee, Science and Music Award; [oth. writ.] I have written several poems the last two years but none of them has been published. All are written about relatives who expired. I wrote one poem to be read as the eulogy at my husband's funeral.; [pers.] I seem to be motivated to write after someone I love and adore departs this life, therefore by expressing my feelings of love, sorrow, sadness, and appreciation in words helps me to face reality and to accept their departure from this life.; [a.] Garnesville, FL

ERSKINE, SUSAN MARRIE-HOLM
[b.] June 9, 1956, Sacramento, CA; [p.] Elaine F. Zielske-Holm; [m.] Randy L. Erskine, March 9, 1989; [ed.] Norte Del Rio High School, Portland Community College, Savannah Technical Institute, Central Texas, U. of Maryland; [occ.] U.S. Army, Military Police, Sergeant; [memb.] Noncommissioned Officers Assoc.; [hon.] (2) Army Commendation Medals, (2) Army Achievement Medals, (2) Overseas Service Ribbons, National Defense Serv. Ribbon, NCO Professional Development Service Ribbon, Army Service Ribbon; [oth. writ.] Unpublished; [pers.] Most of my writings are a reflection of my past childhood and a previous marriage. These were not good times, and writing them helps me to deal with the memories. When someone reads them, maybe it will open their eyes for a better life as well.; [a.] Savannah, GA

ERVIN, DERRICK
[pen.] Derrick Ervin; [b.] February 22, 1977, Lee County, AL; [p.] George and Barbara Ervin; [ed.] Freshman - Southern Union College, Wadley, AL, Beawegard High School; [occ.] Student at Southern Union College; [memb.] Spanish Club, Fellow Christian Athlete, Future Business, Leader's, of America (FBLA); [hon.] Student of the Week, A-B Honor Roll, 3rd Place in Kung Fu Tourn., 4th Place in Beautillion Mu Sigma Omega Chapter of AKA, National Honor Society; [oth. writ.] Several poems published in Church Programs.; [pers.] I strive to reflect my feelings and the feelings of everyone through my writing. I have been greatly influenced by poems that express romance of the young at heart.; [a.] Loachapoka, AL

ESHELMAN, CHAD E.
[b.] January 7, 1972, Salino, KS; [p.] Rex and Cathy Eshelman; [ed.] Southern Nevada, Vocational Technical Center (Vo-Tech); [occ.] Disabled Draftsman; [pers.] Inspiration! Inspiration is needed to write a good poem. So few truly inspiring themes are left in the world. Life is 10% (Ten Percent) what happens to you and 90% (Ninety Percent) how you react.; [a.] North Las Vegas, NV

FAIRFIELD, DOSTON PAUL
[b.] 1967; [a.] Houston, TX

FARAZ, NUMAIR
[b.] December 23, 1984, Bangladesh; [p.] Rubiya Nur, Shafiq Ur Rahman; [ed.] 5th Grade, Elementary School (currently); [occ.] Student; [memb.] The International Society of Poets; [hon.] Young Author's Festival, Kindergarten; [pers.] A start always leads to a stop.; [a.] Diamond Bar, CA

FARNHAM, CARON
[b.] October 29, 1962, Australia; [p.] Joy and Richard Farnham; [ed.] Palm Beach - Currumbin High; [occ.] Commercial Fisherman-Traveller/Surfer; [hon.] In classical R.A.D. Ballet and Olympic Gymnastics; [pers.] To live the life I love, to love the life I live.; [a.] Maleiwa, HI

FARR, VIRGINIA W.
[pen.] Virginia W. Farr; [b.] October 20, 1908; [p.] Allen Gurney and Antoinette Prince Woodruff; [m.] Deceased; [ed.] Northfield Seminary (Northfield, Mass.), Baypath Business Institute (Springfield, Mass.); [occ.] Retired; [memb.] Tuesday Morning Club (A Literary Club), (Honorary Member), Westfield, Mass., St. Petersburg Shuffleboard Club, St. Petersburg, Florida.; [hon.] "Hall of Fame" in International Shuffleboard Assoc. 1994; [oth. writ.] "Montana and the Mesh Bandana" in the Natl. Poetry, Library of Poetry book "Shadows and Light" and words to an anthem entitled "Life's Cycle" (never published but copywrited).; [pers.] Most of my writings are of a humorous nature and what I term as "Doggered" or "Light Verse".; [a.] Saint Petersburg, FL

FAUROT, JULIE ANN
[b.] October 25, 1960, Los Angeles, CA; [p.] Jane and Ben Faurot; [ed.] Associate of Arts Degree in Psychology, Bachelor of Arts Degree in Radio - TV Film, Master of Arts, Degree in Educational Psychology and Counseling; [occ.] Psychotherapist; [memb.] California Association of Marriage and Family Therapists (C.A.M.F.T.); [hon.] Dean's List, Graduated with Honors; [oth. writ.] All of my writings have been personal. This is the first sample I've ever released publically.; [pers.] My poems are strictly bi-products of strong emotions derived from what it is I see...and, then, I interpret. Isn't that what we all do?; [a.] Studio City, CA

FEAL, CHRISTINE M.
[pen.] Andrea Christine Feal; [b.] September 18, 1979, Brooklyn, NY; [p.] Carlos Feal and Awilda Santiago; [ed.] I'm a junior in the Minority Academy in P.R.; [occ.] Student, Poet and Volleyball Player; [pers.] I find inspiration in the problems other people have confronted. The feelings of others, there pains, and worries have always captured my sympathy, and allow me to write.; [a.] Rio Piedras, PR

FEENEY, PATRICIA LYNN
[b.] June 19, 1982, Anniston, AL; [p.] Jeanette and William Feeney; [ed.] I have attended St. Gabriel School (Louisville, Kentucky), St Pius X School (Mobile, Alabama), and Oak Mountain School, Birmingham (Alabama) all for grade school. I am currently at Birmingham, Our Lady of the Valley School (Alabama) and in the 8th grade, I plan on attending John Carroll High School.; [memb.] Our Lady of the Valley Basketball, Volleyball and I am on the Cheerleading Squad. I am also part of Our Lady of the Valley Youth Group.; [hon.] Young Authors Runner Up and Winner of my class 2 times - Principals List (Straight A's); [oth. writ.] None published; [pers.] Trust in God, the helper in need. God shall always protect us, for we are his creation.; [a.] Birmingham, AL

FEIT, ARIELLE LEAH
[b.] February 29, 1988, Los Angeles; [p.] Brenda and Harold Feit; [ed.] Sinai Akiba Academy, Second Grade; [occ.] Student; [a.] Los Angeles, CA

FELICIANO, PAT
[pen.] Pat; [b.] January 14, 1941, Philadelphia, PA; [p.] Edwin and Nancy; [m.] Michael, October 8, 1960; [ch.] Four girls and two boys; [ed.] High School, not graduated; [occ.] Works for large company of hotels; [hon.] Awards in school for writing short stories and poems.; [pers.] I believe in writing what you feel, not what you hear. It has to come from the heart.; [a.] Kissimmee, FL

FERCY, MYRA
[b.] February 17, 1927, Antigo, WI; [m.] Lloyd Fercy, June 11, 1949; [ed.] Antigo High, Langlade County Teachers College, UW Stevens Point; [occ.] Retired School Teacher; [memb.] Member of Provincial Board, Northern Province of Moravian Church, Church Women United; [oth. writ.] "The Moravian" Magazine, July/Aug. '95, column entitled "Words for Women" - My article is "Hot and Now".; [pers.] I like to write about everyday things that are evidence of God's Love.; [a.] Green Bay, WI

FERGUSON, CYNTHIA LISA
[pen.] Lisa Allen, Cynthia L. Claus; [b.] July 17, 1956, New York, NY; [ed.] B.S. NY Institute of Technology, NY, M.A. National University, CA, Hicksville High School, NY; [occ.] Marriage, Family and Child Counselor, Owner, Counseling Center for Growth; [memb.] CAMFT, CERA, ALMA; [oth. writ.] Articles on the struggles of Adult Adoptees; [pers.] My dream is to make a difference by touching the lives of many people.; [a.] San Diego, CA

FERGUSON, LINDA
[b.] December 16, 1943, Alliance, NE; [p.] Alfred and Sophie Iversen; [m.] Don Ferguson, September 7, 1963; [ch.] Brad, Kenny, Robert, Errick, Christopher, Valarie, Eleanor, and Linda; [ed.] Completed High School Alliance Nebraska; [occ.] Housewife, Store Clerk, School Bus Driver, Volunteer Firefighter and EMT; [memb.] Toastmistress - Past President, Jay Ceens - Past Director, Secretary, Vice President, Colorado Certified EMT, EMSAC Member, School Booster Club, Scout - Den Leader; [oth. writ.] None published, but I have a private collection of my writings.; [pers.] That which uplifts, inspires and encourages anyone to be their best, or brings peace or joy in a world of confusion or pain is that which brings life's greatest fulfillment and satisfaction - seek to be such a blessing.; [a.] Elbert, CO

FERGUSON, ROSEMARY
[pers.] In my early years, since I was a child -- which dates back to a long time ago, I have felt a deep reverence for life and awareness of the beauty of nature. I feel deeply the pain and joy of another. I have had no formal training. What I write I write from the heart. I feel almost as if I am the source being used to put into words what has already been. It's as if all the letters of the alphabet are tossing around in space, falling into awards. My poems come to me quickly; I have never sat down and tried to write a poem out of the blue. Sometimes when I am quite busy I find myself singing the words which turn into a poem. The words come quickly; if I am interrupted I lose it all. In "Saga of Man and Dog" I knew nothingas to what the next line would be. I didn't know the ending until he took out his knife and carved into stone "here lies the best friend that I've ever known." The titles of my poems comes after the poem is written. I have written on many subjects. My huband, my friends, keep pressing me to put them into book form and have them published. It's almost as if I feel compelled to do this, yet I get caught up in my everyday living and it's frustrating to me to feel my days are slipping by and I am not accomplishing my goal. I have a vision of my book. As I see it, the cover wouldbe "Rosemary for Rememberance." I envision a spray of the herb rosemary on the cover, which stands for rememberance. [oth. writ.] Our local newspaper, Western World; [a.] Bandon, Or

FERNEAU, MARK
[pers.] Those of us who look for symbolic meanings, fail to see the real poetry in the passage. When we ask, "What does it mean?" We express that everything be understandable. But, if you don't... all the mysteries of the Universe are yours to behold.; [a.] Brandon, FL

FERRIS, JOHN
[b.] February 13, 1957, Berkeley, CA; [p.] Pat Ferris, Bill Ferris; [m.] Laurie Ferris, June 29, 1980; [ch.] John Ferris V, Antionette Ferris; [ed.] Albany High School, Television Production Major A.H.S.; [occ.] Home Remodeler; [hon.] Television Production A.H.S. 1985; [oth. writ.] Published "Letters to Editor" and various Songs copyrighted.; [pers.] I feel real poetry should send a chill up your spine. And make you think. So I strive for this in poetry and song writing.; [a.] Elverta, CA

FERRUZZA, EDWARD J.
[pen.] "Fast Eddie"; [b.] October 2, 1930, Brooklyn, NY; [p.] Anna Crane, Joseph Ferruzza, both deceased; [m.] Barbara Young (Deceased) September 1960; [ch.] Edward Daniel Ferruzza and daughter-in-law Susie Ferruzza; [ed.] High School Graduate and "School of Hard Knocks"; [occ.] Retired, but "Touring" with the Seasoned Citizen's Theatre Company, a group of go plus (Age Wise) Performers, giving a one hour variety show to hospitals, Senior Citizen's Centers and Nursing Homes; [hon.] Good Health Long Life and the fact that I love what I am doing, "Enjoying My Life"; [oth. writ.] Comedy skits and "Gags" for shows;

[pers.] "You don't stop playing because you grow old, you grow old, because you stop laying". "You only live once, but if you work it right, once is enough".; [a.] Brooklyn, NY

FIELDS, BONELL
[b.] June 17, 1941, Calvert, TX; [p.] Andrew and Anna Lawrence Sr.; [ch.] Ann Fields, Pam Fields, Venson Fields Jr.; [ed.] High School Graduate, Practical Nursing School, Courses to become a Registered Nurse; [occ.] LPN - Commercial Review Nurse; [memb.] St. Stephen AME Church, Southern Heights Community Organization, NAACP; [oth. writ.] Several short stories (none published), several poems "How Long", "Mothers", "Willie", "Family Reunion", "Fathers"; [pers.] Hitch your wagon to a star and keep praying. Believe that you can do it and it is done.; [a.] Enid, OK

FILIPOWICZ, ALDONA
[b.] August 20, 1983, Poland; [p.] Alina Filipowicz; [ed.] Bildersee I.S 68, Junior High School; [occ.] A Dressmaker; [hon.] Honor Roll, $50 (Elementary School); [pers.] I tried and tried for once I did. Hurray!!! Now, I believe in Poems and I might succeed.; [a.] Brooklyn, NY

FISHER, CORY LEE
[b.] December 16, 1971, Rapid City, SD; [p.] Gary Fisher, Susanna Bach; [ed.] Faith High School; [occ.] Rancher; [memb.] Faith Volunteer Fire Dept., St. Josephs Catholic Church, Faith High School, Allumni Ass. President; [pers.] We as a people, (Americans), need to start taking responsibility for our actions. We need to stand tall and be proud of who we are.; [a.] Faith, SD

FITZGERALD II, MICHAEL J.
[b.] July 24, 1981, Livonia, MI; [p.] Michael Fitzgerald; [m.] Deborah Fitzgerald; [ed.] Presently 9th Grade, John Glenn High; [occ.] Student; [hon.] School Academic Letter, Governors Award for Math and Science; [pers.] I would like to thank my mother, father, and my 8th grade English teacher, Mr. Downs for all their help and creative guidance.; [a.] Canton, MI

FLAGG, LISA G.
[b.] June 7, 1950; [ed.] B.A. Wesleyan University - (Romance Languages) Graduated Top of Class in my major and also earned CT State Teaching Cert. (Secondary Ed.); [occ.] Design Music and Choreography for Olympic Level Dressage Riders Teach Riding and Train Horses; [hon.] Won Creative Writing Award for Short Story, entitled "Anonymous". My music and choreography has won National Awards and has been used by the U.S. (twice) in the Volvo World Cup; [oth. writ.] Translation (French to English) of "Ecole De La Cavalerie" - has been published. Am presently working on a collection of poetry.; [pers.] Always do unto others as you wish done to you.; [a.] Glastonbury, CT

FLANAGAN, MARY VIRGINIA
[pen.] Mary Virginia Flanagan; [b.] October 11, 1923, Minneapolis, MN; [p.] Paul B. Johnson, Catherine (Clancy) Johnson; [m.] Robert J. Flanagan, April 16, 1977; [ch.] 5 from a former marriage, 3 step children present; [ed.] Annunciation, Academy of Holy Angels Mpls. St. Mary's Hospital School of Nursing, Rochester MN, B.S. of Minn., Mpls. Mn. U of N.M. Post Grad.; [occ.] Retired Public Health Nurse, Community Volunteer; [memb.] Aquinas Neuman Center Lector Albuquerque N.M., Founder and Council Member of Praying Mothers (intercessory group), Amnesty International, Southern Poverty Law Center Supporter; [oth. writ.] Many articles for a quarterly of the Praying Mothers for 10 yrs., one of my poems used in an annual brochure for a statewide Peace Pilgrimage; [pers.] I like to present spiritual awareness as it manifests itself in people, in nature and in my dreams, Wildlife and Nature delights me.; [a.] Albuquerque, NM

FLAVELL, KATRINA
[pen.] Kat; [b.] March 3, 1982, Minot, ND; [p.] Shelley Flavell and Neil Flavell; [ed.] Attending 8th Grade Jr. High; [occ.] Student; [memb.] School Newspaper; [hon.] Music Memory, Horse Show Ribbons; [oth. writ.] "Hopes" was published in River of Dreams in 1994. Other poems have been written just for pleasure.; [pers.] My life has always been hard, complicated, and full of problems. Poems help me escape. I just pour my feelings out on paper.; [a.] San Jose, CA

FLEMING, MARY KAY
[pen.] Mary Kay Fleming; [b.] August 31, 1916, Sharon, PA; [p.] Mary A. and John M. Overfield; [m.] William McIntyre Fleming Jr., December 27, 1941; [ch.] Dian and William III; [ed.] High School - 4, Ballet Training - 15 years, Ballet Teaching - 5 years, Business School - 1 year; [occ.] Retired - Ballerina and Accountant (An unlikely mixture); [memb.] Alpha Chi Omega - Social Sorority, "Write Start" - Florida Jr. College, Sponsor - Hospital Candy Striper Program; [hon.] I really have no awards as such but have done guest readings for library, senior and church groups.; [oth. writ.] Poetry: "Going Home" - U.S. Stars and Stripes, "Solace in the Wind" - Library Benevolent Assoc., "After Thought" - Sparrow Grass. Essays: "Shuffle Off To" - Florida Times Union, "Beyond Second Gear" - Beaches Leader; [pers.] When age persuaded me to take my "Final Curtain Call" - I taught ballet, with my children in the classes, for college tuition - I worked in accounting. I have no adding machines, calculators or computers on my walls - but my first love, pink satin shoes and memories hang on the wall!; [a.] Atlantic Beach, FL

FLETCHER, MARIAN GRACE
[pen.] Marian Grace Johnson; [b.] July 29, 1953, Atmore, AL; [p.] Louiza Rudolph and Robert Johnson Sr.; [m.] Richard; [ch.] Paula Porter, Antre Porter, Eddie Porter, Rashante Porter and Desiree Porter; [ed.] Passaic High School, First School of Paralegal and Southern Career Institute; [occ.] Free Lance Paralegal and Notary Public; [memb.] Daughters of Jeremiah Chapter 236, Library Committee at Grace's Bible Church, Queens and Kings of Hearts Charity Benefits Organizer, President; [hon.] Outstanding Service Award, Best Dressed and Best Twister (Dance); [oth. writ.] Poem published in the Herald and Newspaper. Unpublished Book of Poetry and Book of Fiction; [pers.] I try to bring happiness and laughter to the sad, comfort to the mourners, God to the UnGodly, love to the lonely. I just try to Brighten Everybody's life through my poetry.; [a.] Passaic, NJ

FLORES, JESSE ARIEL
[b.] November 26, 1954, San Antonio, TX; [p.] Mr. Joe Flores and Mrs. Adelita Flores; [ed.] Eastwood High School, El Paso, TX, Long Beach City College Dean's List '83; [occ.] 4 Ray Technologist; [hon.] 1976 JACC Feature Photo Award (1st Place), 1993 William James Association, 3rd Place Artistic Writing; [oth. writ.] The Cross, Mary, Dance of the Black Snake (Child Abuse), Strings, Rape, Circles, The Fee; [pers.] This poem "Yesterdays" is dedicated to my father who struggles with cancer. My writings are meant to awaken lost feelings in a person's soul.; [a.] Yucaipa, CA

FLORES, JOE R.
[b.] August 18, 1956, Las Cruces, NM; [p.] Joe and Angela Flores; [ch.] Joe R. Flores Jr.; [ed.] B.S. Elem. Ed; [occ.] 5th Grade Teacher, Anthony Ind. School District, Texas; [oth. writ.] Several Children's Books and a Novel, all complete, but unsubmitted.; [pers.] I hope the reader enjoys my work as much as I enjoyed writing it.; [a.] Las Cruces, NM

FLOUERS, ANNETTE
[b.] October 30, 1966, Saint Louis, MO; [p.] Emma L. Flouers, Mayne Imes; [ch.] Alexander Raphael Flouers; [ed.] Normandy Sr. High, Forest Park College; [occ.] Management, 9 West Corporation; [oth. writ.] First Publication, The National Library of Poetry; [pers.] I desire to inspire hearts and swoon souls. My inspiration is continuously fed by a soulful food called "Everyday" life.; [a.] Saint Louis, MO

FLURRY, GEORGE E.
[pen.] By George; [b.] October 4, 1947, Marysville, CA; [p.] Clyde B. and Betty M. Flurry; [m.] Faith M. Flurry, March 22, 1992; [ch.] Joshua B. Flurry, Paul L. Flurry, Cynthia A. Harper, Susan M. Daigle and Robert D. Harper Jr.; [ed.] United States Navy: Received G.E.D. 1965, San Joaquin Delta College Stockton, CA 1976; [occ.] Manager, Express One Stop A Division of Sullivan Oil; [memb.] Church of Christ; [oth. writ.] Radio Program (Christmas) in Perry, OK, Poems in local newspapers. Several songs/lyrics copyrighted in the Library of Congress; [pers.] Everything I write is based on life in a poetic form. Through my poems and lyrics, I can release my emotions.; [a.] Baton Rouge, LA

FLYNN, MARY L.
[b.] July 15, 1934; [p.] Van Watson Flynn, Lois Odell Flynn; [ed.] Jackson Memorial Hospital School of Nursing (Miami, Florida), Credits at Orlando Jr. College, Hunter College, University of New Orleans, and Rollins College; [occ.] Retired Nurse; [hon.] Several poems published. Has made the Bush, Quayle, Dukakis, and Bentsen Collections, has had poems and art works put up on display, R. Viosca, has taught many Flynn's poems and literary works at stilled

The Great School.; [pers.] Has worked at Orange Memorial Hospital, De Paul Hospital, Slidell Memorial Hospital, and several other hospitals.; [a.] New Orleans, LA

FOGARTY, COLLEEN C.
[b.] May 2, 1946, Wisner, NE; [p.] Patrick Jr., and Bly McGill; [m.] James D. Fogarty, December 28, 1968; [ch.] Tess, Erin, Adam, Ben; [ed.] Wisner High School, St. Joseph's School of Nursing, enrolled in Graceland Outreach Curriculum; [occ.] Staff Nurse in a Post Anesthesia Care Unit; [memb.] Omaha Press Club, Cast Member Nursing Organizations; [oth. writ.] "Murder in the Nunnery", a play with lines assigned to each individual attending a dinner drama...used as a fund raiser for Duchesnees Academy; [pers.] When life seems complicated and complex, simplify and isolate with paper and pen.; [a.] Omaha, NE

FOLEY, JANETTE LOUISE
[pen.] Lenore Dream; [b.] January 26, 1954, Bay Shore, NY; [p.] Lester and Carolyn Gosier; [m.] Patrick M. Foley, October 30, 1982; [ch.] Wyatt Patrick, Lee Michel; [ed.] Bay Shore High School, West Chester State College; [occ.] Substitute Teacher; [memb.] Church of the Cross, Lakeridge Assc. Board Member; [oth. writ.] Reflections Magazine, Union Life Magazine; [pers.] I attempt to draw from what's real when writing my impressions.; [a.] Denver, CO

FORDHAM, CHRISTA R.
[b.] June 22, 1960, New Brunswick, NJ; [p.] Sylvester and Hazel Williams; [m.] Deceased; [ed.] Famous Writers School (home study), Twins Oaks School of the Bible; [occ.] Writer, Former Foreign Missionary; [memb.] Distinguished Member, International Society of Poets; [hon.] Editor's Choice Award for "Growth", published in A Sea Of Treasures.; [oth. writ.] "Writer's Rap," published in The Path Not Taken; [pers.] I write by the grace of God. "Car Horns" is dedicated to my brother Raymond Eugene Williams, an accomplished artist.; [a.] Bound Brook, NJ

FORNERO, ELAINE
[pen.] Egf; [b.] October 29, 1948, Philadelphia, PA; [p.] Tina and Emilio Fornero; [m.] Joseph Petner; [ed.] Archbishop Prendergast High School; [occ.] Assistant Manager, Computer Operations - Bell Atlantic; [oth. writ.] An annual Christmas Poem to friends and relatives.; [pers.] If you can't make yourself happy, you can never make anyone else happy and no one else can ever make you happy; [a.] Upper Darby, PA

FORRESTER, DOROTHY J.
[b.] July 25, 1915, Vermont; [p.] Clyde and Jessie Joslyn; [m.] Edwin C. Forrester, July 12, 1942; [ch.] 2 - Christine and Lee; [ed.] High School, Art School; [occ.] At home; [memb.] Leagues of Woman Voters, Faith United Church of Christ, Salvation Army Auxiliary, 20th Century Woman Club; [hon.] Scholarship to Art School; [oth. writ.] Have a few poem published in newspaper.; [pers.] Look on the bright side and emphasize the positive.; [a.] Muscatine, IA

FORTNER, SARA JEAN
[pen.] Shorty; [b.] September 12, 1980, Lowell, MA; [p.] Mary Ann Fortner, Robert Fortner; [ed.] A Sophomore at Lowell High School; [memb.] ARCH (Advance and Rise to Challenging Hights) a program through Lowell High and U-Mass Lowell; [a.] Lowell, MA

FOSTER, HATTIE MAE
[b.] January 26, 1954, Green County, AL; [p.] Mrs. Clara Williams; [m.] Mr. Lester Foster Jr., June 17, 1972; [ch.] Latonya S. Foster, Lester B. Foster, DeVanta Freeman Grandson; [ed.] I attended Local Junior and Business Colleges, Shelton Community College, C.A. Fredd, Technical College, Career Training Institute, National Career College, Tus. Al; [occ.] Presently employed by The University of Alabama, I'm a Supervisor for The Abused and Neglected Children; [memb.] A member of The Organization of Jehovah Witnesses; [hon.] I've received the following awards for perfect attendance in high school, Citizenship Award, Employee of the Month four times from the State Employment of Alabama. Recognition for helping some homeless people. Received two scholarships from The State of Alabama.; [oth. writ.] I've written a description of How to be "Thankful" for a local Elementary School paper for a student. Another poem that I've written hasn't been published yet is title "What About The Children"?; [pers.] I try to let my feelings, my love for others relfect in my poems. Also, I try to reflect how others may be feeling. One way to say anything is through a poem; [a.] Fosters, AL

FOX, MONA
[b.] July 25, 1944, Kansas City, MO; [p.] Jane and Frank Barnard; [ch.] Bryan Corey, 25 years, Donna Maureen 19 years; [ed.] Graduated Fremont High School 1962, Certificates from various writing and language Seminars; [occ.] Secretary to the President of a major steel distributorship. Most important occupation is still being a mother and family member.; [pers.] "Never say Never." Go where your heart leads you, and always see and search for the RAINBOWS in life, there are so many that there are always enough to go around, find them and pass them out to those less fortunate.; [a.] San Lorenzo, CA

FRANCO, JIMMY M.
[b.] February 15, 1953, Carlsbad, NM; [p.] Annie L. Duncan; [m.] Linda S. Franco, March 30, 1972; [ch.] Yolanda, Lavonda, Jimmy Jr.; [ed.] High School, U.S. Army Engineer School; [occ.] Potash Miner; [memb.] Church of Christ; [oth. writ.] Numerous poems unpublished. In process of getting a book made of my poems.; [pers.] In my poems I try to write, what I feel, and to feel, what I write.; [a.] Carlsbad, NM

FRAZIER, JANET LEE
[pen.] Janet Lee Frazier; [b.] September 18, 1935, West Virgina; [p.] James and Gertrude Bland; [m.] Ralph, May 23, 1959; [ch.] Annette, Karen, Kenneth; [ed.] AA - Citrus College; [occ.] Retired Registrar, Episcopal Theological School, Claremont; [a.] Claremont, CA

FRENCH, CHRISTINE
[pen.] Christine French; [b.] Providence, RI; [ch.] Two daughters; [ed.] Educated in New England; [occ.] Writer and Presenter; [pers.] When a parent's love is never ending, a child's need is never pending.; [a.] Newark, DE

FRIEDLANDER, FRANK W.
[pen.] North Star; [b.] October 13, 1947, Coulee Dam, WA; [p.] Frank W. Friedlander Sr., Beulah B. Boyd; [m.] Deborah J. Friedlander, August 25, 1965; [ch.] Shelly A. Chaney, Randall S. Friedlander; [ed.] HS, 2 yrs. Technical, 2 yrs. College; [occ.] Public Works and Utilities Director; [oth. writ.] None to date, prior writings primarily shared with friends and family.; [pers.] I write as I receive inspiration from God. I write mainly as therapy for personal well being. Sometimes we need to express inter feelings in ways to externalize daily pressures. Maybe can relate to what we write.; [a.] Nespelem, WA

FRYBERGER, KAMI A.
[b.] July 27, 1965, Wadsworth, OH; [m.] Dennis Blake, February 29, 1996; [ch.] Dustin Ryan, Darrin Reed Bourgeois; [ed.] G.E.D. Private Law Enforcement in College; [occ.] Driver; [hon.] 4.0 and Perfect Attendance Honor Roll; [oth. writ.] A few poems for Dennis and friends. Nothing published. A few children's books for 1st Graders.; [pers.] Personal thanks to my love Dennis for supporting me and my best friend Tony. Keep following your dreams and try to do your best always. Never give up on yourself.; [a.] Marshallville, OH

FRYE, DELENA CHERYL
[b.] April 5, 1953, Logan; [p.] Robert and Gladis Lowe; [m.] Berry Neal Frye, November 4, 1978; [ch.] Jason Robert and Matthew Neal; [ed.] High School Diploma; [occ.] Assistant Store Manager of Consolidated Stores; [hon.] Presidential Physical Fitness Award 12th Grade and 12th Grade Phys. - Ed. Award; [oth. writ.] A poem published in my 12th Grade School Newspaper.; [pers.] Don't take life so serious, it's really simple if you just take time to smell the Roses, then you'll see how precious it is.; [a.] Lyburn, WV

FRYE, DONNA RENEE
[p.] John I. Zink, Geneva Zink; [ch.] Joseph Lancer Frye; [ed.] Albion Jefferson High School, Indiana University; [a.] Clayton, OH

FULLER, ADAM
[b.] July 14, 1977, Biloxi, MS; [p.] Mary Freeman, Hossiena Ghlom Izadi; [ed.] Student at the University of North Carolina at Greensboro; [occ.] Mail Clerk/Student Journalist; [memb.] Hug-A-Greek Society; [oth. writ.] Several articles written for student run newspaper on campus, "The Carolinian" poem, "Teenage Frier", publish in anthology, Shadows and Light.; [pers.] Procrastinate long enough and it will get done.; [a.] Greensboro, NC

GALINTA, ROMEO A.
[b.] Philippines; [p.] Mariano Galinta and Benigna Galinta; [ch.] Romar, Romel, Pamela and Patrick; [ed.] Ll.B, M.A. and Ph.D.; [occ.] Probation and Parole Officer, City of Philadel-

phia; [memb.] Pennsylvania Assoc. of Probation, Parole and Correction, Trinity Methodist Church Administrative Council and Parish Personnel Relation Committee; [hon.] Cotabato City Foundation Award and Bronze, Boys Scout of the Philippines; [oth. writ.] Numerous poems and articles published in APPD Newsletter, PAPPC Quarterly, Philadelphia Observer and MASCA Connection; [pers.] Achieving your goals finds no barriers other than those set by you. I have been deeply motivated/by my brother, Rick, a writer by himself and Olga Mandybura.; [a.] Philadelphia, PA

GALLMEYER, RITA F. DENISON
[pen.] Rita Denison; [b.] August 16, 1942, Chicago, IL; [p.] David and Flora Denison; [m.] Paul R. Gallmeyer, August 3, 1974; [ed.] Gage Park High - 1960, Northern Illinois University, BS in Ed and MS in Ed.; [occ.] Teacher-Reading, Specialist at Madison School Lombard; [memb.] NEA (National Ed Associate), IEA, and LEA, Association of Chapter 1 Teachers, ERIN (Early Reading Intervention Network), Moraine Galley Church Member; [oth. writ.] Many poems, articles and books as yet unpublished, Several Poems have appeared in Kidney Dialysis Newsletter; [pers.] Find Love, receive love, give love.; [a.] Glendale Heights, IL

GALVIN, NATE
[b.] March 21, 1978, Seattle, WA; [p.] J. Gerald Galvin and Laura Galvin; [ed.] Senior at J.F.K. High School; [occ.] Student, Commercial Fisher Man; [pers.] I write about many different things. Never just one subject.. um... Yeah!, something cool like that.; [a.] Seattle, WA

GARCIA, ALAN C.
[b.] May 28, 1970, Stockton, CA; [p.] Bienvenido C. and Judith A. Garcia; [m.] Tami L. Garcia, May 26, 1995; [occ.] Marketing Officer (For C.U.); [pers.] I must escape this Kafkaesque darkness, and the only way to do is to isolate my cultural beginnings, my make up, myself, I search for the link to the motherland!; [a.] Springfield, OR

GARDNER, LORA DYMPHNA
[pen.] Dymphna; [b.] May 21, 1968, Watertown, NY; [p.] John Gardner, Judith Gardner; [m.] Gary Combs Jr, lifetime partner; [ed.] Moravia Central, Onondaga Comm. College; [hon.] Music Scholarship, Dean's List; [pers.] A loved pen never lies.; [a.] Moravia, NY

GARNER, SALLY H.
[b.] September 19, 1932, Boston, MA; [p.] Benjamin and Rebecca Davis; [m.] George H. Garner (Divorced), July 18, 1959; [ch.] Jonathan Michael Garner; [ed.] Norte Dame de Pitie, Cambridge Jr. College, Cambridge, Mass. Golden West College and Cal. State Univ., California; [occ.] Retired Medical, Transcriptionist and Ret. Dance Teacher; [memb.] Past Member: Dance Teacher's Club of Boston, Feb. 25, 1954, Past Member Professional Dance Teacher's Assoc., Inc, 12-31-71, Past Member American Assoc. for Medical Transcriptionists (19957); [hon.] Employee of the month, VIP Award-Anaheim General Hospital (1982), VIP Award-Garden Park Hospital (1974), Graduated with honors from high school; [oth. writ.] I have written several poems six of which will be in various anthologies. Also, I have written over 8 children's books all unpublished.; [pers.] "Writing is a creative adventure." "Poetry touches one's soul."; [a.] Norwalk, CA

GARRETSON, JOHANNA A.
[b.] January 14, 1917, Passuruan, East Java, Indonesia; [p.] Jan Karel van Haastert, Rudolphine, Henderika, Frederika van Olden; [m.] Johnnie Derell Garretson, May 4, 1954; [ch.] 2 sons (adopted); [ed.] Dutch diploma of 5 yrs H.B.S. equal to maybe Junior College was trained for assistant librarian had my training in the library of the city of Surabaia in East Java and worked there till World War II broke out.; [memb.] I was a volunteer in Polomar Hospital in Escondido, Ca. for 15 years. 1977-1992, move to S. Dimas; [hon.] Only a 7,500 hour pin for volunteer work in Polomar Hospital in Escondido Ca. Where I used to live from 1969-1992; [oth. writ.] Just for myself some essays and longer poems. I always loved to write as a teenager, every thing is lost in WW II, in Dutch language; [pers.] I also love to write about nature's wonders. My husband, died in 1976, but he worked for Mobil Oil in Colombia, South - America from 1949-1965 and then we were transferred to Libya, N. Africa where he worked till 1969. I followed him after our marriage in '54. They were eventful years. We went thru 2 revolutions in Colombia and the Middle East war in Tripoli, Libya in '67. I believe in the creative God the Holy Spirit, He also created the first male and female He named God and Goddess. Their first son was, Jesus Christ, the messiah of this World. I am of the Protestant Faith as a child I got my religious education in Passuruan, Indonesia in a Protestant Church. I'm not affiliated with any church here in the USA I do study the bible at home. My husband and I came to live here in the USA officially in July 1969, we settled in Escondido, Ca. North East of San Diego.; [a.] San Dimas, CA

GARRETT, LAVERNE C.
[b.] September 15, 1961, Shreveport, LA; [p.] James and Mary Chreene; [m.] Ronald Garrett, November 19, 1988; [ch.] Bubba, James, Josh, Brandon and Hunter; [ed.] Fair Park High School, Bassier Community College; [occ.] Secretary for Garrett Logging; [memb.] Union Springs Babtist Church; [pers.] I write poems and music in my spare time. I find it relaxing and I enjoy putting my thoughts and feelings to good use.; [a.] Mansfield, LA

GARY, RHONDA
[b.] December 31, 1965, East Chicago, IN; [p.] Katie Gary, Royzel Gary; [ed.] West Side High School, Indiana University Northwest; [occ.] Show Coordinator, Avlon Industries, Bedford Park, IL; [memb.] Alpha Kappa Alpha, sorority, Inc.; [hon.] Indiana, University Northwest, Dean's List; [pers.] Everything I write reflects love, peace and hope. With each morning we awaken our goals can be realized.; [a.] Griffith, IN

GASKIN, ROBERTA KATERI
[b.] June 3, 1977, Jamaica; [p.] Robert Gaskin and Theresa Gaskin; [ed.] Attended Catholic, Elementary and High Schools, in Trinidad, (West Indies) where I grew up.; [occ.] Student at Alabama Aviation and Technical College; [pers.] My poetry is based mainly on society and how I view the world. The wrongs and rights and the many injustices.; [a.] Dzark, AL

GATES, CURTIS O'NEAL
[pen.] Curtis O'Neal Gates; [b.] October 6, 1946, San Angelo, TX; [p.] Ms. La Verne Gates; [ed.] Central High, Henderson County Jr. College, Stephen F. Austin State University; [pers.] The world is not the thing yet a poet will probably say there is life in everything and that words are sometimes somehow somewhere alive and full of light. Certainly it is sayings and songs that light my way and nothing is profane.; [a.] Houston, TX

GAUCK, LINDA A.
[b.] April 14, 1958, New York; [p.] Theresa Rago, Richard Butler; [m.] Arthur J. Gauck, May 11, 1985; [ch.] Kevin Daniel, Matthew Jon; [ed.] Syosset High; [memb.] St. Margaret of Scotland R.C., childrens litergy; [hon.] Home Economics award; [oth. writ.] Published in local newspaper; [pers.] I believe I was born with a pen attached to my heart. I thank God for my gifts.; [a.] Selden, NY

GAUTHIER JR., HARTWELL L.
[b.] October 12, 1947, Norwich, CT; [p.] Hartwell L. Gauthier Sr., Angelica K. Gauthier; [m.] Judy R. Gauthier, April 7, 1968; [ch.] Kimberly, Hartwell III, Eric; [ed.] Quinebaug Valley Community, Technical College and Thames, Valley State Technical College; [occ.] Design/Drafting, Yardney Technical Products, Inc. Pawcatuck, CT; [memb.] Division 101 St. Airborne Association and V.F.W.; [hon.] Dean's List - Quinebaug Valley Community, Technical College and S.M.E. Scholarship - Thames Valley State Technical College; [a.] Plainfield, CT

GEIGER, ASHLEY
[pen.] "Ash"; [b.] March 14, 1983, Atlantic City, NJ; [p.] Donald and Robin Geiger; [ed.] Grammer School 7th grade; [occ.] Student; [hon.] Student of the month finals for book cover for disabled children. A-B honor student.

GELLER, BUNNY
[b.] May 21, 1926, New York; [p.] Herman and Shirley Juster; [m.] Lester Geller, July 7, 1946; [ch.] Judy, Sheryl, Robert, Wayne (also six grandchilren); [ed.] FAIRFAX High School, L.A., Ca., U.C.L.A. (California), (now attending "Elders" classes) Florida International University; [occ.] Poet also (Artist, Sculptor); [memb.] International Society of Poets, Nat'l. Library of Poetry, The National Museum of Women in the Arts, Assoc. Member, Pegasus Mint, Pennington, N.J., Nat'l. Member Smithsonian Assoc.; [hon.] Balfour Medal - American Legion Award - Excellence in Essay, Honorary Art Award, San Francisco World's Fair Exhibit. Distinguished Member I.S.P., Editor's Choice Award, Nat'l. Library Poetry, Invited Guest Internat'l. Art Expo, N.Y., Broward Co. Main Library, Fl., Western Electric, Hopewell, N.J.; [oth. writ.]

Published in newspapers in N.Y. and Florida published: Bunny Geller-Original Poetry, for all ages. Second poetry book, "Choices", to be released in 1996. Have been writing since early childhood.; [pers.] I have faith in the intrinsic good of humanity, and believe that love, compassion, caring and tenderness will continue to develop ever stronger on our planet. My poetry and my art express my deep feelings in these beliefs.; [a.] Hallandale, FL

GENNETTE, ELAINE M.
[pen.] Elaine; [b.] November 4, 1919, San Francisco; [p.] Anna May and James Kiley; [m.] Albert F. Gennette, February 10, 1955; [ch.] I sets twins - 2 singles; [ed.] H. School, 2 yrs. of College; [occ.] Ret. (Air Force Husband); [hon.] Golfing - Oil Painting; [oth. writ.] Story book's for children - have never tried to have them published; [pers.] I also had a pre-school for children for five yrs. Be longed to the San Francisco Batlet School; [a.] San Francisco, CA

GEORGE, LINDA J.
[b.] October 30, 1953, Cleveland, OH; [p.] Joseph Williams, Willa Williams; [m.] Russell A. George, August 24, 1974; [ch.] Ebony S. George, Jamal A. George, Brionna N. George; [ed.] John Hay High School; [occ.] Data Entry Operator, Ft. Myers Police Dept., Ft. Myers, FL; [pers.] Hoping my writing touches the hearts of others, which has experienced so much pain.; [a.] Fort Myers, FL

GEORGE, SEMELE A. CID
[pen.] Semele A. C. George; [b.] Saint Thomas, VI; [p.] Rhudel A. George and Lucia A. Cid George; [ed.] St. Peter and Paul High School, 1989 (St. Thomas), University of the Virgin Islands (St. Thomas), B.S. Point Park College, 1994 (Pittsburgh, PA); [occ.] Probate Officer, Territorial Court of the Virgin Islands; [oth. writ.] Contributed black history profile articles to the Globe (point park college's newspaper), poetry published in the daily news, the cavalcade, the "Poetic Voices of the Caribbean: Virgin Islands, Antigua, Greneda, Trinidad, Jamaica."; [pers.] "I truly believe that a poem has fulfilled its purpose only if the reader, or listener, can understand or relate to its words."; [a.] Charlotte Amalie, VI

GEORGOPOULOS, ARETI
[b.] June 29, 1972, Athens, Greece; [p.] Drs. Angeliki and Apostolos Georgopoulos; [ed.] The Park School, Brown University; [pers.] Writing is a migration of the soul, in poetry, I transcribe the journeys.; [a.] Providence, RI

GERMANY, JOAN
[b.] September 22, 1952, Teaneck, NJ; [p.] Junior and Gertrude Ritter; [ch.] Joamia Mathilda Germany and Jonathan Lloyd Germany; [ed.] M. Katzenbach H.S., N.J., California, State University, Hayward-B.A. in anthropology, 1980, John F. Kennedy University, Orinda, Calif.-currently a graduate in Master of Arts program in Arts and Consciousness; [occ.] Instructional Assistant for Special Ed.-Hearing Impaired, Bret Harte Jr. H.S., Oakland, Calif.; [memb.] Sahara Buddhism; [hon.] Outstanding Young Women of American 1979, Who's Who In California, 1981-1982, Recognition Award from Deaf Community Service 1987; [oth. writ.] Poems published in New Voices in American Poetry 1972 and 1974, an article on anthropological perspective - Deaf and Hearing cultures published in anthropological newsletter at Calif. State U. Hayward - 1980; [pers.] Poetry is a beautiful way to express ability through writing.; [a.] Walnut Creek, CA

GIARRUSSO, DEBRA M.
[b.] May 30, 1953, Troy, NY; [p.] Dorothy and Carmen Mangene; [m.] Joseph A. Giarrusso, April 26, 1986; [ch.] Michelle Tierney, Michael Tierney; [pers.] In loving memory of my beloved husband, Joseph A. Giarrusso, born 9-7-44 died 6-19-92, who taught me the meaning of unconditional love.; [a.] El Cajon, CA

GIBBONS, COLLEEN
[pen.] Gibbons, Colleen; [b.] November 19, 1981, Johnstown, PA; [p.] Michelle/Michael Gibbons; [ed.] Eisenhower Jr. High School; [occ.] Student; [memb.] Dance, Scuba team, Church Sport League, Member of Southside, Baptist Church.; [hon.] I've always wrote when something was bothering me. But this is really my first award and most definitely an honor.; [oth. writ.] Poems and stories are what I like to write most but don't really know what to do with them.; [pers.] I try to make the point clear that life is something no one should take for granite, it's a gift from the Lord above; [a.] Riverview, FL

GIBSON, MARTIN E.
[pen.] Martin E. Gibson; [b.] March 3, 1951, Philadelphia; [p.] George T. Frances; [ed.] North East Catholic High School; [occ.] Laundry, Manager at the Latham Hotel for 25 years; [memb.] Actor's Equity; [oth. writ.] Written over 40 poems; [pers.] Hopefully with God help, the world will finally experience a real love's renaissance.; [a.] Philadelphia, PA

GIGANTINO, SANDI
[b.] October 16, 1987, Plainfield, NJ; [p.] Richard and Terry Gigantino; [ed.] Second Grade at Millstone Elementary School, Millstone, NJ.

GILLAND, ESTHER FRANCES
[pen.] Esther Frances/Esther Frances Villalobos; [b.] February 15, 1951, San Francisco, CA; [p.] Eugene and Abigail Villalobos; [m.] William D. Gilland III, December 22, 1984; [ch.] Shontel Nicole and Leonard Eugene-Andrew; [ed.] Woodrow Wilson High School/San Francisco City College, Western Apostolic Bible College; [occ.] Bank of Santa Maria, Santa Maria, California; [hon.] My honors ..My awards...come from all who enjoy my writing.; [oth. writ.] Poems: "Trust Me", "Prisoner Within", "Promise of Love", A Message to Desiree", and more.; [pers.] Writing allows me to enter the hearts of the unknown.; [a.] Santa Maria, CA

GILLESPIE, JAMES RANSOM JOSHUA
[b.] October 7, 1985, Cortland, NY; [p.] John D. S., and Theresa I. Gillespie; [ed.] I am a 5th grader at F.S. Barry Elementary School - Mrs. Foster my 4th grade teacher taught me how to write poetry; [memb.] Weblos Scout, member of Elementary Select Orchestra; [hon.] Award of Excellence in the NYSSMA Solo Competition for violin solo, Several Principal Awards for Excellent Academic Achievement, World Conservation Award in Cub Scouts. (NYSSMA) New York State School of Music Association; [oth. writ.] 6 other personal unpublished poems.; [pers.] As a 10 year old I try to show others that there really is some good in the youth of today. I am the oldest of 5 children.; [a.] Cortland, NY

GILLESPIE, JOANNE
[b.] August 17, 1957, Detroit Lakes, MN; [p.] Gordon and Arlene Strom; [m.] Daniel C. Gillespie, December 5, 1981; [ch.] Eric, Jeffrey, Jennifer, Kristina, Peter, Kevin and Jessica; [ed.] B.S. degree in Secondary Education in Social Studies at Moorhead State University; [occ.] At night, Nurse's Assistant and full-time Homemaker at daylight.; [memb.] Detroit Lakes Community Alliance Church, Home School Children; [pers.] I pen what I feel at the moment.; [a.] Audubon, MN

GILLIS, DOROTHY M.
[pen.] Dorothy M. Gillis; [b.] May 2, 1933, New Kensington, PA; [p.] Edward and Marie Griffiths; [m.] Robert Glenn Gillis, October 8, 1955; [ch.] 3 girls, Cathy, susan and Judy; [ed.] High School; [occ.] Home maker and volunteer worker at open Door Babtist Church; [memb.] Of open Door Babtist Church, AARP, Christian Women's Assn., Christian singles, Homemaker's Club of Fairfax, Fairfax County Choral Soc., (21 yrs.), Cirpeper Piedmont Choral Society (2 yrs.); [hon.] 2 awards from for Volunteers from Gov., Dough for "Area Agency Wilder on Aging"; [oth. writ.] Children's Book "Peter Rabbits Adventure", "Here's my Life", (My life story) 8 other poems; [pers.] I have spent my Life in music and loved every minute of it.

GINES, KEVIN R.
[b.] June 30, 1969, Stockton, CA; [ed.] Franklin High School, San Joaquin Delta College A.A, Humanities, Saint Mary's College (CA) R.A. Management, Minor Behavioral Science; [occ.] U.S. Postal Service; [memb.] United States Marine Corps, ALPHA GAMMA SIGMA, American Legion, American Manager Association; [hon.] Dean's List; [pers.] Question the absolute and absolutely will you be questioned; [a.] Stockton, CA

GIVEN, MALENA D.
[b.] October 5, 1979, Charleston, WV; [p.] Deborah Rader and Charles Given; [ed.] St. Albans High School; [occ.] In High School; [memb.] Highlawn Presbyterian Church; [pers.] I base all my writings on how I feel at a given time about a situation or a special person in my wife.; [a.] South Charleston, WV

GLASS, MARGARET L. C.
[b.] April 26, 1955, Chester, PA; [p.] Jimmie L. Clemons, Birtha L. Clemons; [m.] Ronald, September 22, 1971; [ch.] Zita, Rodney, Ronetta and Grands, Eric, Erica, NI Jericka; [occ.] Owner of (Justa world of gifts) wholesale-distributor; [memb.] Specialty Merchandise Corporation;

[hon.] His, Hers 1987 1st place, His Hers 1987-1988 most improved bowling awards; [oth. writ.] Abuse right outside my - window my 1st published in treasured poems of America fall 1994 and to be published in poetic voices of America Summer 1996 edition are my poems facing face to claim and regard to HIV; [pers.] There are care takers of children today that have looked to long down yesterdays path of darkness forbidding the children of tomorrow to be color clear to see the light down the path of hope today. For me, to bear witness to life is to live and write.; [a.] Chester, PA

GLASS-NASH, CHERYL
[b.] January 21, 1961, Cleveland, OH; [p.] Melvin Glass Sr., Margie R. Glass; [m.] Divorced; [ch.] Cherae Latrice Nash; [ed.] High School: Suffield Academy, Suffield, Ct. Briefly attended Oberlin College, Oberlin, Ohio; [occ.] Secretary with the Cleveland, Public School System, Cleveland, OH; [memb.] Active Member of Jonas Temple Church of God in Christ in Cleveland, Ohio, where I serve on the Public Relations, Committee and have Participated in Drama Events (Skits, Plays).; [hon.] Was selected as one of the outstanding young women of America, 1993.; [oth. writ.] Several no-published poems.; [pers.] My desire is that my Lord and Saviour Jesus Christ be glorified in the poems that I write because he is the giver of the gift. I have been writing for him for a long time! I also want people to be encouraged. "And we know that all things work together for good to them that love God, to them who are the called according to his purpose." (Romans 8:28, King James Version); [a.] Cleveland, OH

GLICK, HAROLD JAMES
[pen.] Slim Glickman; [b.] October 7, 1949; Goshen, IN; [p.] Andrew and Violet Glick; [m.] Janie Glick, July 7, 1973; [ch.] Tiffany and Tina Glick [ed.] Bachelor Degree, Urbana University, Ohio; [occ.] Dayton Post Office, 23 years; [memb.] Disabled American Veterans, 15 years, Arrow Brook Church - Xenia, Ohio; [hon.] Purple Heart Aaward, Cross of Gallantry, U.S. Marine - Honorable Discharge, 1970; [oth writ.] The New Heroes of the 90's, The Mailman's Gospel Song, songs recorded by Charles Clark, Hollywood Artists Record Co. 1993; [pers.] When I was 19 years old I served a tour of duty in Hell! My patriotic poem (How Many More Walls) is a reminder to all that the price of our freedoms cost many a great expense! [a.] Xenia, OH

GLIDE, SHAWN LESLIE
[b.] July 23, 1968, Detroit; [m.] Kenneth Winton Glide, September 5, 1993; [ed.] Eisenhower H.S., Wayne State University, Travel School; [occ.] Travel Agent/Artist; [pers.] To be in touch with ones soul through any medium is the highest honor of all; [a.] Detroit, MI

GNAU, JASON THOMAS
[b.] July 6, 1970, Winston-Salem, NC; [p.] Janet Coyne (mother), Bryte Fite, (grandmother); [ed.] Bachelor of Music in Music, Education Degree from Appalachian, State University, Boone, North Carolina; [occ.] A Manager at Peaches Music and Video, Winston-Salem, NC; [memb.] Centenary United Methodist Church, Phi Mi Alpha Sinfonia Fraternity, (Professional men's Fraternity); [hon.] Former 1st Chair Trumpet Player of the Appalachian, State University Wind Ensemble.; [oth. writ.] Most all of my writings (Poems/Song Lyrics) have been as a Hobby, Honestly.; [pers.] In my writing I reach for a pure, and sincere reflection of how I think, feel, and imagine things.; [a.] Winston-Salem, NC

GOLDEN, LORRAINE
[pen.] Amelia Francis Rogers; [b.] July 18, 1934, Pensacola, FL; [p.] Loraine and Hillary O. Barnes; [m.] Roger F. Golden, June 9, 1956; [ch.] Gregory C., Stephen J., Richard L., Pensacola High, Fl.; [ed.] 2 yrs Findlay College, Ohio English, Children's Education, no degree; [occ.] First United Methodist Church, Executive Secretary to Senior Pastor; [memb.] Lawyers' Wives Association, American Notaries Association, Christian Writer's Association; [oth. writ.] Several poems published in state publications, local newspapers, church newsletters, short stories christmas plays.; [pers.] Born in the South, raised on the Wilderness Gulf Coast of the Northern Florida Panhandle, a strong love of nature was formed early. My writings acknowledge God and all this Glory!; [a.] Niceville, FL

GOLDSTEIN, ROBERT
[b.] October 8, 1927, Butte, MO; [p.] Ruth and Jacob Goldstein; [m.] Erika Guldstein, August 9, 1986; [ch.] 3, Brenda, Corey, Heidi; [ed.] B.A. Stanford University, M.A. Stanford University, M.E.D. Stanford University, Ph.D. University of Minnesota; [occ.] Retired; [hon.] Dean's List; [oth. writ.] Currently about and publish a book of poems. A book on French-Iruyvois, Relations 1609-1701. Several articles for Social Science Journals; [pers.] Derived great inspiration from the desert and my own life experiences of travel, study, and determination to preserve lifes joys a travails, as well as my wife's goodness and strength.; [a.] Tucson, AR

GOMEZ, ELENA M.
[b.] June 29, 1941; [p.] William and Maria Gomez; [ed.] H.S. Buenavista, Havana, Cuba, B.A. University of Delaware, 1997 M.A. La Salle University; [occ.] Program Administrator, Delaware Prevention Network, Consultant in Private Practice; [memb.] Several Board of Directors and Advisory Boards for Non-Profit Organizations; [hon.] BAUSH and LOMB Distinguished Science Award; [oth. writ.] Over 200 poems 1 Roman-A-Clef short story; [pers.] The progress of creation is the poet's agony, it's the distilled shorthand of the soul.; [a.] Wilmington, DE

GOOD, MARGARET
[b.] February 4, 1933, Torrance County, NM; [p.] Claude and Bertha A. (Crider) Brown; [m.] Paul W. Good, March 16, 1962; [ch.] Dena Sue Roberts, Edward F., Steven W.; [ed.] Ewing School, Torrance Co, NM, Estancia High, Estancia, Nm, Harding University, Searcy, Ark; [occ.] Retired Secretary; [memb.] Church of Christ, International Society of Poets; [hon.] NM Girls State, 1950, High School Salutatorian, Scholarship to Harding U.; [oth. writ.] Published in High School Poetry Anthologies (2 yrs), Sermons in Poetry (2) College Poetry Anthology, (1 yr), Famous Poets Society (2 anthologies), NLP (11 Anthologies including Best Poems of 1995 and 1996), Vessels publishing several poems; [pers.] I credit my 6, 7, 8th grade teacher, Eulah Watson, now deceased, for getting me started writing. My writings generally consist of things with which I am familiar, specific events, people and religion.; [a.] Stephenville, TX

GOODMAN, BRETT
[b.] April 4, 1984, Dunedin, FL; [p.] Thomas and Patricia Goodman; [ed.] Currently in Elementary School; [occ.] Student; [memb.] Maricopa County 4-H; [hon.] Grade level winner in school poetry contest.; [pers.] In my writings, I try to touch people's emotions and make them feel that they are a part of my poems.; [a.] Scottsdale, AZ

GOODWIN, HAZEL J.
[pen.] Rolly Anna Pleasant; [b.] April 15, 1946, East Saint Louis, IL; [p.] Ollie Thomas-Powell and Albert W. Thomas (Dec); [m.] Divorced; [ch.] Arthur L. Goodwin (Dec)., and Kevin Michael Goodwin; [ed.] B.S. Bus Admin., Eastern Ill., University, Charleston, Ill. Lincoln High School (E. St. Louis, Ill.); [occ.] Information System, Independent Consultant, HRD Trainer; [memb.] (1) South Brunswick (Educ., Committee), Concerned Black Parents and Citizens, (2) Religious Affiliation - Unity Center (NYC); [hon.] Who's Who in Finance and Industry (1981-82), Who's Who in the East (1972 then 1980), Carol Chapman Memorial Award, 1982, Outstanding Sales Awards (81-84, 87-88); [oth. writ.] 1) Chapbook of original quotes titled "thoughts to help you ride the Wave of Change", at 1994, 2) Book of Poetry: Skeletons from my Closet" Lay Pollyanna Pleasant, 1995, 3) Chapbook: "You Have My Blessings as you Love"; [pers.] I believe that the natural rhythm of poetry speak and stick with people. Using this Medium I write poetry that ooze from my soul to heal me and then I share the common experience with others; [a.] Kendall Park, NJ

GOOLEY, PATRICK J.
[pen.] Joseph; [b.] December 26, 1978, Tulsa, OK; [p.] Richard and Debbie Gooley; [ed.] Bartlesville Mud-High, Pope John Paul II High School; [occ.] Student; [memb.] The Sunsounds Music Club Drama Club Rights for life Pro-Life Group, Prism Literary Magazine St. Andrew's Catholic Church.; [hon.] 19 medals for superior musical performance. 4 time District Honor choir singer.; [oth. writ.] Several poems published in school news papers. Poem published in school yearbook.; [pers.] A great teacher is the basis of a great writer.; [a.] Coval Spring, FL

GOTTLIEB, MICHAEL
[b.] January 15, 1943, Brooklyn, NY; [p.] Benjamin Gottlieb; [ed.] B.Sc. Brooklyn College, Thomas Jefferson H.S.; [occ.] Nutritional Consultant, Public Speaker (nutrition, stress, reduction, consciousness, expansion, etc.), Health products, salesperson, writer, poet,; [memb.] American WW 2 Orphans, Network, Jewish War Veterans,

ASPCA, Nat'l. Humane Society; [hon.] Marched in 1995 "Nation's Parade", November 11, 1995 to represent 183,000, American WW 2 orphans - Veteran's, Day Parade. Rec'd gold `Jubilee', medal from French gov't and `Front-line Britain' medal from Britain to recognize my dad's WW 2 Service.; [oth. writ.] "Value in american: The Heartless Society,", "The Life of Mother Mary", books. 2 research articles in "Nutrition for Mental Health", newsletter for the Canadian Schizophrenia Foundation".; [pers.] I believe in the innate potential of every individual to overcome emotional and physical handicaps. I believe in balancing physical (worldly) and spiritual pursuits. I believe in God.; [a.] New York City, NY

GRACE, BETTIE
[b.] November 23, 1931, Charlotte, NC; [p.] Wm a. Durean, Virgence Durean; [m.] T. B. Grace (Deceased), June 19, 1948; [ch.] Four; [ed.] High School, have loved operator's and music - like Jeanette McDonald and Nelson Eddie. Have written Poems but never sent them in; [occ.] Homemaker; [memb.] Church - St. Peters, Episcopal; [a.] Jacksonville, FL

GRAHAM, DEBORAH K.
[pen.] Kehaulani (Hawaiian Name); [b.] April 26, 1956, Honolulu, HI; [p.] Mr. and Mrs. Kahaunaele; [ch.] Kuulie, Hoku, Tatiana; [ed.] Kaimuki High, Leeward Community College, Honolulu, Hawaii; [occ.] Black Pearl expert for Tahiti Perles Hon, HI; [memb.] Hawaiian Sovereignty; [hon.] Leeward Community College Poem contest winner in 1984. Title of poem "In The Beginning.; [oth. writ.] My first poem was published in a yearly College magazine "Harvest". Hon, HI 1984; [pers.] On the Hawaiian Islands the Aloha Spirit is alive and well. Aloha!; [a.] Oahu, HI

GRAHAM, KYMBERLY HENDERSON
[b.] June 23, 1965, Riverside, CA; [p.] Travis/Nedra Henderson; [m.] Steve Graham, November 23, 1990; [ch.] Chucky, Gregory, Steven, Derrick, Richard, Angela; [ed.] Attended St. Catherines of Alexandria K-8th Ramona High School, National Education Ctr for Medical Assisting; [occ.] Medical Assistant/Phlebotomist; [memb.] Allied Health National Registry for EKG technician and Phlebotomy, American Heart Assoc. as a C.P.R. trainer; [hon.] Several awards for Public Service, good work and Graduated High Honors from NEC; [oth. writ.] Personal poems for friends and family; [pers.] This poem is dedicated to the memory of Kierin Cauley, age 23 months, and to Peggy Thorson who told me I should submit some of my work.

GRANT, BARBARA J.
[b.] December 26, 1938, North Franklin, NY; [p.] Charles Grant, Marion Grant; [ed.] Franklin Central School, 12th Grade Graduate; [occ.] Burr Hand, Amphenol Corp., Sidney, NY; [memb.] Mustang Club of America, National Arbor Day Foundation; [pers.] The reason I wrote this poem. My Nephew James L. Thomas IV was enlisted in the Marines. While in Boot Camp he was so homesick he wrote and wanted my opinion if he should stay in or try to get out. I could not tell him what to do with his life, so I wrote this Poem and sent it to him. He stayed in the Marine Corps., and I am very Proud to have him as my Nephew!; [a.] Franklin, NY

GRANT, JOAN JULIEN
[pen.] Joan J. Grant; [b.] April 15, 1934, Cornwall, Ontario, Canada; [p.] John Julien, Winnifred Julien; [m.] Douglas Grant, September 24, 1955; [ch.] Stephen Grant, Ann Arakaki, Gail O'Hara; [ed.] West L.A. College, Otis Art Institute, MFA; [occ.] Artist, (Sculpture); [pers.] I try to express how answer to questions concerning "Life" are inherent within the Natural world. I have been influenced by both early and contemporary poets and contemporary poets of Earth-bound genre.; [a.] Los Angeles, CA

GRANT, JUDITH
[b.] July 29, 1963, Jamaica; [p.] Cyril and Enid Grant; [ed.] St. Hilda's High, Brown's Town, Community College, Dental Auxiliary; [occ.] Beauty Consultant; [memb.] Grace Baptist Chapel; [oth. writ.] Poems and short stories songs; [pers.] "The ultimate goal in life is spiritual Growth". Sharing my life and my time with others should be towards that end, short of that it is a waste of time.; [a.] Bronx, NY

GRAVES, APRIL
[b.] March 31, 1982, Burlington, VT; [p.] Steven and Kansas Graves; [ed.] I am a student in the 7th grade. I am presently attending Bellows Free Academy School, located in my hometown of Fairfax, Vermont; [occ.] Poet, student at B.F.A. school; [hon.] This is my first award, to be published! My first publication was in our town newspaper, The Fairfax News.; [oth. writ.] I have written many other poems. A few are, Down The Street, I Am Different, Unique, No Other, Be My Light, and Paper.; [pers.] Thank you Mom, Dad, Shana, Mr. Daniels, and to you Mrs. Nilsson. I owe it all to you! Also Thanks to Denim, Caffeine, and Arizona. The soul is in the eyes.; [a.] Fairfax, VT

GRAY, BUDDY
[pers.] Buddy Gray is a lifelong Cincinnatian who - for 25 years - has devoted his entire adult life to homeless, poor people of the Over-the-Rhine neighborhood. He is one of the founding volunteers of the Drop Inn Center Shelter. Drop Inn shelters 150 to 250 women and per night. It also has a 6 month alcohol and drug recovery program. Buddy and his co-workers als helped found ReSTOC, a low income housing coooperative. Volunteers, homeless people, church and student groups have saved abandoned buildings from the wreccking ball and parking lots and rehabbed them into 111 apartments. He lives a simple lifestyle and receives a monthly stipend of $200 from a local community group.

GREEN, ANNIE LAURIE
[b.] September 10, 1980, Nashville, TN; [p.] Douglas B. Green Cynthia Ann Turner; [ed.] Hume Fogg Academic High School; [occ.] Student; [memb.] B.M.I. (Broadcast Music Incorporated); [hon.] First Place Trash Art Award Metropolitan Nashville Public Schools; [oth. writ.] "My little brother" (co-writer) Song performed on C.B.S. television.

GREEN, HAZEL S.
[b.] July 22, 1909, Provo, UT; [p.] M. Emeline Gay, James C. Show; [m.] Deceased, Ralph C. Hundley (1st married-died) July 15, 1926, David A. Green (second married-died) 1975; [ch.] Ralph James Hundley, Jeanine Hundley, Long-Bryan Patrick Hundley, Colleen Fay Hundley, Ericson-Margaret Kathryn Hundley Sanchez; [ed.] Provo Jr. High 7th Grade - Central U. Vocational Sch. Licensed Practical Nurse 1952; [occ.] Retired, did house work, picked fruit, four yrs. Auditors Office, Four yrs. Treasurer office at City County Bldg, Provo, UT; [memb.] L.D.S. Church - Alpine Country Club - Les Amies Club - Chamber, Commerce Jaycetts. Have written plays, Fashion Shows for Church. Had Leading roles operators, leading role in three play-member of Choir-Singing Mothers. For dress making, quilts, flowers, Beautification of Yard, Trees and Shrubs; [oth. writ] None except for church; [pers.] My mother wrote stories, many readings poems. Several to me personally, which has influenced my life in respect to poetry.; [a.] Highland, UT

GREEN, VERLEEN ROSE FLETCHER
[pen.] V. Rose; [b.] October 27, 1963, Pontiac, MI; [p.] Rev. Eddie Fletcher, Rosie Lee Fletcher; [ch.] Henry L. Green III; [ed.] Pine Bluff, HS Grad., 1981, University Arkansas Pine Bluff, Central Texas College Europe; [occ.] 9 Year U.S. Army Veteran, Inspirational Poet; [memb.] Veteran of Foreign Wars (VFW), (DAV) Disabled Veterans Assoc.; [hon.] (3) Army Good Conduct Medals, Army Achievement Medal (3 Oak Leaf Cluster), (NCOPD-2), NCO Professional Development Ribbons, (NDSM) National Defense Service Medal, (ASR) Army Service Ribbon, (OSR) (2) Overseas Service Ribbon, Vernon L. Bowers Administrative Award of Excellence (88); [oth. writ.] Presently writing two novels "Wrong Side of the Mirror"/"Friendly Deceptions"; [pers.] I strive to up lift peoples spirits with poetry. I am greatly influenced by thought provoking events of everyday life.; [a.] Pine Bluff, AR

GREIWE, SANDRA
[pen.] Sandra Greive; [b.] August 19, 1942, Saint Louis, MO; [p.] EDW and Dorothy Harvey; [m.] Marlin Greiwe, October 24, 1964; [ch.] Deidre, Kristin, Rebecca, Marissa; [ed.] Normandy High, Deaconess College of Nursing, Lindenwood College, MO Univ., St. Louis Campus; [occ.] Self Employed Registered Nurse Prepared, Children Instructor, Founder and Program and Workshop Director of Recycle Roundup, an environmental not for profit arts and science education organization since 1989.; [memb.] Chairman of Home Ec., Advisory, Board School District of City of St. Charles, First Capitol GArden Club MO Federated Garden Club, Holy Cross Evangelical Lutheran Church, AAL St. Charles Branch, (Aid Assoc. of Lutherns), Lutheran Brotherhood Branch 8306; [hon.] PTA, 1979-81, Outstanding Contribution to Monroe Elementary, 1991 MO Waste Control, Coalition Environmental Achievement, 1992 MO DPT of Energy Award,

1993 Tambrands Tampax MO Environmental Woman of Action, 1994 Hardees Hometown Hero for Environmental Awareness; [oth. writ.] Once upon a time in real life, zig, zag and oodles or zoodled, one rainy day, dumping horror, side show (an environmental play); [pers.] I strive to and celebrate encourage mans innate desire to live harmoniously with his natural and manmade world, to conserve natural resources, to develop interdependence in all of his relationship.; [a.] Saint Charles, MO

GRIECO, NICOLE
[pen.] Nicole Grieco; [b.] June 23, 1984, Buffalo, NY; [p.] Augustine Grieco, Barbara Grieco; [ed.] Student at Buffalo Academy for Visual and Performing Arts; [memb.] In cheer leading, dancing; [hon.] Cheer leading, dancing and honor roll awards; [oth. writ.] "On Grandma's Lap", and short stories; [pers.] In reference to my poem, I reflected on the death of my grandpa guss; [a.] Buffalo, NY

GRIFFIN, PAUL
[b.] March 12, 1957, Dublin, Ireland; [p.] Gerard Griffin, Kathleen Griffin; [ed.] Some College, Montgomery, County Community College, Bluebell, PA, Lankenau Hospital Radiology Program, Philadelphia; [occ.] Security Officer and X-Ray File Clerk; [memb.] American Heart Association, American Registry of Radiologic Technologists; [hon.] Dean's List; [oth. writ.] Nothing published, nothing submitted for publication; [pers.] Essentially, at school, I hated poetry. I couldn't understand words worth or Tennyson. Now if the mood takes me I write only in rhyming verse. Some of my work is decades old and all subjects under the sun are written about.; [a.] Spring City, PA

GRIFFITH, PEGGY
[pen.] Pmg; [b.] June 20, 1927, Waco, TX; [p.] Donie Gunn, Luther Gunn; [m.] John Griffith, February 13, 1947; [ed.] Waco Hi-Waco, TX, Walsh College, Canton, OH; [occ.] Retired; [memb.] Order of Eastern Star, Institute Management Accountants, National Smithsonian, Ladies of Canton Elks, AARP; [hon.] (A) EARNED ELA - Institute of Accountants, (B) National and Local Recognition for Revision of G.E. Forms; [pers.] Try to find good things in everybody; [a.] Canton, OH

GRIMALDI, KATHLEEN GALVIN
[b.] March 19, 1942, Waterbury, CO; [p.] Francis Xavier and Margaret Brett Galvin; [m.] Philip Grimaldi, April 4, 1970; [ch.] Lynnette Marie and Joseph Christopher; [ed.] Fordham University, B.A., Stony Brook, M.A., Immaculate Conception, M.A., Seminary; [occ.] Teacher of English, Middle County Sch. Dist., St. Joseph's College; [oth. writ.] Professional Articles - magazines, 1st poem published; [pers.] My poetry represents my personal search, if not always for the Beauty inherent in Life, the essential Harmony, Mystery. All Poets shapes me.; [a.] Port Jefferson, NY

GRIMES, MS. PAMELA EMELIA
[pen.] Maude Weaver; [b.] March 3, Monroe, LA; [p.] Barney and Wanda Neel Grimes; [m.] Divorced; [ch.] Amelia, Adam, Adrienne, Amanda, Alexander; [ed.] B.A. Texas A. and M. University, M.A. Hood College, Fred, MD; [occ.] Teacher - unemployed; [memb.] American So. Political Science; [oth. writ.] Credit and the International Economy (Amex bank review), U.S. Policy and So. Africa, U.S. Policy and the USSR., The Value of NATO, others all technical on environmental issues. Childrens books, vol. of short stories, vol. poetry; [pers.] My writings are directed at global policy and the U.S. They reflect my international view of America and Western Europe with their diverse multicultural entities, which comprise each sovereign national entity.; [a.] Tennessee Colony, TX

GROOMES, ROYAL O.
[pen.] Gy Thomas; [b.] June 29, 1919, Springfield, MS; [p.] Thomas, Eythal Groomes; [m.] Hester S. Groomes, June 29, 1982; [ed.] 3rd year Mich., State, full term High School; [occ.] Rancher - retired; [memb.] Seventh - Day - Adventist Corning, Ca.; [hon.] For sponsoring a program, "Program - Project Last Chance" that addresses the problems of troubled children before they become candidates of State Prison.; [oth. writ.] Unpublished Novel, "Rugged Is My Cross", approximately 300 unpublished poems. Many articles and news commentary.; [pers.] We live in a unforgiving society. Were it not so we (I) would not meet the challenge of salvaging the violation of our social rules of low and order. It is easier for some of us to forget than to forgive; [a.] Corning, CA

GUERCIO, FAYE WEST
[b.] March 31, 1924, Provo, UT; [p.] Edward Lee and Eliza West; [m.] Victor Guercio (Italian), May 6, 1944; [ch.] Betty Jean, Frank Lee, Rick, Gay Lynne; [ed.] Franklin Elementary Dixon Jr., High School, Provo High School; [occ.] Housewife (unemployed), Seamtress, Crafts, Grandmother of 16; [memb.] Daughters of Utah Pioneers, Treble Clef's Ladie's Chorus, L.D.S. Church; [hon.] Award (for writing choral program), Queen of the May (at age 12), Our son, Frank graduated from BYU and is Nurse Anesthetist at American Fork Hospital. (UTAH) our son, Rick also graduated form BYU, and is a Chemical Engineer, with a degree in Corporate Management.; [oth. writ.] Many poems. Poems written in honor of L.D.S. Church President Spencer W. Kimball. Had several poems in my ward's poetry book for our stake.; [pers.] I strive to write poetry in praise of different people's fine attributes and accomplishments. I also write poetry in appreciation of blessings and the beauty of nature! I admire the poetry of Helen Stienez Rice; [a.] Salt Lake, UT

GUERIN, GEORGE JOHN
[b.] November 15, 1922, Puerto Rico; [p.] John Guerin and Petra San Juan Guerin (Deceased); [m.] Alta Guerin (Deceased), April 23, 1943; [ch.] Gina, Mercedes, Jonathan (George (Deceased)), Grandchildren: Noelle, Arielle, Jordan, Zachary, Ryan, Wende, Keith Guerin and Melody; [ed.] Boys High School, City College Brooklyn, N.Y., Fairleigh Dickensen University (Business Adm:), U.S. Army Schools, Instructor, Field Sgt., Artillery, Forward observer school.; [occ.] Retired; [memb.] Cancer Society-American Heart Association 1963 to 1980; [hon.] U.S. Army W.W. II Presidential Citation-The Bronze Star, Received by General George Patton for heroic achieve while in battle with the 36th Infantry, Division in France, Plus two battle clusters for the Italian Campaign and Germany.; [oth. writ.] "Strands of Time and Essence" story of my life. A Manuscript to be published soon in the late spring.; [pers.] "I learned something early in life", there are two great times of happiness, when you are haunted by a dream, and when you realize it. Between the two there's a strong urge to let it all drop. But you have to follow your dreams to the end. There are abandoned bicycles in every garage because their owners' backsides got sore the first time they rode them. They didn't understand that pain is a necessary part of learning. I almost gave up a thousand times before reaching those moments of happiness when I forgot that I was cold. You can accomplish this through painting, music, or writing poetry or anything, as long as you concede that, before you can play a Bach sonata, you must first learn to play the scales.

GUERRA, ISABEL MARIA
[b.] January 12, 1962, Mission, TX; [p.] Leonel Guerra, Aurora Guerra; [ed.] Newman Smith H.S., University of North Texas; [occ.] 911 Telecommunicator; [pers.] Writing for me has always been a release. That which cannot come out out verbally, is said best by my pen.; [a.] Denton, TX

GUILLOD, JEFFREY
[b.] December 21, 1974, Rochester, NY; [p.] Richard and Elaine Guillod; [ed.] High School Grad., Studying Journalism; [occ.] Retail Sales; [oth. writ.] Unpublished writings include, "Love Remembered, "Never Again", and "Granted"; [pers.] "If one man finds hope, friendship and a desire to live, let no other criticize him for the way he went about doing it, for it is a blessed time when a man can find his dream, for he doesn't only make the world a better place but he makes himself a better man."; [a.] Rochester, NY

GURLEY, TONI R.
[b.] August 26, 1961, Pascagoula, MS; [p.] Patricia Hartline English/Derrel Hicks; [ch.] Randy, Casey and Matthew Gurley; [ed.] Pascagoula High School, Delaware Technical College, AA, Wilmington College, BA, Behavioral Science; [occ.] Student; [hon.] Dean's List, Graduated College with Highest Honors; [oth. writ.] My other poems have been used by teachers and mental health professionals for therapeutic situations; [pers.] Love the children, the animals, the less fortunate. You will be blessed in the end.; [a.] Lewes, DE

GURSKY, SANDRA M. WARD
[b.] March 7, 1943, Detroit, MI; [p.] Deceased; [m.] Bernard A. Gursky; [ed.] High School and 2 yrs., of College, studied Accounting; [occ.] Buyer; [oth. writ.] Have never published anything. Am just beginning to try. Have written about 200 poems; [pers.] I always try to write from the heart, whatever subject I am tackling.

Susan Polish Shutz is a poet that has influenced me.; [a.] Missoula, MO

GUTHRIE, BARBARA A.
[pen.] Barbara A. Guthrie; [b.] June 8, 1923, Detroit, MI; [m.] John M. Guthrie, October 31, 1949; [ch.] 3 sons, 1 daughter; [ed.] 2 yrs college (science major), 6 yrs Chinese Painting at Chow Studio of Art Travel Agent Course; [occ.] Domestic Engineer and Great Grandma; [memb.] Miami Springs Woman's Club, (prior) Allied Arts, Miami Art League, Miami Springs-Hialeah Art League, Fla. Federation of Womans Clubs; [hon.] 2 best in show DCFWC poetry and literature, DCFWC 7 blue (1st) in poetry, DCFWC 5 red (2nd) in poetry, 3 3rd in poetry, Articles - 1 red (2nd (3rd) 1 hon. men.; [oth. writ.] 2 poems published at age 10 in Detroit News 1 poem published at age 13 in prudenville times. Two articles published in the Henning Minnesota Advocate; [pers.] Primary interest, nature, childrens poems of insects and "critters" humour in every day life some Nostalgia and observation influences - Robt. Burns. Christopher Morely, Don Marquis, Rbt. Service.

GUTHRIEOH, STEVE I.
[b.] Pittsburg, KS; [p.] Louis T., Jennie N. Mitchell Guthrie; [m.] Janice R. Paulo; [ch.] Amanda Melissa; [ed.] A.A., San Joaquin Delta College, Stockton, Ca.; [memb.] Kansas City Southern, (R.R.) Historical Society, Inc., Shreveport, LA; [pers.] In 1928, Edward Henry Blakeney wrote: "The poet's aim is to please, or to blend in one the delightful and useful." He added, "Every Superfluous, His message: "Be brief." In that regard, my aim is to dispense a little truth from an all-too recent, painful memory - in your 20 lines? I invite you to share that pain. But do it quickly!; [a.] Stockton, CA

GUZMAN, IRVING LAZERUS
[b.] July 28, 1978, Jersey City, NJ; [p.] Carmen M. Guzman; [ed.] Xavier High School; [pers.] Poetry is the expression of what lies deep within your heart. Everyone is a poet in their own unique way; [a.] Guttenburg, NJ

HABERKORN, ANNE
[b.] September 23, 1982, Tampa, FL; [p.] Nancy Haberkorn, Richard Haberkorn; [ed.] Blake Jr. High; [occ.] Student; [memb.] Math League, Orchestra, Video Club; [hon.] The Presidential Recognition Award, Honors Orchestra; [a.] Tampa, FL

HACKNEY, ASHLEY GENE
[b.] September 4, 1984, Chas, WV; [p.] Kelly Hackney, Bobby Meadows; [ed.] 5th grade at Kennay West Virginia in Jackson County; [memb.] Highrisers 4-H Club, Piano at Rodney's School of Music, Gymnastics at Deanna's School of Dance and grade school band; [oth. writ.] A poem called cats; [a.] Kenna, WV

HAFFLEY, LEOLA A. WETZEL
[b.] March 16, 1913, Fairlawn, OH; [p.] Irvin H. and Mary K. Wetzel; [m.] Lloyd E. Haffley, February 9, 1938; [ch.] Elinor, Floyd, Frank, David, Paul, and Carl; [ed.] Graduated from High School May 27, 1932 (Independence, Ohio), as Salutatorian of my class.; [occ.] (No Job) Just occupied at home.; [memb.] Hillview Wesleyan Church, (My husband and I are the oldest couple in our church); [oth. writ.] As a 'teenager', I wrote a few poems including a 'class poem' for our class of 1932.; [pers.] As far back as I can remember I have loved poetry.; [a.] Lock Haven, PA

HAGEN, TAMARA R.
[pen.] Tomorrow Rose; [b.] April 10, 1964, Tacoma, WA; [p.] Caroline and Steven Hess; [m.] Kevin M. Hagen, July 23, 1988; [ch.] Robert, Aaron, Joshua; [ed.] Puyallup High School; [occ.] Home school teacher for kindergarden and first grade; [pers.] My goal in life was to have children, and my teacher in high school said that I would have the happiest children, I pride myself in having happy children and a wonderful husband.; [a.] Okinawa, Japan

HAGESTAD, KRISTIN KELLY
[b.] March 5, 1980, Edison, NJ; [p.] Diane and Gary Hagestad; [ed.] Currently attending Middletown Township High school South; [occ.] Student - Sophomore; [memb.] Eagle Leaders, Thespian Society, Bottlecappers, Friendship Club, Law Explorers, Medical Explorers Dance - Tap and Ballet; [hon.] National Dance Competitions; [pers.] "Learn to listen, opportunity sometimes knocks softly"; [a.] Lincroft, NJ

HAIMOWITZ, ALVIN
[b.] March 5, 1952, Los Angeles; [p.] Irving and Beatrice Haimowitz; [ed.] Excelsior High School, California State University, Long Beach; [occ.] Surgical and Pharmaceutical Purchasing; [hon.] Certificate in Honors, Summa Cum Laude, Cal. State University; [oth. writ.] Poems, short stories, plays, published in various local journals; [pers.] I try to encompass the pain, complexity and sweetness of life in my poetry and writing.; [a.] Long Beach, CA

HAIR, CLAYTON M.
[pen.] Clayton Maxwell IIII; [b.] June 6, 1968, Austell, GA; [p.] Mr. Frank L. Hair, Mrs. Bobbie S. Chafin; [ed.] College Grad. - Chemistry (Kennesan St. College, Kennesan GA), Graduate Student - (currently), University of Tennessee; [occ.] Graduate Teaching Asst. - Chemistry (Organic); [memb.] American Chemical Society, American Institute of Chemists.; [oth. writ.] (None published or publishable); [pers.] "We're all nothing but Maggot food on the hoof - so you might as well enjoy it while you're here"; [a.] Knoxville, TN

HALE, MICHAEL T.
[b.] June 18, 1977; [pers.] I try to accomplish in my writing what all artists try to accomplish, to liberate the mind and enlighten the soul.; [a.] CA

HALL, EMILY
[pen.] Emily; [b.] April 20, 1978, Brooklyn, NY; [p.] Stanley and Evelyn Hall; [ed.] High School Student; [occ.] Student; [memb.] Kiwins - Community Service Club, Bowling Team; [hon.] Athletic Award and block letter for basketball, varsity 1994, Oakland Athletic League Metals for OAL Women All City High Game, Oal Women All City High Average, Oal Athletic Award and block letter for Bowling 1995; [pers.] In times of despair, keep your hopes and dreams alive.; [a.] Oakland, CA

HALSTEAD JR., GERALD
[b.] June 24, 1965, Auburn, NY; [p.] Gerald and Catherine Halstead; [ed.] Cato-Merdian High, Auburn Community College; [occ.] Railroad Field Main; [hon.] High School Top 20, Golden Poet Trophy for 1992; [pers.] The greatest thrill a writer can experience is to make people laugh, cry, or say wow!; [a.] Baldwinsville, NY

HALVERSON, JENNA
[pen.] Kitty; [b.] March 3, 1980, Downers Grove, IL; [p.] Lynn Talarico; [hon.] Target Range, Grade School - Literature Award; [oth. writ.] Black, published in the 1994 edition of Anthology of Poetry by Young Americans; [pers.] I believe a true poet can reach into the heart of an experience, grasp the innermost feelings and put them into wards.; [a.] Missoula, MT

HAMILTON, JODY
[b.] September 22, 1974, Omaha, NE; [p.] Judy and Steve Hamilton; [ed.] Ralston High School, Metropolitan Community College; [occ.] Certified Nurse's Aide; [oth. writ.] Poems published in High School Literary magazine; [pers.] My writing reflects emotions or experiences that I or people I care for have had. I try to recreate that feeling with just a few words.; [a.] Omaha, NE

HAMMONDS, MARK A.
[b.] January 4, 1956, Pratt, KS; [p.] Charlie Hammonds, Patricia Hammonds; [ch.] Clayton Wayne Hammonds; [ed.] Ness High, Ness City Kansas; [occ.] Painter; [oth. writ.] Several poems which remain unpublished; [pers.] I am very honored to have my writings published in a book of such importance; [a.] Abita Springs, LA

HAMMONS, DANA ELIZABETH
[pen.] Dana Elizabeth Hammons; [b.] October 15, 1977, Santa Clara, CA; [p.] David and Norma Hammons; [ed.] Graduated from Los Gatos High school, CA. in 1995 (June), currently attending the University of Nevada at Reno; [occ.] Student (full-time); [memb.] Poetry for Every one in Los Gatos (CA), The Wellness Center at UNR, The Agriculture Club at UNR, Member of Christ Child Church in Los Gatos, CA.; [hon.] Brown Belt in Kiik Siil, 1st place in Los Gatos poetry contest (9/94), most improved employee at Summit Veterinary Hospital in Los Gatos.; [oth. writ.] "Racism", "Words Have No Poetry", "The Beginning of the End," "Beginning", "Life", "Forevermore", "Syd", "Simon", "Gunk", "Sky" (all poems); [pers.] "Who is more foolish? The fool or the fool that follows him?" -Obe won Kanobe (The Empire Strikes Back") Just a thought... How do they handle handicapped parking at the special olympics?; [a.] Reno, NV

HANAN, JULIA C.
[b.] August 16, 1962, Atlanta, GA; [p.] Leah - Bahor Cohen; [m.] Rubin M. Hanan, September 8, 1935; [ch.] Larhti Lapidus, Dr. Lewis Hanan,

Dr. Morris Hanan; [ed.] Business; [occ.] Retired; [memb.] EA Sepsardic Cona; [hon.] Many Religious Citations for Charitable and Civic Contributions; [pers.] Deep believe in God.

HANLIN, LEROY
[pen.] Leroy Hanlin; [b.] November 14, 1978, Canton, OH; [p.] Wayne; [ed.] I am trying to get my G.E.D., I am currently in 10th grade.; [occ.] I am in a treatment facility, I am not insane I just broke the law and I am now rehabilitated and know right from wrong.; [hon.] In 8th grade I got Best Changed Man in school. I get Man of the Week in here and Most Leadership of the Week.; [pers.] I grew up in Ocala FL, I went to school at East Marion Elementary Fort McCoy Middle and Vanguard High. I am now getting A's PB's. I have only one brother no-one else. I did not know of the so-called talent I have until I got locked up and had time to think I'm not a bad person. I assure you, I am also under foster care supervision. I have nothing to my person's no money no nothing.; [a.] Lowell, FL

HANSEN III, GEORGE E.
[b.] December 3, 1945, Escanaba, MI; [p.] Louise Wiessert and George E. Hansen II; [m.] Mary Hansen, March 13, 1971; [ch.] George and Mike; [ed.] 7 yrs College, Bay de Noc Comm., Col., (Assoc. of Science), Washtenaw Com., Col.(Graphics), Univ. of MI, Arch., Land. Arch., and B.S. in Adv. Design; [occ.] Journeyman Painter and Signist; [memb.] Saint Elisabeth Ann Seton Parish, Friends of the Liabrary, Escanaba, and U. of M Alumni, Delta Kappa Epsilon; [hon.] Husband and Father, Lover of God (Good Orderly Direction); [oth. writ.] Many (mostly spiritual and on human Nature), non-published. "Questioning Perspective", "Forgiveness", "What's A Who To Do?", etc...; [pers.] Honesty, openmindedness and willingness to learn. Shakespeare "To thine own self be true and it shall follow as the night does the day that thou can't be false to any man."; [a.] Escanaba, MI

HANSON, JANE L.
[pen.] Jane Hanson-Harris; [b.] December 26, 1905, Nelson, NE; [p.] Mr. and Mrs. Frank J. Potter; [m.] Alfred W. Harris, November 19, 1955; [ch.] Three; [ed.] Scholarship - School of Fine Arts, University of Louisville KY, Northwestern Univ., Clev. School of Art; [occ.] Interior Designer, Painter, Table Designer And Costume Designer For Whealer; [memb.] Clev. Museum of Art., American Society of Interior Design, National Museum of American Women, Cleveland Play-House Club In Art, Fairmount Presbyterian Church; [hon.] Interior Design, Poetry; [oth. writ.] Working on 3 stories for children, Article for Shell Club "Use of Shell in Design" Poetry, Delivers many lectures on Design; [pers.] "Working poetry is like painting a picture" it produces. Many views is an expression of the heart and fun to do!; [a.] Cleveland, OH

HANSON, PATTY
[b.] April 26, 1937, Ventura, CA; [p.] Henrietta and Jesse Hollingsworth; [m.] Marvin L. Hanson, May 4, 1957; [ch.] Tammi Skiba and Lori Hanson; [ed.] Ventura Senior High School and Ventura College; [occ.] Retired Teachers Aide, Meiners Oaks Elementary School; [memb.] Ventura Community Orchestra, Ojai Summer Band - The International Society of Poets; [hon.] Honorary life membership award from the Parent Teachers Association.; [oth. writ.] Poems for several metaphysical newsletters including "Reflections." A poem in the Anthology, "Between The Raindrops" and "The Best Poems of 1996." Published by the National Library of Poetry.; [pers.] Poetry is the way a bliss moment expresses itself.; [a.] Ojai, CA

HARDIN, DUSTIN
[b.] March 13, 1976, Jeffersonville, IN; [p.] Brenda and John Hardin; [ed.] Scottsburg High, Currently a student at Ivy Tech in Madison.; [oth. writ.] Wrote a few poems in High School, Was very much enjoyed by literature Teacher, Debbie Wilson.; [pers.] I write poems straight from the heart. I have been influenced most by the one girl in my life and who will hopefully be there forever, Angela Austin.; [a.] Scottsburg, IN

HARDY, MILDRED M.
[b.] July 29, 1919, Connellsville, PA; [p.] Thos. W. and Veronica Moore (both deceased); [m.] Neil D. Hardy, June 29, 1945 (celebrated 50 years of marriage); [ch.] (1 daughter) Linda; [ed.] Graduated Connellsville High School - class of 1938; [occ.] Busy Housewife; [pers.] "Enjoy life - read a lot and learn all you can", I have many interests, cooking, water colour, painting, sewing, egg decorating. I like keeping busy; [a.] Wilmington, DE

HARGETT, CAROL JANE
[b.] January 12, 1936, E. Bernstadt, KY; [p.] Deceased; [ed.] Two Degrees - B.A. and M.A. in Elementary Education; [occ.] Just retired from teaching, since retiring - I decided to send some of my stories and poems to publishers.; [hon.] Valedictorian in High School - History Award in High school; [oth. writ.] I've written many children's stories and poems but rarely sent them to any publisher. I just used them in the classroom.; [pers.] I like to write stories to entertain children. I like to write poems of goodness and beauty, I try to stay away from violence in writing.; [a.] Richmond, IN

HARKINS, THERESA M. WHEATON
[b.] November 29, 1951, Elmira, NY; [p.] Frank-Helen Wheaton; [m.] William Cary Harkins, June 27, 1981; [ch.] William Wallace and Colleen Marie Harkins; [ed.] State Univ., NY, Univ. of Copenhagen, Denmark, Wheelock College, Boston, Ma.; [occ.] Free Lance Writer; [a.] Fairfax, VA

HARLOW, AUDREY CARTER
[b.] February 6, 1927, Spotsylvania, VA; [p.] Ernest Chester and Bowker Pritchett Carter; [m.] Robert D. Harlow, May 29, 1948; [ch.] Bronwyn Leigh Harlow Ziegler; [ed.] High School; [occ.] I was a housewife and mother until 6 yrs. ago I became a semi-in valid because of extensive surgery.; [memb.] Goshen Baptist Church; [oth. writ.] A few poems, mostly for family and friends.; [pers.] I have a deep faith in God and His word instilled in me by Christian parents and my church. During my 128 days ordeal in the hospital, 67 of them in coronary ICU, I was not expected to live from the beginning. God did what medical science was unable to do. My medical records state that I made a miraculous recovery from the usually fatal circumstances. My poem expresses my philosophy of life.; [a.] Fredericksburg, VA

HARRIS, JEANNE
[b.] May 5, 1961, Salina, KS; [p.] Henry Baltine, Doris Baltine; [m.] Randall Harris, April 18, 1988; [ch.] Michael and Taylor; [ed.] Wichita Falls High School, Midwestern State University; [occ.] Jack County; [memb.] Catholic Church; [oth. writ.] Several poems; [a.] Jacksboro, TX

HARRIS, MRS. HELEN A.
[b.] August 31, 1921, Indian Reservation; [p.] Clara Logan, Frank Davey; [m.] Charles V. Harris—Died February 7, 1995, May 19, 1940; [ch.] 5 - Rosalie, Bruce, Linda, Steven, Tracy; [ed.] Grammer and High school; [occ.] Retired; [memb.] Senior Citizen - NICOA - life member of the V.F.W. John F. Ahrens post 5296 Aux. Salamanca, N.Y. Past Pres. Of The Cattaraugus and Allegany County V.F.W. Auxiliary Member of the Salamanca American Legion Auxiliary.; [hon.] Blue ribbons for Indian craft work, First place for Indian dance competitions.; [oth. writ.] "I would like to see the The Pretty Flowers" printed in your Book. "My Way" for contest also "Running" for contest; [pers.] "Do unto others as you would have them do unto you." "To thine own self be true." I am a full blood Seneca Indian and proud of it!!; [a.] Salamanca, NY

HARTIGAN, GEORGE T.
[pen.] G.T. Hartigan; [b.] April 11, 1936, Brooklyn, NY; [p.] Maurice and Margaret Hartigan; [m.] Eleanor, August 1, 1992, Widowed - 1989; [ch.] 6 children, 3 stepchildren; [ed.] B.A. - History , John Jay College New York, N.Y.; [occ.] Substance Abuse Counselor; [memb.] Marine Corp League, ELKS; [hon.] Magna Cum Laude, John Jay; [oth. writ.] 3 Novel's, several short stories; [pers.] To Tell A Story, That Brings A Smile, A Tear Or A New Adventure; [a.] Staten Island, NY

HARTMAN, JOAN A.
[b.] November 2, 1938, Wadsworth, OH; [p.] Roy and Laura Hartman; [ed.] Highland High Graduate 1957 Granger, Ohio, In time classes in Creative writing: Home Decorating: Flower Arranging: Photography; [occ.] Retired from University Hospitals at Ohio State in Columbus, Ohio; [memb.] Attend Grace Brethren Church where I worship my Lord.; [hon.] Fall 1995 won an Editor's Choice Award for poem published in "At Water's Edge!; [oth. writ.] Two Published poems "At Waters Edge" and "A Muse To Follow"; [pers.] I was born and raised in deeply rural Ohio on land settled by my great-great grandfather. I have always felt close to the land and my ancestors who lived here. In my work I try to capture the essence of fresh air and life and hope, the simple beauties of times past and the extraordinary in things very ordinary.; [a.] Columbus, OH

HARTWIG, EVELYN O. DANSKIN
[b.] April 13, 1914, Zion City, IL; [p.] George and Olo Crosby; [m.] Leonard F. Hartwig; [ed.] College - 3 yrs and Associate Degree Eng. and Hist Music Minor, Certified Christian Education; [occ.] Retired; [memb.] United Meth. Church, PEO Chef BY, Lincoln China Painters, United Methodist Women, Lincoln Quitters Guild.; [pers.] I find music - not necessarily auditory - in all phases of life - musical - poetry - art - nature. Music is the heartbeat of life in all its moods.; [a.] Lincoln, NE

HARVELL, DOLORES S.
[b.] October 19, 1933, Fort Bragg, NC; [p.] Joseph A. and Katherine K. Samons; [m.] J. Lee Harvell, May 30, 1953; [ch.] Deborah Gay, Jennie Lee, Julia Anne and Kimberly Dee; [ed.] Western High School, Georgetown, D.C., University of Maryland; [occ.] Realtor, Prince George's County, Maryland; [memb.] Prince George's County Board of Trade, Business Professional Women's Organization (Previous State and Local Chaplain).; [hon.] Recognized as a leading REALTOR and member of the local community. Received recognition as the Distinguished Sales Associate and Business Woman of the Year by her peers.; [oth. writ.] The Children, The Green Canopy, Grannie, The Pine Tree Forest; [pers.] My compositions are a creation of the moment at hand or drawn upon past experiences. The writing of SARAH, was inspired by a summer picture of my seven years old Granddaughter, Sarah Elizabeth Merchant. These pieces are my legacy to my children and grandchildren.; [a.] Clinton, MD

HASSELL, JENNIFER LYNN
[b.] September 30, 1970, Nashville, TN; [p.] Robert and Winifred Hassell; [ed.] Dickson County Senior High School, Dickson, TN, The University of Tennessee at Knoxville - Degree in Communications w/ concentration in journalism (B.S.); [occ.] Correctional Officer; [a.] Nashville, TN

HATCHER, KENNETH DOANE
[b.] April 27, 1914, Jefferson Co., TN; [p.] George Bert and Sallie Thresher Hatcher; [m.] Berenice Bailey Hatcher, September 30, 1935; [ed.] BS in BA, Univ., Tennessee, summa cum laude; [occ.] Retired; [memb.] United Methodist, Amer. Inst. and TN Soc. of CPA's Mason; [hon.] Phi Eta Sigma, Beta Gamma Sigma, Phi Kappa Phi, Delta Sigma Pi, several scholarships.; [pers.] "All things come from you, O God!"; [a.] Knoxville, TN

HAVENS, WILL H.
[b.] November 21, 1910, Douglas County, MO; [p.] B. Ray and Mary E. (Todley) Havens; [m.] Clara E. (Keeler) Havens, December 2, 1933; [ch.] Ivan, Ruth-Ann-Bill; [ed.] Self Educated beyond High School by home study courses and correspondence; [occ.] Retired Minister; [memb.] Ava Gen. Baptist Church, American Bible Society, International Society of Poets, AARP, Ava Area Ministerial Association, Honorary Member of White River Association Presbytery; [hon.] Editor's Choice Awards for poems Published in "The Desert Sun", Edge of Twilight" and "The Garden Of Life", Award for 50 years Pastoral Ministry Plus an Award for eight addition years Pastoring; [oth. writ.] A book of meditations, three books of poems and three books of essays. Many articles and poems published in are publications; [pers.] I write to offer encouragement to those in need to help them over the rough spots. My pet saying is, "Keep On Keeping On," and it is included in much of my writings. I want to Minister in my poems and essays 'til the Lord calls for me; [a.] Ava, MO

HAVER, LEANNAH P. MAPES
[pen.] Leah; [b.] October 26, 1926, Tenn.; [p.] Lawrence Garner and Bertha; [m.] Ralph Mapes, March 28, 1988, Richard Haver, October 13, 1995; [ed.] Two years of college

HAVER, ORIANA
[b.] June 5, 1982, Highland Park Hospital; [p.] Susan and Stephen Haver; [ed.] Elm Place Middle School; [memb.] Immaculate Conception, Orphans of the Storm; [oth. writ.] Poems printed in school newspaper; [pers.] I am greatly influenced by the holocaust. And the literature about it.; [a.] Highland Park, IL

HAWKINS, JEFF
[pen.] Jeff Hawkins; [b.] December 14, 1968, Grayling, MI; [p.] Margo and Jay Myers, Roger and Vita Hawkins; [m.] Jennifer K. Phillips Hawkins, April 8, 1995; [ed.] Oakland University, Ferris State University, Ypsilanti (Mich.) High School; [occ.] Sports Copy Editor of The News Herald of Panama City, Fla.; [oth. writ.] "Bleacher View" sports column in The News Herald of Panama City, Fla.; [pers.] Silent Rain was one of series I wrote to help gain the love of the girl of my dreams, who is now wife.

HAY, HENRY JAMES
[pen.] Jim Hay; [b.] December 18, 1942, Detroit; [p.] Dallas Hay, Mavis Hay; [ch.] Tony Christine, Robin Aneice; [ed.] Bachelor of Fine Arts, Master of Fine Arts, Michigan State University; [occ.] Artist, Teacher; [hon.] Letter of Congratulations from U.S. President Gerald Ford for "Tree of American" Sculpture, "H. James Hay Day" in Mt. Clemens, Michigan, Key to City of Lansing, Michigan; [oth. writ.] Illustrations for Folk Tales of Japan, illustration for "Koho Magazine" in Japan, Poem in Mirrors of the Soul published by Modern Poetry Society, Dunnellon Florida; [pers.] My artwork is a mixing of sculpture, painting, drawing, light, sound and words. I am doing a lot of writing now because I live in such a small house and have a nice, used computer. I am interested in the "Mie Wo Kiru" poses of the Kabuki actor-moments of perfection.; [a.] Eugene, OR

HEADLY, KIM
[b.] March 30, 1983, Brooklyn, NY; [p.] Sylvia Morales Headley and Roger Headley; [ed.] Fieldston High School, Ethical Culture Elementary School; [occ.] Student; [pers.] Destiny is not a predetermined thing.; [a.] New York, NY

HEALEY, ANNE MARIE
[b.] June 17, 1956, Central Falls; [p.] Raymond and Claire Fournier; [m.] Divorced; [ch.] Jennifer, Christopher, Brad; [ed.] St. Mathieu's Grammar School 1-8, C.F. Nutre Dame High School C.F. 9-12, The Sawyer School Pawt R.I.; [occ.] Secretary to the Chief Central Falls Fire Dept.; [memb.] Committee Chairperson and Fund Rasing for St. Mathieu's, Troop 2 C.F., Parishinor of the Parish for 39 years.; [hon.] Twice awarded the Monsignor Paquin Award for Adult Scout of the Year.; [pers.] This poem is dedicated to my patron St., Saint Anne and The Holy Family. Without my strong Catholic beliefs, I would not have my beautiful 3 children and my fiancee Michael Geoffrey; [a.] Lincoln, RI

HECKER, ANDRES
[b.] March 25, 1977, Caracas, Venezuela; [p.] Johnny and Beatrice Hecker; [ed.] University of Miami; [oth. writ.] Written various articles for local newspaper. A tumultuous amount of poems; [pers.] Innocent in ignorance; [a.] Miami, FL

HEGGINS, MELODY E.
[pen.] Medy Dronet; [b.] September 21, 1961, Lafayette, LA; [ed.] University of Southwestern Louisiana, English Liberal Arts; [memb.] Sigma Tau Delta (English Honor Society), Arts, Humanities, and Behavioral Sciences Alumni; [a.] Lafayette, LA

HEGLUND, SHERRIE
[b.] January 19, 1967, Rolla, MO; [p.] John and Shirley Lauf; [m.] Donald R. Heglund, August 4, 1986; [ch.] Rachel and D.J.; [ed.] KicKapoo High, Draughn Business College - Dean's List and Student Coucil, Ford and Isuzu Diesel Training; [occ.] Jenkins Diesel Power, "Warranty Administrator"; [pers.] I wish to touch the hearts and souls as they read my poetry, in hope they will feel my inspiration. Writing poetry is how I deals with life. I was inspired by the poem "Dawn" by Paul Dunber.; [a.] Pleasant Hope, MO

HEINTZKILL, MARY M.
[b.] November 26, 1954, Green Bay, WI; [m.] Thomas Heintzkill; [ch.] Matthew, Elizabeth, Mary-Therese; [ed.] BA Psychology, Rel. Studies, Secondary Ed from UW - EauClaire, Mths (theological studies) from Saint Norbert College; [occ.] Chaplain at Hospice of Greater Kalamazoo; [hon.] Magna Cum Laude, Graduate, Dean's List; [pers.] My work is often a reflection on the struggles within me between conflicting forces. "Little Girl Within" is a reflection on my struggle to rise out of ashes.; [a.] Schoolcraft, MI

HENDERSON, CAROLYN E. W.
[b.] October 30, Washington, DC; [ed.] Lincoln Hospital School of Nursing, North Carolina Central University, University of North Carolina at Greensboro, University of North Carolina at Chapel Hill; [occ.] Educational Administrator, Durham County Hospital Corporation, Durham, NC; [memb.] American Nurses Asso., American Society for Healthcare Education and Training, Delta Sigma Theta Sorority, Inc., American Society for Training and Development, St. Joseph's AME Church, Chi Eta Phi Nursing Sorority, Inc.; [hon.] Santa Filomena Nursing

Honor Society, Listed in Who's Who of American Women, Outstanding Women of America and Who's Who in Nursing; [oth. writ.] Some articles printed in local newspaper... Carolina Times, The Herald Sun and The Kinston Daily Free Press; [pers.] I believe that writing is one of the true expression of life.; [a.] Durham, NC

HENKEL, JENNIFER KAY
[b.] December 10, 1976, Shakopee, MN; [p.] Daniel H. and Nicolette L. Henkel; [ed.] 12th Grade, I am going to the Courage Center in Golden Valley Minnesota, to help me learn to live more independently.; [hon.] Made the Dean's list 2 times in the 12th Grade.; [oth. writ.] Color Blind World, The Cage, The Egale, Several poems written none have been published; [pers.] The poem Dreamer was inspired because of my disability (Spastic Quadriplegis Cerebal Palsy) which I have had from birth. I have lived in Minnesota, Washington, Florida, California and back to Minnesota. I live at home with Dad and Mom and Sister and have (2) Brothers.; [a.] Chaska, MN

HERNANDEZ, ALVIN ELIAS
[b.] February 19, 1964, Tulare, CA; [p.] Pete and Julia Hernandez; [ed.] Porterville Union High, Porterville College; [occ.] Warehouse Equip. Operator; [memb.] Porterville Believer's Church, Porterville Men's Golf Club; [pers.] I envision the ink from my pen as an artery flowing from my heart, the gift of expressing myself I care to share.; [a.] Terra Bella, CA

HERNDON, CASANYA
[pen.] "Casey"; [b.] November 23, 1935, Riverside, CA; [p.] Joanne Williams and James Herndon; [ed.] Graduate of Brethren Christian High School, currently a Senior at CSU Dominguez Hills as a Pre-Law, Sociology Major and Pol., Sci., Minor; [occ.] Student (full-time), Receptionist/Office Aid)part-time); [memb.] Phi Alpha Delta Pre-Law Frat. State Church of God in Christ Youth choir, So. California Div., From line, Youth Ministries. Singled Out For Christ Ministry.; [hon.] Presidents List at CSU Long Beach, Outstanding Student of Swahili (fall '94); [oth. writ.] My Brother, Chocolate Creams, Little Dancers, and more; [pers.] My eternal Prayer is that we will never forget that the future lies in the hands of the children of the present.; [a.] Carson, CA

HERRING, ANDREW
[b.] December 28, 1983, Denver, CO; [p.] Kathy and Charles Herring; [ed.] 6th grade; [occ.] student; [memb.] Younger Generation Players, Theater; [hon.] title role of "Oliver Twist." Huck Finn in "Tom Sawyer"; [pers.] I want to get further in my acting and poetry career; [a.] Denver, CO

HERRING, NATHALIE
[b.] May 23, 1969, Sacramento, CA; [ch.] Branden Herring; [ed.] College - Bookkeeping/ Accounting; [occ.] Accounting in a corporate environment; [oth. writ.] Writing poetry has been a hobby for a very long time and I have several favorites.; [pers.] I intend to publish several more poems soon. I am pleased with the way a lot of my poems have turned out. I will continue writing them.; [a.] Sacramento, CA

HERRINGTON, SHELIA
[b.] December 10, 1950, Savannah, GA; [p.] Eva Southwood German; [m.] Kenneth Herrington, July 30, 1970; [ch.] Kimberly Canice, Kenneth Benjamin, Keren Denice, Keilah Marie; [ed.] Savannah High School, South College; [occ.] Owner/Operator Sunshine Adventures Travel; [hon.] First Tabernacle Baptist Church Honorary Readings; [oth. writ.] "Born To Be A King", "I Could Have Been So Beautiful", "The Mystery of His Will", "Savannah By The Sea", "A Call To Glory" these poems and several other non-published works; [pers.] Let the words of mouth and the meditation of my heart be acceptable to God.; [a.] Savannah, GA

HERSKOWITZ, THOMAS VON PHILLIP
[b.] December 20, 1971, Charleston, SC; [p.] Anne Osborne, Gifford; [ed.] Montclair Preparatory, Los Angeles, Calif., The Citadel, Charleston S.C., College of Charleston; [occ.] Student; [hon.] Graduated with English Honors from Montclair College-preparatory School. Several short stories published in the literary text: "The Shako". Received Charleston Post Courier Award for "Feature Writer Award of Year". Features Editor and Executive Editor of Citadel Newspaper, "The Brigadier".; [a.] Charleston, SC

HERZBERGER, MAGDA
[b.] February 20, 1926, Cluj, Romania; [p.] Herman Mozes (Deceased) and Serena Vinacour (Deceased); [m.] Eugene E. Herzberger, November 21, 1946; [ch.] Monica Riekoff and Henry Herzberger; [ed.] Bachelor's of Science Degree, One Year Medical School at King Ferdinand University, 1946-1947 in Cluj, Romania; [occ.] Poet, Lecturer, Composer; [memb.] International Society of Poets, Beth El Sisterhood, Women's Club and Kiwanis Club in Fountain Hills, Arizona; [hon.] Personalities of West and Midwest Award, three poetry grants, 1977, 1980 and 1985, Who's Who in Poetry 5th Edition, Cambridge, England, Poet of Merit Award, 1993 (The National Library of poetry, Editor's Choice Award, 1994-1995, and 2nd prized winner of 1994 National Library of Poetry Competition, The International Who is Who of Intellectuals, Cambridge, England, 1978 - 1982; [oth. writ.] Books: Will You Still Love Me? The Walts of the Shadows, Songs of Life Eyewitness to Holocaust, and 300 independent poems published, one short story, two narratives (Poetic), one children's book, one book on the Holocaust in the making.; [pers.] Being a survivor of the Camps, my goal is to keep the memory of the Holocaust alive through my writings and music and to instill a love of poetry in the hearts of all the people. I'm also a hiker, skier and marathon runner.; [a.] Fountain Hills, AZ

HESTER, LOUISE CARLISLE
[pers.] I wrote this poem in honor of my granddaughter whom was killed in a car wreck, February 27, 1994. I can express my true feelings in poetry.; [a.] Laurel, MS

HEWELL, RUTH
[b.] March 3, 1917, Rockdale County; [p.] W. T. and Mary F. Underwood; [m.] Deceased; [ch.] Two; [ed.] Some H.S. and some Night School - Red Cross V. Nursing; [occ.] Q. Control and some Lab. Work; [oth. writ.] Some short stories published in short stories of farm life.; [a.] Porterdale, GA

HEY, DOROTHY KAY
[b.] October 2, 1955, Kingsport, TN; [p.] Morris and Lena Browning; [m.] Anthony Richard Hey, January 26, 1977; [ch.] Matthew Kayne Hey; [ed.] Lake Wales Sr. High, Erwin Technical Institute; [occ.] Home Health Aide; [memb.] St. Clements Catholic Church; [hon.] The biggest honor in my life is to be Mrs. Anthony Richard Hey. Caregiver of the year for 1995.; [pers.] I believe in being good, kind, and honest towards everyone. I love people of all nations and all walks of life.; [a.] Plant City, FL

HICKEY, DANIEL PAUL
[pen.] Daniel P. Hickey; [b.] August 9, 1969, Dayton, OH; [p.] Herbert Hickey, Janet Hickey; [ed.] B.A. in Theatre Arts, Eastern Michigan University; [occ.] Surveyor of Preppy Pizza (Okay I'm a waiter); [memb.] Aside from my gym, I don't really have any.; [hon.] I've received previous awards for speech-writing and delivery, as well as being the recipient of positive theatrical reviews.; [oth. writ.] A lobby for Sisyphus Pebble, Tree and He, Tempest In A Glass of O.J.; [pers.] My advocation of education overwhelms me sometimes. Never arrest learning, a fresh viewpoint beats a day-old roll any day of the year.; [a.] Chicago, IL

HIGGINS, MS. N. LOY KUHU
[pen.] Loy; [b.] August 2, 1944, Louisville, KY; [p.] Arthur Louis Kuhu (Deceased) and Nina Waller Kuhu; [m.] Dr. David Michael Higgins, November 27, 1990; [ed.] DuPont Manual High School, Louisville, KY, Class of '62, Eastern Kentucky State College, Richmond, KY, '62-'64, Miami Dade Junior College, Miami, FL, '73-'74, AA Degree., Fine Arts/General, U of the State of New York, '86, AS Degree, Liberal Arts and General Sciences (Regents Program), conferred January '87, Scottsdale Community College, Scottsdale, AZ, '95, Studio Recording and Electronic Music; [occ.] Writer, Musician, Teacher, Desktop Publisher; [memb.] International Society of Poets, National Authors Registry, Adult Recital Series of AZ State Music Teachers Assn, Alliance Francais, Senior Friends; [hon.] Poems published in the "National Library of Poetry's" antholoy "A Voyage to Remember," the Modern Poetry Society of Dunnellon, FL's volume of modern poetry "Mirrors of the Soul," and Iliad Press Literary Anthology "Crossings," Honorable Mention, Pine Hills, NY Poetry Competition 1995, Superior and Excellent Awards, National Federation Junior Festivals '93, '94, '95, Special Commendation, National Guild of Piano Teachers '93, '94, '95, and membership in the National Fraternity of Student Musicians, Student Division of American College of Musicians and Piano Hobbyists, ASMTA, Central District, 43rd Piano Ensemble,

'95; [oth. writ.] Poems, humorous short stories, songs, and lyrics. Writer and publisher of POETRY LINES series. Arranger and performer of several keyboard cassette recordings, recorded in my home studio in Scottsdale, AZ; [pers.] Creativity is driven by emotion — be it joy, sorrow, love, hate, or fear, therefore, indifference is rarely found in the arts.; [a.] Scottsdale, AZ

HILBERT, MELANIE I.
[b.] November 22, 1943, Shenandoah, PA; [p.] William and Evelyn Purnell; [m.] David E. Hilbert, May 4, 1963; [ch.] D. Jeffrey, Deborah Lynn; [ed.] Mount Penn High School, Attended Kutztown State College, Courses through American Banking Institute; [occ.] Housewife; [memb.] Lititz Woman's Club, Trinity E.C. Church; [hon.] National Honor Society, Dean's List, DAR Good Citizenship Award; [pers.] Many thins change in life, but my family is the one constant I can always count on. I treasure them above all else.; [a.] Lititz, PA

HILL, JEROME
[pen.] Hakim Yamini; [b.] May 4, 1961, Philadelphia, PA; [p.] Fredrick Carrington, Aluna Hill; [ch.] Hakim Gantt, Nasia Hill; [ed.] Benjamin Franklin High, Orleans Technical Institute; [occ.] Carpenter, more than just scenery, Philadelphia, PA; [pers.] I write poetry because I love, I feel. And If I could bring a smile to someone's face. Bring some sunshine into someone's life through my words. To write something that makes a difference to someone, to the world, will always warm my heart.; [a.] Philadelphia, PA

HILLIARD, ELEANOR
[pen.] Dawn Hilliard; [b.] Knapps Creek, NY; [p.] Deceased; [ch.] Carol Carpenter; [ed.] 12 yrs. - 2 yrs. College; [occ.] Retired; [memb.] National Library of Poetry; [hon.] Poetry, Several Silver, Golden, Honorable Mention; [oth. writ.] Short stories, essays.

HILLIMAN, JOY HOWARD
[b.] January 7, 1936, Guyana, SA; [p.] Donald Muriel Howard; [m.] Dennis N. Hilliman, December 21, 1960; [ch.] Dennis, Dorrell, Dudley Hilliman; [ed.] Trinity Methodist, Elementary Arubaanse Academic, Guyana S. America, Plainfield, NJ; [occ.] Social Worker, CSW - Consumer Affairs Investigator; [memb.] Upper Room, Full Gospel Church, Gospel Singer; [hon.] Golden Poet 1991. Many poems published in Local Church Bulletins and Papers.; [oth. writ.] Black Family, Life and Black Fathers.

HINTZ, BLUE JEAN
[pen.] Blu Hintz; [b.] March 22, 1948, Port Huron, MI; [m.] Randy T. Hintz, June 7, 1974; [ch.] Kristy, Steven, Dustin Hintz; [ed.] Midland High; [occ.] Entrepreneur "Cottage, Computer Gifts"; [memb.] Small Business Assoc.; [oth. writ.] Published in Fledgeling Wings 1955 (Pen name - Shirley De Shone); [pers.] To stand tall is to walk on ones own two feet, but never forget to carry you Teddy Bear.; [a.] Midland, MI

HLINKA, GEORGE
[b.] March 31, 1929, Manhattan, NY; [p.] Anna Benyo, Michael Hlinka; [ed.] Franklin K. Lane High, Brooklyn College; [occ.] Goliard; [oth. writ.] The unpublished epic narrative poem, "Amaranthine" (250PP), a romance of Colonial New York during the American Revolution.; [pers.] Poetry is the supreme testament to man's life experience. To be revindicated, it must be made comprehensible and meaningful to the messes.; [a.] Bloomingburg, NY

HOBAUGH, ARLENE
[m.] Ike Hobaugh; [occ.] Elementary English, Teacher; [memb.] Delta Kappa Gamma; [hon.] Listed in Who's Who Among American Teachers, Chamber of Commerce Excellence in Education Award Recipient, Received Commendation from La. House of Representatives for Excellence in Education, Jefferson Parish Teacher of the Year, La. State Finalist Elementary Teacher of the Year, National Finalist in State Farm Good Neighbor Award; [oth. writ.] Poem published in school district's newsletter; [a.] Kenner, LA

HODGE, JASON
[b.] December 21, 1979, Maryville, TN; [p.] Glen Hodge and Sherry Price; [ed.] William Blount High School; [occ.] Electro Polisher; [memb.] Primo's Gym; [hon.] Blount County and Tennessee Honors Diploma, Runner-up in Southeastern Power Lifting Championship; [pers.] Those who are dependent cannot lead themselves. Imagination and memories are the keys to poetry.; [a.] Maryville, TN

HODGES, PAULA NICOLE
[b.] July 10, 1976, Fort Worth, TX; [p.] Dennis and Mary Beth Newland; [m.] Jay Allen Hodges, August 6, 1994; [ch.] Melinda Key; [ed.] Granbury High School; [occ.] Operator at Hood General Hospital; [oth. writ.] Article for the Hood Country News; [a.] Granbury, TX

HOGAN, RHONDA KAY
[b.] March 3, 1968, Fort Worth, TX; [p.] Bill and Mary Lovelady Stepmom - Anita Lovelady; [m.] Christopher French Hogan, July 21, 1995; [ch.] Ricky Joe, Andi Keith, Natalie Nicole Ellen Hogan; [occ.] Data Entry; [pers.] When I lost my mom it hit me hard so my advice to you is keep your family close at heart. Let them always know that no matter what circumstances arise you do love them. You can be rich and not have so much as a penny.; [a.] Hurst, TX

HOGUE, ILA ANN
[b.] August 15, 1948, Harrodsburg, KY; [p.] Jane Geary, M. J. Simpson; [m.] Gerald R. Hogue Jr., October 19, 1971; [ch.] Jeffrey Dale, Kytina Michelle, Karen Anne; [ed.] Non-Graduate, lack 1 yr., Lubbock, Tex.; [occ.] Housewife

HOLLAND, ELIZABETH N.
[b.] July 13, 1940, Talladega, AL; [p.] Jin and Myrtle Holland; [ed.] MD Degree, Univ. of Tenn. 1969, BS Degree, Southwestern at Memphis 1961; [occ.] Physician; [hon.] Volunteer H Year Memphis 1993, DAR Medal of Honor; [oth. writ.] Author of book and workbook, Godly Parenting - poem published by Nat'l Lib. of Poetry - Lord Make Me A Tool; [pers.] I write as a tool to express my Christian commitment - and to help others to understand the love of bad in their lives. This poem - I am a "We" way written 3 days after surgery for breast cancer.

HOLLISTER, CHERYL
[b.] November 14, 1957, Baltimore, MD; [p.] Charles Kidd Jr., Diane Kidd; [ch.] Sarah Lynn, Russell Frank; [ed.] West Carteret High, University of North Florida; [occ.] Health Teacher; [memb.] University of North Florida National Alumni Association, St. Andrews Presbyterian Church, International Society of Poets; [hon.] Phi Theta Kappa; [oth. writ.] 4th poem published by the National Library of Poetry.; [pers.] This poem reflects my thoughts on the changes in the dating system in todays society.; [a.] Jacksonville, FL

HOLM-KNAUS, JACK A.
[b.] June 3, 1948, Walla Walla, WA; [ed.] (2) Associate of Science, (1) Associate of Art., Assoc. of Science Linn Benton Comm. College, Ass. of Science and Art Portland Community Col.; [occ.] Student (disabled vet); [memb.] Phi Theta Kappa

HOLMES, BETTY MAHAIR
[pen.] Betty B. Holmes; [b.] February 16, 1927, Spaulding, OK; [p.] E.R. and Susie Bryant; [m.] Daniel H. Holmes (Deceased T.M. Mahair), December 21, 1994 (1-19-1945, 42 yrs. 21/2 mo.); [ch.] (Thomas Deceased), Judy Lane and Mikeal D.; [ed.] Grade and Jr. High Spaulding, Okla, High School 2 yrs. Tulare, Calif., GED Beaumont, TX. Adult Learning Center 1976; [occ.] Retired - Housewife, Retired Manager Naturalizer shoe store; [memb.] International Society of Poets, Southwest Writers League Inc., Central Church of Christ; [hon.] Honored with aninvitation to become distinguished member of International Society of Poets - Honored with nomination as Poet of the year 1995, and as Poet of Merit for which I was unable to attend - Honored with Editor's Choice Award of which I am very proud.; [oth. writ.] "Quiet Wonders" Sparrow Grass Treasured Poems of America Fall 1995- "Stay Yes-Recycle No" Beyond The Stars "Real Picture" for Sparrow Grass (1996 Summer), "A Sailor's Daydreams" for a Muse to Follow "Messed Up But Good" for Beneath The Harvest Moon; [pers.] I believe that dreams can come true. I've always been told the couldn't but after all the good things that have happened with my writing in 1995 no one can make me believe different. I had never entered a contest until 1995 and it is hard for me to believe the things that have happened; [a.] Lumberton, TX

HOLMES, JAMES P.
[pen.] June 8, 1946; [ed.] BA University Minnesota Morris; [occ.] Managers; [a.] Cyrus, MN

HOLMES, JOSHUA RYAN
[pen.] Josh Holmes; [b.] January 16, 1978, Eglin AFB, FL; [p.] Jim and Brenda Hasson; [ed.] Will graduate High School June, 96 and will obtain

Certificate of Attainment in carpentry from Hazleton Vocational Technical School.; [occ.] High School Senior; [memb.] VICA Member and Vice President of Class for VICA; [hon.] 2nd Honors in Grades and 1st Place in Graphic Design in VICA Poster Contest.; [oth. writ.] No published work.; [pers.] I write to express my opinions.; [a.] Hazleton, PA

HOLMES, TWANNA
[b.] October 2, 1951, Roswell, NM; [p.] James and Alvin Davis; [m.] Russell E. Holmes, April 3, 1969; [ch.] Russell Jr. and Amy; [ed.] Andrews High, Central Texas College; [occ.] Sub. Teacher; [oth. writ.] Many Poems; [pers.] Give me a situation or subject I can write a poem about it. I write from my heart.; [a.] Burnet, TX

HONEYWOOD, JESSIE A.
[b.] November 19, 1951, Chicago, IL; [p.] Enos and Charley Mary Honeywood; [ch.] Hershel, Jesse, King, Natasha, Sheri, Dyer; [ed.] Farragut H.S, Wright College, Chicago State College; [oth. writ.] Poetry and versus under work "White Sugar Melts, Brown Sugar Creams", Short Stories.; [pers.] Touch another life in a positive way. A smile, A squeeze of the hand, a kind word, a vote of confidence, a pat on the back, a shoulder to cry on, an encouraging hug. Something to say "I Care".; [a.] Chicago, IL

HONT, BRETT PAUL S.
[b.] December 27, 1964, Weco, TX; [p.] Nancy Ann Pizzor, Rick Paul Short; [occ.] Party cook, and Chiefs Apprentice.; [hon.] 320 hours of capenters apprentice

HOOSER, ALICE
[b.] July 26, 1978, Utah; [p.] Howard Whitlock, Bonnie Thornock; [m.] Dave Hooser, October 30, 1993; [ch.] Ryan Christopher Hooser; [ed.] Valley High School, graduate 1996, May; [occ.] Daycare Teacher; [hon.] 3.8, GPA, 1995; [pers.] Love is a powerful emotion, it must be treated as such.; [a.] Sandy, UT

HOOVER, JEANNE TYSON
[pen.] The writing Nurse; [b.] July 18, 1914, Penn., U.S.A.; [p.] Eva Lucinda and Maurice Frederick Tyson; [m.] Ray Francis Hoover III, May 7, 1938; [ch.] Marley Shiffert and Sandra Claire; [ed.] After High School with Honor, Registered Nurse, Univ. in Penna. in Phila., Public Health, Maryland - travelling around world with my husband; [occ.] Care-Giver for husband, Conservatrix for daughter Sandy; [memb.] Mark Twain Memorial - Pres. Women's Comm. 2 yrs., V. Pres. 2 yrs., Welles - Turner N/Em. Library - Gl., Pres. Friends of W.T.M., etc. etc.; [hon.] I am a Twin - Honored to Marry Ray F. Hoover and bear his two daughters. It is an Honor to be A Christian; [oth. writ.] Wrote first story age 8, wrote stories for Libertas in High Sch., Article in H.U.P. quarterly, wrote Good Food Column Clastonbury Citizen for five yrs.; [pers.] "Let the beauty we love - be what we do" Rum. "Experience is an archway where through forever fades the vision on the view and I am part of all I have met" - Ulysses. Good Morning, Lord what are you up to today? Can I be a part of"? Thank you. Amen; [a.] Clastonbury, CO

HOPKINS, BEVERLY ANN MARIE
[pen.] Bev; [b.] March 26, 1954, Detroit, MI; [p.] Mary Tierney, Charles Tierney; [m.] Robert J. Hopkins, February 16, 1985; [ch.] Kimberly Elizabeth, Benjamin Joseph, and Brian Robert; [ed.] Eastern Michigan University - B.A. Elem. Education, Teacher Elem. Education, 31/2 years, Insurance Claims Adjuster 7 yrs.; [occ.] Part time - flower shop, housewife, farm wife, volunteer in childrens school and church; [memb.] Farm Bureau, Vantown United Meth. Church; [hon.] National Honor Society; [oth. writ.] Summer articles for a local newspaper, curr. enrolled in a course Children's Institute of Literature, My Own Personal Book titled "Windows to the Soul"; [pers.] For the "Silver Star" in my life who has encouraged, guided and directed me to reach for so much more....; [a.] Webberville, MI

HORTING, CHRISTOPHER R.
[pen.] Christopher Angst; [b.] March 1, 1978, Media, PA; [p.] Reed Horting, Deborah Horting; [ed.] Phoenixville Are High School; [occ.] Cook for Little Caesars; [memb.] S.A.D.D.; [hon.] Who's Who Among, American High School Students for Consecutive Years (1993-1994, 1994-1995); [pers.] Inside of some is a darker side, hidden in the shadows of their subconscious. Only through poems and stories is this side ever brought into the light.; [a.] Malvern, PA

HORTON, SHIRLEY M.
[pen.] Horton, Shirley Campbell; [b.] August 18, 1929, Brockton, MA; [p.] William Macomber, Gertrude Macomber; [m.] Lewellyn R. Horton, November 2, 1991; [ch.] Christopher, Bonnie, Mark, Beth Todd; [ed.] Graduated from Howard High West Bridgewater, MA., Member of Nat'l Honor Society - Graduated from Springfield Training School Springfield, Mass; [occ.] Homemaker; [memb.] Member of West Yarmouth Congregational Church, Served on many Committee, Also was a Deaconess, Song with many chorus on Cape Cod.; [hon.] First poem published 1995, National Library of Poetry "At Water's Edge" Distinguished member of International Society of Poets.; [oth. writ.] Two poems to be published 1996 - Nat'l Library of Poetry, have written for several Christian Newsletters.; [pers.] To me poetry is like a song flowing from your intermost being outward. Iris sharing with the world the things you see and feel in it, hoping perhaps other's will identify with it.; [a.] Taunton, MA

HOUSTON, BILLIE
[pen.] Barri Bryan; [b.] November 24, 1927, Lehman, TX; [m.] M. H. Houston, June 2, 1943; [ch.] Five; [ed.] AA - San Antonio College, BA (History) UTSA, MA (Psychology) UTSA; [occ.] Writer; [memb.] Austin Writers' League, Canyon Lake Writer's Guild; [oth. writ.] Novels poetry anthology essays.

HOUSTON, ROBERT MASO
[pen.] Alan Jonathan Woods; [b.] November 18, 1977, Concord, NC; [p.] Nancy Houston, Garry Houston; [ed.] South Rowan High School, Corriher - Lipe Middle School, Landis Elementary School; [occ.] Student; [oth. writ.] Several other poems; [pers.] "The writing comes from the heart not from the pen."; [a.] Kannapolis, NC

HOWARD, GEORGE O.
[pen.] G.O.H. Gold; [b.] October 26, 1960, Landstuhl West, Germany; [p.] Kathleen E. Francis; [ed.] Frankfurt American High School; [occ.] Dreamer; [hon.] Editor's choice Award 1995, The National Library of Poetry.; [oth. writ.] Published Poems include "Aids", Between The Raindrops", The Road To Knowhere", The Best Poems of 1996; [a.] Garland, TX

HOWARD, GOLDIE ELAINE
[pen.] Goldie Howard; [b.] May 2, 1957, Grayson, KY; [p.] Golden and Evelyn Wilburn; [m.] Brian Howard, February 11, 1984; [ch.] Samantha Howard; [ed.] Bachelor of Social Work, Morehead State Univ.; [occ.] Instructional Assistant, Brookside Elementary; [memb.] Nicholasville United Methodist Church, International Society of Poets; [a.] Nicholasville, KY

HOWE, AMBER
[pen.] Amber Howe; [b.] April 9, 1947, Pennsylvania; [p.] Edith and Roy Howe; [ch.] Todd Austin Howe and Blake Justin Howe; [ed.] University of Pittsburgh, Georgia State, University of Maryland; [occ.] Administrative Assistant and student; [oth. writ.] Previous National Library of Poetry "Editor's Choice Award" recipient and work chosen for the National Library of Poetry "Sound of Poetry"; [pers.] My wish is gladden those hearts in which love grows.; [a.] Bowie, MD

HOWE, LORALIE FRANCES DEARINGER
[pen.] Loralie Frances Dearinger Howe; [b.] November 25, 1925, Lexington, KY; [p.] Julian Lewis and Grace Jack Dearinger; [m.] James Gilbert Howe, December 20, 1945; [ch.] Two Daughter: Susan Stack and Jamie Nichols; [ed.] Graduated Henry Clay High School, Lexington, KY, No formal College Degree, Studied Dance and Theatre Arts - Danced and Sang for U.S.O. During W. W. II, also worked at Oak Ridge, Tenn. on the Atomic Bomb Project. Met my husband there, where he was in service. Army Eng. Corps. belong to Pasadena Presbyterian Church. Pacific Asia Museum in Pasadena California. Pasadena Athletic Club. Dephhium Society; [hon.] Three Silver Cups In Gymnastic Tournaments in High School, Bronze "A Bomb" Medal for working in Oak Ridge, Tennessee to help end W.W. II; [oth. writ.] "A Long Time Longing" published 1995 by National Library of Poetry. Also many poems never published.; [pers.] I believe poetry is in the soul of every person's being, the words "Within" us are by and large never heard. Poetry is as natural as breathing - it is a dance step about to be taken and will soar into the air, once given.; [a.] Pasadena, CA

HOWELL, KENNETH J.
[pen.] Kenneth; [b.] January 18, 1993, Lapel, IN; [p.] Valter and Bernadine Howell; [m.] Engaged to be married, January 18, 1959; [ch.] Malinda, Malissa, Jesse, Dusty; [ed.] 1-12 4 years

trade school Lapelhigh School; [occ.] Pipefitter (PDM), Predictive Maintenance; [oth. writ.] I have around a hundred poems or should I say my sweetie has them; [pers.] Most of my poems came from my heart and my love and happiness for dawn.; [a.] Elwood, IN

HOWES, ANDREW R.
[b.] October 29, 1968, Weymouth, MA; [p.] David Howes, Rita Howes; [ed.] Rockland High School, North Eastern University; [occ.] Army Officer; [pers.] Written to and for Cecilia.; [a.] Haleiwa, HI

HUFSTETLER, DAVID M.
[b.] December 31, 1948, Tampa, FL; [p.] Doris and Harold Hufstetler; [ch.] Joseph and Jennifer; [ed.] High School and 2 yrs Jr. College, RO, Hillsborough High and Hillsborough Community; [occ.] LAB Assistant Manager (Optical LAB); [pers.] I hope my poetry will be an inspiration and help to those who read my message in my poems.; [a.] Tampa, FL

HULLUM, CORI RENAE
[pen.] Teeki; [b.] July 22, 1974, Akron, OH; [p.] Bertha and William Hullum; [ch.] William Shaquille Hullum; [ed.] John R. Buchtel High School, University of Akron; [occ.] University of Akron Bookstore; [oth. writ.] In 2nd Grade I wrote a short story book called "The Girl With Curls."; [pers.] I believe writing is my calling and I hope to fulfill this dream.; [a.] Akron, OH

HUME, HAVAH S.E.
[b.] March 20, 1951, Rochester; [p.] Havah Smith and George Moon; [occ.] Own business; [pers.] This poem is in memory of my brothers Leonard and Joshua Burley who died of aids in my arms of my home with all this family near and mom holding them as they went to me our Lord. Leonard Burley, May 1, 1947 - July 6, 1991, Joshua Burley, July 9, 1951 - April 2, 1993

HUNT, KATHERINE
[b.] April 14, 1961, Portsmouth, VA; [p.] James and Dianna Young; [m.] Anthony Hunt, September 23, 1995; [ed.] Columbus East High, Ohio State University; [occ.] Student Loan Specialist 2, Ohio Student Aid Commission, Columbus, OH; [memb.] National Forencis League, National Honor Society; [hon.] Diploma of Distinction in Music; [oth. writ.] Several poems in employee Newsletters; [pers.] I listen to my heart, it knows the truth. I greatly admire black authors, they say what we feel.; [a.] Columbus, OH

HUNTER, BARRY CLARANCE
[pen.] PP; [b.] December 13, 1951, Philadelphia, PA; [p.] James and Rena Hunter; [m.] Former wife Divorced Lizarine R. Knight (Hunter) Divorced, June 1972, 1978; [ch.] David Demond Hunter, Lisa Nicole Hunter; [ed.] Jones Jr. High School, Thomas Phila., A Edison High School Phila., Morgan State (College) University Balt. Md., Adelphia Business School, Inc., Phila. Charute A.F.B. Weather Observing School Rantool Illinois; [occ.] American Lawman, Retired American DAV. Veteran; [memb.] Masons, Kappa Alpha NAACP, Kappa Morgan State College 1971, Eternal Scroller National Rifle Assn., D.A.V. Disabled American Vets, Former Member U.S. Treasury U.S. Secret F.B.I. Ident Wash. D.C. U.S. Navy, USAF S.A.C. Omahane OSI Office Special Investigation; [hon.] National Honor Society, National Library of Poetry best poem 1994, Valedictorian Jr. High School, Football, Track and Field High School, Motivation High School White, Williams Scholarship Program Edison High School; [oth. writ.] Phila. Daily News, People's Paper Poetry Phila., Tribune Poet's Corner Vantage Press New York City, National Library of Poetry entries poems; [pers.] If loves light of creations shines in man and man kinds heart. Then in that light which is equally the light of Almighty God and heaven and the spirit of angels. If that light known as the light of love which started creation. Shines in the spirit of what love can be. Then in Almighty God heart and heaven's heart, and in man's heart whom believe in love. Even in death as many men would still live in time in the heart of love light called creation. A light of a vision of life can still be seen even beyond death darkness. No parables no ascertainment. In love's light God's light and that light that shines in man's hearts love. Nothing can stop the power of love not even death.; [a.] Philadelphia, PA

HUNTER, CHARLES E.
[b.] July 23, 1920, PaloPinto, TX; [p.] James E. and Minnie C. Hunter (Deceased); [m.] Frances E. Hunter, January 1, 1970 (12:01 am); [ch.] Tom Steder, Joan Barker; [ed.] ABA - South Texas Law and Commerce Correspondence - Texas University, Graduate Draugfins Business College, President, City of Light School of Ministry; [occ.] Retired CPA, Retired Captain US Air Force, President Hunter Ministries (Wife-Co President); [memb.] Texas Society of Certified Public Accountant Trustee, International Charismatic Bible Ministries, The Happy Hunters, Charles Love Frances International Evangelist and Teachers; [oth. writ.] Authors of 39 Christian Books, Video and Audio Bible School, Articles for Charisma Magazine and others, Television and Radio Programs National and International; [pers.] Actively engaged in world evangelism. Opening thousands of churches in Russia, China and other nations. They have videos (15 hours) on HOW TO HEAL THE SICK in languages so that 80% of the world's population can watch them in their own native languages. The companion book is also in the same languages. Charles and his wife Frances are known as the Apostles of Healing.; [a.] Kingwood, TX

HUNTZINGER, DEBBY
[b.] April 21, 1981, Abington, PA; [p.] Doris and David Huntzinger, [ed.] Presently in 9th grade; [occ.] Student; [memb.] National Junior Honor Society and TADA (Teens Against Drugs and Alcohol); [hon.] National Smoke out Poetry Contest for Montgomery Township; [oth. writ.] Numerals poems including: "Growing Up", "There's A Monster In My Closet", and "Differences."; [pers.] I enjoy writing as a means of expressing my feelings about my world and the world around me.; [a.] Jenkintown, PA

HUTCHINS, SHARLEEN
[b.] January 28, 1961, Monroe, WA; [p.] John Hutchins Sr., Patsy Esser-Danhof; [ch.] Sonja Shambaugh, Chris Peterson; [ed.] Snohomish High School; [occ.] Caregiver and owner of TWS, Ltd an errand running Service; [memb.] The International Society of Poets and National Society of Female Executives; [hon.] Commanding Officers Accommodation Awards, Two Editors Choice Award from the NLP.; [oth. writ.] "A Tapestry of Thoughts" the NLP, "Best of '95" the NLP, "Dance on the Horizon" the NLP, "Dusting off Dreams" Quill Books, "Listen With Your Heart" Quill Books; [pers.] Peace and harmony must be reached in the world, if we all work together it can be.; [a.] Snohomish, WA

HUTH, LINDSAY
[b.] February 3, 1977; [p.] Tim and Patty Huth; [occ.] Student At University of Iowa; [a.] Bettendorf, IA

HUTSON, LONA
[b.] December 27, 1916, Garrad Co., KY; [p.] Hunter - Marget Ray; [m.] Cecil Hutson, March 22, 1938, May 3, 1970; [ch.] James R. Cobine; [ed.] Threw 10th grade; [occ.] Retired - was Executive Housekeeper for 23 yrs. for Howard Johnson; [memb.] Northside Church of Christ, Ladies Aid; [hon.] When in school I was first in running and second in State; [oth. writ.] My one and only poem; [pers.] I love nature, and love being a country girl. Most of my life was spent on the form. I loved all phase of form life, I had many many, peta but one I could not tame was an oposson, But I did try. My son was born after 6 yr. of marriage and my husband passed away with that awfull empsenra. I left the form and moved to tje city. There I found it necessary to find work this I did on my first try as executive housekeeper for Howard Johnson Motel there I met many famous people. I spent 23's year there retired when they sold the place. This was a very trying lime in my life. A few year late I met and married my presenr husband.

ILUNGA, KALENGA EMMANUEL
[pen.] RDTRS; [b.] July 22, 1961, Kinshasa/Zaire; [p.] Marie Mwika and Andre Ilunga; [ed.] High school diploma (with emphasis, in Biochemistry) Computer Science student/Utah Valley Community College Orem/Utah; [occ.] A Pepsi employee after a car accident (07/14/94); [oth. writ.] Myself and I, Flake, Solo, Morning Reach, Deer Creek, to set the record straight, etc. unpublished poems.; [pers.] Insight like wine is the fermented juice of sights it intoxicates when not served; [a.] Provo, UT

IRONS, AMY
[b.] April 5, 1969, South Bend, IN; [p.] Kay Shaw, Kenneth Irons; [ed.] John Adams High School, Indiana Vocational Technical College; [occ.] Advertising Dept. at local newspaper and bookseller.; [hon.] Academic Scholarship; [pers.] My goal in life is to find ultimate happiness through the peace I find within myself. My poetry helps to find and reflects that peace. I was inspired to write by Rita Mae Brown and Sylvia Plath.; [a.] South Bend, IN

ISRAEL, MARIA ERITA M.
[pen.] Smile; [b.] November 15, 1961, Philippines; [p.] Alfredo Israel and Milagros Israel; [ed.] B. S. in Mass Communication; [occ.] Pediatric Medical Assistant; [pers.] "Man cannot live by bread alone"; [a.] Riverdale, MD

JACK, BARBARA J. W.
[b.] September 2, 1950, Natrona Hgts, PA; [p.] William and Betty Walker; [m.] Samuel L. Jack, March 29, 1969; [ch.] Joseph O., Frederick O.; [ed.] Highlands High School, Natrona Hgts, PA.; [occ.] Housewife, Poet, Children Stories, volunteer Mountainside Elementary, Ft. Carson, CO.; [memb.] VFW 6461; [hon.] 1987 Honorable Mention Award, 1988 Golden Poet Award 1989 Silver Poet Award, 1990 Honorable Mention and Editor's Choice Award, 1991 Golden Poet Award; [oth. writ.] Several other anologies, newspaper, nursing home newsletter, School District 8 Newsletter; [pers.] To love, to care and to be loved and to be cared for! I am enriched, replenished by the love given by my friends!; [a.] Colorado Springs, CO

JACKSON SR., EDWARD ELLIS
[b.] January 14, 1940, Pittsburgh, PA; [p.] Edward and Lillian (Deceased); [m.] Fifi L. Jackson, August 29, 1990; [ch.] Pandora, Stephanie, Edward Jr., Sean, Selena, Pele and Nakenya; [ed.] Geo. Westinghouse High School, Univ. of Ill Champ/Urbane Law Enforcement Management Course, Loop Jr. College, Johnnie Coleman Institute. Theology United States Army - 10 Military Schools; [occ.] Supervisor Distribution and Operations United States Postal Service Chicago, Ill. MPO; [memb.] National Association of Postal Superv. Christ Universal Temple - New thoughts Alliance Life Member, Christ Universal Temple Assembly; [hon.] United States Army/Reserves 25 yrs. A.A.M. ARCOM w/4 award device, GCM, VSM, OSM, NDSM with 1 Oak Leaf Cluster, AFRM 4 yrs., AFRM 10 yrs. with 2 device, A.S.M., Pres. Cit with 2 award device, Para-chutist wings, Drill Sgt. Badge, Wpn's M. Korea, Sharpshooter Badges.; [oth. writ.] Several shorts stories edited from my autobiography "The Ultimate Trip" publishing pending acceptance.; [pers.] Thoughts, feelings, words, actions and reactions: These five senses, emotions are the core to men's success or failure in his brief existence in this moment. As a man thinketh, so is he! The power of thoughts, through unspoken or spoken words is beyond the comprehension of mortal man.; [a.] Blue Island, IL

JACOBSEN, LINDA LEE
[pen.] Linda Lee Jacobsen; [b.] May 7, 1943, Harlan, IA; [p.] Bernard and Ann Stoltz; [m.] James Jacobsen, October 28, 1961; [ch.] Todd, Troy, Tyler; [ed.] Harlan High Sch., self-taught artist through my library of art books and attending workshops.; [occ.] Freelance artist, painting, V. owner of the art of Linda L.J.; [memb.] Iowa Artists; [hon.] Art Shows; [oth. writ.] Many poems written over the past several years, and writings on hand painted cards.; [pers.] Nature plays an important role in my poems, as does human and animal relationships interacting at times with nature, which creates beautiful thoughts that must be written down and many times painted.; [a.] Harlan, IA

JAMESON, ELIZABETH MARIE
[b.] November 7, 1981, Massachusetts; [p.] Catherine Shook; [ed.] I'm in 8th grade at Southwest Junior High; [a.] Palm Bay, FL

JANES, PATRICIA
[b.] September 10, 1950, Brockton, Mass; [p.] Rita Bousquet; [m.] Richard Janes, June 28, 1985,; [ch.] Candida, Mellisa Rebekah and Dellis; [ed.] High School Diploma CNA nurse training; [occ.] CNA; [hon.] Being a special CNA

JARAMILLO, KIMBERLY CECILIA
[b.] August 11, 1965, Denver, CO; [p.] Fred Pollack, Mary Ellen Pollack; [m.] Marvin Jaramillo, February 14, 1987; [ch.] Jennifer Ashley (10), Brittney Renee (7), Desiree Monique (5); [ed.] Highland High School; [occ.] Cook at Wishbone Restaurant (Westminster Colo.); [hon.] Who's Who Among American High School Students 1984 and several drama awards in high school; [oth. writ.] I've written three other poem's none of which have been published as of yet.; [pers.] All of the poems I have written were inspired by my Grandma Cecilia Ramirez who passed away on May 27, 1995 may her memory live forever.; [a.] Thornton, CO

JARRELL, ANITA LASHON
[b.] December 21, 1977, Baton Rouge, LA; [p.] Rev. and Mrs. Iverson Jarrell Sr.; [ed.] Southern University Honors College, Southern University Laboratory High; [occ.] Poet, Student; [memb.] Gamma Stars of Gamma Alpha Chi Fraternity, Southern University Student Ambassadors, Alumni - America's Homecoming Queen, Inc.; [hon.] Miss Southern High 1994-95, First Place: Sigma Gamma Rho Sorority 1994 Blade History Contest, (essay) Second Place: 1994 Sickle Cell America Foundation Essay Contest, Honorable Mention: Iliad Press Summer 1995 Awards Program (poetry); [oth. writ.] Several poems published in Perspective (an anthology), plays written for Southern University Laboratory High School; [pers.] My writing is a talent granted to me by God. My poetry is anointed and not only does it inspire me, but mostly all who read it. I began writing as a result of influence from Mrs. D. Elliott, my high school honors English teacher. Regret, love and happiness.; [a.] Baton Rouge, LA

JARVIS, NATASHA
[b.] June 22, 1967, Weybridge-on-Thames; [ch.] Cy Fair High, Texas Houston Community College,; [ed.] Executive Assistant; [pers.] My writing continues to open me to new levels of healing within my life.

JEFFERS, JEN
[b.] December 20, 1982, Rochester, NY; [p.] James Jeffers, Marie Jeffers; [ed.] Ontario Primary, Ontario Elementary, TCA Middle School; [occ.] 7th grade student; [hon.] Continental Math League first place, high honor roll; [a.] Ontario, NY

JEFTS, MICHAEL DAVID
[pen.] Michael David Jefts; [b.] August 10, 1959, Manchester, NH; [p.] Thomas J. Jefts Jr. and Carmel Ida Roy; [ch.] Shawnna Lynn Jefts; [ed.] Fort Hill High School Cumberland, M.D.; [occ.] Dispatcher and lighting specialist; [memb.] International Collectors Society; [oth. writ.] Dealing in blood (unsubmitted unpublished), 2. Soul of a vampire short story (unpublished), 3. Return of the Mask (unsubmitted unpublished), 4. Jeremy and Sherlock (A poem for Jeremy Brett); [pers.] Penning this poem was a joy and an inspiration that could only have come from a presence like Jeremy Brett. He touched my soul, the rest was easy.; [a.] Cumberland, MD

JENKINS, COLBY BRADFORD HOLMAN
[b.] March 14, 1977, Raleigh, NC; [p.] Dr. and Mrs. Ronald Bradford Jenkins; [ed.] Home Schooled, grades 4-10, Phillips Exeter Academy, Exeter, NH, grade 11 and Choate Rosemary Hall, Wallingford, CT, grade 13; [occ.] High School Student; [memb.] Georgia College Fencing Team, 1992-93, Phillips Exeter Fencing Team, 1995, U.S. Chess Federation, Vice Pres., Choate Rosemary Hall Chess Club, Milledgeville, GA Chess Club, Choate Rosemary Hall Improv. Club, 1995-96; [hon.] Eagle Scout, 1994, Black Belt in Tae Kwon Do, 1994, U.S. Chess Federation, First Place in Berkman Scholastic Championship, 1988, Atlanta Junior Active Championship, 1988, Georgia Junior Active Championship, 1998, Scholastic South Carolina Chess Association, 1991, Southern Scholastic Speed Tournament, 1991, Southern Scholastic Chess Tournament, 1991, Honorary Page in Georgia House of Representative, 1990.; [pers.] "If the sound of my face is heard hitting the ground, let it be known that it was the fall after an unsuccessful leap for a star."; [a.] Milledgeville, GA

JENSEN, DAMARIS JEAN
[pen.] D. J. Jensen; [b.] October 8, 1983, Tucson, AZ; [p.] Mary Warga and Scott Jensen; [ed.] 6th grade at Four Peaks Elementary School in Apache Junction, Arizona; [memb.] President of the Student Council; [hon.] Student of the Month, Scholar of Distinction; [pers.] I think not of what is bad but of what is good.; [a.] Apache Junction, AZ

JENSEN, SHARON L.
[pen.] Sharon Hansen Jensen, Sharon Lea Hansen; [b.] Gettysburg, South Dakota; [p.] Charles and Lillian Hanson; [m.] Divorced, 1984; [ch.] Eric, Dawn, Charles; [ed.] BS Degree-South Dakota State U. Majors: Secondary Education/ Music added English major 1984-University of Mary-Bismarck, ND; [occ.] Medical Transcriptionist, former music and English teacher; [a.] Bismarck, ND

JERIC, RICK
[pen.] RDJ; [b.] November 20, 1961, Cleveland; [p.] Ernest, Lauerne (Deceased); [m.] Kathy, May 10, 1980; [ch.] Joe, Cindy, Katie; [ed.] Euclid Senior High, Tri C, Lakeland Community; [occ.] Machine Tech. Eye Lighting International (Elina) also Musician at local clubs; [oth. writ.] Three dozen poems and about 50 songs.; [pers.] I

find the beauty of writing in choosing the perfect words in both sound and meaning, whether its in my poetry or my songs.; [a.] Madison, OH

JEZ, FAITH
[b.] November 25, 59, Wilkes-Barre, PA; [p.] Lil and Daniel Tomassacci; [m.] John Jez, August 26, 1978; [ch.] John age 15, Amanda age 11; [ed.] High School Graduate, presently taking College Course for Children's literature; [occ.] Marketing researcher; [pers.] I try to reach the heart in my writing and through the heart the mind. When both the heart and the mind are touched - then you make a difference.; [a.] Plains, PA

JEZ, JENNIFER
[pen.] Jenn Jez; [b.] March 17, 1981, South Hadley; [p.] Steven S. Jez, Shelia L. Scherlin; [ed.] South Hadley High School; [occ.] A student at South Hadly High School, a dancer, at the dance shop.; [memb.] The Dance Shop; [pers.] In my poetry I always write from experience, and my heart. Nothing is ever just thrown together for a piece of poetry. I always say, "It has to come from the Heart."; [a.] South Hadley, MA

JOHNSON, CHARLENE L.
[pen.] Charyl Hobbs; [b.] November 1, 1932, Detroit, MI; [p.] Edward and Alva Hobbs; [m.] Ralph E. Johnson, September 26, 1952; [ch.] Elaine, Ralph, Jean, Richard, Timothy, Kerry; [ed.] Clifton Rural Elementary, Romeo MI Romeo High School, Romeo (Graduate) Eastern Michigan University Ypsilanti MI (Elementary Education - 1 year); [occ.] Secretary, Nebraska State Probation; [memb.] St. Joseph Altar Society, Catholic Daughters of America Yorkshire Playhouse; [pers.] I believe that every heart is a storehouse of treasures longing to be expressed. Thus it is my hope that my verses gleaned from a lifetime of experiences may touch the heart of my readers.; [a.] York, NE

JOHNSON, GEORGE W.
[pen.] George W. Johnson; [b.] August 11, 1936, Goodhue County, Minn; [p.] Erb and Lillian Johnson; [m.] Jolene, July 4, 1994; [ch.] Three; [ed.] High School - (GED); [occ.] Semi-Retired also drive school bus; [memb.] Church; [hon.] 36 year's, driving truck. 1 plague one million miles, numerous awards.; [oth. writ.] 2 Books expressions to share Vol. I and Vol II unpublished, would like to get them published!; [pers.] I make my book's up, in wooden cover's.; [a.] Hot Springs, SD

JOHNSON, GLENDA
[pen.] Hankuf; [b.] March 11, 1965, Chicago, IL; [p.] Jimmy Baxter, Anita Johnson; [ch.] Brian Kortell Johnson; [ed.] Frazier Elementary School; [occ.] Chicago Housing Authority Security Officer.; [oth. writ.] Several other poems that have not yet been read by the public.; [pers.] I write in order to reach people, to make them think and to give them a view on subjects unlike any other.; [a.] Chicago, IL

JOHNSON, GLENN D.
[b.] April 2, 1949, Hellier City, KY; [p.] Frank and Verna; [m.] Lula Sue, December 11, 1993; [ed.] One Year Wayne State U.; [occ.] City of Detroit; [memb.] Southwest Alane Club; [oth. writ.] Point of Touch Wings; [pers.] Wife, kids, 2 dogs birds, house, Mortgage not a philosophical place in my mind; [a.] Detroit, MI

JOHNSON, JEREMY D.
[pen.] Jeremy Johnson; [b.] October 30, 1970, Reno, NV; [p.] Robert Johnson, Tanya McDougall Johnson; [ed.] Reno High School, University of Nevada - Reno, Santa Monica College; [occ.] Instructional Specialist (English), Santa Monica High School; [hon.] Several Scholarships for Journalism a few years ago.; [oth. writ.] Several poems published in small literary magazines across the country.; [pers.] To constantly be putting your ideas, beliefs, your very self on the line daily: That is what a poet does. He cannot hide in books, they consume him, he cannot escape the world, it surrounds him. He lives in the belly of the Gods!; [a.] Los Angeles, CA

JOHNSON, JOSEPH R.
[b.] August 14, 1934, Philadelphia, PA; [p.] Mr. and Mrs. Joseph R. Johnson; [m.] Donna Louise Milan, February 14, 1995; [ch.] Grown and married; [ed.] Atlantic City High School Lincoln University, Penna Pasadena City College; [occ.] Book Seller/Shipping and Receiving Mngr. - Book City - Hollywood, CA, Graphic Arts & Design; [memb.] Omega Psi Phi fraternity, Free & Accepted Mason [pers.] Love is all there is. Love is eternal. Love is law. I wish mankind would learn this. It's almost the 21st century and people are still killing people. The human race is inhabiting the planet Earth.; [a.] Hollywood, CA

JOHNSON, KRISTINA ANN
[b.] May 15, 1985, St. Paul, Minn; [p.] Margaret, Charles (Chuck); [ed.] Started at Creative Center (Pre School) then turning point (Montessori) now in 5th grade at St. Martin of Tours; [occ.] Student; [memb.] National Geographic; [hon.] I won 1st, 3rd, 4th place in track meet; [oth. writ.] "A Rainbow" (poem), "Lonesome Lily" (Haiku); [pers.] I like poems that are calm and gentle.; [a.] Los Angeles, CA

JOHNSON, LAURA L.
[b.] March 26, 1973, Mullins Hospital, SC; [p.] Mrs. Edith Johnson and the late Mr. Miley Johnson; [ed.] Aynor High School Horry Georgetown Technical College; [occ.] Data Entry Operator Canal Wood Industries, Conway S.C.; [memb.] Mount Herman Baptist Church; [oth. writ.] Several writings published in local newspaper.; [pers.] Through my writings I hope to honour and glorify my Lord and Savior Jesus Christ, for His eternal blessings in my life. What a blessing if someone in return should receive a blessing when reading my writings.; [a.] Galivants Ferry, SC

JOHNSON, MARCELLA S.
[pen.] Marci; [b.] August 4, 1977, Fairmont, WV; [p.] Gerald and Deborah Johnson; [ed.] Fairmont Senior High School, Currently attending Fairmont State College; [oth. writ.] Just a personal notebook: It's a collection of thoughts made into poems and prose - a rhyming diary.; [pers.] I love symbolism and deep meaning, making people think about my works: Most people don't get the true meanings - I enjoy explaining them, and watching their faces say, "Ahhh."; [a.] Fairmont, WV

JOHNSON, PAMELA A.
[b.] January 26, 1955, Portsmouth, VA; [p.] Willifrede L. West, Ruby R. West; [m.] Luther Johnson Jr., September 6, 1975; [ed.] Mark Morris High School University of Oregon; [occ.] Supervisor, Postal Service; [memb.] Sergeants Association Ebone Eyes Women's Group University of Oregon Alumni Assoc.; [hon.] Deans List; [pers.] My writings come from the heart. I have been greatly inspired by the writings of Maya Angelou; [a.] Portland, OR

JOHNSON, PENNY
[pen.] Penny Johnson; [b.] July 1, 1940, Danville, KY; [p.] Irene Sebastian, Bufor Dearr; [m.] William Evan Johnson, July 15, 1958; [ch.] William E. Jr. (Buddy) Robert, Anthony (Roggie) Johnson; [ed.] Graduated Famous Writer's School Life: Memember and Graduate Newspaper Institute of America N.Y; [occ.] Free-lance, Writer; [memb.] National Writer's Club International Order of Merit-I.S.O. (advisor) American Biographical Institute; [hon.] Semi-finalist North American Poetry Open, Editors Choice Awards, Who's who in Poetry Woman of the year - A.B.I., Honorary Doct or of letters London, England; [oth. writ.] "Awesome", "A Bouquet of Poet", "Surprise", "Fall's Fabulous Gifts", "The Symbol", "Sensational Season", "I Will", "Comfort from my Grand parents", (All published poems); [pers.] How best to teach a lesson, inspire others, give thanks, ask and answer a question. Search for the truth-send out love to others-beautify the world-"Poetry" is "How"; [a.] Lexington, KY

JOHNSON, RODNEY
[pen.] Sonny Jim, Wane Lake; [b.] April 23, 1963, Los Angeles, CA; [p.] James and Doris Young; [m.] Veronica Avila-Johnson, Nov. 8, 1994; [ch.] Veronica Bridgette, Miles Austin Curtis; [ed.] Eagle Rock High, Pasadena City College, CSULA; [occ.] Pastry Chef, Oaks of Pasadena, CA; [memb.] CCAC, Bean Town Writers Club, Institue of Corrections, ACF; [oth. writ.] Currently working on first novel escape from Paradise not published; [pers.] I seek a delicate balance between the shakes of too little and the Abyss of too much. Influenced by Noir worldwide; [a.] Pasadena, CA;

JOHNSTON, MARGARET
[b.] October 2, 1926, Oakland, CA; [p.] Edgar Turgeon, Margie Turgeon; [m.] Ralph W. Johnston (Deceased), September 13, 1950; [ch.] Peggy Ann, Eileen Kathryn, Carol Mae, Bonnie Lynn, Robert Warren, Betty Jean, David Alan; [ed.] Live Oak Union High School of Morgan Hill, Salinas Jr. College, Samuel Merritt Hospital School of Nursing; [occ.] Retired R.N.; [memb.] Volunteer Driver for

American Dancer Society, San Martin Presbyterian Church and Choir, Flower Lover's Club, Happy Sounds Singing Group; [hon.] Helen Amaro Caregivers' Award, San Jose Mercury News Doer's Profile, Woman of the Year Ann Arbor, Michigan 1968; [pers.] I enjoy writing poetry for my family and friends.; [a.] Morgan Hill, CA

JONES, BOB
[b.] December 17, 1941, Riverside, CA; [p.] Howard and Jean Jones; [m.] Sarah Martin, June 17, 1995; [ch.] Melannie Schliebe, Dennis Jones, Kim Mattingly, Bill Sutherland; [ed.] UC Berkeley, BA Zoology, M.S. Forestry; [occ.] Teacher, Mead Jr. High Mead, WA; [a.] Spokane, WA

JONES, CAROL
[pen.] C. J. Jones; [b.] March 12, 1939, Delaware Co, PA; [m.] John Paul Jones, March 29, 1958; [ch.] Jean, Jotton, Joan, and Jim; [ed.] High School Darby PA; [memb.] Asbury United Methodist Church - Mothers March of Dimes; [oth. writ.] Several poems that I just read to children at home or at my church; [pers.] I just start to write when I am travelling along the highways. And by ways of life.

JONES, CRYSTAL DAVENPORT
[b.] May 25, 1963, Plymouth, NC; [p.] Donald A. Davenport, Joyce J. Davenport; [m.] Claude Byron Jones, December 31, 1988; [pers.] Puddles and Brooks reminds me of God's quiet ways amidst the storms, special thanks to my husband, byron. Thank you for being there.; [a.] Goldsboro, NC

JONES, FLORENCE M.
[b.] April 11, 1939, West Columbia, TX; [p.] Isaiah and Lu Ethel McNeil; [m.] Waldo D. Jones, May 29, 1995; [ch.] Roderick, Wanda and Erna; [ed.] Prairie View A&M University BS (Cum Laude) 1961 and MED 1968 Post Graduate: Rice University, University of Houston and St. Thomas, Univ.; [occ.] 1. Piano Instructor 2. Writer 3. story teller; [memb.] Life Member: Texas Retired Teachers Association, Distinguished Life Member: International Society of Poets, Association for Childhood International, Oak Meadows Church of God, National Women of Achievement National, State and Local Story Telling Associations; [hon.] The National Library of Poetry Editor's Choice Award, Outstanding Achievements in Education, Letter of Recognition: Pres, Bill Clinton, Gov. Ann Richards and George W. Bush, Gold Cup-Music National Women of Achievement and Diamond Key Award; [oth. writ.] (1) Science Modules for Houston Ind. Sch. District, (2) Gifted and Talented Program for Petersen Elem. School, (3) Poems published in several anthologies; [pers.] Poetry writing is a dynamic enjoyable way to write stories in a condensed form. In my poems, I try to convey the idea that our lives powerfully affect the lives of others.; [a.] Houston, TX

JONES, GWENDOLYN
[pen.] Gwendolyn; [b.] January 6, Texas; [m.] Ronald R. Jones; [ch.] Two; [pers.] Rise above yourself - be all that you can be.... fly as an Eagle; [a.] Los Angeles, CA

JONES, MARY LOUISE FREEMAN
[b.] April 6, 1948; Belle Garde, FL; [p.] Jack and Gussie Freeman; [p.] Jack and Gussie Freeman; [m.] John David Jones, December 12, 1971; [ch.] Dameritrais Jones; [ed.] Lake Shore High School, Belle Glade, FL; [occ.] Apartment owner and manager; Mt. Zion Ame Church, Belle Glade, Fl;

JONES, MICHAEL D.
[pen.] Michael D. Jones; [b.] February 17, 1942, Crowell, TX; [p.] George and Bertha Jones; [m.] Frances A. Jones, November 12, 1982; [ch.] Letwixt the two of us 7; [ed.] 7th grade; [occ.] Own my own business; [oth. writ.] I have written over 3,000 poems and 300 songs. With only one poem published, in sea of treasures. Two little doggies. At this place in time I am totally unknown.; [pers.] My philosophy in plain and simple I believe, that of God's word the bible, to have a knowledge. Is for more important than a P.H.D. from th every finest college. I write to the Glory of my God; [a.] Houston, TX

JONES, MICHAEL JAY
[b.] April 9, 1958; [p.] Roy J. Jones/Jean C. Jones; [m.] Monique G. Jones, July 16, 1988; [ch.] Heather Nicole/Jean Elizabeth; [ed.] Perryville High University of Maryland Fire and Rescue Institute.; [occ.] Car Inspector, Amtrak National Railroad Passenger Corp.; [memb.] Community Fire Co. of Perryville Maryland, Inc. The Ashley Alumni Association; [pers.] The poem that I wrote came from the heart. My higher power (GOD) also helped me. "Let Go Let Go"; [a.] Perryville, MD

JONES, PRENTISS
[pen.] Penny Jones; [b.] July 13, 1919, Kenton, TN; [p.] Columbus E. Jones, Molly M. Jones; [m.] Delia Jones, June 5, 1965; [ch.] Two; [ed.] High school graduated 1936 at Roswell high school Roswell, New Mexico.; [occ.] (1949-1979) Retired from Western Greyho Viud Lines (Driver) 30 years of service.; [memb.] Perry Technical Institute; [hon.] French Foreign Legion 1937 to 1941 was discharge at Sidibel-Abbes in North Africa, then entered the U.S. Army Dec. 8, 1941. And discharged October 25, 1945 sworn in at Santa Fe, N.M. discharged at Plattsburg N.Y. (Plattsburg Barracks) (New York); [oth. writ.] This is the first one that I have entered in a contest. I have wrote a number of poems concerning my friends of things that they have done such as trips and vacation and their lives.; [pers.] When I have nothing else to do I love to sit down and do poetry especially in the earthly morning hours with no one to interrupt of hinder my thoughts. I love to think of the good things that I have done in the past.; [a.] Las Cruses, NM

JONES, REGINALD D.
[pen.] Reggie Jones; [b.] October 16, 1959, Berkeley, CA; [p.] Jeanine Jackson; [ed.] Colby Community Juco Kansas State University Hill City High; [occ.] Sales; [oth. writ.] No other poems published at this time; [pers.] Without trying to sound too philosophical, I simply try to write about personal experiences that people can easily relate to.; [a.] Kansas City, KS

JONES, TIFFANY
[b.] September 26, 1983, Laurel, MS; [p.] Walter and Felishia Jones; [ed.] Quitman Lower Elementary, Quitman Upper Elementary, Quitman Junior High School; [hon.] Superintendent Honor Roll, Student of the Month, Attendance Award, Educational Excellence (given by Bill Clinton), USM gifted studies award, High Average Award; [oth. writ.] Written several but haven't sent off to published.; [pers.] I write to express myself and my feelings. When I can't talk to anyone I write.; [a.] Pachuta, MS

JONES, VANN G. C.
[b.] June 15, 1967, Spokane, WA; [p.] Dr. T.C. Jones, Mrs. Cintorie Jones; [ed.] Callaway High School, Togaloo College, BA - Economics; [occ.] Sales and Marketing Analyst; [memb.] Alpha Phi Alpha Fraternity Red Cross of America, Boston Ski Party; [oth. writ.] 'Passion', '1 Nation'; [pers.] I believe you can accomplish anything you want, if you but your mind to it.; [a.] Boston, MA

JONES, WILLIAM H.
[pen.] William Henry Jones, W.H. Jones, Bill Jones; [b.] April 1, 1924, Black Diamond, WA; [p.] Helenor Jones - Father (Deceased); [m.] Barbara A. Jones, May 17, 1960; [ch.] Denise Lynn Williams, Robert Jeffery Jones; [ed.] B.A. San Diego State, Navel School of Hospital Administration; [occ.] Captain, U.S. Navy (Ret); [memb.] (1) Federal Health Care Executives Institute Alumni Assn., (2) Fleet Reserve Assn., (3) Distinguished Member - International Society of Poets; [hon.] Legion of Merit (Navy), Numerous Service Medals and awards, Graduated with honors 5 military schools, Advanced from Apprentice Seaman to Captain during Naval Career.; [oth. writ.] (1) The National Library of Poetry: "Beyond the Stars", "Best Poems of 1996", "Spirit of the Age", (2) Sparrowgrass Poetry Forum, Inc. "Treasured Poems of 1995", "Poetic Voices of America", "Treasured Poems of America", (3) Oroville Register, Oroville, CA. "The Infamous Still in Oroville"; [pers.] I believe in personal achievement, inspiring others to fulfill their dreams, at peace with self and others, all with a sense of humor, dedication and perspective.; [a.] Lake San Marcos, CA

JOOS, STEVE
[b.] February 4, 1955, Peoria, IL; [p.] Charles, Shirley; [ed.] Peoria Public Schools (Richwoods H.S.) Illinois Central College Bradley University.; [occ.] Sports writer, Posey Country News, Poseyville, Ind.; [memb.] Apostolic Christian Church; [hon.] Outstanding Staff writer, Bradley Scout, 1977-78. Honorable mention best column, Inland Press Association, 1994; [oth. writ.] Several poems published invarious anthologies and the entertainment section, of

the Springfield (Ill. Journal-Register; [pers.] My poetry deals with the various sites and sounds of my life and perhaps everyone's life: Faith, Country, surroundings and that certain someone; [a.] Poseyville, IN

JORDAN, KRISTI
[b.] September 8, 1972, Nashville, TN; [p.] Harold and Geraldine Jordan; [ed.] Wellesley College (graduated in 1994), currently enrolled in Doctoral Program at Vanderbilt University; [occ.] Student (graduate); [memb.] Alpha Kappa Alpha Sorority Incorporated, YWCA; [oth. writ.] Poetry (nonpublished) short stories and other writing in the works; [pers.] In all my efforts to attain poetic stature, I have learned that rejection is the bittersweet candy of accomplishment when taken in small doses.; [a.] Nashville, TN

JOYCE, CARRIE
[b.] October 16, 1981, Ellsworth, ME; [p.] Matthew and Candis Joyce; [ed.] Eight grade; [occ.] Student; [hon.] Honor and High Honor Rolls, Local and State essay contests; [a.] Minturn, ME

KAMINSKI, BONNIE
[pen.] Bonnie Seefeldt Kaminski; [b.] February 24, 1950, Marinette, WI; [p.] Lawrence, Adeline; [m.] Donald Kaminski, October 3, 1970; [ch.] Corre Lawrence, Tirsa Adeline; [ed.] Lena High School, NWTC Green Bay, WI; [occ.] Licensed Practical Nurse; [oth. writ.] Mother's Day Poem "M is for the moments brought by Blue Mountains Arts Visions of Boulder Co. 1993-94 was reprinted 1994-95. Collection of poems in Essentials of Mental Health Care, Planning and Interventions 1986, WB Saunders. Also Colors of Beauty, to hide the sorrow, about child abuse. Freedom Prayer, for women of domestic abuse for Rainbow House. Also Dax Bonnie's personal poems from the heart as a hobby.; [pers.] My poems are a gift from God. His gift has brought comfort, happiness, and new understanding to those who have received them.; [a.] Coleman, WI

KASAKOV, VIVIAN
[b.] April 11, 1931, South River, NJ; [p.] Antonina and Prokop Makarus; [m.] Michael Kasakov (Deceased); [memb.] I am a member of the St. Peter and Paul Russian Orthodox Church, South River, N.J.; [pers.] My poems are inspired by the deep feelings within my heart, influenced by the people who have touched my life throughout the years, and by the strong faith that has always been a part of me.; [a.] Spotswood, NJ

KAYE, CAREN
[b.] March 12, 1951, NYC; [p.] Anita and Kenneth Kaye; [m.] Renny Temple, November 15, 1980; [ch.] Jessica Temple age 14, William Temple age 9; [ed.] H.S. of the Performing Arts, NYC, Carnegie-Mellon University, Antioch University; [occ.] I am a mind/body educator, Parent Educator and have a masters in Clinical Psychology.; [memb.] I am a member of: The Screen Actors, The Californian Therapist, Founder of the Academy of Mind-Body Medicine; [hon.] Drama Loque Award for Outstanding Work as an Actress. Written in Who's Who in Entertainment. An Ordained Minister in counseling and Honorary Doctorate in Theology.; [oth. writ.] I have written for several periodicals on parenting and many poems have been printed. I am co-founder and contributing editor to E.P.C. (Educational and Psychological Connecting) Guild.; [pers.] My philosophy subscribes to our personal committed to move from complaisance to resolve - we cannot control our circumstances, only our perceptions.; [a.] Los Angeles, CA

KEEGAN, HEATHER MARIE
[pen.] Heather Marie Keegan; [b.] September 7, 1984, Neptune, NJ; [p.] Gerald Keegan and Susan Keegan; [ed.] Currently attending Walnut Street Elementary School in Toms River, New Jersey; [occ.] Student Walnut Street Elementary School; [memb.] Girl Scout 6 years, Young Astronaut Club, Computer Club, Dance Centre Competition Tap Class, Toms River Girls Softball Team, School Chorus; [hon.] Young Authors 1994, Omni Literature, Omni Math, Omni Music; [oth. writ.] Many other poems, none submitted for publication. I also enjoy writing short stories, none submitted for publication.; [pers.] I like to write poems that make people feel happy.; [a.] Toms River, NJ

KEITH, HARLOW J.
[b.] May 31, 1953, Toledo, OH; [p.] Frank and Barbara Keith; [m.] Mitzi Keith, June 23, 1979; [ch.] Marisa, Heather, Amanda; [ed.] Kenyon College (Undergrad), Old State University (grad); [occ.] Consultant; [hon.] 3rd Degree Black Belt Tae Kwon Do; [pers.] I hope people enjoy reading my work as much as I enjoy writing it.; [a.] Gahanna, OH

KELLER, ESTHER HAHN
[pen.] Esther Hahn Keller; [b.] June 15, 1909, Salem, OR; [p.] Russian; [m.] Del F. Keller, May 1936; [ed.] Salem High School graduate, Monmuth State Teachers College, McKay Business College, Los Angeles; [occ.] Retired; [memb.] Golden Gate Church of Religious Science, Ernest Holmes College Institute R.S., Artists Embassy Int., Beta Sigma Phi, Business Sorority; [hon.] Poetry readings in Golden Gate Church R.S., Poetry readings Spring Gardens; [oth. writ.] Poems in Spiritual Arts, Letter News, Poem, Friendship Circle, Artists International Painting Award; [pers.] My intention is to look for the cold in all my life's experiences I call the process of living adventures in self-discovery; [a.] San Francisco, CA

KELLY, ANNIE L.
[b.] March 17, 1922, Grenada, MS; [p.] Winston Roland, Fannie Roland; [m.] Matt Flowers, August 4, 1939; [ch.] Joanne, Nell, Barbara, Johnny Lee, etc.; [ed.] 10th grade; [occ.] Housewife; [hon.] 90-91 Poet of the Year Merit Award; [oth. writ.] Autobiography, several poems; [pers.] Married twice and mother of 16 children and grandmom and great grandmom of 50 children and love them all!; [a.] Saint Paul, MN

KEMP, ASHLEY
[pen.] Ashley Kemp; [b.] April 1, 1977, Newnan, GA; [p.] Brantley and Brenda Kemp; [ed.] (H.S.) Brentwood Academy in Brentwood TN, University of Alabama (Tuscaloosa) Freshman; [occ.] Student; [hon.] High School Musicals and plays - Academy Singer Award, Peter Jenkins Writer's Award, Volleyball (4 years); [oth. writ.] Poems published in New Girl Times (NY); [pers.] I write about topics that other people my age can relate to. It's basically whatever is on my mind. I believe life is a ball and if you don't look around once in a while - you might miss it.; [a.] Nashville, TN

KENKEL, LAURA
[b.] April 15, 1982, Cincinnati, OH; [p.] Henry and Connie Kenkel; [pers.] In my writing, I draw out my emotions with words. All art is "drawn" with different mediums.; [a.] Cincinnati, OH

KENNEDY, ELVIRA E. STEWART
[pen.] Stewart Kennedy; [b.] September 19, 1945, Raleigh, NC; [p.] Wilma and Lester Stewart; [m.] George Kennedy (Deceased - July 29, 1992), September 20, 1980; [ch.] (Twins) Sean and Troy; [ed.] St. Augustine's College, Raleigh, N.C., B.A. Degree, Long Island University, N.Y., M.A. Pace University, Dean's List, Honors Program, presently attending fashion design school; [occ.] Author and Fashion Designer, Senior Rehabilitation Therapist - 21 yrs., retired 2/91 (from 1/70 - 2/91); [memb.] St. Stephen's Episcopal Church, Pearl River N.Y., Hope Baptist Church, Newark N.J. (presently), National Association of Female Executives - (NAFE); [hon.] Who's Who in American Women 1992, Who's Who in Women Internationally - 1991; [oth. writ.] Many in poetry, novel in completion stages "In Thy Fathers House", short plays.; [a.] Maplewood, NJ

KEPLER, PATRICIA B.
[b.] October 16, 1942, Attica, IN; [p.] Ralph E. and Mary J. Smart; [m.] Rex Frederick Kepler, July 17, 1978; [ed.] Attica High School; [occ.] Taught Communications for Ivy Tech. College, Previous Business Owner, Executive Secretarial Service, District Administrator; [hon.] Writing Safety First Article; [oth. writ.] Short story "All I Got Was A Dozen Eggs and A Head Of Lettuce", `Safety First' article.; [pers.] Look in your heart and lead the way for others.

KERN, THOMAS J.
[b.] April 26, 1974, Marysville, WA; [p.] Scott and Dianne Kern; [ed.] Marysville Pilchuck High School, U.S. Army Infantry — Ft. Benning Georgia, Ft. Hood Texas, Ft. Irving California, Ft. Polk, Louisianna; [occ.] Executive Assistant, Computer Coordinator; [hon.] Battalion Coin (Military), National Defense Ribbon (Military); [oth. writ.] Several unpublished works. Military Articles Future Publication with The National Library of Poetry; [pers.] I try to illustrate the fact that we are a hopeless species. Yet I also try to show that there is still hope if we open our hearts and our minds.; [a.] Everett, WA

KETTERER, IAN L.
[pen.] Kat; [b.] February 2, 1966, Rochester, NY; [p.] Preston and Ellie Ketterer; [m.] Tammy M. Ketterer, August 31, 1985; [ch.] Katherine Louise, Ashlee Nicole; [ed.] Pittsford Sutherland H.S., Park College; [occ.] Military (currently in Sarajevo, Bosnia-Herzegovina); [memb.] Holy Ghost Headquarters, Church of God In Christ, Feagin's #17, Prince Hall Masonic Lodge; [hon.] Various Military Awards; [pers.] Marriage is a sacred union, instituted by God Himself. I strive to convey my beliefs on paper just how much my beloved wife means to me.; [a.] Augusta, GA

KICSOW, HERBERT L.
[pen.] Herbert L. Kicsow; [b.] March 10, 1923, Missouri; [p.] Martin W. and Rena Alice Kicsow; [m.] Betty J. Kicsow (Deceased), December 8, 1945; [ch.] Terry Lee, Rosalie, Marla, Karen; [ed.] 7th grade; [occ.] Retired; [memb.] Moose Lodge, V.F.W., Legion; [oth. writ.] Several; [pers.] Have been writing for about three months. Have written about one hundred seventy poems.; [a.] Bellflower, CA

KIEL, MATHEW K.
[pen.] Matt McGee, M. K. Kiel, Kris Kiel; [b.] March 1, 1950, Augusta, GA; [p.] Deceased - Viola McGee (Native American), Orrie Kiel (Bavarian Immigrant); [m.] Divorced - March 11, 1992, Married - March 26, 1986; [ed.] Graduate of high school, in small town South Carolina, in 1969, I am a loving, laughing, sand and living man (with an excellent mind) who grew up severely abused, impoverished, obese, bi-racial and multi-cultural in the 50's and 60's. Now that is an education only life can provide.; [occ.] Student of everything. (I've been "permanently" and "totally" disabled for the last 9 years by a hereditary spinal cord disease).; [memb.] Humanity, A.S.P.C.A., Animal's Best Friend, National Wildlife Federation.; [hon.] Every moment of sincere, selfless love, I've ever received, three times having held new-born babies, to have once saved a human life, to have twice had my live saved by another, every second of sincere, selfless love I've every given. To have lived as totally as I could every day I have lived. To have been touched by God.; [oth. writ.] A large number of songs, only 4 of which have ever been published, essays, poetry, limericks, ghost-writing of technical articles and some speeches, jokes, puns and humorous, compositions. I am the author of several widely known works of public domain, by the great Anonymous...; [pers.] I want to become educated enough to lose the very ability to hate. To always remember that the real measure of our wealth is in how much we have given, and the truest success is in how often and deeply we have made others feel loved and valued.; [a.] Lawrence, MI

KILLMON, EDITH RODGERS JOYNES
[b.] October 12, 1953, Nassawadox, VA; [p.] Arthur W. Joynes, Sr., Lavinia Ashby Joynes; [m.] Bruce R. Killmon; [ch.] Maria, David, Adam; [ed.] Central High School, Painter, Va., Va. Commonwealth University, Richmond, Va., Peninsula General Hospital School of Nursing, Salisbury, Md., Eastern Shore Community College, Melfa, Va.; [occ.] Registered Nurse, Maternal-Child Health Unit, Northampton-Accomack Memorial Hospital, Nassawadox, Va.; [hon.] Salutatorian of high school graduating class, Certified as an Inpatient Obstetric Nurse (R.N.C.) 12-1-95; [oth. writ.] Have written many other poems, none previously published.; [pers.] My poems express my feelings about life and about living in harmony with nature in a rural setting.; [a.] Eastville, VA

KINARD, CYNTHIA COCHRAN
[b.] December 8, 1952, Columbia, SC; [p.] Thomas L. and Eleanor B. Cochran; [m.] James B. Kinard, April 10, 1976; [ed.] Franklin High, Franklin, NC, Western Carolina University, Cullowhee, NC; [occ.] Portrait Artist (Watercolors); [memb.] Welcome Home Baptist Church, Traphill, NC, Blue Ridge Arts Clan, Alleghany County Arts Council, Friends of the Library; [hon.] Franklin Rotary Club Honors Award and Banquet - all four years high school. Graduated with honors - WCU winner Highlands Art Exhibit Juried Show.; [oth. writ.] My other writings are unpublished at this time - they are poetry and 2 novels (which I am still writing); [pers.] Most of my poetry is spiritual in nature and is intended to honor and glorify Jesus Christ.; [a.] Sparta, NC

KINCAID, CATHIE
[pen.] Cakrak; [b.] November 25, 1959; [ch.] Ryan Kincaid; [ed.] Newark High School, Mt. Summit College; [occ.] State Farm Insurance, Administrative Secretary, Portrait Artist; [memb.] International Training in Communications (ITC Club), Spring Hills Baptist Church, (Drama/Puppet Performing Group); [hon.] Art Awards, H.S. Central Ohio League Doubles Champion (Tennis); [oth. writ.] Short story - Marianna and the Pearl, numerous poems, programs and bulletin design; [pers.] Let a positive outlook be in everything you do, there's already too much sadness in our world. Touch a person's heart with poetry, and you've made a new friend, whether they are near... or far.; [A.] Newark, OH

KINDRED, ALAN DEWAYNE
[pen.] Alan Kindred; [b.] March 6, 1978, DeKalb Co, AL; [p.] Herman and Claudean Kindred; [ed.] 10th grade - age 16 yrs., old; [occ.] Student (Deceased); [hon.] Just school awards; [oth. writ.] Alan was 15 years old in 1993 when he wrote this poem. When he was 16 years old in 1994 he was killed in an automobile accident.; [pers.] As the poem expresses Alan was a very caring person. He especially loved babies and the elderly. Alan was our only child and we gave him a good life, but he was never selfish, he always had a lot of compassion for the under privileged.; [a.] Rainsville, AL

KING, DONNA E.
[b.] September 1, 1965, New Bedford, MA; [p.] Joan and Emil King; [ed.] University of Massachusetts, Dartmouth, Received B.A. in Sociology, University of South Florida working towards M.S.W.; [occ.] State of Florida Public Assistance; [memb.] International Society of Poets; [oth. writ.] Published work includes "First Night", featured in Walk Through Paradise, "Structure" featured in Mirrors of the Soul, "The Edge" featured in Reflections of Life; [pers.] My writing comes from the heart and soul. I want to feel others read. I want to touch the lives of others however distant or near. My poetry is derived from a personal view of my endeavors in my life.; [a.] Sebring, FL

KING, FRANCES H.
[pen.] Fran; [b.] August 31, 1929, Atlantic City, NJ; [p.] John Johnson and the late Mary Johnson; [m.] The late Jerry L. King Sr., July 3, 1954; [ch.] Jerry King Jr., and Donna Mason; [ed.] Graduate of Atl. City High Class of 1947; [occ.] Retired - American General Finance - 21 yrs; [memb.] Main Landers Civic Club, Ivy Leaf Chapter #18 - Order of Eastern Stars, Mount Pleasant Baptist and Church Missionaries, Deaconess, Usher Bd and Coordinators Club; [hon.] Business and Professional Women, State of New Jersey, Black Writers Award - March 1990, Golden Poet 1990 Award, Words of Poetry Merit Certificate - March 1990, Honorable Mention - Words of Poetry; [oth. writ.] 3 poems published in the "Words of Poetry" Anthology 1991, Poetry Readings - January 1995, Mount Zion Baptist Church. Feb 1995 - Pleasantville Public Library and April 1995 - Pleasantville Public Library; [pers.] God is the center of my life and has given me bright hopes for the future. It is from this source I find peace - consolation and inspiration.; [a.] Pleasantville, NJ

KING, LINDA SUE
[pen.] Linda King, L.K.; [b.] February 1, 1954, Dallas, OR (Polk County); [p.] Clarence and Elizabeth Hildebrand (Deceased); [m.] Clarence King, October 5, 1987; [ed.] General Education, Journal Writing, Class in Diabetes Education; [occ.] Home Care Nurse; [memb.] Member of Congregational Church, formerly Christian Women Clubs and TOPS (Take Off Pounds Weight Club), YWCA; [hon.] Former track (running and relays awards), Weight Club - Losing and Achieved Goal Weight (ribbons and a trophy), Arts and Crafts Award for 4-H "Be Kind To Animals"; [oth. writ.] "A Mother". It was read at my mothers funeral service, I prepared it for a "Mothers Day Memory"; [pers.] "I was inspired by my husband love and compassion for people and his positive attitude and way of living"; [a.] Salem, OR

KINSEY, TIFFANY
[b.] November 27, 1982, Shreveport, LA; [p.] Carol and Steven Click; [ed.] 7th grade; [hon.] In 1994, I went to the Young Writers Conference. President's Education Award, Culture Awareness Week Poster and Essay Contests, "A" Honor Roll; [pers.] My granddad (Rio Bruno) can write really well, and I feel that he has taught me a lot of what I know, and not just about writing. Writing is definitely my life.; [a.] Fort Madison, IA

KIRBY, DELMAN
[b.] March 22, Chilhowie, VA; [p.] Dewey Blewins and Rosa L. Green; [m.] Harold W. Kirby, October 17, 1952; [ch.] 5; [ed.] Graduated

from Charleston Beauty Academy and Owner and Mg., the Dilmas Family Hair Care and Hawaii Surf Tanning Salon.; [occ.] Beautician; [oth. writ.] Love writing, songs and poems, plan to write short stories, and writing comes easy for me.; [pers.] Determination and think positive and lots of effort.

KIRSCH, M. KRISTI
[pen.] M. K. Kirsch; [b.] March 17, 1970, Portland, OR; [p.] John Kirsch, Paula Kirsch; [ed.] Westside Christian High, Liberty University, Calvary Chapel Bible College; [occ.] Wedding Coordinator; [hon.] Homecoming Queen 1988; [oth. writ.] Several unpublished poems and other reflective writings.; [pers.] "To know wisdom and instruction, to perceive the words of understanding, to receive the instruction of wisdom, justice, and judgment, and equity" (Proverbs 1:2-3); [a.] Inglewood, CA

KITCHEN, WILLY
[b.] April 3, 1955, MD; [p.] Julie and Sam Ried; [m.] Derrie; [ch.] Julia Liegh; [occ.] Computer Engineer; [memb.] American Society of Manufacturing Engineers, Tennessee Writers Alliance; [pers.] Gangster Girls is the first poem I have completed. I started writing in 1995 and I thoroughly enjoy creating with words. Writing is a new found passion in my life.; [a.] Smyrna, TN

KLEIMAN, JERROLD
[b.] July 2, 1955, Mineola, NY; [p.] Henry Kleiman, Sybil (Ross) Kleiman; [ed.] W. Tresper Clarke High School; [memb.] (Past Membership) - Feingold Association of N.Y. (1978-1984), an Association dedicated to helping children with learning disabilities, such as Attention Deficit Disorder (ADD), without the use of drugs such as Ritalin.; [pers.] I believe that societies will never really be able to overcome racism and other forms of bigotry, as long as they view it as "normal". In my opinion, these irrational hatreds, ought to be regarded and classified as psychological disorders, at least akin to the irrational fears, know as phobias.; [a.] Amityville, NY

KLINE, KEITH
[b.] September 17, 1966, Benton Harbor, MI; [p.] Ralph and Shirley Kline; [occ.] Carpenter for P.A.R. Const. St. Joe, MI; [hon.] Ranked 2nd in the World W.N.W.A. Arm Wrestling, Feather Wt. 1995, Ranked 3rd 1994; [pers.] To my Sis, Kathy Kline. Remember we can do anything we put our minds to, anything!; [a.] Benton Harbor, MI

KNAPP, SUSANNA
[b.] New York, NY; [ed.] BA New York University, MPA New York University; [occ.] Retired from being an Administrator in the health field.; [memb.] MENSA; [oth. writ.] Seashore to be published in "Mirrors Of The Soul", February, 1996; [pers.] Gave the poem Memory to my lover in memory of the death of his wife and, in retrospect, the sense of my own impending loss.; [a.] New York, NY

KNOLL, LEONA ANN
[pen.] Lee or Lee-Ann; [b.] August 2, 1945, Brooklyn, NY; [p.] Edward Oliver Berner, Eva Ann Berner (Nee Anthony); [ch.] Stephanie M. DePalma, Susan M. Knapeck, Heather-Ann Knoll; [ed.] Graduate of Midwood High School, Brooklyn, NY, Insurance School, Secretarial School, current student of Institute of Childrens Literature.; [occ.] Notary Public, Mother and Home-School Teacher, Poet, Writer; [memb.] National Notary Association; [hon.] Editors Choice Award for Outstanding Achievement in Poetry, 1995.; [oth. writ.] Un-named (Poem), The Battle For The Mat (poem), Ode To A Problem Child (poem/ode), Write And Reason (poem), The Presidents' Wives (a short play), for the Girl Scouts.; [pers.] To my children: This one's for you. I'm still useful, no longer misunderstood. Have faith in God and you will, too. You're never too old or sick, don't quit! Walk in faith, live, learn. I love you all.; [a.] Vineland, NJ

KNOWLSON, THOM
[ed.] Philosophy - History: West Virginia, Wesleyan - Dugnesne Universities; [occ.] Transportation Mgr., Freelance gardener.; [oth. writ.] The poem "Jetstreams" included in this volume is part of a greater work: Rhapsodies of Existence of which this submission is only the opening lives of the 8th Rhapsody.; [pers.] As outward reality is oftentimes an ambiguous melange of opposites... so inward reality echoes its substance in vibrant mosaics of intensified, internal colors of passionate perception. It is philosophical poetry's purpose to achieve an ecstatic unity between "the outer and the inner" within the passionate of existence.; [a.] Pittsburgh, PA

KNUTSON, DAWN
[b.] January 25, 1963, Minneapolis, MN; [m.] Eric Knutson, August 19, 1989; [ch.] Brett Anthony and an unborn boy; [ed.] Bachelor of Science Degree in Special Education from St. Cloud State University; [occ.] Early Childhood Educator; [memb.] National Association for the Education of Young Children (N.A.E.Y.C.); [oth. writ.] Two poems published in "I Knew You for a Moment" put out by the Pregnancy and Infant Loss Center (P.I.L.C.) in Wayzata, MN.; [pers.] I write what I feel and I live what I believe.; [a.] Lakeville, MN

KOCH, FREDERICK
[b.] June 13, 1931, Chicago, IL; [p.] Jean and Arthur Koch; [m.] Annabelle Koch (Nee Lewis), August 27, 1950; [ch.] Sara, James, Stephen, Kenneth; [ed.] Wilson J.C., Rochester U., School of Optics (Summer Session), US Army Signal School, Taught Basic Electronics in Adult Ed.; [occ.] Retired Aerospace Program Manager, Engr. Consultant; [memb.] Pres. Home Owners Assoc., Sr. Warden - Church Vestry; [hon.] Company Chairman's Award for joint management of "Star Wars" program.; [oth. writ.] Have file of unpublished works, time now to dust them off and take myself seriously.; [pers.] Spoonful of reality with dash of whimsey and occasional pinch of sugar. I like diversity and believe the sum of all the parts can be greater than the whole man. I like C. S. Lewis and Shakespeare's sonnets. We are surrounded by enough creative material for countless life times.; [a.] Lake Forest, CA

KOCHANY, KATARZYNA
[b.] April 11, 1977, Warsaw, Poland; [p.] Ewa Lipczynska, Jan Kochany; [ed.] Bluevale Collegiate, York University; [occ.] Film and Video Student at York University; [memb.] Cinematheque Ontario, "The Excalibur" Board of Directors, Creative Arts Students' Association at York; [hon.] Beryl Pflug Citizenship Award, York University Entrance Scholarship, Centre in the Square Drama Award; [oth. writ.] Published in Swiat Mlodych, an established Polish Youth Magazine (1990), letters to the editor in The Toronto Star and Kitchener Waterloo Record; [pers.] For too many of us deny that we're all born brilliant artists.; [a.] Ontario, Canada

KOGI, VIOLET WAHITO
[b.] September 3, 1974, Nainbi, Kenya; [p.] Absalom Kabochi and Gladwell Kabochi; [ed.] Pangani Girls High School, Nainbi Kenya, Missiouri Baptist College - MO.; [occ.] Student at Missouri Baptist College - Freshman.; [memb.] Y.M.C.A.; [oth. writ.] One article published in local Kenyan Magazine "Interlude".; [a.] Bridgeton, MO

KOHLMAN, VAL
[pen.] Morning Dawn; [b.] January, Lake Linden, MI; [p.] Reino (Kohlman) Kolehmainen, To Elaine Leroux; [ch.] R. Wolfgang Zientek, Debra Zientek Sydenham; [ed.] Mott College - AD-RN, Mott College - AD-MOA, MSU - 2 yrs; [occ.] Currently Registered Nurse, Geriatrics, previously Genesis Memorial - Flint MI, ICU 2 yrs - Med-Surg 3 yrs., Surgical 3 yrs.; [memb.] Democratic National Comm., International Library of Poetry, Smithsonian Institute of Arts, Public Citizen, National Rifle Assoc.; [hon.] Golf Club Champion 3 yrs, Clio Country Club - Clio, MI, previously to "The Life Style of a Poet", "Dear Old Al" - published in 1995, ED. Beyond The Stars - NLOP; [oth. writ.] Numerous articles for family and friends, enjoy logo's, currently writing a novel; [pers.] "May the seasons awaken the child in you and may the wisdom of God know your heart"; [a.] Dollar Bay, MI

KOKINO, OLGA
[pen.] Aglo Onikok; [b.] May 26, 1955, Istanbul, Turkey; [p.] Gregory Kokino (Deceased), Elsy Kokino; [ed.] Bishop Garcia Diego High, Santa Barbara City College, University California, Santa Barbara, B.A., University California, Riverside, M.A.; [occ.] English Teacher, University High, LAUSD, CA.; [memb.] Southland Council Teachers of English, California Association Teachers of English, Journalism Educators Association, International Reading Association.; [hon.] "Sunspots" newsletter editor, National Standards Committee, NCTE, Western States Conference, Advisory Board, "Read" Magazine, 1994-95; [oth. writ.] Articles in various publications, including:

"Nexus", UCSB, "The Channels", SBCC, "Council Chronicles", NCTE, UCSB yearbook 1976 and 1977, adviser, high school newspaper.; [pers.] "Only those who will risk going too far can possibly find out how far they can go." - T.S. Eliot. "Where there is no vision, people perish." Proverbs 29:18; [a.] Long Beach, CA

KOLAR, KATHLEEN A.
[b.] February 12, 1947, Cleveland, OH; [p.] Walter and Florence Wrobleski; [m.] Frederick, September 30, 1967; [ch.] Christopher, Jeffrey, Loriann; [ed.] Garfield High, Community College; [occ.] Owner Lindy's Beach Resort; [memb.] International Society of Poets, St. Joseph's Church, Chili Cookoff, Ottawa County Visitors, Bureau Port Clinton Chamber Of Commerce, Peninsula Chamber of Commerce; [hon.] Editor's Choice Award; [oth. writ.] The Slate Is Empty Glory, The Little Known Man, The Bouquet, Marble Head, Harmony Court, Cool Waters of Deliverance, What Have You Done For Me Lately?, The Old House Spoke.; [pers.] When we envy, dehumanize or threaten others, we harm ourselves and society because we undermine and destroy human dignity and potential. We blacken the horizons of peace. We need to become each others advocates.; [a.] Marble Head, OH

KOLLAR, JILL
[b.] June 17, 1984, Coon Rapids, MN; [p.] Mark and Sharon Kollar; [ed.] Shepardson Elem. School; [occ.] Student; [a.] Fort Collins, CO

KOONCE, CARLUS D.
[b.] February 23, 1973, Kinston, NC; [p.] Joan Koonce Lewis; [ed.] Clarke Central High School, Truett-McConnell College; [occ.] Student; [pers.] "In everything you do, put God first, and He will direct you and crown your efforts with success" Proverbs 3:6; [a.] Athens, GA

KORASKA, LEANN COLEMAN
[b.] January 1, 1958, Longview, TX; [p.] Bill and Barbara Coleman; [ch.] Brian Keith Koraska; [ed.] Longview High School; [occ.] Bridal Consultant; [pers.] "Sweet pea" - take a chance, make a dream come true!; [a.] Longview, TX

KOSTER, RICHARD
[b.] April 6, 1923, Toledo, OH; [p.] Matthew and Hazel Koster; [m.] Soe Koster, March 31, 1987; [ch.] 3 boys; [ed.] Denison University, Granville, Ohio - major in Philosophy - 2 years only; [occ.] Retired from Kroger Co., 40 years Executive V.P., Food and Manufacturing. Currently Sculptor and poet; [pers.] My carvings in stone and wood reveal my soul - my poetry is a prayer to Almighty God for the gift of life; [a.] Cincinnati, OH

KRAFT, EUGENE
[b.] November 12, 1942, Park, KS; [p.] Deceased; [ed.] B.A., Philosophy, Rockhurst College, M.A., English, University of Kansas, Ph.D., English, University of Missouri; [occ.] Retired; [memb.] National Council of Teachers of English, Modern Language Association, College Language Association; [oth. writ.] More than 100 publications, primarily in the areas of African and African American studies, and in creative writing.; [a.] Grainfield, KS

KRENNING, KELLY
[b.] September 13, 1966, Iowa; [p.] Mike and Karen Gurke; [m.] Tom Krenning, November 7, 1987; [ch.] Elijah, Emily, Caleb, Abigail; [ed.] Bettendorf High, UM-St. Louis; [occ.] Mother and student; [a.] Saint Louis, MO

KRICK, KIRSTEN
[b.] September 30, 1973, Stanford, CA; [p.] James and Ilse Krick; [ed.] Northgate High, Smith College; [hon.] Dean's List, Cum Laude; [a.] Fairhope, AL

KRIEGER, LAURA T.
[pen.] Laura T. Krieger; [b.] October 3, 1930, Union County, NJ; [p.] Edward H. and Frances V. Miller; [m.] George N. Krieger, December 2, 1950; [ch.] Brenda J., Francine J.; [ed.] St. Michael's Elementary, Union High School, Newark Academy of Arts (2 yrs); [occ.] Retired, Accountant, Postmaster Relief, Change Water, NJ; [memb.] Daughter of The American Revolution (Chapter Regent Peggy Warne Chapter), Changewater United Methodist Women, Girl Scouts of America (former leader) 25 yrs and member, St. Anne's R.C. Church, Hampton, NJ; [hon.] State of N.J. "Our Schools", Chairman Warren Co., 4 yrs., Regent, DAR 95-98 yrs., P.T.A. president 8 yrs. Warren Hills Regional High School; [oth. writ.] Poems, essays and short stories. 1 poem published by all state Ins Co., in 1949 newsletter, Newark, N.J.; [pers.] My poems and prayers are inspired by my long standing faith, family support and love. I dedicate this poem to my sister Frances who died April 14, 1991 at age 58 of Leukemia.; [a.] Changewater, NJ

KRUEGER JR., WILLIAM
[b.] April 16, 1959, Springfield, MO; [p.] William and Joan Krueger; [m.] Cindy Krueger, May 25, 1985; [ch.] Ashley Brooke, Jessica Anne, Courtney Michelle; [ed.] Kickapoo High, Southwest Missouri State University; [occ.] Kraft Foods; [memb.] American Heart Ass., Saint Elizabeth Ann Seton; [pers.] My inspiration to write has been influenced by religious studies. To provide and share what has been given to me.; [a.] Springfield, MO

KUCHMAN, MARY ANN
[pen.] Mary Ann Kuchman; [b.] September 3, 1979, Norwalk, CT; [p.] Kathleen and Gary Kuchman; [ed.] Orchard Hills Elementary, East Shore Middle School and Foran High School; [occ.] All for A Dollar - Thanks Tammy and Marissa for your help.; [hon.] Track and Field in 5th and 7th grade. Second honors in High School and Achievement Honors in Elementary. Softball for 6 years.; [oth. writ.] I have written 147 poems since 1993. I started a book titled "When You Live, You Love", which all the poems are written in.; [pers.] Difficult problems in my life made me realize the importance of helping others and myself. Special thanks to two teachers who helped me a lot Mrs. Kuster and Mrs. Castellucci. Mom, I did it and I love you. To my family and friends I love you, too! Thanks; [a.] Norfolk, VA

KUCZMARSKI JR., JEFFREY MICHAEL
[pen.] Ren Escuandolas, Jefe; [b.] July 9, 1974, Tomahawk, WI; [p.] Jeff and Karen Kuczmarski; [ed.] Rhinelander High School, I am currently a senior at St. Norbert College; [occ.] Student; [memb.] I'm a member of the Pi Gamma Mu International Honor Society for the Social Sciences; [hon.] Dean's List, Resident Life Award; [oth. writ.] Several poems published in St. Norbert College's Literary Magazine Graphos; [pers.] I am fascinated by the duality of Human Nature, Mythology, and the mystical aspects of the universe. I hope my works encourage others to dream as much and explore the power of their imaginations, it is the dreamers of today who create our tomorrows; [a.] DePere, WI

KULP, BRENDA A.
[pen.] B. Annie Kulpepper; [b.] May 1, 1961, Allentown, PA; [p.] Madeline Reinert; [ch.] Laura Lindsey; [ed.] Northampton High School, Rethlehem Vocational Technical School; [occ.] Cashier at Pichel's Farm, Market in Bethlehem, PA; [pers.] I am currently devoting most of my free time writing an original screenplay. My long term goal is focused on writing fictional novels. I would also like to try my hand as a songwriter. The sky is the limit, and no one can keep me away from my keyboard!; [a.] Northampton, PA

KUMAR, CHANDA
[pen.] Chanda "Sunir" Kumar; [b.] April 10, 1979, Columbia, SC; [p.] Mr. and Mrs. Suresh Kumar; [occ.] Student; [hon.] Tennis Award, Math Awards, Science Awards

LA MICELA, IVANO G.
[b.] May 25, 1971, Italy; [p.] Antonio and Giovanna La Micela; [ed.] P.S. #5 - Paterson, NJ. Passaic County Tech. and Voc. H. S. four years - US Marines, rank of Corporal. Attending Passaic County Community College, seeking degree in English.; [occ.] Financial Services; [memb.] US Marine Corps. Reserves; [hon.] National Defense Medal, Good Conduct Medal, Arctic Service, Naval Achievement Medal; [oth. writ.] Wrote on topic about teenage drinking for Mothers against drunk drivers in 1989-90, Received 2nd place honors statewide.; [pers.] I say today's generation must live for the future, not the day. We all need a road map to follow, or we head nowhere!; [a.] West Paterson, NJ

LABOLLITA, SHARON A.
[pen.] Sharon A. Schuhmacher; [b.] May 2, 1943, Staten Island, NY; [p.] Mayona Schuhmacher, Charles Schuhmacher; [m.] Joseph LaBollita, May 1, 1965; [ch.] Dean LaBollita, Tiffany LaBollita; [ed.] Curtis High, Drakes Secretarial; [occ.] Retired Executive Secretary, Medical Transcriber; [hon.] One award in high school, freshman year - did not save a copy.; [oth. writ.] Several poems written only for family and close personal friends, however I will be submitting more in the near future. My poem is written about my adopted son "who came to me at age 7". His occupation is a Mental Health Counsellor.; [pers.] I am inspired on the spur of a moment to write about people who have left an impression on me. I always strive to speak the

truth whether good or otherwise. My future goal is to write a short novel.; [a.] Jackson, NJ

LACADIE, CONNIE COLEMAN
[b.] June 15, 1946, Chadron, NE; [p.] Betty Folwell, Lawrence Coleman; [m.] Michael R. Lacadie; [ch.] Gary II and Chad Moon; [ed.] Glenrock High School; [occ.] Office Mgr. Federal Aviation Administration (FAA) Human Resources; [memb.] Federally Employed Women, Inc. (Few), Clover Park PTSA Council, Toastmasters Int'l.; [hon.] Sustained Superior Accomplishment Award (1976 and 1980), Civilian Meritorious Service Award (1987), DOT Federal Women's Program Mgrs. Intra-Dept. Council Secretary of 1992, Essay 1st Place Award (1992), DOT Superior Achievement Award NEED (1994), Regional Administrator's Award for Excellence in Federal Women's Program (ANM) (1994); [oth. writ.] Several unpublished poems, messages about life.; [pers.] I strive to reflect the possible growth achieved from all of life's experiences. I wonder what happened to respect and continually vocalize its importance. Lack of it breeds the atrocities we witness daily; [a.] Tacoma Lakewood, WA

LAKIEN, ATMETA M.
[pen.] Lanie Jordon, Meta; [b.] June 11, 1970, Majuro, Marshall Is.; [p.] Edwin C. Lakien and Tamar Lakien; [ed.] Marshall Islands Mission Academy, Georgia Cumberland Academy, Southern College, and Leewared Community College. And Hawaii Job Corps.; [occ.] Hawaii Job Corps and Tahiti Imports.; [hon.] Honorable Mention in the JAC National Essay Contest.; [oth. writ.] Children's Short Stories. Love Stories. And other poetries.; [pers.] I strive to express my thought and feelings concerning Nature and what mankind is doing to each other.; [a.] Waimanalo, HI

LAL, NEETA
[b.] May 1, 1983, New York; [p.] Rajesh and Shail Lal; [ed.] Seventh Grader, Harbor Day School; [occ.] Student; [oth. writ.] Many other unpublished poems - in my possession currently; [pers.] When I begin to write, my ordinary world is transformed into one filled with adventure, excitement and tranquility.; [a.] Newport Beach, CA

LALLY, MIKE
[b.] February 2, 1938, Galway, Eire; [p.] Thomas and Julia; [m.] Kathleen, November 1990; [ch.] Heather, Niels, George and Thomas; [ed.] High School - St. Mary's College, Galway, BA degree at Univ. of Nevada Reno 1966.; [occ.] Golf Professional at Hillcrest C. C. Leicester, MA and owner, (turned pro. at age 55); [memb.] Unitarian Universalent Church; [hon.] Chosen from the ranks of the enlisted for the West Point Academy at Ft. Stewart, GA 1960 before I became a U.S. Citizen; [oth. writ.] I have written poetry for over 30 years - 'Alone' is the first one I've ever entered and was written at the Univ. of Nev. Reno 30 years ago - while still a student there; [pers.] Many of my writings have been aligned with the peace process in Northern Ireland - Peaceful co-existence is my motto in life - I spring from a most positive fountain!; [a.] Charlton, MA

LAMARCHINA, CAROLYN J.
[b.] December 1, 1946, Burbank, CA; [p.] Joyce and John Bertetti; [ch.] 2 Girls, Cara Mishanne Addis, Tamara Jean Addis; [ed.] High school graduate, full scholarship to Mt. St. Mary's in Los Angeles (Music) - not taken; [occ.] 'Cellist on stage for Wayne Newton; [memb.] Honorary Member: International Society of Poets '94-'95; [hon.] Women's Scholarship (Music), Full Scholarship, Mt. St. Mary's (Music), Winner: Farewell Speech Jr. High, All So. California and All State Orchestra Winner; [oth. writ.] Yesterday's Future; [pers.] God Dictates... I take notes!; [a.] Billings, MI

LAMBERT, JOHN
[b.] September 27, 1971; [pers.] To Susie: I am sorry. (She understands); [a.] Pittsburgh, PA

LANCE, BONNIE JEAN
[b.] October 7, 1926, Ashland County; [ch.] Linda, Barbara, Bobbi, Stephan; [ed.] Ashland High School - 1944, Night Classes Ashland University Technical School - Computer Classes etc.; [occ.] Retired; [oth. writ.] Waiting - published in East of the Sunrise.

LANDIS, MICHELLE
[b.] July 30, 1968, Orange, NY; [p.] Gail and Dennis Soroka; [ed.] Senior at Trenton State College, Finance Major.; [occ.] Office Manager with American Express Financial Advisors

LANE, FRANCHON
[b.] June 5, 1971, Brooklyn, NY; [p.] Anne L. Lane, Robert E. Lane; [ed.] Elementary School P.S. 152, in Brooklyn, NY, attended Brooklyn College for three years.; [hon.] I received an award for creative writing in elementary school. I tutored writing for a semester at Brooklyn College and received an A in Poetry Writing.; [oth. writ.] I've never had any work published prior to this. I've written many poems, but I feel Insomnia, Insomniac is my best piece. Some of my other poems are: Chess and Angels of Darkness. My favorite poem is Eating Poetry, by Mark Strand.; [pers.] I'm a woman of few words. Writing poetry is my vehicle for self expression.; [a.] Brooklyn, NY

LARKIN, SANDRA
[pen.] Sandra Lee; [b.] June 10, 1950, Elgin, IL; [p.] Art Henschel; [m.] Earl D. Larkin, April 22, 1977; [ch.] Susan, Jacks; [ed.] Helix High School, North American School of Accounting Basic Computer Corporation; [occ.] Checker; [memb.] Arthritis Foundation, The Susan G. Komen Breast Cancer, Doris Day Animal League, MADD, Unity School of Christianity; [hon.] Volunteer School Aide Award, Benefactors Award; [oth. writ.] I have written a few article on Oregon Citizens Alliance, The House of Congress in all local newspaper in Oregon; [pers.] Writing my poems was influence by my faith in God, my daily word Booklet I received by Unity School, I read everyday.; [a.] Hillsboro, OR

LAUREL, JOHN E.
[b.] November 30, 1943, Kodiak, AK; [p.] Edward and Valentine Laurel; [ed.] South San Francisco High, City College of San Francisco; [occ.] Saute Chef Ristorante Piatti Sonoma, CA; [oth. writ.] Lyrics and music performed by Rock group 'Fresh Oil'.; [pers.] I once thought I had a pretty good understanding of the English language and the meaning of most words. Today's generation has made me take another look.; [a.] Glen Ellen, CA

LAVEDAS, KRIS
[b.] September 20, 1962, Fort Wayne, IN; [p.] Katherine Lavedas; [ch.] Alysa; [ed.] Northeast High School, Lincoln NE., Univ. of Nebraska - Lincoln; [occ.] Medicaid payment Review Specialist for State of NE.; [oth. writ.] Several poems, novel in progress, articles for a monthly community newsletter; [pers.] The tragedies in our past often prepare us to deal with the future, and to help others along the way. A trial with cancer helped diminish my fear of rejection and reach a life's goal - publication!; [a.] Lincoln, NE

LAWSON, SUSAN
[b.] September 1, 1946, Louisville, KY; [p.] Ray and Dorothy Garrison; [m.] Deceased, May 11, 1979; [ch.] David Lawson, Ona Rae Garrison; [ed.] Boone County High School Graduate Florence, KY.; [occ.] Manual Labor, Data Entry, not currently employed; [hon.] An Award of Merit Certificate. "Dear Mom" Honorable Mention; [oth. writ.] I have go or more poems many are on a relationship of Jesus and God. I have written the words of one song called "Broken Love" based on Alcoholics. I am going to write a book of poems about teens. My son is my inspiration for this book.; [pers.] My inspiration comes from many sources. A movie, a comment made by someone, the news (as this one was) mostly Jesus puts them in my mind.; [a.] Union, KY

LAY, DEENA LEEANN
[b.] September 24, 1980, Sapulpa, OK; [p.] Mr. and Mrs. Bill Lay; [ed.] Talala Christian Academy, Talala, OK; [occ.] High School Student; [memb.] I am a member of Rabbs Creek Baptist Church in Talala, OK.; [pers.] "I press toward the mark for the prize of the high calling of God in Christ Jesus." Philippians 3:14; [a.] Talala, OK

LAY, RONDA
[b.] February 11, 1980, Knoxville, TN; [p.] Ron and Debbie Lay; [ed.] Mount Olive Elementary, South-Doyle Middle and High; [occ.] Childcare Worker, Promises Child Enrichment Center, Knoxville, TN; [memb.] Acteens, Church Youth Group, Church Youth Choir, German Club, Mixed Chorus, and Church Soloist; [hon.] High Honor Roll, Outstanding German Student 'Kee of the Mouth', "Who's Who" Recipient, Tennessee Youth Chorale, Service Aide in Acteens; [oth. writ.] I have, ever since the 6th grade, written poems in my spare time I won an award in 1993 on a state level for a poem I wrote. My poems are occasionally printed in school newspapers.; [pers.] The verses I write come from the inspiration of the Lord and from what I feel in my heart. My poetry allows me to express the thoughts, feelings, and opinions from the depths of my soul.; [a.] Knoxville, TN

LAZZERI, ALICE
[pen.] Alice Carol Lazzeri; [b.] September 2, 1928, Scranton, PA; [p.] Thomas Corcoran, Helen Quinn; [m.] Peter Sam Lazzeri, July 12, 1951; [ch.] 3 Patricia, Paula, Peter Jr.; [ed.] High School; [occ.] Home Maker; [memb.] Altart Rosary Society; [oth. writ.] Poems and songs; [pers.] Since the 50's I have a notebook of poems and songs. Raising a family. I never pursued them.

LEE, DAVID BARTON
[b.] August 13, 1963; [p.] David and Betsy Lee; [m.] Julie M. Lee, October 17, 1992; [ed.] Kinston HS and North Lenior High Schools (Graduated from North Lenior HS); [occ.] Fire Truck Mechanic, Fire Truck and Apparatus, Salesman for Lee Fire Eqpt.; [pers.] A life time is a terrible thing to waste.; [a.] Wilson's Mills, NC

LEE, JOYCE ANN LLOYD
[b.] November 30, 1943, Washington, DC; [p.] Joseph and Ruby Lloyd; [ch.] Cynthia Ann Lee; [ed.] Eastern High School Graduated June 1961, University of the District of Columbia 1982-1983; [occ.] Vice President Love Joy Jewelers - Wash. DC; [memb.] African-American Business Association, District of Columbia Jewelers Guild, Performance, Achievement; [hon.] Numerous Outstanding and Meritorious Awards U.S. Dept. of Justice 1968-1987, African-American Business Association Award - 1994 Chamber of Commerce Business Award - 1992; [pers.] "Do unto others as you would have them do unto you."; [a.] Washington, DC

LEE, YI-HSIN
[pen.] Fly Girl; [b.] October 9, 1971, Taipei, Taiwan; [p.] Ku-Hung Lee, Shu-Chen Lee; [ed.] Grant High School, California State University, of Northridge - BA in Art; [occ.] Restaurant Manager, H. Salt Fish and Chips, W. L.A., Ca.; [hon.] June 1990 - Awarded "Outstanding Work in Painting", Ulysses S. Grant High School, June 1990 - Interviewed for Article. "Bohemians of 1990", Art Department Ulysses S. Grant High School; [oth. writ.] 1992 - An Essay published in New Voices by the C.S.U. of Northridge. Titled "My Father's World." It was my first writing contest.; [pers.] I have visions and dreams, I have all that I need. Dedicated to mom and dad.; [a.] North Hills, CA

LEGRAND, JAMES W.
[b.] April 4, 1970, Summit, NJ; [m.] Michelle J. LeGrand, August 19, 1995; [ed.] Plainfield High School, Seton Hall University, BS in Management, Information Systems; [occ.] Business Systems Analyst for the Metropolitan Life Insurance Company; [oth. writ.] Song Lyrics for accomplished and aspiring artists, and poems to be purchased by those who feel I've captured their thoughts in my writings.; [pers.] All things are truly possible through faith in the Lord. I thank Him for the wonderful life He is guiding me through, and pray others will live as blessed a life as I have.; [a.] Iselin, NJ

LEIK, JOSEPH
[b.] May 2, 1977, Dayton, OH; [p.] Richard Leik, Dorothy Leik; [ed.] Precious Blood, Chaminade Julienne High School; [occ.] Student; [memb.] Precious Blood Church, Trotwood Madison Youth Baseball; [hon.] Youth Ministry Award, Coach's Award; [pers.] So life doesn't get boring, live it with an abundance of energy and excitement. My brothers Robert and Michael have always influenced my writing.; [a.] Trotwood, OH

LEIST, CLEMENTINA CEIDE
[pen.] Clementina Ceide Leist, Clemen; [b.] November 3, 1917, Aguadilla, PR; [p.] Aniceto Ceide, Milagros Veiga; [m.] Leslie Charles Leist, July 9, 1948; [ch.] Leslie Charles; [ed.] Perpetual Help Academy High Sch. PR, Norte Dame College, Balto. Md.; [occ.] Housewife; [memb.] Am. Lung Ass., Boys Town., St. John of God, R.C. Church, Cape May, N.J.; [pers.] The greatness of the Lord inspires most of my writings, in which I strive to emphasize the spiritual side of mankind. My sister Amelia Ceide, a well known poetess in P.R. and abroad was the sparkle of inspiration starting my writings.; [a.] Cape May, NJ

LEITNER, PATTY
[b.] May 27, 1955, Zanesville, OH; [p.] Lloyd Raymond McCoy II; [m.] Scott Robert, October 8, 1983; [ch.] Dane Edward; [occ.] Retired Claims Manager; [memb.] United Methodist Women; [pers.] Don't be guilty of knowing the price of everything and the value of nothing; [a.] Alexandria, VA

LEM, DAISY M.
[b.] April 16, 1932; [m.] Recently widowed, March 1960; [ch.] Arleen, Jocelyn, Mark; [ed.] Commerce High, attended City College of San Francisco and San Francisco State University; [occ.] Retired; [oth. writ.] Composed over a dozen poems but had never tried to publish them. "The Hidden Pain" is my first poem that will be available to the public's eyes.; [pers.] Whatever talent I may have as a poetry writer, comes from a Divine Force who spontaneously inspires me. Poems are the windows of the author's thoughts, emotions and beliefs. It is the most personal of writings as it reveals the author's soul.; [a.] San Francisco, CA

LEONARD, MARY MAY T
[pen.] Mary Leonard; [b.] July , 1916; Essington, PA; [p.] Mary E. Leonard James; [occ.] Homemaker; [memb.] American Legion #144, Disabled American Veterans, La Salle School of Art; [hon.] Red Cross Assoc., Homemaker Year, Best customer of the month; [oth. writ.] Several, but never entered any; [pers.] I think its wonderful that you help talented authors to help themselves, maybe sometimes, make a lifetime career. [a.] Drexel Hill, PA

LEONARD, MELODIE
[b.] March 3, 1982; [p.] Lewis Leonard, Cynthia Leonard; [ed.] Waterville School, currently 8th grade student; [hon.] Principal's List; [pers.] My being but thirteen years of age does not diminish my aspiration to write.; [a.] Orondo, WA

LESSER, FRANK
[b.] January 20, 1980, Columbus, OH; [p.] Brian and Lois Gruhin Lesser; [ed.] 10th grade student, Bexley High School, Bexley, Ohio; [occ.] Student; [memb.] Student Council, Art Club, Lamplight; [hon.] Honor society, over a 43 cumulative average, participated in the 1995 Ohio State University Summer Program for the Academically Gifted and Talented in the Arts, one of three students comprising the 9th grade English team which finished first in the State of Ohio on the Ohio Tests of Scholastic Achievement; [oth. writ.] Winner of two best of rounds and winner of Best of the Best in the Power of the Pen Competitions.; [a.] Bexley, OH

LEWIS, MICHAEL
[pen.] Lewie, Lewie (Baby shoes); [b.] November 30, 1969, Middletown Hospt.; [p.] Richard Lewis, Linda Noble; [occ.] Hamilton Cement Walls and Footers; [memb.] International Society of Poets Distinguished Member; [hon.] Distinguished Member Plague; [oth. writ.] Once Again, Christmas Is Home Cooking, What To Do; [pers.] There comes a moment in time when a man needs a wife to find his life.; [a.] Middletown, OH

LIARAKOS, STEVE
[pen.] Ouzo; [b.] September 14, 1973, Athens, Greece; [p.] Olga and Spiro Liarakos; [ed.] Niles North High School, Southern Illinois University; [occ.] Bartender; [pers.] My hedonism is satisfied, thru my love of women.; [a.] Skokie, IL

LILLY, ARREN RUTH
[b.] August 2, 1980, Kansas City, MO; [p.] Richard and Donna Lilly; [ed.] 9th grade; [occ.] School; [memb.] Civil Air Patrol; [oth. writ.] The Closet, Pandoras Box, both published by the National Library of Poetry.; [pers.] "Never dough the spirit of your imagination"; [a.] Fairborn, OH

LINDQUIST, HARRIET H.
[b.] February 15, 1928, Camden, NJ; [p.] Frederick and Jeannette; [m.] Bruce W. Lindquist, May 13, 1950; [ch.] Norman, Pamela, Jan, Carl, Brian; [ed.] Registered Nurse (now retired), Graduated Thomas Jefferson, University Hospital Feb. 1950; [occ.] Conducting small ceramic classes and making porcelain dolls in my home; [hon.] American Legion Award for all around best student in 9th grade. Several blue ribbons and trophies in ceramic show competitions.; [oth. writ.] Several poems already published by NLP. Feeding the Birds, Adam And I Took A Walk, March, Yard Sale Finds.; [pers.] I try to live by the code of doing each day, what I can to help others and be kind. To guide my children, grandchildren that right way. "For I shall not pass this way again."; [a.] Audubon, NJ

LINDSAY, LINDA R.
[b.] December 21, 1942, Winston-Salem, NC; [p.] Sarah Hart, Robert Long; [m.] Bruce Lindsay, October 14, 1989; [ch.] Kim McKenzie-Banks, 2 grandchildren - Brandon and McKenzie; [ed.] Atkins High School Winston-Salem, NC, Winsalm Business College - Winston-Salem, NC., Stenotype Academy New York, NY; [occ.] Sales Agent USAir TLC Dept. Winston-

Salem, NC; [memb.] "Friends" Community Club - Galilee Baptist Church (Hostess Committee, Children's Church) - Pink Broom Stick (Cancer Services); [oth. writ.] 1. "Color You Mother", 2. "You Can Find Her", 3. "Color You Dad", 4. "I Am A Man", 5. "The Orphan", 6. "Dear Mommy", 7. "Look at Us Now"; [pers.] I would like to thank God for allowing me to express myself through poetry. I also would like to thank my sister Barbara McCracken, Marsha Hemric for their support and Hilda Hodge for believing in me.; [a.] Winston-Salem, NC

LINDSEY, BARBARA J.
[pen.] Barbara J. Black-Lindsey; [b.] January 28, 1940, New York City, NY; [p.] Lola D. Black; [ch.] Kevin, Eric, Nathan, Tamiki and Duane; [ed.] University of Massachusetts-Amtterst and Atlantic City, New Jersey Public Sch.; [occ.] Licensed Practical Nurse, Substitute Teacher; [memb.] Unitarian Society of Hartford, CT; [hon.] Cum Laude - '79 U. Mass., Awarded a plaque from "One Church, One Child" program for participating in adoption video.; [oth. writ.] Poems published in College Magazine - "Drum" U. Mass.; [pers.] Poetry lets my mind soar to worlds yet to be visited. And I write to reveal, to the reader, those worlds. For poetry is differently my yesterdays, my todays and my tomorrows. I wrote this poem in remembrance of Mom.; [a.] Windsor, CT

LINDSEY, GAVIN
[pen.] Gavin Lindsey; [b.] December 29, 1975, Knoxville, TN; [p.] Vernon Lindsey, Norma Lindsey; [ed.] Currently attending the University of Tennessee where I hope to earn my degree in Criminal Justice; [occ.] Stock worker at office Depot; [pers.] This poem will more than likely be my last and only poem I write. I wrote this poem from my tattered heart knowing I will never get to be with my true love again, this was another way to vent my unnoticed love for her.; [a.] Knoxville, TN

LINDSTROM, LISA M.
[pen.] Leo; [b.] August 8, 1961, Minneapolis, MN; [p.] Ward R. Engebrit and Mari Jane Engebrit; [m.] Jeffrey R. Lindstrom, July 25, 1992; [ed.] Institute of Children's Literature Continual Education of Law; [occ.] Poet, Insurance Adjuster, Manager; [memb.] Distinguished Member, International Society of Poetry; [hon.] Editor's Choice Award for poem "Unfantasy" in "At Water's Edge".; [oth. writ.] Anthologies "At Water's Edge", "Best Poems of 1996" and "The Voice Within". Presently working on becoming a publisher so I may get my 1st book of Poetry to press.; [pers.] I gain positive power when releasing negativity in my poetry. It is so important to remain positive. I also feel joy which creeps into my poetry more often as my style reveals itself.; [a.] Yorba Linda, CA

LINGLE, MERLA R.
[pen.] Merla Rose; [b.] February 26, 1949, Oskaloosa, IA; [p.] Merlin and Josephine White; [m.] Harmon K. Lingle, October 16, 1987; [ch.] Michael Spegal and Janette Cable; [ed.] High School, Crowder College; [occ.] Federal Meat Inspector for USDA Govt.; [memb.] Sweet Water Baptist Church, Sherifs Association; [hon.] Penmanship Awards, Award of Merit, Golden Poet Award, Three, Silver Poet Awards 1989, 1990, 1990. Great American Merit Certificate Award, 1987, Newspapers.; [oth. writ.] "My Blue Mustang" Honorable Mention Award 1987; [pers.] I enjoy seeing a person smile, or a tear in their eye, when I know one of my poems have touched someone's heart.; [a.] Neosho, MO

LITALIEN, GERALD
[b.] January 23, 1949, Rumford, ME; [p.] Roland Litalien, Catherin Litalien; [m.] Elizabeth, August 20, 1970; [ch.] Merrie Sue, Joshua; [ed.] Mexico, High School; [occ.] Conductor/Springfield Terminal Railway Co.; [memb.] The American Legion, Post No. 0024, Fraternal Order of Eagles, Aerie No. 1248, The Big Red One, 26th Infantry Regiment Association, Blue Spader; [pers.] I collect and create things from Mother Nature, she speaks to anyone if they listen.; [a.] Mexico, ME

LLANES, ANTHONY MITCHELL
[b.] March 10, 1971, Trenton, MI; [p.] Dolores and Victorio R. Llanes; [ch.] One; [ed.] McMillan Elementary School, Beard Elementary School, Jeffries Elementary, Little Mack Elementary, Wilson Jr. High, South Western High School; [pers.] I have written other poems but I never finished them.; [a.] Detroit, MI

LOCKHART, JOHNNIE
[b.] March 8, 1942, Iaeger, WV; [p.] Carl and Zelphia Phillips; [m.] Ronald Lockhart, January 17, 1959; [ch.] Pamela Guella and Ronald Lockhart II; [ed.] High School Education; [occ.] Secretary/Bookkeeper for Iaeger Intermediate School; [memb.] Born Again Christian and member of Calvary Baptist Church; [oth. writ.] Have written poems for my own enjoyment, but this is the first time I have entered any kind of contest or sent in any to be published.; [pers.] I love to write poetry about God and all His creations. I hope that something that I would write would be a blessing to someone else. I also love romantic poetry.; [a.] Iaeger, WV

LOEB, PNINA TIVONA
[b.] June 24, 1955, Los Angeles, CA; [ed.] B.S. from Cal. State, Northridge Teaching Credentials from Sonoma State University; [occ.] Teacher; [pers.] From a childhood of incest and isolation, through retrieved memories, to conscious life. Poetry has become the expression of my life journey, my voice and declaration in becoming.; [a.] Santa Rosa, CA

LOGAN, SANDRA LEE
[pen.] Sandi; [b.] April 18, 1960, Cheverly, MD; [p.] Mary Proctor and Arthur Seidler; [m.] Ervin T. Logan, June 22, 1991; [ch.] Jessica and Jarren Hall; [ed.] Gwynn Park High School, A.A. degree from PG Community College, pursuing B.S. degree in Psychology at Univ. of MD; [occ.] Computer Systems Analyst, Tsgt. in USAFR; [memb.] Phi Theta Kappa, Expressions of Joy Church Committee, Full Gospel A.M.E. Zion Church; [hon.] Phi Theta Kappa, 1995, Dean's List, 1994-95, Delegates Scholarship Award, Editors Choice Award; [oth. writ.] One poem published and another to be published in the near future; [pers.] This poem is dedicated to one of the joys in my life, my daughter Jessica Shiree', in memory of her first love.; [a.] Upper Marlboro, MD

LONG, ANNA NADINE
[pen.] Nadine Simms Long; [b.] July 10, 1932; Salisbury, MD; [ch.] One daughter - Leslie, 1953 (writer in LA); [ed.] Graduate - 1950, other courses in writing and art on college level; [occ.] Receptionist and guide at art gallery, Salisbury State Univ; [hon.] Many for sales, second in State and you are Beautiful; [oth. writ.] What is this thing - Love? Play - presented 1995 on local stage, Other published articles on subjects of interest. Other poems in collection of works with my daughter. Working on another play and book for new brides; [pers.] It is each person's responsibility to use his talents to improve, the cultureand environment in which we live and show kindness whenever we can.; [a.] Salisbury, MD;

LONG, PATRICIA S.
[pen.] Pat Long; [b.] December 23, 1954, Philadelphia, PA; [ch.] A daughter, a son, (and two cats); [ed.] Will complete my B.A. in English at Muhlenberg College in May '96 (in Allentown, PA); [occ.] Evening College Advisor, full-time student - both at Muhlenberg College, full-time mother and homemaker, and a poet; [hon.] Dean's List at Muhlenberg College, Presidential Assistantship at Muhlenberg College (College President's Scholarship); [oth. writ.] (Poetry about children, nature, and relationship). None other than "Fire" published.; [pers.] I am in awe of the power of life and love, and seek to affirm that which is good, and to disarm pain and fear by facing it. I love to walk in the rain, collect rocks, laugh, talk to my cats, hear the voices of children, cook, write, watch sunsets in Winter, make love, teach, read, grow exotic plants, sing, remember my grandmother, swim in a mountain creek, pray, play, and love my kids.; [a.] Bethlehem, PA

LOPEZ, OLGA RASMUSSEN
[b.] July 2, 1921, New York City, NY; [p.] E. Michael Rasmussen, Marie Elizabeth Rasmussen; [m.] Arthur E. Lopez (Deceased), March 9, 1941; [ed.] At the age of 53 I graduated from New York University with an Associate in Applied Science (Social Work); [occ.] I worked for 30 years for the New York State Dept. of Labor, Head Clerk in the State of NY with my own private secretary and worked on the 71st floor in the World Trade Center Supervising Clerical Supervisors. I retired at the age of 56.; [memb.] International Society of Poet, AARP, Gypsy Carnival Troupe of St. Thomas, Smithsorican Institute - Chamber Member, The Toastmasters Club, National Museum of the American Indians, National Geographic Society, Civil Service Employees Association, St. Thomas St. John Chamber of Commerce, The New York Urban League, NAACP (Chelsea Greenwich Village Chapter), Harlem YMCA, North Shore Animal League, Humane Society of St. Thomas,

The Japanese Society, St. Thomas St John Golf Club, Shibui Condominium Association, COAST (Council on Alcoholism and Drug Dependence), NY Public Library, NY State Gov't. Employees Retirement System, Alumni Association New York University, Marianist Mission, VI Resource Center for the Disabled, The College Fund, (UNCF) United Negro College Fund.; [hon.] I was honored by the State of New York. After 25 years of service. I received a Certificate of Thanks from the United Jewish Appeal 1956 Service Award. And it was certainly an honor to be chosen one of two sent to the VI to set up the VI program; [oth. writ.] My poem about Hugo Hurricane was accepted by the daily news here but after preparing it for publication they decided that it was too long. I have since submitted it to the University of the VI for their 1996 contest. I have too many poems to count that I have written through the years - many are lost. I recently wrote about 25 - my poems are spontaneous and I never know when I'll suddenly start writing; [pers.] I am deeply moved by the greatness of God and the beauty that surround us all. I feed, I love, the animals of all kind I once had 21 cats, I now have 3. I would like to be known as a peace maker.; [a.] Saint Thomas, VI

LORIMER, BARBARA
[b.] March 24, 1927, Portland, OR; [p.] Wilfrid and Anne Lorimer; [ed.] B.S. in Nursing, U. of Portland, BA in History, Boston University, MA in Teaching in Inner City Schools - New York University; [occ.] Attending writing and literature classes at Portland Community College; [memb.] National History Honorary; [oth. writ.] Have been published in various newspapers and Peace Corps. Mag. My goal is to spread understanding and appreciation of other peoples, other cultures.; [pers.] My finest assignment as a worker was that of a Peace Corps. Vol. nurse in British North Borneo later to become Sabah Malaysia. There I worked principally with indigenous peoples, such as the Dusuns.; [a.] Portland, OR

LOW, THAYER SUSANNA
[b.] September 6, 1984, California; [p.] Kerr and William Low; [ed.] St. Andrew's Pre-school and St. Margarets in San Juan Capistrano, California, and Vail Mountain School in Colorado.; [hon.] Two Superior Awards in Suzuki Junior Violin Festivals.; [oth. writ.] Stories published in "Impressions", the VMS sixth grade magazine.; [a.] Edwards, CO

LOWE, LISA H.
[b.] November 13, 1965, Glasgow, KY; [p.] Pamela Tallman and Julian Horton Jr; [m.] P. Wesley Lowe; January 6, 1991; [ed.] Univ. of TN-Martin, BS Meharry Medical College, MD; [occ.] Physician; [memb.] Chi Omega Sorority, Phi Kappa Phi Honor Society, Radiologic Society of North America, Society of Pediatric Radiology; American College of Radiology; American Medical Association American RAEN FGEN Ray Society; [hon.] Certificate of Merit; RSNA; World Peace Scholarship; 1st Place Paper Presentation at Southern Medical Association; See CV for others; [oth. writ.] My Time as a Minority at Meharry Medical College; A Missed Opportunity; Mass Effect in the Renal Sinus; [pers.] I would rather be a dissatisfied woman than a satisfied pig; [a.] Arlington, VA;

LOWRIE, KEITH R.
[pen.] Kip Lowrie; [b.] June 19, 1975, Michigan; [p.] Richard and Barbara Lowrie; [ed.] High School - Orchard Lake St. Mary's, College - Lake Superior State University enrolled in Fisheries and Wildlife Management; [occ.] Student; [hon.] 2nd place English Oratorical Winner and Senior of the Year Award; [pers.] "Times trials essence for humanity has now been filtered and stored for later acknowledgement"; [a.] Rochester Hills, MI

LUCADO, YVONNE S.
[b.] August 24, 1952, West Virginia; [p.] Issac and Ruby Thornton; [m.] Mark A. Lucado, July 1, 1978; [ch.] Michael M., Marc A., and Maurice A.; [ed.] Hughes High School; [occ.] Next Day Air Driver. United Parcel Ser. (Cincinnati, Ohio); [memb.] United Way Sponsor, Women Helping Women Association, First Pentecostal Church.; [hon.] Very Important Parent Award, Honorable Mention Award; [oth. writ.] Poem, song written for Kilgour Elementary School, Cincinnati, Ohio, poems for class reunions and church events.; [pers.] I enjoy writing poems that will reach out and touch someone. My poems are based on real life issues and feelings; [a.] Cincinnati, OH

LUCAS, BENJAMIN W.
[pen.] The Dreamer; [pers.] Enter the dreamland. For without the feelings... The words are meaningless... Embrace the dreams.; [a.] Tacoma, WA

LUETJE JR., MELVIN L.
[b.] July 14, 1961, Hobbs, NM; [p.] Melvin L. (Sr.) and Burnilea Luetje; [m.] Tammy R. Price (Divorced - March 8, 1989), July 8, 1985; [ed.] 12th; [occ.] Mechanic, for Dink Prather; [hon.] I've been in newspapers 5 times, read one at Cinderilla Pageant, and have had 3 read at funerals, now this great honor; [oth. writ.] I have over 300 pages of poetry - so far.; [pers.] I am an unlearned man. This writing is a gift - on loan from God. Out of a class of 45 and I graduated 427th. God has special gifts for each and every one of us.; [a.] Hobbs, NM

LYNCH, CHRISTINA
[pen.] Christina Lynch; [b.] February 2, 1975, San Francisco, CA; [p.] Virgil and Patricia Lynch; [ed.] Vernonia High School Portland Community College; [occ.] Trouble Shooter for Epson Portlan Inc.; [oth. writ.] Several poems and short stories published in small school anthologies and several articles in school newspaper.; [pers.] I write as a stress reliever and believe that writing is a very good form of self expression for those who may have a hard time expressing themselves otherwise.; [a.] Vernonia, OR

LYNCH, ROBERT
[pen.] Rob; [b.] October 1, 1963, Fort Worth, TX; [p.] Robert Lynch I, Lilo Mills; [ed.] Irving High, El Centro Jr. College; [occ.] Retired from Nations Bank; [memb.] Phi Theta Kappa; [hon.] Who's Who Among American Junior Colleges.; [oth. writ.] A very special poem to Jodi called "My Friend"; [pers.] Everybody is dealt a "hand" in life, you can decide either to fold or try to improve it's value - this is my choice! My poems are inspired by the Almighty.; [a.] Dallas, TX

LYNN, IRVING A.
[pen.] I. Astrakhan Lynn; [b.] July 23, 1916, Montreal, Canada; [p.] Benjamin Lynn, Rose Lynn; [m.] Pat Lynn, November 28, 1965; [ch.] Bruce, Dorie, Brenda, Jeffpey; [ed.] South Side High, City College of New York, Rutgers University; [occ.] Retired Supervisory Auditor, U.S. Army Audit Agency, Managed New Audit Agency, N.Y. City.; [memb.] Temple B'nai Shalom; [hon.] Outstanding Awards, Sustained Superior Performance Awards for work performance.; [oth. writ.] Poems, essays and short stories published in local newspapers.; [pers.] My writing focuses on the revelation of feeling, the self discovery, process, the new insights into myself and others which enrich my life and my writing; [a.] Deerfield Beach, FL

LYON, WENDY
[b.] June 10, 1960, Fort Lauderdre, FL; [ch.] Amber Lyon, Aslan Lyon; [occ.] Entrepreneur; [memb.] California Coalition Against Dui, National Association of Female Executives, Child Abuse Prevention Foundation; [oth. writ.] Several recording contracts within the music business; [pers.] "The purest gold is drawn through the hottest fire."; [a.] Encinitas, CA

LYTLE, MICHELLE Y.
[pen.] Michelle Stevans; [b.] September 24, 1955, San Diego, CA; [p.] Ivy and Shirley Beaubouef; [ch.] Daughter - Christin D. Lytle 15; [ed.] Degree in Early Childhood, Education, SDSU '1976', Received Nursing Lincense '1980', Continued with a career in Nursing.; [occ.] Full Time Family Practice Nurse, Del Mar California.; [memb.] National Organization for Young Children, Nature Conservancy, William Holdens Wildlife Reserve, Fund, Kenya, Africa; [oth. writ.] Novel - (1994), "Peaceful is My Soul", Book - Poetry and Prose (1985), "Rose Peddles and Dreams", current work: "Hakuna Mpaka Kesho", "Not Until Tomorrow", Swahili - Poetry and Prose about Africa.; [pers.] My passion for Africa has traveled with me through my life. I have been greatly influenced by the strength and love of the Female African American Authors. Their writings and stories, have touched my heart deeply.; [a.] El Cajon, CA

MACDONALD, COLLEEN
[b.] August 16, 1982, Midland, MI; [p.] Cliff and Peggy MacDonald; [ed.] Home Schooled; [occ.] Student, Multiple Sclerosis Achievement Center Volunteer; [memb.] YMCA Swim Team; [hon.] Youngest speaker at 1993 International Concrete Conference.; [a.] Inver Grove Heights, MN

MACKE, ROBERT
[pen.] Bob Macke; [b.] June 10, 1944, Ann Arbor; [p.] Francis H. Macke, Edith Cox; [m.] Divorced, 1994; [ch.] Robert, Michelle, Tim, Mary; [ed.] B.S. Bus. Admin and Econ B.S. Criminal Justice minor Psy. Culver-Stockton; [occ.] Investigator - offer the stole of Nevada;

[ho.] Honor Society Culver Stockton College Canton MO.; [oth. writ.] A collection of unpublished poems. Call reflection.; [pers.] My writings are a reflection of my intersection with the people who touch my life with this frienship and occasional hardship.; [a.] Boulder City, NV

MACKENZIE, JOAN T.
[b.] March 2, 1926, MA; [p.] Marcy G. and Pierce F. Taylor; [m.] Divorced; [ch.] Emmy L. and Philip E. MacKenzie; [ed.] B.A. and M.A. Stanford Univ., M.B.A. Golden Gate Univ., J.D. Univ. of San francisco; [occ.] Private Investor, Poet; [memb.] Tech. Securities Analysts Assoc. S.F., Save S.F. Bay, Save The Redwood League; [oth. writ.] Techno-Economic Studies; [pers.] Poets who have influenced me: Pope, Cavafy, Plath, Roethke (others too, of course).; [a.] Menlo Park, CA

MACPHETRIDGE, BETTY ANN
[b.] April 3, 1931, La Crosse, WI; [p.] Dan and Cora Young; [m.] Don MacPhetridge, September 10, 1955; [ed.] 12th Grade plus many development seminars throughout my career.; [occ.] My Business Training led me to secretarial duties at Trane Co. in La Crosse WI where I retired in '88 as a Manufacturing Engineering Assistant.; [memb.] 45 Years in PSI (Professional Secretaries International) and am very active in our United Methodist Church.; [hon.] Secretary of the Year in PSI.; [oth. writ.] Being very involved in crafts I design greeting and cards and compose very personal poems to utilize therein. I enjoy coordinating parties form. Have written many Happy Ads for friends that are published in our local paper.; [pers.] Writing poetry, to me, is a neat way of truly expressing oneself and my wish is to inspire hopefuls. My belief in life is to enjoy every moment and to enjoy moment and to accomplish this it is imperative we care and share. But...Most of All...and a daily priority, we must count blessings and Give Thanks!; [a.] Onalaska, WI

MAGATHAN, CHERYL L.
[pen.] "Cheryl"; [b.] March 23, 1953, Wichita, KS; [p.] Joe Leach and Darienc Allen (Deceased); [m.] Joe Magathan, February 19, 1977; [ch.] Erik 21, Troy 19, Jared 17, Rabel 12; [ed.] High School - Cosmetology School Business; [occ.] Teaching Home schooling for 2 youngest children.; [memb.] Jehovah's Christian Witness; [oth. writ.] Several poems on various subjects deadline with life and feelings.; [pers.] Writing, for me, is an out pouring of conscience. It is a way to dream up from oneself the past and present - because behind every line is a part of a persons views in life. It is cleansing and symbolic like our dreams because we were through life's; [a.] Newton, KS

MAHABIR, RAM HARAKH
[pen.] Ramh-mbir; [b.] May 19, 1962, Lautoka, Fiji; [p.] Pandit Dwarka and Sirtaji; [m.] Maren Ingeburg Petersen, September 11, 1964; [ch.] Dirk Petersen Mahabir, Ronald Karsten Mahabir; [ed.] B.A. (English), M.A. (Education), Ph.D. (Bus. in Administration). Studied Gothic, Icelandic, Anglo-Saxon, Middle English, Hindi, Sanskrit, Latin; [occ.] Realtor-Counselor, Appraiser, Tax Preparer; [memb.] Real Estate Certificate Institute, International Certified Appraiser, Graduate of R.E. Institute, Marin, California and National Association of Realtors; [hon.] Teachers "B" Bursary, Wilson and Horton Prize in Journalism, Highest Achievement in R.E. Marketing, Who's Who in California, International Who's Who of Professionals.; [oth. writ.] Articles in magazines and newspapers; [pers.] Every member of human race under the skin is both a human animal and human being. The said race can change for the better and an extensive positive learning throughout life. My sons are prime examples of this philosophy.; [a.] Tiburon, CA

MAHER, JAMES
[pen.] Emerson Bridges; [b.] March 30, 1977, Alexandria, LA; [ed.] Little Rock Catholic High, Catholic University of America; [oth. writ.] Self-published collection, "Phantom."; [pers.] Influenced greatly by the writings of Eliot and Donna, by the teaching of Mr. Stephen H. Wells, by my friend Corey D. Keith 2nd all those I have met.; [a.] Chicago, IL

MAHONEY, DENNIS
[b.] April 23, 1979, Perth Amboy, NJ; [p.] Ellen and Dennis; [ed.] Metuchen High School; [occ.] Student; [oth. writ.] Numerous unpublished poems; [pers.] Live life or die life; [a.] Metuchen, NJ

MAHOVER, MARLA
[b.] August 28, 1973, Philadelphia, PA; [ed.] Indiana University of P.A., major in Mass Communications Media/Spanish, also Universidad de Valladollid, Espana; [occ.] Customer Service Representative with First Union Bank; [memb.] I belong to the Sharon Baptist Church S.W. Philadelphia, Zeta Phi Beta Society Inc., Short Term Missionary with M.I.A. (Mission in Action); [hon.] Received educational honors at Universidad de Valladolid; [oth. writ.] Play writer of "Can You Reach My Friend." Poem entitled "When the Lights Go Off" published in a book called Traces of My Mind. Several articles written for the newspaper "The Penn." in Indiana, PA. (feature writer); [pers.] "For I am not ashamed of the gospel of Christ, for it is the power of God unto salvation... Roman Lilba I like to put myself in other people's shoes, in other people's mind and then, I write.; [a.] Philadelphia, PA

MAIERITSCH, NICHOLAS J.
[pen.] Nick Maieritsch; [b.] November 12, 1984, Chicago, IL; [p.] John and Marge Maieritsch; [ed.] Six years of Elementary Education; [occ.] Student; [pers.] I have always liked the sound of poetry that was read to me. My teacher Mrs. Altman, encouraged me to write.; [a.] Chicago, IL

MAINES, LISA A.
[b.] August 22, 1960, Clearfield, PA; [p.] Rita and James F. Maines; [ed.] High School Graduate; [occ.] Day Care Worker; [oth. writ.] The near completion of a child's book.; [pers.] My inspirations come from nature. The bigger, the better... The smaller, the sweeter...; [a.] Augusta, GA

MALINSKI, KATHLEEN F.
[b.] November 7, 1952, Santa Barbara, CA; [p.] John R. Feehan and Dorothy A. Feehan; [m.] Arthur M. Malinski, October 18, 1985; [ed.] University of Southern California, Bachelor of Arts, English, 1974; [occ.] Freelance Copy writer and owner of a marketing Commnications/copy writing Business.; [oth. writ.] Article published in "Wing World" magazine; [a.] Walnut, CA

MALINSKY, KEITH F.
[b.] February 7, 1960, Amityville, N.Y.; [p.] Kenneth Malinsky, Patricia Malinsky; [ch.] Alfonso Trujillo, Raymond McDaniels II; [ed.] Commack High School South, Suffolk College, Azusa College; [occ.] Child Care Counselor Group Home, Burbank, CA.; [memb.] Foster Care Association, Century Cable Production, Insane Domain Productions.; [hon.] Dean's List; [oth. writ.] Two plays produced in Hollywood, one children's book published, several cable shows produced.; [pers.] I have always tried to capture the beauty of the rose without tainting it. My two main influences in my writing are Walt Whitman and Jack Kerovac-Kindred Spirits.; [a.] Burbank, CA

MALOY, MR. RICK D.
[b.] August 12, 1960, Coshocton, OH; [p.] Larry D. Maloy, Rosalie M. Maloy; [ed.] Newcomerstown High, 1 yr. Kent St. Univ. (Tusc.); [occ.] Senior Embroidery Machine Operator, Bowman Sportswear; [oth. writ.] I have a regular submission to the Newcomerstown News, I have won four (4) times in The Time Reporters Ghost Story Writing Contest.; [pers.] No effort is wasted, if it is the very best you have to offer. Always strive to give your very best, and never look back. You cannot change where you've been, but your future is entirely up to you.; [a.] Newcomerstown, OH

MALTESE, MICHAEL
[b.] April 25, 1979; [pers.] "Nothing stops the man who desires to achieve" - Eric Butterworth; [a.] North Brunswick, NJ

MANFRE, LORETTA LOUISE SALVIO
[pen.] Retta; [b.] June 2, Brooklyn, NY; [p.] Paul and Anna Salvio; [m.] Nicholas, August 14; [ch.] Anthony; [ed.] Christian Grammar School Sacred Heart, John Jay H.S., Cambridge Correspondence; [occ.] Writing at home; [memb.] Various charities concerning children with special needs in what I enjoy spending extra money on.; [oth. writ.] Many unfinished and in production hopefully one day to create a book and publish the many poems I've written my goal to one day write for greeting cards that have true meaning.; [pers.] My ambitions is to reflect real life situations into creative poems and quotes that touch the very soul God is my influence my sons vision gives me direction hopefully if only one person is affected I'm accomplished; [a.] Howell, NJ

MANGER, SANDRA
[b.] January 12, 1958, Hondo, TX; [p.] Pansy Elizabeth Breiten, Edward Breiten; [m.] Henry G. Manger III, July 17, 1976; [occ.] Medical Student; [memb.] Lytle United Methodist Church; [a.] Pearsall, TX

MANN, NANCY E.
[pen.] Kido; [b.] September 4, 1963, Rochester, NY; [p.] Leon James Mann and Carol and Robert Jackman (Deceased); [m.] Divorced Twice; [ch.] Dariel Lee Englert, two children deceased.; [ed.] High School Diploma and 13 years of Mothering Child.; [occ.] Teachers Aid at an Infant Development Center for Physically and Emotionally Handicapped Children.; [hon.] Local County Fair (poem) Blue Ribbon.; [oth. writ.] Several articles written in the local paper about issues in the area, many other poems written, working on my 34th daily Journal since 1985.; [pers.] I've been greatly influenced by the more than usual trauma a person faces in a life time and counting the many supportive and compassionate friends and people in my area.; [a.] Mill Hall, PA

MANN, ROBERTA
[b.] March 24, 1970, Hazel Crest, IL; [p.] Robert Granath and Carol Granath; [m.] Robert J. Mann Jr., December 15, 1990; [ch.] Joseph Robert and Jessica Marie; [ed.] Oak Forest High School; [occ.] Office Representative, State Farm Insurance Crestwood, IL; [oth. writ.] Private Journals; [pers.] To reflect inner peace and strength through writing; [a.] Midlothian, IL

MANNIGAN, MARGARET PRICE
[b.] December 30, 1934, Cleveland, OH; [m.] Divorced; [ch.] Cynthia, Andrew, Dennis, Melinda, Gerald, Donald; [ed.] Cape Vincent Central School, St. Anthony's Parochial School; [occ.] Debt Collector; [memb.] American Legion Auxiliary 40 years post 832, AARP; [hon.] 2nd prize Miss IGA Teenager, Essay Contest 5/51; [pers.] Favorite poet: Rod McKuan; [a.] Watertown, NY

MANTERIS, APRIL LYNN
[b.] April 11, 1979, Metairie, LA; [p.] Gregory J. Manteris, Evelyn C. Manteris; [ed.] Albemarle High School (Junior); [occ.] Student; [memb.] Keywanettes Club, Sierra Club, School Newspaper; [hon.] Freshman Scholar, Most Talented-Drama I, High Honor Roll, Academic Excellence, Who's Who Among American High School Students; [pers.] Through my writing I am able to embark on many journeys through time, love, new worlds, and life. I became capable of facing my greatest dreams and my worst fears. As long as I may write, I shall always be free.; [a.] Charlottesville, VI

MARCOU, DAVID J.
[pen.] Joseph David (no used here); [b.] November 25, 1950, La Crosse, WI; [p.] David A. and Rose C. Marcou; [ch.] Matthew A. Marcou; [ed.] B.A. Un-Madison 1973 History, M.A. Univ. of Iowa 1978 Ama studies, B.J. UM-Columbia 1984 Journalism; [occ.] Teacher and Freelance, Journalist; [memb.] St. Joseph the workman Cathedral, La Crosse, WI; [hon.] Second and third places in Recent Golden Soul writing contests for non-fiction.; [oth. writ.] 1. Calling America, 1980-85, (a book of black and white photographs), 2. More Memoir for Matthew: The Reflections of an American Journalist on his time in fourth Korea, 3. If I Do the Research, The Lord Brings Me Luck: The Plain - Spoken Autobiography of David J. Marcou, 4. Korea 2050: An American Journalist's View of How Age-Old card is Coping with Rapid Change Just West of the Rising Sun, 5. My London Autumn: The Episodes Adventures of an Intinerant American Journalist in 1981 Britain, 6. More Memoirs for Matthew: New Northern South Korean Adventures upon American Journalist in the Mid-19805, 7. Images: The Body of Christ Matthew, and Me Or a Little Bit of Creation, (A Photobook); [pers.] I am a strong believer in the ability of almost any human being to contribute to society with their writing and a photograph. My son is developing his abilities in this regard, and not is becoming and good fledging professional writer and photograph — — as a result.; [a.] La Crosse, WI

MARKS, DAVID J.
[b.] August 13, 1953, Pendleton, OR; [p.] Dr. Tom and Jean Marks; [ed.] M.S.T. 1986, M.A.T. 1993, B.S. 1978, B.A. 1993, A.S. 1995, Portland State University; [occ.] Medical Laboratory Technician; [memb.] Planetary Society; [hon.] Co-captain Reed College Soccer Team; [oth. writ.] Several unpublished books of poetry and novels; [pers.] While we all work to solve the A.I.D.S problem, hope fully the strains of poetic jubilee will uplift our spirits.; [a.] Portland, OR

MARLOWE, LYNN
[memb.] International Society of Poets, Association for Research and Enlightenment; [hon.] Essay Awards including The American Legion.; [oth. writ.] Poems, articles, published in High School newspaper.; [pers.] I have been inspired by the romantic poets. I have an interest in metaphysics, philosophy, psychic sciences and the beauty of life.; [a.] Island Lake, IL

MARQUARDT, JANE
[b.] June 8, 1952, Dayton, OH; [p.] Robert L. Marquardt, Susan R. Marquardt; [m.] Pauline Blanchard; [ed.] University of Utah (B.S., J.D.), University of San Diego (L.L.M.); [occ.] Attorney; [pers.] My family is full of writers and poets. None of us are particularly famous, but our shared fascination with words ties us together through our various walks of life.; [a.] Ogden, UT

MARSH, FREIDA
[b.] August 10, 1931, Arkansas; [p.] Dovie and Virgil Wilson; [m.] Divorced, 1978; [ch.] Eric and Karen Hankins; [ed.] 6 grade I had to go to work in fields at 12 year old; [occ.] Antique Dealer; [pers.] I have always been able to write poetry I should have done something about it. But had to raise my brothers and sister.; [a.] Exeter, CA

MARSHALL, PATRICIA
[b.] March 11, 1946, Hackensack, NJ; [p.] John and Clara Marshall; [m.] Roger G. Marshall; [ch.] John McKinley ("Mac") Marshall; [ed.] Smith College (B.A.), Harvard University (A.M.), Duke University (Ph.D.); [occ.] Professor of Classical Studies University of Richmond; [a.] Richmond, VA

MARTIN, DIANA SIMMONS
[b.] March 14, 1944, Trinidad, West Indies; [p.] Cecil and Eileen Simmons; [ch.] Paul Martin; [ed.] San Juan Gov't. Trinidad W.I. Tottenham Tech. London England Fairfield Hospital Hitchin Herts U.K., Amersham and Wycombe Hops. Bucks U.K.; [occ.] R.N. Geriatrics in ECF.; [hon.] Psychology Award 1967; [pers.] I live by the golden rule. I believe that kindness begets kindness, and love is the most powerful emotion to experience; [a.] Fort Worth, TX

MARTIN, EVELYN RUTH
[b.] January 18, 1935, Austin, TX; [p.] Rev. E. M. Franklin and Alla Franklin; [m.] William Martin Sr., April 9, 1955; [ch.] Five; [ed.] High School graduate (Anderson High) Austin, TX., attended - Huston Tillotson College Austin Texas, attended-Los Angeles City College - L.A Calif., attend-People's Business College, graduated Autis, TX graduated - Austin's College of Business Administration, Austin, Texas, 1970; [occ.] Retired; [memb.] Wives Auxilary - East Austin Optimist Club - Member Vice President - St. James Baptist Church Sanctuary Choir (current) 1995-96, Reporter St. James Music Department, 1995-96, member American Heart Association; [hon.] Award presented (1991) for 25 years of dedicated service from Travis State School. (Employed) Award presented for worker of the month. Travis State School (1990), Award presented (1994) for 30 years of dedicated service from the St. James Baptist Church Choir.; [oth. writ.] For Church functions, such as funerals, newsletters, special activities and special dedications upon request. Reunions and weddings. Oratorical events.; [pers.] I mainly strive to reflect my poems toward memories that the young and old can relate to.; [a.] Austin, TX

MARTIN, JAMES WOODROW
[pen.] J. W. Martin; [b.] August 25, 1942, Okmulgee, OK; [p.] Woodrow and Willena Martin; [m.] Vicki Martin, November 23, 1967; [ch.] James H. Martin and Jedediah P. Martin; [ed.] B. A. Fort Hays Kansas State University, 1969; [pers.] This is a poem of my father's that I have enjoyed reading many times. He died in June of 1974 and I have submitted it on his behalf. His writings have meant a great deal to me.; [a.] Chase, KS

MARTIN, LEONA
[pen.] Ginger Martin; [b.] August 8, 1966, Montabello, CA; [p.] Lou Coleman and Mickie Coleman; [m.] Jim Martin, August 8, 1990; [ch.] Kimberly Ann Martin; [pers.] This is my first poem published and it is dedicated to my father to express my feelings for him that I didn't get a chance to express before he passed away. And has been a way of making peace within myself regarding him.; [a.] Fontana, CA

MARTIN, MICHAEL A.
[b.] February 29, 1940, Akron, OH; [p.] Beatrice M. Gorcoff and Albert L. Martin; [ed.] Diploma in Claim Adjusting and Accident Investigation, Diploma in Hotel/Motel Management - 4 yr. College Equivalent-H.S. (College Entrance Boards Test), Graduate-Passed College GED- Received two Major Educational Awards in U.S.

Air Force, Strategic Air Command-U.S. Air Force Europe Conspicuous Award.; [occ.] Poet-Book and Song Writer, Professional Security Officer Main Job.; [memb.] Master Mason, 32nd Degree Scottish Rite Mason and Shriner - Member Post #8 (American Legion) - Distinguished Member of the International Society of Poets.; [hon.] Nominated as a "Best Poet" 1995 - Presidential Security in U.S. Air Force - Received several Editor's Choice Awards for Outstanding Poetry from the National Library of Poetry, Published Author (Book)-"Atlantis Secrets Revealed" Published Poet, Lyric Writer for Hill Top Records who recorded "To Eva My Love"/In Best Poems of Published Poet by the 1995.; [oth. writ.] Published poet by the National Library of poetry poems in Dance On the Horizon-Echoes of Yesterday Best Poems of 1995 Beyond The Stars Walk Through Paradise A Delicate Balance. Published Book: Atlantis Secrets Revealed Published in Las Vegas, NV by Gorman Inc. Hill Top Records featured "To Eva My Love" in their Album "America:; [pers.] To strive for perfection in all I do. I especially want to make my Book: Atlantis Secrets Revealed very successful and to write the very best lyrics for songs. I do write books - poetry - lyrics for songs.; [a.] Las Vegas, NV

MARTIN, WILLIAM C.
[b.] Utica, NY; [ed.] St. Francis de Sales High School Utica College of Syracuse Univ.; [pers.] For providing me with a reason to write, I shall always be grateful to Brother Owsin, C.F.X. I am indebted to Dr. Norman Nathan for my interest in poetry and fine verse. His readings and lectures and fondly remembered.

MARTINEZ, BERNARD S.
[pen.] Bernie Martinez; [b.] June 15, 1941, Westminster, CO; [p.] Ben and Henrietta Martinez; [m.] Christine Martinez, October 7, 1966; [ch.] Antoinette C. and Miguel Ramon; [ed.] Metropolitan State College-Denver Co., Santa Monica College-Santa Monica Ca., LA Trade-Tech. Los Angeles CA; [occ.] Senior Building Inspector City of Los Angeles; [memb.] International Conference of Building Officials; [a.] Westchester, CA

MARTINEZ, TAMARA
[pen.] Evelyn Itzel; [b.] March 20, 1982, Nicaragua; [p.] Maria Gloribel Martinez; [ed.] Minor (8th grade student); [occ.] Student at Immaculate Conception School; [hon.] Honor roll student, was elected to be a D.A.R.E representative for my old school, and a couple of my poems were published in the school newspaper.; [oth. writ.] Have written several poems and I am in the process of completing my own personal book of poems.; [pers.] Sometimes I feel trapped in my own world, I feel as if I were lost and unable to find my way back, but writing can somehow give me the strength that I need to keep on living.; [a.] Westwego, LA

MARTINKOVIC, MARY LOU
[b.] May 22, 1952, Jersey City, NJ; [p.] Albert and Ada Dice; [m.] John F. Martinkovic Jr., March 7, 1986; [ch.] Christine and Brian; [ed.] Edison High School; [occ.] Administrative Assistant to Director of Engineering-Frigidaire Company, Edison NJ; [memb.] Ladies Auxiliary Jackson Elks #2744; [hon.] 3 years - Past President - Ladies Auxiliary; [pers.] I was inspired by my love for John who is now my husband.; [a.] Jackson, NJ

MASHBURN, CHARLES L.
[b.] August 1, 1950, Borger, TX; [p.] Wilma L. Brown; [m.] Sherry L. Mashburn, August 18, 1995; [ch.] Billy, Wesley, Tracey, James; [ed.] High School - Buckeye Union High Buckeye, Arizona; [occ.] Commercial Construction Superintendent; [oth. writ.] Over 60 poems/songs. Currently writing first novel. 18 poems have been put to music and a collection will be copyrighted in early 1996.; [pers.] All of my writing has been done since I met my wife Sherry in April 1995. Her encouragement and support has inspired me to pursue a talent that I have allowed to remain dormant most of my life.; [a.] Austin, TX

MASTERSON, MRS. CAROL A.
[pen.] Carol A. Masterson; [b.] September 9, 1940, Winnemucca, NV; [p.] Juilio Giusti and Bertha Thomsen Giusti; [m.] William D. Masterson, August 5, 1958; [ch.] Christopher David and William Juilio Masterson; [ed.] Pershing Co. High and Grammar, Lovelock, NV, State and Community Schools - Reno and Carson City, NV, - Vancouver, VA, Portland, OR; [occ.] Investigator, Auto Parts, Owner; [memb.] Oregon Genealogical Forum - Portland, OR Grace Harvey Art Studio - Vancouver, WA, Oali - Portland, OR; [hon.] "Business Women" The Outlook - Gresham, OR; [oth. writ.] Family history; [pers.] People's lives are a creative inspiration to my success. I use my gut feeling and my heart as a guidance.; [a.] Vancouver, WA

MATHEWS, SONDRA S.
[pen.] Marie Saunee; [b.] August 24, 1944, Zanesville, OH; [p.] Mary and Daniel Darst; [m.] Divorced; [ch.] David (Deceased), 1 daughter, Robin Renee; [ed.] R.N., B.S.N. (Ohio University 1986); [occ.] R.N., B.S.N. Cardio Rehabilitation-Bethesda Hospital (Z.O); [memb.] O.U. Honor Society, American Heart Assoc.; [hon.] (1) General Excellence: Physical and Biological Sciences - G.S.M.C. School of Nrsg., (2) National Dean's List 1986, (3) Past Pres. O.C.C.L. Federation, (4) A.H.A; [oth. writ.] I am working on a book "When The Wind Blows" this poems is the first publication. (Lights Of Love); [pers.] My personal strength comes from the "Eternal Light" of our blessed savior.; [a.] Zanesville, OH

MATHIS, JEAN K.
[pen.] Imogene; [b.] July 2, 1920, Dubuque, Iowa; [p.] Rose Rahe and J. V. Vorwald; [m.] F. John Mathis, October 12, 1940; [ch.] 7 children - all professionals; [ed.] Junior College, Advisor City Sports writing classes! I am a ready, history 'Buff in Todays World of Change'; [occ.] Mother/Teacher 20 years writer. Phys Ed. and Competitive Sports; [memb.] Independent Reporter, Teacher (ret.), WW II Vet's. Wife Assoc., "Most Honest Research from 'US News', Tree Farmer Assoc., Coaches Assoc., Landlord in CA, 20 Units Assoc., Business President (office equip.); [hon.] Stock Inv. Woman of the Year, many award from schools as a teacher and trophies plus good sportsmanship awards for my 'Student's of Teens'. I am proud to have had this opportunity.; [oth. writ.] Poems and consumer reports, research writer, politics and financial reports for mags. and newspapers who may or may not use but has benefited me and family; [pers.] Retired in Oregon last 25 years this state is conducive to thinking about who, what, when, and where! Grateful for academia which gave me discipline to knowledge and a hunger for people and places!; [a.] Springfield, OR

MAYER, JACQUELYN ANN
[pen.] Jacque Mayer; [b.] January 7, 1949, San Jose, CA; [m.] Dennis Mayer, December 21, 1970; [ch.] Josh Jennifer, Jori, Jessie and Tammy; [ed.] Del Mar High School '67, Master's PC Design '73, Twin Lakes College of the Healing Arts '92; [occ.] Massage Therapist; [memb.] Associated Body Work and Massage Professionals (ABMP); [oth. writ.] Local newspapers and church news letters; [pers.] My writing is a reflection of my own personal life experiences. I have been greatly influenced by singer/songwriter, Don Rogelberg and Pastor, author and personal friend Peter Wilkes.; [a.] San Jose, CA

MAYLAND, DIANA
[b.] February 28, 1947, Missoula, MT; [p.] Lyle Kenyon, Peggy Kenyon; [m.] Martin R. Mayland, July 20, 1977; [ch.] Wade William, Scott Carsten, Daniel Martin; [ed.] Greybull High, Cosmetology, Northwest Community College; [occ.] Cosmetologist (Hair Dresser), Inn Keeper, Ranch Wife, Artist; [memb.] Wyoming Writers and Poets Ass., Cody Art League, Grace Lutheran Church; [hon.] Nymerous Art Awards, The Jamison Award 1979; [oth. writ.] Art reviews for Wy., artists local news column; [pers.] I strive to reflect the uniqueness of how mankind and our natural world are complementary and inseparable entities.; [a.] Greybull, WY

MAYNARD, JANET KAY MUELLER
[p.] Eugene and Allie Mueller; [m.] William G. Maynard, July 5, 1969; [ch.] James and Denise, Grandchildren, Nicole Maynard, Reyce Maynard; [occ.] Manager; [oth. writ.] Planning to write a book. Many poems written.; [pers.] My grandmother Mabel E. Mueller was also a writer of folk lore and poetry. I'm proud to follow; [a.] Ashland, OH

MAYOL, ELAINE L.
[pen.] Elaine Mayol-Colon; [b.] May 18, 1968, San Juan, PR; [p.] Cristobal and Myriam Colon; [m.] Carlos Mayol, December 20, 1991; [ed.] BA Degree, Education Univ. of Puerto Rico, BA Degree, Industrial Design The Union Institute, Cinci, OH; [occ.] Designer student; [memb.] The Planetary Society; [hon.] (1) Drama highest honor at M. Janer High School. (2) Univ. of P.R. Drama Lider Award. (3) Univ. of P.R. Kerigma (newspapere) editor awards (2); [oth. writ.] (1) Los Bienaventurados (novel), (2) Quien dicta al dictador (novel), (3) Articles for Puerto Rican Newspapers.; [pers.] I've learned that the hardest thing for a human to be is "Humane".

I reflect in my writing my preoccupation about the way that we treat each other, the rudeness, the meanness, the "bad ways" that sooner or later we have to get rid off; [a.] Cincinnati, OH

MAYSE, BERNIE
[b.] March 27, 1958, Clarksburg, WV; [p.] Paul Mayse, Thelma Mayse; [ed.] Roosevelt - Wilson H.S., West Virginia University; [occ.] Retail Management; [memb.] "Friends of Life"; [pers.] The poem was written for Thelma Mayse - Colburn, formerly Thelma - Margarette - Wright of Shinnston W.V., "The only mother I would ever choose."; [a.] Bridgeport, WV

MCARTHUR, FRANCES C.
[b.] December 21, 1924, Fort Lupton, CO; [p.] Charles Wagner, Frances Wagner; [m.] Robert F. McArthur, June 18, 1948; [ch.] Linda Cheryl, Donald Roy; [ed.] San Fernando High School; [occ.] Retired; [memb.] Women's International Aglow Open Door Christian Fellowship Church, VFW Ladies Auxiliary 2468, WOTM #361 Lodge #1037, TOPS #430 Roseburg — TOPS KOPS Society; [hon.] 1992 Chapter Queen TOPS #430 Roseburg; [oth. writ.] A short story and many poems, several published in church bulletins; [pers.] My poems are mostly religious and come to me by inspiration of the Holy Spirit. I strive to exalt the Lord.; [a.] Roseburg, OR

MCBRYDE, FREDERICK VANQUEZE
[pen.] King Frede; [b.] April 14, 1966, Troy, AL; [p.] Johnnie C. McBryde (Deceased), Mary Alice McBryde, Starks; [ch.] (Adopted daughters) Shaneka S. McBryde, Frederica M. McBryde; [ed.] Charles Henderson High School, Troy State University, Troy, B.S. Broadcast Journalism, Criminal Justice (Double Major); [occ.] Correctional Officer I; [memb.] Mason, K.G.L. Model one, First Missionary Baptist Church, Troy; [hon.] ADC-Outstanding Youth-1989, Deans List, Certified Family life-Educator; [oth. writ.] Personal non-published songs, short stories, and poems.; [pers.] I strive to elate, the reader, and I thrive emotionally from the spirit, as the negative is transformed to positive. I give credit for my gift, to me First Missionary Baptist Church, for allowing me to explore the effects of my works by being on numerous church programs.; [a.] Troy, AL

MCCAIN, HOWARD MITCHELL
[b.] August 5, 1935, Cleveland, MS; [p.] Howard McCain, Marguerite McCain (Deceased); [m.] Divorced - February 3, 1989, April 8, 1967; [ch.] Dennis, Bonney, James; [ed.] B.S. Degree Civil Engineering, Miss. State University - 1957, B.S. Degree Business Administration University of Southern Miss. 1962; [occ.] Employed by the U.S. Public Health Service; [memb.] Louisiana Engineering Society, American Society of Civil Engineers; [oth. writ.] Seven contributions to the reminiscences portion of: "Old Main-Images Of A Legend", Harmony House Publishers 502-228-2010, Library Of Congress Catalog No. 95-79213, Hard Cover Intern Standard Book No. 1-56469-018-8, First Edition Fall 1995, Copyright 1995 Ms. State University Alumni Association;

[pers.] Words that rhythm delight the mind, through and through. But a poem must also be clear, and it must ring true.; [a.] Lafayette, LA

MCCARLEY, BECKY
[b.] June 12, 1952, Portsmouth, VA; [p.] Dan McCarley Sr., Dolores K. McCarley; [ed.] M.A. Psychology - West Georgia College; [occ.] Writer, Metaphysical teacher, Massage therapist; [oth. writ.] A book to be published soon, called "The Seven Laws of the Universe - a handbook for Masters" (A meta-physical children's book) and 4 other manuscripts in process.; [pers.] Interested in teaching people about the location of Heaven (within) and the laws required to create the Kingdom in their lives and thus on earth.; [a.] Roswell, GA

MCCARTHY, NANETTE METSKAS
[b.] August 18, 1949, Illinois; [p.] George and Della Metskas; [m.] Gary Olson DDS, 1992; [ch.] Sean, Lauren and Collin McCarthy; [ed.] Riverside-Brookfield High School-Honors in English, Univ of Illinois BA - Honors Las, Northwestern University M.D., Residency in Psychiatry at Michael Reese Hospital, Chicago and Medical College of Wisconsin; [occ.] Psychiatrist - emphasis on Psychotherapy; [oth. writ.] "Custody" poem in The Garden of Life. "To The Mother's Who Have Lost their Children" in Best Poems of 1996 "Today" in The Voice Within.; [pers.] This poem is dedicated to "Truth" because with time it always prevails.; [a.] WI

MCCOY, DANIELLE M.
[b.] July 17, 1966, Cambridge, MA; [p.] Niles G. and Beverly A. Pierre; [m.] Michael V. McCoy, August 25, 1991; [ch.] Michael Jr. (3), Christopher (2), Jocelyn (1); [ed.] St. Louis Academy (high school) Katharine Gibbs School (Associates Degree); [occ.] Mother, Wife; [pers.] Since I was 3 years old, all I've ever wanted to be was a mother. Now, with every chocolate kiss, every sticky finger hug, every crayon drawing, and every "I love you Mumma," my dream comes true again every single day.; [a.] Wilmington, MA

MCCOY, PARKER SHIRLEY J.
[b.] August 8, 1936, Cleveland, OH; [ch.] Four Children, (11) Grandchildren; [ed.] Graduated from John Hay High School at the age of seventeen; [occ.] Retired; [memb.] St. Mark Baptist Church Cleveland, Ohio, National Authors Registry, International Society of Poets, International Society of Authors and Artists, The National Writers Association, The Poets' Guild, And the American Black Book Writers Association; [hon.] Two "Editor's Preference Award of Excellence" 1994 and 1995 from Creative Arts and Science Enterprises for my poems, "Free To Be Me!" and "Prejudice." "Editor's Choice Award" from The National Library for my Poem, "Why Me Lord?"; [oth. writ.] My poems and essays have appeared in the following anthologies: American Poetry Annual, American Poetry Anthology, Voices of Many Lands, A Moment of in Time, Musings, Reflections, Best New Poems of 1994, Poetic Voices of America, Our Captured Moments and Who's Who in Poetry.; [pers.] My goal is to publish short stories for teenagers and pre-teens. I feel that our young black children, and indeed

all children, need guidance and encouragement from an inspirational point of view that gives hope, self-confidence and a sense of pride in who they are. "When we share our thoughts, we have truly given of ourselves."

MCCRAW, MARQUIS RONELL
[pen.] Marquis Ronell; [b.] August 3, 1977, Los Angeles, CA; [p.] Ronell and Donna McCraw; [ed.] High School graduate, attending College (Cerritos College, J.C.); [occ.] Hubperson, UPS; [hon.] Honor student through high school, Most Inspirational in Track and Field, Most Vivid Imagination; [oth. writ.] Space and Our Future, The Time is Now, Paradise, My Heart, Life is Like a Feather, Your Will Be Done, More Than A Friend. None have been published.; [pers.] I like to go deep into the creative part of my brain. To pull out the most colorful imaginary things write about. I don't just write, I become a part of my writing. The people who influenced my writings are my grandmother Oretha Upchurch and Rudyard Kipling; [a.] Lakewood, CA

MCCULLAH, SAMANTHA
[pen.] Sam McCullah; [b.] August 23, 1981, Fort Benning, GA; [p.] Michael and Sheri McCullah; [ed.] Gardner Junior High School; [occ.] Student; [memb.] National Junior Honor Society, River Valley Living History Association; [hon.] Honor Roll three years; [oth. writ.] Two poems published in the "Anthology of Poetry by Young Americans"; [pers.] I think that every person has a degree of badness in them and I try to represent that in my writing. I'm influenced greatly by Edgar Allan Poe; [a.] Russellville, AR

MCCULLOCH, SHARON LILL ANGEL
[pen.] "Angel" and for S.L.G.; [b.] February 21, 1968, Southern Oregon; [p.] Larry and Susan Gallagher; [ed.] Crater High School, Central Point, Ore. returned to finish high school 9 years later at Spokane Community Falls College; [oth. writ.] Have written over 500 poems since 5th grade none published yet; [pers.] My poems are a reflection of my heart and soul. My future plans are to write a book(s) about my life including my poems, which are my life; [a.] Spokane, WA

MCDANIEL, JOYCE H.
[b.] February 9, 1956, Spartanburg, SC; [p.] Jimmy and Gena Hill; [m.] Rickey McDaniel, June 5, 1976; [ch.] Brian, Patrick and Keli; [ed.] Spartanburg High School; [memb.] Member of Zion Hill Baptist Church; [pers.] This poems is dedicated in memory to my grandmother Nannie Fleming who passed away May 29, 1995. She is my inspiration for this poem and taught me to love the Lord and life.

MCDOWELL, BARTHOLOMEW VILLA
[b.] March 21, 1971; [p.] Theresa and Michael Villa-McDowell; [m.] Courtney Chiba; [ed.] UC Santa Cruz; [memb.] Musical Group; [oth. writ.] Novels, plays and songs; [a.] Los Angeles, CA

MCDOWELL, CATHERINE M.
[pen.] Cathy Guerin-McDowell; [b.] November 28, 1949, Chicago, IL; [p.] James R. Guerin and Lucille Ledger; [ed.] Tilden Gen. High, Chicago City College, Texas Southmost College,

Academy of Real Estate, American College of Real Estate; [occ.] Realtor; [memb.] Active member: National Assoc. of Realtors, Texas Assoc. of Realtors, Greater El Paso, Assoc. of Realtors, Women's Council of Realtors, El Paso Chamber of Commerce, Grievance Com.; [pers.] Through the hands of God, I am able to write with feelings using an open mind and heart.; [a.] El Paso, TX

MCGARY, CHARLES S.
[pen.] Charles S. McGary; [b.] June 29, 1963, Old Waverly, TX; [p.] Charles C. and Doris M. McGary; [m.] Fiance Patricia A. Kizzee, June 8, 1996; [ch.] Charles Selwyn, Jazmon Lamar, Eumah Michelle, Enrique Michael; [ed.] Graduate of New Waverly High School 1981, New Waverly, TX; [occ.] Construction worker: Preparing to go to college.; [hon.] None - other than present honor.; [oth. writ.] I wrote a poem, "This is My Country", which is read to every class since 1977 in New Waverly, TX. I have written several but never thought to try to published any.; [pers.] I write what is in my heart, in hopes that my feelings will someday be an inspiration to our younger generation.; [a.] Huntsville, TX

MCGEE, VICKI
[b.] March 19, Oakland, CA; [p.] Thelma McGee and James McGee; [ed.] San Pedro High, Loyola Marymount University, Laney College; [occ.] Motivational Speaker, Actress; [memb.] International Black Writers and Artists; [oth. writ.] The Whitney Houston Thong, The Prophesy, Shock Treatment, (short story) My Daddy and Elsie's Mama, Paradigm Victor (all other poems); [pers.] The vast richness of the human spirit is my greatest source of Inspiration in my writing.; [a.] Emeryville, CA

MCGILL, ERMA LEE RAIBURN
[b.] January 14, 1942, Kiowa, OK; [p.] Ethridge Lee and Allie Raiburn; [ch.] (3) Gloria, Randy, Kimberly, 7 grandchildren; [ed.] Bachelor of Science in Elementary Educ, Early Childhood, and Mentally Handicapped, S.O.S.U. Durant, O.K.; [occ.] Lead teacher in All Day Headstart Program; [hon.] President's Honor Roll at Southeastern OK State University; [oth. writ.] Teaching ideas published in Teacher's Mailbox Magazine; [pers.] I enjoyed poetry as a child. I like all poetry but especially Robert Frost. Poetry is a way to communicate my feelings and tell a story in a few words.; [a.] Kiowa, OK

MCGOWAN, EILEEN
[b.] October 11, 1948, Philadelphia, PA; [p.] Catherine and Francis McGowan; [ed.] MA Bilingwal Bi Cultural Studies, MA Religious Studies; [occ.] Phd. Student Catholic University of America; [memb.] The Sisters of Mercy of the Americas - Philadelphia Regional Community; [oth. writ.] Many none published persons which reflect the pain and the promise of the human condition.; [a.] Mount Rainier, MD

MCGREGOR, MATTHEW W.
[b.] October 15, 1920, Montreal, Canada; [p.] Deceased; [m.] Patricia Ingham McGregor, September 21, 1957; [ch.] Margaret Ellen; [ed.] University of Michigan; [occ.] Retired Journalist; [memb.] Veterans for Peace, Salvation Army, American Friends Committee.; [hon.] A very Hopwood Award, 1951, UM, Pulitzer Nomination for Civil Right Series 1956, Short Story in "Best American Short Stories, 1969," Short Stories in National Journals, poetry in several newspapers.; [oth. writ.] Local and state awards for newspaper work, photography; [pers.] "Poetry, like bread, is for everyone," (Roque Dalton); [a.] Storrs, CT

MCKAY, GREGORY D.
[pen.] Purple Frog; [b.] December 6, 1951, Pullman, Washington; [p.] George and Dolores McKay; [m.] Jiji R. McKay, December 29, 1983; [ch.] Joanna and Matthew; [ed.] United States Air Force Academy, San Diego State, South Western College; [occ.] Electronic Industrial Controls Mechanic; [memb.] Iron Hand Assoc.; [hon.] Freedom Infantalis; [oth. writ.] Published in underground papers: Mad Hatter, Smoke and Colors, Freedom Breeze; [pers.] By my passage through numerous "Hospitals", I have the pleasure to encounter interesting souls that transgress the line between patient and staff.; [a.] San Diego, CA

MCKENNA, BLAKE
[b.] August 13, 1970, Rome, NY; [pers.] This piece is dedicated to the influential genius, Frank Black.; [a.] Chicago, IL

MCKERN, SHAWN P.
[b.] May 13, 1970, Owosso, MI; [p.] Michael McKern, Lynn McKern; [ed.] Michigan Lutheran Seminary; [occ.] United States Navy; [pers.] Real life is the best source of my personal inspiration; [a.] Saint Marys, GA

MCKETHAN, ELIZABETH T.
[pen.] Lib; [b.] September 17, 1921, Lumberton, NC; [p.] Rev. and Mrs. W. F. Trawick; [m.] Kenneth A. McKethan, February 2, 1943; [ch.] K. A. Jr., James and Robert (twins); [ed.] B.A. Degree - some graduate work; [occ.] Retired Educator spend many hours volunteering at V.A. Medical Hospital; [memb.] UDC - Eastern Star, 1. Member and Elder at Reilly Rd. PP Church, 2. Retired educator taught in Elem. Schools for 32 years; [hon.] Teacher of the year - Red Cross Vol. of the year, Vol. of the year at Fayetteville V.A., Medical Center; [oth. writ.] Have written many poems and short stories - some have been published in newspapers; [pers.] I strive to see the best in people to accept people as they are and help when needed. My grandson who died from Protussyndrome was my greatest teacher. My poem is about him!; [a.] Fayetteville, NC

MCKIERNAN, ROBERT D.
[b.] June 13, 1970, Houston, TX; [p.] Robert P. Mckiernan and Patricia Ann Mckiernan; [ed.] Senior Year at Western Connecticut State University; [occ.] Student, Security Officer; [memb.] American Red Cross Volunteer, US Marine Corps Desert Storm Veteran, Western Connecticut State University LaCrosse; [hon.] Letter of Appreciation from Secretary of State, various military decorations; [pers.] Written for C.W.; [a.] Danbury, CT

MCKNELLY, THEODORE TALIAFERRO
[pen.] Ted McKnelly; [b.] October 10, 1923, Pocatello, ID; [m.] Meredith, December 16, 1946; [occ.] Psychologist; [pers.] I enjoy the clear sparse language of haiku and the national human world it reflects.; [a.] La Canada, CA

MCLAIN, MS. DARRYL LYNN
[pen.] M. C. Darryl - "D"; [b.] January 8, 1955, West Chester, PA; [p.] Mrs. Marion L. McLain; [ed.] BA - Christian Education Manna Bible College (Honor Roll); [occ.] Disabled as of 3/95 formerly Staffing Coord. and Nsg. Care Tech.; [memb.] American Heart Assoc. Red Cross, American Diabetic Assoc., Institute of Children's Literature, Smithsonian Institute; [hon.] 1970-72 Library Service Award - Henderson Senior High School Gregg Shorthand Awards 70-72 Community Service - Brotherhood Crusade, and Southern California Gas Company Los Angeles, CA 1992, NCGCC, Inc. Nobel Prize - 1974 "Yes You Can" Stroke Club - Bryn Mawr Rehab. 1980 Employee of the Year - Century City Hosp. 1984; [oth. writ.] "Our Bible Roots", "Advance Toward Peace", "AIDS Is Not" (Documentary), "Black Jews - A Biblical Perspective", "Nobody Told Me" - (A Play), "Are You Saved?" - (A play); [pers.] To live peacefully with all men, to promote goodwill, and to help somebody along life's way, so my living will not be in vain. To spread God's love, and be a witness to live in fellowship.; [a.] Inglewood, CA

MCMILLAN, CYD
[pen.] Cyd Connor, Cyd Ryan; [b.] June 1, 1969, Emmett, ID; [p.] Chet McMillan and Erline Foraker; [oth. writ.] I have written many poems, song, articles, only one has been published. I wrote an article on Aids that a friend of mine sent to the Dean of Education of the University of Maryland which he commended in a personal note.; [pers.] In my writing I find many forms of therapy and for healing the soul there is nothing better than the written word. I find my childhood is a major influence in my writing, both the pain and the joy seem to work together.; [a.] Portland, OR

MCPHAIL SR., DAVID A.
[pen.] David A. McPhail Sr.; [b.] October 28, 1940, Weymouth, MA; [p.] Madeline and Archibald; [m.] Louise, May 18, 1991; [ch.] David Jr.; [ed.] Rockland High School Rockland, MA; [occ.] State Worker with Dept. of Motor Vehicles; [memb.] United States Veterans Vietnam Era Post 2 Abington MA; [pers.] Life is very short so I try to keep a smile all the time.; [a.] Braintree, MA

MEADOWS, MAURICE
[pen.] Maurice Meadows; [b.] December 23, 1960, Frankfurt, Germany; [p.] Chester and Vivian Meadows; [m.] Rebecca Meadows, November 3, 1993; [ch.] Trisha, Range, D'Aryes and Tre'vyon; [ed.] Edmonds C.C. (Computer Science); [occ.] Chef; [oth. writ.] Poems in Christian News Letters.; [pers.] In strange land we all must walk. If we walk with opened my minds you'll find that somewhere soon along the way there will always be a friend...Thank you Kimil Gray for never giving up on me. Luv you; [a.] Lynnwood, WA

MEADOWS, VIRGINIA MARIE
[pen.] Ginny Meadows; [b.] March 29, 1937, Covington, VA; [p.] Bishop L. and Nancy J. Meadows; [m.] Divorced; [ch.] Larny K., Robin C., Donald C., Bonnie M.; [ed.] King George H.S. 12 years KG Va American School Chicago Ill 3 yrs Bible College 4 years. 2 yrs. Nursing School Portland Maine; [occ.] Nursing; [memb.] American Heart Association Nursing Assoc. of America Bible Teaching International Society of poets 1994 and 1995; [hon.] Nursing, Teaching Training Nurses for the future poetry. Editor's Choice Award The National Library of Poetry for 1995; [oth. writ.] Writing songs and poetry for ten years. Poems published in a new release at water's edge.; [pers.] I strive be a blessing to all man kind. In my writings.; [a.] Holiday, FL

MEANEA, KAREN
[pen.] Silver Rain; [b.] August 3, 1954, Portland, OR; [p.] Arnold and Dorene Saucy; [m.] Divorced; [ch.] Duke James; [ed.] James Monroe High, Mt. Hood and Portland Community Colleges; [occ.] I advocate Iaman information specialist for the disabled and homebased working on a houses Hing babysitting, Business-Computer, tutoring local and National organizations; [memb.] Arthritis Foundation, National Organization of Rare Disorders, Fibromyalgia Association, Chronic Pain Association, Chronic National Fatigue Association, Alliance for the Mentally Ill.; [oth. writ.] Corresponding with people from all walks of life throughout the world.; [pers.] My writings enable me to write from my hearts to empower all people in our society that are hurting. My personal experiences allows me to reach out, touch, and bring healing hope, compassion, unconditional love to the broken hearted children, women, men, who are victims of all forms of abuse and chronic diseases.; [a.] Portland, OR

MEDVITZ, LINDA STROM
[b.] August 29, 1943, San Diego; [p.] Marjorie Reed and Thomas Joseph Reed; [m.] Thomas James Medvitz, December 19, 1981; [ch.] Sherry Ann Strom and Michelle Strom; [ed.] Church College of Hawaii which became Brigham Young University; [occ.] C.E.O. of Homeowner Association Management Company called Strom Management Inc.; [memb.] Zoological Society, Association of Research and Enlightment, Community of Community Association Institute, California Association of Community Managers, Sacred Rainbow Circle; [hon.] (PCAM) Professional Community Association Manager, (CCAM) Certified California Association Manager, Iridology Certification; [oth. writ.] "Insights" a series of articles published in the "Light News" and "Sacred Rainbow Circle" news letters.; [pers.] Am here to simply help mankind live in harmony, empower himself or herself through love and healing energies.; [a.] Lakeside, CA

MEEHAN, DOROTHY K.
[pen.] Dorothy K. Meehan; [b.] June 24, 1921, Lowell, MA; [p.] Mabelle Lapham; [m.] William Meehan - Deceased, November 4, 1938; [ch.] Thomas, Dorothy, Robert Sheridan; [ed.] High School; [occ.] Part Time monitor for special need children; [memb.] Eagles Veterans Club Member of Commanders Club Disabled American Veterans; [hon.] Certificate of Achievement in Rra. Electronic Mathematics - awarded by Bunker Hill Community College - Data Printer Corp. June 30 1981; [oth. writ.] I am starting to write and also do the drawings for childrens poems to hopefully be published and sold to the public.; [pers.] I believe that if any one person can write or show their feelings on paper and it turns out good enough to make a better person of who reads it anyone, they deserve lot's of credit.; [a.] Saugers, MA

MEISLOHN, BARBARA JO
[pen.] Bobbi Meislohn; [b.] March 10, 1957, Baltimore, MD; [p.] Edna Wick, John Co. Wick; [m.] Robert Meislohn, October 7, 1977; [ch.] Robyn Leigh; [ed.] Institute of Notre Dame High School; [occ.] Administrative Assistant, NWNC Chapter, American Red Cross; [oth. writ.] Several poems published in high school literary magazine. Currently writing and compiling poems for my own book.; [pers.] I write what I feel, I am influenced by my favorite poets — Poe Whitman and Frost, as well as Maya Angelou and Rod McKuen.; [a.] Winston-Salem, NC

MELICK, CLETUS E.
[b.] August 5, 1926, Tiffin, OH; [ed.] B.S. Agriculture, Ohio State University; [occ.] Retired State of Ohio; [oth. writ.] Books from Eagle's Nest Publishing, Tiffin, Ohio "Expectations" - Poetry "Experience" - Stories "Indiscretions" - Offbeat stories; [a.] Tiffin, OH

MEROLA, P. J.
[pen.] P. J. Merola; [b.] June 6, 1951, NJ; [m.] Kathy, November 11, 1979; [ed.] HS - Some College; [occ.] Lab Tech; [oth. writ.] Hundreds of poems created my own character "The Black Panther" he appears unnamed in many of my poems; [pers.] A leap of the cat, look if you dare, let your eyes focus on hell in mid-air; [a.] Middlesex, NJ

MERRILL, GAIL
[b.] May 5, 1946, Marshall, NC; [p.] George Fisher and Nan Fisher; [m.] John Merrill, April 17, 1965; [ch.] John Christopher and Andrew Dustin; [ed.] Marshall High, Western Academy; [occ.] Artist, Watercolor; [memb.] Art Alliance, Beyond Boundaries Ministries; [hon.] "Best of Show", art 1993, Asheville Symphony Art Competition winner, 1992, first are recognition at age 15; [oth. writ.] Poems published in local newspaper, also in Art Alliance newsletters. Church bulletins and writing that correspond to art work; [pers.] Momentary words may stimulate emotions, challenge intellect or persuade other's will and are soon swept away with th wind but timeless words are those spoken from a heart of love; [a.] Weaverville, NC

MERRITTS, RITA
[pen.] Rita A. Merritts; [b.] October 28, Brooklyn NY; [p.] Eva Mazzaro and Philip; [ch.] Tracy Denise, Dana Nicole and Lomoriello; [ed.] Grover Cleveland H.S., State University of New York: Empire State College, West Chester Community College, Queensborough Community College, Mercy College. Pursuing degrees in Community and Human Services/Therapeutic Recreation. Dance, Liturgical Dance, Music Ministry, and Spiritiual Development Studies, Art, and Therapeutic Recreation. (Youth Ministry, Spiritual Development, and Music Ministry studies were through the Archdiocese of New York educational certifications and seminars); [occ.] Receptionist/Student; [hon.] A.A.S. degree: Performing Arts - General, WCC President's List, Dean's List, Charles H. Dyson Scholarship, Certifications. Youth Ministry Studies, Aerobic and Dance Exercise. Varityper Corporation Scholarship; [oth. writ.] Poem "Family", published in National Library of Poetry's Anthology, "A Voyage To Remember". Poems for Center for Christian Counseling newsletters, Westchester C.C. newspaper, The Viking, and "The Best of the Phoenix" publication; [pers.] The poem, " The choice", is dedicated to Dana, Scott, and to my grandson, Christopher Michael. It is my prayer that every couple and/or female who is faced with "choice" will find the courage and support to "Choose Life" (Deuteronomy 30:19), and that every couple and/or female who have chosen otherwise will receive healing and reconciliation with God. Also, it is my prayer that people struggling with life or death issues, in general, will seek for ways of preserving life; [a.] Tuckahoe, NY

METZNER, RICHARD J.
[b.] February 15, 1942, Los Angeles, CA; [p.] Robert and Esther Metzner; [m.] Leila Kirkley, June 26, 1993; [ch.] Jeffrey, David and Ian; [ed.] Standford University, Johns Hopkins School of Medicine; [occ.] Psychiatrist, Associate Clinical Professor, U.C.L.A.; [memb.] American Psychiatric Association (Fellow); [hon.] Golo Award, American Fun and Television Institute of New York; [oth. writ.] Numerous Articles and Book Chapters, various professional journals; [pers.] Present in the space between is the connection among all things: Sexual, sypnaptic, subatomic, and celestial.; [a.] Los Angeles, CA

MEYER, JILL
[b.] October 30, 1980, Baltimore; [p.] Patricia and Jack Meyer Sr.; [ed.] Grade School Education, Asension School presently in second year of high school at the Institute of Notre Dame; [occ.] Part time secretary; [memb.] 1) Forensics Team, 2) School Literary Magazine (Garland), 3) Students Against Drunk Driving, 4) School Newspaper (Windows), 5) Pep Squad (Spirit Group); [hon.] 1) Optimist Oratorical Zone Winner, 2) Stazioski Scholarship, 3) Two time Optimist Oratorical District Winner; [pers.] Although I am young, I see the pain in the eyes of too many people. I hope that one day we can live in harmony, and enjoy life.; [a.] Baltimore, MD

MICHAELS, OLIVIA
[b.] February 9, 1950, Reidsville, NC; [p.] Charles Delgardo and Thelma Delgardo, Deceased; [m.] Jimmy Allen Michaels, October 25, 1981; [ch.] Michelle Leigh, Michael William; [ed.] High School Business College; [occ.] Designer Top Notch Designs; [memb.] Sec. and Tres. full Gospel Assoc.; [hon.] Sales, Motivational; [oth. writ.] Layouts and Advertisements

in newspapers for various Corp. wrote Sales Motivational Training Materials. Monthly news letter; [pers.] I hope this begins my career as a writer. After all it took me long enough to decide. I feel I have a lot to share with the world.; [a.] Wilmington, NC

MICHELS, JESSICA
[b.] January 9, 1987, Miami; [p.] James J. Michels; [pers.] I think if you work hard and keep it up, and keep on going, then you will do very good (The Bible says don't grow weary of doing good); [a.] Hyde Park, NY

MIELKO, MICHELE
[pen.] Starla; [b.] October 2, 1978; [p.] Laraine Mielko, Michael Mielko; [ed.] Graduating June 1996 from Fair Lawn High School; [pers.] My poem, "Billy" is about a musician I admire for his songwriting and musical ability. He has very much inspired most of my writings and my bass and acoustic guitar playing.; [a.] Fair Lawn, NJ

MIESZKOWSKI, ELIZABETH ELLA
[b.] June 24, 1959, Detroit, MI; [p.] Mike and Irene Mieszkowski; [ed.] Oakland University, Macomb College (Music and Nursing); [occ.] Registered Nurse, San Diego California; [hon.] Vice President Nursing class, several awards in music performance (drumming), currently composing my own original music.; [oth. writ.] In a dream, would I have ever known, little old woman, I've searched this life, a soul's remembrance, Angel; [pers.] Sometimes inspiration lies in those we know. To my mother, I love you. And to my dearest friend, Joanne Muller, I love you too as with the Lord, you'll always be with me.; [a.] San Diego, CA

MILES, VERONICA SUSAN
[b.] November 30, 1959, Manton, KY; [p.] Joseph Julian and Naomi Marie Nalley; [m.] Joseph Daniel Miles, June 17, 1977; [ch.] Rebecca Jo, Daniel Wade; [ed.] Marion County High School; [occ.] Housewife; [pers.] Writing poetry is therapeutic for my soul.; [a.] Loretto, KY

MILLER, ANESA
[b.] June 8, 1954, Wichita, KS; [p.] Ruth W. and Malcolm Miller; [m.] Jaak Panksepp, May 1, 1991; [ch.] Ruth Ellen and Antonia; [ed.] BA- Occidental College MA, PhD - University of Kansas; [occ.] Freelance Writer, Translator and Editor; [hon.] Foreign Language and Area Studies Fellowships (1982-85); [oth. writ.] A Road Beyond Loss: Poems of healing for bereaved parents and other survivors of lost love - $7 ppd (MFLC, 708 E. Wooster Bowling Green, OH); [pers.] Strongly influenced by Russian literary traditions; [a.] Bowling Green, OH

MILLER, DIANE PEMBERTON
[b.] June 13, 1948, Chicago, IL; [p.] William and Kathryn Pemberton; [ed.] Columbia College, School of Broadcasting, Internship - Cox Cable - TV News Anchor, Internship - Centel Cable - TV Producer.; [occ.] Independent Television Producer and Marketing Executive; [memb.] Former Church Librarian (3 years). Church of St. John the Evangelist, Flossmoor, IL, The Espiscupal Church of Flossmoor. (Resided in Flossmoor), Rector, Reverend Thomas A. Vanderslice. I am also the Granddaughter of an Espiscupal Priest, deceased; [hon.] National Honor Society; [oth. writ.] Executive Producer - Produced Television Program Titled "The Law and You". Aired (5) Months, Cable Television (Centel). Program Announcements Published in Star Newspaper (Flossmoor, IL) and other Southern Suburbs of Chicago.; [pers.] The poem encompasses all that is asked from God of man. My extensive reading while Church Librarian greatly expanded my knowledge and awareness of the Holy Spirit. Inspired by Jay Ross, Atty. at Law.; [a.] Chicago, IL

MILLER, DOROTHY C.
[b.] February 4, 1921, Bermuda; [p.] Carl and Eva Hollis; [m.] Alfred P. Miller, January 18, 1947; [ch.] Phyllis, Connie, Judy, Patty, Paul, Nancy, Mary, Mark; [ed.] Whitney Institute and Mt. Saint Agnes Academy in Bermuda; [occ.] Housewife; [oth. writ.] Many poems and stories written as a child and later for my own children and grandchildren. Only 1 poem and a X'mas story published in a local newspaper when I was 13; [pers.] Influenced by the beauty of nature I enjoy writing descriptive poems and I especially love writing for and about children; [a.] Gunnison, UT

MILLER, ELIZABETH MARIE
[pen.] Isabel Martin, Ruriko Mochida; [b.] September 18, 1945, Baltimore, MD; [p.] Albert H. and Angela Miller; [m.] I am single; [ch.] I have no children; [ed.] Lafayette H.S., Brooklyn N.Y., Staten Island Community College, AA, 1969, Hunter College, BA in History, 1975; [occ.] Secretary for the New York City Housing Authority; [memb.] Esperanto League for North America; [hon.] Hunter College Dean's List; [oth. writ.] Poems published in the Housing Authority's "Focus on Women." Three poems published in three National Library of Poetry volumes; [pers.] Poetry is a gift of the Goddess. I hope to serve Her through my life and through my poetry.; [a.] Brooklyn, NY

MILLER, KENNETH L.
[b.] Nov. 27, 1978, Mt. Clemens, MI; [p.] Jerry L. and Catherine O. Miller; [ed.] Henry Ford II. High School; [occ.] student; [memb.] National Honor Society, Macomb Junior Players Drama group, Drum Major of Ford II. High School Marching band; [hon.] Young Author's Awards, Music Scholarship Awards to attend Interlochen Music Camp 2 years, Detroit Free press, 1st place in writing competition. Led band in 1996 Rose Bowl Parade! [oth. writ.] Many short stories and poems; [pers.] My poems and stories are often centered around nature. I am greatly inspired by Romanticism. [a.] Sterling Hts, MI

MILLER JR., ROBERT L.
[pen.] Hyke Lee; [b.] January 26, 1950, Laurens County; [p.] Robert and Nannie Miller Sr.; [m.] Sallie Mae Miller, January 24, 1985; [ch.] Christain, Yvonniza, Ny Roby, Robert III; [ed.] Associates Degree Criminal Justice Senior with course toward Sociology; [occ.] Disabled Veteran; [memb.] Dunn Creek Baptist Church Inspirational Choir, Dunn Creek Lodge #302 Masons Due West Community Action Program; [pers.] It's not enough to live for today, we have tomorrow and yesterday. I've been greatly influenced by Nikki Giovanni and Watts Prophets, last poets and others; [a.] Donalds, SC

MILLER, MARK T.
[b.] March 15, 1967, Covina, CA; [p.] William "Ted" Miller Deanna Yosek Goins; [occ.] Production Leadman Flynn and Enslow Inc. Signal Hill, Calif; [pers.] Humanity has set into motion circumstances and conditions that are controlled by our choices. So choose wisely. I want to thank my parents for without them I would not exist. I will forever be in their debt.; [a.] Rossmoor, CA

MILLETT, KAREN L.
[pen.] Karen L. McGlade; [b.] December 31, 1968, Bryn Mawr, PA; [p.] William and Elizabeth McGlade; [m.] Robert J. Millett, November 7, 1992; [ch.] Thomas James Millett; [ed.] Haverford High; [occ.] Secretary, Shevlin Financial Broomall, PA; [oth. writ.] None that have been published; [pers.] "My poetry comes from the heart and reflects some of my life's experiences. This piece is dedicated in memory of my friends and family who are gone, but not forgotten."; [a.] Drexel Hill, PA

MILLINER, TYRONE
[pen.] T-Bone; [b.] August 5, 1956, Philadelphia; [p.] Eular Borsket, Harry E. Milliner; [m.] April Milliner; [ch.] April Christine Milliner; [ed.] Germantown High School - JNA Food Service School Both in Philadelphia; [occ.] Manager/Cook Zoom Restaurant Phila. PA; [memb.] Member of DVA disabled Veterans of America; [oth. writ.] Oh Lord I Thank You and others in newspapers locally.; [pers.] I think to put in words your inter most feelings in a way that the world can embrace is a gift that only God could have given; [a.] Philadelphia, PA

MILLS, PATSY ANN
[pen.] Pati Mitchell-Mills; [b.] July, Saint Petersburg, FL; [p.] Theodore and Evelyn Mitchell; [m.] Wayne (Divorced); [ch.] Angel, Eric, Jamie and Duke; [ed.] 1st yr Polk Junior College, Winter Haven, FL, Macon, Georgia; [occ.] Ceramic Tile Muralist; [memb.] Executive Business Womens Network (Founder 1988), Executive B.C.N., Pronet; [hon.] Presented Tile Art Miniature to Barbara Bush... scene of "Tallahasee Capitol Building" as a Florida Artist.; [oth. writ.] 1) Are You There? Do You Care?, 2) Angel Feathers, 3) Lady Rhino, 4) Is Noonie A Looney?, 5) Net's A Bet, 6) Pink Marshmellow Sky. ??? each poem with an angel feather; [pers.] I turned off the T.V. and stopped taking the newspapers. Started my day and ended the day with a poem titled Headlines, Morning News and Evening News, wonderful starts and endings...; [a.] Winter Haven, FL

MIN, BYUNG J.
[b.] April 24, 1948, Korea; [p.] Jung S. and Kwang D. Min; [m.] Myung J. Min, January 10,

1981; [ch.] Lisa, Sarah, Christina and Samuel; [pers.] I only write to see the change.; [a.] La Canada, CA

MINJARES, DAVID SAMUEL
[pen.] David Minjares; [b.] September 13, 1966, South San Gabriel; [p.] Luis Minjares Jr., Grace Minjares; [ed.] St. Anthony's School, Don Bosco Technical Institute, Rio Hondo College, California State University Los Angeles; [occ.] Actor, Writer (Poetry, Stories, Plays), Jazz Music Researcher, publisher; [oth. writ.] Mostly self-published anthologies through my publishing company, Oodle Productions: Sepia Token (1994), Mantra (1993), Poltergeist of the Streets (1993), Sympathy (1992), Fool Filter (1992), Warped Hand Memories (1992) (to name a few); [pers.] I approach writing as a constant challenge through natural instinct. I write about life: It's mysteries and revelations, it's darkness and preciousness, and it's controversies and it's less obvious treasures. Those are my influences.; [a.] South San Gabriel, CA

MITCHELL, GRACE R.
[b.] October 30, 1935, Winona, MN; [p.] Grace and Alfred Riebe (Deceased); [m.] Glenn E. Mitchell, December 18, 1955; [ch.] Five daughters; [ed.] Bachelor's in Education Winona State U. 1969, Life Practical Nursing Program Rochester, MN 1983; [occ.] LPN Assisi Heights Rochester; [memb.] President Christ Church United Methodist Woman and S.E. district officer UMW Saturday Meals Program for Needy Cancer Committe United Commercial Travelers Zumbrovalley Snow Mobilers Asso.; [hon.] Graduated with Honors special Mission Recognition - United Methodist Women; [oth. writ.] I tend to write longer poems printing them on "Grace Note Cards" I have composed music to some of them follow your dream - Batterflies Are Free The Cross and the Roses and Christmas Carols Down Bethlehem Way - God's Gift - Glory Glory - Christmas Bells; [pers.] I started writing serious poems about 6 years ago when I couldn't find one I liked for a memorial service. Money I receive for cards is donated to missions. I would like to share my poems with more people but don't know how!! I sang one of my songs at daughter's Wedding and Sister's Funeral; [a.] Lumbro Falls, MN

MIXON, ANTHONY A.
[pen.] Tony; [b.] May 15, 1964, Virginia; [p.] Bobbie J. Mixon and Charles A. Mixon; [ed.] Associates in Criminal Law-Phillips Jr. College; [occ.] Retail Security-Lowe's Home-Improvement Warehouse!; [hon.] Editor's Choice Award or Outstanding Achievement in Poetry the National Library of Poetry - 1994; [oth. writ.] Precious moments, published in The National Library of Poetry's "Songs On The Wind" 1994, "In The Merry Ole' Land Of Lowe's" published in corporate issued periodical 1995. "My Sweetest Dream" published in the Sparrowgrass Forum, 1995; [pers.] "Goodbye To Love" would you have to be the best example of the style of poetry I write. My words come from the heart and my hope is that someone may find strength in these words. If my words help but one person,
then I have ontained my dream in life. I'd like to dedicate this to M. Rousseau, With love; [a.] Goose Creek, SC

MIZE, KATHRYN
[pen.] Kathryn Mize; [b.] June 2, 1923, Seymour, TX; [p.] Mr. and Mrs. C. H. Peek; [m.] Charles E. Mize (Deceased 1989), March 3, 1947; [ch.] John D. Mize, Marilyn K. Lawhen; [occ.] Retired; [memb.] AARP Widowed Person Service, Southwest Cowboy Poets Assn. Amarillo, TX., Westcliff Bible Church; [oth. writ.] Cowboy Poetry - I've had poetry published in 2 Southwest Cowboy Poets Assn. Books.; [pers.] I wrote my first poem in 1992 at the age of 69. I grew up in a Western atmosphere when I saw an advertisement that cowboy poets were to be at the Big Tex. I went for a visit; [a.] Amarillo, TX

MOLNAR, CHLOE POLLOCK
[pen.] Chloe Pollock Molnar; [b.] April 4, 1930, Kittanning, PA; [p.] David and Fannie Pollock; [m.] Ernest S. Molnar, May 17, 1992; [ed.] BFA in Drama-Carnegie-Mellon University 1952-graduated Cum Laude, Kittanning High School; [occ.] Retired; [memb.] Women in film (Former member Bd. of Directors), Carnegie-Mellow University West Coast Drama Clan (Former memeber, Bd of Directors), Huntington Beach Art Center, L.A. and Santa Fe Opera Leagues; [hon.] Phi Kappa Phi, Mortal Board, Carnegie-Mellow University National Service Award-1982; [oth. writ.] None published; [pers.] I have spent my life trying to make this a letter world in which to live and love.; [a.] Huntington Beach, CA

MONEAR, STEPHANIE C.
[pen.] Neysa Meniere; [b.] May 12, 1951, Flint, MI; [p.] Earl and Eleanor Crompton; [m.] Clifford E. Monear, June 10, 1977; [ch.] Karl, Nathanael, Erica, Nicodemus; [ed.] Southwestern High, Mott College; [occ.] Professional Singer; [oth. writ.] A book of poetry and three short stories for children, hopefully soon to be published.; [pers.] In writing I seek to liberate my heart, and if in so doing I can touch the heart of another whose experiences somehow parallel my own, then I am content. (Two of my favorite poets are Tennyson and Walter Benton).; [a.] Flint, MI

MONGIAT, WALTER JOHN
[pen.] Mongiat; [b.] January 2, 1954, Fanna, Italy; [p.] Pietro and Maria Mongiat; [ed.] St. Anthony Catholic School, Boyland Central Catholic H.S.; [occ.] Freelance Illustration Artist; [pers.] Together with our minds the written word and the arts are powerful mediums, which we can influence, communicate and entertain others, just glad to be a small part.; [a.] Rockford, IL

MONTALBANO, ASCENZA
[b.] March 14, 1979, Rochester, NY; [p.] Philip and Ascenza Montalbano; [ed.] Our Lady of Mercy HS; [occ.] Student; [memb.] Campus Ministry Board, Mercedes (Literary Magazine), Veritas (Yearbook); [hon.] High Honor Roll, Honor Roll, Merit Roll, 1994 AIDS Forum 2nd place, 1994-95 Who's Who Among American High School Students; [oth. writ.] Several poems,
essays, short stories; [pers.] There may be problems caused by diversity but there would be more problems if we were all the same. I feel writing, as can any art, brings us unity and a common ground.; [a.] Rochester, NY

MOON, SUSAN MIRIAM
[b.] March 30, 1978; [p.] Dr. Paul R. Moon and Mrs. Betty Froese Moon; [ed.] Currently in 12th grade at Minnechaug, Regional High School, Wilbraham, MA; [occ.] Student; [memb.] Student Gov't. Nat'l. Honors Society, Member of St. Cecilia's Church, Volunteer Teacher of 6th grad CCD, Captain of Girls' Cross Country Team, Nat'l. Youth Leadership Forum on Medicine in Boston July 1, 1995.; [hon.] Winner of the 1995 Achievement Awards in Writing by the Nat'l. Council of Teachers of English. Smith College Book Award Junior English Department Award Massachusetts Interscholastic Athletic Association for (Outstanding Sportsmanship Award-Dec. 7, 1995); [oth. writ.] Was requested by University of Washington to submit to Essay Contest submitted Dec. 95.; [pers.] That of William Blake "To see a world in a gain of sand......"; [a.] Wilbraham, MA

MOORE, JUDY
[pen.] Judith Marie; [b.] August 28, 1946, Harper, KS; [m.] "Shade Tree"; [ch.] Greg, Douglas, Geoff; [occ.] Cross Country Truck Driver; [pers.] I write of my children, my memories and my personal philosophy.; [a.] Wetmore, CO

MORAN, NATALIE
[b.] October 4, 1981, Warren, MI; [p.] Kathleen Moran, Patrick Moran; [ed.] 9th Grade student at Jeannette Junior High and Macomb Mathematics Science Technology Center; [hon.] Honor Roll, Presidential Academic Fitness Award, 2nd place in local VFW Speech Contest; [pers.] Some say the sky's the limit, I believe there are no limits.; [a.] Sterling Heights, MI

MORCOM, GERALD FRANCIS
[pen.] Pen Rose; [b.] November 8, 1931, Jermyn, PA; [p.] Francis, Lillian Moon Morcom; [m.] Alberta Horan Morcom, October 26, 1957; [ed.] Jermyn High, Pennsylvania State University Technical Institute; [occ.] Retired; [memb.] Associate of the Mountain Echo a Local Rural Newspaper published in Clifford Pennsylvania; [oth. writ.] Poems, articles, published in local newspapers, (Arbon Dale News, The Mountain Echo, Scranton Times, Scranton Tribune; [pers.] Inspired to write by the sight of a single red rose on a wall of a small humble country home on a gently sloping mountainside in a beautiful valley of the endless mountains of Pennsylvania; [a.] Fell Township, PA

MORGAN, TOM
[b.] December 18, 1937, Toledo, OH; [m.] Nora Jean, January 25, 1958; [ch.] Todd and Juli; [ed.] University of Toledo, Owens Technical College, U.S. Navy; [occ.] Materials Engineer; [memb.] Toledo Stained Glass Guild, American Society of Materials; [hon.] Past Chairman, Toledo Chapter ASM, Dean's List Owens Tech; [oth. writ.] Technical Reports;

[pers.] My writing springs spontaneously from the heart and tarries but briefly in the brain; [a.] Bowling Green, OH

MORRIS, BRIAN PATRICK
[b.] December 23, 1983, Gallup, NM; [p.] Evelyn and Rogers Morris; [ed.] 6th Grader at Cathedral School in Gallup, New Mexico; [occ.] Student; [hon.] 3 years Academic Excellence, 3 years Science Fair Winner, numerous state, National And International Karate Awards, award for 6 years of School Perfect Attendance (not one day missed since kindergarten); [oth. writ.] Several poems and short stories; [pers.] "To be the best I can be at whatever I do."; [a.] Gallup, NM

MORRIS, CAREY LYNN
[b.] November 3, 1981; [p.] Rick and Debroah Morris; [ed.] Andorson Elementary, Ryan Elementary, Chicago St Elementary, Bronson Jr., Sr. High.; [occ.] Jr. High Student; [memb.] 4-H and track team.; [hon.] Personal success award, The Daily Reporter Certificate of Excellence, Mathematics and Science Center Award, Perfect Attendance Award, Athletics Award, 4-H Award, Sump Rope for Heart, State Board of Educations, Girl Scouts, Book Reading Program Award. And many more.; [oth. writ.] I had a poem published in elementary school in a poem book.; [pers.] I am going to follow in my father and grandfathers foot steps and strive to make a well minored life for me. My grandfather was a hard working former and my fathers an Executive Industrial Engineer.; [a.] Bronson, MI

MORRIS, JAMIE LEE
[b.] February 14, 1981, Portland, OR; [p.] Marshall and Maggie Morris; [ed.] West Powell Hurst Elementary School, Alice Ott Middle School, David Douglas High School; [occ.] School; [pers.] I have never entered my poetry till recently and I have never shared it with anyone, except a fun family members. I think writing helps you understand yourself better and from where your trying to come from, well for me at least.; [a.] Portland, OR

MORRIS, JAY L.
[pen.] J-Boy; [b.] July 10, 1978; [p.] Ernie Morris (Father), Carolyn Morris (Stepmother), Mary Morris (Mother); [ed.] Pearland Senior High School; [memb.] ECOC: Ecology Club; [pers.] I love love stories and hope to find the same love I read, and write about.; [a.] Pearland, TX

MORRISON, MEGAN
[b.] July 4, 1982, Jackson, MS; [p.] Tully Morrison, Margie Morrison; [ed.] Attending the 8th grade at Edinburg High School; [oth. writ.] Three poems being published in an Iliad Press anthology; [a.] Edinburg, MS

MORTIMER, CLAIRE A. E.
[pen.] Solomey; [b.] July 5, 1953, N.O. LA; [p.] Nathaniel & Delores Elmore Jr; [m.] Sept. 1975, married, divorced; [ch.] 3 Orlando, Kelsey and Cira-Maria; [ed.] Dillard University - BSA degree, 28 hrs in Masters of Counseling and Education, MED; [occ.] RN - Supervisor of Cardiac Rehabilatation; [memb.] American Nurses Assoc., LCAPR - Louisiana Cardio Pulmanary, American Heart Assoc, NOMPO, Alph Kappa Alpha Sorority; [hon.] McDonald Award in Nursing, Dillard University 4 yr. scholarship Upward Bound Program Assistant Award; [pers.] Live and give completely and never look back and regret; [a.] N.O. LA;

MOSES, SHANTELLE ANGOVE
[b.] March 17, 1983, Houston, TX; [p.] Janet and Hal Moses; [ed.] Ross Elementary, and Creekside Intermediate; [occ.] Student; [memb.] League City Little League Softball, Jill Rauscher School of Dance, Solo Oboe Player for Creekside Intermediate Concert Band; [hon.] Science Fair 3rd place 1994; [oth. writ.] As of this date none have been published.; [pers.] I'm only 12 right now, so my dreams that I would like to achieve are to receive a scholarship of my writing and music, go to college and make a difference in the world.; [a.] League City, TX

MOSLEY, ELLA MAE
[b.] November 8, 1932, Granby, MO; [p.] Paul Porter, Grace Zarse; [m.] Eugene Mosley, February 25, 1949; [ch.] Phillip E., Delores A., Mark A.; [ed.] Granby High School; [occ.] Housewife; [oth. writ.] Song's we play at church and Granby House (Retirement Home); [pers.] We put on a Mother's Day program for the residents at the Granby House, and I wrote this poem for the Mother's there; [a.] Neosho, MO

MOTEN, MELISHA
[b.] February 25, 1975, Kansas City, KS; [p.] Jean Moten, Griegory Moten; [ed.] Washington High School, Kansas City, Kansas; [occ.] Student - Southern University, Baton Rouge, LA.; [hon.] High School - National Honor Society, Kansas Honor Scholar, Student Council, Mid-America Consortium for Engineering and Science Achievement. College - Dean's List; [oth. writ.] Joy, Wondering, School Days, The Sun, Feelings, Ways, Boring, The Ocean, Music, Dolls, Night, My Grandpa, Kisses, The Wind, A Star, Ersaline.; [pers.] I have written many poems, which I have kept in my personal journal since I was a young child. My poems express my inner feelings about nature, things that are dear to me, and the people I love.; [a.] Kansas City, KS

MOULDEN, DIANN F.
[pen.] Diann Freeman; [b.] December 20, 1955, Knoxville, TN; [p.] William Freeman and Laura Freeman; [m.] Kenneth A. Moulden, March 8, 1992; [ch.] Dermaine R. Freeman; [ed.] Austin-East High School, Knoxville Business College, H&R Black Income Tax School and Pellissippi State, Technical Community College; [occ.] The Fresh Market, Farragut, TN; [memb.] Inner City Church, Creater Ebenezer Baptist Church and St. Joseph's Church; [hon.] The greatest honor was being adopted into the family of God. The greatest award having access to the blood of Jesus Christ; [oth. writ.] I have written and directed several plays and songs at my church. By inspiration of the Holy Spirit.; [pers.] I want to be used by God to each the hearts and souls of many many people then my writings. I have been greatly influenced by the reading of God's word. And life has also been a teacher.; [a.] Concord, TN

MOUSSOURIS, EDWARD
[b.] July 26, 1968, Boston, MA; [p.] Alexander Moussouris; [m.] Helena Reynolds; [ed.] North Eastern University; [occ.] Scuba Instructor on Princess Cruise Lines; [hon.] Who's Who in American Colleges and Universities 1994; [oth. writ.] A letter in a note, Butterfly Song, To Twilight With The Wolf, Wet Tuesday, He Who Understands.; [pers.] Poetry is something that flows like energy. It is an art. It is whatever we create. I believe in poetry where words form sentences. I love to write about love.

MOWRY, S. L.
[b.] April 3, 1944, Woonsocket, RI; [p.] Richmond and Olive Mowry; [m.] Michael J. Meagher, September 1, 1989; [ch.] Kimberly Marlow, Shannon Mohr; [ed.] BS - Psychology 1989 UG College Asssociate Degree's: Sociology, Political Science, Fine Arts (painting, photography, sculpture); [occ.] Psychotherapy; [memb.] International Society of Poets, Southeast writers Association, Dahlonega Art Alliance, North Georgia College Alumni Association; [hon.] Deans List, Outstanding College, Students of America; [oth. writ.] Over 63, publications; [pers.] "If things get dull, create a crisis".; [a.] Dahlonega, GA

MOYERS, JOEL E.
[pen.] Joel; [b.] September 8, 1928, Knoxville, TN; [p.] Fred and Lila Moyers; [m.] Laura Blanche Emert Moyers, March 14, 1952; [ch.] Joe E. and Ella Louise; [ed.] 15 Months College - Mech Engr., 2 correspondence courses; [occ.] Construction/Carpenter and small time farmer - 7 animals; [memb.] Retired National Park Service and Fed. Hwy Adm., and Military 32 yrs Webb Creek U.M. Church; [hon.] Silver Poet Award 1990; [oth. writ.] Stories for children - none published date. Poem to world of poetry; [pers.] Thank you for allowing me to enter this contest and having a poem selected. The opportunity in itself is a motivation. I have 4 grandchildren, ages 3 to 11 and write them separately every two weeks, and include poems to them on occasion.; [a.] Gatlinburg, TN

MOZDYNIEWICZ, WOJTEK
[pen.] Womo; [b.] May 9, 1904, Nowytarg, Poland; [p.] Katarzyna and Stnislaw; [ch.] Dymitr Mozdyniewicz; [ed.] High School Nowytarg, University of (Aviation), Technology - Warsaw, Poland - MSA; [occ.] Mech Eng - Aerospace, (Boeing, McDon. Douglas, Rockwel Int, Bombardier Co.); [hon.] Int Gold Badge with 3 Diamonds - FA1, Saiplanes; [oth. writ.] Techn. Book 1976 Poland, 15 Techn. Papers (USA, Pol), Short 2 novels (pol) over 200 poems never publish, Poem "Tulip" 1987 golden poet - World of Poetry, Sacramento, CA; [pers.] Motivation, Achievements, satisfaction the loop or happiness, many shall less big ones. Expect best, be prepared for worst, take life how is coming!; [a.] Tucson, AZ

MUKY, NORINE
[pen.] Norine Muky; [b.] November 24, 1984, Chicago, IL; [p.] Timothy and Barchara; [ed.] Northwest School 5th Grade, Evergreen Park, IL; [occ.] Elementary Student; [hon.] PTA Reflections Award, Dare to Discover 1994 for music and lyrics; [oth. writ.] Many writings - none published: Optical Illusions, Happy Thoughts, The Forest, Family, Seasons, The Night Rider, Narnia (based on the him the with and the world) and many, many more!; [pers.] I find poetry calming when other things are frustrating me. I write poetry for myself because it makes me feel good inside.; [a.] Evergreen Park, IL

MULLEE, CHRISTIAN ELAINE
[pen.] Kitty; [b.] May 14, 1984, Gainesville, FL; [p.] Dr. R. G. Mullee, Nancy Mullee; [ed.] Brentwood Private School, Gainesville, Fl, gr 1-5 6 Ft. Clarke Middle School; [occ.] Student, Teach Poetry to sick children at the Healing Arts Ctr.; [memb.] Girl Scouts of America, Covenant Presbyterian Church; [hon.] Poet of the year - Brentwood - 4th grade, creative writing award - Brentwood graduation, Brentwood graduation, 5th grade; [oth. writ.] Several poems published in school papers, currently writing my own collection, The Horse 1991; [pers.] Life is like an ocean trying to battle to the place beyond where the waves break. Each wave, like a day, passes.; [a.] Gainesville, FL

MULLINS, CAROLINE BRITT
[b.] December 3, 1946, Annapolis, MD; [p.] Helen Behlke and Charles Britt; [m.] Dallas K. Mullins, April 11, 1991; [ch.] Dawn M. Brown; [ed.] Graduated from Annapolis High School; [occ.] Writer/Owner of Teddy Bear Day Care; [memb.] Edgewater Baptist Church; [oth. writ.] Poem "Why", book "History of Mayo, Md."; [pers.] I strive to be able to give something back to God and mankind for the goodness that has been shown to me.; [a.] Riva, MD

MUNCY, LARRY D.
[b.] May 30, 1954, Logan, WV; [p.] Harold R. Muncy, Ruth Jerrylene (Jeffrey); [m.] Sheila L. Monroe, November 4, 1978; [ch.] Jennifer D., Clint D., Cory D.; [ed.] 1 yr. College - Cuyahoga Community College Clove Ohio.; [occ.] Disabled; [memb.] Life member disabled American Veterans, Amvets; [hon.] Distinguish grad. - U.S. Army Aircraft Maint. Fort Rucker Ala. 1971; [oth. writ.] Evil in the wind (never submitted for Pub.) The Dream of Tears - (never submitted for Pub.); [a.] Kent, OH

MUROSKI, REBECCA ANN
[b.] August 7, 1977, Oswego, NY; [p.] Edmund and Linda; [ed.] Senior in High School; [occ.] Student; [memb.] Girl Scouts, Concert Band, Marching Band, Chorus Cheerleading, Track, Tennis, Ski Club, Member of Saad Tutoring (Host) others with reading problems; [oth. writ.] Has a poem published in famous poems of today by the famous poets society poem title - "Morning Love"; [pers.] Writing seems so easy for me. It's as if someone spiritual or from a past life is helping me. Thoughts are always racing through my head. I can't write them down fast enough; [a.] Pulaski, NY

MURPHY, BETTY
[b.] July 14, 1937, Des Moines, IA; [p.] Marie Hoch and Hollie Shaw; [m.] Larry Murphy, January 7, 1963; [ch.] Gene, Theresa, Patrick, Paula, Barbara; [ed.] 2 Years College - L.P.N.; [pers.] I have always written poetry for friends and relatives. It's something I enjoy. I feel family is very important and children are God's gift to us.

MURPHY, HELEN MARIE
[pen.] H. M. Murphy; [b.] October 19, 1948, Los Angeles, CA; [p.] Herbert and Evelyn Kraus; [m.] Brian M. Murphy; [ch.] Jason and Eric Murphy; [ed.] Harbor Junior College, LA, CA University of Arizona, Tuscon, Arizona; [occ.] Fine Arts, Visual Artist; [hon.] Many honors and awards, works exhibited and collected Nationally and Internationally; [a.] San Francisco, CA

MURRELL, SARAH YVONNE
[pen.] Yvonne K. Murrell; [b.] July 30, 1940, Raleigh; [p.] Norwood King, Catherine King; [m.] Grover Murrell, October 8, 1960; [ch.] Regina Yvette Murrell; [ed.] City College NY, Rutgers N,J Essex College of Business NJ, Phillips Business College NJ, CA State University CA.; [occ.] Network Marketing, and Distribution Administration; [memb.] Nat'l. Female Executive NAFE: Nat'l. Assoc. for Female Executives Women's Club; [hon.] Honor Roll and Honor Society; [pers.] Projection: I strive to be at the center of things in the cosmos. Four more years we will be in the 21st century and all that will be left of the 20th century will be reflections of times past.; [a.] Compton, CA

MUSSELMAN, DORIS
[b.] May 24, 1933, Lancaster, PA; [p.] Hoover Morrison, Ella Morrison; [m.] Charles Musselman, October 6, 1956; [ch.] David, Susan, Mark, Brian; [ed.] Southern Lancaster County Joint High School; [occ.] Homemaker; [pers.] I feel family closeness is invaluable and writing to or about my grandchildren is one way of helping to cement that bond.; [a.] Willow Street, PA

MUTSCHLER, MATTHEW A.
[pen.] Matt; [b.] December 30, 1967, Pgh; [p.] Ralph and Lorraine; [m.] Pamela Sue, March 14, 1992; [ch.] Three; [ed.] Brentwood High School Union Carpentery School; [occ.] Contractor; [memb.] German Clubs; [hon.] Writing award in High School from parkvale saving on "Children: The future of America"; [oth. writ.] Leaflett written in High School given to friends.; [pers.] Although I can be critical, I tend to concentrate on girts we've all been given.; [a.] Pittsburgh, PA

NAFZIGER, ANDREA S.
[b.] June 16, 1977, Wauseon, OH; [p.] Roger and Karen Nafziger; [ed.] Pethsville High School, Goshen College; [occ.] Student; [memb.] North Clinton Mennonite church, National Honor Society, National Wildlife Federation, Wolf Haven International; [hon.] Honors Scholarship to Goshen College, Guardian Angel Publication in "A Celebration of Ohio's Young Poets"; [oth. writ.] Guardian Angel; [pers.] Peace and love to all God's creation; [a.] Archbold, OH

NAHRSTEDT, JANET MICHELLE
[pen.] Janet Nahrstedt; [b.] November 11, 1983, Winter Haven, FL; [p.] William and Susan Nahrstedt; [ed.] Currently attending Avon Park Middle School; [occ.] Student 6th grade; [memb.] Currently studying violin at South Florida Community College; [hon.] Maintained principal's list (4.0) throughout school career, awarded citation for outstanding math student of 1994 by Florida Highlands Chapter of the Air Force Association, fourth place Tropicana-4-H Public Speaking Program Highlands County, FL, Blue Ribbon Avon Park Middle School Science Fair - 1996; [pers.] Avon Park, FL

NASLUND, JANICE JOANN
[b.] May 5, 1942, Gordon, NE; [p.] Mr and Mrs Albert Layton; [m.] Jeams Ross Naslund, July 27, 1979; [ch.] Donald, Patrick Robert, Mark-Kelly; [ed.] High school GED, Hanna Wy; [occ.] Work with the mentally disabled for Beth Page Mission (Community Living Assistant; [oth. writ.] I have written several poems about the people and things in my life that are very important to me but I have never done anything with them.; [pers.] I write about how I feel and try to live my life to be the best I can to every one around me. God is my influence.; [a.] Holdrege, NE

NEAL, CHARLES EDRICK
[b.] March 28, 1969, Houston, TX; [p.] Charles Farrel and DeLois Neal; [ed.] BA in Political Science from Texas Southern University, Houston, Texas, Lamar Sr. High School, Houston, TX; [hon.] National Dean's List 1987-88, 1991-92, and 1992-93; [oth. writ.] Two poems published in college newspaper, The TSU Herald; [pers.] Although our society is played with many vices I try to avoid writing about them. Instead it is my intent to convey to my readers my vision of a society devoid of so much evil and hatred.; [a.] Houston, TX

NEAL, JAMES LEE
[b.] July 7, 1969, Lexington, KY; [p.] Marshall and Judy Neal; [m.] Kelly Neal (Fiancee), May 18, 1996; [ed.] BA in Special Education (Learning and Behavior Disorders), BA in Middle School Science, School: Eastern Kentucky University; [occ.] Special Education Teacher; [pers.] My Fiancee sent this poem in "Kelly, A Beautiful Rose" is one of many poems I wrote to her, including one in which I proposed to her with. She is my inspiration. I dedicate whatever I write not to mention my life to her.; [a.] Lexington, KY

NEDELESCU, LIVIU
[b.] May 15, 1977, Bucharest, Romania; [p.] Iulian and Lidia Nedelescu; [ed.] Senior at Lakewood High, second year in post-secondary option at Case Western Reserve University, Cleveland, OH; [occ.] Student; [memb.] Watter Science Seminar, National Honor Society, American Field Service; [hon.] Celebration of Excellence Award, US First Best Defense Team Award; [oth. writ.] Song lyrics, essays, poems; [pers.] I don't think the power of Romanticism is cute. My new approach, present in the poem "At the End of the World" is to

take serious things as Nature cliches and let the reader think on these backgrounds.; [a.] Lakewood, OH

NEELY, JENNA
[b.] December 9, 1982; [p.] Sheresa Neely; [ed.] 7th (still in school); [occ.] Student; [oth. writ.] Poems top my mom when little; [pers.] I believe that artistic abilities enhances the world around us.; [a.] Lebanon, TN

NELSON, AUDREY M.
[pen.] Audrey Powell Nelson; [b.] January 6, 1930, Sioux Falls, SD; [p.] Mr and Mrs Frank Powell; [m.] Sydney A. Nelson, February 5, 1950; [ch.] Sharyl Lynne Dimpick, Peggy Anne Mines, Scott Allen Nelson; [ed.] Graduated high school (Garretson SD) 1948; [occ.] Retired Secondary School Teacher for Sr. Adults, Chairman of Program Committee; [memb.] Emmanuel Baptist Church; [oth. writ.] I have many poems I've written and articles too but none has won any awards; [pers.] I try to make a moral statement in every poem and article I write. I love to write. I can get rid of a lot of frustration and anxiety when I sit down and write.; [a.] Sioux Falls, SD

NELSON, DONALD
[pen.] Donald Nelson, Walks in Spirit; [b.] August 4, 1945, Billings, MT; [p.] Donald L. and Della M. Nelson; [ch.] Victor J. Nelson (16 yrs) lives with me; [ed.] Billings West High (1963 graduate); [occ.] Trainer for Micron Technology, Inc., a computer chip manufacture in Boise, ID. Camp-On Creations (Native American Art), Note: Camp-On creations is a side business I own, I draw native American art and have the art put on a wearable items; [memb.] National Museum of the American Indian BASS (Bass Anglers Sportsman Society) crafted with the Western Idaho Pow-Wow Assn; [hon.] Employee of the Year twice, Suggestion of the Month, Suggestion of the Quarter, Articles about my native American art in the local paper, my greatest honor - my son Victor, to have one of my poems selected in the National Library of Poetry Contest, and printed; [oth. writ.] My Little Buddy Boo, This Song Ain't About Texas, Life on the Homestead, Set Free, Majestic Protector, My Heart Sings, Chasing Endless Time, Alone in the Storm, Wartermelon Sneakin', Boyhood Find, Spooks in the Closet, Ridin' the Edge, Just a Wooden Pony, Bison's Flight; [pers.] I am very versatile with random thoughts and many past experiences of myself and stories handed down to me by my father, who was very adventurous in his youth. My poetry and songs I write are of these stories and thoughts. Through my poetry and songs I can share this with others, now and in the future.; [a.] Caldwell, ID

NELSON, LOIS J.
[b.] March 25, Wellston, OK; [p.] William Clifford Reed (Deceased), Earla Mae Reed Ross; [m.] James Urschel Nelson (Deceased), October 31, 1958; [ch.] Son Urschel Dino Nelson, grand Dominique Nelson, Dametrius Nelson, Mercedes Shade Johnson, Deion Nelson; [ed.] BS San Francisco State University, MA New College of California; [occ.] Accounting Supervisor; [memb.] Treasurer, Delta Sigma Theta Sorority, San Francisco - Peninsula Chapter: Project Co-chairperson: Delta Sigma Theta Inc, SF-Pen-Alumnae Chapter; [hon.] Bertha Pitts Campbell Award, 1994 - San Francisco-Peninsula Alumnae Chapter of Delta Sigma Theta Sorority Inc.; [pers.] I strive to present the positive aspects of life; [a.] San Francisco, CA

NELSON, MARTIN
[b.] November 11, 1957, Cambridge, OH; [p.] Richard and Francis Nelson; [ed.] Carson-Newman College, Grace Seminary; [occ.] Writer, President Worldwide Goat, Winona Lake, IN; [oth. writ.] Muffy the Goat stories and several poems and books for clients; [a.] Winona Lake, IN

NELSON, TODD
[b.] July 24, 1971, Kansas City, MO; [p.] Jay and Karen Nelson; [ed.] Monroe High School, Bradley University; [occ.] Database Marketing; [memb.] AMA, PRSA, AHA, SHERM; [hon.] State Forensics, General Assembly (church), Intrafraternity Council; [oth. writ.] Newspaper articles, poetry compilations, novel in process; [pers.] Ink and paper are simply 2 dimensional without the mind and heart. I want to touch people with written feelings.; [a.] Peoria, IL

NELSON, WAVA J.
[b.] January 1, 1931, Lake City, AR; [p.] Vercie Morgan and Martha Cook; [m.] deceased, married March 15, 1954; [ch.] 4; [ed.] grade 14; [occ.] retired; [memb.] Phi Beta Sig, wrote articles on brain tumor research and cancer research, LA and San Francisco; [oth. writ.] My One True Love; [Pers.] Studied under Maurice Ogden, award winning author of The Hagman, and the "O.Henry Award;" [a.] Huntington Beach, CA;

NERO, MAXCINE FULLER
[b.] July 31, 1940, Texas; [p.] Malissia Randolph, Paul Fred; [m.] Don Nero, August 20, 1976; [ch.] Beverly, Anita, Tyrone, Crystal; [ed.] HG Temple High, Valrie Hurd, Beauty Business College; [occ.] Custodian DJH; [memb.] ISP Perry Chapel CME Church; [hon.] Editor's Choice Award, the International of Poet Merit Award; [oth. writ.] Angeles Whisper, Illegal Granny, Blues; [pers.] I direct my mind to seek wisdom.; [a.] Diboll, TX

NESLEIN, RONALD R.
[pen.] Ron Neslein; [b.] November 26, 1972, Baltimore, MD; [p.] Shirley Neslein, James Neslein; [ed.] Southern High School, Baltimore, Troy State University, Montgomery Alabama, Community College of the Air Force, Montgomery Alabama; [occ.] Network Systems Analyst; [hon.] 1990 - The National Society of the Sons of the American Revolution Good Citizenship Medal; [oth. writ.] Several poems and song lyrics; [pers.] I have been greatly influenced by Eddie Vedder. We all seem to forget what really matters.; [a.] Baltimore, MD

NETTLES, MINNIE L.
[pen.] Lee; [b.] November 18, 1932, Montgomery County; [p.] Leola B. Nettles and Stokes Nettles; [ed.] George Washington Carver High, Alabama State University 1 yr, Floyd Business School 2 yrs; [occ.] Practical Nurse 35 yrs. will semi retire 1st of the year; [memb.] Southside Church of Christ, Bible Class Teacher; [pers.] I have never had any writings published before. I just like to put some things together when I am just sitting around the house doing nothing. Just trying to see what might happen.; [a.] Montgomery, AL

NEVINS, BARBARA JEAN
[pen.] Barbie; [b.] January 31, 1981, KC, MO; [p.] Phyllis and John Hubbard (Stepdad), Ted Nevins (Dad); [ed.] Freshman at Braymer High School; [memb.] Northland Pentecostal Church of God; [hon.] "B" honor roll; [oth. writ.] Written many other poems, none of which have been acknowledged or published; [pers.] I enjoy writing to express my feelings and beliefs. I hope that one day it will take me somewhere, or that I can influence our younger generations.; [a.] Braymer, MO

NEWMAN, LISA B.
[pen.] Lisa B. Newman; [b.] March 28, 1964, New Haven, CT; [p.] Barbara D. and Joseph D. Florentino; [m.] William D. Newman, September 19, 1992; [ed.] Southern Connecticut State University; [occ.] Graphic Designer, Jewelry Designer, Calligrapher; [memb.] Calligraphers Guild, Hamden Arts Council; [hon.] Art Achievement Award, Dean's List; [oth. writ.] Verse of greeting cards; [a.] Hamden, CT

NEWSHUTZ, DAVID BRADLEY
[pen.] Shutz; [b.] August 29, 1969, Cleveland, OH; [p.] Ronald Newshutz, Karen Kempel; [ed.] Cleve Hts High School, Cleve Inst of Art, Academy of Health Sciences, John Carroll University; [occ.] Medic, Artist, Student; [pers.] I can not live by one philosophy for tomorrow I may be someone else; [a.] Cleveland, OH

NEWTON, ROBERT FRAZIER
[b.] December 7, 1947, Philadelphia, PA; [p.] Edward and Marie Newton; [ed.] MS Industrial Education, Fort Hays State University; [occ.] Cabinet Maker; [memb.] Kansas Emergency Medical Service; [oth. writ.] Several poems published in college newspaper; [a.] Otis, KS

NGUYEN, MATTHEW K. DRAVEN
[pen.] Matt Nguyen, Matt Draven; [b.] May 15, 1974, Saigon, Vietnam; [p.] Thieu Nguyen, Khonh Lai, Mr and Mrs Terry Murphy; [ed.] El Monte High School, Pasadena City College; [occ.] Teacher's Aide St Gertrude Catholic School; [memb.] International Thespian Society, The Adventurer's Guild; [hon.] Hall of Fame for Drama; [oth. writ.] The Song of Joe and many others; [pers.] I believe anything is possible in fantasy and in reality; [a.] Bell, CA

NGUYEN, THUA THI
[pen.] Huong Sa; [b.] October 5, 1938, Hue, Vietnam; [p.] Hoe Nguyen; [m.] Thang Huu Ie, July 11, 1964; [ch.] 5; [ed.] AA in Teaching, had taught 5th grade for 15 years - Accounting 20 years in high school in Vietnam; [occ.] Preparation food at Labou's Restaurant, Sacramento, California; [hon.] Writing essay between classes in PRPC, Philippines topic: "Freedom"; [oth. writ.] Xuan Thanh Binh (Peace New Year),

Nguoi Bao Tro (My Sponsor), Chi Ho Toi (My Cousin), Trung Tam Luyen-Doc (Reading Center), Lop Hoc Computer (Computer Class), Chiatay (Farewell); [pers.] I, my husband and my children came to Sacrament, CA from Vietnam on April 14, 1989. I am working, learning more English, computer and supporting my children: 2 sons are in UC Berkeley, 2 children are in VC Davis, one in college. Hobbies: writing poem, planting flowers; [a.] Sacramento, CA

NICHOLS, MARY
[pen.] May; [b.] Barbados; [m.] Divorced; [ch.] 1 son; [ed.] London England SRN-BA; [occ.] Registered Nurse; [memb.] Church groups, volunteer organizations; [hon.] Blue Ribbons, poetry writing - reading, recognitions in nursing; [oth. writ.] "Universal Love," "NIght of the Storm," "Beauty," "The Butterfly," "The Vision"; [pers.] "Taking life as it comes!"; [a.] Paterson, NJ

NICHOLSON, EDWARD A.
[pen.] Edward A. Nicholson; [b.] October 14, 1936, Glen Cove, NY; [p.] Edward and Annie Nicholson; [m.] Christina, May 21, 1960; [ch.] 1 daughter - Kimberly; [ed.] High school - Glen Cove High, College - University of Hawaii; [occ.] SPC Marketing Public Relations and Advertising, VP Sales and Marketing; [memb.] Reformers Church of Locust Valley, NY; [oth. writ.] None published, first time entrant; [pers.] Poetry brings out within me the intuitive insight of my spiritual soul - that without it remains dormant to myself and the outside world - it provides answers I ask about controversy, the unknown, and to some extent - The Wisdom of God.; [a.] Northport, NY

NIGHTINGALE, WILHELM H.
[pen.] Manfried Swamp Root; [b.] August 10, 1942, Vera Cruz, Mexico; [p.] W. Ed. and Goldie Pearl Nightingale; [m.] Connie Nightingale, January 2, 1960; [ch.] Paula Foster, Laura Eden, Thomas A., Ginger, Margaret and Andy; [ed.] BS and MS Texas A&M, DD Baylor University; [occ.] Minister; [memb.] GLC, TSTA, NEA, Christians Against Satan; [hon.] Alpha Chi, Phi Beta Kappa; [oth. writ.] Novels: Placebo, Dave's Dilemma; [pers.] I strive to follow Cicero's dictum: "Noli me vocare, ego te vocabo."; [a.] Schertz, TX

NIKLAUS, JANET M.
[b.] September 14, 1930, Fall River, MA; [p.] Jessie McIlwaine; [m.] Robert L. Niklaus, August 16, 1958; [ch.] 3 girls - all married; [ed.] High School Gordon-Barrington College, Truesdale Hosp Sch of Nursing School of Tropical Medicine - Antwerp, Belgium; [occ.] R.N., Pikes Peak Hospice; [memb.] My church, Colorado Springs Symphony, Colorado State Nurses Assoc.; [hon.] Nursing Award "The Nurse I Would Choose If I Were Ill" 1989; [oth. writ.] Poem published in hospice publication, other poems - not published; [pers.] I strive to honor God and my country, and serve others to the best of my ability.; [a.] Colorado Springs, CO

NIX, AMANDA SAMANTHA
[b.] January 24, 1958, Madison, IN; [p.] Everett C. Glenn and Edith M. Glass; [m.] Sam Nix Sr., December 1, 1994; [ch.] Ashley, Stacy, Little Eagle, Mariah, Adonis; [ed.] GED; [occ.] Disabled; [hon.] Editor's Choice Award '95; [oth. writ.] Publication in the Garden of Life National Library of Poetry; [a.] Louisville, KY

NOGULICH, NATALIJA
[b.] Chicago; [ed.] BA Lake Forest College; [occ.] Actress, Director, Teacher, Founder of The Grace Players Theatre Company; [memb.] Phi Beta Kappa, Screen Actors Guild, Actor's Equity Assoc.; [hon.] Seven Dramalogue, Critics Awards for Best Actress, Best Director, Best Producer for 3 different stage productions; [oth. writ.] Many unpublished poems, essays and short stories; [pers.] "Beauty is my Aim." Gandhi

NOONAN, D. THOMAS
[b.] March 25, 1957, Castro Valley, CA; [p.] John T. Noonan, Colleen B. Northrip; [ed.] West Valley College, DeAnza Community College, Actors Studio-Epic Norris; [memb.] San Francisco Zoological Society, Monterey Bay Marine Sanctuary, Police Athletic League; [hon.] Dean's List; [oth. writ.] Various plays staged but yet to be published; [pers.] Inspired by P.B. Shelley. There is no greater action than the use of words, and no greater courage than the common man who uses them.; [a.] Santa Clara, CA

NORDMANN, KAREN
[b.] December 30, 1961, Illinois; [m.] Brian G. Nordmann, November 26, 1983; [ch.] Claire Marie, Jacob John, Emily Rose; [pers.] This poem was inspired by and written for Brian, 3 years prior to our marriage he remains my inspiration...; [a.] Elkmont, AL

NORRIS, JOANNE KYNE
[b.] July 26, Galway, Ireland; [p.] Patrick and Sarah Kyne; [m.] Allen Norris, July 7, 1989; [ch.] Jason, Nicole; [ed.] Mercy Convent, Galway, San Francisco State, SF, Univ of San Francisco, SF; [occ.] Language Arts Teacher, ESL Teacher; [memb.] Basel Folk Connection, CATESOL, The Gamma Association of California, Literacy Alliance Southbay, Easy English Program, Phi Beta Kappa; [hon.] Dean's List; [oth. writ.] Several poems published in magazines, newspapers and in school journals, work-in progress: children's book; [pers.] Now I'm tongue tied, know nothing will come out worth writing about, but I've got to keep at it, whether it's worth it or not, that's the secret. And then every once in a while, I'll write something profound, and wrenching, and neat which will please me no end, just like now, no doubt.; [a.] Sunnyvale, CA

NORRIS, ROBERT E.
[pen.] Bob Norris; [b.] January 5, 1929, Lund, UT; [p.] Ollie M. and Violet C. Norris; [m.] Patricia Christensen, February 25, 1956; [ch.] Martin Robert, Camille Patricia, John Howard; [ed.] South Sevier HS, University of Utah BS Mining Engineering; [occ.] Retired from US Forest Service 1984; [oth. writ.] Several poems in church newsletter; [pers.] I strive to capture the inspiration that comes to all people, through my observations of nature and particularly in people's reactions to silence.; [a.] Portland, OR

NORTON, JIM
[b.] July 20, 1976, Marion, IN; [p.] Bill and Janie Norton; [ed.] Presently sophomore in college; [occ.] Student; [hon.] Honors Program IUPFW University (Indiana/Purdue Ft. Wayne, IN); [a.] Marion, IN

O'BRIEN, KERRI
[ed.] Attending University of Maryland - College Park; [occ.] Forbes Newspapers 93-95, Winter Break, January 1995, Cranford, NJ, Twirling Instructor four years after school, recreational, Programs, Township Recreation Office, Bass Shoes Sales Clerk Summers 1992 and 1993, Lord and Taylors -94-95; [memb.] School Paper, Yearbook, JSA, Student Government, Captain Flag Squad, Member Choir, Swim Team, Junior Varsity Volleyball, Freshman and Sophomore Year, Junior Varsity Basketball, Marching Band and Jazz Band, Students concern for the Needy (Treasurer), American Field Service, Society of Professional Journalist, Kappa Delta Sorority, Student Government Assoc., Young Democrats, UMUC (Campus Radio Station), Channel M (Campus Television); [hon.] Who's Who Among American High School Students, Four-time winner New Jersey State PTA Poetry Contest, Second runner-up Miss New Jersey Teen Scholarship and Recognition Pageant 1993, Honor Roll, High Honor Roll - High School, Student Ambassador to Russia, Summer 1991, Twirling, Winner of various County and State Twirling Awards, 94-95 Dean's List (National)

O'DONNELL, CAROL ANN
[pen.] Keecool; [b.] September 13, 1962, Pittsburgh, PA; [p.] Robert and Dorothy O'Donnell; [ch.] Joshua Scott O'Donnell; [ed.] Warwick High School, Palmer Business Institute; [occ.] Secretary, East Lampeter Ambulance Association, Lancaster, PA; [memb.] St James Catholic Church; [hon.] Graduated top of my field (Word Processing) on the Dean's List through Palmer Business Institute; [oth. writ.] As a child I used to write poems and short stories; [pers.] I enjoy writing poetry because I am able to express my true feelings. Someday I would like to published a child's book.; [a.] Lititz, PA

O'NEAL, JOSEPHINE MARIAN LATIMORE
[pen.] Jomarian O'Neal; [b.] March 24, 1932, Atlanta, GA; [p.] Joseph-(Joe) and Sammie Latimore; [m.] William Gilbert O'Neal Jr., 1951; [ch.] William III, Vanessa and Yolanda; [ed.] BS degree Morris Brown College, 1961, MSE-Atlanta University 1975; [occ.] Teacher-APS (Retired) 1989; [memb.] Antioch East Baptist Church

O'NEAL, RAY
[b.] January 11, 1932, Trussville, AL; [p.] James and Pearl O'Neal; [m.] Divorced; [ch.] Teresa, Winifred, Peggy and Fred; [ed.] City College, San Diego, CA; [occ.] Retired; [memb.] Christian Faith and The International Society of Poets; [hon.] Dean's List and several Editor's Awards for poems; [oth. writ.] Published in other books and recorded on tapes; [pers.] Listen to the song of life and share discreetly.; [a.] San Diego, CA

O'NEILL, MEGAN L.
[b.] August 30, 1978, Warren, OH; [p.] Bonnie and Kevin O'Neill; [ed.] North Allegheny Senior High School, 11th grade; [occ.] Student; [memb.] North Allegheny Marching Band, German Band, Christmas Band, Project Earth, Volunteer at Leader Nursing Home and Junior Classical League; [hon.] Straight A student, Honor Role, won 1st place in a Holocaust poetry contest, 3rd place in a Martin Luther King Jr. essay contest = both for the city of Pittsburgh; [oth. writ.] Poems: "A Glimpse Of A Lemon Tree", "Almost A Poem", "A Time Of Innocence", "The Wishing Well"; [pers.] To all of my friends and family, thank you. You are the true treasures of my life.; [a.] Wexford, PA

OBRIEN, KERRI
[pen.] Kerri Obrien; [b.] January 23, 1976, Scotch Plains, NJ; [p.] Anne Obrien; [ed.] Graduate high school I am a sophomore now at the University of Maryland; [occ.] Part time student Fanwood Scotch Plains Press (Forbes News); [memb.] Chorus - VP Society of Professional Journalists - Kappa Delta Sorority (Project Excellence Choir), Young Democrats - Sportscaster WMVC, Campus Station - SGA Student Assoc., Nom Trophies for twirling; [hon.] 1st place 5 times in PTA Poetry Contest = Who, Who Among American High School students 93-94-1995-1995-96, Who Who College Students - New Jersey (Miss Teen Pageant - 2nd Recognition Pageant - also teen representative national pageant; [oth. writ.] Wrote poetry and short stories, won blue ribbons (1st) in PTA Reflections Contest for five years in state and went to ???? wrote for Forbes New-High School; [pers.] I truly believe that love is the answer to changing the world and people. We have to learn to love and tolerate all the differences in all people for a permanent peace; [a.] NJ

OCHILTREE, JOHN M.
[b.] August 10, 1935, Union, SC; [p.] Odis W. and Dollie K. Ochiltree; [m.] Margaret K. Ochiltree, April 19, 1961; [ch.] Terri, Kriss, Eric, Jo Ann, (10 GC); [ed.] BA/English, Wofford College, Spartanburg, SC; [occ.] Security Supervisor; [memb.] VFW, SC Sheriffs Assn.; [hon.] BA degree, Presidential and DA Certificates of Appreciation for Mil. Svc., 3d Brigade 24th Inf. Div. Cert. of Achievement, Milliken M.O.P. Cert.; [oth. writ.] "Rhymes For All Times" a collection of personal unpublished poetry; [pers.] I believe in the here and now. I am here and it is now.; [a.] Chesnee, SC

OCONER, ZENAIDA LAZARTE
[pen.] Zeny; [b.] August 27, 1942, Manila, Philippines; [p.] Feliciano O. Lazarte Sr. and Clara I. Lazarte; [m.] Dr. Virgilio V. Oconer, October 27, 1963; [ch.] Apple married to Willie, Bernadette, and Nino Gil, grandchildren-Aprwil, Marvi, Jofel; [ed.] La Consolacion College, University of Sto. Tomas; [oth. writ.] Several poems written for personal keepsake; [pers.] I express my unspoken words of love, affections, sentiments, and emotions through writing. I usually write what I feel and feel deeply what I write.; [a.] Lakewood, CA

OFFERMAN, VAN P.
[b.] January 3, 1972, Chicago; [p.] Wayne and Charlotte Offerman; [ed.] Graduate of CHIC Culinary College; [occ.] Professional Cook, Southside Bistro, Anchorage, AK

OGDEN, ADREN L.
[b.] March 4, 1952, Little Park, AR; [p.] Arney Golleher and Helen Henry; [m.] Leonard R. Ogden, December 3, 1982; [ch.] Byddy and Michael Collins, Leonard W. Ogden, Karen S. Ogden; [ed.] GED Diploma, Secretarial Sciences at Capitol City Business School; [occ.] Housewife-Raising 2 grandsons; [memb.] None at this time once belonged to Poet's Roundtable of America in Benton, AR; [hon.] 10-1981 - 1st honorable mention - (Saline Co., AR Poetry Contest), Capitol City Jr. College - Dean's list once - honor roll twice; [oth. writ.] Numerous poems published in local paper, personal poems done for friends, family to give others. One published under another name in a school poetry book.; [pers.] For years I made others happy with my writings, and feel it is time to advance and get the most I can from it and share it with others.; [a.] Benton, AR

OJEDA, DANIEL JR.
[b.] May 3, 1942, Minneapolis, MN; [ed.] Miller Vocational High School, University of Minnesota Extension Service, United States Army Infantry School; [memb.] Life Member of: Veterans of Foreign Wars, American Legion, Minnesota National Guard Enlisted Association, Enlisted Association of the National Guard of the U.S., 82nd Airborne Division Association, Military Order of the Cootie, International War Veterans Alliance; [hon.] Combat Foreign, United States and State Awards too numerous to mention; [oth. writ.] Co-Author "A Christmas Promise"; [pers.] I have been influence by Author, Actor, Veteran and Humanitarian, Douglas Fairbanks, Jr. whom I have had the opportunity to meet on several occasions I have given to my God and my Country all that has been asked of me. I continue to serve as citizen of the U.S. and am proud to have been one of the original Skysoldiers in Vietnam 1964-66.; [a.] Minneapolis, MN

OLEMAUN, CHASTITY
[b.] July 7, 1985, Barrow, AK; [p.] George and Pauline Olemaun; [ed.] 5th grade Ipalook Elementary School; [occ.] Student; [memb.] Arctic Slope Regional Corporation; [hon.] Junior Achievement, honor roll student; [oth. writ.] "Spring" Spring In Barrow; [pers.] I enjoy writing poems and other things; [a.] Barrow, AK

OLSEN, ROY EDWARD
[b.] February 16, 1951, Brooklyn, NY; [p.] Andrew and Doris Olsen; [m.] Kathleen Ann Olsen, May 26, 1973; [ch.] Eric, Christopher, Michael, Thomas; [ed.] High school; [occ.] Electrical Mechanic; [oth. writ.] Yes, never tried to publish; [pers.] As long as we are all willing to accept change, we will all keep on learning.; [a.] Brooklyn, NY

OLSON, DONNA J.
[pen.] D. J. Olson; [b.] October 20, 1949, Portales, NM; [ed.] Portales High, Hadley School for the Blind; [occ.] Poet/Author; [memb.] Primitive Baptist Church; [oth. writ.] Multiple poems; [pers.] Due to the recent loss of a great part of my sight I seem to have received more insight.; [a.] Stephenville, TX

OLSON, MELISSA
[pen.] Rebecca Richards; [b.] March 2, 1973, Port Washington, WI; [p.] Patrick Remis and Beverly Remis; [m.] Richard Olson, July 31, 1993; [ch.] Aquinas High, Logan Senior High, University of Wisconsin, La Crosse; [ed.] Nuclear Medicine Technologist; [occ.] National Nuclear Medicine Society; [oth. writ.] Several other poems, essays, and short stories; [pers.] While riding the roller coaster of life, remember that the twists and turns are what make it interesting. Just keep yourself on the right track.; [a.] West Allis, WI

OLSZEWSKI, JEANINE
[b.] February 1, 1982, Flushing, NY; [p.] Frank and Roberta Olszewski; [ed.] P.S. 164, Queen of Peace Grammar Schools; [oth. writ.] Several poems in local and school papers; [pers.] I try to reflect personal heartache and the hate that often exist in love. Often, I try to remind the reader of how short, therefore, precious life is.; [a.] Flushing, NY

OOSTHUIZEN, ANDY
[b.] October 12, 1945, South Africa; [occ.] Director/Producer/Playwright/Artistic Director for Sabona Productions; [hon.] Human Rights Award from Brandeis National Women's Committee, 5 awards from Optimist International, New Jersey, for work done with children; [oth. writ.] Playwright of 15 produced plays, namely "Sabona" "You, Me And Our Skeletons"; [pers.] We are all part of an experiment, so strive to make the experiment a success.; [a.] Adelphia, NJ

ORAM, MILDRED B.
[b.] July 9, 1922, New York City, NY; [p.] Adeline and Christian Beckel; [m.] James R. Oram, September 3, 1944; [ch.] Carol Lorenz, Leonard Oram, Linda Oram; [ed.] Walton High N.Y.C., graduate Germantown High, Germantown, N.Y., 2 yrs. Journalism - Newspaper Inst., Literacy Training; [occ.] Retired Homemaker; [memb.] Lutheran Church of our Savior Tampa, FL, Volunteer Lutheran, Braille Worker, Volunteer Church Office (Girl Friday); [hon.] Stewardship Award, Lutheran Church of our Saviour, Service Award for volunteer- Braille by Lutheran Aid Assoc.; [oth. writ.] Several poems published in poetry magazines and church publications; [pers.] Priorities: God family -3 ch., 7 grands, 5 great-grands volunteer service extra income from - care giving survey participant hopefully writing.; [a.] Tampa, FL

ORCUTT, TREMAINE
[pen.] Tremaine; [b.] July 31, 1953, Fort Worth, TX; [p.] Jewell Sterling and Colle Orcutt; [ed.] Boca Raton High School; [occ.] I share "Super Blue Green Algae" with others; [oth. writ.] I have written many poems and although none of my writing has been published - I recently made

the choice to solicit publication of my poems; [pers.] The poetry that I write comes from the essence that is me. I intend to share my messages with all of mankind.; [a.] Louisville, CO

ORTEGA, ESTHER LAGE
[b.] Havana, Cuba; [p.] Pedro Lage, Italica Fernandez; [m.] Nicanor Ortega, May 31, 1968; [ed.] Elementary School, High School, Havana University, Dr. of Philosophy and Letters, Piano Teacher, graduated at Conservatory of Music in Havanna, Cuba, working in both fields by competition, Master degree of Sciences, Long Island University, Brooklyn Center, School Teacher at Secondary Schools, New York; [occ.] Retiree Teacher; [memb.] The National Library of Poetry, Spanish Publications, Brujula Compas, Anthology Francisco Henriquez, Miami, "Cuba", "Los poetas del Exodo", "Poet from the Exodus", Anthology, "The Inter-American Editor", Miami, Spanish and American Link, Cultural Society, New York, The Newspaper: "The Information" Prof: Emilio Martinez Paula, Texas (Huston); [hon.] Poetry Awards as: Diplomas, Certificates, others; [oth. writ.] Spanish Magazines, own poetry books, two, "Luzy Sombra" Luna en Scorpio, (1988-first, 1994-second); [pers.] The immaterial being today. The great mistake.; [a.] New York, NY

OSBORNE, CARRIE PATRICIA
[b.] July 13, 1984, Charleston, WV; [p.] Thomas R. Osborne and Harriet Nelson Osborne; [ed.] Holz Elementary School, Charleston, WV; [a.] Charleston, VW

OSHIRO, DAY H.
[b.] October 16, 1961, Kauai, HI; [p.] Takeshi and Gladys Oshiro; [occ.] Legal Secretary; [pers.] Through my writing, I allow my guards to fall to the side, exposing my true self. I am thankful for being able to share.; [a.] Honolulu, HI

O'SULLIVAN, BRENDAN
[b.] November 9, 1983, Providence, RI; [p.] Noel & Doraine O'Sullivan; [ed.] Randall Holden Elementary School; [occ.] Student; [memb.] Children's Crusade for Higher Education, St. Timothy Church Youth Group; [hon.] ATAM(Accordian Teachers Assoc. of Mass.) 1993 Standard Piano Solo 2nd Place, ATAM 1995 Standard Piano Solo 1st Place; [pers.] I really enjoy writing poetry, it's a lot of fun. More kids should try it! [a.] Warwick, RI;

OUIMET, MARY
[b.] July 17, 1909, Chicago, IL; [p.] Jacob Keller and Laura; [m.] Deceased, 1933; [ch.] Marlene and Carol; [ed.] Graduated from high school; [occ.] None-retired; [hon.] Poems in Chicago paper, won 2nd prize in School Poetic Entries; [pers.] I enjoy writing poetry. When I give a card everyone asks for a poem; [a.] Marshfield, WI

OWEN, DAVID KENNETH
[pen.] Henry Milam Hollis; [b.] January 8, 1958, Jacksonville, TX; [p.] Mr and Mrs Kenneth Owen; [ed.] Certificate of Technology in Horticulture also some Culinary Arts Certificates; [occ.] Horticulture Sales; [memb.] Junior Achievements, Future Farmers of America, Phi Beta Lambda/Future Business Leaders of America and Houston Orchid Society; [oth. writ.] A Child Is..., The Little Old Clock, Let Me..., It Can Be Seen, and Power; [pers.] I wish to dedicate this poem, "Homesick", to a very sweet and special young lady, Erna Frank. She gave me a place to stay while visiting her country, Switzerland. I felt more at home there than anywhere else. Erna, I miss you. Love You, David Owen; [a.] Frankston, TX

OWENS, DONEEN RAE
[b.] May 6, 1936, Portland, OR; [p.] Roy and Gladys Anderson; [m.] Divorced; [ch.] five daughters: Delani Layne, Jenni Ann, Desiri Jayne, Jodi Lynn, Dori Marie, two granddaughters, one grandson - Franklin; [ed.] High school - one year business school - two years with Institute of Children's Literature in Redding Ridge, CT; [occ.] Gallery Director at Rickert Gallery - Newport, OR 97365; [memb.] Assembly of God Church, Newport Bayfront Merchants Assoc. Secretary; [pers.] My love for people, especially children, and also my love of animals, is the motivating factor in my desire to write.; [a.] Newport, OR

PACHECO, SHERILYNN ROSE
[b.] August 18, 1962, Honolulu, HI; [m.] Derek D. Pacheco, March 20, 1993; [ch.] Charisse, Sheral, Danny; [ed.] Hilo High, University of Hawaii at Hilo, Liberty University, independent study; [occ.] Full time mother; [memb.] Moms In Touch International, New Hope Fellowship; [hon.] Quill and Scroll International Honorary Society for High School Journalist - Award of Honor; [oth.writ.] Inspirational poems for Elementary School children; [pers.] The beauty of poetry is searching deep within myself, and listening to the whispering words of my soul.; [a.] Hilo, HI

PAGE, LOUISE
[b.] March 1, 1917, New Haven, KY; [p.] Richard and Mary Coolee; [m.] William Page, January 3, 1953; [ed.] College; [occ.] During World War 2, I worked at Curtis Wreight Comptometor Operator; [memb.] International Society of Poets; [hon.] Distinguished and Gold Pin Membership; [oth. writ.] I wrote a song, "Life is a Big Game," Tin Pan Alley put the music to the song. Second song Hick 1, Too Many Friends, Zab Records; [a.] Crestwood, KY

PAGE, MARGUERITE
[b.] January 28, 1926, Oklahoma City; [m.] Archie Page, October 9, 1943; [ch.] Son-Archie Dennis (Deceased), daughter and son-in-law Paula and Patrick Prince, grandsons- David Page, Patrick, Michael, Mitchell Prince; [ed.] Kern Country Union High School Class of 1944; [occ.] Retired; [oth. writ.] 1st poem at age 13. Have written many since for family and friends honoring special occasions. Nothing published.; [pers.] Poetry is a reflection of the heart.; [a.] Kernville, CA

PAGE, RICHARD S.
[b.] February 6, 1952, Jacksonville, FL; [p.] Jack and Sarah Page; [m.] Ruth Page, November 25, 1989; [ch.] Kris; [ed.] BBA University of Georgia; [occ.] Department of Defense, Defense Commissary Agency; [memb.] Alpha Kappa Psi Professional Business Fraternity, Civitan, Federal Executive Board, (Previous) - Pennsylvania Food Bank, Board of Directors; [hon.] Federal Executive of the Year (Pennsylvania), Civilian Meritorious Service Medal, Honor Alumni, Alpha Kappa Psi Fraternity; [pers.] To dream of a world of Keats, Byron, and Wordsworth and help to make it so.; [a.] Aiea, HI

PAIGE, NATASHA RENEE
[pen.] Tasha; [b.] October 21, 1982, Washington, DC; [p.] Penny and Mr. Rory Feltow; [ed.] 8th Grade; [occ.] Author (young); [memb.] Do the write thing summer youths organization for writing to stop the (summer of 95) violence in the city (my essay is topic) of father being victim of crime; [hon.] When I was five yrs old in 1st grade Elementary School I was awarded for writing poetry for Amelia Bedelia under short stories for kids at the Martin Luther King Library in Wash. DC; [oth. writ.] Essay for do the wright thing, summer of 95 1987 - Amelia Bedilia short stories for kids Martin Luther King Library; [pers.] My father was victim of gun shot wound to the head he survived two bullets to the brain. It happened in bridgeport connecticut in result I started to write about crime and violence in the city streets; [a.] Washington, DC

PALACIOS, JEANNIE M. LOUIE
[b.] May 7, 1958, Oakland; [p.] Peter Louie and Eleanor Verceles-Louie; [m.] Tyrone K. Palacios, July 17, 1993; [ch.] Tyson A. Palacios 11-18-87 DOB/Tyler A. Palacios 7-23-92 DOB; [ed.] Oakland High - Graduated 1976, Air Force Transportation School - 1978, Member of the Air Force Reserves since 1978, Member of the 45th APS (Aerial Port Squadron), Rank: Staff Sergeant, currently attending Holy Names College (Psychology Major) - as a Junior; [occ.] Member of the Air Force Reserves - 45th Aerial Port Squadron as a Staff Sergeant, Secretary for Pacific Bell and mother/wife, Independent Mary Kay Consultant; [hon.] Plaque from Pacific Bell for serving during Desert Storm, and plaque from Air Force Reserve for Desert Storm; [oth. writ.] I have been writing since my early teenage days, encouraged by an English teacher to keep a journal. Nothing has been published, although I would like to write greetings for cards. I've written many poems and love letters for friends and family. I consider it a great compliment that they can trust me to portray their deepest thoughts and feelings.; [pers.] Tyrone, Tyson and Tyler - I'm so lucky to have you in my life. No matter how difficult things get, there is always a smile or a hug waiting for me when I need it most.; [a.] Tracy, CA

PALEKA, WALTER KALALANI
[b.] March 28, 1978, Maui; [p.] James K. Paleka, Bernadette K. Paleka; [ed.] Hawaii, Molokai High School, and Hawaii Job Corps Center; [occ.] Student at Hawaii Job Corps Center; [memb.] Hawaii Job Corps, Hawaiian Club, and member of musical group called Hawaiian Knights; [hon.] Recognition and academic awards as "Corpsmember of the Month"; [oth. writ.] "Now I know", "Since Hanna Moved Away",

"Patience", and "Dedicated To The One I Love"; [pers.] Writing poetry helps me think clearly about how I feel and also enables me to work out my problems.; [a.] Waimanalo, HI

PAMIN, DIANA DOLHANCYK
[pen.] Diana Dolhancyk; [b.] December 13, Cleveland, OH; [p.] Peter Dolhancyk, Diana Dribus Dolhancyk; [m.] Leonard Pamin; [ch.] Diana Anne, Louis Peter; [ed.] West Tech High, Titus College of Cosmetology; [memb.] Arthritis foundation, nominated into International Society of Poets (a distinguished member) and I've sponsored a young girl in India for the past 15 yrs; [hon.] "Editors Choice Awards", for outstanding achievement in poetry for "The Parting", in Journey of the mind, published by the NLOP for "Stormy" in songs on the wind, also for "Shadow Side" in at waters edge. International poet of merit award (plaque) from ISOP, and was nominated poet of the year for 1995 by ISOP accomplishment of merit award for the poem "Rain" from creative Arts and Science, in journey to our dreams; [oth. writ.] Honorable mention for the poem "The View" from sparrowgrass poetry in treasured poems of America. The poem "Love No More" will be in "Best poems of 1996." The poem "The Parting" was in the Sun Star newspaper, along with a picture and write upon the front page.; [pers.] "Always give someone a smile, you'll never know whose heart you might lighten. I'm inspired by many things in life, a gamut of feelings and thoughts in regards to many things. Poets use words instead of paint brushes."; [a.] North Royalton, OH

PAMPERIN, CARLA SUE
[pen.] Scarlet Carla; [b.] October 30, 1963, Rome, NY; [p.] Beverly Harms/Robert Gump; [m.] James Alan Pamperin, 1st marriage February 16, 1995, 2nd marriage April 17, 1995 (same man); [ch.] Brandon Louis Pamperin, Terry James Pamperin; [ed.] My schooling for kindergarten was in Sioux City, Iowa, 1st grade through 7th was in Clarion Elementary, 8th-11th grade in Clarion Junior High and Clarion Senior High, GED on 4/28/89 through ICCC in Eagle Grove; [occ.] IA 50533/1year of Secretarial at ICCC, I run my own craft business at home called Carla's Creations. I write short stories and poems I'm trying to get published!; [memb.] The fitness center in Eagle Grove, The Church of Nazarene, many craft clubs!; [hon.] Tiny Tot Drawing Contest! My drawings I also do, in art, won me a scholarship to an Art School in 7th grade. My mom couldn't afford to send me though! Physical fitness awards all through school! Most organized girl at Camp for Church!; [oth. writ.] Poems titles I've written are: What's love!, Impressions!, Dreams Are Forever!, Twin Sister!, A Man's World!, My Purpose!, Searching for Identity!, Who Am I!, A Mother's Request!, Softer Petals!; [pers.] The poems I write are from deep within my soul, usually real things that I have experienced in my life! My poetry is how I express my thoughts and feelings-good or bad! I feel that many readers can relate to my words and learn also from them!; [a.] Eagle Grove, IA

PANTANO, DANIEL
[pen.] Jordache; [b.] February 10, 1976, Langenthal, Switzerland; [p.] Giuseppe Pantano-Katharina Wiest-Pantano; [ed.] Kreuzfeld Primar-and Selcundar-Schule, Langenthal, Switzerland, Palmer College Preparatory School, Tampa, USA; [occ.] Student at Palmer College Preparatory School; [oth. writ.] One poem published in Modern Poetry Society called "Shadowlands"; [pers.] This poem was written on August 26, 1995 in Langenthal, Switzerland. I dedicate this poem to my life. A life, so strange and complex that I am not able to find the right answer.; [a.] Tampa, FL

PAREJA, DENISE
[b.] January 23, 1980, Guayaquil, Ecuador; [p.] Sharon and Enrique Pareja; [ed.] Sophomore at College Park High School California, St Mary's Elementary School; [oth. writ.] Poems published anonymously in school literary magazine; [a.] Martinez, CA

PAREJKO, RYAN
[pen.] Homer Jay; [b.] June 16, 1975, Chicago, IL; [p.] Janet Almen, Jim Parejko; [ed.] Pursuing a degree in Education at Valdosta State University, Valdosta GA; [occ.] Student; [oth. writ.] Undisclosed; [pers.] "Life is too short for regrets"; [a.] Oak Forest, IL

PARK, SEUNG
[b.] August 24, 1979, Seoul, South Korea; [p.] Sung Do and KyungLee Park; [ed.] Cronbrook Upper School (ongoing); [occ.] High School Student; [hon.] 2nd place, world Symphony Orchestra Music Competition, Outstanding Fine Arts Student; [oth. writ.] Several poems published in the school literary magazine; [pers.] It is always darkest before dawn, we must strive hardest when our cause seems most desperate.; [a.] Rochester Hills, MI

PARKER, SHARON
[b.] September 3, 1955, Sylacaaga, AL; [p.] Chester and Agnes Pruitt; [m.] Hugh Parker Jr., July 27, 1979; [ch.] Rachael (15), Brandon (14); [ed.] Completed High School, attended Community College; [occ.] Housewife, part time home transcriptionist (medical); [oth. writ.] I have no published works, just a personal collection of my writings kept hidden away to share with family and friends; [pers.] I want to share feelings and a sense of where we're going as a race a people who hold in our hands the responsibility of caring about each other and our world, and am influenced by different poetry styles; [a.] Alpine, AL

PARNOW, JOHN
[b.] August 1, 1940, Jersey City, NJ; [p.] Charles J. and Dorothy C. Parnow; [m.] Sarah Orchid Parnow, April 22, 1976; [ch.] Christopher J.; [ed.] St. Michaels Grammar, Emerson HS, University of Maryland; [occ.] Self employed; [hon.] Military service awards 5X GCM, 13X air medal, meritorious achievement medal, meritorious service medal, Vietnam campaign medal, with 5 oak leaf clusters, meritorious unit citation, presidential unit citation; [oth. writ.] Two years of non-fiction articles about the Soviet Union for local weekly publication with cartoons. Unpublished short stories the Abusement Park - my father's star, the contest, Shoe Makers Boy.; [pers.] I am preoccupied with the stream of time, the psychologist and emotional effect of war and combat on the individual, and the season of a love relationship. The two years I spent in Vietnam and years spent seeing the poverty in foreign countries maker me look deeply at humanity.; [a.] Denville, NJ

PASULKA, SASHA
[b.] March 24, 1982; [ed.] 8th Grade student at Phoenix Country Day School; [oth. writ.] I have been published in "Heliocentric Net", "The Writer's Slate", "Write from the Heart" among others; [pers.] In my poetry, I try to portray, people I know especially teenagers, and their inner thoughts and emotions, which are so often misunderstood by adults.; [a.] Scottsdale, AZ

PATASNICK, TODD GAVIN
[b.] July 1, 1970; [p.] Robert M. and Patricia J. Patasnick; [ed.] Morristown High School, University of Oklahoma, New Jersey Institute of Technology, Art Students League; [occ.] Computer System Consultant; [memb.] Alex Wilkie Freestyle Martial Arts Academy and Royler Gracie Jui Jitsu Academy, Raritan, NJ; [pers.] To draw with words, to design, to uncover, to sculpt the non-physical, the emotion.; [a.] Morristown, NJ

PAUL, JON KELLY
[pen.] Jon Kelly; [b.] August 31, 1963, Athens, Greece; [p.] Bill and Priscilla Paul; [m.] Patricia Shaver Paul, August 1, 1992; [ed.] BS Business Administration Stnayer College in Spring 1996; [occ.] Account Analyst Merkle Computer Systems; [memb.] West Potomac Rugby Club Good Shepherd United Methodist A Club of Brethren; [hon.] "Most Versatile" Timberlake Football Club "Outstanding Lineman" Richland Hills Varsity Football Club; [oth. writ.] A Charlaton's Charade (A composition of all my poetry); [pers.] I like articulating my thoughts through sound and diction. I credit Eddy Vedder Bono Vox, James Douglas Morrison and Lord George Gordon Byron as influences.; [a.] Woodbridge, VA

PAULLE, PHILIP J.
[b.] April 10, 1916, New York City; [m.] Deceased, July 5, 1949; [ch.] Four Daughters; [ed.] High School 2 Year College; [occ.] Retired; [memb.] American Legion Amvets served four years 1914/1945 during WWII two years in US two years in Europe; [pers.] I am four months younger than the great Frank Sinatra I lived on the west side on NYC he was born in Hoboken NJ my mothers family settled in Aloboken NJ migrating; [a.] Odoven, NJ

PAWLEY, SHANNON M.
[b.] September 21, 1973, Norfolk, VA; [p.] Robin U. Johnson, Earline F. Johnson; [m.] Larry W. Pawley, April 8, 1995; [ed.] North Carolina Wesleyan College, Nansemond River High School; [occ.] Office Manager for Clog Busters, Inc.; [memb.] Omicron Delta Kappa, Pi Gamma Mu, Gamma Sigma Alpha, Pi Epsilon; [hon.] Dean's Honor List, Sarah Alexander Tulloss Award, RDTC ribbons, Who's Who

Among American Universities and Colleges, Psychology Departmental Honors, graduated Cum Laud, senior thesis published; [oth. writ.] Keeping up with the Joneses — An examination into the American Cult Phenomena; [pers.] The pocketbook is mightier than the conscience. If you have any doubts, look at America's big business.; [a.] Portmouth, VA

PAYNE, JOANN A.
[b.] May 1, 1942, Denver, CO; [p.] Parks B. VanDolah, Anne T. VanDolah; [m.] June 9, 1973; [ch.] Jon, Mike, Steven, and Daniel Payne; [ed.] BA in Biology Reed College 1968 and Post-Baccalaureate Courses in Psychology; [occ.] Mental Health Therapist; [oth. writ.] Unpublished; [pers.] I believe spirituality and sensuality are closely entwined, and to deny one is to short-circuit the other. Influenced by G.G. Jung, Viktor Frankl, and Amy Lowell; [a.] Gresham, OR

PEARCE, DONALD E.
[b.] June 3, 1951, Winchester, MA; [p.] Warren R. (Sr.) and Bette; [ch.] D. Eric (Jr), Daniel, Denise, and Douglas; [ed.] 1970 NRHS; [occ.] Maint. and Repair Technician ITI Chelus Ford MA; [memb.] International Society of Poets; [hon.] Editors Choice Award National Library of Poet 1995; [oth. writ.] "Witch Woman" published in walk through paradise 1995; [pers.] All great gifts come from God.; [a.] North Reading, MA

PEEBLES, WILMA
[b.] December 17, 1929, Marion, IL; [p.] Arlie and Bessie (Askew) Simmons; [m.] Wallace L. Peebles, August 18, 1951; [ch.] Paul Peebles - Beth Ann (Peebles) Asp; [ed.] Marion High School Adult Business and Computer Classes at John A. Logan Community College; [occ.] Retired - State of Illinois Employee; [memb.] Reorganized Church of Jesus Christ of Latter Day Saints, National Ataxia Foundation AARP; [hon.] Silver Key for Second Highest Student in Sophomore class. (1945), 1982- One of ten outstanding state employees employed by the state of IL; [oth. writ.] Several poems - unpublished; [pers.] To me, life's truths expressed in an artistic but simple way represent the most beautiful poetry. I think there would be no greater satisfaction for a poet than to be able to do this.; [a.] Marion, IL

PENKO, MICHAEL JOHN
[pen.] Michael John Penko; [b.] April 16, 1975, Cleveland, OH; [p.] Cathy Wright, John Miller; [ed.] R.B. Chamberlin High School; [occ.] Sales Clerk; [oth. writ.] Two other poems, as well as "Change", were published in a High School literary magazine. They were "Taken, not his pride" and "Why hate?"; [pers.] Writing is my sole passion. Its my release of how I feel and observe, I plant to make writing my art for my life. I just hope that someday I'll be remembered as a voice from my generation.; [a.] Twinsburg, OH

PENN, LEVAR MICHAEL
[pen.] Var; [b.] May 27, 1977, Wilmington, DE; [p.] Denise Penn; [ed.] 12th Grade student William Penn High School; [occ.] Telemarketer; [hon.] Graduated from John Casablanca's and Barbizon of acting modeling; [oth. writ.] Thunderstorm, Running Hard and Fast, Dearest Love, A Trip to the Soul, Peaceful Journey; [pers.] From a seed to a flower, from a boy to a man I grow and learn therefore I am but who am I? If I don't know myself how can anyone else know, and if no don't exists. My poems are evidence of my existence.; [a.] New Castle, DE

PERERA, GEORGE B.
[b.] February 11; [p.] John Stephen, Mary Margaret Perera; [ed.] St. Aloysius Seminary, Sri Lanka, Aquinas University College, Sri Lanka, National Seminary, Sri Lanka, St. Joseph Seminary, Canada, Fairfield Univ., Ct., USA, Boston University, Boston; [occ.] Priest, Chaplain, Hospice of Hillsborough Inc.; [memb.] Distinguished member of Internat. Soc. of Poets, National Association of Catholic Chaplains, Assoc. of Mental Health Clergy, International Society of Graphoanalysis (life); [hon.] Catholic Writer of the Year 1967 (Sri Lanka), Nominee - International Poetry Award '95, Award for outstanding achievement in poetry '95, (National Library of Poetry); [oth. writ.] Freelance journalist - published in Canada, USA, Sri Lanka, Biweekly Column in Port Charlotte Sun Herald, 'Lord, My Easter Gift' (Poems); [pers.] Life is a gift and not a choice. A gift to be cherished. Live one day at a time and celebrate life.; [a.] Tampa, FL

PERKINS, RICHARD H.
[b.] August 24, 1970, Lower Bucks County, PA; [p.] Judith H. Wentworth, James H. Perkins Jr.; [m.] Jasmin B. Perkins, November 22, 1992; [ed.] Harrison Central High School, Gulport/Miss.; [occ.] Military Service Member (US Army); [memb.] NCOA Member; [hon.] Good Conduct Medal (2 awards), Overseas Medal, Air Assault, Army Commendation, Army Achievement Medal; [oth. writ.] Several poems published in Harrison Central High School Literature Magazine "The Phoenix"; [pers.] When I am far from loved ones, the one way I can always stay close by is thru writing, it helps to deal with emotions even when emotions are hard to realize.; [a.] Bad Kreuznach, Germany

PERLOW, MARY
[b.] May 5, 1910, Lafayette, IN; [p.] Eli Brodsky-Rachelle; [m.] James, May 31, 1931, passed away February 23, 1993; [ch.] Two sons; [ed.] 4 Yr. High, many College Courses I am a Braille Teacher-since 1960 through library of congress. All volunteer.; [occ.] Brailing for blind I do choir music for 6 yrs, I taught "Parenting" for Chicago High Schools - Through Chicago University; [memb.] Cong. Sholom Leisure Wld. Hadassah, Na Mat-Life remembering B'Nai Brith Red Cross, Paralyzed Veterans Cancer Research; [hon.] Too numerous to write speaker's bureau for Braille holy communion for boy (blind) University of Judaism Mull Holland Dr. small-contributions to each a must! Can give you many more all Volunteer; [oth. writ.] Took care of blind girl in Chicago since he was nine. She was graduated from Ill. - passed bar at 1st try-lawyer still keep in touch she lives in Richmond VA, I had 62 years happy ones with husband James; [pers.] Chicago Bd. of Education wanted me to come teach brain. Many of other awards raised Boy-Mark at 13 yrs. now is 62 years old.; [a.] Seal Beach, CA

PERROW II, MELVIN C.
[b.] July 1, 1978, Charlottesville, VA; [p.] Melvin/Josephine Perrow; [ed.] High School Senior Albemarle Country Schools-Charlottesville, VA; [occ.] Student; [memb.] Football Team, Basketball Team, Track and Field, Choir, Peer Counselor, AMEZ, Church, The (Youth) Va. Consort, The Troupe (Performing Arts); [hon.] Sports certificates, letters, and track metals, Choir - Regional Honors, Homecoming King 1995; [oth. writ.] A variety of poems and short stories unpublished

PERRY, CHRISTIE
[b.] December 30, 1976, Caldwell, TX; [p.] Phil and Cindy Perry; [ed.] Graduate from Caldwell High School, now attending Blinn Jr. College; [hon.] Graduated advanced plan. Drama cast and crew award.; [oth. writ.] "Average Joe" previously published, and many other unpublished poems; [pers.] Everyday is a new poem just waiting to be written.; [a.] Caldwell, TX

PERSAUD, ANDRA E.
[b.] April 14, 1956, Trinidad, West Indies; [p.] R. Diptee (Father); [m.] Divorced (1 yr); [ch.] Marcus and Rodney Persaud; [ed.] AS Degree in Nursing; [occ.] Registered Nurse; [pers.] This poem was written for Roger a very dear friend, who got married. Unfortunately he never received it.; [a.] Pinellas Park, FL

PETERSON, RITA WHITMORE
[b.] April 9, 1931, Greenville, OH; [occ.] Professor; [oth. writ.] Author and scientific illustrator. Has published over 30 books, chapters, and articles in the fields of biology, science education and learning.; [pers.] This is my first exploration of poetry as a form for expressing a deep respect for nature. Until now, my expression has been through drawings (published), paintings and photographs (sold).; [a.] Laguna Beach, CA

PETRILLI, ELIZABETH
[b.] September 28, 1962, St. Marys, PA; [p.] Jerome and Kathleen DePrator; [m.] Rocco Petrilli, August 7, 1982; [ch.] John, Alycia; [ed.] St. Marys Area High School, Pennsylvania State University; [pers.] It is a gift to be able to express your thoughts in words.; [a.] Trumansburg, NY

PEYTON, GLADYS M.
[pen.] Gladys Martin Peyton; [b.] September 29, 1921, Winchester, VA; [p.] Albert F. Martin Sr. and Blanche Long Martin; [m.] Deceased; [ed.] Graduated from below standard, Douglas High School, Winchester, VA; [occ.] General House Cleaning; [memb.] A.M.E. Church, Lay Organization, Church Organist, Missionary Society; [hon.] Certificate and plaques from different church organizations; [oth. writ.] Papers (people say they are Sermons) plays, pageants, articles on various subjects and other long poems; [pers.] Would like an appraisal on some of my other work after the contest; [a.] Winchester, VA

PHARIS, VIKI S.
[pen.] Viki S. Pharis; [b.] October 30, 1952, Goshen, IN; [p.] Donald and Betty Herendeen; [m.] Rick L. Pharis, August 5, 1978; [ch.] Joshua 13, Adam and Ashley 11 (twins); [ed.] Concord High School, Indiana University, Bloomington IN. Graduated with degree in Elem. Ed. K-6 with Dual Endorsement in special Ed., Masters in Learning Disabilities; [occ.] Learning Disabilities Teacher at Concord Oxbow Elem. Elkhart, IN; [memb.] St. Mark's Methodist Church, Psi Iota Sorority (locally), Emmaus Community; [hon.] Phi Beta Kappa, Dean's List; [oth. writ.] Personal poems given as gifts; [pers.] I am inspired by the learning disability students I teach each accomplishment no matter how great or small is a gift of hope which is so rewarding. My family is the mot precious gift God has given me. I strive to be the example he wants me to be for them and to others.; [a.] Goshen, IN

PHELPS, EVA MURPHY
[pen.] Eva Murphy Phelps; [b.] May 18, 1940, Slabfork, WV; [p.] Fred and Josephine Murphy; [m.] Sonny Phelps, October 5, 1960; [ch.] Julia Gwen and Brad Glenn; [ed.] Galax High School - Galax, VA; [occ.] Eckerd Drug; [oth. writ.] Many, many poems but none published before now; [pers.] I enjoy writing poems for family and friends for births, birthdays, retirements, marriages, etc. I am mainly influenced and inspired by my love for my family and friends. Many of writings reflect my love for the natural beauty of nature.; [a.] Winston-Salem, NC

PHILLIPS, DELISA I.
[b.] April 17, 1963, Lufkin, TX; [p.] Mr and Mrs Johnnie F. Roberts; [m.] Gregory R. Phillips, October 6, 1984; [ch.] Gregory II and De'von Phillips; [ed.] M.B. Smiley High School Houston Community College; [occ.] Domestic Engineer; [memb.] American Heart Association American Lung Association; [hon.] Great Mothers Award of the Year; [oth. writ.] A Housewife, East of the Sunrise Love is, My Everything Recited by Gregory and De'von Phillips which took 1st place trophies. The Man in my Dream, The Wondering Child.; [pers.] I take one day at a time asking God for strength to do the task of that day to the best of my ability which inspires me to relax and write.; [a.] Houston, TX

PHILLIPS, THOMAS MICHAEL
[pen.] Thomas; [b.] February 24, 1969, Anchorage, AK; [p.] Linda Sedlock, Thomas N. Phillips; [ed.] Flint Northern High, Mott College, McLaren Hospital; [occ.] Paramedic, Iredell Co. North Cardina; [oth. writ.] I have several others, some published, some not, Hangin' On, Suicide, Broken Ties, Nightmare, Down this Road, to name a few; [pers.] My dream is to someday write professionally or do my own book.; [a.] Elkin, NC

PHILPITT, EDWARD
[b.] November 15, 1926, Washington, DC; [p.] Richardo Isabel - Both Quakers; [ed.] Graduate from Benjamin Franklin Univ - 1952 Wash. DC; [occ.] Retired and Poet; [memb.] Int'l Society of Poets; [hon.] Int'l Society of Poets, Poet of Merit 1995 selected six times for "Sound of Poetry" by National Library of Poetry in 1995; [pers.] Newness is our future guideline. Life would not be satisfactory without caring people never knock experience - that what we all need. It's fun to play but, more profitable to work.; [a.] Washington, DC

PHOTIKARMBUMRUNG, ELMA DIEL
[b.] February 26, Philippines; [p.] Alfredo D. Diel, Concepcion D. Diel; [m.] Sam Photikarmbumrung, October 14; [ch.] Nate, Nick, and Neil; [ed.] Dumangas High School, University of the Philippines, Silliman University; [occ.] Part time lecturer, Ofc. Asst.; [memb.] Presbyterian Women's Assoc., Delta Lambda Sorority; [hon.] Class Salutatorian, College Scholar; [oth. writ.] "It Pays To Be Alone At Times", "The Wanton trail", Daydreams '94", "Musings '95", "Alternatives At Daybreak", "Makajawan", "The Awakening '93", and "Eternal Fires"; [pers.] Faith can move mountains, a strong faith overcomes man's limitations.; [a.] Palatine, IL

PICKERING, CORTNEY LAYNE
[b.] December 22, 1979, Ardmore, OK; [p.] David Pickering, Kay Pickering; [ed.] Sophomore at Elmore City Pernell High School (currently); [hon.] National Honor Society, Who's Who Among American High School students (2 years in each) Spanish Award, English Award, Instrumentalist Magazines First Chair Award, Superintendants, Honor Roll, County Poetry Contest, first place; [oth. writ.] Several unpublished poems and a novel in the works; [pers.] I love to laugh and make others laugh.; [a.] Elmore City, OK

PIETROPAULO, JASON
[b.] January 1, 1979, Wilmington, DE; [p.] Larry and Kathy Pietropaulo; [ed.] In High School (11th grade); [occ.] Student; [oth. writ.] None published; [pers.] My poem simply express a flurry of emotions I experienced in my struggle to understand. Many ideas for this and my other writings sprang forth from numerous late - night discussions with Anthony Jeselnik, Brendon Collopy and Brad Church. Thanks mom, dad, Joe and Kate.; [a.] Pittsburgh, PA

PIPER, JO
[b.] April 5, 1929, Lake City, IA; [p.] Ella and Wilber Chase; [m.] Charles M. Piper, March 23, 1951; [ch.] Steven, Kevin, Alan; [ed.] BA in Education at UNI, Writing Seminars, Rebuilding Seminars, Progress while Aging Seminars; [occ.] Homemakers, Writer, Volunteer; [memb.] Honor societies, Senior Transportation Council, RSVP, International Society of poets, McKee Medical Center Service League; [hon.] Editor's Choice Awards from NLP, Distinguished member ISP; [oth. writ.] The word, Whitman's Child, Tokens for Grief, My Meditation in the Mountains, poems in local newspapers and service organizations; [pers.] The joy from my writing is reflected in my face and now I am so proud to be able to read my poetry to various social and nursing home groups; [a.] Loveland, CO

PISANI, LORI E.
[b.] March 10, 1963, New Rochelle, NY; [p.] Dan and Dianne Pisani; [ed.] BA Elem Ed. Fairleigh Dickinson Univ. MS Counseling and Development Long Island University; [occ.] Elementary School Teacher Guest Lecturer - Univ. Level; [hon.] Merit Scholar, University Dean's Award, Summa Cum Laude both undergraduate and graduate studies; [oth. writ.] Currently writing a book about my family and home. Also writing a chapter for book regarding educational philosophy and practice.; [pers.] I believe it is the miles we have walked in life that shape who we are. We must revisit those miles, and draw strength from our journeys.; [a.] New Rochelle, NY

PITTARD, CLARENCE S.
[pen.] C. Sumner; [b.] Munford, TX; [p.] Mr. and Mrs. J. B. Pittard; [ed.] High school - Wolfe City and Kingston Texas Business School, Dallas TX, American Institute of Banking - Dallas, TX, Aerocraft Rudiments Study - Dallas, TX, Study of Telephone Technique - Fort Worth, TX; [occ.] Retired from a career of Banking-Aerocraft and the Federal Government - Dallas, TX; [memb.] Southwest Writers Literary Organization of Dallas, TX, The Composers, Authors and Artists of American, Ft Worth TX, The Poetry Society of Texas Writers Correspondence Chap of St. Louis, MO; [hon.] Received five dozen literary awards during the seventies and early eighties during and one dozen year end selected as outstanding writer member of South West - in years of 1971 and 1973; [pers.] Rapidity in auxiliary work progression however efficiency is what counts most anytime onward, ever and backward never

PIVER, COURTNEY L.
[b.] September 4, 1976, Raleigh, NC; [p.] William C. Piver, Jackie Piver; [ed.] Needham B. Broughton High School, University of North Carolina at Chapel Hill; [occ.] Student; [a.] Raleigh, NC

PLETZ, CYNDE
[b.] December 19, 1955, Columbus, OH; [p.] Bob and Arleen Ord; [m.] Frank Pletz, September 10, 1994; [ch.] Nathan, Jamie Robert, Kaylee, Doug, Jason, Jamie Lynn; [occ.] Office Coordinator CTR Systems, Warrendale, PA; [memb.] Vanport Presbyterian Church; [oth. writ.] Poems published in High School newspaper and in other newsletters; [pers.] This poem is dedicated to my husband and best friend, Frank, my children from whom I learn as well as teach, my parents Bob and Arleen Ord, my brothers Bob, Ron, and Chris, my dear friends Sandi Landers and Madeline Robb, and my grandmother, the late Dorothy Lees Hatchner. Their faith and love are always with me.; [a.] Beaver, PA

PLIMPTON, LESLIE
[b.] September 24, 1959, Chicago, IL; [p.] Bonnie and Charles Plimpton; [ed.] Western Illinois University, De Paul Univ., Loyola Univ., Columbia College; [occ.] Film, Television and Video Producer, Photo Editor; [oth. writ.] Currently writing a book on the life of the late Reverend Mike Matoin, Minister of Unity Church in Chicago; [pers.] I am dedicating my

work to bringing enlightened subject matter to a greater audience.; [a.] Ojac, CA

POEL, CAROL J.
[b.] June 28, 1937, Chicago, IL; [p.] Eugene and Phyllis Springen; [m.] John Edward Poel, June 20, 1980; [ch.] Linda Murray, Brenda Clouser; [ed.] Graduate, Chapman College; [occ.] Writing children's stories, poetry; [memb.] International Society of Poets; [hon.] Editor's Choice Award, given by the National Library of Poetry, published poems in the Garden of Life and Best Poems of 1996; [oth. writ.] Childhood, Ten Thousand Dreams; [pers.] I write about life, especially events concerning my past.; [a.] Ramona, CA

POLIZZI, JAYNE
[b.] March 4, 1977, Blue Island, IL; [p.] Andrew Polizzi, Mary Polizzi; [ed.] California State Polytechnic University, Pomona Arcadia High School; [occ.] Student; [hon.] California Scholarship Federation; [oth. writ.] First publication; [a.] Monrovia, CA

POPE, MARIKO R.
[b.] January 30, 1958, Mt. Pleasant, MI; [p.] Charles Murphy, Mariko Murphy; [m.] David Pope, September 10, 1988; [ch.] Ryan Pope; [ed.] 1995-96 Doctoral student in Management, 1994-1995 MS Systems Management, Colorado Tech, BA International Relations; [occ.] Colorado Tech University Doctoral Student and Consultant in Systems and International Management; [memb.] Society of Logistics Engineers (CT Sole Chair, Vice-Chair Professional Development), Rocky Mountain Jr Chamber of Commerce (VP Community Development, UP Marketing), Japan-America Society, World Trade Org.; [hon.] Who's Who Worldwide, Who's Who American Universities and Colleges; [oth. writ.] Several research and technical reports to include a publication in a Japanese EPDC Journal to create cross-cultural understanding in elective power development and "The Implementation and use of case tools for systems development within Fairfax Country Government"; [pers.] My mission in life is to blend the beauty of art and the logic of science to create harmony and understanding for all people and in all things.; [a.] Colorado Springs, CO

POPOLLA, SABRINA
[pen.] Odessa Zeromus; [b.] January 29, 1980, Chicago Heights; [p.] Robert and Susan Popolla; [ed.] 5 yrs. Greenbriar Elementary 3 yrs. Washington Jr. High, 2 yrs. Bloom HS Junior in Bloom now; [occ.] Student; [hon.] High Honor Roll and Honor Roll in grade school and Jr. High; [pers.] Shakespeare and chickens are cool; [a.] Chicago Heights, IL

PORTER, SCHARLENA ANN
[pen.] Scharlena A. Porter; [b.] July 2, 1950, Indianapolis, IN; [p.] Joe R. Porter and Gertrude Walker; [m.] Divorced, June 4, 1976; [ed.] Rosenwald Elem. Frank Hughes High Cliffon, W. Attended JSCC Jackson TN/TSU Nashville, TN Tennessee Boad of Regents State Vocational Edu. Certification Clerical file and receptionist and songs data entry OPI Nashville, TN; [occ.] Housewife and homemaker; [memb.] Wesley United Methodist Church, SMENC, SNEA and STEA, Certified with American Red Cross Volts; [hon.] American history award 68-4-N Public speach 67 4-N cooking 662 Black American History Awards 76, Certificate Of Appreciation 95 WUMC; [oth. writ.] He had a dream, I can love a valentine, what is love? What is life melody of a song, my sweet lady and Jesus presence several poems published in county news Wayne in Tennessee; [pers.] I feel that my poems and songs should reflect on the nature time with its loveliness, beauty and strength to guide the human nature of past, present and future; [a.] Lorain, OH

POSIN, DAN Q.
[b.] August 13, 1909, Turkestan, Russia; [p.] Abraham and Anna; [m.] Frances "Patsy" Schweitzer-Posin, 1993; [ch.] Dan Jr and Kathryn; [ed.] AB, MA, PLD University of California, Berkeley; [occ.] Prof. of Physics and Astronomy Emeritus and retired to continue teachings; [memb.] Phi Beta Kappa, Sigma Xi, Pi Mu Epsilon, Fellow American Physical Society, Authors Guild, Amer. Feder. of TV and Radio Artists, Amer. Instit. of Physics, Acad. of Televis. Arts and Sciences; [hon.] President Montana Academy of Sciences 1944-46, James T. Grady Award, Amer. Chem. Soc, (1972), Heart Fund Chairman Award, Six Emmy Awards Best Educator and Best Programs, TV, Chicago; [oth. writ.] Many children's books and books on Space and Astronomy: "Life In The Universe", "Life Beyond Our Planet", "Mendeleyev - The Story Of A Great Scientist", "I Have Been to the Village, with introduction by Einstein", "Science in the Age of Space"; [pers.] Campaigner against war, against mis-use of atomic energy, and campaigner for peace - with justice; [a.] Millbrae, CA

POST, FRANK R.
[b.] June 28, 1964, Alexander, NY; [p.] Raymond Post, Patricia Ruge; [m.] Christine Post, June 19, 1993; [ch.] Jennifer Alison; [ed.] Alexander High, Phoenix Institute of Technology, Genesee Hosp. School of Radiologic Technology; [occ.] Registered Radiologic Technologist; [memb.] First Presbyterian Church, ASRT, ARRT, RTSNYS, RSRT; [oth. writ.] Music lyrics; [pers.] I write about feelings, personal experiences, things that make myself or others feel good or can relate to.; [a.] Bergen, NY

POSTEN, MATTHEW SCOTT
[b.] July 30, 1966, Toledo; [p.] William and Marilyn Posten; [m.] Michele Lee Posten, February 18, 1995; [occ.] Merchant Marine on the freighters of the Great Lakes for Oglebay Norton; [pers.] My poems come from my soul and my heart where true words come forth.; [a.] Toledo, OH

PRENTIS, EDNA ZIMMERMAN
[b.] November 15, 1915, Welcome, NC; [p.] Mr. and Mrs. E. J. Zimmerman; [m.] Rev. Robert B. Prentis (Deceased), October 23, 1934; [ch.] Linda Cecil, husband Ron Cecil; [ed.] Welcome High School, 2 yrs. Duke University, Music and Art (private and classes); [occ.] Former Piano Teacher. I write songs (music and lyrics) newspaper column paint water color, acrylic, pastel, oil, colored pencil.; [memb] Davidson County Museum of Art, Welcome Home and Garden Club, welcome 55 and Over Club, Friend of Country Store Group; [hon.] 2 Years won the citizen of the year from the welcome Civitan Club. Honorable mention of Jefferson Award from Winston Salem, NC; [oth. writ.] I hope to write a book of the history of my town and my life.; [pers.] My philosophy is to make the world better and more beautiful that includes environmental problems, have been coordinator of festival for 17 yrs. at the country store, country senior citizen Butley that helps the income of seniors who sell there.; [a.] Welcome, NC

PRESTON, CYNETHEA
[pen.] Nece; [b.] February 1, 1979, Washington, DC; [p.] Susie K. Preston (Mother) and James W. Preston (Father); [ed.] Student at Largo High School in Upper Marlboro, Maryland; [oth. writ.] I have written other poems but I have not published any of them. The One That's Best is the first to be published.; [pers.] My writing is my life. It's about things I go through. As I hear and see different things I write about it in ways I can understand or relate to. It's like someone's talking to me and I'm taking notes. My writing is very important to me because it's my guide in my life. If I'm not writing I have words floating through my mind and it's not a day that that doesn't happen.; [a.] Landover Hills, MD

PRICE, DAVID JOHN
[pen.] David John; [b.] March 20, 1962, San Diego; [p.] Wayne Everett, Mary Ann; [m.] Gwendolyn Joy, December 31, 1994; [ed.] BS Business Admin Marketing, Emergency Medical Technician, River Rescue Technician; [occ.] Ocean Lifeguard; [memb.] Pi Sigma Epsilon, Calif. State Lifeguard Ass. United States Lifeguard Ass.; [oth. writ.] Morning Rose, Stoic History, Flying Free, Pslam to the World, Spirit in my Face, Modern Bondage on this Day, Newest Creation Who Am I, Electric Soul; [pers.] The truth resides within the word. Today we read and hear many words, it is up to each of us to seek that which is true.; [a.] Carlsbad, CA

PRICE, LAFAYE
[pen.] Chee; [b.] June 22, 1950, Travis County; [p.] Jessie J. Sauls and Leslie Faye Sly; [m.] Roy Howard Price Sr.; [ch.] Barry Eugene Yett Jr.; [ed.] GED, UT College, Houston Business College Nixon Business College; [occ.] Fashion designer Author and Song Writer; [memb.] Texas Writer Assoc.; [hon.] Mrs. Black Austin 1987-1988 and Mrs. Black Austin Barber Gueen 1978-1979; [oth. writ.] Songwriting song on an album call Walking with MyMmaster I am author of three books. The books are self publish and copy-righted.; [pers.] I love to sew, horseback ride. I work heard in my church and I sing in a Gospel group call (Sensational Royal Light Singers) as a soloist; [a.] Austin, TX

PRINCE, LILLIAN LESHANDA
[b.] December 5, 1983, Washington, DC; [p.] Herbert and Alice Prince; [ed.] Presently in 7th

grade attended Allenwood Elem. School and presently attending Thurgood Marshall Middle School, Temple Hills, MD; [memb.] Camp Springs Boys and Girls Club, True Deliverance Church of God Youth Choir, Clinton Track Team; [hon.] Honor roll each semester since first grade, Presidential Honor Roll, Music Award, Safety Patrol Award, Plans Recitals, Clinton Track Team; [oth. writ.] Many poems and a few short stories; [pers.] I would like to be able to help someone; [a.] Temple Hills, MD

PROCTOR, NICHOLAS
[pen.] Nicholas Proctor; [b.] 1985, Hertford, NC; [p.] Willis & Debbie Proctor; [oth. writ.] several short stories and poems; [pers.] This poem was written by a 9 yr. old, 4th grade boy, after attempting to prepare mower to cut grass. As the poem indicates he blew a tire (which was flat) when filling it with air and felt he was in trouble;

PRUETT, ASHLEE
[b.] June 30, 1983, Grand Act, CO; [p.] M. Brent and Julie Pruett; [ed.] Concordia Luthern School, Mesa View Elementary School, Life Academy Christian School, and currently homeschooled; [occ.] Student; [memb.] Community Hospital Babysitter's Association, Grand Mesa Youth Soccer Assoc., AAU Junior Women's Basketball Assoc. (Competitive); [hon.] Principal's Honor Roll, several academic achievement awards, United States Achievement Academy National Awards; [oth. writ.] Working on several items in the process of being sent to publishers; [pers.] My family, especially my mother, has greatly influenced and encouraged me. By the grace of God I hope my writings can be helpful to all mankind and influence them dearly.; [a.] Palisade, CO

PRUSA, LOU ANN HATFIELD
[b.] September 10, 1954, Coldwater, KS; [p.] Charles and Beth Hatfield; [m.] Steven J. Prusa, June 2, 1973; [ch.] Steven Jr. and Lori Beth Prusa; [ed.] Bachelors Degree in Human Resources Management From Friends University, Wichita, KS; [occ.] Hatfield-Prusa Funeral Home and Furniture Store Funeral Director and Furniture Dealer; [memb.] Chapter EG PEO sisterhood, Kansas Funeral Directors Association, National Funeral Directors Association, Holy Spirit Catholic Church, Coldwater Chamber of Commerce, Dodge City Chapter Daughter of the American Rev. Eagle Pride Booster Club, Kansas Genealogy Society; [hon.] Graduated with high honors from Friends University (3.75 or above); [oth. writ.] Poem "Have you thought" published in newspaper. Poems submitted for experimental learning project at Friends University.; [pers.] I try to live by the code of ethics from "The Golden Rule." The values of rights us wrong have been well established, since I live in the rural midwest. Making the best choices is the difficult part. I've tried to be committed to love and accept the responsibilities of forgiveness. I hope when I leave this world, people remember me with fondness.; [a.] Coldwater, KS

PRUSIENSKY, PAUL R.
[b.] September 20, 1953, Ridgewood, NJ; [p.] Peter and Edith; [ch.] Paul and Joel; [ed.] John F. Kennedy HS, Totowa, NJ, NJ State Corrections Acad., Essex County Police Academy; [occ.] Sergeant—Ret. (Passaic Co. Sheriff's Dept.); [memb.] Retired and Disabled Policeman of America, Jefferson Youth Soccer League; [hon.] Honors enough to have been included in this anthology; [oth. writ.] "The Birthstones" and two dozen other assorted poems recently compiled for future publication. "Birthstones" is a bound set of 14 poems dedicated to each month of the year.; [pers.] The power of the pen is only as great as the fortune of its wielder. The right words, read by the right person at the right time, often makes all the difference in the world.; [a.] Oak Ridge, NJ

PUCKETT, LANA
[b.] November 14, 1961, Amerillo, TX; [p.] Sam and Cora Puckett; [m.] Frankie Taggett, September 6, 1996, getting married; [ch.] Lance Steven, Brandon Scott, Shanna Lee; [ed.] Fort Kent High; [occ.] Excel Representative; [memb.] Songwriters Club of America; [hon.] Student of the year award M.S.A.D. High School; [oth. writ.] Several poems published in local newspapers. Published song "If my womb had windows" to music city music, Nashville, Tenn. 37217.; [pers.] I strive to reflect the goodness of mankind in my writing I want to touch people's hearts and remind them we are all special and God loves each one of us.; [a.] Fort Kent, ME

PUKACH, JENNIFER
[b.] November 24, 1968, Aliquippa, PA; [p.] Marion Pukach, John Pukach; [ed.] Quigley High Duquesne University Masters Degree in Criminal Justice Duquesne University; [occ.] Retail and Wholesale Business; [hon.] American Legion Award National Honor Society; [pers.] Three statements have helped me in dealing with people and life. You can't change the spots on a leopard. To thine own self be true. Do it now.; [a.] Pittsburgh, PA

PULSNEY, NANCY
[b.] September 8, 1945, Indiana, PA; [p.] John and Mary Hurtack; [m.] Allen Pulsney, June 3, 1967; [ch.] Paula and Jennifer; [ed.] BCI High School; [occ.] Blair Corp, mailing dep; [memb.] Russell U. Methodist Church; [oth. writ.] Two poems published in sparrowgrass poetry forum; [pers.] I strive to reflect meaning in life, simplicity and beauty in nature.; [a.] Russell, PA

PURDUE, TODD
[pen.] Mr. Frost T. S. Puredue; [b.] March 18, 1965, Lincoln, IL; [p.] Steve and Charlene Purdue; [ed.] B.S. Central Missouri State USAF Tech Trug, ATC; [occ.] Engineer (Electronics); [memb.] ARNG; [hon.] Letter of Appreciation, Army Achievement Medal; [oth. writ.] The Indiana Peyote Ritvol, Poe Vs Irving Love Vs Lust. I strive to invigorate people's minds with writing that is both fresh and fun. This I accomplish with on easy to read poem.; [pers.] Have a good day.; [a.] Quincy, IL

PURUSHOTHAMAN, C.
[b.] June 6, 1934, Kalappanayackan Patti, India; [p.] Chennakesavalu and Alamelu Ammal; [m.] P. Chandralekha, September 14, 1960; [ch.] Dhana P. Ganesan, MD (Daughter), Jay P. Kumar, MD (Son), Srilatha P. Athiyaman; [ed.] Pre-University College: National College, Trichy, India, Engineering: Government College of Engineering, Coimbatore, India; [occ.] Retired Superintending Engineer, Government of Tamil Nadu, India; [memb.] Fellow and Chartered Engineer (India) of the Institution of Engineers (India); [hon.] Government of Tamil Nadu, India, awarded two First Prizes for two of my books in 1990 and 1993; [oth. writ.] The Most Economic Way of House Construction, History of Pandya Kings in Tamil Nadu, India (in verse), Comparative Study of Classical "Vasthu Sastra" and Modern Engineering Technology, Estimating and Costing, The World to Exist, Planning of Community Halls-A Superficial Analysis, "Engineering Maintenance-A Case Study", Workshop on Cycle Disaster Mitigation, "Planning of Building with Scientific Sanctity, "The King Karikalan and the Irrigation of Kaveri River"; [pers.] Though I am an Engineer, the study and understanding of the classical writings had made me a poet. I am proud to be called a "Poet". The encouragements that I get from time to time have now made me work hard to elevate myself as one of the first grade poets in the world and to serve the mankind for its prosperity. Though the ocean loses its surface water to the domination of mighty Sun and wearer of the fierce wind, it gets back the entire water lost in course of time by gravitation. Likewise the countries that lost their independence owing to the domination and warfare of an alien nation, got back theirs by the sacrifices of their Sons. Then why the war and domination? I would thrive hard through my writings to deface both, from this world and pave way for peace, as peace alone is eternal.; [a.] Spring Hill, FL

QUEEN, YVONNE JO
[pen.] Yvonne Jo Queen; [b.] February 24, 1952, Dunkirk, NY; [p.] Mother Betty Estes, Dad Harry Estes; [m.] Keith Queen, April, 1990; [ch.] Carrie Hadden, Stephanie Queen; [ed.] GED in 1992; [occ.] Employee of School Board of Manatee County, Bradenton FL; [hon.] I was honored by our school board newspaper Manatee Educator in Sept. 1995, the editor printed The Pioneer Man and congratulated me on my second poem to be published; [oth. writ.] Poetic Voices of America, Spring 1995 - The Pioneer Man, Sparrowgrass Poetry Forum, Inc. also Summer 1996 edition of Treasured Poems of America - Love's Regrets also in the same edition Windows of Perception Within; [pers.] Poetry to me is an avenue of art, that lets your heart express all the encompassing experience life can bring. "Traveling with Clarification by Words".; [a.] Bradenton, FL

QUIJANO, VLADIMIR
[pen.] Vova; [b.] June 15, 1964, San Francisco, CA; [p.] Oscar A. Vladimir, Tania Vladimir; [ch.] Taylor Paul, Keenan Alexander; [ed.] 1st grade OakKnoll, M Park, Pre-School Menlo Park; [occ.] Maintenance Building Engineer, Reserve Police Officer; [pers.] Thank you to my true love, Cindy Sue De Vine. She was my inspiration to write such a poem. A special

thanks to my niece Jackie May Vladimir, for taping the Poetry Contest Ad to my dresser mirror. I love you girls!; [a.] Redwood City, CA

RAGAN, GALE
[b.] April 5, 1956, Miami, FL; [p.] Jerry and Mae Ragan (Both are Deceased); [ch.] Melvin Ted Reid and David John Alexander Reid; [ed.] University of Miami; [occ.] Teacher, Math Curriculum Specialist, College Professor; [memb.] Book Review Club "Between Friends", National Council of Teachers of Math (NCTM), Florida Council of Teachers of Mathematics; [hon.] Fulbright Scholar, Teachers for Africa, Leadership Miami, Teacher Quest Scholarship Program, Alpha Kappa Alpha Sorority Inc., Board of Director, University of Miami, College of Arts and Sciences Alumni Association; [oth. writ.] A book of poems, "In My Room" (being published by Watermark Press, books "Divine" family story (being published Winston-Derek Publishers, Inc.), "Lemonade and Teardrops" fairy tale (to be published - submitted to Winston-Derek, Game Invention "Game of Hearts" (to be submitted to Winston-Derek), songwriting "Whom Can You Trust" (being recorded for the "America" project by Hill Top Records), songwriting "Escape" (being recorded for "America" project by Hill Top Records), poem "Early Morning" (published in anthology "At Water's Edge" by the National Library of Poetry; [pers.] I enjoy writing and creating educational materials. I have been influenced by my mother, a country school teacher.; [a.] Miami, FL

RAGAN, IMOGENE
[b.] February 5, 1922, Pana, IL; [p.] Cyrus and Edith Zahradka; [m.] Maruin R. Ragan (Deceased), August 16, 1943; [ch.] John, William, Cyrus, and Marisue; [ed.] Pana Township High School; [occ.] Retired; [memb.] National Honor Society '40, NRTA of Illinois; [pers.] I try to live a "Christian - Oriented life with a smile on my face, love in my heart, hope for the future - oh yes! And a never ending sense or humor!; [a.] Lafayette, IN

RAGHUNATH, BALA
[pen.] Karthik; [b.] February 9, 1965, India; [p.] Balasubramanian and Jamuna; [m.] Uma, June 24, 1993; [ed.] Chemical Engineer; [occ.] Dir. of Eng./Dev.; [memb.] American Institute of Chemical Engineers; [hon.] Outstanding Teaching Assistant, Univ. of Cincinnati, 1990; [oth. writ.] Poems (in personal notebook); [a.] Wisconsin Rapids, WI

RAMIREZ, GUADALUPE
[pen.] Lupe Ramirez; [b.] December 12, 1959, San Salvador, CA; [p.] Esperanza Guadron; [m.] Sal Ramirez, December 17, 1977; [ch.] Daniel, Marilynn, Sal, Rocio, Edward, Charlie; [ed.] Franklin High, Travel Management Academy Pacific, Real Estate School; [occ.] Real Estate Agent; [pers.] Life is our greatest treasure and the most precious gift from God.; [a.] Los Angeles, CA

RAMSEY, BETSY
[b.] July 10, 1945, Asheville, NC; [p.] Mary Belle Marshall, Walter Alan Marshall (Deceased); [ed.] Lee H. Edwards High School, Biltmore Elementary School, David Millard Junior High; [occ.] Executive Director - Assoc. on Battered Women of Clayton County; [hon.] Realtor of Year, Woman of Year, Public Servant of Year, Community Leader of Year, United Way Volunteer of the Year, Recognition by US Dept of Justice for Assistance to Victims of Crime, TBS Super Citizen of the Week, Resolution Georgia House of Representatives for work with victims; [pers.] Time is a gift, use it wisely, as once it is used it is over. Memories linger forever so remember the laughter so it will live on.; [a.] Clayton County, GA

RANDALL, NATOSHA
[b.] December 5, 1972; [p.] Paul and Mini Reitz; [m.] John Randall, April 16, 1994; [ch.] John Michael Jr.; [ed.] Southern High School 1991; [occ.] Receptionist/Operator; [oth. writ.] None that have been published; [pers.] Clothe yourselves with love, for it is a perfect bond of union. Col. 3:14; [a.] Baltimore, MD

RANDALL, SUSAN L.
[b.] May 21, 1960, Massena, NY; [p.] Anita and Lawrence Beattie; [ch.] Auburn and Adam Randall; [ed.] Findlay University (1978-1980) Findlay, Ohio - 2 years State University of NY., Potsdam, NY - Grad. 1982 degree: English; [occ.] Administrative Assistant (card attached); [memb.] St. Francis Parish Girl Scouts; [hon.] Dean's List, Delta Zeta, Economics Team Excellence Cup (Dec. 1995); [oth. writ.] Several poems published in campus newspapers. Publish a monthly campus newsletter; [pers.] My writings reflect personal feelings and experiences. My favorite poet is Edgar Allen Poe.; [a.] Potsdam, NY

RASHEED, FARAH
[b.] August 24, 1977, Dhahran, Saudi Arabia; [p.] Capt. M.R. Azhar and Vasmeen Rasheed; [ed.] Yanbu International School, Saudi Arabia (K-G-9), Leysin American School, Switzerland (10-12), Hollins College, (Freshman now); [occ.] College Student; [hon.] European Council of International Schools, (ECIS) for International Understanding; [pers.] I dedicate this poem to my family, who understand.; [a.] Roanoke, VA

RASKA, RACHEL FARMER STRATTOR
[b.] July 4, 1912, Near Rosewood, KY; [p.] Cordie Stradert and George Farmer Alonzo Stradert; [m.] Siewin B. Raska, October 28, 1962; [ch.] June Rhea Stratton; [ed.] Graduate Bevier-Cleaton High School 1930, Western KY, State Teacher's Col. - one term 1930, Graduated from Speer Memorial Hospitals 1934; [occ.] Retired nurse; [oth. writ.] The cyclone in "Between The Raindrops"; [a.] Clarksville, TN

RATTI, JODY
[pen.] J.R. Robinton; [b.] October 26, 1978, Fairview, NJ; [p.] Wayne Ratti, Margaret Ratti; [ed.] Bergen Catholic HS; [pers.] Be it the last or the first, the best or the worst, the memories stay forever and a day...; [a.] Fairview, NJ

RAY, LUIS ENRIQUE
[b.] October 19, 1980, California; [p.] Judy Canidos, Carlos Oviedo; [ed.] Currently enrolled in Salesian High School in Los Angeles 10th grade; [occ.] Student; [pers.] I want to thank my mother for encouraging me to follow my dreams and goals.; [a.] Los Angeles, CA

RAY, WYNONA A.
[pen.] Wynona Ray; [b.] April 13, 1948, Hamilton, OH; [p.] Winton Ray and Crystal Brown Ray; [ch.] La Ronda, La Donna Ray, Jalana Ray, Nika Ray, Kenchese Ray; [ed.] Harrisom Elementary, Jr High Roosevelt Hamiltom High; [occ.] Home Maker, Cashier; [oth. writ.] When Our Mother Cries, Streets Of Stone Don't Lead, Back Home; [pers.] When I write my words represent and reflected feelings and thoughts. Of all people. From yesterday, today and from a time to come. Believing we are all connected. Which make us the people of each day to come; [a.] Aurora, CO

RAYMUNDO, NANCY ANN
[b.] February 15, 1945, LI, NY; [m.] George Raymundo, November 14, 1965; [ch.] Two daughters, Nancy Lynn and Dawn Estelle; [ed.] N. Babylon High School, LI, NY; [occ.] Housewife, trying to publish children's books and poetry; [hon.] 1995 Diamond Homer Award from Famous Poets Society Hollywood, California; [oth. writ.] Survival or not published by Famous Poets Anthology; [pers.] Most of my poetry is written from the Heart of my thoughts. Reflecting on issues of everyday life.; [a.] Weaverville, NC

REA, BILLY JOE
[pen.] "B.J."; [b.] October 5, 1976, Waco, TX; [p.] Leonard H. and Laquita Rea; [ed.] High school LaVega; [occ.] Unemployed; [oth. writ.] I have at least 16 more other poetry entry's in my own personal journal and a few short stories.; [pers.] Look at life as a journey not race.; [a.] Greenville, TX

REA, CAROLINE
[b.] November 10, 1978, Baton Rouge, LA; [p.] Catherine Blendeau and Patrick Rea; [pers.] Always remember the value of a peaceful solution to any problem.; [a.] Norfolk, VA

RECK, ADAM L.
[pen.] Dark Wolf; [b.] October 9, 1972, Cleveland, OH; [p.] Richard Reck and Star Zadorecky; [ed.] Brecksville Broadview Hts High School, Cuyahoga Community College; [occ.] Machinist (CNC Operator); [memb.] Pres of Small Artists Guild (after midnight); [hon.] Cleveland Institute of Art 2 key finalists (89, 90), 1 place (91), attended National Competitions 2 years in Rodchester, New York, 1991 Outstanding Graphic Artist by Cleveland Printing Council; [oth. writ.] Currently working on book; [pers.] Prejudice and denial are the soil of a stagnant mind. Because not only is a closed mind ignorant to the world, but is also blind to the beauty of diversity.; [a.] Cleveland, OH

REECE, JANIE DEE
[pen.] Janie Reece; [b.] May 28, 1950, Enterprise, IL; [p.] Dean and Evelyn Reece; [ch.] Shawn, Jason, and Jacob; [ed.] Walla Walla Community College, Portland State University; [occ.] Emergency Dept. R.N. Travel nursing around America; [memb.] Sierra Club; [hon.] Dean's List; [oth. writ.] Several poems and short stories, book in progress; [pers.] Writing is a tool to explore and express the feeling in the minds darkest recesses. Exploring, analyzing and declaring on paper molds one's perception of those thoughts and sheds the brightest light on the darkest feelings. In this light acceptance of self is achieved and thru that, acceptance of all others.; [a.] Los Angeles, CA

REICHERT, GWEN PATTERSON
[b.] January 22, 1946, Moultrie, GA; [p.] James Artist Patterson and Thelma Hobby Patterson; [m.] Allan C. Reichert, April 20, 1968; [ed.] M.Ed., University of North FL, Jacksonville, FL, 1974, B.A., Jacksonville University, Jacksonville, FL, 1968; [occ.] Supervisor of Title I Services for St. Johns County, FL; [memb.] International Reading Assn., FL Reading Assn., St. Johns County Reading Council, Phi Delta Kappa, FL Assn. of state and Fed. Ed. Prog. Administrators, Jane Austen Society, Beatrix Potter Society, Bronte Society, Randolph Caldecott Society of America; [hon.] Honorary Membership in the Caldecott Society of Am., St. Johns County Reading Councils, "Literacy Award, FL Jaycees "Outstanding Young Educator" Award, St. Augustine Jaycees, "Outstanding Young Educator" Award, Listed in outstanding Elem. Teas. of America, Dean's List at JU and UNF; [oth. writ.] Articles: "Objectives and Activities for Location and Study Skills", "Happiness Is Individualized Reading", "A Honey Of An Idea", "Tasha Todur Regards Randolph Caldecott a Genius of Illustration", "Randolph Who? From Where? What Did He Do?" I serve as editor of the title I Handbook And The Caldecott Society Newsletter; [pers.] I cannot imagine a career other than one in the field of Education. I have been an Elem. classroom teacher, elementary principal and serve as an adjunct professor at Jacksonville University. When I do have "freetime" I am involved in the Caldecott Society, genealogical research, writing Haiku, reading nineteenth century literature and spending time with my husband and cat. My favorite travel destinations are England and Scotland. I enjoy facilitating teaching and learning.; [a.] Saint Augustine, FL

REILLY, ANGELA M.
[pers.] I anticipate an age when mankind allows one another to experience their time alone in the open spaces as opposed to backing each other into corners, and forcing the elevation of walls.

REILLY, WILLIAM
[b.] May 13, 1937, Jersey City, NJ; [p.] John F. Reilly, Genevieve Reilly; [m.] August 11, 1962; [ch.] Brian Reilly, Bonnie Reilly; [ed.] Westfield High School 1956, Union County College Engineering Drafting; [occ.] Retired Purchasing Agent; [memb.] Holy Trinity Roman Catholic Church, Knights of Columbus; [oth. writ.] Several poems published in literary periodicals around country, one essay published summer '95, Many Leave One Tree, essay in Dec '95 of Many Voices; [pers.] I strive to bring joy through poetry. I call my writings "feelings on paper". My essays endeavor to enlighten people about abusers.; [a.] Marlboro, NJ

REILY, JESSICA
[b.] December 3, 1978, Gainesville, FL; [p.] Edward and Catherine Reilly; [ed.] Upper Merion High School; [occ.] Student; [memb.] Good Shepard Lutheran Church, Upper Merion Track and Cross Country Team; [oth. writ.] Several other poems and short stories, hopefully a book in the future; [pers.] "Some may say that I'm a dreamer but I'm not the only one" Don't let others tell you that your style is wrong just because they can't see the light.; [a.] King of Prussia, PA

REINCKE, MARTHA J.
[pen.] Martha Jane; [b.] September 21, 1958, Battle Creek, MI; [p.] Gus Adolph Klon - Ruth Marie Klon; [ch.] Daniel Lee; [occ.] Nanny, Boise Idaho; [pers.] I have always love writing poems, short stories, songs and reading other people's poems, I come from a long line of writers in my family; [a.] Boise, ID

RENFRO, CAROLINE MARIE
[pen.] Caroline Renfro; [b.] March 21, 1982, Charlotte, NC; [p.] Diana and Traylor Renfro; [ed.] Currently ('95-'96) in the 8th grade at Piedmont open Middle School; [memb.] Young Writers Workshop (Summer '95, Summer '96....); [hon.] Honor roll (A-B), Awards in NATRC (North American Trail Ride Conference) as a Junior Novice; [oth. writ.] Article for Dilworth Quarterly, "Championships" and "How Much Longer" (poem submitted) published in Exploring Charlottes Web (Publication for a writers workshop) Newspaper for Piedmont Middle School (1 feature, 1 editorial); [a.] Charlotte, NC

RESENBECK, LORETTA
[pen.] Loretta Petry; [b.] September 15, 1966, Huntingburg, IN; [p.] Clarence and Sylvia Petry; [m.] Christopher Resenbeck, October 24, 1987; [ed.] Graduated from Southridge High School, 1995., attended VUJC, for 1 yr. for occupational training; [occ.] Cashier, clerk for energy plus - Co-op; [memb.] I'm a member of Mothers Against Drunk-Drivers (MADD) and I support our American Veterans; [hon.] I haven't received any material honors, but, orally my superiors in high school honored me for my compensational work and poetry.; [oth. writ.] I've written several poems and songs. I have a personal Library. I haven't really submitted anything for publication except 2 books, 1 on child.; [pers.] I believe, that we are part on this earth to love and care for one another. My only hope is that one day everyone will realize this and that there will be great peace.; [a.] Holland, IN

REVIE, JENNIFER
[pen.] Jennifer Anne Revie; [b.] September 19, 1975, Harford, PA; [p.] John and Elaine Revie; [ed.] Freshman at College Misericordia; [occ.] Student; [memb.] Lit Club; [hon.] I was published in my college magazine "Instress"; [pers.] Dedicated to my amiga; [a.] Harford, PA

RHODES, ELAINE
[b.] May 13, 1922, Rhinelander, WI; [p.] Albert and Carrie Petersen; [m.] Harold Rhodes (Dusty), November 28, 1942; [ch.] Gary (50), Donna (44), Mary Anne (37); [ed.] High school; [occ.] Retired; [memb.] Wisconsin Regional Writers Assoc.; [hon.] Poetry published in John Frost's Anthology, My Mom, Harsh Words, Peace on Earth; [oth. writ.] In the process of writing our Family history for our children; [a.] Janesville, WI

RHODUS, CHARLOTTE A.
[pen.] Jo Ann Rhodus; [b.] October 7 1945, Tylertown, MS; [p.] William Rhodus and Basha Rhodus; [m.] Divorced ex-husband - Milo Weber, October 3, 1965; [ch.] Tania Renee, Robert Milo Weber, Jill Ann Rhodus; [ed.] Holden High School, Holden, LA, Baton Rouge Vo Tech, Baton Rouge, LA; [occ.] Secretary, VA Medical Center, No, LA, Sales associate, Sears; [oth. writ.] One poem published in local newspaper, I have other poems that not been published; [pers.] All poems that I write are written to people who are very dear to me and who have touched my heart and life!; [a.] Westwego, LA

RICCA, LAURA
[b.] May 3, 1979, Brooklyn, NY; [p.] Marlene Ricca and Anthony Ricca; [ed.] Jr. in South Share High School; [hon.] Gloria Carnazza Memorial Award, 69th Precint Community Council Award; [pers.] I put all my feelings and thoughts into my writings. If it wasn't for my teachers who worked me to "death", I would have never wrote "All for Nothing"; [a.] Brooklyn, NY

RICE, CHRISTOPHER
[b.] November 19, 1974, St Cloud, MN; [p.] John and Margaret Rice; [ed.] Apollo High School, St. Cloud St. University, Colorado St. University; [occ.] Student, Colorado St. Un.; [memb.] Powder Ridge Alpine Ski Team , Colorado St University Ski Team, Fellowship of Christian Athlete, College Republicans, Premedicia; [hon.] Honors Society; [pers.] I have but one goal in my writing, to give birth to something new, something pure, something true.

RICHARDSON, MICHAEL AARON
[pen.] The Poetic Chef; [b.] May 19, 1959, LA, CA; [p.] Deborah Richardson-Green, Robert Lee Richardson; [ed.] Palisades High School, Pacific Palisades, CA, Laney College, Oakland, CA; [occ.] Owner/chef of Michael's Romantic Interludes; [memb.] The World Stag Poets Workshop LA, CA; [hon.] 3 times Dean's List at Laney College, Oakland, CA; [oth. writ.] 1st book "Feeling In The Extreme"; [pers.] I work for a living, but I live for my muse.; [a.] Los Angeles, CA

RICHBURG, ELIZABETH
[b.] June 8, 1948, Philadelphia; [p.] Elizabeth and Andrew Brewer; [m.] Cornelius Richburg

(Deceased), August 16, 1975; [ch.] Doretha Judy Richburg; [ed.] OverBrook High, Lincoln Prep. College, Computer Data Processing Institution, PWBA LAN Training; [memb.] Pinn Memorial Baptist Church, Director of, Our people Community Development Corporation; [hon.] U.S. Department of Labor Sectary's Exception Achievement Award, (PWBA LAN Administrator's); [oth. writ.] Several other poems, Reflection, Legacy, Heaven and one short story, In between the lines; [pers.] This poems (A lover's rose) was written for my husband Cornelius Richburg. Because their was a time in our marriage that was very stressful financially, and I wanted to give my husbands something to cheer him, so I decided to give my love for him in words. In life this (A lover's Rose) was my gift to him. In death this (A Lover's Rose) is.

RIESTERER, WENDY C.
[pen.] Catherine; [b.] June 16, 1978, Sandusky, OH; [p.] Mary Riesterer, Ronald Riesterer; [ed.] St. Mary's Central Catholic High Attend, Will attend the University of Toledo (fall 1996); [occ.] Student; [memb.] National Honor Society, Key Club, Environmental Club, International Club, Great Books Club, Student Council, Tennis; [hon.] Founder and President of Great Books Club, Vehicle co-editor (literary magazine); Who's Who Among American Students (3 years); [oth. writ.] A collection of the poems by Wendy Riesterer, several loose poems; [pers.] I have found that beauty is in that of which we do not understand.; [a.] Sandusky, OH

RIFFLE, STELLA
[b.] January 3, 1932, Webster Springs; [p.] Lela and Virgil Miller; [m.] Robert Riffle Sr. (Divorced 1976), 1949; [ch.] Shelia, Robert, William, Larry; [ed.] Mat; [occ.] Retired Elementary Teacher; [memb.] Webster Spring Garden Club, Sand Run Baptist Church, Holly River State Park Foundation, Inc, Webster County Assn. Retired School Person, Alpha Delta Kappa, American Baptist Women; [hon.] Portrayed teacher in video "A day in A One-Room School" (shown at holly river park) I am deeply honored to have wealth of friends; [oth. writ.] Have written much! Only submitted for publication 3 times and was included in Anthologies on the threshold of a dream and of Diamonds and Rust; [pers.] I write from "the heart", as feelings are expressed most exclusively through writing easing one through many difficult times as well as happy ones! "My imaginative escape!"; [a.] Webster Springs, WV

RILES, KEVIN H.
[pen.] K.H.R.; [b.] January 15, 1968, Miami, FL; [p.] Laura I. Riles, Bobby Riles; [m.] Adrienne M. Riles, October 16, 1995; [ch.] One son Denzel; [ed.] Miami Carol City Sr High; [occ.] Dade County Court House Traffic Division; [memb.] New Birith Baptist Church (Deacon); [hon.] On my job I wrote a suggestion on how to save money for my job, perfect attendance for five years; [oth. writ.] I'm Free, Black Beauty, Black Butterfly, Beyond the Stars, Sunshine, Ghetto Blues; [pers.] This poem was written when a co-worker was killed by her son. I was hurt and when I prayed that night, the Lord put in my heart to write this to help my spirit understand the pain we all felt; [a.] Miami, FL

RING, SHAWN
[pen.] Shawn Ring; [b.] May 16, 1976, Buffalo, NY; [p.] Timothy Ring, Janis Ring; [ed.] Orchard Park High School Class of '95 (currently attending college); [occ.] Working part-time jobs and is a student; [oth. writ.] In the process of publishing first book of poetry, and is working on a second one; [pers.] A man who has everything, but has not love(d), has nothing. I believe in that, and try to express it in all my poetry. July 9, 1994 is when I wrote this piece.; [a.] Orchard Park, NY

RIOS, AMELIA
[b.] Columbia, South America; [m.] Adan Rios; [ch.] Cynthia, Sylvia; [ed.] University Of WA. Experimental College; [occ.] Medical Clerk; [memb.] Seattle Public Library, PETA (People for the Ethical Treatment of Animals), ASPCA (The American Society For the Prevention of Cruelty to Animals); [hon.] Audubon Society; [oth. writ.] Children's stories Miscellaneous Poetry; [pers.] Mother nature is a great giver or beauty. In it's many gifts, I find wonderful subjects to write about, spiritual enrichment, and never ending hope.; [a.] Seattle, WA

RIPPLEY, DONNA
[pen.] Abbey Guffaur; [b.] February 21, 1959, Cincinnati, OH; [p.] Bob and Audrey Jeanmougin; [m.] William B. Rippley, October 3, 1981; [ed.] Seton High School; [occ.] Executive Assistant to the President, CBIS; [memb.] Humane Society, League of Animal Welfare; [pers.] Life is short — have fun. Find amusement in everyday occurences. Laugh a lot; [a.] Cincinnati, OH

RISING, REBECCA
[pen.] Catalina Devereaux; [b.] February 9, 1981, Holyoke; [p.] Mr and Mrs Edwin Rising; [ed.] Agawam School System, formerly a freshman at Agawam High School; [memb.] Sweet Valley High and Babysitters Club; [hon.] Essay contests in 88 and 87, competition for Junior Great Books in 90, Champion in Partners in Excellence Reading program in 91, Accelerated Reader in 93, and Essay Contest in 93; [oth. writ.] The Mysterious Horse in 93, A Serious Called Black Hill Acres (with friend Sarah Freeman), Meeko at Camp in 95, a few poems, and a writer for a camp newspaper in 95. None of the these have been published.; [pers.] In my stories, I always mix fiction, my life, and what I would like my life to be like.; [a.] Feeding Hills, MA

RITCHIE, CAROL LEE
[b.] July 28, 1944, Perth Amboy, NJ; [p.] Gurdon L. and Mable I. Judge; [m.] Edmond M. Ritchie, December 30, 1974; [ch.] Nine; [ed.] GED 12th grade; [occ.] Parts Packer at Emerson Power Transmission Products, Ithaca, NY; [memb.] Lord Hill Church, Machinists Union, Cajun French Music Assoc.; [hon.] ISO Achievement, 20 years award for working for Emerson Power transmission; [oth. writ.] Numerous poems, often to commemorate special events and occurrences; [pers.] Deeply concerned about people disadvantaged by birth defects. Much writing influenced by contact and experience with these people.; [a.] Newark Valley, NY

RIZZO, TARA BOESCH
[pen.] Tara Boesch Rizzo; [b.] October 18, 1971, Englewood, NJ; [p.] Richard Boesch, Millie Boesch; [ch.] Daniel Nicholas Rizzo; [ed.] Vernon Township High School, Sussex County Community College; [occ.] Student and mother; [memb.] Screen Actors Guild (SAG); [hon.] Phi Theta Kappa, Honor Society, Dean's List and National, Deans List (I am printers in 1994-1995 18th Edition vol. 1), President - Theatre Arts Club at SCCC; [oth. writ.] 3 articles/personal stories published in College Newspaper; [pers.] I strive for truth. Revealing and bringing to light the unseen, yet, the obvious. I love shakespeare where by "Ignorance is as dark as hell".; [a.] Newton, NJ

ROBERSON, NEAL W.
[b.] May 31, 1920, Summer, NE; [ch.] 2 daughters and 3 granddaughters; [ed.] High school by GED tests, mostly self taught; [occ.] Manager of Motel; [hon.] Second World War, Honorable Discharge; [oth. writ.] Autumntide, Harp Song, Bee and the Flowers, Circling in the Sand, A Whisper of Knowledge; [pers.] Before I became blind I used to be an avid reader of Thoreau, Emerson, and Whitman. Took many walks in wilderness to enjoy nature.; [a.] Superior, MT

ROBINSON, DORIS
[pen.] Doris Robinson; [b.] March 24, 1951, Ft. Meade, FL; [p.] Red And Alene Albritton; [m.] Darrell R. Robinson, July 13, 1991; [ch.] 3; [ed.] Fort Meade Jr-Sr High Grades 7-11, GED (Columbia State), Columbia State, Tenn.; [occ.] Poultry Worker and Factory Worker; [oth. writ.] A Mother's Pain (Sept 1990), Pets (1987), I Going Home (1986), Marriage (1987), Sharing (1986), Forgetfulness (1986), Problems (1983), Life (1986), What is Love (1986), Pride (1986), Patience (1986), Second Time Around (1990), Starting Over (1991), Choices (1990), Broken Plans (1991), Loneliness (1990); [pers.] I write poems based on my life and problems faced. I have been writing poems since 1969.

ROBINSON, MICHAEL C.
[pen.] Mr. Robinson, Big Mike; [b.] June 22, 1969, Clinton Hos.; [p.] James and Phyllis Robinson; [hon.] I have won many athletic awards such as all conference etc... and received an award for keeping a GPA of over 3.5, Christian Fellowship award; [oth. writ.] I have many unpublished poems. If you would like to see them, call (864) 833-5881. They have been published in the local newspaper.; [pers.] I was taught that God works miracles through those who believe. So through the poetic talents that he blessed me with I hope to develop curiosity that can only be satisfied by God.; [a.] Clinton, SC

RODGERS, CHRISTINE
[b.] November 23, 1956, Redwood City, CA; [p.] Ernest and Mary Rodgers; [ed.] St. Francis High School, U.C.L.A., Circle in the Square; [occ.] Actress-poet-pilgrim; [memb.] Z Space Studio; [oth. writ.] In progress - solo performance piece called "octave". A book of spiritual poetry

entitled "Shuffling Toward and Place of Grace"; [pers.] For me, poems are windows - a way of looking into things - to see as and painter sees - everything. And to get a glimpse of God.; [a.] San Francisco, CA

RODRIGUEZ, JESSICA ANN
[pen.] Jessica Rodriguez; [b.] July 22, 1984, Odessa, TX; [p.] Jaime P. Rodriguez, Diana H. Rodriguez; [ed.] 6th grade education; [occ.] Student; [memb.] United States Achievement Academy National Honor Roll member, member of The Gifted and Talented Class in Junior High; [hon.] Honor Roll Student; [oth. writ.] Other writings in "Gifted and Talented" class in school; [pers.] I love animals I love everything about them and I try to write strictly about animals, especially their habits.; [a.] Alpine, TX

RODRIGUEZ, NANCY R. L.
[b.] March 21, 1957, Southbridge, MA; [p.] Frank Roso and Nellie Roso; [m.] Gilberto Rodriguez, December 16, 1977; [ch.] Jason and Joshua; [occ.] Providence House, Nursing Home, Southbridge

ROE, RANDY A.
[b.] May 16, 1961, Superior, WI; [p.] Willard and Lucille Roe; [m.] Laurie Jean Roe, August 18, 1990; [ch.] Stepson Jeffery; [ed.] Superior S High School, Superior, WI; [occ.] Printing press operator in Flexography for 12 years; [memb.] Member of Prince of Peace Lutheran church of Spring Lake Park, MN; [pers.] I would someday hope to have my own book of Poetry published, maybe someone who reads this, will contact me and give me some advice on how to get started.; [a.] Fridley, MN

ROFFLER, ILSE
[b.] February 28, 1940, Switzerland; [p.] Hans and Ida Schoedler; [m.] Hans Roffler, June 24, 1961; [ch.] Kathrin, Robert, Jean; [ed.] College and trade school in Switzerland; [memb.] International Society of Poets, San Pedro Writer's Guild; [pers.] In my writings, I like to capture the values and meanings of life.; [a.] San Pedro, CA

ROGERS, AMY L.
[pen.] Amy Rogers; [b.] October 13, 1975, Newport News, VA; [p.] Alice Matheny; [ed.] High School Graduate, Herbert Hoover High Clendenin WV 25045; [occ.] Receptionist for a foot dr.; [memb.] WMCA; [oth. writ.] Romantic poems, nature; [pers.] I've been writing poems since I was a little girl, feelings just pop in my head and I write them down, mostly - how I'm feeling at that particular time.; [a.] Clendenin, WV

ROGERS, BRANDY
[b.] March 23, 1982, Harrison, AR; [p.] James R. and Loretta; [ed.] Bergman High School; [hon.] President's Academic Effort Award signed by President Bill Clinton, (hon.) Junior Beta Club; [a.] Bergman, AR

ROGERS JR., GRANT
[pen.] Lamar; [b.] June 3, 1958, Welch, WV; [p.] Grant Rogers Sr., Carrie Rogers; [m.] Margaret Ann Rogers, April 10, 1995; [ed.] Asst. Degree 2 years; [occ.] Teacher of Life; [pers.] Always treat others better than you would like to be treated yourself, and good things shall always surround you, and your loved ones. The love I have for my wife, influences me.; [a.] Princeton, WV

ROMANETZ, STEPHEN C.
[b.] February 16, 1977, Newport News, VA; [p.] Steve Romanetz and Janet Romanetz; [ed.] Phoebus High, University of Alabama (Freshman); [occ.] Student; [memb.] The Southern League; [oth. writ.] Several unpublished poems; [pers.] I try to promote the qualities of a good Southern Gentleman to anyone, even a Yankee. My teachers at Phoebus High have been my inspiration.; [a.] Hampton, VA

ROMANS, ANN
[pen.] La Vita; [b.] April 3, 1929, Wetumpka, AL; [p.] John Varner and Tumpka Varner; [m.] (Divorced) December 28, 1968; [ch.] Anthony Jones and Annetta Romans; [ed.] BA Knoxville College, MA John Carroll Univer., Case Western Reserve Univer., Alpha Kappa Alpha Sorority, St. Marks Church, Television certificate, Nursing certificate on aging, Real Estate; [occ.] Elementary Teacher, Cleveland, Ohio, Comedienne, Author, Writer, Community Worker, Counselor; [memb.] St. Marks Presbyterian Church, Alpha Kappa Alpha Sorority, 11th District Caucus, GAC-Pac Political Action-Pres. of Cleveland Black Writers, Anti-Basileus Gamma Phi Delta Sorority, Growth Assoc., Board of Education Acknowledgement; [hon.] Certificate of performance Award from President Bill Clinton, and George Bush, Listed In Who's Who Among Black Americans, Research award from Ford and Rockerfeller Foundations to travel around the world, Topic-The Relations of the Black man to the people of the World": Anna Chatman "Greatest Love Award", W.A.V.E. Community Award, Lady D' Drill Team, and Kentucky's Colonels Award; [oth. writ.] Textbook: Michael Jackson, Alphabets Coloring Book with Phonics; [pers.] I believe in caring for others: Love is the greatest.; [a.] Cleveland, OH

ROMERO, ISSAC
[pen.] Zeke; [b.] October 27, 1989, San Jose; [p.] Pete Romero; [ch.] Thomas S. Romero and Krystal; [ed.] San Jose High School, San Jose City College; [occ.] Trasportion Spec., Track Driver; [memb.] I am a member to a Christian Church (family life outreach) of San Jose, I also manage a band called Gypsy Style (Latin Rock); [oth. writ.] I have been published in Poetic Voices of America, Spring 95, (Snow Bird) as well orchard magazine Santa Cruz. I was displayed at Maclart Gallery in San Jose, CA; [pers.] A passage of time is but a moment, compared to a Brand of Self Bondage (Isaac 2 Romer); [a.] San Jose, CA

ROMERO, NESTOR HERNANDO
[b.] September 25, 1961, Bogota, Colombia, South America; [p.] Hernando Romero, Clara Inez Alvarez; [ed.] St Johns HS in Shrewsbury, MA, Tufts University Medford, MA, BA - Int Relations and History (Cum Laude); [occ.] US Army Peacekeeping Force in support of UN in Haiti as well as Intl Business in Mexico from San Diego for Norton Company; [hon.] Various military awards and decorations; [oth. writ.] Several poems and essays presented to friends and family; [pers.] Poems reflect the human endeavor to understand oneself and our role in life using nature as a vehicle toward defining this mystery.; [a.] San Diego, CA

RONDEAU, ROBERTA M.
[pen.] Bobbie, Berta; [b.] July 26, 1963, Keene, NH; [p.] Terrance and Martha Quigley; [m.] Separated going on divorce; [ch.] Chrystal and Eric; [ed.] High school (Dropout) but went back and finally got my GED, 6 years age; [occ.] Unfortunately now a homemaker (I am permanently disabled); [memb.] RSDA (Reflex Sympathic Dystrophy Association, the reason why I'm disabled now) but always hoping for a cure!; [hon.] This is truly an honor and award for me to actually have my poem published; [oth. writ.] I'm Finally Free! (to be published in a Tapestry of Thoughts) (this is great 2 poems both being published!; [pers.] I wrote this for my new "Mom" Ella Miller for when she became ill and was having a hard time with it. I wanted to show her how much I love her! (And she really loves this) (Crazy Redneck family way); [a.] Troy, NH

ROSE, GEORGE E.
[b.] March 16, 1972, Phila, PA; [p.] Sharon, Joseph Quintieri; [ed.] Abraham Lincoln High, College Prep Courses; [occ.] Sampling Director, Cocoa Barry US Inc Pennsauken NJ; [hon.] Graduated with honors in top 5% of class; [oth. writ.] Collection of poems and short stories for my own enjoyment; [pers.] I gather much of my inspiration from nature and the many special women in my life.; [a.] Philadelphia, PA

ROSE, SALLY L.
[b.] October 6, 1939, Culver City, CA; [p.] Jack and Peggy Phen; [ch.] Michael Pamela, Lorraine, Jennifer and 12 grandchildren; [ed.] Washington High, LA, Mt. SAC, Walnut, CA received AA, 2 yrs. at Cal. St. L.A. at Los Angeles, CA; [occ.] Accountant at Jet Propulsion Lab, Pasadena, CA; [memb.] San Bernardino County, Radio Amateur Community Emergency Service; [hon.] Dean's List, Alpha Gamma Sigma Honor Society, Golden Key Honor Society; [pers.] After my mother saw a poem I had written for a friend, she wanted me to write one for her. This was written only a few months before she died. She was a great fan and I miss her.; [a.] Adelanto, CA

ROSENFELD, LINDA
[pen.] France du Beaumont; [b.] September 14, 1949, The Bronx, NY; [p.] Michael and Rosalie Kaplan; [ch.] Stesh and Becky Rosenfeld; [ed.] High School graduate, Cosmetologist; [occ.] Housekeeper; [oth. writ.] Childrens cookbook Eng and Span; [pers.] I have been influenced by lifes romance and hardships. I have lived in a Guatema for several years where my children were born and have delved into the Mayan history.

ROSS, CALVIN
[pen.] Carlos Ross; [b.] August 11, 1950, Washington, DC; [p.] Deceased; [ed.] American

Univ.; [occ.] Bristol Meyers Squibb; [oth. writ.] 4 poems, published in local NY paper "What Magazine"; [pers.] The best, shared and remembered thoughts are the ones that are written down.; [a.] New York City, NY

ROSS, DENNIS JAMES
[pen.] D. J. Ross; [b.] July 21, 1964, Woburn, MA; [p.] James Ross and Theresa Ross; [ed.] 12 yrs. high school grad., Marine Corps, French Foreign Legion, Travel several countries; [occ.] Builder; [oth. writ.] Several poems, short stories, one novel, nothing published, nothing attempted; [pers.] Kipling, Dickens, Longfellow, Poe etc. Sufferers, adventures, dreams. Through words poets and writers are key holders to our imagination. Experience and my mother's inspiration are my tools, in my writing.; [a.] New Orleans, LA

ROSS, LORI
[b.] February 12, 1971, Athens, OH; [p.] William and Judith Ross; [m.] Fiance (Jeff Wells); [ch.] 1 Kayleena Ross; [ed.] Alexander High School, Hocking College; [occ.] Registered Nurse; [hon.] Dean's List in college; [pers.] You supply adequate safety and wellness at my best to each and every patient, and posess a nonjudgemental attitude.; [a.] Athens, OH

ROSSEL, RICHARD
[b.] January 15, 1950, Los Angeles; [occ.] RN; [pers.] In 1969 I drove up the coast accompanied by six or seven hitchikers that I had picked up. We stayed together in big sur, and I wrote this poem one night. I was 19.; [a.] Los Angeles, CA

ROSSMAN, JEANNE LOUISE
[pen.] Jeanne Louise Vane; [b.] January 11, 1941, San Francisco, CA; [p.] Alexander and Mildred Hanson; [m.] Paul G. Rossman, August 11, 1988; [ch.] Kimberly, Rebecca Lyn, Phillip Dylan; [ed.] BSW Social work San Francisco State College and Masters Social Work - MSW - U.C. Berheley Ca; [occ.] Seminary Student Episcopalian; [memb.] NASW - Board Certified Diplomate Clinical Social Work; [oth. writ.] Professional journal; [pers.] Grace for me, is that momentary union with "all that is" what interferes with the experience of my grace has been the source of my life, love and work and it remains, for me, a most valuable effort; [a.] San Anselmo, CA

ROTH, MARVIN P.
[pen.] Marvin P. Roth; [b.] November 1, 1933, Pittsburgh, PA; [p.] David and Freda Roth; [ch.] Peter Joseph Roth-12, Sarah Rebecca Roth-10; [ed.] University of Pittsburgh, BBA Class of 1955; [occ.] Professional Matchmaker for past 15 yrs; [memb.] Kappa Nu Fraternity, Kappa Kappa Psi Honorary Band Fraternity, former member of Pitt Varsity Marching Band; [hon.] Kappa Nu Junior worthy; [oth. writ.] As a professional matchmaker I have been interviewed several times for newspaper and magazine articles and have appeared on radio and television shows in the Pittsburgh area; [pers.] "Things" aren't important... "people" are, "I am an incurable romantic", "Always love your children... they are the most precious gifts you will ever receive"; [a.] Pittsburgh, PA

ROUNDHILL, PEGGY
[m.] Bernard - Graphic Artist - air-brush specialist; [ch.] Son, Simon - song-writer-Guitarist; [ed.] Educated in Auckland New Zealand at primary school, high school, University; [occ.] Partner in Graphic Art Studio; [memb.] Member of I.A.S., International Association of Scientologists, member of Church of Scientology; [oth. writ.] I have had stories poems and articles published in magazines and newspapers in New Zealand. I am writing a biography about Bernard's art career, I am planning to publish a book of my poems illustrated by Bernard.; [pers.] I enjoy expressing in poetry, the life, love, beauty and truth I see and feel around me.; [a.] Los Angeles, CA

ROUSSEAU, MICHELE M.
[b.] April 16, 1995, New Rochelle, NY; [p.] Viateur and Noreen Rousseau; [ed.] Graduated from 4 year college, Iona in New Rochelle, NY, B.A. in English Literature, High School graduate Academy of the Resurrection in Rye, NY; [occ.] Secretary; [hon.] Honor of having high school schetches shown at the Rye Reading Room. Two awards for both poetry and drawings in book titled "Who's Who of American High School Students", (two different years -1976 and 1977); [oth. writ.] Published poem entitled "The Paler Horse". Many other poems too numerous to mention. Currently working on novel called "An Amish Girl's Dilemma".; [pers.] (When my novel becomes complete, I would love one of your publishers to review it for possible help and or final publication (perhaps MR. Ely). Please get back to me on this by way of either phone or address); [a.] New Rochelle, NY

ROY, ROBERT
[b.] June 25, 1976, Lynn, MA; [p.] Rob and Linda Roy; [ed.] Auburndale High School, Tallahassee Community College; [occ.] Student a part time Musician; [hon.] John Phillip Sousa Musicianship Award, Leo Ruckle Musicianship Award, Superior Percussion Ratings at State Solo of Ensamble Festival; [pers.] Set your own goal, be true to yourself and then shall you be happy; [a.] Tallahassee, FL

RUD, TRACY P.
[ed.] BA 1988, Kennesaw State College, Marietta, GA major: English, minor: Music. Currently pursuing MS in Technical Communication Management, Mercer University, Atlanta, GA; [occ.] Information Development Consultant; [memb.] Society for Technical Communication - Senior member; [oth. writ.] Writer of poetry, children's stories and fiction; [pers.] Writer, musician, love a good joke, eclectic, key lime pie, snorkeling, Cape Cod, Ann Rice novels, antiques, ice hockey, petting zoos, fine wine. ("The cure for anything is salt water - sweat, tears, or the sea." Isak Dinesen); [a.] Acworth, GA

RUDLOFF, JOSEPH D.
[pen.] Joey (On love poems); [b.] December 11, 1917, Charles, MO; [p.] Lawrence G. and Emma Jean Rudloff; [m.] Gloria Jean Rudloff, December 10, 1965; [ch.] Linda, Michael, Leo, Lezlie, Steffanie and Karen; [ed.] Soldan High, Washington University, BS degree, St Louis, MO; [occ.] Retired; [memb.] DAV, American Legion, 4th Marine Division Association; [hon.] Honorable Discharge from the US Marine Corps Reserve World War II. Purple Heart Medal, Presidential Unit Citation with 3 stars, Navy Unit Citation, Asiatic-Pacific Ribbon with 4 stars, etc.; [oth. writ.] The National Library of Poetry Anthologies - "Between the Raindrops" (To My Love), "Best Poems of 1996" (Reflections), "A Muse to Follow" (Her Tender Kiss), "Beneath the Harvest Moon" (When You Surf the Internet); [pers.] The rapid growth in communication technology, including computers, and the establishing of NAFTA and GATT, brings the world together in promoting economic growth. Third World countries should show the fastest growth. I am 78. I hope to live to see this.; [a.] Venice, FL

RUSHTON, STEPHANIE
[b.] August 18, 1981, Anderson, SC; [p.] Steve and Susan Rushton; [ed.] Currently a student at Pendleton High School; [occ.] Student; [memb.] Pendleton United Methodist Youth, Pendleton High School Concert Band; [hon.] Junior Scholar, All-American Scholar, United States National Band Award, United States Leadership and Service Award, Distinguished Honor Roll; [pers.] I write to express myself as well as to help others learn about the true meaning of life.; [a.] Pendleton, SC

RUSS, JANICE CALTON
[b.] August 11, 1955, Smithville, TX; [p.] Willie Ray Calton, the late Eunice Calton; [m.] Alex A. Russ Jr.; [ch.] Elbertina Calton, Christopher Russ, Derrick Russ and Alexa Russ III; [ed.] Polytechnic High, Mansfield Business; [pers.] The honor goes to God for putting the words into my heart. I strive to give our youth something to think about. For you because I love you. Straight from the heart. I was influenced by many poets but mostly by my Mom who is my heart.; [a.] Fort Worth, TX

RUSSELL, MAXINE KAISER
[pen.] Maxine Russell, Maxine K. Russell; [b.] February 17, 1912, St. Paul, MN; [p.] Max Kaiser and Klara Treubert Kaiser; [m.] Robert Lee Russell, October 2, 1946; [ch.] James M. Russell, Roberta M. Fraser; [ed.] Graduate U of MN at Minneapolis SLA '32 I'm a perennial student attending many seminars and classes, for the most part, in writing; [occ.] Retired, but writing; [memb.] University of Minnesota Alumni Assoc., Writers Alliance, Brainerd, Central Lakes College and Chair of Heartland Poets, Brainerd, MN, League of MN Poets and National Federation State Poetry Societies, Delta Zeta Alumni Association; [hon.] My poems have been published in poetry magazines, such as The Moccasin and Studio One, also newspapers, NFSPS awards in contests, The Lamp of DeltaZeta, Amana Bulletin; [oth. writ.] Leaves from a Greenhouse, Honey in the Heart, Jungle Angel: Bataan Remembered, Leaves from my Family Tree, Honeybees of Waxcastle; [pers.] Since my childhood spent in our family greenhouses, I have enjoyed writing poetry and short stories. Gardening, and beekeeping have

also brought me inspiration and satisfaction.; [a.] Brainerd, MN

RUTON, MILDRED MARSH
[pen.] Ruton, Mildred Marsh; [b.] November 2, 1906, Bridgeport, OH; [p.] Jos. Clarence Marsh and Pearl Fonner Marsh; [m.] Edgar Ruton (Deceased), November 15; [ch.] 2 boys oldest is deceased; [ed.] High school grad. my education came mostly from travel all over the USA and Canada in show business with my husband Eddie Ruton and from working at various offices in big firms and reading; [occ.] Retired; [memb.] NLP, IPS, Eastern Star, Silver Club (past President of Silver Club and currently Secretary 1996 of same. LCAP. (Leching County Aring Program); [hon.] Award from LCAP for talent (comedy) for improving the quality of life (volunteer my stand-up comedy for shows held for the elderly.) and 4 Editor's Choice Award NLP and award of merit from ISP convention for my poetry 1995; [oth. writ.] I am writing a children's book about the off stage antics of the dogs that performed in our dog act with pictures of the things (tricks) they did. My poetry has slowed me down on that this year.; [pers.] Do right, not wrong, and you will never fail to get along - in life be goos to everyone, they you'll know your life's "Well Done".; [a.] Newark, OH

RYAN JR., FRANK J.
[pen.] F.J.R; [b.] December 3, 1954, Bronxville, NY; [p.] Gloria and Frank J. Sr.; [m.] Jane Joan Ryan, June 26, 1988; [ch.] Lauren Marie born 8/19/93; [ed.] Iona Preparatory School, New Rochelle, NY Concordia College, Bronxville, NY; [occ.] Regional Manager/Circulation Operations for Gannett Co.; [memb.] Westchester County Medical Center Heart Club; [hon.] 1994 and 1995 Winner of the New York Posts Valentines Day Prose Contest; [oth. writ.] Many Editorial Articles published in Major New York Newspaper and National magazines including Time Magazine. Prose and poetry published in New York Post. Current event and sports articles published in The White Plains Reporter Dispatch, Yonkers Herald Statesman and Standard Star.; [pers.] "Writing is the ultimate power to the immortal expression of ones passions and opinion. Time may erase cherished words once spoken, however writing is the indelible stamp of remembrance to those words".; [a.] Yonkers, NY

RYDZEWSKI, NORINE WALSH
[b.] February 21, 1923, Chicago; [p.] Mr. and Mrs Martin Walsh; [m.] Casimer (Casey) Rydzewski, September 7, 1940; [ch.] 8 children, 23 grandchildren, 19 great grandchildren; [ed.] 8 yrs Ephinay Catholic School; [occ.] Retired, 25 yrs at Western Electric; [memb.] Moose; [pers.] I'm hoping in some small way my writing will make a difference in the world, by bringing people closer together. We all have faults but if we work on our own faults maybe we won't have time to find fault in others; [a.] Downers Grove, IL

SAGE, BRADFORD J.
[b.] August 7, 1951, Norwich; [p.] Robert Sage Sr. and Shirley Davis; [m.] Karen Sage, November 3, 1989; [ch.] Montville High School, 2 Years College, No Degree; [ed.] Maintenance Technician at Lutheran Home (Convalescent); [occ.] MVP Track Trophy, Montville High School; [memb.] One Poem Unpublished; [hon.] MVP Track Trophy Montville High School; [oth. writ.] One poem unpublished; [pers.] To my beloved wife, Karen who has brought me from darkness to light, also to the Lord Jesus Christ, who has given us everything.; [a.] Cromwell, CT

SALEH, CAROLE JEAN
[b.] July 22, Santa Barbara, CA; [p.] Hilda M. Jensen and Eugene De Bortoli; [ch.] Sharvin J. Saleh and Shereen J. Saleh; [ed.] San Jose State, Criminology San Jose City College, So. Science Santa Barbara High School; [occ.] Accounting Government Contract Co.; [memb.] Lutheran Church, Danish Lodge Membership, Lions Club, United Way for Multiple Services; [hon.] Lions Club Speech Contest Winner, Poems published in the "Promethean" San Jose City College; [oth. writ.] Gypsy Fire, Lonely People, Love/Lust, Goodbye My Love; [pers.] Whether a poet or not "to write from within" speaks from the heart. How better does one know more about themselves, these feelings, than to express in writing and reflects upon them.; [a.] San Jose, CA

SALES, LEONIDES S.
[pen.] Leo; [b.] April 22, 1936, Baccara, Ilocos, Philippines; [p.] Gregorio Albano Sales and Maria S. Sales; [m.] Divorced, March 3, 1955; [ch.] Victor Sales, Glenda Sales, Anthony Sales, Ferdinand Sales, Geraldine Shimoe, Christopher Sales, Lilibeth Sales and Ronald-Reagan Sales; [ed.] High School - Kabankalan Academy Negros Occidental Philippines, Northwestern College, Laoag City, Philippines, Bachelor of Science in Commerce University of the East, Manila, Philippines, Aircraft Armament Repair Course, U.S. Army Ordinance Center and School, Aberdeen Proving Ground, Maryland 21005 U.S.A. Special Intelligence Operations Course, Philippines; [occ.] Philippine Air Force Armed Forces of the Philippines, Lieutenant Retired, 23 years of Government Service, Former Security Aide of President Ferdinand Edralin Marcos of the Philippines; [memb.] American Association of Retired Persons, May 1986, Filipino American Community of Los Angeles, Inc. 1989-1990, Unites Bacarreneous of Hawaii Inc. 1992, BNCHS Club of Hawaii 1992, Kiss AM Fun Club Hawaii 1992, Filipino Californians Senior Citizens Society Inc. 1993, International Circle Inc. 1993 to present; [hon.] The Philippine Republic Presidential Unit Citation Badge, Commendations, Official Appreciation, Anti-Dissidence Campaign Ribbon etc.; [oth. writ.] Articles published "The Youth Grinder" newspaper - Baccara.; [pers.] "Be nice to people and be humble at all times," "Always be kind and loving to people older than you. You'll soon be rewarded and feel good too." "In order to be a leader you must learn to follow."; [a.] San Francisco, CA

SALIM, KHALFANI
[pen.] Khalfani Salim; [b.] June 18, 1974, Warren, OH; [p.] Marilyn Walker; [ed.] St. Pauls College; [pers.] May the poor break the yoke of their oppression, by either raised voices or raised guns.; [a.] Newport News, VA

SANA, MERCER
[b.] February 4, 1981, Kankakee, IL; [p.] Skip and Mary Mercer; [ed.] Limestone Elementary, Herscher High; [occ.] High School Student; [memb.] High School Rodeo Association; [hon.] Rodeo Competition Awards; [oth. writ.] The Ultimate Sin, Do You Know, Fire, Shot in the Dark, Save Me, Five Minutes Alone; [pers.] I like to write poems on how I feel. If I'm in any kind of mood I write it down instantly.; [a.] Kankakee, IL

SANDERS, JENNIFER
[b.] March 12, 1975; [pers.] I have been writing ever since I can remember and through the years it has become a source of healing.; [a.] Portland, OR

SANDS, MYRA J.
[pen.] Myra J. Sands; [b.] March 27, 1976, Helena, MT; [p.] Vicky Lynn Sands; [ed.] Graduate of West Valley High School Spokane WA; [occ.] Stock Replenishment Associate; [hon.] Senior Art Student of the Year - West Valley High School; [oth. writ.] I had a poem called "the great white bird published in" the quill and scroll of west Valley High School.; [pers.] "What kind of love runs through your heart with a pleasure so close to pain?" What kind of love? The love that I have.; [a.] Post Falls, ID

SANDSTEDT, ELLEN E.
[b.] March 1, 1917, Palo, MN; [p.] John and Anna Liimatta; [m.] Edward Sandstedt, June 10, 1944; [ch.] One Daughter; [ed.] B.S. Degree in Elementary, Education from University of MA, Duluth Branch; [occ.] Retired Elementary Teacher; [hon.] I am considered the family and community poet. I have written and presented poems for birthdays, retirement, anniversaries, funerals, and memorial services. Also for community and church celebrations; [oth. writ.] I have also written poems about my two "dropped off" pets, my dog Buffy and my cat Ginger; [pers.] I love poetry, especially poems that rhyme. Using very few words, the poet can tell a story, paint a picture, or present a viewpoint. It can touch the heart or feed the intellect.; [a.] Aurora, MN

SAPIENZA, STEPHANIE
[b.] August 9, 1977, Southampon, NY; [p.] Carla and Paul Sapienza; [ed.] Blue Valley Northwest High School, Kansas State University; [occ.] Student; [hon.] Several Local Publications, Literary Magazines Head Rush (Editor), and the Muse (Sr. Editor), Potpourri, Dean's List; [pers.] Vision is our most limited resource, there are no hopeless situations, just people who think hopelessly. Influences include C.S. Lewis, Lewis Carroll, Linda Goodman, Eva Peron.; [a.] Stilwell, KS

SARKISSIAN, HENRY A.
[b.] February 16, 1922, Tehran, Iran; [m.] Annik, October 1948; [ch.] Armen and Vahe;

[ed.] High School in Tehran Iran; [occ.] Tax preparer (IRS Enrolled Agent); [memb.] AARP (?) KCET (?); [oth. writ.] "Tales of 1,001 Iranian Days" St. Bk #533-04476-6, Lib. Congress 79-67512

SCHAEFFER, MADELINE
[b.] September 5, 1942, Lancaster, PA; [p.] Marlin and Virgina Frey; [m.] Rodney Schaeffer, September 23, 1962; [ch.] Lorie, Andrew, Sharon and Jeff; [ed.] Freshman at Wichita State - currently enrolled with Berean School of the Bible; [occ.] Housewife; [memb.] Church - Assembly of God - Calvary of Naperville; [hon.] Woman Aglow-Officer, Prayer Chairmen; [oth. writ.] Wrote christian retreat material - news letters - testimony of how Lord works in my life; [pers.] I want the Lord God to use me in whatever way he wants, if it is in writing inspirational material or in doing for others. This is the desire of my heart.; [a.] Oswego, IL

SCHALLERT, PATRICIA V. M.
[b.] August 2, 1952, Coopers Town, NY; [p.] John and Violet Weir Schallert; [m.] Michael E. Phillips, June 27, 1991; [ch.] Heidi, Heather, Mike, Keri, John Zachery, Ashley, Ben (step children); [ed.] Cooperstown Central School, Clark Community College; [occ.] Full time student, tutor for English student and English as a second language students; [memb.] I participate in many fund drives, member of several communities; [oth. writ.] Biographical writings for women of Achievement 1995 Vancouver, Washington, several essays and poems; [pers.] I pride myself with honest, forth rightness, and reliability. Along with great children and a wonderful husband, I consider these my greatest attributes.; [a.] Battle Ground, WA

SCHEEL, ROSE-MARIE
[b.] September 4, 1937, United Kingdom; [m.] Ronald Young, February 6, 1993; [ch.] Sarah Scheel Cook, W. Christopher Scheel; [ed.] Westcliff High School for Girls, Westcliff-on-Sea, Essex, U.K., University De Grenoble, France; [occ.] Head Resident, University of the South; [memb.] Episcopal Church Women, Formerly, "Another Mother For Peace"; [hon.] Honary Testimonial, The Royal Humane Society; [oth. writ.] Several travel articles published: Airline publication/travel magazines; [pers.] Recognizing the needs to defend the principle of freedom I am opposed to acts of aggression that terrorize children and the helpless. I ashore to the concept that we are all citizens of the world.; [a.] Sewanee, TX

SCHEFFLER, HEIDI JOY
[b.] April 18, 1976, Shelbyville, IN; [p.] Saundra S. Walden; [ed.] Shelbyville High School, Blue Rivers VOCA; [occ.] National City Bank Customer Service Rep.; [hon.] Local Fair Art Award, Vocal High School Award; [oth. writ.] Several poems and articles published in local newspapers; [pers.] I write mostly about love life experiences. Children have a lot to talk about and say, if we are willing to listen. The same is true for everything, it just takes that moment to listen.; [a.] Shelbyville, IN

SCHENKELBERG, PAMELA
[pen.] Pam; [b.] December 5, 1957, Carroll, IA; [p.] Bill and Jean Schenkelberg; [ed.] Bachelor's of Science in Nursing (BSN) and Masters in Nutrition (M.S.); [occ.] Nutritional Products Distributor; [memb.] American Holistic, Nurses Association; [hon.] Big Brother Big Sister Program for 5 years; [oth. writ.] I wrote a poem the desert which was published in a book by the Iowa Society of Poets while in High School.; [pers.] I get my ideas in writing poems through life's experiences and creative thinking.; [a.] Carroll, IA

SCHERBERG, GOLDIE R.
[b.] March 14, 1909, Lithuania; [p.] Charles and Ida Esther (Deceased); [m.] Max, January 1, 1930; [ch.] Lee Carl (d), and Neal Hirshel; [ed.] U. of Minnesota - M.S in Hematology, U. of Minnesota Cert. in Soc. Work; [occ.] Retired; [memb.] League of Women Voters of Chicago, Temple KAM Israel, Chicago; [hon.] Honored by Sinclair Community College in Dayton for Originating Mental Health Technology Program - 1st in Country, Weight State School of medicine Bridgeport, Conn. PTA for School Improvement, Ranked First in High School Graduating Class St. Louis, President Dayton LWV, President Bridgeport Conn. PTA, Produced TV Series on Public Issues in Dayton; [oth. writ.] Poetry for drama "The Return" produced in Dayton, Ohio 1991. Pending: Poetry for drama in Chicago.; [pers.] I believe in the promise of America and feel that nothing is more important for our country than striving for our democratic principles and the well being of all our people. Attainment of this will, hopefully, help to spread the message so that the whole world can achieve a durable peace.

SCHLEPER, ALISA
[pen.] Ali; [b.] February 19, 1984, Houston, TX; [p.] Joan and Tom Schleper; [ed.] Woodside Elementary, Oak Grove Middle School; [occ.] Full time student; [memb.] St. Francis of Asisi Parish and Youth Group, Continental Little League; [hon.] Young Authors Award Mt.-Diablo School District; [oth. writ.] Poem published in Contra Costa Times, 2-13-94; [a.] Concord, CA

SCHMIDLAPP, BRYAN
[b.] February 5, 1980, Cincinnati; [p.] Pat and John Schmidlapp; [ed.] Sophomore at Purcell-Marian High School; [occ.] Student; [memb.] Various Role Playing Game Clubs, Hackberry Literary Magazine of Purcell-Marian; [pers.] "Fear not change."; [a.] Cincinnati, OH

SCHNEIDER, KELLY
[pen.] Monica Sarber; [b.] April 19, 1982; [p.] Norman Schneider and Connie Cooper-Schneider; [ed.] Private Schools my Whole Life; [occ.] Student; [memb.] Newspaper Clubs in School; [hon.] Writing and Achievement Awards from Schools; [oth. writ.] Many poems but this is my first published; [pers.] I like to write sad poems because so many others strive to base their on good things. Despite this, I am a very happy person.; [a.] Henrietta, NY

SCHNEIDER, MICKEY L.
[b.] August 22, 1962, New Prague, MN; [p.] Eugene and Joan Schneider; [ed.] Jordan High School, St. Cloud State College, MN; [pers.] My writings reflect the romanticist in me, but the credit goes to Paulette Lebens who encouraged me to write again, my family who gave me all of my heart, and the people who touched my life... if only for a moment.; [a.] Jordan, MN

SCHRAMM, MODINE G.
[b.] September 23, 1917, Lydia, SC; [p.] Duncan and Naoma Galloway; [m.] Dr. Robert J. Schramm (Deceased), March 6, 1943; [ed.] Lydia High School, Lydia, S.C., Bowens Business College (BS), Columbia, S.C., Lake Erie College (BA) Painesville, Ohio, Eastern Connecticut State Univ. MA degree, Willimatic, Connecticut; [occ.] Retired; [memb.] American Name Society, League of Women Voters, Greater Hartsville (S.C) Chamber of Commerce, and AARP; [oth. writ.] Articles in the Willimantic Chronical (newspaper), plus some poetry. Two articles in the Connecticut Onomastic Review, a branch of the American Name Name Society.; [pers.] If life hands you lemons, make sweetened lemonade.; [a.] Hartsville, SC

SCHULMAN, SCOTT C.
[b.] April 20, 1961, Chicago, IL; [ch.] Jessica Nichole; [ed.] Brooks Institute of Photography - BA; [occ.] Photographer; [hon.] Communication Arts Photo, Annual - 90, 92, 93, Communication Arts Advertising, Annual - 92, Advertising Photographers of America Merit Award 92; [pers.] "I am what I give"; [a.] Santa Monica, CA

SCHUMACHER, DONNETTE L.
[b.] January 25, 1972, Warsaw, IN; [p.] Randy and Priscilla Ransbottom; [m.] Ryan E. Schumacher, August 15, 1992; [ed.] Lighthouse Christian Academy High School 1991; [occ.] Home-maker; [memb.] The Free Spirit Pentecostal Church of North Manchester, Indiana; [oth. writ.] I have written over eighty christian poems; [pers.] When I was eleven years old I had a stroke. I had to learn everything all over again. I thank the Lord for healing my body and saving my soul. It's only the Lord which gives me the knowledge to write my poems.; [a.] Warsaw, IN

SCHURADE, RITA MILLER
[b.] February 4, 1942, Oakland, MI; [p.] Hurley and Luretha Miller; [m.] Divorced; [ed.] A.A. Nursing RN License Certificate Family Nurse Practitioner; [occ.] Disabled; [memb.] International Society of Poets, American Nurse Assoc.; [hon.] Editors Choice National Library of Poetry; [oth. writ.] Poems published: Smell The Flowers, Home, Cancer-Stroke, The Outdoors, A Rainbow; [pers.] Enjoy writing poems for friends-poems about love, friendship, nature, outdoors, feelings

SCHWARTZ, NETTIE Y.
[pen.] Nettie Yanoff Schwartz; [b.] October 9, 1919; [ch.] Three - 1 Grand Children 5 - Great Grandchildren; [ed.] B.S. Degree University of Louisville Masters Degree in Education Spalding College - Lousiana KY; [occ.] Retired Teacher, Author - Artist; [memb.] All Organizations

Related to my Work and Helping Others; [hon.] Was state Chairman for Youth Art Month and Placed KY 1st received see Award; [oth. writ.] Double day and Co Painting with a Needle 1972, 2nd Printing 6 months later revised edition 1995. Many craft books with history of each traveled - under title ancient crafts for moderns.; [pers.] Taught student 5 steps of learning: Silence - Listen - Remember practice - Teach other listen to everyone. You'll hear good thing - some rest. But listen - final decision is yours to make!; [a.] Louisville, KY

SCHWARTZ, ZACHARY
[b.] September 28, 1974, Springfield, MA; [p.] Lawrence I. Schwartz, Bunnie, Schwartz; [ed.] Long Meadow High, Marshall University; [occ.] Student; [memb.] Sigma Phi Epsilon Fraternity; [oth. writ.] A collection of copyrighted unpublished poems; [pers.] My hope is to reach out to others through my writing.; [a.] Long Meadow, MA

SCOTT, DEBRA A.
[b.] September 16, 1969, Lansdale, PA; [p.] Albert and Gail Scott; [ed.] North Penn High School, Montgomery County Community College; [occ.] Cashier; [memb.] Trinity Evangelical Lutheran Church Sunday School Teacher; [pers.] I have gotten inspiration from my deceased grandmother, Gwen Bennet, who was also a published writer in the family.; [a.] Lansdale, PA

SEAFAROWICZ, BOGUSZAWA
[pen.] Rusla; [b.] November 24, 1946, Gdansk; [p.] Wladyszawa - Ennamuel; [ed.] Elementary, High School first year Private Church School, Later Committee Highs Medical College, Kins Press, Cerame Sculpture; [occ.] Full time student; [memb.] American Red Cross, SPNTA Movico College Transaction, Womens Group, Top Dog Breacher in Poland; [hon.] I never 6 years ago, blade group give me grany in worsow - inspiration. Don't remember name, big shok. I gave home American Red Cross - Diploma and Honor - Santa Monica; [oth. writ.] I have several short poems from Poland, but don't live polish time and don't want remember his poems.; [pers.] America is the best pleasure on whole inspiration artists. Everybody have own happy time - I have now love, but no so much!; [a.] San Diego, CA

SEAMONS, MOLLY FISHER
[b.] November 2, Ogden, UT; [p.] Burt and Many Fisher; [ch.] Scott and Mandy; [ed.] BS U of Utah; [occ.] Accounting Manager high tech start-up; [memb.] In woman's Club, Chi Omega Sorority; [oth. writ.] Assembled 2 poetry books - Lace Sunlight and hands are held 2 poems published; [pers.] I specially enjoy writing about my romantic feelings; [a.] Saratoga, CA

SEATON, CLYDE C.
[pen.] Clyde C. Seaton; [b.] January 13, 1943; [p.] Roy and Thelma Seaton; [m.] Sadie D. Seaton, March 7, 1976; [ch.] Jermaine Tyrone Seaton; [ed.] Buniwick School and PS 3; [occ.] Safe Deposit Clerk; [memb.] Trinity Community Assembly of God; [hon.] Berean College, The Police Department, Trinity Assembly of God; [oth. writ.] One happy big family and others; [pers.] My poems bring satisfaction to my thought and mind.; [a.] Bronx, NY

SEIGNIOUS, MARLENE MAIS
[b.] February 8, 1978; [p.] Daphane Seignious and Norman Seignious; [ed.] I attended Walton High School. This is my fourth and I am moving on with my life to college to major in Psychology/Nursing; [occ.] I am currently attending in Walton High School; [memb.] I am in a Shakespare Club, Tennese Club, pre-teaching and I also do voluntary work; [hon.] I am in honor classes, and as for awards I have received many merits for English, Science, History, Math, and have received a plaque for getting a 90 on my math regents end a certificate for working; [oth. writ.] I read that rather than lasting your anger out on others, I should take that negative energy and build it into something positive so for I wrote many other poems about sadness, love, and etc; [pers.] In my opinion I feel that there is too much to life than what people make of it. people from other countries come to America to get the wrights that they deserve or in which was owed to them come with nothing; [a.] Bronx, NY

SEKRETA, MEGHAN
[b.] September 26, 1978, Lombard, IL; [p.] Mr. and Mrs. John Sekreta Jr.; [ed.] Eastside Catholic High School; [hon.] National Honor Society; [pers.] I write what I see and feel. That is what makes it mine.; [a.] Redmond, WA

SELLERS, ANDREA D.
[b.] July 10, 1977, Memphis, TN; [p.] Lula B. Turreu Sellers and Mazell Sellers; [ed.] Sophomore at Phillips Count Community College; [occ.] Part-time secretary for Holiness Trinity World Outreach Ministries; [memb.] Phi Beta Lambda the subdivision of Future Business Leaders of America (FBLA); [hon.] I was awarded a trip to Florida for the summer for raising the most money in our chapter (Chi Bho) of Phi Beta Lambda for Arkansas Children's Hospital; [oth. writ.] "See The Unnamable" but it has never been published. I also have other poems that I've not shown or read to anyone.; [pers.] Poetry is the expression of the soul, therefore a poet's writings aren't merely words they're a vital judge of character.; [a.] Helena, OK

SENZ, GORDON S.
[b.] May 9, 1969, Orrville, OH; [ed.] High School Diploma; [occ.] Musician; [oth. writ.] "Cycle of Hate" - song recorded by heavy metal band "Eulogy" on their 1994 album. I have written poetry and song lyric's for nine years, so I have many works that are waiting to be published.; [pers.] My poems and song lyrics are derived from the varied experiences I have survived. The troubles and pain I have endured are often softened by writing poems which deal with my problems, which are like the problems we all deal with in our lives.; [a.] Wellington, OH

SHAFER, SCOTT C.
[b.] May 5, 1978, Fairfax, VA; [p.] Jon Shafer, Lucinda Scott Shafer; [ed.] Anderson High School; [pers.] I don't strive to bring my writing to the world, I strive to bring the world to my writing.; [a.] Anderson, IN

SHANER, MARJORIE E.
[pen.] Marjorie E. Shaner; [b.] November 18, 1919, Shelby, CO; [p.] Joe and Ethel Wells; [m.] Charles R. Shaner, September 12, 1940; [ch.] Six; [ed.] G.E.D.; [occ.] Retired; [memb.] Sigma Beta Sorority, Town and Garden Club, PTA Senior Citizens; [hon.] Senior Citizen 1990, Sr. Citizen Queen 1991, Homemaker of year. Several Times Honorary Education, Taught Public and Private-Teacher; [oth. writ.] Many poems; [pers.] When you are given a talent, you should share it with others.; [a.] Shelbyville, IN

SHARIEFF, NAEEM
[pen.] Naeem Sharieff; [b.] September 12, 1960, Karachi-Pakistan; [p.] A.M. Sharieff and Mumtaz Sharieff; [ed.] B.A. - University Of Karachi, LL.B - S.M. Law College Karachi-Pakistan; [occ.] Security Officer Staff Pro-great Western Forum; [memb.] Sind Bar Council - Pakistan, Karachi Bar Association - Pakistan Notary Home Department - Karachi Pakistan; [hon.] Advocate - Karachi, National Cadet Corps, Certificate - Karachi - Pakistan; [oth. writ.] Several articles published in local and Pakistan Newspapers; [pers.] Beauty of heart is better than face beauty. Face beauty is not lasting. Heart beauty ever lasting. Those who pick heart beauty spend a peaceful life.; [a.] Harbor City, CA

SHARP JR., EUEL E.
[b.] October 17, 1960, Portsmouth, VA; [p.] Euel E. Sharp and Norma Jean Sharp; [m.] Norma Jane Rambo-Sharp, January 13, 1990; [ch.] Ashton Faith Rambo-Sharp; [ed.] Vienna High School, Shawnee College; [occ.] Corrections Lieutenant, Illinois Department of Corrections; [oth. writ.] Several articles published in National Magazines; [pers.] Always strive to be the one who says "I did," not "I could have or should have."; [a.] Vienna, IL

SHARP, JUDITH ANNE
[b.] October 25, 1957, Baton Rouge, LA; [p.] Elizabeth Woodside and O.G. Woodside; [ed.] High school graduation from High Land School, Pocatello Idaho; [occ.] Audit Clerk at National City Processing Company; [memb.] YMCA, I swim and lift weights; [hon.] This will be my first award, is having this poem published. This gift you have given me, came when I needed it most. My mother passed away in June 1995, and my father had stroke Sunday, you have lifted my world, thank you so very much; [oth. writ.] I have written a lot of poems, I am currently trying to put a book of poems together to be published. This same poems was published in the paper where my aunt passed away at Glassgow, KY, that too was no honor.; [pers.] I have found my best work comes from my personal experience in my life, my true feelings come out on paper. The yellow rose came about when my Aunt passed away, yellow rose where her favorite as to are my mothers, and myself.; [a.] Louisville, KY

SHEDOSKY, NINA K.
[pen.] Nin; [b.] April 28, 1955, Logan, WV; [p.] Robert and Bonnie Powers; [m.] Edwin T. Shedosky, August 29, 1994; [pers.] I've written poetry since a young age, and all my poems come to me thru feelings I have involving the circumstances around me.; [a.] Dixon, IL

SHEEHAN, BRENT D.
[pen.] Kennedy Hawkins; [b.] July 17, 1978, San Diego, CA; [p.] David D. Sheehan, Reanay K. Sheehan; [ed.] Columbia Central High School, Michigan State University (2 Years); [occ.] College Student; [oth. writ.] Many unpublished ones; [pers.] Reading is overrated, writing is underrated, write for yourself and others will relate. I have been influenced by circumstances in my life. Note: The world above is under-rated.; [a.] Clarklake, MI

SHEEHAN, HELEN
[pen.] Undecided; [b.] January 29, 1920, New York City, NY; [p.] Sofia and Matthew Sobanko; [m.] Patrick Joseph Sheehan, February 19, 1953; [ed.] Elementary School in Rockland County, N.Y. until 1931 and attended P.S. 60 in Manhattan, then High School (Textile) on W. 18th St., (now dismantled). Furthered studies in Art and Writing at night Schools; [occ.] Retired; [memb.] In the past, I tried Oil Painting at Art Students League, Essay Writing at Fordham H.S. plus drawing, night courses after work. For the present am corresponding with the Long Ridge Writers Group in W. Redding, CT as a prospective Author; [hon.] Gold stars and and mother-of-pearl necklace as top scholar in elementary school, plus two/two and-one-half gold pieces when my sketches and poem was put in school book; [oth. writ.] Poem and sketches entered into P.S. 60 years book. Composed a song from music of Charlie Chaplin and Paulett Goddard's movie "Lime-light" called "Eternity". An almost duplicate wording was published by someone else, - back in the '40's.; [pers.] The arts have always intrigued me. Everything within our senses yields gathering of beauty and knowledge. Discord of wars (ugly) has remarkable photography not to be ignored. History in the making promotes new forms of words. Being a senior I have yet to adopt the modern trend.; [a.] Astoria, NY

SHELBY, NORMA K.
[pen.] Agape; [b.] May 27, 1926, Louisville, KY; [p.] Emma and Patrick Wells Knight; [m.] Joe Shelby Sr.; [ch.] Ten; [ed.] College Credits in Early Childhood Education Missionary of Oak Grove Missionary Baptist Church; [occ.] Self-Employed Child Cane Owner and Director (10 years) Since 1965 (began); [pers.] Sentimental over all the poems and short stories from Paul Lawrence Dunbar" (since High School class of 43 1/2); [a.] Louisville, KY

SHELKSOHN, OWEN WADE
[pen.] Le Chevalier Mal Fait; [b.] September 14, 1976, Varren, MI; [p.] Dr. Oliver Walter, Marilynn Russell; [ed.] University High School, University of Arizona; [occ.] Student; [memb.] Sei Ryu Kan, Kajukenbo Self Defense/Karate; [pers.] I hate humanity. I enjoy paradox and balance, two things embodied by my favorite symbol, the yin yang.; [a.] Tucson, AZ

SHELL, LOIS
[b.] December 10, 1975, Wilmington, DE; [p.] Charles C. Shell (Deceased), Fannie L. Shell; [ed.] Frederick Christian Academy (K-2) Home School (3-12) Applying For My GED; [occ.] Caring for an elderly lady, apprenticing midwife; [pers.] I thank God for giving me the talent for writing poetry. He alone deserves all the credit; [a.] Burnsville, VA

SHELLEY, JEANNINE
[pen.] Elaine Daniel; [b.] November 13, 1955, LaGrange, GA; [p.] Hollis and Cornelia Daniel; [ch.] Holly Myric and Clay Byron; [ed.] I have been to 4 different Colleges, but never finished - Graduated from High School at 16 due to Advanced Reading Skills; [occ.] Administrative, Assistant; [memb.] I work with an organization called end violence now, which works with men to end Domestic Violence. I am also a member of a local business; [hon.] Association for Entrepreneur; [oth. writ.] I have about 15 other poems that have not been published. I'm also writing a book that will take about 2-3 years to research on domestic violence.; [pers.] This poem was written for a cousin who died at a very young age. I only met her once, but her aura and smell stayed with me for years. I can't remember her face, only the way she smelled.; [a.] Lawrenceville, GA

SHERMER II, RICHARD CLAY
[pen.] Serling; [b.] January 10, 1978, Mount View, CA; [p.] Richard Shermer Sr., Diana Nissim; [ed.] Senior at Carlmont High School, Belmont, Calif.; [occ.] Student and soccer player; [pers.] In my writing, I try to capture my feelings on a certain subject, as they happen. Rod Serling has been a large influence, on my need and desire to write. I strive to have his intelligence.; [a.] Redwood City, CA

SHERRITZE, SONJA
[b.] August 29, 1967, Chattanooga, TN; [p.] Mary Sherritze, Dillon Louis Sherritze; [ed.] BA (HIgh Honors) in Journalism and Mass Media, Rutgers University 1989; [oth. writ.] Published in New Jersey's Couner Post, New Yorks the Westsider, and the Journal of Chemical Education.; [a.] Hoboken, NJ

SHETH, SACHIN D.
[b.] November 7, 1971, Bombay; [p.] Dinesh Smeth and Smakuntala Smeth; [ed.] Bachelor's in Petrochemical Engineering currently working towards my Master's in Chemical Engineering Diploma in D Base III plus; [memb.] International Society of Poets, Aiche, Youth Hostel Association of India, Friends of India Association, Ahemdabad Nature Lovers Association; [hon.] Fellowship from Gulf Coast Hazardous Substance Research Center, Texas Merit Scholarship, Editor's Choice Award National Library, First prize, Musical Talent of Poetry Contest; [oth. writ.] The Mirage, Heat And Dust, Euthanasia, A Cold Cold December, The Wall, Kusukshetras Galore; [pers.] If you can't be a peacock then just be a hare if you can't be a deer, if you do something be sure of it and never do anything with fear.; [a.] Beaumont, TX

SHIELA, GERALDIN A.
[pers.] Marches in silver march leader of great books transmuted meditation (T.M.). USN club avid believer. Teacher is the city, (Pruit Igo), before its old victim.; [a.] Solbdu, AZ

SHINE, BAMBI J.
[b.] April 20, 1960, Burlington, VT; [p.] Douglas Beede, Norilla Tisci; [m.] Todd D. Shine, April 16, 1988; [ch.] Shawna Lynn, Sommer Jo, Kristal Brook; [ed.] South Burlington High, Essex Junction Vocational; [occ.] Owner of "Bambi Dear, Co." a create your own T-Shirt Co. Pompano Beach, Florida; [memb.] Children's International, Village United Methodist Church, Junior Chamber of Commerce; [hon.] Numerous Awards and Certificates from the Jaycees, Write-Up Competition Awards, Diabetes Research Awards, State Book Writing Champion; [oth. writ.] Several poems and stories in personal library; [pers.] My writings all come from the heart. Most of them reflect my life, and my family. My family is my life! The creativity in my soul comes from my mother, and for that, I thank her!; [a.] Pompano Beach, FL

SHULER, MISTY LYNN
[b.] June 29, 1975, Swain County; [p.] Jerry and Judy Shuler; [ed.] Graduated from Swain High School in 1994; [pers.] I am pleased at having my poem published and I am looking forward to seeing my words in print. I've always been a fan of poets like Edgar Allen Poe and I am greatly influenced by that type of poetry.; [a.] Bryson, NC

SIEMS JR., RICHARD W.
[b.] Inglewood, CA; [p.] Doris Earlene Siems, Richard Siems Sr.; [ed.] Leuzinger High School Honor Roll Graduate, Associated Technical College Graduate in "Telecommunications" 1993; [occ.] Cal Trans Att. (Ambitious and Hopeful writer!); [hon.] 1974 City Winner in 'Dodgers' Long-throw Distance in their Annual RNN, Hit, and throw contest... 214 feet...; [oth. writ.] Just completed my first novel! (95) yr. finished)... film companies and publishing houses are welcome!; [pers.] "Freedom is the greatest thing and the worst thing that ever happened to man" - R.S. Jr. "Pray for the Lord to guide you in your life and he will...." R.S. Sr. "the greatest feeling in the world is truth" - R.S. Jr.; [a.] Yucaipa, CA

SIKORSKI, KATHRYN A.
[b.] March 28, 1930, New York City, NY; [ed.] M.A. Univ. of Arizona - 1959, Ph.D. Univ. of Penna - 1968, Ethnological Field Work - Ariz., New Mex. and Michigan, Mexico; [occ.] Retired, Instructor (Anthropology) Utah State Univ., Asst. Prof., Hartwizk College, NY; [hon.] Phi Beta Kappa, Cumius Fund Research Craft (U. of Ariz.); [oth. writ.] Books modern hopi pottery, 1968, Utah State Univ., styles of living in Santa De, Michigan, MS-Ph.D. Dissertation - U. of Penna articles in 1959 Ariz., Highways "Zuni Jewelry."; [a.] Homaland, CA

SILVA, JOSEFINA G.
[b.] January 16, 1954, Harlingen, TX; [p.] Miguel and Bertha Garcia; [m.] Mario Silva, October 28, 1972; [ch.] Mario II, Laura, Marcos, Priscilla Marie; [ed.] Rockport-Fulton High, Texas Southmost College; [occ.] Applications Clerk (Government Employee), U.S. Immigration and Naturalization Service; [memb.] Christian Fellowship Church; [pers.] I strive to reflect the goodness of my heavenly father.

SILVERS, KIM
[b.] May 20, 1965, Augsburg, Germany; [p.] Claude Pylant Jr., Pat Vail; [m.] Ken Silvers, January 25, 1988; [ch.] Christian Courtney, Franklin Matthew; [ed.] Marrianna High School, Chipola Jr. College, CNA License; [occ.] Homemaker; [memb.] American Heart Association, American Red Cross, Southside Baptist Church, Florida First Start/Head Start; [pers.] My poetry comes naturally to me and I feel is a gift from God. This is my first poem ever published.; [a.] Marianna, FL

SIMCOX, KATHY A. HOUCK
[b.] May 28, 1950, Roswell, NM; [ch.] Joel Elisha, Blaine Lavaud; [ed.] Medical Lake High, WA, Buena Vista College, IA; [occ.] Excel Corporation Meat Packer; [hon.] Dean's List; [pers.] I believe that we should all strive to be better citizens and get along with those who are different from ourselves.; [a.] Ottumwa, IA

SIMMONS, LISA
[b.] May 17, 1980, Spokane, WA; [p.] Vicki Simmons, Jim Simmons; [ed.] Mullan Road Elem., Moran Prairie Elem., Sacajawea Jr. High, Ferris High School; [memb.] Young Writers Club, MSU (Multicultural Student Union), Drill Team; [hon.] Equity-Diversity Award, Young Writers Award, Piano Composition Award; [oth. writ.] Several poems published in school newspaper; [pers.] My angels are poems from the heart. My first love writing and it will always be my closest friend.; [a.] Spokane, WA

SIMPSON, GALE
[pen.] Stormie, Windy or Daisy Simpson; [b.] November 22, 1956, Philadelphia, PA; [p.] David and Joan Simpson; [ed.] N.E. Standard H.S.; [occ.] Sec. Guard; [hon.] Editor's Choice Award from: The National Library of Poetry of "'95" for "Great And Marvelous Are Thy Works"; [pers.] The more I keep the word of God in my life... I find love, joy, peace, happiness and blessing... almost everyday of the wk... it's just ashame more people don't have what I have in Christ Jesus.; [a.] Philadelphia, PA

SIMS, ANNETTE GILSTRAP
[pen.] Ann; [b.] May 1, 1953, Kingsville, TX; [p.] Tommy and Corinne Gilstrap; [m.] Joe Stenberg, February 21, 1991; [ch.] Travis Black and Kristen Black; [ed.] Bishop High, Texas A and I University; [occ.] Owner of Sims Insurance Agency; [memb.] The Society C.I.S.R. Program; [hon.] A.R.M. agent of the month 1991; [oth. writ.] One published poem in a local newspaper. Numerous other poems written through the last 20 years.; [pers.] "My poems reflect deep heart felt thoughts that merely pass through my mind's given inspiration to my pen."; [a.] San Antonio, TX

SINGHO, BERYL
[pen.] "Precious Gem"; [b.] March 16, 1920, Lynchburg, VA; [p.] Edna and Richard Cardwell; [m.] Rodney Singho, December 28, 1983 and (2nd time) July 15, 1991; [ch.] One son (deceased), one stepdaughter Queens; [ed.] H.S. Graduate - 1 yr Queens College Courses Med. Terminology; [occ.] Retired City Worker Heart and Hospitals (Med. Secretary); [memb.] NAACP, YRBM League AARP, CSREA Mother Hale Aids, Cancer, Research; [hon.] 32 yrs. Service Hearth and Hospitals Vol Schools Pediatric Wards (hosps.); [oth. writ.] Usually writing have other poems, this the first I submitted! My mother and grandparents were educators.; [pers.] I have had a network of sorrow in my life, the worse being the murder of a most worthy son and only son on his birth day. My motto is it can always be worse and to "Forgive the unforgivable" God sent me my husband 2 to the Bate of my sons murder. Our love is unconditional, He is almost half my age we married twice! For love.; [a.] Queens, NY

SINGLETON, CARL RAY
[pen.] Carl R. Singleton (or) Carl Singleton; [b.] November 10, 1968, Dallas, TX; [p.] Berthal Singleton; [ed.] Bachelor's Degree in Engineering, Technology from the University of North Texas (Minored in English) L.G. Pinkston High; [occ.] Mail Sorter (United Parcel Service); [pers.] My future goals are to marry and catch at the college level.; [a.] Dallas, TX

SJURSETH, JANICE L.
[pen.] Jan; [b.] September 28, 1938, Berwyn, IL; [p.] Wesley and Loretta Bruhnke; [m.] (Curtis Eiklor, August 8, 1959) Bruce D. Sjurseth, October 29, 1983; [ch.] Gary, Daniel and Susan Eiklor; [ed.] Luther High School South (graduate) Chicago, IL Several Classes at Elgin Community College; [occ.] Payroll/Benefits Adm. Co. Newsletter Editor and Writer; [memb.] Calvary Lutheran Church, Elgin, EL; [pers.] When creative juices start their flow what should I do then where shall it go - when I neither play a note or sing in fine soprano voice the poetry has thus become my personal instrument of choice. Poets give back some rhyme and reason to a strife turn world.; [a.] Elgin, IL

SKOTNICA, JUDITH A.
[pen.] Judith Simone Skotnica; [b.] June 8, 1941, Buffalo, NY; [p.] Joseph A. Simone Sr., June M. Simone; [m.] William Skotnica, June 21, 1986; [ch.] Dawn A. Souza, Joseph M. Cook; [ed.] Extended Adult Education in Art, Literature, Computers, and Product Assurance; [occ.] Aspiring Artists, Poet, and Writer; [memb.] Ex Libris Artists, Writers and Mythology Group of Morro Bay, American Reflex Sympathetic Dystrophy Association (ARSDA); [hon.] Citation of Merit for Outstanding Performance in the Titan IV Space Program; [oth. writ.] 1) I am currently working on an autobiography about the psychological and physical pain of living with chronic never dystrophy, and the courage of self-discovery, hope and surrender to a higher source. 2) A portfolio of non-published poems.; [pers.] The magic of words open new perspective and are a conduit to personal development that creatively express this author's most intimate thoughts. Words feed the soul.; [a.] Morro Bay, CA

SKYWATER, SHARON
[pen.] Coyote-Skywater; [b.] April 21, 1954, Redding, CA; [ch.] Kriston Joseph and Dylan Shea; [occ.] Addesign - contributing writer - Franklin Banner Trib. (Newspaper); [oth. writ.] Short stories: The Little People, Calling Coyote, Turtle and Coyote's Great Adventure, Poems: Remember, Monkey Climb, many others; [pers.] To have the life we wish to live, we must have the courage and perseverance to Create it!; [a.] Franklin, LA

SLACK, MERRILYN
[b.] September 30, 1942, Los Angeles, CA; [m.] Jerry A. Slack, November 9, 1968; [ch.] Allison and Megan; [ed.] Redondo Union H.S. Elcamino College, V.C.L.A, Union The Logical Seminary Richmond VA; [occ.] Clergy-Presbyterian Church (USA); [memb.] Various Denominational Organizations; [oth. writ.] Various articles for Kansas City Area News papers; [pers.] I believe that the love of the Lord, Jesus Christ, Covers a multitude of sins, and that any and all evil can be made null and void; [a.] Smithville, MO

SLINGERLAND, DOUGLAS A.
[b.] February 19, 1921, Schenectady, NY; [p.] Emma Voegtling and Chester F. Slingerland; [m.] Dodie Kapelle, 1952; [ch.] Stephen, Michael and Sharon (Dede); [ed.] B.S. Union College Schenectady, N.Y.; [occ.] Manager Director/Custodial Services Sanders, A Lockheed Martin Co. Nashua, N.H.; [memb.] Nat'l Exec. H.K. Assoc. - Past V.P. Past exalted Ruler - B.P.O.E. #1317 Cohoes, NY Past V.P. Am Soc. Qual, Cont. Sub Vets WW II Assoc. Mem. AM. Legion; [hon.] WW II Vet. ETO Medal - 8 Battles Stars Soldiers Medal; [oth. writ.] Winder's Training Manual for "Peter J. Scweltzer/NC Lee, MA; [pers.] Poetry is "Internal Thoughts....External Expression, Eternal Display!"; [a.] Nashua, NH

SMITH, ANDREA RENAE
[b.] August 27, 1975, New Albany, IN; [p.] Michael and Mary Ellen Smith; [m.] Engaged to Douglas Myers, August 10, 1996; [ed.] Floyd Central High School Graduate, current College Student at Indiana University Southeast (Marketing Major); [occ.] Advertising Assistant, Tigne Marketing and Communications; [memb.] St. Mary's New Albany Catholic Church; [a.] Georgetown, IN

SMITH, ASHLEY LYNN
[b.] July 3, 1984, Danbury, CT; [p.] Shown E. Smith and Mary R. Smith; [ed.] 6th grade; [occ.] 6th grade student; [memb.] Girl Scouts, Ski Club, Chorus; [hon.] First award I got this poem when I was walking to my bustop and it was raining so I listened to the sounds and made up a poem then I put it on paper.; [oth. writ.] I wrote An Avalanche also and sent that to you; [pers.] If you are aloud to dedicate your poem

to somebody I would like to dedicate it to Karen Sconlon my English teacher who taught me how to write poems.; [a.] Addison, NY

SMITH, CHEVELLE D.
[pen.] Chevelle D. Smith; [b.] December 10, 1972, Philadelphia, PA; [p.] Lana M. Smith, Robert Taylor; [ed.] R.S. Walton Elem., Thomas Fitzsimons Sr. High, Ben Jamin Franklin High; [occ.] Action Cash Clerk, Sands Hotel and Casino; [hon.] Ben Franklin Business Institute - Distinguished Honor Roll Award, Reading Excellence/Mastery Award; [pers.] I love to read poetry. I love to write poetry and short stories. My feelings and emotions of this poem reflects on the strength and togetherness of black women sense the beginning of our existence.; [a.] Atlantic City, NJ

SMITH, CINDA
[b.] July 24, 1960, High Point, NC; [p.] Frank Smith and Ruth Smith; [ed.] Randleman High, Wingate College

SMITH, ELIZABETH ALLEN
[b.] July 15, 1972, Spartanburg, SC; [p.] Ruth Christman, Paul Mason Allen; [m.] Dr. Stokes Jerome Smith, March 31, 1951; [ch.] Stokes Jerome, Jr. Elizabeth C.S. Rous; [ed.] Spartanburg High and Winthrop University graduate; [occ.] Retired-radio and television, bookkeeping; [memb.] The Junior League of Spartanburg, Battle of Cowpens Chapter DAR, Cherokee Chapter of Daughters of the American Colonists, Dance Chairman Debutante Club, past president of Spartanburg; [hon.] Little Theatre, member of Senior Order and Who's Who in American Colleges and Universities, editor of College newspaper, free lance news- paper articles and radio shows; [oth, writ] Songs and skits and poetry for volunteer organizations and entertainment for groups; [pers.] (Thank you for being there to inspire people like me who finally have time to do what they love to do:) My favorite quotation: "Who plants a tree, who writes a book, who bears a child, gives pledges three: to life in faith that life is strong, that earth is sure, and time is long."; [a.] Spartanburg, SC

SMITH JR., REX B.
[pen.] Rex B. Smith Jr.; [b.] January 7, 1951, Huntington, WV; [p.] Buddie R. and Nell M. Smith; [m.] A.J. Thompson, April 27, 1983; [ch.] Jennifer Layne Smith (Previous marriage); [ed.] Graduated - Whitehall yearling High School; [occ.] Florist; [hon.] Just having the love and respect of a wonderful family and so many beautiful friends, who accept me "Just As I Am"; [oth. writ.] No other poems. A small collection of songs none published.; [pers.] I was inspired to write this poem because of all the family and friends that have moved on into the next life. So many friends that have died due to AIDS, and looking into their faces as they said good-bye.; [a.] Dallas, TX

SMITH, LINDA L.
[pen.] Jaz; [b.] August 22, 1963, Albequerque, NM; [p.] Albert and Mattie Leaphart; [m.] Daniel Smith, November 3, 1984; [ch.] Joshua Lee; [occ.] Administrative; [memb.] Zion HIll Baptist Church Children's Director; [oth. writ.] Wrote poems and songs for 20 years; [pers.] I write spiritually enhanced work nd was originally influenced by the writings of Arthur Gordon and like writers.; [a.] Dacula, GA

SMITH, MARLENE M.
[b.] October 11, 1962, Decatur, GA; [p.] F.M. Stafford Smith and Dixie Stewart Smith; [ed.] High School - Shamrock H.S. in Decatur, GA graduated 1980, no college; [occ.] Printer in composing room at Atlanta Journal and Constitution news papers; [oth. writ.] I have written thousands of poems in the past 20 yrs. This is the first time I have entered one in a contest. For me this an especially grand honor; [pers.] I write what I feel. My feelings are very strong and writing is wonderful outlet. Pablo Neruda is my favorite modern poet. Coleridge and Baudelaire have influenced much of my writings as well; [a.] Stone Mountain, GA

SMITH, RENEE MICKLE
[pen.] Renee Falder; [b.] January 28, 1958, Elba, AL; [p.] William E. Mickle Sr., and Ruby Wilkes-Mickle; [m.] Mel, June 23, 1992; [ch.] But my 3 dogs are like my kids; [ed.] 1976 Graduate of Elba High, Alabama; [occ.] Mostly homemaker, but I do prepare resumes, etc. and Custom Frames; [memb.] I was a member of the world of poetry; [hon.] Golden Poet 1986 World of Poetry, Silver Poet 1990 World of Poetry, Award of Merit Certificate - Honorable Mention with Poem Grass of Green Velvet 1985 - World of Poetry; [oth. writ.] Grass of green velvet received merit award. I've written many "books" of poems, lyrics, etc., but as of present I haven't published any yet.; [pers.] I began writing poetry in elementary school and I've haven't finished yet. I try to bring about my hopes and beliefs of the goodness in each of us and that love is our greatest strength, for without love in our hearts, our life is empty.; [a.] Auburn, WA

SMITH, ROSE MARIE
[pen.] Dee Dee Smith; [b.] July 18, 1951, Sacramento, CA; [p.] John Solaja and Rose Marie Solaja; [ed.] Verdugo Hill High School (With Honors), Glendale College; [occ.] Production Manager Xcel Digitran, Ontario, CA; [memb.] Peta, Library of Congress; [hon.] 1987 Chairman's Achievement Award, Xcel Corporation; [pers.] I draw inspiration from the vision of the women's movement, feminist publishing houses and the exploration of the female experience.; [a.] Sun Valley, CA

SMITH, RUTH
[pen.] Emily Smith; [b.] January 9, 1965, Greenville, PA; [p.] John Kristyak and Ruth Kristyak; [m.] David Smith, September 13, 1990; [ch.] Candace Marie; [ed.] Commodore Perry H.S., Kee Business College; [occ.] Secretary/Homemaker; [memb.] Christian Community Church; [pers.] I use writing as a therapeutic way of releasing stress. Coming face to face with your feelings keeps them, feelings, visible and out of harms way.; [a.] Greenville, PA

SMITH, SHELLY L.
[b.] May 11, 1969, Marion, IN; [p.] Jerry D. Smith, Karen S. Smith; [ed.] Oak Hill High, Ball State University; [occ.] Paine Webber, SA, Carmel, IN; [hon.] Alpha Gamma Delta; [pers.] I live by a quote from Robert Fulghum. He couldn't have said it better than "If you are patient long enough, some dreams come true and fate will draft you."; [a.] Indianapolis, IN

SMITH, SHERILYN K.
[b.] March 13, 1971, Dallas, TX; [p.] Mr. and Mrs. Alonza L. Smith Jr.; [ed.] Texas State Technical, College in Waco and the Art Institute of Dallas (Graduated 6/92, Dean's List Award); [occ.] Sports Writer/Photographer; [hon.] Miss 1995 Minority Opportunity News Bachlorette, Miss Up-N-Coming by Jim Jackson Dallas Mauericks, Dean's List Award all Collegiate Years at Institute; [pers.] I feel the talent that I have is a gift from God. I am able to express myself through poetry and photography. I have always viewed my life differently at times I feel I have always looked through a view finder, but not always with a camera.; [a.] Dallas, TX

SMITH, TISHAWNA MARIE
[b.] March 13, 1976, Corona, CA; [p.] Cynthia Rosenberger and Travis Curtis; [ed.] Sky High Continuation/Alternative High School; [occ.] Hawaii Job Corps, Student Employee; [memb.] California Conservation Corps Member Hawaiian Club Member; [hon.] Most Outstanding Student California Conservation Corps, Training Session 116 Hawaii Job Corps, Computers Student of the month; [oth. writ.] Several poems published in school and Corps member newspapers; [pers.] I am greatly influenced by Maya Angelou's beautiful works. I find that writing poetry helps me to better understand the circumstances of life and it brings me inner peace.; [a.] Joshua Tree, CA

SMITH, VIRGINIA LOUISE
[b.] August 27, 1979, Key West, FL; [p.] Flynn and Marian Smith; [ed.] Student at Key West High School. I plan to attend College after high school graduation.; [pers.] Through my poetry I would like people to look at the world in a more reflective way.; [a.] Key West, FL

SMITH, WM.
[pen.] Tyrre Curtis; [b.] August 16, 1931, Marlow, OK; [p.] Henry and Bonnie Smith; [ch.] Crazy, Jun, Kimberly; [ed.] Lindsay Cal. High School; [occ.] Port truck leaving; [memb.] B.P.O.E. Elks First Church of God; [oth. writ.] One book published "Poetry From My Soul" several poems published in newspapers; [pers.] I like to write the new dimensions, I will not honor pre conceptions. The world that I live in is very small, but my mind it knows no bounds at all This is what I am all about I am a constant reaching out; [a.] Napa, CA

SNIEZAK, STEPHEN MARTIN
[pen.] Steve Christy Jr.; [b.] January 3, 1961, Cheektowaga, NY; [p.] Donald Sniezak Sr., Charlotte Sniezak; [ed.] School of Hard Knocks; [occ.] Machine Operator; [memb.] National Rifle Association; [oth. writ.] Piles of tomes in the closet gathering dust; [pers.] In all things there must be balance, never give up when it's for real. "Semper in excretum sumus sed altra veriat."; [a.] Travelers Rest, SC

SNYER, KATHLEEN
[pen.] Kathleen Snyer; [b.] June 4, 1986, Seattle, WA; [p.] Steve Snyer, Crystal Wright; [ed.] South Colby Elementary; [occ.] Student, South Colby Elementary, Port Orchard, WA; [hon.] Good Work Awards, Extra Mile Awards, Awards for Stars (Students that are Reaching Success); [pers.] I try to enjoy each and every day I wish there were more hours in the day! This poem is dedicated to the other writer in our family, my grandfather Duane.; [a.] Port Orchard, WA

SOCHUCK, ALPHONSINA
[pen.] "Alphy"; [b.] December 19, 1964, New Jersey; [p.] Carlo and Mary Ellen Giovannitti; [m.] Stanley J. Sochuck, October 9, 1993; [ch.] Angelo Giovannitti; [occ.] Tenneco Packaging; [pers.] For some of you, may relate this poem to someone you know, and others she may remain as simply Jane Doe, but to me she is not just another lost human being, that is why I refer to her as "Arlene". Please think twice before you tilt that glass, I would hate to read of another Jane Doe that has been forced to pass.

SOHN, PATRICIA L.
[b.] September 7, 1957, Orange, CA; [p.] John and Ivadell Yates; [m.] Robert E. Sohn, May 5, 1984; [ch.] William D. Rash; [ed.] La Quinta High; [occ.] Accountant; [oth. writ.] I have a collection of poem's written over the last (2) two years I hope to have published one day.; [pers.] I hope to make a contribution to all of those great poets I have read and learned so much from. I want to help others discover the "Romantic" that is in us all.; [a.] Buena Park, CA

SOKOLOWSKI, TINA L.
[pen.] Tina Sokolowski; [b.] July 7, 1964, La Porte, IN; [p.] Al J. Kathryn (Thomas) Sokolowski; [ed.] Galena Elem. La Porte, IN, Heritage Christian AC, New Buffalo, Mi, Marquette H.S. Michigan City, IN, Northwest Beauty College, Michigan City, IN; [memb.] Sing Sands Girl Scouts of America, Y.M.C.A., La Porte, IN Cosmetologist Association; [hon.] Awards received as accomplished flutist, and pianist; [pers.] This writing was influenced from memories of early childhood from the love and closeness shared growing up with granpa, father Joseph Gabriel Sokolowski O.S.B., and is dedicated in memory of him.; [a.] La Porte, IN

SOMANI, NITA
[pen.] Nidhi; [b.] July 15, 1965, India; [p.] Dr. G. L. Purohit and Sushila Purohit; [m.] Anil Somani, November 13, 1994; [ed.] B.S. (Pharmacy), M.S. (Medical Chemistry); [occ.] Instructor in Sawyer College, San Jose; [hon.] Won many Awards for Public Speaking, won a Scholarship for M.S.; [oth. writ.] Many poems and articles have been published in leading newspapers and magazines in India; [pers.] A million beautiful thoughts are racing through my heart and mind - and I want to share them all!; [a.] Campbell, CA

SOMMERS, BRIAN K.
[pen.] Daoly Maerc; [b.] February 12, 1976, Baltimore, MD; [p.] Gerry Sommers and Mary Lou Sommers; [ed.] Queen Annes County High, Anne Anundel Community College, English Education; [occ.] Substitute Teacher in Queen Annes County, MD; [hon.] Represented Queen Annes County High School in the Chesapeake College Poetry Festival; [oth. writ.] Publication of other poems "words" and "the spell of the green faerie" in lions tales: The queen annes county high school literary magazine; [pers.] If my poetry serves my purpose at all, it is to carry people out of their ignorance and help them look at things in a positive way. My favorite poets are voltaire, Edgar Allan Poe, and Jim Morrison.; [a.] Stevensville, MD

SORRELLS, JACQUELINE
[pen.] JaQ-5; [b.] October 21, 1963, Nuringburg, Germany; [p.] Thomas and Barbara Sorrells; [ch.] Joequetta Shawneice Jenkins; [ed.] Psychology Major, JFK High Wellingboro, NJ, Barbazon Modeling School, Freedom Theater-Philadelphia, PA; [occ.] Correction Officer for Law Enforcement of NJ; [memb.] PBA; [hon.] Certificate in Completion of Law Enforcement training for State of NJ; [oth. writ.] This poem is my first submitted. I have many more just waiting to be published.; [pers.] I'd rather set the example, then to be the example. Reflect every second of light.

SORVINO, CAROLE M.
[b.] July 15, 1936, Newark, NJ; [p.] Edmund and Rose May; [ch.] Jeffrey, Gina, and Gregory; [a.] Belmont Shore, CA

SPALDO, EUGENIA
[pen.] "Jean"; [b.] May 23, 1923, New York City; [p.] Wilhelmina Rose and Christian Samson; [m.] Louis Spaldo (Deceased 7 yrs), November 4, 1958; [ch.] 1 Ronald Scrivani; [ed.] 3 years High School; [occ.] Home-maker; [memb.] American Legion and Disable American Veterans; [oth. writ.] Poems Thinking of You, What is a Friend, The One I Love; [pers.] I like to write poems out of the space of the moment. Some of my poems fit in with some music tunes. Poems to me have a lot of meaning.; [a.] Paughkeepsie, NJ

SPARROW, BRANDY
[pen.] Brandy Sparrow; [b.] January 10, 1977, Queens, NY; [p.] Wayne Sparrow, Lenora Sparrow; [ed.] Cardozo High, College Student; [occ.] Student in College/Library Assistant; [memb.] Jehobah Witness; [hon.] Basketball honors school service. I have also been awarded with a loving family; [oth. writ.] Several other poems to be published; [pers.] In my poetry I reflect on the simple things in life. My poems reflect my dreams desires and the obstacles that have been put in my way throughout my life.; [a.] Cambria Heights, NY

SPEARS, SANDRA E.
[pen.] S.E. Spears; [b.] October 20, 1946, Norfolk, VA; [p.] Ernest J. Carter Sr. and Alice A. Carter; [m.] June 13, 1970 (Divorced September, 1975); [ed.] Lincoln Elementary School, Roosevelt High School, Gary, Indiana (Diploma), Lincoln University, Jefferson City, Missouri (B.S), University of Michigan, Ann Arbor, Michigan National-Louis University (Currently working on my Masters); [occ.] Training Specialist, The first National Bank of Chicago, Chicago, Illinois; [memb.] Liberty Baptist Church, National ASDT, United Way, Alpha Kappa Alpha Sorority, Incorporated, Roosevelt High School Alumni Association, Lincoln University Alumni Association; [hon.] Dean's List, National Louis University; [oth. writ.] 80 personal poems (unpublished); [pers.] I believe in living life to its fullest every day. Through thoughts and actions demonstrate the positive virtues of a quality life, as they relate to love, charity and courage; [a.] Chicago, IL

SPELLER, TAMAKA
[pen.] Tammy Luv; [b.] August 11, 1973, Philadelphia, PA; [p.] Darlene and Melvin Speller; [ed.] Currently a College Student at the University of District of Columbia (UDC); [oth. writ.] My poems are not published; [pers.] I write from the heart to make my poems true. My words are meaningful and that is what makes all my poems special.; [a.] District Heights, MD

SPENCER, PEARLIE BRIDGES
[pen.] J. P. Me'Velenti; [b.] January 25, 1946, Valdosta, GA; [p.] Daisy and Willie Columbus Bridges; [m.] George S. Spencer, February 24, 1964; [ch.] Joaquin, Juan, Mario, Eric, Perlita; [ed.] Pinevale High, Valdosta Technical Institute Valdosta, Georgia; [occ.] Activity Director - Certified Holly Hill Nursing Home Valdosta, Georgia; [memb.] Thessalonian Baptist Church, Church's Clerk, Women Missionary Society, Anniversary Committee, Georgia Society of Nursing Home Activity Directors, Quality Management, Safety Committees; [hon.] 2nd Place Essay Contest, Employee of Month of November '95, Employee Spotlighted in United health Service Newspaper Dec. '95, Proclamation from the Major, City of Valdosta as the Bridges Family Reunion Weekend Aug 31, 95; [oth. writ.] Several articles for cooperation newsletter, local newspaper (published); [pers.] I strive to reflect a positive image of the inner-peace, knowledge of the Greatest love for all mankind in my writing.; [a.] Valdosta, GA

SPENCER, PORTIA
[pen.] Jennee; [b.] June 6, 1975, Los Angeles; [p.] Katherine Baber; [ed.] Eisenhower High School Graduate "1993," San Antonio Regional Occupational Program; [occ.] Student; [memb.] CEDA, Drama Club, Phemail Lyric, Black Cultural Foundation; [hon.] Certificate of Merit from CEDA, for three years 10th, 11th, 12th grade in the yr of "91," "92," "93"; [oth. Writ.] "So Its The Rain," "Magic Box," "Black Women," "Whisper," "Believers Of Voice," "At Home," "Sunny Days," "Did I," "My Mind," "A Sister To The Black Crow," "Black Two Jupiter."; [pers.] Believers of voice, its your choice! Voice, I feel will come and take you home. If you believe.; [a.] Pomona, CA

SPENCER, TONY
[b.] August 23, 1964, Berkley Springs, WV; [p.] Charles Spencer, Dollie Spencer; [m.] Chuck Andrews, August 25, 1992; [ed.] Paw Paw High School, Potomac State College, Shenandoalt University; [occ.] Sales for Westvaco Corp. Luke, MD; [oth. writ.]

Mythical reality will you? Love will!; [pers.] If my writings open one eye or soften one heart in consider them a success!; [a.] Cumberland, MD

SPIKES, CLYDE
[b.] January 12, 1953, Dequiney, LA; [p.] Sylvester, Eva Spikes; [m.] Kimberly Ann Mayer, October 14, 2001; [ch.] Corey (26), Eva (19); [ed.] G.E.D. 8th Grade Drop out "School of Hard Knocks," "University of Pain and Suffering."; [occ.] In mate at "Oregon State Penitentiary"; [oth. writ.] "Rain to pain," "2 friends too," "20 green door."; [pers.] "Live simply, so others can simple live." "Silence is not always golden but often yellow."; [a.] Salem, OR

SPRINGER, JUDY ANN
[pen.] J. Ann; [b.] September 26, 1950, Cullman, AL; [p.] Worth - Margaret Duckett; [m.] Steve Springer; [ch.] Heath, Daniel, DeAnn, Trey; [ed.] Grand Prairie High School, Grand Prairie Beauty School; [occ.] Housewife, Decorating, Arts/Crafts with Writing Poetry; [memb.] A.B.W.A, First United Methodist Church (GP); [hon.] A beautiful grand daughter born August 18, "Logan Anne" and 4 beautiful healthy children and the best husband in the world, I am truly blessed; [oth. writ.] "The Real Thing," "That Special Feeling," "Longing," "Yearning," "Y-O-U," "Someday."; [pers.] I get ideas and inspiration from real life. The ups and downs that heart ache can bring. happiness over finding your soul mate and your prince charming.; [a.] Grand Prairie, TX

SPRINGER, NORMA
[pen.] Norma Sears Bowen; [b.] December 17, 1937, Guyana, SA; [p.] Aubrey and Winefred Sears Bowen; [m.] Eustace Springer, February 11, 1957; [ch.] 13; [ed.] Buttons High School Guyana, Georgetown Hospital NSG-School, University of Guyana; [occ.] Registered Nurse Song Writer; [memb.] Hilltop Records Music of America; [oth. writ.] "The World Is Beautiful" "Reach For Success" "Don't Give Up" "Look Up" "Our Love Is Now Beginning" "We Need Peace" "Pretty Girl" Thanks To America"

STAMP, JULIE E.
[pen.] Julie E. Stamp (Jes); [b.] May 5, 1980, San Diego; [p.] Bob Stamp; [ed.] Currently Enrolled in El Capitan High School, 10th Grade; [occ.] Student; [memb.] Enrolled in AYSO Soccer 3rd Year; [hon.] I have received One First Place Trophy, 2 Third Place Trophies for Soccer and One Most Outstanding Girl Freshmen in El Capitan Band; [oth. writ.] This poem is just one if many creations; [pers.] To the many writers out there who have this chance they should take it. My friends and family boosted my faith in my talent. Have fun and keep imaging! To my humanities teacher Mrs. Coffin-Prince and to my good friend cash mere, thanks.; [a.] Lakeside, CA

STANTON, CHRIS A.
[b.] March 2, 1949, Portland, OR; [p.] The late William Perrotto and Dolores Cavanaugh; [m.] James F. Stanton, August 30, 1987; [ch.] Linda Johnson, Tami Henkes, Rich Henkes, Granddaughter Cassidy Richard and Step children Cindy, Stephens and Paul Stanton; [ed.] Beaverton High School, Clackamas Community College, AIB; [occ.] Account Service Rep. Citizens First Bank, Arkadelphia, Arkansas; [memb.] M.L. Hummel; [oth. writ.] I have been writing poetry since 1980 and have a large collection.; [pers.] My writings are a reflection of my soul. Sometimes sadness, sometimes happiness, always with true feelings of my heart. They are my way of releasing my feelings to (most of the time) only myself.; [a.] Arkadelphia, AR

STANTON, RICKY J.
[b.] April 8, 1953, Chicago, IL; [p.] Harold and Doris Stanton; [m.] Jama M. Stanton, October 22, 1993; [ch.] (2) Angie and Kris; [ed.] College Graduate; [a.] West Frankfort, IL

STAPLES II, MILTON THOMAS
[pen.] Milton Thomas Staples II; [b.] April 1, 1944, Washington, DC; [p.] Milton Staples and Serena Staples; [m.] Divorced; [ch.] Eric Thomas Staples, (Step-son) Les Couchenour Jr.; [ed.] Suitland Senior High, Anne Arundel Community College, University Maryland; [occ.] TWA Change Team Advisor/ Ramp Service Crew Chief; [oth. writ.] Reader's Digest/various magazines; [pers.] My writings is greatly influenced by my life experiences and the early romantic poets.; [a.] Pasadena, MD

STEDELBAUER, JOYCE CARR
[pen.] Joyce Carr Stedelbauer; [b.] May 17, 1934, Kansas City, MO; [p.] Dan and Rowena Carr; [m.] George Stedelbauer, June 9, 1956; [ch.] 2; [ed.] B.A. English Literature Wheaton College, Illinois; [occ.] Inspirational Speaker and Bible Teacher; [memb.] Virginia Society of Poets, National League of American Pen Women; [hon.] For community service; [oth. writ.] Published in fall of 1995 in "Poet's Domain" Painter, VA; [pers.] My gift of poetry is God given, then I work with careful craftsmanship to bring it to fruition.; [a.] Williamsburg, VA

STEPHENSON, MELANIE
[b.] August 4, 1971, Chester, SC; [p.] Francis and Linda Stephenson; [ed.] Bachelor of Science - Elementary Education from Winthrop University; [occ.] Keyboarding, Word Processing Teacher, Chester Middle School, Chester, SC; [memb.] Parkway Baptist Church; [a.] Chester, SC

STERLING, ANNIE
[pen.] Sylvia Seabon; [b.] December 13, 1937, Montgomery, AL; [p.] Zephaniah Sterling and Ethel Sterling; [m.] Lawrence Seabon; [ch.] One; [ed.] High School; [occ.] Retired; [oth. writ.] Personal poetry relating to those who have touched my life in some heart felt manner. Truly my musings.; [a.] Plainfield, NJ

STEVENSON, CHARLES E.
[pen.] Sha! Sha!; [b.] December 26, 1962, Darlington, SC; [p.] Phyllis Stevenson; [ed.] Pate Elementary School and Bruson Dargan, Junior High and St. John's High School; [occ.] Nein Haven Board of Education; [hon.] 1983 I entered the World's Cooking Fair I won 2nd Place and was Awarded 2 Trophy's and 2 medal's and 1 plaque

STEWART, CLAUDETTE SUZANNE
[pen.] Claudette S. Mautor; [b.] January 23, 1948, East Orange, NJ; [p.] Michael Fred and Helen A. (Margerum Mautor); [ch.] Shaun Renig and Michael Blake; [ed.] DeLand H.S., DeLand FL, BS Rollins College, Winter Park, FL; [occ.] Farmer, Artist, Author; [memb.] Leicester Volunteer Fire Dept., N.C. Search and Rescue Assoc., N.C. Herb Association, High Country Art and Craft Guild; [hon.] 1995-1996 Marquis who's who of American Women; [oth. writ.] Living with Potpourri, 1988 Everlasting Floral Gifts, 1990 Nature at Ground Level, 1993; [pers.] Poeta nascitur, non fit. Faire de la prose sans le savoir.; [a.] Big Sandy Mush, NC

STEWART, LORNA M.
[b.] April 27, 1918, Vernal, UT; [p.] Bernard A. Bell and Fannie E. W. Bell; [m.] Myron Joseph Stewart, July 4, 1946; [ch.] Tracy, Joseph, Linda, John, Lucinda; [ed.] Rossevelt High, Taft Jr. College, University of Utah correspondence courses. Seventy-seven years in the school of life.; [occ.] Retired executive secretary - housewife; [memb.] Daughters of Utah Pioneers, Church of Jesus Christ of Latter-day Saints; [hon.] Shared in group Award of Excellence on the Apollo Space Program. Received "Second Miler" District Award, Boy Scouts of America, Utah National Parks Council; [oth. writ.] Submitted a poem to Ideals Magazine, a copy of which they retained in their permanent file. Have written numerous poems, some of which have been published. Have written articles, none of which have been submitted for publication as yet.; [pers.] My purposes is to use my insight, caring, compassion and love by serving, sharing, and by heart to heart communication both through the spoken and written word to create a world of abundance, peace and unconditional love.; [a.] Mount Pleasant, UT

STITT, DEBORAH
[b.] February 22, 1979; [p.] David and Yamile' Stitt; [ed.] Quisqueya Christian School in Port-au-Prince, Haiti where American and lebanese parents are missionaries; [occ.] Student; [hon.] Honor roll, principal's Award and Creativity Award; [oth. writ.] Articles for school yearbook, autobiographical essay's eulogies and other poems; [pers.] I wish to portray the link between love and nature. Two of the most beautiful aspects in life held together by a rope of thorns, laid on a bed of roses and sprinkled with tears.; [a.] Forth Lauderdale, FL

STOKES, DONNA V.
[pen.] Donna V. Slack; [b.] August 5, 1954, Boston, MA; [p.] Donald and Ruth Slack; [ch.] Diana R. Goodwin (Tibbettes); [ed.] Norcross - So. Boston Thomas Edison Jr. high Massasoit Community College Brockton South Eastern Tech Ins. So Eastern HCC - TPA, Fl A.S. A.A. RN; [occ.] Medical Assistant; [memb.] Girls Club So. Boston - H.E.I.P. So. Boston, Treasure of your City Fla. Alcalde Associ-of Y Bor City-Fla.;

[hon.] Girls Club - Talent Awards 3 Consecutive Yrs - 1968 (TV) Singer Community and of Boston - Two Golden Arrow Head Award the same MO 1967 from Camplapton (record); [oth. writ.] Short stories, many poems, and one world in progress; [pers.] "We are all here for the same reason to live - leave others to do the same, in their own way.; [a.] Tampa, FL

STONE, SHELBY J.
[b.] November 2, 1943, York, PA; [p.] Marie and Joseph G. Newport; [m.] George Stone (Deceased), April 15, 1964; [ch.] Maria Stone-Matthews, Amadeo Stone; [ed.] High School - Eastern H.S. Wrightsville, Pennsylvania; [occ.] Information Specialist, U.S. Department of Education; [memb.] Professional Managers Association; [hon.] Mentor Award - 1990; [oth. writ.] Unpublished poetry; [pers.] My children, grandchildren, parents, and family have inspired me most.; [a.] Washington, DC

STORINO, HENRY E.
[b.] May 7, 1921, Seattle, WA; [p.] Frank and Theresa Storino; [m.] Joan M. Storino, April 24, 1954; [ch.] 4 (2 sons, 2 daughters) 8 grandchildren; [ed.] 5 yrs. College, 4 yrs. Medical School 1949-53, 3 yrs Mayo Clinic (Neurosurgery) 1955-58, 2 yrs. at Univ. or Oregon (Neurology Residency) 1962-64; [occ.] Retired (as of 1987); [memb.] AMA, OMA, American Academy of Neurology; [pers.] I believe that the greatest untapped natural resource in the world today is the Brain Power of the common people.; [a.] Portland, OR

STUART, EVA
[pen.] Eva Stuart; [b.] November 18, 1934, Brown County, TX; [p.] S. J. and Eva Eaton; [m.] Wilbur Ray Stuart, July 1, 1954; [ch.] Carson, Sidney; [ed.] BS Sulross State University, Texas, MSN University of El Paso; [occ.] Retired; [oth. writ.] Several poems published locally; [a.] May, TX

SUAREZ, MEGAN
[b.] May 18, 1983, Forthworth, TX; [p.] Al and Laura; [ed.] Presently completing seventh grade; [hon.] Straight A student chosen to take SAT in 7th grade, Outstanding Tennis Champion, and Church Soloist; [pers.] We cannot lead someone else to the light while we are standing in the dark.; [a.] Grapevine, TX

SULLIVAN, EDWARD THOMAS
[pen.] Et Sullivan; [b.] March 23, 1954, Aberdeen, MD; [p.] Raymond and Esther Sullivan; [m.] Anna Marie Sullivan, November 11, 1980; [ch.] Stacy, Aja, Erik; [ed.] Spring Valley H.S. 1972; [occ.] Regional Operations Mgr., Developers Diversified Realty Corp.; [memb.] Cousteau Society, Save the Manatees, Sherra Club, WUNC Public Radio, PADI Certified Advanced Open Water Diver (Scuba); [oth. writ.] Many poems (unpublished) currently working on first book; [pers.] Take time to listen to others. Go for long walks on quiet beaches or wooded trails. Give something back to the people in your life. Protect the water, the air and the land. The others will listen to.; [a.] Durham, NC

SULLIVAN, SUZY D.
[b.] September 15, 1961, Ellisville, MO; [p.] Walter and Stella Clough; [ed.] Lebanon High; [occ.] Mail Carrier; [oth. writ.] I had written a short poem to honor along time friend that had deceased, published in the local paper.; [pers.] My love and respect me to write "Eternal Love" I hope the words I wrote will inspire others to take time for the elderly and each other.; [a.] Lebanon, MO

SULLIVAN, ZENIA DELL
[b.] February 7, 1965, Monroe, LA; [p.] Roy W. and Lois D. Rice; [m.] Robert Lee Sullivan Jr., May 24, 1985; [ed.] G.E.D. Little Rock, Arkansas BA Degree, English Educ. 1995, University of Arkansas at Monticello; [occ.] Substitute Teacher, Crossett School District, AR; [hon.] Dean's List; [oth. writ.] Several poems and short stories; [a.] Crossett, AR

SUMMERS, LINDA
[pen.] Susan; [b.] January 19, 1946, Austria; [p.] Maria Magdalena and Joseph; [ch.] Travis, Samantha, Kelli; [ed.] High School Irodology Life and Education and the Universe of Life. Taught by the Holy Spirit and God; [occ.] Mother, Educator, Volunteer in Schools; [pers.] I know that we were all created by the beauty of love. That our destination is of place, love and harmony. That the reason me suffer is because of our lack up proper knowledge. We are our brother and sisters keepers for life.; [a.] Breckenridge, CO

SUMRALL, COURTNEY
[pen.] Forrest, Alanis; [b.] January 21, 1980, Methodist Medical Center; [p.] Angela and Paul Sumrall; [m.] 10th Grade Richland High School; [ch.] Student; [ed.] Soccer, Band, Beta Club, U.N. Mock Security Council, Track Volleyball; [occ.] Honor Student; [a.] Richland, MS

SUTHERLAND, GENE N.
[b.] March 1, 1950, Everett, WA; [p.] Norman and Viola Sutherland; [m.] Judi (Joslin) Sutherland, July 3, 1971; [ch.] Jeremy, Jason and Johanna; [ed.] Cascade High (Everett), Northwest College, Cariboo College; [occ.] Electrical/Control Systems Designer, Harris Group Inc. Seattle, WA; [pers.] I write what I am experience and feel. To do anything less would be a lie.; [a.] Everett, WA

SUTTON, ANGIE
[b.] June 19, 1976, Puyallup, WA; [ch.] Kylee Marie Carr; [ed.] Franklin Middle School, A.C. Davis High School; [occ.] Student; [memb.] FBLA; [hon.] Student at the month 3 times, Honor Roll 3 times through High School, Business Certificate for Completing 99 Business Credits; [pers.] Life is only what you make of it. Life is a test of your strength and hope. And with hope there will be a better tomorrow.; [a.] Yakima, WA

SVEDAS, DANIEL MARTIN
[pen.] Dan; [b.] August 4, 1972, Pomona, CA; [p.] Mary and Steve Burton; [ed.] Damien High School, Pitzer College - B.A. Chicano Studies and Psychology; [occ.] Document Clerk; [hon.] Chicano Studies Award for Academic Excellence. Ford Foundation Scholarship for Continuing Education; [pers.] The Chicano/Latino experience has offered me a wonderful view of our society. Giving me a state of its strengths, weakness, and the direction my people need to take to move forward. My brothers and sisters are my greatest influence.; [a.] Altadena, CA

SVEITIS, BARBARA STEFANIA
[pen.] Basia; [b.] June 3, 1940, Chelm, Poland; [p.] Chester and Wincentyna Franecka Glowacki; [m.] Joseph T. Sveitis, September 9, 1961; [ch.] Elizabeth, Carol Ann, Thomas J.; [ed.] Graduated St. Casimir High, Chicago IL Presently Attending Florissant Valley Community College; [memb.] Polish Falcons of America, Polish National Alliance, Distinguished of International Society of Poets; [hon.] Awards in oil Painting. Received two Editor's Choice Awards in 1995; [oth. writ.] My poem "great marriages" published in anthologies "garden of life" and "a path not taken" was dedicated to my husband on our 34th wedding anniversary. A poem was published in my college literary magazine "the voyageur." My latest poem "the journey" will be published this summer in the anthology "spirit of the age."; [pers.] I write for people of all ages. As a poet I like to touch the readers heart and soul and create significance of life. My poems reflect real life experiences. I am dedicating my poem "Internment" in memory of my dearest mother.; [a.] Saint Louis, MO

SWANGIN, TERICA LYNN
[b.] May 12, 1979, Edison, NJ; [p.] Thomas Swangin Jr., and Marilyn Swangin; [ed.] 11th grader at McCorristin Catholic H.S. Hamilton, NJ; [occ.] Student; [memb.] National Honor Society, Key Club, Evironmental Club, French Club, Math League, SADD (Students against Drunk Drivers), year book Club, Mock Trial, Newspaper Staff. Production Crew member of Cable Weekly Show: "Catholic Corner".; [hon.] 1991 Create an Ad winner for the Burlington County Jimes (newspaper) Westampton Middle School Academic Excellence Award, Rogate's Gifted and Talented Award (1993); [pers.] I love to write about nature because it is the only real history book known that allows us to understand the origins of our very existence.; [a.] Westampton, NJ

SWEENEY, SANDRA CHRISTINE
[pen.] Christine Ireland; [b.] July 23, 1956, Margarettville, NY; [p.] Dr Lenemaja Friedman and James Sweeney; [ed.] Los Angeles city College, Los Angeles Valley College, Counselor Hollywood Professional School Teacher; [occ.] Warner Bros Studio Facilities Set Lighting; [memb.] Exolic Feline Breeding Compound, Smithsnian Museum; [hon.] Emergency Warden Warner Bros Studio Emergency Services; [oth. writ.] Last anthology of The National Library of Poetry (1 entry) Local Magazine "In The Hood"; [pers.] Knowledge is the key! Life is my store house of experiences I have to share with you.; [a.] Sherman Oaks, CA

SWEIGART, DENA L.
[pen.] Dena Loree Sweigart; [b.] September 27, 1980; [pers.] To fantasize about one's discontent, to make a memory of frozen beauty. It is an escape and a survival, an insanity and a salvation.

SYUND, ELLIE
[b.] April 10, 1981, Wyoming; [p.] Mr. John and Sheila Syund; [ed.] I went to Overland Elementary and now I'm attending white mountain Junior High; [hon.] I've gotten many Awards for Sports and have been on the Honor Roll Several Times; [oth. writ.] In my free time I love writing other poetry. My poetry is how I've felt about things and had no other way to express except by poetry.; [pers.] All I have to say is hat I believe it's not how some one look it's how good they looks from the inside.; [a.] Rock springs, WY

SZABO, BRENT KELLY
[pen.] "Loks"; [b.] May 15, 1969, Gary, IN; [p.] James Szabo, Denise Mair; [m.] William Walls, November 28, 1994; [ch.] Baxter, Bernie, Pandora, Sly; [occ.] Owner of Design Studio; [memb.] National Forensics League; [hon.] Outstanding contribution for Choreography, 1st place in writing contest sponsored by Inner City in New York; [oth. writ.] Recently published in book entitled "Tomorrow Never Knows" with a poem entitled "Perceptional Thought Process Of a Transparent Nothing!; [pers.] This writing and my little piece of this book is for my father - I'll miss him always - forget him never. For you Dad... James Szabo.; [a.] San Diego, CA

SZULEWSKI, JENNIFER
[b.] October 22, 1980, Morristown, TN; [p.] Paul Szulewski, Karen Reed; [ed.] Nashua, Catholic Regional Junior High School, 9th Grade; [occ.] Student; [memb.] YMCA, Band, Year Book; [hon.] Band, Sports; [oth. writ.] None published; [pers.] I like to write poetry because it gives me a way to express my feelings. I got interested in poetry after reading "The Raven" Edgar Allan Poe, and some of the poetry written by a good friend Beth Guerrette.; [a.] Nashua, NH

TAEGEL, ANDREW ROBERT
[b.] January 30, 1982, Kansas City, KS; [p.] Richard, Tere Taegel; [ed.] Ridgeview Elem., Liberty Middle Sch, Liberty Jr. High; [occ.] Student; [oth. writ.] Several poems unpublished as yet; [a.] Liberty, MO

TAG, AMY
[b.] January 10, 1980, Springfield, MO; [p.] Ronny Tag and Carol Tag; [ed.] Springfield Catholic High School; [occ.] Student; [memb.] National Forensics League, Thespian Society; [hon.] Lettered in Forensics; [oth. writ.] No other published writings; [pers.] I write to evoke deep thoughts and to make people question whether popular belief holds any truth.; [a.] Springfield, MO

TAGER, ROBERT E.
[b.] March 13, 1971, Johannesburg, South Africa; [ed.] Lyttelton Manor High School; [occ.] Screenplay writer; [oth. writ.] I am currently working on my next screenplay, a science fiction thriller; [pers.] I attempt to illuminate the paradox that is mankind. I have been greatly influenced by the poetry of William Blake and Robert Frost, as well as T.S. Elliots' The Wasteland.; [a.] San Diego, CA

TAHFOOT, JONATHAN
[pers.] Student-Montreat College Temporary residence: Black Mountain, NC, Earth.

TALLMAN, EVELYN
[b.] Novemver 13, 1922, So. Westerlo, NY; [p.] Mrs. Hazel F. Mabie; [m.] Deceased, January 23, 1940; [ch.] One; [ed.] Greenville High School, National Baking School, 835 Diversey Parkway Chicago, Illinois; [occ.] Retired I write poetry; [memb.] Social Service by Albany County Social Security Benefits; [hon.] Golden Poetry Gram World of Poetry

TAM, MAXINE
[b.] April 24, 1985, West Shore, OH; [p.] Shirley Tam, Thomas Tam; [a.] Twinsburg, OH

TANCREDI, JANINE
[pen.] Janine Tancredi; [b.] July 23, 1979, Delaware; [p.] Janie Seigfried and Joe Tancredi; [ed.] I plan to successfully complete high-school and attend college with my major being in social sciences; [oth. writ.] "Voices" "Permanent Scars" "Confusion" Only a Friend" Hidden Feelings" Regreted Anger"; [pers.] The only way to overcome life's obstacles is to approach all situations with an open mind. I'd like to give a special thanks to C. Macecevic who has helped me more than she can possibly know.; [a.] Delaware, PA

TAVOULARIS, ORIANA NICOLE
[b.] May 31, 1968, Torrance, CA; [p.] Dr. Tom and Janine Tavoularis; [ed.] High School: Miraleste College: El Camino, U.S.C., California State University Long Beach; [memb.] Greek Orthodox Church in Long Beach CA, Long Beach California Community Playhouse, Who's Who Among American High School Students; [hon.] Won first place in drama festival in college, starred, wrote, choreographed USC student film nominated for a student Academy award, High School varsity track-CIF three years, Presidential athletic award -two years; [oth. writ.] 30 poems, 5 short stories, 1 full length spec-scrip for sit-com "coach", 1 full length dramatic play, sports writer for El Camino newspaper, Staff writer and advertising manager for high school newspaper; [pers.] The beauty of life is in the beauty of the souls that reflects an inner force to reach beyond the mind.; [a.] Rancho Palos Verdes, CA

TAYLOR, STEPHEN ALEXANDER
[b.] May 6, 1964, Anson County; [p.] George and Vangeleen Taylor; [ed.] Bowman Sr High, Anson Community College; [occ.] Artist of Steel Native American Art; [pers.] My inner most feelings and thoughts flow when writing poetry. Due to my native american heritage I realize the feelings of future and past native americans, for this I write.; [a.] Peachland, NC

TELLES, DANIEL
[pen.] Daniel (Dan); [b.] April 3, 1954, El Paso; [p.] Conception M. Limas; [ch.] Jennifer M. Telles, Lisa M. Telles; [ed.] Austin High School Class of 1972; [occ.] Lead Computer Operator A.O. Smith Water Products Corp.; [memb.] National Rose Society, National Geographic Society; [hon.] All league Shortstop and Outfielder Amateur Softball League Foreman for two Federal Cases; [oth. writ.] Poems not mentioned but will be submitted in time; [pers.] I always try to do my best, and don't give up and if you don't try you'll never some day I will be a famous poet!; [a.] El Paso, TX

TEMPLETON, MELISSA
[pen.] Jane Johnson; [b.] January 3, 1978, Flint, MI; [p.] James Rutherford, Cindy Templeton; [ed.] Millington High, Tuscola Technology Center; [memb.] Future Homemakers of America; [hon.] Honor Roll, Perfect Attendance; [oth. writ.] I write poems for myself or for friends. My first poem I sent in will be published by The National Library of Poetry. It is just a sample of my other writings. It is also my most valuable ones too.; [pers.] Life is too short to be serious all the time. Most of life should be lived with a smile and a laugh. You never know when yours will end!; [a.] Millington, MI

TERRELL, MARIE
[b.] August 23, 1939, Poplarville, MS; [p.] Mr. and Mrs. Hubert Cowart; [m.] Tommy Terrell, January 5, 1974; [ch.] Sandra, Shelia, Mary K., John, Cindy; [ed.] 11 Grade and Cosmetology; [occ.] Retired; [pers.] My husband married me with 5 kids and adopted them for his own. He is very special to me.; [a.] Grannis, AR

THATCHER, TODD C.
[b.] January 25, 1980, Woodburym, NJ; [p.] Robert Thatcher and Kim Thatcher; [ed.] Currently in 10th grade at Kingsway Regional High School; [occ.] School; [memb.] School Newspaper; [hon.] Numerous Academic Awards; [oth. writ.] One book, The Slumbering Fire, which is a fantasy novel currently seeking publication; [pers.] I try to always portray accurately the essence of human nature and tell an interesting story in all of my work.; [a.] Mullica Hill, NJ

THEIRER, LUANN
[b.] July 7, 1946, MN; [ed.] A.D. in Nursing, B.S. from College of St. Francis; [occ.] R.N.; [memb.] Ill Nurses Asso.; [hon.] Poem published in Local Religious Mag.; [pers.] Poetry should reflect man's inner conflicts.; [a.] Carol Stream, IL

THOLEN, ANN L.
[ed.] Ph D pending NYU, MA Teaching NYU, BSLL Georgetown; [occ.] Disabled (head injured), Former technical writer; [memb.] AAVW, Moravrain Church; [oth. writ.] Computer manuals, grant proposals, test plans, training manuals; [pers.] I am head injured with poor short term memory and concentration. So, I have switched to poetry.; [a.] Allentown, PA

THOMAS, ARTHUR, R.
[pen.] Art Thomas; [b.] October 7, 1911, England; [p.] Frank Thomas-Rhoda Fisher; [m.] Arline Duerr, April 13, 1946; [ch.] Patricia, Kaye, Peggy; [ed.] Waldo High School, Waldo Florida - 1929; [occ.] Retired; [memb.] Masonic Orders; [hon.] Presidential Citation WW II Bronze Star; [oth. writ.] None published, other WW II poems some 300 letters I wrote to Arline. She saved them all and the make great reading; [pers.] I was communications chief in the radio halftrack, 14th armor DLV which kept me in a forward position which we were in combat.; [a.] Rocherster, NY

THOMAS, JODY D.
[b.] April 12, 1954, North Tonawanda, NY; [p.] Charles and Peggy Drapo; [m.] Jeffrey D. Thomas, April 24, 1976; [ch.] Shannon and Kelly Thomas; [ed.] Tonawanda High School, Doyle Beauty School; [occ.] Child care Worker; [oth. writ.] This is my first one printed; [pers.] I write as an outlet for my feelings and past experiences in hopes of turning then around to speak to someone and help comfort them whether it be laughter or in seriousness.; [a.] Denton, TX

THOMAS, ROSIE M.
[b.] June 13, 1949, Greenville, AL; [p.] Willie and Lola Patterson; [ch.] Christopher and Nicole; [ed.] Asst Degree Nursing University State of New York; [occ.] R.N.; [memb.] New Salem Baptist Church Health Awareness Commit. Association Operating Room Nurses Vol for Domestic Violence Group; [pers.] I believe that my writings express my deep feelings for people and life.

THOMAS, THERESSA LYNN
[b.] January 26, 1959, Houston, TX; [p.] Ruben Harper Jr., Merline Harper; [ch.] Kwjuana La'Shae, Theresa Lynnae'; [ed.] Ross Shaw Sterling High, Houston Community College, TExas School of Business; [occ.] Supervisor of File Clerks/Records, Davis and Shank P.C., Houston, TX; [memb.] New light Christian Center Church, Women of the Word; [pers.] The writing of poetry is a tool for man to get in touch with his emotions, feelings, like and dislikes. Writing it down cures the mind and souls and free the spirit.; [a.] Houston, TX

THOMPSON, CHELSEA
[pen.] Chelsea Thompson; [b.] August 18, 1969, Philadelphia, PA; [p.] Patricia Thompson - Elliot Brown; [ch.] Marian and Patricia; [ed.] Completed High School; [occ.] Homemaker; [oth. writ.] Various Poems; [pers.] My writing reflects my inner feelings.; [a.] Philadelphia, PA

THOMPSON, ESTELLE
[b.] Senior Citizen, Portsmouth, VA; [p.] Rev. and Mrs Major Weale; [ch.] Bob Thompson, Ben Thompson; [ed.] Booker T. Washington High School, Hampton Institute; [occ.] New york city Dept. of Social Services (Retired); [memb.] Mid-West Afro-American Theater Alliance, Brooks Memorial United Methodist church, Richard B. Harrison Players, OASIS, American War Mothers, Women's Society of Christians Service; [hon.] Brooks Memorial United Methodist Church -Service Award, The Youth -Elderserve Pilot Project Certificate; [pers.] I have spent much of my life performing dramatics readings of the literary words of Afro-American Writers. It was this experience that inspired me to try my hand at writing poetry.; [a.] Charlestown, WV

THOMPSON, HEATHER
[b.] August 16, 1971, Provo, UT; [p.] Douglas and Vickie Thompson; [ed.] A.A. from Ricks College (Genera) B.S. From Utah State University in English (Technical/Professional Writing); [occ.] Lockheed Martin of Idaho in document control at the Test Reactor Areg; [hon.] Dean's List; [oth. writ.] Short stories (fiction), poetry, advertisements; [pers.] I have been greatly influenced by Rita Dove and strive to make my poetry as influential and grabbing as hers.; [a.] Idaho Falls, ID

THOMPSON, LEE-ANNE MCGRATH
[pen.] Lee-Anne McGrath; [b.] May 16, 1938, Toronto, Ontario, Canada; [p.] Mr. and Mrs. Donald Brooks; [m.] Thomas W. Thompson, December 14, 1990; [ch.] Choi Shorter, Fred Johnson; [ed.] Danforth High, Det. Police Academy, Det College of Business; [occ.] Fire/Security Supervisor Chrysler; [oth. writ.] "I had a talk with Jesus", "Pictures in the Sky", "God's Wonderful Word", "If God Can Change Me"; [pers.] All of my poems are of a spiritual nature. Inspired by God's beauty in all Natural Settings.; [a.] Detroit, MI

THORN, CYNTHIA AUSTIN
[pen.] Cynthia Fujii, Cynthia Austin; [b.] February 24, 1950, Dallas, TX; [p.] Kenneth Yoshito Fujii and Anita Esperanza Fujii; [m.] George E. Austin (Deceased), Kenneth Wayne Thorn, July 3, 1994; [ch.] Christopher Robin Austin; [ed.] El Centro College: Associate of Arts and Sciences Degree; [occ.] Retail Fashion Industry, writer, housewife, and mother; [memb.] Bryan Adams High School: Parent, Teachers, and Student Assoc.; [hon.] National Collegiate of Social Sciences Award, Phi Theta Kappa Honor, Fraternity, Harry S. Truman Scholarship Nominee, National Alumni Association of Phi Theta Kappa Fraternity; [oth. writ.] "When the Night is over", "For I am like a newborn", "Hello Holy Spirit", "Abba Father I Love You", "That Warrior Boy of Mine", "That Warrior Boy for Christ", "Our Lord Is Coming Back for Us", "Oh, Faithful Loved One Such As I", "A Love That Surpass All Time", "I only wanted to tell them that love was the name of your game", "Lord Let Me hold Fast To Thy Ways", "King David's Cave", "Love Is", "Take Me Anywhere, Lord", and numerous others; [pers.] If I ever had anything to be grateful for my....life, it would be to Our Heavenly Father and His son Jesus Christ, for allowing me to get to know Him and experience his love and Christ Jesus' love, through His sweet Holy spirit who is within us all, and available to all if only for the asking.; [a.] Dallas, TX

THORNTON, ALISON REED
[p.] April 17, 1977, Houston TX; [m.] Sharon W. Thornton and Joseph Thornton; [ed.] High School Education - 2 year Apprenticeship as silversmith; [occ.] Busser; [oth. writ.] 2 Books; [pers.] Within my philosophies I strive to comprehend and experience as much of the/my surroundings as possible sharing much of what I've grown to believe while revealing deep within my count. growth or expansion. Also striving to not obstructing anymore path in a negative or false way.; [a.] Winchester, VA

THORNTON, SARA
[pen.] Bear; [b.] September 24, 1979, Boise, ID; [p.] Kathy Zancher, Jerry Thornton; [ed.] Meridian High School; [occ.] Student, Junior High School, volunteer at Boise V.A. medical center; [memb.] Yough American Bowling Alliance; [hon.] $100.00 Scholarship from Young American Bowling Alliance; [oth. writ.] Written other poetry for own enjoyment; [pers.] Poems reflect my own feelings, and I have been greatly influenced by many poets; [a.] Boise, ID

THUSAT, JOSHUA
[pen.] Horst Thusat; [b.] August 31, 1980, Port Clinton, OH; [p.] Marcina and David Thusat; [ed.] Sophomore in High School; [hon.] Superior Music Award for Solo and Ensemble, Highest in talent for poetry Freshman; [oth. writ.] Several poems written in local and school newspaper. Other stories surely to come in the future.; [pers.] A poet, to me, is a person who puts his hands in the boiling water to tell about it to other people. I am a person who has known what it is like to feel lost, sad, afraid, and many other things. I'm conclude, although the tog pipes play loudly, see everything to the end, so the story has a beginning, turning point, and ending.; [a.] Port Clinton, OH

TICE, BRADLEY S.
[b.] October 6, 1959, Palo Alto, CA; [p.] Mr. L.T. Tice and Mrs. Paula N. Tice; [ed.] San Jose State University B.A. Degree in History 1987"; [occ.] Director of Research Advance Human Design; [memb.] New York Academy of Sciences, The Ohio Academy of Science Cahperd; [hon.] Editor's Choice Award 1995 (The National Library of Poetry), Best Poems of 1996, (The National Library of Poetry); [oth. writ.] (Book), Herbert Hoover's Intellectual Development (New York: Carlton Press, 1996); [pers.] The art of writing is not so much what you put down, as what you do not.; [a.] Cupertino, CA

TIDWELL, JUANITA
[b.] April 23, 1963, Atlanta, GA; [p.] Mr. and Mrs. John H. Strain; [m.] Terreel G. Tidwell, May 21, 1988; [ed.] Adairsville High School, Floyd Junior College, Senior-At Shorter College; [occ.] Customer Service Representative-Shaw Industries; [memb.] First Baptist Church of Canersville; [oth. writ.] Several articles written for college newspaper (Floyd Junior). This newspaper "The Six-Mile Post" was recognized as the best newspaper in a junior college competition.; [pers.] I am deeply moved by events that have occurred to my family members or close friends. This gives me inspired to write.; [a.] Cartersville, GA

TILLEY, JESSICA
[pen.] Ee-ore; [b.] April 23, 1976, Hartford, CT; [p.] Glenda Tilley-Kearns, Robert Keans; [ed.] Eat Hartford High School; [occ.] Photography Lab Technician; [hon.] Crossroads Poetry Award Adele-Lexwe Lewendowsky Literary Award; [oth. writ.] Crossroads literary magazine 91-94 Independent publications; [pers.] If only to make the pain tangible through words, then I have accomplished giving meaning to the memories.; [a.] Hartford, CT

TOCA, TEDI
[b.] November 11, 1961, Albany, NY; [p.] Theodore and Jewel Toca; [m.] Divorced; [ch.] Alexander Schulz; [ed.] Averill Park High, 1979, Degree in Progress, Hudson Valley Community College, plan to major in English and teach creative writing; [occ.] Secretary, State of NY agency; [memb.] Den Leader, Boy Scouts of America, Twin Rivers Council; [hon.] Publication in "A Muse To Follow", semi-finalist in contest, scouting -1 year service award; [oth. writ.] Poetry since 1978 - read at local "open mike" nights; [pers.] Writing has helped me understand my own life for years. The art of communication through reading poems of others and writing my own is my greatest joy and strength.; [a.] Averill Park, NY

TODA, JOY
[b.] June 6, 1976, Honolulu, HI; [p.] Goering Toda, Sharon Toda; [ed.] McKinley High School, Kapiolani Community College; [occ.] Student; [pers.] I would like to thank my mother for her encouragement and George Wn for being my inspiration. Some people express themselves with words, others with pictures. The main thing is to be able to communicate because in life, that is most important. Smile from your heart!; [a.] Honolulu, HI

TONEY, DAVID
[b.] September 10, 1984, Santa Monica, CA; [p.] Linda and Terry Toney; [ed.] Stoney Brooke Christian School Grade 6; [memb.] Soccer, Basketball, and football teams; [hon.] "A" Honor roll, Soccer Championship - 1995 division 4 AYSO, football champions 1995; [oth. writ.] Children's book, "Dinasours" and Assorted poems and short stories; [a.] Mission Veijo, CA

TOOMBS, SHAWN
[pen.] Shawn Michael Toombs Guldenschuh; [b.] March 18, 1970, Warsaw, NY; [p.] Donald Guldenschuh and Mary Toombs; [m.] Patty Toombs, February 14, 1992; [ch.] Stepson Robert Macomber, Son Shawn Toombs Jr., Daughter Ashley Toombs; [ed.] Elementary - #41 Kodak Park-Rochester, NY, Jr High - John Marshall High School - Ridge Way Ave. Rocherster, NY, H.S.-Edison Tech. - Colfox St, Rochester, NY, G.E.D. - Our lady of Mersy (7-92)- Greece, Rochester, NY; [oth. writ.] Many other poems that have not yet been published or seen; [a.] Mount Morris, NY

TORCASSO, MARK STEVEN
[b.] September 7, 1964, Alhambra, CA; [p.] Dominic Torcasso, Valerie Torcasso; [m.] Nena A. Torcasso, February 20, 1993; [ed.] San Marino High School Graduate; [occ.] Building contractor, specializing in framing houses; [memb.] NAUS: Against vivasection: Humane Society, Natural Resources Defense Council, Suspected Child Abuse and Neglect. (S.C.A.N.); [pers.] The world I know is a beautiful place, mostly because I share it with my inspiration, my beautiful wife Nena. Unfortunately there are problems with the world but peace is within all of us, treat all creature big and small with love and respect and we can change the world.; [a.] Greendrier, AR

TOUVILLE, TAMMY DIANE
[b.] December 8, 1969, Guernsey, OH; [p.] Everett Wickham, Linda Diane Clewell; [m.] Nick Allen Touville, November 8, 1991; [ch.] Nichoel Wickham; [ed.] Byesville Elem. Byesville Ohio, Springfield High, Holland Ohio; [occ.] Cambridge Cleaners and Housewife; [pers.] I have been influence by all the early poets and mostly give thanks to all my family who has inspired me to fulfill my dream. Specially my Aunt Vicky Jacobs, and foster mother Alesia Tracy who helped me keep my dreams alive.; [a.] Cambridge, OH

TRACEY, JOHNSON
[b.] May 13, 1969, Kansas City, MO; [p.] Kathy Kay Byrd; [ch.] Aaron, Jermaine and Anthony; [ed.] Van Horn High School, Penn Valley Community College, Concorde Career Institute (college); [hon.] Outstanding student of the month award and the Deans list of the term award at concorde Career Institute; [oth. writ.] Expressions of Love, The Spirit of Love, Stand on Demand, A psalm of dedication, Eyes of love and many others; [pers.] I believe that the expressions of love come in many ways. I strive to express the beauty of life in my poetry, and what I hope to gain through my writing is the hearts of others.; [a.] Kansas City, MO

TRAVELER, CLAIRE W.
[b.] July 30, 1944, Bronx, NY; [p.] Francis Renner and Dolores Schmidt; [ed.] Currently enrolled in Masters Program in Education with concentration in Special Education; [occ.] Teacher of Children with learning disabilities-Escondido, CA; [memb.] Kappa Delta Pi Storymakers-a women's journal writing community chapel of awareness spiritualist church; [oth. writ.] Poetry published in Flatbush Life and Mira Costa College literary Magazine Tidepools, Co Author: When Woman Write Their Lives, and Life Sentences published by Wild Flower Hotline; [pers.] I am a believer in the hopes and dreams of the future - The Children of Today.; [a.] Escondido, CA

TREADWAY, HELENE G.
[p.] George Lester - Sadie Lester (Deceased); [m.] C. James Treadway; [ch.] Bonita, Lester, Phillips, grandchildren: Dustin and Heather; [memb.] 1st Baptist (Erwin) Teacher - Choir Member - P.T.O. - AARP Dist. Mem. ISP; [oth. writ.] Children's stories, and children's poems. Hundreds of other poems. Some published by the National Library of Poetry.; [pers.] My poems address, the greatest influences in my life. My love for God, family, country - friends. It is my way of expressing by appreciation for each of the above. I cannot ever remember not loving poetry. It has always been a vital port of my being.; [a.] Erwin, NC

TREGELLAS, JAN MARIE
[pen.] Jan Marie Tregallas; [b.] March 13, 1970, Grangeville, ID; [p.] Larry and Marilyn Tregellas; [ed.] Graduated 1994 from Boise State Univ. with BA in Business Admin.; [occ.] End user Specialist for a food broker; [hon.] Deans list, nominated to attend Nat'l Youth leadership Council in Washington DC; [pers.] This poem is in memory of my father Larry Tregellas. I wrote it shortly after his death. I hope it will help others with their questions after losing a loved one to suicide.; [a.] Mendian, ID

TRIMBLETT, KIMBERLY
[b.] September 10, 1974, Nutley, NJ; [p.] Catherine and Henry Trimblett; [ed.] Nutely High School, Montclair State University; [occ.] Full time college student, part time receptionist; [oth. writ.] Free Lance writing- (other poems and short stories); [pers.] My writing is a realistic reflection of my experiences and emotions. My poems in essence, are an exploration of life. I have been influenced by such poets as William Blake, Dylan Thomas and Anne Sexter.; [a.] Nutley, NJ

TRIMMELL, JERRY L.
[b.] January 11, 1974, Frankfurt, Germany; [ed.] Wichita high School West, Friends University College; [occ.] Post Office Date Conversion Operator; [oth. writ.] Numerous unpublished poems and short stories; [pers.] Humanity should abandon materialism in exchange for a perfectly formed grapefruit.; [a.] Wichita, KS

TRINQUE, MYRA
[b.] May 9, 1920, Texas; [p.] Claud and Ola Carroll; [m.] Eddie Trinque, June 8, 1952; [ch.] Donald; [ed.] Graduated from Howland High School and Post graduate from Roxton Texas High School. One semester in Western Baptist Bible College; [occ.] Retired; [memb.] Judson memorial Baptist Church - Bowling Leagues in Pinole, CA; [hon.] Valedictorian of High School class; [oth. writ.] Not published; [pers.] "God is my refuge", my friend, my guide I am a born again believer that Jesus Christ is my only way to heaven. His blood covers my sins from the eyes of God. That God for this assurance.; [a.] Richmond, CA

TROTT, JEAN S.
[b.] October 8, 1925, Galesville, MD; [p.] Louis Siegert, Sophie Siegert; [m.] Calvin C. Trott, May 19, 1947; [ch.] Stuart, Bonnie, Chris; [ed.] Southern High School (Lothian, Md.), Strayer's College - Baltimore, MD; [occ.] Retired 1988 as office Services Manager for Central Office of A.A. Co. Public School System, Annapolis; [memb.] Anne Arundel Co. Retired Teachers Assoc., Maryland Retired Teachers Assoc., United Methodist Church; [oth. writ.] Nothing

published (write mostly for my own amusement and other's amazement); [pers.] I have always tried to do my very best at any task no matter how small or large that task might be.; [a.] Galesville, MD

TRUDEAU, MIMI
[b.] March 20, 1942, Saint Paul, MN; [m.] Donald Lee Burg, June 23, 1988; [ch.] Brent and Phillip Griffin; [ed.] B.S. Secondary English Emphasis: Writing University of Minnesota M.E.D. Guidance and Couseling University of Wisconsin; [occ.] Volunteer couseling for chronically ill; [memb.] CFIDS Assoc. of America, Minnesota CFS Association, Wisconsin CFS Association, National Fibromyalgia Assn., National Sjogren's Assn., American Assn. of Counselling, Poets in the Schools Program; [hon.] Graduate Teaching Assistanship 1987, President Graduate Student, Counselling Organization; [oth. writ.] Asst. Editor: Chequamegon Sun, Bayfield County Newspaper, Editor: Various Newsletters, Published: Gypsy Cab Faces of Wisconsin, Numerous public readings; [pers.] I write from my personal experiences touching upon the gamut of human emotions.; [a.] River Falls, WI

TRUONG, ELLEN CRISTINA
[b.] July 19, 1947, Sarasota, FL; [p.] Wilbur and Mildred Witmer; [m.] Hop Van Truong, August 6, 1982; [ed.] Leo High, Goshen College, George Washington University; [occ.] Editor of the Humane Consumer and Producer Guide, Washington, D.C.; [memb.] The Humane Society of the United States, American Society of Notaries, Chancel Choir; [hon.] I am acknowledged in several books by reknown author Dr. Michael W. Fox, which include Inhumane Society: The American Way of Exploiting Animals, Troubled Harvest, Seeds of Hope, The Boundless circle: Caring for Creatures and Creation.; [oth. writ.] National Geographic Society, Akwesasne Notes, Book review for International Network for Religion and Animals News; [pers.] My writings are influenced by native Americans and animal protections.; [a.] Arlington, VA

TUCKER, DANRECO MARTINEZ PEREZ
[pen.] S.A.B; [b.] April 27, 1976, Milledgeville, GA; [p.] Charlie Lester Tucker, Robin Louise Tucker; [ed.] Baldwin County High School, Milledgeville, GA; [occ.] I am studying to become a sports medicine major at Akron Univ.; [oth. writ.] My mother raised 5 children with the help of God Almighty, my great grandmother and my grandmothers. My mother willingness to survive inspired me to strive for my goals that I can. The other women in my life also helped as well.; [pers.] Most of my writings reflect my feelings towards things I loved or loved in the past, My dedication to my great grandmother Lucille Boyer, my Dad Charlie Lester Tucker and to Nocera Preze Tucker.; [a.] Milledgeville, GA

TUCKER, DARLENE M.
[b.] December 16, 1942, Romeo, MI; [m.] Dwayne K. Tucker, July 4, 1960; [ch.] Danae, Deirde, Dwayne II, Dawna; [ed.] Univ. Of Alaska; [occ.] Youth Counselor Family Centered Services/AYI, Fairbanks, Alaska; [memb.] Emer. Medical Tech. II, State of Alaska, CPR/1st Aid Instructor - Amer. Heart Anderson City Council - Land Use Planning Emer. Medical Services Director; [hon.] Fairbanks Community Mental Health Board of Directors '85-'88, Resource Center for Parent and Children Board of Directors '86-'88; [pers.] I believe by faith anything is possible, although often pictured in real life different from what man invisioned.; [a.] Anderson, AK

TUCKER, HANNAH JOY
[pen.] Frances Willard; [b.] December 12, 1940, San Antonio, TX; [p.] Harry Willard, Joy Willard; [m.] Glenn Falkenstien, September 26, 1964; [ch.] Three; [ed.] Mac Arthur High, "Mississippi State College for Women"; [occ.] Partner in Professional Mind Reading/Magic Act - "Falkenstein and Willard"; [memb.] "International Brotherhood of Magicians" "Society American Magicians" "A.F.T.R.A." and "A.G.V.A." "Miss San Antonio" 1959"; [hon.] (S.A.M.) ("Magicians Hall of Fame) and CBS (Magicians Favorite Magicians) "Psychic Entertainers Award" "D.R.A.G.O.N. Award (magic Act) Milbourne Christopher Award Danniger Award Stage Magicians of the Year"; [oth. writ.] Biographical Sketches magic Publications (Screenplay - Optioned by CBS - Life Story) "Gerri Magazine " Feature Article, " The Illusionist" Feature Article "Alexander" - Book on Mentalism introduction only; [pers.] I have always been in the "magic world". I am 4th generation "medium and "magician". I deeply believe that the "arts" is the bridge between the mental and spiritual worlds in which we live.; [a.] Sherman Oaks, CA

TURNER, TRACY
[pen.] Tahirah Turner; [b.] April 17, 1963, Phila, PA; [p.] Clyde J. Turner Sr. and Frances E. Williams; [ed.] U.S. Naval Academy, Phila. H.S. for Girls; [occ.] Commonwealth of PA, Income Maintenance Caseworker, UN. Air Force Reserves, E-5, Staff Sergeant; [pers.] By the power of God I press on day by day to try and record life as poetic as it is lived.; [a.] Philadelphia, PA

UNDERWOOD, JAI
[pen.] Jai Underwood; [b.] August 18, 1964, Plant City, FL; [p.] Wallace and Minnie Underwood; [m.] Julie Taylor, November 19, 1995; [ch.] Heather Nichole, Amber Danielle; [ed.] Plant City High, Business International, St. Pete Jr. College; [occ.] Entrepreneur, Tampa, FL; [oth. writ.] I have other poems, but they have never before been published.; [pers.] The feelings I express come from my heart. I believe the words anyone expresses if it comes from the heart are beautiful and a reflection of your soul.; [a.] Tampa, FL

UNGER, IRENE PERRY
[b.] August 23, 1960, Manhattan, NYC; [p.] Howard J. Perry; [ch.] Virginia Perry Unger; [ed.] Yonkers High School; [occ.] Administrative Assistant NYNEX; [oth. writ.] My life's journals since 1979, forever sweet places - Tomorrow never knows; [pers.] Each time my daughter writes me an "I Love You" note, it's as if I'm being hugged by an Angel. What a precious gift from heaven - my daughter.; [a.] Carmel, NY

URBAN, WILLIAM
[b.] July 15, 1974, Putnam, CT; [p.] Barbara Urban, Ronald Urban; [ed.] Pomfret School, US Naval Academy; [occ.] Midship, USN; [pers.] How do I look this good every single day? God bless America. Hey, for an hour's work I thought this poem wasn't that bad.; [a.] Annapolis, MD

VAN BEERS, KIRSTEN L.
[b.] August 1, 1952, Grand Rapids, MI; [p.] Wallace and Gladys Erickson; [m.] Dennis E. Tsujiuchi; [ch.] Scott, April, Anthony and Erica; [ed.] Canyon Del Oro High School, Long Beach City College; [occ.] Computer Operator, St. Mary Medical Center, LB, CA; [pers.] My thoughts and words have been inspired by my love of life and touched by the love of my dreams.; [a.] Paramount, CA

VAN COUR, ALICE CLEMONS BEYER
[pen.] Alice C. Van Cour; [ch.] Mitch, Ethel, Joanne, and Judy; [ed.] Lester, Carl Beyer and Denise Van Cour; [occ.] Retired ran a small Hotel; [memb.] Cottage Inn in Copenhagen for years which I enjoyed very much doing. Customer's called Ma Alice.; [hon.] When you down and feeling blue published in Famous poems of today, famous poetry Society 1995; [oth. writ.] Poem Our Home published in National Library of Poetry at Water Edge Editions choice award poem Bed of L. Fe published American Poetry, Anthology Summer 1995 by Arcadia poetry press; [pers.] My advise to anyone writing poetry is send it to contest etc - Hey you never know and it's worth a try.; [a.] Copenhagen, NY

VARELAS, DEBBIE G.
[b.] August 29, 1962, Tucson, AZ; [p.] Tony L. Gallego and Christina R. Gallego; [m.] Joseph D. Varelas, February, 1987; [ch.] Sarah Christina; [ed.] Sunnyside High, University of Arizona; [occ.] Accountant; [pers.] I like to write about feelings I have experienced throughout my life. I have been influenced by my Catholic Faith and by Poet James Douglas Morrison.; [a.] Tucson, AZ

VARGO, JUNE K.
[pen.] June K. Vargo; [b.] June 5, 1931, Pennsylvania; [p.] Susan and Michael Kanyan; [m.] Michael H. Vargo, June 30, 1951; [ch.] Susan Denora, Elizabeth Masia and Michael P. Vargo; [ed.] Graduated from Blairsville High School, Blairsville PA. Attended Indiana Hospital Sch. of Nursing Indiana, PA; [occ.] Retired from Monroe Country Health Dept. (School Health) Roch, NY; [memb.] United Methodist Women; [hon.] American Legion School Award. Award of Merit-Inter-National Society of Poets.; [oth. writ.] I completed Novels, 'The Catalpa Tree' and 'What Goes Around' in process of deliberation with agent; [pers.] Someone once said, 'The people who never fail are the people who never tried! I have been writing many years. Sometime success. Sometime not. My Protangist seem like my extended family and I love them.; [a.] Rochester, NY

VARJABEDIAN, LORI
[pen.] Lori Varjabedian; [b.] March 1, 1977, Vero Beach, FL; [p.] Deborah and Sumpad Varjabedian; [ed.] Vero Beach High School Indian River Community College; [occ.] Student at Treasure Coast Massage and Holistic Therapy; [memb.] The Sierra Club; [pers.] I don't write my poems... they write themselves. Inspiration lies in every gift our Mother Earth has to offer.; [a.] Vero Beach, FL

VAZIRI, MAZIAR
[pen.] Cyrus Caesar; [b.] December 15, 1971, Persia; [ed.] Queens College; [memb.] Golden Key National Honor Society; [hon.] Dean's List; [pers.] To enduring Persia, the land of artists and poets, where women are idealized. I hope someday soon you may break free from the chains of fundamentalist religion.; [a.] Fresh Meadows, NY

VEGA, MARILYN
[b.] March, 1973, Puerto Rico; [occ.] Emergency Room Technician, student; [oth. writ.] Personal collection of poems; [pers.] Write about whatever you want, don't worry about who's not going to like it.; [a.] IL

VELMERE, VICKI L.
[b.] July 25, 1954, Seedro Wooley, WA; [p.] Mr. and Mrs. George R. Davidson; [m.] David R. Velmere, October 10, 1993; [ch.] Penny Liebe, Mark Liebe, Jennifer Liebe; [occ.] Equipment Operator; [pers.] I look at nature, respect God's grace and try to reflect all of His glory in poetry. Today's world can be made liveable and the good remembered in poetry for tomorrow's youth.

VENDETTO, ALICE
[b.] August 4, 1917, West Haven, CT; [p.] Walter Squires, Olga Squires; [m.] Michael Vendetto, October 5, 1936; [ch.] Joan Di Mezza, Nicolina Gannon, Dolores Peterson, and Michael C. Vendetto; [ed.] Graduated from Commercial High School; [occ.] Retired. I was in charge of nurses, taking care of children.; [oth. writ.] Poems published by Sparrowgrass Poetry Forum Inc.; [pers.] After raising four children, and caring for my husband who was ill for eleven years, he passed away four years ago. I started to write poems, that I always wanted to do. My compassion for people, and my religion, I try to apply it to my poetry. My father fought me to be kind, and giving toward everyone. This is my goal in life.; [a.] Hamden, CT

VERNON, SHIRLEY MARIE
[b.] October 11, 1957, Jacksonville, AL; [p.] James Vernon and Louise Vernon; [ed.] Jacksonville High School, Jacksonville State University B.S. Degree in Accounting; [occ.] Administrative Assistant Tommy Turpin and Associates, CPA Birmingham, AL; [memb.] Alabama Association of Public Accountants Toastmaster's International, Unity of Birmingham Church, The Women of Vision International Network; [hon.] Dean's List, Magna Cum Laude, Best Student-Literature/College 1987, Best Speaker-Toastmaster's International; [oth. writ.] Two inspirational writings for Women of Vision, three poems written about the "Love and Milk and Honey" Paintings of Nationally recognized artist, John Soloman Sandridge, Short stories, articles and poems including "Beautiful Man, God's Masculine Art."; [pers.] "To write is to inspire, to inspire is to love and to love is to Heal." "When we inspire, love and heal ourselves we inspire, love and heal the world."; [a.] Birmingham, AL

VICK, JASON
[b.] October 6, 1977, Greenville, MS; [p.] Grady F. Vick, Jr. and Cindy Stokes; [memb.] Member of New Life Church of Millbook, AL; [hon.] Awarded "Friendliest" and "Best Christian Attitude" of New Life Academy; [pers.] "He is no fool who gives what he cannot keep, to gain what he cannot loose" -Jim Elliot. Give Jesus your trash, and in return, He will give you treasure, and eternal life.; [a.] Prattville, AL

VICKLES, ELENI
[b.] October 22, 1952, Athens, Greece; [p.] Theodoros Papamihail, Maria Kinigalakis Papamihail; [m.] Harold Darwin Vickles, March 20, 1976; [ch.] Candy Marie, Aaron Matthew; [ed.] Nikea High School, Piraeus, Greece Colorado Christian University Lakewood, CO; [occ.] Student at Colorado Christian Double major Psychology, English; [memb.] Colorado Christian University Literary Club Gathered Cover Book Club Literary evening, Poetry reading at Colorado Chr. Univ.; [pers.] I desire to express into words, pain on paper. Being a bilingual, I have been asked in what language I think my poems. I hear my poems in the language of feelings and emotions which translated in whatever words are available.; [a.] Denver, CO

VIGDORCHICK, INNA RUTH
[b.] May 31, 1984, Riga, Latvia; [p.] Natalya, Leon; [ed.] 6ht grade at Miller Creek Middle School; [memb.] YMCA, SNL (Local Club); [hon.] President's Education Awards Program in Recognition of Outstanding Academic Achievement 1995; [oth. writ.] Several poems and stories (never published); [pers.] I greatly thank my 6th grade language arts teachers, Mrs. K. Phillips, for all of the inspiration and encouragement.; [a.] San Rafael, CA

VILLAVERDE, MARCELLIANO
[pen.] Marcelliano Villaverde; [b.] August 9, 1929, Onomea, HI; [p.] Deceased; [m.] Nani Villaverde, February 9, 1952; [ch.] Six, 18 grand; [ed.] AA, BA, MSW, MBNA-PHSM; [occ.] Retired; [memb.] ASCAP, UH Alumni, ASSN, (Troa) The Retired Officers ASSN, (DAV) Disabled American Veterans, State of Hawaii Constitutional Convention Delegate; [hon.] World of poetry, 7 Academy (As golden poet) awards, Australian Women's Executive Network Poetry Publication. "In Rundle Way", vantage press "New Voices in American Poetry" 1985 pp. 556-557, "Needs", "That's Life," "Gifts With Thanks", Single album, "A Hawaiian Christmas", "The Spirit Of Christmas", 500 Poetry Writings; [oth. writ.] Unpublished Manuscript Biographic Profile and History of ancient Hawaii, America, Spanish in Philippines: "Gold Fever" (Pending Publication), Mango CD: "My Paradise Hawaii", Theme released January 1996; [pers.] Capture the essence of the moment and the world will feel your heart, mind, soul, and "Time's wasted all who waste's time", (An original one liner).; [a.] Hilo, HI

VIRGONA, VALERIE F.
[b.] August 21, 1954, Belleville, IL; [m.] Richard J. Virgona, August 20, 1987; [ed.] A. S. George Washington University, B.S. The University of The State of New York Regents College; [occ.] Small Business owner, Horticultural Nursery; [memb.] Mt. Dora Chamber of Commerce; [oth. writ.] This is my first poem of many more to come; [pers.] I have a lifelong interest in comparative Religions, Spiritual Philosophy and Art. Daily meditation on the unity of all life provides me with much creative inspiration.; [a.] Tangerine, FL

VIX, LLOYD
[b.] June 21, 1931, Houston, MN; [p.] Lloyd and Lula Vix; [m.] June Marie (Ullaw) Vix, February 16, 1952; [ch.] Jacqueline, Betty, Thomas, Timothy, and Jayme; [ed.] Graduate Houston High; [occ.] Retired Manager of Manufacturing Engineering; [oth. writ.] Booklet (Come Along With Me) 99 pages of short stories and poetry, printed for our grand children; [pers.] I have captured my thoughts and with a few written words will attempt to create an image inviting you to understand the purpose of our lives, serving a greater power enjoying special moments with the ones you love.; [a.] Houston, MN

VON LUTZOW, BETTY POYER
[pen.] Betty Poyer von Lutzow; [b.] February 7, 1920, Chicago, IL; [p.] Stephen A. Poyer and Ethel M. Poyer; [m.] Robert W. von Lutzow, March 22, 1941; [ch.] Bonnie Sue, Robyne Lee, Robert W., Jr and Gary Stephen; [ed.] Starrett School for Girls (High), Grinnell College, Vogue School; [occ.] Homemaker; [hon.] Produced and directed 3 plays, "Seventeen", "Tom Sawyer", and "Brother Rat" - to benefit the Spanish American War veterans. My Father was a veteran of this war. A bronze bust of President Reagan I sculptured and was requested (a copy) by the White House. In the Spring of 1978 I was sculpting a bust of Ronald Reagan. It is larger than life-size (26" tall) and is cast in bronze. In April of that year Ronald Reagan, wife Nancy, and father Dr. Loyal Davis came to our home to se the work I was doing in in the clay. We had met him many times in the past at Trunk and Tusk meetings here in Phoenix. Pictures of the bronze sent to the Reagans, after they moved into the White House, brought a call from them requesting a copy of the bronze. The bust is now at the Reagan Library in California. I was honored by the foregoing.; [oth. writ.] Other poems published in local newspapers. "Christmas Scene", "My Love", "MY Friend", "My Way", "Mr. Wonderful", "Morning at Jollywood"; [pers.] My observation of the beauty in nature, and in life, is what inspires my poems.; [a.] Phoenix, AZ

VUCETICH, SHAUNA
[pen.] Shauna Vucetich; [b.] October 11, 1959, Pueblo, CO; [p.] David and Margaret Roscover; [m.] James Joseph Vucetich, April 4, 1981; [ed.] Silver Cord graduate, Pueblo Country High

School Business Certificate, Associate of Arts Degree in Business and Office Education from the University of Southern Colorado, and Continuing Education Courses Trinidad State Junior College; [memb.] American Quarter Horse Association United Church of Walsenburg's Quilter's Group; [hon.] Huerfano Country Certificate of Service on the Library Board, First Place Honor for the 1987 Arkansas Valley Journal Writing Contest, 1989 Colorado Press Association Photo Journalism Feature, Honorable Mention; [oth. writ.] Writing correspondent for the Arkansas Valley for three years. Poems published in the Mile High Society Anthology "Ariel" and previous anthologies of the National Library of Poetry.; [a.] Walsenburg, CO

WALDENMAIER, DAVE
[b.] May 29, 1980, Garland, TX; [ed.] Naaman Forest High School; [occ.] Student N.F.H.S.; [oth. writ.] Basically just a bunch of stuff I keep in folders and notebooks; [pers.] I use poetry to tell people what I believe life is (and Death) and to help myself cope with the fact that we all have to live, and we all have to die someday. I often use my poetry to write music, I have been inspired by Metallica.; [a.] Garland, TX

WALKER, CAROLYN GREENE
[b.] February 9, 1941, Pensacola, FL; [p.] Ed and Pearl Greene; [ch.] Sherri Michelle Walker; [ed.] San Jose State University, University of San Francisco; [occ.] Teacher - grade 3 O.B. Whaley School - Evergreen School District - San Jose, CA; [memb.] Santa Clara County Reading Association, National Alliance of Black School Educators, Emmanuel Baptist Church; [hon.] San Jose Police Department Adopt A School Program Award; [oth. writ.] Composed a variety of poems, have written several short stories based on experiences of self and others, compiled a collection of poems for future anthology publication.; [pers.] The rewards of writing is inspiring because of the audience it can reach which shares many of my personal thoughts and experiences. I am most influenced by Maya Angelou and Langston Hughes.; [a.] San Jose, CA

WALKER, MARGARET NASH
[b.] November 7, 1946, Providence, RI; [p.] Phelps and Maxine Walker; [m.] Richard Fluegel, April 2, 1988; [ch.] Jay Kyle, Krista Walker; [ed.] B.A. - Spanish - Denison Univ., B.S. - Allied Law - Univ. Central Fla., J.D. - Law - Mercer Univ.; [occ.] Lawyer; [memb.] Fla. Bar. Assoc.; [hon.] Dean's List Univ. Central Fla., Finalist Moot Court Competition - Mercer U.; [oth. writ.] Editorials in various local newspapers; [pers.] My poetry is the voice of my personal struggle to grow.; [a.] Saint Petersburg, FL

WALKER, MATTHEW AARON
[b.] September 29, 1971, Pawhuska, OK; [p.] Jack and Hazel Walker; [ed.] Barnsdall High School Oklahoma State University Texas A&M University; [occ.] Student; [memb.] Phi Gamma Delta, Texas Marine Mammal Stranding Network; [hon.] Phi Eta Sigma, Dean's List; [oth. writ.] Several poems published in College literary magazines, Articles in student press bulletin; [pers.] I write about who I really am and what truly feel so that others can make the same discoveries in themselves.; [a.] Galveston, TX

WALKER, VERNA J.
[b.] July 19, 1915, NC; [p.] Finley and Ava McGee Jarvis; [m.] Coleman L. Walker Sr. (Deceased), December 22, 1934; [ch.] C.L. Jr., Sid, Mary, Ava, Howard, Louise, Barbara and Sharon; [ed.] Kings Creek High, Caldwell Community College; [occ.] Retired, do Knitting, Quilting, Crocheting, and other Crafts; [memb.] Hollow Springs Primitive, Baptist Church, Hollow Springs Homemakers, Caldwell County Retired Senior Volunteer Person; [hon.] High School, Valedictorian. Dean's List in College, Graduated with Honors; [oth. writ.] For School publications, RSVP newsletter, and Miss.; [pers.] I must keep busy, I'd rather wear out than rust out.; [a.] Boomer, NC

WALL, EILEEN J.
[pen.] January 3, 1948, England; [ch.] Alex, David; [ed.] BA Classics, London, AS Nursing, BS Computer Science, BSN Nursing, Diploma in Education; [occ.] Clinical Care Coordinator, HIV Clinic; [pers.] My poetry expresses the universal connections between people, their God and their world.; [a.] San Diego, CA

WALLACE, C. GUY
[b.] December 9, 1911, Stephensville, TX; [p.] Myrtle Elizabeth and William Franklin; [m.] Newell May, September 28, 1935; [ch.] Guy Robert and Carl Franklin; [ed.] Frederick High School, Frederick, OK; [occ.] Retired; [memb.] First Baptist Church, Grand Junction, CO; [oth. writ.] Anticipating the publication of my song, "My Colorado Home"; [pers.] My inspiration for writing comes from God's majestic creations. I am especially influenced by the great 'outdoors'.; [a.] Grand Junction, CO

WALLACE, ETHEL BEATRICE
[pen.] Bea Wallace; [b.] October 21, 1919, Mills Co, TX; [p.] John and Nola Randles Long; [m.] John Ray Wallace, February 7, 1948; [ch.] John, Fred, Jim, Royce; [ed.] Goldthwaite High School; [occ.] Retired; [memb.] American Assoc. of Retired People (AARP), Trinity Christian Church; [pers.] Through my writing I strive to reflect my ideas and values about family, reality, personality, and a bit of imagination.; [a.] Ovalo, TX

WALTERS, KELLY
[b.] August 6, 1981, Toledo, OH; [p.] Laurie and Micheal Walters; [ed.] Bowsher High School 1st Year; [occ.] Not old enough; [memb.] Drama Club; [hon.] First One; [oth. writ.] Life, welcome to the world seen through my eyes, an ode to friendship, my little diamond...; [pers.] Poetry is one of the best things in life... your feelings put into words.; [a.] Toledo, OH

WALTON JR., JACK B.
[b.] January 28, 1970, Long Beach, CA; [p.] Jack and Mary Walton; [m.] Loretta Walton, September 16, 1995; [ch.] Nathan Clay; [ed.] St. John Bosco HS, Los Angeles Trade Tech.; [occ.] Service Writer; [memb.] Knights of Columbus, St. John Bosco Alumni Assn.; [hon.] Eagle Scout- Boy Scouts of America, Percussion Precision Award, Community Service Scholarship-Knights of Columbus, Outstanding Customer Service Award from SAAB-SCANIA; [oth. writ.] Anything that pops into my mind that also sounds unique or original.; [pers.] I get great pleasure from expressing my feelings through words and the thought that others may find pleasure from those words is spine-tingling.; [a.] Huntington Beach, CA

WARD, JENNA
[b.] December 20, 1976, Sacramento, CA; [p.] Linda and Gerald Ward; [ed.] High School Grad., Attending Stephen F. Austin State University; [occ.] Waitress; [pers.] I have been writing poetry since I was 10 years old. The first poem I wrote, I have lived by. "Live today, for tomorrow, remember yesterday, to forget the sorrow."; [a.] Lufkin, TX

WARD, TIMOTHY L.
[pen.] Draw Mit; [b.] August 4, 1956, Traverse City, MI; [p.] Carol Jane, Francis Porter; [ch.] Jeromy, Rebekah, Jessica, Jason, Joshua; [ed.] Biology, Chemistry, Bio-Organic Chemistry-Purdue University; [occ.] Pharmaceutical Chemist - Eli Lilly and Co., Instructor - Ivy Tech State College; [hon.] Ellsworth Scholarship, H.C. Brown Wetherill Scholar, Eli Lilly National needs fellow; [oth. writ.] Spectroscope evidence for a spirookirane Intermediate in the synthesis of 4- (Hydroky Methyl) - 2 - (dimethyleamino) methyl thiazole. Biocatalysis and Nineteenth Century Organic Chemistry: Conversion of D-Glucose into Quinoid Organics; [pers.] The past, present and future are now.; [a.] Lafayette, IN

WARE, DAVID CARL
[pen.] David C. Ware and D. C. Ware; [b.] May 4, 1937, Claymont, DE; [p.] Hiram B. and Beatrice Ware Sr.; [m.] Rebecca Louise Ware, November 24, 1984; [ed.] Eddystone High School - Graduate (Eddystone, PA); [occ.] Retired from Super Fresh Food Markets (A and P); [memb.] Granite Corinthian A.F. and A.M. Lodge #34 Talleyville, DE, NUR Temple A.A.O.N.M.S. of Wilmington, DE, Scottich Rite Consistory - Valley of Wilm., DE V.F.W. #5546 - Trainer, PA; [oth. writ.] Ocean Tide (poem), Wedding Night (poem), A Time of Decision (poem), My Mother (poem); [pers.] The first poem I ever wrote was in the first grade for my mother. I still have the original copy - 53 years later.; [a.] New Castle, DE

WARREN, CAROL HUGGINS
[b.] May 2, 1949, Elloree, SC; [p.] George Huggins and Grace Collier Huggins; [ch.] Sheri D. Warren, Jimmie Warren, Fritz Eric Oriol; [ed.] College graduate, Paralegal ABA Lehman College, Bronx, New York; [occ.] Paralegal; [memb.] Board of Directress, Southern Community Economic Dev. Council, President: Federated Youth Club, Columbia, SC; [oth. writ.] Short Story (in my skin) Poems: Dinae, 1955, Again The Dawn, Is God A Dictator, One Black Man's Dialogue; [a.] Columbia, SC

WASHINGTON, FELICIA ANN
[b.] July 18, 1968, Jackson, MS; [p.] Marva Mae Washington; [ch.] Marla Denise Washington; [ed.] BS. N. in Nursing; [occ.] Registered Nurse; [pers.] Every soul has an inner beauty. It is up to each individual the limits to which that beauty is expressed outward.; [a.] Jackson, MS

WATTS, MARGARET
[b.] May 31, 1933, Louisville, KY; [m.] Deceased; [ch.] Seven, eight grandchildren, one great grandchildren; [ed.] "Assoc. Degree of Nursing," Ursuline Academy, Jefferson Community College, Bellarmine College; [occ.] Registered Nurse; [memb.] Collect P.M.'s Precious Moments Club; [oth. writ.] Articles: 1) Feature writer - Bride and Groom, Inc., 2) "Dreams" - Published in Anthology "Tapestry of Words, 3) Church Articles; [pers.] I wrote this poem in tribute to my sister as I helped care for her while dying of cancer. Originally titled "to my loving sister Regine."

WEAVER, ROBIN EMILY
[pen.] Robin Emily; [b.] February 18, 1970, New York; [p.] Mr. Caleb and Rosa Weaver; [ed.] Bisphopville High in SC, Printing Trade School in NYC, Berkeley College in NYC; [occ.] Xerox Operator, Docuprint in New York; [pers.] My writings comes from within my soul and heart. The words and thoughts are about how a person that I love touches my soul.; [a.] New York, NY

WEBER, MICHAEL BRIT
[b.] Febuary 13, 1976, E. Lansing, Mich; [p.] Brit Weber and Ruth Ann Weber; [ed.] GED; [occ.] waiter; [oth. writ.] none published; [a.] Ann Arbor, MI;

WEBSTER, CAMERON S.
[b.] August 2, 1971, Pasadena, CA; [p.] Dan Webster, Deborah Sanger; [ed.] B.A. in Literature, Vanderbilt University; [oth. writ.] Many poems and short stories, with more to come. I will also soon embark upon a novel and a screenplay.; [pers.] Much of my writing involves the relationship between human psychology and the human environment at the turn of the Millennium.; [a.] Portland, OR

WEDDINGTON, LOUISE
[b.] January 1, 1949, Centre, AL; [p.] Charles McBrayer, Mary McBrayer; [m.] David E. Weddington, December 5, 1974; [ch.] Nancy Ann, Casey Lee, Misty Dawn; [ed.] Cherokee Co. High, Centre, AL, Gadsden State College, Gadsden, AL, Ayers State College, Anniston, AL; [occ.] Nurse, Cherokee Co. Nursing Home, Centre, AL; [memb.] A.N.A., A.H.A.; [oth. writ.] Numerous poems I have written fro family and friends; [pers.] I strive to put on paper the feelings in my heart. I have been greatly influenced by my family and friends. Especially my sister Joan Mayhall, she holds a special place in my heart.; [a.] Centre, AL

WEIDENMANN, ELIZABETH
[b.] February 11, 1927, River Forest, IL; [p.] Helen Lucy and Myron Frank Sutherland; [m.] Divorced (February 2, 1988), September 25, 1948; [ch.] Steven Alan, Merri Lee; [ed.] Jr. College, S. Sem; [occ.] Retired; [hon.] Best Sportsmanship; [oth. writ.] "After almost 40 years" a poem printed in "world treasury of golden poems."; [pers.] I have three things I believe "to thine own self be true," the golden rule and that a lady exemplifies "sincere" simplicity, sympathy and serenity.; [a.] Vernon Hills, IL

WEIR, BELINDA C.
[b.] February 25, 1976, Jamaica; [p.] Cecil and Olivine Weir; [ed.] Suncoast Magret High School in Rivera Beach, FL, University South Florida, Tampa, FL; [occ.] Student studying to one day be a successful teacher; [hon.] Campus Compact - Volunteer Program-University of South Florida (USF) Adopt a school; [oth. writ.] Why Do They Wilt, 1993, National Library of Poetry, Tears of Fire; [pers.] With God all things are possible, I hope that I'll continue to make my parents proud and I've learned that good friends are hard to find - love you Christina Platt, forever true blue.; [a.] Tampa, FL

WEISFELNER, SARA R.
[b.] September 16, 1976, New Hyde Park, NY; [p.] Susan and Leon Weisfelner; [ed.] Herricks High School, currently a sophomore at New York Institute of Technology majoring in TV/Radio; [hon.] Awarded public service around November, 1995 for volunteer at the Holocaust Memorial and Educational Center of Nassau County; [oth. writ.] Poem A Lonely Soul Published in National Library of Poetry - Garden of Life.; [pers.] I write from my heart for my love - thank you Jeremy.; [a.] Albertson, NY

WEISS, SONDRA
[b.] November 30, 1936, Westfield, NY; [p.] Theodore and Virginia Peacock Skinner; [ch.] John Mollard, Elizabeth Otander, two grandsons, John and Bobby; [ed.] Long Island University, Pratt Institute, Hood College; [occ.] Retired Librarian; [hon.] University Honors Program, Optimates Honor Society, Albert A. Berman Memorial Senior Honors Award for Short Story "The Mystic Mirrors" Sigma Tau Delta National English Honor Society; [oth. writ.] Published in Journey of the Mind (Night's Bout) and at Water's Edge (Magical Midnight Moment). In the 25th Anniversary issue of Spectrum, Long Island University's Literary Publication of the University Honors Program, short stories, poetry aired on radio, songs.; [pers.] The memory of an intimate word lovingly spoken or unspoken, written or sung that is shared with a friend, will always bring a smile that warms the heart forever.; [a.] Maitland, FL

WELCH JR., ROBERT JAMES
[pen.] Bobby Welch; [b.] June 9, 1982, Long Island, NY; [p.] Robert Welch, Deborah Welch; [ed.] West Hernando Middle School; [occ.] Student; [memb.] The National Junior Beta Club, West Hernando Youth Athletics Club, Young America Bowling Association, YMCA Basketball League, Hernando County Sheriff's Junior Deputy League; [hon.] West Hernando Honor Roll, President Academic Fitness Award, Superintendent's Certificate of Excellence; [oth. writ.] Several poems, some of which were published in local newspapers; [pers.] My poetry allows me to express my thoughts to myself, as well as, to all who may read it.; [a.] Spring Hill, FL

WELLS, LAURENCE K.
[pen.] Laurence K. Wells; [b.] October 31, 1937, California; [p.] Deceased; [m.] Deceased, July 5, 1970; [ch.] Four; [ed.] High School, Some College; [occ.] Disabled; [oth. writ.] Just starting to write to help occupy my time and, keep my brain fresh!; [pers.] Since I love lost my wife and my children are grown, when I became disabled I needed something to do. Writing has always been a dream, and I enjoy it.; [a.] Hayward, CA

WENDT, JULIA
[pen.] Rye Wendt; [b.] August 19, 1981, Milwaukee; [p.] Jennifer and Peter; [ed.] Enrolled at Fred Moodry Jr. High Anaconda, Montana; [occ.] Jr. High School Student; [hon.] Delta Kappa Gamma 2nd Place State at Wisconsin 6th Grade 1993-94; [pers.] "You may say I'm a dreamer, but I'm nothing only one. I hope some day you will join us and the world will live as one."

WERNSTEIN, SONJA
[b.] December 4, 1966, New York; [p.] Martin and Erika; [ed.] BFA/Rhode Island School of Design; [occ.] Freelancer; [oth. writ.] Featured articles and news items for local publications, swiss news and new roots, and also Business Communication texts; [pers.] In poetry, I write about small journeys and events involving people, places, objects and perception.; [a.] Missoula, MT

WEST, CLARA
[b.] July 1, 1919, Terre Haute, IN; [p.] Clarence and Lillie West; [m.] Widowed, November 19, 1945; [ch.] Patrick West; [ed.] Business College, Plus Numerous Correspondence Courses; [occ.] Retired; [oth. writ.] Human interest story in Ocala, FL Star-Banner, (just finished my first fiction novel); [pers.] If the human race were color-blind, our world would be a place of peace and beauty.; [a.] Dale City, VA

WEST, PAMELA S.
[pen.] Pamela S. West; [b.] September 23, 1981, KY State; [p.] David West and Vicki McCoy; [ed.] I am currently a Freshman in High School, Northland High School of Columbus, OH; [hon.] I have gotten several School Awards over the years. However this is my first actual acceptance of any kind outside of School; [oth. writ.] I have several poems and short stories but as I said before this is my first published piece.; [pers.] I would like to dedicate my work to God for always being there for me. And to Mr. Hall my 9th grade health teacher and also Mr. Phillips my 8th grade literature teacher.; [a.] Columbus, OH

WESTOVER III, DAVID A.
[b.] July 6, 1942, Wilmington, DE; [p.] David A. and Evelyn F. Westover; [ed.] B.A. (History): B.A. (Russian), Certificate (Russian Area Studies): Penn State, 1968, Diploma: Defense LAnguage Institute, 1963; [occ.] Front Desk Supervisor, Henlopen Hotel, Rehoboth Beach, DE; [memb.] National Cathedral Association, Penn State Alumni Association, National Geographic Society, The Planetary Society; [hon.] National

Library of Poetry Editor's Choice Award, 1995; [oth. writ.] I have published poetry in PIVOT, the Penn State poetry annual, Morning Breeze, and The National Library of Poetry. I seek a publisher for my novel on the Cold War.; [pers.] I first saw the subject of my poem while serving with the U.S. Army's 78th Special Operations Unit in Berlin, 1963-65. I was struck by the stunning ugliness of the Wall, and of the message it embodied.; [a.] Lewes, DE

WESTSTRATE, SABRINA
[pen.] Nicole Weststrate; [b.] July 31, 1978, Birmingham, AL; [p.] Jerry Weststrate, Brenda Weststrate; [ed.] Moritmer Jordan High School; [memb.] Hag Missionary Baptist Church Youth Group, PALS, FBLA, Concert Band, Marching Band, Majorette, String Orchestra; [hon.] A.B. Honor Roll, Perfect Attendance, Who's Who of National High School Students; [pers.] I think that there is a goodness in my writing. I have been influenced by early Poets.; [a.] Morris, AL

WHETSTONE, ERMA
[b.] January 3, 1976, Goshen, IN; [occ.] Baby Sitting for a School Teacher, Shipshewana, IN; [pers.] I wrote that poem one day out of the blue sky and wrote down on paper how I feel about "the one I love" (my boyfriend) was my first poem written ever.; [a.] Shipshewana, IN

WHITE, BARBARA JEAN
[pen.] Barbara; [b.] May 26, 1943, Des Moines, IA; [p.] Mr. and Mrs. R. G. McCarty; [m.] Divorced; [ch.] Thomas Christopher, James Gregory; [ed.] Graduate of Long Beach Poly High School; [occ.] Graphics Supervisor/Designer; [memb.] Honorary Phi Beta Kappa on Graduation from High School - Graduating in the Top 2% Member/President Phi Gamma Chi; [hon.] Several One-Woman Art Show Exhibits, Owner: Barbara Ink - Wholesale Greeting Card Company; [oth. writ.] "Volumes" of poetry - verse etc. for myself, this was my first attempt at publication, I am most honored; [pers.] "The living of this life is the catalyst to creativity."; [a.] Long Beach, CA

WHITE, DAVID
[b.] April 29, 1957, Saint Louise, MO; [p.] Robert and Betty White; [m.] Carol White, August 19, 1989; [ch.] Tiffany White and Michelle Sexton; [ed.] St. Charles High School. St. Charles Missouri; [occ.] Employed by the Dial Corp.; [oth. writ.] This is my first but not my last; [pers.] I have also played around with poetry concerning my everyday experiences but I have just come to the conclusion that I can write them down and they mean more.; [a.] O'Fallon, MO

WHITE JR., THOMAS LEE
[b.] February 27, 1952, Louisville, KY; [p.] Margareth (Deceased, 1982) and Thomas White Sr. (Deceased, 1984); [ch.] Five; [ed.] GED 1977, Technical Degree in Business Machine Accounting 1982, from Ivy Tech Vocational College; [occ.] Striving Writer; [oth. writ.] I have a manuscript, which my (Lawyer-Agent) promises to be published soon - (Like 1996). It has been copywrited at The Library of Congress in Washington, DC, 1993, My Novel will be a success (Thank you).; [pers.] I would love to dedicate this poem to my deceased mother and father. (Thank you, Jesus). And I would like to say, Family is very important, there is always room for a change.; [a.] Louisville, KY

WHITE, TIMOTHY LAURENCE
[pen.] T. Lawrence White, T. Lipton; [b.] April 21, 1950, Saint Paul, MN; [p.] Alfred and Eva White-Stokes; [m.] Kimaka Ashanti-Stafford White, August 22, 1975; [ed.] Bachelor of Arts Degree from Metro-State University Saint Paul, MN; [occ.] Metro Social Worker for Path; [hon.] Honorable mention for prayer for the poor from the world of poetry; [oth. writ.] Poems Two Broken Hearts (world of poetry) Loving You Is So Right For Me (world of poetry) Yahweh Goes Flowers, Never Ending God's Flowers, Never Ending Glory, Carrousel Of Colors A Harmony Of Humans; [pers.] We are all sub creators from the one true God. We cannot take credit for something that was created before we thought of it!; [a.] Saint Paul, MN

WHITFIELD, GEORGE R.
[pen.] David George Moze; [b.] September 27, 1943, Virginia; [p.] George and Elnora Whitfield; [m.] Rose Whitfield, March 25, 1968; [ch.] Denise, Sonia, Michelle, Michael; [ed.] Pursuing Bachelor of Arts Degree - Pace University; [occ.] Admin. Supervisor, State Dept./Corr.; [memb.] Union Baptist Church, Church Officer-Various Church Committees; [oth. writ.] Numerous poems unpublished - Church News Bulletin and Informational Paper; [pers.] Gratification in writing poetry with the hope that when it is read the reader/s life will be positively changed. All of my inspiration comes from above.; [a.] Greenburgh, NY

WHITMIRE, BONITA D.
[pen.] Pulaski Ethridge; [b.] August 8, 1958, Baltimore, MD; [p.] John and Eva Lee Whitmire; [ed.] Southside High 1976, Greenville Technical College 1979, University of South Carolina 1987; [occ.] Market Research (free lance); [memb.] Edwards Rd. Baptist Church, Mbr. of Chancel Choir. Pleasantburg Lions Club, 1st Female Mbr. 1st Female President (1994-95) 95-96 Zone Chairman-Zone Six; [hon.] Melvin Jones Fellowship 1992, Highest Award that can be received from Lions. ISP-International Poet of Merit Award 1993; [oth. writ.] 2 Poems - Reedy River Review, Poem - Palmetto Lion, poem in East of Sunrise, poem to be published in Best Poems of 1996. Also editor of the Single Adult Ministry Newsletter at Edwards Road Baptist Church.; [pers.] My writing reflects the core of my being. Often, when I write, what I write pours out of me, as if I have no control over it.; [a.] Greenville, SC

WHITMIRE, MATTHEW
[pen.] "Hezakiah"; [b.] December 5, 1974, Phoenix, AZ; [occ.] College Student-U. of A.; [oth. writ.] Runestaff co-authored with Travis Hall; [pers.] I think therefore I am. I have been greatly influenced by J.R.R. Tolkien's writings.

WIER, RUSSELL D.
[b.] December 5, 1944, La Cygne, KS; [p.] Clarence and Wanda Wier; [m.] Divorced; [ch.] Patrick and Heather; [ed.] La Cygne Rural High; [occ.] Paint and Wallcovering Contractor; [memb.] Linn County Fair Board, Linn County Extension Service, Community Leader, Busy Workers 4-H 17 years; [hon.] Serving the Young Adults and Youth of my 4-H Club, Editors Choice Award - the National Library of Poetry. Award of Merit - Holly Woods Famous Poets Society; [oth. writ.] "Friendship" published in the anthology "Famous Poems of Today," "What is love?" published in "Between the Raindrops" the National Library of Poetry; [pers.] My poetry so far has been mainly about the love of people around me, family and friends, but with my love of animals and the West I'm going to incorporate these into my poetry.; [a.] La Cygne, KS

WIESNER, EUGENE F.
[b.] April 22, 1956, Hays, KS; [p.] Mr. and Mrs. Eugene F. Wiesner; [m.] Maria P. Wiesner, May 18, 1988; [ch.] Simon Wiesner; [ed.] Billings Senior High 1974, Billings Vo Tech 1975, Eastern Montana College, completed 1 year 1976; [occ.] Baker. I work for IBC in Billings, MT; [memb.] St. Anthony's Church; [hon.] I received a letter from John Paul II on a poetry book I wrote entitled the "Hundred Songs of Fatima"; [oth. writ.] "The Hundred Songs" a book of 100 poems I wrote in 1982; [pers.] I have had letters of nine published in the Billings Gazette and many others newspapers throughout the Northwest United States. "Love yourself and others."; [a.] Laurel, MT

WILDER, LILLIE DALE
[pen.] Lillie D. Wilder; [b.] August 16, 1920, Baker, FL; [p.] Bennet Hobbs and Lora Hobbs; [m.] Floyd O. Wilder, August 8, 1937; [ch.] Linda A., Sharon O., Teresa G., Floyd O. Jr.; [ed.] Finished High School at Belle Glade High; [occ.] Retired in 1992 after being Secretary in an Elementary School 27 yrs.; [memb.] First Baptist Church, Glades Historical Society, Keen Kids; [hon.] Professional Standard Certificate from A.E.S.O.P., Honored to be Floyd's wide for 45 yrs., until death did us part. Honored to help raise 4 normal, Healthy Children, who have presented us with 4 grand sons, and 1 Great Grand Son; [oth. writ.] Since I started in 1989, I've written 160 songs and a few poems.; [pers.] I've made tapes of a few of my songs for family and friends. I play guitar to accompany my singing. I plan to keep writing songs as long as they come to me free, complete with a tune.; [a.] South Bay, FL

WILHELMY, GUS
[b.] February 17, 1935, Saint Paul, MN; [p.] George Wilhelmy, Emily Wegner; [m.] Mary Rose Vallely, September 1, 1990; [ch.] Rochelle Marie, Todd Jerome, Rebecca Ann; [ed.] B.A. Bellarmine College Louisville, M.A. University of Michigan, Ann Abbor; [occ.] Fund Raising Executive; [memb.] American Marketing Association, American Management Association, National Society of Fund Raising Executives; [hon.] Martin Luther King Community Service

Award, Outstanding Young Man of America, Founder's Award: Safer foundation, Editors Choice Award from NLP; [oth. writ.] Numerous Articles in magazines and newspaper... poetry in other magazines; [pers.] I seemingly write best about the pain, the struggle, the weakness of all of us... yet my view is very hopeful, romantic, touches the light within.; [a.] Chicago, IL

WILLETT, EDWARD F.
[pen.] Edward F. Willett; [b.] August 25, 1933, Maple Rapids, MI; [p.] Frank James and Eleanor Emily; [m.] Betty Ann (Deceased November 17, 1971), July 18, 1958; [ch.] SFC. James E. Willett; [memb.] Lansing Michigan Jaycees 1962-1969, Lansing YMCA Mystic Lake Union, Camp Committee-secretary 5 yrs.; [hon.] Jaycee of the month 1962, Outstanding New Jaycee 1963; [oth. writ.] "Flowers of Time" Published 1993 - National Library of Poetry, "Whispers in the Wind", "My Only Sunshine" Published 1995 - National Library of Poetry, "Best Poems of 1995"; [pers.] Expressions from the pen are never lost!; [a.] Perry, MI

WILLIAMS, BARBARA K.
[pen.] "Turtle"; [b.] May 7, 1951, Pittston Hosp., PA; [p.] Fred C. Williams and Marion Williams; [ed.] 1 yr. Mansfield State College, Mansfield, PA. - 1 yr. Luzerne County Community College, Nanticoke, PA; [occ.] Unemployed - caregiver for sick mother; [memb.] Lifetime member 1 Sp since 1995; [hon.] Award of merit for poem published - "Forever Friends" - 1995; [oth. writ.] Many other poems written - not published as of yet; [pers.] Life is what you make it.; [a.] West Wyoming, PA

WILLIAMS, DANNEISHA
[pen.] Neisha; [b.] April 24, 1979, California Hospital; [p.] Cynthia and Donald Williams; [ed.] I attended Our Lady of Victory Elementary and Junior High School, and graduated with honors and a president certificate. I now attend Long Beach David Starr Jordan High School.; [pers.] I've been into poetry since I was twelve years old. My favorite poet is Maya Angelo.; [a.] Long Beach, CA

WILLIAMS, GREGORY
[b.] February 25, 1976, New Orleans; [p.] Greg Williams Sr. and Beverly Williams; [ed.] Achieved G.E.D. Gretna, LA; [occ.] Winn Dixie Avondale, LA; [oth. writ.] I write about life and how it's touch me, and on visions that I've seen in my dreams.; [a.] Avondale, LA

WILLIAMS III, JOHN T.
[pen.] John T. Williams III; [b.] September 4, 1975, Olongapo, Philippines; [p.] John and Susana Williams; [ed.] 12 yrs. High School with Diploma plus a variety of communications School in Military San Marcos High School; [occ.] Military (Marines); [hon.] Earned two awards for my poetry in Junior High (previous poems); [oth. writ.] Personal writings that are within my possession such as other poems; [pers.] I write poems to express my innermost feelings. It is a way I can release tension, and really say what's on my mind. It's what I feel and think, that's all that matters. Most of my poems are inspired by my father.; [a.] Oceanside, CA

WILLIAMS, JAMES THOMAS
[b.] December 11, 1968, Green Bay, WI; [p.] Phyllis and Henry Smeester; [ed.] High School and N.C.T.C. diplomas; [occ.] Construction/Painter; [hon.] Several certificates, award for track; [oth. writ.] Poems published in local newspapers; [pers.] I write poems based on feelings of my life.; [a.] Green Bay, WI

WILLIAMS, RICHARD LEE
[pen.] "Yarn Spinner"; [b.] November 21, 1946, Louisville, KY; [p.] Mr. and Mrs. Chas J. Williams; [ed.] GED in Army Vietnam era Vet.; [occ.] Retired from Propane Bus. currently recuperating/Hip Replacem.; [memb.] Former Member (years ago) Kentucky Railway Museum, no current memberships; [hon.] Just Safe Drivers Awards and other safety awards through Co.; [oth. writ.] May poems, verse and free-verse and an occasional "yarn" none published - I have one short story in rhyme, which is 240 lines in length.; [pers.] My writings reflect experiences or observations gained during my - many travels and travails. I am also an avid reader of non fiction and or historical works.; [a.] Umatilla, FL

WILLIAMS, SHANE
[b.] May 28, 1970, New Castle, IN; [p.] Mike and Carol Williams; [m.] Jami Williams, August 14, 1993; [ch.] Jeremy; [ed.] B.S. History-Northeast Missouri State Univ., B.A. Education Univ. of MO - Kansas City - Wentzville High; [occ.] 8th Grade Social Studies Teacher - Raytown Middle School, Raytown, MO; [pers.] I write about things that have touched or affected my life.; [a.] Lee's Summit, MO

WILLIAMS, SHANNON F.
[b.] October 27, 1972, Savannah, GA; [p.] Mr. and Mrs. Eugene Williams; [ed.] Bachelor of Arts - Political Science, Bachelor of Science - Education, Valdosta State University, High School Graduate-H.V. Jenkins High Savannah, GA; [occ.] Graduate Student; [memb.] Student Professional Association of GA Educators, Phi-Alpha Delta Pre-Law Fraternity, Senator for Student Government Assoc., V.P. Black Student League, Justice for Judicial Board, Premiere Model, Member-Sylvia's Models and Talent Agency; [hon.] Nominee for Who's Who Among Student in American Colleges and Universities; [oth. writ.] I have written two plays and a book entitled, From Poverty To Prosperity, An Annotation of Prominent Black Americans in Poem Format.; [pers.] I try to broaden my horizons as much as possible. I fervently believe in words of Frederick Douglas, "Without Struggle There Is No Progress."; [a.] Valdosta, GA

WILLIAMS, TWINKLE BRIGGS
[pen.] Twinkle Williams; [b.] March 8, 1958, Lexington, Davidson Co, NC; [p.] Hilda and Dolan Briggs; [m.] Divorced; [ch.] Tyson and Lara-Ashley Hohn Williams; [ed.] B.A. Degree in Elementary Ed.; [occ.] First Grade School Teacher - Davidson, CO; [memb.] Audaboun Society Schools, N.C.P.S. - N.C. Poetry Society, National Story letters Assoc., Professional Clown Assoc., Women of Evangelical Lutheran Church; [hon.] N.C. Zoological Society Chancellors List - Catawba College; [oth. writ.] Children's stories - plays and stories for local Clown Ministry groups - poetry in Davidson Co., writers guild. Local personal interviewers biographical.; [pers.] I strive to reflect the positive qualities in all people. Love and encouragement makes everyone's journey through this life a little easier. I am greatly influenced by the writings of my mother who is an inspirational artist, musician, and lover as life.; [a.] Lexington, NC

WILOWSKI JR., E. J.
[b.] November 21, 1957, Manhasset, NY; [p.] Judge and Mrs. Edmund J. Wilowski; [m.] Heidi M. Wilowski, June 3, 1990; [ch.] Hedy-Helene and Marc; [ed.] Holy Cross High School, Flushing, New York, St. John's University, Jamaica, New York; [occ.] Song Writer, Author; [oth. writ.] Summers Lament, published in East of the sunrise. Numerous songs and music scores, as well as several short stories.; [a.] Locust Valley, NY

WILSON, CHARLOTTE
[pen.] Charlotte Wilson; [b.] October 10, 1942, Chattanooga, TN; [p.] Henry and Hulda Carbine; [m.] Divorced; [ch.] Cynthia Forkner; [ed.] Hi School Graduate and Beauty School Training; [occ.] Disabled but play for elders at the Hospitals; [hon.] Music Award; [oth. writ.] Dear Father Up In Heaven, Get Ready To Go, Prayers Answered and others; [pers.] I play music and enjoy it very much. I have older type music and try to play anything I hear, if I like it. I've been playing since I was about 60 years old.; [a.] Rossville, GA

WILSON, JESSICA
[b.] July 27, 1982, Lawrence, KS; [p.] Greg and Beverly Wilson; [ed.] 7th grade student at Douglas County Christian School, Lawrence, KS; [occ.] Student; [oth. writ.] Writes for personal fun and home work assignments; [pers.] I usually like to write about calm situations. The old without is one of my favorites to write.; [a.] Lawrence, KS

WILSON, NANCY JO
[b.] May 3, 1978, Concordia, KS; [p.] James Wisdon and Shirley Wilson; [ed.] Clay Center High, Cloud County Community College; [occ.] Certified Nurses Assistance; [a.] Clay Center, KS

WINDISH, CATHERINE M.
[b.] October 21, 1959, Queens, NY; [p.] John S. Smith, Catherine A. Henshaw; [m.] William R. Windish, April 28, 1990; [ch.] Alexine Catherine, Sally Carlene; [ed.] Islip High School, St. Catharine Jr. College, Flagler College; [occ.] Mother, Substitute Teacher; [memb.] P.T.A. Board Member, M.L. Pre-School Board Member, Member - Jr. Women's Club, Learn to Read Tutor; [hon.] Who's Who in American Jr. Colleges; [oth. writ.] Nothing published; [pers.] We all carry around baggage. You can keep what's yours if you so desire, but give the rest of it back to who it belongs to, or get rid of it and move on. God will take care of the rest.; [a.] Saint Augustine, FL

WISE, RODERICK L.
[b.] January 7, 1947, Winter Haven, FL; [p.] Buster and Sabra Wise; [m.] Yvonne Hodges Wise, October 28, 1966; [ch.] Dana Yvette, Randall Loren, Stephanie Marie, Bryan Edward; [ed.] Winter Haven Senior High University of Maryland; [oth. writ.] Personal collection of poems; [a.] Yorktown, VA

WISEMAN, JANE L.
[pen.] Jo Margaret McKenzie; [b.] March 27, 1944, Athens, OH; [p.] Margaret, George Parsons; [m.] Rev. David J. Wiseman, May 28, 1961; [ch.] Jana Renee, Evan David, Owen Earl; [ed.] Attended Ohio University, eleven years music instruction. Graduate of Rutland High School.; [occ.] Homemaker, piano teacher. Girl Scout Leader; [memb.] Girl Scouts of America; [oth. writ.] Children's puppet productions, children's stories, poetry, short stories; [pers.] The soul is a "trunk" unlocked by words. May my words be a key that stirs the emotions of my readers, reaching their souls.; [a.] Rutland, OH

WOJAK, MEGAN YVETTE
[b.] September 26, 1978, DeKalb, IL; [p.] Deborah Wojak; [ed.] Thatcher High School (currently enrolled), part-time student at Eastern Arizona College; [occ.] Student; [oth. writ.] Poems and short stories for personal enjoyment and for others to enjoy; [pers.] Great spirits have always encountered violent opposition from mediocre minds. - Albert Einstein; [a.] Thatcher, AZ

WOLFE, TAWNY
[b.] June 25, 1947, Fort Collins, CO; [p.] M/M Lou Samsa; [m.] Ronald J. Wolfe; [ch.] Raleigh Donoran Wolfe; [ed.] Hillsboro or H.S. Coursework Portland Community, Long Beach State; [occ.] Family owned small interstate trucking (juck-of-all-trades); [memb.] Nat'l. Writer's Club, City News Service; [hon.] 1st place, 3rd place with son in Photo Exhibit and '95 Western Idaho Fair; [oth. writ.] "This One's For You, Dad" Chisholm, MN Free Press-Tribune Press June 13, 1991, Written for WWII Rilot Father (B24) as Tribute to his experiences and my memories; [pers.] (Poem "Despair" written at bottom of depression with M.S.) Interest in human nature and mother earth's creatures-If we look out for "earth" she looks out for us.; [a.] Greenleaf, ID

WOLOSS, BOB
[b.] November 4, 1948, Northampton, MA; [p.] Rudy Woloss, Gladys Rattel; [m.] Carol Woloss, April 4, 1987; [ch.] Benjamin and Sarah; [ed.] University of Massachusetts - Amherst; [occ.] Sales/Marketing and Business Development; [memb.] Sigma Phi Epsilon; [pers.] From the miniscule to the grand, see the world around you with all your senses for nothing is insignificant and there is value in every experience. Trust in yourself, persevere, have fun whenever possible and write it all down.; [a.] Hampstead, NH

WONG, JASON ALOYSIOUS
[b.] October 20, 1973, Honolulu, HI; [p.] Aloysious K. B. Wong, Rosemarie Wong; [ed.] St. Theresa's School Damien Memorial High School, University of Hawaii at Manoa; [occ.] Student at University of Hawaii of Manoa; [memb.] The Smithsonian Associates, BEE-net, Catholic Digest Book Club, Book of the Month Club; [hon.] Vice President Legion of Mary; [pers.] God works through my writing so that I can make others feel good about themselves.; [a.] Aiea, HI

WOO, AARON STEPHAN
[b.] November 15, 1979, Seattle, WA; [p.] Arnie and Ardath Woo; [occ.] Current Honors Student Roosevelt High; [memb.] Honor Roll; [oth. writ.] Only for Honors Language Arts Class.

WOOD, BONNIE
[pen.] Bonnie Wood; [b.] August 16, 1948, Tompkinsville, KY; [p.] Lovel and Velma Wood; [ed.] Pompkinsville High Ray Reid Beauty School, Lois Glyn Beauty School; [occ.] Pharmaceutical Wholesale Co.; [memb.] Member of Macedonia Baptist Church near Moss Tennessee; [hon.] Student excellence Award best grades and attitudes; [oth. writ.] I have several poems of different nature birthdays sympathy wedding Christmas just say I was thinking of them I have written few songs; [pers.] I hope that it will be a blessing to each and everyone who reads this poem.; [a.] Fountain Run, KY

WOOD, KATHLEEN
[pen.] Kathleen Wood; [b.] June 27, 1946, Morristown, NJ; [p.] Arthur F. Ringwood (Deceased), Blanche K. Ringwood; [ch.] Peter Shawn Doran; [ed.] BS West Chester Univ., MA U. of Houston, Candidate for Ed. D. at U. of Houston in Educational Leadership; [occ.] Instructor, Consultant-Communications; [memb.] Pasadena Little Theatre, Texas Junior College Teachers Ass'n., National Educational of Educational Leaders; [hon.] Spirit of San Jacinto award for 1990 through 1995, Honorary Sheriff's Deputy in Harris County, appointed Lector of Trainer for Diocese of Galveston - Houston; [oth. writ.] Poems published in the National Library of Poetry Anthologies, various newsletters, lyrics for songs, and working on dissertation; [pers.] Poetry expresses the reflections of the mind, heart, and soul.; [a.] Houston, TX

WOODRUFF, SHIRLEY
[pen.] Shirley T. Woodruff; [b.] June 17, 1950, Trenton, NJ; [p.] William and Mary Jane Travis; [m.] Gerald L. Woodruff, July 4, 1970; [ch.] Susan, Peter, Aaron and Lisa; [ed.] High School graduate, one year college; [occ.] Housewife; [oth. writ.] Poetic Verse in High School digest. Section in Christian newsletter entitled "Through My Kitchen Window."; [pers.] With the realization of my spiritual depravity by the gift of God I have found the greater meaning of life. Through the art of communication, in verse I desire to share life's trials, joys, and beauty. The pictures we leave for others to encourage their lives.; [a.] Swartz Creek, MI

WOODS, HEATHER FAYE
[b.] October 17, 1977, San Mateo, CA; [p.] Marcia Woods, James Woods; [ed.] Crystal Springs Uplands High School, Kenyon College; [occ.] I am a first year student at Kenyon College; [hon.] Currently working as a student associate on the Kenyon Review.; [a.] Gambier, OH

WRIGHT, DAVID
[b.] December 10, 1956, Roanoke Rapids, NC; [p.] Earl and Betty Wright; [ed.] Peterson High, San Jose State University; [memb.] International Society of Poets; [hon.] Editor's Choice Award; [oth. writ.] Poem published in the book - Walk Through Paradise; [pers.] Expressing beauty from the heart.; [a.] Vancouver, WA

WRIGHT, RETA MARIE
[b.] January 14, 1954, Toms Rivers, NJ; [p.] Charles and Ruth Creamer; [ch.] Tanya, Tammy, David and Melissa; [ed.] Central Regional High and World Outreach Bible School; [occ.] Microfilmer; [memb.] Overcomers faith - fellowship church; [hon.] Couple of poems published in books; [oth. writ.] You Cared, The Angels Came, My Mother, My Little Michael, My Friend, In His Eye's, Cinderella; [pers.] I believe that life our God given gift, should be shared to the fullest with others-whether through poetry, an out stretched hand of love, a smile or even a kind word, to a hurting world.; [a.] Bayville, NJ

WRIGHT, TAMARA ANGELIC
[b.] February 26, 1974, Tucson, UMC, AZ; [p.] Betty and Henry Freeman; [ed.] Son-Life Chapel (Middle School)/Amphitheater High School/ University of Arizona (College of Education); [occ.] Full-time Student and Writing Tutor; [hon.] Who's Who Among American High School Students. American Biographical Institute - Distinguished Leadership Award; [oth. writ.] I am currently writing a book of Christian Poetry - the comfort zone: "Poetry from the heart."; [pers.] May all who read my poems be blessed with their messages of love and hope, messages of love and hope, messages written solely by the hand of God upon my heart. Always a Christian and a lady is who I am.; [a.] Tucson, AZ

WYATT, BRIAN L.
[b.] May 6, 1975, Paducah, KY; [p.] Mike Wyatt and Sue Reeves; [ed.] Graduate of Lone Oak High School Currently a Sophomore at Murray State University; [pers.] My family and my close friends make up my life, without their support and love, my life and my heart would be empty.; [a.] Paducah, KY

YANDELL, GAIL
[pers.] My writings have been inspired by Gerald Jampolsky M.D., The center for Attitudinal Healing, Lorrain Campbell and those who have Loved and Supported me. I write from my experiences of growth, which creates an ever changing awareness of myself and others - Learning to see things differently and always knowing love is the answer.; [a.] Yucaipa, CA

YAZINSKY, JOHN T.
[pen.] Baby J. Babyface; [b.] October 17, 1975, Brooklyn, NY; [p.] John W. Yazinsky, Kathy Moore; [ed.] PS 124 For Elementary JH551 Junior High John Kay High School and The

Street of N.Y.; [occ.] Electrician; [memb.] NRA; [hon.] It's been my honor to know Daire Lyons as she has bought me many things about life.; [oth. writ.] I've written many poems about love and its ups and downs but I've only recently started sharing it so hopefully you'll read of me again.; [pers.] I would just like to write the world is a beautiful place to enjoy so I try to bring people together by writing to make them smile cry and most important understand.; [a.] Brooklyn, NC

YEOMAN, BERNICE
[b.] September 3, 1915, Peoria, AR; [p.] William Samuel and Rhoda E. Yeoman; [ed.] Tamaha, Okla. Ardmore, Okla., Prairie View, Okla., Lenapah, Okla, Coffeyville Jr. College and 4 yrs. in Tahlequah, Okla.; [occ.] Retired; [memb.] Church of God; [oth. writ.] Youth for Christ "Conquest" magazines; [pers.] Desire to use every avenue possible to help people become aware of the danger our world faces, because of our rejection of God.; [a.] Coffeyville, KS

YOHE, PATRICIA MELLE
[b.] December 11, 1954, Park Ridge, IL; [p.] Otto Melle, Helen Melle; [m.] Richard L. Yohe Jr., June 20, 1993; [ch.] Melissa, Tina, Michael, Rocco, and Laura Defrenza, Grandchildren: (Shawn and Samantha); [ed.] Fire Academy - Arlington State of Ill, Paramedic Paralegal Institute; [occ.] Fire Fighter, Paramedic; [memb.] American Heart Association - Branch Member Ill. Professional Fire Fighters Assn.; [hon.] Paramedic Cum-Laude Highland Park Hospital Achievement Award for outstanding service Northfield fire/rescue Dept.; [oth. writ.] First poem ever submitted for evaluation!; [pers.] When your struggling, remember the verse, to dream the impossible dream, to fight the unbeatable foe, to bear with unbearable sorrow to run, where the brave dare not go... Yes! This is my quest!; [a.] Round Lake Beach, IL

YONGE, AMELIE C.
[pen.] Amelie; [b.] June 1, 1953, Montgomery, AL; [p.] James and Dutchie Cooper; [m.] Matt Yonge, September 2, 1978; [ch.] Amelia - 14, Chandler - 12; [ed.] H.S. Sidney Lanier - Montgomery, AL, - 1971, Auburn University, Auburn, AL - B.S. in Elem. Education - 1975 Taught - Seventeen yrs. in public and private schools; [occ.] Coordinator of Admissions and Community Relations - Episcopal Day School; [memb.] Tri Delta Sorority - college ADK - Nat. Teacher's Pensacola Jr. Lg. - past Exec. and Board Member Kaleidoscope Dance Theater - former Board Member Episcopal Day School - past Board Member; [hon.] 1st Place in Alabama National Poetry Day Contest - 1969 or '70 Received several grants while teaching Poetry Editor of "North Tower" - literary mag. at sidney Lanier H.S.; [oth. writ.] Years of poetry; [pers.] To make a difference...; [a.] Pensacola, FL

YOST, FAITH DAVIS
[b.] June 19, 1959, Reidsville, NC; [p.] Charles F. and Yvonne M. Davis; [m.] Ed W. Yost; [ch.] Edel, Jaymie, Andrew, Derek, Denise; [ed.] Reidsville High, Robeson Community College; [occ.] Computer Administrator, Lumbee River Legal Services; [memb.] National Notary Assn., Lumberton Optimist Club; [a.] Lumberton, NC

YOUNG, ANGELA
[b.] July 20, 1980, Huntingdon Valley, PA; [p.] Louise and Robert Young; [ed.] A sophomore at Archishop Ryan High School in Philadelphia, PA; [hon.] A Certificate of Outstanding Achievement Awards from NASA; [oth. writ.] In the "Kids Beat" section of the peace officer magazine I wrote an article called "Kids And Crime In America."

YOUNG, CHERYL ANN
[b.] November 18, 1963, Danville, IL; [p.] Kenneth H. Young II, Marcella M. Young; [ch.] One son (Deceased); [ed.] Danville High School, Danville Area Community College; [occ.] Records Technician, Danville Police Department; [memb.] Carter Metropolitan C.M.E. Church; [oth. writ.] "A Years Past"; [pers.] This is dedicated to my darling son in heaven - Travis L. "J.R." McCullough. The expressions of sympathy and love from my family, church, friends, co-workers and community inspired me to write.; [a.] Danville, IL

YOUNG, KEVIN D.
[b.] August 2, 1963, Philadelphia; [p.] Ruby E. Young; [ch.] Nicole Lynn Baldwin; [ed.] West Philadelphia Catholic High School for boys, Lincoln University, B.S. in Business Administration; [occ.] Inventor and entrepreneur; [memb.] Omega Psi Phi Fraternity Inc.; [hon.] Honorable discharge from the United State Marine corpss, Granted a United States Patent/Patent/Pending status on three (3) additional inventions; [oth. writ.] Several articles for local newspapers. Many more unpublished poetry and short stories. Pending publication of a manuscript.; [pers.] One's acceptance of thy own thoughts and perceptions, should not be contingent upon anyone else's approval.; [a.] Daytona Beach, FL

YOUNG, LOIS M.
[b.] October 7, 1923, Boise City, OK; [p.] Martha Wilder Witten and Edwin Witten (Both now Deceased); [m.] Deceased; [ch.] 4 sons, 6 Grandchildren, 4 Great Grandchildren; [ed.] A.A. Degree, R.N. 1961 Worked Many years as a Critical Care Nurse. Specialized in Pediatrics; [occ.] Retired R.N.; [hon.] Alpha Gamma Sigma (1955) (While in a vocational Nursing program) (Orange Coast College); [pers.] I always strive to treat other people as I want to be treated. My Nursing career was very rewarding but now I'm happy to be retired.; [a.] Orange, CA

YOUNG, MAURICE WELDON
[b.] September 20, 1948, Flint, MI; [p.] Ervin and Christeen Young; [ch.] Maurince Jr. Marisha, Amber Young; [ed.] Flint Northern High, St. Paul Technical College, C.S. Mott College; [occ.] Machinist - 3M Minnesota Mining and Manufacturing; [hon.] Honorable Discharge United States Air Force 1994 Minnesota State Fair Talent Competition winner, the Bachelors Vocal Group; [pers.] I wish everyone a life filled with love, family and fun! I have been greatly influenced by the poetry of Walter Benton.; [a.] Eagan, MN

YOUNG, PAULINE
[pen.] Polly Snapp Young; [b.] July 4, 1926, Dandrige, TN; [p.] John Snapp, Rusha Snapp; [m.] Donald E. Young (Deceased), June 11, 1994; [ed.] Maury High, Dandrige, TN, Knoxville Business College, Knoxville, TN; [occ.] Retired; [memb.] Former member of Several Genealogy Societies. Distinguished Member of The International Society of Poets.; [hon.] National Library of Poetry Editors Choice Award, the Amherst Certificate of Achievement. Poems published by The National Library of Poetry, Sparrow grass Forum, and the Amherst Society; [oth. writ.] Letters, short stories, a letter used in "Personality Development Class" in Business College. Short Story used in "Social Study Class" in KY Gramma School (South Shore, KY). Poem pub. in Memory of my Aunt in "Monterrey County (CA) Herald"; [pers.] My poems are inspired, straight from heart, and beauty and Nature.; [a.] Newport, TN

YOUNG, ZACHARY
[pen.] Zach; [b.] March 25, 1979, Winter Park, FL; [p.] Shana Young, Terry Young; [ed.] Junior 11th Grade, Lyman High School, Mascott - Greyhound; [occ.] High School Student; [memb.] Young Life, Northland Community Church; [hon.] Presidential Academic Awards in Elementary and Middle Schools Who's Who Among High Students voted "Mc. Greyhound" - Lyman High School for school year 1995-1996; [oth. writ.] Poem - "Life, Take Control" published in Guarantee Trust Life Ins. quarterly newsletter. Copy sent to President Clinton Aug. 8, 1994, and was acknowledged with a wonderful from the White House.; [pers.] My deepest emotions, values, and thoughts of my life of expressed in my writing. My wish is that one day I would put these words to music for everyone to enjoy.; [a.] Casselberry, FL

YOUNGBLOOD, DOROTHY F.
[b.] September 4, 1925, Philadelphia, PA; [p.] Robert and Marie Fulton (Deceased); [m.] Hubert H. Youngblood (Deceased), January 26, 1952; [ch.] Gina Y. Hatcher, Michael Youngblood; [ed.] Virginia State University Rutgers University (retired 6th grade school teacher); [occ.] Free-lance writing Independent Distributor of Herbalife Weight Management Program; [memb.] Alpha Kappa Alpha Sorority, Tacoma Urban League; [hon.] Outstanding Service Award 1986, '88, '90 - National Sickle Cell Assoc. Represented Rutgers Univ. at United Nations during World Education Week in 1965 at Rutgers Univ. - Best Teaching Voice recorded and buried in time capsule to be opened in 2000 AD; [oth. writ.] Book published 1986.. entitled I Hurried... I Waited... Articles in Gazette Telegraph Newspaper in Colorado Springs, Co 1979, '80, '81, '82 (presently writing a novel); [pers.] For me... "Life is what you make it and I've made mine beautiful. I count my blessings every day. I'm living life to the fullest and I'm happy, healthy and grateful to Almighty God".; [a.] Tacoma, WA

YOUSIF, LAURA
[b.] April 9, 1976, Baltimore, MD; [p.] Nidal Zawaideh (Mother); [ed.] Associates (LIB), Continuing to MSU to study Education; [occ.] Sales Representative; [pers.] Poems are a reflection of ones inner self, and for somebody to share that with others is poetry.; [a.] Troy, MI

ZACKERY, HELEN J.
[b.] February 11, 1946, Green County, NC; [p.] Lillian Edwards and Johnny Edwards; [ch.] Dione Zackery and Inez Zackery; [ed.] Hillhouse High School, BA, Albertus Magnus College; [occ.] Eligibility Services Worker; [memb.] Vital Element Productions, Inc. - A Theatrical Company; [hon.] Whose Who in Community Colleges, Mother of the Year Award and Dean's High List while attending South Central Community College; [oth. writ.] Many unpublished poems, songs and spiritual letters; [pers.] Strive to be your best and from your heart reach out to others so glorious things will happen to you.; [a.] New Haven, CT

ZAKOUR, ZACHARY
[b.] March 28, 1969, Santa Monica; [ed.] B.A. English CSULB, Cum Laude; [occ.] English Teacher, Dawney High School; [memb.] Phi Beta Kappa; [hon.] Cum Laude Golden Key National Honor Society; [pers.] With my writing and in my life I am searching for truth and beauty.; [a.] Long Beach, CA

ZALEVSKY, KENNETH A.
[b.] September 15, 1963, Pittsburgh, PA; [p.] Marvin, JoAnne Zalevsky; [ed.] Carnegie Mellon University, Math/Computer Science; [occ.] Computer Consultant; [hon.] Placed in the Top 5 at the Pennsylvania State Body Building Championships Two Years in a Row; [pers.] I am a competitive body builder who believes that, in addition to poetry and music, the body is also a work of art.; [a.] Pittsburgh, PA

ZANGHI, ANTHONY F.
[b.] May 24, 1925, Philadelphia, PA; [p.] Deceased; [m.] Josephine J. Zanghi, May 28, 1945; [ch.] Three Sons; [ed.] Two Years H.S., Two Years Voc., One Year IBM School; [occ.] Retired; [memb.] AARP - T.C.V., V.F.W.; [hon.] Served in World War II received, Philippine Liberation Medal, also our Unit received 2 Bronze Stars for Battle of Luzon 1st Cavalry Div.; [oth. writ.] I have written various, still hiding in dresser draws. This poem is first I ever submitted.; [pers.] Just as a journey begins with one steep, so does a penny saved, begins a journey to dollars.; [a.] Turnersville, NJ

ZENDEJAS, GILBERT
[pen.] Gil Zendejas; [b.] November 22, 1945, Whittier, CA; [p.] Tony Zendejas, Dolores Zendejas; [m.] Victoria, November 27, 1966; [ed.] Whittier High School; [occ.] Troubleman for Southern Calif. Edition; [oth. writ.] Several poems for personal enjoyment; [pers.] I believe that a poem truly reflects one's true feelings to the world to wear.; [a.] El Monte, CA

ZETT, CRYSTAL
[b.] February 9, 1983, Janseville, WI; [p.] Linda Zett, Robert Zett; [ed.] I am currently in 7th Grade at Edison Middle School; [memb.] Rock County 4-H, First Lutheran Church, Nursery Care; [hon.] Poems in Anthologies, Blue Ribbons, Trophies in 4-H and School; [oth. writ.] Poems, novel, anthology, short stories; [pers.] Every one has a talent and if you don't know what it is yet, try different stuff until you find it.; [a.] Janesville, WI

ZIEGLER, JAMES F.
[pen.] James Francis Ziegler; [b.] September 5, 1950, Minot, ND; [p.] Mr & Mrs Adam Ziegler; [m.] Mrs. Derbara Ziegler; [m.] June 4, 1981; [ch.] Jade, Dianne, Mike & Paul; [ed.] Rochester High School, Bail State University, Associate of Arts (1983); [occ.] Painter; [memb.] Ball State University Alumunus, Sigma Phi Epsila Alumnus, St. Joseph Catholic Church, Former Member USAF (Res) & United States Tennis Assoc; [hon.] Various Sports Awards in several sports; [oth. writ.] Poems published in Newspapers / Gollier's Travels, 'Steve Yoder,' 'Ode to a Champion,' and 'The Passing of Coach'; [pers.] My hope is that those reading my poetry can be inspired to see what they could be when they put their faith in Jesus Christ & put action behind their Faith w/ work & prayer to realize their aspirations. [a.] Rochester, IN;

ZILBA, ZACHARY J.
[pen.] Coy Haizens; [b.] December 13, 1977, Sandusky, OH; [ed.] Home Schooled, preparing for College; [occ.] Writing, Acting; [hon.] Wrote and Directed a Play at Clyde High School, received standing Ovation; [oth. writ.] Just completed first novel entitled "Silent Tears," and an putting finishing touches on feature length screenplay. Ready to start work on "The Pros" my second novel.; [pers.] Even in the coldest silences, they are whispering to me. The voices of a thousand tales yearning to be told.; [a.] Green Springs, OH

ZIMAK, ALICE F.
[b.] January 28, 1966, Newport News, VA; [p.] Gilbert Waller, Barbara Stroup; [m.] Gary Zimak, December 22, 1990; [ch.] Tara Marie, Lindsey Fay; [ed.] Denbigh High, Christopher Newport University, Radford University - B.S. Marketing; [occ.] Material Analyst for Newport News Shipbuilding; [memb.] Junior Women's Club of Newport News; [hon.] Dean's List; [pers.] My poem illustrates an important message that one should consider... the angels are within you.

ZIMMERMAN, ELLEN
[b.] April 1, 1949, Oskaloosa, IA; [p.] Robert and Frances Maxwell; [m.] David Zimmerman, June 20, 1987; [ed.] Montezuma Community Stuarts School of Hair styling, Blackhawk Community College; [occ.] Hair Salon Owner/Operator Part-Time Postmaster Relief; [memb.] United Church of Deep River, American Legion Auxiliary, VFW Auxiliary, Rebekkah Lodge; [hon.] Wrote and Read Poem "World War II Remembrances: At Memorial Day Services; [oth. writ.] Several poems published in local papers, several published in anthologies, write poems for social local occasions.; [pers.] I write from my heart first - then my head.; [a.] Deep River, IA

ZIPPO, GINA A.
[b.] March 22, 1985, Edison, NJ; [p.] Joseph and Valery Zippo; [ed.] I am a fifth Grade Student at Indian Hill School in Holmdel, NJ; [occ.] Student; [oth. writ.] This is my first poem at this time.; [pers.] My purpose for writing this poem is that I like flowers, they look pretty and smell nice and make the world two happy place.; [a.] Holmdel, NJ

ZOU, KELLY
[pen.] Windy Zest; [b.] February 26, 1971, Shanghai, China; [p.] Bao Kang Zou, Li Juan Zou; [ed.] MA - University of Rochester, BA - Chaminade University of Honolulu; [occ.] Ph.D. Candidate in Statistics, University of Rochester; [memb.] American Statistical Association, The International Biometric Society, Statistical Society of Canada; [hon.] Delta Epsilon Sigma, Summa Cum Laude, Presidential Scholarship, 1st Prize, National Writing Contest, China; [oth. writ.] Statistical journal articles appeared in medical decision making, medical imaging, biometrics. Articles for the Youth, Shanghai TV and Radio stations.; [pers.] Have a try.; [a.] Rochester, NY

INDEX OF POETS

Index

A

Aaronson, Sharon 328
Abad, Elsielyn A. 111
Abbott, Joshua 34
Abell, Sandi D. 569
Abney, Modena 200
Abraham, Gary 118
Abrahamson, Roger 276
Abrajano Jr., Cesar M. 56
Ackerman, Heather 411
Ackerman, Morgan 603
Acosta, Gustavo 287
Acosta, Rosenda M. 580
Adam, Jason Patrick 476
Adam, John 137
Adamek, Gene 74
Adams, Elaine M. 34
Adams Jr., Albert J. 359
Adams, Kris 205
Adams, MaryAlice 528
Adams, Robert 268
Adams, Sherry Sue 522
Adamson, Glenn L. 629
Adamus, Carol A. 388
Adcock, Shirley S. 530
Adee, Robert 200
Aderman, Susan M. 295
Adiv, David 79
Adkins, Pauline G. 556
Adler, Benjamin N. 123
Adler, Diane 159
Adler, Jeremy 430
Aguayo, Andrea de 444
Aguilar, Brian 24
Aguilar, Saundra J. 247
Aguilar-Medina, Veronica 279
Aguirre, Francie 418
Ahamed, Smitha 310
Ahearne, Patrick 252
Aherne, Damien 383
Ahmed, Nadine 566
Ahner, Shari Lu 205
Aiken, Elizabeth 126
Aker, Linda L. 336
Akers, Ilia 428
Akin, Alton A. 146
Akin, Robbin C. 211
Akright, Lois 488
Al-Saeed, Aesha 174
Alalamua, Olotania 261
Alan, Robert 208
Alan-Kersh, Todd 346
Albertson, Mary 355
Albertson, Trevor 217
Albin, Raymond F. 488
Albo, Bill S. 401
Albright, Harry T. 7
Albright, Jay C. 77
Albu, Carmen 128
Alderman, Annabel 81
Alders, Nellie M. 268
Alexander, Brent 161
Alexander, Brian 397
Alexander, Ephraim 40
Alexander, Margaret 552
Alexander, Shermaine 562
Alexander, Troy 621
Alford, Betty 10
Alford, Casey 360
Alford, Ricky 620
Algren, Donna Lee (Bromm) 53
Allen, Brian T. 400
Allen, Carol L. 23
Allen, Kandy 514
Allen, Linda 313
Allen, Ronald J. 571
Allen, Ruth 523
Allen, Tracy L. 278
Allen-Smith, Elisabeth 5
Allen-Smith, Marie Anna, 591
Allison, Vivian C. 569
Alt, Brandon C. 105
Althaus, Carol M. 134
Altuner, Conchita 130
Amador, Liliana 302
Amiotte, Billy 68
Amodeo, Jamie 620
Amore, Quirino C. 329
Amper III, Nicanor 344
Amren, Joanna 142
Amrich, Barry 108
Amsden, Jeffery Grant 122
An, David 470
Andersen, Morten 536
Anderson, Anne V. 465
Anderson, Candy 381
Anderson, Chris 461
Anderson, Danny Ray 166
Anderson, Ed 435
Anderson, Jeff 117
Anderson, Jennifer 148, 169
Anderson, Lisbeth 316
Anderson, Matthew L. 293
Andor, Stephanie 316
Andrade, Daniel 149
Andrade, Marlene 578
Andrewlavage, Wanda 209
Andrews, Donnie R. 92
Andrews, Jay 439
Andrus, Sonya 291
Angelini, Eileen M. 415
Angell, Michelle 262
Angers, Allen J. 403
Anguzza, Tonya 533
Annoreno, Nancy L. 319
Anonymous 169
Antaya, Renee 185
Apodaca, Leslie J. 332
Aponte, Norma 281
Applebaum, Rena 606
Applegate, Richard 621
Appleton, Christopher 116
Ardys, Ruth 281
Arends, Neil 223
Arincorayan, Derrick 88
Arioli, Grace 27
Armentrout, William Winfield 257
Armstrong, Belinda 358
Armstrong, Carolyn 408
Armstrong, Chris 148
Armstrong, Darlene M. 111
Armstrong, Joseph 67
Armstrong, L. Kenneth 348
Arnal, Sandra 306
Arndt, Mary A. 554
Arnold, Bill 27
Arnold, Choela Leslie 392
Arnold, Cleotha 471
Arnold, Janelle 357
Arnold, Nathan 294
Arnold, Patrice A. 228
Arnold, Patricia L. 217
Arnold, Shasta 320
Arnold, Shea 312
Arnold, Susan K. 263
Aro, Christine 359
Aronson, Rolann 553
Arrington, Rae 324
Arrowood, Kellie Dawn 250
Arthur, D. V. 599
Arthur, Steven 329
Arviso, Steven H. 277
Asch, Elise 474
Ashby, Virginia 282
Ashe, Tonya 210
Ashforth, Patricia S. 451
Ater, Kathy M. Dolle 502
Atkins, Helen F. 151
Atwell, Allyson 115
Au, Billy S. 140
Auber, Donny 418
Aubuckon, Mickey 190
Auer, Leona M. 235
August, Shoshana 346
Auguste, Carlo 376
Augustine, Diana De 424
Aune, Elsie 154
Austin-Thorn, Cynthia 70
Avalos, Lena M. 586
Avalos, Tonya 505
Ayars, Leona S. 274
Ayers, Debra J. 124
Ayyagari, Usha 507
Azzinaro, George 464
Azzone, Jared 132

B

Babik, Holly 462
Bacon, Kathy 270
Badeaux, Delynda 461
Baez, Nelly 554
Baffes, Thomas 510
Bagsby, Gaila 20
Bailey, Jennifer 150
Bailey, Oneita 523
Bailey, Tammy S. 349
Bain, Brandace B. 363
Baize, Buena Rose Brack 445
Baker, Betty A. 142
Baker, Catherine 87
Baker, Lynda E. 546
Baker, Michelle 620
Baker, Nancy 321
Baker, Sharron 179
Balaban, Jeff 36
Balas, Edward M. 40
Balasa, Andrew 28
Baldine, Laura A. 269
Baldwin, Barbara 136
Balistreri, Sandy 509
Ball, June 62
Ball, Melissa 487
Ball, Nicole 273
Ballou, Mary J. 576
Banker Jr., John C. 67
Bankins, Louise J. 202
Bankston, Sandra 265
Banning, Mary A. 271
Bapst, Julie Ann 141
Baptist, Brenda J. 172
Barb, Lillian 498
Barber, Matthew G. 233
Barbour, Louise H. 245
Barela, Linda 291
Barker, Ryan 552
Barkus, Jason Andrew 107
Barletta, Pamela A. 221
Barltrop, Laura 520
Barnard, Glynnette 336
Barnes, Chris 143
Barnes, Christine Ann 167
Barnes, Curry 423
Barnes, Hadiya S. 20
Barnes, Joe 402
Barnes, Sonya 285
Barnett, Joni Evans 165
Barocas, Edward L. 460
Barr, Anthony Barr 137
Barr, Renee 587
Barrasso, John T. 363
Barrett, Elizabeth 54
Barringer, Bobby 17
Barroso, Oscar 260
Barrow, Andrew 415
Barrow, Barbara S. 104
Barta, Ricki Terese 451
Barthlein, Sandra M. 567
Bartholomew, Daisy D. 434
Bartlett, Patricia Armstrong 498
Barton, Derek 36
Barton, Doris 440
Baschwit, Faye 465
Basheer, Bradine 620
Basinger, Eleanor F. 440
Bass, Amy 460
Bass Jr., Jim 121
Bass, Mona Lisa 620

Bates, Ella Ray Weese   176
Bates Sr., Wesley   564
Bates, Tony   354
Bathke, Christine   391
Batista, Arthur   130
Battersby Jr., William H.   553
Bauch, Mary H.   584
Bauer, Geraldine   425
Bauer, Jami L.   10
Baugh, Cheri R.   143
Baughn, Anadel   125
Baum, Russell A.   483
Baum Sr., Louis F.   212
Baumann, Jeff   110
Bautista, Saul E.   500
Bax, Sheila   190
Bay, Robert   566
Bayer, Katie   525
Bayer, Nicole C.   259
Bazan, AnneMarie K.   165
Beahm, Robin T.   310
Beall, Joanne   362
Bean, Judith   442
Bearden, Teresa   304
Beaty, Jennifer   111
Beaudet, Carolyn M.   13
Beaver, William A.   198
Beck, Larry   529
Becker, Aubria R.   146
Becker, Casey   74
Becker, Jamie Elizabeth   372
Beckham, Elizabeth B.   370
Bednar, Corde Marie   170
Bedsole, Wendy LaCoste   328
Bedwell, Lori   180
Beeson, John F.   28
Beggs, Lacinda   517
Behan, Scott J.   257
Belanger, Cynthia L.   16
Belanger, Susan C.   529
Belicek, Terri L.   559
Beliveau, David L.   46
Bell, Carla S.   429
Bell, Christine E.   383
Bell, Donna Jean   469
Bell, Eva   121
Bell, Jenny   32
Bell, Josephine   145
Bell, Linda A.   315
Bell, Pat   495
Bell, Ron   314
Bellamy, Artha   386
Bellar, Connie   360
Beltrani, Angela   526
Beltz, Hilda   158
Belveal, Adelia M.   165
Belvin, Kay   450
Bembenek, Pauline M.   559
Benanti, Deborah   477
Bender, Dustin L.   76
Bender, Sheila M.   210
Benedetto, Shirley   490
Bengali, Mumtaz   265

Benitez, Linda Marie   235
Bennett, Angela L.   131
Bennett, Danielle   151
Bennett, Glenn Ferris   103
Bennett, Je'Nean   441
Bennett, Russell   580
Bennington, Mary K.   259
Bennion, Pamela   186
Benoit, Bill   460
Benson, Erik   37
Benton, April   142
Berger, Bette   10
Bergthold, Kristen   311
Berker, Michael C.   257
Berkopec, Katrina   327
Berkowitz, James   52
Bernacki, Lindsey   490
Bernal, Richard A.   206
Bernard, Eugene F.   441
Bernhardt, Lance E.   581
Berning, Marilyn Bublitz   598
Bernstein, Herman   440
Berntsen, Thomas   584
Berry, Denise H.   371
Berry, Sean   570
Berry, Vonnie   339
Best, But You Know   109
Bettis, Dina   430
Beuhler, Ethel   90
Beveridge, Macelle   309
Beyers, Jennifer R.   424
Bice, Liola   319
Bickford Jr, William H.   355
Bickford, Pam   265
Bickley, Dixie C.   125
Bielski, Lauren   202
Bierley, Tempo   186
Bietenholz, Peter M.   267
Bighum, Rebecca Marie   546
Birkey, Cheryl   15
Birt, Michelle G.   226
Bisbee, Samantha Mae   538
Bishop III, Neil Eugene   307
Bishop, Indigo   384
Bishop, Michael F.   574
Bishop, Rosemarie E.   196
Bishop, Sandee   230
Black, Barbara J.   412
Black, Eleanor J.   406
Black, Rilla   304
Black, Ruth A.   331
Blackburn, Carol   426
Blackburn, Pearl A.   328
Blacker, Matt   354
Blackman, Melissa Rowell   343
Blackmon, Louis L.   496
Blackwell, Lloyd F.   448
Blackwell, Wanda   256
Blahut, Kenneth M.   185
Blair, Jennifer S.   96
Blake, Jeanne Thomas   428
Blanchette, Robert   622
Blanck, O.   487

Bland, Lora Martin   309
Blankenship, Janice   111
Blankensop, Melissa   532
Blanpied, Gail L.   420
Blanton, A. L.   348
Blasio, Lora De   505
Blevins, Lillian   587
Blevins, Marvin   284
Bliss, Carl Leo   33
Block, Stephen   485
Blommer, Julianne   156
Bloskey, Denise A.   453
Blue, Patricia   619
Blue, Victoria   577
Blumberg, Carolyn   25
Boatwright, Emma Lou   36
Bober, Frank J.   27
Bockbrader, Alyce M.   471
Bockelman, Allma   43
Bodily, Leah M.   258
Boe, Sean   538
Boettcher, Albert P.   95
Bogardus, Christopher   9
Boggess, Sabina Catarina   590
Boggs, Lisa   189
Bogle, Peggy   286
Bogus, Margery Dempsey   502
Bohman, Helen Rose   65
Boldosser, James M.   46
Bolivar-Brauet, Dolores Maria   392
Bolle, Kees W.   312
Bollom, Zane R.   561
Bolton, Ray   570
Bonacum, Donna   116
Bond, Amanda   132
Bond, Amelia   445
Bond, Herquelies   43
Bond, Jamie   364
Bond, Marty Waltman   276
Bond, Mel   203
Bonifacio, Anna   444
Bonner, Thomas   301
Bonvillian, Millie   605
Bonvouloir, Denise   173
Booker, Dorothy R.   124
Booker, Leslie   326
Boone, Kathleen   597
Boortz, Michael   548
Booth, Cherish   13
Booth, Ken   321
Boothe, Jamie   153
Borden, David   78
Borders, Tina   282
Borello, Joanne   103
Borg, Clyde L.   100
Borger, Sophia Simmons   249
Bork, Enid M.   171
Born, Angela   12
Borusky, Paul E.   281
Bosley, Betty May   438
Boswell, David J.   94
Bottger, James   42
Boudreaux, Herbert S.   622

Boudreaux, Lucille J.   284
Bouie, Sonya Renee   566
Bouldin, Della M.   399
Boule, J. Lynne   301
Boven, Michael D.   312
Bowar, William   393
Bowen, Celia   99
Bower, Leslie Anne   261
Bower, Roberta   631
Bowerman, Shirley F.   325
Bowers, Janice   32
Bowman, Christine   431
Bowman, Jason   160
Boyd Jr., Lester W.   297
Boyd, Peggy R.   586
Boykin, Lucy M.   488
Boyle, Robin   187
Bozek, Eliza   150
Bozzelli, Gina   401
Brabham, Debra   63
Bradbury, Susan   482
Bradley, Debbie M.   461
Bradley Jr., Joe A.   445
Bradley, Phyllis Brackett   268
Brancae, Gary Lewis   393
Brandt, Cathy M.   106
Brandt, Karin R.   278
Brant, Donna K.   39
Brant, Gerald B.   616
Brantley, Heather   98
Brasseur, R. Garner   313
Braxton, Lillian L.   220
Braxton, Susan   180
Brazee, April   163
Brazelton, Tom   253
Brazil, Chryssa   51
Brazil, Martina C.   619
Brebner, Elaine E.   27
Breden, Mindy   557
Breding, Miranda   304
Brennis, Diane   135
Brettmann, Paula   510
Breves, Phyllis   293
Brewer, David Allen   406
Brewer, Tracy Shoemaker   330
Brewton, Zonya   534
Bridges, Jackie   30
Bridges, Keith   280
Bridges, Robert   341
Bridick, Carmen S.   67
Brieden, Lee   527
Briedis, John   102
Brigham, Shirley   293
Bright, Denise   417
Brilis, Angela M.   467
Brimsek, John   138
Brisbon, Leonard H.   299
Britt, Donna L.   173
Britt, Gladys L.   94
Britt, Ruby B.   179
Britton, Betty   105
Broadhead, Tamera Dean   539
Brogdon, Margaret A.   187

Brogren, Claire 159
Brom, John 382
Bron, Laura L. 317
Broniman, Carl 102
Brooke, Ashli Turner 136
Brookover, Phyllis 205
Brooks, Anthony D. 23
Brooks, Connie 357
Brooks, David 96
Brooks, Holly 127
Brooks, Mary Frances 578
Brooks, Sheila 200
Brooks, Stella L. 243
Brophy, Matthew L. 302
Brower, Randy 204
Brower, Robert 325
Brown, A. Jean 579
Brown, Byron 93
Brown, Darlene 138
Brown, Donald Comer 49
Brown, Erin Nichelle 460
Brown, Evelyn C. 86
Brown, Gwen 434
Brown, Helen L. 155
Brown, James J. 4
Brown III, James M. 461
Brown, Keith A. 282
Brown, Kristin 355
Brown, L. R. 541
Brown, Mandy Cherie 604
Brown, Marini 244
Brown, Michael James 282
Brown, Naomi Y. 305
Brown, Robbin J. 239
Brown, Stephen C. 347
Browne, Cynthia Yeager 398
Brownlee-Cobb, S. 622
Bruce, Betty G. 415
Bruegger, Mary 619
Brumbaugh, Karen Ruth 211
Brumbaugh, Kathy 194
Bruner, David D. 165
Bruner, Faith E. 72
Bruner, Lorri Ann 202
Brunhoeber, Brenda 478
Bruning, Mary H. 546
Bruno, Christie 125
Bruschi, Geoffrey B. 79
Brush, Kathie 218
Bryant, Brian M. 80
Bryant, Edwina 13
Bryant, Mike 245
Bryant, Pat 251
Bryson, Anna E. 423
Bubb, Aimee 22
Bubnowski, Sherry 493
Bucek, Maureen 186
Buchko, Nicole 542
Buchta, Elizabeth 363
Buck, Joanne Michelle 24
Buckner, Etta Mae 386
Budetto, Charles W. 178
Budjinski, Brenda L. 364

Buehner, Dollie 149
Buel, Carrie 375
Buford, Paul S. 619
Bullard, Winifred 253
Bullock, Dorian R. 114
Bullock, Tippeney 565
Burchette, Christopher Allan 447
Burdick, Bryan J. 419
Burge, Elizabeth A. 404
Burger, Eileen M. 431
Burgess, Amanda 318
Burgess, Leonard 543
Burgos, Federico J. 411
Burgos, Linda E. 306
Burke, Dennis A. 132
Burke, Vicky L. 337
Burke-Warren, Catherine 368
Burks, Bobbie 163
Burnett, Shirley 335
Burns, Alexi 82
Burris, Naomi L. 451
Burroughs, Christine 78
Burrowes, Stephen 486
Burrows, Elizabeth MacDonald 481
Burrows, John L. 68
Burton, Helen 392
Burton, Janet Worrell 178
Burton, Tim 329
Bush, Emma 398
Bush, Josephine M. 373
Bush, R. David 245
Bush, Ryan 258
Bushey, Lisa Greenwood 257
Buskirk, Jamie D. Van 390
Busse, Ronald A. 549
Bussey, Alfred G., 135
Buswell, Shone 511
Butchart, Clare Ventura 14
Butcher, Lorna 508
Butler, Diane E. 619
Butler, Kelly Marie 201
Butler, Linda M. 452
Butler, Teri Richardson 489
Butler, Virginia 490
Butters, Amanda J. 375
Buzzelli, Timothy J. 556
Buzzo Jr., Bill J. 63
Byal, Katherine 198
Byard, Sue 271
Bykens, Hayley 333
Bynum, Aaron Anthony 137

C

Cabak, Karen T. 306
Caddell, William A. 338
Cady, Bonnie K. 107
Caffey, France V. 111
Caggiano, Antonio 72
Cagle, Mary 484
Caguin, Mike A. 283
Cahall, Keith B. 603
Cain, Paulette 340
Calder, Lisa K. 325

Calderon, Margaret 279
Calderone, Allene 140
Calderone, Tiffany 529
Caldwell, John 96
Calhoun, Michelle 288
Callahan, BonnieAnn 16
Callahan, David Glen 164
Callaizakis, Debi 152
Calvert, Sheri 540
Calzadias, Destiny D. 21
Camacho, Lorenzo S. 283
Camacho-Martinez, Marcotulio 292
Camara, Chianti Marie 417
Cameron, Robert W. 182
Cameron, T. James 327
Camhi, Martin 515
Campbell, Aria 144
Campbell, Dennis 367
Campbell, Dottie 154
Campbell, Edna M. 101
Campbell, Helen V. 22
Campbell, James 364
Campbell, Melissa Annette 549
Campi, Florence 156
Canavan, K. 554
Cancel, Jennifer 430
Candelaria, Elizabeth G. 475
Candella, Joseph 421
Cantrell, Teresa L. 330
Cantrelle, Emile A. 121
Capek, Thaddeus 299
Capen, Rose Marie 581
Caponiti, Carol 99
Capps, Michelle 551
Caputo, Michael 533
Cardullo, Allison Hannah 375
Cargill, Jack 478
Carinder, Brent 171
Carlin, Jill 126
Carlisle, Leslie 265
Carnovsky, Jaclyn 363
Caro-Capolungo, Ralph J. 278
Carpenter, Anne A. 380
Carpenter, Barbara Jean 121
Carpenter, Linda G. 353
Carpenter, Richard 284
Carr, David Duane 619
Carroll, Shawn 335
Carrozzi, Nicholas 595
Carson, Jean McKelvey 168
Carson, Stephanie 306
Carson, Ted 490
Carstensen, Velma 263
Carter, Elizabeth M. 131
Carter, Jodie 41
Carter, Kelvin 448
Carter, Kendra 350
Carter, Shaunda 278
Carter, Trisha 341
Carufel, Jammie 106
Carvey, Theresa Anne 299
Casal-Tillman, Yvonne 505
Casarez, Eileen M. 626

Cashner, Matt 517
Caskinette, Ann 454
Castillo Jr., Ramon R. 271
Castlevetro, Carmel 85
Castrejon Jr., Tomas 349
Castro, Sandra I. 585
Catalano, Kristen M. 229
Cathcart, Maria Markovic 293
Caudill, Cynthia 140
Caudill, Sandra Lynn 487
Cauley, O'Neal Sim 601
caulfield, thomas j. 334
Causey, Dorothy 33
Cavanaugh, Dawn 156
Cavanaugh, Melissa L. 325
Cavender, Andrea 402
Cavender, Jeanne M. 142
Caves, Donald W. 5
Cavil, Lillian M. 600
Caywood, John 438
Cea, Vincent 237
Cedarleaf, Dorothy E. 95
Cejner, S. Blake 582
Cepero, Paul 272
Cervantes, Teresa 300
Chadwell, Shannon R. 605
Chafin, Heather R. 81
Chamberlain, Courtney M. 49
Chambers, Deborah Louise 376
Chambers, George 429
Chambers, Michelle 326
Chambliss, Charlotte J. 430
Chandler, Christy 154
Chandler, Kristina M. 330
Chandler, Travis A. 619
Chandless, Kathryn 598
Chapman, Patricia A. 480
Chappel, Rosel I. 591
Chapple, Tonia E. 569
Charles L. Roberts, Jr 152
Charles, Shannon 196
Charlton, Angela 391
Charlton, Caryn 86
Chase, Connie L. 448
Chassion, Michael J. 180
Chastain, Jack F. 459
Chaudhry, Arifa S. 391
Chavez, Alex 379
Chavez, Nicole 312
Check, Wayne A. 289
Checketts, Rosemarie L. B. 326
Chen, Susan Y. 284
Chery, Premil 299
Cheski, Paul M. 535
Chester, Chris 134
Cheverton, Ian 396
Chew, Kim Jin 267
Chiba, Courtney 118
Chikere, Remigius 545
Childs, Emily 407
Childs, Wilbur J. 290
Chinault, Grace H. 148
Ching, Elena 137

Chismar, Yahni 341
Chiu, Pat 284
Chiucchi, Leslie Ann 539
Cho, David 87
Choquette, Gloria Rose 166
Chrisman, Madelyn Marie 579
Chrissos, Lauren 303
Christensen, Daniel 390
Christensen, Kerry 267
Christenson, Laurie 219
Christine, Andrea 178
Christman, Justin Potter 108
Christopher, Charles 378
Christy, Eve 463
Christy, Miranda Rashell 353
Church, Sarah 343
Churion, Susana 191
Ciavarella, Susan 497
Cibas, Ario 89
Ciciarelli, Lucie 294
Cieslewski, Iva 128
Cillo, Edna Elsie 414
Ciresi, Natalie 341
Clannach, Candon Aelfdan 120
Claridge, John 367
Clark, Bessie Soderborg 376
Clark, Bill 41
Clark, Caleb 126
Clark, Carol 434
Clark, Gary L. 387
Clark, George A. 403
Clark, George L. 4
Clark, Joyce M. 86
Clark Jr., Walter V. 218
Clark, Kathleen N. 280
Clark, Lill 299
Clark, Martha R. 286
Clark, Susan Margaret 244
Clark, William 594
Clark, William Nelson 534
Clarke, Evon R. 104
Clarkson, Jennifer 70
Clary, Emmanuel 431
Clay, Kristina 184
Clay, Maritza E. 326
Clayton, Cheryl 107
Cleary, James S. 112
Clegg, Jamie M. 174
Cleland, Joan 173
Clemence, John S. 80
Clement, Marie 585
Clements, Betty 365
Clements, Jan 434
Clendenen, Harvey E. 39
Clifton, Roberta H. 334
Cline, Dawn Lynn 381
Cline, Will 351
Clukie, David R. 41
Clymer, Michelle C. 240
Coble, Casey 88
Coburn, Deas A. 385
Cochenour, Kristin 327
Cochran, Anthony 478

Cockett, J. Uilani 345
Cockriel, Janet 19
Coffee, Della 134
Coffee, Kate 541
Coffey, Doris Aline 417
Coffey, Kenneth W. 493
Coffey, Ryan 266
Cohen, Alecia J. 462
Cohen, Chuck 27
Cohen, Robert 188
Cohen, Timothy S. 548
Coile, LaDon 602
Coiro, Gina Del 424
Cole, Donna 133
Cole, Leslie A. 276
Cole, Nellene 619
Cole, Stephanie 270
Coleman, Carla 366
Coleman, Ebony 101
Coleman, Jennifer S. 17
Coleman, Tangela M. 513
Coleman-Lacadie, Connie 81
Coles, Carol 80
Colie, April L. 446
Collette, Dorothy 469
Collie, Nahshon 216
Collins, David T. 447
Collins, Emily 139
Collins Jr., Herbert 176
Collins, Leanna Mae 214
Collins-Spina, Patricia A. 513
Colombaro, Sherry L. 486
Colon, Anthony 12
Colquitt, Susan Y. 521
Colvin, Ferne I. 420
Combs, Amy Beth 26
Comenzo, Lucy 452
Comiskey, Marguerite 225
Composto, Anthony J. 175
Conley Jr., William H. 255
Conner, Jennifer L. 474
Conner, Sheila Y. Bohler 272
Connolly, Margalo Astrid 251
Connor Jr., Leo J. 349
Constant, G. 316
Conway, Michael F. 273
Conway, Richard William 452
Conway, Das 455
Conway, Toni 339
Cook, Carolyn Gresham 398
Cook, Mary Townsend 297
Cook, Peggy (Anthony) 302
Cooke, Carrie M. 468
Cooke, Harry J. 51
Cooley, Glenn 44
Coolidge, Diane L. 398
Coombs, Eleanor I. M. 133
Cooper, D. Judson 186
Cooper, David James 103
Cooper Jr., Tyrus B. 287
Cooper, Kathleen 541
Cooper, Yvonne 331
Coose, Rebecca 534

Copas, Teresa 246
Copeland, Anne Anderson 76
Copeland, Jimmy 57
Copenhaver, Valerie 594
Copley, Mary F. 243
Coppage, Pauline M. 352
Coret, R. L. 336
Corey, Kelli A. 449
Cornwell, Connie J. 175
Cornwell, Russell C. 257
Corrales, Christina 48
Cortello, Frank 24
Costanzo, Mary Cabrini 270
Costello, Donna 100
Cotey, Jon (Gypsy) 444
Cotton, Rodrick D. 509
Couch, Jimmy G. 471
Coulter, Jennifer 115
Coulter, Patricia 202
Cour, Alice C. Van 155
Courter, Sophie 551
Coville, Doris Dickson 468
Cox, Albert A. 65
Cox, Bradley David 445
Cox, Deidra 460
Cox, Douglas M. 165
Coy, Allen Randy 83
Coyle, Jessica 177
Crabtree, Martha 548
Craft, Reginald 524
Craig, Gerrish 148
Crandall, Bruce 171
Crane, Deanna R. 368
Crane, Trey 241
Cranston, Leona E. 349
Crapo, J. Gregory 253
Crawford, Craig J. 106
Crawford, Eric 398
Crawford, John K. 152
Crawford, Lisa Burk 484
Crawford, Miriam White 570
Crawford, Wanda Jo 530
Cray, Verdell 279
Creamer, Carolyn 98
Creamer, Cortni 71
Creaser, Irina 101
Creech, Kathleen E. 524
Crespo, Margarita 560
Cresta, Joseph M. 112
Crews, Anna Marie 86
Cribb, Wayne 322
Crismond, Dianne 175
Cristanus, Joseph E. 413
Crittenton, Jacque 367
Crockett, Susan E. 288
Cronin, Laura J. 329
Cronk, Lee Ann 604
Crosby, Jessica M. 144
Cross, Kendrick N. 228
Crosta, Dina 426
Crowe, Ann 370
Crowell, Marlene 316
Crownover, Fran 396

Croxson, Denson D. 146
Croyle, Douglas E. 406
Crozier, J. Richard 534
Crumb, Eric T. 436
Cruz, Laura 232
Csupo, Brandon 162
Csupo, Jarrett 78
Cuffee, Marquintala 220
Culla, Kathleen 509
Cummins, Emma 162
Cummins, Jennie 477
Cummiskey, Tom 297
Curley Jr., Robby 529
Currie, Morgan 247
Currier, Alfred 443
Curry, Johanna 116
Curry, Terri 562
Curry, Yolanda 263
Curtin, John-Robert 82
Curtiss, Julie Ann 113
Cushing, Charlotte 175
Cushing, Michael K. 243
Cypert-Arnold, Kathleen 495
Czerwinski, John 19

D

Dagg, Vera 340
Dahlstrom-Roadruck, Erika 114
Daily, Judi 365
D'Alesandro, Nyle Kennerly 345
D'Alessandro, P. A. 320
Daley, Elaine 25
Dalley, Jaimy 378
D'Ambrosio, Tony 276
D'Amico, Jennifer Anne 403
Dammen, Stephanie 344
Dandridge, Ramon T. 541
D'Angelo, Susan 228
Daniel, Elaine 417
Daniels, Donald R. 150
Daniels, Mary A. 226
Daniels, Michelle Yeavon 590
Daniels, Sandee W. 293
Dankers, Judy 122
Danridge, Judy 40
Danskin, Robert W. 324
Daoud, Michel 494
Dare, Jeffrey 89
Darland, Deborah 171
Darling, F. L. 288
Darty, Gregory 115
Dass, Diana 454
Davenport, Melissa Hatten 594
David, Michael 516
Davidson, Brenda Thomas 152
Davidson, Helen Tripp 35
Davidson, J. Corinne 450
Davidson, Jean M. 359
Davidson, Katy 202
Davis, Amanda 94
Davis, Constance 162
Davis, Elnora S. 387
Davis, Etta M. 374

Davis, Gwain Addison 384
Davis, Hillary Rose 168
Davis, Johnnie 447
Davis Jr., Scott 321
Davis, Kathryn J. 284
Davis, Lynda Bryan 496
Davis, Stacey P. 340
Davis-Flint, Joanne 375
Dawkins, Danielle 478
Dawkins, Neva 317
Dawson, Ginny 123
Dawson, Kristi 317
Dawson, Marie H. 255
De Coster, Darryll A. 432
De Marco, Mildred L. 334
de Vries, G. 322
De Witt, Neal C. 264
Dean Jr., Edward M. 364
Dean, Laura 314
DeAndrea, Mary E. 517
DeBey, Rana 501
Debney, John J. 446
DeBord, Leann 352
DeChaine, Myra L. 287
DeClue, Annette D. 7
DeCoteau, Kordai 558
Dee, Michael Coleman 630
Deflavio, Joy 169
Defoor, Joshua 107
DeGrechie, Casey 454
Dehoff, Dale 14
DeJohn, Kathy 598
DeJohn, Linda S. 256
DeJoya, Adee 23
DeKarske, Kathy 550
Del Santo, Thomas W. 325
Delander, Cheryl 15
Delavan, Rayma Dee 567
DeLay, Lea Rene 270
Deleon, Migdalia 601
Delgado, Vernon 596
Delgrego, Kristen 227
D'Elia, Filomena 7
Delker, Eleanor 424
Dell, Steven 520
Dellien, Alyce Marie 6
DeLon, Steven K. 539
Delsanter, Michael B. 331
DeLude, Raymond 350
Demars, Cindy C. 455
Demetriou, Sarah 344
DeMorier, Julie 96
Denette, Trisha 320
Denis, Jheran 442
Denise, J 322
Denison-Gallmeyer, Rita 568
Denmark, Phillis 210
Dennis, Jessie 71
Dennis, Richard S. 594
Denton, Martha McCalister 509
DePierre, Laura 200
DePietro, Joan C. 167
Derian, Kitty 325

DeRocher, Patricia A. 274
Derr, Karen 542
Derwingson, Joni 89
Deserto, Jamie 108
DesLaurier, Mildred V. 276
DeStefano, Anthony 53
Deters, Nicole 314
Detwiller, Cheryl 104
Deusen, Alyson Van 382
Devine, Edith 128
DeVore, Cheryl 133
Dewing, Doug 137
Dexter, Michelle 197
DeYoung, Diane 385
Dhondt, Mildred H. 312
Diaz, Anita M. 49
Diaz, Anna 120
Diaz, Karin 494
Dick Jr., Robert C. 453
Dicke, Robert J. 544
Dickens, Chris 84
Dickerson-Czarnecki, Brenna 126
Dickson, Lawrence Michael 320
DiCristina, Linda 295
Diephuis, Ronald T. 222
Diesch, Christine 369
Dietz, Cindy M. 157
Dietzler, William S. 481
Dill, Edith P. 392
Dillon, Ellen Rose 85
Dimitri, William K. 449
Dimos, John T. 455
Dinardi, Angela Marie 407
Dincognito, Bill 50
Dinsdale, Myra 530
Dioguardi, Gy. 509
DiPietro, Gina 146
Dischinger, Theresa 237
Dittman, Chris L. 165
Ditzler, Derick Dean 28
DiVito, Tim 353
Dixie, Kwaseera 219
Dixon, Jean 74
Dixon, Jesse E. 32
Dixon, Tanya K. 327
Doan, Jacqueline S. 425
Dodge, Oren 201
Doherty, Adedayo 382
Doherty, Debbie 33
Doherty, Mary 558
Dolan, John J. 54
Dolhancyk, Diana 363
Domansky, David W. 131
Domeny, Margaret 219
Donald, James H. 168
Donohoe, Susan K. 279
Donohoo, Carolyn Jane 130
Donohoo, Margie 327
Donovan, Gladys M. 29
Dooley, Nyta 290
Dorsey, Nathaniel Tex 344
Dorval, Lindsey 491
Dosoretz, Lizy 571

Doss, Jeremy 9
Dotson, Lisa L. 529
Doty, David 96
Dougherty, Rhett 353
Doughty, Krissy 268
Douglas, Dawn L. 431
Dover, Ryan 578
Dowd, Patricia 531
Dowdle III, Paul Edward 350
Dowling, Ben 397
Downs, Jay Warren 32
Doxtader, Linda 514
Doyle, Diane 99
Doyle, Laura M. 209
Doyle, Leslie F. 450
Drake, Claudette 145
Dreamer., The 269
Dreier, Donna 104
Dresbach, Brad 172
Dronet, Medy 291
Drop, Patricia 586
Drummond, Judith A. 93
Du Frane, Nicole 348
Dubbs, Junia Lorain 98
Dubovik, G. J. 315
Dubrova, Luba 531
Ducat, Frank 428
Dudley, Kristina Bryn 497
Duefrene, Carol 158
Duffey, Betty 28
Duffin, Ashley 179
Dugal, Lena 310
Dugan, Kyle T. 487
Dugas, Christi 159
Duggan, Robert D. 198
Duggins, Michelle 503
dunaway, d. l. 269
Duncan, David Paul 40
Duncan, Robert M. 451
Dunham, Austin B. 391
Dunkle, Hollie 431
Dunlap, Helen Brown 426
Dunn, Edith A. 104
Dunnagan, Carol K. 162
Dunne, Irene S. 404
Durfee, Sandra J. 517
Durham, Jewell 395
Durnbaugh, Linda 342
Durocher, Marie A. 627
Dusch, Sandra Matteson 312
Dusel, William 568
Duvall, Faith 473
Duvall, Leslie D. 206
Dwyer, Karen 223
Dye, Alma F. 37
Dye, Dorotha W. 166
Dyer, Karen J. 271
Dyke, Claudia Van 94

E

E., Ann 445
Eads, Raymond 264
Eagan, Amy 15

Earles, Cassandra D. 157
Earnest, Arleen A. 402
Eason, Sarah 597
Eastern, Rene 484
Eastman, G. 331
Eastman, Jayne 11
Eastman, Jody 145
Easton, Andrew S., Age 12 418
Eastwood, Suzy 277
Eaton, Kathy D. 183
Ebel, Sandra 299
Eblin, Williadine 273
Echevarria, Elsie 466, 593
Eckard, Julie Diane 148
Eckerle, Philip A. 581
Edgar, Danielle 98
Edmondson, Betty 163
Edward 588
Edward, John Laurel 134
Edwards, Andrew J., 414
Edwards, Chris 15
Edwards, Elizabeth 456
Edwards, James Brian 445
Edwards, Jessica 629
Edwards, Morry 557
Edwards, Norma Elaine 313
Edwards, Pamela J. 623
Edwards, Paul Allen 324
Edwards, Warren P. 494
Eenhuis, Terry 351
Eichner, Michael 499
Eide, Eric 82
Eileen, Alisa 443
Eklund, Janet Lynn 68
Eldred, Richard 250
Elie, Gia 122
Ellegood, Elizabeth 618
Ellerbe, Belinda M. 168
Ellingson, Debra 69
Elliott, Amanda C. 435
Elliott, Edna 137
Elliott, Katherine C. 201
Ellis, Deborah L. 52
Ellis, Katrina W. 243
Ellworth, Diana 107
Elmer, Marion 232
Elmore, Evelyn 70
Elshot, Kitty 305
Elson, Dee 3
Emanuel, LaVerne M. 271
Emerling, Jae 112
Emerson, J. A. 551
Emory, Alyce D. 139
Enage, Danielle 429
Engelman, Amanda 49
England, Nancy 452
England, Tasha 305
Engle, Cheri 592
Engle, Richard W. 523
Engleman, Janet L. 28
Engler, Linda 297
Engstrom, Diane L. 128
Enrique, Leonard 548

Enriquez, Edward 109
Enyart, Kathleen L. 590
Epps, Irma Sun Woman 71
Erb, James W. 618
Erdei, Eunice F. 83
Erickson, Laurie Ann 535
Ernce, Darcianne M. 94
Ernst, Patricia May 543
Erskine, Susan M. H. 296
Ersley, H. 332
Ervin, Derrick 358
Erwin, Adeline C. 12
Erwin, Elaina 361
Eselhorst, Albert R. 433
Eshelman, Chad 480
Eshleman, Michael J. 450
Essary, Mary L. 571
Essi, Martha G. 285
Essler, Susan 479
Estacio, Rudeen 276
Estrada, Amy 379
Ettienne-Modeste, Clyde 401
Etue, Lawrence 334
Eugenio, Giovannie Monica 96
Evanosich, Anna Geary 135
Evans, Cristin 444
Evans, Olive 230
Evans, Tamika J. 556
Everage, Camilla 418
Everett, Christopher 448
Everett, Dan 172

F

Fleischer, Scott Nelson 628
Fago, Heather L. 102
Faille, Shawn 577
Falk, Mary Harding 348
Falter, Donna 125
Fanning Jr., John M. 145
Farahay, M. L. 355
Farber, Eric 129
Farkas, Jay Ann 102
Farler, Patricia M. 449
Farnham, Caron 358
Farr, Larry Shane 335
Farr, Virginia W. 604
Farrell, Amanda 473
Farris, Thomas E. 292
Farrugia, George A. 115
Faucheux, Misty 486
Faulhaber, Travis 241
Faulkner, Barbe 390
Faulkner, Steve 195
Faulstich, Kelly K. 190
Faurot, Julie Ann 445
Favale, Daria 427
Fearnhead, Joy 166
Fedele, Michelina J. 516
Feeney, Patricia Lynn 491
Feig, Elaine E. 104
Feit, Arielle 3
Feldman, Samuel 338
Feliciano, Pat 618

Fenske, Deloris 156
Fercy, Myra 204
Ferguson, Cynthia L. 86
Ferguson, James 404
Ferguson, Linda 276
Ferguson, Scott 539
Fernandez, Carlos 630
Fernandez, Paul 623
Ferneau, Mark 543
Ferriell, Darla 166
Ferris, John 176
Ferruzza, Edward J. 142
Fetler, Erik 382
Fetter, June 366
Fick, Kelly 214
Field, Kim 247
Fielding, Dan 465
Fields, Barbara J. 394
Fields, Bonell 121
Figel, Tiffany 490
Filip, Robert E. 317
Filipowicz, Aldona 618
Fillebrown, Matthew 493
Fillie, Chris 130
Fillmore, Amber G. 395
Finch, Kim 627
Fine, Elmeta 55
Finnegan, Christine 150
Finnerty, John F. P. 82
Firth, Ina A. 106
Fischer, Terrie Mavis 218
Fischetti, Patricia 275
Fisher, Cory L. 77
Fisher, Darwin R. 420
Fishkind, Carole Perrin 141
Fitch, Howard M. 380
Fitzgerald, Cathy 457
Fitzgerald II, Michael J. 327
Fitzgerald, Michael 482
Fitzgerald, Patrick 338
Flaherty, Virgil F. 628
Flanagan, Virginia 533
Flannery, Sean 187
Flaten, Mike V. 555
Flavell, Katrina 338
Fleischer, Herb 480
Fleming, Bill 32
Fleming, Mary Kay 532
Fleming, Patricia A. 263
Fletcher, Grace Weaver 29
Flodquist, Paul 578
Flores, Abel J. 5
Flores, Angelia 149
Flores, Joe R. 618
Flores, Max S. 554
Florio, Frank J. 50
Flournoy, Rachel 306
Flowers, Annette 4
Floyd, Virginia Wray 353
Flurry, George 456
Flynn, Mary L. 342
Flynn, Phyllis 494
Flynn, Ursula A. 296

Focas, Angella A. 111
Fogarty, Colleen C. 373
Folbre, Terri 521
Forbes, Phyllise R. 311
Forbis, Cecilia 101
Forcade, Michele 304
Ford, Daniel 88
Ford, Karin L. 220
Ford, T. C. 531
Fordham, Christa R. 17
Foreman, John R. 57
Formanek, Hedy W. 123
Formica, Joy R. 104
Fornero, Elaine 127
Forney, Jewell 411
Forrest I, Lewis E. 589
Forrester, Dorothy J. 179
Forstrom, Barbara 121
Forthuber, Drena 161
Fortier, E. L. 348
Fortner, Sara 498
Foster, Brian 142
Foster, Donald 98
Foster, Hattie 82
Foster, Stephenie C. 541
Foust, Rebecca 323
Fowler Sr., Thomas S. 562
Fox, Mona 337
Fox, Willard R. 210
Francis, Brad 97
Francis, James G. 107
Francis, Stacy L. 285
Franco, Jimmy M. 91
Frandrup, Dallan 446
Franks, Timothy J. 303
Fraser, Dana 38
Frazier, Janet Lee 168
Frazier, Sharlene 290
Frazier-Allison, Catherine 24
Frechette, Fernand 65
Freedman, Fannie 155
Freeland, Edla Josephine 385
Fregoso, A. 552
French, Christine 11
Friedlander, Frank W. 26
Friedman, Theodore 241
Friesen, Bruce K. 147
Friesen, Molly 571
Frinier, Catherine 110
Frisch, Nadine 332
Frizzle, Christine 443
Frohman, Howard Loeb 465
Frost, Keith R. 323
Frost, Mary Ethel 573
Fryberger, Kami 239, 618
Frye, Delena Cheryl 122
Frye, Donna Renee 44
Fudge, Thomas A. 311
Fuentes, Meliza B. 255
Fularz, T. 301
Fulks, Cindy 159
Fullen, Cindy Sue 116
Fuller, Adam 125

Fuller, Kevin J. 593
Fulton, Toni 342
Fuss, Brianne 125

G

Gabbard, Ruby L. 206
Gaddie, David 168
Gagne, Louise Marie 483
Galbraith, Steven T. 577
Galfano, Rosa Leonora 235
Galindo Jr., Joseph P. 78
Galinta, Romeo A. 344
Gall, Chad 52
Gallar, John 66
Gallas, Betty 115
Gallegos, R. Michael 194
Gallina, Juliane 169
Galvin, Nathan 286
Gamble, Marcia 337
Gandesbery, Jack 506
Garadis, Matt 293
Garber, Davina Lynn 178
Garcia, Amy 75
Garcia, Janie L. 463
Garcia, Lillian Lydia 265
Gardenias, Saundra Coon 207
Gardner, Frank 402
Gardner, Lora Dymphna 449
Garner, Sally H. 280
Garratt, Brittany 6
Garretson, Johanna A. 426
Garrett, Laverne 566
Garris, Amy Elizabeth 404
Gary, David W. 97
Gary, Rhonda R. 210
Gaskill, Larry 192
Gaskin, Kateri 498
Gates, Curtis O. 618
Gauck, Linda 197
Gauld, Laurel 263
Gauthier Jr., Hartwell L. 80
Gbado, Rufin B. 590
Geeting, Christopher 143
Geiger, Ashley 112
Geist, Marsha L. 317
Geller, Bunny 397
Gellings, Mary T. 283
Gelshenen, Linda 249
Gennette, Elaine M. 617
Genszler, C. W. 290
George, Laura 549
George, Sandra 582
George, Semele A. Cid 563
Georgopoulos, Areti 93
Gerhartz, Jennifer 622
Gerhauser, Dina 152
German, Cynthia A. M. 372
Germani, Deena L. 87
Germany, Joan 169
Gerszewski, Thom 308
Giarrusso, Debra M. 475
Gibbons, Cindy 37
Gibbons, Colleen 422

Gibson, Jonelle 169
Gibson, Martin E. 480
Giera, Barbara A. McCoy 52
Gies, Tania 340
Gifford, Cynthia J. 23
Gigantino, Sandi 301
Gilbert, Brenda 69
Gilbert, Cabrina A. 145
Gilbert, Geoffrey 429
Gilbert, Jane Dunnell 550
Gilbert, Margaret 296
Gilbert, Troy 625
Gilchrest, Winniferd 564
Gilchrist, Chad 385
Gill, Anna M. 123
Gill, Kimberly A. 309
Gill, Sharolette Nicole 337
Gillespie, Joanne 47
Gillespie, Joshua 111
Gillette Jr., H. A. 564
Gilliam, Angela G. 437
Gillis, Dorothy M. 100
Gillispie, Nolan 242
Gilman, Melissa 326
Gilmartin, Joseph H. 400
Gilmore, Anna 174
Gines, Kevin R. 232
Gioia, Benjamin 447
Giordano, Shannon Lee 213
Giron, Robert 583
Giuliani, Marilyn Kay 347
Given, Malena 287
Givens, Pamela 342
Gladney, Derrick 31
Gladstone, Lawrence James 183
Glass, Margaret L. C. 536
Gleason, Helen 175
Gleason, Wilma E. 339
Glenn, Jim 140
Glide, Shawn Leslie 482
Gliem, Diana S. 133
Glogowski, Theresa 216
Glover, Charmaine 122
Gnau, Jason Thomas 39
Godbolt, Shirley 338
Godfrey, Cami 432
Goecke, Jane 462
Goen, Suzanne 260
Goerke, Dorothy M. 176
Goff, Jennifer Marie 148
Goff, Nichelle L. 328
Gold, Matthew 186
Golden, Lorraine A. 204
Goldman, Anita 447
Goldsmith, Susan 532
Goldson, Doreen 411
Goldstein, Joy 160
Goldstein, Robert A. 347
Golley Jr., Howard 174
Gomez, Elena M. 454
Gomez, Pedro W. 528
Gonsalves, Jamesy U. 89
gonzales, juan 94

Gonzales, Kristofer G. 325
Gonzalez, Maria 196
Gonzalez, Michelle Martin 200
Gonzalez, Sarah 259
Gonzalves, Krystal 267
Gooch, Bessie Evers 108
Good, Jessie H. 22
Good, Margaret 277
Goodman, Brett 122
Goodwin, Hazel 136
Goodwin, Lillie Mae 335
Goodwin, Mary Alice 496
Gooley, Patrick J. 489
Gore, Kellie D. 601
Gosline, Kristin M. 225
Goston, Patty 196
Gotsch, Ted 332
Gottberg, Greg 70
Gottlieb, Jeanette 440
Gottlieb, Michael 617
Goulet, Jennica 84
Gowan, Faye 153
Grace, Bettie J. 463
Grace, Wanda P. 282
Graham, Debbie Kehaulani 111
Graham, Gloria 159
Graham, Kymberly Henderson 295
Gramlich, William 562
Gran, Stephanie 213
Granholm, Richard A. 604
Grant, Barbara J. 144
Grant, Joan Julien 147
Grant, Judith 405
Grassman, Curtis E. 140
Grasso, Monica L. 339
Graves, April 161
Graves, Melanie K. 599
Gravitt, Betty Chester 35
Gray, Buddy 43
Gray, Tina 321
Grayson, Anna M. 41
Greco, Mary Ann 507
Greco, Vanessa Renee 308
Green, Alice 56
Green, Annie 147
Green, Eric Charles 87, 608
Green, Ernestine 90
Green, Geraldine 132
Green, Louise 508
Green, Verleen R. 495
Green, Vincent E. 260
Greenwell, Heather 12
Gregory, Dan 399
Gregory, Elizabeth Lisa 36
Greisman, Joan 422
Greiwe, Sandra 288
Grenier, Mary A. 555
Gresham, Kathy L. 245
Grieb, Lori Sue 278
Grieco, Nicole 565
Griffin, Carol 478
Griffin, Carolyn 377
Griffin, Geneveive 359

Griffin, Paul 216
Griffith, Peggy 504
Griffiths, Donna T. 153
Grijalva, Arthur A. 399
Grim, Kelly 533
Grimaldi, Kathleen Galvin 291
Grimshaw, Douglas W. 360
Grindell, Mark 324
Grishkevich, Susan 511
Groce, Wade 347
Grogan, Anne 361
Groman, Neal B. 313
Groomes, Royal T. 207
Grosjean, Genevieve 398
Grothjan, Cheryl 75
Grubb, Laurie 272
Guenther, Mel 631
Guenthner, Bernard Scott 162
Guercio, Faye West 399
Guerin, George John 410
Guerin-McDowell, Cathy 155
Guerra, Isabel 382
Guida, Ann 12
Guillod, Jeffrey 617
Guinn, George 378
Guinn, Lori 223
Gulino, Chris 75
Gully, Joan Reego 161
Gum, Rebecca Curry 555
Gunsteen, Sally Vilim 298
Gunther, Paul 597
Gupta, Sabyasachi 530
Gurlacz, Willie Ann 293
Gurley, Toni 280
Gursky, Sandra M. W. 258
Guthrie, Barbara A. 617
Guthrie, Steve L. 539
Guttromson, Michelle G. 326
Guy, Theresa 271
Guzman, Irving Lazerus 470
Gwynn, Shon A. 323

H

Haas, Megan 589
Haberkorn, Anne 107
Hackney, Ashley 467
Hadden, Violet P. 251
Haffley, Leola A. 489
Hagen, William W. 629
Hager, Wendy 498
Hagestad, Kristin 563
Haghighi, Niloufar 234
Hahn, Anita L 19
Haimowitz, Alvin 373
Haines, Lula M. 302
Hair, Max 276
Hale, Michael T. 211
Hall, Donna 137, 167
Hall, Emily T. 175
Hall, Karen A. 208
Hall, Marjorie Guess 567
Hall, Michelle 604
Hallcox, Jarrett 128

Hallenbeck, Judy 476
Hallman, Linell C. 222
Halseth, Kristy J. 208
Halstead Jr., Gerald 447
Halverson, Jenna 432
Ham, La Hom 233
Ham, Natasha 561
Hamilton, Jody 145
Hamilton, Randy 449
Hamilton, Rich 527
Hamilton, Wayne 262
Hamlin, Katie 264
Hamman, Marilyn 349
Hammer, Kenneth 292
Hammonds, Mark Allen 617
Hammons, Dana 414
Hanan, Julia 66
Hance, Becky 465
Handelman, Mika 288
Haney, Nancy L. 269
Hanford, Heather 53
Hanlin, Leroy 491
Hansen, Bart F. 456
Hansen III, George E. 69
Hansen, Laura 532
Hanson, Jane Huelster 117
Hanson, Patty 581
Hanson, Rachel Leigh 522
Harberg, Arthur L 127
Hardell, Peter R. 213
Hardie, H. Ernie 261
Hardin, Dustin 162
Harding, Charles G. 171
Hardison, Mildred 307
Hardy, Mildred M. 340
Hardy, Tese 284
Hargett, Carol Jane 176
Hargis, Ione M. 97
Hariz, Mirna 551
Harlan, Charlie 114
Harlow, Audrey C. 108
Harman, Gregory Lee 399
Harmon, Joane 156
Harmon, Sulesa 544
Harnden, Deb 438
Harney, Elizabeth A. 151
Harnish, Melissa A. 605
Harper, Jennifer 39
Harris, Evan 3
Harris, Helen A. 73
Harris, Jane Hanson 36
Harris, Jeanne 29
Harris Jr., Odio 195
Harris, Kirk D. 233
Harris, Loretta 352
Harris, Mary P. 586
Harris, Matt L. 264
Harris, Tamara L. 355
Harrison, Domeka 177
Harrison, Michael P. 349
Hart, Angela M. 368
Hartigan, George 128
Hartigan, Gertrude 141

Hartley, Callie A. 98
Hartley, Jim 416
Hartman, Charlotte 118
Hartman, Joan A., 129
Hartz, John 122
Haruvi, Jacob 63
Harvell, Dolores 134
Harvey, Elizabeth 415
Harvie, Diana I. 34
Hassan, Angela K. 35
Hassell, Jennifer Lynn 386
Hasson, Christopher 422
Haston, Adrienne 406
Hatalla, Caryn F. 74
Hatcher, Kenneth D. 339
Hathaway, Shirley M. 241
Hatzenbuehler, Jeffrey 433
Hauer, Oriana 314
Havens, Will H. 587
Hawkins, Jeff 150
Hawkinson, Gladys 395
Hawley, Roy G. 201
Hay, Jim 3
Hayes, Eddie 373
Hays, Darla 381
Hazel, Tina M. 346
Headley, Kim 299
Heady, Kenneth Wightman 576
Healey, Anne Marie 360
Healey, Helen V. 368
Heaton, Steven C. 536
Hecker, Andres 93
Hegadorn, Maribeth 239
Hegland, Dagmar 178
Heglund, Sherrie 547
Heilman, Teresa 288
Heim, Sandra Lee 224
Heimeyer, Naomi 185
Hein, Richard A. 559
Heine, Margaret Kleintop 254
Heino, Nicole 209
Heintzkill, Mary 499
Heisler, Stacey 219
Heitsch, Leona Mason 593
Heitzig, Fred F. 113
Heitzman, Christine Anne 477
Helding, Hilary 123
Heller-Church, Carol Lee 8
Helmer, Victoria 192
Hencye, Benjamin Todd 169
Henderson, Carolyn E. W. 30
Henderson, Julie Shockey 35
Henderson, Kathleen J. 286
Henderson-Shepard, Carolyn 66
Hendricks, Amanda 459
Hendrickson, Alvira V. 423
Henkel, Jennifer 104
Hennessey, Chrissy 395
Henry, Norma J. 300
Henry, Pauline 234
Henson, Ginger 438
Hepner, Elizabeth 444
Hepner, Kathleen Steinbacher 521

Heprian, Virginia M. 580
Herbert, Tammy 355
Hermes, Danyel 151
Hernandez, Alvin E. 132
Hernandez, Joshua 119
Herndon, Casanya 144
Herring, Andrew 617
Herring, Lee E. 527
Herring, Nathalie L. 223
Herrington, Shelia 518
Herron, Erica Nicole 285
Herron, Peggy L. 294
Herskowitz, Thomas 510
Herzberger, Magda 302
Hess Jr., James D. 467
Hess, Kelly A. 489
Hessman, Peter 272
Hester, Debbie 386
Hester, Louise 220
Heston, Catherine D. 465
Hewell, Ruth 617
Hewett, Eugene S. 99
Hewitt, Angela Eilene 132
Hey, D. K. 341
Heyden, Katie 626
Hickey, Daniel 57
Hickman, Dan 448
Hicks, Fannie 79
Higgins, N. Loy 296
High, Suzanne K. 255
Highfield, Thomas G. 262
Hilbert, Melanie I. 247
Hilbert, Rebecca 515
Hildebrandt, Sarah 183
Hill, Adrienne 138
Hill, Jerome 174
Hill Jr., Oliver W. 207
Hill, Kela Renee 323
Hilliard, Dawn 409
Hilliard, Donnell 24
Hilliman, Joy Howard 410
Hills, Katherine E. 278
Hilstad, Gordon 395
Hilton, Stacy 313
Himmelsbaugh, Steven D. 285
Hinds, Arlene 371
Hines, Jackie 133
Hines, Thomas N. 203
Hinkle, D. J. Potter 621
Hinkle, Rosemary G. 592
Hinson, Amy D. 77
Hintz, Blu Jean 617
Hinz, Tammy 309
Hirschman, Harry 23
Hirsh, Colette K. 445
Hirst, Douglas B. 98
Hiryovati, Evelyn J. 20
Hiser Jr., Edward G. 57
Hitchen, Audrey D. 23
Hlinka, George 110
Ho, Tony 186
Hoban, Tacey M. 241
Hobaugh, Arlene 90

Hoch, Kristy 601
Hodge, Janice 404
Hodge, Jason 149
Hodges, Pam 329
Hodges, Paula 207
Hodges, Shirley 346
Hoff III, Milton S. 567
Hoffman, Barbara J. 470
Hoffman, Frank G. 476
Hoffman, James G. 85
Hoffman, Susan 522
Hoffmann, Dieter 369
Hogan, Nancy L'enz 333
Hogan, Rhonda K. 287
Hogue, Ila A. 616
Hohmann, Agnes G. 67
Holbrook, Tabitha 321
Holbrook, Virginia W. 218
Holden, Vicki 606
Holdren, Delores 126
Holland, Anne 478
Holland, N. Elizabeth 216
Hollenback, Diana 174
Holley, Lesia 520
Hollingsworth, Gerry M. 464
Hollister, Cheryl 4
Holmes, Betty B. 420
Holmes, Darcy 170
Holmes, J. 351
Holmes, Josh 95
Holmes Jr., Archie 437
Holmes, Robert T. 585
Holmes, Trish A. 295
Holmes, Twanna 519
Holsey, Edna F. 123
Holzkamp, Virginia 294
Holzman, Lena 577
Honeywood, Jessie A. 29
Hood, Mitchell 348
Hood, Orda 271
Hoogland, James 65
Hooks, Jennifer 13
Hooks, John 114
Hooser, Alice 109
Hoover, Allison Christy 179
Hoover, Jeanne Tyson 142
Hoover, Mary 591
Hopkins, Beverly A. 94
Hoppe, Kathleen 567
Hoppe, Melvin 557
Hoppy, Evelyn C. 92
Horn, Bette 388
Horn, David S. 389, 425, 627
Horn, Frank 63
Hornbeak, Joyce E. 421
Horne, Charna M. 137
Horner, Kara 351
Horting, Christopher R. 40
Horton, Shirley Campbell 287
Hoss, Madeleine M. 482
Houck-Simcox, Kathy A. 507
Hourihane, J. Maurice 502
Houser, Ashley 113

Houston, Billie 166
Houston, Robert 584
Howard, Bessie L. 91
Howard, George O. 616
Howard, Goldie 30
Howard, Jonathan L. 409
Howard, Judith Schwartz 356
Howard, Nikki R. 250
Howard, Rachel 236
Howe, Amber 118
Howe, Loralie Frances 314
Howe, Melody J. 540
Howell, Kenneth 574
Hoxie, Michele 314
Hoy, Eleanor Panck Van 65
Hsieh, John En 108
Hsing, Ellis C. K. 5
Hubbard, Luke 215
Hubiak, Diane M. 16
Huckaby, Jeannette 66
Huden, Marjorie W. 598
Hudson, Katy Lynn 247
Hudson, Marie A. 215
Hudspeth, Renee Devere 222
Huenink, Cori L. 76
Huer, Corrine 458
Huff, Kevin G. 335
Huffman, Dana R. 139
Hufstetler, David 20
Hughes, Barbara J. 417
Hughes, C. 349
Hughes, Robert F. 279
Hughes, Tracie 356
Hugunin, Alberta June 87
Hugunin, Sherrie 189
Hulett, Angela 375
Hull, Cassandra 455
Hull, Shane 507
Hullum, C. R. 551
Hulme, Stephanie 572
Hultz, Frankie 11
Hume, Havah Sandra Elaine 440
Hume, Tommie F. 196
Humfleet, Constance 410
Humphrey, Denise Aileen 157
Humphreys, Barbara Ann 131
Humphries, Bridget 139
Humphries, Dorrie 76
Hunniford, Roseanne 307
Hunsberger, Bonnie Lee 225
Hunt, Katherine 322
Hunt, Sherrie C. 516
Hunter, Charles E. 80
Hunter, Jim 132
Hunter, Melvin P. 208
Huntley, Doris L. 103
Huntsman, Marie B. 224
Huntzinger, Debby 384
Huratiak, Nancy J. 188
Hurd, Angelina Paone 89
Hurdle, Linda F. 526
Hurley, Veronica Ann 519
Hurst, Chaxy 77

Huseby, Steven L. 538
Huston, Miriam R. 590
Hutchins, Heather 43
Hutchins, Sharleen C. 320
Huth, Lindsay 304
Hutson, Laura 301
Hutson, Lona 315
Hutton, David R. 57
Hutzel, Christy 81
Huy, Thon 515
Huynh, Vu Tien 560
Huze, Marlena 524
Hvidt, Michael A. 531
Hylton, Elizabeth Anne 360
Hylton, Rosemarie 577

I

Iasiello Jr., Vincent A. 585
Idol, Magdalene 487
Iler, Angie 120
Iles, Helen Marie 115
Ille, Emilie Louise 362
Illuzzi, Michael 515
Im, Sharon 238
Ingle, Barbara 466
Ingles, Michelle 599
Irons, Amy 105
Isenberg, Olivia L. 280
Israel, Frantz Guichard 15
Israel, Maria Evita M. 544

J

Jack, Barbara J. W. 616
Jackimek, Deborah D. 100, 623
Jackson, Brenda K. 118
Jackson, Crystal 364
Jackson, Debbie 110
Jackson, Efrem D. 479
Jackson, Eric 36
Jackson, Ida B. 407
Jackson, Kenya L. 603
Jackson, Sherrie 507
Jackson Sr., Edward Ellis 53
Jackson Sr., William 589
Jacob, Beverly M. 173
Jacobs, Gretta L. 393
Jacobsen, Linda Lee 234
Jacobson, Katelyn Jane 313
Jacquant, Jaclyn De 106
Jade, Sam 294
Jaenicke, Jason 118
Jagusch, Leeanne 618
James, Carlton 456
James, Connie 466
James, Vincent 597
Jamison, Kaye 205
Janardhanan, Neela 331
Jane, Martha 320
Janes, Particia 591
Jaramillo, Kimberly Cecilia 253
Jarrell, Anita 403
Jarvis, Natasha 306

Jasilionis, Mary 345
Jasmine, Albert 129
Javins, Lydia 308
Jeffers, Jen 117
Jefferson, Dotsie 120
Jefferson, Jeanette H. 458
Jeffries, Michelle 254
Jefts, Michael 616
Jenkin, Stacey 521
Jenkins, Colby 372
Jenkins, De'Aundra 407
Jennings Jr., Alfred R. 374
Jensen, D. J. 525
Jensen, Sharon Hansen 278
Jeric, Rick 452
Jernigan, Franchon R. 475
Jester, Dane S. 51
Jetton, B. 316
Jez, Faith 396
Jez, Jenn 363
Jeziorski, Marlene 273
Jimenez, Cary 170
Jimenez, Susanne A. 212
Jo Agro, Nicki 265
Jo Baker, Mary 298
Joe, Billy Rea 131
John, Bess 389
John, Harold 363
Johnee—, Skyline 333
Johnson, Amanda 116, 365
Johnson, Bertha Mae 34
Johnson, Carole L. 110
Johnson, Charlene 45
Johnson, Cyril W. 21
Johnson, Deron 388
Johnson, Don 75
Johnson, Francis B. 383
Johnson, George W. 616
Johnson, Glenda 475
Johnson, Glenn D. 90
Johnson, Gregory J. 411
Johnson, Heidi Lee 132
Johnson, Janey B. 408
Johnson, Jennifer 146
Johnson, Jeremy 377
Johnson, Jessica 153
Johnson, Jill L. 173
Johnson, Joseph R. 153
Johnson, Juanita 462
Johnson, Kathleen J. 483
Johnson, Kristina 334
Johnson, LaLoie 208
Johnson, Laura L. 236
Johnson, Lona 601
Johnson, Marcella 500
Johnson, Marlene N. 304
Johnson, Mary E. 348
Johnson, Matthew 517
Johnson, Rebecca 450
Johnson, Rodney C. 549
Johnson, Ronell 600
Johnson, Shirley M. 181
Johnson, Sue 306

Johnson, Terry 298
Johnson, Tracey 578
Johnston, Dottie J. 120
Johnston, Kathleen 215
Johnston, Margaret 216
Joiner, Destiny 165
Jolliff, Raymond 492, 616
Jones, Abigail L. 366
Jones, Bob 24
Jones, Carol J. 615
Jones, Cherise M. 33
Jones, Crystal Davenport 109
Jones, Cynthia L., M.D. 54
Jones, David 145
Jones, Florence M. 152
Jones, Gwendolyn 9
Jones, Jerry 479
Jones, Joie 174
Jones, Juanita F. 28
Jones, L. Dranae 326
Jones, Mary L. Freeman 506
Jones, Michael C. 319
Jones, Michael D. 227
Jones, Michael J. 588
Jones, Nora 280
Jones, Penny 615
Jones, Reggie 539
Jones, Steven R. 250
Jones, Tiffany 532
Jones, Vann G. C. 182
Jones, Velores (Val) 313
Jones, Virginia A. 306
Jones, William Henry 285
Jones, Wray Christine 295
Jones-Johnson, Beverly 74
Jones-Markwood, Ann 101
Joos, Steve 596
Jordan, John J. 42
Jordan, Kristi 237
Jordan, Mildred L. 324
Jordan, Nancy 256
Jordan, Willie M. 246
Jorgensen, Laverne 199
Joseph Longo, Ed. D. 99
Joseph, Marjorie 500
Joseph, Sheliagh 503
Joshi, Priti 199
Joshi, Vishnu P. 587
Jouget, James C. 158
Joyce, Carrie L. 164
Joyce, Reginald 336
Joyner, Annette N. 71
Joynt, Marion V. 323
Julander, June 105
Julian, Eleanor 390
Jump, Erica 171

K

K., Willy 525
Kabler, Aaron J. 433
Kaczenas, Estelle Lowe 144
Kaffenberger, Tara 192
Kahns, Michelle 324

Kale, Josephine H. 475
Kaliher, Heidi 105
Kallab, Lisa 316
Kalnas, Mary 569
Kaminski, Bonnie Seefeldt 173
Kampf, Hilde 415
Kane, Cindy 110
Kane, Shaun 338
Kaneshiro, Warren A. 554
Kannankeril, Charlene 164
Kapp, Teresa 544
Kappel, Kristen 244
Karafa, Shirley A. 323
Karash, Troy A. 236
Karchinski, Minnie 336
Karlovec, Evie L. 124
Karpinski, Lisa 214
Karstens-Cox, E. 351
Kasakov, Vivian 307
Kasner, Lori 606
Kassan, Elisabeth S. 117
Kaye, Caren 457
Kazantzis, Athena 126
Kearney, Wini 548
Kearsing, Barbara A. 178
Keegan, Heather 125
Keenan, Joseph R. 436
Keese, Maura Leigh 205
Keesee, Valerie D. 338
Kehoe, Timothy J. 629
Keirs, Ronald 344
Keith, Harlow J. 615
Keller, Esther Hohn 371
Keller, Graciela 471
Kellerman, Mary 345
Kelley, Deborah Clark 440
Kelley, Janice 150
Kelley, Mildred 628
Kelley, Stan 580
Kelley, Wendy 238
Kellis, Hilda 172
Kellogg, Thelma 316
Kellum, J. Kent 603
Kelly, A. L. 336
Kelly, Isabella 31
Kelly, Katie Scarlett 315
Kemp, Ashley 422
Kemp, Grace Marilyn 407
Kendall, Lucinda L. 323
Kender, Winnie 535
Kendra, Erika 400
Keniston, Jacob 367
Kenkel, Laura 233
Kenna, Hendryk Zenon 49
Kennedy, Gail Sari 407
Kennedy, Patricia 547
Kepler, Patricia B. 595
Kepple, Dawn 630
Kern, Thomas J. 312
Kernstock, Sandra L. 322
Kerr, Particia Ann 308
Kerr, Terry Lee 195
Kerwin, Judi 359

Kessinger, Joan 443
Kessler, Carol T. 393
Ketterer, Ian L. 16
Key, Brandi 110
Keyser, Tyler 218
Kidder, Tracy Ann 201
Kidwell, Ersel M. 38
Kiel, Mathew K. 224
Kielbowicz, Walter E. 329
Kielty, Sarah 332
Kiesow, Herbert L. 614
Kilchrist, Mrs. Kermick 347
Kilgour, Jan M. 426
Kilkenny, Joyce 71
Killingsworth, Keli Adell 290
Killmon, Edith 156
Kim, Elizabeth 25
Kim, Neal 547
Kim, Ok-Gyung 355
Kimball, George Edward 97
Kinard, Cynthia Cochran 17
Kincaid, Cathie 405
Kindred, Alan 404
King, Donna E. 406
King, Frances H. 459
King, Julia 117
King, Linda 238
King, Raymond E. 328
King, Theresa 249
King, Victoria Clodfelter 492
Kingsley, Anita 139
Kinney, Michael W. 277
Kinney, Tracy 275
Kinsey, Tiffany 525
Kinyon-Wilson, Angela S. 40
Kiper, Janis 165
Kirby, Delma 397
Kirkpatrick, Ellen R. 124
Kirkpatrick, Joyce M. 104
Kirsch, M. Kristi 575
Kirschenmann, Gerald L. 154
Kirschenmann, Isaac 406
Kiser, Adrienne 119
Kiss, Timothy P. 600
Kissinger, Kellee S. 215
Kitagawa, Iris 164
Klassen, Betty 16
Kleiman, Jerrold 14
Klein, W. Richard 483
Kline, Jennifer 400
Kline, Keith H. 252
Kline, Marshall 350
Klotch, Eric 417
Knapp, Susanna H. 314
Knaus-Holm, Jack 430
Knauss, Ernest 445
Knecht, Leonard 449
Knepp, David Lee 145
Knight, Fannie B. 468
Knight, Frances G. 124
Knight, Kelly 500
Knoll, Charles 389
Knoll, Leona 508

Knowlson, Thomas R. 211
Knowlton, Stacey Dawn 197
Knox, Phyllis Wakefield 328
Knudsen, Darwin C. 413
Knutson, Dawn E. 411
Koch, Frederick W. 377
Kochany, Katarzyna 301
Kofoid, Murray 281
Kogi, Violet Wahito 511
Koh, Amy 87
Kohlman, Val 302, 450
Kokino, Olga 232
Kokinos, Larry 560
Kolar, Kathleen A. 504
Kolibaba-Tucker, Jane L. 459
Kolka, Jennifer 432
Kollar, Jill 128
Kollar, Lynn F. 214
Koncikowski, Mark 481
Kondo, Esaku 473
Kontes, Kathy 309
Koonce, Carlus Delonte 83
Koppenhaver, JoAnn 191
Koppert, Susan 354
Koraska, Leann Coleman 325
Korchman, Kerry Ann 338
Korhnak, Michael 224
Korn, Lynn M. 275
Koster, Richard 505
Kotsakor, Dorothea 99
Kouw, Terry 303
Kovar, C. Marek-McConkey 50
Kraft, Eugene 475
Kramm, Stephanie 518
Krause, Genevieve 138
Krazmien, Katherine L.W. 292
Kreher, Paul 530
Krenning, Kelly 292
Krick, Kirsten 497
Krieger, Laura T. 191
Krmpotich, Leslie 627
Krockmalnic, Arnold M. 121
Krueger Jr., William H. 289
Kruse, Marlene 212
Kubiak, Rebecca J. 301
Kubik, Sara 583
Kubus, Patricia Goskowski 342
Kuchman, Mary A. 588
Kuczmarski, Jeffrey 615
Kuecker, Carrie 158
Kulhanjian-Freeland, Virginia 585
Kulp, Brenda A. 477
Kumar, Chanda 84
Kumar, Tobi 242
Kuppenbender, Alvin J. 393
Kushner, Emily Gail 466
Kusmit, Jared 6
Kutemeier, Nathan 274
Kuxhausen, Dorothy 63
Kvingedal, Harriet Trehus 477
Kyle, Lidi Mary 546
Kyzer, Kathryn 533

L

La Micela, Ivano G. 615
La Whon, Theresa 266
LaBollita, Sharon 335
LaDeaux, Terri Jo 450
Laffey, John 397
LaFleur, Gary B. 154
LaFountain, Kristi 529
Lagattolla, Maria Teresa 622
Lake, Claire 424
Lakien, Atmeta Malani 615
Lal, Neeta 603
Lally, Mike 303
Lam, Carmen 389
Lambert, Allan H. 148
Lambert, Christy 446
Lambert, John 614
Lamie, Mary Ellen 602
Lamoreaux, Jim 146
Lampe, Ralph H. 197
Lance, Bonnie Jean 55
Landis, Michelle 182
Landry, Jane Portie 473
Lane, Franchon 149
Lane, Herbert L. 456
Lane, Jack 96
Lane Jr., William H. 588
Lane, Memory C. 219
Lane, Tammy 187
Lang, Lisa 537
Lansing, Clara E. 365
LaPage, Lynette 528
LaPatra, Gary D. 456
Lapayover, Adam 75
LaPlace, Linda 323
Lara, Teresa I. 273
Laramie, Yvonne 568
Laramore, Viv 561
LaRocque, Glenn Lee 117
Larripa, Micah J. 183
Larson, Glenn D. 402
Larson, Victoria 451
Lary, Rhiannon 511
Lasker, Lee Dubin 318
Latzke, JoAnn 162
Laubert, Barbara L. 419
Laumann, Felix 164, 607
Lauro, Alfred 119
Lavala, Pat 530
Lavedas, Kris 532
Lavin, Kelly Ann 252
Law, C. Brian 233
Lawrence, Reno K. 532
Lawshe, Dewey 415
Lawson, Rodney 194
Lawson, Susan 335
Lay, Deena L. 474
Lay, Ronda L. 519
Lazarte-Oconer, Zenaida 573
Lazcano Jr., Fernando A. 442
Lazzeri, Alice Carol 144
Leach, Dean 446

Leader-Picone, Whitney 621
Leahwood, Tatiana 272
Leavitt, Norman T. 250
Leazier, Kaye 282
Lechuga, Alfred 435
Lee, Alexander W. 55
Lee, David B. 468
Lee, Janet 447
Lee, Janet A. 110
Lee, Jordan Hugh 13
Lee, Joyce Ann 432
Lee, Kai 590
Lee, Peter John 451
Lee, Sandra 253
Lee, Sandra L. 329
Lee, Yi-Hsin 333
LeFay, M. Malefica 343
Leflar, Regan 298
Legaspi, Victor E. 586
LeGrand, James W. 157
Leibhardt, Maidi 236
Leik, Joseph 150
Leiker, Garry 65
Leist, Clementina Ceide 18
Leistman, Gale 454
Leitner, Patty 326
Leland, Audra J. 158
Lem, Daisy M. 123
Lemberger, Heidi J. 125
Lenhart, Gerry Anne 435
Lent, Donna E. 7
Lentry, Carl 472
Leon, Douglas 386
Leonard, Melodie 451
Leonardo, Kimerri Noel 251
Lesco, Robert 289
Lesko, Roseanne 199
Lessenthien, Kurt G. 485
Lesser, Frank 47
Lester, Nicole 280
Lester, Tina 191
Lethrud, Jeanine M. 437
Leuz, Millie 296
Levi, Jeff 156
Levine, Rosalind 582
Lewanski, Lori Ann 486
Lewis, Billy 97
Lewis, Carrie 377
Lewis, Escorita 70
Lewis, Evelyn J. 80
Lewis, Kellie 526
Lewis, Lisa 250
Lewis, Mary K. 595
Lewis, Michael C. 353
Lewis, Rychael 261
Lewis, Stacey Ann 198
Lewis-Escalona, Suzan M. 350
Lewis-Ross, Adrienne V. 21
Li, Helen 120
Liarakos, Steve 293
Liberatore, Jill 625
Liegl, Rebecca 344
Lien, Jerry 416

Lieurance, James R.   179
Lightwine, Linnea   595
Ligon, Nancy Ann   208
Liguori, Jennifer   123
Lile, Marshall W.   287
Lilly, Arren   471
Limon, Miriam   244
Lin, David   380
Lind, Dorothy Stanberry   479
Lind, Julia E.   50
Linde, Charles   110
Linder, Cerissa   369
Lindner, Kirk   504
Lindquist, Harriet H.   457
Lindsay, Linda   558
Lindsay, Shantey R.   528
Lindsey, Gavin   48
Lindstrom, Lisa M.   502
Lineaweaver, Iva Nell   469
Lingle, Merla   190
Link, Sylvia   553
Linville, Sandra L.   535
Lippert, Lisa   76
Lipscomb, Audrey   311
Lisa, Margaret   264
Litalien, Gerald   422
Little, Mary J.   354
Liu, Pek Hu   236
Livingston, Amy   436
Livingston, Eddiemae   123
Livingstone, Mirriam   509
Llanes, Anthony   614
Lloyd, Cedric   418
Lloyd Jr., H. V.   242
Lloyd, Regina   355
Loan, Christopher L. Van   139
Locke, Wanda   449
Lockhart, Johnnie   77
Lockwood, Diana   161
Lockwood, Kathryn   571
Lodhi, Rafia   262
Loeb, Pnina T.   192
Logan, Robert   485
Logan, Sandra   334
Logan, Vera L.   303
Logisz, Rosemary   331
Lohner, Kay   238
Lohrer, Travis J.   297
Lombard, Matthew   569
Long, Nadine Simms   452
Long, Pat   182
Long, Rebecca   238
Longanecker, Kari   222
Loomis, Joyce   457
Loomis, Robert   497
Looney, Dale C.   30
Lopatka, Viki   221
Loper, W. F.   491
Lopez, Brynn   360
Lopez, Jennifer   390
Lopez, Louise   318
Lopez, Olga Rasmussen   227
Lorimer, Barbara   382
Lorin, Jason   476
Lou, Bonnie   173
Loube, Emily   126
Louise, Janette Foley   135
Love, Penelope   540
Lovelace, Flora   158
Lovely, Jean   622
Lovette, Malisa   302
Low, Donna Marie   431
Low, Thayer   301
Lowe, Lisa H.   298
Lowe, Mary   508
Lowell, Edna M.   140
Lucado, Yvonne S.   269
Lucariello, Leona   352
Lucas, Ashley   38
Lucas, Brett De'Angelo   463
Lucas, C.   498
Luetje Jr., Melvin L.   336
Lugar, Lilly   510
Lugo, Debbi J.   137
Luke, Tiffany   278
Lull, Avis   459
Lumpkins, Shannon A.   556
Lundberg, Gypsy   147
Lundy, Anna   441
Luong, Saumi   318
Luong-Tran, Harrison   42
Luppino, Michael   331
Lussier, Wanda   226
Lustenberger, Dave   446
Lustgarten, Linda Jill   337
Lutcher, Dane C.   151
Lutty, Jennifer B.   52
Lutz, Millicent E.   258
Lutzow, Betty Poyer von   100
Lynar-Cohen, Eleanor   86
Lynch, Christina R.   14
Lynch, Corbett   161
Lynch, M. S.   524
Lynch, Robert L.   493
Lynn, I. Astrakhan   484
Lynn, Martha   537
Lyon, Wendy   333
Lytle, Dorothy W.   135
Lytle, Joy Stevens   396

M

Maack, Eric D.   128
MacDonald, Colleen   134
Macey, Faye E.   172
Machuca, Daniela   101
MacIntosh, Colleen   463
Mack, Sophia C.   248
Macke, Bob   148
MacKenzie, Joan T.   421
Mackin, Howard   143
MacPhetridge, Betty Ann   392
Madden, Sarah B.   537
Maddocks, David   261
Madison, Wendy   512
Magargee, Jill   427
Magathan, Cheryl   357
Magsarili, Reena   535
Mahabir, Ram   331
Mahan, Dolores   161
Maher, Brian Thomas   50
Maher, James   102
Mahoner, Marla   529
Mahoney, Dennis   405
Maia, Mercedes D.   341
Maiello, Wendy Levinson   226
Maieritsch, Nick   317
Main, Cara D.   101
Maines, Lisa A.   488
Mais, Marlene   229
Maitilasso, Kristi   198
Maitland, Christy   376
Makela, Susan J.   583
Malchow, Ashley   476
Male, Kristen   570
Malinoski, Anna   160
Malinski, Kathy   186
Malinsky, Keith F.   205
Malone, Daniel   34
Malone, Dianna   7
Maloy, Rick   547
Maltese, Michael   492
Mancini, B.   339
Mancini, Denise   131
Mancini, Jenny   163
Manfre, Loretta L.   613
Manfredi, Geraldine   39
Manger, Sandra   604
Mangin, Cheryl   453
Mangold, Bonnie   139
Mann, Kathleen K.   341
Mann, Nancy E.   217
Mann, Roberta L.   614
Mann, Wilma   489
Mannerberg, Eric R.   372
Mannigan, Margaret P.   337
Manoranjan, Susanna   512
Mantas, Dennis   73
Mante, Rowena E.   322
Manteris, April Lynn   170
Manuel, Julia Y.   29
Manzur, Thasneem   182
Mapes, Leah P.   183
Marcelle, June   119
Marchinke, Shanna   530
Marcou, David J.   90
Marinaj, Gjeke   173
Mariner, Jennifer   178
Marino   516
Markaj, Flora   47
Markle, George D.   165
Marks, David   179
Marks, Michelle   275
Marks, Milli   226
Marks, Ruth K.   531
Marlowe, Lynn   214
Marnchianes, Helene   393
Marquardt, Jane   443
Marquez, Manuel   504
Marquis, Carolyn F.   133
Marr, Erin   385
Marsh, Freida   68
Marsh, Hal   163
Marshall, Andy   92
Marshall, Patricia   305
Martagon, Mike   277
Martell, Tami   590
Martin, Dolly Ann   445
Martin, Edith N.   406
Martin, Evelyn   436
Martin, Ginger   19
Martin, Isabel   112
Martin, J. W.   500
Martin, Jean M.   387
Martin, Jeramiah   166
Martin, Karen R.   234
Martin, Lawrence   505
Martin, Marty   300
Martin, Melinda   291
Martin, Michael A.   273
Martin, Rita A.   285
Martin, William C.   184
Martineau, Jessica   129
Martinez, Alexandra   408
Martinez, Bernard   614
Martinez, Katrina   243
Martinez, Steve   575
Martinez, Tamara   612
Martinkovic, Mary Lou   516
Martz, Aaron R.   179
Marvin, Buryle W.   155
Mashburn, Charles L.   448
Mason, Arlene   172
Mason, David S.   47
Mason, Kelsey   308
Massey, Alice J.   145
Massey, David   436
Massey, Myrtle Price   194
Mathews, Sondra S.   242
Mathis, Deniese   66
Mathis, Jean   149
Matlock, Edward J.   621
Matos, Ruben   212
Matsuda, Kelly   256
Matthews, Mary   270
Matthews, Melinda A.   199
Matusewitz, Maria   328
Matzner, Charles   394
Mau, Steven   345
Maull, James   152
Mauro, Marsha M.   194
Mautor, Claudette   138
Maxey, Mary   328
May, Jeffrey   156
May, Joseph Adam   470
May, Stephanie   575
Mayer, Jacquelyn Ann   474
Mayfield, Lynn   564
Mayland, Diana   383
Maynard, Melissa Ann   545
Mayol, Elaine L.   381
Mayse, Bernie D.   461
Maze, Michelle K.   557

Mazloff, Anna L. 475
Mbarga, Monique Z. 289
McAfee, Patsy 246
McArthur, Frances C. 12
McBee, Linda 260
McBryde, Frederick V. 37
McCahan, Lorene Parshall 522
McCain, Amy 474
McCann, Amy G. 416
McCarkindale, Deanna 25
McCarley, Becky 122
McCarthy, Nanette 499
McClairen, Lubertha 227
McClintock, Autumn 113
McClure, Larry Dean 318
McClure, Matt 514
McCollum, Marilyn S. 205
McConnachie, Cathy 149
McConnell, Isabelle 30
McCorkle Jr., W.W. 355
McCormick, Mary Elise 326
McCoy, Danielle M. 11
McCullah, Samantha 341
McCulloch, Sharon Lill 249
McCullough, Carolyn 92
McCune, Lisa 311
McDaniel, Jenny 378
McDaniel, Joyce H. 18
McDay, Tonyell F. 252
McDole, Ian P. 175
McDonald, Charles T. 455
McDonald, Sonya Rebecca 562
McDonough, Catina 372
McDowell, Marcia 623
McEachen, Diane 102
McElhiney, Leda 184
McElroy, K. R. 246
McFarlane, Dar 144
McFarlane, Misty 274
McGarvey, Sean 312
McGarvie, Frances 376
McGary, Charles Selwyn 167
McGee, Vicki 537
McGill, Erma 439
McGilvray, Kristi M. 337
McGowan, Eileen 94
McGrath, Anne D. 423
McGregor, Matthew W. 297
McGregor, Terry 348
McKaig, Heather 27
McKay, Blayne 623
McKay, Gregory D. 25
McKee, Wilson 492
McKenzie, Ethel P. 160
McKeon, Martha A. 347
McKern, Shawn P. 231
McKethan, Elizabeth 172
McKiernan, Robert 515
McKinney, Teresa Dezern 288
McKinstry, Erin 124
McKinstry, Patrick Michael 303
McKnelly, Ted 344
McKnight, J. 247

McLain, Darryl Lynn 370
McLaren, Michele 272
McLaughlin, Hildy 480
McLemore Jr., William R. 582
McLeod, Betty J. 22
McMenamin, Teri K. 299
McMillen, Ruth E. 279
McMillian, Cyd 35
McOlive, Mendi 286
McPhail Sr., David A. 614
McPhillips, William 548
McQueen, Mark 189
McShan, Henry L. 446
McShane, Hazel 443
McVey, Jennifer L. 444
McWilliams, Chris 123
Mead, Jenny 122
Meadows, Connie 94
Meadows, Teresa 335
Meadows, Virginia 336
Mealy, Elaine 119
Meanea, Karen 180
Mednick, Richard 295
Meehan, Dorothy 523
Meeks, Toby Shawn 574
Meier, Jeffery B. 374
Meislohn, Bobbi 149
Melcombe, John 45
Melick, Cletus E. 9
Melle-Yohe, Patricia 231
Melton, Dorothy J. 48
Mendoza, Brianna 94
Mendoza, E. J. 525
Mendoza-Kickham, Piedad 343
Menke, Ken 244
Mercer, Sara 559, 613
Meritt, Ann E. 66
Merkledove, Nicole Ronae 181
Merrill, Gail 72
Merritt, Julie 444
Merritt, Terri Maria 346
Merritts, Rita A. 287
Mesa, John De 414
Messa, Steve 337
Messel, Evelyn L. 20
Messerli, Alexander R. 131
Metz, Brenda 473
Metzger, Phyllis 482
Metzner, Richard J. 349
Meyer, Emily 89
Meyer, Jill 154, 613
Meyer, Kristin 513
Meyer, Rebecca J. 352
Meyer, Scott 353
Meyers, Don 38
Meyers, Sally A. 251
Mezyk, Inez M. 34
Michaels, Olivia 184
Michels, Jessica 44
Micka, Richard G. 291
Micozzi, Jean 382
Middleton, Jeanette 4
Middleton, Nancy 292

Mielko, Michele 606
Mieszkowski, Ella 19
Milburn, Tammy S. 341
Miles, Veronica Susan 604
Miller, Alex 442
Miller, Amanda 97
Miller, Anesa 101
Miller, Audrey Wright 69
Miller, Carl R. 147
Miller, Charles 439
Miller, Charles F. 169
Miller, Crystal K. 373
Miller, Dana Nicole 464
Miller, Diane B. 611
Miller, Dorothy C. 366
Miller, Isaac R. 469
Miller, James D. 178
Miller, Jenna 33
Miller Jr., Robert L. 294
Miller, Julia Fox 379
Miller, Kenneth L. 507
Miller, Lita C. 230
Miller, Madge 511
Miller, Marilaine 539
Miller, Mark T. 275
Miller, Mary R. 499
Miller, Mary T. 337
Miller, Mellie E. 288
Miller, Michael Jason Huls 576
Miller, Nichole 300
Miller, Patsy Louise 621
Miller, Rachelle S. 219
Miller, Roxann 540
Miller, Sharon A. 222
Miller, Sue 572
Milliner, Tyrone 613
Mills, Alice M. 54
Mills, Rian J. 555
Millsaps, Lauren 546
Miltner, Katie 506
Mimna, Shawne Rose 249
Min, Byung J. 442
Mincher, Megean 320
Miner, Meghan 536
Minjares, David S. 410
Minnick, Jessica 177
Minton, Danny 130
Mir, Alex Gonzalez 349
Miranth, Nicole J. 283
Mischke, Charles C. 360
Misener, Joy 434
Mishra, Kunal 621
Mishur, Robert J. 501
Mitchell, Annie 178
Mitchell, Brandi 111
Mitchell, Cathy 100
Mitchell, Christina 370
Mitchell, Grace 106
Mitchell, Linda 234
Mitchell, Lisa 563
Mitchell, Margery Lusk 285
Mitchell, Phillip D. 279
Mitchell, Sherry 483

Mitchell, Simone 625
Mixon, Anthony A. 479
Miyaki, Kim 332
Mize, Kathryn 493
Mizerny, Michael 353
Moccia, Melissa 327
Moffet, Amy 111
Moffitt, C. 228
Mogle, Sean 547
Mohler, Virginia 231
Moir, Marlene B. 272
Molcsan, Stephen Edward 314
Molnar, Chloe Pollock 44
Monear, Stephenie C. 605
Mongiat, Walter J. 453
Monroe, Amanda 375
Monroe, R. Carroll 233
Monson, Gloria 442
Monson, Susan 299
Montalbano, Ascenza 10
Montefusco, Robert 287
Monteiro, Lydia 242
Montello, Ralph 606
Montemarano, Ralph 311
Mooney-Arrington, Courtney 53
Moore, Elaine 109
Moore, Erica 460
Moore, Frances Kinlaw 42
Moore, Freda B. 467
Moore, James N. 135
Moore, Judith Marie 447
Moore, Manda L. 571
Moore, Nona C. 200
Moore, Sandra K. 300
Moore, Troi P. 626
Moraga, Maria 296
Morales, Marian 307
Morales, Nicole 549
Moran, Natalie 550
Morefield, Earlene 373
Moreland, Teresa Joy 235
Moreno, Keli 482
Moreno, Roy 264
Morey, William A. 273
Morgan, Deborah 92
Morgan III, Richard T. 274
Morgan, Mary Antionette 527
Morgan, Tom 315
Morganski, Molly Beth 314
Morgenlender, Elena 421
Moriarty, James 52
Moritz, Donna Long 177
Morris, Brian 461
Morris, Carey 83
Morris, Charles 390
Morris, Irene J. C. 19
Morris, Jamie 41
Morris, Jay L. 613
Morris, Ronald G. 555
Morrison, Gregory S. 475
Morrison, Megan 342
Morrissette, Jennifer K. 112
Morrow, Joe 156

Morsink, Essi 467
Mortimer, Claire Elmore 624
Morton III, Stanley E. 571
Mosley, Ella 373
Mosser, James E. 33
Mosser, Sue A. 517
Moulden, Diann F. 81
Moussouris, Edward 114
Mowry, S. L. 304
Moyers, Joel E. 612
Mozdyniewics, Wojtek 193
Mozenko, Tonya 452
Mpelezos, Jess 122
Mucha, Henry P. 388
Mueller-Maynard, Janet 412
Muis, Shaun 281
Mull, Linda A. 203
Mullee, Christan 379
Muller, Jean 21
Mullins, Caroline L. Britt 414
Mulry, Norine 602
Mumper, Kristin 193
Mumphrey, Nancy 593
Muncy, Larry D. 571
Mungin, Theodore L. 193
Munoz, Aurora 42
Munroe, Val 271
Murdoch, Patsy A. 306
Muroski, Rebecca 134
Murph, Keith 572
Murphy, Betty 68
Murphy, H. Marie 503
Murphy, Jessica 48
Murphy, Lisa 290
Murphy, Michael J. 576
Murray, Janine C. 119
Murray, Louisa M. 330
Murray, Samuel F. 624
Murray, Shari 286
Murrell, Sarah 315
Musselman, Doris 85
Mutschler, Matt 209
Mutz, Violet Loreane 330
Myers, Angel 128
Myers, Kathy 281
Myers, Kathy J. 450
Myers, Rena 300
Myers-Anderson, Christine 388
Myrick, Cheryl L. 167

N

Nackerud, Nola 589
Nacouzi, Dr. Antoine, 64
Nafziger, Andrea 147
Nagamine, Dina 64
Nagata, Stefanie 582
Nahrstedt, Janet 383
Nalin, Maureen H. 592
Nance, Tasneem Taneshia 602
Nardini, Janet 106
Naser, Doreen 94
Nash, Cheryl K. 21
Naslund, Janice 52
Nason, Barbara 409
Nason, Carissa 30
Nassar, Munir E., MD 212
Natale, Susan 501
Nathanson, Julie Ann 396
Nathe, Anthony R. 130
Naylor, Tami 271
Neace, Michelle 563
Neal, Charles Edrick 68
Neal, Robert L. 496
Neal, Sara 536
Nebraska, Leslie Staack 332
Nedelescu, Liviu 267
Nedrow, Michael W. 247
Neely, Jenna 101
Neervoort, Alexander 158
Neese, Sandra 277
Neff, Gregg 158
Neitz, George 366
Nelsen, Danielle 428
Nelson, Audrey M. 474
Nelson, Donald J. 100
Nelson, Esther M. 118
Nelson, Lois 587
Nelson, Martin 519
Nelson, Melissa Beth 255
Nelson, Todd 211
Nelson, Wava J. 301
Nemitz, Tara R. 453
Nerheim, Steven J. 335
Neslein, Ronald R. 292
Ness, Kelly 624
Nesselroad, James F. 109
Nethers, Deana Rae 114
Nettles, Minnie L. 214
Netzel, Candace 159
Neusch, Lisa 549
Nevill, Antoinette 382
Nevins, Barbara 135
Newbill, Yolanda F. 514
Newby, Jan Marie 380
Newhouse, Sharron 564
Newman, Lisa 290
Newman, Lisa B. 241
Newshutz, David B. 391
Newsom, Dorothy A. 135
Newton, Robert F. 343
Neymotin, Florence 381
Nezezon, Manette A. 450
Nguyen, Matt 207
Nguyen, Phu 551
Nguyen, Thua Thi 181
Nicholes, Joseph 433
Nichols, Alan 157
Nichols, John 93
Nichols, Mary 309
Nicholson, Edward A. 405
Nickel, Richard E. 227
Nicklin, Dorothy 55
Nicol, Nancy 303
Nicolelli, Cindy 3
Nielsen, Barbara 152
Nielsen, Peggy 485
Nierman, Marjory 351
Nightingale, Wilhelm 330
Niklaus, Janet M. 165
Nile-Heald, Christin 106
Nimtz, Walt G. 221
Nix, Amanda S. 439
Nogulich, Natalija 278
Noonan, D. Thomas 516
Nordmann, Karen 291
Norman, Bertrand R. 23
Norris, Robert 537
Norton, Daniel 135
Norton, Jim 384
Norton, S. Jeannine 266
Norton-Yetter, Nancy 330
Notaro, Sally 269
Novak, Jessica 357
November, Harry J. 122
Nowlin, Mike 291
Nunez, Mary D. 591
Nunnaley, Laura 528
Nusbaum, Daniel C. 429
Nuz, Bad 416
Nzinga, Kozowali 305

O

O'Brien, Kerri 269
Ochiltree, John M. 133
O'Connor, Dymphna 88
O'Connor, Richard S. 262
O'Dell, Sonya Ann 495
O'Donnell, Carol 143
Oels, Kyle 303
Oertel, Becky 91
Offerman, Van P. 344
Ogden, Adren L. 103
Oglesby, Dorothy W. 409
O'Grady, Anthony N. 112
Ojeda Jr., Daniel 362
Olbrys, Amanda 99
Oldham, Sherry Lee 571
Olds, Geraldine M. 438
Olemaun, Chastity 174
Ollila, Zachary G. 515
Olsen, Roy 613
Olson, Amy 56
Olson, Chip 121
Olson, Denise Auch 156
Olson, Melissa 197
Olson, Patricia 550
Olson, Robert J. 452
Olszak, Sandra L. 626
Olszewski, Jeanine 40
Oltmanns, Anna 358
O'Neal, Dawn 365
O'Neal, Jomarian L. 26
O'Neal, Ray 283
O'Neill, Mary B. 629
O'Neill, Megan 187
Onks, Gary D. 409
Onody, Laszlo 600
Ooley, Matt 310
Oosthuizen, Andy 30
Oram, Mildred 273
Oren, Virginia P. 296
Orosz, Sarah 563
Orr, Ione B. 163
Ortega-Lage, Esther 462
Ortiz, Maria A. 258
Ortiz, Maricarda 451
Ortiz, Victoria 241
Osberg, Nancy 576
Osborne, Carrie 421
Osburn, Irene 155
Oshiro, Day H. 101
Osland, Adrian 108
Osman, Zuhal 262
Osmond, Kimberly Belika 199
Ostendorf, Bernice M. 112
O'Sullivan, Brendan 625
Otoshi, Yoshiyuki 274
Otto, Allison M. 366
Ouellette, Nicole 494
Ouimet, Mary 612
Overmeyer, Norma 245
Overton, Uriel 545
Owen, Christy 176
Owen, David 408
Owens, Doneen 458
Owens, Paige 277
Owens, Priscilla A. 216

P

Pacheco, Sherilynn 253
Page, Benjamin 8
Page, Louise 558
Page, Marguerite 235
Page, Richard S. 480
Paige, Michelle 501
Paige, Natasha Renee 561
Painter, Venus D. 228
Palacios, Jeannie 426
Paleka, Walter 612
Palladino, Matthew P. 266
Palmer, David 151
Palmer, Kathleen Mead 521
Palmer, Penelope 336
Palmer, Scott M. 561
Palmer, Valerie 298
Palmieri, Maria 297
Palumbo, Mary Louise 289
Pamperin, Carla Sue 362
Pananen, Amy 115
Pantano, Daniel 45
Paradise, Jocelyn B. 374
Pardalos, Panos M. 349
Pardue, Michael L. 346
Pareja, Denise 368
Parejko, Ryan 568
Park, Seung 485
Parker, Brian 463
Parker, Reni Lachterman 584
Parker, Sharon 220
Parker, Silvia Cirne 294
Parker, Theodore 341
Parker-McCoy, Shirley J. 488

Parks, Icil Anne 91
Parmer, Rebecca 577
Parnow, John J. 109, 286
Parra, Diego 117
Parsons, Candice 102
Parvis, Michele 281
Pascucci, Edward A. 444
Pasulka, Sasha 302
Patasnick, Todd Gavin 576,
Patel, Kalpesh 335
Patterson, Andre 174
Patterson, Charlene 96
Patterson, Fred I. 117
Patterson, Helen T. 9
Patterson, Jessica 153
Patterson, Melody J. 578
Pattison, Deborah J. 356
Patton, Theresa 505
Paul, Betty 141
Paul, Jon 162
Paulle, Phillip J. 206
Paulsen, Laura 514
Pavlic, Julia Grace 167
Pavone, Teri 483
Pawley, Shannon M. 313
Pawlik, October A. 261
Payne, Daniel Canfield 105
Payne, Joann A. 112
Payne, Ricarda McDonald 451
Peacock, Marjorie M. 254
Peacock, Renee 567
Pearce, Don 429
Pearson, Shayna 484
Pease, Paul Andrew 249
Pease, Sandra K. 220
Pederson, Lois 343
Peebles, Wilma 207
Pekala, Jennifer Ann 458
Pelland, Carrie 160
Pellant, Roberta 569
Pelon IV, Paul A. 295
Pence, Robert W. 540
Pendleton, Boyd D. 107
Penelope, Eileen 585
Penko, Michael John 276
Penn, LeVar Michael 599
Pennington, Janet C. 448
Pennock, Danielle 106
Penny, Denise McVay 46
Pentek, Kathleen 284
Pentleton, Bertha 158
Pereira, Jennifer 358
Perera, George B. 612
Perkins, Richard H. 324
Perkins, Robert L. 311
Perlow, Mary 317
Perrow II, Melvin C. 190
Perry, Christie 374
Perry, Stephanie 213
Persaud, Andra 476
Person, Phillep 502
Peters, Dorothy 126
Peters, Leland E. 194

Peters, Rebecca 340
Peters, Tiffany Beatrice 217
Peters, Tonya 580
Peterson, D. Silas 183
Peterson, Dawn Marie 464
Peterson, Kathy A. 201
Peterson, Lorena 625
Peterson, Rick 531
Peterson, Robert 189
Petitfrere, Julia 126
Petrey, Joellen 151
Petrey, Shelia 292
Petrilli, Elizabeth 472
Petry, Loretta 218
Pevehouse, Betty Rinehart 6
Peyton, Gladys 402
Pfeifle, Linda 180
Pflum, Steve 187
Pham, Rosalyn 537
Pharis, Viki S. 581
Phelan, Anne Marie 420
Phelan, Claudia 361
Phelps, Eva Murphy 14
Phillippi, Meghan 313
Phillips, Barbara A. 428
Phillips, Cheri 176
Phillips, Daphne 11
Phillips, Darlene 118
Phillips, Janelle 119
Phillips, Lisa Helen 320
Phillips, Pamela Kelly 483
Phillips, Susan 243
Phillips, Thomas M. 309
Philpitt, Edward 135
Photikarmbumrung, Elma 134
Piascik, Jackie 105
Pick, Jeremy C. 368
Pickard, Clytie N. 150
Pickering, Cortney 148
Pickett, Charles M. 5
Pieper, Helen 467
Pierce, Grace 153
Pierre, Anne J. 147
Pierre, Enette Charles Jean 72
Pierzchalski, Amy 62
Pietrangelo-Jordan, Toni 602
Pietropaulo, Jason 73
Pike, Rod 283
Pilato, Gabriella Maria 6
Pillsbury, Sally 333
Pinkerton, Edward L. 441
Pinson, Jenny 401
Pionke, James A. 69
Piper, Gary 400
Piper, Jo 4
Pisani, Lori E. 595
Pittman, Naomi O. 490
Pitts, Annette 141
Pitts, Loretta J. 586
Pitts, Muriel 189
Piver, Courtney 163
Piver Jr., Johnny W. 97
Pizzuli, Jessica 46

Pledger, Elizabeth 155
Pletz, Cynde 394
Plimpton, Leslie 523
Ploskonka, Jason 170
Plowden, Melissa L. 274
Plummer, Mary Bernice 567
Poe, Dennis Vernon 160
Poel, Carol 384
Pogue, Michelle 337
Polatsek, Katie 181
Polhkowski, Lisa 347
Polise, Anne 17
Polizzi, Jayne 116
Pollack, Dorianne Gollubier 399
Pollak, Irvin 136
Polson, Daniel 380
Pont, Norita A. 448
Poole, Cheryl 64
Poole, Jenni L. 118
Pooler, Tamatha Anne 182
Pope, Mariko R. 225
Popielski, T. 305
Porter, Betsy Gibson 161
Porter, Brent 151
Porter, Scharlena A. 552, 624
Poscablo, Cristina 75
Posin, Dan Q. 114
Possel, Richard 303
Post, Frank R. 425
Posten, Matt 332
Poteet, Rosemarie 348
Pottharst, Russell C. 347
Potts, John David 384
Potts, Margaret R. 501
Potts, Marjorie 588
Potts, Sheila I. 245
Powell, Chris 143
Powell, Winnie J. 333
Powers, A. Elaine 222
Poyet, Donna M. 93
Pranulis, Trudy 351
Prentis, Edna Zimmerman 40
Preston, Cynethea 612
Price, Bernice 138
Price, LaFaye 234
Price, Pamela E. 235
Pride, Elizabeth 108
Priebe, Theresa 507
Prince, Lillian Le'Shanda 574
Prince-Colbath, Christopher 361
Pringle, Kathryn L. 312
Prisk, David 512
Proctor, Eric 157
Proctor, Gregory L. 385
Proctor, Nickolas 318
Profitt, Alex B. 48
Provost, Thomas 519
Pruett, Ashlee 36
Prusa, Lou Ann 326
Prusiensky, Paul 528
Puckett, Lana 532
Puckett, Laverne 219
Pugh, Tim 498

Puglia, Antonio 362
Pukach, Jennifer 45
Pulsney, Nancy 611
Pulver, Stephen 490
Purcell, Lana 319
Purdue, Todd 611
Purdy, Megann 275
Purushothaman, C. 518
Pusateri, Andrew Charles 472
Pye, Dee 405
Pyle, Amanda 367

Q

Queen, Yvonne Jo 328
Quijano, Vladimir C. 611
Quiles, Christopher 358
Quinn, Joanne 64
Quinn, William J. 484
Quintana, David Robert 11

R

Race, Dottie Macik 481
Racicot, Ann Marie 378
Racin, Brian J. 129
Radloff, Druscilla L. 456
Ragan, Gale 127
Ragan, Imogene 103
Raghunath, Bala 160
Ragland, Alice 359
Ralph, Charlene 121
Ramamurthi, Rekha 588
Ramirez, Lupe 496
Ramnarine, Marlo 281
Ramos, Dawn 367
Ramos, Sharlene 451
Ramp, Robert J. 565
Rampolla, Richard 316
Ramsey, Betsy 88
Ramsey, Kristy 538
Ramsey, Nola G. 287
Ramseyer, Angela 164
Randall, Diana 142
Randall, Natosha 208
Randall, Susan L. 350
Randell, Zenobia 448
Randolph, Allison 171
Randolph, Donovan 161
Rangel, Georgia 127
Rankins, Christina M. 124
Rapp, James M. 389
Rasa, Tatiana 258
Rashbrook-Carlson, Lois 347
Rasheed, Farah 7
Raska, Rachel Farmer 192
Rasmussen, Anders 419
Rasmussen II, Elmer 177
Rathbun, Skylar R. 208
Ratliff, Sissy Temple 284
Ratti, Jody 139
Raumer, Rainer W. 300
Rave, Ordia 575
Rawls, Candice 43

Ray, Wynona 305
Rayburn, Dorrice S. 146
Rayfield, Barbara 8
Raymundo, Nancy Ann 489
RDTRS 283
Rea, Caroline 161
Reade, Michael 626
Ready, Bryan 97
Reaves, John E. 122
Reavis, Kari 535
Reck, Adam L. 392
Recor, Leah 301
Reda, Tony 453
Redding, Barbara 45
Reece, Alethia 463
Reece, Evelyn C. 415
Reece, Janie 433
Reed, Becky 112
Reed, Erica 175
Reed, Janice 113
Reed, Molly 195
Reese, Diane Petitpas 136
Reese, Robert 193
Reese-Howell, Janet O. 430
Reeser, Anabel 356
Reeve, Chester 38
Reeves, Dorothy 611
Reeves, Nell S. 275
Reffett, Kimberly 565
Reichert, Gwen Patterson 436
Reichle, Martha Fowler 259
Reid, DeCha S. 108
Reilly, Angela 443
Reilly, Jessica 153
Reimer, Courtney A. 178
Reindl, Holly 153
Reiswig, Stephanie 320
Remmert, Lisa Michelle 251
Remus, Alice B. 79
Renae, Andrea 42
Renee-Hair, Helen 225
Renfro, Caroline 64
Renwick, Cyra G. 119
Revie, Jennifer Anne 469
Reynolds, Bryan 78
Reynolds, Caitlin A. 444
Reynoldson, Darlene M. 175
Rhodes 339
Rhodes, Elaine 419
Rhodes, Jason Tyler 170
Rhodes, Tiffany 244
Rhodin, Michael 350
Rhodus, Jo Ann 170
Rhoton, Heather 142
Rhyet 246
Ricca, Laura 584
Rice, Arlene B. 113
Rice, Brian 130
Rice, Christopher 115
Rice, Jackie 11
Rice, Maria 518
Rice, Tracey Christopher 283
Rice, Wilma A. 285

Rich, Christie 144
Rich, RoxAnna 597
Richards, David 369
Richards, Phee 288
Richardson, Donna M. 82
Richardson, Karl G. 560
Richardson, Michael A. 206
Richardson, Patricia F. 491
Richburg, Elizabeth 437
Richman, Libbie 189
Richter, John 142
Rickabaugh, Linda S. 314
Riddell, Marie 538
Riddlesperger, Biley 51
Rideout, Christine E. 99
Riedel, Roger G. 277
Rieger, Melanie 299
Riehn, Kathryn 330
Riesterer, Wendy C. 288
Riffle, Stella 329
Riggle, Deanna 51
Riggs, Anne W. 446
Riles, Kevin H. 628
Riley, Tunisia L. 210
Ring, Shawn T. 603
Riobo, Daniel 364
Riojas, Mercedes C. 620
Riola, Sara Hewitt 499
Rios, Amelia 8
Ripley, Nancy 320
Rippley, Donna 419
Rising, Rebecca 575
Ristic, Ankica 383
Ritchie, Carol Lee 107
Rittel, Judi 163
Ritter, Brenda McPeters 371
Ritter, Jared 86
Rivera, Jorge L. 95
Rivera, Luis 557
Rivera, Ricardo 506
Rizzo, Tara 542
Roach, Patt 560
Roads, Spencer N. 545
Roane, Bernett S. 434
Roback, Matthew W. 352
Robbins, Rebekah L. 566
Roberge, Bob 29
Roberre, Marc 338, 630
Roberson, Anna 146
Roberson, Neal 239
Roberson, Renee 560
Roberti, Melissa Leigh 558
Roberts, Amanda Rachael 80
Roberts, David 362
Roberts, Rachel 248
Robertson, Bess M. 113
Robichaud, Janeen 165
Robins, Douglas C. 73
Robinson, Doris 611
Robinson, Heather 163
Robinson, Joy Lee 371
Robinson, Katheen J. 209
Robinson, Meshelle A. 453

Robinson, Michael C. 611
Robinson, Ralph 321
Robinson, Sandy 297
Robinson, Viola 486
Robitaille, Norman A. 340
Roby, Jackie 110
Rocco, Nettie P. 583
Rodger, Sonja S. 318
Rodgers, Christine 120
Rodriguez, Adriana 423
Rodriguez, Anthony 49
Rodriguez, Arlena 140
Rodriguez, Hilda 466
Rodriguez, Loisita 252
Rodriguez, Nancy 596
Rodriquez, Jessica Ann 129
Roe, Randy A. 352
Roesler, Kimberly 597
Roffler, Ilse 109
Rogero, Gerald 394
Rogers, Amy 607
Rogers, Betty 95
Rogers, Brandy 30
Rogers, David 170
Rogers, Mary M. 345
Rogers, Wesley J. 622
Rogers, Wilda Lee 230
Rogerson, Judy Cox 137
Rojas, Mercedes C. 524
Roland II, Peter 330
Rollin, Marty 318
Rollins, Terri 191
Roman, Abimeleth 129
Roman, Debbie 74
Romanetz, Stephen C. 593
Romans, Ann 478
Romanyschyn, Kristen 344
Romero, Evelyn Y 464
Romero, Issac 99
Romero, Joe 71
Romero, Kerwin 272
Romo, Sam C. 303
Romos, Alex 419
Ronell, Marquis 545
Rooks, Lewis H. 270
Roper, Lisa 315
Rose, Brenda K. 420
Rose, Carlos 356
Rose, George 362
Rose, Pen 218
Rose, Ronald D. 263
Rose, Sally 240
Rosenfield, Linda B. 284
Ross, Alex 131
Ross, Andrea 176
Ross, Dennis J. 177
Ross, Harriet Kimball 101
Ross, Janet Marie 389
Ross, Lauren 318
Ross, Lori 535
Ross, Rachel L. 518
Ross, Steve 277
Ross, Valinda 605

Rossetti, Cesarina Maria 172
Rossi, Bridget 401
Rossiter, Helen B. 142
Rossman, Jeanne Louise 394
Roten, Jessica 416
Roth, Marvin 267
Rothenberg, Mary Jo 231
Rotwein, Jerrold Jack 387
Roundhill, Peggy 345
Rousseau, Michele M. 527
Rowbotham, Laura 344
Rowe, Beverly 310
Roy, Andrea 102
Roy, Lisa 289
Roy, Robert 515
Royse, Beverly 144
Roza, Mishalle 249
Rubins, Adam 366
Ruckman, Mel 270
Rud, Tracy P. 188
Rude, Maxine Ilah 276
Rudewicz, Eleanore M. 129
Rudloff, Joseph D. 169
Ruffin, Pauline 321
Ruffing, John 123
Ruhr, Susan 566
Rule, Craig 56
Rumford, Joanne Marie 141
Runkle, Kimberlee 631
Runner, Audra W. 163
Rupp, Jonathon 54
Ruprecht, Albert 438
Rushton, Stephanie 292
Russ, Janice 370
Russell, Maxine Kaiser 589
Russell Sr., James S. 67
Russell-Mannick, Judith 15
Russo, Ann P. 104
Rust, Linda Ruth 450
Rutchick, Harriet F. 98
Rutkowski, Joseph 626
Rutkowski, Joseph J. 157
Ruton, Mildred Marsh 510
Ryan, Arlene 32
Ryan, Edward H. 53
Ryan, Jennifer M. 7
Ryan Jr., Frank J. 469
Ryan, Katherine 558
Ryan, Michele Ann 280
Ryan, Susan Gardner 276
Ryder, Denise A. 154
Rydzewski, Norine 568
Rynders, Sharlotte Jones 307

S

S(Poet Boulter) 627
Saadoon, Kamal A. 195
Sabol, Betty Jane 96
Saephan, Farmmary C. 91
Safeeullah, Gilda Bribieseca 610
Sage, Bradford J. 164
Saige, Charles A. 107
Salaita, Fayez 110

Salas, Larissa 259
Saleh, Carole Jean 150
Sales, Francis de 116
Sales, Leonides S. 239
Salim, Khalfani 611
Sallman, Angela 423
Samano, Lorraine M. 268
Sampson, Harold L. 390
Sanabia, Angela C. 161
Sanders, Christina C. 158
Sanders, Jennifer M. 18
Sanders, Presley R. 575
Sandoval, Espie 64
Sands, Myra J. 333
Sands, Stacy 520
Sands, Stephanie 534
Sandstedt, Ellen 377
Sandusky, Keisha 242
Sandusky, Steve Dean 351
Sanford, Tamyka T. 488
Santana, Melissa 553
Santana, Vanessa 223
Santefort, Sara 491
Santo 253
Santore, J. C. 610
Santos, Sarita DeLos 506
Sarkissian, Henry A. 158
Sarnowski, Robert A. 527
Satriani, Charles C. 457
Satterfield, Mandy 229
Savage, J. Adele 600
Savage, Jane E. 427
Savell, Ruby 297
Sawyer, Sylvia 339
Sayler, Lauree 292
Scannell, Regina 300
Schachl, Simone 506
Schaedla, Yens 578
Schaefer, Duana 17
Schaeffer, Madeline 242
Schaffer, Stacey M. 453
Schallert, Patricia V. M. 514
Scharmen, Karen Sue 607
Schauer, Julius Karl 400
Schaugaard, Carolyn Irene 39
Scheel, Rose Marie 282
Scheffleo, Heidi J. 610
Schell, Mark M. 183
Schenkelberg, Pamela 284
Scherberg, Goldie R. 138
Schetlin, Eleanor M. 82
Schilling, Elmo M. 9
Schladweiler, Leonard J. 322
Schleig, Gerald K. 440
Schleper, Alisa Renee 44
Schlieman, Sheryl 594
Schmerz, Lyle L. 221
Schmidlapp, Bryan 171
Schmidt, K. G. 280
Schmidt, Marjorie 239
Schmidt, Matt 188
Schmidt, Steven T. 503
Schmittou, John W. 433

Schmitz, Sarah 308
Schneider, Kelly 217
Schneider, Mickey 310
Scholl, Margaret 192
Scholz, Ernest G. 45
Schramm, Modine G. 190
Schroeder, Elizabeth 106
Schroeder, Margaret L. 229
Schrom, Susan 230
Schuckmann, Rachel 496
Schuepbach, Lynnette 331
Schuett, Lindsey 310
Schuetze, Kathryn L. 332
Schuld, Debra J. 16
Schulman, Scott C. 453
Schultz, Joelle M. 159
Schumacher, Donnette Lee 408
Schurade, Rita 518
Schwartz, Judith 394
Schwartz, Marcia 237
Schwartz, Nettie Y. 254
Schwartz, Zachary S. 610
Scocozzo, Sylvia B. 268
Scolaro, Dominic 171
Scott, Helen 386
Scott, Debra A. 100
Scott, Harriett 159
Scott, Kathryn 529
Scott, Robyn 221
Scott, Ronald V. 574
Scott, Terri L. 594
Scott, Tyronica 210
Scott-Joynes, BitterHoney 293
Scouler, Amy 432
Scoville, Ryan 223
Scully, Joe 167
Scurti, Jennie 151
Seabon, Sylvia 610
Seamons, Molly F. 227
Sears, Kate 481
Seaton, Clyde C. 369
Seeger, Elizabeth Anne 85
Segers, Olen 252
Seib, Rita R. 524
Seibert, Kathy 497
Seidel, Catherine F. 427
Sekreta, Meghan 513
Sellers, Andrea I. 386
Sellors, David 168
Senz, Gordon S. 168
Serafin, Jason Kenneth 472
Sewell, Dora Jean Muller 478
Sexton, Chuck 422
Sexton, Laura 562
Shaak, Kathryn 204
Shabazz, Kafre 520
Shade, Todd 544
Shafer, Benjamin 103
Shafer, Scott C. 285
Shaffer, William 602
Shaker, Jana K. 379
Shales, Amanda N. 143
Shaner, Marjorie E. 232

Shaner, Suzanne 256
Shannon, Alicia M. 164
Shannon, Bess 84
Shannon, Ethel M. 14
Shapiro, George 138
Sharieff, Naeem 351
Sharp, Norine W. 313
Shaski, Heather 389
Shaw, Fanny Lee Baker 102
Shaw, Susan J. 232
Shearer, Julie 39
Shedosky, Nina 321
Sheehan, Brent D. 177
Sheehan, Helen 63
Sheehan, Richard 221
Shelby, Norma 502
Sheldon, Helen M. 20
Shelksohn, Owen 337
Shell, Lois A. 550
Shelton, Mary L. 288
Shelton, Patricia 248
Shelton, Ruth 354
Shepard, Millie 453
Shepard, Teri Marie 256
Shepard, Valeria F. Seay 630
Sheppard, Jan 470
Sheridan, Joel 22
Sherman, B. J. 266
Shermer Jr., Richard 236
Sherritze, Sonja 481
Sheth, Sachin D. 606
Shibles, Crystal 141
Shields, George 109
Shields, Geraldine Allen 127
Shimkus, Liz 356
Shine, Bambi Joy 88
Shipley, Ami 37
Shipstead, Margaret 552
Shirinian, Emelda Darlene 140
Shirley, Preston 492
Shirley, Willie Lou 538
Shockley, Doris K. 8
Short, Brett P. 15
Short, Jan 27
Shrader, Jo 168
Shuler, Misty 329
Shults, Berniece Doudna 117
Shults, Tina Marie 345
Shultz, Dianne 134
Shultz, J. D. 344
Shy, William WL 305
Sibley III, Alden W. 169
Siddiqi, Nazia M. 196
Siebern, Nancy M. 482
Siegal, Vanessa 536
Siegel, Eric 136
Sieler-Randolph, Kim 273
Siemann, Serah 309
Siems Jr., Richard W. 316
Sievers, Lisa J. 501
Sigmon, Edith McGhee 224
Sikorski, Kathryn A. 491
Silvas, Johnny V. 4

Silver, Kressy 506
Silverman, Ryan 248
Silvers, Kim 311
Silvers, Nicole 486
Simmons, Lisa 302
Simmons, Synell 602
Simmons-Martin, Diana 113
Simms Sr., Donald L. 412
Simon II, Nathaniel Birch 503
Simonsen, Victoria L. 229
Simonton, Melinda 569
Simpkins, Tiffany A. 542
Simpson, G. 557
Simpson, Gale 365
Simpson, H. Labron 312
Simpson, Marian 307
Sineway, Colleen 160
Singh, Shalirita 531
Singho, Mrs. Beryl 542
Singleton, Carl R. 610
Singley, Kathy A. 316
Singley, Lawrence I. 554
Sirek, Heather 405
Sirmon, Lesa 189
Sitton, Sharon 592
Sjurseth, Janice 108
Skog, Lezli 342
Skotnica, Judith Simone 45
Skriapas, Denise 105
Skrine, Joseph A. 404
Skvor, Ernst 441
Skywater, Sharon 188
Slack, Merrilyn 549
Sladky, Joan Marie 119
Slater, Delian B. 447
Slavicek, Margaret 568
Slingerland, Douglas A. 148
Smalkowski, Frances 424
Smeaton, Tony 197
Smeltzer, Susan 318
Smialkowski, Lola M. 512
Smith, —Melody 628
Smith, Ashley 114
Smith, Chevelle D. 462
Smith, Cinda L. 169
Smith, Cindy 120
Smith, Daniel 470
Smith, Dillon 13
Smith, Dorothy 443
Smith, Douglas J. 356
Smith, Evelyn L. 410
Smith, Frankie R. 120
Smith, Gwyndolyn 411
Smith, Jeff 137
Smith, Jennifer 87,
Smith, Joan 387, 518
Smith, Jody 439
Smith Jr., B. Rex 597
Smith, Kellie D. 319
Smith, Kevin 202
Smith, Lekita Ruth 600
Smith, Lillian 573
Smith, Lillian K. 319

Smith, Linda L. 204
Smith, Lloyd W. 353
Smith, Lynda 573
Smith, Mark Samuel 282
Smith, Marlene 479
Smith, Mary L. 449
Smith, Melody 513
Smith, Misty 320
Smith, Rachael Lynn 274
Smith, Randall Lee 198
Smith, Renee Mickle 194
Smith, Robert J. 188
Smith, Roger 510
Smith, Rose Marie 272
Smith, Ruth E. 203
Smith, Shelly Lynn 240
Smith, Sherilyn Kathleen 568
Smith, Ted Michael 352
Smith, Teri K. 555
Smith, Tishawna 524
Smith, Tomeka 234
Smith, Valoria R. 590
Smith, Virginia 500
Smith, Walter E. 328
Smitherman, Doug 364
Smithson, Hazel 112
Smoot, Jacqueline 173
Smythe, Mercedes 304
Snider, Kenzi 451
Sniezak, Steve 282
Snow, Cindy 416
Snyder, Bernice 395
Snyder Jr., Earl 129
Snyder, Michael D. 537
Snyder, Rebecca S. 206
Snyder, Sharlene 338
Snyder, Thomas F. 572
Sobers, Sophie M. 315
Sochuck, Alphonsina 136
Soderquist, Bonnie 12
Sohn, Patricia Linn 582
Sokolowski, Tina Louise 270
Soloway, Matt 502
Somani, Nita 342
Sommers, Brian Keith 379
Sorensen, L. Lee 520
Sorrells, Jacqueline 83
Sorrels, Katie 185
Sorvino, Carole M. 372
Sosa, Cindy 368
Sosa, Margie Romero 243
Sosa, Michael 229
Soter, Anna O. 380
Souders, Glenn A. 147
Souders, Sharlene N. 548
Sousa, Douglas 176
Sowden, Tanya 345
Soyring, Paul 279
Spain, Dyan 145
Spaldo, Eugenia W. 119
Spano, Michelle A. 266
Sparrow, Brandy 155
Spaulding, Patricia 203
Spears, Sandra E. 592, 593
Speight, Julie 94
Speller, Tamaka L. 599
Spence, LaShonda Yvette 313
Spencer, Anita 365
Spencer, Geneva L. T. 463
Spencer, Jeannette 116
Spencer, Kari 329
Spencer, Pearlie B. 505
Spencer, Peggy 283
Spencer, Portia 342
Spencer, Tony 216
Speranza, Sarah 601
Speros, Michelle 271
Speth, Harry L. Vern 162
Spinks, Nellie Johnson 321
Spinosi, Dotty 425
Spivak, Nan 244
Sprabary, Michael S. 301
Springer, J. Ann 562
Springer, Norma 184
St. Kilian, Michael 203
Stafford, Tenna F. 295
Stahl, Marianne 512
Stairs, Laura 596
Stalerman, Ruth 184
Stalter, James J. 70
Stamp, Julie 129
Stamper, R. C. 282
Stanley, Brian 97
Stanley, Jennifer 422
Stanton, Chris 41
Stanton, Ricky J. 495
Staples II, Milton Thomas 298
Stark, Lenora Sullivan 299
Stark, Tammy Marie 187
Starks, Sandra 526
Staub, Angela Conrad 166
Steakley, Germaine 403
Stebor, Austin F. 25
Stedelbauer, Joyce Carr 131
Steele, Danielle 128
Stegenga, Ann 607
Steinbaum, Keith 214
Steinberg, Brandon P. 378
Steindl, Priscilla A. 542
Stephens, Angel M. 115
Stephens, Laurie Ann 543
Stephens, Teresa 323
Stephenson, Melanie 230
Stern, Charles M. 471
Stern, Stella S. 315
Sterr, Dawn M. 101
Stevans, Michelle 610
Stevens, Jodi 408
Stevens, Kate 211
Stevens, Katherine 526
Stevens, Matt 307
Stevenson, Camina 393
Stevenson, Charles E. 159
Stevenson, Julie A. 167
Stewart, Deborah B. 369
Stewart, Del 31
Stewart, Gary 31
Stewart, J. Michael 278
Stewart, Lorna M. 281
Stewart, Robert 206
Stewart-Kennedy, Elvira E. 438
Stiles, Alice A. 130
Stilwell, Robert J. 290
Stinnett, Matthew 260
Stirling, Thomas D. 212
Stirpe, Isabella R. 160
Stitt, Deborah 164
Stoeckel Sr., Peter T. 505
Stokes, Donna V. 60
Stokes, Erica 458
Stone, Rachel 592
Stone, Shelby J. 494
Storino, Henry Enrice 370
Stottman, Thomas W. 308
Stovall, Natalie 627
Strash, Victoria 292
Stratton, Diane C. 387
Strauss, Sheilah 207
Strey, Kathie 562
Strom-Medvitz, Linda 537
Stromeyer, Charles 51
Stromswold, Carol 146
Stuart, Eva M. 432
Stuart, Teresa 510
Stutzbach, Paul 543
Suarez, Megan 237
Sublett, Megan 274
Sucari, Lisette 550
Suchanek, Louis A. 317
Sueiras, Maria R. 629
Sulak, Kat 327
Sullivan, Edward T. 609
Sullivan, Elva I. 38
Sullivan, Jackie 413
Sullivan, James F. 426
Sullivan, Mary 328
Sullivan, Suzy D. 275
Sullivan, Zenia 584
Summerhill, Ashley Brooke 173
Summers, Dorothy 128
Summers, Linda 609
Sumrall, Courtney 364
Suski, Steve 598
Susman, Bertha 76
Sutak, Ivon 167
Sutherland, Gene N. 170
Sutter, Joe 138
Sutton, Angie 149
Sutton, Gale 103
Svedas, Daniel 372
Sveitis, Barbara Stefania 26
Swain, Sharon 553
Swangin, Terica Lynn 223
Swartzendruber, Gary 468
Sweatman, Debbie 439
Sweeney, Sandra Christine 492
Sweigart, Dena Loree 114
Swift, Bunny 376
Swift, Geri 157
Swindell, Tanya Albert 218
Swiontek, Richard 352
Swisher, Gary 630
Swochak, Mary Ann 513
Sylvester, Natalie 493
Syvrud, Ellie 177
Szabo, Brent Kelly 73
Szczublewski Jr., James M. 125
Szumita, Odessa A. 318

T

Taegel, Andrew 17
Tag, Amy 133
Tager, Robert E. 225
Takashima, Gene 367
Tallfoot, Jonathan 168
Tam, Maxine 607
Tancredi, Janine 78
Tanner, Edith C. 375
Tappan, Amber 109
Tarantino, Samuel J. 279
Tarle, Naomi 503
Tarling, Sarah E. 483
Tarros, Victor Frank 201
Tarter, Christine J. 460
Tarver, Ina Hazel 154
Tate, Adam John 6
Tavarone, Robert 328
Tavoularis, Oriana Nicole 560
Taylor, Amy 357
Taylor, Cheryl D. 403
Taylor, Clarance 443
Taylor, Glenda 136
Taylor, Michael 336, 337
Taylor, Pan 181
Taylor, Rossme A. 346
Taylor, Sharon L. 181
Taylor, Stephen Alexander 609
Taylor, T. Marie 275
Taylor, Velande 579
Tebo, Kenneth B. 521
Techmeier, Mary 310
Teets, Virginia P. 550
Teliho, Margaret T. 586
Telles, Daniel 378
Templeton, Melissa 286
Templin, Kylee 190
Tergis, Jane P. 48
Terlizzi, Denise De 148
Terrell, Marie 259
Tesh, Ruby Nifong 294
Tezak, Stephanie 187
Thakoor, Neelum 325
Thatcher, Todd 295
Thattanakham, S. Neena 291
Thayer, Melvin 293
Thibodeaux, Lacreta R. 343
Thiel, Mike 282
Thierer, Luann 352
Thomas, April 377
Thomas, Elene G. 117
Thomas, Gary 132
Thomas, Jody D. 391

Thomas, Joe 471
Thomas, Joyce Smith 472
Thomas, Rosie M. 574
Thomas, Stephen 250
Thomas, Theresa Lynn 598
Thompson, Betty W. B. 413
Thompson, Chelsea 387
Thompson, Chrissy 106
Thompson, Estelle 102
Thompson, Heather 73
Thompson, Helen 155
Thompson, Jane 18
Thompson, K. J. 304
Thompson, Katelan M. 522
Thompson, Kyle 289
Thompson, Marjorie B. 556
Thompson, Micheal A. 563
Thompson, Vernon 546
Thor, Garrett 154
Thorne, Lindsay Sparrow 341
Thornhill, Tad 330
Thornton, Alison 400
Thornton, Sara 452
Thorpe, Eric 113
Thusat, Joshua 418
Tice, Bradley S. 95
Tidwell, Jeanita 157
Tiemann, Georganne G. 95
Tilley, Jessica 609
Tillinger, Mary Lou 294
Tingley, Paula 319
Tinoco, Maria Isabel 333
Tippett, Mary J. 289
Tisler, Mandy Lynn 559
Toca, Tedi 350
Toda, Joy 31
Todd, Leslie N. 240
Tolar, Randy Mark 572
Tolbert, M. 533
Toll, Ralph Winfield 304
Tomes, Amy 474
Tomingas, Emma 83
Tompkins Jr., Robert L. 544
Tompkins, Sheila 525
Toney, David 26
Tonkovich, Valerie Jane 506
Toombs, Shawn Michael 225
Toomer, Jan D. 143
Toop, Leslie K. 561
Torbert, Bertha 111
Torgersen, Chris 127
Toro, Maximino 327
Toro, Susanne C. 233
Torres, Anthony 385
Torres, Darlene 371
Torres, Sandra 343
Toter, Tanya 354
Touville, Tammy D. 511
Townes, Linda A. 534
Townsend, Susan Tice 522
Traveler, Claire W. 50
Travis, Travlen 487
Treadway, Helene 129

Tregellas, JanMarie 609
Tremaine 213
Tremelling, Kenneth 602
Trenary, Christine B. 120
Trent, Steve 354
Trettin, Rosemary 308
Trimblett, Kimberly 264
Trimmell, Jerry 116
Trinque, Myra D. 330
Troia, Barbara H. 164
Troia-Fitchett, Barbara H. 624
Trook, Weigellia G. 540
Trott, Jean S. 151
Trudeau, Mimi 448
True, Audrey M. 89
Trumbull, John 473
Truong, Ellen C. 413
Truss, Krystal 248
Trzaskos, Bernadette 425
Tsosie, Shirley 193
Tucker, Craig Wilton 56
Tucker, Danreco 608
Tucker, Darlene Mae 99
Tucker, DiDama Star 172
Tucker, Virginia Wynne 180
Tummolo, Launi L. 620
Tunis, Mindy 260
Turano, M. Jane 18
Turbyfield, S. Rose 346
Turman, Sheila 336
Turner, Andrea 177
Turner, Helen 92
Turner II, William R. 593
Turner, Jeff 472
Turner, Martha 504
Turner, Tahirah 542
Turner, Temple 266
Tuttle, Sharon M. 331
Tuttle, Tracey 305
Tuzzolino, Christina 140
Tweton, Annie 165
Twyford, Rebecca June 580
Tyner, Doris 446

U

Uetz, Kathy MacLean 579
Uhler, Margaret A. 342
Ulmer, Carolyn 139
Ulmer, Thomas P. 324
Underwood, Don 17
Underwood, Jai 126
Unger, Irene Perry 413
Unruh, Brent 369
Unzicker, Otto 561
Upchurch, Doris 88
Urban, Jessica 104
Urban, William 193
Ureta, N. Ming S. 579
Urias, Lilia 300
Usinger, Rob 331

V

Va. 497
Valdellon, Annabelle 446
Valdivia, Sandra L. 238
Valle, Argelio Del 171
Valore, Michelle 452
Van Beers, Kris 554
van Konijnenburg, Kymberly 185
Van Meter, Malissia 307
Van Wye, Laura 192
Vance, Steven 492
Vandemark, Bianca 464, 591
VanDenBerg, Roland 523
VanderVeer, Jennifer 162
Vandine, Mike R. 277
Vandiver, Jerry 130
Vane, Norman Thaddeus 528
VanGiller, Gene 447
Vanier, Tracy I. 573
VanNess, Jon 90
Vanosdol, Scott D. 346
Vardell, Barney Wayne 95
Varelas, Debbie G. 124
Vargas, Denise 143
Vargas, Raquel M. 310
Varghese, Lynn 311
Varghese, Susan Lorrine 209, 630
Vargo, June K. 308
Varjabedian, Lori 305
Varley, Sarah 570
Vasquez, Rosa 243
Vatalaro, Shannin 185
Vaughn, Stephanie L. 195
Vaziri, Maziar 592
Vazquez, Elsa L. 379
Vega, Marilyn 317
Velmere, Vicki L. 334
Verdon, Michelle 543
Vernon, Shirley M. 346
Vestal-Knight, Mary Beth 585
Vick, Jason 84
Vickles, Eleni 412, 609
Vicol, E. A. 564
Vigdorchik, Inna Ruth 409
Villa, Geraldine 157
Villa-McDowell, Bartholomew 608
Villarreal, Andrew 179
Villaverde, Marcelliano 255
Viloria, Jen 81
Vine, Earle Edward 141
Vineyard, Mark 266
Viola, Patricia 545
Virgona, Valerie F. 541
Viscelli, Anne C. 455
Vittoria, Todd Michael 290
Vix, Lloyd J. 520
Volak, April 416
Voorhes, Wanda L. 487
Vucetich, Shauna 501

W

Wade, Jenny 424

Wadzinski, Arleen J. 31
Wagner, Angela 374
Wagner, Cheryl 136
Wakeland, Sherrie 557
Wakeland, Shukuno S. 340
Waldenmaier, Dave 431
Walker, Donna 435
Walker, Gladys E. 114
Walker, Heather L. 139
Walker, Justine 96
Walker, Lucienne Corriveau 294
Walker, Margaret Nash 485
Walker, Marilyn K. 348
Walker, Matthew A. 261
Walker, Mordecai 565
Walker, Pamela 499
Walker, Toddeanna E. 583
Walker, Verna J. 280
Walker, William 256
Walker-Greene, L. Carolyn 575
Walkup, Regina 311
Wall, Eileen J. 142
Wall, Elizabeth 421
Wallace, Bea 154
Wallace, C. Guy 150
Wallace, Michelle 581
Walls, Alison M. 28
Walls, Gladys 127
Walls, Marian Kelley 281
Walsh, Deborah R. 378
Walsh W., Jay 441
Waltemire, Gary Alton 391
Walter, L. J. 306
Walters, Nancy 587
Walters, Sara 449
Walton Jr., Jack B. 155
Waltz, Terry S. 186
Wang, Philein 248
Wangberg, Elizabeth 427
Ward, Jenna 361
Ward, Karen S. 183
Ward, Linda 496
Ward, Nycki J. 348
Ward, Timothy L. 339
Wardell, Lydia Barnes 566
Ware, David C. 359
Warner, Bea 444
Warner, Kathryn J. 322
Warner, Mary L. 330
Warren, Carol Huggins 608
Warren, Franklin J. 3
Washburn, Janet 425
Washington, Felicia Ann 361
Washington, Wanda Lynn 182
Waters, Lakisha 237
Watson, Elwood 374
Watson, Marva M. 300
Watts, Andrea Lee 84
Watts, Margaret 199
Way, Barbara 401
Weathers, Ryan 229
Weaver, Maude L. 565
Weaver, Robin E. 606

Weaver, Robin 325
Weaver-Duval, Judy 406
Webb, Bethany 127
Webb, Debra 98
Weber, Glenna 461
Weber, Marilyn Goode 500
Weber, Roela 296
Webster, Cameron 432
Weddington, Louise 252
Weeks, Shirley 495
Weese, Georgianna M. 156
Weese, James de 18
Weidemann, Elizabeth 110
Weigner, Edith L. 98
Wein, Bella 148
Weinstein, Sonjia 296
Weir, Belinda C. 412
Weisfelner, Sara 296
Weiss, Ben 5
Weiss, Sondra 314
Welch, Amy 151
Welch, Barbara 395
Welch, Bobby 99
Welch, Candace 31
Welch, NaKesha 298
Welch, Rita 324
Weller, Kay H. 307
Wells, Hallie 147
Wells, Laura 354
Wells, Lawrence 608
Wells, Lisa A. 511
Wells, Melinda 191
Welscher, Bridget 144
Weltz, Mike 343
Wempen, Raechel 289
Wendt, Rye 322
Wengland, Thressa J. 579
Wentzel, Jon H. 10
Weppener, Barbara S. 103
Wermann, Edward J. 24
Werner, Tim 332
Wesolowski, Edward 125
Wesson, Clarence N. 105
Wesson, Sheri L. 290
West, Clara 8
West, Jeanette Kay Labaj 26
West, Pamela 324
West, Todd 215
Westover, David A., III 474
Westover III, David A. 597
Weststrate, Sabrina 555
Wetzel, Rebecca K. 215
Weygandt, Ada 144
Weygandt, Anthony 396
Wheaton-Harkins, Therese 240
Wheeler, Gary L. 399
Whetstone, Erma 3
Whisnant, Michelle 550
Whitacre, Gina A. 458
Whitaker, Cheyney R. 86
White, Barbara Jean 457
White, David 437
White Jr., Thomas 231

White, Kimberly Joan 246
White, Martin 504
White, Matthew J. 572
White, Ruth Ann 519
White, Timothy Lawrence 226
White, Windle 526
Whitehead, Wendy 181
Whitehurst, Amber Leigh 114
Whitfield, George 477
Whitley, Robert H. 538
Whitlow, Heartha 360
Whitman, Veronda 518
Whitmire, Bonita 151
Whitmire, Matthew 232
Whitt, Theresa 300
Wiatrowski, Linda 556
Wicke, Philip 286
Wiechelman, Susan 305
Wiemer, Muriel Krug 319
Wier, Russell D. 488
Wiesemann, Emily 126
Wiesner, Eugene F. 399
Wilbur, Danielle 410
Wilcox, Lisa Ann 224
Wilcox, Teresa 579
Wilcox, Wilmer 317
Wilde, Larkin 270
Wilder, Janice A. 397
Wilder, Lillie D. 254
Wiley, Jennifer 454
Wilhelm, Cora L. 72
Wilhelmy, Gus 9
Wilkerson, Diane J. 436
Wilkins, Angela Cain 153
Wilkins, Victor 275
Wilkinson, Linda 296
Willadson, E. 269
Willard, Frances 383
Willett, Edward F. 125
Willette, Earlene 130
Willey, Mary K. 547
William, Gregg 47
Williams, Alma Ann 79
Williams, Antionette 141
Williams, Barbara 357
Williams, Betty L. 69
Williams, Carol Westbrooks 85
Williams, Christopher J. 54
Williams, Cindy M. 103
Williams, Darryl L. 44
Williams, Donna M. 341, 617
Williams, Donneisha 140
Williams, Eva Forrest 379
Williams III, John Thomas 35
Williams, James Thomas 95,
Williams, Jan 22
Williams, Lakeshia 190
Williams, Marilyn E. 302
Williams, Richard L. 553
Williams, Ruth E. 595
Williams, Shane 308
Williams, Shannon 608
Williams, Tabitha 596

Williams, Thelma 334
Williams, Twinkle 228
Williamson, Dewey E. 95
Williamson, Evelyn 28
Williamson, Ian 113
Williamson, Mark 238
Williamson, Wilson L. 354
Williamson-Ater, Winifred 268
Willis, Jeremy 112
Wilowski Jr., E. J. 339
Wilson, Carolyn 144
Wilson, Charlotte 136
Wilson, Clyde 43
Wilson, Danny 370
Wilson, Grace 68
Wilson, Heaven 133
Wilson, Isedora 55
Wilson, Jeanette A. 149
Wilson, Jessica 77
Wilson, John 308
Wilson, John Paul 355
Wilson, Ken 213
Wilson, Nancy Jo 339
Wilson, Nicole 254
Wilson, Patricia Ann 569
Wilson, Patricia Myatt 512
Wilson, Seneca 622
Wilson, Susan D. 225
Wims, Fannie C. 427
Winburn, D. C. 449
Winbush, Helen J. 384
Winckler, Karen A. 350
Windish, Catherine M. 414
Windle, Michelle 274
Windom, Arlene 109
Wing, Aaron 37
Winkelman, Doris June 455
Winkler, Treica 291
Winspear, William M. 504
Winston, Kathy 573
Wintheiser, R. 552
Wise, Roderick L. 351
Wiseman, Jane L. 98
Wiseman, Mike 574
Wiskochil, James A. 143
Wismer, Loretta M. 319
Wisniewski, Andrea 468
Wisniewski, Scot 279
Witherspoon, Rhenetta 234
Witkin-Kaufman, Laura 293
Wittkopf, Michelle 543
Wittkower, Mary 320
Wofford, Kimberly 334
Wohlenhaus, Grace 90
Wojak, Megan 334
Wolf, Mackensie 282
Wolf, Tawny 271
Wolfe, Kimberly J. 332
Wolfe, Lacey 514
Wolfe, Melba Honey 323
Wolnick, Meridith Anne 508
Woloss, Bob 381
Woloszyn, Jodi 100

Woo, Aaron 10
Wood, Bonnie 361
Wood, Jeanette Cronin 466
Wood, Jo Ann 166
Wood, Kathleen 274
Wood, Leia Kathryn 599
Wood, Michael D. 516
Woodard, Howard A. 54
Woodruff, Elaine 53
Woodruff, Lois J. 310
Woodruff, Shirley T. 340
Woods, Amber L. 72
Woods, Heather Faye 388
Woods, Myrshia L. 214
Woodward, Bethany 13
Woodward, Shannon L. 570
Woolf, Linda L. 484
Woolf, Lynda L. 570
Working, Ella V. 460
Worts, Elna Rogers 166
Wozniak, Jen 66
Wrath, Andres J. 79
Wray, Wendy 262
Wrenn, Brandi 625
Wright, Buck 257
Wright, Erica Evette 363
Wright, Jesse 137
Wright, Reta 335
Wright, Tamara Angelic 559
Wriston, Marlene 340
Wyatt, Brian L. 91
Wykle, Misty Starleen 270
Wynn, Ethel 358
Wyrich, Carlene 12
Wyse, Janet 31
Wysocki, Helen B. 158

X

Xavier, Sabrina 209

Y

Yamasaki, Youko 250
Yancey, Lori 209
Yandell, Gail 124
Yang, Lina 329
Yanibas, Aris F. 147
Yasparro, Rosemary Muntz 309
Yates, Mariann E. Barr 583
Yates, Ruth 316
Yazinsky, John T. 127
Yeager, Addie Hill 372
Yeager, Robert L. 607
Yeoman, Bernice 371
Yerkes, Cecelia R. 467
Yoder, Suzanne 347
Yokely, Gerald 21
Yokley, Jean Henry 435
Yon, Tracy Linette 283
Yonge, Amelie Cooper 98
Yort, Thangsy 217
Yost, Faith Davis 34
Young, Angela 171

Young, Catherine A.   411
Young, Claire   437
Young, Emilie F.   46
Young, Lois M.   333
Young, Maurice Weldon   336
Young, Pauline   204
Young, Zachary   257
Youngblood, Dorothy F.   461
Younger, Patrick A.   272
Youngers, Melinda   596
Youngstrand, Helen L.   160
Yousif, Laura   253
Yundt, Lillian R.   346

Z

Zacherl, Shelley Irene   279
Zachrisson, Christopher   620
Zackery, Helen J.   154
Zaengle, John F.   141
Zaha, Cheryl   428
Zakour, Zachary   240
Zakrajshek, Lynn   278
Zalar, Gertrude P.   357
Zalevsky, Kenneth A.   349
Zanghi, Anthony F.   166
Zaverdas, George   67
Zelkin, Tali   315
Zeller, Bonnie   367
Zeman, Laurel   558
Zendejas Sr., Gilbert   179
Zerin, Edward   18
Zeromus, Odessa   531
Zett, Crystal   117
Ziegler, James Francis   177
Zilba, Zachary   607
Zimak, Alice F.   152
Zimbelman, Treena   230
Zimmerman, Ellen   417
Zimmerman, Myrtle D.   589
Zimpelman, Hillari   47
Zippin, Lawrence I.   503
Zippo, Gina Ann   54
Zou, Hong   427
Zou, Kelly H.   508
Zvonik, Martha   231
Zwack, Cathy Abston   46
Zwank, Cyndi   56